BLUE RIBB🎀N
College Basketball Yearbook

Other sports titles from Brassey's

Blue Ribbon College Football Yearbook: 2001 Edition, edited by Chris Dortch

Playing Hurt: Evaluating and Treating the Warriors of the NFL, by Pierce E. Scranton, Jr., M.D.

Links Lore: Dramatic Moments and Forgotten Milestones from Golf's History, by Peter F. Stevens

Baseball Prospectus: 2001 Edition, by Joseph S. Sheehan et. al.

Jewish Sports Legends: Third Edition, by Joseph M. Siegman

At Speed: Up Close and Personal with the People, Places, and Fans of NASCAR, by Monte Dutton

Rebel with a Cause: A Season with NASCAR Star Tony Stewart, by Monte Dutton

The Most Wanted Series:
Football's Most Wanted: The Top 10 Book of the Great Game's Outrageous Characters, Fortunate Fumbles, and Other Oddities, by Floyd Conner

Golf's Most Wanted: The Top 10 Book of Outrageous Duffers, Deadly Divots, and Other Oddities, by Floyd Conner

Baseball's Most Wanted: The Top 10 Book of the National Pastime's Outrageous Offenders, Lucky Bounces, and Other Oddities, by Floyd Conner

Basketball's Most Wanted: The Top 10 Book of Hoop's Outrageous Dunkers, Incredible Buzzer-Beaters, and Other Oddities, by Floyd Conner

NASCAR's Most Wanted: The Top 10 Book of Outrageous Drivers, Wild Wrecks, and Other Oddities, by Jim McLaurin

Soccer's Most Wanted: The Top 10 Book of Clumsy Keepers, Clever Crosses, and Outlandish Oddities, by John Snyder

Wrestling's Most Wanted: The Top 10 Book of Pro-Wrestling's Outrageous Performers, Punishing Piledrivers, and Other Oddities, by Floyd Conner

College Basketball Yearbook

2001-2002 Edition

Edited by Chris Dortch

BRASSEY'S, INC.

Washington, D.C.

ISBN 1-57488-396-8

Printed in the United States of America.

Brassey's, Inc.
22841 Quicksilver Drive
Dulles, Virginia 20166

First Edition

10 9 8 7 6 5 4 3 2 1

From the Editor

For the last 15 years, Sept. 11 has been a date to remember. Fifteen years ago, on Sept. 11, 1986, my daughter Jennifer was born.

Though the day will always hold a special place for me, Sept. 11 took on new meaning in 2001. On Sept. 11, 2001, I was knee deep in editing copy for the 21st edition of Blue Ribbon College Basketball Yearbook when I got a call from my wife. She sounded frantic. Someone had exploded a bomb at the World Trade Center in New York, she said.

I quickly turned to CNN, just in time to see that my wife had gotten bad information. It wasn't a bomb. Terrorists, as everyone knows by now, had hijacked four jets, two of which were guided into the twin towers at the WTC. Minutes after the attack on New York came news that another plane had been crashed into the Pentagon. The Pentagon! Still a fourth plane—thanks, we later learned, to some remarkable heroes who thwarted the mission—had crash-landed in Pennsylvania, far short of its intended target in Washington.

The devastation that ensued shocked the world.

Like all Americans, Blue Ribbon's team was affected by the tragedy. Several of us found it difficult to work. It was hard for me to stay away from CNN and the broadcast networks. I flipped back and forth between the channels for the next several days, my emotions running the gamut from fear to sadness to anger. Freedom had been challenged on Sept. 11, and the world would be forever changed.

Several Blue Ribbon writers, understand-ably, put their workload on hold in the aftermath of the tragedy. Who could blame them? They obviously felt empathy for those who had been at Ground Zero, plus freedom-loving Americans across the country and the world. Some of our writers even had loved ones in harm's way. Gary Laney who just joined us this year and did an excellent job with the Southland Conference, wrote of that horrifying day in his newspaper, the American Press of Lake Charles, La.

I received the call around 8:45 Tuesday morning. It was the only thing that kept me from being a basket case all day.

It was my sister, calling from a pay phone in Battery Park in New York City, just blocks from the World Trade Center in extreme lower Manhattan. She was calling to tell me she was all right.

She was only on the phone briefly because there was a line of people anxious to connect to loved ones. I got off the phone relieved.

That changed five minutes later when the first of the Trade Center towers collapsed.

I didn't hear from her again until I reached her at her Brooklyn apartment after 3 p.m. Thank God she was all right. Physically, at least.

Emotionally, she'll never be the same. That's what happens when you spend the day in Hell.

She was still in shock when I talked to her Tuesday afternoon. She was reliving the horrors of the day, repeating over and over, "Gary, I thought I was going to die today. I was sure I was going to die."

Cindy Laney saw the Boeing 767 crash into the second World Trade Center tower. She was only blocks away.

"I didn't just see it, it flew right over my shoulder," she said. "It was so low, it was like a crop duster. I watched the plane disintegrate into the building. I watched it put a gaping hole into the building. I watched it and I didn't know what to do. I just cried."

As did we all.

As much as I love college basketball—and that's a lot—I quickly realized how little importance games have in light of the tragedy of Sept. 11. Still, we had a book to get out, and get it out we did. This year more than ever, I hope Blue Ribbon can help college basketball fans enjoy their favorite sport. And I hope that, in some small way, our book can help them re-enter a state of normalcy.

Is that possible? Being a proud American, I believe it is. The incredible show of solidarity by my fellow countrymen after the attacks was enough to convince me of that.

It is to the memory of the many thousands of people—mostly Americans, but many from around the world—who lost their lives that terrible day, Sept. 11, that we dedicate the 21st edition of Blue Ribbon College Basketball Yearbook.

BLUE RIBBON MEDIA, LLC

PRESIDENT—Drew Maddux
EDITOR—Chris Dortch
OPERATIONS MANAGER—Bryan Chance
ASSOCIATE EDITORS—Stan Crawley, Dave Link
CHIEF OF PRODUCTION—Brian Hinchman

EDITORIAL STAFF

AMERICAN EAST—Steve Bradley
ATLANTIC COAST—Al Featherston, Tim Peeler, Bob Thomas
ATLANTIC SUN—Mike Ashley
ATLANTIC 10—Steve Bradley,

Jeff DiVeronica, Bill Doherty, Jim Mandelaro
BIG EAST—Michael Bradley
BIG SKY—Robert Meseroll
BIG SOUTH—Mike Ashley
BIG TEN—Patrick Donnelly, Stewart Mandel
BIG 12—Wendell Barnhouse, Blair Kerkhoff
BIG WEST—Craig Staszkow
COLONIAL—Mike Harris
CONFERENCE USA—Zack McMillin
HORIZON—Mike Strange
INDEPENDENTS—Charlie Creme
IVY—Steve Bradley
METRO ATLANTIC—Steve Bradley
MID-AMERICAN—Rick McCann
MID-CONTINENT—Patrick Donnelly
MID-EASTERN—Mike Gore

MISSOURI VALLEY—Dave Reynolds
MOUNTAIN WEST—Mike Sorensen
NORTHEAST—Charlie Creme
OHIO VALLEY—Dave Link
PAC-10—Jeff Faraudo
PATRIOT—Stan Crawley
SOUTHEASTERN—Chris Dortch, Chris Low
SOUTHERN—Dave Link
SOUTHLAND—Gary Laney
SWAC—Mark Alexander
SUN BELT—Dan McDonald
WEST COAST—Steve Bergum
WESTERN ATHLETIC—Paul Arnette

RPI data supplied by Jim Sukup, The RPI Report

Team Index

Conference Index

Index

2001-2002 Blue Ribbon All-America Teams

FIRST TEAM
Brett Nelson, 6-4 JR, Florida
Jason Williams, 6-2 JR, Duke
Chris Marcus, 7-1 SR, Western Kentucky
Casey Jacobsen, 6-6 JR, Stanford
Tayshaun Prince, 6-9 SR, Kentucky

SECOND TEAM
Frank Williams, 6-3 JR, Illinois
Juan Dixon, 6-3 SR, Maryland
Udonis Haslem, 6-8 SR, Florida
Jared Jefferies, 6-9 SO, Indiana
Kareem Rush, 6-6 JR, Missouri

THIRD TEAM
Troy Bell, 6-1 JR, Boston College
Keith Bogans, 6-5 JR, Kentucky
Carlos Boozer, 6-9 JR, Duke
Lonny Baxter, 6-8 SR, Maryland
Jason Kapono 6-7 JR, UCLA

FOURTH TEAM
Marvin O'Connor, 6-4 SR, St. Joseph's
Mike Dunleavy, 6-8 JR, Duke
Dan Gadzuric, 6-11 SR, UCLA
Sam Clancy, 6-7 SR, Southern Cal
David West, 6-8 JR, Xavier

Preseason All-Conference players not chosen to the above four teams are designated Blue Ribbon honorable mention All-Americans.

PLAYER OF THE YEAR
Jason Williams, 6-2 JR, Duke

NEWCOMER OF THE YEAR
Cedric Bozeman, 6-6 FR, UCLA

Blue Ribbon College Basketball Yearbook Preseason Top 40

1. Duke	21. Georgetown
2. Illinois	22. Cincinnati
3. Kentucky	23. Tennessee
4. Maryland	24. Indiana
5. Florida	25. Arkansas
6. UCLA	26. Boston College
7. Missouri	27. Arizona
8. Kansas	28. Michigan State
9. Virginia	29. Ole Miss
10. Iowa	30. Fresno State
11. St. Joseph's	31. Wyoming
12. Connecticut	32. Ohio State
13. Temple	33. Utah
14. Memphis	34. Alabama
15. Stanford	35. Western Kentucky
16. Oklahoma	36. Purdue
17. Syracuse	37. Southern Cal
18. North Carolina	38. Providence
19. Oklahoma State	39. Wake Forest
20. Texas	40. Xavier

Duke 1

LOCATION	Durham, NC
CONFERENCE	Atlantic Coast
LAST SEASON	35-4 (.897)
CONFERENCE RECORD	13-3 (t-1st)
STARTERS LOST/RETURNING	1/4
NICKNAME	Blue Devils
COLORS	Blue & White
HOMECOURT	Cameron Indoor Stadium (9,314)
COACH	Mike Krzyzewski (Army '69)
RECORD AT SCHOOL	533-164 (21 years)
CAREER RECORD	606-223 (26 years)
ASSISTANTS	Johnny Dawkins (Duke '86)
	Steve Wojciechowski (Duke '98)
	Chris Collins (Duke '96)
TEAM WINS (last 5 years)	24-32-37-29-35
RPI (last 5 years)	9-3-1-2-1
2000-01 FINISH	Won NCAA championship.

COACH AND PROGRAM

Mike Krzyzewski will always remember the spring of 2001.

It was a time when great moments in his personal life were matched by great achievements in his professional life. Within a week at the end of March and the beginning of April, his oldest daughter Debbie delivered his second grandson and his Duke basketball team delivered his third NCAA championship. And two months later, his second daughter Lindy was married the same week as Krzyzewski's first-ballot election to the Basketball Hall of Fame.

Does it get any better than that?

Certainly, there's no higher plateau for Duke basketball to reach. Krzyzewski has taken a proud but second-tier program and lifted it to the pinnacle of the college basketball world. He has put Duke in a class with Kentucky, UCLA, Kansas and North Carolina—indeed, since his breakthrough season in 1986, none of those storied programs have been able to keep up with Coach K's pace. In those 16 years, Duke has:

• Won three national titles. Kentucky is the only other program to win two in that span.

• Played in the title game seven times. Kentucky is second with three.

• Played in the Final Four nine times. UNC is second with six.

• Finished No. 1 in the final regular-season poll five times, including the last three years.

The bad news – for Duke's opponents—is that Krzyzewski is still just 54 years old. He is at the height of his power.

"I still feel like a young guy," he said. "I've got a lot of years left."

There have been times during Krzyzewski's 21 years at Duke when it appeared he wouldn't make it into the 21st century. There were a couple of losing seasons in the early 1980s when only the faith of Blue Devil athletic director Tom Butters stood between Coach K and the school's disgruntled fans. Even after the program took off, Krzyzewski seriously considered leaving Duke in 1990 to become head coach of the Boston Celtics. He looked hard at job offers from the Miami Heat and the Portland Trail Blazers after the 1994 season.

Then there was the infamous back injury and the painful recovery that forced Krzyzewski to take a leave of absence in the middle of the 1995 season.

That could have been the end for the Blue Devil coach. Instead, the months away from the job and the challenge of rebuilding a program that collapsed in his absence seemed to invigorate Krzyzewski.

He returned to his job with the same passion he had shown as a young, unheralded coach from Army. Within two seasons, Duke was back atop the ACC standings. Within three seasons, the Blue Devils had returned to the No. 1 spot in the polls. And last March in Minneapolis, Duke gunned down Arizona in the title game to claim the biggest prize of all for the first time since K's back-to-back titles in 1991-92.

That victory confirmed Krzyzewski's long-term commitment to Duke.

"I wondered, if we did win it again, how would I feel?" he said. "I thought I might feel like, 'That's it, maybe I should do something else.'

"Instead, it was like, 'Let's do this again.' "

That could happen with five of the top seven players from last season's championship team returning. It could happen because, if anything, Krzyzewski seems to be improving as a coach.

Duke's 2001 title was the culmination of one of his most brilliant coaching jobs. All season, critics suggested that the Blue Devils were too thin and too weak up front to go all the way. Then, in the next-to-last regular season game, starting center **Carlos Boozer** suffered a broken foot. Surely, it seemed, that disaster at Duke's most vulnerable spot would cost the Blue Devils any chance in postseason. But the West Point graduate refused to moan about his bad luck—or let his players mourn either.

"I was trained for that," he said. "Whether it's muddy or sunny, let's figure out a way to win."

Outside observers wondered whether Krzyzewski would merely replace the injured Boozer with raw 6-11 sophomore Casey Sanders or if he would insert freshman Chris Duhon, a marvelously talented backup guard, into the lineup and go small.

Krzyzewski did both. He did start Sanders for Boozer, but he also replaced senior guard Nate James with Duhon. He reached deep down his bench for Reggie Love, a little-used 6-4 walk-on from the football team and made Love his first backup in the middle. The insertion of Duhon—Duke's quickest player—energized the Blue Devil defense, while the use the versatile veteran James off the bench, plus the contributions of Sanders and Love, suddenly gave Krzyzewski the depth he lacked before.

"It's weird," point guard Jason Williams said after Duke knocked off rival North Carolina for the second time in eight days without Boozer. "When we had Carlos, everybody said depth was a problem for us. Now different guys are stepping up."

Krzyzewski saw a team that was re-energized by the changes.

"We're more refreshed," he said. "We're on a different energy curve."

It was a curve that carried the Blue Devils to 10 straight victories after Boozer's injury ... and the national title. It was, Coach K admitted, one of his most gratifying achievements.

"I'm glad we won, but I could still be coaching this team," Krzyzewski said after returning from Minneapolis. "I'm anxious to coach our team next year."

The Duke coach understands how hard it is to repeat in this era. But keep in mind, he's the only coach to do it since UCLA's John Wooden won seven straight titles more than a quarter century ago.

"It's a different dynamic," Krzyzewski said. "You don't ever want to feel like you're defending anything. You want to say, 'Hey, this is the next thing. Let's pursue it.' "

Duke's pursuit of the 2002 title got a lot easier when Jason Williams confounded the NBA and returned to Duke for his junior season, passing up an almost sure shot at being the No. 1 pick in the 2001 draft.

But that was merely more evidence of Krzyzewski's still-growing experience as a coach. After losing three underclassmen to the NBA in 1999, he decided he needed to be more proactive in guiding his players to the next level. He and his staff came up with a plan that would allow his top players to graduate in three years, instead of four—offering them the incentive to stay and get their degree before moving on.

Williams and Boozer are both on that path. Duhon appears to be headed that way, too, and is expected to stay through the 2002-2003 season.

So Krzyzewski is once again ahead of the curve in college basketball. It's hard to imagine his program slipping very far—if at all—as long as he remains at the helm.

How long will that be? Will Krzyzewski remain at Duke for the nine or 10 seasons he needs to pass Dean Smith as the winningest coach in college basketball history?

"I don't set timetables for how long I coach," Krzyzewski said. But…

"I feel better right now than I have in maybe eight or 10 years ... just health-wise, my love of teaching. I could see myself doing this for a long time."

Duke fans had better enjoy Krzyzewski's run. It simply can't get any better for the Blue Devils than it is now.

2001-2002 SCHEDULE

Nov.	19-21	#Maui Invitational
	25	Portland
	27	*Iowa
Dec.	2	Clemson
	5	Temple
	8	@Michigan
	16	North Carolina A&T
	18	**Kentucky
	29	San Diego State
Jan.	2	***Davidson
	6	@Florida State
	10	Georgia Tech
	13	@North Carolina State
	17	Maryland
	19	Wake Forest
	24	@Boston College
	27	Virginia
	31	@North Carolina
Feb.	3	@Clemson
	7	Florida State
	9	@Georgia Tech
	14	North Carolina State
	17	@Maryland
	21	@Wake Forest
	24	St. John's
	28	@Virginia
March	3	North Carolina
	7-10	##ACC Tournament

@Road Games
*Big Ten/ACC Challenge
**Jimmy V Classic, Continental Air Arena, East Rutherford, NJ
***Charlotte, NC
#Maui, HI (vs. Seton hall first round); also Ball State, Chaminade, Duke, UCLA, South Carolina, Kansas)
##Charlotte Coliseum, Charlotte, NC

STARTERS NOT RETURNING

F-SHANE BATTIER (6-9, 19.9 ppg., 7.3 rpg., 1.8 apg., 2.1 spg., 2.3 bpg., 34.9 minutes, .471 FG, .419 3PT, .796 FT). Battier ended his storybook career as the poster-boy for NCAA basketball.

Could he have done any more? He was the consensus national player of the year as a senior, MVP of the Final Four, two-time academic All-American, a three-time national defensive player of the year and first chairman of the Student Basketball Council.

Besides all that, Battier was a sports writer's dream, the most articulate college player of his generation.

"He's all-everything," Arizona's Richard Jefferson said before the title game. "Some people rank Shane Battier right below Jesus Christ."

Battier, a religion major at Duke, might have flinched at that comparison, but there's no question that he was often the Blue Devil savior. For instance, in the last five minutes of the title game, he kept Arizona at bay with three straight baskets, including a backhanded tip-in that had to be seen to be believed.

"The one consistent thing [about Duke] is that Shane Battier is going to have a great game because he just makes things happen," Arizona coach Lute Olson said. "I don't think there's any question in anyone's mind about him being the player of the year."

Battier was justly celebrated for his deadly three-point shooting and his amazing defensive prowess—which went far beyond his knack of taking charges, a talent that earned him the derisive nickname "Floppier" from critics.

"They may have the most alert, most aware defensive player that I can ever remember in college basketball in Shane Battier," Kansas coach Roy Williams said after watching Battier's defense make the difference in a 2000 NCAA Tournament loss to the Devils.

Yet, what Krzyzewski expects Duke to miss most is Battier's leadership.

"It's a huge voice that we lose," the Duke coach said. "Every huddle, locker room setting, bus ride—Battier had a huge influence on our team in every way. That's our biggest void, not so much a talent void."

The Blue Devils will be able to replace Battier's three-point shooting. And the Duke defense, while different without one of the best help-side defenders in basketball history, will still be formidable.

But it remains to be seen whether anyone on the Blue Devil roster will be able to step up and fill the leadership void that Shane Battier leaves behind him.

OTHERS NOT RETURNING

G-RYAN CALDBECK (6-3, 0.1 ppg., 0.5 rpg., 2.7 minutes). Caldbeck was a former manager who was strictly a practice player. He played 35 minutes all season, all in mop-up situations.

F/G-NATE JAMES (6-6, 12.3 ppg., 5.2 rpg., 1.6 spg., 27.8 minutes, .494 FG, .314 3 PT, .799 FT). James started 33-of- 34 games as a junior and the first 29 games of his senior season. But he was replaced in the starting lineup by Duhon after Boozer's injury and finished his career as Duke's sixth man.

His reaction to his demotion was instructive—James didn't pout or complain. He continued to be a force off the bench. He was in double figures four times in the postseason and his last-second tap-in beat Maryland in the ACC Tournament.

James was a versatile player. He was Duke's best wing defender. He was a good long-range shooter (88 three-pointers in his last two years), a surprisingly tough offensive rebounder and, most importantly, the player who gave the most consistent effort on the team.

"The fact is that no one is more stable than Nate," Krzyzewski said. "Night after night he gives us a solid effort."

James is the first—and probably the last—player in ACC history to be a part of five regular-season championship teams (he red-shirted after six games in 1998 and earned a hardship year of eligibility). The only ACC players to appear in more career victories than James' 117 were teammate Shane Battier and former Duke star Christian Laettner.

James, the son of a career Marine sergeant, was a prep All-American who endured three injury-plagued seasons before he got his chance to play a significant role. When that chance came, James made the most of it. While Battier was the vocal leader of the Duke team, James was the emotional heart and soul of the Devils. He was, quite simply, the toughest player Duke had.

That toughness will be missed.

G-J.D. SIMPSON (6-4, 1.0 ppg., 0.5 rpg., 3.2 minutes). Krzyzewski said on several occasions that Simpson was a Division I talent, but in four seasons, the guard from California never played a significant minute for Duke.

However, he was a good enough practice player that Krzyzewski made him as tri-captain along with Battier and James in his senior season.

F-ANDRE SWEET (6-6, 4.1 ppg., 2.6 rpg., 11.3 minutes, .481 FG, .333 FT). Sweet was a late recruit from New York who Krzyzewski hoped would mature into a solid wing player, perhaps a defensive stopper in the Brian Davis/Billy King mold.

Sweet showed promise in seven early-season games, especially in an eight point, five rebound effort in 18 minutes against Army. But academic struggles sidelined Sweet after the first semester and finally convinced him to leave the program.

While he was not a factor as a freshman, Sweet's departure—he joined prep teammate Andre Barrett at Seton Hall—leaves Duke with just three scholarship players in the freshman/sophomore classes.

PROJECTED STARTERS

G-JASON WILLIAMS (6-2, 196 lbs., JR, #22, 21.6 ppg, 6.1 apg, 3.3 rpg, 2.0 spg, 31.8 minutes, .473 FG, .427 3PT, .659 FT, St. Joseph's HS/Plainfield, N.J). Which was more remarkable—the sophomore season Williams recorded to lead Duke to the 2001 national title or his postseason decision to pass up the NBA draft and return to Durham for his junior season?

Although Williams vowed late last season that he would return, more than a few commentators refused to take him at his word, especially after NBA sources revealed that the Blue Devil point guard would likely be the first player taken in the draft. One former Dukie in the media even went so far to say he'd eat crow if Williams returned to Duke.

"In today's society, you can say something, but nobody holds you to what you say," Williams said. "I've always been raised that if you say you're going to do something and you commit yourself to doing something, you honor your commitment and stick to your word."

So why did Williams put the NBA millions on hold?

"I feel like there is so much fun in college, especially when you play for a great program like this and be around your peers and just be a kid still," Williams said. "I'm not sure I'm ready to make this a job."

Skeptics pointed out that injury could make Williams' decision backfire, and indeed, that seemed to be happening when the Blue Devil guard broke a bone in his left hand in a pickup game on campus in August. However, the injury turned out to be minor and Williams promised to be back at full speed for the start of the season.

"It's not anything that will keep him from reaching his dreams or keep Duke from winning a national championship," his mother Althea Williams told The Sporting News.

Critics also wondered what else Williams had to prove in college after earning first team All-America honors as a sophomore and winning the NABC National Player of the Year Award—the only major POY honor that didn't go to teammate Shane Battier.

But Krzyzewski believes that one of the qualities that makes Williams special is his determination to refine his talent.

"He's made quantum jumps each year in getting better," Krzyzewski said. "I love it when somebody assesses their strengths and weaknesses and they say, 'I know that I have to get better. I know that I want to achieve some things that require time.' Talent does not require time. The development of talent, the development of leadership, the development of communication can only come through time and experience."

Krzyzewski wants Williams to shoulder the leadership mantle that Battier carried the last two years. He'd like to see his floor leader make better decisions with the ball (he averaged almost four turnovers a game) and to be a better on-the-ball defender.

It's scary to imagine Williams improving his game. He was tough enough to handle last season.

"I think you knew he would be great, but I don't think anybody anticipated him becoming the best player in the country as a sophomore," Missouri coach Quin Snyder, a former Duke assistant who helped recruit Williams, said.

Snyder watched Williams pour in 31 points and pass out nine assists—on a sore ankle—to beat his Missouri team in the second round of the NCAA Tournament. Less than a week later, Williams scored 19 consecutive points in a six-minute stretch against UCLA that effectively buried the Bruins in the Sweet 16. He added 28 points against Southern Cal to propel Duke to the Final Four.

As good as Williams is when he's on, he's just as dangerous when he's not. Even as a freshman, he demonstrated the uncanny ability to overcome a bad game and still make killer plays in the clutch. That attribute came to the fore last season at Maryland, when Williams managed just 10 points, no three-pointers and 10 turnovers in the game's first 38 minutes. But with Duke down 10 with a minute to play, Williams exploded for eight points in 16 seconds, helping tie a game that the Devils won in overtime.

He showed his resiliency again in the national title game. He missed nine of his first 10 three-pointers, but with Duke nursing a 77-72 lead in the final minute, Willams floated behind a Battier screen and nailed the three-point shot that cemented the victory.

"All I care about is winning games," Williams said. "Even when I'm struggling, I have to maintain an aura of confidence."

Williams is on pace to become the leading scorer in ACC history. That isn't likely to happen—he's also on pace to graduate from Duke after this season. Krzyzewski said that even though his star point guard is technically a junior, he's treating him as a senior in his final year of college ball.

That's still one more year than many expected Williams to play at Duke.

PG-CHRIS DUHON (6-1, 186 lbs., SO, # 21, 7.2 ppg, 3.2 rpg, 4.5 apg, 2.0 spg, 27.8 minutes, .424 FG, .361 3PT, .650 FT, Salmen HS/Slidell, La.). It's almost unfair that in an era dominated by point guard play, Duke should possess not just one, but two of the nation's finest points.

Duhon may be even more of a natural playmaker than All-American Jason Williams. The sophomore from Louisiana proved that last summer when he quarterbacked the U.S. National team in the World Championships for Young Men in Saitama, Japan. His play was a revelation for those who saw him as a supporting player for Williams.

"It gave me an opportunity to assert myself at both ends of the court," Duhon said of his summer experience. "If Jason were here, I would have still tried to assert myself as a leader, but not as much as I'm trying to do now. When I go back to Duke and play with Jason, I'll be confident enough to show my leadership on the court."

Confidence is just about the only thing that held Duhon back as a freshman at Duke. He was a little hesitant to assert himself offensively on a team that had so many veteran scorers. Instead, he was content to play defense and distribute the ball. He did both extraordinarily well—sharing the team defensive award with national defensive player-of-the-year Battier and compiling an eye-popping 2.85-to-1 assist/turnover ratio.

But Krzyzewski wanted and needed more from his freshman standout, especially after Boozer was lost with a broken foot late in the regular season. The misfortune convinced the Blue Devil coach to move his rookie sixth man into the starting lineup.

Duke wouldn't lose again.

"That was the change," Krzyzewski said. "It wasn't bringing Casey or Reggie [in at center]. The change was bringing Duhon into the starting lineup."

The impact of the change was immediate. In Duhon's first start at North Carolina, he harassed UNC point guard Ron Curry into seven turnovers. He forced Maryland's Steve Blake—who had a history of success in his matchups with Williams—to six turnovers in an ACC semifinal. He had a lot to do with Jason Gardner's 2-of-11 shooting performance in the NCAA championship game.

"Most players come in thinking, 'How can I score?' " Battier said. "But Chris is thinking about defense and 'How can I impact this team defensively?' "

The irony is that Duhon came to Duke regarded as one of the best shooters in his class after blowing away the field in the three-point shooting contest at the McDonald's All-American game. He showed only flashes of that skill in his freshman season—he made 4-of-6 three-pointers in his second college game, against Villanova, drilled 5-of-6 three-pointers in a close loss at Virginia and foiled Southern Cal's defensive strategy with three second half three-pointers in the East Regional title game.

"Chris' shooting has taken a back seat to some other parts of his game," Krzyzewski said. "When he brings that part up, he'll be the complete player we know he can be."

Duhon appeared to mature into that player with his summer play. This season, Duhon will team with Williams to give Duke the best backcourt in college basketball.

SF-DAHNTAY JONES (6-5, 206 lbs., JR, #30, Steinert HS/Trenton, N.J. & Rutgers). The transfer from Rutgers was a mystery man until last summer's USA Basketball Trials in Colorado Springs.

"He really turned some heads here," Syracuse coach Jim Boeheim said. "He was the best two-guard here—by far. He's not even the same [player I saw at Rutgers]. It's not even close."

Krzyzewski, who got to see the athletic wing man perform in practice all season, admits he was surprised by Jones' development.

"Dahntay did something this year that I didn't know was possible," the Duke coach said. "He's gotten better ... he's gotten a lot better. [St. John's transfer to Duke] Roshown McLeod got better, but not a lot better in the year he was out. The reason for that is you have no way of testing your skills in competition. Somehow, this kid created competition every day. Like he wanted to go after Jason if Jason got hot in practice. He wanted to go after Battier when Battier was dominating practice.

"He'll definitely be our best athlete next year."

Jones wasn't bad in his two seasons at Rutgers, where he averaged 16.0 points and 4.6 rebounds as a sophomore. He was also regarded as an excellent defender—a skill that has Krzyzewski excited.

Williams is excited about the chance to play alongside one of his oldest friends.

"I always wanted to play with Dahntay since I was a little kid," Williams said. "He played for an AAU team that had a lot of big names and I used to go down and see them play and say, 'Whoa, this guy is really good.' "

A lot of Duke opponents may be saying the same thing next year.

"He could be one of the stars of the league," Krzyzewski said. "There's no question about that."

SF-MICHAEL DUNLEAVY (6-8, 220 lbs. JR, #34, 12.6 ppg, 5.7 rpg, 2.6 apg, 1.4 spg, 29.2 minutes, .474 FG, .373 3PT, .694 FT, Jesuit HS/Portland, Ore.). Perhaps the most controversial recruiting decision Krzyzewski ever made involved Mike Dunleavy.

It was late in the summer of 1998, when the Duke coach backed off highly rated shooting guard Casey Jacobsen in order to pursue the gangly son of Portland Trail Blazers coach Mike Dunleavy. Jacobsen has gone on to establish himself as one of college basketball's top players at Stanford. But Krzyzewski's gamble was justified on the night of April 2, 2001, when Mike "Don't call me Junior" Dunleavy scored 21 points and drilled four second-half three-pointers to help Duke edge Arizona in the NCAA title game.

"He carried us tonight," teammate Chrus Duhon said. "He hit some huge shots—they were all net. You could see it in his eyes."

Although Dunleavy's three-point shooting proved the difference in Minneapolis, that's not why Krzyzewski preferred the slender coach's son to the deadly scorer. The Duke coach fell in love with his versatility.

"He's as skilled a basketball player as we've ever recruited," Krzyzewski said. "He can pass. He can dribble. He knows court balance and he's a very graceful player. I'll use him a lot like Grant."

That's Grant as in Grant Hill, another slender 6-8 forward with a wide range of skills. Nobody is comparing Dunleavy to Hill yet, although their sophomore numbers do look very similar. And at least one well-known observer ranks Dunleavy in pretty heady company.

"He'll play in the league, no question," Magic Johnson told Sports Illustrated. "He's got Larry Bird's shot, my passing game and his father's smarts."

Dunleavy is uncomfortable with such comparisons. That's one reason he asked the Duke sports information office to stop listing him as Mike Dunleavy, Jr. He wants to be his own man.

"I really don't like to compare myself with anybody," he said. "But I have watched guys and tried to take things from them. I absolutely consider myself a student of the game."

Dunleavy was at his best in some of Duke's toughest games. He burned Illinois for 21 points in the ACC/Big Ten Challenge. He helped Duke survive a surprisingly difficult trip to Clemson with a 17-point, 17-rebound effort. He stunned North Carolina with 24 points and 13 rebounds in the ACC title game. He had 15 points, hitting 3-of-4 three-pointers, nine rebounds and four assists in Duke's second-round NCAA victory over Missouri.

Is it any wonder that teammate Shane Battier suggested that Dunleavy should be rated a national player-of-the -year candidate in 2002?

"He's as complete a basketball player as you'll find in the country," Battier said. "He can do it all—pass, shoot, dribble, drive."

Dunleavy is likely to play more power forward this season after the departure of Battier. He's added 15 pounds of muscle and he continues to grow. Although officially listed at 6-8, he appears to be almost as tall as the 6-11 Sanders.

Krzyzewski is hoping that Dunleavy can use his breakout performance against Arizona as a launching pad into this season. If Duke hopes to repeat, Dunleavy, one of the game's best complementary players as a sophomore, has to accept a starring role as a junior.

C/F-CARLOS BOOZER (6-9, 270 lbs., JR, #4, 13.3 ppg, 6.5 rpg, 1.3 apg, 0.9 spg, 0.9 bpg, 25.6 minutes, .604 FG, .719 FT, Douglas HS/Juneau, Alaska) Duke probably would not have won the national championship if Boozer had not broken his foot, forcing Krzyzewski to made radical changes in his lineup and rotation.

But it's equally probable that Duke wouldn't have won the title if Boozer had not recovered in time to play a significant role in Final Four victories against Maryland and Arizona. In 25 minutes against the Terps, he had 19 points, making 7-of-8 field goals, and neutralized Maryland big man Lonny Baxter in the middle. He had 12 points and 12 rebounds in 30 minutes in the title game against the Wildcats and kept 7-footer Loren Woods under control.

Boozer is the second Alaskan to made his mark on college basketball in the "lower 48", following in the footsteps of former Duke standout Trajan Langdon.

His career has been marred by two broken bones—one in his left foot just before the start of his freshman season and one in his right foot late in his sophomore year. Despite those problems, Boozer has established himself as one of college basketball's better big men—a physical post player with quick feet and the ability to score with either hand.

He has topped the 20-point mark 17 times in his career and last year led the ACC in field-goal percentage. His 26 points helped Duke edge Temple in the title game of the Preseason NIT. He was a perfect 8-of-8 from the field and 9-of-9 from the line in a 25-point effort against Clemson. And just before his injury, Boozer's 25-point, 13-rebound effort made the difference in a narrow victory over Wake Forest.

Yet, Krzyzewski said that Boozer is still just tapping his potential.

"Carlos is still very much a work in progress," Krzyzewski said. "He's had some outstanding games. In some games he's showed his youth and in some games we haven't learned how to use him yet."

Boozer got something of a wake-up call in the summer before his sophomore year. He showed up at the tryouts for the U.S. national team out of shape and was cut. That failure hit him hard.

"He really wants to be an outstanding player," Krzyzewski said. "He's very willing to learn. He craves instruction and he takes responsibility."

Boozer proved that he's learned from his mistakes when he showed up in Colorado Springs last summer for the 2001 USA Basketball Trials. This time he was in shape, claimed one of the 12 places on the national team for the World Championships for Young Men and was a dominant player on the team that represented the United States in Japan.

The burly Alaskan will enter his junior year at Duke on track to graduate after this season. He understands that he needs a big year to put himself in position to enter the NBA draft.

"I need to have a good year and I'd like to win another national championship," he said. "But I expect a good year."

Boozer, who will be a power forward in the pros, may get a chance to show off his skills at that position this season. Krzyzewski plans to use Boozer and rapidly developing center Sanders together as part of his rotation.

KEY RESERVES

C-MATT CHRISTENSEN (6-10, 247 lbs., SR, #41, 1.6 ppg, 2.3 rpg, 8.4 minutes, .586 FG, .438 FT, Belmont HS/Belmont, Mass.). If it seems like Christensen has been at Duke forever, that's because he has.

Christensen, the nephew of former NBA center Greg Kite, arrived on the Duke campus in the fall of 1995 when Cherokee Parks and Erik Meek were the big men on the roster. After seeing just a little action as a freshman in 1995-96, Christensen took two years off for a Mormon mission in Germany. When he returned to Duke in 1998-99, he took a red-shirt year, battling Elton Brand and Chris Burgess every day in practice.

Christensen finally got a chance to contribute as a 22-year-old sophomore, but his lack of mobility—a problem aggravated by a pair of bad knees—has limited him to spot duty over the last two seasons. There are times when his bulk is useful inside, but Christensen just can't keep up with Duke's normal fast-paced tempo.

His best effort as a junior was a six-point, seven-rebound performance in 23 minutes against North Carolina A&T. He banged with UNC's massive Brendan Haywood for 12 minutes in Duke's late-season victory in Chapel Hill, but that was his high point, Down the stretch, 6-4 walk-on Reggie Love got more minutes in the pivot.

Christensen underwent off-season knee surgery that could help his mobility. Even so, the development of Casey Sanders and the return of Nick Horvath to the roster will cut into Christensen's minutes. He remains a useful player, but only in a limited role.

G-DANIEL EWING (6-3, 175 lbs., FR, #5, 18 ppg, 5.4 rpg, 3.5 apg, 4.0 spg, .512 FG, .440 3PT, .790 FT, Willowridge HS/Sugarland, Texas). Duke's only scholarship recruit is vaulting from a championship high school program to the defending college champs.

Ewing teamed with Texas recruit T.J. Ford and two other Division I prospects to lead Willowridge to back-to-back Texas state championships and a 39-0 record last season. His prep coach Ronnie Courtney (now the head coach at Texas Southern) believes Ewing's experience as part of a great team should help ease his transition from prep stardom to a supporting role at Duke.

"I think he'll adjust well," Courtney said. "Dan is an extremely hard worker and his intelligence will render him playing time."

Krzyzewski can see a role for his freshman guard, even in a backcourt dominated by veterans.

"The way we play and the athleticism we'll have, having him come off the bench will make that better," Krzyzewski said. "We won't have to change styles to make substitutions."

Ewing is a versatile guard, capable of playing both the point and the wing.

"He and T.J. were interchangeable," Courtney said. "It wasn't a situation where we had a definite two guard. We were fine with him at the point."

Ewing was the leading scorer for Willowridge, but it was his role as the team's defensive stopper that might earn him more playing time at Duke.

"When we played teams with a great scorer, it was his job to shut that scorer down," Courtney said. "As defensive-minded as Duke is, that could be a real asset."

F/C-NICK HORVATH (6-10, 230 lbs., SO, #3, 2.8 ppg, 2.3 rpg, 9.0 minutes, .304 FG, .167 3PT, Mounds View HS/ Arden, Minn.). Not everything went right for Duke in 2001. Even in a national championship season, the Blue Devils had to cope with some bad luck. And the loss of Horvath for the season with a bad foot certainly qualifies as misfortune.

The sharp-shooting big man from Minnesota was expected to play a major role off the bench last season. He offers toughness in the post, nice passing skills and a surprisingly good three-point touch.

But the former Minnesota Mr. Basketball was able to limp through just six early season games. He sat out the rest of the season, robbing Krzyzewski of the player he expected to provide frontcourt depth. He'll return this season, still a sophomore after being rewarded with a medical hardship season.

Krzyzewski can only hope Horvath fulfils the promise he showed in 32 games as a freshman in 1999-2000. Called Duke's "secret weapon" by Chris Carrawell, Horvath saved a game against DePaul by banking in a game-winning three-pointer. He hit 3-of-4 three-pointers and scored 13 points in 18 minutes in a victory over Wake Forest that clinched the ACC regular-season title. He hit 2-of-3 three-pointers to help pull out a difficult game at Clemson.

"I think having Nick back will be big," Krzyzewski said. "I think he'll be a solid guy. He can score facing the basket. He has perimeter skills."

Horvath's return should give Krzyzewski a lot of frontcourt options in the coming season. He'll be able to sub for Boozer in the post or to team with another big man if the Duke coach wants to go with a big lineup.

F-REGGIE LOVE (6-4, 225 lbs., SO, #42, 1.3 ppg., 1.6 rpg., 6.2 minutes, .529 FG, .588 FT, Providence Day School/Charlotte, N.C.). Love, with his broad shoulders and long arms, bears a curious resemblance to the last Duke player to wear No. 42—All-American Elton Brand.

Of course, Love is four inches shorter than Brand and not nearly as dominant on the basketball floor. But the Blue Devil football standout—he's a wide receiver with NFL potential—made a surprising impact on the basketball court last season. When Boozer broke his foot against Maryland, Love suddenly went from being a little-used walk-on to Duke's top frontcourt reserve.

Love was surprisingly effective playing in the post against players such as Maryland's Lonny Baxter and UNC's Brendan Haywood. His finest moment came in the ACC title game against the Tar Heels, when he abused the 7-foot Haywood for eight rebounds in 16 minutes and teamed with Casey Sanders to limit the future NBA first-round draft choice to nine points on 4-of-10 shooting.

Love, who will join the team after Duke's football season ends in late November, might have a harder time showing his stuff this season with the return of Horvath and the development of Boozer and Sanders. But his toughness will be put to good use in practice. And if injuries or other disasters do strike, Krzyzewski has to know that he's always got Love to fall back on.

C-CASEY SANDERS (6-11, 230 lbs., JR, #20, 2.5 ppg, 1.8 rpg, 0.9 bpg, 10.7 minutes, .467 FG, .517 FT, Tampa Prep/Tampa, Fla.). The injury that sidelined Boozer was the best thing that ever happened to Sanders.

Before Boozer went down with a broken foot in the next to last regular season game, Sanders was languishing on the Duke bench, his sophomore season as unproductive as his freshman year. The former Prep All-American from Florida remained a tantalizing waste of talent—a tall, quick shot blocker who lacked the strength or the confidence to play in the ACC.

That changed in the final weeks of the season when Boozer's misfortune thrust Sanders into the starting line-up, jump-starting his career.

"I didn't want it to happen this way," Sanders said. "I looked at it like, 'How am I going to handle this?' "

Sanders handled it surprisingly well, stepping into the starting lineup for Duke's final 10 games, including the Blue Devils' successful ACC and NCAA tournament runs. He didn't put up big numbers, but he was effective on defense and occasionally on the boards. He had seven points, four rebounds and two blocked shots—including one crucial block of a Terence Morris lay-up to protect a two-point lead with 97 seconds left—to help Duke edge Maryland in an ACC semifinal.

"I hate to see it happen today, but I like to see a player step up in a big game," Maryland coach Gary Williams said. "He's taken some criticism and it's good for him that he had a big game today."

Sanders' strong finish is something he can build on.

"It's always been a matter of confidence for Casey," teammate Chris Duhon said.

Krzyzewski is looking forward to see how far the bulked-up Sanders—he added 20 pounds to his lanky frame last summer—progressed in the off-season. He'll explore combinations that have the 6-11 Sanders and the 6-9 Boozer in the game together.

"Casey has shown he can play away from the basket," Krzyzewski said.

He's also shown he can block shots. He ranked 11th in the ACC in blocks last season, despite averaging less than 11 minutes a game.

"There are better scorers than me," Sanders said. "Defensively, I'm not concerned."

OTHER RETURNEES

G-ANDRE BUCKNER (5-10, 170 lbs., JR, #15, 0.2 ppg, 0.5 rpg, 0.3 apg, 3.7 minutes, .167 FG, .250 FT, University Heights HS/Hopkinsville, Ky.). The younger brother of former Clemson standout Greg Buckner was planning to walk on at Tennessee until Krzyzewski, scrambling after the unexpected departure of Will Avery to the NBA, offered the small, quick playmaker a scholarship at Duke.

Krzyzewski made it clear that he was bringing Buckner in as a practice player. He's been superb in that role, battling classmate Jason Williams in workouts every day.

His significant game moments have been rare. Usually used as a mop-up player, Buckner did contribute to one hard-fought win in his freshman season, when foul trouble forced him into a game at Clemson. He made 2-of-3 free throws and had a steal down the stretch to help the Blue Devils pull away for the victory.

The presence of Williams and Duhon, plus the addition of Ewing, makes it even more unlikely that Buckner will see significant game action. But he remains a valuable practice player and if Krzyzewski is desperate for some help at the point, Buckner can be counted on as a solid ball handler and a pesky defender.

G-ANDY BORMAN (6-1, 181 lbs., JR, #40, 0.9 ppg, 0.3 rpg, 2.4 minutes, 7 appearances, Bradenton Academy/ Morrisville, N.C.). Krzyzewski's nephew is at Duke on a soccer scholarship and won't join the basketball team until that season is over in late November or early December—unlike the Duke football team, which will send Love to K's squad after its season, the Blue Devil soccer has a good chance for postseason play.

That's no hardship. Borman is strictly a practice player for the basketball team.

OTHER NEWCOMERS

G-MARK CAUSEY (6-4, 184 lbs., FR, #45, 26.9 ppg, 4.6 rpg, 2.8 apg, 3.6 spg, .430 3PT, .780 FT, East Hall HS/Gainesville, Ga.). Georgia's Class AA Player of the Year is an exceptional walk-on, although it's hard to conceive of a walk-on getting playing time in Duke's talented backcourt.

"Mark's willing to take his chances," East Hall coach Seth Vining said. "He knows it's going to be tough. You know that every year, Duke brings in a bunch of All-Americans. But Mark's a pretty good player. I think he'll surprise some people at Duke."

Causey, rated one of the nation's top 20 wing guard prospects by one recruiting service, led East Hall to the first state title in school history.

QUESTIONS

Leadership? Former Wake Forest coach Dave Odom labeled Shane Battier as one of the greatest leaders in ACC history. And fifth-year senior Nate James wasn't bad either. Duke's only senior this season is a little-used reserve center. Can anybody step up and replace Battier and James as the team leaders?

Focus? The starting lineup will contain five potential NBA lottery picks. At least two—and maybe more—will be headed for pro basketball after this season. Will all five be able to focus and sacrifice as necessary to make Duke a championship contender again ... or is there a danger of individuals trying to showcase their skills?

ANSWERS

Talent! Nobody else will start five potential NBA lottery picks. And unlike last season, there's plenty of depth

with Sanders and Horvath providing frontcourt options, while Ewing offers a very talented third guard.

Krzyzewski! The Hall of Fame coach is at the top of his skills. Nobody is better than Coach K at getting his team ready to play night after night and he certainly knows how to win in postseason. If anybody can repeat as national champion, he can—indeed, he's the only coach who has repeated since John Wooden retired.

Defense! Even without Battier, there's a chance that this team could be better than last year's excellent defensive team. Duhon is Duke's best on-the-ball defender since Hurley. Jones is a superb wing defender. Sanders is the best shot blocker Krzyzewski has ever had. Plus, there's enough depth this year to play the all-out pressure that last year's team couldn't.

Backcourt! Williams and Duhon will almost certainly be the nation's best backcourt. But they have a chance to be even better than that—they could turn out to be one of the best backcourts in college basketball history. Not only are both supremely gifted players, there's a chemistry between them that makes them better together than apart. It's no accident that Duke is 10-0 when both are in the starting lineup.

DUKE 2000-2001 RESULTS

#Princeton	87-50
#Villanova	98-85
##Texas	95-69
##Temple	63-61
Army	91-48
###Illinois	78-77
@Temple	98-68
Davidson	102-60
Michigan	104-61
@Portland	97-64
####Stanford (L)	83-84
North Carolina A&T	108-73
@Florida State	99-72
Clemson	115-74
@NC State	84-78
Virginia	103-61
Boston College	97-75
@Georgia Tech	98-77
Wake Forest	85-62
@Maryland	98-96
North Carolina (L)	83-85
Florida State	100-58
@Clemson	81-64
NC State	101-75
@Virginia (L)	89-91
@St. John's	91-59
Georgia Tech	98-54
@Wake Forest	82-80
Maryland (L)	80-91
@North Carolina	95-81
#####North Carolina State	76-61
#####Maryland	84-82
#####North Carolina	79-53
######Monmouth	95-52
######Missouri	94-81
######UCLA	76-63
######Southern Cal	79-69
######Maryland	95-84
######Arizona	82-72

#Preseason NIT in Cameron Indoor Stadium
##Preseason NIT in New York
###ACC/Big Ten Challenge in Greensboro, NC
####Pete Newell Challenge in Oakland, CA
#####ACC Tournament in Atlanta
######NCAA Tournament
@Road Games

BLUE RIBBON ANALYSIS

BACKCOURT	A+
BENCH/DEPTH	A
FRONTCOURT	A-
INTANGIBLES	A

It's not fun being No. 1. But Krzyzewski has been through it before. He's used to the spotlight. He's used to the pressure. His 1991-92 team spent every week of the season atop the polls en route to college basketball's only back-to-back titles since UCLA's seven-year run ended in 1974.

Yet, Krzyzewski would be the first to point out that his 1992 title team needed a miracle just to reach the Final Four. Without Christian Laettner's unforgettable shot in the last second of overtime against Kentucky in the East Regional title game, the '92 Blue Devils would have been

just another unsuccessful title defender.

Will the 2001-2002 Blue Devils need a similar miracle to give Krzyzewski his fourth NCAA championship?

History would suggest that it won't be easy, even for a team as talented as the one Duke will put on the floor this season. But history would also suggest that nobody is better equipped to confront the vicissitudes of fate better than Coach K. He's won as a huge underdog (1991). He's won as the preseason favorite (1992). He even won last season after losing his one supposedly irreplaceable player to injury.

His 2001-2002 team certainly has the talent to repeat. Krzyzewski wonders about leadership, but as long as he is on the bench, that's an empty concern. Duke is as well positioned to make a title run as any team the veteran coach has ever had.

That doesn't mean that the Blue Devils are a lock to cut down the nets in Atlanta. It just means their chances look better going into the season than anybody else's.

(A.F.)

Illinois 2

LOCATION	Champaign, IL
CONFERENCE	Big Ten
LAST SEASON	27-8 (.771)
CONFERENCE RECORD	13-3 (t-1st)
STARTERS LOST/RETURNING	2/3
NICKNAME	Fighting Illini
COLORS	Orange & Blue
HOMECOURT	Assembly Hall (16,450)
COACH	Bill Self (Oklahoma State '85)
RECORD AT SCHOOL	27-8 (1 year)
CAREER RECORD	157-88 (8 years)
ASSISTANTS	Billy Gillispie (SW Texas State '83)
	Wayne McClain (Bradley '77)
	Norman Roberts (Queens College '87)
TEAM WINS (last 5 years)	22-23-14-22-27
RPI (last 5 years)	25-24-63-23-5
2000-01 FINISH	Lost in NCAA Elite Eight.

COACH AND PROGRAM

Bill Self is fresh off a feat never before accomplished by a college basketball coach. He's taken two consecutive teams to the NCAA Elite Eight—at two different schools.

Self is often referred to as your prototypical "hot young coach." If that's true, the last two seasons must be akin to a four-alarm fire.

Of course, Self's present situation is not entirely his doing. Normally when there's a coaching change at a major-conference school like Illinois, it's a pretty good bet the new guy is in for a rebuilding job. But in Self's case, he walked into college basketball's equivalent of a generous Christmas gift.

The 38-year-old Oklahoman was coming off a 32-5 season at Tulsa in 1999-00, one that had earned him several national coach-of-the-year honors, when he was tabbed to replace Lon Kruger upon the departure to the NBA's Atlanta Hawks. What Kruger left behind was a highly talented squad coming off an NCAA second round appearance and primed to achieve exactly the kind of national prominence Self would help it achieve.

With the "Peoria Pipeline" of Frank Williams, Marcus Griffin and Sergio McClain all in their junior or senior years, plus the presence of reigning Big Ten co-freshman of the year Brian Cook (11.2 ppg, 6.1 rpg,), the Illini were destined for preseason Top 10 status no matter who would be coaching.

But Self deserves significant credit for taking over the program just four months before embarking on what would become the school's best season in 12 years: a 27-8 record, a share of the Big Ten regular season title (with Michigan State) and coming within one game of the Final Four, falling 87-81 to eventual national runner-up Arizona.

From his arrival, Self preached tough defense, and the Illini responded by holding opponents to 38.6 percent shooting from the field, third best nationally and the school's top performance since 1955-56. They also led the Big Ten in three-point shooting (.390) and averaged their highest rebounding total (40.0 per game) since 1979.

And Self defeated a problem that can often bring down even the most talented squads: clashing egos.

"When we first got the job, we had been told we had a really good team," Self said. "On the flip side, we knew something was missing. Chemistry, from what I was told, wasn't that strong, and that's something we can take pride in is the guys committed to each other, we liked each other and we became a team."

Illinois didn't have to wait long to find out whether it would become a great team, thanks to a brutal schedule put together by Kruger before he left. ("Lon must have known he was leaving," joked Self.) It began at the Maui Invitational, where the Illini knocked off sixth-ranked Maryland and came within three of then-No. 1 Arizona. Six days later, they again faced the nation's No. 1 team in the nation, this time Duke, in Greensboro, N.C. They lost by only one, and Self began to realize what he was dealing with.

On Dec. 9, the Illini stunned No. 7 Seton Hall by rallying from 21 down to win in overtime. And a week later they avenged their loss to Arizona in a game at Chicago's United Center. Their only remaining non-conference slip was a road loss at Texas. And in Big Ten season, they notched win streaks of four and five games, the watermark coming in their only date of the season with Michigan State, a 77-66 victory at Assembly Hall.

"When we came from 21 down to beat a pretty good Seton Hall team, I knew we would be good, but I didn't know how quickly that would happen," Self said. "It gave us some confidence and let us know we can get this done. That was a huge win."

Yet despite its success and consistency during the regular season, Illinois may have been one of the more anonymous No. 1 NCAA seeds in recent memory heading into the tournament.

In only his second year starting, Williams had become a prolific scorer and the Illini's closest thing to a star, but not necessarily a household commodity like Shane Battier at Duke or Casey Jacobsen at Stanford.

Rather, the team's forte was balance. The roster was one of the deepest in the country, with nine players averaging double-digit minutes.

This year, the Illini lose two of the more valuable guys from that rotation in McClain and Griffin—who had five years' starting experience between them—but still figure to be a very deep team. Three freshmen and a junior college transfer join nine returning letterman to form a fully-stacked roster.

"There's seven guys that, barring injury, will play a lot of minutes," said Self. "Then there's going to be about two other guys who emerge. And it may not be the same two every game, it may vary based on scouting reports and who is playing well."

The Elite Eight was nice, but there's a definite anticipation in Champaign that this will be the team to return Illinois to the Final Four for the first time since Lou Henson's famed 1989 team of Kendall Gill, Nick Anderson and Marcus Liberty.

Self knows it. He also knows the program will lose at least five of its top seven players after the season, including Williams, a fourth-year junior who it's understood will turn pro after another good season.

"I know we had a good year last year, but it was expected," Self said. "The Elite Eight game, other than the national championship, is the toughest one to lose. It's happened to [Self] two years in a row. You're kind of the lost soul, so to speak. People remember Final Four teams and Sweet 16 teams, but very rarely do people talk about the teams that made the Elite Eight, maybe because it's the same weekend [as the Sweet 16]. It's a tough, tough loss, and it was disappointing, because we were right there."

Steps are being taken to ensure a smooth transition after next spring's expected exodus. They include the hiring of a particularly notable new assistant: Wayne McClain, the Peoria prep coach who led future Illini Williams, Griffin and son Sergio to three straight state titles at Manual High School. The Illini also have commitments from standout Chicago point guard Dee Brown and Tobacco Road wing guard J.R. Morris.

In the meantime, though, the wheels are in motion for a memorable 2001-02 season. Self has constructed a schedule equally if not more challenging than last year's— one that includes Arizona, Maryland, Missouri, Georgia Tech, Arkansas and Gonzaga—knowing he has a veteran team that can handle it. And a couple of injury-prone players seemed to be in good shape headed into fall.

"There's no doubt about it this has a chance to be a special team," Self said. "That's on paper, though. If we get a little lucky, keep guys healthy, this could be our year. The pieces are in place, now we've got to make it happen."

2001-2002 SCHEDULE

Nov.	16	Gonzaga
	19	#Eastern Illinois
	22-24	##Las Vegas Invitational
	27	*@Maryland
Dec.	1	Texas A&M-Corpus Christi
	4	**Arizona
	8	***Arkansas
	16	Western Illinois
	18	Illinois State
	22	****Missouri
	29	Loyola-Chicago
Jan.	2	Minnesota
	5	@Wisconsin
	9	@Purdue
	12	Michigan
	15	Iowa
	23	Wisconsin
	27	@Indiana
	29	@Ohio State
Feb.	3	Michigan State
	7	@Michigan
	9	Purdue
	12	@Michigan State
	16	@Seton Hall
	20	Penn State
	23	@Northwestern
	26/27	Indiana
	2/3	@Minnesota
	7-10	###Big Ten Tournament

@Road Games
*ACC-Big Ten Challenge
**Phoenix, AZ
***Chevrolet Shootout at United Center, Chicago
****Braggin' Rights Game, Savvis Center in St. Louis
#First round, Las Vegas Invitational
##Las Vegas, NV (schedule determined after first-round games; Pool 1 includes Georgia Tech, Illinois, Eastern Illinois, Pennsylvania. Pool 2 includes Iowa State, Saint Louis, Hartford, Southern Illinois)
###Conseco Fieldhouse, Indianapolis, IN

STARTERS NOT RETURNING

SF-SERGIO McCLAIN (6-4, 7.5 ppg, 5.5 rpg, 2.9 apg, 1.3 spg, 25.5 minutes, .401 FG, .375 3PT, .552 FT). Of the three members of last year's squad from Wayne McClain's Peoria Manual teams, Sergio was the only one to play in Champaign immediately upon leaving Peoria. Last season was the first since his freshman year an injury didn't slow him for at least a few games.

A scorer McClain was not; he never averaged more than the 8.6 points per game he notched as a sophomore and he shot below 40 percent three of his four seasons. Yet he became universally regarded as the Illini's unsung hero. In three years as a starter, the small forward did all the little things, usually drawing the opposition's top scorer defensively and becoming a master at taking charges.

As a senior, McClain stepped up his rebounding considerably, having averaged 3.4 a game his first three seasons. He led the Illini with 11 rebounds in their game against No. 1 Duke.

C-MARCUS GRIFFIN (6-9, 11.3 ppg, 6.0 rpg, 1.0 apg, 1.3 bpg, 24.7 minutes, .533 FG, .000 3PT, .592 FT). Another of the Peoria triumvirate, Griffin played two years at Lincoln Junior College before arriving in Champaign. Upon doing so, it didn't take long to establish himself as one of the elite post players in the Big Ten.

As a senior, Griffin's production went up in almost every area. He led the Illini in rebounding on seven occasions and, along with Brian Cook, formed a tough inside duo that contributed to Illinois' stout defensive shooting percentage. In a notable performance, he held eventual first round draft pick Samuel Dalembert of Seton Hall to three points while notching 24 points and 13 rebounds of his own.

OTHERS NOT RETURNING

G-NATE MAST (5-11, 0.8 ppg, 0.6 rpg, 3.0 minutes, .357 FG, .571 3PT, .250 FT). A four-year walk-on and Champaign native, the point guard saw his most playing time his sophomore year, appearing in all but one game and starting four. He averaged 2.1 points that season.

But with the arrival of Frank Williams in 1999, Mast's

point guard minutes dried up. He saw action in 20 games as a senior.

G-JOE CROSS (6-0, 1.1 ppg, 0.7 rpg, 2.4 minutes, .333 FG, .182 3PT, 1.000 FT). The walk-on transferred from Florida International in the fall of 1998 and became eligible midseason his junior year. His older brother Dan starred for Kruger on his 1994 Final Four team at Florida.

The younger Cross recorded 10 double-double games his freshman year at FIU but was relegated to reserve duty as a sophomore and played only in mop-up duty in two seasons for the Illini.

PROJECTED STARTERS

PG-FRANK WILLIAMS (6-3, 205, JR, #30, 14.9 ppg, 3.7 rpg, 4.4 apg, 2.0 spg, 32.2 minutes, .410 FG, .320 3PT, .806 FT, Manual HS/Peoria, Ill.). Williams wasted no time dismissing rumors of his possible departure for the NBA, announcing his return in the locker room after Illinois' last game. He did so despite projections he would go high in the first round.

A similar announcement probably won't occur next year, so Self and most fans are planning as if this is Williams' senior season. If it goes like the last one, there will still be plenty left to enjoy.

The 1998 Illinois Mr. Basketball who sat out his first year as a partial qualifier, Williams was the 2001 Big Ten Player of the Year and a third-team All-American. He cut down on many of the rookie mistakes he made the year before, showing more care with his shot selection even while becoming more of an offensive threat.

"We had a lot of balance [last year.] When guys were able to get shots, Frank was very content in [getting them the ball]," said Self. "He thinks like a point guard, but when the game's on the line, he says, 'Now it's time for me to put ball in my hands.' "

For exposure purposes, it helped that many of Williams' biggest games came against Illinois' toughest opponents. His scoring average soared to 19.4 against the Illini's nine Top 25 opponents, including a career-high 30 in the Sweet 16 against Kansas. Williams also seemed to come to life in the second half of games, scoring 61 percent of his points after halftime.

Williams was chosen one of 14 finalists for the USA Basketball World Championship for Young Men team over the summer but had to withdraw after injuring his right wrist during a practice fall.

SG-CORY BRADFORD (6-3, 200 lbs., SR, #13, 9.9 ppg, 2.5 rpg, 1.8 apg, 0.7 spg, 29.8 minutes, .379 FG, .371 3PT, .797 FT, Rraleigh Egypt HS/Memphis, Tenn.). After his first two seasons in which he averaged 15.4 and 15.3 points respectively, it was Bradford, not backcourt mate Williams, who was tabbed preseason Big Ten Player of the Year.

But a knee injury suffered while playing for the USA Basketball select team in Hawaii late in the summer necessitated arthroscopic surgery in September. It didn't keep him out of any action, but it definitely had an effect on Bradford, whose scoring average slipped by more than five points and who finished as the team's fourth-leading scorer.

"He probably showed more toughness than anyone on team," Self said. "Expectations of him were high, but he knew the knee problem wasn't going to heal overnight. He played well through it, but a consistent, healthy Cory is a totally different athlete."

Bradford did make history last season with his first three-pointer against Arizona on Dec. 16. Having hit at least one trey every game since his college debut on Nov. 11, 1998, Bradford broke the NCAA record of 73 straight games, previously held by Virginia Tech's Wally Lancaster (1986-89). The streak would grow to 88 before ending on Feb. 13 against Wisconsin.

As for the knee, doctors told Bradford the best treatment would be rest, which he got plenty of in the off-season. Expect a return to pre-junior year form.

SF-LUCAS JOHNSON (6-8, 230 lbs., SR, #22, 5.0 ppg, 3.3 rpg, 1.7 apg, 0.6 spg, 17.4 minutes, .462 FG, .346 3PT, .747 FT, Maine West HS/Des Plaines, Ill.). With his shaved head and take-no-prisoners aggressiveness, "Luuuuke" has been Illini fans' favorite in the past. Whether their approval continues this year may depend on whether Johnson can acclimate himself to a greater role.

His first three seasons, Johnson has served primarily as McClain's backup, energizing the Illini with his rebounding ability and penchant for diving on the floor. Now, he leads a group also including Damir Krupalija, Sean Harrington, Brett Melton and junior college transfer Blandon Ferguson that will figure into two available starting spots.

"It's a big step going from the role of being the guy who provides a spark off the bench to a guy who can be a major contributor, but I think he's more than capable of handling it," Self said. "He can make open shots, he's a good rebounder for his position. On paper, he would appear to have the best chance to replace Serge."

One thing that will help Johnson is his versatility. While primarily known as a rebounder, he was also the Illini's second-leading three-point shooter. He can also draw fouls and convert at the free-throw line, like he did in a victory over Iowa last season, scoring 16 points on 8-of-9 free throws while also grabbing eight rebounds.

PF-BRIAN COOK (6-10, 240 lbs., JR, #34, 11.2 ppg, 6.1 rpg, 1.2 apg, 1.3 bpg, 24.2 minutes, .546 FG, .368 3PT, .802 FT, Lincoln HS/Lincoln, Ill.). Even with Williams and Bradford, Cook may be the Illini's most skilled player. In a poll of Big Ten players before last season, he was selected the Big Ten's "best future pro" by Sports Illustrated. And he has been selected to U.S. national teams each of the last two summers, averaging 8.0 points and 4.1 rebounds for the club that took gold at the World Championship for Young Men in Japan in August.

While Cook's post skills are obvious, having led the Illini in rebounding and blocked shots, he's also exceptionally versatile for his size. Last season he stepped back and hit 28-of-76 three-point attempts while also shooting nearly 90 percent from the free-throw line (35-of-39) in Big Ten play.

"One thing we'll be getting on Brian about is to become a dominant player for us day in and day out," Self said. "We're going to ask him to do more things because it's his time."

There were flashes of dominance at times last season. Like his 25-point, 11-rebound game against Missouri. Or a 22-point, 10-rebound day at Penn State.

But the Nittany Lion game also exposed Cook's one Achilles heel. That game, like in five others, he fouled out. He committed 118 fouls in 35 games, and managed to play only 10 minutes and take four shots in the season-ender to Arizona. Without Griffin around anymore, the Illini will need Cook to stay in more games, and for longer stretches.

C-ROBERT ARCHIBALD (6-11, 250 lbs., SR, #21, 7.2 ppg, 4.5 rpg, 0.6 apg, 0.8 bpg, 15.1 minutes, .588 FG, .738 FT, Lafayette HS/Ballwin, Mo.). If not for one game, Archibald could have been the Illini's secret weapon this season. But he's not exactly anonymous anymore after scoring 25 points—more than double all but one other game all season—and grabbing seven rebounds in the NCAAs against Arizona. This despite fouling out, something he did quite a bit last season (nine times).

Besides the Arizona game, Archibald's top efforts included 16 points (on 10-of-12 free throws) and 12 rebounds against Illinois-Chicago and 12 points and 12 rebounds against Penn State.

In addition to foul trouble, Archibald has been plagued throughout his career by chronic back pain that sometimes keeps him out of practice and, on a few occasions, games. He's sought opinions from several different doctors, who currently have him on a stretching regimen to try to limit the problem this season.

That could become important if Archibald, as expected, takes over Griffin's spot in the lineup. He started 28 games his first two seasons, and though he won't be expected to pour in 25 every night, his nice array of moves around the basket could come in handy. But he'll need to cut down on the fouls significantly if he plans to get serious minutes in the post.

KEY RESERVES

F-BLANDON FERGUSON (6-4, 220 lbs., JR, #23, 14.4 ppg, 5.6 rpg, .410 3PT, St. Joseph Notre Dame HS/Oakland, Calif. and College of Southern Idaho). Self knew the Illini would miss the unsung hero McClain, so he went out and found a McClain play-alike.

"Blandon reminds me a lot of Sergio," Self said. "He's a jack-of-all trades type player who I think will be a defensive stopper for us."

Ferguson handled that same role in junior college. Southern Idaho coach Derek Zeck buys into the McClain comparison.

"Blandon is a great kid who is big, strong, athletic wing player that can defend the one through four positions," Zeck said. "He can shoot the three and score off the dribble. Brandon's a Sergio McClain type player who can do a lot of things for you to help the team win."

Ferguson was a Top 50 recruit coming out of Oakland, Calif., where he played at Notre Dame High School, Jason Kidd's alma mater. Last year he was a third-team national junior college All-American.

Ferguson has the distinction of being the first California native to play basketball at Illinois since Glenn Potter in 1924.

G-SEAN HARRINGTON (6-3, 185 lbs., JR, #24, 5.7 ppg, 1.4 rpg, 1.2 apg, 0.8 spg, 17.6 minutes, .415 FG, .459 3PT, .692 FT, Elgin HS/Batlett, Ill.). When Harrington comes in the game, it's usually for one reason: to shoot. Despite playing less than half the game on average, he managed to toss up 111 attempts from behind the arc last year, making 51 of them to lead the Big Ten in three-point percentage. At one point last year, he made nine consecutive attempts spanning four games. And in the Maui Invitational against Arizona, he came off the bench to hit 5-of-9 three-point shots.

Harrington will likely play a similar role this year, though he could see more time in the lineup if Self elects to go with a small three-guard set, something he did with some success at Tulsa.

"He's certainly going to be a guy who could give us a spark, but he could maybe be a starter, I don't know," Self said. "You've got Cory and Frank, and then you've got some guys like Sean that could fit in just about anywhere. Somebody's got to emerge from that group. I'm certainly not opposed to playing three small guards if we can rebound, and Frank for one could be a pretty good rebounder."

F-DAMIR KRUPALIJA (6-9, 232 lbs., SR, #33, 4.8 ppg, 3.9 rpg, 0.7 apg, 0.6 spg, 10.4 minutes, .597 FG, .467 3PT, .679 FT, Boylan HS/Rockford, Ill.). For three years now, the Yugoslavian has been a key contributor to the Illini—when he's healthy. Arthroscopic knee surgery the day before practice started last year kept him out of eight of the season's first 14 games. And a laundry list of injuries sidelined him for five games and kept him in pain most others the year before.

"Damir is a guy who seems like he can turn an ankle walking to class," Self said. "He's certainly been injury prone to this point, but when healthy, he's one of the best rebounders around."

Headed into this season, Krupalija was indeed healthy, and if he remains so should push for added playing time in the post. He started slow last year because of the knee injury, but eventually came on strong. He notched a double-double with 15 points and 12 rebounds against Northwestern. Against Iowa, he registered 13 points and nine rebounds in only 18 minutes.

It's scary to think what Krupalija could do if he stays healthy and ever plays more than 20 minutes a game.

C-NICK SMITH (7-2, 240 lbs., FR, #45, redshirted in 2000-01, Bloomingdale HS/Valrico, Fla.). Smith arrived in Champaign last year a very lanky 7-2 and agreed to red-shirt while working to bulk up. That proved tough, as the rigors of practice and effects of the flu made it hard for him to retain weight after he put it on.

But Illinois can't afford to keep its first 7-footer in 13 years on the shelf any longer.

"Nick is a guy that has improved tremendously in the weight room and has increased his strength," Self said. "We'll count on him to give us minutes inside.

"He's very skilled offensively, can certainly alter shots defensively. He's just strength away from really having an impact."

OTHER RETURNEES

G-BRETT MELTON (6-5, 195 lbs., SO, #00, 1.5 ppg, 0.8 rpg, 5.6 minutes, .254 FG, .200 3PT, .625, Mahomet-Seymour HS/Mahomet, Ill.). Melton had all the credentials to be an impact freshman, considering he was ranked among the nation's top 100 recruits by analyst Bob Gibbons. He just picked the wrong time to enter the program.

Melton saw his best playing time early in the season, notching 16 minutes against Wisconsin-Milwaukee, 13 against Kansas State and 12 against Texas Southern. But by Big Ten season, the Illini's guard rotation was set, and Melton didn't even play in seven league games. With Williams, Bradford and Harrington back, it's hard to picture his PT getting significantly better.

G-JERRANCE HOWARD (6-1, SO, #25, 0.4 ppg, 0.4 rpg, 3.4 minutes, .267 FG, .500 FT, Peoria HS/Peoria, Ill.). Another Peoria native, Howard played alongside former Indiana Hoosier A.J. Guyton for one season at Peoria High. He redshirted in 1999-00, becoming eligible halfway through, and played for the first time last year. Like Melton, he found playing time in the backcourt to be sparse. In his best outing, he handed out four assists in 12 minutes against Wisconsin-Milwaukee.

OTHER NEWCOMERS

G-LUTHER HEAD (6-2, 170 lbs., FR, #4, 22.0 ppg, 8.0 rpg, 6.0 apg, Manley HS/Chicago). Amazingly, Head is Illinois' first Chicago Public League recruit since 1994, a drought some attribute to longtime Lou Henson assistant Jimmy Collins not getting the head coaching job upon Henson's 1996 departure. Collins is now the coach at Illinois-Chicago. The last two CPL players to wear the Illinois uniform were Bryant Notree and Kevin Turner.

An exceptional athlete, Head wowed onlookers at campus pickup games this summer with his leaping ability. He figures to be one of the cornerstones of the Illini's future but may play a limited role in a crowded backcourt this season.

"Luther's a really good athlete, just a good all-around perimeter player," Self said. "I'm sure we could go small and play him as the third guard, maybe as the second guard, maybe even the point. He's a very skilled athletic guy."

Head was recruited by former Illinois assistant Rob Judson, who later left to take the top job at Northern Illinois. Still, Self hopes the signing of head can open doors again in talent-rich Chicago.

"We feel that to be as good as Illinois can be, we must recruit the city of Chicago," Self said. "The [signing] of Luther Head to the University of Illinois will hopefully open doors for future recruits as well."

G-ROGER POWELL (6-6, 215 lbs., FR, #43, 20.7 rpg, 9.0 rpg, Joliet HS/Joliet, Ill.). A consensus Top 100 recruit, Powell is more physically ready to play immediately than Head but is not as quick. He was plagued by injuries his senior year but appears to finally be healthy.

"I see him playing primarily at this time as a perimeter player, but he's certainly a guy who could play either inside or outside," Self said. "Roger is an athletic wing player who can play more than one position. He's a good shooter who can become an excellent shooter. He can put the ball on the floor and take it to the basket."

Powell, a good student, committed to Illinois when Kruger was still the coach.

"We're also very excited to recruit a prospect out of the Joliet Township program run by Bob Koskosky," said Self, who has committed to stocking his team with in-state players. "The previous staff had done a great job recruiting Roger and we are very happy he held to his commitment."

G-NICK HUGE (6-5, 200 lbs., JR, #31, 4.6 ppg, 2.6 rpg, 16.0 minutes, .419 FG, .1000 FT, .423 3PT, Charlotte Christian HS/Charlotte, N.C. and Appalachian State). Huge was recruited to Appalachian State by Buzz Peterson, who later replaced Self at Tulsa and is now at Tennessee.

Huge played in just 12 games at Appalachian State, leaving after the Mountaineers' Dec. 21 game against Richmond. He reached double figures twice, scoring 10 points against Richmond and 10 against UNC Asheville.

With his shooting ability, Huge might be able to help the Illini in certain situations. He becomes eligible in December for the spring semester.

QUESTIONS

Foul trouble? One of Illinois' few weaknesses last year was foul trouble, evidenced most notably in the ugly Elite Eight game against Arizona in which the Illini had a whopping 36 fouls. In that game, six players fouled out, putting almost the entire onus on Williams. He made only 3-of-15 shots, and it was amazing Illinois stayed as close as it did. On the season, there were 29 disqualifications among Illinois players. Archibald had nine on his own despite averaging less than 20 minutes a game. Can it be rectified?

Injury woes? Injuries have hovered around the program for what seems like several years. Last year Bradford and Krupalija were hit hardest. This season, 29-year trainer Rod Cardinal would like to take it easy for once. Though this team figures to get the same minutes from its bench as last year, the actual number of players involved will probably decrease. Keeping the main contributors healthy becomes that much more important.

Schedule? Coaches always walk a fine line between under-scheduling and over-scheduling. Last year's brutal non-conference schedule proved the perfect touch for a growing squad. Self hopes the same trick works again this season. "It's a monster schedule, but a lot of it had to do with the type of team we had coming back," Self said. "We have a veteran team, and with guys having gone through it once, should pick it up a little better. But with the type of teams we're playing, you could play well and leave sad with just about every team we play in the non-conference."

ANSWERS

Depth! In a year when Michigan State has only eight scholarship players and Arizona, last year's nemesis, lost four starters to the NBA, the Illini again have one of the nation's most fortified rosters. They may be able to go nine or 10 deep depending on how the freshmen develop.

"I think we'll have a deep bench," Self said. "I can see this team going nine deep, but I don't know if it will be equal minutes nine deep like it was last year. When you look at the roster, you could make a pretty good case for each guy."

Versatility! The Illini possess a little bit of everything. Size? Cook and Smith. Speed? Williams and Bradford. Shooting? Bradford and Harrington. Toughness? Archibald and Johnson.

All of which should create tremendous match-up problems for Illinois' opponents. Looking around the Big Ten, there is plenty of talent but hardly a team that, like Illinois, seems to have everything. Iowa may be the one exception. The Illini and Hawkeyes swapped blowouts on each other's courts last season.

Frank Williams! Having Williams back for a third year should prove huge for the Illini. He could easily wind up a first team All-American just by producing similarly to what he did a year ago. The amazing thing is that, despite considerable buzz surrounding him, Williams never seriously considered the NBA after last season. He immediately announced he was returning, and Self had to convince him just to look into his standing. In an age where far less developed players forsake school—and still get millions—Williams' apparent devotion to improvement is refreshing.

ILLINOIS 2000-2001 RESULTS

Maine	86-57
#UNLV	74-69
#Maryland	90-80
#Arizona (L)	76-79
Texas Southern	86-67
##Duke (L)	77-78
@Kansas State	76-56
Wisconsin-Milwaukee	85-44
Seton Hall	87-79
Arizona	81-73
@Missouri	86-81
@Texas (L)	64-72
Illinois-Chicago	77-64
Minnesota	80-64
Ohio State	83-68
@Iowa (L)	62-78
Michigan	80-51
@Northwestern	63-49
Penn State	92-60
@Mighigan	55-51
@Penn State (L)	95-98
Northwestern	84-59
Michigan State	77-66
@Purdue	82-61
Wisconsin	68-67
@Indiana	67-61
@Ohio State (L)	61-63
Iowa	89-63
@Minnesota	67-59
###Purdue	83-66
###Indiana (L)	56-58
####Northwestern State	96-54
####Charlotte	79-61
####Kansas	80-64
####Arizona	81-87

#Maui Invitational in Maui, HA
##ACC/Big Ten Challenge in Greensboro, NC
###Big Ten Tournament in Chicago
####NCAA Tournament
@Road Games

BLUE RIBBON ANALYSIS

BACKCOURT	A
BENCH/DEPTH	A-
FRONTCOURT	B
INTANGIBLES	A-

The problem with preseason hype is it's hard to exceed. The Illini had their best season in more than a decade last year, yet it was hard for fans to be completely overjoyed with the Elite Eight. After all, that's where they were supposed to be, based on the preseason prognostications.

This year, the expectations aren't any lower. And they shouldn't be. The Illini lost two valuable players in McClain and Griffin, but that's it. Compared with some teams in their league and around the country, that hardly seems critical. Especially when players like Williams, Cook and Bradford return, and when those expected to join them in the lineup, guys like Archibald and Krupalija, already have three years of significant experience behind them.

"I would say that our leadership will stem from what Frank and Cory bring to the table, because those are the two guys that can get anybody to follow them," Self said. "Of course we want our guys to be self-starters and be leaders in their own right, but those two hold the keys to leadership on this team."

There's a sense of urgency to this season, even if Self won't admit it. He knows practically the entire rotation will be wiped out by this time next year. And having been to the precipice that is the Elite Eight in consecutive seasons, he, like Illini fans, thirsts for the Final Four.

To get there, Illinois will need to maintain the kind of defensive intensity it displayed last season. Scoring and rebounding shouldn't be a problem. Bench play obviously won't be a problem. It will be interesting to see how the lineup develops. Last year, McClain and Griffin rounded out five logical starters, from start to finish. This year, Archibald, Johnson, Harrington, Krupalija and Ferguson all could be anything from starters to 10-minute-a-game bench players.

Of course, a lot of teams would love to have that problem. With the ever-growing rash of underclassmen and even high schoolers leaving for the NBA, rosters like the Illini's are hard to come by. They literally have the classic college basketball composition: experienced seniors, budding underclassmen, a junior college transfer and three promising freshmen.

And after last year's schedule, there's hardly a team in the country that should intimidate the Illini. They're the favorite for the Big Ten title. And, barring injury, they should be able to compete for an even bigger title as well.

(S.M.)

Kentucky 3

LOCATION	Lexington, KY
CONFERENCE	Southeastern (Eastern)
LAST SEASON	24-10 (.706)
CONFERENCE RECORD	12-4 (t-1st)
STARTERS LOST/RETURNING	1/4
NICKNAME	Wildcats
COLORS	Blue & White
HOMECOURT	Rupp Arena (23,000)
COACH	Tubby Smith (High Point '73)
RECORD AT SCHOOL	110-33 (4 years)
CAREER RECORD	234-95 (10 years)
ASSISTANTS	Mike Sutton (East Carolina '78)
	Reggie Hanson (Kentucky '91)
	David Hobbs (VCU '71)
TEAM WINS (last 5 years)	26-34-28-23-24
RPI (last 5 years)	2-2-7-5-9
2000-01 FINISH	Lost in NCAA Sweet 16.

COACH AND PROGRAM

There was a time this off-season when it appeared that the Big Blue walls just might be crumbling.

On the heels of a disappointing loss to Southern Cal in the NCAA Tournament's Sweet 16, reports out of Columbia, S.C., had South Carolina aggressively pursuing Kentucky head coach Tubby Smith with a "blockbuster" deal to succeed Eddie Fogler.

South Carolina athletic director Mike McGee received permission to speak with Smith, and the Gamecocks were flashing some pretty serious money.

Nobody at Kentucky really wanted to believe that Smith was interested, but he acknowledged that he was at least listening.

About a month later, both of Kentucky's returning All-

SEC performers—Tayshaun Prince and Keith Bogans—entered their names in the NBA draft. There was reason to believe that both would be first-round picks, too.

If all this wasn't enough, sophomore center Jason Parker tore the anterior cruciate ligament in his right knee in a pickup game in late June. He underwent reconstructive surgery on July 2, and doctors said his recovery time would take four- to six-months.

There was also an arrest of junior center Marvin Stone for public intoxication after he had already been serving a suspension for academic reasons.

Collectively, Kentucky fans asked: What next?

One by one, the answers began to fall into place, and for a change, the news was all good.

Smith said no thanks to South Carolina and signed a new six-year contract with Kentucky that will pay him approximately $1.5 million annually. In addition, he will receive a $1 million loyalty bonus should he remain at Kentucky for the next six seasons.

Following their coach's lead, Prince and Bogans also decided to return to Kentucky and withdrew their names from the NBA draft after participating in the pre-draft camp. Smith had thought all along that both of the players would be back. But his faith was tested when Bogans waited until the final day to pull his name out of the NBA hat.

"I had a good feeling [Bogans] would be back," Smith told The Cats' Pause. "I was the one trying to give him the boost, 'Hey, go up there and give it your best shot.' That's my job to be supportive and do all I can to help him reach his goal."

The latest estimate on Parker is that he could be back in time for the Wildcats' SEC opener against Mississippi State on Jan. 5. As for Stone, he has been reinstated and will be one of the candidates to start at center while Parker is sidelined.

When you throw in the return of junior center Jules Camara, who sat out last season after violating UK's student-athlete alcohol policy, the Wildcats have a chance to put as talented and as deep a team on the floor come January as any team in the country.

"We're looking for good things," Smith said. "We should have a full complement of players. Losing Jason Parker was a big blow, but his surgery and rehab are going well. With Prince and Jules Camara, we have a big plus on the front line. I really like our freshman class and feel they will complement our returnees as well."

It's Smith's way of saying that this is a team with the pieces in place to get back to the Final Four. The Wildcats haven't been there since Smith's first season in Lexington when they won the 1998 national championship.

"We've got so many players coming back, that's why people are projecting us so high," Prince told The Cats' Pause. "We're very deep at every position whereas a lot of teams lost a lot of players from their programs."

Smith will have an endless supply of potential combinations he could put on the floor, especially once Parker returns.

On the perimeter, he could go athletic with Cliff Hawkins, Gerald Fitch and Bogans. There's also the option of going big and athletic with Prince, Camara and Stone as the three forwards and sliding Bogans back to the two-guard position.

Stone and Marquis Estill would start for most teams, and if freshman guard Rashaad Carruth is as good as advertised, he should open up the middle even more with his long-range bombs.

The hard part belongs to Smith. He has to find enough minutes to go around.

2001-2002 SCHEDULE

Nov.	15-16	#NABA Classic
	24	Morehead State
	28	*Kent State
Dec.	5	VMI
	8	North Carolina
	15	Kentucky State
	18	**Duke
	22	***Indiana
	29	Louisville
Jan.	2	****Tulane
	5	@Mississippi State
	9	Georgia
	12	@South Carolina
	15	Ole Miss
	19	@Notre Dame
	22	@Auburn
	26	Alabama

	29	@Florida
Feb.	2	South Carolina
	6	@Tennessee
	9	@LSU
	13	Vanderbilt
	16	@Georgia
	19	Tennessee
	23	Arkansas
	27	@Vanderbilt
March	2	Florida
	7-10	##SEC Tournament

@Road Games
*Firstar Center, Cincinnati, OH
**Jimmy V. Classic, East Rutherford, NJ
***RCA Dome, Indianapolis, IN
****Freedom Hall, Louisville, KY
#Lexington, KY (vs. Western Kentucky, first round; also George Washington, Marshall)
##Georgia Dome, Atlanta, GA

STARTERS NOT RETURNING

PG-SAUL SMITH (6-2, 6.6 ppg, 2.1 rpg, 3.5 apg, 1.5 spg, 29.3 minutes, .373 FG, .345 3PT, .678 FT). He was the point guard the Kentucky fans chided, complained about and wondered aloud if he would be playing so much if his dad weren't the coach.

But Smith (Daddy's Boy to some in the Bluegrass) will be missed more than most people probably realize.

"It'd be really puzzling to see what would happen if I didn't have that 'Smith' on the back of that jersey," Smith told The Cats' Pause last season. "I think it'd be really funny to see. Maybe in the next life."

Smith was an extension of his father on the court, getting the Wildcats in the right sets, keeping them under control and setting the tempo defensively.

Above everything else, Smith played within himself and didn't make mistakes. He had 134 assists last season and only 62 turnovers. He finished fourth in the league in assists and ninth in steals.

In Kentucky's season-ending loss to Southern Cal, he might have been the best Wildcat on the floor. Smith finished with 17 points, including 5-of-7 shooting from three-point range, and handed out four assists.

But over his career, he was an inconsistent shooter from the perimeter and not much of a scorer. In fact, he entered the NCAA Tournament last season having scored in double figures only twice in the previous 23 games.

OTHERS NOT RETURNING

SG-TODD TACKETT (6-2, 0.4 ppg, 0.8 ppg, 0.4 rpg, 0.5 apg, 6.5 minutes, .195 FG, .045 3PT, .556 FT). Tackett sat out last season to rehabilitate his knee, but decided not to return to the Kentucky basketball team. He will instead pursue a professional baseball career.

"Todd has a dream to play pro baseball, and he feels now is the time to pursue that career," Smith said. "We wish him the best of luck."

Tackett, an all-state guard at Paintsville (Ky.) High School, rarely played in his two seasons with the Wildcats. He had surrendered his scholarship to help the Wildcats meet the limit of 13 this year.

PROJECTED STARTERS

PG-J.P. BLEVINS (6-2, 180 lbs., SR, #3, 2.8 ppg, 0.9 rpg, 0.6 apg, 0.8 tpg, 13.4 minutes, .386 FG, .291 3PT, .667 FT, Metcalfe County HS/Edmonton, Ky.). Shoring up the point-guard position could be the difference in the Wildcats joining the Final Four gala as participants this season or sitting at home and watching the festivities on television.

Blevins will get the first shot, but Hawkins will be lurking. Smith has said he intends to at least start out with Blevins, who is coming off a disappointing junior season.

In three of his final six games, Blevins didn't even score a year ago. He also lost his three-point stroke, which had always been a strength. The other area he must improve is his assist-to-turnover ratio. Blevins finished with 28 turnovers and 19 assists.

But getting first dibs on the job should help restore Blevins' confidence. He can't afford to be nearly as erratic this season if he's going to stay in the starting lineup. Ideally, the Wildcats would like to see him return to his sophomore form when he averaged 4.2 points per game and handed out 42 assists as compared to 24 turnovers. He also shot .358 from three-point range.

A better defender than he's given credit for, Blevins saw his minutes decrease last season. That's after playing 16.5 minutes per game as a sophomore. But after starting slowly last season, the two-time Academic All-SEC guard never recovered.

"We have confidence in both J.P. and Cliff, that they can get it done," Smith said. "We need big years out of both of those guys."

SG-GERALD FITCH (6-3, 185 lbs., SO, #4, 6.8 ppg, 4.4 rpg, 1.9 apg, 1.2 spg, 19.8 minutes, .455 FG, .408 3PT, .690 FT, Westside HS/Macon, Ga.). One of the most underrated players in the country, Fitch earned All-SEC Freshman honors last season.

Largely unheralded coming out of high school in Macon, Ga., Fitch moved into the starting lineup in the Indiana game and never came out. Once he became a starter, Kentucky proceeded to win 15 of its next 17 games.

Fitch is one of the best rebounding guards you're going to find, averaging 4.4 per game last season. He attacks the boards like a power forward.

But the thing Smith liked most about Fitch last season was that he didn't play nor think like a freshman. If there was a big shot to take, he didn't hesitate. He wanted the ball in his hands, and knew what to do with it.

Fitch is also one of the better shooters on the team. He was the lone Wildcat last season to shoot 40 percent from three-point land.

His development was also key in being able to move Bogans to small forward and Prince to power forward, which created all sorts of mismatches for opponents.

Fitch's greatest attribute was the bottom line. In those games he started, the Wildcats were 21-5. But before Smith inserted Fitch into the starting lineup, they were just 3-5.

In his last 14 games, Fitch shot 53 percent from the field and 51.4 percent from three-point range. He scored in double figures five of his last eight games.

"We feel extremely good about our wings," Smith said. "We've got two guys, Bogans and Fitch, who are pretty much interchangeable there."

SF-KEITH BOGANS (6-5, 205 lbs., JR, #10, 17.0 ppg, 4.6 rpg, 2.4 apg, 1.0 spg, 2.6 tpg, 30.9 minutes, .473 FG, .361 3PT, .697 FT, DeMatha HS/Hyattsville, Md.). Bogans has that look of a heavyweight fighter, and that's also the way he plays.

One SEC assistant coach mused last year that Bogans played every possession as if it were his last. As it turned out, last season was nearly Bogans' last at Kentucky. He waited until the final day to withdraw his name from the NBA draft.

The ironic thing is that Smith thinks Bogans may have actually hurt himself by participating in the pre-draft camp in Chicago.

"I saw him work out a couple of times in Chicago, and I think he was just a little nervous," Smith told The Cats' Pause. "It's a stressful situation, a lot of pressure. You've got all these NBA scouts and the entire administration from most of the NBA teams sitting there evaluating kids. It's a tough situation."

Nonetheless, Bogans is back for his junior season and should be one of the nation's top swingmen. He was a second-team All-SEC selection last season and led the Wildcats in scoring. Bogans isn't what you would call a pure shooter, but he's capable of scoring points in bunches. He scored 21 points in the second half of Kentucky's loss to Southern Cal last season in the NCAA Tournament. He also exploded for 21 after halftime against Florida and 23 in the second half against LSU.

Bogan's big body allows him to muscle his way inside and maneuver for points. He's also a strong driver to the basket.

"Keith has to continue to work on his outside shot, though he really improved from his freshman to sophomore year," Smith told The Cats' Pause. "If he makes the same type of improvement this year, it would be a great accomplishment."

Also, Smith thinks Bogans will be a more relaxed player, having tested the NBA waters.

"He understands now what he needs to do," Smith told the Lexington Herald-Leader. "He'll come back with renewed vision and re-invigorated."

PF-TAYSHAUN PRINCE (6-9, 215 lbs., SR, #21, 16.9 ppg, 6.5 rpg, 2.9 apg, 0.7 spg, 1.1 bpg, 32.9 minutes, .495 FG, .358 3PT, .843 FT, Dominguez HS/Compton,Calif.). Prince is Kentucky's first returning All-American since Kenny Walker in 1985-86. He's also the best returning player in the SEC.

As the season wound down a year ago, Prince hit one of those strides all players dream about. He scored in every way imaginable, rebounded, blocked shots and hit too many big shots to count. He also played a little defense, holding Notre Dame All-American Troy Murphy to 10 points below his average.

"We didn't know how much he could move our team to another level when he plays like that," guard J.P. Blevins told the Lexington Herald-Leader last season. "We've seen what he can do, and we'll be hard to stop when he produces like that."

Prince would have likely gone in the top half of the first round had he not withdrawn his name from the NBA draft. Physically, he still needs to get a little stronger and could stand to add some weight to his lanky 6-9 frame.

But he's so smooth and has a left-handed baby hook in the low post that is impossible to defend.

"Being a lefty doesn't make him more difficult to guard," Mississippi State head coach Rick Stansbury said. "It's his ability to jump and make shots [and] his ability to put the ball on the floor."

To their credit, the Wildcats weren't shy about feeding Prince the ball last season. The more he got it, the more he produced. His baby hook became his staple.

"I think that's unstoppable," Blevins told the Lexington Herald-Leader. "I don't think anybody in the country can block it. It's a high percentage shot and one he can go to any time he wants to when he needs to score. We don't think anybody can guard Tayshaun on the block."

After playing on the perimeter his first two seasons, Prince moved to the power-forward spot last season and made life miserable for bigger, slower players trying to come out on the floor to defend him.

It got to the point where so many teams were double-teaming him that his teammates were getting wide-open looks.

Barring injury or some type of slump, Prince will be a strong candidate for national player-of-the-year honors.

"He's got the total package," Smith told the Lexington Herald-Leader. "He just needs to refine."

The Prince-Bogans tandem was responsible for 42.5 percent of the Wildcats' scoring last season. Getting them both back from the doorstep of the NBA is something that doesn't happen every day in this era of take the money and run.

But in the end, both players decided they weren't quite ready for the NBA.

"It always helps us when a player decides to return," Smith said. "We recruit players to be a part of a family. Just because they come back to refine their skills, it makes no difference. That is why they are here to start. When they improve individually, it helps the team. Their success means our success, and our success means their success."

C-JULES CAMARA (6-11, 225 lbs., JR, #40, 7.2 ppg, 4.6 rpg, 0.9 apg, 0.5 spg, 1.6 bpg, 20.4 minutes, .481 FG, .167 3PT, .679 FT in 1999-2000, Oak Hill Academy/Mouth of Wilson, Va.). Camara was sorely missed last season. He's the Wildcats' most athletic big man and a one-man zone defense in the middle with his ability to throw back shots.

"Jules gives us the shot-blocking threat we didn't have a year ago," Smith said. "Plus, he runs the floor, has good range on his shot and has as much playing experience as anyone other than Tayshaun."

Camara has played primarily at power forward in his career. But with Parker out for an undetermined time, Camara is certain to see his share of time in the post.

He didn't play last season after falling victim to the school's automatic one-year suspension for a drunken driving conviction. But during the 2000 season, Camara played in 31 games for the Wildcats with 11 starts.

Camara also has international experience after playing for the 2001 Senegalese National Team in the African Games in August. He has great quickness and jumping ability for his height. During his sophomore season, he ranked fifth in the SEC with 1.6 blocked shots per game and swatted away 12 in the last four games.

"He limits layups and limits people from getting easy shots, which will be a big help to us," Smith said.

KEY RESERVES

SG-RASHAAD CARRUTH (6-3, 195 lbs., FR, #2, 18.5 ppg, 4.3 apg, .551 FG, .466 3PT, Oak Hill Academy/Mouth of Wilson, Va.). The Wildcats needed a shooter and went out and got perhaps the best one in the country. Carruth has great range and can fill it up from 25 feet. He may be the best pure three-point shooter Kentucky has signed since Tony Delk.

Ranked as the No. 1 shooting guard in the country last year, Carruth was a McDonald's and Parade All-

American. He still needs to improve his offense off the dribble, but should see considerable playing time on the wing for the Wildcats.

"Carruth gives them what they seem to be lacking, a consistent outside shooter," recruiting analyst Bob Gibbons told the Lexington Herald-Leader. "He's a little undersized to be a wing guard, but he's athletic."

Oak Hill head coach Steve Smith said Carruth also expanded his game last year.

"He can create his own shot," Smith told the Lexington Herald-Leader. "He can score off the dribble. I think he got tired of people labeling him as just a three-point shooter."

Carruth set the school record at Oak Hill for three-pointers made in a game with 12, including eight on consecutive possessions. Carruth played alongside Hawkins as a junior at Oak Hill.

PF-ERIK DANIELS (6-7, 205 lbs., SO, #14, 5.2 ppg, 2.6 rpg, 0.8 apg, 12.9 minutes, .566 FG, .278 3PT, .603 FT, Princeton HS/Cincinnati, Ohio). Daniels epitomizes Kentucky's deep bench. Last year, he averaged less than 15 minutes per game and would have been starting at a lot of other schools. He's a tough player who defends and always seems to come up with a play that makes the difference in a game. Daniels has bulked up to 205 pounds and should be even more consistent on both ends of the court this season. He's also a gamer, meaning he seems to play much better in games than practice.

The start to Daniels' freshman year was sensational. He made 20 of his first 23 shots despite missing some early practices because of arthroscopic knee surgery.

"I didn't think I'd be playing as much as I did with me having surgery before the season," Daniels told The Cats' Pause. "I was just thankful to be out there at all."

Daniels hit an unbelievable growth spurt in high school. He started his freshman year standing 5-10, but had grown to 6-2 by the end of the year. He just kept growing, which took a toll on his knees.

"My muscles caught up when I was able to work out a lot," Daniels told The Cats' Pause. "The pain gradually went away."

PF-MARQUIS ESTILL (6-9, 240 lbs., JR, #50, 7.3 ppg, 3.8 rpg, 0.6 apg, 1.1 bpg, 13.8 minutes, .603 FG, .313 3PT, .731 FT, Madison Central HS/Richmond, Ky.). Estill was the Wildcats' third-team center last season, and at times was the best player on the court. In Kentucky's second-round NCAA Tournament win over Iowa, he scored a career-high 22 points. But that was his first double-digit game since Jan. 31.

"You know, we knew Prince was a great player and we didn't have an answer for him," Iowa head coach Steve Alford told the Lexington Herald-Leader after that game. "And even with that, I thought the difference was Estill."

Estill returns as the best perimeter shooter among Kentucky's post players. He shot .603 percent from the field a year ago, which was tops on the team. He also led the Wildcats in blocked shots with 36. In SEC play, Estill was even better—shooting .639 from the field and .811 from the free-throw line.

Sore knees have hampered Estill, who gave up his scholarship this summer to get the Wildcats back to the NCAA limit of 13 scholarships. Kentucky found itself over the limit after Prince and Bogans decided to return to school.

"Marquis must work as hard as he can to stay healthy," Smith said. "He's always going to be bothered by sore knees, but he's going to have to find a way to fight through it."

Estill's weakness is his defense. He doesn't have the best footwork.

PG-CLIFF HAWKINS (6-1, 190 lbs., SO, #1, 3.0 ppg, 1.1 rpg, 1.6 apg, 1.0 spg, 1.8 tpg, 11 minutes, .390 FG, .231 3PT, .594 FT, Oak Hill Academy/Mouth of Wilson, Va.). Hawkins is easily the most athletic of the Wildcats' two point guards. He plays the game at the speed of light and occasionally gets himself in trouble in always trying to force the issue.

Compared by some in Kentucky to former point guard Wayne Turner, Hawkins relies on penetration and quickness. He's a rugged on-the-ball defender and has also shown signs of being an outstanding passer. Where he needs to tighten up considerably is taking care of the ball.

A year ago, Turner finished with 54 assists and 59 turnovers. Such a ratio isn't going to cut it with Smith. But as last season progressed, Turner began to catch his breath and play a little more under control.

"He's starting to breathe and relax more—and do the

things he's capable of doing," Smith told the Louisville Courier-Journal last January. "He's starting to play to his ability and to his potential. I thought he was outstanding defensively [in the win over Notre Dame], and he's feeling comfortable running our offense now. It just takes time."

Hawkins averaged 13 minutes per game in the SEC Tournament. He played his best basketball late in the season.

Playing more under control should also help Hawkins' shooting. He was just 3-of-13 from three-point range last season and shot less than 40 percent from the field. The only other drawback with Hawkins is his stamina. He suffers from asthma.

C-JASON PARKER (6-8, 253 lbs., SO, #42, 8.6 ppg, 4.7 rpg, 0.6 apg, 0.7 bpg, 1.5 tpg, 19.1 minutes, .552 FG, .398 FT, West Charlotte HS/Charlotte, N.C. and Fork Union Military Academy, Fork Union, Va.). Had he not blown out his knee, Parker would be the starter at center. He could still regain that spot during the SEC part of the schedule if all goes well with his recovery.

The Wildcats hope to get him back by the first part of January. Parker's injury was a bad one. In addition to tearing his anterior cruciate ligament, he also damaged two areas of cartilage.

The injury was similar to the one former Kentucky star Derek Anderson suffered during the 1996-97 season, but the damage to Parker's knee was much more extensive. Anderson actually practiced two months later and even considered playing in the NCAA Tournament.

Smith is optimistic that Parker will also make a speedy recovery, although he won't be rushed by anyone.

"I don't know the exact prognosis," Smith said. "If everything goes well, he could be ready some time in second semester, but that's not the way I want to approach the situation. We have to tell him, 'As soon as you can get back, get back.' We want to continue to motivate him."

Parker, an All-SEC Freshman selection a year ago, is the only Kentucky freshman to start his first game under Smith. He wound up starting all 34 games and was third on the team in scoring and second in rebounding. His best game came in the NCAA Tournament loss to Southern Cal when he scored 22 points and grabbed 13 rebounds. Parker's blend of power and athleticism make him the ultimate low-post player.

When he gets back this season, he will need to shore up his free-throw shooting after shooting just .398 from the line a year ago.

C-MARVIN STONE (6-10, 253 lbs., JR, #24, 6.0 ppg, 4.6 rpg, 0.6 apg, 0.9 bpg, 18.2 minutes, .507 FG, .584 FT, Grissom HS/Huntsville, Ala.). Inconsistency has plagued Stone during his first two years. He's faced distractions off the court, some of them tragic.

In 1999, his father died from a sudden heart attack, and then last season, he lost his sister to a heart ailment. At one point last season, Stone considered transferring after experiencing some academic difficulties and discussed the possibility with Smith.

When Stone went home for Christmas, there were no guarantees he would return. But he did, although he never found any kind of groove.

"Marvin is a young junior who's continuing to improve," Smith said. "He was a starter at the beginning of last year before he went to the bench. Now he looks to come back more focused. He's probably our most complete post player. If he continues to work and improve, he'll have the opportunity to start."

Stone is an accomplished scorer with soft hands and a soft touch. He still needs to become more aggressive inside and stronger on both ends of the court.

Tied for second on the team in rebounding last season, Stone could really solidify Kentucky's frontcourt with a big year. The Wildcats could play around with several different combinations.

OTHER RETURNEES

SG-CORY SEARS (6-6, 193 lbs., SO, #33, 0.2 ppg, 1.1 rpg, 0.4 apg, 3.7 minutes, .400 FT, Hargrave HS/Corbin, Ky.). A former scholarship player, Sears remains on the team as a walk-on. He owns a consistent perimeter jumper, but lacks the speed and quickness to be an impact player.

Sears played in 10 games last season, failing to score in SEC games.

SG-MATT HEISSENBUTTEL (6-4, 188 lbs., SO, #15, 0.9 ppg, 0.3 rpg, 0.2 apg, 3.2 minutes, .222 FG, .200 3PT, .667 FT, Catholic HS/Lexington, Ky.).

Heissenbuttel is a walk-on wing player who can also shoot it from the perimeter. He played in 10 games last season and hit a three-pointer against South Carolina.

While growing up in Lexington, Heissenbuttel was a ball boy for the Wildcats in the 1990s.

OTHER NEWCOMERS

PG-ADAM CHILES (6-0, 192 lbs., FR, #00, 16.1 ppg, 4.5 rpg, 5.1 apg, Ballard HS/Louisville, Ky.). If the Wildcats need a third point guard, Chiles will be the guy. He's a stocky player who's stronger than many of the guards he faces. As a senior at Ballard High School in Louisville, Chiles averaged 16.1 points and 3.1 steals per game on a team that was ranked as high as third nationally by USA Today. Chiles is the first player from Ballard to ever sign with Kentucky.

Chiles, who was impressive in the Derby Classic, signed during the April period. He also considered Cincinnati and Maryland. Chiles has experienced some back problems in the past.

SG-JOSH CARRIER (6-5, 193 lbs., FR, #5, 23.7 ppg, 5.0 rpg, Bowling Green HS/Bowling Green, Ky.). Carrier was selected Kentucky's 2001 Mr. Basketball, becoming the first UK-bound player to win the award since Richie Farmer in 1988.

Carrier has great range on his jumper. He averaged 23.7 points last season while shooting 48 percent from the field. He was also recruited by Louisville, UCLA, Tulane and Colorado.

An injury limited Carrier in the July camps, which made it difficult for many of the analysts to rate him.

"Some think he's really good. Some think he doesn't belong in the top 150," Prep Stars' Rob Harrington told the Lexington Herald-Leader.

PF-CHUCK HAYES (6-7, 237 lbs., FR, #44, 25.0 ppg, 19.0 rpg, 5.0 apg, Modesto Christian School/Modesto, Calif.). If the Wildcats can find the minutes, Hayes could be a factor this season in the frontcourt. He can play either small or power forward. Hayes bench-presses 295 pounds, squats 450 pounds and runs the 40-yard dash in 4.8 seconds. He's a former all-state football player in California and could be the surprise of this class. He's an exceptionally sound player for a rising freshman.

"He's a very intense warrior type," Gibbons told the Lexington Herald-Leader. "He will inspire the kids around him to play that way."

Somewhat limited as a shooter, Hayes was a Parade All-American at Modesto Christian last season. He chose Kentucky over Kansas, Saint Louis and UTEP.

QUESTIONS

Point guard? Do the Wildcats have one good enough to carry them to the Final Four? Between them, maybe Blevins and Hawkins can get it done. But point-guard play is crucial the deeper a team gets in the tournament. See Jason Williams at Duke and Frank Williams at Illinois.

Living up to expectations? Anything less than a Final Four appearance will be met with considerable gnashing of the teeth in the Bluegrass State.

ANSWERS

Frontcourt depth! Tayshaun Prince. Marvin Stone. Jules Camara. Marquis Estill. Jason Parker when he returns from knee surgery. What team in the country can match that kind of depth on the front line? The simple answer: None.

Prince-Bogans tandem! The boys are indeed back and they should be better than ever. It's a tandem that rivals Florida's Udonis Haslem and Brett Nelson as being the best in the SEC and maybe even the best in the country.

Tubby time! Smith specializes in getting every ounce out of his team. It shouldn't be any different this season. And with the talent he has to choose from, the Wildcats are going to put a serious hurt on some foes.

KENTUCKY 2000-2001 RESULTS

#St. John's (L)	61-62
#UCLA (L)	92-97
##Jacksonville State	91-48
Penn State (L)	68-73
@North Carolina	93-76
Eastern Kentucky	94-79
@Georgia Tech (L)	84-86

@Michigan State (L)	45-46
###Indiana	88-74
High Point	102-49
@Louisville	64-62
Georgia	67-63
South Carolina	69-63
Notre Dame	82-71
Tennessee	84-74
@Mississippi (L)	55-65
@Alabama (L)	60-70
Vanderbilt	86-75
@Georgia	85-70
@South Carolina	94-61
Florida	71-70
Mississippi State	76-57
@Tennessee	103-95
@Vanderbilt	79-74
LSU	84-61
@Arkansas (L)	78-82
Auburn	90-78
@Florida (L)	86-94
####South Carolina	78-65
####Arkansas	87-78
####Mississippi	77-55
#####Holy Cross	72-68
#####Iowa	92-79
#####Southern Cal (L)	76-80

#Coaches vs. Cancer Classic in New York
##At Cincinnati
###At Louisville
####SEC Tournament in Nashville
#####NCAA Tournament
@Road Games

BLUE RIBBON ANALYSIS

BACKCOURT	A-
BENCH/DEPTH	A
FRONTCOURT	A
INTANGIBLES	A

Prince and Bogans may have thought they needed a little more seasoning before skipping to the NBA. But their return to the college game also says something about the Wildcats' prospects for this season.

If the point-guard play can hold up, this is a national championship-caliber team with a coach who knows what it takes to get there.

"I'm kind of giddy with Tayshaun and Keith coming back," Smith told the Lexington Herald-Leader. "And I'm excited about the direction of the program."

It's a direction headed due south down Interstate 75, all the way to the Georgia Dome. It's Final Four or bust for the Wildcats.

(C.L.)

Maryland 4

LOCATION	College Park, MD
CONFERENCE	Atlantic Coast
LAST SEASON	25-11 (.694)
CONFERENCE RECORD	10-6 (3rd)
STARTERS LOST/RETURNING	1/4
NICKNAME	Terrapins
COLORS	Red & Black
HOMECOURT	Cole Field House (14,500)
COACH	Gary Williams (Maryland '68)
RECORD AT SCHOOL	242-139 (12 years)
CAREER RECORD	449-267 (23 years)
ASSISTANTS	Dave Dickerson (Maryland '89)
	Jimmy Patsos (Catholic University '89)
	Matt Kovarik (Maryland '98)
TEAM WINS (last 5 years)	21-22-28-25-25
RPI (last 5 years)	23-9-4-117-12
2000-01 FINISH	Lost in NCAA semifinal.

COACH AND PROGRAM

Well, they said it would never happen. They said Gary Williams would never take Maryland to its ever-elusive first trip the Final Four, because the intense coach was too busy yelling at his players to advance beyond the tournament's early rounds.

Last year, the Terps finally proved everybody wrong, as Williams mellowed out and his team advanced to the national semifinals for the first time in school history

before stepping in a big pile of Duke.

But that's OK. For a program that had been hounded by the constant parenthetical—"Maryland, which has never been to a Final Four"—getting to Minneapolis was a great accomplishment.

Williams found out just how great over the summer, as he made the alumni tour and recruiting rounds. He found even more support for a program that sees only limitless possibilities on the horizon, as it begins its final season in the historic hangar known as Cole Field House. Next season, the Terps move into the high-tech Comcast Center.

"The main thing is, right or wrong, the perception of going to a Final Four moves you to a different category of teams, once you get there," Williams said. "I have always wondered why that is, since it is only one or two more games than making it to the Sweet 16.

"I guess it is the right one or two games. The timing of it was pretty good, as far as all the side benefits are concerned."

And that's a real switch for the Terps, who have had miserable timing in the past. Remember in 1974, when Lefty Driesell had the second-best team in the nation, but didn't even get invited to the NCAA Tournament because of the ridiculous rule that limited each conference to only one team in the field?

Remember how close Len Bias came to getting the Terps back to that level, before he crashed himself and the program, taking Driesell with him?

Remember how Williams came along and built a solid program, even while wearing the heavy cape of NCAA probation in his first two years? He developed talent that was rarely rated high among recruiting analysts and put together teams in the 1990s that approached greatness in the regular season, but couldn't perform in the postseason.

Now, in a whole new millennium, things have changed, thanks to a simple appearance in the Final Four.

"As a program, there have been so many times, going back to the '70s, that we have had good teams that didn't make it," said Williams, who graduated from Maryland in 1968. "It was almost like we had a ceiling to crack.

"Now, we feel like anything is possible. There is no more, 'Gee, I wish we could get to the Final Four.' That is gone. Now, let's see how far we can go each year. There is no barrier there."

Williams has built a national championship-caliber program. He has taken the Terps to a school-record eight consecutive NCAA Tournaments. His team has won 25 games in each of the last three seasons. Last year's team matched the school's highest final ranking ever, finishing No. 4 in the nation.

But there is still an obstacle standing in the way: Duke. It's the same problem that, over the last 10 years, several ACC teams have had in football, in trying to catch up with Florida State. Clemson, Georgia Tech and North Carolina all made it to the top 10 in both polls on several occasions, but have never been able to dethrone the Seminoles.

The difference is that Maryland has had sustained success in basketball. Unfortunately for Williams and his charges, Duke has been better. The world seems to love it when Duke and North Carolina are dueling against each other. Only the schools' diehard fans (though there are a lot of them) really care who has the upper hand. The rest of the country seems to be intrigued by the rivalry, the passion and the excitement.

But Maryland has been a better challenger the last two years, beating the Blue Devils twice at Cameron Indoor Stadium. The unfortunate part about last season was not that Maryland lost to the Devils three times in four meetings, including the famous comeback at Cole Field House in which Duke overcame a 10-point deficit in the final minute and won the game in overtime.

No, the unfortunate part came in the Final Four game, when everybody who cared saw Duke beat Maryland for the third time in the season. They automatically assumed the Terps were somehow an inferior product. But that's hardly the case. Williams just wishes that everyone would comprehend that fact.

"Our problem is that everybody says, 'You are not as good as Duke,' " Williams said. "Well, nobody else in the country is either. But because we are in the same league, we have to overcome that. The fact that Duke won, that made them the best. We might have been second best. We beat them once. We have done that more than any other team in the last couple of years.

"We still have some goals that we want to get done

here, but that doesn't make us a bad basketball team because we didn't beat Duke."

Besides, Williams has enough talent and experience possibly to overtake the Blue Devils. With four starters returning—including All-ACC candidates Lonny Baxter, Juan Dixon and Steve Blake—and a solid trio of freshmen to fill in some holes, the Terps have Top 5 possibilities heading into the season.

They have to be more consistent than they have the early parts of the last two seasons, when high expectations were squashed with early losing streaks. Two years ago, the Terps lost their first three conference games. Last year, they lost three of their first four games of the season and suffered another slump after Duke's demoralizing comeback victory.

They also have to find a way to replace Terence Morris, the power forward who never quite lived up to the promise he showed as a sophomore, when he could have left school early and been a lottery pick in the NBA draft. Instead, he stayed in school two more years and was eventually a second-round pick of the Houston Rockets.

They also have to replace Miller's shooting and the inside presence of Mike Mardesich, who was a key frontcourt presence the last three years.

"We lost more than people think," Williams said.

But even Morris was little more than a role player during the Terps' run to the Final Four, and Williams knows his team has all the elements to be even more successful this year.

"This team, if we can replace what we lost and we work as hard as we did last year, can win at the Final Four," Williams said. "Those are big ifs. We were a very good team in terms of work ethic and playing together.

"It was a team that really got it together as the season went along."

Seven of last year's top nine scorers return, and the three incoming freshmen have distinct roles to play. Six-foot-nine forward Ryan Randle, who comes from the same junior college that produced Steve Francis, will help inside; 6-6 swingman Michael Grinnon will try to replace Miller's points off the bench; and 5-9 point guard Andre Collins will back up Steve Blake.

Either junior Tahj Holden or sophomore Chris Wilcox will take over Morris' place in the frontcourt.

Everything else should be in place to get back to, and perhaps even win at, the Final Four.

2001-2002 SCHEDULE

Nov.	8-9	#Coaches vs. Cancer IKON Classic
	17	American
	24	Delaware State
	27	*Illinois
Dec.	2-3	##BB&T Classic
	9	Detroit
	11	Monmouth
	21	@Oklahoma
	27	William & Mary
	30	@North Carolina State
Jan.	3	Norfolk State
	9	North Carolina
	13	@Georgia Tech
	17	@Duke
	20	Clemson
	23	@Wake Forest
	26	Florida State
	31	@Virginia
Feb.	3	North Carolina State
	10	@North Carolina
	13	Georgia Tech
	17	Duke
	20	@Clemson
	24	Wake Forest
	27	@Florida State
March	3	Virginia
	7-10	###ACC Tournament

@Road Games
*Big Ten/ACC Challenge
#Madison Square Garden, NY (vs. Arizona first round; also Florida, Temple)
##MCI Center, Washington, DC (vs. Princeton first round, also Connecticut, George Washington)
###Charlotte Coliseum, Charlotte, NC

STARTERS NOT RETURNING

PF-TERENCE MORRIS (6-9, 12.2 ppg, 7.7 rpg, 1.9

apg, 2.2 blocks, 27.6 minutes, .432 FG, .289 3PT, .795 FT). Why was it that everyone expected so much more out of Morris, who became little more than a decent role player in his final two seasons at Maryland?

Mainly, it was because of his breakout sophomore season, when he was able to slide underneath the radar during the Steve Francis show and put up big numbers for the Terps, earning first-team All-ACC honors.

Had he left school then with Francis, Morris would probably have been a lottery pick. But he opted to stay in his comfort zone. A small-town player who never participated in the summer AAU basketball circuit during his prep days, Morris never liked getting too much attention and was willing to wait for a professional career.

But did he wait too long?

Expectations were extremely high after he averaged 15.3 points and 7.1 rebounds as a sophomore. But his scoring went down his final two years. He improved his rebounding as a junior to 8.6 per game, but dropped back as a senior to 7.7.

It wasn't that Morris turned bad. It was just that he never turned it up, like everyone expected. Williams thinks that Morris was always unfairly criticized during his final two seasons, though there were times when the Terps badly needed Morris' help and didn't get it.

"He's one of the best players to ever play here," Williams said of Morris, who finished his career in ranked in the school's all-time top 10 in five different categories: points (8th), rebounds (4th), blocks (2nd), three-point field goals (8th) and steals (8th).

"He didn't have a good scoring senior season and people judge you on how many points you score. But having a guy with his experience out there, knowing the offense, he was very important to us. I think he has a good future in the NBA."

Especially because he was taken in the second round of the NBA draft by Houston, where he will rejoin Francis. Maybe that will allow him to reach his potential, because he was at his best when he was a complement to Francis.

"I think the thing that hurt Terence was when he got to be the main guy for us," Williams said. "He was always a player who would complement other players and that made him a great team player.

"He could do things to help you score even if he was not doing the scoring. He made great contributions to the team, yet people thought he should be some kind of first-team All-American. That didn't happen."

OTHERS NOT RETURNING

SF-DANNY MILLER (6-8, 4.8 ppg, 2.6 rpg, 2.1 apg, 18.8 minutes, .432 FG, .277 3PT, .556 FT). After starting all 34 of Maryland's games as a sophomore, Miller had to play a different role after losing his starting job to Byron Mouton four games into his junior year.

Miller struggled out of the gate and Mouton, who sat out the 1999-2000 season after his transfer from Tulane, was itching to contribute.

Williams benched Miller after he made only three of his first 12 shots to start the season.

"He is a good player," Williams said. "He just got off to a bad start."

The problem was, he never got any better. Relegated to a reserve role the rest of the season, Miller was clearly affected by his change in status. A 35.1 percent shooter from the three-point line in his first two seasons, Miller struggled with his outside shot all season long, making only 27.7 percent of his three-pointers last year.

And things didn't figure to get much better this year, playing behind Mouton. So Miller, a former McDonald's All-American, opted to leave Maryland and transfer to Notre Dame, where he will have one year of eligibility remaining after sitting out this season.

C-MIKE MARDESICH (7-0, 3.6 ppg, 2.6 rpg, 10.2 minutes, .473 FG, .533 FT). After losing two of his top frontcourt players, Williams knows he is going to miss Mardesich's presence inside. The hulking center didn't really contribute much in the way of scoring or even rebounding last year, but throughout his career he was able to contribute to the Terps on and off the court.

"He kept everything positive in our locker room," Williams said of Mardesich, one of the team's senior tri-captains. "I think our players really respected what Mike was for our team last year. You obviously need great players, but you also need people that you can depend on.

"We had a solid group of players like that and Mike was sort of the leader."

But it was a difficult role to accept. Mardesich saw his rebounding average and his minutes per game go down every year after he averaged 5.4 points and 4.3 rebounds in 18.2 minutes a game as a red-shirt freshman.

The Terps simply found other options in Baxter, Holden, Morris and, last year, Wilcox.

F-LARON CEPHAS (6-7, 1.7 ppg, 0.6 rpg, .526 FG, .429 FT). Cephas never really matured into a contributing player, but Williams always gave him credit for being a productive practice player. A tri-captain with Mardesich and Morris, Cephas played in only 14 games last year, getting a cursory start on senior day. He scored 24 points all season.

PROJECTED STARTERS

PG-STEVE BLAKE (6-3, 160, JR, #25, 6.9 ppg, 3.0 rpg, 6.9 apg, 3.0 tpg, 1.6 spg, 28.8 minutes, .399 FG, .394 3PT, .714 FT, Oak Hill Academy/Miami Lakes, Fla.). Steve Blake is the perfect example of how numbers mean virtually nothing in college basketball. How can someone 6-3 and 160 pounds be physically imposing? How can someone who averages less than seven points a game and shoots less than 40 percent from the field be so dangerous to opponents?

Blake, one of the most dangerous point guards in the game, has answers for those questions. He's a playmaker who gets every one of his teammates involved in the action, as his school-record 248 assists would suggest.

He became the first Maryland player since John Lucas in 1974 to lead the league in assists, averaging 6.9 per game and maintaining an assist-to-turnover ratio of 2.23-to-1.

"He is one of those four-year guys who gets better every season," Williams said of his playmaker. "He's a throwback player, a gym rat. He likes to be in the gym in the summer time."

What Williams wanted Blake to do this summer, however, was work on his shot. The coach believes Blake will have to score more, because defenses are naturally going to sag off him to defend other shooters.

"He showed at times last year that he can be a good shooter," Williams said. "His next development has to be in scoring consistently."

Blake is a great defender, as he showed in the Duke game against Blue Devil All-American Jason Williams, who had only 13 points and committed 10 turnovers against Blake's defense. The Terps' collapse, in fact, came just after Blake fouled out.

Now, Blake enters his third year as the Terps' starting point guard and Williams has high expectations for him.

"Last year, I think he had a great year in getting the ball to Juan Dixon, Lonny Baxter and Terence Morris, and people that could score," Williams said. "He sacrificed his own game in terms of how many points he could score.

"Steve is smart enough, going into his junior season, in knowing that his offensive numbers will go up because not only does he know where the basketball needs to go, but when he is open, he has to shoot the basketball."

Williams is also smart enough to know that Blake is at his best running the Terps' fast-paced offense and leading the pressing defense. With Dixon and Mouton still on the team, Blake doesn't have to be a scoring machine, as long as he can get them the ball or get it inside.

If Blake has proved anything over the last two years, it's that college basketball is not always about the scoring numbers.

SG-JUAN DIXON (6-3, 164 lbs., SR, #3, 18.2 ppg, 4.3 rpg, 2.6 apg, 2.4 tpg, 2.6 spg, 30.5 minutes, .483 FG, .411 3PT, .865 FT, Calvert Hall HS/Baltimore, Md.). We've spent three years waiting for Dixon, a human swizzle stick, to snap in two. It hasn't happened yet and it doesn't look like it is ever going to.

Heading into his senior year, the spindly shooting guard, who arrived with such indifferent expectations, is one of the most dynamic players in the country.

"Nobody thought he could play when he got here," Williams said.

Few people, however, knew about Dixon's desire to separate himself from his difficult upbringing. Both his parents died of AIDS while he was in high school. He had trouble making a qualifying score on the SAT coming out of high school and had to sit out a semester while awaiting the results of two tests he had to retake. He ended up sitting out the 1997-98 season as a red-shirt.

The next year, Dixon was a reserve playing behind the dynamic Steve Francis. All of his experiences made him tougher, and by the time he was a sophomore he was ready to demonstrate his toughness and his talent. He more than doubled his scoring average from 7.4 points a game to 18. He increased that last year by averaging 18.2 points and earning a spot on the first-team All-ACC squad for the second year in a row.

Even Williams is surprised at how well Dixon has played in college. But the coach thought he saw something in the 145-pound guard at Calvert Hall: quickness that nobody else on the floor could match and shooting touch.

All anybody else ever saw was a rail-thin guard who didn't look like he could compete within the rigors of the ACC. But anybody who underestimated Dixon made a serious mistake.

"The thing I like most about Juan is that he has no fear of any body who plays against him," Williams said. "He's not afraid to place himself in pressure situations.

"He is also one of the most positive players I've coached in terms of staying with his shot and not letting slumps or setbacks get in his way. He is very resilient."

Dixon worked hard to get here. When the Terps were going through their post-Duke tailspin last season, he would spend extra time working out and practicing his jumper.

Though he has never been the most gifted ball handler in the world, Dixon has improved enough that Williams might give him a few minutes at the point on occasion. One thing that hasn't changed is his defense. He has led the ACC in steals for two years running and it will be an upset if he doesn't do it again this year.

"Defensively, he likes to steal the ball," Williams said. "He drives me nuts sometimes because he likes to run around on defense. When you need a big steal or a big play, you look towards Juan, because he makes things happen."

Dixon also because a vocal team leader, taking the blame for the Valentine's Day loss to Florida State, then revitalizing his game at the end of the regular season. He averaged 25.5 points in the four games before the ACC Tournament.

He spent the summer with teammate Lonny Baxter starring for the U.S. team in the World University Games, an experience that will only improve his game heading into his senior year.

Dixon led the U.S. in scoring, averaging 19.3 points and 3.8 rebounds a game. He was also the team's top three-point shooter, hitting a team-high 17 of his 46 shots from behind the arc (.370 percent).

SF-BYRON MOUTON (6-6, 215 lbs., SR, #1, 9.6 ppg, 4.0 rpg, 1.2 apg, 0.8 spg, 22.7 minutes, .508 FG, .405 3PT, .779 FT, Rayne HS/Rayne, La.). One of the biggest question marks going into last season, when the Terps returned all five starters, was how the team's chemistry would be affected by Mouton's presence.

He sat out the 1999-2000 after transferring from Tulane, where he led the Green Wave in scoring for two consecutive years. But he also played the same position as Miller, who had started all 35 games of Mouton's red-shirt year, and there were questions about how Mouton would fit in.

Williams solved that problem fairly quickly, though painfully. Miller didn't play well early in the season and the Terps lost three of their first four games. Williams decided he needed to shake things up, and Mouton, as the most energetic player on the team, was able to provide a spark the Terps had been missing.

"We were flat early in the year," Williams said. "Byron gives you the enthusiasm that is really contagious. We put him in the starting lineup and he really changed us in terms of attitude on the court.

"That enthusiasm got through to a couple of other guys."

Mouton went on to start 30 games, providing explosive scoring capabilities from the wing and inside.

Miller, by all accounts, handled the transition well, but apparently didn't want to go through it a second time. In the off-season, he transferred to Notre Dame.

"We will miss Danny," Williams said. "But Byron was good for us, getting us off to some good starts. We had been getting off to some really bad starts. He was a guy we had to get on the court."

Mouton excelled as a starter, hitting 50.8 percent of his shots and finished the year as Maryland's second best shooter in the starting lineup. He improved his shooting dramatically from his gunning days at Tulane, where he made a paltry 36.9 percent of his shots.

PF-TAHJ HOLDEN (6-10, 247 lbs., JR, #45, 4.5 ppg, 2.3 rpg, 0.5 bpg, 12.1 minutes, .494 FG, .480 3PT, .608 FT, Red Bank Regional HS/Red Bank, N.J.). The one spot that Williams isn't sure about heading into the season is where Morris used to play, power forward. He has two good options in Holden, a junior, and Wilcox, a sophomore.

Neither player burned up the baskets last year, but both have lots of ability. Holden actually played better in the NCAA Tournament than Morris did, averaging 6.4 points, 2.8 rebounds and shooting 52.9 percent from the field in the five NCAA Tournament games.

"We have to get them both on the floor this season," Williams said. "It's a nice problem to have to deal with. We have to be creative about it."

Holden is another Williams recruit who wasn't particularly well thought of coming out of high school. Scouting reports said that he was soft and would have a hard time fitting into the ACC.

"To his credit, Tahj has become one of our strongest and toughest players," Williams said. "I can't say enough about him. I never saw as much criticism of a player before he even got a chance to practice by some people, and he just threw it all in their face."

Holden missed nine games during the early part of the season because of a broken foot, which he suffered in practice in early December. He returned to play in each of the Terrapins' final 20 games, showing a nice outside shooting touch and a strong physical presence inside.

His biggest game of the season came in the West Region NCAA Final, when he came off the bench to hit three of four three-points shots, all eight free throw attempts and score a career-high 14 points against Stanford.

"Without Tahj, we would not have been in the Final Four because his inside defense was key against teams like Stanford," Williams said. "I expect Tahj, like Lonny Baxter, to improve each year for us."

"He has a great chance to be a starter for us."

C-LONNY BAXTER (6-8, 260 lbs., SR, #35, 15.6 ppg, 7.9 rpg, 1.5 bpg, 0.9 spg, 26.0 minutes, .566 FG, .500 3PT, .592 FT, Hargrave Military Academy/Chatham, Va. and Anacostia HS/Silver Spring, Md.). Of the many obstacles Lonny Baxter has overcome to turn himself into an All-ACC basketball player, this had to be one of the most satisfying: the school finally got the nameplate on his locker spelled correctly. He was listed as "Lonnie" his first two years. Now, you can just call him a superstar.

Voted the Most Outstanding Player in the NCAA West Region last year and co-winner of team MVP honors with Juan Dixon, Baxter was one of the most important ingredients in the Terps' run at the Final Four. He averaged a double-double in the NCAA Tournament: 16.2 points and 10.0 rebounds.

Mostly what Baxter offered was brute strength inside. He's not tall enough, by most standards, to play center in college basketball. But he is certainly wide enough and strong enough. Few people want to get in his way.

Williams smiles when he thinks about Baxter's success, which began early in his freshman season when starting senior center Obinna Ekezie was lost to an injury. Baxter was forced into the starting lineup and he's been an inside monster ever since.

"In the long run, that was very beneficial for him," Williams said. "He has gotten better each year and we expect him to get better this year with taking jump shots and facing the baskets."

It would be nice to develop those skills, of course, but Baxter didn't become the ACC's third leading rebounder, sixth leading shot blocker and seventh leading scorer by working his way outside. He did it by working hard in the interior, catching Blake's passes for easy shots (hence the 56.6 field goal shooting percentage) and putting back rebounds for dunks and layups.

Williams doesn't want him to get away from those things in his final college season.

"You never want to take away from Lonny what he is good at, which is his ability to catch the ball down low, take it to the basket, take a foul and put the ball in the basket," Williams said. "Lonny is what basketball players used to be, which is to come in for four years and gradually become a very good basketball player."

There is still some room for improvement. Baxter attempted 25 percent more free throws than any other player on the team, yet Juan Dixon made more free-throws than Baxter did. Baxter finished the season shooting 59.2 percent from the line, which will need to improve if the Terps are going to get all the production it needs from inside.

Baxter had a productive summer playing for the bronze-medal winning U.S. team in the World University Games. He was the team's leading rebounder, grabbing 6.3 boards per game, along with his 15.3 points a game. He hit an amazing 69.8 percent of his shots in the tournament's eight games.

KEY RESERVES

G-DREW NICHOLAS (6-3, 160 lbs., JR, #12, 6.6 ppg, 1.6 rpg, 2.4 apg, 16.6 minutes, .494 FG, .420 3PT, .702 FT, Long Island Lutheran HS/Hempstead, N.Y.). Last year, when the Terps were woefully lacking in guards, Nicholas was the team's backcourt depth. He mostly filled in at point guard behind Steve Blake, even though it was not his natural position, but he also logged time at both wing positions, which is why Williams called him one of the team's most valuable contributors last year.

Nicholas was recruited as a shooting guard, but showed the ability to help out anywhere on the court. He was a fairly dangerous ball-handler against the press, but made only one turnover every 13.2 minutes of play, compared to one turnover every 9.3 minutes for Blake.

"Drew can play three positions for us," Williams said. "This year, we want to be able to use his flexibility. He is a very good shooter, even though he didn't shoot it particularly well last year.

"But he was able to play some pressure minutes, and I think he will come back a better player this year. He knows how to score and you can never have too many guys like that."

Nicholas played in every game last year and ended up third on the team in three-point field goals with 34. Despite what Williams said, Nicholas was the Terps' top three-point shooter last year and was among the best long-range shooters in the conference. His best game of the season came in the regular-season finale, when he scored 16 points and had 10 assists in a 102-67 rout of Virginia.

F/C-RYAN RANDLE (6-9, 245, JR, #33, 18.0 ppg, 7.0 rpg, .600 FG, Allegany CC/Cumberland, Md. and Duncanville HS/Duncanville, Texas). With the loss of Morris, Mardesich and the little-used Cephas—who combined for 18.6 points and 11.4 rebounds in 42.2 minutes per game last year—the Terps need immediate help inside.

Baxter, Holden and Wilcox are all certainly capable of picking up the slack, but Williams knows he needs more interior depth if the Terps are going to survive the ACC season and start another run in the NCAA Tournament.

Basically, the coach needed to find the 10 quality minutes a game he got last year from Mardesich.

So, like every other coach in college basketball, Williams went looking for a big man. And, like every other coach in college basketball, he discovered that there weren't many available.

He did, however, find Randle, a 260-pound hulk who just happened to play at the same Maryland junior college that produced one-year Terp star Steve Francis.

Randle helped Allegheny Junior College reach the National Junior College Athletic Association championship game. In his two years at the school, Randle helped the Trojans compile a 60-5 record. But he was not the center of the Trojans' offense in the homestretch of the season. That title belonged to Virginia Tech signee Terry Taylor. But that doesn't mean Randle can't be a good understudy this season for the Terps.

"He's got pretty good skills," Williams said. "Losing Morris and Mardesich, we needed another skilled big guy. I think he gives us that.

"How he will develop once he gets here, we'll have to see."

Williams has a good track record of recruiting guys who aren't highly regarded and turning them into productive players in the ACC. That pretty much describes Randle and the other two Terps' recruits perfectly.

PF-CHRIS WILCOX (6-10, 220 lbs., SO, #54, 3.6 ppg, 2.1 rpg, 0.5 blocks, 8.6 minutes, .580 FG, .606 FT, Enloe HS/Raleigh, N.C.). It took a while for Wilcox to get used to the pace of playing in the ACC. He barely contributed much of anything during the first three months of the season. He scored only 16 points in the Terps' first 11 ACC games. But after watching from the sideline so long, Wilcox started catching on in practice and was gradually worked into the rotation of players.

Williams even put the athletically gifted player into the starting lineup against Florida State in February. Wilcox responded by hitting 6-of-7 from the field and blocking three shots.

He quickly became a crowd favorite for his ability to dunk and block shots, but he had little polish away from the basket, other than an ability to make good interior passes. Williams hopes that will change heading into this year.

"Everybody knows that Chris dunks, and blocks shots, and exciting things like that," Williams said. "Now, Chris' next step as a sophomore is to develop his offensive game to where he can make shots out of the offense, not just follow-ups or fast breaks.

"He's got to be able to help us run the offense."

And while Williams loves Wilcox's shot-blocking abilities, the coach also expects him to play more team defense.

"He has got to become a solid defensive player where his man doesn't beat him off the dribble," Williams said. "He has to be able to keep a guy from catching the ball in the post."

Williams would like to get Wilcox, Holden and Baxter on the floor together whenever possible, giving the Terps one of the most formidable front lines in the conference. It would be a nice change from a lineup that included three quick guards. But Wilcox has to improve on both ends of the floor before he will earn double-digit minutes in the game.

OTHER RETURNEES

G-EARL BADU (6-0, 160 lbs., SR, #4, St. Francis Academy/Baltimore, Md.). After winning a spot on the roster during an open campus tryout in the fall of 1998, Badu begins his third season as essentially a practice player for the Terps. He and McCall mimic an upcoming opponents' backcourt during practice, which Williams calls a "key role" in the Terps preparation.

And while the perks are good, especially on a team that goes to the Final Four, Badu played only three minutes all of last year and did not score a point nor grab a rebound.

G-CALVIN MCCALL (6-3, 200 lbs., SR, #5, 0.5 ppg, 0.8 rpg, .250 FG, 2.8 minutes, Dr. Phillips HS/Orlando, Fla.). McCall seemed to have an extremely promising future at Maryland—as a quarterback for the football team. In fact, he was the Terps' starter for 17 games under previous head coach Ron Vanderlinden. He also joined the basketball team as a walk-on in December, 1999, and contributed some important minutes in his two seasons with the team.

However, when Ralph Friedgen took over the football program, it became apparent to McCall, who set school passing records for a freshman quarterback, that junior college transfer Shaun Hill would be the team's starting quarterback.

Friedgen wanted McCall to stop playing basketball to concentrate on football, something McCall didn't want to do. So he gave up his football scholarship to be a walk-on member of the basketball team. Williams did give him a scholarship, at least for this year.

McCall will still be little more than a practice player and self-described team clown who tries to keep things light in the locker room with his big laugh and frequent jokes. But Williams believes he might be a bigger contributor than most people anticipate.

"This is his first year of not playing football," the coach said. "He has played a lot of basketball that he didn't play before. He [was] in a very good summer league in Orlando with Tracy McGrady and those guys.

"It will be interesting in the fall."

Williams says McCall can shoot, even though he made only 4-of-13 shots last year. He's obviously athletic enough to play strong defense, even though he played the ultimate offensive position in football. His ball handling skills are adequate.

"I think he can really help us," Williams said. "He played quarterback. You have to be pretty intelligent to handle that."

C-MATT SLANNIKA (7-4, 257 lbs., FR, #40, DeMatha HS/Olney, Md.). Although he never started or scored more than 10 points in a single game as a high school senior, Slannika was a risk Williams was willing to take. Five years ago, Mardesich had similarly bad credentials and he proved to be a solid contributor for four years.

"You take a chance on a guy who is 7-4 and see how he is going to be," Williams said. "He has gotten better. Will he be good enough to help us this year? I don't know. But he will be good enough to help us in the future."

While many see Slannika, who red-shirted last season, as a poor man's Serge Zwikker (the former North Carolina center who blossomed enough over five years to get drafted by the NBA), Slannika still needs to develop some other skill than being tall.

Williams said Slannika improved while sitting out last year because he worked hard all year long.

"I know one thing, he is good to have around in practice," Williams said. "He gives you a good look on your second team when you are trying to work on things."

OTHER NEWCOMERS

G-ANDRE COLLINS (5-9, 180 lbs., FR, #10, 15.6 ppg, 6.0 apg, Hargrave Military Academy/Cheatham, Va. and Crisfield HS/Crisfield, Md.). One of the glaring weaknesses the Terps had last year was a replacement for Steve Blake at point guard. Drew Nicholas, a natural shooter, gave his best effort at giving Blake, who logged more minutes on the team than anyone other than Dixon, a little bench time, but the point is not Nicholas' regular position.

Williams hopes that having Collins around will allow Blake to catch his breath or just to give the Terps some flexibility with their lineup. In fact, the coach had hoped Collins would be around last year, but the quick guard needed to spend a year at prep school to become academically eligible.

Now, Williams is simply glad Collins around, even if he is the smallest player on any ACC roster this year.

"We can rest Steve now," the coach said. "There were times last year where Steve had to play tired and if we could have just gotten him out of there for a minute, it would have helped him. We didn't have that luxury."

Collins helped Hargrave Military Academy go 27-1 last year. In high school, he was a scoring machine, averaging 30 points a game as a senior and 29 points as a junior.

Williams won't just use Collins to spell Blake. The coach is already thinking of ways to put Blake, Collins and Nicholas on the court at the same time, giving the Terps the fastest backcourt in the ACC.

"That would make a great ball handling team," Williams said.

Rebounding, though, not so much.

F-MICHAEL GRINNON (6-6, 195 lbs., FR., #21, 19.0 ppg, St. Dominic HS/Oyster Bay, N.Y.). The Terps need someone to take Miller's role as a complementary swingman who can come off the bench and score points quickly.

Williams believes Grinnon is just the person to do that, though he hoped to give the player a year-long apprenticeship. That changed when Miller opted to transfer to Notre Dame.

"Grinnon is a great shooter," Williams said. "I think he will be a good four-year player for us. You need to get some guys who develop while they are in school and he is one of those guys who works very, very hard."

Like many of the recruits Williams has signed over the years, Grinnon wasn't a big name on the summer recruiting circuits. His signing last fall barely caused a ripple in the world of basketball recruiting. But Grinnon had a great senior season at St. Dominic High School, leading his team with a 19-point scoring average.

"He wants to be here and he wants to play," Williams said. "We have always had guys like that, who didn't play a lot in their first year, but wound up as good as some of the big-time recruits that you hear about.

"They were willing to work hard and when they got their turn, they were really good."

Grinnon, by most accounts, has good shooting range with the ability to make spot-up jumpers just about anywhere on the court. He still needs working creating his own shot, but Williams hopes that will come with time.

QUESTIONS

Pressure? The Terps know from the outset of this season that they will be one of the best teams in the country. They haven't fared very well the last two years under those expectations. Will this year be any different?

Depth? The Terps need some production out of a recruiting class that was not all that well thought of. Who is going to step forward and provide some critical off-the-bench minutes now that Mardesich and Miller aren't around any more?

Improvement? Dixon, Baxter and Blake have improved every year they have been on campus. Can they go even farther?

ANSWERS

Experience! With four returning starters, three of whom will get consideration for All-ACC honors, the Terps have one of the most settled lineups of any team

in the country, let alone the ACC.

Backcourt burners! Few teams in the country have a combination of backcourt players who can match Blake at the point and Dixon and Mouton on the wings.

Williams! When things started crumbling last year, Williams calmed down a little, turned down his famous foot-stomping, coat-throwing act and allowed the Terps to get their confidence back. This team should be mature enough not to get yelled at.

MARYLAND 2000-2001 RESULTS

#Louisville	95-73
#Illinois (L)	80-90
#Dayton (L)	71-77
##Wisconsin (L)	75-78
###Michigan	82-51
###George Washington	71-63
Stony Brook	107-59
@Pennsylvania	87-81
Maryland-Baltimore Co.	93-67
Norfolk State	123-78
Chicago State	117-55
UMES	105-53
@Clemson	104-92
Georgia Tech	93-80
North Carolina (L)	83-86
@Florida State	76-55
Wake Forest	81-71
@NC State	75-61
Duke (L)	96-98
Virginia (L)	78-99
Clemson	69-54
@Georgia Tech (L)	62-72
@North Carolina (L)	82-96
Florida State(L)	71-74
@Wake Forest	73-56
NC State	95-66
Oklahoma	68-60
@Duke	91-80
Virginia	102-67
####Wake Forest	71-53
####Duke (L)	82-84
#####George Mason	83-80
#####Georgia State	79-60
#####Georgetown	76-66
#####Stanford	87-73
#####Duke (L)	84-95

#Maui Invitational in Lahaina, HA
##ACC/Big Ten Challenge in Milwaukee, WI
###BB&T Classic in Washington, DC
####ACC Tournament in Atlanta
#####NCAA Tournament
@Road Games

BLUE RIBBON ANALYSIS

BACKCOURT	A+
BENCH/DEPTH	A-
FRONTCOURT	A-
INTANGIBLES	A-

Unfortunately for Williams, the Terps are getting ready to experience the hard part of success: sustaining it.

The hard-luck Terps had every right to celebrate last year's Final Four appearance after finally breaking through that self-installed ceiling. It was amazingly uncharted territory for a program that has had some great teams in the past.

But what should concern Williams is that he loses three senior starters—Baxter, Dixon and Mouton—after this season. It would have been nice to capitalize on last year's success and sign a blue-chip prospect in this year's freshman class, such as Julius Hodge (N.C. State) and Jawad Williams (North Carolina), two players Maryland heavily courted.

That didn't happen. In fact, most recruiting analysts are quite unimpressed with this year's trio of freshmen, as they frequently are with Williams' players. However, they admit that the coach has a good track record of developing lesser recruits and turning them into stars, as he did with Joe Smith, Rodney Elliott, Laron Profit, Terence Morris, Juan Dixon and Lonny Baxter.

But it's hard to sustain Final Four success with players who are projects and sleepers.

"We are fortunate, the way college basketball is these days, to have an experienced nucleus coming back," Williams said. "But our most important recruiting class in a while is going to be the one that arrives in September, 2002."

"I think we have some guys in this class who can help us, but the guys who can play are going to be here next fall."

Williams isn't about to let his team rest on its laurels, and as a recruiter, he doesn't want to either. But he hopes everyone's job will be a little less difficult now that his program has finally hit college basketball's big time.

"We had to get over the stigma of never going to the Final Four," Williams said. "We did that last year and now we have to move on.

"That doesn't guarantee us anything for this year, but it makes it easier to get there again."

(T.P.)

 **Florida 5**

LOCATION	Gainesville, FL
CONFERENCE	Southeastern (Eastern)
LAST SEASON	24-7 (.774)
CONFERENCE RECORD	12-4 (t-1st)
STARTERS LOST/RETURNING	1/4
NICKNAME	Gators
COLORS	Orange & Blue
HOMECOURT	O'Connell Center (12,000)
COACH	Billy Donovan (Providence '87)
RECORD AT SCHOOL	102-56 (5 years)
CAREER RECORD	137-76 (7 years)
ASSISTANTS	John Pelphrey (Kentucky '91)
	Anthony Grant (Dayton '87)
	Donnie Jones (Pikeville '88)
TEAM WINS (last 5 years)	13-14-22-29-24
RPI (last 5 years)	160-75-26-8-19
2000-01 FINISH	Lost in NCAA second round.

COACH AND PROGRAM

For the moment, let's ponder what might have been at Florida. In the aftermath of the 2000 national runner-up season, the Gators lost a pair of players—Mike Miller and Donnell Harvey—who left with two and three years, respectively, of eligibility remaining and were first-round picks in the NBA draft. Miller was the fifth overall selection and one of the top rookies in the NBA last season.

Last May, Florida signee Kwame Brown—a 6-foot-11, 250-pound forward with frightening skills and agility for a player that size—also took his act to the NBA. Brown didn't have to wait long to hear his name called. He was the first overall pick of the draft by the Washington Wizards and became the first high school player to go No. 1 overall.

Then in September came the news that guard Ted Dupay, rumored to be involved in gambling, was dismissed from the team when the rumors turned out to be true.

That's a significant loss of personnel, but don't feel sorry for the Gators, though. They're not exactly hurting.

Billy Donovan, entering his sixth season as the Florida head coach, has assembled a recruiting machine in Gainesville that is second to none. He has signed seven McDonald's All-Americans since 1998. Only Duke's Mike Krzyzewski can match that total during that same span.

Of course, one of those All-Americans was Brown, who had committed to the Gators just before his junior year of high school in Brunswick, Ga. But in the end, the lure of the NBA was simply too strong.

"It's obvious Kwame's decision was based on helping his family," said Donovan, who helped Brown train for the NBA pre-draft camps at Florida's facilities even after Brown spurned the Gators. "It's hard to fault anyone for trying to provide for their family. I certainly respect that decision because family should be the most important thing in everyone's life."

Had Brown not been pulled away by the NBA, he would have punctuated a freshman class that would have rivaled Michigan's Fab Five in the early 1990s as the most heralded of all-time.

Forwards David Lee of St. Louis, Mo., and James White of Kensington, Md., were two of the top 10 prospects in the country a year ago. To give you an idea about their talent, they finished 1-2 in the slam-dunk contest this past year at the McDonald's All-American game.

Donovan also reeled in power forward Adrian Moss, who was ruled eligible after initially signing with Southwest Texas State.

"We've got guys on this team who want to win,"

Donovan told the Gainesville Sun. "We'll lose Brent Wright and Major Parker, two guys who were major ingredients to this team. But with these guys, we'll have the same depth in the frontcourt that we do in the backcourt."

The returning nucleus includes senior center Udonis Haslem and junior guard Brett Nelson—two of the top five players in the SEC—while senior guard Teddy Dupay is certainly one of the grittiest players in the league. When completely healthy, Dupay is a terror from the perimeter.

The future is equally bright. Already, Donovan has commitments from four of the top players in the country for the 2002 signing class. Point guard Anthony Roberson of Saginaw, Mich., small forward Mario Boggan of Oak Hill (Va.) Academy and Matt Walsh of Fort Washington, Pa., are all ranked among the top 40 prospects in the country by Dave Telep of The Sporting News.

Another Florida commitment, shooting guard Rashid Al-Kaleem of Charlestown, Mass., is a Top 100 player nationally.

"All these kids want to go to Florida because there's a great style of play, and coach Donovan is a player's coach," Dupay told CBS SportsLine. "All the players love him, and it's still the University of Florida. There are no negatives about it.

"Top programs are going to lose people to the NBA or graduation, and you have to reload to be successful. He has done it four years in a row."

With that said, the Gators enter yet another season lugging considerable expectations. Donovan likes it that way. It has become the unwritten standard at a school where basketball was once an afterthought, something that passed the time away between football season and spring football.

But not anymore.

Donovan, 36, has the basketball program at Florida booming. The Gators were knocked out in the second round of the NCAA Tournament last season, but lost in the national championship game two years ago to Michigan State.

His recruiting prowess unquestioned, Donovan also proved that he could coach a little bit last season. Injuries hit the Gators like a two-ton truck. Point-guard Justin Hamilton went down. So did Wright, and so did Dupay.

Still, Florida hung on and managed to knock off Kentucky on the final day of the regular season to earn a share of the SEC championship along with the Wildcats. The Gators closed the regular season with seven consecutive wins.

"I don't mind having expectations placed on our program," Donovan said. "High expectations mean you should be in the mix for high seeds in the NCAA Tournament and competing for conference championships every year. That is what we hope to do.

"I hope the expectations people have for us, though, are based on the experience we have returning from last year and not because of the freshmen we have coming in. Our freshmen are certainly talented, but the strength of our club will be in experience."

Indeed, four starters and 10 players from last season's team are back. The Gators, in sweeping to their second straight SEC title, joined Kentucky as the only team in the league to go back-to-back in the last 25 years.

With so many injuries a year ago, Donovan had to pull back the reins a bit on his pressure-until-you-drop style. But the numbers are there this year for the Gators to get back to the up-and-down style that worked so well for them during their run to the national championship game.

"I really think we will be in a position to be 10-deep," said Donovan, who had players miss 33 games with injuries last season. "We didn't play with a full complement of players for the entire SEC schedule last year and we really had to make adjustments in our style of play."

All told, Florida returns 84 percent of its offense and 80 percent of its rebounding.

"With our depth and with our experience, and if we stay injury free, we're a basketball team that can compete with anybody," Donovan said. "But like anything else, we've got to be able to win basketball games. We're a team that has good players and good talent. I just know that on any given night in our league, with the way things are, anything can happen."

2001-2002 SCHEDULE

Nov.	8-9	Coaches vs. Cancer Classic
	16	Florida State
	28	@New Hampshire
Dec.	2	Tulane
	5	Michigan State
	8	@South Florida
	15	*Charlotte
	18	High Point
	22	New Orleans
	28	Stetson
	30	Belmont
Jan.	5	South Carolina
	9	@Tennessee
	12	@Vanderbilt
	16	LSU
	19	Georgia
	26	@Arkansas
	29	Kentucky
Feb.	2	Mississippi State
	5	@South Carolina
	9	Vanderbilt
	12	@Georgia
	16	@Ole Miss
	20	Auburn
	23	@Alabama
	26	Tennessee
March	2	@Kentucky
	7-10	##SEC Tournament

@Road Games
*Orange Bowl Classic, Miami, FL
#New York, NY (vs. Temple, first round; also Arizona and Maryland)
##SEC Tournament, Atlanta, GA

STARTERS NOT RETURNING

SG-TEDDY DUPAY (5-11, 178 lbs., SR, #5, 13.4 ppg, 2.2 rpg, 2.8 apg, 1.5 spg, 29.6 minutes, .407 FG, .371 3PT, .817 FT, Mariner HS/Ft. Myers, Fla.). The gambling investigation by Florida campus police that hung over Dupay's head in the off-season made for some uneasy moments for everyone.

Dupay denied the allegations from the time they broke, but ultimately he owned up to them as Florida had no choice but to dismiss him from the team.

For most of the off-season, Dupay was more worried about returning to the court healthy after fighting through injuries last season. Dupay made a miraculous return from back surgery to help lead the Gators to their second straight SEC title. He did his best to scale it back during the off-season.

"I took a couple of months where I didn't do anything but shoot every once in a while," Dupay told CBS SportsLine. "I needed it mentally and physically. I'm trying to get back into shape so I can hopefully start the season fresh. It was way too early for me to come back [from disc surgery], but it was the right time for us. We won 10 of our last 11 games and were able to turn things around. It was still a rewarding season, but we just ran out of gas [against Temple in the NCAA Tournament]."

Dupay, plagued by a torn rotator cuff in his shoulder as a sophomore, was one of the country's best shooters. He had great range and was equally effective with the ball in his hands. He ranked third in school history with 188 career three-pointers.

SF-MAJOR PARKER (6-4, 5.1 ppg, 3.4 rpg, 1.6 apg, 23.4 minutes, .426 FG, .393 3PT, .565 FT). Parker didn't offer big numbers, but he was one of the Gators' emotional leaders and a relentless defender. He was versatile enough and strong enough to guard out on the perimeter while also dropping back into the paint and leaning on a bigger players when necessary.

Parker was also one of those players who just seemed to find a way to make a big shot or a big play when the Gators needed it most.

While his basketball career at Florida is over, he's giving football a shot this fall as a fifth-year senior. Parker has bulked up to 240 pounds and is playing defensive end for Steve Spurrier's Gators.

OTHERS NOT RETURNING

PF-BRENT WRIGHT (6-8, 12.7 ppg, 6.2 rpg, 1.6 apg, 1.3 spg, 24.4 minutes, .579 FG, .577 3PT, .809 FT). One of the more diverse players on the team and a team captain, Wright simply couldn't shake the injury bug a year ago.

He opened his senior season playing some of the best basketball of his career. His size and ability to shoot from the perimeter made him a difficult cover for any-

body. But Wright suffered a stress fracture in his right foot and had surgery on Jan. 4. He returned four games later, only to break his thumb and undergo a second surgery

Later in the season, Wright re-aggravated his foot injury and underwent a third surgery. He missed the entire postseason, as Donovan didn't want to risk bringing him back and possibly jeopardizing any future Wright might have at the professional level.

Wright began last season as a starter, but was replaced by Matt Bonner after the injuries began to accumulate.

Wright and Parker were the first two players Donovan signed when he came to Florida. Donovan will honor them by hanging their jerseys in the new $10 million practice facility.

G-DAVID KLIEWER (6-2, 0.3 ppg, 0.5 apg, 4 minutes, .250 FG). Kliewer was a walk-on player attending Florida on an academic scholarship. He was forced into action during the rash of injuries last January. But in February and March, he played a total of one minute.

PROJECTED STARTERS

PG-JUSTIN HAMILTON (6-3, 207 lbs, JR, #12, 6.6 ppg, 1.8 rpg, 2.7 apg, 1.3 spg, 22.7 minutes, .402 FG, .258 3PT, .750 FT, Booker HS/Sarasota, Fla.). Hamilton was the Gators' starting point guard in the national championship game as a freshman and was also running the club last season before blowing out his knee.

In a Jan. 17 game against Georgia, Hamilton tore the anterior cruciate ligament in his knee while attempting a layup. He missed the remainder of the season, but has worked his way back. Hamilton returned to the court in June after some intense rehabilitation.

Regarded as one of the SEC's top defenders, Hamilton has rangy arms and is extremely athletic. He also takes care of the basketball. He had 26 assists and just four turnovers in his last nine games before he was injured.

But what Donovan likes most about Hamilton is the way he pressures other teams into mistakes and the way he disrupts. Hamilton is versatile enough to play both guard spots and could also play small forward. He owns a 38-inch vertical leap.

"Everybody wants to play offense ... everybody can play offense," Hamilton said. "But you have to have somebody that can play defense. I am going to be a player who is going to do that. I have always liked to play defense and cause havoc."

Hamilton's efforts on defense haven't gone unnoticed. He was chosen by ESPN analyst Dick Vitale as one of the top five defenders in the country.

"A lot of people don't notice the good things Justin does on the court because he is so quiet," Haslem said. "He has long arms and is very athletic. He is the most active player on the court with his hands and gets a lot of deflections."

PG-ORIEN GREENE (6-4, 200 lbs., SO, #1, 3.4 ppg, 2.3 rpg, 2.7 apg, 1.2 spg, 19.1 minutes, .354 FG, .250 3PT, .750 FT, Gainesville HS/Gainesville, Fla.). This is just a guess on our part. Greene could end up starting as Florida goes with three guards, or Donovan might decide to insert one of his athletic freshmen into the lineup.

Green is a multi-dimensional player, but he will probably see most of his time at point guard this season.

Last season, he was one of five players on the team to play in every game. His strengths are his ability to find the open man and defend. He's also an outstanding leaper, which coupled with his 6-4 frame, can make life miserable for opposing guards.

"The thing about Orien is that when you are playing with him or against him, you don't realize he's [6-4] because he is doing so many things a shorter player can do," Dupay said. "That's when you know a guy is really skilled."

Greene didn't play like a freshman last season, as evidenced by his 85 assists (second on the team) and his ten turnover free games. Green led Florida in assists in four games, and had two seven-assist, no turnover games (against Florida A&M and New Hampshire). "Orien is someone who likes to pass," Donovan said. "He derives a lot of pleasure in that."

Green can also score. He had a career-high 13 point against New Hampshire and 12 against South Carolina in his first SEC game.

Green was a decorated high school player. He was Florida's Mr. Basketball and a third-team Parade All-American. Along with Hamilton, Nelson and Dupay, he gives the Gators one of the deepest backcourts in the nation.

SG-BRETT NELSON (6-3, 182 lbs., JR, #10, 15.3 ppg, 2.7 rpg, 4.3 apg, 1.9 spg, 31.2 minutes, .450 FG, .453 3PT, .800 FT, St. Albans HS/St. Albans, W.Va.). A consensus first-team All-SEC choice last season, Nelson enters this season as perhaps the premier backcourt player in the league. He can do it all—shoot, pass, finish and get to the basket. There were some who thought Nelson would have been a mid first-round selection in the NBA draft had he come out last season. Nelson gave it some thought, but decided to return.

In reality, Nelson still needs to get stronger and put on some weight before he's ready for the NBA rigors. But he should be one of the real difference-makers in college basketball this season.

"He's awesome," said backcourt mate Teddy Dupay after the Gators beat Tennessee last January. "Who's better than him in America right now? We've seen flashes of it, but nobody comes in as a freshman and is great. He had some great spurts, but it's about eight games in a row now where he has been super. And that's a sign of a great player, when he's great every night. You know he's the first one in everyone's scouting report."

Nelson's 17.9 scoring average in league games was tops in the conference last season. He also shot an astonishing .453 from three-point range, and that's after taking 179 three-point shots.

"I'm really, really excited with the improvement Brett made from his freshman to his sophomore year," Donovan told the Gainesville Sun. "He had an outstanding year. A lot of people thought he should have been co-player of the year in the conference, with he and [Kentucky's] Tayshaun Prince. Brett's going to continue to get better because of his love of the game. He's going to work on his shooting and his strength, which will allow him to expand his game."

Nelson was much more under control last season. His quick release enables him to get a shot from just about anywhere, but he's also effective on dribble penetration and pulling up for jumpers on the break.

Nelson led the Gators in scoring 14 times. He scored at least 17 points in 11 straight SEC games and reached double figures in 15 of the Gators' 16 games inside the league.

Nelson can also pass and defend. He led the Gators in assists in 22 games and finished second in the league in assistts. Nelson led the SEC with his average of 2.2 steals in league games only.

PF-MATT BONNER (6-10, 237 lbs., JR, #15, 13.3 ppg, 7.7 rpg, 1.5 apg, 0.8 spg, 0.4 bpg, 28.5 minutes, .514 FG, .381 3PT, .664 FT, Concord HS/Concord, N.H.). Bonner was one of the most improved players in the country last season. An academic All-American, he is a polished shooter for a big man and is capable of scoring from several different spots on the floor. His rebounding a year ago was huge. Bonner averaged 8.6 rebounds in league games, which was second best in the SEC.

"He's got it all, a full package and strong body," CBS analyst James Worthy said. "He can score from a variety of ways and is really a match-up problem for a lot of defenses."

Bonner started in 17 games last season, taking over after Wright ran into his injury problems. Bonner more than picked up the slack with his blend of offense, rebounding and smarts.

During the off-season, Bonner had surgery in June to remove bone chips and correct cartilage damage in his left knee.

C-UDONIS HASLEM (6-9, 246 lbs., SR, #50, 16.8 ppg, 7.5 rpg, 1.0 apg, 0.8 spg, 1.0 bpg, 28 minutes, .597 FG, .709 FT, Miami Senior HS/Miami, Fla.). Haslem looks like he ought to be playing tight end in the NFL. That is, until you see him move in the post and work his bevy of low-post moves. He's almost impossible to stop one-on-one. His touch is as soft as he is strong.

Haslem was a third-team All-America selection by the Associated Press last season. He ranks in the top 10 at Florida in eight different career categories and has started in 68 consecutive games.

Without question, Haslem will be the heart of this team.

"He has a win-first attitude," Donovan said. "I think that made him understand, really understand, what it means to play for a title. At Miami Senior, he didn't average a lot of points or rebounds. But he just won. He's a selfless guy who knows what is best for the team."

Former South Carolina head coach Eddie Fogler said last season that he had seen very few post players cut from the same mold as Haslem.

"He's the best post player I've seen with hands, posi-

tioning, competitiveness, runs the court as good as anybody," Fogler said. "The key is foul trouble. Now we don't intentionally go after him. He's too smart for that ... I don't care what he does for the rest of the year. I think he's the best man in the league."

Haslem has dropped 40-plus pounds and reduced his body fat from more than 15 percent to 9.8 percent since coming to Florida as a freshman.

A sleeker Haslem was too much for the SEC to handle last season, considering he was already stronger than anyone he faced in the league—he was voted the strongest player in the league in a Sports Illustrated poll—and is so crafty in the post. He led the league in field-goal percentage and was third in scoring. He reached double figures in 27-of-31 games and had nine double-doubles.

The Gators really leaned on Haslem in the postseason. He averaged 20 points in the NCAA Tournament, the fifth-highest average in the tournament.

Haslem could be considered undersized for a center, but not in Donovan's opinion.

"He plays taller than 6-8 because he is 6-8 wide," Donovan said. "If he gets position, he plays like he's seven feet. He's always been a very intelligent playe when it comes to gaining position, sealing, posting and catching the ball in the low post. He's very effective."

KEY RESERVES

SF-LADARIUS HALTON (6-4, 200 lbs., JR, #23, 3.2 ppg, 1.5 rpg, 1.4 apg, 0.8 spg, 14.2 minutes, .378 FG, .283 3PT, .682 FT, New Smyrna HS/New Smyrna Beach, Fla.). The Gators have yet to see the best of Halton, who battles a degenerative condition in his right knee. Halton, one of the most explosive athletes on the team, was forced to miss the 1999-00 season after having surgery on his knee. He appeared more comfortable as last season progressed and started in five games.

"He is so athletic, he does things you can't teach," Donovan said.

Halton could fit in at either one of the wing positions and would be a candidate to start early in the season if the Gators want a little more height in the lineup. One of many outstanding leapers on the team, Halton has uncanny body control and goes to the basket with a vengeance. He has gained more than 15 pounds since his freshman season.

Halton's role increased gradually last season. He averaged 15.4 minutes for the last 26 games after averaging just seven the first four. In a five-game stretch in the SEC season, Halton was on the floor an average of 24 minutes.

Halton had season highs of 11 points (against Florida A&m, South Carolina and New Hampshire) and six assists (against Bethune-Cookman).

F-JAMES WHITE (6-6, 172 lbs., FR, #2, 18.0 ppg, 6.0 rpg, Hargrave Military Academy/Chatham, Va. and Newport HS/Kensington, Md.). If Donovan were picking the one true small forward on this team, it would be White. He attended Hargrave (Va.) Military Academy as a senior in high school, but is originally from Kensington, Md. White was rated one of the top three small forwards in the country by The Sporting News coming out of Hargrave.

"He is such an explosive athlete," Donovan said. "You're not going to find a better runner and jumper in the country. He's a guy who handles it, passes it and shoots it very well. There have not been too many guys that I've seen in high school that leave the floor and do the things he can do."

White led Hargrave to a 25-1 record last season against mostly junior colleges and junior varsity teams from four-year universities.

Donovan said White isn't a great shooter, but a very good shooter. And with the way Florida likes to run and press, White should fit in perfectly.

"He's done stuff I've never seen before in my entire life," Donovan said. "Off of one leg off the floor, they've measured (his vertical leap) at 46 inches. He'll jump from the free-throw line. He can do a lot of different things."

F-DAVID LEE (6-9, 224 lbs., FR, #24, 25.0 ppg, 12.0 rpg, 4.0 apg, 4.0 bpg, Chaminade Prep/St. Louis, Mo.). From the time he committed to Florida, Lee has evoked comparisons to Miller. Both are in the 6-9 range and can shoot it from the outside. Both are from the Midwest, and both were heavily recruited by Kansas before ultimately deciding on Florida.

"Plus, we're both white," Lee told the Gainesville Sun.

Recruiting analyst Brick Oettinger called Lee "the best Caucasian prospect we've seen in well over a

decade."

It remains to be seen if Lee can shoot as well as Miller did. But Lee is more equipped athletically to play right now than Miller was when he arrived on campus. Lee weighs 224 pounds, loves to post up players and isn't shy about taking his game out on the perimeter. He's also a dunking machine.

"Do I know David Lee?" Miller said. "Yeah, I know David. He's better than me. Right now."

A natural left-hander, he broke his left arm as a sophomore in high school and played the last four weeks using his right hand.

Lee, who wears his hear long, admits that he doesn't look like a basketball player. It's a look that has lulled some of his opponents to sleep.

"I'm not that strong, so I don't look like I can play," Lee said. "Plus, I have long hair. So I look kind of like the village idiot."

When opponents watch Lee soar over their heads, they don't think he's the village idiot. Like new teammate White, Lee has some serious hops. He won the slam dunk contest at the McDonald's All-American game and again at the Nike Derby Festival.

Lee could have played anywhere in the country—his final choices were Duke, North Carolina, Kentucky, Missouri, Kansas, Illinois and Florida—but he was impressed with his recruitment by Donovan and Florida. During the recruiting process, he began jokingly calling Donovan "The Stalker."

Donovan was glad his hard work paid off. He'll put Lee to good use this season.

"David Lee is a multi-dimensional guy," Donovan said. "he can step out and shoot it, he can put it on the floor. He is extremely athletic and explosive."

OTHER RETURNEES

F-BONELL COLAS (6-9, 205 lbs., SO, #42, 3 ppg, 2 rpg, 8.6 minutes, .583 FG, .731 FT, North Miami HS/Miami, Fla.). Colas arrived at Florida weighing just 190 pounds. But he's already added 15 pounds to his frame and would like to eventually get to 225. He's proven he can run the floor, finish on the break and block shots. But with Haslem prone to foul trouble on occasion, Colas will need to shore up his post defense and ability to rebound in traffic.

Colas showed improvement in his overall game last season and gained confidence on the offensive end. The key this season will be adding strength.

"I'm pretty much on a sight diet," Colas said. "I try to eat everything in sight."

Colas played in 25 of the 31 games last season. Six of his 10 blocked shots came in a five-game stretch late in the season.

G-RONNIE KING (5-11, 178 lbs., JR, #53, 1.7 ppg, 0.4 rpg, 0.7 minutes, Armwood High School/Brandon, Fla.). King was not eligible last season after changing his major and falling below required minimum hours toward graduation progress, although he still practiced with the team.

A fourth-year walk-on, King is a sticky man-to-man defender in the halfcourt and possesses the quickness to keep his man in front of him. He's not afraid to attack the basket and has made 23 trips to the free-throw line despite playing just 49 career minutes.

As a sophomore in 1999-00, King was the only walk-on to see action in the NCAA Tournament. He also played in the SEC Tournament.

OTHER NEWCOMERS

F-ADRIAN MOSS (6-9, 219 lbs., FR, #4, 17.0 ppg, 8.0 rpg, Fork Union Military Academy/Fork Union, Va. and Humble High School/Houston, Texas). He's not Kwame Brown, but when Moss was able to sign a scholarship in late July, he solved some depth problems created when Brown opted for the NBA draft.

There was some uncertainty this summer as to whether Moss would be eligible this season. But after initially signing with Southwest Texas State in 1999, he received a full release from that scholarship after a postgraduate year at Fork Union. Moss has been at Florida since the second session of summer school.

Moss is a relentless rebounder and shot blocker who was one of five Division I signees on a Fork Union team that went 24-7. He runs the floor well, has a good face-up game and is comfortable with his back to the basket. In one game last season, Moss scored 35 points.

Moss went to high school just north of Houston and signed with Southwest Texas in November, 1999. But when that school made a coaching change, Moss had second thoughts and asked out of his scholarship. He was listed as one of the top 12 unsigned seniors in the nation by *The Sporting News* in January of 2001 before settling on the Gators.

"He is a disciplined kid who has improved tremendously in his year at Fork Union Military Academy and he will be an asset in our frontcourt," Donovan said.

QUESTIONS

Dupay's status? How long does this gambling investigation linger, and will there be a hangover effect? Dupay has maintained he has done nothing wrong, and there has been no evidence that he has. The Gators, even with their depth, need him on the floor and need him healthy to be at their best. Haslem is the guy inside who makes it go, but Dupay is that guy on the perimeter.

Backing up Haslem? During his career, Haslem has occasionally run into foul trouble. There's not much behind him this season. Colas is more of a rangy small forward who likes to run the floor. With Brown opting for the NBA, the Gators don't have that other big body who can score, rebound and defend in the post, though freshman Adrian Moss is known as a shot blocker.

ANSWERS

Freshman class! White and Lee have all the tools to be stars. They should also complement each other well, White at small forward and Lee at power forward. Landing just one of them would have been a coup for most programs. But for the Gators to sign both in the same class simply spells bad news for everybody else in the SEC the next few years.

U-D! It's short for Udonis Haslem. As former Gator Major Parker once said, the only person to ever stop Udonis Haslem is Udonis Haslem. When he gets on one of those rolls in the paint, he's something to see. In many ways, he's college basketball's version of Karl Malone. And with Nelson and Dupay bombing away from the perimeter and opening up the paint, Haslem could be in for a colossal year.

Numbers game! Donovan has the depth to play the way he wants to this year, which means the Gators will look to press and run teams into submission. Even the big guys (Lee, Colas, Bonner, Haslem and Moss) run the court well. There's also a whole host of wing players such as Halton, White, Hamilton and Greene who are in that 6-3 to 6-6 range and are blurs up and down the court.

FLORIDA 2000-2001 RESULTS

@Florida State	85-70
Florida Atlantic	100-42
DePaul	83-76
@Michigan State (L)	83-99
Rutgers	79-65
Florida A&M	125-50
#Gonzaga	85-71
Bethune-Cookman	106-64
American University	76-33
@Tulane	103-85
New Hampshire	102-54
@South Carolina (L)	68-69
@Mississippi State	81-80
Georgia (L)	72-75
Vanderbilt (L)	61-63
@Auburn	65-63
South Carolina	69-57
Tennessee	81-67
@Georgia	82-71
@Kentucky (L)	70-71
Arkansas	73-63
@LSU	81-74
@Tennessee	88-82
Mississippi	75-55
Alabama	89-68
@Vanderbilt	72-62
Kentucky	94-86
##Alabama	69-62
##Mississippi (L)	69-74
###Western Kentucky	69-55
###Temple (L)	54-75

#At Sunrise, FL
##SEC Tournament in Nashville
###NCAA Tournament
@Road Games

BLUE RIBBON ANALYSIS

BACKCOURT	A
BENCH/DEPTH	A
FRONTCOURT	A-
INTANGIBLES	A

If Brown hadn't turned pro, the Gators would have been an easy choice for preseason No. 1. They might still warrant some consideration.

This team has a similar make-up to the one that went to the championship game in 2000. In Haslem and Nelson, the Gators have an inside-outside tandem Donovan wouldn't trade for any other duo in the country.

There is also the infusion of new talent, spearheaded by White and Lee, that will make the Gators even more athletic this season.

Though Florida's depth was impacted slightly with the loss of Kwame Brown to the NBA and Donovan to a suspension, the Gators will still have plenty of run/jump athletes to play the style their coach favors. That means Florida will be the aggressor on defense, trying to force turnovers and speed up the tempo of the game. Offensively, Haslem will see a lot of action in the post, but as always, the Gators won't be hesitant to let fly with a three-pointer when they get open looks. And they always work hard for those.

Donovan, already the winningest NCAA Tournament coach in Florida history, is committed to seeing the Gators making deep runs in the tournament every year.

"The University of Florida has enjoyed pockets of success in men's basketball," Donovan said. "Our goal is to bring some consistency to the program.

"The more times you play in the NCAA Tournament, the more chances you have to be successful."

The Gators will be gunning for their fourth straight 20-win season. Kentucky will have something to say about the SEC title, but don't be surprised if Florida is still alive when the Final Four converges on the Georgia Dome in Atlanta.

The Gators are that good—and that deep.

(C.L.)

UCLA 6

LOCATION	Los Angeles, CA
CONFERENCE	Pac-10
LAST SEASON	23-9 (.719)
CONFERENCE RECORD	14-4 (3rd)
STARTERS LOST/RETURNING	1/4
NICKNAME	Bruins
COLORS	Blue & Gold
HOMECOURT	Pauley Pavilion (12,800)
COACH	Steve Lavin (Chapman '88)
RECORD AT SCHOOL	114-47 (5 years)
CAREER RECORD	114-47 (5 years)
ASSISTANTS	Jim Saia (Chapman '87)
	Gerald Madkins (UCLA '97)
	Steve Spencer (Sonoma State '85)
TEAM WINS (last 5 years)	24-24-22-21-23
RPI (last 5 years)	8-13-20-28-7
2000-01 FINISH	Lost in NCAA
	East Regional semifinal.

COACH AND PROGRAM

The days of being too young and too few are over at UCLA. Limited at times in recent years by youth and/or lack of depth, the Bruins rank as the almost unanimous favorite in the Pac-10 because they have experience and numbers.

It's a given that UCLA always has talent.

"I think our team is kind of hungry to get back in the winner's circle in terms of the Pac-10 championship," coach Steve Lavin said. "We've finished strong the last couple of years, but it took a while to adjust both years, first losing [point guard] Baron [Davis after 1999], then last year JaRon [Rush] and Jerome [Moiso].

"Hopefully, from the outset, from start to finish, this is a team with the depth and experience and maturity and leadership to play at a more consistent level."

The Bruins aren't without a few question marks, but there are so many potential answers they cannot be ignored as the conference favorite. Four starters return, including the frontline trio of center Dan Gadzuric and forwards Jason Kapono and Matt Barnes.

Among the top seven scorers on last year's squad, only starting point guard Earl Watson is gone. And the Bruins will replace him with prep All-American Cedric Bozeman, who headlines one of the nation's premier recruiting classes.

The Bruins anticipate sizable contributions from two other players who red-shirted last season—fifth-year senior wing **Rico Hines** and transfer **John Hoffart**, a massive center from Cal Poly.

In all, Lavin can call upon 10 or more capable players, which should dovetail nicely with the switch to the full-court press defensive scheme.

Down at halftime against North Carolina in Pauley Pavilion, Lavin went to the press and the Bruins transformed an 18-point deficit into a two-point lead before succumbing, 80-70. Just 4-4 at that point in the season, with critics at their heels, the Bruins stayed with wall-to-wall defensive pressure the rest of the season and thrived.

They won 19 of their final 24 games, forcing an average of 17.3 turnovers during that stretch while out-shooting foes 47.8 percent to 42.7 percent.

There were a few bumps along the way, such as at Cal, where the Golden Bears dismantled the UCLA press and won, 92-63. But the Bruins rebounded two days later to knock off No. 1 and unbeaten Stanford, 79-73.

In the NCAA Tournament, defense also paved the way for UCLA's dash into the Sweet 16 round for the fourth time in Lavin's five seasons. The Bruins squashed Hofstra, 61-48, in the opening round, then suffocated Utah State, 75-50, marking the first time in 19 seasons UCLA had limited consecutive opponents to 50 points or fewer.

"We'll be deeper at each position and able to plug guys in on the press," Lavin said. "We're probably more athletic and quicker, and we have a year of experience with the press."

Lavin is also becoming more experienced, although some of his experience comes through events he would have preferred avoiding. Two years ago, at the end of the 1999-2000 season, UCLA received an e-mail containing a death threat against Lavin's father, Cap Lavin. An arrest subsequently was made in the case.

Last year, Lavin dealt with the distraction of athletic director Pete Dalis having spoken with Rick Pitino, who had recently resigned his position with the Boston Celtics. Dalis and Pitino both claimed the conversation had nothing to do with Pitino looming as a potential coaching candidate at Westwood, but there was no stopping the rumor mill.

Pitino wound up taking the job at Louisville, and Lavin said he has received support from UCLA chancellor Dr. Albert Carnesale and vice chancellor Pete Blackman, who played for coach John Wooden in the early 1960s, and who oversees athletics.

Finally, last spring, the school, several Southern California newspapers and Arn Tellum, who is Lavin's agent, received copies of a e-mail alleging a series of NCAA violations by Lavin and threatening to expose all of them to the media unless Lavin were fired.

Investigation of the case was not entirely resolved by late August, but no major violations involving Lavin were anticipated.

All three episodes contribute to what Lavin called "a brave new world," but he enters this season feeling somewhat more comfortable with the state of things.

"I don't think at the highest level there's going to be such a thing as smooth sailing. There's always something on the horizon," he said. "But in terms of my situation, because of the support of the chancellor and the vice chancellor, I feel really good about my future."

Not to mention the immediate future of his basketball team.

2001-2002 SCHEDULE

Nov.	19-21	#Houston
	28	Pepperdine
Dec.	5	UC Riverside
	8	*Alabama
	15	UC Irvine
	20	@Washington
	22	@Washington State
	27	Columbia
	29	Georgetown
Jan.	4	Washington
	6	Washington State
	10	@Southern Cal
	12	Kansas

	17	@Arizona State
	19	@Arizona
	24	Stanford
	26	California
	31	@Oregon
Feb.	2	@Oregon State
	6	Southern Cal
	9	@Villanova
	14	Arizona
	16	Arizona State
	21	@California
	23	@Stanford
	28	Oregon State
March	2	Oregon
	7-9	##Pac-10 Tournament

@Road Games
*John Wooden Classic, Anaheim, CA
#Maui, HI (vs. Houston first round; also Ball State, Chaminade, Duke, Kansas, Seton Hall, South Carolina)
##Staples Center, Los Angeles

STARTERS NOT RETURNING

PG-EARL WATSON (6-1, 14.7 ppg, 3.7 rpg, 5.2 bpg, 34.8 minutes, .493 FG, .352 3PT, .636 FT). He played two years at shooting guard in the shadow of classmate Baron Davis, then took over at the point the last two seasons and became a rock of consistency for the Bruins.

Watson is the only four-year player in UCLA history to start every regular-season and NCAA Tournament game (129) and he used that opportunity to set the Bruins' career mark of 235 steals. Watson also ranks No. 4 at UCLA in assists (607), making him only the second player in school history with at least 600 assists and 200 steals.

The Kansas City, Kansas native finished his career with 1,449 points, a four-year scoring average of 11.2 points per game.

As a senior last year, Watson led the Pac-10 with 1.9 steals per game and ranked second in assists at 5.2.

"Earl Watson is the most courageous player I've ever coached," Lavin said. "To start all those games, he played through concussions, eye surgery, stitches and other numerous bumps and bruises. He has been our leader and at my side for the last four years. I will truly miss him."

OTHERS NOT RETURNING

G-RYAN BAILEY (6-3, 2.2 ppg, 1.0 rpg, 12.0 minutes, .351 FG, .200 3PT, .629 FT). The younger brother of former UCLA star Toby Bailey played three seasons for the Bruins after transferring from Penn State. Bailey played 93 games for UCLA, all but 14 of them coming off the bench.

He enjoyed his most productive UCLA season as a junior, averaging 3.2 points and 2.4 assists while playing nearly 17 minutes per game.

G-JASON FLOWERS (6-0, 1.2 ppg, 0.6 rpg, 6.6 minutes, .429 FG, .286 3PT, .750 FT). Flowers played one season at UCLA as a walk-on after transferring from UC Irvine. He was inserted into the starting lineup when the Bruins were 4-4 and about to play at Purdue, and he contributed to an 8-2 stretch as a starter at mid-season.

G-RYAN MOLLINS (6-5, 0.5 ppg, 0.3 rpg, 1.3 minutes in four games, .500 FG). A freshman walk-on last season, Mollins did not return this year.

PROJECTED STARTERS

C-DAN GADZURIC (6-11, 248 lbs., SR, #50, 11.7 ppg, 8.6 rpg, 1.9 bpg, 26.9 minutes, .534 FG, .453 FT, Governor Dummer Academy/Byfield, Mass.). Gadzuric has made steady progress since his debut three years ago as a raw prospect, and UCLA believes he can be one of the nation's most productive big men this season. A soccer player in his native Holland during his youth, Gadzuric averaged 13.3 points, 12.0 rebounds and 2.7 blocks in three NCAA Tournament games last spring.

"He's probably the poster child for staying in school for four years and getting a degree, because he's so dominant," Lavin said. "When Dan is out of foul trouble and injury-free, he's as dominant a low-post player as there is in the country."

Injuries were a problem early, as Gadzuric sat out UCLA's NCAA loss to Detroit his freshman year because of knee problems. Other than a sprained ankle, however, he was healthy last year, and the results were evident.

Gadzuric did accumulate 98 personal fouls last sea-

son, fouling out of four games, but Lavin believes he can limit those problems merely by slowing down a bit.

"He was very raw and athletic when he came to UCLA," Lavin said. "His poise and composure are the areas you see the improvement. When he takes a deep breath and takes his time, his energy and compassion are plusses on defense. Offensively, he needs to play aggressively and hard-nosed, but take his time."

Gadzuric had 11 double-doubles last season, including a 22-point, 17-rebound performance while playing on an injured left ankle in the Bruins' 79-77 overtime victory against Arizona. He had 19 points and 16 rebounds against Washington, and 16 points to go with 14 rebounds in a win over Kentucky.

PF-MATT BARNES (6-7, 230 lbs., SR, #23, 11.6 ppg, 7.3 rpg, 1.6 spg, 30.3 minutes, .478 FG, .574 FT, Del Campo HS/Citrus Heights, Calif.). One of the most-improved players in the Pac-10 last season, Barnes found his niche when the Bruins went to the full-court press in December. Barnes was averaging a modest 8.7 points entering the North Carolina game, when he broke loose for 18 points. He went on to score in double figures in eight of 10 games, and 17 for the season. Barnes, who averaged just 5.6 points as a sophomore, erupted for a career-best 32 in a home defeat to Stanford.

"Even though he's a front line player, he's the point man in our 1-2-1-1 press. He's long and he has a great understanding of every position on the floor and what the coaching staff wants," Lavin said. "Defensively, he has a great ability of reading the situation, knowing when to trap and when to fake and drop back."

Physically, Barnes is far from the prototypical power forward, but his quickness compensates for his lack of size.

"He's a very hard match-up," Lavin said. "He's really improved playing with his back to the basket, and facing people up and driving. Now he's hoping to add the perimeter jumper."

SF-JASON KAPONO (6-7, 199 lbs., JR, #24, 17.2 ppg, 5.7 rpg, 2.3 apg, 1.2 spg, 35.1 minutes, .441 FG, .457 3PT, .869 FT, Artesia HS/Lakewood, Calif.). Kapono is one of the most consistent scorers and dangerous perimeter shooters in the country. Entering his junior season, he already has scored 1,080 career points and has a career .465 accuracy mark from three-point range.

"He's obviously as prolific a shooter as there is in the country," Lavin said of the two-time All-Pac-10 pick who is a preseason Playboy All-American. "When teams prepare to play us, they emphasize cutting down his catches, and that means extending defensively, which is going to open things up inside."

Kapono scored in double figures 25 times last season, going for 18 points or more on 20 occasions. He scored 22 points against Kansas, 21 against Kentucky and equaled his career-high of 28 against Villanova, DePaul and Washington State.

He was held without a three-point basket just three times in 32 games last season, and nine times buried at least four shots from beyond the arc.

Kapono briefly considered bolting for the NBA after last season, which did not surprise or concern Lavin.

"I knew he was a player who each season would consider his options," Lavin said. "Coming out of high school he had clearly expressed his ambition of playing at the next level. But it also wouldn't surprise me if he decided to stay [at UCLA] his entire career."

Kapono played over the summer with the USA 21-and-under team that won a gold medal at the World Championship For Young Men in Saitama, Japan. He averaged 7.0 points in the eight victories, including 14 points against Slovenia and 10 points against Argentina.

Lavin said Kapono also worked hard during the off-season to round out his game.

"He's a basketball gym rat, so he accepts and embraces the challenge of improving in areas where he's deficient," the coach said. "He worked on his overall strength and conditioning, and finishing around the basket.

"And I think his maturity and leadership skills will improve because he's got more experience behind him."

SG-BILLY KNIGHT (6-5, 210 lbs., SR, #3, 7.9 ppg, 1.9 rpg, 17.6 minutes, .460 FG, .421 3PT, .732 FT, Westchester HS/Los Angeles). Knight took over as the starter at UCLA's troubled shooting guard spot for the Feb. 3 game at Stanford, two days after a disastrous defeat at Cal. He responded with 22 points—which exceeded his total of the previous seven games combined—and the job was his.

Knight went on to average 13.1 points as a starter in UCLA's final 14 games, helping the club to an 11-3

record. He shot .496 from the field over that stretch, including .492 from three-point distance.

Curiously, he averaged 19.8 points on the four Saturdays in February, shooting 60 percent from beyond the arc.

"Billy's another player who stretches the defense," Lavin said. "If teams are keying on Kapono, when Billy's left open he's a deadeye shooter. He's developed his mid-range game, and on the back line of our press he anticipates passes very well. We wouldn't have guessed that would be a strength of his."

PG-CEDRIC BOZEMAN (6-6, 183 lbs., FR, #21, 20.0 ppg, 6.0 rpg, 5.0 apg at Mater Dei HS/Santa Ana, Calif.). The Bruins expect Bozeman to earn the starting point-guard assignment, and Lavin doesn't consider the prospect of a freshman in that role to be a hazard.

"Cedric is exceptionally polished for a player his age," Lavin said. "He's a different size but he reminds me of [5-foot-10] Tyus Edney in terms of his disposition and temperament. He's got a tailor-made personality to play point guard."

Lavin said the experience with which Bozeman will be surrounded will be a critical factor in his performance.

"Any freshman, I don't care how talented he is, still will have the natural growing pains that come with the transition," Lavin said. "The fact that he's got four starters returning and seven upperclassmen will kind of help him with his homework assignments."

At Mater Dei, Bozeman was a McDonald's All-America selection and was chosen to the USA Today All-America third team. He was the player of the year in Southern California, according to both the Los Angeles Times and Orange County Register, after leading the Monarchs to a 33-2 record and the state large-school title.

"Listening to the pro scouts talk, they feel he's pretty special, pretty exceptional," Lavin said. "There were some questions about whether he was a pure point guard, but I never had any doubt about that. I've never worried about his decision-making or floor leadership."

KEY RESERVES

F-T.J. CUMMINGS (6-9, 205 lbs., SO, #43, 6.4 ppg, 3.5 rpg, 18.8 minutes, .485 FG, .652 FT, Flossmoor HS/Homewood, Ill.). Cummings burst onto the scene with 24 points and seven rebounds in his collegiate debut against Kansas, and could be ready for another breakthrough this season.

"The summer feedback we've gotten from kids and former players is that he's been as dominant a player as any in the men's gym," Lavin said.

Cummings, the son of former NBA standout Terry Cummings and an All-Pac-10 Freshman selection last year, could be the best non-starter in the Pac-10 this season.

"He had some big games for us last year, gave us kind of a sneak preview," Lavin said, alluding to an 18-point effort against Arizona State and a 13-point outing against Washington.

"All freshmen hit the wall, and you could see it with him," Lavin said. "I think he's hungry, and now has a better idea how to pace himself. He's just stronger with another year under his belt."

G/F-RICO HINES (6-4, 217 lbs., SR, #22, 3.4 ppg, 2.1 rpg, 14.7 minutes in 1999-2000, Hargrave Military Academy/Chatham, Va. And Greenville, N.C.). Hines returns as a fifth-year senior after missing all of last year after knee injury. He tore cartilage in his right knee in practice and underwent season-ending surgery on Nov. 1.

Already the owner of a UCLA diploma, Hines is taking post-graduate classes to maintain his eligibility. Lavin cherishes the experience he brings to the team.

"You feel like asking him, 'Didn't you play with Mike Warren and Curtis Rowe? Weren't you around 20 years ago?' " Lavin joked. "He's someone who aspires to coach, and he's a tough warrior. In the full-court press, he has an understanding of directing traffic."

Hines has appeared in 72 career games at UCLA, averaging just under 13 minutes and 2.7 points. He is just a .276 shooter from three-point range, but Lavin said improving that skill was a major off-season goal.

F-ANDRE PATTERSON (6-7, 210 lbs., FR, #5, 26.8 ppg, 13.0 rpg at Washington HS/Los Angeles). The co-Los Angeles City Player of the Year last season, Patterson will get the chance to contribute at power forward immediately as a freshman.

"He's athletic and quick. He can gives us what Charles [O'Bannon] gave us as a freshman, a kid that goes and gets easy points for you on second shots. He's got to work on his perimeter shot, but he's as athletic as anybody we saw [in recruiting] last year."

Patterson was a Cal-Hi Sports first-team all-state selection and a finalist for the McDonald's All-America Game.

G/F-DIJON THOMPSON (6-6, 180 lbs., FR, #1, 23.0 ppg, 7.0 rpg, .532 FG at Redondo Union HS/Redondo Beach, Calif.). Thompson doesn't arrive at Westwood with the reputation of Bozeman, but Lavin suggested his contributions may rival those of his freshman classmate.

"Don't be surprised if he's as much of an impact player," Lavin said. "We don't want to hold the guy back. He's kind of like Paul Pierce, but a little more mobile and fluid. He shoots the ball well, puts it on the floor. He's just gifted and skilled."

Thompson will play at either of the wing positions, although he had some experience at point guard in high school. He was a Division II all-state selection last year and Southern California Division II Co-Player of the Year.

G-RAY YOUNG (6-3, 210 lbs, SR, #34, 7.0 ppg, 2.2 rpg, 22.8 minutes, .352 FG, .212 3PT, .822 FT, St. Joseph-Notre Dame High School/Oakland, Calif.). Young arrived at UCLA three years ago as a McDonald's All-American, but still has not blossomed into a standout player. Still, Lavin regards Young as very much an asset to the program.

"It's a luxury for us to have a veteran player like Ray," Lavin said. "At different times in his career, he's stepped up and had some big games. He's always had the confidence and belief he's going to turn the corner and have the breakout year.

"We're hoping this year, with his experience and ability, he'll lose himself at the defensive end of the floor and turn it around at the offensive end."

Ironically, Young lost his starting job last season despite the Bruins' move to a pressure game that seems perfectly suited to his skills. He's quick and a tenacious defender, and very dangerous in the open floor.

But Young's shooting eye has deteriorated each year, his three-point percentage reaching a career-low .212 last season when he closed the season just 3-for-23 over UCLA's final 13 games. He did score a season-high 20 points against Kentucky, had a career-best nine rebounds at Arizona and a career-high six assists against UC Santa Barbara.

OTHER RETURNEES

G-TODD RAMASAR (6-5, 204 lbs., SR, #11, 0.7 ppg, 0.8 rpg in 6 games, Riverside North HS/Corona, Calif.). Ramasar is a fifth-year senior walk-on who has played a total of 68 minutes spread over 25 games in his UCLA career. He has scored 15 points as a collegiate player, six of them in one game against Washington State three years ago.

Lavin said Ramasar plans to attend law school, and actually could decide to leave the team this fall and pursue that goal if it's clear his playing time will continue to be minimal.

G-JANOU RUBIN (6-3, 180 lbs., SO, #2, 1.5 ppg, 0.3 rpg in 4 games, James Logan HS/Union City, Calif.). A walk-on, whose father played ball at Santa Clara, Rubin saw action in four games last season, totaling five minutes on the floor. But he made the most of them, hitting all three of his field-goal attempts.

OTHER NEWCOMERS

PG-RYAN WALCOTT (6-2, 175 lbs., FR, #10, 16.2 ppg, 5.4 rpg in 1999-2000 at Shadow Mountain HS/Phoenix, Ariz.). Walcott figures to provide Bozeman with his greatest competition at point guard, and likely will handle the understudy duties at the position.

"I haven't guaranteed Cedric a starting position," Lavin said. "Ryan has quickness and point-guard abilities and he doesn't make any mistakes. There's something to be said for that on a team with a lot of firepower. He doesn't dazzle you, but he's just a solid, low-risk kid."

Walcott, who red-shirted as a freshman last season, is a cousin to NBA standout Mike Bibby, and followed Bibby as the point guard at Shadow Mountain High in Phoenix. He averaged 18 points, nine assists and eight steals as a senior, keying the team's victory in the Arizona 5A state championship game.

F-JOSIAH JOHNSON (6-8, 240 lbs., FR, #54, 24.2 ppg, 12.5 rpg in1999-2000 at Montclair Prep/Van Nuys, Calif.). The son of former UCLA All-America forward Marques Johnson and the younger brother of ex-Bruins star Kris Johnson, Josiah is ready to begin contributing

after sitting out as a red-shirt last season.

Lavin expects good things from Johnson, if not right away.

"If it's not this year, then somewhere down the road," Lavin said. "Like his father and like Kris, he has that element that's difficult to teach, that savvy and a feel for the game that is pretty special."

UCLA's depth at power forward could make it tough for Johnson to break into the rotation this season. But Lavin said Johnson's strength and conditioning are much-improved from a year ago.

C-JOHN HOFFART (6-10, 286 lbs., SO, #52, 2.6 ppg, 2.5 rpg, 11.8 minutes, .441 FG, .485 FT in 1999-2000 at Cal Poly-San Luis Obisbo & Davis HS/Davis, Calif.). Hoffart provides the Bruins with a different look, a physical inside presence whose biggest challenge may be keeping up with the club's fast-paced game.

"He's more in the tradition of a Wisconsin Badger," Lavin said. "But he's got good hands and ruggedness."

Hoffart sat out last season after transferring from Cal Poly, where he had an 11-point game against Northern Arizona and a 12-rebound performance against Cal State Northridge his freshman season.

G-JON CRISPIN (6-2, 185 lbs., JR, 7.2 ppg, 1.6 rpg, 1.7 apg, 1.0 spg, .395 FG, .356 3PT at Penn State/Pitman HS, Pitman, N.J.). Crispin will sit out this season after transferring from Penn State, where he co-starred last year in the backcourt with his older brother, Joe. Joe, who led Penn State in scoring at 19.5 points, signed a contract with the Los Angeles Lakers over the summer.

Jon Crispin, who will be a junior next season when he becomes eligible to play, started 31-of-33 games last year for the Nittany Lions. He averaged 9.3 points, 2.1 assists and 1.4 steals while starting 22 games as a freshman at Penn State.

G-GENE BARNES (5-8, 170 lbs., FR, 18 ppg, 5 rpg, 8 apg, 4 spg, The Branson School/Marin, Calif.). A freshman walk-on, Barnes is scheduled to red-shirt this season after leading his 29-5 high school team in scoring, assists, steals and minutes last season.

G-QUINN HAWKING (6-4, 175 lbs., FR , 25 ppg, 8 rpg, 3 apg, Anaheim High School/Anaheim, Calif.). Also a candidate to red-shirt as a freshman walk-on, Hawking is the son of Bob Hawking, who coached at Cal State Fullerton and developed former UCLA great Don McLean at Simi Valley High.

G-KYLE TAYLOR (6-4, 180 lbs., FR, 20 ppg, 9 rpg, 4.6 apg, Salinas HS/Salinas, Calif.). A freshman walk-on, Taylor is the grandson of Bill Hagler, who was a third-team All-America pick at Cal in 1951.

QUESTIONS

Point guard? Is talented freshman Cedric Bozeman ready to take the reins of the high-powered Bruins? And is there a capable man in reserve at the position?

Contentment? Given the Bruins' extraordinary depth, Lavin will have to juggle substitutions creatively to keep all his players content with their minutes.

The unknown? At UCLA, there's always a surprise lurking around the next corner. Will anxious alums ever be satisfied? Is there another Pitino controversy looming? Will the ceaseless talk radio rabble stir trouble? Or can there be peace and order in Westwood?

ANSWERS

Depth! Lavin has operated with a limited roster for much of his tenure at UCLA, often forced to improvise after unexpected departures. Not now. This team has at least 10 capable players who will wear on the opposition.

Dan Gadzuric! The Pac-10 lost virtually all of its experienced centers after last season. Gadzuric is the exception, and if he can stay healthy and stay out of foul trouble he can dominate.

The freshmen! Lavin signed one of the nation's top recruiting classes, and it's not limited to Bozeman. Don't be surprised if Thompson and Patterson play significant roles this season.

UCLA 2000-2001 RESULTS

#Kansas (L)	98-99
#Kentucky	97-92
Cal State Northridge (L)	74-78
UC Santa Barbara	83-77
##Georgia Tech (L)	67-72
Hawaii	84-64
UC Irvine	65-60
North Carolina (L)	70-80
@Purdue	87-82
Washington	86-64
Washington State	75-57
USC	80-75
Villanova	93-65
@Arizona State	91-83
@Arizona (L)	63-88
Oregon State	67-40
Oregon	98-88
@California (L)	63-92
@Stanford	79-73
@USC	85-76
@DePaul	94-88
Arizona	79-77
Arizona State	73-68
@Oregon	88-73
@Oregon State	68-65
California	79-75
Stanford (L)	79-85
@Washington State	86-76
@Washington (L)	94-96
###Hofstra	61-48
###Utah State	75-50
###Duke (L)	63-76

#Coaches vs. Cancer Tournament in New York
##John Wooden Classic in Anaheim, CA
###NCAA Tournament
@Road Games

BLUE RIBBON ANALYSIS

BACKCOURT	B
BENCH/DEPTH	A
FRONTCOURT	A
INTANGIBLES	B

The Bruins have so many players on their roster Lavin probably could benefit from a football depth chart. Still, he realizes that's only a blessing if he's able to effectively manage his personnel.

"Being able to find a rotation, in terms of a substitution pattern, will be critical," he said.

So will the development of Bozeman, expected to control the reins of a talented squad.

"That's the most natural key, integrating the freshmen, and Cedric in particular because he's at the crucial position at the point," Lavin said. "It's something we have to watch closely."

Bozeman and the Bruins will be tested early and often with a challenging schedule that tips off at the Maui Invitational. UCLA also plays non-conference games against Alabama, Georgetown, Kansas and Villanova.

Lavin believes his club is up for the assignment.

"For the first time during my tenure as head coach we have the balance in each class and the depth at each position that you strive for as a coach," he said.

And, as usual at UCLA, the expectations that go with it.

(J.F.)

Missouri 7

LOCATION	Columbia, MO
CONFERENCE	Big 12
LAST SEASON	20-13 (600)
CONFERENCE RECORD	9-7 (t-6th)
STARTERS LOST/RETURNING	2/3
NICKNAME	Tigers
COLORS	Black & Gold
HOMECOURT	Hearnes Centeer (13,300)
COACH	Quin Snyder (Duke '89)
RECORD AT SCHOOL	38-26 (2 years)
CAREER RECORD	38-26 (2 years)
ASSISTANTS	Marcus Perez (Army '89)
	Tony Harvey (Cameron '83)
	Lane Odom (High Point '89)
TEAM WINS (last 5 years)	20-18-16-17-20
RPI (last 5 years)	80-59-35-44-44
2000-01 FINISH	Lost in NCAA second round.

COACH AND PROGRAM

This could be the season Missouri fans have been craving.

The Tigers have had more success than many, three

straight NCAA Tournament appearances, only a couple of misses from postseason play in the last two decades. Only occasionally, like 1994, has the push gone beyond a couple of victories, but the program always looked forward to March.

But not since the late 1980s will a Missouri team be as highly regarded entering a season. Only twice in the 1990s have Tigers teams been ranked in a preseason poll and neither time higher than No. 15. No Missouri team in the last decade has been picked to win the conference title, and only one Tigers team actually did finish first.

So you understand the feeling; for years Missouri has mostly been good enough to finish in the league's upper division and not good enough to win.

Now, the talk is these Tigers are tops in the Big 12, better than Oklahoma State, Texas, Oklahoma, Iowa State, and dare Missouri think it? Kansas.

The optimism is based on several factors. In the NCAA Tournament, Missouri pushed national champion Duke before falling in the second round. The Tigers' hauled in a recruiting class considered to be one of the nation's best. And four of the top five players return, including All-America candidate Kareem Rush.

"It's gratifying to see your name listed among the top programs in the nation," coach Quin Snyder said. "I think the recognition is an indicator that people believe we're headed in the right direction."

Missouri athletic director Mike Alden believes it, too. In July, he gave Snyder a huge contract boost. The new five-year deal guarantees him $815,000 per year. If he cashes in on all incentives, Snyder could make $1.27 million. That would take winning the Big 12 championship and a national title.

"He's been successful," Alden said. "You want to reward success."

You also want to keep the other programs from making a run at Snyder.

"It does diffuse some of that," Alden said.

Snyder said he had no intention of leaving, and he hasn't interviewed for another job while he's lived in Columbia. But you could see the attraction. He's young—35 on Oct. 30—groomed as a player and assistant coach under Duke coach Mike Krzyzewski and just well-groomed. Snyder's wavy hair continues to be a hot topic.

At Duke, Snyder knew nothing but success. He helped lay the foundation for the Blue Devils' dynasty. Snyder's teams reached the Final Four in three of his four seasons. He was there for Duke's first championship push under Krzyzewski in 1986 and his teams reached the semifinals in 1988 and 1989.

After attending training camp with the Indiana Pacers, Snyder returned to Duke to pursue graduate work. He left after two years to spend a season as an assistant on Larry Brown's staff with the Los Angeles Clippers.

Brown recruited Snyder, a McDonald's All-America from Mercer Island, Wash., heavily while he was the Kansas coach. But Brown remained impressed with Snyder and hired him in Los Angeles. It was then Snyder met and married Brown's daughter, Kristy. They later divorced, and Snyder has since married Helen Redwine, a teacher. Brown and Snyder remained friends, and Brown was one of several who went to bat for Snyder when Alden made the hire.

Experience was the big concern when Snyder was selected over then-Tulsa coach Bill Self. Snyder had never coached a game and now he was being asked to go up against Kansas' Roy Williams, Oklahoma State's Eddie Sutton, Oklahoma's Kelvin Sampson and Texas' Rick Barnes.

"It's hard to apologize for not having experience," Snyder said soon after he was hired. "I'm trying to prepare, to break down every element possible, so there are as few surprises as possible."

Snyder has held his own. He not only beat Kansas and Williams in the first meeting, he crushed them by 22. Missouri beat the Jayhawks again last season. Three years into the job, Snyder has a couple more cagey veterans to combat—Texas Tech's Bob Knight and Baylor's Dave Bliss.

But the experience factor as an issue has quieted and will be non-existent if the drama unfolds as the Tigers dream. What's not being quieted is Missouri's prospects.

Moments after Missouri's loss to Duke, assistant coach Tony Harvey threw down the gauntlet.

"We'll have as good of young talent as probably anyone in the country," Harvey said. "We'll have size. We'll have athleticism. We'll have all the things you need to be

successful. The ball, of course, has to fall your way sometimes. But I think all the potential is there."

It starts with Rush, the 6-6 wing who made all the Mizzou nation happy when he announced he was returning for his junior year. He led the Big 12 in scoring at 21.1 points and is one of the league's top outside shooters, hitting .448 percent from behind the arc.

Rush is a silky smooth player who often requires a double-team, which last season at times worked effectively because Missouri had some holes in the offense. That doesn't appear to be the case this year with a potential starting lineup of Wesley Stokes at the point, Clarence Gilbert at shooting guard, Rush, center Arthur Johnson and possibly Travon Bryant at power forward.

The bench also is deep. Talented players like forward Justin Gage, wing Rickey Paulding and guard Josh Kroenke are experienced, although Kroenke sat out all but one game last year after suffering a concussion early in the season. The rotation also will include newcomers Uche Okafor, a center, and front-liner Jeffrey Ferguson and wings Najeeb Echols and Duane John.

2001-2002 SCHEDULE

Nov.	13	#Tennessee-Martin
	24	*Xavier
	29	Jackson State
Dec.	1	Grambling State
	3	@Saint Louis
	8	Southern University A&M
	15	Iowa
	22	**Illinois
	29	@DePaul
Jan.	2	Coppin State
	5	Nebraska
	9	@Iowa State
	12	@Kansas State
	16	Texas A&M
	19	Colorado
	21	@Oklahoma
	26	Kansas State
	28	@Kansas
Feb.	3	Virginia
	6	Iowa State
	9	@Baylor
	13	@Nebraska
	17	Texas
	20	@Texas Tech
	23	@Colorado
	25	Oklahoma State
March	3	Kansas
	7-10	##Big 12 Tournament

@Road Games
*John R. Wooden Tradition, Conseco Fieldhouse, Indianapolis, IN
**Braggin' Rights game, Savvis Center, St.. Louis
#Guardians Classic (if Missouri wins, it will play either Air Force or Yale on Nov. 14; Semifinals and final are Nov. 20-21 at Kemper Arena, Kemper, MO)
##Kemper Arena, Kansas Cit, MO

STARTERS NOT RETURNING

G-BRIAN GRAWER (6-0, 8.4 ppg, 2.6 rpg, 2.6 apg, 28.4 minutes, .404 FG, .836 FT, .408 3PT). Grawer, a genuine good guy, put in a nice career. He wound up a four-year starter and one of the best three-point shooters in Mizzou history. His .421 career three-point percentage ranks second on the school list to Kareem Rush.

When Rush went down with an injured thumb, Grawer came up big, averaging 15.1 points in seven games, more than doubling his average before the Rush injury. He looked like the player he was as a sophomore when he ranked third in the nation in three-point percentage.

Grawer, the son of former Saint Louis University coach Rich Grawer, played with the savvy and intelligence of a coach's kid. He rarely took bad shots or made sloppy turnovers. Rich Grawer, who was fired in 1992, was a constant presence at Tigers' games.

"It was a blessing in disguise for me," Rich Grawer said. "I feel bad that maybe I didn't spend as much time as I could have or should have because I was so involved with SLU."

Rich made up for lost time by spending hours a day working with Brian on his game as young teenager.

"He pushed me and make me work, and when I wanted to work out he dropped what he was doing to work with me," Brian Grawer said. "When he got out of

coaching that was really the point where my basketball career started to elevate."

It was a proud father that watched Brian help the Tigers to the NCAA second round last season. Now, Brian appears to be headed toward a coaching career. Don't be surprised to see father and son working on the same staff one day, like the Alfords.

C-TAJUDEEN SOYOYE (6-9, 6.9 ppg, 6.6 apg, 26.6 minutes, .449 FG, .780 FT). Soyoye arrived at Missouri from Nigeria by way of Meridian (Miss.) Community College. Before he played his first game in Columbia three years ago, Soyoye amazed fans with his feats of strength and speed. He bench-pressed 400 pounds, a school record for a basketball player, and was the fastest player on the team.

But he never became the basketball player Mizzou envisioned. Soyoye averaged about 7.5 points and 6.5 rebounds in his two-year career. As a junior, he was the only regular taller than 6-6. He figured to be helped by the addition of center Arthur Johnson, a true center who allowed Soyoye to play his more natural power-forward position.

Instead, Soyoye became more of a non-factor on offense. His numbers fell from the previous season.

"I was hoping I could come in and make an impression in the Big 12," Soyoye said. "That didn't happen."

Soyoye will try to make a go of it in pro ball, probably overseas. He got his degree in biochemistry and is interested in becoming a doctor.

OTHERS NOT RETURNING

F-JOHNNIE PARKER (6-6, 1.6 ppg, 1.8 rpg, 10.7 minutes, .395 FG, .143 3PT, .632 FT). Parker was a victim of high expectations. He came out of Webster Groves High in suburban St. Louis and was considered a recruiting coup for the Tigers after leading his school to a state championship as a junior. Parker was a senior the same year as Larry Hughes and there was some feeling that the players were equal in talent.

But it never happened for Parker, who played out of position at power forward. That was necessary because the Tigers while Parker was on the roster were a small team. Parker was more of a big guard/small forward who in high school was considered a good ball handler and three-point shooter.

"I thought it was going to be better than what it turned out to be," Parker said. "I thought things would go a different route, but they didn't."

Parker had his moments. As a freshman he scored 10 second-half points in a victory over rival Illinois. As a sophomore, he started 16 games and once again came up big against the Illini by making a steal with six seconds left.

But as a junior, Parker was suspended for the Iowa game for breaking team rules. As a senior, he got in Snyder's doghouse and missed three games.

In one of them, Snyder chose to play former manager Ryan Kiernan as the last one off the bench.

JUSTIN GAGE (6-5, #11, 1.7 ppg, 1.2 rpg, 13.9 minutes, .286 FT, .333 3PT, .500 FT, Jefferson City HS/Jefferson City, MO). He's listed here, although there's a chance Gage could join the roster. But as one of the league's best wide receivers, Gage is expected to skip basketball and concentrate on becoming an NFL prospect this winter. Besides, Missouri's roster runs deeper than ever. It would be tough for Snyder to find minutes for Gage.

PROJECTED STARTERS

PG-WESLEY STOKES (5-10, 175 lbs., SO, #2, 6.4 ppg, 1.9 rpg, 2.0 apg, 1.2 spg, 19.8 minutes, .382 FG, .386 3PT, .695 FT, Poly HS/Long Beach, Calif.). The first thing Missouri fans knew about Stokes is that he attended the same high school as one of the most notorious names in the school's basketball history, Tyus Edney. But once they got to know Stokes, old Mizzou fell in love with this long dread locked, lefty dynamo.

As the season progressed, Stokes assumed a more prominent role. He was playing more point than Brian Grawer. Stokes started late in the regular season and averaged 12.1 points in a seven-game stretch.

His best game came on a night when Missouri seemed destined to lose. Kansas State came to Columbia the day Kareem Rush was out with his thumb injury and Clarence Gilbert scored only two points. Stokes scored a career-high 19 and had most of the big points down the stretch.

Stokes came up big in several other games—17

points against Texas, 12 points and seven assists against Texas A&M. Over a 15-game stretch toward the end of the season, Stokes made 19-of-40 from behind the arc. He became the team's most reliable outside shooter.

Without Grawer in the lineup, there's no doubt about the point-guard responsibilities.

"He was a key player for us in the second half of the season," Snyder said. "We saw a lot of growth from him throughout the year."

SG-CLARENCE GILBERT (6-2, 194 lbs., SR, #4, 16.5 ppg, 2.7 rpg, 3.5 apg, 1.3 spg, 33.5 minutes, .364 FG, .368 3PT, .806 FT, Dillard HS/Fort Lauderdale, Fla.). On the surface, the season was unfolding nicely for Gilbert. He ranked among the Big 12 scoring leaders and captured the nation's attention for his 43-point output in the four-overtime victory over Iowa State. The production was the fourth most in school history, and tied for the high point mark in the five years of the Big 12. Also in that game, Gilbert recorded nine assists and no turnovers in 56 minutes. The minutes were a league record, as well as field goals attempted (36) and three-pointers attempted (18).

The victory was the Tigers' fifth straight and made them 12-3. Missouri was rolling toward a season greater than what expectations had held. But over the next few games, something wasn't right about Gilbert and the Tigers. The Iowa State victory was grand, but questions arose over Gilbert's gunning. Shooting roles seemed ill defined. Should Gilbert be getting more shots than Kareem Rush?

Missouri lost three straight, all on the road. The Tigers came back and squeezed out a victory over Texas Tech, then pulled off their usual home upset victory over Kansas. The game at Oklahoma State, the Cowboys' first after the tragic plane crash, also became a downer for Missouri when Rush broke his thumb.

That left Gilbert as the main man. And in his first test with Rush out of the lineup, Gilbert was horrible against Kansas State. He scored two points, missed all five shots from the floor and played just 24 minutes. After the game, reporters were told Gilbert suffered from the flu, but that wasn't the only problem.

As the Tigers were putting the finishing touches on a gutsy comeback victory, Gilbert sat on the bench and pouted. Television cameras showed Gilbert not joining a team huddle and slouched on the bench. After the game, he argued with assistant coach Tony Harvey.

That was enough for Snyder. He suspended Gilbert just as Missouri was headed to Iowa State for an important league game. Now, the Tigers would be without their top two scorers. Missouri lost by eight in an excellent effort.

Gilbert returned to the team but not as a starter. He came off the bench for the next five games, regaining his starting role only for the regular-season finale. He appeared to be a changed player. And he was the right guy at the right time in Missouri's first-round NCAA Tournament victory over Georgia. With the game tied in the final seconds, Rush penetrated, drew the double team and kicked over to Gilbert on the right baseline. His 15-foot jumper swished at the buzzer, giving Missouri its first NCAA victory since 1995.

Snyder and Gilbert have cleared up the problems, and Gilbert and Rush have been selected co-captains for this season. But Snyder said the trouble was never between he and Gilbert.

"It was a question of a young man being part of a team," Snyder said. "This had less to do with a player and a coach than with a player and his team."

And Snyder was willing to possibly sacrifice the Tigers' position in the eyes of the NCAA Tournament committee than a principle. At the time, Mizzou was faltering and its at-large chances were not assured.

"We're building a program," Snyder said. "A program includes values, a system, a way of playing, an approach to the game. Individual stuff is great, but a couple of years from now, you don't remember who was first team All-Big 12, you remember who won the conference. That's what's important.

"Clarence needed to develop other aspects of his game. He needed to embrace that. By the end of the season his heart was in the right place."

Gilbert could see more time at the point. That's where he'll play when Stokes isn't on the floor. That moves Rush to the shooting guard and gets more minutes for Rickey Paulding.

SF-KAREEM RUSH (6-6, 218 lbs., JR, #21, 21.1 ppg, 6.7 rpg, 2.0 apg, 0.7 bpg, 1.3 spg, 30.6 minutes, .442 FG, .448 3PT, .800 FT, Pembroke Hill HS/Kansas City, Mo.). Hard to believe, but Missouri has never produced a consensus All-American. The Tigers might have the best program in college hoops history without one.

Mizzou has come close, and the school says 20 of its players have earned All-America honors. There's disputing that fact. But to become a consensus All-American you have to make the majority of first-teams. Nobody had done that. Not Norm Stewart, John Brown, Willie Smith, Ricky Frazier, Steve Stipanovich, John Sunvold, Derrick Chevious, Doug Smith, Anthony Peeler, Melvin Booker or Rush.

Hey, it's not an easy thing being a consensus All-American. You've got to win over a lot of folks.

Rush should do that this year. He's undoubtedly the most talented player on the roster, and probably the Big 12. Rush's game is part perimeter shooter, part slasher, part post-up artist. At 6-6, he can comfortably play two positions, easily play a third and is a point guard on occasion.

That he's left-handed makes everything a little different.

"I'm confident in what I can do," Rush said. "Not overly confident. Not egotistical. Just confident."

National champion Duke saw Rush's confidence first hand. After Rush scored 20 in the 13-point second-round loss to the Blue Devils, Mike Krzyzewski said, "he's as good a player as has played against us all year. He's a beautiful player to watch. I'd love to have coached him."

Duke's Mike Dunleavy might have put it best.

"Kind of slippery," Dunleavy said. "Hard to guard. He's got everything in his arsenal, and he's just really smooth and fun to watch."

And to think Rush hasn't completed a full season in college. NCAA sanctions over benefits he received from a summer-league coach while at Kansas City's Pembroke Hill cost him nine games as a freshman. Rush started only six, but was voted league freshman of the year.

Last season's broken thumb suffered against Oklahoma State cost him another seven. The thumb was encased in a splint, foam and bandages when Rush returned for the regular-season finale, at Kansas. Rush played poorly, and probably shouldn't have returned that day. But from then on, Rush was terrific, and ever since he declared after the Duke game that there was no way he would miss his junior season, Tigers' fans have been salivating over this season's prospects.

"I'm excited along with everybody else," Rush said. "I've added a couple of inches to my vertical. Who knows? By the end of the season I might be dunking on everybody."

But Rush thinks his scoring average may actually decrease this season—and understands that would be a good thing for the Tigers.

"I think we'll have too much power for me to score that many points this year," Rush said. "I don't think we have to have me shooting all those balls. I'm looking forward to that. I'm still probably going to draw the best defender. But I want to make the players around me better, help out my teammates."

Snyder wants to see Rush get a little stronger. The ideal Rush would keep his finesse while adding muscle.

"We want him to develop more power, be more explosive," Snyder said. "He already is an incredible finesse player. We want him to flash more aggressiveness."

No comment on Rush would be complete without comparing his decisions to those of his old brother, JaRon. Growing up in Kansas City, JaRon developed into an outstanding basketball talent at a young age. Adults, some with good intentions, others not, influenced JaRon in ways that have all but killed his basketball career.

Kareem has made some mistakes along the way, none on the scale of JaRon. And now Kareem is positioned to achieve—postseason honors, an NBA career—the riches that have eluded JaRon, who when last seen was bouncing around minor-league basketball.

If you had asked anyone familiar with the Rush brothers five years ago which one would go farther in hoops, the answer would have been JaRon.

PF-ARTHUR "DOCK" JOHNSON (6-9, 270 lbs., SO, #50, 9.0 ppg, 7.8 rpg, 2.0 bpg, 1.1 spg, 24.5 minutes, .518 FG, .544 FT, Pershing HS/Detroit, Mich.). You go back to Missouri teams over the last six or seven years, plug in a guy like Johnson and maybe the Tigers win a league title or two.

The inside presence has been lacking in the program since the days of Jevon Crudup in the early-1990s. It had always been a makeshift situation, and the hole was never more glaring than in Missouri's 2000 NCAA Tournament loss to North Carolina, when the Tar Heels played volleyball on the offensive boards.

Quin Snyder went to Detroit and told Johnson that if he signed with the Tigers he would be the starting center. Johnson was sold. It took a four-game audition to get him the starting lineup, but once it happened, Johnson acted like he belonged.

Johnson finished runner-up in Big 12 Freshman-of-the-Year voting and easily made the league's all-freshman team. He became the first Missouri freshman to lead the program in rebounding since Stan Ray in 1976.

Johnson finished in the top six in the Big 12 in rebounding, offensive rebounding, double-doubles and blocked shots. The school-record 65 blocks were a big deal. In just one season, Johnson joined the school's career top 10 list.

As for his offensive skills, Johnson has a nice touch around the basket and is a put-back artist. He isn't the type who's at his best stepping outside and knocking in 15-footers.

Look for Johnson to get into double digits in scoring and rebounding this season. But it may come from a power forward position if Uche Okafor becomes Missouri's starting center.

If Okafor doesn't start, Johnson remains in the middle and Travon Bryant could move into the starting power forward role.

C-UCHE OKAFOR (6-11, 245 lbs., JR, C, #00, 9.2 ppg, 7.2 rpg, 2.4 bpg, College of Southern Idaho/Anambra State, Nigeria). The Tigers, who always seem to need size, got much bigger when Okafor said he was coming to Missouri.

The native Nigerian stands close to 7-0and owns a wingspan of 7 feet, 7 inches. He's raw and needs work on his offensive skills, but Okafor comes more prepared than many junior college centers. He was rated the No. 2 junior college player in the nation at any position by CBS.Sportsline.com and the No. 6 player by PrepStars.

Okafor helped College of Southern Idaho reach the regional championship game. The team finished 29-4 and was fourth in the final junior college polls.

Okafor was the final player to sign with the Tigers, and it changed the way Snyder looked at his team. Plugging Okafor in the middle will mean sliding Johnson to the power forward.

Now the question is Okafor's eligibility. Before coming to Missouri, Okafor lived in Russia and signed a contract to play for a pro team there. He never played a game and says he didn't receive money. But the school and NCAA are sorting through the issue.

Okafor is enrolled and is practicing. It's a testament to Quin Snyder's recruiting that the Tigers could lose Okafor and not be severely damaged. Johnson would go back to the middle.

KEY RESERVES

PF-TRAVON BRYANT (6-9, 245 lbs., SO, #5, 3.0 ppg, 3.5 rpg, 0.8 bpg, 13.2 minutes, .485 FG, .281 FT, Jordan HS/Long Beach, Calif./Maine Central Institute). Tough year for Bryant, whose admission to Missouri was delayed until he achieved his test scores. He didn't become eligible until the Christmas break, then had to battle his weight and conditioning throughout most of the season.

But after a disastrous opening game in which he committed two turnovers and two fouls in three minutes against Illinois, Bryant showed signs of life. He scored 12 against Colorado, collected 12 rebounds against Kansas State. The minutes increased throughout the season as Bryant became a regular in the rotation.

At times, Bryant played timidly, understandable considering his time table. The three other prized freshmen—Wesley Stokes, Arthur Johnson and Rickey Paulding—got in an entire semester of games, and had been elevated to significant roles when Bryant arrived.

"All the things I went through personally, that was tough," Bryant said. "But I know those things are going to make me stronger down the road."

This season, Bryant will give Missouri more inside muscle. He'll get the time vacated by T.J. Soyoye, and will give Missouri just as much rebounding strength and much more offensive skill.

Bryant, a lefty, possesses a nice touch from 12-15 feet and can play with his back to the basket. He could see some action at center.

G-JOSH KROENKE (6-4, 200 lbs., SO, G, #15, 2.7 ppg, 0.8 rpg, 9.4 minutes, .391 FG, .373 3PT, .600 FT in 1999-2000. No points, one rebound in one game in

2000-2001, Rock Bridge HS/Columbia, Mo./New Hampton Prep, N.H.).

Two seasons ago, Kroenke played in 30-of-31 games and connected on 22-of-59 three-point tries. His best games were against non-league opponents, but Kroenke managed to put up eight points against Texas. During the second half of the 2000 season, Kroenke was playing double-digit minutes.

After sitting out all but one game last season with a concussion, Kroenke might have a harder time getting those kind of minutes. This is the deepest team for which he's played, and the guys who have moved from last season didn't play his position.

As a kid, Kroenke was a ball boy for the Tigers. His dad, Stan, is a longtime Missouri booster and is vice chairman and part owner of the St. Louis Rams.

F-RICKEY PAULDING (6-5, 210 lbs., SO, F, #23, 7.0 ppg, 2.4 rpg, 0.9 apg, 17.2 minutes, .421 FG, .214 3PT, .679 FT, Renaissance HS/Detroit, Mich.). Oh, Rickey, you're so fine ... when you go to the hoop. Paulding is the team's most authoritative and artistic dunker. He can reach 11 feet, 4 inches with a one-step vertical jump.

The problems for Paulding are he's not a good perimeter shooter, although he improved as his freshmen season progressed, and he plays Kareem Rush's position.

"Kareem and Rickey are not the same kind of players," Snyder said. "Rickey is more athletic."

The idea is to translate athleticism into basketball skills, to become less of a dunker and more of a ball-handler. Maybe it's just a matter of letting him play more. Paulding started the games Rush missed with his thumb injury and did well, scoring in double figures in five games. He started making some three-pointers around that time, and while it's easy to criticize his overall three-point accuracy of .214 percent, it went up to .303 in league games.

"College basketball was tougher than I thought it was going to be," Paulding said. "But I got a chance to play through some of my mistakes [when replacing Rush]. You got to go on to the next play. I didn't have time to dwell on things, and that helped."

OTHER RETURNEES

G-RYAN KIERNAN (6-0, 195 lbs., #10, 0.0 ppg., 0.0 rpg, fourgames, Rockhurst HS/St. Charles, Mo.). A former manager who appeared in three games last season for a total of three minutes, Kiernan didn't get off a shot but was credited with one turnover.

G-MICHAEL GRIFFIN (6-3, 180 lbs., #35, 0.0 ppg, 0.0 rpg, 2 games, Holy Innocents' Episcopal/Waycross, Ga.). Griffin is a practice player who appeared in two games for a total of three minutes last season.

OTHER NEWCOMERS

G/F-NAJEEB ECHOLS (6-7, 235 lbs., FR, #33, 25.0 ppg, 12.0 rpg, 8.0 apg, Whitney Young HS and Morgan Park HS/Chicago, Ill.). Now here's a nugget for the 40-somethings. Echols' mom, Sherry Scott, was an original member of the band Earth, Wind & Fire. Echols has a little show time to his credit, appearing regularly on the television show Preps by Fox Sports, which featured the lives of some Chicago area basketball players.

Echols is a slashing-type player, who, despite leading Whitney Young in scoring two years ago, was known for his defense. He's seen as a power forward/small forward type.

Echols spent his first three years in high school at Whitney Young, where he helped his team win a state championship as a freshman. He transferred to Morgan Park as a senior but didn't play because of a knee injury suffered before the season. He served as a coach.

"He can play everywhere," Snyder said.

F/C-JEFFREY FERGUSON (6-10, 230 lbs., #32, 12.2 ppg, 10.1 rpg, 2.8 bpg, Benton Harbor HS/Benton Harbor, Mich.). Like fellow recruit Najeeb Echols, Ferguson didn't play last season. He sat out because of Michigan's transfer rules involving international students. The stats above are from Ferguson's junior season, when he helped Benton Harbor to a state championship.

Ferguson is seen as a big man of the future, unless Uche Okafor is declared ineligible. In that case, Ferguson's time table is moved up and he becomes the top reserve big man behind Arthur Johnson and Travon Bryant.

G-DUANE JOHN (6-6, 190 lbs., #11, 32.5 ppg, 12.1 rpg, 3.0 apg, Berkshire Academy/Berkshire, Fla.). A West Indies native who moved to Canada to live with his mother, John was considered one of the nation's best high school players as a junior before moving to Florida and playing for Berkshire.

"He could be the most athletic player we have," Snyder said.

John was one of seven players for Berkshire to earn Division I scholarships. He was considered a consensus top 50 high school prospect. He's been at Missouri since early summer taking classes and getting acclimated to college life.

John is behind Kareem Rush and Rickey Paulding at the wing.

QUESTIONS

Okafor? His eligibility would change the Tigers' line-up but not their prospects.

Gilbert? Are his pouting problems behind him?

Altitude adjustment? Preseason high rankings are new to the Tigers. Will they have the maturity to handle the expectations?

ANSWERS

Rush! A wonderful talent. One of the college game's top players.

Gilbert! When he's on, he can make shots from Jefferson City.

Snyder! With high hopes for a deep NCAA push, the biggest test of his young career awaits.

MISSOURI 2000-2001 RESULTS

Lincoln University	98-63
Savannah State	90-49
#Rhode Island	70-60
#Valparaiso	77-61
#Syracuse (L)	62-84
Texas-Pan American	78-57
Depaul	99-84
Saint Louis	77-73
@Iowa (L)	94-99
@Indiana	68-63
Illinois (L)	81-86
Stetson	89-64
Coastal Carolina	75-61
Nebraska	68-66
@Colorado	82-76
Iowa State	112-109
@Kansas State (L)	59-80
@Virginia (L)	72-85
@Nebraska (L)	79-85
Texas Tech	66-64
Kansas	75-66
@Oklahoma State (L)	66-69
Kansas State	70-66
@Iowa State (L)	64-72
Colorado	80-69
@Texas A&M	97-90
Oklahoma (L)	61-63
Baylor	69-59
@Texas (L)	61-76
@Kansas (L)	62-77
##Texas A&M	77-62
##Oklahoma (L)	65-67
###Georgia	70-68
###Duke (L)	81-94

#Great Alaska Shootout in Anchorage
##Big 12 Tournament in Kansas City, MO
###NCAA Tournament
@Road Games

BLUE RIBBON ANALYSIS

BACKCOURT	A
BENCH/DEPTH	A
FRONTCOURT	B
INTANGIBLES	B

Ready or not, Mizzou, here it comes. Expectations have exited the interstate and are making a bee line down Stadium Drive right to the Hearnes Center front door. This potentially is the best team Missouri's had since the 1994 bunch went 14-0 in league play.

That was an excellent chemistry team without many stars. This one has stars and will seek chemistry. Missouri will continue to work toward a goal of offensive balance. Once again, the Tigers relied heavily on three-point shots and while they shot a healthy .380 from behind the arc, didn't always shoot wisely.

For the second straight year, Snyder went after big men who could play immediately and landed Okafor, who he'll plug in immediately. Along with Johnson, the Tigers could sport one of the league's best front lines.

They already have the best player in Rush, one of the best shooters in Gilbert and top ball-handler in Stokes. The bench is the deepest it's been in years, so deep that Snyder shouldn't have to rush his freshmen into prominent roles like last year.

"We're getting close, very close," Snyder over the summer. Close to what? A league title. That hasn't happened since '94. A Sweet 16 appearance? Same year. A Final Four. Never happened. The Tigers are closer to those goals than they've been in years.

(B.K.)

 # Kansas 8

LOCATION	Lawrence, KS
CONFERENCE	Big 12
LAST SEASON	26-7 (.780)
CONFERENCE RECORD	12-4 (t-2nd)
STARTERS LOST/RETURNING	2/3
NICKNAME	Jayhawks
COLORS	Crimson & Blue
HOMECOURT	Allen Field House (16,300)
COACH	Roy Williams (North Carolina '72)
RECORD AT SCHOOL	355-89 (13 years)
CAREER RECORD	355-89 (13 years)
ASSISTANTS	Neil Dougherty (Cameron '84)
	Joe Holladay (Oklahoma '69)
	Ben Miller (Luther '91)
TEAM WINS (last 5 years)	34-35-23-24-26
RPI (last 5 years)	1-7-15-19-11
2000-01 FINISH	Lost in NCAA Sweet 16.

COACH AND PROGRAM

Roy Williams arrived at his press conference with a stuffed monkey on his shoulder. It was a gift from his wife, Wanda, so hubby could knock the monkey away as the Jayhawks prepared for the Sweet 16.

Williams and Kansas indeed crossed a barrier and lifted a burden from the coach's shoulders when the Jayhawks crushed Syracuse in the second round to reach the Sweet 16.

In 1997, Kansas owned college basketball's longest streak of consecutive Sweet 16 appearances with five. Since then, the Jayhawks watched the final 16 teams do battle without them.

All the losses hurt, but the 1998 defeat was the most devastating. Top-seeded Kansas fell to Jim Harrick's Rhode Island team in one of that tournament's big upsets. It was the final game for Raef LaFrentz and Paul Pierce, the final season for the Jayhawks as a perennial top five team.

The next two seasons produced no league titles (Kansas had won the final two in the Big Eight and first two of the Big 12), no final top 10 finishes, no All-America players. In those years, the NCAA Tournament actually provided more satisfaction than the regular season.

In 1999, the sixth-seeded Jayhawks had Kentucky on the ropes before falling in overtime. In 2000, eighth-seeded Kansas led top-seeded Duke in the final minute before losing.

Yes, a monkey may have lived on Williams' back, but it wasn't the burden he made it out to be. The bigger problems had come in the regular season. Over the last two years, Iowa State replaced Kansas as the league's top dog.

Not only did the Cyclones rip dominance away from the Jayhawks, they took it to them in their house, becoming the first opponent to beat Williams in Lawrence in successive seasons since Missouri a decade earlier.

Allen Field House, where Kansas once won 62 straight under Williams, was no safe haven when Iowa State came calling. Point guard Jamal Tinsley was especially cruel to Kansas. He never lost to the Jayhawks.

In each season, Kansas was favored to win the Big 12. That's not the case this season. Missouri gets the nod. That's another monkey off Williams' back. He enters the season with a team good enough to make a strong NCAA Tournament push but one that shouldn't be good enough to win the league.

Certainly, the Jayhawks will be different. The new starters are smaller than the people they replace. Gone is 7-0 center Eric Chenowith and 6-5 forward Kenny Gregory. The lineup newcomers will be 6-9 Drew Gooden and 6-9 Nick Collison on a full time basis (only one usually started last season) and probably 6-0 point guard Aaron Miles.

"We will definitely have three more true-guard perimeter players as opposed to a small forward type in the third spot," Williams said.

How will that change the Jayhawks? Williams hopes they'll be better defensively. That end has slipped below Williams' expectations in the last few years. Kansas hasn't pressed effectively since the days of Jacque Vaughn and Jarod Haase in the backcourt. The Jayhawks haven't been a turnover-forcing team, and therefore an easy scoring transition team in years.

"I want us to be able to put more pressure on people," Williams said. "Hopefully, having a little smaller lineup will allow us to pick up farther on the court than the three-point line. Last year, we basically guarded people from the three-point line in.

"I want to push the defense out, extend it. I wanted to do that last year, but early on in practice I saw we weren't able to. The personnel just wouldn't allow it."

Kirk Hinrich and Jeff Boschee gave Kansas ample offense and solid leadership, but they didn't have the foot speed to press the entire floor. If Miles delivers on his promise, he might be the key to Williams' plans. But Williams is quick to keep the pressure off his newcomer. He might not even play point guard, his position last year at Jefferson High in Portland, Ore.

"Aaron's junior year he played half the time he played point and half at shooting guard because they had another who played the point," Williams said "Whatever we do, I've always tried to make sure we don't say 'We have to find somebody to do this.' I don't think I'll be saying 'Aaron's the one [guard], Kirk's the one or Jeff's the one.'

"We will be a better ball-handling team. But another way of looking at it is we won't be as good on the boards. Kenny Gregory averaged seven rebounds as a small forward. That's sensational."

What Kansas has this season is four players—Hinrick, Boschee, Collison and Gooden—who have no offensive weaknesses. Chenowith was never the offensive presence around the basket you'd hoped from a 7-footer. He could hit the medium-range jumper.

Gregory was an athletic wonder, a remarkable leaper and dunk specialist who became a much better perimeter shooter in his senior season. But he never put together a total offense game.

Gooden and Collison are excellent scorers with similar skills. Both have developed half-hooks around the basket and neither mind stepping outside. Gooden is especially strong from the baseline and Collison uses the backboard well.

Both will need to rebound more. Chenowith got his share and Gregory more than his. Now a smaller Kansas has to find somebody to pick up their nearly 15 boards per game.

Hinrich, who set a school record by making 50.5 percent of his three-pointers, will look to shoot more. More shots may be available from the wing. The streaky shooting Boschee will set school records for field goals and attempts behind the arc.

Sheer numbers make the Kansas recruiting class one of the nation's best. The group of high school teammates Miles and guard Michael Lee, wing Keith Langford and power forward Wayne Simien got in most analyst's top five. All of them figure to be in the playing rotation along with senior forward Jeff Carey.

The Jayhawks won't be as highly regarded nationally entering this season as in past years, but this team could be better equipped for a Big 12 championship and longer NCAA Tournament run.

2001-2002 SCHEDULE

Nov.	19-21	#Maui Invitational
	28	Pittsburg State
Dec.	1	@Arizona
	4	Wake Forest
	8	UMKC
	12	@Princeton
	15	South Carolina State
	22	@North Dakota
	29	*Tulsa
Jan.	2	Valparaiso
	5	@Colorado
	9	Nebraska
	12	@UCLA
	15	@Oklahoma State
	19	Oklahoma
	23	@Iowa State
	26	@Texas A&M
	28	Missouri
Feb.	2	Colorado
	4	@Kansas State
	9	Texas Tech
	11	@Texas
	16	Baylor
	18	Iowa State
	24	@Nebraska
	27	Kansas State
March	3	@Missouri
	7-10	##Big 12 Tournament

@Road Games
*Kansas City, MO
#Maui, HI (vs. Ball State in first round; also Chaminade, South Carolina, Seton Hall, Duke, Houston, UCLA)
##Kemper Arena, Kansas City, MO

STARTERS NOT RETURNING

C-ERIC CHENOWITH (7-1, 270 lbs, 9.5 ppg, 7.6 rpg, 1.5 bpg, 22.6 minutes, .457 FG, .648 FT). Probably the most criticized player Roy Williams has coached, Chenowith's big crime was showing promise too early. He made second-team All-Big 12 as a sophomore. The next step naturally is first-team honors while pushing for All-America.

Chenowith went the other way. He dropped from 13 points to 8.6 as a junior. He was yanked from the starting lineup with 13 games remaining in the season as Williams went with his freshmen, Drew Gooden and Nick Collison. Chenowith's off-season work habits were called into question.

The good news for Chenowith was he did improve as a senior. His scoring average increased to 10 points and he added two more rebounds a game. He was a full-time starter until the last few games and the play got him drafted, in the second round by the New York Knicks.

But Chenowith will be remembered for promising career that went largely unfulfilled. He did not become the dominant player in the middle Kansas had hoped. Offensive, he seemed more comfortable away from the basket than beside it. He was easily pushed around, and perhaps the most telling statistic of his career was his 45 percent shooting from the field. That's horrible for a 7-footer.

Chenowith finished second on Kansas' career blocked shots list and fourth in the rebounding list.

F-KENNY GREGORY (6-5, 208 lbs, 15.6 ppg, 7.3 rpg, 2.4 apg, 31.6 minutes, .567 FG, .386 3PT, .424 FT). Maybe too much was expected all along. Gregory came to Kansas as a high-flying wing player who with a little refinement would fashion his game in the mold of Michael Jordan. Not become Jordan, but be like Mike. After all, Gregory had the hops, and, after al,I wasn't that the un-teachable quality that separated Jordan from the rest of the human race?

But Gregory never rounded into the overall talent that others predicted. For three seasons, he couldn't make a shot that wasn't a dunk, and while his perimeter shooting improved dramatically as a senior (38.6 percent from three-point range) his free-throw shooting remained horrible. Gregory finished his career at 43.3 percent.

And that figure killed his game. You can't be a slasher or play above the rim as Gregory did without making free throws. If Gregory had been a 70 percent shooter, he would have added two points to his 15.6 scoring average and probably even more because he wouldn't have passed up scoring opportunities for fear of going to the line.

Remove the expectations and Gregory had a fine career. He stands ninth on the school's career scoring leader list, and because of his work around the boards, finished with a 53.3 career shooting percentage.

Gregory wasn't drafted and is trying to battle onto an NBA roster as a free agent. Overseas or minor-league basketball is probably in his future.

OTHERS NOT RETURNING

C-LUKE AXTELL (6-10, 220 lbs, G-F, 5.3 ppg, 2.6 rpg, 15.2 minutes, .373 FG, .346 3PT, .800 FT). The success of four-year transfers has taken a downward turn at Kansas under Roy Williams. First, there was Ricky Calloway, the Indiana wing who left Bob Knight for Larry Brown but got Williams instead.

Calloway became a starter on Williams' first excellent team in 1990. Then came Rex Walters, who started at Northwestern but became an all-conference guard for the 1993 Final Four Jayhawks.

After that was Jarod Haase, the starting shooting guard for the remarkable three-year run of the mid-1990s.

Then came trouble. Lester Earl transferred from LSU under a cloud of suspicion, was hurt for most of his time in Lawrence and was never a productive player.

Axtell was next. He fled the mess of Tom Penders' final season in Texas and showed up in Lawrence with his hair cut and ready to become a team player. But personal problems forced him to miss the second half of his junior season, and last year he never got his game untracked.

Axtell went from being a member of the All-Big 12 freshman team at Texas to an inconsistent-shooting sub for most of his two years in Lawrence. His three-point touch, Axtell's calling card, was lost most of last season, when his percentage dipped from .392 to .346.

Basketball become secondary to Axtell before the season. On his 22nd birthday last September, he got baptized at an apartment-complex swimming pool.

"Going to the bars and doing whatever I used to do, basically was living in sin," Axtell said.

G-MARIO KINSEY (6-2, 175 lbs, G, 1.9 ppg, 0.6 rpg). Although only a sophomore, don't expect Kinsey to show up for basketball. His battle as the football team's starting quarterback was only one of his off-season concerns.

Kinsey ran afoul of the law for snatching a purse just before football season kicked off. He is not listed on the team's preseason roster.

Kinsey left the team midway through last season to prepare for spring football.

PROJECTED STARTERS

PG-KIRK HINRICH (6-3, 180 lbs., JR, #10, 11.5 ppg, 6.9 apg, 4.1 rpg, 32.7 minutes, .500 FG, .505 3PT, .843 FT, 1.3 spg, West HS/Sioux City, Iowa). The team's most important player. Hinrich makes Kansas go, much the way point guards of Roy Williams' past teams—namely Adonis Jordan and Jacque Vaughn—did. It's no coincidence that Kansas finished with its best record (26-7) in three years in Hinrich' first season as a full-time point guard.

Hinrich isn't smooth, but he is effective and plays intelligently. His assist-turnover ratio is better than 2-1, and that's impressive because he led the Big 12 in assists at 6.9. Kansas shot better than 50 percent from the floor last season and Hinrich gets some credit for that, getting the ball in positions for teammates to score.

Hinrich grew up with the game. His father, Jim, has coached West High in Sioux City, Iowa for 23 years. In grade school, Kirk was the team's ball boy. He rode the team bus and paid attention to the locker room talks. He always challenged the older boys to shooting contests.

"Kirk grew up watching these older kids play and he looked up to them like heroes," Jim Hinrich told the Kansas City Star. "He started to love basketball. It wasn't work for him. We never had to force him to play. By the time he got to high school and got on that same court he grew up on it was almost like living out a fantasy."

In 1999, son led the team to the state championship, dad's first. As a point guard should, Hinrich got more comfortable with every game. He shot only after exhausting all other options. With a 50.5 three-point percentage, Hinrich probably ought to look a little more for points. Last season he finished sixth on the team in field-goal attempts.

"My [freshman] year the rap on me was that I couldn't score," Hinrich said. "That bothered me because I knew I could shoot. I just had to prove it."

One way to get more shots from Hinrich is to change his role in the offense. That might happen if the Jayhawks go with freshman Aaron Miles at the point. Hinrich would move to the shooting guard and Jeff Boschee to the wing.

PG-AARON MILES (6-0, 160 lbs., FR, #11, 20 ppg, 8.0 apg, 6.0 rpg, 5.0 spg, Jefferson HS/Portland, Oregon). Kansas will have a three-guard lineup, and the guess here is that Miles, if he doesn't open the season at the point, will work his way into the starting lineup.

"It'll definitely be more a more guard-oriented lineup than in the past," Roy Williams said. "Which guards it will be I can't say for sure."

Miles is the first high-profile point guard recruited by Williams since Jacque Vaughn who isn't a combo guard.

Vaughn's successors, Ryan Robertson, Jeff Boschee and Kirk Hinrich, all spent some time in the career at shooting guard.

Miles is a pure point, who, like Hinrich, doesn't look to shoot first. But he did average 20 points, along with eight assists, for Jefferson High in Portland, Ore.

The honors rolled in for Miles. He won the Morgan Wooten Award as the national player of the year who combines basketball with academic skills.

Miles owned a 3.7 grade-point average and was student body vice-president last year. He was chosen the fourth best high school point guard in the country and the 11th best high school senior by ESPN.com.

Miles was talked into coming out for the Jefferson High football team as a senior and ended up as the starting quarterback. He led the team to a league title.

Miles, player of the year in Oregon and a McDonald's All-America, turned down offers from Arizona and UCLA.

SG-JEFF BOSCHEE (6-1, 185 lbs., SR, #13, 11.1 ppg, 4.1 apg, 3.5 apg, 33.3 minutes, .427 FG, .360 3PT, .787 FT, 1.2 spg, Valley City HS/Valley City, N.D.). The big difference between Boschee's sophomore and junior season was his hair. He kept his head shaved two years ago, but grew his hair out last year.

"Shaving it was something I started doing as a pregame routine and it just stuck," Boschee said. "But it's been nice to go out with my parents and friends and not have people recognize me."

Last year was something of a turnaround season for Boschee. His three-point shooting dropped from 41 to 36 percent, but his scoring increased from 10 to 11.1 points. It meant Boschee has become a better all-around player, and that he was no longer playing point guard. The move actually was made toward the end of the previous season. Hinrich's move to the point pushed Boschee to the off guard.

But it wasn't like Boschee forgot his skills. His assist-turnover ratio of 115-44 led the Big 12. The big upside last season was Boschee's defense. He earned the team's defensive player-of-the-year award and probably had his best game hounding Jamaal Tinsley at Iowa State. The Cyclones won, but Boschee earned praise for his efforts. He also scored 19 that day.

Boschee has started 95-of-100 games. He has a chance to become the program's career leader in three-pointers.

Boschee's big day this season is Dec. 1. That's when the Jayhawks travel to the University of North Dakota to meet the Fighting Sioux. Boschee grew up in Valley City, N.D., and it's the hometown game that Williams tries to deliver to all recruits. Should be as big as a Fighting Sioux hockey game.

PF-NICK COLLISON (6-9, 250 lbs., JR, #4, 14.0 ppg, 6.7 rpg, 2.2 apg, 27.0 minutes, .596 FG, .400 3PT, .625 FT, 1.6 bpg, Iowa Falls HS/Iowa Falls, Iowa). He's the Jayhawks' most unspectacularly good player. Collison shows little emotion when he plays. No snarls, fist pumps, chest-thumping. Just two points, now go play defense. Perhaps it's a fear-of-failure condition, or just a slight lack of confidence.

"I've never gone out and dominated a game," Collison said. "It's something I think I can do. Someday, I'd like to go out and win a really big game for my team."

The thing is, Collison had to talent to make that happen. At 6-9, he scores around the basket with a variety of moves, most of which end up with his body bent in strange ways. But he's also effective from 10-12 feet and will occasionally pop a three-pointer.

Collison's best game was also one of his most frustrating. He scored a team-high 23 points in Kansas' loss to Illinois in the NCAA Tournament, but went only 6-of-14 from the free-throw line. A little more success there and the Jayhawks would have kept it closer.

The heat is on Collison and Drew Gooden this season. With Kansas moving to a three-guard lineup, the Jayhawks will need more inside muscle from its starting big men. Collison averaged 6.7 rebounds last season, down slightly from the 6.9 per game he grabbed as a freshman.

"We have guys who can shoot from the outside, so it would be stupid for me to shoot from there," Collison said.

But Collison's position on the next level will be small forward, where he'll have to shoot from the outside. Roy Williams said Collison won't be restricted to the paint, but he also mentioned that at least one other play he knew didn't have much trouble moving from the paint to the perimeter.

"It worked for James Worthy," Williams said. "If you're good you can make that switch."

Collison will have nothing to worry about.

PF-DREW GOODEN (6-9, 230 lbs., JR, #0, 15.8 ppg, 8.4 rpg, 1.8 apg, 27.2 minutes, .516 FG, .400 3PT, .648 FT, 1.1 bpg, El Cerrito HS/Richmond, Calif.). Gooden felt compelled to announce that he was returning for his junior season and not casting his lot with the NBA. He might have made some money this year, but not as much has he stands to make by playing at least one more season in college.

Gooden was as much of a go-to guy as Kansas had last season. He led the Jayhawks in scoring and was voted first-team all-conference by the media. Collison made the coaches' first-team.

Gooden strengthened his game as a sophomore by playing smarter. The physical tools were the same, he simply applied them better. As a freshman, Gooden shot 45.1 percent from the floor and often took questionable shots. That happened much less last season and Gooden improved his shooting percentage to 51.6.

"I changed my style a bit," Gooden said. "The year before, I basically shot a jump hook and outside jumpers. Last year I took the ball to the basket more. It made me more of a threat and I was more confident."

As he did with Collison, Williams told Gooden that Kansas needed more production from him in the paint. He talked about how former Jayhawks center Greg Ostertag and then starting center Eric Chenowith were limited by their lack of mobility.

Gooden took it to heart and became a more all-around threat. It also helped him that his playing time increased from 21 to 27 minutes per game. He didn't feel like a part-time player as he did as a freshman.

"I got to play with some security," Gooden said. "[My freshman year] we had a lot of guys rotating at the power forward position. I'd think, 'I'm only going to get 20 minutes, so I better do something.' When you play more often, there's no need to rush around and take bad shots. You know you're going to be out there."

A more relaxed and confident Gooden recorded a team-high 10 double-doubles. He led Kansas in scoring 11 times and in rebounding 13 times, and that's with Gooden missing eight starts, five because of a wrist injury.

Gooden's best shot is a short half-hook from the baseline. It's about the surest thing in the Kansas offense. What Williams would like to see more of is rebounding and post defense. The Jayhawks are smaller than they've been in years and will need all the inside muscle they can muster.

One advantage for Gooden: He stays out of foul trouble. He's fouled out of only two games in two seasons.

KEY RESERVES

G-BRETT BALLARD (6-0, 175 lbs., G, SR, #3, 1.5 ppg, 0.6 rpg, 6.4 minutes, .323 FG, .391 3PT, .857 FT, Hutchinson HS/Hutchinson, Kansas/Cowley County CC/Arkansas City,Kansas and Hutchinson Community College/Hutchinson, Kansas). You've got to admire the walk-on's spirit. In a game at Iowa State, Ballard hacked Cyclones forward Paul Shirley on a rebound. Cyclones guard Jamaal Tinsley got in Ballard's face and Ballard gave it back.

"I'm was tired of this team getting pushed around," Ballard said. "I thought I needed to make a statement. Just because you're an All-American, don't get in my face because I'm a walk-on."

Call it a walk-on Kodak moment.

Ballard got more playing time than a walk-on might expect as Kirk Hinrich's backup. The Jayhawks needed to fill the slot when Hinrich went to the point and Jeff Boschee slid to the off-guard on a full-time basis.

Ballard came out of high school without major Division I skills, but he started 30 games in junior college as a freshman and averaged nine points and six assists for Hutchinson as a sophomore. There, he was a teammate of Chris Zerbe, who also walked on to the Jayhawks' roster.

Ballard's goal is to follow his father's footsteps into coaching. Jim Ballard has spent more than 20 years coaching middle school and sophomore ball in Hutchinson.

C-JEFF CAREY (6-11, 250 lbs., C, SR, #22, 1.5 ppg, 2.0 rpg, 8.3 minutes, .543 FG, .600 FG, Camdenton HS/Camdenton, MO). At mop-up time or playing important minutes, Carey gives Kansas an able body big man off the bench. His role becomes more important this year with the departure of Eric Chenowith.

Carey's numbers have remained steady through his career. He's been good for about two points and two rebounds per game. But while he's not a McDonald's All-American like the players for which he subs, Carey is good enough that when he spells Nick Collison or Drew Gooden, there's no substantial fall off.

Carey plays within himself. He takes only good shots, doesn't mishandle the ball and gets good position for rebounds. He's the kind of guy who, if he played 28 minutes, would averaged a solid 12 points and seven rebounds. If he played at a low-level Division I program, he'd be an all-conference player.

As it is, Carey is the top reserve front-liner on a perennial power, and that's good enough for him.

F-KEITH LANGFORD (6-4, 200 lbs., G-F, FR, #5, 25.7 ppg, 8.6 rpg, 4.2 apg, North Crowley HS/Fort Worth, Tex.). Langford, more than any newcomer, was the talk of preseason workouts and it would not be a stunning development if he eventually found his way into the starting lineup.

Langford was not the most heralded of the Kansas recruits, but he may be the best athlete of the bunch. He's a silky smooth, left-handed shooting wing who can play the big guard or small forward. It's the position that Jeff Boschee plays if Kansas start freshman Aaron Miles at the point.

But if Langford starts, Kirk Hinrich could stay at the point with Langford and Boschee on the wings.

Langford was selected North Texas Player of the Year by the Fort Worth Star-Telegram and all state by the Texas Association of Basketball Coaches.

He originally committed to Mississippi, but backed out to consider Kansas, Oklahoma and Cincinnati. Langford says his favorite player is Jalen Rose, and tries to pattern his game after the Pacers' star.

G-MICHAEL LEE (6-2, 210 lbs., G, FR, #25, 19.7 ppg, 5.0 rpg, Jefferson HS/Portland, Ore.). Kansas had never had a player from Oregon. In one year, Roy Williams got two. Lee was Aaron Miles' teammate at Jefferson High, on the basketball court and football field. It was Lee, a tight end, who persuaded Miles to come out for the football team. All Miles did was start at quarterback and lead Jefferson to the league championship.

Lee played mostly shooting guard for Jefferson, but is a good ball handler who could back up the point. Williams wants to use Lee's quickness on defense.

"Hopefully we'll pick up farther out on the court than the three-point line," Williams said. "Last year, we basically guarded people from the three-point line in. This year we'll push the defense out a little down the floor."

PF-WAYNE SIMIEN (6-8, 245 lbs., F, FR, #23, 19.3 ppg, 10.0 rpg, Leavenworth HS/Leavenworth, Kansas). It's been a decade since Kansas signed a high school player from the Kansas City area. Mostly, recruits have come from California and Iowa. Simien is a terrific catch for the Jayhawks, who looked to add front-line muscle.

Simien was the state's high school player of the year and the top player in the Kansas City area. ESPN.com labeled him the nation's 15th-best power forward. As a junior, he led Leavenworth to the 6A championship.

Simien is a powerfully built forward who gives Kansas much needed frontcourt depth. It's not out of the question that he could work his way into the starting lineup if Kansas wanted to go big. The Jayhawks outrebounded 27-of-33 opponents last year, but the lasting image of the season was Kansas getting out muscled by a more physical Illinois team in the Sweet 16. Simien's the kind of player the Jayhawks can go to war with.

Simien underwent shoulder surgery after last season, but he's expected to join the team at close to full strength when practice opens.

OTHER RETURNEES

G-LEWIS HARRISON (6-0, 165 lbs., G, SR, #2, 0.4 ppg, 0.3 rpg, 2.4 minutes, Piper High School/Kansas City, Kansas/Kansas City Community College/Kansas City, Kansas). A walk-on point-guard who said he was close to quitting competitive basketball when a Kansas assistant invited him to walk-on tryouts. Harrison emerged as the best guard from 70 candidates.

F-TODD KAPPELMANN (6-9, 230 lbs., F, SR, #50, 0.3 ppg, 0.4 rpg, 1.6 minutes, Augusta HS/Augusta, Kansas, Butler County Community College/El Dorado, Kansas). When he shoots inside, Kappelman sometimes hangs to the left before shooting the ball. The reason? He's blind in his left eye and he tilts his head a little to left to get a better aim with his right eye.

Kappelman, a walk-on, appeared in 16 games and made two of his five field-goal tries last season.

F-BRYANT NASH (6-6, 200 lbs., F, SO, #15, 0.7 ppg, 1.2 rpg, 5.1 minutes, .280 FG, .333 3PT, Turner

HS/Carrollton, Texas). Nash's first shot in a Kansas uniform: air ball from three-point land in the opening game.

"I was so nervous out there I was actually shaking," he said.

As the season progressed, Nash lost his jitters and helped Kansas as a reserve small forward. He got minutes when Kenny Gregory and Luke Axtell were hurt. Because he's the only true small forward on the roster, Nash could get more minutes than the five he averaged last season, for defensive purposes if nothing else. Drew Gooden or Wayne Simien may not have the quickness to drop down and guard a 6-6 wing. Defensive specialist is a role that could suit him well.

F-CHRIS ZERBE (6-5, 230 lbs., SR, F, #34, 1.9 ppg, 0.6 rpg, 2.1 minutes, .684 FG, Andover HS/Andover, Kansas, Hutchinson Community College). Zerbe led the Kansas walk-ons in scoring. Why not put it up? He made 13-of-19 from the field. Zerbe played in the paint most of his career. He moved to the perimeter at Kansas.

OTHER NEWCOMERS

G-JEFF HAWKINS (5-11, 155 lbs, FR, #1, 19.6 rpg, 4.5 apg, 4.3 apg, 2.6 spg, Sumner Academy/Kansas City, Kansas). Hawkins red-shirted last season. He attends Kansas on an academic scholarship. He'll get a few minutes at the point and could be used in specific defensive situations.

QUESTIONS

Size? Chenowith might not have been the smoothest of 7-footers, but he was seven feet, and helped Kansas become one of the nation's rebounding leaders.

Rebounding? Gregory was a big part of the rebounding advantage. Kansas no longer has that advantage.

Timid shooting? Hinrich, one of the best shooters in the game, needs to shoot more.

ANSWERS

Hinrich! It's tough to be critical of the guy. With Tinsley gone from Iowa State, he becomes the Big 12's premier point guard.

Gooden/Collison! Great inside punch. As juniors, this may be the last we see of them in college.

Tradition! They say it no longer matters to kids. But playing in Allen Field House and all that means is a huge advantage for the Jayhawks.

KANSAS 2000-2001 RESULTS

#UCLA	99-98
#St. John's	82-74
North Dakota	92-52
Boise State	101-61
Washburn	99-56
Middle Tennessee State	99-66
Illinois State	80-61
@Wake Forest (L)	53-84
@DePaul	75-69
Tulsa	92-69
@Ohio State	69-68
##Southwest Missouri	77-43
@Texas Tech	94-82
@Oklahoma	69-61
Nebraska	84-62
Texas A&M	100-70
@Colorado	85-75
Kansas State	92-66
@Missouri (L)	66-75
Texas	82-66
Iowa State (L)	77-79
Oklahoma State	77-61
@Baylor (L)	77-85
@Iowa State (L)	71-79
Colorado	91-79
@Nebraska	78-74
@Kansas State	77-65
Missouri	75-59
###Kansas State	94-63
###Oklahoma (L)	57-62
####Oklahoma State	69-54
####Boston College	74-71
####Kentucky	80-76
####Duke (L)	69-79
#####Cal State Northridge	99-75
#####Syracuse	87-58
#####Illinois (L)	64-80

#Coaches vs. Cancer Classic in New York
##Spring Shootout in Kansas City, MO
###Big 12 Tournament in Kansas City, MO
####NCAA Tournament
#####NCAA Tournament
@Road Games

BLUE RIBBON ANALYSIS

BACKCOURT	A
BENCH/DEPTH	B+
FRONTCOURT	A
INTANGIBLES	A

Even though it didn't win the Big 12 as expected last season, Kansas made some strides, and more improvement should be in store this season. The Jayhawks will start a senior, three juniors and probably a freshman, making them one of the most experienced teams in the nation. Boschee, Hinrich and Collison have started just about every game they've played. Gooden has played just as many minutes as any of them.

The main challenges in the Big 12 will come from Missouri and Oklahoma State. But don't be surprised to see Kansas back on top for the first time since 1998.

(B.K.)

 # Virginia 9

LOCATION	Charlottesville, VA
CONFERENCE	Atlantic Coast
LAST SEASON	20-9 (.690)
CONFERENCE RECORD	9-7 (4th)
STARTERS LOST/RETURNING	1/4
NICKNAME	Cavaliers
COLORS	Dark Blue & Orange
HOMECOURT	University Hall (8,392)
COACH	Pete Gillen (Fairfield '68)
RECORD AT SCHOOL	53-37 (3 years)
CAREER RECORD	327-165 (16 years)
ASSISTANTS	Tom Herrion (Merrimack '89)
	Walt Fuller (Drexel '87)
	Scott Shepherd (Robert Morris '91)
TEAM WINS (last 5 years)	18-11-14-19-20
RPI (last 5 years)	29-91-93-73-36
2000-01 FINISH	Lost in NCAA first round.

COACH AND PROGRAM

Will this be the year that impish Pete Gillen finally grows up? OK, that might be asking a little too much for the ACC's biggest kid since Jim Valvano. But going into his fourth year at Virginia, this should at least be the year Gillen's program matures, if not the coach himself.

He has a solid foundation built around three seniors, three juniors and a red-shirt sophomore who was injured a year ago.

There is a total of four starters returning from last year's 20-9 team, making the Cavs one of the most experienced teams in the league, behind only league power Maryland.

Considering where Gillen started—with six healthy scholarship players and seven walk-ons in his first season after taking over for Jeff Jones—it's a well-stocked pantry that should keep the Cavaliers among the best teams in the nation, as they were for most of last season.

"I think we have a chance to be an exciting team," said Gillen, who was rewarded by the school with a new contract worth a reported $9 million over the next 10 years. "I never try to make predictions or promises of that nature, because we are in the premier basketball conference in the country and I know you can get humbled in a hurry.

"But I think we can compete at a high level. We have a chance to be better than we were last year."

The Cavs have improved steadily the last three years, starting with a surprising 14-16 debut for Gillen, who inherited a limited number of scholarships and a general lack of talent. The next season, the Cavs won 19 games in the regular season and went to the National Invitation Tournament.

And last year, Gillen took the school to the NCAA Tournament for the first time in four years. At times last year, the Cavs were unbeatable, especially when they played in rocking University Hall, where they compiled an ACC-best 14-1 home record. They were ranked all

season and spent six weeks in the Top 10 in January and February, during which time they beat three teams ranked in the Top 5 for the first time in school history. They finished fourth in the nation in scoring (third in the ACC behind Duke and Maryland) with 85.0 points a game.

March, however, was not kind to the Cavaliers, beginning with a regular season-ending 35-point loss at Maryland, continuing with a narrow loss to Georgia Tech in the first round of the ACC Tournament and a last-second loss to Gonzaga in the first round of the NCAA Tournament.

It was just the culmination of the same problem the Cavaliers had all year long: the inability to win on the road. The Cavs were 6-8 away from U-Hall last year, not a good sign for a team that wants to earn some national respect and stay at the top of the ACC ladder.

"We need to do a better job on the road, especially against the elite teams in our conference," said Gillen, who has won six ACC road games in his three years at the school.

There are other areas where the high-scoring Cavaliers need to improve. With only one little-used player taller than 6-8 on his roster, Gillen has had to make do with junior Travis Watson as his center for the last two years.

That doesn't mean the Cavaliers didn't get good production out of their interior players. Watson was second in the league with 9.1 boards a game, while the team finished first in the league in offensive rebounds (15.1), rebounding margin (+5.6) and rebounding defense (33.4). But Virginia also gave up a lot of easy shots that left no opportunity for rebounds, and a post presence would have helped.

Like everybody else who tried to get a big man in recruiting this year, Gillen came up empty. His primary target, 7-footer DeSagana Diop of Oak Hill Academy in Virginia, went straight to the NBA, going with the No. 8 pick to the Cleveland Cavaliers.

Gillen did find a big man willing to come to Charlottesville in 6-10 center Nick Vander Laan. Trouble is, Vander Laan played at the University of California last year and must sit out this season under NCAA transfer rules. Ditto for Rutgers transfer Todd Billet, a point guard.

That means the Cavaliers will have a misplaced frontcourt for the third year in a row, one of the reasons they were last in the ACC in field-goal percentage defense last year. Watson is a power forward who has had to play center and senior Chris Williams is a small forward who has had to play the power slot.

And the two frontcourt recruits Gillen brought in this year, 6-8 Elton Brown and 6-8 Jason Clark, won't really alleviate that lack of size. But maybe they and 6-8 sophomore J.C. Mathis can spell Watson long enough to let him heal from the nagging injuries he accumulated through the ACC season. He played through five different injuries, but was so beaten up by the end of the season that he lost his effectiveness as a rebounder and a scorer.

With more inside help this year, the Cavaliers could be a serious force in the ACC this season.

More inside bodies would also help the Cavaliers' defense, which tuckered out at the end of last season.

"Early in the season, when we beat teams like Purdue and Tennessee and got off to a 10-1 start, I thought our pressure was very good," Gillen said. "As the season went on, since we weren't very big we got a little tired and teams also made adjustments, so our pressure wasn't quite as effective."

Overall, with the addition of four freshmen who can contribute immediately, the Cavaliers will be quicker and more athletic this season. They will have more options, if not more size, underneath. And they will have more experience than just about any other team in the league.

"I think our chemistry should be good," Gillen said. "We know each other well, played a lot of games together. We are fairly experienced.

"We have a chance to be a very competitive team, an exciting team and potentially a special team."

2001-2002 SCHEDULE

Nov.	16	Wagner
	18	East Tennessee State
	21	Howard
	28	*Michigan State
Dec.	1	Virginia Tech
	8	@Auburn
	17	Charleston Southern
	20	**Georgetown

	23	Rutgers
	30	Grambling
Jan.	5	North Carolina State
	8	@Clemson
	12	@North Carolina
	15	Wake Forest
	19	Florida State
	22	@Georgia Tech
	24	VMI
	27	@Duke
	31	Maryland
Feb.	3	@Missouri
	6	@North Carolina State
	10	Clemson
	12	North Carolina
	17	@Wake Forest
	20	@Florida State
	23	Georgia Tech
	28	Duke
March	3	@Maryland
	7-10	#ACC Tournament

@Road Games
*ACC/Big Ten Challenge at Richmond, VA
**John Thompson Classic, Washington, DC
#Charlotte Coliseum, Charlotte, NC

STARTERS NOT RETURNING

G-DONALD HAND (5-11, 12.6 ppg, 3.2 rpg, 6.0 apg, 3.13 topg, 31.7 minutes, .366 FG, .282 3-PT FG, .813 FT). When Gillen dreamed of his perfect point guard, Donald Hand was not among the finalists. Hand, a lightly regarded recruit coming out of Paterson, N.J., was a scoring point guard who looked to shoot first and ask questions (like, "How many points did I score") later. At times during his four years as a starter, he was brilliant. At times, he was booed by his own fans.

Just look at the stretch he had in the middle of last season: He scored 20 or more points in four consecutive games, a career first. He followed it up by hitting only 3-of-23 shots, including 1-of-9 from three-point territory, and committing 17 turnovers in the next four games, a February swoon like the one he suffered as a junior.

And just about the time Gillen was ready to pull every hair out of his big old head, Hand came back to play one of his best games of the season, helping the Cavs whip No. 4 North Carolina at home with 17 points.

When his wildly inconsistent career came to an end, Hand ranked in the school's top five in four categories: assists, steals, three-point field goals and free throws made. But he also spent plenty of time in the doghouse.

"Donald did a great job for us and we will miss him," Gillen said. "He was criticized, sometimes unfairly. He was very talented, very quick. He was a concern for the other team.

"He wasn't always consistent, but teams had to find a way to stop him."

Hand made his biggest offensive contribution as a sophomore, when he averaged 17.1 points as the top scoring option on Gillen's first team. But as Gillen was able to lure better talent to Charlottesville, Hand's productivity necessarily waned.

Though he was a second-team All-ACC pick as a junior, his scoring dipped to 15 points a game, second on the team behind Williams. As a senior, Hand's scoring fell even more, as Roger Mason Jr. and Travis Watson became the team's primary offensive weapons. But Hand was also playing a much different role. With Majestic Mapp lost for the season after knee surgery, Hand was required to run the offense. He averaged a career-high six assists a game, finishing third in the ACC in assists per game and 10th in assist-to-turnover ratio.

And, even though it was a wild roller-coaster ride, Hand had plenty of experience playing in big games. He started 110 times in his 120-game career for the Cavaliers.

OTHERS NOT RETURNING

G-KEITH FRIEL (6-4, 8.4 ppg, 1.0 rpg, 17.9 minutes, .399 FG, .428 3PT, .903). Friel's purpose was simple: Come off the bench and score points in bunches. For two years, he did that. He didn't have a lot of assists or rebounds or steals. But he could score with a deadly three-point shot. Last season he led the ACC in three-point shooting, and would have been at the top in free-throw shooting had he gotten to the line enough times to qualify.

Friel finished his short career ranked eighth on Virginia's all-time list of three-pointers made with 107, even though he played for only two years.

Friel transferred to Virginia after spending two years at Notre Dame, where he was one of the best shooters in the Big Ten.

"We'll miss Keith because even when he didn't score, he attracted so much defensive attention and emphasis it made other people's jobs easier," Gillen said.

F-STEPHANE DONDON (6-9, 4.6 ppg, 3.2 rpg, 14.1 minutes, .400 FG, .333 3PT, .745 FT). Recruited from a Texas junior college to shore up Virginia's lacking inside game, Dondon provided some rebounding and scoring off the bench.

The native of Touluse, France started the first three games of his career as a junior, but then served as a reserve the rest of the time. He was hampered last season when he suffered a sprained foot against North Carolina.

And while Dondon never contributed as much as Gillen hoped, the Cavs could use someone of his height this year to help Watson and Williams inside.

G-JOSH HARE (6-2, 0.5 ppg, 0.7 rpg, .444 FG, .500 3PT, .000 FT). When Gillen inherited the job from Jones, there weren't enough players on the roster to practice five on five. Hare was one of seven players who earned their way onto the team in an open tryout in October, 1998. He in fact became a reliable contributor in his first season, playing more than 20 minutes a game. He averaged 3.6 points, 2.5 rebounds and 2.0 assists for a team that went 14-16, but Gillen was grateful to have him.

As the Cavs recruited better players and the program improved, Hare's time on the floor dwindled, down to 3.2 minutes a game as a junior to 2.1 minutes as a senior. He scored only 10 points in his senior season, but again, Gillen would not have gotten his program off the ground in that first season if he hadn't gotten solid contributions from players like Hare.

G-GREG LYONS (6-4, 0.9 ppg, 0.2 rpg, 1.5 minutes, .500 FG, .500 3PT). After playing as a walk-on for two seasons then taking a year off, Lyons rejoined the team last season, primarily to help the Cavs in practice. Lyons wasn't really a contributor, but he was a shooter. All four of his field goals last year were from beyond the three-point line, and in his three-year career he made 10-of-21 three-point shots.

Nto bad for someone who earned his way on the team in an open tryout.

STARTING LINEUP

PG-MAJESTIC MAPP (6-2, 183 lbs., R-SO, #11, 5.3 ppg, 0.9 rpg, 2.2 apg, 1.7 topg, 0.7 spg, 18.7 minutes, .335 FG, .320 3PT, .604 FT in 1999-2000, St. Raymond's HS/Harlem, N.Y.). With his passing and play-making abilities, Mapp is more the kind of point guard Gillen likes to have running his team, one who thinks pass first, points second.

And with the departure of four-year starter Donald Hand, Mapp is slated to step in immediately in the point-guard position, assuming his reconstructed knee allows him to play when practice starts in October.

Mapp blew his right knee out last August while playing in a pickup game on campus, tearing the anterior cruciate ligament and forcing him to miss all of last season. That left the Cavaliers with only Hand at the point-guard position. He handled those responsibilities capably, but Mapp is more suited to Gillen's style.

"Majestic is a classic point guard in that he has a great feel for the game," Gillen said. "He was well coached in high school, shares the ball very well and has very good vision. I think he's at his best when he's pushing the fast break because he sees the floor well and gets the ball out to players.

"He needs to continue to work in his perimeter shooting."

During his freshman year, Mapp played in all 31 games as a reserve point guard. He didn't shoot well, making only 33.5 percent of his field-goal attempts and scoring only 5.3 points a game. But he was second on the team in assists with 69, and Gillen was ready to gradually give him more responsibilities.

This year, Gillen has no choice. Mapp is his starting point guard, with some help from Mason and freshman Keith Jennifer.

"When he is healthy and playing the way he is capable, he is our starting point guard," Gillen said. "He has the experience, strength and the savvy to do the job."

"He has poise. He is not afraid. He really sees the floor well. He makes a lot of other players better. He might not be the scorer that Donald was, but I think he will distribute the ball very well and get guys involved."

Gillen compared Mapp to some of the other point guards he has developed over the years: Jamal Walker at Xavier and God Shamgod and Michael Brown at Providence.

"They were great scorers, but they made other players better," Gillen said. "That's more our style."

SG-ROGER MASON JR. (6-5, 201 lbs., JR, #21, 15.7 ppg, 3.7 rpg, 2.5 apg, 2.3 topg, 1.1 spg, 32.0 minutes, .476 FG, .442 3PT, .884 FT, Good Counsel HS/Silver Spring, Md.). Just as quickly as the Cavaliers moved up in the national polls, Mason became the team's offensive centerpiece. The athletic guard with the sweet shot more than doubled his freshman scoring average, jumping from 7.6 points a game two years ago to a team-leading 15.7 points a game last season, good enough for sixth in the ACC.

And the good thing for the Cavaliers was that Mason kept getting better and better, averaging more than 18 points over the Cavs' last 10 games and scoring a season-high 30 in the season-ending NCAA loss to Gonzaga.

"He was our go-to guy down the stretch," Gillen said. "I think he has a chance to be a special guard. He was our co-MVP with Travis Watson. This year, I think he has a chance to be an elite player.

"I think he is one of the top 10 players in the ACC as we go into the season."

Mason's shooting abilities were apparent from the three-point line and the free-throw line. He led the league with an 88.4 free-throw percentage, at one time hitting 45 consecutive free throws. And he would have been at the top of the league's three-point shooters if he had made six more long-range shots.

Gillen believes that all Mason—a third-team All-ACC selection as a sophomore—needs is a little more experience in big-time game situations, which he got this summer as a member of the USA Basketball team that won the bronze medal in the World University Games in Beijing, China.

Mason was the U.S. team's third-leading scorer, averaging 13.0 points and 4.8 rebounds in eight games while shooting 51.9 percent from the floor.

While Mason spent most of his time playing the two-spot last year, he also spent some time backing up Hand at the point, which is how he led the team in minutes played. He will likely do more of the same this year, as Mapp slowly works his way back into game shape.

Playing the point last year improved Mason's ball-handling abilities.

"That made him a better player," Gillen said. "He did a very good job. Going into this season, he's gotten a little stronger and his perimeter shooting has improved."

SF-ADAM HALL (6-5, 200 lbs., SR, #31, 10.1 ppg, 5.5 rpg, 1.2 apg, 1.6 topg, 1.2 spg, 26.8 minutes, .506 FG, .269 3PT, .642 FT, Katy HS/Katy, Texas). There's probably no better defensive player in the ACC and only a few better in the country than Hall, the athletic small forward who loves to play a 94-foot game.

In fact, most players in the ACC know they have really arrived when they find out they will be going one-on-one against Hall.

"He will be our defensive stopper again this year," Gillen said. "He is certainly someone who can slow down a tremendous player on the other team."

Duke's Jason Williams found that out when he was only 5-for-21 against Virginia's defense, with Hall drawing the primary assignment of covering the Blue Devil All-American. Clemson's Will Solomon found out how good Hall is when he went 2-for-14 and scored only 10 points against Hall's defense.

But Hall has some offensive skills, too. He's been a steady contributor for three years, averaging 10.8 points as a freshman and 10.1 points in both his sophomore and junior seasons. He led the team in field-goal percentage at 50.6 percent, but that almost seems low considering how many of Hall's baskets were swooping, crowd-pleasing dunks. He used his athletic ability particularly well on the offensive end, finishing in the league's top 10 in offensive rebounds. None of them were more important than his game-winning tip-in against the Blue Devils on Valentine's Day.

"I think he is the best athlete in the ACC as far as running and jumping and athletic ability," Gillen said. "I haven't seen an athlete like him."

Few people have ever seen a 6-5 wing player grab 17 rebounds in a game, as Hall did against Wake Forest last season, the most boards by a Virginia player in six years.

Gillen would like to see Hall celebrate his final collegiate season by improving his offensive productivity.

"He is an important cog in our team," Gillen said.

PF-CHRIS WILLIAMS (6-7, 206 lbs., SR, #33, 14.5 ppg, 6.7 rpg, 2.0 apg, 2.0 topg, 0.7 bspg, 1.5 spg, .503 FG, .395 3PT, .760 FT, Minor HS/Brimingham, Ala.). Headline writers really don't know much about Williams, whose game has been loud for the last year while his demeanor has remained quiet.

"He's a quiet player and a quiet person," said Gillen, who calls Williams the 'Silent Assassin.' He is not real comfortable talking about himself and not real big on talking to the media. I think because of that, he is a very underrated player."

Which is odd because Williams has been a model of consistent excellence during his career. Last year, he was third in the ACC in field-goal percentage; 10th in scoring, rebounding and defensive rebounding; 11th in free throw percentage and 13th in steals.

In other words, Williams does a little bit of everything, even while playing out of position at power forward.

"He is the glue in a lot of ways that holds things together," Gillen said. "He is so steady. He is going to get 11 or 12 points every game, six or seven rebounds. Last year, he had a better year than people thought."

"I don't think he got the respect he deserved."

Perhaps that's because Williams' role has changed over the years. As a freshman, he and Hand were the Cavaliers' best scoring options. Williams, one of Jeff Jones' final recruits, averaged 16.8 points and 7.5 rebounds a game and was selected ACC Freshman of the Year. But as a sophomore and junior, that load has been spread around to others as Gillen has amassed more talent. Williams scoring average has gone down by a point or more in each of the last two seasons.

"As our team has gotten stronger, Chris has not been called on to be Hercules or Atlas and carry the world," Gillen said. "That does not diminish how good a player he is. Some people read that wrong."

Playing out of position takes its toll, too.

"Chris has had to sacrifice like Travis Watson and has had to play a lot at the four position," Gillen said. "That means he's had to guard the power forward on the other team, and I think he has gotten beat up and worn down a little for the offensive end."

Still, Williams has improved his three-point shooting every year, making an impressive 39.5 percent of his shots behind the arc last year.

"That's excellent for a guy who isn't considered a shooter, really," Gillen said.

C-TRAVIS WATSON (6-8, 254 lbs., JR, #35, 12.3 ppg, 9.1 rpg, 1.2 bspg, 1.0 spg, 28.4 minutes, .497 FG, .617 FT, Oak Hill Academy/Mouth of Wilson, Va. and Brookneal, Va.)

Even shoulders as broad as Watson's can't carry a heavy load forever. The undersized but productive center gamely carried the bulk of the Cavaliers' inside dirty work.

Like Maryland's Lonny Baxter, he was outsized almost every night, though rarely ever out-worked. He always managed to get his points and his rebounds, accumulating more double-doubles (13) than any player in the league. He finished second in the ACC in rebounding to Georgia Tech 7-footer Alvin Jones and made second-team All-ACC.

"He was our inside scorer last year," Gillen said. "He could go inside and score or get fouled. He did a marvelous job."

But those poundings by taller players frequently took a toll. Watson was bothered at times by a variety of injuries, especially in February. His laundry list of injuries included a sprained knee, a hip pointer, a strained hamstring and a sprained ankle. He missed about 14 days of practice during the ACC season, but never missed a game and was only out of the starting lineup on Senior Night.

Watson was clearly bothered by injuries in the Cavaliers' 90-80 loss at N.C. State, when he was held to a season-low five points and four rebounds.

"He had five significant injuries that would have prevented a lot of guys from playing," Gillen said. "He overcame all of that and played. Without him playing we probably would have lost some more of those games and not had as good a year. He stepped up.

"I think our fans really appreciated what a warrior Travis was, how courageous and tough he was last season."

But if the Cavaliers are going to have the kind of season Gillen and Cavalier fans are hoping for, Watson needs some help. He needs Elton Brown and Jason Clark to absorb some of the pounding he took inside. If

J.C. Mathis and even Jason Rogers could contribute, it would be a huge plus for Watson's weary body.

KEY RESERVES

F-ELTON BROWN (6-8, 250 lbs., FR, #42, 28.4 ppg, 9.8 rpg, Warwick HS/Newport News, VA). Virginia needs exactly what Brown offers: a bulky inside presence. The height-impaired Cavs have had to rely on Travis Watson and Chris Williams playing out of position for the last two years and were desperately seeking a big man throughout the fall and spring recruiting periods.

They fell short, so to speak, when most of their top targets went elsewhere or directly to the NBA. But Brown, the best prospect in the Cavs' well-regarded class, can take up just as much room as Watson inside and should be a force in the middle.

"He is an excellent offensive player in the low post," Gillen said. "He's a wide body who's very strong and has excellent moves. He'll be one our top scorers in the low post because he has excellent moves, good hands and a great feel for scoring down close to the basket.

"He's also a good rebounder and a tremendous competitor."

Brown was a three-year starter and three-year MVP at Warwick High. He was also a standout for Boo Williams' AAU team, where he was a teammate of fellow Virginia freshman Jason Clark.

The two have been buddies ever since and are looking forward to playing together in college.

"Elton is mature beyond his age," Gillen said. "He was still 17 until his birthday in September, but he plays like he's a lot older."

F-JASON CLARK (6-8, 225 lbs., FR, #34, 17.0 ppg, 10.0 rpg, 4.0 bspg, Hargrave Military Academy/Chatham, Va. and Kellam HS/Virginia Beach, Va.). Though he wasn't the most widely recruited player on Hargrave Military's 27-1 team last year—that honor went to Florida signee James White—Clark was one of the most valuable players on the team.

Playing slightly out of position as a power forward, something he better get used to at Virginia, Clark was a consistent, if not flashy player who was a key to Hargrave's success.

"Jason plays bigger than his size," Gillen said. "He is a tremendous athlete who does a lot of the dirty work. He does whatever it takes to win."

In his two years at Hargrave, Clark also got to know incoming Cavalier point guard Keith Jenifer, who played at the school last season.

More important, however, was that Clark maintained a long-time friendship with Elton Brown. The two were teammates on Boo Williams' successful AAU team from the Virginia Beach area.

The two players never said they wanted to attend the same school, and Clark signed with the Cavaliers in November. But there's no doubt that his commitment to the Gillen's program helped get Brown on board.

The two have completely different but complementary games. Clark is strong and athletic, with the ability to defend all three interior positions.

"Right now, his defense is his strength," Gillen said. "He may be the second-best athlete on the team. He'll be able to score points on stick-backs and tap-ins, so a guy like him is going to be very important in our style.

"He can get up and down the floor. He is going to play a lot of minutes."

G-JERMAINE HARPER (6-3, 170 lbs., FR, #24, 21.2 ppg, 5.7 rpg, 4.3 apg, 2.3 spg, Blue Ridge School/Gardena, Calif.). Gillen can't wait to see how Harper plays in Virginia's up-tempo offense. Gillen believes that Harper might be the best athlete on the team, with all proper respect to Adam Hall and fellow freshman Jason Clark.

"He will be very good in our up-tempo game," Gillen said. "He is a very quick, explosive athlete and a great defender."

Harper grew up in California, but played for three years at a private school in the Virginia mountains, where he was a three-time Division I Independent Schools all-state selection. Harper graduated as the school's all-time leading scorer (1,658), rebounder (551), assist-maker (433) and three-point shooter (102).

Because of his versatility, Harper can play either guard position and maybe even small forward, though he is primarily a two-guard. However, he is an inconsistent shooter who mostly relies on his athletic ability to slash and score, instead of his skill to stop and shoot.

"He has to continue to work on his consistency from the perimeter," Gillen said. "But he can score in a lot of

different ways. I think he is going to be a significant contributor as a freshman."

G-KEITH JENIFER (6-3, 165 lbs., FR, #10, 13.0 ppg, 6.0 rpg, 11.0 apg, Towson Catholic HS/Hargrave Military Academy/Chatham, Va. and Towson, Md.). Though he is primarily a point guard, Jenifer will get the opportunity to play both backcourt positions this year as an understudy to Mapp and Mason.

"He is going to play a lot this year," Gillen said.

Jenifer came to Charlottesville from Towson, Md. after a one-year detour to Hargrave Military Academy, where he was a teammate with incoming freshman Jason Clark on a team stocked with Division I basketball talent. He graduated from Towson Catholic High School two years ago after averaging 18.8 points, six assists and seven rebounds as a senior.

"I think his game took a step up during that year at Hargrave," Gillen said. "He worked on his strength and had an opportunity to improve in all areas of his game.

Jenifer is a penetrator who likes to mix it up inside and get the ball up and down the floor, which Gillen believes will be perfect for his team's style. He plays strong defense and Gillen will have no trouble working him into the lineup immediately as one of many players providing backcourt depth.

"He will be an important asset to our team," the coach said.

F-J.C. MATHIS (6-8, 231 lbs., SO, #32, 3.4 ppg, 2.1 rpg, 11.9 minutes, .422 FG, 1.000 3PT, .500 FT, John F. Kennedy HS/Brooklyn, N.Y.). By the end of his freshman season, Mathis was a regular off the bench. He played in all 29 games, contributing where he could at the power forward and center positions. He began to get more time midway through the year after Stephane Dondon suffered a sprained foot and missed three games.

This year, Gillen expects Mathis to improve and become more productive as he gains some experience.

"J.C. is one of our hardest workers," Gillen said. "He spent the whole summer and spring working on his strength and agility. He is going to be a big factor for us at the No. 4 position."

Mathis, like Watson, will have to get used to being out-sized just about every night, something he handled better as the season went along last year. Mathis, the fundamentally strong son of a high school coach, also has motivation to come back strong as a sophomore. He was on the free-throw line with 21.4 seconds to play in Virginia's NCAA Tournament game against Gonzaga, shooting a critical one-and-one. He missed his first shot, Gonzaga got the rebound and went on to score the game-winning basket, handing the Cavaliers their third consecutive defeat in the month of March.

Those kinds of memories tend to stick with a player over the summer. Gillen just hopes it is positive motivation for the upcoming year.

"I think his minutes are going to go up this year," Gillen said. "He is very important to our team. He will go to the offensive boards. He will take a charge. He is a solid basketball player.

"He's not really flashy, but he plays the game. He does all the little things that thrill a coach."

F/G-MAURICE "MO" YOUNG (6-4, 200 lbs., SO, #23, 2.6 ppg, 1.3 rpg, 6.7 minutes, .444 FG, .154 3PT, .615 FT, Bishop McNamara HS/Mitchellville, Md.). Most of Young's contributions came early in the season. That's when he was twice chosen ACC Rookie of the Week, for performances against non-conference competition.

But he scored only 15 points in ACC play, eight of which came during mop-up duty in the Cavaliers' 103-61 loss at Duke. He didn't play in four ACC games and was held scoreless in 10 others.

This year, however, with the loss of Friel on the wing, Young will be asked to come off the bench and offer more offense as a small forward.

"We are hoping he will give us some offense off the bench," Gillen said. "He is not the same type of player Keith Friel was, but we are hoping he can have the same kind of productivity off the bench."

Friel was a gunner who led the ACC in three-point shooting, while Young is a slasher who can penetrate and draw the foul.

"I think Mo can pick up some of the scoring we lost with Keith and Donald," Gillen said. "He is going to have a great opportunity to be an impact guy for us."

OTHER RETURNING PLAYERS

C-JASON ROGERS (6-10, 230 lbs., JR, #30, 1.9 pga, 0.9 rpg, 3.6 minutes, .429 FG, .591 FT, Robert E. Lee HS/Staunton, Va.). Gillen keeps waiting for Rogers, the only player on the roster taller than 6-8, to get strong enough to contribute. That may happen now that the lanky center has added around 10 pounds of muscle to his stringy frame, but he spent most of last year on the bench, playing in only five of the Cavaliers final 18 games.

"He can give us some minutes," Gillen said. "Hopefully, he can come in and guard a center or a power guy inside so Travis Watson doesn't get into foul trouble.

"His biggest problem has always been his lack of strength, but I think he is doing what he can to address that issue."

Rogers, who blocked 362 shots during an all-state high school career, has swatted 10 shots at Virginia. Gillen would love to see him come off the bench and do a little more of that.

"He is big and he can block some shots, maybe even hit a basket or two," Gillen said. "We have some other options, but we would love to see him come in and contribute."

G-JASON DOWLING (6-3, 201 lbs., SR, #5, 0.6 ppg, 0.2 rpg, 2.0 minutes, .400 FG, .250 3PT, .250 FT, Xaverian HS/Brooklyn, N.Y.). Dowling is the last remaining walk-on that Gillen found in a campus-wide tryout in October, 1998. He made his biggest contribution in his freshman season, averaging nearly three minutes a game for a team with a short roster. He won't get much more than some scrap time on the court this year, but that doesn't mean Gillen isn't appreciative of his four-year contribution to the program.

"I am glad to have him back for a fourth year," Gillen said. "He makes a very valuable contribution to our team. He's very quick and pushes our guards in practice."

QUESTIONS

Outside shooting? With the loss of Keith Friel, the Cavaliers have lost their only sure-bet three-point shooter. Developing a replacement for the deadly bomber will be a key goal for Gillen in preseason practice.

Size? The Cavs have only one player on the roster taller than 6-8 and, so far, he hasn't contributed much. They will have to rely on a slew of 6-8 interior players to face off against bigger competition.

Road worriers? The Cavaliers were 6-8 away from University Hall last year (5-6 on the road and 1-2 at neutral sites). In his three years as the Cavs' head coach, Gillen has won a total of six ACC road games. Those numbers will have to improve if Virginia wants to be among the national elite.

ANSWERS

Speed! No team in the ACC, except for maybe Maryland and new-look Wake Forest, plays a more up-tempo game than the Cavaliers. With a handful of more athletic players, the Cavs should be even more fun to watch this year.

Mason, Watson! Maryland changed its fortunes in recent years on the rise to stardom of Juan Dixon, a slashing shooting guard, and Lonny Baxter, an under-sized, but beefy post man. Roger Mason Jr. and Travis Watson are built from the same molds, and they should keep the Cavs near the top of the league for the next two seasons.

Gillen's guidance! The Cavs have improved every year under the frenetic red headed coach. No reason to think he can't squeeze a few more wins out of his charges this year.

VIRGINIA 2000-2001 RESULTS

Long Island	96-50
Coastal Carolina	117-78
@Virginia Tech	64-48
#Purdue	98-79
@Virginia Military	89-70
Ohio University	90-71
##Tennessee	107-89
Maryland-Baltimore Co.	85-69
Bucknell	99-49
@Dartmouth	102-56
@Wake Forest (L)	73-96
NC State	88-81
Georgia Tech (L)	68-73
@Duke (L)	61-103
Florida State	89-71
Missouri	85-72
@North Carolina (L)	81-88

@Clemson	104-76
Maryland	99-78
Wake Forest	82-71
@NC State (L)	80-90
@Georgia Tech (L)	56-62
Duke	91-89
@Florida State	69-66
North Carolina	86-66
Clemson	84-65
@Maryland (L)	67-102
###Georgia Tech (L)	69-74
####Gonzaga (L)	85-86

#ACC/Big Ten Challenge in Charlottesville, VA
##Jimmy V Classic in Syracuse, NY
###ACC Tournament in Atlanta
####NCAA Tournament
@Road Games

BLUE RIBBON ANALYSIS

BACKCOURT	A
BENCH/DEPTH	A-
FRONTCOURT	B+
INTANGIBLES	B+

Gillen has gotten Virginia's program back in the arena. Now he has to get it back in the game.

It's been six years since the Cavaliers have won a game in the postseason, a span of 10 straight losses that includes three ACC tournament games, one NIT game and one NCAA Tournament game under Gillen.

So Cavalier fans don't have to wonder what Gillen is talking about when he says he wants his team to go to the next level. He simply means that his team can't be satisfied just getting into the postseason, as it was the last two seasons. He has now gotten the program back to the level where it should expect to succeed in the post-season by winning games and establishing itself among the national elite.

This year's team is good enough to do that. Perhaps even to get back to the Sweet Sixteen or beyond. One good way to assure that success on the neutral courts of the postseason is to start winning some regular season road games, something the Cavs have not been good at so far under Gillen.

After all, it is called ""The Road to the Final Four."

(T.P.)

 # Iowa 10

LOCATION	Iowa City, IA
CONFERENCE	Big Ten
LAST SEASON	23-12 (.657)
CONFERENCE RECORD	7-9 (t-6th)
STARTERS LOST/RETURNING	1/4
NICKNAME	Hawkeyes
COLORS	Gold & Black
HOMECOURT	Carver-Hawkeye Arena (15,500)
COACH	Steve Alford (Indiana '87)
RECORD AT SCHOOL	37-28 (2 years)
CAREER RECORD	193-105 (10 years)
ASSISTANTS	Rich Walker (Bowling Green '71)
	Greg Lansing (South Dakota '90)
	Brian Jones (Northern Iowa '94)
TEAM WINS (last 5 years)	22-20-20-14-23
RPI (last 5 years)	34-74-13-56-24
2000-01 FINISH	Lost in NCAA second round.

COACH AND PROGRAM

Steve Alford is an avid golfer, so when looking for a metaphor to describe the upcoming season, naturally he turns to the links.

"Saturday is 'moving day' on the PGA Tour," Alford said. "You know, you've made the cut and on Saturday you're either going to move yourself into contention for the championship or you're going to drop out of the running.

"Well this season is our 'moving year.' We've had two years here, we've put the players in place, put the system in place ... we've made the cut, so to speak. We've done everything we can to put ourselves in position to be playing for the Big Ten championship in late February and make a long run in the NCAA tourney in March."

There was a point last season when you might have wondered whether Alford indeed had put Iowa in position

to make the leap to the elite of the Big Ten this year. Despite starting the year 17-4, the Hawkeyes struggled down the stretch after suffering some key injuries, and finished the regular season on a 1-7 run that dropped them to a tie for sixth in the Big Ten.

But with a berth in the NCAA Tournament resting squarely on their performance in the Big Ten Tournament, Alford's Hawkeyes stepped to the tee and played it like like Tiger Woods on the 18th hole of a major:

1. Tee shot knocked stiff down the middle of the fair-way—a 72-55 win over Northwestern in the first round, behind Reggie Evans' 20 points and 14 rebounds.

2. Second shot, a fairway wood to the apron of the green—a 75-66 win over Ohio State in a quarterfinal, behind a season-high 18 points from freshman Glen Worley.

3. Approach, a feathery wedge to within five feet of the cup—a 94-74 blowout of fellow upstart Penn State in a semifinal, behind 30 and 14 from Evans, fast making a name for himself in the conference and the nation.

4. And finally, the knee-knocking five-foot birdie putt with the entire nation looking on—a 63-61 victory over Indiana in the Big Ten championship game with fresh-man guard Brody Boyd (of Dugger, Ind., fittingly) leading the way with 22 points.

You remember Indiana, of course. Alford sure does. The 2000-01 season was the year he finally, definitively severed ties with his alma mater and ended any specu-lation that he would return to Bloomington to prowl the sidelines as the most powerful man in the state—the head basketball coach at IU.

The job surely could have been his when the Indiana administration fired Bob Knight last fall, but Alford was quick and decisive when he renewed his commitment to Iowa after one year on the job. IU hired Mike Davis, and Alford's Hawkeyes ended the Hoosiers' Cinderella run to the Big Ten title with a glass-slipper fitting party of their own.

Alford couldn't have asked for a better situation, actu-ally. As long as Knight was the head coach at Indiana, opposing coaches would batter Iowa recruits with claims that Alford was merely biding his time in Iowa City until the General bequeathed his red sweater to his former point guard. Now Alford has proof to back his claims that he's going nowhere any time soon, and the future has never looked brighter for Iowa basketball.

And the Hawkeye fans have responded in a big way. Alford said that when he travels throughout the state to "I Club" gatherings, he's greeted with nothing but enthusi-asm for the program.

"I've been to just about every corner there is in Iowa, and the reception has been incredible," Alford said. "The fans are excited for a lot of reasons—one, for the suc-cess we've been having, and two, for the success they foresee us having this year. But mostly, it's an apprecia-tion of how we're doing it and the people we're doing it with."

Boosters aren't the only fans to throw their support squarely behind the Hawkeyes. Students are scooping up season tickets at an unprecedented rate. When Alford arrived on campus, there was no official student section at Carver-Hawkeye Arena. But since the creation of the "Hawks Nest," the number of students purchasing sea-son tickets jumped from 300 to 500 last year, and this season at least 2,000 students are expected to fill their special section.

The Hawkeye faithful should have plenty to cheer for this year, as Alford brings an experienced, talented team back to defend their Big Ten postseason title.

"The key is, we're going to be deep," Alford said. "This is the deepest team we've had since I've been here, and trying to find a 9-to-10 man rotation will be dif-ficult because of the talent and depth we have."

Once again the Hawkeyes will be playing one of the toughest schedules in the nation. For the third straight year they'll take on the defending national champs—this time playing Duke at the United Center in the Big Ten-ACC Challenge. They have road games at Iowa State and Missouri, host Kansas State and a tough Louisiana Tech squad, and play in two tournaments—their own Gazette Hawkeye Challenge (vs. SMU, LaSalle and Alabama State) and the Guardians Classic, where they could end up facing the likes of Memphis, Missouri or Alabama.

"Our schedule strength was top 15 last year and top 10 two years ago," Alford said. "This year I think it's back to top 10 with the teams we play and the number of road games we have in the non-conference. Hopefully our seniors have the experience to get us through this. We play a lot of major programs before getting to the Big Ten, with a number of road games."

"We tasted some success last year, but then the injury bug hit us and we had to relearn how to do things. Then we tasted success again at the end of the year, and that got everybody fired up.

"In the off-season, we've worked awfully hard, and the kids have done a good job in individual workouts. They've all been here this summer working on their games. We're looking forward to seeing that improvement, seeing how these young kids develop into the mix," he said.

2001-2002 SCHEDULE

Nov.	13	#Maryland-Eastern Shore
	17	Louisiana Tech
	27	*Duke
	30	##Hawkeye Challenge
Dec.	1	##Hawkeye Challenge
	4	@Northern Iowa
	8	@Iowa State
	12	Drake
	15	@Missouri
	22	Kansas State
	28	Mercer
Jan.	2	Wisconsin
	5	@Ohio State
	9	Northwestern
	13	Indiana
	15	@Illinois
	19	@Northwestern
	22	Michigan State
	26	@Purdue
Feb.	2	Penn State
	5	@Indiana
	9	Minnesota
	13	@Penn State
	16	Ohio State
	19	@Wisconsin
	23	Michigan
March	2	@Michigan State
	7-10	###Big Ten Tournament

@Road Games
*ACC-Big Ten Challenge, United Center, Chicago
#Guardian Classic (If the Hawkeyes win, they will play either Boston University or New Orleans on Nov. 14; semifinals and final are Nov. 20-21 at Kemper Arena, Kansas City, MO)
##Iowa City, IA (vs. Alabama State, first round; also LaSalle, Southern Miethodist)
###Conseco Fieldhouse, Indianapolis, IN

STARTERS NOT RETURNING

PG-DEAN OLIVER (5-11, 14.9 ppg, 4.8 apg, 2.8 rpg, 1.4 spg, 1.7 tpg). Oliver was the main man at point guard for the last four years at Iowa. He started all but two games in his career and piled up some eye-popping career numbers.

He was one of just three players in Big Ten history to pile up 1,500 points, 500 assists and 200 steals in his career. He also led the Hawkeyes in scoring in 1999 and 2000, and he finished in the top ten in school history in three categories—scoring (seventh), assists (second) and steals (second).

Last year Oliver earned third-team All-Big Ten honors as the team's third-leading scorer (14.9) and top assist man (4.8). In Big Ten games he averaged 5.2 assists, becoming the fourth Hawkeye to lead the league in assists, joining Andre Woolridge (1996-97), B.J. Armstrong ('89) and Cal Wulfsberg ('76).

Oliver was the team's leading scorer in 11 games last season, scoring a season-high 27 points in a home loss to Ohio State. That started a streak of four straight games in which he led the Hawkeyes in scoring. But he saved his best for last, dropping 26 on Kentucky in Iowa's second-round loss in the NCAA Tournament.

OTHERS NOT RETURNING

G-KYLE GALLOWAY (6-6, 1.3 ppg, 0.7 rpg). Galloway played just 13 games last season before calling it a career due to a back injury.

As a junior, he started 18 games and averaged 8.5 points a game, scoring a career-high 30 at Minnesota. His outside shooting ability and experience were missed down the stretch.

G-JASON SMITH (6-3, 1.5 ppg, 0.8 rpg). Smith was

another senior guard who provided depth and leadership in the backcourt. He played in 19 games last year, scoring a season-high six points in the victory over Penn State in the Big Ten semifinals.

PROJECTED STARTERS

PG-BRODY BOYD (5-11, 155 lbs., SO, #11, 5.8 ppg, 1.3 rpg, 1.5 apg, 16.7 minutes, .392 FG, .373 3PT, .675 FT, Union HS/Dugger, Ind.). There should be a three-man battle to replace Oliver in the starting lineup. The leading candidate will be Boyd, who gained valuable experience in starting the final 12 games at off-guard last year.

He averaged 9.3 points in the six postseason games last year and was the star of the Big Ten championship game with 22 points on 8-of-12 shooting (4-for-8 beyond the arc). His two free throws with 22 seconds left were the final margin of the 63-61 victory over his homestate Hoosiers.

Boyd's three-point percentage last year (.373) was the third best all-time for an Iowa freshman. He scored in double-figures eight times in his rookie season, including a streak of five straight games after Recker went down.

Boyd was a big help to the Hawkeyes, replacing first Recker and then Ryan Hogan when the two shooting guards were lost to injuries. With both of them back and Oliver departed, Boyd will get a chance to move back to his natural position of point guard, but don't expect him to be shy about taking his shot if it's open.

SG-LUKE RECKER (6-6, 210 lbs., SR, #24, 18.1 ppg, 3.9 rpg, 2.6 apg, 33.6 minutes, .439 FG, .431 3PT, .856 FT, DeKalb HS/Auburn, Ind. and University of Arizona and Indiana University). The other Hawkeye player who could have drawn interest from the pros if not for a series of injuries is Recker.

"When you look at all the power forwards and shooting guards in the country, it's hard to find anybody better than those two," Alford said of his dynamic senior duo.

The Indiana transfer (by way of Arizona, where he never played a game) was midway through a strong junior season when a cracked kneecap sidelined him for the remainder of the year. But now the 6-6 senior is back to finish what he started last year.

"Luke is healing well," Alford said late in the summer. "He's been released to do individual workouts, and I think he's going to have a huge year. He saw what he could do last season on one leg. He was starting to get the national attention when he was injured. He's motivated to do well for the Iowa program and to do well for his professional future. He's a special shooting guard who has great leadership potential."

Recker had a solid half season. He twice earned Big Ten Player of the Week Honors, the second time after he dumped 27 points and eight rebounds on his old school (Indiana) and 17 points, three rebounds and three assists on Minnesota. Recker also scored 27 points against Illinois (on 10-for-10 free-throw shooting), notched his season high of 28 against cross-state rival Iowa State, scored 26 against Drake, 25 against Kansas State and 23 against Missouri.

A healthy Recker can do even more damage this season, given Iowa's depth and array of offensive weapons. Teams will try to key on Recker, but if they do, one of his teammates will step up.

SF-DUEZ HENDERSON (6-7, 200 lbs., SR, #23, 6.3 ppg, 3.4 rpg, 21.0 minutes, .514 FG, .345 3PT, .761 FT, River Rouge HS/Detroit, Mich.). The Hawkeye offense should get a boost from the continued development of Henderson, who started 29 games last season. Alford lauded Henderson for doing many of the little things that made the Hawkeyes successful.

"Duez was probably our most improved player last year, improving in leadership and the role he was settling in to," Alford said. "He was probably the biggest key in our run through the Big Ten tourney, making big shots and big defensive plays in every game."

In the Big Ten championship game, Henderson scored with 1:42 remaining to put the Hawkeyes on top, then grabbed the rebounds on each of Indiana's final two missed field goals, securing the victory. He also scored in double figures in each of the first three games of the tournament, including a five-for-five performance from the field against Penn State.

Then in the NCAA Tournament, he played a career-high 36 minutes and scored a season-high 16 points in Iowa's opening-round victory over Creighton. Clearly as the season evolved, so did Henderson's confidence and his role in the offense. As a senior, he'll be a legitimate third option, taking pressure off Recker and Evans.

PF-REGGIE EVANS (6-8, 245 lbs., SR, #32, 15.1 ppg, 11.9 rpg, 34.9 minutes, .475 FG, 1.000 3PT, .630 FT, Woodham HS/Pensacola, Fla. and Coffeyville JC/Coffeyville, Kansas). Evans had as much or more impact than any newcomer in the country last season, leading the nation in four major categories—rebounding, free throws (218), free throw attempts (346), and double-doubles (22). He was voted national Newcomer of the Year by ESPN.com, made the national All-JUCO transfer team selected by collegeinsider.com, and earned honorable mention All-America honors from the Associated Press.

"I've been in college basketball for a long time and followed it as a fan before that, and I don't know if there's ever been a player in his first year of Division I play to lead the country in four statistical categories," Alford said.

Evans was one of 12 players selected to play for Team USA in the FIBA junior world championships in Saitama, Japan, this August, where he helped lead the U.S. to the title with an all-star roster of teammates that included Troy Bell, Carlos Boozer, Chris Duhon and Nick Collison. Evans was fifth on the team in scoring and third in boards in the eight-game tournament, and—predictably—he led the team in free throws attempted and made.

"I see Reggie being a real leader," Alford said. "Everyone respects him for the year he had last season and I think he will step up his leadership. He has to continue to progress—he will be the focus of our opponents this year. But he's a warrior, and when he gets on a mission, he gets it done."

That Evans is back for his senior season is no small feat in itself. After his breakout junior year, he caught the attention of NBA scouts and drew the interest of more than a few agents who tried to persuade Evans to turn pro. Even though Evans eventually decided to return to campus, the process left a bad taste in Alford's mouth.

"I've never had to deal with what I dealt with when the season was over from the standpoint of agents," Alford said. "It opened my eyes as to what is going on out there with our game, and it's the part I disliked the most—I wish there's something that could be done.

"Talking to a kid who has completed his eligibility or has declared that he's leaving early is one thing. But [agents] calling kids in their dorm rooms when they have not declared? It's unethical.

"The good thing about it is when I talked to Reggie about it, I was able to tell him, 'You've made the decision to stay in school and now you know who not to talk to next year.' Because if they're going to be unethical now, that's obviously how they conduct their business."

Evans, whose game is aggressive and physical, had some monster games last season. His season high of 30 points came against Penn State. He also had a season-high tying 18 boards in that game. Evans grabbed 18 rebounds in three other games.

C-JARED REINER (6-11, 255 lbs., SO, #5, 3.1 ppg, 2.9 rpg, 12.7 minutes, .411 FG, .673 FT, Tripp-Delmont HS/Tripp, S.D.). In the middle, Alford brings back two 6-11 sophomores who earned invaluable playing experience last season. The leading candidate to start is Reiner, who also started 23 games last year and led the team with 20 blocked shots.

Reiner is an honor roll student, so he should be smart enough to know that he won't be the focus of the offense this season. However, he should be able to gobble up any rebounds that manage to slip past Evans, and his presence down low will take some pressure off the all-everything power forward.

Reiner had some moments last season. He scored a season-high nine points (with four rebounds and three blocks) against Wisconsin-Milwaukee, and grabbed seven boards against Illinois.

KEY RESERVES

F-GLEN WORLEY (6-7, 220 lbs., SO, #4, 7.5 ppg, 3.8 rpg, 22.9 minutes, .449 FG, .250 3PT, .722 FT, West HS/Iowa City, Iowa). Another freshman who played some key minutes last year was Worley. He had the big game against Ohio State (18 points) in the Big Ten tournament and should be counted on to back up both forward positions this year.

"Glen could really explode this year," Alford said. "He has worked hard since the end of last season and can play both inside and on the perimeter."

Worley shot 45 percent (89-for-198) from the field, and his 72.2 percent mark from the free-throw line was the fourth-best ever for a Hawkeye freshman.

Worley started 15 games last year and was the

team's second-leading rebounder and shot blocker. He was also invited to the USA Basketball national team trials in the off-season, one of only 10 freshman to earn an invitation.

C-SEAN SONDERLEITER (6-9, 225 lbs., SO, #53, 2.0 ppg, 1.9 rpg, 7.7 minutes, .548 FG, .650 FT, Christian Academy/Des Moines, Iowa). The other freshman to see duty in the middle last year was Sonderleiter. He comes back after a season that was hampered by nagging ankle injuries.

Sonderleiter earned his first career start at Michigan State, where he scored four points and grabbed five boards, and he dropped in a season-high nine points at Michigan.

G-RYAN HOGAN (6-4, 185 lbs., SR, #2, 7.2 ppg, 2.6 rpg, 21.0 minutes, .348 FG, .362 3PT, .742 FT, Deerfield HS/Deerfield, Ill. and the University of Kentucky). Recker should get excellent support from Hogan, who filled in when Recker went down last year until he, too, suffered a season-ending knee injury that knocked him out of the Hawkeyes' final 10 games.

Hogan sat out 1999-2000 after transferring from Kentucky. He was a member of the Wildcat team that won the 1998 NCAA championship. Last year his best game came at home against Minnesota, when he totaled 12 points, four boards, three assists and four steals. He also had 13 points, six rebounds and four assists in a win over eventual NIT champion Tulsa.

OTHER RETURNEES

F-ROD THOMPSON (6-6, 230 lbs., SR, #25, 1.8 ppg, 1.2 rpg, 5.0 minutes, .395 FG, .278 3PT, .615 FT, Galesburg HS/Galesburg, Ill.). Another reserve who can play both forward positions is 6-6 senior Thompson. He scored a season-high 11 points, including 4-of-5 field goals and two three-pointers, in Iowa's NCAA Tournament loss to Kentucky.

F-CORTNEY SCOTT (6-6, 245 lbs., SO, #52, 2.5 ppg, 2.1 rpg, 8.9 minutes, .485 FG, 1.000 3PT, .636 FT, Lansing Waverly HS/Jackson, Mich.). Adding some muscle down low is Scott, who'll back up Evans at the power-forward spot. He started two games as a freshman, scoring four points and grabbing five boards in his first career start against Northwestern. He had a season-high nine points in Iowa's double-overtime victory over Missouri.

NEWCOMERS

G-PIERRE PIERCE (6-4, 180 lbs., FR, #3, 36.4 ppg, 9.1 rpg, 5.2 apg, Westmont HS/Westmont, Ill.). The battle to replace Oliver in the starting lineup could boil down to Body and Pierce, who brings great size and a scoring mentality to the position. Pierce was the runner-up to NBA top-five pick Eddie Curry in the Illinois Mr. Basketball voting, and was a two-time all-state selection in Illinois.

Alford calls him "a true point guard who can push the ball. Brody and Pierce give us a different dimension in that they are guys who can score from the point guard position."

Pierce can really score. His career scoring total of 2,931 points ranks seventh best in state history. He set Westmont records for points in a career and one game (52). He also holds school records for career rebounds, assists and steals.

Pierce made a clean sweep of the major all-state honors in Illinois, being chosen first team by the Champaign News Gazette, Chicago Tribune, Illinois Basketball Coaches Association and Associated Press.

G-CHAUNCEY LESLIE (6-2, 165 lbs., JR, #1, 10.1 ppg, 3.1 rpg, 2.6 apg, 1.5 spg Marshall HS/Rochester, N.Y. and Indian Hills CC/Ottumwa, Iowa). Leslie could also find himself in the point guard mix. The Rochester, N.Y. native is a winner, having helped lead Indian Hills to a fourth-place finish at the Junior College National Tournament.

"Chauncey gives us a veteran player in the backcourt with his two seasons at the junior-college level," Alford said. "He adds athleticism to both ends of the floor. With his quickness, he can break down defenses off the dribble and get our offense started by getting past people. Defensively, he can stop the ball and get the other team under control."

Leslie was a big-time athlete in high school, starring for Marshall's football, basketball and track teams. He was an all-state pick in football, but decided to concentrate on basketball and picked one of the most successful junior college programs in the country.

"Chauncey comes from a great program, a tradition-rich school in Indian Hills," Alford said. "We always like to add student-athletes to our program who have already been involved in successful, winning programs."

Leslie was a big reason Indian Hills was 32-5 a year ago. He shot 44 percent from three-point range, and if he could come anywhere close to that figure in the Big Ten, he'd be a valuable addition.

F- MARCELLUS SOMMERVILLE (6-6, 210 lbs., FR, #15, 20.0 ppg, 9.3 rpg, Central HS, Peoria, Ill.). Another small forward who could get some minutes this year is Sommerville, an all-state player in Illinois.

Sommerville played with his back to the basket his first three years at Central, but in his senior season he worked on his perimeter game and stepped outside to do some damage.

"I've been working on my outside shot since before my senior season," Sommerville told the Iowa City Press-Citizen. "I did workouts with our shooting coach [at Central]. It's worked, and I'm starting to hit it."

Sommerville, a consensus Top 80 player, was ranked No. 22 in the country by recruiting analyst Bob Gibbons. Sommerville should justify that lofty status, especially if he can continue to improve his perimeter game.

"I'm kind of a tweener right now," Sommerville told the Press-Citizen. "I need to work on my ball handling a little more. Once I can handle the ball, I'll be more of a perimeter player. But if I could get a smaller guard on me, I have the ability to take him down low and post him."

Sommerville was selected to the Illinois Basketball Coaches Association top five all-state team and was voted to the AP Class AA all-state first team as a senior. He was also chosen the Mid-State Six Conference Player of the Year.

C-EREK HANSEN (6-11, 205 lbs., FR, #34, 15.0 ppg, 9.9 rpg, Trinity HS/Bedford, Texas). Hansen desperately needs to gain size and strength, but he comes to Iowa with some defensive ability. He was selected his high school district's defensive player of the year the last two years, averaging five block shots a game as a junior and 5.8 blocks last year. True, he was probably stuffing a lot of 6-1 centers, but he has the frame to alter shots in college.

Hansen was a first-team all state pick and was ranked the ninth-best player in Texas last season. He's a good athlete, having competed in the sprints, hurdles and high jump. He brings more than enough tools for Alford and his staff to work with.

The possibility exists that Hansen could red-shirt this season, though that wouldn't be his first choice.

"I want to play," Hansen told the Iowa City Press-Citizen. "But if I'm going to red-shirt this year, I'm going to make sure that they know I red-shirted and worked hard, so I can get a lot of playing time that next season."

QUESTIONS

Point Guard? Oliver was a four-year starter, meaning nobody on the roster has experience running the show at the Division I level. That's a tough hurdle for a team that hopes to contend for a Big Ten championship.

Defense? Opponents topped 80 points on the Hawkeyes eight times last season, and Iowa was 2-6 in those games. Without Oliver setting the pace, look for opponents to try to push the ball even more against the slower Hawks this season.

ANSWERS

Stars! Nobody in the Big Ten can match the 1-2 punch of Recker and Evans. Both players are legitimate NBA prospects, and they're both seniors, which goes a long way in today's underclassmen-dominated college game.

Balance! Shut down the outside game, and Evans will blow up down low. Plug up the middle, and Recker will kill you from the perimeter. Find a way to take them both out of the flow, and Henderson and Boyd will find plenty of openings. It will be tough to guard the Hawkeyes this year.

Coaching! If you were starting a program from scratch, your choice for coach would be Alford, a former Big Ten star and all-around student of the game, a coach who's young enough to relate to his players but forceful enough to command their respect.

IOWA 2000-2001 RESULTS

Wisconsin-Milwaukee	83-79
@Drake	73-71
Georgia Tech	85-67
#Tennessee-Chattanooga	66-65
#Tulsa	79-60
Northern Iowa	74-42
Iowa State	80-68
Missouri	99-94
Centenary	72-52
@Kansas State (L)	78-86
##Detroit	69-68
##Tennessee (L)	68-80
St. Louis	68-56
@Penn State	86-85
Illinois	78-62
@Purdue	83-73
@Wisconsin (L)	54-67
Michigan (L)	69-70
@Minnesota	87-74
Indiana	71-66
Minnesota	64-55
Ohio State (L)	68-69
@Northwestern (L)	61-69
@Michigan (L)	85-95
@Michigan State (L)	70-94
Purdue	78-72
@Illinois (L)	63-89
Penn State (L)	73-78
Wisconsin (L)	57-59
###Northwestern	72-55
###Ohio State	75-66
###Penn State	94-74
###Indiana	63-61
####Creighton	69-56
####Kentucky	79-92

#Gazette Hawkeye Challenge in Iowa City
##Rainbow Classic in Honolulu, HI
###Big Ten Tournament in Chicago
####NCAA Tournament
@Road Games

BLUE RIBBON ANALYSIS

BACKCOURT	B+
BENCH/DEPTH	B+
FRONTCOURT	A-
INTANGIBLES	A

Alford has been a huge shot in the arm to this program, and his presence on campus vaults Iowa into the top 10 of programs to watch for in the next decade. He's a dynamite recruiter and a dynamic presence on the sideline. He is the face of Iowa basketball, plain and simple.

This year he's got two All-America candidates in Evans and Recker, and that can go a long way toward winning the Big Ten. It's a rough-and-tumble conference, and Evans is the premier banger in the league, so if he gets any help from the young centers, he could actually improve on last year's performance.

Henderson could be a sneaky scorer who ought to draw enough attention to allow Recker to get his points. And the young point guards won't be asked to do too much but get the ball to the scorers and pop the occasional three.

No doubt about it, the Hawkeyes are a legitimate favorite to win the Big Ten and advance to at least the Sweet 16 this season.

(P.D.)

St. Joseph's 11

LOCATION	Philadelphia, PA
CONFERENCE	Atlantic 10
LAST SEASON	26-7 (.788)
CONFERENCE RECORD	14-2 (1st)
STARTERS LOST/RETURNING	4/1
NICKNAME	Hawks
COLORS	Crimson & Gray
HOMECOURT	Alumni Memorial Fieldhouse (3,200) and Palestra (8,722)
COACH	Phil Martelli (Widener '76)
RECORD AT SCHOOL	107-78 (6 years)
CAREER RECORD	107-78 (6 years)
ASSISTANTS	Matt Brady (Siena '87)
	Monte Ross (Winston-Salem '92)
	Mark Bass (Saint Joseph's '96)
TEAM WINS (last 5 years)	26-11-12-13-26

RPI (last 5 years)   12-138-140-120-32
2000-01 FINISH   Lost in NCAA second round.

COACH AND PROGRAM

It was one of the greatest seasons in Phil Martelli's long career at St. Joseph's: a school-record 26 victories, an Atlantic 10 Conference title and a berth in the NCAA Tournament. The Hawks' season ended with a 90-83 loss to powerful Stanford in the second round, but even that had positive vibes as Martelli's resilient team wiped out a 14-point deficit and took the lead in the second half.

Four starters return for St. Joe's, but Martelli is taking a what-have-you-done-for-me-lately approach heading into the season.

"It's exciting for the players and the fans," he said of the great expectations facing the Hawks this year. "But to me, it doesn't really impact what we have to do. Six games last year were won on the final possession. It's not like we were clearly dominant other than in the win-loss category."

Of course, that's the only category that really counts, and Martelli's team will put up far more Ws than Ls this year. The main reasons are senior Marvin O'Connor and sophomore Jameer Nelson, who just might be the top backcourt in the nation.

"It's a tremendous backcourt," Dayton coach Oliver Purnell said. "Nelson is one of the top three or four point guards in the country. And O'Connor can score points in bunches as well as anybody. He proved that in the NCAAs last year."

Martelli says O'Connor and Nelson "go together like peanut butter and jelly. When you think of Marvin, you think of Jameer. They deserve the mantle of being one of the best backcourts in America."

Martelli, one of the most affable coaches in Division I, was wooed by Rutgers after last season but eventually signed a four-year extension with St. Joe's, with a two-year option following that.

"I see it as a six-year deal unless [the administration] decides they don't want me anymore," he says. "There's no place else my family or me want to be."

Martelli has become synonymous with St. Joe's, having spent 10 seasons as an assistant there before succeeding John Griffin in 1995. He is the fifth-winningest coach in school history, and his teams have made two trips to the NCAAs, including a Sweet 16 appearance and a No. 12 final ranking in 1997.

"People need to remember that we're not too far removed from three consecutive losing seasons," he said, referring to the three years preceding last year.

That's typical cautious coach-speak, of course, but Martelli is no fool. He knows the talent is there, and it extends beyond his terrific backcourt.

"We have the potential to be very good," he said. "The talent is there, no doubt."

In addition to O'Connor and Nelson, the Hawks return senior guard Na'im Crenshaw, 6-10 senior forward Bill Phillips and 6-9 senior center Damian Reed, a fourth-year starter. Crenshaw was voted Atlantic 10 Sixth Man of the Year.

"I'm going to start four 23-year-old guys," said Martelli, the 2001 Eastern College Coach of the Year. "And they're all fifth-year players. That's going to be very important for us this year, all that experience and maturity."

Not since the All-America tandem of Cliff Anderson and Matt Guokas, Jr., led the Hawks to a No. 1 preseason ranking by Sports Illustrated in 1965-66 has there been as much national attention surrounding St. Joe's basketball team heading into a season.

The Hawks have been ranked as high as ninth by ESPN.com, are 10th in the foxsportsnet.com preseason poll, 11th by Blue Ribbon and 15th by college basketball analyst Dick Vitale.

2001-2002 SCHEDULE

Nov.	15-16	#BCA Classic
	25	Colorado
	28	@Delaware
Dec.	1	Canisius
	8	@Pennsylvania
	10	Drexel
	21-22	##Tournament of Champions
	31	Gonzaga
Jan.	5	@Massachusetts
	9	@Rhode Island
	13	St. Bonaventure
	16	Fordham
	19	George Washington
	23	@Duquesne
	26	@Pennsylvania
	28	@Villanova
	31	Rhode Island
Feb.	2	@Temple
	6	*LaSalle
	9	@Fordham
	13	@Richmond
	16	@Xavier
	19	Massachusetts
	23	Dayton
	28	@St. Bonaventure
March	3	*Temple
	6-9	###A-10 Championship

@Away Games
*The Palestra, Philadelphia, PA
#Berkeley, CA (vs. Eastern Michigan; also California, Princeton)
##Charlotte, NC (Georgia State; also College of Charleston, North Carolina)
###First Union Spectrum, Philadelphia, PA

STARTERS NOT RETURNING

F-FRANK WILKINS (6-9, 5.8 ppg, .417 FG, .683 FT, 20.2 minutes). Wilkins was a two-year starter whose career spanned the great 1997 St. Joe's team and last year's NCAA participant. The former all-Massachusetts high school star was a swingman who gave Martelli depth last year. He played in 115 games in his career with St. Joseph's but started only 39, finishing with a 6.4 scoring average.

OTHERS NOT RETURNING

G-ERICK WOODS (6-5, 3.9 ppg, .417 FG, .765 FT, 11.1 minutes). Woods started at two guard his freshman but relinquished the job with seven games left in the season. He would play in 80 more games over his final season but start just three of them. A versatile athlete—he also played for the St. Joseph's baseball team—Woods was an aggressive perimeter defender and a team captain last year. He ranked fifth on the team in three-point shooting (.333) and scored 11 points in his lone start against Western Kentucky.

F-LIONEL NGOUNOU (6-8, 1.8 ppg, .556 FG, .857 FT, 3.9 minutes). A team captain who played sparingly throughout his career. Ngounou missed 14 games at mid-season last year because of a slight tear of the meniscus. He scored a career-high four points against West Carolina, Colorado and Duquesne but played in only eight games. Chosen the team's Most Improved Player after his junior year, this native of Cameroon arrived in the United States in August 1996.

PROJECTED STARTERS

PG-JAMEER NELSON (6-0, 190 lbs., SO, #2, 12.5 ppg, 4.0 rpg, 6.5 apg, 1.67 spg, 33.8 minutes, .461 FG, .373 3PT, .820 FT, Chester HS/Chester, Pa.). He turned in the best freshman season in the history of St. Joseph's basketball, earning National Freshman of the Year honors by Sports Illustrated, ESPN.com's Dick Vitale, CBSsportsline.com and collegeinsider.com.

Nelson also was a second-team all-district pick by the NABC and second-team All-Atlantic 10 and became just the third St. Joseph's player to lead the A-10 in assists while setting a school record with 213 (the previous record was Matt Guokas Jr.'s 176).

"He is a true point guard and there aren't enough of them in college basketball," Martelli said. "He's beyond his years in terms of understanding. It's repetitious to say, but he's a better kid than he is a basketball player. He's someone you want on your team at all times."

Nelson experienced more success this year at the USA Basketball World Championships for Young Men, where he helped his team earn a gold medal.

Nelson earned first team all-state accolades in high school after averaging 21 points, seven assists and six rebounds and leading Chester to the state championship his senior season. He was chosen Delaware County Daily Times Player of the Year and schoolsports.com State Player of the Year and chose St. Joseph's over A-10 rival Temple.

Nelson started all 33 games last year, leading the team with 55 steals and finishing second in scoring and three-pointers. He showed a flair for the dramatic, too, nailing a pair of free throws with 5.4 seconds left to beat

St. Bonaventure and then hitting a 35-footer at the buzzer to send the second game with the Bonnies into overtime.

"Jameer plays a huge role in what we do," O'Connor told CBSsportsline.com. "He takes a lot of pressure off me and (Na'im) Crenshaw. He's important to the team.

Nelson, who turns 20 on Feb. 9, nearly pulled off a triple-double in the loss to Stanford during last year's NCAA Tournament. He finished that game with 14 points, nine assists and nine rebounds, giving opponents a strong signal that the best is yet to come.

SG-MARVIN O'CONNOR (6-4, 190 lbs., SR, #11, 22.1 ppg, 3.7 rpg, 2.6 apg, 1.1 spg, 33.5 minutes, .465 FG, .374 3PT, .676 FT, Simon Gratz HS/Philadelphia, Pa. and Villanova). A 2002 Blue Ribbon and Playboy All-American, O'Connor became one of the East's most explosive scorers last year. Fans and sportswriters are still talking about his incredible performance against LaSalle, when he scored 18 points in the final 57.5 seconds and finished with a career-high 37.

"The first thing that stands out about Marvin is his fierce desire to win," Martelli said. "A lot of guys in Division I want to win. With Marvin, his desire is off the charts."

O'Connor is wise beyond his years, too, Martelli said. "He recognized that when he had over 30 points six times last year, we lost five of those games," he said. "He understands that we have to have some balance."

O'Connor was voted the Atlantic 10 Conference Player of the Year by the media, and was chosen both the A-10 and Philadelphia Big 5 Player of the Week three times.

He set single-season St. Joseph's records for points (706) and three-pointers (99) and became the first Hawk to average more than 20 points per game since 1973.

That scoring continued in the postseason, where O'Connor was the leading scorer in the NCAA Tournament with 29 points per game over two games. His 37 points in a second-round loss to Stanford were the most in the tournament.

"I'd never heard of him before we drew St. Joseph's," Stanford All-America swingman Casey Jacobsen told reporters afterward. "That was the most amazing performance of anyone I've guarded. I worked my butt off out there to try to be where he was."

O'Connor is dangerous from anywhere, including three-point range. He is seventh on St. Joseph's all-time list with 164 in just 58 games.

The Philadelphia native set a school scoring record by tallying 706 points over 32 games, breaking the 34-year mark held by Cliff Anderson (690, 1966-67). The Philadelphia Big Five Co-MVP also became the first St. Joseph's player to average over 20 points for a season (22.1 ppg) since Mike Bantom and Pat McFarland did it identical 20.3 averages in 1972-73.

Selected the 1997 High School Player of the Year by the Philadelphia Inquirer after averaging 20.9 points and 9.4 rebounds), O'Connor originally played at Villanova and averaged 4.7 points in 21 games (five starts) during his 1997-98 freshman season. He had to sit out the following year after transferring to rival St. Joseph's but was chosen team MVP in 1999-2000 after leading the Hawks in scoring with 16.6 per game.

"He's gone beyond my expectations of him," Martelli said. "I always thought he would be a guy who would fight hard, but I never would have said to you that he can get 30 points in an NCAA game, or 37, or all the things he's done.

"He's the right player for our style of play, that's for sure."

SF-NA'IM CRENSHAW (6-5, 190 lbs., SR, #20, 11.4 ppg, 3.3 rpg, 2 apg, 0.3 spg, 27.2 minutes, .418 FG, .398 3PT, .759 FT, Overbrook HS/Philadelphia, Pa.). Crenshaw was voted the Atlantic 10's top sixth man last year but should move back into the starting lineup. He started his first two seasons but sat out the first 10 games last year because of a team-imposed academic suspension.

Crenshaw has been a reliable scorer throughout his career, averaging 10.7, 11.7 and 11.4 in his first three seasons.

"He's also arguably the best defender in the Atlantic 10," Martelli says. "He's our best three-point shooter, and he had a lot to do with us winning last year."

The versatile Crenshaw, who can play either guard or small forward, hit a team-high 39.8 percent from three-point range (39-for-98) last season. For his career, the southpaw has made 123 three-pointers, ranking No. 10 on the school's all-time list.

PF-BILL PHILLIPS (6-10, 240 lbs., SR, #24, 11.6

ppg, 8.9 rpg, 3.4 apg, 1.3 spg, 0.45 bpg, 34.7 minutes, .548 FG, .323 3PT, .660 FT, Archbishop Carroll HS/Collegeville, Pa.).

One of the top power forwards in the Atlantic 10 returns. Phillips moved into the starting lineup last year but played the second half of the season with a stress fracture in his foot. He still was good enough to earn third team all-Atlantic 10 honors.

"He was arguably our most valuable player," Martelli said. "First in rebounding, second in assists ... people talk about our backcourt first, and then they talk about Phillips."

Phillips is an intelligent player—he's the first St. Joseph's basketball player ever selected Academic All-American—with a shooter's touch. He connected on 32-of-99 three-point shots last year.

C-DAMIAN REID (6-9, 225 lbs., SR, #25, 9 ppg, 6.5 rpg, 0.9 apg, 0.45 spg, 0.51 bpg, 23.2 minutes, .615 FG, .250 3PT, .625 FT, Bethune Collegiate HS/Scarborough, Ontario). Reid returns for his fourth year as a starter and joins the 6-10 Phillips to form the tallest front line in St. Joseph's history. Reed split time last year with 7-1 Alexandre Sazonov, but when his numbers are extrapolated over 40 minutes, he averaged 15.5 points and 11.3 rebounds per game.

"He continues to do the smaller things for us," Martelli said. "On a team with a lot of scoring, he's invaluable because he just fits. He doesn't have a lot of demands."

Reed has led the Hawks in field-goal percentage for three consecutive seasons and is third all-time in that department (.536). He set a single-season Hawks record last season, hitting 110-of-179 for .615.

Nicknamed "Little Admiral" because of his resemblance to NBA star David Robinson, Reed was one of Canada's top-scoring players in high school, averaging 26 points in 1996-97. He originally enrolled at Dawson College in Lennoxville, Quebec, before signing a letter-of-intent with St. Joseph's in spring 1998. He was a member of the Atlantic 10 all-rookie team the following season.

KEY RESERVES

C-ALEXANDRE SAZONOV (7-1, 235 lbs., JR, #51, 4.9 ppg, 3.5 rpg, 0.30 apg, 0.06 spg, 1.9 bpg, 15.2 minutes, .560 FG, .630 FT, Cardinal O'Hara HS/Springfield, Pa.). The Russia native played in all 33 games but made zero starts. His role was filling in for Reed, yet his 65 blocks last season rank sixth all-time at St. Joseph's.

"Each year he has made a monumental jump in his game," Martelli said. "He really gives us a presence in the lane."

Sazonov, who worked out with the Russian National Team this summer, needs to work on committing less fouls. He was called for a team-high 113, resulting in five disqualifications.

Sazonov underwent surgery on both legs in August to correct exertional compartment syndrome (ECS), an exercise-induced pain and swelling. Unfortunately, the only remedy is rest.

Sazonov made the most of his time on the floor a year ago. He blocked those 65 shots despite averaging just 15.2 minutes.

Sazonov averaged 13 points, 13 rebounds and a phenomenal nine blocks as a senior for Cardinal O'Hara High, earning second-team all-Philadelphia Catholic League honors as a senior (third team as a junior).

He played in 30 games for St. Joseph's as a freshman in 1998-99 and was second on the team in field-goal percentage (.480). He red-shirted the following year but became one of the East's most improved players last year.

He will be a key player for the Hawks this season, especially if Reed gets into foul trouble.

PG-TYRONE BARLEY (6-1, 185 lbs., SO., #12, 1.4 ppg, 0.5 rpg, 1.2 apg, 0.4 spg, 9 minutes, .406 FG, .333 3PT, .556 FT, Seton Hall Prep/Newark, N.J.). Barley is an excellent defensive player who spelled Nelson at the point last year and will be called upon for the same role this season.

"I say this in an affectionate way: He's a very mean-spirited player," Martelli said. "He's the toughest guy on our team and he's totally willing to accept his role."

Barley averaged 10 points, six rebounds and six assists as a high school senior at nationally-ranked Seton Hall Prep and became the fourth player from his team to earn a Division I scholarship.

Last year, he played a season-high 26 minutes against George Washington and recorded five points and four assists. He led the team with a 1.94-1 assist-to-

turnover ratio.

SG-DELONTE WEST (6-3, 180 lbs., FR, #15, 20.3 ppg, 6.5 rpg, 5 apg, 4 spg, Eleanor Roosevelt HS/Greenbelt, Md.). West was chosen the 2001 Metro Player of the Year by the Washington Post. The left-hander is a slasher-type guard who scores most of his points driving to the basket.

"He's a fierce competitor and a very explosive player," Martelli said. "We're going to improve his perimeter shot, but he makes everyone around him a better player."

Martelli says West's time will come.

"He's a backup now and a star in the future," the coach said.

SG-JEFF MILLER (6-6, 215 lbs., SO, #2, 1.5 ppg, 1.2 rpg, 0.4 apg, 0.1 spg, 4.7 minutes, .333 FG, Interboro HS/Prospect Park, Pa.). A perimeter shooter with excellent range, he worked hard in the off-season in an effort to improve his playing time. Miller averaged 19 points and nine rebounds during his senior year of high school. Last year, he scored 15 points in 53 minutes of action.

"He's a deep shooter and probably our best post passer," Martelli said. "He'll be in that mix for backup minutes."

SG-MIKE FARRELLY (6-1, 175 lbs., JR., #3, walk-on who scored four points and recorded five assists during season, Clarkstown North HS/New City, N.Y.). This walk-on earned a spot on the team during the 2000-01 workouts, becoming just the fourth St. Joseph's player to move from junior varsity to varsity since the junior varsity program was reinstated in 1992-93. He played in 10 games last year (14 total minutes).

SG-PHIL MARTELLI, JR. (5-10, 155 lbs., JR, #10, walk-on who played in eight games , St. Joseph's Prep/Drexel Hill, Pa.). He's part of the first father-son combination in St. Joseph's basketball history. He scored his first collegiate points by hitting his only field-goal attempt at Rhode Island. Finished the season 2-for-3 from the floor. He averaged two points and one rebound as a high school senior.

OTHER NEWCOMERS

C-DWAYNE JONES (6-11, 225 lbs., #21, 25.8 ppg, 17.8 rpg, 6.4 bpg, American Christian Academy/Chester, Pa.). Jones was a three-time first team All-Tri-State Christian Athletic Conference selection in high school and the 2001 TSCAC Player of the Year. He scored more than 1,700 points and grabbed more than 1,200 rebounds in his career but will have to bide his time behind an extraordinary group of big men.

"He's a shot blocker, long and lanky," Martelli said. "It will take him a while to get his feet underneath him now that he's in college, but eventually he will be a big impact player."

F-JAMAL NICHOLS (6-8, 225 lbs., FR, #23, 14.9 ppg, 13.5 rpg, Ben Franklin HS/Philadelphia, Pa.). Martelli won a recruiting battle with new Villanova coach Jay Wright and a few Pac-10 teams for this gifted player.

Nichols was awarded the 2001 Markward Award, given to the Philadelphia Public League Player of the Year. He also earned four-team all-state honors. He's a versatile player who will become even more well-rounded under Martelli.

"He's more inside than outside, but he'll become more outside than inside with us," the coach said. "He's a sponge in terms of learning what we want him to do, and he plays a really tough-minded game."

Nichols will watch and learn this year, but he should be a three-year starter for the Hawks.

G-F PAT CARROLL (6-5, 190 lbs., FR, #33, 15.7 ppg, 6 rpg, Hatboro-Horsham HS/Horsham, Pa.). Carroll joins the Hawks after a terrific high school career, where he helped his school post a 105-23 record over four seasons. He earned second-team all-state honors as a senior.

"Pat is a kid who is wise beyond his years," Martelli said. "He has a great work ethic and only takes good shots."

F-JOHN BRYANT (6-7, 220 lbs., FR, #34, redshirted in 2001-01, Woodbridge HS/Woodbridge, Va.). Bryant is an athletic power forward who sat out last season after he fractured the growth plate of his right foot. He's healthy again and will be coming off the bench this season. He had modest numbers in high school (9.9 ppg, 7.8 rpg, 3.7 bpg as a senior) but Martelli considers him a "late bloomer."

QUESTIONS

Overhyped? The Hawks doubled their win total from

the previous year and fans have been itching for the new season to begin ever since St. Joseph's was eliminated by Stanford in the second round of the NCAA Tournament last March. But Martelli worries about "human nature" and how his team will handle the role of favorites in the Atlantic 10.

Failing their boards? Martelli says there's a simple reason St. Joseph's didn't advance to the Sweet 16 last March. "It's our rebounding," he said. "We weren't physical enough, and part of the problem was with our wings. They must contribute on the glass."

Outside shooting? The Hawks were not overwhelming from three-point range last year (.356) and Martelli says that could hurt this season. "Our perimeter shooting is a question mark," he said. "I love the three-point shot, but we don't shoot it easily and comfortably."

ANSWERS

PB&J! Martelli calls his outstanding backcourt duo of O'Connor and Nelson "peanut butter and jelly," but opponents may be calling them other things. They have a chemistry that belies their age and Nelson is the perfect point guard for the high-scoring O'Connor.

Bench! Not many teams can boast of having a 7-1 center on the bench with as much game experience as Sazonov, or a reserve guard who is as defensive-minded as Barley. If foul trouble crops up, as it is sure to do, Martelli has go-to players who can get the job done.

Generation Next! Martelli will lose some top players after this season, but he's already reloading with future stars such as Nichols, Jones and West.

ST. JOSEPH'S 2000-2001 RESULTS

#Western Carolina	103-53
#South Carolina State	84-71
#Vanderbilt (L)	76-78
@Colorado	97-78
Old Dominion	70-65
@Rutgers	67-65
Drexel	68-54
Villanova (L)	75-78
@DePaul (L)	76-80
@Western Kentucky	74-68
St. Peter's	79-69
Delaware	72-67
Duquesne	75-60
@Rhode Island	92-67
@George Washington	76-71
Dayton	84-71
@Temple	73-51
@Xavier (L)	73-86
@St. Bonaventure	78-76
Temple	71-62
Fordham	88-78
@Dayton	82-72
@Duquesne	90-70
Massachusetts	84-69
@LaSalle (L)	90-91
##Massachusetts (L)	70-75
###Georgia Tech	66-62
###Stanford (L)	83-90

#America's Youth Classic in Nashville
##Atlantic 10 Tournament in Philadelphia
###NCAA Tournament
@Road Games

BLUE RIBBON ANALYSIS

BACKCOURT	A
BENCH/DEPTH	B
FRONTCOURT	B+
INTANGIBLES	B+

There's plenty of reason to be optimistic on Hawk Hill, where Martelli's team has experienced success and yet remains hungry for more. O'Connor is a national player of the year candidate and a favorite to lead the NCAA in scoring. Point guards don't come much sharper than Nelson, and the frontcourt is solid and intimidating.

St. Joseph's loses only one starter (Wilkins) and he started only 34 percent of the time during his career. It appears that only injuries and overconfidence can derail the Hawks this season, but anything less than a trip to the Sweet 16 will be considered a down year by most of their fans.

That's a lot of pressure for a team that suffered through three consecutive losing seasons before last year.

The Hawks must be more consistent than last year. Yes, they ripped off winning streaks of eight and 10 games to climb into the top 25 of both major polls by the end of February. But they also lost to LaSalle in the regular-season finale, then stumbled against Massachusetts in the Atlantic-10 Tournament semifinals. That late-season slumped dropped them to a ninth seed in the NCAA Tournament, leading to that second-round match-up with Stanford instead of perhaps landing a fourth seed and an easier path through the tournament.

The quick-witted Martelli hosts a weekly TV show in Philadelphia which features a popular skit called "Martelli the Magnificent," a takeoff on Johnny Carson's old "Carnac" routine. This year, don't be surprised if the rest of the nation starts calling him magnificent. And he won't need to open an envelope to discover the two most important answers—O'Connor and Nelson.

"St. Joe's is a top 15 or even top-10 ballclub," Dayton's Purnell says. "They have all the ingredients, including real, real, good size. This club is for real."

(J.M.)

Connecticut 12

LOCATION	Storrs, CT
CONFERENCE	Big East (East)
LAST SEASON	20-12 (.625)
CONFERENCE RECORD	8-8 (3rd)
STARTERS LOST/RETURNING	3/2
NICKNAME	Huskies
COLORS	Blue & White
HOMECOURT	Gampel Pavilion (10,02)
	and Hartford Civic Center (16,294)
COACH	Jim Calhoun (American International '68)
RECORD AT SCHOOL	349-142 (15 years)
CAREER RECORD	599-279 (29 years)
ASSISTANTS	Dave Leitao (Northeastern '83)
	Tom Moore (Boston University '87)
	George Blaney (Holy Cross '61)
TEAM WINS (last 5 years)	18-32-34-25-20
RPI (last 5 years)	65-2-2-14-62
2000-01 FINISH	Lost in NIT second round.

COACH AND PROGRAM

We're not going to go overboard here, but when most teams win 20 games, it's an occasion for celebration and even vindication. It's a job well done and proof positive that the current administration knows what it's doing.

With such prosperity often comes postseason success, or at least an invitation. Coaches sign extensions. Recruits pour in. Season ticket applications expand. The whole program is generally considered in good shape.

Sometimes, 20 isn't such a magical number. When a team wins, say, a combined 93 games the previous three years, 20 can actually be a step back, a reason for concern. Or, at least, people wonder whether it was a one-year correction or a true step back. That was Connecticut's story last year.

The Huskies went 20-12, good numbers for about 95 percent of all Division I teams. But not good for UConn, which is used to operating with the other five percent, atop the rankings and in the second weekend of the NCAA Tournament. The alarm is not sounding in Storrs, not two years removed from a national title, but nobody wants a repeat of last season. It's all relative. If Virginia Tech wins 16 this year, Hokie fans will be encouraged. If the Huskies win "only" 20 again, their partisans will start to worry. If you haven't known prosperity, you can't understand what it's like to take a step away from it.

Just don't make a big deal about it to Jim Calhoun. He'll cite the storied recent history of his program, with its wins, titles, All-Americans, draft choices and other assorted hosannas. And he should. Connecticut is an elite program, and one year that takes it to the NIT isn't about to change that.

"We lost three players early [to the NBA] in the past four years—Ray Allen, Richard Hamilton and Khalid El-Amin," Calhoun said. "We had 20 wins last year, and if we had Khalid, that total would have been higher. The year before, we won 25, and that would have been considerably higher with Richard Hamilton."

As Calhoun sees it, last year's problems weren't caused by a lack of talent, rather a dearth of leadership. Connecticut bolted to a 10-1 start, with a win over Arizona the prime scalp. Things looked good. But a five-

game January losing streak torpedoed the good times and started the Huskies on a tough trip that improved some as the year went on but eventually crash-landed after a first-round Big East Tournament loss to Syracuse and a second-round NIT defeat at the hands of Detroit. Not the best way to go out.

"I was disappointed that our guys—Edmund Saunders, Albert Mouring and Souleymane Wane—didn't carry on the torch," Calhoun said. "We had that 10-1 start and were looking pretty good, but to finish with just 20 wins was tough.

"Winning 20 games accomplished something, but I think we were capable of more. We kind of played like a Connecticut team, but not quite."

Connecticut fans shouldn't be too worried about their team, no matter how last year ended. The Huskies could be the best team in the country that must replace three starters. Although Mouring, Saunders and Wane had talent, none was the kind of charismatic player who could lead and provide dependable crunch-time production. There should be no problem with that this year, because sophomore Caron Butler appears ready to step up and stop deferring to his elders, a maddening practice he developed last year. Still, he was to be applauded for very un-freshmanlike behavior at a time when most 18-year old collegiate newcomers believe they are the second coming of Bill Walton.

Butler had the talent necessary to be the big producer on the Huskies. His anticipated willingness to accept that mantle this year will help Connecticut immensely.

Connecticut will also be aided by the continued growth and maturity of point man Taliek Brown, who was given so much responsibility on the ball last year that he was practically assured of some form of struggle. Now a year older and stronger, Brown should be much better prepared for his job, particularly because it appears as if the Huskies have a player—freshman Ben Gordon—capable of giving him some support.

In fact, the Huskies should have a much deeper bench this year, something that should make Calhoun happy and allow his team to play a style that much more resembles the old Connecticut teams.

"I'd love to get back to playing nine or 10 kids a game and pressing," Calhoun said.

The arrivals of Gordon, rebounding forward Mike Hayes, swat-happy center Emeka Okafor and guard Chad Wise, plus the healthy return of Scott Hazelton, who red-shirted last year to allow his broken foot to heal, should give the Huskies a much deeper lineup and more flexibility for Calhoun.

Connecticut is perhaps a year away from making a deep tournament run, but it has the components to be extremely dangerous come March, particularly if Butler and Brown are ready to shoulder a huge portion of the load. Each has the talent to thrive. Now, they need the attitude.

Nobody will have to worry about Connecticut winning a measly 20 games this year. Count on at least 25, although that hasn't been so well received in the past, either. When you set a standard as high as Calhoun has, there are bound to be some runaway expectations. After last year, the coach probably won't mind hearing how everybody wants his team to win big. At least that means the possibility for huge success is there. Like it or not, that's the reality at a program like Connecticut.

2001-2002 SCHEDULE

Nov.	19	Vanderbilt
	26	New Hampshire
Dec.	2-3	#BB&T Classic
	8	Northeastern
	11	@Massachusetts
	21	Quinnipiac
	28	St. Bonaventure
Jan.	2	@Virginia Tech
	5	Miami
	7	Oklahoma
	10	Virginia Tech
	13	@Villanova
	16	North Carolina
	23	St. John's
	26	@Arizona
	30	Rutgers
Feb.	2	@Miami
	5	Providence
	9	@St. John's
	11	Villanova
	16	Boston College
	19	@Georgetown
	23	West Virginia
	25	@Boston College
March	2	Seton Hall
	6-9	##Big East Tournament

@Road Games
#Washington, DC (vs. George Washington first round; also Princeton, Maryland)
##Madison Square Garden, New York, NY

STARTERS NOT RETURNING

SG-ALBERT MOURING (6-3, 15.1 ppg, 3.2 rpg, 1.7 apg, 34.4 minutes, .437 FG, .374 3PT, .889 FT). Mouring had a solid senior season, but he never developed into the threat that many thought he would become. Though still deadly from the outside and also more willing to take the ball to the basket, Mouring didn't display the attitude necessary to be a first-rate two man.

Sure, he scored 31 against Virginia Tech, but he had only six at Villanova. He was erratic in Big East play and crash-landed in the NIT, scoring a total of 15 points in the Huskies' two games. Mouring was better suited for an auxiliary role, which is unfortunate, because the Huskies needed more from him last year.

PF-EDMUND SAUNDERS (6-8, 9.9 ppg, 7.2 rpg, 1.0 apg, 28.5 minutes, .530 FG, .679 FT). Saunders filled his role well last year, banging on the boards and scoring close to the basket. Although some may have had grander plans for him, his ability dictated that he should not be counted on for much more.

Saunders did improve his rebounding numbers last year and was a big reason the Huskies owned the boards against most rivals. But like his fellow seniors, he was not a rock during Big East competition and actually saw his numbers drop. Though he could have graduated this year and petitioned the NCAA for an extra season of eligibility, Saunders and the program decided it was time for him to move on.

C-SOULEYMANE WANE (6-11, 4.6 ppg, 4.8 rpg, 0.7 apg, 20.4 minutes, .482 FG, .591 FT). Give Wane credit for being consistent. Two years ago, he averaged 4.3 points and 4.8 rebounds. Those numbers didn't change much last season.

Although he was counted on heavily to step up after the graduation of Jake Voskuhl, Wane gave the Huskies what he had always given them: steady, unspectacular play that included plenty of fouls and not an overwhelming amount of playing time.

Wane always looked the part, but he never blossomed into more than that. There were moments when he contributed mightily, like his 11-point, 14-rebound effort against Villanova and his 13 points and 10 boards in the win over Notre Dame. But there were not enough highs like that for the Huskies' needs.

OTHERS NOT RETURNING

G-MARCUS COX (6-4, 2.7 ppg, 1.7 rpg, 1.4 apg, 11.0 minutes, .359 FG, .294 3PT, .625 FT). Cox struggled on and off the court last year. He never became comfortable on it, shooting poorly from the field and failing to give the kind of help at the point Brown needed. Off it, he was suspended for nine games because of various violations of team policies and closed the season off the active roster. He moved on to Massachusetts, where he hopes to recapture the form that made him the 1999 Connecticut Prep Player of the Year.

F-AJOU DENG (6-10, 4.8 ppg, 4.7 rpg, 0.5 apg, 14.8 minutes, .476 FG, .750 FT). Once heralded as the next great Connecticut player, Deng lasted just six games in 2000-01 before transferring after the first term of classes to Fairfield.

Deng seemingly had it all. He could run, he had a nice shooting touch and was well skilled. But he never adapted to the speed or the toughness of the Big East game and will be better suited at a mid-major level.

PROJECTED STARTERS

PG-TALIEK BROWN (6-1, 185 lbs., SO, #12, 8.1 ppg, 2.5 rpg, 4.9 apg, 1.7 spg, 28.1 minutes, .430 FG, .250 3PT, .545 FT, St. John's Prep/Queens, N.Y.). Brown had a solid freshman season, but he was certainly not a sensation. He improved as the season went on, producing more points and assists in Big East games than in non-conference games and certainly improving his free throw percentage. In conference play, Brown made 70.8 percent of his free throws.

As Calhoun said, Brown was given too much ball

handling responsibility. If El-Amin had stayed, Brown would have been a good apprentice and partner to the burly guard. But El-Amin's departure forced Brown into 30 minutes a night. At the point, that's going to take a toll.

"He got hit by being the Lone Ranger with the ball, on a team without great leadership," Calhoun said. "He was handling the ball too much. I think he will be better this year."

Brown showed flashes of serious potential. He had 12 assists against St. John's in January and 10 four nights later against Pittsburgh. But his shooting must improve. He attempted only 20 three-pointers all year, something that allowed teams to play off him. His overall percentage of 43.0 percent wasn't all that helpful, either. He must be a more complete offensive threat this year, to complement Butler. He should do that. Brown has good size and enough talent to thrive. Last year was tough, but it will help.

SG-TONY ROBERTSON (6-2, 200 lbs., JR, #32, 7.2 ppg, 2.2 rpg, 1.5 apg, 0.5 spg, 20.2 minutes, .452 FG, .326 3PT, .769 FT, St. Andrew's HS/East Providence, R.I.). Mouring loved to sit outside the line and fire away, but that's not Robertson's style. He's more happy going to the basket than staying away from it, though his perimeter game is improving.

"We all expect him to burst onto the scene this year," Calhoun said.

The problem that Robertson must overcome is more mental than physical. Calhoun said that the junior has a tendency to lose confidence when things don't go well and can get down on himself. That's not the attitude a two man needs. Robertson must work to be fearless and willing to dominate—or at least try it. He has potential and skill.

There were some nights last year when Robertson looked ready. He had 14 against Arizona and 15 against Dayton. He scored in double figures in four straight Big East games, with a 14-point effort in the big win against Boston College the crowning moment.

SF-CARON BUTLER (6-7, 235 lbs., SO, #3, 15.3 ppg, 7.6 rpg, 3.1 apg, 2.2 spg, 32.8 minutes, .435 FG, .304 3PT, .754 FT, Maine Central Institute/Racine, Wisc.). Syracuse fans may not want to hear this, but it was Orangemen coach Jim Boeheim who was most responsible for any increased confidence Butler may have this year. As coach of the U.S. team that won the World Championship for Young Men Tournament in Japan, Boeheim spent his time with Butler trying to convince the sophomore forward to be more assertive. If the counsel stuck, the Huskies will be in great shape.

Butler has all the tools to be a standout three man. He scores, attacks the backboards, has excellent size and strength, good quickness and jumps well. He led the Huskies in scoring and rebounding last year but could have been even more impressive, had he not deferred to his elders.

"He's a powerful kid and has good hands," Calhoun said. "But he didn't take over games last year. He played well in the under-20 tournament, but he didn't always dominate. [Boeheim] pushed him in that direction. Caron understands that he needs to do that."

The key with Butler is his outside game. He took the requisite 300-to-500 jump shots a day during the off-season, realizing that an improved three-point shot will make him especially potent and the Huskies particularly lethal. His mid-range game is tremendous, and he can bang away inside.

There were times when Butler was overwhelming. He had 29 points and 13 rebounds against Boston College and 25 and nine against Miami. But those outings were few and far between. For the most part, Butler was content to score in the mid-teens and grab a good share of rebounds. This year, he gets to take over. Connecticut needs him to do that.

PF-JOHNNY SELVIE (6-7, 235 lbs., SR, #44, 10.9 ppg, 5.5 rpg, 0.3 apg, 0.6 spg, 23.7 minutes, .547 FG, .670 FT, Southeastern (IA) CC/Flint, Mich.). Calhoun doesn't hold back at all when it comes to Selvie.

"This is a big year for Johnny," Calhoun said. "He's on a team where he's the only senior, and this is it for him. He doesn't have a chance to come back. He's terrifically talented, but he has to score 16-17 points a night for us. We're going to ride him through the month of December, and it's up to him whether we'll keep doing it. He needs to be a second or third option for us offensively."

Selvie had a solid major-college debut last year after a big career at Southeastern (Iowa) Community College. He scored well close to the basket and rebounded ferociously at times, but he was inconsistent. One night, he would score 26 against St. John's. The next, he would get six at Providence. He needs to find an in-between and give the Huskies reliable interior scoring and board work. That's where he lives, and it's where he needs to thrive. If he can't do it, Selvie will lose time to Hayes, a banger and solid defender.

C-JUSTIN BROWN (7-0, 245 lbs., SR, #20, 1.2 ppg, 1.2 rpg, 0.2 apg, 5.4 minutes, .517 FG, .308 FT, Australian Institute/Perth, Australia). Brown may just be renting this spot for a bit, while Okafor gets comfortable, because unless the Aussie makes a huge jump, he will see most of his time as a reserve.

Calhoun has had luck in the past developing centers into solid competitors. His work with Travis Knight and Jake Voskuhl bear that out. But Brown hasn't come along that much and has struggled to match his skills with the spirit and toughness necessary to play big-time college basketball.

"This is his year," Calhoun said. "He's worked hard and gotten stronger. He's talented."

KEY RESERVES

G-BEN GORDON (6-2, 185 lbs., FR, #4, 24.1 ppg, 4.9 rpg, 5.4 apg, 3.6 spg, .530 FG, .390 3PT, .800 FT, Mount Vernon HS/Mount Vernon, N.Y.). Gordon will see time at both backcourt spots, giving much-needed assistance to Brown and some more perimeter pop, in the event Robertson struggles with his role. It's not unreasonable to believe that Gordon could grab a starting spot by mid-season.

"He's an immensely talented kid," Calhoun said. "He jumps, shoots and works hard. I always catch him in the gym. He has a great work ethic. He's going to challenge Tony Robertson and make [Robertson] a better player."

Gordon helped Mount Vernon to the 2000 New York class A state title and an '01 state semifinal, while averaging 27.3 points during the final two postseasons of his career. He led the'00 ABCD camp in three-point shooting.

C-EMEKA OKAFOR (6-9, 240 lbs., FR, #50, 22.0 ppg, 16.0 rpg, 6.0 bpg, Bellaire HS/Houston, Texas). Here's another freshman who could have a starting job before long. Calhoun absolutely gushes about Okafor's defensive ability and rebounding potential. It won't even matter if he doesn't score. Okafor is that imposing that his offensive game doesn't matter now.

His performance in the 2001 Pittsburgh Hoops Classic was jaw dropping. Okafor had 26 points, 12 boards and 10 blocks and simply dominated a collection of prep all-stars. He's quick, strong and not afraid. Unlike many Connecticut big men who need time to develop, Okafor should have an immediate impact.

"He's cut," Calhoun said. "He's a bigger version of [former Husky interior force] Kirk King. He has wide shoulders and is quick. He is physically ready to play now. His offense is behind his defense now, but he can be one of those guys who can change the game with his size."

F-MIKE HAYES (6-8, 215 lbs., JR, #25, 13.7 ppg, 11.4 rpg, 59.8 FG, Cowley County (KS) CC/Hartford, Conn.). There are no illusions here. Hayes is a rebounder who will support Selvie at the four spot and give the Huskies some more baseline defense.

"He knows what he is, and that's terrific," Calhoun said. "He can jump and rebound. He has great size."

Hayes led Cowley County in scoring and rebounding last year. His offensive game is limited primarily to layups and put-backs. He runs the floor well but can bang in the halfcourt.

F-SCOTT HAZELTON (6-8, 215 lbs., R-FR, #21, 28.8 ppg, 12.2 rpg in 1999-2000, Central Catholic HS/Lawrence, Mass.). Hazelton missed all but five games of last year nursing a broken foot that dates back to his senior year of high school. Calhoun believes the wing is completely clear of trouble now and should add some athletic ability to the frontcourt. A good athlete, Hazelton won the team's preseason mile run and has added 15 pounds to his frame since arriving in Storrs.

Hazelton has fine skills and was a highly regarded recruit, thanks in large part to his big junior season. If healthy, he has a chance to be a factor in the coming years.

G-CHAD WISE (6-5, 190 lbs., FR, #5, 22.0 ppg, 6.0 rpg, 6.0 apg, Lonoke HS/Lonoke, Ark.). Wise is a fine athlete who could see time at both backcourt spots this season. He passes and handles well and can drill it from deep. Wise was also an all-state quarterback as a senior in high school, although he has no plans to join the Huskies' gridders.

"He can really shoot," Calhoun said. "He's very interesting."

Although Wise isn't expected to play huge minutes this year, he can give Calhoun options, particularly against zones and in games that require more halfcourt offense, thanks to his shooting.

OTHER RETURNEES

G/F-SHANNON TOOLES (6-5, 210 lbs., SO, #30, 0.1 ppg, 0.3 rpg, 0.1 apg, 2.6 minutes, .500 FG, Coatesville HS/Coatesville, Pa.). Tooles is an athletic wing who saw time in 17 games last year but attempted only two shots. He hails from the same high school as former Connecticut standout Richard Hamilton. Though he has a good game for the open court, Tooles won't get much more time until he can step up in more structured situations.

G-ROBERT SWAIN (6-4, 205 lbs., SO, #2, 1.5 ppg, 0.5 rpg, 0.2 apg, 3.9 minutes, .429 FG, .571 3PT, Tri-Cities HS/College Park, Ga.). Swain didn't join the team until the second semester of last year, because he had to take the Georgia state Regency examination during the fall, in order to complete his academic work as a high schooler.

He saw spot action last year and impressed with his outside shooting ability. Swain isn't going to start, but he has the ability to be an offensive weapon in certain situations.

G-KWASI GYAMBIBI (6-0, 175 lbs., SR, #10, 0.4 ppg, 0.3 rpg, 0.0 apg, 1.6 minutes, .000 FG, .750 FT, Church Farm (PA) School/Norwalk, Conn.). A walk-on, Gyambibi played in seven games last year and scored all three of his points on free throws. He also grabbed a pair of rebounds.

G-MIKE WOODWARD (6-5, 215 lbs., JR, #35, 0.3 ppg, 0.3 rpg, 0.0 apg, 1.3 minutes, .000 FG, .500 FT, Rocky River HS/Rocky River, Ohio). A walk-on, Woodward played three times last year and scored his sole point on a free throw. He pulled one rebound.

QUESTIONS

Scoring? Butler will get his, but at least one other player must step up and become a reliable weapon.

Leadership? Selvie is the only scholarship senior on the team, and he is in just his second year in the program. He has a chance to show the way, but Butler must take charge, too.

Youth? By season's end, the Huskies could be starting two sophomores, two freshmen and a senior. There's talent throughout the lineup, but is it too young?

ANSWERS

Butler! Get out of his way. It's time for Butler to be a big-time Big East player. He has the tools, and it appears as if he has the desire.

Depth! The Huskies can use 10 players again, which means more pressing and fast breaking, just like Calhoun prefers.

Freshmen! The newcomers could all make significant contributions right away. Look for Gordon and Okafor to vie for starting time.

Selvie! The senior has the ability to be a major factor, and now he'll have the opportunity. Calhoun expects him to take advantage.

CONNECTICUT 2000-2001 RESULTS

Quinnipiac	86-72
#Dayton (L)	66-80
#Chaminade	77-61
#Louisville	83-71
Brown	88-78
Houston	72-60
New Hampshire	97-70
Arizona	71-69
Massachusetts	82-67
Fairfield	100-66
Rhode Island	87-76
Stony Brook	67-58
@Boston College (L)	68-85
St. John's	82-80
Pittsburgh	73-53
@Providence (L)	68-81
@Texas (L)	56-60
@Miami (L)	74-77
Villanova (L)	59-70
@St. John's (L)	55-60
Virginia Tech	85-72

Providence	83-68
@Villanova (L)	60-74
Boston College	82-71
@Virginia Tech	61-46
@Syracuse (L)	60-65
Miami	60-53
Notre Dame	75-59
@Seton Hall (L)	63-65
##Syracuse (L)	75-86
###South Carolina	72-65
###Detroit (L)	61-67

#Maui Invitational, Lahaina, HI
##Big East Tournament, Madison Square Garden, NY
###NIT

BLUE RIBBON ANALYSIS

BACKCOURT	B
BENCH/DEPTH	B+
FRONTCOURT	B+
INTANGIBLES	A-

OK, so Connecticut won "just" 20 games last year. The Huskies appear ready to put that disappointment behind them and challenge for the Big East title again. There is enough talent on board, but Calhoun must find some standard-bearers, something last year's team lacked.

Butler has the potential to break out this season—and then leave town. If he learned how to dominate over the summer, he could be unstoppable. No other player in the league has his combination of size and skill. He has improved his outside shot and can be expected to average about 20 points.

Expect improvement in Brown, too. He has the skills, and now he has a year's experience. If he can shoot better, teams will play closer to him, and he'll be able to penetrate more. That will help everyone. Better production can be also looked for in Selvie and Robertson, who no longer have to wait their turns. Robertson had better be ready, because Gordon could take his job.

The interior situation looks good, provided Okafor is as talented as advertised, and Brown can be more than an ancillary player. Selvie should be a big board man, and Hayes has the ability to make big contributions in that area, too.

We joke about Connecticut's mini-slide, but the Huskies aren't accustomed to having so much trouble. Calhoun wants to get back to the old pressing style that was so successful before, and he has the numbers and athletes to do it. If Butler and Selvie become leaders, and Brown is more consistent on the ball, then 25-30 wins are possible. Connecticut will be quite good, but it's a question of whether it happens this season or next.

(M.B.)

Temple 13

LOCATION	Philadelphia, PA
CONFERENCE	Atlantic 10
LAST SEASON	24-13 (.649)
CONFERENCE RECORD	12-4 (3rd)
STARTERS LOST/RETURNING	1/4
NICKNAME	Owls
COLORS	Cherry & White
HOMECOURT	The Liacouras Center (10,206)
COACH	John Chaney (Bethune-Cookman '55)
RECORD AT SCHOOL	431-179 (19 years)
CAREER RECORD	656-238 (29 years)
ASSISTANTS	Nate Blackwell (Temple '90)
	Dan Leibovitz (Pennsylvania '96)
TEAM WINS (last 5 years)	20-21-24-27-14
RPI (last 5 years)	37-30-21-9-23
2000-01 FINISH	Lost in NCAA regional final.

COACH AND PROGRAM

Just take a look at John Chaney. Do you think he cares much about what he sees in the mirror?

The Temple coaching legend has the same philosophy about this basketball team. Do you think he cares much about the Owls' record in November, December or January? Of course he doesn't.

That's why it seemed so puzzling that during the Christmas season last year—when Temple was in the

midst of losing seven straight, its worst slide in Chaney's 19 years and longest since dropping 11 straight in 1975—everyone was again turning Chaney into Scrooge, making him huff and puff about what was wrong with his underachieving club.

Never mind that in that losing streak, Temple lost games to eventual national champion Duke (twice), Villanova, Miami of Ohio, Penn State, Wisconsin and Wake Forest. Only one of the setbacks—a 93-68 crushing by Duke at First Union Center—was by more than eight points.

"My zone has worked for 35 years and it still works when they know what they're doing," Chaney chirped after his Owls allowed Wisconsin to badger Temple with 14-for-28 shooting from beyond the arc in a 66-58 loss on Dec. 14 at home.

Abandon his trademark zone? What, are you crazy, Chaney thought.

"I've played man, zone, triangle-and-2. I've done it all," he said. "It has nothing to do with it. They run good stuff and they put shooters on the floor. Kids today can make threes, I don't care whether you play man or zone.

"I could have scheduled Ramapo or Little Sisters of the Poor, but I schedule the tough teams and I'll continue to do that as long as I'm here. We've been through this before, maybe not losing this many, but if we stay healthy, we'll be all right. You win now for next year."

You think he might know what he's talking about now, folks?

Temple recovered with a mini-roll to start the A-10 season, then found itself as a team. It qualified for the NCAA Tournament for the 17th time in 19 seasons and 12th consecutive time—think about that consistency for just a second—and won 10 straight to capture the conference tournament and reach the Elite Eight. Again, Chaney was on the brink of reaching his first Final Four.

But again, the missing piece on a coaching resume that needs no defending was not achieved. The Owls, Cinderellas as a No. 11-seeded team, just like they were as a 10th-seeded team in 1991 when they reached the regional final, losing 69-62 to defending national champion Michigan State in the South Region championship game in Atlanta. It was Chaney's fifth Elite Eight (1988, '91, '93 and '99) in what was possibly his least talented team.

It's mostly good news for Chaney again this year. In addition to his induction into the Basketball Hall of Fame in October, his Owls return four starters, including national player-of-the-year candidate Lynn Greer, and should have a little bit better depth thanks to a few talented newcomers. Four starters—Greer, backcourt mate Quincy Wadley, center Kevin Lyde and swingman David Hawkins—averaged more than 34 minutes last year and the fifth, athletic 6-6 forward Alex Wesby, averaged more than 31. Eventually, his team just ran out of gas. Not that you'd get Chaney to use that as an excuse.

"With every step forward that we take, I think we become a scarier team for other guys to deal with," Greer, last year's catalyst along with Wadley, told CBS Sportsline.com during the NCAA run. "We just have so much confidence right now that we expect to win and keep moving ahead. If other people are surprised we're still standing, that's on them, man. We're not shocked by what we're accomplishing now."

And those goals were reached because of Temple's typical treacherous schedule.

"It seems like every year we somehow manage to play a lot better basketball in late January and early February," Chaney said this fall [he had to be smiling as he uttered those words]. "I think those games prepare us and really help the kids grow."

Greer, a first-team all-conference pick who averaged 18.2 points, 5.5 assists and 2.0 steals, will again be the one to make Temple go this season, but losing Wadley's 15.1 points and usual dose of leadership will be tough. A third-team all-conference selection, he and Greer each made more than 80 treys and connected on nearly 38 percent from three-point land. But Wadley is the only significant loss from last year.

"I don't think you can replace leaders, but you have to have other players who want to take on the challenge and stand tall," Chaney said.

Temple won't have Hawkins to help out until the second half of the season. He's out for academic reasons. He was an all-rookie team pick in the conference last year and gave Temple four perimeter threats and another swift defender and decent rebounder.

Lyde, a second-team all-conference pick last year and fourth-year starter, should continue to be a force on both ends of the floor. The 6-10 Lyde averaged 12.9

points, 8.9 rebounds and 2.0 blocks. The 6-6 Wesby is the type of wing sniper the Owls love. He averaged 10.1 points and 5.5 rebounds last year, while making 33 percent from beyond the arc—a figure that needs to improve.

Look for beefy Ron Rollerson (3.1 ppg, 4.2 rpg), a 6-10 senior center, to get more minutes until Hawkins returns. Rollerson averaged 16 minutes last year. Junior forward Greg Jefferson is another returnee who could see more time and three newcomers have to make an impact.

Up front, Chaney likes the look of 6-9, 235-pound Glen Elliott, a freshman from Jacksonville, Fla. Nile Murry, a 6-4 freshman from Houston, should see time at point guard, and sophomore Brian Polk, who sat out last year, could also contribute.

Any way you look at it, though, Temple will be deeper than last year. Then again, its bench couldn't have gotten any shorter.

The rumors are that Chaney, who turns 70 this year, could be calling it quits after this season after the departure of at least three key seniors. But you know he won't let up, not for a second. Hall of Famers don't do that, and Chaney took his place among immortals this October. The early morning practices, part of what reportedly drove talented freshman forward Carlton Aaron and guard Ronald Blackshear from the team last year, will continue. After 656 victories, why would Chaney change his style?

"I don't try and relax my guys," Chaney told CBS Sports line. "I tell them, this is hard work. You hear a lot of guys say, 'We're going to play and we're going to have fun.' You're [expletive] not going to have fun playing for me. It's hard work. Now, fun comes when your work is done."

When Chaney decides to step down, he is likely to turn the program over to his longtime assistant and former player, Nate Blackwell.

2001-2002 SCHEDULE

Nov.	8-9	#Coaches vs. Cancer Classic
	29	Charlotte
Dec.	1	Penn State
	3	@Wisconsin
	5	@Duke
	8	*Villanova
	18	**Alabama
	20	Memphis
	22	DePaul
	30	Pennsylvania
Jan.	6	@Fordham
	9	Duquesne
	12	Rhode Island
	16	@St. Bonaventure
	19	@Massachusetts
	23	Richmond
	26	@North Carolina State
	30	Fordham
Feb.	2	St. Joseph's
	6	@Rhode Island
	9	@George Washington
	13	@LaSalle
	16	Massachusetts
	20	Xavier
	23	St. Bonaventure
	27	@Dayton
March	3	*@St. Joseph's
	6-9	##A-10 Tournament

@Road Games
*The Palestra, Philadelphia, PA
**Jimmy V Classic, East Rutherford, NY
#New York (vs. Florida first round; also Arizona, Maryland)
##First Union Spectrum, Philadelphia, PA

STARTERS NOT RETURNING

SG-QUINCY WADLEY (6-4, 15.1 ppg, 4.6 rpg, 2.3 apg, 1.5 spg, 1.8 tpg, 31.2 minutes, .413 FG, .379 3PT, .738 FT). A former football player, Wadley provided a sense of toughness that has been a staple of Temple teams. He also covered a ton of ground in Chaney's match-up zone and was never afraid to make a play in crunch time, whether slashing to the hole or stepping back and drilling a three-pointer.

That type of leadership and court savvy isn't easy to replace.

A fifth-year senior, Wadley came alive in March after

returning from a shoulder sprain, and it's no coincidence that his presence helped the Owls fly higher. Wadley scored 16 points or more in six straight games, including a 24-point, 10-rebound effort in a rout of Florida in the NCAA Tournament. He drained 5-of-10 treys in that game, too, and in fact had a torrid March streak in the tournament, going 12-for-19 until putting up an 0-for-7 night against Michigan State in the regional final.

In 16 of his 33 games, Wadley made at least three shots from beyond the arc—a nice security blanket for any team to have. Finding someone to duplicate that this season will be tough. That's why veterans Wesby and Hawkins need to step up their game to assist Greer, who also might get help from talented freshman Murry and sophomore Polk.

OTHERS NOT RETURNING

F-MAMA CELLOU BARRY (6-8, 0.9 ppg, 0.8 rpg, 4.6 minutes, 16 games, .438 FG, .250 FT). Barry saw action in 16 games, mostly as a way for Temple to eat up space in the middle. His job was simple: set a lot of solid screens to help free up the team's shooters. In a pinch—when Lyde or Rollerson got in foul trouble—Barry gave Temple enough minutes off the bench to get by.

PROJECTED STARTERS

PG-LYNN GREER (6-2, 175 lbs., SR, #14, 18.2 ppg, 3.6 rpg, 5.5 apg, 2.0 spg, 2.2 tpg, 39.6 minutes, .401 FG, .379 3PT, .868 FT, Engineering and Science HS/Philadelphia, Pa.). Reggie Jackson once said that he was the straw that stirs the drink for the New York Yankees.

That's exactly what Greer does for Temple. There was some doubt if he would be able to run the team after Pepe Sanchez graduated, but Greer came through with a stellar season. With the arrival of freshman point man Murry, it's possible Chaney will move Greer to shooting guard. But one wonders if he'll mess with a good thing.

Greer has been one of Temple's top shooters the last two seasons, and his assist-to-turnover ratio last year (5.5 to 2.2) was solid.

"When you have a three-guard offense like we do, all three roles are similar," Chaney said. "You have to be able to dribble, pass and shoot. We've had good guards around here for a lot of years and that's what we expect from Lynn this year."

Chaney likes to call Greer "Little Boy," because of his baby face, but Greer became The Man last year. He was selected first-team A-10 and in the Owls' last 11 games he was nearly unstoppable. A finalist for the Wooden Award this year and a member of last summer's U.S. World University Games team, he scored 20 or more points nine times, including 19, 20, 21 and 22 in four NCAA Tournament games.

This year he might even have a little more bounce in his step late in the game if Temple can give him a breather once in awhile. He was a workhorse last year. Greer led the nation in minutes played, but he had fair warning before the season.

"During the off-season coach told me that I would be playing 40 minutes a game," Greer said. "I prepared myself by running a lot, lifting weights. That is part of the game, we don't have many subs and we don't have any subs for Quincy and me."

All those minutes gave Green time to build some stats. He was first in the league in free-throw percentage, seventh in scoring, 11th in field-goal percentage, third in three-point percentage, third in assists and second in steals.

Greer's first-team All-Atlantic-10 selection was well deserved as he carried on a Temple tradition. The Owls have had at least one A-10 first-team member since 1993.

SG-DAVID HAWKINS (6-5, 215 lbs., SO, #34, 10.4 ppg, 4.4 rpg, 1.2 apg, 1.5 spg, 1.4 tpg, 34.1 minutes, .398 FG, .286 3PT, .646 FT, Archbishop Carroll High School/Washington, D.C.). Put an asterisk next to his name. Academic problems will keep Hawkins out until January and that hurts. It means Chaney has to either go with a bigger lineup and start Rollerson or bring a inexperienced player such as one of the incoming freshman in off the bench.

Hawkins, an A-10 All-Rookie team pick last year, is a great third-guard in Temple's scheme. He's hardly a great shooter, but he excels by slashing and getting into the lane. He's not afraid of contact, either, but needs to play a little more under control. Also a hard worker on defense and rebounding, his absence will be felt early.

If there is a silver lining it's that without Hawkins some of the newcomers and backup Greg Jefferson will get more minutes and more time to develop until he returns.

Out of Washington, D.C., where he was an AAU teammate of Lyde, Hawkins initially signed a national letter of intent with Tulane. But he was allowed to wiggle out of that when coach Perry Clark left for Miami (Fla.) and was succeeded by Shawn Finney. He was considered one of the top 100 prep recruits in the country.

SF-ALEX WESBY (6-6, 190 lbs., SR, #23, 10.1 ppg, 5.5 rpg, 1.0 apg, 1.0 spg, 0.6 tpg, 31.3 minutes, .393 FG, .325 3PT, .654 FT, Ben Franklin HS/Philadelphia, Pa.). Wesby averaged just 3.5 points as a sophomore, but last year was one of the major reasons Temple made its NCAA run. Without Wadley around, he'll be counted on for even more this year, including some big shots late in games.

A good rebounder for his size (5.5 per game) and a defender who covers plenty of ground, he emerged at times as a defensive stopper and on the other end he was a viable offensive option. Wesby was afforded open looks because of the attention paid to Greer and Wadley and made 74 treys, including a career-high four twice. Driving up his percentage from downtown (.325) also will be key.

PF-KEVIN LYDE (6-10, 260 lbs., SR, #42, 12.8 ppg, 8.9 rpg, 2.0 bpg, 1.3 apg, 0.5 spg, 34.6 minutes, .515 FG, .561 FT, Oak Hill Academy, Va./Washington, D.C.). Lyde thought about leaving for the NBA but after announcing he reversed his decision, and with him back, it makes Temple again an A-10 and national power.

"We played with four guys out on the perimeter and one guy inside so he had to do everything for us," Chaney said. "I think he's one of the best rebounders in the country and when he gets the ball down low I haven't seen anyone who can stop him."

Lyde is the type of powerful, low-post threat every great team needs. He's a wide body who is a presence defensively. He alters shots and relies on strength and good positioning to seemingly always be around the ball when it comes off the glass. Chaney says Lyde's the best rebounder he's ever had.

"He has the best hands I've ever seen," Chaney said after Lyde announced his intentions to turn pro last spring. "[The team that drafts him] won't have to worry about his rebounding ability; he's the best we've ever had. And if he's in good health, he can block shots, too."

Lyde's offensive game is solid, too. Last year, Chaney had to get creative to get the most out of Lyde, pulling the big man from games after he committed his first foul. Limited to eight minutes in the first half after picking up a foul against Fordham, personal foul, Lyde played the entire second half and finished with a career-high 27 points and 10 boards.

"Kevin Lyde is the most important player on our ball club," Chaney said after that game. "We take him out when he picks up his first foul now. Every one of them has come because of some guard letting his man penetrate. He won't let anybody by without a challenge, and that's how he gets fouls."

Lyde's teammates knew what he meant to their success.

"It means a lot for our team for him to be on the floor," Wadley said. "He's our inside presence, both scoring and blocking shots. When he's out of the game, we struggle offensively and defensively."

Last season, Lyde was second in the A-10 in field-goal percentage, double-figure rebounding games (16) and double-doubles (14). He was third among A-10 rebounds.

Temple will need as much or more form the big man this season.

At the next level, Lyde will need to develop more face-up moves to be a contributor because he'll find fewer match-up deficiencies.

After announcing in April that he was opting for the NBA draft, Lyde changed his mind. He would have been just the fourth player to leave Temple early during Chaney's 19 seasons. But Donald Hodge (1991), Marc Jackson ('97) and Mark Karcher (2000) all found out that the NBA considered them unworthy of being first-round picks.

With a solid senior season and some offensive polish, Lyde has the chance to go high in the draft.

C-RON ROLLERSON (6-10, 295 lbs., SR., #30, 3.1 ppg, 4.2 rpg, 0.6 tpg, 0.8 bpg, 16.0 minutes, .562 FG, .528 FT, Faith Christian Academy/Pennsauken, N.J.). A big body that was valuable coming off the bench last season, Rollerson might be needed for more minutes this year, especially early with Hawkins out because of academics.

He isn't as good as Lyde defensively or grabbing rebounds, but he sure does take up space and with him and Lyde in the paint, there isn't much room for opponents to operate. He'll be called upon this year for more than the occasionally dunk or stick-back. Chaney seems to like him more coming off the bench, and that might eventually be his role again, but maybe not until Hawkins returns.

KEY RESERVES

F-GREG JEFFERSON (6-5, 200 lbs., JR, #1, 2.0 ppg, 2.5 rpg, 9.5 minutes, .561 FG, .571 3PT, Philadelphia Christian Academy/Los Angeles, Calif.). Jefferson saw action in 28 games last year, but his one shining moment came in the NCAA regional semifinals. Jefferson scored a career-high15 points and grabbed seven rebounds in an 84-72 victory over Penn State. He had scored 40 points all season before that, but made seven of his nine shots in 21 minutes of action.

He gave the Owls something they hadn't had throughout the tournament—bench points. That's right, until that game, no Temple reserve scored in the Big Dance. He'll need to the same this season.

F-GLEN ELLIOTT (6-9, 235 lbs., FR, #4, 19.0 ppg, 12.0 rpg, 3.0 apg, Jacksonville Bolles HS/Atlantic Beach, Fla.). A McDonald's All-America nominee, Elliott could be a factor very soon off the bench for the Owls, whom will need some frontcourt help.

His AAU, the Tallahassee Wildcats won AAU championships over the summer, including the Great American Shootout in Texas and the Junior Men's National Pro-Am Tournament in Jacksonville.

G-BRIAN POLK (6-4, 210 lbs., SO, #3, 30.0 ppg, 13.0 rpg, in 1999-00 at Sussex Tech/Harbeson, Del.). Polk missed last year, sitting out because of academic reasons, but should help Temple off the bench this season. He was selected to the Delaware All-State team after his junior year and capped a great prep career by earning the Delaware State Player of the Year award in his final season. He amassed 2,056 points over his four-year career.

PG-NILE MURRY (6-4, 200 lbs., FR, #21, 18.0 ppg, 6.0 rpg, 6.0 apg at Klein Forest HS/Houston, Texas). Touted as Greer's eventual replacement, he could see big minutes this winter as a true freshman. Murry fits right into the mold of classic, bigger guard for the Owls. He was chosen first-team all-state as a senior. His team produced three Division I recruits.

OTHER RETURNEES

F-ROULDRA THOMAS (6-5, 205 lbs., SR., #40, 0.2 ppg, 0.7 rpg, 4.9 minutes, 12 games, .111 FG, Natchez HS/Natchez, Miss). Coming out of high school, he was a USA Today honorable mention All-American. But Thomas didn't like his first stop, North Carolina State, and transferred to Temple. He sat out the 1998-99 season after transferring and hasn't made much of an impact with the Owls, either. He did play in 12 games last year and has the opportunity to give the Owls frontcourt help once again.

OTHER NEWCOMERS

G-JAY JAMESON (6-0, 170 lbs., SR, #22, averaged 0.6 ppg in 1998-99 at Long Island University, 1,274 career points at North Penn HS/Lansdale, Pa. and Long Island University). You don't call too many college kids journeymen, but this will be Jameson's third college stop. He sat out last year after transferring from Montgomery County Community College, despite not even playing hoops there.

Jameson did play one year at Long Island in Brooklyn as a walk-on and saw action in nines games. Before that, he enrolled at Philadelphia Textile, but didn't play there, either. He pushed plenty of guys in Temple practices last year and might be able to help the Owls this season off the bench.

"I don't do real well with All-Americans. I like kids who shovel their way out of trouble. I just like blue-collar kids," Chaney told the Philadelphia Inqurier, referring to Jameson.

F-HAWLEY SMITH (6-6, 210 lbs., FR, #15, 16.5 ppg, 10.0 rpg, 4.0 apg, .560 3PT, Jacksonville Bolles HS/Jacksonville, Fla.). Another newcomer, Smith was voted Class AAA Player of the Year and MVP in all classifications in the Northeastern Region by the Florida Coaches Association.

The stat that pops out is his three-point shooting percentage. If he hits anywhere close to that for the Owls, he'll see minutes.

QUESTIONS

Adios? Is this Chaney's last year? And if so, it might be an extra boost for an already talented team to take their veteran coach to a place he's never been—the Final Four. Chaney wouldn't coach differently if the building was on fire, so don't expect any decision he has made about his future—even if it's in his own mind only—to affect him.

Depth? The Owls were thinner than Calista Flockhart last year and lost Wadley and Hawkins (half the season) for this winter. There is a good group of newcomers, but are they ready for prime time and will they be able to adjust to Chaney's basic training?

Schedule? Once again, Chaney will prepare his team with a brutal schedule with home games against Memphis, Cincinnati, DePaul, Villanova and Penn State and road games at Duke, N.C. State and Wisconsin and a season-opening game against Florida in the Coaches vs. Cancer tournament. The next game would be against either Arizona or Maryland. Will the Owls learn from those stern tests?

ANSWERS

Go-to guy! Greer shouldered the load of the point guard position last year and blossomed into one of the country's best players. A resourceful player indeed, at 6-2 he makes things happen.

Let's be up front! Chaney calls Lyde the best rebounder he's had, and that's saying something. If Lyde has worked on some post moves so he can be a 15-to-18 points-per-game player instead of 13, that'll help immensely.

The maestro! You can't argue with the man's success. Chaney goes out, gets players who fit his style and molds them into winners. If 17 NCAA appearances in 19 years aren't enough proof, what is?

TEMPLE 2000-2001 RESULTS

Delaware	56-49
New Mexico	61-49
@Memphis	67-62
#Indiana	69-61
#Duke (L)	61-63
@Miami, Ohio (L)	58-66
Duke (L)	68-93
@Villanova (L)	62-69
@Penn State (L)	60-66
Wisconsin (L)	58-66
Wake Forest (L)	65-73
Cleveland State	73-46
@Pennsylvania	74-60
@LaSalle	75-61
St. Bonaventure	63-43
@Dayton	68-58
Fordham	77-70
St. Joseph's (L)	51-73
@DePaul (L)	64-65
@Fordham	90-72
Massachusetts (L)	64-65
@Duquesne	84-58
Rhode Island	77-47
George Washington	91-58
@Xavier (L)	71-78
@St. Joseph's (L)	62-71
@Massachusetts	84-52
Dayton	70-62
LaSalle	60-58
@George Washington	92-88
##Dayton	76-63
##George Washington	77-76
##Massachusetts	76-65
###Texas	79-65
###Florida	75-54
###Penn State	84-72
###Michigan State (L)	62-69

#Preseason NIT in New York
##Atlantic 10 Tournament in Philadelphia
###NCAA Tournament
@Road Games

BLUE RIBBON ANALYSIS

BACKCOURT	A-
BENCH/DEPTH	B
FRONTCOURT	B
INTANGIBLES	A

If the returning starters—Greer, Lyde and Wesby (for now)—improve at all, Temple would be good enough to win plenty of games. Yes, the dynamic is different with the graduated Wadley—whose absence last year because of injury was part of the reason for Temple's seven-game losing streak—and Hawkins (out till January for academic reasons) gone, but Chaney has a bunch of gamers.

Elliott will be a key, backing up Lyde and Rollerson in the frontcourt, and Murry and Polk could play huge roles in just their first college seasons. Jameson could be a sleeper in the backcourt and might provide valuable minutes off the bench.

Temple will struggle again during the regular-season playing one of the country's toughest schedules, and that could hurt it in the A-10 race. But just like last year, expect the Owls to come together at the right time and give Chaney a nice farewell run. It just won't take him to the Promised Land (Final Four).

(J.D.)

Memphis 14

LOCATION	Memphis, TN
CONFERENCE	Conference USA (National)
LAST SEASON	21-15 (.583)
CONFERENCE RECORD	10-6 (2nd)
STARTERS LOST/RETURNING	2/3
NICKNAME	Tigers
COLORS	Royal Blue & Gray
HOMECOURT	The Pyramid (20,142)
COACH	John Calipari (Clarion State '82)
RECORD AT SCHOOL	21-15 (1 year)
CAREER RECORD	214-86 (9 years)
ASSISTANTS	Tony Barbee (UMass '93)
	Steve Roccaforte (Lamar '89)
	Derek Kellogg (UMass '95)
TEAM WINS (last 5 years)	16-17-13-15-21
RPI (last 5 years)	76-68-125-130-68
2000-01 FINISH	Third place in NIT.

COACH AND PROGRAM

Never doubt the basketball fanaticism of those who follow the University of Memphis.

This summer, word broke out that anyone could enter the Larry O. Finch Center, where the U of M basketball team trains, and watch noontime pickup games. Most days, every University of Memphis player—freshmen included —were involved in the games.

Pro players and former U of M players like Cedric Henderson, Elliot Perry, Chris Garner, Penny Hardaway, Daryl Wilson, Tyrone Washington and Lorenzen Wright also played. It was the best pickup game in town.

And so the fans came, first in pairs, then in dozens and, on some days, as many as 100 people would be in the gym watching pickup ball. Some actually took notes and then posted long narratives of the games on message boards, detailing who played well, who looked good, who didn't look so good. Some even called into radio talk shows to discuss a player's personality based on behavior in pickup games.

It was ridiculous in a lot of ways, and the U of M players, impressed as they were at the devotion of the fans, thought it humorous that people were actually putting stock in what happened in meaningless pickup games.

There was, however, reason for some excitement. The fans got to see newcomers like Chris Massie, the massive power forward who punished some of the pro players with his strength and skills. They got to see that Dajuan Wagner's jumper had an almost classic look to it, that freshman Anthony Rice was better than advertised, that center Earl Barron had improved dramatically, that incoming point guard Antonio Burks was able to rocket up and down the court and play rugged defense.

The fans began formulating starting lineups based on the games, began wondering how far the Tigers could go in the postseason.

One thing about pickup ball, though. Games go to eight, by ones. Everyone gets to play significant minutes. If your best buddy is running at guard, you probably get the ball a lot. If you charge into the lane leading with your

shoulder, nobody steps in for a charge.

U of M coach John Calipari knows all this, however, and he must realize the risks of heightened expectations based on pickup games, even ones with some structure and a whole host of big men.

"We have eight guys who all could start," Calipari said. "That's when I come back to, 'Are you willing to step back so this team can go huge, instead of scoring 17 a game score 13?' That's going to be the hardest part. It's going to be the toughest challenge I have in my coaching career."

How about that? Remember, Calipari got to spend time coaching the New Jersey Nets.

Yes, the Tigers have more guarantee games than usual on the schedule, but these are real opponents. The pickup games are over, Tiger fans. All that talent must find a way to coalesce. The sum needs to be better than the parts.

Last season, with five returning starters on a team that had won six games in a row to finish the season, the Tigers struggled early and only made the NIT. Then they made a nice run to Madison Square Garden and eventually finished third.

This team's schedule is more gentle, so a big early stumble is not likely, and hence should not derail what can be a conference championship team. The key is building chemistry early so momentum can be built late.

This team will unquestionably be built around a freshman, Wagner, even with a senior, Kelly Wise, who is considered one of the five best players in his league. Wagner averaged more than 40 points a game in high school and his skills will translate just fine to the college game. He is very strong, very explosive and very grounded in the fundamentals of the game.

But he is one of six newcomers on the roster, many of whom will play serious minutes. Most likely, the backcourt will consist of Wagner and Burks, neither of whom has had to play a Division I game, neither of whom has tasted 40 minutes of Division I intensity.

It won't be easy, but it could be spectacular.

"If you say to everyone on the team, 'Do you want to win a national championship, compete for the Final Four?' Yes," Calipari said. "Are you willing to give up three or four points, are you willing to give up three or four minutes, are you willing to come off the bench versus starting?' Now it's, 'Whoaaaaa.' Different question."

There are, actually, lots of questions this team must answer. It will resemble a team more in the Calipari mold. How quickly he can bring the squad together, and place everyone in their rightful roles, will determine this team's ultimate success.

2001-2002 SCHEDULE

Nov.	13	#Wofford
	18	Northwestern State
	24	Southeastern Louisiana
	28	Christian Brothers
Dec.	1	Eastern Kentucky
	7	@Ole Miss
	15	Tennessee
	20	@Temple
	22	Austin Peay
	28	Tennessee-Martin
Jan.	2	Arkansas
	5	Southern Miss
	12	@Tulane
	15	South Florida
	18	@Southern Miss
	23	UAB
	26	@Houston
	30	Louisville
Feb.	2	TCU
	4	Tulane
	8	@UAB
	13	@Charlotte
	16	Houston
	20	@South Florida
	23	DePaul
March	3	@Cincinnati
	6-9	##C-USA Tournament

@Road Games
#Guardians Classic (if Memphis wins, it will play on Nov. 14 against either Sacramento State or Old Dominion; semifinals and final are Nov. 20-21 at Kemper Arena, Kansas City, MO)
##Firstar Center, Cincinnati, OH

STARTERS NOT RETURNING

PG-SHYRONE CHATMAN (6-4, 209, 9.2 ppg, 3.1 rpg, 4.6 apg, 30.1 minutes, .413 FG, .753 FT, .406 3PT) All Shyrone Chatman did was save John Calipari's first season as head coach at the University of Memphis. Without him, an early disaster would have become much worse. Without him, there would have been no battle for the conference title, no hope for an NCAA Tournament bid, no eventual NIT bid, no run to Madison Square Garden.

Chatman entered his senior season having averaged 3.9 points and 1.7 assists over three previous seasons at Memphis. He had started the final six games of the 1999-2000 season, at his natural position, shooting guard, and he began last season as a shooting guard and backup point guard.

Then, the U of M began last season going 2-5 against a schedule that included five Top 25 teams in the first seven games. Then, starting point guard Courtney Trask (see below), a C-USA All-Freshman team member the year before, was suspended for academic misconduct, along with small forward John Grice.

With the season slipping away, Chatman stepped in and became a leader. More than that, he became a producer, a playmaker, a defensive stopper, a crowd favorite. Because Chatman played so seldom in the first four games, his true stats come from Conference USA play (11.0 ppg, 2.8 rpg, 5.6 apg (2.9 tpg), .355 3PT, .758 FT).

SF-SHANNON FORMAN (6-5, 9.8 ppg, 4.4 rpg, 2.1 apg, 29.6 minutes, .453 FG, .676 FT, .355 3PT). Another one of four seniors who made real contributions last season, it took Forman until the fourth game of the season to finally prove to Calipari he was the team's small forward. Calipari probably cost the Tigers a few wins because of his early allegiance to Grice, playing him over Forman in many crucial situations because he knew that Grice's athleticism and shooting made him potentially very valuable to the team.

Calipari had actually begun his coaching stint at Memphis by saying, repeatedly, that the team desperately needed a small forward. That was in the face of Forman being the only returning player who had started every game the prior season, in the face of solid stats that got much better as his junior season progressed.

Forman was the team's second leading scorer in conference games, at 11.1 points per game. He was the defensive stopper on the wing, the toughest player on the roster and he did not mind doing dirty work. His value to the team was best personified in the NIT semifinal loss to Tulsa, when he single-handedly brought the Tigers back to life they went down 20 in the second half.

The deficit would be cut to four after Forman's energy and will sparked his teammates, though Memphis did eventually lose.

OTHERS NOT RETURNING

PG-COURTNEY TRASK (6-3, 4.9 ppg, 2.7 rpg, 2.3 apg, 20.1 minutes, .318 FG, .731 FT, .275 3PT). This is Calipari's take on Trask's decision to leave the program two weeks after the fall semester began to transfer to LSU: We want guys willing to compete and, besides, we won without him and we will win again.

Make no mistake, Calipari was disappointed to see him leave. Trask was the only experienced point guard on the roster and one of two guards with any kind of Division I experience. Again, he was not an NBA prospect like some others, but is well suited to the college game. He is a fine three-point shooter, has a strong handle and good understanding of the game.

Because of his outside shooting, he would have started at point guard for most of the season.

Trask did not want to go into full detail about the reasons for his leaving, but it was clear he was no longer happy in Memphis. He tried. He stayed for the summer, he went through two weeks of tough workouts and, in his final workout, even brought his teammates back to center court for one of those unity chants.

SG-MARCUS MOODY (6-5, 10.1 ppg, 2.1 rpg, 2.2 apg, 24.0 minutes, .414 FG, .627 FT, .355 3PT) The roller coaster ride that was Marcus Moody's career at Memphis is over.

Moody, you may recall, had a magical night at Oklahoma as a freshman, when he scored 41 points and set all kinds of Memphis freshman scoring records. Some say it was the worst thing to happen to Moody's long-term prospects, but those people are wrong. Moody would have been a streaky shooter his entire career if he

had scored two points that night. It would have taken a coach as stubborn as Calipari to get Moody going defensively if he had not played that night. And even if he had stayed home and watched that game on TV, Moody still would have finished his college career without having taken one charge.

But Moody, for his faults, made his hometown program better for playing four years. He finished his career with 1,206 points, putting him 19th on the all-time U of M scoring list. He also finished with 163 three-pointers to become the all-time leading three-point shooter in Tiger history.

Moody and Calipari never clicked. Moody and his father felt he deserved a spot in the starting lineup, and Calipari disagreed. So Moody quit, just before a crucial two-game road trip to Arkansas and to Tennessee (Memphis lost both games).

He would rejoin the team, however, and finish out his season to a huge ovation on Senior Night. A Memphis native who seems to know everyone in the city, it was the right way for Moody to finish his career.

PF-SHAMEL JONES (6-9, 5.8 ppg, 3.7 rpg, 1.0 apg, 16.6 minutes, .531 FG, .712 FT). Jones served as Memphis' tough guy last year, an inside enforcer willing to quarrel with anyone who wanted to start playing rough against the Tigers. Jones began his career at Georgetown, transferred to Memphis and started playing small forward. By his senior season, it was clear that although he had some perimeter skills, he was better utilized inside. He was really more of a reserve center for the Tigers last season.

Jones showed his true value in the postseason, when he averaged 9.2 points, 5.4 rebounds and blocked 13 shots in seven games. Jones bought into Calipari's preaching about effort and toughness, and played the best game of his career in a narrow home loss to Cincinnati. Jones had 17 points, 10 rebounds and three assists in that game, and the fact that those kinds of occasional numbers earned him only a reserve role says something about Memphis' frontcourt strength.

Jones can be replaced, but someone has to embrace the role he accepted as team toughman.

PF-PARIS LONDON (6-8, 3.9 ppg, 2.5 rpg, 0.7 apg, 10.4 minutes, .378 FG, .773 FT). It looked as if Paris London had finally broken through. He dropped 30-plus pounds in the off-season. For the first time in his career, he scored in double figures in three straight games: 11 at Tennessee, 15 versus Ole Miss and 15 versus Arkansas State. Even, after an ankle injury, he had a 12-point, four-rebound night against Houston.

But London was never able to secure a full-time spot on the floor under Calipari, and he missed the entire NIT run because of an inner-ear problem.

In the summer, he finally left the team for good, announcing he was transferring from Memphis to Arkansas State, where he will have one year of eligibility after sitting out this season.

London cited the need for a change of scenery after a disappointing career at Memphis that included three different head coaches.

PROJECTED STARTERS

PG-ANTONIO BURKS (5-10, 185, SO, #10, 14.2 ppg, 4.2 rpg, 3.6 apg, 3.9 spg at Hiwassee [Tenn.] College in 1999-2000 and Booker T. Washington HS/Memphis, Tenn.). Burks is a jet. That's all you need to know about the Tigers' probable starting point guard.

In a summer-league game with other college and pro players, Burks scored 55 points. Asked how he did it, Burks replied, "Basically, I just kept outrunning everybody."

In pickup games, Burks stayed with speedy NBA players like Chris Garner, Elliot Perry and Jason Williams. He has added strength since leaving high school as a quick but scrawny point guard, and now loves bodying up opposing point guards on both ends of the floor.

Burks won't see many point guards quicker than him, but he will see many with more experience. His challenge, with Courtney Trask no longer on the team, is to learn Calipari's system and earn the faith of his teammates.

"He's got size, but also speed and quickness," Calipari said. "Now the key is, will he be able to use that for his teammates. You cannot drive in like you are playing in the summer league and there are 6-1 guys in there. When there are five guys back and two of them are 6-10, you are just not driving in.

"I'm telling him, if the floor is open, two or three men

are back, make a play because your speed and quickness will take over. If there are five guys back there, you have to get us started in our offense."

Burks is a Memphis native who signed with Liberty out of high school but never had a chance of qualifying academically. After a nice freshman season in junior college, his coach left the program and, instead of following, Burks chose to come home. He showed up at the U of M and asked Calipari and his staff if he could join the team, informing them he had enrolled and was paying his own way.

Burks could not join the team until he had completed two semesters at Memphis. He did spend a lot of time around the practice facility, and Calipari and staff did everything they legally could to make him feel like a part of the program.

Burks is still technically a walk-on, though he will receive a scholarship by next season. He comes from a tough part of Memphis, but fans will love his endearing personality and tough-minded play.

The questions Burks must answer are the following: 1) Can he consistently knock down open jumpers, because Dajuan Wagner and the frontcourt will create plenty? 2) Because he has never played at this level, does he know what it means to play hard every second he is on the floor and never take off a possession? 3) Can he learn Calipari's system and make it go from the point guard spot?

"It'll be hard for Antonio if he is open and cannot make shots," Calipari said. "Because he is going to be open."

SG-DAJUAN WAGNER (6-1, 197, FR, 42.5 ppg at Camden High/Camden, N.J.). If you want to irritate John Calipari, then suggest that Dajuan Wagner was merely the fourth-best high school player in America last season, behind the likes of Kwame Brown, Eddy Curry and Tyson Chandler.

Calipari's scoffs at the notion, and points to the Atlanta Tipoff Club's Naismith Award for male prep player of the year.

"There were some great big guys but when you talk about playing basketball, he had the best skills ... handling skills, shooting skills and passing skills," Calipari said.

Wagner is a genuine basketball prodigy, and many people were stunned when he did not enter the NBA draft. A local celebrity in Camden since he was a sixth-grader, Wagner has a mastery of the sport at 18 that many current pros will never have.

He is a commanding ball handler. He is fearless in attacking the basket, and has a defensive back's body, enabling him to finish no matter how hard the contact. His first step is devastating, his second step is conclusive. He can pull from 30 feet if you give him room, and his jump shot has developed each year.

He is refined and is ready for the college game.

"The thing that you see most that people would have an impression because he was so highly thought of," Calipari said. "No. 1, that he would come in with an arrogance that no one could deal with, and that is so far from the truth. He's very receptive to the weight room and very receptive to conditioning. And his teammates know he will be a good teammate."

Wagner set a New Jersey record by scoring 3,462 career points, and, in becoming a McDonald's All-American, he joined his father, Milt, as the first father-son duo to accomplish the honor.

Wagner and Calipari met when the coach was an assistant under Larry Brown with the Philadelphia 76ers. Calipari began going to Camden games and, because Wagner came to many 76ers games, the two of them gained a rapport.

By the time Calipari agreed to become Memphis' coach, Wagner had all but pledged to follow the coach wherever he ended up in college.

Even with that, Calipari took no chances. He signed Wagner's best friend, Camden forward Arthur Barclay, while Wagner was still a junior. He hired Milt Wagner and made him an administrative assistant on his staff. At the end of Wagner's junior year, he committed.

Wagner signed, he turned down the NBA and he arrived in time to take a summer class at Memphis.

Wagner does have weaknesses. When Larry Brown was in town for a few days in late summer, he preached to Wagner about defense and consistent effort. Calipari believes Wagner has only scratched the surface of his potential, which is saying something for a player who scored 50 or more points in nine games as a senior (including 100 in one game).

"The greatest thing in all this is that as he has begun to condition, he has never really had his heart rate where it needs to be," Calipari said. "Which means it's scary when he gets his heart to 18 vs. 160, after conditioning, this all may be to another level."

Calipari prefers to use Wagner as a shooting guard, but Trask's departure means Wagner must play some at the point (though he'll be more of a lead guard from the spot, looking to score first). After watching Brown steer Iverson to success as an undersized two, Calipari believes Wagner can do similar things from the position.

There are some differences. Iverson is quicker. Wagner is much, much stronger (think Ronnie Lott). Wagner is a better shooter right now than Iverson was at the same age, and is more in control on the court.

"He scores the ball," Calipari said. "And you are going to cheat your team and cheat him if you put him at point and say, 'OK, run the club.' What he does naturally and he's done his whole life is score the ball. I think you put him at the position he is most comfortable with. Can he play point? Absolutely. He can handle the ball well enough. He understands the game, he reacts to the game.

"He can do that, and he can do that at the next level, but you are going to take away the thing he does best, which is score the ball."

Calipari is realistically hoping to keep Wagner for two seasons, though he is prepared to get only one from him. With Yao Ming probably entered in the draft and Western Kentucky's Chris Marcus possibly becoming a No. 1 caliber pick, there is hope. Jason Williams of Duke presumably will be the first point guard chosen, and Illinois guard Frank Williams would be a consideration, too.

SF-SCOOTER McFADGON (6-5, 190, SO, #3, 9.3 ppg, 3.3 rpg, 1.3 apg, 24.6 minutes, .398 FG, .358 3PT, .775 FT, Raleigh-Egypt HS/Memphis, Tenn.). Nobody surprised Calipari more than Scooter McFadgon. The first time Calipari saw him play, in a loss at the Tennessee state high school tournament, he wondered if McFadgon could play at a high enough level.

It took two practices to make Calipari realize he had underestimated McFadgon, who had signed with the previous Tiger staff. McFadgon became a full-time starter and was probably the most clutch player on the team.

In Memphis' first win of the season, McFadgon hit the game-winner, a little putback to beat Miami (Ohio). He drained a late three-pointer and then hit the game-winner in the final minute of a win at DePaul. He forced overtime with a three-pointer in the final minute of regulation against Saint Louis, and allowed Memphis to steal a win at UAB with another put-back late in the game.

Memphis' bid to win a Conference USA title died when McFadgon left halftime of the Southern Miss game with a high-ankle sprain. Remarkably, he came back to play in the Conference USA Tournament a week later, scoring 17 gutsy points in a loss to Cincinnati.

McFadgon averaged 10.8 points and 4.1 rebounds in league play, and was voted to the Conference USA All-Freshman squad. He enters this season as the only proven three-point shooter on the team. McFadgon's jump shot is just a tad awkward, though it is looking smoother every time he lets fly. Calipari likes to say McFadgon plays old-school basketball, and often compares him to Dave Debuscherre with his running scoop shots and one-handed leans.

Most likely, McFadgon will play small forward, though shooting guard is his more natural position.

"He can play the three; we are not in the NBA," Calipari said. "Most threes we play will be his size or smaller."

McFadgon was the one player on Memphis' team last season willing to put the ball on the floor and attack the basket, even if he didn't have a great breakdown move. His overall shooting percentage suffered some as a result, but he always seemed to make shots when they were needed the most.

"Scooter is going to find the game is easier," Calipari said. "As a freshman, we put him in positions where how many times did he have an open shot? He had to go create one because we had no one to break down on the dribble. We had to throw the ball to the post every single play last year, and, a guy like Scooter, that's an issue. Now, we get a breakdown dribbler, Scooter's man helps, he's getting open shots."

PF-KELLY WISE (6-10, 217, SR, #45, 15.3 ppg, 10.1 rpg, 1.9 apg, 1.6 bpg, 1.2 spg, 30.8 minutes, .481 FG, .504 FT, .000 3PT, Choctawhatchee HS/Ft. Walton Beach, Fla.). Wise seriously considered turning pro. Coming back was the right decision.

Now is his chance to really make some money, though Wise cannot contract the senioritis that sometimes inflicts players looking to be drafted very high. That means using only the refined small forward skills he has and not trying to force a game he does not yet master.

The reason he is a prospect has to do with his speed, quickness, soft hands and nose for the basketball. Because he has never shown any commitment to putting on extra weight and strength, Wise has made the decision for NBA teams: He will play small forward on the next level.

In college, however, he is a perfect power forward. Despite his size, he is very strong in the post and getting better each year and taking contact and making shots. At times last season, the Tigers simply went to Wise time after time to win games.

"He was tremendous for us last year," Calipari said. "There were times when he absolutely carried the team, where we could throw it to the post and he would score. But he was a little streaky. I expect this year coming back he will be more consistent."

Wise led the league last season with 17 double-doubles, and he scored in double-figures in all but three games.

His most impressive performance last season came against South Florida in Tampa, when he scored a season-high 24 points on 9-of-12 shooting. His 23-point, seven-rebound, five-block performance in the NIT consolation game against Detroit had to win him a few fans among NBA scouts.

Wise had, Calipari said, a "spotty" off-season, though he has always seemed to come back better and more poised each season at Memphis. Wise does play with a quiet arrogance; his game would benefit from a little more emotion, and, while that is a quibble, he does have a responsibility, as a senior, to be the team's leader.

Twice last season, he grabbed 21 rebounds in a game, first at Tennessee and then two weeks later at Miami; both times he set an arena record for a college player. It seems possible that, with breakdown dribblers in the backcourt this season, Wise could challenge for the national lead in rebounding all next season; he rarely got easy put-backs last year because defenses did not need to collapse on penetrating guards.

Calipari said he will allow Wise to play some small forward this year, though his ball handling and instincts do not make him a great fit at the position. His shot seems to have improved somewhat, though he must become a better free throw shooter after barely converting half of his attempts last season.

"He can play that position if he has the skills," Calipari said. "He can guard it, but, skill wise, can he step out on the floor and play the position? We have to wait to see that."

C-EARL BARRON (6-11, 240, JR, #30, 8.3 ppg, 4.7 rpg, 0.4 apg, 1.3 bpg, 19.2 minutes, .541 FG, .583FT, Clarksdale HS/Clarksdale, Miss.). Tiger fans are hoping Earl's excellent summer yields a most dominating winter.

Upon earning a surprise invite to USA Basketball's junior men's trials, Barron ran and blocked shots and used his little canny post moves to make the finalist list of 16.

When he returned to Memphis from Colorado, he was a different player. Barron always had the skills and even the athleticism (for a 7-footer—and Calipari swears he's all of it—Barron can jump rope like a welterweight and he played high school tennis), but he has always lacked the arrogance of a great player. As one former U of M player put it while watching the Tigers run pickup games before the trials: "If Earl was a dawg, he'd be a lottery pick."

Meaning, if Barron showed the same disdain for opponents as Wise or Wagner, he could dominate.

When he returned this summer, Barron began showing disdain. Arrogance, even. He talked back to the big, beefy interior players who once muscled him around. With 245 pounds packed onto his once scrawny frame (Barron was 195 when he signed with Memphis), Barron pushed back. He shot three-pointers like a young Arvydas Sabonis. And he dunked. Did he ever dunk.

Earl the Meek had turned into Earl the Merciless.

That should be a scary thought for opponents.

A clue to why Barron is so good inside comes when you watch him perform the old Mikan drill. He is nimble off either foot and has dexterity with both hands. He is best on the right block, where the only way to stop him is to literally shove him either as he is catching the ball or shooting it.

Calipari's biggest frustration last season was Barron's inability to hold onto passes at times. Cincinnati completely neutralized Barron by smashing him whenever the ball came to his hands. He often had trouble holding the ball while on the move.

Playing against a high level of competition all summer—in pickup games and for the World University Games team—Barron no longer seemed to have that trouble.

Defensively, he is a very good shot blocker who is also probably the best on the team at drawing charges.

"He is a quietly driven player," Calipari said. "The guys that are driven and have played for me in the past, they really take it to another level. Now you are looking at one of the better shooters. That's because he goes into the gym and works on it. Now he's gaining confidence, 'Hey, I can go make these teams and do other things.' "

KEY RESERVES

PF-CHRIS MASSIE (6-8, 260, JR, 18.0 ppg, 12.0 rpg, Oxnard College/Oxnard, Calif. and Arcola, Texas). When Calipari signed Massie, he invoked one name: Anthony Mason.

It is a very good way to describe Massie and his game. He is not quite to Mason's level, but his game is very similar. His body is cut out of stone. His arms are long and huge. His legs are like tree trunks. And he moves around the court with the agility and confidence of a small forward.

Massie also has nice touch and confidence on his three ball and doesn't mind putting it on the floor to go by his man. That'll be OK so long as he doesn't get carried away with roaming the perimeter.

"What he does around the basket, he's just a monster," Calipari said. "You've gotta foul him. My question now is that he's got to be shooting a lot of free throws, because it'll be Shaq attack. … You'll find out, he's able to shoot it, able to make threes, but his game is get it to him close to the basket and he's going to score. He's powerful."

Massie, who is 25, has an interesting story. He did not play high school basketball while growing up in Arcola, Texas. After high school, he worked as an electrician's apprentice for a company in Houston, installing fixtures and outlets. He played pickup games at a local gym, where a friend of a friend of a junior-college coach saw him playing and asked if he would be interested in college ball.

Massie, who earned his GED, said he was, and wound up at Oxnard. He had some minor troubles there, including last winter when he failed to show up when the second semester began, but surprised a lot of people by finishing school and by not entering the NBA draft.

Massie admits he has never played in a system that demands maximum effort at all times, and he trails the big men on that count. Calipari will love the arrogance Massie brings to the court, and opposing big men will likely react to the way he flat muscles and challenges them.

Massie could well start. He's certainly one of the five best players on the team, but this is not a draft. This is a team. He will start some this season, but, for now, we stick with Barron inside because of his experience.

SG-ANTHONY RICE (6-4, 185, FR, North Clayton HS/North Clayton, Ga.). Rice was going to play no matter what, but Trask's departure means his minutes will increase. The Tigers will need his shooting and playmaking skills.

Rice has not yet stopped surprising the Memphis coaching staff. He won them with a devastating shooting performance at a camp the summer before his senior season, then went to the Nike camp and ditched the shooting act to prove he could be a playmaker. His senior season in high school was underrated by too many recruiting observers.

When he arrived for the summer in Memphis, flamboyant afro setting him apart, Rice took on the likes of Cedric Henderson and Penny Hardaway and held his own. He makes shots, and he is athletic enough to slice into a defense to create his own shot or one for a teammate.

He is very similar to McFadgon, maybe a little more advanced offensively than McFadgon was at the same stage and a little less advanced defensively. Still, his long arms and athleticism will make him a great defender.

"I'm not saying he is this good, but he reminded me of Clyde Drexler," Calipari said. "Really long, long muscles, fairly good skills with the ball, explosive, tough, hard-nosed and will go at you. I don't like soft guys, and he has a toughness to him."

C-MODIBO DIARRA (6-10, 235, SO, #43, 2.7 ppg, 2.6 rpg, 0.2 apg, 9.8 minutes, .508 FG, .548 FT, .000

3PT, Notre Dame Prep/Fitchburg, Mass. and Mali in West Africa). Diarra never quite became what Tiger coaches hoped for as a freshman, though that did not decrease their long-term enthusiasm for the genial big guy.

Diarra just clearly needs more everyday work in the gym against competition. Calipari told Diarra he should play in Memphis's up-and-down summer league because he wants Diarra to become quicker to the ball and more instinctive on the court.

Renowned as a defensive prodigy in high school, Diarra never quite became the dominating defender last season. He always seemed one step too late getting to the spot he needed to occupy. Daily battles with the likes of Barron, Massie and Wise should continue his improvement.

"He just hadn't played that long," Calipari said. "He wants to get good, he wants to get better. Feel for the game happens over a period of time."

It is possible that the Tigers could red-shirt either Diarra or freshman big man Duane Erwin because of all the frontcourt strength. Calipari is hoping Diarra can show rapid progress in the preseason; with his size and strength, he could be a valuable reserve.

Diarra actually started 24 games last season, but he usually came out of the game and never returned. His best games came against truly inferior competition, but he did show, in those performances, he has a lot of competitive will about him.

"He's got ice water in his veins," Calipari said. "He's tough to the ball. He's got to work on quickness to the ball more than anything."

PF-DUANE ERWIN (6-9, 220, FR, 14.0 ppg, 11.0 rpg, 7.0 bpg, Lee HS/Huntsville, Ala.). Diarra and Erwin would play lots of minutes for lots of teams in Conference USA, but that is not necessarily going to be the case with the Tigers. At least not this season.

"When you add Duane and Dibo, it becomes, are we playing a bigger lineup?" Calipari said. "If we play a bigger lineup, those two will have minutes there. And if we play a smaller lineup, they may have less minutes."

As for Erwin, Calipari loves his potential. Erwin almost signed with UAB last season, and he would be a very valuable member of that team, serving as the inside enforcer the Blazers need.

He decided to come to Memphis in large part because he felt his chances of making the NBA were better under Calipari and against serious competition every day.

Erwin put on 20 pounds while in Memphis for the summer, and he, too, played in those daily pickup games against professionals. Somewhat timid at first, Erwin was blocking shots and tracking down every rebound in sight by the end of the summer.

He owns a nice little jumper out to 17 feet, and handles it very well for someone his size. Like Wise, Erwin is probably a small forward down the road, and, unlike Wise, he seems willing to put in the off-season work necessary to make the transformation.

For Erwin and Diarra, this season will be about getting ready for next season. And the one after that.

"This is about three years from now, not this year," Calipari said. "This is a process for them. Where are these two? Do they have an opportunity to keep playing [beyond college]? That's what they have to keep in mind. They are going against guys every day who will in all likelihood play in the NBA. Are you going to get better? Absolutely. And then when they leave, it's you."

PG-NATHANIEL ROOT (5-11, 170, JR, #4, 2.1 ppg, 0.6 rpg, 1.1 apg, 5.7 minutes, .303 FG, .667 FG, .296 3PT, Adamsville HS/Adamsville, Tenn.). A former walk-on who was awarded a scholarship after the season, Root could see more minutes, especially if anything happens to Burks or if he is less effective than Tiger coaches hope.

There are reasons Root had to walk on. His three-point shot is streaky at best, though it's getting better. He is not swift of foot, nor much of a leaper. He is not very good with his left hand.

Still, he almost always makes good decisions. He runs the team with a sense of command. He is not afraid to get into an opponent on defense, and is not afraid to take important shots.

His greatest value is the energy and enthusiasm he brings to practice. He challenges his teammates and could care less if he seems corny and goofy while exhorting teammates to increase their own energy and enthusiasm.

In the Ole Miss game last season, it was actually Root who got the Tigers back into the game in the first half, going at it with little Jason Harrison and hitting a shot near the end of the half that drew a roar from the crowd.

Though he will still be a seldom-played reserve, Root has proven he can stand the pressure of big games and tough opponents. If needed, he can be called upon.

OTHER RETURNEES

SF-JOHN GRICE (6-6, 205, SR, #20, 4.0 ppg, 1.6 rpg, 0.7 apg, 14.2 minutes, .207 FG, .833 FT, .097 3PT, Southwest Tennessee CC and Central HS/Memphis, Tenn.). Grice is ineligible to play the first semester and has a lot of work to do to gain eligibility for the second semester. The Tigers are preparing as if Grice will have to sit out this season.

Grice's academic difficulties are in part because of his involvement in academic misconduct that also affected Courtney Trask.

Grice was a heralded recruit, a local junior-college all-American who turned down Kentucky and Ole Miss to sign with Calipari. And Calipari honestly thought Grice could be his best player.

It was clear from the start of practice that Grice was going to struggle to conform to Calipari's dictates. Grice loves to be flashy, loves to look smooth, loves to work on crazy shots in practice rather than the ones that win games.

He has a world of talent and is very pleasant to be around but just never seemed to find a comfort level last season. He barely played after missing 16 games because of suspension.

When he did play early, and Calipari deserves credit for more than giving Grice a chance to prove himself, he was ineffective to the point of being a disservice to the team. He was 3-of-31 from three-point range, 12-of-58 overall and he grabbed more than two rebounds on only one occasion.

"He struggled when he had to play within a structure," Calipari said. "He struggled on what was a good shot and what was not. He struggled on when he should take his man and when not."

"People see him play in the summers and say, 'Boy, he is really good.' Think about it. He's 6-6, can guard a point guard, can dunk the ball, can shoot the hell out of it, handles it and passes it OK but he's a little sloppy with the ball. But when you look at it, he should be performing better than he is performing. He has the tools. ... I haven't been able to push the buttons and figure it out."

OTHER NEWCOMERS

PF-ARTHUR BARCLAY (6-8, 222 lbs., SO, 24.0 ppg, 17.8 rpg, 4.0 bpg in 1999-2000 at Camden HS/Camden, N.J.). Barclay's signing with Memphis ensured that Wagner would also be coming, a year later, but Calipari believes he found a glue type of player in the scrappy power forward.

Barclay is a true blue-collar player, although he has worked enough to show some small forward skills. His role on this team, however, will be to go in, set screens, get loose balls and rebounds and inflict some punishment on defense.

Barclay has a charismatic personality and could emerge as a leader in his career at Memphis, even if he never gets huge playing time.

Though Calipari won't come out and say it, he is also hoping Barclay's presence will be a factor when Wagner has to make a decision about the NBA next spring. Barclay and Wagner are really like brothers, having lived together in Camden throughout high school.

Barclay was a non-qualifier who enrolled in school last season but could not be an official part of the team. Like Burks, he hung around the Larry O. Finch Center and knows what Calipari's system is about and can counsel Wagner on what to expect.

Knee surgery in the off-season corrected persistent problems Barclay had since a freshman in high school, and he says he feels better than he ever has about his game.

"The players tell me he is rebounding the ball [in pickup games]," Calipari said. "That's what he does. If you get a guy that will go in and rebound, run the floor and defend, there is always a spot for that."

QUESTIONS

Point the way? Burks appears to have all the tools of a successful point guard, but he has no experience in Division I and did not play or practice with a team at all last season. When a player doesn't play in meaningful games for a year, the Memphis hoops culture actually has a tendency to completely exaggerate that player's potential value. Burks could be very good, but Wagner could also wind up spending more time at the point than Calipari would like.

Who's the man? OK, that's easily answered; Wagner is the man. But who else? Do you start Massie over Barron? Do you dare bench Massie, a 25-year-old with NBA aspirations? Do you limit Wise's exposure at small forward, the position he knows he must play on the next level? Do you make sure McFadgon gets enough touches? It will be an interesting preseason, to say the least.

Is he really that good? Wagner has yet to let anyone down, despite the enormous expectations always heaped upon him. But you have to wonder if, maybe, too much is being expected of a true freshman. All indications are that Wagner is prepared for the leap to Division I, but freshman success is never, ever a sure thing.

ANSWERS

Dajuan! Wagner is a prodigious scorer who values winning above all else. He has the ability to dazzle the city of Memphis and become one of college basketball's dominant players.

Wise man! No, Wise did not have a good off-season. And, yes, the scenario actually exists whereby he spends more time on the bench. This team does not need Wise so much for survival anymore, but it does need him to thrive. Throughout his career, he has exceeded expectations for the season, and there is no reason to believe he will be any less of a gamer than he has always been.

Balance! Once Memphis got rolling under Calipari, you could just about guarantee five players scoring in double figures. In fact, five players averaged in double figures in C-USA games last season. When Calipari's teams play at their best, there is a lot of sharing and spreading of wealth. If the many talented players on this team buy into that concept, watch out come March.

MEMPHIS 2000-2001 RESULTS

Temple (L)	62-67
#Miami (Ohio)	60-59
#Stanford (L)	60-83
#Utah (L)	58-61
Tennessee-Martin	81-49
@Arkansas (L)	68-74
@Tennessee (L)	76-86
Mississippi (L)	56-64
Arkansas State	83-60
Christian Brothers	98-54
@Miami (L)	57-66
Southern Miss (L)	67-75
Kansas State	81-58
Howard	112-42
@Houston	86-78
@DePaul	72-68
St. Louis	72-63
Houston	72-68
@Tulane	91-69
@UAB	76-73
Marquette (L)	65-71
@South Florida	100-89
Tulane	91-64
Cincinnati (L)	65-66
@Charlotte (L)	76-83
UAB	86-69
South Florida	79-61
@Southern Miss (L)	55-74
@Louisville (L)	56-65
##Marquette	71-64
##Cincinnati (L)	79-89
###Utah	71-62
###Texas-El Paso	90-65
###New Mexico	81-63
###Tulsa (L)	64-72
###Detroit	86-71

#Puerto Rico Shootout, San Juan, PR
##Conference USA Tournament, Louisville, KY
###NIT

BLUE RIBBON ANALYSIS

BACKCOURT	A-
BENCH/DEPTH	A-
FRONTCOURT	A
INTANGIBLES	B

Here is Calipari, speaking in that Western Pennsylvania accent: "Agendas got to be thrown out."

There it is. That is the mission. This is not to suggest any of his players have agendas; it's just that they cannot develop as so many newcomers try to become integral parts of a whole that is right now only a vision.

In Wagner and Wise, the Tigers have two legitimate C-USA Player-of-the-Year caliber players. In Barron and Massie, they have two big men who could start for anyone in the country. Those are the four players upon whom the foundation must be built. Calipari is talking about seriously installing a zone for the first time in his career, in large part because of unbalanced lineups that may result from the several big men and true guards. There really aren't many swingmen, and DePaul coach Pat Kennedy can tell Calipari how that can hurt a team. That is one area that teams can attack, and it is why Calipari will use some zone.

Calipari will not come right out and say it, but much of his preseason work was geared toward getting Wagner ready to play at this level. Defense. Effort. Attention to detail. Those are the things to which the national high school player of the year must accustom himself.

Ultimately, Calipari's teams are built on hard-nosed defense, rebounding and post presence. This team should have all of that, with the defense the biggest question mark of the three.

Everyone in the program—staff and players included—signed a document in the preseason devoting themselves to winning a national title. To Calipari, that means more than playing great basketball.

"My issue is, 'What are you willing to give up and sacrifice for us to be something special?' " Calipari said.

That is Calipari's challenge. There is abundant talent, and more on the way for this program. Last season's team made a nice run to the NIT Final Four. This team wants to make the real Final Four, but that would be a surprise on the order of Florida's march to Indianapolis in 2000.

Memphis will return to the NCAA Tournament for the first time since 1996, and the Tigers won't lose in the first round. This is a team that should have Final Four aspirations; it is just too young to expect anything more than the Sweet 16.

(Z.M.)

Stanford 15

LOCATION	Stanford, CA
CONFERENCE	Pac-10
LAST SEASON	31-3 (.912)
CONFERENCE RECORD	16-2 (1st)
STARTERS LOST/RETURNING	4/1
NICKNAME	Cardinal
COLORS	Cardinal & White
HOMECOURT	Maples Pavilion (7,391)
COACH Mike Montgomery (Long Beach State '68)	
RECORD AT SCHOOL	319-146 (15 years)
CAREER RECORD	473-223 (23 years)
ASSISTANTS	Tony Fuller (Pepperdine '83)
	Eric Reveno (Stanford '89)
	Russell Turner (Hampden-Sydney '92)
TEAM WINS (last 5 years)	22-30-26-27-31
RPI (last 5 years)	19-5-6-15-2
2000-01 FINISH Lost in NCAA West Regional final.	

COACH AND PROGRAM

It's safe to say coach Mike Montgomery never has suffered such huge personnel losses in any of his 23 seasons as a Division I head coach. Of course, he's never had so much talent to lose, either.

Four starters departed from a program that compiled a four-year record of 114-19 with three Pac-10 Conference titles and a trip to the 1998 Final Four. By historical standards, what the Cardinal has achieved since the mid-1990s is borderline science fiction.

Twins Jason and Jarron Collins, wing Ryan Mendez and point guard Michael McDonald arrived as freshmen that magical Final Four season and helped run Stanford's string of consecutive NCAA Tournament appearances to seven.

Before 1989, remember, Stanford hadn't been to the tournament once since 1942.

Stanford isn't exactly starting from scratch. Junior

guard Casey Jacobsen is an All-America selection, and Montgomery's recruiting has netted a higher level of player in recent years than ever before at the school.

Still, the Cardinal enters the season without four players who combined in their careers to score 2,637 points and grab 1,331 rebounds.

"There is a great deal of uncertainty as to who's capable of stepping up," Montgomery said. "We finished the last two years as the No. 1 team in the country and a No. 1 seed in the tournament. I don't expect that's going to happen this year."

It's a tribute to Montgomery's program that rivals will shed few tears over his personnel departures. Stanford won't be the premier team in the country, but it won't be anyone's victim, either.

"There's turnover in every program," Montgomery said. "We've got some young kids and we're going to have to give them an opportunity, let them develop and see what they can do.

"It's not a question of whether they're competitive. It's whether they can win close games, do those things that are intangible, that you just don't know about."

Stanford experienced similar losses from its starting lineup two years ago when the senior class of Tim Young, Arthur Lee, Pete Sauer and Kris Weems graduated. Those four had been the cornerstones for a team that was 99-28 over four years and, in 1999, won the school's first Pac-10 title.

With question marks and inexperience everywhere, the 2000 team merely improved on that with a 27-4 record and another Pac-10 crown.

Can Curtis Borchardt become Jason Collins? Will Justin Davis capably replace Jarron Collins? Will one of three point guard candidates step forward to fill the shoes of Michael McDonald?

Those are among the questions that loom regarding this club. Curiously, this Stanford team will depart from its recent tradition of strength and numbers up front. For a change, there is not great depth on the front line.

At the same time, Montgomery figures to rely more heavily on youngsters than in the past, including at point guard, where freshman Chris Hernandez will battle for a significant role.

Said Montgomery with his typical deadpan sarcasm, "I have concerns about every position on the floor ... the coaching staff, the media and the league."

2001-2002 SCHEDULE

Nov.	17	@New Mexico
	20	Southern Utah
	24	*Purdue
Dec.	1	**Texas
	15	Long Beach State
	18-19	#Stanford Invitational
	22	***BYU
	29	****Michigan State
Jan.	4	California
	6	@California
	10	@Oregon State
	12	@Oregon
	17	Washington State
	19	Washington
	24	@UCLA
	26	@Southern Cal
	31	Arizona State
Feb.	2	Arizona
	7	Oregon
	9	Oregon State
	14	@Washington
	16	@Washington State
	21	USC
	23	UCLA
	28	@Arizona
March	2	@Arizona State
	7-9	##Pac-10 Tournament

@Road Games
*Wooden Tradition, Indianapolis
**Children's Charity Classic, Chicago
***Las Vegas Shootout, Las Vegas
****Pete Newell Challenge, Oakland, CA
#Maples Pavilion (vs. Belmont, first round; also Portland, Santa Clara)
##Staples Center, Los Angeles

STARTERS NOT RETURNING

C-JASON COLLINS (7-0, 14.5 ppg, 7.8 rpg, 1.3 bpg, 26.3 minutes, .613 FG, .462 3PT, .784 FT). Collins

posed the Cardinal's primary off-season question: Would he elect to join twin brother Jarron in the NBA draft or return for another season? Technically, Collins probably was eligible for two more collegiate seasons. He spent his first two years at Stanford shelved by injury, and could have petitioned for a sixth year, had he so desired.

Collins made the decision to leave, and no one really expected otherwise, given that his health stabilized and his pro stock probably reached a peak. Still prevented by his troublesome knee from practicing on consecutive days, Collins nonetheless became a serious inside force for the Cardinal.

He was a first-team All-Pac-10 selection and a third-team All-America pick by the National Association of Basketball Coaches. Other honors included the Pete Newell NABC Big Man of the Year, and selection to the U.S. Basketball Writers Association All-District 9 team.

A Stanford co-captain, Collins also shared the team's MVP award. Remarkably efficient, Collins shot 50 percent or better in 30-of-34 games, finishing his career with a school-record .608 field-goal accuracy. He had eight double-doubles last season, and scored a career-high 33 points against Washington.

Said Montgomery, referring to both brothers, "The value of those two guys is going to be hard to evaluate because they were so steady. They gave you great size, they passed the ball, they just knew how to play."

PF-JARRON COLLINS (6-11, 12.8 ppg, 6.7 rpg, 28.3 minutes, .558 FG, .687 FT). Overshadowed a bit last season by his more physical brother, Jarron steadily developed during four productive, winning seasons. He wound up with 1,081 career points and 534 career rebounds in 129 games.

A first-team All-Pac-10 selection last season, Jarron was a finalist for the Naismith Player-of-the-Year award and a member of the 10-man John Wooden All-America team. He was MVP of the Cable Car Classic, scoring 25 points in the title-game victory over host Santa Clara. He had 22 points and nine rebounds in a key early-conference win at Arizona, and was an all-tournament pick at the Puerto Rico Shootout.

SF-RYAN MENDEZ (6-7, 11.4 ppg, 3.3 rpg, 2.2 apg, 28.1 minutes, .476 FG, .400 3PT, .931 FT). Mendez also finished his career among Stanford's all-time greats, totaling 1,032 points in 127 games. He enjoyed his finest season as a senior, starting all 34 games and serving as a team co-captain.

Mendez ranks third on Stanford's career list with 178 three-point baskets, hitting .420 from beyond the arc for his career. Gradually during his career he became more than merely a perimeter shooter, improving his passing, rebounding and overall floor play. He scored in double figures 19 times as a senior.

Mendez converted 94-of-101 free throws for a .931 mark that is second best all-time at Stanford and No. 3 on the Pac-10 list. He made 49 straight free throws to set a Pac-10 record, 46 of them in conference games, setting another record. Mendez's six straight free throws in the final 33 seconds at Oregon helped seal a 69-62 victory.

PG-MICHAEL MCDONALD (6-1, 8.0 ppg, 2.8 rpg, 4.9 apg, 27.0 minutes, .490 FG, .514 3PT, .724 FT). McDonald was as big a contributor as anyone to the Cardinal's success. A question mark entering his first year as the starting point guard his junior season, McDonald developed into a superb floor leader last year.

His assist-to-turnover ratio of plus-3.06 per game was the best in the Pac-10 and ranks as the second-best mark in school history, better than any assembled by his recent predecessors, Arthur Lee and Brevin Knight. He had five games where he had no turnovers and 12 others with just one.

A career .317 shooter from three-point range entering his senior season, McDonald converted a conference-best .514 last season, the third-best single-season mark in Pac-10 history. He scored 18 points against USC, all of them coming on six three-pointers, and had a career-high 19 points against San Francisco State.

McDonald earned honorable mention All-Pac-10 honors, and was the team's winner of the Howie Dallmar Coaches Award.

OTHERS NOT RETURNING

None.

PROJECTED STARTERS

PG-TONY GIOVACCHINI (6-2, 180 lbs., SR, #25, 2.0 ppg, 1.0 rpg, 2.0 apg, 12.3 minutes, .345 FG, .182

3PT, .600 FT, Judge Memorial HS/Salt Lake City, Utah). Giovacchini will get the first shot at winning the vacant point guard slot, and it's likely he'll be in the starting line-up for the opening of the season. He is steady and competent, knows the system, and he's a senior.

Giovacchini enhanced his position with a solid performance during the Cardinal's summer tour of Australia. He averaged 6.5 points, 3.8 rebounds and 2.0 assists in the five games, pleasing the coaching staff.

"Tony played very well," Montgomery said. "Of all the guys, Tony stepped up from a leadership standpoint. Typically, the seniors have done that."

Giovacchini is limited in that he's not extremely quick or athletic. Montgomery is aware of that, but prefers to dwell on Giovacchini's assets.

"Tony's tough, he's strong, he's got the experience, and he knows what his job is," Montgomery said. "We need him to have the confidence. But in pressure situations, we don't want to just hang him out there. Typically in the past, teams have kind of attacked him."

Giovacchini has played 88 career games, all of them off the bench. He had a career-high seven points against both Memphis and UNC-Greensboro, and had an eight-assist, zero-turnover effort against Cal.

SG-CASEY JACOBSEN (6-6, 210 lbs., JR, #23, 18.1 ppg, 4.0 rpg, 2.3 apg, 31.7 minutes, .508 FG, .472 3PT, .813 FT, Glendora HS/Glendora, Calif.). Jacobsen is the Cardinal's lone returning starter, but he's a terrific starting place. He was a consensus All-America selection as a sophomore, getting the nod from The Associated Press, The Sporting News, John Wooden and the U.S. Basketball Writers Association.

Jacobsen was the third-leading scorer in the Pac-10, but it's his willingness to take—and make—the big shots that separates him. He vaulted into the national spotlight when he scored 26 points and made the winning basket with 3.6 seconds left in a December win over Duke.

Jacobsen led the Cardinal in scoring 20 times, reaching double figures 33 times in 34 games. He scored a career-high 27 points against Cincinnati in an NCAA Tournament game, one of 14 games he notched at least 20 points.

A superb perimeter shooter, Jacobsen led Stanford with 84 three-pointers and was fourth in the nation at .472 from beyond the arc. He had 14 games with at least three three-point baskets.

Jacobsen augmented his game last year with an improved ability to put the ball on the floor and pull up for the medium-range shot. He also has worked hard to become a more effective passer and defender. And Montgomery believes Jacobsen's best days are ahead.

"I expect him to be better because he's got another year under his belt," Montgomery said. "His ability to make others better has continued to improve. He can draw lots of attention, and it's really important for him to draw that second or even third guy and find his teammates and make them better players."

Without Mendez and McDonald to draw defensive attention on the perimeter, Jacobsen is likely to see even more of the opposing defense's focus.

"Now, most certainly, they're going to force other players to prove their ability," Montgomery said. "He's going to have to be patient and be better. It's a challenge he'll relish."

Jacobsen announced before the end of last season he planned to return for his junior year, but he did give the topic some additional thought before the NBA draft last spring.

"It's very fashionable—that's what everybody is thinking,"

Montgomery said. "With the number of players going early, there aren't the seniors left. They've already been taken.

"I'm sure Casey had some thoughts about it. We had a conversation, and that was the end of it."

SF-JOSH CHILDRESS (6-7, 190 lbs., FR, #1, 24.0 ppg, 8.0 rpg, 5.0 apg, 3.0 bpg at Mayfair HS/Lakewood, Calif.). A McDonald's All-America selection, Childress ranks among the most coveted players Stanford has recruited.

Although Montgomery anticipates a training camp battle for the small forward spot, it will be surprising if Childress doesn't eventually earn the starting role.

"The adjustment's going to be the big key for him, because the college game is more physical," Montgomery said. "But he's certainly a very talented kid. He's got long arms, he's fairly explosive, can play above the rim. He's a bit of a glider in that he's slender, but that's deceptive because he's pretty quick off his feet.

"No question, Josh has to help us. He's capable of

putting up some numbers."

Childress had a 39-point, 22-rebound effort in a triple-overtime game against Long Beach Poly. He was an all-state selection and was voted MVP of Suburban League. As a junior, he averaged 22 points and seven rebounds, helping his team to a 27-3 record. He had a 40-point, 20-rebound game in just three quarters of play as an 11th grader.

His high school coach, Dave Breig, said of Childress, "Josh has the talent, the grades, the manners, the morals, the ethics. You really couldn't ask for more out of Josh. He's polite. Nothing gets to his head."

PF-JUSTIN DAVIS (6-8, 230 lbs., SO, #22, 3.9 ppg, 3.0 rpg, 11.6 minutes, .514 FG, .442 FT, St. Joseph-Notre Dame HS/Berkeley, Calif.). The Cardinal expects Davis this season to blossom into a physical and explosive presence at power forward. He red-shirted two years ago because of the team's glut of big men, then missed the first six games last season with a strained abdominal muscle and ankle sprain.

Those injuries, combined with plain rustiness, prevented Davis from showing his dynamic qualities on a consistent basis last season. But there were encouraging glimpses.

Davis had nine points and nine rebounds in 19 minutes against Fordham in a non-conference game, and had 10 rebounds, seven points, three steals and a block at Oregon. In a career-high 21 minutes, he had eight points, three rebounds and two blocked shots against UCLA.

Over his final 15 games, Davis made 61 percent of his shots from the floor.

Davis played with the team on its Australian summer trip, then had surgery to remove bone spurs from his ankle and clean out some floating cartilage. He was expected to be healthy in plenty of time for the start of practice.

"If he does what he can—rebound the ball, explode, get to the basket with his quickness—he'll give us a lot of help inside," Montgomery said. "He's hard to guard because he's so quick."

C-CURTIS BORCHARDT (7-0, 230 lbs., JR, #11, 6.4 ppg, 4.2 rpg, 1.1 bpg, 16.5 minutes, .534 FG, .429 3PT, .768 FT, Eastlake HS/Redmond, Wash.). Stanford fans are holding their breath that Borchardt's delicate right foot holds up this season. If it does, the Cardinal may be capable of another special season.

"We're not very big without him," Montgomery said. "He's a long, 7-foot kid who can block shots and he's got skills. He's just a good player."

Borchardt missed the final 14 games of last season and the last 11 as a freshman after sustaining separate stress fracture injuries in the foot. He had surgery last spring, with two screws implanted into the navicular bone to help stabilize the area.

"He's made great strides in every area," Montgomery said in early August. "Strength-wise, he's worked real hard on the weights to get his legs balanced up. He's always had one leg bigger than the other because he didn't use the one."

Borchardt did not play on the team's Australian summer tour, but began playing half-court games in August. Montgomery said the team expects him to be ready for the season.

"It's a matter of getting him in game shape and getting him some confidence," Montgomery said. "I don't think you can spend all your time worrying about things. I have to assume he's had all the bad luck he needs. We're banking on him having a normal junior year."

In just 37 career games, Borchardt already has blocked 61 shots to rank seventh on Stanford's all-time list. Borchardt also is a competent passer and good mid-range shooter.

KEY RESERVES

G-JULIUS BARNES (6-1, 180 lbs., JR, #24, 4.4 ppg, 1.4 rpg, 1.0 apg, 14.6 minutes, .381 FG, .317 3PT, .727 FT, Rowland HS/Rowland Heights, Calif.). Originally recruited as a quick and explosive athlete with the potential to become a point guard, Barnes still is learning the position.

As a result, his role this season is most likely to play as a backup at both guard positions.

Asked if Barnes has developed a point guard mentality, Montgomery conceded, "Not yet. A point guard has to think team first. 'How do I get Casey involved? How do I get Curtis involved?' He's still working on that."

In addition, Barnes needs better consistency with his shot.

"He's a bit of a feast or famine guy," Montgomery said. "He needs to understand good shot, bad shot."

Still, Barnes gives the Cardinal a dimension of speed and aggressiveness. He was voted his club's most improved player last season, when he played double-digit minutes in 26 games.

Barnes had his best game against Duke, contributing nine points, three rebounds, two assists and a blocked shot in 17 minutes. He scored a career-high 15 points in a win over Oregon State.

PG-CHRIS HERNANDEZ (6-2, 180 lbs., FR, #11, 16.7 ppg, 6.9 apg, 5.0 rpg, .510 FG, .830 FT Clovis West HS/Fresno, Calif.). Touted as the Cardinal's point guard of the future, that future could arrive quickly if Hernandez develops.

Hernandez led his high school team to 134 wins in four seasons, including a 31-3 record and a trip to the Southern California final his senior year. Clovis West was ranked as high as No. 2 in the state and No. 12 in the nation last season.

"He's a tough kid and he understands his job," Montgomery said. "He's not looking to score unless he needs to. He takes charges, gets loose balls, plays very hard."

A nominee for the McDonald's All-America game, Hernandez had a 29-point effort against powerhouse Modesto Christian and helped engineer wins during his career against the likes of Dominguez and Mater Dei, two of Southern California's premier programs.

Montgomery rarely has hustled freshmen into the spotlight, but he said Hernandez will get a long look.

"Logically speaking, you prefer the seniors or upper-classmen to have first opportunities. But we're in a situation where there's been a lot of turnover, and it could be the style changes. Everybody is going to have that opportunity."

C-ROBERT LITTLE (6-10, 265 lbs., FR, #42, 17.0 ppg, 14.0 rpg, .600 FG at Paul VI HS/Fairfax, Va.). Little will get the chance to show what he can do early because of the Cardinal's shortage of post players. But Montgomery said Little has work to do before he's ready to fulfill his collegiate potential.

"He's got to change his body, and he's in the process of doing that," Montgomery said of the weight loss Little is experiencing. "He's got great hands. He just needs to pick up his work ethic a little bit, needs to adjust to playing at this level. He's going to be thrown into it."

Little was all state in Virginia, putting together a 22-point, 22-rebound effort in one game. He averaged 15 points and 10 rebounds as a junior.

G/F-MATT LOTTICH (6-4, 190 lbs., SO, #33, 2.7 ppg, 0.8 rpg, 6.9 minutes, .489 FG, .407 3PT, .833 FT, New Trier HS/Winnetka, Ill.). Lottich will compete for the small forward spot after a solid freshman season. He played in 25 games last season, averaging nearly seven minutes per outing on a veteran squad.

"He's gotten stronger through weights. He needs a little more consistency on his shot, but strength has helped him," Montgomery said. "He'll compete, for sure. He's got a year under his belt and he'll stick you on defense. He's not the quickest kid, but we've always dealt with that."

Montgomery believes Lottich will begin to blossom now that he's concentrating solely on basketball. He was a big-time three-sport star in high school, batting .480 as a baseball first baseman and passing for more than 2,000 yards and 20 touchdowns as a football quarterback.

OTHER RETURNEES

F/C-JOE KIRCHOFER (6-9, 240 lbs., SO, #OO, red-shirted in 2000-2001, 1.3 ppg, 1.2 rpg, 5.6 minutes, .435 FG, .667 FT in 1999-2000, Laguna Creek HS/Elk Grove, Calif.). Kirchofer comes off a red-shirt year, sitting out to develop while Montgomery shuffled in a deep stable of big men last season. Now the Cardinal needs some contribution from him.

"Joe's definitely improved," Montgomery said. "He played pretty well in Australia, rebounded the ball well. He had a nice spring in terms of weightlifting. He should be able to be a rebounder and defend and be a presence in there."

Kirchofer played in 22 games as a freshman, twice scoring six points in a game.

F-TEYO JOHNSON (6-6, 256 lbs., SO, #5, 4.1 ppg, 2.2 rpg, 9.8 minutes, .513 FG, .455 3PT, .650 FT, Mira Mesa HS/San Diego). A gift from the Stanford football team, Johnson played a key role off the bench last season, providing a quick, physical inside presence.

Johnson's availability this year depends on when the Stanford football team winds up its season.

"The earliest we're going to get him is the first of December," Montgomery said. "But he has a little bit of a different sort of skill. He's really athletic, runs the floor. He's undersized as a post, but that's where we needed him, and that's where we need him again."

Extremely confident, Johnson was happy to mix it up inside with taller players, using his muscle and quickness to give them fits. He played double-figure minutes in 10 of Stanford's final 12 games, contributing eight points, four rebounds, an assist and a block in 20 minutes against UNC Greensboro in the NCAA Tournament.

He had eight points and six rebounds in a win at Cal, and hit two three-pointers in the second half of a win at Oregon.

G/F-KYLE LOGAN (6-5, 202 lbs., JR, #3, 1.6 ppg, 0.7 rpg, 4.5 minutes, .455 FG, .500 FT, Mercersburg Academy/Hagerstown, Md.). Montgomery isn't sure what he can expect from Logan, who has been limited to 101 minutes in 22 games over the last two seasons because of injury.

"He's just had a whole series of mishaps," said Montgomery, noting that Logan injured his shoulder in the spring. "Certainly he has the ability. At this point he should be able to help us compete. He's just not ever been able to get himself in a sustained situation where he's able to do that."

Blessed with good quickness, Logan had a career-high six points to go with three rebounds and three assists in 12 minutes against Washington last season.

G/F-TYLER BESECKER (6-6, 205 lbs., SO, #14, 1.2 ppg, 0.6 rpg, 3.6 minutes in 5 games, .500 FG, 1.000 FT, Mercer Island HS/Bellevue, Wash.). A walk-on who led his high school team to back-to-back state championships in Washington, Besecker has struggled since developing an arthritic condition in his joints.

"It's a pretty tough deal, but he's bouncing back," said Montgomery, alluding to a summer-league game in which Besecker scored 25 points. "For him to even play a game means he's making progress."

Besecker and his high school team compiled an 81-9 record in three seasons. He averaged 18 points as a senior and had 17 points and 12 rebounds in the state title game that season.

OTHER NEWCOMERS

F/G NICK ROBINSON (6-6, 195 lbs., FR, #21, 13.4 ppg, 5.4 rpg, 3.3 apg, .510 FG in 1998-99 at Liberty HS/Liberty, Mo.). Robinson red-shirted last year after returning from a two-year Mormon mission to Maceio, Brazil. He is expected to compete for some playing time this season.

"He's a pretty good athlete, pretty explosive," Montgomery said. "He needs some more consistency on his shot, but he's mature. [The mission] doesn't change their initial ability, but that first year back is tough because they haven't done anything in two years."

Robinson, now nearly 22 and married, enjoyed a storybook high school career. He was a 4.0 student and helped his team to a 31-0 record his senior season, hitting a game-winning, fade-away shot to capture the state title.

QUESTIONS

Borchardt's health? If Borchardt can make it through the season on both feet, Stanford may be better than some expect. He is a player whose timing and shot blocking can change the game on defense, and he has offensive skills as well.

Point guard? Stanford has enjoyed a run of eight years with excellent point guard play, beginning with four-year starter Brevin Knight, followed by two-year stints each from Arthur Lee and Michael McDonald. Now there's no obvious and immediate heir to the job, so a given becomes an unknown.

Experience? Here's a scary reality—aside from Jacobsen, no one in the Stanford program ever has started a college game. Four starters who combined to average nearly 47 points and 20 rebounds won't automatically be replaced.

ANSWERS

Casey Jacobsen! In Jacobsen, Stanford not only has one of college basketball's brightest stars, it has a player unafraid to make the big play when it matters most.

Recruiting class! Stanford's three-man recruiting

class is excellent, and it addressed needs. Don't be surprised if Childress and Hernandez eventually give the Cardinal two freshmen starters, something that never has happened in Montgomery's 15-year tenure.

Momentum! For years, Stanford's mediocrity was an inescapable pattern. Now Montgomery has this program rolling at a high level, and that confidence and expectation should pay some positive dividends.

STANFORD 2000-2001 RESULTS

San Francisco State	100-49
#Old Dominion	84-60
#Memphis	83-60
#Georgia	71-58
UC Riverside	84-41
@Long Beach State	86-63
##Sacret Heart	94-52
###Duke	84-83
####Fordham	86-60
####Santa Clara	78-63
@Arizona State	94-77
@Arizona	85-76
Oregon State	73-49
Oregon	100-76
California	84-58
New Mexico	75-44
@Washington	94-63
@Washington State	72-61
USC	77-71
UCLA (L)	73-79
@Oregon	69-62
@Oregon State	82-63
@California	88-56
Washington State	75-64
Washington	99-79
@USC	70-68
@UCLA	85-79
Arizona (L)	75-76
Arizona State	99-75
#####UNC Greensboro	89-60
#####St. Joseph's	90-83
#####Cincinnati	78-65
#####Maryland (L)	73-87

#Puerto Rico Shootout in San Juan
##Deutsche Banc Alex Brown Invitational in Stanford, CA
###Pete Newell Challenge in Oakland, CA
####Cable Car Classic in Santa Clara, CA
#####NCAA Tournament
@Road Games

BLUE RIBBON ANALYSIS

BACKCOURT	A-
BENCH/DEPTH	B
FRONTCOURT	B+
INTANGIBLES	B

It's easy to look at what Stanford lost from a year ago and discount the Cardinal as a serious threat to win the Pac-10 title. But Montgomery is among the nation's top coaches—in his 24th season, he needs 27 victories to reach 500—and he is working with a better caliber athlete the last few years than ever before.

Jacobsen's evolution will be interesting to watch. He was so good, so cool under pressure as a sophomore last year it's sometimes hard to imagine him getting much better. But Montgomery expects more and Jacobsen's fire burns so intensely he should take his game up another step this season.

Without question, there are issues.

"Certainly depth at the post has got to be a consideration," Montgomery said. "We can't afford to lose people there. We just don't have alternatives.

"Our perimeter will be fine. The development of freshmen kids will be critical."

If Borchardt and Davis remain healthy, and if Childress and Hernandez are able to deliver as freshmen, Stanford will be a handful. The three-time defending Pac-10 champs aren't ready to concede their title just yet.

(J.F.)

Oklahoma 16

LOCATION	Norman, OK
CONFERENCE	Big 12

LAST SEASON	26-7 (.787)
CONFERENCE RECORD	12-4 (t-2nd)
STARTERS LOST/RETURNING	3/2
NICKNAME	Sooners
COLORS	Crimson & Cream
HOMECOURT	Lloyd Noble Cener (12,000)
COACH	Kelvin Sampson (Pembroke State '78)
RECORD AT SCHOOL	159-69 (7 years)
CAREER RECORD	332-217 (17 years)
ASSISTANTS	Ray Lopes (College of Idaho '87)
	Jim Shaw (Western Oregon '85)
	Bennie Seltzer (Washington State '97)
TEAM WINS (last 5 years)	17-22-23-27-26
RPI (last 5 years)	46-33-48-16-15
2000-01 FINISH	Lost in NCAA first round.

COACH AND PROGRAM

For most of the 1990s, while the Oklahoma football team struggled, the Sooners' basketball program was the only reason for an OU fan to get excited about winning. Since the 1994-95 season, Oklahoma has been led by Kelvin Sampson, a shirt sleeves, lunch pail type coach who consistently turns out gritty teams.

Now, though, Oklahoma's football program is back where the fans believe it belongs. When the Sooners won the 2000 national championship under second-year coach Bob Stoops, OU had its seventh national championship.

Nearly three months later, the Sooners' basketball team had its fifth first-round NCAA Tournament loss in seven seasons under Sampson.

You can see where this could be headed, can't you? Successful, hard-working coach. Winning teams. Not enough championships or postseason success. It's a formula that has sent many a good coach screaming and running way—or being chased away—from a good job.

"We were a No. 4 seed in the NCAA Tournament and finished the year ranked 13th in the country," Sampson said of last year's team. "I think we had a great year and made huge strides. Our goal this year is to improve. I think it gets harder to improve the higher you go, but it's fun to sit back and try. I can honestly say we have a chance to get better. And I think our best basketball is ahead of us."

Yes, last year was a success. After losing heart-and-soul forward Eduardo Najera from a team that won 27 games (the most under Sampson's watch), OU slugged its way through the Big 12 Conference, won 26 games and the Big 12 tournament title (the first regular or post-season championship for Sampson).

But in our what-have-you-done-for-me lately society, the Sooners' first-round loss to Indiana State was a stinger.

Athletic director Joe Castiglione, one of the best in the business, is not putting any pressure on Sampson. In fact, Castiglione specifically made sure that a new practice facility and improvements to Lloyd Noble Center were budgeted. After being mentioned in connection with every major job opening over the last few seasons, Sampson had a quiet off-season.

But Sampson's apparent interest in other jobs, plus OU's inability to consistently advance in the NCAA Tournament could cause Sooners fans to start complaining if Oklahoma trips over its own shoe laces next March.

"We've consistently been a top 20 team," Sampson said. "Across the board, I think this will be our most athletic team. I think you'll see us more creative on defense. I think you'll see us trap more, whether it's running and jumping in the halfcourt or extending our pressure. It's hard for a coach who doesn't press to become a pressing coach.

"Another thing we have is depth. I don't know that we've ever had as solid a group of 10 as we have with this group. If we get these 10 to the starting gate in September and October and finish the race with them in February and March, I think this team has the chance to be really, really, really good."

If that happens, it will probably be because Sampson will again do a great job of coaching. The Sooners must replace three starters, but they have one of the nation's top recruiting classes to provide an infusion of talent. And while the top half of the Big 12 figures to be another dog fight—Kansas, Missouri, Texas and Oklahoma State all have potential to be top 25 teams—Oklahoma has to be considered a team that will challenge for a spot near the top of the standings.

"If I'm a fan at the University of Oklahoma, I'm getting

really, really excited about watching this group," Sampson said. "They're going to be fun to watch. This is a great group of kids that will compete its butt off and play its heart out. Who knows? We think we're going to be pretty good."

Among coaches, Sampson is one of the straightest shooters. If he believes the Sooners are going to be pretty good, it's hard to doubt him.

2001-2002 SCHEDULE

Nov.	12	#Central Connecticut
	28	Central Michigan
Dec.	1	@Arkansas
	5	St. Bonaventure
	8	Louisiana Tech
	15	High Point
	16	Bethune-Cookman
	18	Eastern Illinois
	21	Maryland
Jan.	5	Texas A&M
	7	@Connecticut
	12	Texas Tech
	16	@Nebraska
	19	@Kansas
	21	Missouri
	26	@Texas Tech
	30	Oklahoma State
Feb.	2	@Texas
	6	Baylor
	9	@Texas A&M
	13	@Oklahoma State
	16	Kansas State
	19	@Baylor
	23	Texas
	26	Iowa State
March	2	@Colorado
	7-10	##Big 12 Tournament

@Road Games
*All College Classic, Oklahoma City, OK
#Preseason NIT (if Oklahoma wins, it will play either Michigan State or Detroi on Nov. 14; semfinals and final on Nov. 21 and 23 at Madison Square Garden, NY)
###Kemper Arena, Kansas City, MO

STARTERS NOT RETURNING

PG-J.R. RAYMOND (6-2, 11.3 ppg, 3.5 rpg, 27.2 mpg, .442 FG, .400 3PT, .762 FT). For the first part of last season, Sampson played Hollis Price at the point and J.R. Raymond on the wing. Then, in mid-January, the Sooners lost three-of-four games. Sampson decided to switch Price and Raymond. With the ball in his hands, Raymond started to dominate. Over the next 10 games, Raymond averaged more than 18 points. And the Sooners won nine of those games.

But before the Sooners traveled to face Maryland in a big non-conference game in late February, Sampson suspended Raymond. The team chemistry that was starting to develop was wiped out. Sampson eventually dismissed Raymond from the team.

SG-NOLAN JOHNSON (6-4, 13.2 ppg, 4.9 rpg, 30.2 mpg, .449 FG, .297 3PT, .826 FT). Johnson led the Sooners in scoring and he got his points the hard way. A slashing driver, the left-handed Johnson was at his best when the Sooners would clear out and let him work one-on-one. He had the size, quickness and ball-handling ability that made him hard to guard.

Johnson wasn't a particularly great shooter and he was below average from three-point range, but he was adept at putting points on the board. He led the Sooners in free-throw attempts and makes.

Over the last seven games, after Raymond's suspension, Johnson raised his game. He averaged nearly 17 points a game down the stretch.

SF-JAMEEL HAYWOOD (6-6, 3.8 ppg, 4.6 rpg, 18.8 mpg, .437 FG, .660 FT). This guy was a typical worker bee. An undersized back-to-the-basket player, Haywood started 17 games last season. He was often Aaron McGhee's frontcourt partner in the Sooners' three-guard lineup. Haywood scored a season-high nine points in two different games—against Texas and at Missouri.

The high point of his season came in the game in Columbia when his buzzer-beating shot from just inside the free-throw line gave the Sooners a 63-61 victory.

OTHERS NOT RETURNING

SG-TIM HESKETT (6-1, 3.7 ppg, 0.7 rpg, 13.4 mpg, .319 FG, .308 3PT, .733 FT). Before last season, Sampson joked that Heskett "came in with Wayman [Tisdale]." Certainly, Heskett was one of those players whose career seemed to last forever. He made an impact as a freshman with his outside shot, but a bad back forced a red-shirt season in 1997-98.

Heskett's mobility was severely hampered and he became little more than a spot-up three-point specialist. He was a defensive liability, so that also limited his playing time.

SG-KELLEY NEWTON (6-2, 9.8 ppg, 2.5 rpg, 23.9 mpg, .463 FG, .434 3PT, .763 FT). A larger, more mobile version of Heskett, Newton got plenty of playing time as one of Sampson's first backcourt options off the bench. Newton scored a career-high 26 against Coppin State and had 20 against SMU.

After Raymond was off the team, Newton had to step in as a starter. He scored 14 in his first start against Maryland. Over the last seven games, he averaged 13 points, highlighted by a 26-point effort in the Sooners' final game.

PROJECTED STARTERS

PG-QUANNAS WHITE (6-1, 190 lbs., JR, #4, 17.0 ppg, 4.0 rpg, 5.0 apg at Midland [Texas] Junior College and Augustine HS/New Orleans, La.). White is expected to be the Sooners' point guard, allowing Price to play on the wing. While the junior-college to Division I transition often can be a difficult one, White has two advantages—he'll be playing alongside Price, his former high school teammate, and he'll be running a familiar offense.

"The good thing about Quannas is that his team at Midland ran the same offense as us," Sampson said. "He's been running this system for two years. He knows how to run our box stuff, our set plays and our 1-4."

White will no doubt draw comparisons to another Midland product who became a star guard for the Sooners in the late '80s—Mookie Blaylock.

"When we signed Quannas White, we envisioned him being our starting point guard on a full-time basis," Sampson said. "We envision a quicker team, a more athletic team. And the person we think can make us a quick team by getting the ball up the court is Quannas.

"He's got a good feel for the game and can score the ball better than you think. He's a good three-point shooter, not a great one. But the thing I like is that he's a winner."

SG-HOLLIS PRICE (6-1, 165 lbs., JR, #10, 11.8 ppg, 2.6 rpg, 4.6 apg, 33.2 mpg, .433 FG, .342 3PT, .811 FT, St. Augustine HS/New Orleans, La.). Price should be a main cog for the Sooners, but Sampson is concerned whether the junior will be 100 percent to start the season.

Price's 2000-01 season ended much like the team's season ended—painfully. In OU's NCAA Tournament first round loss to Indiana State, Price collided with a Sycamore player late in the game. The Indiana State player lost a tooth when his mouth crashed into Price's arm. Price suffered a gash so severe that he suffered a torn triceps tendon in his right arm.

"Hollis' injury turned out to be more severe than we first thought," Sampson said. "He had three different surgeries. They cleaned and irrigated the wound twice and then fixed the severed tendon. There was severe atrophy with the arm."

While he rehabbed the injury, Price made the best of a bad situation.

"The byproduct of this is that Hollis has worked harder with his left hand," Sampson said. "And that's something he knew he was going to have to do anyway. He's really worked hard with his left hand and that will help him have a great junior year."

The spindly Price has started 54-of-67 games, including all but one last year (he didn't start in deference to Tim Heskett on Senior Night).

Last season, he started the first 16 games at point guard before moving to shooting guard when J.R. Raymond took over at the point. When Raymond was suspended, Price had to move back to the point for the last seven games.

Price, though, is more comfortable at off-guard. Despite his lack of size, his quickness allows him to slash to the basket and get open for mid-range jumpers. Sampson wants Price to be more assertive this season, especially when it comes to attacking the rim and getting fouled.

"His quickness is a factor in transition," Sampson said. "If we can get him up the court to receive the pass then we think we can put more pressure on the defense. We'd like Hollis to be able to get the pass and attack the rim. We think that'll get him to the free-throw line more and it'll put more pressure on the defense to get back."

If there is one player who figures to be the focal point of the Sooners this season, it will be Price.

"I want Hollis to force himself on this team," Sampson said. "We tell our kids that as a leader they'll invoke a response, either a negative one or a positive one. We want Hollis to get this team behind him and go."

SF-DARYAN SELVY (6-6, 215 lbs., SR, #24, 6.9 ppg, 5.2 rpg, 21.8 mpg, .459 FG, .642 FT, 78 offensive rebounds, Carl Albert Junior College, Okla./West Memphis, Ark.). Selvy is one of those players who defy description. He doesn't really have a position. He's not a particularly effective shooter and his numbers don't overwhelm you. But he can create headaches for the other team.

"I don't know if I knew how to coach him last year," Sampson said. "I struggled with where to play him because, conventionally, he doesn't have a position. He's not a two, not a three and not really a four or a five. He's a guy that you have to force on the opposition and say, 'Match up with him.'

"He's a hard match-up because he can put the ball on the floor so well and get to the basket."

Selvy played the fifth-most minutes on the team last season, but he led the Sooners in rebounding. Selvy was particularly hard working on the offensive glass, with 78 of his 166 boards keeping OU possessions alive. He also tied for the team lead with 23 blocked shots.

"When we lost J.R. Raymond, I thought it positively affected Daryan Selvy because it gave him opportunities he wasn't getting before," Sampson said. "At the end of the year I thought he was our best guy at creating shots for others. He would drive and kick it out to our guards for a lot of open three-pointers."

Selvy was a major factor in the Sooners' triumph in the Big 12 Tournament. He averaged 26.7 minutes per game and scored 29 points in the three games.

Selvy's playing time increased when the Sooners' rotation was whittled to seven players late in the season. This year, he'll probably see most of his time on the wing. While he's not a three-point threat, Sampson likes Selvy's ability to exploit the defense.

"He'll have a much bigger role this year in terms of scoring and being one of our primary players," Sampson said. "He's really improved since the season ended. I want him to live on the edge more. I want him to play with abandonment. The more he plays like that, the harder match-up he'll become."

PF-AARON McGHEE (6-8, 250 lbs., SR. #13, 12.9 ppg, 4.8 rpg, 24.1 mpg, .460 FG, .489 3PT, .770 FT, Cincinnati/Vincennes Junior College, Ind./Aurora HS, Aurora, Ill.). As the replacement for Najera, McGhee did a nice job handling that considerable pressure. He was Oklahoma's second-leading scorer and third-leading rebounder. And while his numbers didn't approach those of Najera, he did what was needed—give the perimeter-oriented Sooners a low-post threat that helped keep defenders honset.

"Aaron stayed here when the season ended and went straight to work," Sampson said. "Since then I think he's worked as hard as any of the returning players. We expect him to be one of our leading scorers, to rebound better and to defend better."

One problem that McGhee needs to rectify is foul trouble. He committed at least four fouls in 19 games and fouled out six times. That's a major reason he averaged just 24 minutes a game. Also, he had some nights when he was a non-factor. McGhee had 14 games where he scored nine or fewer points. In the Sooners' last three games, he scored a total of 19 points.

"I expect him to be a senior, and that means I expect consistency," Sampson said. "I don't expect my seniors to be up and down. I expect them to be leaders and to be consistent."

With Jabhari Brown expected to take over at center, McGee also might have to adjust his offensive game; there might not be as many touches in the low post as there was last season when he was basically the first and last option on the blocks.

C-JABAHRI BROWN (6-10, 210 lbs., SO, #21, 8.6 ppg, 6.3 rpg, 2.3 bpg, 24.3 mpg at Florida International/St. Thomas, U.S. Virgin Islands). During Sampson's tenure, the Sooners have basically "made do" at center. They've never had a shot blocker or consistent rebounder playing the position. That could change this season.

During 1999-00, Brown played his freshman season at Florida International. He played 24.3 minutes a game, averaging 8.6 points, 6.3 rebounds and 2.3 blocked shots. Because he transferred from FIU to Oklahoma in mid-semester, Brown won't be eligible to play for the Sooners until mid-December.

Sampson is very enthusiastic about Brown.

"He's a high-level athlete," Sampson said. "He can really run and he's a smart kid—extremely intelligent with a high basketball IQ. He gives us something we haven't had since I've been here and that's an athletic big man on offense and defense. And he'll run the floor as well as any of our guys. Jabahri's upside is high, he has a high ceiling above him."

However, playing well for FIU in the Sun Belt Conference is slightly different than playing in the Big 12 Conference, where the big men like to bang bodies like it's the WWF.

"Jabahri needs to get bigger and stronger, but he's proven he can play on this level," Sampson said. "We're working with Jabahri on different ways for him to be effective. When the ball hits the rim and goes straight up, he has as good a shot of getting it as anyone."

While Brown is not a polished offensive player, if he can rebound and block shots, he'll provide a safety net for the rest of the Sooners' defenders. And McGhee's presence as a low post scorer could mean that Brown won't be under pressure to score.

KEY RESERVES

PF-JOHNNIE GILBERT (6-8, 230 lbs., SO, #32, 2.3 ppg, 4.3 rpg, 16 mpg, .389 FG, .523 FG, .523 FT, 23 blocked shots, Patrick Henry HS/Minneapolis, Minn.). Gilbert proved to be a solid front-court reserve a year ago. As a freshman, he made six starts and played in 26 games. Even though he averaged just 16 minutes a game, Gilbert averaged 4.3 rebounds and tied for the team lead with 23 blocked shots.

"Johnnie's kind of like a snake in the grass," Sampson said. "He doesn't say much and you don't really see him until you walk by him. And then he just jumps out at you. That's the way he plays. If he was ice cream, he'd be vanilla. He's just solid. He's one of those kids who could lead the league in rebounding if he gets the minutes.

"He has to improve his offensive skills, improve with the ball in his hands and be able to make plays. His free-throw shooting has improved, and so has his ability to hit the 15-foot baseline jumper. We told him he has to be a threat from 15 feet and in. I think he's our best overall rebounder and our best overall shot blocker coming back."

Until Brown becomes eligible at the end of the first semester, Gilbert is a candidate to be a starter.

C-JOZSEF SZENDREI (6-9, 240 lbs., JR, #42, 15.4 ppg, 14.8 rpg, .610 FG, .740 FT in 1999-2000 at Northeastern Junior College, Colo./Budapest, Hungary). Szendrei (pronounced ZEND-ray) is an expert on knee surgeries and rehabilitating injuries. He tore the anterior cruciate ligament in his right knee in June of 2000 and his left ACL in April of 2001. That calamity limited him to two games last season before he decided to red-shirt.

"He's worked his butt off in that weight room and in rehab," Sampson said. "I think you're going to see a mentally tough, hungry Jozsef Szendrei. I think he's going to be a tremendous help for us. How much playing time he'll see depends on his recovery. Right now I would say he's our fifth post. But he's a kid who can move up."

Szendrei's strength is his ability to rebound. If he's able to contribute, he'll serve as a frontcourt reliever for Brown and McGhee.

G-BLAKE JOHNSTON (6-1, 180 lbs., FR #12, 23.3 ppg, 4.8 rpg, 8.0 apg in 1999-2000 at Midland HS/Midland, Texas). Johnston sat out last year because of a hip injury and a respiratory condition. A flashy playmaker who could wind up as White's primary backup, Johnston spent his red shirt season working on his outside shot.

"Blake's one of those kids who will work to improve in the areas you challenge him," Sampson said. "I'm anxious to see Blake compete against Hollis and Quannas on a daily basis to determine how far he's come. I know he's improved a lot. I love his attitude, his grit and his toughness. Blake Johnston is going to help us win games."

OTHER RETURNEES

G-MICHAEL CANO (6-1, 180 lbs., SR, #3, 2.3 mpg, 2-5 FGs, 0-2 3PTS, 2-2 FTS, Tom C. Clark HS/San Antonio, Texas). Cano is one of the practice fodder, end

of the bench players coaches love to have around. In fact, Cano's attitude is such that, after last season, Sampson awarded him with a scholarship.

"Michael Cano has earned the right," Sampson said. "We awarded him a scholarship when the season ended and I can't tell you how proud I am of him and the progress he's made. Michael's a huge, huge part of our success. He really understands Sooner basketball, he's a leader and he cares. He won our practice team player award last year and that's a reflection of his attitude and personality."

Cano has played in 30 games during his first three seasons. Last season, he played in nine games, averaging just over two minutes a game.

G-RICHARD AINOOSON (6-3, 185 lbs., JR, #20, Midwest City HS, Oklahoma City, Okla.). He returns to the team as a walk-on player. A local product, he sat out last season to work on his academics. Ainooson is a management information systems major, meaning he's taking high-level computer and math classes. While he took the year off from basketball, Sampson says he improved his GPA and now it's over 3.0.

SG/SF-JASON DETRICK (6-5, 210 lbs., JR #5, 23.0 ppg, 5.7 rpg, 2.3 apg, 2.2 steals per game at Southwest Missouri State-West Plains Junior College, Mo./Newport News, VA.). When the Sooners want to go with a three-guard look, Detrick might be one of the players Sampson calls on. And, with Price and White being undersized starters, Detrick can add some size to the backcourt.

A first-team junior college All American last season, Detrick is a slasher who likes to take the ball to the rim. Tom Barr, his junior-college coach said that Detrick, "Just has that knack for scoring."

He's also a solid defensive player. Last season at Southwest Missouri State-West Plains, he set school records for deflections and charges taken.

"His coach had me at 'Hello' when he started talking about Jason taking charges and getting his hands on loose balls and diving on the floor," Sampson said. "Then we saw him play against the No. 1 team in the nation and he had 42 points and was absolutely the best player on the floor.

"He has a love affair with basketball. This kid is infatuated with the game. He's a gym rat. Like all junior college kids, he'll undergo an adjustment period. But we think he's going to be an outstanding wing for us."

SG-EBI ERE (6-5, 215 lbs., JR, #2, 25.5 ppg, 7.6 rpg, 1.7 apg, 1.8 steals, 1.6 blocks per game at Barton County Community College, Kansas/Tulsa, Okla.). The name is pronounced EBB-ee EAR-ee. Get used to it. Sampson is convinced the Ere era could be exciting.

"Ebi is a prolific scorer," Sampson said. "He has great size for a wing and he can put the ball in the hole. I think he has the potential to come in and impact our team right away."

Ere is from Tulsa. He signed with Oklahoma out of high school, but had to attend junior college when his grades didn't measure up. In last year's National Junior College Athletic Association national tournament, Ere averaged 32.3 points in four games, including a 52-point outburst.

"I loved Ebi in high school," Sampson said. "But his improvement maturity-wise and personality-wise has been great. He's a much better player than he was in high school. He's way more mature and more physically developed. And he's got an air of confidence about him. Ebi Ere thinks he's pretty good."

SF/SG-MATT GIPSON (6-9, 205 lbs., FR, #15, 23.4 ppg, 9.2 rpg, 2.7 blocked shots per game at Burkburnett HS/Burkburnett, Texas). An intriguing player who has Sampson gushing, Gipson helped make the Sooners' recruiting class one of the nation's best. However, considering that he's more comfortable playing on the wing and the glut of players on the perimeter, it's not clear if Gipson will wind up as a contributor or as a red-shirt.

"We may red-shirt Matt or he may come in and beat someone out," Sampson said. "He's got a big heart with a great attitude. He's a bright kid with an unbelievably bright future here."

Sampson is particularly enamored with Gipson's versatility and with his hard-nosed attitude.

"He competes hard and has a lot of Eduardo Najera's characteristics when it comes to effort," Sampson said. "He's not a guy you can slip into a category. He's not a post man and he's not a guard. Matt can bounce it, he can shoot it and he can pass it. He can defender smaller players but he can also go inside and rebound.

"If he was a stock I'd call all my best friends and tell them to buy it because he's blue chip. I think he's going to be terrific."

QUESTIONS

Point guard? Quannas White will have to make the move from junior college to Division I ball, but another Midland product (Mookie Blaylock) had little trouble making a similar adjustment about 15 years ago. White's ability to handle the point is crucial. If he can, Hollis Price will be free to play shooting guard.

Scoring? Oklahoma lost a significant amount of its firepower from last season. A particular concern is having players who can create their own shots and slash to the basket.

Postseason? The Sooners finally won the Big 12 Tournament, but that was blotted out by a first-round loss in the NCAA Tournament. Despite his ability to mold a team, Sampson's biggest bugaboo is that the Sooners turn March Madness into March Sadness.

ANSWERS

Effort! There might be nights when the shots don't fall and there might be nights when the other team is just better. But there is almost never a game when Sampson's Sooners get beat in the effort department. Sampson gets his teams to play all out from November to March.

Quickness! Sampson believes he has one of his most athletic teams. While Sampson is not known for full-court pressure defense, this team should be able to extend its pressure. Combining the speed with the effort could mean some long nights for the opposition.

Sampson! Here's the bottom line: This guy can coach.

OKLAHOMA 2000-2001 RESULTS

#Alcorn State	73-56
#LaSalle	89-72
##Montana State	84-76
##Tulane	83-69
##Oregon State	78-60
@Mississippi (L)	55-60
North Texas	100-72
Coppin State	103-49
Southwest Texas	96-48
Arkansas	88-79
###Oral Roberts	84-51
###SMU	79-78
@Iowa State (L)	80-100
Texas A&M	78-65
Kansas (L)	61-69
@Texas Tech (L)	59-60
@Kansas State	64-63
Texas	75-68
Nebraska	77-66
@Baylor	65-51
@Texas A&M	72-63
Texas Tech	80-72
@Texas	75-54
@Oklahoma State (L)	44-72
Baylor	82-60
@Missouri	63-61
@Maryland (L)	60-68
Colorado	86-67
Oklahoma State	68-56
####Missouri	67-65
####Kansas	62-57
#####Texas	54-45
######Indiana State (L)	68-70

#Sooner Holiday Classic in Norman
##Big Island Invitational in Hilo, HI
###Touchtone Energy All-College Tournament in Oklahoma City
####Big 12 Tournament in Kansas City, MO
#####NCAA Tournament
@Road Games

BLUE RIBBON ANALYSIS

BACKCOURT	B+
BENCH/DEPTH	B
FRONTCOURT	B
INTANGIBLES	B+

Sampson's OU teams have either been built around stars—Ryan Minor, Eduardo Najera—or they've been a bunch of hard working over achievers. The 2001-02 edition will be something completely different. There is no one player who will contend for All-America or player-of-the-year honors. But Sampson has a roster full of talent.

Price will be a key, but he'll need to get help from his fellow guards.

"Ebi Ere and Jason Detrick will be major factors for us all year," Sampson said. "We're going to be really dependent on both of them to have big years. We need them both. Whether it's together or if one comes off the bench. I prefer to start Hollis because he's a returning veteran. But both these guys are capable of starting. That's why we brought them in here."

The Sooners will be deeper and will have more size than any team Sampson has had. If Brown is as good as Sampson says, he'll be the first legitimate center Oklahoma has had in years. If Brown can shake the rust accumulated as a transfer, he could be a nice fit between bookend forwards McGhee and Selvy.

Only two seniors—McGhee and Selvy—will get much playing time. While this year's Sooners are headed for 20 victories and an NCAA Tournament bid, the future looks bright in Norman.

(W.B.)

Syracuse 17

LOCATION	Syracuse, NY
CONFERENCE	Big East (West)
LAST SEASON	25-9 (.735)
CONFERENCE RECORD	10-6 (2nd)
STARTERS LOST/RETURNING	2/3
NICKNAME	Orangemen
COLORS	Orange & Blue
HOMECOURT	The Carrier Dome
COACH	Jim Boeheim (Syracuse '66)
RECORD AT SCHOOL	600-208 (25 years)
CAREER RECORD	600-208 (25 years)
ASSISTANTS	Bernie Fine (Syracuse '67)
	Mike Hopkins (Syracuse '93)
	Troy Weaver (Prince Georges CC '91)
TEAM WINS (last 5 years)	19-26-21-26-25
RPI (last 5 years)	19-26-21-11-25
2000-01 FINISH	Lost in NCAA second round.

COACH AND PROGRAM

It might not make a lot of sense to say this, especially about a team that has won 25 or more games in three of the last four years, but Syracuse has been down. Not bottom-of-the-barrel, woe-is-me down or anything. But certainly a step or two removed from its once dominant status, when it could be counted on for a spot in the top two or three (at worst) in the Big East and a legitimate shot at the Final Four, provided it could escape a first-round blunder.

That isn't the case anymore. Hasn't been for a long while, in fact. The 'Cuse did author a Cinderella run to the Finals in 1996 (thank you, John Wallace), but that was entirely unexpected. It's been a long time since the days when we could put the Orangemen among the nation's top 10 in the fall and then watch them fulfill their destiny by March. That's not awful news to the rest of the Big East, but for those of us who believe in continuity and like to see traditional powers in their rightful positions, the Syracuse slide has been a little upsetting.

"We had seven or eight years there, where we were pretty dominant," said Syracuse coach Jim Boeheim, who no doubt longs for those days, just as he pines for a full crop of hair. "That's a long period."

The point of all this nostalgia is to warn the basketball world that Syracuse is on its way back to that old level. After about a decade of getting by with short benches, zone defenses and Boeheim's coaching skills (yes, that's right, his coaching skills), the Orangemen look about ready to get back to their old ways. There hasn't exactly been a talent drought in upstate New York, but there haven't been the old teams that featured three and four future NBA players, either. Nobody should cry for Boeheim—his teams have made it to 17 of the last 19 NCAA Tournaments, a record that most coaches would love to have. But it has been a long time since the Orange was seeded higher than fourth (its '97 status). It's all about to change.

Syracuse needed talent, and it has brought it in. This year's recruiting class is loaded. Next year's, though only three men deep, is also packed with talent. Boeheim promises to use "at least" nine players on a regular basis this season. The number could well swell to double figures next season. The Orangemen will be able to run

and press or drop back into that maddening zone that regularly limits opponents to about 40 percent success from the field. And when the time comes to play teams like Kansas, which dumped Syracuse, 87-58, in the second round of last year's NCAA Tournament, the Orangemen won't be overmatched. They'll be able to hang—and then some.

"We needed a big recruiting class this year, and we got it," Boeheim said. "And we still have four or five good players coming back. We have a good group of freshmen who are ready to contribute. We could be in our best position since 1989."

The newcomers give Syracuse instant help at its most vulnerable positions. Damone Brown is gone from the power-forward spot, but 6-8 freshman Hakim Warrick steps right in. Boeheim can't stop gushing about him.

"He's going to be really good," the coach said.

There is a hole at point guard, thanks to Allen Griffin's departure. It would have been filled by Billy Edelin, a highly touted freshman from Oak Hill Academy, but he was suspended from school for one year in last September because of alleged sexual misconduct.

Inside production has been a problem for the Orangemen for a while, with Etan Thomas about the only big man of note in the program for about the last decade.

That's why the arrivals of 7-0, 255-pound freshman Craig Forth and 6-10, 235-pound first-year player Mark Konecny are making Boeheim smile. Forth will probably start right away and give the Orangemen a real, low-post scoring threat. Konecny has promise on the boards and defensively and gives Syracuse plenty of muscle.

"We got some size and some stuff we haven't had," Boeheim said. "We haven't had size or depth for a long time. We've been playing seven guys. We had to play zone, because you can't play man with seven guys. Now, we have three big guys and some perimeter players who can move around some."

Wait, there's more. The Syracuse staff had a productive summer, grabbing commitments from three top-flight high school seniors. That gave the Orangemen eight recruits in two years, the NCAA maximum. It's time to look at prep juniors and smile about what's to come. It's hard to know which of next year's newcomers will be better, point man Jerry McNamara, from upstate Pennsylvania, or wing forward Carmelo Anthony, from Washington, D.C. Count on this: Both will be stars.

Add in 6-9 Matt Gorman, from Watertown, N.Y., and Syracuse's depth could rival that of just about any other program. But we get ahead of ourselves. And we haven't even mentioned this year's projected stars. There's senior Preston Shumpert, who became a force last year by averaging 19.5 points at the three-spot, and junior DeShaun Williams, a great three-point shooter who should improve on last year's 12.4 ppg while helping Edelin handle some of the work at the point. Their presence takes scoring pressure off the newcomers and gives the Orangemen some veterans to lean on when the big games crop up. Syracuse isn't quite ready to go back to its days as a perennial powerhouse, but woe to the Big East in the next few years, when these young players develop, and Boeheim gets things rolling again. If you thought things were tough the last few years, when the Orangemen still managed to win 25 games without a surfeit of NBA-ready talent, look out. It's time to go back to the gold old days.

2001-2002 SCHEDULE

Nov.	12	#Manhattan
	18	Binghamton
	27	Colgate
	29	Cornell
Dec.	2	@Albany
	4	Hofstra
	8	North Carolina State
	16	*Georgia Tech
	20	South Florida
	29	Buffalo
Jan.	2	Rutgers
	5	@Providence
	8	Seton Hall
	12	@West Virginia
	14	Notre Dame
	19	@Tennessee
	22	@Pittsburgh
	26	Virginia Tech
	28	@Georgetown
Feb.	2	@Rutgers
	4	West Virginia
	10	Pittsburgh
	17	@Notre Dame
	21	@Seton Hall
	24	Georgetown
	28	@Villanova
March	3	Boston College
	6-9	##Big East Tournament

#Preseason NIT (if Syracuse wins, it will play again on Nov. 15 against Fordham or DePaul; semifinals and final Nov. 21 and 23 at Madison Square Garden in NY)
*Peach Bowl Classic, Atlanta,GA
##Madison Square Garden, New York, NY

STARTERS NOT RETURNING

PG-ALLEN GRIFFIN (6-1, 10.8 ppg, 3.3 rpg, 6.5 apg, 2.0 spg, 36.7 minutes, .383 FG, .244 3PT, .711 FT). Griffin had a strong season for the Orangemen last year, distributing the ball as well as any other point in the Big East and improving his offensive output dramatically. After spending the early part of his career as Jason Hart's understudy, or at times next to Hart in the miscast role of a two-guard, Griffin emerged as a confident leader last year and even stepped out of character on occasion, like when he scored 31 in the win at St. John's and 20 against Seton Hall.

Though never a great marksman, Griffin improved his shooting last year. But most impressive was his assist-to-turnover ratio, which was well above 2:1. That's tremendous for a college guard. While most basketball fans will consider—correctly—Brown a huge loss for the Orange, Griffin's departure will leave a similarly huge void.

PF-DAMONE BROWN (6-9, 16.4 ppg, 8.8 rpg, 1.8 apg, 1.6 spg, 1.4 bpg, 35.9 minutes, .492 FG, .791 FT). Brown never became "the next Louis Orr," but he certainly concluded his career at Syracuse in fine style, giving the Orange a formidable baseline producer, a reliable rebounder and strong defender.

After spending his first three seasons as a fourth (or lower) offensive option, Brown became a valuable weapon last year. He was a strong offensive board man, scored well close to the hoop and could step away from the basket and provide some more shot-blocking help, next to Jeremy McNeil.

And Brown did have some explosions, like his back-to-back, 26-point, 13-rebound performances against Niagara and Notre Dame and his 26-point, 11-board effort against Virginia Tech. Brown scored 27 against Rutgers and had 23 points and 12 rebounds in a win over Georgetown, no mean feat, given the Hoyas' size.

PROJECTED STARTERS

PG-BILLY EDELIN (6-4, 195 lbs, FR, #14, 21.2 ppg, 4.4 rpg, 8.2 apg, Oak Hill Academy/Mouth of Wilson, Va. and DeMatha HS/Silver Spring, Md.). Edelin, one of the nation's top-rated prospects, was suspended from school for one year for his role in an alleged sexual assault.

A female freshman accused Edelin, a point guard from Silver Spring, Md., of assaulting her in August while both were attending summer school at the university.

Edelin remains in school, pending an appeal of the judicial board's decision. His father said that if the ruling stands, his son will transfer.

Coach Jim Boeheim would not discuss Edelin's case on Tuesday, saying it was "a student's private matter."

Edelin's father said his son admitted to engaging in consensual sexual activities with the female student, but insisted the activity did not include intercourse and was initiated by the woman. However, the judicial board ruled in favor of the female student.

Obviously, Boeheim is hopeful of a favorably ruling in Edelin's appeal.

Edelin wouldn't have had to dominate the game from the point, but he would have been counted on for 25-30 minutes a night, and he has more than enough talent to handle that workload.

He'll get support from sophomore James Thues and even Williams, who averaged 3.4 assists last year, something that should help him adjust well to big-time life.

"It's hard for any freshman to take over the point, but I think DeShaun can play some there, and James Thues is a pretty good little guard," Boeheim said. "Billy is a penetrator and a passer. He's a physical player."

Edelin's 6-4 frame should serve him well during a long season. He can get into the lane and set up others.

He'll also draw some fouls and get his share of points. Not yet a great three-point shooter, he won't be called upon to score all that much, particularly if Shumpert and Williams are doing their jobs. His arrival is perfectly timed and should allow the Orangemen to challenge for the Big East crown.

The Edelin bio is an impressive one. After helping DeMatha to back-to-back 28-5 years, Edelin led Oak Hill to a 33-0 record and the top spot in the USA Today prep rankings. He was selected third-team All-America by both Parade and USA Today and earned a spot over the summer on the U.S. under-18 world championship team. In the final, against Canada, Edelin scored 22 points and had eight assists, keying a 102-99 American win.

SG-DESHAUN WILLIAMS (6-3, 202 lbs, JR, #21, 12.4 ppg, 2.9 rpg, 3.4 apg, 2.0 spg, 32.9 minutes, .369 FG, .335 3PT, .756 FT, Paterson Catholic HS/Paterson, N.J.). The key for Williams this year is whether he becomes a more complete offensive player. His three-point shooting numbers last year were solid, but his overall field-goal percentage was extremely low. In fact, it was the lowest among any of the regulars on the team. Boeheim expects it to improve.

"He has gotten better going to the basket," Boeheim said. "He had 20 points against Kansas [in the NCAA Tournament] and showed he could score against big guys. He has lost 14 pounds from last year and look like he wants to be a player. He wasn't in shape before and admits it. He's getting there."

Williams has the capability to get at least 15 a night, if not more. He scored 24 against Ohio State in Alaska last year and 26 against Virginia Tech. When he came to Syracuse, he was expected to be a big-time scorer, and this could be the year. He could help himself immensely by getting to the free-throw line more. He shot just 82 free throws last year, way too few for a two-man. If Williams becomes more aggressive—and successful—at going to the basket, the Orangemen will have two potent perimeter weapons at their disposal.

SF-PRESTON SHUMPERT (6-6, 198 lbs, SR, #3, 19.5 ppg, 5.9 rpg, 1.6 apg, 1.9 spg, 36.5 minutes, .437 FG, .386 3PT, .763 FT, Fort Walton Beach HS/Fort Walton Beach, Fla.). Boeheim wanted to see Shumpert do more things last year, and he got his wish. Shumpert nearly doubled his points output—for the second straight year—became more aggressive on the boards and played pretty good defense. His outside shooting has improved tremendously over the last two seasons, to the point where he is a threat to launch from almost anywhere.

Now Shumpert takes the lead. Brown is gone, so the Orange will need Shumpert every night. He was there last year, just about every night. He carried a big bit of the scoring load and had a huge start, a big reason the 'Cuse bolted from the blocks 15-1. Most impressive was his 36-point explosion against DePaul, at a time when the Blue Demons were considered formidable.

"We knew Preston could shoot it," Boeheim said. "He did more things for us last year. He has to keep doing that."

Expect it to happen, although the emergence of Williams and the freshmen might keep his average from moving beyond 20 points per game. Still, the Orange attack will start with Shumpert, and there's no reason to believe he won't rise to the occasion again.

PF-HAKIM WARRICK (6-8, 185 lbs, FR, #1, 15.6 ppg, 13.0 rpg, 4.8 bpg, Friends Central School/Wynnewood, Pa.). Although Warrick played for a tiny Quaker school on the outskirts of Philadelphia, often against below-average competition, he distinguished himself on the camp and AAU circuits and comes to Syracuse with a fine resume and a bright future.

"He shoots it, he dunks from the foul line, and he's athletic," Boeheim said. "He's thin, and he might get pushed a little, but he'll hold his own."

Warrick is skinny, but that hasn't been a problem for Syracuse before. Neither Louis Orr nor Brown were husky, but they did just fine. Warrick should fill out as he gets older, and he brings the kind of athletic package to the team that should make it more versatile and difficult to handle, particularly in the open court. Boeheim received rave reviews from other Syracuse players about Warrick's performance in fall pickup games, so it's reasonable to believe he will step in right away and make a significant contribution.

C-CRAIG FORTH (7-0, 255 lbs, FR, #00, 19.2 ppg, 14.5 rpg, 5.0 bpg, Columbia HS/East Greenbush, N.Y.). It may surprise some to see Forth in the starting lineup, giving the Orangemen three freshman among its first five, but Boeheim believes this big man has tremendous potential and the savvy to make an immediate impact.

"He's a real good passer, and he understands the game," Boeheim said. "He knows how to play, and he's pretty quick. He ran two miles in 12 minutes. We've never had a center who could run it under 15 minutes. He's a special player and really good. He didn't have a real fire inside until the summer before his senior year. Then he got it, and he started dunking on people."

Forth joined Edelin on the under-18 team that won the title, scoring six points and grabbing seven boards in the final. Because Shumpert and Williams will be the main scoring options, Forth doesn't have to worry too much about points. If he brings boards and defense to the team, along with a low-post presence that commands the occasional double-team, he'll be doing his job. Boeheim expects to see all that this year.

KEY RESERVES

G/F-KUETH DUANY (6-6, 190 lbs, JR, #13, 5.5 ppg, 3.3 rpg, 0.9 apg, 0.9 spg, 18.4 minutes, .437 FG, .276 3PT, .640 FT, Bloomington North HS/Bloomington, Ind.). One of the three reserves who received reasonably large minutes last year, Duany gets the chance to contribute even more this season. He'll have to, or risk losing his spot in the rotation this season or most definitely next.

"I'd like to see some consistency from him," Boeheim said. "He can score, and he has become stronger, and he should be ready to do a little more for us."

Duany is a lively body who can handle work at a pair of positions. He scores well close to the hoop and from the mid-range, but his long-distance shooting needs to be improved. Duany is a strong offensive rebounder and pretty diligent defender who must give Syracuse help every night, rather than sporadic assistance, as he did last year. It's a big season for Duany, because he has an opportunity and people arriving who can push (or replace) him, should he fail to capitalize.

F-JEEREMY MCNEIL (6-8, 257 lbs, SO, #34, 2.5 ppg, 3.1 rpg, 0.1 apg, 1.9 bpg, 15.9 minutes, .653 FG, .568 FT, Sam Houston HS/San Antonio, Texas). Don't be surprised if McNeil begins the year in the middle, ahead of Forth, or at the four-spot, next to him. Boeheim is impressed with McNeil's off-season development, which has included an increase in his strength and bulk. Those traits will serve him well.

The key is whether McNeil can translate that into increased production, particularly on the backboards, where Syracuse will definitely need it.

McNeil isn't going to score much, and that's OK. But if he can rebound successfully and continue to block shots as well as he did—nearly a two a game in just an average of 15 minutes—then Syracuse will have one of the league's most imposing interior profiles.

C-BILLY CELUCK (7-0, 213 lbs, SR, #35, 4.3 ppg, 3.9 rpg, 0.6 apg, 1.2 bpg, 17.9 minutes, .577 FG, .474 FT, Valley View HS/Jessup, Pa.). Celuck went from long-term bench-warmer to productive interior player last year, grabbing some significant minutes and adding needed help on the backboards.

Celuck isn't overpowering (and never will be) and don't count on him for much offense. His value will be his sheer height, which helps in the rebounding area. He'll also block a shot or two. It will be interesting to see how he is used this year, because Forth is expected to get a good amount of minutes. Celuck will be valuable, but perhaps not every night.

G-JAMES THUES (5-10, 172 lbs, SO, #15, 1.6 ppg, 0.5 rpg, 1.3 apg, 0.5 spg, 7.7 minutes, .387 FG, .481 FT, Martin Luther King/Detroit, Mich.). Edelin is going to need some help, and that means Thues has to continue his development. He showed some signs last year of being able to distribute the ball, take care of it and run the team.

"He's athletic and tough," Boeheim said. "He should be able to give us 10 to 15 minutes a night."

Thues has good quickness and the ability to get into the lane. He shouldn't be asked to score, but he must provide some stability on the point, particularly those nights when Edelin struggles. He is developing according to schedule and should be able to help this year.

F-MARK KONECNY (6-10, 235 lbs, FR, #4, 24.8 ppg, 11.6 rpg, 2.2 bpg, Holy Cross HS/Southbury, Conn.). Although Warrick and McNeil are expected to hold down the four-spot most of the time, Boeheim is eager to see what Konecny can do. The freshman will no doubt be brought along somewhat slowly, but he has the talent to make some contributions, and his future is quite bright.

At times, you'll see him and Warrick in the lineup together, perhaps even with McNeil. It can be done, and Syracuse won't lose too much giddy-up in the process.

"Konecny is a good athlete," Boeheim said. "He's big, and he runs pretty good. He can be a good rebounder."

Konecny was the Gatorade Player of the Year in Connecticut and led Holy Cross to the state finals and a 22-2 record his senior year.

OTHER RETURNEES

C-ETHAN COLE (6-9, 244 lbs, SR, #32, 1.0 ppg, 1.2 rpg, 0.2 apg, 6.2 minutes, .368 FG, .667 FT, New Hampshire/Concord HS/Canterbury, N.H.). The New Hampshire transfer got a chance to grab some pivot time last season, but he lost out to Celuck and McNeil and will have even less chance to get significant playing time this year, barring injury.

Cole is slow and methodical and doesn't possess much of a shooting touch. He's a fair rebounder and average defender. He played in 18 games last year but attempted just 19 shots.

F-GREG DAVIS (6-7, 219 lbs, SO, #33, 0.2 ppg, 0.3 rpg, 0.3 apg, 3.0 minutes, .167 FG, Booker T. Washington HS/Tulsa, Okla.). Davis went to the same high school as former Syracuse standout Etan Thomas, but don't expect a reprise of Thomas' strong career. Davis played in just nine games last year and can't be expected to get on the floor much more this year. He could be an adequate rebounder but lacks a polished offensive game.

G-RONNEIL HERRON (5-11, 158 lbs, JR, #11, 0.0 ppg, 0.0 rpg, 0.0 apg, three appearances, Vanden HS/Warner Robins, Ga.). A walk-on who saw only two minutes of action last year, Herron missed the one shot he took, a three-pointer. He'll help the point guards as a practice player.

G-ANDREW KOUWE (6-0, 170 lbs, SO, #10, 0.0 ppg, 0.2 rpg, 0.0 apg, five appearances, Tampa Prep/Tampa, Fla.). Kouwe is a walk-on who played a total of six minutes last year and missed all three of his shots. Like Herron, he'll contribute as a practice player.

OTHER NEWCOMERS

F-JOSH PACE (6-6, 190 lbs, FR, #5, 26.0 ppg, 9.7 rpg, 3.0 spg, Griffin HS/Griffin, Ga.). Although Boeheim believes Pace will some day be a contributor, it's unlikely he'll grab too much playing time this season. Though athletic and certainly capable of scoring—as his 2,427 career points proved—Pace needs to become more of a perimeter force before he can break the logjam in front of him.

Pace will be good in up-tempo settings and should be able to grab a rebound or two. He was a fine defender in high school and also showed some passing skills.

QUESTIONS

Point Guard? Edelin brings fine prep credentials with him, but he has to deliver big right away.

Rebounding? The Orangemen were out-boarded with Brown. They need the newcomers and big returnees to step up.

Leadership? The losses of Griffin and Brown could cause problems in this area, unless Shumpert is ready to show the way.

ANSWERS

Shumpert! He scored big last year, and even if his numbers sag this year because of improved depth, he has the potential to be an All-America.

Williams! Now is his time to blossom into a strong scoring weapon to complement, and at times supplant, Shumpert.

Freshmen! This is Syracuse's most talented and deepest class in years, and it should help bring the Orange closer to big-time national prominence once again.

Boeheim! Go ahead and make jokes, but Boeheim has 600 career wins, a great defensive mind and an apparently renewed vigor for recruiting. Not a bad combination.

SYRACUSE 2000-2001 RESULTS

St. Francis	73-53
#DePaul	92-84
#Ohio State	77-66

Missouri	84-62
Colgate	73-65
##Akron	81-51
##Virginia Tech	88-68
Albany	105-75
Wisconsin-Greey Bay	69-57
Tennessee (L)	70-83
Columbia	61-47
Niagara	95-69
Notre Dame	79-70
@Pittsburg	71-66
@Rutgers	64-63
West Virginia	86-80
@Seton Hall (L)	65-77
@Notre Dame (L)	60-74
Rutgers	68-54
Georgetown	70-63
@North Carolina State	54-53
@Boston College (L)	63-65
Seton Hall	63-62
Miami (L)	57-68
@West Virginia (L)	76--87
Connecticut	65-60
@Georgetown (L)	61-72
Pittsburgh	80-69
@St. John's	93-91
###Connecticut	86-75
###Providence	55-54
###Pittsburgh (L)	54-55
####Kansas	58-87

#Great Alaska Shootout in Anchorage
##Carrier Classic in Carrier Dome
###Big East Championship in New York
####NCAA Tournament
@Road Games

BLUE RIBBON ANALYSIS

BACKCOURT	B
BENCH/DEPTH	B+
FRONTCOURT	B+
INTANGIBLES	B+

The Orangemen aren't there yet, but they have enough talent on this year's team to cause some big troubles for opponents. In the coming years, they may be simply dynamite. This year's class, coupled with the three projected newcomers for 2002, give the 'Cuse the kind of talent it hasn't had in a while.

For now, it's up to Shumpert and Williams to score, and the rest to fill in. That can be done, particularly if Williams gets to the basket more, and Shumpert continues to develop into a full-fledged offensive force. If they go one-two every night, Syracuse will be mighty tough to handle.

Edelin, of course, is a big key, if his suspension for alleged sexual misconduct is lift. He must handle 25-30 minutes a night at the point and show savvy. He doesn't have to get more than 10 points a night, although he's capable of more, but he must distribute, defend and take care of the ball. He's capable, but he'll have his freshman moments.

The frontcourt will be sturdy, thanks to the arrivals of Warrick, Forth and Konecny and the expected improvements of McNeil and Celuck. If Duany chips in on the wing, and Thues can play 10 minutes a night of reliable ball, the Orangemen will be dangerous. Like we said, this year is just an appetizer, although it could be quite satisfying. The real fun is yet to come. Again.

(M.B.)

North Carolina 18

LOCATION	Chapel Hill, NC
CONFERENCE	Atlantic Coast
LAST SEASON	26-7 (.788)
CONFERENCE RECORD	13-3 (t-1st)
STARTERS LOST/RETURNING	3/2
NICKNAME	Tar Heels
COLORS	Light Blue & White
HOMECOURT	Smith Center (21,750)
COACH	Matt Doherty (North Carolina '84)
RECORD AT SCHOOL	26-7 (1 year)
CAREER RECORD	48-23 (2 years)
ASSISTANTS	Doug Wojik (Navy '87)
	Fred Quartlebaum (Fordham '89)

Bob MacKinnon (King's College '82)

TEAM WINS (last 5 years)	28-34-24-22-26
RPI (last 5 years)	4-1-9-25-6
2000-01 FINISH	Lost in NCAA second round.

COACH AND PROGRAM

Heading into only his third year as a head coach, Matt Doherty is at a crossroads.

Can this relative neophyte take a team that lost five of its top seven players and return to the elite status that has been reserved for only one team from North Carolina in recent years, cross-town rival Duke?

Can he, with the potential of three freshmen in his starting lineup, sustain the success that the program has been known for over the last four decades? You know, the 20-win seasons, the third place or better finishes in the ACC, the NCAA bids that are practically seen as a birthright for the Tar Heels?

Can the experience-thin Tar Heels challenge the Blue Devils and Maryland for the ACC Championship? That's what Tar Heel fans and detractors will be looking for this season.

To be honest, that might be asking a lot of this team, which has to replace two first-round NBA draft picks in, a pair of two-sport stars who were big contributors and a couple of role players who were at least serviceable.

What is left with are two returning starters and a lot of question marks. Sure, Doherty put together what is arguably the best recruiting class in the country, with three players ranked in the top 30 signing up to play for a UNC team that Doherty promises will be more athletic and more fluid than recent teams.

But how will Melvin Scott, Jackie Manuel and Jawad Williams fare when they are immediately thrown into the fire of ACC competition, especially because Doherty couldn't land a big man that would have made all their jobs easier?

Where will the points come from on a team that lost more than 60 percent of its scoring from last year? Can seniors **Jason Capel** and **Kris Lang**, a pair of role players so far in their careers, provide ample leadership for a team in transition?

"People aren't expecting a lot from this team," Doherty said. "People are saying we probably won't finish in the top three of the ACC, that we probably won't win 20 games and we might not make it to the NCAA Tournament. That's fine with me. That's great bulletin board stuff."

Let's get real here: no one is really saying that. What they are saying is that Doherty needs to prove himself in this year of transition. That he needs to make changes quickly so that Carolina can continue to compete with the best teams in the nation.

No one doubts that the Tar Heels will have to scramble to reach their perpetual goals, but there is also an expectation that those things will happen. If they don't, Doherty's honeymoon will end soon.

This isn't the first time the Tar Heels have had to replace so much. Dean Smith did it in his next to last year, right after Jerry Stackhouse and Rasheed Wallace left early for the NBA. The next season, 1995-96, Smith at times started three pretty good freshmen (Antawn Jamison, Ademola Okulaja and Vince Carter) and the Tar Heels went 21-11, finished third in the ACC and were eliminated in the second round of the NCAA Tournament.

The next season, led by the three sophomores, the Tar Heels made Smith the winningest coach in Division I history and advanced to the Final Four.

Doherty's biggest problem is that he doesn't have the 34 years of coaching experience Smith had when he rebuilt his 1995-96 team. But that's not to say Doherty can't do it.

Last season, he was two-thirds of the way to the greatest debut since Orson Welles released Citizen Kane. Even though he wasn't the Heels' first choice to replace the retired Bill Guthridge—Roy Williams famously turned his alma mater down—Doherty arrived in July, 2000 and took charge.

He succeeded by shaking things up in Chapel Hill, where things had gotten as stale as a 25-cent loaf of bread. He was open with the fans and hard on his players. He was a burst of energy who cried after big wins and big losses. He was candid with his team—Duke had the ugliest cheerleaders in the ACC, he said once—and open with the media. He brought his own staff and turned up the volume on the team's strength and conditioning program.

Unlike Guthridge, he didn't do things exactly the

same way Smith did. But after losing twice in the first five games of the season, the Tar Heels took off, a rise that coincided with the return of Ronald Curry and Julius Peppers from the football team.

They won 18 straight games, the longest such streak in more than a decade. They reached the top of both national polls. Doherty even won his first game against Mike Krzyzewski, at Cameron Indoor Stadium, no less. But somewhere in February, the chemistry that every local and national writer had noted began to fall apart. Doherty had built his first team around the scoring of sophomore Joseph Forte and the defensive presence of 7-1 center Brendan Haywood.

Teams learned that Forte was the only real scoring threat, and by slowing him down, the Tar Heels were vulnerable, especially because point guard Curry was limited in his ability to get the ball to other players.

Lowly Clemson was the first to prove this, and Virginia followed suit as the Tar Heels lost five of their final 10 games of the season. Duke not only beat the Tar Heels in the regular-season finale, the Blue Devils embarrassed their biggest rival in the ACC Tournament Championship game, 79-53 in Atlanta. And Penn State ousted the Heels from the NCAA Tournament in the second round.

Still, the Tar Heels finished tied for first in the ACC's regular season, making Doherty the first coach in league history to win that title in his rookie year. He was selected the Associated Press' National Coach of the Year for leading the Tar Heels to a 26-7 record.

The fact is, however, Doherty engaged in a summer-long lessons-learned program. He acknowledges that he made mistakes last year. He may have pushed his team too hard. He may have relied too heavily on Forte's scoring, causing internal tension on the team.

"The No. 1 thing I learned as a coach [last] year was the importance of team chemistry," Doherty said. "You're always learning as a coach, and that's an important lesson I learned."

He has a better relationship with his players this year, a stronger foundation because three of the players are his own recruits and the rest of the team knows what he expects from them.

"Last year, I got the job in July and practice started in October," he said. "I didn't have a foundation that I maybe would have had if I was coaching here longer or if I had recruited the players. We went through some things.

"This year, they know me better and I know them better."

And, while he inherited great personnel when he arrived, Doherty will have talent more suited to his style this time around. He wants a smaller, more athletic team—sort of like you-know-who down the road. That's why he made three incredible athletes his primary recruiting targets.

Scoring will be spread around more this year. Capel and Lang will be expected to provide not only points, but also guidance to the new guys, at least until they develop their games a little.

"This year, it is a different team," Doherty said. "We will have five or more guys who are capable of hitting 20 points in a game. Last year, people were able to zoom in on Brendan [Haywood] or Joe. Now, I think we can get some scoring from a lot of different positions."

But can this team keep the schools strings of 27 consecutive NCAA Tournament berths, 31 consecutive 20-win seasons and 37 consecutive years of finishing in the ACC's top three alive? Doherty isn't making any promises, but he will make sure that his bevy of new personnel strives for that.

"I wouldn't say I am worried, but I am concerned," Doherty said. "You're always concerned. You always want to get better. We have to see a lot of improvement from a lot of people, but we'll work hard at it. We'll see to it that they work hard at it."

2001-2002 SCHEDULE

Nov.	16	Hampton
	20	Davidson
	28	*Indiana
Dec.	2	Georgia Tech
	8	@Kentucky
	16	Binghamton
	21-22	#Tournament of Champions
	27	North Carolina A&T
	30	Texas A&M
Jan.	5	Wake Forest
	9	@Maryland

	12	Virginia
	16	@Florida State
	19	@Connecticut
	23	North Carolina State
	27	@Clemson
	31	Duke
Feb.	2	@Georgia Tech
	6	@Wake Forest
	10	Maryland
	12	@Virginia
	17	Florida State
	20	Ohio
	24	@North Carolina State
	27	Clemson
March	3	@Duke
	7-10	##ACC Tournament

@Road Games
*ACC/Big Ten Challenge
#Charlotte Coliseum, Charlotte, NC (vs. College of Charleston first round; also St. Joseph's, Georgia State)
##Charlotte Coliseum, Charlotte, NC

STARTERS NOT RETURNING

PG-RONALD CURRY (6-2, 5.5 ppg, 3.4 rpg, 4.3 apg, 27.8 minutes, .431 FG, .351 3PT, .574 FT). Once football season ended and he finished his duties as UNC's starting quarterback, Curry was the immediate and clear leader of the Tar Heel basketball team, bringing a quick calm to the Heels that wasn't there with either freshmen Adam Boone or Brian Morrison running the point.

He didn't score a lot, but he didn't have to. All he needed to do was knock down an occasional three-pointer to keep defenses from sagging in on behemoth center Brendan Haywood. His game was a big surprise, and he might have been the Tar Heels' most valuable player until things started falling apart in late February and the team went into a slump.

For much of the season, he made all the right moves, getting the ball into the right hands, running the team without making many mistakes and using his outstanding athletic ability to play great defense. He was seventh in the ACC with 4.25 assists per game. He wasn't exactly the best ball handler in the world—he averaged more than three turnovers a game—but he did a passable job of running the team.

However, Curry's weaknesses were exposed. As athletic as he was, he wasn't a great open-court ball handler. Had he been able to get the ball inside to other players better, the Tar Heels might not have relied so much on Forte.

Curry still had two years of eligibility remaining, thanks to the medical red-shirt he took in 1999-2000. But he was a football senior this fall and despite his struggles on the gridiron, he should know by now that any hope he has for a career in professional sports will come in football. In the summer, he left the door open for a return to basketball, but if he is going to make it in football, he will need to participate in the NFL combines and in individual workouts. That just doesn't leave enough time for basketball.

SG-JOSEPH FORTE (6-4, 20.9 ppg, 6.0 rpg, 3.5 apg, 2.5 topg, 2.1 spg, 34.7 minutes, .450 FG, .377 3PT, .853 FT). For a player that came in with such exciting prospects and contributed All-America numbers for two seasons, Jospeh Forte finished his UNC career under an ugly cloud.

Was the one-time All-American too selfish for the Tar Heels to succeed in the NCAA Tournament? Did he take too many shots? And how exactly did his mother get a job with the sports agency that eventually ended up signing Forte after he decided to leave school after his sophomore season?

No one around Chapel Hill likes to hear those questions. And Forte wasn't exactly pleased that after all the hand-wringing about whether he should go pro or return, he didn't even make lottery status in the NBA draft. He was the 21st pick in the first round, going to the Boston Celtics.

But for two seasons in baby blue, Forte was instant offense for the Tar Heels, earning ACC Rookie of the Year as a freshman and sharing the ACC's Player-of-thepYear Award with Duke's Shane Battier.

He had the highest scoring average for a freshman in school history and, in his second season, he finished second to Duke's Jason Williams. And the combination of his outside shooting and 7-0 center Brendan Haywood's inside presence gave the Tar Heels, who averaged 79 points a game, plenty of scoring.

But Forte also developed into the kind of player Dean Smith always avoided: a primary scoring option who held the fortunes of his team in his shooting hands. He averaged nearly 17 shots per game, a total of 558 in the season, more than any UNC player since Charlie Scott took 611 in 1970.

Smith always said it was easy to shut down one player, which is why he always tried to spread the scoring around. But as the season rolled along, Doherty had little choice but to become more and more dependent on his young shooter.

Haywood was a great inside presence on defense, but was limited to one move on offense. Lang, often hampered by injuries, contributed some, but not frequently. Capel, irked by Forte's shooting and his own lack of attention, wanted to shoot more, but never could. And Curry was a playmaker, not a scorer.

So Forte was Tar Heels' best option, and that is what hurt Doherty's team down the stretch. Forte forced more and more shots, making fewer and fewer of them.

C-BRENDAN HAYWOOD (7-0, 12.3 ppg, 7.3 rpg, 1.3 apg, 3.6 bpg, 27.3 minutes, .592 FG, .516 FT). Possibly no one benefited from Doherty's get-tough approach with the Tar Heels last year more than Haywood, a massive presence inside who was always considered too soft and puffy to become a superstar. He never reached that status in college, even though he was a second-team All-ACC pick who was the most imposing defensive obstacle in the league, if not the country. But he was far more consistent as a senior, as he buckled down in his last opportunity to impress the NBA scouts.

He led the league with a school-record 120 blocked shots, finishing as North Carolina's all-time leader with 304 and becoming only the seventh player in ACC history to surpass 300 career blocks.

"I believe he is the best defensive player in the country," Doherty said late in the year. "He is the anchor of our defense."

He also became the league's all-time leader in career field-goal percentage at 63.9, surpassing Rasheed Wallace's mark of 63.5 percent. Still, it was a productive but frustrating senior season for the big man.

Not as frustrating as his first three years, when he would unaccountably disappear for long periods of time. How could a guy so big be so unnoticeable? How could he not dominate every game he played? After all, he is big, he is athletic and he can jump. It's not like he was Serge Zwikker.

Those were questions that dogged Haywood his entire career. Critics—and there were many of them during his four-year career—called him soft. However, he didn't get as many "Brenda! Brenda" chants as a senior because Doherty arrived and immediately challenged the big man to get into better shape and become the great player every one always expected him to be.

With Forte around, that didn't happen. Haywood's scoring and rebounding numbers actually went down as a senior. Doherty and his coaching staff were frustrated that Haywood wasn't more aggressive inside, but they loved the way he played defense. He tended to get the ball inside, wait for the inevitable double or triple team, then kick it back out to Forte rather than taking on the defenders.

Maybe it was because he was such a poor free-throw shooter—he made only 59.4 percent of his free throws in his career—and he didn't want to risk going to the line.

The fact is, he had such a high shooting percentage because he never strayed far enough away from the basket to take any miss-able shots. Most of his field goals were dunks, easy layups and put-backs. But height is not something that can be developed and Haywood will likely get his chance to contribute for awhile in the NBA. He was drafted with the 20th pick by the Cleveland Cavaliers, then traded in a draft-night deal to the Orlando Magic. In July, he was traded again, going to Washington, where he will play for UNC alumnus Michael Jordan.

OTHERS NOT RETURNING

G/F-MICHAEL BROOKER (6-6, 1.2 ppg, 0.6 rpg, 0.6 apg, 6.6 minutes, .300 FG, .235 3PT, .625 FT). He arrived on campus five years ago with a bad knee, a pickup game injury that had to be repaired before he ever matriculated. He got a medical red-shirt for his first season. But after that, Brooker's career just limped along. He scored in double figures only once in four seasons.

Though he had a reputation as a reliable outside shooter, he hit only 23.2 percent of his three-point shots in his career. He was rarely more than a role player who came off the bench late in games. As a senior, he played in just 17 games, starting two. His biggest contribution of the season was five points in the loss to Kentucky.

G/F-MAX OWENS (6-5, 5.7 ppg, 1.4 rpg, 0.7 apg, 14.1 minutes, .407 FG, .304 3PT, .838 FT). Haywood may have benefited the most from Doherty's devotion to fitness, but Owens benefited the most from Doherty's arrival as head coach. He was pulled from the deep end of the Tar Heel bench and played a greater role during his senior season than he did at the end of his junior year. Only Julius Peppers played more minutes as a reserve.

Owens waited patiently to become a starter for the Tar Heels, hoping as a sophomore to earn the spot vacated by Shammond Williams. But Jeff Capel came in as a freshman and took that job.

In 1999-2000, Capel moved to his natural small-forward position, but Owens was displaced from the shooting-guard position by freshman Joseph Forte. He started a dozen games in a three-guard rotation that Guthridge used while Kris Lang was out, but when Lang returned, Owens saw increasingly less time.

Last year, Owens really had no chance to start, except for the traditional Senior Night. But he came off the bench to supply instant offense at shooting guard or small forward. His scoring average actually went down from his sophomore and junior seasons, but he seemed to get more important minutes last year than he did in the previous two.

Owens was frequently in the lineup when games were on the line and he delivered. He hit three three-point shots in the Tar Heels' victory over Maryland and had a season-high 17 points against Georgia Tech.

"I had pretty high expectations when I got here," said Owens, who played with Tracy McGrady at Durham's Mt. Zion Academy. "I wanted to be a starter. But I don't feel bad about anything. I've learned a lot about the game."

F-JULIUS PEPPERS (6-7, 7.1 ppg, 4.0 rpg, .643 FG, .520 FT). One of the best decisions Bill Guthridge during his three-year tenure as head coach was allowing Peppers to walk on to the basketball team, after getting a strong recommendation from former point guard Ed Cota. Peppers, an All-America defensive end on the Tar Heel football squad, was a key reason Guthridge's last team advanced to the Final Four after a disappointing regular season.

Last year, Peppers took a little more time off than Curry after football season ended to work on some academics. But when he did arrive just before Christmas, he continued his bruising play off the bench. His biggest contribution was never really scoring. He just gave the Tar Heels an athletic big man who was the obvious foil to Haywood's sometimes less aggressive play. But he did hit double figures in scoring and grabbed a half-dozen rebounds four times during the regular season.

But, like Curry, Peppers slowed down considerably at the end of the basketball season. He barely even played in the ACC Tournament in Atlanta, a total of 19 minutes in three games, and admitted that he was at the end of his rope. But who could blame him for being worn out?

However, he came back strong in the NCAA Tournament. He seemed to be the only Tar Heel with spring in his legs in the Heels' second-round loss to Penn State, scoring a career high 21 points and grabbing 10 rebounds.

However, that was the end of Peppers' basketball career, even though he has another year of eligibility remaining. He committed himself in the off-season to becoming the best defensive player in college football, with the hope of being the top pick in the NFL draft. He will likely spend this basketball season attending NFL combines and participating in individual workouts for various teams.

F-JIM EVERETT (6-8, 0.3 ppg, 0.5 rpg, 1.6 minutes, .200 FG, 1.000 FT). Everett was a former walk-on who played on the varsity team for two seasons. He scored only 14 points in his Tar Heel career, four of which came last season.

STARTING LINEUP

PG-ADAM BOONE (6-2, 182 lbs., SO, #31, 1.5 ppg, 0.9 rpg, 1.2 apg, .300 FG, .323 3PT, .750 FT, Minnetonka HS/Minneapolis, Minn.). Doherty said several times over the summer that the point-guard position is wide open, that any one of four players could win the position if

Ronald Curry doesn't return.

Among the returning veterans, our bet is on Boone, who was overwhelmed early in the season when he stepped in immediately to replace the departed Ed Cota, becoming only the 16th player at UNC to start his first game as a freshman since freshmen became eligible to play in 1972. No wonder he seemed timid.

It was a difficult position for any freshman to be in, especially one with modest though solid point-guard skills. Boone, generally considered a Top 50 prospect after his senior season in high school, arrived in Chapel Hill with a decent jump shot and good passing abilities, but he is probably a step slow for the kind of game Doherty wants to play.

Those things were evident from the first game. So being replaced by Curry in the starting lineup wasn't the worst thing that happened to Boone or the Tar Heels.

"That really took the load off of him," Doherty said. "He was thrust into a pretty tough situation, to be thrown in at Michigan State as a point guard. To go against Kentucky at home.

"That's pretty tough for a freshman. Once Ronald joined the team, he was able to grow at his own pace and learn what he needed to learn. I thought he did a remarkable job."

Boone continued to contribute off the bench. His second-half performance at UCLA helped the Tar Heels win at Pauley Pavilion and his three assists and three rebounds were critical in the Tar Heels' win over Duke in February.

Boone turned an ankle before the Clemson game and wasn't the same the rest of the season, but his experiences last year should give him a slight advantage at winning the position going into the season.

SG-MELVIN SCOTT (6-2, 175 lbs., FR, #1, 19.5 ppg, 5.0 rpg, 5.0 apg, 4.0 spg, Southern HS/Baltimore, Md.). Doherty and his staff recruited Scott when they were still at Notre Dame. And when Doherty got the call home to Chapel Hill, it couldn't have made Scott any happier.

"I've wanted to go there since I was a kid," Scott said after Doherty's in-home visit. "I used to always see Carolina, the championships and all that. That's what I wanted."

It didn't hurt that Scott played at the same Baltimore high school as North Carolina director of basketball operations David Cason.

Scott is a great outside shooter who worked hard his senior season to improve his point-guard skills. There's an obvious opening there if Ronald Curry does not return to the basketball team, as he said in the summer. But there is also an opening at shooting guard, with Forte's early departure for the NBA.

Without Forte, the Tar Heels need a shooter and a scorer, two things Scott can do well. One of only two four-year starters at Southern (John Salley was the other), Scott averaged at least 19 points a game his first three seasons. He reached his peak as a junior, when he averaged more than 25 points.

But he concentrated more on being a point guard as a senior, though he was never exactly a pure point guard. He was more in the Donald Hand/Randolph Childress mold of points who like to shoot.

SF-JAWAD WILLIAMS (6-9, 205 lbs., FR, #21, 22.0 ppg, 11.0 rpg, .530 FG, .390 3PT, .760 FT, St. Edwards HS/Lakewood, Ohio). Is this a bad sign or what? In Williams' first appearance at Cameron Indoor Stadium, he suffered a broken nose during the McDonald's All-Star Game. Was it a Blue Devil jinx? Probably not, for this consensus Top 20 prospect figures to step in immediately and play for the Tar Heels.

He's a not-so-small forward who can play inside or outside, a la Duke's Mike Dunleavy. Possibly the most athletic player on the team, he's the prototype player for Doherty's more athletic style he wants to implement for the Tar Heels.

"He explained my role to me," Williams told the Raleigh News and Observer this spring. "He wants me to bring athleticism and quickness so he can go to a smaller lineup and we can really push the ball."

But Williams wasn't really Doherty's first choice to fill that role. Doherty first went after Deerwood, Md., prospect James White, who shocked many recruiting analysts by choosing Florida. It was widely seen as a great payback for Doherty stealing wing prospect Jackie Manuel from West Palm Beach, Fla., earlier in the summer.

So Doherty out-recruited Maryland's Gary Williams to bring in Williams, who held off making a commitment to the Terrapins after Doherty got the UNC job, on the chance that Doherty would come calling. Doherty, who

had recruited Williams for Notre Dame, did and Williams jumped at the chance to wear baby blue.

As a natural small forward, Williams should be able to step into the Heels' cut-down starting lineup from the beginning of the season. Williams is looking forward to being the centerpiece in Doherty's charged lineup.

"I'm really comfortable with it," Williams told the News and Observer. "Me, Jackie and Melvin Scott, we all play run-and-gun type of games. Coach Doherty couldn't do that this year because he had so many big guys. But we're going to come in and change that."

As a senior, Williams averaged 22 points and 11 rebounds. As a junior, he averaged 16.5 points and 8.0 rebounds. His high school coach, Eric Flannery, said Williams' biggest improvement as a senior was on the defensive end, where he paid more attention than he had in the past, and in rebounding.

Still, Williams says he needs to get stronger and develop a more consistent shot before the season starts.

"He is a very versatile player," Doherty said. "He can play inside or outside. He can handle the ball. I think he has a lot of upside to become a very good basketball player.

"I think he will play a significant role on our team."

PF-JASON CAPEL (6-8, 224 lbs., SR, # 25, 11.4 ppg, 7.3 rpg, 3.4 apg 1.6 topg, 31.7 minutes, .470 FG, .418 3PT, .785 FT, St. John's Prospect Hall HS/Fayetteville, N.C.). Doherty is looking to run more set plays to this senior, who has been a steady contributor, but not a star, during his first three years on campus. That's because there was always someone else getting all the attention.

This year, it's the former McDonald's All-American's turn to be one of the primary focal points of the Tar Heels' offense. He's waited long enough.

One of the main reasons for Capel's lack of star status is that he has nearly always played out of position, first as a shooting guard in his freshman season and a power forward as a sophomore and junior. That's where he will be again this year, as Doherty tries to develop a smaller lineup, something he knew he needed after the Tar Heels took their whipping in the ACC championship game.

Capel's numbers have always been steady. He's averaged between nine and 12 points his first three years, but never more. He's scored in double figures in 61 of his 95 career games, but in only five of those has he scored 20 or more.

He's a great rebounder for his size, tying 7-1 center Brendan Haywood for the team lead last year with 242. And, as the son of a coach, he does all the little things that coaches love. Few players in the league could finish sixth in rebounding and 12th in assists, as Capel did last year. He also led the Tar Heels with a 41.8 shooting percentage from the three-point line (he didn't have enough baskets to qualify for ACC rankings).

"I do what I do," Capel told the Raleigh News and Observer last season. "I go out there and score and rebound and pass the ball and play defense. I want to get recognized for it, but it's hard to be recognized when Joe's putting up 30."

But Capel bristled when that particular story called him a "role player."

"I am a player," said Capel, who had just put up 27 points and eight rebounds against in a 96-82 victory over Maryland. "I'm a player and that's it. I don't want to be put in any category, saying I am this or that."

There was a lot of talk last year about a possible rift between he and Forte, which had its genesis in some things Capel said out of frustration after a couple of disappointing losses late in the season. He and Forte both insisted there was no tension between them, but something ruined the Tar Heels' chemistry last year.

So for Capel, this year is a fresh start, with he and Lang as the possible centerpieces on a team that desperately needs scoring.

"Cape will be asked to score some more," Doherty said. "There will be more set plays for him this year than last year."

C-KRIS LANG (6-11, 243 lbs., SR, #42, 11.3 ppg, 5.7 rpg, 0.7 apg, 0.7 bspg, 0.6 spg, .550 FG, .520 FT, Hunter Huss HS/Gastonia, N.C.). Doherty not only wants this oft-injured senior to be a leader on this year's team, he wants him to play a slightly different game.

With Haywood gone, Lang is the Tar Heels' most experienced inside player. But he's always played power forward. This year, he'll likely take over the center position, as Doherty tries to get his best five players on the court.

And Lang has both experience and the ability to run

the floor on his side. However, Lang hasn't always been able to showcase his abilities. He had a great debut season, averaging 10.4 points and 5.4 rebounds as a freshman. But heading into his sophomore season, Lang suffered from shin splints and a mysterious illness that hampered his development and his numbers dropped to 9.5 points and 4.6 rebounds as his playing time fell.

He returned at full-strength last season and made solid contributions in scoring and rebounding. He scored in double-figures in 16 of the Tar Heels' first 18 games, including a career-high 22 points against both Michigan State and Buffalo.

Lang had a sore ankle late in the summer, but stayed relatively healthy all season.

This year, Doherty expects Lang to be more versatile and more vocal on a team that needs on-court and off-court leadership. The coach had Lang working on his outside shot during the off-season, trying to get him to stray as far as 18 feet away from the basket.

That may not be the wisest move for a guy who has never attempted a three-point shot in his career and has made only 62.8 percent of his free throws in college.

"I think that will be important for his development and our development," Doherty said. "It'll also open things in the middle for us and let us have more interchangeable players. It'll allow more movement and open up the floor a little bit."

KEY RESERVES

F/C-BRIAN BERSTICKER (6-10, 232 lbs., SR, #50, 1.5 ppg, 1.0 rpg, 4.2 minutes, .382 FG, .500 FT, Kempsville HS/Virginia Beach, Va.). Like the rest of the Tar Heels, Bersticker found out there were consequences for not abiding by Doherty's desires. The coach wanted Bersticker, an athletic big man known for his emotion, to get stronger and play more aggressively.

When that didn't happen, Bersticker found himself on the end of the Tar Heel bench, getting only marginal playing time. He played in each of the Tar Heels' first 10 games, but saw limited action after that.

"The biggest thing with Brian last year was his strength," Doherty said. "I wanted him to be stronger and more aggressive and have more of a presence in the post."

Bersticker will get a final opportunity to follow the coach's wishes during his senior year. Doherty gave him a handful of suggestions on how to get better.

"I really asked him this summer to work harder on his body," Doherty said. "We'll see if he did that or not. If he did, he can have a big impact on the team. If he did not, then I don't know where he will be."

Doherty admits that the Tar Heels need production out of Bersticker. In the off-season, he called the 6-10 forward "as important as any player we have coming back."

The Heels certainly have an opening for a big man, because Haywood is gone, Jason Parker never arrived and Doherty couldn't land a big man in this year's recruiting class.

So there is little doubt that Bersticker will play more than just four minutes a game.

"Brian can run the floor pretty well and he is a really good shooter," Doherty said. "He can stretch the defense on the floor. I think this year, we will be more open in transition."

Which means Bersticker can contribute, if he follows Doherty's instructions.

G-JACKIE MANUEL (6-6, 185 lbs., FR, #5, 20.8 ppg, 11 rpg, 4.5 apg, Cardinal Newman HS/West Palm Beach, Fla.). Practically the first thing Doherty did after being hired as Bill Guthridge's successor was call on Manuel, a highly regarded swing player who seemed a lock to stay in-state and play for Billy Donovan's Florida Gators. But Doherty called right after the press conference to announce his hiring was over, and Manuel changed his mind quickly.

"I never talked about it, but I always wanted to go to Carolina," Manuel told the Herald-Sun of Durham, N.C.

He committed to the Tar Heels less than a week later, kicking off what Tar Heel fans hope will be a long string of recruiting triumphs for UNC's young coach.

Where Manuel will play this season is a big question. He fits the mold that Doherty wants for the Tar Heels, a great athlete who can run the floor and play great defense. He has long arms, with great quickness and leaping ability.

"I think Jackie is a guy who can play a couple of positions," Durham, N.C.,-based recruiting analyst Dave Telep said. "He's extremely explosive, very athletic and he's a perimeter shooter. He's a guy who's carved out a reputation of playing defense."

But the Tar Heels need a shooter this year to replace Forte's scoring. So Doherty might look first at fellow freshman Melvin Scott or sophomore Brian Morrison, who both have better developed shooting skills than Manuel at the moment.

Manuel, however, will play frequently, as Doherty makes use of what many consider to be one of the best recruiting classes in the nation.

G-BRIAN MORRISON (6-2, 175 lbs., SO, #3, 3.0 ppg, 1.2 rpg, 1.1 apg, 1.2 topg, 9.1 minutes, .330 FG, .378 3PT, .629 FT, Lake Washington HS/Redmond, Wash.). Maybe it was unfair that Morrison tried to play point guard early last year. What else was a freshman who is a natural shooting guard to do when playing behind Joseph Forte? Besides, the Tar Heels had the critical need for a point guard last season.

So he competed with Adam Boone for the starting job. Boone won, and Morrison came off the bench to provide a boost in athletic ability. He hit double figures in two of his first three games, against Winthrop and Appalachian State, but not again after that.

Morrison is more athletic than Boone, with better jumping ability and shooting skills. But he's also not really a point guard, as he showed many times last year, racking up 38 turnovers in 291 minutes of action with ill-advised and forced passes that drove Doherty nuts.

That inability to hold on to the ball and an ankle injury he suffered in practice before the Florida State game cut Morrison's playing time significantly in the second half of the season. He played in 32 games and scored 66 points in the Tar Heels' first 16 games, but only 31 in the final 16.

"My biggest concern with Brian was taking care of the basketball," Doherty said. "He is a great athlete and he can score. He can guard. But he needs to get stronger and he needs to make better decisions with the basketball. If he does that, he will play a lot.

"He will likely play some at the two-guard and some at the point."

As a veteran, Morrison may have the edge going into preseason practice at winning the starting shooting guard position. But the two freshmen coming in—Scott and Manuel—are talented.

Whatever the case, Morrison will get time at both guard positions at times this season. Maybe, if he doesn't try to make too many wild passes, he can even earn a starting job.

OTHER RETURNING PLAYERS

F-ORLANDO MELENDEZ (6-8, 200 lbs., SR, #32, 0.8 ppg, 0.8 rpg, 2.1 minutes, .500 FG, .500 3PT, 1.000 FT, McDowell County HS/Juana Diaz, Puerto Rico). Melendez has one distinction in his career so far: he's the last player signed by Dean Smith before the legendary coach retired in 1997.

Other than that, the athletic Melendez is known for making spectacular dunks in practice and mostly bad decisions on the basketball floor. He has contributed little during his career. Last year, he played in a total of 10 games, with a season-high of five points against Massachusetts.

Will he contribute more this year? Maybe, Doherty says.

"If he really dedicates himself to the defensive end, he can be a great defender," the coach said. "He has good size and great athleticism. On offense, if he would make better decisions with the basketball and be a more consistent shooter, he could certainly help us on the floor.

"He is one of the best athletes we have."

G-JONATHAN HOLMES (6-0, 175 lbs., JR, #14, 1.6 ppg, 0.8 rpg, 0.7 apg, 4.1 minutes, .500 FG, .500 3PT, .923 FT, Bloomington South HS/Bloomington, IN). Doherty doesn't immediately discount the possibility that Holmes will challenge for the starting point-guard position.

"Every one will get their chance," the coach said.

Last year, Holmes was the only returning player with point-guard experience, but Adam Boone won the starting point-guard position in the preseason, before giving way to Ronald Curry. Holmes played in only 14 games, handing out 10 assists with only four turnovers. He is a good outside shooter, who hit three-of-six three-point shots and 12 of his 13 free throws on the year. But he is hardly the kind of athletic player that Doherty wants to build his team around, now that the coach is bringing in his own talent.

But Doherty learned diplomacy from Smith, so

Holmes will get a chance to earn playing time.

"He has worked hard over the summer," Doherty said. "We will see how he stacks up."

F-WILL JOHNSON (6-8, 211 lbs., JR, #44, 1.5 ppg, 1.2 rpg, 0.4 apg, 6.4 minutes, .450 FG, .286 3PT, .722 FT, Hickory HS/Hickory, N.C.). To look at him, Johnson doesn't seem to be the kind of player Doherty is looking for to build his program. But to tell the truth, the coach kind of likes the rangy Morehead Scholar (UNC's most prestigious academic scholarship) who was a recruited walk-on by Bill Guthridge two years ago.

Johnson played in 22 games last year, as a substitute for the oft-injured Kris Lang. He played in 24 as a freshman. He still needs to be stronger to be able to fight for rebounds, but he is one of the deadliest outside shooters on the team, which might earn him more playing time.

But the biggest reason he may get on the court is that the Tar Heels are desperately into shape.

"I expect him to contribute a whole lot," Doherty said. "He is a guy who can shoot the ball and is a tough kid."

OTHER NEWCOMERS

C-NEIL FINGLETON (7-5, 295 lbs., RS-FR, #13, 15.0 ppg, 12.0 rpg, 5.0 bspg, Holy Name Central Catholic HS/Durham, England). No one can teach height, and this former McDonald's All-American has more of it than just about any player in college basketball. He's the tallest player in school history and matches former N.C. State player Chuck Nevitt as the tallest guy to ever play in the ACC.

But can he contribute in Doherty's system, which the coach hopes to make faster and more athletic this year? That is the key to Fingleton's UNC career.

Like Dean Smith said many times about Serge Zwikker, the serviceable 7-2 Dutch center of a few years back, the Tar Heels won't wait for Fingleton to get up and down the floor. Fingleton will have to work hard to get his lumbering body moving.

"A lot depends on Neil's ability to run the floor," Doherty said. "I told him if he was able to run the floor, he'll have a chance to contribute a lot."

Doherty didn't get much of a chance to see what Fingleton, a native of Durham, England, could do last year, because the big man had back surgery in November and sat out as a medical red-shirt. But the coach saw enough to know that Fingleton needs to improve a lot before he will get on the floor.

"I don't want him to make us wait on offense," Doherty said. "Defensively, I want him to be a factor. His reactions to the ball on offense and defense need to improve and that will come when he gets into better shape."

Smith said similar things about Zwikker. But Zwikker worked hard to develop the few skills that he had, and after watching from the bench for two years (one as a red-shirt), he was able to contribute as a junior and senior.

Doherty was pleased with Fingleton's progress during spring workouts and he is anxious to see what the big man learned during his summer abroad with Great Britain's national team. Fingleton was a starter for the team in the World University Games in Beijing.

He played more than 20 minutes a game in seven games, averaging 6.6 points, 4.9 rebounds and one blocked shot.

"This summer was big for him," Doherty said. "He showed in the spring that he is dedicated to becoming a better player. He put his legs to work, running and doing other things. This is a big year for him and he has a great opportunity."

QUESTIONS

Scoring? Who is going to provide the offense on a team that lost a whooping 62 percent of its scoring, including the explosive Forte?

Experience? Could the Tar Heels start three freshmen this year? Would Dean Smith roll over in his grave? (Oops, he's not dead.)

Style? Doherty doesn't really know what kind of offense he wants his team to play. He wants to be fast-paced and spread all over the court, but there are still some things he has to figure out, such as, say, a starting lineup.

ANSWERS

Tradition! All the streaks are still intact, and this model of consistent excellence has still not been broken.

Believe it or not, the Tar Heels have faced greater transition before and still managed to finish in the top three in the ACC, get their 20 wins and make it to the NCAA Tournament.

Coaching! For two-thirds of the season, Doherty was on his way to having a great debut year. It ended on a fairly sour note, but he knows what he wants to do. And if he has problems, Dean Smith is only a phone call away.

New blood! The Tar Heels were a surly bunch at the end of the year and nobody on or around the team liked how they plummeted at the end. A fresh start might not be a bad idea.

NORTH CAROLINA 2000-2001 RESULTS

#Winthrop	66-61
#Tulsa	91-81
Appalachian State	99-69
##Michigan State (L)	64-77
Kentucky (L)	93-76
Miami (Fla.)	67-45
@Texas A&M	82-60
Buffalo	95-74
@UCLA	80-70
###Massachusetts	91-60
###College of Charleston	64-60
@Georgia Tech	84-70
Wake Forest	70-69
@Maryland	86-83
Marquette	84-54
Clemson	92-65
@Florida State	80-70
Virginia	88-81
@NC State	60-52
@Duke	85-83
Georgia Tech	82-69
@Wake Forest	80-74
Maryland	96-82
@Clemson (L)	65-75
Florida State	95-67
@Virginia (L)	66-86
NC State	76-63
Duke (L)	81-95
####Clemson	99-81
####Georgia Tech	70-63
####Duke (L)	53-79
#####Princeton	70-48
#####Penn State (L)	74-82

#NABC Classic in Chapel Hill, NC
##ACC/Big Ten Challenge in East Lansing, MI
###Tournament of Champions in Charlotte, NC
####ACC Tournament in Atlanta
#####NCAA Tournament
@Road Games

BLUE RIBBON ANALYSIS

BACKCOURT	B+
BENCH/DEPTH	B
FRONTCOURT	B+
INTANGIBLES	A

Doherty has many questions facing him in his sophomore season as the Tar Heels' coach, the biggest of which is just how well he can handle the massive turnover from a team that spent several weeks atop the national polls last year.

The obvious solution, of course, is not to rely on one player to replace Forte's scoring or Haywood's defense. The Tar Heels will have to be more balanced, like some of Smith's teams from years past.

"This team could be like the Rick Fox-Pete Chilcutt teams," Doherty said. "Those teams had balance, like when Hubert Davis was here. We want teams to wonder who they are going to have to cheat off of. I would like to think that teams will have a hard time cheating off anybody from this year's team. Last year, they could cheat off several different guys. You can't zero in on as many people this year."

That's not exactly an admission that he handled last year's team incorrectly. Forte and Haywood were two first-round picks in the NBA draft. They were obviously talented players. But "Coach D'oh" learned at the end of last year what Smith always said throughout his career: you can't rely on just one person to provide scoring.

Doherty is still a young coach, one who hasn't even celebrated his 40th birthday. Give him this year to learn a little more and recruit his type of players. Then watch out.

(T.P.)

Oklahoma State 19

LOCATION	Stillwater, OK
CONFERENCE	Big 12
LAST SEASON	20-10 (.667)
CONFERENCE RECORD	1-6 (5th)
STARTERS LOST/RETURNING	0/5
NICKNAME	Cowboys
COLORS	Orange & Black
HOMECOURT	Gallagher-Iba Arena (13,611)
COACH	Eddie Sutton (Oklahoma State '58)
RECORD AT SCHOOL	249-105 (11 years)
CAREER RECORD	679-269 (31 years)
ASSISTANTS	Sean Sutton (Oklahoma State '92)
	Glynn Cyprien (Texas-San Antonio '90)
	Kyle Keller (Oklahoma State '90)
TEAM WINS (last 5 years)	17-22-23-27-20
RPI (last 5 years)	46-33-48-18-49
2000-01 FINISH	Lost in NCAA first round.

COACH AND PROGRAM

Gallagher-Iba Arena was renovated before last season. The roof was literally raised and the best little bandbox of a basketball arena was expanded from 6,381 cozy seats to 13,611 seats. Basically, the construction project involved taking the roof off the arena and building a second deck above the original first level of seating.

There was speculation that the expansion would rob Oklahoma State of its home-court edge. That didn't happen. The Cowboys won 11 of their 12 games in Stillwater last season.

But something that no one could have expected happened to Gallagher-Iba. For one terrible week in late January, the basketball arena became a memorial and, ultimately, a symbol of triumph and perseverance.

On Jan. 27, Oklahoma State lost at Colorado, 81-71. The Cowboys' traveling party had flown to Boulder on three planes—two private jets and one Beechcraft Super King Air 200 propeller plane. On the return trip to Stillwater in that late winter afternoon, the Beechcraft crashed after 15 minutes of flight. All 10 aboard—including players Nate Fleming and Dan Lawson—died. Also killed was Will Hancock, the team's young and talented sports information director, and student manager Jared Weiberg, nephew of Big 12 Conference commissioner Kevin Weiberg.

Oklahoma State coach Eddie Sutton, 64 years old at the time, had no experience call on.

"Coaching 101 doesn't prepare you for anything like this," Sutton said several times after the tragedy.

That Saturday night, still stunned by the news, Sutton was up until 1 a.m. calling family members of the victims to deliver the news personally.

The town of Stillwater and a state that has endured the tragedies of killer tornadoes and the Oklahoma City Federal Building bombing had to absorb another body blow.

In the lobby of refurbished Gallagher-Iba, a 60-foot long by seven-foot high wall displaying the handwritten remembrances of fans and friends. On the Wednesday after the crash, a memorial service was conducted at the arena.

And nine days after the crash, on Feb. 5, Oklahoma State returned to the court to face Missouri in a rescheduled game. Tears turned to sweat. Competition replaced sorrow. Sobs became cheers. All the counseling, all the hugs, all the choruses of Amazing Grace were replaced by a 69-66 Big 12 Conference victory that was important from a sports and basketball standpoint but was also a cleansing catharsis for a team that has been asking "why" and finding no answers.

"All of us, we live baskeball, it's something we do day in and day out," Oklahoma State junior Fredrik Jonzen said after the game. "This week has seemed like an eternity. It was a relief to start playing basketball again."

"Losing never crossed my mind," said Andre Williams, who chased down two crucial offensive rebounds in the final minute. "It was hard to just focus on basketball. I'm used to looking over there (on the bench) and seeing faces that weren't there. We needed this game. It's a win I'll never forget."

It was Sutton's 673rd victory. None of the previous 672 has meant so much. As he walked off the floor after a post-game television interview, his head was bowed and his eyes were moist.

"I don't think I've ever wanted to win a game any more than tonight," Sutton said. "It would have been devastating not to win. It continues the healing process we're all going through. The past few days have been brutal for the players and the coaching staff. We've got a long ways to go, but we took one step closer to being well."

The victory over Missouri lifted Oklahoma State's record to 14-4. Over their next 11 games, the Cowboys went 6-5. They managed to squeeze an at-large bid to the NCAA Tournament, where they lost to Southern Cal in the first round.

Winning 20 games and getting into the NCAAs would have been an accomplishment no matter what. The 1999-2000 Cowboys won 27 games with four senior starters.

Last season was designated as a rebuilding year, with only one starter returning and no seniors. Add in the lasting emotional scars of a mid-season plane crash and Oklahoma State's performance on the court was truly remarkable.

Sutton, who turned 65 on March 12, looked at least 10 years older during the season's final six weeks. From Jan. 27 on, he tried to be a rock for his players, coaches and program. Lost in the sadness was the fact that he was again a rock-solid coach. He was able to mold a team that overachieved in the face of adversity.

"It was a tough, tough year for us. One we'll never forget," said Sutton, whose team returns all five starters. "After last year, I think we're all excited about this season and what it could hold. After all we went through last year, I wouldn't have wanted to go into this season without some good players. That would have made it difficult. But we should be pretty good."

2001-2002 SCHEDULE

Nov.	16	Cincinnati
	17	#Austin Peay
	19-21	##Las Vegas Tournament
	24	North Texas
	29	New Orleans
Dec.	1	Wichita State
	8	Jackson State
	17	Northwestern State
	19	@UMKC
	22	*Arkansas
	29	**Ball State
Jan.	5	Texas
	8	@Baylor
	12	@Iowa State
	15	Kansas
	19	@Texas Tech
	23	Nebraska
	26	Colorado
	30	@Oklahoma
Feb.	2	@Kansas State
	6	Texas Tech
	10	@Fresno State
	13	Oklahoma
	16	@Texas A&M
	20	@Texas
	23	Baylor
	25	@Missouri
March	2	Texas A&M
	7-10	###Big 12 Tournament

@Road Games
*ALLTEL Arena, Little Rock, AR
**All-College Classic, Myriad Convention Center, Oklahoma City, OK
#First round Las Vegas Tournament
##Las Vegas, NV (also UTEP, Providence, TCU, Northwestern State, Oklahoma State)
###Kemper Arena, Kansas City, MO

STARTERS NOT RETURNING

None

OTHERS NOT RETURNING

C-JASON KEEP (6-10, 3.6 ppg, 2.0 rpg, 8.7 mpg, 541 FG, .485 FT). Keep was quickly becoming a cult figure before he was kicked off the team for disciplinary reasons. The 290-pound Keep, who had "Big Daddy" tattooed on one arm, broke a rim with a dunk during the first game played in Gallagher-Iba Arena. He started six games and saw action in 17 others.

F-DAVID ANDERSON (6-8, 0.9 ppg, 1.0 rpg, 5.6 mpg).

Anderson decided to leave the team after playing in 18 games, with one start, as a freshman.

G-ELLIS KIDD (6-4, five minutes in two games). Kidd, who figured to get some playing time in the backcourt, left the program early last season. The departures of Anderson and Kidd allowed Sutton to recruit junior-college replacements.

PROJECTED STARTERS

PG-VICTOR WILLIAMS (5-10, 185 lbs., JR, #5, 33.5 mpg, 11.5 ppg, 2.8 rpg, .365 FG, .280 3PT, .745 FT, 110 assists, 102 turnovers, Illinois State/Kansas City, Kansas). After sitting out two seasons ago after his transfer from Illinois State, Williams quickly immersed himself back into Division I basketball. While Baker spent a lot of the time with the ball in his hands, Williams technically was Oklahoma State's point guard.

He was second on the team in assists with 110, but like Baker he turned it over too much (102 times). The Kansas City product needs to improve on his outside shooting. He was second on the team in three-point shots (125), but shot just .280 from behind the line.

Sutton would gladly take more games form Williams like the one he produced in an important, mid-February victory over Oklahoma. Williams scored a career-high 26 points and was equally impressive on defense. Williams, scored 18 points in the first half, matching the Sooners' total. He also hounded Oklahoma's J.R. Raymond all night. Raymond, who had averaged 20 points during Oklahoma's winning streak, finished with just seven.

"My first shot kind of felt good," said Williams after his career night [his previous best of 25 came while he was at Illinois State]. "The basket just kept getting bigger and bigger for me and I just kept knocking them down."

Sutton encouraged Williams all season to work on his perimeter game. After making a clutch three-pointer in a win over Arkansas in December, Williams mentioned Sutton's good-natured prodding.

"Coach really emphasized this week that I needed to make my shots," Williams said. "He jokingly said that it looked like my shot took its Christmas vacation already. When I
got the open shot I was fortunate enough to make it."

With attention focused on Baker, Williams will get more open shots this season. If he can make a higher percentage of them, it will take some heat off his backcourt mate.

SG-MAURICE BAKER (6-1, 175 lbs., SR, #1, 19.8 ppg, 6.7 rpg, 4.2 apg, 37.4 mpg, .525 FG, .408 3PT, .806 FT, Dixie Community College, Utah/Granite City, Ill.). There were plenty of points to replace from the previous season's team and Baker was more than happy to help pick up the slack.

Baker, a transfer from Dixie Community College in Utah, was one of the biggest surprises in the Big 12. He wound up as a first team all-conference pick and was selected the Big 12 Newcomer of the Year by the league's coaches after finishing second in the conference in scoring, fourth in steals, eighth in three-point percentage and three-pointers per game (2.13), ninth in assists and an impressive 16th in rebounding.

Baker led Oklahoma State in five statistical categories—scoring, three-point shooting, free-throw shooting, assists and steals. On Jan. 3 against UT-San Antonio, Baker had the second triple-double in school history when he had 19 points, 14 rebounds and 10 assists. (Joe Baker had the first with 10 points, 11 rebounds and 10 blocked shots against New Orleans on Jan. 5, 1985).

"It's amazing that with all the great players that have come through this institution—boy we've had a lot of them—that's only the second triple-double," Sutton said after Baker's great night. "[Baker] is a special player. If our big guys could have finished shots, he would have had about 15 assists."

Not just a scorer or passer, the aggressive Baker can also rebound better than any player his size in the country. Baker grabbed an eye-catching 6.7 rebounds a game; 74 of his 202 rebounds came on the offensive end.

"He's unbelievable, isn't he?" Sutton said after Baker scored 25 points and grabbed 10 rebounds in a win over Iowa State. "He rebounds that way in practice, too. I think I embarrassed my big guys by saying, 'How can this little guy lead the team in rebounding?' But he's aggressive, quick and has a nose for the ball."

And perhaps equally impressive to Baker's rebounding was the fact he shot .525 from the field.

"I don't think any of us projected Mo would have the

season he did," Sutton said. "Normally, when you get a player from community college it takes an adjustment. But he had a sensational year and I'd think he can equal or surpass it his senior year."

Baker is an atypical guard in Sutton's system. For his game to flourish, he needs the ball. Baker led the Cowboys in minutes played, shots attempted and turnovers. He had just two more assists than turnovers, a ratio Sutton would certainly want improved this season. However, if Baker had not taken control of the offense, it's doubtful Oklahoma State would have won 20 games.

Consider some of Baker's bigger games. In the first round of the Big 12 Tournament, he scored a career-high tying 31 against Texas Tech. He followed that with a 20-point, 10-rebound effort against Texas, his fifth double-double of the season. In the regular-season finale, he scored 31 points and grabbed nine boards against Oklahoma. Baker scored 26 points in an earlier game against the Sooners as the Cowboys won, 72-44, Oklahoma's worst loss in 20 years.

Baker scored 29 against Baylor, knocking in six-of-10 three-pointers. He scored 27 against Colorado and came up with 22 points and 10 boards in a regular-season win over A&M.

Baker was chosen College Hoops Insider's JUCO Transfer of the Year, and few could argue.

As evidenced by Baker's Big 12 newcomer award, the league's coaches, who watch more tape than anyone and have a better appreciation for who makes plays, were impressed.

"[Baker] is an excellent basketball player," said A&M's Melvin Watkins. "He plays with a lot of emotion, and having a player around that gives you that kind of emotion is a great thing."

SF-MELVIN SANDERS (6-5, 215 lbs., SO, #34, 8.0 ppg, 4.4 rpg, 29.1 mpg, .425 FG, .333 3PT, .590 FT Seward Community College, Kansas/Liberal, Kansas.). For a player who still is adjusting to big-time basketball, Sanders had a solid sophomore season. He started all 30 games and was the Cowboys' defensive stopper.

His offensive numbers were solid. Sanders was third on the team in three-pointers made, but he attempted just 39 free throws. Clearly, he needs to be more aggressive attacking the basket.

That's because Sanders has some serious athletic ability. At Liberal High School in Kansas, he had a high jump of 7-2, a 25-foot long jump and a 52-foot triple jump. Sutton has a history of harnessing athletic ability and turning it into basketball skill. Don't be surprised if Sanders has a breakout season.

PF-ANDRE WILLIAMS (6-7, 210 lbs., JR, #40, 29 mpg, 6.8 ppg, 7.7 rpg, 2.2 blocks per game, .503 FG, .442 FT, Maine Central Institute, Kansas City, Kansas). Two years ago, Williams' freshman season was truncated when he was involved in the Myron Piggie saga that also cost the Rush brothers time in NCAA purgatory. However, by the end of the season that saw Oklahoma State lose to Florida State in the East Regional final, Williams was proving to be a dynamic off-the-bench rebounder.

While most players hunger to hear their names announced as a starter during pre-game ceremonies, Williams prefers to come off the bench. Preferences aside, Williams probably will start up front this season.

At 6-7 and 210 pounds, Williams isn't a prototypical power foward. However, his long arms and leaping ability makes him a terrific rebounder and shot blocker. Last season, Williams was seventh in the Big 12 in rebounding and third in blocked shots. He was voted to the Big 12's all-defensive and all-bench teams.

Williams' biggest shortcoming is on the offensive end. He's not much of a low-post threat; most of his points come from offensive rebounds. And his free-throw shooting was atrocious (.442). If Williams can start to assert himself on offense by developing a consistent move or two, he'll become a star.

PF/C-FREDRIK JOHNZEN (6-10, 230 lbs., SR, #12, 15.0 ppg, 6.5 rpg, .520 FG, .639 FT Katedralskolan/Uppsala, Sweden). Smooth. That's the best description of this stoic Swede. After spending most of his freshman and sophomore seasons as a role player, Johnzen started to come on at the end of the 1999-2000 season. He was perhaps Oklahoma State's most consistent player down the stretch as the Cowboys reached the East Regional final. Johnzen earned All East Regional honors for his efforts.

That solid play continued last season as Johnzen was chosen second-team All-Big 12 by the league's coaches and third-team by the Associated Press. Johnzen, who has range out to the free-throw line, shot 52 percent and was the Cowboys' third-leading rebounder. For his career, he enters this season making 51.4 percent of his shots. That's among the best field-goal percentage marks in school history.

Like Baker, Johnzen saved some of his better performances for the end of the season, when the Cowboys made their drive to the NCAA Tournament. He scored a career-high tying 26 points against Iowa State and equalled that against Missouri. He reached double figures in Oklahoma State's final six games before the NCAAs.

Like Baker, Johnzen has a well-rounded game. He came close to his own triple double, with 13 points, nine boards and seven assists in an 82-76 win over Texas A&M. A good passer, Johnzen handed out a career-high eight assists against Baylor.

Johnzen is also up to making plays at crunch time. His 16-foot jumper with 36 seconds left gave OSU a lead in a win over Kansas State.

Look for Johnzen to continue that strong play, if his summer exploits were any indication. Playing for Sweden in the World University Games, Johnzen had some strong performances. He scored 21 points and grabbed 12 boards against South Korea, had 21 and six against Russia and 13 and 11 against Germany.

KEY RESERVES

F-TERRENCE CRAWFORD (6-6, 235 lbs., SO, #14, 3.5 ppg, 2.4 rpg, 18.7 mpg, .400 FG, .263 3PT, .657 FT, Bishop McGuinness HS/Oklahoma City, Okla.). Crawford's freshman season was wrecked when he suffered a knee injury on Dec. 19. He missed the next eight games before returning to action. Crawford and Sanders are the only small forwards on the roster, so if Crawford is healthy he should get any minutes that don't go to Sanders.

C-JACK MARLOW (7-0, 330 lbs., SO, #55, 1.8 ppg, 1.7 rpg 5.9 mpg, Union HS/Tulsa, Okla.). Marlow is a space-eater (at 330 pounds, he apparently eats everything). As a freshman, he played in 27 games and averaged 5.9 minutes a game. He's a definite project, but he's got the raw ability that indicates eventually he could become a solid contributor. Despite his bulk, Marlow is surprisingly mobile.

F/C-ANTOINE BROXSIE (6-10, 240 lbs., SR, #21, 3.5 ppg, 2.4 rpg, 9.2 mpg, Minnesota/Tampa, Fla.). Broxsie, who played his freshman and sophomore seasons at Minnesota before transferring to Oklahoma State, had a nice debut season as a frontcourt reserve. He started four games—the first four starts of his 75 game collegiate career—while Andre Williams was recovering from an ankle sprain.

Broxsie has a seven-foot, three-inch wingspan, so he's a good rebounder and shot-blocker.

OTHER RETURNEES

F-IVAN McFARLIN (6-7, 210 lbs., SO, #23 Willow Ridge HS, Sugar Land, Texas). Last season, Oklahoma State hoped that McFarlin would be a contributor in its frontcourt rotation. But he failed to qualify academically and spent the season practicing with the team as a partial qualifier. If he stays in school for four seasons and shows the necessary academic progress, he could earn back his fourth season of eligibility.

As a high school senior, the left-handed McFarlin was regarded as a consensus top 40 prospect. He could wind up being a significant player this season.

"Ivan's a fierce rebounder at both ends of the floor," Sutton said. "He's such a hard worker and plays so hard. That should allow him to be a good defender as well."

G-GUY IKPAH (6-0, 165 lbs., FR, #13, Williamstown, N.J.). A walk-on, Ikpah sat out last season as a red-shirt.

OTHER NEWCOMERS

G-CHEYNE GADSON (6-3, 210 lbs., JR, #30, 22 ppg, 5.7 apg, 4.5 apg, Westchester CC, N.Y./Jamaica HS, Jamaica, N.Y.). Gadson will be expected to add some depth at the point-guard position. Last season at Westchester Community College, he averaged 22 points, 5.7 assists and 4.5 rebounds. He's a good passer and his size will be valuable, considering that starting guard Baker and Williams are not that tall.

"Cheyne is a very skilled player," OSU assistant Glynn Cyprien said. "He is a strong, mature player who passes well and can score when needed. Cheyne should come in and challenge for playing time immediately."

Gadson was an honorable mention NJCAA All-American after leading WCC to an 18-14 record.

"Cheyne is an all-around good athlete who was an effective point/combo guard for us," WCC coach Winston Nicholas said. "His strength is getting to the basket and he also has an excellent mid-range game."

G-AARON HILL (6-4, 180 lbs., SO, #2,12.1 ppg, .448 #PT at Salt Lake City CC, Utah/Gunnison Valley HS, Gunnison, Utah). Hill could be the answer to provide another consistent outside shooter. He's particularly adept at stroking the jumper after coming off a screen. He played the 1999-2000 season at Salt Lake City Community College and after one season there was recruited by Gonzaga, Utah State, Utah and Brigham Young. He sat out last season as a red-shirt at Oklahoma State and will have three seasons of eligibility with the Cowboys.

In his only collegiate season, Hill knocked down 100-of-223 shots from behind the arc.

"Aaron is a really great shooter who has the ability to change the game with his shooting touch," Cyprien said. "We expected him to contribute right away and challenge for a starting role."

C-FRANS STEYN (7-2, 295 lbs., FR, #44, Waterkloof HS, Pretoria, South Africa). If Bryant Reeves was Big Country, then Steyn has the chance to be ... Big World?

Steyn (pronounced STAIN) is a project. He'll sit out this season as a red-shirt because he'll be learning the game. He played rugby in high school.

Steyn has never played organized basketball, but he came to the United States last January and spent five months working out with R.C. Buford of the San Antonio Spurs organization.

QUESTIONS

Guard depth? Last season, Maurice Baker and Williams were worn down by playing too many minutes. Newcomers Gadson and Hill should address that problem, but the Cowboys definitely need to expand their guard rotation.

Outside shooting? Baker is a nice spot-up shooter from behind the three-point line, but he's more effective as a penetrator. The Cowboys were tied for 10th in the Big 12 in terms of three-point field goals made.

Ball handling? Despite having two point guard types in the backcourt, the Cowboys committed 506 turnovers last season (their opponents committed 513).

ANSWERS

Baker! He's a player capable of dominating a game in several ways. He can make the three pointer, penetrate and score and even chase down offensive rebounds.

Gallagher-Iba! While the arena expansion might have made the place a little less noisy, it's still one of the toughest places for a visiting team to play. With that sort of homecourt edge, Oklahoma State starts each season with nearly a dozen guaranteed victories.

Sutton! He might never win a national championship, but he is one of the game's great workmanlike coaches. Year in, year out, his teams are knocking on the 20-win door.

OKLAHOMA ST. 2000-2001 RESULTS

UMKC	69-46
@North Texas	94-56
UNLV	77-69
@Wichita State (L)	59-61
Arkansas	74-73
@Northwestern (La.) State	73-59
Arkansas-Little Rock	70-60
Lamar	86-45
@San Diego State (L)	66-87
Texas-San Antonio	88-63
@Texas (L)	71-78
Iowa State	88-80
Texas Tech	65-46
@Baylor	76-65
St. Gregory's	74-58
Texas A&M	76-64
@Colorado (L)	71-81
Missouri	69-66
@Nebraska (L)	75-78
@Kansas (L	61-77
Oklahoma	73-44
Texas (L)	69-80
@Texas A&M	82-76

Kansas State	52-47
@Texas Tech	66-58
Baylor	71-68
@Oklahoma (L)	56-68
#Texas (L)	54-55
##Southern Cal (L)	54-69

#Big 12 Tournament in Kansas City, MO
##NCAA Tournament
@Road Games

BLUE RIBBON ANALYSIS

BACKCOURT	A
BENCH/DEPTH	B
FRONTCOURT	B
INTANGIBLES	B+

Baker is the kind of dynamic player who can dominate games by ripping off points in bunches. Jonzen provides a nice complementary scoring threat on the front line.

If Oklahoma State can shore up its depth in the backcourt, it should challenge for the top of the Big 12 Conference race.

Sutton never has the same All-America talent that the Dukes and Kentuckys of the world enjoy. But give him a bunch of good players and he knows how to mold a winning team. Sutton's holy trinity of basketball involves defense, good shots and taking care of the ball. His teams invariably adhere to all three principals, which is a major reason Sutton's teams are successful.

The tragedy of last season aged Sutton. This might be his last good-to-great team and there's this gut feeling that he soon might decide to hang 'em up.

If this year's team can play up to its potential and make a deep run in the NCAA Tournament, don't be surprised if Sutton steps down and hands the keys to the program to his son Sean, the team's associate head coach.

(W.B.)

Texas 20

LOCATION	Austin, TX
CONFERENCE	Big 12
LAST SEASON	25-9 (.735)
CONFERENCE RECORD	12-4 (2nd)
STARTERS LOST/RETURNING	2/3
NICKNAME	Longhorns
COLORS	Burnt Orange & White
HOMECOURT	Erwin Center (16,496)
COACH	Rick Barnes (Lenoir-Rhyne '77)
RECORD AT SCHOOL	68-31 (3 years)
CAREER RECORD	270-165 (14 years)
ASSISTANTS	Brian Cousins (Providence '91)
	Frank Haith (Elon '88)
	Russell Springmann (Salisbury State '90)
TEAM WINS (last 5 years)	22-23-19-24-25
RPI (last 5 years)	32-110-57-10-9
2000-01 FINISH	Lost in NCAA first round.

COACH AND PROGRAM

King Football is not abdicating the throne any time soon. The sport played with pads and the pointy oblong ball is still the one that stirs the passions of fans in the Lone Star state.

For a basketball coach born and raised in ACC country, Rick Barnes continues to fight the good fight. He believes the Longhorns' basketball program can be one of the nation's best. And never mind the fact that he is trying to create the sort of emotional following in Austin that he witnessed growing up in the shadow of Tobacco Road's hoops giants.

"The question is, can we generate the same passion for basketball that they have over there?" Barnes asked, referencing the passion plays staged annually by the likes of Duke and North Carolina. "Do I want the passion here? No question. I want people to be excited."

Other than when UT is playing a home football game, that's a tough task. Texas students apparently have more important things to do than camp out waiting for tickets to see Texas A&M's basketball team play. And Austin residents are either too involved in state politics or stuck in the city's horrendous traffic to want to invest a

few hours watching the Longhorns who don't wear helmets.

Barnes is not facing a unique problem. The personable Abe Lemons developed some exciting teams and always provided some color during the Southwest Conference days.

Bob Weltlich, a solid coach, was the exact opposite of Lemons. His "Kaiser Bob" approach rubbed people the wrong way and overshadowed the fact that he's a solid coach.

Tom Penders appeared to have the right stuff. His shoot first, play defense later playing style took UT within a basket of the 1990 Final Four. But, as evidenced by his messy departure from George Washington, The Tan Man likes to build program on weak foundations.

Barnes came to Texas from Clemson and in three seasons his 38-10 record in league games is the best in the Big 12 Conference. Barnes' first three UT teams have been successful because of rock-solid defense and a pound-it-inside offensive philosophy. While it produces victories, that style doesn't attract fans. In three years under Barnes, UT has had one sellout.

Last season, Texas averaged 9,081 fans in the 16,715-seat Erwin Center. And that was with a team that deserved some love—the Longhorns had to replace three starters plus NBA early entree Chris Mihm and still won 25 games, the second-most in school history.

Barnes' dilemma was underlined last Dec. 16. Texas played host to Texas A&M-Corpus Christi. A crowd of 4,753 fans showed up for the Longhorns' 79-71 victory. In the Erwin Center's 23-year history, that's the second-smallest crowd—3,442 showed up for a game on Feb. 17, 1988, Weltlich's final season.

One reason for the low turnout was the fact that the game occurred during finals week and that many of the students had wrapped up their tests and departed for Christmas break. The other reason might have been a bit more galling. A few blocks away at Darrel K. Royal/Memorial Stadium the Texas Class 5A high school state championship game was being played. Midland Lee running back Cedric Benson, who had committed to play for UT coach Mack Brown, was on display and many Horns fans were at the stadium, checking out the second coming of Earl Campbell. Not that Barnes cared much for excuses.

"I don't care if it means me getting on the phone and asking people why they aren't coming," said Barnes, who spent 30 minutes after the game letting reporters watch the steam coming out of his ears as he ranted about basketball attendance.

"We're begging people to come. I don't want people turning on the TV and seeing that no one is at our games. We should be embarrassed. Some things have got to change."

And changes have been made.

First, Texas has spent $2.7 million on a renovation of the Erwin Center. A round, multi-purpose facility, the "Super Drum" has never made any one compare it to Cameron Indoor Stadium. For basketball, it's a round peg in a rectangular hole. The court is placed in the middle of the circular theater seating. Fans are as comfortable as if they were at their local multiplex.

In order to get more students closer to the action, the re-figured seating has added 1,162 seats behind each baseline.

"It will give us a totally different atmosphere," Barnes said. "For the first time, we have something we can give the students that will really make them feel a part of the game and the team."

Second, Texas figures to have a player who plays the kind of dazzling, game-stopping ball that should have fans standing at games and buzzing amongst themselves between games. Freshman point guard T.J. Ford is considered the most ballyhooed recruit in Texas' 95-year basketball history.

"We're going to have some fun this year," Barnes predicted. "The bottom line is winning, but I do expect we'll have a different team. I always coach to my team. My job is to put my players in the best spots for us to win. I expect us to play much quicker, to get it out and go. T.J. will play a big part in that. He's defined by winning."

And if Barnes continues to have his way, Texas could wind up being defined by more than football and spring football.

2001-2002 SCHEDULE

Nov.	17	Jacksonville
	21-24	#Great Alaska Shootout
	28	Arizona

Dec.	1	*Stanford
	5	Texas A&M Corpus Christi
	10	Washington State
	19	McNeese State
	22	**UNLV
	29	@Utah
Jan.	2	Texas-Pan American
	5	@Oklahoma State
	7	Providence
	12	Baylor
	14	@Texas Tech
	19	Nebraska
	23	Texas A&M
	26	@Baylor
	30	@Kansas State
Feb.	2	Oklahoma
	6	@Texas A&M
	9	Colorado
	11	Kansas
	17	@Missouri
	20	Oklahoma State
	23	@Oklahoma
	26	Texas Tech
March	2	@Iowa State
	7-10	##Big 12 Tournament

@Road Games
*Classic 4 Kids, United Center, Chicago, IL
**Las Vegas Showdown, Thomas & Mack Center, Las Vegas, NV
#Anchorage, AK (vs. Oregon State first round; also Alaska Anchorage, Gonzaga, Indiana, Marquette, Oregon State, St. John's, Tennessee)
##Kemper Arena, Kansas City, MO

STARTERS NOT RETURNING

SF-MAURICE EVANS (6-5, 15.6 ppg, 5.3 prg, 33 mpg, .440 FG, .389 3PT, .757 FT, 5.3 rpg, 44 steals, 21 blocks). Evans, who transferred to Texas after leading Wichita State in scoring as a sophomore, had a disappointing season. Texas fans expected Evans to approach his 22.6 points a game average he posted for the Shockers. However, the transfer season after sitting out plus the step up in competition appeared to take its toll on Evans' game.

The 220-pound Evans never seemed comfortable last season. Perhaps it was Texas' offensive struggles without a true point guard. Perhaps Evans found the level of play in the Big 12 Conference—especially the bare knuckles defensive approach—too difficult to overcome.

Playing at small forward and shooting guard, Evans did lead Texas in scoring. Perhaps the expectations were too high. Evans wound up as a third-team All-Big 12 choice by the coaches, but this was a Longhorns team that needed a star. Evans was too inconsistent to fill that role. In Texas' nine losses, Evans averaged 12 points.

While he made nearly 39 percent of his three-point shots, Evans shot just 44 percent from the field. Despite having quickness and strength, Evans didn't attack the basket nearly enough; he finished fourth on the team in free throws attempted but led the team in three-point field- goal tries. Evans' decision to leave after his junior season to enter the NBA draft was a surprise. His decision to hire an agent, thereby blocking any chance he might have of testing the draft waters and then returning for his senior season, was a shock. Evans was not selected in the two-round draft. If ever a player needed another year of honing his skills, it was Evans.

G-DAREEN KELLY (6-3, 34.6 mpg, 15.3 ppg, 4.6 rpg, .360 FG, .276 3PT, 76 assists, 84 turnovers). Kelly missed the first eight games while getting his academics in order. While that might have limited his and the team's offensive growth, the biggest problem that Kelly and the Longhorns had was the lack of a point guard.

Kelly wound up playing too much at the point. He was much more comfortable at shooting guard, but his time there often put him in conflict with Evans, who was interested in raising his NBA stock by playing shooting guard.

From the wing, Kelly was a dangerous weapon because he could shoot the three and also penetrate to get his shot. When forced to play the point, Kelly's game withered.

But don't think that Kelly had a bad year. He led the team in minutes played and assists (his total of 76 gives you some idea of how limited UT was in terms of ball handling and play making). He scored 20 or more points five times and was second on the team in scoring at 15.3 points a game.

OTHERS NOT RETURNING

G-CHRIS McCOLPIN (6-0, 10.1 mpg, 1.4 ppg, 1.0 rpg, .286 FG, .880 FT). An example of what was good and bad about the Longhorns the last few seasons. A former walk on, McColpin was on scholarship his last three seasons.

Intelligent on and off the court (twice a first-team Big 12 All-Academic selection), McColpin lacked size and ability. He made up for that with hustle, an accurate outside shot (all six of his field goals were three-pointers) opponents had to respect, and the ability to get the ball to the right player at the right time. The downside was that Texas' offense usually ran more efficiently with McColpin on the court. A player like T.J. Ford should put an end to that sort of thing.

G-YAIR HARARI (6-1, 1.0 mpg, 0.0 ppg, 0.0 rpg).

A three-year walk on, Harari saw action in eight games during his career. The last two seasons, he was selected winner of the Jack Gray Award that goes to the player who exhibits outstanding character, citizenship and academic achievement.

PROJECTED STARTERS

PG-T.J. FORD (5-11, 165 lbs., FR, #11, 12 ppg, 9.4 apg, 7.8 spg, Sugar Land Willowridge HS/ Houston, Texas). Last spring, Texas was worried that Ford was going to need neck surgery to correct spinal stenosis, a condition that causes abnormal narrowing of the openings in the spinal column that the spinal cord runs through. While Ford is not cured, he's not expected to experience any problems.

And for the next few seasons, the Longhorns hope that Ford is a pain in the neck for opponents.

One of the highest-rated recruits ever to sign with the Longhorns, Ford was tabbed as a consensus top 20 national prospect by all the major recruiting services and ranked as the best pure point guard prospect in the nation by Bob Gibbons' All Star Report. The third McDonald's All-American in school history, he averaged 12 points, 9.4 assists and 7.8 steals per game while leading Sugar Land Willowridge High School to a 39-0 overall record, the Class 5A state title and a final national ranking of No. 2 in his senior season.

Texas fans are buzzing about Ford almost as much as they buzzed about the arrival of freshman running back Cedric Benson. Barnes said he could hardly finish a meal in a restaurant this summer without someone asking about Ford.

"Unbelievable expectations lead to disappointments," Barnes said. "Fans can be unrealistic. But I don't think that T.J. or this team or I are being unrealistic in what we expect. T.J. doesn't want to be treated in any way other than what every other freshman is treated."

And Ford appears to be the right player at the right time. Texas' offense needs a jolt and Ford should provide it. In three previous seasons, Barnes has made do without a point guard. Now, he's got a player who can break down defenses and deliver the ball to the right player at the right time.

"I want to bring leadership," said Ford [the T.J. stands for Terrance Jerod]. "That's what we're missing. We're getting no easy baskets."

SG-BRANDON MOUTON (6-5, 210 lbs., SO, #3, 20.2 mpg, 5.4 ppg, 2.3 rpg, .394 FG, .373 3PT, .500 FT, St. Thomas More HS/Lafayette, La.). Mouton is the leading candidate to take over for Maurice Evans at shooting guard. He is particularly adept at slashing to the basket, but last season he showed that he could be a reliable three-point threat.

An athletic player who can score by slashing to the goal as well as spotting up from three-point range, Mouton played in all 34 games in his freshman season. He ranked sixth on the squad in scoring and fifth in assists (43) and blocked shots (10). Mouton posted seven double-digit scoring performances during the season and was the second-best three-point shooter on the squad.

If Mouton plays like he did against eventual national champion Duke last season, he could give the Horns the scoring punch they need on the perimeter.

In Texas' NIT semifinal loss to the Blue Devils at Madison Square Garden, Mouton had a career-high 18 points on 8-of-16 shooting, five rebounds, three assists and three steals in 31 minutes off the bench.

SF-BRIAN BODDICKER (6-9, 225 lbs., SO, #33, 19.6 mpg, 5.7 ppg, 3.9 rpg, .365 FG, .355 3PT, .694 FT; Duncanville, HS/Duncanville, Texas). With the addition of Ford, the Horns have two McDonald's All-Americans on the roster for the first time in school history. Boddicker, a former McDonald's All-American who was also voted UT's Most Improved Player last year, is a solid inside-outside scoring threat who has made great strides in his post defense.

In addition to skills that earned him national recognition as a high school player, Boddicker is developing a tough mental outlook. Fans around the Big 12 decided to single out Boddicker last season, turning his last name into "Booooooodicker."

"I like being a person nobody likes," Boddicker said. "I want to be a player that people hate around this league."

The Texas coaching staff is trying to make Boddicker into an inside-outside threat. Barnes likes the fact that Boddicker can be a difficult match-up for opponents. Boddicker has spent considerable time studying tapes of former Notre Dame star Troy Murphy and former Oklahoma star Eduardo Najera.

Unfortunately last season, the match-up problems Boddicker caused opponents also worked against him. He had a team-high 114 personal fouls and fouled out of five games. He began last season by coming off the bench for the first five games, before making 14 consecutive starts at center from early December through late January. Boddicker then returned to his sixth-man role and played his best ball during the team's late-season surge, averaging 9.5 points while hitting 9-of-16 (.563) three-pointers during the final six games of the regular season.

Boddicker ranked fifth on the squad in scoring (5.7 ppg) and rebounding (3.9 rpg) while hitting 35.5 percent from three-point range. He posted 10 double-figure scoring performances, tops among the talented Texas freshman class.

Boddicker also earned Big 12 Rookie-of-the-Week accolades (Jan. 8) for his efforts in the home win against Oklahoma State, when he posted a career-high 17 points on 6-of-12 shooting and six rebounds in 35 minutes of work.

PF-CHRIS OWENS (6-8, 245 lbs., SR, #20, 30.5 mpg, 14.4 ppg, 7.9 rpg, 2.7 bpg .391 FG, .641 FT, Duncanville HS/Duncanville, Texas and Tulane). Texas' coaching staff believes the foundation for this season's team—and for Owens' senior season—was laid at halftime of the Longhorns' 79-65 loss to Temple in the first round of the NCAA Tournament.

At halftime, Texas trailed 41-22. The Horns had played poorly. They appeared intimidated by the Owls' match-up zone and their relentless effort. But before Barnes or any of his assistants could say a word in the locker room, Owens was standing tall. For five minutes, Owens asked his teammates why they were playing scared. Then he begged them to play better and harder in the second half.

"No one would take ownership of their actions," Owens said. "I think everyone in the locker room at the time thought I was trying to motivate, which was not necessarily my mindset. The only reason I got so upset was because the way we played in the first half seemed to be a reflection of our entire season."

Owens should be one of the top power forwards in the nation. As a member of the USA World University Games team, Owens earned a starting role last summer. One of 50 returning players across the country to be selected to the Wooden Award Preseason Watch List, Owens is a powerful two-way player.

His 92 blocked shots last year set a single-season record at Texas, breaking the mark held by Chris Mihm. Owens also led the team in rebounding (7.9 rpg, fifth in the Big 12) and double-doubles (nine) and ranked second in steals (35) and third in scoring (14.4 ppg). A great nephew of Olympic track and field legend Jesse Owens, the sculpted senior needs to improve his ability to finish plays inside. While he can rebound and block shots like an All-America power forward, his scoring touch is barely all-conference. Last season, he made just 39 percent of his field-goal attempts and shot 64 percent from the free-throw line.

"I expect Chris Owens to make a big push for All-America honors," Barnes said. "He's really turned the corner. He has simplified his game offensively, finding two or three go-to moves that he can use from 15 feet and in. Chris doesn't just want to play well this year, he wants to dominate. And he wants to dominate every time he steps on the floor. We're going to need Chris to be that type of player."

C-JAMES THOMAS (6-8, 220 lbs., SO, #0, 7.0 ppg, 6.5 rpg, .484 FG, .457 FT, 20.7 mpg, Schenectady, N.Y. and Hargrave Military Academy/Chatham, Va.). When Chris Mihm opted to pass on his senior season and make himself eligible for the NBA Draft, Texas lost the best big man—and one of the best players—in school history.

For most of last season, Mihm's replacement in the middle of the Texas offense was a player few Horns fans knew much about.

Thomas, a broad-shouldered man-child, had a solid rookie season. His hard work, particularly in offensive rebounding, made Thomas a fan favorite in the Erwin Center.

Thomas made 20 starts and became the first freshman to start a season opener since Terrence Rencher in 1991-92. Thomas ranked second on the team in rebounding (6.5 rpg), blocks (28) and field-goal percentage (.484) and fourth in scoring (7.0 ppg).

Thomas credits his year at Hargrave Military Academy with helping turn his life around. He admits that he was a head case as a youngster, running with the wrong crowd on the mean streets of Schenectady.

"I learned how to be a man there, how to be responsible," Thomas said. "I'm very proud of myself for making it through that year and getting my grades."

Thomas holds himself to high standards and often gets angry with himself if he doesn't play well. If he continues to improve—like most of his teammates, he needs to improve his shooting percentages from the field and at the line—Texas should have a solid low post presence for the next few seasons.

KEY RESERVES

G-ROYAL IVEY (6-3, 190 lbs., SO, #24, 15.8 mpg, 2.8 ppg, 1.6 rpg, .365 FG, .659 FT, Blair Academy/Queens,N.Y.). While Mouton is expected to step in for Maurice Evans at shooting guard, he probably will get plenty of competition from Ivey, who moves back to the off-guard spot after playing out of position as a point guard last season.

Despite never having played the position before coming to Austin, Ivey took over the starting duties at point guard and wound up making 26 starts.

Ivey had his best game against eventual national champion Duke. He posted a career-high 11 points on 5-of-9 shooting, three steals and two boards in 23 minutes off the bench. That performance in a losing effort convinced Barnes to start him in the next game against Indiana.

If Texas has a defensive stopper on the perimeter, it's Ivey. Even as a freshman, he was one of the team's top on-the-ball defenders. When Texas knocked off fifth-ranked Illinois, Ivey was a key factor, holding Illini point guard Frank Williams to just eight points on 1-of-14 shooting.

G-FREDIE WILLIAMS (6-1, 178 lbs., SR, #10, 3.7 ppg, 1.4 rpg, .516 FG, .562 3PT, .588 FT, 15.0 mpg, 60 assists, 30 turnovers; Evans, Ga. and Mississippi Delta CC). The player who probably will be negatively impacted by T.J. Ford's arrival is Williams. However, if he is relegated to a backup role, Williams has shown resilience. And if he winds up sharing time with Ford at point guard, Williams has proven that he is capable of being a winner at the Division I level.

Williams began last season as Texas' starting point guard. He then lost the job to Royal Ivey in game four (Indiana), and was relegated to the bench for spot duty during much of the middle portion of the season.

Williams proved to be a study in perseverance. The sparkplug for the Horns' late-season surge, he averaged 6.0 points while posting 34 assists against just 12 turnovers with a team-high 16 steals during the final 10 games of the year.

In Texas' victory over sixth-ranked Iowa State, Williams simply dominated Cyclones' All-American Jamaal Tinsley. Williams posted a season-high 14 points, five assists against one turnover and three steals. He also held Tinsley to 6-of-15 shooting and forced four turnovers, before Tinsley fouled out with almost eight minutes remaining.

If, as expected, this becomes Ford's team, Williams should be able to provide solid play when Ford is on the bench. And having Williams around in practice should help Ford's transition from high school to college. No matter the way the playing time is divided, Texas probably has more quality depth at the point guard than it has ever had.

F-WILLIAM WYATT (6-8, 222 lbs., JR, #2, 7.3 mpg, 1.3 ppg, 1.6 rpg, .314 FG, .737 FT, 16 steals, South HS/ Grand Prairie, Texas). A fundamentally sound player,

Wyatt does a nice job as a spot player at power forward.

Wyatt has undergone four knee surgeries since the middle of his junior year in high school. Basically, he has no cartilage left in either knee. His knees make him a mystery and thus make it difficult for Barnes to know when or for how long he should play. When Wyatt's knees aren't aching, he's a solid defender and rebounder. However, when his knees are too swollen to function properly, Wyatt can barely walk, much less play basketball.

Last year, Wyatt saw action in 31 of the 34 games and played double-digit minutes in 11 games. When Wyatt was playing well, Barnes was inclined to leave him in the game because when Wyatt warms up and then cools down, his knees start aching.

Wyatt is a player who even the most objective observer wants to succeed. He received the team's Jay Arnette Coaches Award last season, presented to a player for his behind-the-scenes efforts and contributions to the squad. Texas nominated Wyatt for the 2000-01 Big 12 Conference Male Sportsperson of the Year award, Wyatt is one of the school's most active community service participants who has regular speaking engagements around Austin.

G/F-CHRIS OGDEN (6-7, 215 lbs., JR, #45, 2.2 ppg, .382 FG, .341 3FG, .700 FT, 8.6 mpg, Seminole HS/Seminole, Texas). Ogden, who played at the Class 3A level in high school, is still struggling with the transition to Division I. He's a fine shooter, but that's not enough. His minutes played decreased from his sophomore season. Ogden isn't quick enough to defend the wing players he is often matched against. And, as his 10 free-throw attempts in 248 minutes suggest, he doesn't do much other than shoot jumpers.

OTHER RETURNEES

C-JASON KLOTZ (6-10, 235 lbs., FR, #21, 2.0 mpg, 3 games, Forest HS/ Klein, Texas). Instead of James Thomas taking over for Chris Mihm as UT's center, most thought Klotz would be the man in the middle.

If Klotz is able to stay healthy, he gives Barnes another big body to use on the front line. Klotz saw a combined total of six minutes of action in three of UT's first six games last year. He suffered a sprained right ankle during practice on Dec. 4 and did not see any game action following the injury.

Klotz ranked as the No. 5 high school prospect in the state of Texas by Mike Kunstadt's Texas Hoops after his senior year at Klein Forest High School. He averaged 17 points, 10 rebounds and two blocks as a senior while leading his team to a 32-5 record and a runner-up finish at the Class 5A state tournament.

G-DREW GRESSETT (6-1, 162 lbs., SO, #32, 2 minutes played in 2 games, Westlake HS/ Austin, Texas). A sophomore walk-on, Gressett figures to take over the role filled the last few years by Yair Harari. In other words, when Gressett plays, the Longhorns are ahead by 30.

OTHER NEWCOMERS

F-DEGINALD ERSKIN (6-6, 220 lbs., JR, #15, 18.9 ppg, 5.2 rpg in 1999-2000, Gonzales HS/Gonzales, Texas and North Texas). An intriguing addition to the roster, Erskin is a walk-on who can play either forward position. During the 1999-2000 season at North Texas, he played for former UT assistant coach Vic Trilli. As a sophomore, he averaged 18.9 points and 5.2 rebounds per game and was a second team Big West Conference selection.

While it is uncertain how Erskin will adjust after sitting out last season or to the move up in competition, if he can become a reliable player off the bench, he would provide Barnes some options on the front line. Despite his lack of height, Erskin might be able to see some action as a post player. That would allow Barnes to move around versatile front liners like Chris Owens and Brian Boddicker.

G-TERRELL ROSS (6-4, 190 lbs., JR, #23, 9.3 ppg, 7.7, 6.3 rpg, 7.7 apg, Meade HS/Laurel, Md. and Allegany College/Laurel, Md.). Ross figures in the mix at shooting guard, even though he was a two-year starter at point guard while in junior college. With players like Ford, Williams and Ivey on the roster, it seems unlikely that there will be much time for Ross at the point.

Last year, Ross was a first-team NJCAA All-America selection as Allegany finished second in the national junior college championship.

"Terrell is a versatile player with good size who can help our backcourt play in many ways," Barnes said. "He

handles the ball and sees the floor well, can score and defend, and is a good worker. The most attractive thing about Terrell is that he comes from one of the most storied junior college programs in the nation and received great coaching while at Allegany."

F-SYDMILL HARRIS (6-6, 190 lbs., FR, #13, Hoofddorp, The Netherlands/Caland Lyceum). A small forward, Harris is interesting mostly because he's the first European-born male (born in Amsterdam) to play basketball at the University of Texas. With the glut of players on the wings, Harris would appear to be a red-shirt candidate.

F/C-CHRIS WRIGHT (6-10, 235 lbs, FR #44, Redwater HS/Redwater, Texas). Rated as the 25th-best high school center prospect in the nation by Bob Gibbons' All Star Report heading into his senior year at Redwater High School, Wright tore his ACL in his knee during the middle of his junior season and did not play competitive basketball as a senior. Before his injury, he averaged 20.6 points, 12.8 rebounds and 7.0 blocks in his junior year.

Wright is a likely red-shirt candidate, although he's an above-average prospect. He has the size to play inside and the shooting touch to score from the perimeter.

QUESTIONS

Scoring? Somehow, some way, Barnes has got to find some guys who can get the ball in the basket. Scan last year's statistics and there are way too many players with shooting percentages below 40 percent.

Ball handling? Texas had 502 turnovers compared to 414 assists last season. Only Kansas, Oklahoma State and Nebraska had more turnovers in the Big 12.

Right mix? No doubt, many teams will be following the Duke offensive system by using four perimeter shooters with one big man playing in the middle. Texas has a lot of big-bodied athletes, but they resemble more of a power team than a sleek bunch of three-point shooters.

ANSWERS

Defense! With Barnes' teams, it's a given. Texas will always be tough to beat because it is tough to score on. Barnes has the depth, the size and the quickness to defensively grind teams.

Leadership! Owens and senior reserve Fredie Williams have the right kind of personalities to fit the leadership profile. They'll need to come through in those roles because having a freshman point guard as the team's leader can be a dangerous thing.

T.J. Ford! A lot is expected of this first-year player, but he appears to have The Right Stuff. He'll be expected to distribute the ball, limit his mistakes and break down defenses. Ford probably won't have a scoring burden. If he can penetrate and create opportunities for his teammates, he'll be doing his job.

TEXAS 2000-2001 RESULTS

#Navy	79-65
#California	57-54
##Duke (L)	69-85
##Indiana	70-58
Texas-San Antonio	70-51
SW Texas State	90-60
###Sourth Florida (L)	69-87
Texas A&M-Corpus Christi	79-71
@Houston	71-60
Illinois	72-64
UNC Asheville	74-43
Utah	70-59
Oklahoma State	78-71
Kansas State	63-41
@Nebraska (L)	67-80
Connecticut	60-56
@Texas A&M	60-56
Baylor	73-66
@Oklahoma (L)	68-75
@Arizona (L)	52-80
Texas A&M	81-61
@Kansas (L)	66-82
@Colorado	77-72
Oklahoma (L)	54-75
Texas Tech	73-58
@Oklahoma Statte	80-69
@Baylor	69-59
Iowa State	94-78
Missouri	76-61
@Texas Tech	78-55
####Oklahoma State	55-54
####Oklahoma	54-45
#####Temple (L)	65-79

'#Preseason NIT in Texas
##Preseason NIT in New York
###Dodge Shootout in Tampa, FL
####Big 12 Tournament in Kansas City, MO
#####NCAA Tournament
@Road Games

BLUE RIBBON ANALYSIS

BACKCOURT	B
BENCH/DEPTH	B
FRONTCOURT	B+
INTANGIBLES	B+

Texas appears to have the makings of the best team in school history. The Longhorns return 58.6 percent of their scoring and 72.9 percent of their rebounding from last year's team.

"We've got strong senior leadership in Chris Owens and Fredie Williams, and lots of talented, athletic guys who can make plays," Barnes said. "Offensively, we're going to play quicker. Truth be known, we will probably resemble some of our teams at Providence that got up and down the floor. We've got players at every position who can run and finish plays. Defensively, we'll keep our same philosophies, which have worked pretty well lately."

The 2000-01 edition finished with 25 victories, just one shy of the school record. And that despite the fact that for much of the season, the offense was dysfunctional.

"There's no doubt that if I was playing Texas, I'd probably pack everyone inside of 20 feet and make us hit shots," Barnes said after his team's season-ending loss to Temple in the NCAA Tournament's first round. "We have to hit shots and we have to penetrate. I can't tell you how many times we penetrated and got the ball stripped. That comes down to ball handling. That's the next step we have to take with the program."

Barnes is a clever one. He knows what he's got, and that's a solid program. Texas has had one of its best and most consistent stretches of basketball under Barnes' leadership. The Longhorns are a gritty, defensive-oriented team. They're always tough to beat.

Now, Barnes knows what comes next. To make the move from a top 25, NCAA Tournament program to a top 10 Final Four program, Texas needs to learn how to score points while not giving up its defensive mindset.

"We've accomplished some very big things as a program during our first three years," Barnes said. "Are we where we want to be? Absolutely not, but we're getting there. We want the University of Texas to climb into the Top 10 early in the year and stay there for the duration of the season.

"And we need to make some noise come March. That's what I want. That's what our players want. And I hope that's what our fans want, because that's where this thing is headed."

Ford's arrival should provide a boost to the attack, but turning the ball over to a freshman doesn't always guarantee consistency. Barnes is not the kind of coach who will suffer turnovers and mistakes gladly. If Ford struggles to get his game together at times, Barnes will have to grin and bear it.

(W.B.)

Georgetown 21

LOCATION	Washington, DC
CONFERENCE	Big East (West)
LAST SEASON	25-8 (.757)
CONFERENCE RECORD	10-6 (2nd)
STARTERS LOST/RETURNING	2/3
NICKNAME	Hoyas
COLORS	Blue & Gray
HOMECOURT	MCI Center (20,600)
COACH	Craig Esherick (Georgetown '78)
RECORD AT SCHOOL	52-33 (3 years)
CAREER RECORD	52-33 (3 years)
ASSISTANTS	Mike Riley (Georgetown '78)
	Ronny Thompson (Georgetown '92)
	Chip Simms (Georgetown '92)

TEAM WINS (last 5 years)		20-16-15-19-25
RPI (last 5 years)		57-115-97-70-41
2000-01 FINISH		Lost in NCAA Sweet 16.

COACH AND PROGRAM

All those who doubted whether Craig Esherick was the man to lead Georgetown back to national prominence need only look at last season, when the Hoyas bolted to a 16-0 start, finished with 25 wins, hung in the Top 25 for most of the season and then advanced to their first Sweet 16 since 1996.

Not bad, eh?

Esherick, who took over in mid-ride when John Thompson decided to abandon coaching for a career as a radio host and part-time college athletics conscience, was originally viewed as a Bill Guthridge-style compromise candidate, called upon to lead only because it would have been impossible to find someone more "qualified" during the middle of a season.

Even though he had been a trusted Thompson lieutenant for years and had performed countless important tasks—on and off the court—for the program, many considered Esherick a stopgap. He would coach for a few seasons until things became so bad that a big name would be recruited to stop the bleeding and bring Georgetown back to its rightful position atop the Big East.

Shows how much we know. Just because a man hasn't directed a program doesn't mean he isn't capable. And during his two-plus years in the top job, Esherick has proven himself more than capable, building the team from a national afterthought into a program now which deserves some serious consideration. The Hoyas aren't yet back to their fire-breathing, mid-'80s days and probably will never repeat that run, when they played in three NCAA championship games in four years. That's magical stuff. But a quick look at the team's roster and its most recent recruits would indicate that plenty of good times are ahead.

Last year was proof of that. Using a deep rotation filled with mix-and-match parts, Esherick brought Georgetown to the next logical step, after its strong 2000 NIT showing. The Hoyas played outstanding defense, limiting foes to a meager 38.8 percent success rate from the field, locked down the backboards, to the tune of a plus-9.3 rebounding margin and scored an unheard-of (for Georgetown, at least) 78.0 points per game.

Even though four major components of that team are gone, the Hoyas remain in good shape, thanks to the returns of three starters and three more key reserves and the arrival of a recruiting class that Esherick believes will eventually produce four starters, not a bad success rate for any newcomer crop. While it's hard to predict another Sweet 16 berth, given the unpredictability of the NCAA Tournament, it isn't hard to forecast another trip to the NCAA Tournament and perhaps even a Big East title, especially given the conference's lack of overwhelming favorite.

"At the beginning of last year, I was not predicting a Sweet 16 performance, but I did think we would make the NCAA Tournament," Esherick said. "This year, we have the capability of making the tournament again. We've had teams here that I knew were capable of making the Sweet 16. In '85, I thought we'd get back to the championship game, and we did."

A funny thing happened last season, as the Hoyas rollicked to their 16-0 start, Esherick's expectations rose. The same thing could happen this season, if Georgetown can get off to a quick start. Even though the Hoyas have a good nucleus of returning talent, there is no guarantee how it will blend together, particularly with the unexpected, late-summer loss of guard Demetrius Hunter, who started all 33 games last year—Esherick used the same starting lineup for every game in 2000-01—and was expected to be a major backcourt contributor this season.

Hunter transferred to UNLV, so that he could be with his girlfriend and their son. Not the best news for Hoya fans but certainly a gold star for Hunter, who must be applauded for his responsible behavior, even if it does bring some short-term misery to Georgetown's program.

Without Hunter—who scored 11.1 points in conference play last year, was Georgetown's most reliable three-point shooter and had the ability to pass, as well as score—the onus falls on sophomore power forward Mike Sweetney and senior guard Kevin Braswell. They are the only proven statistical producers from last year and perhaps the Big East's most formidable inside-outside pairing.

"If I had to predict, I would say Mike and Kevin would score more, in relation to the rest of the guys on the team," Esherick said. "They'll average more points. I think we have other people capable of scoring. But I don't think the scoring will be anywhere near as balanced as it was last year. It got to the point where I didn't know who the leading scorer was after games. Some games, we had six guys in double figures."

Although Braswell and Sweetney will lead the way, Georgetown will again feature an egalitarian approach behind them. Perhaps swingman Gerald Riley will score 10 a game. Then again, it could be forward Courtland Freeman, who is finally healthy. Big center Wesley Wilson has potential, as do incoming guards Tony Bethel and Drew Hall. Like last year, Esherick has a versatile roster and the ability to adapt to any lineup a rival uses—or dictate tempo himself by using myriad on-court combinations.

"That's the kind of team we have," Esherick said. "We can keep people off-balance. We're not predictable. Playing a lot of people makes practice more productive."

The only givens at Georgetown this year are Braswell and Sweetney, who will own spots in the starting lineup as long as they are healthy. After that, Esherick could go big, with the 6-9 Freeman and the 6-11 Wilson flanking Sweetney. He could go smaller, with Freeman in the middle and 6-8 junior Victor Samnick at the small forward. He might use Riley at the two spot, or perhaps one of the freshman guards. Don't expect the same five starters to trot out for every opening tip this year. That just won't happen. Do anticipate another year with eight or nine players who average double-figure minutes.

"I like playing a lot of people," Esherick said. "It's beneficial in a lot of ways. We can fast break and press, and that's the style of play I'm most comfortable with."

If Esherick is comfortable, that's a good thing, because he has proven himself to be a worthy successor to Thompson. The Gregory Peck look-alike (think To Kill a Mockingbird) has lifted Georgetown back to the rare air occupied by tournament successes, and he doesn't plan on stopping. If this recruiting class is as good as advertised, the Hoyas will be in good shape for a long time, since Braswell is the only senior on the team. Those who fretted when Thompson left can relax. Esherick is in charge, and he knows what he's doing.

2001-2002 SCHEDULE

Nov.	16	Marymount
	19	*Georgia
	21	Coastal Carolina
	24	Towson
	26	Grambling
	28	Bethune Cookman
Dec.	1	Houston
	6	@South Carolina
	10	Morgan State
	17	Howard
	20	**Virginia
	29	@UCLA
Jan.	2	Miami
	5	@Rutgers
	12	@Boston College
	16	Seton Hall
	19	Pittsburgh
	21	@Notre Dame
	26	@Pittsburgh
	28	Syracuse
Feb.	2	West Virginia
	9	Notre Dame
	12	@Seton Hall
	16	@Villanova
	19	Connecticut
	24	@Syracuse
	27	@West Virginia
March	2	Rutgers
	6-9	#Big East Tournament

@Road Games
*Hall of Fame Tip Off Classic, Springfield Civic Center
**John Thompson Classic, Washington, DC, MCI Center
#Madison Square Garden, New York, NY

STARTERS NOT RETURNING

C-RUBEN BOUMTJE BOUMTJE (7-0, 9.1 ppg, 6.8 rpg, 0.3 apg, 1.1 bpg, 21.6 minutes, .517 FG, .718 FT). Although Boumtje Boumtje's career was plagued by injury, it became clear that he was not going to blossom into the interior force many had predicted he would become. Long and gifted athletically, Boumtje Boumtje simply lacked the offensive skills necessary to become a consistent scorer at the collegiate level.

A strong rebounder and capable shot blocker, Boumtje Boumtje ran the floor well and contributed plenty at the defensive end. The Portland Trailblazers thought enough of him to make him a second-round draft pick, but that was a step below where many thought Boumtje Boumtje might land, when last year commenced. After an injury-plagued junior year, he was expected to blossom last season. Though he did remain healthy enough to play every night, Boumtje Boumtje gave the Hoyas more of the same, only in a full-season package. His season averages of 9.1 and 6.8 were right on his career numbers (9.6, 7.0), showing his skills but also his limitations.

G-DEMETRIUS HUNTER (6-2, 7.6 ppg, 2.4 rpg, 2.2 apg, 1.0 spg, 24.8 minutes, .433 FG, .389 3PT, .654 FT). Hunter's departure was a shocker, especially because he had completed a term of summer school and had not given any indications that he would not return when he left for Vegas after classes. But, on a two-day bus ride from D.C. to the desert (who says college athletes are spoiled?) Hunter changed his mind.

"When his girlfriend had the baby last August, I was concerned that the emotional roller-coaster he was on could have an effect on whether he came back to school," Esherick said. "When he went back to Vegas at the end of summer school, he decided he couldn't be away from his baby anymore."

Unlike the old days, when Hunter's return to his hometown school might have raised some eyebrows, given the program's reputation for shady dealings, Hunter joins a Rebel program that is now under the control of venerable Charlie Spoonhour, who is not running a basketball-style casino.

"I like Charlie Spoonhour," Esherick said. "I think Demetrius will be fine."

The Hoyas, however, will miss the guard, especially because there is little proven depth in the backcourt now. Hunter was a fine long-range shooter, a good ball handler and productive defender. He was primed to become a force in the Big East and would have complemented Braswell. His loss forces the Hoyas to use their freshmen more and hope that Riley can become a strong wing.

OTHERS NOT RETURNING

F/G-NAT BURTON (6-4, 5.1 ppg, 3.5 rpg, 1.3 apg, 1.0 spg, 16.4 minutes, .569 FG, .603 FT). Burton's numbers shrank some last year, but that didn't minimize his contributions to the team. He was the one who hit the game-winning, buzzer-beating layup against Arkansas in the opening round of the NCAA Tournament. That play showed two things about Burton. First, his reliability and status as a senior leader led Esherick to put him on the court so late in such a big game. It also proved that while he wasn't much of an offensive force, Burton could deliver.

A defensive specialist who could handle assignments to guard any kind of perimeter player, Burton was excellent in the press and good on the backboards. He wasn't much of a shooter (the layup was on the outskirts of his range), but he could handle the ball and distribute it. On a team that had plenty of scoring options, Burton was a perfect complementary player, the kind most successful teams need. Though his numbers don't suggest it, Burton will be missed.

F-GHARUN HESTER (6-4, 0.4 ppg, 1.0 rpg, 0.0 apg, 5 appearances, .333 FG). A deep reserve who played wide receiver on the Hoya football team, Hester saw a total of 18 minutes last season and made one shot. He never came close to duplicating his strong board work during the 2000 NIT, when he pulled down 10 rebounds in two games.

G-ANTHONY PERRY (6-3, 6.7 ppg, 2.3 rpg, 1.1 apg, 1.4 spg, 41.1 FG, 17.4 minutes, 35.8 3PT, 67.6 FT). Once considered the Hoyas' two man of the future, Perry slumped tremendously during the end of the 1999-2000 season and never completely recovered. Esherick's goal for him last year was to hit open shots, and while Perry did flash some long-range success, improving his three-point percentage mightily, he was not a primary scoring option for the Hoyas and was relegated to sixth man status.

But the development of Braswell and Hunter as the team's backcourt starters didn't completely drench Perry's hopes. He averaged more minutes than any other reserve, showed his commitment to the program and Esherick by playing good defense (he was second on the team in steals) and finishing second to Hunter in three-point percentage. Although Perry's career didn't end with the same status as it began—when he averaged more than 30 minutes a night as a freshman—it was an improvement on the second half of his junior year and therefore closed on a high note.

C-LEE SCRUGGS (6-11, 7.5 ppg, 4.4 rpg, 0.6 apg, 1.0 bpg, 13.7 minutes, .376 FG, .329 3PT, .750 FT). Last year was supposed to be a point-scoring, rainbow-shooting bonanza for Scruggs, who had been the scourge of the Hoyas' 2000 postseason and who had set NBA scouts a-drooling with his smooth shot and lanky frame. They saw a modern-day Bob McAdoo. By the end of the year, Georgetown fans were seeing red.

Scruggs loved the outside shot, so much so that he reduced his 6-11 frame by several inches, thanks to his insistence on hanging out on the perimeter at all times.

"Lee Scruggs was able to do what he did, because we had Wesley, Ruben and Mike inside," Esherick said. "He could step out and shoot."

And shoot Scruggs did. Though he missed the first nine games of last season because of academic troubles, Scruggs got his share of shots. Problem was, he didn't make many of them. His sub-40 percent field-goal percentage dried those scouts' mouths up right quick, and his wayward three-point shooting didn't help much, either. Scruggs went from a potential star to a reserve who averaged just 13.7 minutes a game. Though Esherick has a more enlightened view of scoring than did his predecessor, he wasn't going to tolerate a 6-11 player who wanted to be a guard.

PROJECTED STARTERS

PG-KEVIN BRASWELL (6-2, 190 lbs., SR, #12, 11.5 ppg, 3.4 rpg, 6.1 apg, 2.9 spg, 31.5 minutes, .378 FG, .302 3PT, .742 FT, Maine Central Institute/Baltimore, Md.). With Hunter gone, Braswell becomes the Hoyas' top backcourt weapon. Although he would appear to have that title by default, Braswell would have been looked at as a huge contributor, even if Hunter had not headed back to Glitter Gulch. Despite struggling with his shooting percentage last year, Hunter was a second-team All-Big East selection who fills a stat sheet like few other guards in the country. He can score, pass, defend and rebound. And, if Esherick's prediction comes true and Braswell shoots better, he might threaten the all-conference first team and be one of the more productive guards in the nation.

As it is, Braswell is already one of the more underrated backcourt performers. That should change, because the Hoyas are without any other real scoring options, besides Sweetney. The key, of course, to increased production is improved accuracy from the outside.

"He worked hard on his shot last summer," Esherick said. "I think he's capable of being a very good three-point shooter. He had an awful lot of pressure his freshman and sophomore years as far as doing a lot of ball handling. I don't think he'll have as much pressure to do that this year. [Freshmen] Tony [Bethel] and Drew [Hall] and Gerald Riley and Ramell Ross can handle it, and our big people can handle the ball on the perimeter."

Braswell had some big games last year. He scored 26 at Seton Hall and 23 against Syracuse, in the Carrier Dome. He was also the leading scorer in all three of the Hoyas' NCAA Tournament games.

SG-TONY BETHEL (6-2, 160 lbs., FR, #22, 18.0 ppg, 7.0 rpg, 5.0 apg, 5.0 spg, Montrose Christian/Fort Washington, Md.). Although Esherick must rely on both Bethel and Hall, it's more likely that the skinny Bethel would get the start, because he could play both guard spots. Of course, it's also possible that Esherick might swing Riley to the two and employ one of his many forwards at the three spot. For now, we'll go with Bethel.

Bethel underwent wrist surgery during the summer, but he's expected to be fine by the start of the season. He's aggressive and energetic and can score inside and out.

"He's an explosive scorer who is very athletic," Esherick said. "He can also shoot the three-pointer."

If Bethel doesn't start this year, he'll be in the first unit next, when Braswell is gone, and he and Hall step up.

SF-GERALD RILEY (6-6, 205 lbs., SO, #32, 6.7 ppg, 2.8 rpg, 0.9 apg, 0.7 spg, 17.8 minutes, .357 FG, .261 3PT, .731 FT, Baldwin HS/Milledgeville, Ga.). Riley had what Esherick considers a "normal" freshman year, suffering many of the same ups and downs that other first-year players endured last year. Unlike Sweetney, who was a rock throughout the season, Riley had trouble shooting for much of the year. Expect that to change.

One thing that won't change is Riley's ability to defend. He'll also become a better rebounder; he's already pretty good on the offensive boards. Riley can play the two or the three, and he has the ability to defend bigger men, too. He blocks shots and can pass pretty well. As Esherick said, he can also handle it. A role-player who could blossom into more as he gains experience, Riley is a nice fit for the Hoyas' style.

PF-MIKE SWEETNEY (6-8, 260 lbs., SO, #34, 12.8 ppg, 7.4 rpg, 1.8 apg, 0.7 spg, 24.2 minutes, .516 FG, .619 FT, Oxon Hill HS/Oxon Hill, Md.). Now for the "abnormal" freshman. Sweetney made a huge impact last year, and not just because of his super-sized, 260-pound frame. He led the Hoyas in scoring, and what was even more impressive was that his scoring average swelled to 14.0 points in Big East play. For a freshman to improve like that in league play is nothing short of remarkable.

That doesn't mean Esherick hasn't found things for Sweetney to work on.

"Anybody that's a freshman has things to work on," the coach said.

The main thing is conditioning. Sweetney played only 24.2 minutes a game last year, a number that must swell, if the Hoyas are to be a powerhouse.

"He has to be in better condition at the beginning of the season than he was last year," Esherick said.

Sweetney also needs to improve on last year's 61.9 percent free-throw accuracy. He shot 168 times from the free-throw line last year, easily the most on the team. If he can get up to 70 (and beyond), he could be a more productive point producer. He could also improve his shooting range, something which Esherick believes is certainly possible. Still, it's hard to argue with what Sweetney was able to do last year. He had a great debut and will be a standout in the Big East for as long as he wants to stay in school.

C-WESLEY WILSON (6-11, 235 lbs., JR, #50, 5.5 ppg, 3.3 rpg, 0.3 apg, 0.9 bpg, 12.1 minutes, .482 FG, .554 FT, Maine Central Institute/Vallejo, Calif.). With Boumtje Boumtje gone, it's Wilson's time to step up in the pivot. After sitting out the 1999-00 season, because of NCAA Clearinghouse problems, Wilson had a solid debut last year. He didn't overwhelm anyone, but he did have moments when he proved he could be a force. Now, Wilson needs more consistency.

"There were some games last year, when Ruben got in foul trouble, and Wesley came in and played well," Esherick said. "There were five or six games last year that we might not have won if Wesley didn't play as well as he did. With Ruben leaving, I expect Wesley will give us more."

Wilson is a mobile big man who can defend well and runs the floor like someone a few inches shorter. He'll get a stiff challenge from Freeman during the preseason camp and will likely split the center position with him, but Wilson must step up, especially on the backboards, if the Hoyas are to compete for a tournament berth.

KEY RESERVES

F/C-COURTLAND FREEMAN (6-9, 222 lbs., JR, #2, 2.7 ppg, 3.2 rpg, 1.0 apg, 1.0 bpg, 11.8 minutes, .357 FG, .462 FT, Socastee HS/Myrtle Beach, S.C.). Two years ago, Freeman was plagued by hand and knee problems but still played in every game. Last season, foot and back problems were the culprits, and this time, he couldn't go. Freeman played just six games and contributed little to the Hoya cause.

"After a while, it seemed almost like he was trying to invent new injuries," Esherick said. "But he handled sitting out well."

Freeman is an athletic big man who can play two positions and should factor greatly into the Hoyas' frontcourt plans. He should be a good board man and block a couple shots a game. Don't expect too much offense, but he will trigger the break and could even finish a few.

F-VICTOR SAMNICK (6-8, 208 lbs., JR, #13, 3.8 ppg, 3.4 rpg, 0.5 apg, 14.1 minutes, 40.5 FG, 64.1 FT, Newport (Md.) Prep/Doala, Cameroon). Esherick goes back in time to find comparisons for Samnick's defensive abilities and comes up with some old-school Hoya heroes.

"Victor is as good a defender as we have had at the forward position ever here," Esherick said. "That's going back to Bill Martin and Reggie Williams. He's also an excellent rebounder who can play the three or four. He's improved his offense, too."

Samnick doesn't have much shooting range, but he can hit a baseline jumper and finish close to the basket.

He should also grab about five or six rebounds a game, something that will help out greatly.

G-DREW HALL (6-2, 170 lbs., FR, #5, 15.0 ppg, 9.0 rpg, 5.0 apg, Montrose Christian Academy/Silver Spring, Md.). A true point guard, Hall is absolutely being groomed for future starting assignments. He may even get some time with the first unit this year, if Esherick decides to use Braswell at the two spot, the better to take advantage of his scoring.

"Drew does not look to score," Esherick said. "He wants to penetrate and set up others. He's athletic and, like Tony, takes pride in his defense."

That's the magic phrase at Georgetown, and because of that, and Hall's unselfish play, he'll get minutes this year. He's quick, has good size for the point and he'll fit into the Hoya style of play quite well. Next year, he takes over the job. For now, he'll get 15-20 minutes of good apprentice work.

F-HARVEY THOMAS (6-8, 210 lbs., FR, #15, 19.0 ppg, 14.0 rpg, 8.0 bpg in 1999-2000, Hamilton HS/Memphis, Tenn/Frederick, Md.). Thomas is expected to make more of an immediate impact than the other Hoya frontcourt newcomer, Darrel Owens. Esherick describes Thomas as "explosive" and can see him contributing in the open court and on defense, particularly blocking shots. With so many frontcourt players in front of him, Thomas isn't going to gobble up minutes, but the possibility is there for some time, thanks to his offensive hybrid game, which combines the ability to slash to the hoop and his long-range shooting.

G/F-RaMELL ROSS (6-4, 185 lbs., SO, #10, 2.0 ppg, 1.3 rpg, 1.0 apg, 6.9 minutes, .316 FG, .700 FT, Lake Braddock HS/Fairfax, Va.). Ross made only 12 appearances last year but figures to see more time this season. He missed his senior year of high school with a shoulder injury, and the rust was evident last season.

But Ross has some potential. He's a good ball handler and can shoot the ball well. He'll also play good perimeter defense and guard a couple different positions.

OTHER RETURNEES

F-OMARI FAULKNER (6-6, 215 lbs., SO, #3, 1.2 ppg, 0.5 rpg, 0.2 apg, 4.8 minutes, .375 FG, .500 FT, Hamilton HS/Memphis, TN). Faulkner played in only six games last year, thanks to Burton's presence, but could move up the team hierarchy some. One thing to keep in mind is his number–3. It belonged to Allen Iverson and probably isn't just doled out to anybody, so it's possible Faulkner could become something.

A pure shooter, Faulkner no doubt spent last year learning the finer point of defense. Expect that education to continue this year, and if it takes, Faulkner will find himself on the court more.

G-TRENTON HILLIER (5-9, 165 lbs., JR, #11, 1.0 ppg, 0.4 rpg, 0.7 apg, 5.2 minutes, .450 FG, .500 FT, Kenston HS/Chagrin Falls, Ohio). Hillier plays wide receiver on the Hoya football team and joins the Georgetown hoop unit in late November. But he isn't just a practice player. Hillier saw time in 24 games last year and provided some depth at the point. He's quick and can distribute the ball well. He'll even hit the occasional three-point shot. Though not a big-time producer, Hillier does contribute.

OTHER NEWCOMERS

F-DARREL OWENS (6-6, 205 lbs., FR, #20, 21.0 ppg, 8.0 rpg, 5.0 apg, Assumption HS/Napoleanville, La.). Owens has plenty of skills, but he played at a small school in Louisiana and is expected to need some time to acclimate himself to the high-Division I level.

"He's a wing player who can handle the ball well," Esherick said. "He's a good shooter and can play forward and guard. He just has to get a little more comfortable with this level of competition."

QUESTIONS

Backcourt depth? Esherick may sound confident that his newcomers can fill in for Hunter, but the guard's decision to leave forces the youngsters to step up immediately.

Rebounding? Losing Boumtje Boumtje, Scruggs and Burton will hurt on the boards. Can the mix-and-match forwards make up for lost production?

Pivot? Boumtje Boumtje may have been oft injured, but he was a rock in the middle when healthy. It's up to Wilson or Freeman to take over.

Scoring? Esherick is convinced a two-man nucleus of Braswell and Sweetney, with several others orbiting it, is enough. But last year's balance was hard to beat.

ANSWERS

Braswell! A lot of people don't know how talented and productive he is, but he should be quite popular around the country by March.

Sweetney! The big sophomore is powerful and athletic. There's always the possibility of a sophomore slump, but he has too much talent for that.

Depth! The Hoyas can play big, small, fast or slow. They have the talent and numbers to dictate tempo and overwhelm many opponents.

Freshmen! Esherick needed reinforcements, and he got them. Hall, Bethel and Thomas should make immediate impacts, and Owens has a big upside.

GEORGETOWN 2000-2001 RESULTS

Bethune-Cookman	85-75
#Central Florida	77-65
#College of Charleston	79-68
#Minnesota	76-60
Nicholls State	90-48
@Louisville	70-63
Grambling State	88-51
Coastal Carolina	78-60
Howard	123-90
Maryland-Eastern Shore	75-51
@Houston	79-63
@West Virginia	90-66
Seton Hall	78-66
Morgan State	86-68
Virginia Tech	96-68
@Seton Hall	99-91
Pittsburg (L)	66-70
UNLV	79-62
Notre Dame (L)	71-78
@Syracuse (L)	63-70
West Virginia	94-77
@Pittsburgh	81-67
@Providence (L)	79-103
Villanova (L)	56-59
@Rutgers	76-73
@St. John's (L)	70-73
Syracuse	72-61
Rutgers	74-58
@Notrre Dame (L)	72-79
##Seton Hall (L)	40-58
###Arkansas	63-61
###Hampton	76-57
###Maryland	66-76

#Hawaii Pacific Thanksgiving Classic at Blaidsdale Center
##Big East Tournament in New York
###NCAA Tournament
@Road Games

BLUE RIBBON ANALYSIS

BACKCOURT	B-
BENCH/DEPTH	A-
FRONTCOURT	B+
INTANGIBLES	B+

The Hoya basketball prospectus quotes ancient classic rockers Thin Lizzie to herald "the Hoyas are back in town..."

OK, so that doesn't score many points with today's alternative crowd (or with anybody under 35, for that matter), but we get the point. After struggling on the national fringes for the late 1990s, Georgetown is again a major player.

Esherick has done a good job improving recruiting and installing a system which actually embraces scoring the basketball. That's something old Blood and Guts Thompson didn't exactly care for. Because the Hoyas will run and shoot now, some talented recruits are filling the program's roster, most notably Sweetney, who has the potential to be a dominant collegiate player, should he stick around another couple years. Even if this is his last season, Sweetney should be highly productive.

Still, Braswell is the key. His mission is to continue distributing the ball well while improving his shooting accuracy, and thus, his point output. He's a talented player who can be extremely disruptive defensively and hurt rivals many ways with the ball. If he's healthy and gets some ball handling support, the Hoyas will be dangerous.

It's hard to predict from where the main assistance will come. Riley has experience and could sneak into double figures, while Freeman has potential up front. Both Hall and Bethel will have their moments, but it's tough to predict sustained success for freshmen. Figure on a group effort, with plenty of different lineups and new supporting heroes every night. Esherick will milk the Braswell/Sweetney axis for all he can and help the complementary parts come through. If they do, the Hoyas have a good shot at another solid tournament run. Though title contention is a ways off, the Hoyas have returned. Thin Lizzie fans are waiting anxiously for a similar resurrection by their heroes.

(M.B.)

Cincinnati 22

LOCATION	Cincinnati, OH
CONFERENCE	Conference USA (American)
LAST SEASON	25-10 (.714)
CONFERENCE RECORD	11-5 (1st)
STARTERS LOST/RETURNING	1/4
NICKNAME	Bearcats
COLORS	Red & White
HOMECOURT	Shoemaker Center (13,176)
COACH	Bob Huggins (West Virginia '77)
RECORD AT SCHOOL	301-94 (12 years)
CAREER RECORD	469-168 (19 years)
ASSISTANTS	Keith LeGree (Cincinnati '99)
	Andy Kennedy (UAB '91)
	Dan Peters (Kent State '76)
TEAM WINS (last 5 years)	26-27-27-29-25
RPI (last 5 years)	16-18-9-1-26
2000-01 FINISH	Lost in NCAA
	West Regional semifinals.

COACH AND PROGRAM

Cincinnati is still the team to beat in Conference USA. Still the king of the hill. Still the benchmark of success in the league. Still the team with the biggest bulls-eye etched onto its back.

Yes, Final Four coaches the likes of John Calipari and Rick Pitino and Billy Tubbs are now in the league, and up-and-comers like Bobby Lutz at Charlotte and Tom Crean at Marquette are doing more than just challenging Cincinnati's invincibility. And, yes, the Bearcats did only tie for the league title last season with Southern Miss, while failing to win the conference tournament title for the third straight season.

But rumors of this king's demise are being exaggerated. Until someone proves otherwise, Cincinnati rules the roost.

Every year, it seems, Cincinnati coach Bob Huggins finds a new player to take the lead. Last year it was Steve Logan, who became the C-USA Player of the Year. The year before that, it was Kenyon Martin, the national player of the year. This is a program that made Bobby Brannen a legit league player-of-the-year candidate a few seasons back.

"We'll be fine," Huggins told the Cincinnati Enquirer in the off-season. "We'll find a way to keep our head above water. We always have. I don't know how it happens. ... But somebody always steps up."

Who will it be this season? Well, Logan is back, for one, but his backcourt mate, Kenny Satterfield, decided to forego his final two seasons of eligibility so he could be picked late in the second round of the NBA draft.

That loss stunned Huggins, and began a tumultuous off-season that means the preseason begins with uncertainty for the six-time defending C-USA champs.

Young assistant coach Mick Cronin, who got his start under Huggins and built a solid reputation, bolted to coach under Pitino at Louisville.

Donald Little, the one returning frontcourt player with lots of promise, got into misdemeanor scrapes with the law and was booted from the team.

Antawn Jones, a talented but erratic junior-college transfer, quit the team for a second time, this time for good.

The Cincinnati Post ran a feature story about the program's difficulties.

With Little hoping to be reinstated for the season, and with challengers to Cincinnati's throne, Huggins can't wait to get back to his refuge: the basketball court.

"I never know [how good his team is] until we go out

there and start running up and down," Huggins said.

Last season was strange in many ways for the Bearcats. They dropped out of the Top 25 for the first time in forever. They had lost for only the second time ever in Conference USA play at home [to Louisville] and then were swept by Marquette. Charlotte dismantled the 'Cats in the championship game of the C-USA Tournament in Louisville.

Yet, the NCAA Tournament, which had been the program's bugaboo, made everything seem just peachy. Playing out west, Cincinnati disposed of BYU and Kent State before losing in the Sweet 16 to Stanford.

The second-round jinx had been broken by the most unlikely of teams, one that had only two players average in double figures after December. Even with the loss to Stanford, the Bearcats seemed poised for another long season camped in the Top 25, if not the Top 10.

When Satterfield left, unexpectedly, it changed things.

"It was a surprise, because from everything he said, he was going to stay," Huggins said.

Even without Satterfield, the backcourt should be a strength for this Cincinnati team. And promising newcomers will make the inside game more effective.

Huggins will play it low key. He will say he thinks Memphis is the team to beat, and he would probably say that even if he didn't think it was true, just to put the weight on Calipari's shoulders. He will say the league is much improved. And he will openly question his team.

"I don't know how we stack up as a team this year," said Huggins, in his 13th season as Cincinnati coach. "We've got so many question marks."

For those who aren't aware, check out the number of wins over the last five seasons for this program. Consider that last year was a "down" season, and that produced 25 wins. Consider that Huggins has 301 wins as Cincinnati head coach and a .758 winning percentage.

Yeah, there are lots of questions.

This program has proven it can produce even more answers.

2001-2002 SCHEDULE

Nov.	16	@Oklahoma State
	20	Wright State
	24	UNLV
	28	Dayton
Dec.	1	Duquesne
	8	Coppin State
	10	Toledo
	14	@Xavier
	17	Richmond
	20-22	#Las Vegas Classic
	29	*Akron
Jan.	5	@East Carolina
	8	Charlotte
	12	@Houston
	16	DePaul
	19	Louisville
	22	@Saint Louis
	29	East Carolina
Feb.	2	@Marquette
	6	@Charlotte
	9	@Wake Forest
	12	Saint Louis
	15	Southern Miss
	19	@DePaul
	22	Marquette
	27	@Louisville
March	3	Memphis
	6-9	##C-USA Tournament

@Road Games
*Rock-N-Roll Classic, Cleveland, OH
#Las Vegas, NV (vs. Mississippi State, first round; vs. Louisiana-Monroe second round)
##Firstar Center, Cincinnati, OH

STARTERS NOT RETURNING

PG-KENNY SATTERFIELD (6-2, 14.4 ppg, 4.7 rpg, 4.9 apg, 3.1 tpg, 1.7 spg, 34.4 minutes, .388 FG, .788 FT, .333 3PT). After showing that he was one of the, oh, 10 best players in his own conference, Satterfield decided he must be good enough to merit NBA first-round draft status. Or perhaps his agent, Dan Fegan, assured him there weren't enough point guards to choose from, and that waiting a year, when Jason Williams and Frank Williams and Dajuan Wagner would likely be available, would be costly.

By all accounts, Satterfield was in good shape academically, and there is no question that he was improving by leaps and bounds on the court. Once a streaky player, both as a shooter and decision-maker, Satterfield had become a rock in the backcourt and his on-court charisma drove the Bearcats.

Nonetheless, he is gone. The 54th pick (of 58) in the draft, Satterfield enters the winter trying to survive as a professional rather than preparing to make a run at a seventh Conference USA championship that surely would have boosted his stock among NBA teams.

Huggins admits this caught him by surprise. After Huggins convinced Satterfield a year earlier that his career would be better served by becoming a complete college player, the New York point guard made a huge leap as a sophomore. He would likely have been on that large early season watch list for the Wooden Award, and he and Logan would have been featured as one of the best backcourts in the country.

That is what is most disappointing about Satterfield's decision to enter the NBA draft. He and Logan had become a duo capable of slaying the most imposing of opponents. Like two great jazz artists trading riffs, Lo and Satt (as Huggins called them) shredded defenses and set the tone out front for Cincinnati's own brand of suffocating, jujitsu defense. As Huggins grew more confident in his team in general, he was letting Satterfield and Logan gear the running game, and that surely would have continued this season.

When Satterfield struggled early in the Conference USA season—single-digit points in four of six games in one stretch—the Bearcats struggled, too. When he found himself again, the Bearcats caught fire. He scored in double figures in 14 of the final 15 games, finally relieving some of the pressure on Logan and thus turning Cincinnati into a Sweet 16 team.

Alas, he is gone, and the lessons Huggins taught almost seem wasted.

"There's a guy who you've kind of taught what you want to have done for two years," Huggins told the Cincinnati Enquirer after Satterfield turned pro. "At the end, he got to where he was actually starting to understand and do some things. I think it's harder most of the time to train, to teach, point guards than it is anything else."

OTHERS NOT RETURNING

SF-ANTWAN JONES (6-8, 5.3 ppg, 2.4 rpg, 0.5 apg, 13.9 minutes, .376 FG, .727 FT, .300 3PT). This just never really worked out. Jones was supposed to be the answer to Cincinnati's interior scoring. An inside-outside threat known for his energy in the paint, Jones injured his foot in the preseason. His game—and his psyche—never recovered. He left the team midway through the season, but was allowed to return. He left after the season and Huggins seemed only too happy to let the former junior college All-American leave the program.

Jones had his moments, going for 16 points and five rebounds against Youngstown State and 15 points and six rebounds against UAB. But he did not score in double figures in the final six games of the regular season, when he had earned a spot in the Huggins doghouse.

Jones could have made a huge difference in this program, and, had he avoided that foot injury, maybe he would have done more. Cincinnati will not miss his presence so much as his promise. He was a good enough three-point shooter who could bring great energy to his game all over the court, and he was gifted with great athleticism.

PROJECTED STARTERS

PG-STEVE LOGAN (6-0, 196 lbs., SR, #22, 17.6 ppg, 2.4 rpg, 2.4 apg, 1.0 spg, 32.5 minutes, .423 FG, .880 FT, .391 3PT, Lakewood St. Edward HS/Cleveland, Ohio). Anything you think he can't do, Steve Logan can do better. Play point guard? Yes, he can (190 assists, 84 turnovers for his career).

Play shooting guard? Oh, he can do that, too. Logan averaged 20.9 points in C-USA play, with 47 three-pointers on .456 shooting from three-point range.

Lead a team? Oh, yeah (Conference USA Player of the Year as a junior).

This has been Logan's M.O. since he arrived from Cleveland as, well, let Huggins tell the story.

"He just has a great understanding of how to play," Huggins said. "I saw him play as a freshman or a sophomore at St. Ed's and he had a great understanding of how to play back then. … I couldn't believe a fat guy could play that good."

Logan said at last year's Conference USA Tournament that he had lost a total of 26 pounds since high school.

"They used to call me Fat Boy," Logan said. "You reach a point where you just want to shut everybody up."

Logan has done everything a 6-0 point guard prone to weight gains must do to play in Division I. That he has prospered and enters the season as a national player-of-the-year candidate says much about his drive and Huggins' ability to pull the best out of players.

"I can't explain to you how Steve Logan goes from being our third guard to being the player of the year in the league," Huggins told the Cincinnati Enquirer.

We can.

Logan is quicker than he appears, and as shifty and difficult to guard on the perimeter as any small guard in the country. He is kind of a reverse Kevin McHale, a small guy who uses his body and positioning and his own understanding of defenders to find gaps and openings and to release his shot.

He is both reliable from long range—172-for-452, .391, for his career—and crafty inside the three-point line. A .422 career field-goal percentage is a nice number for a little guy unafraid to drive. He is at his best stopping and popping or throwing up high, soft floaters while moving to either side.

Last season, Logan shot 150 free throws, and knocked down 88 percent of them. He is a complete player in every sense, and can hold his own as a defender despite the size. Logan is plenty strong.

"He is probably the most skilled guard I have had other than Nick [van Exel] in terms of just being able to do a lot of things," Huggins said.

With Satterfield's departure, Logan will have to move back to point guard, though the term lead guard is more apt. He played the position as a freshman and sophomore, and has a great sense of how Huggins wants things to run.

"He understands what's supposed to happen and where the ball is supposed to go," Huggins said.

Logan had actually considered transferring after his sophomore season, when Satterfield had supplanted him as a starting point guard. It took him midway through last season to figure out he was capable of dominating games; after scoring in single figures in six of the first 13 games, Logan scored in double figures in every game thereafter. Averaging 12.7 points in mid-January, Logan averaged 20.6 over the remaining games. He led the team in scoring in 11 straight games.

At the C-USA Tournament in March, Marquette coach Tom Crean, emotional after his team's loss to Memphis, tried to make a point about the value of Brian Wardle to his program and ended up directing a less-than-subtle verbal jab at Logan.

He said, "It's an absolute joke that Brian Wardle is not player of the year in this conference."

Huggins, after his team defeated Memphis thanks to Logan's 32 points, shot back, unprompted.

"To make a statement like that is ridiculous," Huggins said. "I don't know what anybody else would want him to do."

SG-IMMANUEL MCELROY (6-4, 195 lbs., SR, #23, 7.0 ppg, 3.3 rpg, 1.7 apg, 22.3 minutes, .557 FG, .547 FT, .300 3PT, Tyler JC/Tyler, Texas, and Lincoln HS/Port Arthur, Texas). No other Cincinnati player can make as big a difference for this team.

McElroy came into the program known as a ridiculously talented athlete, a strong and explosive wing who was clearly destined for a role as defensive stopper on the perimeter. Problem was, he might have embraced that role too much; at the very least, he allowed himself to defer more than his coaches or teammates wanted him to on offense.

"I hope he shoots it a little more," Huggins said.

McElroy—Huggins calls him "Mac"—was a junior college All-American who averaged 21.0 points, so he can clearly score. He had committed to Memphis as a freshman—he never signed—and Tiger coaches saw him as a franchise kind of player. That may have been a little too exuberant for someone without great shooting skills from beyond 17 feet, but there is clearly more offensive game than McElroy chose to display last season.

"He's tremendously unselfish and we've got to get him more offensive minded," Huggins said.

McElroy did score in double figures in six of the final 11 games last season, and he had a terrific Conference USA Tournament. Against Memphis, he scored 13 points and had a monster alley-oop dunk that changed the complexion of the game. His 13 points against UAB prevented an upset in a quarterfinal game.

McElroy can play the two or the three, and could even direct things from point guard, if absolutely necessary. You could even see him at the four if Huggins goes with a four-guard lineup—he says he will—on occasion.

Still, his best contributions will be on defense and in intangible areas.

"He is the one guy who is tough enough to kind of stand up when things get physical," Huggins said midway through last season. "His understanding of play is really great."

McElroy is married and has two children, and, along with Logan, he can be a kind of rock for this team, which must develop some new stars.

"To say Mac is a lot more mature than the rest of our guys is an understatement," Huggins said last season. "He is one of the most responsible people I have ever been around. He comes to play every day and gives you an honest effort every day."

SF-LEONARD STOKES (6-6, 202 lbs., JR, #13, 10.1 ppg, 3.9 rpg, 1.2 apg, 25.1 minutes, .443 FG, .771 FT, .320 3PT, Turner Carroll HS/Buffalo, New York). Enigma, thy name is Leonard.

Here we have a player capable of getting 23 points and six rebounds against UNLV, 18 points and seven rebounds against South Florida, 17 points and fur rebounds against DePaul, and yet ...

And yet, he also goes oh-fer against Memphis and Marquette in back-to-back games. He can score 16 points in 27 minutes on one night (against UAB in the C-USA Tournament) and then come back the very next night and get two points in 22 minutes (against Memphis).

"He's got to be more consistent," Huggins said. "He's too good a guy, so when he didn't shoot it well, he let it bother him."

Stokes tends to raise expectations early in the season, then only occasionally meet them. Last season, he scored in double figures in 10 of the first 12 games, then managed double figures in only nine of the final 23 games. In seven games last season, he scored two or less points.

Stokes was as good as anyone on the team at earning free-throws, and he dropped 91-of-118 for the season. That is in part due to his ability to slash into the lane; it also comes when he is active in the lane, going to the boards as a swingman.

Huggins is happy with Stokes's defensive progress, and that is no small matter. He and McElroy can combine to make life very difficult for opposing wings.

Perhaps his finest moment last season came in a comeback win over Saint Louis, when he scored 12 points in the final 9:44 to rally Cincinnati to a victory.

That, however, was more the exception than the rule for Stokes. Too often, if he misses a few early opportunities, he becomes invisible.

Huggins likes to point to all the players in his program who became difference-makers in the course of one season. Logan is one. Bobby Brannen was another. Even Martin made unimaginable progress from his junior season to his senior season.

"Somebody always steps up," Huggins said.

If Stokes can be that player, then Cincinnati could be on its way to another C-USA title.

PF-JAMAAL DAVIS (6-9, 227 lbs., SR, #1, 6.7 ppg, 4.2 rpg, 1.0 apg, 24.2 minutes, .528 FG, .569 FT, Barton County JC/Great Bend, Kansas and Merrillville HS/Gary, Ind.). Davis has never been the flashiest player. He has never been the undisputed star. He is a workhorse, a blue-collar player who brings his hard hat to every game and practice.

And when he is on his game, it's not a bad idea to bring a hard hat with you to the lane.

Davis started all but one game last season at power forward, though his numbers are more those of a reserve player. He was efficient if not prolific offensively, and productive if not dominating on defense and on the boards.

On a team that badly needed a standout interior player, Davis was adequate. That may not be good enough this season, so use a pencil to jot down Davis's name as a starter.

"He's going to have to play a whole lot better than last year because we've got a lot more depth now," Huggins said.

Davis showed early promise, getting 13 points and eight rebounds against Marshall and 16 points and seven rebounds against Youngstown State, but he never could sustain those kinds of numbers. His best games of the year came in the NCAA Tournament against Kent State (16 points, 10 rebounds, 8-of-9 shooting) and in the crucial mid-season win over a Wake Forest team then ranked in the Top 10 (11 points, eight rebounds, two steals).

Davis, who played as a freshman at Purdue before transferring to a junior college, is good fundamentally, but he will not be a great rebounder unless he gained a lot of strength in the off-season.

"Strength has a lot to do with it," Huggins told the Cincinnati Enquirer midway through last season. "Lack of aggression has a lot to do with it. He blocks out. You watch him, he puts a body on people. They just throw him out of the way."

The emphasis this off-season has been to improve Davis' base of skills. Even if he does enter this season stronger, his minutes will be earned by proving he can hit open jumpers from inside 15 feet and doing more pure low-post scoring.

"He's got to be more consistent at everything," Huggins said. "He's not a power guy. He's got to be a skill guy. His skills have got to be more consistent."

C-DEREK HOLLMAN (6-10, 265 lbs., JR, 19 ppg, 11 rpg, Panola JC/Carthage, Texas and Laflore HS/Itta Bena, Miss.). As with Davis, use a pencil when throwing Hollman into the lineup. The guess here is that Huggins will want defense and strength in the middle after watching the Bearcats finish with a negative rebounding margin, the first time that has happened in Huggins's coaching career.

According to the Cincinnati media guide, Hollman has aspirations of playing professional football, and he certainly has the size. Also, Huggins hopes, the mentality.

At Laflore High in Itta Bena, Miss., Hollman was an all-state pick as a tight end/defensive end.

At Panola, Hollman was an all-region pick, and, though not a prolific scorer, he averaged a double-double.

"He's a big strong guy, has got great strength," Huggins told the Cincinnati Enquirer when Hollman signed. "He's tough, physical."

The scouting report indicates that Hollman's specialty will be defense, though Huggins is not discouraged with his offensive skills. Though the Bearcats still played physically last year, there was no true enforcer inside.

Hollman needs to be that enforcer.

"He's a lot of the things we didn't have," Huggins told the Enquirer. "He's a good defender in the post. He can score a little bit in there. He'd better [help right away]."

KEY RESERVES

C-DONALD LITTLE (6-10, 224 lbs., JR, 6.0 ppg, 5.6 rpg, 1.9 bpg, 0.5 apg, 23.0 minutes, .506 FG, .515 FT, .000 3PT, Winchendon Academy, Mass./Augusta, Ga.). In a tumultuous off-season, perhaps nothing affected Huggins as deeply as the bad spot his talented junior got himself into. Little had never posted great numbers, but he has always seemed 10 percent away from being a legitimate inside force, on offense and defense. Little also knew drastic improvement was possible after seeing Kenyon Martin's transformation as a senior at Cincinnati.

So why did Little allow himself to be kicked off the team just when he had a chance to emerge as one of Cincinnati's lead players?

Good question. But in late September, Little was reinstated.

"I think he showed his commitment to returning to the program by remaining in Cincinnati and getting his priorities straight and his personal house in order," said athletics director Bob Goin.

"He completed course work and paid for his summer school classes to keep him on schedule to graduate before his eligibility expires."

Little, 23, was charged with misdemeanor assault after an incident in May at a bar where he was accused of kicking a female employee in the ribs. Little would plead guilty to a lesser charge of persistent disorderly conduct, and claims he did not kick the woman.

Two weeks later, Little was charged for speeding in a work zone, driving under the influence of alcohol, driving with a suspended license and possession of marijuana. He pled guilty to lesser charges of reckless driving, having an open container of alcohol in his vehicle and not having his license in his possession when stopped by police. The marijuana charge was dismissed as unfounded.

"The things I was accused of, I didn't do," Little told Cincinnati Enquirer beat writer Michael Perry. "I was mad at myself, really. I put myself in bad situations. ... I really want to apologize as far as the program, the university and to Bearcat fans.

"Coach Hugs, he's gone to bat for a lot of guys and he's gotten to the point where he's tired of it. He's tired of everybody looking down on the program. I want to apologize to him. Everybody's going to beat him up now for what I did."

Little will probably eventual start for at center, and the guess is that, if he is truly contrite, he would be a much better player. He is strong and agile, if a little slow getting to the ball at times. After blocking 66 shots last season, he could have provided coverage again for a team that could go with four players 6-5 or under on the court at times.

Little had taken a red-shirt season when he first arrived in the program, and thus got to practice two seasons against Martin. A confident shooter from 15 feet and in, Little took often took off on certain possessions, and Huggins punished many a scorer's table after watching Little fail to go and retrieve rebounds.

His most significant contributions of the season probably came at Memphis, when he made three clutch jumpers to help the Bearcats hold off the Tigers at The Pyramid.

At one point last season, Little had a string of 18 straight games with a blocked shot and 12 straight with two or more.

Huggins told the Enquirer he wanted to "do the right thing" for Little and for the basketball program.

With Little reinstated, this basketball team becomes much better. Huggins knows doing so would invite some scorn from outside the program, but that does not seem to be his motivating concern.

"The easiest thing to do is say, 'Go, get out,' " Huggins said. "That's not hard. ... All those people who make decisions about people they don't know, if it were their kids, they wouldn't make those decisions. You do discipline people, but you don't over-discipline people ... when you are dealing with people's lives."

PF-JASON MAXIELL (6-7, 230 lbs., FR, #54, 22.5 ppg, 13.3 rpg, 5.7 bpg, Newman Smith HS/Carrollton, Texas). That same pencil you are keeping handy for those we have listed as starters? Be prepared to use the eraser, and then break out a pen. Because once Jason Maxiell finds his way into the starting lineup, he could be there a long time.

It might be a four-year stay.

There have been more talented freshmen to enter this program under Huggins's watch—Danny Fortson and DerMarr Johnson come to mind—but Maxiell enters at a time and place when the Bearcats desperately need an inside player to emerge as more than just a contributor.

Maxiell may be that guy. It won't be a shock if he does start the first game, but we're keeping Davis ensconced because he started all but one game last year.

Huggins is sure proud of his recruit.

"I think he is going to be really good," Huggins said. "We haven't had an explosive athlete like we had in the past, and he is like that. I really like him and he's gotten better and better [since signing]."

Maxiell was ranked as the 18th-best senior in the country by recruiting analyst Bob Gibbons last season. He doubled his scoring average as a senior, and was able to spend the summer in Cincinnati getting acclimated to school and learning what it takes to compete against bigger, stronger, faster athletes.

Maxiell had game highs of 37 points and 21 rebounds and had a pair of triple doubles (points, rebounds, blocks), so he can explode on a given night. He was also an all-tournament player at the U.S. Olympic Festival. He was first-team all-state in Texas' highest classification.

If Huggins has the same success with Maxiell as he had with Kenyon Martin, another Dallas-area player, the Bearcats should be able to thrive in that part of the country recruiting.

SG-FIELD WILLIAMS (6-3, 190 lbs., SO, #2, 3.2 ppg, 0.6 rpg, 0.4 ppg, 7.5 minutes, .434 FG, .800 FT, .438 3PT Waltrip HS/Houston, Texas). Before he is finished, Field Williams will be a star. Maybe not a great all-around player, maybe a shooting specialist, but mark it down: Williams will emerge as the kind of player people go out of their way to see play basketball.

The kid can flat shoot the ball. From deep. From deeper. From deepest. He also has a charisma about him on the court that will, at the very least, endear him to his own student section. He is also not afraid to be a little flamboyant; after going with cornrows, Williams let them loose and sported a massive, disco-era afro that would have humbled Oscar Gamble.

You could say he lacks a conscience, because he pulls from anywhere, but that is not true. He hit above 50 percent from long range in high school and was better than 40 percent as a freshman in limited duty.

There's no reason to have a heavy conscience if you aren't doing anything wrong, anyway. The theory here is that when Williams gets consistent minutes, watch out. When he is allowed to find his shooting rhythm, he will have a six, seven or eight three-pointer kind of night.

"I think he is going to be much better," Huggins said. "He shot the ball really will last year as little time as he got."

Huggins really likes the way Williams works. Becoming so numbingly accurate from three-point range requires time in the gym, and Williams devotes himself to developing as a player. Huggins said he is handling the ball better and his shot has become even quicker and more refined.

"He's really a great kid and he's had a great summer," Huggins said.

With Logan, a consummate winner and underrated playmaker, Williams should get plenty of opportunities to launch from deep.

"He's going to be like LaZell Durden and Darnell Burton and those guys," Huggins said. "Unlimited range."

C-B.J. GROVE (6-11, 270 lbs., JR, #44, 4.2 ppg, 3.8 rpg, 0.4 apg, 0.2 bpg, 16.2 minutes, .488 FG, .471 FT, .000 3PT, George Jr. Republic HS/Grove City, Pa., and Cincinnati, Ohio) His full name is actually John L. Grove. As a kid, however, Grove was called Baby John because of his baby-faced appearance, and the nickname was shortened to B.J.

Unfortunately for B.J. and the Bearcats, Grove has had trouble shedding the baby fat. Or, rather, keeping it off.

"I hope he's about 60 pounds less when we start the season," Huggins said late in the summer. "B.J. didn't have a very good summer. His weight ballooned up again. He was down to 10-percent body fat and let himself go. He's going to have to lose 50 pounds."

With Little's status in doubt, this is a serious matter. Grove started 21 games last season on a less-than-stellar front line, and showed some signs that he could be a nice Division I big man.

In a Conference USA Tournament semifinal against Memphis, he played a career-high 35 minutes, scoring six points and pulling eight rebounds. He had a double-double in league play (12 points, 10 rebounds) against UAB. In the NCAA Tournament, Grove had just his second double-figure scoring game of the season, getting 11 points to go with five rebounds.

When Grove shows more self-discipline, he improves. It certainly did not help him when he had to miss most of preseason conditioning as a freshman, and he has battled to find himself since.

Entering January last season averaging 1.5 points and 1.7 rebounds, he began a daily 30-minute personal workout session devoted to post skills last season, and tripled his averages. He is not a great athlete—only eight career blocks in 640 minutes—so the skill sessions are imperative.

Like Little, however, just being a contributor won't be enough to gain significant playing time on this squad.

Grove will have to sit out the conference opener after striking UAB guard LeAndrew Bass with his elbow during a game in the league tournament's quarterfinals.

"Striking at or about the head of a player is not part of basketball and will not be tolerated," C-USA commissioner Mike Slive said.

PG-TARON BARKER (6-0, 190 lbs., JR, #11, 12.8 ppg, 6.7 apg, 3.3 spg, Odessa JC/Odessa, Texas and Case HS/Racine, Wisc.) Some people like to throw jabs at Huggins by saying he fields a football squad. Look at big Derek Hollman and B.J. Grove, and you see their point.

But it's the shorter guys who are really the specimens built for football. Steve Logan is a fire hydrant who could throw on a Dallas Cowboys uniform and pass for Emmitt Smith.

Barker, most likely a bench player who will see a lot of time as a combination guard, can bench-press 350 pounds. That is remarkable for a basketball player his size.

"Taron is a strong, tough player who loves to win," Huggins said.

Barker could start, but it is more likely that Logan will

serve as a lead guard and Barker will provide relief and allow Logan to move to shooting guard. Barker was also pursued by Connecticut and Auburn, so he clearly can fit into a big-time program.

Satterfield's late departure made Cincinnati scramble late to find another point guard, and Barker was still available.

"The door was wide open for me," Barker told the Cincinnati Enquirer. "They told me what I wanted to hear: They're going to put the ball in my hands and go from there. … My intentions? I'm trying to get to the Final Four."

Barker isn't necessarily an explosive point guard, but Huggins sees him filling a role.

"He's not going to break down anybody and go by you," Huggins said. "He's good at running a team and getting the ball where he wants it to go."

OTHER RETURNEES

SF-RODNEY CRAWFORD (6-5, 220 lbs., SR, #30, 0.5 ppg, 1.8 rpg, 0.2 apg, 8.0 minutes, .308 FG, Bakersfield JC/Bakersfield, Calif. and Withrow HS/Cincinnati, Ohio). Crawford joined the Bearcats as a walk-on last fall and, though he was not eligible to play until mid-December. Before fracturing his ankle and missing 13 games, Crawford had games of nine rebounds (against Xavier) and 10 rebounds (versus Youngstown State).

His energy was invaluable in practice.

Crawford should be a guy who plays 10-15 minutes per game, depending on the match-ups. He can defend and rebound and do all the dirty work some don't like. And many big guys didn't seem to like it last season.

"I think we win a couple more games last year if he doesn't break his ankle," Huggins said. "He was really coming on for us."

SF-ROD FLOWERS (6-8, 225 lbs., SO, #30, 1.2 ppg, 1.1 rpg, 0 apg, 4.6 minutes, .304, .500, .444 3PT, Butler HS/Huntsville, Ala.). Flowers is built like a prototypical Cincinnati big man, but what are we to make of last season, when he failed to gain much playing time despite a horrific Cincinnati front line?

The media guide tells us: "The best part of Rod Flowers' basketball career lies ahead of him."

Hope so. Flowers never scored more than five points or pulled more than four rebounds in any given game.

He does, however, come from one of America's most under-rated hoops cities, Huntsville, where he averaged 22.1 points and 14.5 rebounds as a senior. Clearly, he can produce.

After a year of adjustment, Flowers needs to prove he can contribute. Huggins likes his shooting for a big man, and that could be his niche.

OTHER NEWCOMERS

SF-JIMMY HUBBARD (6-6, 210 lbs., JR, 15.0 ppg, 6.1 rpg, 3.8 apg, 74 three-pointers, Johnson County JC/Overland Park, Kansas and Belton HS/Belton, Mo.). Hubbard is a natural wing whose versatility is probably his strength. He was a two-time All-American at Johnson County and he led the team to the NJCAA Division II national title.

Huggins likes him a lot.

"Jimmy is a skill guy and I think he will make up for his lack of athleticism," Huggins said. "I think he's got toughness and he will really help us."

QUESTIONS

Where is Logan? Huggins has to figure out where Logan will play. He's the team's best point guard, would be very good as the lead guard and would allow Huggins to put his three best, most experienced players on the court at the same time in Logan, McElroy and Stokes. However, Logan proved last season he can be one of the best shooting guards in the country, despite his height.

Who comes up big? It is hard to believe that a Cincinnati team coached by Huggins had a negative-rebounding margin for the season and that the point guard was the second-leading rebounder on the team. Huggins likes his new big guys, and there will be genuine competition for playing time. Expect the Bearcats to improve down low.

Will Mac attack? McElroy is capable of averaging 12-15 points per game if he asserts himself, and this team very much needs him to score. His partner on the wing, Leonard Stokes, has no problem developing an offensive mindset, but he must become more consistent.

ANSWERS

Logan's run! Logan played inspired, old-school basketball last winter, and he has enough game and savvy to lead a Top 25 team. His will to win may be the most significant part of his personality, and, if this team follows this leader, it will not lose many games.

Find a way! Someone always seems to emerge out of Huggins' system, and there are plenty of candidates for belated stardom, from Stokes and McElroy to sophomore Field Williams and freshman Jason Maxiell. History suggests that someone on the Bearcat roster will make an unexpected leap forward.

Run, Baby! Run! There is more overall athleticism on this team, which has big men who can get out and run. They also have some skills. Expect Huggins to open things up a bit more.

CINCINNATI 2000-2001 RESULTS

Boise State	73-61
Marshall	79-75
#Notre Dame (L)	51-69
@Dayton	82-76
Oakland	97-58
##Xavier (L)	67-69
###UNLV	90-72
####Youngstown State	74-65
####Clemson	88-80
####Alabama	77-74
UNC Wilmington	65-55
#####Toledo (L)	66-69
Charlotte	76-66
@Marquette (L)	44-47
@Louisville	72-52
UAB	90-83
@Saint Louis (L)	62-71
Louisville (L)	54-63
Wake Forest	78-72
Tulane	105-57
@Charlotte (L)	58-60
DePaul	91-70
@Southern Miss	64-52
@Memphis	66-65
Marquette (L)	63-66
St. Louis	68-61
Houston	85-50
@South Florida	77-66
@DePaul	75-62
######UAB	73-70
######Charlotte (L)	72-80
######BYU	84-59
#######Kent State	66-43
#######Stanford (L)	65-78

#John Wooden Tradition in Indianapolis
##Skyline Chili Crosstown Shootout in Cincinnati
###Las Vegas Shootout
####Puerto Rico Holiday Classic in San Juan
#####Rock-N-Roll Shootout in Cleveland, OH
######Conference USA Tournament in Louisville, KY
#######NCAA Tournament
@Road Games

BLUE RIBBON ANALYSIS

BACKCOURT	A-
BENCH/DEPTH	B+
FRONTCOURT	B
INTANGIBLES	A-

Please forgive us the stock market terminology, but here goes.

It is possible that this Cincinnati team is a little overvalued. The price-to-earnings ratio is a little steep for this kind of pricing, perhaps, but Huggins has delivered huge results year after year after year. There's no reason to believe he won't get the maximum use out of his resources, even if they aren't all proven.

Logan is the best player in Conference USA until proven otherwise, and he ought to take umbrage at folks picking Memphis's Dajuan Wagner—or South Florida's Altron Jackson—to supplant him as league player of the year.

It is hard to believe Logan was able to carry Cincinnati so often last season, but few players in the country did so much for their teams. He led the team in scoring in 11 consecutive games at one point.

"If you've got a leader who's coming out and playing every game like it's his last, it should rub off on every-

body on the team," Field Williams said toward the end of last season. "He approaches practices like a game, which is what all the great players do. Every time he steps on the court, he takes it seriously."

That attitude should infect the rest of the team, and guys like Williams are poised for breakout seasons.

The biggest difference from last season should be the frontcourt. Maxiell could become one of those freshman phenoms who elevates his team to another level, and Hollman and Hubbard will add to the mix.

How bad was the frontcourt last season?

This was Huggins after the Charlotte loss in the C-USA Tournament, "Next year, I think I am going to institute a rule that every time [the post players] stand and don't go rebound the ball, they lose meal money. Because they ought to have to pay like everybody else to watch. And we're letting them in free."

If Little is back, the frontcourt will be even better, but, even without him, it will be improved. Guys like Jamaal Davis and B.J. Grove, regulars last season, could become bit players this year.

The old maxims that defense wins championships and guards get you through tournaments bodes well for this Bearcat squad. Another second-round NCAA Tournament appearance should be in the offing, and the Sweet 16 is attainable again. Anything past that is icing, but it is possible.

(Z.M.)

Tennessee 23

LOCATION	Knoxville, TN
CONFERENCE	Southeastern (Eastern)
LAST SEASON	22-11 (.666)
CONFERENCE RECORD	8-8 (4th)
STARTERS LOST/RETURNING	3/2
NICKNAME	Volunteers
COLORS	Orange & White
HOMECOURT	Thompson-Boling Arena (25,981)
COACH	Buzz Peterson (North Carolina '86)
RECORD AT SCHOOL	First year
CAREER RECORD	105-50 (5 years)
ASSISTANTS	Chris Ferguson (Cumberland '81)
	Al Daniel (Furman '79)
	Kerry Keating (Seton Hall '93)
TEAM WINS (last 5 years)	11-20-21-26-22
RPI (last 5 years)	139-26-25-12-18
2000-01 FINISH	Lost in NCAA first round.

COACH AND PROGRAM

In late February, former Tennessee coach Jerry Green startled the hosts of Vol Calls by announcing, "Tonight, we're going to do something different."

With that warning, Green launched into a diatribe about his status and rapidly declining popularity. Stung by criticism from fans and the media after his team had taken a nosedive from 13-1 and a No. 4 ranking in both polls by losing eight of 10 Southeastern Conference games, Green lashed out, daring Tennessee's administration to fire him.

In April, he got his wish.

Of course, Tennessee's spin meisters didn't call it a firing. But when athletic director Doug Dickey, at the behest of former school president J. Wade Gilley, asked to meet with Green after the Vols were unceremoniously dumped from the NCAA Tournament in the first round, it wasn't to exchange pleasantries. Dickey wanted to see whether Green would accept a buyout of the remaining four years of his contract and walk away quietly.

After some haggling over price, Green did just that, taking with him a guarantee of $1.1 million. Green pocketed $300,000 on March 31, and will get a check for $200,000 on Jan. 1 for the next four years. Happy New Year, Jerry, courtesy of Tennessee's suddenly impatient fans and administration.

After years of languishing in mediocrity, Tennessee basketball—with an assist by the recruiting of former coach Kevin O'Neill—had been lifted up by Green and his staff. But 22 victories a year and four straight NCAA Tournament appearances weren't enough for Vol fans, many of whom believed the program was stuck in a rut under Green's leadership. Without question, it was a rut in which 90 percent of Division I teams would love to be stuck. But each of Green's four seasons ended badly in the NCAA Tournament.

The critics cried loudly after the first three of those losses, but last season they didn't wait for the NCAA Tournament to voice their complaints. The Vols' puzzling midseason spiral started a fire Green couldn't extinguish. Most blamed his lack of discipline for the decline—which saw the Vols deteriorate into a disoriented, uninspired bunch that just wanted to get the season over.

Gilley, who had taken at least partial credit for the hiring of a then 29-year-old Billy Donovan at Marshall, wanted another Donovan type at Tennessee. Of course, Tennessee fans knew Billy the Kid, who eventually moved to Florida, where he and his Gators have regularly kicked the Vols' tail, including twice a year ago.

Thus, it was no surprise that Tennessee's list of coaches centered around three young, rising stars: Buzz Peterson of Tulsa, Jeff Lebo of Tennessee Tech and Gregg Marshall of Winthrop.

Any of those three might have been a good choice, but Peterson's stock was boosted by an NIT run that saw Tulsa, in the course of one week, beat three teams Tennessee plays every year—Mississippi State, Memphis and Alabama. That last win gave the Golden Hurricane the NIT title, and all but secured Peterson's candidacy at Tennessee.

It didn't hurt that Peterson has some connections. His roommate during his playing days at North Carolina was Michael Jordan. Peterson's references on his resume weren't too shabby either: Dean Smith, Roy Williams and Eddie Fogler.

After a fairly quick search, Peterson got the job in early April. A resident of Asheville, N.C., just a short hop over the Great Smoky Mountains from Knoxville, Peterson said all the right things at his press conference the day he was hired. He longed to be back in familiar territory, Peterson said, where he could see his family more often and munch on such Southern treats at Krispy Kreme donuts and Krystal hamburgers. And as for competing against the powerful draw of Tennessee football, well, Peterson wanted 50-yard line seats negotiated into his contract.

Those words did much to endear him to the orange-clad masses.

After reviving a fallen program at Appalachian State and carrying on the good work of former coach Bill Self at Tulsa, Peterson was deemed ready for the step up to the SEC. Suffice to say he was thrilled with the opportunity.

"When I called coach Smith about the job, he said it was the perfect fit for me, a no-brainer," Peterson said. "I know we've got a little work to do, or I wouldn't be here. But this is a dream job, the place where I could stay the rest of my life. I can't wait to get started."

2001-2002 SCHEDULE

Nov.	16	Tennessee Tech
	21-24	#Great Alaska Shootout
	29	Appalachian State
Dec.	6	@SMU
	15	@Memphis
	17	Radford
	20	@Louisville
	22	West Virginia
	29	@Wisconsin
Jan.	6	Ole Miss
	9	Florida
	12	@Georgia
	16	@Mississippi State
	19	Syracuse
	21	Middle Tennessee State
	23	South Carolina
	27	Auburn
	30	@LSU
Feb.	2	@Vanderbilt
	6	Kentucky
	9	@South Carolina
	13	Arkansas
	16	@Alabama
	19	@Kentucky
	23	Vanderbilt
	26	@Florida
March	2	Georgia
	7-10	##SEC Tournament

@Road Games
#Anchorage, AK (vs. Marquette, first round; also Alaska-Anchorage, Gonzaga, Indiana, Oregon State, St. John's, Texas)
##Georgia Dome, Atlanta, GA

STARTERS NOT RETURNING

PG-TONY HARRIS (6-0, 11.4 ppg, 2.0 rpg, 3.8 apg, 28.5 minutes, .358 FG, .346 3PT, .774 FT). Seldom has a player's stock fallen so drastically in the course of a single season. Harris was a preseason All-America pick, Wooden Award nominee and first-team All-SEC selection. After watching Harris play flawlessly (20 points, 12 assists, one turnover) against Austin Peay last November, NBA super scout Marty Blake declared Harris a solid prospect.

From that high point in just the season's fourth game, Harris plummeted. A variety of injuries (the severity of which were questioned by fans and even teammates) kept Harris out of four key SEC games. A messy incident where a supposedly injured Harris sprinted—in street clothes—toward the Kentucky bench to jump in the middle of a brief skirmish involving teammate Isiah Victor brought torrents of criticism.

After that, Harris didn't seem to be the same player. He shot poorly, turned the ball over more often and generally seemed as though he was going through the motions. Consequently, Blake's prediction never came true. Harris wasn't drafted.

Harris' arrival—he was signed by former coach Kevin O'Neill—was heralded by Tennessee fans four years ago. His departure was applauded by some, even though Harris was an exciting, if erratic performer. Was Harris guilty of reading his clippings and looking past college to an NBA career? Was he hampered by Green's hands-off discipline policy? Those questions will never be answered.

C-CHARLES HATHAWAY (6-10, 5.1 ppg, 4.8 rpg, 1.4 bpg, 19.8 minutes, .649 FG, .603 FT). Given the fact Hathaway was a Parade and McDonald's All-American and a consensus top 10 player coming out of his school, his Tennessee career would have to be considered disappointing. The big man never developed enough offensively to be a real factor.

True, Hathaway had some decent games, most particularly in his freshmen season, when he gave a tantalizing glimpse of his physical tools. But a blood clot in his right shoulder and subsequent surgery to remove it in his sophomore year derailed Hathaway's progress.

He started last year, but at times seemed to disappear on the floor, no small feat for a man so big. In five years (including his aborted sophomore season and subsequent medical red-shirt), Hathaway never did display a strong offensive move, even though his coaches implored him to learn the jump hook. Though Hathaway was an occasional strong defender and rebounder, those skills weren't enough to earn him more than 20 minutes

PF-ISIAH VICTOR (6-9, 12.8 ppg, 6.6 rpg, 0.9 apg, 1.0 bpg, 26.3 minutes, .543 FG, .267 3PT, .621 FT). Victor had a solid career at Tennessee, but his contributions in five years (he was forced to red-shirt his first season in Knoxville) were a far cry from what was predicted. Former Tennessee coach Kevin O'Neill was fond of calling Victor a future NBA lottery pick. Despite a good showing in the first NBA tryout camp in Portsmouth, Va. last April, Victor wasn't even drafted.

He will no doubt play for pay somewhere, but the NBA might never be a reality given the fact he's basically a man without a position. Victor is too slight to be a power forward and not a good enough perimeter shooter or ball handler to be a small forward. Green experimented with Victor at a wing position, but he never got enough extended time at the position to learn it.

Victor put together some good games at Tennessee and was a crowd pleaser with his dunks and blocked shots. But his contributions will be replaced by junior Marcus Haislip.

OTHERS NOT RETURNING

G-HARRIS WALKER (6-1, 4.5 ppg, 1.4 rpg, 2.0 apg, 1.8 tpg, 12.7 minutes, .473 FG, .387 3PT, .583 FT). Walker was dismissed from the team in late July for a violation of team rules. Published reports said that he failed multiple drug tests. Peterson wouldn't comment on the exact reason for the dismissal of Walker, who eventually turned up at Tennessee-Chattanooga.

Walker is a great athlete who can run and jump with the best of them. But he often played out of control and did more harm than good. A year ago, he had 67 assists, but 62 turnovers. Despite playing less than 13 minutes a game, he averaged nearly two turnovers.

Peterson would have given Walker a chance to play the point, but with the addition of Thaydeus Holden, his minutes wouldn't have increased drastically this season.

G-TERRENCE WOODS (6-3, 5.9 ppg, 1.3 rpg, 0.9 apg, 0.9 tpg, 12.8 minutes, .370 FG, .384 3PT, .800 FT). Woods was booted along with Walker, and for the same reason. Like Walker, Woods has some useful skills, but he was limited. Woods is a great shooter and he hit some big shots for the Vols last year. He made an improbable game winner in the closing seconds against South Carolina that might have saved an NCAA Tournament bid for the Vols.

For the most part, though, Woods had a sub-par shooting year. And when his shot wasn't falling, there wasn't much more to be extracted from Woods' game. He's not a particularly good ball handler or defender. He can shoot free throws, but he seldom drove to the basket so he could pick up fouls and get to the line.

Woods' minutes will be hungrily gobbled up by seniors Del Baker and Jenis Grindstaff. And Woods will sit out the season after transferring to Florida A&M.

PROJECTED STARTERS

PG-THAYDEUS HOLDEN (6-0, 180 lbs., JR, #10, 22.2 ppg, 4.2 rpg, 2.5 apg, Silsbee HS/Silsbee, Texas; Lamar University/Beaumont, Texas; Seward County CC/Liberal, Kansas). Hired just days before the state of the NCAA's spring signing period last April, Peterson had to make a decision. Should he burn a scholarship or hold it until the following November? Given the shaky status of Jon Higgins, who was deciding whether to transfer after Green's ouster, Peterson and assistant Chris Ferguson—the lone holdover from Green's staff—decided to go after a guard, and preferably one who could help right away.

While at Tulsa, Peterson had seen Holden play.

"Buzz really didn't need a guard at Tulsa," Seward County coach Dave Brown told The Tennessean, "but when he got the job at Tulsa, he was on Thaydeus the very next day."

Peterson and Ferguson thought they had to hurry and get involved with Holden, who had several scholarship offers from the likes of Wichita State and Creighton and was also starting to get phone calls from Michigan State and Michigan.

As it turned out, the Tennessee coaches didn't have to lay any hard-sell tactics on Holden. The player had kept up with Peterson at Tulsa. And he liked Tennessee. Holden signed without visiting Knoxville.

"I couldn't believe it," Peterson said. "So I said to Thaydeus, 'I've got one question. I know Tennessee is one of the best programs in the country, but for us to make one phone call and less than a week you're ready to come, why?' He said 'Coach let me tell you, I'm from Silsbee, Texas, outside of Beaumont, but for some reason I watched SEC football. Tennessee was on a lot. And I grew to love that orange.'

"When I interviewed for this job, people said 'Why do you want to coach at a football powerhouse?' Well, right there we got our first recruit because he had seen Tennessee play football on TV. It's a great advantage."

Peterson couldn't have known it at the time, but the acquisition of Holden became huge after the dismissal in late July of veteran guards Harris Walker and Terrence Woods.

Though Holden was Seward's top scorer (fifth nationally) and three-point shooter (he made 85 threes last season while shooting 40 percent from beyond the arc), he'll start out at the point for Tennessee. Peterson likes his size and strength (Holden bench-presses 300 pounds) and thinks Holden can be a disruptive force defensively.

Holden brings some experience. Having red-shirted at Lamar in 1998-99, Holden is older than most juniors; he turns 22 in February. As a freshman at Lamar, Holden was the Cardinals' third-leading scorer (8.1 ppg) and helped led them to their first NCAA Tournament appearance in 17 years. Lamar, seeded 16th in the East Regional, played mighty Duke in the first round. The Cardinals lost by 30 points, but Holden led them in scoring with 14.

By all accounts, Holden is cut from the same mold as Higgins in that he's coachable, team oriented and versatile.

"I'll bring leadership and whatever it takes to win," Holden told The Tennessean. "I feel comfortable at both guard positions."

SG-JON HIGGINS (6-3, 190 lbs., JR, #42, 6.5 ppg, 3.5 rpg, 2.4 apg, 1.0 tpg, 1.0 spg, 28.1 minutes, .467 FG, .486 3PT, .645 FT, Shaker Heights HS/Shaker Heights, Ohio). After Green's departure, Higgins seriously thought about transferring. He kept Peterson—and Vol fans—anxiously waiting for more than a month before announcing that he would stay in Knoxville.

"You could understand what he was going through," Peterson said. "Jerry Green and [former Tennessee assistant] Byron Samuels recruited him, and all of a sudden they were gone. He's probably thinking, 'Those guys have left me and I don't know this new guy.' But I'm glad he thought about it and gave us a chance."

Higgins has started the last two years, thanks in large part to his steadiness, defensive ability and uncanny knack for three-point shooting. But despite those skills, Higgins always had to play a subordinate role to Tony Harris and others. This year, Higgins will step out of the shadows and into a premier role for the Vols.

Though Higgins has played the point at various times in his career, Peterson wants him to concentrate on shooting. And with good reason. Last season Higgins led the Vols and the SEC in three-point shooting. His unreal .556 from behind the arc in SEC games also led the league. He set a school record for three-point percentage, smashing the old standard of .434 set by Mark Griffin in 19988-89.

One of the first things Peterson did when he got the job was look at a stat sheet. He couldn't believe Higgins averaged just 4.5 shots per game.

"That number's got to go up, way up," Peterson said. "I'd like him to take 10, 12 shots a game. I've told Jon not to worry about what his teammates are thinking. He's got to take that big shot for us."

Higgins took his share of big shots last season, when he evolved into the SEC's best shooter. In one two-game stretch against Vanderbilt and South Carolina, he was 8-for-8 from the floor and 7-of-7 from three-point range. Higgins reached double figures eight times, with a season high 18 against Iowa.

Higgins could also be counted on to defend. He routinely faced the likes of Preston Shumpert (Syracuse), Luke Recker (Iowa), Trenton Hassell (Austin Peay) and Jeryl Sasser (SMU) and made everyone he guarded work for his points.

Higgins is also thrifty with the basketball and seldom makes mistakes that lose games. His assist-to-turnover of 2.88 in SEC games led the league.

Above all else, Higgins is an all-world person. He always does the right thing, on and off the floor.

"He's just a great, great kid," Peterson said. "It was a big day when he said he was staying. I want him to take on a bigger role for us. Not just in taking a big shot. I want him to become a leader. He can handle it."

SF-VINCENT YARBROUGH (6-7, 210 lbs., SR, #22, 13.9 ppg, 7.4 rpg, 2.5 apg, 2.2 tpg, 1.3 bpg, 1.6 spg, 31.7 minutes, .443 FG, .339 3PT, .638 FT, Cleveland HS/Cleveland, Tenn.). Yarbrough got some good advice after his junior season, and he was smart enough to heed it. After briefly looking into his NBA draft potential, Yarbrough decided it would be in his best interests to hang around for his senior season.

That decision was also in Tennessee's best interests. Now that Tony Harris had departed, Yarbrough will be the unquestioned star of this team. Always talented, but never seemingly fully motivated, Yarbrough has one last chance to show the college basketball world that he really was the No. 1 player in his high school class, as one recruiting service anointed him.

Without question, Yarbrough has some physical skills. He has great leaping ability, quickness and stamina. He possesses long arms and is a pesky defender who gets to a lot of errant passes. He can score inside or out—though he relies too much on his jumper—pass and rebound as well as any small forward in the country. When he puts his mind to it.

Some think Yarbrough has underachieved in his first three years. That might be an easy contention to support, but it isn't fair to blame Yarbrough or his former coaching staff for failing to get the most from him. Often in Yarbrough's first three seasons, he wasn't the focal point of the offense. There are some who believe Yarbrough was never going to be the No. 1 option as long as Tony Harris was the point guard. Harris had a penchant for calling his own number, probably too often. That left a lot of players standing around, and at times, one of them was Yarbrough.

That will change this season.

"Vincent is a great player, but there's a little bit more in there we can find," Peterson said. "We asked him to take some of his weaknesses and work on them over the summer.

"I'd like to see Vince do some more creating off the dribble. He can do it. He also needs to become a little bit more consistent with his shooting. If he can do those things, he'll be tough to stop. He can do some amazing stuff. You throw that ball up around the glass, and good gosh, he's gonna go get it. If he puts in the work, he'll have a great senior year.

PF-RON SLAY (6-8, 225 lbs., JR, #35 12.9 ppg, 5.3 rpg, 0.5 apg, 1.9 tpg, 0.3 spg, 0.2 bpg, 22.7 minutes, .502 FG, .356 3PT, .702 FT, Oak Hill Academy/Mouth of Wilson, Va.; Pearl-Cohn High School/Nashville, Tenn.). Some folks around the SEC, most notably fans, have tried to paint Slay as some sort of thug. And given his particular brand of showmanship—which by comparison would make a young Muhammad Ali look shy—it's easy to see why Slay could become the man SEC fans love to hate.

But those who know Slay well speak of a different side of his character. Hidden behind his trash talking, hand waving and Oscar-nominated pratfalls lies the heart of a lion. Slay is a competitor, a team player, a hard-worker in practice and a stand-up guy. Consider that Slay's best friend on the team is Jon Higgins, who displays all those qualities and probably wouldn't associate with anyone who didn't.

If Higgins gives his stamp of approval, then Slay is OK.

That's the way Peterson sees it. And if he needed any more positive feedback, he got some from a credible source before he even took the Tennessee job.

"[Illinois coach] Bill Self told me if he could take another player from another team in the country, Slay would be the first one he'd take, just becomes he comes ready to play every night," Peterson said.

Of that there can be no doubt. But Peterson, a retiring guy himself, would like Slay to dial back his antics a bit, if for no other reason than to keep him from becoming a lightning rod for criticism from opposing fans.

"You've got to love Ron's enthusiasm," Peterson said. "I watched [tape] of a lot of games from last year, and he got himself into trouble at times. We just need to channel some of that enthusiasm in a different direction. He's good for the young guys, because every day in practice, this kid is fired up and ready to work hard."

Lest we forget to mention it, Slay's game isn't solely based on emotion. He can play, and might have a chance to do so for pay some day. He's a crafty low-post scorer and loves to step outside and make three-pointers, which he can do at a passably consistent rate. Few players in the country can get to the rim with more authority than Slay, who can power dunk in traffic or as a finisher on the break. He had a couple of broken backboards to his credit in high school, and it's only a matter of time until he rips one down in some SEC arena.

If Peterson can indeed channel Slay's emotions and get him to cut back on his turnovers, he can elevate his All-SEC status (he was third team a year ago) and become a star. Slay already has a leg up on that status, having been anointed last season as ESPN analyst Dick Vitale's top sixth man in the country. Slay was also a third-team All-SEC pick.

Dickie V will have to find another sixth man to praise this season, for Slay will become a starter after two years of caddying for Isiah Victor and Vincent Yarbrough. He earned that on the strength of his play in postseason games a year ago. After a pair of sub-par games to end the regular season, Slay hit Auburn with 22 points and 11 rebounds in the second round of the SEC Tournament and had 20 points and five boards against Ole Miss the next day. Many of his teammates seemed to be eager to get what had become a disappointing season over with, but not Slay.

If Peterson can indeed channel Slay's boundless energy, he's capable of putting up those sorts of numbers on a regular basis.

C-MARCUS HAISLIP (6-10, 230 lbs., JR, #12, 5.8 ppg, 2.5 rpg, 0.7 apg, 0.6 tpg, 0.2 spg, 1.5 bpg, 13.2 minutes, .516 FG, .359 3PT, .757 FT, Marshall County HS/Lewisburg, Tenn.). We list Haislip as the starter, but he won't be for at least the first five games of the season. Haislip was declared academically ineligible for the first semester. Tennessee coaches aren't concerned about him doing the required work in the classroom and regaining his eligibility.

That's a good thing, for Haislip might be the most gifted athlete on a team that has athletes in abundant supply. That also might have been true the previous two years, but playing behind C.J. Black, Charles Hathaway and Isiah Victor, Haislip's minutes were sporadic.

There were those who wondered why Green didn't try to use Haislip more often last season, especially when Hathaway and Victor were ineffective. But Haislip made the most of his time. Despite averaging just 13 minutes, he led the Vols in blocked shots. His 51 blocks were the fifth-highest single-season total in school history. His average of 1.5 blocks per game ranked third in the SEC.

Haislip can do more than turn back shots. He can score inside—more because of his leaping ability and quickness than brute strength—and also make enough three-pointers to keep defenses honest. He's a good free-throw shooter and can finish on the break with acrobatic slam dunks.

Haislip had some big individual games as a sophomore. In a career-high 24 minutes, he scored 16 points on six-of-eight shooting against Georgia. He lit up SMU for 14 points in just 11 minutes. Against Auburn in the SEC Tournament, Haislip showed his mettle after getting hammered in the mouth in the first half. He was led off the floor and had to get 10 stitches, but returned and scored all 11 of his points in the second half.

Peterson is going to ask Haislip to alter his game slightly this season.

"In high school, he played a lot out on the perimeter," Peterson said. "We're asking him to take his game inside because of his height and jumping ability. It'll be an adjustment, but I want him to get more physical."

Haislip has committed himself to the weight room and has actually become the Vols' strongest player in the bench press. His added strength helped him get more active and absorb more pounding in the post last year. He'll be asked to do even more damage down low this season, as he becomes a starter.

"It's all up to Marcus," Peterson said. "He's got amazing athletic ability. The talent's there. If he'll continue to work hard, he's got a tremendous upside."

KEY RESERVES

F-DEL BAKER (6-5, 200 lbs., SR, #32, 3.5 ppg, 1.1 rpg, 1.0 apg, 0.7 tpg, 0.5 spg, 0.4 bpg, 11.8 minutes, .415 FG, .267 3PT, .412 FT in 1999-2000, Cleveland HS/Cleveland, Tenn.). No one can say Baker isn't thorough. Late in his junior season, Baker broke his right foot and was lost for the remainder of the year. After working hard to rehabilitate his foot in the off-season, Baker broke his left foot before last season began.

Though Green hoped to be able to get Baker back on court, the injury was slow to heal and Baker eventually decided to red-shirt. That gave him the opportunity to close out his career along with his half brother Vincent Yarbrough, who came to Knoxville a year after Baker.

Nobody has ever accused Baker of playing the same kind of game as his brother. He wasn't highly recruited by upper-level Division I schools. Baker was signed by former Vol coach Kevin O'Neill in hopes of attracting Yarbrough. The plan worked, but O'Neill never hung around long enough to reap the benefits of his recruiting ploy, or to find out that Baker really could play big-time Division I basketball.

In Baker's injury-plagued four seasons, he's made some strides. His jump shot was erratic his first two seasons and he was often turnover prone. Baker eventually decided his best chance of making significant contributions was as a defensive stopper.

With his height, long arms and leaping ability, Baker can make it tough on an opposing shooter. Vol fans wonder if a healthy Baker could have shut down North Carolina's Joseph Forte and prevented a heartbreaking loss in the NCAA Tournament's Sweet 16 in 2000.

Peterson is glad to have Baker on his side. The senior is a lock to log significant minutes this season, especially after the dismissal of guards Harris Walker and Terrence Woods.

"I've been real impressed with Del," Peterson said. "He's come off the injury fine. And he's worked really hard. You can tell he wants to make his senior year a special year.

"He'll be a wing player for us, and I've told him he's got to look at his offensive game as a weapon and make people guard him. I feel confident that when we're on the road, Del's not going to get rattled. He's been around."

C-BRANDON CRUMP (6-10, 230 lbs., FR, #33, 15.8 ppg, 10.2 rpg, 2.9 bpg in 1999-2000, Klein HS/Klein, Texas). Crump terrorized his teammates in practice last season, which he served out as a red-shirt. That was his choice, given the fact he showed up in Knoxville as a skinny 17 year-old. The time on the sidelines was good for Crump, as it allowed him to add 15 pounds of muscle and hone his skills.

By the end of the year, Crump was drawing attention. One NBA scout who witnessed a March practice session said that Crump and Marcus Haislip were the Vols' two best NBA prospects.

Crump is a long way from the NBA, but Peterson is glad to have him. Crump won't be a starter right away, but he fits into the Vols' four-man post rotation. He's not a banger, but he's got a lot of skills that will serve him well. Crump has developed a jump hook and he can also step outside and shoot medium-range jump shots. He's a good passer from the high post and seems to have a natural instinct for how the game should be played.

"Crump is really a disciplined kid," Peterson said. "I know he'll do the right things on and off the floor. On the floor, he's worked really hard. This kid just needs experience. He's got a nice little mid-range game, and he can alter some shots. He's grown since he's been here. He's got tons of potential."

G-JENIS GRINDSTAFF (6-2, 185 lbs., SR, #24, 3.1 ppg, 1.4 rpg, 1.6 apg, 1.0 tpg, 0.5 spg, 0.0 bpg, 11.7 minutes, .313 FG, .255 3PT, .765 FT Spruce Pine HS/Spruce Pine, N.C.; Virginia Tech). Few players have had to deal with the hardships Grindstaff has endured the last two years. His trials and tribulations have been well documented. In the summer of 1999, Grindstaff lost both parents to cancer. Basketball was about all Grindstaff had to help him through that ordeal, but in the first game of the 1999-2000 season, that was taken from him when he went down with a serious knee injury.

Grindstaff lost the entire year, after having sat out the previous year as a red-shirt when he transferred from Virginia Tech. Thus, when Grindstaff took the floor last season, he was two years removed from his freshman year with the Hokies, when he averaged 10.5 points and was chosen to the All-Atlantic 10 freshman team.

Grindstaff never totally shook the rust off his game, and his knee injury had robbed him of some speed and mobility. Green played him sporadically, and Grindstaff found himself pressing when he did get in games, trying to make something happen.

Most of the time not much happened. But Grindstaff had his moments. He had a Tennessee career-high 11 points and six rebounds in 20 minutes of work against Syracuse. In a huge come-from-behind win at South Carolina, Grindstaff knocked down a three-pointer that trimmed the Gamecocks' lead to three. In the SEC Tournament, Grindstaff had seven points and three assists in 11 minutes against Ole Miss.

Peterson, like Grindstaff a former Mr. Basketball in North Carolina, hopes he can coax a bit more out of Grindstaff in his senior season.

"I'm going to expect him as a senior to step it up," Peterson said. "I want him to be a leader and be more vocal. I've seen this kid play since he was in high school. He's got a lot of potential, but nobody's had as tough a time as Jenis has. I'm really hoping he can have a big senior year."

Grindstaff has appealed to the NCAA for another year of eligibility, but Peterson doesn't hold out much hope that the appeal will be granted.

F-DEREK STRIBLING (6-6, 185 lbs., FR, #21, 20.0 ppg, 8.0 rpg, 4.0 apg, Rickards HS/Tallahassee, Fla.). There was never any doubt that Stribling wanted to come to Tennessee, even after Green left and was replaced by Peterson. Stribling was recruited as the heir apparent to Yarbrough.

"I hope to give them a lot of the same things Vincent Yarbrough does," Stribling told The Tennesseean. "I love to go to the basket, run the break and play good defense."

Like fellow Vol freshman Elgrace Wilborn, Stribling showed up on the top 100 lists of some recruiting analysts. He certainly had his pick of upper-echelon Division I schools—Stribling chose Tennessee over Georgia and was also recruited by Georgetown, Maryland, DePaul and Connecticut. Hometown Florida State apparently put in a strong bid for Stribling's services as well.

Peterson plans to throw Stribling into the mix early. After the July ouster of guards Harris Walker and Terrence Woods, Stribling picked up some minutes without raising a finger. Peterson can easily switch Yarbrough to the shooting guard spot and play Stribling at small forward.

"He's very athletic," Peterson said of Stribling. "He's very similar to Vincent. He just needs to get more consistent with his outside shot."

When Tennessee signed Stribling, he wasn't a consistent three-point shooter. But he's put in a lot of work on his jump shot and isn't afraid to take it.

"I don't expect too many people to leave me open," Stribling told The Tennessean. "If they do, that's their fault."

F-ELGRACE WILBORN (6-8, 210 lbs., FR, #15, 11.6 ppg, 13.1 rpg, 6.6 bpg, South HS/Springfield, Ohio). There were some anxious moments last spring when Wilborn, after first stating that he wanted to play for Peterson, changed his mind and wanted out of his scholarship. He blamed Green's ouster for his abrupt change of heart, but more likely he saw an opportunity for instant playing time at the school many thought he wanted to sign with all along, Michigan State.

After the Spartans unexpectedly lost sophomore forward Jason Richardson and freshman center Zach Randolph to the NBA draft, they had some openings in the frontcourt. NCAA rules prevented Michigan State from recruiting Wilborn, so it was left up to the player to make contact with the Spartans. Apparently, he was dissuaded from that by Peterson's stern proclamation that he wasn't about to grant Wilborn a release from his scholarship.

Peterson really wanted Wilborn, who, depending on what recruiting guru you favor, was ranked among the nation's top 100 players. It would have been next to impossible to get a decent big man last spring had Wilborn bolted. And Peterson really likes Wilborn's upside.

"Right now, his defense is better than his offense," said Peterson, who recruited Wilborn when he was at Tulsa. "He's going to come in here and just get better every day. With playing time, he's going to be right in the mix."

Wilborn is a tremendous athlete who has recorded a vertical leap of 44 inches.

"He can get up," Peterson said. "He plays taller than 6-8. He can really alter some shots."

Wilborn led the state of Ohio in blocked shots, and also averaged a double double. Most recruiting analysts question Wilborn's range past a dunk, but his defense will earn him immediate playing time at Tennessee and give the Vols—along with Yarbrough, Crump and Haislip—a potent shot-blocking foursome.

"I think I bring a tenacity to the court, especially defensive-wise, and a little bit of show time, too," Wilborn told The Tennessean when he signed last November. "I look at the SEC, and there's nothing but athletes in that conference. That's my game and where I fit in best."

Wilborn might have forgotten those words last April, but Peterson's not-so-subtle reminder that the player cast his lot with the Vols first was enough to keep him in Knoxville.

OTHER RETURNEES

F-ANDY IKEAKOR (6-8, 245 lbs., SO, #34, 0.8 ppg, 0.5 rpg, Westbury Christian/Houston, Texas). Ikeakor was a bust last season, and many thought that had Green and his staff stayed around, they would have encouraged the youngster to transfer to a school at a much lower level of Division I.

Ikeakor was suspect from the outset, when he showed up on campus at 285 pounds. He looked so massive, plodding and earthbound some sports writers wondered whether he could jump over the free-throw line. Despite daily workouts, Ikeakor's weight didn't seem to dip so much as a pound all season.

As if the added weight wasn't enough of a problem, Ikeakor also displayed a lack of good judgement when he got into into a fight before the season began with Tennessee football player Kevin Burnett, a rugged, future All-SEC linebacker from Compton, Calif. Ikeakor suffered a broken hand in the fracas and missed a lot of preseason drills.

Luckily for Ikeakor, with a new regime comes a new attitude from the head coach. Peterson wants to try and give Ikeakor a chance. If he doesn't show some progress, even the patient, kind-hearted Peterson might have to show him the door.

F-ZACH TURNER (6-7, 230 lbs., JR, 0.2 ppg, 0.5 rpg, Christian HS/Charlotte, N.C.). Turned played in eight games a year ago, usually when the Vols were way ahead. In many instances, he slipped into the late-game action ahead of scholarship teammate Andy Ikeakor.

Even though the Vols don't have as much depth and strength up front as they did in the days of C.J. Black and Charles Hathaway, Turner doesn't figure to play any more this season than he did a year ago.

OTHER NEWCOMERS

F-MICHAEL COLLINS (6-6, 215 lbs., FR, #3, 28.0 ppg, 10.0 rpg, Commerce HS/Nicholson, Ga.). When Collins signed a football scholarship with Tennessee last

February, he said that Vol coach Phil Fulmer had given him permission to play basketball as well. Blue Ribbon decided to list Collins on the Vols' roster, but Tennessee fans won't believe he's a basketball player until they see him in baggy shorts.

Over the years, several excellent two-way players have signed with Tennessee. All were football players first, and most said they wanted to give basketball a try. All-America defensive tackle John Henderson is one recent example.

Somehow, though, none of those players ever made it to the basketball court. The last football players to also play basketball for the Vols were Ron Widby and Bill Young—35 years ago.

One reason Tennessee doesn't produce good two-way players is the fact the football team almost always plays in a late-December or early January bowl game. By the time a football player can join the basketball team, it's mid January, which means he's missed three months of practice. It would be hard for anyone to make up that much ground and have any significant impact.

Collins was a first-team all-state pick in football and basketball and was ranked by some recruiting analysts among the top 100 players in the country in both sports. He had a great senior season on the court, leading Commerce to the state tournament.

Though Collins had good statistics as a basketball player, these are the numbers that stand out to Fulmer, who has first dibs on the youngster: In his four-year career, Collins accounted for 79 receptions for 2,339 yards and 27 touchdowns, 1,343 rushing yards and 24 touchdowns, 379 tackles and 13 interceptions.

If Collins doesn't break in the Vols' five- or six-man receiver rotation as a freshman, he could be red-shirted. And if he is, expect Collins to suit up for the basketball team.

G-DRIONNE MAJOR (6-2, 170 lbs, FR #5, 27.2 ppg, 6.0 apg St. Bernard HS/St. Bernard, La.). After the late-July dismissal of guards Harris Walker and Terrence Woods, Peterson said he hoped he could find a walk-on point guard from the student body. "I'm hoping that with 22,000 students, we can find somebody who can handle the ball," Peterson told the Knoxville News-Sentinel.

Peterson never had to conduct tryouts. The day after it was announced that Walker and Woods were gone, Major told the News-Sentinel he was walking on at Tennessee.

Major isn't your ordinary every day walk-on. Oddly, though he's a Louisiana native, he followed Tennessee as a youngster, paying particular attention to former Vol All-American Allan Houston. Considering how bad Tennessee was back then, even with Houston scoring tons of points, Major must have been a big fan.

"It's been a lifelong dream [to play for Tennessee], ever since I was in middle school," Major told the News-Sentinel. "I even used to watch them play on TV when Allan Houston was playing."

Unlike most walk-ons, Major could have gotten a scholarship to a Division I school. New Orleans, Tulane, North Texas and Louisiana-Lafayette all offered. Notre Dame recruited him when Matt Doherty was coaching there but backed off when Doherty left for North Carolina and Mike Brey took over.

Major, who can play either guard spot, was a first-team Class 3A all-state pick in Louisiana and was the New Orleans metro player of the year in the small-school division.

QUESTIONS

New coach? How well will the Vols adapt to the philosophies of Peterson, who will instill discipline in the program not seen in the Green era?

Leadership? Who will take over this team and be an extension of Peterson on the floor?

Point guard? Can Thaydeus Holden handle this all-important position?

ANSWERS

Talent! The Vols are still one of the most talented teams in the country, despite the loss of three seniors.

Athleticism! Tennessee isn't physically imposing, but the Vols have plenty of players who can run and jump. Shot-blocking will be a strength.

New coach! The Vols clearly needed a change, and Peterson is just the guy to give it to them. Though he has installed some rules (curfews, study halls, etc.), Peterson is generally considered a player's coach.

TENNESSEE 2000-2001 RESULTS

UT-Chattanooga	88-66
East Tennessee	102-76
Wisconsin	66-56
Austin Peay	98-65
UNC-Asheville	85-59
@West Virginia	79-78
Memphis	86-76
Southern Methodist	85-76
#Middle Tennessee	99-83
##Virginia (L)	89-107
@Syracuse	83-70
###George Washington	92-81
###Iowa	80-68
###Hawaii	69-58
@Auburn	96-88
South Carolina	79-71
@Kentucky (L)	74-84
Mississippi State	84-79
@Georgia (L)	75-77
@Florida (L)	67-81
Vanderbilt	72-50
@Arkansas (L)	77-82
@Mississippi (L)	71-87
Kentucky (L)	103-95
Florida (L)	82-88
Georgia (L)	76-88
@Vanderbilt	78-70
@South Carolina	68-67
LSU	78-71
####Auburn	73-66
####Mississippi (L)	73-86
#####Charlotte (L)	63-70

#At Nashville
##Jimmy V Classic in Meadowlands, NJ
###Rainbow Classic in Honolulu, HI
####SEC Tournament in Nashville
#####NCAA Tournament
@Road Games

BLUE RIBBON ANALYSIS

BACKCOURT	B-
BENCH/DEPTH	B
FRONTCOURT	A
INTANGIBLES	B

Tennsssee basketball has been on an upswing the last four years, but apparently that improvement wasn't enough. It's going to be Peterson's job to see that the Vols take their game to the next level.

Does Peterson have the talent to do that? Certainly, Tennessee doesn't have the array of weapons it did a year ago, but then again, none of the three departed seniors—Harris, Victor and Hathaway—did anything that can't be duplicated by Yarbrough, Higgins or Haislip.

There are two keys for the Vols in their quest to put together a fifth straight 20-win season and earn a fifth straight NCAA Tournament bid. Someone has to play the point, whether its Higgins or newcomer Holden. And Tennessee, with just 11 scholarship players on the roster, needs to stay healthy, or depth could be a real problem.

Our prediction is that Tennessee will play a lot harder and smarter under Peterson than it did for Green, who had apparently lost the respect of his players. That probably won't translate into a higher finish in the SEC East standings, as Florida and Kentucky loom large.

(C.D.)

 **Indiana 24**

LOCATION	Bloomington, IN
CONFERENCE	Big Ten
LAST SEASON	21-13 (.618)
CONFERENCE RECORD	10-6 (4th)
STARTERS LOST/RETURNING	1/4
NICKNAME	Hoosiers
COLORS	Cream & Crimson
HOMECOURT	Assembly Hall (17,484)
COACH	Mike Davis (Alabama '83)
RECORD AT SCHOOL	21-13 (1 year)
CAREER RECORD	21-13 (1 year)
ASSISTANTS	John Treloar (Bellhaven '78)
	Jim Thomas (Indiana '83)

	Ben McDonald (UC Irvine '84)
TEAM WINS (last 5 years)	22-20-23-20-21
RPI (last 5 years)	21-21-14-22-16
2000-01 FINISH	Lost in NCAA first round.

COACH AND PROGRAM

Want to take a look back at the last year of Mike Davis' life? Make sure you're sitting down. This is going to be dizzying.

Before Sept. 8, 2000, Davis was just an assistant coach getting ready for another season. But then an Indiana student asked the now historic question, "What's up, Knight?" to which the Hoosiers' coach of 29 years responded unfavorably. Within four days, Bob Knight was deemed in violation of the "zero tolerance" policy placed on him by the university the previous spring. After undeniably the most controversial coaching change in recent sports history, Davis was suddenly interim head coach, entrusted with taking over the team only a month before the start of practice.

In the year to follow, Davis would hit the lowest of lows (losing to Indiana State to fall to 2-3, suffering an NCAA first-round upset against Kent State) and the highest of highs (beating No. 1 Michigan State, upsetting top-seeded Illinois in the Big Ten Tournament). He would suffer the wrath of skeptics, IU traditionalists and Knight himself with some of the changes he made. And he would be forced to wait until after season's end to finally get the interim tag removed and officially become the next head coach of Indiana basketball.

Not that things ended there. Next came the unexpected departure of center Kirk Haston to the NBA draft, followed almost immediately by the rigorous summer recruiting circuit and finding replacements for two assistant coaches. Finally, heaven forbid he take a break, Davis spent a few weeks coaching the Big Ten touring team in England and Ireland, returning to Bloomington in time for individual conditioning drills in late August—just under a year since his original ascension.

"I want to take a vacation," Davis said. "But that Big Ten tour kind of took its place."

Looking back, Davis survived a nearly impossible situation and has come out of it golden. In the days surrounding IU president Myles Brand's much-debated decision to fire Knight, there were many times when it appeared the program might undergo a complete whitewash. Players like Dane Fife and prized freshman Jared Jeffries threatened to quit. Davis' rapid appointment was done in large part to appease the players, who all but demanded an internal promotion.

But there was one factor weighing heavily against the 40-year-old Davis: He was not a Hoosier. Far from it, Davis was born in Fayette, Ala., played for the Crimson Tide and came to IU in 1997 from a stint as assistant at his alma mater. Surely the school would not entrust its sacred basketball legacy—five national championships, 19 Big Ten crowns—to a man with more connection to Bear Bryant than to Bob Knight? Popular speculation had the school waiting until after the season, then tapping one of Knight's many young coaching disciples, mainly Iowa coach and star of the Hoosiers' 1987 national title team, Steve Alford.

Whether IU officials ever actually made an offer to Alford—as was reported in several media outlets—may forever remain a mystery. The school denies it. Alford raised a stink at the mere mention of his alma mater during an NCAA Tournament press conference.

But what is clear is that Indiana would have had a hard time letting Davis go after the job he turned in under incredible circumstances last season. His 21 wins were second only to Butler's Thad Matta (23) among the nation's 17 first-time head coaches. The Hoosiers' two Big Ten Tournament wins were their first in the four-year history of the event. Their No. 4 seeding in the NCAA Tournament was their highest since 1993.

"Last year when I got the job, everything happened so quick, I was just trying to make sure I was prepared for the season," Davis said. "Now as I look back on it, it kind of scares me a little. Not really aware of the position I was in, it was high pressure. But I didn't realize that at the time, I just wanted to coach basketball, prove to everybody I could do a good job."

Both Davis and the players were still quite obviously in a haze from the Knight fallout when the season began, and it showed. After beating Pepperdine and South Alabama at home to begin the Preseason NIT, the Hoosiers looked barely into it during losses in New York to Temple (69-61) and Texas (70-58), then came back to Indiana only to suffer their second straight heartbreaker

to the cross-state Sycamores, 59-58. A downtrodden Davis heaped the blame on himself during post-game press conferences, after one of which, when there were no more questions, Davis sat for nearly 10 minutes in silence before returning to the locker room.

Things started to turn, though, in December, with wins over No. 10 Notre Dame and No. 24 Charlotte. On Jan. 7, IU shocked the then top-ranked Spartans 59-58 on a Haston buzzer-beater and for the first time, the Assembly Hall faithful embraced the new Hoosiers. IU would play .500 ball for most of the rest of Big Ten season but scored important wins at Ohio State, Penn State and Purdue. Even though no assurances had been made about Davis' future, things were looking good by the time IU rolled off five straight wins, culminating with the Big Ten semifinal upset of No. 4 Illinois.

"Once we got to Big Ten play and we beat Michigan State, I knew we could beat people," Davis said. "I was starting to feel good, and then when we went on the road and beat Ohio State and Penn State. I felt like after winning two big road games like that—it was my job. The last three [regular season] games, that was just like icing on the cake, then we go into the Big Ten Tournament and win a couple games."

The only blip on Davis' otherwise successful debut came at the end. After losing 63-61 to a surprising Iowa team in the Big Ten final, the Hoosiers continued a disturbing trend that had punctuated Knight's latter years, bowing out in the NCAA first round to 13th-seeded Kent State. The loss marked IU's fifth first round exit in the past seven years.

But anyone who watched Davis' team knew this was by no means Knight's Hoosiers. Davis stressed more motion on the court—not to mention more freedom. The type of mistake that in the past would instantly get a player yanked and, most likely, an earful, like fouling the three-point shooter, merited only a cold "don't do it again" stare from Davis. The players particularly clicked on defense, holding opponents to the lowest field-goal percentage (.382) since the Big Ten started keeping the statistic in 1974.

This year, with a full off-season to prepare, Davis is looking forward to further putting his stamp on the program. Filling Haston's All-Big Ten caliber production will be a challenge, but the Hoosiers should be able to contend with most anyone in the conference, but may still be looking up at loaded Illinois and Iowa. After winning Big Ten Freshman-of-the-Year honors, Jeffries is considered one of the best players in the country. It will be the sophomore's team to carry.

In the meantime, Davis has been busy assembling what could wind up one of the nation's top recruiting classes, part of his larger—and lofty—vision for the program.

"If I can get a top four, top five recruiting class every year, we'll have the personnel we need to put on the floor every night and compete, like the Dukes and North Carolinas," Davis said. "We're trying to win national championships."

2001-2002 SCHEDULE

Nov.	18	@Charlotte
	21-24	#Great Alaska Shootout
	28	*North Carolina
Dec.	1	@Southern Illinois
	4	Notre Dame
	8	Ball State
	15	**Miami
	22	***Kentucky
	28-29	##Ameritech Hoosier Classic
Jan.	2	@Northwestern
	5	Penn State
	8	Michigan State
	13	@Iowa
	19	@Ohio State
	23	@Penn State
	27	Illinois
	31	Purdue
Feb.	2	@Minnesota
	5	Iowa
	9	Louisville
	13	Wisconsin
	17	@Michigan
	20	Ohio State
	24	@Michigan State
	26/27	@Illinois
March	2	Northwestern
	7-10	###Big Ten Tournament

@Road Games
*Big Ten/ACC Challenge
**Orange Bowl Classic
***RCA Dome, Indianapolis, IN
#Anchorage, AK (vs. Alaska Anchorage first round; also Gonzaga, Marquette, Oregon State, Texas, St. John's, Tennessee)
##Conseco Fieldhouse, Indianapolis, IN (vs. Eastern Washington first round; also Butler, Samford)
###Conseco Fieldhouse, Indianapolis, IN

STARTERS NOT RETURNING

C-KIRK HASTON (6-10, 19.0 ppg, 8.7 rpg, 1.2 apg, 1.1 bpg, 1.1 spg, 30.8 minutes, .469 FG, .377 3PT, .687). The 6-9 Haston was truly IU's most valuable player in 2000-01, a warrior who improved tremendously from the time he arrived on campus, nearly doubling his scoring average from his freshman year while battling a knee injury. His ability to play both around the basket as well as step back and take a shot proved a great threat to defenses, often opening up the lane for IU's other players.

Haston often garnered the "underrated" label during his three seasons at IU, leading the Hoosiers in scoring and rebounding last season but slipping under the radar of those who vote on All-America and other such honors. The Charlotte Hornets certainly took notice, though, selecting Haston with the 16th overall pick in June's NBA draft after his impressive performance at the Chicago pre-draft camp.

Haston's college coach knew well his value but never actually expected him to leave, not even after the player put his name on the underclass list in May without hiring an agent in order to "test the waters."

"We had no idea we were going to lose Kirk," Davis said. "I didn't think he was going to do it up until the day [June 15] he said he was going to do it."

OTHERS NOT RETURNING

G-ANDRE OWENS (6-2, 4.7 ppg, 1.4 rpg, 14.1 minutes, .453 FG, .389 3PT, .742 FT). Owens' freshman season at IU didn't go quite as planned. The projected starter at point guard in these pages before last season, the 6-2 Indianapolis native was instead turned into more of a swingman, a role with which he was never quite comfortable. Though it can't be said for sure, Owens may have fared better under Knight, the man who recruited him, who put less emphasis on athleticism and was said to admire Owens' defensive tenacity.

Owens announced in May he was transferring to play for one of his former recruiters, ex-Ball State coach Ray McCallum, at Houston. He said he did not consider reuniting with Knight at Texas Tech.

PROJECTED STARTERS

PG-TOM COVERDALE (6-2, 200 lbs., JR, #3, 10.7 ppg, 3.4 rpg, 4.8 apg, 1.5 spg, 34.1 minutes, .454 FG, .356 3PT, .663 FT, Noblesville HS/Noblesville, Ind.). Coverdale's emergence as the Hoosiers' floor leader last season was stunning, considering he had played a total of only 41 minutes as a freshman. After the exit of backcourt veterans A.J. Guyton, Michael Lewis and Luke Jiminez, the Hoosiers were desperate for one of the youngsters to step up, and Coverdale answered the call, starting all but two games.

Despite being more of a true off-guard, Coverdale handled point duties respectably, maintaining an assist-to-turnover ratio of nearly two-to-one. But he also made and attempted the most three-pointers on the team (52-of-146), and the arrival of freshman point guard Donald Perry may allow him to play the two more often.

"No one really knew what he could do, but he was fantastic for us last year," Davis said. "And in individual workouts, I've never seen him work as hard as he's doing. He's a very tough minded kid."

Coverdale's biggest negatives have come off the court. The 1998 Indiana Mr. Basketball arrived at IU out of shape after a year of prep school, contributing to his season on the pine. He didn't do anything to endear himself to Hoosier fans by garnering two citations for underage alcohol consumption last year, one in May and one in December, just three days before scoring 30 points in IU's upset of 10th-ranked Notre Dame.

Davis did not suspend Coverdale, but placed him under a 10 p.m. curfew and ordered him to move into a dorm and seek counseling. The coach sent him another message after showing up late for the Big Ten team's final practice before departing for England. Davis left Coverdale off the trip. The incident garnered some headlines and elicited some grumbling from fans with a long memory, but another good season should move him quickly back into their good graces.

SG-DANE FIFE (6-4, 200 lbs., SR, #11, 5.1 ppg, 2.8 rpg, 3.2 apg, 1.4 spg, 32.9 minutes, .374 FG, .306 3PT, .629 FT, Clarkston HS/Clarkston, Mich.). Fife, a former McDonald's All-American, was one of the most visibly upset players after Knight's firing, going so far as to announce he was leaving the team before reconsidering. If Fife's displeasure reared its head in any way during the season, it was his miserable shooting numbers. But scoring is also not what the Hoosiers look for from him.

Fife is considered one of the conference's better defenders, gluing in on opponents' top shooting threat and getting a hand in his face at all times.

"He just hates for people to score," Davis said. "He takes it personally if somebody scores on him."

In retrospect, Fife's elite status coming out of high school in Clarkston, Mich., was probably overstated, due largely to his two-sport stardom (Fife was coveted by Michigan and others as a quarterback) and his coming to play for Knight. But he's spent the off-season working on his shooting and Davis would not be surprised to see him have a memorable senior season.

"Fife right now is playing lights out, he's a different player than he's ever been," Davis said. "Offensively, he's improving well. That's what I've been impressed by with him. He's going to really surprise some people this year."

SG-KYLE HORNSBY (6-5, 205 lbs., JR, #32, 6.9 ppg, 2.0 rpg, 1.0 apg, 19.6 minutes, .432 FG, .426 3PT, .710 FT, Anacoco HS/Anacoco, La.). Like Coverdale, Hornsby's contributions increased dramatically from his freshman to sophomore year, though he had shown signs of what was to come. After red-shirting in 1998-99 with a knee injury and seeing limited action the first half of 2000, Hornsby came on late, scoring a then-career high 15 points in IU's NCAA Tournament loss to Pepperdine. He finished that year averaging 3.4 points.

Last season, Hornsby started 11 games, leading the team and ranking fourth in the Big Ten in three-point field-goal percentage. His role diminished slightly during conference season, when he averaged 5.8 points and shot .370 from behind the arc.

Whether he becomes a permanent member of the starting lineup this season may depend on factors out of his control. If George Leach emerges as a capable center, the Hoosiers would probably only start two guards, Coverdale and Fife, with Hornsby providing an offensive spark off the bench like much of last season. Hornsby doesn't get to the basket often, and it is still a question whether he can match up defensively with often quicker wing players. He's been plagued by a host of injuries, most recently a late-season ankle sprain that limited him in the postseason.

But there's no underestimating his ability as an outside marksman.

"Hornsby's probably the best shooter on the team," Davis said. "He's got to knock down shots for us to win. Our guards had more opportunities to shoot, they just didn't shoot. I expect them to take more shots this year."

SF-JARED JEFFRIES (6-10, 215 lbs., SO, #1, 13.8 ppg, 6.9 rpg, 2.4 apg, 1.2 bpg, 32.6 minutes, .442 FG, .245 3PT, .620 FT, North HS/Bloomington, Ind.). At first glance, the lanky Jeffries would hardly seem fit to take over a basketball game. He's a deceiving 6-10, more of a face-forward post player than a true big man. But if you're a defender, don't spend too long observing his wiry frame. He's liable to be three steps past you and on his way to a dunk before you can blink.

The hometown hero was bound to be under pressure upon his long-awaited arrival at IU, having gained a reputation as one of the nation's top five incoming freshmen after leading Bloomington North High School to the state championship game. But then before even having his first college practice, the man Jeffries had grown up watching was unceremoniously removed.

In retrospect, Davis' ascension was probably the best thing that could have happened to Jeffries' career. The two had developed quite a kinship during Jeffries' recruitment, and that affection carried over to the season, where Davis was far more forgiving of his many freshman mistakes than Knight would have been. Jeffries was too talented not to start under any coach, but it's doubtful he would have had the freedom to develop into such a go-to guy so early in his career.

"I think early on he played like he had the weight of world on his shoulders," Davis said. "There was the hometown pressure, plus with me getting the job, I thought he was trying so hard at first to help me keep the job. I had to get him to relax a little."

Jeffries' potential is unlimited, but IU fans better enjoy it while they can. After pondering the NBA after just one season, Jeffries seems likely to jump if he has the type of sophomore season most are expecting of him. With Haston gone, the team will most definitively run through Jeffries, whose explosiveness, unselfishness and defensive ability make him extraordinarily well rounded for his size.

"He's the guy we're really depending on," Davis said. "He averaged 13 points a game last year, but he could have averaged 20 if he hit more free throws, took more three-pointers. He's picked up some weight, he's stronger. He's a great player, I think he'll be a lottery pick."

PF-JEFF NEWTON (6-9, 210 lbs., JR, #50, 6.1 ppg, 4.8 rpg, 1.2 apg, 1.7 bpg, 21.6 minutes, .517 FG, .529 FT, Mays HS/Atlanta, Ga.). Dick Vitale tabbed Newton one of the country's "six significant players" who needs to step up in 2001-02, and rightfully so. Newton is a lanky power forward who will be asked to be a de facto center in Haston's absence.

A modest surprise as a freshman two years ago after a largely unheralded high school career in Atlanta, Newton seemed to level off as a sophomore. Part of it was the arrival of Jeffries, who suddenly crowded the previously barren frontcourt. But part of it was an extremely laid-back demeanor that has contributed to his getting a "soft" reputation.

"Newton is probably the key for us," Davis said. "He's laid back, but he's playing hard right now. He's got to continue to do that for us to be successful. He's athletic, he's so quick, and now he's getting stronger. It's a matter of understanding his role."

His role is to block shots—he has 104 in two seasons—and provide IU with an offensive threat in the post. Newton is quick and can create his own shot in the lane. If he can become a double-digit scorer, the combination of Newton and Jeffries could ease the loss of Haston, at least a tad.

KEY RESERVES

C-GEORGE LEACH (6-11, 220 lbs., SO, #5, 1.8 ppg, 1.5 rpg, 1.0 bpg, 6.6 minutes, .375 FG, .478 FT, Olympic HS/Charlotte, N.C.). Leach was a project from the get go, sitting out his first year as a red-shirt when the NCAA ruled him a partial qualifier (his 810 SAT score was 10 points shy, but a high school guidance counselor erroneously told him he didn't have to retake the test). That said, his first year playing was a bit of a disappointment for IU fans who had waited anxiously for his arrival while watching an undersized team get dominated at times in 1999-00.

Much of Davis' plans will depend on how far Leach can develop between his freshman and sophomore seasons. In the little action he did get, the only ability he showed was being able to block shots. If that continues, Davis will have no choice but to go with a three-guard lineup and no true center.

But if Leach can develop some semblance of an offensive game, it would take a lot of pressure off Newton as well as allowing Jeffries to become more of a perimeter player.

"It all depends on how George Leach develops," Davis said. "He's really, really worked hard, picked up 15-20 pounds. If he continues to improve and develop, he'll be able to give us a different look."

G-DONALD PERRY (6-2, 170 lbs., FR, #12, 29.6 ppg, 8.6 apg, 7.5 spg, McCall HS/Tallulah, La.). Davis speaks very highly of last year's Louisiana Mr. Basketball, so highly in fact as to suggest Perry could win the Hoosiers' starting point-guard job as a freshman. That would allow Tom Coverdale to move over to his true position, shooting guard, while giving IU a fairly strong backcourt rotation of Coverdale, Perry, Dane Fife, Kyle Hornsby and A.J. Moye.

"We've got Donald Perry now to be the point guard," Davis said. "He'll give us a different look. I'm not sure how it will play out. They'll all compete for the position."

Perry is not as highly regarded by national recruiting experts, many of whom don't list Perry among the top 100 prospects. His primary suitors besides IU were Saint Louis and Tulane of Conference USA.

G-A.J. MOYE (6-3, 215 lbs., SO, #2, 3.3 ppg, 2.4 rpg, 9.3 minutes, .466 FG, .737 3PT, Westlake HS/Atlanta, Ga.). Moye was a top 75 prospect coming out of

Atlanta's Westlake High School but did not contribute as much as expected after arriving overweight and not as quick as needed to run the floor. But his days at IU are far from doomed. An emotional and outspoken player who doesn't take well to losing, Moye has clearly drawn the admiration of Davis.

"He shot 1,000 balls a day this summer. He's improved from last year, and his conditioning is a lot better from when he came in overweight," Davis said. "He's going to compete for playing time. He's a warrior, he's a blue-collar player and he's a guy you've got to put on the court."

F-JARRAD ODLE (6-8, 220 lbs., SR, #43, 3.3 ppg, 2.8 rpg, 11.2 minutes, .484 FG, .588 FT, Oak Hill HS/Swayzee, Ind.). Odle is a strong, gritty player and Indiana native whose main roles are primarily hustle and defense. In the past, he's been good for a stick-back or two a game. But in his final season, he may finally be called on for more extensive duty in all areas as the Hoosiers work to fill Haston's minutes in the post.

"Odle is going to be a front-line guy who comes in and bangs, gets loose balls," Davis said. "He had a great game against Illinois in the Big Ten Tournament last year [29 minutes, five points, seven rebounds]. If he gives us that same effort every night, we're going to be really good."

OTHER RETURNEES

F-MIKE ROBERTS (6-9, 210 lbs., SO, #33, 1.7 ppg, 1.3 rpg, 10 games, 4.0 minutes, South Eugene HS/Eugene, Oregon). Roberts has put on 20 pounds since arriving a year ago from New Hampton (N.H.) Prep School, but he's still not particularly strong for a frontcourt player. Though he should see more time than last year, it will be hard for the Eugene, Ore., native to work his way into the regular rotation.

OTHER NEWCOMERS

F-SEAN KLINE (6-8, 210 lbs., FR, #23, 20.5 ppg, 7.4 rpg, North HS/Harrington, Ind.). A first team all-state selection as a senior, Kline is the only native Hoosier among IU's three recruits this year. He brings much needed size to the frontcourt and could become an instant contributor if he can get his body into Big Ten shape.

"Sean's a hard-nosed kid, [but] his conditioning is not great right now," Davis said. "He's getting there, working out twice a day."

Kline originally committed to the Hoosiers in June, 2000, against the wishes of his mother. Then his father told reporters after Knight's firing that Kline was backing off his commitment. But he indeed signed and arrived on campus over the summer for individual workouts.

G-MARK JOHNSON (6-2, 170 lbs., FR, #21, 22.9 ppg, Oregon HS/Oregon, Wis.). Johnson is considered a good outside shooter but didn't register on most recruiting experts' radars. He does not appear on analyst Brick Oettinger's list of the top 300 seniors in the class of 2001.

G-SCOTT MAY (6-0, 165 lbs., FR, #15, North HS/Bloomington, Ind.). May is a high school teammate of Jeffries and son of the former IU great of the same name, who starred on Knight's 1976 undefeated national championship team. While this May might not contribute much for the Hoosiers, they were hopeful he'd be joined by another who might. Younger brother Sean May is a senior at Bloomington North and considered one of the top 20 prospects in the country.

QUESTIONS

Leach? The 6-11 sophomore is by far the biggest question on the team, and one that has far-reaching implications on the rest of the squad. While the Hoosiers had modest success as a perimeter team last season, their real strength was being able to go to Haston inside. They also led the conference in shots blocked per game (5.24). Leach doesn't necessarily have to morph into Haston overnight, but he does need to become somewhat of a factor for IU to be successful.

Perry? IU thought it would have a freshman point guard last year, Andre Owens, but that didn't pan out. A year later, Owens is at Houston and the Hoosiers are looking to another freshman. Certainly the emergence of Coverdale last year makes point guard less of a concern, as he could man the position full-time if needed. There's also the possibility Jeffries, who has hands like a guard, could become somewhat of a Grant Hill-type point forward. But being able to utilize a true floor leader like

Perry would open up so many other worlds for the Hoosiers.

Free throws? Knight would have been particularly ornery if he had been forced to watch last year's edition of the Hoosiers. They were an absolutely abysmal foul-shooting team. Their .636 team percentage was by far the Big Ten's worst, trailing Northwestern's .671 by a considerable margin. IU was still able to win a number of close games last season, but it can't afford to hope that would trend continue if the shooting problem remains status quo.

ANSWERS

Jeffries! The kid is for real, and this is his year. Most instant-impact players make significant strides between their freshman and sophomore seasons, like last year with Frank Williams at Illinois, Jason Williams and Carlos Boozer at Duke, Gilbert Arenas at Arizona and Casey Jacobsen at Stanford. Jeffries is a talent along their lines.

Defense! The Hoosiers' penchant for glove-tight defense wasn't just a catch phrase last season. There was documented proof. No Big Ten team in the last quarter-century held opponents to a lower field goal percentage than the Hoosiers. Either everyone happened to have really bad days when they played IU, or Davis had his players doing something right.

Time! An entire year has passed since the Knight saga. No longer will the comparisons be hanging over Davis and the players. The reporters and their endless questions about the man and his methods have headed south to Lubbock, Texas. But more than that, the program is Davis' to keep and do what he wants with. He's had a full year to prepare for this season, rather than a month. And he doesn't have to go through the schedule worrying whether one embarrassing loss to Ball State or Wisconsin is going to cost him his job.

INDIANA 2000-2001 RESULTS

#Pepperdine	80-68
#South Alabama	70-62
##Temple (L)	61-69
##Texas (L)	58-70
@Indiana State (L)	58-59
Southern Illinois	85-61
@NotreDame	86-78
###Western Michigan	87-59
###Ball State	65-50
Charlotte	76-62
Missouri (L)	63-68
####Kentucky (L)	74-88
Northeastern	103-65
Valparaiso	63-60
Wisconsin (L)	46-49
Michigan State	59-58
Michigan (L)	64-70
Penn State	77-69
@Minnesota (L)	74-78
Purdue	66-55
Iowa (L)	66-71
Ohio State	70-67
@Penn State	85-78
Michigan	72-59
Northwestern	78-54
Illinois (L)	61-67
@Michigan State (L)	57-66
Wisconsin	85-55
Minnesota	86-53
@Purdue	74-58
#####Wisconsin	64-52
#####Illinois	58-56
#####Iowa (L)	61-63
######Kent State	73-77

#Preseason NIT in Indianapolis
##Preseason NIT in New York
###Ameritech Indiana Classic in Bloomington, IN
####At Louisville, KY
#####Big Ten Tournament in Chicago
######NCAA Tournament
@Road Games

BLUE RIBBON ANALYSIS

BACKCOURT	B
BENCH/DEPTH	C+
FRONTCOURT	B+
INTANGIBLES	A

Last season ushered in a new era in Indiana basket-

ball, but one gets the sense we didn't get to see completely what it will look like.

"Our season, at the beginning, was like a circus," Davis said. "I didn't really have time to get in everything I wanted, I was just teaching basics. It took time. By the end of the year, we were really good offensively. We led the Big Ten in field goal percentage defense and shot blocking, yet I think we could still improve defensively. That is scary."

There's no doubt the Hoosiers have the ability to scare a lot of people in the conference and the nation, but a thin line stands between competing for a title and slipping into the middle of the pack. A lot is being placed on the shoulders of Jeffries, a bona fide star but one that still shows signs of youth and immaturity.

Guys like Coverdale and Hornsby improved by leaps and bounds last season but whether they can go any higher remains to be seen. And there are literally no proven bench threats, with IU counting on either or both Leach and Moye to step up or for Kline and Perry to make impacts as freshmen.

If Haston had returned, this would unquestionably be a Top 10 team. Instead, Indiana will start out fighting for a spot in the Top 25. The Hoosiers should get off to a much better start than last season, its biggest challenges coming in the Great Alaska Shootout against Tennessee, Texas, St. John's or Gonzaga, the ACC/Big Ten Challenge at reloading North Carolina and the annual December date with Kentucky.

The Hoosiers will grow over the course of the Big Ten season, likely finishing among the top three or four. But, as always, the team's success will be measured in March, which has not been kind to the program in a long, long time. Davis has visions of Final Fours and national championships, but first things first: IU needs to make it out of the NCAA's first weekend.

(S.M.)

Arkansas 25

LOCATION	Fayetteville, AR
CONFERENCE	Southeastern (Western)
LAST SEASON	20-11 (.645)
CONFERENCE RECORD	10-6 (2nd)
STARTERS LOST/RETURNING	1/4
NICKNAME	Razorbacks
COLORS	Cardinal & White
HOMECOURT	Bud Walton Arena (19,200)
COACH	Nolan Richardson (UTEP '63)
RECORD AT SCHOOL	376-155 (16 years)
CAREER RECORD	495-192 (21 years)
ASSISTANTS	Mike Anderson (Tulsa '82)
	Brad Dunn (Western Illinois '81)
	Wayne Stehlik (Nebraska-Wesleyan '79)
TEAM WINS (last 5 years)	18-24-23-19-20
RPI (last 5 years)	58-20-29-49-46
2000-01 FINISH	Lost in NCAA first round.

COACH AND PROGRAM

Like so many other teams in the Southeastern Conference, Arkansas was plundered by the NBA last spring.

Not that anyone connected to the program thought that Joe Johnson wouldn't one day be playing at the highest level. It's just that Arkansas fans, coaches and players hoped the 6-9, versatile forward would hang around a while longer than he did, at least one more year.

Instead, after his sophomore season, Johnson decided he was ready for the NBA. And the draft bore out that contention. Johnson was a lottery pick, chosen 10th in the first round by the storied Boston Celtics. So, just like SEC Western Division brethren Auburn (point guard Jamison Brewer), Alabama (Gerald Wallace) and LSU (Kedrick Brown), Arkansas lost a great player, a player who might have made the difference in winning the division or finishing considerably farther down the pack.

Then again, the Razorbacks, with one of the deepest teams in the SEC, might just have the rest of the Western Division teams right where they want them.

"That's what we want [people] to say," guard Jannero Pargo told the Arkansas Democrat-Gazette when it was suggested the Hogs might not even be an NCAA Tournament team this season. "We can build off that. We can use that to motivate us, to show teams that, yes, we did lose a great player in Joe, but we can still be a great team, and every year we're going to be in the NCAA Tournament regardless of who we lose."

Last year, a defensive lapse allowed Georgetown to steal a victory from Arkansas in the first round of the NCAA Tournament. The Hogs were crushed by the defeat, but in retrospect, their late-season drive to secure a tournament berth was nearly as impressive as their four-wins-in-four-days run to the SEC Tournament title the year before.

Last season, Arkansas got off to a puzzling 0-3 start in SEC play, but rallied with five straight league wins in the final two weeks to claim second place in the West and a first-round bye in the league tournament. Included in that stretch was a big homecourt victory over Kentucky and road wins at South Carolina and Alabama.

There was no magic in the tournament in 2001—Kentucky saw to that—and the Hogs fell flat in the NCAAs, too, uncharacteristic for them.

Despite that early exit from the Big Dance, and despite the loss of Johnson, there is still a lot to like about this team.

Consider that Johnson's second season in Fayetteville was hampered by injury. Not that his contributions weren't significant, but it seems likely veteran coach Nolan Richardson can find a way to replace a 75-percent effective Joe Johnson.

He'll do that with depth, and with athleticism. Perhaps only Kentucky among SEC teams has a larger assortment of interchangeable parts. True, Arkansas doesn't have a dominating presence in the post, but the way Richardson likes to play—turning games into ugly, helter-skelter affairs with intimidating full-court defensive pressure—this team seems perfectly suited.

"Our strengths are experience and quickness," Richardson said. "We know how we're going to play and what we're going to do from the first day of practice. They know what they have to do and that they need to get in shape. We have to rebound and it will have to be by committee. We don't have a great rebounder. If we can do a better job, by committee, that will make us a very good team."

2001-2002 SCHEDULE

Nov.	12	#Maine
	18	Oral Roberts
	28	@Tulsa
Dec.	1	Oklahoma
	4	Southwest Texas State
	8	*Illinois
	10	UNC Greensboro
	20	Tennessee-Chattanooga
	22	**Oklahoma State
	29	Elon
Jan.	2	@Memphis
	5	@Auburn
	8	Mississippi State
	13	@LSU
	16	South Carolina
	19	Ole Miss
	23	@Georgia
	26	Florida
	30	@Alabama
Feb.	2	Auburn
	9	@Ole Miss
	13	@Tennessee
	16	LSU
	20	Alabama
	23	@Kentucky
	27	@Mississippi State
March	2	Vanderbilt
	7-10	##SEC Tournament

@Road Games
*United Center, Chicago, IL
**Alltel Arena, Little Rock, AR
#Preseason NIT (if the Razorbacks win, they will play either UNC Wilmington or Wake Forest on Nov. 14 or 15. Semifinals and finals are Nov. 21-23 at Madison Square Garden, NY)
##Georgia Dome, Atlanta, GA

STARTERS NOT RETURNING

JOE JOHNSON (6-9, 14.2 ppg, 6.4 rpg, 2.5 apg, 2.3 tpg, 0.4 bpg, 1.4 spg, 29.1 minutes, .468 FG, .443 3PT, .747 FT). Joe Johnson, we hardly knew you. That's the feeling Arkansas fans must have had after Johnson declared for the NBA draft last spring. His freshman sea-

son was abbreviated because he was academically ineligible at the start, and his sophomore season was hampered by injury. Still, Johnson showed enough talent to lead the Razorbacks in scoring both seasons and pick up an armload of accolades, including the 2000 SEC Newcomer of the Year, Basketball Times Freshman All-America, SEC All-Tournament and second-team All-SEC.

Hog fans can only wonder how good Johnson would have been this year, and how much he would have lent to a team that's already the deepest and most athletic in the SEC. Clearly, Johnson was one of the best players to ever don an Arkansas uniform.

Unfortunately for the Hogs, Johnson is that rare player who didn't need a lot of college seasoning to be ready for the pros. Everybody knew that. Johnson looks forward to his time in the NBA, and he caught a break by getting drafted (as the 10th pick in the first round) by Boston, a team that is eager to return to its glory days and will do everything possible to field a winner.

"Playing at Arkansas has gotten me ready for what I need to do [in the NBA]," Johnson said. "Getting up at 5:30 in the morning for practice has mentally prepared me for what's about to happen, and coach Richardson's system of getting up and down the floor and getting after it on both ends of the floor has helped me out. I'll take it on to the professional level now."

"I'm just so very proud of Joe," Richardson said. "He went in the top 10. When he first decided to go, he was projected in the 15- to 17 range, but he went to the various camps and worked hard, and it paid off.

"Every NBA scout was impressed with his work ethic and made statements that he worked hard. He will be a good pro. He will find his niche and Boston saw that in him."

Boston also had the 11th pick and took forward Kedrick Brown of Okaloosa-Walton (Fla.) Junior College. Later in the first round, the Celtics grabbed North Carolina guard Joseph Forte.

"I'm ecstatic about the 10th and 11th picks, Joe Johnson and Kedrick," Celtics coach Jim O'Brien said. "I wanted three-point shooters that are athletic and can handle the basketball. I think people like that are exactly what we needed. With both picks, especially Joe, we wanted people that could shoot the long ball, create their own shot at the end of the shot clock and are willing to pass the basketball and are unselfish players."

"Joe is a versatile player," Richardson said. "There are players who can score and then there are players who make others around them better players. Joe makes other people better. He's a rare commodity."

OTHERS NOT RETURNING

BRANDON DAVIS (6-4, 3.0 ppg, 2.4 rpg. 1.1 apg, 0.8 tpg, 0.6 spg, 10.3 minutes, .417 FG, .270 3PT, .706 FT). Davis was a veteran player who knew what Richardson wanted, but his contributions, given the Hogs' depth at the perimeter positions, were not all that substantial and will be replaced easily enough by newcomers or existing personnel.

Ironically, though Davis never played a minute of football at Arkansas, he signed a free-agent contract with the NFL's Cleveland Browns. He's a former all-state football player at Fairview High School in Camden, Ark.

PROJECTED STARTERS

PG-JANNERO PARGO (6-2, 165 lbs., SR, #12, 12.3 ppg, 2.1 rpg, 2.3 apg, 1.9 tpg, 1.5 spg, 23.9 minutes, .449 FG, .417 3PT, .878 FT, Neosho CC/Chanute, Kansas and Robeson HS/Chicago, Ill.). It's a testament to Pargo's talent and his worth to Arkansas that last season, along with Tennessee's Ron Slay, he was the only other player to earn All-SEC honors (third team) without being a full-time starter.

We're listing Pargo, who came off the bench 16 times and started 15 times last season, as the starting point guard, but that's subject to change. Save for T.J. Cleveland, the Hogs don't have a true point guard. And Pargo could end up a reserve again, given Richardson's penchant for shuffling his starting lineup.

It's far more likely, though, that Pargo will continue his strong play from a year ago, remain a fixture in the starting lineup and lead Arkansas in scoring.

A year ago, Pargo was second on the team in scoring behind Joe Johnson, but in league games only, he paced the Hogs with his 14.2 average. He was also one of the SEC's most prolific three-point shooters, and wound up ranked fourth in the league in three-pointers

per game (2.35) and fourth in three-point percentage. It came as no surprise that Pargo led Arkansas with six 20-point scoring games.

It was also no shocker that, despite the presence of eventual NBA lottery pick Johnson, Pargo was voted the team's MVP.

"Without Pargo, we probably would not have won more than 12 games last year," Richardson said. "If he gives any indication that he can improve on what he brought to the table last year, then he will be a tremendous player for us."

Pargo, as the numbers would suggest, was at his best against SEC competition. The two Mississippi schools found that out in successive league games. Pargo torched Mississippi State with 28 points in an 83-72 Arkansas win, knocking down six three-pointers in 12 attempts. The six threes were a team season high. At Ole Miss, Pargo was scoreless in the first half, but finished with 20 points.

Pargo enjoyed being a pain in the backside to the SEC's ranked teams. He scored 24 points and had four steals in an 87-58 win over Alabama, then ranked No. 12. In an 82-77 overtime win over then-No. 8 Tennessee, Pargo made 5-of-9 three-pointers and scored 17 points. He made three more three pointers and scored 16 points in an 82-78 late-season win over then-No. 13 Kentucky that helped seal the Hogs' invitation to the NCAA Tournament.

Lest we focus too much on Pargo's scoring ability, it's only fair to point out he's also a strong defender who last season was second on the team and eighth in the SEC in steals (47). He's also a playmaker; Pargo handed out 72 assists, third among the Razorbacks.

Look for Pargo to earn even higher All-SEC recognition this year as he becomes the unquestioned star of this team.

SG-BRANDON DEAN (6-1, 200 lbs., SR, #13, 8.2 ppg, 2.2 rpg, 1.8 apg, 0.9 tpg, 1.2 spg, 18.8 minutes, .431 FG, .362 3PT, .618 FG, Ouachita Parish HS/Monroe, La.). Dean was the MVP of the 2000 SEC Tournament, but as he found out last season, there's no resting on laurels at Arkansas.

After a loss to Auburn in mid-February, Richardson called out Dean and Teddy Gipson for a lack of work ethic.

"It ain't what you did last year," Richardson said.

It didn't take long for Dean to get the message. Dean scored 12 first-half points in the Hogs' next game, against LSU, and Arkansas won easily.

"You never know what coach is going to do," Dean told the Arkansas Democrat-Gazette. "You've just got to be prepared whenever your opportunity comes."

Clearly, Arkansas is a better team when the athletic Dean plays well. He's scored in double figures 30 times in his Arkansas career, and the Razorbacks won 25 of those games.

Dean struggled early in SEC play last year, but the wakeup call provided by Richardson helped get him untracked. He averaged just 5.4 points in league games, but that figure improved to 9.2 over the last five games and 12.5 in the SEC Tournament.

Dean can obviously answer the call as the season gets down to crunch time. And with his gifts—speed, quickness, leaping ability—he's more than capable of averaging double figures through the course of this season.

Part of the reason Dean has never averaged more than the 8.5 points a game he scored as a sophomore is depth. Arkansas has had plenty of guards to run in and out of games. But Dean can be a special player, whether its driving the ball to the rim, making three-pointers or being sure-handed (his 2.0 assist to turnover ration in league games ranked No. 2 in the SEC last season).

Along with Gipson and Pargo, Dean will be a go-to scorer for the Hogs.

"Brandon is a guy we need to pick up his game," Richardson said. "Not so much towards the end of the season, but at the beginning. I think he will."

SF-TEDDY GIPSON (6-4, 170 lbs., SR, #23, 8.1 ppg, 2.1 rpg, 1.6 apg, 1.4 tpg, 1.1 spg, 19.0 minutes, .503 FG, .302 3PT, .718 FT, Farmerville HS/Farmerville, La.). Like Dean, Gipson needed a late-season challenge from Richardson to recharge his batteries for the Hogs' stretch run. Also like Dean, Gipson responded. In Arkansas' last five games—against Alabama, Georgia, LSU, Kentucky and Georgetown—he averaged 11.4 points. 2.6 rebounds, nearly two assists and two steals while shooting 54 percent from the field and 50 percent from three-point range.

Arkansas will need that kind of effort from Gipson all

season. As one of five seniors, he'll be expected to shoulder his share of the scoring load and provide leadership.

Gipson can handle the responsibility. He's one of the best athletes on the team and the SEC. Gibson is a little on the lean side, but he has that rare combination of being able to slash to the basket and shoot from the perimeter. He's a career 36 percent three-point shooter, good enough by anyone's standards. Last year, he slipped a bit from three-point range, but he made up for it by getting to the basket more often and shooting 50 percent from the field.

Gipson scored in double figures 11 times, including a career-high 20 against LSU. He also scored 16 against Georgia, 14 against Mississippi State and 13 in a return, late-season match-up with LSU.

Points don't reflect Gipson's value to the team, though. A game that might be more indicative of that came against Grambling, when he scored just eight points, but matched his career highs with six assists and four steals. He also grabbed a season-high six rebounds.

The rangy Gipson is a solid defender who has 100 career steals. With his long arms, he makes it tough for guards to drive around him.

Given Gipson's varied skills and value to the team, Richardson is just hoping for a bit more consistency from him in his senior year.

"He had an up and down junior season," Richardson said. "I think now he's settling in and is ready to be the kind of player I think he can be where he's taking more responsibility with the experience he has."

PF-CARL BAKER (6-8, 210 lbs., JR, #4, 5.2 ppg, 4.0 rpg, 0.9 apg, 1.0 tpg, 0.8 spg, 21.2 minutes, .374 FG, .444 3PT, .725 FT, Palestine-Wheatley HS/Palestine, Ark.). The versatile Baker's worth was never more apparent than at the start of the SEC season a year ago. Baker missed four straight games with an injury, including three league games. Arkansas lost them all. When he returned, the Hogs closed out the season 11-5.

Why is Baker so important? As the team's utility man, he does a little bit of everything. Richardson would have no qualms about letting Baker guard a point guard or a center. He runs as well as any big man in the league. He's a willing rebounder and a good passer. And Baker can also drift out to the perimeter and shoot; he's a career 45 percent three-point shooter.

Once Baker returned to the lineup, he turned in some big games. His 16 points, eight boards, two assists and a career-high three steals were key in a win over Tennessee. He scored 13 points and grabbed five rebounds against Ole Miss and turned in 12 points, six rebounds and three steals against Georgetown in the NCAA Tournament.

With Joe Johnson having departed to the Boston Celtics, Baker's contributions will be relied upon even more heavily. Together with Larry Satchell, he's got to provide interior defense. And with his ability to shoot from distance and draw defenders away from the basket, Baker is an important piece in Arkansas' offense.

C-LARRY SATCHELL (6-9, 220 lbs., JR, #50, 3.7 ppg, 3.5 rpg, 0.4 apg, 1.1 tpg, 0.6 spg, 1.4 bpg, 13.9 minutes, .408 FG, .636 FT, Waco HS/Waco, Texas). Satchell is one of Arkansas' most important players. On a team that isn't overloaded with size and physicality, Satchell is a fearsome interior defender. And he isn't just tough on opponents. When Satchell has some constructive criticism for a teammate, he isn't afraid to voice it.

"I think Larry's been the difference maker for us," Richardson told the Arkansas Democrat-Gazette. "Why? Because Larry is tough and will say what he has to say, and everybody is going to listen.

"I put him in the starting lineup because you had to have him on the floor so he can say something and the other players respect it."

"Larry is our emotional leader," guard Brandon Dean told the Democrat-Gazette. "He gets everybody enthused."

Satchell was a key player in Arkansas' stretch run. After joining the starting lineup in a mid-January game against Auburn, Satchell helped lead the Hogs to an 11-5 record the rest of the way.

Satchell hasn't been called on to do much scoring, though he's capable of reaching double figures, as he did with a career-high 12 points against Maryland-Eastern Shore. His most important contribution is defending the paint.

A year ago, Satchell was third in the SEC in blocked shots and second in league games only. His 30 blocks in league games rank as the third-best effort in school history. He blocked 45 shots on the season, 10 of them coming in two games where he registered a personal-best five blocks. One of those five-block victims was Auburn. Satchell chipped in eight points and six rebounds in that game.

Richardson would love to get that kind of performance from Satchell every night. He's hoping Satchell elevates his game a notch or two this season.

"The improvement Larry showed from his freshman year to his sophomore year was tremendous," Richardson said. "All he has to do is improve 20 percent this year and I'll be happy."

KEY RESERVES

G-T.J. CLEVELAND (6-1, 168 lbs., SR, #5, 7.5 ppg, 2.3 rpg, 2.6 apg, 1.5 tpg, 1.9 spg, 22.1 minutes, .411 FG, .361 3PT, .750 FT, Minor HS/Birmingham Ala.). Cleveland has started only 21 times in his Arkansas career—just nine a year ago—but he might be the Razorbacks' MVP. Why? He's an old-fashioned, throwback style of player who does everything well. Cleveland is a career .401 shooter from three-point range. He's a playmaker (team-high 83 assists last season). He's sure-handed (team-best 1.77 assist to turnover ratio). He can defend (61 steals, tops on the team and second in the SEC). He's fearless (Cleveland won the 2000-2001 "Hogman Award" for giving up his body for the team).

Best of all, Cleveland is an extension of the Arkansas coaching staff on the floor. On a team without a true point guard he comes the closest.

Given his worth to the team, a casual fan might ask why Cleveland didn't start more than nine times last year. The answer to that question is simple. Arkansas coaches think Cleveland gives the team a lift as a sixth man. And check out where Cleveland is at the end of games. It isn't on the bench.

Cleveland's contributions came in a variety of ways last season. Against LSU, Cleveland scored a season-high 19 points. In a win over Tennessee State, Cleveland handed out a career-high matching eight assists. He made seven steals in a win over Maryland-Eastern Shore. Cleveland can also put games away from the free-throw line; he was third in the SEC in free-throw percentage in league games only.

"We count on T.J.," Richardson said. "Because were the ball is, that's where T.J. is."

G-BLAKE EDDINS (6-7, 220 lbs., JR, #21, 3.9 ppg, 1.6 rpg, 0.4 apg, 0.7 tpg, 0.5 spg, 10.0 minutes, .400 FG, .387 3PT, .680 FT, Trinity HS/Montgomery, Ala.). Arkansas' depth and a nagging lower back strain combined to hold down Eddins' minutes last season, but he's a valuable presence who contributes timely three-point shooting, hustle and toughness. When Richardson gives him the call, Eddins is always ready to rumble.

Arkansas was 6-1 when Eddins was in the starting lineup, but he's become useful off the bench. With his long-range shooting, he can rack up points in a hurry. Eddins reached double figures five times last year, leading the team with 15 points (on five-of-seven shooting) in just 16 minutes against Memphis. He also tagged Georgia for 12 points in just 11 minutes.

Eddins' role probably won't be drastically altered this year, but he could see some more minutes as Richardson relies on his experience.

F-MICHAEL JONES (6-9, 210 lbs., FR, #22, 14.3 ppg, 6.8 rpg, 2.8 bpg, in 1999-2000, Parkview HS/Little Rock, Ark.). Jones took advantage of a red-shirt year, adding 20 pounds of muscle. He also grew two inches, so Richardson is getting a different player than the one who showed up on campus a year ago.

"We felt a year of weight training and practicing would help make him a very good player," Richardson said. "His future is very bright. He is long and is going to be 6-10, he can run and he enjoys playing. He plays with enthusiasm for a big kid, and I really like him."

The only evidence Arkansas fans have of Jones' ability is last year's Red-White intra-squad game, where Jones scored seven points and added five rebounds, one assist and a blocked shot in 19 minutes.

F-ALONZO LANE (6-7, 250 lbs, JR, #31, 6.9 PPG, 3.2 RPG, 0.6 apg, 1.1 tpg, 0.6 spg, 0.5 bpg, 18.9 minutes, .515 FG, .514 FT, Canton HS/Canton, Miss.). Last season Lane's playing time decreased from his freshman year, but he was still Arkansas' most proficient inside scorer. He's undersized for a post player, but Lane uses his speed to get past taller defenders and can also step outside to make medium-range jump shots.

Lane led the Hogs in field-goal percentage last season. If he'd had enough attempts to qualify, Lane would have been fifth in the SEC in that department, third in league games only. For his career, Lane is shooting .538. He's made 50 percent of his shots in 40-of-65 career games.

Lane reached double figures nine times a year ago and paced the Hogs in scoring three times. He had a season-high 17 points against Ole Miss, also adding five boards and two blocked shots in that game. Lane scored 16 points against Louisiana-Monroe and 15 (on 6-of-7 shooting) against Auburn.

Richardson is planning on going to Lane more often this season as Arkansas seeks to establish an inside game to open up things for its perimeter scorers.

"Lane is the type of kid we have to get going early," Richardson said. "He worked extremely hard in the off-season to get stronger. This could be the year he breaks out and has a tremendous season."

G-J.J. SULLINGER (6-5, 195 lbs., FR, #0, 21.4 ppg, 7.5 rpg, 6.0 apg, 2.1 bpg, 1.8 spg, Worthington HS/Columbus, Ohio). Sullinger was the Razorbacks' only signee of the fall recruiting period, and he was a good one. Sullinger went on to win co-player-of-the-year honors in Ohio. Richardson loves his versatility.

"[Sullinger is a] swing guard who can play three positions [point guard, shooting guard, small forward]," Richardson said. "He's going to be an outstanding player for us. He's a slasher. He has great instincts, makes good passes, has good quickness and great awareness. He's in the same mode as Teddy Gipson and Brandon Dean. He understands the game and will fit in very well."

OTHER RETURNEES

F-DIONISIO GOMEZ (6-8, 215 lbs., SR, #33, 1.5 ppg, 2.1 rpg, 0.4 apg, 0.7 tpg, 0.3 bpg, 8.7 minutes, .294 FG, .176 3 PT, .400 FT, Fayetteville Christian HS/Fayetteville, Ark. and Panama City, Panama). Gomez is an example of how the NCAA's system of academic eligibility should work. A non-qualifier his first season, he's since become a two time member of the SEC's Academic Honor Roll. If Gomez graduates in four years—and it seems likely he will—he can claim another year of eligibility and return next season.

Gomez—who started 12 games a year ago—is limited offensively, but he's active for his size and is a good rebounder and defender. He led the Hogs' in rebounding four times last season and finished the year as their fourth-leading rebounder. Gomez was also second on the team with his 17 blocked shots.

Gomez did begin to show signs of life as a scorer last year, increasing his point total from 47 his first season to 103 despite playing four few games. He scored a career-high 10 points five times, against Jackson State, Louisiana-Monroe, North Texas, Grambling and Mississippi State.

Richardson would love it if Gomez could duplicate his performance against Mississippi State more often. In that game, Gomez was three-for-three from the field and four-of-six from the free-throw line. He also chipped in seven rebounds, two assists and two steals.

G-CHARLES TATUM (5-10, 175 lbs., JR, #3, 5.7 ppg, 0.8 rpg, 0.3 apg, 0.8 tpg, 0.8 spg, 10.4 minutes, .392 FG, .312 3 PT, .952 FT, Midland HS/Midland, Texas). Tatum hasn't played all that many minutes in his Arkansas career, but he's been a handy guy to have around. In his reserve role, Tatum has given the Hogs instant offense and intense defense. He was voted Arkansas' defensive player of the year, a sure sign his efforts in that area haven't gone unappreciated.

Tatum made the most of his time last season. He scored a career-high 18 points in 19 minutes against Grambling, had 12 points in 14 minutes against Jackson State, 14 points and four steals in 16 minutes against Louisiana-Monroe and 13 points in 14 minutes against North Texas.

Tatum didn't reserve his higher-scoring games for non-league opponents. He scored 11 points in just eight minutes in a big win over Alabama. In that game, he sunk the then-No. 12 ranked Crimson Tide with consecutive threes—only 20 seconds apart—from the same spot on the right baseline. He also had 14 points and a career-high-tying four steals in 15 minutes against LSU and nine points in 14 minutes in a win over then-No. 13 Kentucky.

"We will depend on his jump shot and his attacking the basket, and we will certainly depend on his tenacity on defense," Richardson said of Tatum.

OTHER NEWCOMERS

G-JAMAR BLACKMON (6-1, 200 lbs., SO, #20, 2.1

ppg, 1.4 rpg, 8.1 minutes in 1999-2000, Mississippi Valley State and McClellan HS/Little Rock, Ark.). Blackmon left Mississippi Valley State and the SWAC behind for tougher competition in the SEC. Can the walk-on hang? Don't be surprised if Richardson finds a way to use him.

"One of his strengths is that he will guard you," Richardson said. "Another strength is he is a physical kid who can make a difference on the offensive end and the defensive end."

Blackmon might earn a few useful minutes helping harass opposing ball handlers in Arkansas' famed "40 Minutes of Hell" full court defensive scheme.

F-BERRY JORDAN (6-7, 215 lbs., FR, #22, 16.8 ppg, 13.6 rpg, 6.1 bpg, Arlington Country Day HS/Jacksonville, Fla.). Assuming last spring that Joe Johnson was going to take his act to the pros, Richardson and his staff began searching around for a replacement. At the Pittsburgh Hoops Classic, Richardson spotted Jordan and knew he'd found his man.

"He's a jumping jack with a lot of athletic ability," Richardson said. "He's a good offensive rebounder, and he's had good rebounding stats throughout his career. And he's a good shot blocker. I was really impressed when I saw him at the all-star game. He runs the floor very well and has tremendous jumping ability."

Did you notice Richardson mentioned Jordan's hops a couple of times? He's not exactly Air Jordan, but the youngster has a 39-inch vertical leap, and he puts it to good use. Jordan won the dunk contest at Pittsburgh, his third such title of the year.

His jumping ability helps him defensively, too. As a junior, Jordan set a Florida single-season record with 169 blocks.

QUESTIONS

Size? The Razorbacks don't have a huge physical presence in the post. Alonzo Lane comes the closest, but he's only 6-7. Will the lack of size hurt Arkansas if an opponent can force the game into the half court?

Rebounding? This was a problem area a year ago and the Razorbacks weren't able to address it through recruiting. Arkansas was out-rebounded by 7.3 boards per game in SEC play and 5.7 per game overall.

ANSWERS

Depth! Arkansas is one of the few teams in the SEC that has the full complement of 13 scholarships. Richardson's system requires having a lot of bodies to run in and out of the game, so he'll take full advantage of his numbers.

Athleticism! The Razorbacks have tons of quick, athletic guards and forwards who can help apply defensive pressure and score in transition.

Three-point shooting! Last season, Arkansas led the SEC and was seventh in the nation in three pointers per game (8.8) and was third in the league in three-point percentage (.368). Except for Joe Johnson, all of the Hogs' long-range bombers return.

ARKANSAS 2000-2001 RESULTS

#Tennessee State	90-68
#Southern Miss (L)	54-63
Jackson State	107-78
Louisiana-Monroe	99-59
Centenary	88-57
Memphis	74-68
North Texas	97-77
@Oklahoma State (L)	73-74
Northwestern State	115-47
@Oklahoma	79-88
Grambling State	121-66
Maryland-Eastern Shore	100-40
@Mississippi State (L)	73-87
Mississippi (L)	48-53
@Vanderbilt (L)	64-81
Auburn	82-72
Alabama	87-58
@LSU	59-52
@Mississippi (L)	73-84
Mississippi State	83-72
Tennessee	82-77
@Florida (L)	63-73
@Auburn (L)	63-71
LSU	87-70
@South Carolina	69-67
Kentucky	82-78
@Alabama	66-63
Georgia	82-67
##Kentucky (L)	78-87
###Georgetown (L)	61-63

#John Thompson Classic in Fayetteville
##SEC Tournament in Nashville
###NCAA Tournament
@Road Games

BLUE RIBBON ANALYSIS

BACKCOURT	B
BENCH/DEPTH	A
FRONTCOURT	B
INTANGIBLES	B+

Several SEC teams were hurt by the NBA draft, and Arkansas was one of them, losing Johnson, taken 10th in the first round by the Boston Celtics.

Johnson will be missed, but Arkansas has enough depth to cover for him.

Richardson has said in the past that he would almost rather not have a star player, preferring a roster full of hungry over-achievers who covet playing time and expend a lot of energy when they get it. That describes this team perfectly.

Pargo, third-team All-SEC a year ago, is the closest thing to a star on the roster. There are other solid players—Dean, Gipson, Satchell, Baker, Cleveland among them—but what Richardson has is 14 players of fairly equal ability. The veteran coach will try and blend those players together, calling on them at various times of the season.

Richardson loves to juggle his starting lineup and considers it a challenge to try and push the right buttons and fit his players into game situations where they can best help the team. If he does that to perfection this season, Arkansas can reclaim the SEC Western Division title, be a factor in the SEC Tournament and earn a high seed in the NCAA Tournament.

(C.D.)

Boston College 26

LOCATION	Chestnut Hill, MA
CONFERENCE	Big East
LAST SEASON	27-5 (.847)
CONFERENCE RECORD	13-3 (1st-East)
STARTERS LOST/RETURNING	2/3
NICKNAME	Eagles
COLORS	Maroon & Gold
HOMECOURT	Silvio O. Conte Forum (8,606)
COACH	Al Skinner (Rhode Island '74)
RECORD AT SCHOOL	59-62 (3 years)
CAREER RECORD	197-187 (13 years)
ASSISTANTS	Bill Coen (Hamilton '83)
	Ed Cooley (Stonehill '94)
	Pat Duquette (Williams '93)
TEAM WINS (last 5 years)	22-15–6-11-27
RPI (last 5 years)	28-121-212-145-10
2000-01 FINISH	Lost in NCAA second round.

COACH AND PROGRAM

Al Skinner refuses to consider last year's 27-win, out-of-nowhere, surprise-'em-all, defy-the-experts, reinvigorate-the-program season anything other than the obvious next step in his regime and the expected outcome of his players.

Once the Eagles started the year 11-0, the shock was gone, and BC was expected to receive the same notice and consideration as any other big-conference power.

And after the final bell rang, and Boston College had fallen to Southern California in the NCAA Tournament, there was no talk about overcoming expectations this coming season, as opposed to sneaking up on people, as some (not Skinner) thought the Eagles did last year.

"[The players] all came here with the attitude that they wanted to be successful," Skinner said. "So, this should not be a surprise to them. This is where they wanted to be. I've talked with them about being successful and competitive in this league, and that's where we've come to.

"Once the season began, we weren't sneaking up on anybody. Of course, the public perception was different."

It remains a little contrary to what Skinner is preaching to his team. That makes sense. Any coach who follows up big success with talk of "hoping" that his team can repeat or improve, is sowing the seeds of doubt and perhaps failure. Of course Skinner should be telling his players that last season was expected. Of course he should be telling them that more is in store for the 2001-02 campaign. That's what coaches do.

Writers don't always think that way. That's why we're left with the tough question of whether the Eagles will approach what they did last season, particularly after sustaining some significant graduation losses and needing to rely on untested newcomers. That doesn't even begin to address the team's interior, which looks even more vulnerable than last year's did. Skinner did a great job last year putting together a team that worked selflessly together and sacrificed almost totally for the whole. That's how the Eagles won. His challenge this year is to integrate new key components into that philosophy and to keep any holdovers from taking prosperity for granted.

While Boston College has the potential to be formidable again, it isn't operating under the illusion that it will simply overwhelm people with superior talent. While the Eagles have some top-flight players, most notably guard Troy Bell, they can't pile on the high school All-Americas and win with pure ability.

"Everybody accepted their roles last year," Skinner said. "We hadn't been in an environment before [17 wins in the previous two seasons; 32 in the three before last year] where we were very successful, and the guys wanted to change that. They did everything they had to be successful.

"They sacrificed to win. The players were more open with each other. Sometimes people get defensive, but there wasn't any of that. We were at the bottom, and we couldn't be too sensitive about things. Everybody was open to constructive criticism."

That was great last year. But BC has now fed at the victory trough and pushed away with a full belly. The Eagles won the Big East's East Division. They won the conference tournament. They made it back to the NCAA show. Can a team that accomplished so much last year again be selfless? Does it have to?

Boston College ought to enter this year filled with confidence. Even though two starters and a key reserve are gone from what was essentially a seven-man rotation, the holdovers—most notably Bell, forward Uka Agbai and guard Ryan Sidney—are proven winners and made significant contributions last year.

"The nice thing is that we have some talented people coming back," Skinner said. "I'm happy about that. We have a nucleus to work with. It depends on how well the younger people mature and fill the roles we need them to fill."

Bell and Sidney are expected to form a dynamic backcourt duo, with help from touted freshman Jermaine Watson. Anybody who saw Sidney play last year knows how effective he is defensively and in the open court. He improved as the year went on, showed the ability to penetrate and score close to the basket. If Watson can rise to the challenge, the Eagle backcourt could be even better than last year's that went four deep and was clearly the engine of the championship train.

Things should be even better up front, which means Agbai won't be going it alone against some pretty big, deep opponents. He did a great job of that last year but had little help. Skinner expects a healthy Kenny Walls, experienced Brian Ross and rehabbed Andrew Bryant to provide needed depth.

And that doesn't even take into account what 6-11 freshman Nate Doornekamp or 7-1 newcomer Kirsten Zoellner can do.

Yep, things could keep on rolling at BC. Experience, depth and confidence may all conspire to keep the Eagles at or near the top of the Big East standings. Skinner must guard against a breakdown in the principles of openness and selflessness, which played such big roles in last year's success. If that happens, we won't be asking any more questions. Well, maybe a few.

2001-2002 SCHEDULE

Nov.	18	Boston University
	21	New Hampshire
	24	Penn State
	28	St. Bonaventure
Dec.	1	@Michigan
	4	Morris Brown
	8	Massachusetts
	11	Iowa State

	16	Holy Cross
	20-22	#Rainbow Classic
	31	@Seton Hall
Jan.	5	Pittsburgh
	9	@Villanova
	12	Georgetown
	17	St. John's
	20	Virginia Tech
	24	Duke
	29	@Miami
Feb.	2	@Providence
	6	@Virginia Tech
	10	Miami
	13	Providence
	16	@Connecticut
	18	*St. John's
	23	Villanova
	25	Connecticut
March	3	@Syracuse
	6-9	##Big East Championship

@Road Games
*Madison Square Garden, NY
#At Honolulu, HI (vs. Miami, OH first round; also Hawaii, Portland, Iona, Holy Cross, Georgia, Arkansas State)
##Madison Square Garden, NY

STARTERS NOT RETURNING

SG-XAVIER SINGLETARY (6-6, 11.7 ppg, 5.2 rpg, 1.6 apg, 30.3 minutes, .404 FG, .311 3PT, .676 FT). Singletary never became the big-numbers guy the Eagles anticipated he would be after the big guard transferred from Howard. But his senior season was an improvement on the previous one, and that helped the BC cause considerably.

Singletary finished as the team's second-leading scorer but again struggled from the field, particularly in Big East competition, when his percentages dropped both inside and outside the three-point line. Singletary was big early, and stung Massachusetts (22 points) and Quinnipiac (23) in back-to-back games. He had 18 against Connecticut and 16 against Virginia Tech but moved into the background offensively some, as Sidney emerged. Still, Singletary played good defense and rebounded well.

SG-KENNY HARLEY (6-5, 10.7 ppg, 5.6 rpg, 2.4 apg, 1.6 spg, 32.1 minutes, .440 FG, .422 3PT, .633 FT). Last year marked the end of a wild career for Harley, who emerged as a potential standout as a sophomore, sagged considerably in '99-00 and then rebounded well in his senior season.

The biggest improvement for Harley came in his marksmanship. He made more than three times the number of treys he did as a junior and shot a career-high 42.2 percent from behind the arc. Harley was a steady performer who finished second on the team in rebounds, defended enthusiastically and provided consistent offense that actually improved as the season went on.

Though not a star, Harley was a solid, veteran performer who will be missed.

OTHERS NOT RETURNING

F-JONATHAN BEERBOHM (6-7, 6.4 ppg, 3.7 rpg, 1.1 apg, 17.7 minutes, .510 FG, .632 FT). Beerbohm came to Boston College as a raw inside player who had been able to overwhelm smaller foes in high school. He made a gradual transition into more of a wing player but never was quick enough to play full-time at the three-spot. He wasn't big enough to bang inside, either.

Beerbohm's numbers sagged a bit last year, but he filled a role of a willing, hustling inside player capable of playing good defense, scoring a bit and grabbing a few rebounds. That was important on a team that lacked interior heft.

F-ANDREW DUDLEY (6-11, 0.4 ppg, 2.0 rpg, 0.2 apg, 7.4 minutes, .333 FG). After appearing in just five games last year, the sophomore decided to transfer to St. Peter's. He'll be eligible after the first semester and will give the Peacocks some interior size.

Dudley should be more successful at the MAAC level, which won't require him to be as quick as the Big East did.

G-JON EKWEOZOR (6-1, 0.4 ppg, 0.1 rpg, 0.1 apg, 1.3 minutes, .500 FG). A walk-on, Ekweozor played in 11 games last year and made two of the four shots he attempted. He had two points and one rebound against Pittsburgh and two points against Brown.

PROJECTED STARTERS

PG-TROY BELL (6-1, 171 lbs., JR, #2, 20.4 ppg, 4.3 rpg, 4.2 apg, 2.7 spg, 34.2 minutes, .459 FG, .391 3PT, .857 FT, Academy of Holy Angels/Minneapolis, Minn.). There is no way the Eagles even sniff success without Bell, who has been tremendous his first two years with the program and should continue to improve. An excellent all-around player who can score, get others involved, shoot well from all over the place and apply significant defensive pressure, Bell is on the verge of making a big national breakthrough.

"He can still improve," Skinner said. "He needs to get to the point where he totally controls the game, scoring and the way he directs the other individuals on the team. He had help last year from Kenny, X and Jon, since they had played a lot. Now, he has to shoulder more of the responsibility and give direction."

It's hard to believe Bell—a third-team preseason All-American pick by Blue Ribbon—isn't ready for the challenge. He's capable of some mammoth scoring outputs, as his 32-point effort against Southern California in the second round of last year's NCAA Tournament proved. Bell had nine other games in which he scored 25 or more. He's tough to guard, because he penetrates so well but can also drill it from deep. As a result, Bell takes a lot of free throws, often in clumps of three, after someone fouls him on a shot from behind the arc.

"He can shoot the ball so well, and if you don't guard that shot, he'll make it," Skinner said. "If you get too close, he'll penetrate and score. He's a very difficult player to defend."

SG-RYAN SIDNEY (6-2, 195 lbs., SO, #5, 9.4 ppg, 4.7 rpg, 1.6 apg, 1.7 spg, 22.2 minutes, .490 FG, .275 3PT, .567 FT, Pioneer HS/Ann Arbor, Mich.). After watching Sidney's strong debut, fans of Michigan and Michigan State are no doubt wondering why their teams didn't recruit the wing more diligently. Sidney was a high-energy, open-court player who excelled in fullcourt defensive sets and was practically impossible to stop off the dribble.

Sidney now moves into the starting two spot, barring an insurrection by Watson, and should be even more dangerous. After a relatively slow start, save a 12-point effort in the opener against St. Peter's, Sidney demonstrated his skills in Big East play, scoring in double figures 11 times, with an 18-point effort at Connecticut and twin 17-pointers against Villanova and Providence the highlights. The challenge now for Sidney is to improve his outside shooting. He made only 11-of-40 shots from behind the arc and needs to become more of a threat from the perimeter, the better to keep opponents from sagging on him, the better to defend the drive. Skinner doesn't want to force Sidney into anything that isn't in his repertoire, but would like to see an improvement.

"We don't emphasize one area that a guy needs to get better in," Skinner said. "We're going to ask Ryan to do what he's most comfortable with. If he works on his shooting, and it improves, we'll ask him to do more of it.

"Kenny Harley was a 30 percent [three-point] shooter as a freshman and made 40 percent as a senior, because of the hard work he put in."

SF-KENNY WALLS (6-5, 194 lbs., SR, #21, 7.3 ppg, 3.3 rpg, 1.6 apg, 0.7 spg, 22.6 minutes, .395 FG, .307 3PT, .800 FT, Galileo HS/San Francisco, Calif.). This is a big year for Walls, who struggled with tendinitis in his right knee last year and had sporadic success. He'll need to improve a shooting eye that has been somewhat wayward the past couple years. Walls has excellent athletic skills and could be a big contributor.

"He saw what the seniors did last year, how they finished up," Skinner said. "I'd like to think he wants to be in that position. He's working at getting his body healthy."

Walls had a pretty good second half of the season. He scored 16 against Villanova, 15 against West Virginia and 10 in the first-round NCAA game against Southern Utah. If healthy, Walls can be an active rebounder and a good defender.

PF-BRIAN ROSS (6-8, 240 lbs., SR, #45, 2.9 ppg, 1.7 rpg, 0.3 apg, 9.0 minutes, .525 FG, .462 FT, North Quincy HS/North Quincy, Mass.). Here's another key to the Eagles' success. Ross must be able to replicate his strong freshman and sophomore seasons, when he appeared to be on the verge of making a major contribution. Last year, he was nagged by back and foot problems that prohibited him from playing to his potential.

"He needs to get back in great shape," Skinner said. "Obviously, he's not the best athlete, so he has to work extra hard to compete. He extends himself and becomes vulnerable to injury."

Ross is not quick, but he is big and could be a strong positional rebounder, particularly against the bigger teams on the BC schedule. He scores well close to the basket and actually can step behind the line to hit some long-range shots. If healthy, he'll be a factor.

PF-UKA AGBAI (6-8, 245 lbs., JR, #00, 9.1 ppg, 3.9 rpg, 0.7 apg, 25.8 minutes, .530 FG, .684 FT, Archbishop Molloy HS/Queens Village, N.Y.). As the sole interior weapon for the Eagles last year, Agbai had some pretty heavy responsibilities. He had to handle just about all the major defensive work against enemy big men, hold down the rebounding fort when said tall fellows crashed and provide the BC perimeter army with some interior support. Simple, eh?

Not really. That's why Agbai's numbers aren't so great. At least, that's what Skinner says. He believes that had Agbai not had to occupy so many opponents inside, he could have scored and boarded more.

"He allowed the other people on our team to get to the backboard," Skinner said. "If he was just chasing down rebounds, maybe he wouldn't have occupied the other big guys, and we wouldn't have gotten so many rebounds as a team. His numbers are misleading."

Agbai didn't have too many dominating nights last year. His signature efforts were a 16-point, seven-rebound outing against Providence, followed by a 15-point, three-board night against Morris Brown. For the most part, Agbai hovered around or just into double figures and could usually be counted on for five or six boards a night. That should continue to be his M.O. this year, although he might be asked to rebound more, thanks to the losses of Singletary and Harley, each of whom had more boards than Agbai.

Agbai is pretty quick, despite his heft. He shoots pretty well from the field, although his numbers fell off in Big East play, when opponents crowded him, and he was facing a steady diet of taller pivots. He'll be effective again, but it's unlikely he'll become a huge point producer. If he gets 10-15 a night, the Eagles will be fine, particularly if some of their other big men step up.

KEY RESERVES

G-JERMAINE WATSON (6-3, 190 lbs., FR, #4, 28.5 ppg, 5.0 apg, Tabor (Mass.) Academy/Thayer (Mass.) Academy/Lincoln-Sudbury HS/Dorchester, Mass.). Some might look at Watson as this year's version of Sidney, but he's a different kind of player. The combination guard shots it a little better than Sidney and can handle more work at the point. But there are similarities.

"He's a very fine penetrator and handles the ball extremely well," Skinner said. "He's a fine defensive player, and I think he'll fit in well. He's physical."

Watson finished with more than 2,000 career points during his three prep stops and played in the Capital Classic and Pittsburgh Hoops Classic last spring. Expect him to get about 20 minutes a game at both guard spots and add plenty to the BC rotation.

F-ANDREW BRYANT (6-7, 224 lbs., FR, #34, 23.2 ppg, 9.2 rpg in 1999-2000, Denison HS/Denison, Texas). Bryant could have played last year, but Skinner didn't want to waste a year of eligibility, when it was clear the forward wasn't going to get a lot of minutes. So, he'll take the wing into battle this year, hoping he can get some inside-outside help from him.

"He shoots the ball extremely well and is a pretty good rebounder," Skinner said.

Bryant has a chance to be a valuable component this year, because of his versatility. And, if Walls or Ross struggles, there could be some starting time available, too.

C-NATE DOORNEKAMP (6-11, 245 lbs., FR, #13, 27.0 ppg, 15.0 rpg, Ernestown Secondary School/Odessa, Ontario). One of two big men imported this year by Skinner, Doornekamp is expected to give the Eagles much-needed heft inside and allow Agbai to play along the baseline at times, rather than always in the pivot. He played on the 2001 Canadian World University Games team in Beijing and impressed. Though not totally polished, Doornekamp will get an immediate chance to prove himself.

"We brought him in to play," Skinner said. "He has good lateral quickness and a good head for the game. I like what he has to offer."

G-UDO HADJISOTIROV (6-2, 190 lbs., SO, #3, 2.3 ppg, 0.5 rpg, 0.8 apg, 6.6 minutes, .394 FG, .333 3PT, .737 FT, Winchendon (Mass.) Academy/Sofia, Bulgaria). Although Hadjisotirov didn't show it last year, he is a big three-point weapon who has a chance to step up this season. He played in 19 games in 2000-01 and showed some flashes by scoring 12 points against Wofford and nine against Vanderbilt. He was largely invisible in Big East play.

A big part of Hadjisotirov's development will be based on his ability to stay in good condition. He struggled with that last year, but his summer spent with the Bulgarian team at the World University Games helped.

"He shoots the ball well, and he has improved his quickness," Skinner said. "I'm excited about his improvements physically."

OTHER RESERVES

G-ADAM DEMONG (6-2, 175 lbs., JR, #40, 0.6 ppg, 0.4 rpg, 0.0 apg, 1.5 minutes, .000 FG, .700 FT, Glenbard West HS/Glen Ellyn, Ill.). A walk-on who didn't make a shot from the field but converted 7-of-10 free throw tries, DeMong will provide practice depth in the backcourt.

OTHER NEWCOMERS

C-KIRSTEN ZOELLNER (7-1, 260 lbs., FR, #12, 14.0 ppg, 10.0 rpg, Institute School of Hannover/Hannover, Germany). Zoellner will get some minutes this year, if only because of his size, but he remains raw and likely won't have a big role for a couple more years. Still, he brings some size to the Eagle roster, and that's what the team needs.

"I think he's improving," Skinner said. "The one thing he does well is catch the ball around the basket. He has to learn our style and learn how to play up-and-down. He has to push himself and play at our speed."

Zoellner played for the Hannover Club Team for three years and spent the 1997-98 season in Wapello, Iowa, as an exchange student. His brother, Klaas, played four years for Akron and graduated last spring.

QUESTIONS

Depth? The Eagles have some talent, but their primary bench players are either freshmen or inexperienced sophomores.

Size? Agbai is a hoss inside, but Doornekamp and Zoellner must give him some support.

Encore? Last season was a great bolt of lightning, but the Eagles must sustain the success now that everyone will be gunning for them from the start of the year.

ANSWERS

Bell! He's one of the elite players in the Big East and should receive considerable national mention this year. He does it all.

Agbai! Don't look at his numbers. Focus on his value inside and the little things he does to help the whole team.

Sidney! He had a big debut and appears ready to take a much larger role on the team.

BOSTON COLLEGE 2000-2001 RESULTS

St. Peter's	100-75
Brown	81-52
Marist	74-65
Wofford	71-57
Holy Cross	77-48
Youngstown State	93-65
@Massachusetts	74-65
Quinnipiac	88-55
Vanderbilt	97-74
Connecticut	85-68
@Miami	73-72
@St. John's (L)	71-73
Miami	82-73
@Duke (L)	75-97
Rutgers	77-51
@Villanova	90-80
Virginia Tech	83-61
Villanova	89-74
Syracuse	65-63
@Virginia Tech	83-59
@Connecticut (L)	71-82
Providence	81-73
Notre Dame (L)	75-76
Providence	59-58
Morris Brown	84-63
St. John's	67-62
@West Virginia	96-65
#Villanova	93-79
#Seton Hall	75-48

#Pittsburgh	79-57
##Southern Utah	68-65
##Southern Cal	71-74
#Big East Tournament in New York	
##NCAA Tournament	
@Road Games	

BLUE RIBBON ANALYSIS

BACKCOURT	A-
BENCH/DEPTH	B-
FRONTCOURT	C+
INTANGIBLES	B

Good college teams need good guards, and that's why Boston College was successful last year. If Watson steps up and Walls plays the way he can, then BC should enjoy more prosperity this year, because its pressure defense and up-tempo offensive style are conducive to thriving in the Big East.

Bell is the star, and Skinner finds plenty of ways for him to score. Bell helps out, too, by setting up his teammates and playing the kind of defense that leads to easy baskets. He and Sidney should be a dynamic backcourt combination, with Walls a worthy wing and Watson a strong complementary part off the bench.

We all know Agbai carries a big load up front. He hopes to have some help this year from Ross and Bryant, while the two big newcomers will likely make sporadic contributions, depending a lot on who the opposition is. The bottom line is that this is a good team. Boston College probably won't win 27 games again, but the Eagles are threats to win the Big East's East Division and should grab another NCAA Tournament berth. That's what the players came to do, and after a couple tough seasons, they're doing it.

(M.B.)

 Arizona 27

LOCATION	Tucson, AZ
CONFERENCE	Pac-10
LAST SEASON	28-8 (.778)
CONFERENCE RECORD	15-3 (2nd)
STARTERS LOST/RETURNING	4/1
NICKNAME	Wildcats
COLORS	Cardinal & Navy
HOMECOURT	McKale Center (14,545)
COACH	Lute Olson (Augsburg '58)
RECORD AT SCHOOL	447-133 (18 years)
CAREER RECORD	639-225 (28 years)
ASSISTANTS	Jim Rosborough (Iowa '66)
	Rodney Tention (San Francisco '88)
	John Jay (Arizona '81)
TEAM WINS (last 5 years)	25-30-22-27-28
RPI (last 5 years)	16-5-17-7-3
2000-01 FINISH	Lost in national championship game.

COACH AND PROGRAM

Coach Lute Olson lost four starters from last year's national finalist to the NBA draft, then lost an appeal to the NCAA to get scholarship relief. None of it compares to the truly significant loss he suffered last season, the death of his wife of 47 years, Bobbi.

Everything the Wildcats overcame and achieved last season—suspensions, injuries, the distraction of the looming NBA draft, and ultimately a charge into the Final Four—was played out under the dark cloud cast over the program by Bobbi's death after a long battle with ovarian cancer.

She died on Jan. 1, two days after Olson told his players in an emotional meeting that he was taking a leave of absence from the team. His players all knew what that meant.

Surrounded by family, Olson stayed away from the team for nearly three weeks as the Pac-10 Conference season began. The entire Tucson community grieved for a woman who was much more a part of the basketball program than most coach's wives. Her seat at McKale Center was left vacant, a lone rose sitting in her place.

The fact is, the Wildcats missed Mrs. Olson, but badly needed their coach. The team struggled with the loss and without their coach, finally beginning a march toward the Final Four with a run off 11 straight victories, eight of

them against teams bound for the NCAA Tournament or in the event itself. All that transpired after Olson returned to the team.

In the end, the Wildcats lost in the national final to Duke in a battle of the teams picked Nos. 1 and 2 by Blue Ribbon months before. Simply getting to the season's final game was a remarkable achievement for a team with as much talent as any in the nation. But given the pall cast over the program after the death of Bobbi Olson, the run was amazing.

This will be a dramatically different season for Olson and the Wildcats. He has had the off-season to gradually begin adjusting to life on his own. And his team will be without familiar faces, too.

With the four starters gone to the NBA, Olson will build his club around starting point guard Jason Gardner, fellow juniors Luke Walton and Ricky Anderson and a slough of youngsters.

Arizona has less experience than any team projected to finish among the top seven or eight in the Pac-10, but Olson's Wildcats have finished lower than fourth place in the conference just once since his second season in Tucson, way back in 1985. That was in 1997, when the 'Cats were fifth in the Pac-10 with freshman point guard Mike Bibby, then raced to the national championship.

Long-time Arizona associate head coach Jim Rosborough suggested that this season poses a scenario where Olson can be at his most dangerous.

"In 21 years with Lute, absolutely, unfailingly, we have been at our best at underdogs," Rosborough said.

Of course, that rarely has been the case, given just how good the Arizona program has been. The Wildcats have won at least 22 games for 14 consecutive seasons, actually averaging just under 27 victories during that stretch.

Olson said the Wildcats are conceding nothing entering this season, despite the fact their roster of 10 scholarship players includes five freshmen and another rookie who was red-shirted a year ago.

"It's not a case where we relish not being as good as we've been," Olson said. "Our guys are going to battle hard to make sure we aren't stepping away from that contenders' position."

Arizona signed a highly regarded five-man freshman class, but when senior Loren Woods was joined in the NBA draft by juniors Michael Wright and Richard Jefferson and sophomore Gilbert Arenas, Olson wanted to add more personnel to his roster.

A new NCAA rule that limits schools to signing five players in a year and eight over a two-year span prevented the Wildcats from bringing in additional recruits. Olson filed an appeal to the NCAA, but was turned down.

"It's one of the few rules they've ever put in where they didn't give you a year to adjust," Olson said. "The rule is not a good rule, period. But if they'd given us a year to adjust, they would have found out it's not a good rule."

Rosborough suggested that Arizona's situation—with three underclassmen leaving for the draft—was somewhat unique and deserved special consideration.

"The bottom line is that the rules, as they are written, can put us at a competitive disadvantage through no fault of our own," Rosborough said. "We had a number of players who decided to turn professional, and there is nothing we can do about it."

2001-2002 SCHEDULE

Nov.	8-9	#Coaches vs.Cancer IKON Classic
	27	@Texas
Dec.	1	Kansas
	4	*Illinois
	8	**Purdue
	15	@Michigan State
	20	@Oregon State
	22	@Oregon
	28-30	##Bank One Fiesta Bowl Classic
Jan.	4	Oregon
	6	Oregon State
	10	@Washington State
	12	@Washington
	17	Southern Cal
	19	UCLA
	23	@Arizona State
	26	Connecticut
	31	@California
Feb.	2	@Stanford
	7	Washington
	9	Washington State

	14	@UCLA
	16	@Southern Cal
	20	Arizona State
	28	Stanford
March	2	California
	7-9	###Pacific-10 Tournament

@Road Games
*Phoenix, AZ
**Wooden Classic, Anaheim, CA
#At Madison Square Garden, New York (vs. Maryland, first round; Florida, Temple)
##Tucson, Ariz. (vs. Pepperdine first round; also Valparaiso, West Virginia)
###Staples Center, Los Angeles, CA

STARTERS NOT RETURNING

C-LOREN WOODS (7-1, 13.2 ppg, 6.5 rpg, 2.9 bpg, 2.1 apg, 30.3 minutes, .504 FG, .830 FT). Woods closed out his sometimes rocky, sometimes brilliant college career with a tumultuous senior season. A transfer from Wake Forest after two years there, Woods sat out the first six games of the season while serving an NCAA suspension for accepting "excessive" gifts from a family friend.

He returned for a road game against Connecticut, where he scored nine points but was whistled for a controversial goal-tending call on what turned out to be the game-winning shot by UConn's Tony Robertson with 1.8 seconds left.

Woods had 15 points and 10 rebounds in his next game, but Arizona lost again, falling to Illinois in Chicago. Two games later, in a win over Butler, Woods had a season-high 25 points to go with nine rebounds and three blocks.

But he was ejected from the Pac-10 opener against Cal after receiving two technical fouls, then strung together a series of uneven performances, mixing strong games with unproductive efforts.

His talent never was an issue. In a win over Washington, Woods joined Jason Kidd as the only Pac-10 players with more than one career triple-double, collecting 13 points, 10 rebounds and 10 blocked shots.

But after a loss at Oregon, in which he shot 4-for-14 and scored 11 points, Woods was suspended by Olson for the Oregon State game two days later for his conduct in practice. A month after that, he had just two points in a win over OSU, prompting him to tell reporters he was disgusted by his own play and had regrets that he didn't leave school for the NBA after his junior season.

Olson, obviously facing his own much greater personal issues, seemed to grow weary of the problems Woods mostly brought on himself. He finally addressed the topic, suggesting his center was old enough to speak for himself, but would have to live with the consequences of his words.

That seemed to energize Woods, who finished the season with a flurry, averaging 16.9 points and 7.9 rebounds over the final seven games, including the six-game NCAA Tournament run. He was selected to the All-Final Four team after setting an NCAA Tournament record with 24 blocks in six games.

Projected as a mid-to-late first-round NBA pick, Woods slipped to the second round, where the Minnesota Timberwolves took him with the 46th pick.

"Everyone I spoke with said that Loren had great workouts," said Olson. "Going to Minnesota will give him a good chance to show what he can do. Minnesota got a steal in Loren Woods."

PF-MICHAEL WRIGHT (6-7, 15.6 ppg, 7.8 rpg, 27.9 minutes, .594 FG, .797 FT). Wright bolted for the NBA draft after earning his second straight All-Pac-10 selection as a junior. A powerful low-post presence in college, Wright was one of the most consistently productive players Olson has had in years.

Wright was voted to the Associated Press All-America third team, was MVP of the Maui Invitational and was a John Wooden Award finalist.

At Maui, Wright averaged 16.3 points and 13.7 rebounds, helping the Wildcats to victories over Chaminade, Dayton and Illinois. He scored in double figures 32 times in 36 games, including 28 points in an unstoppable performance against Cal and 26 points at Washington.

Wright was chosen with the 39th pick in the second round by the New York Knicks.

"Everyone I heard from loved Michael's work ethic and attitude," Olson said. "It will be difficult not to keep him on any roster due to his attitude and work ethic. There is no question that he can shoot the ball. Michael's success will be determined by how well he can defend."

SF-RICHARD JEFFERSON (6-7, 11.3 ppg, 5.4 rpg, 2.7 apg, 27.5 minutes, .479 FG, .344, 3PT, .655 FT). Jefferson joined the mass exodus of Arizona players from the collegiate ranks despite a less-than-overwhelming junior season.

An explosive player, Jefferson scored in double figures 23 times, including 18 points in the Maui title-game win over Illinois and 20 points in a victory over Gonzaga. He scored 20 points in Arizona's loss to Mississippi State that snapped the team's 31-game win streak in its own Fiesta Bowl Classic tournament.

But Jefferson disappeared on occasion, too. He was scoreless on 0-for-6 shooting and fouled out in a loss to Purdue, and had just three points before fouling out of an early Pac-10 defeat to Stanford that set the tone for the remainder of the conference season.

Jefferson gave a better sampling of his capabilities in the Final Four, averaging 18 points and eight rebounds against Michigan State and Duke, earning all-tournament honors for the weekend. He also displayed impressive defensive potential, limiting Big Ten Player-of-the-Year Frank Williams of Illinois and soon-to-be lottery pick Jason Richardson of Michigan State to a combined 15 points on 5-for-26 shooting.

Jefferson was chosen 13th by Houston, which traded him on draft night to New Jersey.

"Richard is such a talented player that he will make an impact with the New Jersey Nets," Olson said.

SG-GILBERT ARENAS (6-3, 16.2 ppg, 3.6 rpg, 2.5 apg, 1.8 spg, 29.0 minutes, .479 FG, .416 3PT, .734 FT). Arenas earned All-Pac-10 honors before departing after his sophomore season for the NBA. In many ways, he seemed the best prepared of any of the four Wildcats to make the transition.

Arenas enjoyed an excellent final college season, improving by leaps and bounds his three-point shooting from .292 the year before. In Pac-10 games, Arenas averaged 18.0 points, and he was voted Most Outstanding Player of the NCAA Midwest Regional, averaging 16.3 points in four victories, including 21 in the regional final against Illinois.

Arenas scored 27 points in Arizona's 105-61 rout of USC, hitting 8-of-9 shots, including all five from beyond the arc. He scored 22 points in the Wildcats' late-season victory at top-ranked Stanford.

His most productive game was a career-high 30-point outburst at UCLA, in which he scored 19 points after halftime to bring the Cats back from a 13-point hole in an eventual overtime defeat.

Arenas was drafted 31st by the Golden State Warriors.

"I think this is a good fit for Gilbert," Olson said. "He's a California kid and Golden State features a style that he plays best in."

OTHERS NOT RETURNING

F-EUGENE EDGERSON (6-6, 4.6 ppg, 4.0 rpg, 12.9 minutes, .576 FG, .686 FT). A fifth-year senior, Edgerson returned to the club last season after taking off 2000-01 to complete his student teaching. He started twice last year—when suspensions prompted the need—and provided the Wildcats with the same qualities he always had: defense, rebounding and muscle.

F-JUSTIN WESSEL (6-8, 2.6 ppg, 1.6 rpg, 11.1 minutes, .467 FG, .724 FT). A senior last season, Wessel earned five starts—all when Woods was sitting out—and gave the Wildcats hustle and grit. His talents didn't compare to those of Arizona's high-profile starters, but Olson appreciated his work ethic and versatility.

G-LAMONT FRAZIER (6-3, 2.4 ppg, 1.3 rpg, 10.3 minutes, .377 FG, .543 FT). Frazier provided the Wildcats with backcourt help off the bench during his senior year. He played in 32 games, a vast improvement over his junior year when he saw action in just seven games because of a medical condition. Frazier was limited by poor shooting, but at least he knew his limits. The guard did not attempt a three-point shot all season.

G-JOHN ASH (5-10, 1.1 ppg, 0.8 rpg, 3.6 minutes, .300 FG, .571 FT). A fifth-year senior walk-on, Ash appeared in 12 games, all of them off the bench.

PROJECTED STARTERS

PG-JASON GARDNER (5-10, 181 lbs., JR, #22, 10.9 ppg, 3.0 rpg, 4.1 apg, 1.6 spg, 32.4 minutes, .381 FG, .367 3-PT, .809 FT, North Central HS/Indianapolis, Ind.). Clearly, the Wildcats become Gardner's team this season. The only holdover from last year's starting five, he will be given a good deal of freedom, but also a large share of responsibility for directing a young squad.

"The big thing is leadership," Olson said. "Jason's always been a good player under pressure. It's encouraging to have him out there when games are on the line. Our guards have always had a lot of freedom. It's not going to be a case where we tell him to do whatever he wants. Our system is pretty well established. Our guards have had freedom, but it's not going to be him just going out and jacking the ball up whenever he wants to."

Make no mistake, though, Gardner will have a fair share of latitude, provided he doesn't get carried away.

"Turn Jason loose like Duke does Jason Williams, and you'll see that kid average 20 points a game," Rosborough said. "He'll be the type of player Damon Stoudamire and Khalid Reeves were as seniors when they did come back."

There was some question as to whether Gardner would be back this season. He entered his name in the NBA draft pool and attended the pre-draft camps. He did not hire an agent, however, leaving him the option to return. It's a good thing, because Gardner did not impress scouts at the camps. Several scouts advised him he was unlikely to be drafted.

Finally, Gardner made the decision to remove himself from the draft.

"It's a dream of mine to play in the NBA," Gardner said at the time. "I enjoyed the pre-draft experience and learned a lot from it. I'm looking forward to the season with a great group of teammates."

Gardner was selected national freshman of the year by the U.S. Basketball Writers, Basketball Times, Basketball News, ESPN.com and Dick Vitale two years ago, when he averaged 12.9 points, 4.8 assists and 3.7 rebounds. But he did not shoot particularly well either of his first two collegiate seasons, and that shortcoming showed up at the pre-draft camps.

"They indicated he needed to become a more consistent shooter," Olson said. "And he's got to be able to create his own shots. Those are probably the two main things. As I told Jason once he came back, we've had great guards that have gone in the lottery that would not have been ready after their sophomore year, either.

"Damon Stoudamire was not ready, and ended up being the [NBA] Rookie of the Year after putting in four [college] years. Jason Terry is another example of a guy who would not have been ready after two years. It's just getting crazy now, so many guys being told by people who really don't know anything that they're going to be drafted in the first round."

Gardner played well down the stretch last season, averaging 12.5 points in six NCAA games, including 28 points, six rebounds and six assists in wins over Mississippi and Illinois. He had five games with at least 20 minutes and zero turnovers, and the Wildcats are 24-5 in two years when Gardner hands out at least five assists.

SG-TRAVIS HANOUR (6-6, 189 lbs., SO, #5, 3.1 ppg, 1.4 rpg, 8.8 minutes in 20 games, .339 FG, .185 3PT, .900 FT, Laguna Beach HS/Laguna Beach, Calif.). Hanour is the most veteran of a group of young players competing for the starting shooting guard spot. He played somewhat sparingly last season, and rarely seemed to play with much confidence.

"Travis is a very good shooter and also very athletic," Olson said. "The biggest thing with him is once he gets the confidence, knowing the minutes he's going to play. That part of his game will come together quickly. Defensively, he still needs to get better, but that's generally true of younger players."

Hanour enjoyed his best game as a freshman at Oregon State, scoring a season-high 11 points on 4-for-5 shooting, including 3-for-4 from three-point range. He was 2-for-23 from beyond the arc in all other games.

As a senior in high school, Hanour averaged 25.7 points, 9.7 rebounds and 5.4 assists, and shot 40 percent from three-point range.

SF-LUKE WALTON (6-8, 233 lbs., JR, #4, 5.5 ppg, 2.2 rpg, 3.2 apg, 1.1 spg, .420 FG, .220 3PT, .672 FT, University HS/San Diego, Calif.). The youngest of legendary UCLA center Bill Walton's four sons, Luke will be asked to be more than the role player he was his first two seasons. Although he is more physical than Ricky Anderson, the coaching staff likes Walton on the wing because of his vision and passing ability. He is a smart player with a good understanding of all that goes on during the game.

"He'll be key with leadership," Olson said. "Luke, with the time he's going to get this year, I think will turn in consistent numbers. He's a good, solid player—nothing flashy. He's been one of our leading assist guys, one of our leading rebounders for minutes played.

"He has to have a good year for us to be good. He needs to stay healthy."

Walton had at least five assists in eight different games last season, and was selected Pac-10 Player of the Week after averaging 13.5 points, 10.0 rebounds, 5.5 assists and 4.5 steals in wins over Gonzaga and St. Mary's. He had four points, three rebounds and four assists in the national championship game against Duke.

PF-RICKY ANDERSON (6-9, 220 lbs., JR, #33, 4.5 ppg, 2.2 rpg, 13.6 minutes, .414 FG, .277 3PT, .769 FT in 1999-2000, Long Beach Poly HS/Long Beach, Calif.). Anderson red-shirted last season to gain strength and improve his skills, and the coaching staff expects him to be one of the biggest surprises in the Pac-10.

"Rick is a wonderful player and I think before he leaves, he'll be an All-American," Rosborough said.

Olson said added strength and weight will benefit Anderson, who could play at either of the forward spots.

"He's very slender, but now he's strong and slender," Olson said. "We've lost a lot of production, not only from a scoring standpoint but from a rebounding standpoint. He's going to have to be a big factor on the boards. Ricky's been one of our best shooters since he arrived on campus, but we need him to step up big-time."

Olson said match-ups, more than anything, will dictate at which spots Anderson and Walton are used.

Anderson, whose father played for Olson at Long Beach City College in the early 1970s, played every game but one two seasons ago, and started twice. He had the best game of his career in the final game of the 1999-2000 season, scoring 12 points on 4-for-5 shooting in an NCAA Tournament game against Wisconsin.

C-ANDREW ZAHN (6-9, 254 lbs., FR, #13, 17.2 ppg, 11 rpg, 4 apg, 3 bpg in 1999-2000 at Redondo Union HS/Redondo Beach, Calif.). Zahn sat out last season as a red-shirt, but will come into training camp as the lead candidate to win the low-post job. He is far from a sure bet to hold off Arizona's talented incoming freshmen.

Zahn actually is more of a power forward than a center, but Olson needs only to look back to the national championship team of 1997 for an example of a club that thrived without a true center.

"In '97 we had A.J. Bramlett playing center, and our Final Four team of '88 we had [Tom] Tolbert and [Anthony] Cook [inside]. Neither of those classified as centers," Olson said. "Andrew's got a big body and had a year of practice. He should have the advantage of that year.

"We haven't see him in a game situation, but he has good hands and a good shooting touch. The key thing with him is to refine his offensive skills in terms of actual game experience. He's one of the guys who's going to get a good, solid look."

Zahn started every game for four years in high school, helping Redondo Union to an 81-15 record, including 25-5 his senior season. As a prep player, he played two years in Paris on a Nike summer touring team.

KEY RESERVES

G-WILL BYNUM (5-10, 180 lbs., FR, #3, 27.0 ppg, 6.0 rpg, 6.0 apg at Crane Tech Prep/Chicago, Ill.). Bynum is a dynamic combination guard who eventually will be groomed as Gardner's replacement at the point.

"He's a great athlete and he's very strong, and he's got a 42-inch vertical leap," Olson said. "I think any of our young guards will play well with Jason. Will scored a lot of points [in high school] against box-and-ones and all sorts of defenses. But we've never believed a point guard shouldn't be a scorer also. If you're a scorer, that opens up driving lanes and passing lanes."

Bynum was rated as a Top 50 national recruit by Bob Gibbons' All-Star Report and Hoop Scoop. He played in the Wendy's All-Star Shootout in Chicago and the Nike Derby Festival Classic in Louisville, Ky. He was a Chicago Tribune all-state selection.

A four-time All-Chicago Public League pick, Bynum was twice voted to the all-state team.

G-SALIM STOUDAMIRE (6-2, 175 lbs., FR, 28.5 ppg, 6.0 rpg, 3.9 apg at Lake Oswego HS/Lake Oswego, Ore.). A cousin of ex-Wildcats star Damon Stoudamire, Salim brings the skills to play either guard position, although he is first and foremost a scorer.

Stoudamire is the Oregon Class 4A all-time leading scorer with 2,219 career points. A McDonald's All-American, Stoudamire was an all-state pick in Oregon as

a junior and sophomore. He averaged 23.0 points as a junior, 28.6 points as a sophomore and 21.7 points as a freshman.

"He's an outstanding shooter, he can handle the ball and he's a good competitor," Olson said. "The biggest thing with freshmen is how they're able to adjust to the defensive end. You don't know until they get there, but I think both [Stoudamire and Bynum] have the capability of being very good defensive players."

C-ISAIAH FOX (6-9, 260 lbs., FR, #52, 20.0 ppg, 12.0 rpg at Crossroads HS/Santa Monica, Calif.). Fox is a wide-body athlete who will get the chance to demonstrate if he can contribute right away. Rated as the No. 60 prospect in the nation by Fast Break Recruiting Service, Fox led Crossroads to a 28-6 record and a berth in the California Division IV state final.

"I think he's going to be a very solid player," Olson said. "With freshmen, we have to see what takes place in a practice situation. We have a good idea from what they did in high school, and certainly one of those inside positions is really wide open. That position needs to be a solid defender."

Fox averaged 23.0 points and 19.0 rebounds in the state playoffs last season, including 30 points and 21 rebounds in the state final loss. As a junior, he averaged 25 points and 13 rebounds. He led Crossroads to a four-year league record of 55-1.

C-CHANNING FRYE (6-10, 230 lbs., FR, #45, 22.0 ppg, 15.0 rpg, 6.0 bpg, 3.0 apg at St. Mary's HS/Phoenix, Ariz.). Quick and agile, Frye reminds some Arizona onlookers of ex-Wildcats star A.J. Bramlett. Of the Cats' five incoming freshmen, however, he may be the one who contributes the least at the start.

"He runs well and he made great progress last year as a senior," Olson said.

But Frye is thin and does not have great strength yet. Last season, he led his high school team to a 30-3 record and the Arizona Class 5A state title. He was the state player of the year, according to the Arizona Republic, and was the Arizona Gatorade Player of the Year, along with a fourth-team Parade magazine All-America selection.

His prep team was 26-7 two years ago and was ranked No. 19 in the nation by USA Today.

F-DENNIS LATIMORE (6-8, 230 lbs., FR, #34, 24.0 ppg, 11.0 rpg, 3.0 apg, 2.0 bpg at Halsted HS/Halsted, Kan.). Rated as the No. 27 prospect in the country by Fast Break Recruiting Service and a Top 50 pick according to Bob Gibbons' All-Star Report, Latimore returns to Arizona after spending his final two high school seasons in Kansas.

He was the Kansas Class 3A state player of the year last season, and was the Kansas Gatorade Player of the Year as a junior after averaging 25.0 points and 13.3 rebounds. He played his sophomore year at Mountain View High in Mesa, Ariz., leading the team to the Class 5A state crown.

"He has good versatility, and we could use him a lot facing the basket. He could be a swing forward," Olson said.

Latimore even could wind up playing essentially the center spot, if the Wildcats decide to go small and utilize a quick alignment.

OTHER RETURNEES

F-MIKE SCHWERTLEY (6-5, 224 lbs, SO, #14, 1.1 ppg, 0.9 rpg, 4.1 minutes in 10 games, .300 FG, .571 FT, Brophy Prep HS/Phoenix, Ariz.). A walk-on who red-shirted in 1999-2000, Schwertley saw limited action a year ago. He had his most extensive and productive outing in a rout of St. Mary's, contributing seven points and four rebounds.

Schwertley, the son of former NBA player Leonard "Truck" Robinson, likely will remain primarily a practice player for the Wildcats.

G-JASON RANNE (6-4, 200 lbs., SO, #11, 0.0 ppg, 0.1 rpg, 2.3 minutes in nine games, Bishop Kelly HS/Tulsa, Okla.). Ranne is a walk-on who averaged 18 points as a high school senior two years ago. Both of his parents are Arizona alums, his father having played basketball in 1971-72 before attending medical school.

OTHER NEWCOMERS

None.

QUESTIONS

Depth? Because of defections to the NBA and the

NCAA's 5-and-8 scholarship limitations, the Wildcats have just 10 scholarship players. If they lose more one or two to injury, their ranks will be dangerously thin.

Youth? Five of the Cats' 10 scholarship players are freshmen and two others are second-year players who combined to score 61 points a year ago. Are Olson's youngsters ready to make sizable contributions now?

Defense? Olson always has said success begins at the defensive end, and Arizona is so inexperienced at the post position he must be concerned about just how well his club will stop opponents inside.

ANSWERS

Jason Gardner! Essentially spurned by the NBA last spring, Gardner may play this season with a chip on his shoulder. If he uses that as a positive motivation, the Wildcats will have a driven team leader.

Lute Olson! Having now taken Arizona to the Final Four on four occasions since 1988, Olson clearly has established himself as one of the greatest coaches in Pac-10 history. And he's sometimes been at his best with a young team facing modest outside expectations.

Tradition! No one who has been paying attention for the last 15 years or so can reasonably expect the Wildcats to slink off into the Arizona sunset. These guys have won too much, for too long to disappear. McKale Center remains a huge asset, and Olson's young talent is just that—talented.

ARIZONA 2000-2001 RESULTS

#Chaminade	97-57
#Dayton	75-69
#Illinois	79-76
##Purdue (L)	69-72
Gonzaga	101-67
St. Mary's	101-41
@Connecticut (L)	69-71
@Illinois (L)	73-81
LSU	88-75
###Butler	72-60
###Mississippi State (L)	74-76
California	78-75
Stanford (L)	76-85
@Washington State	84-51
@Washington	89-64
USC	71-58
UCLA	88-63
Arizona State	86-75
Texas	80-52
@Oregon (L)	67-79
@Oregon State	68-41
Washington	82-62
Washington State	86-51
@UCLA (L)	77-79
@USC	105-61
@Arizona State	88-58
Oregon State	65-54
Oregon	104-65
@Stanford	76-75
@California	78-76
####Eastern Illinois	101-76
####Butler	73-52
####Ole Miss	66-56
####Illinois	87-81
####Michigan State	80-61
####Duke (L)	72-82

#Maui Invitational in Maui, HI
##John Wooden Tradition in Indianapolis
###Bank One Fiesta Bowl Classic in Tucson
####NCAA Tournament
@Road Games

BLUE RIBBON ANALYSIS

BACKCOURT	B+
BENCH/DEPTH	B-
FRONTCOURT	B
INTANGIBLES	A-

This may not be one of Olson's best teams at Arizona, but it could be one of his most intriguing. No one is more curious about how the team might evolve than Olson.

"There are a lot of question marks right now with this team," he said. "We're going to have to answer those questions as we go through the season. I think we've got guys who will be hard workers, team-oriented guys who will adjust well to our style.

"As long as we stay healthy, I think we can be pretty

good."

While several of the newcomers must show they can contribute immediately, Olson will count most heavily upon his three most experienced returnees—Gardner, Walton and Anderson.

"It's obvious our three juniors have to stay healthy and I think they're capable of giving us excellent years," Olson said. "Jason Gardner will give us an experienced guy at the point and that's going to be important with our young guys. Those three [older] guys need to have big years."

Olson has put together his typically challenging non-conference schedule, which might scare off some teams but could have the effect of hardening this group for the Pac-10 campaign.

Don't look for these Wildcats to make a return trip to the Final Four. But don't expect them to sail off the radar screen, either.

(J.F.)

 ## Michigan State 28

LOCATION	East Lansing, MI
CONFERENCE	Big Ten
LAST SEASON	28-5 (.848)
CONFERENCE RECORD	13-3 (t-1st)
STARTERS LOST/RETURNING	4/1
NICKNAME	Spartans
COLORS	Green & White
HOMECOURT	Breslin Center (14,759)
COACH	Tom Izzo (Northern Michigan '77)
RECORD AT SCHOOL	148-53 (6 years)
CAREER RECORD	148-53 (6 years)
ASSISTANTS	Brian Gregory (Oakland '90)
	Mike Garland (Northern Michigan '77)
	Mark Montgomery (Michigan State '92)
TEAM WINS (last 5 years)	17-22-33-32-28
RPI (last 5 years)	70-11-3-3-4
2000-01 FINISH	Lost in NCAA Final Four.

COACH AND PROGRAM

The Michigan State Spartans are in the midst of a run unmatched by anyone in the country over the same time period, save defending national champion Duke.

Consider these accomplishments: Four consecutive Big Ten titles. Three straight Final Fours. And the 2000 national title to boot.

The man who succeeded his mentor and 19-year MSU staple Jud Heathcote in 1995 has taken the program to heights even Heathcote couldn't. Tom Izzo, the first coach in school history to produce four straight 20-win seasons, is one of the hottest names in coaching—at any level. In fact, it's hard to tell who is more popular these days: Izzo, or high school buddy Steve Mariucci, who happens to coach one of the NFL's most recognizable franchises, the San Francisco 49ers.

Izzo, 46, came darn close to leaving the Spartans after the championship season. That's when the moribund Atlanta Hawks made a lucrative offer to entice the Iron Mountain, Mich., native to join the NBA ranks. He wound up turning it down, and appears unlikely to leave East Lansing any time soon. When his most logical NBA suitor, the Detroit Pistons, found themselves with a job opening last spring, Izzo made it clear he wasn't interested.

Izzo was coming off perhaps his finest coaching job yet. MSU's 2000 title run, as well as the Final Four season that preceded it, were almost to be expected, that's how seasoned and talented the Spartans had become. But the way they played during last year's encore, despite having lost four-year stars Mateen Cleaves (now with the Pistons), Morris Peterson (Toronto Raptors) and starting power forward A.J. Granger, was at least a little surprising. The Spartans were in many ways their most dominating yet, handling their typically brutal battery of non-conference opponents (North Carolina, Florida, Kentucky, Seton Hall) to start 12-0 and increasing their nation's-best rebounding margin of the year before from 11.7 to 15.4.

MSU shared the Big Ten regular-season crown with Illinois, falling 77-66 to the Illini in their only regular-season matchup on Feb. 6. There was much anticipation for a possible rematch in the Big Ten Tournament final, but Penn State, which would go on to the Sweet 16, surprised the Spartans, 65-63, in their first game. MSU

recovered to win its first four NCAA Tournament games by an average 18-point margin before running into a torrid Arizona squad in the Final Four, falling 80-61. But the loss did little to diminish their overall accomplishments.

"To be in three straight Final Fours says something about consistency," Izzo said after beating Temple, 69-62, in the South Regional final in Atlanta.

"Is our program looked at the same way as Kentucky and Duke and North Carolina? Maybe not. But we're trying to get there."

Said senior Andre Hutson, "I never though we would do it three years in a row. You have to consider us an elite program now."

Even elite programs must rebuild from time to time, and that's just what Michigan State faces this season. Izzo terms the challenge ahead "total reconstruction." As if losing Hutson, fellow four-year starter Charlie Bell and key role players David Thomas and Mike Chappell wasn't enough, both sophomore Jason Richardson and freshman Zach Randolph bolted early for the NBA, the school's first early entrants since Magic Johnson in 1979. Richardson went No. 5 overall to the Golden State Warriors, Randolph No. 19 to Portland.

"It's one of those strange things," said Izzo. "Losing those two guys, it wasn't totally surprising, but kind of. We probably should have planned for both [to leave], but I thought during the season both would come back for another year."

Over the last two off-seasons, the program has bid farewell to seven players who started at least their final season and 10 scholarship players overall. Even top assistant Stan Heath left after last season for the top job at Kent State.

Izzo is left with a shell of his typical roster: eight scholarship players, none of them seniors, and two walk-ons. And Izzo's teams had become accustomed to going eight- or nine-deep most games.

Any last-minute efforts to add a couple more recruits in the spring were basically rendered impracticable by the new 8/5 scholarship rule, with Izzo reluctant to take a chance on the type of periphery prospects still available so late.

Unfortunately, the schedule was designed for a team that wouldn't be so overtly young. Izzo has never been one to shy away from a challenge, and this year those challenges come in the form of games against Florida, Arizona, Virginia, Stanford and Seton Hall, plus a preseason NIT field that includes Oklahoma, Syracuse, Arkansas, Fresno State and USC. Only the Arizona and Seton Hall games are in the comforts of the Breslin Center, where MSU holds a nation's-best 44-game home winning streak.

But no one, including Izzo himself, seems to be writing off the potential of this team. He likes the fact that all five of his returning scholarship players gained overseas playing experience this summer. And for his part, the always light-hearted coach is choosing to focus on the positives.

"Some of it is going to be kind of fun," he said. "At least you don't have to worry about playing time."

2001-2002 SCHEDULE

Nov.	13	#Detroit
	28	*@Virginia
	30	##Spartan Coca-Cola Classic
Dec.	1	##Spartan Coca Cola Classic
	5	@Florida
	9	Nicholls State
	15	Arizona
	17	UNC Asheville
	19	Oakland
	22	Seton Hall
	29	**Stanford
Jan.	5	@Minnesota
	8	@Indiana
	12	Wisconsin
	16	Purdue
	19	@Penn State
	22	@Iowa State
	30	Michigan
Feb.	3	@Illinois
	6	@Northwestern
	10	Ohio State
	12	Illinois
	16	@Purdue
	21	Minnesota
	24	Indiana
	26	@Ohio State
March	2/3	Iowa

7-10	###Big Ten Tournament

@Road Games
*Big Ten/ACC Challenge
**San Francisco, CA
#Preseason NIT (if Michigan State wins, it will play Connecticut or Oklahoma on Nov. 15 or 16; semifinals and final Nov. 21 and 23 at Madison Square Garden, NY)
##East Lansing, MI (vs. Indiana Purdue-Fort Wayne first round; also Lamar, Maine)
###Conseco Fieldhouse, Indianapolis, IN

STARTERS NOT RETURNING

SG-JASON RICHARDSON (6-6, 14.7 ppg, 5.9 rpg, 2.2 apg, 1.2 spg, 28.5 minutes, .503 FG, .402 3PT, .689 FT). Richardson made as giant a leap between his freshman and sophomore years as is seemingly possible, going from a reserve playing 15 minutes a game to an All-American and NBA lottery pick. Not that it was entirely surprising after his storied high school career in Saginaw, Mich., capped by the 1999 Mr. Basketball Award.

Richardson's sophomore breakthrough began the summer before, when he starred for the U.S. national team that broke in the Olympic Dream Team, scoring 20 points against the NBA players. His most marked improvement during the season came in his shooting, going from just under 30 percent on three pointers to more than 40 percent on 65 attempts. His ability to score both from outside and on the drive, where he could make use of his tremendous leaping ability, caused headaches for defenders.

Richardson's only negative was he did seem to cool off a bit as the season went on, most notably in the season-ending loss to Arizona, when he made only 2-of-11 shots and finished with six points.

PG-CHARLIE BELL (6-3, 13.5 ppg, 4.7 rpg, 5.1 apg, 1.0 spg, 31.3 minutes, .402 FG, .342 3PT, .770 FT). In preparation for the season-ending barrage of award and All-America voting, Michigan State touted Bell with posters declaring him "America's mot complete guard." Considering Duke's Jason Williams, among others, hadn't left the country, it may have been a stretch, but there was some evidence to support it.

Bell may not have been MSU's first or even second offensive option sometimes, but few if any 6-3 guards are capable of averaging nearly as many rebounds as assists. And his ability to match up with taller players defensively was key for the Spartans.

Richardson's ascension meant that Bell didn't gain as much of the spotlight as he had been expecting his senior year. He had already shared it for three years with fellow Flint natives Cleaves and Peterson. He also wasn't quite the outwardly emotional floor leader that Cleaves was, but Izzo is uninhibited in his praise of Bell's character.

When it came time for the NBA draft in June, Bell's size and lack of a true position may have played a factor. He was overlooked through both rounds and ended up signing a free agent contract with the Phoenix Suns.

PF-ANDRE HUTSON (6-8, 13.8 ppg, 7.6 rpg, 1.9 apg, 0.8 spg, 29.9 minutes, .622 FG, .725 FT). Hutson was the leading rebounder on the best rebounding team in the country. Enough said.

Like Bell a starter since his freshman year, Hutson was tenacious on the glass and led with his hustle. His offensive production went up every year, from 7.5 points a game as a freshman, and his rebounding presence remained strong despite the ever-changing post players around him, from Granger and Antonio Smith early to Zach Randolph and Aloysius Anagonye later.

Hutson came up especially big in MSU's four NCAA Tournament wins last year, averaging nearly a double-double (14.3 points, 9.8 rebounds). He was the Spartans' leading scorer in the loss to Arizona with 20 points. And in his most impressive performance of the season, Hutson notched 11 points, 16 rebounds, four assists and three steals in a Feb. 24 road win at Penn State.

SF-DAVID THOMAS (6-7, 5.4 ppg, 4.7 rpg, 1.9 apg, 1.1 spg, 22.4 minutes, .493 FG, .167 3PT, .903 FT). The consummate role player, Thomas finally gained some much-deserved notoriety during last year's Final Four run.

Having recently visited his 37-year-old cousin Wayne Thomas, bedridden with terminal cancer, in Canada, Thomas turned in two of the biggest performances of his life during the tournament. First came a career-high 14 rebounds in the second round against Fresno State. A week later, he helped the Spartans break Temple's tenacious matchup zone, scoring a career-best 19 points in a 69-62 Elite Eight victory.

The fifth-year senior was one of Izzo's favorite players, the only one on the roster still around from MSU's last non-Big Ten title team. Thomas' complete absence of complacency made him work even harder, and Izzo rewarded him with a starting job when there were probably more talented guys to choose from.

OTHERS NOT RETURNING

C-ZACH RANDOLPH (6-9, 10.8 ppg, 6.7 rpg, 1.0 apg, 0.7 spg, 19.8 minutes, .587 FG, .635 FT). Randolph was always one of the most acclaimed prospects in the country in high school. But with a host of dominating performances in the McDonald's All-Americaa game (23 points, 15 rebounds) and Nike Hoop Summit (24 points, eight rebounds) the spring of his senior year, Randolph had risen to No. 1 on most recruiting lists by the time he arrived in East Lansing.

In today's age of instant gratification and sped-up development, it was to be expected a player of Randolph's stature would start immediately. For an eight-game stint in January, he did, but as Izzo found out, even the best freshmen make freshmen mistakes.

It was a season of highs and lows as Randolph struggled with both his weight (he dropped 20 pounds from high school but still clocked in at 260) and Big Ten interior defenses. He dazzled in December's title-game rematch against Florida, scoring 27 points in 23 minutes. But he hit bottom in a Jan. 27 loss to Ohio State, managing only two points and one rebound against Buckeye big man Ken Johnson. Randolph's struggles earned him a return trip to the bench, though his actual minutes played barely changed.

Clearly, Randolph is immensely talented, but many wondered whether he was ready for the NBA. That didn't stop the Marion, Ind., from leaving after one season, despite his mother, high school coach and Izzo's best efforts to dissuade him.

G/F-MIKE CHAPPELL (6-9, 4.7 ppg, 1.9 rpg, 0.7 apg, 13.6 minutes, .443 FG, .311 3PT, .757 FT). In his two years in East Lansing, Chappell never quite achieved the level of play expected of a former Duke Blue Devil. But he did provide quality minutes off the bench at both forward and guard.

During his sophomore season at Duke in 1997-98, Chappell played 14.4 minutes a game and shot an impressive 43.4 percent from three-point range. His minutes stayed about the same in his first season with the Spartans two years later, but his shooting touch did not, dropping to 31.6 percent (37-of-117) on treys. He did come up big, though, in the national championship game against Florida, filling in when Mateen Cleaves went down briefly with an ankle injury and scoring five straight points to extend MSU's lead from 50-44 to 55-44.

Chappell's production remained relatively low again last season, his 4.7-point scoring average his lowest since his freshman year.

PG-BRANDON SMITH (5-10, 0.4 ppg, 6.3 minutes, 18 games played). A transfer from Coastal Carolina, Smith played three years in East Lansing, earning limited playing time.

His first two seasons, there was a certain Mr. Cleaves hogging most of the PT at point guard. And last year, heralded freshman Marcus Taylor arrived. When Smith was on the court, Izzo could at least count on a tough-minded defensive performance.

PROJECTED STARTERS

PG-MARCUS TAYLOR (6-3, 190 lbs., SO, #1, 7.4 ppg, 1.3 rpg, 3.6 apg, 22.0 minutes, .396 FG, .271 3PT, .744 FT, Waverly HS/Lansing, Mich.). A Lansing native, Taylor's first brush with Spartan greatness came at 10 years old, when he attended Magic Johnson's summer camp in Los Angeles, even staying at the superstar's house. As young as junior high, he was playing pickup games with active MSU players.

In other words, his eventually suiting up for the Spartans was inevitable.

Upon his arrival last season, Taylor did not disappoint. Izzo was content to break him in as Cleaves' successor slowly, starting him in only nine games. But considering Taylor's experience, Izzo considers him "a returning starter."

"He could have started even more," Izzo said. "When we did start him, the problem wasn't him starting but sud-

denly we didn't have any scoring punch coming off the bench."

Taylor played 22 minutes a game and turned in a decent 1.75 assist-to-turnover ratio. He showed exactly the kind of ball-handling and defensive skills expected of a McDonald's All-American.

But where Izzo expects to see Taylor step up this season is in scoring. With the exception of a 15-point, seven-assist performance against Florida, Taylor was mostly an afterthought in the offense, but that wasn't the role asked of him. Just like Richardson, who went from seventh man as a freshman to top scorer as a sophomore, Izzo foresees Taylor exploding this season. And just like Richardson the summer before his sophomore year, Taylor earned a spot on the USA Basketball team that captured the World Championship for Young Men in Japan. Playing alongside guards like Duke's Chris Duhon and Boston College's Troy Bell, he averaged 5.7 points, 1.3 rebounds and 2.8 assists in six games.

"I could see Taylor having the same breakthrough year," he said. "He made the same team that Richardson did last summer ... And I think he's better than some guys who left [for the NBA] this year."

Of course, the only problem with that is if Taylor winds up one of those leaving next year.

SG-KELVIN TORBERT (6-4, 220 lbs., FR, #23, 26.0 ppg, 8.2 rpg, 3.5 apg, 2.5 spg, Northwestern HS/Flint, Mich.). Losing Richardson is made slightly less painful by the addition of Torbert, similar in playing style and, by all indications, athletic ability. Just as Richardson was one of the nation's top recruits his senior year, Torbert was a USA Today first team All-American and the Gatorade national player of the year.

His jumper is deadly, his explosiveness to the basket unmatched among the nation's incoming freshmen. He lit up the McDonald's All-America game with 21 points.

Logically, with Torbert's talents and MSU's glaring need for a scorer, expectations will loom large for him to emerge as an immediate superstar. But Izzo remains cautious.

"He's got strength, many different kinds of skills," Izzo said. "But just like other great players around the country, just like Richardson and other kids that have been here, there's an adjustment all freshmen have to make.

"Everyone looks at these players coming in just like they do in the pros—who's gonna help you? But tell me a team going to the Final Four, winning their conference, where those freshmen are really dominant. For example, I really like [Duke's Chris] Duhon. What did he average last year? No more than most other freshmen because he was on such a great team with so many other great players."

SF-ADAM WOLFE (6-9, 215 lbs., SO, #3, 1.7 ppg, 1.7 rpg, 6.0 minutes, .273 FG, .167 3PT, .875 FT, South HS/Westerville, Ohio). Wolfe's biggest obstacle as a red-shirt freshman wasn't Big Ten competition. It was headaches.

Throughout the season, Wolfe suffered from migrane headaches, a condition that has plagued him since childhood. Some of the headaches were debilitating enough to keep him laid up in his room for two days at a time. This obviously put a crimp on his development.

Izzo says doctors finally have the problem under control, and Wolfe figures to have a shot at taking over one of the starting forward positions, if he can hold off incoming freshman Alan Anderson. The Westerville, Ohio, native draws comparisons to former Spartan A.J. Granger in terms of his ability to both bang underneath and step back for the occasional outside shot.

"I don't look at him as being a complete rookie, but he has to make a big jump," said Izzo. "Both [Adam] Ballinger and Wolfe bring something different in that they can shoot the ball. This year, we might play more with the high-low."

Wolfe showed some encouraging signs playing for the Big Ten Men's Basketball Foreign Tour team on its trip to England and Ireland. He was the team's leading scorer (14.3 ppg) and rebounder (6.5 rpg). He also shot .586 (34-of-58) from the field and .412 (seven-of-17) from three-point range.

PF-ADAM BALLINGER (6-9, 250 lbs., JR, #55, 1.9 ppg, 1.6 rpg, .4 blocks, 8.2 minutes), .465 FG, .727 FT, Bluffton HS/Bluffton, Ind.). Like several teammates, Ballinger was limited by injury last year. He missed the first eight games of the season with a broken thumb. But he also made the first start of his career on Jan. 21 against Ohio State and took full advantage, scoring a career-high 10 points.

Like Wolfe, he has decent offensive moves, but will be counted on more for his strength. It will be tough replacing a rebounder the caliber of Hutson, but

Ballinger will get the first shot.

"We've led the country in rebounding margin two years in a row with two completely different teams," Izzo said. "Granger hardly liked to post up at all, Last year, we went to more of a post-up team with Randolph. Yet we led the nation in rebounding both years. This will again be a little bit of a different team, but hopefully the rebounding will continue like it has. It's been very important for us."

C-ALOYSIUS ANAGONYE (6-8, 255 lbs., JR, #25, 4.7 ppg, 3.1 rpg, .5 blocks, 17.7 minutes, .624 FG, .714 FT, DePorres HS/Detroit, Mich.). Despite averaging less than 20 minutes a game last season, Anagonye becomes the most experienced player on the team this year. He did start 24-of-33 games and led MSU by shooting 65.8 percent (25-of-38) from the field in Big Ten play.

By default, Anagonye must become the Spartans' main defensive presence in the paint. But he has actually been more impressive on the offensive end thus far, gaining more offensive (57) than defensive (46) rebounds last season. Some of his best games came against teams with quality big men, like his 10-point, 12-rebound effort against Samuel Dalembert and Seton Hall and his 5-of-7, 13-point day against Marvin Ely and Fresno State in the NCAAs.

"We're hoping he becomes even more offensively skilled," Izzo said. "He has some offensive weapons he can use."

Of course, Anagonye was helped last year by the presence of Randolph, who was more of a true center. At 6-8, Anagonye will be giving up inches to many of his counterparts on the schedule this season, like Purdue's 6-11 John Allison and Michigan's 7-2 Josh Moore. A good early test will come in December against Florida's Udonis Haslem, quite possibly the nation's top center.

KEY RESERVES

C-JASON ANDREAS (6-10, 240 lbs., SO, #44, 0.5 ppg, 1.0 rpg, 4.8 minutes). Andreas joined Wolfe this summer on the Big Ten Foreign Tour Team that played in England and Ireland and went 6-0. In fact, the Ohio pair's development has been closely linked throughout their MSU careers. Both arrived in 1999 and red-shirted during the national championship season.

After waiting their turns for two years, Adreas, Wolfe and Adam Ballinger will be asked to step into much larger roles this season. But Andreas' experience this far has been more limited than the other two, so despite being MSU's tallest options, he will at least start the season as a likely reserve.

The closest thing to a moment of glory for Andreas last year was logging 11 minutes against Ohio State, grabbing three rebounds. But behind the scenes, he is obviously making strides, earning MSU's most improved player award last season.

Andreas showed promise on the summer tour, averaging 3.8 points and 4.2 rebounds while shooting 11-of-25 from the field (.440 percent). He was six-for-six from the field and scored 12 points in the fourth game, a victory over the Waterford Crystal Basketball Club.

"He's got great toughness and incredible intelligence," Izzo said. "He can play a role, can bang, can defend. He's like Antonio Smith, who did so much without doing much on the stat sheet."

G/F-ALAN ANDERSON (6-6, 230 lbs., FR, #15, 21.2 ppg, 5.1 rpg, 7.2 apg, DeLaSalle HS/Minneapolis). A Top 50 recruit who burst onto the scene at the summer 2000 Nike All-America camp, Anderson could find himself pressed into the starting lineup sooner than expected because of MSU's mass attrition. Izzo thinks he may be even more talented than most recruiting analysts realized.

Anderson was a first team all-state performer his junior season before an injury-plagued senior year limited him to city honors. He's an impressive shooter who was lighting it up in summer pick-up games with MSU teammates in East Lansing.

"We think he's got a chance to be awfully good as a swing guy/small forward," Izzo said. "He got hurt, missed some time last year. But he's been very well coached in high school by Dave Thorson, a former assistant at Minnesota. He understands working hard. He's not great at any one thing, but good at a lot of little things."

A year ago, Anderson was ranked No. 22 in the country by recruiting analysts Bob Gibbons and Dave Telep.

G-CHRIS HILL (6-3, 180 lbs., FR, #5, 19.8 ppg, 5.5 rpg, 4.0 apg, Lawrence North HS/Indianapolis). The Spartans think they may have found a hidden gem in Hill, who wasn't rated nearly as highly as Torbert and

Anderson. Izzo raves about his outside shooting ability, which has been likened to former MSU great Sean Respert.

"We're very happy with Chris Hill," he said. "He's probably one of the best shooters we've had here since I've been head coach."

Hill shot 48 percent from the field, 39 percent on three-pointers and 89 percent at the free-throw line last year. After a bout of mononucleosis that caused him to miss just two games, he returned to score 22 points and notch eight rebounds in a 57-53 upset of No. 1 Pike High.

He probably needs to add some strength to adjust to college ball. Izzo thinks he can be versatile.

"Chris Hill can play the combo-guard position, meaning he has the ability to play some point guard and shooting guard with his strength being the ability to put the ball in the basket," Izzo said. "I think he could be one of the best pure shooters we've had in our program since guys like Shawn Respert."

OTHER RETURNEES

G-MAT ISHIBA (5-10, 155 lbs., SR, #11, 0.3 ppg, 17 games, 35 minutes, Seaholm HS/Sugar Creek, Ohio). Ishiba has played 75 minutes of mop-up duty in two seasons of college basketball. But hey, he has a national championship ring, and he can boast the Spartans almost always win (34-1) when he plays. Never mind that's because they're already up big, but the outgoing walk-on is beloved by teammates and a favorite of the "Izzone" student section.

OTHER NEWCOMERS

G-TIM BOGRAKOS (6-2, 180 lbs., FR, #30, 13.0 ppg, 6.0 rpg, 4.0 apg, 2.0 spg, Central HS/Flint, Mich.). Bograkos is a walk-on from Flint, Mich. (where else?), who red-shirted last year. He was a three-sport star in high school, earning all-state honors in baseball and basketball and all-league in football.

Bograkos is a legacy. His father, Tim, played basketball and baseball for Michigan State, earning two letters in hoops.

QUESTIONS

Enough bodies? Having only eight scholarship players leaves little room for injuries. And it doesn't help that so few have actually proven they can be regulars in a Big Ten rotation, let alone for a team accustomed to Final Fours.

True freshmen? It's clear the Spartans will need immediate contributions from their three recruits, especially Torbert. An adjustment period is to be expected, but Torbert may need to have the kind of impact seen last year from Seton Hall's Eddie Griffin or St. Joseph's Jameer Nelson.

Too much, too soon? Izzo's treacherous non-conference schedules the last few years have served to fortify his teams for the rigors of the Big Ten and postseason tournaments. This year, he hopes it doesn't have an adverse effect if MSU loses some early games, like wrecking the confidence of a young and growing club.

ANSWERS

Taylor made! If MSU's sophomore point guard blossoms like expected, the bumps in the road could lessen. By all indications, Taylor is ready to become one of college basketball's elite point guards and help make some of the young players better.

Unbeatable at Breslin! The enthusiasm of Michigan State's student section—collectively known as the "Izzones"—gives the Spartans a tremendous homecourt advantage. They haven't lost at the Breslin Center since the last game of 1997-98. The streak may end this year, but MSU may also be able to pull out some games it otherwise wouldn't.

Tom terrific! Izzo has proven himself one of the top coaches in the college ranks, both for his on-court management and the way he relates to and unifies his players. This season could prove his biggest challenge yet, but it's one he's more than likely up to.

MICHIGAN STATE 2000-2001 RESULTS

Oakland	97-61
#Cornell	89-56
#Eastern Washington	83-61
##North Carolina	77-64
Illinois-Chicago	97-53

Florida	99-83
@Loyola	103-71
Kentucky	46-45
@Seton Hall	72-57
@Bowling Green	85-69
Wright State	88-61
Penn State	98-73
@Indiana (L)	58-59
Northwestern	84-53
Wisconsin	69-59
Ohio State	71-56
@Northwestern	74-58
@Ohio State (L)	55-64
@Michigan	91-64
Purdue	72-55
@Illinois (L)	66-77
@Minnesota	94-83
Iowa	94-70
Indiana	66-57
@Penn State	76-59
@Wisconsin	51-47
Michigan	78-57
###Penn State (L)	63-65
####Alabama State	69-35
####Fresno State	81-65
####Gonzaga	77-62
####Temple	69-62
####Arizona	61-80

#Spartan Coca-Cola Classic in East Lansing, MI
##ACC/Big Ten Challenge in East Lansing, MI
###Big Ten Tournament in Chicago
####NCAA Tournament
@Road Games

BLUE RIBBON ANALYSIS

BACKCOURT	B+
BENCH/DEPTH	D
FRONTCOURT	B-
INTANGIBLES	B

Rebuilding, reloading, call it what you want. But this will definitely be a transition year for the Spartans. They are basically looking at two stars, Taylor and Torbert—the latter of whom has yet to play a collegiate game—and a thin supporting cast filled with more questions than answers. It's still enough to keep them in the upper half of the Big Ten, but the run of four consecutive league titles is likely over.

But that's not to say Izzo's mini-dynasty is dead. It didn't end with the loss of cornerstones Cleaves and Peterson, and it probably won't end as long as he's the coach. But he is the first to admit that after failing to properly prepare for losing Richardson and Randolph so soon, he needs to adjust to the times.

"It used to be you signed a great class, you said to yourself, 'Whatever else we do, for the next four years we have a chance to be really good.' Now it's different," he said. "It makes recruiting harder. But at least now I can start preparing for it a little better. I'm not sure I did a good job of it last year."

Izzo did end up landing replacements for Randolph and Richardson, if a year late. A pair of Top 30 prospects that play their positions, 6-10 Paul Davis (Rochester Hills, Mich.) and 6-4 Maurice Ager (Detroit), will arrive next fall. If he can keep Taylor and Torbert too, the Spartans' talent level should return quickly to form.

As for this year, it will all depend on what, if anything, he gets from previous non-factors like Wolfe, Ballinger and Andreas, and if Anagonye can take his game to the next level. Izzo talks about the need for the team to "get better every week," to take its lumps early against the non-conference titans but turn the experiences into a positive come January.

But he also looks around his league and sees teams that made out much better in the annual NBA defection derby. Frank Williams came back to Illinois. Luke Recker and Reggie Evans returned to Iowa. Kirk Haston left, but Jared Jeffries stayed at Indiana. All of which leaves the Spartans a non-favorite for the first time in four years.

(S.M.)

 Ole Miss 29

LOCATION	Oxford, MS
CONFERENCE	Southeastern (Western)

LAST SEASON	27-8 (.771)
CONFERENCE RECORD	11-5 (1st)
STARTERS LOST/RETURNING	3/2
NICKNAME	Rebels
COLORS	Cardinal Red & Navy Blue
HOMECOURT	Tad Smith Coliseum (8.700)
COACH	Rod Barnes (Ole Miss '88)
RECORD AT SCHOOL	66-35 (3 years)
CAREER RECORD	66-35 (3 years)
ASSISTANTS	Marc Dukes (Mississippi College '73)
	Eric Bozeman (Arkansas Tech '81)
	Wayne Brent (Northeast Louisiana '89)
TEAM WINS (last 5 years)	20-22-20-19-27
RPI (last 5 years)	48-16-46-66-8
2000-01 FINISH	Lost in NCAA Sweet 16.

COACH AND PROGRAM

It's a good thing preseason predictions mean absolutely nothing. If they did, basketball coaches at Mississippi would be coming and going like pizza delivery men at an all-day, all-night fraternity party.

Since the SEC expanded to 12 teams during the 1991-92 season, the Rebels have been picked at the bottom or near the bottom of the Western Division every year. But what's real and what's perceived are two entirely different things.

Rod Barnes, in his fourth season as the Ole Miss head coach, has taken what his former boss, Rob Evans, started and elevated it to an even loftier perch.

Last season was a magical ride. The Rebels won a school-record 27 games, garnered the program's third SEC West title in the last five years and went to the Sweet 16 for the first time in school history.

Keep in mind, too, that Ole Miss has never been confused for hoops nirvana. The interest, facilities and tradition leave much to be desired.

Don't tell that to Barnes, who has his alma mater in pretty exclusive company. Mississippi is one of only three SEC teams that has made five consecutive postseason appearances (four NCAA and one NIT). The other two are Arkansas and Kentucky.

During the last five years, Ole Miss' three SEC West titles are the most of any team in that division and tied for tops in the conference overall with Kentucky.

"What we've strived to do here is build a total program," said Barnes, who moved from assistant to head coach after Evans bolted for Arizona State. "Winning breeds winning. We've made a commitment here that we want to be one of the best teams in the country. Every day, we've had that commitment from the players and the coaches.

"But for the first time, we're getting that commitment in every aspect—players, coaches and the administration. It makes a big difference."

The smartest thing the Ole Miss brass did was to lock up Barnes to a new four-year contract after last season. It was a good thing, too, because South Carolina, Michigan and Tennessee all sent feelers his way. South Carolina even made official contact.

Barnes said his new financial package will place him financially in the middle of the pack among SEC coaches.

"Now that we've established our program, we've got to start taking steps to take the program to another level," said Barnes, the 2001 Naismith Coach of the Year. "We're expecting to have a good season next year, every year. I feel the same way about other things. I want improvements on the coliseum this year, next year, the year after that. There's something you can do all the time."

The first wave of upgrades on Tad Smith Coliseum should be completed in time for this season. The current seats will be replaced by upholstered, chair-back seats—all in blue—and capacity will increase from 8,135 to 8,700.

In addition, a large video board will be installed, as well as two full display scoreboards and a state-of-the-art sound system.

As Barnes has noted, Ole Miss drew as few as 3,000 fans for some non-conference games last year. He wants to see the fan support match what the Rebels have done on the court.

"I'm trying to get our fans to understand the importance of not only buying season tickets, but also coming to every game," Barnes said. "We need to fill the coliseum up every time we play. That's what happens at a lot of other places. We're not talking about 20,000. We're talking about 8,000 or 9,000.

"Until we do that, we can't say we're there yet. To

have 13th-ranked Oklahoma State come in here on a Saturday night and only draw 5,500, that tells me we're not there yet ... We've got to get all of our people coming to the games in larger numbers."

The Rebels return just two starters from last season's Sweet 16 team, but seven players from the regular rotation a year ago are back. Barnes believes deeply in playing a lot of players, too.

What's more, he has proven in his three years at Ole Miss that there's a certain continuity about the program. When Evans left, there was no drop off. The system now is pretty much the same as it was under Evans.

"We made a few changes, but not many," Barnes said. "At the great programs, like Duke and North Carolina and Kansas, when one of the coaches leaves or retires, it's handed over to someone else in the family.

"When I took over for Rob, I was very familiar with the system and the transition was much easier. I can't say I will always be at Ole Miss. You never say never. But the thing that excites me the most is that I know beyond a shadow of a doubt that this program, in all aspects, is better than it was when I got here."

2001-2002 SCHEDULE

Nov.	15-18	#Top of the World Classic
	25	@Kansas State
	28	Morris Brown
Dec.	1	George Mason
	3	Louisiana-Monroe
	7	Memphis
	16	*Tennessee-Martin
	21-22	##Sun Bowl Classic
	29	Arkansas-Pine Bluff
Jan.	2	David Lipscomb
	6	@Tennessee
	9	Auburn
	12	Mississippi State
	15	@Kentucky
	19	@Arkansas
	23	LSU
	26	South Carolina
	30	Vanderbilt
Feb.	2	@Georgia
	6	@Alabama
	9	Arkansas
	13	@Auburn
	16	Florida
	23	@Mississippi State
	27	@LSU
March	2	Alabama
	7-10	###SEC Tournament

@Road Games
*DeSoto Civic Center, Southaven, MS
#Fairbanks, AK (vs. Bowling Green, first round; also Alaska-Fairbanks, Butler, Delaware, Radford, Washington, Wichita State)
##El Paso, TX (vs. IUPUI, first round; also Mississippi Valley State and UTEP)
###Georgia Dome, Atlanta, GA

STARTERS NOT RETURNING

PG-JASON FLANIGAN (6-1, 7.1 ppg, 3.1 rpg, 2.2 apg, 0.8 spg, 27.2 minutes, .389 FG, .355 3PT, .679 FT). The Rebels' starter at point guard in all 35 games last season, Flanigan was part of a one-two punch running the club that also included Jason Harrison.

Flanigan and Harrison—high school teammates at Parkview High School in Little Rock, Ark.—made each other better. Flanigan was the starter, while Harrison provided instant energy off the bench.

Flanigan's specialty was his defense. He was a tenacious defender, one of the best in the SEC, and he also took care of the ball. He had 41 assists compared to 24 turnovers in SEC games last season and was very good in transition.

Like Lockhart, Flanigan exuded the kind of on-court presence that Barnes demands. He got the ball to the right people, always guarded the other team's best perimeter scorer and played within the framework of what Barnes wanted.

SF-JASON HOLMES (6-5, 6.3 ppg, 2.6 rpg, 1.8 apg, 0.9 spg, 21.4 minutes, .376 FG, .347 3PT, .769 FT). The third senior in the starting lineup last season, Holmes split time with Aaron Harper at one of the wing positions.

Holmes wasn't a prolific scorer, but he was capable of big nights. He poured in a career-high 26 points against Alabama in the regular-season finale as Ole

Miss blasted the Crimson Tide, 105-71, and won the SEC's Western Division title outright.

Holmes recovered from a miserable junior season to make a significant contribution last year. He was one of the Rebels' best three-point shooters and made his share of big shots. It was a far cry from his junior season when he went 3-for-42 at the end of the season. He had reported to Ole Miss in terrible playing shape that year after transferring from Southwest Mississippi Community College.

C-RAHIM LOCKHART (6-8, 13 ppg, 8.1 rpg, 0.9 apg, 1.4 spg, 1.4 bpg, 27.3 minutes, .554 FG, .478 FT). Lockhart was the Rebels' enforcer last season, and at times, carried the team on his massive shoulders.

At 6-8 and 255 pounds, Lockhart was an intimidating presence defensively and never shy about going to the boards. His offense also came around to the point where he was en effective insider scorer.

Lockhart led Ole Miss in scoring, rebounding, steals and blocked shots last season. He was a first-team All-SEC selection by the coaches and a second-team All-SEC selection by the media.

As good as he was on the court last season, Lockhart will probably be missed most when it comes to leadership. He was the guy the younger players looked to any time things got tight. His mental toughness rubbed off on the rest of the team.

"We won't have that one strong leader like Rahim, which is why we will have to get it from several different people," Barnes said.

The one area where Lockhart struggled was the free-throw line. He shot just .478 from the stripe, making him an inviting target to foul in the waning minutes of close games. Lockhart was also foul prone, fouling out of five games last season.

OTHERS NOT RETURNING

C-JOHN ENGSTROM (7-0, 1.0 ppg, 0.8 rpg, 0.4 apg, 4.4 minutes, .556 FG). Engstrom played sparingly last season. He saw action in only two SEC games, starting the final game of his career against Alabama on Senior Day.

Knee injuries plagued Engstrom throughout his career. He underwent two different surgeries on his right knee, including one to repair an ACL tear.

PROJECTED STARTERS

PG-JASON HARRISON (5-5, 155 lbs., SR, #11, 7.1 ppg, 1.9 rpg, 2.9 apg, 1.3 spg, 21.3 minutes, .362 FG, .379 3PT, .833 FT, Parkview HS/Little Rock, Ark.). He might be one of the smallest players in college basketball, but Harrison clearly has one of the biggest hearts. The Rebels' lone senior, Harrison will take over the point-guard duties on a full-time basis now that Flanigan is gone. Suffice to say Barnes has supreme confidence in Harrison, who has a way of making plays when the Rebels need them most.

"Certain people have that knack of getting you to a certain point and then getting you over that point," Barnes said. "I've never coached a guy or played with a guy who's made as many big plays in crucial situations as Jason has. Sometimes you can't figure out how it happens. It just happens."

The impressive thing about Harrison last season was that he had a knack of making big shots even when he was struggling with his shot. Case in point: His clutch three-pointer against Notre Dame with 46 seconds remaining to propel Ole Miss into the Sweet 16.

"We've all seen guys who don't make shots, and then right when they need to, they make them," Barnes said. "It's like a guy in baseball. He may not hit a lot of home runs, but hits the one to win the game. That's the way Jason has been. Against Notre Dame, he had not been shooting the ball well. But at the biggest moment and at the biggest time, he knocks down the big three."

Harrison, accustomed to taunts from opposing fans concerning his diminutive 5-5 frame, is the ultimate pest with his on-the-ball defense. He's also adept at penetrating defenses and has handed out 100 assists in each of his last two seasons. The last Ole Miss player to do that was Barnes during the 1987 and '88 seasons.

"I just go out and do whatever I have to do to help my team win," Harrison said. "I really don't worry about what other people say. As long as my team wins, I'm happy."

SG-DAVID SANDERS (6-3, 185 lbs., JR, #15, 6.9 ppg, 2.7 rpg, 1.9 apg, 0.8 spg, 23.1 minutes, .503 FG, .219 3PT, .669 FT, Tallahassee CC/Tallahassee, Fla. and Provine HS/Jackson, Miss.). Barnes believes the

strength of his team this season will be on the wings. He has a nucleus of returning perimeter players who've played quality minutes.

Sanders is back at the shooting guard spot after starting 28 games there last season. He's an explosive player who needs to be a little more consistent with his shot. He shot just .219 from three-point range a year ago.

What Sanders does best is get to the hoop. One of the top athletes on the team, he's ultra quick and excels in the open court. He's also one of the team's top finishers on the fast break.

On the defensive end, Sanders will inherit Flanigan's role of guarding the other team's best perimeter scorer. He blocked a shot with seven seconds remaining last season to seal the NCAA victory against Notre Dame.

"David Sanders is ahead of everyone right now at the two-spot, but the good thing is that we have a lot of guys there," Barnes said. "We could play a ton of people on the wings this year if we wanted to, and a lot of it will depend on how the game is going and who's playing well.

"One night, Sanders may get 22 or 23 minutes. The next time, he may get 16 minutes, especially if Emmanuel Wade is playing well. We have some options there, which is nice."

Sanders, a member of the Rebels' "Provine Posse," played his first season at Ole Miss last year. He attended Northwest Mississippi Community College in 1999-2000, but did not play basketball. During the 1998-99 season, Sanders played at Tallahassee (Fla.) Community College.

SF-AARON HARPER (6-7, 205 lbs., SO, #5, 9.2 ppg, 2.9 rpg, 2.0 apg, 0.8 spg, 23.1 minutes, .352 FG, .354 3PT, .750 FT, Provine HS/Jackson, Miss.). The Rebels will never be known for their abundance of jump shooters, but Harper gives them great range from the perimeter.

He was third on the team in scoring last season and returns as the Rebels' top three-point threat. His size (6-7) makes him a difficult cover, especially when he has his stroke going from the perimeter.

Although he didn't make the SEC's All-Freshman team a year ago, Harper probably had the numbers. His 63 three-pointers were the third most for a single season in Ole Miss history.

As a rule last year, when Harper had it going offensively, so did the Rebels. They were 15-1 when he scored in double figures. He will become the first or second option on offense this season.

"The thing about Aaron is that he doesn't fear shooting it," Barnes said. "He's not one of those guys who misses two or three shots and then gets hesitant about shooting. If he's open and he's got room, he's going to shoot. Shooters have to have that kind of confidence."

Barnes said Harper, who started 15 games, was even better in practice a year ago.

"I hope that's because he was only a freshman," Barnes said. "We had some practices where he was unbelievable. I want to see him bring that to more of the games. If so, it's going to open up lanes for other people because they won't be able to leave him."

Harper's top-scoring game last season came against Tennessee in the regular season when he drilled five three-pointers and finished with 23 points. He also scored 21 points against the Vols in the SEC Tournament.

Harper originally signed with Ole Miss in November of 1998, but didn't qualify academically. He re-signed in 1999 and was able to enroll in January of 2000. He practiced with the team during the final part of that season, which helped his development last year.

"Sitting out was a big plus for me because I believe I would have just lost a year," Harper said.

PF-JUSTIN REED (6-8, 225 lbs., SO, #23, 11 ppg, 5.9 rpg, 0.8 apg, 1.3 spg, 24.6 minutes, .478 FG, .549 FT, Provine HS/Jackson, Miss.). Reed came to Ole Miss last year as perhaps the most heralded recruit in school history. He did nothing to dispel that distinction on the court.

Like Sanders and Harper, Reed also hails from Provine High School in Jackson, Miss. He and Harper combined to form the best one-two freshman punch in the league last season.

Reed started in 32-of-35 games and rarely played like a freshman. He was voted the 2001 SEC Freshman of the Year by the coaches and the SEC Newcomer of the Year by the Associated Press.

"He's got a chance to be a great player," Barnes said. "He's the kind of player you win with and can cause confusion for teams in a lot of different ways."

Reed spent the summer playing for Team USA in the World University Games. Barnes was an assistant on that staff, headed up by Penn State's Jerry Dunn.

"Justin's one of those guys that we'll have to do a lot of things this year that go through him," Barnes said. "That can be a concern because it's the first time we've asked a sophomore to carry the bulk of the team. But Justin has everything it takes to be that kind of player. He's very coachable and has a great work ethic. He works on his game and plays the game with great intensity."

As an example, Reed averaged 200 outside shots a day this summer. His perimeter game a year ago wasn't what Barnes or Reed wanted.

Barnes said Reed is a cross between former Rebels Ansu Sesay and Keith Carter in terms of natural ability and work ethic.

"Justin just has that killer instinct where he's going to do whatever he has to to beat you," Barnes said.

Reed was a Parade All-American in high school and rated by most recruiting services among the top 25 prospects in the country.

C-JOHN GUNN (6-10, 250 lbs., JR, #31, 2.8 ppg, 1.2 rpg, 0.2 apg, 6.8 minutes, .541 FG, .926 FT, Oxford HS/Oxford, Miss.). Gunn will get the first crack at replacing Lockhart in the post. But in reality, Barnes will look to three players to fill that void—Derric Allen, Richard Kirklin and Gunn.

Barnes likes Gunn's skill level. He just doesn't have much experience. Versatile enough to play center or power forward, Gunn is pretty mobile for a big man.

"He plays better facing the basket than he does with his back to the basket," Barnes said. "He's a good free-throw shooter and a good shooter from 12-to-15 feet. He has a lot of offensive skills, but needs to get better on defense."

Gunn was behind to start last season. He missed the second half of his freshman season with mononucleosis. That illness slowed his progress in the off-season.

"The good thing is that we're not going to ask one person to do it in the post for us," Barnes said. "We'll do it by committee. When we need offense, it might be John. When we need a more athletic guy in there, it might be Richard. If we need more power or defense or more toughness, it might be Derrick.

"We've got three different types of players there."

KEY RESERVES

G-JUSTIN JOHNSON (6-0, 185 lbs., FR, #12, 20.6 ppg, 4.2 rpg, 3.8 apg, Seventy-First HS/Fayetteville, N.C.). Barnes worried very little about his point-guard position a year ago. He had two—Harrison and Flanigan.

Harrison, as seasoned and clutch as he is, will need help. That's where Johnson comes in.

"Justin has to establish himself there, and we need that to happen fairly quickly," Barnes said. "We're not asking him to be the go-to guy, but we do need him to be an SEC-caliber point guard."

That's a tall order for a freshman, but Johnson has the credentials. He led his high school team to a 27-2 record last year.

"Justin's a natural scorer and shoots the three well," said Bernie Poole, who coached Johnson at Seventy-First High School. "He also shoots the 15-footer about as well as anyone, and he's gotten better.

"He's a real physical kid, built kind of like a running back. He was a great leader, and the younger players really looked up to him. I believe he would have gotten a lot of attention [from other schools] if he hadn't signed early."

Johnson signed with the Rebels during the early signing period in November of 2000.

G-EMMANUEL WADE (6-3, 185 lbs., JR, #32, 4.4 ppg, 1.8 rpg, 0.9 apg, 0.4 spg, 14.8 minutes, .424 FG, .333 3PT, Lee HS/Marianna, Ark.). Wade played well for the Rebels to close last season. He had a pair of three-pointers in the NCAA Tournament that were huge. The first one tied the Iona game at 70 with 1:56 remaining, and Ole Miss hung on to win, 72-70. Wade finished with a career-high 19 points in that game. He also connected from three-point range to break a tie at 51 against Notre Dame with 4:04 remaining. The Rebels won, 59-56.

"Emmanuel played well in the postseason last year," Barnes said. "He has a bunch of potential. He just hasn't been as aggressive offensively as I would need for him to be. I think that could happen this season. He's a junior and has been working very hard. The more we get

out of him this season, the better we'll be."

Wade started five games last season. He's a slasher to the basket who also defends well. He and Sanders should complement each other well at the shooting guard spot.

C-DERRICK ALLEN (6-8, 230 lbs., JR, #40, 19.1 ppg, 9.7 rpg, Southern Union State CC/Wadley, Ala. and Gadsden HS/Gadsden, Ala.). Physically, Allen is probably the closest thing the Rebels have to Lockhart. He's big, physical and not adverse to mixing it up in the middle.

Of course, Allen has yet to play in his first SEC game. He did not play last season after battling tendinitis in his knee. Allen received a medical red-shirt for the 2000-01 season and still has two years of eligibility remaining.

Allen transferred to Ole Miss from Southern Union State (Ala.) Community College. He knows the Rebels' system, though, having practiced with the team last season.

"He doesn't make a lot of mistakes and is always attacking," Barnes said. "He's not a great athlete, but a good athlete. The thing he does, though, is fight you to the very end."

In some ways, Allen reminds Barnes of former Georgia post player Anthony Evans with his ability to maneuver for points inside. If Allen can provide the same kind of contributions Evans did for Georgia, Ole Miss won't miss Lockhart as much as some might think.

F-RICHARD KIRKLIN (6-9, 210 lbs., JR, #45, 1.9 ppg, 0.9 rpg, 0.2 apg, 6.6 minutes, .431 FG, .346 3PT, .667 FT, Watson Chapel HS/Pine Bluff, Ark.). The most athletic of the Rebels' post players, Kirklin could also play power forward if needed. He runs the floor well and can also defend on the perimeter.

He just hasn't played very much and is still developing physically. He spent the summer playing on the Planet Basketball squad that toured New Zealand.

"He will be more of a defender and shot blocker for us," Barnes said. "He can shoot the three, which makes him difficult to defend. He'll give us a guy out there who's very athletic."

F-CHRIS RHODES (6-7, 215 lbs, FR, #33, 20.4 ppg, 10.7 rpg, 1.9 bpg, Westbury Christian HS/Stafford, Texas). A spring signee, Rhodes adds to what Barnes thinks will be a deep rotation on the wing. A true small forward, Rhodes knows a thing or two about winning. He was a member of four consecutive state championship teams at Westbury Christian.

"I think he's a guy who can help us immediately with his ability to get rebounds, play strong around the basket and defend," Barnes said. "He's an athletic guy who plays extremely hard."

Barnes sees a lot of the same qualities in Rhodes that he saw in Reed at this time last year.

F-JOSH HAYES (6-7, 195 lbs., SO, #30, 2 ppg, 0.6 rpg, 0.2 apg, 5 minutes, .526 FG, .429 3PT, .667 FT, Parkview HS/Little Rock, Ark.). Hayes is another player who could help at either shooting guard or small forward. He had his moments last year after sitting out the 1999-2000 season with a stress fracture in his right foot. Hayes increased his strength and gained more confidence as last season progressed. Barnes loves his versatility.

"He's another one of the reasons I like our wings so much," Barnes said. "The wing spots are where we'll have to win a lot of ballgames. We feel like our two, three and four people can match up with anybody."

OTHER NEWCOMERS

G-JONATHAN LOE (6-3, 175 lbs. FR, #44, 20.9 ppg, 3.6 apg, 3.4 spg, Bartlett High School/Memphis, Tenn.). Loe has the makings of a combo guard capable of playing both positions. He probably leans, though, to being more of a shooting guard. He led his Bartlett High School team to the Tennessee Class 3A state championship last year. Loe was among the three finalists for Mr. Basketball in Class 3A.

"We'll start him off the ball, but he could make the adjustment to the point," Barnes said. "We just want to start him off where he's most comfortable, and that's trying to create and score."

F-KENDRICK FOX (6-7, 195 lbs, FR, #4, 15.2 ppg, 7.4 rpg, 2.1 bpg, Lafayette High School/Oxford, Miss.). Fox suffered an ACL knee injury in October last year as a high school senior, but played in 16 games without surgery. He later underwent surgery in March, meaning that it could take him a while to get all the way back.

Barnes sees Fox developing into the kind of player who can score from the perimeter and also take his man inside. On the defensive end, Fox is also an accomplished shot blocker.

"He's really different than anybody else on our team, a guy who can do a lot of different things," Barnes said.

QUESTIONS

Void in the post? Barnes is hoping to go the three-headed route in replacing Lockhart in the post. Lockhart was the heart and soul of the team last season. It's doubtful that five players could replace him when you start adding up everything he meant to the Rebels.

Leadership? Lockhart and Flanigan made it their team a year ago. Whose team will it be this season?

Depth at point guard? The Rebels are in big trouble if something should happen to Harrison. Barnes is counting on Johnson being an immediate factor. But leaning on freshman point guards in the SEC is risky business.

Long range bombing? Harper potentially is a great perimeter shooter. He needs help, though. Guys like Sanders, Wade and Hayes need to knock down more jumpers this season.

ANSWERS

Defense, defense, defense! With Barnes, it's pretty simple. If you don't play defense, you don't play. The Rebels play the kind of in-your-face defense that teams hate playing against.

Strength in numbers! Barnes is optimistic that different people will step up big on different nights.

"Our first five isn't going to beat a lot of other people's first five," Barnes said. "But we're going to play nine and 10 men, pressure you and try to force you to do what you're not comfortable doing. And over the period of the game, we feel like we've got different people who can make a play to help us win."

Justin Reed! Don't be surprised if Reed emerges as one of the best players in the SEC this season. He has all the tools, not to mention the body, and the kind of drive you can't teach.

OLE MISS 2000-2001 RESULTS

Arkansas-Pine Bluff	98-47
Sam Houston State	71-65
@Virginia Commonwealth	88-84
Louisiana-Monroe	76-62
Oklahoma	60-55
Kansas State	60-46
@Memphis	64-56
Southeastern Louisiana	58-46
Troy State	92-65
#Southern Illinois	70-66
#USC	84-83
#Iowa State (L)	68-73
Morris Brown	94-59
@Vanderbilt	81-68
@Arkansas	53-48
Georgia (L)	66-70
@Alabama (L)	63-82
Kentucky	65-55
@Mississippi State (L)	69-79
Arkansas	84-73
@Auburn	74-70
LSU	50-33
Tennessee	87-71
Mississippi State	51-48
@South Carolina	67-61
@Florida	55-75
Auburn	64-62
@LSU (L)	77-78
Alabama	105-71
##Tennessee	86-73
##Florida	74-69
##Kentucky (L)	55-77
###Iona	72-70
###Notre Dame	59-56
###Arizona (L)	56-66

#Pearl Harbor Invitational in Laie, HI
##SEC Tournament in Nashville
##NCAA Tournament
@Road Games

BLUE RIBBON ANALYSIS

BACKCOURT	B-
BENCH/DEPTH	B+
FRONTCOURT	B
INTANGIBLES	B+

Barnes thinks Ole Miss has safely established itself as one of the top 50 basketball programs in the country. His goal now is to make the Rebels a top 30 team.

"There is a group of top 15 programs in the country," Barnes said. "They can recruit anybody anytime. Everybody knows them. The next 15 are schools that can compete with those schools ... That's what we're trying to establish, that top 30 position for this program.

"The top 30 programs have a chance every year to go deep into the NCAA Tournament."

The Rebels are gunning for their sixth consecutive postseason appearance. Even without Lockhart and Flanigan, another trip to the NCAA Tournament seems well within their reach, especially if Reed, Harper and Sanders develop the way Barnes thinks they will.

Moreover, no other coach in the SEC gets as much out of their players as Barnes, the ultimate overachiever when he played for the Rebels.

"I've always told them that the little things are what count," Barnes said. "That's the way I tried to play. I wasn't going to out-jump anybody. But as long as you take good shots, shoot a good percentage and play as a team, you're going to win a lot of games.

"Our kids have bought into what we're doing."

(C.L.)

Fresno State 30

LOCATION	Fresno, CA
CONFERENCE	Western Athletic
LAST SEASON	26-7 (.788)
CONFERENCE RECORD	13-3 (1st)
STARTERS LOST/RETURNING	2/3
NICKNAME	Bulldogs
COLORS	Red & White
HOMECOURT	Selland Arena (10,220)
COACH	Jerry Tarkanian (Fresno State '55)
RECORD AT SCHOOL	134-65 (6 years)
CAREER RECORD	759-187 (30 years)
ASSISTANTS	Danny Tarkanian (UNLV '84)
	Wil Hooker (Fresno State '92)
	John Welsh (UNLV '87)
TEAM WINS (last 5 years)	20-21-21-24-26
RPI (last 5 years)	61-76-71-25-20
2000-01 FINISH	Lost in NCAA second round.

COACH AND PROGRAM

For those who had Fresno State shooting the moon at this season's NCAA Tournament, they can only hope the Bulldogs' re-entry into the Earth's atmosphere doesn't burn off any more key pieces as veteran head coach Jerry Tarkanian tries to right the ship.

He knew all the talk this summer of having the most talented team since his 1990 national championship squad at Nevada-Las Vegas was just that—a lot of talk.

True, the Bulldogs have a legitimate lottery pick in center Melvin Ely. And small forward Chris Jefferies' perimeter game is a perfect complement to the big man underneath.

But what caused Fresno State to fall off the radar was the loss of point guards Tito Maddox and Nick Irvin, and shooting guard Dennis Nathan. They won't return for a variety of reasons, leaving Tarkanian's backcourt suddenly skinny.

Transfer Chris Sandy said all along he would beat Maddox where it counts—on the court. Now, his only concern is learning to live life as a starter without having to really earn it.

Maddox was shown the door during the dog days of summer after it was confirmed he had accepted gifts from an agent. At the time, Maddox believed the hype that he was ready for the NBA. He even went so far as to declare his willingness to enter the draft.

This proved a costly decision for Maddox and Tarkanian. The Los Angeles resident eventually saw the light and decided to return to school. But by then his transgressions were complete. It was only a matter of time before Tarkanian had to cut Maddox loose.

To compound the problem, Irvin, perhaps the best passer on the team, wasn't academically sound. His senior leadership will be missed almost as much as the depth he provides. Tarkanian already spent the summer figuring a way to replace the dearly departed Demetrius Porter.

Last season, the senior shifted to the two spot after

Maddox became academically eligible after eight games. It was a seamless transition that allowed the multi-faceted Maddox to strut his stuff.

Problems occurred late into the WAC season when Maddox decided to take on a more dominant role. It upset the balance Tarkanian had worked so hard to achieve during the season and resulted in second-round exits at the WAC and NCAA tournaments.

Tarkanian survived a key battle after Ely graduated in time to earn an extra year of eligibility. The long time head coach also had a solid, if small, recruiting class, proving he can still attract talent.

The problem comes when so many incidents off the court detract from what's happening on it. Had Maddox been an isolated incident since Tarkanian took over the program, it wouldn't be so problematic. But it wasn't an isolated incident.

Tarkanian has put out his share of fires since returning to his alma mater. Perceived scandal, fair or not, seems to follow Tarkanian wherever he goes. Many believe this will be his final year Fresno State.

Next season, the Bulldogs will be in a new arena, and the feeling around this thriving community on the edge of the desert is Tarkanian can be replaced. They thought the same thing at UNLV and look what has happened there the last decade. A steady decline that Tarkanian once predicted.

"People here think this school will thrive after I'm gone," Tark said shortly after securing his national championship with a 30-point win over Duke in 1990. "The Georgetown of the West. But they couldn't be more wrong. This program will struggle after I'm gone."

It's equally hard to imagine that players such as Ely, Jefferies, Maddox and current Dallas Maverick guard Courtney Alexander would work their way to Fresno State without Tarkanian, new arena or not.

But if this is his last go-round, look for Fresno State to remain the class act of the Western Athletic Conference. The Bulldogs have enough talent in Ely and Jefferies to more than dominate the other nine teams in the league.

"The one thing that can get you in this league is the travel," Tarkanian said. "There's no other conference in the country that has to play in San Jose on Thursday and Honolulu on Saturday.

"We also had two-day trips to SMU and TCU, or Houston and then Tulsa. It absolutely amazes me what these kids have to go through on the road."

But for Fresno State to hold the national attention it thinks it deserves, road wins at such outposts as Ruston, La., Boise, Idaho, and Honolulu are a must. Fresno State also has to do well in the preseason NIT.

The Bulldogs open at home against Montana State. Win there and Fresno State will take on either Wyoming or talented Southern California. That winner advances to the preseason NIT final four in New York's Madison Square Garden.

"This is a great way to start the season," Tarkanian said. "It's exciting for our players and our fans. If you do well here, you can get some recognition nationally. We played in the preseason NIT several times when I was at Vegas and it was always a great experience for our players."

Tark would have liked to have had Maddox with him, although there are several coaches around the WAC who believe the sophomore was a distraction. With him gone, and Sandy more than just an adequate fit, Fresno State might wind up a better team.

And that's not good news for the WAC. Barring any more last-second transactions, the Bulldogs could make it two titles in a row.

2001-2002 SCHEDULE

Nov.	13	#Montana State
	28	@Pacific
	30	##Fresno State Invitational
Dec.	1	##Fresno State Invitational
	4	San Francisco
	8	@San Diego State
	11	@California
	15	Pepperdine
	20	Savannah State
	27	@Hawaii
	29	@San Jose State
Jan.	3	Rice
	5	Tulsa
	12	@Nevada
	17	@Boise State
	19	@UTEP
	24	SMU
	26	Louisiana Tech
	31	@Tulsa
Feb.	2	@Rice
	7	Nevada
	10	Oklahoma State
	14	UTEP
	16	Boise State
	21	@Louisiana Tech
	23	@SMU
	28	San Jose State
March	2	Hawaii
	5-9	WAC Tournament

@Road Games
#Preseason NIT (if Fresno State wins, it will play Southern Cal or Wyoming on Nov. 14 or 16; Semifinals and final on Nov. 21-23 at Madison Square Garden, NY)
##Fresno, CA (vs. Air Force first round; also Montana State, UC Riverside)
###Reynolds Center, Tulsa, OK

STARTERS NOT RETURNING

PG-TITO MADDOX (6-4, 13.5 ppg, 5.8 rpg, 8.0 apg, 1.6 spg, 0.2 bpg, 32.2 minutes, .391 FG, .703 FT). If there's a better judge of talent in the WAC than Tarkanian, the other league coaches would like to know who he is. No matter what else you say about the 30-year veteran head coach, when he sees someone he believes is ready to take the next step, he's the first one to tell them.

So when everybody and his mother started talking up Maddox midway through last season and how one year of college should turn the NBA trick, Tark was one of the first to disagree.

Talented, perhaps. A lottery pick, no, and that was one reason Maddox decided to come back and play another season in Fresno. Instead, Maddox accepted a gift from an agent, forcing Tarkanian to cut him loose and play this season without him.

What does Tark lose? Well, only the best assists player in the WAC who could create off the dribble. Not a bad shooter, Maddox took it upon himself to prove to everyone he was great from downtown, but that sadly was not the case.

"You saw how Fresno State faded down the stretch," one WAC coach said. "The chemistry was ruined. Maddox got outside his role and it hurt. They weren't nearly as good. Everybody filled Maddox's head with how great he was. I know it upset Tark because he became a distraction. Who knows? They may be better off without him."

Perhaps, but if Maddox had learned to fit back in and let big man Melvin Ely run the show from in low as he did the first part of his freshman season, then the Bulldogs could have got a lot farther in the postseason.

As it stands, the former first team All-CIF selection who was ranked among the top 10 guards in the country by several recruiting services in 1999 can only hope to catch on at the professional level.

"Obviously, we're disappointed at what happened,"" Tarkanian said. "It's unfortunate when something like this occurs. Kids have to be so careful these days who they associate with and what they do.""

Life goes on for Maddox and Tark, but each man suffers because of the loss.

PG-DEMETRIUS PORTER (6-0, 15.2 ppg, 2.3 rpg, 3.0 apg, 1.8 spg, 0.3 bpg, 31.2 minutes, .440 FG, .387 3PT, .771 FT). When last season began, everyone said Demetrius Porter was the finest point guard in the WAC. Not only could he distribute the basketball at all the right moments, he could pull up and shoot a jumper with anyone on the floor.

Then along comes Tito Maddox, who gains his eligibility a third of the way into the season. He immediately has an impact, forcing Porter to reassess his role with the team. True, he's a fierce competitor who plays unselfish basketball, but he doesn't have the same kind of flare or size of the more physically imposing Maddox.

But instead of fighting change, Porter played the counter-puncher for Maddox. When he was needed at the point, Porter took charge and directed traffic like a New York cop in rush hour. When Maddox ran the show, which was as often as not, Porter shifted easily to the two spot, providing a better outside percentage than Maddox and more points a game.

"Demetrius was a tremendous basketball player for us,"" Tarkanian said. "He was a playmaker who could hurt you from the outside. We're going to miss him on the floor."

Even more so, now that Maddox is gone. Porter and Maddox accounted for 11 assists and 29 points a game. They were good defensively, able to create fast break buckets with steals out front. Born in Fresno, Porter was the consummate guard. It's bad enough losing Maddox unexpectedly. Porter's departure will be missed even more. He wound up ranked second on the team in career steals, third in career assists, fourth in career three-point field goal attempts and goals, and second in career three-point percentage. Over the last two seasons, no player in the WAC has been ranked in the top 15 in as many statistical categories and yet he failed to receive at least second-team All-WAC in either season.

OTHERS NOT RETURNING

SG-DENNIS NATHAN (6-6, 5.6 ppg, 2.9 rpg, 2.3 apg, 17.0 minutes, .447 FG). Another guard bites the dust, and that's not a good thing for the Bulldogs. Nathan decided not to return over the summer.

It's a shame, for Nathan gave Fresno State a physical presence that allowed him to play guard and forward with equal success. Tark would have likely looked at him at the point had he returned.

True enough, he probably would have settled in at forward. But the Contra Costa (Calif.) College product could score from in close and provide the kind of depth needed when injuries or foul problems come along.

Nathan would have been a senior. His leadership would have come in handy, but Tarkanian can't worry about that now. He has to develop depth with the players he has at this point. Unfortunately for him, Nathan would have been a fine addition to what was once a deep and talent-laden ball club.

PG-SCOTTY GRAHAM (6-5, 0.0 ppg, 2.0 rpg, 1.0 apg, 7.0 minutes, .000 FG). This was another of Tark's finds who never had time to blossom within the system. Looking for playing time and not really seeing any, Graham was in for only one game. This year, Tark expects several walk-ons of Graham's caliber to take a chance on the Bulldog merry-go-round. The only bad thing here is Graham is one of several guards who have left the program over the last few months.

PG-NICK IRVIN (5-11, 234 1.9 ppg, 0.6 rpg, 1.8 apg, 6.6 minutes, .250 FG). Irvin isn't the prototype point man. He is short and rather stocky, but much like some of the other wayward guards who have left the program this year, Irvin had a special gift. He could pass the basketball in a crowd like no other on the squad. Sometimes, he'd make Tark flash that foolish grin of his with one of his specialties down low.

"The big guys loved him because he passed the basketball," Tarkanian said.

Irvin did lack consistency, but he could have provided valuable minutes off the bench, the kind needed to win championships. Perhaps Tark will find a suitable replacement for Irvin, perhaps not. He gave the team the much-needed chemistry for championship drives. He's another lost senior who could have helped make sure this talented team found its way to the big dance in March.

PROJECTED STARTERS

PG-CHRIS SANDY (6-2, 180 lbs., SR, 16.0 ppg, 3.0 rpg, 6.0 apg, Westark CC/Fort Smith, Ark. and New Town High School/Brooklyn, N.Y.). The signing of Chris Sandy proved to be a good one for Tarkanian, who lost five point guards along the way this summer. Sandy had hoped to prove his worth against the likes of Tito Maddox and Nick Irvin, but will have to be satisfied with practically being handed the starting job at the point.

Not that there's anything wrong with that. Tarkanian is confident Sandy will handle himself not only adequately, but perhaps as well as Maddox given the time and the circumstances needed to develop the A game.

"The kid is versatile and that's what we need," Tarkanian said. "He can play the point or the two spot. I like this kid. I really wanted him to be a part of this basketball team because of the things he said while we recruited him. He reminds me of Larry Johnson. He's that kind of kid."

Sandy's eligibility problems may leave him with only a single season with Tark, but it will be a crucial one if the head coach wants to exit the center stage in style. Signed in April, Sandy almost wound up in Hawaii before Tarkanian convinced him that Fresno was the place to be. Sandy is now glad he made the choice because he has a chance to make an immediate impact with a team that could advance deep into the NCAA Tournament.

"He gives our team great chemistry and leadership,"

Tarkanian said. "He's also a very smart basketball player. He can pass and shoot. We need him to step up right away now that Tito won't be with us."

Maturity will be a factor. For Sandy to fit into Fresno State's plans, he will have to learn on the fly. He believes he can do that. He just wishes Maddox were still around to help make the transition to Division I a smoother one than it will be now.

SG-TRAVIS DEMANBY (6-4, 200 lbs., JR, #22, 4.6 ppg, 1.3 rpg, 1.5 apg, 1.0 spg, 14.8 minutes, .455 FG, .411 3PT, .714 FT, South Medford HS/Medford, Ore.)

This is one guy who will see extended playing time, especially in the early going. How long he stays near the top of the leader board depends on how often he hits the outside shot. One thing DeManby can do is shoot. He hits from long range almost as well as he does from the free-throw line.

"But we also need him to be able to play defense better and pass the basketball," Tarkanian said. "In our offense, the guards have to force turnovers to create fast breaks. That's what we need out of those guys."

Tarkanian is a stickler for defense. He believes it's a good way to create easy baskets and get teams that like to play halfcourt out of their comfort zone. This is one area where DeManby needs work or risk losing a possible starting job.

SF-CHRIS JEFFERIES (6-8, 216 lbs., JR, #1, 15.6 ppg, 4.9 rpg, 1.9 apg, 1.5 spg, 0.9 bpg, 30.7 minutes, .442 FG, .368 3PT, .688 FT, Washington Union HS/Fresno, Calif. and Arkansas). If it weren't for Tito Maddox out front and Melvin Ely down low, perhaps swingman Chris Jefferies would be viewed as the leading actor on the stage.

Instead, the transfer from Arkansas who spent most of last season as the team's leading scorer often took a lesser part for the Bulldogs on game days.

But not any more. With Tito Maddox gone and a host of new guards scrambling to take his spot on the floor, Tarkanian will turn more to Jefferies to pick up the slack in scoring and rebounding.

Last year, Jefferies faded down the stretch, but still managed a healthy shooting percentage from in close and beyond the three-point stripe. If he can get into a rhythm, one that involves Ely and new point guard Chris Sandy, then Jefferies may finally fill the shoes of the departed Terrance Roberson.

"We're going to need everybody to play better," Tarkanian said. "Chris is a good player who can do a lot of things on both ends of the floor. He's a tremendous defender and can score from the outside and driving to the basket. I like the way he defends. That's what makes him special."

He was good enough to be among the top newcomers in the Southeastern Conference for the Razorbacks. He scored 16 points in an NCAA Tournament game as a freshman before deciding to leave Arkansas and join Tarkanian in California. If he regains the confidence he lost late last year, this could be a dangerous player. There isn't a better small forward in the WAC. Tark hopes he proves that this season.

PF-SHANNON SWILLIS (6-7, 221 lbs., SR, #3, 7.0 ppg, 6.2 rpg, 1.2 apg, 1.9 spg, 1.0 bpg, 27.3 minutes, .599 FG, .600 FT, Bullard HS/Long Beach, Calif. and Southern Cal). Swillis is one of those players who receives very little publicity but is the key component for the team. This power forward is one of those table setters, the guy who does the dirty work and cleans up after himself.

Tarkanian loves this guy, who was a star in high school who found out life at Southern California wasn't to his liking. So instead of sticking around and hoping for as many minutes as he could get, Swillis transferred out and joined Tark's troop at Fresno State.

"Shannon does a lot of things to help make Ely look good," Tarkanian said. "You need a strong guy in the post to go hard to the basket, get the loose balls and rebounds, and help your team make plays. We need him in there."

Swillis finished second to Ely in rebounding last year, almost grabbing as many boards as points. His job is not to score. More importantly, he tries to draw away the double teams from Ely or make a team pay for that strategy. This isn't a fancy ball player worried about how he looks rather than how effective he can be.

Teams with a lot of stars need players like Swillis. He doesn't have an ego, accepts the role he has been given and can score when it counts the most. Swillis played in 15 games with the Trojans as a freshman, but wasn't that much of a force. At Fresno State, he has found a comfortable home.

C-MELVIN ELY (6-10, 256 lbs., SR, #33, 16.0 ppg, 7.5 rpg, 1.4 apg, 0.9 spg, 2.7 bpg, 30.5 minutes, .583 FG, .671 FT, Thornton Township HS/Harvey, Ill.). If anyone doubted Melvin Ely's ability to compete with the game's best, they saw why Tarkanian calls him one of the best around during the World Games in China over the summer. Not only did Ely score consistently in the paint, he also rebounded with authority, leading the USA team in that category several times during the course of the competition.

Not only did Ely score on the court this summer, he also scored in the classroom in the spring. He graduated on time, meaning the non-qualifier out of high school earned another year of eligibility. Granted, Tark lost a battle when Tito Maddox was declared ineligible, but he won the war keeping Ely around for another season.

"He's one of the best big men in the country," Tarkanian said. "He's not only a good offensive player and rebounder, but he defends as well as anyone. He's a potential All-American who did a great job getting that extra year by performing in the classroom. He is a great, great kid."

He's also one outstanding basketball player who has blocked 273 shots in his collegiate career, averages nearly 60 percent from the field and has had to overcome leg injuries to become an instant NBA lottery pick next summer.

For now, the 2000-2001 WAC Player of the Year will be content bringing another championship to Fresno State. He did his part last year and figures to be counted on even more with all the comings and goings over the summer. He's a great player, but also the team leader on and off the court.

Entering his senior season in high school, he was rated the No. 1 center in the country by Athlon, No. 2 by BlueChip and No. 5 by Dick Vitale's. Sports Illustrated called him the most sought after player in the 1997 class.

KEY RESERVES

C-MUSTAFA AL-SAYYAD (6-9, 225 lbs., SO, #55, 2.3 ppg, 2.4 rpg, 0.2 apg, 0.2 spg, 0.5 bpg, 9.4 minutes, .558 FG, .531 FT, Washington College Academy/Limestone, Tenn.). How quickly this big man can develop could be one of the keys to Fresno State's success. Something of a project last year, Al-Sayyad is steadily improving under the tutelage of Melvin Ely. He doesn't have the knowledge or skills of the big center he spells from time to time, but he could potentially be one of the better backup big men in the league. He's had some problems learning the American game. But in time, he could be just what Tark is looking for should Ely be tired or get into foul trouble.

F-ANDREA BONA (6-6, 224 lbs, SR, #23, 1.4 ppg, 0.6 rpg, 0.4 apg, 0.0 spg, 0.0 bpg, 4.9 minutes, .400 FG, .429 3PT, .000 FT, Rome, Italy, Redemption Christian Academy). Playing behind Jefferies isn't exactly the way to make it into the starting lineup and that's OK with Tark.

Like Al-Sayyad for Ely, Tark would love Bona to develop into a solid backup player who could last on the floor more than just five minutes. True, Bona will never replace Jefferies. But he can provide some pivotal minutes in a close game. Last year, he played sparingly. That might change this season, given Fresno State's lack of proven depth. What Tark likes about Bona is his defensive skills.

F-NOEL FELIX (6-9, 220 lbs, JR, #12, 3.0 ppg, 2.9 rpg, 0.2 apg, 0.6 bpg, 0.4 spg, 12.6 minutes, .462 FG, .609 FT, Inglewood HS/Los Angeles, Calif.). Felix and Swillis share playing time because they are so much alike in body types and athletic skill. Felix still has the potential to make a bigger name for himself in this program. He is very athletic, with good size down low. He can position himself for rebounds and score from inside when called upon.

This could be a breakout season for Felix. Last year, Swillis saw the majority of playing time at the power-forward spot, but that could change if Felix continues to mold himself into a good Division I basketball player.

G-DAMON JACKSON (6-4, 196 lbs, SR, #4, 4.0 ppg, 1.9 rpg, 0.4 apg, 0.5 spg, 8.4 minutes, .373 FG, .328 3PT, .750 FT, Perris HS/Perris, Calif. and College of the Sequoias). If Travis DeManby winds up at the point behind Chris Sandy, Jackson could be the beneficiary of this move. Not an automatic starter by any means, what Jackson does provide is a lanky frame that can pass, shoot and defend.

With the recent defection of guards, Jackson has a chance to show why he was so effective at junior college under the watchful eye of Tarkanian's son, George, who isn't a bad basketball coach himself. Jackson has a decent eye from long range and can play the point if needed.

OTHER NEWCOMERS

F-HIRAM FULLER (6-9, 235 lbs., JR, Wabash (Ill.) Valley College, Modesto (Calif.) Junior College and Stadium High School/Tacoma, Wash.). Considered one of the top junior college recruits in the country, Tarkanian locked up the power forward last November. A year later, the former Modesto Junior College standout is even better than before, averaging in double figures in scoring and rebounding his two years through the junior college ranks. Many figure him to be the WAC's Newcomer of the Year and the perfect scoring and rebounding complement for center Melvin Ely.

He was rated the second-best power forward in the country last season by several national recruiting magazines and can only make Fresno State that much better. Tarkanian is very high on Fuller, who was one of only two recruits Tark signed in the off-season. The other was guard Chris Sandy.

"Hiram is a great player," Tarkanian said. "He can play at the next level. We've been after him for three years. To finally have him in our program is good for us because he's a great person. He's also big and strong, and tremendous in the post. We're very fortunate to have him."

QUESTIONS

Backcourt losses? The real question is how well the team responds to the loss of several guards during the off-season. Tito Maddox's departure is obviously a key.

Can Sandy run the point? Junior college transfer Chris Sandy could grow into those pointy shoes, but that figures to take some time. Who will replace those eight assists and 14 points a game Maddox contributed? Who has the defensive skills that produced nearly two steals a game? Even if Sandy fits in, what about some of the other young players hoping to crack the starting lineup?

ANSWERS

Defense! Tarkanian believes defense will go a long way in determining whether the Bulldogs are a viable team come NCAA Tournament time. Yes, they will win the WAC, with or without Maddox. But that isn't enough. Tark wants to advance beyond the second round of the Big Dance.

Melvin Ely! The big senior is one of the top centers in the game, able to impact games on either end of the court.

FRESNO STATE 2000-2001 RESULTS

#Saint Mary's	104-66
#St. Bonaventure (L)	74-87
##North Carolina State	82-63
San Diego State	70-62
Pacific	66-55
@San Francisco (L)	89-90
@Santa Clara	64-51
UAB	87-67
###Toledo	88-72
###Louisiana-Lafayette	85-69
Georgia	80-61
South Carolina State	84-59
Norfolk State	107-80
@Rice	69-58
@Tulsa	93-79
TCU	94-82
SMU	92-86
@Nevada	72-69
UTEP	108-56
@Hawaii (L)	73-91
@San Jose State	86-75
San Jose State	82-57
Hawaii	86-63
@TCU (L)	88-102
@UTEP (L)	61-80
@SMU	77-64
Nevada	91-68
Rice	79-74
Tulsa	84-77
####Rice	60-52
####Hawaii (L)	67-76
#####California	82-70
#####Michigan State (L)	65-81

#Hispanic College Fund Classic in Fresno, CA
##Tip-Off Classic in Springfield, MA
###Trend Homes Classic in Fresno, CA
####WAC Tournament in Tulsa, OK
#####NCAA Tournament
@Road Games

BLUE RIBBON ANALYSIS

BACKCOURT	B
BENCH/DEPTH	B-
FRONTCOURT	A-
INTANGIBLES	B+

This is a talented if troubled basketball team. As has been the case for several seasons, Tarkanian attracts gifted players, but they often come at a price.

Off-the-court problems—case in point Tito Maddox, who was kicked off the team after accepting a gift from an agent—seem to happen with a great deal of regularity, often distracting the team from the task at hand.

Through the first half of last season, Fresno State often dominated its non-conference and league opponents, but as soon as Maddox heard how he was a lottery pick in the making, he upset the balance of the team. Twice, the Bulldogs lost to Hawaii, including in the second round of the WAC Tournament. That defeat dropped Fresno State down the seeding chart, resulting in a second-round NCAA Tournament loss to defending national champion Michigan State.

This year, Tark had hoped to run right through the WAC as merely a proving ground for his talent-packed team. The loss of Maddox and several other role players during the off-season have left things stretched a bit thin.

Yes, the Bulldogs should be favored to win the WAC. They have talented post players Ely, Jefferies and Swillis to turn to down low. Sandy is a promising point guard, but unproven at the Division I level. DeManby has a strong outside game, but has yet to prove consistency over the course of a long season. When you ask reserves to fill the holes left by starters, you don't always know as a coach what you will get.

Still, Ely and junior college transfer Fuller offer plenty of points in the paint. Even an average outside shooter should have good looks on the perimeter and hit them often enough to unclog the middle. Despite the loss of Maddox, Tark and Fresno State will make their third consecutive NCAA appearance and could advance to the Sweet 16.

(P.A.)

Wyoming 31

LOCATION	Laramie, WY
CONFERENCE	Mountain West
LAST SEASON	20-10 (.667)
CONFERENCE RECORD	10-4 (t-1st)
STARTERS LOST/RETURNING	0/5
NICKNAME	Steve McClain (Chadron State '84)
COLORS	57-32 (3 years)
HOMECOURT	57-32 (3 years)
COACH	John Giannini (N. Central College '84)
RECORD AT SCHOOL	37-49 (3 years)
CAREER RECORD	205-87 (10 years)
ASSISTANTS	Leroy Washington (Montana '88)
	John Adams (Iowa State '95)
	Heath Schroyer (Armstrong '94)
TEAM WINS (last 5 years)	12-19-18-19-20
RPI (last 5 years)	158-56-74-100-67
2000-01 FINISH	Lost in conference semifinal.

COACH AND PROGRAM

Since coming to Wyoming three years ago, Steve McClain has breathed new life into a program that had been stagnant for most of the previous decade.

His infectious enthusiasm and optimism combined with his ability to attract talented players to the plains of Laramie has turned the Cowboys into a consistent winner with high expectations for the future.

For the second straight year, the Cowboys have very high expectations heading into the season. This time around they hope to turn those expectations into reality with a league championship and an NCAA Tournament berth.

Like last year, they have most of their starters return-

ing, including a couple of All-Mountain West players in Josh Davis and Marcus Bailey. In fact, they have all five starters and eight of their top nine players returning. They also have several top recruits who figure to play important roles on the team.

However, the optimism is tempered with caution because of what happened last year.

In 2000-2001, the Cowboys fully expected to be good enough to gain an NCAA berth for the first time since 1988. And they ended up having a pretty good season, winning 20 games for the first time in a decade and tying for the Mountain West regular-season championship with Utah and BYU. A loss to the Cougars in the MWC tournament, however, relegated the Cowboys to the NIT, where they were upset in the first round by Pepperdine.

"These guys tasted it last year with an excellent season and they earned some rewards like a conference title and postseason play," McClain said. "I believe they are hungry for more."

What happened in 2000-2001 was that Davis, despite earning all-league honors, didn't quite have the season most folks expected after his fine sophomore season. Davis saw his numbers fall as his scoring went from 14.3 points to 13.5 points, his field-goal shooting declined from 49.9 to 48.5 percent and his three-point shooting went way down.

Then there was Ugo Udezue, who was a mere shadow of himself after coming back from knee surgery after an outstanding 1998-1999 season when he averaged 20.5 points and 7.4 rebounds per game and was first-team all-league. He had sat out most of the '99-'00 season after sustaining his knee injury, but last year couldn't even crack the starting lineup and averaged just 3.8 points and 3.0 rebounds.

The heralded transfers didn't turn out to be so great either. Scottie Vines, who was expected to fill a void at shooting guard, couldn't shoot worth a darn and rarely saw action in the second half of the season, ending up with an abysmal 22.5 field-goal percentage, including 10.5 from three-point range. The last anyone saw of Vines, he was trying to make the Cowboy football team as a defensive back.

In fact, shooting, particularly three-point shooting, was the biggest hindrance to the Cowboys having a championship season and gaining an NCAA berth. The Cowboys shot just 44.7 percent from the field as a team and a dreadful 28.5 percent from three-point range. To correct that, McClain recruited a couple of sharp-shooting junior college transfers and has had his players working hard on their outside shooting during the off-season.

While certain players didn't live up to expectations, the Cowboys had a couple of players who greatly exceeded expectations in Marcus Bailey and Uche Nsonwu-Amadi.

Bailey had started as a freshman, but he made a huge leap during his sophomore season as he led the team in scoring with 17.4 per game and made the top 10 in the MWC in seven different categories, while earning first-team All-MWC honors.

"Marcus is another year older and it's fun to think about how much better he will be as a junior," McClain said.

Nsonwu-Amadi took over for his fellow Nigerian and distant cousin Udezue in the starting lineup and compiled some impressive stats, averaging 11.8 points and 8.3 rebounds per game. He also led the league in field-goal percentage (.602).

"Uche is much stronger," McClain. "With Ugo, Josh and Uche, we're pretty good up front."

As for Udezue, McClain said, "I think Ugo has made great progress during the summer. He feels better about himself and has much more confidence in that knee. If he can come back strong, he adds so much more to our attack."

Besides Vines, the only player the Cowboys lost from last year was guard Brett McFall, who was a valuable player off the bench for the Pokes because of his hustle and outside shooting.

The three new players who will try to find playing time on the Cowboys' talented roster are junior college guards Brandon Dickerson and Donta Richardson and freshman point guard Jason Straight.

McClain has improved by one victory in each of his three years and could move up another notch or two this year. He brought the high-pressure defense and run 'n gun offense he learned from Billy Tubbs as an assistant for four seasons at TCU, and uses it to full advantage at the 7,200-foot altitude of Laramie.

His first two years, the Cowboys were ranked in the top 10 in scoring in the country—10th in 1998-99 and fifth in 1999-2000. Last year, because of injuries and some players not playing up to expectations, the Cowboys had to adjust their style a bit and play a more patterned offense, but they still averaged 76 points per game.

The Cowboy program is in the best shape its been since the late 1980s when Eric Leckner and Fennis Dembo led the team to back-to-back NCAA berths. It hit a lull in the early 1990s under Joby Wright when the Cowboys averaged only 13 wins a year. But McClain has amassed more victories in his first three seasons (57) than any coach in Wyoming history.

The fans are also coming back since McClain took over. Last year, attendance jumped 2,073 per game over the previous year, including a record 15,456 for the Colorado State game. It was the third-best attendance year in Arena-Auditorium history and was the sixth biggest increase in the NCAA last season.

"Our attendance is certainly an indication of how our fans feel about the program," McClain said. "It took a little while for them to buy into what we were doing. But I believe they are committed because they see the great commitment of our players and coaches. They have a great attitude about our program, which is extremely important. I could see a similar jump in attendance this season.

McClain has excellent help from assistants Leroy Washington and John Adams and has a valuable new addition to the coaching staff in Heath Schroyer, who has been an assistant at BYU the last four years. Schroyer was given much of the credit for the Cougars' strong defense under Steve Cleveland the last four years. If Schroyer can make similar progress with the Cowboys, who are known as an offensive-minded team, it could make the difference in a few extra victories for Wyoming.

Unlike many coaches who try to downplay their chances in order to look better if they exceed expectations, McClain always likes to play up his team and its potential. He's tempered the optimism a bit this year because of last year's disappointment of not making the NCAAs, but he's still looking forward to a successful season.

"We are certainly aware of what the expectation will be and we look forward to that challenge," McClain said. "This is a veteran team and I think this team is ready for it. Their attitude and work ethic have been unbelievable. Guys like Chris [McMillan], Josh [Davis] and Ugo [Udezue] have been around a long time. They understand there will be higher expectations for this team than for any Cowboy team for a long time."

2001-2002 SCHEDULE

Nov.	13	#@USC
	19	Arkansas-Pine Bluff
	24	Eastern Kentucky
	26	@Denver
	28	@Detroit Mercy
Dec.	1	Cal State Fullerton
	6	Cal State Northridge
	12	@Boise State
	15	Montana State
	19	Indiana State
	22	Alaska-Anchorage
	29	Portland State
Jan.	1	@Texas Tech
	5	@UNLV
	12	Colorado State
	21	@San Diego State
	28	New Mexico
Feb.	2	@BYU
	4	@Utah
	9	@Colorado State
	16	UNLV
	18	San Diego State
	23	@Air Force
	25	@New Mexico
	28	BYU
March	2	Utah
	7-9	##Mountain West Tournament

@Road Games
#Preseason NIT (If Wyoming wins, it will play Montana or Fresno State on Nov. 14 or 16; semifinals and final on Nov. 21 and 23 at Madison Square Garden, NY)
##Thomas & Mack Center, Las Vegas, NV

STARTERS NOT RETURNING

None

OTHERS NOT RETURNING

G-BRETT McFALL (6-0, 7.7 ppg, 2.4 rpg, 3.3 apg, 21.5 minutes, .358 FG, .290 3PT, .808 FT). McFall was a sparkplug off the bench throughout his four-year career at Wyoming, a guy who could get the team moving with his hustle and outside shooting ability. However, his shooting fell off drastically his senior season from 46.0 percent from three-point range to 29.1 percent as the whole team struggled from the outside. He was also a good passer, averaging more than three assists each of his last three seasons in Laramie. He started just one game in four years, but was a consistent scorer who averaged 6.1 points over four years.

G-SCOTTIE VINES (6-2, 1.9 ppg, 1.3 rpg, 0.9 apg, 7.9 minutes, .226 FG, .105 3PT, .545 FT). Vines came to Wyoming after an all-conference year at Eastern Utah Junior College and was expected to challenge for the starting off-guard spot. The only problem was, he couldn't shoot the ball. He had shot 48 percent from the field and 38 percent from 3-point range in junior college, but in his first game at Wyoming he went 1-for-12 and went downhill from there. He still has eligibility left, but decided to try out for the Cowboy football team instead this year.

PROJECTED STARTERS

PG-CHRIS MCMILLAN (5-10, 180 lbs., SR, #10, 6.9 ppg, 2.6 rpg, 4.2 apg, 32.0 minutes, .372 FG, .351 3PT, .654 FT, Brea Olinda HS/Brea, Calif.). Since the day he stepped on the Wyoming campus, McMillan has been the Cowboys' starting point guard. For 86 straight games, McMillan has been the starter at the point, playing 31 minutes per game. He ranks No. 3 on the all-time Wyoming assist list with 369 and with 134 more assists this year, he would pass Sean Dent (1984-88) and become the school's all-time assist leader.

His streak of consecutive starts came into question this summer when he broke his left leg just above the ankle in a summer league softball game, of all things. The injury happened in late July and he was supposed to keep weight off his leg for six weeks. However, McClain is counting on his reliable point guard to be ready when practice starts in mid-October.

"He'll be back to practice full speed by Oct. 13," McClain said. "Chris has improved each season, so we expect him to be even better his final year. We expect him to run the team more effectively and become an even better leader. You've got to have a veteran point guard to be good."

McClain said McMillan "has never cared about scoring," which is one reason his scoring dipped from 9.7 two years ago to 6.9 last year when Bailey's scoring shot up. But McClain says he wants his point guard to look to the basket more.

"He needs to start to shoot the ball more to go along with our inside game," McClain said. "We've got to have him do that."

SG-MARCUS BAILEY (6-5, 190 lbs., JR, #44, 17.4 ppg, 4.1 rpg, 3.2 apg, 1.2 spg, 31.9 minutes, .470 FG, .326 3PT, .853 FT, Cheyenne East/Cheyenne, Wyo.). For much of last season, Bailey looked like the best player in the Mountain West Conference. One thing is certain—he was easily the most improved player in the league. After a solid freshman season when he started most of the games and averaged 7.8 points, Bailey exploded last year, more than doubling his average to 17.4, tops in the Mountain West Conference. He finished in the Top 20 in the league in five other categories.

Even McClain has shown surprised by the rapid development Bailey has shown. He envisioned him being more of a role player when he signed him in 1999, hoping perhaps Bailey could contribute in his junior and senior seasons. Instead he became the Cowboys' go-to guy last year with Ugo Udezue still recovering from a knee injury and Josh Davis struggling through an off season.

"He had a great sophomore season," McClain said. "He led the conference in scoring from Day One until the end and he proved his ability all year. He gives us that threat on the perimeter with his range. I expect the same kind of production from him as last year."

Bailey has played small forward and big guard for the Cowboys, but with several talented big men and with Davis playing mostly at small forward, Bailey will play the big guard position this year. A Mormon, he considered leaving on a two-year church mission, but will probably see how far his basketball career will take him at this point.

SF-JOSH DAVIS (6-8, 235 lbs., SR, #22, 13.5 ppg, 9.4 rpg, 1.8 apg, 28.4 minutes, .485 FG, .203 3PT, .733 FT, Salem Academy HS/Salem Ore.). For two years, Davis has been a first-team All-MWC selection, although even Davis might admit that last year's award was based more on his reputation from the previous year. Still, the Wyoming sports information department is pushing Davis for All-America honors in hopes that he will have a breakout year that many experts believe he's capable.

McClain says one of the reasons for Davis' struggles last year was that he didn't know his role on the team. With Udezue not recovering from his injury as expected, Davis played more at power forward, although he also swung back and played the small forward position.

"I expect him to have a big year for us," McClain said. "Last year we were forced to play Josh inside and it changed his game. He wasn't getting the shots he normally gets. This year he won't have to bounce back between the three and four spots."

Davis became the 27th player in Wyoming history to score 1,000 points in his career and ranks 24th with 1,077 points. With approximately 500 points this year, he'll move into the top 10 scorers all-time at Wyoming. He'll finish even higher on the rebounding list as he currently ranks 10th with 712. He's also third on the blocked shots list with 128 and though he won't catch NBA star Theo Ratliff's 425 total, he could catch Eric Leckner (164) for second place.

PF-RONELL MINGO (6-9, 245 lbs., SR, #00, 6.6 ppg, 4.1 rpg, 1.6 apg, 1.5 bpg, 16.4 minutes, .487 FG, .701 FT, Compton CC/Compton, Calif. and Fremont HS/Los Angeles, Calif.). After joining the Cowboys as a junior college transfer, Mingo experienced an up-and-down-and-up season for the Cowboys. He began the season as a starter playing a lot of minutes, highlighted by his first game, a 15-point outing on 7-of-8 shooting against UC-Riverside. Gradually his minutes began to decline, until he was playing single-figure minutes, bottoming out with a three-minute stint against Colorado State. However, the next game at BYU, he played 21 minutes and scored a career-high 18 points and he was re-inserted into the starting lineup for the final seven games.

McClain said Mingo made the adjustment from junior college well last year and thinks he'll be even better this year with 20 additional pounds and increased confidence.

"He's not only an offensive threat, but a defensive threat because he can block shots," Mingo said. "He can move well for a big guy and fits in well to our running game."

C-UCHE NSONWU-AMADI (6-10, 260, JR, #5, 11.7 ppg, 8.4 rpg, 0.8 bpg, 27.4 minutes, .606 FG, .566 FT, Indian Hills Community College/Ottuma, Iowa and Enugu, Nigeria). Talk about a pleasant surprise. Before last season, the man known simply as "Uche" was almost an afterthought when talking about the Cowboys' top prospects. He came to Wyoming on the recommendation of Cowboy center Ugo Udezue, a distant relative of his from Nigeria. Nsonwu-Amadi had played one year at Indian Hills and posted modest numbers of six points and five rebounds per game.

But when Udezue wasn't able to perform as well as expected after knee surgery, Nsonwu-Amadi filled in wonderfully for the Cowboys, leading the MWC in field-goal percentage, while posting impressive numbers of 11.7 points and 8.4 rebounds. He was voted MWC Newcomer of the Year by both the coaches and the media and also earned All-MWC second-team honors.

"He just got better and better as the year went along," McClain. "He has size and strength and he's difficult to guard. We've been working on moving his game out to 15 feet. I expect him to have a big year for us."

KEY RESERVES

F/C-UGO UDEZUE (6-9, 245 lbs., SR, #4, SR, 3.8 ppg, 3.0 rpg, 13.2 minutes, .395 FG, .554 FT, Riverdale Baptist High School, Mitchelville, Md./Enugu, Nigeria). After averaging just 3.5 points and 4.2 rebounds as a freshman, Udezue came from nowhere to put in an all-league season in 1998-99 when he averaged 20.5 points and 7.4 rebounds for the Cowboys. However, the following year, he injured his knee severely enough in the fifth game that he required surgery that forced him out for the season with a medical hardship. When he came back last year, everyone expected Udezue to pick up where he left off the season before when he was all-conference. Instead he was a mere shadow of himself as his numbers reverted back to his freshman season and his knee bothered him all year.

"We've got Ugo back healthy again, his weight is down and he's running without favoritism [to the knee]," McClain said. "He never had the confidence that he was OK last year. But I've seen some flashes of the old Ugo this year. Maybe we'll get to see the real Ugo again."

G-PARIS CORNER (6-1, 193 lbs., SR, #24, 4.1 ppg, 1.3 rpg, 0.9 apg, 13.3 minutes, .339 FG, .270 3PT, .649 FT, Iowa State and West Brook High School/Beaumont, Texas). The guy with one of the greatest names in college basketball hopes to make more of an impact than he did last year after transferring from Iowa State. At ISU, he saw little action, but showed his potential during one three-game stretch during his sophomore season when he scored in double figures in three straight games. After sitting out a year as a red-shirt, he saw spotty action for the 'Pokes last year, playing as many as 27 minutes and scoring 14 points against BYU, but also playing less than 10 minutes on nine occasions.

"Last year he was coming off a year of sitting out," McClain said. "He can knock down the threes and gives us a lot of depth on the perimeter. We expect a lot from Paris."

G/F-DAVID ROTTINGHAUS (6-5, 210 lbs., SO, #20, 3.5 ppg, 1.9 rpg, 12.2 minutes, .408 FG, .316 3PT, .625 FT, Charles City HS/Charles City, Iowa). Coming out of high school, where he once made 10 three-pointers in a game, Rottinghaus was listed among the top 75 recruits in the nation. He quickly made an impression on the Cowboy coaches and by midseason, Rottinghaus found himself in the starting lineup as a true freshman with a 16-point performance at LSU to his credit. However, his playing time dwindled as the season progressed and the Cowboys went with a bigger lineup that included Ronell Mingo. Rottinghaus is a swingman who is valuable when he's shooting well, and his numbers (40.8 percent from the field, 31.6 percent from three-point range) should improve this year.

"Like any freshman, he slipped during the second half of the season," McClain said. "He's gained 15 pounds and is up to 210 and really looks good. He gives us some good depth."

G-JASON STRAIGHT (5-11, 165 lbs., FR, #3, 29.8 ppg, 7.0 apg, Dunbar HS, Chicago, Ill.). He starred for three years at Dunbar High, earning all-state honors his last two years and was ranked among the top 75 players in the nation by All-Star Scouting Service. He wasn't highly recruited by many top programs, but McClain is thrilled to have snagged him.

"He's definitely a steal for us, no question," McClain said after seeing Straight work out late in the summer. "He's a true point guard who can shoot and distribute the ball. The signing of Jason is great for our program because it will give us a freshman point guard to come in and compete with Chris McMillan and give him an opportunity to grow and learn our system from a senior who knows what it's like to play at the college level."

G-DONTA RICHARDSON (6-2, 170 lbs., JR, #1, 22.0 ppg, 4.0 rpg, 7.0 apg at Sheridan College/Sheridan, Wyo. and Liberty HS/Colorado Springs, Colo.). Richardson is a versatile player who can play either guard position or the small forward spot. He earned first-team NJCAA All-America honors last year and led his high school team to a 30-2 record and a state championship.

"Donta is a young man who we've had our eye on the last two years," McClain said. "He is ideal for our system because he can play either the point, two-guard or small-forward spots for us. I like the fact that he will come to us as a mature player who can really shoot the ball."

OTHER RETURNEES

F-JOE RIES (6-8, 225 lbs., SO, #25, 1.6 ppg, 1.0 rpg, 6.1 minutes, .480 FG, .565 FT, DeSmet Jesuit HS/St. Louis, Mo.). Ries came to Laramie as one of the Pokes' more high-profile recruits in many years, having ranked among the nation's top 125 players after helping lead his team to the finals of the state tournament. Last year he played in 22 games, but played less as the season progressed, with several DNPs in league play. It will be tough finding much playing time until Josh Davis and Ugo Udezue graduate.

"He's capable of being a strong contributor for us," McClain said. "He will play more, depending on how well Ugo is this year."

F/C-ALEX DUNN (6-10, 220 lbs., FR, #13, 24.0 ppg, 11.0 rpg, 3.0 bpg at Sioux Central High School, Sioux Rapids, Iowa). After an outstanding high school career, Dunn impressed the Cowboy coaches in fall practice last

year, but they decided to red-shirt him because they had other big men such as Uche Nsonwu-Amadi and Ugo Udezue. He could back up both the Nigerians this year. Dunn grew seven inches his senior year and has excellent perimeter skills for his height.

OTHER NEWCOMERS

G-BRANDON DICKERSON (6-4, 200 lbs., JR, 18.0 ppg, 6.0 rpg, Copiah-Lincoln Junior College/Wesson, Miss. and Baton Rouge, La.). Because of their three-point shooting woes last year, the Cowboys were determined to pick up another shooter and found a good one in Dickerson. He shot 40 percent from three-point range last year and even better as a freshman when he shot 45 percent and ranked among the top 10 in the country.

"We were looking for another guard who could shoot the three, and as we evaluated the people available Brandon became the individual who we felt best fit the need," McClain said. "We feel he is a young man who will make our program better."

QUESTIONS

Ugo or No-go? Three years ago, Ugo Udezue was an all-conference performer who averaged 20 points a game. Since his knee injury, however, he's never been close to the same. If he can play like he did in '98-99, the Cowboys will have one more weapon inside to go with Uche Nsonwu-Amadi, Ronell Mingo and Josh Davis.

Three-point shooting? Last year, the Cowboys couldn't hit their three-pointers and finished with a terrible 28.5 percentage. Nobody was immune from the three-point plague, as Chris McMillan's 35.1 percent was best on the team. The Cowboys will need to shoot considerably better this year from three-point land this year.

Which Josh? Even though he earned all-league honors and was even chosen league player of the year by the media, Josh Davis had an off-year in 2000-2001. His scoring and shooting percentage fell off and he didn't seem the same player as the previous year as he shifted between the small and big forward spots. If he can put a big season together, the Cowboys could go places.

ANSWERS

Depth! With eight of their nine top players back, plus several good recruits, the Cowboys should have talent coming out of their ears. All five starters return along with a couple of part-time starters.

Coaching! Steve McClain is one of the bright young coaches in the game and his enthusiasm rubs off on his players and helps fuel their run 'n gun game. He also pulled a coup of sorts by getting a top assistant, Heath Schroyer, away from fellow conference rival BYU.

Double U! They may not be the Twin Towers, but Nigerians Uche Nsonwu-Amadi and Ugo Udezue give the Cowboys a couple of the top post men in the Mountain West, especially if Udezue is able to regain his all-league form from 1998-99.

Marcus! Last year Marcus Bailey made a remarkable improvement, going from a seven-point scorer to 17.9 and leading the Mountain West Conference. If he shows similar improvement this year, watch out.

WYOMING 2000-2001 RESULTS

Cal Riverside	77-59
Denver	70-55
Creighton	78-74
@Montana State	77-62
@Cal State-Northridge (L)	71-74
@Cal State-Fullerton	78-61
Oregon State	65-53
Delaware State	92-64
@South Carolina (L)	67-78
@Akron	81-73
Wichita State	72-65
@LSU (L)	69-73
@Utah (L)	71-83
@Colorado State	70-69
Utah	78-77
Brigham Young	85-78
@Air Force	71-56
@New Mexico	82-78
San Diego State	101-66
UNLV (L)	78-80
Colorado State	72-70
@Brigham Young (L)	63-79
@Creighton (L)	72-84

Air Force	82-70
New Mexico	81-61
@San Diego State	69-62
@UNLV (L)	102-106
#San Diego State	73-58
#Brigham Young (L)	66-77
##Pepperdine (L)	69-72

#Mountain West Conference Tournament, Las Vegas, NV
##NIT

BLUE RIBBON ANALYSIS

BACKCOURT	B
BENCH/DEPTH	A-
FRONTCOURT	B+
INTANGIBLES	B

The Wyoming program has made steady progress through McClain's three years and could be ready to make a national splash this year with a senior-dominated team and talented players at every position. Just look at a possible starting lineup with four-year starter McMillan at the point, Bailey, the leading scorer in the MWC last year, at off-guard, two-time all-league performer Davis at small forward, former all-league player Udezue at big forward and Nsomwu-Amadi, last year's newcomer of the year, at center.

The reserves would include forwards Mingo and Rottinghaus, who both started several games last year, three sharp-shooting guards in Corner, Richardson and Dickerson and heralded freshman point guard Straight.

"There's no question this is the most talented team we've had since I've been here," McClain said.

Except for the Preseason NIT, the Cowboys should breeze through their non-conference schedule, with the toughest game being a New Year's Day match-up against Texas Tech and new coach Bobby Knight. They could even make their mark in the NIT, if they can get by USC on the road in the opener, and could end up in New York.

Once they get to the league portion of the schedule, the Cowboys should be confident and ready to challenge Utah and New Mexico for the championship. In fact, the regular-season championship could very well be decided March 2 when Utah visits Laramie. Even if they don't win the conference tournament championship in Las Vegas, watch for the Cowboys to be headed to the NCAA Tournament for the first time in 13 years with another 20-plus victory season.

(M.S.)

 # Ohio State 32

LOCATION	Columbus, OH
CONFERENCE	Big Ten
LAST SEASON	20-11 (.645)
CONFERENCE RECORD	11-5 (3rd)
STARTERS LOST/RETURNING	1/4
NICKNAME	Buckeyes
COLORS	Scarlet & Gray
HOMECOURT	Value City Arena (19,200)
COACH	Jim O'Brien (Boston College '71)
RECORD AT SCHOOL	78-49 (4 years)
CAREER RECORD	313-266 (19 years)
ASSISTANTS	Bruce Parkhill (Lock Haven '71)
	Paul Biancardi (Salem State '85)
	Dave Spiller (Canisius '78)
TEAM WINS (last 5 years)	10-8-27-23-20
RPI (last 5 years)	132-176-12-24-37
2000-01 FINISH	Lost in NCAA first round.

COACH AND PROGRAM

Whatever prediction you're thinking about making for Ohio State's season, you might want to reconsider. The Buckeyes aren't exactly known for fulfilling prophecies.

Three years ago, OSU was coming off an 8-22 season and seemed a logical pick to remain at or near the cellar of the Big Ten. Despite the addition of highly touted transfer point guard Scoonie Penn from Boston College, no one in their right mind would have guessed the Buckeyes would improve by 19 wins and play in the 1999 Final Four.

Last season, OSU seemed hardly in condition to

compete for a second straight Big Ten title, having just lost stars Penn and Michael Redd and key starter George Reese. But the Bucks again defied expectations, going 11-5 in the conference and returning to the NCAA Tournament despite the presence of three first-year starters. They beat four of the last five ranked opponents they faced. Even a first round NCAA upset at the hands of 12th seeded Utah State hardly seemed to damper things.

"That's over with," assistant coach Paul Biancardi said. "When you really look back at the entire season, it was very successful from beginning to end. We really improved as a whole, it just didn't end the way you wanted it to."

This year, the Bucks could fly under the radar yet again. For a second straight year, the focal point of the team has moved on, this time in the form of All-Big Ten center Ken Johnson, but 80 percent of last year's scoring returns.

It's doubtful anyone in Columbus foresees this team rolling over without Johnson. If anything, fans have come to expect a Jim O'Brien-coached team to defy expectations. The Scarlet and Gray faithful may have just run their football coach out of town, but they've got no complaints about the man in charge in hoops.

"The present state of basketball at Ohio State is impeccable," Ohio State AD Andy Geiger said. " ... Under Jim's leadership, the program will do well, compete for the Big Ten title and challenge for national honors and recognition."

In 1997, after 11 years at Boston College, O'Brien and his staff brought their East Coast know-how to a Midwestern program steeped in history but stuck in a rut. After decent success in the early '90s with players like Jim Jackson and Chris Jent, the Buckeyes had slipped to the bottom of the Big Ten in Randy Ayers' waning years.

O'Brien had taken three of his last four BC teams to the NCAAs. He instantly tapped his East Coast roots for the rebuilding job, not just with the arrival of his former BC player Penn, but in recruiting. In fact, five current scholarship players hail from New York, Pennsylvania or Massachusetts, the same number as from Ohio.

The Bucks' recent success is obviously starting to carry weight in the Midwest as well. Their first recruit for 2002, Detroit native Ricardo Billings, chose OSU over homestate Michigan State. Highly touted point guard Ja'Quan Hart, a partial qualifier who will practice with the team this season, picked OSU after failing to gain admission to original top choice Michigan.

While making the Final Four in just his second season greatly accelerated O'Brien's rebuilding effort, the slate wasn't wiped completely clean. It would have been easy for the Bucks to slip back down after Redd and Penn's departure. Instead, OSU is coming off three straight seasons among the top three in the Big Ten standings, with a good chance of making it four in 2002.

Now O'Brien is on the verge of doing something unprecedented at OSU. The program has played in 21 NCAA Tournaments, but this could be the first time in history it has done so for four seasons in a row. O'Brien, who earned his second Big Ten Coach of the Year award last season, owns the second-best winning percentage during league games in school history at .578 (37-27).

"We've gotten ourselves into the position we want to be, a program that goes to the [NCAA] tournament every year, competes for the Big Ten title every year. We're at that stage now, and we want to continue that," Biancardi said. "It will all depend on the development of our post players, how quickly the freshmen come in and give us some depth. There are a multitude of things that have to go right for us to be successful."

There isn't one particular post player on the roster who is going to replace Johnson, and certainly not a shot blocker of his caliber. But then, OSU didn't exactly live and die by Johnson last season.

In reality, the Bucks were a three-guard team that liked to light things up from the perimeter, shooting 38.1 percent as a team from three-point range. Four different players attempted at least 99 shots from behind the arc.

But with the good among the guards came the bad, like turnovers. In the Bucks' 77-68 loss to Utah State in the NCAA first round—a game in which Johnson dominated with 14 points and 14 rebounds—OSU coughed up the ball 21 times to only five by the underdog Aggies.

"Turnovers hurt us all season long," O'Brien said. "We were not good with the basketball all year."

The Bucks had ample opportunity to work on the turnover problem, as well as develop some post players, during a 16-day trip through Europe that wrapped up Sept. 4. The seven-game swing through Switzerland, France, Belgium and The Netherlands, along with the practices in Columbus leading up to it, allowed an already veteran-intensive club to gain even more experience together.

The last time O'Brien took a club overseas was at Boston College in 1994. That year's team, led by stars Howard Eisley and Bill Curley, would end up making a surprise run to the Elite Eight.

OSU fans hope it's an indication of things to come.

2001-2002 SCHEDULE

Nov.	18	Winthrop
	20	Albany
	27	*North Carolina State
Dec.	2	UNC Wilmington
	9	IUPUI
	12	Santa Clara
	15	@Louisville
	19	Pittsburgh
	22	Eastern Illinois
	29	UNC Greensboro
Jan.	2	@Purdue
	5	@Iowa
	9	@Massachusetts
	12	@Northwestern
	16	Penn State
	19	Indiana
	24	Michigan
	26	@Minnesota
	29	Illinois
Feb.	2	Northwestern
	6	@Wisconsin
	10	@Michigan State
	16	@Iowa
	20	@Indiana
	23	Purdue
	26	Michigan State
March	2/3	@Michigan
	7-10	#Big Ten Tournament

@Road Games
* Big Ten/ACC Challenge
#Conseco Fieldhouse, Indianapolis, IN

STARTERS NOT RETURNING

C-KEN JOHNSON (6-11, 12.5 ppg, 7.3 rpg, 0.8 apg, 4.0 bpg, 29.5 minutes, .578 FG, .711 FT). That Johnson's services would be available in 2000-01 was hardly a given. The four-year starter had been a Prop 16 his freshman year and lost that season of eligibility. But in April after his junior year, the NCAA granted him an extra year after OSU appealed on proof he had a learning disability. Johnson gladly delayed his NBA entry to return to Columbus for another year.

He led the team in scoring in only seven games, but the nation's premier shot blocker cleaned up once again on the defensive end, a major reason opponents shot only 40.3 percent from the field against OSU.

If an opposing player tried to score inside, there was a good chance his shot was going to get altered by Johnson. He finished his career as the No. 4 all-time shot blocker in NCAA history (444), behind only Adonal Foyle, Tim Duncan and Alonzo Mourning. His 161 rejections as a junior set a Big Ten record.

"I've never had a player come as far as Ken Johnson," O'Brien told the Akron Beacon Journal. "The whole concept of him leading the conference in blocked shots, considering where he was when I got here, is just off the charts."

Despite all this, Johnson wasn't drafted until the late second round (No. 49 overall) by the Miami Heat. It was a bit of a surprise considering he had been a projected mid-to-late first round selection in most mock drafts beforehand. But such is the disturbing trend in the NBA, where four high school centers went among the draft's first seven picks, but a seasoned four-year college guy like Johnson nearly went undrafted.

OTHERS NOT RETURNING

SF-COBE OCOKOLJIC (6-8, 1.6 ppg, 1.5 rpg, 0.3 apg, 6.5 minutes, .353 FG, .154 3PT, .588 FT). The native of Kraljevo, Yugoslavia transferred after seeing his playing time dwindle from starting 13 games as a freshman to playing in only 22 as a sophomore, all off the bench. He did not play in either of the Buckeyes' post-season games, against Iowa in the Big Ten Tournament and Utah State in the NCAAs.

SF-KEL FRAZIER (6-3, 1.4 ppg, 0.3 rpg, 0.1 apg, 0.1 spg, 3.9 minutes, 1.000 FG, 1.000 FT). Frazier appeared in only seven games as a senior but made the most of them, connecting on all four field-goal attempts and both free throws he shot.

PROJECTED STARTERS

PG-BRIAN BROWN (6-4, 200 lbs., SR, #13, 14.5 ppg, 4.4 rpg, 4.1 apg, 1.4 spg, 33.8 minutes, .446 FG, .404 3PT, .710 FT, Bishop Loughlin HS/Brooklyn, N.Y.). After two seasons in the shadows of Penn and Redd, Brown emerged last season as OSU's top scorer while sharing point guard duties with Brent Darby. In fact, his 449 points exceeded the combined total of his first two seasons (415).

Brown reached double figure scoring in 27-of-31 games. In his top performance of the year, he registered a career-high 25 points in leading the Buckeyes to a 64-55 upset of Michigan State. He led the team in scoring on 14 other occasions.

Brown will enter 2001-02 in his second season as team captain and the undisputed first option on offense.

"He improved his three-point shooting," Biancardi said, "and when he does that, he's tough, because he can already score a lot of points by going to basket. He's just such a good all-around guard, he can do a little bit of everything, and he's just now coming to the forefront in scoring."

Brown first entered the Buckeyes' starting lineup as a freshman during their five-game run to the 1999 Final Four. He has remained ever since. Yet he was still overlooked to a degree last season considering his production, garnering only third team All-Big Ten honors from the league media, honorable mention from the coaches.

SG-BRENT DARBY (6-1, 195 lbs., JR, #4, 9.6 ppg, 2.5 rpg, 2.3 apg, 0.6 spg, 26.6 minutes, .411 FG, .351 3PT, .766 FT, River Rouge HS/Detroit, Mich.). After playing sparingly as a freshman, Darby was one of four regular guards who rotated among three positions last season, starting 16-of-31 games. He shared point-guard duties with Brown, but like Brown is more of a scorer.

His inconsistent play also had him scuttling in and out of the lineup. Darby started the season among the first five, then played behind Sean Connolly for three games in December, returned for 11 more, returned to the bench for 12 more, then started the last game of the season.

Before being yanked midway through Big Ten play, Darby appeared to lack confidence, his head sinking upon nearly every missed shot or bad pass.

"It's hard to be the point guard after Scoonie Penn has been the point guard," Biancardi said. "He put a lot of pressure on himself in feeling that he had to fill Scoonie's shoes right away, but Brent did terrific job in his dual role."

Darby's best outing of the season came in the Great Alaska Shootout against Florida State with 18 points and five assists. But he also ended the season on a high note with nine consecutive double-figure scoring games, prompting his brief return to the lineup against Utah State. Over one three-game span in February, Darby averaged 15.5 points, 4.5 assists and five rebounds.

"My game is being aggressive and getting into the lane," Darby told the Akron Beacon Journal. "Whenever someone tries to step up on me, I'm going to blow by them with a dribble."

SF-BOBAN SAVOVIC (6-5, 240 lbs., SR, #21, 8.9 ppg, 3.8 rpg, 3.5 apg, 1.1 spg, 30.0 minutes, .439 FG, .390 3PT, .739 FT, East Side HS/Newark, N.J. and Montenegro, Yugoslavia). In O'Brien's three-guard set, Brown and Darby share point-guard duties and rotate into the shooting guard spot with Sean Connolly. Savovic, then, is the "big" guard, usually matched up with the opponent's small forward defensively, where he shut down several capable scorers last season. He's able to get some rebounds for a guard, and he's also capable of bringing the ball up the floor and setting up teammates. And he's become one of the team's main leaders.

Savovic's junior season served as somewhat of a redemption for the Yugoslavia native, who appeared in just 16 games the year before because of leg and ankle injuries. He also ballooned to as much as 260 pounds as a sophomore after a freshman year when he played all 34 games for OSU's Final Four team, and concern over his family back in war-torn Kosovo weighed heavily.

"The biggest change has been my mental outlook on things," Savovic told the Akron Beacon Journal. "I would come out on the court [as a sophomore], and worry about hurting myself. Every practice and every game, I couldn't run around without thinking I was going to hurt myself again."

In particular, he showed some clutch scoring ability in the regular-season finale, when OSU rallied from 20 down to top Penn State 93-87 in State College. With OSU playing four guards during the comeback, Savovic hit 6-of-7 field goals en route to 17 second-half points and 23 overall.

But Savovic also suffers from inconsistency. During one eight-game stretch last season he shot 29.5 percent from the field and made only two of 20 three-pointers.

PF-ZACH WILLIAMS (6-7, 230 lbs., SO, #33, 6.6 ppg, 3.8 rpg, 0.5 apg, 0.3 spg, 20.7 minutes, .503 FG, .655 FT, Christ the King HS/Middle Village, N.Y.). Williams was a pleasant surprise as a freshman, stepping in for the departed George Reese and starting all 31 games. Although he shot above 50 percent from the floor, he'll never be the caliber shooter Reese was. But he shows obvious rebounding ability and can earn his points under the basket.

"Zach was a guy who came in and really provided us with some energy," Biancardi said.

A Brooklyn, N.Y., native, Williams is a product of two prolific hoops programs, Christ the King High School and the Riverside Church AAU team, playing alongside ex-St. John's star Omar Cook on both.

With so many hot-shooting guards and the presence of Johnson inside, Williams wasn't asked to score much last year. That may or may not change after Johnson's departure. But he will need to become more of a defensive presence in the veteran center's absence.

C-WILL DUDLEY (6-8, 230 lbs., SR, #43, 4.9 ppg, 2.1 rpg, 0.5 apg, 0.3 bpg, 11.0 minutes, .533 FG, .655 FT, Bishop Loughlin HS/Brooklyn, N.Y.). Another Brooklyn native, Dudley's elevation to starting center was delayed by a year when Johnson was granted his extra season of eligibility. And even now, he will be pushed by 7-2 Velmir Radinovic to keep the job. He is easy to overlook considering his extremely quiet nature—he's rarely likely to run his mouth, on the court or in the locker room.

But Dudley has shown flashes of what he can do in Johnson's place, stepping up with eight points in 26 minutes when Johnson was in foul trouble against Iowa in the Big Ten Tournament. Against Purdue, he grabbed a rebound off high school teammate Brown's miss and made a last-second game winner.

Dudley has improved every season since arriving in 1998, having played only 96 minutes in a freshman year that ended with Jan. 21 foot surgery. His minutes and stats have improved every year, though nowhere near a starter's production.

OSU runs the risk of being too small if Dudley plays with Williams and three guards. He's able to compensate offensively with a nice jump hook that falls over bigger centers. But he'll need to become a force in the paint defensively or opposing guards will feed to their big men all night.

KEY RESERVES

G-SEAN CONNOLLY (6-5, 210 lbs., JR, #3, 7.6 ppg, 3.0 rpg, 2.0 apg, 0.7 spg, 24.5 minutes, .412 FG, .417 3PT, .840 FT, Bishop Fenwick HS/Peabody, Mass. and Providence). Big things were expected of Connolly after his transfer from Providence, where he started all 30 games and averaged 11.0 points as a freshman, but what appeared to be a stress fracture in his foot suffered while sitting out a year kept him from contributing as heavily as possible.

Then after the season, doctors determined the stress fracture had healed but that it was strained ligaments from a preseason ankle sprain that had caused him pain throughout the season. Surgery was performed to tighten the ligaments and he is now fully recovered.

Nonetheless, Connolly started 15 games and, despite having little lift off his foot, shot an impressive 41.7 percent (45-of-108) on three-pointers. In his finest moment of the season, he hit the game-winning three-pointer with 29 seconds left to give OSU a 63-61 upset of No. 3 Illinois on Feb. 22.

Now healthy, if Connolly's production continues to go up, O'Brien will be hard-pressed to keep him out of the starting lineup.

C-VELMIR RADINOVIC (7-0, 235 lbs., SO, #14, 2.6 ppg, 1.4 rpg, 0.3 apg, 0.2 bpg, 5.9 minutes, .517 FG, .645 FT, T.A. Blakelock HS/Toronto, Ontario Canada). Radinovic is the wild card in OSU's equation. The Bucks could really use him to emerge as the low-post replacement for Johnson. But the Toronto native played sparingly in only 19 games last season while adjusting to the speed and strength of the Big Ten. It would take a giant leap his sophomore year to become a regular contributor.

"I think he'll be a very good player, especially in last two seasons. This year is a year where he's going to be up and down," Biancardi said. "He needed to put on weight, and he's up to 235. Last year he struggled to get to 220. He's got skills, but he needs to learn how to play with his back to the basket. Right now, he'll catch ball, then he's really not sure what move to make yet."

G-BRANDON FUSS-CHEATHAM (6-1, 190 lbs., FR, #2, 27.9 ppg, 7.0 apg, 4.0 spg, Blackhawk HS/Beaver Falls, Pa.). Fuss-Cheatham finished as the all-time scoring leader at his high school (2,281 points) and earned all-state honors as a junior and senior. He is considered by many to be one of the top 10 point guards nationally among incoming freshmen.

Last year, Brown and Darby shared ball-handling responsibilities in the absence of a true point guard on the roster. Fuss-Cheatham is a true point guard. Whether he can progress rapidly enough as a freshman to become the full-time point guard remains to be seen, but he does possess the court vision and ball distribution skills needed of the position.

"Brandon is everything we were looking for," O'Brien said. "He is the ultimate point guard. He is an extension of the coaching staff on the floor and an outstanding floor leader with the ability to score. He has been associated with winning his entire career."

F-MATT SYLVESTER (6-7, 190 lbs., FR, #40, 21.3 ppg, 8.0 rpg, 3.0 apg, Moeller HS/Loveland, Ohio). Sylvester comes from good genes. His father, Mike Sylvester, was a standout in the early '70s for Dayton, scoring 36 points in a classic triple-overtime game against Bill Walton and UCLA in the 1974 NCAA regionals. He went on to play professionally in Italy for 17 years.

Mike's son is the classic swingman, taking smaller guards one-on-one off the dribble. He figures perfectly into OSU's three-guard system and could see time as a freshman spelling for Savovic.

"Matt is throwback player," O'Brien said. "You don't find kids who play his style anymore. He has an understanding of how to play. Matt is a multi-skilled player who can do it all. I love his fiesty-ness."

OTHER RETURNEES

F-TIM MARTIN (6-6, 240 lbs., SR., #44, 2.6 ppg, 3.0 rpg, 0.6 apg, 0.3 spg, 11.8 minutes, .681 FG, .000 3PT, .425 FT, Dunbar HS/Dayton, Ohio and Kent State). A former transfer from Kent State, Martin walked on at OSU in 1998 but didn't play until last season. He became a regular part of the frontcourt rotation and was chosen the team's most improved player. He plays with a warrior mentality but is limited offensively and will be counted on mainly as a rebounder.

G-DOYLAN ROBINSON (6-4, 210 lbs., SR, #10, 1.1 ppg, 1.1 rpg, 0.8 apg, 5.4 minutes, .308 FG, 1.000 FT, Buchtel HS/Akron, Ohio). Robinson was set back last year by a serious car accident on Dec. 3. He played in just nine games and is only now becoming fully healthy again.

But Robinson set himself back again over the summer, his academic standing becoming a question. He stayed home from OSU's trip abroad to concentrate on a summer course he needed to pass to be eligible for fall semester.

G-SHAUN SMITH (5-10, 170 lbs., JR., #24, 0.6 ppg, 0.5 rpg, 0.5 apg, 3.2 minutes, .200 FG, .500 3PT, .667 FT, Walnut Hills HS/Cincinnati, Ohio). The Cincinnati native walked on as a sophomore, appearing in 12 games. He showed his ball-handling ability with three assists in seven minutes against Coppin State on Dec. 30.

G-RYAN HEFLIN (5-10, 180 lbs., JR., #23, #23, 0.6 ppg, 0.3 rpg, 0.2 apg, 2.2 minutes, .200 FG, .667 3PT, .500 3PT, Meadowdale HS/Dayton, Ohio). Another sophomore walk-on, Heflin appeared in 14 games. He notched two assists, two rebounds and a steal in four minutes against Eastern Kentucky.

OTHER NEWCOMERS

F/C-TERENCE DIALS (6-9, 240 lbs., FR, #34, 18.0 ppg, 12.0 rpg, 4.0 bpg, Boardman High School, Youngstown, Ohio). Dials will probably see minutes as a freshman because of the Buckeyes' dearth of big bodies. Physically, he has the size to play in the Big Ten but is coming off a senior year of high school where he was limited to less than half a season due to knee surgery.

"Terence will bring us rebounding and scoring in the front court," O'Brien said. "He is athletic with a nice touch and good hands. He will add a tough presence and is physically mature, which will help him down low in the Big Ten. I look at Terence as someone who will bring toughness and a competitive spirit to our team."

C-MATT MARINCHICK (6-10, 240 lbs., FR., #54, red-shirted in 2000-01, Hudson HS/Hudson, Ohio.). The Hudson, Ohio, native sat out last season because he needed to gain strength. Buckeye coaches hoped to use the European trip to find out whether Marinchick could figure into their big-man rotation. In his senior year at Hudson High School, Marinchick earned third team all-state honors, averaging 19.8 points, 9.0 rebounds and 4.0 blocks.

QUESTIONS

Center? As of now, the Buckeyes plan to start the 6-8 Dudley in place of Johnson, with the 7-2 Radinovic maybe waiting in the wings. It remains to be seen whether that will cut it in the Big Ten.

OSU doesn't necessarily need someone to come in and dominate in the low post like Johnson did. But Johnson's presence was enough to keep defenses from spreading out to contain the Bucks' perimeter guys. That might not happen this year if teams don't think OSU can hurt them in the paint.

Freshmen? From Redd and Johnson to Brown and Williams, OSU has counted on freshmen to start throughout O'Brien's tenure. This year's lineup seems set, but the coach will want to find a way to mix Fuss-Cheatham and Sylvester's ingredients into the mix.

Both, along with Dials, are some of O'Brien's most touted high school recruits since he arrived in Columbus. They hold the key to OSU's future.

Got the point? Running the point guard position by committee seemed to work last year. But with the addition of Fuss-Cheatham and a glut of guards on the roster, OSU may want to think about a more definitive approach to that position.

Darby, in particular, struggled with the burden of trying to replace the all-everything Penn. He was at his best coming off the bench as an offensive sparkplug. If he resumes that role this year, O'Brien will have to decide between an established senior, Brown, and an unproven freshman, Fuss-Cheatham, in that spot.

ANSWERS

Seniors rule! In college basketball, you can't go wrong with a team led by seniors. The Buckeyes have a good nucleus in Brown, Savovic and Dudley, none of whom knows what it's like to win less than 20 games.

Brown and Savovic are unquestioned leaders. Brown does it with his gaudy numbers. Savovic is the emotional type who leaves it all on the court. Dudley is far quieter and has yet to play a full-time role during his career but has gained valuable experience backing up a player like Johnson for three seasons.

Sean song! If injuries hadn't slowed him last year, the Providence transfer Connolly would be a star for the Bucks by now. It's not too late for him to catch up with the plan.

Connolly certainly showed flashes of greatness last year and, if healthy, could even emerge as the Bucks' No. 2 scorer behind Brown. The only question is whether he can get the ball enough what with Brown, Savovic and Darby all on the perimeter as well.

It's the coaching, stupid! O'Brien has proven a master at taking the hand dealt him each season and building a team accordingly. Replacing Johnson is this year's challenge, one O'Brien will probably turn into a positive.

On paper, last year's team had no business finishing as high as it did. Losing Redd, Penn and Reese was a dagger, and the roster left in their wake lacked a true point guard or a second big man behind Johnson. Yet O'Brien molded that team into a winner just like he did during the Final Four season.

OHIO STATE 2000-2001 RESULTS

Yale	65-45
#Florida State	90-65
#Syracuse (L)	66-77
#Valparaiso (L)	64-67

Eastern Kentucky	90-44
Denver	83-46
Massachusetts	54-51
St. John's	71-58
Morehead State	93-62
Robert Morris	88-46
Kansas (L)	68-69
Coppin State	80-42
Northwestern	73-56
@Illinois (L)	68-83
Penn State (L)	75-78
Minnesota	75-72
Michigan	78-61
@Michigan State (L)	56-71
@Wisconsin (L)	42-57
Michigan State	64-55
Indiana (L)	67-70
@Minnesota	73-66
@Iowa	69-68
Wisconsin	63-58
@Purdue	65-64
@Alabama (L)	67-85
Illinois	63-61
@Northwestern	69-57
@Penn State	93-87
##Iowa (L)	66-75
###Utah State	68-77

#Alaska Shootout in Anchorage
###Big Ten Tournametn in Chicago
###NCAA Tournament
@Road Games

BLUE RIBBON ANALYSIS

BACKCOURT	A-
BENCH/DEPTH	B
FRONTCOURT	B-
INTANGIBLES	B+

Last year, we guessed, would be a transition year for the Buckeyes. We've changed our mind; it's this year.

Not that the Buckeyes are going to fall apart without Johnson. Hardly. Brown is a legitimate star, and Connolly, Darby and Savovic make for a deadly perimeter game. A return to the NCAAs and a run at the top of the Big Ten is to be expected.

But this is also a roster whose potential has a clear ceiling. Playing with an ever-changing guard lineup and no proven big man can get O'Brien only so far. They will excel against teams similar in style but may get overwhelmed if an opponent has more than one capable post player. Williams is too small to play power forward and Dudley is too small to play center. Radinovic is certainly tall but just not ready.

Like he's done so many times before, O'Brien will likely maximize the performance of his veterans while grooming the next generation for its eventual takeover. Radinovic, by all indications, could one day be dominant. And Connolly and Darby are only juniors.

Meanwhile, Sylvester, Fuss-Cheatham and Dials were talented enough to comprise a consensus Top 20 recruiting class. And that was before the addition of Hart, higher rated than any of them but not available to play until next season. The sleek point guard from Flint, Mich. was labeled "the George Gervin of the millennium" in high school, no small comparison. After Hart couldn't gain admission in Ann Arbor, OSU was able to win out over Michigan State for his services because of a glut of perimeter players on the Spartans' roster.

O'Brien has built a program that should maintain its current level of success for years to come. Therefore, we should no longer act surprised when, come March, we hear Ohio State's name being called on Selection Sunday.

(S.M.)

Utah 33

LOCATION	Salt Lake City, UT
CONFERENCE	Mountain West
LAST SEASON	19-12 (.613)
CONFERENCE RECORD	10-4 (t-1st)
STARTERS LOST/RETURNING	0/5
NICKNAME	Utes
COLORS	Crimson & White
HOMECOURT	Jon M. Huntsman Center (15,000)

COACH	Rick Majerus (Marquette '70)
RECORD AT SCHOOL	262-73 (12 years)
CAREER RECORD	361-125 (17 years)
ASSISTANTS	Dick Hunsaker (Weber State '77)
	Jeff Strohm (Eastern Illinois '88)
	Kerry Rupp (Southern Utah '77)
TEAM WINS (last 5 years)	29-30-28-23-19
RPI (last 5 years)	5-14-18-47-54
2000-01 FINISH	Lost in NIT first round.

COACH AND PROGRAM

Coach Rick Majerus is not only one of the biggest coaches, literally, in college basketball at 300-plus pounds, he has become one of the biggest coaches in all of college basketball because of his success at Utah over the last 12 years.

He has won 78 percent of his games at Utah with a 262-73 mark, won nine regular-season league titles, advanced to the NCAA Tournament eight times, including four Sweet 16 appearances and back-to-back Elite Eight appearances. The highlight of his tenure at Utah was the 1998 NCAA championship game in San Antonio, where his Utes led Kentucky most of the way before faltering at the end. During the decade of the 1990s, Utah ranked eighth among NCAA Division I programs in both wins (250) and winning percentage (.767). Over the last five seasons, the Utes have the seventh-best winning percentage in NCAA Division I at .791 with a 129-34 record.

Majerus has earned widespread recognition at Utah, winning five national coach-of-the-year awards (Basketball Times 1991, UPI 1991, Playboy in 1992 and 1998, and John Wooden 1998), seven district coach-of-the-year honors and Western Athletic Conference Coach of the Year fives times.

Because of his success, Majerus has been a hot commodity for other positions, but he seems to become more comfortable the longer he stays at Utah. This past off-season was one of the quietest for the coach, who got some attention from UNLV for the third time in the last decade and from Wisconsin for the second time. This time, Majerus pretty much squelched any speculation early in the search process.

But 2000-2001 was not a usual season for Majerus, who ended up coaching just one regular-season game for the Utes before a variety of problems kept him on the sideline.

First, he left the team just before its trip to Puerto Rico because he wasn't fully recovered from an off-season knee operation and needed to take six weeks off for rehabilitation. Then the week he was supposed to re-join the team in early January, he went into the hospital for a heart procedure, which set him back another week. Then he announced he would be taking the rest of the season off to go back to Wisconsin to be near his mother, who was undergoing cancer treatments.

Through all these ups and downs, assistant coach Dick Hunsaker, who was a successful head coach at Ball State for several years in the early 1990s, guided the Utes and did a decent job. After a shaky non-conference season when the Utes lost home games to Weber State and Southern Utah and went just 8-6, they caught fire midway through the Mountain West Conference season. After losing three straight at the end of January, the Utes ran off seven straight wins in February and tied for the MWC title with BYU and Wyoming. Hunsaker ended up being voted MWC Coach of the Year.

However, the season ended on a sour note when the Utes dropped their opening game in the MWC Tournament to New Mexico and then lost in the first round of the NIT to Memphis, which went on to the NIT Final Four.

Majerus rejoined the team for practices in May before their once-every-four-years trip to Europe, but he suffered one more setback when he received a severe cut on his leg in a freak accident on a rental car van in Los Angeles. The injury was serious enough that Majerus' doctors advised him not to accompany the team to Europe, and once again Hunsaker took over the controls, as the Utes went 4-4 in games in France and Spain.

After hardly coaching for a year, Majerus is excited to finally get back to doing what he loves most. He said he feels bad for his players who came to Utah to play for him and says there might be a bit of a readjustment period.

"This will be somewhat of a rebuilding year and certainly a get-acquainted year for me," Majerus said. "I'm excited and optimistic to see how the players respond and the attitudes they display. I expect that we'll be good

defensively and that we'll have good depth."

The Utes have all five starters back from last year along with Jeff Johnsen, who has started several games over the past two years. Utah lost only one senior in Nate Althoff, who started almost half the games after starting the two previous years. They also lost the leading scorer, Kevin Bradley, who couldn't make it academically.

As far as their four new recruits are concerned, there shouldn't be any problem academically as all four were honor students in high school. Martin Osimani is a point guard from Florida who played on the Uruguayan National Junior Team, while 6-11 center Chris Jackson was the top player in New Mexico. The other two, guard Eric Osmundson and center-forward Cameron Goettsche, are talented players who may red-shirt but have great potential.

The Utes made another change in their coaching staff in the off-season, adding Salt Lake high school coach Kerry Rupp to take the place of Jason Shelton, who took a job at Colorado.

2001-2002 SCHEDULE

Nov.	16	St. Francis (Ill.)
	20	Boise State
	23	Utah State
	26	@Alabama
Dec.	1	Pepperdine
	4	*Arizona
	8	Troy State
	15	@Weber State
	18	Southern Utah
	21	Idaho State
	29	Texas
Jan.	2	Whitworth
	7	@St. Mary's
	12	UNLV
	14	San Diego State
	19	@Air Force
	21	@New Mexico
	28	Brigham Young
Feb.	2	Colorado State
	4	Wyoming
	9	@San Diego State
	11	@UNLV
	16	Air Force
	18	New Mexico
	23	@Brigham Young
	28	@Colorado State
March	2	@Wyoming
	7-9	#Mounain West Tournament

@Road Games
*America West Arena, Phoenix, AZ
#Thomas & Mack Center, Las Vegas, NV

STARTERS NOT RETURNING

None

OTHERS NOT RETURNING

C-NATE ALTHOFF (6-11, 8.1 ppg, 3.2 rpg, 17.5 minutes, .612 FG, .743 FT). After starting the previous two seasons, Althoff lost his starting job to Chris Burgess midway through last year. At 6-11, he had developed a nice inside game with a variety of jumpers and soft hooks and was an excellent free-throw shooter for a man his size. However, he never developed into a solid rebounder, actually falling from 4.7 his junior year to 3.2 last year, and wasn't much of a shot-blocking threat. Majerus also was frustrated because of his constant nagging injuries.

G-KEVIN BRADLEY (6-1, 10.7 ppg, 3.3 rpg, 2.3 apg, 22.3 minutes, .416 FG, .386 3PT, .723 FT). The transfer from Compton Community College ended up as the leading scorer for the Utes last year, despite coming off the bench for most of the season after beginning the year as a starter. Bradley could get hot and fill it up from outside, but also had a hard time fitting in to the team concept and playing defense. He was benched by Hunsaker in mid-season, but he came back to help the Utes during their league championship run. When he couldn't keep up academically, his scholarship wasn't renewed for this season.

F-MIKE PUZEY (6-8, 1.6 ppg, 1.7 rpg, 8.6 minutes, .542 FG, .812 FT). Known as a scrappy player who wasn't afraid to put a body on an opponent, but Puzey was never much of an offensive threat. Puzey saw his minutes diminish last year under Hunsaker and with the prospect of even fewer minutes this season with all the big men in the program, he transferred up the road to Utah State.

G-MARC JACKSON (6-0, 1.2 ppg, 0.9 rpg, 0.7 apg, 6.0 minutes, .211 FG, .773 FT). The reserve point guard played some key minutes during the first half of the season, but didn't see much action in the second half of the season. He left on a Mormon mission after the season, and will return for the 2003-2004 season.

F/C-JON GODFREAD (6-10, red-shirted in 2000-2001). Like Puzey, he couldn't see much future at Utah with all of the other big men in the Ute program so he transferred to Northern Iowa last spring after sitting out as a red-shirt.

PROJECTED STARTERS

PG-TRAVIS SPIVEY (6-1, 205 lbs., SR, #11, 5.2 ppg, 2.8 rpg, 3.5 apg, 0.8 spg, 24.8 minutes, .411 FG, .250 3PT, .739 FT Salt Lake Community College and Georgia Tech/Myrtle Beach, S.C.). The Utes' fortunes this year could very well hinge on the play of Spivey at the point-guard position. Spivey came to Utah as a heralded point guard because of his play at Salt Lake Community College, where he was the conference player of the year with some gaudy statistics. Before that he had started for a season at Georgia Tech in the powerful Atlantic Coast Conference.

However, he got off to a slow start at Utah and didn't establish himself as the starter until near the end of the non-conference schedule. Spivey wasn't known as a great outside shooter and he lived up to that reputation, rarely taking shots and finishing just 8-for-32 from three-point range. His forte was driving to the basket and passing off to the open man. He got more comfortable with the offense as the season progressed, and after some early games when he committed a slew of turnovers, he settled down and completely turned around his assist-turnover ratio. Over the final six games of the Mountain West season, Spivey handed out 36 assists while committing only 10 turnovers.

Unfortunately he saved his worst game for last, when he went scoreless with five turnovers and just two assists in the Utes' first-round NIT loss to Memphis.

What worries many Ute fans going into this season is which Spivey will they see this year. Even Majerus shows his concern by saying, "It's going to be an adventure for me with Spivey."

SG-NICK JACOBSON (6-4, 200 lbs., SO, #15, 7.9 ppg, 1.4 rpg, 1.1 apg, 23.6 minutes, .459 FG, .381 3PT, .806 FT, Roseville (Minn.) HS/Fargo, N.D.). After coming out of high school with high credentials as a deadly outside shooter, Jacobson ended up sitting out his first year as a red-shirt when the Utes figured they had enough bodies at that position. Then last year after Majerus left the team after the first game, Jacobson nearly got buried on the bench early in the season by Hunsaker, playing just three minutes against USC and nine against Georgia and Utah State.

Suddenly in game eight against Weber State, Hunsaker inserted Jacobson into the starting lineup and he responded with 12 points. Although he had some ups and downs the rest of the season, Jacobson started every game from then out and finished with a respectable 7.9 scoring average on 46 percent shooting. In the early going, fans wondered as Jacobson shot an abysmal 20 percent (4-for-20) from three-point range in his first 10 games. However, he got better as the season progressed and finished with a flourish over the final 13 games, going 23-for-43 from behind the arc (53.5 percent).

With no other point guards on the trip, Jacobson was able to play some valuable minutes at the position during the Utes' eight-game summer trip to Europe. One of Jacobson's drawbacks as a freshman was his defense, but he got better as the season progressed and you can be certain he worked on it during the off-season now that Majerus is back running the show.

"I like Nick," Majerus said. "He's a good shooter and a competitor. He's going to play a lot for us this year."

SF-BRITTON JOHNSEN (6-9, 205 lbs., JR, #31, 9.2 ppg, 5.4 rpg, 1.5 apg, 22.1 minutes, .455 FG, .426 3PT, .650 FT, Murray HS/Murray, Utah). Probably the most gifted of all the Ute players, Johnsen is still trying to live up to the potential he showed during the 1998 NCAA Tournament when he helped the Utes on their run to the finals. He actually only saw limited action that season because of an early-season injury, but his moments in the NCAAs opened up some eyes and increased expectations for the 6-9 stringbean.

After his freshman season when he averaged just 3.5 points and 1.6 rebounds, Johnsen left on a two-year church mission. When he came back, he was slowed by knee problems and though he had a decent season as a sophomore last year, he showed his mission rustiness at times. Johnsen ended up second on the team in both scoring and rebounding and was also a surprising second in three-point shooting, hitting 20-of-47 shots. However, he also had a propensity to make turnovers and finished with 73, just two behind point guard Travis Spivey, who handled the ball a lot more. He gets compared to former Ute All-American Keith Van Horn, because of his ability to score inside and outside, and he may even be more athletic than Van Horn. He needs to get his game more under control and perhaps with Majerus cracking the whip, that will happen this season.

Majerus said Johnsen has done a good job of "hitting the weights" during the off-season to get bigger and stronger. He expects Johnsen to play a key role for the Utes this year, but he believes some people expect too much of him.

"Lots of guys have potential," Majerus said. "Britton's potential certainly took a hit last year and he's going to see if he can play up to those expectations."

PF-PHIL CULLEN (6-9, 215 lbs., SR, #40, 9.1 ppg, 4.4 rpg, 23.5 minutes, .413 FG, .378 3PT, .661 FT, Chelan HS/Chelan, Wash.). When he arrived from Washington as a freshman, many folks noticed how much Cullen looked like Keith Van Horn, the former Ute All-American, not only because of his haircut, but his body size. Unfortunately, some fans expected Cullen to play like Van Horn, which never happened over his first three years.

Cullen has a similar outside game to Van Horn, with an uncanny ability to knock down three-pointers, especially from the corner. That stretches the opponents' defense to have to go out and guard Utah's four-man outside, but the problem with Cullen is that he has never developed a strong inside game like Van Horn. Some folks have even said Cullen is a shooting guard in a power forward's body. He didn't even average as many as three rebounds per game his first two seasons at Utah and last year improved only to 4.4 per game while starting 26 games.

There are questions surrounding Cullen as he prepares for his senior season. He spent the summer playing baseball in the Seattle Mariners' organization and appears to have a future as a pitcher. Majerus wonders how good Cullen will be if he's made up his mind to pursue baseball as a career. But he's trying to look at it as a positive.

"I'm sure he hasn't picked up a basketball all summer," he said. "But in a way it could be refreshing for him not to play. I don't know where his head's at. But I'm sure he'll give us a good effort."

C-CHRIS BURGESS (6-10, 245 lbs., SR, #34, 7.8 ppg, 5.9 rpg, 1.2 bpg, 21.6 minutes, .543 FG, .435 FT, Duke University and Woodbridge HS/Irvine, CA). For a guy who thought he'd be playing in the NBA by now, it's been a rocky path for Burgess ever since leaving high school as the national player of the year by one publication (The Sporting News). Burgess played two years at Duke, and although he was a part-time starter, he never came close to matching the exploits of fellow classmates Elton Brand, William Avery and Shane Battier. After two years and sitting out nearly the whole national championship game loss to Connecticut in 1999, Burgess decided to transfer to Utah, where he had relatives and where he could learn under the tutelage of Majerus, who is known for developing big men.

During the year he sat out as a red-shirt, Burgess developed back problems and didn't practice much of the season. He went to a back clinic and got his problems straightened out, but last year he had other concerns, including a health condition that drained his energy and an ankle injury that caused him to miss four games. Burgess showed flashes during the year and was especially effective for the Utes with his shot-blocking ability on defense and his overall rebounding ability. He had off-season surgery on his ankle and expects to have a big senior season. He must if he still has dreams of playing in the NBA. One aspect of Burgess' game that must improve is free throw shooting, which was an abysmal 43.5 percent last year, or else Majerus will be tearing out what little hair he has left on his head.

"Chris has to have a good senior year for us to be good this year," Majerus said. "He seems to be in good shape and lost some weight like I asked him to do. He showed a lot of enthusiasm when I coached him before."

KEY RESERVES

G/F-JEFF JOHNSEN (6-4, 200 lbs., SR, #35, 8.6 ppg, 3.4 rpg, 2.2 apg, 1.0 spg, 21.9 minutes, .495 FG, .404 3PT, .756 FT, Murray High School/Murray, Utah). A two-time Mr. Basketball in Utah in high school, Johnsen is still trying to find his niche as a collegian. Johnsen, a year older than Britton, is an athletic, scrappy player, who can do many things on the court. Unfortunately, at his size, Johnsen is a bit too small for the small-forward spot, and he hasn't been quite good enough in his outside shooting to be a shooting guard. Just like the last two years, he'll be used at both positions, although he won't be the main man at either spot.

Last year, Johnsen started nine games early in the season before settling into a role as one of the first men off the bench like he did his first two seasons. Johnsen worked hard on his outside shooting before last year and he improved his range, finishing at just under 50 percent for the season. Johnsen isn't afraid to mix it up inside and to drive to the basket, but he sometimes makes poor decisions resulting in turnovers.

"Jeff has got to end his reckless turnovers," Majerus said. "He's a good defender and will be important to our success as a senior this year."

G/F-TRACE CATON (6-4, 215 lbs., JR, #21, 2.2 ppg, 0.7 rpg, 0.5 apg, 9.6 minutes, .510 FG, .462 3PT, .600 FT, Alamosa HS/Alamosa, Colo.). As a freshman, Caton played a big role in the Utes' drive to the national championship game, often being the first man off the bench and being voted as the top sixth man in the WAC in a media poll that year. He averaged 4.0 points and more than a rebound per game, while shooting 46 percent from the field. After that season, he left on a church mission for two years and last year with Majerus gone, Hunsaker didn't know what to do with Caton. He played a lot of minutes in some early-season games, even leading the Utes in scoring with 19 points on 5-of-6 three-point shooting against American-Puerto Rico. However, he only hit double figures twice the rest of the season as his minutes diminished substantially.

Majerus is expected to give him more of a chance, but he may find playing time hard to find with Jeff Johnsen playing the same position and freshman Martin Osimani able to play the big guard as well as point.

"We'll have to see if Trace can perform somewhat reminiscent of his freshman season," Majerus said.

G-MARTIN OSIMANI (6-3, 205 lbs., FR, #3, 13.8 ppg, 8.2 rpg, 10.8 apg, Champagnat Catholic HS/Halleah, Fla./Montevideo, Uruguay). The Utes went far out of their usual recruiting area to pluck Osimani from big schools in the South that coveted his services. Osimani played on the Uruguayan National Under 21 Team and helped lead it to a third-place finish in the South American Tournament as the starting point guard, averaging 12.2 points and 5.8 assists. He came to the United States and played two years for Champagnat Catholic High School in Halleah, Fla., where his team was ranked No. 15 in the nation last year by USA Today.

He's known as a tough player who can run the floor well and is an excellent passer. He's more mature than most freshmen, as he is already 20 years old and has valuable experience in international competition.

C/F-LANCE ALLRED (6-10, 240 lbs., SO, #41, 2.2 ppg, 1.8 rpg, 5.6 minutes, .609 FG, .500 FT, East HS/Salt Lake City, Utah). With Burgess and Nate Althoff both playing last year, there wasn't much time left for Allred in the post. The times he did get in the game, particularly in the middle of the year when Burgess was injured, he showed some offensive ability as well as some feistiness out on the floor. Unfortunately he's been slowed by back problems, serious enough that Majerus wonders if he can play much this year or down the line. "He's got a chronic back problem and I don't know how much he can give us," he said.

OTHER RETURNEES

C-CAMERON KOFORD (7-0, 215 lbs., SR, #13, 2.2 ppg, 1.6 rpg, 5.3 minutes, .529 FG, .444 FT, Fremont HS/Plain City, Utah and Weber State,). The Utes picked up Koford virtually at the last minute last year, stealing him from right under the noses of Utah State, which thought he had committed. The Utes had a late scholarship opening and decided to give Koford a try, figuring you can't go wrong with a 7-footer. He saw limited action last year, but he played a lot on the Utes' European trip and he may end up as the backup center behind Burgess if Allred's back doesn't improve.

OTHER NEWCOMERS

C-CHRIS JACKSON (6-11, 240, FR, #30, 20.0 ppg, 9.7 rpg, 4.9 bpg, Los Alamos HS/Los Alamos, N.M.). In high school, Jackson was regarded as perhaps the top player in New Mexico and one of the Top 100 seniors in the nation. He selected Utah over New Mexico, Purdue and Stanford, partly because both sets of grandparents live in Salt Lake City. He led his school to two district titles and a third-place state finish last year. However, he played among smaller teams in New Mexico and hasn't really been tested much against players his size. Besides his talent on the basketball floor, he is an exceptional student, scoring 1580 on his SAT. Jackson was an National Merit finalist.

"He's a kid who's big and rangy and raw," Majerus said. "He's done a good job with his body, but he played against terrible competition last year, so it's hard to tell how he'll be."

G-ERIC OSMUNDSON (6-4, 195, FR, #32, 23.1 ppg, 6.0 rpg, 8.0 apg, St. Augustine HS/Carlsbad, Calif.). Majerus loves signing players like Osmundson, a late-bloomer the Utes picked up on before a lot of other major schools took notice.

In years past, Majerus has found little-recruited players such as Keith Van Horn, Andre Miller and Michael Doleac and turned them into all-Americans. Osmundson may never reach those heights, but he does show a lot of potential after growing four inches and 20 pounds his junior year and impressing recruiters in summer camps. He can play either guard position for the Utes and could red-shirt his first year because of the wealth of talent already in place.

F/C-CAMERON GOETTSCHE (6-8, 215, FR, #43, 18.4 ppg, 10.4 rpg, 2.7 apg, Thunder Ridge HS/Highlands Ranch, Colo.). The Utes signed him in the spring after he was selected to Colorado's all-state team as a senior. Goettsche is an all-around athlete who can jump well and also starred in baseball, football, track, volleyball and soccer, where he led his school to the state title. In high school he mostly played center with his back to the basket, but will be counted on to play more forward in college. How he makes that transition will determine how much action he'll see as a freshman.

QUESTIONS

Coach? After Majerus left the team three different times last year, for a bad knee, his mother's health and a bad cut on his leg, some folks wonder what may pop up to keep him from coaching again this year. He acts like he's planning to coach all season and for many seasons to come, based on the recruits he has committed already for next year. However, he also says he'll quit in a minute if his mother's health deteriorates. Some skeptics won't believe Majerus will actually be coaching again this year until they actually see him on the floor.

Chemistry? The Utes may have their most talented team ever, even more so than the NCAA runnerup team of 1998. They don't have any real stars, however, and with several players of similar ability, it may be hard to mesh the team into a 25-30-game winner Ute fans were used to in the late 1990s.

Turnovers? For the first time since Majerus came to Utah, the Utes finished the season with more turnovers than assists. Part of the problem was breaking in a new point guard in Spivey, but even after he cut his turnovers drastically as the season progressed, other players were prone to turning the ball over. Majerus is big on assist-to-turnover ratio and will make a point of correcting last year's problem.

ANSWERS

Rick Majerus! Assuming nothing crops up in the fall, Majerus' presence on the bench this year should make a huge difference for the Utes. Nothing against Hunsaker, who guided the unsteady ship last year as well as he could, but all of the players were recruited to play for Majerus and they should respond better to his leadership. Majerus should be able to fix some of the problems that plagued the Utes in their 19-12 season.

Height! Chris Burgess, 6-10, is expected to start at center this year and play a lot of minutes, but if he can't, there are plenty of big bodies to bring in. Lance Allred is also 6-10, while Cameron Koford measures 7-0. Then there's 6-11 freshman Chris Jackson and 6-8 freshman Cameron Goettsche. Don't forget about 6-9 Britton Johnsen and 6-9 Phil Cullen. That's seven players 6-8 or taller, and waiting in the wings is 6-10 Tim Frost, who is

sitting out this year after transferring from the University of Portland.

Depth! The Utes are deep at every position, so much so that some talented players won't see much playing time and a couple of freshman may end up red-shirting. Having veterans like Jeff Johnsen and Trace Caton coming off the bench will make the Utes a better team this year.

UTAH 2000-2001 RESULTS

Idaho State	71-65
#American Puerto-Rico	94-37
#Georgia (L)	60-65
#Memphis	61-58
Cardinal Stritch	93-47
##Southern Cal (L)	60-65
@Utah State (L)	57-58
Weber State (L)	77-79
Washington State	87-63
@Pepperdine	69-56
Southern Utah (L)	70-77
Concordia	88-37
@Texas (L)	59-70
Long Beach State	80-67
Wyoming	83-71
UNLV	79-70
San Diego State	58-39
@Wyoming (L)	77-78 (OT)
@Colorado State (L)	65-73
@BYU (L)	61-69
Air Force	63-58
New Mexico	80-69
@San Diego State	76-63
@UNLV	85-77
Louisville	84-67
Colorado State	67-45
BYU	82-75
@Air Force (L)	60-71
@New Mexico (L)	66-61
###New Mexico (L)	61-66
####Memphis	62-71

@Road games
#Puerto Rico Shootout
##Wooden Classic
###Mountain West Tournament
####NIT

BLUE RIBBON ANALYSIS

BACKCOURT	B
BENCH/DEPTH	B+
FRONTCOURT	B+
INTANGIBLES	A-

After what the Utes went through last year with all of Majerus' troubles, anything that goes wrong this year should seem like a piece of cake. When it was all said and done last year, the Utes still had another league co-championship to add to their collection, but their 19-12 mark was the worst for a Utah team in seven years and the team played uninspired in their first-round NIT loss to Memphis.

Having Majerus coaching for the whole year should make a big difference for the Utes, as should the extra year of experience for players such as Burgess, Johnsen and Jacobson, who had all sat out the season before, as well as Spivey, who came in as a junior college transfer.

With no preseason tournament and only two tough road games (Alabama and Arizona State), the Utes should build up a glossy non-conference record as they head into Mountain West Conference play. That could be as tough as ever with Wyoming and New Mexico fielding strong teams, San Diego State being vastly improved and the others capable of winning seasons.

Look for the Utes to climb back above the 20-win plateau and into the NCAA Tournament again. If things really mesh, the Utes have the talent to make another deep run into the tournament like they did more than once in the late 1990s.

(M.S.)

Alabama 34

LOCATION	Tuscaloosa, AL
CONFERENCE	Southeastern (Western)

LAST SEASON	25-11 (.694)
CONFERENCE RECORD	8-8 (3rd)
STARTERS LOST/RETURNING	0/5
NICKNAME	Crimson Tide
COLORS	Crimson & White
HOMECOURT	Coleman Coliseum (15,043)
COACH	Mark Gottfried (Alabama '87)
RECORD AT SCHOOL	55-42 (3 years)
CAREER RECORD	123-66 (6 years)
ASSISTANTS	Philip Pearson (Alabama '93)
	Orlando Early (Gardner-Webb '90)
	T.R. Dunn (Alabama '77)
TEAM WINS (last 5 years)	17-15-17-13-25
RPI (last 5 years)	87-84-72-93-42
2000-01 FINISH	Lost in NIT championship game.

COACH AND PROGRAM

Alabama coach Mark Gottfried doesn't even want to think about what kind of team he could have put on the floor this season. It's too painful.

Not that the Crimson Tide won't be good. With All-SEC players Rod Grizzard and Erwin Dudley and a stable of quality guards, Alabama will be hard to handle. But Alabama could have trotted out a potential Final Four team. Academics and defections have cut into the Tide's numbers, to the point where depth—or a lack thereof—could become a real problem.

That's particularly true in the frontcourt. Gerald Wallace, last year's heralded freshman, decided he needed only one year of college seasoning before jumping to the NBA. And junior college forwards Kei Madison and Rodney Bias, both 6-9, didn't qualify academically. Even 6-8 senior Sam Haginas, who barely played last year but could have helped bang inside this season, decided in July to quit the team.

"We've got to find a way to play with very little options around the basket," Gottfried said.

Either that, or Gottfried has to hope Dudley and 6-9 Kenny Walker are tireless, don't get injured and stay out of foul trouble. After the 6-8 Grizzard, who's a wing player, Alabama has a lot of guards. No player besides the 6-7 Reggie Rambo is taller than 6-3.

"We could have had a really solid front line," Gottfried said. "But now our concern is depth behind Erwin and Kenny. We feel like we may have to play three guards at times. It'll be like the South Carolina teams of a couple years back, when Eddie Fogler played those three great guards [Larry Davis, B.J. McKie and Melvin Watson]."

It just so happens Alabama has three guards who can potentially be as good as that trio in rookies Maurice Williams and Earnest Shelton and junior Terrance Meade.

Gottfried will need some firepower to face a schedule that he vastly improved from a year ago. Alabama took a lot of heat for playing a weak non-conference schedule (the Tide's final strength of schedule ranked 231 out of 319 Division I teams, even taking into account the NIT run). When it came time to handing out NCAA Tournament bids, the selection committee agreed with the critics, leaving out Alabama despite a 21-win season.

This time around, Gottfried has loaded up. Alabama will play—along with Missouri, Iowa, Memphis and 12 others teams—in the inaugural Guardians Classic. There's also a home-and-home arrangement with Utah, a match-up with UCLA in the John Wooden Classic, a game against Temple in the Jimmy V Classic and another against Notre Dame in the Sugar Bowl Classic.

Gottfried thinks his team can handle those games, even taking into consideration Alabama's dismal road record the last three years. During that time the Tide won just two SEC road games. A year ago, the Tide was 17-1 at home, but 2-7 on the road.

But Alabama might have gotten a lift with its play in the NIT. The Tide reeled off four straight wins—two away from home—to reach the championship game. Alabama didn't play all that well in losing the title match to Tulsa, but Gottfried was pleased at how well his team regrouped after the disappointment of not playing in the NCAAs.

A key win in the Tide's NIT run came at Purdue.

"Winning at Purdue was definitely a good mental step for our guys," Gottfried said. "It was pretty hostile in there. Our team took a lot from the whole NIT experience. I think our young guys, the nucleus of this team, are now juniors. We've got to be careful not to use [youth] as an excuse [for the road record]. We should be old enough and mature enough to do better away from home."

That's as long as no one gets hurt or in foul trouble. Alabama enters the season with just nine scholarship players (11 if you count former walk-on Antoine Pettway and partial qualifier Lucky Williams).

"We don't have much margin for error," Gottfried said.

2001-2002 SCHEDULE

Nov.	13	#Mississippi Valley State
	26	Utah
	29	McNeese State
Dec.	3	Tennessee-Chattanooga
	8	*UCLA
	14	Jacksonville State
	18	**Temple
	21	Alabama A&M
	27	***Notre Dame
	31	Florida A&M
Jan.	2	Bethune-Cookman
	5	LSU
	9	Vanderbilt
	12	@Auburn
	16	@Georgia
	19	Mississippi State
	26	@Kentucky
	30	Arkansas
Feb.	2	@LSU
	6	Ole Miss
	9	@Mississippi State
	13	@South Carolina
	16	Tennessee
	20	@Arkansas
	23	Florida
	27	Auburn
March	2	@Ole Miss
	7-10	##SEC Tournament

@Road Games
*John Wooden Classic, Anaheim, CA
**Jimmy V Classic, Meadowlands, NJ
***Sugar Bowl Classic, New Orleans, LA
#Guardians Classic (if the Crimson Tide wins, it will play either Samford or Loyola-Marymount on Nov. 14. Semifinals and finals are Nov. 20-21 at Kemper Arena, Kansas City, MO)
##Georgia Dome, Atlanta, GA

STARTERS NOT RETURNING

None

OTHERS NOT RETURNING

F-SAM HAGINAS (6-8, 1.4 ppg, 1.2 rpg, .304 FG, .706 FT, 5.1 minutes). After making some key contributions as a freshman, Haginas played sparingly the last two seasons. He left the team last year, only to change his mind and return.

Ironically, though he stood to significantly increase his minutes this season, Haginas quit again. Gottfried was disappointed, especially given the lateness of Haginas' decision. Alabama had virtually no chance to recruit a replacement.

"I thought he had a great opportunity," Gottfried said. "We were really counting on him, and I told Sam that. He called in July to tell me he was quitting. That really left us shorthanded."

C-JEREMY HAYS (6-10, 4.4 ppg, 3.0 rpg, .444 FG, .750 FT, 9.6 minutes in four games). Hays' injury plagued career ended after four five games last season. After having sat out the previous year rehabilitating a serious knee injury, Hays had high hopes for 2000-2001. But a puzzling leg injury made it too painful for him to play, and he reluctantly gave up the game.

"A lot of people forget last year that we didn't have Jeremy Hays," Gottfried said. "You take one of the SEC's best centers away from any team in the league and it's going to hurt them."

G-TARIK LONDON (6-1, 2.6 ppg, 1.4 rpg, 2.7 apg, .405 FG, .231 3PT, .684 FT, 16.9 minutes). London led Alabama in assists last season (100), but shot the ball so poorly Gottfried had to take emergency measures and throw Travis Stinnett into the fray, making him a starter. London was a solid four-year contributor, but his efforts can more than be replaced by freshman Maurice Williams.

G-DOC MARTIN (6-3, 5.4 ppg, 3.0 rpg, .365 FG, .340 3PT, .722 FT, 21.4 minutes). Like London, Martin was a four-year player who made his share of contributions to Alabama's rebuilding efforts. But Martin struggled with his shot at times. Freshman Earnest Shelton, one of the top shooters in the high school ranks last season, should step in and give Alabama a bit more firepower off the bench.

F-ALFRED MOSS (6-8, 1.4 ppg, 1.4 rpg, .611 FG, .722 FT, 4.9 minutes). A year ago, Moss regained a lost season of eligibility by earning his degree. Gottfried thought Moss would help the Tide more than he eventually did. Moss logged all of 122 minutes, little of it when the outcome of a game was in doubt.

This is the year Alabama could have really used Moss.

F-GERALD WALLACE (6-7, 9.8 ppg, 6.0 rpg, 1.2 apg, .438 FG, .175 3PT, .568 FT). Wallace started his college career in fine fashion and gave Tide fans reason for excitement after a 27-point outburst against Grambling and a 26-point effort against Akron. That latter performance came on Dec. 9. It was the last time Wallace led the Tide in scoring.

Indeed, as the competition got better, Wallace's contributions lessened. By the end of the year, he was barely scratching, scoring one point against Florida and none against Ole Miss. No one in the Alabama camp thought Wallace was ready to jump to the pros, but he declared for the NBA draft and was chosen by the Sacramento Kings as the 25th pick in the first round.

Clearly, that was another example of the NBA recent trend of drafting on potential, for Wallace's game needs some work, despite his amazing athleticism.

"When we recruited Gerald, we knew he wanted to get to the NBA quickly and was going to have opportunities to do so," Gottfried said. "But I felt like in this conference he still had a lot to prove. Losing him hurts our team. You just don't replace a guy who ends up a first-round draft pick."

PROJECTED STARTERS

PG-MAURICE WILLIAMS (6-1, 183 lbs., FR, #25, 26.9 ppg, 4.2 rpg, 8.6 apg, 3.4 spg, Murrah HS/Jackson, Miss.). Some long-time observers of Mississippi high school basketball are calling Williams the most polished guard to come from the state since Chris Jackson. Murrah coach Bob Frith says Williams is the best player to come from the school that has also produced James Robinson, Ronnie Henderson, Othella Harrington and Jesse Pate. That's high praise, but Williams is worthy of it.

We're listing Williams as the probably starter at point guard, but that's hardly a reach. Chances are good he'll be the best guard on the floor from Alabama's first practice. Yes, he's a freshman, but Williams is no ordinary freshman.

"I think he can be an impact player," Gottfried said. "All freshmen obviously go through transition periods. Until those players get on the floor, you never know. But Mo has all the potential to be a fabulous player. Just his presence here is going to make our other guards better."

How? Williams is one of those rare players who has the gift of being a blender. He does so by getting everyone involved. Or by becoming a scoring machine and attracting so much defensive attention some of his teammates are wide open. Whatever he has to do, Williams does it.

"He can go out and get you 50, he's fully capable of that," said Mark Alexander of the Jackson (Miss.) Clarion-Ledger and Blue Ribbon. "But if you tell him to go out and get everybody else involved and get 15 assists, he can do that, too."

Williams, a Parade and McDonald's All-American, had a storied career at Murrah, where he scored 2,433 career points, fifth on the school's all-time list. But numbers don't come close to measuring his worth.

"Point guard is a tough position," Frith told the Clarion-Ledger. "Maurice just knows the game—how the flow is going, who's open—and when you're open, he's going to try to get the ball to you. His second option is to shoot, because he wants to pass the ball if he can."

Williams is a great playmaker, but he can be just as deadly shooting. He set a school record with 103 three-pointers in 202 attempts last season. Yes, he shot 51 percent from behind the arc. He also shot 59 percent from the floor. Williams doesn't have to rely on his perimeter shot; he's quick enough to blow by defenders and is an explosive jumper who can dunk in a hurry.

With all the firepower Alabama has, Williams won't have to score, which is fine with him.

"He'll do well at the next level," Frith told the Clarion-Ledger. "He's going to a situation where he doesn't have to score for a team to win. There won't be all those double teams. Now his man can't leave him, you can believe that."

SG-TERRANCE MEADE (6-2, 180 lbs., JR, #14, 10.8 ppg, 2.9 rpg, 1.2 apg, 1.9 tpg, 0.8 spg, 28.2 minutes, .408 FG, .345 3PT .758 FT, Scottsboro HS/Scottsboro, Ala.). It's a tribute to Meade's talent that in a year where he didn't shoot the ball as well as he had as a freshman, he still reached double figures 22 times and finished as Alabama's third-leading scorer.

Meade struggled with his shot at times, perhaps frustrated by the high standard he'd set for himself the year before (43 percent from three-point range). But undaunted, Meade kept plugging away.

"At the end of the year he started to play better," said Gottfried, who wasn't all that worried about Meade. Why?

"He is the hardest worker you could have," Gottfried said. "I'm not sure there's a guy in America who can work any harder than Terrance. His year was frustrating, because he never did get into a groove shooting the ball like he did his freshman year. But it wasn't because he didn't work at it. This guy is tireless. At the end of year, he got his confidence back. Still, you've got to think the kind of year he had last season would make him hungry to get back out there this year."

Alabama is dangerous when Meade's three-point shot is falling. Meade can do a lot to open the inside for Dudley and Walker, and he can take pressure off Grizzard, who is more of a slasher than a shooter.

In the postseason, Meade's play contributed to a decent Alabama run. He scored 20 in a crucial SEC Tournament win over Vanderbilt, and had 14 big points in a key NIT road win at Purdue. He also scored 14 in the NIT final against Tulsa.

Meade produced some high-scoring games earlier in the year, though they didn't come against the best of competition. He scored a season-high 25 against Arkansas-Pine Bluff and 21 against Grambling. Not long after, his shot stopped falling, but as Gottfried said, Meade worked hard to solve the puzzling slump and kept on shooting. For the season, he cranked up 168 three pointers, second on the team behind Grizzard, and made 58, also second to Grizzard.

Alabama will need Meade to be more consistent this season. And with five scorers on the floor at all times, he's likely to sneak free more often for open jump shots. If he can get his three-point average back into the low 40s, the Tide will be tough to stop.

SF-ROD GRIZZARD (6-8, 210 lbs., JR, #21, 17.0 ppg, 6.1 rpg, 2.0 apg, 2.5 tpg, 1.1 spg, 1.0 bpg, 31.8 minutes, .398 FG, .327 3PT, .812 FT, Central Park Christian/Birmingham, Ala.). Unlike some of his peers in the SEC (Georgia's D.A. Layne comes quickly to mind), Grizzard wasn't about to make a mistake and declare too early for the NBA.

"I know I'm [coming back]," Grizzard said last March. "I haven't thought much about the NBA thing. I know there's a lot I've got to improve here, so I kind of let that go and focused on [summer] to get better and come back here."

Smart move, for as talented as Grizzard is, he does have to improve a few things. His jump shot could use some work, and he could stand to get bigger and stronger. That in turn might improve Grizzard's stamina. Last season he hit a wall while having to play 32 minutes a game. While Alabama was squandering its chances for an NCAA Tournament bid with a late-season four-game losing streak, Grizzard's shot went AWOL. In one two-game stretch, he was 5-for-24 from the field.

"I just know I haven't had the season here that lets everyone know that I'm ready to leave," Grizzard said before the NIT. "I've done some good things here, but ultimately it's not been to my liking where I think I can make that next step. I've got to get stronger."

Just as he'd hoped, Grizzard made some strides during the summer. He spent a lot of time in the weight room and pushed his weight up to 210. That hardly qualifies him for Mr. Universe competition. "But you've got to remember, when he came here, he was like 175," Gottfried said.

Theoretically, the added weight will make Grizzard a little tougher to slow down on his forays to the basket. The truth is, Grizzard needs to take it to the rack more often. He tossed up 214 three-pointers last year, making 70. Considering 33 percent is acceptable, Grizzard's shooting percentage from behind the arc wasn't bad. But he'd improve his overall field-goal percentage (which was ninth among Tide regulars) by exploiting his athleticism and jumping ability and getting to the rim.

"He knows I don't mind him shooting it," Gottfried said. "But I also like him to attack the rim. He went to the free-throw line more often [181 times] than anyone else in the conference last year. He can exploit that by getting to the rim."

Grizzard had a breakout season in 2000-2001. He was chosen to the All-SEC first team after narrowly missing out on the league's scoring title (by three-tenths of a point to LSU's Ronald Dupree). Grizzard's well-rounded game showed up in the SEC's stats. He was 17th in rebounding, third in free-throw percentage and eighth in three-pointers made. Grizzard led Alabama in scoring, steals (40) and blocked shots (38) and was second in rebounds and assists (75).

Still, Gottfried wants more.

"For two years, he was fabulous, terrific," Gottfried said. "But he got a little tired at the end of the year and faded some down the stretch. Rod's had to work at getting rid of some bad habits as far as how hard he works and practices. Now he understands how to do that."

"We need Rod to step up even more this year and play like a senior," Gottfried said. "He's capable of that. We need him to be consistent, especially through the stretch run."

PF-ERWIN DUDLEY (6-8, 258 lbs., JR, #35, 14.4 ppg, 10.0 rpg, 0.7 apg, 0.6 spg, 1.5 tpg, 0.4 bpg, 30.6 minutes, .529 FG, .606 FT, AC Hatch HS/Uniontown, Ala.). Dudley made a selfless decision over the summer. He was one of 16 finalists for a spot on the U.S. World University Games team, but chose not pursue the opportunity because of tendinitis in his left foot. "I want this to be a big year for Alabama, and I want to be 100 percent," Dudley said.

Dudley stood a good chance of making the team—Ole Miss coach Rod Barnes was an assistant coach and likely would have put in a good word—giving him an opportunity to fine-tune his game and showcase his skills. But he passed.

Gottfried was grateful. Had Dudley aggravated the injury, the Tide could really be hurting this season. Already down to two post players because of academic problems and defections, Alabama would have been desperate without Dudley.

After a solid debut as a freshman, when he showed he was perhaps the best rebounder in the SEC, Dudley became a star last season. He was the only player in the league to average a double-double. He led the SEC in rebounding by a large margin, was 10th in scoring and third in field-goal percentage. Dudley was 12th in Division I in rebounding and piled up 15 double doubles, tops in the SEC.

For his efforts, Dudley was chosen to the All-SEC second team.

Dudley has a natural inclination to rebound, but he's helped his cause through intense weight room work.

"He's getting to be more of a bruiser," Gottfried said. "He came in at 220 pounds. Right now he's close to 260. He has really improved his body. He's worked extremely hard at it."

The extra size and strength has allowed Dudley to do some damage in the post.

"He's really improved offensively," Gottfried said. "His freshman year, he wasn't sure what to do with the ball. Now he's very confident and wants the ball because he feels like he can score."

Dudley does so with post moves and brute strength, but he's also developed a jump hook that's hard for defenders to stop. He gets more than his share of garbage baskets because of his relentless rebounding.

"Too bad he's never been able to play his true position for us," Gottfried said. "He's a four man. But obviously, a lot of guys who are four men wind up playing the post in college."

Dudley was consistent all season, but he saved his best for last. He was chosen to the NIT All-Tournament team after averaging 17.8 points and 13.8 rebounds in Alabama's five games. He started the tournament in fine fashion with 22 points and a career-high 19 boards against Seton Hall. He followed that with 10 and seven against Toledo, 20 and 16 against Purdue, 20 and 16 against Detroit and 17 and 11 against Tulsa in the championship game.

Dudley will have to deliver like that night after night for the Tide this season, and he better not get tired or in foul trouble. Gottfried has no options if Dudley isn't on the floor.

C-KENNY WALKER (6-9, 214 lbs., JR, #42, 6.7 ppg, 4.6 rpg, 0.4 spg, 0.6 bpg, 18.2 minutes, .486 FG, .739 FT, Wolfson HS/Jacksonville, Fla.). Walker's injury-plagued freshman year was a letdown, and his sophomore year was becoming a disappointment, too, before Gottfried sat him down in early February and asked him to become more aggressive. Walker had tended to sit

back and let some of his teammates do the scoring. Gottfried convinced Walker he had to shoulder his share of the scoring load.

The pep talk worked wonders. After a long dry spell during which he didn't reach double figures in 14 straight games, Walker responded with 12 points and seven boards against Mississippi State. Over a seven-game span, he averaged 11.1 points and 7.2 rebounds.

Walker's contributions tapered off a bit after that, but he came alive again in the NIT. He led Alabama with a career-high 24 points in a big road victory at Purdue. He came up with 13 points and seven rebounds in an NIT semifinal victory over Detroit.

"He's another guy [along with Demetrius Smith] who didn't have a full freshman year," Gottfried said. "He broke his leg as a freshman and obviously was bothered by it when he came back. Last year, he really came on at the end of the year when we needed him.

"Kenny's got a lot of skills, and he's a great, great person—very coachable. Sometimes he just needs to be more aggressive. He needs to be on the attack mode more. He can shoot the ball. He's very quick and hard to guard; he's got a few post moves, but he's not a banger-type player. I was really proud of him at the end of the year."

Walker will have to elevate his contributions a notch this season, and, like Dudley, do his best to stay on the floor.

KEY RESERVES

G-ANTOINE PETTWAY (6-0, 165 lbs., SO, #50, 2.9 ppg, 1.1 rpg, 1.6 apg, 0.8 spg, 1.6 tpg, .412 FG, .333 3PT, .586 FG, 12.4 minutes, Wilcox Central HS/Camden, Ala.). Alabama's guard play was inconsistent last season, so Pettway, who came to Alabama on an academic scholarship and was an invited walk-on, wound up playing a lot more than a typical walk-on.

Pettway appeared in 29 games and averaged more than 12 minutes. He proved to be a catalyst off the bench, once scoring 19 points against Ole Miss. Pettway handed out a career-high six assists in Alabama's victory over Louisville.

Over the summer, Pettway was rewarded with a scholarship.

"I've really wanted this," Pettway said. "I'm really excited about my athletic scholarship. I was hoping to get it, praying to get it and now it has finally happened."

Pettway grew up an Alabama fan, and though he had full scholarship offers from other Division I schools, he elected to try and walk-on at Alabama.

Gottfried is glad he did.

"He reminds me of [former UCLA point guard] Cameron Dollar," Gottfried said. "He's just tough and hard nosed—he has no fear. His dad's a high school coach, so he's got a feel for the game. He's a guy you want to jump in a foxhole with, no question."

G-EARNEST SHELTON (6-3, 190 lbs., FR, #5, 27.0 ppg, 5.0 rpg, 4.0 apg, White Station HS/Memphis, Tenn.). The acquisition of Shelton was a positive byproduct of Gottfried's hiring last year of former University of Memphis assistant and interim head coach Johnny Jones, who helped lure the sharp-shooting Memphian away from his hometown school. Jones won't be around to see Shelton shine, however; he took the head-coaching job at North Texas last April and was replaced by former Charlotte assistant Orlando Early.

Alabama might not have many post players, but with Shelton, Williams, Stinnett, Smith and Meade, the Tide has the best-shooting group of guards in the SEC, and maybe the country.

"[Shelton's] probably the best shooter I've ever coached," said White Station coach Terry Tippett, who also coached former Wake Forest star Robert O'Kelley.

If Shelton can have the same sort of impact at Alabama that O'Kelley did at Wake Forest, the Crimson Tide got a real bargain. Gottfried already knew that Shelton was a solid citizen who makes great grades, is coachable and works hard to get better. And Shelton isn't an overpowering athlete who will bolt for the NBA after one season. More likely, he'll be around four years, making solid contributions each year.

Gottfried knows what he's going to get with Shelton. He's not a three-man or a backup point. He's strictly a shooter.

"He's got a super-quick release, a refined motion, knows how to read screens and works tirelessly to get open," said Zack McMillin of the Memphis Commerical-Appeal and Blue Ribbon. "He's a little slower afoot than you'd like to see, but he knows how to play the game and

he knows how to score."

Shelton was a two-time player of the year (as chosen by the Commerical-Appeal) in talent-rich Memphis, no small accomplishment in itself. He was offered a scholarship by the hometown school and new coach John Calipari, who actually turned down eventual Kentucky signee Rashaad Carruth to wait on Shelton. But when Calipari tired of waiting and went another direction, the player trimmed his choices to Wake Forest, Tennessee and Alabama.

Gottfried is glad Shelton picked the Tide. In Gottfried's mind, he can never have too many shooters.

"Earnest can certainly make shots," Gottfried said. "Last year he was one of the best shooters in the class. How quickly he transitions to the SEC, you never know. But we're excited about having Earnest on our team."

G-DEMETRIUS SMITH (6-3, 215 lbs., SO, #23, 0.0 ppg, 0.7 rpg, 0.2 apg, 3.7 minutes, Calloway HS/Hogansville, Ga.). Alabama fans didn't get to see the real Smith last season. He came in out of shape, and by the time he started rounding into form, he broke his foot. That was in early December. Smith returned in January, but wound up playing in just 10 games. He didn't score a point. "He never really got into the groove at all," Gottfried said.

Now Gottfried thinks Smith, a former Top 100 recruit, can be a secret weapon for Alabama. He can play either guard spot, giving the Tide plenty of depth behind probably starters Williams and Meade. Smith should see plenty of action, and not just because Alabama is so thin in numbers.

"He's a versatile guard," Gottfried said. "He can do a lot for us."

G-TRAVIS STINNETT (6-0, 170 lbs., JR, #10, 6.8 ppg, 1.8 rpg, 1.7 apg, 1.6 tpg, 0.5 spg, 17.2 minutes, .419 FG, .442 3PT, .820 FT, Alcoa HS/Alcoa, Tenn.). Stinnett finally got to play after a two-year hiatus, and he made the most of his opportunity.

That opportunity seemed forever in the making for Stinnett, who missed his first two seasons at Alabama while battling a pelvic injury. After surgery corrected the problem, Stinnett showed up last year in top physical condition for the first time in his collegiate career.

Still, some of the same questions remained about Stinnett, who originally signed with Gottfried when the latter was coach at Murray State. Stinnett would surely have been a star in the Ohio Valley Conference. But was he too small and too slow to make contributions at the SEC level?

Stinnett answered those questions after Gottfried, almost in desperation, turned to him in a game against Auburn in late January.

"With our personnel, at times we had some guys on the floor who weren't great shooters," Gottfried said. [Opposing teams] were using triangle and twos and box and ones on us. We were looking at junk defenses every night. Some teams were not even guarding our perimeter players."

Enter Stinnett, who astounded everyone by coming off the bench and scoring a team-high 17 points as the Tide outlasted Auburn.

He wasn't a one-game wonder. Stinnett proved to be the perimeter scoring threat the Tide had been lacking. He led Alabama in scoring in several other games, including against Seton Hall in the NIT when he torched the Pirates for a career-high 22 points, all of them coming in the first half. Stinnett also scored 16 against Georgia and Arkansas, both team-high efforts.

Stinnett finished the season third in the SEC in three-point percentage. He was also third in league games only (.458).

"He played very well," Gottfried said. "I was very proud of Travis. He went through two years of injuries, and I'm sure there were times when he thought about whether or not he should continue.

"We're glad he hung in there. He can really shoot the ball. And he's a smart player, too."

Stinnett ended up starting 14 games. He probably won't be a starter this season, but because the Tide's only real depth is in the backcourt, he'll still play a lot of minutes as Gottfried tries to exploit his team's strengths.

OTHER RETURNEES

F-SOLOMON DAVIS (6-6, 215 lbs., SO #3, 1.0 ppg, 0.7 rpg, .267 FG, .400 3PT, .333 FT, 3.1 minutes in 1999-2000, LeFlore HS/Mobile, Ala.). When Davis heard from Gottfried during the summer about Alabama's personnel shortage, he decided to rejoin the basketball team. Solomon is in school on a President's scholarship and walked on to the team two years ago. Despite that, Gottfried sweetened the deal by placing Davis on athletic scholarship.

Davis sat out his first year (1998-99), and as a red-shirt freshman played in just 14 games, not enough to make him think too seriously about continuing his basketball career. An engineering major, Davis instead decided to give up basketball so he could focus on his studies.

Davis—a former all-state player at LeFlore—comes from good basketball stock. His father Solomon Sr. played at Kentucky State and was drafted by the Phoenix Suns. The younger Davis might not play a lot this year, but then again, Gottfried just might have to call on him.

In the brief time he spent on the floor as a freshman, Davis showed he could do one thing—he knocked down four-of-10 three-pointers.

F-REGGIE RAMBO (6-7, 230 lbs., SO, #4, 0.4 ppg, 0.4 rpg, 2.0 minutes, Peabody HS/Lena, La.). Rambo passed up scholarship offers from other SEC schools to sign at Alabama, but he must have wondered last year whether he might the right move. Rambo saw the court in just 10 games for a total of 20 minutes.

If the Tide didn't need him last year, it certainly will now, given the threadbare depth situation in the front-court.

Rambo's attitude wasn't affected by his lack of playing time, and he dedicated himself to the weight room, bulking himself up to 230 pounds.

"He's done a great job getting bigger and stronger," Gottfried said. "He's got to provide depth for us. He can shoot well, rebound well and plays hard. He's very active."

OTHER NEWCOMERS

G-LUCKY WILLIAMS (6-6, 220 lbs., FR #13, 19.2 ppg, 8.0 rpg, Central Park Christian/Birmingham, Ala.). Williams is in school, but wasn't eligible for the first semester because he hadn't achieved an NCAA-required score on a standardized test. Given his team's lack of depth, Gottfried is hoping to gain Williams' services for the second semester. In recent years, several SEC West players—among them Joe Johnson (Arkansas) and Stromile Swift (LSU)—have gained eligibility for the second semester of their freshman season after earning the required test scores.

Williams isn't a Joe Johnson or Stromile Swift, but he's capable of helping the Tide in certain situations. He's a native of Nigeria who played one season for the same high school that produced Grizzard. Before that, he played high school basketball in New Jersey. Central Park finished 26-2 last season with Williams and Auburn signee Marco Killingsworth leading the way.

"He's quick, he's a jumping jack and he shoots the three well," Central Park coach Levan Parker told the Huntsville Times. "I think Alabama is the perfect place for him."

Williams shot 56 percent from the field and 84 percent from the free-throw line last season. If he become eligible, he'll get some playing time in conference play.

"I think Lucky is going to be nice addition to our team," Gottfried said when Williams signed last May. "He's talented. He's athletically gifted. His best basketball is ahead of him. Hopefully he can emerge as a shutdown defender during his career here."

QUESTIONS

Depth? Defections and academic troubles have combined to thin out Alabama's roster.

Size? Gottfried doesn't have a lot of height or bulk to turn to off the bench. He has three players 6-8 or taller, all of whom start, and no post reserve on the bench save Reggie Rambo.

Point guard? Will freshman Maurice Williams live up to his billing and take over at the point?

ANSWERS

Grizzard and Dudley! The Tide has two All-SEC players in the acrobatic Grizzard and the hard-working Dudley.

Athletic ability! Even with the loss of Wallace, Alabama has a lot of run-jump athletes who can finish plays.

Scoring punch! Alabama needed to recruit some players, particularly in the backcourt, with some scoring ability, and it succeeded.

ALABAMA 2000-01 RESULTS

Troy State	92-64
Arkansas-Pine Bluff	110-53
Louisville	100-71
Grambling	107-61
Wofford	68-64
#Akron	73-59
#North Texas	94-55
##Northern Iowa	64-56
##Washington	69-60
##Cincinnati (L)	74-77
Alabama State	82-56
Southeastern Louisiana	92-63
@LSU	82-73
@Tennessee (L)	69-86
Mississippi State	72-59
Mississippi	82-63
@Arkansas (L)	58-87
Kentucky	70-60
Auburn	81-80
@Vanderbilt (L)	62-68
LSU	76-66
@Mississippi State	84-70
Georgia	76-68
South Carolina	60-55
Ohio State	85-67
@Auburn (L)	69-72
@Florida (L)	68-89
Arkansas (L)	63-66
@Mississippi (L)	71-105
###Vanderbilt	78-59
###Florida (L)	61-69
####Seton Hall	85-79
####Toledo	79-69
####Purdue	85-77
####Detroit	74-63
####Tulsa (L)	60-79

#Arby's Hardwood Classic, Birmingham, Ala.
##Puerto Rico Holiday Classic in San Juan
###SEC Tournament, Nashville, TN
####NIT

BLUE RIBBON ANALYSIS

BACKCOURT	B+
BENCH/DEPTH	C
FRONTCOURT	B
INTANGIBLES	B

Had Gottfried been able to get 6-9 junior college recruits Madison and Bias in school, Alabama would have been a clear-cut favorite to win the SEC's Western Division championship. But neither player qualified academically, and to make matters worse, 6-8 senior Haginas called Gottfried in July to tell him he was quitting.

By that time, it was far too late to find any replacements, which means Dudley and Walker, the Tide's only true post players, are going to have to shoulder a huge load this season.

If Dudley and Walker prove durable and they don't get into foul trouble, Alabama will still be hard to handle, given the presence of All-SEC forward Grizzard and a stable of quality guards. Gottfried might have to put a smaller, quicker lineup on the floor and offset any defensive size mismatches with quickness mismatches on the other end.

We still think Alabama is a quality, postseason team, given the maturity of the Tide's strong junior class and the addition of guards Williams and Shelton. Alabama won't be as dominant without the size and bulk of Madison and Bias, but the Tide, if it holds up against a greatly improved schedule, should be able to earn enough brownie points with the NCAA Tournament selection committee to receive a long-awaited Big Dance ticket.

(C.D.)

Western Kentucky 35

LOCATION	Bowling Green, KY
CONFERENCE	Sun Belt (East)
LAST SEASON	24-7 (.774)
CONFERENCE RECORD	14-2 (1st)

STARTERS LOST/RETURNING	1/4
NICKNAME	Hilltoppers
COLORS	Red & White
HOMECOURT	E.A. Diddle Arena (8,100)
COACH	Dennis Felton (Howard '85)
RECORD AT SCHOOL	48-41 (3 years)
CAREER RECORD	48-41 (3 years)
ASSISTANTS	Pete Hermann (SUNY-Genesco '70)
	Ken McDonald (Providence '92)
	Bert Tucker (Maine-Farmington '94)
TEAM WINS (last 5 years)	12-10-13-11-24
RPI (last 5 years)	176-209-149-202-79
2000-01 FINISH	Lost in NCAA first round.

COACH AND PROGRAM

The long and storied tradition of Western Kentucky basketball may have had its renaissance last season, but the groundwork of the Hilltoppers' return to prosperity in 2000-01 was set one year earlier.

Surprised? After all, WKU went from an 11-18 record the previous year all the way to the 24-7 mark that included the Sun Belt Conference regular-season and tournament titles and the 'Toppers' first trip to the NCAA Tournament since 1995.

You've got to look a little more closely at the end of that 1999-2000 season, though. That year, Western won three straight games near the end of the regular season, and then made it to the semifinals of the league tournament before falling by three points to top-seeded South Alabama.

"We knew we had accomplished a lot, growing up with a very young team," said coach Dennis Felton, who took over the Hilltopper program before the 1998-99 season. "By the end of the year, we felt like we were a pretty good basketball team, about as good as anybody in the league."

Then, the 'Toppers took a spring trip to Europe, playing four games of international competition in France and Switzerland and getting even more of an opportunity to grow as a unit.

"That gave us a lot of constructive time together when we were able to do that in the spring," Felton said. "The 10 days of practice time was every bit as valuable as the four games we played.

"We had a lot of first-year players that had a lot of learning to do, but they got a lot done during the season. And when we came back in the spring, we were a second-year team and the guys came to practice with a new sense of experience and expectation. They weren't the big-eyed group that we had a year earlier."

In that short period of time, WKU went from an unaccustomed spot of also-ran in the Sun Belt race to a dominant force in the league—but it wasn't easy.

In fact, the Hilltoppers struggled at the start of last year. After three opening wins, Western literally gave away a nationally televised decision to Vanderbilt, and followed that with road losses at New Mexico and Murray State. The stretch gave Felton cause to wonder about a team that he envisioned heading for greater things.

"Looking back, it was a part of getting better," he said. "We played well enough to beat Vanderbilt … we led wire-to-wire until the very end, but we got excited and basically coughed up a win. We were still learning, and we didn't know how to close a team out."

That 70-66 loss was followed by a humbling 18-point setback at New Mexico, and then a two-point loss at in-state rival Murray.

"The New Mexico game was the toughest we played all year," Felton said. "We struggled from start to finish. But the Murray game was the most difficult loss we had all year because we played so poorly and didn't come out ready to play."

More trouble loomed on the horizon with a battle against Louisville in Freedom Hall, and WKU's struggles continued with a double-digit deficit early. But the 'Toppers rallied to take a 68-65 victory, and went on to win 21 of their next 24 games, including a stellar run through the Sun Belt Conference.

Western's only conference losses came on hostile courts at South Alabama (74-66) and Louisiana Tech (73-72), both in overtime, and toward the end of the year the squad took five straight league wins by double-digit margins. Three straight wins in the league tournament—with a last-minute semifinal win over Louisiana-Lafayette the only test there—gave the Hilltoppers their third Sun Belt Tournament crown.

But Felton said the Louisville win was the key to all of that success.

"That was pivotal for us," he said. "We had lost a lot of the confidence that we had built up and we didn't have anything to be confident about the way we played at Murray, and then we came out and didn't play well in the first half. Our team just decided at halftime that enough was enough. Losing is one thing, but not playing with aggressiveness and confidence was no longer acceptable.

"That game gave us the experience of inching our way back into it, taking the lead and having to fight and hold on to win it."

A disappointing loss to Florida in the first round of the NCAA Tournament didn't take much of the luster off a season that saw WKU rank seventh in the nation in scoring margin (+13.4 ppg), second nationally in rebound margin (+9.6 rpg) and 11th in scoring defense (60.9 ppg).

"You tell fans that a season like that doesn't come along too often," Felton said. "Rarely do you dominate a conference the way we did. We beat our conference opponents by over 15 points per game, and that's just total domination."

It was also a bit of redemption for WKU supporters who had struggled in a series of non-Western-like years. The Hilltoppers have posted 63 winning seasons in 82 years, made 17 NCAA Tournament and 11 NIT appearances and have recorded 32 20-win seasons. However, the previous five years were a lost cause with five straight sub-.500 marks.

Felton's first two seasons included records of 13-16 and 11-18.

"When I got here, the program was probably in the worst shape it has ever been," he said. "We had a very ambitious plan on how we wanted to see this program get re-established and become champions. This program has as much tradition as anybody in the country, and for the team to win a championship in our third year, it couldn't have come at a better time."

The rebirth coincides with an upcoming renovation of venerable E.A. Diddle Arena, which has been the 'Toppers' home for 38 years. The facility will host the Sun Belt Tournament in both 2003 and 2004.

But Felton's not resting on any laurels, and has high and hardy hopes for the future.

"We expect to be better than last year, that's for sure, but there's a whole new set of challenges," he said. "We're a big game for everybody we play this time, starting with Kentucky on down. All of our opponents understand that they better bring their 'A' game with them, and a year or two ago that wasn't how we were perceived and wasn't what we faced every night."

2001-2002 SCHEDULE

Nov.	15-16	#NABC Tournament
	20	*Evansville
	26	Murray State
	27	@Creighton
Dec.	2	**Vanderbilt
	5	@Akron
	8	@Austin Peay
	15	West Alabama
	19	Creighton
	22	@Southern Miss
	28	@New Orleans
	30	@South Alabama
Jan.	2	@Florida International
	5	Austin Peay
	10	Louisiana-Lafayette
	13	New Mexico State
	16	@Middle Tennessee
	19	@Denver
	24	Arkansas-Little Rock
	26	Arkansas State
	31	Florida International
Feb.	3	Morris Brown
	7	@Arkansas-Little Rock
	9	@Arkansas State
	16	North Texas
	19	Kentucky State
	23	Middle Tennesee
	28	##Sun Belt Tournament
March	1-5	##Sun Belt Tournament

@Road Games
*Area Bank Classic, Bowling Green, KY
**Gaylord Arena, Nashville, TN
#Lexington, KY (vs. Kentucky first round; also George Washington, Marshall)
##Lakefront Arena, New Orleans, LA

STARTERS NOT RETURNING

G–NASHON McPHERSON (6-4, 10.4 ppg, 3.6 rpg, 1.6 apg, 1.0 spg, 24.0 minutes, .383 FG, .365 3PT, .741 FT). A starter at Western's third guard spot in all 31 games last season, McPherson graduated last May after starting for much of his four-year career. He came back from a preseason cardiac irregularity, was cleared to play before the start of the year and finished as the squad's second-leading scorer and most prolific three-point threat. More than his numbers, he was the unquestioned team leader and was the proverbial "coach on the floor."

"He was the biggest reason for our turnaround," Felton said. "He took this team by the throat and coached it. There's a major void left there."

OTHERS NOT RETURNING

F–RAIMONDS JUMIKIS (6-8, 2.7 ppg, 1.6 rpg, 0.7 apg, 8.1 minutes, .422 FG, .706 FT). Jumikis played in 29 games as a freshman after coming from his native Latvia. The former member of the 19-under Latvian Junior National Team returned home in August, just before the start of the fall semester, with what were described as "critical family issues that will not allow him to continue his college career." Jumikis averaged just more than eight minutes per game as a reserve on the front line, after averaging 14 per game in helping his team finish ninth in the FIBA Junior World Championships in the summer of 1999.

C–BRIAN ALLENSPACH (6-11, 2.0 ppg, 1.0 rpg, 0.3 apg, 6.5 minutes, .417 FG, .667 FT). A backup center, Allenspach appeared in 20 games during his junior season. He had started four games and played in 27 in his sophomore year after transferring from Davidson after his freshman season, and averaged 2.8 points and 11.8 minutes per game as a sophomore. He completed his B.S. degree in business in May and decided against an option of graduate school, which would allow him to play his final year of eligibility.

PROJECTED STARTERS

PG–DEREK ROBINSON (6-1, 185 lbs., SR, #23, 8.9 ppg, 3.0 rpg, 3.9 apg, 1.3 spg, 25.9 minutes, .430 FG, .345 3PT, .708 FT, Bourbon County HS/Paris, Ky.). Robinson may well have been what has held the Hilltoppers together during the struggles of two seasons before last year. The former Sun Belt Freshman of the Year has run the point on a full-time basis for two seasons, and there's nobody with more confidence in him than Felton—and nobody who is a bigger supporter.

"I was just devastated that he or any other player we have besides Chris [Marcus] didn't made all-conference," Felton said. "We dominated the league, so that just doesn't make any sense. I think Derek's the best point guard in the league. He's run our team with such great efficiency, and he's one of the best defenders in the league. It's great to have him back."

Robinson is far from being just a ball distributor and quarterback. He scored double figures in 11 of the final 21 games of the 1999-2000 season when WKU started its resurrection, and followed that with 15 twin-digit games last year. He has 715 career points, going over the 700 mark in the Sun Belt title game, and he had 14 points in that season-turning game against Louisville.

In that same game, he came close to a triple-double, with eight assists and eight rebounds, and it was his two free throws with 11 seconds left that locked up the win. His three-pointer with 3:09 left in the Sun Belt title game erased South Alabama's final lead and started the 'Toppers on an 11-0 run that locked up the tournament crown and the NCAA Tournament berth.

Robinson is also a former Kentucky state scoring champion, averaging 32 points per game as a senior at Bourbon County, where he set school records for career points (2,372) and assists (587).

The first WKU player in six seasons to surpass 100 assists in back-to-back seasons, Robinson was third in the league in assists and his assist-per-minute mark was second (and is the top mark among returnees). The by-minute marks are a better indicator of his worth, because newcomer Raynardo Curry also saw extensive time at the point-guard slot, especially late in the season.

"It's just bizarre that he doesn't get more credit than he does," Felton said.

SG–FILIP VIDENOV (6-4, 200 lbs., JR, #13, 6.5 ppg, 2.4 rpg, 1.8 apg, 0.9 spg, 18.6 minutes, .460 FG, .410 3PT, .815 FT, Washington College Academy/Limestone, Tenn. and Kozloduy, Bulgaria). Videnov started 11 games for the Hilltoppers two years ago and moved into a regular spot in the lineup last year, becoming a solid scoring threat and providing an athletic presence in WKU's three-guard attack. He's also a competent defender with good size for a guard, but his stock rises most when he has the ball in his hands.

"He can score in a variety of ways," Felton said. "He's an explosive driver who can finish with a dunk over your center, but he's also a very effective three-point shooter. He can create and he can finish ... he's got a good mid-range game and can take it to the rim."

Videnov, only the second non-U.S.-born player ever to start for the Hilltoppers, shot almost 43 percent from three-point range in the regular season and holds a two-year-career .868 mark from the free-throw line, having missed only seven free throws in two seasons.

He nursed an injury early in the conference season, but came on strong late, including a career-best 18 points (six-of-eight field goals, 3-of-4 treys) in WKU's home finale against Middle Tennessee. His minutes were up-and-down for much of the season, because the 'Toppers had a wealth of wing players.

The native of Sofia, Bulgaria was a member of the Bulgarian Junior National Team that was runner-up in the European Championships before he came to the U.S. to attend prep school at Washington College.

"Very athletic and very creative," is Felton's description.

SG–TREMAIN ROWLES (6-4, 200 lbs., SR, #42, 6.0 ppg, 2.3 rpg, 1.6 apg, 1.3 spg, 18.3 minutes, .425 FG, .368 3PT, .650 FT, Gwynn Lake Prep/Landover, Md. and Parkdale HS/Landover Hills, Md.). Yes, he's listed as a second guard along with Videnov, because that comes closer to describing Western's normal three-guard alignment. Rowles joins with Robinson as the only fourth-year performers on the team, and has been a solid part of the WKU backcourt since hitting The Hill.

He has averaged at least 15 minutes per game in all three of his collegiate seasons and has 19 starts, including 10 last year, so it's not much of a stretch to envision Rowles taking McPherson's role in the regular starting lineup.

"We think we've got eight or nine starters," Felton said, "because we really do have that many guys that can play and contribute. But Tremain's a starter whether or not he comes off the bench. He's a Mr. Fix-It for us ... he can fill any gap that we need him to. Whether it's rebounding, defending a great scorer, or even running the point some because he can make the extra pass to get our offense going."

Rowles may be the most distinctive player in the Sun Belt because of his throwback Afro 'do, but his game is definitely not retro. In fact, he scored half of his season's 185 points in the final 10 games of last season, averaging 9.2 per outing down a stretch that also included three of his four double-figure games. He had 18 points against both North Texas and Arkansas-Little Rock and 20 at Arkansas State in that run.

He also hit more than 50 percent on both field goals and three-pointers in that late run, and it was his steal and layup with 27 seconds left that broke open a two-point game in an 82-75 win over Louisiana-Lafayette in a Sun Belt semifinal.

Rowles finished second on the team in steals and third in assists despite playing 18.3 minutes per game and had a 2-to-1 assist-to-turnover ratio, committing less than one turnover per game.

"He's played everything for us from point to center—literally," Felton said. "He's a jack of all trades, and his value to us is that he's so versatile plus he's smart in knowing what to do in all of those positions."

PF—DAVID BOYDEN (6-8, 230 lbs., JR, #34, 7.4 ppg, 5.1 rpg, 1.0 apg, 0.5 spg, 25.3 minutes, .461 FG, .328 3PT, .545 FT, Fork Union Academy/Fork Union, Va. and Hermitage HS/Richmond, Va.). Some might say that the job of the other frontcourt player at WKU this year is to stay out of Chris Marcus' way. While there's some merit to that, Boyden's contributions to the Hilltoppers over the last two seasons make him much more than the "other" red jersey near the basket.

He was the second-leading rebounder on a Western squad that finished second in the nation in rebound margin, and he scored in double figures six times in the last 14 games of the season. He also shot more than 57 percent in his nine twin-digit scoring games and, most surprisingly, he bounced outside to hit 13-of-28 from past the three-point arc in those same nine games.

"He's been a starter from day one because he's very intelligent and very solid, and maybe the best defensive forward in the league," Felton said. "But he's also developed into a really good three-point shooter, and that's important, because that helps us space the floor for Chris to have room to operate inside. We wanted him to go from a 12-foot shooter to a three-point shooter between his freshman and sophomore seasons, and he did that."

Boyden has started 58-of-60 games in his career and has always been a solid defender—he held Evansville preseason Missouri Valley Conference Player-of-the-Year Craig Snow to 10 points and six rebounds in 31 minutes in last year's season opener—but his shooting came as a surprise. He still has a long way to go from the free-throw line, hitting only .545 last year and .517 in his career.

But there's no question that he'll battle inside. Almost 50 percent of Boyden's rebounds last year (73-of-159) came on the offensive end.

"He becomes more and more aggressive as a player the more he plays," Felton said, which may explain why Boyden's turnovers more than doubled from his freshman to his sophomore year despite only slightly more playing time. "He's close to turning that next corner."

C–CHRIS MARCUS (7-1, 285 lbs., SR, #21, 16.7 ppg, 12.1 rpg, 0.9 apg, 0.6 spg, 29.5 minutes, .547 FG, .639 FT, Olympic HS/Charlotte, N.C.). It starts and stops in the middle for the Hilltoppers. While WKU would be a very solid team without the big-bodied Marcus in the middle, there is no question that he is the biggest man on The Hill.

If there were any questions about his talents by the end of last season, they were quickly quashed during the Sun Belt Tournament when he crushed everything placed before him.

He opened the tournament with 22 points and 14 boards against Florida International, and followed that with a career-high 33 points and 13 rebounds in a close win over Louisiana-Lafayette (the only close call for the 'Toppers after Feb. 15). He came close to 20-20 vision with 20 points and 18 rebounds in the title game win over South Alabama.

His 25.0 and 15.0 averages—and the fact that he missed only 12 shots in the entire tournament—made Marcus probably the easiest tournament MVP selection in Sun Belt history.

"He was an absolute beast in the tournament," Felton said. "He answered the call in every game. Against frontcourts like UL-Lafayette and South Alabama had, both of them with terrific size and talent, it was really impressive to see the success he had with so much on the line.

"Teams are competing as hard as they can at that point, with all the passion they have to play in the national tournament, and mistakes are really critical then. He just kept making big shot after big shot. That's his most impressive stretch of basketball ever. He carried a load."

Impressive may be the best adjective to describe Marcus, but shocking may be a better one to describe how far he's come in such a short time. This season will be only his fourth to play organized basketball after only one year of high school action.

But that's been enough to earn him Associated Press honorable-mention All-America honors, Sun Belt Player of the Year and Defensive Player of the Year accolades and a host of other awards. He's mentioned prominently on most of this year's preseason All-America listings.

"The thing that makes me most proud is that he's become an All-American the old-fashioned way," Felton said. "He earned it on the court. He didn't have all of those rankings coming out of high school, so he's not a paper All-American. We haven't spent a dime on any kind of All-America campaign. Everything he's received has been based entirely on his performance on the floor."

Marcus led the nation in rebounding last year, and "double-doubles" literally became everyday occurrences for him (he had 20). He narrowly missed the first "triple-double" in WKU history with 12 points, a career-high 21 rebounds and a school-record nine blocked shots against Tennessee State.

Marcus also had several runs at "20-20" games, including a 27-point, 19-rebound effort against South Alabama. At one point, he had eight straight double-digit point and rebound efforts, and he's done that trick 29 times in 56 career starts.

Marcus was the Sun Belt's Newcomer of the Year and Defensive Player of the Year as a sophomore in 1999-2000, his first year of collegiate play, and he led the league in both rebounding and blocked shots. He would also have ranked in the top ten nationally in shooting (.596) but did not attempt enough shots to qualify.

His 97 blocked shots last season broke his own school record, and that doesn't come close to including the shots that were altered because of his presence.

"Western could have easily won some games in the [NCAA] tournament," New Mexico State coach Lou Henson said, "and that's because of Chris Marcus. He's just tremendous."

"A lot of us in the league are pretty similar," UL-Lafayette head coach Jessie Evans said. "The difference in them is that the rest of us don't have a lottery pick back there under the basket."

"He is made of sterner stuff than the average basketball star his age," said Pat Forde of the Louisville Courier-Journal. "He's blessed with two preciously rare commodities: patience and perspective."

His rapid improvement doesn't come as a surprise to Felton, who saw much more than a large body coming out of the Charlotte area, where Marcus played his first organized basketball in a summer 1997 AAU tournament. He had averaged only eight points and nine rebounds in his one season at Olympic High.

"The best thing about Chris is that he picks up things very quickly," he said. "He challenges you as a coach because he wants to know the finer points of what you're talking about. He's really, really smart, and he doesn't take long to figure things out and put information to use. Sure, he works hard, but his intelligence is his greatest attribute."

KEY RESERVES

PG-RAYNARDO CURRY (6-0, 180 lbs., JR, #11, 4.7 ppg, 2.2 rpg, 2.2 apg, 1.5 spg, .19.4 minutes, 429 FG, .313 3PT, .722 FT, East HS/Memphis, Tenn.). Even with the solid backcourt that the Hilltoppers had returning, Curry still established himself as a regular presence in his first season. After sitting out his freshman year, he played in every game, starting five and averaging more than 19 minutes per game. He had provided a preview of that success on the team's European tour one spring earlier, averaging 12.3 points, 3.5 assists and 3.8 steals in four games.

He then played 23 minutes in his first college game at Evansville, and late in the season he averaged double figures in WKU's final four games while hitting 61 percent from the field.

"He was a rookie last year and learned a lot," Felton said. "He'll be a much more forceful and consistent player this year. He's got great speed and quickness and needs to get that speed under control, but he may be the best on-ball defender in the league. He can really harass people and create a lot with his defense."

Curry led the Hilltoppers in steals (44) as a sophomore, but needs to improve his shooting (5-of-16 three-pointers last year after hitting almost six treys per game in high school).

G-MIKE WELLS (6-3, 190 lbs., JR, #15, 5.2 ppg, 2.5 rpg, 0.7 apg, 0.4 spg, 14.7 minutes, .406 FG, .277 3PT, .875 FT, Todd County Central HS/Elkton, Ky.). Wells had an inconsistent season for the Hilltoppers as a sophomore after sitting out his freshman year. He showed flashes of big things, earning Sun Belt Player-of-the-Week honors for his play in late December when he averaged 12.5 points and 3.8 rebounds off the bench in two wins. He made four straight free throws to lock up one win and seven points in one minute of play in the other victory. He also struggled at times, finishing with more turnovers than assists for the season.

"He's going to be a talented off guard," Felton said. "He had some good games, games in which he looked like a veteran, and made some big plays. He made an impact, and even when he had the ups and downs it wasn't that bad."

A rangy player, Wells finished last year with almost as many blocked shots (10) as steals (12), and had a career-high 16 points in an early-season league win at Denver.

The genes are in the right place. Older brother Bubba led the nation in scoring and earned All-America honors at Austin Peay before a brief career in the NBA.

F–NATE WILLIAMS (6-8, 240 lbs., JR, #30, 4.6 ppg, 2.6 rpg, 0.3 apg, 0.3 spg, 14.5 minutes, .490 FG, .667 FT, Ravenscroft HS/Raleigh, N.C.). Felton said that Williams may have been Western's most improved player last year, and he may be right. He showed big improvement in every statistical category as a primary reserve on the WKU front line, especially from the free-throw line.

In his freshman year, Williams averaged less than two shots per game even though he played more than 10 minutes per outing, perhaps showing offensive timidity because of his struggles at the line. He hit under 35 percent from the line that season.

Last year, he virtually doubled his success rate.

"He developed a lot more confidence on the court," Felton said. "I think he rushed things offensively because he didn't want to get fouled, but last year he did a good job of getting to the line and then making them. He's very strong and athletic around the basket, and we need him to be more of a force inside."

Williams had career highs of 15 points twice during the season and three double-digit scoring games in what was obviously a happier season than his first.

"The great thing is that he's enjoying the fact that his game and his offensive range is improving," Felton said. "He's a much better all-around player from a year ago."

F–TODOR PANDOV (6-9, 230 lbs., SO, #45, 2.6 ppg, 1.9 rpg, 0.3 apg, 10.7 minutes, .446 FG, .296 3PT, .419 FT in 1999-2000, Washington College Academy/Limestone, Tenn. and Plovidv, Bulgaria). Pandov returns to active duty after red-shirting in the 2000-01 season, and he's expected to provide help at several slots once he shakes off the rust of a year of inactivity. He had played in 27 games, earning one start, in his freshman year.

That season, he came on at the end of the year, hitting 27 of his last 44 field goal tries, including seven of his last 18 outside the arc. Pandov had a high game of nine points late in the season.

"He's our best pure athlete," Felton said. "He's a 6-9 guy that can play anywhere on the court. He can shoot the three and he can put it on the floor, he's got great explosiveness. He just needs more time to learn the game and learn how to put his athleticism to use more efficiently with nine other players on the floor."

G–NATHAN EISERT (6-5, 200 lbs., SO, #4, 0.9 ppg, 0.3 rpg, 1.4 minutes, .750 FG, Seneca HS/Louisville, Ky.). A walk-on, Eisert played in nine games as a freshman and picked up late-game minutes. He hit three-pointers against Arkansas State and Savannah State.

"He's worked hard to try to get in the mix more," Felton said. "He put on about 25 pounds last year and got much stronger, which is going to be a major help to him."

OTHER NEWCOMERS

F-CALEB HALCOMB (6-10, 220 lbs., SO, #33, 9.0 ppg, 4.0 rpg, Lincoln Trail College/Robinson, Ill. and Bowling Green HS/Bowling Green, Ky.). A former hometown hero in Bowling Green, Halcomb comes to the Hilltopper program after a year at Lincoln Trail. where he worked on developing his game to go with his physical skills. He has three years of collegiate eligibility.

"He's a long guy," Felton said of the Bowling Green native who has a 7-6 wingspan. "He's very good at blocking and altering shots. He's more of a defensive and rebounding presence right now, but has the potential to turn into a really good player."

G–PATRICK SPARKS (6-1, 170 lbs., FR, #22, 31.4 ppg, 7.0 rpg, 6.1 apg, Muhlenberg North HS/Central City, Ky.). Sparks developed a cult following among Kentucky prep basketball followers during his four-year career as a prolific scorer and all-around player for Muhlenberg North. He's probably one of the few guards in Kentucky history to lead his team to the state championship tournament three straight years, and came within one game of making that four tournament appearances in a row. He led the state in scoring as a senior but was also a standout passer.

"He's extremely creative and has terrific vision. He loves passing the ball," Felton said. "He got standing ovations in both games in the Kentucky-Indiana all-star series, and he was close to a quadruple double in both games. We're pretty solid at guard, but I expect him to come in and make an impact and do a lot of good things as a freshman."

F-KALIN HOLLAND (6-7, 225 lbs., FR, #25, Bowling Green HS/Bowling Green, Ohio and Bowling Green, Ky.). Holland, a walk-on, is a hometown product, but he played his high school ball at Bowling Green High in Ohio, meaning that his name, hometown and high school will look confusing on Western's roster all season.

"He's a big body and has some tools," Felton said, "but he has a lot to learn."

QUESTIONS

Leadership? McPherson was the inspirational leader of the Hilltoppers, and his departure leaves a hole that someone will have to fill in a hurry. There are only three seniors on what still is a young team, and the two that have played the most—Marcus and Robinson—have been leader-by-example performers.

Backing up the big guy? Marcus hasn't been plagued by fouls, which is the bane of many big centers. He's fouled out only twice in two seasons and averaged only 2.3 fouls per game last season. With Allenspach not returning, there are no other pure centers on the WKU roster.

Can they run-run-run? The Hilltoppers worked hard on developing a running game last year and averaged more than 75 points per game in Sun Belt play, but were not really a fast-breaking team. Some clubs tried to push the tempo against Western during the season, with inconsistent results.

ANSWERS

Lock 'em down! Led by shot-blocking machine Marcus and a lot of in-your-face guards, WKU was one of the nation's top defensive teams last year, and all of the stoppers are back. The Hilltoppers allowed only 60.9 points per game, the country's 11th-best mark, and foes hit only 40.7 percent of their shots. Those numbers were even better (59.8 ppg, 40.2 percent FG) in league play.

Throw bodies at them! Nine different players played double-figure minutes last year, both overall and in Sun Belt play. And nobody averaged as many as 30 minutes per game (even Marcus was at 29.5). Felton is not afraid to play a lot of people, and he's fortunate to have good depth.

Look for the biggest thing in sight! Marcus was one of only three players in the country to get 19 rebounds in a game more than once, and only two players nationally had more double-double games. And he has guards that know when to get the ball into his hands.

W. KENTUCKY 2000-2001 RESULTS

@Evansville	61-59
Union College	75-45
Tennessee State	90-66
Vanderbilt (L)	66-70
@New Mexico (L)	57-75
@Murray State (L)	81-83
@Louisville	68-65
Akron	73-58
Savannah State	103-60
St. Joseph's (PA) (L)	68-74
@New Orleans	68-63
@Denver	80-61
Ashbury College	81-29
Louisiana Lafayette	79-62
@South Alabama (L)	66-74
Arkansas-Little Rock	59-49
New Mexico State	72-61
Louisiana Tech	55-47
Arkansas State	79-61
@Florida International	55-46
@Middle Tennessee	71-63
North Texas	107-63
@Louisiana Tech (L)	72-73
Florida International	69-49
@Arkansas-Little Rock	86-73
@Arkansas State	100-60
Middle Tennessee	92-51
#Florida International	68-51
#Louisiana Lafayette	82-75
#South Alabama	64-54
##Florida (L)	56-69

#Sun Belt Tournament in Mobile, AL
##NCAA Tournament
@Road Games

BLUE RIBBON ANALYSIS

BACKCOURT	A-
BENCH/DEPTH	A-
FRONTCOURT	A-
INTANGIBLES	B

Felton is already on record talking about how seasons like last year's 24-win campaign don't come along very often, but he, his staff and players, and everybody in southern Kentucky will be hugely disappointed if the Hilltoppers don't show some more magic this season. Five straight losing seasons before last year's turnaround made even the most diehard fans antsy for success, and now that success is supposed to perpetuate

itself.

Fortunately for WKU, those expectations are reasonable. Western had the second-biggest turnaround in the 82-year history of Hilltopper basketball last year, and all but one of the major cogs in that revitalization are back with another year's experience. A team that won as many games last year as the previous two years combined has a chance to win even more if it can improve its postseason performance.

That may be the only rap on this team. The 'Toppers did not play well in an NCAA Tournament first-round loss to Florida after going into the postseason with high hopes.

"We would have felt better if we'd played the way we had been playing and still lost," Felton said of the loss to the Gators. "We've had a nasty taste in our mouths all spring and summer. We want to get back there and stay longer." The first task is to get back to the NCAAs, and an improved Sun Belt may make that a little tougher than Western's blitzkrieg through the league last year. With the much-improved non-conference schedule, though, WKU should earn an at-large bid even if the Hilltoppers are surprised in the league tournament.

After that, Felton's not bashful about setting higher goals.

"We want to play for the national championship," he said. "The problem is that there are a whole lot of other teams that will have something to say about that. There are literally hundreds of very good teams out there. You can be terrific and still get beat by another terrific team. But we're going to try to do some special things this year."

(D.M.)

Purdue 36

LOCATION	West Lafayette, IN
CONFERENCE	Big Ten
LAST SEASON	17-15 (.531)
CONFERENCE RECORD	6-10 (8th)
STARTERS LOST/RETURNING	1/4
NICKNAME	Boilermakers
COLORS	Old Gold & Black
HOMECOURT	Mackey Arena (14,123)
COACH	Gene Keady (Kansas State '58)
RECORD AT SCHOOL	456-206 (21 years)
CAREER RECORD	494-225 (23 years)
ASSISTANTS	Jay Price (Kansas '91)
	Cuonzo Martin (Purdue '95)
	Todd Foster (Purdue '96)
TEAM WINS (last 5 years)	18-28-21-24-17
RPI (last 5 years)	20-8-23-27-53
2000-01 FINISH	Lost in NIT quarterfinal.

COACH AND PROGRAM

During Gene Keady's 21 years as head coach, the Purdue Boilermakers have been one of the Big Ten's most consistent programs. They've made 20 postseason appearances—16 of them in the NCAA Tournament. Going into 2000-01, Keady's teams had finished third or higher in the Big Ten for seven consecutive seasons—including three straight titles from 1994-'96. They reached the NCAA Sweet 16 or Elite Eight four of those years.

All of which made last season hard to bear in West Lafayette.

At times, it was a typical Keady season: An upset of No. 1 Arizona on Thanksgiving weekend. A seven-game winning streak in December. A 3-0 start to the Big Ten season.

But the bitter taste left in Purdue fans' mouths after 2000-01 has little to do with those accomplishments. They remember seven losses in nine games, settling for the NIT for the first time since 1992 and, most telling, the Boilers' worst Big Ten record (6-10) and standing (eighth place) of Keady's career.

Not that the coach had complete control over what transpired. Already a young team playing without four major contributors from the previous season's Elite Eight team, the Boilers were devastated by injuries in 2001. Center John Allison was quickly developing into one of the league's premier post players when he went down with a stress fracture in his foot on Feb. 2. On Feb. 9, a similar fate befell forward Rodney Smith, who broke his foot.

Within a week, the team had lost its top two rebounders and two of its top three scorers, not to return until March. By then, the Boilers' NIT fate had been sealed. And after wins over Illinois State and Auburn, their season ended in fittingly painful fashion: by blowing an 11-point lead with 15 minutes to play and falling to Alabama in double overtime in a home game that would have sent them to the NIT semifinals in New York.

"We went through a rough season," Keady said after that game. "Hopefully from this rough season, the young kids will have learned something and helped build themselves up to where they can compete with this type of team [Alabama]. They had too many horses for us."

Despite the club's struggles, the Boilermakers did exhibit several traits characteristic of Keady's best teams. They were tenacious on defense, ranking second in the Big Ten in turnover margin (+2.88) and opponents' three-point shooting percentage (.321). They shot well from outside, ranking second in the league in that category as well (.380).

But the Boilers also showed a couple frustrating trends. They often dug holes too deep to overcome even with tremendous rallies, like their 17-point deficit UCLA, the 35-18 halftime margin at Minnesota, the 21-4 eyesore at Iowa and the 14-point second-half bulge against Ohio State. Purdue would lose all four games by six points or less.

"I don't think we took the right type of pride on defense," Keady said. "I don't think they knew how to do that because they were so young."

And then there were the fouls. So many fouls. The Boilers saw 27 players disqualified in 32 games, compared with nine the year before.

"We have to learn how to win close games," Keady said. "We have to learn how to take care of the basketball at critical parts, and start to find ways to win. I think championship teams play to win."

The good news for Keady is that last year's youngsters are this year's veterans. Four of the regulars are now seniors, which, based on the recent past, is a good indicator of success. In 1995-96, a cast of six seniors led Purdue to a 26-6 record and Big Ten title. Four years later, it was seniors Brian Cardinal, Jaraan Cornell, Greg McQuay and Mike Robinson pacing an Elite Eight finish.

The bad news is, the injury bug hasn't entirely subsided. While four returning starters dot this year's roster, one of them, guard Kenneth Lowe, underwent shoulder surgery in August and may miss the season.

Keady doesn't seem fazed by Lowe's status. The squad is particularly deep at guard, welcoming junior college sensation and likely instant starter Darmetreis Kilgore. Preserving Lowe's junior season with a red-shirt may make sense considering the roster will once again be young in 2002.

It's clear Keady expects this season's edition to return Purdue to its proper place in the polls and league standings. But his club's potential may not seem that obvious to outsiders. Like most of his recent squads, this is a blue-collar team that plans to achieve its goals without any noticeable stars.

In fact, not since Glenn "Big Dog" Robinson took his skills to the Milwaukee Bucks in 1994 has Purdue had a true All-America-type player. Keady always gets great mileage out of talented but unheralded guys like Cardinal, former center Brad Miller and current assistant coach Cuonzo Martin. All three would go on to play professionally, but not before staying all four years at Purdue, something Keady values. He tries to avoid situations like the one Tom Izzo presently faces at Michigan State, where sophomore Jason Richardson and freshman Zach Randolph bolted after last season, leaving Izzo with only eight scholarship players.

Then again, Izzo is coming off three consecutive Final Fours, a destination Keady has yet to reach despite his many accolades, which include six Big Ten titles and seven league coach-of-the-year honors.

"We've had a top 10 team here seven times in the last 21 years, and I want to get to that level again," Keady said. "We need to redo some things, get better players, and get a little better work ethic and stop some teams on defense."

With his sixth win of this season, Keady will reach his milestone 500th victory. In March, his contract was extended through 2005. Purdue fans clearly adore him. They treasure all those Big Ten title rings—not to mention all those wins over Indiana.

But they also crave that one elusive symbol of national superiority, to reach the Final Four, something most would deem unlikely without the McDonald's All-America-type players that litter the rosters at places like

Duke and North Carolina. But Keady has a lot of faith in his returning roster and has high hopes for Kilgore as a potential scoring machine.

"Our goal here is always to win the Big Ten, Go to the NCAAs, go the Final Four if we can," Keady said. "Last year, when we didn't have many seniors and guys were getting hurt, it was just impossible. It's frustrating. This year, if we stay healthy, we should be as good as anybody, next to maybe Illinois and Iowa."

2001-2002 SCHEDULE

Nov.	16	@Valparaiso
	21	Radford
	24	*Stanford
	27	Butler
	30	#Purdue Classic
Dec.	1	#Purdue Classic
	5	Xavier
	8	**Arizona
	15	***Dayton
	17	##UIC
	20-22	###Las Vegas Invitational
	29	Robert Morris
Jan.	2	Ohio State
	5	@Michigan
	9	Illinois
	12	Minnesota
	16	@Michigan State
	19	@Wisconsin
	23	Northwesrn
	26	Iowa
	31	@Indiana
Feb.	6	@Penn State
	9	@Illinois
	13	Michigan
	16	Michigan State
	20	@Northwestern
	23	@Ohio State
March	2	Penn State
	7-10	####Big Ten Tournament

@Road Games
*Wooden Tradition, Conseco Fieldhouse, Indianapolis
**Wooden Classic, Anaheim, CA
***Boilermaker BlockBuster, Indianapolis, IN
#West Lafayette, IN (vs. William & Mary first round; also Akron, Oakland)
##First round Las Vegas Invitational
###Las Vegas, NV (schedule determined after first-round games; Pool 1 includes Georgia Tech, Illinois, Eastern Illinois, Pennsylvania. Pool 2 includes Iowa State, Saint Louis, Hartford, Southern Illinois)
####Conseco Fieldhouse, Indianpolis, IN

STARTERS NOT RETURNING

PG-CARSON CUNNINGHAM (6-1, 9.8 ppg, 1.8 rpg, 4.4 apg, 26.4 minutes, .372 FG, .339 3PT, .860 FT). Cunningham was an outstanding floor general for the Boilers, the prototype for an old-school point guard. He was very much the glue during last year's struggles, entering the season Purdue's leading returning scorer (11.0 ppg as a junior) and only returning starter.

But he also battled injuries throughout his career. Not only did his scoring drop a tad from his junior year, but his three-point shooting percentage came in far below his .400 career clip previously.

"I think you can say that he is pretty courageous," Keady said. "He had an elbow surgery last year, got that well. He had two knee operations and was just getting that well when John and Rodney went out. He had some tough luck here injury wise."

Cunningham showed his offensive ability when the two starters were injured, scoring a season-high 25 points in an 82-61 loss to Illinois and averaged 17.3 points over a six-game span. But Purdue will miss him more for the intangibles. Cunningham was a third-team Academic All-American as a senior.

OTHERS NOT RETURNING

F/C-ADAM WETZEL (6-9, 3.4 ppg, 3.2 rpg, 13.5 minutes, .431 FG, .541 FT). After being academically ineligible for fall semester and missing the season's first 13 games, the sophomore played the final 19 and started four times in place of the injured Allison. But he struggled mightily on offense, making only four of 14 shots. He fell behind freshman Kevin Garrity on the depth chart behind Allison.

In his best performances, Wetzel scored nine points off the bench against Minnesota and grabbed nine rebounds against Wisconsin. After the season, he transferred to be closer to his home in Keokuk, Iowa.

PG-TRAVIS BEST (6-1, 0.7 ppg, 0.6 rpg, 4.2 minutes, .182 FG, .333 3PT, .615 FT). As a junior, Best made little impact following his transfer from Louisville, where he played sparingly in 1997-98 and 1998-99. The native of Frankfort, Ky., did not have his scholarship renewed for this season and will finish his career at NAIA Wesleyan University.

PROJECTED STARTERS

PG-AUSTIN PARKINSON (6-0, 183 lbs., SO, #11, 1.4 ppg, 1.1 rpg, 2.3 apg, 11.1 minutes, .400 FG, .188 3PT, .609 FT, Northwestern HS/Kokomo, Ind.). Parkinson's point-guard abilities are apparently genetic. His father, Bruce, played for Purdue from 1973-77 and remains the school's all-time assists leader (690).

Now, his son is listed as the frontrunner to replace another prolific passer, the departed Cunningham, though he'll face competition from junior Willie Deane and freshman Brandon McKnight.

Parkinson appeared in all 32 games as a freshman and had the most assists on the team outside of Cunningham with 73. He struggled with his shot and showed little scoring ability but does deliver a little bit of everything else.

In a performance typifying his season, the Kokomo, Ind., native notched four assists, four steals and two rebounds against Penn State. His top assist game came against Northwestern, with seven—and five points—in 18 minutes.

SG-DARMETREIS KILGORE (6-5, 202 lbs., JR, #33, 21.4 ppg, Washington HS/South Bend, Ind. and Tyler JC/Tyler, Texas). Kilgore is a proven scorer who was a consensus junior college All-American at Tyler and the No. 2 scorer in his conference. He is an inside-outside player who can get to the basket in a hurry and possesses impressive leaping ability but can also pull up from outside.

Junior-college recruiting expert Rick Ball rated Kilgore the nation's No. 3 JC wing guard prospect going into last season. Recruiting analyst Brick Oettinger rated him the Big Ten's fourth best incoming player this year. CBS Sportsline chose Kiglore No. 8 among junior college transfers entering Division I.

All this despite the fact Kilgore barely registered a speck on the recruiting radar during his career at Washington High because of poor grades.

Along with the other newcomers, Kilgore arrived on campus over the summer and instantly wowed onlookers. Even before the start of fall practice, Keady expected him to earn the starting shooting guard spot and become one of the focal points of Purdue's offense.

"Junior college players sometimes take time to adjust, but he was here all summer lifting weights," Keady said. "He's very quick, but when he got here he was like a string-bean. But he's developing strength though his weightlifting. He's gotten a lot better ball-handling wise. We'd like to get up and down more, and he's quick. He'll be able to play the kind of up-tempo style we like to play here."

SG-MAYNARD LEWIS (6-1, 187 lbs., SR, #12, 9.9 ppg, 3.5 rpg, 1.1 apg, 22.2 minutes, .405 FG, .398 3PT, .779 FT, South HS/Terre Haute, Ind.). Lewis' .398 shooting percentage from behind the arc (47-of-118) ranked ninth in the Big Ten. But he was far from Purdue's first option on offense, finishing as the team's fourth-leading scorer.

After scoring in double-figures five straight games in December and then reaching the 14-point plateau three straight games around New Year's, Lewis went cold when the calendar turned to Big Ten season. After making only four of 22 field goals (.182) over a four-game span in early January, he was scratched from the lineup and would remain a reserve for eight of the next 11 games while Keady struggled to maintain a consistent lineup because of injuries.

Lewis would end up starting 19-of-32 games as a junior but should finally settle into a full-time starter's role this season, especially if Lowe sits out. Keady seems to be comfortable playing with a small lineup, something inevitable if the 6-1 Lewis and 6-0 Parkinson both start in the backcourt. Lewis and Kilgore will likely both pose as wing players in Keady's three-guard set.

"Lewis, he'll mostly be a shooting guard," Keady said. "He and Joe Marshall we're counting on a lot for leadership. He's really solid leadership-wise, the ultimate in

team player."

PF-RODNEY SMITH (6-6, 231 lbs., SR, #31, 13.9 ppg, 4.8 rpg, 1.0 apg, 1.0 spg, 1.0 bpg, 26.6 minutes, .540 FG, .443 3PT, .625 FT, Pike HS/Indianapolis, Ind.). Smith stepped up his production significantly last season, making the broken foot that shortened his season that much more disappointing. In addition to dealing daily with asthma, Smith was finally beginning to realize his full strength after spring knee surgery when he went down Feb. 7 against Wisconsin. Doctors operated on him the next day and he was able to play again within a month.

Though he technically missed only six games before returning for the Big Ten Tournament, he was limited to reserve duty the rest of the way and was far from the player who emerged as Purdue's leading scorer after averaging only 5.1 points as a sophomore.

Before the injury, Smith was averaging nearly three times that at 14.8 per game. He was also he team's leading shooter from both the field and behind the arc and ranked second behind Allison in both rebounds and blocked shots. The tri-captain was selected as the team's MVP.

"He really developed his shooting between sophomore and junior year," Keady said. "We're counting on him to be a great player in this league."

C-JOHN ALLISON (6-10, 242 lbs., SR, #54, 10.2 ppg, 5.3 rpg, 1.2 apg, 2.7 bpg, 24.5 minutes, .533 FG, .674 FT). Allison was also making tremendous strides before his injury. After playing only 8.1 minutes per game as a sophomore and scoring just 2.6 points per game, Allison had little trouble easing into a starter's role last season, ranking second in the Big Ten in blocked shots and ninth in field-goal percentage.

The problem was that injury. He missed virtually the entire month of February and didn't return to his starter's role until the NIT.

But now that Allison is healthy, Keady has lofty expectations for his senior season. He's obviously an elite post defender and shot blocker. Now Keady wants him to take the next step in scoring and rebounding.

He's shown flashes, scoring 29 points against Appalachian State, putting together a double double with 18 points and 12 rebounds at Northwestern and collecting 15 points and eight rebounds against Minnesota. But the Boilers could really use performances like those on a regular basis.

"He's stronger this year," Keady said. "He could be one of better shot blockers in the nation. But he needs to step up offensively. I told him the year before to shoot 500 jump shots a day, and I think he did that. Now, I think he needs to average in double figures scoring or rebounding."

KEY RESERVES

F-BRETT BUSCHER (6-8, 239 lbs., SO, #3, 4.7 ppg, 3.8 rpg, 19.0 minutes, .439 FG, .660 FT, Chesterton HS/Chesterton, Ind.). Buscher was Purdue's top recruit coming out of Chesterton, Ind., a year ago, ranking as high as the top 50 nationally by some recruiting experts. His freshman year was a bit quieter than might be expected of someone with his credentials, but the injuries to Allison and Smith did allow him to start the season's final 11 games. He showed good aggressiveness and intensity on defense but struggled offensively and sometimes got muscled around in the paint.

"He's a lot like Brian Cardinal was at that stage," Keady said. "He dives, takes charges, can shoot, is a good rebounder. From what I hear, he's really improved [over the summer]. Plus, I think he was homesick last year."

Over the summer, Buscher played for the NIT All-Star Team on a four-game tour of Slovakia, Austria and Hungary, averaging 7.0 points, 5.8 rebounds and 3.5 assists. Buscher had a double double (10 points, 10 boards) against Slovakia.

If he's improved as much as anticipated, Keady will count on him as the first option off the bench when the Boilers need size. The coach also hasn't ruled out starting him.

G-WILLIE DEANE (6-1, 196 lbs., JR, #0, 8.6 ppg, 3.1 rpg, 1.4 apg, 1.0 spg, 20.3 minutes, .427 FG, .377 3PT, .704 FT, Schenectady HS/Schenectady, N.Y. and Boston College). Deane is probably among the most talented players at Purdue. And he could very well be the starting point guard by the season's opening.

But first, he needs to get into Keady's good graces.

"Willie Deane could be one of the top point guards in the country if he can learn to stop fouling 84 feet from the basket," Keady said. "He's OK, he's just trying to learn to play. He plays wild, and we don't play wild here."

A transfer from Boston College, Deane fouled out of six games last year, quite odd for a mostly backup guard. But when he was in the game, he showed a capability to score, especially against tough competition. He led the Boilers with 16 points in their upset of then-No. 1 Arizona. And his career-high of 20 came on 6-of-8 three pointers against Michigan State.

"He's probably one of the best create-your-own-shot guys we've had since Glenn Robinson," Keady said. "We'll probably give him a little more freedom, but his problem is staying in the game."

G-JOE MARSHALL (6-2, 200 lbs., SR, #15, 6.9 ppg, 2.9 rpg, 1.1 apg, 21.3 minutes, .401 FG, .377 3PT, .650 FT, LeFlore HS/Mobile, Ala., Southern Idaho JC and Mississippi State). A fifth-year senior, Marshall is entering his second season at Purdue after transferring from Mississippi State. In the first, he started five games though mostly provided a quick spark off the bench.

A decent outside shooter, Marshall's best effort of the season came with 19 points on 4-of-5 treys and 7-of-8 free throws against Virginia. He notched 16 points and 17 against Michigan.

With Lowe missing, Marshall's role at shooting guard will likely increase. And if his summer stint with the Big Ten foreign tour team is any indication, Marshall may be ready. He averaged 12.2 points, 3.7 rebounds and 4.3 assists for the team, which went 6-0. Marshall was chosen the game's MVP in the Big Ten's first victory, and he scored a game-high 17 points in the team's fifth win.

OTHER RETURNEES

G-KENNETH LOWE (6-3, 199 lbs., JR, #20, 11.3 ppg, 2.9 rpg, 1.8 apg, 1.0 spg, 26.5 minutes, .479 FG, .407 3PT, .865 FT, West HS/Gary, Ind.). Lowe is one of four returning starters for the Boilermakers. The only problem is, he might not be returning this year.

The junior underwent shoulder surgery on Aug. 9 to correct a problem he's had since high school and will likely be sidelined until January. At that point, a decision will have to be made whether he should resume playing or take a red-shirt year.

"If ever there was a year you wanted to red-shirt someone like Kenny Lowe, this would be the year you could do it," Keady said. "If we get into January, and he feels comfortable doing that, we'll probably do it. A year out would really help him. This is his second time getting operated on it, and he came back too fast the first."

Lowe can play either point guard or shooting guard. He improved his shooting tremendously as a sophomore last season, including going from a less-than 70 percent free-throw shooter to nearly 87 percent, good for third in the conference. He led Purdue in scoring on six occasions.

C-KEVIN GARRITY (6-11, 253 lbs., SO, #34, 0.8 ppg, 1.3 rpg, 9.8 minutes, .346 FG, .313 FT, Hun School/Princeton, N.J.). Garrity certainly has a Big Ten body. It didn't seem to help much, though, during his limited playing time as a freshman. He struggled offensively and, despite being logically suited to bang the glass, never collected more than three rebounds in any one game.

But Garrity did gain valuable experience, starting five times in place of the injured Allison. In his longest stint of the season, he played 30 minutes against Illinois.

OTHER NEWCOMERS

F-MATT CARROLL (6-8, 221 lbs., FR, #32, 14.5 ppg, Smoky Hills HS/Aurora, Colo.). The newcomer should provide some frontcourt depth for the Boilers, possibly in a similar role to Buscher's last year. He was an honorable mention all-state selection both his junior and senior years of high school and possesses good speed for a big man. He should be well suited to running the floor in Purdue's up-tempo offense.

"Matt Carroll could be a good rebounder for us," Keady said. "We expect big things from him."

A National Honor Society member and honor roll student in high school, Carroll has already decided to major in management at Purdue.

G-BRANDON McKNIGHT (6-2, 172 lbs., FR, #10, 28.6 ppg, 7.8 rpg, 8.0 apg, LaSalle High School/South Bend, Ind.). Indiana's Mr. Basketball runner-up is the classic pass-first, shoot-second point guard.

He will compete with Parkinson and Deane for minutes at that position. He needs to put on some size and will likely need time to adjust to the speed of the college

game but possesses exactly the type of ball-handling flair Purdue is losing with the graduation of Cunningham.

"The thing I liked about Brandon when I watched him was his fast-break judgment," Keady said. "You need to either shoot it or kick it, don't try to force it, and that's what he does."

G-ANDREW FORD (6-2, 188 lbs., FR, #4, redshirted in 2000-01, 18 ppg, .410 3PT in 1999-00, West Lafayette HS/West Lafayette, Ind.). A local product with a lifelong devotion for Purdue, Ford's father Bob starred for Purdue from 1969-72 and ranks 19th on the school's all-time scoring list (1,244 points).

Ford sat out as a freshman after leading West Lafayette High to sectional titles as a junior and senior.

C-IVAN KARTELO (6-11, 247 lbs., JR., will sit out 2001-02, 0.8 ppg, 1.4 rpg, University of Notre Dame/Split, Croatia). Kartelo transferred last spring after an injury-plagued sophomore season that limited him to 16 games with the Irish. He was developing nicely before the injury, though, having played in all 37 games as a freshman coming out of Winchendon (Mass.) Academy. He should be a decent addition in 2002 for the Boilers, who by then will have lost Allison.

QUESTIONS

Healthy? The Boilers were hit unusually hard by injuries last year and have already been struck again this year, losing Lowe. One wonders whether they'll be able to keep the trainers less busy this season.

This is a deep squad, so asking certain reserves to fill in for a game or two isn't the end of the world. But losing your top two rebounders for a significant period of time—as was the case last year—spells doom in the Big Ten.

Point guard? In Keady's up-tempo, fundamentally sound system, a reliable floor leader is a must. Cunningham filled that role nicely the last couple years. There is no shortage of candidates to replace him, but each has his questions.

Deane is talented but sloppy and constantly draw's Keady's ire. Parkinson shot horrendously as a freshman. McKnight seems to have the goods but is only a freshman. One will emerge as the man.

Rebounding? Keady doesn't mind playing with a small team, but it needs to be able to grab boards. Last year's club got out-rebounded by an average 3.0 per game—a number that grew to 4.8 in Big Ten play.

The one proven commodity is Allison, though even he needs to step up his totals this season. Smith does well for his size but will always be more of a small forward. That leaves the Boilers hoping Buscher, Carroll or Garrity can blossom into the kind of second rebounder they need to contend.

ANSWERS

Experience! Keady loves seniors, and this team has four of them playing considerable roles. The way Purdue is able to contend for Big Ten titles without the raw talent of their competitors is by working harder and playing smarter.

Is Allison/Smith/Lowe/Marshall as formidable a group as those before it in '95-'96 and '99-'00? Hard to say. Most have had only one year in the forefront and have yet to prove themselves over a sustained period. But it beats the situation they were in a year ago.

Shooting! The Boilers have their weaknesses, but knocking it down from outside is not one of them. Five returning players shot 38 percent or better from behind the arc last season, and the team finished second overall in the Big Ten.

One of Purdue's best shooters, Lowe, will be on the sidelines this season, but with the addition of Kilgore, this should continue to be the team's strength, especially if it can develop the inside game necessary to keep its wing players open.

Kilgore! Keady doesn't want to jinx him, but he's having trouble hiding his enthusiasm for the junior college import. He is a proven scorer who's already been on campus for a summer lifting and working out with teammates.

Purdue is not the type of program inclined toward a newcomer showing up and instantly scoring 20 points a game—though Keady wouldn't dissuade him from doing it. The team obviously lacked a go-to guy last season and Kilgore could fill that void.

PURDUE 2000-2001 RESULTS

Central Michigan (L)	66-67
#Arizona	72-69
##Virginia (L)	79-98
Appalachian State	79-65
Duquesne	78-52
Alabama A&M	79-51
###Valparaiso	73-46
Santa Clara	98-52
Florida International	93-48
@Akron	98-67
UCLA (L)	82-87
Michigan	80-60
@Northwestern	69-61
Wisconsin	73-67
Iowa (L)	73-83
@Minnesota (L)	67-70
Northwestern	78-59
@Indiana (L)	55-66
Minnesota	83-68
@Michigan State (L)	55-72
@Wisconsin (L)	54-73
Illinois (L)	61-82
Ohio State (L)	64-65
@Penn State (L)	71-92
@Iowa (L)	72-78
@Michigan	78-59
Indiana (L)	58-74
####Minnesota	91-77
####Illinois (L)	66-83
#####Illinois State	90-79
#####Auburn	79-61
#####Alabama (L)	77-85

#John Wooden Tradition, Indianapolis, IN
##Big Ten/ACC Challenge, Charlottesville, VA
###Boilermaker Blockbuster, Indianapolis, IN
####Big Ten Tournament, Chicago, IL
#####NIT

BLUE RIBBON ANALYSIS

BACKCOURT	B+
BENCH/DEPTH	B
FRONTCOURT	B
INTANGIBLES	B

One below-par season did little to hamper Purdue's reputation as a Big Ten power. The fact is, despite their stellar record over the last decade, the Boilers barely have one.

"It's always been amazing to me how, when Purdue wins the Big Ten, the league must be down," a sarcastic Keady said. "It always tickles me when they say that. Just once we'd like to get in the race and have people say the league's up!"

Misnomer or not, the "down" label usually gets applied to a league when it's been drained of star power. But with the exception of Michigan State, most Big Ten teams survived the spring NBA exodus relatively unscathed. So how, then, one might ask, can the starless Boilers be deemed a factor in this year's race?

Because we've learned better by now than to pick against a senior-laden Purdue team, no matter how bland it might appear. Even in a clear rebuilding year, the Boilers were probably one less injury away from returning to the NCAAs last year. With a clean bill of health and a bevy of experience, making the field probably won't be a problem this season. It's a question of how far the Boilers can advance.

Purdue's success will depend partly on improved rebounding, partly on how its backcourt gels. Out are Cunningham and, at least until January, Lowe. In is a point guard to-be-announced and Kilgore, who could have a tremendous impact offensively.

Keady will probably experiment with different lineups during a non-conference schedule that includes games with Arizona (in Anaheim, Calif.), Stanford (in Indianapolis), Xavier, Dayton, Butler and Valparaiso. But by January, he'll probably unlock the right combination. And even if they struggle at times in Big Ten play, that doesn't rule out a run in March. The 1999 Sweet 16 team went 7-9 in the conference.

Chances are, this team will not stoop anywhere close to that level, but it probably won't be earning Keady a seventh ring either. There are no athletes on this club the caliber of Iowa's Reggie Evans or Illinois' Frank Williams, both of whose teams will be favored to contend for the league title. The Boilers, though, can be competitive at the next rung, fighting with Indiana, Ohio State and perhaps Minnesota for the third seed in the Big Ten Tournament and jostling for NCAA seeding.

"I think one of the three new guys coming in has to

step up and do something for us. I'm not sure if we can be a rated top 10 team with the [returning] players ... We need some depth," Keady said. "If [the players] make the same improvement this year that they did last year, we'll be alright."

(S.M.)

Southern California 37

LOCATION   Los Angeles, CA
CONFERENCE   Pac-10
LAST SEASON   24-10 (.706)
CONFERENCE RECORD   11-7 (t-4th)
STARTERS LOST/RETURNING   2/3
NICKNAME   Trojans
COLORS   Cardinal & Gold
HOMECOURT   L.A. Sports Arena (16,161)
COACH   Henry Bibby (UCLA '72)
RECORD AT SCHOOL   81-67 (5 years)
CAREER RECORD   81-67 (5 years)
ASSISTANTS   Damon Archibald (Boise State '95)
              Kurtis Townsend (Western Kentucky '82)
              Eric Brown (Cal State Northridge '98)
TEAM WINS (last 5 years)   17-9-15-16-24
RPI (last 5 years)   54-177-85-76-14
2000-01 FINISH   Lost in NCAA East Regional final.

COACH AND PROGRAM

For Henry Bibby, this was old, familiar territory. But his USC players weren't quite sure just what they were getting in to.

Now the Trojans understand the NCAA Tournament. The trepidation is gone, but the wonderful taste lingers, and they want another big spoonful.

The 2000-2001 season was a breakthrough for USC, which won a school-record 24 games and forged deeper into the current NCAA Tournament format than ever before.

USC had twice before (1940 and '54) played in the Final Four, but never had won three games in the NCAAs. Last spring, the Trojans raced to a 48-19 halftime lead on the way to beating Oklahoma State in the opening round, upended No. 3 seeded and Big East champion Boston College two days later, then roared to a 43-24 halftime margin on the way to beating second-seeded Kentucky.

Only a 79-69 loss to eventual national champ Duke kept the Trojans out of the Final Four.

Bibby, of course, participated in three Final Fours, winning all three as a star guard with John Wooden's UCLA teams of the early 1970s. But for his players, this was heady stuff.

"These guys started to believe in themselves," Bibby said. "They believed they had a good basketball team last year, but they were probably a little hesitant at first when we got into the tournament."

USC, after all, hadn't played in the NCAAs since 1997, and hadn't won a tournament game since '92.

"After we beat Oklahoma State—they've always been a great team—the players started to believe a little bit," Bibby said. "To play the Big East champs and beat them, that really took us to another level. And then to jump on Kentucky the way we did ... "

With three starters back from a year ago, USC should be prepared to maintain what it achieved. Or build upon that success.

"I've never seen guys work as hard during the summer since I've been here," Bibby said. "When we first got here [six years ago], you couldn't get them in the gym. Now you can't get them out of the gym.

"I think they realized what we've talked about all along. If you get to the tournament, the exposure you're looking for will be there. They see that. They like that fanfare they were getting. It's something that really hadn't been here."

Bibby had guided the Trojans to the NCAAs once previously, in his first full season with the program in '97. A year later, USC fell off to 9-19. But don't expect a repeat of that disastrous encore. This team has experience at key places and talent virtually everywhere.

At the heart of things is 6-7 senior forward Sam Clancy, who evolved into one of the Pac-10's best players last season. Senior point guard Brandon Granville has started 89 games in his USC career, and senior for-

ward David Bluthenthal is at once among the conference's better three-point shooters and rebounders.

Bibby called the trio the "cornerstones" of his program, adding, "They are a testament to the statement that hard work pays off. I expect them to bring the seriousness back, to try to pick up where we left off."

Sophomore Desmon Farmer, who started 16 games last season before Jeff Trepagnier became eligible, is virtually a fourth returning starter. And twins Errick and Derrick Craven are promising backcourt players for the near future.

Bibby believes future recruiting will benefit from the success last year's squad enjoyed.

"It makes the program more recognizable," he said. "It helps get us in the homes of some of the top players in the country. More high schools know about us now, and people back east have a new respect for us. It was a major step."

Taking the next step isn't automatic, and the Trojans do have some obstacles. Would-be starting center Kostas Charrissis was ruled ineligible by the NCAA and will miss the first 15 games. That makes a small team even smaller, at least for a while.

USC has plenty of depth and versatility in the backcourt, but Bibby has fewer options up front.

What he does have is significant: players who have done it before, who believe they can do it again.

2001-2002 SCHEDULE

Nov.	13	#Wyoming
	26	UC Santa Barbara
Dec.	1	@Bradley
	3	Rhode Island
	6	*Pepperdine
	12	@Long Beach State
	16	Miami (Ohio)
	20	@San Diego
	22	@Loyola Marymount
	29	@Washington State
Jan.	4	*Washington State
	6	*Washington
	10	*UCLA
	17	@Arizona
	19	@Arizona State
	24	California
	26	Stanford
	31	@Oregon State
Feb.	2	@Oregon
	6	@UCLA
	14	Arizona State
	16	Arizona
	21	@Stanford
	23	@California
	28	Oregon
March	2	Oregon State
	7-9	##Pac-10 Tournament

@Road Games
*Los Angeles Forum
#Preseason NIT (If the Trojans win, they will play either Montana State or Fresno State on Nov. 14 or 16. Semifinals and finals are Nov. 21-23 at Madison Square Garden, N.Y.)
##Staples Center, Los Angeles

STARTERS NOT RETURNING

F/C-BRIAN SCALABRINE (6-9, 14.7 ppg, 5.9 rpg, 2.8 apg. 0.9 bpg, 32.8 minutes, .478 FG, .303 3PT, .801 FT). An All-Pac-10 selection as a junior, Scalabrine did not play quite to that level a year ago but still was a key man for the Trojans. A versatile, crafty big man, Scalabrine was an awkward match-up for most teams.

He was a skilled low-post player but was also able to step away from the basket and provide a shooting or passing threat. A .403 shooter from three-point range as a junior, Scalabrine cooled off considerably last season, although he still had his moments.

At the Yahoo! Sports Invitational in Hawaii, Scalabrine scored 28, 27 and 26 points on consecutive days. He had four 20-point performances in Pac-10 play, along with an 11-point, 15-rebound game against Washington.

Scalabrine averaged 10.3 points in four NCAA games, then was taken in the second round of the NBA draft by the New Jersey Nets.

G-JEFF TREPAGNIER (6-4, 9.0 ppg, 5.1 rpg, 1.5 spg, 29.6 minutes, .453 FG, .235 3PT, .607 FT). Perhaps the best athlete in the Pac-10 last season, Trepagnier

experienced what cannot be labeled as anything but a bizarre season.

He sat out 13 games, the result of two separate NCAA infractions. First, Trepagnier was suspended for violating the extra benefits rule when he accepted a fall trip to Las Vegas from the runner of a sports agent.

The NCAA went after him again because of a car loan co-signed by the father of his girlfriend. The problem there was that his girlfriend's mother was a part-time track coach at USC, so once more the arrangement was deemed inappropriate.

Trepagnier solved the problem by getting married on the eve of the Pac-10 Conference season—in Las Vegas.

Once back on the court, Trepagnier gave the Trojans a different dimension. A 7-foot high jumper on the track team, he showed off his remarkable leaping ability in a game at Cal when he soared above Clancy for a spike-tip that Bibby said compared to anything he saw Julius Erving pull off during his playing days.

In that win at Cal, Trepagnier had his best game of the year, totaling 19 points, 11 rebounds, five steals, four assists and two blocked shots. He had 22 points in a win at Washington, and averaged 15.0 points and 5.8 rebounds in four NCAA Tournament games.

Trepagnier was picked in the second round of the NBA draft by the Cleveland Cavaliers.

OTHERS NOT RETURNING

F-JARVIS TURNER (6-7, 3.6 ppg, 2.4 rpg, 9.9 minutes, .557 FG, .429 3PT, .568 FT). Turner returned unexpectedly last season after being granted an extra year of eligibility after an ankle injury the year before.

It turns out Turner played less last season than in 1999-2000, when he averaged 14 minutes per game. Still, he saw action in 28 games and was productive, given his limiting playing time.

C-LUKE MINOR (7-3, 0.5 ppg, 0.5 rpg, 2.2 minutes in 10 games, .400 FG, .250 FT). Perhaps the largest athlete ever to suit up for USC, Minor's role for the Trojans was just that—minor. He left USC with plans to transfer to another school after the season.

G-TYLER MURPHY (6-2, 2.2 ppg, 1.4 rpg, 11.3 minutes, .420 FG, .343 3PT, .688 FT). A senior transfer shooting guard from the University of Vermont, Murphy averaged 7.3 points over the season's first four games, notching 10 points in a win over Loyola Marymount.

Murphy scored 10 points again in a win over Long Beach State in late December, but his role and his production dwindled to almost nothing in Pac-10 action.

PROJECTED STARTERS

PG-BRANDON GRANVILLE (5-9, 175 lbs., SR, #5, 12.4 ppg, 2.7 rpg, 6.1 apg, 1.7 spg, 34.4 minutes, .428 FG, .372 3PT, .791 FT, Westchester HS/Los Angeles). A starter in all but three games of his college career, Granville holds the throttle on the Trojans' attack. Poised to become USC's first four-year starting point guard since Jacque Hill (1980-83), Granville is first on the school's career assist list (595), third in three-pointers (162), fourth in steals (175) and 12th in free-throw percentage (.785).

"Brandon Granville has improved every year and has really become a leader for us," Bibby said. "I expect him to continue to improve and bring up his level of intensity. I'd like to see him be a little more aggressive offensively and a little more creative this year.

"Everything starts with Brandon. Every night he comes ready to play, ready to give us everything he has."

Granville dealt out at least five assists in 26 different games last season, including 11 against BYU-Hawaii and 10 against Cal. He scored 22 points against both Arizona State and Cal, had 21 against Long Beach State and scored 20 against Washington.

With 216 assists, Granville will move to third on the all-time Pac-10 list, behind only Gary Payton (938) and Pooh Richardson (833).

SG-DESMON FARMER (6-4, 225 lbs., SO, #33, 6.4 ppg, 2.8 rpg, 1.0 apg, 18.8 minutes, .419 FG, .338 3PT, .557 FT, Northwestern HS/Flint, Mich.). Farmer should step in seamlessly as the full-time starter at shooting guard after keeping the spot warm early last season for Trepagnier.

"He was one of our go-to guys as a freshman," Bibby said. "I don't think there's any better one on one player in the conference than Desmon Farmer. If people leave him open, he'll make shots.

"He plays with a lot of enthusiasm and has been

good defensively for us."

Farmer scored a season-high 24 points against Washington last season, and scored in double figures seven times in USC's first 13 games, all of them as a starter. He had a 21-point, nine-rebound game against Cal State-Northridge and scored 14 points against Arizona.

"He's reckless on the floor and I kind of like that," Bibby said. "He's gotten stronger over the summer. He's basically a fourth returning starter for us. He's also probably our best passer."

SF-DAVID BLUTHENTHAL (6-7, 220 lbs., SR, #34, 13.5 ppg, 6.8 rpg, 1.5 spg, 1.4 apg, 31.3 minutes, .472 FG, .409 3PT, .786 FT, Westchester HS/Los Angeles). A surprise two years ago, Bluthenthal has become a dependable, productive player with great versatility. He arrives at his senior season needing just 82 points to join Clancy and Granville as 1,000-point career scorers.

An excellent rebounder, Bluthenthal may best be known for having corralled 28 boards against Arizona State his sophomore season. He also is a dangerous perimeter player who has made 109 three-point baskets the last two years after making none as a freshman.

"David was an inside player in high school and also said he wanted to go to a school where he could go outside," Bibby said. "He's one of the best shooters I've ever seen. He shoots it deep as well as anyone.

"But he's also been our best post-up player. He's got a jump hook, a turn-around, face-up jumper and a fade-away jumper. I think he's one of the best three men in the country."

He scored in double figures 21 times last season, including 29 points each against Oregon and Cal State Northridge. He also had seven double-doubles, highlighted by a 17-point, 13-rebound performance against Duke in the East Regional final.

Bluthenthal was in early foul trouble and held scoreless in USC's opening-round NCAA game against Oklahoma State, then averaged 21.3 points over the next three.

PF-JERRY DUPREE (6-7, 200 lbs., SO, #31, 7.2 ppg, 3.2 rpg, 13.2 minutes in 1999-2000 at College of Southern Idaho). Dupree is the most likely candidate to fill out the starting frontcourt at the season's outset. He played two years ago on a 29-7 team that featured six players averaging in double figures, then finished his two-year degree as a student only last year at San Bernardino Junior College.

"He's going to come in and play. I can't see this kid not playing in this program," Bibby said. "I love his athleticism."

Dupree arrives at USC with three years of eligibility. Although he is slight of build, Dupree is quick and a good jumper and likely will be used near the basket. When Charissis returns and if Bibby decides to go with a bigger lineup, Dupree figures to come off the bench at either of the forward spots.

C-SAM CLANCY (6-7, 240 lbs., SR, #50, 17.3 ppg, 7.5 rpg, 2.4 bpg, 1.1 spg, 33.2 minutes, .501 FG, .659 FT, St. Edward HS/Fairview, Ohio). Last season is viewed as Clancy's breakthrough year, but Bibby prefers to look a year earlier.

"Last year was a very, very good year for him, but the year before he was having a great year when he got hurt," Bibby said, alluding to a broken foot Clancy suffered three weeks into the 2000 Pac-10 season. "We were 6-0 in the Pac-10 and we were playing as well as we did in the tournament [this past year] when he broke his foot."

Clancy was good enough last year that he considered leaving school for the NBA draft, then decided against it. Bibby believes good things will come to the senior who waited.

"Sam just dominates," Bibby said. "He's a shot blocker, he can go outside or inside, he rebounds, he's a smart, smart kid. I expect him to be a lottery pick this year."

A natural power forward, Clancy may have to play the center position for USC, at least early in the season while Charissis is out. Bibby doesn't expect that to make a difference.

"We didn't think Brian [Scalabrine] was a true center last year and he played a lot at that spot," Bibby said. "Sam has played a lot on the block. I don't think you really have to have a true center. You coach according to the players you have in your program. We will be a little smaller this year."

Clancy's scoring and rebounding numbers have improved each year, and he has worked to hoist himself from a .476 free-throw shooter as a freshman to a competent level last season.

Clancy was overpowering at times as a junior. He scored in double figures 30 times in 34 games, including a 31-point, 13-rebound performance against UCLA. He had 28 points against Arizona State and scored 25 at Cal.

In NCAA play, Clancy averaged 18.0 points and 10.8 rebounds.

KEY RESERVES

C-KOSTAS CHARISSIS (6-11, 250 lbs., JR, #15, 1.2 ppg, 1.2 rpg, 4.7 minutes, .444 FG, .625 FT, Bachlitzanaki HS/Athens, Greece). Charissis might have been USC's starting center had he not been suspended for 15 games after the NCAA's recent crackdown on foreign players with experience on professional teams.

Charissis played as an unpaid member of the Papagou-Athens club in his native Greece in 1999, averaging 3.0 points and 3.0 rebounds. NCAA rules always have prohibited players from participating in a league or on a team with professionals, but until this summer the NCAA had not concerned itself with athletes who did not accept a salary.

USC was awaiting word on an appeal to the NCAA as school began.

"He's an experienced player who has started in this program," said Bibby, referring to the fact that Charissis started 13 games as a freshman and one last year. "We need him."

Charissis saw fairly limited playing time last year, never playing more than 12 minutes in a game. He was more involved as a freshman, when he averaged close to 10 minutes over 26 games, and had a nine-point, eight-rebound effort against Arizona.

PG-ROBERT HUTCHINSON (6-1, 195 lbs., JR, #4, 1.2 ppg, 0.6 rpg, 7.4 minutes, .324 FG, .273 3PT, .692 FT, Okaloosa-Walton Junior College/Niceville, Fla. and Westover HS/Albany, Ga.). Hutchinson saw action in 33-of-34 games last year, providing the Trojans with a solid player off the bench.

"He will probably be a backup player, but he's a steady, good backup," Bibby said. "If you had more guys like that, you'd be able to play a little. He brings a lot of steadiness to the team."

Hutchinson enjoyed his finest moment in the second-round NCAA game against Boston College, stepping in at the point when Granville fouled out. He shot 5-for-6 from the free-throw line in the final 77 seconds, helping to secure the victory.

"The Boston College free throws gave him a lot of confidence," Bibby said.

G-ERRICK CRAVEN (6-2, 170 lbs., FR, #22, 19.9 ppg, 6.8 rpg, 4.4 apg, 2.6 spg, .530 FG, Bishop Montgomery HS/Torrance, Calif.). Regarded as the slightly more accomplished of the twin brothers, Errick was rated the No. 10 shooting guard prospect in the country by ESPN.com.

He and his brother led Bishop Montgomery to consecutive California state Division III titles their final two seasons. Errick became the first player since Paul Pierce in 1994-95 to win the South Bay Daily Breeze Player-of-the-Year Award for two straight seasons.

"Errick is a great athlete who can handle the ball well and really likes to play defense," Bibby said. "He can get to the basket and dunk on you. He's exciting. He's physical and has quick feet. He's very aggressive and plays hard."

Errick is one minute older than Derrick.

Bibby said he's never coached twins, and still is figuring out how this will work.

"They do most of the same things. They both drive, both shoot outside, they're both very physical players," Bibby said. "I like the intensity they bring. And they bring something we haven't had—physical play at the guards."

G-DERRICK CRAVEN (6-2, 170 lbs., FR, #24, 16.4 ppg, 6.4 rpg, 5.6 apg, 1.9 spg, .560 FG at Bishop Montgomery HS /Torrance, Calif.). Derrick shared CIF Division III Player of the Year and Del Rey League MVP honors with his brother each of the last two years.

Perhaps best suited to play point guard, Derrick can handle either backcourt position, as can his brother, Bibby said.

"Derrick has improved his shooting, and he can defend and drive," Bibby said. "He's very similar to his brother. He's not getting as much credit as he deserves. We think he can help us."

OTHER RETURNEES

G-GENNARO BUSTERNA (6-3, 205 lbs., SR, #14, 0.0 ppg, 0.3 rpg, 1.9 minutes in 8 games, McCook College/McCook, Neb. and Manual HS/Denver, Colo.). Busterna arrived last season from junior college and rarely saw any meaningful playing time. Bibby hopes that changes this season.

"He's a shooter and last year we wanted him to shoot the basketball," Bibby said, alluding to the fact that Busterna attempted just seven shots, and did not make any.

"Hopefully, this year he'll get more playing time. He can be a steady shooter and he's a good one-on-one player."

As a sophomore at McCook College, Busterna averaged 20.8 points and shot .491 from three-point range.

G-NATE HAIR (6-4, 200 lbs., JR, #1, 1.7 ppg, 1.4 rpg, 9.9 minutes, .200 FG, .222 3PT, .500 FT, Capistrano Valley HS/Mission Viejo, Calif.). Hair's status for this season still was uncertain as school began. He was contemplating a red-shirt year while settling matters in a grievance he filed against former USC assistant coach David Miller.

Hair missed the first five games last season with a strained knee tendon, then had difficulty working his way into the playing rotation. After an 0-for-5 shooting effort in his debut against UC Santa Barbara, Hair made 5-of-12 attempts the next two games.

He then made just 2-of-18 shots the remainder of the season, playing a total of 37 minutes in Pac-10 action.

As a freshman, Hair averaged nearly 17 minutes in 27 games, scoring 4.2 poin5w, including 14 points against Oregon State, 13 against Oregon and 12 against Stanford.

OTHER NEWCOMERS

C-RORY O'NEIL (6-11, 220 lbs., FR, #21, 25.1 ppg, 13.5 rpg, 3.0 bpg, Burroughs HS/Ridgecrest, Calif.). O'Neil is likely to get a good look early in the season, with Charissis sidelined. Bibby views him as a hybrid big man, able to play either the power forward or center spot.

"He's the next Brian Scalabrine. I think he can be better than Brian at an early age," Bibby said. "He's very skilled offensively, can shoot it outside, runs the floor, and knows the game. We've got to get him to be a little tougher, physcially."

O'Neil was a Student Sports magazine fourth-team All-America pick and an All-CIF Division III first-team selection. He also was the Desert Sky League Player of the Year and was selected the sixth-best prep center in the country by ESPN.com.

F-NICHOLAS CURTIS (6-8, 220 lbs., FR, #44, 19.9 ppg, 14.8 rpg, 3.6 bpg, .680 FG, .790 FT, Oxnard HS/Oxnard, Calif.). Curtis is a combination forward who Bibby believes is something of a sleeper.

"Nicholas is young and he's still growing. He'll be closer to 6-11 by the time he gets out of here," Bibby said. "He's an excellent rebounder and he can handle the basketball. He was kind of overlooked, but I think he'll surprise a lot of people. We expect him to contribute."

Curtis is Oxnard High's career leader in points (1,215), rebounds (1,003) and blocked shots (244). He was selected to the Los Angeles Times first-team All-Ventura County team and helped his club to a 24-0 record in Pacific View League games his three seasons on the varsity team.

QUESTIONS

Depth? Bibby simply doesn't have lots of bodies, especially among frontcourt players. An injury at the wrong place or time could spell trouble.

Size? The Trojans have no experienced player taller than 6-7. Charissis is huge, but has no track record and likely won't be available until January. The only other players in the program with any height are freshmen.

Expectations? USC charted new territory last season, and suddenly more will be expected . The Trojans will be hungry for more, but so will fans and media. Do the they have the savvy to handle all the attention?

ANSWERS

Sam Clancy! The son of a former NFL lineman, Clancy is as tough as any player in the Pac-10. He improved his offensive skills last season to the point that at times he almost could not be stopped.

Experience! The Trojans enter this season with three seniors who have combined to start 221 college games. Clancy, Granville and Bluthenthal return with the confidence of having come within one step last season of reaching the Final Four.

Young Talent! The Trojans have three superb seniors, but Bibby also is building for the future with players like Farmer and a promising freshman class. There will be moments they play like kids, but the newcomers should blend nicely with the veterans on this club.

SOUTHERN CAL 2000-2001 RESULTS

Bradley	107-92
San Diego	78-67
LMU	91-68
#Utah	65-60
Cal State Northridge	99-90
@UC Santa Barbara	75-73
Pepperdine	76-73
##Brigham Young	86-74
##Mississippi (L)	83-84
@Northwestern (L)	61-63
Long Beach State	95-73
Washington State	82-59
Washington	87-61
@UCLA (L)	75-80
@Arizona (L)	58-71
@Arizona State	77-58
Oregon	78-74
Oregon State	73-47
@Stanford (L)	71-77
@California	80-66
UCLA (L)	76-85
Arizona State	80-68
Arizona (L)	61-105
@Oregon State (L)	52-67
@Oregon	87-80
Stanford (L)	68-70
California	74-69
@Washington	85-56
@Washington State	78-63

#John Wooden Classic in Anaheim, CA
##Pearl Harbor Invitational in Laie, HA
@Road Games

BLUE RIBBON ANALYSIS

BACKCOURT	A-
BENCH/DEPTH	B-
FRONTCOURT	B+
INTANGIBLES	B

It's easy to tell Bibby likes this team, and there are good reasons for that. He also knows the Trojans are not without flaws.

"My concern is are we going to have enough bodies up front? Do we have enough big bodies to go at people?" he said. "We know Sam is big, but Sam is 6-6, 6-7."

A lack of experience off the bench also concerns Bibby, but there are things his Trojans will do well. One of them should be scoring.

"I love that. We can shoot the basketball with anybody," he said. "Hopefully, we can finish in the top half of the Pac-10."

The expectations from virtually everyone will be that the Trojans should be considerably better than that.

(J.F.)

Providence 38

LOCATION	Providence, RI
CONFERENCE	Big East (East)
LAST SEASON	21-10 (.677)
CONFERENCE RECORD	11-5 (2nd)
STARTERS LOST/RETURNING	2/3
NICKNAME	Friars
COLORS	Black & White
HOMECOURT	Dunkin' Donuts Center (12,993)
COACH	Tim Welsh (Potsdam State '84)
RECORD AT SCHOOL	48-43 (3 years)
CAREER RECORD	118-65 (5 years)
ASSISTANTS	Steve DeMeo (SUNY-Buffalo '87)
	Phil Seymore (Canisius '88)
	Bob Walsh (Hamilton '94)
TEAM WINS (last 5 years)	24-13-16-11-21
RPI (last 5 years)	31-76-91-175-39
2000-01 FINISH	Lost in NCAA first round.

COACH AND PROGRAM

Those in the know didn't have to be convinced that Providence had made the right coaching choice when Pete Gillen continued his wanderings and moved on from Rhode Island to Virginia.

Tim Welsh had been a successful coach at Iona, and before that, a proven assistant at Syracuse. Yep, it was just a matter of time. That time has come.

The Friars ended three years of poor play and ugly basketball last year by authoring the Big East's second-biggest surprise. As interesting as Providence's 21 wins were, they were no match for what went on at that "other" New England Big East school. BC's run to the top 15 and a league title was just too weird and unpredictable to be supplanted, no matter how encouraging Providence's play was.

Those who know Welsh understand that he wasn't going to succeed the way he wanted until he had a roster with enough depth for him to employ his up-tempo system. For a while, it looked as if the Friars wouldn't have enough people to start a game, much less send waves of players onto the court. Defections and dismissals had killed continuity and left Welsh with a pair of patchwork clubs his first two years at Providence. Last year, the turmoil settled, and PC was able to rely on the players it had recruited.

No more injuries to vital players. No more mid-summer bolts to Columbus, while the coach was away. No more academic troubles or off-court shenanigans. Providence had a nucleus, fortified it with some newcomers and went to work.

No one paid much attention during the Friars' 9-3 non-conference start, probably because losses to Maine and Creighton were included. But when PC beat Connecticut, 81-68, on Jan. 13, people began to take notice. Forget that the Huskies weren't their usual full-strength selves. Providence had won a big game over an established conference team. Perhaps Welsh had turned things around.

It's hard to imagine Welsh won't succeed. He is intense but gregarious enough to woo recruits, media and fans with his personality. He may not have the television recognition quotient of some other coaches, but that doesn't matter in the Big East any more, where only UConn's Jim Calhoun, Syracuse's Jim Boeheim and St. John's Mike Jarvis can be picked out of a lineup by more than just the rabid fans.

Go ahead, paint a mental picture of what Virginia Tech's Ricky Stokes looks like. Or Miami's Perry Clark. Unless you are an ESPN devotee, you're not going to recognize them. That's good for Welsh, who comes into the league at a time when even the dwindling number of well-established bosses is struggling to remain powerful. He can put together a team that includes a strong group of freshmen, some Europrospects, a junior college newcomer and a transfer or two and then flood the floor with constant substitutions.

That's what he did last year and how he was able to win 11 league games with a team that included four new players, each of whom saw double-figure minutes. Welsh's style of play was heavy on defense and made considerable use of charismatic point man John Linehan, whose groin injury was a big reason Providence struggled so mightily during the 1999-00 season. With Linehan keying the defense and running the team with his trademark intensity and unflagging mental toughness, the Friars set upon helpless rivals.

A perfect example was their 76-67 win at Villanova. The Wildcats were helpless offensively, thanks to the different types of pressure exerted by Providence. Of course, Villanova was capable of turning it over at any time last year, but the 'Cats were completely embarrassed on their home court by a Friar team that smelled blood and then drank from 'Nova's open wounds for 40 minutes.

Here comes the encore. It should feature more of the same. Even though warhorses Erron Maxey and Karim Shabazz are gone from the front line, Welsh expects new faces (there are six of them this year) to fill in and keep the parade moving along.

"Everyone around the country loses people every year," Welsh said. "(Maxey and Shabazz) were very good players for us. Someone will have to step up and fill their roles. That's what you do in recruiting. You get freshman who can step in."

Providence is moving ahead off the court, too. The program's entire nerve center was gutted and replaced during the off-season. The Friars have new offices, player lounges and locker rooms. The practice court was re-

done. That should help when the prospects come through. They'll like what they see on the floor and then relish the creature comforts back on campus.

About the only bad news during the off-season was some genius' decision to sell naming rights to the Providence Civic Center to Dunkin' Donuts. Aside from the lame tie-ins with dunking donuts and dunking basketballs, the move can't help the team's reputation much. Let's see, now. St. John's plays at Madison Square Garden, the nation's most famous arena, and Providence plays at the Dunkin' Donuts Center. Somehow, it's not the same.

But the Friars' 2001-02 outcome should be similar to its immediate predecessor. Providence has good depth around Linehan and a nucleus that includes guards Romauld Augustin and Abdul Mills and forwards Christopher Anrin and Maris Laksa, as well as center Marcus Douthit. All have the potential to be big-time contributors. Add in junior college import Garnet Thompson and freshman Ryan Gomes, the two gems of the six-man crop of newcomers, and Providence should be able to run and press and harass just about everybody on the schedule. It's a good time to be a PC fan, and that should continue, as long as Welsh sticks around.

2001-2002 SCHEDULE

Nov.	16	#Las Vegas Invitational
	19-22	##Las Vegas Invitational
	24	Columbia
	28	Brown
Dec.	1	@Rhode Island
	3	@South Carolina
	8	George Washington
	19	Sacred Heart
	22	Boston University
	30	Central Connecticut
Jan.	2	@Villanova
	5	Syracuse
	7	@Texas
	12	St. John's
	16	Connecticut
	19	@Miami
	22	Rutgers
	26	@St. John's
	30	@West Virginia
Feb.	2	Boston College
	5	@Connecticut
	9	Virginia Tech
	13	@Boston College
	19	Villanova
	23	@Virginia Tech
	26	Miami
March	2	@Notre Dame
	6-9	###Big East Tournament

@Road Games
#First round TBA
##Las Vegas, NV (also UTEP, Austin Peay, TCU, Northwestern State, Oklahoma State)
###Madison Square Garden, New York, NY

STARTERS NOT RETURNING

F-ERRON MAXEY (6-6, 11.4 ppg, 6.4 rpg, 0.6 apg, 1.1 spg, 25.0 minutes, .475 FG, .686 FT). Maxey was never a dominant force, but he was a senior, a four-year college performer and one of the cornerstones of last year's team. He led the team in scoring, was second in rebounding and played some pretty good defense. Although Maxey never wowed anyone with his skill level —he turned it over way too often and didn't have the greatest shooting range—he was a solid Big East player whose consistent contributions will be missed.

Maxey's high-point effort last year was 19, against Rhode Island. But he came on late and led the Friars in scoring in their last three games, including 16 against Penn State in the NCAA Tournament loss.

C-KARIM SHABAZZ (7-2, 8.9 ppg, 7.4 rpg, 1.6 apg, 2.3 bpg, 24.9 minutes, .558 FG, .638 FT). Once Shabazz became comfortable at Providence after transferring from Florida State, he became a solid rebounder and an above-average shot blocker.

Long and athletic, Shabazz wasn't going to overpower too many people, but his sheer height made him imposing. He didn't possess that spectacular an offensive game, although he did blossom into a solid interior scorer last year, particularly in Big East games, when his scoring average swelled to 10.3 points per game. During league play last year, he shot 62.1 percent from the field and had some memorable nights. Chief among them was his 22-point, 11-rebound effort in the 103-79 home rout of Georgetown. Shabazz also had 17 points and eight boards in a win over Pittsburgh.

Though the Friars are counting on talented sophomore Marcus Douthit to take over in the middle, Shabazz will be missed, thanks to his defense and emerging offense as the year moved along.

OTHERS NOT RETURNING

G-CHRIS ROGERS (6-4, 2.5 ppg, 1.6 rpg, 1.5 apg, 0.5 spg, 12.8 minutes, .411 FG, .813 FT). Welsh referred to Rogers as a "utility infielder" last year, and he was right. Rogers did a lot of little things for the Friars last year and filled his role willingly, despite seeing his minutes drop nearly six a game from the 1999-00 season.

Rogers was able to play both guard positions and scored nine points twice, against Rhode Island and Binghamton. He had eight in the home win over St. John's.

PROJECTED STARTERS

PG-JOHN LINEHAN (5-9, 165 lbs., SR, #12, 10.7 ppg, 2.4 rpg, 4.0 apg, 3.1 spg, 26.2 minutes, .416 FG, .417 3PT, .856 FT, Winchendon (Mass.) School/Chester HS/Chester, Pa.). Everything you need to know about Linehan comes courtesy of Welsh's opinion of the fiery point man's best game ever at Providence.

"It came when he did not score a basket," Welsh said, referring to Linehan's five-point (all free throws), six-rebound, six-assist, six-steal effort in the win at Villanova.

Linehan is clearly the heart of the Providence team, even if he isn't a dominating scorer. He controls tempo, plays aggressive defense and allows the Friars to be the go-get-'em type of team that they are. Linehan is as tough as someone a foot taller—as evidenced by his history of playing through injuries—and has improved his shooting to the point where opposing teams can't leave him alone from long range anymore. He was second on the team in three-point shooting last year and was deadly in Big East play, making 44.6 percent of his shots from behind the arc.

"His toughness and energy trickle down to the other guys on the team at practice every day," Welsh said. "You hear stories about [Michael] Jordan as a competitor in games, and obviously in practice, where he was legendary. If somebody didn't play, he got in their face, even at the end of a three-hour practice. That's the way John is. He plays the same way all the time."

Linehan did have some big games last year, statistically. He scored 22 points against Boston College and had 20 the second time, against Villanova. His 18 points and 10 assists keyed the win over Georgetown, and he had back-to-back 17-point efforts in wins over Rhode Island and Massachusetts.

SG-ABDUL MILLS (6-3, 190 lbs., JR, #11, 10.9 ppg, 3.0 rpg, 2.9 apg, 1.5 spg, 26.4 minutes, .403 FG, .355 3PT, .627 FT, Milford (CT) Academy/Brooklyn, N.Y.). Expect Mills to continue his development into a solid Big East scoring guard. Though he struggled with inconsistency last year, he showed signs of becoming the kind of productive wing that all good teams need. Now in his third year as a starter, Mills could be ready to break out.

Of course, that comes with a qualifier. On the balanced Friar club, there isn't too much room for a 20-a-night man, so Mills may have to be happy with 12-to-15 each game. That's fine, particularly if Romauld Augustin, Linehan and low-post newcomer Garnett Thompson get theirs, too. Welsh isn't too concerned about having a "go-to" player, so long as he has four or five solid offensive options.

Mills had two separate stretches last year when he was quite strong. The first was an eight-game string, when he hit double figures in all but one game and had 25 in a win at George Washington. He heated up again in Big East play, scoring more than 10 in six-of-seven games, with a 19-point outburst against Virginia Tech and a 20-point effort against Binghamton, two days later, the highlights.

Mills is a pretty good shooter who needs only to improve his shot selection and get a little stronger physically to improve his percentage. He also needs to boost his free-throw numbers, particularly because he was second on the team in attempts from the stripe last year.

SF-ROMAULD AUGUSTIN (6-7, 205 lbs., JR, #4, 9.2 ppg, 2.7 rpg, 2.6 apg, 0.9 spg, 26.9 minutes, .446 FG, .402 3PT, .684 FT, Youngstown (Ohio) Rayen HS/Montreal, Quebec). The third member of the Friar perimeter brigade, Augustin is a smooth three-man with a sharp shooting eye and good handling skills who ought to author the same kind of improvement that is expected of Mills.

The key for Augustin this year is how well he handles Big East life. Although his scoring average improved in league play, his shooting from the field and three-point range fell when the big games began. After starting strongly against conference foes, with six double-figure efforts in his first seven games, Augustin topped 10 only one more time in Big East play, with 22 against Connecticut. His expected maturity and increased strength should help him become more reliable in January and beyond.

We saw a glimpse of what may lay ahead during the summer, when Augustin averaged 21 points a game as a member of the Canadian national team in the World University games. Included was a 35-point outburst against China, which beat the U.S. for the gold medal.

PF-GARNETT THOMPSON (6-9, 215 lbs., JR, #23, 24.0 ppg, 12.0 rpg, 5.0 apg, 6.0 bpg, Suffolk (N.Y.) Community College/Central Islip HS/Islip, N.Y.). Welsh isn't particularly fond of junior-college players, unless they can fill a need. The departures of Maxey and Shabazz created a hole up front, and Welsh believes Thompson can help fill it.

"He has enough skill and can be a good shot blocker and rebounder for us," Welsh said. "He is athletic and likes to face the basket."

Thompson was a first-team Division III JC All-American last year, his first at Suffolk, and was rated one of the top 25 junior college players in the country by Prep Stars. He grew three inches during the last two years and has a chance to make an immediate contribution.

C-MARCUS DOUTHIT (6-10, 215 lbs., SO, #21, 5.4 ppg, 4.0 rpg, 1.0 apg, 1.7 bpg, 15.6 minutes, .483 FG, .750 FT, Notre Dame Prep/Syracuse, N.Y.). Anybody who saw Douthit play last year understands why Welsh isn't all that torn up about Shabazz's departure. Although he'll miss the senior's reliability, he knows Douthit can be something special.

"He's shown he has tremendous talent," Welsh said. "He can block shots and has good passing skills around the basket. He can change a game and be dominant inside. You can't double down on him, because he's such a good passer."

The key for Douthit this year is a to handle a big jump in minutes, from his 15.6 last year to nearly double that. Though not imposing physically, he moves well and has excellent instincts. Douthit has a solid shooting touch and is long enough to rebound well and cause problems defensively. He must, however, cut back on his fouls. He was disqualified from five games last year, quite a feat when averaging 15 minutes a night.

KEY RESERVES

F-MARIS LAKSA (6-9, 212 lbs., SO, #22, 9.0 ppg, 3.2 rpg, 1.2 apg, 0.6 bpg, 19.9 minutes, .410 FG, .458 3PT, .882 FT, Latvian Junior National School/Ventspils, Latvia). Laksa should continue to play a key role on the Friars, unless the NCAA finds out that he played opposite a professional during a club game or two or accepted a cheese sandwich as remuneration for playing in a game. Then, he might be suspended—or worse.

Like all European players, Laksa's past is being called into question by the organization which permits organized graft among the AAU summer circuit and permitted members of USA Basketball teams to receive payment for fine performances this past summer.

Laksa is like most European players. He's a solid shooter with good ball handling skills who needs to work on his defense and rebounding. The rebounding aspect will be particularly important this year, with Shabazz and Maxey gone. At 6-9, Laksa will be counted upon to provide some interior heft and production. But he can score. He had 24 against Boston University and 18 against GW, among his 11 double-figure efforts.

F-CHRISTOPHER ANRIN (6-7, 220 lbs., SO, #20, 5.8 ppg, 1.7 rpg, 0.9 apg, 0.3 spg, 13.0 minutes, .396 FG, .364 3PT, .821 FT, Alvik HS/Varmdo, Sweden). An even better shooter than Laksa, Anrin is a largely one-dimensional European player who could be in the same boat as his fellow world traveler, if the NCAA finds something it deems fishy.

Anrin took only 29 shots that weren't behind the arc last year and displayed little proclivity for defense or rebounding. Though Welsh promises he'll get better, expect to see Anrin lurking behind the arc, looking for a kick-out or skip pass to launch a three-pointer. Anrin can be a big weapon. He had 18, including four three-pointers, against Miami and scored 15, with four more treys, against Binghamton.

G–SHEIKU KABBA (6-2, 185 lbs., SO, #13, 4.6 ppg, 1.9 rpg, 1.7 apg, 0.7 spg, 15.3 minutes, .470 FG, .465 3PT, .636 FT, Bronx Regional HS/Bronx, N.Y.). Kabba enjoyed a strong debut season last year, backing up both backcourt spots and providing a look into what life will be like next year, when Linehan is gone.

Kabba isn't a classic point man; in fact, Welsh prefers to see him off the ball. But that doesn't mean Kabba can't handle the job. He had a solid assist to turnover ratio that was above 1:1 and showed he could distribute the ball early, when he had seven assists against Missouri-Kansas City and six against Auburn.

"He's more of a shooter and a scorer than a point, but he has to be our backup point this year," Welsh said. "He shoots the ball well and is a better 'push' point guard than [Linehan]. But when we had Sheiku and John in the game together, we moved John to the two spot."

F-LELAND ANDERSON (6-7, 245 lbs., SO, #34, 2.1 ppg, 1.4 rpg in 1999-2000, University of Michigan/Attleboro HS/Attleboro, Mass.). The question isn't whether Anderson will contribute, once he gets onto the court, it's if he gets onto the court. He has been injury-prone since his high school days and missed considerable practice last year with the Friars because of an assortment of leg and back problems.

"He's got to stay healthy," Welsh said. "He gets healthy every fall and then starts practice and gets hurt. He looks the part. He's big and strong. The question is, 'Can he give us production?' "

Anderson could provide some vital interior help for the Friars, who need some big bodies. But, like Welsh said, he has to be healthy, or he won't get into the main rotation.

F-RYAN GOMES (6-7, 235 lbs., FR, #3, 26.9 ppg, 16.0 rpg, 5.0 apg, 3.0 bpg, Wilby HS/Waterbury, Conn.). Welsh calls Gomes a "sleeper" and is intrigued by his blend of size and skill.

Gomes is a strongman inside who grabs offensive rebounds and converts them. He had 30 or more points in 10 games last year and was the MVP of his league. Though not a highly recruited player, Welsh thinks Gomes will surprise some people.

F-ROB SANDERS (6-6, 205 lbs., FR, #33, 22.0 ppg, 10.0 rpg, St. Thomas More (CT) Prep/New London HS/New London, Conn). Sanders may have the body of a perimeter player, but he belongs closer to the basket.

"He's a high-jump type guy, real athletic," Welsh said. "He's a rebounder and a runner who plays along the baseline."

Sanders was a star on the St. Thomas More team which captured the New England Prep School title, not an easy thing to do, given the stout competition. As a senior at New London, he was a first-team all-state performer and the Eastern Connecticut Player of the Year in 2000.

G-DONELL ALLICK (6-4, 195 lbs., SO, #10, Winchendon (MA) School/Hillhouse HS/Riverside Academy/New Haven, Conn.). The well-traveled Allick missed last year as a partial qualifier but was able to practice with the Friars. He'll fight for time in a crowded perimeter group that includes plenty of depth and experience.

"He can play the three or two positions," Welsh said. "He's got to work on his scoring. He has some questions about how he'll perform in certain situations. He has defensive toughness and is a hard-nosed kid. He brings energy and is strong."

OTHER RETURNEES

G-KAREEM HAYLETTS (6-0, 160 lbs., SR, #15, 1.1 ppg, 0.3 rpg, 0.2 apg, 12 appearances, .545 FG, .250 FT, Bergenfield HS/Bergenfield, N.J.). A walk-on who has been a strong practice partner for Linehan, Hayletts scored five points against Binghamton and four against Brown and Virginia Tech.

F-STEPHEN TRAUGOTT (6-5, 195 lbs., JR, #35, 1.0 ppg, 0.3 rpg, 0.7 apg, three appearances, .167 FG, .500 FT, Iona Prep/New Rochelle, N.Y.). Traugott played a total of 11 minutes last year at the small-forward position and scored three points. One came against Brown, and two were scored in the rout of Binghamton.

F-BRIAN SCHNURR (6-7, 220 lbs., SR, #45, 1.0 ppg, 0.0 rpg, 0.0 apg, 2 appearances, .507 FG, Fairfield Prep/Fairfield, Conn.). A walk-on forward, Schnurr played three minutes last year and scored his only basket of the season against Rhode Island.

OTHER NEWCOMERS

F-TUUKKA KOTTI (6-9, 205 lbs., FR, #25, 15.1 ppg, 7.6 rpg, 2.2 apg, 2.0 spg, Salon Sarga Salo/Forssa, Finland). A skilled forward with good shooting range, Kotti hit 39.1 percent from behind the arc and 45 percent from the field in helping his team to the prep semis in Finland last year.

Kotti is expected to struggle for time early behind Laksa and Anrin, because each performs a similar service for the Friars and has a year of experience.

QUESTIONS

Rebounding? Even with Maxey and Shabazz last year, the Friars could do no better than a push on the boards. Douthit and the newcomers must be able to provide help on the interior.

Inside scoring? The same thing goes for this category. Maxey led the team in points per game last year and was reliable close to the hoop, and Shabazz got better as the year went on.

Expectations? The Friars must now deal with being hunted by other Big East teams, after their NCAA season in 2000-01. How they handle the pressure will determine if they return to the Madness.

ANSWERS

Depth! Welsh likes to play 10 or 11 people, and he certainly has enough candidates to feature a number of different combinations.

Linehan! The senior is a tremendous leader and the spark for the Friars' defense and fast break.

Shooting! Providence made 40 percent of its three-point attempts last year, a great figure for anybody. It could be even better this year.

Defense! Opponents made just 40 percent of their field-goal tries in 2000-01 and were a putrid 29.8 percent from behind the arc. It's hard to lose playing that kind of "D."

PROVIDENCE 2000-2001 RESULTS

Holy Cross	63-57
Maine (L)	71-80
#UMKC	60-53
#Creighton (L)	51-63
#Auburn (L)	69-80
Florida International	74-55
Rhode Island	95-72
@Massachusetts	85-70
@George Washington	93-80
Brown	110-59
Boston Un iversity	73-49
South Carolina	60-55
@Seton Hall (L)	80-87
@Villanova	76-67
Connecticut	81-68
Miami (L)	64-78
@Virginia Tech	75-60
Pittsburgh	77-61
@Miami	80-70
Villanova	84-64
St. John's	75-63
@Connecticut (L)	68-83
Georgetown	103-79
@St. John's	64-53
@Boston College (L)	73-81
Virginia Tech	96-56
Binghampton	119-58
Boston College (L)	58-59
Rutgers	69-66
##Pittsburgh (L)	54-55
###Penn State	59-69

#Energia Systems Thanksgiving Tournament in Kansas City, MO
##Big East Championship in New York
###NCAA Tournament
@Road Games

BLUE RIBBON ANALYSIS

BACKCOURT	B+
BENCH/DEPTH	B+
FRONTCOURT	B-
INTANGIBLES	B+

This group of Friars isn't all that well known, but

Welsh has built a strong foundation for what looks like seasons of success. There is depth, versatility and plenty of perimeter strength. Those are good ingredients for winning plenty of games.

The big question this year is up front, where Douthit, Thompson, Anderson and Gomes must emerge as a formidable interior group, the better to prevent teams from slogging it inside offensively and then attacking the perimeter. If they deliver—and they don't have to be fire-breathers—the Friars will be dangerous.

Of course, Linehan is the trigger man. He'll keep everything rolling and get his perimeter mates involved. The Friars have wing men who can attack the rack and also fall back to launch long-range missiles. It's a great combination.

The NCAA Tournament is a completely realistic goal this year, and a couple of wins aren't out of the question, either. Providence snuck into the national eye last year but begins this season with plenty of people watching it. That's as it should be and how Welsh wants it.

(M.B.)

 # Wake Forest 39

LOCATION	Winston-Salem, NC
CONFERENCE	Atlantic Coast
LAST SEASON	19-11 (.633)
CONFERENCE RECORD	8-8 (t-5th)
STARTERS LOST/RETURNING	2/3
NICKNAME	Demon Deacons
COLORS	Old Gold & Black
HOMECOURT	Lawrence Joel Memorial Coliseum (14,407)
COACH	Skip Prosser
	(U.S. Mercant Marine Academy '72)
RECORD AT SCHOOL	First year
CAREER RECORD	165-78 (8 years)
ASSISTANTS	Jeff Battle (Marshall '85)
	Dino Gaudio (Ohio '81)
	Chris Mack (Xavier '93)
TEAM WINS (last 5 years)	24-26-17-22-19
RPI (last 5 years)	7-37-60-34-29
2000-01 FINISH	Lost in NCAA first round.

COACH AND PROGRAM

New Wake Forest head coach Skip Prosser didn't mind picking up the phone a couple times in the last six months and calling new South Carolina head coach Dave Odom.

Where better to get information than his predecessor?

Prosser left Xavier to coach the Demon Deacons after Odom bolted for the Gamecocks. Odom had spent a dozen years building a successful program at the small private school in Winston-Salem, but felt the need to move on. It didn't help that Wake Forest athletics director Ron Wellman wasn't offering Odom a contract extension beyond this season. So he was lured away by the promise of a bigger, more secure paycheck and the opportunity to work at a larger public university, one that was not hamstrung by private-school admissions policies.

There always seemed to be tension on the sub-surface of the Odom-Wellman relationship. There was also tension between Odom and some of Wake's most devoted fans, who always wanted him to be more successful than the small school was willing to commit to be.

Odom took the Deacons to the NCAA Tournament eight times in 12 years. He was smart, funny and had a healthy respect for the history and importance of the ACC. He was loved by the media for his candid answers to every question that was ever asked of him and many of those that weren't. But even with his best teams he could never get beyond the Elite Eight. His only championship in 12 years was the 2000 National Invitation Tournament, which was important, but hardly the kind of thing that gets a coach a lengthy contract extension.

In the post-Tim Duncan era, the Deacons made it to the NCAA Tournament only once in four years, and any benefit it gained from making the field last year was certainly and permanently erased after a disastrous first half against Butler, in which the Deacons trailed 43-10 at the half.

Odom's departure left Wellman needing a quick solution for a difficult position. He found Prosser, a Pete

Gillen protégé who had established a good program at Xavier, another small school with similar academic hurdles.

"The two schools are very similar: small private schools that both have a tremendous commitment to educating and graduating its student athletes," Prosser said. "Of course, no place is better than any place else, but there were kids who liked Xavier because it was a small school that played basketball on the highest level.

"There are a lot of kids who like Wake Forest for the same reason, a small school academically that plays basketball in the best conference in the country."

Still, most coaches might not pick up the phone to share notes on players, even if Prosser was asking Odom about players the latter had recruited to Wake Forest. But Prosser was fairly desperate. He and Odom couldn't have more different coaching styles. Prosser likes to get up and down the floor, stretching the game 94 feet on offense and defense. Odom liked to stay in the halfcourt, playing hard-nosed defense and a set offense.

So, with five returning seniors, a high flying junior and five new players (including two who practiced with the team last year) coming in, Prosser needed reliable information about his new charges.

"I actually talked to Dave before I even took the job," Prosser said. "We talked a couple of times afterwards and even had breakfast during the July recruiting period. He is a good friend.

"And, from my point of view, it's hard to have too much information. I am trying to get as much information about Wake Forest and this team as I can."

Well, coach, here are a few tidbits: The Demon Deacons have two exceptional players in senior power forward Darius Songaila and junior swing man Josh Howard. Senior Craig Dawson, who played sixth man for the last two years as a substitute for Robert O'Kelley, won't have any trouble stepping into the starting lineup.

The trouble is, the Deacons have very little height, with only one player on the roster taller than 6-9. Losing center Josh Shoemaker and Rafael Vidaurreta will hurt the Deacons' defense and rebounding.

Under Odom, those players and O'Kelley soared to the Top 5 of both major polls last year, after winning their first dozen games, including a 31-point victory over Kansas at home. Then, with no real explanation, things began to fall apart. Wake never recovered from a one-point loss at North Carolina in January. It ended up losing 11 of its last 18 games, including the first-round embarrassment in the NCAA Tournament.

Prosser certainly didn't spend much time thinking about what went wrong last year. All he knows is that he has inherited a team with five seniors who have never won a game in the NCAA Tournament. He believes they are anxious for postseason success.

To get there, they will have to play under Prosser's philosophy, which is vastly different than Odom's.

"We are just going to try to push the ball at every opportunity," Prosser said. "The hardest defense to play is transition defense. We are going to try to attack teams in transition before they set up.

"If it is a sumo wrestling match down in the blocks, that is not good for us, because we are not that big. But I think the more free-flowing the game is, the better for us. I think we have some guys who hopefully can score in the open court and get open shots in transition."

The Deacons, with their lack of size, must find some help underneath, even if Prosser can keep the team moving. The only player taller than 6-9 on the team is red-shirt freshman **Dshamal Schoetz**, who isn't really expected to contribute this year.

"That is my biggest concern," Prosser said. "Shoemaker and Vidaurreta were two of the best rebounders in the league.

"I think if we can find a way to rebound effectively, I think we have the ability to score some points."

Songaila and Howard, the team's top two scorers last year, will certainly help there, especially in an up-tempo game. The athletic, fluid Howard could become a superstar in this system, with his shooting and scoring abilities. And Songaila has always been able to put the ball in the basket.

Prosser doesn't know if he will build his team around either of those players.

"At this point, I can't think whether we are going to have one or two players who we are going to build around," Prosser said. "I think it will have to be more of an 'equal-opportunity' offense to start with, and then we will see how it plays out."

2001-2002 SCHEDULE

Nov.	13	#UNC Wilmington
	18	Elon
	27	Minnesota
Dec.	4	@Kansas
	7	South Carolina State
	16	Florida State
	20	St. Francis
	19	@St. John's
	29	Marquette
Jan.	2	Richmond
	5	@North Carolina
	7	@Navy
	12	Clemson
	15	@Virginia
	19	@Duke
	23	Maryland
	26	Georgia Tech
	30	@North Carolina State
Feb.	2	@Florida State
	6	North Carolina
	9	Cincinnati
	13	@Clemson
	17	Virginia
	21	Duke
	24	@Maryland
	27	@Georgia Tech
March	2	North Carolina State
	7-10	##ACC Tournament

@Road Games
#Preseason NIT (if Wake Forest wins, it will play again on Nov. 16 against Arkansas or Maine; semifinals and final Nov. 21 and 23 at Madison Square Garden, NY)
##Charlotte Coliseum, Charlotte, NC

STARTERS NOT RETURNING

G-ROBERT O'KELLEY (6-1, 185 lbs., 12.6 ppg, 1.5 rpg, 1.9 apg, 28.6 minutes, .418 FG, .351 3-PT, .730 FT, 25 steals). One headache Prosser won't have to deal with—as Odom did for the last two years—is where to play O'Kelley, the former ACC Rookie of the Year and second-team All-ACC selection who never really seemed to fit in after his successful debut.

Odom played him as a shooting point guard as a sophomore and halfway through his junior season. But as the team's only consistent offensive threat, O'Kelley was drawing all the attention of the defense and a lot of iron on his shots. He went through a horrific shooting slump, during which time Josh Howard and Darius Songaila became deadly offensive weapons.

Odom finally pulled the trigger on the long-awaited move to shooting guard midway through O'Kelley's junior year, and the Deacons went on to win the NIT championship. But O'Kelley had a down year, dropping off more than four-and-a-half points from his sophomore scoring average and plummeting to 35.1 percent from the field.

As a senior, O'Kelley played a different kind of role. Odom even pulled him from the starting lineup during a six-game stretch midway through the ACC season, when O'Kelley missed 18 consecutive three-point shots. It was the first time in O'Kelley's career he didn't start for the Deacons. His minutes dropped precipitously, but his production did not improve as Odom had hoped. At the end of his career, he was hardly the offensive centerpiece that he was early in his career.

Still, O'Kelley left as one of the school's top 10 leading scorers and is second all-time with 282 three-point field goals.

C-JOSH SHOEMAKER (6-9, 238 lbs., 6.0 ppg, 7.4 rpg, 1.7 apg, 26.3 minutes, .529 FG, .500 3PT, .739 FT, 20 steals, 20 blocked shots). After spending his first three years on campus as a productive and well-liked sixth man, Shoemaker was thrown into the starting lineup at the beginning of last year when Rafael Vidaurreta suffered a preseason knee injury.

To the surprise of many, Shoemaker responded brilliantly and was the Deacons' most improved player through the first half of the season. He led the ACC in rebounding the first two months of the season, after grabbing at least nine boards in nine of the Deacons' first 12 games.

Shoemaker's role was diminished some when Vidaurreta returned, but he was still a solid contributor throughout the season and finished as the team's leading rebounder. He had a solid shooting touch, making a team-high 55 percent of his field-goal attempts.

But his biggest contribution for four years was being a tough-nosed rebounder. He averaged more rebounds than points in each of his four years.

Wake fans will realize just how important and improved Shoemaker was last year as they watch the Deacons' undersized frontcourt this year.

OTHERS NOT RETURNING

C-RAFAEL VIDAURRETA (6-9, 268 lbs., 3.2 ppg, 3.6 rpg, 16.1 minutes, .447 FG, .563 FT, 10 blocked shots). After suffering a knee injury in late September, Vidaurreta never really returned to the physical presence he had been in his first three years on campus. He missed the first seven games of the season while recuperating from the surgery, and when he returned, he barely managed double-digit minutes.

In Vidaurreta's absence, Shoemaker came out of his shell, leading the team in rebounding all season long. It was a disappointing and frustrating end to a career in which Vidaurreta, the most popular player on the team, became one of the top 10 rebounders in school history.

"It was frustrating," Vidaurreta said. "Everybody looks forward to their senior season and being a leader, but there was nothing I could do."

Vidaurreta returned to the starting lineup for the final four games of the year, but that did not turn things around the way Odom had hoped.

PROJECTED STARTERS

PG-BRODERICK HICKS (6-1, 171 lbs., SR, #3, 6.9 ppg, 1.9 rpg, 2.6 apg, 20.4 minutes, .405 FG, .378 3PT, .771 FG, 37 steals, Strake Jesuit HS/Houston, Texas). Most of last year, Odom employed a two-player point guard system that seemed to be effective. Hicks, a pusher who likes to score, and Murray, a pace-setter who likes to pass, combined for 161 assists and only 68 turnovers.

Murray had a calming influence on the Deacons. He started 18 times and was in charge of the offense the most often. But Hicks, who opened and ended the season as the starter, provided instant offense, scoring a season-high 18 points against Clemson and Cincinnati.

Hicks, however, is more suited to Prosser's style, and while the coach won't give any of his potential four point guards an advantage for the starting job heading into the season, he definitely believes Hicks has the skills necessary to get the job done.

"Broderick is the main lynchpin if we are going to play the way we want to play," Prosser said. "He has shown the ability to rush the ball up the court and the ability to have good defensive pressure going the other way.

"In certain games, he shoots the ball well."

And there's the problem. Prosser needs more consistency out of his point guard, and Hicks has been anything but during his career. He's a streaky shooter, one who made 10-of-15 three-pointers during one stretch of January, but also was only 8-for-26 from beyond the arc in the Deacons' last 10 games.

"With Broderick, the thing is that he is going to have to be consistent," Prosser said. "I try to put a lot of responsibility on the point guard. I try to get him to run the team for 40 minutes."

From everything the coach has learned about Hicks, he believes the senior can handle the responsibility.

"He is a senior and he has good experience," Prosser said. "He has had some very good moments at times. He should be able to do this. He is a bright kid. It won't overtax him mentally.

"His success at the point will really go a long way in determining how successful we are as a team."

SG-CRAIG DAWSON (6-5, 205 lbs., SR, #42, 12.5 ppg, 2.2 rpg, 2.0 apg, 24.8 minutes, .454 FG, .379 3PT, .667 FT, Kinston HS/Kinston, N.C.). Sometimes, it's nice to have a good lineage, for genes and for practice. Dawson has both in uncle Jerry Stackhouse, the former North Carolina All-American and star of the Detroit Pistons. Dawson grew up playing against him, and spent the last couple of off-seasons working out with him and his professional teammates.

And last year, Dawson began to shine. Early in the year, he was the Deacons' leading scorer, a guy with a deadly shooting touch and the ability to score points in a hurry. He proved that in the whipping of Kansas when he had 20 points in 24 minutes. Dawson also dropped 23 points in 23 minutes against Temple and a career-high 29 points in 33 minutes against uncle Jerry's alma mater, North Carolina.

But most of Dawson's work came off the bench last year. He started only eight games all year, playing mostly behind O'Kelley at the shooting-guard position. In the end, he proved to be a more consistent and more productive player, even though he suffered through a mid-season shooting and scoring slump.

As with almost every player on the roster, Prosser is concerned about Dawson being more consistent this year. He's also interested in seeing how he handles being a starter his senior year.

"At times, he is lights out," Prosser said. "He shoots the ball great."

What the new coach worries about is Dawson's condition. In his first year-and-a-half at Wake, Dawson was injured. He was limited by a stress fracture his entire freshman season and a sprained ankle as a sophomore. He was 100 percent as a junior, but the inability to properly condition himself because of earlier injuries may have contributed to Dawson's inconsistent play down the stretch. Prosser says that won't be the case this year.

"He is going to have to get into unbelievable condition," Prosser said. "He has the ability to get the ball up the court and get himself open for shots, then turn around and guard on a full-court basis. I think he could have a terrific year if he gets into that kind of condition."

SF-JOSH HOWARD (6-6, 191 lbs., JR, #5, 13.6 ppg, 5.9 rpg, 1.8 apg, 27.2 minutes, .490 FG, .391 3PT, .685 FT, 58 steals, 32 blocked shots, Hargrave Academy/Glenn HS/Winston-Salem, N.C.). An explosive and athletically gifted player, Howard might benefit the most from the change in styles between Odom and Prosser. Odom was a huge fan of Howard, the kind of slicing wing forward that the Deacons had never really had before. After watching Howard score 18 points and grab nine rebounds against Georgia Tech, Odom beamed about Wake's rare homegrown talent.

"I think right before our very eyes, Josh Howard is emerging as one of the very best players in this league," Odom said. "I don't want to go overboard or anything, but he certainly has the ability to change the game when he is playing like [this]."

Howard did emerge as one of the league's best players, and the change in style may benefit him even more. Prosser, for one, is excited to see how Howard will play in a 94-foot game.

"He can score in the open floor," Prosser said. "He can be an excellent offensive rebounder and an excellent defender. He needs to become a more consistent three-point shooter, and if he does that, he will be really hard to guard.

"I think he will be terrific in the press, because he has long arms. He has worked hard in the off-season on his strength and his stamina. He has set himself up for a big year, but again, it has to come to fruition."

Prosser is looking for more consistency from everyone on the roster, and from Howard in particular.

"There are games where he is absolutely brilliant," Prosser said after watching tapes in the summer. "But he has the same question that so many of our players have: Can he be consistent?"

Howard was the team's leading scorer, second-best three-point shooter, third-leading rebounder and second-best shot blocker last year, but his leadership abilities go far beyond the numbers.

As a freshman, he made public comments about how some of his teammates were mailing in the season. Not long afterwards, the Deacons went on a roll and won the NIT championship.

Prosser wants to see the same kind of vocal and aggressive behavior this year, on the floor and off.

PF-ANTWAN SCOTT (6-8, 197 lbs., SR, #34, 6.8 ppg, 3.6 rpg, 16.2 minutes, .487 FG, .250 3PT, .731 FT, 12 steals, 38 blocked shots, Oak Hill Academy/New Bern, N.C.). Few players can excite a home crowd the way Scott, an athletic leaper capable of making thunderous dunks, can. He owns the team's best standing-still vertical jump (35 inches), which he used to block a team-high 38 shots last year.

When he was on, he was extremely productive, averaging 6.8 points in only 16.2 minutes a game. And he was on most of the early part of the season, coming off the bench to hit double figures in seven of the Deacons first 14 games. But that productivity declined as the Deacons slowly slid from the Top 10 onto the NCAA Tournament bubble. He scored in double figures only once in the team's last 16 games, a 10-point performance at Virginia.

"From everything I have heard, he has been an enigmatic player at Wake Forest," Prosser said. "You see some things that he does and you say, 'Wow, that is impressive.'

"And then other games he doesn't play a lot. Antwan and I have talked about that at length. I told him that coach Odom is a great coach and has won a lot of games, and if he didn't play you a lot, then there must be a reason."

So Prosser left it up to Scott to figure out what that reason was over the summer.

"I asked him to investigate in his own heart what he hasn't done here and why he hasn't played more," Prosser said. "He is obviously very gifted athletically. He is going to have to play a lot for us, because we don't have a lot of options inside. This may be the first time since he has been at Wake Forest that he is really going to be counted on.

"In the past, if he played great, then well great. If he didn't, then coach Odom would find someone else. This year, he is a necessary commodity. He is going to have to play well for us down low."

Because, the coach knows, there really aren't a lot of other low-post options.

PF-DARIUS SONGAILA (6-9, 245 lbs, SR, #25, 13.2 ppg, 6.0 rpg, 1.7 apg, 25.5 minutes, .500, .444 3PT, .816 FT, 26 steals, 22 blocked shots, New Hampton School/Marijampole, Lithuania). Prosser has heard plenty about Songaila's game. He knows that Songaila can be brilliant at times, stupid at others. He heard all about how the Lithuanian star hit the wall midway through last year, after spending all last summer trying out for, then playing on, his country's bronze-medal-winning team at the 2000 Sydney Olympics.

Prosser doesn't want to hear any more. He knows how good Songaila can be. He was, after all, Wake's second-leading scorer, rebounder and shooter last year. The coach has seen the tapes.

Prosser also knows that Songaila can be a reasonable and engaging person, one who can agree during a June meeting with a coach to take it easy on the aggressive play away from the basket. But that's in June.

Prosser's job is to keep Songaila in games, something that the gifted big man was able to do a little better last year, after leading the ACC in fouls his first two years on campus.

"Darius is a great kid, very bright and very talented," Prosser said after meeting Songaila in the summer. "I heard all about his year last year, about how he didn't get back to school until October and how he hit the wall and ran out of gas.

"I don't know all that. I wasn't here to see him. But we have talked and he is really determined to come back and have a great senior year."

Songaila—nicknamed the "Baltic Bear" by his girlfriend—started slowly last year after returning from his summer of duty to his country. He didn't score more than 20 points in a game until he posted a career-high 27 in the Deacons' ACC opener against Virginia, Wake's 12th game of the season. Songaila broke the 20-point barrier only twice more all season. His foul trouble in the North Carolina game in Chapel Hill allowed the Tar Heels to make a season-altering comeback on the Deacons. Odom eventually got fed up with Songaila's play and stopped his preaching.

To be fair, Songaila reduced his ACC leading foul total from 118 in 2000 to 98 in 2001. Prosser, who knows how valuable a weapon Songaila can be, wants that number reduced even more, which may be hard in a run-and-gun system that creates more possessions per game.

The good thing for Songaila is that those possessions tend to be shorter. Most of his problems occur deeper in the 45-second clock.

"He is a bright kid and he knows that some of the fouls he commits are unintelligent," Prosser said. "Some of the fouls I have seen him take are situations where he fouled someone back, that sort of thing.

"He understands what I am telling him. It makes perfect sense to him and he agrees with it all. But those conversations are in June. In the heat of battle, we'll see."

Songaila is a bright player, one who learned immensely from his Olympic experience and one who could be a star in the ACC. As a senior, he has to put that knowledge to good use by staying in as many games as possible.

KEY RESERVES

F-VYTAS DANELIUS (6-8, 228 lbs., FR, #13, 19.0 ppg, 14.0 rpg, .702 FG, Park Tudor HS/Indianapolis). When Prosser heard Dave Odom was leaving Wake Forest, he got on the horn to coach Ed Kelly at Park Tudor High School in Indianapolis. Prosser had seen Daneluis play while recruiting his high school teammate,

forward Will Caudle, and thought, "this kid can play."

Prosser figured he would find out if Daneluis, who had given Wake Forest a commitment in the spring, might be interested in changing his mind.

So for a couple of weeks, Prosser sung the praises of Xavier University, telling Daneluis how nice it would be to rejoin Caudle in college. Then, in an odd twist, Prosser was hired by Wake Forest, and he had to start recruiting Daneluis for the Demon Deacons all over again.

"One day I was telling him what a great place Xavier was, and the next I was telling him to go with his initial gut feeling and go to Wake Forest," Prosser said.

It didn't hurt that Songaila, who like Daneluis is from Lithuania, kept sending the young big man e-mails encouraging him to come down to Wake Forest and join the Deacons.

Daneluis, who speaks five languages, has some of the size Prosser is looking for inside and what the coach calls "deceiving athletic ability."

"I was impressed with his skills for a guy of his size," Prosser said.

But that was an instant-analysis that came from the one game Prosser saw Danelius play in high school.

G-TARON DOWNEY (6-2, 171 lbs., FR, #4, Fork Union Military Academy/Fork Union, Va. and Oxford, N.C.) In nearly all of his interviews over the summer, Prosser emphasized how important he thinks the point-guard position is and how wide open the position is going into the season.

Obviously, Hicks and Murray have the edge on the position with their three years of experience, but Prosser is also thinking about the program's future. And he won't be able to run the kind of fast-pace offense until he has a point guard who can do what he wants.

That's why Downey, who signed with the Deacons last fall, will get plenty of opportunity to show off his advanced abilities to the new coaching staff.

Downey, who spent last year honing his skills at Fork Union, is a dynamite scorer who led all high school players in the state of North Carolina two years ago with a 30.7 point scoring average.

But he spent last year learning how to run an offense, at the suggestion of the previous Wake staff, which wanted him to learn more about the position before he became a Deacon.

Prosser noticed those abilities when he was recruiting other players at Fork Union for Xavier, seeing him play on three or four occasions.

"I didn't really watch him that closely because I knew he was already coming to Wake Forest," Prosser said. "He is a guy who is in that mix for those very, very important point guard minutes. I understand that he can shoot the ball really well and he has really good quickness.

"We are counting on him. I think he is going to have to play for us. He can push the basketball. He has good quickness and we can shoot the ball. He has decent size. He will be in that point guard mix."

G-A.W. HAMILTON (6-3, 176, SO, #11, 1.8 ppg, 0.4 rpg, 0.8 apg, 6.8 minutes, .355 FG, .267 3PT, .667 FT, Hargrave Military Academy/Chatham, Va., and Georgetown, Ky.). In Prosser's system, the point guard is one of, if not the, most important positions on the court and the Deacons are going to need someone to guide them this year and in the future.

But is Hamilton capable of doing what Prosser wants? Hamilton was so lightly regarded coming out of Kentucky as a high school senior that he opted to go to prep school just to improve his chances of getting a Division I scholarship.

Hamilton's game improved, but Prosser admits that he knows very little about the sophomore's abilities. He played sparingly last year, averaging only 6.4 minutes in 19 games, the only scholarship player on the team who didn't average in double digits. Hamilton hardly showed up in the few game tapes Prosser watched this summer.

Hamilton also hurt his wrist during off-season workouts and needed surgery, severely limiting his conditioning. Prosser is willing to give Hamilton the benefit of the doubt, however.

"I saw his former coach at Hargrave over the summer and he told me 'Skip, he is really going to surprise you,'" Prosser said. "But he has basically been hurt since I got here, so I don't know much about him.

"I do know that the point-guard position is so important to us and there I no heir-apparent after the seniors are gone. There is a great opportunity for him to play, and he will be in the mix for point guard minutes."

G-STEVE LEPORE (6-5, 199, JR, #23, 9.2 ppg, 3.7 rpg, 29.0 minutes, .369 3PT in 1999-2000, St. Edward HS/North Olmstead, Ohio and Northwestern). Prosser's

style calls for athletic players who have the ability to get up and down the floor. That's not exactly Lepore's game. The three-point shooter who spent last season sitting out as a transfer from Northwestern is more of a spot-up jump shooter, maybe in the mold of former Wake Forest guard Rusty Larue.

"I'm not the most athletic guy, but I play hard and I think I can guard people," Lepore said when he arrived at Wake Forest. "What I lack in athleticism I try to make up for with my mind."

Prosser will give Lepore every chance to earn playing time, because the coach likes how he has prepared himself during the off-season.

"He may be the hardest worker on our team," Prosser said. "He is extremely dedicated. You never know how a kid is going to come off a sit-out year, but I think he took great advantage of that year."

Lepore started every game of his sophomore season at Northwestern and led the Wildcats with 66 three-pointers. But he became frustrated with the team's 5-23 record and wanted to join a winning program. He came to Wake Forest after spending a summer traveling with a U.S. junior national team, for which Odom was an assistant coach. Now, he knows he will have to adapt to fit into Prosser's system.

"He wants to win," Prosser said. "He'll do what ever it takes. I think he'll be in really good condition. He is a good, intelligent player who will be able to play well defensively, be able to rebound. You don't want your whole playing time to depend on your ability just to make shots because sometimes that doesn't happen.

"I think he is working hard to do other things other than just shooting the ball."

F-JAMAL LEVY (6-9, 177 lbs., FR, #10, Panama City, Fla./Berkshire Academy). Going into fall practice, Prosser had never seen Levy play, either in person or on tape. But the two met before summer break to talk about Prosser's expectations.

According to the reports the coach got back from his players, who participated with Levy in summer pickup games, the young freshman seemed to be progressing.

"Like all freshmen, he is going to have to learn that he has to play very hard for a long period of time," Prosser said. "But I think he looks like a guy who could be at the front of the press, like an Antwan Scott or a Josh Howard. I could see him swinging back and forth between the four and the three positions."

On a team that is lacking in height and frontcourt depth, Prosser has no doubt that Levy will contribute immediately.

Levy, a native Panamanian who was a standout on his country's national junior team, played two years of high school basketball in South Florida, where he earned a reputation as a quick leaper and decent shooter.

G-ERVIN MURRAY (6-5, 189, SR, #31, 2.2 ppg, 2.8 rpg, 2.9 apg, 18.5 minutes, .426 FG, .231 3PT, .778 FG, Wallace-Rose Hill HS/ Wallace, N.C.). Though not the typical kind of point guard Prosser uses to lead his style of press, Murray still has plenty of ways he can contribute. He can spell Hicks at the point or play either wing spot.

"I remember him from the tape two years ago when [Xavier] played [Wake Forest] in the NIT," Prosser said. "He sort of does a great job of helping out where ever he is needed.

"I hesitate to call him a utility man, but that is kind of what he is."

Murray is a solid ball-handler who turned the ball over only 26 times to go with his team-leading 84 assists. He's a pass-first point who started 12 games last year, before giving up the job to the run-and-shoot Hicks in the latter half of the season, as Odom tried desperately to get his team going again.

Murray isn't much of a long-range shooter, as his 23.1 success ratio from the three-point line suggests, but Prosser thinks Murray might be able to develop a consistent mid-range jumper that could be dangerous.

"To me, he is a great complement to all of the perimeter guys," Prosser said. "His is a different type point guard than Broderick and a different type two or three than Josh or Craig."

OTHER RETURNING PLAYERS

G-ALAN WILLIAMS (6-3, 176, SO, #20, 0.8 ppg, 0.6 rpg, 2.1 minutes, .375 FG, 1.000 FT, Briarcrest Christian/Memphis,Tenn.). A walk-on that Prosser will likely invite back for practice purposes only. He played in 10 games last year, scoring eight points, though none in ACC play.

G-MATT LINEBERGER (6-3, 203 lbs., SO, #10, 0.1 ppg, 0.1 rpg, East Grand Rapids HS/Grand Rapids, Mich.). A walk-on that Prosser will likely invite back to the squad for practice purposes. He played in 10 games also last year, scoring his only point of the season on a free throw against Georgia.

OTHER NEWCOMERS

C-DSHAMAL SCHOETZ (7-0, 261, R-FR, #53, 20.1 ppg, 10.1 rpg, 4.0 bpg, .650 FG in 1999-2000, Wesleyan Academy/High Point, N.C. and Cottbuss, Germany). One thing everybody agrees on regarding Schoetz: he's tall. Odom knew it when he recruited him and Prosser recognized it almost immediately. Schoetz kind of sticks out on a team where the next tallest player on the roster is only 6-9.

But can he help the Deacons' lacking inside game? Prosser doesn't know yet.

"I know when I first got the job and we had a few weeks to work with the kids, individual improvement, he worked hard at those things," Prosser said. "No one has really seen him play, but he is working hard to improve.

"If he can contribute, that will be a big, big plus. He could give us a low-post presence, which at the moment we just don't have."

When former coach Odom signed Schoetz, a native of Germany who played at a nearby private school in High Point, N.C., the coach knew he was a project. Schoetz had been playing basketball for only three years when he arrived in Winston-Salem from Germany and spending a year working against Vidaurreta, Shoemaker and Songaila had to have toughened him up. But Schoetz still may be a year or two away from being a contributor, especially in a new system that requires a little more movement up and down the court.

QUESTIONS

Size? The Deacons have only one player—7-0 red-shirt freshman Schoetz, a poster child for the word "project"—taller than 6-9. They have to find some way to compete on the boards.

Transition? Under Odom, the Deacons played a completely different style than they will under Prosser. How they adjust to that change will be the key to the season.

Consistency? Prosser has some key questions about every player on his roster in terms of playing the same every night out.

ANSWERS

Experience! The Deacons return six players who averaged more than 16 minutes a game last year and three players who averaged in double-digit scoring.

Depth! Prosser has more options than he cares to think about going into the season, including five new players at his disposal. He just has to find the right five players who play at their highest level every night.

Final go-round! Last year at Georgia Tech, Paul Hewitt inherited five seniors who wanted badly to go to the NCAA Tournament. Guess what? That's what Prosser has this year.

WAKE FOREST 2000-2001 RESULTS

#Mount St. Mary's	108-61
#Air Force	84-44
@Richmond	69-61
Campbell	86-47
##Michigan	71-60
South Carolina State	66-55
Kansas	84-53
Georgia	75-57
Radford	92-52
@Temple	73-65
Navy	90-58
Virginia	96-73
@North Carolina (L)	69-70
Florida State	76-53
@Georgia Tech (L)	89-95
@Maryland (L)	71-81
Clemson	71-63
@Duke (L)	62-85
@Cincinnati (L)	72-78
NC State	74-69
@Virginia (L)	71-82
North Carolina (L)	74-80
@Florida State	71-65
Georgia Tech	81-65

Maryland (L)	56-73
@Clemson	92-60
Duke (L)	80-82
@NC State	76-58
###Maryland (L)	53-71
####Butler (L)	63-79

#BCA Classic in Winston-Salem, NC
##ACC/Big Ten Challenge in Ann Arbor, MI
###ACC Tournament in Atlanta
####NCAA Tournament
@Road Games

BLUE RIBBON ANALYSIS

BACKCOURT	B+
BENCH/DEPTH	A-
FRONTCOURT	B
INTANGIBLES	B+

Wake Forest, despite what fans may have thought at times, had a great basketball coach in Odom. He took a program that had long suffered in the shadows of its three Tobacco Road counterparts—Duke, North Carolina and N.C. State, which have won eight NCAA titles between them—and made the Deacons competitive.

He went to the NCAA Tournament eight times in 12 years, no small feat for the second smallest school in Division I's six major basketball conference (only Providence is smaller).

He found some gems along the way: Rodney Rogers, Randolph Childress and a former swimmer from the Virgin Islands named Tim Duncan. But fighting the battle against those three traditional giants takes a lot out of a man. Add to that the fact that Odom didn't get the contract extension he needed from his own school, and the battle just didn't seem worth it any more. So it's easy to see why he would leave an ACC school for an SEC school that hasn't had much tradition of success since Frank McGuire retired.

What, then, should we say to Prosser, who inherits a program deep with experience? Knock yourself out, coach.

Coming from Xavier, Prosser knows the difficulties of coaching at a small, academic-minded institution. He knows what it's like to be in the shadow of bigger in-state schools, like he was with cross-town rival Cincinnati and Ohio State.

And he knows how to beat them. He owned a 4-3 record against the Bearcats during his tenure at Xavier. So playing in the shadow of Tobacco Road giants doesn't intimidate Prosser, and he certainly won't let it intimidate his team.

"We always thought it was a positive to go against a team that was big, a Final Four-caliber program," Prosser said. "We never got caught up in being poor little Xavier. We wanted to make a fight out of it."

This year, with a team mostly recruited by Odom, Prosser has the talent and experience to beat North Carolina and N.C. State and maybe even Duke. He's off to a good start in rebuilding the program with impressive recruiting, which he will need next year after losing five seniors and possibly Howard, if the junior swingman has a great season.

Prosser, a well-liked and much-respected member of the coaching community, seems up for the challenge.

(T.P.)

Xavier 40

LOCATION	Cincinnati, OH
CONFERENCE	Atlantic 10
LAST SEASON	21-8 (.724)
CONFERENCE RECORD	12-4 (t-2nd)
STARTERS LOST/RETURNING	2/3
NICKNAME	Musketeers
COLORS	Navy, Blue, Gray & White
HOMECOURT	Cintas Center (10,250)
COACH	Thad Matta (Butler '90)
RECORD AT SCHOOL	First year
CAREER RECORD	24-8 (1 year)
ASSISTANTS	Sean Miller (Pitttsburgh '92)
	Alan Major (Purdue '92)
	John Groce (Taylor '94)
TEAM WINS (last 5 years)	23-22-25-21-21

RPI (last 5 years)	30-31-49-88-47
2000-01 FINISH	Lost in NCAA first round.

COACH AND PROGRAM

When it came to the category of "dream job," you'd think Thad Matta would already have checked the box last year, next to "Butler," right?

The Illinois native was in his first season as head coach of a Division I team and it was his alma mater. At 32, he was one of the youngest head coaches in America and Butler is a place where hoop dreams come to life. In Hoosiers, the Bulldogs' homecourt of Hinkle Fieldhouse was immortalized in a heartwarming classic set in America's heartland.

Even before taking over at Butler, Matta already had a hand in some magical stuff as an assistant on different staffs that went to four straight NCAA Tournaments. It started with Miami (Ohio) under Herb Sendek in 1994-95, then to Western Carolina in '95-96, then back to Miami when Charlie Coles took command in '96-97 before landing at Butler in '97-98.

When Butler head coach Barry Collier bolted for Nebraska after the 1999-00 season, Matta was the man. He had his first program to run and it was a team for which he had a huge hand in recruiting. The Bulldogs turned in a storybook season in Matta's rookie year in charge, winning the Midwestern Collegiate Conference (11-3) regular-season and tournament championships and going 24-8. He was chosen the MCC Coach of the Year and earned National Rookie Coach of the Year by CBS SportsLine and College Insider.

Butler won 13 of its last 15 games, including a 58-44 upset at then 10th-ranked Wisconsin and a 79-63 bashing of then 23rd-ranked Wake Forest in the first round of the NCAA Tournament. The win over Wake Forest was Butler's first NCAA Tournament victory since 1962. Eventual NCAA runner-up Arizona ended its run in the second round of the tournament, but what a first season, huh?

"It was kind of a dream come true," Matta said. "That was really special because I recruited all of those guys."

But dreams change.

Xavier came calling, looking for someone to replace Skip Prosser, and Matta—considered one of the bright young coaching candidates in the country—had to consider the Musketeers, who have become a perennial Atlantic 10 power.

Prosser was 148-65 (.695) in his seven years at Xavier and became the second-winningest coach in school history, leading Xavier to five straight postseason tournaments and six in seven years and four consecutive 20-win seasons. But Prosser, just like his predecessor, Pete Gillen, who left for Providence after the 1993-94 season, departed for a bigger school in a bigger conference—Wake Forest in the Atlantic Coast Conference.

Enter Matta, who said he couldn't turn down trying to continue to build the tradition that Prosser and Gillen had built at Xavier.

"I am very comfortable with the overall mission of the university," Matta said the day he was introduced as coach. "I support the vision to build a national program the right way without losing sight of the integrity and academic reputation that have become synonymous with Xavier.

"It's very hard not to get excited about this program and its potential. How can you not get excited when you walk through the Cintas Center?" he said of the facility that opened last September. (The Musketeers won 13-of-14 games there last season.) "But it's more than just a building. You can feel the excitement about the program throughout the Xavier community and the city of Cincinnati. … I love where this program is but I'm even more excited about helping to realize its potential."

Throughout the late 1980s and early '90s, Xavier was considered one of those "sleeper" teams that no one wanted to play come NCAA Tournament time. But now the Musketeers think they're ready to become a national power and they have the man to lead them there. The question is, will Matta have enough manpower? A strong nucleus returns, but he'll have only nine scholarship players.

Xavier has been rated as high as 25th in the country (by Dick Vitale) in preseason rankings and might just have the X-factor every team that wants to keep playing deep into March needs. That is an often-unstoppable force—6-8 junior forward David West. The reigning A-10 Player of the Year is one of the best players in the country. He flirted with leaving early for the NBA, but returned. West averaged a double-double last year.

He anchors the lineup along with two other starters: A-10 All-Rookie team member Romain Sato is a versatile 6-5 shooting guard who led the team with 65 treys and will need to make an even bigger contribution, and senior forward Kevin Frey.

Gone are two starters, solid senior point guard Maurice McAfee and shooting guard Lloyd Price, who each averaged about nine points, along with backup big men Reggie Butler and Marcus Mason and a few others that either transferred or graduated early and opted not to come back. But junior Lionel Chalmers seems ready to shine at the point and 6-4 guard David Young also is back, along with senior guard Alvin Brown.

Last season ended with a bitter taste for the Musketeers. After a sparkling regular season (24-6), they were seeded second but were upset in an A-10 Tournament quarterfinal by No. 7 George Washington, 84-74, and the lost in the first round of the NCAA Tournament to Notre Dame, 83-71.

Depth, particularly in the frontcourt behind West and Frey, could be a big problem this year and that might force Xavier to play a slower pace. That hasn't been its style or Matta's.

"We'll have to stay injury free and also stay away from foul trouble," Matta said.

Both big men are coming off surgeries—West's toe, Frey's ankle—and the only other scholarship post player is 6-9 freshman Anthony Coleman. Freshman Will Caudle, a 6-9, 220-pound prep star from Indianapolis, has been a big letdown. He is appealing an academic credit problem that most likely will keep him out this season.

Caudle is a physical inside player who runs the floor well and has earned a reputation for hard, aggressive play on defense. He averaged 13.0 points, 7.0 rebounds, 1.2 blocks and 1.0 assists a game as a senior at Warren Central, while shooting 64 percent from the field and 67 percent from the free-throw line.

"It's a pretty dramatic loss," Matta said. "That's a big body that could have come in and given us some quality minutes off the bench."

Xavier also lost out on Vytas Danelius, a Lithuanian native who played at Indianapolis Park Tudor. The 6-7, 210-pound small forward is with Prosser at Wake. He considered Wake, South Carolina, Notre Dame and Butler while Matta was there. Matta and Park Tudor coach Ed Kelley were college teammates at Butler.

But Matta has landed a solid recruiting class for next year, packed with big men to address the thin frontcourt, but by then Frey will have graduated and West might be in the NBA. Headed to Xavier next season are 6-9, 235-pound junior-college forward Anthony Myles, a Chicago native playing at Olney (Ill.) Central College; 6-10, 235-pound junior-college forward/center Randy Holbrook; 6-8, 210-pound forward/center Angelo Smith; and 6-7, 225-pound power forward Brandon Cole. The other signee is 6-foot point guard Dedrick Finn.

"If they wanted to rebuild their front court, they were able to do it and do it in a year when that wasn't easy," Dave Telep of BlueChipHoops.com told the Cincinnati Enquirer. "... There isn't another school in the country that got four post guys. Not only that, but they got guys who are pretty good."

But that's the future. For now, Matta's main concern is a thin bench.

"The number one strength I see in the tapes I've watched is that these guys play with a great passion," said Matta, who at 33 is the ninth-youngest Division I head coach in the country and the youngest in Xavier history. "The key will be getting our new guys to understand and accept a role. We have to find what they do well off the bench and put them in a role where they can succeed. I've been fortunate to be with teams in the past that have had good defenders, so that's something I'll put a lot of stock in. If you can shut someone else down, you can play for us."

2001-2002 SCHEDULE

Nov.	17	Coastal Carolina
	24	*Missouri
	28	@Miami OH
Dec.	1	@San Francisco
	5	@Purdue
	8	Long Island
	10	Wisconsin
	14	Cincinnati
	20	Kent
	22	@Creighton
	31	@Siena
Jan.	5	@Dayton
	9	Fordham
	12	Richmond
	17	@George Washington
	19	@LaSalle
	23	@Rhode Island
	26	Dayton
	30	Duquesne
Feb.	2	@Richmond
	9	@St. Bonaventure
	14	George Washington
	16	St. Joseph's
	20	@Temple
	24	@Duquesne
	28	LaSalle
March	2	Massachusetts
	6-9	#A-10 Tournament

@Road Games
*John R. Wooden Tradition, Conseco Fieldhouse, Indianapolis, IN
#First Union Spectrum, Philadelphia, PA

STARTERS NOT RETURNING

PG-MAURICE McAFEE (6-0, 9.6 ppg, 2.7 rpg, 1.2 spg, 4.8 apg, 3.0 tpg, 34.2 minutes, .368 FG, .265 3PT, .723 FT). Following in the footsteps of former Xavier stars such as James Posey and Gary Lumpkin, McAfee acquitted himself rather well over two years as a starter.

After playing the perfect role as third guard as a sophomore, he became a solid starter and quite a leader. He was a co-captain last year and sacrificed some scoring to get others involved.

"Maurice just wants to win," Prosser told the Cincinnati Enquirer after a win last season over St. Joseph's. "If that means scoring baskets, he'll do that. If that means taking charges, he'll do that. If it means guarding [Marvin] O'Connor and [Jameer] Nelson, he'll do that.

"This team in many ways will be remembered as his team. He relishes that."

G/F-LLOYD PRICE (6-5, 9.2 ppg, 4.4 rpg, 1.6 apg, 3.0 tpg, 34.2 minutes, .400 FG, .250 3PT, .651 FT). Academic woes—at least at Xavier's standards—cost Price his scholarship and senior season. A solid three-man, he was selected second-team all-league after his sophomore year before taking a step back last season. The school announced April 2 that he would not return for "academic reasons."

Important footnote: Xavier has not had one of its basketball players not earn a diploma since 1985.

"Privately, some in XU's program view this as addition by subtraction. Price was maddeningly inconsistent and often played out of control," wrote Neil Schmidt of the Cincinnati Enquirer. "He never lived up to his billing as the highest-rated recruit in XU history [No. 17 by The Sporting News]."

Price averaged 13 points and six rebounds as a sophomore, but had an injury-filled junior season and shot a career-low 40 percent from the field, including 25 percent on three-pointers.

OTHERS NOT RETURNING

C-REGGIE BUTLER (6-10, 2.9 ppg, 2.4 rpg, 1.1 tpg, 11.6 minutes). Averaged 7.5 minutes as a junior and just slightly more last year. Butler was an adequate low-post backup, but not much more. Put it this way: If you went to the Cintas Center last year and missed some of the action, very rarely would someone said, "The Butler did it," although he did make two starts.

C-MARCUS MASON (6-9, 0.5 ppg, 0.3 rpg, 2.6 minutes, 13 games played). With the emergence of West (as a sophomore) and Frey (as a junior) last year, Mason was never really a factor in his senior season.

F-KHALIL NIXON (6-7, 1.2 ppg, 1.6 rpg, 5 games played). The Brooklyn, N.Y., native transferred in from the College of the Sequoias in Visalia, Calif., before last season but left the team Dec. 22 after little playing time, then in early January declined an invitation to try out for the team and return. So much for Xavier's recent success importing transfers from the California junior-college circuit.

Looking for a silver lining? Nixon's departure gave freshman walk-on Tom Compton, a 6-10 center, a locker. Compton had practiced during most of the early season without one.

G/F-BRANDON McINTOSH (6-5, 0.6 ppg, 0.4 rpg, 4.2 minutes, 14 games played). McIntosh, who played

high school ball in the Cincinnati area, struggled to find many significant minutes behind players such as Price, Sato and Young. He could have returned for his senior season as a graduate student, but instead graduated last summer.

PROJECTED STARTERS

PG-LIONEL CHALMERS (6-0, 178 lbs., JR, #0, 8.9 ppg, 1.9 apg, 1.5 tpg, 2.2 rpg, 1.3 spg, .365 FG, .302 3PT, .671 FT, 26.7 minutes, Albany HS/Albany, N.Y.). A partial qualifier as a freshman, he could only practice with the team, but the time served Chalmers well. He played in all 29 games last year, starting eight, and is primed to succeed McAfee as the point guard.

"In our system, we need a point guard to run the team," Matta said. "From what I've seen in Lionel I'm pretty confident that he has the ability to run our team. He's improved his outside shot and we're hoping he can have a big year."

Another bonafide outside threat with Sato would make life so much easier for West and Co., but Matta will make sure Chalmers keeps his assist-to-turnover ratio in good shape first. A very quick, aggressive player, he's a pest defensively pressuring the ball.

He scored 18 points in a win over Temple last year, one of 10 double-digit games he posted. He also showed he's not afraid to take the big shot if West gets bottled up.

Chalmers was the hero of the second half at Toledo, scoring all 12 of his points to go with two rebounds, two assists and two steals in 11 minutes of action on the road. You may actually have seen the most memorable play of his career that night—a game-winning three-pointer at the buzzer that led "Plays of the Day" on SportsCenter.

SG-ROMAIN SATO (6-4, 195 lbs., SO., #10, 10.7 ppg, 5.4 rpg, 1.4 apg, 1.8 tpg, 0.9 spg, .386 FG, .374 3PT, .730 FT, 30.2 minutes, Dayton Christian HS/Dayton, Ohio/Central African Republic). There's not much Sato can't do and last year, his rookie season, was proof of that. He was voted to the A-10's All-Rookie team after being third on the team in points and rebounds and leading the way with 65 treys. His perimeter shooting will be absolutely crucial this year to help free up West and Frey.

An explosive athlete, his vertical leap is measured at 38 inches. He grabbed 16 rebounds in a game. Oh yeah, he also speaks six languages.

"He's going to be a star," ESPN's Tim McCormick said. "The kid's a chiseled athlete. ... He's from the Central African Republic so he doesn't have a lot of the bad habits that kids develop here."

His defense is improving, too. Sato played for the African National Team over the summer, representing the Central African Republic.

Sato scored 31 points to mark the second-highest point total ever by a Xavier freshman and his eight three-pointers in a game tied the best ever total by an A-10 freshman and were just one shy of the A-10 single-game record (nine). He broke the Xavier record of seven treys that was shared by Maurice McAfee and Jamie Gladden (twice).

"He's a guy who gets better every day," Matta said of Sato, who has lived in America for just two years. "He's still just learning the game and he has a great work ethic. He just loves the game."

A former "Mr. Basketball" in Ohio, Sato averaged 26.4 points, 15.6 rebounds and 5.3 assists as a senior.

SG/SF-KEITH JACKSON (6-5, 196 lbs., FR, 16.7 ppg, 6.7 rpg, Purcell Marian HS/Cincinnati, Ohio). If Matta decides to stay more up-tempo, he might go with a three-guard lineup and Jackson is a candidate to step right in. Senior returnee Alvin Brown is another, but Matta said "he likes Jackson's capacity to learn." The Sporting News rated him No. 39 nationally in last year's senior class.

This, however, is the spot where the loss of Caudle might hurt.

A good athlete, Jackson worked a lot in the fall on his jump shot. He was twice chosen the Cincinnati Enquirer's Division II Player of the Year and was a second-team all-state pick by The Associated Press. He was among ESPN.com's top 20 small-forward prospects.

PF-KEVIN FREY (6-8, 235 lbs., SR, #3, 11.4 ppg, 6.3 rpg, 1.2 apg, 2.1 bpg, 1.4 spg, 2.7 tpg, .430 FG, .258 3PT, .770 FT, Maine West HS/Chicago, Ill.). You want someone to do the dirty work—and then some—for your team? Frey is your man. He can bang with the best of them and has a hunger for the ball.

"He's a guy that it seemed every time he played well Xavier won," Matta said. "He has to have a good year for us. He's a tough, physical competitor and defensively has the chance to be one of the better players in the A-10."

Frey is rehabbing from tendon damage and bone spurs in his foot, but Matta said he expects his work-horse to be at full strength by the time the season starts.

Matta was right. Frey is a great barometer for Xavier: Over the last two seasons, when Frey scores in double figures, Xavier is 23-4, including 14-2 last season. A huge plus is his accuracy at the free-throw line, a team best 77 percent. Also, for the second straight year Frey was one of the big heroes in the win over Cincinnati. He contributed 15 points and seven rebounds.

F/C-DAVID WEST (6-8, 232 lbs., JR, #30, 17.8 ppg, 10.9 rpg, 2.0 apg, 1.4 spg, 2.1 bpg, 2.7 tpg, .551 FG, .740 FT, 33.7 minutes, Hargrave Military Academy, Va./Garner, N.C.). He's baaaack.

West thought about the NBA, especially with an off-season coaching change, but decided to return for what could be his final college season. Not only was he voted the Musketeers' Most Improved Player last year, he won A-10 Player of the Year honors, was selected to the A-10's All-Defensive team and begins this season as a second team All-America selection by Dick Vitale. He is one of the 50 preseason finalists for the 2002 John R.Wooden All-American Team and Player-of-the-Year Award and a member of the 10-player preseason Playboy All-America team. He participated in the USA Men's National Team Trials and was a finalist before withdrawing his name because of injury.

He was second in the nation last year with 20 double-doubles and his rebounding average was fourth in the country. West, who draws comparisons to former Xavier and current Miami Heat star Brian Grant, led the A-10 in field-goal percentage, rebounding and blocks, His 61 swats were a school record, breaking the mark of Aaron Williams (New Jersey Nets), who had seasons of 57 twice. He also led the X-men in steals and was second in assists and free-throw percentage.

Talk about a tenacious rebounder. Check out these monster efforts: a career-high 21 against George Washington, 15 against Temple, 17 against Kent State and a game-high 13 in the win at cross-town rival Cincinnati.

Rest assured, Matta knows how important West is to everything—repeat—everything that Xavier will do.

"Coaching a guy liked David West, you have to find ways to get him the basketball in positions where in can succeed," Matta said. "But we have to get guys to buy into the team concept."

It's pretty nice knowing, though, that if you get the ball to West, something good is usually going to happen.

Matta said at first he was worried that the coaching change might cause West to leave, but then they talked.

"It was the first question I asked him," Matta said, "but he said he loved Xavier and that this place has been good to him."

But West isn't just gifted. He works hard at his game.

"I've never coached a guy that has his work ethic and his capacity for work," Matta said. "He goes hard in everything he does. You couple that with his skill level and you've got a great player. He's very patient in the post and can pass and makes good decisions."

Xavier can't keep up with the praise around the country for West, who averaged nearly a double-double as a freshman before breaking out last year.

Said Vitale, "You are talking about a physical presence around the basket with great moves. He's got those long arms, good timing and he anticipates well."

Said Prosser, "Dave handled all of the increased attention very well. He's unselfish. He listens. He has a tremendous passion for the game. He's getting better and better. He's just scratching the surface of his talent."

Said St. Joseph's coach Phil Martelli, "He's almost like a point center. A lot of big guys will throw it only to the person who passed it to them, but David finds guys all over the floor."

Enjoy him while you can, Xavier fans, this might be your last season with West.

KEY RESERVES

G-DAVE YOUNG (6-4, 210 lbs., JR, 2.5 ppg, 1.1 rpg, 0.2 apg, 1.1 tpg, .371 FG, .323 3PT, .455 FT, 11.6 minutes, New Castle HS/New Castle, Pa.). Young really came on as the season wore on last year, but was plagued by inconsistency.

"He's added some strength and worked on his jump shot," Matta said. "We need him to help us on the boards this year."

Young missed his freshman season to concentrate on his academics, but last year played in each of the last eight games and scored a career-high 10 points, including 2-of-2 shooting from three-point range, in the win over St. Bonaventure.

G-ALVIN BROWN (6-3, 180 lbs., SR, 1.7 ppg, 4.6 minutes, 19 games played, Gonzaga High, Washington, D.C.). Brown was used sparingly at both guards positions last year, but will need to expand that role this season as one of only two seniors on the team.

Said Matta, "We need him to be a leader for us. We also need him to be a great defender and come in and knock down some open shots."

Brown, a graduate student, averaged 6.5 points and 17.8 minutes as a sophomore as the first guard off the bench but saw his minutes diminish last year with the arrival of Sato, Chalmers and Young. He hit for double figures nine times, so he can score. What he must improve on to be a real contributor is shooting the ball. He made 13-of-25 field goals last year but was just 0-for-3 from beyond the arc.

F-ANTHONY COLEMAN (6-10, 210 lbs., SO, #21, 12.0 ppg, 14 rpg, 5 apg, 3.5 bpg in 1999-00 at Centennial HS/Carson, Calif.). Coleman practiced with the team last year but red-shirted.

"He doesn't have a lot of bulk to him but he's a tremendous athlete," Matta said. "He's still learning to play at his height."

Coleman was 6-4 as a junior in high school but went through a dramatic growth spurt and was 6-9 as a senior.

G-JAISON WILLIAMS (6-3, 182 lbs., FR., # N/A, 17.0 ppg, 4.0 rpg, 4.0 apg, 4.5 spg in 1999-00 at Hinkley HS/Aurora, Colorado). Williams didn't play high school ball last year because of state rules in Ohio after his transfer from Colorado to Columbus. He was a second-team all-state selection as a sophomore and junior in high school.

Most recruiters had him as a top-150 pick. He will play both guards positions for Xavier, and Matta said is a good athlete who has the ability to make three-pointers.

OTHER RETURNEES

G-ANDRE JOHNSON (5-9, 158 lbs., JR., #22, 0.5 ppg, 1.0 tpg, , 1.8 minutes, Union (Pa.) HS/Youngstown, Ohio). A walk-on with good quicks whom Matta hopes pushes Chalmers and other guards in practice. He played in just four games last year (five minutes) and made one field goal.

F-JAMES BARONAS (6-8, 240 lbs., SR., #45, 0.0 ppg, 1.3 rpg, Mount St. Joseph HS/Baltimore, Md). Headed to medical school next year, this fourth-year walk-on played in four games last year (seven minutes). His size will help in practice toughening up others.

F-TOM COMPTON (6-10, 220 lbs., SO., #54, 2.0 ppg, St. Xavier HS/Cincinnati). Another walk-on, Compton played in one game last year (one minute) and converted his only field-goal attempt.

F-RYAN CALDWELL (6-5, 245 lbs., JR, #50, 0.0 ppg, 1.0 rpg, McNicholas High School/Cincinnati). Another local product and walk-on, he played in only one game last year.

QUESTIONS

Inexperience? Xavier has four solid players, but after that the Musketeers are mightily challenged to produced anyone with significant minutes at this level. Backup guard David Young's 6.9 minutes per game last year are the most of any returnee, and the frontcourt is just as green.

Doctor's orders? Matta said his razor-thin team has to avoid injuries, a tall order. If one of the Big Four goes down, look out. Foul trouble also could be a stumbling block. West fouled out three times last year and Frey twice. That'd be five too many times this winter.

Schedule? It's one of the toughest in school history, featuring 13 games against 2001 postseason qualifiers, including seven NCAA Tournament teams. Matta said he doesn't mind losing a few games, as long as it prepares the team for March, but the losses will affect Xavier's postseason seed.

ANSWERS

The man! West is good enough to keep his team in just about any game, and as one of the top players in the

country, just might have to do that quite a bit.

Keep coming! If Frey and Sato show more than last season, it will make West doubly more dangerous. Their improvement, along with Chalmers running a steady ship in his first full-time college duty at point, is crucial.

Matta matters! Let's face it, the guy has won at whatever program he's been a part of, but his second season as a college head coach—if he's thrown a couple of curveballs—could really test him.

XAVIER 2000-2001 RESULTS

Miami (Ohio)	68-54
Eastern Kentucky	93-75
Samford	65-55
Louisiana-Monroe	86-68
@Wisconsin-Madison (L)	46-61
San Francisco	75-49
@Princeton (L)	52-58
@Cincinnati	69-67
Marquette	75-59
@Toledo	63-61
#Kent	71-60
@Fordham	82-71
LaSalle	81-66
Massachusetts (L)	64-75
@Rhode Island	99-82
@George Washington	76-74
St. Joseph's	86-73
@Duquesne	81-48
Daayton	82-72
George Washington	71-63
@St. Joseph's (L)	76-79
Temple	78-71
@Massachusetts (L)	49-59
Rhode Island	79-65
St. Bonaventure	77-60
@LaSalle	79-55
@Dayton (L)	62-65
##George Washington (L)	74-83
###Notre Dame (L)	71-83

#Rock and Roll Shootout in Cleveland, OH
##Atlantic 10 Tournament in Philadelphia
###NCAA Tournament
@Road Games

BLUE RIBBON ANALYSIS

BACKCOURT	B
BENCH/DEPTH	C-
FRONTCOURT	B+
INTANGIBLES	B

Not exactly the grades of a potential Sweet 16 team, which Matta has said is his goal in his rookie season. The reason? Unless one of the newcomers is dynamite, this team is very fragile.

West will cover up a lot and could put up huge numbers, but he'll need support from Frey, Sato and Chalmers. If Sato can step up to another level, that might take this team to where it wants to go. But one injury or recurring foul trouble and Xavier's depth will be put to the test. The Musketeers were ranked highly by a lot of preseason publications, mostly on the basis of West, one of the nation's top players.

"The biggest thing we have to overcome is putting in a new system," said Matta, whose up-tempo style might have to be tempered because of a lack of depth. "Xavier has been successful, so I want to keep some things but I want to coach to my strengths. Playing the schedule we do, there may be some hard times, but it's all about playing our best ball in late February and March."

The Cintas Center, the school's two-year-old home-court, was kind to Xavier last year. It won 13 out of 14 there. It'll need that kind of dominance again. If everything goes to plan, the Musketeers should return to the NCAA Tournament. But things don't always go to plan, so it might be a tougher road than it looks right now.

(J.D.)

AMERICA EAST

BLUE RIBBON FORECAST
1. Boston University
2. Maine
3. Vermont
4. Northeastern
5. Stony Brook
6. Hartford
7. New Hampshire
8. Albany
9. Binghamton

ALL-CONFERENCE TEAM
G Huggy Dye, SR, Maine
G Charles "Ricky" Cranford, SR, Northeastern
F Jason Grochowalski, SO, Boston
F Trevor Gaines, SR, Vermont
C Justin Rowe, JR, Mainel

PLAYER OF THE YEAR
Charles "Ricky" Cranford, SR, Northeastern

NEWCOMER OF THE YEAR
Justin Rowe, JR, Maine

2001-2002 CONFERENCE TOURNAMENT
March 2-3, Matthews Arena, Boston, MA
March 9, Championship game at homecourt of higher remaining seed

2000-2001 CHAMPIONS
Hofstra (Regular season)
Hofstra (Conference tournament)

2000-2001 POSTSEASON PARTICIPANTS
Postseason Record 0-1 (.000)
NCAA
Hofstra

TOP BACKCOURTS
1. Maine
2. Boston University
3. Northeastern

TOP FRONTCOURTS
1. Vermont
2. Boston University
3. Maine

INSIDE THE NUMBERS
2000-2001 conference RPI: 17th (of 31)
Conference RPI (last five years): 13-17-16-21-17

DID YOU KNOW?
Delaware, Drexel, Hofstra and Towson left the America East to join the Colonial Athletic Association and Albany, Binghamton and Stony Brook have joined the league this season. Binghamton, which is in its first full season of Division I competition, will play a full regular-season schedule but is not eligible for the conference tournament until 2004. ... Hofstra, Delaware and Drexel were the top three teams in the America East last season and Boston University is the last current member of the conference to play in the NCAA Tournament (1997). ... Ron Everhart (Northeastern) joins Scott Beeten (Albany), Al Walker (Binghamton) and Nick Macarchuk (Stony Brook) as new coaches in the league, although Macarchuk isn't really new. He coached Canisius for 10 seasons and was chosen the America East (then North Atlantic Conference) Coach of the Year in 1984. ... Northeastern guard Charles "Ricky" Cranford, a third-team selection, is the only returning member of the all-league team. ... Boston University junior Paul Seymour is the grandson of former NBA All-Star Paul Seymour (Syracuse Nationals (1946-60) and the nephew of former NFL tight end Pete Holohan (San Diego Chargers, Los Angeles rams 1982-90). ... Northeastern freshman forward Meshak Burke-Bennett, also a wide receiver for the football team, will be the first Husky to play both football and basketball since Jim Murphy in 1993-94. ... Maine will play at Arkansas on Nov. 12 in the first round of the Preseason NIT. ...Cleveland State coach Rollie Massimino (Vermont '56) returns to Patrick Gym on Nov. 24 to coach against his alma mater for the first time in 10 years. Massimino, a member of the UVM Athletic Hall of Fame, brought Villanova to Burlington in 1991 and the Catamounts pulled off a 70-68 victory. ... Northeastern will play host to the quarterfinals and semifinals of the conference tournament in 2002 and Boston University will do the same thing in 2003. Delaware had served as quarterfinal and semifinal host since 1996.

(S.B)

Albany

LOCATION	Albany, NY
CONFERENCE	America East
LAST SEASON	6-22 (.214)
CONFERENCE RECORD	NA
STARTERS LOST/RETURNING	0/5
NICKNAME	Great Danes
COLORS	Purple & Gold
HOMECOURT	Recreatin and Convocations Center (5,000)
COACH	Scott Beeten (Lehigh '71)
RECORD AT SCHOOL	6-22 (1 year)
CAREER RECORD	6-22 (1 year)
ASSISTANTS	Will Brown (Dowling College '95) Frank Ross (American '87)
TEAM WINS (last 5 years)	17-19-14-11-6
RPI (last 5 years)	NA-NA-NA-293-317
2000-01 FINISH	Lost in regular-season finale.

After Albany finished last season with just seven scholarship players and a laundry list of needs in order to be a more competitive Division I team, its head coach knew what route the program needed to take.

The Beeten path. The Scott Beeten path, that is.

Never heard of it? Well, it takes 30 years of basketball coaching to find and runs through New York City, Philadelphia and other hoops hotbeds like Ventspils, Latvia, and Urk, The Netherlands.

"I had to go back to my roots," said Beeten, who earned many frequent flier miles as the top assistant at California and George Washington before taking over at Albany on Aug. 1, 2000.

Those roots stretch far and wide and allowed Beeten to address several areas of concern as the Great Danes, a third-year Division I team, prepared to enter their first season of America East play.

The first objective was to get bigger—fast. Albany was out-rebounded by an average of 5.6 rebounds per game and often started a front line of players listed at 6-7, 6-5 and 6-3.

"We got pounded on the boards last year," Beeten said. "I think the one area we did really concentrate on is getting some people who can help us inside."

And Beeten went halfway around the globe to do it. He used the contacts he initially established from 1990-97 while working under Mike Jarvis at GW. They helped him land Jan van den Berg, a 6-10 center who was playing club ball in his native Netherlands, and Janis Pipikis, a 6-8 power forward from Latvia.

"I'm very fortunate that I have some very, very good friends that are very, very knowledgeable in a certain field," Beeten said.

It also doesn't hurt that he keeps in regular contact with them and can recite phone numbers, fax numbers and e-mail addresses off the top of his head.

Beeten also signed players closer to home, landing forwards Rasheed Peterson and Chris Wyatt from his home state of Pennsylvania and point guard Earv Opong from Brooklyn. He also attracted three quality walk-ons,who should do more than fill the traditional role of practice players.

"We got a little bit of everything and some much, much needed size," Beeten said.

The newcomers join a core group that fought an uphill battle last season, but never gave in despite closing the season with 12 losses in the final 14 games.

"We were consistently playing from a position of weakness rather than a position of strength," Beeten said. "But, it helped us develop three or four guys that can help us this year. We have more size and more depth and some of the guys that played some major minutes won't have to play as much this year, but will be more effective."

One of whom is sophomore guard E.J. Gallup (17.4 ppg, 3.4 rpg, 1.6 apg, 1.9 spg, 37.8 mpg), a slender 6-4, 185-pound shooting guard who began to impress Beeten shortly after individual workouts began in the fall.

"He gives you everything he's got every night," Beeten said. "He's a very good shooter and he's gotten better at moving without the ball and taking people off the dribble."

Those improvements were almost out of necessity once opponents figured out who Gallup was and the number of outside shots (.410, 93-of-227 3PT) he made.

"He became a marked man," Beeten said. "He was playing with a target on his back because teams knew that if you stopped him, you had a real good chance of beating us."

Those chances improved even more when Antione Johnson (11.5 ppg, 3.0 rpg, 3.1 apg, 1.0 spg) had an off game, but, fortunately for Albany, that didn't happen very often. Johnson, a 6-0 junior, is more of a combo guard, but he was forced to run the point last season and he hardly left the floor (37.8 mpg), playing 14 games of 40 minutes or more, including all 55 in a triple-overtime loss to Maryland-Eastern Shore.

"Antione probably improved more during the course of the season than any kid I can remember in a long time," Beeten said. "The kid just improved by leaps and bounds, he just kept getting better and better and better. I think now that we've gotten more good players that his life is going to be made a lot easier."

Can you say Opong?

The 5-7 junior refined his game at Rucker Park in Harlem and led Sullivan County (N.Y.) Community College (12.8 ppg, 8.6 apg, 3.4 spg) to a 30-2 record and the NJCAA Division III title game last spring.

"He's quick, he has a great handle, he can pass and he's a better scorer than people think," Beeten said.

Opong is also a demon on defense.

"The hardest guys to play are the ones smaller than you because they are always at your feet," Beeten said.

Sequon Young, a 6-0 freshman walk-on, brings additional depth to the position. Young (7.0 ppg, 3.2 rpg, 4.3 apg) directed nearby Schenectady (N.Y.) High School to the New York State Public High School Athletic Association Class A championship.

"We've gone from having no point guards to having two-and-a-half," Beeten said.

The Great Danes also have more depth on the wing with juniors Sam Hopes (11.2 ppg, 4.0 rpg, 2.0 apg, 1.7 spg) and Alex Barnhill (7.8 ppg, 5.8 rpg, 1.2 apg, 1.3 spg) return and freshman Peterson figures to work his way into the mix. Hopes, 6-3, made 23 starts and Barnhill, a 6-4 transfer from Canisius, became a regular contributor after gaining his eligibility second semester. Both may take on different roles with more talent around them this season.

Peterson, a graduate of University City High School in Philadelphia, spent the last two seasons at Kansas City (Kansas) Community College. A 6-7 slasher, Peterson followed up his all-conference selection as a freshman (19.2 ppg) with a strong sophomore season (15.0 ppg, 3.2 rpg) and could step in right away.

"He gives us size, offense and athleticism on the wing," Beeten said "He's got a good pull-up game, he can shoot the ball from three and really plays well in the open court."

Junior Brian Barnes (0.2 ppg), a 5-10 walk-on, rounds out the returnees in the backcourt.

"He's what you consider the perfect walk-on," Beeten said. "He does nothing but help you win."

Senior Will Brand (14.0 ppg, 6.9 rpg, 2.3 apg, 1.2

spg) increased his point production by nearly three points per game despite playing out of position most of the time. The 6-5 Brand, a natural small forward, was forced to play center at times because of the Great Danes' lack of size but should return to his natural spot this year.

"He was consistent," Beeten said. "He scored night in and night out and he led us in rebounding. Unfortunately, he had to guard players much bigger than him, but I think it was a learning experience that will help us in the long run."

Senior **Joe Vukovic** (6.3 ppg, 4.0 rpg), an under-sized center at 6-7, played through a rash of nagging injuries last season but should be able to spend more time at his natural power forward this year.

"He's a very tough kid and probably has a higher threshold of pain than any kid I've ever coached," Beeten said. "What he lacks in talent, he makes up for in aggressiveness and hard work and he's going to get some minutes.

"You've got to find a place for a kid like him, and we're going to."

Pipikis, who enjoyed a solid tour of the United States with the Latvian Ventspils Club last fall (10 ppg), and Wyatt will also see time at power forward.

"He's a true old-fashioned power forward," Beeten said of Pipikis, a freshman. "He can bang and score around the basket. Basically his game is from 15 feet and in."

Wyatt, a 6-6 freshman, is a fundamentally sound player and somewhat of a late bloomer who came on strong last season (10.0 ppg, 6.5 rpg) for Hatboro-Horsham High School in Horsham, Pa.

"He's a big strong kid with a tremendous body and some really good upside," Beeten said.

The same is true for van den Berg, a 21-year-old sophomore. He was a reserve (1.9 ppg, 2.4 rpg, 1.2 bpg) for Zwolle, a first division club team in The Netherlands, but has the natural ability to develop into a legitimate player.

"Right now he's a little bit raw offensively, but he's a very, very good defender, a good rebounder and a good shot blocker," Beeten said. "He's athletic and he's very, very active."

The Great Danes will also have **Karim Ouattara** (1.9 ppg, 3.0 rpg), a 6-7 senior, back in the frontcourt but may be without Steve Albany (2.8 ppg, 2.8 rpg), who missed the last 24 games of last season with a knee injury. Albany, a 6-9 sophomore, has had surgery on both knees and his career could be in jeopardy.

Albany could also receive some frontcourt minutes from **Andrew Marsh** (18 ppg, 8 rpg, 4.6 apg) and **Jemel Williams**, a pair of freshman walk-ons. Marsh, a 6-6 native of Yankers, N.Y., comes from The MacDuffie School in Springfield, Mass.

"He's athletic, he's long and he's a skilled kid," Beeten said. "He can score, he can pass and he can rebound. He can do just about everything."

Williams, 6-3, led Aquinas Institute in Rochester (N.Y.) to the Section V Class BB championship (18.6 ppg, 7.3 rpg) and scored more than 1,300 points in his career.

"He's young and a little raw, but he's got a chance," Beeten said.

2001-2002 SCHEDULE

Nov.	17	Lafayette
	20	@Ohio State
	24	@Quinnipiac
	27	@Siena
Dec.	2	Syracuse
	5	@Bucknell
	8	@Yale
	11	Army
	23	@Robert Morris
	31	@Vermont
Jan.	2	@Maine
	7	Binghamton
	13	Maine
	15	Columbia
	18	@Dartmouth
	20	@New Hampshire
	24	Boston University
	26	Northeastern
	30	New Hampshire
Feb.	2	@Stony Brook
	5	@Binghamton
	8	@Hartford
	10	Vermont
	12	@Northeastern
	16	@Boston University
	22	Hartford
	24	Stony Brook
March	2,3,9	#America East Tournament

@Road Games
#Matthews Arena, Boston, MA (Championship game at homecourt of highest seeded team.)

BLUE RIBBON ANALYSIS

BACKCOURT	C
BENCH/DEPTH	C
FRONTCOURT	D+
INTANGIBLES	B

When you have coached basketball for 30 years like Beeten, you know when your team is not good.

Such was the case last season, Beeten's first as head coach at Albany, when the Great Danes gutted out a long season in which they were hampered with limited talent and finished with just seven players.

Although it would have been easy to do, Albany's core group of players did not give up, and several of them took advantage of the opportunity to play major minutes and improved. The result is a solid nucleus consisting of Brand, Johnson and Gallup.

Beeten also tapped into his vast basketball network to bring in players who will make immediate contributions. He brought in Pipikis and van den Berg from Europe, Opong and Peterson from junior colleges and forward Wyatt from high school.

The newcomers will all have a chance to compete for playing time, along with three walk-ons.

"What we're trying to do is integrate the eight new players with several players who performed well for us in the past," Beeten said.

It will take the Great Danes, who are in just their third year of Division I, time to adjust to their new personnel, and more growing pains can be expected. The upgrade in personnel will allow Albany to play a more aggressive style and the program should begin to look more like the team Beeten envisioned when he came to New York's Capital District last summer.

"For the first time since I've been here, I feel like we are building a program rather than just having a team," Beeten said. "We've got more numbers, we've got more size, we've got more depth and we've raised the talent level."

There's little doubt the Great Danes will be a better team this season, but the program is still in its infancy and has plenty of growing to do.

(S.B.)

Binghamton

LOCATION	Vestal, NY
CONFERENCE	America East
LAST SEASON	14-14 in Division II (.500)
CONFERENCE RECORD	NA
STARTERS LOST/RETURNING	1/4
NICKNAME	Bearcats
COLORS	Dark Green, Black & White
HOMECOURT	West Gymnasium (2,275)
COACH	Al Walker (Brockport State '81)
RECORD AT SCHOOL	14-14 (1 year)
CAREER RECORD	27-51 (3 years)
ASSISTANTS	Lawrence Brenneman (Geneva '85)
	Randy Dunton (Baptist Bible College '84)
	Marcell Fisher (Brockport '94)
TEAM WINS (last 5 years)	8-17-13-14-14
RPI (last 5 years)	NA-NA-NA-NA-NA
2000-01 FINISH	Lost in regular-season finale.

With 13 years of head coaching experience at Division I, II and III programs, Al Walker has a working knowledge of what it takes to succeed at each level.

He knows it will not be easy taking a .500 Division II team into a mid-major Division I conference and being competitive in a transition year, like he try to will do with Binghamton this season. He also knows the difficulty of playing as a Division I independent, something the Bearcats will avoid by making the quick jump to the America East. Binghamton will play a full conference schedule this season but is not eligible for the America

East Tournament and a possible NCAA bid until 2004.

"I'm optimistic because we have such good people who we hope turn into good players," said Walker, who directed programs at Colorado College, Cornell and Chaminade before returning to his native New York in 2000.

Some may think hearing a college basketball coach say his players are good people first is akin to having your teen-age buddy tell you the girl you are double dating with Friday night has a nice personality, but Walker believes in the way he's shaping his program.

The Bearcats bring in nine new players this season, including two UConn transfers, and are joining a league that saw its top three teams from last season jump to the Colonial Athletic Association.

"We know where we are and what we are trying to do," Walker said. "We're trying to be a good team in the America East Conference and hopefully some day we will be."

It just may take some time for that day to arrive. Binghamton has beaten just one Division I opponent in its history (72-55 over Army).

Walker, who played alongside Miami Heat assistant coach Stan Van Gundy (the older brother of New York Knicks coach Jeff Van Gundy) for Stan's father Bill at Division III Brockport State, is following the same formula he used to turn things around at his previous stops. He has scoured the country for players and he'll use whatever combination is necessary to get the job done.

"We'll try to defend you, first and foremost," Walker said. "We'll run on misses and we might run on makes, too."

How often will depend on the Bearcats' ability to cut down on turnovers after committing 18.3 per game last season.

"Taking care of the ball, which was a problem last year, has a chance to be something that is done effectively this season," Walker said.

The bulk of the ball handling responsibility will fall on junior transfers **Anthony Green** and **Charles Baker**, who played together for Binghamton assistant Randy Dunton at Marshalltown (Iowa) Community College two seasons ago.

The 6-1 Green led the city of Philadelphia in scoring (24.0 ppg) his senior year at Germantown High School before spending a season at Marshalltown. He spent last season at Gloucester County (N.J.) College (14.2 ppg, 6.0 apg) and should help solidify things.

"He's a Philly kid, which is indicative that he knows how to play," Walker said. "He's one of those junkyard-dog point guards. He's one of those kids whose whole life is wrapped up in that orange ball and you're going to have to beat him up to take it away from him."

Baker, originally from Houston, is a fiery competitor whose teams at Westbury Christian High School won four consecutive private school championships. He earned first-team all-region honors at Eastern Wyoming Junior College (12.0 ppg, 5.5 rpg, 4.1 apg) last season.

"He's just one of those guys that we absolutely had to have in the locker room and on the floor—he's a tremendous leader," Walker said. "He does everything coaches like in order to have a chance to win. He competes until he drops."

The arrival of Green and Baker means a new role for 5-10 senior **Mike Wright**, the Bearcats' most valuable player each of the last two seasons. Wright (11.4 ppg, 2.8 rpg, 3.0 apg, 2.1 spg) is a solid shooter and defender who played point guard by default the last two seasons. Already the school's all-time steals leader, he should continue to contribute either as a third guard or reserve.

"I think he'll be much more productive as a two than he was as a one because he can shoot it, he's fast, has good feet and can defend," Walker said.

Sophomore transfer **Brett Watson**, a 6-0 walk-on who saw action in seven games for Connecticut1s 1999-2000 team, will also compete for minutes.

"He will work and work and work and he1s athletically gifted," Walker said. "He suits this team well and it1s just a matter of him knocking shots down and taking care of the ball."

Freshman walk-ons **Dani Wohl** (18.2 ppg, 4.1 rpg, 11.0 apg, 3.4 spg), 6-0, from West Bloomfield (Mich.) and 6-1 **Louie Karis** (14 ppg), a sharp-shooter from Xaverian High School in Queens (N.Y.) round out the frontcourt.

Another newcomer, 7-0 freshman center **Nick Billings**, could be the key to the frontcourt. The Bearcats seemingly stole Billings, USA Today's Player of the Year in Alaska, out of Anchorage and his presence and shot-blocking ability will be an immediate boost to Binghamton's defense.

"He has a physical package that high-major programs across the country would be attracted to," Walker said. "He's 7-feet and very, very good athletically. He will try and block every shot and dunk every ball on your head."

Billings (17.0 ppg, 10.0 rpg, 5.0 bpg) led Kodiak High School to its first state championship since 1952, averaging 19 points and eight blocks in the state final four.

The Bearcats also welcome forward **Stanley Ocitti** from Connecticut. Ocitti, a native of Uganda, grew up in Holland and saw action in four games as a freshman on UConn's 1999 national championship team and played in three games as a sophomore. Ocitti is a very long 6-8 and the junior could be a key contributor if he shakes off the rust of a long layoff from competitive basketball.

"He has the physical tools to be a very nice mid-major player," Walker said. "He just hasn't played competitively in a structured program very much."

Binghamton also returns three starters in the frontcourt who played at least 24.8 minutes per game, including junior **Jeffrey St. Fort**. The 6-6 St. Fort (13.0 ppg, 4.4 rpg) has led the team in scoring the last two seasons, but needs to turn up the intensity—especially on defense—to be as successful at a higher level of competition.

"If he can continue learning how to play basketball and not relying on just playing with his physical gifts, he will be an effective mid-major player," Walker said.

Senior center **Joost Ooms** (8.5 ppg, 5.8 rpg), a 6-8 transfer from Three Rivers (Mo.) Community College, led the team in rebounding and won Bearcat fans over with his work ethic last season. He excels at doing the little things, like setting screens, and should benefit from having less pressure to score and more talent around him.

"He's a very good garbage guy and he's good off the bounce," Walker said.

Jeffrey Daws (7.7 ppg, 2.3 rpg, 2.0 apg) is good from the wing. The 6-4 senior from Vestal stayed at home and has made his living from the outside, as 53 of his 65 field goals last season came from behind the three-point arc. He also made .839 of his free-throw attempts.

"Jeff is our best spot-up shooter," Walker said. "He can really stretch the defense. We need him strong, confident and comfortable on the floor."

Six-foot-five senior **Kyle Washington** (2.2 ppg), a three-year letter winner, played in 26 games last season and also returns. The Bearcats are also hoping for some minutes out of 6-9 sophomore **Joe White** (1.8 ppg, 2.2 rpg), a reserve center who needs to increase his strength to be a reliable Division I player.

Walker is also high on incoming freshmen **Andy Hannan** and **Sebastien Hermenier**. Hannan, a 6-6 late bloomer, signed early before turning heads at larger programs with a strong season (23.0 ppg, 8.0 rpg, 3.3 apg) at Academy of Holy Angels in Minneapolis. He could challenge for immediate minutes at small forward.

"He has great handle and a great ability to see the floor," Walker said.

Walker also likes the athleticism of the 6-6 Hermenier, who was selected one of the top five forwards in the Washington, D.C., area by DC Hoops despite missing the last seven games of his senior season at the Maret School with a concussion. Hermenier (22.0 ppg, 15.0 rpg, 6.0 apg, 4.0 spg, 2.0 bpg) chose the Bearcats over Loyola, Drexel and Albany.

2001-2002 SCHEDULE

Nov.	16	Dartmouth
	18	@Syracuse
	23-24	#Red Auerbach Classic
	27	Oral Roberts
	30	##Ball State Tournament
Dec.	1	##Ball State Tournament
	8	@Army
	16	@North Carolina
	29	@Stony Brook
Jan.	2	Hartford
	4	Quinnipiac
	7	@Albany
	10	@Boston University
	12	@Northeastern
	15	Stony Brook
	20	Maine
	24	Northeastern
	26	Boston University
	28	Colgate
	31	@Maine

Feb.	2	@New Hampshire
	5	Albany
	8	Vermont
	13	@Vermont
	18	@Hartford
	21	@St. Francis
	24	New Hampshire
March	2,3,9	###America East Tournament

@Road Games
#Washington, DC (vs. Stony Brook first round; also George Washington, Yale)
##Muncie, IN (vs. Ball State first round; also Austin Peay, Elon)
###Matthews Arena, Boston, MA (Championship game at homecourt of highest seeded team.)

BLUE RIBBON ANALYSIS

BACKCOURT	C-
BENCH/DEPTH	C-
FRONTCOURT	D
INTANGIBLES	C

Not to be negative, but it's just too much to expect an average Division II team to be competitive in an established Division I conference, regardless of how much change the league has undergone.

This program has potential, but it will take time. Binghamton broke ground on a $38.3 million, 6,000-seat field house in June of 2000 and with no football program to compete against, men's basketball will be at the center of the Bearcats' athletic program for years to come.

Walker also has a history of building successful teams from humble beginnings, so give him time. He points to Oakland's grand entrance into the Mid-Continent Conference two years ago as the ultimate success story, but that scenario seems too good to be true here.

With six returning lettermen and nine newcomers, Binghamton could be a very good Division II team this season, but it will struggle in Division I. Any success is dependent on the team gelling quickly and improving throughout the season.

"If they do come together, we can be good," Walker said. "If they don't, we'll get spanked just like everybody expects us to."

Green and Charles, former junior-college teammates, will improve the backcourt, and two-time MVP Wright will continue to contribute. The frontcourt is full of questions, including how fast 7-0 freshman Billings adjusts to college and how soon UConn transfer Ocitti can work out the rust after three years of limited playing time. Ooms, St. Fort and Daws all started last season, but must improve for this team to stay in, and win, a few games.

(S.B.)

Boston University

LOCATION	Boston, MA
CONFERENCE	America East
LAST SEASON	14-14 (.500)
CONFERENCE RECORD	9-9 (5th)
STARTERS LOST/RETURNING	5/0
NICKNAME	Terriers
COLORS	Scarlet & White
HOMECOURT	Case Gymnasium (1,800)
COACH	Dennis Wolff (Connecticut '78)
RECORD AT SCHOOL	107-97 (7 years)
CAREER RECORD	107-97 (7 years)
ASSISTANTS	Larry Greer (Northeastern '89)
	Orlando Vandross (American International '92)
	Jason Williford (Virginia '95)
TEAM WINS (last 5 years)	25-19-9-7-14
RPI (last 5 years)	38-88-242-275-187
2000-01 FINISH	Lost in conference quarterfinal.

If one thing has remained constant in this year of continuous change for the America East Conference, it is the Boston University men's basketball team.

The Terriers return each of their 11 letter winners and all five starters from a squad that showed plenty of grit to overcome injuries to win three of their last four games to finish .500 last season. Factor in the impact of three quality recruits and BU fans may be cheering loud enough to

raise "The Roof"—the nickname for Case Gymnasium—as their team makes a strong run for its first NCAA bid since 1997.

"I feel that we have everybody back and we have good players," BU coach Dennis Wolff said. "We have some good versatility and can score from different positions. We've also seemed to have regained the toughness that we lost in the previous couple of seasons."

Injuries and other obstacles have slowed the Terriers a bit in recent seasons, but Wolff believes if his team stays injury free and maintains a healthy attitude, the program can return to its 1995-98 level, where it won 62 games and finished no worse than second in the conference.

"We're really excited about where we're at right now," said Wolff, who surpassed St. John's coach Mike Jarvis as the winningest coach in BU history last season. "I feel pretty good about our team and what we can do if we work hard and stay semi-OK health-wise."

Only two players, senior **Stijn Dhondt** and sophomore guard **Kevin Fitzgerald**, started all 28 games last season, but with junior tri-captain **Billy Collins** and sophomores **Ryan Butt** and **Jacob Kudlacz** all recovered from season-ending foot injuries, the Terriers should have plenty of players to run at people.

"In regards to top-to-bottom depth, I don't think we've ever had so much depth and stability," said Wolff, who received a contract extension through 2005-06 in the offseason.

The abundance of depth and stability will give Wolff several options this season, but one thing he isn't bending on is having a strong inside game.

"We still need to have a more established post presence," Wolff said. "We need to be able to throw the ball inside to get baskets when we need to."

Sophomore **Jason Grochowalski**, who was selected BU's most valuable player as a red-shirt freshman last season, should get a lot of looks. The 6-6 Grochowalski (12.7 ppg, 4.3 rpg) came on strong the second half of the season to earn a spot on the America East's All-Rookie team while leading the conference in free-throw shooting (.860).

"Jason couldn't be tougher," Wolff said. "He's very hungry to score every time he touches the ball."

Grochowalski made 38-of-92 three-pointers last season (.413), but is also an aggressive player who isn't afraid to mix things up. If his ball handling and decision-making improve, he should be in line for another solid season.

A healthy Kudlacz (2.5 ppg, 1.5 rpg) will also help inside. Kudlacz played just six games before being sidelined with an ankle injury. A 6-8, 225-pound native of Poland, Kudlacz has fully recovered from surgery on both ankles. If he comes back aggressively, he should build on the solid foundation he set as a freshman (6.7 ppg, 4.3 rpg) two seasons ago.

"He could be a good player," Wolff said. "A lot of it is up to him."

Dhondt, a 6-6 native of Belgium, won his teammates and coaches over with his all-out play last season. His numbers (7.8 ppg, 4.3 rpg, 1.4 apg, 1.0 apg) weren't overwhelming, but his willingness to rebound, defend and run down loose balls earned him the team's "Friends of Basketball Award" for last season and tri-captaincy this season.

"He's a strong, tough basketball player who goes to the basket hard," Wolff said. "He has really added to our competitive level."

Butt (12.7 ppg , 4.3 rpg) is one player who should benefit from being pushed by Dhondt in practice every day. A solid 6-7 and 240, Butt put up solid numbers before a foot injury suffered on Feb. 17 forced him out of the team's final four games. When he is ready to play, he can be a difference-maker for the Terriers.

"He is as skilled a post player as we have," Wolff said. "His ability to be effective is predicated on his conditioning and strength."

Seniors **Jerome Graham** and **Ignacio Rodriguez** give BU added experience. Graham (5.8 ppg, 3.8 rpg), a 6-7 forward, should continue to be a solid player off the bench while Rodriguez (2.2 ppg, 2.5 rpg), a 6-9 center who made five starts in 2000-01, may see a reduced role with everyone around him healthy again.

Sophomore **Daniel Daccarett** (0.6 ppg), a 6-9 walk-on, saw action in 10 games last season and also returns.

The BU frontcourt should also benefit from the addition of freshmen **Rashad Bell**, a 6-6 forward, and center **Matt Czaplinski**, a 6-9 center.

Bell (27 ppg, 12 rpg, 4.5 bpg) scored 52 points against Archbishop Molloy during his senior season at

St. Francis Prep in Queens, N.Y.

"He's a slashing 6-7 player, who is extremely athletic," Wolff said. "He's a little bit different than a lot of guys on our roster."

Czaplanski (12.0 ppg, 8.0 rpg, 5.0 bpg) led Bunnell High School in Stratford, Conn., to just its second trip to the state Class L quarterfinals and was chosen the best shot blocker in Connecticut last year by the New Haven Register. He has the size and strength to help out and should benefit from a very competitive practice setting.

Collins (7.6 ppg, 4.8 rpg, 1.0 apg) and junior **Paul Seymour** (12.0 ppg, 4.4 rpg, 1.5 apg,), a pair of swing players, will help in both the frontcourt and backcourt.

The 6-7 Collins transferred from Rutgers. He sat out the 1999-2000 season under NCAA transfer rules and played just 12 games before a stress fracture in his left foot cut last season short. He is versatile enough to play shooting guard or either forward spot.

"I really don't think people have had a chance to see what he can do," Wolff said. "He's the type of guy that can play several positions and can help us in a lot of ways." Wolff said.

Seymour, the 2000 America East Rookie of the Year, finished second in scoring and led the Terriers in minutes played last season. Although he didn't get the open looks he did his first year, Seymour finished with similar statistics as the team's starting shooting guard. He may also see time at small forward this season.

"He's a very smart player," Wolff said. "He has some creativity in his ability to get free and score off the dribble and, I think, with some added strength he will improve."

Guard **Matt Turner** may have made the biggest impression of any Terrier last season. Turner (11.5 ppg, 2.2 rpg, 2.0 apg), a 5-9 junior, hit four three-pointers in a 1:17 span late in the game as BU overcame a 10-point deficit to force overtime against Maine in a conference tournament quarterfinal game. Turner, whose primary role was to provide offense off the bench, finished with 35 points in the Terriers' overtime loss.

The game served as a positive finish to an up-and-down season for Turner. He was suspended for two games in January, but came back strong (15.2 ppg) over the final 11 games and scored in double figures in seven of the last eight.

If all of the positives carry over and Turner learns to finish his drives to the basket better, he could dominate.

"Matt has the ability to be an unstoppable player," Wolff said. "If he improves his decision-making and he has the mindset that he is going to be a factor on defense on every play, then he's going to be one of the best players in the league."

Leadership is the main reason Fitzgerald, a last-minute signee Wolff believes was under-recruited, won the starting point guard spot as a freshman.

"He defends well and really knows how to play," Wolff said.

Fitzgerald (4.9 ppg, 3.0 rpg, 3.1 apg, 1.7 spg) finished second on the team in minutes played and was voted the Terriers' best defensive player and rookie of the year.

The arrival of 6-0 freshman **Chaz Carr** (22.0 ppg, 3.0 rpg, 3.0 apg, 1.5 spg) from Manchester (Conn.) High School will ease some of the burden placed on Fitzgerald last season.

Mark Michalek (0.5 ppg, 1.0 apg), the team's other tri-captain, also returns. Michalek, a 6-0 senior, received the team's Reggie Stewart Award for his commitment to the program and will be one of the Terriers' leaders regardless of how much action he sees in games.

2001-2002 SCHEDULE

Nov.	13	#New Orleans
	18	@Boston College
	25	St. Peter's
	28	George Washington
Dec.	1	@Holy Cross
	4	Harvard
	8	@Columbia
	12	Dartmouth
	22	@Providence
	28-29	##Oneida Bingo and Casino Classic
Jan.	2	@New Hampshire
	5	Vermont
	7	@Hartford
	12	Stony Brook
	20	@Northwestern
	24	@Albany
	26	@Binghamton
	29	Hartford
Feb.	2	@Vermont
	8	@Maine
	10	New Hampshire
	14	Northeastern
	16	Albany
	21	@Stony Brook
	24	Maine
March	2,3,9	###America East Tournament

@Road Games
#Guardians Classic, Iowa City, IA (If Boston University wins, it will play either Maryland Eastern Shore or Iowa; Semifinals and final are Nov. 20-21 at Kemper Arena, Kansas City, MO)
##Green Bay, WI (vs. UWGB first round; also Lipscomb, UC Irvine)
###Matthews Arena, Boston, MA (Championship game at homecourt of highest seeded team.)

BLUE RIBBON ANALYSIS

BACKCOURT	B+
BENCH/DEPTH	A
FRONTCOURT	A
INTANGIBLES	B+

Boston University is not a lock for the top spot in the America East, but they certainly have the most—and best—reasons to be considered the preseason favorite.

First and foremost, every player returns from last season. Granted, the Terriers were not world-beaters, but they did come on strong near the end and should make a natural progression through experience.

Second, BU is healthy. Having Collins, Butt and Kudlacz back from foot injuries makes the Terriers a deeper and stronger team. Not that anyone likes to lose players to injury, but BU also knows what the players forced into increased action last season can do.

Third, Turner and Seymour team with Fitzgerald to form a solid backcourt, and the frontcourt, headed by Butt and Grochowalski, is as deep as any in the league.

Fourth, a strong recruiting class adds depth at point guard with Carr, on the wing with Bell and in the paint with Czaplinski.

Fifth, Hofstra, Delaware and Drexel are now in the Colonial Athletic Association. The Terriers may have been strong enough to challenge even if the league stayed the same, but the changes certainly don't hurt their chances.

The one knock against BU could be the fact it has only four seniors, but the Terriers do have experienced players who have learned on the fly. In fact, that supposed weakness could turn out to be a strength if the Terriers are able to contend for the league title during the next few seasons.

"My thinking is we are heading into two or three years where we can be very competitive in our league," Wolff said.

He may be right.

(S.B.)

Hartford

LOCATION	West Hartford, CT
CONFERENCE	America East
LAST SEASON	4-24 (.143)
CONFERENCE RECORD	1-17 (10th)
STARTERS LOST/RETURNING	1/4
NICKNAME	Hawks
COLORS	Scarlet & White
HOMECOURT	Chase Family Arena (4,475)
COACH	Larry Harrison (Pittsburgh '78)
RECORD AT SCHOOL	4-24 (1 year)
CAREER RECORD	4-24 (1 year)
ASSISTANTS	Al Seibert (Fredinia State '85)
	Chris Pompey (Pittsburgh '84)
	John Yablonski (Seton Hall '97)
TEAM WINS (last 5 years)	17-15-11-10-4
RPI (last 5 years)	128-153-208-233-310
2000-01 FINISH	Lost in conference first round.

Larry Harrison has long been regarded as one of the best recruiters in basketball. He landed the likes of Danny Fortson and Kenyon Martin for Bob Huggins at Cincinnati and Quentin Richardson and Bobby Simmons for Pat Kennedy at DePaul.

This year it was time for Harrison to take care of himself. Harrison's first season as head coach at Hartford didn't quite go as well as he or his staff had hoped. The Hawks struggled to a 4-24 record, the worst in the school's 52-year history, and ended the season on a 16-game losing streak.

Injuries and misfortune played a part, but the hard truth is Hartford didn't have the horses to be much more than competitive. Such shouldn't be the case this year. Harrison and his staff brought in five new players, three freshmen and two transfers, and with them the dark cloud that hung over last season has made way for a silver lining.

"There was excitement last year, too, but this is a lot different," Harrison said. "I know the league, I know what our players can do and I know what the players we are bringing in can do."

Harrison and Co. hit the road looking for players who could score and rebound and those who possessed mental and physical toughness. He thinks he found them in early signees **Shaun Swan** and **Trevor Goode**, freshman guard **Charles Ford**, junior college transfer **Junior Amous** and former American University forward **Deon Saunders**, who will be eligible to play in January.

The newcomers bring depth to a scrappy unit that didn't give up last season, despite its inability to produce points. Hartford finished last in the America East in offense (65.0 ppg) and scoring margin (-11.1).

"At times we did a good job defensively, but we just didn't have the bodies to throw at people to play the way we wanted to play," Harrison said.

Now they do. The Hawks plan to play a full-court game and wear down their opponents with pressure and traps a la Cincinnati.

The influx of talent won't stop sophomore **Ryan Stys** from being Hartford's focal point. Though only 5-10 and 160 pounds, Stys went from being New Hampshire's "Mr. Basketball" as a high school senior to an unlikely BMOC with the Hawks. He surprised almost everyone by earning all-rookie honors and finishing second on the team in scoring (11.9 ppg, 3.3 rpg, 3.3 apg, 1.4 spg).

"He is going to be the symbol of what we do," Harrison said.

Stys led the team in minutes played (34.6) while shooting 43-for-103 (.417) from three-point range. With more talent around him, Stys shouldn't see so many double teams or have to do as much.

"I'm really looking forward to seeing what he can do," Harrison said. "I think his scoring is going to go up, but more importantly, I think his assists are going to go up."

Senior **Mantas Storpirstis** (9.3 ppg, 1.8 rpg, 1.1 apg) should be a frequent recipient. The 6-4 Storpistis shot .387 from behind the arc while making 60 three-pointers last season.

"He's going to be our designated shooter," Harrison said. "He can shoot off the dribble and has gained more confidence in his shooting ability."

Junior combo guard **Wayne McClinton** (6.4 ppg, 3.4 rpg, 3.0 apg) also logged a lot of minutes in the backcourt and should have more energy as the team's defensive stopper.

"He's got enough quickness and physical strength where he should be able to guard both the one and two positions," Harrison said.

The 5-11 Ford (10.0 ppg, 5.0 rpg, 4.0 apg) was one of 10 Division I players at Notre Dame Prep in Fitchburg, Mass. He will put plenty of pressure on opposing guards.

"He plays a lot bigger than he is, he plays like he's 6-2 or 6-3," Harrison said. "He can really get up and down the floor and jump."

Swan's job will be to boost the offense. A prolific scorer (31.7 ppg, 8.2 apg), he led Coastal Christian Academy of Virginia Beach, Va., to the Christian School National Championship and was chosen most valuable player at the championship tournament.

"Shaun's going to score, that's his forte," Harrison said. "He's very quick, very tough and can get to the basket and draw fouls."

Harrison also has big plans for Saunders, a 6-7 swingman who put up modest numbers (2.4 ppg, 2.2 rpg) in five games at American last season. The Hawks will use him at both the three and four spots and isolate him in certain situations.

"He's a complete player that can do a lot of things," Harrison said.

Power and hustle made the 6-7 Amous famous at Connors State (Okla.) Junior College. In addition to scoring and rebounding (12.0 ppg, 7.0 rpg), Amous is relentless in doing the little things it takes to win, something he learned while earning two state championships at Bishop McGuinness High School in Oklahoma City.

"He knows how to play," Harrison said. "He doesn't mind banging and he can wear you down. He also likes diving on the floor and into the stands, and I like that."

Saunders and Amous will join four returnees in the frontcourt. All can contribute.

Josh Odugbela (7.4 ppg, 5.0 rpg, 1.0 apg, 1.0 spg), a 6-8 junior, continued to develop and led the team in rebounding during conference play. He should be able to use his athleticism to get points inside.

Injuries got the best of 6-6 junior **Pierre Johnson** last season; he played in only 15 games. Johnson (7.7 ppg, 4.1 rpg), played his best game of season, contributing 16 points and 11 rebounds in a double-overtime win at Rhode Island in December, but was in and out of the lineup most of the rest of the way.

"He's our quickest inside player and a great offensive rebounder who can defend," Harrison said.

Defense is also the calling card for senior **Todd Jones** and sophomore **Louis Bosley**. The 6-9 Jones (1.5 ppg, 2.4 rpg) is a banger and the 6-6 Bosley (4.0 ppg, 3.5 rpg) is a developing talent who gained valuable experience as a freshman.

"His best assets are blocking shots and rebounding," Harrison said of Bosley. "He's a quick jumper who needs to finish better inside."

More inside scoring should come from Goode (22.7 ppg, 10.2 rpg, 5.2 bpg), a solid 6-9 power man who helped Cape Henry (Va.) High School to the Tidewater Conference Championship.

2001-2002 SCHEDULE

Nov.	16	@Delaware State
	19	#@Iowa State
	23-24	##Las Vegas Invitational
	29-30	###Phoenix Classic
Dec.	3	@Manhattan College
	8	Fairleigh Dickinson
	11	@Siena
	13	@Rutgers
	28	Clemson
Jan.	2	@Binghamton
	5	Northeastern
	7	Boston University
	12	New Hampshire
	17	@Maine
	20	Vermont
	22	@Dartmouth
	24	@New Hampshire
	26	Stony Brook
	29	@Boston University
Feb.	1	@Northeastern
	5	Maine
	8	Albany
	13	Maryland-Eastern Shore
	15	@Stony Brook
	17	Binghamton
	22	@Albany
	24	@Vermont
March	2,3,9	####America East Tournament

@Road Games
#First round, Las Vegas Invitational
##Las Vegas, NV (schedule determined after first-round games; Pool 1 includes Georgia Tech, Illinois, Eastern Illinois, Pennsylvania. Pool 2 includes Iowa State, Saint Louis, Hartford, Southern Illinois)
###Phoenix, AZ (vs. Central Connecticut first round; also Niagara, Winthrop)
####Matthews Arena, Boston, MA (Championship game at homecourt of highest seeded team.)

BLUE RIBBON ANALYSIS

BACKCOURT	B-
BENCH/DEPTH	C
FRONTCOURT	C
INTANGIBLES	B

Even though his team lost its final 16 games last season, Hartford coach Larry Harrison said he never questioned its effort.

"Even up through the conference tournament, we felt we could win," Harrison said. "We never doubted we could beat teams, we just couldn't get over the hump. We just couldn't make that next pass or make that next shot or get that next rebound."

That won't happen all the time this season. Harrison and his staff have brought in five new players who could make an impact in practice and games. Last season the

Hawks were nursing injuries, this year they'll be competing for playing time.

"It will be a different look because we have additional players and we have players who can push each other in practice," Harrison said.

Stys had an outstanding freshman season and leads the seven returning players. Stys shouldn't have to carry such a large burden this year with newcomers Swan, a freshman guard, and power forward Amous, a junior college transfer, providing offensive help. Saunders, a transfer from American University, will provide more assistance when he becomes eligible in January.

The Hawks will be much improved, but it may take some time for all the new personnel to adjust. With only two seniors on the roster this season and 6-4 guard Jerell Parker, a transfer from Loyola, waiting to join the team next fall, the best days are certainly ahead. Hartford may have to wait a year to have a legitimate chance to win the conference, but don't expect any prolonged losing streaks to end the season, either. A finish somewhere in the middle of the nine-team pack is a reasonable expectation.

(S.B.)

 # Maine

LOCATION	Orono, ME
CONFERENCE	America East
LAST SEASON	18-11 (.621)
CONFERENCE RECORD	10-8 (4th)
STARTERS LOST/RETURNING	2/3
NICKNAME	Black Bears
COLORS	Blue & White
HOMECOURT	Alfond Sports Arena (5,712)
COACH	Dr. John Giannini (N. Central College '84)
RECORD AT SCHOOL	79-67 (5 years)
CAREER RECORD	79-67 (5 years)
ASSISTANTS	Ted Woodward (Bucknell '86)
	Ed Jones (Maine '94)
	Randy Lee (South Carolina '95)
TEAM WINS (last 5 years)	11-7-19-24-18
RPI (last 5 years)	207-259-128-113-130
2000-01 FINISH	Lost in conference semifinal.

With 61 victories in the last three seasons, Dr. John Giannini has established Maine as one of the more consistent programs in America East, but there is still something missing.

Despite all of its success, Maine still has not broken through and advanced to the NCAA Tournament. With the departure of Hofstra, Delaware and Drexel—the three teams that finished above the Black Bears in the conference standings last season—that could change this year.

"We'll have a chance to compete for the championship again," said Giannini, whose team has lost in the semifinals of the America East Tournament three straight times. "We've done that the last three years, but we would like to win that NCAA berth instead of being just a contender for it."

Maine will have to do it without Carvel Ammons and Julian Dunkley, a pair of forwards who earned all-conference honors. But, if college basketball truly is a game of guards, you've got to like the Black Bears' chances, because the entire starting perimeter returns.

Senior **Huggy Dye**, a preseason all-conference selection, struggled to find his shot last season (.401 FG) but still posted decent numbers (13.3 ppg, 2.6 rpg, 2.4 apg) despite pressing himself to play better.

"He's the kind of kid that loves basketball so much that when he struggles he has a hard time dealing with it," Giannini said.

At 6-3, Dye has a well-rounded game. A second-team all-conference pick as a sophomore, Dye had a strong off-season and should be one of the top backcourt players in the league again this season if he relaxes and lets the game come to him.

"He's very complete, he's very good at everything," Giannini said. "I think sometimes he puts too much pressure on himself and he doesn't have to do that."

Having running mates **Errick Greene** and **Derrick Jackson**—two of the Black Bears' three captains—back should ease any of that tension. Greene, a 6-3 senior, recovered from a foot injury that cost him all but two games in 1999-2000 to have a solid junior season (10.6 ppg, 4.9 rpg, 2.5 apg, 1.2 spg). Expect Greene, who

deferred a bit to Dye and Maine's established frontcourt players last season, to be more of a scorer this year.

"He had a phenomenal off-season," Giannini said. "He's a better shooter, he's more athletic and he really sees himself as more of an offensive threat."

Jackson, a 6-2 junior, is a reliable ball handler who led the team in minutes (30.3 mpg) last season. He doesn't score a lot (6.3 ppg, 3.4 rpg, 1.2 spg), but is a strong perimeter defender and team leader.

"Derrick really is a great defender and a flat-out warrior," Giannini said.

The backcourt suffered a blow when Tory Cavalieri (7.9 ppg. 2.9 rpg, 4.3 apg, 1.5 spg), a member of the America East All-Rookie Team, decided to transfer closer to his home in New Jersey. Cavalieri's departure leaves the Black Bears without a true point man, but Dye, Greene, Jackson and junior-college transfer **Ricky Green** are combo guards who should be able to get the job done.

"We don't have that real floor general, but we have four guys who can handle the ball, pass, shoot and defend," Giannini said.

Giannini compares Green, a 6-0 junior who played at Shawnee (Ill.) Community College, to former Black Bears Marcus Wills and Fred Meeks, junior college players who came in and made immediate contributions. As a sophomore, Green had a productive season (21.1 ppg, 3.0 rpg, 2.1 apg, 2.2 spg, .465 3FG).

"We think that Ricky could be very similar to them in terms of scoring ability," Giannini said.

Junior **Rickey White** and freshman **Alfredus Petkus** could also be factors on the wing.

White, an athletic 6-4 swingman, showed flashes of brilliance in practice last season but didn't get much playing time. White (2.1 ppg, 1.2 rpg) is not a great outside shooter but can get to the rim and make things happen.

"If you put him out there, all he's going to do is get rebounds, play well and make a high percentage of his shots," Giannini said.

Petkus, a 6-5 native of Lithuania, spent last season at New Hampton (N.H.) Prep. His outside shooting prowess should be a boost for the Black Bears, who struggled from three-point range (.339) last season.

Without a doubt, the biggest questions for the Black Bears this season are in the frontcourt. Ammons and Dunkley combined for 32.1 points and 14.5 rebounds per game and were first- and second-team all-conference, respectively. While their loss is significant, Giannini thinks he has able replacements ready.

The biggest is **Justin Rowe**, a 7-0 transfer from Clearwater (Fla.) Christian College who was able to practice with the Bears as he red-shirted last season.

"He was as dominant in practice as any player I've had in the last five years," Giannini said.

Rowe, a junior, gives Maine a huge presence inside. Already a strong defender and rebounder, his offense progressed last season and he should be an immediate force.

"He is just one of those special kids who got bigger, stronger and better older, rather than younger," Giannini said.

Clayton Brown, a 6-7 junior, should also be ready to step in. Stuck behind Ammons last season, Brown (3.2 ppg, 1.4 rpg) showed most of his skills in practice, but took advantage of an opportunity to play in the regular-season finale and contributed 14 points and nine rebounds in 22 minutes.

Seniors **Jamar Croom** and **Todd Tibbetts** could also play greater roles. At 6-9 and 250, Croom (0.0 ppg, 0.2 rpg) has good size and is a strong inside post player but has been slowed by knee surgery. He is also a respected leader as evidenced by his selection as the Black Bears' third captain.

Tibbetts, 6-7, has seen his playing time decrease throughout his career after missing the 1998-99 season with a knee injury, but could finish on an upswing. Tibbetts (1.7 ppg) has increased his strength and may be able to shoot his way to more playing time.

"He could be hard to keep on the bench because he plays well in practice," Giannini said. "He could be a good player."

Freshmen **David Dubois** and **Mark Flavin** will also push for time.

The 6-9 Dubois, a Quebec native, attended College Montmorency. Dubois has a great deal of natural talent and could develop into a key player for Maine.

"Athletically and physically, he is as good as anyone we've had up here," Giannini said.

The 6-10 Flavin red-shirted last season. He is a good ball handler and passer for a player his size and brings solid credentials (20.0 ppg, 15.0 rpg, 5.0 apg) from Weymouth (Mass.) High School.

Maine also signed **Joe Campbell**, a 6-6 forward from Bangor, Maine, but he is expected to red-shirt this season.

Two other players, guard Tom Waterman and forward Andre Riley, have left the program to seek more playing time. Waterman transferred to Franklin Pierce College and Riley has moved on to American International College.

2001-2002 SCHEDULE

Nov.	12	#@Arkansas
	16-17	##Florida International Tournament
	20	Delaware State
	25	Troy State
	30	###Spartan Classic
Dec.	1	###Spartan Classic
	9	@Sacred Heart
	11	@Norfolk State
	23	@Massachusetts
	30	Brownw
Jan.	2	Albany
	6	@Stony Brook
	11	@Vermont
	13	@Albany
	17	Hartford
	20	@Binghampton
	26	@New Hampshire
	31	Binghampton
Feb.	3	@Northeastern
	5	@Hartford
	8	Boston University
	10	Stony Brook
	14	New Hampshire
	17	Vermont
	21	Northeastern
	24	@Boston University
March	2-3	####America East Tournament
	9	#####America East Tournament

@Road Games
#Preseason NIT (if Maine wins, it will play UNC Wilmington or Wake Forest on Nov. 14 or 16; Semifinals and final are Nov. 21 and 23 at Madison Square Garden, NY)
##Miami, FL (vs. Texas-San Antonio first round; also Florida International, St. Peter's)
###East Lansing, MI (vs. Lamar first round; also IUPU-Fort Wayne, Michigan State)
####Matthews Arena, Boston, MA (quarterfinals and semifinals)
#####At home court of higher seeded team

BLUE RIBBON ANALYSIS

BACKCOURT	A
BENCH/DEPTH	B
FRONTCOURT	B
INTANGIBLES	B+

Having led Rowan College to three Division III Final Four appearances and the 1996 national championship, Giannini certainly knows what it takes to build a winning basketball program. Giannini has spent the last five seasons putting the pieces in place at Maine, and the Black Bears certainly appear poised to make another run at the America East's NCAA Tournament bid.

The Black Bears return their starting backcourt of seniors Dye and Greene and junior Jackson, but must replace two top-level forwards

At 7-0, Rowe gives Maine a legitimate big man, unlike any other in the league, and certainly has the ability to make an immediate impact.

The three main issues for the Black Bears are finding effective frontcourt players, developing depth at guard and having Dye return to the form that earned him second-team All-America East as a sophomore.

Rowe and Clayton Brown could answer the first question by playing the same way in games as they did in practice last season. Green and freshman Petkus could provide the necessary backcourt depth and Dye's natural ability and attitude indicate last year's problems could have been an aberration.

"If two of those three things happen, we are right up there at the top," Giannini said. "If we get three of those three to happen, we are going to be tough to beat."

None of the three is impossible, so figure on the Black Bears being right in the hunt all the way through-

out the season.

(S.B.)

New Hampshire

LOCATION	Durham, NH
CONFERENCE	America East
LAST SEASON	7-21 (.250)
CONFERENCE RECORD	6-12 (9th)
STARTERS LOST/RETURNING	1/4
NICKNAME	Wildcats
COLORS	Blue & White
HOMECOURT	Lundholm Gymnasium (3,500)
	and Whittemore Center (7,200)
COACH	Phil Rowe (Plymouth State '74)
RECORD AT SCHOOL	10-46 (2 years)
CAREER RECORD	10-46 (2 years)
ASSISTANTS	Darryl Hilliard (Maine-Farmingham '88)
	Cory McClure (Westbrook College '96)
	Jim Woods (Boston College '98)
TEAM WINS (last 5 years)	7-10-4-3-7
RPI (last 5 years)	237-231-298-310-264
2000-01 FINISH	Lost in conference first round.

Phil Rowe would be the perfect pitchman for Pontiac. Not only is he building a basketball program, he's building excitement.

It hasn't been easy. Rowe took over the struggling Wildcat program in June of 2000 and has instilled an all-out hustle at all times in his players that has generated a groundswell of support in the Granite State without an abundance of victories. Home attendance increased 27 percent last season for a team that won 5-of-11 games in Lundholm Gymnasium and was a combined 2-15 on the road.

The numbers, both at the gate and in the standings, should increase this year. The attendance will be boosted by Florida's Nov. 28 visit to the 7,200-seat on-campus Whittemore Center. Although the Gators figure to roll over the Wildcats, like they have the last two seasons, a sellout crowd is expected to watch Concord native Matt Bonner in his return to his home state.

Improvement on the court doesn't come with the same guarantee, but the Wildcats should continue to progress. Two solid recruiting classes give the team more depth and the returning players spent the off-season in the weight room and working on individual skills.

"I think the guys are taking more personal pride in their workouts," said Rowe, a New Hampshire native who compiled a 183-174 record at Division III Plymouth State before being hired to rebuild the Wildcats.

Playing with pride hasn't been a problem in Rowe's first two seasons, but matching up with talent has. Opponents averaged 82.1 points and outscored the Wildcats by 9.6 per game. New Hampshire got pounded on the boards and struggled on offense, shooting just .388 from the field.

The Wildcats often resembled a hockey team during the second half of last season, as Rowe divided up the minutes to evaluate his players and often employed 5-for-5 substitutions. The strategy didn't lead to an abundance of wins as New Hampshire lost 10 of its last 12, but it did offer experience to a team that returns 11 of its 13 letter winners and has just three seniors on this season's roster.

"The nice part is that because we are so young and have so many freshmen and sophomores that we are all on the same page," said Rowe, who has his top six scorers and 83 percent of his point production back.

Austin Ganly, a 6-6 senior swingman whose 25.6 scoring average led the country after five games, leads the returnees. The gangly, 195-pound Ganly (13.3 ppg, 3.4 rpg, 1.1 apg) tailed off in the middle of the season before regaining his form late.

"He can shoot the ball with anybody in the country," Rowe said.

Ganly worked on improving his strength and creating shots off the dribble in the off-season.

"That's where his game is starting to take shape," Rowe said.

Marcus Bullock (9.1 ppg, 3.4 rpg, 2.0 apg, 1.4 spg), a 6-0 combo guard, led the team in three-pointers with 59 and finished second in scoring and minutes as a freshman. His emphasis this season will be on shooting and refining his overall skills.

Allen Gould, a 6-6 swingman, also contributed as a

freshman despite being slowed by a knee injury that required surgery at the end of the season. Gould (7.4 ppg, 3.4 rpg) scored in double figures nine times but fouled out five. He went through eight weeks of rehabilitation on his knee and is back at full speed, which should lead to more production this season.

"He's a long, gangly three-four man that creates problems for opponents," Rowe said. "He's tough to handle because he shoots the three-pointer and is pretty good in the post."

Senior **Assane Faye** (5.5 ppg, 3.3 rpg) showed improvement over the second half of last season and comes off a summer tour with Senegal's national team. The 6-7 Faye overcame injuries to average 8.6 points in New Hampshire's final 14 games.

Junior shooting guard **Shawn Collette** (3.5 ppg), 6-0, also had his moments last season, highlighted by 17 points in an 89-87 loss to Towson on Jan. 28. **Brady Catlett**, a 6-4 freshman who red-shirted last season, adds another shooter on the wing. Catlett, whose great uncle Gale is the head coach at West Virginia, averaged 22 points and 11 rebounds during his senior season at Hedgesville (W. Va.) High School in 1998-99.

The big question in the backcourt will be at the point, which was thought to be in good hands before last season. Marcelle Williams averaged 13.6 points as a freshman and earned a spot on the America East All-Rookie Team in 1999-00, but left the team because of personal reasons last fall and withdrew from school in January, leaving the Wildcats short-handed all season.

Senior Colin Donahue (5.4 ppg, 3.4 rpg, 4.82 apg, 1.2 spg) filled in admirably, but his graduation leaves the position in the hands of freshmen **Ronnie Dennis** and **Roland Williams**.

Rowe hit the recruiting trail knowing he needed a point guard, but will he have one ready to start Nov. 16 at Notre Dame?

"We're going to find out," he said. "It's a situation where we needed to bring people in who could play right away."

It's a situation where the coach hopes the newcomers will bring out the best in each other. Competition breeds success.".

The 5-11 Williams (28 ppg, 5.0 apg) hails from Elgin Air Force Base in Florida and is the all-time leading scorer at Rocky Bayou Christian School. The 6-3 Dennis (18.0 ppg, 8.0 apg) led Abbeville (Ala.) High School to the state playoffs in each of his three seasons, earning league MVP honors as a senior.

Junior **John Dullea** (4.5 ppg, 1.4 rpg, 1.4 apg), 6-0, adds depth and experience at the point.

Now comfortable that he can go two deep at each position, Rowe doesn't plan on slowing his team down.

"We press all the time and we're not bashful about diving on the floor," he said. "We create havoc and it's a style that's fan friendly."

It's also player friendly, as long as no one takes plays off.

"The bench is a great motivator," Rowe said without hesitation.

So is team captain **Chris Brown**, a fifth-year senior who could have signed a contract to play professionally overseas but decided to return to the program.

The 6-4 Brown (7.1 ppg, 4.0 rpg, 2.0 apg, 1.3 spg) missed the first four games of last season with a torn tendon in his ring finger and saw his production drop, but is one of the top rebounders in the conference when healthy.

"He's more of a power player, but he can knock down the three," Rowe said of Brown.

Brown averaged 10.7 points and was third in the league in rebounding as a sophomore, so his numbers should be up if he stays healthy. His fearless attitude will also shape an otherwise young and inexperienced frontcourt.

Junior **Jeff Senulis**, the team's fifth-leading scorer last season, also figures to play a larger role. The 6-8 Senulis (7.0 ppg, 3.1 rpg) has bulked up and had a strong summer playing in Boston's Beantown League.

"He probably made the most strides of anyone in the weight room." Rowe said.

The Wildcats also need more out of sophomores **Matt Kauderer** and **Kyle Peterson**. The 6-5 Kauderer (5.0 ppg, 3.0 rpg) played well early in the season but was an academic casualty and missed the final 20 games. He gained experience over the summer playing for the gold-medal USA team at the Maccabiah Games in Israel. The 6-9, 255-pound Peterson (1.5 ppg, 1.4 rpg) hit the camp trail hard during the summer and has the size and strength to contribute inside.

Help should also come from a trio of 6-7 freshmen—**Ben Sturgill**, **Brandon Krug** and **David Sands**.

Sturgill (14.3 ppg, 9.8 rpg) led Hamilton (Ohio) High School to sectional and district championships as a senior and should offer the most immediate help.

"He's an inside-outside guy," Rowe said. "He's adept in the post, can score with either hand and runs the floor well."

Krug (22.4 ppg, 10.5 rpg) owns the career records for rebounds and blocks at Dwight Township (Ill.) High School and Sands (13.3 ppg, 11.7 rpg) led Tabor Academy of Marion, Mass., to the 2000 New England Prep B championship as a junior and a second-place finish as a senior.

2001-2002 SCHEDULE

Nov.	16	@Notre Dame
	21	@Boston College
	24	Dartmouth
	26	@Connecticut
	28	Florida
Dec.	1	@Buffalo
	6	New England College
	8	@Lehigh
	12	Harvard
	29	Northeastern
Jan.	2	Boston University
	5	Colgate
	7	Army
	12	@Hartford
	14	@Vermont
	18	@Stony Brook
	20	Albany
	24	Hartford
	26	Maine
	30	@Albany
Feb.	2	Binghamton
	5	@Northeastern
	8	Stony Brook
	10	@Boston University
	14	@Maine
	22	Vermont
	24	@Binghamton
March	2-3,9	#America East Tournament

@Road Games
#Matthews Arena, Boston, MA

BLUE RIBBON ANALYSIS

BACKCOURT	C
BENCH/DEPTH	C
FRONTCOURT	C
INTANGIBLES	C+

After two seasons of juggling and shuffling just to stay afloat, Rowe finally has "his" team in place.

His newest challenge will be breaking in two freshman point guards and letting his young, talented players learn on the go.

"The biggest thing is guys getting playing time and experience," Rowe said. "It's very important for our young point guards to develop as quickly as possible."

Those freshman point guards, Dennis and Williams, join a team that returns its top six scorers from last season and has been characterized by a refusal to cave against more talented opponents.

Rowe employs a frenetic, full-court style that both Dennis and Williams like to play, but their job as freshmen will be to take care of the ball and get it into the hands of seniors Ganly and Brown and sophomores Bullock and Gould.

New Hampshire's style has troubled opponents in the past and the players also believe in the program, as evidenced by the commitments they made in the off-season.

There is also excitement among the coaching staff and fans as the season approaches, but this team's best days are still ahead of it. The Wildcats will fight to the end every night, but still will probably lose more than they win.

(S.B.)

Northeastern

LOCATION	Boston, MA
CONFERENCE	America East
LAST SEASON	10-19 (.345)
CONFERENCE RECORD	8-10 (6th)
STARTERS LOST/RETURNING	3/2
NICKNAME	Huskies
COLORS	Red & Black
HOMECOURT	Cabot Center (2,000)
COACH	Ron Everhart (Virginia Tech '85)
RECORD AT SCHOOL	First year
CAREER RECORD	92-104 (7 years)
ASSISTANTS	Julius Allen (Southern Nazarene '81)
	Frank Martin (Florida International '93)
	Adam Ginsburg (Buffalo '97)
TEAM WINS (last 5 years)	7-14-10-7-10
RPI (last 5 years)	257-186-228-296-214
2000-01 FINISH	Lost in conference semifinal.

After five years of unfulfilled promise under Rudy Keeling, the task of bringing the team with the most America East titles and NCAA appearances (including six in seven seasons from 1981-87) falls squarely on the shoulders of Ron Everhart, who scripted a successful rebuilding story in his seven seasons at McNeese State and was hired to replace the fired Keeling in April.

"I think it's going to be a challenge, but I'm looking forward to it," said Everhart, who played for the legendary Morgan Wootten at Dematha High School in Hyattsville, Md. He also had the unenviable task of guarding Dell Curry in practice throughout his playing career at Virginia Tech.

"It's a program that hasn't had a great deal of success in the recent past, so our challenge will be to go out and compete and get some local guys to stay at home and play," Everhart said. "It's a great school in a great basketball city."

Everhart's McNeese team went 22-9 last season and earned an NIT berth. The Cowboys also led the Southland Conference in scoring (83.2 ppg) and Everhart plans to employ the same three-guard, up-tempo, full-court pressure system with the Huskies.

"We will play that way and we have the tools to do it," he said.

Ideally Everhart would like to play an 11-man rotation, but it may be difficult to cultivate that kind of depth, particularly in the backcourt, this season.

"That would be the way our guys would work best— to keep coming at you on offense and to keep coming at you on defense," Everhart said.

Everhart has already installed the type of intensity and desire he demands in individual workouts. Players stayed on campus to lift weights this summer for the first time in memory and practices will be conducted at a crisper pace than some of the holdovers are accustomed.

The Huskies will also be young with five freshmen and just three seniors on the roster, but that youth may help facilitate the transition to Everhart's style.

"The biggest thing I'd like to see change is the defensive mentality," Everhart said. "When we walk onto the floor we should have a little swagger in our step in knowing that we can stop some people."

Northeastern's opponents should also have a tough time stopping senior guard **Charles "Ricky" Cranford**, the conference's top returning scorer. The well-traveled Cranford (16.6 ppg, 3.7 rpg, 1.6 apg), who originally signed with Saint Louis and also attended Coffeyville (Kansas) Community College, carried the Huskies through the second half of last season while shooting .494 from the field.

"He's very talented offensively," Everhart said of the 6-5 Cranford. "He can shoot the perimeter shot, he can slash and finish on the back end and I really think can score in the system we are going to play."

Cranford, who some say has slid by on talent in the past, also showed signs of maturing into more of a senior leader during the off-season.

The Huskies also have a leader in 5-11 senior point guard **Jean Bain**, their only other returning starter. Bain (7.8 ppg, 1.9 rpg, 4.2 apg, 1.6 spg) returned from a torn ACL that cost him the second half of the 1999-2000 season to finish strong. Bain, who also lost seasons to Hodgkin's Disease (1995-96) and a broken wrist (1997-98), is a distributor who takes care of the ball (122 assists to 59 turnovers) and can shoot the three (.333). His challenge this season will be defending the entire court.

"He's a very heady guy who is quick on his feet and a good perimeter shooter who can get to the basket," Everhart said. "He really is an amazing kid and I think he's done a remarkable job of turning up the intensity."

The return of sophomore **Toby Brittian**, who missed last season because of personal reasons, will also pro-

vide a boost. The versatile 6-4 Brittian (10.1 ppg, 2.4 rpg, 1.4 apg, 1.6 spg in 1999-2000) made the conference's all-rookie team two years ago and may be well served by the coaching change after clashing with Keating. He can play anywhere from shooting guard to power forward and has the athleticism to excel in Everhart's system.

"Since I've been the coach at Northeastern, the kid has been a tremendously hard worker and a model citizen," Everhart said. "I expect that if he continues to do these things that he could be one of our better defenders. He could be our most explosive athlete."

The remainder of the backcourt responsibilities will fall to three freshmen—**Antonio Johnson**, **Aaron Davis** and **Dennis D'Addezio**.

The 6-3 Johnson (16.1 ppg, 6.7 rpg, 3.3 apg, 3.6 spg), a late signee from Salem High School in Virginia Beach (Va.), is a strong defender and good deep shooter.

"He can also take it to the basket and score," Everhart said.

Davis, also 6-3, was one of the top outside shooters in New Jersey for Bishop Francis Essex Catholic in East Orange. He was listed in the Newark Star Ledger's "Bomb Squad" as one of the state's top three-point threats. Not long after signing with Northeastern, Davis earned MVP honors over three Big East recruits in a New Jersey AAU Tournament.

"He's long, he can score and he can play defense," Everhart said. "He can play the two or the three, slash and beat you off the dribble."

Both Johnson and Davis will make an immediate impact.

"I'm counting on it," Everhart said. "I'm excited about Antonio and Aaron playing right away mainly because they are such tenacious defenders."

Defense seems to be the biggest question regarding the 6-6 D'Addezio, who has played for his father on one of the top amateur clubs in his hometown of Caracas, Venezuela. D'Addezio is a good shooter who can handle the ball, but hasn't had much experience playing against American college players. He joins Hector Romero (New Orleans), Victor Luces (UTEP) and Juan Manaure (Hawaii) as the only Venezuelans in NCAA Division I basketball.

"He's the unknown piece to the puzzle," Everhart said.

Change will also be the operative word in the frontcourt, where center George Aygar and Tyrone Hammick have exhausted their eligibility and Jean Francois (8.2 ppg, 4.3 rpg) transferred to Georgia Southern after a promising freshman season that saw him start six games and finish fourth on the club in scoring.

Red-shirt freshman **Lunzaya Nlandu** and transfer **Quilninious "Q" Randall** seem anxious to fill the void and have already impressed Everhart enough to be dubbed "warriors."

The 6-7, 230-pound Nlandu, from Montreal, missed last season with a broken left wrist, but played with the Canadian National Team over the summer. He will bring much-needed size and strength to the Huskies, who were out-rebounded by an average of 5.8 boards per game last season.

"He's a tremendously hard worker and a very proud kid who has had success through international basketball," Everhart said. "He's a kid who expects to be good and I expect him to be good."

Nlandu played three seasons at Vanier College, a prep school in Quebec and is an explosive leaper with a good touch around the basket.

Randall, a Boston native, spent a season and a half at George Mason before leaving the school eight games into his sophomore season to seek a school closer to home. Although Randall, a 6-5 junior, didn't put up big numbers at George Mason (1.6 ppg, 1.2 rpg in 23 games as a freshman), Everhart has high expectations for him.

"He may be one of the best rebounders I've ever been around," Everhart said. "I expect him to be a double-digit rebounder for the remainder of his two-year career here."

Immediate help should also come from Odessa (Texas) College transfers **Sylbrin Robinson** (11.0 ppg, 11.7 rpg, 3.7 rpg) and **Cornelius Wright** (7 ppg, 4 rpg), who both played high school ball for NU assistant Frank Martin at Miami (Fla.) Senior High. Both are juniors.

Robinson, a 6-9 forward/center, gave an early commitment to Florida in high school, but ended up at Florida International before landing at Odessa. Some recruiting services ranked him only slightly behind Southern Cal All-American Sam Clancy and ahead of Luke Walton

(Arizona) and David Bluthenthal (USC) as a power forward prospect coming out of high school. He should come in and contribute immediately. Robinson averaged 5.5 points and 6.6 boards as a part-time starter at Florida International.

"We are getting a kid who can really come in and fit our style real well," Everhart said. "He runs the floor real well and, from a front line perspective, he adds a degree of depth and a degree of athleticism that can help us play the way we want to play."

The 6-6, 235-pound Wright returned from an ACL injury to help Odessa return to the NJCAA Tournament for the first time since 1997.

"He's a real athletic 6-6 and is someone that we can count on to score inside and finish with his jump hook," Everhart said.

More help could come from **Meshak Burke-Bennett**, a 6-6 freshman from Dorchester, Mass. and a dual recruit who also plays wide receiver for the football team. Bennett (19.7 ppg, 9.4 rpg at Sharon High School in 1999-2000) attended Notre Dame Prep in Fitchburg (Mass.) last season.

"He's a very tough kid and a very good rebounder," Everhart said. "He's been playing some pickup ball with some of our upperclassmen and all they are talking about is how hard he plays. When upperclassmen are saying that about an incoming freshman, that's quite a statement."

Questions surround returnees **Tim West** and **Jesse Dunn**. West, a 6-5 senior, played in 23 games last season (2.4 ppg, 1.7 rpg) had knee surgery in the off-season and may not be ready to return. Dunn, a 6-7 junior walk-on, missed all of last season with a broken ankle. He is a good shooter, but it is uncertain how he will fit in.

2001-2002 SCHEDULE

Nov.	16-17	#:Pepsi Shootout
	20	Brown
	24	Northern Arizona
	27	@Harvard
	29	@Virginia Tech
Dec.	3	@Loyola
	8	@Connecticut
	17	@Drexel
	20	Rider
	22	@Rhode Island
	29	@New Hampshire
Jan.	5	@Hartford
	7	Vermont
	10	Stony Brook
	12	Binghamton
	17	@Vermont
	20	Boston University
	24	@Binghamton
	26	@Albany
Feb.	1	Hartford
	3	@Maine
	5	New Hampshire
	12	Albany
	14	@Boston University
	17	@Stony Brook
	22	Maine
March	2-3	##America East Tournament
	9	###America East Tournament

@Road Games
#Poughkeepsie, NU (vs. Columbia first round; also Drexel, Marist)
##Matthews Arena, Boston, MA (quarterfinals and semifinals)
###At home of higher seeded team

BLUE RIBBON ANALYSIS

BACKCOURT	B
BENCH/DEPTH	C
FRONTCOURT	B-
INTANGIBLES	B

There's no disputing that Northeastern has struggled in recent seasons, but there are certainly reasons for optimism. Everhart promises to inject new life into the program with his high-speed, full-court system. It's a style players enjoy playing and spectators enjoy watching.

The Huskies also have talent. There's no reason Cranford shouldn't make the all-conference team and contend for player of the year. Bain adds stability in the backcourt and the multi-talented Brittian could be a huge

boost if he returns to form after missing last season because of personal reasons. The Huskies' lack of depth will force their three freshmen guards to enter the mix and contribute from the outset. Northeastern should get something out of a group that includes Nlandu and transfers Randall, Robinson and Wright.

The defection of the league's top three teams to the Colonial Athletic Association also increases the likelihood for improvement. Caution is still advised, but a fresh start will probably do the program well. If things fall into line favorably, this is a team that can hang with anybody in the league.

(S.B.)

Stony Brook

LOCATION	Stony Brook, NY
CONFERENCE	America East
LAST SEASON	17-11 (.607)
CONFERENCE RECORD	NA
STARTERS LOST/RETURNING	2/3
NICKNAME	Seawolves
COLORS	Scarlet & Gray
HOMECOURT	USB-Sports Complex (4,103)
COACH	Nick Macarchuk (Fairfield '63)
RECORD AT SCHOOL	23-34 (2 years)
CAREER RECORD	333-354 (24 years)
ASSISTANTS	Nick Macarchuk III (Canisius '88)
	Edgar De La Rosa (St. Francis NY '83)
	Brian Blaney (Roanoke '94)
TEAM WINS (last 5 years)	10-13-11-6-17
RPI (last 5 years)	NA-NA-NA-264-205
2000-01 FINISH	Lost in regular-season finale.

Nick Macarchuk admits he's a pessimist.

Remind him that his Stony Brook squad was the best independent in the country last season and he's quick to point out the Seawolves were 5-0 against non-Division I opponents, played 14 home games and rode the broad shoulders of Leon Brisport—a former Big East player who dominated the inside—to a surprising 17-11 record in their second season of Division I play.

He'll also tell you things will be different this season. The schedule, which includes three Big East opponents and only one non-conference home game (Cleveland State on Dec. 4), will be much more difficult and Brisport (16.6 ppg, 8.8 rpg, 1.5 bpg) has graduated, leaving Stony Brook with a big hole in the middle.

Factor in all of the things associated with joining a conference for the first time and the fact the Seawolves don't have a senior on their roster and Macarchuk's concerns start to seem more valid. Then, like a savvy defender working through a screen, he hedges.

"I don't like to be right," the Independent coach of the year in 2000-01 said. "My assistants say we have a good team and our attitudes our good. The players feel good and I think we have enough pretty good players where we can do some things."

One thing Macarchuk doesn't back away from is his joy of being back in the America East.

"It's a wonderful fit for us," the former Canisius and Fordham coach said. "It's right where we belong."

The play of junior transfer **Larry Jennings** and sophomore **D.J. Munir** in the backcourt will go a long way in determining how well the Seawolves fit.

The 6-1 Jennings (6.3 ppg, 2.8 apg) started 28-of-29 games for St. Joseph's in 1999-2000 and had 25 games where he turned the ball over two or fewer times. He brings leadership and stability to the point on a team that didn't determine its starter until late last preseason.

"He's just a tough customer," Macarchuk said. "He's a tough, hard-nosed player."

The addition of Jennings will also allow the 6-3 Munir (10.8 ppg, 3.3 rpg, 4.0 apg, 1.3 spg) to slide back to his natural shooting guard spot after taking over the point last fall.

"He was our biggest surprise last year," Macarchuk said. "He was supposed to back up [departed shooting guard] Josh Little, but after we made the switch we never took him out unless he got in foul trouble.

"Composed is the word. He's very composed."

Munir, who weighs just 175 pounds, did wear down toward the end of the season, but should flourish with

Jennings as a running mate.

"If he comes back with his head screwed on straight, he's a good player in this conference," Macarchuk said.

Six-foot Sophomore **Lee Church** (1.6 ppg, 1.2 apg), considered a candidate to start at the point last season, will back up both guard spots. Sophomore **Trevor Bryant**, who missed last year with a broken foot, and junior **Patrick Spitler**, a transfer from Canisius, are walk-ons who provide depth in practice.

The addition of Jennings, coupled with the loss of Brisport, means the Seawolves could abandon the deliberate style they played last season and push things a bit more. Several players long on athleticism and short on experience will compete for time on the wing and, in all likelihood, determine how fast and high the Seawolves will fly.

Sophomore **Jairus McCollum** (8.3 ppg, 3.5 rpg, .527 FG) made 18 starts and gained valuable experience last season. A powerful dunker and good mid-range shooter at 6-5, McCollum needs to put forth a more consistent effort to raise his game.

"He's a highlight-film guy," Macarchuk said. "Hopefully he's matured and grown up a little bit."

The Seawolves are also hoping to get some production from sophomore **Aeneas Middleton** (2.2 ppg, 1.6 rpg in 20 games in 1999-2000), a 6-5 transfer from Manhattan.

"He's very athletic," Macarchuk said of Middleton, who is also an aspiring rapper. "He's not a prolific scorer, but he plays with a very high level of energy."

Freshmen **Mike Orfini** and **Pieter Nieuwenhuyzen** will also compete for time on the wing. The smooth-shooting 6-5 Orfini (16.0 ppg, 7.0 rpg) led Gonzaga (Va.) High School to the Washington Catholic Conference championship game. The 6-4 Nieuwenhuyzen (8.0 ppg, 4.0 rpg) is a rugged inside player who prepped at Maine Central Institute last season. He put up solid numbers (15.0 ppg, 8.0 rpg, 6 apg) in 1999-2000, his senior season at Branson (Calif.) High School.

Brisport's departure will be difficult to overcome inside, but the Seawolves return three players and boast a promising freshman to pick up the slack.

Sophomore **Mike Konopka** (6.7 ppg, 3.8 rpg, 1.1 apg) was Stony Brook's best player last preseason before a broken finger sidelined him for seven weeks. At 6-8 and 215, Konopka can put the ball on the floor, but needs to bulk up a bit to withstand the pounding he'll take inside.

"He could be huge for us if he continues to put on weight," Macarchuk said.

A strong finish to his freshman year led to high expectations for **Joakim Eriksson** last season, but injuries contributed to a disappointing season. The 6-8 Eriksson (2.4 ppg, 1.3 rpg) can be an effective high post player when healthy and must play a bigger role for the team to succeed.

"He's a good, solid defensive player," Macarchuk said. "He's very smart and a good passer."

Sophomore **J.B. Bennett** (1.9 ppg, 1.8 ppg) can get up and down the floor and will figure into the mix if he can gain get bigger and stronger.

"He's going to fight for a position," Macarchuk said. "He's 6-7 or 6-8, weighs about six pounds and runs like the wind."

Jon Paul Kobryn, a 6-9 freshman, could turn out to be a pleasant surprise. Kobryn played for Bob Hurley at St. Anthony's of Jersey City (N.J.). He didn't post big numbers, but brings size and an inside presence.

"He's a big, strong kid who never got to shoot the ball," Macarchuk said. "He got the ball off the boards for put backs and shot free throws, that's it. But we're hoping he's going to be able to help us."

2001-2002 SCHEDULE

Nov.	17	@St. John's
	19	@Sacred Heart
	23-24	#George Washington Tournament
	28	@Rutgers
Dec.	1	@Harvard
	4	Cleveland State
	8	@Hofstra
	11	@Villanova
	13	@Army
	22	@Providence
	29	Binghamton
Jan.	2	@Vermont
	6	Maine
	10	@Northeastern
	12	@Boston University

	15	@Binghamton
	18	New Hampshire
	24	Vermont
	26	@Hartford
Feb.	2	Albany
	8	@New Hampshire
	10	@Maine
	15	Hartford
	17	Northeastern
	21	Boston University
	24	@Albany

@Road Games
#Washington, DC (vs. Binghamton first round; also George Washington, Yale)

BLUE RIBBON ANALYSIS

BACKCOURT	B
BENCH/DEPTH	C
FRONTCOURT	C-
INTANGIBLES	C

When Macarchuk heard the announcement that Stony Brook would be joining the America East Conference this season, he called his core group of players together and thanked them for having faith in his program.

Macarchuk told the players when he recruited them that some day they would join a league, and this was their moment to celebrate a promise delivered. After two seasons as an independent, the Seawolves finally had a league to call their own.

"It's a great feeling going into the season knowing we are going to be playing for something," Macarchuk said. "It gets hard to motivate kids in February when you've got nothing to play for."

Having lost its best player, Brisport, to graduation, Stony Brook enters its initial conference season with questions in the frontcourt, where Eriksson and Konopka will need to be more productive. The guard positions should be solid with St. Joseph's transfer Jennings at the point and Muir at the two spot. Jairus, McCollum and Middleton offer plenty of explosiveness on the wings, which could make the Seawolves fun to watch.

"It's an interesting team," Macarchuk said. "I think we can be OK, but we don't know the league."

With nary a senior on its roster, Stony Brook doesn't have the proven performers of Boston University, Maine or Vermont, but could compete if its young players mesh together. The Seawolves' will need to grow up fast in order to win in a season with one non-conference home game and road games at St. John's, Rutgers, Hofstra and Villanova.

"To win on the road, you've got to be good and you've got to be experienced," Macarchuk said. "I don't know if we are going to be good, but I do know that we are not going to be experienced."

The Seawolves will probably be good enough to finish somewhere in the middle of the conference, which isn't a bad debut.

(S.B.)

Vermont

LOCATION	Burlington, VT
CONFERENCE	America East
LAST SEASON	12-17 (.414)
CONFERENCE RECORD	7-11 (t-7th)
STARTERS LOST/RETURNING	1/4
NICKNAME	Catamounts
COLORS	Green & Gold
HOMECOURT	Roy L. Patrick Gym (3,228)
COACH	Tom Brennan (Georgia '71)
RECORD AT SCHOOL	175-240 (15 years)
CAREER RECORD	221-298 (19 years)
ASSISTANTS	Jesse Agel (Vermont '84)
	Pat Filien (College of St. Rose '93)
	Jeff Rush (Richmond '01)
TEAM WINS (last 5 years)	14-16-11-16-12
RPI (last 5 years)	197-173-234-278-221
2000-01 FINISH	Lost in conference quarterfinal.

Some people around America East may hesitate to discuss the status of the conference now that last season's top three teams, Hofstra, Delaware and Drexel,

have left (along with Towson) for the Colonial Athletic Association.

Tom Brennan isn't one of them.

"For me it's like getting a new job," Brennan said. "It's like getting a shot in the arm."

The excitement builds with each word Brennan speaks, and you can't blame him. The dean of America East coaches leads a squad that returns nine lettermen, three starters and the bulk of its scoring and rebounding.

Vermont, which has never made an NCAA or NIT appearance, would have been competitive with the aforementioned defectors. Without them the Catamounts need to be considered contenders, even though they will be without starting center Matt Sheftic (10.0 ppg, 5.3 rpg, 1.1 apg, 1.4 bpg) who decided in September not to return to the team.

Basically a half-court team that runs selectively, the Catamounts don't have a great deal of quickness and will need to work together in order to shut opponents down and move toward the top of the league.

"We've really got to get better defensively," said Brennan, whose team gave up 77.6 points per game last season. "We're going to change defenses more and we're going to take more chances."

They'll be able to, thanks to an experienced and talented group of big men led by returning starters **Trevor Gaines** and **Grant Anderson**, the top two returning rebounders in the conference.

The 6-7 senior Gaines (12.9 ppg, 7.6 rpg, 1.3 apg, .505 FG) is a two-year co-captain who enters his third season as a starter ranked second in points and first in rebounds among the league's active players.

"He's a warrior," Brennan said. "He's a tremendous defender. He's the one guy we've got that can really, really guard."

Gaines can also step out and make shots. His only glaring weakness is at the free-throw line, where he is a career .569 shooter.

Anderson, a 6-7 junior, overcame a slow start (1.8 ppg, 3.2 rpg) where he played just 10 minutes per game to become one of Vermont's better players (5.7 ppg, 5.9 rpg, 1.3 apg, 1.0 spg). He is also best near the basket (.541 FG) where he can convert offensive rebounds into points.

"He's very solid," Brennan said. "He's a great offensive rebounder with a real nose for the ball."

Sheftic (10.0 ppg, 5.3 rpg, 1.1 apg, 1.4 bpg), a local product from nearby Essex, Junction, Vt., is certainly doing everything he can to be the best he can be.

Senior co-captain **Corry McLaughlin**, junior **Scotty Jones** and freshmen **Taylor Coppenrath** and **Germain Njila** provide the depth up front. The loss of Sheftic will mean McLaughlin, Jones and Coppenrath will need to take on larger roles.

The 6-9 McLaughlin (3.4 ppg, 2.4 rpg,) is a shot maker who has embraced his role as a reserve and become a solid leader and contributor. The transfer from Fordham is in line to become just the second five-time member of the America East's academic honor roll and is an example of the progress Vermont basketball has made.

"Ten years ago he would have been a star for me here," Brennan said. "But what he's become is a tremendous leader who has never quit or complained and has set an example for everyone else to follow.

The 6-7 Jones (4.4 ppg, 5.1 rpg, 1.0 bpg) has also learned to make the most of his time and provide valuable minutes. He has played in 57 straight games and will take over the starting center spot vacated by Sheftic.

The 6-8 Coppenrath, Vermont's high school player of the year at St. Johnsbury Academy (25.0 ppg, 10.0 rpg) in 2000, red-shirted last season to build his strength and could push for minutes.

"I think he was the steal of the draft last year," Brennan said.

Njila, from Cameroon, is the first African native to play for the Catamounts. A good leaper at 6-5, he put up big numbers at The Master's School (21.0 ppg, 14.0 rpg) in West Simsbury, Conn., and could contribute on the glass.

T.J. Sorrentine (14.8 ppg, 2.9 rpg, 5.5 apg, 1.6 spg), a 5-11 sophomore, staked his claim at the point as a freshman last fall and should follow in the Catamounts' fine tradition at that position. The America East Rookie of the Year, Sorrentine debuted with 24 points at Cleveland State, and led the league in assists.

"He's a stud," Brennan said.

Sorrentine also showed uncharacteristic poise for a freshman by taking better care of the ball than expected. He was the only Vermont player to start all 29 games.

"He really bought into what we were doing and was as solid as a rock," Brennan said. "He really protected the ball and his understanding of the game and his play was better than I thought it would be as a freshman."

Expect Sorrentine's scoring to increase with the graduation of shooting guard Tony Orciari (17.7 ppg), a member of the All-America East first team the last two seasons.

Junior **Corey Sullivan** (3.6 ppg, 1.2 rpg) could be the favorite to replace Orciari, Vermont's No. 2 all-time scorer with 1,743 points. Sullivan, 6-6, added 25 pounds of muscle in the off-season and is a dangerous long-range shooter (.343 3PT).

Andre Anderson could be the man at shooting guard. The 6-1, 170-pound Anderson (2.0 ppg) has good quickness and can also play the point. Vermont's depth took a hit when Jed Thibault (1.7 ppg), a 5-11 junior, also left the team in the off-season.

Freshmen **Mike Goia** and **David Hehn** both have good size and range that could earn them playing time on the wing. Goia, 6-4, starred at Somerville (N.J.) High before attending Blair Academy (16.0 ppg, 6.0 apg) last season. Hehn, 6-5, was rated the top shooting guard in Canada by Cage Canada magazine after a big senior season (22.0 ppg, 8.0 rpg, 8.0 apg, 4.0 spg) at St. Christopher's High School in Sarnia, Ontario.

Sophomore walk-on **Jack Phelan** (0.2 ppg), the son of former Hartford coach Jack Phelan, played in 13 games as a freshman and rounds out the backcourt contingent.

2001-2002 SCHEDULE

Nov.	16-17	#Mohegan Sun Classic
	20	@Dartmouth
	24	Cleveland State
	26	@Duquesne
Dec.	2	Lehigh
	5	@Sacred Heart
	18	Harvard
	27-28	##Florida International Tournament
	31	Albany
Jan.	2	Stony Brook
	5	@Boston University
	7	@Northeastern
	11	Maine
	14	New Hampshire
	17	Northeastern
	20	@Hartford
	24	@Stony Brook
	26	@Michigan
Feb.	2	Boston University
	8	@Binghamton
	10	@Albany
	13	Binghamton
	17	@Maine
	22	@New Hampshire
March	2,3,9	###America East Championships

@Road Games
#New Britain, CT (vs. Brown first round; also Bucknell, Central Connecticut)
##Miami, FL (vs. Florida International first round; also Long Island, Ohio)
###Matthews Arena, Boston, MA (Championship game at homecourt of highest seeded team.)

BLUE RIBBON ANALYSIS

BACKCOURT	B
BENCH/DEPTH	B+
FRONTCOURT	A
INTANGIBLES	B+

Given all of the changes—personnel and otherwise—in the league this season, you've got to like Vermont's chances for success.

The Catamounts return three starters from a team that closed last season 8-3 after losing 11 in a row. Gaines and Anderson provide a solid foundation in the frontcourt. Add Sorrentine, last season's America East rookie of the year, at the point, and the nucleus appears very solid.

The graduation of Orciari, a Vermont icon, leaves a void that's not easily filled. Sorrentine and others can pick up the scoring slack, but they will also need to perform when teams are not designing their defenses around stopping someone else.

Speaking of defense, the Catamounts also need to do a better job of playing it. Opponents put the ball in the basket too frequently last season, but this area can be improved through hard work and cooperation.

This is a team with far more positives than negatives. The Catamounts have many reasons to be optimistic. They just have to do it on the floor.

"We've played 100 years and we have not won yet, but we're close," Brennan said. "Coaches say it doesn't mean anything, but if we were ever picked first in our league I would get my wall papered with it because it's something that's never been done here."

There's no need to redecorate the office yet, but Brennan's team certainly has the players to challenge for the top spot in the conference during the regular season and string together three wins in the tournament. As he says, they just haven't done it yet.

(S.B.)

Clemson

LOCATION	Clemson, SC
CONFERENCE	Atlantic Coast
LAST SEASON	12-19 (.387)
CONFERENCE RECORD	2-14 (9th)
STARTERS LOST/RETURNING	1/4
NICKNAME	Tigers
COLORS	Orange & Purple
HOMECOURT	Littlejohn Coliseum (11,020)
COACH	Larry Shyatt (College of Wooster '73)
RECORD AT SCHOOL	42-54 (3 years)
CAREER RECORD	61-53 (4 years)
ASSISTANTS	Darren Tillis (Paul Quinn College '96)
	Matt Driscoll (Slippery Rock '92)
	Bobby Hussey (Appalachian State '63)
TEAM WINS (last 5 years)	23-18-20-10-12
RPI (last 5 years)	11-28-98-168-168
2000-01 FINISH	Lost in conference quarterfinal.

Larry Shyatt came to Clemson three years ago with his eyes wide open.

"When I took the job, no one had a clearer picture than me of the problems," he said. "No one knew the Clemson history, the current program better than I did. We had a nice six-senior, two-junior team. We knew that within two years, we would have to replace 11 of the 13 players."

Shyatt, an assistant at Clemson under Rick Barnes before taking the head-coaching job at Wyoming for one year, also understood that he was inheriting a team with some serious off-court problems, problems he still won't discuss. It's taken Shyatt three seasons to not only replace the talent, but to clean up the behind-the-scenes mess.

Apparently, those problems disappeared in the off-season with the departure of four upperclassmen. Junior Will Solomon, the team's top scorer and a two-time All-ACC player, jumped to the NBA, while veterans Dustin Braddock, Pasha Bains and Chucky Gilmore all transferred.

Their exit, combined with the graduation of injury-plagued center **Adam Allenspach**, leaves Shyatt with a team that's painfully young.

"We have eight underclassmen," he said. "I like it. I like them. We've eliminated some serious problems in our program. Because of that, it's the best summer we've experienced socially, academically and most of all basketball-wise. It's the first summer since I went to Wyoming that I enjoyed for 12 weeks. Every player was here, in school full time, without problems and healthy.

"That's something for us to start with."

But is Shyatt starting in time? After two lackluster seasons—seasons marked by injuries and those off-the-court problems—how good is his job security?

"If your goal is to be a high echelon team for a long period of time, rather than a short period of time, probably the most important items are patience and stability," he said. "I'm not a quick fix guy."

Shyatt is also an optimist who insists that the Tigers have better players—and better people—coming into the program than ever before. In fact, he claims that his last two recruiting classes stack up with anybody in the ACC.

"As a group, I wouldn't trade with any team in the ACC," Shyatt said. "In the eight [freshmen and sophomores] we have, we've combined not only a higher level of talent, but also a far better group of individuals off the floor."

ATLANTIC COAST

BLUE RIBBON FORECAST
1. Duke
2. Maryland
3. Virginia
4. North Carolina
5. Wake Forest
6. North Carolina State
7. Georgia Tech
8. Florida State
9. Clemson

TOP 40
Duke, Maryland, North Carolina Virginia and Wake Forest are ranked among the 2001-2002 *Blue Ribbon* Top 40. Extended profiles can be found in the Top 40 section of *Blue Ribbon*.

ALL-CONFERENCE TEAM
G-Jason Williams, JR, Duke
G-Juan Dixon, SR, Maryland
F-Josh Howard, JR, Wake Forest
F-Travis Watson, JR, Virginia
F/C-Lonny Baxter, SR, Maryland

PLAYER OF THE YEAR
Jason Williams, JR, Duke

NEWCOMER OF THE YEAR
Julius Hodge, FR, North Carolina State

2000-2001 POSTSEASON PARTICIPANTS
Postseason Record: 11-5 (.687)
NCAA
Duke (National champion)
Maryland (Final Four)
North Carolina (Second round)
Georgia Tech
Virginia
Wake Forest

TOP BACKCOURTS
1. Duke
2. Maryland
3. Virginia

TOP FRONTCOURTS
1. Maryland
2. Duke
3. Virginia

INSIDE THE NUMBERS
2000-2001 Conference RPI: 3rd (of 31)
Conference RPI (last five years): 1-1-2-4-3

DID YOU KNOW?
Last season, Duke won its third national championship (eighth in league history) and Maryland made its first-ever trip to the Final Four. It was the third time since 1990 that the ACC has sent two teams to the national semifinals. Georgia Tech and Duke both went in 1990 and North Carolina and Duke went in 1991. ... Only two players return from last year's first-team All-ACC unit, Maryland's Juan Dixon and Duke's Jason Williams. Gone are ACC Co-Players of the Year Shane Battier of Duke and Joseph Forte of North Carolina, and Georgia Tech center Alvin Jones. It was the first time in league history that two players shared the player-of-the-year award. ... Georgia Tech coach Paul Hewitt was chosen the ACC Coach of the Year, after leading the Yellow Jackets to a 17-13 mark in his first year as head coach. Interestingly enough, another first-year coach in the league, North Carolina's Matt Doherty, was chosen the Associated Press National Coach of the Year. Doherty became the first rookie coach in league history to lead his team to the ACC's regular-season championship. ... The ACC will have a record 145 games televised this year, including the league's unusual Sunday night package on Fox Sports Net. A total of 19 games will be shown on Sunday nights, including some men's and women's double-headers. In all, 70 of the league's 72 regular-season games will be televised as well as all eight games in the ACC Tournament.

(T.P.)

Last year's three freshmen performed at a very high level—in some cases out of necessity. A combination of Allenspach's back problems, a broken foot that sidelined Gilmore and off-season knee surgery that limited 6-8, 260-pound junior **Ray Henderson** (5.4 ppg, 4.8 rpg) to sporadic duty, forced 6-7, 265-pound **Chris Hobbs** (7.3 ppg, 6.3 rpg) to shoulder most of the inside scoring and rebounding load.

Hobbs, coming off an ACL injury that forced him to sit out most of his senior year at East Chapel Hill (N.C.) High School, responded with an impressive effort that earned a spot on the All-ACC Freshman Team. He recorded six double-doubles and led all ACC freshmen in rebounding.

Shyatt believes Hobbs can be even better.

"I don't think Chris played to his strengths last season," Shyatt said. "He had an outstanding freshman season in some people's eyes, but not mine. Chris, coming off an entire year of rehab, was probably close to 25 pounds overweight and six months behind in conditioning. Clearly, his next three years could be even more outstanding. When this guy gets in condition, look out."

Shyatt expects to give Hobbs and a healthy Henderson (who has gotten his weight down from 288 to 260 pounds) help from his latest recruiting class. **Sharrod Ford**, a 6-9, 210-pound shot blocker who averaged 16 points and 12 rebounds at Hargrave (Va.) Military Academy, is the most heralded, especially after turning in an impressive performance for the United States team at the World Global Games in Dallas in July.

"Sharrod Ford is probably the best inside athlete we've recruited in the last decade," Shyatt said. "Someone like Sharrod Ford can make a difference."

But Shyatt warned that 6-8 freshman **Jemere Hendrix**, a late pickup from Covington, Ga, who originally signed with Notre Dame, might be the surprise of the group with his ability to go inside or outside.

"He is probably our best athlete coast to coast," Shyatt said. "He's really a multi-dimensional athlete, a guy who can rebound and bring it and also quite capable of hitting the three."

In contrast to last season, Shyatt has plenty of frontcourt depth this year. He has 6-10, 240-pound freshman **Steve Allen** of Ft. Lauderdale, Fla., and 6-6, 260-pound **Olu Babalola** from London, England, to provide inside muscle. And 6-10 junior **Tomas Nagys** (3.7 ppg, 4.1 rpg) from Lithuania will be trying to build on a late-season surge that saw him improve his scoring from 1.8 a game to 7.1, his shooting from 26 percent to 47 percent and his rebounding from 3.2 to 5.7—all over the last 10 games.

"Tomas was named our most improved player by unanimous vote," Shyatt said. "He seemingly came to life in that North Carolina game and from that point has a much higher level of confidence in his offensive skills. But it was on defense and his ability to control his emotions that made the difference in his last eight to 10 games."

The North Carolina game mentioned by Shyatt may turn out to be a key moment in the program. The Tigers, buried in the ACC basement, stunned the nation's No. 1 ranked team in Littlejohn on Feb. 18. Significantly, the Tigers did it without a major contribution from Solomon. Instead, Shyatt got contributions from a lot different players—most of them back this year.

"That game should be a strong signal sent that not only can it happen, but it should happen ... and it should happen more often with the young people we have," Shyatt said. "That should place expectations on them that they're readier than people think."

Shyatt's expectations are high because he's finally got the kind of backcourt he wants to play with, one that features two or even three primary ball handlers in the lineup at one time.

The nominal point guard is 6-0 junior **Edward Scott**

(7.3 ppg, 3.4 rpg, 4.2 apg), appointed as Clemson's first captain since Terrell McIntyre and Tom Wideman shared the job in 1999.

"He represents everything I'm looking for in a Tiger," Shyatt said. "He's done an outstanding job through difficult time."

Scott had to play as a freshman with a pin in his broken foot. He never complained and never made excuses. That's what impresses Shyatt most.

"For the next two years, we have a terrific role model and a good focal point for a young group," the Tiger coach said.

Scott, a good defender who's careful with the ball, offers a sharp contrast to his running mate in the backcourt. The only thing holding back 6-1 sophomore **Tony Stockman** (12.0 ppg, 1.9 rpg, 2.6 apg) is, in Shyatt's words, "his carelessness."

"That's the only thing separating him from stardom," the Clemson coach said. "Carelessness did not allow him that stardom. I equate that to youth and immaturity. I think he has the capability of exploding on the scene this year."

Stockman, the leading freshman scorer in the ACC, finished second to Chris Duhon in the ACC rookie of the year voting and joined Hobbs on the league all-freshman team. He's a natural point guard—maybe even more creative than Scott. But to achieve the stardom Shyatt predicts, the Ohio native will have to improve his 37.4 percent shooting and his 1.2 to 1.0 assist-to-turnover ratio.

If Clemson needs more ball handling help, Shyatt can turn to his most heralded recruit—6-4 **Chey Christie**. The younger brother of former Clemson standout Tony Christie averaged 25.4 points and 7.8 rebounds as a senior at Biloxi (Miss.) High School. But he really established himself after the season, earning MVP honors at the Capital Classic and for the U.S. team in the World Global Games.

"He really gives us two assets we haven't had—size in the backcourt and athleticism," Shyatt said. "He's capable of a 360 or a lob dunk, someone who can rebound and start a break."

Christie will play in the backcourt and will share some time on the wing with 6-5 sophomore **Dwon Clifton** (3.9 ppg, 2.6) who came to Clemson from High Point, N.C., with the reputation as a great long-range shooter, but made just 17-of-58 three-point shots. Clifton played well enough in the other phases of the game to start 18 games as a freshman, but he'll need to find his shooting touch to become a quality ACC player.

"Dwon got what every kid coming into college wants—immediate time," Shyatt said. "But he also was not on an overly successful team. That probably played into his lack of confidence at times."

Shyatt believes that the time Clifton spent working out over the summer with such former Clemson standouts as Greg Buckner, Merle Code and Tony Christie helped restore his confidence.

"That's played a very important role in his maturity," he said. "I look for Dwon to have a chance to grow."

The only senior on the roster is 6-5 **Jamar McKnight** (3.4 ppg, 1.3 rpg), who is in just his second year at Clemson after transferring from Northeast (Miss.) Community College. The high-flying wingman had some spectacular dunks last season, but he'll have to elevate his shooting and his defense to take minutes away from Clifton and Christie on the wing.

Walker Holt (0.3 ppg, 0.1 rpg), a 6-3 junior, is a former walk-on who has earned a scholarship in each of the last two seasons. He and 6-3 junior walk-on **Jermel Douglas** (0.1 ppg, 0.1 rpg) are likely to make their contribution in practice.

2001-2002 SCHEDULE

Nov.	17	#Morris Brown
	24	Wofford
	27	@Penn State
	29	Coastal Carolina
Dec.	2	@Duke
	5	Appalachian State
	8	South Carolina
	15	Elon
	18	Winthrop
	22	Charleston Southern
	28	@Hartford
Jan.	2	Yale
	8	@Georgia Tech
	12	@Wake Forest
	15	North Carolina State
	20	@Maryland
Feb.	3	Duke
	10	@Virginia
	13	Wake Forest
	16	@North Carolina State
	20	Maryland
	23	Florida State
	27	@NorthCarolina
March	7-10	##ACC Tournament

@Road Games
#Paradise Tournament, Virgin Islands (vs. LaSalle in second round on Nov. 19; also Eastern Michigan, Miami, FL, UAB ; championship and two consolation games on Nov. 20)
##Charlotte Coliseum, Charlotte, NC

BLUE RIBBON ANALYSIS

BACKCOURT	B
BENCH/DEPTH	B
FRONTCOURT	B-
INTANGIBLES	B

No team in the ACC has a more dismal basketball heritage than Clemson. The Tigers have never won an ACC championship, have never gone to the Final Four and have finished in the league's top three just six times in 48 years—and never twice in a row.

Shyatt is trying to lay the foundation for a program that can go where no Clemson team has ever gone before. But to do that, he needs time for his youngsters to mature.

"What you'd love to have in your program is a combination of talent and maturity," Shyatt said. "We lack maturity."

It's going to be difficult for the Tigers to climb very far out of the ACC basement with such a young team. But Clemson should be a much more difficult hurdle for the league's upper echelon than a year ago. Although Will Solomon was an NBA talent, his unbalanced a young team. Shyatt, reluctant to criticize his star, nevertheless believes the Tigers will be better without him.

Clemson will clearly be better with the addition of so much frontcourt depth. And if youngsters such as Stockman, Hobbs and Clifton blossom in their sophomore seasons as Shyatt hopes, the Tigers may make real progress.

(A.F.)

Florida State

LOCATION	Tallahassee, FL
CONFERENCE	Atlantic Coast
LAST SEASON	9-21 (.300)
CONFERENCE RECORD	4-12 (8th)
STARTERS LOST/RETURNING	4/1
NICKNAME	Seminoles
COLORS	Garnet & Gold
HOMECOURT	Tallahassee-Leon County Civic Center (12,500)
COACH	Steve Robinson (Radford '81)
RECORD AT SCHOOL	52-67 (4 years)
CAREER RECORD	98-87 (6 years)
ASSISTANTS	Coleman Crawford (North Alabama '75)
	Rob Wilkes (Stetson '93)
	Stephen Giles (North Carolina '90)
TEAM WINS (last 5 years)	20-18-13-12-9
RPI (last 5 years)	42-40-55-122-172
2000-01 FINISH	Lost in ACC play-in game.

At some point, Florida State's basketball free-fall must end. In a span of four seasons, the Seminoles' basketball fortunes have plummeted precipitously from 18 wins and a surprise NCAA Tournament berth in 1998 to nine wins and the most losses (21) in school history last season.

"I think the ball's got to bounce our way a little bit," FSU coach Steve Robinson said, knowing that if it doesn't, his tenure in Tallahassee could end in March after five seasons.

Based on the preseason smile Robinson has been flashing with regularity—a sight mostly unseen over the last three seasons—the ball may already be bouncing the Seminoles' way.

For the first time since his inaugural FSU team came within overtime of advancing to the Sweet 16, Robinson has a reason to smile other than blind optimism. From his potentially precarious perch, Robinson likes the look of his team, which was fortified by a second consecutive strong recruiting class.

"There are certainly some positive signs out there with our ball club," Robinson said. "The last two years, certainly everybody's concern was quality of players, or level of talent. I think the last two years—we've brought in two classes that have helped fill the need. We have good players in our program."

That may come as a surprise to those who haven't been watching carefully. Robinson's first two recruiting classes were filled with projects, 'tweeners and players who weren't capable of lifting the Seminoles from the ACC's second division. Gradually he's made in-roads on the recruiting trail, first adding depth, followed by front-line talent. Still far removed from the upper reaches of the league—namely Duke, Maryland and Virginia—the Seminoles appear to have enough parts to pull together their first winning season since '98.

And make no mistake, securing a winning season was foremost on Robinson's mind when he put together a schedule that's embarrassingly soft by ACC standards, though certainly understandable. Florida, whom the Seminoles visit in the season-opener, is the lone team among 11 non-conference opponents that advanced to the NCAA Tournament last season.

With eight home dates in the first six weeks of the season against the likes of Savannah State, Elon, Western Carolina and Campbell, Robinson will have ample opportunity to shake down his deepest squad to date.

"There's enough interchangeable parts there that we're going to have to go with the five guys that are going to do the best job of playing together," said Robinson, who has vowed to scrap the systematic position-by-numbers terminology. "I think that can be a big strength of this team."

Of course there will be one exception to that rule. Senior point guard **Delvon Arrington** (11.5 ppg, 4.8 apg.), a partial qualifier who has been with Robinson since Day One, earned his fourth year of eligibility by graduating over the summer. Barring injury the 5-11 speed-merchant will become FSU's all-time assists leader, providing the engine that drives the 'Noles for a fourth consecutive year.

"Going into last season we felt like we had a lot of guys who had a little time, but we didn't know how they were going to respond," Robinson said. "Delvon is pretty solid and steady, but you don't know about the other four spots. That's the way the year went. Going into this year, looking at the guys returning who played and played a lot—you've got eight guys right there who all got their feet more than wet."

Though Arrington has cemented the only starting spot, six others have earned at least one start in their career. That said, it may well be the five newcomers who nudge the 'Noles into the positive side on the won-loss ledger.

Robinson's recruiting class could be his strongest to date. The group was given a major lift with the addition of 6-8 freshman swingman **Anthony Richardson**. Richardson, the first McDonald's All-American signed by FSU since 1994, is a partial qualifier whose appeal to the NCAA for immediate eligibility was granted in late September.

The potential addition of Richardson, who averaged 18 points and nine rebounds last season for Leesville Road (N.C.) High, could substantially enhance the Seminoles' standing in the ACC.

Even if Richardson had been forced to sit, the Seminoles made significant gains. FSU gained length and athleticism with the addition of 6-11 junior college center **Trevor Harvey**, who averaged 13 points and 6.5 rebounds for Marshalltown (Iowa) Community College last season. Freshman forward **Adam Waleskowski** (6-9) is expected to provide some much-needed toughness and scoring in the post, after averaging 15.1 points and 10 rebounds at Kettering (Ohio) Bishop Alter last season.

Sophomore **J.D. Bracy**, who sat out last season as a partial qualifier, is expected to immediately challenge for a starting spot in the backcourt with the graduation of lone senior Adrian Crawford. A prolific high school scorer (27.3 ppg) out of Kissimmee (Fla.) Osceola, Bracy is a serious upgrade athletically from Crawford. Robinson said Bracy was the one of the team's "hardest workers" in the off-season, adding 15 pounds to his 6-4, 205-pound frame.

The wildcard among newcomers is freshman football quarterback **Adrian McPherson**. A coveted two-sport recruit by North Carolina, the 6-4 McPherson averaged 35 points for Bradenton (Fla.) Southeast last season, en route to becoming the first athlete in Florida history to win Mr. Football and Mr. Basketball honors. McPherson's contributions, however, figure to be limited by his backup status for the bowl-bound football team, which may keep him off the court until early January.

While there will be significant early contributions from the newcomers, the continued development of the returnees will undoubtedly be key if the 'Noles are to make a move. Among that group, no player has made more significant move than junior center **Nigel "Big Jelly" Dixon**. By paring nearly 90 pounds from his massive 6-10 frame, the 330-pounder is no longer a novelty act only capable of providing assistance in hockey shift-like spurts. Dixon could double his 6.7 point, five rebound output of a year ago merely by increasing his minutes.

"He's a different player; a different person," said Robinson, who expects to get more from Dixon, now that there is less of him.

This time last season sophomore **Michael Joiner** was faced with the prospect of living up to his reputation as the best recruit Robinson had signed to date. Joiner did just that. Despite playing out of position as a 6-7 power forward through much of the year, he became the first Seminole since Bob Sura to land a spot on the ACC's All-Rookie team, averaging 9.3 points and a team-leading six rebounds a game.

With the addition of Harvey and Waleskowski in the post, Joiner should become even more productive with extended minutes on the wing.

Joiner wasn't the only first-year FSU player to prove that he could play in the league. After sitting out his freshman season as a partial qualifier 6-10 junior **Mike Mathews** came into his own down the stretch last season. The ACC's top returning shot blocker (44), Mathews averaged 7.3 points and 3.1 rebounds despite making only nine starts. A solid shooter in the 15-foot range from either the high post or along the baseline, Mathews' .466 field-goal percentage was second best on the team.

"They [Joiner and Mathews] have proven they can play in this league," Robinson said.

So, too, has senior guard **Monte Cummings**. Coming off the bench in 28-of-29 games, the junior college transfer established himself as the league's top sixth man, averaging 10.7 points and 1.8 assists, which ranked second on the team.

A slasher with quick hops, Cummings provided the 'Noles with much-needed energy. Though his mid-range jumper is solid, the 6-4 senior must improve his three-point shooting (.214) to have a realistic shot at grabbing a starting spot.

Consistency will also be a key for senior co-captain **Antwuan Dixon**, a 6-5 wing player who has established himself as the Seminoles' top defender. Perhaps the team's top athlete, Dixon has improved steadily at the offensive end throughout his career, capped by last season's bests of 8.7 points, to go with 5.8 rebounds. Still, he's been known to go extended stretches without significant scoring contributions, then break out with a big performance, as he did in the season finale with 23 points against Clemson in the ACC Tournament.

Sophomore wing **Andrew Wilson** (4.3 ppg., 1.7 rpg.) may have his minutes squeezed with the influx of talent on the perimeter, unless he can bolster his .336 field goal (.217 3PT) shooting. One of the team's top shooters in practice, the 6-6 Wilson must carry that over to game time. If not, his high-energy play on the defensive end may be his most significant contribution.

Robinson has no idea what to expect from 7-0 senior **David Anderson** (1.1 ppg, 1.2 rpg.), who never recovered from a preseason hamstring tear. Unless Anderson can regain his confidence, he will be relegated to the end of the bench, watching Nigel Dixon, Mathews and Harvey down on the low block.

If the Seminoles have one glaring weakness, it's the lack of a proven backup to Arrington at the point. Six-foot-two sophomore **Ryan Lowery** (0.5 ppg, 1.4 apg) was not the answer in his first season, eventually losing his backup role to 5-11 junior walk-on **Marcell Haywood** (0.6 ppg, 0.6 apg) over the final weeks of the season. Haywood will likely get the first crack at spelling Arrington, but someone must step up here.

2001-2002 SCHEDULE

Nov.	16	@Florida
	20	Savannah State
	23	Elon
	28	@Northwestern
Dec.	4	Birmingham Southern
	8	Western Carolina
	16	@Wake Forest
	19	Cleveland State
	22	American
	27	Virginia Tech
	29	Campbell
Jan.	2	@South Florida
	6	Duke
	8	@North Carolina State
	16	North Carolina
	19	@Virginia
	24	Clemson
	26	@Maryland
	30	@Georgia Tech
Feb.	2	Wake Forest
	7	@Duke
	10	North Carolina State
	17	@North Carolina
	20	Virginia
	23	@Clemson
	27	Maryland
March	2	Georgia Tech
	7-10	#ACC Tournament

@Road Games
#Charlotte Coliseum, Charlotte, NC

BLUE RIBBON ANALYSIS

BACKCOURT	B
BENCH/DEPTH	B
FRONTCOURT	C+
INTANGIBLES	C+

There is no denying the Seminoles' improvement in terms of talent. A stellar recruiting class—especially after super recruit Richardson was declared eligible in late September—is proof of that. And with 10 other returnees, experience becomes a positive for the first time since Robinson's initial year.

"I look at our potential to have very solid depth," Robinson said. "I think we can be as athletic as any team on the floor we play."

On the surface, that comment would seem to be a reach, but there is little doubt that the 'Noles should be able to run and jump with just about everyone in the league. But if FSU is going to turn things around, it must improve its field goal percentage—.427 from the field and .319 from three-point range—and field-goal percentage defense (.453 and .395).

Robinson is hopeful that last season has strengthened his team's resolve. To his credit, there were very few nights the out-manned 'Noles just failed to show up. And it's not a total reach to say the season may have turned out modestly better had FSU not suffered consecutive five-point home losses to Minnesota and Furman.

"We just never seemed to get regrouped enough," Robinson said. "I think it [past adversity] can be a positive factor for us [depending on] how we channel it. Hopefully we can use those things in a positive fashion."

Robinson won't allow off-the-floor distractions to derail this team, particularly his job status should the 'Noles struggle in ACC play.

"As I look at this season, it's not about me," he said. "It's about our players and our team and how well they can perform. I'm going to coach them as hard as I've ever coached. Whatever I have to give, I give that. I've always based my life on being a guy that was not afraid to work hard."

That hard work has already paid off in some ways. The Seminoles are beginning to attract the kind of talent necessary to compete, and the university has not backed off its commitment. A new basketball practice complex is under construction.

Ultimately the Seminoles' performance on the floor will determine whether Robinson ever has the opportunity to direct a workout in that building.

(B.T.)

Georgia Tech

LOCATION	Atlanta, GA
CONFERENCE	Atlantic Coast
LAST SEASON	17-13 (.567)
CONFERENCE RECORD	8-8 (5th)
STARTERS LOST/RETURNING	3/2
NICKNAME	Yellow Jackets
COLORS	Gold & Black
HOMECOURT	Alexander Memorial Coliseum (10,000)
COACH	Paul Hewitt (St. John Fisher '85)
RECORD AT SCHOOL	17-13 (1 year)
CAREER RECORD	83-40 (4 years)
ASSISTANTS	Dean Keener (Davidson '88)
	Willie Reese (Georgia Tech '89)
	Cliff Warren (Mount St. Mary's '90)
TEAM WINS (last 5 years)	9-19-15-13-17
RPI (last 5 years)	100-62-57-149-39
2000-01 FINISH	Lost in NCAA first round.

Paul Hewitt was not Dave Braine's first choice to replace Bobby Cremins when the silver-haired one departed after the 1999-2000 season. But after watching the relatively unknown young coach work miracles in his first season at Georgia Tech, the Yellow Jackets' athletic director must have sent thank-you notes to the big names who turned him down a year earlier.

How many coaches could have taken the remnants of a 13-17 team—one that lost a first-round draft pick to the NBA, plus its No. 2 scorer—and produced a 17-13 NCAA Tournament team in his first season in Atlanta? Hewitt not only did it, but he did it by beating seven NCAA Tournament teams, including Maryland, Kentucky, UCLA and Virginia—the latter twice!

Is it any wonder Hewitt outdistanced another first-year coach (UNC's Matt Doherty) as the ACC Coach of the Year?

It was a dramatic turnaround for a school that was desperate to stop its slide toward basketball oblivion. Cremins, who made the Yellow Jackets a national power in the '80s and early '90s, lost his recruiting magic and endured a string of sub-par seasons before being forced into retirement after the 1999 season. He didn't leave Hewitt a lot to work with. There were no Kenny Andersons, no John Salleys, no Stephon Marburys on the roster.

All Hewitt inherited was a talented, but underachieving big man, an erratic point guard and a bunch of non-descript players who had never won anything significant before he got there.

Even less remains this season. No ACC team lost more to graduation than the Yellow Jackets—three starters and five of the top seven scorers are missing from last year's team. Even with five freshmen entering the program, Hewitt has just 11 players on scholarship and one of those may not be able to play this season.

"We were definitely strapped by the 5/8 rule," said Hewitt, who made an unsuccessful appeal to the NCAA to get a waiver to bring in another big man who wanted to play for the Jackets.

What Hewitt does have going for him is the memory of last year's success.

"Last year, we had to convince our players that some of the things we were asking them to do were necessary," Hewitt said. "Now there's no doubt in anybody's mind. They had a great experience last year and now they believe in us."

Hewitt is curious to see how his second Georgia Tech team performs. He has upgraded his talent, but at the cost of considerable experience.

"We have more depth than we had last year, more athleticism overall," he said. "I like the talent, but it's going to take time to mature and grow. Obviously, we lost a tremendous defensive and offensive presence in the low post with Alvin Jones."

Jones, a 6-11 center who blossomed as a first-team All-ACC player under Hewitt's tutelage, will leave the biggest hole in the Georgia Tech lineup. His 13.4 points a game won't be that hard to replace, but his ACC-best 10.4 rebounds a game and his 101 blocked shots will be.

"You can't replace what Alvin gave us on defense," Hewitt said. "What we certainly can do is be a better unit defensively and not reply on one person."

Hewitt originally signed prep big man Michael Southall to replace Jones. But Southall, a former Kentucky recruit before getting into trouble with the law, was cut loose by the Jackets last spring after he ran into more legal trouble. That left Hewitt with a huge hole in his recruiting class. He filled it midway through the summer when he landed **Luke Schenscher**, a 7-0, 230-pound Australian who was thought to be headed for Boise State.

"He's a long, skilled player," Hewitt said. "He'll be a rugged-type player."

Schenscher, a 19-year-old from Hope Forest, Australia, was the youngest member of Australia's Gold Medal team in the East Asian Games in Osaka, Japan last spring. He also made summer trips to Croatia, the United States and another trip to Japan.

"He's a very finesse, offensive-type player," Frank Arsego of the Australian Institute of Sports told the Macon Telegraph. "You're looking at a guy with a range of post moves, including jump hooks and a sky hook. He runs the floor well for a big guy. And he's got really good hands."

Hewitt has no doubts about Schenscher's ability. His big concern is keeping the young big man fresh.

"He's good enough to help us," Hewitt said. "I just don't know how he'll hold up physically. He's played a lot of basketball in the last year and I have to be careful not to wear him down in preseason."

If Schenscher has any trouble establishing himself as a major contributor right away, Hewitt may have to use 6-5, 225-pound sophomore **Clarence Moore** (4.8 ppg, 3.9 rpg as a freshman in 1999-2000) as a post player. Moore, a strong leaper who plays bigger than his height, missed last season with a broken foot. In an ideal world, he would perform as an oversized wing, rather than as an undersized power forward.

But Hewitt's options are limited in the post. His best big man might turn out to be 6-8, 245-pound freshman **Ed Nelson** of Ft. Lauderdale, Fla. Voted Florida's prep player of the year by USA Today, Nelson averaged 26 points and 11 rebounds as he helped St. Thomas Aquinas to the state 5-A title.

"Ed Nelson is a classic four man," Hewitt said. "He shoots the ball very well, he's extremely athletic and he works very, very hard. Because of circumstances, he will have to play. He's a big, strong kid. He can hold his own."

Hewitt also believes that 6-7, 215-pound sophomore **Robert Brooks** (2.8 ppg, 3.0 rpg) can elevate his contributions after being a spot player as a freshman. The slender forward from Saginaw, Mich. has added 20 pounds to his frame in the off-season, but Hewitt said he still needs to get stronger.

"Nobody works harder than him, but he's still got a ways to go," Hewitt said. "If he can put on the weight where he can get down there and bang a little bit and rebound a little better, he's going to be a very good player in this program."

The Tech coach is hoping that 6-8 senior **Michael Isenhower** (0.9 ppg, 1.0 rpg) will also be able to provide some solid minutes in the post.

Unfortunately, the former transfer from the Air Force Academy is still having trouble with the nerve problem in his leg that limited him a year ago. Even off-season surgery failed to correct the problem.

"He is still not healed," Hewitt said. "I don't know that he'll be able to play."

The Georgia Tech coach has a lot more options on the perimeter—so many, in fact, that he might use four small guys with one post player at times.

"You may see some unusual lineups," Hewitt said. "Versatility is something we like. We can play a lot of different combinations."

That's part of the running, pressing style that Hewitt used to average 22 wins a year at Siena. He wants to bring the same style to Georgia Tech and with the addition of three physically gifted freshmen wing players to the roster, he's getting the kind of athletes who can execute his system.

"The roster may be more suited for my style, but it's also very, very young," he said. "There's a reason why people favor senior dominated teams."

It's the same reason Hewitt is so enamored by the one senior who will play a major role for the Jackets this season—senior point guard **Tony Akins** (14.5 ppg, 3.5 rpg, 4.3 apg). The 5-11, 182-pound native of Lilburn, Ga., was a wild, erratic player in his first two years, but has developed into a steady, smart playmaker with a deadly three-point touch.

"He's matured as much as anybody I've ever been around," Hewitt said. "To see him go from being a quiet person to a leader ... it's just great to see."

Akins improved his consistency last season, hitting double figures in 24-of-30 games and producing more assists than turnovers 20 times. He shot a career best .419 on three-pointers, ranking third in the ACC.

"I think we've got one of the best point guards in the country," Hewitt said. "Particularly the second half of last season, he showed everybody in the ACC the quality of point guard he can be. We're going to need him to pick

up where he left off in order for us to be successful."

The graduation of part-time point guards Darryl LaBarrie and T.J. Vines leaves Hewitt without an experienced backup for Akins. However, versatile 6-6 freshman **Anthony McHenry** (known as Anthony Vasser when he averaged 14 points and six rebounds to lead Woodlawn High School in Birmingham to the Alabama 6-A title) counts point guard as one of his three positions, along with wing guard and small forward.

"He can do a lot of things," Hewitt said of McHenry. "He's very unselfish and he loves to pass the ball. We're starting to get more of the look we're trying to recruit in the long perimeter players and the versatile players. We're going to be the type of team, as this program evolves to where we want it that has great depth and versatile players."

Two more members of Hewitt's latest recruiting class also qualify as multi-position players. **Barry Elder**, a 6-4 wing from Madison, Ga., and **Isma'il Muhammad**, a 6-6 wing player from Atlanta, should fit Hewitt's plan perfectly. Elder, who averaged 26 points, six rebounds and two steals as a senior at Morgan County High School, is a physically gifted wing with a three-point shooting touch and the strength (he benches more than 300 pounds) to score down low. Muhammad, who averaged 28 points, 14 rebounds, six assists and four steals as a senior at W.D. Muhammed High School, may be the best leaper entering the ACC this season.

"He can run, jump and do a lot of things with sheer athleticism," Hewitt said. "Hopefully, we'll use his athleticism to bolster our defense—our press, our man-to-man and things like that."

The newcomers will have to compete with last year's two freshman surprises to win playing time. **Marvin Lewis** (8.8 ppg, 4.5 rpg) started 29-of-30 games as a freshman. The 6-3 guard from Germantown, Md., proved a good three-point shooter (.374) and was the team's best wing defender as he was selected to the ACC's All-Freshman team.

"He can be even better this year," Hewitt said. "He's worked hard in the weight room and he's worked on scoring off the dribble."

Halston Lane (6.8 ppg, 2.4 rpg) was an explosive scorer as a freshman. The 6-4 wing from Oak Ridge, Tenn., had some of his best performances in Georgia Tech's toughest games. He poured in 23 points in 17 minutes to help upset Kentucky and hit 3-of-5 three-pointers in the upset of UCLA.

"He benefited a lot from playing the post spot and having bigger players chase him," Hewitt said. "We've got to figure ways to keep getting him favorable matchups. He can score."

Walk-on **Winston Neal** (0.5 ppg, 0.6 rpg) played in just eight games a year ago. The 6-1 senior is a valuable practice player, but is unlikely to be a factor in games.

2001-2002 SCHEDULE

Nov.	16	Florida A&M
	19	#Pennsylvania
	22-24	##Las Vegas Invitational
	28	*Wisconsin
Dec.	2	@North Carolina
	9	@Georgia
	16	**Syracuse
	19	***Davidson
	21	Wofford
	23	Tulane
	29	IUPU
Jan.	2	Cornell
	5	Clemson
	10	@Duke
	13	Maryland
	19	@North Carolina State
	22	Virginia
	26	@Wake Forest
	30	Florida State
Feb.	2	North Carolina
	6	@Clemson
	9	Duke
	13	@Maryland
	16	@Saint Louis
	20	North Carollina State
	23	@Virginia
	27	Wake Forest
March	2	@Florida State
	7-10	###ACC Tournament

@Road Games
*ACC/Big Ten Challenge
**Chick-fil-A Peach Bowl Classic
***Charlotte Coliseum
#First round, Las Vegas Invitational
##Las Vegas, NV (schedule determined after first-round games; Pool 1 includes Georgia Tech, Illinois, Eastern Illinois, Pennsylvania. Pool 2 includes Iowa State, Saint Louis, Hartford, Southern Illinois)
###Charlotte Coliseum, Charlotte, NC

BLUE RIBBON ANALYSIS

BACKCOURT	B
BENCH/DEPTH	B+
FRONTCOURT	C
INTANGIBLES	B+

Hewitt wants to run and press. He inherited a team that was ill suited for that purpose, yet still managed to somehow manufacture a successful team in his first season at Georgia Tech.

He's rapidly remaking the roster in his own image. Georgia Tech has lost a good deal of experience and one of the nation's best big man in Jones, but the Jackets have added four very athletic recruits—three of them wing players. They'll team with last year's two talented freshmen wings, plus Moore, to give Hewitt a deep collection of versatile young wing players that few programs can match.

Georgia Tech may be too inexperienced and too thin in the post to exploit its new strengths this season. However, it's clear Hewitt knows where he's going and is well on the way to getting there. In one year, the unheralded successor to Cremins has succeeded in putting the buzz back in the Jackets' program.

(A.F.)

North Carolina State

LOCATION	Raleigh, NC
CONFERENCE	Atlantic Coast
LAST SEASON	13-16 (.448)
CONFERENCE RECORD	5-11 (7th)
STARTERS LOST/RETURNING	3/2
NICKNAME	Wolfpack
COLORS	Red & White
HOMECOURT	Entertainment and Sports Arena (19,722)
COACH	Herb Sendek (Carnegie Mellon '85)
RECORD AT SCHOOL	86-74 (5 years)
CAREER RECORD	149-100 (8 years)
ASSISTANTS	Larry Hunter (Ohio '71)
	Larry Harris (Pittsburgh '78)
	Mark Phelps (Old Dominion '96)
TEAM WINS (last 5 years)	17-17-19-20-13
RPI (last 5 years)	59-55-56-64-89
2000-01 FINISH	Lost in conference semifinal.

For a man standing at the end of a shaky plank, blindfolded with a final cigarette hanging out his mouth, Herb Sendek is surprisingly optimistic.

The sixth-year N.C. State coach, flanked by the most heralded recruiting class of his Wolfpack tenure, is supremely confident that his program will turn things around this season, though he's not guaranteeing that his team will make it to the NCAA Tournament.

The Wolfpack, of course, has been absent from the big tournament since 1991, which is one of the reasons Sendek got pushed to such a precarious perch. Going 13-16 and finishing seventh in the ACC last season didn't help either.

But with the long-awaited arrival of McDonald's All-American **Julius Hodge** and four other talented freshmen, Sendek is eager to get started on his most critical season in Raleigh.

"I am optimistic and enthusiastic," Sendek said during the summer. "I like the dynamics of our team. I think we go into the season with an enthusiasm and eagerness that we have not had."

And he won't let talk of his possible demise temper that enthusiasm.

"I cannot and will not coach under a veil of fear," Sendek said. "I want our team to have a quiet confidence. I want them to be fearless and relentless."

That's a difficult expectation for a program that experienced its share of turmoil over the last calendar year. But Sendek believes that having some amount of pressure on his program is not necessarily a negative.

"A certain amount of stress is good in any walk of life because it helps you reach your potential," Sendek said. "Some amount of pressure or stress, whatever you want to call it, is good. Too much, like with anything, is not good."

Last year was a prime example of the latter. It was a disaster—Sendek prefers to call it a "detour"—pretty much from the moment practice started. That's when senior Damon Thornton was arrested for driving while intoxicated after plowing the car of one of his teammates into another car. It was the third arrest of his career. Sendek suspended him for the first semester.

Forward Damien Wilkins, the one-time savior of the program, was hampered by an early injury, and senior center Ron Kelley had continuing knee problems.

Then, after Thornton finally returned to action, another legal problem disrupted the season. Guard **Anthony Grundy**, the team's leading scorer, was arrested the day before the Wolfpack played North Carolina for assaulting a former girlfriend. He was later found not guilty of that charge, but it was an inopportune time for such a big distraction.

On the court, things were going poorly. The Wolfpack lost seven of its nine ACC games and needed overtime to beat Florida State. State lost a heartbreaking overtime game at Wake Forest, then collapsed against Syracuse at home in its most important non-conference game of the season.

Two days after the Wolfpack pulled off an 90-80 upset of top 10 Virginia, N.C. State athletics director Lee Fowler tried to head off any further speculation about Sendek's future by announcing that the coach, who has four years remaining on his contract, would return for the 2001-02 season.

Thus inspired, the Wolfpack raced out and lost six of its final eight games to finish out the program's first losing season under Sendek.

Over the summer, the Wolfpack program continued to look like a sinking ship. Wilkins, a former McDonald's All-American who was once called the school's most important recruit since David Thompson, declared for the NBA after his sophomore season, hoping to find the success that his father, Gerald, and uncle, Dominique, had experienced during long professional careers.

Assistant coach Sean Miller, after pursuing several head-coaching positions, left to become an assistant coach at Xavier, a move that couldn't even graciously be called lateral. Miller, the older brother of Wolfpack senior guard **Archie Miller**, had been with Sendek all five years at N.C. State.

Freshman Trey Guidry, one of the few bright spots during the Wolfpack's dismal season, announced that he would transfer, joining a long list of players who have left Sendek's program seeking other opportunities. Guidry, who averaged 3.1 points a game and started six times as a freshman, wound up at Illinois State.

And then came the kicker: Wilkins finally realized what others had been saying all along, that his game was not nearly ready for the NBA. He sprained an ankle during the NBA's prospect camp in Chicago and got only tepid responses from workouts at Orlando, Miami and Charlotte. But about the same time Wilkins was making his final decision to return to school, Sendek decided that Wilkins wouldn't be allowed to return to the team.

It was a bold move for a coach whose job was on the line, but Sendek had the full support of the N.C. State administration and, for the most part, Wolfpack fans. It seems Gerald Wilkins demanded that Sendek build his team around Damien, a laughable request considering Wilkins' 41 percent shooting from the field and his inconsistent abilities. That Gerald wanted Damien moved to shooting guard, the position Hodge plays, made any chance of reconciling with the family impossible.

Though the elder Wilkins denies that he ever demanded anything from Sendek, the coach told Damien that he could not return to the team. Wilkins ended up enrolling at Georgia, where he will have to sit out the season under NCAA transfer rules.

Wilkins' departure increased the number of transfers to 10 during Sendek's five years at the school.

"We took a detour last year, and that's been documented over and over again," Sendek said during a summer news conference. "Now, it is time to move on with excitement and anticipation for next season. Our recruiting class is very heralded. The returners have rededicated themselves and worked exceptionally hard this spring."

The Wolfpack's quintet of freshmen was ranked No. 1 in the nation by InsidersReport.com, No. 3 by Sports Illustrated, No. 5 by Prepstars.com and No. 6 by both ESPN.com and The Sporting News.

Hodge, the highest rated recruit coming into the ACC this season, is the primary reason for that, of course. The 6-6 McDonald's All-America shooting guard from St. Raymond's High School in the Bronx showcased his abilities for Wolfpack fans during the annual all-star game, which was played for the first time at nearby Duke in Cameron Indoor Stadium. He scored 17 points in the high-scoring game, and learned a little about what he needed to do to compete at the highest level of college basketball.

Hodge (23 ppg, 8 rpg, 4 apg), after leading his team to both the city and state titles as a senior, arrived early in Raleigh to get to know his new teammates. He enrolled in summer school in June and spent much of the summer playing with the other four freshmen—forwards **Levi Watkins** and **Josh Powell**, wing player **Ilian Evtimov** and center **Jordan Collins**—in a well-known Raleigh adult summer league that has been stocked for years with NBA and ACC talent.

Hodge, who enters school as a 17-year-old freshman, knows that he and his fellow freshmen are coming in with great expectations, and more than a little amount of pressure. So he spent the summer working with weights and trying to add some muscle to his spindly frame. He worked on his ball handling in case he needs to be more of a playmaker.

"There is going to be a lot of pressure on me," Hodge said. "[But] we have a really good recruiting class coming in with me. We will have a lot of young guys coming in to help change things."

Sendek acknowledged the need for immediate change when he hired former Ohio University head coach Larry Hunter to replace Miller. Hunter, 52, was fired after a 19-11 season at Ohio, but has 509 victories as a Division I head coach, more than three times as many as Sendek. His arrival ratcheted up talk of going to a more wide open, high-scoring style that Sendek once used when he was competing against Hunter as the head coach at Mid-American Conference rival Miami.

"I think we have done some of that, more than we have really gotten credit for or been recognized for," Sendek said. "When I first got here, it was such a different and unusual team and style that we had to play. Since then, we have tried to run more, but we haven't been recognized for it."

There's a reason for that: The Wolfpack's scoring offense has increased only slightly over the last couple of years because of the team's inability to make shots. Last year's team shot a mere 41.3 percent from the field in ACC games, and that included two curve-busting performances against Virginia, in which the Wolfpack made an uncharacteristic 60 of its 102 shots. Otherwise, State would have been last in all of the ACC's shooting statistics.

Sendek's team shot under 40 percent from the field 11 times last season, was last in the ACC in three-point shooting in conference games only and seventh overall in free-throw shooting.

"We really haven't been associated as a team that was playing fast because we were just scoring in the 60s," Sendek said. "I am very confident that we are going to be able to shoot the ball better this year. If nothing else, just from the free-throw line.

"That's not to say we are going to be like Arkansas, completely helter-skelter. But the truth, I think, or reality of our style hasn't been accurately depicted."

Sendek's team never really evolved over the last two years. Wilkins (11.7 ppg, 5.8 rpg) was supposed to be the centerpiece as a small forward, but that proved to be a load he was unable to carry. The frontcourt rotation of Thornton, Kenny Inge, Ron Kelley and Cornelius Williams was always expected to play better than their limited skills would let them. Inge and Thornton were great athletes, but mediocre basketball players. Kelley was the team's best frontcourt scorer, but he was hampered with knee injuries during his final two years on campus.

That left most of the offense up to 6-3 Grundy (13.6 ppg, 3.9 rpg) or the diminutive (5-9), injury-plagued Miller (9.3 ppg, 1.3 rpg), who missed nine games last season with a hairline fracture in his leg. Those two seniors will be the leaders of a team that has all of its experience in the backcourt and must replace some 60 percent of its rebounding from a year ago.

Junior **Clifford Crawford** (7.7 ppg, 3.2 rpg, 3.5 apg,), a 6-3 point guard, is supposed to run the show, though Sendek says he will refuse to label any of his players this year with nominal position titles.

"With this team, I am not going to circle anybody and say you are a point guard," Sendek said. "I want our guys to play a lot of different positions. I want them to be flexible enough to execute and perform at any different position.

"We may have five players on the court that have a perimeter flavor to them. I don't think we are going to have five guards on the floor—I hope we aren't reduced back to those days—but we should have five players who can pass, dribble and shoot on the floor."

That means Hodge, Grundy, Crawford and Miller will get the bulk of the scoring opportunities for the Wolfpack, with an additional spark provided by former McDonalds All-American **Scooter Sherrill** (4.2 ppg, 1.7 rpg), a 6-3 sophomore shooting guard who did not have the kind of impact he expected in his first college season.

Evtimov, the younger brother of former UNC player Vasco Evtimov, played high school basketball in Winston-Salem and is expected to provide some of the shooting that recent Wolfpack teams have lacked.

The rebounding and inside muscle, however, will have to come from elsewhere.

Sophomore **Marcus Melvin** (4.3 ppg, 2.9 rpg), a 6-8 power forward, has the only real frontcourt experience returning from last year. But he played sparingly, averaging only 11 minutes a game. Red-shirt freshman **Michael Bell**, a 6-9 forward, is back in action after sitting out last year with an injury and long-term project **Kris Jensen**, a 7-1 center who enrolled at State after two years as a reserve at Southeastern Community College, will also provide some inside depth.

But three freshmen forwards will certainly get their chance to contribute. Collins, a 6-10 product of DeMatha High School in Hyattsville, Md., is the latest in a long line of players from that school to play for the Wolfpack. He is the biggest and strongest of the Wolfpack's three freshmen, though hardly the most athletic.

Powell, a 6-9 forward from Riverdale (Ga.) High School, might be the most versatile of the newcomers. He held his own against the NBA's No. 1 pick, Kwame Brown, during a state high school playoff game, scoring 16 points and grabbing 12 rebounds while Brown had 26 points and 11 rebounds.

Finally, 6-7 swing forward Watkins of Rockville (Md.) Montrose Christian Academy has experience playing inside, but he transformed himself into a wing player during his senior season after losing about 25 pounds. He averaged 23.2 points and 11.2 rebounds during his final prep season and will likely benefit immediately from Wilkins departure.

2001-2002 SCHEDULE

Nov.	14-16	#BCA Classic
	20	James Madison
	23	The Citadel
	27	*@Ohio State
Dec.	1	UMass
	5	Wofford
	8	@Syracuse
	15	UNC Asheville
	19	Charleston Southern
	23	@Houston
	30	Maryland
Jan.	5	@Virginia
	8	Florida State
	13	Duke
	15	@Clemson
	19	Georgia Tech
	23	@North Carolina
	26	Temple
	30	Wake Forest
Feb.	3	@Maryland
	6	Virginia
	10	@Florida State
	14	@Duke
	16	Clemson
	20	@Georgia Tech
	24	North Carolina
March	2	@Wake Forest
	7-10	##ACC Tournament

@Road Games
*Big Ten/ACC Challenge
#Raleigh, NC (vs. Prairie View A&M, first round; also East Carolina, Fairleigh Dickinson, High Point, Northwestern, Rutgers, San Jose State, VCU)
##Charlotte Coliseum, Charlotte, NC

BLUE RIBBON ANALYSIS

BACKCOURT B-

BENCH/DEPTH	B
FRONTCOURT	B-
INTANGIBLES	C

Yes, the Wolfpack has a great recruiting class coming in. And Sendek just might be able to turn things around this season, by listening to Hunter and letting those young guys and his perimeter veterans get up and down the floor in a fast-paced stampede.

But this is clearly the most critical year of Sendek's career at N.C. State. The school, with its gleaming new arena, cannot afford to keep paying a coach around $800,000 per year if he cannot field a team that can qualify for the NCAA Tournament.

At a school with two national championship banners hanging from the rafters, a full decade of struggling to reach mediocrity is more than enough patience. If this had happened a few miles down the road, at either Duke or North Carolina, there might have been riots in the streets years ago.

This is Sendek's sixth season. He's got all the amenities he needs. He even has enough players. What this year's team doesn't have, however, is much experience. The good news is that with so many early entries into the NBA, experience is not a requirement for college basketball success anymore.

And while some have been saying this for two years now, this truly is Sendek's final chance to turn things around: Win, or leave.

(T.P.)

Belmont

LOCATION	Nashville, TN
CONFERENCE	Atlantic Sun
LAST SEASON	13-15 (.464)
CONFERENCE RECORD	NA
STARTERS LOST/RETURNING	1/4
NICKNAME	Bruins
COLORS	Navy, Red & Blue
HOMECOURT	Municipal Auditorium (8,354)
COACH	Rick Byrd (Tennessee '76)
RECORD AT SCHOOL	318-164 (15 years)
CAREER RECORD	410-219 (20 years)
ASSISTANTS	Casey Alexander (Belmont '95)
	Brian Ayers (Lipscomb '93)
	Roger Idstrom (Mars Hill '89)
TEAM WINS (last 5 years)	15-9-14-7-13
RPI (last 5 years)	NA-NA-NA-280-268
2000-01 FINISH	Won regular-season finale.

Finally.

After a five-year wait for complete Division I membership, the Belmont Bruins are cleared to compete as a full member of the Atlantic Sun Conference. They're eligible for the league's postseason tournament and the trip to the NCAA Tournament that goes along with an ASC title.

"If you've never lived it, you don't know how long that seems," 16th-year coach Rick Byrd said. "It's been five years since we've had the chance to play postseason. We've got a goal now at the end of the year and you just can't even measure the difference it makes in recruiting."

The Bruins became an NAIA powerhouse under Byrd and have had moderate success since opting for Division I competition in 1996-97. They were 13-15 last year and return four starters, so they may be a surprisingly strong new member of the Atlantic Sun.

Byrd's Belmont teams are a system-based program ala Samford. The Bruins run an open-post, motion offense that relies on lots and lots of three-pointers. In fact, Belmont was second only to Duke last year in threes made per game (10.3).

It's no fluke either. Belmont is the only team in the country to rank in the top three nationally in that category the last three seasons.

"We knew what we were getting into and we made a decision to get skilled guys that could shoot it because it's just so hard to get big men," Byrd said. "We're a motion offense with a lot of good shooters."

And Byrd has a nest full of those type players returning, beginning with 6-5 senior forward **Wes Burtner** (20.1 ppg, 5.1 rpg), who earned All-Independent honors last season.

"Wes is almost the prototype of the guy we were looking for when we decided how we were going to attack recruiting in Division I," Byrd said. "He's a very skilled,

mentally tough Kentucky high school player. He's very intelligent and a great shooter, even though he's more than a half step slow. He doesn't have the quickness of a lot of guys he matches up with, but he's a very effective college player."

Burtner was 10th in the nation last year with 3.3 three-pointers per game. He has scored in double figures 69 times in 82 games, and he led the Bruins in 12 statistical categories last season.

The only other senior in the rotation is 6-2 **B.J. Proffitt** (9.3 ppg, 1.5 rpg, 4.1 apg), who has started the last 42 games for the Bruins, primarily at point guard. The third-leading scorer on the team last season, Proffitt slumped in his long-range shooting, from .357 beyond the three-point arc in 1999-00, to .299 last season.

Sophomore **Steve Drabyn** (8.6 ppg, 2.0 rpg, 3.9 apg) led the team with .395 percent shooting last year from three-point range, and turned into the team's steadiest ball-handler. The 6-0 guard registered an 11-to-1 assists to turnovers ratio in the final three games and also holds the national high school free-throw percentage record at .921 (397-of-431) in his career at LaPorte (Ind.) High School. He will again plug in alongside Proffitt to give the Bruins a solid backcourt tandem.

Jese Snyder (18.2 ppg, 5.2 rpg, 2.6 apg) will have a say in that mix, too. The 6-2 freshman, from Lenoir City (Tenn.) High School is Belmont's most athletic perimeter player and the team's best on-the-ball defender. He redshirted last season as a freshman to learn the system and get stronger.

"We thought a red-shirt year would be good for him, and it was, but he's a better player than we thought he was," Byrd said. "He can play either guard spot and he

can beat his man off the dribble which is something we're not very good at."

Another sophomore, **Wil Howard-Downs** (2.1 ppg, 1.1 rpg) came on strong late last year and should again see action. Howard-Downs is a 6-4 guard with a nose for the ball. He had six steals in the final three games last season.

Little-used senior **Matt Roberts** (0.0 ppg, 0.0 rpg) also returns on the perimeter.

A major reason Belmont could turn some heads this season in the conference, though, is inside, where 6-8 junior **Adam Sonn** (14.2 ppg, 9.4 rpg) has emerged as the program's first legitimate Division I post threat. His prolific rebounding ranked him 24th in the nation a year ago and he earned second-team All-Independent honors while shooting a team-high .477 percent from the field.

"Adam gave us a real inside scoring threat," Byrd said. "He's an effective scorer and he's got three-point range. He gave us an inside dimension we lacked and that has made us a better team."

That inside game has gotten stronger as 6-8 sophomore **Adam Mark** (6.8 ppg, 4.8 rpg) has come on. Mark started 11 of the last 14 games last season as a freshman, averaging nine points and 5.8 rebounds over that stretch. Not quite as thick as Sonn, Mark is "more of a face the basket guy," Byrd said. "But he's probably our best rebounder for his size and he's got a great nose for offensive rebounds."

The inside game should get another lift from the return of 6-10 sophomore **Scotty Blackwell** (14.6 ppg, 8.0 rpg in 1999-2000). Blackwell originally signed with the Bruins out of Tioga High in Pineville, La., but he was

---

ATLANTIC SUN

BLUE RIBBON FORECAST
1. Georgia State
2. Jacksonville
3. Troy State
4. Central Florida
5. Samford
6. Stetson
7. Mercer
8. Belmont
9. Florida Atlantic
10. Jacksonville State
11. Campbell

ALL-CONFERENCE TEAM
G-Ravii Givens, JR, Stetson
G-Robert Rushing, SR, Troy State
G-Jay Heard, JR, Jacksonville State
F- Scott Emerson, JR, Mercer
F- Thomas Terrell, SR, Georgia State

PLAYER OF THE YEAR
Thomas Terrell, SR, Georgia State

NEWCOMER OF THE YEAR
Jay Heard, JR, Jacksonville State

2001-2002 CONFERENCE TOURNAMENT
Feb. 28-March 2, UCF Arena, Orlando, FL

2000-2001 CHAMPIONS
Hofstra (Regular season)
Hofstra (Conference tournament)

2000-2001 POSTSEASON PARTICIPANTS
Postseason Record: 1-1 (.500)
NCAA
Georgia State

TOP BACKCOURTS
1. Stetson
2. Troy State
3. Georgia State

TOP FRONTCOURTS
1. Mercer
2. Georgia State
3. UCF

INSIDE THE NUMBERS
2001-2002 RPI: 21st (of 31)
Conference RPI (last five years): 30-25-22-27-21

DID YOU KNOW?
Now in its 24th season, the Trans America Athletic Conference officially became the Atlantic Sun Conference this past June. ...The league's highest RPI ever (21st) helped land champion Georgia State an 11th-seeded team in the NCAA Tournament, where the Panthers upset Wisconsin. ...With Belmont coming into the league this season, only the top eight ASC teams will be invited to the conference tournament. ...The format will be changed again after next season when Samford and Jacksonville State leave for the Ohio Valley Conference. ... New Division I program Gardner-Webb is headed into the league but has to wait five years to be eligible for the conference tournament, the process Belmont just completed. ... Georgia State coach Lefty Driesell is only two wins behind Bobby Knight as the NCAA's winningest active coach (764). Driesell should pass Knight and Hank Iva (767) this year and move into third place all-time behind only Dean Smith (879) and Adolph Rupp (876). ...Jacksonville's Hugh Durham is 12th among active coaches with 573 career victories. ... Junior Ed Dotson, eligible as a transfer at UCF this season, has the rare opportunity to add the conference newcomer of the year award to his collection after earning freshman-of-the-year honors two years ago for former-TAAC member Centenary. ...The newcomer of the year award will be one of the most hotly-contested fights in years, with several talented transfers coming into the league or becoming eligible, including two legitimate candidates at Jacksonville in juniors Calvin Warner (Eastern Michigan) and Travis Robinson (Barton County [Kansas] Community College). ... Belmont has ranked among the top three in the nation in three-point field goals made per game the last three years.

(M.A.)

red-shirted and then left the program last season before having a change of heart and returning this year. Because he didn't play anywhere else, he's immediately eligible.

"He's 6-10 and 245 pounds so he's the first guy we've had with a real presence inside," Byrd said. "We're definitely counting on him."

Ronnie Colbert (10.0 ppg, 10.1 rpg) is a 6-6 freshman out of Decatur (Ala.) High School, and probably the best athlete on the team.

"He may choose to red-shirt and add some weight and strength," Byrd said. "He can impact the game more than anybody we have with his athleticism. He's a leaper and we just don't have many of those."

Steve Strickland, a 6-9 junior forward, will be eligible second semester after transferring last spring from a junior college where he did not play. A left-hander, Strickland has offensive skills that can help. He averaged 17.5 points and 9.0 rebounds at Mt. Vernon (Ill.) High School two years ago.

Two other freshmen, 6-4 **Chad Caterson** and 6-4 **Nick Otis**, round out the team. Caterson is a 21-year-old freshman from Montreal, and averaged 16 points and six rebounds at Champlain College prep school. Otis played for his father at LaPorte (Ind.) High and averaged 20.6 points and 7.8 rebounds.

2001-2002 SCHEDULE

Nov.	16	@Southern Illinois
	19	Valparaiso
	24	@Jacksonville
	26	Middle Tennessee
	29	Campbell
Dec.	1	Georgia State
	16	@Stetson
	18-19	#Stanford Invitational
	28	@Navy
	30	@Florida
Jan.	5	Troy State
	7	Mercer
	10	@Jacksonville State
	12	Samford
	17	@Central Florida
	19	@Florida Atlantic
	26	Central Florida
	28	Florida Atlantic
Feb.	2	@Samford
	4	Jacksonville State
	7	@Mercer
	9	@Troy State
	14	Stetson
	16	Jacksonville
	21	@Georgia State
	23	@Campbell
	28	##A-Sun Tournament
March	1-2	##A-Sun Tournament

@Road Games
#Maples Pavilion, Palo Alto, CA (vs. Stanford first round; also Portland State, Santa Clara)
##UCF Arena, Orlando, FL

BLUE RIBBON ANALYSIS

BACKCOURT	B-
BENCH/DEPTH	C
FRONTCOURT	C+
INTANGIBLES	C

Belmont has enough veterans and a solid enough system to cause some trouble for fat-cat ASC teams that might take the Bruins lightly. Trouble is, most conference teams won't take them lightly for just those reasons.

Burtner and Sonn are a couple of solid players, but on the whole, the Bruins don't match up well athletically with most of their new conference rivals. Coach Byrd has been doing something right all these years to win more than 400 games, so figure Belmont can hang around with most of the teams in the league and maybe even win more than it loses.

That would be a heck of a season for Belmont, and playing in a conference tournament is the icing on the Division I cake that they finally get to stick a finger in.

(M.A.)

Campbell

LOCATION	Buies Creek, NC
CONFERENCE	Atlantic Sun
LAST SEASON	7-21 (.250)
CONFERENCE RECORD	5-13 (8th)
STARTERS LOST/RETURNING	1/4
NICKNAME	Camels
COLORS	Orange & Black
HOMECOURT	Carter Gymnasium (945)
COACH	Billy Lee (Atlantic Christian '71)
RECORD AT SCHOOL	203-245 (16 years)
CAREER RECORD	324-333 (23 years)
ASSISTANTS	Cliff Dillard (Campbell '89)
	Joe Gallagher (Pembroke State '68)
	Matt Allen (Wofford '95)
TEAM WINS (last 5 years)	11-10-9-12-7
RPI (last 5 years)	248-266-263-228-300
2000-01 FINISH	Lost in conference first round.

The Camels have been in a veritable desert the last few seasons in the league formerly known as the Trans America Athletic Conference.

Since joining the TAAC (nee Atlantic Sun) in 1994, Campbell has posted one winning season and that was six years ago. Last season, 16th-year coach Billy Lee guided one of his most inexperienced teams to a 7-21 mark, his worst season ever.

The Camels seemed to be nearing an oasis late last season, winning three of their last four after a disastrous 14 losses in 15 games stretch. One of those losses was in overtime and five more defeats were by eight points or less.

"We had so many new players we never really developed the consistency you need," said Lee, who remains the most popular man on the small campus. "We've got a chance to be better this year, particularly if we can get more consistent outside shooting.

"Actually, we've got the shooting. We just need the making now."

The Camels shot .427 percent from the field last year as a team, a dismal mark by Campbell's previous efforts in Lee's patented motion offense. Even more galling, the normally high-scoring Camels dropped all the way to last in the conference in scoring (65.0).

Don't blame senior sharpshooter **Adam Fellers** (15.5 ppg, 2.4 rpg). The 6-2 guard led the conference in free-throw percentage (.844) and three-pointers made per game (3.07). His statistics were close to his 1999-00 numbers, a testament to his steadiness despite the personnel flux around him.

"What makes Adam so valuable," Lee said, "is his work ethic. He's here early every day shooting 300–to-500 shots, and the other guys on the team see that. If I had my way, we'd name a building for him when he leaves."

One of the bright spots for CU last year was at the other guard spot, where then-freshman **Emory Walton** (7.6 ppg, 3.1 rpg, 3.4 apg) earned league all-rookie honors. The 6-2 guard just kept getting better every game, doubling his assists to turnovers over the last 21 games.

The support behind that starting duo should be improved this year, too. Sophomore **Tarik Johnson** (5.3 ppg, 2.0 rpg) also came on strong last year as a freshman. The 6-3 guard scored in double figures in four of the last six games, including 14 points in the regular season finale against Central Florida.

"Tarik is going to surprise a lot of people this year," Lee said. "I don't know whether he's a small forward or a big guard. I don't know what to call him, but he's a good basketball player."

Another sophomore, 6-0 **Derek Gray** (3.0 ppg, 0.9 rpg), is an athletic guard candidate, but he's still learning the game. His best basketball is ahead of him, but possibly not this season.

That rounds out the backcourt returnees, but there's another candidate for playing time who has more experience with this system than any other player on the team. Transfer **Brooks Lee** (5.1 ppg, 1.9 rpg, 1.8 apg at High Point in 1999-00) has been in the system since he was five years old. The coach's son sat out last season as a transfer. He not only brings knowledge of the playbook but a deadly three-point stroke. He hit 42 percent behind the arc as a sophomore for the Panthers.

Lee could be one answer to the perimeter-shooting problem that plagued Campbell last season. Another

solution may be a strong senior season from 6-5 **Zydrunas Stankus** (7.9 ppg, 2.9 rpg), The Lithuanian small forward looks to improve on last season's .351 shooting, and become more of an offensive threat.

Lee has options at the position if "Z" doesn't come up big. Sophomore **Brad McKeiver** (3.8 ppg, 1.8 rpg, 1.6 rpg) is a little taller at 6-6, and he's the hard-nosed kind of player Lee has thrived with in the past. He's a good passer and he makes those around him better, though he needs to improve his shooting touch (.362), too.

Another possibility is junior transfer **Solomon Yearby** (15.2 ppg, 4.0 rpg) from Wallace (Ala.) State Junior College. Only 6-2, Yearby is more naturally a guard, but his shooting stroke could earn him a starting berth as Lee tries to open up his offense again.

Up front, the Camels have a solid three-man rotation at power forward and center. **Jonte' Edwards** (8.0 ppg, 5.4 rpg), a 6-7 junior, is coming off a career year but the feeling around "The Creek" is he can do more.

"He a real competitive kid and he plays with a lot fire," Lee said. "We were expecting big things of him last year and we are again this season."

Bobby Jones (2.6 ppg, 4.5 rpg) held down the power forward slot next to Edwards at center last year. The 6-6 senior does the dirty work, setting screens, hitting the boards and defending.

Jay Carter (6.8 ppg, 3.9 rpg) backs up both positions and does it well. A 6-8 senior, Carter gives CU size, rebounding, scoring and defense off the bench. Carter shot 47 percent from the field last year and was eighth in the league in blocked shots (0.9 bpg).

The front-line rotation could get a big addition this season if 6-11 freshman **Tim Summa** (10.0 ppg, 10.0 rpg) of Salyersville (Ky.) High School comes along quickly. He's the tallest Camel player in 20 years, and Lee has high hopes for him, though he certainly may need polish as a rookie.

Another candidate but even more of a question mark is 6-6 **Dominique Klein**, a freshman import from Hamburg, Germany. The athletic Klein averaged 27 points and nine rebounds in a German league, but it remains to be seen how that translates to the American college game. His availability may also be in doubt as the NCAA is cracking down on foreign players who have played in leagues with other players who received pay. Klein did not, but he still may be ineligible under tighter rules unless Lee wins his appeal to the NCAA.

As always, though, the coach is upbeat about the coming season.

"We've brought in some players that can help us," Lee said. "The thing I like is we've got 10 players who are familiar with our system. That's a much better situation than we had last year."

2001-2002 SCHEDULE

Nov.	17	@LSU
	20	UNC Pembroke
	24	UNC Asheville
	26	Furman
	29	@Belmont
Dec.	1	@Furman
	12	@Georgia State
	19	Troy State
	21	*Coastal Carolina
	29	@Florida State
Jan.	2	Mercer
	5	@UCF
	7	@Florida Atlantic
	10	Jacksonville
	12	Stetson
	17	@Samford
	19	@Jacksonville State
	23	Georgia State
	26	Samford
	28	Jacksonville State
Feb.	2	@Stetson
	4	@Jacksonville
	7	Florida Atlantic
	9	UCF
	14	@Troy State
	16	**Mercer
	23	Belmont
	28	#A-Sun Tournament
March	1-2	#A-Sun Tournament

@Road Games
*Myrtle Beach Convention Center
**Macon Centreplex
#UCF Arena, Orlando, FL

BLUE RIBBON ANALYSIS

BACKCOURT	B
BENCH/DEPTH	C
FRONTCOURT	C
INTANGIBLES	D

No doubt the Camels can be better than last year, but they aren't over the hump, yet. The Atlantic Sun Conference is getting stronger, too, and looking at the CU program, you wonder if the Camels can compete year-in, year-out with Georgia State, Troy State and the other league bullies.

Their location in (stop the presses) now two-stoplight Buies Creek is a severe disadvantage in this far-flung league. Every trip is a long one, and the more urban schools in the league—and every school is more urban than Campbell—have distinct recruiting advantages.

Not the least of those advantages is that everyone plays in a bigger, nicer facility than Campbell's 48-year old Carter Gymnasium, a 945-seat, wooden-raftered pit. The talent disparity between the Camels and Atlanta-based Georgia State, the Atlantic Sun's top team, is growing wider.

Lee used to say he was "in a sword fight with a pocket knife" when the odds were stacked against his team. That adage seems more and more apt.

(M.A.)

 UCF

LOCATION	Orlando, FL
CONFERENCE	Atlantic Sun
LAST SEASON	8-23 (.258)
CONFERENCE RECORD	3-15 (10th)
STARTERS LOST/RETURNING	2/3
NICKNAME	Golden Knights
COLORS	Black & Gold
HOMECOURT	UCF Arena (5,100)
COACH	Kirk Speraw (Iowa '80)
RECORD AT SCHOOL	108-126 (9 years)
CAREER RECORD	108-126 (9 years)
ASSISTANTS	Chris Mowry (St. Ambrose '84)
	Jorge Fernandez (Stetson '85)
	Craig Brown (Florida '95)
TEAM WINS (last 5 years)	7-17-19-14-8
RPI (last 5 years)	301-169-102-208-270
2000-01 FINISH	Lost in conference quarterfinal.

It's déjà vu all over again at Central Florida, where the Golden Knights will be predicted to have the kind of year that they were supposed to have last season.

A funny thing happened on the way to the Golden Knight's predicted upper division finish. They were actually last in the conference, buried under an avalanche of near misses, nagging injuries, poor defense, poor perimeter shooting and crunch-time collapses.

The Knights lost six games by five points or less, including two in overtime. Twelve of 15 conference setbacks were by nine points or less, and UCF was dismal late in close games, losing 21 times when the team trailed with five minutes to play.

Opponents shot 45 percent from the field and seemed to snag all the key rebounds. Many of the problems stemmed from just how young the Knights were, particularly on the perimeter. UCF's three-point field goal shooting dipped from nearly 40 percent two years ago to .319 last season.

Four freshmen figured into the rotation, and veteran coach Kirk Speraw hopes the trial by fire last year has forged a new attitude among his players. That attitude and some talented additions just may make last season's predictions come true this season.

"We'll be much improved with the experience our youth gained a year ago," Speraw said. "They were forced into playing a lot of quality minutes and that will greatly benefit us this season. Last season, some of our guys had to grow up fast."

Junior guard **Al Miller** (4.6 ppg, 2.8 rpg, 4.8 apg) already had some experience and is back for his third season as a starter. Speraw jokes the 6-0 Miller would have averaged 10 assists per game last season if the Knights had hit shots. Miller does a great job of distributing the ball and Speraw is counting on him to be a leader on the team this season.

Alongside Miller, the Knights are counting on junior **Jason Thornton** (6.3 ppg, 1.8 rpg) to bounce back from the nagging shoulder injury that hampered him a year ago. Thornton, a 6-5 swingman, averaged 12.7 points per game as a freshman and ranked second in the nation with his .495 shooting from three-point range. Last season, he underwent arthroscopic surgery on his shooting shoulder the first day of practice and lost the arc on his shot, plummeting him into a shooting slump that lasted all season. He hit just 34 percent last year but Speraw is counting on the trying season to become a plus for Thornton.

"He has regained some of his confidence," the coach said. "I think he will be a much stronger competitor this season, having gone through what he did."

Thornton's troubles pushed **Joey Graham** (8.6 ppg, 3.8 rpg) into the spotlight last season, and the 6-6 sophomore took advantage as a freshman. He started 19 games and scored in double figures 13 times, including a 21-point effort against Troy State in the Atlantic Sun Tournament.

Opponents could have double trouble this season as Joey's twin brother, **Stephen Graham** (3.6 ppg, 1.3 rpg), continues to improve. Two of his best games came in the conference tournament, and he is emerging as an offensive threat. If he can improve his defense to the level of his brother's play, he'll see even more action.

Speaking of defense, 6-4 junior guard **Marius Boyd** (2.4 ppg, 1.4 rpg) should play more this season, too. Boyd's calling card is defense and UCF coaches love his toughness and competitive nature. And even if he doesn't improve his offensive game, Thornton and Joey Graham can handle that aspect and let Boyd concentrate on defense.

Another possibility is junior transfer **Ray Abellard**, who averaged double figures last year at Pensacola (Fla.) Junior College. He has all the tools to be a big-time guard, including a sweet shot and great quickness. He's generously listed as 5-10 on the CFU roster.

"We're deep and I think there will be some tough decisions in regards to minutes," Speraw said.

Up front, 6-8 senior power forward **Paul Reed** (14.0 ppg, 7.4 rpg, 1.8 bpg, 1.2 spg) led the team in four categories, scored in double figures 27 times, and had six double-doubles last year.

He can play either the four or five position, but UCF coaches are counting on Reed to improve on his tendency to play well in the first half and not as well in the second.

"I think teams defended him better in the second half but the bottom line is Paul has to step up and have a great senior year," Speraw said.

Speraw has an ace in the hole in his plans to make Reed more effective this year. Junior **Ed Dotson** (14.7 ppg, 5.7 rpg in 1999-00) is eligible this season after transferring from Centenary, and he will have an immediate impact if he is fully recovered from a stress fracture suffered in the spring.

The 6-7 forward was an All-Independent second team selection two years ago. He's an explosive scorer on the low block, has tremendous athleticism and should blossom into a great rebounder.

Another injury question mark for the Knights is 6-10 senior **Evandro Moretti** (2.4 ppg, 1.6 rpg), who was limited to 18 games last year with nagging knee problems. In fact, UCF saw five of the top eight players a year ago undergo arthroscopic surgery.

Moretti never got into a rhythm last season and the Knights need his size—240 pounds—around the basket.

Sophomore **Josh Bodden** (3.8 ppg, 2.9 rpg) contributed last year as a freshman, and at 6-9, he can play underneath or on the wings. Bodden played extremely well down the stretch last season, and improved his game over the summer, getting stronger and adding some more explosiveness offensively.

Senior **Baronti Simms** (6.5 ppg, 1.4 rpg) is another player who struggled last season. Coming off ACL surgery after missing the entire 1999-00 campaign, Simms had trouble finding a niche. He has a pure shooting stroke and at 6-8 and 230-pounds, can help the team up front, if he can bounce back and regain his confidence.

Freshman **Jamon Hard**, a 6-5 forward from Fort Walton Beach, Fla., rounds out the scholarship players. **Tim Kiscaden**, a 6-0 point guard from nearby Oviedo High School, and **Brian Graham**, the brother of the Graham twins and a 6-4 junior wing who transferred from Florida College in Tampa, are also available, though all three are unlikely to see much action this season.

2001-2002 SCHEDULE

Nov.	16	Puerto Rico Mayaguez
	19	@Hampton
	24	@East Carolina
	29	Jacksonville
Dec.	1	@Florida Atlantic
	8	Florida A&M
	13	Chicago State
	17	@Jacksonville State
	19	@Samford
	22	@Marist
Jan.	2	Stetson
	5	Campbell
	7	Georgia State
	10	@Troy State
	12	@Mercer
	17	Belmont
	22	Florida Atlantic
	26	@Belmont
	29	South Florida
Feb.	2	Mercer
	4	Troy State
	7	@Georgia State
	9	@Campbell
	14	Samford
	16	Jacksonville State
	21	@Stetson
	23	@Jacksonville
	28	#A-Sun Tournament
March	1-2	#A-Sun Tournament

@Road Games
#UCF Arena, Orlando, FL

BLUE RIBBON ANALYSIS

BACKCOURT	B
BENCH/DEPTH	A
FRONTCOURT	B+
INTANGIBLES	C

The Golden Knights have a first seven as strong as anyone in the league. Hey, they did last year, too, on paper. But things didn't quite work out for good guy Speraw.

Open shots were missed. Key rebounds lost. Young defenders out of position. Injuries. Famine. Plague. You get the idea.

If the bad karma carries over, this team will again struggle with confidence and that's a killer in a league with so many teams bunched evenly talent-wise. Speraw knows. He has shored up some holes with Abellard and Dotson, but the onus for improvement rests with the attitude of the returnees.

"We have to dig deep and fight our tails off every possession," Speraw said of a characteristic last year's team was missing. "That's a tone we have to set early on in practices. I think the talent is there. It's a belief in themselves we have to get."

One edge for UCF this year is that the Atlantic Sun Conference comes to Orlando, Feb. 28-Mar. 2. After last year, any break looks like a good one for the Knights.

(M.A.)

 Florida Atlantic

LOCATION	Boca Raton, FL
CONFERENCE	Atlantic Sun
LAST SEASON	7-24 (.226)
CONFERENCE RECORD	5-13 (9th)
STARTERS LOST/RETURNING	1/4
NICKNAME	Owls
COLORS	Blue & Gray
HOMECOURT	FAU Gymnasium (3,000)
COACH	Sidney Green (UNLV '83)
RECORD AT SCHOOL	9-52 (2 years)
CAREER RECORD	58-112 (6 years)
ASSISTANTS	Ken Huber (Ohio State '96)
	Omar Cooper (St. Andrews '99)
	Mark Wade (UNLV '98)
TEAM WINS (last 5 years)	9-16-6-2-7
RPI (last 5 years)	257-263-215-315-266
2000-01 FINISH	Lost in conference quarterfinal.

Rebuilding a down-and-out program isn't easy. Last

season, Florida Atlantic coach Sidney Green had to spend much of the preseason just figuring out who all these new players were. He had only two returnees from the previous year.

Apparently, Green found some guys who could play because the Owls more than doubled their win total from 1999-00. If they do that again this year, Green will really have accomplished something.

And that notion may not be that far-fetched, which is the real testament to Green's rebuilding efforts. The Owls return one of the league's best backcourt combinations in sophomore **Jeff Cowans** (13.7 ppg, 4.3 rpg), senior **John Smart** (5.5 ppg, 2.4 rpg, 3.9 apg) and sophomore **Earnest Crumbley** (11.7 ppg, 3.3 rpg). And they certainly have a serviceable game in the paint with two key returnees up front.

"Our freshmen are now sophomores and we know what they can do," Green said. "We've also added four junior college players that will help bring more leadership."

The 6-2 Cowans really showed what he could do as a freshman, winning Atlantic Sun Rookie-of-the-Year honors and turning into one of the league's most explosive perimeter scoring threats.

"He's a scorer, he can score at will," Green said. "He knows how to set his teammates up, too, and he's still improving."

The 5-10 Smart provides leadership but he may have to fend off a severe challenge to hang on to his starting point guard job. Crumbley was another dynamite freshman last season, earning league all-rookie honors despite starting just 12 games. A 5-10 whirlwind, he finished second on the team in scoring to Cowans and averaged 1.7 three-point field goals per game.

Another possibility is junior transfer **Anthony Slater**, who led the national junior college ranks with 10.5 assists per game at New Mexico Junior College. The 5-9 Slater also averaged 8.2 points and 3.3 steals.

"Our point-guard position is going to be very competitive," Green said.

On the front line, Green returns two starters, both seniors. **Daryl Dingle** (7.6 ppg, 5.7 rpg) is a 6-7, 225-pound power forward who hit 47 percent of his shots last year to lead the team. He was even better in conference play, shooting .515 percent and averaging 8.8 points, and he has added a jump shot out to 15 feet for this season.

"He adds a lot strength and leadership for us in the post area," Green said. "He's a very good offensive rebounder and he's the kind of guy that gets you 10-12 points and 10-12 rebounds and nobody notices it until the game is over."

Raheim Brown (9.3 ppg, 5.5 rpg) is the other senior returnee in the paint. At 6-10, he gives FAU good size around the basket, and he could be primed for a big year.

"Raheim injured his knee midway through the season last year and it hampered him [the rest of] the year," Green said. "He's stronger now, though, and he has worked hard rehabbing. He's a senior and he knows this is it for him."

The Owls would have all their starters back had sophomore Clay Fuller chosen to stay in the program instead of transferring. The FAU coaches were ready, though, and have a much more than adequate replacement.

Andre Garner (20.7 ppg, 7.9 rpg) is a 6-4 junior transfer from Consumnes River (Calif.) College who can step right in and provide more fire power inside and out.

"I'm still surprised we were able to land him," Green said. "He's strong, a leaper, can shoot the three. He liked the idea of being a part of something that was building and growing and he wants to help put us on the map."

Sophomore **Pierre Downing** (4.8 ppg, 2.8 rpg) is another option at the three-spot as a 6-6, 225-pound sophomore. **Jeff Hamilton** (3.8 ppg, 1.4 rpg) is a 6-7 sophomore also in the mix.

The Owls also have some depth and experience behind their big men with 7-0 **Nick Neumann** (5.0 ppg, 4.8 rpg) back as a junior, and 6-8 **Robert Williams** (5.5 ppg, 4.1 rpg) returning for his sophomore season. Green would love for Neumann, a fourth-year junior, to "crack that starting five and average 20-25 minutes."

Newcomer **Avery Headley** could work into some serious playing time this year, too, as a junior transfer from Sierra (Calif.) College. Last season, he averaged 17 points and 8.9 rebounds per game, and at 6-7, 245 pounds, he's a force inside.

"Avery is a Charles Oakley-type player with more of an offensive game," Green said. "He can shoot out to 17 feet but he plays above the rim and he knows how to finish and that's something we didn't have last year."

Junior **Antoine Stevens**, a 6-1 guard from Daytona Beach Community College, rounds out a quality recruiting class that thankfully didn't have to match the quantity of last season's 10 newcomers.

"We're counting on every last one of these guys to provide leadership and help for this team," Green said. "If everyone stays healthy, I'm very optimistic. The attitude is there and these guys have come back in great shape so I can see the commitment."

Green is as pleased with the program's progress off the court as what has transpired on it. The basketball team's cumulative grade-point average last season was 2.65, the highest in the program's history. Green inherited a team that posted below a 2.0 three years ago.

On the court, the Owls have players who can run the up-tempo offense and pressure defense Green favors.

"The big thing is we've got more maturity and more guys who believe in the system," Green said. "We've got the bodies. We've got to just keep taking control of the minds. We've come a long way."

2001-2002 SCHEDULE

Nov.	17	@Hofstra
	20	St. Mary's
	26	@Miami
	29	Stetson
Dec.	1	Central Florida
	4	@Liberty
	8	VCU
	17	@Samford
	19	@Jacksonville State
	27	Drake
Jan.	2	Jacksonville
	5	Georgia State
	7	Campbell
	10	@Mercer
	12	@Troy State
	16	@Birmingham-Southern
	19	Belmont
	22	@Central Florida
	28	@Belmont
Feb.	2	Troy State
	4	Mercer
	7	@Campbell
	9	@Georgia State
	14	Jacksonville State
	16	Samford
	21	@Jacksonville
	23	@Stetson
	28	#A-Sun Tournament
March	1-2	#A-Sun Tournament

@Road Games
#UCF Arena, Orlando, FL

BLUE RIBBON ANALYSIS

BACKCOURT	B+
BENCH/DEPTH	B
FRONTCOURT	C
INTANGIBLES	B

Florida Atlantic won two games in 1999-00. Last year, it won seven, including conference games against Troy State, Mercer, Jacksonville, Central Florida and Jacksonville State. The Owls lost twice during the regular season to Campbell, then beat the Camels in the first round of the tournament before Georgia State bumped them off.

Green, the former UNLV forward who knows a thing or two about tournament success, kept his team in Atlanta for the duration of the 2001 TAAC Tournament.

He wanted them to experience the weekend and watch and learn.

Now Green can put one of the new Atlantic Sun Conference's best backcourts out on the floor, and he's got a solid rotation of big bodies in the paint. Cowans has the makings of a big-time player, and if transfers Garner, Headley and Slater live up to their clippings, the Owls just might emerge as a league darkhorse.

The Owls haven't attracted as much attention around the league the last few years, a by-product of their previous talent-level and their location, but that could all change this season if this young team is ready to take another step up the conference ladder.

With the new eight-team conference tournament format, they'll have to improve again just to get a shot in the tournament. If they are there again at the end, this might just be a team no one wants any part of come late

February.

(M.A.)

Georgia State

LOCATION	Atlanta, GA
CONFERENCE	Atlantic Sun
LAST SEASON	29-5 (.852)
CONFERENCE RECORD	16-2 (1st)
STARTERS LOST/RETURNING	2/3
NICKNAME	Panthers
COLORS	Royal Blue, Red & White
HOMECOURT	GSU Sports Arena (5,000)
COACH	Lefty Driesell (Duke '54)
RECORD AT SCHOOL	79-42 (5 years)
CAREER RECORD	762-377 (39 years)
ASSISTANTS	Michael Perry (Richmond '81)
	Travis Williams (Georgia State '96)
	Bobby Champagne (South Alabama '90)
TEAM WINS (last 5 years)	10-16-17-17-29
RPI (last 5 years)	186-195-175-160-33
2000-01 FINISH	Lost in NCAA second round.

The trouble with taking a downtrodden program to its best season ever is that a year later, you gotta start all over and do it again.

Such is the case at Georgia State, where coach Lefty Driesell guided the Panthers to the most wins in the nation last year, conference regular season and tournament titles and a berth among the final 32 teams in the NCAA Tournament.

"None of that will win us a game this year," said Driesell, ready to stomp up and down the sidelines for a 40th season. "It probably did help us in recruiting and it shows the guys more of what it takes to win and be a top-ranked team."

League MVP Shernard Long and fellow first-team all-conference guard Kevin Morris are gone, but Driesell can still put the deepest, most talented team on the floor in the newly-christened Atlantic Sun Conference.

Seven lettermen, including three starters, retur. To that mix has been added another five junior college recruits—Lefty's trademark in rebuilding the GSU program—to restock the Panther roster.

"We've added more size and skill, so we know we'll be a better rebounding team," Driesell said. "We hope the competition within our roster will spur everyone to the highest level. The depth of the roster is the best we've ever had here at State."

And that's bad news for Atlantic Sun rivals, who already were struggling to match up with Lefty's collection of talent. The Panthers appear primed for another run through the league and a shot at more NCAA Tournament glory.

Those plans depend on 6-7 senior forward **Thomas Terrell** (16.4 ppg, 7.5 rpg). Terrell transferred from Copiah-Lincoln (Miss.) Junior College last year and was fourth in the TAAC in scoring, sixth in rebounding and was second team all-conference.

He played more minutes than any other Panther and he scored in double figures in 28-of-34 games. Terrell saved his best basketball for the TAAC Tournament, though, earning MVP honors. He's a match-up nightmare, the team's leading rebounder and a big man who popped out to make 83 three-pointers last season.

"He's our Shane Battier," Driesell said. "We'll make sure he gets the ball on offense and he'll make sure he gets it on defense."

The other returning starters are 6-5 senior forward **"Bam" Campbell** (5.8 ppg, 4.9 rpg) and 6-3 junior guard **Darryl Cooper** (12.7 ppg, 3.2 rpg, 72/34 apg, 1.6 spg). Campbell, a transfer from Northeast Mississippi Community College, was second on the team in rebounding and led the squad in field-goal percentage, hitting .507 percent from the field. He had 11 rebounds in the first-round NCAA Tournament win over Wisconsin, and provided a strong, physical presence in the paint all season.

Cooper, a transfer from LSU, is acknowledged as the top defender on the team, and he's a threat from the perimeter (43 three-pointers) or on drives to the basket (134 free throw attempts). He was 12-for-12 from the line against Florida Atlantic last season to set a school record, and he could step into the all-conference shoes left by Long and Morris.

Lamont McIntosh (2.0 ppg, 0.8 rpg) showed he was

ready to move into a starting role with his key performance off the bench in the TAAC title game. The 6-3 sophomore chipped in 11 points in 10 minutes to help beat Troy State and he has the ball-handling skills and defensive prowess to break through this season, Driesell thinks.

Two newcomers could also figure prominently. **Leroy Davis**, a 6-4 junior transfer from Southern Union (Ala.) Junior College, was regarded as one of the top wing prospects available last year. He originally signed with Louisville but was released from his commitment when Denny Crum left the program.

Davis averaged 15.5 points and 5.5 rebounds last year for 21-6 Southern Union, and has won raves with his defense.

The other backcourt addition is 5-11 **Bayi Handy**, a sophomore transfer from Hagerstown (Md.) Community College who began his collegiate career at Delaware State. Handy scored 8.0 points and handed out 4.2 assists per game for the 28-6 Hawks, and he's a scrappy hustler.

Returning wing **Cedric Patton** (2.9 ppg, 1.2 rpg), a 6-7 transfer from Alabama, is a junior now and has already proven valuable as a versatile inside-outside performer. He had two double-figure scoring games off the bench but he may be hard-pressed to find more playing time this year.

Senior **Donnie Davis** (5.3 ppg, 2.9 rpg) lost his starting job last season with the influx of transfer talent, but he emerged as a top sixth man, playing in every game and playing the fifth most minutes of anyone on the team. The 6-8 forward is a renowned leaper, noted for highlight reel dunks. Davis will set a school record for career games played if he gets into 28 games this year.

Senior **James Gilchrist** (2.1 ppg, 1.9 rpg), a 6-6 transfer from Polk (Fla.) Junior College, saw limited duty. He missed six games with a hip pointer at mid-season but came back to contribute during the tournament run.

Otis Donald will have a chance to work into a role. He practiced with the team last year after transferring from Tennessee-Chattanooga, where he set several blocked-shot records. The 6-8, 225-pound senior is just the kind of defender Driesell likes around the basket. He averaged 3.7 points and 3.9 rebounds, but blocked 118 shots in three seasons at UTC. Donald had a school-record 66 blocks in 1998-99, including another record of seven in a game.

Beyond Donald, Driesell has imported even more size this season, including junior **Kendrick Alloway**, a 6-8 transfer from Northeast Mississippi Community College. Recruited by Tulane, Charlotte and Murray State, Alloway averaged 14.9 points and 11.9 rebounds last season, and he's likely to work into the rotation.

Likewise, 6-11 sophomore **Nate Williams** (16.0 ppg, 9.0 rpg) led Highland (Ill.) Community College to a 29-5 record last season and he has the tools to step in and make an impact.

Another big man, 6-10, 245-pound junior **Andre Tooks**, is more of a wide-body and he can help if he's fully recovered from surgery to repair a chipped bone in his foot. Tooks missed 10 games at Fort Scott (Kan.) Community College but still averaged 8.0 points and 7.5 rebounds for the Greyhounds. He also played football his freshman year at Fort Scott.

2001-2002 SCHEDULE

Nov.	17	Valdosta
	24	@Central Michigan
	27	Charleston Southern
Dec.	1	@Belmont
	4	*Georgia
	6	Mercer
	12	Campbell
	16	**Mississippi State
	21-22	#Raycom Sports Tournament
Jan.	2	Troy State
	5	@Florida Atlantic
	7	@UCF
	10	Stetson
	12	Jacksonville
	17	@Jacksonville State
	19	@Samford
	23	@Campbell
	26	Jacksonville State
	28	Samford
Feb.	2	@Jacksonville
	4	@Stetson
	9	UCF
	9	Florida Atlantic
	14	@Mercer
	16	@Troy State
	21	Belmont
	28	##A-Sun Tournament
March	1-2	##A-Sun Tournament

@Road Games
*Georgia Dome, Atlanta, GA
**Peach Bowl Classic, Phillips Arena, Atlanta, GA
#Charlotte Coliseum, Charlotte, NC (vs. St. Joseph's first round; also College of Charleston, North Carolina)
##UCF Arena, Orlando, FL

BLUE RIBBON ANALYSIS

BACKCOURT	B
BENCH/DEPTH	A
FRONTCOURT	A-
INTANGIBLES	A

When you're hot, you're hot. And Georgia State is hot right now, riding the wave of last season's two-game visit to the NCAA Tournament. The payoff was another banner recruiting class that should again help Driesell heft a championship trophy in March.

It's too simple to say Lefty wins because he gets the best players. His team worked hard last year—on both ends of the court. The Panthers led the TAAC in scoring (79.4 ppg) but were third in defense (68.7 points allowed) and led the loop in steals (10.3).

Some of that perimeter firepower and defense is gone, but it seems the Lefthander has replacements ready to step in. Terrell will push for Atlantic Sun Player-of-the-Year honors and Cooper has a chance to step out of the shadow cast by Long and Morris.

Nobody casts a larger shadow than Driesell, though, and he's only two wins behind Bob Knight as the NCAA's winningest active coach. Overall, Driesell should move into third place all-time this year behind only Dean Smith and Adolph Rupp.

Apparently, Lefty can coach. He'll be back center stage at the NCAA Tournament come March.

(M.A.)

Jacksonville

LOCATION	Jacksonville, FL
CONFERENCE	Atlantic Sun
LAST SEASON	18-10 (.643)
CONFERENCE RECORD	11-7 (t-3rd)
STARTERS LOST/RETURNING	2/3
NICKNAME	Dolphins
COLORS	Green & White
HOMECOURT	Swisher Gymnasium (1,500)
COACH	Hugh Durham (Florida State '59)
RECORD AT SCHOOL	46-63 (4 years)
CAREER RECORD	573-374 (33 years)
ASSISTANTS	Doug Durham (Georgia Southern '92)
	Bobby Kennen (Palm Beach Atlantic '93)
	Ivin Gunder (Jacksonville '00)
TEAM WINS (last 5 years)	5-8-12-8-18
RPI (last 5 years)	274-248-244-306-189
2000-01 FINISH	Lost in conference quarterfinal.

It took veteran coach Hugh Durham only three years to rebuild Jacksonville's basketball program to an-ultra competitive level in the tough Atlantic Sun Conference. The Dolphins had never finished higher than sixth since joining the league in 1998, before last year's third-place tie with Stetson.

And now—at least on paper—Durham faces another rebuilding task with the core of his 18-10 team of a year ago now graduated. Center Kris Hunter and veteran guards Shawn Platts and Brandon Williams will be hard to replace, but not impossible.

A veteran of 33 years, Durham has a trick or two up his sleeve, including a great recruiting class that will provide immediate impact at all the right spots.

"On paper we've got talent and I think we can bring it together and compete for a championship," Durham said. "What concerns me is we're new. It wouldn't be accurate to say we're young but we're new as far as playing together."

The 6-11 Hunter was fifth in the nation in blocked shots last year and his presence allowed Durham to extend the Dolphin defense. Before Hunter became eligible, Jacksonville allowed opponents to shoot .482 percent from the field in 1999-00. Last year, with the big fella in the middle, foes hit just .408.

But the Dolphins have some key pieces to help rebuild, including junior point guard **Kevin Sheppard** (9.2 ppg, 2.0 rpg, 2.8 apg). The 6-0 Sheppard won the job midway through last season, emerging as one of the top on-the-ball defenders in the conference. His quickness is his calling card, and he's capable of scoring in bunches. He nearly scored in double figures despite averaging just 22 minutes played per game. Sheppard spent the summer touring with the Virgin Islands national team, gaining more experience.

He and junior **Tabari Brown** (3.8 ppg, 2.9 rpg) are the only returning starters. Brown sat out the first nine games a year ago thanks to eligibility complications after his transfer from Coffeyville (Kansas) Community College. By mid-season, though, he was starting at power forward where his 6-7, 230-pound frame made him a force. As his defensive intensity continues to improve, the big junior can have an even greater impact, though Durham might opt to put more of a scorer in this position.

Junior **Calvin Warner** (14.6 ppg, 7.0 rpg at Eastern Michigan in 1999-00) sat out last season, but there's no doubt he'll fit into the Dolphin lineup somewhere. At 6-7, 220, he's a natural low post player with great mobility and ability to pop out and shoot from 15-feet.

Another transfer, 6-6 junior **Travis Robinson**, should fit in at small forward or big guard. Robinson averaged 18 points and six rebounds last year in an abbreviated season (he quit the team) at Barton (Kansas) Community College. Robinson is a definite perimeter threat who is deadly off the dribble. He averaged 14.9 points in eight games as a freshman at Fresno State, including a 33-point outburst against LSU.

"Travis is a complete player who can play all three perimeter positions for us," Durham said. "We're excited about having him and I think the people of Jacksonville will enjoy watching him play."

A native of Gastonia, N.C., Robinson played his prep ball at Mount Zion Christian Academy, where he was rated the top player in the nation his sophomore year. He was tabbed A Top 20 player as a senior after averaging 26.2 points, 6.3 rebounds, 3.2 assists and 3.1 blocks.

Junior **Antwan Robertson** (4.2 ppg, 2.1 rpg) was steady off the bench last season and has a chance to blossom into a great perimeter defender. The 6-6 small forward's athleticism also makes him a threat to take the ball to the basket on the other end.

The team's lone senior, **Toby Frazier** (4.1 ppg, 1.4 rpg, 2.6 apg) gave way to Sheppard last year at the point after starting 16 games. He provides stability off the bench and looks to pass first, score second.

Junior **James Daniels** (4.0 ppg, 1.9 rpg) averaged 14 minutes a game last year as a reserve at shooting guard, and he has experience and a knack for taking the ball inside against taller foes. The 6-2 Daniels also has impressed the coaches with his defensive work, including 24 steals in his 21 games last year. He sat out seven games because of a clerical error from his admittance to the university in 1999.

Senior **Ali Kaba** (4.8 ppg, 6.2 rpg) is a blue-collar worker around the basket who gets most of his shots in second-chance situations. The 6-8 power forward began last season as a starter and was a key performer until a broken hand sidelined him in early February.

Along with Kaba, another wide-body, 6-9, 235-pound **Jeff Howard** (0.4 ppg, 0.9 rpg) returns as a junior. Howard caddied for Hunter last year but has displayed a nice shooting touch around the basket.

The opposite extreme inside for the Dolphins is 6-4 junior walk-on **Johnny Jones** (3.0 ppg, 2.9 rpg), who has given the team a lift off the bench with his ability to battle inside with taller opponents.

Durham is confident he has the answer inside in 6-9 transfer **Ryan Lewis** (6.0 ppg, 6.0 rpg, 2.3 bpg) from Chipola (Fla.) Junior College. The 230-pound junior started his career at Georgia before transferring to Chipola, where he shot 57 percent from the field last year and helped the team to a 20-10 record.

"I told Ryan if he thinks he's as good a player as we think he can be, he'll do well here," Durham said. "He can give us rebounding, shot-blocking and a presence in the paint, and anything he does offensively is a plus."

One of the more interesting additions to the Jacksonville roster this season is also at center, where 6-9, 235-pound **O.J. Gilmore** (12.0 ppg, 10.0 rpg) of Jacksonville's Arlington Country Day High School will battle for playing time as a freshman. Gilmore's father

Artis is regarded as the best player in JU history, but his son doesn't seem to be shying away from the challenge of wearing the same uniform.

"I was very impressed that he wanted to come here," Durham said. "He played on such a talented high school team, his statistics don't look very good but he's got good hands and moves pretty well."

Brian Novitsy, a 6-6 freshman small forward from Horsham, Pa., averaged 10.5 points and 3.5 rebounds at Hatboro-Horsham High for a team with five double-figure scorers. He has a sweet stroke from the perimeter but he may not be ready to help much this season.

David Lee (24.6 ppg, 5.2 rpg) is a 6-2 freshman who could work into playing time immediately at the shooting guard spot. As a senior at Hardaway High, Lee was the Columbus (Ga.) Player of the Year.

2001-2002 SCHEDULE

Nov.	17	@Texas
	19	@New Orleans
	24	Belmont
	29	UCF
Dec.	1	Stetson
	4	Florida Tech
	8	Savannah State
	17	@Wichita State
	20-22	#San Juan Shootout
	29	@Savannah State
Jan.	2	@Florida Atlantic
	5	Jacksonville State
	7	@Samford
	10	@Campbell
	12	@Georgia State
	17	Mercer
	19	Troy State
	22	@Stetson
	26	@Mercer
	28	@Troy State
Feb.	2	Georgia State
	4	Campbell
	7	@Samford
	9	@Jacksonville State
	16	@Belmont
	21	Florida Atlantic
	23	@UCF
	28	##TAAC Championship

@Road Games
#San Juan, Puerto Rico (vs. Oral Roberts first round; also Baylor, Puerto Rico, Coppin State, Florida International, Niagara, Texas-Pan American)
##UCF Arena, Orlando, FL

BLUE RIBBON ANALYSIS

BACKCOURT	C+
BENCH/DEPTH	B
FRONTCOURT	B
INTANGIBLES	A

Even with some huge pieces from last year missing, this a team that turned the corner a year ago and returns a nucleus that knows what it take to win. And in Durham's book that ingredient is defense.

The Dolphins led the league in defensive field-goal percentage and blocks last season and were third in steals and fourth in rebounding margin. Hunter made a lot of that possible, but the work ethic Durham instilled and the confidence positive results brought are still with this squad.

Sheppard is back to pressure the ball out front, and Durham still has quickness on the perimeter and some tantalizing size in the paint. If transfers Warner and Robertson pick up the scoring slack left by Platts and Williams, the Dolphins can keep right on swimming with the Atlantic Sun sharks this season.

(M.A.)

Jacksonville State

LOCATION	Jacksonville, AL
CONFERENCE	Atlantic Sun
LAST SEASON	9-19 (.474)
CONFERENCE RECORD	6-12 (7th)
STARTERS LOST/RETURNING	2/3

NICKNAME	Gamecocks
COLORS	Red & White
HOMECOURT	Pete Mathews Coliseum (5,500)
COACH	Mike LaPlante (Maine '89)
RECORD AT SCHOOL	9-19 (1 year)
CAREER RECORD	9-19 (1 year)
ASSISTANTS	Jeff Maher (Penn State '85)
	Michael White (Mississippi '99)
TEAM WINS (last 5 years)	10-12-8-17-9
RPI (last 5 years)	270-275-188-199-251
2000-01 FINISH	Lost in conference first round.

Quick, name a returning player for Jacksonville State. It's tough. There are only four to choose from, and none of them were among the Gamecocks' top four scorers a year ago.

It sounds like the formula for disaster for a program that was 9-19 last year in coach Mike LaPlante's first season. Gone are the talented tandem of Mike McDaniel and Brant Harriman, along with six other letter winners. But don't shed any tears for the Gamecocks. They should be better this season.

"We've definitely improved our talent pool but at the same time, it's a lot of new faces," LaPlante said. "It's a challenge to get them all on the same page but I really don't think people realize the talent we've got coming in."

The Gamecocks return three starters, but they'll all have to fight to keep their jobs this year with the group LaPlante and assistants Jeff Maher and Michael White have brought in. Chief among those newcomers is at least one familiar name to basketball fans in the Southeast, former Auburn guard **Jay Heard** (3.6 ppg, 1.1 rpg, 1.2 apg in 1999-00). The 6-3 swing guard may just be as good as any transfer coming into the league this year but for some reason, his name isn't regularly being mentioned among the top newcomers. People seem to have forgotten about him while he spent a year practicing with the team last season.

"When he was a freshman at Auburn he put 18 [points] on Florida on CBS," said LaPlante, who was an Auburn assistant at the time. "I like that people aren't talking about him. He's a talent, a major college player. We were 29-4 at Auburn and he was playing."

Heard will likely displace either two-guard **Emerson Brown** (6.4 ppg, 2.8 rpg, 1.1 apg) or swing-guard **Ryan Chambless** (3.9 ppg, 1.4 rpg). Brown is a quick, 6-2 sophomore and the team's top returning scorer. He plays all out all the time and the coaches are hoping to rein him into the system a little bit more this season. The 6-1 senoir Chambless started 20 games last season after beginning his career as a walk-on. He's on scholarship now and LaPlante loves the work ethic and dedication he brings to the team.

"He's a chemistry guy," said the coach, referring to his effect on the team, not an academic major.

Chambless was actually a small forward in the perimeter-oriented Gamecock system. He shared time there with **Josh Perry** (2.3 ppg, 1.9 rpg), a 6-3 sophomore. A "high-octane" athlete, in LaPlante's words, Perry is still learning the game and needs to cut down on his fouls. Heard could play this position, too, in LaPlante's scheme.

Scott Watson (5.4 ppg, 2.4 rpg, 3.8 apg, 1.2 spg) is another key returnee as a 5-11 sophomore point guard. A hard-nosed defender, Watson won't surrender his point position without a fight.

"Scott was a freshman last year and got a chance to play in 28 games," LaPlante said. "He basically started the whole season and even though he took some lumps at times, that experience has made him better."

Junior college transfer **Cornelius "Poonie" Richardson** (14.8 ppg, 3.5 rpg, 7.8 apg) was a star last season at Lawson State (Ala.) Community College, and he will play somewhere immediately this season at JSU. A good shooter, Richardson could play alongside Watson if LaPlante wants extra ball handling. Richardson will likely be given an opportunity to run the offense.

"We can run a lot of different lineups with those guys," LaPlante said. "I don't know who's going to win all the spots, but we'll have great competition. I know Jay Heard is going to be in there and I know Poonie is going to be in there and I know **Omar Bartlett** is going to be in there."

The 6-8, 235-pound Bartlett (15.2 ppg, 8.3 rpg, 2.6 bpg) is a junior transfer from Jones (Miss.) Community College. "He's another guy who I think has a chance to be an impact player in our league," LaPlante said. "He's multi-dimensional, can play a lot of different positions and he's got a great work ethic."

Bartlett has been playing organized basketball for only three seasons, one in high school in Miami, Fla., and two more at Jones. He's still learning the game and has a chance to blossom into a low-post monster at JSU.

Bartlett will be backed at power forward by two 6-7 freshmen, **Carl Brown** and **Travis Billings**. Brown averaged 19.6 points, 9.6 rebounds and 3.6 blocks at Birmingham's Jackson-Olin High School and he's already 226 pounds.

Billings can play either post spot in JSU's interchangeable system at power forward and center. He's already 245 pounds. Billings averaged 14.4 points, 7.9 rebounds and 2.2 blocks at Monroe High in Albany, Ga.

Another freshman swingman, 6-5 **Marcus Brown** (22.5 ppg, 8.5 rpg, 2.1 bpg), was a standout at Bannekar High School in College Park, Ga. He can play small forward or move up to the four-spot.

Chris Bruce (14.1 ppg, 10.3 rpg, 3.0 bpg) is a 6-8 red-shirt freshman from West High School in Morristown, Tenn., and the only center listed on the roster. He red-shirted last year because of the depth the Gamecocks enjoyed inside.

"The way we play, the four and the five [positions] are basically the same," LaPlante said. "Our rotation inside will be Bruce, Omar Bartlett, Travis Billings, Carl Brown and Josh Perry can even slide into some forward. We can also move Jay Heard down and go four-and-one."

Little-used 5-10 junior guard **Neal Barker** (0.0 ppg, 0.0 rpg, 0.5 apg), who played in four games last year, is also back.

"We've only got four returnees but that's a little deceiving because we had two guys [Heard and Bruce] who were with us last year in practice," LaPlante said. "We've got a lot of mixing to do to find the right guys. That's our biggest concern."

2001-2002 SCHEDULE

Nov.	18	@Auburn
	21	@Birmingham Southern
	29	@Troy State
Dec.	1	@Mercer
	14	@Alabama
	17	Central Florida
	19	Florida Atlantic
Jan.	2	@Samford
	5	@Jacksonville
	7	@Stetson
	10	Belmont
	17	Georgia State
	19	Campbell
	22	Samford
	24	@Savannah State
	25	@Georgia State
	28	@Campbell
Feb.	2	Savannah State
	4	@Belmont
	7	Stetson
	9	Jacksonville
	11	@Morris Brown
	14	@Florida Atlantic
	16	@Central Florida
	18	Morris Brown
	21	Mercer
	23	Troy State
	28	#A-Sun Tournament
March	1-2	#A-Sun Tournament

@Road Games
##UCF Arena, Orlando, FL

BLUE RIBBON ANALYSIS

BACKCOURT	B
BENCH/DEPTH	C+
FRONTCOURT	C-
INTANGIBLES	C

Jacksonville State struggled last year with two freshmen in the backcourt. The front line play was solid, but the Gamecocks were a little one-dimensional offensively, relying too heavily on seniors McDaniel and Harriman.

Some of the youngsters LaPlante landed were unhappy they didn't get more playing time behind the veteran duo and have since transferred, effectively blowing up the team the coach first envisioned.

Then again, that might not be such a bad thing.

Heard will step right in and be one of the top players in the Atlantic Sun, and Bartlett and Richardson just may make names for themselves, too, this year.

Despite all the new faces, the new guys that really need to come through, are juniors. JSU can be a lot better in a hurry if the new mix jells. And a lot of opposing coaches and JSU fans may know their lineup by the end of the season.

(M.A.)

Mercer

LOCATION	Macon, GA
CONFERENCE	Atlantic Sun
LAST SEASON	13-15 (.464)
CONFERENCE RECORD	10-8 (6th)
STARTERS LOST/RETURNING	3/2
NICKNAME	Bears
COLORS	Black & Orange
HOMECOURT	Porter Gym (500),
	Macon Coliseum (8,500)
COACH	Mark Slonaker (Georgia '80)
RECORD AT SCHOOL	38-75 (4 years)
CAREER RECORD	38-75 (4 years)
ASSISTANTS	Mike Gillespie (Morehead State '95)
	Cleveland Jackson (Georgia '96)
	Jeremy Luther (North Greenville '96)
TEAM WINS (last 5 years)	3-5-8-12-13
RPI (last 5 years)	186-195-175-160-216
2000-01 FINISH	Lost in conference quarterfinal.

In a guard-driven league, Mercer boasts the Atlantic Sun Conference's best frontcourt. Coach Mark Slonaker hopes that asset and a rebuilt backcourt will propel the Bears to the upper echelon of the league.

For two years in a row, the Bears have finished the regular season strong. Last season, they won six of their last nine games before falling to Stetson in a conference quarterfinal, and their 10-8 ASC mark was their first winning record in league play in nine seasons.

More importantly, the improving Bears still have two years to ride the skills of talented big man **Scott Emerson** (16.4 ppg, 7.5 rpg), a serious candidate for ASC Player-of- the-Year honors this season.

The 6-9, 235-pound junior is already acknowledged as one of the league's top performers and he ranked in the league's top 10 in four categories last season, finishing sixth in scoring, fourth in rebounding, eighth in field goal percentage (.488), and sixth in free-throw percentage (.800).

"He's a force to be reckoned with and the best returning big man in the league," Slonaker said. "There are some kids coming in and getting eligible this year [around the conference], but as far as returning, he's the best."

Emerson added three-point range to his game last year, tripling his three-pointers made to 27-of-70 .(386 percent). Those numbers could increase again, and Slonaker said the versatile forward has improved his passing skills and his ability to work off the dibble.

In Mercer's triangle offense, Emerson plays the forward position ala the Los Angeles Lakers' Robert Horry. He has the green light to shoot threes, but the Mercer coaches would also like to see him aggressively go to the basket, too.

"Last year his free throws went down a little bit," Slonaker said. "I don't mind a 6-9 guy out there on the wing if he shoots 39 percent from three, but I think Scott became a little too enamored with being out there. He's too good a post player to spend all his time out there."

Emerson has that freedom at Mercer thanks to 6-11 junior center **Justin Howard** (5.9 ppg, 4.7 rpg), who makes that Jared guy on the Subway sandwich commercials look like a slacker. Howard, who entered college at more than 330 pounds, is down below 280, and a lot of that remaining bulk is added muscle.

Howard had several huge games last year, but as his final averages indicate, he also had several games where he didn't produce much at all. Slonaker looks for him to become more consistent.

"I'd like [Howard] and **Bobby Hansen** to combine for about 16 or 17 points and eight or nine rebounds together as a tandem to complement Emerson," Slonaker said. "Howard blocks shots, takes up space and what he really does is take on the big, strong kid for the other team and gets Emerson out of that. That keeps Emerson out of foul trouble."

Hansen (3.2 ppg, 3.5 rpg) is a 6-9 sophomore forward who can spell both Emerson and Howard at the

four and five positions. He averaged 13.1 minutes per game as a freshman last year.

Sophomore **Andrew Walker** (1.7 ppg, 0.7 rpg) should see more duty this year. A 6-9 finesse forward despite his 245 pounds, Walker has the size to help inside despite appearing sparingly in just 17 games last season.

Another option is 6-10 freshman **Will Emerson** (19.0 ppg, 10.0 rpg), Scott's younger brother fresh out of Camden County (Ga.) High School. He can shoot the three, is solid inside that range facing up, has proven a good passer and is not afraid to bang in the paint.

"With another Emerson in there, we feel like we have five pretty good inside guys," Slonaker said.

What the Bears don't have is the explosive, play-above-the-rim athlete they lost when sophomore Wesley Duke (8.0 ppg, 3.6 rpg) went down with his third ACL knee injury last year at the conference tournament. The 6-5 Duke, Slonaker hopes, can join Danny Manning as one of the few players to ever come back from three ACL re-constructions. A member of the ASC All-Freshman team last season, Duke had gone down the year before in the season opener and had to red-shirt. He will take a full year off this time to let the injury completely heal.

Along with Duke, Mercer lost three key seniors from the perimeter—all-conference guard Rodney Kirtz, steady Korey McCray and three-point marksman Josh Sagester. The return of red-shirt junior **Aleem Muhammad** (4.9 ppg, 2.8 rpg in 1999-00) will help offset some of those losses.

The 6-4 Muhammad used the year off to put on 15 pounds of muscle and Slonaker hopes he can burst back upon the scene like Kirtz did last year.

"I don't know if [Aleem] can go out and get 18 a game like Kirtz did in conference games, but I hope he can be a kid who can get us some points on the perimeter," the coach said. "He has played two years. He's long. He can score off the dribble. He knows the offense. This can be his year."

Like Kirtz, Muhammad will play that Michael Jordan, Kobe Bryant—i.e. scoring—role in the triangle.

Junior college guard **Clarence Baker** (10.4 ppg, 7.3 apg) steps in from Kankakee (Ill.) Community College to run the point. The 5-9 Baker slipped through the cracks a little bit as a late signee thanks to the NCAA's "five-eight" rule, in which colleges can only sign five players in any one year, eight over any two year period.

"A lot of people had already signed their five by late May," Slonaker said. "We were able to sneak in there and get him. His speed and quickness help us match up with the better teams in the league."

Freshman **Tyler McCurry** (15.6 ppg, 7.3 apg) out of Abingdon (Ill.) High School, will back Baker. Another cat-quick guard, the 5-10 McCurry can score with either hand and has a penchant for knocking down the big three.

Junior **Noel West** (4.1 ppg, 2.7 rpg) is one of the team's best athletes, but hasn't put it all together to consistently win playing time. The 6-2 West will duel 6-1 freshman **Jay January** for the two spot. January, a military brat, settled at Burkburnett (Texas) High School last year, where he averaged 22 points and made two all-star games in an almost unheard of feat playing just one season in the state.

Freshman **Brad Authur** is a 6-5 sharpshooter from the same Abingdon (Ill.) High School that produced McCurry, and his long-range shooting could earn him playing time. Arthur scored 16 points per game and shot nearly 45 percent from three-point range.

Several walk-ons round out the roster. Junior **John Chvatal**, a 6-7 forward, played in one game last year. **Eddie Holland**, a 5-11 sophomore guard, also made one appearance, while 6-3 junior **Jay Vickers** got in two games, though none of them registered any statistics. **David Matthews**, a 6-0 sophomore, and 6-2 **Melvin Harris**, another sophomore, didn't see any action last year, but Harris is a skilled enough athlete that if he improves his defense, he could contribute.

2001-2002 SCHEDULE

Nov.	16	Howard
	17	@Minnesota
	23-25	#Big Island Tournament
	29	Samford
Dec.	1	Jacksonville State
	6	@Georgia State
	8	@Georgia Southern
	20	Fort Valley State
	28	@Iowa

	30	@South Carolina
Jan.	2	@Campbell
	7	@Belmont
	10	Florida Atlantic
	12	Central Florida
	17	@Jacksonville
	19	@Stetson
	23	@Troy State
	26	Jacksonville
	28	Stetson
Feb.	2	@Central Florida
	4	@Florida Atlantic
	7	Belmont
	11	Troy State
	14	Georgia State
	16	Campbell
	21	@Jacksonville State
	23	@Samford
	28	#A-Sun Tournament
March	1-2	#A-Sun Tournament

@Road Games
#Hilo, HI (vs. Hawaii-Hilo first round; also South Carolina State, Wisconsin, LSU, Weber State, Hawaii, Colorado State)
#UCF Arena, Orlando, FL

BLUE RIBBON ANALYSIS

BACKCOURT	C
BENCH/DEPTH	C+
FRONTCOURT	A-
INTANGIBLES	B

Mercer, with it's tough academic standards, will never compete on the same recruiting plane with several of the league's better basketball programs. Slonaker has opted to pursue a Samford-like approach, depending on a system and veteran players working within that system to make the program competitive.

In this case, the system is the triangle offense, and while Mercer boasts the ASC's top returning front line, headlined by Scott Emerson, the Bears are suspect in the backcourt until the new guys prove themselves. Slonaker thinks they're all good shooters, a requirement in the triangle the Bears didn't meet last season.

The schedule—including Minnesota, Iowa, South Carolina and Hawaii—is tough and could cause the Bears to again start slowly. But don't count them—and particularly Emerson—out down the stretch.

(M.A.)

Samford

LOCATION	Birmingham, AL
CONFERENCE	Atlantic Sun
LAST SEASON	15-14 (.517)
CONFERENCE RECORD	12-8 (5th)
STARTERS LOST/RETURNING	2/3
NICKNAME	Bulldogs
COLORS	Red & Blue
HOMECOURT	Seibert Hall (4,000)
COACH	Jimmy Tillette (Our Lady of Holy Cross '75)
RECORD AT SCHOOL	74-44 (4 years)
CAREER RECORD	74-44 (4 years)
ASSISTANTS	Mike Morris (UAB '91)
	Paul Kelly (Tulane '87)
	Tristan Tillette (Berry '98)
TEAM WINS (last 5 years)	19-14-24-21-15
RPI (last 5 years)	222-225-76-134-180
2000-01 FINISH	Lost in conference semifinal.

It's a funny thing about Samford. The Bulldogs were just a notch above .500 last year, and 10 of their 13 players this year are either freshmen or sophomores. So why does Samford come up whenever the discussion among Atlantic Sun Conference coaches turns to the teams to watch out for this season?

The Bulldogs won league titles in 1999 and 2000, and though they dropped back to the pack last year, they're still the team no one in the league enjoys playing.

The Princeton offense coach Jimmy Tillette runs at Samford makes for some long nights for opponents at the defensive end, given all the screens, constant motion and backdoor cuts. It's no fun to try to defend, and when it's on, it's nearly impossible to stop.

Trouble is, players don't just step off the street and know how to run this offense. It takes time to get the timing down, and that's one reason you don't see a whole lot of transfers coming to Samford.

"You can't expedite the learning of the offense," Tillette said. "I'd like to get a 'Princeton For Dummies' book for them. Learning the offense will be particularly challenging for us this year because we're so young."

Tillette does have some experience coming back at key positions, though. Senior **Chris Weaver** (10.1 ppg, 5.0 rpg, 3.7 apg) is back as a combination guard and his 36 minutes played a game led the team last year. He's the team's leading returning scorer, and well versed in the system after playing extensively as a sophomore and again last year.

Along with the 6-2 Weaver, Tillette has his starting point guard back, too. Junior **Cornell Felton** (6-2 ppg, 2.1 rpg, 2.5 apg) started all 29 games last year, taking over from the sainted Mario Lopez, Samford's point guard on the back-to-back title teams. The 5-11 Felton led the conference in three-point percentage, hitting .472 (34-for-72).

"By the end of the year, Cornell was doing a real nice job," Tillette said. "He took over for a guy that started three years and because of the intricacy of what we do, it took Cornell about 20 games to get a feel for it."

The Bulldogs think they have another starter coming back in **Corey Green** (6.4 ppg, 3.2 rpg, 1.6 apg). A 6-3 senior swingman, Green suffered a stress fracture in the first game and played with the painful injury all year until off-season surgery. He had red-shirted the previous season because of a logjam of talented players on the wing.

"Corey was at about 75 percent all of last year," Tillette said.

Sebastian Sachse (4.6 ppg, 3.3 rpg) started 25 games last year as a red-shirt freshman, and he's his own worst enemy at times, said Tillette, because he's such a perfectionist.

"He's a German kid with a big heart and works so hard," the coach said. "I told him he didn't really have basketball instincts and he asked me, 'Coach, can you teach me how to develop my instincts?' I had to explain to him instincts don't work like that."

The 6-8 Sachse fits in as a power forward, and after a slow start last year, he came on to shoot .387 percent from three-point range, including .416 in conference games.

"I thought he had some particularly good moments for us last year," Tillette said. "He works hard and he's gotten stronger. He's got some good basketball ahead of him."

The Bulldogs lost their two leading scorers in all-conference center Marc Salyers and talented swingman Derrick Jones.

"That's the difficult part, replacing those two," Tillette said. "But I think we've got a guy that can step in and start and play a lot of minutes for us."

That would be 6-10 sophomore **Phillip Ramelli** (0.7 ppg, 1.0 rpg), who now has a year in the system, and who, potentially, can bring some things to the low post even Salyers couldn't.

"Phillip is a post player where Marc was really a perimeter player we stuck down there," Tillette said. "So Phillip's a little ahead in post skills and has a knack for defending down in the post. He also has a knack for being 6-10, which is nice."

Ramelli played in a similar motion system in high school, so he's a little ahead of the learning curve, though he hasn't shot any three-pointers in a game yet.

"He has a pretty good touch," Tillette said. "He hits them in practice. He just needs to get game experience."

The Bulldogs are thin in big men behind Ramelli and Sachse, so look for 6-8 freshman **Bryan Boerjan** to see some action. Boerjan averaged 17.1 points and 9.6 rebounds last season at Rock Falls (Ill.) High School, earning a McDonald's All-America nomination. Boerjan, who has already shown he can shoot the three-pointer, was only the third player in Illinois history to play on four I-A sectional championship teams.

Rounding out the regular player rotation are sophomores **Tyson Dorsey** (3.8 ppg, 0.3 rpg), and **Eddie Harper** (1.8 ppg, 1.5 rpg). Dorsey was fourth in the conference in three-point field goal percentage at .431 (25-for-58), and was even better in league play, hitting 50 percent. The 6-3 guard is a native of Brantford, Ontario, and his biggest adjustment was improving his defense, which he has done.

Harper, a 6-5 guard, will play behind Green, and Samford coaches like his potential. They brought him along slowly last year but he's capable of being another

lethal perimeter threat.

Red-shirt freshman **Jon Mills**, a 6-6 forward who will back Sachse, is the best pure shooter in the program, Tillette said. A high school quarterback, he also averaged 24 points, 12 rebounds and six assists for the Winfield (Ala.) High basketball team two years ago.

Another player who could work into the picture is 6-1 sophomore **Will Gardner** (1.0 ppg, 0.5 rpg). If Gardner can contribute some minutes at the point, it could free up Weaver to play more at two guard. Gardner needs to get stronger and tougher to make that scenario work.

Freshman **Anthony LoPiano** is a 6-1 point guard from St. Dominic High School in Long Island, N.Y., where he was an all-league performer. He probably has too much to learn to help much this season. Likewise, 6-6 **J. Robert Merritt**, a left-hander with a soft outside touch, probably won't see much action this year if the Bulldogs stay healthy. Merritt was all-state at Bishop McGuinness High in Oklahoma City, Ok.

Josh Hare, a 6-6 transfer forward from Appalachian State, will have to sit out a year. He averaged 3.5 points and 1.9 rebounds per game last year in 30 games at ASU.

2001-2002 SCHEDULE

Nov.	13	#Loyola Marymount
	17	Louisiana-Monroe
	26	@Georgia
	29	@Mercer
Dec.	1	@Troy State
	6	North Georgia
	8	@Illinois State
	17	Florida Atlantic
	19	Central Florida
	21	Morehead State
Jan.	2	Jacksonville State
	5	@Stetson
	7	@Jacksonville
	17	Campbell
	19	Georgia State
	22	@Jacksonville State
	26	@Campbell
	28	@Georgia State
Feb.	2	Belmont
	7	Jacksonville
	9	Stetson
	14	@Central Florida
	16	@Florida Atlantic
	21	Troy State
	23	Mercer
	27	##A-Sun Tournament
March	1-2	##A-Sun Tournament

@Road Games
#Guardians Classic at Tuscaloose, Ala.; vs. Alabama or Mississipppi Valley in second round; semfinals and final on Nov. 20-21 at Kemper Arena, Kansas City, MO)
##UCF Arena, Orlando, FL

BLUE RIBBON ANALYSIS

BACKCOURT	B-
BENCH/DEPTH	C
FRONTCOURT	C-
INTANGIBLES	B+

"We're gonna be young," Tillette said. "I've got 10 freshman and sophomores. So we're gonna to rediscover that the most important implement I can bring on a road-trip is a night light."

No, coach, the most important thing Samford can bring is that Princeton offense, and players who know how to run it. Weaver, Felton and Green are up to speed on the perimeter. Sachse is getting there and Ramelli could surprise folks this year, stepping in for Salyers.

The Bulldogs are so young they might be a year away from really causing some trouble around the league, ala two years ago. And they're so young and thin they really can't afford injuries. Then again, they've got some red-shirts, so those years listed on the roster are a little misleading.

Imagine that, Samford with its Princeton Chinese fire drill of an offense and backdoor wizardry, misleading folks a little bit.

Watch out, Atlantic Sun.

(M.A.)

Stetson

LOCATION	DeLand, FL
CONFERENCE	Atlantic Sun
LAST SEASON	17-12 (.586)
CONFERENCE RECORD	11-7 (3rd)
STARTERS LOST/RETURNING	2/3
NICKNAME	Hatters
COLORS	Green & White
HOMECOURT	Edmunds Center (5,000)
COACH	Derek Waugh (Furman '93)
RECORD AT SCHOOL	13-8 (1 year)
CAREER RECORD	13-8 (1 year)
ASSISTANTS	Wylie Tucker (Montevallo '78)
	Jon Coffman (Washington & Lee '96)
	Nate Dixon (UNC Wilmington '94)
TEAM WINS (last 5 years)	9-11-14-13-17
RPI (last 5 years)	295-235-225-270-202
2000-01 FINISH	Lost in conference semifinal.

When Derek Waugh took over the Stetson program in late December, he hit the ground running. And so did his team.

Eschewing Murray Arnold's half-court schemes, the Hatters hit the gas and ran away to a 13-8 record under Waugh, including a third-place finish in the Atlantic Sun. Now minus two front-line starters, including all-conference forward Sebastian Singletary, what does Waugh plan to do?

Put the pedal to the metal, of course.

The youngest Division I coach in the country—he'll be 30 in October—Waugh took over after Arnold's sudden retirement Dec. 27 of last season. The players obviously took to the youthful leader, winning their first conference tournament game in seven years and finishing with the most victories since the 1988-89 season.

"Losing Sebastian and Will [Robertson] we lose some scoring, but the big key is rebounding," Waugh said. "We're going to look to run a little bit more to take a little heat off the other team going to the offensive boards."

That seems like a good plan with Stetson returning arguably the Atlantic Sun's top backcourt combination in **Ravil Givens** (12.6 ppg, 2.6 rpg, 5.9 apg) and **Eugene Ambrose** (11.5 ppg, 2.8 rpg). Givens is a 5-9 junior point guard who has improved each year. He really seemed to blossom last year after Waugh gave him the green light to run. Givens led the conference and was 25th nationally in assists.

"I think he averaged 14 points and seven assists in the second half of the season," Waugh said. "I think this could really be his break-out year and he's come back in the best shape he's ever been in."

The 6-4 sophomore Ambrose was voted to the league's all-rookie team last season, and may have been the best freshman by the end of the year. He's certainly one of the Atlantic Sun's most explosive players, as his 27-point outburst against Belmont indicates. Ambrose also became a solid one-on-one defender and he'll have an expanded role this year as he's called on to rebound more.

Singletary tied for the conference rebounding lead with teammate **Santos Hampton** (12.7 ppg, 9.2 rpg). A senior, the 6-7, 260-pound Hampton is certainly capable of shouldering more of the load in the paint and he seems to be rising to the occasion.

"He has really embraced a leadership role," Waugh said. "In terms of individual improvement in a four-year span, the way he has rounded into shape has just been incredible."

Santos improved his free-throw percentage from .397 two years ago to .511 last season. He enters this year 250 rebounds shy of Ken Showers' Stetson career mark of 980 boards.

Rebounding is also a concern at the 6-6 Robertson's vacant small-forward spot. Sophomore **Derrick DeWitt** (10.2 ppg, 1.8 rpg in 1999-00) will likely move in and at 6-4, he has a completely different game. Before red-shirting last season because of preseason ankle surgery, DeWitt made 61 three-pointers in 1999-00.

The time off allowed DeWitt to add strength, and his athletic ability and skillful but sometimes streaky shooting will make him a major factor this season.

Singletary's power-forward position may go to senior **Ricky McConnell** (4.4 ppg, 2.3 rpg), a 6-8 forward/center with a nice touch from the perimeter. Problem is, sometimes McConnell is a soft touch in the paint, too.

"He's one of the best shooting big men in our league but he really needs to work on his aggressiveness," Waugh said. "When he's aggressive, he's a good player but when he gets shy, he's not."

McConnell will also back Santos as Stetson suffers a shortage of big men. In fact, Waugh may just chuck the whole power-forward thing all together.

"We might even go to four guards around a center," Waugh said. "Actually a lot of teams have moved to that because teams are realizing that big guys are at such a premium that if you can just get four good guards who can play and go a little up-tempo, that's not a bad way to go."

Particularly if you've got the perimeter players to pull it off. Stetson is adding that kind of player in junior college All-American **Alexis McMillan** (17.8 ppg, 6.4 rpg, 3.8 spg) from Wallace (Ala.) State. McMillan, a 6-4 junior, was Alabama Junior College Player of the Year and led WSCC to a 30-5 record.

"The best thing about him is that he makes everyone else around him better," Waugh said. "He doesn't do one thing incredible but he does everything well. I think the guys are really going to enjoy playing with him."

Van Morris (3.6 ppg, 1.9 rpg) is a valuable combo guard on the perimeter. A 6-4 junior, Morris plays either guard spot and plays with a lot of emotion. He provides solid defense and leadership off the bench.

Josh Reasor (3.8 ppg, 1.4 rpg), **Joe McNeal** (1.9 ppg, 1.6 rpg) and **Craig Butts** (1.7 ppg, 1.8 rpg) round out the returnees. All sophomores, only Reasor saw appreciable time off the Stetson bench last season. Reasor, a 6-5 swingman, played in every game last year.

At 6-4, McNeal can play big guard or either forward spot, though he played in only seven games last year. Butts, a 6-6 forward/center, saw action in just six games but the Hatters' lack of size could force him into action if he's ready.

The recruiting class yields only freshman **Mark Stiles** as help up front this year. Stiles averaged 21 points and nine rebounds at Bishop Kenny High School in Jacksonville, but at 6-8, 215, he needs to put on some more muscle to have much impact.

Kevin Craig, a 6-6 swingman from Sugar Land, Texas, averaged 3.5 points and 2.8 rebounds per game last year at Rice. He'll have to sit out a year at Stetson to become eligible, but Waugh is confident he can step right in and help.

Craig won't help this year and Stetson's streak of three straight years ranking in the top 15 in the country in rebounding margin is in jeopardy.

"We're going to shoot the ball better and get out on the break a little better so if we can rebound, I think we've got a chance to win the conference," Waugh said.

2001-2002 SCHEDULE

Nov.	17	Webber
	19	@College of Charleston
	24	@Birmingham-Southern
	29	@Florida Atlantic
Dec.	1	@Jacksonville
	6	Western Carolina
	16	Belmont
	22	@Texas Tech
	28	@Florida
Jan.	2	@UCF
	5	Samford
	7	Jacksonville State
	10	@Georgia State
	12	@Campbell
	17	Troy State
	19	Mercer
	22	Jacksonville
	26	@Troy State
	28	@Mercer
Feb.	2	Campbell
	4	Georgia State
	7	@Jacksonville State
	9	Samford
	14	@Belmont
	21	UCF
	23	Florida Atlantic
Feb.	28	#A-Sun Tournament
March	1-2	#A-Sun Tournament

@Road Games
#UCF Arena, Orlando, FL

BLUE RIBBON ANALYSIS

BACKCOURT	A
BENCH/DEPTH	C+
FRONTCOURT	B-
INTANGIBLES	A

Waugh changed the whole dynamic at Stetson last winter, putting his own mark on the program after a mid-season coaching switch. All he did was take the Hatters to their best record in 12 seasons. One league insider said Waugh's players "would eat glass for him," they seem to play so hard.

Stetson had five players scoring in double figures last season and the Hatters were one of only two conference teams to knock off Georgia State. That's a lot of positive karma for a program that hadn't made many waves in recent years.

Givens and Ambrose may comprise the Sun Atlantic's best backcourt and Waugh sounds like he has a plan to overcome the lack of size and depth in the paint. Hampton is one of the league's better big men and Waugh has proven his mettle on the bench. Still, McMillan had better emerge as a big-time scorer to help offset the losses of Singletary and Robertson or Stetson will be all hat and no cattle this season.

(M.A.)

Troy State

LOCATION	Troy, AL
CONFERENCE	Atlantic Sun
LAST SEASON	19-12 (.613)
CONFERENCE RECORD	12-6 (2nd)
STARTERS LOST/RETURNING	3/2
NICKNAME	Trojans
COLORS	Cardinal, Silver & Black
HOMECOURT	Trojan Arena (4,000)
COACH	Don Maestri (Southern Miss '69)
RECORD AT SCHOOL	316-222 (19 years)
CAREER RECORD	316-222 (19 years)
ASSISTANTS	David Felix (Troy State '77)
	Billy Jeffcoat (Troy State '94)
	Kobie Baker (Talladega '98)
TEAM WINS (last 5 years)	16-7-9-17-19
RPI (last 5 years)	155-297-270-181-126
2000-01 FINISH	Lost in conference final.

What do the Troy State Trojans do for an encore in 2001-02?

Well, one more win would be nice. The Trojans stormed to the second-best record in the conference last season and reached the tournament championship game before falling to Georgia State on the Panthers' home floor.

"Last year we had a lot of success," said 20th-year coach Don Maestri, who knows a little about such things. "The players are returning have a lot of confidence from last year but you can't believe that you are going to have success this year because we had success last year."

Maestri, who has won 316 games (an average of more than 16 per season) at the school, has a few holes to fill in the starting lineup, but he also has two starters and seven letter winners returning. "We lost a lot of key players and we're going to have to get some guys some experience early so that they can contribute at the end of the year," Maestri said. "We have to go out there and create our success."

Creating is what second-team all-conference point guard **Robert Rushing** (14.5 ppg, 3.7 rpg, 4.4 ppg, 2.6 spg) is all about. The 6-1 senior went from shooting guard and sixth man to "the man" last year at point, scoring in double figures in 23 games, with 20 or more points seven times.

Maestri thinks opponents will focus on stopping Rushing more this season, and he's happy his point guard put in extra work this summer to rise to the challenge. "Robert's a joy to coach," said Maestri. "He has really grown into a very good basketball player."

Matt Holman and his 14 points per game are gone from the second guard spot, and a couple of newcomers are the favorites to replace him. Junior **Ben Fletcher** averaged 17.3 ppg at Enterprise (Ala.) Junior College last season and he has a reputation as an explosive scorer.

"Ben was one of the top scorers in the junior college ranks last season," Maestri said. "He can shoot the three, but he's got a physical presence that will help us offensively and defensively."

Along with the 6-3 Fletcher, freshman **Jacob Hazouri** is another possibility. Hazouri, from Milton, Fla., is a 6-2 long-distance shooting specialist. He was a standout in the Florida High School All-Star game, pumping in 26 points, including six three-pointers.

Rushing will also see some action at shooting guard as 6-2 sophomore **Herbert Evans** (2.6 ppg, 1.7 rpg, 2.0 apg) continues to emerge at the point. Evans appeared in 28 games last season, averaging 13 minutes, and he will see more action this year.

Senior guard **Eddie Morris** (1.2 ppg, 1.1 rpg), 6-2, missed the first five games last year with a fractured foot though he came back to appear in 18 games. He still seems buried on the depth chart.

The battle to replace swingman Derrick Davis at small forward is wide open. The early favorite is 6-6 senior **Donnie Pemberton** (3.7 ppg, 2.7 rpg), who battled through a back injury last season to play in 30 games. The hard-nosed Pemberton was limited to 18.5 minutes per night but won friends and influenced Maestri's thinking with his gutty performance.

"He's the hardest competitor in the conference," the coach said. "He has played four years and his leadership ability will be a key factor on our team."

Converted post player **Marcus Millhouse**, another transfer from Enterprise Junior College, is also a candidate. The 6-4 junior averaged 12 points a game last year at EJC, his first season as a perimeter performer.

"Marcus played out of position in junior college," Maestri said. "He played inside more than on the perimeter. How fast he reacts to playing the perimeter again will determine his contribution."

Red-shirt sophomore **Rob Lewin** (3.9 ppg, 3.6 rpg) got some experience last season, averaging 10.8 minutes in 23 games. The TSU coaches love his versatility.

"He can step out and play at the three, as well as move inside and play the four and five positions," said Maestri of the 6-7, 230-pound Lewin. "His game experience is going to help him a lot this year."

The Trojans are set at power forward, where **Lemayn Wilson** (14.6 ppg, 5.9 rpg) returns after a stellar junior season in which he led the team in scoring and rebounding. The 6-8, 210-pound transfer from Pearl River (Miss.) Junior College scored in double figures in 26 games and came on to earn first-team all-tournament honors in TSU's run to the title game. He's deadly on the low block or from three-point range, where he hit a team-high 1.9 treys per game.

"I think Lemayn has worked very hard in the weight room and on his game," Maestri said. "I'll be very disappointed if he isn't a more complete player than last year."

Lewin, who is 20 pounds heavier than Wilson, offers another dimension at power forward. **Lovell Craig** (0.8 ppg, 0.4 rpg) provides further depth. The 6-9 junior appeared in just 12 games last year, but has shown potential as a shot blocker. Maestri likes Craig's work habits and he's one of the key players the coach wants to see play a lot early this season so he can help more down the stretch.

If Craig does develop, Lewin would likely see more time at center, where he is the team's only experienced candidate in the wake of Jacova Jenkins' graduation. Jenkins averaged 9.6 points and 5.1 rebounds last year and leaves big shoes to fill.

Along with Lewin, two junior college centers will compete for the job. Junior **Lacedrick "Ced" Pettway** averaged 14 points at Jones County (Iowa) Community College last year and at 6-6, is very athletic and plays with great desire, Maestri said.

The other candidate is 6-6, 245-pound junior **Willie Bynum**, who averaged 12 points and eight rebounds last year at Marshalltown (Miss.) Community College on a team that sent three post players to Division I. Bynum plays with a savvy and effectiveness that belies his height, and he's comfortable facing the basket or with his back to it.

2001-2002 SCHEDULE

Nov.	16	@Kansas State
	23	@Marshall
	25	@Maine
	29	Jacksonville State
Dec.	1	Samford
	8	@Utah
	15	Nicholls State

	19	@Campbell
	29-30	#Touch America Classic
Jan.	2	@Georgia State
	5	@Belmont
	10	Central Florida
	12	Florida Atlantic
	17	@Stetson
	19	@Jacksonville
	23	Mercer
	26	Stetson
	28	Jacksonville
Feb.	2	@Florida Atlantic
	4	@Central Florida
	9	Belmont
	11	@Mercer
	14	Campbell
	16	Georgia State
	21	@Samford
	23	@Jacksonville State
Feb.	28	##A-Sun Tournament
March	1-2	##A-Sun Tournament

@Road Games
#Bozeman, MT (vs. Montana State first round; also Hampton, San Diego)
##UCF Arena, Orlando, FL

BLUE RIBBON ANALYSIS

BACKCOURT	B+
BENCH/DEPTH	C+
FRONTCOURT	B-
INTANGIBLES	B

In Rushing and Wilson, Troy State has a one-two punch that can again propel the Trojans to the upper reaches of the league. They're a little thinner than last year, though, and the early schedule—eight of the first 11 games are on the road—is brutal.

Some tough times early might shake the team's confidence, but down the road, the experience should help, though the Troujans still don't match up man for man with Georgia State.

Maestri does have enough parts to keep the Trojans on the run that has seen them win 36 games the last two years. The winningest coach in school history, Maestri did some of his best work two years ago when TSU was picked sixth and went on to earn a share of the regular-season conference title.

Now, though, the other A-Sun teams are gunning for Troy State, and that's a new challenge for the team. If Rushing and Wilson are up to the challenge, then so are the Trojans.

(M.A.)

 # Dayton

LOCATION	Dayton, OH
CONFERENCE	Atlantic 10
LAST SEASON	21-13 (.618)
CONFERENCE RECORD	9-7 (t-5th)
STARTERS LOST/RETURNING	4/1
NICKNAME	Flyers
COLORS	Red & Blue
HOMECOURT	Dayton Arena (13,455)
COACH	Oliver Parnell (Old Dominion '75)
RECORD AT SCHOOL	110-99 (7 years)
CAREER RECORD	211-174 (13 years)
ASSISTANTS	Ron Jirsa (Gettysburg '81)
	Frank Smith (Old Dominion '88)
	Josh Postorino (Dayton '99)
TEAM WINS (last 5 years)	13-21-11-22-21
RPI (last 5 years)	173-61-161-51-57
2000-01 FINISH	Lost in NIT quarterfinal.

With four starters returning from a 21-13 club that made a run at the NIT title, Dayton coach Oliver Purnell has plenty of reasons to be optimistic.

"We have lots of quality players and quality depth," he says. "These guys have been there. They know what it takes. The key will be making sure we can stay consistent."

The top returnee is 6-8, 230-pound sophomore center **Keith Waleskowski** (11.3 ppg, 7.7 rpg), who made the Atlantic 10 All-Rookie team last year. Waleskowski has a reputation for being a blue-collar, grinder-type play-

 # ATLANTIC 10

BLUE RIBBON FORECAST

East
1. St. Joseph's
2. Temple
3. Massachusetts
4. St. Bonaventure
5. Fordham
6. Rhode Island

West
1. Xavier
2. Dayton
3. Richmond
4. LaSalle
5. Duquesne
6. George Washington

ALL-CONFERENCE TEAM
G-Lynn Greer, SR, Temple
G-Marvin O'Connor, SR, St. Joseph's
G-J.R. Bremer, SR, St. Bonaventure
F-Rasual Butler, SR, LaSalle
F-David West, JR, Xavier

CO-PLAYERS OF THE YEAR
Marvin O'Connor, SR, St. Joseph's and David West, JR, Xavier

NEWCOMER OF THE YEAR
Keith Jackson, FR, Xavier

2001-2002 CONFERENCE TOURNAMENT
March 6-9, First Union Spectrum, Philadelphia, PA

2000-2001 CHAMPIONS
St. Joseph's (Regular season)
Temple (Conference tournament)

2000-2001 POSTSEASON PARTICIPANTS
Postseason Record: 7-6 (.538)
NCAA
Temple (Elite Eight)
St. Joseph's (Second round)
Xavier
NIT
Dayton (Third round)
Richmond (Second round)
St. Bonaventure

TOP BACKCOURTS
1. St. Joseph's
2. Temple
3. LaSalle

TOP FRONTCOURTS
1. Massachusetts
2. Xavier
3. St. Joseph's

INSIDE THE NUMBERS
2000-2001 conference RPI: 8th (of 31)
Conference RPI (last five years): 8-7-10-8-8

DID YOU KNOW?
After playing last season as a one-division, 11-team conference, the Atlantic 10 has switched back to two six-team divisions for this season. The change is a result of Richmond's move from the Colonial Athletic Association. ...The addition of Richmond isn't the only change in the league this season, as seven of the 12 teams have new head coaches patrolling their sidelines. Perhaps the most interesting scenario is at Rhode Island, where former St. Bonaventure coach Jim Baron was lured away from his alma mater after nine seasons. The Bonnies replaced Baron with Pepperdine coach Jan van Breda Kolff. The other new coaches: Danny Nee (Duquesne); Karl Dobbs (George Washington); Billy Hahn (LaSalle); Steve Lappas (Massachusetts) and Thad Matta (Xavier). ... The Atlantic 10 was 81-66 (.559) in non-conference games last season. ... You've got to like St. Bonaventure's chances in a two-on-two tournament of the league's assistant coaches. The Bonnies' assistants include Kenny Blakeney and Billy McCaffrey, who both played on national title teams at Duke ...George Washington meets Connecticut on Dec. 2 in the first round of the BB&T Classic at the MCI Center in Washington, D.C. George Washington's first-year coach is former Connecticut point guard and long-time assistant Karl Hobbs. ... LaSalle is one of 17 schools that has won both the NIT and NCAA championships. ... UMass has made at least one three-pointer in 93 straight games, since a 1998 first-round NCAA Tournament loss to Saint Louis, but new coach Steve Lappas' club isn't expected to have many sharpshooters this winter. ... Lappas, who led Villanova to the 1994 NIT title, and Duquesne's Danny Nee, who guided Nebraska to the 1996 NIT crown, are the only active coaches in the Atlantic 10 to win a postseason NCAA or NIT tournament championship. ... Only in 1988 (Temple, Rhode Island) and 1993 (Temple, George Washington) has the A-10 sent multiple teams to the Sweet 16. ... The most overachieving A-10 team in NCAA Tournament play, without question, is Temple. In 1991 (No. 10 seed) and last year (No. 11), the Owls reached the regional finals. Coach John Chaney, who was inducted into the Basketball Hall of Fame in October, has never reached the Final Four and this might be his last season (19 years, 431-179; 29 years overall, 656-238). ... New Xavier coach Thad Matta, who led Butler to the second round of the NCAA Tournament in his rookie season last year, was an assistant at different schools (Miami of Ohio, West Carolina and Butler) that made it to the Big Dance in four consecutive seasons (1994-98).

(S.B., J.D.,J.M.)

er who can score. He led Dayton in rebounding, field-goal percentage (.552) and free-throw percentage (.843) and was second in scoring to Tony Stanley (15.9), the lone departed starter from last year's team.

Waleskowski made a dent in the program's record book. He was just the third UD freshman to lead the team in rebounding and the third to lead in free-throw percentage. His 385 points were third best by a Flyer freshman, behind only Tony Stanley (431) and Johnny Davis (415). Waleskowski's free throws, free-throw attempts and free-throw percentage were all freshman records, as were his 261 rebounds and 94 offensive rebounds.

"Keith is just a solid player," Purnell said. "We expected him to be improved over last year because he's such a hard worker. He also works very hard in the weight room, and on individual skills."

Waleskowski looked terrific in Dayton's five-game

Australian tour last May, averaging a team-high 18.6 points. He averaged 24.3 over the final three games, providing what Flyers fans hope is a sneak preview of things to come this winter.

Also back is three-year starter **Brooks Hall**, a 6-6 junior wing who averaged 9.2 points despite suffering a stress fracture in his right tibia. He came back for the final five games and actually increased his scoring to 12 points per game in that span.

"He was banged up all year and he still contributed," Purnell said. "If we can get him healthy and keep him healthy, our perimeter play is going to be pretty good."

David Morris, a 5-10 junior guard, is back for his second year as Dayton's starting point guard. He has led the Flyers in assists the last two seasons (5-1 last year, 3.5 in 1999-2000) and was second in the Atlantic 10 in assist-to-turnover ratio last year (2.12-to-1).

Nate Green, a 6-6 junior forward, was one of five

Flyers to average at least nine points last year and will start for the third consecutive year. Green led Dayton in field-goal percentage at .565 and was voted its defensive player of the year.

Yuanta Holland (9.1 ppg, 5.3 rpg) thought he had played his last game for the Flyers last year, but the 6-7, 225-pound senior forward regained a year of eligibility after graduating from Dayton last May. Holland was second on the team in rebounding. He started 19 games last year.

"Green and Holland both started for us a number of games last year," Purnell said. "They've proven over time that they're both pretty good Atlantic 10 players."

Holland is the first Dayton player to take advantage of the NCAA rule—which passed in 1999-2000—that allows Prop 48 players ineligible as freshmen to regain a fourth season of eligibility. The legislation that eventually became the rule was originally sponsored by the Atlantic 10.

Ramod Marshall was a solid fill-in during Hall's absence last year, averaging 8.6 points. The 6-2 sophomore guard really picked it up down the stretch, averaging 12.3 over his final 12 games. He will provide Purnell with a quality reserve with experience.

"He was our best all-around guard coming down the stretch," Purnell said. "He played both the one and two. We're looking at him for the two-guard spot with Stanley gone. He can give you some firepower there."

Sean Finn is the only Dayton holdover without starting experience, but the 6-11 sophomore center raised a few eyebrows when he averaged 10.4 points and shot .786 from the field during Dayton's Australian tour in May. Quite an improvement over last year, when he averaged a meager 1.1 points and 1.7 rebounds.

The final holdover from last year's team is 6-5 swingman **Sammy Smith** (1.4 ppg, 1.6 rpg). Last spring, Smith told Purnell that he wanted to transfer. In July, he called the coach and said he had made a mistake and asked to return. Purnell said yes.

"He is the type of student-athlete we want in our program," Purnell said "I'm pleased for him that he realizes this is a place he can continue to grow and mature."

Smith was humbled by the turn of events.

"I know not everyone gets a second chance," he said after being reinstated, "and I feel very blessed that I am getting one."

Newcomers **Jason Osborne**, **Mark Jones** and **D.J. Stelly** round out the scholarship roster. Osborne, a 6-7 forward-center, red-shirted last season after knee and shoulder surgeries. He averaged 13.1 points and 14.2 rebounds as a senior in high school and worked hard in the off-season to shed some of his 260 pounds.

Jones is a 6-1 point guard who signed last fall and then led Norwich (Conn.) Free Academy to the state championship game. He was chosen Connecticut's top prep player by the Hartford Courant after averaging 16.4 points and 5.3 rebounds.

"We'll try to work him in at the point," Purnell says. "There's nothing wrong with having two quality point guards."

Stelly, a 6-4 wing, was voted to the all-region team at Northeastern Junior College in Sterling, Colo., averaging 17 points and 7.1 rebounds.

"He's a slasher and a very good athlete," Purnell said. "It looks like he can also be an excellent defender."

Purnell has methodically built Dayton into a contender. In his first three seasons, the Flyers were 35-48. Since then, Dayton has won 75 games in four years and been invited to two NIT Tournaments and one NCAA Tournament.

The Flyers are battle-tested. They finished third in the Maui Invitational—the premier preseason tournament in college basketball—and beat two of the three ranked teams they played there, including eventual Final Four participant Maryland. They also went 9-4 in non-league play, and they beat a ranked team (Connecticut) to open the regular season and another ranked team (Xavier) to close it.

With an experienced team returning, Dayton looks to make its fourth postseason appearance in five years, something not seen at the school in three decades.

2001-2002 SCHEDULE

Nov.	18	Toledo
	21	Central Michigan
	24	@Villanova
	28	@Cincinnati
Dec.	1	Morehead State
	5	@Marquette
	8	Eastern Kentucky
	15	*Purdue
	18	Austin Peay
	22	Saint Louis
	29	Miami (OH)
Jan.	5	Xavier
	9	George Washington
	12	@Duquesne
	19	Richmond
	23	@LaSalle
	26	@Xavier
	29	@Massachusetts
Feb.	3	St. Bonaventure
	6	@Fordham
	10	@Richmond
	13	Duquesne
	16	Rhode Island
	21	@George Washington
	23	@St. Joseph's
	27	Temple
March	2	LaSalle
	6-9	#A-10 Tournament

@Road Games
*Conseco Fieldhouse, Indianapolis, IN
#First Union Spectrum, Philadelphia, PA

BLUE RIBBON ANALYSIS

BACKCOURT	B-
BENCH/DEPTH	B
FRONTCOURT	B+
INTANGIBLES	B

The question mark going into last year was the inside game. But all Green, Holland and Waleskowski did was average a combined 29.4 points and 17.2 rebounds while shooting .548 from the field. And all three return this year.

Morris and Marshall are solid but unspectacular guards. Their job will be getting the ball inside and letting the big men do their job.

The Flyers ended last season with three straight sell-outs, and their regular-season average of 12,718 is the school's highest since 1971-72.

Marshall coach Greg White would sooner have a root canal than play in Dayton.

"I've been at every arena in the country with the exception of North Carolina," he said, "and this is, without a doubt, in the top five or six."

Last January, The Sporting News selected Dayton's fans the best in college basketball in a vote of coaches, media members and sports information directors.

There's a positive vibe about this team, and with good reason. With a veteran lineup and a seasoned coach, Dayton appears headed for another 20-win season. The Flyers will play in the West Division as the Atlantic 10 splits in two, and they should give Xavier a run for the division title.

Dayton went deep into the NIT last year. This time, with one of the most veteran clubs in the Atlantic 10, the Flyers' sights are on the NCAA Tournament.

"Consistency, period, is our question mark," Purnell said. "We had some great moments last season, but we weren't consistent.

"Now the guys are a year older. They have the ability. So now it's a question of commitment—and consistency."

(J.M.)

Duquesne

LOCATION	Pittsburgh, PA
CONFERENCE	Atlantic 10
LAST SEASON	9-21 (.300)
CONFERENCE RECORD	3-13 (t-10th)
STARTERS LOST/RETURNING	2/3
NICKNAME	Dukes
COLORS	Red & Blue
HOMECOURT	A.J. Palumbo Center (6,200)
COACH	Danny Nee (St. Mary's of the Plains '71)
RECORD AT SCHOOL	First year
CAREER RECORD	368-278 (21 years)
ASSISTANTS	Charles Cunningham (North Alabama '73)
	Randy Roth (Ohio '83)

John Mahoney (Robert Morris '98)

TEAM WINS (last 5 years)	9-11-5-9-9
RPI (last 5 years)	174-149-269-216-219
2000-01 FINISH	Lost in conference first round.

Duquesne athletic director Brian Colleary and the powers-that-be at Duquesne obviously believe that there's no substitute for experience.

On April 4, 2001, the school signed 55-year-old Danny Nee to a five-year contract. Nee replaced the 32-year-old Darelle Porter as Duquesne's coach. Porter had no previous head coaching experience when he took over the Dukes, and it showed in the team's lack of discipline—both on the court and in the classroom.

Duquesne is coming off three consecutive 20-loss seasons under Porter and seven losing seasons in a row and hasn't been to the NCAA Tournament in 24 years.

It's ancient history now, but Duquesne was a national power way back in the 1950s, making a succession of Top 10 finishes with players such as Dick Ricketts. The Dukes' success continued into the 1960s, but they have floundered most of the last 20 years. The team's last NCAA trip was in 1977; their most recent NIT invite came in 1994.

Most people forget it in the avalanche of losses, but Porter got off to a good start on the recruiting trail. His first full recruiting class, a five-man group, was ranked the finest in the Atlantic 10 in 1999 by the Basketball News. However, 6-5 guard/forward **Brad Midgley** is the only one of the five players that did not experience a serious academic problem—a fact that was blamed on Porter's inexperience and the fact that he was viewed, rightly or wrongly, as the players' buddy, not an authority figure. In the end, that may be why the school opted for the no-nonsense ex-Marine Nee over Bruiser Flint, who like Porter is a young thirty-something coach.

Despite the mess that Porter left and the program's lack of recent success, Nee isn't pessimistic.

"I look at Duquesne and say, 'Why not?' " said Nee, who coached seven NCAA Tournament teams at Nebraska and Ohio University. "They've underachieved for years, but it can be done."

Anything is possible, of course, but the questions facing Duquesne are: 1) Is the school committed to winning? 2) Is Nee the right man for the job? 3) Can Nee change the mindset of his current players and attract enough A-10 caliber ballplayers to turn things around?

On the first point, the school does seem more committed to winning under Nee. They're not paying him Coach K money, but Nee is making a decent buck (a reported $250,000 per season). What's more, the school has vowed to pump more resources into the program—which if it happens, should help recruiting. How bad were things under Porter? Nee's predecessor once complained that Duquesne was so tight-fisted the administration wouldn't spring for cell phones for his assistant coaches—something that's unheard of in 21st century basketball recruiting circles. So, Porter bought the phones for them.

Questions two and three are connected.

Sure, Nee, the tough-minded, Irish-Catholic from New York City, has 21 seasons of coaching experience and a track record of turning programs around. He is 368-278 with seven NCAA and seven NIT appearances at Ohio University, Nebraska and Robert Morris. But his stay at Robert Morris wasn't quite as successful as his previous stops—the Colonials were 7-22 in 2000-20001, his only season there.

Before that, Nee was fired at Nebraska amid slumping attendance and fan discontent after an 11-19 season. So, will potential recruits—and their parents and AAU coaches—see Nee as the guys who worked wonders at Nebraska or the guy who was fired by the Huskers and then had his problems at Robert Morris?

Nee, whose wife is a Pittsburgh native, jumped at the chance to upgrade his job and still stay in the Steel City. He beat out Flint, the former Massachusetts coach who eventually accepted the head coaching position at Drexel, and East Tennessee State coach Ed DeChellis for the job. While most onlookers see clouds over the program, Nee—a glass-is-half-full kind of guy—sees a bright future for the Dukes.

"I want kids who want to wear that jersey and be proud of playing at Duquesne," Nee told the Pittsburgh Post-Gazette. "It's going to be my job to build the perception of it. I think now the players are beaten dogs. I think they are really down. I don't think they're self-perception is real high. They are looking for some leadership and discipline, and I can provide those things. That is part of a winning program."

Nee will follow the same plan for rebuilding programs that worked for him at Ohio and Nebraska.

"I rebuild basketball programs. I know I can do it. I've done it before," Nee said. "And if you've done it before, you can do it again. I look at Duquesne, and I don't see any reason why we can't be successful."

It will take a few solid recruiting classes to get the job done, and that's why Nee hired Charles Cunningham and Randy Roth as his top assistants. Cunningham and Roth have good track records in recruiting. Cunningham, who went to two NCAA tournaments while an assistant under Clem Haskins at Minnesota, has recruited and/or coached players such as Bobby Jackson, Sam Jacobson, Joel Pryzbilla and Popeye Jones. Roth recruited Michael Redd and Ken Johnson, one of the premier shot blockers in the country last season, to Ohio State.

The hiring of Cunningham, who was at UNLV last year, paid quick dividends as he was able to help Nee land freshman **Simplice Njoya**, a 6-10, 225-pound center from Cameroon and The Masters School in Dobbs Ferry, N.Y., during the late signing period. Cunningham was recruiting Njoya for the Runnin' Rebels. Njoya is raw, but brings much-needed size to a team that started three guards and two forwards last season.

Because of the sorry state of the program, Nee probably doesn't have any choice but to plug the raw recruit in at center from Day One and let him learn the hard way—by trading elbows with the David Wests and Kevin Lydes of the A-10. He'll struggle, but learn. Njoya averaged 19.0 points, 10.0 rebounds and 2.5 blocked shots last season.

Njoya isn't the only new foreign import Nee will count on. Nee also signed **Aly Samabaly**, a 6-3 point guard from Akron, Ohio St. Vincent-St. Mary, the same school where the nation's best high school player, 6-7 junior LeBron James, currently stars.

"Simplice and Aly give us a solid base for building our program," said Nee. "They will have a positive impact and should be able to help us both inside and on the perimeter. I know they were both impressed by the quality of the academic programs at Duquesne as well as the city of Pittsburgh. Our staff and players did a great job of recruiting."

Samabaly, a native of Mali, grew up in France before coming to the United States and enrolling at St. Vincent-St. Mary. In his only two seasons of organized basketball, he helped St. Vincent-St. Mary to a 53-1 record and back-to-back Division III state championships. Samabaly averaged 17.1 points as a junior and 12.0 points and 5.0 rebounds last season for a team that finished the season ranked No. 5 by USA Today.

"Aly has only played the game of basketball for five years," said his high school coach Keith Dambrot, whose father Sid played for the Dukes from 1952-54. "His game is only in the 'infant' stages. He is an Atlantic 10-type athlete. He is very, very good defensively. Offensively, he has to get better instinctively. He sacrificed a lot of individual things for the good of our team. He is going to be a credit to Duquesne."

While players like Njoya and Samabaly represent the future of Dukes basketball, Nee's first Duquesne team will be built around 6-7 senior scoring machine **Wayne Smith**. Pretty much since he arrived from Toronto three-plus years ago, Smith has replaced Molson as the most popular Canadian import on Duquesne's campus.

How did he end up with the Dukes? Porter, then an assistant under Scott Edgar, first laid eyes on Smith at the ABCD Camp. And he loved his game, so he set out to sell Smith on Duquesne. Easier said than done. Smith could read. He knew the Dukes weren't exactly Duke and, all the while, his mailbox was filling up with recruiting letters from colleges all over the states.

But then it happened. Smith broke his foot and most teams backed off with one major exception—Duquesne. The loyalty paid off as the Dukes landed Smith, despite the fact that Kentucky, Wake Forest and Boston College all got involved late after it became obvious that he would be A-OK.

Smith enters his senior season at Duquesne as the school's 13th all-time leading scorer (1,377 points). He averaged 16.2 points over his first three seasons. All the losses have taken their toll on Smith, who at times last year seemed more interested in putting up his own individual numbers than helping the team win. Still, on a team crying out for talent, Smith is a guy with skills. Smith, who needs 587 points to pass Ricketts as the school's all-time scoring leader, doesn't need a compass to find the basket. And he's a pretty darn good rebounder for his size (5.7 rpg in 2000-01), which appears clos-

er to 6-5 than the 6-7 at which he's listed.

Smith will need to hit the glass with even more verve this winter. The reason? Dukes forward Jack May, a starter and one of the team's top rebounders, withdrew from school during the summer and will not return. May, a 6-8 power forward, was the second academic casualty from former Darelle Porter's much-ballyhooed 1999 recruiting class.

"Jack had the opportunity to rectify his academic situation during the summer session, but didn't do it," Nee said. "He had numerous things he needed to do. When it became evident we weren't going to get things done, he came to me and said, 'Coach, I'm just going to go to a junior college.' "

May is the second player from Porter's first recruiting class to leave school because of academics. Last spring, Devin Montgomery, who became a starter midway through his freshman season, failed out of school. Montgomery has enrolled at Pepperdine and will be eligible in 2002-2003.

But, May is a much bigger loss. May averaged seven points and 5.6 rebounds last season and was one of three players to play in all 30 games for the Dukes, starting 24 times. May led the Dukes in rebounding a team-high 13 times. Nee had expressed a strong interest in keeping May eligible as he believed May could be a strong player in the conference for the next two seasons.

"We lost a damn good player," Nee said. "I wanted him. He is a good, hard-nosed, tough rebounder."

Making matters worse in Duquesne's frontcourt is the fact that 6-10 junior forward **Chris Clark**, who became a starter near the end of last season, failed an accounting course in the spring semester and will be ineligible for the first seven games of 2001-02 season.

Clark, who averaged 1.4 points and 1.1 rebounds per game, can practice with the team, but the first game of the 2001-02 season he could be eligible is Dec. 22 against Pitt at Mellon Arena.

Clark is yet another academic casualty of the heralded recruiting class that included May, Montgomery, 6-4 junior **Kevin Forney** and Midgley.

Once it became apparent that Clark, who started the final five games of last season, would be ineligible for the first semester, he had surgery to stabilize his injured right ankle.

So, at least until Clark returns, it appears that Nee will go with a starting five containing one tall freshman in the 6-10 Njoya and a bunch of mid-sized veterans (Smith, Forney, 6-5 senior **Jamal Hunter**, and 6-5 senior **Aaron Lovelace**).

The return of Forney, who has experienced a series of personal setbacks since coming to Duquesne, and Hunter might surprise some folks. Over the summer, Forney (9.1 ppg, 2.7 rpg, 55 assists) was in serious academic peril. He wasn't able to get eligible until late summer. He's an A-10 caliber athlete and player, but he sometimes gets too out of control on the wing.

Hunter is back after he was granted a fifth season of eligibility by the Atlantic 10 Conference.

Hunter, from Rocky Hill, Conn., will be a senior and will have a different role this season. Hunter, who played exclusively at the off-guard position for Porter, is learning how to play point guard.

A transfer from Loyola College in the middle of the 1998-99 season, Hunter averaged 2.6 points per game in 18 games in 1999-00. Last season, Hunter started the final six games and averaged 5.9 points. During the final eight games, he averaged 14 points. During his time at Duquesne, Hunter has 55 turnovers and 29 assists. He had 40 turnovers and 20 assists last season.

"We think it's a real positive," Nee said of Hunter's return. "We think he is a young man who can help us win. He's an older guy with a lot of experience. I am very impressed with him. We're going to make him a combo guard. We're going to play him some at the point and some at the off-guard."

Nee doesn't really have any choice. Without a pure Atlantic-10 level point guard on his 2001-02 roster, Hunter is the best option he's got right now. While not a pure point, at least Hunter has some experienced hands to share the ball handling chores with in Forney and the Lovelace, who missed 14 games due to injury last year. When healthy, Lovelace can be an asset. He averaged 5.4 points and 3.2 rebounds last season and made six starts.

During the summer, Nee got some addition help at point guard when **Tyler Bluemling**, a 6-2 freshman from Mt. Lebanon (Pa.) High school, backed out of a commitment to Navy and signed with the Dukes. Navy athletes don't sign letters of intent, so Bluemling wasn't held to a

scholarship, freeing him to sign with Duquesne. He will probably red-shirt this season.

Midgley (4.6 ppg, 2.5 rpg), a junior, can play small forward or shooting guard. He enters the season with a team-high streak of 59 consecutive games played.

Jon Pawlak, a 6-9 freshman, is painfully thin but is a good shooter and could get some backup minutes in the frontcourt.

2001-2002 SCHEDULE

Nov.	18	Maryland-Eastern Shore
	26	Vermont
	29	@Ohio
Dec.	1	@Cincinnati
	5	Bowling Green
	8	@UNC Wilmington
	19	@West Virginia
	22	*Pittsburgh
	27	@Cleveland State
	29	Liberty
	31	George Mason
Jan.	6	@George Washington
	9	@Temple
	12	Dayton
	16	LaSalle
	19	@St. Bonaventure
	23	Saint Joseph's
	26	@Richmond
	30	@Xavier
Feb.	2	Fordham
	6	Massachusetts
	9	@Rhode Island
	13	@Dayton
	16	George Washington
	19	@LaSalle
	24	Xavier
March	2	Richmond
	6-9	#Atlantic 10 Tournament

@Road Games
*Mellon Arena, Pittsburgh, PA
#First Union Spectrum, Philadelphia, PA

BLUE RIBBON ANALYSIS

FRONTCOURT	C
BACKCOURT	C-
BENCH/DEPTH	D+
INTANGIBLES	C

Nee begins this season with high hopes.

"We have to aim high," Nee said. "Our goal is not be .500. I don't like the word average. Average means 50 percent is above you and 50 percent is below you. It means mediocre. I don't want to have a mediocre basketball team. You don't want an average meal. You don't go out and buy an average suit. I don't want them to be average. I want 100 percent of what they're doing. If they have A or B ability and they're giving me C effort, it won't be tolerated.

"We have to sell the kids on being the best they can be. We're going to crawl, walk and then run. That's the journey. Success is not a journey, it's a destination."

The destination could take longer to reach than Nee envisions. But given his track record (and overlooking the previous two years), this program bears watching over the next couple of years.

(B.D.)

Fordham

LOCATION	Bronx, NY
CONFERENCE	Atlantic 10
LAST SEASON	12-17 (.414)
CONFERENCE RECORD	4-12 (9th)
STARTERS LOST/RETURNING	2/3
NICKNAME	Rams
COLORS	Maroon & White
HOMECOURT	Rose Hill Gym (3,470)
COACH	Bob Hill (Bowling Green '71)
RECORD AT SCHOOL	26-32 (2 years)
CAREER RECORD	26-32 (2 years)
ASSISTANTS	Mike Brown (Vermont '73)
	Shay Berry (Central Connecticut '89)
	Cameron Hill (Trinity '99)

TEAM WINS (last 5 years)   6-6-12-14-12
RPI (last 5 years)   243-223-198-136-147
2000-01 FINISH   Lost in conference first round.

Can you blame Bob Hill if he was a little too concerned about making sure his Fordham team had plenty of big men down low? After all, he's an NBA guy, a league in which you get nowhere near the postseason without a strong low-post presence. His center with the San Antonio Spurs, you may recall, was a player by the name of Robinson, as in "The Admiral," David Robinson.

"The lesson I've learned is that if you don't have good guards you don't win in college hoops," said Hill, who begins his third season as a college coach hoping the Rams can rebound from a 12-17 record—a definite step back after going 14-15 two years ago. "With so many big guys going to the NBA early, it has watered down the front lines in college basketball."

It's not as if Fordham didn't have any good guards last year. In fact, its two top scorers were senior guards Bevon Robin and Jason Harris. The problem was the Rams were a little too reliant on Robin (14.3 ppg, 5.1 apg, 4.1 rpg) and the 5-9 Harris (11.2 ppg, 2.5 spg) and they lacked backcourt depth, a bad combination for sure. That meant foul trouble was big trouble.

Fordham bolted to an 11-6 record, including wins over St. John's (at Madison Square Garden, no less), Iona and George Mason, but faded fast. Its last win of a season that mercifully ended on March 7 at LaSalle was Feb. 18. The Rams dropped 11 of their last 12 games and six straight (five by double-digits) to close the season. Contributing to that was an injury to Robin and a shooting slump by Harris (26.3 percent in A-10 play), who had been one of the league's best long-range shooters as a junior.

"They had nice careers," Hill, who didn't recruit either and reportedly had differences with Robin, said politely.

Arseni Kuchinsky, a 6-7 forward who averaged 8.3 points off the bench, is the other key loss.

After solidifying the frontcourt with the addition last year of 6-8, 250-pound sophomore **Jeff McMillan** (10.0 ppg, 7.8 rpg, 25 blocks), who had a strong rookie season, Hill has looked to bolster the backcourt.

Mark Jarrell-Wright, a 6-5 senior, is a welcome transfer from Providence College. He practiced with the team last year during his red-shirt season. Two other newcomers who could have a major impact are 6-4 sophomore **William "Smoosh" Parker** and 6-2 freshman Adrian Walton. They are both from the Bronx area and have had their share of experience on New York City playgrounds.

Parker averaged 11.7 points and 6.0 assists last year at Southern Idaho Junior College, and Walton, who plays the point, averaged 26 points and 10 rebounds for Bronx Regional. He was recruited by schools such as Miami and Fresno State.

Michael Haynes (5.6 ppg, 2.3 rpg), a 6-8 sophomore, also returns and should help in the backcourt.

The Rams are going to be much younger than a year ago, and that will certainly hamper them early. But their newfound depth will allow them to change from their laid-back defensive style and become more aggressive.

"Bevon and Jason were all we had last year, so we were limited with what we could do," Hill said. "I expect us to extend more defensively on the perimeter and to press more."

Another highly regarded newcomer who had to sit out last season after tearing his ACL in a summer league game is **Cori Spencer**, a 6-7, 250-pound red-shirt freshman. At Peekskill (N.Y.) High, he played one season with former Duke star Elton Brand. The knee injury came while he was playing in the prestigious Rucker League in New York City.

The season before that, Spencer was one of the top players in the New England Prep School Athletic Conference, along with Fordham teammates McMillan and 6-8 sophomore forward **Liberto Tetimadingar**. Spencer was a first-team All-New England Prep pick.

Much was expected last year of Tetimadingar (2.7 ppg, 2.0 rpg), a native of France whose game is centered on mid-range and pull-up jumpers. But after averaging 21 points, 12 rebounds and two blocks at Worcester (Mass.) Academy in 1999-00, he didn't adjust well to the college game.

"He could be an X-factor for us if he comes into his own," Hill said. "He can run, he can jump and he's very intelligent."

Unlike Tetimadingar, McMillan's transition was much smoother. He came in as arguably the most heralded big man in Fordham history—of course, it's a history that includes just four NCAA Tournament berths in 98 years—and didn't disappoint. He earned A-10 All-Rookie team honors.

"He can still improve by leaps and bounds," Hill said. "One of the things that shocks me about young guys is that with camps and AAU teams, the landscape has changed so much, and I don't know if it's for the better. AAU kids sometimes lack basic fundamentals. You have to work with them a lot on pivoting and balancing."

Hill and his staff helped McMillan polish post moves last year and that helped. But "as good as he was," Hill said, "Jeff can still get significantly better."

Duke Freeman-McKamey did that in his sophomore year and won the A-10's Most Improved Player Award. The 6-9 senior averaged 11 points and eight rebounds as a sophomore, and while those numbers diminished just a bit last year (10.5 ppg, 6.9 rpg), Hill said by working on his game Freeman-McKamey kept improving.

"So often in life you have to take a step backward to take a bigger step forward," Hill said.

Forward **Teremun Johnson**, a 6-6 senior, is the other returning starter for Fordham, with Freeman-McKamey and McMillan. They make up a solid front line, but unless the academic problems of 6-11, 315-pound behemoth **Glenn Bateman** are taken care of, no Ram will be listed on the roster as a center. He's a wide-body with soft hands.

Hill said Bateman, who played high school ball in Detroit and comes to Fordham from a Bronx prep school, is in the midst of an appeal for eligibility. He definitely would add some bulk down low. Bateman once ripped down a backboard at an Adidas ABCD camp.

The versatile and athletic Johnson (9.8 ppg, 3.6 rpg, 2.3 apg) is a much different post presence, but Hill loves his tenacity. "He's a defensive back playing basketball," Hill said.

True, Johnson was an all-state football player in high school. "He's so tough. He finds ways to score and he has the courage to take the big shots," Hill said.

Also back is 6-6 senior forward **Steve Canal** (4.0 ppg, 4.1 rpg), a useful role player the last two years who will be counted on for more minutes. **Chris Duckrey**, a 6-6 sophomore guard from Marlton, N.J., 6-3 junior guard **Tyrone Stallings**, out of the Bronx, and 6-4 sophomore guard **Alessandro Acquaviva**, who hails from Napoli, Italy, saw little action a year ago but round out the list of nine returnees.

2001-2002 SCHEDULE

Nov.	12	#@DePaul
	19	@South Florida
	24	Siena
	28	@Iona
Dec.	1	*St. Johns
	8	@Marquette
	19	Delaware State
	22	*Northwestern
	27-28	#ECAC Holiday Festival
Jan.	2	@Holy Cross
	6	Temple
	9	@Xavier
	12	Massachusetts
	16	@St. Joseph's
	20	@Rhode Island
	23	St. Bonaventure
	26	LaSalle
	30	@Temple
Feb.	2	@Duquesne
	6	Dayton
	9	St. Joseph's
	13	Rhode Island
	16	@St. Bonaventure
	23	@Massachusetts
March	2	George Washington
	6-9	###A-10 Tournament

@Road Games
*Madison Square Garden, NY
#Preseason NIT (If Fordham wins, it will play Manhattan or Syracuse on Nov. 14 or 16; Semifinals and final on Nov. 21, 23 at Madison Square Garden, NY)
##New York, NY (vs. Manhattan first round; also Iona, Seton Hall)
###First Union Spectrum, Philadelphia, PA

BLUE RIBBON ANALYSIS

BACKCOURT	C
BENCH/DEPTH	B
FRONTCOURT	B+
INTANGIBLES	C+

The Rams had big plans last year. They had a veteran backcourt and blossoming front line. They thought, after going 14-15 in 1999-00, it would be the next step back to respectability in Hill's rebuilding process after former coach Nick Macarchuk's three final seasons of 4-23, 6-21 and 6-21.

They were wrong.

A season of regression for Harris, whose scoring average (15.2 to 11.3) and shooting averages (39.1 to 26.3 3PT) dipped, and an injury that kept Robin out helped ruin the Rams' 11-6 start, and losing became contagious once again at a less-than-rosy Rose Hill Gymnasium.

"It's all about changing the culture," Hill said. "It's not always just about talent. You have to believe you can win first before you can win. But we're not as fragile as we were last year."

This team will be younger, bigger (if Bateman is cleared to play), faster, more athletic and most importantly deeper. That will allow the Rams to play more uptempo and try to force mistakes that could turn into easy transition baskets. But there will be plenty of growing pains. The backcourt is young, and you don't walk into a league like the A-10 as a guard and expect immediate success. With McMillan, Johnson and Freeman-McKamey, the frontcourt will be strong—if not spectacular. But plenty of questions remain.

Will Spencer bounce back from the ACL injury and have the type of rookie season many thought he could?

Will Tetimadingar, who can play all five positions, be a consistent contributor?

Will Bateman be around to eat space, block shots and hit the boards, or will he be hitting the books?

And most importantly, will Fordham be able to make some outside shots? Harris, Robin and Kuckinsky combined for 162 of the team's 199 shots from behind the three-point line last year. All are gone.

You know that next step Fordham expected to take last year? This should be the season that happens. It better be, or Hill might start wondering why he took himself out of the running for the Cleveland Cavaliers' head-coaching job last off-season. An NCAA Tournament berth isn't likely, but a winning record—Fordham's first since its last trip to the Big Dance in 1992—and the school's first A-10 postseason victory since it joined the league in 1995 is a realistic goal.

(J.D.)

George Washington

LOCATION	Washington, DC
CONFERENCE	Atlantic 10
LAST SEASON	14-18 (.438)
CONFERENCE RECORD	6-10 (7th)
STARTERS LOST/RETURNING	1/4
NICKNAME	Colonials
COLORS	Buff & Blue
HOMECOURT	Charles E. Smith Center (5,000)
COACH	Karl Hobbs (Connecticut '85)
RECORD AT SCHOOL	First year
CAREER RECORD	First year
ASSISTANTS	Kevin Broadus (Bowie State '90)
	Darrell Brooks (Bowie State '79)
	Steve Pikiell (Connecticut '90)
TEAM WINS (last 5 years)	15-24-20-15–14
RPI (last 5 years)	86-38-42-125-121
2000-01 FINISH	Lost in conference semifinal.

Shortly after being hired as the head coach at George Washington University in May, Karl Hobbs announced that he would build his offense around high-scoring guard **Chris Monroe**.

Hobbs didn't have much choice. Not after high scoring guard SirValiant Brown declared for the NBA draft with two seasons of eligibility remaining. And not after guards Mike King (11.7 ppg) and Bernard Barrow (5.2 ppg) graduated.

The cupboard became even more bare in July, when Hobbs suspended center Attila Cosby, who averaged 8.4 points and 7.2 rebounds, for failing to meet academic standards. Cosby eventually left school.

That left Monroe as the sole returning starter from last year's 14-18 team.

"Are we rebuilding? Oh yeah, oh yeah," Hobbs said with a laugh. "I think we're the epitome of a team that is rebuilding."

Hobbs joins GW after eight seasons as an assistant coach at Connecticut, where he helped recruit Huskie stars such as Richard Hamilton, Khalid El-Amin and Kevin Freeman—all starters on UConn's 1999 national championship team.

Hobbs himself was a four-year starting point guard for UConn from 1981-84. He was hired at GW after a burned-out Tom Penders resigned April 20 with three years left on his contract. Days before, the university had announced that possible NCAA violations were pending that involved long-distance calls made by several players. Cosby also was facing nine new misdemeanor charges in connection with a felony rape charge that had been previously dismissed.

"Obviously I'm very thrilled to get the job at George Washington," Hobbs said, "but I know I walked into a tough situation."

In addition to the previously mentioned departures, Hobbs will be without sophomore forward **Marquin Chandler** (2.0 ppg) for 11 games and sophomore guard **Darnell Miller** (1.4 ppg, 35 assists) for three. They are under NCAA-imposed suspensions, leaving Hobbs with 10 scholarship players.

The best of the bunch is Monroe, a versatile athlete who led the Colonials in scoring (18.7 ppg) and was second in rebounds (6.1) while earning a spot on the All-Atlantic 10 third team. The 6-3 junior is capable of hitting a three-pointer or taking it to the basket. He's also a strong free-throw shooter, making 77 percent of his attempts his first two seasons.

"He's the kind that brings a certain work ethic to the game," Hobbs said. "He's got an incredible amount of hustle.

"People heard so much about SirValiant Brown last year, but Chris shot the ball well, rebounded well and did so many different things for this team. Now I'm going to ask him to do even more."

The Colonials' inside game will be anchored by senior **Jaason Smith**, a 6-8 leaper who averaged 5.7 points as a junior. Smith appeared in 30 of GW's 32 games last year and led the team with 30 blocked shots.

"He's a senior and a captain," Hobbs said. "He hasn't had a lot of playing experience, but he's been around. I'm expecting some leadership from him. He needs to become a rebounder who can get me points in transition and around the basket."

Manning the middle will be senior **Albert Roma**, a 7-footer who was chosen the Colonials' Most Improved Player last season. Roma averaged only two points and 1.7 rebounds in limited action but will be given additional responsibilities this season.

Roma and Smith will be spelled by **Matija Debevec**, a 6-11 freshman center from Slovenia who is on a crash course of learning American basketball.

"He's a work in progress," Hobbs said. "He's a little raw, but he's working hard. He's still a couple of years away from what we want him to be, though."

Greg Collucci, a 6-3 sophomore guard, will be counted on to provide outside scoring. He hit 31 three-pointers last year, making 43.7 percent of his treys while averaging 3.9 points. A coach's son, Collucci can expect to see plenty of action this winter.

"He's going to be able to have to make the three-point shot for us," Hobbs said. "He shot the ball exceptionally well last year and we need more of that from him."

Newcomers include **Tamal Forchion**, a 6-6, 225-pound freshman power forward out of Roman Catholic who was selected the Philadelphia Inquirer's City Boys Player of the Year after averaging 18 points, 11 rebounds and three blocks. **Darrio Scott**, a 6-6 freshman forward who was Hobbs' first recruit, also could see action. Scott averaged 24.5 points, 9.6 rebounds and 3.1 steals while shooting 57 percent from the field at Virginia Episcopal School in Lynchburg, Va.

Local standout **T.J. Thompson**, from Germantown, Md., also joins the young Colonials. Thompson is a 5-11 freshman point guard who averaged 14 points and eight assists for the Newport School.

The Colonials' biggest setback came in May, the week before Hobbs was hired. That's when Brown declared early for the NBA draft after his sophomore season. The 6-1 shooting guard was a third-team NABC All-American and finished his career with 1,274 points, which ranks 19th in school history. His 20.9 career scoring average is the second-highest in Colonials history.

As a freshman, Brown averaged 24.6 points and nearly became the first freshman to lead the NCAA in

scoring, finishing one-tenth of a point behind Fresno State's Courtney Alexander.

"It's never easy losing a player as talented as SirValiant Brown," Hobbs said, "but that's in the past. We need to focus on the job at hand, because we have a very young team."

Hobbs hopes to play an up-tempo style, but he'll wait until the season begins to see how that fits in with his raw team.

"I want to be able to run and fast break. Will I be able to play like that this year? I'm not sure."

Either way, it appears Monroe will be a one-man show going into this season.

"He's up to it," Hobbs said. "He's excited about the chance. "Having Chris is the strength of this team. Collectively, I hope we'll be a team that will defend you and rebound the basketball consistently."

The new coach's biggest worry is a roster that already is thin.

"My No. 1 concern is going into a season with just 10 scholarship players and trying to get through the whole year," he says. "Hopefully we'll get through it."

When Hobbs was introduced as GW's new coach in May, he credited his mother Evelyn—who sat in the front row that day—with instilling in him the values he will bring to Washington.

"Those are some of the same things I'm going to pass to my players," he said. "It's going to be a program that's going to have communication, trust, caring and teamwork."

One thing it probably won't have much of, at least this year, is victories.

2001-2002 SCHEDULE

Nov.	15-16	#NABC Classic
	19	@Texas A&M
	23-24	##Red Auerbach Colonial Classic
	28	Boston University
Dec.	2-3	###BB&T Classic
	5	@Old Dominion
	8	@Providence
	29	Charlotte
Jan.	3	St. Bonaventure
	6	Duquesne
	9	@Dayton
	13	LaSalle
	17	Xavier
	19	@St. Joseph's
	23	@Massachusetts
	26	Rhode Island
	30	@Richmond
Feb.	2	@LaSalle
	9	Temple
	14	@Xavier
	16	@Duquesne
	21	Dayton
	23	Richmond
March	2	@Fordham
	6-9	####A-10 Tournament

@ Road Games
#Lexington, KY (vs. Marshall first round; also Kentucky, Western Kentucky)
##Washington, DC (vs. Yale first round; also Binghamton, Stony Brook)
###Washington, DC (vs. Connecticut first round; also Maryland, Princeton)
####First Union Spectrum, Philadelphia, PA

BLUE RIBBON ANALYSIS

BACKCOURT	B
BENCH/DEPTH	C-
FRONTCOURT	C
INTANGIBLES	C-

The Colonials must improve on the road, where they were only 2-8 last season, and they must keep their heads above water until Chandler and Miller return. The team will be hard-pressed to match last year's scoring average of 77 points per game.

Monroe is ultra-talented, but how well he fares with teams keying on him all season will be the big question. He'll get his points, but will Smith be able to provide the balance GW needs with inside scoring?

The Colonials made an unexpected but electrifying run in the Atlantic 10 Tournament last year, finally falling to Temple in a semifinal. A similar run this season would be even more unexpected. Hobbs has a reputation for

being an excellent instructor, but he inherited a mess and will need time to forge his own identity on the team and to build chemistry.

Penders' abrupt—and late—departure did not give George Washington much time to perform an extensive search for a coach. In fact, Hobbs is the first coach with no prior college head coaching experience hired by George Washington since Gerry Gimelstob in 1981.

Hobbs' main job now is restoring order. The wins, he hopes, will come later.

(J.M.)

La Salle

LOCATION	Philadelphia, PA
CONFERENCE	Atlantic 10
LAST SEASON	12-17 (.414)
CONFERENCE RECORD	5-11 (8th)
STARTERS LOST/RETURNING	2/3
NICKNAME	Explorers
COLORS	Blue & Gold
HOMECOURT	Tom Gola Arena (4,000)
COACH	Billy Hahn (Maryland '75)
RECORD AT SCHOOL	First year
CAREER RECORD	42-46 (3 years)
ASSISTANTS	John Gallagher (St. Joseph's '99)
	Roland Houston (Rhode Island '82)
	Joe Lombardi (Youngstown State '81)
TEAM WINS (last 5 years)	10-9-13-11-12
RPI (last 5 years)	178-183-171-173-146
2000-01 FINISH	Lost in conference quarterfinal.

It didn't take Billy Hahn long to solidify his reputation as a terrific recruiter. Just three weeks after being hired as head coach of LaSalle University in April, the longtime Maryland assistant signed four top high school seniors to national letters of intent.

"Billy Hahn always has been one of the best recruiters in the East and this recruiting punctuates it," said Dick "Hoops" Weiss, the New York Daily News' national college basketball writer. "To get this caliber of players this late in the year is unbelievable. His recruiting may change the face of LaSalle basketball."

It's a face that needs changing, but it won't happen overnight. Hahn inherits a team that was 12-17 under 15-year coach "Speedy" Morris and finished eighth in the Atlantic 10 Conference. Morris was fired last spring and Hahn signed a five-year contract.

Only two starters return, but one of them is leading scorer and second-leading rebounder **Rasual Butler**, a 6-7 senior forward from Philadelphia's Roman Catholic High. Butler came into his own as a sophomore, averaging 18.4 points to lead the Philadelphia Big Five. He only improved last year (22.1 ppg, 6.4 rpg) and should be one of the top players in the Atlantic 10 again this season. Butler scored in double figures in 28-of-29 games last year and enters his final season at LaSalle 17th on the school's all-time scoring list.

"Just watching him in preseason workouts and seeing what he's brought to the table so far, he has every possibility of being a first-round NBA pick," Hahn said. "Comparing him to some of the players I've been able to coach in the past who went on to the NBA, he's along those same lines. He has that pedigree."

In addition to being an excellent outside shooter, Butler is a slasher who creates opportunities for himself and his teammates. He'll be counted on more than ever to provide the bulk of the scoring for LaSalle.

"He's a guy that can score plenty of points," St. Joseph's coach Phil Martelli said. "He's improved and his shot selection has gotten better. He has the look that the next level is looking for."

The other returning starter—and the only other senior on the roster—is 6-2 point guard **Julian Blanks**, who averaged 12.2 points and six assists last year (his 174 assists ranked third in the Atlantic 10). Blanks is a workhorse who has started all 95 games since joining the Explorers three seasons ago. He scored in double-digits in 18 games last season.

"He's been tremendous," Hahn said. "He has a great work ethic and he can really shoot the basketball. And it's all about making shots in this game."

Blanks enters the season with 406 assists, which ranks seventh all-time at LaSalle and puts him on pace to finish second. He is also 12th in career steals with 122, having led the team in each of his first three seasons with the Explorers.

Hahn will bring Maryland's up-tempo offense and pressing defense to LaSalle.

"I'm familiar with it, and it worked when I was at Maryland," he said. "It might need some tweaking, but it's the system we'll use."

The Explorers must replace 6-7 forward Victor Thomas (10th in school history with 1,765 points) and 6-11 center Garrett Bragg, who averaged 6.2 points and 5.3 rebounds. James Jordan, a 6-8 forward who started 17 games, is also gone.

The new coach is counting on 6-3 sophomore guard **Rasheed Quadri**, a defensive specialist, and freshmen guards **Mike Cleaves** and **Sean Mulholland** to provide depth in the backcourt. Quadri started nine games last year, scoring nine points in wins over nationally ranked St. Joseph's and Fordham late in the season.

Cleaves is a 5-10 guard who was voted MVP of the Hoopfest AAU Tournament in Providence, R.I. He averaged 16 points and six assists at Notre Dame (Mass.) Prep. Mulholland is a 6-1 red-shirt freshman who sat out last season after undergoing knee surgery in the fall. He scored 1,191 points at Shawnee (N.J.) High School.

The big question for LaSalle is in the paint, where Hahn will rely on three relative newcomers. **Reggie Okosa** is a 6-9 junior who sat out last season after transferring from Virginia Commonwealth. He'll be expected to make an immediate impact.

Okosa averaged 6.7 points and 6.6 rebounds at VCU two seasons ago. Before college, he was selected the Gatorade Player of the Year in Delaware after averaging 21 points and 10 rebounds at Claymont High.

"He has great potential," Hahn said.

Joining Okosa underneath will be 6-9 sophomore forward **Joel-Jean Baptiste** and 6-8 freshman **Dzflo Larkai**. Baptiste is a work in progress. He played in 17 games last year but scored in only six of them. He is listed at 270 pounds, or as Hahn said, "He's a real large human being. He's not fat, but he needs strength and stamina. With improved conditioning, he can provide us with some real minutes."

Larkai is a versatile athlete from England who also played football and was a member of the rowing team in high school. He averaged 12 points, nine rebounds and four blocks at The Gunnery School last season.

LaSalle suffered a hit underneath when 6-8 Anwar Wilson decided to enter medical school rather than return for a final season at LaSalle.

"That was a big setback for us," Hahn says, "but it's hard to blame him."

Hahn decided not to view any tape of his new team when he took the job last April, wanting everyone to start with a clean slate. But the Explorers' strengths—and question marks—are obvious.

"We have quality perimeter people but our big question mark will be our big men," he said. "There are times when you might see one big guy and four perimeter-type people out there on the court for us."

LaSalle won the NIT in 1952 and the NCAA championship in '54, but has not reached the NCAA since 1992 or posted a winning record since finishing 14-13 in 1993.

This will be Hahn's second stint as a head coach. He was 42-46 at Ohio University from 1986-89, then began a 12-year stint as Gary Williams' assistant at Maryland, helping guide the Terps to eight consecutive NCAA appearances and a Final Four berth last March.

Hahn's recruiting prowess is well known. He was chosen one of the top 10 recruiters in the eastern United States by Eastern Basketball and helped recruit players such as Steve Francis, Laron Profit, Steve Blake and Exree Hipp.

History is on Hahn's side this season. The previous five LaSalle coaches won at least 20 games in their first season, and 14 of the last 15 Explorers' coaches posted winning records in their inaugural season.

"I think we're going to be OK on the perimeter," the new coach said. "My concern is, 'Will we be good enough inside? Can we defend and rebound?'"

2001-2002 SCHEDULE

Nov.	18-20	#Paradise Jam
	24	@Delaware
	27	@Villanova
	30	##Iowa Tournament
Dec.	1	##Iowa Tournament
	5	Rutgers
	8	*Drexel
	15	@Seton Hall
	22	UAB
	28	@Marist
Jan.	5	@Richmond
	10	St. Bonaventure
	13	@George Washington
	16	@Duquesne
	19	Xavier
	23	Dayton
	26	@Fordham
Feb.	2	George Washington
	6	*@St. Joseph's
	9	@Massachusetts
	13	Temple
	16	Richmond
	19	Duquesne
	23	Rhode Island
	28	@Xavier
March	2	@Dayton
	6-9	###Atlantic 10 Tournament

@Road Games
*The Palestra, Philadelphia, PA
#St. Thomas, Virgin Islands (vs. Morris Brown, first round; also UAB, Eastern Michigan, Clemson, Miami)
##Iowa City, IA (vs. SMU first round; also Alabama State, Iowa)
###First Union Spectrum, Philadelphia, PA

BLUE RIBBON ANALYSIS

BACKCOURT	B+
BENCH/DEPTH	C
FRONTCOURT	C-
INTANGIBLES	B+

The exciting Butler is one of the Atlantic 10's top players and will be able to shoulder the load on most nights. He'll form a potent Killer Bs combination with Blanks, but the rest of the lineup could be shooting blanks most games.

Hahn is woefully thin underneath and will have to rely on a transfer who missed last season, an inexperienced and (perhaps) out of shape sophomore and a freshman. Hahn wants to improve on last year's 69.3 scoring average with his up-tempo offense, but it could be a challenge in what could be a year filled with growing pains.

The bench is young and not very deep. One player to watch is 6-5 freshman guard **Jeff Farmer**, who averaged 24.5 points, 12 rebounds and seven assists last season at The Morgan School in Connecticut. But give Hahn time. His recruiting skills are terrific, and he should return LaSalle to the national prominence the school enjoyed in the early 1990s. It just won't happen overnight.

(J.M.)

 **Massachusetts**

LOCATION	Amherst, MA
CONFERENCE	Atlantic 10
LAST SEASON	15-15 (.500)
CONFERENCE RECORD	11-5 (4th)
STARTERS LOST/RETURNING	2/3
NICKNAME	Minutemen
COLORS	Maroon & White
HOMECOURT	Mullins Center (9,493)
COACH	Steve Lappas (CCNY '77)
RECORD AT SCHOOL	First year
CAREER RECORD	230-172 (13 years)
ASSISTANTS	John Leonard (Manhattan '82)
	Andrew Theokas (William & Mary '92)
	Chris Walker (Villanova '92)
TEAM WINS (last 5 years)	19-21-14-16-15
RPI (last 5 years)	47-28-106-116-64
2000-01 FINISH	Lost in conference final.

From 1996-2001, Steve Lappas' teams at Villanova produced six players taken in the NBA draft, including lottery picks Kerry Kittles and Tim Thomas. That figure is equal to what Connecticut and Kansas turned out for the next level, one shy of what Duke and Cincinnati produced and half of what Lute Olson developed at Arizona, all in that same span.

But what separated Lappas and Villanova from those other programs? Each, except for Kansas, reached at least one Final Four in that time frame. Not a big crisis for Kansas coach Roy Williams, who made it there in 1991

and '93. But it became quite an issue for some Wildcats fans who thought Lappas had stopped molding a Super 'Nova.

So on Friday, March 23, Lappas resigned after nine mostly successful seasons at Villanova. Three days later, he was introduced as the new coach at Massachusetts, which saw the James "Bruiser" Flint Era end on March 12.

Like Lappas, Flint was forced out. He saw his Minutemen finish 15-15 and out of any postseason tournament despite having one of the best players in A-10 history, three-time all-conference guard Monty Mack. It was a UMass team many thought could challenge for the A-10 title, and the Minutemen proved that by making a run to the conference championship game before succumbing to Temple, 76-55. But rebounding from a 2-9 conference start to finish fourth (11-5) wasn't enough. For the third straight season, the Minutemen weren't going to be a part of March Madness and Flint had to go. He's now in Lappas' old city, coaching at Drexel in Philadelphia.

It was even more of a "What Have You Done For Me Lately?" exit for Lappas at Villanova. The Wildcats went 8-19 in his first season but then won 20 or more games in six of the next seven and reached the NCAA Tournament four times. The last two seasons, though—with records of 20-13 and 18-13—put Villanova on the NCAA bubble and it burst—just like his job security.

"We won 20 games a year but there's always pressure to win," Lappas said. "That's the way it is."

So it was on to UMass, which chose Lappas, 47, over UNC Greensboro's Fran McCaffery, Jim Larranaga of George Mason and Jim Baron of St. Bonaventure.

"This was the perfect job at the perfect time," Lappas said at the press conference when he was introduced as coach. "It was the perfect time for a change for me and my family and when this opportunity came along, I knew it was something special."

He won't have the services of Mack, who carried the Minutemen at times last year and made more career three-pointers (331) than any player in A-10 history, but three starters return to a team with one of the league's tallest frontcourts.

Lappas teams have always been perimeter oriented, but this season UMass might have to look inside first.

Senior **Kitwana Rhymer** (9.9 ppg, 7.3 rpg, 2.1 bpg), a 6-10 center and third-year starter, and 6-11 junior forward **Micah Brand** are back. They shared the league's most-improved-player award last season, while Ryhmer also was selected the defensive player of the year. Last season, the third-team all-conference choice was the team's second-leading scorer and top rebounder and shot blocker. His scoring averages have increased each season, from 2.5 to 7.8 to 9.9.

"He's a strong kid, he works very hard and I like what I've seen so far," said Lappas, who got an early look at his new teram during a trip to Greece in late August.

That journey was originally set up for his Villanova team, but the switch was made to his new school.

"It was a tremendous help to me," said Lappas, whose club will encounter UMass' traditionally tough schedule, including non-conference match-ups with Boston College, Connecticut and Ohio State. "Not just basketball-wise, but culturally, it was a good trip. I got to see that these guys like to compete, they play hard. I saw a lot of spirit."

Brand earned his first career start in the sixth game last year and went on to start 22 of the last 24. He averaged 8.4 points and 4.7 rebounds while blocking 33 shots.

"As he gets stronger I'd like to see his rebounding numbers go up even more than his points," Lappas said.

A trio of 6-8 seniors—**Eric Williams** (3.8 ppg, 3.5 rpg), **Jackie Rogers** (6.6 ppg, 3.9 rpg) and **Ronnell Blizzard** (1.6 ppg, 1.6 rpg)—should compete for the other frontcourt spot, unless Lappas opts to go with a smaller and more inexperienced lineup. Williams is in his second season after transferring from Syracuse. Since coming out of Paul Robeson High in Brooklyn, he's had the body of a big-time college player but failed to live up to his potential. Lappas, however, saw good things in Greece, where Williams averaged nine points and eight rebounds.

"Maybe he's ready to emerge," Lappas said.

Another transfer from a Big East school, former St. John's guard **Shannon Crooks** (9.0 ppg, 3.5 rpg, 3.0 apg, 1.6 spg) has found a home in Amherst. A third-year starter, the 6-2 senior last year he became the first UMass player since Edgar Padilla in 1996-97 to lead the team in assists and steals. Crooks made 18 of his 74 three-point shots last year and is the team's top returning long-range threat.

That could be a problem in Lappas' offense.

"This is the first time I've had a team that doesn't look like a terrific shooting team," said Lappas, whose past clubs have relied on the three-point shot. "I'm concerned about that."

Neither Flint nor his predecessor, John Calipari, emphasized three-point shooting, and Flint even referred to it at times as "fool's gold" which tempted offenses to become stagnant.

Don't be surprised if forwards like Williams (2-for-8 last year) or Blizzard (5-for-17) try to get into the long-range shooting act now that Flint's more structured offense isn't a harness.

Three sophomore swing players—6-4 **Jameel Pugh** (1.2 ppg), 6-6 **Willie Jenkins** and 6-0 **Dwayne Killings** (1.0 ppg)—round out the returnees. They saw limited action last year.

The newcomer who could have the most impact is 5-11 sophomore guard Anthony Anderson. Lappas probably will hand over the point-guard reins to him, while sliding Crooks to the two-guard slot. Anderson, who sat out last year because of academics, averaged 24 points and 10 assists as a senior at Boston's English High School.

Raheim Lamb, a 6-5 sophomore forward who also missed last season because of academics, will be eligible. He averaged 21 points and 12 rebounds, also at English High School.

Kyle Wilson, a 6-2 freshman from White Rock Christian Academy in Vancouver, British Columbia, and 6-6 freshman forward **Brennan Martin** out of Hargrave (Va.) Military Academy via California are true freshmen. Wilson might be a big help from the outside. He was considered Canada's top prep point guard and once made 12 treys in one game. He averaged 25 points and 9.5 assists per game last year.

Martin averaged 14.5 points and 4.0 rebounds for Hargrave while shooting 53 percent from three-point range. He had committed to Villanova while Lappas was the Wildcats' coach.

2001-2002 SCHEDULE

Nov.	16	Arkansas-Little Rock
	24	Marist
	27	*Oregon
Dec.	1	@North Carolina State
	4	Holy Cross
	8	@Boston College
	11	Connecticut
	15	**@Central Connecticut
	23	Maine
	29	@Marshall
Jan.	5	St. Joseph's
	9	Ohio State
	12	@Fordham
	16	@Richmond
	19	Temple
	23	George Washington
	26	@St. Bonaventure
	29	Dayton
Feb.	2	@Rhode Island
	6	@Duquesne
	9	LaSalle
	13	St. Bonaventure
	16	@Temple
	19	@St. Joseph's
	23	Fordham
	27	Rhode Island
March	6-9	#A-10 Tournament

@Road Games
*Springfield Civic Center, Springfield, MA
**Mohegan Sun Classic, Uncusville, CT
#First Union Spectrum, Philadelphia, PA

BLUE RIBBON ANALYSIS

BACKCOURT	C
BENCH/DEPTH	C
FRONTCOURT	A-
INTANGIBLES	B

Say this for Lappas: He didn't waste any time trying to shape this team for the future around his philosophy of using the three-point shot as a weapon. If freshman Wilson or Martin can surprise by knocking down a few shots and Anderson can handle the point with Crooks helping him along, the Minutemen have a chance to be

better than many people think.

The frontcourt will be the buoy that keeps this team afloat. The backcourt, with only Crooks having any significant minutes at this level, is what will determine UMass' success.

"I think we have a pretty athletic team, so we'll have to run and push the ball a little," Lappas said, knowing full well that when UMass does get caught in a slower game he has horses like Rhymer and Brand to go to.

Their continued development as offensive players also will be key, but with Mack around to command so much attention from the defense, everyone's job will be tougher. If Williams can cash in on the potential people have been saying he's had for years, this will be one of the league's better frontcourts.

But if the outside shots aren't falling, well, that changes everything.

"You have to get guys in here to play the style you want and our administration understands that," Lappas said. "I told them when we came in that it's going to take a little time. I'm not worried about that."

Twenty wins would be a great start for the Lappas Era at UMass. It'd also be pretty similar to what he did at Villanova, but the win total won't matter. Just find a way into the NCAA Tournament and it won't matter.

(J.D.)

Rhode Island

LOCATION	Kingston, RI
CONFERENCE	Atlantic 10
LAST SEASON	7-23 (.233)
CONFERENCE RECORD	3-13 (t-10th)
STARTERS LOST/RETURNING	3/2
NICKNAME	Rams
COLORS	Light Blue, Dark Blue & White
HOMECOURT	Kearney Gymnasium (3,385)
	and Providence Civic Center (12,641)
COACH	Jim Baron (St. Bonaventure '77)
RECORD AT SCHOOL	First year
CAREER RECORD	206-202 (14 years)
ASSISTANTS	Dan Theiss (Plattsburgh State '81)
	Desmond Oliver (Dominican '92)
	Tyrone Weeks (Massachusetts '98)
TEAM WINS (last 5 years)	20-25-20-5-7
RPI (last 5 years)	35-19-67-240-233
2000-01 FINISH	Lost in conference first round.

A lot of people believe the beauty of college basketball is found in the names found on the front of the uniforms, rather than those on the back. That's especially true at Rhode Island, where even the most die-hard fans will have a hard time recognizing the Rams this season.

The program was expected to undergo a facelift after Jerry DeGregorio announced his resignation in February, but as time went on it became apparent Rhody received the Phyllis Diller Special as only five players from last year's team will open this season with the Rams.

The biggest change comes at the top, where Jim Baron, who has made his name rebuilding programs at St. Francis (Pa.) and St. Bonaventure, his alma mater, has taken over as head coach. A tireless worker, relentlessly upbeat person and seasoned recruiter, Baron has already had most of his skills tested during the early stages of his new job.

Soon after taking over, Baron learned that Tavorris Bell (19.6 ppg, 5.7 rpg, 1.2 apg, 2.1 spg) and Zach Marbury (16.9 ppg, 4.0 rpg, 2.6 apg, 1.6 spg) the team's two top returning scorers, had basically dropped out of school. Both applied for the NBA draft, but neither was selected.

At the end of spring semester senior Marcus Evans (4.3 ppg, 5.1 rpg) and sophomore Andre Scott (4.0 ppg, 4.2 rpg), both 6-9 post players, were declared academically ineligible. Evans will miss at least the first semester of this season and Scott was dismissed from the team in September, but could return in the future if he makes enough academic progress.

The problems weren't limited to the players. In July assistant coach Shawn Hood, who Baron had hired away from Wisconsin, was charged with inappropriately touching a nine-year-old girl. He was placed on administrative leave by the university and eventually resigned in early September.

Later in the summer Baron learned freshman guard Dawan Robinson, a 6-3 dynamo from Philadelphia, did not meet eligibility requirements and would have to sit out this season. On July 31 the university also did not admit Chaz Briggs, a 6-7 power forward who helped Wabash Valley (Ill.) College to the national junior college championship. Briggs, who would have been an immediate inside presence, ended up at West Virginia.

Through it all Baron remained upbeat. Despite its recent troubles, Rhode Island has a storied basketball tradition and is building a new $54 million, 8,000-seat Convocation Center scheduled to open on July 4, 2002. The Rams also caught a couple of breaks toward the end of the summer when they signed forward **Marcel Momplaisir** and **Lazare Adingono**, who left Rhode Island in June but transferred back from Xavier College in Louisiana without losing any eligibility.

"Things are looking positive and bright, but it is going to take some time," Baron said.

How long is anybody's guess.

"I don't know," Baron added. "I'm not putting any stipulations on when, where and how long it's going to take."

He's just doing everything he can to make it happen. In addition to pitching his program to potential recruits, Baron has hit the road to talk with fans and boosters to rejuvenate interest in the program. He even has the Rams starting several home-and-home series on the road this season, so the schedule in the new building will be all the more attractive next season.

As for this season, Baron admits "we have a lot of work to do."

The Rams do return their top two playmakers, senior **Dinno Daniels** and junior **Howard Smith**.

The 6-0 Daniels (11.6 ppg, 2.1 rpg, 3.3 apg, 1.0 spg) showed dramatic improvement while starting 29-of-30 games during his first season in Kingston. He is a dependable ball handler and free-throw shooter (.779 FT) who should be a leader on the floor for the Rams.

Smith (4.4 ppg, 2.9 rpg, 3.5 apg, 1.5 spg), also 6-0, led the team in assists despite making just nine starts and playing only 23.3 minutes per game.

Knee injuries limited guard **Brian Woodward** (13.9 ppg, 4.9 rpg, 3.0 apg, 1.5 spg) to just eight games last season, but the 6-3 junior is the team's leading returning scorer. Woodward, a Top 100 recruit from Cardozo High School in Queens, N.Y., also tore up his knee in high school, but enters this season healthy and could be a productive player if he remains that way.

Steve Mello, a 6-1 sophomore who joined the team at the end of first semester last season, also returns. Mello (3.4 ppg, 1.3 rpg, 1.0 apg) made .353 of his three-point shots and is the Rams' top returning long-range threat.

Adingono, a 6-6 native of the Cameroon, walked into Baron's office in June and said he was leaving for Xavier, an NAIA school in New Orleans, but returned to Rhode Island and re-enrolled this fall. The junior played in 10 games after joining the Rams in January and posted modest numbers (2.0 ppg).

Evans will help the Rams inside if he is cleared to return. Basically a banger, he uses his 250 pounds to clear out space inside, which is an area of the floor where the Rams don't have much size, depth or experience.

The rest is up to the newcomers, who are being counted on for immediate help.

"There's no question," Baron said. "You better be able to be able to come in and contribute when you've only won 12 games in two years. That's what we are pitching to all of our recruits—that this is a great opportunity to come in and play right away."

Guard **Emmett Murphy**, a transfer from Monroe College in the Bronx, and forward **Troy Wiley**, from Paris (Texas) Junior College, have the most experience. Murphy, a 5-11 junior (13.7 ppg, 2.3 apg), helped the Mustangs to a 19-9 record last season while finishing second on the team in assists. The 6-8 Wiley (13.4 ppg, 5.4 rpg, 1.0 apg) is a face-up player who led Paris in scoring and handles the ball well in traffic.

Dustin Hellenga, a 6-4 shooting guard from Centerville, Va., is the first recruit of the Baron era. Hellenga caught the attention of Rhody assistant Desmond Oliver at Villanova's Charlie Webber Tournament and attended South Lakes High School, the alma mater of Grant Hill, in Virginia and prepped at the Winchendon School in Massachusetts (17.2 ppg, 5.2 rpg, 2.2 apg).

"He can drain three-pointers and is athletic enough to dunk without a running start," said Michael Byrnes, his coach at Winchendon.

Baron's memory paid off in landing **Jamaal Wise**, a 6-5 forward from Maryland. Rhode Island hadn't even contacted Wise until Baron took over, but the coach remembered seeing him play in the Reebok League in 2000 and was able to land him. Wise (24.7 ppg, 11.7 rpg) dominated at Paint Bridge High School in Burtonsville and has made himself a better ball handler and shooter.

Forwards **Derrick Dale** and Marcel Momplaisir and guard **Jeff Kalapos** round out the freshman class. The 6-6 Dale (17 ppg, 4.0 rpg, 6.0 apg) earned all-conference honors at Bogan Tech in Chicago and the 6-7 Momplaisir is from New York. An athletic wing, Momplaisir did not play high school ball last season, but drew attention at the Las Vegas Big Time Tournament. He is thin and considered a bit unpolished. Kalapos is a 6-5 guard from Stradford Conn .

2001-2002 SCHEDULE

Nov.	20	@Virginia Tech
	24	Iona
	27	@Fairfield
	29	Buffalo
Dec.	1	*Providence
	4	@USC
	8	@Valparaiso
	11	@Yale
	15	@Pittsburgh
	22	Northeastern
	28	@Brown
Jan.	6	@St. Bonaventure
	9	St. Joseph's
	12	@Temple
	20	Fordham
	23	Xavier
	26	@George Washington
	31	@St. Joseph's
Feb.	2	Massachusetts
	6	Temple
	9	Duquesne
	13	@Fordham
	16	@Dayton
	20	Richmond
	23	@LaSalle
	27	@Massachusetts
March	2	St. Bonaventure
	6-9	#A-10 Tournament

@Road Games
*Providence Civic Center
#First Union Spectrum, Philadelphia, PA

BLUE RIBBON ANALYSIS

BACKCOURT	C-
BENCH/DEPTH	D
FRONTCOURT	D-
INTANGIBLES	C

It's hard to believe it's only been three years since Rhode Island came within a basket of knocking off Stanford in the 1998 Midwest Regional Final and advancing to the Final Four, because these Rams are light years away from the likes of Lamar Odom and Cuttino Mobley.

Baron made St. Francis (Pa.) and St. Bonaventure into NCAA Tournament teams and expects to do the same with the Rams. He just happens to be starting from the bottom because academic ineptitude has left him very little to work with.

The backcourt is serviceable when Woodward is healthy. Daniels and Smith are decent players, but won't win many games on their own. The frontcourt is a mess with Scott off the team and Evans out until at least the end of first semester.

Baron knows how to build a program, but needs time to put in a foundation before much can be expected.

"A lot of it is just reinvigorating a program with your attitude and that's what I'm doing," he said. "You've just got to stay at it. A lot of it is bringing in your own players and putting in your own system, but it has to be calculated and you have to do it the right way."

Which means the Rams won't be taking any shortcuts to the top of the conference. They might get there again someday, but it won't be this year.

(S.B.)

Richmond

LOCATION	Richmond, VA
CONFERENCE	Atlantic 10
LAST SEASON	22-7 (.759)
CONFERENCE RECORD	12-4 (1st Colonial)
STARTERS LOST/RETURNING	2/3
NICKNAME	Spiders
COLORS	Red & Blue
HOMECOURT	Robins Center (9,171)
COACH	John Beilein (Wheeling Jesuit '75)
RECORD AT SCHOOL	78-39 (4 years)
CAREER RECORD	167-101 (9 years)
ASSISTANTS	Jeff Neubauer (LaSalle '93)
	Mike Jones (Howard '90)
	Matt Brown (Shippensburg '94)
TEAM WINS (last 5 years)	13-23-15-18-22
RPI (last 5 years)	167-66-164-94-48
2000-01 FINISH	Lost in NIT second round.

Richmond may have a lot of new concerns this season, its first as a member of the Atlantic 10, but at least the Spiders don't have to worry about being invited to their conference tournament.

Despite rolling to a first-place finish in the Colonial Athletic Association with a 12-4 conference record last season, the league did not allow Richmond to play in its tournament because it didn't want the league's automatic NCAA Tournament bid going to a lame-duck team. This meant the Spiders had to earn an invitation to the Big Dance during the regular season, and they came darn close before being left on the other side of the fence on Selection Sunday.

This year the Spiders start almost all anew, but with the same objective. They have a new league, several new players, new offices in the Robins Center and the same goal of making the NCAA Tournament.

Shifting to the Atlantic 10 provides Richmond with stiffer competition on a regular basis, which could help (better chance at an at-large bid) and hinder (possible worse record) its case.

"The two words I use to describe the move most are opportunity and challenge," Richmond coach John Beilein said. "It's an opportunity for us and it will be a challenge."

Many players in the Atlantic 10 are bigger and quicker than those Richmond faced in the CAA, but that doesn't mean Beilein is going to change the way he does things. The Spiders had the 10th-best scoring defense in the nation (60.8 ppg) last season and were fourth in fewest turnovers per game (10.9). Richmond will look to upgrade its recruiting in the future, but Beilein also realizes his perimeter-based offense can frustrate opponents from the outside in.

"We've got the pieces in place, it is just going to take some time," Beilein said. "We are going to need to get some taller players, but we're trying to find kids that still play our style."

Richmond lost nearly half of its scoring to graduation, including forward Greg Stevenson, who led the CAA in scoring (19.1 ppg), three-point shooting (.500 3PT) and was fourth in rebounding (7.7 rpg). Forwards Kinte Smith (9.5 ppg, 4.9 rpg, 2.7 apg) and Rick Houston (7.7 ppg, 4.0 rpg) will also be missed, but the Spiders do not come into the Atlantic 10 devoid of talent.

"We lost some great seniors that contributed on and off the court in many ways," Beilein said. "But we still have a foundation of players that have never experienced losing at the college level.'

Senior **Scott Ungerer** is the cornerstone of that foundation. The 6-7 Ungerer is the consummate Beilein player, someone who does all of the little things so well that they become big things. A three-year starter, Ungerer's statistics (6.4 ppg, 3.5 rpg, 4.4 apg, 1.1 spg) don't wow you until you take a closer look. His 2.84-1 assists-to-turnover ratio led the CAA and his value as a defensive stopper is enhanced by his ability to defend any position on the floor.

"He just plays anywhere," Beilein said. "He does whatever we need. He probably would score much higher if he weren't so unselfish. He's probably one of the best passers in the country."

Junior **Reggie Brown** got off to a fast start last season, averaging 20 points through the first six games, but struggled to remain consistent the rest of the way. Brown (10.1 ppg, 1.6 rpg, 2.6 apg, 1.0 spg), a 6-0 guard, has

added 20 pounds in his two years in the program and that should help him stay stronger throughout the season.

Brown finished as the team's second-leading scorer last season and is one of several players Beilein hopes will share the load on offense.

"This year will be more scoring by committee than last year when Greg was so dominant," Beilein said.

Sophomore **Tony Dobbins** is expected to be a key member of that committee. A 6-4 transfer from Virginia Tech (4.7 ppg, 1.8 rpg in 1999-2000), Dobbins has some Atlantic 10 experience and plenty of talent, having been ranked among the Top 100 prospects by recruiting analyst Bob Gibbons when he came out of high school. Although he wasn't able to play last season, Dobbins made a good impression on the coaching staff with his performance in practice.

"He's got a lot of the intangibles that we are looking for with good skills and intensity," Beilein said. "He may be the hardest working player that I've ever coached. He has a chance to be a special player."

Junior **Jeff Myers** (2.4 ppg, 1.1 rpg, 1.9 apg) is another player who doesn't make many mistakes. Consistent play earned the 6-1 Myers a starting job in the Spiders' final 11 games last season, a stretch where Richmond closed 9-2. He also went 11 games without committing a turnover and has shown a penchant for making big plays.

"He's like the Doug Flutie on our team," Beilein said. "He doesn't have the computerized things as far as stats and numbers go, but when he's in the starting lineup, we win."

Richmond may also receive immediate contributions from **Jason Morton** (24.0 ppg), a 6-1 freshman combo guard and natural scorer who played for former North Carolina and NBA great Bobby Jones at Charlotte (N.C.) Christian High School last season.

"He's got great quickness and he can shoot it," Beilein said. "He gives us the athleticism that we need to play some of the quicker guards in the Atlantic 10."

Walk-on **Justin Lay** (0.9 ppg), a 6-2 junior, returns after seeing limited action in eight games last season.

The Spiders do not have a great deal of bulk in the frontcourt, but they do have some experience in returning centers **Eric Zwayer** and **Tim Faulconer**.

Zwayer, a 6-9 junior, started the last eight games last season and averaged 10.3 points and shot .604 from the field in his new role. Zwayer (7.7 ppg, 4.0 rpg) has worked hard on his game and picked up additional experience while playing on a tour of Iran over the summer.

Faulconer, a 6-11, 225-pound senior, was selected to the CAA All-Defensive team the last two seasons and already holds Richmond's career record with 165 blocked shots. Faulconer (4.1 ppg, 3.5 rpg, 2.2 bpg) is not a refined offensive player, but he led the conference in blocked shots and is one of the reasons the Spiders limited opponents to .404 shooting from the field.

"He changes a lot of people's directions on their shots," Beilein said.

The Spiders will have a much different look without mainstays Stevenson and Smith at the forward spots.

Mike Skrocki, a 6-6 sophomore, could be ready to step into a starting role after displaying some Ungerer-like qualities while playing in all 29 games as a freshman. Skrocki (3.1 ppg, 1.1 apg) is versatile enough to play any position except center and his 1.7-1 assist to turnover ratio was impressive for a first-year frontcourt player.

"He shoots it really well and he also sees the floor," Beilein said.

Junior **Jonathan Collins** (0.6 ppg) saw limited minutes last season but could contribute on the defensive end this season. At 6-9 Collins has the size to play both forward and center. He also runs the floor well and is adept at blocking and changing shots.

Freshmen **Patrick O'Malley** and **Jermaine Bucknor** could also see minutes at forward.

The 6-8 O'Malley was selected captain of West Virginia's Class AAA all-state team after capping a standout career at George Washington High School in Charleston. O'Malley (21.0 ppg, 11.0 rpg) plays mostly power forward, but has the ability to step out and make jump shots.

Bucknor (20.0 ppg, 8.0 rpg) is an athletic 6-7 forward from Edmonton who does not turn 18 until November and could possibly red-shirt. An All-Alberta selection at Ross Shepard High School, Bucknor's calling card is versatility.

"He is the type of player that is comfortable at nearly every position on the floor," Beilein said. "We love to recruit versatile players like Jermaine who can shoot, rebound and really pass the ball."

2001-2002 SCHEDULE

Nov.	16	Appalachian State
	24	*@UAB
	28	@Radford
	1	VCU
	5	Mississippi State
	8	@Charlotte
	17	#@Cincinnati
	20-22	##Las Vegas Invitational
	28-29	###Spider Invitational
Jan.	2	@Wake Forest
	5	LaSalle
	12	@Xavier
	16	Massachusetts
	19	@Dayton
	23	@Temple
	26	Duquesne
	30	George Washington
Feb.	2	Xavier
	6	@St. Bonaventure
	10	Dayton
	13	Saint Joseph's
	16	@LaSalle
	20	@Rhode Island
	23	@George Washington
	27	Fordham
March	2	@Duquesne
	6-9	####A-10 Championship

@Road Games
*UAB Classic, Birmingham, AL
#First round Las Vegas Invitational
##Las Vegas, NV (also Mississippi State, Purdue, Illinois-Chicago, SW Missouri, Cincinnati, Texas A&M, Louisiana Monroe)
###Richmond, VA (vs. VMI first round; also Cornell, James Madison)
####First Union Spectrum, Philadelphia, PA

BLUE RIBBON ANALYSIS

BACKCOURT	B
BENCH/DEPTH	B-
FRONTCOURT	C
INTANGIBLES	B

Richmond's sports information department bills this season as "A Whole New Ballgame," and the description is nothing short of accurate.

The Spiders have moved from the Colonial Athletic Association to the Atlantic 10, one of the nation's top conferences year in and year out. Richmond also must replace nearly half of its offense after the graduation of Stevenson, Smith and Houston. The new league will present physical challenges for the Spiders, who will strive to get bigger and stronger to build on the successful foundation Richmond has established over the years.

Ungerer is Richmond's unquestioned leader. He doesn't score a lot, but is one of the nation's top passers and defenders. He may have to be a bit more selfish with the ball this season and will get offensive help from guards Brown and Dobbins.

Zwayer and Faulconer have been an effective tandem at center, but will be challenged by the bigger, stronger players in the Atlantic 10. Stevenson and Smith dominated the minutes at forward so Richmond will need someone to step up immediately, with sophomore Skrocki leading the list of candidates.

Richmond has averaged 19.5 wins in Beilein's four seasons and should make most of the necessary adjustments to continue building on its success. Repeating last year's accomplishments might be a bit much to ask, but the Spiders should still be a solid team that contends for a postseason berth.

(S.B.)

St. Bonaventure

LOCATION	St. Bonaventure, NY
CONFERENCE	Atlantic 10
LAST SEASON	18-12 (.600)
CONFERENCE RECORD	9-7 (t-5th)
STARTERS LOST/RETURNING	3/2

NICKNAME	Bonnies
COLORS	Brown & White
HOMECOURT	Reilly Center (6,000)
COACH	Jan van Breda Kolff (Vanderbilt '74)
RECORD AT SCHOOL	First year
CAREER RECORD	174-128 (10 years)
ASSISTANTS	Kenny Blakeney (Duke '95)
	Billy McCaffrey (Vanderbilt '94)
	Kort Wickenheiser (Muhlenberg '95)
TEAM WINS (last 5 years)	14-17-14-21-18
RPI (last 5 years)	104-117-165-46-74
2000-01 FINISH	Lost in NIT first round.

On April 10, the day he was introduced as the 17th head coach in the history of St. Bonaventure basketball, Jan van Breda Kolff promised to bring a new, faster brand of play to the quiet campus nestled in New York state's southwestern corner.

"We want to play an up-tempo style and take advantage of our athleticism and try and get in the open court and create opportunities to shoot three-pointers," van Breda Kolff said in his first news conference.

The Bonnies gave a sneak preview of what to expect this season during an 11-day, six-game trip to Europe in August. If the feature is anything like the preview, van Breda Kolff and his team will get two thumbs up from the raucous Reilly Center faithful.

St. Bonaventure posted a 4-2 record and averaged 98 points per game while playing club teams from England, Belgium and France on its tour. The Europeans don't play defense like Temple and the other top teams in the Atlantic 10 are noted for, but at least these new-look Bonnies should be entertaining to watch.

"It's nice to be exciting," said van Breda Kolff, who left Pepperdine and the beaches of Malibu for the Allegany Mountains of Olean, which are much closer to his family. "It's the way the players like to play, it's what the fans like to watch and, as a coaching staff, it's a style that we like to coach. So it should be a win-win situation for everybody."

Winning is something both van Breda Kolff and the Bonnies have done their share of lately.

Van Breda Kolff led Pepperdine to 47 wins in his two seasons there, including a victory over Indiana in the first round of the 2000 NCAA Tournament in what turned out to be Bob Knight's last game as coach of the Hoosiers. He also averaged 17 victories in his six seasons at Vanderbilt and led Cornell to a 16-10 record and second-place finish in the Ivy League in the second of his two seasons in Ithaca.

St. Bonaventure enjoyed a resurgence in the final years of Jim Baron's tenure, earning postseason bids in three of the last four seasons. While last season ended with a loss to Pittsburgh in the first round of the NIT, the Bonnies very nearly captured the hearts of college basketball by upsetting Kentucky in the first round of the 2000 NCAA Tournament. The fifth-seeded Wildcats prevailed, 85-80, in two overtimes, but the message was clear: The Bonnies were back.

They'll just look a little different this season. Baron left his alma mater for A-10 rival Rhode Island and last year's inside-outside combination of center Peter Van Paasen (14.6 ppg, 4.0 rpg) and forward Kevin Houston (19.5 ppg, 6.9 rpg) has graduated.

But all is not lost. Senior guard J.R. Bremer averaged 36 points per game in Europe and is ready to build on last year's breakout season and become one of the premier players in the league. Senior forward Vidal Massiah, the team's other returning starter, looks to continue his pattern of improving each season and guards Marques Green and Patricio Prato are ready to establish themselves as solid college players. Van Breda Kolff and his staff are also out to make a good first impression and they are bringing in a talented batch of newcomers to help them pick up the pace.

"What we are trying to create is a team that controls the tempo and makes the opponent play our style," van Breda Kolff said. "For the most part we will be an up-tempo team that presses for most, if not all, of the game."

The new system plays right into the hands of Bremer, a dynamic 6-2 senior who earned third-team all-league honors and may have been the most improved player in the Atlantic 10 last season. Bremer (16.6 ppg, 3.9 rpg, 4.2 apg, 1.6 spg) improved his scoring average by almost seven points last season and could challenge for the league scoring title because of his ability to finish strong inside and bury the outside shot. He topped the 40-point mark twice during the Bonnies' European tour.

"He's a guy that can put up big numbers because he can score in bunches," van Breda Kolff said. "He's also a good passer and a good rebounder. He does a lot of

different things well for us."

Green, a 5-7 sophomore who will start at the point, should also thrive. He made solid contributions (6.2 ppg, 1.6 rpg, 4.7 apg, 1.7 apg) while playing 25.2 minutes per game as a freshman and should be more productive in his increased role. He had 38 assists and just 12 turnovers in six games overseas.

"He'll spearhead our attack both offensively and defensively," van Breda Kolff said. "He's very fast with the ball and he can get it up and down the court. He's also a very good on-the-ball defender, he's quick and he's got good hands."

Prato, who struggled last season after a strong freshman season, will be looking to bounce back in 2000-2001. The 6-4 native of Argentina missed nine games after breaking his wrist at Cleveland State Jan. 16 and struggled to regain top form. Prato (6.0 ppg, 3.4 rpg, 1.2 apg) has the reputation for being a deadly outside shooter, which he is, but he can also put the ball on the floor and create.

"He's got deceptive quickness," van Breda Kolff said. "He can get to the basket, he finishes well and he's an excellent shooter."

One of the Bonnies' fiercest competitors, Prato appears to be back on track after averaging 21 points per game in Europe.

Three newcomers, junior Joe Shepard and freshmen Mike Gansey and Patrick Methot-Lottin, will bolster the backcourt.

Shepard, a 6-2 native of Springfield, Mich., led Owens (Ohio) Community College to a 30-7 record fifth-place finish in the 2000 National Junior College Athletic Association Division II Tournament. Shepard (16.5 ppg, 4.6 rpg, 4.2 apg, 2.1 spg) was selected a third-team All-American for his efforts.

Shepard did not play while completing his associate's degree last season, but is a slasher who can create his own shot, as well as a strong defender.

"He's probably our best overall athlete," van Breda Kolff said. "He can run the floor, he jumps well and he can rebound off the wing. He's got really good defensive instincts and will fit into our system well."

The 6-4 Gansey (27.2 ppg, 10.5 rpg, 3.2 apg, 3.3 spg, 1.6 bpg) was runner-up for Ohio's Mr. Basketball award while starring at Olmstead Falls High School near Cleveland last season. Gansey finished his high school career with 1,909 points in 91 career games (20.9 ppg). He has the ability to get to the basket and score with either hand and can also shoot well from the outside.

"I really like his attitude, his effort and his maturity," van Breda Kolff said. "He's going to step in and play right away for us."

Methot-Lottin, a 6-6 swingman from Cameroon, played at Maine Central Institute last season (17.0 ppg, 8.5 rpg) after attending Archbishop Carroll High School in Washington, D.C., for two seasons and is a skilled offensive player with NBA shooting range and the knack for making big plays.

"He's kind of like a smaller version of Jalen Rose," van Breda Kolff said. "He has the uncanny ability to get around his man and make shots."

The Bonnies will miss the size, experience and maturity of Van Paassen, who is now playing professionally in Belgium, and the frontcourt will need to follow Massiah's hard-working lead in order to succeed.

Like Bremer, Massiah (9.1 ppg, 4.6 rpg, 1.0 apg) came into his own last season, increasing his scoring by 6.6 points and doubling his rebounding. Although he's a bit undersized, Massiah is a capable power forward with above average ball handling skills and shooting range.

"He's a veteran player that has gotten better each year that he has been here," van Breda Kolff said.

The other forward spot appears to be up for grabs with seniors Robert Cheeks and Elton Ruddock, juniors Marlon Miller and Orion Garo and freshman Saulis Dumbliauskas all in the mix.

The 6-6 Cheeks suffered through a disappointing junior year (1.9 ppg, 2.9 rpg). He battled knee and thumb injuries early in the season before being forced to the sidelines after suffering an MCL tear in a loss to Massachusetts at the A-10 Tournament.

The 6-8 Ruddock (1.0 ppg, 1.3 rpg) has worked hard to increase his strength and was rewarded with more playing time toward the end of last season. He made his first career start in the NIT loss at Pittsburgh and comes into this season on a bit of an upswing. Ruddock's strengths are defense and rebounding, two areas where the Bonnies will need help this season.

The 6-9 Miller sat out last season after transferring from Nevada, but did practice with the Bonnies. He posted modest numbers as a freshman (1.8 ppg, 1.9 rpg) before getting lost on the bench and leaving the team for personal reasons nine games into his sophomore season. He has the body to be a player and could factor into things before the season is over.

Garo, also 6-9, is a native of Albania who is still adjusting to the American game. He saw limited action in four games last season (0.8 ppg) but will get a chance to show his abilities with the new coaching staff.

The 6-8 Dumbliauskas , a native of Lithuania, has shown tremendous promise (18.5 ppg, 12.8 rpg, 3.8 apg, 2.9 bpg, .500 3FG) during his one season in the United States. The son of a coach, he runs the floor well and has good hands. He led Lynchburg (Va.) Christian Academy to a 19-9 record and can play either power forward of center.

"He can get to the basket and score," van Breda Kolff said. "He also can shoot the three, has good moves around the basket and is a good passer."

2001-2002 SCHEDULE

Nov.	20	@Cleveland State
	24	Niagara
	28	*Boston College
Dec.	1	@Toledo
	5	@Oklahoma
	8	Wisconsin-Green Bay
	12	Ohio
	15	@Canisius
	20	@Siena
	31	@Kent
Jan.	3	@George Washington
	6	Rhode Island
	10	@LaSalle
	13	@Saint Joseph's
	16	Temple
	19	Duquesne
	23	@Fordham
	26	Massachusetts
Feb.	3	@Dayton
	6	Richmond
	9	Xavier
	13	@Massachusetts
	16	Fordham
	23	@Temple
	28	Saint Joseph's
March	2	@Rhode Island
	6-9	#Atlantic 10 Tournament

@Road Games
*HSB Arena, Buffalo, NY
#First Union Spectrum, Philadelphia, PA

BLUE RIBBON ANALYSIS

BACKCOURT	B
BENCH/DEPTH	C
FRONTCOURT	C-
INTANGIBLES	C

Change, and a lot of three-point shots, will be in the air as van Breda Kolff takes over at St. Bonaventure this season.

Van Breda Kolff inherits a team with talent, particularly Bremer, and plans to implement a fast-paced system that should be both fun and exciting to watch.

If Bremer and Green click like they did during a tour of Europe this summer, the Bonnies will put up plenty of points. Additional scoring could come from Prato, Massiah and newcomers Shepard and Gansey.

The post is the biggest question for the Bonnies, who allowed opponents to shoot .455 from the field and were out-rebounded by 3.2 boards per game last season. Massiah has shown steady improvement over the years, but the rest of the frontcourt is unproven, especially with the graduation of leaders Kevin Houston and Peter Van Paassen.

The Bonnies did have a chance to bond during an 11-day trip to Europe in August, but still need to work on all of the traps, rotations and presses the new staff is putting in, and that will take time.

"We just need to get more efficient in what we do," van Breda Kolff said. "The only way you become more efficient is through repetition."

Saint Bonaventure is aiming for a third straight post-season bid for just the second time in school history. A solid foundation is in place and van Breda Kolff is a proven winner, but all of the changes may make improving on last season difficult. The Bonnies will be entertaining and another trip to the NIT isn't out of the question.

(S.B.)

BIG EAST

BLUE RIBBON FORECAST

East Division
1. Connecticut
2. Boston College
3. Providence
4. Villanova
5. St. John's
6. Miami
7. Virginia Tech

West Division
1. Syracuse
2. Georgetown
3. Notre Dame
4. West Virginia
5. Seton Hall
6. Pittsburgh
7. Rutgers

TOP 40

Boston College, Connecticut, Georgetown, Providence and Syracuse are ranked among the 2001-2002 Blue Ribbon Top 40. Extended profiles can be found in the Top 40 section of Blue Ribbon.

ALL-CONFERENCE TEAM

G - Troy Bell, JR, Boston College
G - Preston Shumpert, SR, Syracuse
F - Caron Butler, SO, Connecticut
F - John Salmons, SR, Miami
C - Mike Sweetney, SO, Georgetown

PLAYER OF THE YEAR

Preston Shumpert, SR, Syracuse

NEWCOMER OF THE YEAR

Jonathan Hargett, FR, West Virginia

2001-2002 CONFERENCE TOURNAMENT

March 6-9, Madison Square Garden, New York, NY

2000-2001 CHAMPIONS

Boston College, Notre Dame (Regular season)
Boston College (Conference tournament)

2000-2001 POSTSEASON PARTICIPANTS

Postseason record: 7-10 (.412)
NCAA
Georgetown (Sweet 16)
Syracuse (Second Round)
Boston College (Second Round)
Notre Dame (Second Round)
Providence
NIT
Pittsburgh (Second Round)
Connecticut (Second Round)
Villanova (First Round)
Seton Hall
Miami

TOP BACKCOURTS

1. Syracuse
2. Boston College
3. Providence

TOP FRONTCOURTS

1. Connecticut
2. Notre Dame
3. St. John's

INSIDE THE NUMBERS

2000-2001 conference RPI: 5th (of 31)
Conference RPI (last five years): 4-4-5-3-4

DID YOU KNOW?

The Big East coaching carousel took a few more turns during the off-season, with three schools making changes. Jay Wright takes over at Villanova after a successful tenure at Hofstra. Wright, a former VU assistant, succeeds Steve Lappas, who moves on to Massachusetts. At Rutgers, Kevin Bannon is out and Gary Waters is in. The architect of a resurgence at Kent State that resulted in two NCAA Tournament berths in three seasons, Waters is expected to make the Scarlet Knights a much tougher defensive team. Third is former Big East All-Star Louis Orr, who steps in for Tommy Amaker (Michigan) at Seton Hall. Orr was head man at Siena for a year, before moving on to the Hall. He was a standout player and later an assistant at Syracuse. ... Villanova was scheduled to take a summer trip to Greece, but when Lappas—who has Greek ancestors—moved on to UMass, new man Wright decided to head to Italy. ... Two Big East schools (Pittsburgh and Miami) are expecting to move into new homes next year. Each will be a state-of-the-art, on-campus arena, so say good-bye to Fitzgerald Fieldhouse, the Igloo and Miami Arena. ... As usual, a group of Big East teams will take part in early-season tournaments that put them in action in early November. Syracuse is playing in the Preseason NIT. St. John's heads up to The Great Alaska Shootout. Seton Hall is in the Maui Invitational, and Rutgers will play in the BCA Classic in Raleigh, N.C.

(M.B.)

 ## Miami

LOCATION	Coral Gables, FL
CONFERENCE	Big East (East)
LAST SEASON	16-13 (.552)
CONFERENCE RECORD	8-8 (3rd)
STARTERS LOST/RETURNING	1/4
NICKNAME	Hurricanes
COLORS	Orange, Green & White
HOMECOURT	Miami Arena (15,388)
COACH	Perry Clark (Gettysburg '74)
RECORD AT SCHOOL	16-13 (1 year)
CAREER RECORD	201-158 (12 years)

ASSISTANTS	Dwight Freeman (Western State '82)
	Greg Gary (Tulane '92)
	Brock Kantrow (LSU-Shreveport '92)
TEAM WINS (last 5 years)	16-18-23-23-16
RPI (last 5 years)	90-50-10-30-84
2000-01 FINISH	Lost in NIT first round.

You can't blame us for having questions about these Miami Hurricanes. Heck, even coach Perry Clark is wondering about this year.

So much could go right. So much could go wrong. This team might be exciting and dangerous or blow up because of some potentially huge deficiencies.

Miami rebounded from last year's ugly (0-4) start in Big East play to finish a solid 8-8 in conference games and earn an NIT berth. It wasn't quite on par with the team's success the previous two seasons, when the

'Canes won 23 games two times and played in a pair of NCAA Tournament games, but it could have been worse. This year might be better. Looking for a sleeper team for those preseason chat-room discussions? Try Miami, which brings back four starters and supplemented those players with newcomers whose talents fill specific needs, rather than offer all-around skills.

Forward **Rafael Berumen**? He's an inside scorer, something Miami desperately needs. Guard **Kahleaf Watson**? Quick as they get and able to bring some pressure on both ends. If they do their jobs, and the returnees deliver, Miami will be formidable. If not … well, you know what happens.

"We're in a unique position," Clark said. "We've got some veteran guys we're going to count on, so we didn't recruit to supplement them but for needs.

"In this day and time, I think that impact players want to come in and play a lot of minutes right away. If we brought in someone like that and didn't give him time, that might cause some problems."

So, Clark is going with his core group of holdovers and hoping the new faces are happy with filling their roles. Chemistry is important to him, so playing time will go to those who are willing to be part of a team, not individual stars. It looks as if the veterans on the Miami team understand that, a good start. If the others sign on, Miami could have a deep team, although it will be hard for Clark to play mix and match combinations.

"We don't have all-around depth that maybe some other teams have, but we have people who can come in and do certain things," Clark said. "Our emphasis will be on our starting five."

Perhaps the most important member of that group is 6-7 senior forward **John Salmons** (13.3 ppg, 6.0 rpg, 3.9 apg, 2.0 spg, .474 FG, .793 FT), a multi-dimensional player who can handle work at three positions and defends all five. He led the 'Canes in rebounding, assists and steals last year and posted the best field-goal percentage of any regular. Though largely overlooked because he isn't a huge scorer, Salmons is a star.

"He is the most versatile player I have ever coached," Clark said. "He is such a caring and giving guy to have. I have to prod him to be more aggressive offensively. His development last year was instrumental to our success. He scored more than 50 points (53) in our last two regular-season games. He's very coachable.

"It's hard for me to imagine a more versatile player in the Big East."

Clark is right, but it was Salmons' late offensive outbursts that make him so intriguing this year. He had 30 in a win over West Virginia and 23 three nights later in the triumph over Villanova, shooting a combined 14-of-24 from the field and 22-of-25 from the line in the process. If Salmons becomes a 15-to-20 points-per-game man for the 'Canes, they will be a dangerous offensive team.

His emergence would give Miami a pair of potent forces, because it's expected that 6-10 sophomore shooter **Darius Rice** (14.1 ppg, 4.9 rpg, 1.1 apg, 1.1 spg, .398 FG, .339 3PT, .720 FT) will be even more effective than he was as a freshman. He displayed some true greatness at times and struggled on other occasions. Rice is a silky swingman with unlimited shooting range and scored in double figures on 20 occasions, with a 28-point outburst at Villanova particularly impressive. But he struggled down the stretch, as Big East rivals understood his game better. He had five points in three of the team's last four games.

"We have to help him," Clark said. "When you come in as a shooter, it's tough in this league. Everybody in this league can coach, and the first thing they do is take a shooter's shots away. He has to get himself into position to get good shots. We worked with Darius to get good shots, and when he had them, he knocked them down.

"We have gotten him stronger, and he can put the ball on the floor a little better. He'll get some good shots."

While Salmons and Rice are expected to be the main scorers, don't forget about 6-8 junior forward **James Jones** (11.9 ppg, 5.9 rpg, 1.2 apg, 1.2 spg, 1.6 bpg), who blossomed in Big East play, scoring in double figures in all but four games and hitting Seton Hall for 21. In the Hurricanes' NIT loss to Auburn, Jones had 20 points and 15 rebounds. Jones has the chance to establish himself as one of the Big East's top forwards this year, and Clark expects him to take that step.

"He can shoot the ball and put it on the floor," Clark said. "He's getting stronger, so he can be more physical inside. He's also a calming influence on the team."

The Hurricanes should have some good depth inside, thanks in part to the return of 6-9 senior center/forward **Elton Tyler**, who missed last season because of academics. Tyler averaged 10.1 points and 5.5 rebounds two years ago and showed signs last year in practice of becoming a more complete player. Though not able to play, Tyler practiced during the second semester and impressed some with his ability to guard people. He is in perhaps the best shape of his time at Miami and will be counted up on for production in the middle.

He'll likely team with the 6-9, 255-pound junior Berumen from Los Angeles City College and Simi Valley (Calif.) High School, who averaged 18.0 points, 9.0 rebounds and 3.0 assists last season.

Berumen played a season at New Mexico (1999-00), before transferring to LA City College. Though big, he is skilled and should be able to score in the paint.

"He can pass, catch and understands the game," Clark said. "He can make plays. He's a smart player and moves well. He's fluid."

If the action is fast and up-and-down, the Hurricanes will get some fireworks from 6-7 sophomore **Rodrigue Djahue** (4.1 ppg, 2.7 rpg), whom Clark insists was the team's most impressive player during last preseason. He showed that his coach may have been right during the first few games of the year. He had 11 points and eight boards against Florida Atlantic and 16 points against Northeastern. But when the games slowed down, and the patterns started, Djahue struggled.

"He'll be much better having played a year," Clark said. "He'll understand the system and where to go. Last year, he did more thinking than playing. He's another one of those question marks. If he's on the plus side, we can be very dangerous."

Joining Berumen as an up-front newcomer is 6-8, 220-pound sophomore **Wil Frisby**, from Fresno City College and Bay Shore High School in New York. Frisby averaged 18.5 points, 10.8 rebounds and 1.6 blocks during his one year at Fresno and is expected to bring some rebounding help to the Hurricanes.

"He's more an athlete now than a skilled player," Clark said. "He has skills, can get to the glass and runs the lanes. He can be explosive."

Rounding out the frontcourt is 6-6 senior walk-on **Jerry Schlie** (0.3 ppg, 0.3 rpg), who saw a total of 23 minutes of play in nine games last year and scored his only basket of the season at North Carolina.

The point spot should be manned by 6-0 junior **Michael Simmons** (2.5 ppg, 1.7 rpg, 2.5 apg, 1.1 spg), a reliable ball handler and distributor who is short on flash but has the ability to be a solid Big East point man.

"He's capable of giving us what we need at the point," Clark said. "He's got to play with confidence all the time, though. As far as understanding how to run a team and mechanically doing what a point guard needs to do, he's fine. But he needs to play with confidence and consistency."

Simmons will be pushed, however, by the 6-2 Watson, a freshman from Blue Ridge High School in Dyke, Va. Watson averaged 18.1 points, 4.5 assists, 3.5 rebounds, and 3.0 steals last year. He's a fine defender who can run the break and will be fun to watch.

Joining Rice on the wing is 6-2 sophomore **Marcus Barnes** (7.2 ppg, 1.2 rpg, 1.9 apg), who needs to improve his shooting eye drastically. He made just 32.3 percent of his field-goal tries and only 30.5 percent of his three-point attempts. He will be helped considerably by the departure of Joe Gordon, who wanted more minutes at the two-spot than Clark was willing to commit. That means Barnes will have a shot at plenty of burn and many shots. Now, he has to make them. He had some fine moments last year, scoring 20 or more points on three occasions, including a team-high 24 against Connecticut.

"When I gave him meaningful minutes last year, he stepped up and played well," Clark said. "We were a different team when that happened. When he gets on a roll, he gives us another dimension."

The Hurricanes could get some perimeter help from 6-2 junior **Paulo Coelho**, who missed last year with a torn ACL. He can hit some long shots and provide help at the point, provided his knee is ready.

The two remaining backcourt performers are walk-ons **Danny Marakovits** (0.6 ppg, 0.0 rpg), a 6-4 sophomore, and **Brandon Okpalobi** (0.1 ppg, 0.6 rpg), a 6-2 sophomore.

2001-2002 SCHEDULE

| Nov. | 16-20 | #Paradise Jam |
| | 24 | Lafayette |

	26	Florida Atlantic
	29	Howard
Dec.	3	Florida International
	8	@Texas A&M
	15	*Indiana
	18	Florida A&M
	22	Charlotte
	27	**LSU
	30	St. Francis (Pa.)
Jan.	2	@Georgetown
	5	@Connecticut
	8	@St. John's
	12	@Virginia Tech
	15	Pittsburgh
	19	Providence
	24	Villanova
	29	Boston College
Feb.	2	Connecticut
	5	@Villanova
	10	@Boston College
	13	St. John's
	17	@Rutgers
	26	@Providence
March	2	Virginia Tech
	6-9	##Big East Championship

@Road Games
*Orange Bowl Classic, American Airlines Arena, Miami, FL
**Sugar Bowl Classic, New Orleans, LA
#Virgin Islands (vs. Eastern Michigan on Nov. 18 in first round; vs. UAB on Nov. 19 in second round; consolations and championship on Nov. 20)
##Madison Square Garden, New York, NY

BLUE RIBBON ANALYSIS

BACKCOURT	C+
BENCH/DEPTH	B
FRONTCOURT	B+
INTANGIBLES	B

The Hurricanes have an opportunity to do some good things this year, provided they shoot the ball better (41.3 percent FG in 2000-01) and hit the backboards.

It all comes down to consistency. If their big guns do it every night, they'll be dangerous, because this is a talented team. If they continue to show up erratically, it's hello NIT again.

Salmons is a fine talent who does many things. He plays great defense and leads the way fearlessly. But he needs help. Rice had some magical moments last year, but he has to understand that missing three-pointers isn't as exciting as making two-point baskets. Or passing the ball. A true talent with a good demeanor, Rice can be a big-time pro some day. For now, he has to concentrate on being a complete player, not just a gunner.

There is hope up front, thanks to the return of Tyler and the arrivals of Frisby and Berumen. Those three could give the Hurricanes the interior punch they lacked at times last year. And don't forget about Jones. He has great potential, particularly if his inside game blossoms this year, as Clark expects it to.

Simmons is competent, but he might have trouble fighting off Watson if the newcomer is consistent and under control. Together, they must give the Hurricanes 40 quality minutes at the point, or everything else will suffer.

And Barnes has quite an opportunity, especially if he can play like he did against Connecticut and Providence last season, rather than how he performed against many of the Hurricanes' other foes.

This could be a good year. Clark knows that. But there are a lot of questions. So, we'll split the difference. Figure on about 17 regular-season wins and a fairly impressive NIT run. That's not bad. And it could be better, if Clark gets the right answers.

(M.B.)

 **Notre Dame**

LOCATION	South Bend, IN
CONFERENCE	Big East (West)
LAST SEASON	20-10 (.667)
CONFERENCE RECORD	11-5 (1st)
STARTERS LOST/RETURNING	2/3

NICKNAME	Fighting Irish
COLORS	Blue & Gold
HOMECOURT	Joyce Center (11,418)
COACH	Mike Brey (George Washington '82)
RECORD AT SCHOOL	20-10 (1 year)
CAREER RECORD	119-62 (6 years)
ASSISTANTS	Sean Kearney (Scranton '81)
	Anthony Solomon (Virginia '87)
	Lewis Preston (VMI '93)
TEAM WINS (last 5 years)	16-13-14-22-20
RPI (last 5 years)	64-98-122-52-27
2000-01 FINISH	Lost in NCAA second round.

Nobody was all that surprised when Troy Murphy announced he wouldn't be returning for his senior year at Notre Dame. He had flirted with an early exit after the 1999-00 season, and his performance during Mike Brey's debut had kept his draft stock in the late-lottery range. It was time to move on.

Still, Brey didn't consider "Life Without Murphy" until the big forward made his announcement. Then, he acted. He summoned the Irish players to his house for an informal meeting and issued the challenge. It was time for seniors **David Graves**, **Ryan Humphrey** and **Harold Swanagan** to assume the leadership role they had deferred to Murphy for the last three seasons. If Notre Dame was to make a run at a third-straight 20-win season, something it hadn't accomplished since the Irish had gone five straight seasons with that many from 1983-89, then the seniors in the program would have to take charge.

"It was always Troy's program, and rightly so," Brey said. "When Troy announced, we met, and I said I was excited for Ryan, Harold and David. They were going to get more of the stage, but now they have to back it up."

They certainly must. Without Murphy, the Irish have no proven commodity, only a group of strong complementary parts who distinguished themselves at times last year but offered no evidence that any would be able to carry a team, the way Murphy had. That's why Brey was careful to put the onus on his three seniors, who along with junior wing **Matt Carroll**, will be asked to do the heavy lifting this season. If there were just one individual asked to assume the spotlight, Brey might feel a little shaky. Because he has four veterans, he can head into the season confident the Irish have the ability to contend in the Big East's West Division.

"When I think about our team, what helps me sleep better is that we have four men who have been part of a championship [last year's division title]," Brey said. "When you look at the West, we've got some experienced guys, and Georgetown has lost some guys and Syracuse has lost some guys. Last year, we got picked third and won it. Why can't we make a run for first and second?"

At the risk of deflating Brey's balloon, here's why: The Irish have no go-to scorer and will likely be handing the reins of the team to a freshman point guard. That's not an indictment, merely fact. It's possible that Graves or Carroll could each blossom into 18-points-a-night men on the perimeter, and Humphrey could do the same inside. And if Brey is right about the skills and potential of freshman point **Chris Thomas** from Pike High School in Indianapolis, Ind., the Irish might just be all right at the point.

Notre Dame does have some good points, too, beyond the experience factor. The team will be big—all over. With the exception of Thomas, who goes 6-1, 165, every scholarship player on the roster is at least 6-4. The Irish also have, in Graves, Carroll and probably Thomas, some excellent three-point shooters. And unlike last year, when Notre Dame employed a tight, seven-man rotation, there could be some improved depth, the better to extend the team's defense some and end the constant reliance on half-court basketball.

"We should get down the floor a little quicker this year," Brey said. "We can get some easy baskets."

The key to that will be how well Thomas adapts to 30 minutes a night with the ball. He certainly has the potential. The first-ever Indiana Mr. Basketball to enroll at Notre Dame, Thomas averaged 23.4 points, 3.9 rebounds, 5.7 assists and 3.7 steals last year while playing predominantly the two-guard spot.

Thomas played in the McDonald's All-America game and scored 11 points in 20 minutes of action. Thomas is quick in transition and capable of driving to the basket. Unlike Martin Inglesby, who started the last four years and brought steady play and reliable shooting, Thomas is more of a new-school point.

"He can create a lot," Brey said. "His biggest adjust-

ment will be how he relates to the other four guys. Can he come down and involve them first, and then get his? He's a special talent, and we want to give him the freedom to play. We can do some things with him, like put four on the baseline and let him go. We can ball screen for him up top, and he can come down the lane and create."

The backup situation should be in the hands of 6-4 sophomore **Chris Markwood** from South Portland (Maine) High School. He underwent knee surgery last September to repair some damage at the top of his tibia that included some nerve trouble and was given a 50-50 chance of playing ball again. Brey reports that he looked good in scrimmages toward the end of last year and was fine this summer, so he should be able to give the Irish some minutes.

"I'm interested in watching him run a team," Brey said.

The 6-6 Carroll (12.4 ppg, 5.0 rpg, 3.8 apg) shot .409 from three-point range last year and has the ability to be a deadly scorer. But he must get a little more selfish at times and avoid deferring to his teammates. Perhaps with Murphy gone, Carroll will do that. He had 21 in the first-round NCAA win over Xavier and 20 against Rutgers.

The Irish are hoping to get some help behind Carroll from 6-4 sophomore **Torrian Jones** (1.3 ppg, 0.7 rpg), who saw only 6.9 minutes a game last year and rarely had an opportunity to show what he could do.

"It was a tough situation for him last year," Brey said. Jones is an athletic player who can get to the basket and should be able to defend, particularly in trapping, full-court situations. That should be good enough to get him some time, although he can't be expected to supplant Carroll.

Walk-on **Charles Thomas** (1.8 ppg, 0.2 rpg), a 6-1 junior, rounds out the backcourt picture.

Graves (13.8 ppg, 4.7 rpg) goes 6-6 and has been in Murphy's shadow since arriving at Notre Dame. That's not such a bad thing, because it has allowed him to develop gradually to the point where he can be counted on for consistent, big-time production. Though Graves will never approach Murphy's numbers, he does have a good outside shot and can make some things happen off the dribble.

"I think Graves will have a real big senior year," Brey said. "Murph not being here has helped Graves become a better leader. Watching him talk to the young guys has been fun. He's come out of his shell a little.

"He's a talented offensive player. He can shoot and slash and get to the hole. He offensive rebounds and can get into the lane and finish."

Graves will team with the 6-7 Swanagan (4.1 ppg, 3.4 rpg) and the 6-8 Humphrey (14.1 ppg, 9.0 rpg, .505 FG) in the starting frontcourt. Humphrey had a nice debut for the Irish, after sitting out the 1999-00 season after his transfer from Oklahoma. A powerful inside player who can step out, Humphrey must become more consistent this year, now that Murphy is gone.

"He has to keep it simple and remember who he is," Brey said. "When he starts to shoot jump shots early and not establish himself inside, then it's not one of his better nights. If he goes inside early and then moves out to 10 feet or the foul line, then he'll have a good night."

Swanagan is a great screener, a hustling defender and a solid physical presence who has dropped some weight and should be able to play 30-35 minutes a night, something his flagging stamina prevented him from doing last year.

The two players with the best shots of seeing double-figure minutes up front are 6-9 freshman **Jordan Cornette** from St. Xavier High School in Cincinnati and 6-9 junior **Jere Macura** (1.9 ppg, 1.6 rpg).

Cornette was initially recruited by former Notre Dame coach Matt Doherty and decided to honor his commitment to the school, after meeting the affable Brey. He averaged 14.0 points, 7.1 rebounds and 4.0 blocks last year. He had his knee scoped during the summer and should be ready to practice. Brey would like him to defend a variety of frontcourt positions and bring some quickness to the front line.

Macura can step out on the wing and shoot some, although he made just one of 14 three-point shots last year. He averaged 7.7 minutes last year but could see that total fade, if he doesn't defend better and hit the boards some.

Brey also would like to see 6-11 sophomore **Tom Timmermans** (0.9 ppg, 0.7 rpg), who saw only 36 minutes of playing time last year, exert himself somewhat inside. Though not possessing much offensive polish,

Timmermans is a bruising 248-pounder with the ability to bang with the Big East's beefier players. Don't expect a lot from him, but he has the potential to help out some on the boards.

2001-2002 SCHEDULE

Nov.	16	New Hampshire
	19	Cornell
	23-25	#Hawaii Pacific Thanksgiving Classic
	18	Army
Dec.	1	*DePaul
	4	@Indiana
	8	@Miami, OH
	22	@Canisius
	27	**Alabama
	30	Colgate
Jan.	6	Villanova
	9	@West Virginia
	12	@Pittsburgh
	14	@Syracuse
	19	Kentucky
	21	Georgetown
	26	Seton Hall
	30	Pittsburgh
Feb.	3	@Seton Hall
	6	Rutgers
	9	@Georgetown
	14	@Rutgers
	17	Syracuse
	20	West Virginia
	23	@Miami
	27	@St. John's
March	2	Providence
	6-9	##Big East Tournament

@Road Games
*Children's Charity Classic, Chicago
**Sugar Bowl Classic, New Orleans, LA
#Honolulu, HI (vs. Hawaii-Pacific first round; also Akron, Hampton, Liberty, Monmouth, Tennessee-Chattanooga, Vanderbilt)
##Madison Square Garden, New York, NY

BLUE RIBBON ANALYSIS

BACKCOURT	B-
BENCH/DEPTH	B
FRONTCOURT	B
INTANGIBLES	B+

Murphy may be gone, but the Fighting Irish are not destitute. The return of four experienced hands gives Notre Dame the potential to play some smart, team-oriented basketball.

Meanwhile, the arrivals of Thomas and Cornette and expected health of Markwood could bring some needed depth and quickness to the team.

Humphrey, Graves and Carroll may not be able to put up 20 every night, but they will force defenses to guard the whole floor. If Humphrey works the baseline early, there will be three-pointers available on the wings, and Notre Dame could score a bunch of points.

Of course, all of this depends on whether Thomas is able to distribute, as well as create for himself. The freshman needs to realize that there are some offensive options around him and that feeding them is the first priority. If that happens, the Irish will be all right.

The first year post Murphy should be fine in South Bend. There is experience. There are some scoring options, and even though Murph has moved on, Notre Dame will be able to rebound. Notre Dame will look a little different and should be more willing (and able) to run some. That third-straight 20-win season might be tough to negotiate, but Notre Dame could make a real run at an NCAA Tournament berth.

(M.B.)

Pittsburgh

LOCATION	Pittsburgh, PA
CONFERENCE	Big East
LAST SEASON	19-14 (.576)
CONFERENCE RECORD	7-9 (5th West)
STARTERS LOST/RETURNING	2/3

NICKNAME		**Panthers**
COLORS		**Blue & Gold**
HOMECOURT		Fitzgerald Fieldhouse (6,798)
COACH		Ben Howland (Weber State '80)
RECORD AT SCHOOL		32-29 (2 years)
CAREER RECORD		111-88 (7 years)
ASSISTANTS		Jamie Dixon (Texas Christian '87)
		Barry Rohrssen (St.Francis NY '83)
TEAM WINS (last 5 years)		18-11-14-13-19
RPI (last 5 years)		62-129-118-121-55
2000-01 FINISH		Lost in NIT second round.

Ben Howland can't wait for that new arena to open up at Pittsburgh. It's going to be great. There will be luxury suites on the court level. It will seat 12,600, nearly twice what creaking Fitzgerald Field House can accommodate.

Yes, sir, the John and Gertrude Peterson Events Center will be state-of-the-art. In fact, it will be the best on-campus arena in the Big East.

"It will be spectacular," Howland said.

If things keep going the way they are, Howland will have a team quite worthy of its new digs. After just two seasons at Pitt, the former Northern Arizona boss has created some excitement in a program that had stagnated for several years. And while contention for the Big East title and the magic of an NCAA Tournament run remain off in the future, the Panthers have served notice that they can become something formidable, in time.

Pittsburgh made a resounding statement in last year's Big East Tournament, with a four-day run that almost ended in miraculous fashion. The Panthers defeated Miami, Notre Dame and Syracuse to reach the tournament final, against Boston College. Although BC prevailed in the title game, 79-57, over a Pitt team that was clearly out of gas, the late run secured an NIT berth for Howland and Co. and provided a nice send-off for seniors Ricardo Greer and Isaac Hawkins. Despite playing with a short bench and an extremely young roster (Greer and Hawkins excluded), the Panthers were able to stage a pretty impressive late rally and grab some postseason time.

"We were a team that had some adversity but kept working hard," Howland said. "We came together at the right time and played our best basketball at the end of the season. You always want that. We couldn't get past BC, but I'm proud of the way we played in the Big East Tournament and in the NIT.

"I plan on having it carry over. We have a number of players back from last year's team, and they have seen what happens when they play well together and are focused. We're turning the corner, but we have a long way to go. We are headed in the right direction and on an upward swing."

One of the reasons for optimism this year is the return of 6-0 junior point man **Brandin Knight** (9.2 ppg, 3.3 rpg, 5.5 apg), entering his third year as a starter. This year's challenge for him will be to become a more potent offensive weapon. He continued to struggle from the field (38.7 percent), three-point range (25.8 percent) and the free-throw line (60.9 percent) last year, numbers which all must come up considerably, if the Panthers are to be capable of beating the league's better teams on a consistent basis.

Knight is a strong defender and a war horse capable of handling many minutes. It's possible his production and percentages will improve this year, thanks to the arrival of freshman **Tony Tate**, who should be able to log some minutes at the point.

"Knight was thrown into a tough situation as a freshman, and he handled it very well," Howland said. "He has matured. He has a good feel for the game and is very bright. I'm excited about the fact that we have a point guard with two years of starting experience."

The 6-0 Tate, from Marist High School in Jersey City, N.J., played two years at St. Anthony High School in Jersey City, before transferring to Marist where he was an all-county selection. He's not a future star, but he could be a solid player.

The Panthers would like to have added 6-2 freshman Carl Krauser, from St. Thomas More (Conn.) Prep and Notre Dame Prep in the Bronx, to the roster. But Krauser is a partial qualifier who can practice this year but not play.

The two-spot belongs to 6-3 sophomore **Julius Page** (9.1 ppg, 1.8 rpg), who flashed the ability to score well last year as a complement to Greer. Page had 18 at Georgetown and 17 against both Penn State and Robert Morris. Page needs to improve his accuracy and get to the free-throw line more. He could improve once there,

too, because he made just 62.3 percent of his tries. Howland likes his potential.

He is also impressed with 6-4 sophomore **Jaron Brown** (4.8 ppg, 2.4 rpg). Though more of a slasher than a scorer, Brown is good on the boards and on the defensive end.

"He can defend three positions," Howland said.

With Greer gone, Brown has a chance to grab a starting spot on the wing, provided he improves his offensive repertoire.

Expect to see rugged 6-5 senior **Chad Johnson** (4.5 ppg, 2.4 rpg) on the wing, too. The Nebraska transfer struggled some last year but never quit on the defensive end. His challenge in his final year of college ball is to become a more consistent offensive player.

The Panther perimeter gets a boost from 6-4 red-shirt freshman **Yuri Demetris**,

From Shaler Area High School in Glenshaw, Pa., Demetris sat out last year because the Panthers had depth on the wing, and Howland didn't want him to waste a season on the bench. Demetris certainly has the credentials to help the Panthers. He averaged 30.7 points as a senior and demonstrated a tremendous shooting range. He also added 6.8 assists per game and 5.0 rebounds for a team that won its sectional championship. While Howland is impressed with Demetris' shooting touch, he is more excited about his passing skills.

"He can feed the post and make some plays for other people," Howland said.

The loss of Hawkins puts pressure on the two frontcourt holdovers and makes it essential that newcomers **Chevy Troutman** and **Mark McCarroll** step up immediately. The one proven commodity up front is 6-8 junior forward **Donatas Zavackas** (7.9 ppg, 3.3 rpg). Zavackas got stronger over the spring and has the potential to become a 10-15 points per game man. Howland doesn't have to worry about the Lithuanian's heart, however.

"He's unique," Howland said. "When you think about foreign players, you think they can just shoot. Zavackas can defend, and he busts his butt. He understands how important it is to work. He doesn't force shots, and I would actually like to see him take more three-pointers."

The other returnee is 6-10, 280-pound sophomore **Toree Morris** (2.2 ppg, 2.4 rpg), who scored 10 points and grabbed 10 rebounds in his one start last year (Seton Hall).

"I'm hoping that's a sign of things to come," Howland said.

By the end of last season, Morris was seeing about 15 minutes a game and helping out in the middle. His challenge this year is to improve his conditioning so he can stay on the floor longer.

The inside game gets a big boost from Troutman—from Williamsport Area High School in Williamsport, Pa.—who sat out last year to help his conversion from an inside banger to more of a wing. Though 6-7 and 230 pounds, Troutman showed he could shoot it from the outside during his season off and could have a big impact in 2001-02. Troutman scored 1,563 points and grabbed 1,128 rebounds during his prep career.

"He is going to be good," Howland said. "He can play the three, four or five and defend any of those three. He's a relentless rebounder."

The final piece up front is 6-10 red-shirt freshman McCarroll from Milford (Conn.) Academy and Christ the King High School in Queens, N.Y. McCarroll played 10 minutes of one game last year before succumbing to a knee injury that kept him out for the rest of the season. Lean (210 pounds) and skilled, McCarroll decided against surgery for the knee and strengthened the area through weight work and conditioning. He'll be expected to block shots and score some from 10 feet and in.

2001-2002 SCHEDULE

Nov.	16	Morgan State
	20	Northern Arizona
	23-25	#Robert Morris Thanksgiving Classic
Dec.	1	Savannah State
	5	St. Francis
	8	Penn State
	15	Rhode Island
	19	@Ohio State
	22	Duquesne
	29	St. Francis, NY
Jan.	2	St. John's
	5	@Boston College
	8	Rutgers

	12	Notre Dame
	15	@Miami
	19	@Georgetown
	22	Syracuse
	26	Georgetown
	30	@Notre Dame
Feb.	2	Seton Hall
	7	Villanova
	10	@Syracuse
	16	@West Virginia
	21	Rutgers
	26	@Seton Hall
March	2	West Virginia
	6-9	##Big East Tournament

@Road Games
#Moon Township, PA (vs. Oakland first round; also UC Irvine, Illinois State, Kent State, Hofstra, Robert Morris, South Florida)
##Madison Square Garden, New York, NY

BLUE RIBBON ANALYSIS

BACKCOURT	C+
BENCH/DEPTH	C+
FRONTCOURT	C+
INTANGIBLES	B+

The Panthers may have to step back a bit this year with a young team that features just one senior and only 10 scholarship players on the bench.

Although Howland is happy with all the components on the team, he doesn't have that many bodies available. And those that are available are quite young. With four freshmen and three sophomores among his main men, Howland will have to be patient.

The wing brigade of Knight, Page, Brown and Demetris has promise, but it needs to be consistent and handle the responsibilities of leading the way on the perimeter. Without Greer, Pitt has no main scorer, so someone must step up, or a committee has to be formed.

Troutman will team with Zavackas up front in a good starting forward tandem, but McCarroll and Morris have to provide some stability and minutes, or the Panthers will be worn down inside by most of their Big East rivals.

Howland is right to be excited, particularly after what the Panthers accomplished last year, but the program needs some more time to grow and mature. Another recruiting class, followed by continued experience, will help Pittsburgh become a Big East competitor. The new building beckons, but Pitt isn't quite ready for those bright lights. Chances are, however, it will be. Just wait.

(M.B.)

Rutgers

LOCATION	New Brunswick, NJ
CONFERENCE	Big East (West)
LAST SEASON	11-16 (.407)
CONFERENCE RECORD	3-13 (7th)
STARTERS LOST/RETURNING	3/2
NICKNAME	Scarlet Knights
COLORS	Scarlet & White
HOMECOURT	Louis Brown Athletic Center (8,500)
COACH	Gary Waters (Ferris State '75)
RECORD AT SCHOOL	First year
CAREER RECORD	92-60 (5 years)
ASSISTANTS	Kevin Heck (Wayne State '92)
	Garland Mance (St. Bonaventure '94)
	Larry DeSimpelare (Spring Arbor '91)
TEAM WINS (last 5 years)	11-14-19-15-11
RPI (last 5 years)	119-73-47-102-85
2000-01 FINISH	Lost in regular-season finale.

When Gary Waters describes the players he has inherited from former Rutgers coach Kevin Bannon, his voice is noticeably brighter for those he can say have "bought into the program."

Before his first season even started, Waters could already claim a few unofficial victories that may eventually lead to success down the line. Since taking over the Knights in early April, Waters has devoted many of his efforts to convincing his players—old and new—that he has a plan for success. He has a blueprint that must be followed.

Those who climb on board will be rewarded with playing time. Those who don't are likely to be riding the bench and looking for somewhere else to play. This isn't some young, up-and-coming coach making another resume stop.

Waters is 50. He logged 22 years as an assistant coach at Ferris State and Eastern Michigan before taking over at Kent State in 1996. He has been in basketball longer than all of his players have been alive. He knows what he wants. He's going to get it.

Waters is committed to creating an identity for Rutgers. That's what he did at Kent, where he took the Golden Flashes to a pair of NCAA Tournament berths and an NIT spot in just five years running the show. His teams played relentless, pressure defense and worried about scoring points later. They did so in front of raucous crowds that helped foster a tremendous home-court advantage. They may have succeeded under the national radar, but they succeeded. Now, Waters wants the same thing for the Scarlet Knights.

"When people say the name of a program, you want them to know who you are," Waters said. "When they said, 'Kent State,' they said, 'You're going to get pressured.' We've got to do that here."

It won't be easy. Bannon's tumultuous tenure ended with an 11-16 thud that included a 3-13 league mark. Worse than the problems on the court were the high-profile allegations that Bannon forced a former player to run sprints naked as punishment for not doing well during a practice drill. That certainly didn't help Bannon's case.

Whether that happened has no bearing on Waters. His mission is to make Rutgers win basketball games, and he is the latest in a long line of coaches charged with recreating the magic of 1976, when Rutgers made it to the Final Four. Implicit in that mission is the successful recruitment and signing of top players in the state. That hasn't happened for a while at Rutgers.

Who's the best college basketball player in America right now? Well, it might not be Jason Williams, Duke's off-guard from Metuchen, N.J., but he's in the top two or three, to be sure. Where did last year's top high school prospect (non-NBA division) play his high school ball? DuJuan Wagner played in Camden, NJ. Now, he's playing at Memphis. Think either of those two could help Rutgers?

If you don't, then you're not thinking. Worse still, the one player they had who could be considered top-notch, wing Dahntay Jones, will suit up for the Blue Devils this year, after sitting out last season after his transfer from Rutgers. And even before Waters took the job at Rutgers, last year's leading scorer, Todd Billet (16.6 ppg, 4.2 apg), left the program, bound for Virginia.

As you might expect, Waters isn't predicting a victory parade along the banks of the Old Raritan River. He is, however, promising a few things.

"The biggest thing I've got to change is this team's mentality," Waters said. "We've got to play hard on every possession. They didn't do that last year. They played in spurts. As a result, of their 13 conference losses, nine [actually, seven] were by seven points or less."

Waters does have some things going for him as his new regime commences. One is the "sleeping giant" status of the program. Rutgers is in a fertile recruiting area. The Louis Brown Center is a loud, potentially imposing homecourt. The Knights are in a great conference. It's all there, and he has to find a way to unlock the secret to creating the proper synergy for wins.

"The program is not in great condition," he said. "It's going to be a growing process. It's going to take some time to get back to the level where we can compete in the Big East. The tools are here. With time and some strong recruiting, I think we can get back to the level."

The Knights lost their two top scorers from last year, Billet and forward Jeff Greer (14.3 ppg, 4.5 rpg), but do have some players capable of succeeding in the Big East. One is 6-1 sophomore point man **Mike Sherrod** (7.2 ppg, 3.2 rpg, 2.8 apg), who averaged nearly 30 minutes a game last year and displayed the ability to run the team. Although he did defer at times to Billet, who played a combo role, Sherrod has the potential to handle the position quite well.

"I expect him to do a good job," Waters said. "He's an excellent ball-handler, and I really like his ability to apply defensive pressure. I've always had point guards who can score, and he's average at that."

Expect to see 6-3 freshman **Juel Wiggan**, from Notre Dame (Mass.) Academy and Columbus High School in the Bronx, spelling Sherrod. Wiggan is a classic "New York City" type who can play both positions, and he impressed Waters with his defensive skills.

Although the coach doesn't describe Wiggan as a "slouch" at the other end, Wiggan is better at stopping opponents, a trait that will earn playing time in the Waters world.

There will also be an opportunity for 6-1 senior **Connor Fox** (1.1 ppg, 0.1 rpg) to grab some minutes, although he'll have to match his knowledge of the game with some increased athletic ability.

The two-spot should have belonged to Billet (or Jones), but it will probably be manned by 6-2 junior college import **Jerome Coleman**, from Cecil (Md.) Community College and Robeson High School in Brooklyn, N.Y. He's a fine shooter who averaged 23.5 points last year en route to second-team NJCAA all-America honors. He scored 1,232 points in two years at Cecil Community College and made 202 three-pointers.

Because the Scarlet Knights return a grand total of three (three!) made treys from last year's team, Coleman's range will come in quite handy.

"When we found out we lost Billet, we identified the top three junior-college three-point shooters in the country," Waters said. "He was the second-best. He can also put it on the floor. That's what makes him different from other guards. He can put it down and can shoot it. He can defend, too."

Another newcomer, 6-4 freshman **Ricky Shields**, from Hargrave (Va.) Military Academy and Parkdale High School in Upper Marlboro, Md., will see plenty of time at the two-spot. Shields averaged 17.1 points and 6.2 rebounds last year at Hargrave and impressed Waters with his ability to play big-time defense. During his senior season at Parkdale, he scored 23.2 points per game and averaged 5.1 rebounds. He gets to the rim and is excellent in transition.

Walk-on **Mitch Garrett** (0.0 ppg, 0.0 rpg), a 5-10 sophomore, rounds out the backcourt picture.

Up front, there is some experience, mostly in the persons of **Rashod Kent** and **Eugene Dabney**. Throw in part-time starter **Kareem Wright** and a trio of newcomers, and Waters has some options.

The 6-6, 275-pound Kent (9.8 ppg, 9.3 rpg, .643 FG) is a senior fixture in the program and a big plug in the middle. Quicker than his stout body might indicate, he is a first-rate board man and reliable interior finisher with one vice—foul trouble.

"He played a lot of half-court defense last year, so teams could isolate on him," Waters said. "Our style of play will prevent some of that and perhaps cut down on fouls. He can rebound the basketball with the very best of them."

Dabney (7.4 ppg, 4.7 rpg) is a 6-10 junior who has yet to live up to the huge promise he had when he arrived on campus. He has the skills to be a frontcourt force in the Big East, but he needs to improve his strength and become more committed to full-time excellence. Waters reports that Dabney had a fine summer, both in the classroom and on the court, and could become quite a factor.

The 6-9 Wright (4.6 ppg, 3.5 rpg), meanwhile, appears finally ready to make a big contribution. Now free of some 25 pounds of lard that he brought with him to campus two years ago, the junior could become a defensive stopper and a semi-reliable scorer.

"I expect him to contribute immensely to us," Waters said.

Two players who sat out last year could make big impacts up front, too. One is 6-8, 235-pound junior **Shawn Hampton**, a Virginia Commonwealth transfer who averaged 10.1 points and 6.8 rebounds for the Rams in 1999-00. He was expected to blossom further last year as a practice player, but chronic problems with a dislocated shoulder forced him to undergo surgery and robbed him of all but a few weeks of workouts with the team. Still, he has the potential to give the Knights another inside force.

The most intriguing member of the team is 6-10 sophomore **Herve Lamizana**, from St. Patrick's (N.J.) High School and Abidgen, Ivory Coast. The spindly (215 pounds) forward was the jewel of Bannon's recruiting class last year, but his academic woes forced him to sit out last year and prevented him from practicing.

Worse yet, Lamizana hurt his foot in the spring and spent several weeks with a pin in it to facilitate healing. He was cleared for work in August but will need time to get in shape. He is also not guaranteed to be eligible, pending some summer course work.

"I have no clue what to expect from him," Waters said.

There are three candidates for work at the small forward position, led by 6-7 sophomore **Sean Axani** (2.9

ppg, 3.3 rpg), who showed some signs of potential last year, most notably in a 10-point, seven-rebound effort against Pittsburgh. Another possible contributor is 6-7 senior **Mike Tompson** (1.5 ppg, 1.7 rpg).

"We're going to have to use Tompson in our scheme," Waters said. "He's very athletic and can go outside. We have to work with his confidence."

A 6-9, 205-pound freshman, **Jason McCoy** from Milby High School in Houston, is more of a project. He's young (just 17) but has excellent athletic skills, and Waters says he is a fine offensive rebounder. McCoy averaged 13.7 points and 8.8 rebounds last year.

Rounding out the frontcourt is 6-7 sophomore walk-on **Justin Piasecki** (0.7 ppg, 0.2 rpg), who played in six games last year and scored baskets against Bucknell and Notre Dame.

2001-2002 SCHEDULE

Nov.	14-16	#BCA Classic
	24	Auburn
	28	Stony Brook
Dec.	1	Loyola, MD
	5	@LaSalle
	8	Wagner
	13	Hartford
	15	UMBC
	23	@Virginia
	29	Princeton
Jan.	2	@Syracuse
	5	Georgetown
	8	Pittsburgh
	11	@Seton Hall
	16	West Virginia
	22	@Providence
	27	@West Virginia
	30	Connecticut
Feb.	2	Syracuse
	6	@Notre Dame
	11	St. Peter's
	14	Notre Dame
	17	Miami
	21	@Pittsburgh
	23	Seton Hall
	27	@Virginia Tech
March	2	@Georgetown
	6-9	##Big East Tournament

@Road Games
#Raleigh, NC (vs. East Carolina in first round; also Fairleigh Dickinson, North Carolina State, Northwestern, Prairie View A&M, San Jose State, VCU)
##Madison Square Garden, New York, NY

BLUE RIBBON ANALYSIS

BACKCOURT	C
BENCH/DEPTH	C+
FRONTCOURT	C+
INTANGIBLES	B+

The Knights are starting over again, but they made a good choice in Waters to run the latest rebuilding program. He has the experience and strength of will to create a team that will make the best use of its talents and potential. That's a good starting point. His mission will be to keep the better players in the state home, create some continuity in the program and win in the crowded Big East. Piece of cake.

This year's team will need big help from youngsters and newcomers. The Sherrod-Coleman backcourt has talent but little experience. And there isn't a lot of depth along the guard line, either. There are plenty of bodies up front but no big-time interior scorer. It looks like a committee of six or seven will have to make due there.

Don't expect Waters to predict win totals or postseason berths, but do expect him to promise an all-out pressure-defense feeding frenzy. Rutgers will bother a lot of teams, and it will win some close games, provided the youngsters stay focused. Waters wants the program to have an identity, and it will. Whether that means Rutgers will win big remains to be seen. At least the man has a plan. Those who buy into it should be pleased.

(M.B.)

Seton Hall

LOCATION	South Orange, NJ
CONFERENCE	Big East
LAST SEASON	16-15 (.516)
CONFERENCE RECORD	5-11 (6th West)
STARTERS LOST/RETURNING	3/2
NICKNAME	Pirates
COLORS	Blue & White
HOMECOURT	Continental Airlines Arena (20,029) and Walsh Gym (2,600)
COACH	Louis Orr (Syracuse ('80)
RECORD AT SCHOOL	First year
CAREER RECORD	20-11 (1 year)
ASSISTANTS	Brian Nash (Keene State '92)
	William Garrett (Illinois State '88)
	John Dunne (Ithaca '92)
TEAM WINS (last 5 years)	10-15-15-22-16
RPI (last 5 years)	136-102-92-35-72
2000-01 FINISH	Lost in NIT first round.

Well, here we are, back to square one for the Pirates and in-state rival, Rutgers. Remember when we were firing the starter's pistol to commence the battle between the schools' new coaches, Scarlet Knight boss Kevin Bannon and slick Tommy Amaker?

It was only four years ago, and everybody in the Garden State wanted to see which new man would fare better. At first, it looked as if Bannon would prevail. Then, Amaker took the lead, thanks to the Hall's improbable 2000 Sweet 16 run.

In the end, the race was a dead heat—at least for the programs. Each is starting anew, trying to regroup after disappointing 2000-01 seasons and curious about whether their latest hires are indeed the men capable of leading them to sustained success. The two coaches took different paths. Amaker moved on to Michigan, to help rescue the Wolverines, while Bannon resigned from Rutgers, unable to quell the disappointment among the school's athletic constituencies. Consider Amaker the big winner in that contest.

But what of Seton Hall? In steps Louis Orr, former Syracuse frontcourt legend and extremely successful one-year wonder at Siena, where he replaced another shining coaching star, Paul Hewitt. He must now guide the Pirates back to contention in the Big East, after a 2000-01 season that was filled with controversy, unmet expectations and some truly uninspired play.

Everything that was accomplished by the Sweet 16 club was torn asunder by last year's unit, which was torpedoed by internecine squabbles and petty jealousies. Even though Seton Hall managed a modest run at the end of the season, winning two Big East Tournament games, it couldn't erase the bad taste of a 2-8 regular-season finish and the team's perceived lack of focus.

Orr must repair any bruised egos that still exist and turn what appears to be a talented group of individuals into a team.

"We have to develop chemistry," he said. "We have to work hard. I'm preaching family and team. These guys have to improve their chemistry from last year."

On the court, the Pirates will be an aggressive, uptempo bunch, eager to take advantage of their quickness and depth. And, when things get a little slower, and half-court ball prevails, the Hall will rely on its expected strong outside shooting. It's not a bad combination, and one that could result in a pretty good season.

Although only two starters return, both are guards, an excellent step-off point for any successful team. Sophomore point man **Andre Barrett** and senior wing **Darius Lane** are one of the league's best backcourt pairings and have the potential to be much better. The 6-4 Lane (16.9 ppg, 4.8 rpg, 2.4 apg, 1.7 spg, .395 3PT) is a complete package, capable of scoring from all over the floor. He can be a good passer and strong defender who can get to the backboards. He was an All-Big East honorable mention pick last year and should attract more notice this season, particularly if he concentrates on his complete game for the whole year.

Lane had some big games at big times last year, hitting Illinois for a career-high 31 and scoring 21 against Alabama in the first round of the NIT. He drilled seven treys against West Virginia and Clemson and scored 29 in the win over the Tigers. Orr will ask even more of him this year.

"He's a senior now, so he's got to lead, on and off the court," Orr said. "He has to set the tone for the young guys and want to go out a winner. Everybody knows what kind of an offensive player he can be. We need him to contribute in every area—defending, making plays for others, rebounding and leadership."

The 5-8 Barrett (10.2 ppg, 3.3 rpg, 5.5 apg) was a highly-regarded newcomer last year who was supposed to team with Lane and Eddie Griffin to bring Seton Hall to the Final Four. That didn't happen, but Barrett did have a strong debut. Most impressive was his 2:1 assist to turnover ratio, excellent for a collegiate player.

Barrett did convert only 36.3 percent of his field-goal tries and was a tepid 30.1 percent from behind the arc. Those numbers should improve, thanks to added maturity that ought to result in better shot selection. Unfortunately, Barrett's touch didn't improve this summer, as he played for the bronze medal-winning U.S. team in the World University Games. He averaged 5.5 points and 1.9 rebounds and was second on the team in assists, but shot .357 from the field and just .211 from the three-point line.

Still, Barrett is jet quick and capable of breaking down practically any defender. And, when Amaker headed to Michigan, Barrett decided to stay at Seton Hall, rather than transfer west.

"Having Andre as a point guard, one of the best in the country, is a huge plus," Orr said. "We expect greater leadership and maturity from him. He'll have much more experience and be much more aware."

As if Barrett and Lane aren't enough, the Pirates can call on 6-0 senior **Ty Shine** (9.6 ppg, 1.9 rpg, 2.5 apg), a combination guard with great shooting range who can sit on the wing and fire or run the show. He wasn't thrilled by the arrivals of Barrett and Griffin last year, but he should be happier this year, because Orr is not wedded to any of the team's players and is only looking for leadership and production.

"Ty is experienced and versatile," Orr said. "He can create off the dribble and make big plays and big shots."

Expect to see 6-4 junior **Desmond Herod** (1.8 ppg, 0.9 rpg) in the mix. Herod played in 19 games last year after transferring from UNLV and flashed some athletic ability. Now, he must display more basketball skill. He's a slasher and a leaper who could fit in well with Orr's full-court style.

"Herod's been one of the hardest workers since I've gotten here," Orr said. "We play nine or 10 people, and he has a chance to be one of them, because he has a lot of energy. He can score and defend and is long and athletic."

Rounding out the backcourt is 6-3 senior walk-on **Raheem Carter**, who sat out last year after transferring to Seton Hall from Monmouth. He's a point guard who isn't expected to see all that much time. He did average 4.5 points and 1.2 assists at Monmouth in 1999-00 and had 14 points against Fairleigh-Dickinson.

Although Griffin and 7-0 center Samuel Dalembert—both first-round NBA draft picks—are gone up front, the Pirates have added some talented newcomers, most notably 6-5 freshman **John Allen** from Coatesville (Pa.) High School. Expect Allen to make an immediate impact. A second-team Parade All-America and a USA Today third-teamer, Allen averaged 26.0 points last year and led Coatesville to the Pennsylvania Class AAAA title.

Allen was Coatesville's all-time leading scorer, with 2,372 points, breaking UConn and current Washington Wizards star Rip Hamilton's record. Allen signed early, while Amaker was still coaching the team, but stuck around after Orr took over. He will provide some more wing scoring, and though he might have to defer to Lane somewhat this year, could be a big-time force in the coming years.

"He's a warrior," said Orr, who recruited Allen while an assistant at Syracuse. "He gets after it. He's tough, versatile and efficient. He can score inside and out and is a hard worker. He's a complete player."

The Hall has plenty of options at the forward spots besides Allen. Holdover **Greg Morton** (1.9 ppg, 3.8 rpg), is a 6-7 sophomore who demonstrated the ability to rebound last year. Now, he must display the ability to score somewhat or be relegated to special situations.

Sophomore **Marcus Toney-El** (6.7 ppg, 4.0 rpg) was the least heralded of the three newcomers last year, but the 6-6 sophomore is a nuts-and-bolts player who can help out on the wing or closer to the hoop. Though relatively one-dimensional (off the dribble) offensively, Toney-El is athletic and should flourish at times when the tempo increases.

Orr will be interested to see what 6-7 sophomore **Damion Fray**, from Walt Whitman High School in Huntington, N.Y., can do. Fray sat out last year as a partial qualifier, but is extremely athletic and has potential. He practiced with the team last year but missed six weeks at the outset, because of a fractured wrist. He averaged 19.0 points and 12.0 rebounds as a prep senior but is strong and capable of being hard to handle inside.

"He has a great deal of athletic ability," Orr said. "He's physical and has a chance to be good. He's an explosive athlete who can get to the rim. He's a good offensive rebounder and a high-energy guy. He has plenty of skills with the ball and has a huge upside."

Another new forward who can play the three or four is 6-8 freshman **Mauricio Branwell**, from Notre Dame (Mass.) Prep. Branwell isn't going to score a lot, but he will rebound and defend.

Orr says Branwell "doesn't mind doing the little things," a valuable trait on a team with as much depth as the Pirates have.

The middle could belong to 6-10 senior **Charles Manga** (2.0 ppg, 1.8 rpg), who started four times last year. Manga is a strong player with limited scoring ability who will be called upon largely to defend and rebound. If he can handle those assignments and stay out of foul trouble, he could get 20 minutes a night. If not, he'll be replaced by a rotating forward line that will feature Fray or Branwell in the middle.

Don't expect to see 7-0 freshman **Alexander Gambino** from Long Island Lutheran in the middle for too long. He averaged 10.0 points and 10.0 rebounds last year as a senior and needs plenty of polish.

Though he possesses good hands and a fine shooting touch, Gambino needs to add strength to his 235-pound frame, the better to handle the rough stuff inside. He is likely a project.

2001-2002 SCHEDULE

Nov.	16	@San Francisco
	19-21	#Maui Invitational
	29	Monmouth
Dec.	5	@Rider
	11	St. Peter's
	13	Fairleigh Dickinson
	16	LaSalle
	22	@Michigan State
	27-28	##ECAC Holiday Festival
	31	Boston College
Jan.	5	@Virginia Tech
	8	@Syracuse
	11	Rutgers
	16	@Georgetown
	18	West Virginia
	26	@Notre Dame
	29	St. John's
Feb.	3	Notre Dame
	7	@Pittsburgh
	9	West Virginia
	12	Georgetown
	16	Illinois
	21	Syracuse
	23	@Rutgers
	26	Pittsburgh
Mardh	2	@Connecticut
	6-9	###Big East Championship

@Road Games
#Maui, HI (vs. Duke first round; also Ball State, Chaminade, Kansas, UCLA, South Carolina, Houston)
##Madison Square Garden, New York (vs. Iona first round; also Fordham, Manhattan)
###Madison Square Garden, New York

BLUE RIBBON ANALYSIS

BACKCOURT	B+
BENCH/DEPTH	B
FRONTCOURT	B-
INTANGIBLES	B

Last year, many predicted a Final Four run and a Big East title for the Pirates. What they got were plenty of problems and an ugly, late-season slide.

Amaker is now gone to greener pastures, and Orr will try to build a program that can one day meet those expectations. He'll begin with more discipline, a popular style and a talented backcourt.

Those are three strong foundation pieces. If Barrett and Lane mesh well together, provide leadership and play for the team, rather than their stats, the Hall is off to a good start. Add in Shine, and Orr has some intriguing and explosive options.

The frontcourt will be interesting. Allen has the potential to score a lot, but the Hall needs the other newcomers to team with Morton and Manga in a productive forward wall that defends to the death, crashes the boards and provides enough interior scoring to keep opposing defenses from crowding the perimeter. That could happen, particularly if the Pirates can get the tempo pulsing.

Orr was a good choice for the Pirates, because he'll be happy to stay in South Orange and the Big East for a while—unless Jim Boeheim decides to leave Syracuse in a couple years, and the folks in the Snow Belt turn to one of their own.

Orr will recruit well and put forth teams that are aggressive and smart. But he has a challenge in state, because Rutgers made a good hire with Gary Waters. The race is on again, and Jersey fans hope that the outcome this time is different.

(M.B.)

St. John's

LOCATION	Jamaica, NY
CONFERENCE	Big East (East)
LAST SEASON	14-15 (.483)
CONFERENCE RECORD	8-8 (3rd)
STARTERS LOST/RETURNING	1/4
NICKNAME	Red Storm
COLORS	Red & White
HOMECOURT	Alumni Hall (6,000)
	Madison Square Garden (19,876)
COACH	Mike Jarvis (Northeastern '68)
RECORD AT SCHOOL	67-32 (3 years)
CAREER RECORD	320-173 (16 years)
ASSISTANTS	Kevin Clark (Clark '81)
	Mike Jarvis II (Northeastern '92)
	Dermon Player (St. John's '01)
TEAM WINS (last 5 years)	13-22-28-25-14
RPI (last 5 years)	83-32-6-6-70
2000-01 FINISH	Lost in conference first round.

Well, that didn't quite turn out the way we thought, now, did it?

The arrival of heralded guard Omar Cook was supposed to turbo-charge the Red Storm, bringing it to hurricane status and then setting it loose throughout an undermanned Big East. It didn't matter that three starters were gone from the 1999-00 St. John's edition, or that the team would be starting as many as four new players, the Storm would continue to thrive.

Although Cook had a strong debut, leading the team in scoring (15.3 ppg) and piling up 8.7 assists per game, he was erratic at times, shooting just 36 percent from the field and only 30.9 percent from three-point range.

And the rest of the team was no more complete. While the Red Storm did thrive offensively, it was awful at the other end, allowing rivals to make 44.9 percent of their field-goal tries, and not much better on the backboards, where it fought opponents to a tie. The result was an extremely unfulfilling 14-15 season that brought the Red Storm back—at least for one season—to the unhappy times that preceded Mike Jarvis' arrival. Things became worse soon afterward, when Cook played his one-and-done card and headed to the NBA.

Although there is a collection of familiar names around Jamaica this year, there is a dearth of star power. Even forward **Anthony Glover**, who was expected to be a monster inside, looked rather mortal last year. There are quality newcomers on the horizon, but it remains to be seen whether they have enough to make the instant impact the Red Storm needs.

St. John's is unlikely to slip below .500 again, but the program is well removed from its successes the first two years of Jarvis' tenure.

The backcourt has candidates but few early answers at the point. Perhaps 6-4 junior **Sharif Fordham** (4.8 ppg, 4.9 rpg, 1.2 apg) can do that job, although he proved last year to be more comfortable in a combination role, with plenty of work at the two-spot. Fordham is a good defender but lacks shooting range and will most likely be the third guard used by Jarvis.

The point could be Marcus Hatten, from Tallahassee (Fla.) Community College and Mervo High School in Baltimore, Md., a 6-2 junior who hails from the same junior college that produced former high-scoring St. John's

guard Bootsy Thornton. Hatten was a first-team NJCAA All-American last year after scoring 24.1 points per game and averaging 5.0 rebounds and 3.6 steals. He left Tallahassee with school records for single-season scoring average (breaking Thornton's mark) and steals in a year. Though known for scoring first and foremost, Hatten could get the ball.

The third candidate at the point is 6-1 freshman Tristan Smith from Amityville (N.Y.) High School, who averaged 24.0 points last year and left as the school's all-time leader in points, assists and steals. He led Amityville to a pair of New York Class B titles and was a key member of last season's 27-1 team.

Could Jarvis go with a Smith/Hatten backcourt? Absolutely. That would allow him to use 6-6 sophomore **Willie Shaw** (13.8 ppg, 3.3 rpg, .379 3PT) at the three, although Shaw's shooting ability makes him valuable on the perimeter at the wing-guard position, too. Shaw was the second-leading Red Storm scorer last year and swung between the two and three positions, which are interchangeable in Jarvis' system.

Two more guards in the program are walk-ons **Christian Diaz** from George Washington High School and Santo Domingo, Dominican Republic, a 6-3 junior, and 6-1 freshman **Jon Schelman** from LaGuardia High School in New York, N.Y.

Figure plenty of wing time for 6-6 junior **Alpha Bangura** (6.4 ppg, 2.6 rpg), who made a successful transition to the Big East after transferring to St. John's from Monmouth. His challenge is to improve his shooting range, which is limited, and to improve his rebounding and defense. Another forward with the potential to play significant minutes is 6-6 freshman **Eric King**, from Milford (Conn.) Academy and Lincoln High School in Brooklyn, N.Y. King averaged 22.0 points and 8.0 rebounds last year at Milford after being voted the New York PSAL Player of the Year by the New York Post, after his senior season at Lincoln. He's a physical player who can help inside, something the Red Storm needs.

There are plenty of bodies and experience to man the four and five positions. The question is whether any of them is ready to be a major producer. The 6-6 Glover (13.7 ppg, 5.9 rpg), now a senior, has the potential, no question about it. Though shorter than the average pivot, he has tremendous strength and the desire to hit the boards. Though not expected to be a huge scorer, the Red Storm would like to see him push his rebounding work up to eight or nine a game. He'll get plenty of help from 6-8 sophomore **Kyle Cuffe** (8.3 ppg, 4.4 rpg, .519 FG), who had a fine debut and should use his considerable offensive skills to blossom into a double-figure scorer this season.

Donald Emanuel (3.4 ppg, 2.7 rpg) returns for his senior season at the four and five spots, providing solid rebounding in spurts and some fairly solid defense. The 6-8 banger is a good role player.

When it comes to pure size, few teams can touch the Johnnies, who have three players 6-11 or taller. Unfortunately, none was all that impressive last year. The best of the bunch was 6-11 sophomore **Mohamed Diakite** (2.3 ppg, 1.5 rpg), whom Jarvis likened last year to Patrick Ewing. Diakite is athletic, but he is thin and needs plenty of polish. Sophomore **Curtis Johnson** (1.0 ppg, 1.0 rpg) played just one game last year and continues to grapple with his weight. The 7-3, 320-pounder needs to improve his conditioning and strength to make a significant contribution.

Another 6-11 player, junior **Abe Keita** (0.9 ppg, 1.1 rpg), struggled to find a spot in the rotation last year. Though athletic, with good hands, he has little offensive polish and is still adjusting to the collegiate game.

2001-2002 SCHEDULE

Nov.	17	Stony Brook
	22-24	#Great Alaska Shootout
Dec.	1	Fordham
	8	@Manhattan
	11	@Niagara
	16	Hofstra
	20	St. Francis, NY
	22	Wake Forest
	29	Quinnipiac
Jan.	2	@Pittsburgh
	5	West Virginia
	8	Miami
	12	@Providence
	17	@Boston College
	20	Villanova
	23	@Connecticut
	26	Providence
	29	@Seton Hall
Feb.	3	@Virginia Tech
	6	Fairfield
	9	Connecticut
	13	@Miami
	16	Virginia Tech
	18	Boston College
	24	@Duke
	27	Notre Dame
March	3	@Villanova
	6-9	##Big East Tournament

@Road Games
#Anchorage, AK (vs. Gonzaga first round; also Indiana, Alaska-Anchorage, Tennessee, Marquette, Oregon State, Texas)
##Madison Square Garden, New York, NY

BLUE RIBBON ANALYSIS

BACKCOURT	B-
BENCH/DEPTH	B
FRONTCOURT	B-
INTANGIBLES	B+

This St. John's team has potential, but whatever it accomplishes, it will have to do so by committee, because there is no standout. Maybe that's not a bad thing, after the disappointment the Red Storm endured last year with Cook.

Although one of the newcomers could emerge as a big-time scorer, it will be incumbent upon Shaw, Glover and Cuffe to have big seasons. There is still a question at the point, where any of three players could start—with no guarantee of finishing. After having Cook and Erick Barkley during his three years at St. John's, Jarvis has no such cinch at the team's most important position. How well he fills that spot will determine whether the Red Storm can make a run at an NCAA berth.

The defense and rebounding have to improve, too. Just about everybody scored on the Red Storm last year, taking advantage of the team's desire to run and gun. Expect things to tighten up considerably this year, because Jarvis has plenty of bodies available and can mete out playing time according to the desire to defend.

There won't be another slide below .500, but 25 wins aren't in the offing, either. Still, this is a fairly young team, and plenty will return next year, perhaps even Glover, if he graduates by the end of summer. The 2001-02 season could be a good step toward future success, provided the questions are answered.

(M.B.)

Villanova

LOCATION	Villanova, PA
CONFERENCE	Big East (East)
LAST SEASON	18-13 (.581)
CONFERENCE RECORD	8-8 (t-3)
STARTERS LOST/RETURNING	2/3
NICKNAME	Wildcats
COLORS	Blue & White
HOMECOURT	The Pavilion (6,500)
	and First Union
	Center (19,010)
COACH	Jay Wright (Bucknell '83)
RECORD AT SCHOOL	First year
CAREER RECORD	122-85 (7 years)
ASSISTANTS	Brett Gunning (UNLV '94)
	Joe Jones (Oswego State '87)
	Fred Hill (Montclair State '81)
TEAM WINS (last 5 years)	24-12-21-20-18
RPI (last 5 years)	10-86-43-39-51
2000-01 FINISH	Lost in NIT first round.

It's hard to argue with anybody that says Steve Lappas has a special guardian angel looking after him and his career. Just days before having to endure a meeting with Villanova administrators, in which he was likely to be told he had better return the Wildcats to the NCAA Tournament—fast—Lappas landed a five-year deal to coach Massachusetts at a reported $600,000 per year.

Talk about last-minute reprieves. Villanova had as much chance of making the big tourney this year as

Lappas does getting invited to the Big East referees' Christmas party. So, off Lappas shuffled to Amherst, the beneficiary of some good fortune.

And in comes Jay Wright, a former Villanova assistant, who no doubt believes he has the same special heavenly emissary watching out for him. Wright built Hofstra into a two-time NCAA Tournament participant but could not have imagined jumping to his dream job this year. Lappas had a few years left on his contract, and Villanova was in no position to fire a coach, just because he had won "only" 18 games in a season. Wright was hot, all right, but the timing was not right for him to move where he wanted to go. Or so he thought.

When Wright was announced as Villanova's new coach on March 27, he couldn't contain his emotions. In front of an SRO crowd that included friends, family and former players in the Wildcats' Pavilion homecourt, he cried. Why not? A former Rollie Massimino assistant, Wright grew up in suburban Philadelphia, went to Massimino's hoop camps as a youngster and even married a VU grad (Patricia, class of '83). This was a homecoming for Wright, and he couldn't contain his emotions—at first.

When he finally settled down, Wright spoke about pride. About passion. About how he wanted players to put on the Villanova uniform and then sweat blood for the school. He was promising a team that would play with the same enthusiasm Wright would be displaying from the coaching box. He didn't promise any win totals or guarantee a trip to the tournament in X years. Wright just wanted to have people at the school who wanted to be there as much as he did.

So far, so good. Wright was able to convince all the holdovers of consequence to re-up for another season, even if he did lose the battle to keep last year's top player, pivot Michael Bradley, to stay for his final year. Gone, too, is forward Aaron Matthews, who ran afoul of the school's disciplinarians and has transferred to Delaware State. Bradley is a huge loss. The one-dimensional Matthews, who played aggressive defense and dunked well, is not so big. And, given Wright's early recruiting returns, the best is yet to come.

This summer, Villanova received commitments from a pair of top-50 players, 6-2 guard **Allan Ray**, from St. Raymond's in the Bronx, and 6-7 swingman **Curtis Sumpter**, from New York's Bishop Loughlin. Each played on the Long Island Panthers' AAU club and serve as an excellent example of Wright's ability to recruit New York. For all the trouble Lappas' New York roots caused him in parochial Philadelphia, he never really tapped into the fertile Big Apple recruiting soil. His one big recruit from the north was Tim Thomas of Paterson, N.J., and that was accomplished in part because of Lappas' willingness to hire Thomas' uncle as an assistant. In less than five months, Wright had shaped Villanova's future considerably.

"It's great to call a recruit or talk to a recruit and represent Villanova," Wright said. "Recruits can tell how proud I am to be part of this program. It's nice to be out on the recruiting trail and wear 'Villanova' on your chest."

Wright is effusive in his praise for the school, its tradition and everybody who came before him, but the fact is that Villanova had gone two seasons without a trip to the NCAA Tournament and has fallen into the middle of the Big East pack. Despite Lappas' impressive record of six 20-win seasons in eight years at the school, alumni and fans were increasingly dissatisfied with his ability to win in the tournament (2-4) and hang with the league's big boys. Wright's charge will be to do that. Winning 20 games is nice, but the postseason is everything in college basketball, especially for Villanova's quiet supporters, whose placid behavior at home games belies their great expectations.

The school's 1985 national title was great, but it spawned a culture that might just be unreasonable for a small, private school in the NCAA's current climate. VU's 1985 title was a wildly improbable run that will likely never be duplicated by a school that isn't among the NCAA's football-playing hierarchy. But that doesn't mean Wright can't make it into mid-March's magical time on a regular basis and win some games. If he keeps adding players of Sumpter and Ray's caliber, that should happen.

Just don't expect that much this year. Villanova enters the year with some serious question marks at guard and in the middle. The Wildcats may be more passionate and enthusiastic than ever before, but they still have some holes. Those gaps may even prohibit Wright from installing his system completely, because there may not be the depth or talent to play the up-tempo, pressure defense style he prefers.

"I'm not sure we can play the way I want to," Wright said. "We have some very skilled offensive guys, but in terms of defense and rebounding, that's not our strength. We want our team's strengths to be defense and rebounding. We're probably going to have to meet in the middle somewhere. I'd be lying if I said I knew where that was."

There is experience, but precious little depth, in the backcourt. One returning starter is 6-3 junior **Gary Buchanan** (13.4 ppg, 4.8 rpg, 3.3 apg, .341 3PT, .942 FT), a wing with unlimited shooting range. But Buchanan has to become more than just a stand still gunner. There were times last year when teams controlled him by shadowing his perimeter movements and preventing any passes from finding their way to him. Buchanan would drift around the three-point arc, rather than going to get the ball and then breaking his man down. Buchanan showed little in-between game last year and displayed a distaste for any kind of physical play. That's too bad, because he made nearly 95 percent of his free throw attempts last year but shot only three a game from the stripe.

"I think he can become a complete player, offensively and defensively," Wright said. "He has great potential be a very good rebounder, too. His goal in the off-season was to become a complete player. He's working on putting it on the floor and getting to the foul line more."

The only true point guard in the program right now is 6-0 sophomore **Derrick Snowden** (4.2 ppg, 1.4 rpg, 2.0 apg), who started 12 times last year. Snowden is quick and can penetrate, but he struggled with his ball handling and decision making last year. Though the Wildcat faithful screamed for Lappas to use Snowden more last year, the rookie wasn't up to big minutes. He had some big problems with the press—along with the rest of the Wildcats, who at times looked like a high school team (at Boston College, Feb. 4) when confronted by full-court pressure—and also committed some silly fouls.

Snowden averaged 22.0 minutes in Big East play and showed the ability to score well at times, but he has a big jump to make this year. On pure talent, he should be OK.

But he will need more than that to thrive.

Snowden will team with Buchanan and 6-2 **Reggie Bryant** (5.7 ppg, 1.7 rpg, 28.6 3pt), another sophomore who struggled some last year. Bryant missed seven games with a stomach muscle pull and needed considerable time to get back. He has a good mid-range game, is quick and can pass the ball pretty well. Lappas raved about Bryant's skill package, but the injury and the presence of Buchanan and senior Jermaine Medley made it hard for Bryant to develop any momentum. This year, he'll get plenty of opportunity to play.

"I like the guards a lot," Wright said. "I like the commitment they made in the off-season. I like their toughness, and I like them for this style of play. They need experience and need to play in the Big East. They need to become leaders. One of the question marks on the team is how they will fit into that role. We don't have any other options. They know it, and we know it."

The other guard in the program is 6-3 senior walk-on **B.J. Johnson** (0.3 ppg, 0.0 rpg), who played a total of eight minutes last year.

There are many options up front, although there is nobody with any proven scoring ability. Senior **Brooks Sales** (9.0 ppg, 6.2 rpg, 1.0 bpg, .599 FG) missed five games last year with a broken hand. He has played in the shadow of Malik Allen and Bradley and now gets a chance to assert himself as a force. Although Wright raves about Sales' commitment, the 6-10, 220-pounder has yet to show the requisite strength to be a force inside offensively or as a rebounder. Although Sales should see the ball more and should push his scoring average into double figures, it's unlikely he'll become a standout.

The power forward should be 6-7 junior **Ricky Wright** (8.6 ppg, 4.2 rpg, 58.4 FG), who emerged during the second half of last year as a valuable frontcourt asset. Wright started eight Big East games and showed the potential to be an active four man. Wright can play inside and can step away a bit from the basket, but he does need to work on his mid-range shooting touch because he isn't big enough to do all his business inside.

A pair of freshmen—6-9 **Marcus Austin** from St. Patrick's High School in Irvington, N.J., and 7-0 **Chris Charles** from Crispus Attucks High School in Milwaukee, Wisc.—will have the opportunity to make significant contributions right away. Austin missed a good portion of last year because of mononucleosis, but is a strong interior player who can score close to the basket. He has low-post skills and the power to be a good rebounder.

Charles, meanwhile, is a lean 220-pounder who didn't play ball last year after his school de-emphasized the sport. There will be some rust, but Wright is impressed with Charles' skills.

"He can shoot the ball, has great footwork and great hands," Wright said. "He just needs strength. He's a basketball player, not just a post player. He can feed the post from up high and put the ball on the floor. We're not talking Tim Duncan here, but he's not a project."

Wright would like to find a way to unlock 6-7 junior **Andrew Sullivan**'s (1.7 ppg, 1.3 rpg) potential. A fine athlete who can run and jump, Sullivan has yet to display a full range of basketball skills and has suffered in games that require significant amounts of half-court play. If Sullivan can develop an intensity that matches his athleticism, Wright may have something.

Another holdover with a need to become more of an all-around basketball player is 6-8 sophomore **Andreas Bloch** (2.1 ppg, 0.8 rpg, .419 3PT), a great long-range shooter who has shown little desire to do anything else on the court. Another good athlete with a need to develop his on-court skills more is 6-10 sophomore **Jair Veldhuis** (0.3 ppg, 0.2 rpg), who impressed at times in practice last year but played only 11 minutes. On a team with just 10 scholarship players, however, Veldhuis has a chance to get onto the court.

2001-2002 SCHEDULE

Nov.	21	Grambling State
	24	Dayton
	27	LaSalle
Dec.	1	Bucknell
	5	@Pennsylvania
	8	@Temple
	11	Stony Brook
	22	VMI
	28	Delaware State
Jan.	2	Providence
	6	@Notre Dame
	9	Boston College
	13	*Connecticut
	15	@Virginia Tech
	20	@St. John's
	24	@Miami
	28	St. Joseph's
	30	Virginia Tech
Feb.	2	@Pittsburgh
	5	Miami
	9	UCLA
	11	@Connecticut
	16	*Georgetown
	19	@Providence
	28	*Syracuse
March	3	St. John's
	6-9	#Big East Tournament

@Road Games
*The United Center
#Madison Square Garden, New York, NY

BLUE RIBBON ANALYSIS

BACKCOURT	B-
BENCH/DEPTH	C
FRONTCOURT	B-
INTANGIBLES	B+

Wright doesn't have to worry about a tournament-or-bust mandate this season, but Villanova fans are expecting a greater excitement from the team and are looking to big things in the future from their hometown hero. Wright is a Philly guy who will fit in well with the city's basketball community while still mining New York for talent. It's a great combination that should pay off big in the future.

For now, Villanova must get great play from its guards. That means Snowden and Bryant must be consistent and reliable, while Buchanan has to find that the area inside the three-point line is not filled with poisonous snakes and kimono dragons. If the backcourt delivers, Villanova can be a dangerous team, because Wright knows how to craft a style that plays up a strong perimeter. If they struggle again, then Villanova is in huge trouble.

The frontcourt could be solid, although it's unlikely anybody will emerge as a star. Wright and Sales should be good, while Austin and Charles will be able to contribute. Anything that comes out of the other three—Sullivan, Bloch and Veldhuis—will be gravy.

Lappas has moved on and is in a good spot. Wright has moved in and is in a perfect position—for him. The honeymoon is on, and Wright knows it. This year should feature a return to the NIT, with a brighter outlook predicted for down the line.

(M.B.)

Virginia Tech

LOCATION	Blacksburg, VA
CONFERENCE	Big East (East)
LAST SEASON	8-19 (.296)
CONFERENCE RECORD	2-14 (7th)
STARTERS LOST/RETURNING	4/1
NICKNAME	Hokies
COLORS	Maroon & Burnt Orange
HOMECOURT	Cassell Coliseum (10,052)
COACH	Ricky Stokes (Virginia '84)
RECORD AT SCHOOL	24-34 (2 years)
CAREER RECORD	24-34 (2 years)
ASSISTANTS	Mark Cline (Wake Forest '88)
	Steve Lytton (East Tennessee State '68)
	Randy Peele (West Virginia Wesleyan '80)
TEAM WINS (last 5 years)	15-10-13-16-8
RPI (last 5 years)	125-144-190-141-194
2000-01 FINISH	Lost regular-season finale.

At least Ricky Stokes has some players now. He has a roster that features some performers with track records, along with a few newcomers who might be able to make an immediate impact. It's not like last year, when a preseason conversation with Stokes went something like this:

Renowned Basketball Writer: "Coach, what can you tell us about your backcourt?"

Ricky Stokes: "We'll be using guards there."

RBW: "Who will be starting up front?"

RS: "Most likely, tall people."

RBW: "Do you have any feeling for how the season will go?"

RS: "Yes."

RBW: "Can you elaborate?"

RS: "No, it's too painful to talk about."

And so it went. After leading the Hokies to a respectable, 16-15 record in their 1999-00 Atlantic 10 swan song, Stokes and Tech entered the Big East without leading scorers and top rebounders Rolan Roberts and Dennis Mims, each of whom transferred. Without guard Tony Dobbins, who had transferred to Richmond. Without forwards Rodrigo Viegas (Florida International) and David Wahley (Auburn-Mobile). When the exodus was completed, and Stokes rolled out the balls for the first day of practice, he was looking at a team that had just two returnees from the previous season and enough questions to fill a whole season of The Weakest Link.

In Big East circles, nobody had to guess whom Ann Robinson would be telling to go swimming while wearing a cement Speedo or try walking through South Central LA with an "I Love Mark Furhmann" T-shirt on. The Hokies were indeed the league's weakest link.

Good-bye.

"We knew it would be difficult," Stokes said. "Looking back, we had two players, 12 points and three rebounds [a game] returning. Everybody looking at that knew how difficult it was going to be."

The prophets were correct. Although the Hokies had a few near misses and even beat St. John's and Miami, success was generally limited to the likes of High Point, Elon and Fairfield. Ugly was a kind word for the season. Last year was brutal.

But it's over. The Hokies head into 2001-02 with a much brighter outlook and a real, live college basketball roster. Even though Stokes had to add two junior-college transfers to last year's three junior college newcomers, Tech does have the foundation of a program that could, in a few years, become competitive in the conference. When the Hokies add four new players for next year, they will have just about completed the rebuilding cycle.

The team will still be young, but it will be relatively talented (if Stokes can continue adding some strong players). And it will be a long way from last year, when a trip to Blacksburg, as unpleasant as it might be, given the various twists and turns of the terrain, was practically a guaranteed win, and a visit from the Hokies was a tonic

for any struggling team's ailments.

"It's like the difference between a ninth-grade player and a senior in high school," Stokes said. "We're starting to build a team and a program, but we need consistency."

During the past recruiting cycles, Stokes was able—he thinks—to address the Hokies' primary needs: point guard and low-post scoring. The former was solved by the arrival of 5-11 **Eric Branham** from Hagerstown (Md.) Junior College by way of Cardoza High School in Washington, D.C.. The latter need could be met by 6-8, 280-pound **Terry Taylor** from Allegany (Md.) Junior College by way of Tallwood High School in Chesapeake, Va.

Branham averaged 15.3 points and 5.4 assists last year for Hagerstown and is a quick distributor with above-average defensive skills. He solves a huge problem for the Hokies, who last year had to use **Brian Chase** or 6-7 **Carlos Dixon** at the point. Chase is a scorer, while Dixon is a swingman. Neither embarrassed himself there, but Tech did average a meager 12.2 assists as a team, a big reason they scored only 65.8 points per game. Branham should help improve that.

"I like him," Stokes said. "We listed the things on our board that we wanted a point guard to do, and he met all the criteria. He's a winner. He's competitive. He makes the easy play. He sets things up. He has leadership, too, because he has played for two years."

Branham's arrival allows Chase (12.9 ppg, 2.9 rpg, 2.3 apg, .468 3PT) to become a full-time two man. The 5-10 junior has the potential to become the league's best three-point shooter. It would be nice if he also was able to work more on his off-the-dribble game. Chase is an active defender and quick, so he and Branham should allow the Hokies to press more. There is one question: How will a sub-six-foot backcourt fare in the big Big East? Stokes, a sub-six footer himself, has an answer.

"Twenty years ago, Othell Wilson and I played at Virginia in the backcourt," Stokes said. "Not many people thought we could play together. We definitely played well together."

He's right. The Cavaliers made it to the Final Four in '81, with Stokes and Wilson teamed in the backcourt, and missed the Final Four again two years later by one point. So, Stokes should be confident that the Branham/Chase combo will work.

Not that he doesn't have some other options. Dixon (11.0 ppg, 3.6 rpg, .347 3PT) is a 6-7 sophomore who was the team's second-leading scorer last year. Though not so strong of stature, he is a proficient scorer and good defender whose 47 steals led the team last year. Expect him to start on the wing and then slide into the backcourt with Chase or Branham, when the substitution pattern begins. Dixon was one of the league's top rookies last year and has the opportunity to be an all-star down the road.

"He played tons of minutes and tons of games last year," Stokes said. "It's too bad he had to do that. He's small and has a slight build, so he wore down. He has to be stronger with the ball this year."

It will be interesting to see how Stokes handles the minutes of 6-7 sophomore swingman **Bryant Matthews** (9.1 ppg, 5.2 rpg), who started all but two games last year. The addition of Branham could make Matthews a sixth man. Or, he could start and Chase could come off the bench. Matthews fans shouldn't worry, though. He averaged 27 minutes a game last year and will get that many this season, no matter how he is deployed. His presence and versatility give Stokes some needed flexibility in the league.

Another guard with promise is 6-6 senior **Joe Hamilton** (8.9 ppg, 2.9 rpg), a mid-season addition last year from junior college. He had trouble with his shot, but because he couldn't practice with the team until late December, Stokes is willing to overlook some of his troubles. He also thinks Hamilton will be more successful, particularly from mid-range, this year.

Rico Murray (0.3 ppg, 0.3 rpg), a 6-1 senior, rounds out the backcourt picture. He played in just seven games last year.

The main returnee up front is 6-11, 205-pound senior **Carlton Carter** (7.8 ppg, 6.2 rpg), who had a solid debut for Tech after transferring from Colorado. He showed the potential to score a little in league play, when he had 17 points against Notre Dame, but Carter lacks the strength to dominate inside. Like Hamilton, he didn't start playing until December, so he had some rust. Stokes expects him to improve this year.

"He is skilled, and he showed some flashes toward the end of last year," Stokes said. "He can step out and

face and has gotten stronger. He should have a good senior year."

The spindly Carter is quite a contrast to Taylor, a super-sized pivot who will most likely start immediately for Tech and has the strength and finishing skills to command double teams inside, thereby creating room on the perimeter. As a sophomore at Allegany, Taylor averaged 16 points and 10 boards while shooting .662 from the field. He led his team to the finals of the NJCAA Tournament and was chosen all-tournament. Allegany finished 32-3.

"He gives us a proven inside scorer," Stokes said. "He has a great scoring touch. You think guys as big as him can score only around the basket, but he can step out. He shoots the ball well, and he can move."

Two other newcomers will bring some inside power, but because each is a freshman, Stokes can't expect too much too soon. The more prepared of the two is 6-7, 220-pound forward **C.J. Pigford** from Hargrave (Va.) Military Academy and East Columbus High School in Riegelwood, N.C. Pigford is strong and mature and will give the Hokies another big body who can rebound and defend inside.

Pigford can play both forward positions, as can 6-6 freshman **Harding Nana** from Notre Dame Prep in Middlesburg, Mass. and the Newport School in Kensington, Md. More of a project than Pigford, Nana, a native of Cameroon, averaged 12.3 points and 8.0 rebounds last year at Notre Dame Prep.

"Nana has a good upside," Stokes said. "He's very aggressive and relentless. A guy who works as hard as he does could give us minutes right off."

The new faces up front will allow 6-9, 245-pound senior **Mibindo Dongo** (5.9 ppg, 4.8 rpg, .558 FG) to fill his role as a banger inside. Stronger than most of the other forwards in the league, Dongo has just to improve his shooting touch to thrive. That may not happen, but he will be counted on for muscle inside.

The main casualty in the frontcourt revival could be 6-8 junior **Jon Smith** (3.6 ppg, 2.8 rpg), who averaged 18.3 minutes last year but could see his time diminished. A good open-court player and wing shooter, Smith fills a role, but he might not be able to find significant minutes, if everybody is healthy.

2001-2002 SCHEDULE

Nov.	17	Mount St. Mary's
	20	Rhode Island
	24	@Old Dominion
	27	East Carolina
	29	Northeastern
Dec.	1	@Virginia
	3	VMI
	7-8	#Jim Thorpe Classic
	12	Western Michigan
	15	Radford
	27	@Florida State
Jan.	2	Connecticut
	5	Seton Hall
	10	@Connecticut
	12	Miami
	15	Villanova
	20	@Boston College
	26	@Syracuse
	30	@Villanova
Feb.	3	St. John's
	6	Boston College
	9	@Providence
	13	@West Virginia
	16	@St. John's
	23	Providence
	27	Rutgers
March	2	@Miami
	6-9	##Big East Tournament

@Road Games
#Louisville, KY (vs. Murray State first round; also Louisville, Wisconsin-Milwaukee)
##Madison Square Garden, New York, NY

BLUE RIBBON ANALYSIS

BACKCOURT	B-
BENCH/DEPTH	C
FRONTCOURT	C+
INTANGIBLES	B-

The Hokies will be better than last year. That's a given. Tech has more talent, and Stokes has more options with which to work. A real, live point guard is on campus, as is a post scorer. Those are two big differences from last year, when Tech had to do it all with wing players, some of whom played out of position.

Stokes takes heart in the turnaround authored by Boston College last year. If the Eagles can go from the league's bottom to the NCAA Tournament, anybody can do it, right? Maybe. Tech needs much to go right, in order for it to chase a .500 season, much less go to the big show. Branham must be able to play 30-35 minutes a night and not wear down. Dixon and Chase have to improve their scoring, and Taylor must be as good as advertised. That's a lot of variables.

So, expected about 12-14 wins, not a bad jump from last year. Tech could grab five or six Big East triumphs, too, provided everybody is healthy and produces the way they can. Most importantly, the program is headed in the right direction. If Stokes backs up this year's crop of newcomers with two more good classes, then we can talk tournament contention. And the coach will be able to think back to 2000-01 and smile, knowing that he has withstood the worst of it.

(M.B.)

West Virginia

LOCATION	Morgantown, WV
CONFERENCE	Big East (West)
LAST SEASON	17-12 (.586)
CONFERENCE RECORD	8-8 (4th)
STARTERS LOST/RETURNING	1/4
NICKNAME	Mountaineers
COLORS	Old Gold & Blue
HOMECOURT	WVU Coliseum (14,000)
COACH	Gale Catlett (West Virginia '63)
RECORD AT SCHOOL	431-261 (23 years)
CAREER RECORD	557-305 (29 years)
ASSISTANTS	Drew Catlett (Randolph-Macon '85)
	Chris Cheeks (Virginia Commonwealth '92)
	Lester Rowe (West Virginia '85)
TEAM WINS (last 5 years)	21-24-10-14-17
RPI (last 5 years)	44-39-172-91-73
2000-01 FINISH	Lost in NIT first round.

If somebody wants to make friends with the West Virginia basketball players, he will get a copy of the videotape from Gale Catlett's whitewater rafting excursion during his summer trip to Oregon.

The 59-year-old coach acquitted himself well on the rapids, which weren't overwhelmingly dangerous but had enough kick to cause some problems. And, yes, that was Catlett who was dumped from the raft into the froth and had to hoist himself back to safety. Imagine the laughter and catcalls from the Mountaineers when they saw that.

"I'm sure it will be shown at the appropriate time," said Catlett, no doubt cringing at the tape's blackmail potential.

If Catlett can climb into a raft and hurdle down some raging waters, then he still has enough verve to lead WVU into postseason contention. Even though the rapids took a round or two from Catlett, he emerged smiling and intact at the end of the journey. That's how it might be for the Mountaineers this season. A smooth ride can hardly be predicted, but by season's end, West Virginia could be in pretty good shape. With four starters returning, some good depth and a true gem—freshman point guard **Jonathan Hargett**—entering the program, WVU appears to be in pretty good shape.

"For the first time, since we went to the Sweet 16 three years ago, there's going to be great competition at every position," Catlett said. "We haven't had that kind of depth in a while."

The roster numbers will also allow the Mountaineers to play Catlett's preferred style—pressing and running. The past few WVU editions have been more halfcourt-minded, thanks to a lack of overall speed and depth. Now, with the potential that 10-11 Mountaineers could be playing every night, Catlett is looking for a return to the old days.

A key will be the emergence of Hargett, a 6-0 freshman blur who could unseat incumbent **Tim Lyles** at the point from the moment the balls are rolled out for the first practice. The explosive newcomer is well traveled, having played previously at National Christian (Md.) Academy, Mt. Zion Christian (N.C.) Academy and

Highland Springs (Va.) High School. He averaged 22.5 points and 6.0 assists last year and was rated among the top 50 players in the country by most scouting services.

Credit Hargett's arrival to Catlett's decision to hire former VCU assistant Chris Cheeks. Cheeks is a Virginia native who knows Hargett's family well and was able to sell them on Morgantown and Catlett. It's a huge step for West Virginia, which can boast of having one of the Big East's best newcomers.

"He's as good as it gets out there," Catlett said. "No one in the league or in the country has a player coming in as good as he is. He has all the tools."

Perhaps the only person not thrilled with Hargett's arrival is 5-11 junior Lyles (11.5 ppg, 3.6 rpg, 5.5 apg), who didn't acquit himself poorly at the point last year but has some clear holes in his game, particularly his shooting. Lyles made just 32.5 percent of his field-goal attempts last year and was a weak 22.3 percent from behind the arc. Although he had some big games early on, most notably a 26-point outburst against UNC-Greensboro and 23 in a win over American, he cooled considerably, and during one five-game stretch of Big East play shot just 12-for-52 from the field (23.1 percent).

Lyles also must improve his defensive production. Though quick, he averaged just one steal per game. A change in scheme will help, but he must become more aggressive. Finally, Lyles has to make better decisions off the dribble. Last year, he trapped himself close to the basket too much.

"He is as tough as they come," Catlett said about Lyles. "He's a gamer and a winner. But he doesn't like to practice. You can't get the ball from him, but he doesn't shoot too well. He mashes the ball in there too much. You can't do that in the Big East."

"He has to come back in great condition and has to have a great year, because if there's any slippage, Hargett is right there. Without question [Hargett] has the most skill of anyone on the team."

While Lyles finds himself in a fight for his job, 5-11 senior **Lionel Armstead** (14.3 ppg, 3.2 rpg, 1.2 apg, .392 3PT) is entrenched at shooting guard. Even though his presence ensures the Mountaineers of a small backcourt, no matter who is at the point, Armstead is a deadly long-range shooter who led the Big East with a 46.4 percent three-point success rate in conference play. Last year, however, he shot only 64 times from beyond the arc in league games. That's a number that must increase considerably.

Armstead is quick and can leap, but his 5-11 frame can be a liability in a halfcourt defensive setting. That's another reason Catlett would like to go with an up-tempo strategy this season.

Armstead will get some backup from 6-6 sophomore **Jay Hewitt** (3.0 ppg, 1.3 rpg), who struggled some last year but has potential. He'll fill the two and three spots after being forced to play some point last season, thanks to a lack of depth. Though not that quick or overly athletic, Hewitt has a good feel for the game and gives the Mountaineers some height in the backcourt.

"He's a good ball handler and passer and understands the game better than anybody on the team," Catlett said.

Catlett expects 6-3 freshman Drew Schifino from Bridgton (Maine) Academy and Penn Hills High School in Pittsburgh, Pa. to provide scoring off the bench. He averaged 28.3 points and 5.2 rebounds last year, after lighting it up for 30.2 points during his last year at Penn Hills.

"He's a slashing scorer who is athletic and a jumper," Catlett said. "He can get to the basket."

The rest of the backcourt picture includes 6-0 sophomore **Tobias Seldon** (0.5 ppg, 0.6 rpg), a point who played in just 15 games last year, and 5-10 senior walk-on **Jeff Davis** (0.4 ppg, 0.0 rpg).

The Mountaineers have improved themselves in the backcourt, but they must make up for the loss of inside producer Calvin Bowman, who averaged 17.6 points and 9.7 rebounds last year, as a senior. Although no one player will step in and make up for Bowman's production, WVU does have some options, beginning with 6-8 senior **Chris Moss** (10.7 ppg, 7.9 rpg), who can play forward or center.

Moss isn't going to overwhelm people, but he is a strong presence near the basket. He shot 50.9 percent from the field and blocked 1.3 shots per game a year ago.

For sheer power, there is 6-10, 260-pound sophomore **Chris Garnett**, a transfer from Eastern Kentucky who sat out last year and averaged 7.4 points and 5.4 rebounds during the 1999-00 season with the Colonels.

Garnett has shed 30 pounds since arriving on campus and was too big to handle in WVU scrimmages last year. He may not score as much as Bowman did, but he'll certainly help on the boards and defensively.

"He's as wide and strong as anybody in the league," Catlett said. "He's a rough, tough guy who can run the court. He has a great body."

Catlett also expects to get some help from 7-1 junior **Ales Chan** (1.1 ppg, 1.7 rpg). Chan will be used primarily as a defensive stopper this season but can't be expected to be an offensive threat. Still, Catlett is pleased with his progress and expects Chan to be tougher than he was last year and capable of blocking some shots.

Another role player in the middle should be 6-9, 235-pound senior beast **John Oliver** (3.3 ppg, 3.2 rpg, 50 FG), a weightlifting devotee who won't be pushed around. He isn't too skilled, but he can add some muscle when the situation calls for it.

The Mountaineers have a couple of options at the three spot, beginning with 6-6 junior **Josh Yeager** (8.1 ppg, 3.8 rpg), who started 14 games last year. Yeager is a good long-range shooter who can also pass. But his defense and rebounding need improvement. Catlett believes the extra strength Yeager added during the off-season will help in those areas this year.

Newcomer **Tyrone Sally**, who played Emmanuel (N.C.) Academy, Mt. Zion (N.C.) Academy and Meadowbrook High School in Chesterfield, Va., is also in need of some muscle buildup. The 6-7, 190-pounder has plenty of skill, though. "He just oozes quickness," Catlett said. "He runs the floor and blocks shots. He brings some athletic ability to the three-spot."

Because Yeager and Sally have questions, Catlett imported 6-7, 210-pound forward **Chaz Briggs** from Wabash Valley (Ill.) Junior College. While not a huge offensive force, Briggs can rebound and block shots. He can run the floor and will provide some depth up front.

Rounding out the forward line is 6-6 senior walk-on **Warren Coates** (0.0 ppg, 0.0 rpg).

2001-2002 SCHEDULE

Nov.	16	UNC Asheville
	23-24	#Hispanic College Fund Classic
Dec.	5	@James Madison
	8	Florida International
	15	Robert Morris
	19	Duquesne
	22	@Tennessee
	28-30	##Bank One Fiesta Bowl Classic
Jan.	5	@St. John's
	9	Notre Dame
	12	Syracuse
	16	@Rutgers
	18	@Seton Hall
	23	Marshall
	27	Rutgers
	30	Providence
Feb.	2	@Georgetown
	4	@Syracuse
	9	Seton Hall
	13	Virginia Tech
	16	Pittsburgh
	20	@Notre Dame
	23	@Connecticut
	27	Georgetown
March	2	@Pittsburgh
	6-9	###Big East Tournament

@Road Games
#Albuquerque, NM (first round vs. Southern Miss; also New Mexico, Pacific)
##Tucson, AZ (vs. Valparaiso first round; also Arizona, Pepperdine)
###Madison Square Garden, New York, NY

BLUE RIBBON ANALYSIS

BACKCOURT	B-
BENCH/DEPTH	B
FRONTCOURT	B-
INTANGIBLES	B

Catlett is right to be excited about this season. The Mountaineers have the best talent and depth they've enjoyed since their first year in the Big East. If everybody stays healthy and eligible, West Virginia will return to its pressing style and have a chance at shaking up the Big East some, particularly because the league is without dominant teams this year.

Hargett is a key. If he is as good as advertised, the Mountaineers become a much quicker team and a more dangerous offense, because he can get his points and also set up his teammates. His potential is huge, and West Virginia's ability to land him is a coup for the program, which is trying to improve its status within the Big East.

Catlett will have to be creative at the other spots, because the rest of the Mountaineers have liabilities, along with their strengths. Armstead can shoot and get to the hoop, but he's only 5-11 and can be abused on defense.

The frontcourt has some size and strength, but there isn't a lot of offensive skill. The forwards can score, but they don't defend all that well.

It could be a good year in Morgantown. The Mountaineers aren't title contenders, but they could approach the 20-win mark and make a run at an NCAA berth. If somebody emerges as a reliable frontcourt scorer, West Virginia should be there.

(M.B.)

Eastern Washington

LOCATION	Cheney, WA
CONFERENCE	Big Sky
LAST SEASON	17-11 (.608)
CONFERENCE RECORD	11-5 (2nd)
STARTERS LOST/RETURNING	3/2
NICKNAME	Eagles
COLORS	Red & White
HOMECOURT	Reese Court (6,000)
COACH	Mike Burns (Central Washington '97)
RECORD AT SCHOOL	17-11 (1 year)
CAREER RECORD	65-44 (4 years)
ASSISTANTS	Mike Burns (Central Washington '97)
	Mike Score (Washington '96)
	Ryan Orton (Eastern Oregon '96)
TEAM WINS (last 5 years)	7-16-10-15-17
RPI (last 5 years)	276-164-231-129-170
2000-01 FINISH	Lost in conference final.

Eastern Washington played the transition game to near perfection last season. The Eagles never skipped a beat in their climb up the Big Sky ladder under new coach Ray Giacoletti, who took over for Steve Aggers after the 2000 season.

Eastern lost the Big Sky Conference regular-season title on the last day of the 2000 season under Aggers, then lost in a tournament semifinal.

Enter Giacoletti.

Eastern again finished second in the regular season, but made it to the tournament championship game before falling to Cal State Northridge, which has moved on to the Big West Conference this season.

"I was very pleased with the way things went last year," said Giacoletti, who came to Eastern after three winning seasons at North Dakota State.

"Obviously, we came up a game short in the regular season and the conference tournament," he said. "The kids really bought into what we were trying to do."

Seniors such as Chris White, Aaron Olson and Jamal Jones made the transition easier. White and Olson earned first-team all-league honors and Jones was honorable mention.

"I never like to speak in terms of I. I'd rather say we, but for me it was as gratifying a year as I've had in coaching," Giacoletti said. "Those seniors bought into what we were trying to do, and I know how hard it is to gain trust, to get everybody on the same page. I've been in college coaching for 16 years and it's a challenge in any sport getting people to buy in. We really had 14 kids do that and hopefully it set the tone for the future."

To put Eastern's recent success in perspective, consider this: From 1991 to 1997 the Eagles went 16-88 in league games. Eastern won 23 games over the last two years with White, Olson and Jones leading the way.

"Those kids can walk away with their heads held high, knowing they put their stamp on something," Giacoletti said. "The players with years left need to maintain this program and we need to take one more step. But when you lose three seniors like that you lose experience and a number of intangibles."

That's not to say the Eagles will be hurting this season. Eastern returns a solid pair of starters in 6-3 senior

BIG SKY

BLUE RIBBON FORECAST
1. Weber State
2. Northern Arizona
3. Montana State
4. Montana
5. Eastern Washington
6. Idaho State
7. Portland State
8. Cal State Sacramento

ALL-CONFERENCE TEAM
G - Jermaine Boyette, JR, Weber State
G - Justin Brown, SR, Montana State
F - Dan Trammel, SR, Montana
F - Ryan McDade, JR, Northern Arizona
C - Stephan Bachmann, JR, Weber State

PLAYER OF THE YEAR
Jermaine Boyette, JR, Weber State

NEWCOMER OF THE YEAR
David Bell, JR, Montana

2001-2002 CONFERENCE TOURNAMENT
March 7-9 at home of regular-season winner

2000-2001 CHAMPIONS
Cal State Northridge (regular season)
Cal State Northridge (conference tournament)

2000-2001 POSTSEASON PARTICIPANTS
Postseason record: 0-1 (.000)
NCAA
Cal State Northridge

TOP BACKCOURTS
1. Weber State
2. Montana State
3. Montana

TOP FRONTCOURTS
1. Weber State
2. Northern Arizona
3. Montana

INSIDE THE NUMBERS
2000-2001 conference RPI: 25th (of 31)
Conference RPI (last five years): 22-21-18-16-25

DID YOU KNOW?
The Big Sky Conference returns to an eight-team league this season after Cal State Northridge's departure for the Big West. The league began play in 1963. Montana, Montana State, Weber State and Idaho State are the only remaining members from that first season. ... Idaho State's 10 wins in conference play last season equaled its best total in the last 22 years. The Bengals swept the Montana-Montana State road trip for the first time since 1977. ... Sacramento State's Jerome Jenkins, the interim head coach last season, had the interim label removed in March and was given a one-year contract extension. ... Weber State's win over nationally ranked Utah last season was its first in Salt Lake City since the 1977-78 season.

(R.M.)

point guard **Jason Lewis** (7.4 ppg, 4.3 apg) and 6-9 senior center **Jason Humbert** (8.0 ppg, 3.4 rpg).

Lewis quickly found his way into the Eagles' starting lineup after transferring from Southwestern Oregon Community College, perhaps given to the fact he had played a year of Division I ball at Jacksonville State.

"He's someone, to me, who brought everybody together, the glue of all the pieces," Giacoletti said. "Having the year at Jacksonville State, he knew what to expect and wasn't intimidated."

Lewis is a heady player who knows how to draw a foul and how to take one. Lewis shot 81 percent from the free-throw line last season, including a league-record 16-of-16 against Weber State, and took just five fewer free throws than White, the team leader.

"That's a feel for the game that he's been able to find," Giacoletti said of Lewis' knack for getting to the line. "Taking charges, that's something we talked about from day one. He really bought into that."

Darren Cooper (15.3 ppg, 3.7 apg), a 6-3 freshman from Benson High School in Portland, Ore., could be called on to back up Lewis.

"We were very fortunate to pull in a player like him," Giacoletti said of Cooper, a second-team all-stater.

Humbert was a pleasant surprise for the Eagles last year. He sat out 2000 after suffering a knee injury just four games into the 1999 season. He worked his way into the starting lineup by the beginning of the conference play, allowing White to play his more natural power forward position.

"I really think with the year he had he has a good chance to be as good a post player as there is in league," Giacoletti said. "One thing I'll be looking for is consistency."

Junior Chris Johnson (1.8 ppg, 1.4 rpg) left the program, leaving the Eagles green behind Humbert at center. **Gregg Smith** (5.6 ppg, 3.9 rpg at NDSU)—a 6-10 red-shirt sophomore who came to Eastern along with Giacoletti from North Dakota State—and transfer **T.J. Williams** (18.5 ppg, 11.3 rpg), a 6-8 junior from Edmonds (Wash.) Community College, figure into Giacoletti's plans at the post.

"Williams is extremely athletic," Giacoletti said. "He's the piece we're missing with the post players. He's a guy who can touch both hands on the top of the square on the backboard.

"Smith doesn't need to get any stronger, he needs to get more athletic. He's as big as a house."

Marco Quinto (4.9 ppg, 1.7 rpg), a 6-6 senior, is an unlikely power forward but will probably get the call. Quinto holds the school record for three-point percentage (.508), although he attempted just 34 last season.

"Unless I screw up, I hope he can do the same things this year," Giacoletti said. "He kind of found his niche playing the four for us last year. Hopefully with a year in our system under his belt, his numbers can improve."

Jeremy McCulloch (16.0 ppg, 11.0 rpg), a 6-11 red-shirt freshman from Ladysmith, British Columbia, is another unconventional power forward.

"He's more of a face-up player than a back-to-the-basket guy," Giacoletti said.

Transfer **Keith Browne** (16.1 ppg, 6.1 rpg), a 6-5 junior from Tacoma (Wash.) Community College, will see time at power forward as well. Also figuring into the mix will be **Marc Axton** (11.4 ppg, 4.2 rpg), a 6-7 freshman from Federal Way, Wash.

"Browne's a tough, hard-nose player that's versatile enough to shoot the three, or put it on the floor and make decisions," Giacoletti said.

Giacoletti can pick from among five players on the wings, three of whom saw considerable action last season. **Alvin Snow** (7.4 ppg, 2.5 rpg), a 6-2 sophomore, started 16 games as a freshman and is at the top of his coach's list.

"The best word I can use to describe Alvin is that he's a winner," Giacoletti said of Snow, who led the Eagles in steals last season with 43. "He's someone I really grew to appreciate over the year because of how tough he is."

Eddie Lincoln (2.0 ppg, 1.3 rpg), a 6-4 sophomore, and **Clint Hull** (2.2 ppg, 0.3 rpg), a 6-2 sophomore, are the other two returning letter winners at wing.

"Eddie has 27 games worth of experience now and has a pretty good feel for what the Big Sky's all about," Giacoletti said. "He has the versatility to do a number of different things."

Hull made 13-of-37 three-point shots while averaging just 5.5 minutes a game last season, but ranks behind only Quinto among the Eagles returning.

"Clint can really shoot the three," Giacoletti said. "He's someone we obviously need. One of the things we need to work on is shooting."

Brendon Merritt (18.3 ppg, 4.9 rpg), a 6-4 junior transfer from Tacoma (Wash.) Community College, and **Chris Hester**, a 6-3 junior from Southeastern Iowa Community College, round out the wings. Hester came to Eastern two years ago, but had to sit out last season for academic reasons.

Giacoletti has set up another challenging non-conference schedule that includes trips to Minnesota and Gonzaga, as well as a first-round match-up against Indiana in the Hoosier Classic. It was a game against then defending national champion Michigan State that jump-started the Eagles last year, Giacoletti believes.

"Our trip to Michigan State was the turning point," said Giacoletti, whose Eagles beat Butler before falling to the Spartans, 83-61. "We were very competitive with them. Coming out of that weekend our guys thought there was no reason we can't be successful."

Giacoletti doesn't want the Eagles to slip back down the ladder now.

"With the success that Eastern has had, there's two things this program has never done: win an outright Big Sky title and go to the NCAAs," Giacoletti said. "Those are two steps that need to be taken."

2001-2002 SCHEDULE

Nov.	15-16	#Black Coaches Classic
	19	Northwest College
	24	@Minnesota
	29	Boise State
Dec.	1	St. Martin's College
	4	@Gonzaga
	6	@Idaho
	9	Cal Poly
	15	@Portland
	21	@Saint Mary's
	23	@San Diego State
	28-29	##Hoosier Classic
Jan.	11	Montana
	12	Montana State
	19	Portland State
	25	@Weber State
Feb.	1	Northern Arizona
	2	Cal State Sacramento
	8	@Montana State
	9	@Montana
	16	@Portland State
	22	Idaho State
	23	Weber State
March	1	@Cal State Sacramento
	2	@Northern Arizona
	7-9	###Big Sky Tournament

@Road Games
#Berkeley, CA (vs. St. Joseph's first round; also California, Princeton)
##Indianapolis, IN (vs. Indiana first round; also Butler, Samford)
###Home of regular-season champion

BLUE RIBBON ANALYSIS

BACKCOURT	B
BENCH/DEPTH	C
FRONTCOURT	B
INTANGIBLES	B

Eastern's cupboard might not be as bare as some suspect. Lewis is a player fans will love to hate and coaches will envy. His ability to draw contact will put him at the line as much as any player in the league and for that reason, the Eagles will have a good shot in tight games. He's also a natural leader on a team that will be looking for someone to fill the void left by last year's seniors.

Humbert is a solid center who might look better than that in a league shy on true post players.

The supporting cast is unproven, but guys like Snow and Lincoln proved last year that they're ready to step up.

Eastern went 6-2 on the road in Big Sky play last season, including a win at league champion Cal State Northridge, but just 5-3 at home. The Eagles won't win

that many road games this season, so they better win the ones they should at home.

(R.M.)

Idaho State

LOCATION	Pocatello, ID
CONFERENCE	Big Sky
LAST SEASON	14-14 (.500)
CONFERENCE RECORD	10-6 (3rd)
STARTERS LOST/RETURNING	3/2
NICKNAME	Bengals
COLORS	Black & Orange
HOMECOURT	Holt Arena (8,000)
COACH	Doug Oliver (San Jose State '73)
RECORD AT SCHOOL	28-53 (3 years)
CAREER RECORD	28-53 (3 years)
ASSISTANTS	Jay McMillin (Nebraska-Wesleyan '88)
	Louis Wilson (William Jewell '88)
TEAM WINS (last 5 years)	14-6-6-8-14
RPI (last 5 years)	236-289-272-251-193
2000-01 FINISH	Lost in conference semifinal.

Jordie McTavish played for just one year at Idaho State. Coach Doug Oliver hopes the effect McTavish had on the program will last much longer.

The Bengals won seven league games in the two years McTavish waited on the ISU bench, first as a transfer from Utah and then with a knee injury. With the point guard in the lineup, the Bengals went 10-6 in league, finished third in the regular season and went back to the Big Sky postseason tournament for the first time in four years.

"He exposed the returning players to what it takes to prepare yourself for a long season," Oliver said of McTavish, who led ISU in scoring at 15.6 points per game in his senior season. "Where he had an impact was the emotional lift he gave us on the floor, sometimes good, sometimes bad. He was so competitive. In the spring and fall workouts, he raised the bar a little bit. That impact is as great as any he will have."

ISU asked the NCAA for another year of eligibility for McTavish, but the appeal was denied.

"And to make matters worse, he re-injured his knee playing with the Canadian National Team," Oliver said. "Poor kid. He went through a lot."

Still, McTavish will be on the Bengals' bench as a graduate assistant this season while he earns his degree.

Oliver will also have to replace departed seniors Tim Erickson, the team's leading three-point shooter; center Doug Silva, the team's leading rebounder; and Chad Tracy, Silva's backup. Those four seniors represented 58 percent of ISU's offense last season. Erickson and McTavish combined for 157 three-pointers, which helped the Bengals rank 17th in the nation in treys per game.

The returning starters are **D'Marr Suggs** (11.8 ppg, 5.1 rpg), a 6-3 senior guard, and **Rashad Kirkland** (10.8 ppg, 5.7 rpg), a 6-5 senior forward. Suggs hoisted his share of three-pointers, making 54-of-138, and will give the Bengals a deep threat this season.

"He had off-season surgery to repair a stress fracture in his lower leg," Oliver said. "I expect him to be much better just by the fact that he'll be pain free. He should be one of our leading scorers."

Kirkland is another candidate to pick up his offensive production.

"We're going to try to make a change of philosophy on the offensive end to a four out, one in basketball team," Oliver said. "We'll have to watch his transition from having his back to the basket to facing the basket. Rashad and D'Marr, I expect them to be our anchors."

Suggs will have plenty of help at wing. **Alvin Brooks** (6.7 ppg, 0.7 rpg), a 6-2 junior in eligibility, will return to action. Brooks was granted a medical red-shirt after foot problems limited him to just three games last season.

Arzelle Lewis, a 6-2 red-shirt freshman, could work his way into the lineup.

"He's an excellent defender," Oliver said. "He's an unknown quantity to most people in the conference. He's the type of young man who will force me to play him and then take advantage of it."

Oliver is excited about the potential of another wing, **Jeremy Brown**, a 6-5 junior transfer from Scottsdale (Ariz.) Community College who was academically ineligible last season.

"He could make as much difference in our program as any player we have," Oliver said. "He can play the one, two or three. He's as good a player as we've had in this program since I've been here, maybe a special type of player."

Danny Boticki (3.5 ppg, 1.3 rpg), a 6-4 junior, backed up McTavish at the point last season, but will probably see more time on the wing this year.

"He's an all-purpose perimeter player," Oliver said. "His M.O. is that he's a good perimeter shooter. Last year he had a stretch where the ball wouldn't go in and it affected his confidence. We're hoping that area improves."

Aaron Bradley (2.0 ppg, 0.9 rpg), a 6-5 junior, was injured in a car accident near the end of conference season last year but will be back in the mix at wing.

Mamo Rafiq (2.3 ppg, 1.8 rpg), a 5-10 sophomore, was injured in the same car accident and will compete for the starting point guard position.

"He made strides as a freshman," Oliver said. "He's a little bit of an unknown quantity, but he's a pure point guard."

Rafiq will battle **Dion Jackson**, a 5-10 junior transfer from Casper (Wyo.) Community College, for the starting job.

"He's an excellent athlete and he has that personality that could replace some of the things Jordie brought," Oliver said.

Joining Kirkland at power forward will be **Ruwhabura Barongo "Ray" Munyagi** (18.0 ppg, 11.0 rpg), a 6-5 junior transfer from Peninsula (Wash.) College who originally hails from Tanzania.

"I'm excited to watch him do some things around the basket," Oliver said. "He's a 12-feet-and-in type of shooter but can defend anyone on the floor. The presence of he and Jeremy Brown will force me to play a more up-tempo brand of basketball."

J.T. Nelson (3.0 ppg, 2.4 rpg), a 6-10 senior, will likely get the nod at center.

"It's his time to ante up, if you will," Oliver said. "He's capable when given the opportunity."

Oliver is anxious to see the progress of **Jesse Smith**, a 6-9 red-shirt freshman. Smith is a raw talent who won the state high hurdles in his senior year in high school in Mackay, Idaho.

"The biggest question mark, but the guy who could have the most positive influence could be Jesse Smith," Oliver said. "He's as athletic a young man at that size as I've ever coached in 27 years of coaching. His basketball background is limited, but he could influence a lot of basketball games. It's my job to teach him how to play."

With the loss of Erickson and McTavish, and the addition of players like Brown and Munyagi, Oliver sees an opportunity for change.

"We're somewhat upbeat around here right now," Oliver said. "People say we lost Jordie and Tim Erickson, but we're going to be different. We shot a ton of three-pointers last season. This year we might be more of a mid-range, slashing type of team. And with our depth and athleticism, we should be able to extend pressure.

"If the Smiths and Browns fit right in and we get good guard play and Suggs and Kirkland step up, we can be as good as anybody on a given night."

2001-2002 SCHEDULE

Nov.	17	@Loyola Marymount
	21	@Portland
	24	Southern Utah
	28	@Utah State
Dec.	1	Montana Tech
	7-8	#SW Missouri Tournament
	10	@Southern Utah
	15	Montana Western
	21	@Utah
	28-29	##Utah State Classic
Jan.	2	Portland
	11	Sacramento State
	12	Northern Arizona
	18	@Montana State
	19	@Montana
	25	Portland State
	26	Eastern Washington
Feb.	2	Weber State
	8	@Northern Arizona
	9	@Sacramento State
	15	Montana
	16	Montana State
	22	@Eastern Washington
	23	@Portland State

March	2	@Weber State
	7-9	###Big Sky Tournament

@Road Games
#Springfield, MO (vs. Texas San-Antonio first round; also Southwest Missouri, Southern)
##Logan, UT (vs. Birmingham-Southern first round; also Centenary, Utah State)
###Home of regular-season champion

BLUE RIBBON ANALYSIS

BACKCOURT	C
BENCH/DEPTH	B
FRONTCOURT	B
INTANGIBLES	C

There are a lot of "ifs" in Oliver's assessment of how good his team could be this season.

It isn't possible to overstate the positive influence McTavish had on the Bengals last season. Without him, ISU would have been a sub-.500 team.

And the falloff at point guard this year will be dramatic, regardless of who wins the starting job. On the other hand, Suggs has proven he can score and Kirkland is battle tested.

Oliver is high on transfers Brown and Munyagi, but it usually takes a year for junior college players to adjust to Division I. Unless their learning curve is steep, the Bengals will find it tough to duplicate last year's success.

(R.M.)

Montana

LOCATION	Missoula, MT
CONFERENCE	Big Sky
LAST SEASON	11-16 (.407)
CONFERENCE RECORD	6-10 (7th)
STARTERS LOST/RETURNING	1/4
NICKNAME	Grizzlies
COLORS	Maroon & Silver
HOMECOURT	Dahlberg Arena (7,500)
COACH	Don Holst (Northern Montana '75)
RECORD AT SCHOOL	41-41 (3 years)
CAREER RECORD	41-41 (3 years)
ASSISTANTS	Jim Sampson (Wartburg College '81)
	Todd Schmautz (Montana Tech '92)
	Pryor Orser (Montana State-Billings '90)
TEAM WINS (last 5 years)	21-16-13-17-11
RPI (last 5 years)	121-145-230-119-257
2000-01 FINISH	Won regular-season finale.

A couple of statistics nicely sum up Montana's 2000 season.

"We shot six percentage points less [last year] in conference from three-point range than we did when we won the conference championship in 1999," coach Don Holst said. "And we shot a worse percentage [68 percent to 72 percent] from three free-throw line. Those are the areas that help you win close games."

Of the Grizzlies' 17 losses—their most since 1977—eight came by fewer than 10 points and three were in overtime. The result was that the Griz failed to make the Big Sky Conference postseason field for just the second time since 1978.

"That was frustrating for our kids," said Holst, beginning his fourth year. "We want to take that out on our opponents next season."

That's exactly what the Griz did two years ago. Montana failed to make the postseason in Holst's first year, then charged back to win the regular-season title the following year. After another sub-par year, can the Griz repeat the pattern?

"That's what we're shooting for," Holst said. "We feel with the seasoning those kids had last year, the lessons they learned and all those close losses will be better. The addition of some new players and the vets we have returning give us a chance to be a good basketball team."

The Griz have a chance to have one of their most experienced and deepest teams in years. Four starters return along with another part-time starter and a player coming off of red-shirt who averaged 14 minutes as a freshman.

Point guard **Shane Christensen** (9.6 ppg, 4.6 apg), a 6-1 senior, has started 53 games over the last two sea-

sons and played in all of Montana's games for his first three years in Missoula.

"He's a great leader, a very good defender and pushes the ball well," Holst said of Christensen, who had a team season-high 33 points against Eastern Washington a year ago. "He's been through the ups and downs as a starter. I think you'll see a more relaxed but focused Shane Christensen."

Christensen, an erratic shooter who shot 38 percent from the field last season, will be challenged at the point by **Sam Riddle** (3.0 ppg, 3.1 apg), a 6-0 sophomore who red-shirted last season. Riddle played in all 28 games as a freshman, averaging 13.6 minutes a game.

"As a freshman, he was in the top 10 in the league in assists," Holst said. "He's grown up a lot. With the addition of him, we're very strong at the point."

Riddle shot just 37 percent from the floor as a freshman, but worked with a shooting coach for two weeks this summer.

"He's a guy who works strictly on shooting," Holst said. "[Riddle] spent a couple of weeks in Seattle working with him on three-point shooting. He did that last summer and you could see a marked difference."

Holst's toughest personnel decisions might come at the wings, where there could be as many as eight players to choose from. The incumbents are **Ryan Slider** (7.3 ppg, 4.6 rpg), a 6-5 senior, and **Brent Cummings** (5.7 ppg, 3.0 rpg), a 6-7 junior.

Slider started 15 games last season and came on strong down the stretch, averaging 10.7 points and 5.7 rebounds over the final seven games.

"If he wants to, he can be the best player at his position in the league," Holst said. "If he does, look out."

Cummings shot a team-best 42 percent from three-point range and had a career-high 24 points midway through the league season against Portland State.

"He led the team in three-point shooting, but he probably didn't know that," Holst said. "He probably didn't take enough attempts. He's also probably our best shut-down defender."

Holst recruited **David Bell** (17.0 ppg, 3.0 apg), a 6-1 junior transfer from Porterville (Calif.) College, to bolster the Grizzlies' outside threat. Bell shot 51 percent from three-point range last season.

"He looks great on paper, but he hasn't made a basket for the Griz yet," Holst said. "He knows how to score and has done it. He has a quick release, is good off the dribble and can catch and shoot. He might be an impact player for us."

Deidre Carr (2.3 ppg, 0.9 rpg), a 6-2 senior, and **Matt Luedtke**, a 6-2 red-shirt freshman, are also deep threats but will have several players in front of them, at least at the start of practice.

Two in-state recruits, 6-4 **Jeff Hays** (14.8 ppg, 9.3 rpg) and 6-2 **Kevin Criswell** (33.5 ppg, 12.2 rpg), will also compete on the wings.

"The more I see of Hays, the more I think he'll find a way to play," Holst said. "He's a good passer. He just needs to think in terms of shooting the ball first."

"I think we got lucky to get Criswell. He was under-recruited. He can shoot the heck out of it."

The final candidate at the wing is **Ryan Pederson** (2.7 ppg, 1.4 rpg), a sophomore who at 6-9, but only 195 pounds, is a classic tweener.

"I don't know if he's a four or a three," Holst said. "He can step away and feel comfortable shooting it from three. We'll see how he comes back before we make decisions."

The Griz have a pair of starters returning at the two post positions—**Dan Trammel** (12.4 ppg, 7.8 rpg), a 6-6 senior, and **Travis Greenwalt** (12.1 ppg, 4.4 rpg), a 6-8 senior.

Trammel had three double-doubles in Montana's final five games last season and averaged 15.8 points in that stretch.

"He's a super athlete who had a wonderful year," Holst said. "He can go get rebounds that are out of his area. I always tell him if he gets double digits in rebounding he'll get double digits in scoring because he'll get some easy put-backs.

"Greenwalt is a solid guy who you can count on to do the right thing in the right situation. He's our mental anchor. He maybe needs to concentrate on rebounding a little more."

There will be several new faces backing up Greenwalt and Trammel. Transfers **Victor Venters** (15.0 ppg, 7.0 rpg), a 6-7 sophomore from Diablo Valley (Calif.) College, and **Marcus Rosser** (14.6 ppg, 9.6 rpg), a 6-7 junior from Kansas City Community College, might have immediate impacts.

"Venters is a smart player," Holst said. "He's skilled enough that he can take you off the dribble. He can shoot jump hooks with either hand and he's strong.

"Rosser gets better and better every time out. He can catch the ball and check shots."

Corey Easley (13.8 ppg, 7.6 rpg), a 6-8 freshman, and **Chris McKay** (27.5 ppg, 15.0 rpg), a 6-10 freshman, will likely need seasoning.

Holst wants his team to be tough enough to win the close games this year.

"That was mental toughness," Holst said. "We need to be good enough to go on the road and win games despite any circumstances. We didn't do that last year, the year before we did.

"When we have a team down, we've got to keep them down. It's a few possessions every game."

2001-2002 SCHEDULE

Nov.	16	Evergreen State, WA
	18	@Gonzaga
	20	@Northern Iowa
	23	Concordia
	28	Washington State
Dec.	2	Pacific
	5	Nevada
	8	@Idaho
	10	@Colorado
	20-22	#Yahoo Sports Invitational
	30	Loyola Marymount
Jan.	5	@Weber State
	11	@Eastern Washington
	12	@Portland State
	18	Weber State
	19	Idaho State
	25	@Northern Arizona
	26	@Cal State Sacramento
	31	@Montana State
Feb.	8	Portland State
	9	Eastern Washington
	15	@Idaho State
	22	Cal State Sacramento
	23	Northern Arizona
March	2	Montana State
	7-9	#Big Sky Tournament

@Road Games
#Lale, HI (vs. Navy first round; also BYU, Hawaii, Buffalo, Columbia, New Mexico State, Tulsa and Valparaiso)
###Home of regular-season champion

BLUE RIBBON ANALYSIS

BACKCOURT	B+
BENCH/DEPTH	B
FRONTCOURT	B
INTANGIBLES	B-

The Griz will play six of their first eight conference games on the road and will face league favorite Weber State twice during that stretch. Those first eight games will determine how high Montana can finish in the league standings.

If the Griz can get a couple of road breakthroughs and hold serve at home, then they'll have a chance to make some noise when they play five of their final six at home.

The Griz could be a surprise team this year. Junior college players always look good on paper, but this year's crop of Bell, Venters and Rosser looks legit. Add them to a roster that includes four returning starters and a handful of veteran role players and the Griz could be salty.

If Montana can get out of the early season in good shape, it could contend for one of the top spots in the league.

(Rs.M.)

Montana State

LOCATION	Bozeman, MT
CONFERENCE	Big Sky
LAST SEASON	16-14 (.533)
CONFERENCE RECORD	8-8 (t-4th)
STARTERS LOST/RETURNING	1/4

NICKNAME	Bobcats
COLORS	Blue & Gold
HOMECOURT	Worthington Arena (7,250)
COACH	Mick Durham (Montana State '79)
RECORD AT SCHOOL	172-145 (11 years)
CAREER RECORD	172-145 (11 years)
ASSISTANTS	Jerry Olson (Minnesota-Morris '81)
	Scott Carson (Mesa State '79)
TEAM WINS (last 5 years)	16-19-16-12-16
RPI (last 5 years)	183-145-162-223-223
2000-01 FINISH	Lost in conference first round.

Montana State coach Mick Durham feels much more settled than he did a year ago. Last season at this time, Durham was dealing with the loss of starting point guard Jermaine Walton to academics, leaving the Bobcats without an experienced floor leader.

"We were starting with a freshman point guard and a junior college point guard," said Durham, himself a point guard in his playing days at MSU.

This year, **James Clark** (5.3 ppg, 2.8 apg), a 5-11 senior, and **Jason Erickson** (6.0 ppg, 2.5 apg), a 6-3 sophomore, have a year behind them, helping Durham relax a little bit.

"That right there helps my mindset, we're established at point," Durham said. "We have two point guards in the program now who have played a whole year in the Big Sky."

Not that the Bobcats suffered last year. They finished with a winning record, an 8-8 league mark and returned to the Big Sky's postseason tournament after a one-year absence.

"We lost a couple of games that could have made it a real good season," Durham said. "There were a couple of games that when you look back it was disappointing to lose. But for a year when we had one senior, we made some pretty good strides."

The Bobcats led the Big Sky and were fifth in the nation in three-point field-goal percentage (.415) and were 12th in the country in field-goal percentage (.486). And the Cats lost just one player—forward John Lazosky (13.5 ppg, 3.3 rpg)—from that team.

Clark and Erickson split time almost evenly at the point last year.

"That is still the quarterback, the coaching position on the floor," Durham said. "We run our program through our point guards."

Erickson is the better shooter of the two, hitting 43 percent of his shots to just 38 percent for Clark. Clark had more assists (86-79), but also more turnovers (57-44).

"I was really pleased with both of them in their first year," Durham said. "They had some very good moments, but in their second year I would expect they'll be much more consistent.

"Erickson is taller and probably a little more steady. Clark gives us a burst of speed; he has more energy. I like the contrast between them. They're both capable of hitting the outside jumper, so you have to guard them."

And that goes double for shooting guard **Justin Brown** (11.8 ppg. 2.6 rpg), a 6-4 senior. Brown was fourth in the league in three-point field goal accuracy at 46 percent. But Brown is still recovering from off-season ankle surgery.

"He's having a tough time with his ankle," Durham said. "He may not be ready to go at the start. He's not back playing yet and may be slowed early on."

That could mean an increased role for **Pete Conway** (7.1 ppg, 1.4 rpg), a 6-5 junior. Conway shot 40 percent from three-point range last season.

"Off-guard is our most experienced position," Durham said. "Pete's close to breaking loose. He can be very explosive offensively and he made strides on defense. He can score in a variety of ways."

Luke Anderson (22.0 ppg, 5.0 rpg), a 6-6 freshman from Eagan, Minn., will back up Brown and Conway. Anderson had committed to Minnesota, but decided against walking on for the Gophers and came to Bozeman instead.

"He's kind of a long kid who can shoot it," Durham said. "In time he'll be an excellent Big Sky player."

Durham has a couple of experienced players at small forward in returning starter **Aaron Rich** (9.7 ppg, 4.9 rpg), a 6-6 senior, and **Danny Faaborg** (3.4 ppg, 1.7 rpg), a 6-5 sophomore.

"We really expect Aaron to have a solid senior year," Durham said. "He does a lot of things for us offensively and defensively. He's our best offensive rebounder.

"Danny played 10 to 12 minutes a game and I was really pleased with those minutes. I'm curious to see his

development."

Kenny Plummer (6.2 ppg, 4.1 rpg), a 6-5 senior, will inherit Lazosky's job at power forward.

"He's our most athletic player," Durham said. "He brings a bunch of energy."

Three newcomers will provide depth at power forward. **Damir Latovic** (11.0 ppg, 6.5 rpg), a 6-8 junior transfer from Pensacola (Fla.) Junior College; **Casey Reynolds** (18.5 ppg, 11.7 rpg), a 6-6 junior transfer from Olympic (Wash.) Junior College; and **Jeff Williams** (17.0 ppg, 11.0 rpg), a 6-8 freshman from Salem, Ore., have joined the Cats this year.

"Damir has three-point range," Durham said. "He played center as a freshman and power forward as a sophomore. He could be versatile.

"I'm curious to see what Casey can bring. He's a player that plays pretty well facing the basket. That's pretty much what he'll do for us. Jeff Williams is an athletic young prospect."

Returning at center is **Tom Duffy** (6.6 ppg, 3.6 rpg), a 6-11 junior.

"He's made some great strides," Durham said. "He led the league in blocked shots and gives us an inside presence."

Duffy, however, won't play on Friday nights for religious reasons. He'll miss five league games because of that.

"The players have to understand Tom's situation and I thought they did a great job of that," Durham said.

Filling in for Duffy will be **Bo Segeberg** (15.6 ppg, 7.3 rpg), a 6-9 junior transfer from Antelope Valley Community College. Segeberg is no stranger to the Big Sky, having played at Sacramento State as a freshman.

"Last year he got his confidence back," Durham said of Segeberg's year in junior college. "We're excited about what he can bring."

Durham's teams are nearly always explosive on the offensive end. The key this season, he says, will be at the other end of the floor.

"The years we've been successful have been the years we score points, yet play good defense and rebound the ball," Durham said. "We don't want to hang our hats on one or the other. This team is capable of doing that. If we're up there in scoring and somewhere near the top in defense, we have a shot at the title."

2001-2002 SCHEDULE

Nov.	13	#@Fresno State
	17	Utah State
	26	Jamestown
	30	##Fresno State Invitational
Dec.	1	##Fresno State Invitational
	4	@Utah State
	8	Montana State-Northern
	13	@Arizona State
	15	*Wyoming
	22	IUPU-Fort Wayne
	29-30	###Touch America Classic
Jan.	3	@Weber State
	5	@Portland
	11	@Portland State
	12	@Eastern Washington
	18	Idaho State
	25	@Sacramento State
	26	@Northern Arizona
	31	Montana
Feb.	8	Eastern Washington
	9	Portland State
	16	@Idaho State
	22	Northern Arizona
	23	Sacramento State
March	2	@Montana
	7-9	####Big Sky Tournament

@Road Games
*at Casper, WY
#Preseason NIT (If Montana State wins, it will play Wyoming or Southern Cal on Nov. 14 or 16; semifinals and final will be Nov. 21 and 23 at Madison Square Garden, NY)
##Fresno, CA (vs. UC Riverside first round; also Air Force, Fresno State)
###Bozeman, MT (vs. Troy State first round; also Hampton, San Diego)
####Home of regular-season champion

BLUE RIBBON ANALYSIS

BACKCOURT	B+

BENCH/DEPTH	B+
FRONTCOURT	B
INTANGIBLES	B

The Bobcats have a chance to have one of the best backcourts in the league, IF Brown is healthy. Brown is a team leader and is someone opponents have to keep track of at every moment. If his ankle doesn't come around, Pete Conway is a capable backup, but he's not the leader Brown is nor has he proven to be the consistent threat.

The tandem of Clark and Erickson at point guard should work well for the Bobcats. They bring different styles to the floor and have the ability to keep opponents on their heels.

If there's a question for the Bobcats, it's probably up front. Aaron Rich is the leading returning rebounder, but he does it from his small-forward position. Plummer and Duffy are going to need to step up their rebounding and play good defense to take the Cats to the next level.

Durham has a seasoned bunch. If everyone's healthy and the Cats get the right breaks, they could challenge for the league crown.

(R.M.)

Northern Arizona

LOCATION	Flagstaff, AZ
CONFERENCE	Big Sky
LAST SEASON	15-14 (.517)
CONFERENCE RECORD	8-8 (t-4th)
STARTERS LOST/RETURNING	2/3
NICKNAME	Lumberjacks
COLORS	Gold & Blue
HOMECOURT	Walkup Skydome (7,000)
COACH	Mike Adras (UC Santa Barbara '83)
RECORD AT SCHOOL	35-25 (2 years)
CAREER RECORD	35-25 (2 years)
ASSISTANTS	Eugene Casaus (Northern Arizona '94)
	Dennis Cutts (SUNY-Albany '90)
TEAM WINS (last 5 years)	21-21-20-15
RPI (last 5 years)	107-126-123-78-244
2000-01 FINISH	Lost in conference semifinal.

Northern Arizona plays at Pitt and in The Pit this season.

"And I hope that's not where our season stays—the pits," third-year coach Mike Adras said.

Fat chance.

The Lumberjacks have become one of the premier programs in the Big Sky Conference over the last five years. During that time the Jacks have won 98 games, 11 more than the next best team in the conference.

They've done it by shooting the lights out. NAU was 21st in the nation last season in three-pointers per game at 8.2 and sixth in three-point accuracy at .415. The Jacks made 20 treys in a game against Cal Poly, including 11 by sharpshooter Cory Schwab, who ranked fourth in the nation in three-pointers made. Schwab was one of the few known quantities Adras had returning last season.

"In a transition year, 15 wins is pretty good," Adras said. "It's not 20 wins like we've grown accustomed to. I'm hoping that guys who gained a lot of experience last year will improve and play better this year. We were going through a lot of growing pains."

Schwab's shooting carried the Jacks through some of those pains, but he's gone after a senior season in which he hit a league-record 105 three-pointers. For the first time in recent memory, the Jacks don't have an obvious heir apparent for their gun-slinger role.

"We're not sure who that's going to be," Adras said. "We're kind of hoping **Matt Gebhardt** will be the guy who plays that role."

Gebhardt (7.2 ppg, 3.5 rpg), a 6-4 senior, had just 22 three-pointers last season while shooting 33 percent from beyond the arc. Gebhardt had a knee scoped over the off-season and Adras isn't quite sure what to expect.

"We've got to wait and see," Adras said. "I'm really counting on him. He's got to be a leader and he's got to be able to knock down some big shots. It's different when you're the No. 2 option versus the No. 1 option. We're hoping he'll be the No. 1 option."

If it's not Gebhardt, then point guard **Adam Lopez** (11.0 ppg, 4.5 apg), a 6-0 senior, could step up. Lopez isn't listed as one of the Jacks' three returning starters, which is deceiving. Lopez started 19 games as a sophomore after transferring from Kansas State, but just seven games last season after Rod Hutchings returned to the team.

"Adam has been in the program for four years and has made a lot of big shots in his career," Adras said of Lopez, who was the team's third-leading three-point shooter last season with 43.

Lopez will be spelled by **Chris Ferguson** (14.2 ppg, 3.9 apg), a 6-2 junior transfer from Irvine Valley (Calif.) Community College who played one season at San Diego.

"Ferguson is a very bright young man," Adras said. "It will be interesting to see how well he adapts from junior college to Division I."

Ferguson could also play on the wing, Adras said, along with Gebhardt, **Kody Yazzie** (2.9 ppg, 1.6 rpg), a 6-3 sophomore, and **Joel Rieck** (3.4 ppg, 3.0 rpg), a 6-6 senior.

"Rieck can knock down threes and grab boards for us," Adras said. "I hope we'll see some improved numbers out of him. Yazzie understands how we play very well."

The Jacks also recruited another wing in 6-6 freshman **Eric Patrick** (25.2 ppg).

The strength of this year's NAU team might very well be inside, where a trio of seasoned vets returns. Power forward **Ryan McDade** (10.6 ppg, 8.3 rpg), a 6-7 junior, ranked second in the league in rebounding last season behind only league MVP Brian Heinle of Cal State Northridge. McDade played the last 12 games of last season on a broken ankle that required off-season surgery.

"He's got to be one of the best rebounders in the country for his size," Adras said. "It's a tremendous gift that he has."

McDade, however, has had trouble at the free-throw line, where he made just 38 percent as a freshman and 45 percent last season while taking more attempts than anyone on the team.

"We need him to make a few more," Adras said. "At practice, he gets himself into a nice rhythm and feels good going into the next game. Then in the game he starts talking to himself."

Casey Grundman (11.3 ppg, 5.5 rpg), a 6-9 senior, returns as the starting center. Grundman shot 53 percent from the field last season, eighth best in the league.

"He has the ability to score inside and out," Adras said. "He didn't show great outside touch last year but he has the ability for putting the ball in the basket."

Grundman fouled out of seven games last season.

"We're hoping his understanding of the game will be better than it was last year," Adras said. "He got silly fouls called on him. If he can learn not to do that and play more minutes, I think his numbers can be pretty good."

Brian McHugh (4.3 ppg, 2.8 rpg), a 6-8 senior, is the third returning inside presence for the Jacks. McHugh will play behind McDade, but can also spell Grundman.

"He has nice touch from 15 feet in," Adras said.

Waiting in the wings behind Grundman are **Chris Bennett** (0.9 ppg, 1.2 rpg), a 6-9 sophomore, and **Justin Garcia**, a 7-1 red-shirt freshman.

"Chris seemed to struggle most of last season, but he's very athletic and has great balance in his game," Adras said. "Justin Garcia has improved dramatically, but didn't get a lot of reps in practice last season. But like they say, you can't teach height."

Adras is a little concerned about the non-conference schedule that includes the previously mentioned games at Pitt and New Mexico, as well as road games at Oregon and Boise State. The game at Pitt will match the Jacks against their former coach Ben Howland.

"I'm not excited about playing my former boss," Adras said. "My philosophy is to play as tough a preseason schedule as I can. If we survive that non-conference season, what are we going to see in league that could be much tougher? A lot of my coaching fraternity brothers would think I'm crazy, but the guys look forward to it."

Don't expect the Jacks to get away from doing what they do best, which is shoot the three-pointer.

"We have to replace our leading scorer," Adras said of Schwab. "The way I look at it, that should happen every year. That's what we've done and that's what we'll continue to do—hit the three."

2001-2002 SCHEDULE

Nov.	16	Cal Poly
	18	@Pittsburgh
	20	@Colgate
	24	@Northeastern
	30	New Mexico Highlands
Dec.	6	@Lipscomb
	8	@Tennessee-Martin
	16	@Oregon
	18	@Boise State
	21	Montana Tech
	29	Cal-State Fullerton
Jan.	2	Air Force
	5	@New Mexico
	11	@Weber State
	12	@Idaho State
	19	@Sacramento State
	25	Montana
	26	Montana State
Feb.	1	@Eastern Washington
	2	@Portland State
	8	Idaho State
	9	Weber State
	16	Sacramento State
	22	@Montana State
	23	@Montana
March	1	Portland State
	2	Eastern Washington
	7-9	#Big Sky Tournament

@Road Games
#Home of regular-season champion

BLUE RIBBON ANALYSIS

BACKCOURT	B
BENCH/DEPTH	C
FRONTCOURT	B
INTANGIBLES	B

Including Lopez, the Jacks essentially return four starters, which should be good enough to make them a team to reckon with. If Gebhardt or Rieck can step up and give NAU the outside presence it's had the last five years, the Jacks could be more than that.

McDade is a load around the basket, but he's going to have to improve his free-throw shooting in order for Adras to be able leave him on the floor late in a tight game.

Grundman is capable, although he must play smarter to stay out of foul trouble.

Much beyond the starting five, the Jacks are untested.

Northern Arizona is always tough at home and that will be amplified this season when the league goes to a Friday-Saturday schedule for conference games. Besides dealing with the 7,000-foot elevation at Flagstaff, the Jacks' Saturday opponents will be arriving after playing at Sacramento the previous night.

If the Jacks can improve on their 2-6 league road mark of last year, they should easily be in the top half of the league.

(R.M.)

Portland State

LOCATION	Portland, OR
CONFERENCE	Big Sky
LAST SEASON	9-18 (.333)
CONFERENCE RECORD	6-10 (t-7th)
STARTERS LOST/RETURNING	2/3
NICKNAME	Vikings
COLORS	Green & White
HOMECOURT	The Rose Garden (19,980)
	and Memorial Coliseum (12,000)
COACH	Joel Sabotka (Arizona State '93)
RECORD AT SCHOOL	41-43 (3 years)
CAREER RECORD	41-43 (3 years)
ASSISTANTS	Lorenzo Hall (Cal State Hayward '93)
	Zac Claus (Eastern Washington '98)
TEAM WINS (last 5 years)	9-15-17-15-9
RPI (last 5 years)	NA-NA-NA-192-281
2000-01 FINISH	Lost regular-season finale.

By the time the Portland State Vikings got their bags unpacked last year, they had dug themselves a deep hole. The Vikings played 13 of their first 17 games on the road. They won all four of those home games, but lost all 13 on the road. The murderous schedule also left them 1-5 to start the Big Sky league schedule.

"It was a tough start," fourth-year coach Joel Sobotka said. "We might have lost some confidence early on with a number of those losses."

The Vikings went 5-5 in league from that point on, but failed to qualify for the league postseason tournament for the first time since becoming eligible for the event.

"I would call it a frustrating season," Sobotka said.

"By the end of conference season we were playing pretty well, but unfortunately it didn't kick in until the end."

The Vikings will start this season with another ambitious schedule that will take them on the road for eight of their first 11, including stops at Arizona State, Gonzaga and Stanford's tournament. Portland State, which averages just 790 fans per home game, must schedule guarantee games to generate revenue.

"It's always going to be tough from the standpoint of being competitive," Sobotka said. "Being a mid-major program, there are not a lot of schools below you to schedule.

"We look forward to a competitive non-conference schedule. It prepares you for conference and I tell the guys that if we go to the NCAAs, that's the type of team you're going to be playing. You're going to have more road games than home games against high majors at our level. That's just a fact of life."

Sobotka will have league player-of-the-year candidate **Anthony Lackey** (14.5 ppg, 5.9 rpg), a senior, to help get the Vikings through the tough early-season schedule. At 6-5, 220 pounds, Lackey has the size to post up but also has the range to shoot the three.

"If we have the year we're capable of, Anthony will be a player-of-the-year candidate," Sobotka said.

Lackey shot 41 percent (52-of-128) from three-point range last season, while leading the team in scoring and rebounding. And he did that despite starting the year with a sore knee, which he had scoped last spring.

"He looks great," Sobotka said. "He's able to do things now I haven't seen him do in a while. He understands this is his year to shine. Not only that, he knows it's his last year to go to the NCAA Tournament. He's real excited and this year he has some people around him."

Sobotka would like to play Lackey at the small forward position.

"He can get some mismatches there," Sobotka said. "And he's very unselfish."

Sobotka is also excited about last season's league co-freshman-of-the-year **Seamus Boxley** (7.4 ppg, 4.3 rpg), a 6-7 sophomore who started 16 games at power forward. Boxley led the Vikings in rebounding in four of their final six games and had a career-high 19 points against Sacramento State during that same stretch.

"He surpassed a lot of people's expectations, but not mine," Sobotka said. "He has an incredible work ethic. I knew he was going to help us."

The Vikings lack a true center, so Boxley will have to pull his weight down low.

"He's a presence for us inside," Sobotka said. "It's tougher at our level to get 6-9, 6-10 kids. Seamus is a kid who plays bigger and will outplay most people."

Billy Feeney (15.1 ppg, 7.9 rpg), a 6-9 freshman from Monarch High School in Louisville, Colo., could see time right away behind Boxley.

"He's extremely skilled," Sobotka said. "He was 5-11 as a freshman in high school and played point guard. He needs to put a little weight on. In a year or two, he's going to be fun to watch."

The Vikings are pretty well set at shooting guard with returning starter **Kevin Briggs** (5.4 ppg, 3.0 rpg), a 6-2 junior, and **Charles Madison** (9.6 ppg, 1.6 apg), a 6-1 senior who started 16 games last season while seeing a lot of time at the point.

Madison was the team's leading deep threat, making 58 three-point shots while shooting 36 percent from beyond the arc.

"He's one of the better shooters returning in the conference," Sobotka said of Madison. "It will help him with his focus knowing when he's just playing the two. He's definitely a guy that you have to know where he is."

Briggs, who began his career as a walk-on, could be the Vikings' stopper.

"He's one of the better defenders in the league," Sobotka said. "I'm counting on him to be the guy to match up with the best perimeter player we're facing."

Newcomers **Jeb Ivey** (18.0 ppg, 5.0 rpg), a 6-2 junior transfer from West Valley (Calif.) Junior College, and **Troy DeVries** (15.0 ppg, 5.0 rpg), a 6-3 freshman from Mount Vernon, Wash., will add depth at the wing.

"Ivey is a kid who will help us right away," Sobotka said. "He really shoots the ball well and is a very tough kid who will come in and be an immediate leader.

"DeVries shoots it extremely well and has a great feel for the game. In a pinch, he could probably be a point guard."

Portland State will be relatively untested at both the point and in the middle.

Aaron Fitzgerald (26.7 ppg, 5.0 rpg), a 6-2 freshman from Seattle's Kennedy High School, and **John Glaser** (4.7 ppg, 7.5 apg), a 5-11 sophomore transfer from Cochise (Ariz.) Community College, will battle for the starting job at the point. Glaser helped Cochise reach the junior college national tournament last season.

"Fitzgerald's a tremendous, tremendous competitor," Sobotka said. "I'm expecting him to step in and play right away and contribute.

"Glaser is a true point guard in every sense of the word. He's a guy who delivers the mail, he knows where people are."

Walk-on **John Olinger**, a 6-1 freshman from Salem, Ore., will also get a look at the point.

Another Viking to come on strong down the stretch last season was **Jerrohn Jordan** (1.7 ppg, 1.2 rpg), a 6-8 senior who looks like the favorite to start at center.

"He's really got to provide us with another presence inside," Sobotka said. "He didn't come in last year in great shape, but he committed himself this summer. The light went on about halfway through last season.

"You know what Lackey's going to give you night in and night out. What Jerrohn gives us is a huge key for the season."

Steven Hamilton (0.5 ppg, 0.3 rpg), a 6-11 sophomore, and **Jeff Eischen**, a 6-8 freshman from Hillsboro, Ore., will back up Jordan.

The Vikings had a number of underclasmen leave after last season. Jamaal Thomas (3.3 ppg, 2.2 apg), Felix Lang (1.8 ppg), Heath Bailey (0.9 ppg, 0.8 rpg) and Jelani Williams (0.7 rpg) all left before completing their eligibility.

"Thomas and Lang went down a level," Sobotka said. "Bailey was looking for a better situation. That happened pretty late in the spring. He was a guy I was counting on for quality minutes. But I've always contended that I want people who want to be at Portland State."

Once again, Sobotka will be faced with the challenge of blending a lot of new faces in with his returning players.

"I like the group we have coming back, it's a close-knit group," Sobotka said. "We have some senior leadership and I like the group we have coming in. From a toughness standpoint, we're way ahead of where we were last year."

One positive note the Vikings will carry over from last year is their continuing strong play at home, particularly their on-campus arena, the Stott Center. Over the last five years the Vikings are 24-3 on campus, but just 15-8 at the Rose Garden, home of the Portland Trail Blazers.

"It's a place that you work at all year and in the off-season," Sobotka said of Stott, which is scheduled for some improvements next summer. "That's your home and you have a lot of pride in that. Last year we started to establish a tradition with the students. We're going to continue to develop that college basketball atmosphere."

2001-2002 SCHEDULE

Nov.	17	@Boise State
	20	@Arizona State
	24	San Diego
	27	@Cal Poly
Dec.	1	@Gonzaga
	8	Portland
	12	Oregon State
	15	@Nevada
	18	@Santa Clara
	29	@Wyoming
Jan.	2	Concordia
	5	Loyola Marymount
	11	Montana State
	12	Montana
	19	@Eastern Washington
	25	@Idaho State
	26	@Weber State
Feb.	1	Sacramento State
	2	Northern Arizona
	8	@Montana
	9	@Montana State
	16	Eastern Washington
	22	Weber State
	23	Idaho State
March	1	@Northern Arizona
	2	@Sacramento State
7-9		#Big Sky Tournament

@Road Games
#At home of regular-season champion

BLUE RIBBON ANALYSIS

BACKCOURT	C
BENCH/DEPTH	C
FRONTCOURT	B
INTANGIBLES	B

How far can Lackey take the Vikings? He and Weber State's Jermaine Boyette are probably the two players in the league most capable of dominating a game. But unless players like Boxley, Madison and Jordan can carry their weight, Lackey will be hounded by the opposition. So the better question might be, how much help will Lackey get?

Another question mark for the Vikings is at the point. Glaser has stellar credentials and Fitzgerald gets nothing but praise from Sobotka. But so did Dony Wilcher last year and still the Vikings finished next to last in the league in assist-to-turnover ratio.

On the plus side, the Vikings will play all their Big Sky home games in Stott Center. With the Big Sky switching to a Friday-Saturday schedule for all league games, the Vikings will be tough to beat on their home court. What they get done away from home will determine how high they finish.

(R.M.)

Sacramento

LOCATION	Sacramento, CA
CONFERENCE	Big Sky
LAST SEASON	5-22 (.185)
CONFERENCE RECORD	2-14 (9th)
STARTERS LOST/RETURNING	5/0
NICKNAME	Hornets
COLORS	Green & Gold
HOMECOURT	Memorial Auditorium (2,603)
COACH	Jerome Jenkins (Regis '90)
RECORD AT SCHOOL	5-22 (1 year)
CAREER RECORD	5-22 (1 year)
ASSISTANTS	Bob Canty (Chapan '97)
	John Dahlager (San Francisco State '95)
	Greg Lockridge (Brandon '99)
TEAM WINS (last 5 years)	3-1-3-9-5
RPI (last 5 years)	283-305-297-263-318
2000-01 FINISH	Lost regular-season finale.

At any school other than Cal State Sacramento, this would be called a rebuilding year. At Sacramento, it's simply a building year.

Since joining the Big Sky Conference for the 1996-97 season, the Hornets are 21-111 overall and 10-70 in league games, including an 0-40 mark on the road.

Add to those woeful numbers this fact: The Hornets lost all five of their starters from a year ago.

"I think last season was a season of ups and downs," second-year coach Jerome Jenkins said. "We lost three or four games at the buzzer and we lost quite a few games [three] less than 10 points. We just couldn't get over the hump. I thought we were better than five wins."

Jenkins, an assistant before taking over for Tom Abatemarco last season, said he learned a few things in his first trip around the league as head coach.

"I did a lot of studying of film in the off-season to see where as a young head coach I could've helped the team more," Jenkins said. "My staff and I discussed a lot of basketball over the summer. I think we're on the right track."

Specifically, where the Hornets are at their best is on the defensive end. Sacramento led the league in steals (9.96) and turnover margin (+2.22). But the Hornets ranked last in scoring (70.6), points allowed (78.1), free-throw shooting (.641) and field-goal percentage (.426).

As Jenkins begins to put his stamp on the program, look for more tough defense.

"With the type of guys we've got coming in, you will see the style of play change," Jenkins said. "With my type of guys playing, we want to be up-tempo and pressure you all over the floor. We're improving that way with the athletes we're bringing in.

"Defensively, we want to be able to get after you and

force our opponents to make plays. We were the best defensive team in the league last year ... and forced the most turnovers. We just couldn't score."

The five departed seniors accounted for 52.7 of Sac State's 70.6 points a game last season and 30.3 of the Hornets' 32.3 rebounds.

"I'm very happy with the guys we've got coming back," Jenkins said. "It will take us a while in the preseason, but we will be ready to go."

A pair of players who have never taken a shot for the Hornets will vie for the starting point-guard position. **Ronnie Walton**, a well-traveled 6-3 senior with previous stops at Oregon State and Detroit Mercy, and **Rashaad Hooks** (12.0 ppg, 8.0 apg), a 6-3 junior transfer from West Valley (Calif.) Junior College, will take the Hornets' reins.

"Ronnie gives us leadership and stability on the basketball floor," Jenkins said. "He will be the leader. Rashaad, at one time, was rated as one of the top point guards in junior college. He's very hard-nosed and active defensively."

Rene Jacques (7.2 ppg, 1.2 rpg), a 6-1 senior, is the Hornets' leading returning scorer. He tied for second on the team with 32 three pointers last season and will be the Hornets' chief deep threat this season from his shooting-guard position.

"He's a senior and I expect him to make shots," Jenkins said. "He did a decent job last year, but I think with better point guards he'll get better looks at the basket."

Derek Lambeth (2.7 ppg, 1.6 rpg), a 6-5 junior, and **David Joiner** (2.6 ppg, 1.8 rpg), a 6-6 sophomore, return on the wing.

"We like to post Lambeth up," Jenkins said. "But he can also shoot the open three-pointer. Joiner has very long arms and can put it on the floor and attack the basket."

Jenkins has a pair of new players to choose from at the wing in **Joel Jones** (15.6 ppg, 7.2 rpg), a 6-5 junior transfer from Grossmont (Calif.) Junior College, and **Leo Cravey**, a 6-7 junior transfer from Sierra (Calif.) Junior College.

"Joel could create some problems in the Big Sky," Jenkins said. "He is big for a two-guard in this league and he can dribble, pass, shoot and create his own shot.

"Cravey is a scorer from everywhere on the floor. He can shoot the three and get to the basket."

Jenkins has six big bodies to choose from for his two inside positions. **Cedric Thompkins** (4.1 ppg, 2.8 rpg), a 6-7 sophomore, started five games for the Hornets last season.

"I'm expecting big things out of Cedric for the next three years," Jenkins said. "Rebound, rebound, rebound is what he does. He's very good around the basket."

Tony Champion (1.4 ppg, 1.2 rpg), a 6-9, 290-pound sophomore, is a wild card for the Hornets. With his size, he could give people fits.

"He stayed here all summer long and played in the college league here," Jenkins said. "He lost a little weight. He's starting to turn the corner, starting to dedicate himself to the game. He has great hands and can finish around the basket. When he turns the corner, he'll be a force to reckon with in the Big Sky."

Jay Richardson (2.1 ppg, 1.7 rpg), a 6-8 senior, and **Troy Selvey** (0.5 ppg, 1.0 rpg), a 6-8 senior, are the other returning big men.

"All Richardson wants to do is shoot, so I let him do that," Jenkins said. "Selvey is just a good role player for us. He will rebound very well."

The newcomers down low are **Jimmy White** (21.8 ppg, 7.8 rpg), a 6-6, 235-pound junior transfer from Antelope Valley (Calif.) Junior College, and **Chris Lange**, a 6-8 freshman from Albuquerque, N.M. Jenkins said White was headed to Rutgers until a change in the coaching staff there.

"He's very good around the basket," Jenkins said. "We're hoping he can come to the Big Sky and have a big impact."

Jenkins said White reminds him of former Cal State Northridge power forward Jeff Parris.

"And nobody wanted to play against Parris," he said.

Lange should get plenty of opportunities to play this year.

"No question," Jenkins said. "He's very skilled."

If nothing else, Jenkins wants to have a team that no one in the Big Sky will enjoy facing.

"We want to dictate the game to our style of play," Jenkins said. "Limit teams to one shot. Offensively, we want to be able to out run other teams."

Do the Hornets have the horses to pull it off?

"If we don't quite have them, we're on our way," Jenkins said. "You're starting to see a different kind of athlete at Sacramento State."

2001-2002 SCHEDULE

Nov.	17	Menlo
	21	@San Jose State
	27	@Saint Mary's
Dec.	3	Southern Utah
	6	Cal State Fullerton
	8	@Loyola Marymount
	13	#Old Dominion
	15	@Cal State Fullerton
	17	Lipscomb
	27	@UC Riverside
	30	Idaho
Jan.	3	Texas A&M-Corpus Christi
	7	Dominican
	11	@Idaho State
	12	@Weber State
	16	@Cal Poly
	19	Northern Arizona
	25	Montana State
	26	Montana
Feb.	1	@Portland State
	2	@Eastern Washington
	8	Weber State
	9	Idaho State
	16	@Northern Arizona
	22	@Montana
	23	@Montana State
March	1	Eastern Washington
	2	Portland State
	7-9	#Big Sky Tournament

@Road Games
#Guardians Classic at Memphis (if Sacramento State wins, it will play either Memphis or Wofford on Nov. 14; Semifinals and final are Nov. 20-21 at Kemper Arena, Kansas City, MO)
##At home of regular-season champion

BLUE RIBBON ANALYSIS

BACKCOURT	D
BENCH/DEPTH	D
FRONTCOURT	C
INTANGIBLES	D

The fact that Sacramento State lost five starters is not the big blow it would be to many schools. We're talking about five starters from a team that won just five games.

But the Hornets have as many newcomers (seven) as they do returnees. That's just too much turnover to expect the team to come together anytime soon.

Jenkins is on the right track with the aggressive brand of defensive basketball he teaches. He has to preach defense to keep his team in games without a proven scoring threat.

Jacques is the team's leading returning scorer at 7.2 points per game. He shot just 34 percent from the field last season. And he's the only proven commodity the Hornets have on the offensive side.

The new players Jenkins has brought in—five from the junior-college ranks—could turn out to be good players. Even so, it's too soon to expect the Hornets to get it turned around this season.

(R.M.)

Weber State

LOCATION	Ogden, UT
CONFERENCE	Big Sky
LAST SEASON	15-14 (.517)
CONFERENCE RECORD	8-8 (5th)
STARTERS LOST/RETURNING	3/2
NICKNAME	Wildcats
COLORS	Purple & White
HOMECOURT	Dee Events Center (12,000)
COACH	Joe Cravens (Texas-Arlington '77)
RECORD AT SCHOOL	33-24 (2 years)
CAREER RECORD	88-76 (6 years)
ASSISTANTS	Kirk Earlywine (Campbell '87)
	John Stroia (Wisconsin-Whitewater '81)
TEAM WINS (last 5 years)	14-14-25-18-15

RPI (last 5 years)	149-152-52-104-179
2000-01 FINISH	Lost in conference semifinal.

Weber State Coach Joe Cravens suffers from Februphobia, the fear of February. It's hard to blame him.

The Wildcats cruised into last February with a 6-2 mark in Big Sky Conference play, apparently ready to battle Cal State Northridge for the league title. Five losses in the month of February relegated the Wildcats to also-rans.

"In the month of February we had a little bit of sickness and some injuries, but more than anything our youth showed," said Cravens, entering his third year as head coach of the Wildcats. "We weren't seasoned enough to know how tough the month of February is in college basketball. One of my players came to me last February and said, 'I'm not having much fun.'

"I asked him, 'What did you think we'd be doing, going to Disneyland?' "

The Wildcats won't be any Mickey Mouse team this season; most coaches agree they're the league favorites. But to earn their 16th Big Sky regular-season title, the Wildcats will have to overcome a grueling February schedule.

Because Weber's home arena, the Dee Events Center, will be one of the 2002 Olympic Games media venues, the Wildcats won't play a home game in February, facing five straight opponents on the road. Weber will go from Jan. 26 to March 2 without a home game.

"We'll be the only team in the nation that won't have a home game in February," Cravens said. "I don't know what effect that will have. You combine that with the genius move of playing our conference games on back-to-back nights—I don't see how any college president in his right mind could be in favor of that—and I don't know if we can overcome that tough schedule.

"I don't know if I've ever seen a league with as uneven a playing field. We'll pick you to win the league, but let's see you win it with this schedule. You kind of want a level playing field. To continually have to overcome scheduling hurdles is challenging, to say the least."

Cravens won't get a lot of sympathy from the rest of the league's coaches, not with the talent the Wildcats have returning. Standing at the head of the class is point guard **Jermaine Boyette** (19.1 ppg, 4.2 apg, 3.4 rpg), a 6-2 junior who was second in the league in scoring last season.

"Things will get a little tougher for him as he gains a reputation and has a target on his chest," Cravens said. "He's at his best in the open court, in fast-break situations. To get him the ball, we have to rebound so he can create his own offense. We run very few set plays for him. What he gets, he gets on his own."

Although Boyette led the league in steals at 2.1 a game, Cravens wants his floor general to improve on the defensive end.

"The improvement we need to make on the defensive end begins and ends with him," Cravens said. "His effort and consistency on that end mirrors our team. I'm really counting on him."

Stevie Morrison (8.4 ppg, 1.5 rpg), a 6-0 junior, started alongside Boyette in the backcourt for much of last season, but suffered a serious groin injury in the off-season that might require surgery.

The Wildcats signed **Jamaal Jenkins**, a 6-3 freshman out of Arlington, Texas, and **Marlon Carter**, a 6-6 junior transfer from Southern Mississippi, to add depth in the backcourt.

"Jenkins ha a chance to help us, but he's a freshman," Cravens said. "Carter can play the one, two or three."

Returning at shooting guard is **John Hamilton** (5.7 ppg, 1.9 rpg), a 6-4 sophomore who averaged 15.1 minutes as a freshman. Hamilton's 31 three-pointers were second on the team only to Morrison's 41.

"He has a chance to really take off this year," Cravens said. "He was a pretty big get for us out of Indiana. He's a shooter and a scorer."

Chris Woods (7.5 ppg, 4.5 rpg), a 6-4 senior, will likely be the starter at small forward.

"He's kind of the ultimate role player—he's tough, he rebounds and he plays defense," Cravens said of Woods, one of just two seniors on the roster. "He is THE leader of the team. He's worked as hard as any kid I've been around since last year."

Behind Woods will be **Brad Barton**, a 6-3 junior transfer from BYU-Hawaii, and **Nic Sparrow**, a 6-4 sophomore who returns to the lineup after a two-year

LDS church mission and a red-shirt season.

"At times, he's the best shooter on the team," Cravens said of Sparrow. "He may be a little inconsistent in that it's been three years without playing in front of a crowd. Barton is probably the strongest kid on the team and maybe the toughest."

The power forward and post positions are interchangeable in Cravens' system, and he has plenty of talent to work with. Heading the list inside is **Stephan Bachman** (10.3 ppg, 3.9 rpg), a 6-10 junior who was the league's top freshman two years ago.

"He's really improved defensively," Cravens said. "If nothing else, he was a pretty stable, consistent player. I'd like to think he can take the next step up in his scoring average. But he may just always be one of those 10- to 11-point a game guys, which isn't all that bad."

But Bachman is one of 63 foreign-born players nationwide whose eligibility is being questioned by the NCAA.

"It is absolutely ludicrous to say he was a pro," Cravens said. "If he was a pro then I was a Hollywood movie star. We have to gather the information and present it to the NCAA. They're going over it case by case."

Pat Danley (6.3 ppg, 5.1 rpg), a 6-8 sophomore, started three games last season, averaged 16.6 minutes and displayed plenty of raw talent.

"He had very impressive flashes," Cravens said. "He has the potential to be one of the top rebounders in the league. He and Hamilton have a chance to take a quantum leap."

Marc Thurig (0.9 ppg, 1.9 rpg), a 6-10 senior, should give Cravens valuable minutes off the bench.

"Like Chris Woods, he's the ultimate role player," Cravens said. "He plays hard, defends, rebounds and sets a great example."

Thurig and Woods, the only two seniors, will be co-captains.

"In my years as head coach, I'm as excited as I've ever been about my two seniors," Cravens said. "They're not stars, but they understand their roles and they're the hardest workers on the team."

Talmage Eyre, a 6-9 junior transfer from Salt Lake Community College, will help fill the void left by Jake Shoff (7.4 ppg, 6.0 rpg), who transferred to BYU.

"He's more athletic than Jake," Cravens said. "He can really run, defend and rebound."

The Wildcats were second in the league in scoring (77.8 ppg) and second in rebounding margin (+4.5), but ranked seventh in points allowed (76.7 ppg).

"We weren't always pretty on offense last year, but we were always able to score," Cravens said. "We have to improve defensively. Even during the course of a game, we would hold an opponent to 33 percent in the first half and they'd shoot 66 percent in the second half. That was experience, not being mentally tough enough. If we cut out one mistake per person, we go from middle of the road to leading the league."

Cravens is in the enviable position of having to sift through his talent to find his best five players.

"An old coach once told me that if you don't have a first team, you have two second teams," Cravens said. "We have a chance to be deep, but we have to identify our starting five, develop team chemistry and turn the corner defensively."

2001-2002 SCHEDULE

Nov.	16	@Illinois State
	19	Concordia
	23-25	#Big Island Invitational
	30	Western Montana
Dec.	5	@Brigham Young
	8	Utah State
	15	Utah
	18	Savannah State
	22	Southern Utah
	28	##Dr Pepper Classic
Jan.	3	Montana State
	5	Montana
	11	Northern Arizona
	12	Sacramento State
	18	@Montana
	19	@Montana State
	25	Eastern Washington
	26	Portland State
Feb.	2	@Idaho State
	8	@Sacramento State
	9	@Northern Arizona
	22	@Portland State
	23	@Eastern Washington

March	2	Idaho State
	7-9	###Big Sky Tournament

@Road Games
#Hilo, HI (vs. LSU first round; also Colorado State, Hawaii, Hawaii-Hilo, Mercer, South Carolina State, Wisconsin)
##Chattanooga, TN (vs. Sam Houston State first round; also Bradley, Chattanooga)
###Home of regular-season champion

BLUE RIBBON ANALYSIS

BACKCOURT	A
BENCH/DEPTH	B+
FRONTCOURT	B+
INTANGIBLES	B

If the Wildcats can turn the corner this season, watch out, because they have just two seniors on the roster and both of them are role players.

Boyette is the odds-on favorite to give the Wildcats their third league MVP award in the last four years. He's an explosive scorer who can find his way to the free-throw line if his shot is not falling. If Hamilton takes the step Cravens is looking for, his three-point shooting ability will be the perfect complement to Boyette's penetration.

Danley and Woods give the Wildcats the strong presence inside to be a top rebounding team and Bachman provides polished skills from 12 feet in.

The only question will be how the Wildcats handle the adversity of the odd schedule. Even so, they're a lock to get to the league tournament—wherever it's played. With their talent, the Wildcats should be able to win on anyone's court.

(R.M.)

 Birmingham Southern

LOCATION	Birmingham, AL
CONFERENCE	Big South
LAST SEASON	17-9 (.654)
CONFERENCE RECORD	NA
STARTERS LOST/RETURNING	3/2
NICKNAME	Panthers
COLORS	Black, Gold & White
HOMECOURT	Bill Battle Coliseum (1,750)
COACH	Duane Reboul (New Orleans '72)
RECORD AT SCHOOL	315-71 (12 years)
CAREER RECORD	315-71 (12 years)
ASSISTANTS	Mitch Cole (Montana Sate '92)
	Scott Stapler (Auburn '96)
	Dexter Williams (Tuskeegee '91)
TEAM WINS (last 5 years)	28-28-25-26-17
RPI (last 5 years)	NA
2000-01 FINISH	Won regular-season finale.

This Division I thing certainly didn't seem so hard to the folks at Birmingham-Southern, the Big South Conference's latest addition. The Panthers rolled to a 17-9 record last year in their first season playing with the big boys.

That's the good news. The bad news is the schedule—which still doesn't include full membership in the Big South—is a lot more difficult this season and the Panthers lost their entire front line from last year. BSC will sorely miss Joe Ransom's 19 points and 7.4 rebounds per night, not to mention Adrian Pryor and his 10.2 points and Neal Broome's 13.9 points.

"There's no question, the whole key for us is how fast our unproven guys up front come along," said veteran coach Duane Reboul, who has never had a losing season at the school. "We've got a lot of options, but they're all unproven."

Reboul rests easier thinking about his veterans on the perimeter. Point guard **Rashard Willie** (9.5 ppg, 3.0 rpg, 4.8 apg) returns to run the show, and he'll again team up with surprising **T.R. Reed** (9.0 ppg, 3.6 rpg, 1.8 spg) in the backcourt. **Corey Watkins** (8.7 ppg, 4.0 rpg) is also back, and the senior trio will likely force Reboul to run a three-guard attack.

The 5-10 Willie was a key to BSC's success last year. Reboul often found he needed Willie to put the brakes on the Panthers' up-tempo game to better compete with more talented Division I teams. The Panthers scored a

BIG SOUTH

BLUE RIBBON FORECAST
1. Winthrop
2. Radford
3. UNC Asheville
4. Elon
5. Coastal Carolina
6. Liberty
7. Charleston Southern
8. High Point

ALL-CONFERENCE TEAM
G-Brendon Rowell, SR, Elon
G-Torrey Butler, SR, Coastal
C-Andrey Savtchenko, SR, Radford
F-Greg Lewis, SR, Winthrop
F-Marcus Stewart, SR, Winthrop

PLAYER OF THE YEAR
Andrey Savtchenko, SR, Radford

NEWCOMER OF THE YEAR
Travis Eisentrout, FR, Liberty

2001-2002 CONFERENCE TOURNAMENT
Feb. 28-March 1, Roanoke Civic Center, Roanoke, VA

2000-2001 POSTSEASON PARTICIPANTS
Postseason Record: 0-1 (.000)
NCAA Play-in
Winthrop

TOP BACKCOURTS
1. Radford
2. Winthrop
3. Elon

TOP FRONTCOURTS
1. Winthrop
2. Radford
3. Elon

INSIDE THE NUMBERS
2001-2002 RPI: 31st (of 31)
Conference RPI (last five years): 23-30-30-26-31

DID YOU KNOW?
Fifth-year Division I members Elon and High Point are finally eligible for the Big South Conference Tournament. … Former Division II powerhouse Birmingham-Southern will play a full conference schedule next year but won't be eligible for the conference tournament until 2005-06. … Rumors are circulating that Southern Conference member Virginia Military Institute is headed to the Big South next year, a move that would benefit basketball (especially Virginia rivals Liberty and Radford) as well as the conference's fledgling football programs. Basketball coaches have been told to schedule accordingly. … Winthrop senior center Eyo Effiong was chosen 2001-02 recipient of the Anson Mount Scholar/Athlete Award by Playboy magazine. … Coastal Carolina senior forward Torrey Butler was an honorable mention Associated Press All-American last season. … Radford and Winthrop continue to dominate BSC regular season play. The Highlanders and Eagles are both 32-6 over the last three years, but Winthrop is also 6-0 in the conference tournament under coach Gregg Marshall. … Winthrop became the first BSC team to win three consecutive conference crowns. Before Winthrop's streak, seven different teams represented the league in the NCAA Tournament in the years the Big South was eligible. … The Big South is 0-9 all-time in the NCAA Tournament and 1-1 all-time in NCAA Tournament play-in games. … The only collegiate basketball player to ever earn conference player-of-the-year honors four times was Coastal's Tony Dunkin (1989-93).

(M.B.)

20-point victory at Texas A&M early last year and also knocked off three-time Big South champ Winthrop. Willie proved masterful at the helm of the variable speed control and Reboul's only complaint is he wishes Willie would shoot the ball more.

"When the ball's in his hands, I don't worry," Reboul said. "I can look at other things going on out on the floor. I hardly watch him. He always seems to make the right decisions."

The 6-0 Reed was projected as a backup to Willie but has blossomed into a solid off-guard.

"He's physical and he became an anchor for us defensively," the coach said. "He just outplayed everyone and won a spot in the lineup. He's turned into a good three-point shooter, too."

In fact, all three senior guards can knock it down from behind the arc. Reed shot .429 percent (24-of-56) from long range. Willie shot 42 percent (47-of-112) and Watkins was even more accurate, hitting .467 (46-of-63).

The 6-3 Watkins gives Reboul great versatility. He played point guard as a sophomore, and he's working at small forward now. Watkins can play and guard all three perimeter positions and he's strong enough to hold his own when he gets forced inside.

Up front where the questions begin, the two most intriguing answers are a mouthful—6-11, 255-pound sophomore **Michael Bilostinnyi** (4.0 ppg, 2.0 rpg) and 6-11 red-shirt freshman **Shema Mbyirukira**.

Bilostinnyi played on a gimpy ankle last season that has Reboul lamenting the fact the coach didn't opt to red-shirt him. The Iceland native has since dropped about 20 pounds and looks more ready to contribute on the low block at center.

"He's coming along," Reboul said. "Michael is thick and strong and he's a natural low post."

Mbyirukira is taller than Bilostinnyi. He is now nearly

7-0, but he's also much thinner at 210 pounds and runs the floor more like a forward. BSC coaches love his work ethic and they think he's going to be a good one, though the question is whether that prediction comes true this year or in the future.

So enter 6-7 junior college transfer **Josiah James**, who has the size to play power forward and the athleticism to play small forward. James averaged 17 points and 10 rebounds at Bacone (Okla.) Community College last season.

Reboul has two returnees battling for time up front, too. **Matt Burke** (2.2 ppg, 1.6 rpg) appeared in 26 games last year as a red-shirt freshman. At 6-8, 235, he's a physical option at center and has a great understanding of the Panthers' schemes.

Senior forward **Michael Anspach** (4.2 ppg, 2.5 rpg), 6-7, will also figure into the mix. A committed student, Anspach nearly left the program this year to concentrate on academics but he'll return to lend depth at both forward spots with his shooting ability and defensive prowess.

Little-used 6-2 junior guard **Barry Moss** (1.3 ppg, 0.9 rpg) is the only other returnee, so there are opportunities for freshmen to work into playing time. In the backcourt, two international imports, **Jakob Sigurdarson** and **Andrius Monrtrimas** head the list.

Both 6-4, they each can play both guard positions. Sigurdarson, a member of the Swedish Senior National Team, averaged 19.2 points, 6.1 rebounds and 5.4 assists at Westminster High in Lakeland, Fla., displaying a versatile all-around game.

Monrtrimas, a member of the Under-18 Lithuanian National Team, averaged 20.8 points, 11.4 rebounds and 4.0 assists last season at Norfolk (Va.) Collegiate High School. He's an excellent passer and has great shooting range.

Michael Hubbard and **Jimmy Amerson** round out a deep recruiting class. The 6-5 Hubbard, out of Orlando's Lake Highland Prep, is another perimeter threat from the small forward spot. He may need time to develop, though.

The 6-4 Amerson, a local product from Birmingham's Minor High School, averaged 17 points and eight rebounds last season and could be the most athletic of the freshmen. He has a knack for coming up with rebounds and can play guard or forward.

Reboul is beginning to stockpile size. In late August, he announced that 6-10, 240-pound center Will Scherling will transfer to BSC from Lehigh. Scherling, a Highland Park, Texas native and prep standout at Marine Military Academy, will be eligible next season.

"Will's physical strength and size will be a great asset to our program," Reboul said. "He is a tremendous young man with great potential on and off the court."

Scherling averaged 1.7 points and 0.9 rebounds in just 15 games played as a freshman for the Mountain Hawks. He shot 56.3 percent from the field and blocked two shots.

2001-2002 SCHEDULE

Nov.	16	@Southeast Missouri State
	21	Jacksonville State
	24	Stetson
	27	@Winthrop
Dec.	1	@Butler
	4	@Florida State
	6	Texas College
	9	@Louisiana-Lafayette
	18	Elon
	20	University of the South
	28-29	#Utah State Classic
Jan.	2	Alabama State
	5	Liberty
	12	High Point
	16	Florida Atlantic
	19	@Coastal Carolina
	21	@Charleston Southern
	26	@Savannah State
	29	Charleston Southern
Feb.	2	@Elon
	4	@High Point
	7	Winthrop
	13	Coastal Carolina
	16	@East Carolina
	19	@Liberty
	23	Savannah State

@Road Games
#Logan, UT (vs. Idaho State first round; also Centenary, Utah State)

BLUE RIBBON ANALYSIS

BACKCOURT	B+
BENCH/DEPTH	C+
FRONTCOURT	D
INTANGIBLES	A

The Tougalous, Reinhardts, Berrys and Trevecca Nazarenes have been replaced on the schedule with more D-I opponents, including most of the Big South members. Birmingham-Southern won't play a full conference schedule until 2003, and won't be eligible for the league tournament until 2005-2006.

Last year, the Panthers beat the Big South's best, Winthrop, and they certainly would have been an upper echelon team in the league. They've got lots of holes up front this season but look for Reboul to figure it all out.

Reboul's teams took six straight trips to the NAIA national tournament before moving to the NCAA last year, and Reboul's squads actually went to the NAIA's Big Dance nine times in 11 years, winning the 1992 national championship.

Long story, short: this guy knows how to coach. He's got his veteran floor leader, Willie, back, along with two other senior guards and enough parts to make for some long nights for more-established Division I opponents.

Bill Battle Coliseum is getting a facelift and it's obvious this is a program that "gets it" in terms of the financial support necessary to compete at the Division I level.

While it may not live up to the College of Charleston blueprint it's following, Birmingham-Southern is worth keeping an eye on the next couple of seasons.

(M.A.)

Charleston Southern

LOCATION	Charleston, SC
CONFERENCE	Big South
LAST SEASON	10-19 (.345)
CONFERENCE RECORD	7-7 (t-4th)
STARTERS LOST/RETURNING	3/2
NICKNAME	Buccaneers
COLORS	Blue & Gold
HOMECOURT	CSU Fieldhouse (1,500)
COACH	Jim Platt (Concordia '73)
RECORD AT SCHOOL	10-19 (1 year)
CAREER RECORD	66-78 (5 years)
ASSISTANTS	Jermaine Scott (USC Aiken '96)
TEAM WINS (last 5 years)	17-5-12-8-10
RPI (last 5 years)	143-301-259-298-299
2000-01 FINISH	Lost in conference semifinal.

The Charleston Southern Buccaneers might as well wear orange construction zone jackets and hard hats this season. Second-year coach Jim Platt has certainly put up "Under Construction" signs all over this school's proud program.

Platt pretty much played the hand dealt him last year in coming over from the top assistant's job at Florida State. He had three key seniors lead the team to an amazing 7-7 mark in league play and then to the brink of a berth in the Big South championship game before the game Bucs were finally subdued by top-seeded Radford, 65-62.

In the process, his squad played as hard as anyone in the league and Platt proved expert at creating difficult match-ups with his undersized forwards and a diverse cast of unproven veterans and unknown newcomers.

But Platt, the 2000-01 Coach of the Year in the Big South, doesn't care to dwell on last year's surprising results.

"We're building this program in two stages right now," Platt said. "The first stage is the six juniors who I believe are going to give us a chance to be competitive and then we have this group of [four] young freshman who can grow and improve."

Ironically, those two distinct groupings leave out probably the team's best player, sophomore point guard **Ed O'Neil** (5.6 ppg, 2.6 rpg, 3.2 apg), who burst upon the scene last season to earn Big South All-Rookie honors.

O'Neil wrested the point-guard spot away from junior college transfer **Quinton Gilmore** (2.6 ppg, 1.5 rpg) last season and turned into one of the league's top defenders, registering two steals a game in conference contests. He created havoc on the other end with his fearless drives to the basket, a trademark of his upbringing in the tough New York high school game at Archbishop Molloy High.

"Ed is the kind of guy that can make us competitive in this league," Platt said. "He just loves the game and he knows how to play. He's got the potential to be a great leader for us."

The 6-0 O'Neil has continued to work on his perimeter shooting. He shot .319 (93-of-166) percent from the field last year overall, but his percentage was up to 36 percent in conference games.

Junior **James Segars** (7.2 ppg, 3.4 rpg) at the other guard slot is a player who may really benefit as O'Neil matures. Platt thinks the 6-3 Segars' skill level is catching up to his athleticism and Segars, a BSC All-Rookie selection two years ago, may blossom into a top-rate scorer in the league.

Last season, 6-3 **Gene Granger** (7.7 ppg, 2.0 rpg) worked into the mix as an often-deadly perimeter shooter and he's another important cog in that junior class. Unlike the other two returning backcourt starters, though, Granger is not adept at creating his own shot.

Gilmore provides depth at the point, and don't think Platt is down on the 5-11 senior guard. It's just O'Neil came on that strong and that fast last year.

"We've got a really good situation there," the coach said. "Two point guards like that give us a really solid backcourt."

Senior **Mirko Mandic** (1.5 ppg, 0.2 rpg) rounds out the guard returnees. Nagging injuries have taken a toll on the tough, 6-1 Yugoslavian, but he could work his way back into the rotation this year with his tough defense and ability to score from long distance.

Another intriguing possibility on the perimeter is 6-6 freshman **Trent Drafts** (16.0 ppg, 8.0 rpg) of Battle

Creek High School in Burton, S.C. Drafts has shot up quickly from 6-2, and it looks like he could grow to 6-8 while maintaining his skills as a guard. He will work at small forward to begin his career and Platt loves his savvy and versatility.

CSU has only two returning forwards, 6-6 junior **Charles White** (3.9 ppg, 2.0 rpg) and little-used 6-6 senior **Namiah Williams** (2.4 ppg, 1.8 rpg). White appeared in all 29 games last year and he's an explosive athlete with no position to call home. He's not really big enough to play power forward and he's not a natural small forward, either. Still, he should emerge as a key player this season.

Williams appeared in just nine games last year but did hit a 15-foot buzzer beater to best Anderson College, 90-88. He may not factor in much this season.

The opposite is true of 6-9 senior center **Nikola Pejovic** (4.1 ppg, 2.8 rpg). Pejovic played in every game last year as graduated senior Ivica Perica's sub, and he has the size and developing offensive skills to be a breakthrough player.

"He has a chance to be one of the better centers in the league," Platt said. "He just needs to sustain his effort better. I expect him to make a quantitative leap this season as a player."

The Bucs have some insurance behind him, too, with the addition of 6-9, 250-pound junior college transfer **Chris Warzynski** of Alpharetta, Ga. Warzynski averaged 12 points and nine rebounds last season at Coastal (Ga.) Community College. He will team with the 235-pound Pejovic in the pivot to battle against the likes of Radford's 7-0 Andrey Savtchenko, the Big South's top big man.

The CSU coaching staff liked Warzynski so much they also signed his "little" brother, 6-8, 225-pound **Kevin Warzynski** (18.8 ppg, 8.3 rpg) out of Chattahoochie High School in Alpharetta. Kevin is more of a forward, but he's still growing.

The 2001 recruiting class also yields two more freshmen: 6-8 **Nathan Ball** and 6-8 **Ferdinand Cain**. Ball averaged 12 points and eight rebounds at Page High School in Greensboro, N.C., and he's still growing, too. Cain averaged 11 points and 11 rebounds a game at Northwest Catholic High in Hartford, Conn.

"We really target guys that we feel are being under-recruited," Platt said. "There are guys out there that for whatever reason may not attract as much attention but have an excellent chance to keep developing and turn into solid college players. That's what we're after."

2001-2002 SCHEDULE

Nov.	16	College of Charleston
	19	Anderson College
	24	William & Mary
	27	@Georgia State
Dec.	1	@The Citadel
	12	@VMI
	15	North Greenville
	17	@Virginia
	19	@North Carolina State
	22	@Clemson
	28	@South Carolina
Jan.	2	@UNC Asheville
	5	@Elon
	7	@High Point
	12	Liberty
	14	Radford
	21	Birmingham Southern
	24	@Winthrop
	26	Coastal Carolina
	29	@Birmingham Southern
Feb.	2	@Liberty
	4	@Radford
	7	High Point
	9	Elon
	12	@Fairfield
	16	Winthrop
	21	UNC Asheville
	23	@Coastal Carolina
	27	#Big South Tournament
March	1-2	#Big South Tournament

@Road Games
#Roanoke Civic Center, Roanoke, VA

BLUE RIBBON ANALYSIS

BACKCOURT	B
BENCH/DEPTH	C

FRONTCOURT	C
INTANGIBLES	B

Platt took over late last season and slowly molded a disparate Buccaneer team into the kind of team no one wanted to play late in the year. All-Conference selection O.J. Linney and versatile scorer Nick Mitchell are gone off that dangerous team and it's hard to look at the 2001-02 roster and figure where all the points and rebounds and leadership are going to come from.

Start with O'Neil, who could be the best at his position in the Big South, before this season's over. If big center Pejovic gives CSU an inside presence and Seegars and Granger continue to improve, the Bucs could again throw a scare into the league's top teams.

Charleston Southern beat Winthrop last year and lost three games to Radford by a total of eight points. Platt will have to mix up a new formula this season, but if he gets his team to play as hard as it did night-in, night-out last season, the Bucs will again surprise folks around the league.

They still don't look like one of the conference's most talented teams and a non-league schedule that includes Virginia, Clemson, South Carolina and N.C. State will again ruin their record. That's life when you're a program under construction.

(M.A.)

Coastal Carolina

LOCATION	Conway, SC
CONFERENCE	Big South
LAST SEASON	8-20 (.286)
CONFERENCE RECORD	6-8 (t-4th)
STARTERS LOST/RETURNING	1/4
NICKNAME	Chanticleers
COLORS	Coastal Green, Bronze & Black
HOMECOURT	Kimbel Arena (1,037)
COACH	Pete Strickland (Pittsburgh '79)
RECORD AT SCHOOL	25-58 (3 years)
CAREER RECORD	25-58 (3 years)
ASSISTANTS	Enda Byrt (U. College of Cork '73)
	Don Burgess (Radford '94)
TEAM WINS (last 5 years)	11-8-7-10-8
RPI (last 5 years)	225-300-304-252-289
2000-01 FINISH	Lost in conference quarterfinal.

Coach Pete Strickland says he's "guardedly optimistic" about the 2001-02 season and that's probably good when you trot out a lineup with four starters 6-4 or shorter.

The Chanticleers—ahem—came up short a lot last year, posting an 8-20 mark, including dropping six of their last seven games. But that stretch was a microcosm for this team. Four of the losses were by three points or less and another setback was by six points.

Earlier in the season in more lopsided setbacks, the Chanticleers fought gamely until a lack of size and then a lack of depth because of persistent injuries took a toll against a grueling schedule that included Virginia, Georgia, Georgetown, Clemson and Missouri.

Coastal was often out-manned but rarely out-hustled. Now Strickland has his most experienced team ever, headlined by returning All-American Torrey Butler, an honorable mention selection last season by the Associated Press.

The 6-3 Butler averaged 19.4 points, 5.8 rebounds and shot .523 percent from the field in earning Big South Conference Player-of-the-Year honors. The senior small forward is simply too quick for big men to cover and too strong for guards to handle. Numbers-wise, that meant someone on the opposition had to match up with a guy who led the team in three-point shooting (.476 on 50-of-105) and was second in rebounding.

"It's so hard to get the attention to become an All-American at our level," Strickland said. "But Torrey just kept impressing people night after night. People couldn't help but notice what he was doing."

This Butler did it, all right. He had 28 points at Virginia, 29 in a win at American, 25 at Clemson, and then averaged 21.1 points per game against Big South opponents. He spent the off-season working against the double-teams he's sure to see this season. Butler is becoming a better passer and he is learning to hold his dribble so he can beat the second defender to make his move to the basket.

Book-end Derrick Robinson (11.1 ppg, 4.8 rpg) returns as the power forward. The 6-4 junior enjoyed his finest season despite often filling in at center. The coaching staff hopes those days are over with the return of two foreign centers who have been as hard on team physicians as they have on public address announcers.

Anthony Susnjara (3.3 ppg, 1.6 rpg in 1999-00) missed all of last season after injuring his knee on the first day of practice. A 6-8 sophomore banger, he's got a smooth post-up game that could take some of the heat off the perimeter players.

Junior Mihai Raducanu (5.4 ppg, 2.2 rpg) is the tallest player on the team at 6-9, but he's more of a European-style wing player with a soft touch from the outside, though he's rarely played enough to show what he can do. The big junior was literally snake-bit during preseason his freshman year and also missed time after hitting his head on a Coke machine while diving for a loose ball.

Last year, his injuries continued head to toe as he had ankle, groin and back problems to go with a root canal. Raducanu still managed to average 13.4 minutes per night in 23 games.

If Coastal is to improve this season, one of the centers must step forward to battle the strong inside games of the league's perennial top contenders Winthrop, Radford and UNC Asheville. The other key for the Chants' chances is improvement from the young backcourt.

Junior Brandon Newby (10.9 ppg, 2.2 rpg) could be poised to become an all-conference performer and 5-9 sophomore Alvin Green (6.2 ppg, 3.0 rpg, 4.0 apg) turned heads a year ago, earning a spot on the BSC All-Rookie team.

The 6-2 Newby suffered nagging knee and ankle injuries last year but rarely came out of the lineup. He plays all-out and is "a long 6-2" said Strickland, who cites his long arms and ability to get to the rim.

"If he can stay healthy, I think he can show he's one of the best guards in the league," the coach said. "Brandon has an attitude this year that it's 'my turn'. He wants to show what he can do."

The cat-quick Green could be a budding star, too. He had typical freshman ups and downs most of the year, but then he committed only four turnovers in the last five games. Strickland essentially has another starter returning in the backcourt, too, with 5-10 Justin Burton (4.5 ppg, 1.8 rpg, 2.8 apg) back for his senior season.

A transfer from Owens (Ohio) Community College last season, Burton was slowed in the preseason with a groin injury but came on strong down the stretch, starting the last six regular season games and averaging 7.3 points and 3.7 assists over that span.

"Justin is quick, too, and when we have him and Alvin out there together, we can really defend full court," Strickland said.

Antonio Darden (7.2 ppg, 6.0 rpg) rounds out the backcourt. The 6-2 red-shirt junior's toughness is the stuff of legend. He joined the team as a walk-on, came back the following season with no guarantee he'd make the team and was red-shirted. Last year, he was back again and played so well in the preseason, Strickland gave him a full ride.

Darden played in all 28 games, started 10 times, and led the height-challenged Chants in rebounding.

Kelvin Coggins, a 6-4 sophomore swingman, sat out last season as a Prop 48. He's an explosive athlete and could work into the mix this season.

The injury bug has already struck again this year, too. Junior forward Clint Reed (5.4 ppg, 2.2 rpg) underwent surgery to fix a foot fracture which had become a chronic problem for the sharp-shooting Australian. His cumulative statistics don't do his value justice. He had 16 points and six rebounds at Georgetown, six points and a team-high seven rebounds at Virginia, and 15 points against The Citadel and Liberty. He won't play this season.

Strickland has two freshman with size coming in to help in 6-7 Clinton Nagel (12.0 ppg, 9.0 rpg) of Loveland, Ohio, and 6-5 Matthew Horne (15.0 ppg, 9.0 rpg) of Fort Washington, Md. Horne is more athletic but Nagel is bigger, more physical and likes to battle around the basket, all traits the Chants need.

Coastal was seventh in the league last year in rebound margin (-3.8) and even more to the point, the Chants were last in scoring defense (77.6 ppg allowed) and field-goal percentage defense (.491).

"We can spread some people out and cause trouble sometimes," said Strickland of Coastal's 70.9 points per game (2nd in the league) scoring average. "But defense

is where the lack of size really shows up."

Strickland hopes his team is more experienced and now deep enough without being forced to press freshman into important roles this season.

"For the first time, we've got guys coming back at every position and we've got a little experience," he said. "If the freshmen are too good to keep on the bench, that's great. If not, we should be OK, anyway."

2001-2002 SCHEDULE

Nov.	17	@Xavier
	21	@Georgetown
	24	Western Carolina
	29	@Clemson
Dec.	1	*College of Charleston
	4	East Tennessee State
	9	South Carolina State
	15	@Old Dominion
	21	Campbell
	29	@The Citadel
Jan.	2	@Navy
	5	@High Point
	7	@Elon
	12	Radford
	14	Liberty
	19	Birmingham Southern
	23	UNC Asheville
	26	@Charleston Southern
	31	Winthrop
Feb.	2	@Radford
	4	@Liberty
	7	Elon
	9	High Point
	13	@Birmingham Southern
	16	@UNC Asheville
	20	@Winthrop
	23	Charleston Southern
	28	#Big South Tournament
March	1-2	#Big South Tournament

@Road Games
*North Charleston Coliseum, Charleston, SC
#Roanoke Civic Center, Roanoke, VA

BLUE RIBBON ANALYSIS

BACKCOURT	B
BENCH/DEPTH	C+
FRONTCOURT	C
INTANGIBLES	B+

Coastal can be better this season, but this seems a fatally flawed team without the size around the basket to move past the league's better squads, much less compete against big-time non-conference opponents.

Butler is a big-time talent but the classic "tweener" with no place to play at a higher level of competition. Newby and Green can develop into one of the league's top guard combos but that doesn't help control the paint or the backboards.

Straight arrow Strickland has cleaned up a once sloppy program and he gets the most out of his charges. Trouble is they're still literally coming up short.

(M.A.)

Elon

LOCATION	Elon, NC
CONFERENCE	Big South
LAST SEASON	9-20 (.310)
CONFERENCE RECORD	4-10 (7th)
STARTERS LOST/RETURNING	2/3
NICKNAME	Phoenix
COLORS	Maroon & Gold
HOMECOURT	Koury Center (2,000)
COACH	Mark Simons (Aquinas '72)
RECORD AT SCHOOL	84-138 (8 years)
CAREER RECORD	179-240 (14 years)
ASSISTANTS	James Johnson (Ferrum '93)
	Eric Richardson (Milligan '97)
	Jonathan Tsipis (North Carolina '96)
TEAM WINS (last 5 years)	16-13-11-13-9
RPI (last 5 years)	NA-NA-NA-236-313
2000-01 FINISH	Lost regular-season finale.

The Phoenix may be the most appropriately named team in the Big South this year. From the ashes of a 9-20 season emerges a serious contender for the league crown.

Elon, under-sized, under-manned and over-scheduled last year, is ready to make a mark in its first season of eligibility for the Big South Tournament. And the Phoenix' timing is impeccable.

"It's been like four years of purgatory," coach Mark Simons said of the school's transition to Division I and full Big South membership. "It's a very exciting time for us and the kids are just feeling great about the chance."

They should.

Simons and his staff have put together the program's top Division I recruiting class, adding needed size and talent up front to complement 6-3 senior guard **Brendon Rowell**, one of the top players in the country you haven't heard about.

Rowell (18.8 ppg, 3.4 rpg, 2.5 apg) was first team all-conference last season despite a nagging, often painful shoulder injury that required off-season surgery. The silky smooth Rowell hit .513 (181-of-353) percent of his shots from the field but couldn't really bang inside with the shoulder. Teams were physical with him defensively and aimed multiple defenders at him often.

Rowell was also guilty of sacrificing his own offense to try to further involve teammates, particularly early in games. The results—as Elon's record attests—were not good.

"Brendon can post up and score, bounce out and hit the three and he's as good as anyone off the dribble," Simons said. "There are times when I don't think anyone can stop him."

Senior guard **David Hall** (6.4 ppg, 4.1 rpg) and junior forward **Shamar Johnson** (5.3 ppg, 3.1 rpg) also return on the wings. The 6-4 Hall had a disappointing season last year as the third guard in the undersized Phoenix lineup. He has added 10 pounds of muscle, and Simons says he is primed for a big senior season.

Johnson, a 6-5 junior, is a perfect fit at small forward in Elon's up-tempo game, and he is capable of blossoming into a top scorer. He will share the spot with 6-6, 220-pound **Chris Adams** (3.1 ppg, 4.7 rpg). Adams, one of the team's top defenders, led the squad in rebounding last year.

The question for the Phoenix on the perimeter is at point guard where junior **Ross Sims** (4.0 ppg, 1.0 rpg, 2.6 apg) will battle freshman **Steven Harvin** for the bulk of playing time. Sims led the team in assists last year, caddying for graduated senior Dennis Gaskins, and he has put in extra work this off-season to rise to the occasion.

The problem is Simons likes Sims at the receiving end of passes, though the 6-0 junior must improve his .196 percent shooting from three-point range.

The 5-11 Harvin was a standout at Centreville (Va.) High School, where he averaged 15 points, four rebounds and 6.2 assists per game. Harvin can penetrate and create, though he's not a picture-book jump-shooter.

"He lacks an outside shot," Simons said. "But we don't care. We've got guys that can do that."

Up front, little used sophomores **Matt Backs** (2.5 ppg, 1.6 rpg) and **Cameron Kirby** (0.3 ppg, 1.1 rpg) return, but they aren't likely to see much more action if some of the newcomers are as good as advertised.

The 6-6 Backs had an up-and-down freshman year, but he can contribute at both forward spots. The 6-7 Kirby has added weight to bring him up to around 200 pounds, but he'll be hard-pressed to see much more action.

Another member of that class, 6-6 red-shirt freshman **Gary Marsh**, is going to get lots of work. He would have last season, too, had he not broken his leg in the pre-season. Simons called him one of the best athletes Elon had ever recruited last year and he says Marsh has come all the way back.

"He's a pogo stick," Simons said. "He can play the three, four or five."

Marsh could be joined up front by 6-6, 230-pound freshman **Jackson Atoyebi** of Chicago, Ill., by way of Culver (Ind.) Military Academy. Atoyebi is a "stud," says Simons, pointing out he was recruited by Big Ten football programs as a tight end.

Atoyebi may be a bookend alongside 6-5, 235-pound junior transfer **Quinton McCleod** of Deerfield, Fla., and Broward (Fla.) Community College. A big scorer, McCleod has the athleticism to play small forward if his weight doesn't become an issue. He was all-conference pick for two seasons at Broward

Two swingmen round out the newcomers. **Carlos Moreira** is a 6-3 sophomore transfer from Pawtucket, R.I., transferring in from Community College of Rhode Island. He helped CCRI to a 21-8 record last year and a berth in the NJCAA-II Tournament, where he scored 34 points in a first round loss. Speed and defense are his trademarks.

Sean Newton, a 6-5 sharpshooter from Oak Ridge High in Orlando, Fla., averaged 24 points per game last season, and was simply too good to pass up, though he will have to wait to get his chance to put up points at Elon.

"We're more talented and much deeper than last year," said Simons. "Now we can get back to the tempo we like to play and we can do more defensively."

2001-2002 SCHEDULE

Nov.	16	North Carolina A&T
	18	@Wake Forest
	20	Lynchburg
	23	@Florida State
	27	UNC Greensboro
	30	#First Merchants Classic
Dec.	1	#First Merchants Classic
	4	@Davidson
	6	Bluefield
	15	@Clemson
	18	@Birmingham Southern
	29	@Arkansas
Jan.	2	Radford
	5	Charleston Southern
	7	Coastal Carolina
	12	@Winthrop
	19	@UNC Asheville
	21	Liberty
	26	@High Point
	29	@Liberty
Feb.	2	Birmingham Southern
	4	Winthrop
	7	@Coastal Carolina
	9	@Charleston Southern
	13	UNC Asheville
	16	@Radford
	23	High Point
	28	##Big South Tournament
March	1-2	##Big South Tournament

@Road Games
#Muncie, IN (vs. Ball State first round; also Austin Peay, Binghamton)
##Roanoke Civic Center, Roanoke, VA

BLUE RIBBON ANALYSIS

BACKCOURT	B
BENCH/DEPTH	B
FRONTCOURT	C+
INTANGIBLES	A

The Phoenix will be fun to watch again this season. Simons' teams enjoy playing a full-court brand of basketball that turned the Big South on its ear two years ago when the then-Fighting Christians went a surprising 7-7 in their first full tour through the conference.

Last year, Simons didn't have the personnel, particularly on the front line, to implement his fast-paced attack and full-court pressure, and Elon struggled. The Phoenix were seventh in the league in rebounding margin (-4.0) and Simons' normally high-scoring squad averaged just 64.6 points per game, sixth in the loop.

The schedule is actually tougher this year with Wake Forest, Florida State, Clemson and Arkansas on the non-conference schedule, but Elon is much better equipped to compete this time around. While still not overpoweringly large up front, the team is more athletic and deeper than it has been in their brief Division I history.

Inexperience at point and in the paint could be a problem early, but Elon has the horses to make some waves in the league again.

More importantly, for the first time, the Phoenix has that Big South Tournament pot of gold at the end of the season. With Rowell leading the way, and possibly making a name for himself on the national level, the Phoenix do indeed have a shot at whatever postseason fate the Big South winner earns.

And for four years, that's all they've wanted at Elon—a shot.

(M.A.)

High Point

LOCATION	High Point, NC
CONFERENCE	Big South
LAST SEASON	8-20 (.286)
CONFERENCE RECORD	3-11 (8th)
STARTERS LOST/RETURNING	1/4
NICKNAME	Panthers
COLORS	Purple & White
HOMECOURT	Mills Athletic Center (2,565)
COACH	Jerry Steele (Wake Forest '61)
RECORD AT SCHOOL	452-385 (29 years)
CAREER RECORD	603-459 (37 years)
ASSISTANTS	Brett Reed (Eckerd '95)
	Stephen Barber (Radford '92)
TEAM WINS (last 5 years)	18-12-11-11-8
RPI (last 5 years)	NA-NA-NA-276-316
2000-01 FINISH	Won regular-season finale.

High Point basketball fortunes have seemed at a low point the last two years. Veteran coach Jerry Steele had guided several NCAA Division II powerhouse teams at the school before the Panthers leaped into Division I competition in 1997.

His first two D-I teams were certainly respectable but two years ago when junior big man Geordie Cullen left school early to play professionally in his native Australia, the Panthers went from Big South contenders to pretenders. Last year, the preseason loss of guard J.R. Thompson, who opted to leave school, left the Panthers in another lurch.

Now it's the magical 2001-02 season, High Point's first year of full Big South membership, including a chance to play in the conference tournament for the first time.

"It's the first time in five years we know we're going to be playing at the end of February," Steele said. "That means so much to the players. By design, the NCAA makes it tough on you when you want to come into Division I, and where it really hurts you is in recruiting."

As if the dark clouds were parting, though, this year's High Point recruiting class is the school's best since moving up to Division I. The incoming class alone would be reason for optimism, but there's more. High Point has four starters and eight of the team's top nine scorers back.

And no one should be happier to see help on the way than **Mantas Ignatavicius** (7.3 ppg, 4.4 rpg, 2.5 apg). The 6-3 senior has filled in at every perimeter position, including seeing lots of duty at point guard the last three years. Steele opted to bring him off the bench more last season but the versatile Lithuanian was still third on the team with an average of 28.5 minutes played per night. Two years ago, even with the presence of all-conference performer Cullen, Ignatavicius was selected team MVP.

"He should be an off guard by nature but he's performed that [point-guard] role for us," Steele said. "He's just done whatever we've needed."

Leading scorer **Dustin Van Weerdhuizen** (11.8 ppg, 4.9 rpg, 2.2 apg) is a 6-2 junior wing guard who led the team with 1.8 three-pointers made per game but hit just .273 percent from long range.

"He'll probably play more minutes than anyone because he can do so many things for us," Steele said. "Dustin can bring it down against pressure but he's more natural on the wing. I think he'll have a better year this year."

Senior **Doug Alves** (9.1 ppg, 2.7 rpg) is back and he's an even more deadly shooter on the perimeter after hitting .365 from behind the arc and connecting on 1.5 threes per game. Van Weerdhuizen and Alves each played more than 34 minutes per game last year, and finding them more rest could help the Panthers improve.

Derek Van Weerdhuizen (7.5 ppg, 3.6 rpg, 2.2 apg) is a 6-4 senior forward and Dustin's older brother. Derek has been a spot starter throughout his career, and he'll again be in the mix on the perimeter this season.

Brent Halsch (4.3 ppg, 2.3 rpg) played very little early last year as a freshman but had worked into the rotation by the last five games. The 6-5 Halsch has "three size but we play him at four." Steele said

The incumbent at power forward is **Valdas Kaukenas** (6.7 ppg, 3.5 rpg), a 6-8 senior from Vilnius, Lithuania. Kaukenas started 13 games last season and averaged 15.3 minutes, not that High Point wouldn't have liked to see him on the floor more.

"He's been in foul trouble since he got off the plane," Steele said.

Kaukenas will have help this season as junior college transfer **Ron Barrow** will see considerable action. An athletic 6-6 forward, Barrow averaged 17 points and 10 rebounds last year at American River (Calif.) Junior College. He has impressed with his athleticism and defensive abilities.

The Panthers' best returning athlete is 6-7 senior **Jermaine Wallace** (11.2 ppg, 6.7 rpg), who had a stellar season after transferring from Lincoln (Ill.) Junior College. He missed a lot of early season work last year when family problems forced him to go home briefly. The High Point coaches are working to make him more of a back-to-the-basket low post threat to take advantage of his athleticism.

Sophomore **John Stonehocker** (6.3 ppg, 2.3 rpg) started the first three games last year at center but then broke his wrist and missed the rest of the season. It was a doubly bad break for the 6-9 Stonehocker, who red-shirted the year before as a 17-year-old freshman.

"He really hasn't played at all in two years now," Steele said.

Steele thought he had post help on the way this season in 6-10 freshman Jeremy McCall of London, Ontario. McCall averaged more than 30 points and 15 rebounds at Mt. Calm Secondary School but injured an ACL, underwent surgery and then sustained a staph infection. He'll be forced to red-shirt this season.

The team's two other freshmen scholarship recruits, though, should play a lot this season and should have an impact. **Joey Knight**, a 6-1 guard from Columbia, Tenn., and **Steve Cornette**, a 6-4 guard from Fayetteville, N.C., will both fit right into the backcourt rotation and take some of the pressure off the veterans.

Knight averaged 19 points, six rebounds and seven assists at Columbia Central High School, while Cornette, a long-range bomber, scored 30 points per game and grabbed eight rebounds a night at Terry Sanford High School.

"They make us a little bit better athletically," Steele said. "We haven't been able to out-quick many people. I think by being a little more athletic, we'll be able to run and get a few more easy baskets and create some turnovers."

There's some more help in the backcourt, including 5-11 sophomore **Dan Kalbaugh** (1.0 ppg, 0.7 rpg) and 6-4 freshman walk-on **Franklin Johnson** from Forrestville, Md. Kalbaugh, a good shooter, probably won't see much action. Johnson averaged 17 points and eight rebounds at Bishop McNamara High School, and could have a bright future.

Another signee, 6-5 sophomore transfer Danny Gathings, averaged nine points and three rebounds last season at Virginia Tech before leaving the program at mid-season. He will have to sit out this year, but he's another player capable of making High Point much more competitive.

2001-2002 SCHEDULE

Nov.	16	@Auburn
	20	William & Mary
	24	UNC Wilmington
	27	Warren Wilson
Dec.	1	Brown
	4	Eastern Kentucky
	6	Delaware
	8	Wright State
	15	@Oklahoma
	18	@Florida
Jan.	3	Covenant College
	5	Coastal Carolina
	7	Charleston Southern
	12	@Birmingham Southern
	16	@UNC Asheville
	19	@Radford
	21	Winthrop
	24	@Liberty
	26	Elon
	29	@Winthrop
Feb.	2	UNC Asheville
	4	Birmingham Southern
	7	@Charleston Southern
	9	@Coastal Carolina
	13	Radford
	16	Liberty
	23	@Elon
	28	#Big South Tournament
March	1-2	##Big South Tournament

@Road Games
#Roanoke Civic Center, Roanoke, VA

BLUE RIBBON ANALYSIS

BACKCOURT	C
BENCH/DEPTH	D+
FRONTCOURT	C
INTANGIBLES	C

The Panthers were 4-2 early last season before injuries and a rugged travel schedule took a heavy toll. An overtime loss at Eastern Kentucky and a double-overtime setback at Virginia Tech seemed to take the steam out of the team.

Steele is hoping the roof doesn't cave in again.

"We have more experience, but a lot depends on how we play early," he said. "Not necessarily whether we win or lose but if we play hard and smart."

Some quickness and athleticism in the form of Knight and Cornette and Barrow should help. Ignatavicius and the Van Weerdhuizen brothers, among other returnees, have taken their lumps the last two years, and they'd like to dish out some punishment this year.

The Panthers look better but they—as much as any team in the Big South—know how quickly fortunes can change. They can't afford any injuries up front and even with a lot of bodies on the perimeter, they still don't match up with the league's top backcourts.

Don't discount the progress, though, that Steele and assistant coaches Brett Reed and Stephen Barber are making. High Point is finally starting to look like a team on the way back.

(M.A.)

Liberty

LOCATION	Lynchburg, VA
CONFERENCE	Big South
LAST SEASON	13-15 (.464)
CONFERENCE RECORD	5-9 (6th)
STARTERS LOST/RETURNING	4/1
NICKNAME	Flames
COLORS	Red, White & Blue
HOMECOURT	Vines Center (9,000)
COACH	Mel Hankinson (Indiana-Pa. '65)
RECORD AT SCHOOL	31-52 (3 years)
CAREER RECORD	356-328 (24 years)
ASSISTANTS	Chad Hankinson (West Virginia '94)
	Ty Nichols (Cal State-San Marcos '95)
	Mike Doig (Clearwater Baptist '93)
TEAM WINS (last 5 years)	23-22-4-14-13
RPI (last 5 years)	115-282-310-254-285
2000-01 FINISH	Lost in conference semifinal.

One of these years, the Liberty Flames are going to live up to the preseason hype.

To read the press releases and hear the talk around the league, fourth-year coach Mel Hankinson has been stockpiling top-notch recruits and is getting closer and closer to having the horses to run his multiple-defense, fast-paced offensive schemes.

For two straight seasons, the Flames have lit up their pre-conference schedule only to have trouble once league play started. But Liberty finished fast last year, upsetting UNC Asheville in the Big South Tournament and stretching eventual champion Winthrop to the limit. Liberty led the Eagles by 16 points late in the second half before succumbing in double overtime.

"We've been in a transition, mixing junior college and high school players the last two years after that first season," Hankinson said, "I felt like last year, before some injuries, we really had a chance to go to the [NCAA] tournament, but we had very little offensive punch down the stretch."

Injuries contributed to the Flames' offensive woes, but so did dreadful shooting. Liberty was dead last among 319 Division I teams, hitting just 58 three-point field goals and connecting on just .251 percent of the squad's three-point attempts.

Now subtract four starters from that group, including second team all-conference forward Nathan Day, and one just has to wonder why are they so optimistic in Lynchburg heading into this season?

"We've got more players that know and fit in our sys-

tem," Hankinson said. "And we're starting to get the blend you need. We've got five freshmen, four sophomores, two juniors and two seniors."

One of those seniors and the lone returning starter, second team all-conference guard **Chris Caldwell** (16.7 ppg, 2.9 rpg, 2.5 apg) is a pretty good building block.

"He has always had the skills," Hankinson said. "But the greatest thing about him has been his maturation and leadership. He called every player this summer. He worked very hard on the court and off, and he'll definitely be one of the league's best guards."

The 6-1 Caldwell can play either guard spot and has become one of the Big South's top defenders.

It's likely Caldwell will team with high-scoring freshman **Travis Eisentrout** of Berlin, Pa, in the backcourt. The 6-2 Eisentrout averaged 33 points per game at Berlin Brothers High, and finished 11th in Pennsylvania high school history with 2,824 points, passing Wilt Chamberlain on that list. Most importantly, a good portion of Eisentrout's points came from behind the three-point arc, where he hit 37 percent and became the most prolific three-point shooter in state history.

A year ago, the new backcourt phenom was supposed to be 6-4 red-shirt freshman **J.R. Nicholas** (4.0 ppg, 1.4 rpg), but he appeared in just five games before an ankle injury sidelined him and then personal issues caused him to leave the team. He's back this year.

Little-used **Freddy Williams** (0.5 ppg, 1.8 rpg) and **Eric Johnson** (1.5 ppg, 0.2 rpg) are the only other returnees for Liberty at guard.

The 6-1 Williams is a sophomore who appeared in four games last year, while Johnson, a senior, played in six games after transferring in from Tennessee-Martin last season.

Hankinson has much more experience back at forward and center. Senior **David Watson** (2.3 ppg, 2.3 rpg) is coming back from two knee operations but at 6-8, he's projected by Hankinson as one of the top defenders in the league this season in the post. A warrior, Watson has played with injuries—the knees, a broken wrist—throughout his career.

Injuries moved 6-6 junior **Rob Attaway** (3.7 ppg, 2.5 rpg, 1.5 apg) into the starting small forward position last season, and he'll contend again this year. A heady player, he was third on the team in assists.

Louvon Snead (2.3 ppg, 1.9 rpg) is a 6-7 sophomore power forward who provided solid reserve minutes last season all along the front line. He played at famed St. Anthony's High in New Jersey his senior year in high school.

Philip Ward (3.0 ppg, 3.0 rpg) played in 25 games last season, but the 6-7 sophomore may have difficulty finding playing time this year if the newcomers come along as fast as Hankinson predicts.

Red-shirt freshman **Glynn Turner** isn't exactly a newcomer, but he missed all of last season with a back injury. He's back with that 6-8, 235-pound frame that made him a top prospect a year ago out of Highview Baptist High in Louisville, Ky., where he averaged 14.2 points and 10.6 rebounds.

The guy to keep an eye on, though, should be 6-7 junior **Vincent Okotie**, a transfer from San Diego State. Okotie, at 230 pounds, is a natural small forward with a deep shooting range. He averaged 6.6 points and 4.7 rebounds at SDS before sitting out last year at Liberty.

Jason Sarchet (15.3 ppg, 9.9 rpg at Indian Hills Junior College in Iowa) is another big body who can challenge for a starting berth. At 6-10, 235, he was recruited by Hankinson at West Virginia, where the coach was an assistant four years ago. Sarchet is a "big time player," Hankinson said. He left Indian Hills early and has three years of eligibility left for the Flames.

Mats Persson, a 6-8, 230-pound forward, is another three-years-of-eligibility transfer, coming over from San Diego College, and he's fundamentally sound.

Hankinson is also high on two new swingmen, 6-6 **Torin Beeler** of Huntington Beach, Calif., and 6-7 **Fred Oguns** of Lagos, Nigeria. Beeler averaged 16 points and 12 rebounds at Ocean View High and is a tough kid with a 44-inch vertical leap. Oguns is a solid athlete with great skills that make him a big guard but he's less experienced than Okotie.

Rounding out the newcomers are 6-5 sophomore guard **Brett Lilly**, another transfer from Indian Hills; 6-1 freshman guard **Mike Johnson** from Life Center Academy in Philadelphia; and 6-6 junior **Mark Manley**.

"This is unquestionably the base team you can build a program with," said Hankinson. "Unquestionably, it's the highest skill level since I've been here."

2001-2002 SCHEDULE

Nov.	16	@Vanderbilt
	19	Shenandoah
	23-25	#Hawaii Pacific Thanksgiving Classic
Dec.	1	@Appalachian State
	4	Florida Atlantic
	8	James Madison
	14	Tusculum
	17	@Northwestern
	22	Air Force
	29	@Duquesne
Jan.	2	@American
	5	@Birmingham-Southern
	8	UNC Asheville
	12	@Charleston Southern
	14	@Coastal Carolina
	19	Winthrop
	21	@Elon
	24	High Point
	26	@Radford
	29	Elon
Feb.	2	Charleston Southern
	4	Coastal Carolina
	9	@UNC Asheville
	14	@Winthrop
	16	@High Point
	19	Birmingham-Southern
	23	Radford
	27	#Big South Championship
March	1-2	#Big South Championship

@Road Games
#Roanoke Civic Center, Roanoke, VA

BLUE RIBBON ANALYSIS

BACKCOURT	B-
BENCH/DEPTH	C+
FRONTCOURT	C-
INTANGIBLES	C

The Flames already have a couple of big men committed for next season and their surprise trip to the conference tournament semifinals last year could signal the beginning of a three-or-four-year window for Liberty as a serious contender.

Stop us if you've heard this before.

Somehow, all the great players Liberty has signed the last two years either haven't produced, haven't stayed healthy or haven't shown up at all. Coaches around the league annually agree the Flames are hoarding up good players but somehow that hasn't translated into much success on the court thus far.

Maybe this is the year.

If it is, at least a couple of news guys—likely high-scoring guard Travis Eisentrout, versatile forward Vincent Okotie and big forward Jason Sarchet—are going to have to play major roles.

Only all-conference guard Caldwell turns heads among the returnees and that just doesn't seem enough to reverse the Flames' fortunes this season. Liberty will again play tenacious defense and come at opponents with a deep bench, but until the new guys prove their mettle, it's hard to imagine the Flames as better than middle-of-the-pack in the Big South again this year.

(M.A.)

 **UNC Asheville**

LOCATION	Asheville, NC
CONFERENCE	Big South
LAST SEASON	15-13 (.536)
CONFERENCE RECORD	9-3 (3rd)
STARTERS LOST/RETURNING	2/3
NICKNAME	Bulldogs
COLORS	Royal Blue & White
HOMECOURT	Justice Center (1,100)
	Asheville Civic Center (6,000)
COACH	Eddie Biedenbach (NC State '68)
RECORD AT SCHOOL	74-59 (5 years)
CAREER RECORD	103-120 (8 years)
ASSISTANTS	Thomas Nash (Vanderbilt '95)
	Nick McDevitt (UNC Asheville '01)
TEAM WINS (last 5 years)	18-19-11-11-15

RPI (last 5 years)	106-131-264-219-238
2000-01 FINISH	Lost in conference quarterfinal.

A winning record last season was little consolation for UNC Asheville, which was bounced out of the Big South Tournament in the first round for the first time in six years.

The question is was that early exit part of a continuing downward spiral for the program, or a glitch for a team that has annually been among the Big South's top three since coach Eddie Biedenbach came aboard in 1996?

The low-key Biedenbach said his Bulldogs will be picked anywhere from second to fifth in the league this season, but that he faces the same challenge at the school he faces each season.

"We've got to put the pieces together," Biedenbach said. "I like our team, but I always do. The problem we have is that our most athletic players don't shoot well and our good shooters aren't as athletic. We have to piece it together." The Bulldogs still size up well in the Big South, where only Winthrop and Radford have consistently finished ahead of UNCA the last four years. The Bulldogs have been to two Big South title games in Bidenbach's five years and have established a reputation as a tough team come tournament time.

That image took a hit last season when the 'Dogs dropped four of their last five games, including a first round tournament exit at the hands of Liberty. An overall winning record for the first time in three seasons was of little consolation after that early exit, but Biedenbach is hoping that memory adds fuel to the fire this season.

Bulldog fans are hoping to see more firepower from junior **Andre Smith** (10.4 ppg, 2.6 rpg, 3.7 apg). The 6-2 Smith was the BSC Rookie of the Year in 2000, earning second team all-conference honors, too. Last season, he didn't earn anything as his play noticeably slipped. By contrast, graduated senior Brett Carey, a classic overachiever, was second team all-conference after averaging 13.3 points.

"Andre has been reflecting on last season quite a bit," Biedenbach said. "He's a wonderful athlete with a wonderful attitude but things may have come too easy for him as a freshman. We've talked about that."

If Smith responds to the challenge of improving—and playing without Carey alongside him—he will be the top 'Dog, and a lot of the pieces will fall into place for UNCA. With Carey gone, a starting spots opens but it may not automatically go to athletic junior **Brandon Carter** (3.6 ppg, 1.8 rpg). The 6-3 Carter may have to fend off a challenge from junior college transfer **Alex Kragel**, who averaged 10.5 points and 3.3 assists last year at Walters State (Tenn.) Community College.

Kragel, a 6-2 natural shooter, is more in the mold of Carey, but Biedenbach has also said he may move one of his more athletic forwards to the off-guard spot.

One thing is certain. Steady junior **Colin Shaw** (8.8 ppg, 4.9 rpg) will start somewhere. He's the Bulldogs' 6-5 jack-of-all-trades, able to play anywhere on the floor but point guard. Likely, he'll end up back at forward, but Biedenbach is toying with the idea of playing him at guard.

"He's a good rebounder, but he's not our best; he's a good shooter, but we have others; he's a good passer, but not the best on the team," said the coach. "He does a little of everything well and he just plays with a real joy. He's kind of the glue that holds us together."

Sophomore **Billy Allen** (6.0 ppg, 3.9 rpg) could push into the starting lineup if his shoulder is fully healed from off-season surgery. He has good size at 6-5, and is a solid athlete with a penchant for defense.

Allen could split time with the team's lone senior, offense-minded **Robby Joyner** (6.4 ppg, 4.3 rpg). The 6-5 Joyner started 15 games a year ago but has never been the same since hurting his back in a nasty spill earlier in his career. With Allen providing much of the defensive support, the two veterans can man the small forward position by committee.

If Shaw doesn't settle in at power forward again, 6-7 sophomore **Michael Harper** (2.4 ppg, 1.7 rpg) or a freshman will have a chance to step in. Harper has grown a little more since last year, bulking up to 200 pounds, but freshman **Joseph Barber**, at 6-9, 210, has impressed the coaching staff with his shooting touch and confidence. Barber was a standout at Terra Ceia Christian School in Panlego, N.C.

Barber can also play center, but 6-11, 250-pound junior **Ben McGonagil** (6.0 ppg, 4.8 rpg) should have a lock on that job if he continues to develop like he did last season. McGonagil provides a physical presence in the paint many Big South teams lack.

He'll have company, too, with 6-10, 250-pound freshman **Jon Higginbotham**, a big, active product of Auburn (Ala.) High School joining the program this season. Along with 6-5 swingman **Julian Capel** and 6-6 **Bryan McCullough**, Higginbotham and Barber constitute a heck of a recruiting class.

"All of our four freshmen are good enough that they could be counted on on a regular basis," said Biedenbach, not prone to hyperbole about newcomers. "Some will emerge better than others, but they'll get a chance. We typically play eight or nine players, sometimes 10."

Capel is a cousin of the other basketball-playing Capels. He averaged 16 points a game last year at Pine Forest High in Fayetteville, N.C., and he could work into playing time on the wings. McCullough could be the best of the lot. He's a strong inside force and averaged 20 points, nine rebounds and two assists at North Rowan High in Spencer, N.C. Don't be surprised if he emerges at forward and quickly becomes a potent scorer.

Red-shirt walk-on freshman **Walt Dickinson**, a 6-1 guard from Asheville, and late recruit **Marcus Reddick**, a 6-3 guard from Spencer, round out the team.

2001-2002 SCHEDULE

Nov.	16	@West Virginia
	19	UNC Greensboro
	21	@Minnesota
	24	@Campbell
	28	East Tennessee State
Dec.	1	@Western Carolina
	4	@Furman
	8	Montreat College
	15	@North Carolina State
	17	@Michigan State
	20	@Auburn
	30	Appalachian State
Jan.	2	Charleston Southern
	6	@Radford
	8	@Liberty
	13	Brevard College
	16	High Point
	19	Elon
	23	@Coastal Carolina
	26	Winthrop
	30	Radford
Feb.	2	@High Point
	9	Liberty
	13	@Elon
	16	Coastal Carolina
	20	@Charleston Southern
	23	@Winthrop
	28	#Big South Tournament
March	1-2	#Big South Tournament

@Road Games
#Roanoke Civic Center, Roanoke, Va.

BLUE RIBBON ANALYSIS

BACKCOURT	B-
BENCH/DEPTH	B+
FRONTCOURT	C
INTANGIBLES	B

It's hard not to root for a coach who says of last season's collapse down the stretch: "It was a combination of injuries, attitude and bad coaching."

Biedenbach's teams annually seem to be among the Big South's best, though the grueling non-conference schedule he plays—without complaint—to put money in the UNCA athletic department coffers kill his overall record.

When Smith and Carter, didn't continue to blossom last season, the Bulldogs were exposed as less talented than the league's elite teams and quite frankly, UNCA didn't match up inside or outside with some of their chief rivals.

The bitter taste of last season's unusual poor finish—generally the Bulldogs are playing as well as anyone come tournament time—and an influx of new talent could propel UNCA back into the championship picture.

Only Smith and Shaw are assured a starting berth heading to October practices, and the scrapping this team is going to do to find itself early may be just what this program needs.

Nothing's meaner than a hungry Bulldog.

(M.A.)

Radford

LOCATION	Radford, VA
CONFERENCE	Big South
LAST SEASON	19-10 (.655)
CONFERENCE RECORD	12-2 (1st)
STARTERS LOST/RETURNING	1/4
NICKNAME	Highlanders
COLORS	Red, Blue, Green & White
HOMECOURT	Dedmon Center (5,000)
COACH	Ron Bradley (Eastern Nazarene '74)
RECORD AT SCHOOL	178-108 (10 years)
CAREER RECORD	274-159 (15 years)
ASSISTANTS	Bill Lilly (Glenville State '82)
	Byron Samuels (UNC Asheville '86)
	Chibi Johnson (Radford '98)
TEAM WINS (last 5 years)	15-20-20-18-19
RPI (last 5 years)	182-170-187-159-167
2000-01 FINISH	Lost in conference final.

Radford has won more games than any other conference team in the Big South's 18-year history. Recently, the Highlanders posted two 20-win seasons and then "slumped" to 19 and 18 wins the last two years.

And for all that, Radford has one Big South championship to show for it.

That's the rub under the inflatable Dedmon Center dome. The Highlanders captured their third regular-season title in four years last season and then fell in overtime in the championship game of the league tournament in Roanoke, Va.

Close but no cigar. Again.

The Highlanders last won the championship in 1998, earning the right to get thumped by Duke in the first round of the NCAA Tournament, and then Winthrop started stacking up championship trophies. Three in a row, to be exact. Twice the Eagles beat RU in the championship game.

Now minus a former Big South Player of the Year, indomitable coach Ron Bradley is quietly thinking he may have one of his best teams. He'd better. Radford plays 10 opponents this year ranked in the top 105 in RPI last season.

Oh yeah, and Winthrop has its best team ever, too.

The former player of the year is Jason Williams, who won the honor in 1999-00 and was all-conference last year averaging 17 points. He hit one of the most memorable shots in league history when his driving jumper at the buzzer tied the BSC title game and sent it to overtime.

Likewise, no one is likely to forget some of his antics, which included a technical foul once while he was shooting a free throw. An undeniable talent, Williams' actions divided the team on and off the court the last three years, and while his talent will be missed, his demeanor won't be.

There's another big reason RU will survive. A 7-0, 265-pound reason. That would be senior **Andrey Savtchenko** (15.4 ppg, 10.0 rpg, 1.2 bpg), who nearly transferred last season because of Williams. Instead, Savtchenko earned first team all-conference honors and initiated the process of other BSC programs scrambling to find big bodies to match up with him.

Big Andy hit .545 percent from the field, .574 in conference games and was virtually unstoppable in the league tournament, where he earned MVP honors.

"Andy's game really blossomed," Bradley said. "He's so big and so strong. I think he's the best big man this league has ever seen and he's going to improve practicing against the size we've brought in with our freshmen."

Savtchenko will also benefit from the return of guys who know how to get him the ball. Senior point guard **Mike Hornbuckle** (7.1 ppg, 2.5 rpg, 3.9 apg) and junior **Raymond "Peanut" Arrington** (12.7 ppg, 2.8 rpg) are back to form one of the league's better backcourts.

The 6-1 Hornbuckle played some of the best basketball of his career in an August tour of Russia, Bradley said, and he'll have the ball in his hands more this year with Williams out of the picture. Arrington was sensational as a freshman and solid last season but Bradley got on him about settling for jumpers instead of driving to the basket. The 6-3 Arrington, a defensive stopper, has taken to the idea of attacking the basket and there will be opportunities, again now that Williams is gone.

B.J. Haigler (1.8 ppg, 1.5 rpg, 1.9 apg) became a fan-favorite with his end-to-end play. The 5-10 sopho-

more takes Radford's up-tempo game to another gear when he enters the fray.

Correy Watkins (11.2 ppg, 7.5 rpg) always plays in high gear. The 6-7 power forward is one of the league's most underrated performers.

"I wouldn't trade him for anybody," hoops purist Bradley said. "He does the little basketball things you can't teach. He's a tremendous offensive rebounder. He gets loose balls. He screens. He passes. He plays [power forward] but he can play on the perimeter, too."

Watkins, with 15 new pounds of muscle, will again play power forward, but someone still has to fill Williams' basketball shoes. A likely candidate is athletic 6-6 sophomore **Aaron Gill** (1.0 ppg, 1.5 rpg), who has shown flashes of a big-time offensive game. He didn't play well on the foreign tour and that's opened the door for tinkering by Bradley.

"We could move Correy there, but I don't know if our freshmen are ready up front," he said. "We may run a lot of three guard and we don't have a problem with that."

Haigler would benefit from that last scenario. Junior **Jesse Seamon** (1.5 ppg, 0.4) would have, too, had he not injured his knee on the Russian tour. His sterling play had earned the former walk-on a starting job on the trip before an untimely trip on the court sidelined him, possibly for the season.

Ray Noiles (1.1 ppg, 0.7 rpg) a 6-4 sophomore, who is still trying to find a comfort zone in the college game, rounds out the backcourt returnees.

A junior college transfer, 6-2 **Jason Cornute** (20.0 ppg, 6.0 rpg, 4.0 apg) of Genessee (N.Y.) Community College, will likely see playing time. Freshman **David Popoola** (14.5 ppg, 4.6 rpg, 3.2 apg) a 6-3 point guard from the same Blue Ridge (Va.) High School that produced Savtchenko, is another option.

One other returnee will definitely fit in the rotation up front. Senior **Nosa Obasuyi** (2.3 ppg, 3.0 rpg) is the returning blocked shots leader in the Big South with 1.4 per game, and he's a 6-10 jumping jack, backing Savtchenko. Bradley would have loved to red-shirt Obasuyi at some point in his career but injuries and the loss of a couple of big recruits forced him into action.

Now Obasuyi isn't even the second biggest center on the team, though he is the most experienced reserve. Freshmen **Jason Bees**, a 7-foot, 255-pounder from Russell, Pa., and **Kyle Zaharias**, a 6-9, 240-pounder from Midlothian, Va., give the Highlanders their biggest and deepest front line since their championship season.

Bees averaged 21.4 points, 9.5 rebounds and 4.6 blocks at Eisenhower High. Zaharias averaged 15 points and 14 rebounds at Clover Hill High, the same program that produced former RU great Ryan Charles.

While not as big as that imposing duo, 6-7, 220-pound **Marcus Johnson** is the freshman who could have the biggest impact. He missed much of his senior season at Bishop McNamara High in Mitchellville, Md., with an achilles injury. An explosive leaper, he averaged 15 points and eight rebounds in 15 games.

The freshman who would have had the biggest impact was 6-5 Estonian Jesper Parve, who after signing with Radford, ultimately signed to play professionally in his homeland. He would have fit right into Williams' spot.

2001-2002 SCHEDULE

Nov.	15-17	#Top of the World Shootout
	21	@Purdue
	26	UNC Wilmington
	28	Richmond
Dec.	1	Middle Tennessee
	4	American
	6	Marshall
	8	@East Tennessee
	15	@Virginia Tech
	17	@Tennessee
	22	@East Carolina
	28-29	##State Farm Good Neighbor Classic
Jan.	2	@Elon
	6	UNC Asheville
	9	Winthrop
	12	@Coastal Carolina
	14	@Charleston Southern
	19	High Point
	26	Liberty
	30	@UNC Asheville
Feb.	2	Coastal Carolina
	4	Charleston Southern
	9	@Winthrop
	13	@High Point
	16	Elon
	23	@Liberty
	27	###Big South Tournament
March	1-2	###Big South Tournament

@Road Games
#Fairbanks, AK (vs. Butler first round; also Ole Miss, Wichita State, Delaware, Alaska-Fairbanks, Butler, Bowling Green)
##Johnson Center, Charleston, SC (vs. Holy Cross first round; also Louisiana-Monroe, College of Charleston)
###Roanoke Civic Center, Roanoke, VA

BLUE RIBBON ANALYSIS

BACKCOURT	B+
BENCH/DEPTH	C
FRONTCOURT	A-
INTANGIBLES	B

Bradley has contended in the Big South with less talented teams than this one. He's got the best center in the Big South, and quite possibly in league history.

Savtchenko looks primed for a run at player-of-the-year honors. Hornbuckle is a senior point guard and Watkins is another senior, and arguably the team's most valuable player. Arrington is an emerging star and if not for the hole at small forward, Bradley could have his best team ever.

He's got one of his toughest schedules ever and the Highlanders could be hard-pressed to duplicate the gaudy won-loss records of the last few years. The rest of the league is getting better, too. .

Still, the Highlanders will be near the top of the league, and then they'll technically host the Big South Tournament in Roanoke, 45 miles from the campus. It's a plus—particularly now that the Highlanders have played a few games in the facility. Any extra help is appreciated, and one of these years, things are bound to break for Radford in the tournament. Right?

(M.A.)

Winthrop

LOCATION	Rock Hill, SC
CONFERENCE	Big South
LAST SEASON	18-13 (.581)
CONFERENCE RECORD	11-3 (2nd)
STARTERS LOST/RETURNING	1/4
NICKNAME	Eagles
COLORS	Garnet & Gold
HOMECOURT	Winthrop Coliseum (6,100)
COACH	Gregg Marshall (Randolph-Macon '85)
RECORD AT SCHOOL	60-30 (3 years)
CAREER RECORD	60-30 (3 years)
ASSISTANTS	Barclay Radebaugh (ETSU '84)
	Shaun Golden (Georgia '93)
	Damon Stephenson (Pikeville '92)
TEAM WINS (last 5 years)	12-7-21-21-18
RPI (last 5 years)	249-294-144-142-190
2000-01 FINISH	Lost in NCAA play-in game.

Maybe the secret to Winthrop's unprecedented back-to-back Big South Conference championships is that the Eagles certainly don't talk like a team that has dominated the league for three years.

An August trip to South America gave coach Gregg Marshall his first look at the 2001-02 Eagles, the go-ahead-and-send-it-in favorites to capture a fourth BSC crown, and all the young coach saw was problems.

"On paper, we've got a pretty good team, but what I discovered is that we've got a ton of deficiencies we need to address quickly," Marshall said. "Foremost, we've got guys that haven't played in this system that we need to work into it. It's a team game. It's not a matter of the five best players winning. We've got a long way to go to perform well as a team."

That assessment sounds strange from the leader of a team that simply willed itself to a third conference crown last March. Injuries took away key players and hampered other stalwarts, but when crunch time came, no one in the Big South could put away the gutty Eagles. Liberty blew a 16-point, second half lead and fell in double-overtime of a conference tournament semifinal and regular-season champion Radford saw Winthrop erase an eight-point deficit in the final six minutes of the championship game and prevail in overtime.

And now the Eagles return four starters and seven of the top eight players off that team, plus 2000 tournament MVP and 2001 preseason player-of-the-year **Greg Lewis** (7.7 ppg, 4.8 rpg), who ended up red-shirting last year when a foot injury just wouldn't heal.

Now Lewis must work back into the framework of a team that won a title without him. He averaged 15.7 points and 6.7 rebounds in 1999-00, but played in just six games last season. Marshall estimates he's still only at about 95 percent.

So deep and talented were the Eagles, though, that versatile senior **Derrick Knox** (11.5 ppg, 4.6 rpg) replaced Lewis and Winthrop didn't seem to miss a beat. All the 6-3 Knox did was earn second team all-conference honors, hit .408 from three-point range, make good passes and come up with key rebounds all season.

A big guard with a power forward mentality, Knox struggled on the Chilean tour as Winthrop went 1-7 against South American professionals. He's the likely candidate to move into the two-guard spot vacated by the graduation of the steady Roger Toxey, thus allowing Lewis to return to starting small forward.

But Knox's slump and the emergence of 6-2 junior walk-on **Tyron Myers** (0.9 ppg, 0.4 rpg) may complicate matters. Myers played in just 14 games last year, but Marshall said he "couldn't keep him off the court" on the tour. A backup point guard last year, Myers is big and athletic and proved a solid complement to injured starting point **Pierre Wooten** (8.5 ppg, 3.3 rpg, 3.8 apg).

The 6-3 Wooten is already noted as one of the Big South's top defenders and Myers alongside him sharing point duties seem to free Wooten up to do more things offensively. Marshall loved the way Wooten filled a lane on the break with Myers pushing the ball.

And the options don't end there. Senior **Tywan Harris** (7.1 ppg, 1.1 rpg) is also available, though Marshall stresses he must improve. The 5-11 Harris came off the bench and earned a reputation for hitting big shots, including key threes in the closing minutes of both tournament rallies.

Transfer **Lavar Hemphill**, a 6-3 junior, is eligible after sitting out after his exit from Old Dominion. Hemphill played in 25 games at ODU in 1999-00, averaging 4.2 points and 1.9 rebounds, and he could ease past Harris in the rotation. Knox, too, could see his playing time affected.

Anthony Moore (4.5 ppg, 2.6 rpg) may not be playing much at all. The 6-6 sophomore swingman burst upon the scene last year, earning BSC Rookie-of-the-Week honor three times before suffering a knee injury. One doctor has told him his career is over but another is hoping surgery to remove scar tissue will allow him to return.

When Moore went down with his injury, it allowed 6-6 forward **Tyrone Walker** (7.5 ppg, 4.0 rpg) more minutes and Walker took advantage. He earned BSC rookie-of-the-week honors five times and ran away with the league's rookie-of-the-year award.

"He's got a feathery touch, he can put the ball on the floor and he rebounds a little," Marshall said. "He's got long arms and his body is still developing. He's got a chance to be all-conference, if not this year, then certainly as a junior and a senior."

Marcus Stewart (12.2 ppg, 6.7 rpg) knows all about all-conference. The 6-6 senior was a first team selection last season and added to his resume with the game-winning basket with six seconds left in the BSC title game.

Stewart, one of four fifth-year seniors on the team, is a highly effective combination of physical skill and sheer desire. He had knee surgery during his red-shirt year after coming over from Coastal Carolina, and last season, the knee bothered him so much he had to have fluid drained three times. He had more surgery in the off-season, didn't play very much on the August tour and didn't practice at all.

He's not the only health concern up front. Senior center **Eyo Effiong** (4.3 ppg, 3.7 rpg), 6-9, has never fully recovered from a back injury suffered last preseason. He averaged 8.2 points and 6.2 rebounds as a sophomore and looked on his way to becoming one of the league's premier post players. Now he can't get elevation on his shot against other big players and he plays with constant pain, sharing the post with Stewart.

Red-shirt freshman **Josh Grant** is a 6-8 backup center who is trying to get stronger and adjust to Marshall's demands for constant, passionate effort—"playing with your hair on fire," is how the coach puts it.

Sophomore guard **Bryant Latimer** (1.2 ppg, 0.7 rpg),

a 5-11 backup point, is also back, as is walk-on **Gabe Leventis** (0.3 ppg, 0.3 rpg), a 6-7 sophomore.

Freshman **Sheldon Bailey**, a 6-6 forward, averaged 10 points and 10 rebounds at Southview High in Fayetteville, N.C., before moving on to powerful Mt. Zion Christian Academy in Durham.

"He fits right in here at Winthrop since he's coming off a major knee surgery," Marshall said.

Point guard **Ivan Jenkins**, a 5-11 dynamo who averaged 24 points, 9.8 assists and two steals at Southern Durham High last year, is the other big freshman recruit. Walk-on transfer **Alex English**, a 6-2 guard and the son of another more famous Alex English, is eligible after Christmas. He injured his ankle at William & Mary before his freshman season and never played there.

Another walk-on freshman, 6-6 **Jared Weeks** of Columbia, S.C., is also slated to join the program.

2001-2002 SCHEDULE

Nov.	16	Lander
	18	@Ohio State
	24	@Nebraska
	27	Birmingham Southern
	29-30	#Phoenix Classic
Dec.	15	Marshall
	18	@Clemson
	21-22	##Winthrop Shootout
	28	*George Mason
Jan.	9	@Radford
	12	Elon
	15	Randolph-Macon
	19	@Liberty
	21	@High Point
	24	Charleston Southern
	26	@UNC Asheville
	29	High Point
	31	@Coastal Carolina
Feb.	4	@Elon
	7	@Birmingham Southern
	9	Radford
	14	Liberty
	16	@Charleston Southern
	20	Coastal Carolina
	23	UNC Asheville
	27	###Big South Tournament
March	1-2	###Big South Tournament

@Road Games
*Rogers AT&T NCAA Basketball Showcasse in Halifax, Nova Scotia
#Hartford, CT (vs. Niagara first round; also Hartford, Central Connecticut)
##Rock Hill, SC (vs. Tennessee-Martin first round; also West Virginia State, South Carolina State)
###Roanoke Civic Center, Roanoke, VA

BLUE RIBBON ANALYSIS

BACKCOURT	A
BENCH/DEPTH	A-
FRONTCOURT	B
INTANGIBLES	B

Any other coach in the Big South would kill for Marshall's kind of problems. The three-time defending champs' biggest concern could be that they're too deep. There may not be enough playing time for a veteran corps of players, including seven players in their fourth or fifth year of college basketball.

Of course injuries may already be eating away at some of that depth. Moore may not be ready for preseason and all-conference selection Stewart and starting center Effiong are still battling back. Marshall still doesn't know what to expect from Lewis and there's a real log jam at two guard.

Marshall's track record indicates he'll push the right buttons and have the Eagles soaring again. He's certainly got a motivational tool—playing time.

"Whoever's out there will be going 100 percent," Marshall said. "If not, they'll be sitting beside me. The bench is a great motivator. If we're healthy, we'll have the most depth and possibly the most talent we've had."

(M.A.)

Michigan

LOCATION	Ann Arbor, MI
CONFERENCE	Big Ten
LAST SEASON	10-18 (.357)
CONFERENCE RECORD	4-12 (10th)
STARTERS LOST/RETURNING	1/4
NICKNAME	Wolverines
COLORS	Maize & Blue
HOMECOURT	Crisler Arena (13,562)
COACH	Tommy Amaker (Duke '87)
RECORD AT SCHOOL	First year
CAREER RECORD	68-55 (4 years)
ASSISTANTS	Charles Ramsey (Eastern Mich. '92)
	Chuck Swensen (Indiana '76)
	Billy Schmidt (Wake Forest '92)
TEAM WINS (last 5 years)	24-25-12-15-10
RPI (last 5 years)	22-10-80-79-131
2000-01 FINISH	Lost in conference first round.

Quick. Who won the first Big Ten Tournament in 1998?

Michigan State? Purdue? Illinois?

No, Michigan.

Somehow, that was only three years ago. It was also Brian Ellerbe's first season at the helm of the Wolverines. You'll recall Brian Ellerbe, who took over when Steve Fisher resigned just weeks before the season and steered a Robert Traylor/Louis Bullock-led club to a 25-9 record. Ellerbe's teams subsequently slipped to 12-19 in 1998-99, 15-14 in 2000 and 10-18 last season. After a long year of rumors, Ellerbe was fired March 14.

"I did not see the improvement in the program over the past four years that I hoped for and that I believe is possible," Michigan athletic director Bill Martin said at the time.

So what led to the Wolverines' downfall? Scandal, for one thing. The cloud of a federal investigation into banned booster Ed Martin's gambling ring and alleged connection to UM players has hung over the program for nearly three years.

Second, competition. Michigan State's Tom Izzo has built a mini-dynasty in East Lansing, and UM no longer enjoys a monopoly on the state's talent like it did in the Fab Five days of the early '90s.

Finally, and most directly, came a slew of defections. Jamal Crawford and Kevin Gaines, Ellerbe's talented freshman guard duo in 1999-00, would have been juniors this year. But Crawford, who missed half that season because of various NCAA violations, was gone to the Chicago Bulls by that summer. Gaines was dismissed last fall for repeated run-ins with the law.

Whether Ellerbe could have avoided any of this is open to debate, but in college sports, when there needs to be a scapegoat, it's usually the coach. The school saw its basketball program slipping from the status it enjoyed in the Fab Five era, when the Chris Webber-led Wolverines played in consecutive national championship games. A change was in order—and not a small one, either.

The first name on Martin's list was Rick Pitino, only the most sought-after coaching candidate in the country after his mid-season exit from the Boston Celtics. But neither party got particularly serious. Pitino, who was moonlighting as an NCAA Tournament analyst for CBS at the time, had already visited the school he would end up choosing, Louisville. And the glitzy coach's seven-figure asking price would force Michigan to pay its basketball coach more than its football coach, Lloyd Carr—not likely at a school with impeccable football tradition and a 110,000-seat stadium.

But the man Martin would turn to was himself a hot commodity. The 36-year-old Tommy Amaker had wasted no time making his mark during four years at Seton Hall, his first head-coaching stop. In the summer of 1999, the former Duke star and top assistant under Mike Krzyzewski convinced the nation's top recruit, Eddie Griffin, and two other prep standouts to play college ball in New Jersey. And in the year between their recruitment and their arrival, Amaker took a young Pirate team to the Sweet 16, earning the Hall acclaim as one of the nation's rising programs.

Things didn't go as planned when Griffin and Co. got to town last year. A lack of chemistry and some noted off-court troubles, including a post-game locker room brawl between Griffin and a teammate, doomed the Pirates to

BIG TEN

BLUE RIBBON FORECAST

1) Illinois
2) Iowa
3) Ohio State
4) Indiana
5) Michigan State
6) Purdue
7) Minnesota
8) Michigan
9) Penn State
10) Wisconsin
11) Northwestern

TOP 40

Illinois, Indiana, Iowa, Michigan State, Ohio State and Purdue are ranked among the 2001-2002 Blue Ribbon Top 40. Extended profiles can be found in the Top 40 section of Blue Ribbon.

ALL-CONFERENCE TEAM

G – Luke Recker, SR, Iowa
G – Frank Williams, JR, Illinois
F – Jared Jeffries, JR, Indiana
F – Reggie Evans, SR, Iowa
F – LaVell Blanchard, JR, Michigan

PLAYER OF THE YEAR

Frank Williams, JR, Illinois

NEWCOMER OF THE YEAR

Kelvin Torbert, FR, Michigan State

2001-2002 CONFERENCE TOURNAMENT

March 7-10, Conseco Fieldhouse, Indianapolis, IN

2000-2001 CHAMPIONS

Michigan State, Illinois (co-regular season)
Iowa (conference tournament)

2000-2001 POSTSEASON PARTICIPANTS

Postseason Record: 13-9 (.591)
NCAA
Michigan State (Final Four)
Illinois (Elite Eight)
Penn State (Sweet 16)
Iowa (Second Round)
Ohio State
Indiana
Wisconsin
NIT
Purdue (Quarterfinals)
Minnesota (Second Round)

TOP BACKCOURTS

1. Illinois
2. Ohio State
3. Michigan State

TOP FRONTCOURTS

1. Iowa
2. Illinois
3. Minnesota

INSIDE THE NUMBERS

2000-01 conference RPI: 1st (out of 31)
Conference RPI (last five years): 3-3-1-2-1

DID YOU KNOW?

The Big Ten placed seven players among the 50 pre-season candidates for the Wooden Award: Recker, Williams, Jeffries, Evans, Blanchard, Illinois' Brian Cook and Michigan State's Marcus Taylor. ... Michigan State's Jason Richardson was picked fifth overall by the Golden State Warriors in June's NBA draft, the third time in four years the Big Ten has had at least one top 10 selection. ... New Wisconsin coach Bo Ryan won four Division III national titles and notched a 314-37 record (.895) at Wisconsin-Platteville from 1984-99. He spent the last two seasons at Division I UW-Milwaukee. ... Purdue coach Gene Keady, entering his 22nd season, is the only league coach who predates 1995. ... The Big Ten Tournament moves to Indianapolis this season after conducting its first four tournaments at Chicago's United Center. Its four-day average attendance in 2001 (21,954) trailed only the 48-year-old ACC Tournament. ... The Big Ten was 116-40 (.744) in non-conference play last season, including 15-15 against ranked foes. ... The league's three 2001 NCAA Tournament Sweet 16 teams (Michigan State, Penn State, Illinois) trailed only the Pac-10's four.

(S.M.)

a disappointing 16-15 year. But it didn't seem to reduce the buzz around Amaker, who turned down several overtures before accepting Michigan's reported $700,000-a season offer on March 29.

His mission is clear: Restore the Maize and Blue to the level expected of a program with 20 NCAA Tournament appearances.

"I think everyone wants to see us regain our credibility and regain our place among the nation's elite programs," Amaker said. "We want that obviously, that's what we're striving to do. I think it's absolutely essential that all our people be on board with us and not wait to see how we're going to do it, but to help us do it."

Michigan's recruiting didn't exactly fall off under Ellerbe. Crawford and Gaines were both highly regarded prospects, as are several members of the current roster. But the talent is not at the level of Big Ten rivals Michigan State and Illinois. And it's nowhere near that of Ellerbe predecessor Steve Fisher, who as an assistant in the late '80s helped recruit players such as Glen Rice and Rumeal Robinson, and in eight years as head coach brought in the likes of Webber, Jalen Rose, Juwan Howard and Maurice Taylor.

"We want to identify and target the kids we feel are going to understand and embrace what it means to be at Michigan," Amaker said. "What it means to represent Michigan and what it means to wear the Michigan uniform."

Amaker inherits a squad with 13 returning lettermen and three talented freshmen, but the attrition problem didn't immediately recede upon his arrival.

First to go was backup point guard Maurice Searight, who was already in Ellerbe's doghouse for missing practices and whom Amaker dismissed in May. Then recruits Kelly Whitney and JaQuan Hart failed to qualify academically.

Still, some talent remains. The only starter from last year to graduate is center Josh Asselin, Michigan's third-leading scorer (9.6 points per game) and second-leading rebounder (6.0). The onus of replacing him falls squarely on the massive shoulders of 7-2 sophomore **Josh Moore**, a former Rutgers and UCLA recruit who landed in Ann Arbor last season after a year away from school and basketball.

Moore averaged only 12 minutes and 4.4 points as a freshman, shooting an impressive 54.6 percent from the field and showing flashes of his considerable potential. But he also wasn't the defensive force expected of someone his size, and staying out of foul trouble could be a real issue with increased minutes.

"Josh being the size that he is, and the fact that we don't have many big guys on our roster, becomes a very important player for us," Amaker said. "He's coming off a year where I'm sure he was fairly disappointed in his pro-

duction, but he came off a year prior to that where he sat out a whole year. I think he was working his way back, feeling his way back into things."

The unquestioned star of the Wolverines is 6-7 junior forward **LaVell Blanchard**, a second team All-Big Ten pick last season when he averaged 17.6 points and 7.9 rebounds, both team highs. Blanchard runs the floor and shoots like a small forward but can also post up and bang under the boards with taller power forwards.

The Ann Arbor native joined the Wolverines in 1999 at the same time rival state prep star Jason Richardson arrived at Michigan State. While Richardson was an All-American last year, played in two Final Fours and was the fifth pick in this year's NBA draft, Blanchard's college tenure has been far less glamorous.

"I think he's a very talented player, a local kid, and I think a lot has probably been placed on his shoulders to kind of revitalize our program," Amaker said. "Sometimes that's a lot to ask of a young kid, but I admire how he's handled some things, how well he's played."

Besides Blanchard, Michigan's most impressive performer last year was 6-6 swingman **Bernard Robinson Jr.**, a sophomore who averaged 14.4 points and shot 80.2 percent from the free-throw line. Robinson runs the floor well and serves as the closest thing to a defensive stopper on this team, leading the club with 33 steals last year.

"I think a lot of times when kids come in as freshmen and they have a very good initial year, I think sometimes, subconsciously, they don't realize how much harder it's going to be the next year," said Amaker. "I've talked to Bernard about that, about how much more difficult it's going to be for him as a sophomore, and how much more work he's going to have to put in."

Robinson could either team with Blanchard in a small frontcourt, or move to the backcourt in favor of 6-9 senior captain **Chris Young** (8.6 ppg, 4.9 rpg). After two years in part-time duty, Young started every game as a junior, shooting 64 percent.

Freshman **Chuck Bailey**, a 6-7 all-state forward from Detroit's Martin Luther King High School, will be counted on to provide some much-needed depth up front.

The pint-sized (5-7) **Avery Queen** beat out Searight to become the Wolverines' starting point guard as a freshman last season. Queen compensates for his lack of height with quickness and ball-handling ability, averaging 4.3 assists and a nearly 2-to-1 assist-to-turnover ratio a year ago. In Michigan's 95-85 upset of No. 24 Iowa on Valentine's Day, Queen broke out with 18 points to go with four assists.

Other veterans in the backcourt are 6-5 junior **Gavin Groninger** (5.6 ppg) and 6-4 senior Leon Jones (2.7), but the guy to watch is incoming freshman **Dommanic Ingerson**. The 6-4 Santa Barbara, Calif., native was rated the No. 3 senior guard by recruiting analyst Brick Oettinger.

"Dommanic Ingerson is a very talented young man, a very talented offensive player," Amaker said. "We're going to certainly need his capabilities within this season to provide some much-needed help in the backcourt, where we are potentially not as strong as we like to be."

With the loss of both Hart and Kelly Whitney, a Chicago big man who signed with the Wolverines but will instead attend prep school, Amaker added Detroit Renaissance High School guard **Marcus Bennett** to the class on July 18. Bennett was a first-team Class B all-state pick by the Detroit News and Detroit Free-Press after averaging 23.0 points and 7.0 rebounds as a senior.

2001-2002 SCHEDULE

Nov.	16	Oakland
	20	Fairfield
	23	@Western Michigan
	28	@Bowling Green
Dec.	1	Boston College
	4	IUPU-Fort Wayne
	8	*Duke
	22	Eastern Michigan
	29	**San Francisco
Jan.	2	@Penn State
	5	Purdue
	9	@Minnesota
	12	@Illinois
	16	Northwestern
	19	Minnesota
	24	@Ohio State
	26	Vermont
	30	@Michigan State

Feb.	2	Wisconsin
	7	Illinois
	9	Penn State
	11	@Colorado State
	13	@Purdue
	17	Indiana
	23	@Iowa
	27	@Wisconsin
March	2/3	Ohio State
	7-10	#Big Ten Tournament

@Road Games
*Big Ten/ACC Challenge
**Oakland, CA
#Conseco Fieldhouse, Indianapolis, IN

BLUE RIBBON ANALYSIS

BACKCOURT	C+
BENCH/DEPTH	C-
FRONTCOURT	B
INTANGIBLES	B+

There's an aura of freshness surrounding the Wolverines, with the perpetual lame duck Ellerbe finally put out of his misery and the genial Amaker on board. Despite all the criticism, Ellerbe managed to recruit fairly well, even if not all the star recruits are still there. The ones who are, mainly Blanchard, Robinson and Ingerson, are unquestioned talents well worth building around.

The Wolverines were often competitive last year—though rarely away from home. Their confidence was shattered early on by an 82-51 defeat to Maryland in Washington D.C. and a 104-61 embarrassment against No. 1 Duke at Cameron. Amaker could really use a win early on over a high-profile opponent to set a tone for the new regime.

The Wolverines are undersized and lack proven scorers beyond Blanchard and Robinson. But there's plenty of quickness and athleticism to go around. If players like Moore and Queen develop, and the team buys into Amaker's system, a return to the postseason—most likely the NIT, though possibly the NCAAs—is probable.

(S.M.)

Minnesota

LOCATION	Minneapolis, MN
CONFERENCE	Big Ten
LAST SEASON	18-14 (.563)
CONFERENCE RECORD	5-11 (9th)
STARTERS LOST/RETURNING	2/3
NICKNAME	Golden Gophers
COLORS	Maroon & Gold
HOMECOURT	Williams Arena (14,625)
COACH	Dan Monson (Idaho '85)
RECORD AT SCHOOL	30-30 (2 years)
CAREER RECORD	82-47 (4 years)
ASSISTANTS	Mike Peterson (Northwest Chr. '83)
	Art Prevost (Lamar '90)
	Bill Walker (Missouri-Rolla '87)
TEAM WINS (last 5 years)	18-21-19-17-13
RPI (last 5 years)	142-63-146-148-257
2000-01 FINISH	Lost in NIT second round.

The winters can get pretty cold in the upper Midwest, and for years the heat generated by wild nights at Williams Arena has helped get Golden Gopher fans through those frozen months.

The last few years have not been as kind to the Gophers, who were rocked by the academic scandal that resulted in the dismissal of former head coach Clem Haskins in 1999. Just two years after the proudest moment in the program's history—the Big Ten title-winning 1997 squad reaching the Final Four—all that glory was washed away in a sea of shame.

But new head coach Dan Monson has reason to believe that the hardest days are over, and the sun is about to shine on his program again. Monson, who came to Dinkytown from Gonzaga to replace Haskins, has his most talented group in three years at Minnesota, and once a few new faces gain some experience, he thinks he's got a team that will return the sizzle to the elevated court at Williams Arena.

"We're very talented, but it's young talent, and that's

a big difference," said Monson, who took the Gophers to the NIT last year after spending his first season on NCAA probation. "When I got here, we had a number of pretty good, experienced players. The image of our program was down, the national perception was that we were down ... but last year, for example, we were 15-3 before the injuries hit us.

"We've got some players with some ability this year and the attitude around here is different than it's been in my time here."

Landing a blue-chip recruit will do wonders to that attitude, and the Gophers did just that when they signed 6-10 forward Rick Rickert of Duluth (Minn.) East High School. Rickert—a consensus national Top 20 player—was possibly the hottest recruit in the state's history and has a chance to be the best player Minnesota has developed since Kevin McHale.

Rickert averaged 25.7 points, 11.6 rebounds and 6.9 blocks a game in taking his high school team to the state big-school final as a senior, and he earned All-America honors from McDonald's, Parade and Gatorade. He won Minnesota's Mr. Basketball award and was a finalist for the Naismith Award, given to the best prep player in the nation.

But Rickert didn't just waltz down I-35 and hand Monson his letter of intent. He originally committed to Arizona, but his parents refused to sign the letter without further discussing Minnesota. Eventually the young Rickert relented, and Monson couldn't be happier.

"Rick is a very special player," Monson said. "He really fits into the way we like to play. His versatility will be a big strength for us—he can play inside against smaller players, and he can take bigger players outside. He only lacks on-court experience, and it's just a matter of how long it takes him to make the adjustment. With some kids it takes two weeks, two months, two years ... but as hard as he works and with his basketball IQ, I think it will happen quickly."

The other newcomer who will have a major impact on the team this year is junior Jerry Holman, a 6-10 banger who transferred from Minneapolis Community and Technical College. Holman was a junior college All-American last year when he averaged 19.5 points, 11.3 boards and 6.3 blocks.

"Holman adds a dimension we haven't had since I've been here," Monson said. "He's an inside presence who can block shots and run the floor as well as any big man I've ever coached. And as a juco transfer, I think his transition period will be a little less difficult than for a high school player."

Monson has also brought in a pair of freshman guards who will try to replace some of the zip provided by the departed Terrance Simmons (14.3 points, 2.9 assists as a senior). Maurice Hargrow is a 6-4 slasher who should see time at the two- and three-spots and will help out on the defensive side of the ball.

Aaron Robinson—a 5-8 freshman from Rockford, Ill.—is the only true point guard in the program. Monson compared Robinson to his former Gonzaga point guard Quentin Hall, another sub-six-footer who made a big name for himself in the Bulldogs' recent NCAA runs.

"Aaron gives us that point guard you look to who can change the tempo of the game, immediately speed it up, but he's also a good shooter and at 5-8 he can really pressure teams on both ends of the court," Monson said.

This rapid-fire accounting of the newcomers isn't to suggest the Gophers will be relying solely on new faces to carry the season. Monson has got a solid group returning, including seven letter winners and three players who started throughout last season. Leading the way is the consummate lunch-pail kid, 6-7 senior forward Dusty Rychart (14.6 ppg, 7.7 rpg last year). Rychart came to Minnesota as a walk-on, but as a red-shirt freshman he opened his future coach's eyes when he scored 23 and grabbed 17 boards in a first-round NCAA loss to Monson's Gonzaga squad. Despite the lack of a NBA-caliber body, jumper or vertical leap, Rychart continues to be an indispensable player.

"You look at him, and you just marvel at how he's produced," Monson said. "And that's how you have to measure him too—by his production. He just gets the job done. He's the kind of blue collar player every coach wants in their program."

Another forward with a chance to drop some jaws around the Big Ten is sophomore Michael Bauer (11.4 ppg, 4.8 rpg, 1.5 bpg). Last year the 6-8 Bauer started 13 games at small forward but his season ended early with a broken forearm in a Jan. 27 loss to Purdue. Bauer received a medical red-shirt in 2000 after suffering a severely sprained ankle early in the season.

If Bauer can stay healthy, he will be a key component in the Gopher offense this season. He's a bit like Rickert in that he's got the size to get to the basket, but the touch to play on the perimeter. And as Monson says, he's the kind of player whose enthusiasm is infectious.

"He's got the will to win, and that gravitates to the other players," Monson said. "He's fearless and he doesn't look back at the injuries. With his added strength and maturity he's got a better chance to stay healthy, and when he is healthy we're a much better team."

A pleasant surprise last year was the play of senior Travarus Bennett (5.4 ppg, 4.2 rpg). The 6-7 forward stepped in when senior co-captain J.B. Bickerstaff broke his leg at Northwestern on Feb. 6 and immediately started making an impact, including 16 points and 11 boards in that game, and a season-high 18 in his next game at Michigan.

"He's the best defender on the team," Monson said, "and you've got to manufacture minutes for a player like that. This year we'll get him minutes at both forward positions and at off-guard."

Sophomore Steve Esselink could be something of an X-factor this year. The 6-6 forward sat out last year after transferring from Augustana (S.D.) College, and Monson says he will challenge for time at the two- and three-spots.

"He's an integral part of what we're going to do this year," Monson said. "He's an athletic player who can score points in bunches."

The other front-liner who could see some playing time this season is 6-11 sophomore Jeff Hagen (1.9 ppg, 1.2 rpg). Because of scholarship limitations, the Gophers were thin at the post last year, and the freshman was forced into action. This year Monson would like to be able to red-shirt Hagen and let him gain some needed experience, but he might not have the luxury to do that.

Three guards from last year's team will join the two freshmen in the backcourt mix. Junior Shane Schilling (8.4 ppg, 2.8 rpg) is a 6-6 swingman who started 31-of-32 games at the two-guard last year. He ranked in the top 15 in the Big Ten in three-point percentage (.388) and played for the Big Ten all-stars in their summer tour of Ireland and the U.K.

Kevin Burleson (6.3 ppg, 1.7 rpg, 2.3 apg) is a 6-3 junior who shared the team's point-guard duties last year. He has played both guard positions, although Monson had him concentrating on the point in the offseason.

"He has added strength and the point guard mentality and skills and we hope he will solidify that position," Monson said. "He'll also play some off-guard—we're relying very heavily on Kevin with the departure of Simmons."

Kerwin Fleming (6.8 ppg, 1.5 rpg, 1.0 apg) is a 6-3 senior who came to Minnesota last year out of Kennedy-King Junior College in Chicago. Fleming is an explosive player who dropped 31 on Purdue in the Big Ten Tournament—just two points shy of the tourney single-game scoring record—and he's yet another Gopher who will compete for time at both guard spots.

Monson said he's glad to see that fans and his own players are starting to put the academic scandal behind them and are looking forward to starting over.

"The people in this state love Gopher basketball, and everybody's excited about the newness of this team," he said. "They're all ready for the past to be over with and the present to begin. I think this is the first team to have it totally behind them."

2001-2002 SCHEDULE

Nov.	17	Mercer
	21	UNC Asheville
	24	Eastern Washington
	27	*Wake Forest
Dec.	1	Texas Pan-American
	4	UNC Wilmington
	7	@Georgia
	10	Oregon
	13	Maryland-Eastern Shore
	22	Nebraska
	30	@Texas Tech
Jan.	2	@Illinois
	5	Michigan State
	9	Michigan
	12	@Purdue
	16	@Wisconsin
	19	@Michigan
	26	Ohio State

	30	Penn State
Feb.	2	Indiana
	9	@Iowa
	13	@Northwestern
	16	Wisconsin
	21	@Michigan State
	23	@Penn State
	27	Northwestern
March	2/3	Illinois
	7-10	#Big Ten Tournament

@Road Games
*ACC/Big Ten Challenge
#Conseco Fieldhouse, Indianapolis, IN

BLUE RIBBON ANALYSIS

BACKCOURT	C
BENCH/DEPTH	B+
FRONTCOURT	B-
INTANGIBLES	A-

This could be a true coming-out year for the Golden Gophers. What they lack in experience they more than make up for in potential. Their guards are nothing exciting, but if they can limit the turnovers and get the ball consistently to players like Rickert, Bauer, Rychart and Holman, good things will happen.

Monson is one of the most respected young coaches in the game. He demands toughness, loyalty and commitment from his players on the court and in the classroom—in other words, he was the perfect man to walk into the hornet's nest that was Williams Arena after the Haskins scandal.

And landing a blue-chipper like Rickert was a real coup for Monson. If his staff continues to have that kind of recruiting success, the lean years will soon be long forgotten in Gold Country. In fact, don't be surprised if an NCAA berth this year helps wipe away the bitterness of the academic scandal once and for all.

(P.D.)

 # Northwestern

LOCATION	Evanston, IL
CONFERENCE	Big Ten
LAST SEASON	11-19 (.367)
CONFERENCE RECORD	3-13 (11th)
STARTERS LOST/RETURNING	1/4
NICKNAME	Wildcats
COLORS	Purple & White
HOMECOURT	Welsh-Ryan Arena (8,117)
COACH	Bill Carmody (Union College '75)
RECORD AT SCHOOL	11-19 (1 year)
CAREER RECORD	103-44 (5 years)
ASSISTANTS	Paul Lee (Columbia '86)
	Craig Robinson (Princeton '83)
	Mitch Henderson (Princeton '98)
TEAM WINS (last 5 years)	7-10-15-5-11
RPI (last 5 years)	204-188-83-244-133
2000-01 FINISH	Lost in conference first round.

When Northwestern hired Princeton's Bill Carmody to take over its dilapidated basketball program on Sept. 6, 2000, speculation immediately arose as to how an Ivy League guy would fare in the Big Ten.

Would he try to implement the infamous Princeton offense, with its back-door cuts and perceived slow-down tactics? Would his players all carry 1,500 SAT scores and read Tolstoy on the bench? Did he realize the Big Ten was filled with roaming behemoths just waiting to crush his little Ivy League schoolboys into pieces?

Apparently, observers spent far more time analyzing the situation than the coach himself, who describes his philosophy toward basketball thusly: "We basically put four guys around the center and tell them, 'The first open shot you get, put it in.'

"People talk about [the Big Ten] being more physical or what not, I just still think it's basketball," Carmody said. "People talk about all these different offenses, but at the end of all these offenses, it really comes down to if the guy gets open, he's got to put it in."

Indeed, Carmody's biggest adjustment at his new school wasn't the level of competition. It was the losing. In four years as head coach at Princeton, Carmody went 92-25 with four postseason appearances; his 1998 club

was 27-2 and reached the second round of the NCAA Tournament. This after 14 years as an assistant under Pete Carrill, whose teams every powerhouse in the country dreaded playing in March.

Northwestern, on the other hand, has never even reached the NCAA Tournament. Three NIT appearances, in 1982, '94 and '99, represent its sole basketball highlights. One after another, coaches arrived in Evanston with visions of becoming the one who finally brightens the program's miserable history. None have lasted long enough to see that day, with Carmody's immediate predecessor, Kevin O'Neill, high-tailing it out of town just six weeks before the start of practice for an assistant's job with the New York Knicks.

In retrospect, Carmody is far better suited for academic-minded Northwestern than the high-strung, foul-mouthed O'Neill, who ditched the Wildcats just three years after doing the same to Tennessee. Despite plenty of evidence to the contrary, Carmody believes good grades and a good jump shot can co-exist in major college basketball. And while no one expects Northwestern to reach the same level of success on the court as places like Duke and North Carolina, Carmody would like the program to share at least one common trait: an identity.

"I was a college coach, and even I didn't know what Northwestern stood for really," said Carmody. "That's what I'm trying to instill."

The last couple years, Northwestern has stood mostly for being extremely young, undersized and barely competitive. Though still on the wrong end of too many blowouts last year, the Wildcats did show significant improvement from O'Neill's 5-25 farewell tour.

The players took well to Carmody's more disciplined system, improving their turnover margin from minus-23 the year before to plus-83 and finishing fourth nationally with an assist-to-field goal ratio of .680. In December, they upset a 16th-ranked USC team that would later reach the NCAA Elite Eight, 63-61. On Feb. 10, they beat Iowa, 69-61, to snap an astounding 32-game Big Ten losing streak, and would later knock off Penn State, 62-61, and Michigan, 75-70—the latter their first road win in more than two years.

In addition to being by far the smallest team in the Big Ten—with only two players taller than 6-5—the Wildcats were also officially the youngest team in the country, with freshmen and sophomores playing 84.9 percent of the minutes (down from 99.9 percent in '99-'00). Amazingly, this season will mark NU's first in three years with any seniors (two).

One of those is 6-8 forward/center **Tavaras Hardy** (10.7 ppg, 5.7 rpg), NU's most experienced player after having started 84-of 89 career games. Though he is the team's leading rebounder and closest thing to an inside presence, Carmody would like to see Hardy rely more on his jumper.

"All we did all spring was work on that guy's shooting," Carmody said. "He's always been the big man going back to high school. But when we worked out, it was astounding to me how quickly he started making shots."

Hardy got to put his newfound shooting prowess to the test playing for the Big Ten foreign tour team this summer, and the results were good. He was the squad's third-leading scorer (12.3 ppg), shooting .409 from three-point range (9-of-22).

"Tavaras is a natural shooter," said Carmody. "I just wish we had a center right now that allowed him be a forward."

The only true center on NU's roster is 6-11 junior **Aaron Jennings** (5.4 ppg, 2.4 rpg), who started 13 games as a freshman but couldn't crack the lineup last year despite the Wildcats' desperate need for size. He played only 15 minutes a game, shooting a miserable 40.9 percent from the field.

"We need him to play more and do more, but at times last year it was better not to have him out there," Carmody said. "There's got to be a fire burning him in a little bit. Of course, it's pretty hard to change a guy's personality."

Carmody's quest for some new frontcourt bodies took on drastic proportions this summer. And that meant some serious frequent flier miles. After failing to sign any recruits during the school year—the staff's late arrival last September put them behind the eight ball from the start—Carmody decided to go international.

The first addition was lanky 6-10, 215-pound **Thomas Soltau** of Denmark, who visited NU in June and committed after his first choice, St. Joseph's, rescinded his scholarship offer after another signee

unexpectedly qualified. (Players cannot sign letters of intent after the spring signing period and cannot join the roster officially until enrolling in late September).

In July, Carmody found himself in Split, Croatia—hometown of Toni Kukoc and Goran Ivanesivic—acting on a tip about a couple undiscovered gems. He indeed came away impressed by 6-7 **Vedran Vukusic** and 6-8 **Davor Duvancic**, both of whom visited the NU campus in early August and also committed.

All are essentially mysteries but presumably fit the mold of European big men who run the floor like guards, a la Kukoc, Dirk Nowitzki and this year's draft sensation, 7-1 "small" forward Pau Gasol.

"I don't know who we sent over there 40 years ago to teach them to play, but whoever it was taught them fundamentals," Carmody said. "They can dribble the ball, pass the ball, can take long shots. Their bodies don't look as great, but with just a little weight training, they'll come on."

Finding enough bodies may always be a problem for NU. As far back as the early '90s, when star Rex Walters departed for Kansas, the program has been constantly rocked by attrition. In the spring before Carmody's arrival, four players—most notably current Wake Forest guard Steve Lepore—escaped O'Neill's sinking ship.

This year, it was starting guard Ben Johnson (10.7 ppg) departing for hometown Minnesota. Johnson was tied for second on the team in scoring as a sophomore but was also a poor defender who never really jived with the new coach. While NU's frontcourt wouldn't be able to survive losing someone like Johnson, the backcourt is in relatively good shape.

Carmody calls 6-2 senior **Collier Drayton** (5.4 ppg, 3.7 rpg) the team's undisputed leader. He's hardly a scorer—Drayton is a .394 percent career shooter—but the two-year starter led the team with 101 assists in 30 games and ranked fourth in the Big Ten with 1.6 steals per game. This despite a rather glaring hindrance.

"It's kind of amazing, he's blind in one eye, and he's out there running your team," Carmody said. "He's not a good shooter, but he runs the team, tells people what do. He's a coach on floor kind of guy ... He's worked hard on his shooting, and I hope we see some improvement there."

Junior **Winston Blake** (11.9 ppg, 3.2 rpg) is coming off a remarkable sophomore season in which he led the team in scoring while improving his shooting dramatically, from .298 to .383 on field goals and from .258 to .376 on three-pointers. The 6-5 Blake, who had played less than 15 minutes a game as a freshman, started all 30 games a year ago. His 221 three-point shots set a school record.

"As soon as I saw him, the first day, I knew this guy was going to be a pretty good player," Carmody said. "I'm just surprised he didn't have a better freshman year. He's kind of a suburban jump-shooter right now; he's got to expand his game, drive to the basket more."

In terms of raw talent, the Wildcats' best player may be 6-2 sophomore **Jitim Young** (8.8 ppg, 3.8 rpg). The only Chicago native on NU's roster, Young started all 30 games as a freshman and finished fifth in the Big Ten in steals (1.57 per game). He struggled with his shot, though, hitting only 20-of-83 treys (.233)

"Jitim is chomping at the bit, he really worked hard this summer," said Carmody. "He knows he's good at getting around his man, but in college, you get there and find out it doesn't always pay off. Sometimes you have to pull up."

Off the bench, 6-7 junior **Jason Burke** (3.0 ppg, 1.5 rpg) can play either forward or guard. And Carmody says sophomores **Ed McCants** (4.1 ppg, 2.1 rpg), 6-5, and **Drew Long** (0.8 ppg) may be the team's best shooters. The 6-2 Long played in only six games as a freshman before breaking his foot.

2001-2002 SCHEDULE

Nov.	14-16	#BCA Classic
	24	Chicago State
	28	Florida State
Dec.	8	Kansas State
	15	Florida A&M
	17	Liberty
	22	*Fordham
	28-29	##ASU/az central.com Holiday Classic
Jan.	2	Indiana
	9	@Iowa
	12	Ohio State
	16	@Michigan

	19	Iowa
	23	@Purdue
	26	@Buffalo
	30	Wisconsin
Feb.	2	@Ohio State
	6	Michigan State
	9	@Wisconsin
	13	Minnesota
	16	@Penn State
	20	Purdue
	23	Illinois
	27	@Minnesota
March	2	@Indiana
	7-10	###Big Ten Tournament

@Road Games
*Madison Square Garden, New York
#Raleigh, NC (vs. Virginia Commonwealth first round; also East Carolina, Fairleigh Dickinson, North Carolina State, Prairie View A&M, Rutgers, San Jose State)
##Tempe, AZ (vs. Canisius, first round; also Louisiana-Lafayette, Northwestern)
###Conseco Fieldhouse, Indianapolis, IN

BLUE RIBBON ANALYSIS

BACKCOURT	C+
BENCH/DEPTH	C-
FRONTCOURT	D+
INTANGIBLES	B-

In year two of the Northwestern's Ivy League experiment, the 'Cats should inch closer toward respectability. How much better depends quite literally on some big unknowns—three, in fact, hailing from Denmark and Croatia.

Carmody's system, when executed well, should in itself be good. NU can create turnovers, even against the Big Ten's best, and has some decent shooters in Blake and Hardy who can be dangerous when hot. With a year of experience behind him, Young should be much better.

But the 'Cats won't move above the bottom rung of the league without some size, which means either Jennings drastically improving or at least one or two among the trio of Soltau, Vukusic and Duvancic panning out. Even then, it's doubtful their bodies will be developed enough to pound inside.

"We just want to be competitive, don't want to have any more of those games where after 10 minutes you're down 14," Carmody said. "You're in the game with five minutes to go if you're still within six or so. But if you're down 18 at the half, like we were a few times last year, that's when you know you need players."

(S.M.)

Penn State

LOCATION	State College, PA
CONFERENCE	Big Ten
LAST SEASON	21-12 (.636)
CONFERENCE RECORD	7-9 (6th)
STARTERS LOST/RETURNING	4/1
NICKNAME	Nittany Lions
COLORS	Blue & White
HOMECOURT	Bryce Jordan Center (15,261)
COACH	Jerry Dunn (George Mason '80)
RECORD AT SCHOOL	103-79 (6 years)
CAREER RECORD	103-79 (6 years)
ASSISTANTS	Christian Appleman (Penn State '90)
	Mike Boyd (Northern Michigan '70)
	Rick Callahan (Salem '80)
TEAM WINS (last 5 years)	10-19-13-19-21
RPI (last 5 years)	133-83-87-54-21
2000-01 FINISH	Lost in NCAA Sweet 16.

At some schools, a season that ends in the NCAA Sweet 16 is hardly something to shout about. For a select few—Duke, North Carolina, Kentucky, etc.—it could even be considered a disappointment.

But at Penn State, where just such a thing occurred last season, a Sweet 16 trip is a big deal. Big enough to cause school icon Joe Paterno to declare it, "One of the memorable highlights of our athletic program in my 51 years here."

Happy Valley didn't earn its nickname based on being a basketball school. It has been Paterno's football teams to quite literally put the central Pennsylvania school on the map and define its athletic image. Last March was perhaps the first time since before Paterno's ascension that the basketball team took center stage in State College.

"The football program is much-deserving of their high status," senior guard Titus Ivory said. "They've won national championships. They've been in the spotlight for a number of years, so no, we haven't felt intimidated by any of that. And now that we're putting our name on the map, we're much deserving."

For PSU to continue putting itself on the map, it will need to cash in on last year's success during recruiting. The Sweet 16 team, like most Nittany Lion squads before it, banked on leadership and teamwork to compensate for a lack of athleticism. Few true blue-chip prospects tend to look at the school for basketball. And the trend continued with Penn State's top target for 2002. Gerry McNamara, a 6-1 point guard from Scranton, Pa., generally considered among the nation's top 30 players, ended up choosing Syracuse over the Nittany Lions.

But McNamara may have been too far along in his recruitment to be swayed by the memory of PSU's March run. That might not be the case much longer.

That the Nittany Lions would accomplish anything remotely resembling their second-round upset of second seeded North Carolina—a team that stood No. 1 in the country only a month earlier—seemed unimaginable much of the season. Penn State was, by all indications, an average team, one that went 7-9 in Big Ten play, lost to Northwestern and could have missed the NCAAs altogether if not for Gyasi Cline-Heard's last-second reverse layup to stave off 10-18 Michigan in the first round of the Big Ten Tournament.

PSU entered that game "on the bubble" at 17-10, and wouldn't solidify its tournament status for sure until the following night's 65-63 quarterfinal upset of Michigan State. On the court in the moments immediately afterward, a triumphant Cline-Heard carried the Nittany Lion mascot on his shoulders, while normally reserved head coach Jerry Dunn raising his arms in victory and hugged family members

His jubilation centered around more than just the one win. Dunn had coached the entire season in the final year of his contract, the subject of constant rumors and speculation. Most observers agreed that anything less than an NCAA berth—the school's first since 1996—would cost the sixth-year coach his job. In recent years, Penn State had become recurring visitors to the second-tier NIT and couldn't seem to get over the hump. It often played before half-of-capacity crowds at the sparkling 15,621-seat Bryce Jordan Center.

But after his team's deepest postseason run in 46 years (ending in an 84-72 loss to Temple in the South Regional in Atlanta), Dunn's job is more than a little safe.

"I guess maybe I became a genius overnight," Dunn said at his season-ending news conference. "But I think that's the nature of the business.

"I've spent my whole life trying to prove myself. I always believed I was a good coach and worked hard every day. I think it's flattering to hear other teams and people speak of you in terms of other programs, but like I've said all along, this stems from winning and that's nice to hear."

After being mentioned as a candidate for jobs at South Carolina, George Washington and Rutgers, the fastest coach to both 50 and 100 wins in PSU history signed a five-year contract on May 10, albeit after prolonged negotiations. That security will come in handy this year, because chances of a return trip to the Sweet 16 seem awfully slim.

Penn State is essentially starting over, having lost star guard Joe Crispin (19.5 ppg), his brother and fellow starter Jon Crispin (7.2 ppg)—who transferred to UCLA—starting point guard Titus Ivory (15.8 ppg) and dominating power forward Cline-Heard (16.0 ppg, 8.2 rpg).

Another player who probably would have started this season, 6-10 sophomore Marcus Banta (1.7 ppg, 1.8 rpg), flunked out of school in the spring. He had improved throughout the season, grabbing five rebounds in 10 minutes of action against the Tar Heels.

What's left to carry on the 2000-01 team's legacy? One senior starter, five underclassmen of limited experience and four freshmen.

"I certainly don't want to put any pressure on our players," Dunn said. "The pressure I keep in myself is to continually get better. I understand what pieces of the puzzle are needed to surpass past accomplishments as well as what we will have to acquire."

The lone returning starter is 6-8 senior forward/center Tyler Smith (7.6 ppg, 4.5 rpg). Though he will be counted on to fill much of the void left in the post by Cline-Heard, he is also a decent shooter who shot 51.4 percent from the field and 38.9 percent from three-point range.

"Tyler has to be able to direct and guide on the floor, that is very important, and I think he is very capable of doing that," Dunn said.

Junior B.J. Vossekuil (1.0 ppg, 0.8 rpg) is a 6-9 forward who can also play multiple positions. He will probably be used more as a wing player. Vossekuil appeared in 23 games, averaging only one point and one rebound, but Dunn insists "he's capable of being one of our better offensive performers and rebounders."

Also factoring into the picture in the frontcourt are 6-7 sophomore Ndu Egekese (1.4 ppg, 0.7 rpg)—whose slight minutes increased over the course of last season—and a pair of freshmen. Six-foot-seven Darren Tielsch, a Pennsylvania prep star last season, and 6-9 Jason McDougald, who won two small-school state titles at Reynolds High in Lewisville, N.C., will get a chance to play right away.

The wildcards in the equation are 6-11 Jan Jagla and 6-10 Kevin Fellows, Dunn's other two freshmen. Jagla hails from Germany, where he started for a team that won the world Under-20 championship. Fellows brings an impressive 245-pound frame but played his high school ball in not-exactly-loaded-with-talent Idaho, where he was state player of the year.

The most experienced guard is 6-0 junior Brandon Watkins (3.2 ppg), the main backup to Joe Crispin the last two seasons. Watkins notched 37 assists and shot 42.9 percent on three-pointers, playing 12 minutes a game. His most impressive figure: eight assists and only one turnover in the three NCAA Tournament games. Watkins also scored a career-high 12 points in the finale against Temple.

"Brandon Watkins has the ability to take his game to another level, run this basketball team successfully and make the players around him better," Dunn said.

Likely to join Watkins in the backcourt is 6-5 sophomore Jamaal Tate (2.4 ppg, 1.2 rpg), who played in all 33 games as a freshman, starting two. He saw significant minutes in Penn State's postseason games, notching a season-best 12 points in the Big Ten Tournament win over Michigan.

"I think his playing time last year, particularly down the stretch, was very important to both his confidence, as well as the confidence of his teammates in his ability at crunch time," Dunn said. "He became a guy who made big plays at very critical times in key games."

The Nittany Lions will need Tate to provide help at guard, but he is big enough to play wing forward and should be able to grab rebounds.

How shallow is Penn State at guard? The only other scholarship player at the position is 6-1 sophomore Sharif Chambliss (1.3 ppg), though he can play at either spot. Dunn expects him to provide speed and energy off the bench.

2001-2002 SCHEDULE

Nov.	18	Yale
	21	Lafayette
	24	@Boston College
	28	*Clemson
Dec.	1	@Temple
	5	Lehigh
	8	@Pittsburgh
	19	James Madison
	22	Bucknell
	28-29	#Golden Bear Classic
Jan.	2	Michigan
	5	@Indiana
	9	Wisconsin
	16	@Ohio State
	19	Michigan State
	23	Indiana
	26	@Wisconsin
	30	@Minnesota
Feb.	2	@Iowa
	6	Purdue
	9	@Michigan
	13	Iowa
	16	Northwestern
	20	@Illinois
	23	Minnesota
	2	@Purdue
March	7-10	##Big Ten Tournament

@Road Games
*Big Ten/ACC Challenge
#Berkeley, CA (vs. Coppin State first round; also California, Harvard)
##Conseco Fieldhouse, Indianapolis, IN

BLUE RIBBON ANALYSIS

BACKCOURT	C
BENCH/DEPTH	D
FRONTCOURT	B
INTANGIBLES	B

With all the enthusiasm generated in Happy Valley by the basketball team's unlikely breakthrough in 2001, it's a shame most of the players who contributed to it have moved on. Any dividends the Sweet 16 trip might pay in recruiting won't show up for another year, and in the meantime, this season's overly young squad may go through the kind of struggles that can kill momentum in a hurry.

Penn State's non-conference schedule isn't particularly daunting, aside from a Thanksgiving weekend trip to Big East champion Boston College and a road rematch against Temple. But the Big Ten isn't getting any weaker, and the schedule includes a three-game road swing in late January/early February to Wisconsin, Minnesota and Iowa.

A return to the NIT would be disturbingly familiar territory for Dunn's Lions. But it also wouldn't be that bad an accomplishment for a rebuilding club.

"I would think Brandon Watkins, Jammal Tate, Ndu Egekeze and some of the other guys will step up and take on [bigger] roles," he said. "We have a nice group of guys here and I think we'll be fine."

(S.M.)

Wisconsin

LOCATION	Madison, WI
CONFERENCE	Big Ten
LAST SEASON	18-11 (.621)
CONFERENCE RECORD	9-7 (5th)
STARTERS LOST/RETURNING	4/1
NICKNAME	Badgers
COLORS	Cardinal & White
HOMECOURT	Kohl Center (17,142)
COACH	Bo Ryan (Wilkes College '69)
RECORD AT SCHOOL	First year
CAREER RECORD	383-103 (17 years)
ASSISTANTS	Rob Jeter (Wisconsin-Platteville '91)
	Tony Bennett (Wisconsin-Green Bay '92)
	Greg Gard (Wisconsin-Platteville '95)
TEAM WINS (last 5 years)	18-21-19-17-13
RPI (last 5 years)	142-63-1466-148-257
2000-01 FINISH	Lost in NCAA first round.

Like most basketball coaches, Wisconsin's first-year coach Bo Ryan has plenty of people giving him advice. But the one tip he hopes to remember throughout his rookie year at Wisconsin is the one given him by the woman he married.

"My biggest challenge this year is to heed my wife's advice," said Ryan, who comes to Madison after a 15-year run at UW-Platteville and two years at UW-Milwaukee. "She reminded me the other day, 'Patience isn't your strongest suit.' And it's true—I've got to remember that we've got a ways to go. I've got to keep reminding myself to stay patient, and a couple of years down the road we've got a chance to get some things done. But I think with our experience and schedule, it's going to be a challenge this year."

Indeed, the deck appears to be stacked against the Badgers, who lost five of their top six players to graduation, another to a transfer, and return only five letter winners from last year's fifth-place team in the Big Ten.

Gone are forwards Andy Kowske, Mark Vershaw and Maurice Linton, and guards Roy Boone, Mike Kelley and Ricky Bower (a sophomore who transferred to Brigham Young). That represents 73 percent of the Badgers' scoring and 68 percent of their rebounds from last season, along with 80 percent of their steals and 75 percent of their assists.

And that's a pretty big hole to fill.

"When you lose a lot of seniors you lose game experience," Ryan said. "Not just on-court experience, but how many guys have been to Indiana and been there when the ball is tipped? Or Michigan, or Purdue, or Iowa? Then when you factor in a new coach with a little bit of a different system, it makes for an interesting challenge."

Ryan is going to attack the season with only 11 scholarship players, holding back two grants until next year when he's gotten to know his players better and assessed the team's needs. Consider that four of the scholarship players are freshman who weren't in camp this spring, and it made for a lot of "Hello, my name is . . ." name tags this summer in Madison.

Not that Ryan is a stranger to transitions. After winning four Division III national titles at Platteville, he took over a UW-Milwaukee program that had never had back-to-back winning seasons. But in his two years there the Panthers went 15-14 and 15-13 and he caught the eye of the Wisconsin brass with a sparkling résumé that includes a career .788 winning percentage.

Ryan is replacing Dick Bennett, a legend in Wisconsin who stepped down early last season, a victim of stress and burnout. But this is Ryan's second tour of duty in Madison—he was an assistant under Bill Cofield and Steve Yoder from 1976-84. And he's got Bennett's son, Tony, on his staff to further ease the transition.

On the court, the lone holdover from last year's starting lineup is junior **Kirk Penney** (11.2 ppg, 3.0 rpg, 1.1 apg). The 6-5 guard is one of the top shooters in the conference—he's already cracked the top 10 in the school's career three-pointer list, and he led the Big Ten with a .478 percentage from behind the arc in conference games last year. He played for his native New Zealand in the 2000 Olympic Games, becoming the first basketball Olympian in school history.

"He works extra hard away from the ball," said Ryan of the key to Penney's success. "He's got a good feel for reading screens. He's going to do more from inside 15 feet this year—he's got to get more physical and step away from being a one-dimensional player. That will make him tougher to guard. He's bigger and thicker this year, and he'll get to the free-throw line more often."

Joining Penney in the backcourt could be point guard **Travon Davis** (2.2 ppg, 1.6 rpg, 1.3 apg). The 5-10 senior missed the start of last year because of the NCAA violation that struck throughout the Badger athletic program—a number of athletes received discounted shoes and apparel at a local retailer. Davis came back with a solid conference season as the backup point guard, compiling a 2.63-to-1 assist-to-turnover ratio in Big Ten games, and he enters the season as the leading candidate to succeed Kelley at the point.

"We hope Travon is ready," Ryan said. "Some new coaches wouldn't even play a senior at the point—they'd rather groom their own guy there. But if he's ready and performs the way we'd like to see him perform, he'll get a lot of minutes." Davis excels in the Wisconsin-style pressure defense, so if he improves his offensive performance, he's the most likely man for the point.

His main competition will be freshman **Devin Harris**, a 6-3 guard from Milwaukee's Wauwatosa East High School. He has played the point in high school and AAU ball and flew under the national radar because he was injured much of the summer before his senior year and didn't attend the usual round of national camps and tournaments.

"He's wiry and has good court instincts," Ryan said of his freshman point guard. "The only way for him to improve now is to get him some experience, to get him some scars out there on the floor."

Others in the backcourt mix are 6-3 freshman **Latrell Fleming** and 6-5 freshman **Neil Plank**, players Ryan says are hungry, eager and looking to settle into the right position for his system. **Freddie Owens**, a 6-2 sophomore, is a returning letterman at guard as well.

On the front line, 6-8 senior **Charlie Wills** (4.2 ppg, 3.0 rpg, 0.7 apg) returns with 29 games of starting experience in his career. He's a fifth-year senior who hasn't missed a game in his career, and his toughness will be needed on this young squad.

"He's really responded this spring in stepping up and being a leader on this team," Ryan said. "He had a good summer on the [Big Ten all-star] tour, and he's got a good feel for the game. He's very active, he loves playing the game and he brings an enthusiasm to the court that I like. He typifies that old coaching adage—you want your best players to be your hardest workers."

In the middle, look for 6-11 junior **Dave Mader** (1.1 ppg, 1.6 rpg) to earn some key minutes this year. Ryan said his staff is working with Mader to improve his later-al movement, but he's hungry and worked hard in the off-season on perfecting some of his post moves.

Freshman **Andreas Helmigk**, a 6-10 Austrian who enters the program this year, could battle for time on the front line. **Mike Wilkinson**, a 6-8 red-shirt freshman, and 6-6 sophomore **Julian Swartz** are also in the mix.

While Ryan knows he's got to remain focused on the big picture, he's not worried about pressure from boosters to win immediately.

"It's amazing—the people around here keep asking me, 'What kind of smoke and mirrors are you going to use to win this year?' They are intelligent fans here, and they know there's a learning curve with these young players."

And as for his bosses, the Badger athletic administration? "They've got faith in me that I've got the foresight to build a winning program, I think because I'm a guy who's done it at different levels," Ryan said. "You know, anybody who's ever hired me for a nickel, I give 'em a dime."

2001-2002 SCHEDULE

Nov.	17	@UNLV
	23-25	#Big Island Invitational
	28	@Georgia Tech
Dec.	1	Wisconsin-Green Bay
	3	Temple
	8	@Ohio
	10	@Xavier
	15	Furman
	22	Marquette
	27	@Wisconsin-Milwaukee
	29	Tennessee
Jan.	2	@Iowa
	5	Illinois
	9	@Penn State
	12	@Michigan State
	16	Minnesota
	19	Purdue
	23	@Illinois
	26	Penn State
	30	@Northwestern
Feb.	2	@Michigan
	6	Ohio State
	9	Northwestern
	13	@Indiana
	16	@Minnesota
	19	Iowa
	27	Michigan
March	7-10	##Big Ten Tournament

@Road Games
#Hilo, HI (vs. Hawaii-Hilo first round; also Colorado State, Hawaii, LSU, Mercer, South Carolina State, Weber State)
##Conseco Fieldhouse, Indianapolis, IN

BLUE RIBBON ANALYSIS

BACKCOURT	C
BENCH/DEPTH	D
FRONTCOURT	D
INTANGIBLES	C+

Ryan has his work cut out for him in his first year at Madison. While he's got some potentially strong guards, there's not much raw material up front for him to work with right now. With such a short-handed team, the Badgers will take their lumps this year.

However, enthusiasm should not be a problem, as Ryan is an energetic, upbeat motivator. He'll keep the Badgers playing their trademark scrappy defense, and being the consummate coaches' coach, you can bet that Dick Bennett fans won't even miss a beat.

Oh, they'll miss going to the NCAA Tournament once again, especially after getting pounded by a brutal non-conference schedule that includes UNLV, Georgia Tech, Temple, Tennessee and Xavier. But in the long run—when Ryan has more players and his players have more experience—the Badgers will be just fine, thank you.

(P.D.)

BIG 12

BIG 12 CONFERENCE

BLUE RIBBON FORECAST

1. Missouri
2. Kansas
3. Oklahoma
4. Oklahoma State
5. Texas
6. Iowa State
7. Colorado
8. Texas A&M
9. Baylor
10. Kansas State
11. Texas Tech
12. Nebraska

TOP 40

Kansas, Missouri, Oklahoma, Oklahoma State and Texas are ranked among the 2001-2002 Blue Ribbon Top 40. Extended profiles can be found in the Top 40 section of Blue Ribbon.

ALL-CONFERENCE TEAM

G-Maurice Baker, SR, Oklahoma State
G-Kareem Rush, JR, Missouri
F-Nick Collison, JR, Kansas
F-Drew Gooden, JR, Kansas
C-Chris Owens, SR, Texas

PLAYER OF THE YEAR

Kareem Rush, JR, Missouri

NEWCOMER OF THE YEAR

David Harrison, FR, Colorado

2001-2002 CONFERENCE TOURNAMENT

March 7-10, Kemper Arena, Kansas City, MO

2000-2001 CHAMPIONS

Iowa State (Regular season)
Oklahoma (Conference Tournament)

2000-2001 POSTSEASON PARTICIPANTS

Postseason record: 3-7 (.300)
NCAA
Kansas (Sweet 16)
Missouri (Second round)
Iowa State
Oklahoma
Oklahoma State
Texas

NIT
Baylor

TOP BACKCOURTS

1. Oklahoma State
2. Missouri
3. Kansas

TOP FRONTCOURTS

1. Kansas
2. Texas
3. Missouri

INSIDE THE NUMBERS

2000-2001 Conference RPI: 6th (of 31)
Conference RPI (last five years): 2-6-7-5-6

DID YOU KNOW?

The Big 12 Tournament will leave Kansas City after this season's event. It will be played at the American Airlines Arena in Dallas (the women at Reunion Arena) for the 2003 and 2004 season. After that, another year at Kemper Arena, then the bidding is expected to be wide open. By then, arenas less than five years old will exist in Dallas, San Antonio, Oklahoma City, Denver, St. Louis and Omaha. Just about every significant Big 12 city except Kansas City. ... Baylor coach Dave Bliss' 498 career victories would put him at the top of just about any conference. He's third in the Big 12 behind Tech's Bob Knight (763) and Oklahoma State's Eddie Sutton (697). ... Iowa State's 57 victories over the last two years rank third in Division I behind Duke (64) and Michigan State (60). Only the Spartans' 44-game home floor winning streak is longer than the Cyclones' 36. ... Kansas has won at least 20 games in 12 straight seasons. Roy Williams' first team went 19-12 and was not eligible for the NCAA Tournament because of probation. ... Kansas State's streak of not having a losing record at home is 55 years. The Wildcats haven't been to the NCAA Tournament in five years, matching the school's longest drought. ... Plans for a new $75 million basketball arena at Missouri are moving forward. The university received the OK for state funding in the spring. Tough to beat the Hearnes Center, though. The Tigers have won five straight home games against top 10 teams. ... Nebraska guard Cary Cochran has made at least one three-pointer in 23 straight games. ... Kelvin Sampson hasn't missed the NCAA Tournament as Oklahoma's coach. He's seven for seven. ... No Big 12 school has advanced to the Final Four. Oklahoma State's trip in 1995 was the last by a current member of the conference. ... Nebraska has the longest championship drought of a league school—51 years. ... By two years, Roy Williams is the dean of the Big 12 coaches. He's beginning his 14th season. ... When Bob Knight replaced James Dickey, that left Williams, Sutton, Kelvin Sampson and Colorado's Ricardo Patton as holdovers from the league's inaugural season, 1996-97. ... For the fifth straight year, the Big 12 player of the year will not return. Jamaal Tinsley was a senior at Iowa State. He follows former teammate Marcus Fizer, Nebraska's Venson Hamilton, Kansas' Raef LaFrentz and Jacque Vaughn who made their best seasons their last.

(B.K.)

Baylor

LOCATION	Waco, TX
CONFERENCE	Big 12
LAST SEASON	19-12 (.612)
CONFERENCE RECORD	6-10 (8th)
STARTERS LOST/RETURNING	2/3
NICKNAME	Bears
COLORS	Green & Gold
HOMECOURT	Ferrell Center (10,284)
COACH	Dave Bliss (Cornell '65)
RECORD AT SCHOOL	33-27 (2 years)
CAREER RECORD	498-298 (26 years)
ASSISTANTS	Doug Ash (Hanover College '71)
	Kevin Lewis (SMU '86)
	Brian O'Neill (Eastern New Mexico '88)
TEAM WINS (last 5 years)	18-14-6-14-19
RPI (last 5 years)	93-99-254-133-101
2000-01 FINISH	Lost in NIT first round.

With a degree in marketing and an MBA from Cornell, Dave Bliss knows something about product names. Sometimes, the name is as important as the product. A Snickers bar would taste the same, but would you buy one if it was called a Nickers bar?

That said, it's worthwhile to understand that the 26-year head-coaching veteran has a name that is a headline writer's dream. However, it is more important that his product, coaching basketball, has been successful. No need to headline stories "A State Of Bliss" when the team is winning eight games a season.

In stops at Oklahoma, SMU and New Mexico, the results have been, well, Bliss-ful.

With the Sooners, the Mustangs and the Lobos, Bliss won conference championships. He made hoops important in Norman, setting the stage for a successful run by Billy Tubbs. He took a woebegone SMU program and built it into a Southwest Conference factor. At New Mexico, he took a program that was already in good shape and made it better.

While his beloved New York Yankees know how to win the World Series, Bliss' mission statement his simple: He knows how to coach.

When Bliss left Albuquerque for Waco in the spring of 1999, it wasn't a move to just simplify the spelling of his home address. Bliss though he had one more career move remaining. After coaching at SMU—and recruiting well in Texas while at New Mexico—Bliss felt he was familiar with Baylor's program and the surrounding area. And never mind that the program he was commandeering was at the bottom of the Big 12 Conference.

In two seasons, Bliss has served notice that the Bears no longer belong in the basement. After a 14-15 inaugural season, Year Two saw Baylor roar to a 12-0 record (OK, so it was a Charmin-soft schedule) and finish a respectable 19-12 that included a trip to the NIT—the Bears' first postseason experience in 11 years.

Two victories were especially significant. On Feb. 12, Baylor played in its first Big Monday ESPN game. Mighty Kansas was the opponent, and the home-standing Bears roared to a 25-point first half lead and hung on for an 85-77 victory. Then, in the Big 12 Conference Tournament, Baylor proved the upset of the Jayhawks was no fluke. The Bears, after winning their first-round game in overtime, stunned seventh-ranked Iowa State, 62-49. The loss probably knocked the Cyclones out of a No. 1 seeding in the NCAA Tournament.

Bliss knows the next step is probably the toughest. Baylor is on the cusp of evolving into a solid Big 12 team, a team that could be in the running for an NCAA bid each season. But for Bliss to win another conference championship at his fourth coaching stop? Well, in a league that includes Kansas, Iowa State, Missouri Oklahoma, Oklahoma State and Texas, the line forms to the rear. The Bears are headed for a bit of a transition season.

Two of the main factors in last season's success were the play of seniors Terry Black and DeMarcus Minor. Black, a swooping forward, averaged 15.4 points and 8.4 rebounds in gaining first-team all-conference acclaim. Minor, a steady guard, averaged 15.2 points and 4.6 rebounds and was a second-team all-league selection.

"We've got to take the next step by committee," said Bliss, who needs just two victories to reach the .500 level and should record that milestone when Baylor plays host to Texas-Arlington on Nov. 21.

"In all the years that we've coached, this might be the most competition for positions of any team we've had," Bliss said. "I think the competition for positions will affect how we play, because with greater depth we can increase the tempo, knowing that fatigue isn't necessarily a factor. And fatigue is a great way to substitute.

"Last year one of the things the team did is play very hard and what we want to do is get back to playing hard with that depth and hopefully the style of play will allow that."

A solid recruiting class, the eligibility of two transfers from New Mexico who sat out last season and the return of six players who saw significant playing time should give Bliss a deep roster for game substitutions and provide plenty of playing time competition in practice.

"Whereas the talent has improved," Bliss said, "I also believe that the experience that we had [in two-year starters Black and Minor] will be sorely missed until we get some games under our belt. At which time again I think we should be able to make some strides and really be a better team at the end of this season than we've been thus far."

The top returning players are 6-2 junior guard **Wendell Greenleaf** (27.4 mpg, 10.5 ppg, .366 FG, .286 3PT, .607 FT, 58 steals) and 6-9 senior forward/center **Greg Davis** (32.4 mpg, 9.2 ppg, .531 FG, .310 3PT, .618 FT, 6.1 rpg, 38 blocks, 36 steals).

Greenleaf, who started 30 games at the shooting guard spot last season, is an active player. He was fifth in the Big 12 in steals. The opportunity for playing time is there, but Greenleaf needs to be a more reliable performer.

"Wendell played sporadically last year," Bliss said. "He needs to work on his consistency, not only in his decision-making, but in his shooting and his defense. But he has the strength and competitive zeal that we're looking for with our program."

Davis, who played his first season in Waco last season after sitting out a year after his transfer from New

Mexico, had to log a number of minutes at center. This season, he should be able to return to his more natural power-forward position.

"Greg played some of his best basketball down the stretch last season," Bliss said. "There is no doubt that he will play more comfortable at his 'four' spot. As a defensive player and a rebounder we think Greg is very important to the way we play."

The top candidate to take over for Minor at point guard is 6-3 sophomore **Matt Sayman** (4.9 ppg, .410 FG, .377 3PT, .837 FT). Last season, he played in all 31 games as a freshman. However, he logged most of his 17 minutes per game at shooting guard. Sayman will have to make the transition back to point guard, a position he hasn't played since early in his career at The Colony (Texas) High School.

Sayman had a 1.77 assists-to-turnover ratio last season. Also, he worked hard in the off-season to increase his quickness by dropping 15 pounds. He expects to play at about 180 this season.

"His quickness I think will improve dramatically," Bliss said. "We also think that the smart plays that Matt made throughout his freshman year will allow him to really be a good point guard."

Another candidate at the point is 5-10 freshman **John Lucas III**, who averaged 30.3 points and 11 assists per game at Houston's Bellaire High School. If he plays anything like his father—current Cleveland Cavaliers coach and former NBA guard John Lucas—the Bears should be set at the point-guard position.

Six-foot junior **Andre White** (1.3 mpg, 1.0 ppg), a walk-on, is also available for backup point-guard duties.

No matter who is running the offense, Bliss wants him to keep the pedal to the metal.

"Offensively we really want to quicken the pace," Bliss said. "By the end of the year last year by having DeMarcus [Minor] go as fast as he could I thought that really afforded us a much more aggressive offense."

While Greenleaf is the incumbent at shooting guard, he had best watch his back. **Kevin Henry**, a 6-2 senior, and 6-3 freshman **Kenny Taylor** both are capable of grabbing plenty of playing time.

Henry sat out last season after transferring from New Mexico. Bliss hopes he can boost Baylor's three-point shooting, which was a dismal 29 percent last season (and, hard to believe, a drop from the below average 32.4 percent of the previous season). Playing for the Lobos, White started 66 games. He made 197 three-pointers, including a school-record 102 as a sophomore under Bliss in 1998-99.

"I think his ability to understand our system having run it before should allow him a lot of playing time," Bliss said. "We're hoping that the year off has helped his strength and not diminished his skills."

Taylor played on back-to-back state championship teams at Houston's Willowridge High School.

When Bliss wants to increase the size of his backcourt, he can call on 6-6 senior **Chad Elsey** (17.3 mpg, 6.8 ppg, .321 FG, .259 3PT, .742 FT, 1.9 rpg). Elsey, though, is expected to see most of his playing time at small forward. His ability to shoot from the outside, however, gives Bliss another lineup option.

Bliss has high hopes for his frontcourt. He envisions Davis at power forward with 6-10 sophomore **R.T. Guinn** at center and 6-8 freshman **Lawrence Roberts** at small forward. Guinn (4.6 points, 4.8 rebounds, 13 games started in 1999-2000) sat out last season after transferring from (where else?) New Mexico.

"At his height, R.T. is an amazing outside shooter," Bliss said. "I think his scoring really improved during his red-shirt year. I think he'll be the type of player that very definitely will fit into our way of trying to distort defenses by having big people that are able to shoot outside. I look for him to be a strong rebounder."

Roberts, who was rated as the fifth-best high school prospect in the state by TexasHoops, is capable of playing either forward spot. He's got the power game and rebounding to play power forward and the outside shot and finesse game to handle small forward.

"Lawrence has worked very hard on his game," Bliss said. "And he has a chance to compete for a starting role. I think he'll be one of the players that has a chance to really be a surprise player in the Big 12 as a freshman."

In addition to Elsey, minutes at the small-forward spot could go to 6-6 junior-college transfer **Rod Nealy**, who averaged 19 points and eight rebounds at McLennan (Texas) Community College. As a freshman in 1999-2000, he played in 22 games at Arkansas-Little Rock before transferring. He is a rebounder who is somewhat

reminiscent of Black's playing style.

With Davis able to play some center, Bliss has a versatile front line. Also, Bliss has another option in the middle with 6-10 junior **Steven Othero** (12.5 mpg, 4.9 ppg, 3.4 rpg, .681 FG, .531 FT). He missed nine games because of injuries, but when he became a starter late in the season, he averaged 5.4 points and 5.4 rebounds over the last 10 games.

"Steven may have been one of the surprise players last year for us," Bliss said. "Steven has done a good job of learning and developing over the last year and a half. He has rebounded very well, played defense very well and only promises to get better."

Kind of like the Baylor program under Bliss.

2001-2002 SCHEDULE

Nov.	17	Hardin-Simmons
	21	Texas-Arlington
	24	Sacred Heart
	27	SMU
	29	Cal State Fullerton
Dec.	1	@Rice
	8	North Texas
	17	Centenary
	20-22	#San Juan Shootout
	29	@TCU
Jan.	2	Colorado State
	5	Iowa State
	8	Oklahoma State
	12	@Texas
	16	Kansas State
	19	@Texas A&M
	26	Texas
	30	@Colorado
Feb.	3	Texas A&M
	6	@Oklahoma
	9	Missouri
	12	@Texas Tech
	16	@Kansas
	19	Oklahoma
	23	@Oklahoma State
	27	@Nebraska
March	2	Texas Tech
	7-10	##Big 12 Tournament

@Road Games
#San Juan, PR (vs. Puerto Rico Mayaguez; also Coppin State, Florida International, Jacksonville, Niagara, Oral Roberts, Texas Pan American)
##Kemper Arena, Kansas City, MO

BLUE RIBBON ANALYSIS

BACKCOURT	B+
BENCH/DEPTH	B
FRONTCOURT	B
INTANGIBLES	B+

With this roster, Bliss is closing in on the style of team he wants—quick, athletic players who can make things happen on offense and who have the versatility to befuddle defenses. This team would be very intriguing if the steady Minor was around for one more season of running the team.

"This year we are probably working with better overall basketball talent than in the past couple of years because we've recruited better and better each year," Bliss said.

Baylor's 2001 recruiting class was rated 25th nationally by Rivals100Hoops.com and No. 32 in the nation by HoopScoop. The Sporting News rated Baylor's class as the third best in the Big 12.

Despite the improvements, Baylor will be hard-pressed for a first-division Big 12 finish. Kansas, Missouri, Oklahoma, Oklahoma State and Texas all figure to be Top 25 caliber teams. And one never wants to count out Iowa State.

The Bears, though, have proven they are capable of competitive play. The year before Bliss arrived, that wasn't the case (a winless league season). Sayman will have to prove he's a full-time point guard and Roberts will need to prove he's an impact player.

The non-conference schedule, which Bliss says is tougher, doesn't provide much RPI juice. To reach the NCAA Tournament for the first time since 1988, Baylor will need a nearly perfect non-conference run plus a break-even or better Big 12 record.

(W.B.)

Colorado

LOCATION	Boulder, CO
CONFERENCE	Big 12
LAST SEASON	15-15 (.500)
CONFERENCE RECORD	5-11 (9th)
STARTERS LOST/RETURNING	2/3
NICKNAME	Buffaloes
COLORS	Black & Gold
HOMECOURT	Coors Events Center (11,076)
COACH	Ricardo Patton (Belmont '80)
RECORD AT SCHOOL	90-77 (5 years)
CAREER RECORD	90-77 (5 years)
ASSISTANTS	Terry Dunn (Northern Colorado '77)
	Larry Gay (Florida State '73)
	James Shelton (David Lipscomb '91)
TEAM WINS (last 5 years)	22-13-18-18-15
RPI (last 5 years)	39-120-80-84-109
2000-01 FINISH	Lost in conference first round.

There is no denying it. Colorado took a step back last season. Coming off a pair of 18-victory seasons, the Buffs looked to make a push toward the league's upper half and earn their first NCAA Tournament berth since 1997. Or at least land in the NIT for the third straight year.

"At this point of the year, this is the best I've felt," coach Ricardo Patton said last November.

After a December of inspired ball, postseason seemed like a foregone conclusion. Not that the Buffs had beaten anybody you would likely see deep into March, but a couple of quality victories gave hope entering Big 12 play.

The way they were playing was also inspiring. The Buffs were running, make that sprinting, to victories. They topped 100 points four times before Christmas and were leading the nation in scoring. The most satisfying victory came over state rival Colorado State. The Rams had defeated Colorado in nine straight events like football, volleyball, women's basketball—stuff that only a rival would rub in.

After the Buffs demolished Colorado State, 109-86, Patton added gas to the fire by declaring the victory was personal because he claimed the Rams had tampered with one of Colorado's recruits.

Patton also made some noise later in the month when he griped about the Buffs' paltry crowds. Colorado had just lost at California before 9.300 and the Buffs weren't getting more than 3,000 at home games. Patton's point was the program had improved to a point—and now were playing a running style—where more than a few students should wander in.

The concern, of course, was recruiting. How could Colorado expect to land top prospects when they look around and see 8,000 empty seats?

It all made for an interesting non-conference portion of the schedule. Unfortunately for Colorado, the Big 12 season started. The Buffs expected to continue their winning ways in the opener at Baylor. But they played like they were stuck in mud, losing 61-56. The game seemed to set the tone for the rest of the season.

Colorado got to 5-6 in the league, still in the hunt for an upper division finish, or, with Nebraska and Kansas State visiting, at least two more victories to match the Big 12 record of the previous two seasons. But the Buffs didn't get those. They lost the final five games and fell again to Baylor in the first round of the league tournament. The six-game losing streak was the longest in the Patton era.

It turned out, the team probably wasn't as well equipped to run as Patton originally thought. He added a couple of shooters, but Colorado finished in the middle of the pack in field-goal percentage and three-point percentage. Also, he didn't seem to have from his players the commitment to defense needed to make things work.

Colorado heads into this season without one of the better players to pass through the program lately, power forward Jamahl Mosley, who has graduated, and last season's top assist man, Jose Winston. The Buffs got hardly any offense from Winston, and he announced he was transferring after the season.

But enough talent returns to believe Colorado will be better this season. Not a force. But better.

It starts with the Harrison brothers. Senior small forward **D.J. Harrison** transferred from Aquinas Junior College in Tennessee and made an immediate impact by scoring 38 points against Austin Peay in the second game of the season. For a while, Harrison was leading the league in scoring.

The 6-7 Harrison joined the program two years earlier and sat out the 1999-2000 season to improve his outside game. Patton, who coached a Big 12 all-star team during a tour of Europe, selected Harrison to the squad. He entered the season not as inexperienced as he might have been.

But while Harrison led Colorado in scoring at 15.1, and he shot a solid 39-percent on three-pointers, both figures dipped in league play. Harrison didn't make more than half his shots in any Big 12 game. He hit for 20 or more points in four of 14 non-league games and only twice in the league.

A year of Division I experience should help Harrison. So should the presence of younger brother **David Harrison**, the Buffaloes' prize recruit. David Harrison is a 7-0, 240-pound center who picked Colorado over Duke, North Carolina and Vanderbilt. He's the program's most heralded recruit since Chauncey Billups.

David Harrison averaged 28.5 points, 13.1 rebounds and 5.6 blocks for Brentwood Academy in Nashville. He made the All-America teams of McDonald's and Parade Magazine. One recruiting analyst rate Harrison as the top freshman center in nation after Eddie Curry, Tyson Chandler and Dasagana Diop went pro.

All of a sudden, Colorado has a player who can score in the middle and be a potential force on defense. It also gives the Buffs a front line that eventually can match up with any in the Big 12.

"He should give us a bigger athletic presence in the middle," Patton said of the younger Harrison. "He is a true center."

Patton hopes Harrison could have an impact off the floor as well.

"Any time you're able to recruit at a high level against some of the best competition in the country, I think it speaks volumes for your program," Patton too CNN/Sports Illustrated.com. "What it says to a lot of kids across the country is, 'Hey, if a kid as highly regarded as David Harrison can go to the University of Colorado, boy, maybe I ought to take a look.' I think that's the effect it will have."

The signing of Harrison was a real coup for Colorado. Harrison's father, Dennis, is an assistant football coach at Vanderbilt. Commodore coach Kevin Stallings had recruited the younger Harrison heavily, and most people in Nashville assumed he'd pick his hometown school. As it turned out, family ties did help Harrison make his college choice.

"In the end, playing with D.J., even for one year, was the overriding factor," Harrison said when he announced his decision to sign with Colorado.

Playing next to Harrison will be 6-9 junior forward **Stephane Pelle** (11.3 ppg, 7.5 rpg), the team's leading rebounder and one of the Big 12's most improved players. Pelle started the second half of the season averaging 13.8 points in the final 12 games. He logged 26 points and 17 boards in a loss to Nebraska.

Patton went for size in recruiting and added 6-9 forward **Jason Carter** from Bishop Gorman in Las Vegas. Carter averaged 14 points and nine rebounds a year ago. Another newcomer, **Amadou Doumbouya**, a 6-9 native of West Africa, averaged six points and six rebounds for Eastern Oklahoma State Junior College last season.

Winston was the starting point guard, but late in the season Patton went with 5-11 rookie **Chevis Brimmer** in the final minutes of close games. Brimmer responded with three of his four double-digit games in the last three games. Brimmer didn't hesitate to shoot, but his percentages (31.4 on all shots, 25.6 behind the arc) hurt the Buffs.

Brimmer won't get the job without a battle. Enter **Mookie Wright**, a 6-2 junior from Compton (Calif.) Junior College, the same school that produced recent Colorado star Jaquay Walls. Wright averaged 17 points and seven assists and picked Colorado over Iowa State, Minnesota and Southern Cal. He was a Top 50 high school player out of Manual Arts/Los Angeles three years ago.

"James is a point guard with a lot of game experience," Pataton said. "He is as quick as any guard I've seen in the open court and gives us a second left-hander on the squad."

Nick Mohr (8.7 ppg, 2.1 rpg), a 6-5 senior shooting guard, is the team's most experienced player. He has started 32-of-72 games and his improved his outside shooting each season, peaking at 37.6 percent last season.

All other wing candidates are good shooters with other specialties. **Blair Wilson** (4.4 ppg, 1.8 rpg) started four games as a freshman and goes to the boards well. He led the Buffs in free-throw shooting at 81 percent.

Michel Morandais (5.1 ppg, 2.9 rpg) started three games and hit 41 percent from behind the three-point line. The 6-6 sophomore is also a slasher who often gets to the free-throw line.

Justin Harbert (6.7 ppg, 1.3 rpg) got worn down as the season progressed. He made 30-of-54 three-pointers in non-league games and one of his final 14 over the final nine regular season games and Colorado's season unraveled. The 6-1 sophomore finished as the team's top scorer off the bench.

2001-2002 SCHEDULE

Nov.	17	Arkansas-Pine Bluff
	19	Regis
	22	Rice
	25	@St. Joseph's
Dec.	1	@Georgia
	5	@Colorado State
	10	Montana
	12	Southern
	30	Wisconsin-Milwaukee
Jan.	2	St. Mary's
	5	Kansas
	9	Morris Brown
	12	@Nebraska
	16	Iowa State
	19	@Missouri
	22	Kansas State
	26	@Oklahoma State
	30	Baylor
Feb.	2	@Kansas
	5	Nebraska
	9	@Texas
	13	@Iowa State
	16	Texas Tech
	20	@Kansas State
	23	Missouri
	26	@Texas A&M
March	2	Oklahoma
	7-10	##Big 12 Tournament

@Road Games
#Kemper Arena, Kansas City, MO

BLUE RIBBON ANALYSIS

BACKCOURT	C
BENCH/DEPTH	C
FRONTCOURT	B+
INTANGIBLES	C

Every year we say Colorado is ready to take the next step, and we've only been right once in the last four years. We're going for two-for-five.

The addition of David Harrison is huge. Not just his size, but Colorado's ability to land a prize recruit should do wonders for future recruiting.

Sure, the Buffs had an advantage with older brother D.J., but the younger Harrison turned down much bigger names to make a name for himself in Boulder.

The other plus could be Wright. Colorado gets a cat-quick point guard who not only gets the ball in the shooters' hands but is willing to score a few himself. The competition between Wright and Brimmer should make both better.

So, does Patton turn the Buffs loose like last year? He should craft to his player's abilities and with a 7-footer in the middle, a slower pace could be the way to go. Look for an NIT appearance at least for Colorado.

(B.K.)

Iowa State

LOCATION	Ames, IA
CONFERENCE	Big 12
LAST SEASON	25-6 (.806)
CONFERENCE RECORD	13-3 (1st)
STARTERS LOST/RETURNING	4/1
NICKNAME	Cyclones
COLORS	Cardinal & Gold
HOMECOURT	Hilton Coliseum (14,092)

COACH	Larry Eustachy (Long Beach State '79)
RECORD AT SCHOOL	72-26 (3 years)
CAREER RECORD	72-26 (3 years)
ASSISTANTS	Randy Brown (Iowa '81)
	Bob Sundvold (South Dakota State '77)
	Lance Irvin (Idaho '92)
TEAM WINS (last 5 years)	23-12-15-32-25
RPI (last 5 years)	24-133-116-4-15
2000-01 FINISH	Lost in NCAA first round.

Twice in the last year, Iowa State increased Larry Eustachy's compensation package, and with an annual income of $1.1 million he ranks among the nation's richest coaches. But Eustachy is also one of the most deserving.

It had been five decades since the Cyclones won a Big 12 championship, and now they've won two in a row. In neither year was a title expected, adding to the fans' joy.

For two years, Iowa State supplanted Kansas as the Big 12 kingpin, and its success over the Jayhawks was directly responsible for last season's title. The Cyclones defeated Kansas for a second straight year at Allen Field House, the only opponent to win there, which gave Iowa State its one-game margin over Kansas.

Eustachy's winning streak over the Jayhawks is five, the longest string of success ever against a Roy Williams-coached team. Iowa State withstood the Jayhawks' best shot twice last season.

How and Iowa State and Eustachy done it? Predecessor Tim Floyd laid the foundation, and his ability to cash in on a family friendship and lure Marcus Fizer from Louisiana gave the program its pivotal figure. Iowa State rode Fizer to the Elite Eight in 2000.

What nobody fully understood as Iowa State made that run was the importance of point guard Jamaal Tinsley, the Eustachy recruiting find. Tinsley was the most unstoppable player in the Big 12 for most of last season and gave Iowa State its second All-American in two years.

The players bought into Eustachy, as much as task master as there is college basketball. He runs a tight ship and at times a loud practice. His methods have gotten results.

At least they did until the end of last season.

The Cyclones' golden two-year run ended suddenly and painfully. Second-seeded Iowa State got on the wrong end of an NCAA Tournament magic moment when it lost in the first round to Hampton.

Astonishingly, Tinsley's open layup at the buzzer missed, securing the Cyclones' place in tournament lore.

"It had started before then," Eustachy said. "By the end of the season we were an average team."

True. A week earlier, Iowa State had become the first Big 12 top-seeded team to lose its first league tournament game. It had played unevenly in victories over Nebraska and Texas Tech and was blown out at Texas in the final regular-season games.

The wheels had come off and all Iowa State fans could do was live in the recent past. They'll always have the conference championship, and that's worth savoring. But to have followed its glorious 2000 postseason run with last year's effort left a bitter aftertaste. You just never know when those opportunities will present themselves again.

It doesn't appear to be the case this year. Four starters, including Tinsley, are gone. Kantrail Horton, Martin Rancik and Paul Shirley all were double-figure scorers and worthy of all-conference consideration. Eustachy faces a rebuilding season. But there are a few experienced players that will spur the regeneration.

Guard **Jake Sullivan** (11.4 ppg, .480 FG, .449 3PT, .879 FT), a 6-1 sophomore, was voted Big 12 Freshman of the Year. All the stories you heard about the guy are true. He took thousands of shots—on the driveway—during the winter months in Oakdale, Minn., pausing only to get warm and dry his wet gloves in the oven. He slams down Oreos and ice cream before games.

Sullivan was a relative unknown when he committed to Iowa State before his senior season. Then he starred at a Nike camp and everybody was on his trail. But Sullivan stuck to his word and emerged as one of the nation's top shooters. He buried six-of-eight behind the line in a victory over Kansas that all but sealed the league championship.

"You name the best teams in the country," Eustachy said. "They'd all take him."

But Iowa State has him, and Eustachy toyed with the idea of moving the Sullivan to the point. That won't happen. Sullivan is too dangerous on the wing. He's ISU's leading returning scorer, and last year, he ranked third in the Big 12 in three-point percentage.

Sullivan's wing partner is 6-5 sophomore **Shane Power** (4.7 ppg, .382 FG, .444 3PT, .721 FT), who also can be a deadly shooter. Power also came up big against Kansas, sinking five-of-six shots and notching a season-best 18 points. He also make a season-high three steals in that game.

Power is the team's top perimeter defender, but Iowa State will seek more offense from him this season.

The third and final returning veteran is senior forward **Tyray Pearson** (8.4 ppg, 4.4 rpg, .645 FG, .691 FT). Pearson came to Iowa State as a junior college All-American, but his offensive game wasn't polished and he was often plagued by foul trouble. The 6-7 Pearson figured to start entering last season but couldn't push Horton or Rancik out of the lineup. He'll be counted on to be one of the team's top rebounders and post defenders.

None of Iowa State's other returning players logged much court time last season. The most intriguing is 7-1 sophomore center **Andrew Skoglund** (1.2 ppg, 1.5 rpg, .333 FG), who appeared in nine games. To have an expanded role, Skoglund needs to flex more muscle.

Junior **Omar Bynum** (2.2 ppg, 1.3 rpg, .563 FG) is in line for more playing time at power forward. The 6-7 Bynum played in 12 games in his first year out of junior college and showed good leaping ability. Outside shooting is his weakness.

Others with playing experience are walk-ons—6-2 junior **Brad Davis** (0.9 ppg in five games), 6-2 junior **Justin Fries** (0.7 ppg in six games), 6-3 junior **Brandon Nicol** (1.0 ppg in five games) and 6-4 junior forward **Clint Varley** (0.8 ppg in six games). Which means newcomers will fill out the playing rotation.

The point guard will be 6-0 freshman **Ricky Morgan**, a cat-quick playmaker from Pontiac, Mich. Morgan led Northern High to state's large class state championship averaging 15 points and 8.9 assists.

Morgan is in the mold of Tinsley, who would have preferred to have averaged more assists than points. Eustachy is putting plenty of faith in Morgan. The Cyclones did not sign another point guard.

Iowa State landed one of the top junior college talents in 6-7 junior small forward **Tommie King**, who averaged 20.6 points and 5.6 rebounds for Western Nebraska last season. He also shot .476 from the field and .390 from behind the arc.

Another newcomer looking to start is 6-5 sophomore small forward **Marcus Jefferson**, who started his career at Providence two years ago. Jefferson averaged 3.5 points and 2.6 rebounds in 17 minutes a game for the Friars. He practiced with Iowa State last season.

Jared Homan is a 6-9 freshman center who, in another year, would probably watch much of the season unfold from the bench. But Iowa State lists only Homan and Skoglund as the centers, which means Homan will play plenty. He averaged 22.8 points, 12 rebounds and 6.1 blocks for St. Mary's High in Resmen, Iowa, and was a first-team all-state selection. He's the kind of player Cyclones fans will adore—a lifelong Iowa State fans whose dream was to wear the cardinal and gold.

Iowa State will get more front line help from 6-9 freshman forward **Adam Schaper**, who averaged 21.1 points and 11.2 rebounds for Kankakee Valley High School in Wheatland, Ind. Schaper is a solid offensive player away from the basket, but the concern is his weight. He's about 210 pounds.

2001-2002 SCHEDULE

Nov.	19	#Hartford
	22-24	##Las Vegas Invitational
	27	Savannah State
	30	###Cyclone Challenge
Dec.	1	###Cyclone Challenge
	4	Arkansas-Pine Bluff
	8	Iowa
	11	@Boston College
	16	@Drake
	23	Maryland-Eastern Shore
	29	Northern Iowa
	31	Morris Brown
Jan.	5	@Baylor
	9	Missouri
	12	Oklahoma State
	16	@Colorado
	19	@Kansas State
	23	Kansas
	26	@Nebraska
	29	Texas A&M
Feb.	2	@Texas Tech
	6	@Missouri
	13	Colorado
	16	Nebraska
	18	@Kansas
	23	Kansas State
	26	@Oklahoma
March	2	Texas
	7-110	####Big 12 Tournament

@Road Games
#First round Las Vegas Invitational
##Las Vegas, NV (schedule determined after first-round games; Pool 1 includes Georgia Tech, Illinois, Eastern Illinois, Pennsylvania. Pool 2 includes Iowa State, Saint Louis, Hartford, Southern Illinois)
###Ames, IA (vs. Wisconsin-Milwaukee first round; also Nebraska-Omaha, San Jose State)
####Kemper Arena, Kansas City, MO

BLUE RIBBON ANALYSIS

BACKCOURT	B
BENCH/DEPTH	D
FRONTCOURT	B
INTANGIBLES	C

We talk about this plenty, but Iowa State has been the most difficult program in the Big 12 to predict. When you'd think the Cyclones would suffer, they thrived. When you'd thought they contend, they floundered.

The thinking this time is a down year. With four lost starters, a freshman point guard and at least one other newcomer in the starting lineup, Iowa State can't win the league title for a third straight year. Can it?

If that happens, hand Eustachy national coach-of-the-year honors as soon as the season ends. But underestimate Iowa State at your peril. The Cyclones have made prognosticators look foolish for years. So think of them as an NCAA Tournament team until proven otherwise. They've been good enough under Eustachy and Floyd to deserve the benefit of the doubt.

(B.K.)

Kansas State

LOCATION	Manhattan, KS
CONFERENCE	Big 12
LAST SEASON	11-18 (.370)
CONFERENCE RECORD	4-12 (10th)
STARTERS LOST/RETURNING	2/3
NICKNAME	Wildcats
COLORS	Purple & White
HOMECOURT	Bramlage Coliseum (13,500)
COACH	Jim Woolridge (Louisiana Tech '77)
RECORD AT SCHOOL	11-18 (1 year)
CAREER RECORD	240-165 (14 years)
ASSISTANTS	Mike Miller (East Texas '87)
	Robbie Laing (Troy State '81)
	Charles Baker (Eastern Kentucky '90)
TEAM WINS (last 5 years)	10-17-20-9-11
RPI (last 5 years)	112-81-73-144
2000-01 FINISH	Lost in conference quarterfinal.

If the fans didn't roll out the purple carpet when Jim Wooldridge was announced to replace Tom Asbury a year ago, understand where they were coming from.

The once-popular Asbury never really won back fans after interviewing at California a few years back and his teams didn't make much headway in the Big 12. By the end of his stay in 2000, the fans, what few were attending home games wanted a change.

Thoughts turned to a K-State man. After all, Asbury had come from Pepperdine and had no connection to Kansas State. It was time to dip into the program's proud past. Names like Mike Evans and Rolando Blackman surfaced. There was even a rumor that Tex Winter could sign on for a year or two and groom a successor from the bench.

Wooldridge wasn't on the early radar screen. But then-athletic director Max Urick like what heard about this Chicago Bulls assistant, and he liked what he saw at Iowa State, where Bulls' head man Tim Floyd had previously coached. It wasn't Winter, but Wooldridge had worked with Winter for a year in Chicago.

So it was without much enthusiasm that Wooldridge

entered his first year in Manhattan, and some of the early results weren't encouraging. The Wildcats lost at Wichita State and needed a buzzer beating three-pointer to force overtime against Tennessee State. K-State won that game, but lost the next three.

A third crippling lost came at Old Dominion, a game in which the Wildcats led in the second half. A few of the players grumbled afterward about the team's deliberate style and triangle offense. Wooldridge and K-State needed something good to happen, and opportunity didn't seem to arrive with the 19th-ranked Iowa Hawkeyes two days before Christmas.

But K-State played exceptionally. Guard **Larry Reid** scored 31 as the Wildcats won going away. It was the first victory over a ranked non-league opponent during the regular season since 1981, and the purple people finally took plenty of cheer into the holidays.

A few weeks later, K-State knocked off ranked Missouri. Throughout the Big 12 season there were some lopsided losses, but not as many as in the recent past. When the season ended, the Wildcats had lost just as many as the previous year, but there were signs of life from Wooldridge's program.

The off-season would be critical. Wooldridge didn't hesitate to make changes. He overhauled, adding eight new players. The ones who return form a good nucleus.

Matt Siebrandt, a 6-8, 240-pound junior, became the Wildcats' most consistent inside scoring threat (9.7 ppg, 3.8 rpg). He topped 20 points three times. Siebrandt is right-hander, except around the basket where his most effective move is to get a defender on his hip and go up strong with his left.

Travis Reynolds, a 6-7 senior, was selected to the Big 12's all-bench team after averaging 10.5 points and 7.7 rebounds. He led K-State with a 52.3 shooting percentage and had the team's best power moves. Reyolds also led the Wildcats and was tied for seventh in the Big 12 in rebounding. He had six double doubles in 2000-2001, tied for fifth in the league. Reynolds had 17 double-figure scoring games.

Reynolds' high school teammate at Junction City High School in Junction City, Kansas, 6-7 junior **Quentin Buchanan**, is the Wildcats' best wing defender. He improved his scoring by three points to 7.3 last season and tried to provide more offense down the stretch when he averaged more than 11 field-goal attempts per game over the final four games.

Croatian **Ivan Sulic** (0.6 ppg, 1.4 rpg) is a third-year project who had one shining moment last season—eight rebounds and four points against Kansas. Both were season highs for the 6-9 junior.

Wooldridge brought in five newcomers to fight for spots up front, the best of whom are 6-9 junior forward **Pervis Pasco** and freshmen **Travis Canby** and **Marcelo Da Barrosa**.

Pasco averaged 18.9 points and 8.6 rebounds at Pensacola (Fla.) Junior College, where he was regarded as one of the Top 20 junior college sophomores last season. Pasco also shot 61.5 percent from the field.

The 6-9, 233-pound Canby comes to Kansas State from a year at prep school at Fork Union (Va.) Military Academy, where he averaged 10 points and seven boards. Before then Canby played at Holy Innocents Episcopal School in Atlanta. Canby's grandfather, Vern Schwentfeger, played for Hank Iba at Oklahoma State in the 1940s.

The biggest unknown of the recruiting class is the 6-7, 220-pound Da Barrosa, who averaged 23 points and 11 rebounds at Colegio Santo Americo in Sao Paulo, Brazil in 1999. Da Barrosa enrolled at Kansas State last spring and practiced with the Wildcats during the final two weeks of the season. He's been a member of Brazilian national teams since 1997.

How did K-State land Da Barrosa? One of his club coaches in Brazil was former Wildcat Eduardo Galvao.

The top wing addition is junior **Janerio Spurlock**, a 6-6 slasher from Chipola (Fla.) Junior College. Spurlock averaged 20.2 points and shot 41.2 percent on three-pointers last season. He was selected one of the top 60 junior college players by one service. Spurlock is from Cincinnati.

Wooldridge wants to add a Kansan to the roster every year, even if there isn't one worthy of a Division I scholarship. **Richard Nolan**, a 6-9, 190 pound left-handed freshman from Scott City High School, averaged 21 points and 8.8 points last season.

K-State's most valuable player a year ago was Reid (11.2 ppg, 3.2 rpg), a 6-0 senior. In his first season after transferring from Northern Oklahoma Junior College, Reid became the Wildcats' second leading scorer. He averaged 3.8 assists and his 34.8 minutes per game was the third highest mark in the Big 12. Reid was an honorable-mention All-Big 12 choice last year, and also made the league's all-newcomer team.

The high points for Reid came against Iowa schools. He led the upset over Iowa with 31 points, and he almost brought the Wildcats back from a double-digit second-half deficit at Iowa State with 30 points.

"Larry has been a scoring point guard throughout his career," Wooldridge said. "We don't want to take that away from him. But we hope that by adding the players we have in the backcourt that we have improved his overall skill level and shooting ability."

Those additions are three shooting guards who will fight for playing time. **Gilson DeJesus**, a 6-5 junior and left-handed shooting specialist, is also originally from Sao Paulo, giving the Wildcats more players from Brazil than Kansas on roster. DeJesus averaged 21.4 points for Trinidad (Colo.) Junior College, while shooting 52 percent from the field and 44 percent from behind the arc.

Marcus Hayes averaged 18.1 points, 6.1 rebounds and 3.1 assists for Oviedo (Fla.) High School last season and was chosen to the 6A all-state team. The 6-4 Hayes will walk on this season with the idea of getting a scholarship down the road.

Nick Williams a 6-4 freshman was selected the eighth best recruit in Texas after averaging 17.6 points for Mansfield High School.

All of them will battle veteran **Phineas** (pronounced, for some reason, FINE-us) **Atchison**, a 6-1 senior who led K-State with an 11.7 scoring average. Atchison started the first six games and came off the bench for the final 22, averaging about 24 minutes per appearance. He was the team's most reliable three-point shooter at 40.5 percent. He joined Reynolds on the Big 12 all-bench team.

2001-2002 SCHEDULE

Nov.	16	Troy State
	20	Wisconsin-Green Bay
	24	Mississippi
	27	Tennessee State
Dec.	1	Gardner-Webb
	8	@Northwestern
	15	North Texas
	19	Western Carolina
	22	@Iowa
	29	Fairleigh Dickinson
Jan.	6	@Texas Tech
	12	Missouri
	16	@Baylor
	19	Iowa State
	22	@Colorado
	26	@Missouri
	30	Texas
Feb .	2	Oklahoma State
	4	Kansas
	9	@Nebraska
	12	Texas A&M
	16	@Oklahoma
	20	Colorado
	23	@Iowa State
	27	@Kansas
March	2	Nebraska
	7-10	#Big 12 Tournament

@Road Games
#Kemper Arena, Kansas City, MO

BLUE RIBBON ANALYSIS

BACKCOURT	B
BENCH/DEPTH	C
FRONTCOURT	C
INTANGIBLES	C

Wooldridge has upgraded the Wildcats with a recruiting class that got in most top 50 national rankings just on the sheer numbers. Getting the newcomers to blend with the veterans, naturally, is a concern.

But Wooldridge is also looking for a better shooting team. Last season, K-State shot 41.2 percent from the field and 32.8 from behind the three-point line. Those numbers fall in line with previous Kansas State teams, but Wooldridge didn't coach those teams. He demands better.

"No question about it, we have to improve our field-goal percentage," Wooldridge said. "We hope our overall skill level has improved."

It has. Enough to make a push to the upper division? Probably not. But enough for Kansas State to grab five or six league victories and return to the NIT.

(B.K.)

Nebraska

LOCATION	Lincoln, NE
CONFERENCE	Big 12
LAST SEASON	14-16 (.467)
CONFERENCE RECORD	7-9 (7th)
STARTERS LOST/RETURNING	4/1
NICKNAME	Cornhuskers
COLORS	Scarlet & Cream
HOMECOURT	Devaney Sports Center (13,500)
COACH	Barry Collier (Butler '76)
RECORD AT SCHOOL	14-16 (1 year)
CAREER RECORD	210-148 (12 years)
ASSISTANTS	Dave Campbell (Catawba '66)
	Reggie Rankin (Ohio '89)
	Kevin Mouton (San Francisco '89)
TEAM WINS (last 5 years)	18-20-20-11-14
RPI (last 5 years)	53-41-53-157-96
2000-01 FINISH	Lost in conference second round.

Barry Collier inherited a team that he would not have recruited. Many of the players did not fit his philosophy, and the players were reluctant to change their game.

From this round peg in a square hole season, Nebraska managed to squeeze out 14 victories, improving on the previous year's total under Danny Nee, who's on his second job after getting booted from Lincoln (taking over Duquesne this season after one year at Robert Morris).

Nebraska won the San Juan Shootout. The Huskers beat Texas, Missouri and Oklahoma State. They had Iowa State beaten, only to lose when the Cyclones threw in a pass and scored in seven-tenths of a second.

There were three one-point losses. If they all go the other way, the Cornhuskers are in the NIT. But it could have been more. Nebraska started four seniors, one (center Kimani Ffriend) good enough to get drafted and another (guard Cookie Belcher) who finished among the national career leaders in steals. It was a team with talent but mostly without the will to change.

So Collier should have. No, playing a running, less disciplined style isn't how he won at Butler. And, to be honest, Nebraska didn't win that way before Collier arrived.

But such a style, with a healthy Belcher back in the lineup after sitting out as a medical red-shirt with a broken wrist, might have fit the personnel better. And it would have given players who had been in the program for several years a chance to leave on a higher note.

For reference, Nebraska only had to look at its neighbor to the East. In 1995, first-year Iowa State coach Tim Floyd inherited a team that had been built on offense and quick shots, a system that repulsed Floyd. But he worked with his players, gave them a few more defensive principles, insisted they handle the ball better and turned them loose.

The result was an NCAA Tournament season led by senior guard Fred Hoiberg. That team started four seniors. The next season, Floyd recruited athletes more to his liking and shifted the philosophy entirely. This team, led by guard Dedric Willoughby, won the Big 12 Tournament.

Two teams, two lineups, two philosophies, one coach. It can happen. But there's no use looking back for Collier. He's got plenty of issues this season.

Nobody who averaged in double figures in scoring returns. The top returning rebounder averaged 2.8 boards. The cupboard appears bare. Collier insists it is not.

"We should be a better shooting team on the perimeter and have a better understanding of what we need to do to win," he said. "We will not be blocking shots or rebounding quite the same as last season, but I do think we'll play better defense overall."

Let's start with the shooting. The top returning player is 6-1 senior guard **Cary Cochran** (pronounced CO-horn), a wonderful shooter who cannot be left open anywhere on his side of mid-court. Cochran (9.6 ppg, 2.4 rpg, 2.1 apg, .460 FG, .473 3PT, .871 FT) took 200 shots from the field, 165 from behind last season. He tied the team record with 78 three-pointers last season and was the

big reason that Nebraska set a mark by shooting .383 as a team on threes.

Cochran was third in the nation in three-point percentage a year ago and is the nation's leading returning shooter, but Nebraska will need more than his perimeter shooting. He'll be asked to be more of a leader and all-around player.

Cochran will keep his off-guard position and the point will be run by 6-1 senior **John Robinson**, a New Mexico transfer who became eligible after the first semester last season. Robinson (3.1 ppg, 1.0 rpg, 1.8 apg) is a proven scorer, averaging 10.2 points in 34.4 minutes a game for Dave Bliss' team in as a freshman in 1999. He connected on 35 percent of his three-point shots and was the starting point in the Lobos' two NCAA Tournament games.

Robinson is sure-handed; he was fourth in the Big 12 in assists to turnover ratio (1.9 to 1) a year ago.

The rest of the backcourt minutes will go to 6-2 senior **Kendrick Ford** and newcomers. Ford (1.1 ppg, 0.3 rpg) played in 13 games in his first year after transferring from Neosho (Kansas) Community College. He played in 13 minutes in the opener and only six the rest of the season.

Freshman **Jake Muhlheisen**, a 6-4 guard, was one of the top prospects in Nebraska last year when he averaged 16 points, 3.7 assists and 2.5 steals. He also shot .403 from behind the arc. Muhlheisen was a shooting guard at Southeast High School in Lincoln, Neb., but will play both guard positions this season.

Brennon Clemmons, a 6-2 junior, averaged 14 points and five rebounds for Olney Central (Ill.) Community College. He's seen as a defensive specialist at both guard positions.

Cochran's top backup could be **Corey Simms**, a 6-5 freshman from Normandy High School in St. Louis, Mo. He averaged 22 points, 6.6 rebounds and 3.1 steals as a senior. Defense also is Simms' forte. He finished third in his conference in blocked shots.

So guard-oriented is Nebraska that its best big man, 6-11 sophomore **Brian Conklin**, is one of the team's top outside shooters. Conklin (4.0 ppg, 2.8 rpg, .431 FG, .426 3PT, .588 FT) took more shots outside the arc (54) than inside (48). Conklin weighs a mere 220 pounds, and it's uncertain whether he has the physical capability to pound inside. But he did grab 17 rebounds in a game against Kansas State, including 14 on the defensive end.

"As I gain strength and experience I hope to develop my inside game enough to where I can take a little guy inside and still bring a big guy outside," Conklin said.

It's not like Conklin isn't trying to get bigger. He's been eating four and five meals a day.

As for other frontcourt starters, throw a dart. The first look goes to veterans **Ross Buckendahl**, **Justin Boeker** and **Ben Chesnut**. Buckendahl, a 6-5 senior, didn't play last season while recovering from knee ligament damage. He came to Nebraska as a walk-on out of Northeast (Neb.) Community College and has been awarded a scholarship. Buckendahl played a total of 94 minutes in 2000.

Boeker, a 6-9 senior, averaged 1.1 points and 0.7 rebounds in 15 games. He started his career at Manhattan College, where he averaged 1.4 points and 1.5 rebounds for the Jaspers in 1999. He's a big-body 240-pounds, the heaviest player on the roster. Chesnut, a 6-6 sophomore, played in three minutes of four games last season.

Once again, playing time beckons newcomers. **Dan Heimos**, a 6-11 freshman, averaged 14.1 points, 9.5 rebounds and 4.1 blocks last season for Gilbault High School in Waterloo, Iowa. Like Conklin, he's on the lean side at 215 pounds.

John Turek is a 6-9 freshman from Abraham Lincoln High School in Council Bluffs, Iowa, where he averaged 18 points, 12 rebounds and three blocks for a team that finished 21-1.

Already in the program was **Marques McCarty**, a 6-5 freshman from Fort Bend Austin High School in Sugarland, Texas. McCarty sat out as a red-shirt last season but practiced with the team. He's slated to play small forward.

2001-2002 SCHEDULE

Nov.	20	North Carolina A&T
	24	Winthrop
	28	Texas-San Antonio
Dec.	2	Wofford
	5	Western Illinois
	8	Oral Roberts

	12	@Creighton
	15	Sam Houston State
	22	@Minnesota
	29	@Pacific
Jan.	2	Savannah State
	5	@Missouri
	9	@Kansas
	12	Colorado
	16	Oklahoma
	19	@Texas
	23	@Oklahoma State
	26	Iowa State
	30	Texas Tech
Feb.	5	@Colorado
	9	Kansas State
	13	Missouri
	16	@Iowa State
	20	@Texas A&M
	24	Kansas
	27	Baylor
March	2	@Kansas State
	7-10	#Big 12 Tournament

@Road Games
#Kemper Arena, Kansas City, MO

BLUE RIBBON ANALYSIS

BACKCOURT	C
BENCH/DEPTH	D
FRONTCOURT	D
INTANGIBLES	C

It had been eight years since Collier suffered a losing season. His fourth Butler team went 11-17 in 1993. His next seven turned in winning records, four played in the postseason, three in the NCAA Tournament.

It's not like the guy doesn't know how to win. He has a team more to his liking, with players more willing to buy into the system. He has terrific shooters in Cochran and Conklin, and now he needs them to expand their games.

If Nebraska is to be successful, players nobody outside of Lincoln know much about will have to step forward. Robinson could be one of those players. Perhaps Simms or Muhlheisen, McCarty or Heimos could, too.

Whoever it is, it will be somebody who hasn't faced the competition seen in the Big 12. Nebraska seems to be headed farther away from its days as a postseason regular. Collier won with lesser talent at Butler. If he pulls off a winning season this year, it will be because the whole is greater than the sum of the parts and he'll be a candidate for league coach of the year.

(B.K.)

Texas A&M

LOCATION	**College Station, TX**
CONFERENCE	**Big 12**
LAST SEASON	**10-20 (.333)**
CONFERENCE RECORD	**3-13 (t-11th)**
STARTERS LOST/RETURNING	**1/4**
NICKNAME	**Aggies**
COLORS	**Maroon & White**
HOMECOURT	**Reed Arena (12,500)**
COACH	**Melvin Watkins (UNC Charlotte '77)**
RECORD AT SCHOOL	**30-55 (3 years)**
CAREER RECORD	**72-75 (5 years)**
ASSISTANTS	**Tom Billeter (Illinois '83)**
	Lew Hill (Wichita State '88)
	Bobby Kummer (UNC Charlotte '96)
TEAM WINS (last 5 years)	**11-7-12-8-10**
RPI (last 5 years)	**137-237-157-196-178**
2000-01 FINISH	**Lost in conference first round.**

Of the four Texas schools in the Big 12 Conference, Texas A&M is finding itself an afterthought.

Texas hired Rick Barnes in 1998, within a few days of the Aggies' hiring of Melvin Watkins. Since arriving in Austin, Barnes has turned the Longhorns into a hard-playing group that has made the NCAA Tournament three consecutive seasons. Baylor hired Dave Bliss a year later and in two seasons he has turned the Bears into a solid, dangerous team.

And out in Lubbock, the message of "we're serious" was heard loud and clear last March when the Red Raiders hired Bob Knight.

So that leaves Watkins and A&M pedaling as fast as they can to keep up. College Station has never been a hoops hotbed. Oh, sure, when the folksy Shelby Metcalf was running in junior-college players, old G. Rollie White would rock at times, particularly when the hated Longhorns came to town. But there's just not much basketball tradition in the A&M history books.

The memory of that fabled double-overtime defeat of North Carolina in the 1980 NCAA Tournament is fading. The Aggies' last NCAA trip came in 1987. And junior Bernard King is being touted as an All-America candidate this year. If that turns out, he'll be the school's first basketball All-American since ... 1966?

In his three seasons, Watkins' teams have been cursed by bad luck. Last season, trainer Mike "Radar" Ricke said he had never seen an epidemic of injuries like the ones suffered by the basketball team. A&M lost three returning starters to injuries and a fourth was hobbled and eventually had to quit the sport.

By the end of last season, just seven scholarship players were available. That, coupled with the fact the Aggies lacked senior leadership, resulted in a 10-20 record including a 3-13 conference mark.

"We were very excited going into last season, but it was disappointing to have so many injuries before the season even started. I really felt like the kids were ready to get off to a good start," said Watkins, who is 30-55 at A&M, including descending records of 5-11, 4-12 and 3-13 in Big 12 play. "Obviously, we were disappointed in the number of wins we had last season."

Watkins still jokes about the fact that when he was hired, a thunderstorm was pounding College Station, but when he drove up to the arena for his press conference, the skies cleared and the sun was shining. For the last three seasons, there has been nothing but storm clouds. This season, there might be some silver linings finally starting to shine through.

Watkins has recruited well and there is talent on the roster. For the first time, Watkins believes the Aggies have a competent backup player at each position.

"It's critical for us to stay healthy and somehow have consistency throughout the course of the season," Watkins said. "We know that sometimes things happen, but if we look at it on paper right now, we feel good about where we are. It's the most secure I've felt about our roster since I've been here.

"That's been one of our issues, to have enough players to have competition in practice. That means that every day in practice we will have to compete and that's just something we haven't had."

Watkins hopes that the improved depth will allow the Aggies to be more aggressive and versatile on both ends of the court.

"Any time you have players that versatile, it makes you a team that is a little more difficult to scout because we can change up things," Watkins said. "And it also allows us to play guys at different positions because of match-ups.

"We'd like to extend the defense a little more and be a little bit more aggressive. To do that, you have to play at a high level, which means you can't play as long. That's where that depth will come in. You'll probably see more faces out there, but we'll probably get more things done."

Two of last year's key players who were knocked out by injuries return—**Andy Slocum** and **Tomas Ress**.

The 6-11, 275-pound Slocum started 14 games as a freshman in 1999-2000. But before last season he suffered a shoulder injury lifting weights. Surgery was required to insert two pins. Slocum, who averaged 4.9 points a game as a freshman, spent his second summer in Hawaii at Pete Newell's Big Man Camp. He also has continued to pound away in the weight room.

"I think the football coaches have been following Slocum because he's gotten so big," Watkins joked. "I'm a little concerned because I don't want him so big that's he's stiff and can't run the floor, but he's gained more confidence because he feels stronger."

Ress, also a 6-11 sophomore, played in two games but was sidelined with a staph infection that weakened him before the season, then shelved entirely when he was diagnosed with an infection in his pelvic bone. In 1999-2000, Ress started 12 games and averaged 4.6 points a game. His illnesses caused him to lose 30 pounds, but he has regained that and then some. He expects to play this season at 240.

"Tomas definitely needed to put some weight on and he has built himself up to about 240," Watkins said. "We're excited about that because we knew he needed to bulk up some.

"Their height, as well as the depth they bring in the post area, was missed and we look forward to having them back. They both seem to be doing awfully well and seem to be healthy."

Without Slocum and Ress, A&M often had to rely on 6-8 junior **Keith Bean** (22.3 mpg, 7.0 ppg, 5.5 rpg, .497 FG, .518 FT) at center. Bean will now be able to shift back to his natural power-forward spot.

In addition to Slocum and Ress, Watkins has two other inside players—6-10 sophomore **Nolan Butterfras** (2.4 ppg, 2.0 rpg, .490 FG, .571 FT) was forced to play as Bean's backup as a freshman and 6-10 **Brian Brookhart** (1.1 ppg, 1.4 rpg) is a walk-on who makes solid contributions as a practice player. He transferred from TCU after a messy misunderstanding with the coaching staff there regarding a scholarship offer that never materialized.

But while a lack of a true post presence was a problem, A&M's biggest shortcoming last season was at point guard. In 30 games, the Aggies had 395 assists and 487 turnovers, a horrible ratio. And the average of 13 assists per game suggests that A&M too often relied on one-on-one moves instead of team play to create offense.

Jamal Gilchrist, who as a sophomore made nine starts and played in all 30 games, decided to transfer. That left Watkins with little choice but to go the junior-college route. He signed 5-10 sophomore **Michael Gardener** (13.4 ppg, 7.7 apg) from Garden City (Kansas) Community College and 5-11 junior **Bradley Jackson** (4.5 ppg, 4.6 apg) from College of Southern Idaho. Based on their junior college performances last year, Gardener appears slated to be the starter with Jackson as the backup.

"The point-guard position is where we really had a big void and we think we addressed that with the two young men we signed," Watkins said. "Michael has the potential to really put his fingerprints on the team at the point position. We will definitely welcome what he brings to the team. His biggest strength is running a team."

The arrival of the junior college guards means that **Andy Leatherman** (23.6 mpg, 6.3 ppg, 2.9 rpg, .331 FG, .292 3FG, 57 assists, 57 turnovers) can move back to shooting guard. The 6-3 senior is a former walk-on who is a solid player. Forced to play point guard last season, Leatherman did the best he could, but he had a break-even assist/turnover ratio and he averaged 6.3 points a game.

If the Aggies' talent level has increased as much as Watkins believes, then Leatherman should fill the role of "solid backup."

This season's firepower should come from **Bernard King** and **Nick Anderson**, who if nothing else give the Aggies some NBA flair. A 6-5 junior guard, King (18.0 ppg, 3.8 rpg, 144 assists, 44 steals, .404 FG, .316 3PT, .679 FT) was one of Watkins' first major recruiting gets. Last season he became a solid player by leading the Aggies in scoring despite the dismal record. In just two seasons, he has totaled 1,014 points and should wind up as A&M's career scoring leader if he stays all four years.

"He feels like he has something to prove," Watkins said. "When a player of his ability feels they have something to prove, look out. The sky is the limit for Bernard."

To reach the sky, King needs to improve his shooting percentages. He was one of the Big 12 leaders in free-throw attempts, but he shot a mundane .679 from the line.

A 6-6 sophomore forward, Anderson (10.3 ppg, 5.2 rpg, .455 FG, .231 3PT, .641 FT, team-high 29 blocks) has the bulk (225 pounds) to play the "four" but he's probably more suited to small forward. He was second on the team in offensive rebounds as a freshman. Despite operating around the basket, he struggled with his shooting percentage. If he's going to prove he can play the "three," he's going to need to improve his touch and range.

A 6-7 sophomore, **Jesse King** (4.6 ppg, 3.4 rpg, .333 FG) became eligible after the first semester last season. Watkins likes his athletic ability and his versatility.

"He could be that player that could surprise a lot of people," Watkins said. "He's going to be on the floor for us in some kind of way."

A 6-6 junior guard/forward, **Larry Scott** (1.8 ppg, .364 3PT) never recovered from a severe ankle sprain in late November. As a freshman, Scott led the Aggies in three-point shooting. If he can regain his health and his confidence, he could help A&M as a zone buster or provide an offensive spark off the bench.

A 6-4 sophomore guard, **Dylan Leal** (1.6 ppg, .300 3FG) is a walk-on noted for his shooting ability.

There are two freshmen on the A&M roster. A 6-6

guard/forward, **Daryl Mason** is a local product (Bryan High School) who has the athletic ability to contribute in practice. Unless the Aggies suffer another wave of injuries, Mason is a likely red-shirt candidate. A 6-8 freshman from Arlington (Texas) Lamar High School, **Jared Hall** is a walk-on who will see practice time banging on the front line.

2001-2002 SCHEDULE

Nov.	19	George Washington
	24	@Lamar
	26	Davidson
	30	Long Beach State
Dec.	2	Loyola Marymount
	6	Southeastern Louisiana
	8	Miami
	14	*Tulsa
	17	#Southwest Missouri State
	20-22	##Las Vegas Invitational
	30	@North Carolina
Jan.	3	@Centenary
	5	@Oklahoma
	9	Texas Tech
	16	@Missouri
	19	Baylor
	23	@Texas
	26	Kansas
	29	@Iowa State
Feb.	3	@Baylor
	6	Texas
	9	Oklahoma
	12	@Kansas State
	16	Oklahoma State
	20	Nebraska
	23	@Texas Tech
	26	Colorado
March	2	@Oklahoma State
	7-10	###Big 12 Tournament

@Road Games
*Compaq Center, Houston, TX
#Las Vegas Invitational, Las Vegas, NV
##Las Vegas, NV (schedule determined after first-round games; Pool 1 includes Georgia Tech, Illinois, Eastern Illinois, Pennsylvania. Pool 2 includes Iowa State, Saint Louis, Hartford, Southern Illinois)
###Kemper Arena, Kansas City, MO

BLUE RIBBON ANALYSIS

BACKCOURT	C+
BENCH/DEPTH	B
FRONTCOURT	C+
INTANGIBLES	C

Watkins has proven that he can recruit and sign good players. In late summer, the Aggies received a non-binding oral commitment from Antoine Wright, a 6-7 forward regarded as one of the best high school wings in the country.

But while the talent level has improved in College Station, nothing much else has. Basketball remains an after thought. Fans have not exactly flocked to the impressive Reed Arena. A winning season or two, though, could change that. As the football team proves each fall, there is passion in Aggieland as long as A&M is on the winning side of the scoreboard.

If the new point guards can run the attack, the two Kings and Anderson should be able to provide the offense. There's enough size to allow the Aggies to bang on a more even basis than they have in recent seasons.

Watkins and A&M are due some luck. If the Aggies' top players stay healthy, they might start to see a little light at the end of the tunnel ... and not immediately assume it's an oncoming train.

"A&M is an amazing place," Watkins said. "We have a heck of an alumni base. The Aggies, they love this place like nothing I've ever seen. We'll get it going here. We'll get it going and we'll get all those Aggies out and into Reed Arena. And it's going to be special.

"With the facilities we have here, with the university we have to sell, with the resources we have to sell with, there is no reason it can't be done here basketball-wise. There is a lot to sell here and I believe I'm the man to do it. We are building from the ground up."

(W.B.)

Texas Tech

LOCATION	Lubbock, TX
CONFERENCE	Big 12 North
LAST SEASON	9-19 (.321)
CONFERENCE RECORD	3-13 (12th)
STARTERS LOST/RETURNING	3/2
NICKNAME	Red Raiders
COLORS	Scarlet & Black
HOMECOURT	United Spirit Arena (15,050)
COACH	Bob Knight (Ohio State '62)
RECORD AT SCHOOL	First year
CAREER RECORD	763-290 (35 years)
ASSISTANTS	Bob Beyer (Alfred '83)
	Pat Knight (Indiana '95)
	Chris Beard (Texas '95)
TEAM WINS (last 5 years)	20-17-13-12-9
RPI (last 5 years)	33-105-160-156-182
2000-01 FINISH	Lost in conference first round.

He has a new job. At a new school. In a new state. But he gets the chance to keep his wardrobe.

Bob Knight, new coach at Texas Tech? Bob Knight, changed man? Hardly. At the press conference/pep rally conducted on March 16 to announce Knight's hiring, the former Indiana coach couldn't help but fire a shot across the bow of the school that had dismissed him seventh months before.

"This is without question the most comfortable red sweater I have had in six years," he said, indicating the Red Raider sweater he had donned moments before.

Knight then turned the "news conference" into Gladiator and the United Spirit Arena into the Roman Coliseum. Against the wishes of Tech's administration, Knight invited the 7,500 fans to stay for the question and answer period.

Whenever a reporter asked a question related to Knight's transgressions/problems/controversies, the reporter was booed and Knight was cheered when he answered with a non-answer.

One reporter tried to ask Knight about the infamous practice film clip that was one of the final straws in his dismissal at Indiana.

"As far as those tapes, I think the fans have no interest in seeing or discussing them," he said.

"When the horse is dead, get off of it," Knight said at one point to stop the line of questioning. "The horse is dead. Get off."

As his wife Karen put it, Knight still has a "passion for living."

Oh, so now we get it. Knight's "passion for living" explains all that has come before during his stormy, successful, controversial and legendary career. After a year out of the spotlight, Robert Montgomery Knight will be back on the sideline. His hiring at Tech poses questions by the basket-ful.

Has Tech "sold its soul" to compete in the Big 12? How long before Knight blows a gasket? Working with a revamped roster, how successful will Knight be in his first season? How long will it take for Knight to pass Dean Smith on the all-time victories list?

There are partial answers to some of those questions. There is little doubt that Tech President David Schmidly and athletic director Gerald Myers did a poor job of handling the transition from former coach James Dickey to Knight. Dickey, a good and honorable man, was left twisting in the wind for a few days as it became apparent that Schmidly and Myers were wooing Knight and gauging his interest.

"I never would've envisioned that I'd be able to say that Bob Knight is the basketball coach at Texas Tech," said Myers, who became friends with Knight 30 years ago when both were starting their coaching careers. "I never would have imagined [it].

"He is quite simply one of the best coaches who has ever been involved with the game of basketball. There aren't many people at all who can equal him in terms of his accomplishments both as a coach and as an educator. There's not anybody whose credentials compare to his in the game today."

In his first six months on the job, Knight's famous (infamous?) temper was nowhere to be seen. Knight has stormed the state, appearing at dozens of booster club functions. Along with women's coach Marsha Sharp (herself a national championship winner), the school billed the schmooze fests as "A Sharp Knight Under The

Texas Stars."

And inevitably, there would be Knight, spending an hour posing for pictures with Red Raiders fans. But some cynics would say that even if he appears to be a changed man, he's still the same Bobby Knight. Asked what adjustments he would have to make to his new team, Knight said, "When you are in charge, there is not a whole lot of adjusting that needs to be done."

And that became painfully evident five days after Knight took over. He called in three Tech players—Jamal Brown, Brannon Hayes and Rodney Bass—for a meeting. Knight, with Myers in attendance, told the players that he would be the only one talking during the meeting. Then Knight told the three that they were no longer on the team.

As freshmen last season, neither Hayes nor Bass saw much playing time. Both players thought Knight was kidding.

The next day, Hayes asked Brown, a junior guard who started all 28 games last season, if he was going to the afternoon's scheduled workout.

"He said, 'What for? We're not on the team anymore,'" Hayes said. "I didn't believe him at first. I didn't believe it until I saw my face on SportsCenter."

Knight's purge of last year's team left the Raiders with just four scholarship players at one point. The NCAA's relatively new—and extremely controversial—"five and eight" scholarship rule figures to limit Knight's rebuilding. The rule limits a school to signing five scholarship players in one year and no more than eight during two years. The intent of the rule was to increase graduation rates by forcing coaches to keep the players they sign.

Tech's appeal for a waiver of the rule was denied.

The 60-year-old Knight signed a five-year contract that has an estimated base salary of $250,000 that could get to $400,000 with incentives. In 36 seasons of coaching, Knight has won 763 games and three national championships.

Knight's victory total is fifth in Division I history and he needs 117 victories to move past former North Carolina head coach Dean Smith for first place on the list.

Five years ago, Texas Tech appeared to be in good shape under Dickey. In back-to-back seasons, the Red Raiders won 50 games. But an academic scandal that rocked the athletic department also sent the basketball team into the ditch. Over the last four seasons, Tech has won 51 games. Despite his good guy, hard working image, Dickey became the fall guy as Texas Tech decided that it was sinking fast and deep.

"Coach Knight wins basketball games, and he does it the right way," Schmidly said. "Winning is important, but not as important as educating student athletes and running a clean program. His reputation in those two areas is impeccable."

Knight claims his year off from coaching has left him eager to return.

"When you have coached as long as I have and worked with developing players, it is something you really miss," he said.

Knight's first team in Lubbock will be built around **Andy Ellis** (14.2 ppg, 6.3 rpg, 31.8 mpg, .444 FG). The 6-11, 225-pound senior has skills similar to former Indiana player Kirk Haston. He can be a solid inside scorer and rebounder and can also score from the perimeter.

The other returning starter is 6-4 sophomore **Mikey Marshall** (22.4 mpg, 3.5 ppg, 3.8 rpg). Six-foot-five sophomore **Andre Emmett** (20.5 mpg, 7.7 ppg, 3.6 rpg) is a backcourt reserve capable of scoring. Six-foot sophomore **Marcus Shropshire** (17.1 mpg, 5.3 ppg) should compete for the playing time created by Jamal Brown's departure. Brown last season led the team in minutes played and assists while averaging 10.7 points.

With just a handful of players returning, the newcomers figure to get lots of playing time. **Will Chavis**, a 5-10 junior guard from Panola (Texas) Junior College, is a Philadelphia native who could wind up as the starting point guard.

Seven-foot freshman **Mickey Michalec**, from Skiatook High School in Tulsa, and 6-8 junior **Pavel Storozynski**, from Dodge City (Kansas) Community College, should help on the front line.

Nick Valdez, from Northeastern (Colo.) Junior College, is a 6-6 junior who could compete for playing time at shooting guard or small forward.

"I've never promised anybody what we will do because I don't know," Knight told the fans on the day he was announced as the coach. "But you will be proud of the players. I expect more out of them in the classroom than you do."

2001-2002 SCHEDULE

Nov.	16-17	#Red Raider Classic
	20	@SMU
	24	Sam Houston State
	26	UTEP
	28	@New Mexico State
Dec.	1	TCU
	3	Texas-Arlington
	14	@Houston
	17	Louisiana-Lafayette
	22	Stetson
	30	Minnesota
Jan.	1	Wyoming
	6	Kansas State
	9	@Texas A&M
	12	@Oklahoma
	14	Texas
	19	Oklahoma State
	26	Oklahoma
	30	@Nebraska
Feb.	2	Iowa State
	6	@Oklahoma State
	9	@Kansas
	13	Baylor
	16	@Colorado
	20	Missouri
	23	Texas A&M
	26	@Texas
March	2	@Baylor
	7-10	##Big 12 Tournament

@Road Games
#Lubbock, TX (vs. William& Mary first round; also Northern Iowa, San Diego State)
##Kemper Arena, Kansas City, MO

BLUE RIBBON ANALYSIS

BACKCOURT	C
BENCH/DEPTH	C-
FRONTCOURT	C
INTANGIBLES	B+

Those who believe in Knight's genius as a coach are anxious to see if it still exists. He'll likely need all of his talents and wiles to get Tech through this season.

In the Big 12, the top teams are Kansas, Missouri, Iowa State, Texas, Oklahoma and Oklahoma State. Baylor is a solid mid-level program. That leaves Texas Tech to battle with Nebraska, Kansas State, Colorado and Texas A&M for the table scraps.

And that's exactly the reason why the school turned to Knight. He is a proven winner, a Hall of Fame coach. But does he still have what it takes? His recent teams at Indiana struggled to compete in the Big Ten. Knight no doubt will lure some talented players to Lubbock. What will be interesting to see is whether he can mold those players into a winning team and whether he can keep from erupting into Mount Bobby.

At his introductory press conference, he asked for patience from the media.

"Let's start from scratch and see where we go," he said. "If you have a problem with me, come talk to me before you write about me."

Knight believes he's turned a new leaf. We'll have to wait to see if it's the same old book.

(W.B.)

 ## UC Irvine

LOCATION	Irvine, CA
CONFERENCE	Big West
LAST SEASON	25-5 (.833)
CONFERENCE RECORD	15-1 (1st)
STARTERS LOST/RETURNING	3/2
NICKNAME	Anteaters
COLORS	Blue & Gold
HOMECOURT	Bren Events Center (5,000)
COACH	Pat Douglass (Pacific '72)
RECORD AT SCHOOL	54-57 (4 years)
CAREER RECORD	54-57 (4 years)
ASSISTANTS	Todd Lee (South Dakota '86)
	Len Stevens (Sacramento State '71)
	Tim Cleary (Carroll College '94)

 # BIG WEST

BLUE RIBBON FORECAST
1. Pacific
2. UC Santa Barbara
3. UC Irvine
4. Long Beach State
5. Utah State
6. Cal State Northridge
7. Idaho
8. Cal State Fullerton
9. Cal Poly
10. UC Riverside

ALL-CONFERENCE TEAM
G - Jerry Green, SR, UC Irvine
G - Markus Carr, SR, Cal State Northridge
F - Travis Reed, SR, Long Beach State
F - Adame Ndiaye, SR, UC Santa Barbara
C - Adam Parada, SO, UC Irvine

PLAYER OF THE YEAR
Jerry Green, SR, UC Irvine

NEWCOMER OF THE YEAR
Desmond Penigar, JR, Utah State

2001-2002 CONFERENCE TOURNAMENT
March 7-9, Anaheim Convention Center, Anaheim, CA

2000-2001 CHAMPIONS
UC Irvine (Regular season)
Utah State (Conference tournament)

2000-2001 POSTSEASON PARTICIPANTS
Postseason record: 1-3 (.250)
NCAA
Utah State (Second round)
Cal State Northridge
NIT
UC Irvine

TOP BACKCOURTS
1. UC Santa Barbara
2. Pacific
3. (tie) Long Beach State
3. UC Irvine

TOP FRONTCOURTS
1. Long Beach State
2. UC Santa Barbara
3. (tie) Utah State
3. UC Irvine

INSIDE THE NUMBERS
2000-2001 conference RPI: 18th (of 31)
Conference RPI (last five years): 14-18-19-19-18

DID YOU KNOW?
The Big West lost Boise State to the Western Athletic Conference this season but picked up Cal State Northridge from the Big Sky and UC Riverside from the Division II ranks. ... Just two league schools, Idaho and Utah State, are located outside the state of California, with five of the 10 conference schools (UC Riverside, Northridge, Cal State Fullerton, UC Irvine and Long Beach State) within a few minutes' drive, depending on L.A. traffic, of course. ... Five conference coaches lead teams for which they once played. They are Donny Daniels (Fullerton '77), John Masi (Riverside '71), Leonard Perry (Idaho '95), Bob Thomason (Pacific '71) and Bobby Braswell (Northridge '84). ... A sixth, Irvine's Pat Douglass, played in the Pacific backcourt alongside Thomason in the early '70s. ... Perry is the conference's only rookie coach, though Cal Poly's Kevin Bromley is about as close as you can get. He took over mid-season in 2000-01 after the firing of Jeff Schneider. ... Two of the conference's most successful coaches received lengthy contract extensions during the summer. Douglass, after a 25-victory season and trip to the NIT, signed on at Irvine through 2007-08. Utah State's Stew Morrill, riding 56 victories in two seasons, signed a new 10-year deal. ... Irvine assistant coach Len Stevens has previously been a Division I head coach at both Washington State (1983-87) and Nevada (1987-93). ... Newcomer UC Riverside went 2-10 against conference opponents last season, while Northridge did not play a Big West opponent in 2000-01. ... Only one Big West team has won a national championship—UNLV in 1990. ... The Big West has sent just one representative to the NCAA Tournament each of the past eight years. Utah State's victory over Ohio State in the first round of last year's tournament is the conference's only victory in that stretch. ... Pacific and Utah State have each appeared in three of the last five conference tournament title games. ... Northridge reached the Big Sky conference tournament title game three of the past five years.

(C.S.)

TEAM WINS (last 5 years)	1-9-6-14-25
RPI (last 5 years)	302-241-289-199-78
2000-01 FINISH	Lost in NIT first round.

How good was UC Irvine last season? By Irvine standards, incredibly good.

The Anteaters set a school record with 25 victories, won 21 of their final 24 games, earned the program's first Big West Conference regular-season championship and set school records for consecutive victories with 13 and for home victories with 14.

Irvine's 25 victories nearly equaled the 30 victories the team earned the previous four years combined. Toss in a trip to the NIT where they played eventual champ Tulsa toe-to-toe before falling, 75-71, and you've got all the makings of a dream season.

Next question.

What do the Anteaters do for an encore?

"I don't think we're going to win 25 games," fifth-year coach Pat Douglass said.

Douglass is probably right. A lot of things went Irvine's way last season, and more than a few times the Anteaters escaped with victory when either outplayed or out-hustled. The team won 14 games by five or fewer points.

The Anteaters will not be a one-hit wonder, however. Not by a long shot. The team returns the conference's best player in 6-3 guard Jerry Green (19.0 ppg, 4.8 rpg, 3.0 apg), the conference's best true post player in 7-0 Adam Parada (7.6 ppg, 6.2 rpg) and a player who could be the conference's best newcomer in 6-5 junior forward Jordan Harris, a former All-Patriot League second-team pick at Colgate. Put quite simply, Irvine is not going away.

"Last season didn't just happen," Douglass said. "It took time, and our good young players developed. I think we've developed a solid program. We're hungry to succeed and should continue to be successful."

The Irvine magic will continue to center on Green, a senior who has grown up with Douglass and the Anteaters, having started since he arrived at Irvine in 1998-99.

Green won conference freshman-of-the-year honors that season, and has gradually gotten better; a year ago he was the Big West Player of the Year. He's put on muscle—which allows him to drive, post up and get to the free-throw line more often—and he's developed better confidence in his three-point shot.

Because of that versatility, Green has played considerably at both guard spots, but will likely run the show from the point this season.

"When we put him back at the point last season, that's when he really took off," Douglass said. "It's a lot easier to get him the ball that way."

Douglass almost didn't have Green for his senior season. Green opted to make himself available for the NBA draft, but he wisely didn't sign with an agent. He wasn't chosen, and thus had the option to return to UC Irvine for his season year.

"I am excited about returning to UCI for my senior year and helping the team make another run at a conference title and a postseason berth," Green said after the draft. "This has been a positive experience for me and I thank everyone, especially my family and coaches, for being supportive of my aspirations. I am looking forward to finishing my college career and gaining my degree. Hopefully, I will have an opportunity to achieve my goal of playing professional basketball a year from now."

Suffice to say Douglass was delighted with the turn of events.

"We respected and supported Jerry's decision to pursue [the NBA]," Douglass said in late June. "This has been a good experience for him and has raised awareness of him with the NBA personnel. At the same time, it is great to have the conference MVP returning to the program."

Green's presence should prove a calming force in what would otherwise be a relatively inexperienced backcourt.

Aras Baskauskas (1.3 ppg, 1.1 rpg, 1.2), a 6-3 sophomore, played sparingly but well last season, and will once again be counted on to defend and be a "role guy," Douglass said.

Red-shirt **Mike Hood**, a 6-4 junior from the College of Southern Idaho, will be expected to make an immediate impact, especially with his outside shooting. He sat out last season with tendinitis in his knee, but shot 48 percent from three-point range at CSI.

A pair of 6-3 freshman could also battle for playing time in the backcourt. **DeVaughn Peace** was an all-state pick for a Bishop Montgomery (Torrance, Calif.) High School team that finished 30-2 and won a state title. **Jeff Gloger** averaged 13 points, 5.5 rebounds and 4.8 assists his senior season at Capistano Valley (Mission Viejo, Calif.) High School.

Julian Blake is a 6-3 red-shirt freshman walk-on who averaged 16 points and eight rebounds as a senior at Dorsey High. Ross Schraeder, a 6-5 freshman from Denver's East High School, is a likely red-shirt.

Even with Green in the backcourt, the Irvine strength could be in the paint. The Anteaters will rely heavily on Parada in the post, and Douglass thinks the big man is ready for the added pounding and strength. He's added some weight since last season—up from 240 to 245—which should help survive longer stints during the rugged conference season. He averaged just more than 20 minutes as a freshman, shot a team-high 56 percent from the floor and led the Anteaters in rebounding and in blocked shots with 41.

"We're looking for him to show more quality minutes," Douglass said. "He's still developing, but he has a good touch and is not afraid to take the big shot."

Irvine boasts another pair of big men who may lack Parada's scoring punch. But each has been known to change a shot or two on defense. **J.R. Christ** (4.4 ppg, 3.7 rpg), a 6-9 senior, is a bruiser with considerable experience. **Dave Korfman** (1.6 ppg, 1.6 rpg), a 7-2 senior, has slow feet but long arms. He is expected to fully recover from a head injury that forced him to miss several games last season.

"Those two will be physical enforcers for us," Douglass said. "We only need them to do a couple of things really well, defend and rebound."

A pair of talented sophomores also return for the Anteaters in the paint. The 6-10 **Stanislav Zuzak** (4.9 ppg, 3.3 rpg) was voted to the conference all-freshman team last season despite averaging just 15 minutes per game. His mid-range jumper is his biggest weapon, but he'll need to add some bulk if he plans to mix it up inside.

The 6-7 **Matt Okoro** (3.1 ppg, 3.4 rpg) red-shirted last season after playing as a freshman. The Anteaters simply needed the bodies two season ago, but the year off gave Okoro a chance to bulk up and mature in practice.

"He's one of the high flyers on this team," Douglass said. He gets up quick. Rebounding is his strong suit."

Ryan Codi, a 6-11 freshman post player from Prairie (Vancouver, Wash.) High School, is expected to red-shirt. He averaged 18.2 points, 10.5 rebounds and five blocks per game as a senior.

Harris is the final piece to the Irvine puzzle and he could be the most crucial. He averaged 13.9 points and seven rebounds per game as a sophomore at Colgate. He will give the Anteaters experience and explosiveness at the wing spot and should be able to keep defense from keying on Green on the perimeter.

"He'll go inside and outside ... he plays very athletic," Douglass said of Harris.

While the Anteaters look balanced and deep, Douglass does have a short laundry list of concerns, with three-point shooting at the top of that list. The Anteaters lost their two most productive long-range bombers in Sean Jackson and Ben Jones.

2001-2002 SCHEDULE

Nov.	16	St. Mary's
	20	Pepperdine
	23-25	#Robert Morris Thanksgiving Classic
	28	@Loyola Marymount
Dec.	1	UC Davis
	11	@San Diego
	15	@UCLA
	22	Long Beach State
	28-29	##Oneida Bingo & Casino Classic
Jan.	3	Cal State Fullerton
	5	UC Riverside
	10	@Utah State
	12	@Idaho
	17	Pacific
	19	Cal State Northridge
	24	@UC Santa Barbara
	26	@Cal Poly
	31	@UC Riverside
Feb.	2	@Cal State Fullerton
	7	Idaho
	9	Utah State
	14	@Cal State Northridge
	16	@Pacific
	21	Cal Poly
	23	UC Santa Barbara
March	2	@Long Beach State
	6-9	###Big West Tournament

@Road Games
#Moon Township, PA (vs. Illinois State first round; also Hofstra, Kent State, Oakland, Pittsburgh, Robert Morris, South Florida)
##Green Bay, WI (vs.Libscomb first round; also Boston University, Wisconsin-Green Bay)
###Anaheim Convention Center, Anaheim, CA

BLUE RIBBON ANALYSIS

BACKCOURT	B
BENCH/DEPTH	B-
FRONTCOURT	B
INTANGIBLES	A-

While the Anteaters may not be as strong top to bottom as they were last season, they'll be darn close.

With Green running the show, Irvine can never be overlooked. The returning conference player of the year earned the title for good reason and has gotten stronger and more productive every season under Douglass.

With some consistency and added confidence, Parada should be the conference's top post player while Colgate transfer Harris gives Irvine an experienced scorer and tough rebounder at small forward.

One question mark is in the backcourt, where the Anteaters lack a designated three-point shooter. Douglass does not expect another 25-victory season from this bunch, but anything less than 20 wins could be considered a disappointment.

(C.S.)

Cal Poly

LOCATION	San Luis Obispo, CA
CONFERENCE	Big West
LAST SEASON	9-19 (.321)
CONFERENCE RECORD	3-13 (8th)
STARTERS LOST/RETURNING	4/1
NICKNAME	Mustangs
COLORS	Forest Green & Gold
HOMECOURT	Mott Gym (3,032)

COACH	Kevin Bromley (Colorado State '83)
RECORD AT SCHOOL	4-12 (1 year)
CAREER RECORD	4-12 (1 year)
ASSISTANTS	Tim Murphy (Colorado State '84)
	Bob Lowe (George Fox College '85)
	Kevin Brown (UC Santa Cruz '94)
TEAM WINS (last 5 years)	14-14-11-10-9
RPI (last 5 years)	218-228-251-261-180
2000-01 FINISH	Lost in conference first round.

If ever a team needed a new direction, it's Cal Poly.

Kevin Bromley begins his first season as head coach of the conference's most blatant underachiever three years running. Bromley was handed the interim label last season after the mid-season firing of Jeff Schneider, and he earned the permanent spot after the Mustangs went 4-12 to close the season.

The Mustangs lost in the first round of the conference tournament. There was no miracle turnaround under Bromley, but Schneider's last two teams failed to reach the postseason despite high expectations and sparkling individual talent. Under Schneider, the Mustangs averaged just 10 wins per season since 1998-1999 despite being picked by coaches and media to finish near the top of the conference each season.

Bromley was Schneider's top assistant since 1995. His new staff includes no holdovers from the Schneider era.

"There is a definite newness to the program—a tremendous new feeling among the players," Bromley said. "Team chemistry will ultimately determine how we do this season."

You can't knock team chemistry, but Cal Poly will need much more if it hopes to climb the ladder in the Big West. The Mustangs lost three starters to graduation including the school's all-time leading scorer, Chris Bjorklund (18.1 ppg, 4.9 rpg).

Cal Poly took an additional hit when conference freshman- of-the-year Jamaal Scott (15.1 ppg, 5.9 rpg) transferred to Richmond.

What's left is a largely untested backcourt and a relatively talented frontcourt with a troubling history of injury. Bromley is high on several newcomers, but this team will have plenty to prove.

"I think it's safe to pick us in the middle of the pack," Bromley said.

If there was one player to build around, senior forward **Brandon Beeson** (8.2 ppg, 7.5 rpg) would be it. He's a warrior in the paint who plays as hard as anyone in the conference. Though not a gifted scorer, his relentlessness on the boards and nose for the ball make him a threat.

The downside on the 6-6 Beeson? Health. He missed the final month of last season with a knee injury. This after red-shirting the previous year because of injury and missing much of his sophomore season with a bad shoulder. Fluctuating weight also has been a concern for Beeson.

"He's lost a lot of weight and has done a lot to strengthen his knee," Bromley said. "But I worry about him when we get into the blood and guts part of the season."

Like Beeson, **Varnie Dennis** (8.7 ppg, 4.4 rpg) has the talent to be a force inside if his body cooperates. The 6-7 sophomore struggled with knee problems and conditioning last season but made the most of his minutes. He was an all-conference freshman team pick despite limited practice time and relatively short stints off the bench.

"He was very productive at times but at other times, he hid," Bromley said. "A lot of that was due to his conditioning."

Dennis had knee surgery in the spring, and the physicians "did a lot of work," Bromley said. "Will [his knee] ever be 100 percent? That I can't say. It will be 30 to 60 percent better than last year."

David Henry (4.5 ppg, 3. rpg) is a versatile 6-8 senior forward who has started portions of the last two seasons for the Mustangs and brings a solid inside-outside game.

"He can really shoot it, pass it and put it on the floor," Bromley said. "He also brings maturity and leadership."

James Grace III, a 6-5 junior, (2.5 ppg, 1.8 rpg) has experience and a big body and could be expected to up his scoring production this season, though his minutes may not increase dramatically if Bromley's inside recruits mature quickly.

"James is very athletic and uses both hands well around the basket," Bromley said. "I expect him to be a leader and to contribute when he's in there."

Bromley is high on his recruiting class and thinks he has three inside players who can make an impact early in their Cal Poly careers. The first is 6-11 post **Phil Johnson**, a freshman from Arroyo Grande (Calif.) High School. Johnson signed early with the Mustangs.

"He runs, has a soft touch, makes his free throws and is a shot blocker," Bromley said. "He needs to get acclimated to the Division I game, but I'm anxious to see how he scores the ball."

Yugoslavian native **Vladimir Lisinac**, a 6-9 freshman from Mt. Zion Christian Academy in Durham, N.C., is a complete package who averaged 14.4 points, eight rebounds and three assists last season on a Mt. Zion team that went 35-6.

"He can shoot it, he can pass it," Bromley said.

Cal Poly also landed 6-7 junior **Jared Patterson** from American River College in Sacramento, Calif. Bromley said Patterson has a "granite-type body" and will be a workhorse for the Mustangs.

"He has range to 17 feet," Bromley said. "He'll be productive in this league."

The Mustangs also have red-shirt 6-5 freshman forward **Mike Titchenal** on the roster. A good long-range shooter, Titchenal will be a situation player for the Mustangs—most likely finding time as a zone buster.

The Mustangs' backcourt is not likely to be as explosive as it was last season with Watende Favors (13.8 ppg, 3.8 rpg) having graduated, but roles should be better defined.

At the point, 5-11 red-shirt junior **Steve Geary, Jr.** will finally get his chance after sitting out last season with a back injury. A Carl Albert (Okla.) Junior College product, Geary was the projected starter last season before his injury.

The backup at the point will be another junior college transfer, 6-1 junior **Jason Allen** from Eastern Oklahoma College, where he averaged 6.2 points and 7.5 assists. Allen can also score when needed. He averaged nearly 23 points as a prep standout at Piedmont (Okla.) High. Bromley likes Allen's experience and size and would feel comfortable with him at the point should Geary continue to have back trouble.

"He's got a bigger, stronger body and he knows how to play," Bromley said. "In the Big West, he'll be a good-sized point guard."

Erick Jackson, a 22-year old sophomore from Utah Valley Junior College, looks to be the team's best true shooting guard. The 6-4 Jackson served on a Mormon mission last season and arrives at Cal Poly with added maturity. Jackson averaged 19 points and shot 42 percent from three-point range in high school.

The team's other guards—6-4 **Steve McClean** (0.8 ppg) and 6-3 **Bryan Brown** (0.8 ppg, 0.2 rpg)—are senior walk-ons expected to play little more than a bit part for the Mustangs.

Portland transfer Diaby Kamara, a versatile 6-7 forward who can shoot, rebound and pass, will sit out this season for the Mustangs.

Bromley's demeanor aside—he is considerably more mellow than the often high-strung Schneider—the first-year coach plans to tweak the way Cal Poly recruits. Freshmen were a priority for Schneider, which did not always translate to victories in the junior college-reliant Big West.

"I need a mixture here," Bromley said. "We can get junior college transfers but we need to do our homework."

2001-2002 SCHEDULE

Nov.	16	@Northern Arizona
	24	St. Mary's
	27	Portland State
	29	@Vanderbilt
Dec.	1	@Lipscomb
	9	@Eastern Washington
	15	Oregon State
	20	@Cal State Fullerton
	22	@UC Riverside
	30	Cal State Stanislaus
Jan.	3	Utah State
	5	Idaho
	10	@Pacific
	12	@Cal State Northridge
	16	Sacramento State
	19	UC Santa Barbara
	24	Long Beach State
	26	UC Irvine
	31	@Idaho
Feb.	2	@Utah State

	7	Cal State Northridge
	9	Pacific
	16	@UC Santa Barbara
	21	@UC Irvine
	23	@Long Beach State
	28	UC Riverside
March	2	Cal State Fullerton
	6-9	#Big West Tournament

@Road Games
#Anaheim Convention Center, Anaheim, CA

BLUE RIBBON ANALYSIS

BACKCOURT	C-
BENCH/DEPTH	C
FRONTCOURT	B-
INTANGIBLES	D

If Bromley does little more than provide stability to a wayward program, his first season at Cal Poly will be considered a success.

For starters, Bromley is realistic about his team's chances, which should take some of the pressure off a relatively young team.

The season hinges on the health—and the weight—of forwards Beeson and Dennis. The duo has the skills to be one of the best inside tandems in the conference, but nagging injuries and conditioning issues continue to be of concern.

Plenty will be expected of Geary, who leads a group of three junior college transfers in the backcourt.

Don't look for huge strides this season, but baby steps should work just fine for a team that has seen its win total stay the same or drop every season since 1995-96.

(C.S.)

UC Riverside

LOCATION	Riverside, CA
CONFERENCE	Big West
LAST SEASON	8-17 (.320)
CONFERENCE RECORD	NA
STARTERS LOST/RETURNING	2/3
NICKNAME	Highlanders
COLORS	Blue & Gold
HOMECOURT	Student Recreation Center (3,168)
COACH	John Masi (UC Riverside '71)
RECORD AT SCHOOL	First year
CAREER RECORD	First year
ASSISTANTS	Rusty Smith (Cal State Northridge '71)
	Reggie Howard (UC Riverside '84)
	Darren French (Cal State Bernardino '98)
TEAM WINS (last 5 years)	19-16-14-15-9
RPI (last 5 years)	NA
2000-01 FINISH	Lost regular-season finale.

For all his success as head coach at UC Riverside, it's entertaining to know John Masi once was a professional loser.

Masi played for the New York Nationals in 1970-71 and was regularly made to look foolish on tour with the Harlem Globetrotters.

While Masi's professional career was somewhat of a joke, his coaching career at Riverside has been the polar opposite. In 21 years at Riverside, Masi's record of 428-187 (.685) includes 11 appearances in the Division II NCAA Tournament, highlighted by a runner-up finish in 1996.

Masi's coaching journey takes a huge step forward this season as Riverside makes its debut in the Big West Conference and as an official Division I institution. Significant? You bet, especially after two seasons in limbo between Division II and Division I.

Last year's team went 8-16 against a Division I schedule but was considered a Division II independent. The 1999-2000 version played a Division II schedule but was ineligible for the postseason.

The Highlanders' chances at immediate success in the Big West Conference aren't great, but Masi is already reaping rewards of the switch.

"It's a big relief in terms of the scheduling," Masi said. "The Big West means 18 games in conference ... more than half the season. [Playing in a conference] should give the players a sense of accomplishment. Last year

we played but weren't anywhere. We did get the lay of the land."

The land, as might be expected, was rocky. The losing record marked the first in Masi's Riverside career. Before last season the team's worst finish under Masi had been a .500 showing in 1980-81.

Masi relished the season despite the ups and downs. The Highlanders were 2-10 against Big West competition, beating Cal State Fullerton and UC Santa Barbara at home. The season's biggest victory came on the road at Oregon State in early December.

"I didn't look at wins and losses because we were in so much of a developmental stage," Masi said. "We were into improvement. We got a little experience and in the next year or two we'll get over the hump. In a lot of people's eyes we were competitive and played hard."

In terms of personnel, Riverside will be one of the youngest teams in the conference, with its top five returning scorers either juniors or sophomores.

"We'll have pretty much the entire team back for the next two years," Masi said.

The strength of the Highlanders will be at the forward spot, where 6-6 junior **Mark Miller** (13.2 ppg, 3.6 rpg) and 6-8 sophomore **Vili Morton** (8.5 ppg, 7.2 rpg) each return.

Miller is a third-year starter who led the Highlanders in scoring each of his first two seasons. He can step outside and shoots free throws adequately, which makes him tough to defend, especially with his good size for a small forward.

"Mark's always been good on offense, but we need him to be a more complete player," Masi said. "He needs to be a leader and improve on defense."

Morton was the surprise of last season, starting 23-of-25 games and leading the team in rebounds and blocked shots as a freshman power forward.

Morton was a red-shirt candidate when he arrived at Riverside at the age of 17 but when a recruit fell through, Masi said he had no choice but to give Morton the minutes.

"He showed he can play," Masi said. "The big thing for him this year will be endurance and strength."

Scrappy 6-7 junior **Aaron Hands** (5.9 ppg, 5.7 rpg) returns and will fight for playing time in the paint, as will 6-6 senior **Lloyd Cook** (4.4 ppg, 3.7 rpg), 6-10 junior **Mike Zepeda** (1.3 ppg, 1.3 rpg) and newcomer **John Galbreath**, a 6-6 junior out of Big Bend Community College in Moses Lake, Wash.

Of that group, Galbreath is the most intriguing. He averaged 30 point per game at Big Bend as a sophomore, shooting 65 percent from the field and 42 percent from three-point range. He also shot 85 percent from the free-throw line.

"He's got the firepower," Masi said.

Hands and Zepeda are expected to be role players, Masi said, playing quality minutes for Miller and Morton.

Cook is one of the team's two seniors and is a journeyman of sorts, beginning his college career at Centenary College before transferring to Fresno State for a quarter then landing at Riverside.

Riverside's remaining inside players are 6-11 sophomore project **Jake Dederer** (1.1 ppg, .6 rpg), **Christian Ebenrecht**, a 6-11 freshman from Germany who is a likely red-shirt, and **Cedric Lusk**, a slim 6-8 junior swingman from Cerritos (Calif.) Junior College, where he averaged 16 points, seven rebounds, four assists and three blocks as a sophomore. Lusk sat out last season at Riverside to concentrate on his grades.

The Riverside backcourt does not boast a true point guard but features a handful of players who can do a little of everything. The two top returners are 6-3 sophomores **Ted Bell** (7.5 ppg, 1.2 rpg) and **Kevin Butler** (5.9 ppg, 1.8 rpg, 1.9 apg). Bell shot a team-best 41 percent from three-point range last season and Masi expects him to mature into a dependable double-digit scorer for the Highlanders.

"Defensively, he occasionally got a little confused," Masi said. "But when we needed a big shot on offense, he was the one to take it."

Butler had his good games and bad, Masi said, but his athleticism will always earn him good minutes.

"He can defend," Masi said. "He has the athletic ability to play in this league."

Jason Perkins (4.1 ppg, 1.6 rpg), a 6-4 senior, and **Zadkiel Elder** (2 ppg, 0.5 rpg), a 6-2 junior, are Riverside's other backcourt players with experience. Perkins averaged 14.6 minutes per game last season, seeing his production decrease dramatically from the 1999-2000 season, when he averaged 7.1 points and four rebounds. Elder averaged just 8.4 minutes per game and shot poorly from the field (29.4 percent) and free-throw line (40 percent).

The ineffectiveness of Perkins and Elder could mean immediate playing time for a pair of newcomers in 6-4 junior **Jake Wessel** from Indian Hills (Iowa) Community College and 6-3 freshman **Rickey Porter** from California prep power Mater Dei High School in Santa Ana.

Masi said both can provide scoring punch. Wessel started his college career at Western Illinois, where he averaged 2.8 points and 1.3 rebounds in 12.7 minutes per game.

Porter averaged 12.3 points, 3.2 rebounds and 2.1 assists for Mater Dei in helping lead the Monarchs to a state title and national ranking.

2001-2002 SCHEDULE

Nov.	17	@Portland
	27	@Arizona State
	30	#Fresno State Tournament
Dec.	1	#Fresno State Tournament
	5	@UCLA
	8	@Southern Utah
	15	UC Santa Cruz
	20	UC Santa Barbara
	22	Cal Poly
	27	Sacramento State
Jan.	3	@Long Beach State
	5	@UC Irvine
	12	Cal State Fullerton
	17	Utah State
	19	Idaho
	24	@Pacific
	26	@Cal State Northridge
	31	UC Irvine
Feb.	2	Long Beach State
	9	@Cal State Fullerton
	14	@Idaho
	16	@Utah State
	21	Cal State Northridge
	23	Pacific
	28	@Cal Poly
March	2	@UC Santa Barbara
	6-9	##Big West Tournament

@Road Games
#Fresno, CA (vs. Fresno State first round; also Air Force, Montana State)
##Anaheim Convention Center, Anaheim, CA

BLUE RIBBON ANALYSIS

BACKCOURT	D
BENCH/DEPTH	D+
FRONTCOURT	C+
INTANGIBLES	C

Riverside, making the jump from Division II, has a winner on the bench in veteran coach Masi. On the court, however, the Highlanders don't look to have the talent or depth to make an immediate splash in the Big West.

That doesn't mean Riverside will be outclassed. It was 2-10 against conference teams last season and with Masi at the helm should be able to hang with, and beat, several of the conference's second-division outfits. Talented forwards Miller and Morton will make sure of that.

Masi's biggest task this season could be finding the eight or nine players he can rely on to produce. Last season Masi spread minutes by design, with 10 players seeing between 14 and 26 minutes. This season, expect a tighter rotation and a little more aggressiveness on offense.

"Last year we were checking out the weather, so to speak," Masi said.

(C.S.)

UC Santa Barbara

LOCATION	Santa Barbara, CA
CONFERENCE	Big West
LAST SEASON	13-15 (.464)
CONFERENCE RECORD	9-7 (4th)
STARTERS LOST/RETURNING	0/5
NICKNAME	Gauchos

COLORS	Blue &Gold
HOMECOURT	The Thunderdome (6,000)
COACH	Bob Williams (San Jose State '76)
RECORD AT SCHOOL	42-42 (3 years)
CAREER RECORD	42-42 (3 years)
ASSISTANTS	Marty Wilson (Pepperdine '89)
	David Campbell (St. Mary's '80)
	Mark Amaral (College of Idaho '90)
TEAM WINS (last 5 years)	12-7-15-14-13
RPI (last 5 years)	212-272-189-206-196
2000-01 FINISH	Lost in conference first round.

UC Santa Barbara coach Bob Williams is quick to correct those who think he has six starters returning for the 2001-2002 season.

"We've got seven," Williams said.

Darn it if the coach isn't right.

After three seasons of .500 basketball on the California coast, Williams and the Gauchos appear primed to take a huge step forward. Dangerous and young, they have to be considered among the conference's upper crust.

The team returns all five starters and an experienced sixth man who started eight times a year ago. Toss in senior **Adama Ndiaye**, a bulked-up big man who sat out last season with a fractured finger, and the Gauchos are, well, stacked.

"It's really different this year," Williams said. "The first year here we had nothing. The next year we lost two of our best post players to injury. Last year we played with basically three freshmen. This year is the first time we come back with a veteran at every position. That should help us a great deal."

It won't hurt, that's for certain.

While there are plenty of reasons for optimism, the bulk of the good vibrations come from the return of the 6-9, 245-pound Ndiaye, who averaged 9.3 points, 7.5 rebounds and 1.7 blocks per game during his junior season in 1999-2000. He fractured the ring finger on his left hand just before the 2000-2001 season opener and red-shirted.

His finger is completely healed, and an extra season in the weight room and a summer playing for Senegal's national team should make Ndiaye one of the best post players in the conference. He's an adequate scorer, but does his best work on the boards and on defense, where his long arms will change more than a few shots.

Ndiaye will have some talented company in the paint with 6-9 senior **Mike Vukovich** (11.1 ppg, 5.7 rpg), who made dramatic strides in Ndiaye's absence, earning second-team all-conference honors. When asked if Vukovich was expected to produce the way he did, Williams replied with an emphatic "absolutely not."

Vukovich and Ndiaye are expected to play side by side in Williams' two-post offensive scheme.

"We had [Vukovich] slated to play 10 minutes a game off the bench," Williams said. "He ended up playing 23 minutes and had an all-league type of year. He has a knack for catching and scoring. He's confident and assertive."

Vukovich's breakout season included a monster game against Pacific, where he scored 27 points on a perfect 12-of-12 shooting from the field.

Backups at the post include a pair of injury-plagued sophomores. The 6-11 **J.J. Todd** (0.6 ppg, 1.6 rpg) was used sparingly last season but boasts good size and potential if his body holds up. A herniated disc problem could limit his playing time.

Transfer **Bryan Whitehead** is a 6-8 sophomore who played limited minutes as a freshman at Washington State. He's suffered from shoulder problems, and that took a mental toll, Williams said.

"I think he's a whole lot better than he showed [at WSU]," Williams said. "He's a prime example of player who needs to find his comfort zone. We think he'll find that here. He should be good to play some minutes."

Casey Cook (4.1 ppg, 3.1 rpg), a 6-8 sophomore, also returns, but Williams hopes the health of Todd and Whitehead holds up, allowing for Cook to red-shirt. The injury to Ndiaye last season forced Cook to play perhaps more than Williams had hoped.

Scott Rainey, a 6-10 freshman from Astoria (Oregon) High School, is a likely red-shirt.

At the wing, **Mark Hull** (13.9 ppg, 4.1 rpg), a 6-7 junior, is the team's top returning scorer and a returning all conference second-team pick. Hull played more of a power-forward spot the last two years, but Williams said he should see more time on the perimeter this season.

Hull's 679 points as a Gaucho mark the second-highest combined freshman and sophomore year total in

school history. He was an all-conference freshman team pick after averaging 10.3 points and five rebounds and leading the team in minutes played.

"He poses problems," Williams said. "He's the guy we need to have on the floor."

Two of last year's super freshmen, 6-4 **Branduinn Fullove** (12.2 ppg, 5.0 rpg, 3.2 apg) and 6-4 **Nick Jones** (9.8 ppg, 4.2 rpg, 1.2 apg), will be tough to keep off the court. Both were all-conference freshman team picks and both are pictures of versatility. Each recorded double-doubles last season, and Fullove, in addition to leading the team in assists on the season and scoring during conference play, twice led the team in scoring, rebounding and assists in one game.

"[Fullove] can play the one, two or three, but he's probably best at the wing," Williams said. "He's a good scorer, passer, defender and rebounder."

Williams called Jones the team's "warrior."

"He just got better and better," Williams said.

Like every other spot on the court, the point should be in good hands with the return of 6-1 sophomore **Jacoby Atako** (4.7 ppg, 2.3 rpg, 2.9 apg) and 6-1 junior **B.J. Ward** (4.5 ppg, 3 rpg, 2.9 apg, 1.4 spg). Atako registered more starts than Ward but the two finished the year with nearly the same number of minutes. Atako is penciled in as the starter this season.

"I don't think it's a big deal for them who starts," Williams said. "They're good friends. They push each other."

Three other freshman guards are on the Santa Barbara roster, but it's not likely they are to see much time right away. The most promising is **Cecil Brown**, an explosive 6-4 shooting guard from Canoga Park (Calif.) High School can play if needed, Williams said, but may red-shirt. Brown averaged more than 32 points per game as a senior at Canoga Park.

Chris Newell, a 6-4 product from Eastside Catholic (Bellevue, Wash.) High School and Chrisman Oliver, a 5-8 point guard from St. Bernards (Los Angeles) High, are walk-ons.

2001-2002 SCHEDULE

Nov.	17	Westmont
	24	@San Francisco
	26	@USC
	28	BYU
Dec.	1	St. Mary's
	5	@Loyola Marymount
	8	Pepperdine
	20	@UC Riverside
	22	@Cal State Fullerton
	28-29	#Cable Car Classic
Jan.	3	Idaho
	5	Utah State
	10	@Cal State Northridge
	12	@Pacific
	19	@Cal Poly
	24	UC Irvine
	26	Long Beach State
	31	@Utah State
Feb.	2	@Idaho
	7	Pacific
	9	Cal State Northridge
	16	Cal Poly
	21	@Long Beach State
	23	@UC Irvine
	28	Cal State Fullerton
March	2	UC Riverside
	6-8	##Big West Tournament

@Road Games
#Santa Clara, CA (vs. Detroit first round; also Maryland, Santa Clara)
##Anaheim Convention Center, Anaheim, CA

BLUE RIBBON ANALYSIS

BACKCOURT	B+
BENCH/DEPTH	B+
FRONTCOURT	A-
INTANGIBLES	B

Coaches dream of having six—or even seven—starters returning and Williams is living that dream. The Gauchos boast a potent 1-2 punch in the paint with 6-9 bookends Ndiaye and Vukovich, but are equally as strong on the perimeter with three versatile sophomores who shined as starters last season.

Toss in perhaps the team's most skilled player in

small forward Hull and the Gauchos have all the ingredients for a run at a conference title.

Something to work on? The Gauchos are notorious slow starters and would do themselves a favor by picking up some victories in November and December. The last three seasons, the Gauchos have begun the year with records of 0-8, 2-7, and 2-7.

That said, anything less than a 20-win season could be considered a disappointment.

(C.S.)

Cal State Fullerton

LOCATION	Fullerton, CA
CONFERENCE	Big West
LAST SEASON	5-23 (.179)
CONFERENCE RECORD	3-13 (t-7th)
STARTERS LOST/RETURNING	0/5
NICKNAME	Titans
COLORS	Navy, Orange & White
HOMECOURT	Titan Gym (3,500)
COACH	Donny Daniels (Cal State Fullerton '77)
RECORD AT SCHOOL	5-23 (1 year)
CAREER RECORD	5-23 (1 year)
ASSISTANTS	Jason Levy (Cal State Northridge '93)
	Rob Orellana (Regents College '87)
	Mark Maki (Wyoming '97)
TEAM WINS (last 5 years)	13-12-13-3-5
RPI (last 5 years)	251-202-220-294-293
2000-01 FINISH	Lost in conference quarterfinal.

To his credit, Fullerton head coach Donny Daniels makes no excuses for his first season at his alma mater.

Due to recruiting sanctions stemming from violations back in 1993, Daniels' team was thin to begin with, and grew thinner as injuries and eligibility problems hit. The Titans limped through the season, playing several February games with just eight eligible and healthy athletes.

The result was a 5-23 record, the program's second consecutive single-digit victory season. It was not the type of debut a coach hopes for, especially Daniels, who had been turned down twice in prior attempts to land the Fullerton job.

"Things happen in every program, it just happened in my first year," Daniels said. "We just have to deal with it. You can't say 'Woe is me.' You can't feel sorry for yourself. As I tell my team, if this is the worst things that happens in your life, you'll have a good life."

Fullerton remains under NCAA recruiting sanctions until Dec. 1. Those sanctions limit Fullerton to 11 scholarships and prohibit the recruitment of junior college players. The junior college players on the roster all were walk-ons, and weren't confirmed by the university until late August.

"Probation does exactly what it's supposed to do," Daniels said. "It cripples and hurts you. But it's good to see that cloud lifting. We need to regroup and get recruiting."

Hurdles aside, the Titans did make dramatic strides late last season by winning two of their final four regular season games. The two losses in that stretch—to Long Beach State at home and UC Irvine on the road—were by a total of four points.

Fullerton's improvement at season's end should carry over, especially for a backcourt that returns intact. The most versatile of the returning guards is 6-5 senior **Kevin Richardson** (11.6 ppg, 2.7 rpg), who played both the point and shooting-guard spots and occasionally filled in at small forward. He averaged better than 30 minutes per game.

David Castleton (7.8 ppg, 1.8 rpg, 3.4 apg), who missed the first eight games of the season for academic reasons, quickly became a fixture at the point and seemed to get better all season. The 6-2 senior started 19 times and averaging 32 minutes per game.

Ryan Dillon (8.7 ppg, 2.7 rpg), a 6-2 sophomore, matured quickly as a shooting guard and became the team's most potent three-point threat. He finished the season at 36.8 percent from long range and in conference play averaged a Big West-best 2.8 threes per game.

Dillon showed his explosiveness in a Jan. 31 game against Boise State, where he made a school-record 10 three-pointers and finished with 27 points.

A fourth returning guard, 5-9 sophomore **Chris**

Smith (3.7 ppg, 1.4 rpg) was a competent reserve averaging 16 minutes per game.

Newcomers in the backcourt are **Chris Alexander**, a 6-3 freshman from Price High School in Los Angeles; **Derick Andrew**, a 6-1 sophomore from Rancho Cucamonga (Calif.) High School; **Denver Lopez**, a 6-1 sophomore transfer from Cal State University-Dominguez Hills; **Andrew Maxie**, a 6-4 freshman from LaPuente (Calif.) High School; **Daniel Ryan**, a junior transfer from Chaffey Junior College in Rancho Cucamonga, Calif.; and **Montelle Williams**, a 6-3 freshman from Dominguez Hills High in California.

Daniels said Andrew and Lopez have the best shot at contributing immediately, but Daniels hesitated in ruling out any player's potential worth, especially after the roster gymnastics of last season.

"I don't want any player losing the mental edge, thinking, 'I'm going to red-shirt this year anyway,' " Daniels said.

At small forward, the athletic but injury-bitten **Brandon Campbell** returns to provide some stability to a frontline with more than its share of questions marks.

Campbell, a 6-4 junior and conference high jump and long jump champion, suffered a knee injury in the season-opener last season and made a brief but ineffective comeback several weeks into the season before taking the medical red-shirt. He was effective the previous season, averaging 10.7 points and 4.7 rebounds.

The other returnees to the Fullerton frontcourt are 6-11 junior **Babacar Camara** (7.5 ppg, 4.4 rpg) and 6-9 senior **Josh Fischer** (6 ppg, 3.4 rpg). Camara, a native of Senegal and transfer from Cheickantadiop University in Dakar, was a pleasant surprise for the Titans. He's raw, but moves well for a big man and will only get better.

Fischer is a three-year letter winner who didn't shoot the ball well from the field last season (.382) but isn't afraid to step outside the three-point line and let fly.

A fourth returning front line player, 6-8 senior **Daniel Kohn** (3.9 ppg, 4.0 rpg), suffered a severe knee injury in the final weeks of last season and will miss all of this season after major reconstructive surgery.

As is the case with the backcourt, a slew of newcomers will be in the hunt for playing time. They are 6-6 **Amir Bar-Netzer** and 6-9 **Derrick Franklin**, both juniors from Southern California's Santa Monica Community College; **Wagner Moreno**, a 6-8 junior from Hope University in Fullerton, Calif.; and **Pape Sow**, a 6-10 junior out of Chaffey Junior College in Rancho Cucamonga.

Of the new big men, Daniels said Sow and Franklin have the skills to contribute right away. Sow, like Camara, is a native of Senegal.

Daniels said the key to improving this year lies with three things: improved assists-to-turnover ratio, field-goal percentage defense and rebound margin.

"I never measure improvement on wins and losses," Daniels said. "We're going to measure improvement on effort on a daily basis."

2001-2002 SCHEDULE

Nov.	17	@Pepperdine
	19	San Francisco
	24	Loyola Marymount
	29	@Baylor
Dec.	1	@Wyoming
	6	@Sacramento State
	8	Point Loma
	15	Sacramento State
	20	Cal Poly
	22	UC Santa Barbara
	29	@Northern Arizona
Jan.	3	@UC Irvine
	5	@Long Beach State
	12	@UC Riverside
	17	Idaho
	19	Utah State
	24	@Cal State Northridge
	26	@Pacific
	31	Long Beach State
Feb.	2	UC Irvine
	9	UC Riverside
	14	@Utah State
	16	@Idaho
	21	Pacific
	23	Cal State Northridge
	28	@UC Santa Barbara
March	2	@Cal Poly
	6-9	#Big West Tournament

@Road Games
#Anaheim Convention Center, Anaheim, CA

BLUE RIBBON ANALYSIS

BACKCOURT	B-
BENCH/DEPTH	C
FRONTCOURT	C-
INTANGIBLES	C

Fullerton should be better this season, but don't expect improvement in leaps and bounds. The Titans should feel comfortable with the returning talent and depth in the backcourt, where the versatile Richardson should complement playmaker Castleton and shooter Dillon.

A trio of experienced inside players return in Campbell,

Camara and Fischer, but that trio lacks the firepower to compete with the big front lines of the conference.

Because of lingering NCAA sanctions for past recruiting violations, Fullerton remains a work in progress.

Daniels cut his teeth as a recruiter under Rick Majerus at Utah, and his direct, no-nonsense approach to the game should help him build a winner at his alma mater, just not this year.

(C.S.)

Cal State Northridge

LOCATION	Northridge, CA
CONFERENCE	Big West
LAST SEASON	22-10 (.688)
CONFERENCE RECORD	13-3 (1st Big Sky)
STARTERS LOST/RETURNING	3/2
NICKNAME	Matadors
COLORS	Red, White & Black
HOMECOURT	The Matadome (1,600)
COACH	Bobby Braswell (CS Northridge '84)
RECORD AT SCHOOL	85-63 (5 years)
CAREER RECORD	85-63 (5 years)
ASSISTANTS	John Dahlager (San Francisco St '94)
	Kenya Wilkins (Oregon '97)
	Danny Sprinkle (Montana State '00)
TEAM WINS (last 5 years)	14-12-17-20-22
RPI (last 5 years)	194-242-154-95-82
2000-01 FINISH	Lost in NCAA first round

Bobby Braswell and Cal State Northridge left the Big Sky Conference exactly where they hoped to be. On top.

The Matadors, who have increased their victory total every season since 1997-98, finished the 2000-01 season with a school record 22 wins, a first-ever Big Sky regular season championship (13-3), a first-ever Big Sky Tournament title and first-ever trip to the NCAA Tournament as the Big Sky's automatic berth.

Another big first awaits the Matadors in 2001-02—their debut in the Big West Conference. Northridge is one of two new teams in the conference. UC Riverside is the other.

"I think we had a great run in the Big Sky," Braswell said. "It was a great experience, but at the same time I really believe the new conference is right for us."

While it hasn't always been the case, Northridge's jump from the Big Sky to the Big West will be considered a move up the food chain in terms of conference strength. The Big West's conference RPI last season was 18, while the Big Sky's was 25.

Another pair of plusses associated with the move? Travel and rivalries. Finding the path of least resistance to road games—no more Bozeman, Mont., in the middle of a January snowstorm—should be a breeze with eight of the conference's 10 teams located in California. With seven of those 10 in Southern and central California, regional rivalries will be easy to foster than with Eastern Washington or Northern Arizona.

"The natural rivalries will be great," Braswell said. "It will give our fans a reason to come out and pack the place."

On the court, the Matadors may begin the season as a bit of a mystery. The team lost seven letter winners, three starters and 79 percent of last season's scoring. What's left is one full-time starter and just three others who averaged more than eight minutes per game in 2000-01. Braswell believes he has a handful of newcomers who should be able to step right in.

"I like that not too many folks know too much about us," Braswell said. "I've always said we can play with anybody, and we've never shied away from playing big names."

One of the conference's top perimeter players will be 6-1 senior guard **Markus Carr** (8.7 ppg, 2.3 rpg, 8.9 apg, 1.8 spg), an All-Big Sky first-team pick who led the country in assist average last season. With the loss of so much offensive firepower, expect Carr to score a little more this season and pass a bit less. The Matadors can't afford to go long stretches without him pushing an offense designed to score in bunches.

"He's one of the top point guards in the country," Braswell said. "He's very mature … very talented. We'll ask him to do a lot more in terms of scoring. He could always score when he wanted, and this year he will get more of a chance."

Backing up Carr could be 6-0 junior college transfer **Edward Estevan**, a walk-on from Los Angeles City College who was not heavily recruited but won 64 games in two years at LACC and shoots 48 percent from three-point range.

Keith Jackson (0.3 ppg, 0.3 rpg), a 6-0 sophomore who played a total of 19 minutes last season, is the only other point guard on the roster.

A late roster addition is **Steve Moore**, a 6-3 freshman guard from nearby Dominguez High School.

The shooting guard and small-forward spots should be rich in terms of depth, but where the bodies fall may not be decided until late in the fall.

Perhaps the most intriguing of the bunch is 6-7 sophomore **Curtis Slaughter**, who averaged 10.2 points and 3.8 rebounds at Loyola Marymount in 1999-2000 before jumping a then-sinking ship. Slaughter can do a little of everything, potentially even some point, and does bring a full season of Division I experience, which may give him the edge at earning the start in the backcourt.

Others to keep an eye on at the shooting guard or small-forward spots include a pair of red-shirts in 6-4 freshmen **Gene Myvett** and **Sidney Hampton**. Both were proven scorers in high school and benefited from an extra season to prepare.

Newcomers at the two or three include two freshman, 6-3 **Joseph Frazier** from John Muir High School in Pasadena, Calif., and 6-6 **Ian Boylan** from Norman (Okla.) High School. Frazier averaged 16 points and seven rebounds per game as a senior while Boylan poured in 27.4 points, grabbed eight rebounds and had five assists per game at Norman.

"Boylan has the chance to be a really good player," Braswell said. "Frazier is one of the toughest guys I've ever recruited. He's quick and explosive."

The Matadors will be hard pressed to replace the scoring punch of departed Brian Heinle (20.2 ppg) and Jeff Parris (14.0 ppg) inside, but Braswell recruited well at the power forward and center spots, which should help things.

At power forward, 6-8 senior **Joey Busch** (3.9 ppg, 3.3 rpg) is back and comes off a solid debut season. Busch averaged just 12 minutes per game last season but shot well (.526) from the floor and finished fourth on the team in rebounds.

Pushing Busch will be 6-9 junior **Armand Thomas**, a 225-pounder who averaged 14 points and nine rebounds at Los Angeles' Compton College. Thomas is a Crenshaw High product, as are two other Braswell recruits.

"He's just a beast inside," Braswell said of Thomas. "He's the type of kid who wants to dunk everything … and he loves to rebound."

The other Crenshaw products are **Chris Davis** and **Ryan Sims**. Davis, a 6-8, 230-pound freshman, averaged 15 points and six boards at Crenshaw last season. Sims, a 6-9, 220-pound junior, spent two seasons at Los Angeles City College, where he averaged 12.3 points, 9.1 rebounds and four blocks as a sophomore. Sims should battle 6-10 junior **Dan Read** (1.1 ppg, 1.2 rpg) for the starting post spot.

Lionel Benjamin (2.5 ppg, 1.7 rpg), a 6-3 junior, and Jermar Welch (2.8 ppg, 2 rpg), a 6-6 senior, each averaged about eight minutes per game last season and played a lot of forward, though they may be a bit undersized. Benjamin started nine games for the Matadors last season and shot the ball superbly (.733) in limited minutes.

"A few of the coaches I've talked to think we will have the most athletic big men in the conference," Braswell said. "We like the luxury of having guys who can run."

2001-2002 SCHEDULE

Nov.	17	Nevada
	19	Dominican
	26	@Howard
Dec.	1	@San Diego State
	4	@Wyoming
	8	@Nevada
	16	Southern Illinois
	20	@Utah State
	22	@Idaho
	27	@BYU
Jan.	3	San Diego
	5	Pacific
	10	UC Santa Barbara
	12	Cal Poly
	17	@Long Beach State
	19	@UC Irvine
	24	Cal State Fullerton
	26	UC Riverside
	31	@Pacific
Feb.	7	@Cal Poly
	9	@UC Santa Barbara
	14	UC Irvine
	16	Long Beach State
	21	@UC Riverside
	23	@Cal State Fullerton
	28	Idaho
March	2	Utah State
	6-9	#Big West Tournament

@Road Games
#Anaheim Convention Center, Anaheim, CA

BLUE RIBBON ANALYSIS

BACKCOURT	B
BENCH/DEPTH	B-
FRONTCOURT	B-
INTANGIBLES	C

While Northridge isn't considered among the conference's big five—Long Beach, Pacific, Irvine, UC Santa Barbara and Utah State—this season, the Matadors are a step above the conference's bottom dwellers and should be disappointed with anything less than a mid-pack finish.

The one known commodity is at the point, where Carr's stamina and creativity will be tested. Braswell has cashed in recent successes and a berth in last year's NCAA Tournament by landing some solid transfer and junior college talent, but with so many new faces it may take time for everyone to get on the same page.

Watch out for former Loyola Marymount player Curtis Slaughter, who at 6-7 can handle the ball and mix it up inside. He's a sophomore with experience who should make an immediate impact.

(C.S.)

Idaho

LOCATION	Moscow, ID
CONFERENCE	Big West
LAST SEASON	6-21 (.222)
CONFERENCE RECORD	3-13 (t-7th)
STARTERS LOST/RETURNING	2/3
NICKNAME	Vandals
COLORS	Silver & Gold
HOMECOURT	Cowan Spectrum (7,000)
COACH	Leonard Perry (Idaho '95)
RECORD AT SCHOOL	First year
CAREER RECORD	First year
ASSISTANTS	Donny Tyndall (Morehead State '93)
	Mark Leslie (Idaho '98)
	Jason Ficca (Idaho '94)
TEAM WINS (last 5 years)	13-15-16-12-6
RPI (last 5 years)	196-142-153-195-282
2000-01 FINISH	Lost regular-season finale.

For all his reputed talent as an Xs and Os coach, Dave Farrar never really caught on at Idaho. His teams enjoyed mild success—averaging 14 victories his first three seasons in Moscow—and Farrar even had a certain flair for recruiting junior college standouts.

It was Farrar's inability to keep those recruits, or keep them happy, that ultimately sealed his fate. Farrar was fired in March following a dreadful 6-21 season preceded by the departure of a handful of disgruntled players.

Leonard Perry was hired several weeks later to pick up the pieces. It's a dream job and huge challenge for the 32-year-old Perry, who played two seasons at Idaho as a point guard in the early 1990s.

Perry most recently served as the top assistant to Larry Eustachy at Iowa State. Perry played for Eustachy for one season at Idaho and also served on Eustachy's staff at Idaho and Utah State.

"This is a great opportunity and what a fantastic place to have that opportunity," Perry said. "It is something I have worked hard for and I hope I've learned the right things. There are many challenges with this program, but there is all the optimism in the world as to the direction we're headed."

Given where they were last season, it would be tough for the Vandals to go anywhere but up.

"We've got a huge goal of putting [last year] behind us," Perry said. "The guys returning have been very receptive to that idea."

Idaho's seven returnees include three starters and three others who saw quality minutes last season. The most intriguing of the veterans is 6-5 junior shooting guard **Jerald "Moe" Jenkins** (10.6 ppg, 3.1 rpg), who played in the team's final 14 games and earned the Big West Conference's sixth-man award.

What Jenkins lacked in fundamentals he made up for in energy and athleticism. He finished the season second on the team in field-goal percentage (.421) and first in blocked shots (12). His ability to slash to the basket and create shots inside made him a fan favorite. His tendency to get out of control earned him frequent trips back to the bench.

"We certainly have high expectations for Moe," Perry said. "He's a young man who is still learning. The experience last season was invaluable. He needs to be a better defender and rebounder with his athleticism."

The only other two guard on the Idaho roster is 6-4 senior **Nate Watson** (1.9 ppg, 1.7 rpg), a career bit player who averaged 10 minutes per game as a junior before his season ended with a ruptured spleen.

Given Jenkins' rawness and Watson's physical limitations, don't be surprised if the team's most versatile player and top returning scorer, 6-6 senior **Matt Gerschefske** (11 ppg, 3.6 rpg), sees more time at the big-guard spot. Gerschefske has range past the three-point line and takes good care of the basketball. While he may lack Jenkins' flair, he always finds a way to score.

"Matt will play wherever we need him to play, from the two to the five," Perry said. "I know he's worked his butt off and is looking forward to the season."

The point guard position looks to be in capable hands with the return of 6-1 senior **Bethuel Fletcher** (7.3 ppg, 3 rpg, 3 apg), 6-0 junior **Justin Logan** (1.8 ppg, 1.7 apg), and the addition of 6-0 freshman **Tanoris Shepard**.

Fletcher led the Vandals in minutes played last season despite shooting just 35 percent from the field and hitting just 17-of-58 (.293) three-point attempts in conference play.

Logan, a solid if unspectacular reserve, rarely looked to score and played solid defense.

Shepard, who Perry described as a "talented, true point guard," prepped at Saginaw (Mich.) High School.

"We just need those guys to steady the ship, take care of the ball and make good decisions," Perry said. "Everything starts with those guys. We can't limit our chances on offense."

Down low, the Vandals will once again lack a true big man, something they've gone without the last two seasons. They'll make due with four undersized players led by returners **Rodney Hilaire** (7.9 ppg, 4.5 rpg) and **Marquis Holmes** (3.9 ppg, 3.2 rpg).

Hilaire, a 6-6 senior who saw his minutes and production increase dramatically during conference play, proved he could score and rebound against bigger opponents. Quick off his feet, he turned in an 18-point, 11-rebound performance against Long Beach State. Holmes, also 6-6, held his own in relatively limited action last season and should see considerably more time this season. Nearly half of Holmes' 72 rebounds last season were on the offensive end.

Perry also will need quality minutes inside from 6-6 junior college transfers **Tyrone Hayes** and **David Howell**.

Hayes was a first-team All-Panhandle Conference pick as a sophomore at Florida's Okaloosa-Walton Junior College, where he scored better than 15 points per game while shooting 60 percent from the field.

"Tyrone is probably the X-factor as to how much success we are going to have," Perry said. "I think we're in a situation where he can breathe some fresh air into the program immediately."

Howell is a 26-year-old from Chipola (Fla.) Junior College who spent time in the armed services.

"He'll provide leadership right away because of his age and work ethic," Perry said. "He's a hard-nosed player. He is tough, competitive and a very strong defender."

Two talented recruits will be academic red-shirts this season. They are 6-4 guard Sam Jackson from Valley High School in Las Vegas, Nev., and 6-1 point guard Walker D. Russell from Rochester Hills High School in Pontiac, Mich.

Another highly touted recruit, third-team NJCAA All-America guard Barrie Whitley from Copiah-Lincoln Community College, failed to make required academic progress during the summer and apparently won't be coming to Idaho.

2001-2002 SCHEDULE

Nov.	16	Western Montana
	24	@Boise State
	28	Portland
Dec.	1	Boise State
	4	@Washington State
	6	Eastern Washington
	8	Montana
	12	Pacific
	15	@BYU
	22	Cal State Northridge
	30	@Sacramento State
Jan.	3	@UC Santa Barbara
	5	@Cal Poly
	10	Long Beach State
	12	UC Irvine
	17	@Cal State Fullerton
	19	@UC Riverside
	26	Utah State
	31	Cal Poly
Feb.	2	UC Santa Barbara
	7	@UC Irvine
	9	@Long Beach State
	14	UC Riverside
	16	Cal State Fullerton
	23	@Utah State
	28	@Cal State Northridge
March	3	@Pacific
	6-9	#Big West Tournament

@Road Games
#Anaheim Convention Center, Anaheim, CA

BLUE RIBBON ANALYSIS

BACKCOURT	C
BENCH/DEPTH	C-
FRONTCOURT	C
INTANGIBLES	B-

Perry brings some excitement and enthusiasm back to a program that floundered under the temperamental reign of Farrar.

The Vandals will feature two of the more versatile players in the conference in 6-6 swingman Gerschefske and 6-5 shooting guard Jenkins. That's a good thing, as is the return of point guard Fletcher and forward Hilaire, two starters who should benefit greatly from experience gained last season.

The Vandals, however, have no player taller than 6-6, and while the team will be more athletic, the lack of size should be a decided disadvantage against many of the conference's better teams.

"People will pick us at the bottom of the heap and that's probably where we belong," Perry said. "It's up to us to move up from there."

(C.S.)

Long Beach State

LOCATION	Long Beach, CA
CONFERENCE	Big West
LAST SEASON	18-13 (.581)
CONFERENCE RECORD	10-6 (3rd)
STARTERS LOST/RETURNING	2/3

NICKNAME	49ers
COLORS	Black & Gold
HOMECOURT	The Pyramid (5,000)
COACH	Wayne Morgan (St. Lawrence '73)
RECORD AT SCHOOL	78-67 (5 years)
CAREER RECORD	78-67 (5 years)
ASSISTANTS	Reggie Warford (Kentucky '76)
	Ronnie Dean (Harris-Stowe State College '90)
	Brent Bargen (Doane College '93)
TEAM WINS (last 5 years)	13-10-13-24-18
RPI (last 5 years)	115-251-200-86-166
2000-01 FINISH	Lost in conference first round.

For those on the outside looking in, the highlight of Wayne Morgan's five-year tenure at Long Beach State would be 1999-2000. That squad, led by Big West Player-of-the-Year Mate Milisa, won 24 games and advanced to the postseason for the first time since 1994-95.

In terms of outright success, there would be no argument. In terms of pure coaching, however, Morgan may have outdone himself in 2000-2001.

Piloting a team sent reeling by early-season injury, Morgan and the 49ers gutted their way to 18 victories and a third-place finish in the combined Big West with a record of 10-6.

The 49ers still had a pair of all-conference performers in 6-4 senior guard Ramel "Rock" Lloyd (19.4 ppg, 3.8 rpg, 2 apg) and 6-8 junior power forward Travis Reed (14.5 ppg, 8.7 rpg), but the loss of James "Rudy" Williams, Vance Lawhorn and Tadeu Souza made a potentially dynamite frontline merely mortal. It also transformed a conference favorite into a talented but ultimately overmatched also-ran that was crushed, 95-70, by Boise State in the first round of the conference tournament.

This year's squad has the same potential as the last, with the wild card being the health of the same inside trio that sat out last season.

"We have a chance to have a decent year," Morgan said. "The key is the guys who are injured coming all the way back. None will begin the school year at 100 percent."

The gem of the trio is Williams, a 6-9 senior post voted second-team all-conference in 1999-2000 after averaging 12.2 points and a team-high 7.3 rebounds that season. Off-season surgeries to cure stress fractures in both tibias were initially unsuccessful, as Williams played in six games in 2000-2001 but decided to red-shirt after averaging 8.7 points and 3.7 rebounds.

In late February, Williams had steel shanks driven into both legs from ankle to knee, and recovery has been slow but steady.

The same goes for Lawhorn and Souza. Lawhorn, a 6-8 junior from Dixie Junior College in St. George, Utah, had knee surgery in October after seeing action in the two games for the 49ers. Lawhorn was a proven commodity in the junior college ranks, averaging 18.6 points and 7.5 rebounds at Dixie his sophomore season while logging almost 35 minutes per game.

Souza is a 6-8 junior from Mineral Area Junior College in Flat River, Mo., where he averaged 11.1 points and 6.9 rebounds. A native of Brazil, Souza tore the ACL and MCL in his right knee last spring and was not fit to play in the fall. Reconstruction of the knee continues to limit his mobility, Morgan said.

"He was very explosive—a good, skilled four-man," Morgan said. "Now it's a matter of getting up and down the court."

If one, or all of the threesome can return to their old form, they will have the opportunity to play alongside one of the conference's best in Reed, the 6-8 UCLA transfer who took the conference by storm last season.

A dogged banger, Reed led the conference in rebounding—the first 49er to do so in 20 years. Reed was even more impressive in conference play, averaging 15.3 points and 9.8 rebounds while shooting 55 percent from the field.

"Obviously I was pleased with his play," Morgan said. "He is very rugged, very tough and very difficult to handle."

Morgan said Reed's work ethic appeared to rub off on another of Long Beach's talented forwards, 6-8 sophomore Kevin Roberts (4.9 ppg, 3.5 rpg). Pressed into service perhaps sooner than expected, Roberts improved significantly as the season progressed and averaged 6.9 points and 4.7 rebounds in conference play.

"Kevin, like Travis, is durable and tough," Morgan said. "Both of those guys went through the entire year

without complaining about anything."

Long Beach State has a pair of talented freshmen on the inside who may not see much action if injuries heal with the upperclassmen. Then again, they just might be good enough to earn time regardless.

Alex Graham is a 7-1 post from Redlands (Calif.) High School who averaged 17 points, 12 rebounds, 4.5 blocks and four assists as a senior.

Chris Jenkins, a 6-7 small forward from Sandia High School in Albuquerque, N.M., was an explosive prep scorer and rebounder whose time will come at Long Beach.

"I think we've signed some good freshmen who could start if we asked them to," Morgan said. "But we don't need them to do that."

At the wing, all eyes will be on 6-6 senior Lemi Williams (11.7 ppg, 3.8 rpg), who proved he could score last season but also proved he couldn't.

While Williams started and finished the season strong, he endured a brutal midseason shooting slump and finished the year making just 38 percent of his shots from the field. Morgan defended the play of Williams, who should benefit from playing an average of almost 29 minutes per game.

"I don't think he had an unbelievable year, but most coaches would take a first-year player who averages [11.7] points per game," Morgan said.

In the backcourt, the 49ers' point-guard situation is in great shape with the return of two part-time starters. Ron Johnson (8.7 ppg, 3.0 rpg, 3.2 apg, 2.3 spg), a 6-1 senior, and Michael Darrett (5.7 ppg, 2.6 rpg, 3.4 apg, 1.7 spg), a 6-2 senior, are two of the more complete playmakers in the conference, and both have shown the ability to score when asked. That's important with the departure of Lloyd, which leaves an almost 20-point hole in the backcourt.

Joining Johnson and Darrett in the backcourt will be a trio of newcomers, one expected to contribute right away in 6-4 shooting guard Tony Darden from Dodge City (Kansas) Community College. Darden averaged 15 points and four rebounds as a sophomore and was a 44 percent threat from three-point range.

Anthony Davis is another shooting guard with good size and ability. The 6-5 freshman from Centennial High School in Los Angeles averaged 18.9 points and 6.2 rebounds as a senior.

Freshmen Mark Bowens, a 6-1 product from Cactus High School in Peoria, Ariz., is a point guard unlikely to see much time right away behind Johnson and Darrett, though his 25.5-point per game average his senior season proves he can score.

2001-2002 SCHEDULE

Nov.	15	*Western Michigan
	16	*Alabama State
	17	*Oregon
	24	Charlotte
	26	CS- Monterey Bay
	30	@Texas A&M
Dec.	4	@Pepperdine
	12	USC
	15	@Stanford
	18	Loyola Marymount
	22	@UC Irvine
	29	IPFW
Jan.	3	UC Riverside
	5	Cal State Fullerton
	10	@Idaho
	12	@Utah State
	17	Cal State Northridge
	19	Pacific
	24	@Cal Poly
	28	@UC Santa Barbara
	31	@Cal State Fullerton
Feb.	2	@UC Riverside
	7	Utah State
	9	Idaho
	14	@Pacific
	16	@Cal State Northridge
	21	UC Santa Barbara
	23	Cal Poly
	28	UC Irvine
March	6-9	#Big West Tournament

@Road Games
*America's Youth Classic, Eugene, OR
#Anaheim Convention Center, Anaheim, CA

BLUE RIBBON ANALYSIS

BACKCOURT	B-
BENCH/DEPTH	B
FRONTCOURT	A-
INTANGIBLES	B-

Above the knee, no team in the conference boasts the talent of Long Beach State. Below the knee, the jury is still out.

If the 49ers expect to win a conference title, they will need a slew of players to return from injury, most notably Williams. He's a proven star in this conference, but if his shin problems don't heal, he will be of little help to Reed, who shined for the 49ers last season.

Another key for the 49ers is the maturation of Williams, an athletic scorer who needs to shoot better than 38 percent from the floor. Period.

The 49ers boast two of the conference's most complete guards in Darrett and Johnson but may lack some depth in the backcourt.

The upshot? This team will be good. Whether it is conference-title good be decided in the trainer's room.

(C.S.)

Pacific

LOCATION	Stockton, CA
CONFERENCE	Big West
LAST SEASON	18-12 (.600)
CONFERENCE RECORD	8-8 (5th)
STARTERS LOST/RETURNING	2/3
NICKNAME	Tigers
COLORS	Orange & Black
HOMECOURT	Alex G. Spanos Center (6,150)
COACH	Bob Thomason (Pacific '71)
RECORD AT SCHOOL	202-175 (13 years)
CAREER RECORD	202-175 (13 years)
ASSISTANTS	Ron Verlin (Sacramento State '90)
	Calvin Byrd (Villanova '93)
	Ray Buck (Hawaii '75)
TEAM WINS (last 5 years)	24-23-14-11-18
RPI (last 5 years)	79-82-211-250-139
2000-01 FINISH	Lost in conference final.

Pacific coach Bob Thomason says the 2001-02 Tigers have the potential to be one of the three best teams he's ever put on the floor at the school. That's not-so-secret code for "the best since Michael Olowokandi."

Thomason, beginning his 14th year in Stockton, averaged a respectable 15 victories per season his first eight years at Pacific. That was before the lanky 7-foot walk-on from England found his groove, put on some muscle and powered the Tigers to back-to-back Big West Conference divisional titles and seasons of 24 and 23 victories in 1996-97 and 1997-98.

Olowokandi's departure to the NBA—he was the first pick overall by the Los Angeles Clippers in 1998—brought a familiar calm back to the Pacific program. The team won 14 games the following year, 11 the next and 18 last season, scratching to within one victory of a berth in the NCAA Tournament.

With three starters, a handful of key reserves and at least one impact newcomer suiting up this season, the Tigers appear poised to again make Olowokandi-like waves in the Big West.

Pacific lacks a superstar of Olowokandi's stature, but in terms of depth and balance there may be no team to match it in the Big West. Thomason says his second string will be "better than any in the conference."

"I think we're going to be in the hunt," Thomason said of Pacific's chances of winning a conference title. "There's five teams with a real shot and we're going to be one of them."

The Tigers' strength, both literally and figuratively, will be in the paint, where four players return to form a bruising front line. The most polished of the bunch is 6-7 senior **Mike Hahn** (10.2 ppg, 4.9 rpg), an all-conference honorable mention pick last season. He was second on the team in scoring, led the team in rebounding and minutes played and shot 59.6 percent from the field. He brings a streak of 59 consecutive starts into the 2001-02 season.

A banger with limited range but a nose for the basket, Hahn will need to keep his weight up this season, Thomason said. Hahn began last season at 225 but by

season's end had dipped to 207.

Joining Hahn in the paint will be three returning veterans, each listed as post players but each of whom Thomason said can play the power-forward spot as well. **Mike Preston** (6.8 ppg, 3.7 rpg), a 6-9, 235-pound senior, started just two games last season but averaged better than 19 minutes per game in conference.

Thomason has Preston penciled in as the starter at the post, though he will be pushed by 6-10, 265-pound junior **Tim Johnson** (3.8 ppg, 2.8 rpg) and 6-10, 260-pound senior **Ross Mills** (3.9 ppg, 2.2 rpg).

Thomason said Mills has dropped about 20 pounds from last season and should be a tad more nimble. Mills and Johnson attended the Pete Newell Big Man Camp in Hawaii last summer.

Pacific's other frontcourt veteran is 6-6 senior **Eli Kiedrowski** (2.8 ppg, 2.4 rpg), effective in limited minutes off the bench last season. Dan Masters (2 ppg, 0.7 rpg), a 6-7 senior, is not expected to play this season due to injuries.

There are three newcomers to the Pacific frontcourt and one could be a very good one. **Christian Maraker**, a 6-9 freshman from Varberg, Sweden, has the potential to be better than any of Pacific's current big men, Thomason said. Maraker's weight—he's just 205—is a concern right now, but his talent is not.

"He's my type of four-man," Thomason said. "He could be a (Keith) Van Horn type player once he gets his weight up to 225."

Even without the pounds, Maraker's ability to score could earn him minutes immediately. He averaged 20.3 points and 10.1 rebounds in the Swedish Club league last season and scored 12 points in a head-to-head match-up against Pacific during the Tigers' 2000 tour of Scandinavia.

Miguel Flores, a 6-9 freshman from Woodland (Calif.) High School, is expected to red-shirt as is **Matt Stricker**, a 6-7 transfer from Delta College in Manteca, Calif.

Thomason expects to play a three-guard set, but the combination of players at those spots is far from determined.

"Every position is really up for grabs," he said.

That said, the perimeter players with the most experience are 6-2 senior **Maurice McLemore** (9.9 ppg, 4.5 rpg, 3.3 apg), and 6-1 senior **Jono Metzger-Jones** (7.0 ppg, 2.5 rpg).

McLemore was an all-conference honorable mention pick last season and should land a starting spot at the one, two or three.

Metzger-Jones came on strong at the close of last season, starting seven of the team's last eight games. He's the designated sharpshooter, having made a team-high 53 three-pointers.

Other returnees expected to play limited roles in the backcourt are 6-2 senior **Nathan Davis** (2.1 ppg, 1.7 rpg), 6-1 senior **David Bunts** (1.9 ppg, 0.6 rpg) and 5-9 sophomore **Bradley Bland** (0.7 ppg, 0.3 rpg).

Tossed into the backcourt mix will be a trio of newcomers who will fight for playing time immediately. The first is 5-10 junior college transfer **Demetrius Jackson**, who put up blinding numbers at Shasta College in Redding, Calif. Jackson led all California junior college players with 9.8 assists per game, but also ranked third in the state in scoring (24.4 ppg) and steals (3.6 spg). It will be tough for Thomason to keep Jackson on the bench.

"He can play," Thomason said. "He can pass, he can score. There's also a certain toughness about him."

Thomason also is high on 6-5 swingman **Eli Nolan**, who red-shirted last season but has the mentality to contribute on both ends of the court.

"He's a junkyard dog-type player," Thomason said. "He has a great feel for the game."

The third potential contributor in the backcourt is 6-6 freshman **Jasko Korajkic**, a teammate of Maraker in Sweden.

"He's wiry and clever," Thomason said of Korajkic.

Miah Davis, a 6-1 transfer from Cal State Stanislaus, will red-shirt this season after earning second team all-California Collegiate Athletic Association honors last season.

"We've got more depth and more seniors," Thomason said. "Hopefully we can wear people out."

2001-2002 SCHEDULE

Nov.	17	@Santa Clara
	20	CS Monterey Bay
	23-24	#Hispanic College Fund

		Tournnament
	28	Fresno State
Dec.	2	@Montana
	8	San Jose State
	12	@Idaho
	15	@San Francisco
	22	@Utah State
	29	Nebraska
Jan.	5	@Cal State Northridge
	10	Cal Poly
	12	UC Santa Barbara
	17	@UC Irvine
	19	@Long Beach State
	24	UC Riverside
	26	Cal State Fullerton
	31	Cal State Northridge
Feb.	7	@UC Santa Barbara
	9	@Cal Poly
	14	Long Beach State
	16	UC Irvine
	21	@Cal State Fullerton
	23	@UC Riverside
	28	Utah State
March	3	Idaho
	6-9	##Big West Tournament

@Road Games
#Albuquerque, NM (vs. New Mexico first round; also Southern Miss, West Virginia)
##Anaheim Convention Center, Anaheim, CA

BLUE RIBBON ANALYSIS

BACKCOURT	B
BENCH/DEPTH	B+
FRONTCOURT	B+
INTANGIBLES	B+

An 18-game winner last season, the Tigers are more experienced, deeper and more athletic this season, prompting coach Thomason to predict this team will be one of the three best in his 13 years at Pacific.

That's a good thing for Pacific, but the conference also is improved with as many as five teams with a legitimate shot at a title.

The frontcourt is typical Pacific—blue-collar, tall and deep—anchored by senior power forward Hahn, an improved scorer who has started 59 straight games for the Tigers.

The backcourt is loaded with good athletes, led by returners McLemore and Metzger-Jones, but the real gem of the group could be Jackson, who put up huge numbers in the junior college ranks and could provide the Tigers the explosive offensive threat it has lacked.

Pacific is primed for a big season, but the real key could be returning to its winning ways at home. The Tigers have dropped a combined 10 games at the Alex G. Spanos Center the last two seasons. Between 1991 and 1999, the Tigers never lost more than three games in a season at Stockton.

(C.S.)

Utah State

LOCATION	Logan, UT
CONFERENCE	Big West
LAST SEASON	28-6 (.824)
CONFERENCE RECORD	13-3 (2nd)
STARTERS LOST/RETURNING	4/1
NICKNAME	Aggies
COLORS	Blue & White
HOMECOURT	Dee Glen Smith Spectrum (10,270)
COACH	Stew Morrill (Gonzaga '74)
RECORD AT SCHOOL	71-25 (3 years)
CAREER RECORD	289-163 (15 years)
ASSISTANTS	Randy Rahe (Buena Vista '82)
	Don Verlin (Cal State Stanislaus '89)
	Tim Duryea (North Texas '88)
TEAM WINS (last 5 years)	20-25-15-28-28
RPI (last 5 years)	96-51-170-33-56
2000-01 FINISH	Lost in NCAA second round.

After back-to-back 28-victory seasons—the most successful two-year period in Utah State basketball history—the Aggies lost four of their top five scorers and the heart and soul of the program's back-to-back appearances in the NCAA Tournament.

Given that, fourth-year coach Stew Morrill doesn't hesitate to say his team probably won't win 28 games in 2001-02. Opposing Big West coaches may not be so sure.

The Aggies remain one of the most feared teams in the conference and the reason is Morrill, who has quickly built a winning program at Utah State, where team looms larger than individual talent. Last year, the Aggies knocked off fifth-seeded Ohio State in the first round of the NCAA Tournament. That was the school's first win in the Big Dance in 32 years. School officials are so delighted with the state of the program they signed Morrill to a 10-year deal that takes him through 2011.

Morrill probably could start four walk-ons and a kicking donkey and be a threat to the conference title. Of course, there are no kicking mules on this team. The losses are great, but Morrill has reloaded with three junior college players who could start immediately—two in the frontcourt and one at the point-guard spot.

Talent is only part of the equation. Unselfishness and defense were cornerstones to last year's success, as four players finished the season with double-figure scoring totals and the Aggies led the country in scoring defense, allowing an average of 56.8 points per game.

Given the look at the top teams in the conference, holding your own in the paint will be as important as ever in 2001-02. Long Beach, Pacific, UC Santa Barbara and UC Irvine each have at least two talented and experienced big men.

Utah State, for its part, may be short on Division I experience inside but should not want for talent. Morrill's ability to get the most out of that talent on both ends of the court could be key for the Aggies.

At power forward, where two-time all-conference first teamer Shawn Daniels most recently roamed, the Aggies will insert junior college transfer Desmond Penigar, a 6-7, 240-pounder who averaged 27.8 points and 11.4 rebounds as a sophomore at Ventura Junior College in California. Penigar was a two-time runner-up for state player of the year at Ventura, and averaged 23 points and 12 rebounds as a freshman.

Pushing Penigar will be 6-5 senior Brennan Ray (3.3 ppg, 2.3 rpg) and 6-6 freshman Nate Harris. Ray is a physical player who has made a name for himself as a key role player off the Aggie bench. Harris is the team's blue-chip freshman recruit from Sky View High School in Smithfield, Utah. Harris averaged 23 points and 13 rebounds as a senior and was selected by the Salt Lake Tribune as the state's player of the year.

Like the power-forward spot, the post position could well be filled by a junior-college player with sparkling credentials. That would be 6-9 junior Mike Ahmad from Irvine Valley Junior College in Southern California.

Ahmad was an all-state pick at Irvine his sophomore season after averaging 18 points—on 64.7 percent shooting—and 9.7 rebounds.

To earn the starting nod, Ahmad will need to outplay a pretty fair talent in 6-9 senior Jeremy Vague (3.8 ppg, 2.5 rpg), a good shot blocker who also shot 51 percent from the field.

Mike Puzey, a 6-9 senior transfer from Utah, will sit out this season. The post averaged two points and 2.1 rebounds in 2000-01 for the Utes, so it won't be hard to find improvement at the position.

The Aggies' most accomplished returnee is 6-3 junior shooting guard Tony Brown (11.7 ppg, 3.2 rpg), who will carry much of the load in terms of experience and leadership. Brown was a second-team all-conference pick last season and has 82 starts at Utah State. A proven three-point threat, Brown also has the best assist-to-turnover ratio in school history at 2.18-to-1.

"If you've got only one returning starter, it's good to have Tony Brown in that spot," Morrill said. "Tony's like a coach on the floor. He's gotten better every year and we expect one more jump this season."

Aside from Brown, the Aggies don't have much in the way of a proven commodity at the two-guard. Ryan Wheeler, a 6-4 sophomore out of Tyler (Texas) Junior College, missed most of his sophomore season with an injury after averaging 10 points as a freshman. He's a good shooter who needs work on defense.

"We felt like the priority this spring was to add a shooter and certainly that is Ryan's biggest asset as a player," Morrill said. "With three years of eligibility remaining, Ryan has an excellent upside and will only grow in all aspects of his game."

Another possibility off the bench is 6-3 freshman Mike Stowell, a rugged red-shirt who impressed in practice last year. He averaged 17 points, eight rebounds,

six assists and three steals as a senior at Capistrano Valley (San Juan Capistrano, Calif.) High School.

There will be no lack of pressure on 6-0 junior guard Ronnie Ross, expected to fill the shoes of departed Bernard Rock, who, as his name suggests, was the foundation of the Aggie backcourt the last two seasons.

Ross averaged better than 19 points, four rebounds and three assists in his two seasons at John Wood (Ill.) Community College. He was a preseason junior college all-American as a sophomore at John Wood and has the athleticism and physical maturity to step right in at Division I.

The Aggies also have 5-10 sophomore Thomas Vincent (2.4 ppg, 0.6 rpg, 1 apg) and 5-10 freshman Calvin Brown at the point. Vincent, who played at least 10 minutes in 18 games last season, should be a solid backup to Ross. Brown red-shirted last season after averaging 17 points and 3.5 assists as a senior at Eastside Prep in Palo Alto Calif.

Last year's starting small forward duties were handled by all-conference honorable mention pick Curtis Bobb, with Dion Bailey serving as a more-than-adequate backup. Playing in the shadow of Bobb and Bailey was 6-4 junior Toraino Johnson (2.5 ppg, 1.3 rpg), a gifted athlete whose time has come. Johnson was limited to eight minutes a game last year but had season highs of 15 points and five rebounds against Albany and scored 11 points in the Aggies' first-round victory over Cal State Fullerton in the conference tournament.

Others expected to battle for time at small forward include a pair of 6-7 sophomores in Chad Evans (1.3 ppg, 0.8 rpg) and Spencer Nelson. Evans saw limited time last season. He originally signed with Loyola Marymount before leaving on an LDS Church mission and ending up at Utah State. Nelson, the big school player of the year in Idaho in 1998, returns to Utah State after a two-year mission of his own. He played in all 28 games as a freshman, averaging 4.5 points and 3.3 rebounds. Both players can also play the power-forward spot.

Walk-on Jason Napier (1.3 ppg, 0.2 rpg), a 6-5 sophomore, could see limited time at small forward.

2001-2002 SCHEDULE

Nov.	17	@Montana State
	24	@Utah
	28	Idaho State
Dec.	1	BYU
	4	Montana State
	8	@Weber State
	15	Western State
	20	Cal State Northridge
	22	Pacific
	28-29	#Utah State Classic
Jan.	3	@Cal Poly
	5	@UC Santa Barbara
	10	UC Irvine
	12	Long Beach State
	17	@UC Riverside
	19	@Cal State Fullerton
	26	@Idaho
	31	UC Santa Barbara
Feb.	2	Cal Poly
	7	@Long Beach State
	9	@UC Irvine
	14	Cal State Fullerton
	16	UC Riverside
	23	Idaho
	28	@Pacific
March	2	@Cal State Northridge
	6-9	##Big West Tournament

@Road Games
#Logan, UT (vs. Birmingham Southern first round; also Centenary, Idaho State)
##Anaheim Cenvention Center, Anaheim, CA

BLUE RIBBON ANALYSIS

BACKCOURT	B-
BENCH/DEPTH	B
FRONTCOURT	B+
INTANGIBLES	A-

Utah State appears to have found solid footing under Morrill, who has quickly built a perennial contender in the Big West Conference. How else can you explain the Aggies being among the conference favorites this season after losing four-of-five starters?

Above all, Morrill preaches unselfishness and defense, two things past squads have bought into big time. The program's 56 victories the past two seasons are proof.

The Aggies have reloaded with three impact junior college players in Penigar, Ahmad and Ross.

Morrill's biggest task could be melding their talents into a cohesive unit. If Morrill can get it done, this team could be as dangerous as the previous two.

(C.S.)

Delaware

LOCATION	Newark, DE
CONFERENCE	Colonial Athletic
LAST SEASON	20-10 (.667)
CONFERENCE RECORD	14-4 (2nd, America East)
STARTERS LOST/RETURNING	3/2
NICKNAME	Blue Hens
COLORS	Royal Blue & Gold
HOMECOURT	Bob Carpenter Center (5,000)
COACH	David Henderson (Duke '86)
RECORD AT SCHOOL	20-10 (1 year)
CAREER RECORD	20-10 (1 year)
ASSISTANTS	Josh Oppenheimer (Northern Ariz. '92)
	Billy Martin (UNC Wilmgton '78)
	John Moseley (East Carolina '99)
TEAM WINS (last 5 years)	15-20-25-24-20
RPI (last 5 years)	154-95-61-89-96
2000-01 FINISH	Lost in conference final.

Welcome to the Colonial Athletic Association, Delaware. Go into your first year in your new league without a senior. See the sights quickly. Five of your first six CAA games are on the road. Play at UNC Wilmington, the toughest place to play among the "old" CAA schools, and two nights later play at Virginia Commonwealth.

Four straight 20-victory seasons marked Delaware as one of the nation's top mid-major programs. The Blue Hens are established. Their entry into the CAA was hailed by the old guard as significant, with good reason. It may take some time to show why.

"Just because of my location, I've been aware of the CAA schools for a long time," said Delaware coach David Henderson, a former player and assistant at Duke. "I think it is a big step up from where we're coming from in the America East. One of the big differences is we've had some games in the past where we felt we could put them in the win column. In the CAA, you have to play every night. You play at UNC Wilmington, get one day off and have to play at VCU. That's a really difficult task for us. If you're not able to get back up, you can drop three or four [games] in a row very easily. We have to get to that point."

Henderson's second Delaware team and first CAA team will be missing some pretty key elements. Any team that loses 6-8 Ajmal Basit (15.2 ppg, 9.8 rpg and he only made SECOND TEAM All-AE), 6-0 Billy Wells (13.7 ppg) and 6-4 Greg Miller (7.2 ppg) is going to feel the effects.

The Hens' two returnees are a solid duo. Junior guard Austen Rowland, 6-1, averaged 11.6 points and 4.3 assists. Junior Maurice Sessoms, a 6-8 forward, averaged seven points and 4.2 rebounds. Junior guard Ryan Iversen, 6-3, is not a returning starter, though Henderson considers him one. He averaged 9.2 points and 1.3 steals.

"Rowland is a very good point guard," Henderson said. "He had a great second half of the season. "Sessoms was really playing his first full season in college after transferring from Wisconsin. For all practical purposes he was a freshman and I'm expecting a lot more out of him this year. They have to immediately become leaders of this ball club.

"Ryan is also a great leader, an intangibles guy. He gives us a lot of things."

Henderson has five other lettermen and two redshirts at his disposal. Among the lettermen, 6-7 sophomore Robin Wentt won't be available until second semester for academic reasons. He averaged three points and 1.8 rebounds.

The other returnees are 6-1 sophomore guard Mike Ames (4.1 points), 6-8 sophomore forward Sean Knitter (3.3 points, 1.6 rebounds), 6-8 sophomore forward Dave Hindenlang (1.6 points, 2.3 rebounds) and 6-5 sopho-

COLONIAL

BLUE RIBBON FORECAST
1. UNC Wilmington
2. Virginia Commonwealth
3. Delaware
4. George Mason
5. James Madison
6. Hofstra
7. William and Mary
8. Old Dominion
9. Drexel
10. Towson

ALL-CONFERENCE TEAM
G- Brett Blizzard, UNCW
G -Rick Apodaca, Hofstra
C - Jesse Young, George Mason
F - Willie Taylor, Virginia Commonwealth
F - Tim Lyle, James Madison

PLAYER OF THE YEAR
Brett Blizzard, UNCW

NEWCOMER OF THE YEAR
Vohn Hunter, Delaware

2001-2002 CONFERENCE TOURNAMENT
March 1-4, Richmond Coliseum, Richmond, VA

2000-2001 CHAMPIONS
Richmond (regular season, ineligible for tournament)
George Mason (tournament)

2000-2001 POSTSEASON PARTICIPANTS
Postseason record 1-3 (.250)
NCAA
George Mason
NIT
Richmond (Second Round)
UNC Wilmington

TOP BACKCOURTS
1. UNC Wilmington
2. Virginia Commonwealth
3. Hofstra

TOP FRONTCOURTS
1. UNC Wilmington
2. James Madison
3. George Mason

INSIDE THE NUMBERS
2000-2001 Conference RPI: 13th out of 31
Conference RPI last 5 years: 12-15-17-15-13

DID YOU KNOW?
Who are these guys? This definitely isn't last year's CAA. The league has grown from six to 10 teams with the addition of Delaware, Drexel, Hoftra and Towson from the America East. To recap quickly: American (Patriot), East Carolina (Conference USA) and Richmond (Atlantic 10) all bailed on the CAA last year. The league put together the deal to bring in the four newcomers, with the start date two years away. That left the Standing Six scrambling to fill schedules with only 10 league games. Then the timetable was moved up a year. Then it was moved up another year. Suddenly, everyone had 18 league games and new rivalries to pursue. All 10 teams will qualify for the league tournament. "The fact that they've come on board obviously helps from a scheduling standpoint," Virginia Commonwealth coach Mack McCarthy said. "I'm excited about the long-term prospects of how good the league can be. From a practical standpoint, it's going to be darn tougher to win the league. But I think multiple bids is a realistic possibility right away." … Three of the four newcomers and holdover Old Dominion have new coaches this season. Tom Pecora takes over at Hofstra, James "Bruiser" Flint at Drexel and Michael Hunt at Towson. Blaine Taylor, a former head coach at Montana, left a seat on Mike Montgomery's bench at Stanford to become head coach at Old Dominion. … Jeff Capel III, son of former ODU coach Jeff Capel, has moved from his dad's side to McCarthy's staff at VCU. … Style reigns in the CAA. One publication chosen JMU coach Sherman Dillard as the best-dressed coach in Division I. Another picked Flint, who was at Massachusetts before moving to Drexel. … JMU went to Europe in August (as did the school's women's team). Coach Sherman Dillard wasn't allowed to take his newcomers, but thought the trip would be an excellent chance for the team's 10 returnees to get some additional experience. … UNCW snapped two notable streaks last season: Butler's 18-game home winning streak and George Mason's 17-game conference home winning streak. … If UNCW runs the table in league play this season, coach Jerry Wainwright will tie Lefty Driesell for second place in all-time league victories. Dick Tarrant (Richmond) leads with 106, Driesell (JMU) has 98, Wainwright has 80. Among active coaches, only George Mason's Jim Larranaga joins Wainwright in the top 10 with 47.

(M.H.)

---

more **Anthony Thomas** (1.0 points, 0.5 rebounds).

David Lunn, a 6-4 swingman, and 6-5 forward Mark Curry sat out last season with injuries. Both have freshman eligibility. Lunn, from Baltimore, scored 1,410 points at McDonough High (tops in school history). Curry played at Seton Hall Prep in East Orange, N.J.

"Curry is a solid player with some explosiveness in the paint," Henderson said. "I expect him to be able to contribute right away. Lunn is a tough player and a good defender. We think he can really help us in that aspect.

"Knitter came on late in the season after being injured early. Ames is a great shooter and I think he's more comfortable at this level now. Wentt has come a long way as a player and a person and he'll help us when he gets back."

Delaware is bringing in three new players. The school didn't learn for sure that 6-5 swingman **Vohn Hunter** would qualify. Hunter, from the Bronx, is coming in from Champlain Junior College in Burlington, Vt. He averaged 18.8 points and 4.4 rebounds as a freshman there. Last season, his numbers jumped to 25.6 points and 5.0 rebounds.

Hunter originally signed with Texas, then went the JUCO route after the Longhorns had a coaching change.

"He's a key player," Henderson said, "with his level of

maturity and ability to score. I really believe he has a chance to be an all-conference type player."

Delaware's other recruits are freshmen: 6-0 guard **Mike Slattery** of Wildwood, N.J., and 6-5 forward **Calvin Smith** of Norfolk, Va. Slattery was his league MVP as a senior. Smith was an All-Tidewater choice whose team won a state title when he was a junior.

Slattery will enable Henderson to use Rowland some off the ball.

"We expect Mike to step in and be ready to go," Henderson said. "He's our second ball handler. Rowland is our leader. He can really shoot the basketball also. We don't want to lose the ability of having that outside threat.

"Calvin is a good athlete and a good defensive player. I think he'll be able to help us, too. I don't think we have a lot in terms of experience but I think we'll be a deep ball club."

2001-2002 SCHEDULE

Nov.	15-18	#Top of the World Classic
	24	LaSalle
	28	St. Joseph's
Dec.	6	@High Point
	8	@UNC Greensboro
	15	*Rider

	22	@George Mason
	30	Loyola College
Jan.	3	James Madison
	5	@William & Mary
	7	@Old Dominion
	12	@UNC Wilmington
	14	@VCU
	17	@Pennsylvania
	19	Drexel
	23	Towson
	26	@Hofstra
	30	VCU
Feb.	2	Old Dominion
	6	George Mason
	9	@Drexel
	13	@Towson
	16	UNC Wilmington
	20	William & Mary
	23	Hofstra
	25	@James Madison
March	1-4	##CAA Tournament

@Road Games
*Sovereign Bank Arena, Trenton, NJ
#Fairbanks, AK (vs. Witchita State first round; also Ole Miss, Butler, Washington, Bowling Green, Radford, Alaska-Fairbanks)
##Richmond Arena, Richmond, VA

BLUE RIBBON ANALYSIS

BACKCOURT	B
BENCH/DEPTH	B-
FRONTCOURT	C+
INTANGIBLES	B-

It may not be too long before Delaware is back in its customary position as a challenger for league titles. Of course it would have been better for the Blue Hens to take their maiden voyage in the CAA with a little more experience, but this is not a team to take lightly.

The team will be very solid in the backcourt with Rowland, Ryan and Slattery. Slattery will free Rowland up from total responsibility for running the show. Iversen, as Henderson said, is an "intangibles" guy who does the little but important stuff. Rowland's shooting fell off late last season, but that shouldn't be a problem this year.

Getting Hunter was huge. Delaware found out in late August that he was indeed qualified as it expected and he'll immediately be a force. The swingman can shoot and rebound.

Up front, the Hens have some questions. Henderson has three sophomores between 6-7 and 6-9 who got some experience last year. At least one, probably two, of them have to become dependable regulars. If that happens, Delaware will be better than expected. If it doesn't, well, the Hens may be picked too high.

(M.H.)

Drexel

LOCATION	Philadelphia, PA
CONFERENCE	Colonial Athletic
LAST SEASON	15-12 (.555)
CONFERENCE RECORD	12-6 (3rd East)
STARTERS LOST/RETURNING	4/1
NICKNAME	Dragons
COLORS	Blue & Gold
HOMECOURT	Physical Education Athletic Center
	(2,300)
COACH	James "Bruiser" Flint (St. Joseph's '87)
RECORD AT SCHOOL	First year
CAREER RECORD	86-72 (5 years)
ASSISTANTS	Geoff Arnold (St. Joseph's '87)
	Mike Connors (Ithaca '83)
	Joe "Chuck" Martin (Monmouth '93)
TEAM WINS (last 5 years)	22-13-20-13-15
RPI (last 5 years)	72-156-100-194-144
2000-01 FINISH	Lost in conference first round.

James "Bruiser" Flint is a Philadelphia guy.

He was born there, educated there (Episcopal Academy, St. Joseph's University). Though he's been gone for 14 years, he still considers it home.

Now he's back, trying to turn the Drexel Dragons into a force in a new league: The Colonial Athletic

Association. Drexel is one of four teams coming from the America East to the CAA this season.

Flint still has plenty of family and plenty of friends in Philly. He knows where to get a good cheese steak and, most important, where to find the good basketball players.

"The reception has been unbelievable," said Flint, whose five-year run as head coach at Massachusetts ended last season. He was immediately snapped up by Drexel.

"I hope that is because I'm from Philadelphia. I hope I will be able to get some more players. The biggest difference is that I can have guys on my campus all the time. Guys from the city can come and play here. You get kids in your place more than you did at a place like Massachusetts.

"I think this is a great city. It has really progressed since I left. It's been a terrific opportunity to come back and get reacquainted."

Drexel is pretty serious about the CAA. Steve Seymour, the man Flint replaced, was only in the job two years. He went 28-29. Not great, but not terrible. The Dragons went 15-12 last season and finished third behind Hofstra and Drexel in the America East.

That wasn't good enough, not for what Drexel thought it was getting into with the CAA. Seymour was out. Flint was in.

Gone, too, is almost everyone from last season. Mike Kouser, Joe Linderman and Stephen Starks all made one of the America East's honors teams. Gone. Drexel loses 77 percent of its offense, 60 percent of its rebounding and 45 percent of its assists.

"Thanks for reminding me," Flint said with a laugh. "We knew that coming in, though. We talked about how it is going to be totally new. Everybody who is back, really, didn't play much and they knew we were taking a big step up in competition."

One Dragon does have experience. **Ashley Howard**, a 6-0 junior guard, started 21 games last season. He averaged 8.9 points, 2.9 rebounds and 4.8 assists.

"Ashley was the point guard and everybody thought if he played well, the team played well," Flint said.

That's about it when you talk about serious experience at Drexel.

Jamil Moore, a 6-4 sophomore, averaged 18.7 minutes and 3.5 points. **Robert Battle**, a 6-8 junior, averaged 9.6 minutes, 1.7 points and 2.3 rebounds.

"Jamil had some flashes in what I watched. He's athletic and I think he can be pretty good," Flint said.

Drexel's six other "veterans" made barely a statistical blip. They are 6-4 junior **Henry "Doug" Fairfax**, 6-3 junior **Jay Overcash**, 6-6 sophomore **Tim Whitworth**, 6-3 junior **Eric Schmieder**, 6-6 sophomore **Sean Brooks** and 6-8 sophomore **Pat Deveney**.

Whitworth averaged 2.8 points in five appearances as a freshman and 1.8 in 10 last season. Deveney averaged 1.7 points in 13 games last season.

"One of the kids I've been surprised with is Deveney," Flint said. "He got hurt and didn't play a lot. I think he can be a pretty good player for us."

One interesting "newcomer" is 6-4 senior guard **Julius Williams**. He didn't play the last two seasons but averaged 3.0 points in 36 career games the previous two years.

Flint's freshman class features five players—6-9 center **Steve Showers** of New Tripoli, Pa.; 6-1 guard **Phil Goss** of Temple Hills, Md.; 6-2 guard **Jeremiah King** of Paterson, N.J.; 6-8 **Anthony Lalor** of New York; and 6-6 swingman **Danny Hinds** of Bethlehem, Pa.

Hinds averaged 23 points as a prep senior. Showers averaged in double figures in points and rebounds. King was going to go to Massachusetts and switched to Drexel when Flint moved there.

"Hinds we got late and I think we were lucky," Flint said. "I think he can be a pretty good player. Showers has a chance, though he has to work on some things. Goss has been lighting it up in the Philly summer league. We got Lalor late and I think he could be a good addition."

Flint couldn't even begin to guess at a lineup, though he's certain it will be a young one.

"It is definitely going to be a learning experience for all of us," Flint said. "When I talked to the kids about playing for me and how things would be different, most of them came up and said they'd never played much and that this was a new opportunity.

"Everybody is starting from ground zero."

2001-2002 SCHEDULE

Nov.	16-17	#Marist Classic
	24	@Rider
	28	Pennsylvania
Dec.	1	@James Madison
	5	Lafayette
	8	LaSalle
	10	@St. Joseph's
	18	Northeastern
	23	Hofstra
	29	Niagara
Jan.	3	VCU
	5	@Old Dominion
	7	@William & Mary
	12	@Towson
	16	James Madison
	19	@Delaware
	23	@Hofstra
	26	George Mason
	30	William & Mary
Feb.	2	@VCU
	4	@UNC Wilmington
	9	Delaware
	11	Old Dominion
	16	@George Mason
	18	UNC Wilmington
	23	Towson
March	1-4	##CAA Tournament

@Road Games
#Poughkeepsie, NY (vs. Marist first round; also Columbia, Northeastern)
##Richmond Coliseum, Richmond, VA

BLUE RIBBON ANALYSIS

BACKCOURT	C
BENCH/DEPTH	C-
FRONTCOURT	C-
INTANGIBLES	C

Flint is comfortable at home, which is good because it could be a while before his Drexel Dragons become a comfortable fit in their new league. Drexel lost just about everything.

Howard, by far the team's most experienced player, is a pretty good assist man (4.8 per game) and not much of a shooter (39.5 percent). The 32.4 minutes per game he played last season may look like downtime compared to what he'll be expected to log this season.

Battle is the "vet" up front with all of 9.6 minutes per game on his log last season. He will have to triple his playing time and multiply his scoring (1.7) and rebounding (2.3) averages by more than that. Is it possible?

Look for Hinds to become a big part of Drexel's rotation. He could end up the team's leading scorer.

Is the addition of Flint on the bench a good thing? He's intelligent (a degree in financial management) and personable. It's never a bad thing to have a good guy around. But Massachusetts faded under his watch. He took over after a 35-2 season that saw the Minutemen in the Final Four. His first two teams made the NCAA and lost in the first round. His final three made one postseason appearance, in the 2000 NIT. UMass' record in his final three seasons was 46-47.

Perhaps being at home will help him land players for his new program. But there are a bunch of schools in Philly trying to do the same thing—his alma mater one of them. Flint was fortunate to get a quick second chance. Many folks hope he makes it work this time.

(M.H.)

George Mason

LOCATION	Fairfax, VA
CONFERENCE	Colonial Athletic
LAST SEASON	18-12 (.667)
CONFERENCE RECORD	11-5 (t-2nd)
STARTERS LOST/RETURNING	3/2
NICKNAME	Patriots
COLORS	Green & Gold
HOMECOURT	Patriot Center (10,000)
COACH	Jim Larranaga (Providence '71)
RECORD AT SCHOOL	65-52 (4 years)
CAREER RECORD	262-221 (17 years)

ASSISTANTS	Bill Courtney (Bucknell '92)
	Mike Gillian (NorthAdams State '86)
	Scott Cherry (North Carolina '93)
TEAM WINS (last 5 years)	10-9-19-19-18
RPI (last 5 years)	219-202-107-92-92
2000-01 FINISH	Lost in NCAA first round.

George Evans was 30 by the time he finished at George Mason, and many around the Colonial Athletic Association will tell you that it seemed like he spent all 30 years in a Patriots' uniform.

Evans won the CAA's Player-of-the-Year Award three years running. The Army veteran (hence his late start) had as much of an impact on the league as anyone ever has (including David Robinson) or likely ever will.

For so long, he was Mason basketball. And now he's gone.

Replacing him is enough of a challenge. Mason has to fill some other major gaps as well.

Gone, too, is all-CAA guard Erik Herring.

Also out of eligibility is underrated point guard Tremaine Price, the CAA's assist leader last season and perhaps the perfect point guard for Mason last year. He got the ball where it needed to be.

"How do you replace that kind of talent?" Mason coach Jim Larranaga asked. "Really, you don't. What you have to do is look at the talent you have returning and the incoming talent you have and try to build a team around that.

"You have the foundation. Now you need to change the roles of players who were asked to do one thing when George, Erik and Tremaine were around. It will take time, but that's the process we have to go through."

The process will start with a pair of juniors, the remaining 40 percent of Mason's starting lineup from last season. One is **Jesse Young**, a 6-10 Canadian who averaged 8.2 points and 5.9 rebounds. He came in with much promise and showed flashes of why last season. Mason needs him to take a bunch of the load that Evans carried inside last season. Doubters say he won't be able to do too much without Evans around to take some of the load off.

"The biggest thing Jesse needed when he came in was to get strong," Larranaga said. "He's worked very hard at that the past two years. Toward the end of last season, he began to see the benefits of that work. We do believe the progress will continue.

"He has to go from being George's support player to being the go-to guy. He has to go from eight points a game to 15-16 a game. He is capable of that."

The other junior is **Jon Larranaga**, the 6-6 son of the coach who was a bit of a do-it-all guy last season (8.0 ppg, 4.9 rpg, 1.7 spg, 1.6 apg).

"Jon's contribution is actually greater than his numbers," his dad/coach said. "He gets his hands on a lot of balls, comes up with steals, makes plays that often go unnoticed by the public. From a coaching standpoint, we really appreciate that. On the offensive end, he does a lot of things people take for granted, like in-bounding the ball. This year, he has to be able to do more on the offensive end. It's one thing to average eight, it's another to average double figures."

At least early in the season, the rest of Mason's starters figure to come from last year's reserves. Look for 6-4 sophomore **Raoul Heinen** on the point, 6-5 senior **Rob Anderson** on the wing and 6-6 senior **Terrence Nixon** inside. Anderson averaged 4.8 points last season. Heinen wasn't eligible until the second semester. He averaged 3.1 points and 0.6 assists.

"Rob and Terrence are very capable physically," Larranaga said. "We're expecting Rob to become a major contributor rather than a support player. Terrence is very capable of scoring in double figures. It's his defense that we need him to improve. We need him to become a true 'four' man—battle the post players, rebound well from that position and guard guys who are 2-3 inches taller."

Heinen, Larranaga said, "will be a very solid player as a sophomore. He lost a lot of valuable time and had to play on just his physical ability."

Mason also returns three sophomores in 6-0 guard **Rob Sullivan**, 6-4 guard **Richard Tynes** and 6-9 center **Deon Cooper**. Sullivan was the most productive last season with a 2.2 scoring average.

"Rob and Richard just need more experience, need to get a little bit better at the things we do," Larranaga said. "Cooper is my pet project. I've explained to Deon that the role Jesse had as a freshman and sophomore is one he now inherits. He has to be a support player for Jesse. He's not going to be expected to get 15-16 [points], but we do expect him to hit double figures once in a while."

The Patriots' incoming class is an interesting mix of two freshmen, a junior college transfer and one now-eligible Division I transfer. **Dereck Franklin**, a 6-0 guard, has junior eligibility. He started his career at Boston University.

"He came to Mason because he wanted to be closer to home," Larranaga said of Franklin, who is from nearby Chantilly. "He's learned a lot from being in our program a year."

The freshmen are 6-1 guard **Lamar Butler** of Ft. Washington, Md., and 6-8 **Colin Wyatt** of Williamsburg, Va. Butler averaged 19.3 points at Oxon Hill High. Wyatt averaged 22.1 points and 12 rebounds at Jamestown High.

Darren Tarver, a 6-3 guard, averaged 16.7 points at Wabash Valley (Ill.) Community College. Another signee, 6-6 forward Steve Bonner, didn't gain eligibility. He averaged 21 points at North Idaho Junior College.

"It is my belief [a junior college player] will take almost a full year before they're able to do the things we expect," Larranaga said. "Division I basketball is a lot different than junior college basketball, especially in our situation where things are based on defense rather than offense.

"Our freshmen are in the same boat. The biggest adjustment they'll have to make is on defense."

2001-2002 SCHEDULE

Nov.	17	@Niagara
	19	@Miami (Ohio)
	24	Toledo
	28	Coppin State
Dec.	1	@Ole Miss
	5	Central Michigan
	8	Southern Illinois
	22	Delaware
	28	*Winthrop
	31	@Duquesne
Jan.	3	William & Mary
	5	Towson
	9	@UNC Wilmington
	12	Old Dominion
	14	Hofstra
	19	@Towson
	23	@VCU
	26	@Drexel
Feb.	2	James Madison
	6	@Delaware
	9	@Hofstra
	11	UNC Wilmington
	16	Drexel
	18	@William & Mary
	20	VCU
	23	@James Madison
	25	@Old Dominion
March	1-4	#Colonial Athletic Tournament

@Road Games
*Halifax, Nova Scotia
#Richmond Coliseum, Richmond, VA

BLUE RIBBON ANALYSIS

BACKCOURT	B
BENCH/DEPTH	B-
FRONTCOURT	B
INTANGIBLES	B

It says something that a team that lost as much in a season as any CAA team in recent years—including a three-time player of the year—is still so well regarded by rivals and the media.

That is a reflection of respect for the job Larranaga has done at Mason and the high regard for Mason's reserves of last season and recruits for this season.

Heinen was considered a plum recruit when Mason signed him, and missing the first semester last season hurt his progress. He should be much better this year.

Young, too, was a ballyhooed recruit and Mason needs him to live up to that promise this season in a big way.

If those two have good years, Mason has enough pieces elsewhere to match the preseason predictions. Mason knew it needed immediate help when it recruited a pair of junior college players. Only one got in school, though, so the burden falls on guard Darren Tarver to provide a quick fix. Boston College transfer Dereck Franklin has Division I experience and should be able to

help right away as well.

After a rough first season, Mason put together three strong years under Larranaga. That was with George Evans in uniform. Evans helped set Mason's bar very high, but it is a bar the Patriots should be able to clear.

(M.S)

Hofstra

LOCATION	Hempstead, NY
CONFERENCE	Colonial Athletic
LAST SEASON	26-5 (.838)
CONFERENCE RECORD	16-2 (1st America East)
STARTERS LOST/RETURNING	4/1
NICKNAME	Pride
COLORS	Gold, White & Blue
HOMECOURT	Hofstra Arena (5,124)
COACH	Tom Pecora (Adelphi '83)
RECORD AT SCHOOL	First year
CAREER RECORD	62-24 (3 years)
ASSISTANTS	Tom Parrotta (Fordham '88)
	David Duke (Albany '97)
	Van Macon (Southampton '94)
TEAM WINS (last 5 years)	12-19-22-24-26
RPI (last 5 years)	195-140-81-59-49
2000-01 FINISH	Lost in NCAA first round.

Hofstra has been one of the better mid-major success stories in recent years.

A doormat early in its life in the America East Conference, the Pride became a force. In Hofstra's first three years in the league, it went 19-33 in conference games. The last four years? How about 57-15?

Hofstra has won 20 games in a season only five times in its 27-year Division I history and three of them have come the last three seasons. Hofstra has boosted its victory total in each of the last five seasons.

The basketball class of 2001 was a part of 91 victories. The previous best total for a single class was 63. Hofstra has become an outstanding program.

But the Hofstra that will move into the Colonial Athletic Association this season (along with Delaware, Drexel and Towson) isn't the Hofstra of recent years. Seven players are gone from last year's team, including three who averaged in double figures in points and two who averaged at least six rebounds.

Coach Jay Wright is gone, too, thanks to his new job at Villanova. Back to square one? Probably not.

"This is a big change," said Tom Pecora, the former Hostra assistant who moved into Wright's chair. "Last year, we had seven seniors. This year we have none. Late in games, with the score tied, you can usually look to see who has more seniors on the floor and figure out who is going to win the game.

"Plus, we have the new league situation. The America East was great for us, but this is the right step for the university at this time. We wanted to step it up a notch. I think from top to bottom this is a very competitive league, one where we have to re-establish ourselves over time. It took us time in the America East. I don't think this is going to be any different."

Two of Hofstra's four veterans are guards. They are good ones, too. Junior **Rick Apodaca**, 6-3, is the lone returning starter. He averaged 12.1 points, 3.5 rebounds and 2.8 assists. Six-foot sophomore **Joel Suarez** averaged 6.5 points and one assist.

"Rick is our most experienced player and a guy who can score in a lot of ways," Pecora said. "We'll need him to step up not only physically but mentally as well. We're depending on him a lot.

"Suarez made the all-rookie team. He can play with the ball in his hands or off the ball. Once again, it's time for another guy to step it up."

The other veterans are 6-11, 270-pound junior center **Lars Grubler** and 6-6 junior forward **Danny Walker**. Each averaged 4.4 points. Grubler averaged three rebounds.

"Lars is physical. He has to rebound the ball a little better," Pecora said. "He's a hard-working kid and he's going to be a key for us. Danny saw a lot of minutes coming off the bench. He can do a lot of things well on the court."

Hofstra has three players available who took red-shirt seasons in 2000-2001—6-8 junior forward **Marc Petit**, 6-7 junior forward **Osei Millar** and 6-5 freshman swingman **Mike Radziejewski**.

Millar is a transfer from Boston University. Petit has been bothered by a variety of injuries.

"I think whenever a player sits, he'll have difficulty in the beginning," Pecora said. "It's hard to come back and bring your 'A' game.

"Millar is very athletic and active. Radziejewski is a very good catch/shoot guy who has gotten himself bigger and stronger. Marc could be a leader. He's had an eye injury, an ankle injury, a knee injury. Physically, I can't root for anyone more than him. We want him to rebound the ball and be durable enough to stick out the season."

Hofstra didn't leave New York to reel in its four-player recruiting class. The new faces are 6-8 forward **Kenny Adeleke**, 6-7 forward **Wendell Gibson**, 6-4 swingman **Chris McRae** and 5-11 guard **Woody Souffrant**.

"They're pretty good players, I hope, but once again they're freshmen," Pecora said. "The majority of our players are from established programs, so they're used to working hard. They know what it's all about. I wouldn't be shocked if one of these guys ended up starting or getting a ton of minutes. Wendell can score with his back to the basket. That's his strength and it's very hard to find nowadays. Every time I saw him play, he had a double-double.

"Adeleke [who averaged 19 points and 13 boards a year ago] is big and left-handed, very active on the glass. He can score a little bit with his back to the basket. McRae is just a physical three man. The one thing about most of our guys is they can play multiple spots. Woody is a point guard, a little jet. He can get other people shots and he likes to defend. He's a talented young guy and we may need him a lot."

Pecora especially likes the versatility of his new players.

"They all did what their teams needed for them to win," he said. "McRae played center. They've all made sacrifices for their teams and I think that's a special trait for young guys to have."

Hofstra, without a senior class, will use its two remaining scholarships this recruiting season and then get ready for a big haul the next year.

In the meantime, Pecora will hope his young team gets comfortable quickly in its new home.

"We've got to make them old," he said. "The only way to do that is get them a lot of minutes and let them make their mistakes."

2001-2002 SCHEDULE

Nov.	17	Florida Atlantic
	23-25	#Robert Morris Tournament
Dec.	1	*Iona
	4	@Syracuse
	8	Stony Brook
	16	@St. John's
	21	@Manhattan
	23	@Drexel
	28-29	##USF Shootout
Jan.	3	Old Dominion
	5	UNC Wilmington
	9	VCU
	12	@James Madison
	14	@George Mason
	19	William & Mary
	23	Drexel
	26	Delaware
	30	@Towson
Feb.	2	@UNC Wilmington
	4	@VCU
	9	George Mason
	13	James Madison
	16	@William & Mary
	18	@Old Dominion
	23	@Delaware
	25	Towson
March	1-4	###CAA Tournament

@Road Games
*Madison Square Garden, NY
#Moon Township, PA (vs. Kent first round; also Pittsburgh, Oakland, UC Irvine, Illinois State, Robert Morris, South Florida)
##Tampa, FL (vs. Illinois-Chioago first round; also South Florida, Bucknell)
###Richmond Coliseum, Richmond, VA

BLUE RIBBON ANALYSIS

BACKCOURT	B+
BENCH/DEPTH	B-

FRONTCOURT	B-
INTANGIBLES	B

Last year's Hofstra team would have been the best in the CAA by a wide margin. Its final number in the Ratings Percentage Index report was 43 spots better than any team in the CAA. That was last year.

This year, Hofstra won't be anyone's favorite. But the Pride won't lick the bottom like it did at the start of its life in the America East. A backcourt of Apodaca and Suarez is a good place to start. Hofstra won't take a backseat to many in the CAA with those two.

Up front, 6-11, 270-pound center Grubler gives the Pride size it won't find elsewhere in its new league.

The recruiting class is highly regarded and figures to make its presence felt right away.

With no seniors, the Pride will have plenty of time to grow together. It shouldn't be too long before Hofstra finds itself one of the best in its new home.

As for intangibles, the "original" CAA members are used to long travel and a tough place to play at UNC Wilmington. Wait until they venture to Long Island, where Hofstra is 36-1 in its last 37 home games.

(M.H.)

James Madison

LOCATION	Harrisonburg, VA
CONFERENCE	Colonial Athletic
LAST SEASON	12-17 (.413)
CONFERENCE RECORD	6-10 (t-7th)
STARTERS LOST/RETURNING	0/5
NICKNAME	Dukes
COLORS	Purple & Gold
HOMECOURT	JMU Convocation Center (7,612)
COACH	Sherman Dillard (JMU '78)
RECORD AT SCHOOL	59-53 (4 years)
CAREER RECORD	88-105 (7 years)
ASSISTANTS	Kenny Brooks (JMU '78)
	Ben D'Alessandro (Providence '95)
	Tom Sorboro (Bowling Green '92)
TEAM WINS (last 5 years)	16-11-16-20-12
RPI (last 5 years)	129-197-178-111-198
2000-01 FINISH	Lost in conference semifinal.

A scientist, maybe it was Newton or some other dude, pointed out years ago that every action has an equal but opposite reaction. Surely you've seen those toys with the bouncing balls? Drop two from one direction and two more go in the other direction?

The James Madison basketball team is another example of that theory at work.

Two years ago, everything fell into place for the Dukes. They weren't expected to do much and they ended up tying for the Colonial Athletic Association regular-season championship. JMU coach Sherman Dillard was the league's coach of the year.

Last year, the opposite happened. Nothing fell into place for the Dukes. Some games, it was guesswork as to what players would be available. Dillard learned more about medical terms than he desired. It led to a seventh-place finish. This year?

The juggling had one benefit in that a lot of players ended up with a lot of time. Some had to learn to play multiple positions. This is the year Dillard hopes to see some positive effects of all the negative happenings of last season.

"I'm really excited about our team," Dillard said. "I think we have a chance to be very solid.

"I think our experience shows right now. It's refreshing to see guys out there who know what we're doing."

The starting lineup JMU was using at the end of last season returns intact and Dillard will have four other players on his roster with starting experience. JMU will add two freshmen along with transfer Kenny Whitehead, a 6-10, 240-pound junior who formerly played at Charlotte.

Returning starters at guard are 6-2 sophomore Chris Williams and 6-0 junior David Fanning. The forwards are 6-8 senior Tim Lyle and 6-6 senior Ron Anderson. Ian Caskill, a 6-10, 245-pound junior, is the center.

Lyle was the team's leading scorer (11.6) and rebounder (6.2) last season. Fanning averaged 11 points and 3.2 assists. The other three all averaged between 5.2 and 5.5 points. Caskill averaged 5.4 rebounds.

"Chris has demonstrated he can be a capable point

guard in this league," Dillard said. "He's pretty heady, has some moxie, isn't afraid to mix it up. Fanning is as good an athlete as there is in the league. I think you'll see a little more consistency in his ability to score, especially from the perimeter.

"Tim is a workaholic. He'll be our captain this year. He can step out on the perimeter and he can battle down low. Ian has made significant improvement since he's been here and I think he's playing with a lot more confidence."

Anderson is the one whose numbers figure to jump. A highly touted transfer from N.C. State, he was slowed by a broken foot last season and never got totally comfortable. He did hit 10-of-13 shots in a victory at East Carolina late in the season.

"From the start, there was talk about what Ron could mean to this team," Dillard said. "I think this year you'll see a different Ron. I think the injury really set him back. He'd never use that as an excuse. If he can stay healthy, it will be a big plus for us. I sense that he will have a really good year. He's a solid athlete and, even though you can't tell by looking at him, one of my strongest players."

Pat Mitchell, a 6-7 junior, started 13 times last year and averaged 8.4 points and 6.1 rebounds. Junior Jerian Younger, a 6-9 forward, averaged 5.5 points. Sophomore swingman Dwayne Broyles and junior guard Charlie Hatter—both 6-4—also saw time in the starting lineup.

"There's a great deal of competition for playing time and that will be good," Dillard said. "It's a good problem to have to figure out the best way to rotate guys in and out, particularly inside. It will be a challenge to make sure we get good minutes for all those guys. Timmy and Jerian are capable of moving out to the wing to give other guys some time inside.

"Dwayne has the makings of being a pretty good shooter and he'll get some time at the 'three.' I'd still like to see him get a bit stronger."

JMU's two freshmen are 6-0 guard Daniel Freeman of Waynesboro, Va., and Fork Union (Va.) Military Academy and 6-5 swingman Todd Moret of Peachtree City, Ga. Whitehead will be a factor, too. He averaged 2.2 points and three rebounds as a sophomore at Charlotte.

"Todd is an explosive wing player," Dillard said. "From what I've seen so far, he's a pretty good defender. Daniel Freeman is a combo guard, which gives us a lot of options. Both those guys are physically ready to play right now. Understanding what it takes in other areas is what's going to take some time. I wouldn't be surprised to see both of them contributing in some way.

"Whitehead is a competitor and his forte is rebounding. He'll help us with interior defense. We'll see how a year off affects him. I know it will take a few games for him to get comfortable on the court. We're fortunate to have him. He gives us added depth and added bulk."

The Dukes' other player is 6-7 sophomore forward Kevin Bower, who got in one game a year ago. Dillard said he doesn't anticipate Bower's role changing much.

Dillard was able to get an early look at this team. The Dukes returnees went to Europe in August for a series of games.

"That gave us a good chance to get to see the guys and get some work in," Dillard said.

2001-2002 SCHEDULE

Nov.	20	@North Carolina State
	24	Gardner-Webb
Dec.	1	Drexel
	5	West Virginia
	8	@Liberty
	15	@East Tennessee State
	19	@Penn State
	22	Morgan State
	28-29	#Spider Invitational
Jan.	3	@Delaware
	5	@VCU
	12	Hofstra
	16	@Drexel
	19	@UNC Wilmington
	23	@William & Mary
	26	Towson
	30	Old Dominion
Feb.	2	@George Mason
	4	William & Mary
	6	VCU
	9	UNC Wilmington
	13	@Hofstra
	16	@Old Dominion
	20	@Towson
	23	George Mason
	25	Delaware
March	1-4	##CAA Tournament

@Road Games
#Richmond, VA (vs.Cornell first round; also VMI, James Madison)
##Richmond Coliseum, Richmond, VA

BLUE RIBBON ANALYSIS

BACKCOURT	B-
BENCH/DEPTH	B-
FRONTCOURT	B-
INTANGIBLES	B-

With the right kind of luck—that would be good rather than bad—this can be a pretty good team.

The coaches' preseason All-CAA team included two JMU players (Lyle and Fanning). That might be a little ambitious, but it shows that the Dukes' players are held in high regard.

Just about every coach in the league would trade for Lyle if allowed. He is an all-academic team member and veteran who has started 70 times in 84 career games. He's become dependable inside and is capable of going outside (21 three-pointers last season). He should continue to improve.

Anderson was bothered by his injury all last season and showed toward the end why JMU was so excited to have him. A healthy year makes him a much better player.

Fanning and Williams make for a strong backcourt. Both are capable passers.

Dillard will also be able to bring four guys off the bench who have starting experience. He'll be able to tailor his lineup to the match-up of the game.

JMU has something to prove this season. The Dukes are much closer to the team of two years ago than to the team of last year.

(M.H.)

UNC Wilmington

LOCATION	Wilmington, NC
CONFERENCE	Colonial Athletic
LAST SEASON	19-11 (.633)
CONFERENCE RECORD	11-5 (t-2nd)
STARTERS LOST/RETURNING	2/3
NICKNAME	Seahawks
COLORS	Green, Gold & Navy Blue
HOMECOURT	Trask Coliseum (6,100)
COACH	Jerry Wainwright (Colorado College '66)
RECORD AT SCHOOL	113-93 (7 years)
CAREER RECORD	113-93 (7 years)
ASSISTANTS	Brad Brownell (DePaul '93)
	Mike Winiecki (Richmond '89)
	Rodney Terry (St. Edward's '90)
TEAM WINS (last 5 years)	16-20-11-18-19
RPI (last 5 years)	113-79-191-118-95
2000-01 FINISH	Lost in NIT first round.

UNC Wilmington coach Jerry Wainwright is a naturally funny guy and it's no surprise that he's able to reel off a few one-liners about the lofty predictions for his Seahawks in 2001-02. He also knows it's no joke. Wainwright is sitting on a gold mine this season.

"Obviously there has to be a substance in the air with whomever was making these picks," he said. "I guess they figure I'm the oldest one in the league, they might as well retire this guy by putting a bulls eye on him.

"I'm not going to run from the fact that I think we can be a good basketball team. We have a proven go-to guy, a tremendous junior college point guard coming in, some experience and some really good young players."

Yeah, that does sound like a winning combination all right. Those substances in the air are talent and experience. UNCW was an easy choice for the favorite's tag in the Colonial Athletic Association.

Any discussion of the Seahawks has to start with 6-3 junior guard Brett Blizzard, the preseason CAA Player of the Year. He's twice been all-league and was MVP of the CAA Tournament as a freshman. He averaged 13.8 points last season, not an eye-popping number but pretty strong when you consider UNCW averaged only 61.4

per game. A mid-season cold spell (4-of-24 from three-point range over four games) hurt Blizzard's percentage (.394 for the year). He went 21-for-30 over a five-game stretch later in the season.

"The next thing for Brett is to prove himself to be a leader," Wainwright said. "With only two seniors on our team, he certainly has the most minutes. It is time for him to step up and say, 'This is my team.' He can't just lead by example, which he's always done. He's a good defender, rebounder and probably our best passer. I would hope his assists go up [from 2.5 per game] into that 4-6 range."

UNCW's point guard will be 6-0 junior **Lou Chapman**, who played at Colby (Kansas) Community College last season. He averaged 4.5 assists, to go along with 12.4 points and 2.7 rebounds, as a sophomore.

"He's our biggest addition, without question," Wainwright said. "I've had some good guards here and I really do believe he has a chance to become the best point guard we've ever had. He's quicker than anybody we've had at that spot and he can pass. I think Lou and Brett will play well together. He immediately gives our team personality."

Chapman started 60 straight games in his junior college career, so he comes in with plenty of experience. He wasn't called on to be Colby's leading scorer but proved he could handle his share of the load. Chapman shot 40 percent from three-point range (72-of-180) and 75 percent from the free-throw line a year ago. He led his team in scoring 11 times, with a season high of 24.

Though his frontcourt situation isn't as settled, Wainwright still has some attractive options. One definite is 6-6 senior **Ed Williams**, who averaged 12 points and six rebounds last season. He struggled later in the season after opening with 10 straight games in double figures, including one with 28 points.

"Eddie was probably the smallest four man in the league," Wainwright said. "I think he wore down. If we're able to play him at the small forward spot on a regular basis, that's what will make us a good team. I would anticipate his numbers would only increase. I think he can play at the all-conference level."

Craig Callahan is a 6-8, 245-pound junior who will be a power forward with small forward skills. He was 5-of-5 from the floor in the CAA championship game. Senior **Stewart Hare**, an inch shorter and 35 pounds lighter than Callahan, gives Wainwright a backup option at guard and forward.

"Hare has been on three postseason teams," Wainwright said. "The biggest problem with him has been keeping weight on. If we can use him as kind of a sixth starter, that would be to our advantage. Callahan is a 6-8 guy with a jump shot. You have to guard him. He's the type of guy everyone would like to have."

Options inside are 6-11, 235-pound freshman **Aaron Coombs** and 6-9, 225-pound red-shirt freshman **Brandon Clifford**. Coombs averaged 12 points and eight rebounds at Fort Bend Austin High in Sugarland, Texas. Clifford played five games last season before injuring an ankle.

"We're kind of back to having a big thumper in there," Wainwright said. "For us to fulfill whatever people say about us, we have to be able to throw it inside and get a basket. We weren't able to do it last year. [Coombs] is huge; he's going to be 250 pounds by the time the season starts. He has a chance to be a really good player and I think he can be a defensive factor in there early on."

Bench options are 6-1 sophomore guard **Tim Burnette** and 6-6 sophomore forwards **Joel Justus** and **Anthony Terrell**. Other newcomers are 6-4 sophomore guard **Andy Gunn** and 6-2 freshman guard **Joseph King**.

Terrell made 11 starts last season and averaged 3.3 points. Gunn comes in from Iowa Western Community College, where he averaged 10 points, three boards and two assists last season).

"The guy who had the best year off the bench for us was Tim Burnette," Wainwright said of the player who averaged only 2.2 points. "He's had a great off-season. Gunn is a swing-type player, a big-time athlete. Terrell might be pound-for-pound the best athlete I've seen in my life. If he or Clifford can get it up to 20 minutes a game and be productive, we've got a chance to be really good."

"We have a lot of guys who have played even though they're young. If you had to pick one word to characterize our team, I'd say versatile."

2001-2002 SCHEDULE

Nov.	12	#@Wake Forest
	17	Miami, OH
	24	@High Point
Dec.	2	@Ohio State
	4	@Minnesota
	8	Duquesne
	10	@Bowling Green
	15	@College of Charleston
	21	@Old Dominion
	28	Fairfield
	30	Towson
Jan.	5	@Hofstra
	9	George Mason
	12	Delaware
	16	@William & Mary
	19	James Madison
	23	Old Dominion
	26	@VCU
	28	@Towson
Feb.	2	Hofstra
	4	Drexel
	9	@James Madison
	11	@George Mason
	13	William & Mary
	16	@Delaware
	18	@Drexel
	23	VCU
March	1-4	##CAA Tournament

@Road Games
#Preseason NIT (if UNC Wilmington wins, it will play Arkansas or Maine on Nov. 16; semifinals and final Nov. 21 and 23 at Madison Square Garden, NY)
##Richmond Coliseum, Richmond, VA

BLUE RIBBON ANALYSIS

BACKCOURT	A
BENCH/DEPTH	B+
FRONTCOURT	B+
INTANGIBLES	B+

Any backcourt—at least at the CAA level—that includes Blizzard is going to be pretty good. Some folks like to say he's merely a shooter. They're not paying attention. He averaged four rebounds and 2.5 assists last year.

Chapman, the junior college transfer Wainwright brought in to run the point, is apparently the perfect complement to Blizzard and the entire team. One CAA assistant not at UNCW called him an ideal point guard. He won't look to score and UNCW doesn't need him to do that. He'll get the ball to the right place.

Williams had a better year than people realized, and figures to get better. Hare and Callahan give the Seahawks two bigger guys who can step outside and shoot. At 6-11, Coombs is one to watch. All UNCW needs, with its plethora of shooters, is a big guy to dump it in to for easy baskets. Clifford (6-9, 225) played only five games last season before injuring an ankle. Healthy, he'll be a factor.

As for intangibles, nothing beats UNCW's home court. It has earned a reputation as the toughest place to play in the CAA. UNCW was 11-1 there last season and 19-1 in its last 20 games. Over the last three seasons, UNCW is 18-4 in league play at home and 33-4 in the last five seasons. Richmond, which owns two of those four victories, is no longer in the league.

UNCW is the only CAA team with at least 10 league victories in eight straight seasons. That streak will definitely live another year.

(M.H.)

Old Dominion

LOCATION	Norfolk, VA
CONFERENCE	Colonial Athletic
LAST SEASON	13-18 (.419)
CONFERENCE RECORD	7-9 (t-5th)
STARTERS LOST/RETURNING	2/3
NICKNAME	Monarchs
COLORS	Slate Blue & Silver
HOMECOURT	Norfolk Scope (10,239)
COACH	Blaine Taylor (Montana '81)

RECORD AT SCHOOL	First year
CAREER RECORD	142-65 (7 years)
ASSISTANTS	Jim Corrigan (Duke '80)
	Kenny Gattison (Old Dominion '86)
	Larry Kristkowiak (Montana '86)
TEAM WINS (last 5 years)	22-12-25-11-13
RPI (last 5 years)	91-174-90-232-176
2000-01 FINISH	Lost in conference semifinal.

Blaine Taylor had a pretty good thing going. A former head coach at Montana, he was one of Mike Montgomery's assistants at Stanford. As assistants' gigs go, Stanford has to rank pretty high.

He's been a west-of-the-Mississippi guy, but things he saw right smack on the East Coast changed his life direction.

Fortunately for Old Dominion, Taylor was willing to look at the not-too-distant future rather than the not-too-distant past and agreed to take over the Monarchs' program.

ODU has been pretty darn good for a long time, but the slippage had started in recent seasons. The Monarchs have had three losing seasons in the last four. Interest, and attendance, had been waning.

But there's a new arena on the horizon (next season) and reason to believe ODU isn't that far away from being good again. Just maybe not as close as this year.

"The future here, being a part of what's going to happen is really exciting," Taylor said. "The new arena is great, really perfect. They made a lot of good decisions with that building.

"I know we have our work cut out for us on the court. A lot of good players walked out the door and I inherited somewhat of a younger group. The majority of what they lost was in the paint and that leaves a lot of questions on the front line.

"I know we haven't challenged for the top recently, but I think if things fall together and we stay healthy, we can be pretty doggone competitive. There are others in this league race that would certainly be able to talk more confidently about being near the top."

Gone from last year are reliable Andre McCullum (12.5 points) and rugged Clifton Jones (9.3 rebounds). The Monarchs return three pretty good starters, but there is a massive hole in the middle.

The returning starters are 6-2 senior guard **Pierre Greene** (11.7 points, 3.5 assists), 6-7 junior forward **Ricardo March** (9.4 points, 4.4 rebounds) and 6-5 junior forward **Rasheed Wright** (9.8 points, 4.0 rebounds).

"Pierre is a kid we will lean on," Taylor said. "Rasheed and Ricardo have had good moments. We're going to need a lot more consistent play out of them to stick our nose in this conference race. They've had enough bright moments to kind of tease people. You need more consistent efforts night after night."

ODU's most proven reserves are, unfortunately for Taylor, guards. Sophomores **Troy Nance** (3.6 points, 3.5 assists), 5-10, and **John Waller** (2.8 points), 6-4, are capable, though probably not yet ready for prime time.

Inside, Taylor will have his pick from a trio of sophomores—6-9 **Charles Dunnington** (1.7 points, 1.9 rebounds), 6-11 **Clay McGowen** (1.0 points, 1.2 rebounds) and 6-10 **Joe Principe** (1.7 points, 1.5 rebounds).

"It's really an unproven bunch. I'll be the most interested observer of any," Taylor said. "I think Troy Nance learned some things last year and it will be interesting to see how he performs in the second go-round.

"With the young post kids, it's kind of time. There's opportunity there for one or all of them to step forward and help us. People keep asking what we're going to do in that area. We're going to have to coach. We have to get some performance out of them."

ODU has four newcomers and it looks to be a good recruiting class. But no one in the class will provide the answer in the middle.

James Smith, a 6-7, 185-pounder, averaged 17.4 points at Cape Henry Collegiate in Virginia Beach, Va. **Kiah Thomas** is a 6-4 swingman who signed late. He averaged 14.1 points, 7.3 rebounds and 4.2 assists at Norfolk's Granby High. **Alan Treese** is a 6-8 forward from Delaware, Ohio (12.5 points, 8.3 rebounds). **T.J. Waldon**, a 6-5 forward, averaged 18.8 points and 9.7 rebounds at Kathleen High in Lakeland, Fla.

"I think we have a nice freshman corps to work with," Taylor said. "There's some substance to start some things for the future.

"That group will challenge our rotation. They'll cause some guys to have to show up every day. These kids can certainly make their presence felt in a big way."

Also on ODU's roster is 6-5 swingman **Andreas Themistocleous**, a sophomore walk-on who averaged 0.7 points.

2001-2002 SCHEDULE

Nov.	13	#Sacramento State
	24	*@Virginia Tech
	26	Delaware State
Dec.	1	Illinois-Chicago
	5	George Washington
	8	@East Carolina
	15	Coastal Carolina
	18	Hampton
	21	UNC Wilmington
	30	@UNLV
Jan.	3	@Hofstra
	5	Drexel
	7	Delaware
	12	@George Mason
	14	@Towson
	19	VCU
	23	@UNC Wilmington
	26	William & Mary
	30	@James Madison
Feb.	2	@Delaware
	4	Towson
	9	@VCU
	11	@Drexel
	16	James Madison
	18	Hofstra
	23	@William & Mary
	25	George Mason
March	1-4	##CAA Championship

@Road Games
*Norfolk Scope Arena, Norfolk, VA
#Guardians Classic at Memphis Pyramid; vs. Wofford or Memphis in second round; semifinals and final on Nov. 20-21 at Kemper Arena, Kansas City, MO)
##Richmond Coliseum, Richmond, VA

BLUE RIBBON ANALYSIS

BACKCOURT	B
BENCH/DEPTH	C
FRONTCOURT	C-
INTANGIBLES	C

You won't find too many coaches in the CAA who wouldn't be glad to take Old Dominion's three starters and call them their own.

Greene, who will be the team's lone senior, has developed into a solid point guard. Junior forwards Marsh and Wright both can be a handful, when they're on their game. They never seem to be at the same time, though, and it is imperative for that to happen this year if ODU is going to have any chance of being any good.

It's what is on the table beyond the three returnees that makes ODU's prospects this season a bit troublesome. There is precious little experience inside. The CAA has become a bigger league in recent years. Just about every team has a player who is at least solid in the middle. If you don't have one, you can get overwhelmed pretty quickly.

ODU doesn't have anyone who has proven to be that, not at this point. Someone from among the trio of Dunnington, McGowen or Principe—sophomores all—is going to have to have a much bigger year than anyone expects.

The hiring of Taylor was a good move. He has a track record with his success at Montana and he brings a fresh perspective to a school that needs one. Outgoing coach Capel was a good man and a better coach than people gave him credit for, but it was clearly time after seven years for a new face. ODU had reached a point where it looked stagnant. With a new building coming and a need to generate rather than lose enthusiasm, the time was right for a change.

(M.H.)

 **Towson**

LOCATION	Towson, MD
CONFERENCE	Colonial Athletic
LAST SEASON	12-17 (.413)

CONFERENCE RECORD	7-11 (8th East)
STARTERS LOST/RETURNING	2/3
NICKNAME	Tigers
COLORS	Gold, Black & White
HOMECOURT	Towson Center (5,000)
COACH	Michael Hunt (Furman '85)
RECORD AT SCHOOL	First year
CAREER RECORD	First year
ASSISTANTS	Dino Presley (Kutztown '93)
	Rob Senderoff (Albany '95)
	Daniel Searl (Northeastern '95)
TEAM WINS (last 5 years)	9-8-6-11-12
RPI (last 5 years)	220-238-262-237-235
2000-01 FINISH	Lost in conference quarterfinal.

Ah, summertime, when the living is supposed to be easy.

Towson coach Michael Hunt hopes it wasn't too easy for his players. It's doubtful anyone around the country was more eager to see the summer end than Hunt, who takes over an America East bottom feeder just as it makes the jump into the Colonial Athletic Association.

This is Hunt's first time as a head coach and he wasn't hired until close to the end of the school year. He hasn't had much time to get to know any of his players.

"It made it tough as far as having extensive off-season workouts," said Hunt, who has been an assistant at Towson, Tennessee and Georgia, among other places. "I did get a couple of workouts in before they went away for the summer.

"We have three guys who have played a lot of minutes, started a lot of games and have college experience under their belts. My hope is they worked hard over the summer and improved as individuals so they can provide leadership to the new players."

The veterans Hunt speaks of are 6-4 senior forward **Sam Sutton**, 5-11 junior guard **Brian Allen** and 6-3 sophomore guard **Tamir Goodman**. Allen started 29 times, Sutton 28 and Goodman 23 last season. Sutton was the Tigers' No. 2 scorer at 13.6 per game. He led the team with a 6.2 rebounding average and with a 4.3 assists average. Allen averaged 10.8 points and 4.2 rebounds. Goodman averaged 6.0 points, 2.5 rebounds and 4.0 assists.

"Sam's assists stood out. That made a significant impression on me," Hunt said. "If our basketball team can come together and be willing to share the ball and make plays for each other, it will help us be more competitive as a team.

"Obviously, Sam is our leader in the frontcourt and on our basketball team. We're expecting a good year out of him."

Goodman and 7-0 freshman **Derrick Goode** are two of the more interesting players anywhere. Goodman is a devout Orthodox Jew whose recruitment was the subject of national interest. He had a flirtation and falling out with Maryland before heading to Towson.

Goode, who red-shirted last season, weighs 355 pounds.

"I've been very impressed with Tamir as a person and with his dedication to his religious beliefs," Hunt said. "He's a good ambassador for our university and our team.

"When I got this job, Derrick was 385 pounds. With increased weight loss, he'll see his production rise as a player. You can't teach height and he gives us something maybe other people don't have, and that's a big, wide-bodied guy."

Mohamed Fofana is another red-shirt freshman who is a beanpole to Goode's wide boy. He's 6-8, 185.

Other Towson veterans are 6-6 senior **Kerry Augustus**, 6-7 senior **Mike Shin**, 6-7 sophomore **Marijan Spalevic** and 6-3 junior **Gerald Weatherspoon**.

Weatherspoon made four starts last season and averaged 7.4 points. Shin averaged 3.8 points and 2.0 rebounds. Augustus also made three starts and averaged 2.0 points.

"Kerry and Mike Shin are seniors," Hunt said, "and will be counted on for leadership as well as quality playing time. Spalevic will be counted on to provide depth at the forward position."

Towson's newcomers are 6-9 forward **Tony Dixon** of Jackson, N.J.; 6-3 guard **Calvin Dotson** of Baltimore; 6-8 forward **Jerome Matthews** of Lanham, Md.; and 6-2 **Justin Reaves** of Oxon Hill, Md.

Dotson is a sophomore who played last season at Mott Community College in Flint, Mich. Matthews is a junior walk-on who sat out last season after transferring from Concordia College. The others are freshman.

Reaves is a walk-on. Dotson averaged 9.7 points and 4.0 steals last season.

"We're very excited about Dotson," Hunt said. "He was our first signee. Dixon is a late-bloomer and someone who has the potential to grow literally and figuratively. I think he'll be 6-10 or 6-11 by the time his career is over."

Hunt sounds realistic when he assesses Towson's immediate future.

"We're moving into a more competitive league," Hunt said. "This is an exciting time to be joining the CAA. Nothing is going to happen overnight. It is going to be anywhere from a 3-5 year process to reshape this program."

2001-2002 SCHEDULE

Nov.	17-19	#Battle of Baltimore
	24	@Georgetown
	28	@LSU
Dec.	1	Rider
	5	@VCU
	8	Morgan State
	11	@Maryland Eastern Shore
	20	*Howard
	22	@UMBC
	30	@UNC Wilmington
Jan.	2	Delaware State
	5	@George Mason
	12	Drexel
	14	Old Dominion
	19	George Mason
	23	@Delaware
	26	@James Madison
	28	UNC Wilmington
	30	Hofstra
Feb.	2	@William & Mary
	4	@Old Dominion
	9	William & Mary
	13	Delaware
	16	VCU
	20	James Madison
	23	@Drexel
	25	@Hofstra
March	1-4	##CAA Tournament

@Road Games
*MCI Center
#Baltimore, MC (vs. Coppin State first round; also Loyola, UMBC)
##Richmond Coliseum, Richmond, VA

BLUE RIBBON ANALYSIS

BACKCOURT	C-
BENCH/DEPTH	C-
FRONTCOURT	C-
INTANGIBLES	C-

Sad as it sounds, last year's 12 victories were the most at Towson in the last five years. Still, this is a team that struggled in a league that isn't as good as the one the Tigers play in now. Towson went 2-7 in its final nine games.

As Hunt says, someone told him its good having nine players back. And bad. The experience is good. If those players don't improve, it will be bad.

Sutton had a good year in his first season with the Tigers after transferring from St. Francis. He's the Tigers' best player. Towson's best defender is probably Allen, who will find himself on the short end of many a match-up in the CAA.

Is Goodman really a prime time player? "The Jewish Jordan" wasn't consistent last season. He'll be counted on for more this season.

It's a good thing Hunt is patient. He says this is a process that will take 3-5 years and he's probably right. The CAA is nobody's idea of a powerhouse, but it is higher-rated than the America East. Players coming in will find things move just a tad quicker and they'll find a number of teams that play very good defense. A team that has struggled in the AE doesn't figure to flourish too soon.

(M.H.)

Virginia Commonwealth

LOCATION	Richmond, VA
CONFERENCE	Colonial Athletic
LAST SEASON	16-14 (.533)
CONFERENCE RECORD	9-7 (4th)
STARTERS LOST/RETURNING	3/2
NICKNAME	Rams
COLORS	Black & Gold
HOMECOURT	Stuart C. Siegel Center (7,500)
COACH	Mack McCarthy (Virginia Tech '74)
RECORD AT SCHOOL	45-44 (3 years)
CAREER RECORD	292-170 (15 years)
ASSISTANTS	Mike Ellis (North Carolina '88)
	Gerald White (Auburn '88)
	Jeff Capel III (Duke '97)
TEAM WINS (last 5 years)	14-9-15-14-16
RPI (last 5 years)	131-245-194-172-139
2000-01 FINISH	Lost in conference first round.

When **L.F. Likcholitov** first came to Virginia Commonwealth University three years ago, he knew little English. His basketball skills needed some translating, too. The man was definitely a project.

Likcholitov proved to be an extremely hard worker and today, the results show. He's a pleasant conversationalist, comfortable in English. And, he's a college graduate. A partial qualifier when he came, Likcholitov earned a degree in three school years plus a summer.

Thanks to a relatively new NCAA rule, that earned Likcholitov the year of eligibility he lost on the front end. In any language, that's big for VCU.

Likcholitov (9.6 ppg, 7.0 rpg) is a 6-10, 250-pound senior who has made steady progress on the court. He doesn't need to make dramatic progress this season, he needs only to continue to improve at the same level. If VCU can get 12 points and eight boards out of him on a consistent basis, that will be plenty.

The Rams are rich in slashers and shooters and they'd love to have a dependable big man to deflect some of the defensive attention.

"L.F. is certainly a dimension that we can focus on and the real key thing about him is the amount of improvement he's shown each year," VCU coach Mack McCarthy said. "If he does that again, it's pretty exciting. Last year, he just kept getting better and better."

The off-season never seems to be quiet at VCU, and this year was no exception. Likcholitov's graduation was the good news. There was also some bad.

Forward Johnnie Story, a member of the CAA's All-Freshman team last season when he averaged 7.5 points and 4.7 rebounds, didn't cut it academically and is gone. Also, the Rams finally got recruit Antonio Hargrove eligible. He enrolled in summer school, but was dismissed from the team in August for what McCarthy called "a violation of teams rules."

Apparently, Hargrove was lackadaisical toward his classwork and other requirements. McCarthy figured if the 6-5 swingman was that much trouble now, he wasn't worth having around during the season.

But there's still plenty of reason for optimism at VCU.

Two who will join Likcholitov for sure in the Rams' starting lineup are 6-1 sophomore guard **Domonic Jones** and 6-5 junior forward **Willie Taylor**. Jones averaged 8.6 points in a reserve role last season. Taylor averaged 12.6 points and 4.3 rebounds as a starter, including a high of 41 against Evansville. Taylor was inconsistent and sometimes out of control.

"Domonic probably has the biggest role change," McCarthy said. "Now instead of plugging him in and letting him play if he's playing well, he's going to be the guy out there all the time. I think he's ready to do that. He got valuable experience last year and was able to play both guard positions. I don't think point guard is the best description for what he'll do. I think lead guard is what he'll be.

"We thought Willie would be erratic last year and he was. I fully expect him to be more consistent this year. I think he took a backseat to the seniors last year, but now he and L.F. should be the guys we count on."

This is McCarthy's fourth year at VCU, and he dipped into the junior college ranks this year for the first time. It should provide him with his other two starters. **Josh Clark**, from Dixie (Utah) Junior College, is a 6-7, 210-pounder who will take Story's spot and do much the

same thing. He doesn't figure to be a big scorer, but he should rebound well. **Antoine Willie**, who averaged 24 points at Columbia (Calif.) Junior College, will be on the wing. The 6-2 Willie can also play the point.

Willie to Willie?

"I expect Antoine to have an immediate impact," McCarthy said. "He's a proven scorer. Josh Clark is very athletic, a good rebounder and defender and an adequate scorer. He played on a great junior college team."

Last season, VCU pretty much had two complete units that were interchangeable. Many games, the second five was on the court late. That could be the case at most positions this year as well.

Emanuel Mathis, 6-3, will have junior eligibility after transferring from Florida State. He can back up both guards. "Mathis is probably our most cerebral player," McCarthy said. "He really knows how to play. I have high expectations for him."

Junior **Matt Treadwell** (2.5 ppg, 2.6 rpg), who is 6-11, backs up Likcholitov and sometimes plays with him to give the Rams a twin-towers thing. Juniors Josh Graham (3.2 ppg, 3.0 rpg), 6-5, and **Konstantin Nesterov** (5.5 ppg, 3.7 rpg), 6-8, can come in at the forward spots. Nesterov is a power forward who can shoot from long range.

Walk-on guard **Alex Shtam** (1.3 ppg, 0.7 rpg), 6-3, is also back and McCarthy said he could play more this season.

"From day one, Josh Graham has been one of our better defenders and more savvy players," McCarthy said. "Now I think the maturity factor will be a big plus for him. He's a guy who can literally play three positions out there.

"Treadwell has had a good summer and I think he'll be able to maintain his strength better this season. We know he's capable of having a big impact. I look for Nesterov [one of four Russians on the roster] to make the biggest improvement just because he's acclimated. I think Alex finally sees some opportunity."

VCU has another big man in 7-2 Russian **Denis Orlov**, who saw very limited duty last season.

The Rams also have two freshmen in 6-1 guard **Mark Adams** and 6-8 forward **Derrick Reid**. They were teammates at Meadowbrook High in suburban Richmond. Adams averaged 5.6 assists as a senior. Reid was the Central District Player of the Year with averages of 14.9 points, 9.8 rebounds and 2.1 blocks.

"Denis has gained some weight and gotten stronger. He still has a ways to go," McCarthy said. "Mark Adams, from a numbers standpoint, has a chance to play right away. Derrick can score and play all three front line spots. They come from a very good program, so they'll be well prepared."

2001-2002 SCHEDULE

Nov.	14-16	#BCA Classic
	20	East Tennessee State
	27	Tulane
	29	North Carolina A&T
Dec.	1	@Richmond
	5	Towson
	8	@Florida Atlantic
	15	UAB
	18	Gardner-Webb
	22	@Wagner
Jan.	3	@Drexel
	5	James Madison
	9	@Hofstra
	12	@William & Mary
	14	Delaware
	19	@Old Dominion
	23	George Mason
	26	UNC Wilmington
	30	@Delaware
Feb.	2	Drexel
	4	Hofstra
	6	@James Madison
	9	Old Dominion
	16	@Towson
	20	@George Mason
	23	@UNC Wilmington
	25	William & Mary
March	1-4	##CAA Tournament

@Road Games
#Raleigh, NC (vs. Northwestern first round; also East Carolina, Fairleigh Dickinson, High Point, North Carolina State, Prairie View A&M, Rutgers, San Jose State)
##Richmond Coliseum, Richmond, VA

BLUE RIBBON ANALYSIS

BACKCOURT	B
BENCH/DEPTH	B+
FRONTCOURT	B
INTANGIBLES	B-

This COULD be a very good team. Or not. Bet on good, but there are plenty of questions.

Can Jones do as well in a full-time role as he did in a part-time role? Can either one of two transfers—Mathis or Willie—provide consistent scoring at wing guard?

Can Taylor be more like the guy who scored 41 against Evansville? Or will he be the guy who hit double figures only twice in the past seven games?

Will Likcholitov continue his improvement at center?

Can yet another transfer, Clark, handle power forward?

VCU should be plenty deep and provide McCarthy with some flexibility. There's no need for this team to get worn down. VCU could have the quickest team in the league.

McCarthy and the Rams need a big year to break the cycle of mediocrity they've fallen into in recent years. The material appears to be on hand. Once again, the Rams are breaking in a lot of new players. There's only one senior—Likcholitov—on the roster.

"It's an interesting mix of new people and experience," McCarthy said. "It might be just the right mix. Or, we might struggle for a while. I would think by the end of the year we would be the best that we've been since I've been here."

(M.H.)

William & Mary

LOCATION	Williamsburg, VA
CONFERENCE	Colonial Athletic
LAST SEASON	11-17 (.392)
CONFERENCE RECORD	7-9 (t-5th)
STARTERS LOST/RETURNING	2/3
NICKNAME	Tribe
COLORS	Green, Gold & Silver
HOMECOURT	William and Mary Hall (8,600)
COACH	Rick Boyages (Bowdoin '85)
RECORD AT SCHOOL	11-17 (1 year)
CAREER RECORD	56-66 (5 years)
ASSISTANTS	Jamie Kachmarik (Bowling Green '97)
	Pat Sherry (Tufts '92)
	Milan Brown (Howard '93)
TEAM WINS (last 5 years)	12-20-8-11-11
RPI (last 5 years)	186-106-293-177-217
2000-01 FINISH	Lost in conference first round.

Rick Boyages spent time as an assistant coach in the Big East and the Big Ten. One of the first things he noticed when he became head coach at William and Mary was the physical difference between the majors and mid-majors.

He immediately put an intense weight program in place, and the results were noticeable. The Tribe was a stronger team last season.

But muscles didn't put the ball in the basket. If the Tribe can add a little shooting to the mix, Boyages' second year should be much better than his first.

William and Mary led the CAA in field-goal defense and rebounding margin last year. But it was next-to-last in scoring, seventh in field goal percentage and eighth in turnovers.

"We'll be better, I think," Boyages said. "We played as well defensively last year as we could. Turnovers were the killer. We just didn't have any backcourt. We have five new guys coming in and they should help us be a better shooting team on the perimeter.

"We've been getting up less shots night after night because we cough it up 20 times a game. We need to get that down into the 12-15 range."

Junior **Sherman Rivers**, 6-0, returns at point guard, but Boyages is thinking he might be exclusively a point guard this season. Rivers averaged 9.0 points, 4.5 rebounds and 2.6 assists last season. He also had three more turnovers than assists. He rarely got a break.

"I had no sub for him," Boyages said.

Look for 6-0 freshman **Nick D'Antoni** to help there. From Socastee High in Myrtle Beach, S.C., he averaged

22 points as a prep senior. He can spell Rivers at point. Or he can take over for Rivers at the point and push Rivers to the wing.

"I think the two of them could be a real nice tandem," Boyages said. "Nick could take a lot of pressure off Sherman. Nick is going to have to play."

The Tribe's roster remains top heavy with big folks. The other guards are 6-3 senior **Cody Carbaugh** (3.4 points, 1.9 assists) and 6-2 sophomore **Reid Markham** (1.9 points).

William and Mary's best shooters could turn out to be forwards. **Adam Hess**, a 6-7 sophomore, will be eligible at the start of the second semester after transferring from Eastern Michigan. He averaged 10 points there.

Boyages is also excited about 6-9 freshman **Thomas Vilgianco** of Madison, Ala. and Bob Jones High. He averaged 20 points last year.

"Adam is our best shooter. He could challenge to start as soon as he gets back," Boyages said. "Vilgianco has a chance to crack the starting lineup. We need help at the 1, 2 and 3 spots and they are guys who can factor in right away."

William and Mary has so much size it's absurd.

Senior **Mike Johnson** is a 6-7, 240-pounder who is the team's leading returning scorer (12.0) and rebounder (7.3). He also averaged 1.7 assists. He can step out and hit the three. His 50 made bonus shots were tops on the team by a wide margin.

Tom Strohbehn is a 6-9 senior with plenty of experience, though he's never had a breakthrough year. He averaged 6.6 points and 4.8 rebounds last year.

"Johnson and Strohbehn are similar in that they're big guys who can come away from the basket," Boyages said. "Tommy has a little more inside presence than Mike. They're both very experienced and very physical kids."

Junior **Adam Duggins**, a 6-11, 250-pounder, missed 13 games last season with a broken left hand. He averaged 4.7 points and 3.0 rebounds. Senior **Bill Davis**, 6-7, did a nice job (2.3 points, 2.9 rebounds) in a limited role (11 minutes) last season. **Zeb Cope**, a 6-9 sophomore, started twice and finished with averages of 2.2 points and two rebounds.

"Throw Duggins in for a whole season and it's a very nice mix," Boyages said.

Big newcomers are 6-10 **Nate Loehrke** of Mattawan, Mich., and 6-8, 220-pound **Steve Sorenson** of Hudson, Ohio.

Kori Brown is a 6-6 senior who played in only four games last season.

"We'll be as big and physical as anybody in the conference," Boyages said. "We'll be deep up front and we'll have a lot of flexibility."

William and Mary's increased emphasis on shooting doesn't mean the Tribe has ignored the weight room. Boyages hopes his team is stronger this year than it was last.

"We've made some great strides in that area," he said. "These guys have conditioned like they've never conditioned before. Most of the guys back have been here through the summer. I've seen big transformations in guys like Duggins, Rivers, Carbaugh and Johnson. They'll be starting out in great shape."

2001-2002 SCHEDULE

Nov.	16-17	#Red Raider Classic
	20	@High Point
	24	@Charleston Southern
	26	@The Citadel
	28	Washington & Lee
	30	##Boilermaker Invitational
Dec.	1	##Boilermaker Invitational
	27	@Maryland
Jan.	3	@Maryland
	5	Delaware
	7	Drexel
	12	VCU
	16	UNC Wilmington
	19	@Hofstra
	23	James Madison
	26	@Old Dominion
	30	@Drexel
Feb.	2	Towson
	4	@James Madison
	6	Hampton
	9	@Towson
	13	@UNC Wilmington
	16	Hofstra
	18	George Mason
	20	@Delaware
	23	Old Dominion
	25	@VCU
March	1-4	###CAA Tournament

@Road Games
#Lubbock, TX (vs. Texas Tech; also Nothern Iowa, San Diego State)
##West Laffayette, IN (vs. Purdue first round; also Akron, Oakland)
###Richmond Coliseum, Richmond, VA

BLUE RIBBON ANALYSIS

BACKCOURT	C+
BENCH/DEPTH	B-
FRONTCOURT	B-
INTANGIBLES	C

Less should mean more for Rivers, who was an iron man last season. He averaged 34 minutes per game and ended the season with more turnovers than assists. Not a good number for your point man.

With some added depth, Rivers won't have to wear himself out. D'Antoni is key here. If he can play 10-12 minutes per game at the point, that may be all the rest Rivers needs.

The Tribe also needs to find someone it can rely on at wing guard. Carbaugh? It's his final season and he needs to produce more than the three double-figures scoring games he had last season.

William and Mary shot only 41 percent from the floor and only 31.8 percent from three-point range last season. It won't get better unless those numbers get better, no matter how well it plays defense.

Up front, William and Mary has plenty of size to go around. The team has nine players 6-7 or taller, including four members of its new class. Of them, only Johnson has shown any reliability. That has to change.

William and Mary won eight of its 12 games at home, a decent showing considering William and Mary Hall doesn't provide much of a home-court advantage. The team averaged only 2,120 fans there. Among the victories was a 20-pointer over UNC Wilmington.

(M.H.)

UAB

LOCATION	Birmingham, AL
CONFERENCE	Conference USA (National)
LAST SEASON	17-14 (.548)
CONFERENCE RECORD	8-8 (4th)
STARTERS LOST/RETURNING	2/3
NICKNAME	Blazers
COLORS	Green, Gold & White
HOMECOURT	Bartow Arena (8,500)
COACH	Murry Bartow (UAB '85)
RECORD AT SCHOOL	90-66 (5 years)
CAREER RECORD	90-66 (5 years)
ASSISTANTS	Thomas Johnson (Montevallo '77)
	Matt Bowen (Indiana '95)
TEAM WINS (last 5 years)	18-21-20-14-17
RPI (last 5 years)	115-95-64-103-101
2000-01 FINISH	Lost in conference quarterfinal.

Meet your Conference USA darkhorse, the team most likely to pull off upsets, generate momentum and qualify as the surprise of the league.

Said one C-USA coach in the preseason: "If somebody puts them in their Top 25 or Top 30, they could really look smart."

We seriously considered the Blazers for our Top 40, but, ultimately questions about the quality of their defense kept them out. We will not be surprised to see UAB prove us seriously wrong, especially with a schedule that could land UAB in the Top 25 before conference play begins.

Injuries derailed UAB last year before the season even began, when its best player, **Myron Ransom**, and sixth man, **Morris Finley**, suffered season-ending injuries, Ransom to a torn anterior cruciate ligament and Finley to a broken vertabrae.

UAB's media contact for basketball, Jack Duggan, points out that, for the season, UAB lost a total of 85 player games. Though UAB never challenged for the C-USA title, the Blazers won eight league games and very nearly upset Cincinnati in the C-USA Tournament.

Memphis coach John Calipari was adamant that UAB coach Murry Bartow deserved consideration for league coach-of-the-year honors for his efforts.

Finley is back. So is Ransom. And though the Blazers lost two key components in forward David Walker and point guard LeAndrew Bass (with Bass the most damaging departure) the roster is filled with players who can match the best at their respective positions in Conference USA.

"The thing that jumps out is we can be much better offensively than the last couple of years," Bartow said. "Last year, our team had two or three options and that was it, and we had some real droughts. This year, instead of two or three options, we believe we can have six or seven."

The first option will be senior shooting guard **P.J. Arnold** (13.4 ppg, 2.9 rpg), an energetic 6-5, 205-pound Memphis native who led the Blazers in scoring (14.4 ppg) in C-USA play. Arnold struggled with consistency all season, but was much more steady once league play began.

He scored in double figures in 12 of UAB's final 16 games; he scored 22 points against Marquette, had 30 at DePaul and nearly drove UAB to an upset of Cincinnati with 21 points in the Conference USA Tournament.

"We think he will have an awful good senior year," Bartow said. "The thing he can do is score. I want him to be more well rounded in terms of rebounding better and defense."

Arnold was one of the league's most dangerous three-point shooters, hitting at a .433 clip in conference games. But he was extremely erratic. In the final regular-season game, against Saint Louis, he scored just two points.

"We know he can score," Bartow said. "He just needs to be more consistent."

Arnold's running buddy at UAB is senior **Eric Batchelor** (11.5 ppg, 4.1 rpg), another Memphis native who entered the program as a junior-college transfer with Arnold. A 6-7, 210-pound swingman, Batchelor's biggest strength is his shooting and scoring ability, though he was even more maddening than Arnold with his inconsistency last season.

For instance: In the first meeting with Cincinnati, Batchelor scored 20 points, but, in the C-USA Tournament with the season on the line, he had no points. Zero. After scoring 16 or more points in 10 of the first 17 games of the season, Batchelor had only a pair of 17-point games in the final 14 games.

Batchelor is a better pure shooter than Arnold, but his shot selection helped create a .327 percentage from three-point range. His .831 free-throw percentage is more indicative of his sweet stroke, and he would do well to go inside and use his post-up game to earn more free throws this season.

"I think he's one of the best catch and shoot three-point shooters in the league," Bartow said. "His big strength is that he can make shots and that's what he needs to do. I just expect a little more out of him from the defensive end and rebounding standpoint."

Arnold and Batchelor will not have Bass to set them up anymore, however. His ability to penetrate and score inside helped free them up, and now that task belongs to junior-college transfer **Eric Bush** (18.2 ppg, 6.5 apg, 3.3 spg at Barton County [Kansas] Community College), a 5-10 junior point guard.

A very good playmaker and adequate shooter from three-point range, Bush was highly regarded and heavily recruited.

"It doesn't mean he'll start, but we are certainly expecting a lot out of him," Bartow said. "He makes a lot of things happen. He probably has a few too many turnovers for my liking, but he gets a lot of assists. He's really a great on-the-ball defender.

"The biggest thing with him, if you look at his winning percentage at Barton and then four years [of high school ball] at Anderson, Indiana, his winning percentage is off the charts. He's been a winner."

Finley (6.3 ppg, 1.3 rpg in 1999-2000) is UAB's other player listed under 6-feet, but he is not a point guard. Finley, 5-11 and 165 pounds, will be a red-shirt sophomore after missing last season with the back injury. He scored 36 points in a game against Fresno State as a freshman, and can be a Vinnie Johnson-like scorer at the shooting guard position.

"He's a combo, not a pure point or a pure two," Bartow said. "The thing he can do is create shots. We didn't have many weapons and he could've made some shots for us. He'll have something to say about who starts. He's a really hard worker, and, even if he doesn't start, he'll get starter's minutes."

Asa Woods (2.4 ppg, 1.0 rpg, 0.9 apg), a sopho-

CONFERENCE USA

BLUE RIBBON FORECAST

American
1. Cincinnati
2. Charlotte
3. Marquette
4. Louisville
5. DePaul
6. Saint Louis
7. East Carolina

National
1. Memphis
2. UAB
3. South Florida
4. TCU
5. Tulane
6. Houston
7. Southern Mississippi

TOP 40

Cincinnati and Memphis are ranked among the 2001-2002 *Blue Ribbon* Top 40. Extended profiles can be found in the Top 40 section of *Blue Ribbon*.

ALL-CONFERENCE TEAM

G-Dajuan Wagner, FR, Memphis
G-Steve Logan, SR, Cincinnati
F-Altron Jackson, SR, South Florida
F-B.B. Waldon, SR, South Florida
F-Kelly Wise, SR, Memphis

PLAYER OF THE YEAR

Dajuan Wagner, FR, Memphis

NEWCOMER OF THE YEAR

Dajuan Wagner, FR, Memphis

2001-2002 CONFERENCE TOURNAMENT

March 6-9, Firstar Center, Cincinnati, OH

2000-2001 CHAMPIONS

Cincinnati (American)
Southern Mississippi (National)
Charlotte (Conference tournament)

2000-2001 POSTSEASON PARTICIPANTS

Postseason record: 7-4 (.636)
NCAA
Cincinnati (Sweet 16)
Charlotte (Second Round)

NIT
Memphis (Third Place)
Southern Mississippi

TOP BACKCOURTS

1. Charlotte
2. Memphis
3. Cincinnati

TOP FRONTCOURTS

1. Memphis
2. South Florida
3. Marquette

INSIDE THE NUMBERS

2000-2001 RPI: 10th (of 31)
Conference RPI (last five years): 9-8-6-7-10

DID YOU KNOW?

Cincinnati and Memphis helped the conference improve its postseason record, with the Bearcats breaking the two-and-out jinx that had plagued the program in the NCAA Tournament and the Tigers making their first NIT Final Four appearance since 1957. Cincinnati lost in the Sweet 16 out West and Memphis finished third in the NIT. ... Even so, most thought the league would put four teams in the NCAA Tournament last season. It got only two bids—Cincinnati and Conference USA tournament champ Charlotte—and the NIT invited only two Conference USA teams. The league is now 11-16 in the last five NCAA Tournaments and 9-14 in the last five NITs. ... Cincinnati did continue one notable streak, winning an NCAA Tournament first-round game for the seventh consecutive season. Only Kansas, Kentucky and Stanford can make the same claim. ... The National Division closed the gap a little last season, and will make more strides this season with TCU going into the National and East Carolina into the American. After managing to go 20-26 (.434) in intra-divisional games against the American Division teams last season (including the league tournament), the National now sports a 50-117 (.299) record against the American Division since the league went to the two-division alignment in 1997-98. Of the league's 20 tournament bids since inception, only two—UAB in 1999, Memphis in 1996—have gone to current members of the National Division. ... Cincinnati coach Bob Huggins is the only coach who was on board for the first C-USA season, in 1995-96. He is one of four Conference USA coaches with a Final Four on his resume, having gone in 1992. Memphis coach John Calipari took UMass in 1996, TCU's Billy Tubbs took Oklahoma in the '80s and Louisville's Rick Pitino did it at Providence in the '80s and Kentucky in the '90s. ... South Florida's dynamic duo of B.B. Waldon and Altron Jackson should both surpass all-time C-USA scoring leader DeMarco Johnson of Charlotte (1,763 points in three C-USA seasons) by the end of the season. Waldon is in fifth-place all time with 1,455 career points, followed closely by Jackson with 1,401. ... Charlotte's Jobey Thomas can put the league's career three-point shooting records almost out of reach. He already is first all-time in three-pointers made (236) and three-pointers attempted (630) and should easily surpass 300 career three-pointers and could threaten 900 attempts. ... Memphis senior Kelly Wise should finish his career second in career blocked shots in Conference USA (tied for second with 176, or 116 less than Kenyon Martin) and first in rebounds (745 in 92 games, 124 behind Martin). ... With point guard Courtney Trask transferring to LSU and swingman John Grice ineligible for the fall semester, Memphis will enter the season with only three players on its roster who have attempted three-point shots in a Division I game. One of them is junior center Earl Barron, who is 0-for-4, and the other is former walk-on Nathaniel Root, who has taken most of his 31 attempts in mop-up time. Sophomore Scooter McFadgon connected on 29-of-81 (.358) from long range as a freshman. ... There was something of an assistant coaching carousel in Conference USA in the off-season, with the most notable moves being Mick Cronin (from Cincinnati to Louisville) and Andy Kennedy (from UAB to Cincinnati). ... Conference USA's new television package with ESPN should get terrific ratings in Fond du Lac, Wisc. There are three Dieners from Fond du Lac on different Conference USA rosters: brothers Drake (DePaul) and Drew (Saint Louis) and their cousin, Travis (Marquette).

(Z.M.)

can play the two or three. Johnson, hampered by a stress fracture during the season, started 17 games last season and averaged 27 minutes per game, while Ball, who was hampered with a knee injury, averaged just 14.4 minutes.

Bartow on Johnson: "He's had a good summer. The two big things with him, he had to get stronger and become a better shooter. He is a real low-risk guy and probably the smartest guy on the team from a basketball standpoint."

Bartow on Ball: "He's been hurt and has just never gotten into the rotation. He is a great kid to coach because he is very versatile, and he is a better shooter than we give him credit for being. Whether he plays five minutes or 30, he's totally for the team and he's a high-energy guy."

Jeffrey Collins (21.0 ppg as a senior at Birmingham Ramsay), a 6-4 freshman guard, will occupy a role similar to Ball and Johnson as a versatile athlete in the mold of former UAB guard Torrey Ward.

Bartow will have some interesting choices to make on the interior. Ransom (11.4 ppg, 5.9 rpg in 1999-2000), a senior, is back after missing last season with the torn ACL, and, at 6-5, 225, will likely play an undersized power forward.

If Ransom is fully healed and back in shape, he can make a big impact. He is a good enough outside shooter to take defenders to the three-point arc, but is a determined inside scorer who knows how to take contact and finish. He must improve his free throw shooting, and he can be a defensive liability against a team like Memphis with several tall forwards.

A heralded local recruit, Ransom did not blossom until midway through his junior season, when he became a legitimate leader and go-to player.

"He's a real tough kid who competes hard," Bartow said. "He should be one of our best scorers."

Will Campbell (8.7 ppg, 8.1 rpg), a 6-8, 245-pound senior, showed last season he can man the pivot with the best in C-USA. He averaged nearly a double-double in league games (10.8 ppg, 9.6 rpg) while hitting .576 from the field.

Campbell developed a reputation as one of the league's brashest players. Against Memphis, Campbell kicked away the end of the little carpet used in pre-game warm-ups to introduce the Tigers, and he was never afraid to verbally and physically challenge opposing big men.

Campbell, like Arnold and Batchelor, struggled to grasp consistency, but he scored in double figures in 11 of his final 16 games last season.

"He's a guy we're counting on to have a big year," Bartow said. "I would rate him very highly among the big men in this league."

The most intriguing newcomer for the Blazers is 6-5, 230-pound **Antonae Roberson** (22.0 ppg, 10.0 rpg) from San Jose City College. Bartow compares Roberson's game to former Memphis scoring champ Omar Sneed, if a little less commanding than Sneed.

Other C-USA coaches who saw Roberson believe he will have an impact on the league.

"Not saying he's as good, just that he has a lot of similarities," Bartow said. "He's just got a knack for scoring the ball. He's real efficient and a very good athlete and we're expecting really big things out of him."

Cedric Davis (16.0 ppg, 8.9 rpg), a 6-8, 225-pound junior from Sinclair (Ohio) Community College, is similar to Campbell in physique and will be counted on mainly for defense and rebounding.

"He's probably the strongest guy on our team," Bartow said.

Tom Frericks (2.1 ppg, 2.4 rpg), a 6-9, 250-pound sophomore, is another in the defense-and-rebounding mold who could be an occasional enforcer inside. Frericks, who averaged a personal foul every four minutes as a freshman, can provide offensive rebounding and a junk basket or two.

2001-2002 SCHEDULE

Nov.	17-20	#Paradise Jam
	24	*Richmond
	27	Bradley
Dec.	1	@Murray State
	4	Alcorn State
	8	**Hardwood Classic
	15	@VCU
	19	Louisiana Tech
	22	@LaSalle
	29	Jackson State
Jan.	2	Florida A&M
	5	Louisville
	8	East Carolina

more, is the polar opposite of Finley—he's a 6-5 combo guard who is more of a point than a shooter. Playing behind Bass, Woods never really adjusted as a freshman, but could see playing time this season.

"He's very athletic, a great runner and probably the best ball handler on our team," Bartow said. "He needs to get stronger and improve his perimeter jump shot."

It always seems hard to distinguish between **Tony**

Johnson (4.0 ppg, 3.3 rpg) and **Sidney Ball** (4.0 ppg, 3.9 rpg). Both are juniors, both entered the program at the same time, both are from small southern towns and both have essentially been honest, hard-working role players in their two seasons.

Johnson is 6-5, 180, and can play the one, two or three (he averaged 3.3 assists per game) and is probably UAB's best perimeter defender. Ball is 6-5, 185, and

	12	@Southern Miss
	15	@Marquette
	19	Houston
	23	@Memphis
	26	Tulane
	29	@TCU
Feb.	5	@South Florida
	8	Memphis
	12	TCU
	16	@Tulane
	19	@Saint Louis
	23	South Florida
	26	Southern Miss
March	2	@Houston
	6-9	##Conference USA Tournament

@Road Games
*UAB Classic, Birmingham, AL
**Birmingham Civic Center
#Virgin Islands (vs. Eastern Michigan first round; vs. Miami, second round; championship and consolations on Nov. 20)
##Firstar Center, Cincinnati, OH

BLUE RIBBON ANALYSIS

BACKCOURT	B+
BENCH/DEPTH	A-
FRONTCOURT	B+
INTANGIBLES	B+

This is indeed a solid B-plus team, meaning if the Blazers just exceed expectations a little, they will mess up a lot of predictions in a lot of preseason magazines. UAB won nine of its final 15 games last seasons, with three of the losses by three points or less and two of them slipping away on the final possession or regulation. That was with all the injuries.

UAB has more depth at every position, and, in Campbell and Arnold, two players that should be all-conference by the end of the season. Ransom, before his injury, was developing into an all-league caliber player. They will be good. If Batchelor, Roberson and Bush live up to expectations, Memphis may be the only team in the conference with more firepower than the Blazers.

This is not a great-looking defensive team, however, especially inside. If the Blazers had been successful in the recruitment of Memphis freshman Duane Erwin—the 6-9 center from Huntsville backed off a commitment to UAB in November—this would be as formidable a team defensively as it is offensively. Expect UAB to use a press that was very effective for the Blazers at times the last two seasons.

It is a commonly held assumption that Bartow is on at least a very warm seat in Birmingham, though there is no denying his penchant for winning and fielding more-than-competitive teams. If he can create strong team chemistry and cajole a consistent effort from a roster filled with talent, this could be Bartow's best season.

UAB won't be on anyone's short list of potential NCAA Tournament at-large teams. It should be. This Blazer team could be the biggest surprise in Conference USA, and, with all its offensive ammunition, should be mighty entertaining to watch.

(Z.M.)

Charlotte

LOCATION	**Charlotte, NC**
CONFERENCE	**Conference USA (American)**
LAST SEASON	**22-11 (.667)**
CONFERENCE RECORD	**10-6 (2nd)**
STARTERS LOST/RETURNING	**2/3**
NICKNAME	**49ers**
COLORS	**Green & White**
HOMECOURT	**Dale E. Halton Arena (9,105)**
COACH	**Bobby Lutz (UNC Charlotte '80)**
RECORD AT SCHOOL	**62-38 (3 years)**
CAREER RECORD	**203-102 (10 years)**
ASSISTANTS	**Kevin Nickelberry (Virginia Wesleyan '86)**
	Rob Moxley (Pfeiffer '94)
	Benny Moss (Charlotte '92)
TEAM WINS (last 5 years)	**22-20-23-17-22**
RPI (last 5 years)	**26-25-22-69-45**
2000-01 FINISH	**Lost in NCAA second round.**

As the final seconds ticked away in Charlotte's commanding 80-72 whipping of Cincinnati in the Conference USA championship game last season in Louisville, the Charlotte fans began chanting, "One more year! One more year!"

The cries were directed at Rodney White, the magnificent 6-9 forward who averaged 18.7 points as a freshman. It was, however, a foregone conclusion that White was going to apply for the NBA draft, and, when he did, his decision was vindicated: He went in the top 10.

"I would do it again in a heartbeat," Charlotte coach Bobby Lutz said of his decision to rely on a player who likely was leaving after one season. "Where our program was and is, we have to take the best players who want to come and play for us."

The departure of White seems to leave Charlotte without the dynamic player it needs to compete for a C-USA regular-season title.

The 49ers, however, have a penchant for proving themselves better than perceived and making others look bad for underestimating them. The void White leaves is huge, but the 49ers did not make the second round of the NCAA Tournament without other talented players and a proven system.

Three starters are back from last season's team, and the 49ers will feature what Lutz believes is perhaps the school's best-ever backcourt. The three-balls will be flying, but this team also has several players capable of breaking a defense down and making inside players very effective.

Charlotte, a fixture in the C-USA championship game, is conceding nothing. Lutz loves the versatility of this squad, and believes he has the kind of athletes who can ratchet up the defense, both the halfcourt and full-court variety.

"I hope we can get after people more," Lutz said. "We had so many young guys last year who didn't understand defenses. You'll see us go after people and change defenses more, which is what we always like to do."

Of Conference USA's potential stars, senior shooting guard **Jobey Thomas** (14.0 ppg, 2.8 rpg) may be the least regarded nationally. A 6-4 gunslinger, Thomas possesses the quickest outside release in the league and is relentless running through a gauntlet of screens, like a skier slicing through a slalom course.

Thomas already owns the C-USA record for three-pointers made (236), and he raised his accuracy considerably last season, hitting 40.2 percent from long range for the season and a remarkable 45.5 percent in league games. He also broke Conference USA's record for threes in league games (56 for 3.5 per game) and twice tied the league record for threes made in a game with seven against DePaul and Louisville.

And, Lutz said, Thomas has become an even better shooter. On a European Tour with an NIT all-star team over the summer, Thomas averaged 17.8 points and hit 51.5 percent of his three-point shots from the international range.

Lutz said Thomas has greatly improved his in-between game and the respect for his dribble should make him even more effective from outside. Opponents know not to send him to the line: He hit 80-of-88 (90.9 percent) from the stripe last season.

"He's benching 300 pounds and shooting from NBA range with ease now," Lutz said.

Thomas was lost somewhat in the early-season rotation, struggling in December, but he shared responsibility with White for the late-season charge to the finish. In the final 13 regular-season games, Thomas averaged 17.9 points while shooting .474 from the floor and .477 from three-point range.

"Part of that December was things were going so well we forgot him a little bit," Lutz said. "He carried us when Rodney was hurt. We've challenged him to be a leader. It needs to be his team in a lot of ways and he's ready for that."

Demon Brown (11.7 ppg, 2.5 rpg, 4.0 apg), a 6-1 junior, started the first half of the season at point guard and looked a sure bet to make an all-league team of some sort. For Brown, last year was a rookie season after sitting out his freshman year as a non-qualifier, and his struggles after the New Year made him a sixth-man.

At times, Brown simply got too far ahead of himself and his teammates with his desire to score and create pace. He had only 77 turnovers, but he too often rushed up the first shot available or tried to use his breakdown abilities to go one-on-one instead of letting the multi-layered Charlotte offense develop.

He hit .353 from three-point range, but needs to do better than .384 overall. His demeanor and role in Charlotte's stretch run, while backing up Diego Guevara, suggested a maturing player who can be a great leader once he is fully in charge up top.

Brown is also a beast in the weight room, benching more than 300 pounds. That strength makes him even more effective when he pushes into the lane and on defense.

"He grew up a lot in understanding what we needed to do," Lutz said. "We like the fact that he can score, but we need him to run the team. I think he can have a special year."

Lutz and staff made sure the 49ers will continue to stay potent from the perimeter by signing **Mitchell Baldwin** (17.7 ppg, 5.1 agp), a 6-2 freshman from Rural Hall, N.C. The Winston-Salem Journal selected Baldwin its player of the year two straight years, making him only the fifth player to earn the honor—and the first to play outside the ACC.

Baldwin, who has a 36-inch plus vertical leap, is a combination guard who will see minutes at both guard spots and has the ability to become one of Charlotte's best perimeter defenders. Lutz says Baldwin is quicker than Brown, and rivals Thomas in his ability to get a shot off from the outside.

A streaky shooter, Baldwin will nonetheless earn big minutes as a freshman.

"He gives us a different dimension of quickness," Lutz said. "He needs to be a more consistent shooter to be an outstanding college player."

Eddie Basden, a 6-5 freshman from Upper Marlboro, Md., and **Curtis Nash**, a 6-6 junior transfer from Dallas and Hill (Texas) Junior College, bring athleticism on the wing and will more than fill the void left by James Zimmerman on the wing.

Nash (16.0 ppg, 9.0 rpg, 5.0 apg) can play the one-, two- or three-spots, but needs to add strength.

"He's very versatile and his best position may be the point," Lutz said. "He can really shoot it from deep but he is a great passer. He possesses a great understanding of the game."

Basden (18.5 ppg, 7.5 rpg) was headed to UMass until Bruiser Flint was fired, and Lutz believes he could make an immediate impact on the wing. He's more of a forward, with Nash more of a guard.

"He's in the mold of Galen Young and James Zimmerman," Lutz said. "He can guard people. He's a great finisher near the basket, and can really drive the basketball."

Charlotte's interior will be held together by senior **Cam Stephens** (7.8 ppg, 7.8 rpg), the former Purdue big man who, at 6-8, 240, established himself as a very effective blue-collar player in White's shadow. He had the same number of rebounds (248) as points (248).

Stephens had shoulder surgery in the off-season, but is full recovered. Lutz said he has also slimmed down some.

"He's in the best shape he's ever been in," Lutz said. "He seems to be a little quicker. He'll have more opportunities to score, and he's another guy we need to become a leader."

Kevin "Butter" Johnson (3.5 ppg, 2.7 rpg), a 6-8 sophomore, showed steady progress throughout the season, and was a valuable role player during Charlotte's stretch drive. Johnson saved his best for last, producing career highs in points (nine) and rebounds (eight) in the NCAA Tournament win over Tennessee. In the last five games of the regular season, Johnson averaged 5.8 points while hitting .688 from the field.

A versatile and athletic forward, Johnson can play the three or the four. Most likely, you'll see him out in a 4-1 set as the power forward and Stephens inside as the center.

"He can rebound the ball and he's a very hard match-up at the four," Lutz said.

Matas Niparavicius (0.9 ppg, 0.9 rpg), a 6-9, 220-pound sophomore from Lithuania, has more potential than he showed in his initial season. Injuries derailed him whenever Lutz and staff were getting ready to show him more minutes.

"He's 6-9 at least and he can really shoot it," Lutz said. "He struggled with physical play like a lot of foreign players and he has worked on that. He went up against Rodney every day in practice and that was a beneficial experience."

Sophomore **Tory Reed** (2.5 ppg, 1.4 rpg), like Johnson, spent a season at prep school before arriving as a freshman last season. Reed battled tendinitis early in the season and never really became a factor. At 6-8, 240, Reed can help inside, especially on defense, though Lutz sees him as "probably our best low-post scoring option."

"If you get him the ball on the box, he's pretty good at putting it into the hole," Lutz said.

Senior **Jermaine Williams** (1.2 ppg, 2.1 rpg), at 6-10, 240, should also get a chance to become a consistent player inside.

"He can help us more than he did a year ago," Lutz

said.

David Hardy is a 6-8 red-shirt freshman from Harrisburg, N.C., who walked on last season but will not likely be a factor, though he was a team captain for a state championship team as a senior at Central Cabarrus High School.

2001-2002 SCHEDULE

Nov.	16	Davidson
	18	Indiana
	24	@Long Beach State
	26	Appalachian State
Dec.	1	@Temple
	8	Richmond
	15	*Florida
	18	UTEP
	22	@Miami
	29	@George Washington
Jan.	5	Marquette
	8	@Cincinnati
	12	East Carolina
	15	Saint Louis
	18	@South Florida
	23	Louisville
	26	East Carolina
Feb.	2	@Houston
	6	Cincinnati
	9	@Saint Louis
	13	Memphis
	16	DePaul
	19	@Marquette
	23	Tulane
March	2	@Louisville
	6-9	#C-USA Tournament

@Road Games
*Orange Bowl Classic, Miami, FL
#Firstar Center, Cincinnati, OH

BLUE RIBBON ANALYSIS

BACKCOURT	A
BENCH/DEPTH	B-
FRONTCOURT	B-
INTANGIBLES	B+

With Brown and Thomas starting and guys like Baldwin, Nash and Basden supporting, the 49ers will feature one of the best backcourts in Conference USA and the nation. Thomas and Brown are tough and fiery leaders, and this 49er team should warm to their personalities.

"I think the perimeter is the best it has ever been," Lutz said. "We have six guys who can really play at those spots."

This does not mean Charlotte will rely solely on the outside shot, though Thomas will cause nightmares with his range and hustle and consistency.

"We have people who can break people down on the dribble," Lutz said. "We're more athletic with guys who can really get it to the paint, aside from just pitching it from three-point range."

Inside, Lutz is very confident that Stephens and Johnson will contribute and make the 49ers competitive in a physical, athletic league. And though there isn't great interior depth or vast experience to choose from inside, Lutz does like the versatility his big men will provide.

"Cam is gonna play and Butter is gonna play," Lutz said. "After that, we can go a lot of ways, and I like that."

Charlotte needs one of the wings, Nash or Basden, to develop quickly and provide the hinge an excellent backcourt needs with a less reliable frontcourt.

Can Charlotte compete for another C-USA title? This is yet again a 49er team with some very good elements and lots of role players, and that formula has been successful in the past.

This is a team that, with great defense, could emerge as an NCAA Tournament contender and legitimate threat to Cincinnati in the American Division. We'll call Charlotte an early favorite for the first NIT bid from Conference USA, while refusing to eliminate the possibility of a spot in the Big Dance.

(Z.M.)

DePaul

LOCATION	Chicago, IL
CONFERENCE	Conference USA (American)
LAST SEASON	12-18 (.400)
CONFERENCE RECORD	4-12 (6th)
STARTERS LOST/RETURNING	2/3
NICKNAME	Blue Demons
COLORS	Royal Blue & Scarlet
HOMECOURT	Allstate Arena (17,500)
	and United Center (21,500)
COACH	Pat Kennedy (Kings College '75)
RECORD AT SCHOOL	58-66 (4 years)
CAREER RECORD	384-257 (21 years)
ASSISTANTS	Tracy Dildy (Illinois-Chicago '91)
	Brian Kennedy (Monmouth '90)
	Jim Todd (Fitchburg State '76)
TEAM WINS (last 5 years)	3-7-18-21-12
RPI (last 5 years)	231-193-51-40-151
2000-01 FINISH	Lost in conference first round.

You really needed Al McGuire to properly describe DePaul's team last season. It was a team that defied traditional labels.

McGuire might have said the Demons had guys who shopped Big-and-Tall or in the Juniors department, that there weren't enough guys who could be fitted in the regular men's store. And he might have described the disastrous results of 2000-01 as a burst-balloon kind of year.

Picked by most preseason publications as a Top 25 team, DePaul slipped in the first game of the season and never really recovered. This was a team that could beat St. Joseph's, narrowly lose to Florida and Kansas and then fall apart in league play.

The 4-12 C-USA mark was injurious enough. To see Bobby Simmons, Steven Hunter and recruit Eddy Curry leave for the NBA draft, that only made the season more painful for coach Pat Kennedy. DePaul enters this season having lost four underclassmen to the NBA draft the last two off-seasons.

"It was a Murphy's Law situation from start to finish," Kennedy said.

All is not lost. Kennedy says he accepts full responsibility for last year's debacle, at the same time asserting that this squad is better equipped for consistent success. That is in large part because this season's roster actually includes some in-between players, the versatile 6-4 through 6-6 players that expand a coach's toolbox.

To fully understand how oddly manned DePaul was last year, one needed only to see the backcourt. Kennedy often played **Rashon Burno** and **Imari Sawyer** together.

Burno, a senior, is 5-7, 175. Sawyer, a sophomore, is 6-2, 170. The partnership presented a defensive liability, to say the least. It didn't exactly make for an offensive juggernaut, either.

Sawyer, a product of Chicago's public league, had a fine freshman year on paper. He averaged 11.7 points, set the school record for assists by a freshman with 179 (6.0 per game), averaged 35-plus minutes per game and grabbed 2.4 rebounds per game, besides. But there were 126 turnovers (4.2 per game), a .369 shooting percentage overall (.282 three-point percentage) and poor decision-making at the worst of times.

Sawyer appears to be a difference-making kind of point guard, one who can command a game and a team with his playmaking. But he must learn to direct all his instincts to winning purposes, not just to impress the Bulgarian judge with some flashy move.

"He's got to really control his assist to turnover ratio," Kennedy said. "He's got to play the time-score theory of basketball. He's got to understand that a mistake made at the four-minute mark is the same as one in the final minute."

Sawyer often shared the court with Burno, but he should be the starter this season, with the ever-unselfish Sawyer coming off the bench as a reserve. Sawyer should be a better guard by just being around Burno, who never does more than he can and is always aware of situations.

"For Imari, this is more just learning the game of basketball," Kennedy said. "He's got all the tools and the physical abilities."

Burno (6.7 ppg, 3.7 rpg, 2.9 apg), part of Kennedy's first true senior class, is a bulldog of a player for whom last season must've been agony. Kennedy says he'd like to make sure Burno goes into coaching, and hopes to eventually put him on his staff one day.

Only an adequate shooter (.379 from the field, .340 three-point range, .653 FT), Burno is a leader and his toughness personified DePaul when the Demons resurged his first two seasons. He is the only three-year captain in the history of DePaul basketball.

"He has been plagued with a lot of nagging injuries which is an extension of how hard he plays," Kennedy said. "We tried to play he and Imari together, but that was

simply out of necessity. You will never see the two of them out there together."

Joe Tulley, a 6-2 junior from Rockford, Ill., spent the most time at shooting guard last season, though he will be challenged strongly for time on the court this season. Tulley (7.6 ppg, 2.2 rpg, .362 3PT) is a defensive liability as well, but he earned a reputation last season as a clutch shooter and was very productive near the end of the season.

"Joe kind of blossomed in the last 14 or 15 games," Kennedy said. "He got a tremendous amount of game experience, and he should see quality minutes."

The more likely starter at shooting guard is **Marlon London**, a 6-5, 200-pound junior who transferred from Kansas and sat out last season. London (3.6 ppg, 2.3 rpg in two seasons at Kansas) could play the three, as well.

London has the potential to become an all-league player; if he does, DePaul will surprise lots of folks.

"He's going to be a huge key for us," Kennedy said. "He's got a Quentin Richardson type body, big strong legs and is quick off his feet. He's a little more of a perimeter player. He really has been one of our best players in practice. He's really utilized this year in the weight room."

Kennedy went to the junior-college ranks to find **Marlon Brooks** (17.0 ppg, 4.5 apg at Lincoln [Ill.] Junior College), a 6-1 combination guard who played in high school at Peoria Manual. Brooks' strength is his quickness, and his versatility gives Kennedy his strongest blend of guards since he arrived.

Drake Diener, another freshman who will be in the mix, averaged 20 points, eight rebounds and four assists as a senior in Fond du Lac, Wisc., and the 6-5 guard brings a much-needed sniper's mentality to DePaul. His long-range shot should earn him playing time; after setting the high school record for free-throw percentage in a season, he should at least get to shoot a few technicals.

"He's a dribble-pass-shoot guy we have not had," Kennedy said.

Want more versatility? After a year without many interchangeable parts at all, Kennedy not only gets London but he has an impact freshman available in 6-7, 220-pound freshman **Quemont Greer** from Milwaukee.

Greer (19.0 ppg, 10.0 rpg, 3.0 apg for his high school career) was a fourth-team Parade All-American and he can play two, three or four, with more athleticism than Simmons offered (and perhaps more zeal for winning).

"He's a Bobby Simmons type player," Kennedy said. "He was a real good get for us."

Another nice get came in the form of 6-4 freshman **LaVar Seals** (22.0 ppg, 8.0 rpg as a junior) from Chicago. Seals was very highly regarded but slipped in various rankings after missing most of his senior season because of a broken ankle.

"He's extremely athletic," Kennedy said. "We want to get more up-tempo in terms of pressure defense and he helps us do that."

DePaul's big men come in two shapes and sizes: rangy and athletic and big and wide.

The most experienced—and enigmatic on the court—is 6-9, 250-pound senior **Lance Williams** (10.7 ppg, 5.8 rpg), one of the final remaining members of the much-ballyhooed class that included Richardson and Simmons.

Williams' best season was as a freshman. He broke his foot as a sophomore, and it was a very bad break that Kennedy said Williams has only recently fully recovered from. Williams has always featured a soft touch in close; he knows how to use his body and is quite agile despite his size.

"This has got to be Lance's year," Kennedy said. "He's lost 24 pounds and had a great summer."

Joining Williams in the wide-body club is junior-college transfer **Sam Hoskin** (24.0 ppg, 10.0 rpg at Schoolcraft [Mich.] Junior College), a 6-9, 260-pound load originally from Detroit. Hoskin will spend most of his time as a center, though he may be more of a pure power forward.

Kennedy sees Hoskin as one of the keys to the season and is counting on him for immediate production, both as a scorer and a rebounder. Hoskin spent his freshman season at Eastern Kentucky, where he averaged 15.7 points and 8.0 rebounds while hitting 51.7 percent of his shots from the field.

"He's so thick, he reminds you of a Jeff Ruland," Kennedy said. "He is so thick from head to toe, yet he can play a little away from the basket. When he gets to the basket, he is just a horse."

Andre Brown (6.5 ppg, 5.9 rpg), another Chicago native, was a prep All-American who had a solid but otherwise undistinguished freshman season. A high-energy player who needs to refine his skills away from the basket, the 6-8 Brown is a jumping jack inside who Kennedy believes will blossom as a sophomore.

"Everybody is looking forward to seeing how he will develop," Kennedy said. "He was benching 90 pounds when he came in and now he's up to 290. For Andre, he had to learn like Imari, but did not get the minutes Imari got. I think he was trying to change too much, playing against Steven Hunter every day. He is back to playing the way Andre can play."

Jon Oden (2.2 ppg, 1.8 rpg), a 6-8 junior, doesn't seem like a player who will ever emerge as a star, but that's not necessarily a bad thing. He's an athletic player who can come in as a designated defensive stopper or rebounder if he is willing to embrace such a role.

"If we press and run a little more, he can play a little more," Kennedy said. "It's interesting. We are going to have two bulls and two gazelles out there. Which will be nice."

2001-2002 SCHEDULE

Nov.	12	#Fordham
	25	Youngstown State
Dec.	1	*Notre Dame
	5	Ohio
	8	@Fairfield
	11	Murray State
	16	Long Island
	18	Chicago State
	22	@Temple
	29	Missouri
Jan.	5	Tulane
	8	@Saint Louis
	12	South Florida
	16	@Cincinnati
	19	Marquette
	23	@East Carolina
	26	@Louisville
	29	Charlotte
Feb.	3	@UNLV
	6	@TCU
	9	East Carolina
	12	Louisville
	16	@Charlotte
	19	Cincinnati
	23	@Memphis
	26	Saint Louis
March	1	@Marquette
	6-9	##Conference USA Tournament

@Road Games
*Children's Charity Classic, Chicago
#Preseason NIT (if DePaul wins, it will play Manhattan or Syracuse on Nov. 14 or 16. Semifinals and final are Nov. 21 and 23 at Madison Square Garden, NY)
##Firstar Center, Cincinnati, OH

BLUE RIBBON ANALYSIS

BACKCOURT	B
BENCH/DEPTH	B
FRONTCOURT	B-
INTANGIBLES	B-

There may be more to like about this team in the preseason than last year's preseason Top 25 bunch. There are interchangeable parts. There is real depth. There is versatility. If a few players can become reliable outside shooters, Kennedy may have something.

Kennedy sounds serious about going to more of a fullcourt game, and that certainly is a welcome development.

"We got too much into the halfcourt last season," Kennedy said. "There was too much of me standing up and calling plays."

That kind of game would suit Sawyer, and, presumably, London. It is London, more so than Sawyer, who holds the key to this season. If he can come in and replace Simmons' numbers and surpass his instinct for making winning plays, DePaul won't miss Simmons.

Sawyer must spend more time running his team and less sizing up situations for the flashiest possible maneuver. Some restraint is called for, and much attention to detail could put Sayer back on the track with many of his highly recruited cohorts.

For Williams, this is his year to distinguish himself as a better-than-adequate collegiate player. With his body and soft touch, he could certainly make himself some money by starting the season in tip-top shape and finishing it with consistent numbers and effort. The presence of Hoskin should help him down low, though it's hard to see how DePaul will press with those two serving as final guardians of the basket.

As surprising as it was to see DePaul's descent to last place in the American Division last season, the Demons could offer as big a surprise this season by emerging as a factor in the championship race in C-USA.

The Demons are one of several C-USA teams who begin the season already on the NIT's board of potential postseason picks.

(Z.M.)

 **East Carolina**

LOCATION	Greenville, NC
CONFERENCE	Conference USA (American)
LAST SEASON	14-14 (.500)
CONFERENCE RECORD	6-10 (Colonial)
STARTERS LOST/RETURNING	0/5
NICKNAME	Pirates
COLORS	Purple & Gold
HOMECOURT	Williams Arena at Mingers Coliseum (8,000)
COACH	Bill Herrion (Merrimack '81)
RECORD AT SCHOOL	24-32 (2 years)
CAREER RECORD	191-103 (10 years)
ASSISTANTS	Greg Herenda (Merrimack College '83)
	Richard Morgan (Virginia '89)
	George Stackhouse (East Carolina '91)
TEAM WINS (last 5 years)	17-10-13-10-14
RPI (last 5 years)	97-217-206-220-182
2000-01 FINISH	Lost in conference first round.

As humbling experiences go, the night of Nov. 25, 2000, in St. Louis had something of the feel of a rookie fast-baller trying to sneak a few pitches past Mark McGwire.

That's the night East Carolina and then second-year coach Bill Herrion came into the Savvis Center to take on Saint Louis University, a member of the conference the Pirates would be joining as full-time basketball members. They came to discover how they might stand in the new league. They came in hopes of at least earning some respect from a future C-USA colleague.

Saint Louis had none of it. The score at halftime was 45-20. The final: 90-54.

"We got physically pounded around the building by Saint Louis," Herrion said. "From that standpoint, we know what we are getting into. But we are building."

How far does ECU have to go? Consider that when Herrion left Drexel, the program he was taking over was inferior to the one he had left. Consider that ECU has averaged 12 wins per season the last four years playing in the Colonial Athletic Association. Consider that Saint Louis needed to win its final three regular-season games to reach 8-8 in the league.

Herrion is brutally frank.

"You are talking about a team that was middle of the pack in the Colonial making the jump to Conference USA," he said. "Our situation is much different from TCU."

While it is no stretch to say ECU will have trouble winning even one conference game this season, Herrion doesn't enter the new league without some ammunition. The Pirates return their top seven scorers from last season, and lose only one player who averaged better than 10 minutes last season (reserve forward **Vinston Sharpe**). Herrion also believes he has a crop of newcomers that will move ECU closer to competing in C-USA.

Gabriel Mikulas (15.0 ppg, 5.7 rpg), a 6-8, 220-pound sophomore from Argentina, was the Colonial's Freshman of the Year last season. Mikulas does most of his work around the basket, and he is very crafty and efficient. He hit 59.5 percent of his shots from the field last season and converted 144-of-181 (.796) from the free-throw line.

Herrion would like to see Mikulas increase his rebounding on the offensive end—he had only 49 last season—and cut down on all his turnovers (3.3 per game). Mikulas's biggest challenge this season will be adjusting to C-USA's bigger, stronger post players; his defense will be tested on every possession.

"You are talking about a kid that has a lot of international basketball experience so he is kind of a veteran player," Herrion said. "Last year, he exceeded even our expectations. He is very good around the basket, kind of a shorter, poor man's Kevin McHale. He's a very smart, efficient basketball player."

Mikulas's fellow sophomore, **Erroyl Bing** (10.4 ppg, 7.8 rpg), is also a little unconventional, bringing 250

pounds on a 6-6 frame. Bing is a good offensive rebounder (65 last season) who must become more effective as a three-point shooter (.382 from long range), but not enough to excuse so many misses inside 19 feet by an accomplished offensive rebounder.

"When you throw a freshman into the fire, you hope it will pay off down the road," Herrion said. "He's just a solid power forward, a real hard worker. He does a lot of work, and is the kind of guy who will have a good career. He is the one guy we have that can physically play in the league. His adjustment will be OK because he is a very strong, physical kid."

Brahin Howard, **Jonathan Moore** and **Moussa Badiane** are all newcomers to Division I, and they will be counted on to shore up the frontcourt. With so little depth up front, Herrion will have to figure a way to prevent opponents from wearing down the ECU big men.

Moore is a 6-8, 195-pound sophomore from Raleigh, N.C., who sat out last season. Moore can contribute, though he will be pushed around by the more physical Conference USA big men.

"He's a Conference USA athlete," Herrion said. "He's long and rangy and lanky and really runs the floor. Offensively, he shoots the three and he can score. You get concerned when kids sit out a full year, they can get that rust on them. We've got to be a little bit patient with him."

Badiane a 6-10, 215-pound freshman from France by way of Senegal, brings an advanced defensive game and an offensive potential Herrion hopes to eventually tap into. Badiane, 20, averaged 14 points, nearly 10 boards and five blocked shots for a club team in France.

"He's very athletic and a shot blocker, and that's something we haven't had," Herrion said. "He's got to put on weight and strength. We think the upside and potential is big with this kid."

Howard, a 6-10 freshman, was signed in August and should see action with the lack of frontcourt players available. Last season, Howard played at Cheltenham High School in Wyncote, Penn., outside of Philadelphia. As a senior, Howard averaged seven points, nine rebounds and two blocks.

"He's very skilled, and we've been very, very excited about him in the preseason," Herrion said.

Jason Herring, a 6-9, 215-pound freshman, is a highly rated freshman from Brooklyn who must sit out this season.

The top returning perimeter player is **Fred Primus** (13.1 ppg, 3.1 rpg), a 6-3 senior from Washington, D.C., who was a junior-college transfer last season. Primus had played at Pitt before leaving when Ralph Willard left the program.

Primus led the squad in three-point shooting, converting 80 of his 218 attempts (.367), though he too was not the world's best finisher. Primus hit only .367 of his shots from inside the three-point line. A shooting guard should also do better than .658 from the free-throw line.

"He's a very streaky shooter," Herrion said. "He can score points quickly, but he has to get better with his shot selection."

Travis Holcomb-Faye (9.3 ppg, 4.1 apg, 3.8 rpg), a 6-0, junior from Winston-Salem, N.C., was second on the team in minutes played last season and is the likely starter at point guard.

Holcomb-Faye was just the opposite of Primus. He hit 54.5 percent of the shots he took inside three-point range, but converted only 16 of the 48 three-pointers (.333) he attempted. Like so many other ECU players, Holcomb-Faye was an excellent free-throw shooter (he hit .743 last season and, as a team, ECU hit 72.5 percent from the line).

His versatility will mean big minutes again this season.

"He's very solid as a point guard and might be our best competitor," Herrion said. "He really understands the game, and came from a very successful high school program. He's got to become a better shooter from the perimeter."

Brandon Hawkins (8.9 ppg, 2.3 pg), a 6-2 senior from Morganton, N.C., is another three-point specialist. Hawkins converted 65-of-167 (.389) from three-point range, but—and this is astonishing—was only 7-of-28 (.250) from inside the line. It's safe to say opposing guards will dare him to drive to the goal, and that Herrion will run him through screens looking for openings from deep.

Hawkins and Primus often coexisted together in the backcourt, but will likely share minutes and battle for the shooting guard position.

"He has the most experience on our team in terms of games and minutes," Herrion said. "He's streaky from outside and has to shoot it more consistently. He's probably our best perimeter defender."

Kenyatta Brown (6.7 ppg, 3.0 rpg), a 6-4 senior from Brooklyn, has one last season to fulfill the promise he brought to ECU. Highly skilled, Brown can compete with Conference USA players but he must become a more reliable presence for the Pirates.

"He came out of high school with a really big reputation, and fair or unfair you expect big numbers," Herrion said. "He's just had a good career. He's probably our hardest worker. We need a big year out of him if we are going to have a good basketball team. He plays very hard and he's a good athlete."

Jimmy Bishop (4.0 ppg, 1.5 rpg), a 6-5 sophomore guard, got the most out of his 11 minutes per game last season, putting up about a shot per minute. Herrion expects to see a few more of the long-distance shots fall this season after a 16-of-48 effort last season.

Backcourt newcomer **Devin Boddie**, a 6-2 freshman from Jordan High School in Durham, N.C., was a recruiting priority for the Pirates, and Herrion hopes the huge amount of time and energy invested will result in a high-caliber instate player for the Pirates.

"He's just a real solid kid, good head on his shoulders and plays hard," Herrion said. "He's physically gifted for a freshman, and we see him able to guard people right away."

Craig Savage (1.3 ppg, 0.5 rpg) is a 6-5 junior walk-on who could possibly serve as a zone-buster from outside but won't likely play much. **Bryan Foxx** (0.9 ppg, 0.4 rpg), a 6-1 senior, falls into the same category.

2001-2002 SCHEDULE

Nov.	14	#BCA Classic
	19	@Appalachian State
	24	Central Florida
	27	@Virginia Tech
Dec.	5	@UNC Greensboro
	8	Old Dominion
	15	USC Spartanburg
	19	Middle Tennessee State
	22	Radford
Jan.	2	Lees-McRae
	5	Cincinnati
	8	@UAB
	12	Charlotte
	16	Louisville
	19	@Saint Louis
	23	DePaul
	26	@Charlotte
	29	@Cincinnati
Feb.	2	Saint Louis
	6	@Marquette
	9	@DePaul
	12	Southern Miss
	16	Birmingham Southern
	19	@Louisville
	23	Houston
	26	Marquette
March	2	@TCU
	6-9	##Conference USA Tournament

@Road Games
#Raleigh, NC (vs. Rutgers first round; also Fairleigh Dickinson, North Carolina State, Northwestern, Prairie View A&M, San Jose State, VCU)
##Firstar Center, Cincinnati, OH

BLUE RIBBON ANALYSIS

BACKCOURT	D+
BENCH/DEPTH	C
FRONTCOURT	C-
INTANGIBLES	D+

Herrion was smart to schedule weaker non-conference opponents, because this team has no NCAA Tournament aspirations this season. It needs to learn how to compete, then how to win against mid-range competition before expecting to win much in Conference USA.

It's hard to recall a program attempting a larger leap than the one ECU must take this season. The Pirates struggled in the Colonial Athletic Association, and now must figure a way to compete in a high-major conference. This won't be easy, but Herrion is well suited to guiding this team through adversity.

"From the talent standpoint, there is a gap," Herrion said.

Expect the Pirates to open up their offense more, in part to avoid playing physical, grind-it-out games, and in part to take advantage of the athleticism that is available. Herrion also believes a more wide-open system could provide a recruiting advantage in a region that has more than a few coaches scouting for talent. Herrion could walk the ball upcourt and, as he puts it, "ugly up the game," but knows that could hurt the program in the long term.

There are components around which to build. Mikulas and Bing probably provide the best combination on the team, and it is largely up to them to make ECU competitive in C-USA. It's possible that the Pirates could lose all C-USA games, but not probable. There should be nights when the three-point gunners are all finding a rhythm and the Mikulas and Bing find a higher energy level inside. Even so, anything more than two conference wins would be gravy.

For ECU, this season is kind of a stress test. Herrion gets to find out just where the program stands, and where—and how far—it has to go.

(Z.M.)

Houston

LOCATION	**Houston, TX**
CONFERENCE	**Conference USA (National)**
LAST SEASON	**9-20 (.310)**
CONFERENCE RECORD	**6-10 (5th)**
STARTERS LOST/RETURNING	**1/4**
NICKNAME	**Cougars**
COLORS	**Scarlet & White**
HOMECOURT	**Hofheinz Pavilion (8,479)**
COACH	**Ray McCallum (Ball State '83)**
RECORD AT SCHOOL	**9-20 (1 year)**
CAREER RECORD	**129-106 (8 years)**
ASSISTANTS	**John Fitzpatrick (Bowling Green '80)**
	Jerry Francis (Ohio State '91)
	Brian Hacker (Indiana '90)
TEAM WINS (last 5 years)	**11-9-10-9-9**
RPI (last 5 years)	**152-224-166-185-208**
2000-01 FINISH	**Lost in conference first round.**

Something is building very quietly down in Houston.

After making a huge splash by hiring Clyde Drexler as coach, the administration went another direction when Drexler left after two lackluster years.

It hired Ray McCallum, who had run a fine program at Ball State but was otherwise indistinguishable from a horde of other successful mid-major coaches. It seemed somewhat odd—the Midwestern-raised McCallum put in talent-rich Houston to rebuild a once-proud and mighty program.

But the things McCallum is doing seem right. Last season, he harped on defense, stressing the need to establish a foundation that did more than give up 80 points a game, as was the case under Drexler.

The result? Opponents averaged 71.6 points per game, down 12 percent from the season before. Opponents hit only 43.4 percent of their shots after toasting the Cougars for 45 percent the season before. Houston also managed a 5-3 Conference USA record at Hofheinz Pavilion, the first time the Cougars produced a winning league season at home since joining the conference in 1996-97.

It is on such small victories that one builds a program.

This year's goal? McCallum stays modest.

He's pushing his team to earn a spot in the Conference USA Tournament, which means being in the Top 12 of the 14-team league.

Honestly. That's the main goal. McCallum would obviously love to far surpass it, but there is some sense to his keeping expectations light.

When Houston won a wild home game against Charlotte in early February, in McCallum's 20th game as coach, it was possible to go back 100 games, to the final season under Alvin Brooks, and see this: Houston had won only 26 games out of its last 100.

That's 26-74 for those of you keeping score at home. When you have a .260 winning percentage, it's hard to seem credible if you start talking about winning championships.

There are signs, however, that Houston is ready to crawl out of the morass of losing that has become the program's fate. The Cougars won four of their final six games last season. They earned impressive wins over Saint Louis, Charlotte and Marquette, and even gave conference co-champ Southern Miss a scare at Hofheinz.

While talent may not be abundant, it is readily available. McCallum has used his Midwest roots to lure transfers who will help the program keep pace in Conference USA.

The best player, however, is homegrown, and one McCallum inherited thanks to Drexler's recruiting efforts.

George Williams (13.5 ppg, 7.3 rpg, 27 blocks), a 6-8, 220-pound junior from the metro Houston area, has started all 58 games he has played. His scoring and rebounding averages dropped by a few ticks—0.8 less points per game, 1.2 less rebounds per game—but that was due in part to a slower tempo, more defense and a better supporting cast.

Williams has inside-outside ability, as evidenced by his 26-of-68 (.382) shooting from three-point range for his career. Inside three-point range, he has hit 52.8 percent of his shots; he is a strong finisher, though he does sometimes fade and float on shots.

Williams has not asserted himself as the team's lead dog, and that needs to change this season. His talent and athleticism make him a potential all-conference player, and you will see him listed on many preseason publications' all-league lists. Maybe he deserves such accolades, but he could do much more than he has done. The quiet way he sometimes goes about his on-court business needs some force; it's time to turn up the volume for Mr. Williams.

Alongside Williams is **Patrick Okafor** (10.7 ppg, 8.6 rpg), a 6-8, 240-pound senior who established himself as one of the league's best offensive rebounders last season, leading C-USA with 4.46 offensive retrievals per game.

Okafor, a junior-college transfer originally from Westbury High School in Houston, had a good enough field-goal percentage—.495—but he is much worse a shooter than that stat indicates. Most of his shots come within eight feet, and he has been known to miss more than a few put-backs. If he were a stronger finisher, Okafor would average 14 points per game.

Defensively, Okafor is a better position defender, and, really, that is also how he gets his rebounds. He moves his feet very well, but is not explosive by any means, with only eight blocked shots and nine steals last season.

Okafor had nine double-doubles last season, with the 15-point, 13-rebound effort against Saint Louis in the Conference USA Tournament personifying how this program has changed. On one possession, Okafor tracked down one rebound and nearly maimed himself going out of bounds for a loose ball. McCallum has ingrained effort into his players, and the leadership from Okafor, a psychology major, is very much of the active variety: he prefers to walk the walk.

He and Williams averaged 31 and 34 minutes per game, respectively, last season, and will have to play huge minutes again. There are only two other true frontcourt players on the roster.

One is **Louis Truscott**, a 6-7, 215-pound junior transfer who averaged 8.2 points and 5.7 rebounds while a sophomore at Nebraska in 1999-00. A Houston native (Milby High School), Truscott was considered a consensus Top 100 player as a senior.

Truscott is active and strong for his size. One presumes he worked to improve his three-point shot in the year off after going 5-of-27 as a sophomore at Nebraska. He blocked 24 shots as a sophomore, not bad for a bench player, and Houston needs the athleticism.

Like Okafor, Truscott is a psychology major. Better not play mind games with that Houston frontcourt.

Jeremee McGuire, a 6-10, 215-pound center, comes from Tyler Junior College in Texas, where he averaged 8.6 points and 6.2 rebounds as a sophomore. Those seem like modest numbers, but consider that McGuire averaged only 2.9 points and 2.6 rebounds as a freshman; McCallum hopes the rapid improvement continues.

McGuire's most valuable contribution will probably be defensively. He averaged 2.0 blocks per game at Tyler, and will be needed to help against a conference loaded with good big men this season.

Houston will likely spend a lot of time running three-guard sets this season. There are plenty of perimeter players from which to choose.

The team's best overall player last season was **Dominic Smith** (12.6 ppg, 2.7 rpg, 3.8 apg, 2.3 spg), a fiery 5-10 senior point guard who came to the Cougars out of Paris Junior College. Originally from Coatsville, Va., Smith led the league in steals per game (he had eight in one game, against Charlotte) and ranked 10th nationally—second in the league—in free-throw shooting, hitting .887 from the line.

Smith has breakdown ability, and he took advantage of his quick feet and crossover dribble, earning 160 free throws last season. He was a streaky outside shooter, but did connect on 36-of-101 (.356) from three-point range; he must be more efficient inside the line after hitting .386 from the field for the season. He also needs to be more efficient with the ball after giving up 106 turnovers last season.

Smith seemed to tire near the end of the season, which would make sense for someone who averaged 33 minutes and played with abandon. In the final 11 games, he hit only 33-of-102 (.323) from the field and 9-of-40 (.225) from three-point range.

He will have more help this season. The most significant addition to the team is former Michigan point guard **Kevin Gaines**, a 6-4, 180-pound sophomore from Las Vegas who was one of the nation's top recruits in 1999. Gaines averaged 11.7 points, 3.8 rebounds and 4.6 assists as a freshman at Michigan before running into troubles off the court and being kicked off the team by former coach Brian Ellerbee. Gaines was involved in a drinking-and-driving incident on Labor Day of 2000, and, after his blood-alcohol level tested .17, Ellerbee kicked him off the team.

It was a terrible turn of events for a player ranked by most recruiting observers as one of the Top 40 players in the country, and one of the top five point guards. He was named the best playmaker and best defender at the prestigious Five-Star camps before his senior season.

McCallum chose to give Gaines, who was 19 at the time of his troubles, a chance. He does not become eligible to play until mid-December, and McCallum is trying to downplay expectations of Gaines.

However, as a former co-MVP on a Big 10 team, Gaines should step in and make a huge impact. He and Smith will be able to break down defenses and loosen things up all over the court. Gaines' size and quickness make him a potentially great defender, so opposing guards will know pressure from the Cougars' backcourt.

Although **Marcus Oliver** (5.9 ppg, 3.2 rpg, 1.5 apg) will never be accused of having overwhelming basketball talent, he has managed a solid career at Houston. A 6-3, 200-pound junior, Oliver could spend time at any of three guard positions, with the wing the most likely destination.

Oliver must improve his shooting. A good defender and good rebounder from the guard spot, Oliver has hit only 31.8 percent of his shots in two seasons, and is 22-of-100 from three-point range.

A native of Charlotte, Oliver scored in double figures only four times last season, and was prone to some truly abysmal shooting performances: 0-for-10 vs. Texas Southern, 0-for-5 vs. SE Missouri (the very next game), 2-for-11 vs. DePaul. Not only must he improve his accuracy, his shooting conscience needs cleansing.

Jarrett Sidney, a 6-1 junior guard, is another Houston native who comes back to town from a junior college, in this case Northland Pioneer Community College in Arizona. He averaged 15.7 points as a sophomore after averaging 10.8 points as a freshman at Frank Phillips College in Border, Texas. Sidney was a high school teammate of George Williams.

Bryan Shelton, a 6-3 freshman guard, averaged 18 points at Clear Brook High School in Friendswood, Texas. He's a decent rebounder with potential to be a three-point specialist.

The only other returning player for the Cougars is walk-on Terry Price, a 6-4 senior who has played in only six games in his career.

One practice player available this season is **Andre Owens**, the former guard at Indiana who transferred after his freshman year. An Indianapolis native, he averaged 4.7 points for Indiana last season.

2001-2002 SCHEDULE

Nov.	19-21	#Maui Invitational
	29	Rice
Dec.	2	North Texas
	4	@Texas Southern
	14	Texas Tech
	16	Southwest Texas State
	21	@LSU
	23	North Carolina State
	30	Tennessee State
Jan.	1	@Georgetown
	5	@Saint Louis
	8	@Tulane
	12	Cincinnati
	15	TCU
	19	@UAB
	23	Southern Miss
	26	Memphis
	29	@San Diego State
Feb.	2	Charlotte
	5	@Southern Miss
	9	@TCU
	12	South Florida
	16	@Memphis
	19	Tulane
	23	@East Carolina
	26	@South Florida
March	2	UAB
	6-9	##C-USA Tournament

@Road Games
#Maui, HI (vs. UCLA first round; also Kansas, Ball State, Chaminade, Duke, Seton Hall, South Carolina)
##Cincinnati, OH

BLUE RIBBON ANALYSIS

BACKCOURT	B
BENCH/DEPTH	D
FRONTCOURT	B
INTANGIBLES	C

There is talent on this squad, but it will take some coaching to figure out how best to utilize it. McCallum has five players—Smith, Gaines, Truscott, Williams and Okafor—who could start for most teams in Conference USA, but there is not a whole lot behind them.

If the newcomers can accept roles and give those five some relief, Houston has a chance to make a little more progress. Oliver needs to be an energetic sixth man.

The key to the season could well be how Gaines adjusts. He will have missed a season and a half by the time he hits the court, though he has been practicing full-time with Houston. He and Smith will make for a deadly duo in the backcourt, with both of them able to penetrate, to set up big men and to hit open jumpers. Smith should reduce his turnovers this season, and he should avoid some of the burnout that crept into his game at times a year ago.

Gaines' presence should also help Williams realize he must become this team's main threat, and his contributions must come at significant times. Gaines is a savvy enough point guard to know Williams needs the ball, and Williams should know by now that he can create terrific match-up problems for opponents because of his inside-outside abilities.

McCallum has indicated he wants to open up Houston's offense some, and he probably needs to, if nothing else for recruiting purposes. That may not be the best way to win games this season, because of the poor depth. Most of the big men can run, however, suggesting that up-tempo at the right moments will make for an effective strategy.

Houston will indeed be battling the likes of Tulane, Saint Louis and possibly TCU for the final spot in the Conference USA Tournament. For Houston, making the little dance would be more confirmation that McCallum has the team on the right track.

(Z.M.)

Louisville

LOCATION	**Louisville, KY**
CONFERENCE	**Conference USA (American)**
LAST SEASON	**12-19 (.387)**
CONFERENCE RECORD	**8-4 (t-4th)**
STARTERS LOST/RETURNING	**2/3**
NICKNAME	**Cardinals**
COLORS	**Red & Black**
HOMECOURT	**Freedom Hall (18,865)**
COACH	**Rick Pitino (UMass '74)**
RECORD AT SCHOOL	**First year**
CAREER RECORD	**352-124 (15 years)**
ASSISTANTS	**Mick Cronin (Cincinnati '96)**
	Vince Taylor (Duke '82)
	Kevin Willard (Pttsburgh '98)
TEAM WINS (last 5 years)	**26-12-19-19-12**
RPI (last 5 years)	**17-90-28-38-122**
2000-01 FINISH	**Lost in conference first round.**

It is still hard to believe. Denny Crum is no longer the coach at Louisville. Rick Pitino is his successor.

The current Hall of Fame coach yields to the future Hall of Fame coach. A program that truly had become moribund in Crum's final years is injected with verve and enthusiasm with the arrival of Pitino.

Give Louisville credit: The Cardinals and their fans gave Crum the proper sendoff, full of respect and admiration and appreciation, while greeting Pitino, the once-hated coach of the rival Wildcats, with open arms.

Conference USA needs Louisville to occupy its once-perennial role as a serious factor on the national scene, just as it needs Cincinnati and Memphis to keep their respective cities enthralled with college basketball. No college venue is superior to Freedom Hall when the joint is packed, the fans are rockin' and the Cardinals are on a roll.

The question is: How soon can Pitino get these Cardinals rolling?

You have to listen real close to hear Pitino predict his first team at Louisville could be pretty doggone good. Real close.

"I think if we can get to the .500 mark, it would be a good barometer," Pitino said. "Hopefully we can do better. Looking at the team at this stage, we have the makings of a .500 team. We have a lack of frontcourt depth. We have a lack of precision from the outside. We've got weaknesses."

Pitino would not be Pitino if he didn't think he could do better. This is a guy who went 219-50 at Kentucky. No, he didn't have the success he wanted with the Boston Celtics, but every coach in Conference USA believes Louisville will play at a very high level.

"He thinks they are going to be really good," Memphis coach John Calipari said. "I always call him Mr. Opposites. Whatever he is saying, it's absolutely the opposite."

When it comes to personnel, however, Pitino is brutally honest. He's saying many of the same things Crum said about this team last year: The shooting is horrible, the entire frontcourt is a collective project and the skills need constant nurturing.

Pitino is not shy about declaring junior guard **Reece Gaines** his best player. At 6-5, Gaines (13.9 ppg, 3.3 apg, 3.5 rpg) is tall for a point guard, his natural position, and Pitino will deploy Gaines at both the one and the two spots this season. He should thrive in Pitino's run-and-shoot system; last season he made 42.6 percent of his three-point shots, making him one of Conference USA's best from long range.

Exect Gaines to be more of a shooting guard this season.

"He's my best player and he's a very, very hard worker," Pitino said. "He's very good defensively."

Gaines is also the most experienced player on the roster, by far. He has started 58 of the 61 games he has played at Louisville after establishing himself as a solid C-USA player his freshman season. He became a much steadier player last season and learned how to take over games when it was needed: 22 points against Maryland, 16 against Loyola-Chicago, 28 against Tulane, 23 against Memphis.

His ability to handle the ball and get by people in the fullcourt and halfcourt make him a difficult match-up. His assist-to-turnover ratio—98 assists, 73 turnovers—could be better, and he must become a better free-throw shooter: .675 overall, .609 in Conference USA.

Pitino said he has altered Gaines's shooting form a little, getting Gaines to focus on keeping the ball in front of his head more.

"He's been working on his shooting every day," Pitino said.

After Gaines, Louisville's most veteran player is 6-5 junior swingman **Erik Brown** (10.3 ppg, 3.9 rpg), a transfer from Moorehead State who became eligible midway through last season. Though Brown started just four games all season, he trailed only Gaines and now-departed shooting guard Marques Maybin in total points scored for the season.

Expect Pitino to use Brown and Gaines as post-up options in his high set offense. At 205 pounds, Brown is strong enough to take defenders down low and a good enough shooter to keep them honest from the outside.

That shooting stroke also needs work, however. He hit only 26.9 percent from three-point range and was 31.1 percent from deep in C-USA games. His finishing ability is evident in that he hit 54.9 percent of his shots inside the three-point arc in C-USA games.

"He's got a ways to go," Pitino said. "Erik is a good, solid player. He is good at many different aspects of the game, but not so good at a lot of different areas."

Does Pitino like having the big guards, and will he employ them as he often did at Kentucky?

"They help you defensively with pressure," Pitino said. "They help you offensively with posting up."

The newcomer from whom the most is expected this season is the confident and quicksilver 6-1 freshman **Carlos Hurt**, a Houston native who played his senior season at Louisville Moore. When Hurt committed to the Cardinals, it was seen as a huge step for Crum and his staff in their quest to rebuild the program.

Hurt predicted that many young stars would follow. The Cards certainly put together a more-than-respectable recruiting class, but not one of the nation's best.

Hurt is the best of the bunch. His trash-talking battles with Memphis freshman Dajuan Wagner at summer camps should continue into this season. Hurt is not as advanced as Wagner, though he has plenty of game to back up his talk.

Hurt, who averaged 24.6 points and 7.0 assists as a senior, is a pure point guard who will allow Pitino to move Gaines to shooting guard. Pitino likes Hurt's potential, but is less than effusive about his freshman point.

"He has to improve his defense, his strength has got to get better," Pitino said. "When his strength gets better, he will be a better athlete, though he is a very good athlete for a college freshman."

Bryant Northern (3.5 ppg, 1.3 rpg, 1.2 apg) is a 6-1 sophomore who played 12.3 minutes per game after joining the team as a walk-on last season. He wasn't shy about shooting the ball, and will probably have the opportunity to shoot plenty this season. If so, his effectiveness needs to improve, because he hit only 32.1 percent from the field, 28.4 percent from three-point range and 60.7 percent from the free-throw line for the season.

Northern had assorted outings that showed potential: 13 points against Dayton, 12 against Charlotte, 10 against Utah. He is very strong—he bench press more than 300 pounds—and seems like the kind of gritty, hard-working player that Pitino will like on the floor.

Northern will battle for playing time with 6-1 junior-college transfer **Junior Mohammed**, the much-shorter brother of former Kentucky center Nazr Mohammed. Pitino is fond of Mohammed and expects him to contribute.

"He's a very good athlete," Pitino said. "He's very quick, an average shooter, but he's got a great attitude."

There is no shortage of frontcourt players on the Louisville roster, though some—including Pitino—might argue that quantity does not at all mean quality. Louisville's frontcourt was constantly under construction last season, with no single player or collective players providing reliable production. Crum complained about the frontcourt from start of the season until the very end, and he had much to gripe about (except for the fact that he was responsible for assembling the players; it wasn't like they were assigned to the Cardinals).

This is Louisville's glaring weakness again this season, and the situation was made even worse when the most talented (but also inconsistent) big man, Muhammed Lasege, was ruled officially and finally ineligible after a ruling of the Kentucky state supreme court.

(Aside: The Louisville-Courier Journal pointed out, in a story after the court's ruling, that all members of the voting majority were University of Kentucky graduates.)

The most productive member of the frontcourt was **Ellis Myles** (6.1 ppg, 5.5 rpg), a 6-8 sophomore who enters this season in much better shape. Pitino said Myles has lost 25 pounds (down to 225) and reduced his body fat from 18 percent to nine percent.

"It has made him a better athlete," Pitino said.

Myles hit 48.1 percent of his shots last season, which isn't bad for a freshman big man. The .536 free-throw percentage, however, is more indicative of his touch. He did have 55 assists, a high number for a big man who was not a scoring target.

"He is a smart basketball player," Pitino said. "He has to improve his shooting, but he's got a chance to start at the power forward position."

Joseph N'Sima (2.6 ppg, 5.6 rpg), a 6-8, 215-pound senior from France, played the most minutes of any big man last season, and, though he didn't have huge numbers, showed the most savvy of any of them. He was a good low-post defender who led the team with 55 blocks, and his 44 assists represented a nice number for a big guy.

His shooting, however, was abysmal: .352 (25-of-71) from the field. He did improve to .425 in Conference USA play, where his rebounding average also jumped, to 6.2 per game. He also averaged nearly two blocks per game in the league.

Crum always praised N'Sima for his leadership abilities, and he should become a reliable presence for Pitino.

"Joseph may win one of the frontcourt spots by default," Pitino said.

Luke Whitehead (5.6 ppg, 3.1 rpg), a 6-7, 215-pound sophomore, was last year's marquee incoming freshman, but he never emerged as anything more than an occasional contributor. His father, Eddie, played at Louisville in the '60s, and Whitehead was a standout player at Oak Hill Academy as a senior. His best game last season came against Tulane, when he scored 16 points and pulled seven rebounds. That suggests he can adjust well to Pitino's system, because Tulane forced a running tempo.

Whitehead had other notable performances as well (12 points, 10 rebounds against Georgetown, 14 points against Maryland) but, after scoring in double figures in six of his first eight college games, he did so just three times the remainder of the season.

In the final 12 games, Whitehead played more than six minutes just once and never hit more than a field goal in any of those games.

Pitino needs to coax more of the early-season Whitehead and lose the late-season version. Whitehead could make a big difference as a swingman if he becomes a reliable contributor, because he is an athlete on par with other Conference USA players at his position.

"He's a good athlete who has to improve his shooting," said Pitino, and if you are sensing a trend, it's because Pitino said everyone on the team was woefully deficient in shooting. "He's athletic. He runs and jumps well and he's a hard worker."

Hajj Turner (3.2 ppg, 2.2 rpg) is not physically suited to the Pitino system, but he will make contributions. Two knee surgeries before last season set him back, but he showed he is scrappy and can be a good offensive rebounder.

A 6-8, 220-pound senior, Turner's deficiencies are the same as most of Louisville's frontcourt players.

"Shooting and ball handling are his weaknesses," Pitino said. "He's got a long way to go in every area."

Mack Wilkinson and **Simeon Naydenov** do not project as anything more than spot contributors, with the five minutes per game of last season about right, if that much. Wilkinson, a 6-8, 235-pound sophomore from Louisville and Naydenov, a 6-7, 200-pound sophomore from Bulgaria, each averaged less than two points and two rebounds per game last season when they did play.

How much will Pitino get out of the two late freshman signees, local products **Brandon Bender** (6-9, 245) and **Larry O'Bannon** (6-5, 200)? Some, but not a lot. He is a little higher on O'Bannon, who averaged 21.5 points, 6.8 rebounds and 2.3 assists last season at Louisville Male High School than Bender at this point.

Pitino on O'Bannon, a swingman who could really make an impact if he gives Pitino another outside shooter: "I think he'll play as a freshman. His conditioning is not good now, but that will come. I see him backing up Reece Gaines [at shooting guard]."

Pitino on Bender, a highly rated recruit whose effort and conditioning have always been questioned: "Brandon is sort of like Nazr Mohammed at Kentucky; he's going to be a project. It may be his junior year before you see any major contribution. He's a very poor athlete, he's way out of shape ... but he has potential."

A year ago, Bender averaged 18.1 points, 10.9 rebounds, 2.8 assists and 2.5 blocked shots at Louisville Ballard. He was ranked among the nation's Top 50 high school players and was Kentucky's Gatorade Player of the Year. Bender's 1,860 career points were second all-time at Ballard to current New York Knicks guard Allan Houston. He was the school's all-time rebounding (1,178 career rebounds) and blocked shots (260) leader.

2001-2002 SCHEDULE

Nov.	18	South Alabama
	24	@Oregon
Dec.	1	Tennessee State
	7-8	#Jim Thorpe Classic
	12	Coppin State
	15	Ohio State
	17	Tennessee Tech
	20	Tennessee
	26	Eastern Kentucky
	29	@Kentucky
Jan.	5	@UAB
	9	Marquette
	12	TCU
	16	@East Carolina
	19	@Cincinnati
	23	@Charlotte
	26	DePaul
	30	@Memphis
Feb.	1	South Florida
	5	Saint Louis
	9	@Indiana
	12	@DePaul
	16	@Marquette
	19	East Carolina
	22	@Saint Louis
	27	Cincinnati
March	2	Charlotte
	6-9	##Conference USA Tournament

@Road Games
#Louisville Freedom Hall (vs. Wisconsin-Milwaukee first round; also Murray State, Virginia Tech)
##Firstar Center, Cincinnati, OH

BLUE RIBBON ANALYSIS

BACKCOURT	B+
BENCH/DEPTH	C
FRONTCOURT	D+
INTANGIBLES	B

On paper, Louisville rates as a .500 team, if that. Or, let's say a .500 team that is more likely to go south than to exceed expectations.

But you must factor in Pitino's remarkable college coaching record. He gets players to exceed what had been their best basketball. He runs a high-octane system that produces better-than-expected performances, from talented and non-talented players alike. He will have Louisville's players conditioned as well as any team in the country.

The key, says Pitino, will be defense. The Cardinals will press and they will run. They will also focus on shutting down the halfcourt. His preparation for games will benefit from the presence of assistant coaches who have been in Conference USA for several years.

"We've got to become a great defensive team," Pitino said. "If we can't, we won't win. If we can become a great defensive team, maybe we can exceed .500."

Conference USA coaches expect Louisville to be a great defensive team. And they know that Gaines was already on the verge of becoming one of the best guards in the league, that Brown showed potential but never really looked comfortable last season and that Hurt is one of the most skilled freshmen in the country.

Louisville must get something out of the frontcourt on a consistent basis. Of all the things that sabotaged Crum's last season, it was the frontcourt's unreliablity that dogged the Cardinals most. When the frontcourt did produce, as in a masterful performance against Memphis, with one of the league's best frontcourts, the Cardinals won handily.

Whatever the final record, Cardinal fans should have more fun than they have had at least since the Final Eight run in the mid-90s. There will be no questions about the coach's retirement, no wondering about the future, no doubt that this program is headed in a winning direction.

So buckle up Card fans. Expect a lot of early turbulence and then watch as the Cardinals pull off an upset or two in January or February. The Cards won't win Conference USA, but they will have something to say about who does.

(Z.M.)

Marquette

LOCATION	**Milwaukee, WI**
CONFERENCE	**Conference USA (American)**
LAST SEASON	**15-14 (.517)**
CONFERENCE RECORD	**9-7 (3rd)**
STARTERS LOST/RETURNING	**2/3**
NICKNAME	**Golden Eagles**
COLORS	**Blue & Gold**
HOMECOURT	**Bradley Center (19,150)**
COACH	**Tom Crean (Central Michigan '89)**
RECORD AT SCHOOL	**30-28 (2 years)**
CAREER RECORD	**30-28 (2 years)**
ASSISTANTS	**Dwayne Stephens (Michigan State '93)**
	Darrin Horn (Western Kentucky '95)
	Tod Kowalczyk (Minnesota-Duluth '88)
TEAM WINS (last 5 years)	**22-20-14-15-15**
RPI (last 5 years)	**56-62-133-85-106**
2000-01 FINISH	**Lost in conference quarterfinal.**

Marquette's first two seasons under Tom Crean have followed a similar pattern.

First, there is early success, followed by some gritty, hard-luck losses to solid non-conference foes. Then comes an opening, surprising burst into Conference USA that establishes the Golden Eagles as title contenders. Next is a late-season fade that usually includes an agonizing close defeat. In Crean's first season, Marquette opened Conference USA play 4-1 but lost six of its final eight games.

Last season, Marquette jumped to the front of C-USA with a 5-1 start, but, again, caught the late-season blahs, losing four of its final five games. That inability to finish has prevented the program from making an extraordinary leap forward in Crean's first two seasons. As it stands, Marquette has earned respect and stayed in the mix in C-USA while rebuilding itself in a more athletic, more dynamic image.

In his third season at Marquette, Crean has a mix of players he believes will elevate Marquette's level of play. The paradox is that, even though the talent may be better, the Eagles could struggle more this season than in the past.

There are eight freshmen or sophomores on the roster, and most of them will be counted on for contributions. Oh, and Marquette must find someone to replace shooting guard Brian Wardle, who quite literally carried the Eagles at times the last two seasons (he scored 29 percent of Marquette's points last season).

"We will have to live with mistakes because many of [the younger players] will play significant minutes," Crean said. "It could take a while this year, because the young guys are going to have to play."

Fortunately for Crean, his most experienced player is the guy who runs the show—senior point guard **Cordell Henry** (12.9 ppg, 3.3 rpg, 4.4 apg), a whirling 5-10 dervish from Chicago. Henry has started all three seasons at Marquette, and he blossomed into one of the league's best point guards last season, averaging 14.5 points and 5.1 assists in league play. His emergence gave Marquette a reliable weapon apart from Wardle, and he enters this season as the lead dog.

"He has gotten a little better every year," Crean said. "He's got to take a leap in different areas this season."

Defensively, Henry must become more effective, especially against bigger, more physical opponents. Crean needs Henry to improve his post passing, and his scoring efficiency outside the three-point line (.316 overall, .276 in C-USA play) must come closer to his efficiency inside the three-point line (.495 overall, .531 in league play).

Henry may not be the fastest small point guard in the world, but he's a master of pace, using hesitation moves, head feints and sharp cuts to create room for little runners and pull-up jumpers.

Crean believes Henry will benefit from the arrival of 6-0 freshman point guard **Travis Diener** (21.2 ppg, 3.2 rpg, 7.5 apg) from Fond du Lac, Wisc. Diener, a Parade All-American last season, is a better outside shooter than Henry and he has great floor vision, an attribute Crean believes will help the Eagles better in the open court. He sees Diener and Henry playing together for stretches; at the least, Diener will provide much needed relief for Henry, who averaged nearly 37 minutes per game in C-USA play.

"Travis is going to bring a steadiness to that position," Crean said. "He's a tremendous passer who sees the floor very well. We are trying to become a good fast-break team and he will definitely add to that. He'll definitely create scoring opportunities with his outside shooting."

Crean also likes Diener's competitive nature: He was the MVP of three different summer events before his senior season, he won a state title and was even an all-state player in baseball.

"He's got a great presence on the floor and brings a real toughness," Crean said.

Marquette fans are eagerly awaiting the first game of **Dwayne Wade**'s Eagles career after hearing about his exploits in practice last season as a partial-qualifier. A 6-4, 210-pound guard from Oak Lawn, Ill., Crean gives Wade, who averaged 27.0 points, 11.0 rebounds and 2.7 assists as a senior at Richards High School, some credit for Wardle's fabulous senior year. He believes Wade's play this season will have something to do with his daily practice battles against Wardle.

Wade should play the two, but can swing to the three if needed. He has the potential to be Marquette's best player and one of the best freshmen in Conference USA.

"He's got great body control and balance and I think he's a guy that can get to the basket and score some points," Crean said. "He's got to become a more consistent defender. That's where not having the game experience is a factor. And he's got to be a consistent outside shooter."

David Diggs (0.6 ppg, 0.6 rpg) rarely played last season but Crean hopes the 6-4 senior shooting guard can improve his defense and shooting enough to be a factor.

"No one has done a better job of accepting his role and being a team guy," Crean said. "This summer, he was definitely one of the guys to be a leader on the team."

Ron Howard (17.0 ppg, 5.0 rpg in high school), a rangy 6-5 freshman from Chicago Whitney Young, may be the best athlete on Marquette's roster. Until he gains more strength, his playing time may be limited, but Crean loves his potential.

"Not a lot of people are fast and quick, but he is both," Crean said. "I see him causing great havoc defensively."

Oluoma Nnamaka (10.2 ppg, 5.2 rpg), a 6-7, 225-pound senior forward from Sweden, is the player who could make the biggest difference for Marquette. Nnamaka is more comfortable as a power forward, but has skills and certainly the body and athleticism of a small forward.

Nnamaka has added some strength, and Crean is anxious to see if Nnamaka's ball handling and shooting have improved enough to allow him to play more at small forward.

"When he shoots only a little, we do not win," Crean said. "We've gotta find him shots."

Two of Nnamaka's best games came at Memphis and at Cincinnati. Against the Tigers, he continually took Kelly Wise outside and juked past him to create inside opportunities. Nnamaka is a terrific free-throw shooter (.783 last season), and can help win games by drawing fouls and going to the line.

He can shoot the three (9-of-26 in C-USA play) but needs to make more shots overall (.434 shooting percentage).

"He's got to become more aggressive for a consistent period of time," Crean said.

Last season's biggest surprise, **Odartey Blankson** (6.1 ppg, 5.5 rpg) created expectations he must fulfill as a sophomore. Blankson was solid in every category (.449 from the field in C-USA, .356 from three-point range overall) except rebounding—where he was exceptional (3.8 offensive boards per game)—and free-throw shooting, where he was awful (.556).

At 6-7, 215, Blankson mixes athleticism, toughness and tenacity. He and Crean are a perfect fit for one another.

"He's a guy who has to score more points," Crean said. "We've got to get more production, and that's one of the reasons he played so many minutes last season, because we knew we would need him. What he brought rebounding wise and toughness wise and presence wise was certainly worth the playing time."

Scott Merritt (6.0 ppg, 3.6 rpg), the 6-10, 245-pound sophomore center from nearby Wauwatosa, Wisc., played last season with a hurting back that limited his impact. A highly regarded recruit, Merritt could easily double his averages this season.

"He's one of the keys to our team," Crean said.

Merritt should benefit from practicing against big 6-8 Robert Jackson, a transfer from Mississippi State who must sit out this season. He added strength in the off-season, and Crean expects him to be a more reliable true center: scoring in the post, blocking shots and owning the lane, keying the rebounding effort.

"He surprised me in some areas, playing with toughness and showing he really wanted to win," Crean said.

The production of 6-7, 225-pound senior **Jon Harris** (4.4 ppg, 4.1 rpg) fell last season, especially on the boards. Marquette needs him to get back to the six or seven boards a game he is capable of. If he can become a relentless, eight or nine rebound per game kind of guy, then good luck playing Marquette; that would be a very difficult team to pull away from.

"He's got to be the blue-collar workhorse," Crean said. "He needs to be a more legitimate threat to score and finish, and we need him to be one of our best low-post defenders."

Because of injuries and illness, 6-8, 220-pound sophomore **Terry Sanders** (2.1 ppg, 1.3 rpg) saw a promising freshman season derailed quickly. He was developing as rapidly as Blankson when he contracted mononucleosis early in the season.

"At some point, he is just going to take off," Crean said. "He's got to get a nasty streak in him in terms of rebounding and defending. He has such an ability to get to the basket."

Crean's challenge in terms of creating roles, distributing playing time and finding his best rotation can be seen in two final freshmen—6-7, 215-pound **Todd Townsend** from Chicago (via a New Hampshire prep school) and 6-6, 210-pound **Kevin Menard** from Frankfort, Ill.

Both could fight for playing time and earn significant minutes. Townsend averaged 16.0 points, 9.0 rebounds and 3.0 blocks in prep school last season and Crean loves the way he has battled and overcome personal adversity. Menard (18.0 ppg, 7.0 rpg as a senior) is someone Crean said "needs to take a pillow to the weight room" but could overcome the lack of bulk by showing he can defend and rebound.

"Those are the things that make it hard for us not to play you," Creans said.

2001-2002 SCHEDULE

Nov.	17	Loyola-Chicago
	18	Chicago State
	21-24	#Great Alaska Shootout
	30	##Marquette Blue and Gold Classic
Dec.	1	##Marquette Blue and Gold Classic
	5	Dayton
	8	Fordham
	19	Arkansas-Pine Bluff
	22	@Wisconsin
	29	@Wake Forest
Jan.	2	Morris Brown
	5	@Charlotte
	9	@Louisville
	12	Saint Louis
	15	UAB
	19	@DePaul
	23	TCU
	26	@Saint Louis
	29	@Tulane
Feb.	2	Cincinnati
	6	East Carolina
	9	@Southern Miss
	16	Louisville
	19	Charlotte
	22	@Cincinnati
	26	@East Carolina
March	1	DePaul
	6-9	###C-USA Tournament

@Road Games
#Anchorage, AK (vs. Tennessee first round; also Indiana, Alaska-Anchorage, Oregon State, Texas, St. John's, Gonzaga)
##Milwaukee, WI (vs. Northern Illinois first round; also Texas Southern, Sam Houston State)
###Firstar Center, Cincinnati, OH

BLUE RIBBON ANALYSIS

BACKCOURT	B+
BENCH/DEPTH	B
FRONTCOURT	B-
INTANGIBLES	B-

Marquette will look to run more than in the past and utilize the athletic talent Crean has targeted with his recruiting. Still, expect to find a complicated system of sets and an ultra-prepared squad nearly every game. Marquette may be more up-tempo than in the past, but it still will not likely be a team that beats itself, especially with a four-year starter (Henry) running the point.

With apologies to Rodney White and Charlotte, no team has a bigger void to fill than Marquette does now that Wardle is gone. Wade has the talent to become a star in his own right, but he will probably need at least half the season to adjust and to shake off the rust of not playing for a season. He and Diener are the perfect blocks on which Crean can build a program to compete with the ever-more powerful Memphis, Louisville and Cincinnati.

Replacing Wardle, however, is probably more of the frontcourt's responsibility. It was Wardle who bailed out the inconsistent frontcourt so often the last two seasons; now, guys like Nnamaka and Blankson and Merritt must expand their games by at least 25 percent to give the Eagles any kind of chance at contending for the C-USA title.

Crean has pushed Marquette into the title race in surprising fashion both seasons as coach, but he had Wardle helping him out. There are too many unanswered questions with this squad to take a chance on a bold prediction. Let's just say the Eagles appear to be capable of a 9-7 league record, and could compete for an NIT bid. Crean has to find a way to prevent the late-season slides of the first two seasons, whether it means backing off earlier in the season or making sure the squad builds to a peak after late January/early February.

Marquette will stun a team or two this season. Whether the young talent can stay consistent enough to become C-USA's most stunning team is another matter. This should, at the least, be a fun team to watch evolve.

(Z.M.)

Saint Louis

LOCATION	**St. Louis, MO**
CONFERENCE	**Conference USA (American)**
LAST SEASON	**17-14 (.548)**
CONFERENCE RECORD	**8-8 (t-4th)**
STARTERS LOST/RETURNING	**3/2**
NICKNAME	**Billikens**
COLORS	**Blue & White**

HOMECOURT	**Savvis Center (20,000)**
COACH	**Lorenzo Romar (Washington '80)**
RECORD AT SCHOOL	**36-28 (2 years)**
CAREER RECORD	**78-72 (5 years)**
ASSISTANTS	**Brad Soderberg (Wisconsin-Stevens Point '85)**
	Lance LeVetter (Northern Arizona '92)
	Cameron Dollar (UCLA '97)
TEAM WINS (last 5 years)	**11-21-15-19-17**
RPI (last 5 years)	**172-42-94-42-114**
2000-01 FINISH	**Lost in conference quarterfinal.**

This year is all about next year.

Not to discount the chance Saint Louis has at success in 2001-02, but it's hard not to look at the roster and wonder what kind of team Lorenzo Romar has built for the following year, when he will have been at Saint Louis for four seasons.

There is not one senior on the roster. There are five juniors, meaning there will be five seniors the following season. Each Romar recruiting class has worked to add more athletic talent to the roster. With seven freshmen and sophomores on the squad, this year's mistakes will serve as lessons for the following year.

But who's to say Saint Louis can't arrive one year ahead of schedule? If these guys are going to be good a year from now, won't they be pretty decent this year?

"It would be really easy to say this is a trial run," said Romar, always the optimist. "That's not how to approach it. Let's try to get good now, let's try to grow up as quick as we can."

There is no more motley a collection of players in Conference USA. There is homegrown talent, there are West Coast transfers, there is a guy coming back from a Mormon mission in Latvia, there is one of those point guards Chicago is so famous for producing.

It is that point guard, junior **Marque Perry** (10.1 ppg, 3.5 apg, 2.4 rpg), who is charged with leading this young squad. A starter since his freshman season, the 6-1, 175-pound Perry broke his foot midway through his freshman season and, said Romar, had not fully recovered until after last season.

"He went from February to October of last year and didn't do anything," Romar said of Perry's post freshman off-season. "You take anyone who doesn't do much and then jump into the first day of practice, they will be rusty. People felt like, 'Boy, he improved,' but I still think he could be that much better."

Perry's strength is his ability to break down defenders with his dribble and disrupt a defense. He hit 44.8 percent of the shots he took inside three-point range, and was one of the better free-throw shooters in C-USA, hitting .756 overall for the season and .811 in C-USA play.

League opponents, however, learned that Perry wasn't going to beat you from long range. He hit just .306 from three-point range for the season and was 9-of-33 in C-USA play, where he was also only .396 from inside the arc.

Perry will not have NBA draft pick Maurice Jeffers helping him carve up defenses with slashes into traffic; he must become a more accurate outside shooter.

"I really think he will shoot the ball better, distribute the ball better and will create more havoc for the opposition," Romar said.

Randy Pulley, a strapping 6-2, 205-pound point guard from Raleigh, N.C., will be expected to serve as Perry's backup as a freshman. Recruiting analyst Bob Gibbons rated Pulley as a Top 100 player, and his averages were eye-popping: 26.5 points, 5.8 assists and 4.9 rebounds per game and .626 shooting from the field, including .592 from three-point range.

In one game last season, Pulley was 25-of-27 from the field for 52 points; Pulley also played football at Word of God High School.

"He is kind of a bigger Marque," Romar said. "He can pass the ball and really score the ball. He is really more of a pure point guard."

Could he start?

"It's definitely a possibility," Romar said. "This is a situation where you figure Marque will start and, after that, it is up for grabs."

The stat sheet would confirm Romar's figuring: No other returning payer averaged even seven points per game last season.

Josh Fisher, a 6-2 junior from Washington state, is the most likely companion for Perry in the backcourt. A transfer from Pepperdine, where Romar worked before coming to Saint Louis, Fisher played a reserve role last season behind Jeffers, averaging 5.0 points, 1.8 rebounds and 2.9 assists.

He received SLU's sixth-man-of-the-year award, and could play that role again. However, if he can stay consistent from long range— as he was last year in shooting .390 for the season and .455 in C-USA—Fisher should have a fulltime gig out front with Perry.

Like many of Saint Louis's guards, Fisher is versatile, able to play at the point or off-guard spot. That should allow Romar flexibility with his sets, adjusting to allow Perry to concentrate on scoring if need be.

"He is extremely steady," Romar said of Fisher. "He does a lot of things good, does nothing great. He's probably our best passer. He is a very tough kid, has a big heart and he's a real winner."

Drew Diener (4.5 ppg, 1.2 rpg), a 6-5 junior, should serve as SLU's best three-point shooter. He led the team from long range last season, connecting on 22-of-56 (.393), and was one of many solid free-throw shooters, hitting .805 from the line last season.

Diener is technically a red-shirt junior, and he has made great progress each year. C-USA will see plenty of the Diener family this season. His cousin, Travis, is a freshman at Marquette, and his brother, Drake, is a freshman at DePaul.

"Drew is feisty," Romar said. "He's got some experience, he can really shoot the ball and he's a smart player."

Romar believes 6-4 sophomore swingman **Floyd McClain** (2.0 ppg, 1.2 rpg) will show great progress with his knees finally healed. The sophomore played in only 21 games last season, but made appearances in the final 14.

McClain certainly needs to improve his shooting, which was weak a year ago—.295 from the field, .182 from three and .560 from the free-throw line.

"Floyd is probably our best athlete," Romar said. "It took him until the end of the year to get back on track [because of his knees]. He's a very strong guard and could become a very good defender. We'd like to see him be one of our defensive stoppers, and he has the potential to be one of our leading scorers."

Jason Edwin and **Chris Sloan**, both sophomores, are similar to McClain in that they can play the two or the three position.

Edwin (4.3 ppg, 2.0 rpg), 6-5 and 205 pounds, saw more playing time as a freshman, getting 13.5 minutes per game. He hit 44.4 percent of his shots from three-point range after missing his senior season in high school in Warsaw, Ill.

"He came on like gangbusters," Romar said.

Sloan (1.4 ppg, 1.5 rpg), at 6-7 and 205 pounds, had shoulder surgery in the off-season and will not begin full workouts until practice begins. He played last season despite the tendency of the left shoulder to pop in and out during games. He started 16 games for the Billikens, though he only averaged 10.1 minutes per game; Romar liked the defense Sloan provided from the tip.

"He has proven he can defend and rebound in the tough games," Romar said. "He plays so hard and so intense."

Phillip Hunt is a 5-11 sophomore guard from St. Louis who made only three appearances last season, and won't see much action.

Saint Louis's frontcourt was decimated. The Billikens lost 23.1 points per game, 13.4 rebounds and, maybe most important, 54 blocked shots with the departures of Justin Tatum, Matt Baniak and Chris Heinrich.

Rapidly-improving **Chris Braun** (6.1 ppg, 3.6 rpg), a mobile 6-10, 235-pound junior, should emerge as a very solid Conference USA big man. The very definition of an inside-outside big man, Braun hit 50.0 percent from the field and 39.3 percent from three-point range last season, and showed some athleticism with 22 blocks and 46 offensive rebounds.

Braun, a fourth-year junior, played only 17.1 minutes per game, and was very productive with his time. If he doubles his time and output, Romar would be very happy, indeed.

"Maurice Jeffers averaged six points a game as a junior and 17 as a senior, and I think Chris Braun will do something similar," Romar said.

The rest of the frontcourt is inexperienced, which will likely mean a lot of three-guard alignments for the Billikens. Which is not to say the three newcomers down front can't play.

Kenny Brown (11.9 ppg, 8.0 rpg, 1.9 bpg at Western Iowa Junior College), a 6-9, 260-pound junior originally from Hazelwood West High School in St. Louis, must be the inside enforcer.

"He provides some of the girth and physical play we had lost," Romar said. "We're excited with what he can bring."

John Seyfert (16.0 ppg, 12.0 rpg, 7.0 bpg at Stevensville High), a 6-9, 235-pound forward from Montana, could also bring some intimidation inside, and, with the lack of front line depth, he will have opportunity to prove his worth.

A good all-around athlete, Seyfert lettered in golf, track and baseball in high school. He will have to adjust to a much higher caliber of play, however.

"He's just a banger," Romar said. "He's ready to defend and rebound right now. Offensively, he needs some work, but this is a guy that doesn't mind mixing it up."

Saint Louis's most intriguing newcomer is 6-7, 220-pound forward **Ross Varner** (2.7 ppg, 2.7 rpg at Pepperdine in 1998-99), another Pepperdine transfer who came to Saint Louis after completing a Mormon mission in Latvia.

A sophomore, Varner is origingally from Holladay, Utah. He is a versatile player and has nice athleticism.

"He is the guy people will be pleasantly surprised with," Romar said. "He is the consummate winner. I don't think you'll see rust. He will find a way to get in shape and do everything we ask of him."

2001-2002 SCHEDULE

Nov.	19	#Southern Illinois
	22-24	#Las Vegas Tournament
	30	UALR
Dec.	3	Missouri
	6	@California
	9	Denver
	15	Southeast Missouri State
	19	Furman
	22	@Dayton
	29	Washington
Jan.	2	@Southwest Missouri State
	5	Houston
	8	DePaul
	12	@Marquette
	15	@Charlotte
	19	East Carolina
	22	Cincinnati
	26	Marquette
	29	@Southern Miss
Feb.	2	@East Carolina
	5	@Louisville
	9	Charlotte
	12	@Cincinnati
	16	Georgia Tech
	19	UAB
	22	Louisville
	26	@DePaul
March	2	@Tulane
	6-9	###C-USA Tournament

@Road Games
#First round Las Vegas Invitational
##Las Vegas, NV (schedule determined after first-round games; Pool 1 includes Georgia Tech, Illinois, Eastern Illinois, Pennsylvania. Pool 2 includes Iowa State, Saint Louis, Hartford, Southern Illinois)
###Firstar Center, Cincinnati, OH

BLUE RIBBON ANALYSIS

BACKCOURT	B
BENCH/DEPTH	B-
FRONTCOURT	C
INTANGIBLES	C+

Only Southern Miss lost more key players than Saint Louis in Conference USA, and, as positive as Romar is, this team will struggle.

Though two starters are listed as returning, Perry is really the only true starter back. Sloan started 16 games, but played a very limited role. Braun is the only frontcourt player with any Division I experience, and much of his production will come more than 15 feet away from the basket.

Romar needs someone to emerge a la Maurice Jeffers, who turned himself into an NBA draft pick with a superb senior season. Perry has the ability to be one of the best point guards in Conference USA, but he will find things more difficult without Jeffers creating opportunities. Perry's production should increase, but can he provide as much as the young Billikens will need?

One of the best additions to this team is assistant coach Brad Soderberg, the interim coach at Wisconsin last season. He will provide another head coaching voice from the bench, which is already considered one of the best in the league at making adjustments.

Romar said he would like to take advantage of a more athletic roster to get out and run, and maybe press more than in the past. C-USA, as a league, may force the Billikens to involve themselves in a faster pace, which may be the best thing to happen to the program. With the limited frontcourt, this team is not as prepared to grind out games as it had been in the past.

This year really is about next year, no matter how strong a Norman Vincent Peale impression coming from Romar. Breaking even in C-USA would be a huge accomplishment, but postseason hopes would be a little too high for this young team.

(Z.M.)

 ## South Florida

LOCATION	Tampa, FL
CONFERENCE	Conference USA (National)
LAST SEASON	18-13 (.581)
CONFERENCE RECORD	9-7 (3rd)
STARTERS LOST/RETURNING	1/4
NICKNAME	Bulls
COLORS	Green & Gold
HOMECOURT	Sun Dome (10,411)
COACH	Seth Greenberg (Farleigh-Dickinson '78)
RECORD AT SCHOOL	74-73 (5 years)
CAREER RECORD	179-143 (11 years)
ASSISTANTS	David Zimroth (Florida State '78)
	Clyde Vaughn (Pittsburgh '84)
	Brian Yankelevitz (Long Beach St. '97)
TEAM WINS (last 5 years)	8-17-14-17-18
RPI (last 5 years)	213-119-132-137-97
2000-01 FINISH	Lost in conference quarterfinal.

If Blue Ribbon were a brokerage firm, and you an investor, we'd owe you one when it comes to South Florida. We were bullish on the Bulls the last two seasons, throwing them into our Top 40 because of the high esteem we held for Seth Greenberg's rising program, and especially for guys like **B.B. Waldon** and **Altron Jackson**.

The Bulls was ranked 29th in Blue Ribbon's Top 40 in the fall of 1999. They lost four of their final five games and lost in the first round of the NIT. The Bulls rated No. 31 in BR last fall. They lost their final three games of the regular season and did not even rate an NIT bid.

So we are downgrading the Bulls, from BUY, down past HOLD, past ACCUMULATE and all the way down to NEUTRAL.

We realize the Bulls may find a place in the Top 25 or Top 40 in other places. We've been burned too many times, so we're even downgrading South Florida to third place in its own division.

Prove us wrong, you Bulls. We just can't prop you up any longer. There may not be a better-scoring duo than Waldon and Jackson, but we've been down this road before and seen the Bulls trying to fix a flat tire come March.

All that said, Greenberg deserves serious credit for establishing South Florida as a potential contender in Conference USA. The talents of Jackson and Waldon notwithstanding, his challenge this season is finding a way to replace a class of seniors who provided most of the leadership and guts the last three seasons.

People who look up and see the dynamic duo of Jackson and Waldon and immediately call the Bulls contenders do not realize what the departed Cedric Smith, Chonsey Asbury, Artha Reeves and Sam Sanders brought to this team.

Smith started 100-plus games. Asbury was the team's defensive stopper. Reeves was the consummate role player who could have been a star at a lower-level program. Sanders was a tremendous perimeter defender.

"We will replace it by committee," Greenberg said. "We are a quicker team. We will be an attacking team."

Yes, South Florida will put five guys on the court, even though opposing coaches will spend 80 percent of their time focusing on two: Jackson and Waldon.

Jackson averaged 18.9 points, 4.9 rebounds and hit 48.4 percent of his shots from the field. Waldon finished the season averaging 17.1 points, 7.2 rebounds and hit 54.3 percent of his shots from the field and 50.0 percent from three-point range.

Jackson is the better player and better pro prospect. A 6-6, 186-pound senior swingman with long arms and blazing speed, Jackson averaged 20.0 points and 5.7 rebounds in conference play. He is automatic on the break, has a fabulous in-between game and is nearly unstoppable one-on-one.

He needs to improve his long-range shooting (.311 3PT percentage) and, like so many other Bulls, his free-throw percentage needs improvement (.674 overall and .615 in league games).

"He had an outstanding summer," Greenberg said.

"He's gotten stronger and really concentrated on the weight room. He's worked on his dribble drive game as opposed to just his pull-up game. He's going to continue to be effective and make other people better because he attracts so much attention."

Jackson considered a jump to the NBA after last season, but decided the best career move was another year at South Florida, where he could raise his stature.

"He's very poised now," Greenberg said. "His game is very mature."

Waldon has been an enigma since arriving as a freshman and immediately bolstering the program's profile in the league. But Waldon has actually regressed since the first semester of his sophomore season, and the 6-8, 210-pound senior is often a victim of his own best intentions.

What makes Waldon so good, his aggression and relentless desire, has also conspired against him. Waldon is the king of silly fouls. Last season, he earned a technical foul from the bench, and, because it was his fifth foul, he was done. Fouling out from the bench isn't easy to do.

Waldon has also displayed a tendency to provide dominant performances early in the season (27 points and 10 rebounds against Texas and 21 points and eight rebounds against Wisconsin) before fading when conference opponents put their knowledge of him in the scouting reports.

In conference games last season, Waldon's scoring average dropped by five points per game, his rebounding by three boards per game and his shooting percentage by 7.5 points.

As a sophomore, Waldon averages had dropped by 4.0 points and 0.6 rebounds in league play, with his shooting percentage 13 points and his three-point percentage by 19 points.

"He's a guy that needs to be more consistent and he knows that," Greenberg said. "That's the most important thing."

Because he does so much damage from the inside, using his strong legs and quickness to the rim, Waldon's horrible free throw shooting is inexcusable. Waldon hit only 51 percent of his free throws last season. As a team that is a huge concern; South Florida hit only 60.2 percent from the line last season.

"That is the focal point of our preseason," Greenberg said. "If we hit 64 percent, we win 22 games."

Now, for all the rest.

Gerrick Morris (3.6 ppg, 3.2 rpg, 2.4 bpg), a 6-10, 218-pound red-shirt sophomore, was the most improved player on the team last season. He established himself as a premier shot blocker, getting 11 against George Washington and eight against Wisconsin. He scored in double-figures only twice last season—12 points against Louisville and 12 against Houston—and his .413 shooting percentage cannot be tolerated from a 6-10 center.

Nor can his .478 free throw shooting.

"He affects the game defensively without a doubt," Greenberg said. "He's got to be a threat offensively. He's got to play with more confidence. He's so quick to block a shot, and he's got to use that same quickness to rebound the ball."

Greenberg continues to hold high hopes for senior **Mike Bernard** (2.7 ppg, 1.4 rpg), a 6-11 center from England who has trimmed down some from his playing weight of 280 pounds a year ago. For such a large man, Bernard is very agile and has quick feet and soft hands around the basket.

At times, however, he very much looked like an international player unable to adjust to the more athletic, more physical game in America. Bernard did hit 54.1 percent of his shots while connecting on 73.1 percent from the line.

Bernard played for England's World University Games team over the summer, and had a 19-point, 13-rebound game against Team USA.

Bernard might not get in a full season, however, as he faces an NCAA suspension for an indeterminate amount of games because of his involvement with a foreign club team.

"He'll be on our team, it's just going to depend on how many games," Greenberg said. "He really made a commitment to getting into great shape and did an unbelievable job. He was playing with a tremendous amount of confidence."

Will McDonald (3.2 ppg, 2.6 rpg), a 6-11 junior center, trimmed his body fat from 21 percent down to 12 percent in the off-season and could get serious minutes in the post.

Brandon Brigman (15 ppg, 11 rpg, 3 bpg), a 6-9, 240-pound freshman center from Philadelphia, could be a very productive player if he can learn to play with consistent effort. He earned a reputation as a player who

doesn't always play hard in high school; if Greenberg can change that, he may have a recruiting steal.

"He's got a big, huge freaking body and unbelievable hands," Greenberg said. "He's got great skills. He may remind you a little of Mario Bland, who played at Miami."

Terence Leather (24.8 ppg, 8.6 rpg as a senior at Tampa Robinson) is a 6-9 200-pound freshman forward who red-shirted last season but could earn regular playing time, especially if he can provide better interior rebounding and defense.

Kelvin Brown (17 ppg, 14 rpg) is a 6-7, 220-pound freshman who fits the mold of a South Florida forward: strong, physical and skilled. He could help replace the defensive presence provided by Asbury.

South Florida's backcourt is entirely unsettled, other than the preseason certainty that **Reggie Kohn** (6.5 ppg, 3.7 apg, 2.2 rpg), a 6-1 junior, will play a lot of minutes. Kohn has served as the Bulls' primary point guard the last two seasons, but is only adequate as a floor leader.

He earned his playing time with toughness and an ability to hit clutch shots, but he must improve on the .341 shooting percentage from the field and the .302 three-point percentage from long range. It is also telling that Kohn, while playing more than 900 minutes, attempted only 20 free throws all season.

Kohn is quick, but not quick enough. He's stronger than he looks, but not strong enough. He handles the ball well, but not well enough. That he has contributed says a lot about what a gritty player he really is.

"He's got to make better decisions," Greenberg said. "His risk-reward mentality has got to improve. He's got very good hands, he's very tough and he's added strength."

In 5-10 freshman **Brian Swift** (21 ppg, 4 apg) the Bulls think they have found a point guard for the long term. Greenberg expects Swift to challenge and possibly supplant Kohn as the point guard, which would mean sharing minutes or possibly playing on the floor together.

Greenberg said Swift is somewhat similar to Marquette's Cordell Henry, though he may be a tad slower and a better shooter.

"He's good and he's always been a point guard," Greenberg said. "He shoots the ball with some range. He's low to the ground and strong. He'll be fine in our league."

Jimmy Baxter (2.3 ppg, 0.7 rpg), a 6-5 sophomore, had few opportunities because of last season's veteran team. He'll get his chances this season. A tremendous athlete (he's an all-American high jumper who cleared 7-3 in the NCAA Championships), Baxter can be one of the best defenders on the team (especially if South Florida shows more full-court press, which Greenberg has hinted at). If he finds his shot, he could really contribute.

Baxter averaged 20 points in high school, so he does know what to do with the ball.

"He is a much more confident player," Greenberg said. "He has made a commitment to getting into the gym and putting in the work. He's got to learn where his shots are coming from. ... If he had been a part of our first recruiting class, he would've played a ton of minutes as a freshman."

Greg Brittian, a 6-6 transfer from Central Florida Community College (19.4 ppg as a sophomore, 7.1 rpg as a freshman), will also help the Bulls if they do indeed employ the press.

"He's a mature kid and a mature player," Greenberg said. "He'll be very good when we press. He handles it pretty well and is an excellent passer."

Marlyn Bryant, a 6-4, 200-pound freshman, will contribute. He too helps make this a team that needs to press a lot, and Greenberg compares his game to Cedric Smith. Bryant was the Florida 5A state player of the year after leading his high school Wildwood (Fla.) Leesburg team to a 28-6 record.

"He is probably the best athlete on our team, just ridiculously explosive," Greenberg said. "He is as ready to defend at this level as anyone we've had."

2001-2002 SCHEDULE

Nov.	19	Fordham
	23-25	#University Hoops Classic
	28	Prairie View
Dec.	1	California
	4	@Northern Illinois
	8	Florida
	20	@Syracuse
	28-29	##USF Shootout
Jan.	2	Florida State
	5	TCU
	8	Southern Miss
	12	@DePaul

	15	@Memphis
	18	Charlotte
	23	@Tulane
	26	Cincinnati
	29	@UCF
Feb.	1	@Louisville
	5	UAB
	9	Tulane
	12	@Houston
	16	@TCU
	20	Memphis
	23	@UAB
	26	Houston
March	2	@Southern Miss
	6-9	###C-USA Tournament

@Road Games
#Pittsburgh, PA (vs. Robert Morris first round; also Kent State, Hofstra, UC Irvine, Illinois State, Oakland, Pittsburgh)
##Tampa, FL (vs. Bucknell first round; also Illinois-Chicago, Hofstra)
###Firstar Center, Cincinnati, OH

BLUE RIBBON ANALYSIS

BACKCOURT	B-
BENCH/DEPTH	B-
FRONTCOURT	A-
INTANGIBLES	B-

Jackson and Waldon will make the Bulls more than competitive, and, yes, this could be a very good team just based on their talents. But last season's squad had a lot more talent and experience surrounding the same two guys and managed an 18-13 record that did not earn an invite to the NIT.

To be fair, South Florida would have won 20-plus games if it had shot free throws with anything resembling competency. The Bulls were worse than even the 60-percent rate indicates, missing pressure free throws and getting into prolonged funks that very clearly affected all aspects of their game.

Replacing last year's senior class won't be an easy task. It brought experience, hunger and nice talent. Waldon and Jackson now carry a much larger share of the burden, and if they thought they had seen double-teams and gimmick defenses, just wait until they see what C-USA coaches throw at them with this supporting cast, which is offensively challenged to say the least.

If Greenberg really does make this a more fullcourt team with an all-out press mentality, it will be certainly be entertaining to watch. Jackson is a terrific scorer who is a legitimate threat to lead the nation in scoring with so few other options outside of Waldon.

Waldon, if he has matured on the court, could make a huge difference with consistency and a more focused effort. He's a potential 20-point, 10-rebound per game guy, and, with his strong base, can be a much better defender.

Swift is probably the key to this team. If he emerges as a commanding, dynamic point guard, that will give the Bulls a direction they have lacked in previous seasons. It would also allow Kohn to move to shooting guard, and, while he might be a defensive liability there, would certainly add to this team's offensive firepower.

How much can the Bulls can get from their mixed-bag interior? Morris needs to add offense to his game and become an intimidating defensive player, and either Bernard or McDonald—or both—must establish post scoring.

In Waldon and Jackson, the Bulls know just what they are getting. Outside that, South Florida is a hard team to figure. If this team is more successful than last year's disappointing bunch, then Greenberg should be a candidate for coach of the year in the league.

Our guess is third in the National Division and a possible NIT bid because of Waldon and Jackson.

(Z.M.)

Southern Mississippi

LOCATION	**Hattiesburg, MS**
CONFERENCE	**Conference USA (National)**
LAST SEASON	**22-9 (.710)**
CONFERENCE RECORD	**11-5 (t-1st)**
STARTERS LOST/RETURNING	**5/0**
NICKNAME	**Golden Eagles**
COLORS	**Black & Gold**
HOMECOURT	**Reed Green Coliseum (8,095)**
COACH	**James Green (Mississippi '83)**
RECORD AT SCHOOL	**87-63 (5 years)**
CAREER RECORD	**87-63 (5 years)**
ASSISTANTS	**Luster Goodwin (UTEP '86)**
	Jeff Norwood (Mississippi State '86)
	Kyle Roane (Southern Miss '94)
TEAM WINS (last 5 years)	**12-22-14-17-21**
RPI (last 5 years)	**142-71-134-65-60**
2000-01 FINISH	**Lost in conference semifinal.**

James Green was Conference USA's Coach of the Year in 2000-2001, and deservedly so. His team tied with Cincinnati for the C-USA title, narrowly missed on a rare (at least for this program) NCAA Tournament bid and hit 20 wins for only the seventh time in the last 40 seasons.

For Green to repeat as coach of the year, well, that will take some doing. That, really, ought to mean they name the trophy after him.

Because this Southern Miss team is definitely embarking on a rebuilding season. No reloading, no team in transition. Vital pieces of the Southern Miss puzzle have departed, some on schedule and some not, leaving Green and his staff with the monumental task of defending a championship with a thin cache of resources.

The worst piece of off-season news for the Eagles involved **Kilavorous Thompson**, a senior who tore his anterior cruciate ligament in a summer league game. A well-rounded 6-7, 220-pound forward, Thompson averaged only 7.6 points and 5.2 rebounds, but Green envisioned him putting together an all-league senior year similar to Vandarel Jones, the big senior center who was C-USA's defensive player of the year last season, as a senior.

Thompson had graduated on time, thus earning an extra year of eligibility after sitting out his freshman season as a non-qualifier, and now his career appears to be over.

"That puts a knot on our head," is how Green put it.

Indeed it does.

It also puts even more weight and pressure around the neck of 6-5, 205-pound senior forward **Elvin Mims** (10.0 ppg, 5.4 rpg). It is a measure of how much there is to rebuild that Mims figures to be the focal point of everything Southern Miss does.

Mims is a prototypical inside-outside player, strong enough and explosive enough to score inside but skilled enough to drop from three-point range (.406 for the season). A junior-college transfer, Mims was far too inconsistent last season, scoring 18 points against Iowa State early in the season and following with four against New Orleans. Late in the season, he sandwiched a 22-point breakout against Memphis between a four-point game against Tulane and a six-point game against South Florida.

Southern Miss needs Mims to be consistent and effective from the first game to the last, especially without Thompson to add production. Often last season, Mims deferred to Jones and Wall—and others—instead of creating offense for himself.

Mims also needs to develop his in-between game. He's more naturally suited to playing small forward, but often served as a power forward. Green said he is tinkering with going to a small, quick lineup, in which case Mims would be an under-sized power forward.

"He's got to be the guy that steps up for us and comes up big, for us to have a chance," Green said. "He'll understand more this year he is the guy and has to step up. ... Last year Van and David probably had it in their minds and Elvin in his mind that they were the guys, and that limited him at times."

There will be a plethora of players battling for the spot left open by Thompson's departure, but the early guess here is that freshman **Jasper Johnson** (27.2 ppg, 12.5 rpg, 5.3 apg, 2.3 spg), a 6-7, 230-pound freshman from Simmons High School in Hollandale, Miss., claims the position.

Johnson can play inside or outside, and he is one of the best freshman recruits Green has lured to Hattiesburg. He will certainly earn experience in his first season, and, though there may be early growing pains, Johnson and the Eagles will be better for it in the long term.

"He's very skilled for his size," Green said. "Jasper's problem is going to be making the transition to this level and the intensity, things like running the court, staying down in your stance and moving your feet. He's one of the best-shooting big guys I've ever seen."

Ben Lambert, a 6-8, 240-pound junior from Okaloosa-Walton (Fla.) Community College, is the probable starter at center. A strong player who signed early—USM finished its entire signing class in the fall—Lambert must provide the physical force now that Vandarel Jones is no longer around to muscle Conference USA's big men. His blue-collar approach will mesh nicely with Green's coaching philosophy. Last year, Lambert, a consensus Top 100 junior college sophomore, averaged 13.0 points and 10.5 rebounds.

"We're going to be caught comparing him a lot to Vandarel, but he's a different type player," Green said. "He can step away and shoot it outside. He won't be flashy. He's just a workhorse type of guy."

Carey Rigsby (17.0 ppg, 8.0 rpg), a 6-9, 230-pound junior from Western Oklahoma Junior College, will most likely serve as Lambert's backup, though he can also play some power forward.

"He's a little raw offensively, but he's a banger, a defender, a rebounder," said Green. "He's a hard working guy who is going to do everything you ask of him."

David Haywood (24.3 ppg, 9.5 rpg, 5.3 apg as a senior at Natchez High School), a 6-4, 190-pound freshman, sat out last season and is a red-shirt freshman. He is listed as a forward, and will likely play on the wing.

"He's rangy, he's athletic and he understands how to play," Green said. "He's an adequate shooter, not great, but at the same time he knows how to score. He will be a consistent guy in practice, which will give him an opportunity to play some minutes."

Brandon Gay (22.0 ppg, 15.0 rpg), a 6-7, 205-pound sophomore from Stafford High School in Houston, sat out last season.

"He's one of those 6-7 guys who is skilled," Green said. "He's put on some pounds and is getting bigger. He can score inside and outside, and, with his long arms, we will see how good he can be defensively."

Other than Mims, the Southern Miss player with the best credentials entering this season is senior point guard **Brad Richardson** (5.1 ppg, 3.2 apg, 1.1 rpg). Though the 6-1, native of New Orleans averaged less than 20 minutes per game last season and hit only 34.5 percent of his shots from the field, Green likes the way he runs the offense. He really appreciates the way Richardson gets into opposing guards and defends.

Though Richardson didn't get huge minutes, he probably earned more time than was expected in the preseason because he gave the Eagles a nice defensive dimension in relief of four-year starter Mel Cauthen at the point.

"I think he could be one of the better guards in the league if he can adjust to being a guy who is counted on for a lot of things,'" Green said. "He has what I like in a point guard. He is a good on the ball defender to get you started, and, offensively, he's always a threat to break you down and get into the paint.

"How the people around him shoot the ball will have a lot to do with his success."

Dante Stiggers, a 6-2, 160-pound freshman from Alief-Hastings High School in Houston, is the most likely backup for Richardson. How much Stiggers plays as a freshman will depend on his defense.

"He's very, very quick," Green said. "He has the ability to break you down off the dribble and he's another good on the ball defender that I think will have a really good future here. If Brad were not in our program, we would need him to come along a lot faster."

James Pattman (10.0 ppg, 6.0 apg), a 6-1 freshman from Berkmar High School in Lilburn, Ga., is another option at the point. Green said Pattman is similar to Cauthen, which may mean he surprises and earns good playing time. **Terrell Bolton** (0.5 ppg, 0.3 rpg) is a 5-10 junior walk-on who seldom plays.

The depth at shooting guard will be one of Southern's strengths this season.

If Green chooses to go with a pure shooter on the wing, he can throw senior **Pete Meneses** (3.7 ppg, 0.8 rpg) onto the floor and know he will get solid production.

Green may use three guards all season, meaning the 6-4, 205-pound Meneses would more likely become a specialist. He hit 33.3 percent from three-point range last season, with his best games against Western Illinois (5-of-7 on threes), at Marquette (2-of-4) and against UAB (4-of-7).

Take away those three games, and he shot only 18.5 percent from long range. He must be more reliable, and, with more consistent minutes, he should be.

"He will be better," Green said. "He will have a nice understanding of his role, which is to get open and make baskets. I think he is going to be a better defender than he was a year ago because he knows the importance of doing that so he can be on the floor shooting the ball."

Bernard Duncan (2.6 ppg, 1.5 rpg), a 6-4 senior from Memphis, never found a rhythm last season. He is an instinctive scorer who brings tenacity to the floor that endears him to Green. He is a better shooter than he showed (.373 overall, .188 from three) in limited minutes last season as one of many reserves at guard.

"At times last year, he just came in and he made the plays," Green said. "Defensively, he needed to be better. He had it settled in his mind he wasn't going to get playing time, and he was not as keen in his focus as he needed to be. I hope he will really come in and fight for a spot."

Clement Carter (2.7 ppg, 1.7 rpg) and **Mario Myles** (6.1 ppg, 3.9 rpg) are similar players who can man the two- or three-spots. Myles, a 6-5 junior, started 29 games last season and was very efficient, shooting .474 overall and .380 from three-point range. He was also one of the team's best perimeter defenders.

"We expect a good solid year out of Mario," Green said. "He needs to up his level of play. He's a guy with great experience and great energy. If he can improve in some areas, [such as] ball handling and shooting, he can be very, very solid. He just plays hard."

Carter will give Green lineup flexibility because of his versatility. Like Duncan, the sporadic playing time meant poor shooting stats (.337 overall, .222 on threes) that belied practice performances from outside.

Carter, a 6-5, 220-pound sophomore, is very skilled for his size. If he can display more understanding of Green's system, he could win regular minutes. Like Duncan, he needs to hit shots when given the opportunity.

"A lot will depend on match-ups with Clement," Green said. "He didn't play for a year, and so he was cast in and made some mistakes but also made some contributions. His understanding has really increased."

2001-2002 SCHEDULE

Nov.	17	Jackson State
	23	Hispanic College Fund Classic
	27	Alcorn State
Dec.	1	Arkansas State
	5	@South Alabama
	15	Morris Brown
	18	Millsaps
	22	Western Kentucky
	29	@Auburn
Jan.	5	@Memphis
	8	@South Florida
	12	UAB
	15	Tulane
	18	Memphis
	23	@Houston
	26	@TCU
Feb.	2	@Tulane
	5	Houston
	9	Houston
	9	Marquette
	12	@East Carolina
	15	@Cincinnati
	23	TCU
	26	@UAB
March	2	South Florida
	6-9	##C-USA Tournament

@Road Games
#Albuquerque, NM (vs. West Virginia first round; also New Mexico, Pacific)
##Firstar Center, Cincinnati, OH

BLUE RIBBON ANALYSIS

BACKCOURT	C+
BENCH/DEPTH	B-
FRONTCOURT	C-
INTANGIBLES	B-

It is easy to gloss over the loss of Thompson, but the less-than-stellar statistics do not tell the whole story. Thompson would have been this team's leader, and he was talented enough to embrace a role as go-to player.

That means Mims must have an exceptional season for Southern to have any kind of chance. This is legitimately a team that could sink from first to worst in one season, though it's not probable, not with the way Green gets his players to go all out and pay close attention to detail on defense.

This is a much quicker team than Green has had, one that will likely do more pressing and push the ball in transition more often. Richardson is as steady a point guard as you will find, and much will depend on his growth as a senior.

Green also likes the competition created at each position. Last season, the rotation was pretty well set up to the top seven, and he wasn't always happy with the effort he saw in practice.

"We have a lot of guys similar in abilities, and that

should create a situation where practices are more competitive," Green said. "If we have a strength, that's what it's going to be."

The Eagles need for one or two players to come in and make the same kind of impact Wall made his first season. Johnson certainly has the talent and high school credentials to suggest a heavy freshman contribution, and Green will give Lambert every opportunity to succeed.

Still, there are only a few players—Richardson, Mims, Myles—with substantial experience, and that will make things challenging, to say the least.

"It's going to be tough as we go through it because we are gonna have a lot of guys who haven't played much," Green said. "We have to see who emerges."

Southern Miss should do its usual thing, which is make games very difficult to play while displaying a dogged toughness no matter the circumstance. The only team to consistently handle Southern with ease has been Cincinnati, long the stalwarts for physical toughness in C-USA.

Southern Miss will show fight, count on that. But this Eagle team is limited, and will do well to stay ahead of Tulane and Houston in the National Division.

(Z.M.)

Texas Christian

LOCATION	Fort Worth, TX
CONFERENCE	Conference USA
LAST SEASON	20-11 (.645)
CONFERENCE RECORD	9-7 (WAC)
STARTERS LOST/RETURNING	5/0
NICKNAME	Horned Frogs
COLORS	Purple & White
HOMECOURT	Daniel Coliseum (7,200)
COACH	Billy Tubbs (Lamar '58)
RECORD AT SCHOOL	140-80 (7 years)
CAREER RECORD	579-282 (27 years)
ASSISTANTS	Brian Fish (Marshall '88)
	Rob Flaska (Michigan State '82)
	Scott Edgar (Pittsburgh-Johnston '78)
TEAM WINS (last 5 years)	22-27-21-18-20
RPI (last 5 years)	45-23-40-81-65
2000-01 FINISH	Lost in conference first round.

Eighth-year Texas Christian coach Billy Tubbs, one of four Final Four coaches in Conference USA, was scanning the offensive statistics of his future C-USA opponents. He saw that Memphis averaged 75.1 points per game.

"Ol' Johnny's got 'em running," Tubbs said, and if you couldn't hear the slight touch of sarcasm in his voice, you would as he found other schools.

"Look at Marquette," he said. "Sixty-five points a game."

"What's Louisville? Seventy?" Tubbs said. "Ricky will get them going."

Eventually, Tubbs got to Charlotte, the C-USA scoring champ in 2000-01.

"They are getting up and down the floor in Charlotte," Tubbs said. "Seventy-eight-point-three. How 'bout that?" How 'bout it?

How about meeting Conference USA's new scoring champ, the Horned Frogs of TCU? Make predictions about a league champion, about the player of the year, about the coach of the year all you want. One prediction almost certain to come true is that no team will score as many points this season as TCU.

The nation's leading scoring team last season, TCU's run-it and gun-it style will be something of a shock to the C-USA system.

"We led the nation in scoring last year at 94 points," Tubbs said. "It's embarrassing."

Embarrassing? You mean you'd rather be known for defense?

"Naw," Tubbs said. "You need to be up there dancing with 100 a game."

If the Horned Frogs dance with 100 this season, it will be with a drastically different lineup than last season.

Tubbs lost more than three-quarters of his scoring from a year ago, with five of the Frogs' top four scorers no longer on the roster. The departing players contributed 213 of TCU's 268 three-pointers a year ago, and the club's remarkable .747 free-throw shooting percentage was owed in large part to them.

Tubbs thinks this squad is more rugged and will be better rebounding and defending the interior. He remains confident he has players capable of ringing up the kinds

of huge scoring numbers for which the Frogs are best known.

The most promising returning player is versatile 6-8, 225-pound forward **Bingo Merriex**, a senior whom Tubbs believes will significantly raise his averages of 11.5 points and 4.8 rebounds, if he recovers from a broken right foot suffered in a pickup game in late September. TCU forward Merriex will be out action up to eight weeks.

Merriex averaged 21.7 points over the final seven games of last season, and Tubbs is up front about his expectations for the Wichita Falls, Texas native.

"He's a guy that can put an average of 20 points a game on the board," Tubbs said.

Merriex connected on 52-of-142 (.366) three pointers last season, which allows Tubbs to play him at power forward or center and create match-up headaches for opponents.

"For his size or any size he can really go outside and shoot the ball," Tubbs said. "He's a guy that can stroke it from any place on the floor."

Although he won't score as many points as Merriex, 6-9, 230-pound senior center **Marlon Dumont** enters the season with the same kind of high expectations. Though he averaged only 6.0 points and 4.3 rebounds last season, Dumont is an athletic interior player whom Tubbs believes will make TCU a much better rebounding team.

More than half of Dumont's rebounds last season were on the offensive end, and, if you consider he averaged just 14.1 minutes per game, Tubbs's expectations seem realistic. Dumont was efficient shooting the ball—.518 from the field, .709 from the line—and had 33 blocks in 30 games.

"I think a lot of our season is going to ride on him," Tubbs said. "He's a good rebounder and probably our best shot blocker. He's a guy that runs the floor really well."

Dumont had a rib removed before his junior season, and Tubbs said it affected him.

"He is just now getting back to his normal weight," Tubbs said. "He's just gained back his strength. I see a much better year for him."

Junior-college transfer **Jamal Brown**, a 6-7, 228-pound forward, earned a reputation as a tenacious rebounder at Seward (Kansas) Junior College last season. Tubbs is excited about the potential of Brown, a native of Baltimore who averaged 21.9 points and 14.1 rebounds last season.

"He comes in with that warrior type of mentality," Tubbs said. "The best thing he does is he's just a relentless rebounder."

Brian Carter, a 6-11, 210-pound center, spent last season at Winchendon (Mass.) Prep, but, like so many TCU players, is originally from Michigan (he averaged 19.0 points and 13.0 rebounds as a senior). He brings good skills with him, but his shot blocking and rebounding will be most useful this season.

"He has a good presence on the floor," Tubbs said. "He'll fight for playing time, and I think, in time, he's going to be a really good player."

Rebel Paulk, at 6-10, 240-pounds, could provide a nice inside presence, but he has never given Tubbs much of a reason to play him consistent minutes. He averaged just 0.7 points and 1.1 rebounds last season in 18 games.

"He's a guy we are hoping some day will step up and do something," Tubbs said. "We'd like for him to come around and be a factor. But it's one thing to hope ... "

Marcus Sloan (20.0 ppg, 11.0 rpg, 3.0 bpg), a 6-8, 204 pound freshman from Houston, could contribute at power forward, but will likely serve as more of an apprentice this season.

Sophomore **Chris Campbell** and senior **Colin Boddicker** seldom play, but do provide two more big bodies—6-11 and 6-8, respectively—for practice.

The two players who could most determine TCU's direction this season, **James Davis** (25.1 ppg, 11.0 rpg at Detroit Murray Wright as a senior) and **Corey Valsin** (18.0 ppg, 10.0 rpg at Dallas Lincoln as a senior), are both red-shirt freshmen whom Tubbs said proved to be among the best players in practice late last season. Tubbs said he gave the red-shirts to Davis and Valsin, 6-4 1/2 and 6-5 1/2, respectively, because of TCU's backcourt depth and experience last season.

Their abilities, he believes, will keep TCU's high-powered offense revved sufficiently.

"Davis did a good job for us last year and could very well be our leading scorer this year," Tubbs said. "He will play the two or the three and he can score. When he played against our first team last year, we had a hard time stopping him. He's very good around the basket but is a very good three-point shooter."

Tubbs likes Valsin, too.

"After we red-shirted him, we were wondering why we did it," Tubs said. "I call him a man-child. He's a youngster that is very, very strong physically. He's tough around the basket, and his strength could mean he'll be our best defender. Ryan Carroll was our best offensive player last year, and, when we put Corey on him in practice, Ryan would always struggle."

The perimeter will be held together by—who else?—**Nucleus Smith**, a 6-2 sophomore who averaged 6.9 points, 1.9 assists and 1.9 rebounds last season. Smith played right at 20 minutes per game, and hit 51.5 percent of his shots, including 54.6 percent from inside three-point range.

A strong finisher and another of TCU's Michigan Mafia, Smith can play either the one or the two this season.

"He was a starter for us late in the season," Tubbs said. "He made a lot of progress. He wasn't called on to do a lot of scoring. He's just a real sound player who doesn't make a lot of mistakes."

The most likely complement to Smith in the backcourt is a freshman, 6-2 Corey Santee from Flint, Mich. Santee averaged 20.0 points and 7.0 assists as a senior at Flint Northwestern (and was runner-up for Michigan Mr. Basketball). He and Smith can alternate running the point, with Santee the better pure shooter.

"He was one of the highest-rated point guards in Michigan," Tubbs said. "I think Corey is a little more able to play the point [than Smith]. He's got to earn it."

Alan "Junior" Blount, a slight 6-0, 155-pound junior, will also be a factor on the perimeter. A transfer from Connors (Okla.) Junior College, where he averaged 20.1 points, 4.0 rebounds and 3.1 assists last season, Blount could play either guard position. He fits at the two because of his shooting and despite his size.

"We expect a lot out of Junior," Tubbs said. "The best part of his game is that he's a very good, accurate shooter. We will need his scoring."

J.R. Jones, a 6-1 junior, is a former walk-on from Ft. Worth who played in only six games last season and will make most of his contributions in practice.

2001-2002 SCHEDULE

Nov.	16	#Northwestern Louisiana
	19-21	##Las Vegas Invitational
	25	Louisiana-Monroe
	28	Southwest Texas State
Dec.	1	@Texas Tech
	4	Creighton
	8	South Alabama
	15	Texas-San Antonio
	18	SMU
	20	Appalachian State
	29	Baylor
Jan.	5	@South Florida
	9	Memphis
	12	@Louisville
	15	@Houston
	19	Tulane
	23	Marquette
	26	Southern Miss
Feb.	2	@Memphis
	5	DePaul
	9	Houston
	12	@UAB
	16	South Florida
	23	@Southern Miss
	26	@Tulane
March	2	East Carolina
	6-9	###C-USA Tournament

@Road Games
#First round Las Vegas Invitational
##Las Vegas, NV (also UTEP, Providence, Austin Peay, Oklahoma State)
###Firstar Center, Cincinnati, OH

BLUE RIBBON ANALYSIS

BACKCOURT	B-
BENCH/DEPTH	B
FRONTCOURT	B
INTANGIBLES	B+

Tubbs said coaches at the Conference USA spring meetings told him his club would find running more difficult in C-USA.

"Someone said, you will not run on Southern Miss," Tubbs said. "Well, what if we don't guard them? Are they going to turn down a layup? If they do, their crowd's going to boo them."

This is the kind of brash approach C-USA needs, and Tubbs should have another entertaining and competitive team, no matter the lack of substantial experience on the roster. Tubbs says the newcomers, as a group, are as good as any class he has recruited to TCU, and his coaching style always seems to bring out the best in players.

The question is: Can TCU handle C-USA's more physical style?

Tubbs said he has watched tapes all summer, and calls C-USA a "bang-bang" type conference.

"Physically, we'll be a better team, but physically compared to what?" Tubbs said.

Tubbs doesn't mind the lack of experience, and says he actually likes young teams because there are usually fewer agendas.

TCU will also have to adjust to a wider variety of defenses, with most C-USA coaches willing to mix in zone or at least employ trapping halfcourt systems to disrupt offensive rhythm.

Merriex will carry a heavy load of expectations into the season, and Smith must provide the stabilizing influence in the backcourt. Tubbs will need Dumont to establish himself as the kind of strong inside player who can compete in C-USA, and TCU must become physically tougher in this new league.

If Davis and Valsin have the kinds of impacts Tubbs foresees, then TCU will be a factor in C-USA's National Division.

With a team so young, however, this is more of a transition year. An NIT bid would qualify as an excellent season. Anything more than that and Tubbs will have done one of the best coaching jobs in his illustrious career.

(Z.M.)

Tulane

LOCATION	New Orleans, LA
CONFERENCE	Conference USA (National)
LAST SEASON	9-21 (.300)
CONFERENCE RECORD	2-14 (6th)
STARTERS LOST/RETURNING	1/4
NICKNAME	Green Wave
COLORS	Olive Green & Sky Blue
HOMECOURT	Fogelman Arena (3,600)
	and New Orleans Arena (17,632)
COACH	Shawn Finney (Fairmount State '85)
RECORD AT SCHOOL	9-21 (1 year)
CAREER RECORD	9-21 (1 year)
ASSISTANTS	Wade O'Connor (Bridgewater St. '94)
	Jeff Reynolds (UNC Greensboro '78)
	Steve Snell (Radford '88)
TEAM WINS (last 5 years)	20-7-12-20-9
RPI (last 5 years)	66-220-141-90
2000-01 FINISH	Lost in conference first round.

Tulane could have won more games last season. Shawn Finney, knows this. He knows his first season as head coach would have had double-digits in wins, would have included far fewer fatigue-induced breakdowns, would have looked much better in the record books, if he had chosen a different tactic.

The thin team he inherited from Perry Clark really had only seven legitimate Division I players, though, as it turned out, all of them were pretty fair players. So Finney could have chosen a grind-it-out, shorten-the-game, smash-'em-in-the-mouth halfcourt style and stolen a win here and there.

Instead, Finney, a protege of Tubby Smith's, chose to install the system he believes will eventually push Tulane back to the top of Conference USA. Even with the point guard he inherited not playing because of academics, Finney chose to run and to gun and to establish the Green Wave as an exciting, up-tempo basketball team.

The result? Nine wins, 21 losses and an eight-game losing streak to finish the season. Look closer at the losses though, and you discover that eight were by 10 points or less, five of which were by five points or less and three of which went to overtime.

Even in some of Tulane's more lopsided losses, the Green Wave was even for 35 minutes. One five-minute stretch might produce a 19-2 run and finish the game.

"Last year, guys had to rest on the court," Finney says. "When you [run a style] that tries to wear teams down and you have short numbers, it's hard to do."

Last season's growing pains should yield success this season, especially with that point guard, 6-2 junior **Waitari Marsh** (8.0 ppg, 4.3 apg, 3.7 rpg in 1999-2000)

back in the lineup and 6-6 Minnesota transfer **Nick Sinville** (4.2 ppg, 4.0 rpg in 1999-2000 at Minnesota) ready to play after spending last season as a practice player along with Marsh.

Marsh played nearly 30 minutes a game as a sophomore, and he is perfectly suited to the press-and-run system. He was one of the best in the league at forcing turnovers, with 48 steals, and Finney said his shooting is much improved after the year out of action.

"Wat is great," Finney says. "I really think he can be one of the best point guards in the league. He's got the ability, and he's a great athlete. Now he's got to take that out on the court. He's gained so much maturity, physically and emotionally, and I think people will be very surprised."

It says something about Tulane's talent level this season that Sinville, a junior, cannot be viewed as an automatic starter. The 230-pound native of Shreveport spent much of his time last season playing the wing in practice, diversifying what had been mostly a power game. Finney sees Sinville as a natural—though undersized—power forward who will also be an option at small forward.

"He can be an inside-outside guy for us," Finney said. "He's undersized as a four-man but he's got good strength. He's a quick jumper around the basket."

As for the players coming back, they prospered individually in Tulane's systems. While the inflated possessions of a typical Tulane game last season (average score in league play—85-70) may have conspired against short-term success, there were benefits for Tulane's regulars.

All four returning starters averaged 30 minutes or more per game. Three of them scored in double figures, and no team had more players with multiple double-double games.

"You've got to take a negative and make it a positive," Finney says. "There's nothing more valuable than actual game experience ... When they play major minutes, you see them continue to develop."

Brandon Spann (15.9 ppg, 4.8 apg, 2.6 rpg), a 6-2 junior guard and New Orleans native, was more than adequate as a point guard last season, but Marsh's presence means he can move back to his natural position, shooting guard. Spann must become more efficient as a shooter (.318 from three-point range) and ball handler (4.3 turnovers per game), but he showed plenty of grit last season.

Spann's shooting should benefit from more stand-still, spot-up looks, and Finney is looking forward to putting two guards on the court who can break down a defense off the dribble and wreak havoc defensively (Spann had 51 steals).

"He did a tremendous job last year playing the number of minutes he played," Finney said. "He fought through fatigue. He was just a leader on the court and got us into our offense and really matured as the season went on."

Wayne Tinsley (7.8 ppg, 3.8 rpg, 2.3 apg), a 6-5 sophomore, manned the shooting guard position for most of last season, though his long-range shooting (.143, 4-of-28) left much to be desired. He showed toughness on defense and scoring inside the three-point line (.405 overall shooting percentage, .443 inside the arc), and benefited as much as anyone from the short bench.

Tinsley almost certainly would not have averaged 30 minutes per game if Finney had more options, but the time helped Tinsley.

"He was solid," Finney said. "He had an opportunity to play through a lot of mistakes. He's continued to develop his shot and I see him being a solid Conference USA player."

Of two Tulane walk-ons, 6-0 sophomores **Justin Amick** and **Marc Siegel**, it was Amick (1.7 ppg, 1.3 rpg) who may have made the difference between a struggling Tulane team and one that could have been truly awful.

Amick played 15 minutes per game and provided much needed relief, especially for Spann. He ran the club, he defended and his poise on the court belied his junior-high look in warmups.

"He played within himself and didn't try to do more than he was capable of," Finney said. "He really stabilized us when we became erratic. Other teams look at him and think he can't play, but he just finds a way. I expect him to contribute this season."

All five of Tulane's newcomers are perimeter-oriented. The best of the bunch is probably **Karl Hollingsworth**, a 6-5 freshman swingman from Jonesboro, Ga. Hollingsworth, a solid-looking forward at 220 pounds, averaged 29.5 points and 14.5 rebounds last season, and had 22 points and 13 rebounds in the Georgia-Tennessee all-star game. His size and athleticism suggest he can make a difference defensively.

"He can play the two, the three or the four," Finney said. "He's very versatile and has a great understanding of the game. He's a workhorse, will do whatever it takes to win and Karl has a chance to really contribute."

Byron Parker (7.5 ppg, 4.0 apg at Tyler [Texas] Junior College), a 6-2 junior guard, could shored up Tulane's perimeter defense.

Ben Benfield (25.7 ppg as a senior and 2,800 career points at River Ridge [La.] John Curtis) could fill a sniper's role off the bench. He's known more for his shooting ability, but Finney says the 6-4 freshman is "more athletic than people give him credit for."

Ben Bowling (21.0 ppg, 7.0 rpg, 6.0 apg at Westminster Christian in Florida), a 6-3, 185-pound freshman, became acquainted with Finney when he was at Kentucky. Originally from Hazard, Ky., Bowling is a solid athlete who Finney sees helping at any one of three positions.

"He gives us a lot of flexibility," Finney said.

The point guard of the class is 5-11 **Marcus Kinzer** from Nashville; Kinzer (23.0 ppg, 9.0 apg, 2.5 spg) spent one season at Solebury Prep in New Hope, Pa. after his senior year at Glencliff High School.

"He brings a lot of stability to the point," Finney said. "He's a point guard's point guard. He reminds me of G.G. Smith when we had him at Georgia."

While Tulane may not be very deep inside, there is plenty of talent to go with Sinville. Foremost is senior **Linton Johnson** (13.1 ppg, 8.1 rpg, 2.5 apg, 1.9 bpg), a highly talented 6-8 forward who cleaned up the boards and hit 36 percent of his three-point shots last season. After averaging 11.1 minutes per game as a sophomore, Johnson got 33 minutes per game last season (35 minutes in C-USA games) and developed into one of the league's budding stars.

Johnson should be a candidate for preseason honors this season in the league, and Finney expects him to improve as much this season as he did in his junior year.

"He loves the individual workout," Finney said. "We expect him to continue to mature and develop. He's a guy who just loves making his game better."

Johnson suffered a stress fracture in the off-season and had a pin inserted into his foot, but is expected to have no lingering effects. Finney compares Johnson's game to Shandon Anderson's, and that is about right.

"Shandon might be a little better," Finney said. "Linton is just so long. He gets his hands on a lot of balls and with that long reach can come up with plays."

Brandon Brown (11.8 ppg, 6.6 rpg), a 6-8, 230-pound junior, had played more minutes after three games of his sophomore year than he did his entire freshman season. Like Spann and Johnson, the extended time on the court translated into warp-speed development.

Brown was one of the best offensive rebounders in the league, with 98 of his 197 total boards coming off the offensive glass. Brown could play center if Finney goes with an undersized lineup, but he's a more natural power forward.

"He's a tremendous workhorse," Finney said. "He just finds a way to get it done. He does the dirty things people don't like to do."

Ivan Pjevcevic (1.3 ppg, 0.9 rpg), a 6-10, 220-pound sophomore center from Belgrade, has the potential to be the biggest surprise on this team. A classic European big man—he'd just as soon roam the perimeter as bang inside—Pjevcevic played last season despite a painful knee injury. Pjevcic hit 8-of-16 shots from long range last season.

"He is as skilled a guy as we have," Finney said. "He needs to be more physical and more aggressive. He's got all the tools. It's time for him to apply them."

George Brown (1.6 ppg, 1.3 rpg), a 6-10 sophomore center from Nashville, averaged only 10 minutes per game last season and definitely qualifies as a project. But Finney likes the raw material.

"He's a big guy with great hands and a great work ethic," Finney said. "He's still learning the game."

2001-2002 SCHEDULE

Nov.	16	Loyola, New Orleans
	20	Centenary
	24	Norfolk State
	27	@VCU
Dec.	2	@Florida
	5	New Orleans
	10	Vanderbilt
	21	Lipscomb
	23	@Georgia Tech
	29	Mississippi State
Jan.	2	*Kentucky
	5	@DePaul
	8	Houston
	12	Memphis
	15	@Southern Miss
	19	@TCU
	23	South Florida
	26	@UAB
	29	Marquette
Feb.	2	Southern Miss
	4	@Memphis
	9	@South Florida
	16	UAB
	19	@Houston
	23	@Charlotte
	26	TCU
March	2	Saint Louis
	6-9	#Conference USA Tournament

@Road Games
*Freedom Hall, Louisville, KY
#Firstar Center, Cincinnati, OH

BLUE RIBBON ANALYSIS

BACKCOURT	B
BENCH/DEPTH	B
FRONTCOURT	B
INTANGIBLES	C+

All the above grades could be higher; they could not be lower, which should tell you something about Tulane's potential.

If Marsh is able to return without any rust and flourish as Finney believes he will in an up-tempo system, the backcourt will be dangerous. If Spann is indeed a tough spot-up shooter from the two spot, then Tulane will threaten 80 points per game.

If Johnson improves as much this season as he did last, he'll be an NBA draft pick and play the kind of inside-outside role that Antoine Walker once played at Kentucky, if not on that same level of play. If Sinville can have a huge impact in his new environment, Tulane will be undersized, yes, but its versatility will create some tantalizing matchups.

Those are the four variables for Tulane. If Marsh, Spann, Johnson and Sinville have solid but unexceptional seasons, the Green Wave will be much improved and much more competitive this season. If those four exceed expectations, then Tulane will be a surprise challenger in the National Division.

Finney is emphatic about the press-and-run system he prefers, and there are now enough athletes and basketball players to make it work effectively. Tulane should be able to wear people down with the press this season, rather than wearing itself out as happened so many times last season.

As for launching three-pointers, another component of the system Finney believes in, there may not be enough great shooters on the perimeter to make it work. There is good inside-outside play, however, which should work to stretch defenses.

Finney put together a brutal non-conference schedule, so it will be hard to know how good or bad Tulane can be at lest until mid-January. We will begin to find out this season what kind of coach Finney is.

In a conference stricken with so much parity, only a few teams cannot aspire to some kind of postseason. Tulane was one of them last season, but the Green Wave will challenge for a winning record and possible NIT bid this year.

(Z.M.)

Butler

LOCATION	Indianapolis, IN
CONFERENCE	Horizon League
LAST SEASON	24-8 (.750)
CONFERENCE RECORD	11-3 (1st)
STARTERS LOST/RETURNING	1/4
NICKNAME	Bulldogs
COLORS	Blue & White
HOMECOURT	Hinkle Fieldhouse (11,043)
COACH	Todd Lickliter (Butler '79)
RECORD AT SCHOOL	First year
CAREER RECORD	First year
ASSISTANTS	Jeff Meyer (Taylor '78)
	Mike Marshall (Butler '00)
	Brad Stevens (Depauw '99)
TEAM WINS (last 5 years)	23-22-22-23-24

RPI (last 5 years)	88-52-59-57-29
2000-01 FINISH	Lost in NCAA second round.

They proudly call it "The Butler Way," and it works. What is the Butler way? First of all, it's winning.

The Bulldogs have strung together five straight 20-win seasons. They've been to the NCAA tournament four of the last five years. But "The Butler Way" is also about how to win. Butler wins with hard work and unrelenting defense.

The Bulldogs loved the double-page-spread photo in Sports Illustrated last March of Brandon Miller diving for a loose ball in the NCAA Tournament.

Butler wins with unselfishness. It's always team first, individual second. Six players averaged between 13.0 and 7.8 points last year. And Butler wins with class and humility.

Todd Lickliter understands "The Butler Way," and that's primarily why it took fewer than 48 hours for the school to hire him as Thad Matta's successor last May. Matta lasted only one year after being bumped up to replace Barry Collier, who left for Nebraska after the 1999-2000 season. Xavier snapped up Matta, who guided the Bulldogs to a 24-8 record and another (ho-hum) MCC conference title.

Like Collier and Matta, Lickliter is a former Butler player, and he served as an assistant the last two years, one season under each.

Athletics director John Parry said he had every intention of searching for a replacement for Matta who had head-coaching experience. After all, Butler isn't necessarily a stepping-stone job any more. But after Parry met with Lickliter and listened to the strong recommendations of the players, the search was over.

"I was prepared to take advantage of the enormous interest in the Butler head-coaching position and hire someone with head-coaching experience," Parry said. "However the players made a logical and cogent argument that I should strongly consider assistant coach Lickliter. I did, and they were right.

The Bulldogs didn't need a fresh start. They didn't need rebuilding. Lickliter inherits a team with four returning starters and a strong bench. The Indianapolis native grew up watching Butler basketball before he played it. During his third stint as a Butler assistant, he was a valuable behind-the-scenes strategist, a perfect complement to the emotional Matta.

Promoting Lickliter should maintain the momentum that has kept Butler atop the conference the last two years.

"We've had success and I've been part of that success,' Lickliter said. "Barry and Thad and I all graduated from Butler and played here, so I think there's obviously a family atmosphere here. But I haven't just been waiting my turn. I've enjoyed my work here."

Last year, the Bulldogs recorded the phenomenal statistic of starting the same five players in all 32 games. All five averaged at least 30 minutes a game. The only starter Lickliter has to replace is guard LaVall Jordan, who was second-team all-conference and was the MVP of the MCC Tournament. He averaged 12.4 points and was a defensive stopper.

However, a former starter, 6-11 center **Scott Robisch** (8.0 ppg, 3.7 rpg in 1999-2000) returns for a final season after an injury-plagued season. Robisch, the son of former Kansas star Dave Robisch, was expected to have a big season last winter, but instead had knee surgery in November just before the opener. He was thought to be lost for the year but returned to the team, although he was never the player Butler had hoped. Robisch appeared in 19 games but averaged only 1.9 points. His rehab has continued and he played well over the summer.

"Hopefully, we'll see him for an entire season," Lickliter said, "which would be a first for him since he's been in college. I think he's earned that. He gives us another senior who's been through some adversity and kept battling. He ought to be able to bring some great perspective and that's huge."

The Bulldogs already have a competent big man in 6-10 junior **Joel Cornette** (9.1 ppg, 5.9 rpg). Cornette blossomed as a sophomore, giving Butler an athletic inside presence for 31 minutes a game. His .583 shooting percentage was second best in the league.

"He's extremely unselfish and he's very active [40 blocked shots]," Lickliter said. "That makes for a nice combination."

If Cornette and Robisch are on the court together in a twin-towers alignment, 6-6 senior **Rylan Hainje** (10.9 ppg, 5.4 rpg) could shift from power forward to small forward and give Butler a big lineup. The athletic Hainje averaged 30.7 minutes, mostly at power forward last year. His three-point stroke (.412) was a nice complement to his jumping ability, and that made him an effective weapon around the glass. Hainje is also a strong defender and displayed a toughness reminiscent of former Butler star (and current assistant coach) Mike Marshall.

A couple of other Bulldogs could get more minutes in the Butler rotation this year, including 6-5 sophomore forward **Duane Lightfoot** (1.1 ppg, 1.0 rpg) and 6-5 junior **Rob Walls** (1.7 ppg, 1.1 rpg). Last season Walls, a junior college transfer, averaged 10 minutes, mostly at small forward. His minutes could increase now that he's had a year of indoctrination as to what's expected of a Butler player. He has huge hands (a la Connie Hawkins) and athletic moves but needs to work on his range. He could fill Jordan's role as defensive stopper.

Lightfoot, a lefty, might have to wait to find his niche on an experience-laden roster.

Lewis Curry (2.4 ppg, 0.6 rpg) is a 6-6 junior forward who was seeing playing time early before he hurt his knee. He'll try to get back in the mix. Two big men, 7-0 sophomore **Ben Grunst** (0.5 ppg, 0.4 rpg) and 6-10 junior **Mike Moore** (0.7 ppg, 0.5 rpg), will be battling for whatever minutes are left in the post by Robisch and Cornette. **Andrew Grunst**, a 6-8 forward, is the only freshman in the incoming class and won't be expected to have an impact.

The newcomer of note is **Mike Monserez**, a 6-5 guard who transferred from Notre Dame. Monserez, whose dad played at Butler, could help fill the niche vacated by Jordan at a shooting guard. He's got range and showed in practice last year that he has the necessary toughness to earn minutes at Butler. He is a sophomore and played in all 37 games as a freshman at Notre Dame.

The remainder of the backcourt roles are filled with proven veterans. Even after losing Jordan, this could be the league's best backcourt.

Senior point guard **Thomas Jackson** (13.0 ppg, 3.4 rpg, 4.4 apg) is a candidate for player-of-the-year honors. **Brandon Miller** (11.7 ppg, 2.5 rpg) was a huge contributor after transferring from Southwest Missouri State. **Darnell Archey** (7.8 ppg, 1.2 prg) will reprise his instant-offense role off the bench.

Jackson, a 5-9 senior, ran the Butler offense last year (137 assists/80 turnovers) in addition to being the leading scorer. That combination makes him the near-perfect point guard.

"Leadership is a process," Lickliter said, "and Thomas has earned that. He's earned his teammates' respect. Without a doubt, he could lead this team and wouldn't have to say a whole lot. He's very, very dependable and the other players respect him tremendously."

Miller, a 6-0 junior, led the team with 33.3 minutes per game last year. He can handle the ball and will probably be the point guard in 2002-03 after Jackson is gone. Miller hit .400 from three-point range and .809 at the free-throw line. His 98 assists and 43 steals further indicate that he is a complete player.

Archey, a 6-1 junior, is almost automatic at the free-throw line, with a league-best .952 mark. He also ranked among league leaders from three-point range at .424. He averaged 14.4 minutes and has long, long range, somewhat a surprise for his slight frame.

Nick Gardner (0.7 ppg, 0.5 rpg) is a 6-4 sophomore walk-on who appeared in 11 games last year.

The Bulldogs open the season in the Top of the World tournament in Alaska. Before they get into Horizon League play, they have to run a gauntlet of in-state rivals: Indiana State, Purdue, Evansville and Ball State, as well as an appearance in the Hoosier Classic.

Butler stepped up the tempo a bit under Matta and may do so again this year. The Bulldogs held (only) five opponents below 50 points last year, down from 10 the previous year. Seven opponents scored at least 70 points, up from four the year before. But at crunch time, in the championship of the conference tournament, Butler's defense was vintage in a 53-38 win over Detroit in which the Titans shot 24 percent from the field. The Bulldogs also went to Wisconsin and shut down the 10th-ranked Badgers, 58-44.

2001-2002 SCHEDULE

Nov.	16-18	#Top of the World Tournament
	25	Indiana State
	27	@Purdue
Dec.	1	Birmingham Southern
	3	@Lipscomb
	8	Evansville
	15	Northern Iowa
	17	@Mount St. Mary's
	19	@Ball State
	28-29	##Hoosier Classic

HORIZON

HORIZON LEAGUE

BLUE RIBBON FORECAST

1. Butler
2. Cleveland State
3. Detroit
4. Wisconsin-Milwaukee
5. Illinois-Chicago
6. Wright State
7. Loyola
8. Youngstown State
9. Wisconsin-Green Bay

ALL-CONFERENCE TEAM

G-Thomas Jackson, SR, Butler
G-David Bailey, JR, Loyola
F-Theo Dixon, SR, Cleveland State
G-Willie Green, JR, Detroit
F/G-Clay Tucker, JR, Wisconsin-Milwaukee

PLAYER OF THE YEAR

Thomas Jackson, SR, Butler

NEWCOMER OF THE YEAR

Cedric Banks, SO, Illinois-Chicago and Cain Dolabao, SR, Wright State

2001-2002 CONFERENCE TOURNAMENT

March 1-4 Goodman Center, Cleveland, OH

2000-2001 CHAMPIONS

Butler (Regular season)
Butler (Conference tournament)

2000-2001 POSTSEASON PARTICIPANTS

Postseason record: 5-3 (.625)
NCAA
Butler (Second Round)
NIT
Detroit (Final Four)

TOP BACKCOURTS

1. Butler
2. Cleveland State
3. Wright State

TOP FRONTCOURTS

1. Butler
2. Detroit
3. Cleveland State

INSIDE THE NUMBERS

2000-2001 conference RPI: 11th (of 31)
Conference RPI (last five years): 24-10-14-13-11

DID YOU KNOW?

The league has a new name and a new member. Formerly the Midwestern Collegiate Conference, the new moniker is the Horizon League. Youngstown State joins as the ninth member and third from the state of Ohio. Why did the league change names? The main reason was to avoid confusion with all those other "Mids"—the Mid-America and the Mid-Continent. Youngstown is a logical addition. The Penguins had scaled to near the top of the far-flung Mid-Continent, which stretched all the way to Southern Utah and Oral Roberts. Youngstown and Cleveland State should have no trouble kindling a Horizon League rivalry. ... Butler, still the cream of the crop, has its third new coach in three years. Thad Matta, who moved up when Barry Collier went to Nebraska, has gone to Xavier, winning MCC Coach-of-the-Year honors in his only season as head man. The Bulldogs' administration once again promoted from within, giving the job to Todd Lickliter. The league's other new coach is Bruce Pearl at Wisconsin-Milwaukee. The Panthers lost Bo Ryan to Wisconsin (Madison) after Rick Majerus and a couple other candidates declined to replace Dick Bennett. Pearl, who got his start with Dr. Tom Davis at Boston College, ran a Division II powerhouse at Southern Indiana for nine years and won a D II national championship in 1995. Pearl won't have to do a lot of recruiting this year. The Panthers don't have a senior. ... The Horizon Player-of-the-Year honor is a wide-open race now that two-time winner Rashad Phillips of Detroit is gone. Alas, the NBA apparently had too many questions about Phillips' size and he wasn't drafted. Thomas Jackson may have a difficult time standing out on a balanced Butler team, but any coach in the league would love to have him. Theo Dixon of Cleveland State is the best returning big man in the league and he'll make a run at the scoring title and player of the year. ... The race for newcomer of the year will be interesting as well. Cain Dolobao comes to Wright State from Dayton. Mike Monserez transferred from Notre Dame to Butler. Illinois-Chicago unveils three acclaimed high school signees who had to sit out last year. Cedric Banks was the Chicago Sun-Times City Player of the Year in 2000. ... Wisconsin-Milwaukee is still looking for its first NCAA Tournament bid. This year appears to be building toward 2002-03 when the Panthers will be loaded with seniors, have Colorado transfer Jose Winston eligible and plays host to the Horizon League Tournament in the Klotsche Center. ... Coach Rollie Massimino has improved Cleveland State's record for five consecutive years. He'll need 20 wins to make the same claim after this season. The Vikings got a head start in August when they toured Italy and Switzerland.

(M.S.)

Jan.	2	Wright State
	7	@Cleveland State
	10	@Detroit
	12	@Youngstown State
	17	Wisconsin-Green Bay
	19	Wisconsin-Milwaukee
	23	Loyola
	26	@Illinois Chicago
	30	@Wisconsin-Milwaukee
Feb.	2	@Wright State
	7	Detroit
	9	Cleveland State
	14	@Wisconsin-Green Bay
	16	Youngstown State
	20	@Loyola
	23	Ilinois Chicago
March	1-5	###Horizon Tournament

@Road Games
#Fairbanks, AK (vs. Radford first round; also Ole Miss, Wichita State, Delaware, Alaska-Fairbanks, Butler, Bowling Green)
##Indianapolis Classic (vs. Samford first round; also

Indiana, Eastern Michigan)
###Convocation Center, Cleveland, OH

BLUE RIBBON ANALYSIS

BACKCOURT	A
BENCH/DEPTH	B+
FRONTCOURT	A-
INTANGIBLES	B+

Lickliter becomes the third Butler head coach in three years, but his experience in the program should minimize the transition adjustment. So should the return of four starters who averaged at least 30 minutes a game.

Butler has a system and both Lickliter and the players know it backward and forward. The league may have a new name but Butler is still the team to beat. Jackson, Miller, Hainje and Cornette are proven iron men and Archey is a potent sixth man. If senior center Robisch regains his pre-injury form and stays healthy, and if Notre Dame transfer Monserez contributes as expected, the Bulldogs have all the bases covered. The first-round NCAA Tournament win over Wake Forest last year was no fluke.

Butler will be back in the Big Dance this year with a sixth consecutive 20-win season and should be feared.

(M.S.)

Cleveland State

LOCATION	Cleveland, OH
CONFERENCE	Horizon
LAST SEASON	19-13 (.593)
CONFERENCE RECORD	9-5 (3rd)
STARTERS LOST/RETURNING	2/3
NICKNAME	Vikings
COLORS	Forest Green & White
HOMECOURT	Goodman Arena (13,160)
COACH	Rollie Massimino (Vermont '56)
RECORD AT SCHOOL	70-75 (5 years)
CAREER RECORD	495-353 (28 years)
ASSISTANTS	Mitch Buonaguro (Boston College '77)
	Frank "Happy" Dobbs (Villanova '84)
	Paul Molinari (Villanova '90)
TEAM WINS (last 5 years)	9-12-14-16-19
RPI (last 5 years)	233-127-169-154-100
2000-01 FINISH	Lost in conference semifinal.

All those long bus rides on the Italian highways and cold-shooting nights in hot, suffocating gyms just might pay off with some benefits for coach Rollie Massimino's Vikings this winter.

On the face of it, Cleveland State didn't fare particularly well on its August tour, going 2-4 and laying enough bricks to prop up the Leaning Tower of Pisa for the next century. But Massimino has been around the block a few times and he knows how to put a positive spin on adversity and put the rest in perspective.

"We had a lot of fun over there," Massimino said. "We learned we've got a lot of work to do if nothing else.

"We learned we certainly have to defend better, and we have to rebound better, but those pro teams over there are very, very physical. And you've got to consider we were playing about every night, traveling, no air-conditioning. It was almost 105 degrees on the court at one game we played at 4 o'clock in the afternoon."

The environment will be more conducive back home in Goodman Arena, where the Vikings are shooting for a 20-win season with the knowledge that the Horizon League Tournament will be played on their homecourt.

Somewhere in December, Massimino should join the elite 500-victory club. He starts the season 495-353. This should also be the year he gets above .500 in his tenure with the Vikings. He is 70-75 in five years and has improved Cleveland State's win total in each of those five years. By last year, the Vikings finished 19-13, so keeping that impressive streak alive won't be easy.

"We're very proud of that [streak]," Massimino said. "We definitely have to hit that two-oh mark, but it will be hard because our schedule is very difficult."

Twenty wins is within reach, if, that is, Cleveland State can replace three key veterans—Kevin Ross, Doc Taylor and Anthony Jackson. None of the three were big scorers, but Ross and Jackson added muscle to the inside game and Taylor was capable of getting double-figures on a given night.

The Vikings won't be lacking for veteran leadership, though, in their quest to penetrate the stranglehold on the league's top two spots held by Butler and Detroit. Cleveland State was an impressive 10-4 in games decided by four or fewer points last year. One of those wins was a double-overtime 87-85 thriller over Florida State, the program's first victory over an ACC team.

Nobody was better at crunch time than **Theo Dixon** (18.0 ppg, 4.8 rpg), a 6-6 senior who will make a run at Horizon League Player-of-the-Year honors.

Dixon shot only .405 from the field, but was an impressing .794 at the free-throw line, an asset for an active offensive player. Consider some of his heroics: He swished a 15-footer, was fouled and completed a three-point play with 1.6 seconds to play to deliver a 63-60 win at Wisconsin-Green Bay. He hit a three-point shot with one second left to sink Loyola, 73-70. He hit another three-pointer with 18 seconds left that was critical in a 69-67 win over Detroit. In an early-season 57-55 win over Missouri-Kansas City, Dixon hit five treys, a career best.

"We expect him to be a go-to guy in a lot of ways," Massimino said, "as he was last year. We expect him to defend the other team's best player. He has to really come to the top of the ladder, so to speak."

Massimino wouldn't mind seeing Dixon hit for 18 points a game again this year, as long as he stays in the

team concept. Dixon launched 184 three-point tries last year, and this winter, Massimino hopes the Vikings will have a better inside presence that might reduce the long-range attempts.

The other senior leader is 6-1 guard **Jamaal Harris** (15.3 ppg, 3.4 rpg). Harris was even better in league play, averaging 16.4 points. Harris didn't shoot well in Italy, but the Vikings know what he can do. Harris handed out 71 assists last year, second on the team to **Jermaine Robinson** (10.6 ppg, 2.8 rpg), a 6-1 junior who ran the offense (84 assists, 73 turnovers) in his first season of eligibility.

Robinson launched 140 treys and hit a respectable .371 from behind the arc. Robinson missed the end of the season because of torn knee cartilage and was still limping a bit on the Italian tour. That didn't stop him from making five three-point shots in a seven-minute stretch as Cleveland State concluded the tour with a 79-75 win over the Italian junior national team.

"We're certainly counting on him, though," Massimino said. "He'll be back 100 percent. He's a very good ball-handler and can shoot fairly well for a point guard."

Robinson came out of the well-known Gratz High School program in Philadelphia. This year he'll be joined by former Gratz teammate **Percell Coles**, a 6-3 guard, who had to sit out last winter to get eligible, just as Robinson did in 1999-2000. Coles had a couple of double-figure scoring games in Italy.

"He's a legitimate two-guard," Massimino said. "He's a very talented young man. He just has to learn the system, and he has to learn to defend better."

The Vikings played at times last year with four guards. That might not happen this year often, but two freshmen hope to get in the mix. **Jack Higgins**, a 6-5 shooting guard averaged 16.0 points and 6.0 rebounds at Schenley High School in Pittsburgh, where he was the Pittsburgh Post-Gazette City League Player of the Year. **Walt Chavis** is a 5-11 point guard from Steelton, Pa. who played on a team that won multiple Class 3A state championships. Chavis has established that he can distribute the ball but isn't sure about his eligibility this winter.

Jerrod Calhoun is a 6-3 guard who came to school as an invited walk-on and isn't a bad player. He joins a cast of practice players—**Joe Rogers** (0.4 ppg, 0.2 rpg), **Paul Bosela** (0.0 ppg) and **James Henson** (0.0)—who hope for a little mop-up time.

When the Vikings look inside, **Tahric Gosley** (6.5 ppg, 4.8 rpg) and **Andre Williams** (4.2 ppg, 4.9 rpg) are veterans. Gosley, a 6-8 junior, is the third member of the Gratz High alumni club. His biggest contribution was a league-record 61 blocked shots last year. Gosley might be the Vikings' best overall athlete, in Massimino's opinion. At 6-5, Williams, a junior, isn't tall, but his .532 field-goal percentage last year indicates he choses his shots well.

The departed Ross was the leading rebounder (6.4 rpg) on a team that led the league in rebounding margin at plus-3.9 per game, thus Gosley and Williams need to improve their figures.

After Gosley and Williams, the elevation climbs significantly to a trio shrouded in mystery as to how much contribution can be expected. Sophomore **Pape Badiane** (0.9 ppg, 0.7 rpg), a 6-11 French import, appeared in 19 games last year as a freshman, but averaged less than four minutes per outing. He was only 5-of-12 from the field, but showed signs in the summer tour that he is ready to make more of an impact this year. How much, remains to be seen. He isn't going to score in double figures, but he could make a presence on the boards.

"He played well [in Italy] and got a lot more comfortable," Massimino said.

Freshman **John Rabb**, a 6-11 Cleveland product, sat out last year and wasn't able to practice because of academics. He runs the floor well for a big man and is comfortable facing the basket. The Vikings got their first look at him on the Italian tour. **Pete Ritzema** is a 7-2 center, who also sat out as a freshman, but was able to practice. He worked hard on improving his quickness and agility. Both are still projects.

"Ritzema needs to get quicker and Rabb needs to be more physical," Massimino said.

Tyler Reynolds is a 6-9 freshman from Athens, Pa., who hopes to get in the mix.

Massimino thinks the Vikings' schedule will be a challenge. There is a return game at Florida State and a date against tough Kent State in the Rock & Roll Classic in Gund Arena. Siena and St. Bonaventure, two teams Cleveland State lost to last year, are back on the docket. California will also pay a visit to Goodman Arena this year, giving the Vikings an incentive to claim a Pac-10 scalp to go with the one from the ACC they got last year.

2001-2002 SCHEDULE

Nov.	16	@IUPUI
	20	St. Bonaventure
	24	@Vermont
Dec.	1	Siena
	4	@Stony Brook
	15	Akron
	19	@Florida State
	22	Prairie View A&M
	27	Duquesne
	29	*Kent State
Jan.	3	@Loyola
	5	@Illinois-Chicago
	7	Butler
	10	Youngstown State
	14	Wright State
	19	@Detroit
	24	Wisconsin-Milwaukee
	26	@Wisconsin-Green Bay
	30	Loyola
Feb.	2	Illinois-Chicago
	7	@Wright State
	9	@Butler
	14	@Youngstown State
	16	Detroit
	21	Wisconsin-Milwaukee
	23	Wisconsin-Green Bay
March	1-5	#Horizon Tournament

@Road Games
*Rock-N-Roll Shootout, Gund Areana, Cleveland, OH
#Convocation Center, Cleveland, OH

BLUE RIBBON ANALYSIS

BACKCOURT	B
BENCH/DEPTH	C
FRONTCOURT	B-
INTANGIBLES	B

In Dixon, Harris and Robinson, Cleveland State has a strong nucleus. The flashy Dixon is a candidate to lead the Horizon League in scoring and push for player-of-the-year honors. Harris is a solid backcourt scoring threat who needs to cut down on his turnovers. Robinson ran the team reasonably well last year considering he was a rookie coming off an idle season.

Coles should be a worthy addition to the perimeter rotation. The Vikings need a stronger inside presence, but there are possibilities. Gosley and Williams are capable of boosting their numbers. Badiane looks like the best hope among the Triple Towers to make a meaningful contribution in the paint.

Cleveland State is one of a select few programs that can boast it has improved its win total each of the past five seasons. However, when you're up to 19 wins, keeping that streak alive won't be easy. It will be imperative that the Vikings keep winning the close games.

The Horizon League Tournament comes to Goodman Arena this year, preceded by three home games to end the regular season. The stage is set for a big finish. Second place in the league behind Butler is a niche Cleveland State could reach if enough factors fall into place.

(M.S.)

Detroit

LOCATION	Detroit, MI
CONFERENCE	Horizon
LAST SEASON	25-12 (.675)
CONFERENCE RECORD	10-4 (2nd)
STARTERS LOST/RETURNING	1/4
NICKNAME	Titans
COLORS	Red, White & Blue
HOMECOURT	Calihan Hall (8,837)
COACH	Perry Watson (Eastern Michigan '72)
RECORD AT SCHOOL	178-98 (8 years)
CAREER RECORD	178-98 (8 years)
ASSISTANTS	David Greer (Bowling Green '83)
	Mickey Barrett (Xavier '90)
TEAM WINS (last 5 years)	15-25-25-20-25
RPI (last 5 years)	151-36-44-131-70
2000-01 FINISH	Lost in NIT semifinal.

Every other coach in the Horizon League couldn't be blamed much for looking at Perry Watson and thinking,

"Hey, welcome back to the reality of not being able to hand the ball to the conference player of the year and say, 'Go run the show.' "

For the last two years, Titans point guard Rashad Phillips was a well-deserved conference player of the year. And in 1999, it was Jermaine Jackson winning the recognition. That makes a three-year run of Detroit point guards winning POY honors.

No more. Phillips is gone and the issue of who will replace him in the Detroit lineup is the million-dollar question. Fortunately for Watson, it's the only burning personnel question. Everybody else is back, except for reserve center Walter Craft, and the Titans are so deep in the post he won't be missed.

Detroit, even without Phillips, should be able to keep the heat on defending champion Butler. Last year, the Titans finished second to the Bulldogs in the regular season (by one game) and also in the conference tournament. The latter was a painful experience. With an NCAA bid on the line and a national ESPN audience watching, the Titans got shut down, 53-38, and had a miserable time, shooting .241 percent from the field.

Fortunately, an NIT bid offered some postseason redemption. The Titans went on the road for three consecutive wins, at Bradley, UConn and Dayton, to earn a trip to Madison Square Garden, where they lost in a semifinal. It all added up to a 25-12 record, Detroit's fourth consecutive 20-win season.

Replacing Phillips will take a committee. He averaged 22.5 points, dished out 145 assists and played 34 minutes a game. He was a deadeye at the free-throw line, hitting .910 percent and once making 49 in a row.

"One thing about having a little fellow like that," Watson said, "as good as he was, the other players felt they had to make some sacrifices because he sometimes had the ball in his hands the whole possession.

"If the shot clock was running down, he was the guy with the ball in pressure situations. A lot of times, that's a two-edged sword. Now with him gone, it gives the other guys a chance to step up and show what they're capable of doing."

One such guy is **Greg Grays** (8.9 ppg, 2.7 rpg), a 6-0 senior who made the league's all-newcomer team last year after transferring from Penn State. Grays brought a reputation as a guy who could score points in a hurry. He started 13 games and averaged 25 minutes, but, inevitably, deferred to Phillips while shooting only .370 from the field.

"Greg had a lot of physical problems last year," Watson said. "Then when he's trying to get in a rhythm, he's playing with a guy like Rashad—who is supremely confident—and Rashad figures, 'I can do it.' This year, Greg will be physically back on top and his consistency should be better. He'll be a big-time player."

When Phillips was hurt last year and missed the Central Michigan game, Grays stepped up with 26 points, seven assists and only one turnover. The question is whether he can play the point the majority of the game.

"He's done it before," Watson said. "But what he is, is a great shooter. So a lot of times you don't want him not doing the things he does well. There may be situations where he initiates the offense and then becomes a scorer when the ball comes back to him. We've got to make sure he's comfortable with that."

Another candidate is 6-0 junior **Jimmy Twyman** (1.2 ppg, 0.7 rpg). Twyman is more of a pure point, but didn't shoot the ball with authority last year (.340) and has only one college season behind him. Watson is a firm believer in the value of experience. **Bernie Fuhs** (1.3 ppg, 0.3 rpg) is a 6-0 junior who takes care of the ball well but doesn't generate enough of an offensive presence to get significant minutes.

"Greg and Jimmy Twyman are definitely in the mix," Watson said, "and there could be situations where **Willie Green** will have the ball in his hands because he's very good with the ball."

Green (13.2 ppg, 5.0 rpg) developed into the No. 2 scoring threat behind Phillips last year. The 6-3 junior demonstrated he's a well-rounded player at the shooting -guard position by hitting a .474 percentage from the field and handing out 80 assists. Green is another guy who will be looking for his shot more often now that Phillips is gone.

Darius Belin (4.6 ppg, 2.9 rpg) defended his way into the starting lineup last year, at Gray's expense. Belin, a 6-3 senior, is acknowledged by many as the toughest defender in the league.

"Darius is one of those guys coaches just love," Watson said. "He's like a Michael Cooper. Any perimeter guy we feel can cause us some problems, Darius does a great job, not only making life difficult for them after they get the ball, but making them work extremely hard just to get the ball."

On the offensive end of the court, Belin understands the system and plays within himself.

Another Titan cut from a similar mold is **Hilton Napolean** (1.6 ppg, 1.2 rpg), a 6-5 junior who expends a lot of energy on defense and scrapping for rebounds. Napolean is valuable because he can defend on the perimeter or go inside and guard a smaller post player.

Terrell Riggs (10.1 ppg, 6.5 rpg) is a 6-7 senior who holds down the power-forward spot. Riggs has improved every year and can pose match-up problems because he can step outside if the occasion arises. He's gotten better at putting the ball on the floor and could be poised for a big senior season. Riggs shot .520 from the field last year and joined Belin on the league all-defensive team.

One area Riggs needs work is at the free-throw line. A spotty shooter there as a sophomore, he fell off even more to .527 last year.

Once again, the Titans will be tall in the paint. Unlike some Horizon League teams, Detroit could be mistaken for an NBA team passing through an airport. **Mike Harmon** (3.6 ppg, 4.0 rpg) is a 6-11 senior who tag-teams with 6-10 Marc Mazur (3.6 ppg, 3.1 rpg). **Mark Maxwell** (2.6 ppg, 2.8 rpg) carries 290 pounds on his 6-8 frame. **Clark Headen** is a 6-9 red-shirt freshman who will be hard-pressed to get minutes as he continues to recover from knee surgery. Headen, in fact, has had two surgeries on the knee in question and didn't begin playing pickup games until August.

Mazur, who began his career at Division II Wayne State, wound up as the starter most of the time last season because he was the most complete package. He shot .639 from the field to lead the conference in that department, although he took only 91 shots.

"He continually gave us a presence, offensively and defensively," Watson said. "He's a very intelligent player."

Mazur, however, is an even worse free-throw shooter than Riggs, hitting only .460 last season. Harmon, a lefty, is more athletic. He blocked 46 shots and runs the floor well for a near-7-footer.

"He's more of a finesse player," Watson said. "This year, he could win the job."

Maxwell's challenge is getting in condition and keeping his weight under control. If he does that, he has the catch-and-shoot presence to be the best offensive weapon of the three big men. Watson would like to see what Maxwell could do playing at 280.

Detroit has depth elsewhere as well. **Thomas Dillard** (1.0 ppg, 0.6 rpg) is a 6-6 sophomore who could see action at small forward or shooting guard if he takes a step forward. Dillard was a touted recruit who struggled with the adjustment to the intensity of the college game. He reportedly had a good summer playing against tough pick-up competition.

David Baxter is a 6-3 red-shirt freshman who was a terrific shooter in high school, but finds himself stuck behind more experienced players for the moment. Watson thinks Baxter, whose dad was a star at Michigan, will be a valuable perimeter player down the road after he gets stronger.

Willie Wallace is a 6-6 forward who sat out last year after transferring from Central Michigan, where he averaged 6.4 points two years ago. He could find a niche giving Riggs a breather.

With Baxter and Headen both being red-shirted last year, Watson opted not to sign anyone in the last recruiting season. He'll have five seniors to replace after this year.

The Titans' search to replace Phillips will get national exposure early. Detroit plays Michigan State on Nov. 13 (ESPN) in the Preseason NIT. The Titans have won the last three games against the Spartans, but this will be the first meeting since 1997.

One thing is certain: The Titans will be tough to beat in Calihan Hall. Their 31-game home-court winning streak ranks fourth in the nation.

"The key for us is who emerges as our leaders," Watson said, "and our ability to keep improving. We've got a number of areas that have to be established because of the loss of Rashad."

2001-2002 SCHEDULE

Nov.	13	#@Michigan State
	24	Alabama A&M
	28	Wyoming
Dec.	1	Western Michigan
	3	@Eastern Michigan
	6	@Oakland
	9	@Maryland
	15	Toledo
	19	@Central Michigan
	22	@Bowling Green
	28-29	##Cable Car Classic
Jan.	3	@Illinois-Chicago
	5	@Loyola
	10	Butler
	12	Wright State
	17	@Youngstown State
	19	Cleveland State
	24	@Wisconsin-Green Bay
	26	Wisconsin-Milwaukee
	31	Illinois-Chicago
Feb.	7	@Wright State
	9	@Butler
	11	Wisconsin-Green Bay
	14	Loyola
	16	@Cleveland State
	18	Youngstown State
	23	Wisconsin-Milwaukee
March	1-5	###Horizon Tournament

@Road Games
#Preseason NIT (if Detroit wins, it will play Central Connecticut State or Oklahoma on Nov. 15 or 16; semifinals and final are Nov. 21 and 23 at Madison Square Garden, NY)
##Santa Clara, CA (vs. UC-Santa Barbara first round; also Santa Clara, UMBC)
###Convocation Center, Cleveland, OH

BLUE RIBBON ANALYSIS

BACKCOURT	B+
BENCH/DEPTH	B+
FRONTCOURT	B
INTANGIBLES	B

The adjustment to life after Phillips can't be minimized. The two-time conference player of the year is gone, and with him a ton of leadership, firepower and crunch-time savvy.

Coach Watson is hoping Grays can take the lead role in running the offense and still maintain his shooter's touch.

With four starters back, Detroit will be able to spread some of the load Phillips carried the last two years. Green and Riggs are proven quantities any team in the league would like to have in the lineup. Belin is a defensive stopper and the same journeyman cast is back to work the post-by-committee approach.

If Phillips' floor leadership doesn't prove impossible to replace, Detroit has the horses to stay in contention for the championship, certainly to hold on to the No. 2 spot in the pecking order behind Butler. But that's no small "if."

(M.S.)

Illinois-Chicago

LOCATION	**Chicago, IL**
CONFERENCE	**Horizon**
LAST SEASON	**11-17 (.393)**
CONFERENCE RECORD	**5-9 (6th)**
STARTERS LOST/RETURNING	**2/3**
NICKNAME	**Flames**
COLORS	**Navy Blue & Fire Engine Red**
HOMECOURT	**UC Pavilion (8,000)**
COACH	**Jimmy Collins (New Mexico State '70)**
RECORD AT SCHOOL	**66-78 (5 years)**
CAREER RECORD	**66-78 (5 years)**
ASSISTANTS	**Mark Coomes (Western Illinois '74)**
	Gene Cross (Illinois '94)
	Lynn Mitchem (Butler '83)
TEAM WINS (last 5 years)	**15-22-7-11-11**
RPI (last 5 years)	**157-34-241-234-164**
2000-01 FINISH	**Lost in conference first round.**

The winds of change are definitely howling at one Windy City college basketball program. Coach Jimmy Collins and Illinois-Chicago fans have been waiting for a year to finally cash in on the fruits of what was a banner recruiting class in 2000. Three touted recruits had to sit out a year to become eligible and another had to rehab from knee surgery.

Now that the Flames' version of a Fab Four is ready to suit up, the program has to recover from the loss of three veterans it hoped to have back. The Flames petitioned for an extra hardship season of eligibility for playmaker Joel Bullock (8.9 ppg, 126 assists), who had experienced health problems of his own earlier in his career, but the NCAA said no. Bullock, a member of the league's all-defensive team, will be missed for his leadership.

Academic woes claimed forward Maurice Brown (10.4 ppg), who last season was the leading rebounder in the conference at 8.4 per game. Grades also eliminated guard Taurus Cook (5.7 ppg), who made 13 starts.

"It's a big loss," Collins said. "Joel Bullock played more minutes than anybody else on the team. We thought we had a chance with the petition for the extra year. He had only played one full season and that was last year, but they didn't give it to him.

"Maurice will be a hard loss to make up and Taurus had started to play really well at the end of the year. They just didn't take care of their business. And then Dick Nagy, our most experienced assistant coach, retired. Those are four pillars in our establishment."

Illinois-Chicago is coming off an 11-17 season that was marred by too many close losses and health problems that sidelined two players. There are several problems to be addressed. The Flames ranked last in the conference in field-goal percentage (.398) and free-throw percentage (.653) and were next to last in scoring (67.9 ppg) and three-point shooting (.383). At the other end, Illinois-Chicago ranked next to last in scoring defense (71.5 ppg) and field-goal defense (.452).

An influx of new talent and the return to health of a couple of veterans might go a long way toward addressing those problems. Collins is cautious about putting too much pressure on the newcomers, but it's hard not to get excited, particularly about **Cedric Banks** and **Martell Bailey**.

Banks, a 6-3 wing man, was the Chicago Sun-Times City Player of the Year in 2000 after averaging 21.2 points and 8.4 rebounds at prep power Westinghouse High School. His signing with UIC was a coup, but one that had a delayed effect. He wasn't even able to practice with the team last winter.

"It was a good experience, knowing I had to sit out and I had to try my best in the classroom," Banks said. "I've done all of my work and now I have a 3.6 grade-point average."

What kind of numbers can he put up on the court after a layoff?

"Banks was a top 30 player in high school," Collins said, "and we're not talking state, we're talking nation. He has that Allen Iverson-type quickness. He scored 65 points in a summer pro-am league against some pretty good players.

"He's just a scorer. He's left-handed and he can start off looking like he's off-balance, taking a bad shot and it ends up swishing. But the thing he brings as a freshman is on the ball defensively, he's a tremendous player."

Bailey, a 5-10 point guard, was also an all-stater at Westinghouse. With Bullock gone, he could be running the Flames' offense sooner rather than later. He practiced with the team early last season, but then Collins pulled him off the court to concentrate on class work.

"He was a starting point guard on a Westinghouse team that won a lot of games and lost something like four [actually 132-3]," Collins said. "He definitely understands how to get other people involved."

Armond Williams, a 6-5 guard, is another good recruit from Chicago's Public League who sat out last year. He had to play intramural basketball in his down time. Collins thinks he will be a hard-nosed addition to the rotation.

"He'll dive on the floor and take charges," Collins said. "He's also very quick to the ball so I think he'll get a lot of rebounds. And he's quick enough to get on the perimeter and check people when we're pressing."

William Lewis, a 6-4 swingman, sat out last year for a different reason. He had ACL surgery after averaging 21.3 points and shooting .450 from three-point range in high school. Lewis might not be 100 percent yet, and has other players in front of him at the small forward position.

"I expect these guys to play," Collins said of his rookies-in-waiting, "but I'm always hesitant to put guys in the starting lineup [off the bat]. There's a lot of things you see guys do in pick-up games that once you start teaching in an organized structure, some of them don't do as well."

Collins is optimistic the Flames will be able to look in the paint for offensive production this winter. **Joe Scott** (10.4 ppg, 5.1 rpg) shared team scoring honors last year with the departed Brown. The 6-9 junior will be a perfect complement to 6-11 senior **Thor Solverson** (6.8 ppg, 7.0 rpg), who is back after missing all but four games last year because of a knee injury.

Solverson suffered a medial-collateral ligament tear on Nov. 29. He was able to return to practice by late in the season, but Collins took the cautious route and didn't play him.

"We could have taken a chance and probably won a few of those close games at the end," Collins said. "Physically he was OK, but when you have an injury of that sort, you have to heal mentally and he was very protective of that knee.

"Thor's in great shape now. He's running hard, hitting the weights and playing a lot of basketball. Maybe it was a blessing in disguise he got hurt because he's a better player than he was last year."

Collins would like to see Solverson score in double figures and average seven or eight rebounds. The 6-9 Scott has also been working hard in the weight room. An able defender and shot blocker, Scott also looks for his shot, which Collins loves.

"My philosophy," Collins said, "is that the way to the basket is through the post. If you get the inside people involved first, good things happen."

Providing depth inside are 6-10 sophomore **Jabari Harris** (1.8 ppg, 2.2 rpg) and a couple of newcomers. Harris is fluid, blocks shots and needs to play with more confidence on offense. **Josh Williams** is a 6-8 freshman who averaged 11.0 points and 10.0 rebounds at Chicago's Whitney Young High School.

"Josh is definitely going to get some time," Collins said. "He's had very good coaching in high school and he's working hard in the weight room. Once he gets stronger, he can really help us."

Kyle Kickert is a 6-8 wide body known as "the Beast" to his teammates. He sat out last year after transferring from league rival Wisconsin-Milwaukee, where he saw little action.

Cory Little (2.8 ppg, 3.0 rpg) is a 6-5 swing man who brings experience off the bench. Little, a senior, was rewarded with a fifth year of eligibility because he completed his degree after entering school as a partial-qualifier.

As for bolstering the weak perimeter shooting, maybe the best plan is to get the ball to 6-2 senior **Jordan Kardos** (9.5 ppg, 1.7 rpg) more often. Kardos shot .468 from three-point range on the season. He started 16 games, but missed the last five with an abdominal injury. The Flames lost their final two games by a combined three points.

"This is Kardos' fifth year and he's just a tremendous shooter," Collins said. "The ones that he didn't hit went in and popped out. He's always around the cylinder. I was surprised when he missed."

Jon-Pierre Mitchom (10.3 ppg, 3.0 rpg) is a 6-2 senior guard who started most of the season and played a variety of perimeter positions, including the point. He's a big-time athlete who went off for 33 points in a January game against Wisconsin-Milwaukee. His role this year could depend on how quickly Banks and Bailey fit in the rotation.

T.J. Mixson (2.1 ppg, 0.4 rpg) joins Solverson in returning from the injured list. The 6-3 guard started the final 10 games of the 1999-2000 season at the point, but played only nine games last winter because of heart complications.

Aaron Carr (5.6 ppg, 2.7 rpg), a 6-4 sophomore, got six starts as a freshman at a wing. He averaged 17 minutes a game, but Collins said with the newcomers on hand, Carr will have work to do to get than much court time this year.

"Aaron is definitely starting to understand the game better," Collins said, "but he's got to get more understanding of what we're trying to do and to see people better. He just has to put it all together and step it up a notch."

John Schneiderman (4.3 ppg, 0.9 rpg) is another perimeter option. The 6-1 junior made three starts last year and averaged 13.9 minutes. He needs to get his shooting percentage out of the 30s, but is clutch at the free-throw stripe (.808).

Collins thinks he will have a better substitution pattern this year, thanks to the influx of new faces. Even without Bullock, Brown and Cook, there is no lack of experience returning.

"What we can do is what I've always wanted to do," Collins said. "We can concentrate on defense more and get after people with the press. On offense, I think we can use our creative instincts more than we have in the past. We've got guys who can penetrate and shoot, and I think we've got some toughness.

"We've got a great combination of talent of size, talent and experience. It's just a matter of jelling."

2001-2002 SCHEDULE

Nov.	18	Indiana State
	21	St. Joseph's, IN
	27	Evansville
	29	@Southern Illinois
Dec.	1	@Old Dominion
	8	North Central
	15	Northern Illinois
	17	#@Purdue
	21-23	##Las Vegas Invitational
	28-29	###USF Holiday Classic
Jan.	3	Detroit
	5	Cleveland State
	10	@Wisconsin-Green Bay
	12	@Wisconsin-Milwaukee
	17	@Loyola
	19	@IUPU-Fort Wayne
	21	Youngstown State
	26	Butler
	28	Wright State
	31	@Detroit
Feb.	2	@Cleveland State
	4	@Youngstown State
	7	Wisconsin-Milwaukee
	9	Wisconsin-Green Bay
	16	Loyola
	21	@Wright State
	23	Butler
March	1-4	####Horizon Tournament

@Road Games
#First round Las Vegas Invitational
##Las Vegas, NV (schedule determined after first-round games; Pool 1 includes Georgia Tech, Illinois, Eastern Illinois, Pennsylvania. Pool 2 includes Iowa State, Saint Louis, Hartford, Southern Illinois)
###Tampa, FL (vs. Hofstra first round; also South Florida, Bucknell)
####Convocation Center, Cleveland, OH

BLUE RIBBON ANALYSIS

BACKCOURT	B
BENCH/DEPTH	C
FRONTCOURT	C+
INTANGIBLES	C

Illinois-Chicago was stuck on 11 wins for the second year in a row. An influx of new talent should be sufficient to push the total upward this winter. If Brown and Cook hadn't flunked out, and if Bullock had been granted a hardship year of eligibility, the Flames would have an enviable blend of talented veterans and potent newcomers.

Who knows? The formula could have added up to getting the program back to where it was in 1997-98 when it racked up 22 wins and an impressive RPI (No. 34). However, remove the above-mentioned veterans from the equation and the young studs will have to produce more and sooner.

Banks could be a threat for league newcomer-of-the-year honors and Bailey will probably take over the playmaking duties. If Kardos and Mitchom can provide perimeter scoring to complement Scott and Solverson inside, the Flames won't be the lowest-scoring team in the league again.

(M.S.)

Loyola

LOCATION	**Chicago, IL**
CONFERENCE	**Horizon**
LAST SEASON	**7-21 (.250)**
CONFERENCE RECORD	**2-12 (8th)**
STARTERS LOST/RETURNING	**3/2**
NICKNAME	**Ramblers**
COLORS	**Maroon & Gold**
HOMECOURT	**Gentile Center (5,200)**
COACH	**Larry Farmer (UCLA '73)**
RECORD AT SCHOOL	**30-53 (3 years)**
CAREER RECORD	**125-130 (9 years)**
ASSISTANTS	**Lance Irvin (Idaho '92)**
	Scott Spinelli (Boston University)
	Bill Wuczynski (UNLV)
TEAM WINS (last 5 years)	**12-15-9-14-7**
RPI (last 5 years)	**259-171-229-198-242**
2000-01 FINISH	**Lost in conference first round.**

Larry Farmer and long-suffering Loyola Rambler fans thought a talent upgrade would translate into a less-distasteful bottom line last year.

Unfortunately, the Ramblers' record tumbled from 14-14 in 2000-01 to 7-21 in Farmer's third season. Loyola finished the season with a seven-game losing streak and enters the new season with a 21-game road losing streak. The high-water mark was a solitary two-game winning streak over Eastern Kentucky and Saint Mary's in December. Once January rolled around, the Ramblers managed only two league wins and a non-conference victory over Belmont.

After another off-season of personnel turnovers, Farmer is back hoping for better chemistry and better results.

Loyola brought in six newcomers. This time around, five new players—and possibly a sixth—will replace five departures, only two of whom were seniors who played out their eligibility. Gone are seniors Schin Kerr, a veteran forward who was the No. 2 scorer at 13.3 points, and Wayne Plowman, a backup forward. Jerrell Parker (6.9 ppg), a starting two guard, transferred to Hartford. Hubert Radke (5.0 ppg, 3.3 rpg), a native of Poland who started 16 games in the post, got homesick and left. Terry Grant (7.3 ppg), a strong defender who made 10 starts in the backcourt, came up short academically.

Although he didn't plan it this way, Farmer faces yet another season of blending inexperienced players into the rotation and expecting at least a couple of them to play major roles.

For all the transition, Farmer has one stud to hang his hat on. Ironically, the smallest man on paper is the biggest Rambler on the court. **David Bailey** (17.2 ppg, 4.3 rpg), all 5-8 of him, had a breakout sophomore season. Now that Detroit's Rashad Phillips has finally moved on, Bailey becomes the league's resident "Little Big Man."

Bailey does it all. He obviously scores, but just as important, he averaged 6.1 assists per game last year. He hung 25 points on Michigan State and notched a career-high 35 against Belmont. He had 10 rebounds against Cleveland State, and 12 assists against Eastern Kentucky.

"He was all-conference as a sophomore and we expect him to improve," Farmer said. "Our defense this year will start with him. We're going to pressure the ball a lot more than we did last year.

"That will be David's role. It will be vital that he pressures the ball. So from that standpoint, more will be expected of him at that end of the floor. Of course, what he does offensively is why he's all-conference."

Asking more of Bailey on the defensive end could be detrimental to his offensive energy.

"We'll see," Farmer said. "He's going to have to concentrate a little more on the defensive end. If he truly wants to be a great player, I don't think he can be one-dimensional, especially because of his size."

Bailey shot a creditable .435 from the field, a tribute to his quickness and courage taking the ball into the paint. But he still needs to work on his three-point stroke. It boosted from .286 as a freshman to .328 last year, but there's room for improvement. Bailey is also hoping the strength he added through weight-room work over the summer will help him stand up to the physical defense that teams learned was effective against him as the year went along. Bailey played at about 155 pounds last year and could be up to as much as 160-165 as a junior.

Bailey played 33 minutes a game last year, with his primary relief coming from freshman **Jason Telford** (1.2 ppg, 1.1 rpg). The 6-2 Telford got 8.4 minutes a game last season and earned Farmer's praise for his off-season work ethic.

"He's relentless," Farmer said. "You almost have to be careful what you tell him to do. If you tell him to make 1,000 shots a day, he's going to make 1,000 shots every day."

Two newcomers could take some of the ball-handling burden off Bailey this year. Junior-college transfer **Vasilis Tsimpliavides** is primarily a shooter, but he's comfortable with the ball in his hands. "Vas" is a 6-3 native of Greece who played at North Idaho College last year. A clue to his instant-offense capabilities is the fact that he averaged 14.1 points in only 18 minutes a game. He also shot .410 from three-point range.

"He's got the gift," said Farmer. "He can really shoot the ball and he shoots it from anywhere."

The other newcomer who has more experience at the point is **DaJuan Gouard**, a 6-2 combo guard from Danville (Ill.) High School. Gouard averaged 19.8 points, 6.0 rebounds and 6.0 assists as a senior.

"When the smoke clears, he'll be a two guard," Farmer said, "but as a freshman, he'll have to play the one [point]. He's a great ball handler and passer who can defend. And he can shoot. We envision him playing the point some and moving David to the two spot."

Louis Smith (3.8 ppg, 1.3 rpg) finished last year starting at the two-guard spot. The 6-4 Smith was, predictably, inconsistent as a freshman, but Loyola likes his upside. He has a condor-like wing span, which is a good thing on defense. His comfort zone should expand this

year after a season of adjustment to the college game and his shooting percentages should rise from .319 overall and .266 from behind the arc.

"He ended up starting eight or nine games at the end," Farmer said, "because we really needed scoring and weren't getting it. We recruited Louis and thought he'd be able to come along slowly, but we had to push him in the lineup.

"He didn't respond well at first, but then he started to shoot it with confidence. He'll be an excellent jump-shooter."

With Kerr gone from the small-forward slot, the door is open for 6-8 junior **Cory Minnifield** (5.5 ppg, 3.2 rpg). A terrific leaper, Minnifield began to find his footing later in the season. Like Smith, he has a big upside to improve his scoring once he harnesses his moves.

"He had a great summer," Farmer said. "Word has it he got a broken nose and continued to play [in a pickup game]. That's definitely a step in the right direction for him. With Schin having graduated, he's got a great opportunity."

Ryan Blankston (5.9 ppg, 5.3 rpg) was a junior college transfer who carved a niche last year, starting 20 games at power forward. Though only 6-6, Blankston is a battler who doesn't mind mixing it up on the glass.

"Last year was a learning experience," Farmer said. "Juco guys have to make just as many adjustments as high school kids, but in most cases, they're put on the floor right away. He's worked hard in the off-season on his weights. He's a paint player, a banger. I think with a year under his belt he'll be more comfortable understanding his role and doing all the blue-collar things."

Jonathan Freeman (3.0 ppg, 2.2 rpg) is a 6-7 senior forward who has started here and there. He'll fit in as a reserve at both interior spots.

With Radke's decision to return to Poland, another European import's role becomes more important. Senior **Silvije Turkovic** (7.0 ppg, 5.5 rpg) stands 6-10 and has two years experience. Turkovic, from Croatia, has been a starter. Like many European big men, he is comfortable facing the basket on the perimeter. But with Radke gone, he probably has to become more of a conventional center.

That is, until **Reo Logan** gets eligible. Logan is a 6-11 Chicagoan who began his career at Miami but left after a semester and came home to Loyola. Logan could be eligible by mid-December if he gets his academics in order.

"We're cautiously optimistic," Farmer said. "We won't know until the end of the first semester.

"He's 6-11 so he obviously brings a very physical presence that can do a lot of different things to the game. He's got a nice medium-range shot and he's a good passer."

Three freshmen are being counted on to solidify the inside game. **Joe Evert** is a 6-8 forward from Wanamingo, Minn., where he averaged 12.6 points as a senior. Farmer compares him to a young Tom Chambers, who had a long career in the NBA. Evert was something of a steal for Loyola because he missed much of the early (2000) AAU summer season because of an injury.

"For 6-8, he's a terrific athlete," Farmer said. "He'll play the four for us and eventually some three."

Farmer went to Kirkwood, Mo., and signed a pair of identical twins, **Anthony Smith** and **Antoine Smith**. Anthony is the bigger at 6-9, and averaged 19.0 points as a senior. He could find his way into the lineup at power forward before the season is done. Antoine is 6-7 and averaged 13.6 points. He could play small or power forward.

"We liked Antoine first when we went to scout," Farmer said, "because with his ability to put it on the floor and shoot we thought he would be excellent in our system. Then his brother came in and was a big-time athlete and good rebounder and he had a little nasty in him. We were lucky to find out they wanted to go to the same place. We had the scholarships and the need."

The Ramblers need a scorer or two to step up and take some pressure off Bailey. Somebody has to knock down a perimeter shot. Loyola was last in three-point shooting last year in the league at a frigid .302.

"A lot of teams would pack it in and play David tough when he gave it up and then not let him get it back," Farmer said. "We didn't have that other player who could get 12 or 14 or even 18 on a good night.

"We played good enough defense. We could get open and just not be able to finish. I think we've addressed that in recruiting."

2001-2002 SCHEDULE

Nov.	17	@Marquette

	24	Northern Illinois
	29	Texas A&M-Corpus Christi
Dec.	2	@Central Michigan
	8	Maryland-Eastern Shore
	15	@Eastern Illinois
	18	@St. Mary's
	22	Chicago State
	29	@Illinois
Jan.	3	Cleveland State
	5	Detroit
	10	@Wisconsin-Milwaukee
	12	@Wisconsin-Green Bay
	17	Illinois-Chicago
	19	Youngstown State
	23	@Butler
	26	Wright State
	31	@Cleveland State
Feb.	2	@Youngstown State
	4	Wisconsin-Milwaukee
	7	Wisconsin-Green Bay
	9	IPFW
	14	@Detroit
	16	@Illinois-Chicago
	20	Butler
	24	@Wright State
March	1-5	#Horizon Tournament

@Road Games
###Convocation Center, Cleveland, OH

BLUE RIBBON ANALYSIS

BACKCOURT	B-
BENCH/DEPTH	C
FRONTCOURT	B-
INTANGIBLES	D

Loyola is again a team in transition. For the second consecutive year, Farmer has six newcomers to blend in, and when you're coming off a 7-21 season, at least a couple of them better make an immediate impact. Bailey is coming off a breakout season but he can't carry the Rambler offense by himself.

Returnees like Minnifield, Smith and Turkovic need to provide more help and Tsimpliavides better live up to his reputation for instant offense from the perimeter. If Logan gets eligible for the second semester, Loyola becomes more problematic for Horizon League opponents.

The stats make it clear what Loyola has to do to turn things around. The Ramblers ranked last in the league in scoring defense (76.6 ppg) and field-goal defense (.468). The most damning stat, though, was Loyola's 2-9 record in games decided by four or fewer points. This year, the Ramblers ought to be able to turn a few of those nail-biters the other way and get out of the league cellar. The program's first postseason bid since 1985, though, is still down the road.

(M.S.)

Wisconsin-Green Bay

LOCATION	Green Bay, WI
CONFERENCE	Horizon
LAST SEASON	11-17 (.393)
CONFERENCE RECORD	4-10 (7th)
STARTERS LOST/RETURNING	2/3
NICKNAME	Phoenix
COLORS	Green, Red & White
HOMECOURT	Brown County Arena (5,600)
COACH	Mike Heideman (Wisconsin-Lacrosse '71)
RECORD AT SCHOOL	101-74 (6 years)
CAREER RECORD	167-99 (10 years)
ASSISTANTS	Bob Semling (Wisc.-Eau Claire '81)
	Ben Johnson (Wisc.-Green Bay '92)
	Woody Wilson (Wisc.-Oshkosh '65)
TEAM WINS (last 5 years)	13-17-20-14-11
RPI (last 5 years)	166-100-121-152-159
2000-01 FINISH	Lost in conference first round.

Back on Jan. 22, the Brown County Arena was rocking and rolling. Wisconsin-Green Bay had just knocked off Butler, 69-68, for its sixth win in eight games.

The previous five wins had been stacked end-to-end over Gonzaga, Samford, Youngstown State, San Francisco and MCC rival Wisconsin-Milwaukee. Maybe the gloomy prognostications were wrong after all. Maybe a youthful Green Bay team would defy the odds.

Alas, that night was the Phoenix' high-water mark of the 2000-2001 season. Wisconsin-Green Bay won only two of its final 10 games and finished 11-17, the program's worst record since 1985-86.

On coach Mike Heideman's scorecard, there were too many days and nights of giving up 76 points here, 91 there, 78 over there. Take the home finale against Cleveland State as a microcosm of the season. The Phoenix scored 60, which should have been good enough to win by conventional UW-Green Bay defensive standards. However, the Vikings got out of Green Bay with a 63-60 win.

"As a team," Heideman said, looking to the new season, "we've got to become better defensively. That was my biggest disappointment coaching this group. I didn't think we made it difficult enough for people to score. And that's what we're about."

The Phoenix allowed "only" 63.0 points a game last winter, second-lowest in the league behind champion Butler's 60.3. Still, it was a significant—and fatal—increase from the year before when the Phoenix allowed only 57.8 points. As Heideman said, keeping the score in the 50s is what UW-Green Bay is all about. Along the same lines, the Phoenix finished only sixth in the eight-team league in field-goal defense as opponents shot a healthy .440.

For the first time since 1995, the Phoenix didn't have a player picked on the conference all-defensive team.

Part of the problem—a big part of the problem, in fact—was inexperience. Four freshmen played significant minutes last year, including two that started. It's difficult for a rookie to acquire the mental toughness and focus required to play vintage Phoenix defense.

"We were slow on the perimeter," Heideman said, "and we were playing young kids against some men and the men won. When you've got freshmen going against seniors, that's not what you want.

"Either we can learn from the tough times or we can be dumb. In my opinion, these kids want to be smart and put what they learned to good use."

For the offensively challenged Phoenix, the fact that leading scorer Chris Sager (11.8 ppg, 3.8 rpg) decided to transfer to UNC Charlotte after his freshman year isn't good news. However, to put a positive spin on it, UW-Green Bay might be better defensively on the perimeter with someone else in Sager's minutes.

With Sager gone, the leading returning scorer is **Mike King** (9.6 ppg, 3.6 rpg), a 6-8 junior power forward. King is a banger who isn't designed to lead a team in scoring but would be a nice complementary scorer. His sophomore year got only so-so reviews from Heideman because King was battling a persistent back injury. A member of the Canadian national team, King hadn't really gotten any break from basketball during the last couple of summers. However, this past summer, his back dictated that he take extended time away from the court.

"He worked with a physical therapist three times a week," Heideman said. "We'll have to see where we are and what we need to do in preseason to get him ready to play for us."

Joining King in the paint is 6-10 junior **Greg Babcock** (4.2 ppg, 3.7 ppg). Babcock was one of the most improved players on the team last winter and averaged 17.3 minutes a game. Now, he has to keep his upward spiral intact.

"Greg is one of the keys for us," Heideman said. "He's got to see if he can take it that next significant step and if he does we'll have a good post player. He needs to score better and he needs to make sure he impacts the game on the defensive end more than he did last year."

The Phoenix found another banger in junior-college transfer **Slaven Markovic**. The 6-8, 235-pound Markovic moved from Bosnia to Iowa in high school, teaming with Kansas guard Kirk Hinrich on a state-championship team.

Markovic then went to Southeastern Community College, and averaged 8.7 points and 5.5 rebounds last year.

"He's just a tough kid who competes and bangs around inside," Heideman said. "He really plays outstanding defense."

Kevin Hughes (2.0 ppg, 1.2 rpg) is a 6-7 sophomore forward cut from a different mold. A walk-on who earned a scholarship, Hughes has more of a finesse game and he needs to get stronger to play more than the 10.3 minutes per game he logged a year ago.

The leading candidate at the small-forward spot is 6-4 junior **Chancellor Collins** (4.8 ppg, 3.6 rpg). Collins is coming off a nice season in which he started five games and averaged 16 minutes. He can do more.

"He's probably our best athlete," Heideman said. "He really started to find out how he could impact games with his athleticism and became more confident as the season went on. My hope is he makes a huge step."

Aaron Shaw (4.4 ppg, 1.8 rpg), was one of the freshmen thrown into the mix last year. He averaged 14 minutes a game and shot 40 percent from three-point range. The 6-5 Shaw could really help the Phoenix by being consistent with his long-range stroke, but needs to tighten up on defense.

"He's our best shooter," Heideman said. "And that's one area we have to become much, much better. Aaron was a scorer in high school and he has that mentality."

Aaron Jessup (6.4 ppg, 3.4 rpg) is a 6-4 senior who got off to a great start last year. Then he hurt his ankle and took on a lesser role as Heideman opted for a youth movement. Jessup is sort of a wild card this year. He has the ability to get to the hole and could go out with a bang. **Ryan Mueller** (2.3 ppg, 1.8 rpg) is a 6-6 senior, who, like Jessup, can fit in several positions. Both Jessup and Mueller can win Heideman's heart by showing senior leadership.

Greg Monfre (4.2 ppg, 1.2 rpg) started 17 games as a freshman, running the point. His 49 assists don't sound like a lot, but they were tops on the team. He and **DeVante Blanks** (6.0 ppg, 1.2 rpg), a 5-10 senior, can handle the ball and run the offense. Blanks sometimes doesn't take over the ball until the offense is already in motion, but he has the quickness to make things happen. Monfre has worked on getting stronger in the offseason, Blanks on being more consistent with his scoring. Monfre and Blanks are both dependable at the free-throw line, each hitting 82 percent.

Gene Evans, who didn't figure to get many minutes at the point, transferred to Division II powerhouse Kentucky Wesleyan.

Derek Scheidt (1.9 ppg, 1.0 rpg) is a 6-3 sophomore who earned 8.6 minutes a game last year just by being a hard-nosed defender on the wing. A walk-on, Scheidt could earn even more minutes if he proves he can get a basket every now and then.

UW-Green Bay's major impact newcomer could well be guard **Calix N'diaye**, who probably has the distinction of being the only African-Norwegian playing college basketball. N'diaye is a 6-3 athlete who averaged 15.8 points on his club team in Norway last year while completing a year of military duty. His father is from Senegal and his mother from Norway and N'diaye grew up in the land of the Vikings.

"He's 20 years old," Heideman said, "and is a smart, complete player. He has great leadership, he can handle it, can shoot it a little bit and he can bring it to the rack. We view him as a player who will get substantial time as a freshman."

The only cloud over N'diaye is the NCAA's current crackdown on foreign athletes and whether they compromised their amateur status playing on club teams, particularly in Europe. The governing body of college sports is considering cases of more than 300 foreign basketball players and might levy penalties (sitting out games, etc.).

"We've submitted all the information and we're very hopeful," Heideman said.

The Phoenix have two other newcomers. One will help this year and one will have to wait. **Matt Rohde** is a 6-1 guard from Weyauwega, Wis., who was a prolific high-school scorer with more than 2,600 points. Rohde didn't play against the strongest competition and will have to develop as a defender. By 2002-03, Marshall Williams should be ready to help UW-Green Bay. The 1999 Wisconsin high school "Mr. Basketball" from Milwaukee Vincent began his career at North Carolina State, then transferred to Vincennes College, a strong two-year program. A high-caliber athlete, the 6-4 Williams will have to sit out this year and recover from knee surgery.

"We knew that when we signed him," Heideman said. All in all, it's a decent incoming class, with N'diaye and Markovic capable of challenging for starting jobs. When Williams gets healthy next year, the Phoenix will be more competitive on an athletic basis with the rest of the league.

"This year's freshman class alone are not conference champions," athletic director Otis Chambers told the Green Bay Press-Gazette. "But with these freshmen, with another class or two, we'll be right there."

When the hometown newspaper is quoting the athletic director, it usually means the head coach is feeling some heat. Heideman needs to get the program turned back in the direction when Dick Bennett was in Green Bay before he left for UW-Madison.

Heideman loses two starters, Sager and senior guard Paul Kraft, but no positions are guaranteed this year. King, if healthy, and Babcock are likely starters, but the other jobs especially are up for grabs.

"We're going to see what develops," Heideman said. "I'm not big on saying the positions are the one, two,

three, four or five. I'm more of a guy who finds the five best guys and then we'll see where they play."

2001-2002 SCHEDULE

Nov.	17	UMKC
	20	@Kansas State
	25	Northern Iowa
	27	Chicago State
Dec.	1	@Wisconsin
	8	@St. Bonaventure
	11	Eastern Michigan
	15	@Missouri-Kansas City
	22	@Evansville
	28-29	#Oneida Bingo & Casino Classic
Jan.	5	UW-Milwaukee
	10	Illinois-Chicago
	12	Loyola
	17	@Butler
	19	@Wright State
	24	Detroit
	26	Cleveland State
	28	Youngstown State
Feb.	2	@UW-Milwaukee
	7	@Loyola
	9	@Illinois-Chicago
	11	@Detroit
	14	Butler
	17	Wright State
	21	@Youngstown State
	23	@Cleveland State
March	1-5	##Horizon Tournament

@Road Games
#Green Bay, WI (vs. Boston University first round; also Lipscomb, UC Irvine)
##Convocation Center, Cleveland, OH

BLUE RIBBON ANALYSIS

BACKCOURT	C-
BENCH/DEPTH	C
FRONTCOURT	C-
INTANGIBLES	C

Wisconsin-Green Bay is coming off its worst record in 15 years in part because it paid the price of having to play too many youngsters too many minutes. Four freshmen were big contributors and the good news is that the three who return are sophomores who have been through the wars.

Another plus, unlike last year: The Phoenix will have more senior leadership this time around. That said, the Phoenix will have a tough time moving up in the conference standings unless several players make a significant offensive leap forward.

The only double-figures scorer last year, Sager, transferred. King is the only returnee who averaged more than 9.0 points, and a persistent back injury is a concern. Babcock, Collins and Shaw are three players who need to take their offensive game up a notch. N'diaye could be another offensive weapon who will boost the club's athleticism.

But UW-Green Bay isn't going to turn into a scoring machine and Heideman knows that the Phoenix could help itself tremendously by getting back on par at the defensive end. With a more veteran rotation this year, that's an achievable goal.

(M.S.)

Wisconsin-Milwaukee

LOCATION	Milwaukee, WI
CONFERENCE	Horizon
LAST SEASON	15-13 (.464)
CONFERENCE RECORD	7-7 (5th)
STARTERS LOST/RETURNING	1/4
NICKNAME	Panthers
COLORS	Black & Gold
HOMECOURT	Klotsche Center (5,000)
COACH	Bruce Pearl (Boston College '82)
RECORD AT SCHOOL	First year
CAREER RECORD	First year
ASSISTANTS	Tony Jones (Concordia '85)
	Ken Johnson (Albertson College '91)
	Ryan Swanson (Kansas State '89)
TEAM WINS (last 5 years)	8-3-8-15-15
RPI (last 5 years)	253-244-260-135-124
2000-01 FINISH	Lost in conference first round

It was a compliment to the University of Milwaukee-Wisconsin program when the big boys in Madison came and got their basketball coach last spring. It was also a blow, losing popular Bo Ryan to the Badgers just when he was getting the Panthers a foothold on the local sporting map.

The caliber of candidates interested in succeeding Ryan was also a compliment to the program. In the end, perhaps mindful of the success Ryan had managed stepping up from a Division III program (Wisconsin-Platteville), the administration had no trepidation in plucking Bruce Pearl out of Division II power Southern Indiana.

Pearl, a Boston College man and disciple of Dr. Tom Davis, has great credentials. He was 231-46 at Southern Indiana, bringing home an NCAA title to the Evansville school in 1995. He was ready to tackle his first D-I head-coaching job when Milwaukee came open.

"I saw a great league with great coaches, people that do it right, on and off the court," Pearl said. "I saw a great city, a great state institution. And I was attracted by the fact that it had never been done. This school has never been to the NCAA Tournament and had never had a winning record in Division I conference play.

"The greatest negative is following a guy like Bo Ryan, who was a great coach and a good guy. But I knew he'd have it positioned for success."

Pearl didn't take long to realize he'd made a good move. He loves the campus and the city. UMW won the conference all-sports trophy. Now if Pearl can only get men's basketball in the Horizon League's upper echelon. The Panthers went from 6-8 in league play to 7-7 last year, notching 15 wins for the second year in a row.

Pearl hopes to use Detroit as a model: "Perry [Watson] has done a marvelous job putting players from Detroit on his roster. Milwaukee has got good basketball and tough kids, both of which will fit our style."

Pearl has signed a Milwaukee athlete who wanted to come home, but 6-0 senior Jose Winston will have to sit a year after transferring from Colorado. The former Wisconsin "Mr. Basketball" will have one year of eligibility in 2002-03.

The Milwaukee product who had a big impact last year was sophomore forward **James Wright** (6.7 ppg, 6.2 ppg). Wright, who originally signed with Oklahoma, got his release and was able to play for the Panthers last winter. The 6-6 Wright is a warrior on the boards and plays hard-nosed defense. The only limitation is on offense.

"He loves to defend," Pearl said. "He is a few offensive skills away from being one of the better players in our league. He plays so hard and he wants to win."

Wright might be the most athletic player on the team and loves to block shots. Offensively, Wright has to continue to develop. Once outside of dunking range, his effectiveness falls off considerably.

The best all-around player on the team, as was the case last year, is 6-3 junior wing **Clay Tucker** (13.9 ppg, 4.4 rpg). On a team with no seniors, Tucker is the elder statesman, based on experience. The three-point shot is a viable weapon in Tucker's arsenal. Last year, he shot .407 from behind the arc, compared to .382 overall. He also blocked 23 shots and had 34 steals and is the team's most reliable free-throw shooter (.808).

"He needs to have a big year if we're going to step up to the upper division of the conference," Pearl said. "He's very physically capable of that. He has a pro-style body."

Dan Weisse (8.1 ppg, 2.6 rpg) runs the offense with a steady hand. Not flashy, the 5-11 junior is a gym rat who treats the basketball like an antique vase. He went through a six-game stretch last year without a turnover and played 11 turnover-free games on the season. Where Weisse runs into problems is defending the quicker point guards in the league.

"To fit our style," Pearl said, "he'll need to push the ball harder."

Pearl brings an up-tempo offense and a pressing defense. With a posse of veteran guards, he thinks the current talent will be able to adapt.

"I've got a team right now with eight juniors, including six junior guards," he said. "We've got guards who have played a lot of basketball the last couple of years. I think we've got the backcourt depth to play the way I want to play."

The 6-2 **Kalombo Kadima** (6.2 ppg, 3.3 rpg) is another junior guard and another Milwaukee public-league product. He's not spectacular in any phase of the game, but is physical enough and versatile. Kadima defends well and shot .431 from three-point range year.

"He's an athletic over-achiever," Pearl said. "He's strong as an ox, and can play anywhere from a two to a four. If you play him at the four, his shooting range will extend a defense."

Wright, Tucker, Weisse and Kadima are four returning starters. The fifth starter last year was center Chad Angeli (10.5 ppg, 4.2 rpg). The other loss was 6-9 center Mike Sowder.

Although Wright and Tucker appear to be certain starters, Pearl says all jobs are up for grabs.

"That's one of the great things about being a new coach," he said. "It's a whole new ball game. I wouldn't be surprised if the lineup changes because I've got no preconceived notions on how good these guys are. The strong will survive."

Jason Frederick (11.0 ppg, 2.5 rpg) is like a returning starter and is a candidate to crack the lineup this year. The 6-4 junior guard averaged 25 minutes and led the team in scoring in six games. Frederick has decent range (.374 from three-point range) and can take the ball to the basket. One of his best games was a 17-point effort in a 64-63 MCC Tournament loss to Wright State. When the Panthers need offense, Frederick is usually on the floor. Defense isn't his forte, but he improved last year and the result was increased minutes.

Ronnie Jones (6.4 ppg, 1.6 rpg) is yet another junior guard who earned 17.4 minutes last season, backing up the point and shooting guard spots. The 5-10 Jones started every game as a freshman two years ago and averaged 9.3 points, but was replaced at the point by Weisse last year. He is quicker than Weisse and is a better defensive match-up against quick play makers. His .317 mark from three-point range might have prevented him from playing even more.

Challenging Jones for the back-up point job is freshman **Chris Hill**, a 5-10 recruit from a strong Whitney Young High School program in Chicago. Another recruit from Illinois, 6-3 **Mark Pancratz**, will likewise challenge for a slot in the rotation. Playing the up-tempo game, Pearl likes to use as many as 10 players.

Pancratz gained notice leading his Schaumburg team to a surprising state title upset of NBA draft pick Eddie Curry's team.

"Mark was the best player on his team and Hill was probably the second-best point guard in Chicago," Pearl said. "They both come from great programs with great coaches."

Another recruit and possibly two are set to help Wright in the interior. **Adrian Tigart**, a 6-7 forward from Oshkosh, was a gift left over from Ryan's last signing class. Tigart is an all-stater who can score, handle the ball and pass, all attributes that should add up to significant playing time.

"I would say if you polled all the coaches in the state of Wisconsin and said, 'Which one player would you take out of this senior class?', I think it would be Adrian Tigart," Pearl said. "We hope he will not play like a freshman. He's strong enough to hold his own. I think he's got a chance to play a lot."

Derek Huff is a 6-8, 245-pound power player from Marshalltown (Iowa) Community College, whom Pearl was able to add in the spring. Huff was being recruited by several SEC schools, but a broken bone in his foot was a factor in him sliding to Milwaukee. Huff had surgery in the summer and it's still questionable when he'll be ready to contribute.

Last season, despite limited playing time, Huff averaged 10 points, seven rebounds and three blocked shots.

"He's never been healthy," Pearl said. "This is the second time he's broken his foot. We took a chance on him, but at this level, you have to take a chance to get this kind of player."

Three returning Panthers hope to carve out a niche in the frontcourt. **Justin Lettenberger** (3.1 ppg, 3.4 rpg) is a hard-nosed junior walk-on who hustled his way into 16 minutes a game last year. The 6-5 Lettenberger was out-muscled and out-sized at times, but found a way to hang on and played better than anyone expected.

Dylan Page (2.2 ppg, 0.7 rpg) is a 6-8 sophomore who played in only 16 games as a freshman because of a stress fracture in his foot. Page has a nice upside if he can get stronger and fare better in defensive match-ups with more physical post players. **Nathan Mielke** is a 6-11 sophomore center who was hurt all of last year. He had shoulder surgery and could get some minutes if he can stay healthy. On the thin side, Mielke has to prove he isn't injury-prone.

Ben Brey and **Will Ryan** (Bo's son) are walk-on guards who will help at practice.

Pearl inherits a schedule that includes Iowa State and Louisville, plus a trip to Madison to play Ryan's Badgers.

2001-2002 SCHEDULE

Nov.	17	Concordia-St. Paul
	21	@Western Michigan
	24	@Valparaiso
	30	#Tribune Cyclone Challenge
Dec.	1	#Tribune Cyclone Challenge
	4	@Chicago State
	7-8	##Jim Thorpe Classic
	15	Western Michigan
	22	Wisconsin-Parkside
	27	Wisconsin
	30	@Colorado
Jan.	5	Wisconsin-Green Bay
	10	Loyola Chicago
	12	Illinois-Chicago
	17	@Wright State
	19	@Butler
	21	@Lipscomb
	24	Cleveland State
	26	Detroit
	30	Butler
Feb.	2	@Wisconsin-Green Bay
	4	@Loyola
	7	@Illinois-Chicago
	9	Youngstown State
	14	Wright State
	21	@Cleveland State
	23	@Detroit
March	1-5	###Horizon Tournament

@Road Games
#Ames, IA (vs. Iowa State first round; also San Jose State, Nebraska-Omaha)
##Louisville, KY (vs. Louisville first round; also Virginia Tech, Murray State)
###Convocation Center, Cleveland, OH

BLUE RIBBON ANALYSIS

BACKCOURT	C+
BENCH/DEPTH	C
FRONTCOURT	D+
INTANGIBLES	C

Pearl brings a terrific track record from Division II Southern Indiana to follow in the footsteps of Ryan, who moved up to Wisconsin-Madison. Ryan had done a good job solidifying a wobbly program and building local interest. The Panthers set records for home attendance last year and lowered their RPI from 260 two years ago to 124 last year.

Pearl will speed up the tempo with full-court pressure and go 10 deep in the rotation. His system will be an adjustment for the players, but having six junior guards should help. Tucker, Kadima, Frederick and Weisse have plenty of experience. Tucker and Kadima, in particular, should be able to play the kind of defense Pearl wants.

The situation in the frontcourt is more iffy. Wright is a warrior, but one without a developed offensive game. The departure of senior Angeli leaves an offensive void. Page needs to take a big leap forward and recruits Tigart and Huff find an opportunity for immediate playing time.

This isn't the year the Panthers make their first NCAA Tournament, but they could have a winning conference record if enough chips fall the right way.

(M.S.)

Wright State

LOCATION	Dayton, OH
CONFERENCE	Horizon League
LAST SEASON	18-11 (.621)
CONFERENCE RECORD	8-6 (4th)
STARTERS LOST/RETURNING	2/3
NICKNAME	Raiders
COLORS	Hunter Green & Gold
HOMECOURT	Ervin J. Nuter Center (10,632)
COACH	Ed Schilling (Miami-Ohio '88)
RECORD AT SCHOOL	48-64 (4 years)
CAREER RECORD	48-64 (4 years)
ASSISTANTS	Will Rey (NE Illinois '76)
	Rod Foster (UCLA '83)
	Clay Nunley (Goucher '98)
TEAM WINS (last 5 years)	7-10-9-11-18
RPI (last 5 years)	265-185-255-222-122
2000-01 FINISH	Lost in conference semifinal.

Although this will be a very different Wright State team with a different style of play, first a word about last year. The Raiders jumped from 11 wins in 1999-2000 to

18 last winter, best at Wright State since 1992-93. The 9-1 start (the only loss was to South Alabama) was a school-best and an 8-6 conference finish was program's best in the MCC era.

"We did a lot of good things," coach Ed Schilling said, "and considering the strength of the conference last year, we had a real quality year."

One explanation for the improved results was that the Raiders returned virtually everyone from the previous season. That's not the case this time around. Forward Kevin Melson, an All-MCC first-teamer, and center Israel Sheinfeld, an All-MCC second-team pick, are gone. Melson, one of the league's premier players, ran out of eligibility, while Sheinfeld, a 25-year-old native of Israel, opted to pursue a professional career rather than play a final season in the college ranks. He signed his first pro contract with a Puerto Rican league.

The duo was the heart and soul of Wright State's inside game. Melson averaged a team-best 15.0 points and 6.4 boards. The 6-11 Sheinfeld was the No. 2 scorer at 14.7 points and averaged 6.0 rebounds. Sheinfeld was one of the few bona fide centers in the league and his departure means, in essence, the Raiders will more closely resemble their competition, relying on a smaller, quicker frontcourt.

"Hardly anybody," Schilling said, "played with a true center. In some respects, you're at a disadvantage at one end of the court playing a true center and at the other end you have an advantage. Our league is such a guard and speed league. We're going to play a lot differently than we did with Israel inside."

Now, there is one theme Schilling and Wright State would like to carry over from last year—the impact transfer. **Jesse Deister** (13.7 ppg, 2.5 rpg) proved last year that he knew what he was doing when he transferred from little Cedarville (Ohio) College to Wright State after the 1998-99 season. Diester, now a 6-3 senior guard, had to sit out a year but introduced himself to the MCC last year by winning league newcomer-of-the-year honors. He made .472 percent of his shots, including .413 from three-point range. He was deadly at the free-throw line, shooting .934, second-best in the league. He also snatched a team-best 37 steals.

"When he first came to me and talked about transferring, I told him I wasn't giving him a scholarship," Schilling said, "because I didn't want to give the appearance of taking players from local schools. He got his release and I still almost tried to talk him out of coming. I told him all I would give him is an opportunity as a walk-on.

"He took right up where he left off after sitting out the year. He broke the school record for consecutive free throws and hit the game-winning jump shot in the conference tournament (a 64-63 win over Wisconsin-Milwaukee). He's a big-time shooting guard with great range and he's very athletic."

The Raiders are excited about this year's transfer, which is actually a two-for-one brother act. **Cain Doliboa**, a 6-7 senior, has a year to play after transferring from the University of Dayton. His brother, **Seth Doliboa**, a 6-8 sophomore, transferred from Bowling Green with three years to play.

The brothers are from Springboro, Ohio. Cain Doliboa played 60 games in an injury-shortened career at Dayton, with 14 starts.

"He's a big-time shooter," Schilling said. "He was one of the top shooters in the Atlantic 10 Conference at Dayton. Seth is just a terrific athlete. He can play inside and outside, the three or the four, perhaps even the five if we go with a small lineup."

Cain Doliboa was averaging 9.7 points before an injury ended his 1999-2000 season at Dayton after seven games. Seth averaged 1.3 points in 17 games at Bowling Green two years ago.

"I had recruited Seth very hard at Springboro," Schilling said. "He had a good experience at Bowling Green, but he wanted to come back to Dayton and the opportunity to play with his brother is something he had always dreamed of. In high school they didn't play together because Seth was a late-bloomer. They had followed our program and liked what we were doing. I really think those two guys will help a lot."

Deister wasn't the only impact newcomer last year. **Vernard Hollings** (9.6 ppg, 4.9 rpg) lived up to billing with a solid year. Hollings, a 6-3 junior guard, had to sit out his first year to get eligible. That first year on campus, he and Deister had to be content with a winter of making practice Interesting.

"They dominated practice," Schilling said. "The second team beat the first team darn near every time."

So it was no surprise to Schilling to get the kind of production out of the duo that Wright State got last winter, with each averaging better than 30 minutes a game.

Hollings is a versatile player who can help at the point, the shooting guard or even at small forward. He started at the point most of last year and notched 108 assists and 33 steals. Schilling isn't sure where Hollings will be most needed this year. He's not a great outside shooter, but Schilling expects dramatic improvement on Hollings' .133 accuracy from three-point range.

"He's a good enough shooter that you have to guard him," Schilling said. "As he moved to the point last year, scoring became more of an afterthought, but his role is changing. We may use him to score more this year. He was a very good shooter in high school. And he's so strong. He can post up a point guard."

Hollings is adept at going to the basket, which usually means drawing fouls. It would be a shame if he didn't improve on his .540 free-throw mark.

Joe Bills (4.0 ppg, 1.1 rpg) is a 6-0 junior who is a veteran at the point and could start if needed. He started two years ago but settled into a sixth-man role when Hollings became eligible. Bills hit .422 of his three-point shots last season and is comfortable running the team. He played 21 minutes a game as a sophomore and was frequently on the floor in the late going.

Tyson Freeman (2.5 ppg, 1.1 rpg), a 6-0 junior, earned a scholarship and 10 minutes a game last year. Being a good defender and boasting a league-best .480 mark from three-point range, it's a wonder he didn't play even more.

The odd man out is Mark May, a former starter who decided to transfer after seeing his minutes decline. **Braden Bushman** (1.6 ppg, 0.7 ppg), a 6-5 sophomore guard, appeared in only 12 games last year, but Schilling likes his future.

"He's a kid we think will be good on down the line," Schilling said. "He's making the transition from a five [post] in high school to a two-guard in college. By his junior year, he'll be a key player for us."

Malcolm Andrews, a 5-10 point guard from Cincinnati, will be the only freshman. Considered in some circles the second-best point prospect in the state of Ohio last year, he probably won't see much action this winter as long as Hollings spends significant time at the point.

With Melson and Sheinfeld gone, plus big Bruno Peterson, who played 13 minutes a game, where will the interior scoring come from? Good question.

Thomas Hope (4.4 ppg, 5.6 rpg) is a 6-9 junior who started at power forward and averaged 25 minutes a game. In his first two years, Hope didn't have to think of himself as a scoring option. That changes now. It would be a stretch to project him as scoring machine, but he could approach double figures.

"He'll probably be our starting center," Schilling said. "He's put on about 40 pounds since he got to Wright State and he's probably our best rebounder in traffic. The thing about him is he's fundamentally sound. He boxes out and he's where he's supposed to be. When it comes to execution and fundamentals, he's a coach's dream."

Hope is also mobile. He even ran cross-country as a high schooler in Canada.

Ross McGregor, a 6-9 red-shirt freshman, will probably emerge as the backup center. He dedicated his red-shirt year to getting stronger. Rebounding is his strong suit and he can come off the bench and match up with a big post player.

Michael Doles (2.8 ppg, 1.4 ppg) is a 6-7 sophomore who's ready to take a big step forward. He averaged only 5.6 minutes in 16 games as a rookie, but with Melson gone, the door of opportunity is open.

"He really came on at the end of the year and had his best game in the conference tournament," Schilling said. "We've got high expectations for him."

The Raiders led the MCC in scoring (71.1 ppg), a huge jump from seventh the previous season. They also topped the league in field-goal percentage (.477) and free-throw percentage (.728). At first glance, the first two categories could be hard to match this season without Melson and Sheinfeld. On the other hand, Wright State will have a different look. so it's hard to say.

Hollings should move up to double figures. Hope will pad his average. Doles might make a significant leap from his freshman to sophomore year. The wild card is the Doliboas. If both turn out to be offensive options, the Raiders might pack plenty of punch.

Aside from Deister, Hollings and Hope, it's hard to say what the rest of the lineup will be. Bills, Doles and the Doliboas will certainly be in the mix somewhere, with Bushman, McGregor and Freeman also possibilities.

Wright State had the second-best rebound margin in the league last year, but will have its work cut out to be as strong a presence on the boards this year.

"That's our biggest concern," Schilling said.

The non-conference schedule is greased for another fast start. Michigan State, which pounded the Raiders, 88-61, last year, is replaced by Cincinnati as the bully on the pre-Horizon League slate.

"We feel good about our improvement and the direction we're going," Schilling said, "but in our league, it's going to be just as tough as it was last year. We [the MCC] were ranked 11th in the final computer ranking and it's going to be even better this year.

"Our backcourt is as good as anybody's, with Vernard and Jesse, and even if you put Joe Bills or Seth Doliboa in there, we're as good a backcourt as there's going to be in the league.

"We have the potential to have more firepower than we've ever had, but we also have a glaring need to improve our inside play."

2001-2002 SCHEDULE

Nov.	17	@St. Francis NY
	20	@Cincinnati
	24	IPFW
	28	Tennessee State
Dec.	1	@Miami OH
	5	@Morehead State
	8	@High Point
	11	Oakland
	15	Santa Clara
	20	Prairie View
Jan.	2	@Butler
	5	@Youngstown State
	12	@Detroit
	14	@Cleveland State
	17	Wisconsin-Milwaukee
	18	Wisconsin-Green Bay
	23	Texas-Pan American
	26	@Loyola
	28	@Illinois-Chicago
	31	Youngstown State
Feb.	2	Butler
	7	Cleveland State
	9	Detroit
	14	@Wisconsin-Milwaukee
	17	@Wisconsin-Green Bay
	21	Illinois-Chicago
	24	Loyola
March	1-5	#Horizon Tournament

@Road Games
#Convocation Center, Cleveland, OH

BLUE RIBBON ANALYSIS

BACKCOURT	A-
BENCH/DEPTH	B-
FRONTCOURT	C
INTANGIBLES	C

Wright State is a team in transition because of the departure of inside war horses Melson and Sheinfeld. The Raiders will become smaller, but quicker, which fits more closely with the style of play in the newly dubbed Horizon League.

Over the last two years, Wright State has clawed its way into being competitive in the league. But the Raiders need several players to make strides this year to avoid losing the ground they have gained.

With impressive rookie years behind them, Deister and Hollings are poised to give Wright State strong backcourt play. If the Raiders can hit the jackpot with newcomers—transfer brothers Cain and Seth Doliboa—for a second year in a row, good things are in store.

Another key is having Hope and Doles filling a void in the paint.

(M.S.)

Youngstown State

LOCATION	**Youngstown, OH**
CONFERENCE	**Horizon League**
LAST SEASON	**19-11 (.579)**
CONFERENCE RECORD	**11-5 (3rd)**
STARTERS LOST/RETURNING	**2/3**
NICKNAME	**Penguins**
COLORS	**Red & White**
HOMECOURT	**Beeghly Center (6,500)**
COACH	**John Robic (Denison '86)**
RECORD AT SCHOOL	**31-27 (2 years)**
CAREER RECORD	**31-27 (2 years)**

ASSISTANTS Eric Skeeters (Coppin State '97)
Andy Johnston (New Hampshire '87)
Gary Grzesk (WIsconsin-Green Bay '94)
TEAM WINS (last 5 years) 9-20-14-12-19
RPI (last 5 years) 277-137-199-248-176
2000-01 FINISH Lost in conference first round.

If you ever questioned the logic of why schools in Youngstown, Ohio, and Cedar City, Utah, played in the same league, worry no more. Youngstown State has abandoned the Mid-Continent League, and with it, torturous road trips to Southern Utah.

This season the Penguins become the ninth member of the Horizon League, a much more apt geographical fit. Still, while Butler and Detroit may be closer than Southern Utah and Oral Roberts, Youngstown coach John Robic knows his road trips aren't about to get easier any time soon.

"We moved up from the league ranked 22nd in the country to the 11th-ranked league in the country," Robic said. "I'm not going to miss that trip to Southern Utah, but I don't know if I'm looking forward to Butler and Detroit."

The Penguins challenged for the Mid-Continent title last year, finishing 19-11 overall, 11-5 in the league, and return three starters for their Horizon debut.

"That was a strange league to be in," Robic said. "There were no easy road trips. We played Thursday and Saturday, regardless, and you might get Chicago State and Southern Utah in the same swing. The travel would wear you out."

Looking around for a new home, Youngstown had two possibilities, the MCC (now the Horizon) or the Mid-America Conference. The MAC already had too many teams.

Now, the Penguins can build natural rivalries with Cleveland State, Detroit, Wright State and Butler, among others.

"It's a tremendous move for us," Robic said, "but it's going to take some time to get our program to the level where the upper echelon teams of the Horizon League are. I think our administration is aware of that.

"We made good strides in my two years here in the Mid-Continent, but now it's time to accept a new challenge. I'm realistic in knowing we could take our lumps, but it's like a new beginning. It's like I just got the job over again."

Robic, a former assistant to John Calipari at UMass, was able to prod the Penguins into what would have to be regarded as an overachieving year last winter. This year they will have to make do without MVP Craig Haese, forward Desmond Harrison and two other veterans who played key roles, center Dave Brown and forward Andrew Hannan.

Youngstown got good news on Aug. 9 when senior point guard **Ryan Patton** (10.6 ppg, 5.7 apg) was certified to graduate. Huh? As a freshman partial-qualifier in 1997-98, Patton was ineligible. However, taking advantage of an NCAA rule that rewards partials who earn a degree in four years, Patton gets that fourth year of eligibility restored. Thus, he can play this year.

The 5-11 Patton, who averaged 35.8 minutes a game last year, solidifies the Youngstown backcourt. In one six-game stretch of conference play last winter, Patton averaged 20 points, with a career-high 32 points in one outing.

"You're talking about a young man who really overachieved and had a terrific year," Robic said. "I believe he got snubbed on the all-conference team."

With Haese, and his 14.1 point average gone, the two-guard spot is open. Senior **Rafael Cruz** (10.1 ppg, 2.1 rpg) is the logical replacement. The Puerto Rico native was a big contributor last year off the bench after sitting out a transfer year from Massachusetts. The 6-2 Cruz is capable of improving his 30-percent mark from three-point range.

"Sitting out is always hard, so he had a pretty productive year," Robic said. "He can shoot the three and he can put it on the floor and create on his own. When we got him to slow down and not play at warp speed, he was effective. He's going to have to have a big year for us because we lost an all-conference player in Craig Haese."

If Patton hadn't gotten the extra year, **Marlon Williamson** (1.3 ppg, 0.7 rpg) would have been handed the point guard job. Williamson, a 5-11 senior, will now come off the bench and annoy people with his quick hands. He averaged only 4.3 minutes in 21 games last year and shot only 16 percent from three-point range.

"He's a terrific defender who has worked on his offensive game," Robic said. "He's got a good feel for the game. He's a good extension of me on the floor. We just have to keep him under control a little bit on the defensive side. He tends to put a little too much pressure on

the ball and gets in foul trouble."

Doug Underwood is an incoming freshman for whom Robic has high hopes. The 6-2 Annapolis, Md., product will bring quickness to the backcourt. He averaged 20.8 points as a senior. The backcourt depth was depleted somewhat when sophomore Brian Woodson left the Penguins after one year. **Bill Mallernee**, a 6-6 sophomore walk-on, will help in practice.

Depth is better elsewhere. **TeJay Anderson** (7.1 ppg, 3.8 rpg) was an impact freshman, moving into the starting lineup and averaging 22.7 minutes a game. The 6-6 Anderson is the best athlete on the team.

"He's been working hard on his perimeter game," Robic said, "to give himself another option how to score. He's got great knowledge of the game and good anticipation."

Stephen Flores (7.9 ppg, 5.4 rpg) followed Cruz' route last year. The 6-8 senior sat out in 1999-2000 after transferring from Pittsburgh, then made an immediate impact at Youngstown. He started and averaged 25.3 minutes a game.

"He didn't shoot the ball as well as he would have liked [.253 from three-point range]," Robic said, "but he scraps. He's not an explosive jumper. He's more of a step-out four man."

Patton, Cruz, Anderson and Flores project to give the Penguins four veterans in the starting lineup. The question is, who's the fifth starter?

One candidate is 6-10 **Jeff Ball** (0.7 ppg, 0.3 rpg). Ball, a junior-college transfer, appeared in only nine games a year ago, with primarily mop-up duty. He has worked on his strength but has a ways to go.

"I'm hoping he can give us eight points, six rebounds a game," Robic said. "That would be a good goal for him."

Khari McQueen (1.8 ppg, 1.2 rpg) could be the big man in the lineup—if he's not too big. McQueen, a sophomore, packs up to 300 pounds on a 6-5 frame. If he can get down to 270, Robic likes McQueen's chances of helping the Penguins.

"What's scary is he may be the second most athletic person on the team," Robic said, "but conditioning is a big factor. He did a good job losing weight last year, then injured his ankle and put the weight back on.

"He knows he has to be in better shape. He's athletic at 300, but at 270, he becomes a better athlete."

Virtually an unknown factor is **Sean Johnson**, a 6-8 transfer from Allegheny College in Maryland. Johnson had injury problems last year and didn't get much of a chance to show what he could do. A former all-city player out of Baltimore, Johnson needs to get stronger.

"He's athletic and he shoots the ball well," Robic said. "He'd be another person who could play at the four and maybe some three. He could not defend a center right now."

Two other freshmen will get a chance to help. **Jimmy Moore** is a 6-5 forward whom Robic recruited out of his old stomping ground, Worchester, Mass. **Brian Radakovich** is a 6-6 forward from nearby Steubenville (Ohio) High School. Radakovich averaged 20.1 points and 12.4 boards as a senior.

"Jimmy is hard-nosed and works his tail off," Robic said. "He's the type kid you love to have on your team. Brian is left-handed. I love his work ethic. He's a four man and we might get by using him a few minutes at the five. He's very skilled."

A fifth signee, 6-5 forward Kenneth Lampley of Gary, Ind., will have to sit out this year to get eligible.

Whether the Penguins are ready for their first foray into their new league remains to be seen. Robic preaches hard work and defense, which fits right in with teams like Butler, Detroit and Wisconsin-Green Bay.

"We pride ourselves on our defense," Robic said. "That's what you build on. We'll run when the opportunity is given but we won't force the break. We're organized with it. I want to give the players some freedom and they have it. But I want a little say on who takes the shots.

"We've got a lot out of our players these first two years, but none of these kids were signed with the knowledge that we were moving into a new league. Therefore, we're going to really have to overachieve. Now we're saying we're playing with the big boys, so we've got to go out and get some bigger players with bigger reps. But I just want guys who want to win. I'll take a little less skilled player who is a good person than a top-flight player. That's what I learned from John Calipari."

The Penguins got a taste of their new league last year. They lost a 54-53 heartbreaker to Detroit, which turned out to be the second-best team in the MCC. They also went to Wisconsin-Green Bay and lost in overtime.

In addition to the 16 Horizon League games, Youngstown has to play road games against several teams from its old league, part of what might be called

the divorce terms.

"I haven't dissected the new league yet," Robic said, "but they say everyone in the league is getting better. We have a heck of a climb. It's going to take some time."

2001-2002 SCHEDULE

Nov.	17	@Evansville
	20	Slippery Rock
	25	@DePaul
	29	@Valparaiso
Dec.	1	@Chicago State
	8	@Toledo
	15	Kent State
	19	Robert Morris
	22	@UMKC
	30	@Western Illinois
Jan.	2	Wisconsin-Milwaukee
	5	Wright State
	10	@Cleveland State
	12	Butler
	17	Detroit
	19	@Loyola-Chicago
	21	@Illinois-Chicago
	28	@Wisconsin-Green Bay
	31	@Wright State
Feb.	2	Loyola-Chicago
	4	Illinois-Chicago
	9	@Wisconsin-Milwaukee
	14	Cleveland State
	16	@Butler
	18	@Detroit
	21	Wisconsin-Green Bay
	23	IPFW
March	1-5	#Horizon Tournament

@Road Games
#Convocation Center, Cleveland, OH

BLUE RIBBON ANALYSIS

BACKCOURT	B
BENCH/DEPTH	D
FRONTCOURT	C
INTANGIBLES	C

Moving from the far-flung Mid-Continent to the Horizon League, the Penguins are stepping up in class, at least if the comparative RPIs are accurate.

Robic doesn't argue the point and says Youngstown will have to recruit on a higher plane to compete in the upper echelon of its new home. The Penguins made an impressive step last year, from 12 to 19 wins. But without Haese firing in jumpers, several other Penguins will have to step up their offensive game this year.

The backcourt looks set with Patton and Cruz, and Anderson and Flores will also start. But the fifth starter, presumably in the paint, remains a mystery. The Penguins will have trouble matching up on the boards with several Horizon opponents. This winter will be a learning process as Youngstown gets acclimated. There are dues to be paid.

(M.S.)

Brown

LOCATION	Providence, RI
CONFERENCE	Ivy
LAST SEASON	15-12 (.556)
CONFERENCE RECORD	9-5 (t-2nd)
STARTERS LOST/RETURNING	0/5
NICKNAME	Bears
COLORS	Seal Brown, Cardinal Red & White
HOMECOURT	Pizzitola Sports Center (2,800)
COACH	Glen Miller (Connecticut '86)
RECORD AT SCHOOL	23-31 (2 years)
CAREER RECORD	23-31 (2 years)
ASSISTANTS	Kevin Jaskiewicz (E. Conn. State '88)
	Andy Partee (Monmouth '92)
TEAM WINS (last 5 years)	4-6-4-8-15
RPI (last 5 years)	266-277-301-304-191
2000-01 FINISH	Won regular-season finale.

It's probably a safe assumption that no team in the country took its league by more surprise than Brown did last season.

The young Bears roared to 15 victories and their first winning season since 1986, finishing with just three fewer wins than they had in the previous three seasons combined. The stunning improvement allowed Brown to tie perennial power Pennsylvania for second place in the Ancient Eight, two games behind Princeton.

"We made some major strides, but I think taking the next step will be harder," said Brown coach Glen Miller, who orchestrated the turnaround in just his second season in Providence.

With an astounding 15 letter winners returning and a heralded recruiting class coming in, the Bears certainly have the personnel to contend again. Juniors **Earl Hunt** and **Alaivaa Nuualiita** also give Brown as potent a one-two combination as you'll find in the Ivy League.

"We play nine to 11 guys every single game and our practices are very, very competitive," Miller said. "We place a lot of emphasis on practice performance. It's very possible to go from the seventh or eighth guy into the starting lineup and it's very possible to go from the 15th guy into the rotation. It's also possible to get demoted."

One player who doesn't run much risk of a demotion is the multi-talented Hunt. With 993 points in two seasons, Hunt (19.7 ppg, 6.2 rpg, 2.5 apg, 1.4 spg) has scored more points than any sophomore in the history of the Ivy League. He already ranks 17th in all-time scoring at Brown and his 533 points last season were the sixth best single-season total in school history.

"He scores off the dribble, he can shoot the jump shot and he can post up inside," Miller said of Hunt, a unanimous first-team All-Ivy selection. "I don't know if I've ever coached a player that has worked on his game as hard as Earl."

The 6-4 Hunt, who can play any of the three guard positions in the Bears' system, has stepped up his game by improving his range. His consistency maxed out at 15-16 feet when he arrived at Brown, but last season he finished fourth in the conference in three-point shooting (.410) and third in overall field-goal percentage (.487). Hunt, who scored 20 or more points 15 times, also benefits from being able to invert and post up smaller opponents in Brown's motion offense.

"We have the flexibility in our system to take advantage of mismatch situations and we'll certainly do that with Earl," Miller said.

Though a bit undersized to play center, the 6-7 Nuualiitia used his athleticism to present his share of match-up problems for Brown opponents while earning second-team All-Ivy accolades. Nuualiitia (11.7 ppg, 7.9 rpg, 1.6 apg) owns a variety of post moves and led the league in shooting percentage (.588) while finishing second in rebounding.

"He has a great knack for knowing where the defense is," Miller said. "He can go around or go up and over."

Nuualiitia, who was a high school teammate of Kobe Bryant's at Lower Merion High School near Philadelphia, has also improved his outside shooting and is now more comfortable facing the basket and shooting from the outside.

"It's nice that he can step out and shoot it, but you don't want to take him away from the basket too much because that's what he does best," Miller said.

The improved play of senior point guard **Omari Ware** down the stretch was also critical to Brown's success last season. The 6-2 Ware (7.5 ppg, 3.2 rpg, 3.9 apg, 1.1 spg) averaged 10.8 points as Brown won eight of its last nine games.

"He's very, very quick baseline to baseline," Miller said. "If we get into an end-to-end game, he's most effective."

Although he started all 26 games he played in, Ware could be pushed for minutes or playing alongside another point guard this season. The Bears landed **Jason Forte**, the younger brother of Boston Celtics rookie and former North Carolina star, Joseph Forte. The younger Forte, 6-0, put up huge numbers (30.0 ppg, 10.0 rpg, 7.0 apg) at The Heights School in Maryland last season and will be difficult to keep out of the lineup.

"He's the type of point guard that I like," Miller said. "I like to have a point guard that can also score. He's athletic and he's explosive and he gets his nose right in the middle of things."

Another freshman, **Jordan Jhabvala**, also brings impressive credentials to Brown. Jhabvala (17.8 ppg, 5.0 apg) led Athens Drive High School in Apex, N.C., in scoring and was one of the top-rated prep point guards in the Tar Heel state.

Mike Martin, a 6-4 sophomore, returns as the starting two guard. Martin (6.5 ppg, 2.2 rpg, 2.0 apg) endured a bit of a shooting slump last season (.351 FG), but Miller expects the former three-sport high school star to make strides now that his focus is solely on basketball.

"His scoring output will improve and his shooting percentage will improve," Miller said.

Jesse Wood, a 6-2 senior co-captain, lends experience off the bench. Wood 6.6 ppg, 1.4 rpg, 1.0 apg) can open up things with his three-point shooting ability (.383)

and is a clutch player from the free-throw line at the end of games (.821), as evidenced by his ability to make three free throws with one second left to lift the Bears to a 60-59 win over Columbia.

Sophomores **Matt McCloskey** (1.6 ppg), 6-2, and **Ramel Carrington** (1.2 ppg, 1.2 rpg), 6-4, also return in the backcourt after seeing limited action last season.

There are also plenty of choices in the frontcourt in addition to Nuualiitia. The most experienced is 6-7 senior **Shaun Etheridge**, a three-year starter. Etheridge (9.0 ppg, 5.5 rpg, 1.5 apg, 1.4 spg) contributes in a number of areas and used his awareness to lead the team with 38 steals last season.

Miller is looking for some of last year's newcomers to step things up to help the Bears improve as a team. Sophomores **Jaime Kilburn** (3.3 ppg, 2.2 rpg) and **Patrick Powers** (3.1 ppg, 1.3 rpg) both have shown the ability to warrant consideration.

Kilburn, 6-5, became more of a contributor late in the season and, as an undersized power forward, gives Brown flexibility on defense.

"He can cover guards on the perimeter and is strong enough and quick enough to guard some post players inside," Miller said.

The 6-6 Powers has the ability to shoot from the outside and can also get to the basket. If improves his physical strength, he may warrant more playing time.

"He's athletic and knows how to create his own shot," Miller said. "Looks are deceiving. He doesn't look athletic, but he is."

Brad Simpson (1.6 ppg), a slender 6-8 sophomore,

added 11 pounds in the off-season and could work his way into the mix if he gets stronger.

Six-foot-six senior **Josh Meyer** (1.9 ppg), 6-5 junior **Brandon Howard** (3.2 ppg, 2.1 rpg) and 6-8 sophomore **Will Collier** (1.6 ppg, 1.9 rpg) also return at the forward spots.

Sophomore **Matt McCleggon** (1.6 ppg), Brown's tallest player at 6-10, had his season cut short by mononucleosis after eight games, but could develop with more experience.

The Bears will also have two freshmen in the frontcourt, **Nathan Eads** and **G.J. King**. Eads, a 6-8 forward/center, is a native of Ellicott City, Md. who played at the McDonough School (14 ppg, 8 rpg). King, a 6-7 forward, averaged a double double (19 ppg, 11 rpg) his senior year at Hinsdale (Ill.) High School.

IVY

BLUE RIBBON FORECAST
1. Princeton
2. Brown
3. Pennsylvania
4. (tie) Columbia, Harvard
6. Yale
7. Cornell
8. Dartmouth

ALL-CONFERENCE TEAM
G Earl Hunt, JR, Brown
G Ahmed El-Nokali, SR, Princeton
G Elliott Prasse-Freeman, JR, Harvard
F Craig Austin, SR, Columbia
F Ugonna Onyekwe, JR, Pennsylvania

PLAYER OF THE YEAR
Earl Hunt, JR, Brown

NEWCOMER OF THE YEAR
Edwin Draughan, FR, Yale

2000-2001 CHAMPIONS
Princeton

2000-2001 POSTSEASON PARTICIPANTS
Postseason Record 0-1 (.000)
NCAA
Princeton

TOP BACKCOURTS
1. Harvard
2. Brown
3. Princeton

TOP FRONTCOURTS
1. Columbia
2. Pennsylvania
3. Princeton

INSIDE THE NUMBERS
2000-2001 conference RPI: 28th (of 31)
Conference RPI (last five years): 15-20-26-28-28

DID YOU KNOW?
How's this for domination? The last team to win the Ivy League championship other than Princeton or Pennsylvania was Cornell, in 1988. ... Wisconsin ended Princeton's streak of leading the nation in scoring defense at 11 years. The Badgers allowed 56.6 points per game last season. Utah State (57.6) was second and Princeton (58.1) third. Columbia (58.9) was sixth. The Lions were seventh in field-goal percentage defense. ... Los Angeles Lakers star Kobe Bryant never went to college, but his high school, Lower Merion, is well represented in the Ivy League. Brown standout Alaivaa Nuualiitia, was a teammate of Bryant's and Cornell freshman Kevin Farley also attended Lower Merion. ... Brown's NBA connections don't end there. Freshman point guard Jason Forte is the younger brother of former North Carolina standout and Boston Celtics' rookie Joseph Forte. ... Former Cornell coach Scott Thompson, who resigned last summer because of health reasons, is still contributing to the program. Thompson is working in development at the University. ... Columbia's last Ivy League title came in 1968, the last year the Lions had a 7-footer (Dave Newmark) on the team. Incoming freshman Dave Bizgia is listed at 6-11, but some think he may be closing in on 7-feet. Could both streaks end this season? ... Dartmouth senior Flinder Boyd set the school's single-game assist record with 15 in a game against Holy Cross during his sophomore season. He increased the mark by one with 16 against Albany last season. Do we hear 17? ... Only three teams—Pennsylvania, Princeton and Harvard—have finished in the top four every season since 1996. The Crimson is also seeking a seventh straight season with a double-digit win total. If Harvard is successful, it will set a program record. ... Speaking of records, no player in the history of the Ivy League has scored more points in his first two seasons than Brown's Earl Hunt (993). ... With 360 assists in his first two seasons, Harvard junior Elliott Prasse-Freeman is more than half way to the league record of 611 held by 1987 Yale graduate Peter White. ...Yale's prized freshman Edwin Draughan played alongside Stanford recruit Josh Childress at Mayfair High School in California. ... Cornell, with an enrollment of 13,300, is the largest Ivy League institution. Dartmouth (4,300) is the smallest. Harvard, which was founded in 1636, is the oldest institution. Cornell (1865) is the youngest.

(S.B.)

2001-2002 SCHEDULE

Nov.	16-17	#Central Conn. Tournament
	20	@Northeastern
	24	Wagner
	28	@Providence
Dec.	1	@High Point
	6	@Holy Cross
	22	Stony Brook
	28	Rhode Island
	30	@Maine
Jan.	2	Army
	5	Navy
	7	US Coast Guard

	11	Cornell
	12	Columbia
	19	@Yale
	26	Yale
Feb.	1	@Harvard
	2	@Dartmouth
	8	Princeton
	9	Penn
	15	@Columbia
	16	@Cornell
	22	@Penn
	22	@Princeton
March	1	Dartmouth
	2	Harvard

@Road Games
#New Britain, CT (vs. Vermont first round; also Central Connecticut, Bucknell)

BLUE RIBBON ANALYSIS

BACKCOURT	A-
BENCH/DEPTH	B+
FRONTCOURT	B
INTANGIBLES	B

Ask any coach and they will tell you it is more difficult to stay at the top than it is to reach the top. Brown hasn't reached the top of the Ivy League yet, but the Bears are headed in the right direction.

Hunt and Nuualiitia have already established themselves as All-Ivy caliber players, so they won't catch any teams by surprise. Ware and Etheridge, both seniors, have been durable contributors throughout their careers, so the real key lies in how well and how many young players progress.

Martin, Powers and Kilburn could be keys and freshman Forte, the younger brother of Boston Celtics rookie Joseph Forte, could make an immediate impact.

"They'll make a major difference in whether we're able to take that next step," Miller said of his youngsters.

Hunt and Nuualiitia will do enough to keep the Bears in most games. If the underclassmen can contribute on a consistent basis, this season could mirror last, when Brown entered the final weekend with a chance at the league title.

(S.B.)

Columbia

LOCATION	New York, NY
CONFERENCE	Ivy
LAST SEASON	12-15 (.444)
CONFERENCE RECORD	7-7 (t-4th)
STARTERS LOST/RETURNING	0/5
NICKNAME	Lions
COLORS	Columbia Blue & White
HOMECOURT	Levien Gymnasium (3,400)
COACH	Armond Hill (Princeton '85)
RECORD AT SCHOOL	59-99 (6 years)
CAREER RECORD	59-99 (6 years)
ASSISTANTS	Bill Johnson (Nebraska '88)
	Walt Townes (Clark '84)
	Lyman Casey (Santa Clara '93)
TEAM WINS (last 5 years)	6-11-10-13-12
RPI (last 5 years)	284-239-265-238-258
2000-01 FINISH	Won regular-season finale.

Don't try using numbers and statistics to tell Armond Hill how good his Columbia basketball team will be this season.

The Lions return 12 letter winners, all five starters and Ivy League Player-of-the-Year Craig Austin, but that doesn't mean much to their head coach. They also feature Chris Wiedemann, possibly the best true center in the Ancient Eight, a class of seven experienced seniors and welcome back guard Treg Duerksen, a double-digit scorer in 1999-2000 who missed all of last season with a torn anterior cruciate ligament in his knee and stress fracture in his foot.

Convinced yet that the Lions are contenders for their first conference championship since 1968? Hill isn't saying, at least publicly.

"I'm not expecting anything," said Hill, who starred at Princeton in the mid-1970s and played eight seasons in the NBA. "Just show up, baby, and we'll take our chances."

There are two main reasons for Hill's cautiousness. The first is experience. If there is one thing his 35 years

in organized basketball has taught him, it's that you can't take anything for granted. The second is wisdom. The Lions suffered enough injuries last season that nobody associated with the team is naïve enough to think the dreaded bug can't bite again.

"The most important thing for us is to field a healthy team," Hill said.

That being said, the Lions will be contenders if they can avoid the infirmary. Their combination of experience, depth and talent should keep them within reach throughout the season.

Columbia also plays Princeton-like defense, which doesn't hurt.

"We have to," Hill said. "We don't possess a couple of 7-footers that are going to erase the mistakes we make."

The Lions finished second in the league (behind who else, Princeton) and sixth in the country in scoring defense (58.9 ppg) while finishing first in the Ivy League and seventh in the nation in field-goal percentage defense (.391). Ironically, Hill credits a Nebraska man, his top assistant Bill Johnson, for Columbia's defensive success.

"He's the one that has instilled that mentality," Hill said. "But the players, each and every one of them, are the ones who have bought into it."

Take Austin (18.4 ppg, 4.6 rpg, 2.3 apg, 1.4 spg) for example. The 6-6 senior led the conference in scoring in league games (20.1 ppg) and finished in the top 10 overall in steals and blocked shots (0.6 bpg). He is the first Lion to be voted Ivy League Player of the Year on his own.

"He's a tough kid that has made himself into a player with hard work," Hill said. "He plays both ends of the floor. Obviously, he's one of our go-to guys, but at the same time we ask him to defend."

Things will be even more difficult for Austin, who this seeason could become just the fourth Columbia player to be selected All-Ivy four times. In addition to being a player who opponents will build their defensive schemes around, he has been slowed a bit by tendonitis in his knee throughout the off-season.

"It was an honor for him to be player of the year, but now he's got a huge bull's eye on his back," said Hill, a unanimous choice as the league's top player in 1976.

Fortunately for Austin, Columbia has other targets. The biggest is Wiedemann, a 6-9 sophomore center who led the Ivy League in blocked shots (64) and made 64 percent of his field-goal attempts in league play. A youngster with a wide range of interests, Wiedemann (8.0 ppg, 6.3 rpg, 1.6 apg, 1.7 bpg) is a hard worker who will only improve as he continues to mature.

"If he ever commits himself to basketball, you don't know how good he can be," Hill said.

Senior forwards Joe Case, 53 career starts, and Mike McBrien, 50 career starts, also return with a wealth of starting experience. The 6-8 Case (9.2 ppg, 5.0 rpg, 1.4 apg) enters his third season as a starter after finishing second on the squad in both points and rebounds despite struggling (.344 3PT) to find the outside shooting touch he displayed as a sophomore (.421 3PT).

"Good things are going to happen to him because he puts the work in," Hill said.

The 6-7 McBrien (8.4 ppg, 3.6 rpg, 1.9 apg, 1.5 spg) missed nine games with injuries last season, but is a well-rounded player who makes those around him better.

"Our most versatile player is Mike McBrien," Hill said. "When he first came here as a freshman, he played center for us. Last year he was guarding two guards."

Marc Simon (0.9 ppg, 1.1 rpg), a 6-8 senior, and 6-3 junior Marco McCottry (2.0 ppg, 1.5 rpg) also return at forward. Grant Clemons, a 6-8 sophomore, missed all of last season with an ankle injury, but has a complete game and may be able to contribute.

The return of Duerksen (10.2 ppg in 1999-2000), a 6-3 shooting guard, is a three-point shooting whiz who should ease the offensive burden placed on Austin, Wiedemann and Case. Just as he is with his team, Hill isn't pinning overly ambitious expectations on his players.

"I just hope he gives us a lot leadership," he said of Duerksen.

Seniors Derrick Mayo and Victor Munoz give Hill two experienced options at point guard. The 6-1 Mayo (3.7 ppg, 2.9 rpg, 2.9 apg) is a dependable ball handler who delivers results—the Lions were 9-6 when he was in the starting lineup. The 6-0 Munoz (6.0 ppg, 2.6 rpg, 2.1 apg) started the first 26 games before missing the finale with a knee injury. He has been slowed with tendinitis, but Columbia hopes to have him ready to go at the start of the season.

Juniors Jaime Irvin and Egan Hill also return at

guard. The 6-4 Irvin (1.8 ppg) is a proficient shooter who showcased his skills by hitting three-of-four three-pointers for nine points at Villanova. The 6-3 Hill (0.5 ppg) also played in 17 games and is hoping to transfer his natural athletic ability into more success on the court.

Sophomore Maurice Murphy (2.7 ppg, 1.2 rpg, 1.0 apg), 6-1, saw action in 24 games last season. He has good shooting range and provides depth at the point. Jeff Peate, a 6-1 junior, sat out last season after transferring from Miami (Ohio) and is ready to play.

Having learned a lesson from all of last season's injuries, Hill and his staff brought in seven newcomers—six freshmen and a junior college transfer—this season. Not all will make an impact, but if Columbia gets something from two or three of them, it will be a bonus.

"We're not expecting them to come in and save the program," Hill said. "We're asking them to come in, learn and help out."

Center Dave Bizgia may be the most intriguing newcomer. At 6-11, the product of John F. Kennedy High School on Long Island gives the Lions added size on the front line.

The recruiting class also includes forwards Colin Davis, Jeff Kirkeby and Matt Preston and guards Jeremiah Boswell, Tito Hill and Allan MacQuarrie.

Davis, a 6-5 small forward, ranks second in career scoring at Notre Dame Academy in Green Bay, Wisc. Kirkeby (21 ppg), also 6-5, was one of the nation's best three-point shooters (.520 3PT) at Glendale Community College in Phoenix. Preston, 6-6, was the Nassau County (N.Y.) Player of the Year and All-Long Island twice at St. Mary's High School in Manhasset.

Boswell, a 6-4 shooting guard, scored more than 2,000 points at Pickens High School in Jasper, Ga. Hill, a 6-4 swingman, starred at St. Andrew's School in Florida and combines the grace of a guard with the power of a forward. MacQuarrie a 6-0 shooting guard, totaled 2,243 points in his career at Pine-Richland High School near Pittsburgh.

2001-2002 SCHEDULE

Nov.	16-17	#Pepsi Marist Classic
	20	Haverford
	24	@Providence
	27	Lehigh
Dec.	1	Lafayette
	5	@Army
	8	Boston University
	20-22	##Yahoo Sports Invitational
	27	@UCLA
	31	@San Diego State
Jan.	11	@Yale
	12	@Brown
	15	@Albany
	18	Cornell
	24	@Cornell
Feb.	1	@Princeton
	2	@Pennsylvania
	8	Harvard
	9	Dartmouth
	15	Brown
	16	Yale
	22	@Dartmouth
	23	@Harvard
March	1	Pennsylvania
	2	Princeton

@Road Games
#Poughkeepsie, N.Y. (vs. Northeastern first round; also Drexel, Marist)
##Laie, HI (vs. Brigham Young-Hawaii first round; also Buffalo, Montana, Navy, New Mexico State, Tulsa, Valparaiso)

BLUE RIBBON ANALYSIS

BACKCOURT	B-
BENCH/DEPTH	B+
FRONTCOURT	A
INTANGIBLES	B

If strength through numbers guaranteed success, the 2000-2001 Ivy League title would belong to Columbia.

The Lions return 12 letter winners and started the preseason with 21 players on their roster, but it's really not about what the Light Blue has, it's who they have. Austin, the Ivy League Player of the Year last season, leads a veteran group that has its sights set on the school's first Ancient Eight crown since 1968.

Austin, who was slightly hobbled by a knee injury in the off-season, does a little bit of everything, but can score from the inside, outside or off the dribble when his team needs it. Wiedemann should be among the league's top post players if he continues to develop and seniors Case and McBrien are proven performers.

The backcourt has two dependable point men in Munoz and Mayo and will get a tremendous boost if senior Duerksen can overcome an ACL injury and return to his old form.

The Lions were a stingy ball club last year, but need to do a better job of protecting the basketball (-2.0 turnover margin). Hill will need to establish roles early so all of the players on his roster, even the freshmen sent down to the junior varsity, know where they stand. It would also be helpful if the Light Blue could avoid the injuries of last season.

Columbia certainly has the talent and experience to be in the conference race. If they hold up physically, the Lions even have a shot at winning it.

(S.B.)

 **Cornell**

LOCATION	Ithaca, NY
CONFERENCE	Ivy League
LAST SEASON	7-20 (.259)
CONFERENCE RECORD	3-11 (t-7th)
STARTERS LOST/RETURNING	3/2
NICKNAME	Big Red
COLORS	Carnelian Red & White
HOMECOURT	Newman Arena (4,473)
COACH	Steve Donahue (Ursinus '84)
RECORD AT SCHOOL	7-20 (1 year)
CAREER RECORD	7-20 (1 year)
ASSISTANTS	Mike Burden (Rowan '95)
	Joe Burke (Ursinus '96)
	Izzi Metz (Hobart '98)
TEAM WINS (last 5 years)	15-9-11-10-7
RPI (last 5 years)	168-257-248-288-312
2000-01 FINISH	Lost in regular-season finale.

Steve Donahue placed a special order when Newman Arena, the home of Cornell basketball, was renovated over the summer.

Donahue, who made five trips to the NCAA Tournament during his 10-year tenure as an assistant at Pennsylvania, asked for a large, red-and-white mural bearing the words "Create The Future" to be painted over the entrance to the locker room. It's one of his ways of jump-starting a program that has suffered seven losing seasons in the last eight years and has not won the Ivy League since 1988.

"You can't worry about the past," said Donahue, who took over the Cornell program Sept. 6, 2000. "We're going to try and get this program where we want it to be and focus on the future and we want them to be reminded of that every day."

Cornell was almost forced to take things day by day last season. Donahue was hired after the July resignation of former coach Scott Thompson, who is being treated for colon cancer and is still employed by the university. Cornell played its first game Nov. 18, less than 10 weeks after Donahue came on board.

"It's not the way you plan it," Donahue said. "But, I think it was a great learning experience. ... I think it was rough on everybody—my players, my staff and myself. We had to go to war together and we survived, but we are much more comfortable now."

Cornell has just two seniors on its roster and returns eight letter winners, five of whom averaged less than three points per game. Donahue also welcomes a class of eight freshmen, including 6-10 freshman center **Chris Vandenberg**. Although the Big Red do not have a great deal of experience, Donahue's team is made up of players swho have the first quality he looks for when recruiting.

"Kids who have a passion for the game," Donahue said. "I think with the players that we have left and the new players we have now, that's what we have."

They also have played in Donahue's system for a year, so look for Cornell to apply more defensive pressure and play at a faster pace on offense, pushing the ball up the court and spreading the floor with four on the perimeter. This requires the outside players to pass, dribble and shoot well in order to be effective. You can also look for the Big Red to go deeper than they have in the past and use 10 or 11 players in most games.

Wallace Prather (8.1 ppg, 2.5 rpg, 2.3 apg, 1.7 spg), at 5-9, will be one of the biggest keys. It took Prather, who is entering his third season as a starter, time to adjust to Donahue's system last season, but once he did

the Big Red started to click.

"I'd like him to continue that progress," Donahue said. "I'd like to see him score in the open court, shoot it better and make the people around him better and I think he's capable of doing that."

Prather, a standout defender, needs just 136 points to become the 17th Cornell player to reach 1,000 and is 13 steals away from setting a school record.

Sophomore **Ka'Ron Barnes**, a 6-0 combo guard, brings his all-around game back for a second season on the East Hill. Barnes (10.3 ppg, 2.7 rpg, 2.1 apg, 1.3 spg) led all Ivy League freshmen in scoring last season and topped the Big Red in assists and blocked shots (five). He worked on becoming a more consistent jump shooter and ball handler in the off-season and should be the Big Red's most complete player this season.

"He's very, very consistent and very, very mature for his age," Donahue said. "He's someone who I think can be very, very good in our league. He's got all-league ability and attitude."

Jacques Vigneault, a 6-1 junior, will be looked to provide more minutes this season. Vigneault (2.2 ppg), a dangerous outside shooter, has attempted only two field goals from inside the three-point arc during his Cornell career. He could become a regular contributor if he continues to develop his defensive skills and becomes more adept at taking opponents off the dribble.

"You really have to guard him," Donahue said. "You can't leave him alone."

David Muller, a 6-6 junior, may also fit into the picture at shooting guard. Mueller (1.6 ppg) has good size and gets after it defensively. He also needs to be more effective closer to the basket, as 10 of his 11 field goals last season came from beyond the arc.

Senior **Pete Carroll** (0.7 ppg) also has a solid work ethic. The 6-0 Carroll has proven himself as a valuable contributor off the bench over the last three seasons and can provide valuable minutes behind Prather as well as leadership away from the floor.

Backcourt help could also come from freshmen— **Cody Toppert**, **A.J. Castro** and **Steve Cobb**.

Toppert, a 6-4 left-hander from Albuquerque (N.M.) Academy, put up big numbers in high school (24.3 ppg, 8.6 rpg) and should provide immediate help. He is a smooth outside shooter and determined young man.

"He really plays hard and can really score the ball," Donahue said. "He's a terrific shooter and the thing I really like about him is that he really competes."

Castro (18.7 ppg, 7.0 apg) was a Class 5A first-team all-state performer at Miami's Southwest High School. The 5-9 dynamo is considered Cornell's point guard of the future and will learn a great deal playing behind Prather. Castro has good quickness and a nice outside touch, but may be limited a bit by his stature.

Cobb (17.9 ppg, 7.3 rpg), a 6-4 combo guard, hails from Gonzaga High School in Washington, D.C. He has good athleticism and could develop into a valuable player over time.

The graduation of Ray Mercedes, the second-leading scorer in school history, leaves a hole in the frontcourt that will be difficult to fill.

Much of the responsibility will fall to junior **Jake Rohe**, the only Cornell player to start all 27 games last season. The 6-7 Rohe (7.7 ppg, 5.6 rpg, 1.3 apg,) more than tripled his scoring last season, but is more of a blue-collar player than someone who can carry a team on his back.

"He gets the most out of his ability and playing hard all the time," Donahue said.

Rohe will look to do more facing the basket this season and could see his statistics benefit from his hustle.

"He has the ability to help us in transition because he does run well, and he does all of the dirty work," Donahue said.

Beyond Rohe, the Big Red frontcourt may as well be known as the Big Green, because it has such limited experience.

Justin Gabler, a 6-9 junior, has seen limited action the last two seasons but offers plenty of potential. Donahue says Gabler (1.7 ppg, 1.6 rpg) is Cornell's most improved player since he arrived and is counting on him to produce this season.

"He's getting better and we're hoping he can give us valuable minutes up front," Donahue said. "He can score on the low block, he knows where he's supposed to be on defense and he makes the right decisions with the ball."

Brian Williamson, another 6-9 junior, could also contribute. Williamson (0.8 ppg, 1.0 rpg) has played in just nine games his first two seasons, but has a big body that allows him to be a presence in the defensive paint and on the glass.

Vandenberg, a native of Harley, Ontario, offers the

most hope for immediate help. He averaged a double double (16.0 ppg, 10.0 rpg) at Burford (Ont.) High School and chose Cornell over the likes of Illinois State and Richmond. Vandenberg helped Canada to a sixth-place finish at the World University Games in China over the summer.

"He's a terrific athlete," Donahue said. "He runs the floor, he plays extremely hard, is a good shot blocker and is developing as an offensive player. He also understands the game and knows what to do with the ball."

The same is true for incoming freshmen **Gabe Stephenson** and **Grant Harrell**, who are both three-point threats. The 6-8 Stephenson (15.1 ppg, 5.5 rpg), from J.K. Mullen High School in Denver, has the body of a power forward and a smooth touch, while Harrell (21.1 ppg, 8.3 rpg), from F.W. Buchholz High School in Gainesville, Fla., is a standstill shooter and active defender on the wing.

Kevin Farley and **Eric Taylor**, both 6-7 forwards, round out the freshman class. Farley (16.1 ppg, 7.5 rpg) attended Lower Merrion, the same high school as Kobe Bryant, and brings an athletic style of play from just outside of Philadelphia. Taylor (15.7 ppg, 8.6 rpg) attended Worcester (Mass.) Academy and spends most of his time within 15 feet of the basket.

"I love his work ethic," Donahue said of Taylor. "He's a no-nonsense guy, he works hard, defends well and plays with extreme enthusiasm, which I love."

Donahue also loves to challenge his team to improve, which is one of the reasons he scheduled road games at NCAA Tournament participants Syracuse, Notre Dame and Georgia Tech.

"I want to be able to continue to improve and hopefully when the league comes along we'll be ready," Donahue said.

With a full off-season to prepare under Donahue and a deeper talent pool, Cornell is already far ahead of last year.

2001-2002 SCHEDULE

Nov.	19	@Notre Dame
	26	@Bucknell
	29	@Syracuse
Dec.	1	Colgate
	3	Ithaca College
	5	Buffalo
	8	@Lafayette
	22	Lehigh
	28-29	#Spider Invitational
Jan.	2	@Georgia Tech
	5	Army
	11	@Brown
	12	@Yale
	19	@Columbia
	26	Columbia
Feb.	1	@Pennsylvania
	2	@Princeton
	8	Dartmouth
	9	Harvard
	15	Yale
	16	Brown
	22	@Harvard
	23	@Dartmouth
March	1	Princeton
	2	Pennsylvania

@Road Games
#Richmond, VA (vs. James Madison first round; also Richmond, VMI)

BLUE RIBBON ANALYSIS

BACKCOURT	B
BENCH/DEPTH	C
FRONTCOURT	C
INTANGIBLES	B

Donahue knows what it takes to build a winning program in the Ivy League. He also knows it doesn't happen overnight, or in most cases, within a year or two.

Donahue, a longtime assistant at Pennsylvania, is working hard to point Cornell in the right direction. One of his first tasks is to change the mindset of a program that has five Ancient Eight championships since 1902, the same number Penn won in his decade there.

"We've got to really believe in what we are doing and start something special here every time we walk on the court," Donahue said.

The attitude change is already under way, as is a talent upgrade. Cornell brought in eight freshmen this year and at least two—Vandenberg and Toppert—could play significant roles right away. The Big Red can also build around Prather, Rohe and Barnes.

Donahue wants to play 10 or 11 players and force the tempo. Almost any positive changes will be the result of better defense and patience on the offensive end, where Donahue would like to see his team improve its execution and make better passes to set up easier baskets.

Cornell is going about things the right way with Donahue, but with so many Ivy teams returning so much this season, it will probably take another year or two until the progress pays off with a significant jump in the standings.

(S.B.)

Dartmouth

LOCATION	Cambridge, MA
CONFERENCE	Ivy
LAST SEASON	8-19 (.296)
CONFERENCE RECORD	3-11 (t-7th)
STARTERS LOST/RETURNING	3/2
NICKNAME	Big Green
COLORS	Dartmouth Green & White
HOMECOURT	Leede Arena (2,100)
COACH	Dave Faucher (New Hampshire '72)
RECORD AT SCHOOL	116-146 (10 years)
CAREER RECORD	116-146 (10 years)
ASSISTANTS	Mike Maker (California Baptist '88)
	Jay Tilton (Hobart '92)
	Chris Leazier (Miami '92)
TEAM WINS (last 5 years)	18-7-14-9-8
RPI (last 5 years)	117-271-203-293-304
2000-01 FINISH	Lost regular-season finale.

Most people look at Dartmouth's roster and see a team loaded with underclassmen that returns just 31.6 points per game from last season.

Dave Faucher doesn't share that view. Faucher, the Big Green's coach, prefers to look at the ability of the players who are on his team, rather than the statistics they've posted in the past.

"The way that scouting services and coaching services evaluate teams is by calculating how many returning points a team has," Faucher said. "I don't think that's the way to properly judge this Dartmouth team because we have a talented group of sophomores who are working extremely hard along with a strong class of incoming freshmen.

"Time will tell how they fit in with our returnees. This year I'm looking for better shot selection, quicker ball movement and a game more suited for the interior."

Which is all fine and good, but the plain truth is the three starters Dartmouth lost leave major holes to fill in the lineup if the Big Green hopes to compete with the better teams in the Ivy League.

Scoring and rebounding are the top concerns. Dartmouth was last in the conference in both scoring (-6.1) and rebounding (-6.3) margins last season and lost its top two scorers and rebounders from that club.

Shooting guard Greg Buth (16.2 ppg, 4.1 rpg, 1.7 qpg, 1.5 spg) finished his Dartmouth career with 1,437 points, seventh most in school history. Center Ian McGinnis will be equally, if not more, difficult to replace. McGinnis (10.0 ppg, 9.6 rpg, 3.2 apg) led the league in rebounding and is the first Ivy Leaguer since Princeton's Bill Bradley (1965) to finish with more than 1,000 career rebounds (1,028). The Big Green suffered an additional blow when starting power forward Mark Kissling (8.5 ppg, 5.3 rpg, 1.3 apg) elected to forego his senior season to focus on academic pursuits.

With so many changes, Dartmouth will find comfort in the consistency of 5-11 senior point guard **Flinder Boyd**, who is entering his fourth season as a starter. Boyd (8.5 ppg, 2.2 rpg, 5.2 apg, 1.7 spg) is a true push point who breaks down defenses with his quickness and needs just 16 assists to become the Big Green's career leader.

"He's the whole package," Faucher said. "We're tough to press because he just accelerates through the defense. He's one of the quickest kids we've ever had here."

Vedad Osmanovic (8.8 ppg, 2.0 rpg), a 6-5 senior, is a talented offensive player who is expected to inherit Buth's shooting guard spot.

"He can really score," Faucher said. "He can put it down and he can create his own shot. He's just capable of doing some real good things on offense."

He will likely be backed up by 6-6 sophomore **Jordan Naihe** (0.4 ppg), who saw limited action last season.

Junior **Greg Friel** (1.6 ppg) knows Dartmouth's system well and could see action at both shooting guard and small forward.

"He's a good spot-up shooter who adds intensity," Faucher said of Friel.

There are many more questions up front, where potential far outweighs proven performance.

"I'm intrigued by the inside people," Faucher said. "We haven't had a real strong inside presence as of late."

Scott Klingbeil (1.1 ppg, 1.0 rpg), a 6-11 sophomore who played about five minutes per game last season, is the likely replacement for McGinnis at center.

"He's coming on and he's a talent," Faucher said. "He has some adjustments to make, but he has talent."

Brendan Herbert (3.0 ppg, 3.1 rpg), a 6-8 sophomore, and 6-9 freshman **David Gardner**, a strong offensive player from Hopkins High School in Minnetonka, Minn., could also be in the mix at center. **Jay Jenckes** (0.0 ppg), a 6-11 senior who played just 11 minutes last season, adds depth.

"I like the center position a lot, but we've still got to get some points and rebounds from it," Faucher said.

Charles Harris (6.4 ppg, 3.0 apg, 1.0 apg) could be the answer at small forward. The 6-7 junior was used as both a starter and sixth man last season and is considered the best athlete on the team. Harris, who took a year off after the 1999-2000 season, returned to form last year and was honored with the team's award for hustle, drive and determination at the postseason banquet.

Sophomore **Tyler Davis** (1.8 ppg), also 6-7, also owns a great deal of athletic ability and could emerge as a contributor on the wing.

Dartmouth's freshman class, which includes Gardner and four others, will go a long way in determining the success of the program this season and in years to come. Their range of abilities will present Faucher with several options as he pieces together his team.

"We have a lot of flexibility because of the talent of the freshman class," Faucher said. "We're kind of hoping someone steps up and surfaces as a player."

There are plenty of candidates, including **Michael McLaren**, a 6-5 swingman from Memphis University School in Memphis, Tenn. The 185-pound McLaren may not look imposing, but he has skills. He earned the most valuable player award at the Colonnade All-Star Camp in Birmingham before his senior season.

The Big Green adds depth at guard with **Steve Callahan** and **Michael Liddy**. The 6-3 Callahan (9.4 ppg, 2.2 rpg, 1.7 apg, 1.6 spg) earned first-team Greater City Catholic League honors at St. Xavier High School in Cincinnati and can also play shooting guard. The 6-2 Liddy is a point man from Lake Forest (Ill.) High School.

Brandon Smith, a 6-8 forward from Western Alamance High School in Elon, N.C., adds a bit of mystery to the mix. A talented athlete and dominating post player in high school, Smith could come in and be a contributor for the Big Green.

2001-2002 SCHEDULE

Nov.	16	@Binghamton
	20	Vermont
	24	@New Hampshire
	27	Holy Cross
	30	Lehigh
Dec.	11	@Boston University
	15	@Harvard
	19	@Quinnipiac
	21	@Colgate
	28-29	#Lobo Classic
Jan.	5	Harvard
	11	Pennsylvania
	12	Princeton
	18	Albany
	22	Hartford
Feb.	1	Yale
	2	Brown
	8	@Cornell
	9	@Columbia
	15	@Princeton
	16	@Pennsylvania
	22	Columbia
	23	Cornell
March	1	@Brown
	2	@Yale

@Road Games
#Albuquerque, NM (vs. Southeast Louisiana first round; also New Mexico State, St. Mary's)

BLUE RIBBON ANALYSIS

BACKCOURT	B-
BENCH/DEPTH	C
FRONTCOURT	D
INTANGIBLES	C

With just five upperclassmen on his 14-player roster, Faucher knows his freshmen and sophomores will play a great role in the success of his team.

Having lost his top two scorers and rebounders, Faucher will be leaning on several unproven players in the frontcourt. The Big Green does have size, and Faucher said they are committed to establishing an inside game. But it's uncertain who will carry the load and how well Dartmouth's young players will handle playing against some of the league's more experienced and talented teams.

In addition to finding scorers and rebounders, Faucher is looking for his team to play tighter defense and improve its ball movement to create better shots on offense. Team chemistry will play a great role in this because so many new and different players will be given opportunities.

Boyd has been a rock the last three seasons and his legacy may be helping the younger players develop so Dartmouth can become more of a factor in the conference in the coming years.

Osmanovic will fill some of the void left on offense, and Harris could be a consistent factor at small forward. Beyond that, nobody is sure what Dartmouth will get from its other players.

"We've got to do all of the little things that win games," Faucher said.

As well as a couple of big things, like score and rebound. Dartmouth has some young talented players, but will probably need to overachieve in order to avoid a third straight season with single-digit victories.

(S.B.)

Harvard

LOCATION	Cambridge, MA
CONFERENCE	Ivy
LAST SEASON	14-12 (.538)
CONFERENCE RECORD	7-7 (t-4th)
STARTERS LOST/RETURNING	1/4
NICKNAME	Crimson
COLORS	Crimson, Black & White
HOMECOURT	Lavietes Pavilion (2,195)
COACH	Frank Sullivan (Westfield State '73)
RECORD AT SCHOOL	111-150 (10 years)
CAREER RECORD	111-150 (10 years)
ASSISTANTS	Bill Holden (Bentley '90)
	Lamar Reddicks (Bentley '00)
TEAM WINS (last 5 years)	17-13-13-12-14
RPI (last 5 years)	130-207-237-272-231
2000-01 FINISH	Won regular-season finale.

When people talk about the pressure associated with Harvard, basketball isn't necessarily the first thing that comes to mind. Maybe it should be.

No team in the Ivy League comes after its opponents harder than coach Frank Sullivan's Crimson, a squad that forced a school-record 517 turnovers and led the Ancient Eight in turnover margin (+2.6) and turnovers forced per game (19.9) last season.

Bringing the ball up won't be much easier this season, even with all-everything forward Dan Clemente having graduated. Harvard returns its three starting perimeter people, all of whom finished in the top eight in the conference in steals, and doesn't plan on changing things much as it takes aim at a seventh consecutive finish in the top half of the league standings.

So, is it the system or is it the players?

"It's really the personnel," Sullivan said.

Team captain **Andrew Gellert**, the Crimson's only senior, is also the system's chief engineer. The 6-1 Gellert (7.5 ppg, 3.9 rpg, 3.0 apg, 2.8 spg) has excellent hands and finished first in the league and eighth in the country in thefts. With 179 steals, he is 34 away from becoming the school's career leader and he has also made himself into an opportunistic offensive player who can knock down open shots (.480 FG).

"He's probably one of the most respected players in the league because of his work ethic and leadership," Sullivan said. "He's effective and can beat people off the dribble."

So can junior guard **Elliott Prasse-Freeman**, who has led the league in assists each of his first two seasons and does it all. At 6-3, Prasse-Freeman (9.8 ppg, 4.3 rpg, 6.3 apg, 1.5 spg) is tall enough to see over defenders and quick enough to take them off the bounce.

With 360 assists already, Prasse-Freeman is on pace to surpass Yale's Peter White (611) and become the Ivy League's career leader. He also shares the school record for assists in a game with 15, something he has done twice.

But that's not all.

Last season Prasse-Freeman increased his scoring by 2.6 points over his freshman year. He also led the league in three-point shooting for much of last season before cooling off at the end (.379 3FG) and is only the second player in Harvard history to have more than 100 rebounds and 100 assists in a season, something he has done twice.

"He really works pretty hard at defensive rebounding," Sullivan said. "He does a good job defensive rebounding and getting himself near the rebound angle and he's very good at getting to long rebounds at both ends of the court."

The 5-11 **Pat Harvey**, also a junior, took an academic leave in 1999-2000 and returned with a vengeance after shaking the rust off last season. Harvey (13.8 ppg, 2.8 rpg, 1.8 apg, 1.7 spg) finished second on the team in scoring and second in the league in steals. A strong catch-and-shoot player, he also won three games for the Crimson in the final 10 seconds.

"He's a deadeye three-point shooter," Sullivan said. "He probably will take as many three-point shots as Dan [Clemente, 14 per season] took the last three years."

Junior **Brady Merchant** (5.7 ppg, 2.3 rpg, 1.0 apg) averaged 15.1 minutes per game last season and should be ready to contribute more. A long 6-4, Merchant plays solid defense and can stroke it from the outside.

"He's been an excellent complementary player and we have got to find a way to get him on the floor more than last year," Sullivan said.

Three freshmen—**Jason Norman**, **Kevin Rogus** and **David Giovacchini**—also join the backcourt ranks. Norman, a 6-3 wing from Bellarmine Prep in San Jose, Calif., has great jumping ability and quickness and could contribute immediately on both ends of the floor.

"He's a slashing, athletic guard and the type of player we haven't had for the last couple of years," Sullivan said. "He can go up around the rim and put back the basketball and he can drive it hard."

Giovacchini is a 6-1 combo guard from Salt Lake City, Utah whose older brother Tony is a senior guard for Stanford. Rogus, 6-4, is a catch-and-shoot guard who will add depth to the sharpest shooting three-point team in the Ivy League last season (.366 3FG).

Three-point shooting was just one of the many things Clemente, a two-time, first-team All-Ivy League player did well. Harvard's all-time three-point shooter with 220 and third-leading career scorer (1,484 points) led the team in both scoring (18.7 ppg) and rebounding (6.9 rpg) as a senior and will be difficult to replace. His athleticism and anticipation at power forward was one of the keys to the Crimson's pressure defense.

"We're going to have to learn to play without him, that's for sure," Sullivan said.

Clemente's departure leaves major questions in the frontcourt, but the return of senior **Tim Coleman** could make things smoother. The 6-8 Coleman averaged 11.9 points and 7.6 rebounds in 1999-2000, but took last year off. He is an inside presence and can shoot the three, and his level of play will be a key to Harvard's success this season.

Brian Sigafoos, a 6-11 junior, is also important. Sigafoos (6.8 ppg, 4.4 rpg) spent his freshman season on the Crimson's junior varsity team and progressed enough to start the final 12 games last season. He has a nice touch around the basket, as evidenced by his .632 shooting percentage, but needs to avoid getting pushed around in the paint. He averaged just 15.4 minutes last year, mainly because he was in enough foul trouble to be disqualified seven times.

Like many developing big men, his physical abilities alone offer plenty of reasons for optimism.

"He can run and catch and put the ball back in the basket," Sullivan said. "Just his mere presence around the rim helps us because he gets his hands on the ball."

Junior forward **Sam Winter** (4.3 ppg, 2.3 rpg) also has promise. The 6-6 Winter played well while starting 11 games for an injured Clemente two years ago and has packed some muscle onto his frame, which should make him more effective in the post.

"This is a big year for him," Sullivan said. "We are hoping for a repeat performance (of 1999-2000)."

Junior **Onnie Mayshak**, a 6-8 center, has a limited amount of starting experience. Mayshak (3.2 ppg, 3.0 rpg) split time with Sigafoos the first half of last year before losing the starting job. He has been a bit inconsistent and needs to rebound better, but has enough

physical ability to be a contributor.

Sophomore **Kam Walton** (0.0 ppg), the 6-8 nephew of the omnipresent Bill Walton, returns after a rather uneventful freshman season with hopes of working his way onto the floor.

Graham Beatty, a 6-8 freshman from Mundelein (Ill.) High School, rounds out the recruiting class. He has a good basketball body and a decent mid-range jump shot that could help him get some early time.

2001-2002 SCHEDULE

Nov.	16	Fairfield
	20	@Holy Cross
	24	@Lehigh
	27	Northeastern
Dec.	1	Stony Brook
	4	@Boston University
	8	Colgate
	12	@New Hampshire
	15	Dartmouth
	18	@Vermont
	21	Sacred Heart
	28-29	#Golden Bear Classic
Jan.	5	@Dartmouth
	11	Princeton
	12	Pennsylvania
Feb.	1	Brown
	2	Yale
	8	@Columbia
	9	@Cornell
	15	@Pennsylvania
	16	@Princeton
	22	Cornell
	23	Columbia
March	1	@Yale
	2	@Brown

@Road Games
#Berkeley, Ca (vs. California first round; also Penn State, Coppin State)

BLUE RIBBON ANALYSIS

BACKCOURT	A
BENCH/DEPTH	B-
FRONTCOURT	C
INTANGIBLES	B

Harvard is one of three Ivy League teams that have finished in the top four in the conference standings each of the last six years, so Sullivan must be doing something right.

The Crimson have just never (and we mean never) broken through and won the league. Their standout perimeter players give them a shot, albeit a three-point one, this year, but the lack of an established inside game at the start of the season could hold Harvard back.

You won't find a group of guards in the Ivy League better than Gellert and juniors Prasse-Freeman and Harvey. The trio keys Harvard's pressure defense and each one finished among the top eight in the Ivy in steals last season. Prasse-Freeman is one of the most complete players in the league and could be an emerging star. Norman could also provide immediate help and excitement.

"We've got some experienced players who have really distinguished themselves individually and that's a real plus for us," said Sullivan, who played high school basketball for Rollie Massimino.

The Crimson also have some real question marks in the frontcourt after the departure of Clemente, an all-league forward each of the last two seasons.

Coleman returns after a year away and Sigafoos is blessed with potential, but they'll both have to prove themselves first.

"Everything in the frontcourt is truly a question for us," Sullivan said.

With the level of play from top to bottom improving each season, the Crimson could finish almost anywhere. History says they'll be closer to first than last, but won't have quite enough to wear the crown.

(S.B.)

Pennsylvania

LOCATION	Philadelphia, PA
CONFERENCE	Ivy
LAST SEASON	12-17 (.414)

CONFERENCE RECORD	9-5 (t-2nd)
STARTERS LOST/RETURNING	2/3
NICKNAME	Quakers
COLORS	Red & Blue
HOMECOURT	The Palestra (8,700)
COACH	Fran Dunphy (LaSalle '70)
RECORD AT SCHOOL	206-122 (12 years)
CAREER RECORD	206-122 (12 years)
ASSISTANTS	Gil Jackson (Elizabethtown '69)
	Dave Duke (Villanova '74)
	John Krikorian (Pennsylvania '96)
TEAM WINS (last 5 years)	12-17-21-21-12
RPI (last 5 years)	153-125-58-75-210
2000-01 FINISH	Lost in regular-season finale.

To the surprise of absolutely nobody, the 2001 Ivy League championship came down to the final night of the regular season and a game between perennial powers Penn and Princeton.

And, also to the surprise of nobody (because it has happened 10 of the last 11 years), the team that won the first game was also victorious in the second.

This was not good news for the Quakers, who saw their bid for an Ancient Eight three-peat end with a 68-52 loss at Jadwin Gym. But just being there again was a testament to a Penn program that dropped its first eight games and entered Ivy League play with a 1-9 record.

Penn did a lot of growing up last season and, despite the loss of Lamar Plummer and Geoff Owens to graduation, that experience should serve the Quakers well this season with nine letter winners, including three starters, returning.

The Quakers, who suffered through their first losing season since 1997, will also receive a boost from eight newcomers, including junior transfer **Andy Toole**.

While last season may have been a transition year for the Quakers, this should be a transition year—literally. Look for Penn, which averaged just 66.4 points per game and shot .421 from the floor, to push the ball a bit more to force the tempo.

"We need to ply a little bit faster this year," Penn coach Fran Dunphy said. "We just got no easy baskets last season."

Many of those points should come from junior forwards **Ugonna Onyekwe** and **Koko Archibong**, both returning starters.

The powerful 6-8 Onyekwe (13.8 ppg, 7.4 rpg, 2.0 apg, 1.0 bpg) followed his Ivy League Rookie of the Year season in 1999-2000 with a solid year that earned him second-team All-Ivy accolades. The athletic Onyekwe, who honed his skills in Philadelphia's Sonny Hill League over the summer, is a strong defender with a good touch around the basket. His primary focus in the off-season has been improving his range.

"His shooting form is very good," Dunphy said. "Now we just need that thing to drop a little bit."

The 6-7 Archibong (10.0 ppg, 4.3 rpg) made strides last season and continues to refine his game, but needs to become a more consistent defender.

"He's getting better," Dunphy said. "We expect big things from Koko. He's a good shooter and very good defender. Hopefully he'll get better in all areas."

Andrew Coates, a 6-8 junior, and **Jan Fikiel**, a 6-10 freshman, back up Onyekwe at the power-forward spot.

Coates (0.5 ppg) has been limited by injuries his first two seasons. Fikiel, a native of Ulm, Germany, moved to Florida and starred at Westminster Academy in Fort Lauderdale. Fikiel (21.3 ppg, 8.8 rpg) is a good shooter and strong passer who led Westminster to a 29-2 record and was voted first-team all-state as a senior.

Jon Tross (0.2 ppg), a 6-7 senior, and 6-5 freshman **Greg Kuchinski** will push Archibong. Kuchinski is an explosive offensive player from St. Joseph's High School (Metuchen, N.J.)—the alma mater of Duke star Jason Williams—who scored 48 points against Woodrow Wilson (Camden, N.J.).

Although oft injured, Owens (9.6 ppg, 6.9 rpg, 1.4 apg, 1.5 bpg, .596 FG) was a presence in the middle and earned second-team All-Ivy last season. **Adam Chubb**, a 6-10 sophomore, is the likely successor. Chubb (3.7 ppg, 3.1 rpg) played in every game last season and shot .479 from the field. A heady player, he also is athletic enough that he earned second-team All-Ivy in the high jump at the Outdoor Hectagonal Championships.

"I don't know that any kid knows how to play the game better than Adam," Dunphy said.

Another high jumper, 6-9 newcomer **Nameir Majette** will also look for time in the pivot. Majette (9.0 ppg, 7.0 rpg) also won a state high jump title at Hertford County (N.C.) High School. **Conor Tolan**, a 7-0 freshman from Ireland, also could be in the mix at center. Tolan (14.0 ppg, 11.0 rpg) prepped at the Berkshire School in Massachusetts last season.

Penn, which struggled to find the proper balance between the frontcourt and backcourt last season, will face a similar challenge in 2001-02.

Junior **David Klatsky** (7.1 ppg, 4.1 rpg, 5.6 apg, 1.5 spg) settled into the point-guard role last season and finished second in the league in assists.

The 5-11 Klatsky needs to become a better playmaker and more consistent shooter (.406 FG), although it can be difficult for him to get open looks because of his stature.

The offense of Plummer (15.1 ppg, 2.7 rpg, 1.1 apg), who filled Matt Langel's role at shooting guard well during his only season as a starter and earned first-team All-Ivy honors, must be replaced. The 6-3 Toole transferred from Elon College (15.0 ppg) after the 1999 season and is the likely replacement for Plummer. He practiced with the team last season and has the ability to play either guard spot.

"We are very excited about Andy joining us on the court this season," Dunphy said. "He has already shown this team what he can do on the court, and his leadership and scoring ability will be a huge asset to us in the backcourt."

Another newcomer, 6-5 freshman **Tim Begley**, should also help right away. Begley (14.2 ppg, 6.5 rpg, 4.5 apg, 1.6 spg) led Christian Brothers Academy in Lincroft, N.J., to a 52-2 record during his two seasons as a starter while hitting more than 50 percent of his shots.

"He's a real good basketball player," Dunphy said. "There are probably guys that are better athletes that are not better players. He's a real good decision maker who can make shots."

Senior **Dan Solomito** (2.6 ppg), a 6-6 swingman, provided a spark off the bench last season and could fill a similar role this season. **Duane King**, a 6-5 junior, also returns after a disappointing sophomore year. King (3.3 ppg, 1.6 rpg) made great strides in the preseason, but missed the first two months of the season with a stress fracture and played nine games before suffering a season-ending knee injury. He has rehabilitated the knee aggressively and expects to be ready to return in October.

Sophomores **Jeff Schiffner** and **Charlie Copp** are also looking to take on increased roles. The 6-5 Schiffner (2.4 ppg, 1.3 rpg, 1.2 apg) has the ability to make plays and scored 15 points in a loss at Brown. The 6-0 Copp (1.7 ppg) is still developing his court awareness and decision-making abilities.

Two other freshmen, both 6-2, hope to find their roles. **Patrick Lang**, a combo guard from Atlanta, played in the state championship game in both of his last two seasons at Marist High School. Lang's team won the title his junior season and was runner-up last season when he was its leading scorer (20.0 ppg). **Mike Barker** (17.6 ppg, 7.0 rpg, 6.0 apg), a point guard from St. Joseph's Prep in Philadelphia, has strong leadership skills and will back up at the point.

2001-2002 SCHEDULE

Nov.	19	#@Georgia Tech
	22-24	##Las Vegas Invitational
	28	Drexel
Dec.	1	@American
	5	Villanova
	8	St. Joseph's
	22	Davidson
	30	@Temple
Jan.	5	@Lehigh
	7	Florida International
	11	@Dartmouth
	12	@Harvard
	17	Delaware
	21	Lafayette
	24	@LaSalle
	28	St. Joseph's
Feb.	1	Cornell
	2	Columbia
	8	@Yale
	9	@Brown
	12	@Princeton
	15	Harvard
	16	Dartmouth
	22	Brown
	23	Yale
March	1	@Columbia
	2	@Cornell
	6	Princeton

@Road Games
#Las Vegas Invitational, Las Vegas, NV (first-round game)
##Las Vegas, NV (schedule determined after first-round

games; Pool 1 includes Georgia Tech, Illinois, Eastern Illinois, Pennsylvania. Pool 2 includes Iowa State, Saint Louis, Hartford, Southern Illinois)

BLUE RIBBON ANALYSIS

BACKCOURT	B
BENCH/DEPTH	B
FRONTCOURT	B
INTANGIBLES	B

With six Ivy League championships in Dunphy's 12 seasons, you can never count Pennsylvania out of the league's title hunt.

Although not the overwhelming favorite they were while running off 48 straight conference wins in the mid-1990s, the Quakers certainly have the potential to contend this season. Toole, a transfer from Elon College, should step into a starting guard spot and pick up the scoring void left by the graduation of Plummer.

Klatsky is an effective point man and fellow juniors Onyekwe and Archibong are solid forwards whose best days are still ahead of them. Chubb is primed to take over as the starting center and guard Begley heads a strong crop of incoming freshmen.

Penn, as always, should be a solid defensive club and the offense should flow smoothly with a more-experienced Klatsky running the show. With seven players having competed in the Jersey Shore and Sonny Hill Leagues, the Quakers should be ready to hit the floor running.

"We need to do a better job of making plays," said Dunphy, who withdrew his name from consideration for the head coaching job at La Salle, his alma mater, in the off-season and decided to stay at Penn. "Our shooting has to improve and we need to make better decisions and better plays."

Once again the Quakers will be tested early, playing a difficult non-conference schedule that opens with NCAA Tournament participant Georgia Tech on Nov. 21. The competition should help prepare them for another strong run in the Ancient Eight, which will, once again, be a surprise to absolutely nobody.

(S.B.)

Princeton

LOCATION	Princeton, NY
CONFERENCE	Ivy
LAST SEASON	16-11 (.593)
CONFERENCE RECORD	11-3 (1st)
STARTERS LOST/RETURNING	1/4
NICKNAME	Tigers
COLORS	Orange & Black
HOMECOURT	Jadwin Gym (6,854)
COACH	John Thompson (Princeton '88)
RECORD AT SCHOOL	16-11 (1 year)
CAREER RECORD	16-11 (1 year)
ASSISTANTS	Mike Brennan (Princeton '94)
	Robert Burke (Haverford '88)
	Howard Levy (Princeton '85)
TEAM WINS (last 5 years)	24-27-22-19-16
RPI (last 5 years)	40-22-84-101-127
2000-01 FINISH	Lost in NCAA first round.

When John Thompson III was introduced as Princeton's new coach on Sept. 8, 2000, he was asked if his father, former Georgetown coach and Basketball Hall of Famer John Thompson, offered him any advice.

"He told me to win games," Thompson told the group gathered in the Class of '56 Lounge at Princeton Stadium.

In a season where numerous obstacles gave the Tigers plenty of reasons not to, Thompson's team pulled together and followed those words of wisdom to its 34th Ivy League championship.

Princeton's challenges began on Aug. 30, when Chris Young, a 6-11 center widely regarded as the best player in the Ancient Eight, decided to give up his final two years of eligibility in favor of a $1.65 million signing bonus to pitch for the Pittsburgh Pirates' organization.

Less than a week later, former coach Bill Carmody decided to leave Princeton and replace Kevin O'Neill at Northwestern. Thompson, at age 34, was chosen to lead the Tigers. Then, on the first day of classes, Spencer Gloger, who averaged 12.1 points and made 65 three-pointers as a freshman, decided to transfer to UCLA.

Just when you thought it couldn't get worse, there was more. Starting point guard **Ahmed El-Nokali** under-

went groin surgery and missed two months. Next, **Chris Krug**, the projected starter at center, decided to take a leave of absence from the team and then starting forward Eugene Baah left after 11 games.

The loss of any one of those people, let alone all of them, would rattle most programs, but it didn't even shake Princeton. The Tigers struggled early and entered Ivy League play with a 4-7 record, but won their first four conference games before losing by a point at Dartmouth on Feb. 9. With Princeton seemingly destined for another loss the next night, **Kyle Wente** made a desperation three-pointer at the buzzer to beat Harvard and spark a 7-2 closing run that ended with a 68-52 victory over Pennsylvania to clinch the conference championship.

Princeton advanced to the NCAA Tournament for the 22nd time and lost to North Carolina, 70-48, in the first round of the South Regional, ending a satisfying and successful first season for Thompson.

"It definitely was a pretty good year looking back at the situation as it played out," Thompson said. "It was a very, very good year and it was good to see our team grow. We were a real team at the end and we finished much better than we started."

Having accomplished so much under last year's difficult circumstances raises the bar even higher for the Tigers this season. Princeton loses just one starter, All-Ivy center Nate Walton, and there have been no surprise changes in personnel.

"Going into this year we have more of a feel for who's coming back and where we stand," Thompson said. "We are going to have a nice mix of maturity and youth.

"We have a freshman class that should increase our talent base and we have a good nucleus returning."

The core of that nucleus is El-Nokali (8.6 ppg, 1.9 rpg, 2.0 apg), a 6-4 senior and three-year starter.

"He is a very good ball handler who made strides as a scorer last season," Thompson said. "He's going to control the game for us and the ball is going to be in his hands. He's the head."

And Wente is the heart. The one picture from last season hanging in the basketball office shows his heroic three-pointer—a basket that changed the fortunes for both Princeton and Harvard.

"If that shot doesn't go in, who knows what happens?" Thompson said.

As dim as things looked for Princeton when Wente (8.0 ppg, 3.1 rpg, 2.0 apg, 1.3 spg) was forced to take his 25-foot heave, the outcome isn't atypical for the 6-4 junior, who can play either shooting guard or small forward.

"He's a basketball player," Thompson said of Wente, who played just 18 minutes as a freshman but was honorable mention all-league last season. "He just has a knack for making plays."

As do forwards **Konrad Wysocki** and **Andre Logan** and guard **Ed Persia**, each of whom played a critical role as freshmen last season.

"They all contributed," Thompson said. "They weren't just out there running around, they helped us win games."

The 6-1 Persia (5.5 ppg, 1.7 rpg, 1.5 apg, 1.2 spg) started 23 games and grew up a great deal. A standout quarterback and guard at Monsignor Kelly High School in Beaumont, Texas, Persia will be a better player and leader as he matures.

All of the changes forced the Tigers to lean on the 6-7 Logan (6.9 ppg, 2.8 rpg, 1.6 apg), and the former high school star proved to be durable, if not spectacular.

The 6-8 Wysocki (5.5 ppg, 3.7 rpg) started just one game but provided energy and solid minutes off the bench, often as an undersized center. The Tigers were 10-0 in Ivy League play when he played more than 20 minutes and he was voted the league's Rookie of the Year.

"He's just a competitor," Thompson said. "He's a worker."

Mike Bechtold (8.5 ppg, 2.4 rpg), a 6-6 senior forward, was slowed by a foot injury last season and should be one of the Tigers' top offensive threats this season.

"He's just a terrific shooter," Thompson said. "He makes shots when you need them."

The Tigers will also benefit from having **Ray Robins**, a 6-7 junior forward, back. Robins, who averaged 7.8 points per game in 1999-2000, took last year off from school.

The 6-10 Krug has also returned and will compete with 6-9 senior **Heath Jones** (0.0 ppg) for the starting center spot.

Other returnees are 6-8 senior forward **Conor Neu** (0.8 ppg) and junior guard **Pete Hegseth** (0.2 ppg).

The Tigers should also get help from their five freshmen—centers **Dominick Martin** and **Mike Stephens**, forward **Judson Wallace**, swingman **Tom McLaughlin** and guard **Will Venable**.

"I wouldn't be surprised if any one of them, or all of them, end up contributing," Thompson said.

Martin and Stephens could make the biggest impact, and not just because both are 6-10.

Martin (20.0 ppg, 12.0 rpg, 3.0 bpg) led A.C. Reynolds High School in Asheville (N.C.) to a 24-3 record and its district tournament championship. He has three-point range and is a good free-throw shooter (70 percent), but needs to bulk up from his high school weight of 225 pounds to avoid getting pushed around.

Stephens, from Napa (Calif.) High School, also has the shooting and passing skills to be a "point" center. He has added about 50 points in the last two years, but is still only 230 and may be hitting the nearby buffets with Martin to bulk up.

The 6-4 McLaughlin hails from Andover, Mass., and was getting looks from Stanford, Villanova, Kentucky, Virginia and UMass before he injured a knee and missed his senior season. He poured in 40 points in a game as a sophomore in 1999 and has good bloodlines—his father Tom played at Tennessee and UMass and is a sports agent, and his brother Corry plays at Vermont.

The 6-8 Wallace is a late bloomer who played at Westminster Academy in Georgia. He handles the ball well, and can run the floor and shoot the three. His ability to move without the ball is a plus, but Wallace is a little light at 210 pounds.

Venable, 6-2, brings a great deal of quickness across the country after starring at San Rafael, Calif.

2001-2002 SCHEDULE

Nov.	15-16	#BCA Classic
	24	@Florida International
	28	Rider
Dec.	2-3	##BB&T Classic
	8	Monmouth
	12	Kansas
	21	Lafayette
	29	@Rutgers
Jan.	5	Holy Cross
	11	@Harvard
	12	@Dartmouth
Feb.	1	Columbia
	2	Cornell
	8	@Yale
	9	@Brown
	12	Pennsylvania
	15	Dartmouth
	16	Harvard
	22	Yale
	23	Brown
March	1	@Cornell
	2	@Columbia
	5	@Pennsylvania

@Road Games
#Berkeley, CA (vs. California, first round; also St. Joseph's vs. Eastern Washington)
##MCI Center, Washington DC (vs. Maryland first round; also Connecticut, George Washington)

BLUE RIBBON ANALYSIS

BACKCOURT	A-
BENCH/DEPTH	B
FRONTCOURT	B
INTANGIBLES	B+

Thompson appreciates history, but the Princeton basketball coach just can't afford to live in the past.

While he would like to see his Tigers develop the same sense of unity and togetherness that helped power last year's squad to the Ivy League championship, he isn't banking on it.

Princeton surprised many last season by overcoming the adversity of losing two of its best players and its head coach within two weeks en route to its title run. This year, the Tigers enter the season as one of the favorites in the Ancient Eight, but repeating won't be easy given the balance of the league.

"We have to have the same desire that we had last year," Thompson said.

Princeton returns four starters, including spiritual leader and point guard El-Nokali, one of just three seniors on the team. Wente has proven to be a clutch performer and sophomores Persia, Logan and Wysocki come off solid first seasons where they learned to win. The Tigers add size with freshman recruits Martin and Stephens and welcome back juniors Robins and Krug to boost the frontcourt.

Although it is difficult, Princeton also can't waste time wondering what this year would be like if star center

Young stuck with basketball and Gloger didn't head home to UCLA.

"We just have to figure out how to win games with the people we have," Thompson said.

Those people are good players. If they are the same kind of teammates they were last season, they will be difficult to supplant as conference champs.

(S.B.)

 # Yale

LOCATION	New Haven, CT
CONFERENCE	Ivy
LAST SEASON	10-17 (.370)
CONFERENCE RECORD	7-7 (t-4th)
STARTERS LOST/RETURNING	3/2
NICKNAME	Bulldogs
COLORS	Yale Blue & White
HOMECOURT	John J. Lee Amphitheater (3,100)
COACH	James Jones (Albany '90)
RECORD AT SCHOOL	17-37 (2 years)
CAREER RECORD	17-37 (2 years)
ASSISTANTS	Curtis Wilson (Adelphi '91)
	Ted Hotaling (Albany '95)
	Josh Bland (Fort Lewis '98)
TEAM WINS (last 5 years)	10-12-4-7-10
RPI (last 5 years)	241-218-308-302-255
2000-01 FINISH	Lost in regular-season finale.

The actions of two players this summer told Yale coach James Jones all he needed to know about the direction his program is heading.

Junior guard **Chris Leanza**, the team's leading scorer last season, delivered the first message by starting his days with 6 a.m. workouts in an effort to recover from a shoulder injury that prevented him from practicing much of last season.

The second message came from incoming freshman **Mark Lovett**, who at 6-6 and 220 pounds, trained for and completed a triathlon.

The determination displayed by both is welcome news to Jones, who is trying to resurrect a program that hasn't had a winning season in 10 years. It also shows the Bulldogs are not content with last season, when they finished .500 in the Ivy League and were in the running for the conference championship until the final weekend of the season.

"A lot of teams are talented enough to win, but you have to be mentally tough enough," Jones said. "That's really what you want to be."

Not that Jones is satisfied with being in the middle of the pack.

"We've taken some steps," Jones said. "Our guys had a taste of what it's like to be in the hunt in the last weekend, and that can only help us."

So will having a healthy Leanza (13.3 ppg, 2.3 rpg, 3.5 apg, 1.5 spg), who was in chronic pain with a tight shoulder throughout last season, and had surgery in the off-season.

"He's just a tough player," Jones said. "He hates to lose and he does what it takes to win."

With no seniors on the roster, the 6-1 Leanza (.405 3FG) will undoubtedly be a leader for the Bulldogs. With 121 three-pointers in two seasons, he already ranks fifth in school history and he hit 70 threes last season, just two shy of the single-season mark. In addition to scoring, Leanza, who earned honorable mention All-Ivy honors, topped the Bulldogs in steals, assists and minutes played (36.4 mpg).

"He's got the heart of a lion," Jones said. "Sometimes wonderful things come in small packages."

Jones has upgraded Yale's talent level with two strong recruiting classes and that should ease the load for Leanza, who wore down a bit at the end of last season.

"He may play a few less minutes, but we may get more out of him," Jones said.

Jones is also banking on a big season from junior guard **Ime Archibong**, the Bulldogs' captain. The 6-3 Archibong (9.1 ppg, 3.8 rpg, 1.6 apg, 1.1 spg) may have been the Ivy League's most improved player last season, making 22 starts after playing less than five minutes per game as a freshman.

"Ime's really taken off," Jones said. "He's really started to shine in the last year."

Archibong, who bench presses 350 pounds, is strong off the dribble and is the Bulldogs' top defender who made himself into a player last off-season. His dramatic improvement caught many by surprise, so what hap-

pens if his summer of 2001 was anything like the summer of 2000?

"It's over," Jones said. "He had stages of brilliance last year as a sophomore and if he has a summer like last summer, he is going to be a very special player."

One area where Archibong could improve is in taking care of the ball. He committed almost three turnovers (67) to every two assists (42) last season.

Highly touted freshman **Edwin Draughan** (18.0 ppg, 5.0 rpg, 5.0 apg) will make the backcourt even stronger. The 6-5 Draughan played alongside Stanford recruit Josh Childress at Mayfair High School in Lakewood, Calif. and chose the Bulldogs over the likes of Rutgers and Providence.

Draughan is an excellent shooter with outstanding court presence and can play every position but center.

"He's a kid that can do a lot of different things," Jones said. "He's a special player."

"He's a steal for Yale," David Telep, a recruiting analyst for The Sporting News said. "Especially in that league, he has the chance to be a big-time scorer. He's a little on the light side, but he's a catch-and-shoot type guy. After playing in Josh Childress' shadow, he'll be looking to have a breakout career at Yale."

Alex Gamboa, a first-team all-state selection from Reno (Nevada) High School, also hopes to come in and play. The 6-0 Gamboa (19.0 ppg, 8.0 rpg, 8.0 apg) is a strong set-up man who will find open looks for his teammates.

"He's a solid kid and a great leader," Jones said. "He's a good shooter and can drive and make things happen."

Sophomore **Matt Minoff** (3.6 ppg, 2.7 rpg, 2.3 apg) adds more versatility in the backcourt. The 6-6 Minoff played more than 30 minutes per game for the U.S. team coached by Philadelphia 76ers assistant coach Herb Brown in the Maccabiah Games in July.

Scott Gaffield, another 6-6 sophomore from Canada, also can play guard or forward. Gaffield (3.9 ppg, 2.0 rpg, 1.0 apg) is a hard worker who has gotten stronger. Twenty-seven of Gaffield's 34 field goals last season were three-pointers.

"He's probably the best catch-and-shoot guy we have on the team," Jones said. "He's got good range and we're looking forward to him adding depth."

The major challenge Yale faces in the frontcourt is replacing its top two rebounders—6-11 Neil Yanke (12.5 ppg, 6.7 rpg, 1.0 apg), a second-team All-Ivy selection, and 6-10 Tom Kritzer (5.4 ppg, 4.1 rpg,).

"We'll be smaller, but we'll be quicker to the ball and a better rebounding team," Jones said. "All of our players, one through five, will be chasing the ball."

Some of the rebounding responsibility will fall to juniors **T.J. McHugh** (3.9 ppg, 2.9 rpg) and **Bill Parkhurst** (2.7 ppg, 1.4 rpg).

The 6-8 McHugh started 12 games last season and is coming off an emergency appendectomy in July. A rugged 235 pounds, he should be at full strength when the season opens.

"He has great hands and feet," Jones said. "He can catch anything around the basket."

The 6-7 Parkhurst is far from flashy, but he gets the job done.

"He's a great garbage man," Jones said. "He picks up charges, blocks shots, has long arms and a knack for getting rebounds."

Paul Vitelli, a 6-7 sophomore, will also pitch in. Vitelli, who suffered a meniscus tear in his knee over the summer, was Yale's best freshman (5.7 ppg, 3.4 rpg, 1.4 apg) in 2000-2001 and will be ready for the season. Vitelli prefers to face the basket, but could become a real threat on offense if he develops some more post moves.

Sophomores **Josh Hill** (1.9 ppg, 1.6 rpg), **Mike Smith** (0.0 ppg) and **Justin Simon** (1.4 ppg) also return up front.

The 6-7 Hill has been relentless in his efforts to be a key member of the team and should see more minutes this season.

"He's just a tough, hard-working guy that does everything you need to win basketball games," Jones said. "Josh is a winner."

The 6-5 Smith is a bit of a wild card. A prized recruit, he suffered an ACL injury in high school and had last season cut short after four games because of a torn meniscus. He enters this season at 100 percent and could contribute if he stays healthy and finds the range on his shot.

"He's a guy that's explosive off the dribble going to the basket," Jones said. "He's the best athlete we've got on the team. He's a Big East-type athlete and we're hoping he can become a Big East-type shooter."

The 6-9 Simon appeared in 12 games as a freshman and made the Maccabiah Games team, but his development has been slowed by an injury. He dislocated his ankle and is expected to be out of the lineup until January.

Lovett and fellow freshman **Jerry Gauriloff** will also have the opportunity to play. Lovett (22.5 ppg, 9.5 rpg) is a rugged sharp shooter who can play both inside and out and will not be pushed around.

"He's just one tough son of a gun," Jones said. "He's really a kid that wants to be special."

The 6-9 Gauriloff (20.5 ppg, 12.0 rpg, 3.0 bpg) comes from Minisink Valley High School in Middletown (N.Y.).

"Jerry's a very solid inside player," Jones said. "He's got a lot of heart and he's going to get better, too."

2001-2002 SCHEDULE

Nov.	13	#Air Force
	18	@Penn State
	23-24	##Red Auerbach Classic
	23	Sacred Heart
Dec.	3	@Colgate
	5	@Long Island
	8	Albany
	11	Rhode Island
	29-30	###Furman Tournament
Jan.	11	Columbia
	12	Cornell
	18	Brown
	26	@Brown
Feb.	3	@Harvard
	8	Pennsylvania
	9	Princeton
	15	@Cornell
	16	@Columbia
	22	@Princeton
	23	@Pennsylvania
March	2	Dartmouth

@Road Games
#Guardians Classic (If Yale wins, it will play either Missouri or Tennessee-Martin on Nov. 14. Semifinals and final are Nov. 20-21 at Kemper Arena, Kansas City, MO)
##Wshington, DC (vs. George Washington first round; also Binghamton, Stony Brook)
###Greenville, SC (vs. Gardner-Webb first round; also Furman, MacAlester)

BLUE RIBBON ANALYSIS

BACKCOURT	B+
BENCH/DEPTH	B
FRONTCOURT	C
INTANGIBLES	B

After years of foundering, the Bulldogs appear to be heading in the right direction.

Yale stayed in the hunt almost all of last season even though junior guard Onaje Woodbine, the team's leading returning scorer, decided not to return to the team. With Woodbine out of the picture many thought the backcourt would struggle, but the emergence of Archibong allowed it to flourish.

Archibong and Leanza, who is finally healthy, provide the Bulldogs with an experienced tandem to build their team around. Archibong lends the strength and defense and Leanza is a deadeye shooter from the outside. Freshmen Draughan, who was listed among the Top 100 preseason prospects by CNNSI.com last year, and Gamboa add talent and depth.

The graduation of twin towers Neil Yanke and Tom Kritzer leaves a big void in the frontcourt. The Bulldogs, who were out-rebounded by 2.1 boards per game last season, will need all five players to crash the glass in order to be effective this season. Coach James Jones has recruited more athletic players, and is certainly hoping bigger doesn't mean better, or else his team could be in trouble.

With no seniors on their roster, the Bulldogs are quite young, but they do have an experienced player in Leanza. The key will be getting effective play from a young, unproven frontcourt.

Jones has said he wants his team to build a program that can compete for league championships, something Yale has not won since 1962. The Bulldogs are gathering the pieces to challenge, but may be another year away.

(S.B.)

Canisius

LOCATION	Buffalo, NY
CONFERENCE	Metro Atlantic Athletic
LAST SEASON	20-11 (.645)
CONFERENCE RECORD	9-9 (7th)
STARTERS LOST/RETURNING	2/3
NICKNAME	Golden Griffins
COLORS	Blue & Gold
HOMECOURT	Koessler Athletic Center (1,800)
COACH	Mike MacDonald (St. Bonaventure '88)
RECORD AT SCHOOL	58-47 (4 years)
CAREER RECORD	58-47 (4 years)
ASSISTANTS	Terry Zeh (St. Bonaventure '90)
	Adam Stockwell (LeMoyne '96)
	Chris Moore (Daemen '90)
TEAM WINS (last 5 years)	17-13-15-10-20
RPI (last 5 years)	124-135-155-226-135
2000-01 FINISH	Lost in conference final.

An optimist will look at the Canisius roster and tell you the Golden Griffins return six of their top nine players from the end of last season. A pessimist will look at the Canisius roster and conclude the Golden Griffins lose their top two scorers and top two rebounders. A realist looks at the Canisius roster and sees both.

Consider Golden Griffins coach Mike MacDonald—who took his team within seven points of an NCAA berth last season—a realist who chooses to focus on the first conclusion.

"We can't worry about the guys we don't have, so we're going to worry about the guys we do have," said MacDonald, who received a contract extension through 2005-06 after directing his team to the progam's sixth 20-win season since it started playing basketball in 1903-04.

So, forget about the 36.9 points and 17.6 rebounds per game provided by Darren Fenn, Clive Bentick and Tory Jefferson and consider the contributions of returning starters **Brian Dux** and **Toby Foster** and key reserves **Andrew Bush**, **Hodari Mallory**, **Dewitt Doss** and **Richard Hampton**.

"Every one of them played a big part in winning a game or in helping us build a winning streak," MacDonald said. "These six guys expect certain things."

Like constant improvement. Getting better as the season progresses has been a staple of the MacDonald era, and one of the main reasons for Canisius' success last season was a 6-3 record in February.

The Griffs also pulled together and learned to play as a team when Fenn, their clear go-to guy early in the season, recovered from a knee injury suffered in a Dec. 19 loss to Notre Dame. Although initial reports said Fenn would be out four to six weeks, Fenn missed just two games. Fenn wasn't full strength when he returned and the other Canisius players learned to assert themselves and make plays which made the Griffs a better team the rest of the way.

No player seized the opportunity presented by Fenn's injury more than Bush, a 6-8 senior. The epitome of a self-made player, Bush has climbed the ladder from red-shirt to starter during his tenure.

"I can probably count on one hand the number of bad practices he's had in four years," MacDonald said. "He's what's right with college basketball. He worked hard, he did what he was supposed to do and he definitely progressed."

Some people may have scoffed when MacDonald said Bush would be a key part of any success Canisius enjoyed last season, but he made believers out of them by scoring a career-high 25 points in a win at St. Bonaventure in the first game after Fenn's injury.

The Griffs will lean heavily on Bush (10.0 ppg, 3.2 rpg), who earned his bachelor's degree in physical education and is pursuing his master's, even more this season with top rebounders Fenn and Jefferson gone. Fenn (13.8 ppg, 8.0 rpg, 1.0 apg, 1.2 bpg) graduated and is playing in France and Jefferson (9.5 ppg, 6.3 rpg1.7 apg) did not return for his final season because of personal reasons.

"He gives us a low-post scorer and his jump shot has gotten better," MacDonald said of Bush. "I think he's the kind of player who has to rebound better and stay out of foul trouble while still playing aggressively."

He'll get help from Foster (10.2 ppg, 4.8 ppg, 2.1 apg), a 6-6 junior who led the conference by hitting .443 (70 of 158) from beyond the three-point arc. Foster's shot makes him a tough match-up for opponents because he can also put the ball on the floor and score. He doesn't have the size of some power forwards in the

league, but has started 56 games his first two seasons and learned how to play the position.

"He's got to rebound better and continue to be the best jump shooter on the East Coast," MacDonald said.

Mallory (6.9 ppg, 3.3 rpg, 1.0 apg) will also be a key. Although only 6-3, Mallory plays bigger and provided a boost off the bench when he was healthy last season. He can create problems on the wing and help on the boards, but needs to avoid the foul trouble and injuries that have held him back a bit in his first two seasons.

"He's like [Buffalo Bills quarterback] Rob Johnson, he's got to stay healthy," MacDonald said.

Sophomores Hampton and **Jon Ferris**, both 6-7, also return. Hampton (1.2 ppg, 2.4 rpg) isn't a polished scorer, but could provide valuable minutes as a backup to Bush, especially if Bush gets in foul trouble. Ferris (2.0 ppg, 1.0 rpg) has the ability to score and could become this year's Bush if he is able to step up his rebounding and defense.

Freshmen **Richard Jones** and **Luke Hedges** could contribute in their first seasons.

The 6-6 Jones (17.8 ppg, 10.1 rpg, 6.3 apg) led his Charlestown (Mass.) High School team to a 57-1 record and back-to-back state titles in his final two seasons. Jones is a dangerous outside shooter who made seven three-pointers and scored 25 points in the state final.

The 6-11 Hedges, a native of Canberra, Australia, is more of a project who is adjusting to the college game. He enrolled in school last January and will not be eligible to play until Dec. 22, the day the Griffs host Notre Dame at HSBC Arena.

"He's big," MacDonald said. "He needs to improve his footwork, but he's becoming more Americanized and more comfortable."

Junior **Tom Perkovich** (0.0 ppg), a 6-5, 250-pound offensive lineman on the football team, is also back for his third season as a walk-on forward.

Like Foster, Dux (9.9 ppg, 2.9 rpg, 4.1 apg, 1.0 spg) needed to grow up fast as a freshman and that experience is being rewarded. Dux, a 6-2 junior, is a solid combo guard who fits perfectly into MacDonald's system with an assists-to-turnovers ratio of nearly 3:1. He led the team in minutes played last season and made the MAAC All-Tournament Team.

"He's going to have to score a little more for us and he's got to continue to play mistake-free basketball," MacDonald said.

Doss (2.2 ppg) is the logical choice to step into Bentick's starting spot. After struggling with inconsistency as a junior, Bentick (13.6 ppg, 3.3 rpg, 4.0 apg, 1.4 spg) finished his career with a flourish and was one of the main reasons for the Griffs' turnaround from 10-20 to 20-11.

Defense has never been a concern with Doss, a 5-10 dynamo. His offense was a pleasant surprise last season, although he will need to take better care of the ball in an increased role.

"I think he really evolved into a guy who could make some shots," MacDonald said.

Damon Young (0.5), a 6-2 fifth-year senior, and freshmen **Kevin Downey** and **Chris Ravello** will also compete for time.

Downey, a coach's son, was the co-player of the year in Rochester (N.Y.) after leading Livonia High School to an undefeated regular season and a sectional championship. At 6-3, Downey (25.4 ppg, 8.5 rpg, 5.1 apg) can shoot from the perimeter and also put the ball on the floor.

"I think he's smart, he knows how to play and he'll be able to help us," MacDonald said.

Canisius expects the same things from the 6-3 Ravello (10.7 ppg, 2.6 rpg, 2.5 apg), who played at Archbishop Spalding High School in Severn, Md.

2001-2002 SCHEDULE

Nov.	16	Cornell
	24	@Buffalo
Dec.	1	@St. Joseph's
	7	Rider
	9	@Iona
	15	St. Bonaventure
	22	Notre Dame
	28-29	#ASU/azcentral.com Holiday Classic
Jan.	3	Fairfield
	5	Bucknell
	7	Marist
	9	@Morgan State
	11	@Rider
	19	Siena
	21	@St. Peter's
	26	Loyola

	28	@Siena
	30	Iona
Feb.	1	@Loyola
	6	St. Peter's
	8	Manhattan
	11	@Marist
	13	@Manhattan
	16	Niagara
	18	@Fairfield
	23	@Niagara
	28	##MAAC Tournament
March	1-4	##MAAC Tournament

@Road Games
#Tempe, AZ (vs. Arizona State first round; also Louisiana Lafayette, Northwestern)
##Pepsi Arena, Albany, NY

BLUE RIBBON ANALYSIS

BACKCOURT	B
BENCH/DEPTH	B-
FRONTCOURT	C
INTANGIBLES	C

Canisius expected to lose seniors Fenn and Bentick, but the departure of senior forward Jefferson in the off-season was a surprise. Jefferson, a transfer from Rhode Island, was not a star for the Golden Griffins but was a solid rebounder and decent scorer. Not having Jefferson means Canisius returns just two starters and loses its top two scorers and rebounders from last season, and those losses may be too severe to make a strong run at the top of the conference.

The good news is the Griffs return proven performers in senior Bush and juniors Dux and Foster. Mallory can be a force when healthy and sophomores Hampton and Doss gained valuable experience last year.

Still, outside of Bush, Dux and Foster, there are no guarantees where the points and rebounds will come from. In order to contend, Canisius will need a couple of its lesser heralded players to step forward and at least one of its freshmen to emerge as a dependable player early in the season.

The MAAC is far too competitive to count the Griffs out before the season starts, but it's also not reasonable to expect too much from this team. Canisius won 20 games last season after losing 20 in 1999-2000. Expect this group to wind up somewhere in between those totals.

(S.B.)

Fairfield

LOCATION	Fairfield, CT
CONFERENCE	Metro Atlantic Athletic
LAST SEASON	12-16 (.414)
CONFERENCE RECORD	8-10 (8th)
STARTERS LOST/RETURNING	2/3
NICKNAME	Stags
COLORS	Cardinal Red & White
HOMECOURT	Bridgeport Arena at Harbor Yard (10,000)
COACH	Tim O'Toole (Fairfield '86)
RECORD AT SCHOOL	38-46 (3 years)
CAREER RECORD	38-46 (3 years)
ASSISTANTS	Jerry Hobbie (Fordham '85)
	Matt Roe (Maryland '91)
	Andy Buzbee (Fairfield '00)
TEAM WINS (last 5 years)	11-12-12-14-12
RPI (last 5 years)	227-175-159-149-220
2000-01 FINISH	Lost in conference first round.

Fairfield, Conn. is known more for its beaches than its tall buildings, but that doesn't mean the city won't ever be famous for its skyline. In fact, it could happen sooner than you think.

Fairfield coach Tim O'Toole has assembled a front line that could be as formidable as any in mid-major basketball.

The Stags return 6-5 senior forward **Sam Spann**, an All-MAAC first-team selection last season, and 6-10 sophomore center **Rob Thomson**, a member of the MAAC's All-Rookie team in 2000-01, and also add Sudanese cousins **Deng Gai** and **Ajou Deng**. Deng Gai, a 6-9 freshman, was rated among the top 50 recruits in the country by several college scouting services, and Ajou Deng, is a 6-10 junior transfer from Connecticut who will not be eligible to play until the end

METRO ATLANTIC

BLUE RIBBON FORECAST
1. Iona
2. Marist
3. Fairfield
4. Niagara
5. Siena
6. Manhattan
7. Rider
8. Canisius
9. Loyola
10. St. Peter's

ALL-CONFERENCE TEAM
G Sean Kennedy, SR, Marist
G Daryl Greene, SR, Niagara
F Sam Spann, SR, Fairfield
F Mario Porter, SR, Rider
F Dyree Wilson, SR, Iona

PLAYER OF THE YEAR
Mario Porter, SR, Rider

NEWCOMER OF THE YEAR
Deng Gai, FR, Fairfield

2001-2002 CONFERENCE TOURNAMENT
Feb.28-March 4, Pepsi Arena, Albany, NY

2000-2001 CHAMPIONS
Iona, Niagara, Siena (regular season)
Iona (conference tournament)

2000-2001 POSTSEASON PARTICIPANTS
Postseason Record 0-1 (.000)
NCAA
Iona

TOP BACKCOURTS
1. Marist
2. Niagara
3. Iona

TOP FRONTCOURTS
1. Fairfield
2. Iona
3. Siena

INSIDE THE NUMBERS
2000-2001 conference RPI: 14th (of 31)
Conference RPI (last five years): 21-13-13-20-14

DID YOU KNOW?
Even though Louis Orr left Siena after just one season to become the head coach at Seton Hall, the story in the MAAC this season is about what coaches are staying rather than leaving. Jeff Ruland, who has led Iona to back-to-back NCAA appearances, signed an eight-year contract extension to remain coach of the Gaels through 2008-2009. Mike MacDonald, who took seventh-seeded Canisius to the MAAC Tournament championship game, agreed to a new contract that will keep him on the Golden Griffins' bench until 2006. Joe Mihalich, who has enjoyed great success in his three seasons at Niagara, will remain coach of the Purple Eagles through 2007. Dave Magarity, the 2001 Spalding MAAC Coach of the Year, is locked up through the 2004-05 season at Marist and Bobby Gonzalez, who has rejuvenated Manhattan's program, received an extension to stay with the Jaspers through 2004-05. "I think it's great for the league," MacDonald said. "I think when you identify with the Big East you identify with Jim Boeheim at Syracuse and Jim Calhoun at Connecticut and I think now you'll start to identify the MAAC with people like Jeff Ruland at Iona and Joe Mihalich at Niagara. It also helps defuse the win and move up or lose and get fired mentality." … The MAAC has also decided to break the pattern of alternating the conference tournament between Albany (even years) and Buffalo (odd years) that it has followed since 1996. Siena and Marist will play host to the 2002 and 2004 tournaments in Albany, but the 2003 tournament will be at Sovereign Bank Arena in Trenton, N.J. Rider, Loyola College and St. Peter's will serve as hosts. The tournament will return to Buffalo in 1995. … No team has won three straight MAAC Tournament championships since Lionel Simmons led LaSalle to the 1988, '89 and '90 titles. Iona can equal that feat this spring. … The last MAAC team to win an NCAA Tournament game is Manhattan, which defeated Oklahoma in 1995. Iona lost a 72-70 heartbreaker to Mississippi in the first round last March. … The last three MAAC Rookies of the Year—Jermaine Clark (Fairfield, 1999), Bruce Seals (Manhattan, 2000) and John Reimold (Loyola, 2001)—are no longer with their teams. … Siena coach Rob Lanier is a cousin of Hall of Famer Bob Lanier. … Fairfield newcomers Deng Gai and Ajou Deng, a transfer from Connecticut, are cousins. … Loyola has lost 28 consecutive road games dating back to Feb. 14, 1999 at St. Peter's.

(S.B.)

of first semester.

"We're a different type of team because we've got size," O'Toole said.

They've also got talent. Even though Deng Gai and Ajou Deng have never suited up for the Stags, they are already being mentioned as candidates for first-team all-league honors by opposing coaches.

"He's an absolute animal, he's the real deal," Rider coach Don Harnum said of Deng Gai. "He does not belong in our league. He belongs at Kentucky or somewhere like that."

Gai, who came to the United States just more than a year ago, made a fast impression on the camp scene during his first summer here. He had coaches drooling over him after winning most-valuable-player honors at the Eastern Invitational Camp and earned role player of the week after helping the Orange to victory in the Orange-White Classic at Five-Star Camp.

"He's relatively new to the game, but he picks things up quickly," O'Toole said.

Gai continued to develop at Milford (Conn.) Academy, where he averaged a double-double (18.0 ppg, 10.0 rpg, 3.0 bpg) last season. Hoop Scoop rated him the No. 7 fifth-year high school recruit and O'Toole loves his versatility and potential.

"He's a very talented player," O'Toole says. "He runs, he shoots, he blocks shots and he dunks everything around the basket."

Deng owns the same type of ability, although his lack of strength held him back at Connecticut. Deng, who turned heads while practicing with the Huskies at the 1999 Final Four, played in 35 games, starting 12, for UConn as a sophomore in 1999-2000 (4.5 ppg, 3.5 rpg, 1.3 bpg). He put up similar numbers (4.8 ppg, 4.7 rpg, 1.0 bpg) in six games as a reserve last season before deciding to transfer to Fairfield on Dec. 22, the night the Huskies beat the Stags, 100-66.

"He's a very skilled player," O'Toole said. "He can pass, shoot, rebound and block shots. He does a lot of little things that might go unnoticed until you look at the stat sheet and see he's putting up some pretty good numbers."

No one in the league, with the possible exception of Niagara's Demond Stewart and Rider's Mario Porter, did put up better numbers than Spann last season. The Syracuse transfer emerged from the shadow cast by former Fairfield star Darren Phillip to finish eighth in the league in scoring (15.0 ppg), second in rebounding (9.5 rpg), second in field-goal percentage (.539), fourth in steals (1.7 ppg) and 11th in blocked shots (0.8 ppg).

"Sam had a phenomenal year for us and I expect him to have another phenomenal year for us," O'Toole said.

In addition to everything else he does, Spann can also pass (1.7 apg) and play defense.

"If he wasn't the best defensive player in the league, he was the second-best and I don't know who was No. 1," O'Toole said. "He has tremendous size, strength and speed and he can guard anybody. He's quick enough to step out and guard a two [guard] and strong enough to go inside and guard a four [power forward]."

A solid freshman season by Thomson (8.0 ppg, 5.5 rpg, 2.0 bpg) helped offset the loss of Phillip, who led the nation in rebounding in 1999-2000. Thomson, the team's only true center, finished second in the conference in blocked shots and gained valuable experience playing on a travel team led by Lamar coach Mike Deane this summer. Thomson, who was often guarded by the 6-3 O'Toole in practice, should benefit from having better big players around him every day.

"As long as his confidence level doesn't go down, he's going to learn a lot in practice every day," O'Toole said.

Oscar Garcia (5.5 ppg, 3.4), a 6-8 junior, and **Brad Feleccia**, a 6-7 freshman from Bishop Hannan in Scranton, Pa., provide additional depth and toughness inside. Feleccia (17.0 ppg, 13.0 rpg) was a high school teammate of guard Jerry McNamara, one of the stars of Syracuse's 2002 recruiting class.

Sophomore walk-ons **Matt Colford** (1.0 ppg) and **John Morin** (1.0 ppg) also return at forward for the Stags.

Juniors **Jeremy Logan**, the Stags' second-leading returning scorer, and **Nick Delfico** (5.1 ppg, 2.4 rpg, 1.1 apg) are both veteran 6-5 players who can play either shooting guard or small forward. The Stags will miss 1999 MAAC Rookie of the Year Jermaine Clark (11.6 ppg, 3.7 rpg, 2.9 apg), a 6-5 swing player who did not return to the team.

Logan (11.8 ppg, 3.9 rpg, 1.7 apg) made the MAAC All-Rookie team in 2000, but struggled a bit last season, missing half the year with injuries and academic issues.

"He's back and we're excited about him," O'Toole said. "He's worked a great deal on his shot and can play either the two-guard or swing-spot."

Delfico will also compete for time at the two-spot, along with 6-1 senior **Dan Galvanoni**. Galvanoni (4.6 ppg, 2.2 rpg, 1.9 apg), a transfer from Moorpark (Calif.) Junior College is a solid long range shooter who battled injuries last season. He struggled a bit while playing out of position at the point last year, but could emerge as a key contributor this season.

Seniors **Kyle Walsh** (0.7 ppg) and **Keith Urgo** (0.5 ppg) also return. The 6-3 Walsh has made some contributions over the years and is a team captain. Urgo spent two years with Fairfield's lacrosse team before joining the basketball team last season.

Point guard looms as the biggest question for the Stags and a pair of freshmen, **Tyquawn Goode** and **Kudjo Sogadzi**, hope to provide the answers. O'Toole isn't looking for a savior, just someone to take care of the ball, get it to the right people and play solid defense.

The 5-7 Goode (11.5 ppg, 7.5 apg, 5.3 spg) led Grady High School in Brooklyn to New York's PSAL title and earned first-team postseason honors from both Newsday and The New York Daily News.

"He's a very, very good passer and that's what we've needed the last few years," O'Toole said.

Sogadzi, 6-1, will push Goode. He led Nyack (N.Y.) to the state semifinals, where he scored 23 points, and was selected the most valuable player in Rockland County.

The Stags have something more than new players to get used to this season. The team will leave behind the rowdy "Sea of Red" student section at Alumni Hall and play its home games at the brand new 10,000-seat Bridgeport Arena at Harvard Yard.

2001-2002 SCHEDULE

Nov.	16	@Harvard
	20	@Michigan
	27	Rhode Island
Dec.	6	Iona
	8	*Depaul
	11	St Francis (N.Y.)
	28	@UNC Wilmington
Jan.	3	@Canisius
	5	@American
	8	St. Peter's
	10	@Manhattan
	12	@Niagara
	14	Rider
	18	@Iona
	20	@Loyola
	23	Loyola
	26	@Marist
	29	Niagara
Feb.	2	Manhattan
	6	@St. John's
	8	@Rider
	10	Siena
	12	Charleston Southern
	14	Marist
	16	@Siena
	18	Canisius
	23	@St. Peter's
Feb.	28	#MAAC Tournament
March	1-4	#MAAC Tournament

@Road Games
*At Madison Square Garden, New York, NY
#Pepsi Arena, Albany, NY

BLUE RIBBON ANALYSIS

BACKCOURT	C
BENCH/DEPTH	B
FRONTCOURT	A
INTANGIBLES	B+

The excitement surrounding Fairfield in the off-season is not without justification, but it does come with some degree of uncertainty.

Sure, the Stags bring in Gai and Deng—two players with star potential—but both are still relatively unproven commodities. Both have the talent to dominate at the mid-major level, but it may take some time for Fairfield to fit all of the pieces together properly.

Spann was one of the best all-around players in the conference last season and should be even better with more talent around him. The same is true for Thomson, who stepped in admirably despite having limited experience against players his size.

Fairfield's huge front line should make things easier on the perimeter defenders because it has four skilled shot blockers. It should also improve a defense that finished ninth in a 10-team league in scoring defense (76.82) and opposing shooting percentage (.469) last season.

"We've got some stability and size," O'Toole said. "We should be able to stop people from driving because there are not a lot of places for them to go inside."

The Stags also have Logan back after a troubled sophomore season that limited him to 14 games. If he returns to form, the Stags should be able to score in a variety of ways.

The key to the season will be the performance of freshman point guards Goode and Sogadzi. Neither Goode nor Sogadzi will be called upon to win games for the Stags, but if they can avoid turnovers and provide stability, Fairfield should be a team to contend with.

"We've got some guys that have played pretty well," O'Toole said. "Hopefully we'll get some guard play and we'll be OK."

(S.B.)

Iona

LOCATION	**New Rochelle, NY**
CONFERENCE	**Metro Atlantic Athletic**
LAST SEASON	**22-11 (.667)**
CONFERENCE RECORD	**12-6 (t-1st)**
STARTERS LOST/RETURNING	**3/2**
NICKNAME	**Gaels**
COLORS	**Maroon & Gold**
HOMECOURT	**Mulcahy Center (2,611)**
COACH	**Jeff Ruland (Iona '91)**
RECORD AT SCHOOL	**58-36 (3 years)**
CAREER RECORD	**58-36 (3 years)**
ASSISTANTS	**Craig Holcomb (Brockport State '86)**
	Tony Chiles (Columbia '89)
	Rob O'Driscoll (Villanova '94)
TEAM WINS (last 5 years)	**16-27-22-21-22**
RPI (last 5 years)	**103-43-120-99-105**
2000-01 FINISH	**Lost in NCAA first round.**

All-league center Nakiea Miller, the player who carried Iona to its second consecutive conference championship is gone, but the Gaels still have a big man who wore No. 43 to lead their NCAA charge.

After having his name churned through the rumor mill for various openings last spring, head coach Jeff Ruland signed an eight-year contract extension in March. The move should do at least two things: 1) Keep a prominent name off of the list foundering Big East and Atlantic 10 programs turn to when they go searching for a coach the next eight springs; 2) Guarantee Iona has a competitive team and legitimate shot at making the NCAA Tournament each year through the 2008-09 season.

"My goal is to, before I leave, get this program back to what it was when I was here," said Ruland, who played three seasons (1978-80) at Iona for the late Jim Valvano before leaving early to embark on an all-star career in the NBA. "To play nationally ranked teams in Madison Square Garden and to beat nationally ranked teams in Madison Square Garden."

Ruland knows all about that.

A former All-America center, he scored 30 points and pulled down 21 rebounds as the Gaels defeated eventual national champion Louisville, 77-60, on Feb. 21, 1980.

Now, he's trying to score similar victories as a coach. Ruland has led the Gaels to back-to-back conference titles and successive NCAA Tournament appearances. Iona, the No. 14 seeded team in the Midwest, came within a made shot on its final possession of knocking off No. 3 Mississippi last March, but coming close isn't good enough for this program any more.

"We've really set our goals high," Ruland said. "Only one team in the history of the conference has gone to three straight NCAA Tournaments and that's LaSalle when they had Lionel Simmons."

And that was from 1988-90 when the current crop of Iona players was in grade school. The Explorers also had a superstar in Simmons. The Gaels have a deep, talented team that doesn't rely too heavily on one player. They also must replace the production and leadership of Miller (15.1 ppg, 8.8 rpg, 3.1 bpg), MVP of the MAAC Tournament, and the starting backcourt of fellow departed seniors Earl Johnson (12.8 ppg, 2.7 rpg, 4.0 apg) and Phil Grant (8.5 ppg, 3.7 rpg, 2.7 apg).

"Obviously we lost a lot, but we have good players coming back," Ruland said. "We've got some weapons, but it's the same old situation—how well do the pieces to the puzzle fit together?"

Senior **Dyree Wilson** (12.5 ppg, 4.7 rpg, 2.0 apg) will be one of the cornerstones. Wilson, a 6-5 forward, was MVP of the 2000 MAAC Tournament, earned third-team all-conference honors in what some people termed a "down" year.

Wilson does not have great range, but has worked hard to improve his jump shot. He may need to score more with Miller and Johnson gone, but his most important task will be maintaining his composure and staying within the team concept.

"He's very, very talented," Ruland said. "It's just a case of recognizing and being focused on the task at hand."

Greg Jenkins, Iona's other returning starter, played just two seasons of high school ball, but that didn't stop him from making an impact as a freshman (8.6 ppg, 4.6 rpg, .581 FG). Jenkins, 6-9, played only 21.4 minutes per game and needs to improve his rebounding, but has the potential to put up big numbers this season.

The same could be true for versatile 6-9 junior **Courtney Fields**, who shook off a year of inactivity to put together a solid first season (7.7 ppg, 5.7 rpg, 1.5 apg, 1.5 spg). Fields can play almost any position on the floor and needs to step up his rebounding and cut down on his turnovers, even though he takes better care of the ball than most players his size.

"He needs to be more consistent and a little more dominant around the rim," Ruland said. "He's 6-9 and can really handle the ball and create some mismatches."

Ramel Allen, a transfer from Monroe Community College in Rochester (N.Y.), will be charged with assuming a large part of Miller's role inside. Allen, who enrolled at Iona in January, averaged a double-double (14.4 ppg, 12.0 rpg, 4.5 bpg) and shot better than 60 percent from the floor while leading the Tribunes to a 27-3 mark in 1999-2000.

"He's long," Ruland said. "He's a very good rebounder and shot blocker. He's got a ways to go on offense, but he's got a nice touch around the basket."

More inside help will come from junior **Kenya Carruthers** and sophomore **Charles Henson**. Carruthers, a junior-college transfer, made minimal contributions (2.7 ppg, 1.7 rpg) last season but has the size (6-6, 245) to be a force inside. Henson, a non-qualifier according to the NCAA's initial eligibility requirements, sat out last season but brings more size (6-9) and athleticism to the Gaels. He played at both All Hallows and St. Raymond's high schools in the Bronx, and won the city championship at St. Raymond's his senior season (6.2 ppg, 8.0 rpg).

Drago Pavlovic (1.9 ppg), a 6-7 sophomore, saw limited time as a freshman but adds another dimension to the frontcourt with his shooting ability and range.

Newcomers **Eddie Starks** and **Solomon Brown** bring a great deal of talent to the backcourt, but must fit in quickly for the Gaels to avoid missing a beat.

Starks, a 6-2 sophomore, originally signed with Rutgers and sat out last season as a non-qualifier. The Bronx native was a fourth-team *Parade* All-American (17.1 ppg, 5.6 rpg) coming out of Northwest Christian (Fla.) High School and can play either guard spot.

"He can handle the ball and really has the ability to score," Ruland said. "He's like a baby bull around the rim. For 6-3, he's pretty strong."

Brown, 6-1, is a combo guard with outstanding court awareness. The California native played last season at St. Thomas More (Conn.) Prep (11.0 ppg, 3.0 rpg, 3.5 apg, 2.5 spg) and led his team to the New England Prep Championship.

"He has a great, great feel for the game and really excels at seeing things before they happen," Ruland said.

Starks and Brown will join veterans **Maceo Wofford** and **Leland Norris**, both of whom have starting experience, in the backcourt. Although none of the four has shown the ability to dominate at the college level, each has the skills and the Gaels certainly have strength in numbers.

Wofford, a 5-10 junior, was a prolific scorer (2,259 points) at Jamestown (N.Y.) High School, but his carved his niche in college on defense. Wofford (5.5 ppg, 1.7 rpg, 1.4 apg, 1.1 spg) is tenacious on the ball and can change the tempo of the game with his energy and aggressiveness.

"There's no better defender," Ruland said. "He needs to be a little bit more like he was in high school in terms of scoring more and having confidence he can make shots."

That's not the case with Norris (6.5 ppg, 1.4 rpg, 1.6 apg, .410 3FG), a 6-2 senior, who is comfortable shooting the ball and opens things up inside because defenses must respect his ability to knock down jumpers.

"He's our instant offense, a guy that can really come in and hit the three," Ruland said.

Sophomore walk-on **Randy Williams** (1.1 ppg) saw action in seven games last season and provides depth.

2001-2002 SCHEDULE

Nov.	17	Akron
	20	@Bethune-Cookman
	24	@Rhode Island
	28	Fordham
Dec.	1	Hofstra
	4	@Wagner
	6	@Fairfield
	9	Canisius
	19-22	#Rainbow Classic
	27-28	##ECAC Holiday Festival
Jan.	3	Siena
	5	@St. Peter's
	9	Rider
	13	@Loyola
	15	@Marist
	18	Fairfield
	21	@Siena
	25	Manhattan
	30	@Canisius
Feb.	1	@Niagara
	3	St. Peter's
	6	Marist
	10	Loyola
	13	@Rider
	20	Niagara
	22	@Manhattan
	28	###MAAC Tournament
March	1-4	###MAAC Tournament

@Road Games
#Honolulu, HI (vs. Holy Cross first game; also Arkansas State, Boston College, Georgia, Hawaii, Miami, OH, Portland)
##Madison Square Garden, NY (vs. Seton Hall first round; also Fordham, Manhattan)
###Pepsi Arena, Albany, NY

BLUE RIBBON ANALYSIS

BACKCOURT	B
BENCH/DEPTH	A
FRONTCOURT	A
INTANGIBLES	A

Last season Iona learned how difficult it is to repeat as conference champions. The Gaels rebounded from a three-game losing streak at the end of the regular season in time to win the MAAC Tournament and enter this season with enough talent to make a strong run at a third title.

Wilson is the closest thing Iona has to a star, but Ruland's real formula for victory is strength in numbers. The Gaels will play at least 10 players and will come after opponents from all directions.

"I can envision us playing a lot of pressure defense," Ruland said in a classic understatement.

Wofford gets after it as well as any point man and Allen will make up for a lot of mistakes with his shot blocking on the back end. Guards Starks, Brown and Norris and forwards Fields, Henson, Jenkins and Carruthers will all play key roles in between.

With three MAAC titles in four seasons, the Gaels have momentum on their side. The returning players are also driven by a disappointing two-point loss to Mississippi in the first round of last year's NCAA Tournament, a game that everyone associated with the program believes Iona should have won.

The biggest question is in the backcourt, where starters Johnson and Grant must be replaced. Iona's top four players are talented, but unproven. If they can mesh together and get the ball into the hands of the right players up front, these Gaels will also be good.

"There's no doubt in our minds that the road to the MAAC title goes through New Rochelle," Ruland said.

A third straight title won't come without a fight, but the crown belongs to the Gaels until someone takes it away from them.

(S.B.)

Loyola College

LOCATION	Baltimore, MD
CONFERENCE	Metro Atlantic Athletic
LAST SEASON	6-23 (.207)
CONFERENCE RECORD	2-16 (t-9th)
STARTERS LOST/RETURNING	3/2
NICKNAME	Greyhounds
COLORS	Green & Grey
HOMECOURT	Emil G. Reitz Arena (3,000)
COACH	Scott Hicks (LeMoyne '88)
RECORD AT SCHOOL	6-23 (1 year)
CAREER RECORD	17-40 (2 years)
ASSISTANTS	Bill Geitner (Hamilton '87)
	Byron Thorne (Penn State-Behrend '94)
	Gallagher Driscoll (St. Rose '92)
TEAM WINS (last 5 years)	11-12-13-7-6
RPI (last 5 years)	191-171-184-295-276
2000-01 FINISH	Lost in conference quarterfinal.

Scott Hicks admits the 2000-01 season was a learning experience for the entire Loyola College program.

The Greyhounds learned one of their more difficult lessons—just how competitive the level of play in the MAAC is—firsthand. Despite playing most of its conference rivals tight, Loyola won just two regular-season games and finished tied with St. Peter's at the bottom of the conference standings.

"Last year we were very competitive, but we didn't win as many games as we had hoped," Hicks said. "We were close, but when it came down to the last four minutes we didn't make enough baskets."

The Greyhounds did receive a late reward for their efforts—a 60-58 victory over Fairfield in the opening round of the MAAC Tournament—but will need to be a more efficient offensive club in order to show significant improvement this season.

Loyola allowed only 70.8 points per game, third best in the league, but scored a conference-worst 62.0. The Greyhounds' focus this season will be improving their shooting percentage (.412) and cutting their turnovers (15.9).

The challenge will be made greater by the loss of seven letter winners, including departed senior Brian Carroll (10.3 ppg, 10.6 rpg, 1.3 apg, 1.9 bpg), the conference's leading rebounder, and MAAC Rookie of the Year John Reimold (15.5 ppg, 5.0 rpg, 2.0 apg), who transferred to Bowling Green.

Loyola enters the season with a young team that features 10 underclassmen and a desire to reverse the fortunes of a team that went 3-9 in games decided by 10 points or less and hasn't had a winning season since 1994.

"They're hungry to turn things around," Hicks said. "The big factor for us is we are going to have to have excellent chemistry. We're going to have to share the ball and have our young players step up."

The good news for the Greyhounds is **Damien Jenifer**, the team's only senior, is back to man the point-guard spot, arguably the most important position on the

floor. The 6-0 Jenifer (8.6 ppg, 3.3 rpg, 4.4 apg, 1.9 spg) was expected to have a breakout season last year but was slowed by a knee injury that cost him seven games. He has recovered from surgery and should be back doing what he does best—harassing opponents on defense and getting the Greyhounds running on offense.

"He may be the quickest point guard in the league," Hicks said. "He's got experience which is invaluable in this league."

Jenifer also has a capable running mate in 5-11 sophomore **B.J. Davis**, a member of the MAAC All-Rookie team last season. Davis (12.4 ppg, 2.5 rpg, 2.5 apg, 1.3 spg) can play either guard position and is a dangerous outside shooter (.392 3PT). He also led the team in steals and minutes played (35.9 mpg).

"He's really grown up as a player," Hicks said. "He's just extremely complete. He shoots off the dribble, he can get to the basket and he makes shots, too."

Sophomore **Dennis Desmond** (1.6 ppg, 1.0 apg in 1999-00), a 6-0 transfer from New Mexico State, will back up Jenifer at the point. Desmond will be eligible after the first semester.

Additional depth will come from freshman **Lucious Jordan** and 6-0 sophomore walk-on **Ryan Dickey** (1.3 ppg). The 6-2 Jordan (21 ppg, 7 apg) played at Colonie (N.Y.) High School, not far from where Hicks used to coach at the University at Albany. He is a strong guard and natural scorer who should contribute right away.

The Greyhounds were disappointed to lose Reimold, but Hicks thinks he has a solid replacement ready in 6-5 sophomore **Lindbergh Chatman**, a transfer from Robert Morris (2.6 ppg in 1999-00).

"He's very solid and very skilled," Hicks said. "He can score off the pass and score off the dribble. I think he can come in and provide a good power punch at the swing spot. He's a very good offensive player."

Loyola is also excited to have **Donovan Thomas** back healthy. Thomas, a 6-7 sophomore forward, entered last season on a high after making the MAAC All-Rookie Team in 1999-2000 (8.2 ppg, 4.7 rpg) and averaging a double-double during a summer tour of Europe. But he suffered a torn quad muscle early in the season and had to red-shirt after playing just four games (2.3 ppg, 3.3 rpg).

"He's a tremendous athlete," Hicks said. "He's good defensively, he's a very good rebounder and a quick jumper."

Delonnie Southall, a bruising 6-8 junior, also returns. Southall (3.8 ppg, 3.1 rpg) played in all 29 games last season and has the body to be an inside presence.

Irakli Nijardze, a native of the former Soviet Republic of Georgia, dominated his competition at Holy Cross Regional High School in Lynchburg, Va., and was rated by some to be among the top 30 center prospects in the country.

"He's 6-10, 250 and ready to go," Hicks said.

Nijardze (15.0 ppg, 14.0 rpg in 1999-2000) was selected to the Virginia Independent Schools Division III first team after his senior year and Hicks is confident he will be able to step in, despite not having played against many players his size in high school.

"He's really good," Hicks said. "He's just a skilled offensive player and has got a feel for the game. He scores, he finishes and he should help us."

Bernard Allen, a 6-5 freshman from AWTY International School, is one of the best athletes in the history of his high school and the first to accept a Division I basketball scholarship. Allen (20.0 ppg, 13.0 rpg) is a strong defender and good rebounder for a small forward.

Jim Chivers and Sean Corrigan, also members of the incoming freshman class, provide more depth in the frontcourt.

The 6-8 Chivers, a native of Detroit Lakes, Minn., spent last season prepping at St. Thomas More in Connecticut. The all-time leading scorer at Detroit Lakes, Chivers has good shooting range for a power forward.

At 6-11 and 250 pounds, Corrigan has the ability to play power forward and center. Corrigan averaged double figures in points and rebounds his final two seasons at Holy Tinity High School in Hicksville (N.Y.).

2001-2002 SCHEDULE

Nov.	17,19	#Battle of Baltimore
	26	@Fairlelgh Dickinson
Dec.	1	@Rutgers
	3	Northeastern
	6	@Niagara
	9	St. Peter's
	15	@Mount St. Mary's
	22	@Central Connecticut State
	30	@Delaware

Jan.	2	Manhattan
	4	@Santa Clara
	10	Siena
	13	Iona
	17	@Rider
	20	Fairfield
	23	@Fairfield
	26	@Canisius
	30	@Marist
Feb.	1	Canisius
	3	Marist
	7	@Siena
	10	@Iona
	13	Niagara
	16	@St. Peter's
	23	Rider
Feb.	28	##MAAC Tournament
March	1-4	##MAAC Tournament

@Road Games
#Baltimore, Md (vs. UMBC first round; also Coppin State, Towson State)
##Pepsi Arena, Albany, NY

BLUE RIBBON ANALYSIS

BACKCOURT	B
BENCH/DEPTH	C
FRONTCOURT	D+
INTANGIBLES	C

With just one senior and one junior on its roster, Loyola College will have to grow up fast if it hopes to compete with the top teams in the MAAC this season.

The Greyhounds, who have lost 28 consecutive road games, will have plenty of opportunities to end that streak early this season, because seven of their first 10 games will be played away from Reitz Arena.

Loyola will lean heavily on Jenifer, the only senior on the squad. Davis established himself last season and will be a mainstay for the next three seasons. Transfer Chatman is poised to step in for Reimold at small forward.

The big questions are in the frontcourt. Thomas has the ability to be a cornerstone, but is coming off a quad injury that forced him to red-shirt last season. Mijardze, a solid 6-10 freshman from the Republic of Georgia, is a skilled offensive player who is expected to play right away. Thomas and Nijaradze have the potential to be effective, but there are no guarantees with them at this point.

The two keys will be offensive execution and playing together. The Greyhounds averaged just 62 points per game last season and head coach Hicks hopes having a deeper, more talented team will lead to more makes and, subsequently, more points.

Jenifer's role is also key. Although he won't be around to enjoy the fruits of this season, he can help lay the foundation for the future by sharing his experience with Loyola's younger players and the program can grow.

The Greyhounds have some talent, but it will be difficult for a team with seven newcomers and a suspect front line to seriously challenge the league's top teams this season.

(S.B.)

Manhattan

LOCATION	Riverdale, NY
CONFERENCE	Metro Atlantic Athletic
LAST SEASON	14-15 (.483)
CONFERENCE RECORD	11-7 (t-4th)
STARTERS LOST/RETURNING	2/3
NICKNAME	Jaspers
COLORS	Kelly Green & White
HOMECOURT	Draddy Gymnasium (3,000)
COACH	Bobby Gonzalez (Buffalo State '86)
RECORD AT SCHOOL	26-30 (2 years)
CAREER RECORD	26-30 (2 years)
ASSISTANTS	Mike Bramucci (Ramapo '90)
	Travis Lyons (Manhattan '98)
	Steve Masiello (Kentucky '00)
TEAM WINS (last 5 years)	9-12-5-12-14
RPI (last 5 years)	235-168-291-221-169
2000-01 FINISH	Lost in conference quarterfinal.

No team epitomizes the balance of the MAAC more than Manhattan did last year.

The Jaspers led Niagara by 10 points at Draddy Gymnasium with 4:48 to play last Feb. 2 before the Purple Eagles staged a furious rally, capped by Michael Schmidt's three-pointer at the buzzer that gave Niagara an 81-78 win.

As disappointing as the loss was at the time, no one knew exactly how damaging it was to the Jaspers. When the regular season ended just more than three weeks later, Manhattan found itself in a three-way tie with Marist and Rider with an 11-7 record as Iona, Niagara and Siena sat atop the conference at 12-6. If everything played out the same, with the exception of the Niagara-Manhattan game, the Jaspers would have been seeded first in the conference tournament instead of sixth.

"It's so balanced," Manhattan coach Bobby Gonzalez said of the conference. "If we win that game, we win the league. Instead, we finish sixth.

"I think it's going to be even more balanced this year. You can probably make a case for eight different teams finishing in the top four spots."

Fortunately for him, Gonzalez isn't concerned with eight teams. His focus is on continued improvement for a Jasper program that has finished 9-9 and 11-7 in the conference in his two seasons after going 3-15 in 1998-99.

"We've come a long way in the last two years and we keep adding to what we've got," said Gonzalez, who signed a two-year contract extension through the 2004-05 season in May.

Still, Manhattan is not where it wants to be yet. The Jaspers return three starters and Gonzalez is bringing in a talented group of recruits and transfers, but there are still questions. First and foremost: Who will fill the void left by two-time All-MAAC forward Durelle Brown (17.8 ppg), who finished his career No. 3 on the school's all-time scoring list and is now playing professionally in Spain?

"You don't really replace guys like that," Gonzalez said. "We probably won't have a Durelle Brown, we've got to make up for it in other areas."

With so many players at his disposal this season, Gonzalez will need to experiment to find the most effective combination for the Jaspers. Regardless of what he comes up with, sophomore **Dave Holmes** and junior **Jared Johnson** figure to be in the mix at forward.

The 6-7 Holmes (9.0 ppg, 6.0 rpg), a top recruit from Oak Hill (Va.) Academy, missed the start of last season while an eligibility issue was resolved but still managed to lead the team in rebounding. He did that despite playing less than 20 minutes per game and struggling to get into top playing shape throughout the season. With all systems go from the start, the MAAC All-Rookie team member could break through at power forward this season.

"He's different than Durelle because he's probably more of a rugged guy," Gonzalez said. "He's more of a lunch bucket guy. He's an underneath guy and a guy who can hang around the basket and get the job done."

The 6-7 Johnson (6.7 ppg, 3.9 rpg, 1.2 spg) may have been Manhattan's most improved player last season. Like Holmes, Johnson gets the job done inside.

"Jared has a chance, he could be a good player," Gonzalez said. "He could step up and take over some of the things Durelle did."

Both Holmes, who fouled out eight times, and Johnson, who was disqualified from six, need to do a better job on defense in order to stay on the floor for longer stretches.

Their jobs will become much easier if junior-college transfer **Darnell Tyler** delivers in the middle. The 6-9, 260-pound Tyler originally committed to Rhode Island last fall, but reconsidered after the Rams changed coaches and ended up Manhattan.

"We thought he was a little bit of a steal for us," Gonzalez said.

Tyler, the Jaspers' first true center under Gonzalez, has all of the physical tools to be a force in the MAAC. He comes from Tallahassee (Fla.) Community College, which has sent the likes of Bootsy Thornton and Jason Cipolla to the Big East. Tyler did not play last season, but was solid for the Eagles in 1999-2000 (12.0 ppg, 8.0 rpg).

The Jaspers also have high hopes for 6-6 sophomore **Jason Bennett**, a physical forward from Connecticut who did not qualify to play last season. The lefty's style reminds some of Anthony Mason or former Florida star Donnell Harvey, now of the Dallas Mavericks.

"We're hoping he can be that type of explosive athlete for us," Gonzalez said.

Willie Haynes, a 6-8 senior, also possesses a great deal of athleticism. Haynes (2.4 ppg, 2.2 rpg) showed speed and jumping ability last year while making the adjustment from junior college to Division I.

"He's a little bit raw, but he gave us good energy off the bench," Gonzalez said.

The Jaspers again lost senior Noah Coughlin, who has been limited by injuries the last two seasons, again this year because of a groin injury. The 6-5 Coughlin (8.8 ppg, 4.5 rpg, 1.8 apg) is a strong outside shooter who scored 24 points in 27 minutes against Hartford, but played only four games last season after he was injured.

Freshmen **Charus Moore** and **Kareem Grant** could also see time in the frontcourt. The 6-7 Moore (17.0 ppg, 9.0 rpg) runs the floor well and was selected the most valuable player at Worcester (Mass.) Academy last season. The 6-6 Grant (12.0 ppg) helped St. Thomas More (Conn.) to the New England Class A prep championship. He can apply strong pressure on the wing and can score in a variety of ways.

The task of running the team falls into the hands of savvy senior point guard **Von Damien "Mugsy" Green**. Green, a transfer from San Jacinto (Texas) Junior College, stepped in right away last season and didn't let up.

"Mugsy's a tough New York City guard," Gonzalez said. "He gets in the lane and he does the things that make us go."

The 5-10 Green (9.8 ppg, 3.3 rpg, 5.7 apg, 1.8 apg) played almost 36 minutes per game and finished second in the conference in both assists and steals while shooting .402 from the floor and .805 from the free-throw line. If he can cut his turnovers (3.4) down a bit, the Jaspers should function even better.

The versatility of 6-2 junior **Justin Jackette** is another key for Manhattan. Jackette (11.5 ppg, 3.9 rpg, 1.7 apg, 1.5 spg), a transfer from William & Mary, enjoyed a solid first season with the Jaspers and is a well-rounded player who can handle the ball, pass, rebound and get to the free-throw line, where he is almost automatic (.882 FT).

"I think Justin will probably be the unofficial leader of the team because he really plays hard and he can really defend," Gonzalez said.

Jackette, who missed the MAAC Tournament with a partial MCL tear, is also quite scrappy, and that mentality may allow him to succeed at the small forward spot and make room for transfer **Luis Flores** at shooting guard. Flores sat out last season after playing at Rutgers in 1999-00, where he averaged 3.9 points and 1.4 rebounds in 29 games.

"He can really score," Gonzalez said. "If he can make his shots, he makes us dangerous. He's terrific off the dribble."

The addition of Flores will help offset the loss of Bruce Seals, the MAAC Rookie of the Year in 1999-2000 who failed to make the grade in the classroom. Seals (8.4 ppg, 3.4 rpg, 1.1 apg, 1.1 spg) struggled through his sophomore season, but was still a threat to score for the Jaspers.

Freshman **Justin Gatling**, a combo guard from Largo, Md., will back up Green at the point. Gatling (15.0 ppg, 3.0 rpg, 6.0 apg, 2.0 spg) played for Joe Wootten at Bishop O'Connell High School.

Additional depth will come from three walk-ons, sophomore **Sean Kelly** (0.0 ppg) and freshmen **Junior Clayton** and **Pat Cremen**. Clayton played at Avon Old Farms (Conn.) and Cremen is from Christian Brothers Academy in Lincroft, N.J.

2001-2002 SCHEDULE

Nov.	12	#@Syracuse
	23	Holy Cross
	26	@Long Island
	30	Denver
Dec.	3	Hartford
	5	@St. Peters
	8	St. John's
	21	Hofstra
	27-28	##ECAC Holiday Festival
Jan.	3	@Loyola
	7	Niagara
	10	Fairfield
	12	@Marist
	17	@Siena
	19	Rider
	22	Marist
	25	@Iona
	30	St. Peter's
Feb.	2	@Fairfield
	8	@Canisius
	10	@Niagara
	13	Canisius
	15	@Rider
	18	Loyola
	22	Iona
	28	###MAAC Tournament
March	1-4	###MAAC Tournament

@Road Games
#Preseason NIT (if Manhattan wins, it will play again on Nov. 15 against Fordham or DePaul; semifinals and final Nov. 21 and 23 at Madison Square Garden, NY)
##Madison Square Garden, NY (vs. Fordham first round; also Iona, Seton Hall)
###Pepsi Arena, Albany NY

BLUE RIBBON ANALYSIS

BACKCOURT	B
BENCH/DEPTH	B+
FRONTCOURT	B
INTANGIBLES	B

Gonzalez admits to being a bit of a sandbagger. Although this is clearly his deepest and most talented team during his tenure with the Jaspers, it is also a bit unproven.

The backcourt is solid with Green and Jackette returning, and Flores should provide a boost offensively. The Jaspers have plenty of talented players up front, but none who have proven they can be consistent game in and game out.

The loss of Brown, the school's No. 3 career scorer, means Manhattan will need to find other sources for points and rebounds. Holmes, Bennett and Johnson should be productive and Tyler, a transfer from Tallahassee Junior College, could be a real find at center.

The challenge for Gonzalez is finding the right mix. He is a coach who likes to play up-tempo, aggressive basketball but has been a bit restricted in his first two seasons. That shouldn't be the case this year because the Jaspers begin the season with 12 healthy scholarship players.

"It's taken us two and a half years to get the roster this way, and I'm excited about it," Gonzalez said. "I feel like we well be able to play the style that we've wanted to the last two years, but haven't been able to because we've been short-handed.

"We've got more choices and more bodies. We just have to develop some guys early in the year."

It may take time for Manhattan to mold its lineup together, but the Jaspers should improve throughout the season and be a difficult match for anyone in the league by the time January and February roll around.

(S.B.)

 **Marist**

LOCATION	Poughkeepsie, NY
CONFERENCE	Metro Atlantic Athletic
LAST SEASON	17-13 (.567)
CONFERENCE RECORD	11-7 (t-4th)
STARTERS LOST/RETURNING	1/4
NICKNAME	Red Foxes
COLORS	Red & White
HOMECOURT	McCann Center (3,944)
COACH	Dave Magarity (St. Francis, Pa. '74)
RECORD AT SCHOOL	215-212 (15 years)
CAREER RECORD	275-288 (20 years)
ASSISTANTS	Stephen Sauers (Albany '90)
	Eugene Burroughs (Richmond '94)
	Kyle Mostransky (Marist '01)
TEAM WINS (last 5 years)	6-11-16-14-17
RPI (last 5 years)	289-203-136-191-143
2000-01 FINISH	Lost in conference semifinal.

If there is one thing you should know about Marist this season, this is it: The Red Foxes are not going to sneak up on anybody in the Metro Atlantic Athletic Conference.

After being picked to finish seventh and eighth, respectively, in the last two MAAC preseason coaches polls, Marist has been near the top of the conference for the majority of the last two regular seasons, earning the fourth seed in the conference tournament each year.

Given the competitive balance of the MAAC (the top six teams finished within a game of each other last season), forecasting the correct order of finish is about as easy as being an accurate weatherman in Buffalo. But most coaches around the league are mentioning Marist as one of the top contenders.

There are two reasons the Red Foxes should stay in the hunt from start to finish: senior guards **Sean Kennedy** and **Rick Smith**, who are starting side by side for the third straight season.

"When you have good guards you are going to be able to be in just about every game," said Marist coach Dave Magarity, who received league several coach-of-the-year honors and a new four-year contract after last season.

It all starts with Kennedy (9.2 ppg, 3.1 rpg, 8.1 apg, 2.4 spg), a wispy 6-2, 170-pound gym rat from Long Island who doesn't stop until his team prevails. Kennedy, the first Red Fox to earn first-team All-MAAC honors, led the conference and finished third in the country in assists last season. He also topped the conference and ranked 23rd in the nation in steals.

"He's the head, he's the one that runs our team," Magarity said. "He knows he has the confidence of the coaching staff to run the show and he's proved that he can do that and he's earned that right."

Kennedy already ranks fourth on Marist's career list with 448 career assists and should finish second all time if he stays healthy this season. But he's more than just a playmaker. He is a clutch player with a flair for the dramatic, having closed the 1999-2000 regular-season with a half-court heave at the buzzer to beat rival Siena.

"He's just a special, special player," Magarity said. "He's not just a passer and he's not just a scorer. He is such a leader and he is such a winner."

As is Smith, who has been a presence for the Red Foxes ever since he stepped in for an injured Bo Larragan and started the first nine games of his freshman season.

"From that point on he has made it clear that he could compete physically with any guards in the league," Magarity said.

One of the MAAC's top backcourt defenders, the 6-3 Smith (11.3 ppg, 4.3 rpg, 2.2 apg, 1.4 spg) has also made steady progress on offense throughout his career. He has the physical strength to post up and the range to hit outside jump shots (.333 3PT).

"I think Kennedy is a special player, but Smith is a guy that has always been overlooked and overshadowed," Magarity said. "Smith is just one of those guys that gets it done every night. He's our best defender and he's a warrior."

Smith averaged 20 points in Marist's two MAAC Tournament games and was the only player who did not play in the championship game to make the all-tournament team. He also showed his leadership during a December win over Siena and road loss to Richmond when Kennedy was out with an injury.

"He's irreplaceable," Magarity said. "He just does so many things that help you win."

Just having Kennedy and Smith would make the Marist backcourt good, but there is also strength in numbers.

The Red Foxes were most effective last season when 6-7 junior **Nick Eppehimer**, who plays any position from shooting guard to power forward, was on the floor. Eppehimer (7.4 ppg, 3.4 rpg) made 25 starts and is effective as both a long-range shooter and trail post.

"He's really versatile and has really worked hard," Magarity said. "He's kind of a Wally Szczerbiak, Dan Majerle type."

Marist has also added three backcourt players, all with the ability to contribute.

Brandon Ellerbee, a 5-11 point guard from Plano, Texas, is the heir apparent to Kennedy at the point. Ellerbee (13.0 ppg, 8.0 apg) attended Plano East High School, the same school that produced Michigan "Fab Five" member Jimmy King, and was rated among the 31st best player in Texas and the fifth best point guard.

"He's a steal for us," Magarity said. "He's about as close as you can get athletically to [former Loyola College star] Jason Rowe."

The Red Foxes could turn up the pressure by playing Kennedy, Smith and Ellerbee together and also have the option of turning to experience by inserting transfers **Anthony Walker** and **David Bennett** into the lineup.

Walker's name may be familiar to MAAC followers because the 6-3 junior spent his first two seasons at Loyola College. A member of the 1999 MAAC All-Rookie Team, Walker (7.5 ppg, 2.6 rpg) was Loyola's second-leading three-point threat as a sophomore. In addition to his outside shooting, Walker should provide solid defense on the wing.

"He'll fit in well," Magarity said. "He gives us experience and depth."

Bennett, a 6-1, 235-pound combo guard, is one of the latest members of Marist's pipeline to Snow (Utah) College. Bennett (10.7 ppg, 3.0 rpg, 4.4 apg, 1.1 spg), who played with fellow newcomer **Jared Hunsaker** and holdover **Matt Tullis** at Snow, gives the Red Foxes another shooter. Bennett led the Scenic West Athletic Conference in both three-point (.444) and free-throw (.863) shooting percentage last season.

"He's a very good penetrator and he shoots the ball very well," Magarity said. "He's just an all-purpose type of guard."

Eric Sosler (0.3 ppg), a 6-3 sophomore walk-on, also returns after seeing action in 10 games last season.

The Red Foxes did lose Sherman Whittenburg (5.0 ppg, 1.1 rpg), who transferred to Division II Adelphi, but the addition of Ellerbee, Walker and Bennett should more than offset his departure.

Many teams with such a strong backcourt might suffer in the frontcourt, but that shouldn't be the case with Marist. The Red Foxes will miss Drew Samuels, a second-team All-MAAC forward, but have plenty of players ready to step up, led by the 6-9 Tullis.

After taking some time to adjust from junior college to Division I, Tullis (7.3 ppg, 4.9 rpg,), a senior, emerged as a consistent performer down low. His leadership and performance earned enough respect from his teammates and coaches that he was selected a team captain.

"He's very athletic and very, very good," Magarity said. "He's not a traditional post-up guy, but if he gets you down there he can score because he's got good athletic ability and instincts."

He also has a trusted friend in the 6-8 junior Hunsacker, his former teammate at Snow and Mount View High School in Orem, Utah. Hunsacker (9.6 ppg, 5.3 rpg, 1.8 apg) was an inside force for the Badgers last season, making 124-of-192 shots (.646) from the field.

"He's just a real good low-post player," Magarity said. "He's just a smart, strong, physical kid. He was exactly what we were looking for."

Sophomore **Dennis Young** (2.4 ppg, 1.5 rpg) showed flashes of what he can do during spot duty last season and Magarity is counting on the 6-8 Georgia native to be more of a consistent contributor this season.

Two players, red-shirt freshman **Steve Castleberry** and late signee **Jack Watson**, will add depth at center. The 6-11 Castleberry (18.1 ppg, 9.2 rpg, 2.5 bpg in 1999-2000) played at Solebury Prep in New Jersey and spent last season adding strength.

"He hit the weights hard and had a good summer," Magarity said. "I think he's got a chance, he really does."

Watson, a 6-7 junior from Fort Scott Junior College in Kansas, is a Dallas native whose forte is physical play in the paint. Last season, he averaged 12.0 points, eight rebounds, two assists and two steals per game.

"He's a real physical kid, a space eater," Magarity said. "By adding him it gives us another body in there and some insurance."

Although nobody in the frontcourt aside from Tullis has proven themselves in Division I yet, Magarity is confident he can find enough help for the Red Foxes to be effective and improve on rebounding, their main shortcoming last season.

"We've got to rebound better," said Magarity, whose club was out-rebounded by 1.6 boards per game. "That was one thing we didn't do a great job of last year."

Given the strength of its backcourt, any improvement in the frontcourt could help Marist make an even stronger push in 2001-02.

2001-2002 SCHEDULE

Nov.	16-17	#Pepsi-Marist Classic
	21	South Alabama
	24	@Massachusetts
	29	@Lafayette
Dec.	1	@Bowling Green
	6	Siena
	9	*Rider
	22	Central Florida
	28	LaSalle
	30	@Army
Jan.	2	@St. Peter's
	5	Niagara
	7	@Canisius
	12	Manhattan
	15	Iona
	17	@Niagara
	22	@Manhattan
	26	Fairfield
	30	Loyola
Feb.	3	@Loyola
	6	@Iona
	11	Canisius
	14	@Fairfield
	17	Rider
	21	St. Peter's
	23	@Siena
	28	##MAAC Tournament
March	1-4	##MAAC Tournament

@Road Games
*Sovereign Bank Arena
#Poughkeepsie, NY (vs. Drexel first round; also

Columbia, Northeastern)
##Pepsi Arena, Albany, NY

BLUE RIBBON ANALYSIS

BACKCOURT	B
BENCH/DEPTH	B+
FRONTCOURT	B
INTANGIBLES	B

MAAC backcourts just don't get much better than Marist's Kennedy and Smith, especially now that both are seniors with three years of starting experience.

The combination of Kennedy and Smith gives the Red Foxes stability few teams in this guard-oriented conference can match. Marist should be able to withstand almost any defense opponents come up with and just having Kennedy and Smith around should make things easier on their teammates in terms of getting open shots and handling pressure. Newcomers Walker, Bennett and Ellerbee add depth at the guard spot that makes Marist all the more dangerous.

Tullis and Eppehimer also return and know their roles in the system. Young and newcomers Hunsacker and Watson should provide the help on the glass that the Red Foxes need. The challenge is having the right group of players on the court at the proper time.

"We just have to get everybody on the same page and playing together," Magarity said. "The guards have to buy into it and the posts have to buy into it."

If that happens, the Red Foxes should be able to compete with every team in the league on most nights and may be ready to break through with a trip to the conference tournament championship game and, maybe, an NCAA Tournament berth.

(S.B.)

Niagara

LOCATION	Lewiston, NY
CONFERENCE	Metro Atlantic Athletic
LAST SEASON	15-13 (.536)
CONFERENCE RECORD	12-6 (t-1st)
STARTERS LOST/RETURNING	1/4
NICKNAME	Purple Eagles
COLORS	Purple & White
HOMECOURT	Gallagher Center (2,400)
COACH	Joe Mihalich (LaSalle '78)
RECORD AT SCHOOL	49-37 (3 years)
CAREER RECORD	49-37 (3 years)
ASSISTANTS	Mike Elfers (Wittenberg '85)
	John Coffino (Iona)
	Akbar Waheed (Niagara '99)
TEAM WINS (last 5 years)	11-14-17-17-15
RPI (last 5 years)	217-128-127-146-148
2000-01 FINISH	Lost in conference quarterfinal.

Want to know what the Niagara Purple Eagles will be like this season? Get your hands on a tape of their regular-season finale, a 69-65 victory at Siena last Feb. 24, and your questions will be answered.

Niagara played without MAAC Player-of-the-Year Demond Stewart, who missed the game with a foot injury, and didn't miss a beat as **Michael Schmidt** scored 20 points and **Daryl Greene** and **Tremmel Darden** each hit for 18. The Purple Eagles won and prevented the Saints from earning the top seeding in the conference tournament.

So, Niagara's as good as anyone in the league this year, right? Well, it isn't that simple, but it might not be that far off. Fact is, the only player the Purple Eagles don't return is Stewart (19.6 ppg, 7.7 rpg, 1.7 apg, 1.7 spg), but one game does not provide enough evidence to suggest Niagara can just plug in a replacement and zoom to the top.

"Everyone says, 'You only lost one player,' " Niagara coach Joe Mihalich said. "But, we lost Demond Stewart, who was player of the year in our conference, and there are some intangibles we lose in trying to replace him."

Things like Stewart's leadership, steals and assists will be missed, but so will the nearly 20 points he scored game in and game out. Most of the burden will fall to seniors Greene (10.6 ppg, 3.5 rpg, 5.0 apg, 1.1 spg) and Schmidt (14.8 ppg, 4.5 rpg, 2.6 apg, 1.4 spg), talented players who often took a backseat to Stewart.

"Last year they had a tendency to play off of Demond, this year they are going to step to the forefront," said Mihalich, who has led the Purple Eagles to three straight

winning seasons and received a contract extension through 2006-07 in the off-season.

Although both were effective last season, Greene and Schmidt also return with something to prove.

Greene, a preseason All-MAAC selection who averaged 17.5 points as a sophomore, battled foot injuries throughout last season and didn't have the quickness that usually sets him apart from most opponents. The point guard enters his final season healthy and ready to return to his old form and make up for lost time, including the three games he was forced to miss last season.

"He has an uncanny way of doing the right thing at the right time, and he makes the big shot," Mihalich said of Greene, who still finished third in the conference in assists.

Schmidt, a 6-5 wing, earned third-team All-MAAC accolades, while still showing the effects of sitting out a year after transferring from Texas A&M. His biggest moment came on Feb. 2, when he sank a three-pointer at the buzzer to beat Manhattan on the road. A Toronto native, he played with the Canadian National Team over the summer and should show even more this season.

"He's a real talented guy," Mihalich said. "Obviously he can shoot it and he can score."

So can **James "Mook" Reaves**, a 6-8 sophomore forward who is the likely candidate to be Niagara's third option on offense. Reaves (9.3 ppg, 7.7 rpg, 1.3 bpg) emerged in the second half of the season, averaging 12.6 points in the final five games of the regular season, and earned a spot on the MAAC's All-Rookie team.

Reaves dedicated himself to a training program and lost about 30 pounds before last season. If he stays in shape, he will be a tough match-up for most post players in this league.

"He's got a chance to be a real, real special player," Mihalich said. "He's got great hands, great feet, he's a tough kid and he's real, real strong."

More inside help will come from seniors **Shey Cohen** and **Christos Defoudis**, junior **Luis Villafane** and sophomores **Tomas Kukla** and **Paul de Wet**.

Every team needs players like the 6-8 Cohen (4.4 ppg, 4.2 rpg), who does whatever it takes to win regardless of the pain involved.

"He's got absolutely no regard for his body," Mihalich said of the 26-year-old native of Israel. "He just goes out there and throws it all around. He also gets 'opportunity' baskets and guards the opponent's toughest post player."

Defoudis (5.3 ppg, 3.1 rpg) and Villafane (1.0 ppg, 1.6 rpg) both played in every game last season and can help Niagara improve its rebounding. To a lesser degree, so can de Wet (1.2 ppg) and Kukla (0.4 ppg). Both are foreign-born players who need more experience to contribute in games, but will push the players ahead of them in practice.

"It will be Social Darwinism," Mihalich said of the physical play he expects from his postmen in practice. "Only the strong will survive."

Which is also true in the backcourt, where junior **Rhossi Carron** (4.0 ppg, 1.6 apg) and sophomore Darden (8.4 ppg, 3.1 rpg) proved their value, particularly when Greene struggled, last season.

With Greene coming off such a solid sophomore season, not much was expected of the 5-10 Carron, who played just 6.5 minutes per game as a freshman. His inexperience wasn't a factor down the stretch as Caron scored in double figures in three straight games while running the team.

"The bell went off and he really answered it," Mihalich said.

The same can be said for Darden, a 6-4 dunking machine who was expected to need time to adjust to the college game. Instead, he contributed right away and improved the second half of the season. He made 12 starts and averaged 11.6 points over the final seven games.

"Sometimes you get lucky and we did with him," Mihalich said. "He's an exceptional, electric athlete and he's going to continue to do good things for us."

Senior walk-on **Rauly Leino** (0.0 ppg), a former team manager, returns for his second season with the squad.

Niagara will also have the services of three freshmen, including high school teammates **Alvin Cruz** and **Juan Mendez** from Florida Air Academy in Melbourne, Fla. Cruz (16.1 ppg, 7.5 apg), a 6-1 point guard, and Mendez, a 6-7 forward, led their team to the Florida Class 3A title. Mendez averaged 12.3 points and 7.3 rebounds during the playoff drive. **David Brooks**, a 6-3 shooting guard from Philadelphia, rounds out the incoming recruiting class.

2001-2002 SCHEDULE

Nov.	17	George Mason
	19	Buffalo

	24	@St. Bonaventure
	29-30	#Phoenix Classic
Dec.	6	Loyola
	8	@Siena
	11	St. John's
	20-22	##San Juan Shootout
	29	@Drexel
Jan.	2	@Akron
	5	@Marist
	7	@Manhattan
	12	Fairfield
	17	Marist
	19	@St. Peter's
	24	Rider
	26	Siena
	29	@Fairfield
Feb.	1	Iona
	3	@Rider
	8	St. Peter's
	10	Manhattan
	13	@Loyola
	16	@Canisius
	20	@Iona
	23	Canisius
	28	###MAAC Tournament
March	1-4	###MAAC Tournament

@Road Games
#Phoenix, AZ (vs. Winthrop first round; also Central Connecticut, Hartford)
##San Juan, PR (vs. Texas-Pan American first round; vs. Jacksonville/ORU winner; finals, consolation on Dec. 22)
###Pepsi Arena, Albany, NY

BLUE RIBBON ANALYSIS

BACKCOURT	B+
BENCH/DEPTH	B
FRONTCOURT	B
INTANGIBLES	B

Niagara has emerged as a consistent force in the MAAC during Mihalich's three-year tenure and the same should be true this season.

The Purple Eagles do lose their best player, Stewart, but have talent and experience coming back in a league where success is often marked by a core group of seniors.

If Greene stays healthy, he should return to the form that earned him second-team All-MAAC honors as a sophomore. Schmidt, a transfer from Texas A&M, should also take on more of a load in his second season with the club.

Carron and Darden gained valuable experience last season and give Niagara several options in the backcourt. Reeves has the potential to dominate the post and seniors Cohen and Defoudis can also be productive. Villafane provides shot blocking and experience. Cruz could be the biggest contributor in the freshman class.

Add it all up and Niagara has another solid team. The Purple Eagles need to find consistent scoring and rebounding, but have enough proven players to finish near the top if they play up to their potential and avoid injuries.

"We all need help from two special women in our life—Mother Nature and Lady Luck," Mihalich said. "We need to stay healthy and catch a couple of breaks."

(S.B.)

Rider

LOCATION	Lawrenceville, NJ
CONFERENCE	Metro Atlantic
LAST SEASON	16-12 (.571)
CONFERENCE RECORD	11-7 (t-4th)
STARTERS LOST/RETURNING	2/3
NICKNAME	Broncs
COLORS	Cranberry & White
HOMECOURT	Alumni Gymnasium (1,650)
COACH	Don Harnum (Susquehanna '86)
RECORD AT SCHOOL	62-52 (4 years)
CAREER RECORD	62-52 (4 years)
ASSISTANTS	Jim Engles (Dickinson '90)
	Tony Newsom (Niagara '93)
	Mike Spisto (Oneonta '97)
TEAM WINS (last 5 years)	14-18-12-16-16
RPI (last 5 years)	188-113-188-180-137
2000-01 FINISH	Lost in conference quarterfinal.

Want to see what the prototypical mid-major star looks like? Point your compass toward Lawrenceville, N.J., and get a load of **Mario Porter**.

Porter, Rider's 6-6 senior forward, just might be the guy Clark Kellogg had in mind when Kellogg coined the phrase "stat-sheet stuffer supreme."

You want scoring? Porter can stick the three, stuff a lob or pull up and bury his jumper somewhere in between.

How about rebounding? With above average strength and leaping ability, he can pull the ball down in traffic to start the break or stick it back for an easy basket.

Defense? Porter can step out to defend on the wing or bang bodies in the post.

Toughness? Porter played the last six weeks of last season with a stress fracture in his leg that prevented him from practicing, but still finished second in the Metro Atlantic Athletic Conference in scoring (19.2 ppg), 10th in rebounding (6.8 rpg), third in field-goal percentage (.527), sixth in steals (1.6 spg) and 12th in free-throw percentage (.739).

"I'm not so sure he knows how good he is," Rider coach Don Harnum said. "He's so humble that I almost want him to be more arrogant."

Porter, who also passes well (1.2 apg), certainly has reason to be. He made the MAAC's All-Rookie team as a freshman, earned second-team All-MAAC honors as a sophomore and was first-team as a junior.

Could player of the year be next? Certainly. Especially if Porter, whose improvement comes mainly from hard work in the weight room and on the court in the off-season, is able to dominate more games for even longer stretches than he did last season.

"He's the most explosive player in the league," Harnum said. "He's a 6-6 kid that plays like he is 6-10 at times. He jumps out of the gym and he's explosive. When he was younger, he got away with just using his athleticism, now he's more of a complete player."

He is also the only proven commodity the Broncs have in the frontcourt after the departure of Jonathan McClark (12.8 ppg, 8.6 rpg, 1.9 apg), who is now playing professionally in Spain. Juniors **Brandon "Tank" Wahlmann**, **Robert Reed** and **Vitor Goncalves**, and freshman **Armel Minyem** will try to fill McClark's role by committee.

Wahlmann (2.6 ppg, 2.2 rpg), 6-9, has the most experience and had a strong summer. He has also added about 25 pounds to his frame to help warrant his nickname, which is derived from his middle name—Tankard.

"He's mobile, he's gotten stronger and he's good defensively," Harnum said. "He's an opportunistic scorer, but he's not a polished back-to-the-basket scorer."

Reed (1.9 ppg, 1.8 rpg), a native of England, has some natural shooting ability and understands the game well, but is still adjusting to college basketball in America.

"He's been a little bit of a project, but he still has a chance," Harnum said.

Goncalves, a sturdy 6-9 and 245 pounds, comes to Rider via Utah Valley State College. Goncalves (3.6 ppg, 2.2 rpg) played just over 11 minutes per game, but Harnum believes he will be able to come in and contribute immediately around the basket and from beyond the arc.

"He's just a wide-bodied banger with a nice shooting touch," Harnum said.

At 185 pounds, the 6-9 Minyem is anything but a wide body. A native of Cameroon, Minyem still needs to add 15-20 pounds but played on a solid team at Notre Dame Academy in Middleburg, Va.

"He can shoot threes, put the ball on the floor and he's not as weak as his weight would indicate," Harnum said.

Despite returning two starters, senior **R.J. Wicks** and junior **Mike Wilson**, the competition in the backcourt will be fierce. Harnum has brought in three new players, junior-college star **Rich Baker** and freshmen **Robert Taylor** and **Jerry Johnson**, to challenge the incumbents.

"We didn't get very good guard play," Harnum said, referring to a team that finished ninth in the league in turnover margin (-1.5). "We didn't have the consistency that you need to be successful at this level."

Not many players enjoyed more success than Baker did at his level, NJCAA Division II, last season. Baker (22.5 ppg, 6.25 rpg, 7.25 apg), a 6-0 junior, finished second in the country in scoring and earned third-team All-America honors while leading Lackawanna (Penn.) Junior College to a 19-9 record and the Region XIX championship.

"It was an honor and a privilege to coach Rich Baker for two years," Lackawanna coach Eric Grundman said. "He's the best player I have ever coached."

Baker finished his Lackawanna career with 1,105 points and a 46-14 record.

"He can pretty much do it all," Harnum said. "He can score, he can pass and he can keep people out of the lane."

So can Taylor, who some considered to be the best defensive guard in Philadelphia last season, his senior year at St. John Neumann High School.

"He's got all the defensive instincts," Harnum said. "He's 6-2 with very, very long arms and gets his hands on a ton of passes."

Taylor is also a good offensive player, but needs to further develop his outside shot.

The 6-0 Johnson, who starred at J.P. McCaskey High in Lancaster, Pa., also has game.

"He's almost like a smaller model of Rich Baker, only two years younger and not as filled out," Harnum said.

Which doesn't mean he can't light it up.

"Jerry's got ridiculous range on his jump shot. He has literally got 25-foot range."

The recruits have two things in common: penchants for defense and winning.

"They will be able to keep guys in front of them," Harnum said. "Yeah, we got good defenders, but it's not like they've got other glaring weaknesses in their game."

Or a free ride. Wicks and Wilson won't give up their spots willingly, senior **Mike Scott** has shown an ability to score, and sophomore **Laurence Young** expects to be in the mix after a solid freshman season.

Wilson (6.7 ppg, 1.4 rpg, 2.0 apg, .378 3FG), a 6-2 shooting guard, started to come into his own last season and Wicks (4.0 ppg, 3.4 rpg, 1.6 apg, 1.1 spg), who can play outside at 6-4, does his job in workmanlike fashion. He will be expected to score more this season.

"He does all the little things that don't wow you," Harnum said. "He's the ultimate complementary player. He'll take a charge, come up with loose ball and guard the other team's best player on the wing."

At 6-3 Young (5.4 ppg, 1.5 rpg) will wow you, but he doesn't do it all the time.

"He's a better shooter than we expected," Harnum said. "He can also get in the lane and dunk. He's got a pretty complete game, it just needs to come together a little bit more."

The same is true for the 6-4 Scott (7.2 ppg, 3.4 rpg), who can score in bunches but struggles to take care of the ball at times.

Alwyn "Junior" Curtis also returns. The 6-0 Curtis (4.8 ppg, 1.7 rpg, 2.4 apg), a junior, is a good creative point guard who played in all 28 games last season.

"When the tempo is at a higher pace, he's very, very good," Harnum said.

With so many guards used to playing, practices figure to be intense as Harnum sorts out his rotation. One player he won't have to worry about finding time for is Sam Rotsaert, a seldom-used shooter from Belgium who left after his freshman season to play professionally in his home country.

2001-2002 SCHEDULE

Nov.	17	@Monmouth
	20	Bucknell
	24	Drexel
	28	@Princeton
Dec.	1	@Towson
	5	Seton Hall
	7	@Canisius
	9	Marist
	15	Delaware
	20	@Northeastern
Jan.	2	@Lafayette
	5	@Siena
	9	@Iona
	11	Canisius
	14	@Fairfield
	17	Loyola
	19	@Manhattan
	24	@Niagara
	27	St. Peter's
Feb.	1	@St. Peter's
	3	Niagara
	8	Fairfield
	13	Iona
	15	Manhattan
	17	@Marist
	20	Siena
	23	@Loyola
Feb.	28	#MAAC Tournament
March	1-4	#MAAC Tournament

@Road Games
#Pepsi Arena, Albany, NY

BACKCOURT	B-
BENCH/DEPTH	C
FRONTCOURT	B
INTANGIBLES	C

Rider is a tough team to figure. The Broncs will be able to ride Porter, arguably the league's best player, but it isn't easy to gauge how far he can carry them.

Porter is a monster, but right now he is alone in the frontcourt. Goncalves, Wahlmann, Reed and Minyem may develop into reliable players, but they haven't done it yet. Depth will also be a concern, especially if Porter encounters foul trouble.

Depth, albeit in a different form, may also be an issue in the backcourt where eight players will battle for time. Even with five starters returning to last year's team, the Broncs struggled at the guard spots. This year it will be a daily struggle to fill them.

"Last year was a year where everyone came back and everyone kind of knew where they fit in," Harnum said. "Coming into practice this year no one aside from Mario is guaranteed a spot."

Competition in practice is generally a healthy thing and often sorts itself out. The Broncs have many talented players and it will be Harnum's job to mix and match the right combinations.

Considering all of the question marks, with the exception of Porter, less will be expected of the Broncs this year but the ingredients are there to exceed projections if they mesh properly.

(S.B.)

St. Peter's

LOCATION	Jersey City, NJ
CONFERENCE	Metro Atlantic Athletic
LAST SEASON	4-24 (.143)
CONFERENCE RECORD	2-16 (t-9th)
STARTERS LOST/RETURNING	2/3
NICKNAME	Peacocks
COLORS	Blue & White
HOMECOURT	Yanitelli Center (3,200)
COACH	Bob Leckie (St. Peter's '69)
RECORD AT SCHOOL	4-24 (1 year)
CAREER RECORD	4-24 (1 year)
ASSISTANTS	Dennis Cook
	Devon Smith (Ohio State '00)
	Joe Palermo (St. Michael's (Vermont)
TEAM WINS (last 5 years)	13-8-14-5-4
RPI (last 5 years)	205-243-151-291-259
2000-01 FINISH	Lost in conference first round.

Bob Leckie did not take over as basketball coach at his alma mater to make quick fixes. He's in it for the long haul.

"I don't intend to use St. Peter's as a stepping stone," said Leckie, a 1969 St. Peter's graduate and member of the school's Athletic Hall of Fame. "I want to end my basketball career at St. Peter's and I intend on doing that on a successful note."

In order to do that, Leckie understands every aspect of the program needed to be changed and that what he plans on doing. An ultra-successful high school coach at Bishop Loughlin Memorial High School in Brooklyn, Leckie has brought structure and discipline to a team that had begun to accept many of the habits associated with losing.

He has the Peacocks up early with off-season weight training sessions that begin at 6 a.m. They also run together in the afternoons and attend study sessions at night.

The changes did not lead to more victories last season, but Leckie isn't panicking.

"I don't think anybody is going to put more pressure on me than I put on myself," said Leckie, who played on three NIT teams for the legendary Don Kennedy when St. Peter's basketball was at its peak.

Leckie knows he needs to recruit better players, but he isn't going to bring in just anybody who can help the Peacocks on the court. He wants well-rounded people who will succeed in the classroom and make positive contributions on campus.

The roster has undergone many changes and Leckie thinks the program is shifting back in the direction he wants it to go. Junior forward **Melvin Robinson** is the only player who played all of last season and was on the team two years ago.

"I think we are in better shape than we were last year and I think we've got a little more depth," Leckie said. "Hopefully we can stay healthy and win some more games."

Injuries were an issue last season as St. Peter's lost forward **Kamaal McQueen** to an ACL tear after just four games and junior-college transfer **Marvin Benjamin** battled a herniated disc in his lower back that cost him several games and limited his effectiveness. Both McQueen and Robinson are back for this season and the Peacocks are counting on them because they lost last year's leading scorer Keith Sellers (18.7 ppg) and rebounder Rodney Rodgers (14.2 ppg, 8.2 rpg) to graduation.

McQueen has also graduated, but he decided to come back for one more season. The 6-5 McQueen (12.5 ppg, 4.3 rpg) has rare skills for a player his size and has battled his weight throughout his career at St. Peter's.

"He is virtually unstoppable when he gets the ball inside because people can't get around him," Leckie said. "But, it limits his minutes and the number of times he can get up and down the court."

McQueen received full medical clearance from doctors late in the summer and could provide the team with a boost if he gets in shape. He nearly carried St. Peter's to victory in the 1999 MAAC Tournament as a sophomore and knows what it takes to win. Unfortunately for the Peacocks, he hasn't been healthy since. McQueen did not miss attending a practice or game after he was injured last season and Leckie says he is the most popular athlete on campus with both students and staff.

"He's a great leader," Leckie said. "He's kind of quiet and doesn't like to take the bull by the horns, but he leads by example."

Leckie, who coached against Robinson in high school, remembers the 6-5 junior as a high-flying forward at Cardozo High School. Injuries have taken away some of that athleticism, but Robinson (8.9 ppg, 4.0 rpg, 1.1 apg) still has some game left in his legs.

"He's had some great moments for us," Leckie said. "He needs to be more consistent but he can be an effective player for us."

A healthy Benjamin (4.5 ppg, 4.2 rpg) would also be beneficial. After making stops at Liberty and Marshalltown (Iowa) Community College, the 6-7 senior came to St. Peter's last season, but his health limited his ability to contribute.

Juniors **Corien John** and **Devin Thompson** are both transfers from Monroe College in the Bronx. The 6-4 John attended Erasmus Hall High School in Brooklyn and is strong around the basket. He was selected to Rick Ball's junior college honorable mention All-America list after last season (12.0 ppg, 6.0 rpg).

"He's a great finisher," Leckie said. "He's in great shape. He looks like a world-class sprinter."

The 6-5 Thompson doesn't have a great deal of basketball experience, but has raw ability that Leckie is hoping to tap.

"He's got incredible athletic skills, he can jump out of the gym," Leckie said. "Now we've got to harness that energy and turn him into a productive player."

The Peacocks also signed Ivan Bozoviz, a 6-8 forward from Yugoslavia via New Hampton Prep, but he must sit out this season as a partial qualifier.

The addition of centers Mike McKie and Andrew Dudley, both junior transfers, will also help a team that finished last in the MAAC in scoring defense (81.0 ppg) and rebounding margin (-4.5).

The 6-9 McKie, a Brooklyn native, played one season at Buffalo (8.7 ppg, 5.9 rpg) before transferring. He led the Bulls with 63 blocks in 1999-2000, which is five more rejections than the entire St. Peter's team had last season.

"He's a legitimate defensive center," Leckie said. "He's a shot blocker and has some talent."

The 6-11 Dudley is not eligible to play until the end of first semester. He transferred to St. Peter's after seeing limited action during a year and a half at Boston College. Dudley appeared in five games for the Big East regular-season champions last season (0.4 ppg, 2.0 rpg). A highly rated prospect coming out of high school, the 250-pound Dudley should provide immediate help up front.

"He's athletic and he's strong," Leckie said. "He could be a force in this league somewhere down the line."

Amir Ali, a 6-11 sophomore, also returns to compete at the center spot. Ali (1.5 ppg, 1.7 rpg) struggled with a broken bone in his foot last season and is working to get back in playing shape.

A lack of talent and depth in the backcourt will be the Peacocks' biggest problem this season, especially in a league chock full of good guards.

Much of the burden will fall on senior **Nate Brown**, another Monroe College alum. The 6-0 Brown (5.5 ppg, 2.8 rpg, 2.5 apg, 1.4 spg) started 18 games last season but often deferred to his teammates. He will be counted on for more production and leadership.

"I'm definitely looking at him to improve," Leckie said.

Corey Hinnant, a red-shirt freshman, will also see time at the point. The 5-10 Hinnant, a native of Bay Shore, N.Y., spent last season building strength to prepare for the college game. He was an All-Suffolk County selection at Bay Shore High School as a senior (16.0 ppg) and is also a solid student.

"He's got a great body and he's well ahead of most freshmen," Leckie said.

Regis Devonish, a 6-5 sophomore, showed promise as a freshman and will take over the shooting-guard spot. Devonish, who has just eight percent body fat on his 185-pound frame, added 18 pounds of muscle in the off-season. Devonish (5.1 ppg, 2.2 rpg, 1.0 apg) is also a steady ball handler and smooth long-range shooter (.395 3PT). The highlight of his first season was hitting the winning three-pointer in a 70-68 win over Fairfield.

Jeffrey Prosdocimo, a 5-10 sophomore, walked onto the team after last season started and played in five games (2.7 ppg).

With only three scholarship guards listed on their preseason roster, the Peacocks must avoid foul trouble and fatigue. Brown, Hinnant and Devonish need help handling the ball or else they will wear down and opponents will feast on St. Peter's with pressure defense.

2001-2002 SCHEDULE

Nov.	16-17	#Florida International Tournament
	21	@St. Francis, NY
	25	@Boston University
	27	@Lafayette
Dec.	1	@UNC Greensboro
	5	Manhattan
	9	*Loyola
	11	@Seton Hall
	14	Monmouth
Jan.	2	Marist
	5	Iona
	8	@Fairfield
	13	@Siena
	19	Niagara
	21	Canisius
	27	@Rider
	30	@Manhattan
Feb.	1	Rider
	3	@Iona
	6	@Canisius
	8	@Niagara
	11	@Rutgers
	14	Siena
	16	Loyola
	21	@Marist
	23	Fairfield
	28	##MAAC Tournament
March	1-4	##MAAC Tournament

@Road Games
*Sovereign Bank Arena
#Miami, FL (vs. Florida International first round; also Maine, Texas-Arlington)
##Pepsi Arena, Albany, NY

BLUE RIBBON ANALYSIS

BACKCOURT	F
BENCH/DEPTH	D
FRONTCOURT	D
INTANGIBLES	C

It takes time to rebuild a program, and Leckie is going about things at his alma mater the right way.

St. Peter's isn't in a position to pick and choose its players right now, but Leckie is pursuing athletes with potential who are also solid people. Some will turn out to be good basketball players, others will not, but they will all add to the program.

The Peacocks have some talent in the frontcourt with forwards McQueen, Robinson and Benjamin and incoming centers McKie and Dudley, but there are questions about all of them. It would be nice to see McQueen return to his 1998-99 form, but it's difficult to know what kind of toll injuries have taken on him and what kind of playing condition he will be able to maintain.

The backcourt is barren. Brown is a decent player and Devonish has potential at shooting guard, but that's it. Beyond them the Peacocks are left with a red-shirt freshman and walk-on. The guards need help, but bar-

ring a huge surprise, there doesn't look like any is on the way.

Leckie admits he needs to recruit better players for this program to turn around. As the former coach at Bishop Loughlin in Brooklyn, he is plugged in to the New York City scene and needs to use his connections to upgrade the talent level.

It isn't easy to build from the bottom up, and just getting out of the basement (its home for the last two years) would be an accomplishment for St. Peter's this season.

(S.B.)

Siena

LOCATION	Loudonville, NY
CONFERENCE	Metro Atlantic
LAST SEASON	20-11 (.645)
CONFERENCE RECORD	12-6 (t-1st)
STARTERS LOST/RETURNING	2/3
NICKNAME	Saints
COLORS	Green & Gold
HOMECOURT	Pepsi Arena (15,500)
COACH	Rob Lanier (St. Bonaventure '90)
RECORD AT SCHOOL	First Year
CAREER RECORD	First Year
ASSISTANTS	Rob Jackson (Northeastern '74)
	Steve Seymour (Bridgewater State '81)
	Neil Berkman (Maryland '91)
TEAM WINS (last 5 years)	9-17-25-24-20
RPI (last 5 years)	245-123-41-80-117
2000-01 FINISH	Lost in conference semifinal.

Big shoes are nothing new in the Lanier family, where Bob Lanier used his size-22 feet to get out of Buffalo and carry St. Bonaventure to the 1970 Final Four and himself to a Hall-of-Fame career in the NBA.

Now, there's another Lanier with big shoes to fill. Rob Lanier, Bob's 32-year-old cousin and a former St. Bonaventure player, is following in the significant footsteps of Paul Hewitt and Louis Orr as the head coach at Siena.

"I think it goes with this particular job that the expectations are built in," said Rob Lanier, who was announced as the Saints' top man on April 18. "You want the expectations to be met at the same level as the commitment, and the commitment is very strong here."

Indeed it is. The Saints have averaged 23 victories over the course of the last three seasons and managed 20 and a tie for first place in the MAAC last year despite being picked seventh in the coaches' preseason poll.

With Hewitt now enjoying success at Georgia Tech and Orr on the sideline at Seton Hall after just one season at Siena, the torch fueled with another season of high expectations has been passed to Lanier and he is eager to hold it even higher.

"The good news is they haven't won a national championship and they didn't win the league last season," said Lanier, a 10-year assistant who spent the last two seasons on Rick Barnes' staff at Texas. "As good as they have been, there's room for improvement and they haven't lost their focus."

Lanier is hoping his players keep their focus, because it will make his job of building on past success easier. However, that task will be made a bit more difficult after the graduation of Scott Knapp (13.1 ppg, 2.4 rpg, 3.3 apg) and Isaiah Stewart (8.1 ppg, 2.0 rpg, 3.6 apg), the Saints' starting guards last season.

"They won with the last two coaches, so there are some basic things about winning that they already understand," Lanier said of his returning players. "They know how to win, now we want to win at a higher level."

Lanier knows defense is the ticket. He saw first-hand what good defense can do at Texas as the Longhorns won 49 games the last two seasons despite struggling on offense. Siena led the MAAC in scoring last season (77.68 ppg), but was sixth in scoring defense (73.68) despite finishing second in field-goal percentage by limiting opponents to .422 shooting.

"Ultimately, our goal is to be the best defensive team in our league," Lanier said.

Lanier's commitment to defense is apparent when he talks about his players, even the established veterans like senior **Dwayne Archbold**, a second-team All-MAAC selection last season.

"Defensively, I think people are going to be impressed with the mentality he brings," Lanier said.

They are also likely to be impressed with the 6-5 swingman's offense. Archbold (14.9 ppg, 6.0 rpg, 2.1 apg), one of three returning starters in the frontcourt, is a dangerous outside shooter (.418 3FG) who can also get to the basket.

Senior **Andy Cavo** (8.1 ppg, 4.4 rpg, 1.2 apg) needed some time to overcome the effects of a one-year layoff after transferring from New Hampshire, but settled in as a dependable player. The 6-6 Cavo started 20 of the last 21 games, but had shoulder surgery after the season and could not participate in the team's off-season workouts.

"He's definitely a superstar of a kid," Lanier said. "I know that much, and, he can shoot the ball."

Sophomore **Justin Miller** played exceptionally well for a freshman, starting the final 22 games of last season at power forward after **Dale Taylor** was lost for the season with a stress fracture in his left foot. The 6-8 Miller (8.2 ppg, 4.0 rpg) showed an ability to score inside and blocked twice as many shots (29) than any other Saint.

"If he makes natural progress, he should play a prominent role," Lanier said. "He can score inside and do some things facing the basket, which is what you want from a power forward."

Taylor (4.3 ppg, 4.1 rpg), a 6-9, 220-pound senior, has good range for a big man and also moves well to block shots on defense. He is expected back at full strength to start the season.

"He gives us a strong physical presence and a mature individual that can be counted on," Lanier said.

The same is true for **James Clinton**, another 6-9, 220-pound senior, who missed 14 games last season with a stress fracture. Clinton (7.2 ppg, 3.4 rpg) is one of the most athletic players in the conference and his ability to pass and handle the ball allows him to play at almost every spot on the floor.

"He's a guy with a lot of talent and I think right now he's starting to develop a sense of urgency," Lanier said. "If he plays to the level of his potential, he could have a very successful season and help separate our team from some of the other teams in our league."

Junior **Michael Buhrman** (4.5 ppg, 4.0 rpg), 6-9, provides the Saints with toughness and experience. He came back to play in 24 games last season despite tearing cartilage in his left knee and has surprising range on his jump shot. He also missed the spring workouts after having his knee scoped.

"His reputation is that of a tough, hard-nosed guy that every coach wants on his team," Lanier said. "I expect him to be right in the middle of it making plays to help us win games."

All of the injuries in the frontcourt forced **Austin Andrews**, an athletic 6-9 sophomore forward, to forego his red-shirt and enter the lineup after sitting out the first nine games last season. Andrews (2.8 ppg, 2.4 rpg) runs the floor well and has a great deal of confidence in his jump shot. Although the plan was to hold Andrews out last season, he should benefit from his playing experience. Expect him to come off the bench and play a role in the Saints' pressure defense schemes.

"He has the potential to be a guy that really energizes our team," Lanier said.

The Saints are expecting a big season from 6-7 junior **Prosper Karangwa** (7.8 ppg, 2.4 rpg, 1.5 apg, 1.2 spg) to offset the loss of Stewart, a two-year starter at the point.

Nicknamed "Half a Penny" by the Canadian press, the Montreal native creates match-up problems with his height and gained valuable experience playing in the Tournament of the Americas and Goodwill Games with the Canadian National team. Talent has never been an issue with Karangwa, and he could earn a place among the league's elite players with more consistency.

"He really distinguished himself as a guy who wants to take that next step and take advantage of the enormous talent that he possesses," Lanier said.

With so many options in the frontcourt, Lanier may play Archbold at Knapp's two-guard spot. Sophomore **J.J. Harvey** (3.1 ppg, 1.6 rpg, 1.4 apg), a 6-4 swing player who is skilled enough to play the point, is one of the team's best on-the-ball defenders and should also work himself into the rotation.

"He's got the potential to be a special player on the defensive end," Lanier said of Harvey, who also had his knee scoped in the off-season.

The Saints may have found their solution at the point from a surprising source—former Fairfield guard **Mark Price**. Price (5.9 ppg, 1.4 rpg, 1.0 apg in 1999-2000), a 6-1 sophomore, left the Stags before last season and has joined Siena as a walk-on.

Siena fans also can't accuse Orr of leaving the cupboard bare. The former Syracuse star signed four players last November. The prize may be **Brent Sniezyk**, a 6-10, 240-pound center from nearby Broadalbin-Perth High School.

"He brings the kind of size and physique that we would have liked to have had at Texas," Lanier said

The Saints also landed **Tommy Mitchell**, a 6-3 guard from Tyler, Texas, **Cantrell Fletcher**, a 5-7 point guard from St. John Neumann in Philadelphia, and **Gary Holle**, a 6-8 forward from Troy, N.Y., Catholic.

Lanier admits he doesn't know a lot about the incoming players because they were recruited by Orr, but he likes what he's seen from Mitchell, who enrolled last January, during individual workouts.

"He's a good athlete and a hard-working kid," Lanier said. "His time is definitely going to come because he works at it and he's going to be quite a leader."

Lanier hopes he is, too. Although he has never been a college head coach before, he has taken several teams overseas and doesn't fancy himself as overly demonstrative on the sideline.

"I try to coach like I understand that the players are the ones that win games," Lanier said.

Considering the talent and tradition at Siena, he should get plenty of opportunities to demonstrate that belief.

2001-2002 SCHEDULE

Nov.	24	@Fordham
	27	Albany
Dec.	1	@Cleveland State
	4	Toledo
	6	@Marist
	8	Niagara
	11	Hartford
	20	St. Bonaventure
	29	@Rice
	31	@Xavier
Jan.	3	@Iona
	5	Rider
	10	@Loyola
	13	St. Peter's
	17	Manhattan
	19	@Canisius
	21	Iona
	26	@Niagara
	28	Canisius
Feb.	5	@Manhattan
	7	Loyola
	10	@Fairfield
	14	@St. Peter's
	16	Fairfield
	20	@Rider
	23	Marist
Feb.	28	#MAAC Tournament
March	1-4	#MAAC Tournament

@Road Games
#Pepsi Arena, Albany, NY

BLUE RIBBON ANALYSIS

BACKCOURT	B
BENCH/DEPTH	B+
FRONTCOURT	A-
INTANGIBLES	B

Plenty will be made about the fact Lanier is Siena's third men's basketball coach in three seasons. People should save their breath.

Sure, college basketball is a coaches' game, but not even the best coaches can win without players. Suffice to say that Siena has players and Lanier isn't about to come in and tear up a successful formula. Tweak, yes. Tear up, not on your life.

At 32, Lanier is young enough to remember what it's like to be a player and experienced enough to know what needs to be done to direct a winning program.

The Saints need to settle their backcourt situation, but Karangwa has the talent to be one of the league's best point men and Archbold has the versatility to move from small forward to shooting guard.

If Archbold shifts to the backcourt, Siena will be able to play more of its athletic forwards and apply more pressure. Lanier is a coach who believes in defense first and will drill his system into his players' heads until it becomes automatic. He'll also coach offense, but figures that will come easier if the defensive system is mastered.

Lanier knows a lot will be expected of his team and plans on doing everything he can to have it ready to make plays and continue to be successful in a very even league.

"You need to win when it's time to win," he said. "You have to be effective on offense in the halfcourt late in the game and you need to get stops on defense."

If the Saints continue to do those things, the wins will keep coming. Regardless of who's wearing the suit on the sidelines.

(S.B.)

Akron

LOCATION	Akron, OH
CONFERENCE	Mid-American
LAST SEASON	12-16 (.429)
CONFERENCE RECORD	9-9 (6th East)
STARTERS LOST/RETURNING	2/3
NICKNAME	Zips
COLORS	Blue & Gold
HOMECOURT	James A. Rhodes Arena (5,942)
COACH	Dan Hipsher (Bowling Green '77)
RECORD AT SCHOOL	75-87 (6 years)
CAREER RECORD	201-132 (12 years)
ASSISTANTS	Brian Donoher (Dayton '92) Keith Dambrot (Akron '82) Lannis Timmons (Central State '75)
TEAM WINS (last 5 years)	8-17-18-17-12
RPI (last 5 years)	229-134-99-124-181
2000-01 FINISH	Lost in conference first round.

Akron finished .500 in Mid-American Conference play last season, a pretty nice accomplishment considering everything that went wrong for the Zips. It's also a credit to coach Dan Hipsher for holding the ship together.

The Zips lost their leading scorer and the coach's son, forward **Andy Hipsher**, after six games because of two bulging discs in his back. The 6-8, 203-pound Hipsher (14.2 ppg, 4.3 ppg, .463 FG, .791 FT) had off-season surgery and is expected back at full strength. He took a medical red-shirt and has three years of eligibility remaining.

Forward **David Falknor**, a 6-7, 245-pound senior, dislocated his right big toe while running sprints near the end of a February practice and missed six games. Falknor (9.4 ppg, 3.7 rpg) finished second in the nation and led the MAC in three-point shooting accuracy, making 47-of-87 for a .540 percentage. He also had off-season surgery.

Last season's squad also lost 6-9 center Marco Morgan (3.9 ppg, 2.7 rpg) who was declared academically ineligible after seven games and didn't return this year. Others not back with the Zips are Bruce Weinkein (6.6 ppg, 3.8 rpg, 29 blocks), Klaas Zollner (1.3 ppg, 1.5 rpg), David Kalb (0.3 ppg, 0.4 rpg) and Julius Payne (0.5 ppg, 0.2 rpg).

Having Hipsher and Falknor healthy will strengthen Akron's frontcourt production. Hipsher is an all-conference candidate who can play multiple positions. He is probably best suited for the small-forward spot but has the ability to score around the basket and rebound. With his long arms and ball handling skill, he also can play on the perimeter.

"Andy is our most flexible guy," Hipsher said. "He can go anywhere from two to four [positions]. We really don't have another guy like that."

Falknor's return to full speed is still questionable for the early season. But, when Falknor is healthy and in good physical condition, he's someone other teams can't ignore. It's not difficult to find Falknor on the court. Last season, 47 of his 68 field goals were of the three-point variety.

"David is as good a shooter as there is anywhere in the country," Hipsher said. "Every time he shoots it you kind of expect it to go in."

Falknor was the leading sniper on the NCAA's top three-point shooting team. Akron shot almost as well from behind the three-point line as it did on conventional field-goals, connecting on 189-of-436 attempts for .433 percent.

The Zips return three of their top four long-range shooters and have five of their top six scorers back. The most important loss was senior guard Nate Schindewolf (14.6 ppg, .441 3PT, .870 FT), an All-MAC honorable mention selection.

Coach Hipsher fully expects the Zips to bounce back from a sixth-place finish in the MAC East Division.

"When you throw Andy back in the mix with the recruits coming in I think we're in pretty good shape," he said.

Akron's starting backcourt returns intact with **Rashon Brown** and **Emmanuel Smith** establishing themselves there last year. The 6-1 senoir Brown (12.5 ppg, 2.3 rpg, .480 FG, .846 FT) led the team with 92 assists (4.1 apg) after sitting out a year as a transfer from Western Kentucky. Brown became eligible at the end of the first semester and started all 22 games he appeared in.

"Early in the year we had trouble getting the ball to mid-court and Rashon has no problem there," Hipsher said. "He gives us speed and quickness on the offensive and defensive ends."

Brown and 6-3 junior starter Smith (10.7 ppg, 3.0 rpg, 2.5 apg, .420 3PT) shared the team lead with 31 steals apiece. Smith was uncomfortable playing point guard before Brown gained eligibility, but made nice progress during the latter stages of his debut season.

Smith was the 1999 Mr. Ohio Basketball award winner at Euclid High School, where he averaged 28.4 points and attracted the interest of Big Ten, Big East and ACC schools. He sat out the 1999-2000 season at Akron for academic reasons.

Another good outside shooter in the backcourt mix is 6-0 sophomore Andre Sims (7.9 ppg, 2.3 rpg, .458 3PT), who played 23.1 minutes per game and started five times. Sims started his career in the MAC at Akron neighbor Kent State.

"Andre is a quick-thinking guard," coach Hipsher said. "He's a strong defender, applying good pressure in the backcourt, and has great range offensively."

Akron anticipates continued growth from two sophomore wing players—6-6, 210-pound **Byron Thompson** (3.6 ppg, 4.6 rpg) and 6-7, 195-pound **Larry Penn** (2.4 ppg, 1.3 rpg). Thompson started the majority of last season at power forward and led the team in rebounding. Penn received 10.9 minutes of playing time per game.

The tallest Zip is 7-1, 210-pound sophomore center **Matt Seibert** (2.7 ppg, 1.5 rpg). Akron also has some newcomers who will get extensive playing time and could break into the lineup.

Courtney Jones, a former All-Detroit star at MacKenzie High School, sat out last season with the Zips. Jones, a 6-3 sophomore, averaged 19 points and 12 rebounds as a high school senior.

Freshman guard **Brian Wood** comes in as the all-time leading scorer (2,551) and assist man (648) in Colorado high school history. Wood, 6-4, played for his father, Bob, at Buena Vista High School. As a senior he averaged 29.5 points, nine rebounds, seven assists and four steals. He was voted All-Colorado first team for all classes.

"Brian's numbers speak for themselves," coach Hipsher said. "He's been a producer as a player and is just as strong academically."

Nick Meyers, a 6-9, 230-pound freshman from Jefferson High School in Bloomington, Minn., will beef up the interior game. Meyers averaged 14 points, eight rebounds and three blocked shots as an all-state honorable mention choice.

Hipsher said Meyers will be heavily relied upon to help outinside.

MAC schools hit Cincinnati's Western Hills High School team hard this year, with 6-5 bookend forwards Danny Horace signing with Miami (Ohio) and **Darryl Peterson** joining the Zips.

Peterson, a 220-pounder, made the All-Cincinnati team with averages of 19 points, 10 rebounds and four assists a game.

"Darryl has a great feel for the game and has the ability to contribute on the perimeter or on the inside," coach Hipsher said. "He can shoot, drive to the hoop and rebound and has the ability to be a strong defender."

On a team with several versatile players, 6-9, 195-pound freshman **Rob Preston** is a perfect fit. Preston played at a small southern Ohio high school, Lynchburg-Clay, where he scored 21.5 points per game. He also averaged 9.8 rebounds, 6.5 blocks and 4.5 assists.

Akron basketball is truly a family, with 6-4 freshman **Bryan Hipsher** joining his father and older brother in the program. Bryan Hipsher played at Akron's Archbishop Hoban High School and was an All-Cleveland Plain Dealer first-team member. His senior numbers were 17.5 points, eight rebounds and six assists.

The extremely large freshman class also includes 6-2 **Ken Kowall**, a 20-point scorer at Valley Forge High School in Parma, Ohio, and non-scholarship player **Jeff Penno**, a 6-4 guard from Archbishop Alter High School in Dayton, Ohio. Penno scored 10 points a game for Ohio's Division II state champions.

2001-2002 SCHEDULE

Nov.	17	@Iona
	23-25	#Hawaii Pacific Tournament
	30	##Boilermaker Invitational
Dec.	1	##Boilermaker Invitational
	5	Western Kentucky
	8	@Buffalo
	15	@Cleveland State
	22	Mount Union
	29	*Cincinnati
Jan.	2	Niagara
	5	Ohio

MID-AMERICAN

BLUE RIBBON FORECAST

East Division
1. Marshall
2. Kent State
3. Miami (Ohio)
4. Bowling Green
5. Ohio
6. Akron
7. Buffalo

West Division
1. Ball State
2. Central Michigan
3. Toledo
4. Western Michigan
5. Eastern Michigan
6. Northern Illinois

ALL-CONFERENCE TEAM

G - Trevor Huffman, SR, Kent State
G - David Webber, SR, Central Michigan
G - Keith McLeod, SR, Bowling Green
F - Tamar Slay, SR, Marshall
C - Brandon Hunter, JR, Ohio

PLAYER OF THE YEAR

Brandon Hunter, JR, Ohio

NEWCOMER OF THE YEAR

Ronald Blackshear, SO, Marshall

2001-2002 CONFERENCE TOURNAMENT

March 4, First-round games at campus sites
March 7-9, Gund Arena, Cleveland, OH

2000-2001 CHAMPIONS

Kent State (East Division)
Central Michigan (West Division)
Kent State (conference tournament)

2000-2001 POSTSEASON PARTICIPANTS

Postseason record: 2-2 (.500)
NCAA
Kent State (Second Round)
NIT
Toledo (Second Round)

TOP BACKCOURTS

1. Kent State
2. Bowling Green
3. Central Michigan

TOP FRONTCOURTS

1. Ohio
2. Marshall
3. Ball State

INSIDE THE NUMBERS

2000-2001 conference RPI: 15th (of 31)
Conference RPI (last five years): 11-14-11-12-15

DID YOU KNOW?

Last year's Mid-American Conference tournament championship game between Kent State and Miami (Ohio) drew a league-record crowd of 12,172 at Gund Arena in Cleveland. The previous mark was 7,349 set in the 1995 title game between Ball State and Eastern Michigan played at Savage Hall in Toledo. Also, last year's MAC championship was the sixth best-attended league final in the nation. ... Miami (Ohio) coach Charlie Coles is closing in on 200 career wins. Coles has guided two MAC schools—Central Michigan from 1986-91 and Miami from 1996-present—to a 186-144 record in 11 seasons. With 14 more wins Coles will become the fifth coach in MAC history to reach 200. Coles is 94-60 in five Miami seasons. The RedHawks made it to the conference final all five years. ... Since the MAC went to an East-West division format in the 1996-97 season, no team has won both the regular-season title and the tournament. ... A No. 1 seeded team hasn't won the MAC Tournament since Eastern Michigan in 1996. ... Toledo coach Stan Joplin's contract extension through the 2005-06 season pays him a base salary of $115,000 for the first two years and $127,000 beginning in the third season. The deal has some interesting added perks that include a five percent bonus of base salary for winning the MAC West Division title and a five percent bonus for winning the MAC championship. Joplin will receive a 7.5 percent bonus for earning an NCAA Tournament berth. ... Central Michigan guard David Webber was given the 2001 Bill Boyden Leadership Award, a prestigious honor presented annually to a letterman entering their final year of eligibility. Webber was the 2001 MAC Player of the Year and is an English major with a 3.22 GPA. Boyden was a football and track star for the Chippewas and served as president of the student council. He was a longtime member of the University Development Board until his death in 1980. ... Eight-of-10 players chosen to the All-MAC first or second teams are back. Webber was a first-team selection and the league scoring champion (18.4 ppg). Other returnees on the first team are Marshall center J.R. VanHoose, the rebounding champion (11.1 rpg); Kent State guard Trevor Huffman (16.8 ppg), the MAC Tournament MVP; and Ohio power forward Brandon Hunter (18.1 ppg, 9.4 rpg). VanHoose also led the league in field-goal percentage (.578). Hunter was the only MAC player ranked in the top five for scoring, rebounding and field goal percentage (.510). ... Driving the lane will be tough this season with the league's top six shot blockers back on the court. Ohio's Patrick Flomo led with 105 rejections, followed by Ball State's Lonnie Jones (76), Marshall's Latece Williams (48), Central Michigan's Chris Kaman (45), Eastern Michigan's Ryan Prillman (35) and Northern Illinois' Marcus Smallwood (30). ... Miami has retired the jersey No. 32 of Wally Sczcerbiak, who led the RedHawks to the NCAA Sweet 16 in 1999. Miami beat Washington and Utah in the 1999 NCAA Tournament and fell in the third round to Kentucky. Sczcerbiak scored 90 points in the three games. He now plays for the NBA's Minnesota Timberwolves.

(R.M.)

	7	Eastern Michigan
	12	@Miami
	16	Kent State
	19	@Abll State
	23	Bowling Green
	26	Central Michigan
	30	@Ohio
Feb.	2	Buffalo
	5	@Marshall
	11	Western Michigan
	13	@Toledo
	16	@Eastern Michigan
	20	Northern Illinois
	23	@Bowling Green
	25	@Kent State
March	2	Marshall

4	###MAC Tournament
7-9	####MAC Tournament

@Road Games
*Gund Arena
#Honolulu, HI (vs. Monmouth first round; also Liberty, Tennessee-Chattanooga, Liberty, Hawaii Pacific, Notre Dame, Hampton, Vanderbitl)
##West Lafayette, IN (vs. Oakland first round; also Purdue, William & Mary)
###At campus sites
####Gund Arena, Cleveland, OH

BLUE RIBBON ANALYSIS

BACKCOURT   A

BENCH/DEPTH	C
FRONTCOURT	B
INTANGIBLES	C

Akron has done pretty well in Mid-American Conference play, going 45-27 over the last four seasons. In 1997-98 the Zips recorded a first-place finish in the East Division.

The MAC Tournament is another story. Since joining the league for the 1992-93 season Akron has yet to win a tournament game. Akron didn't qualify for the tournament at all in its first five seasons as a MAC member. Coach Hipsher's teams have since gone 0-4 in postseason play.

Obviously, clearing that hurdle has to be the goal this year.

Hipsher's son, Andy, is a 6-8 sophomore wing player who can lead the Zips if he's fully recovered from off-season back surgery. Falknor's injured big toe is another question mark. Akron also has a quality point guard in Brown and a recruiting class with impressive credentials.

The Zips will be improved, but there's not much room to move up in the crowded MAC East standings.

(R.M.)

 ## Ball State

LOCATION	Muncie, IN
CONFERENCE	Mid-American (West)
LAST SEASON	18-12 (.600)
CONFERENCE RECORD	11-7 (3rd)
STARTERS LOST/RETURNING	2/3
NICKNAME	Cardinals
COLORS	Cardinal & White
HOMECOURT	John E.Worthen Arena (11,500)
COACH	Tim Buckley (Bemidji State '86)
RECORD AT SCHOOL	18-12 (1 year)
CAREER RECORD	18-12 (1 year)
ASSISTANTS	Scot Bunnell (Ball State '96)
	Angres Thorpe (St. Leo '90)
	Tracy Webster (Wisconsin '95)
TEAM WINS (last 5 years)	16-21-16-22-18
RPI (last 5 years)	108-77-117-48-144
2000-01 FINISH	Lost in conference semifinal.

Tim Buckley brought a different coaching philosophy and style to Ball State last season and it took a while to sink in.

Once it did, the Cardinals got right back to their winning ways.

"The team responded very well and we were able to achieve some success," said Buckley, 37, a Ball State assistant previously (1994-99), who returned as head coach after spending the 1999-2000 season as the top assistant at Marquette. "Winning 18 games was a very positive aspect of what we did last year. College basketball is a very competitive environment, and there are over 300 NCAA Division I teams trying to win games."

The 18 wins were the second-highest total for a first-year coach in Ball State history. Only Dick Hunsaker won more with 26 in 1989-90. Ball State recorded its 13th consecutive winning season.

"Last year was a good season," Buckley said. "However, this program is about more than just winning basketball games, and that is where the Ball State program made great strides."

Buckley wants his players to enjoy their college experience, earn degrees, become productive members of the community—and win games.

With four returning starters led by All-MAC second team performer **Theron Smith** and a quality recruiting class, more good things are in store for the Cardinals.

The 6-8, 225-pound Smith returns as a junior with two solid seasons behind him. Smith (16.3 ppg, 8.1 rpg, .462 FG, .360 3PT, .701 FT) improved his first-year production of 12.2 points and 7.6 rebounds when he was voted MAC Freshman of the Year.

Smith scored in double figures 27 times in 30 games, highlighted by a 40-point burst against Texas Tech at the Indiana Classic. And, he was the team academic award winner.

Other starters back are 6-11, 210-pound senior center **Lonnie Jones** (9.4 ppg, 6.6 rpg, 2.5 bpg, .513 FG, .534 FT), an asthma sufferer who carries a device he can breathe into when he feels an attack coming on; 5-10 senior guard **Patrick Jackson** (13.9 ppg, 4.1 apg, .428 3PT); and 5-9 senior **Billy Lynch** (2.5 ppg, 3.5 apg).

Jones started the first two games of the season, and

the final 18. A coach-player meeting in early January was followed by better production from Jones, the school career record-holder with 212 blocked shots.

"We sat down and talked about what he needed to do to be more consistent," Buckley said.

Jackson walked away from the postseason team banquet with most-valuable-player honors after a season when he was the second-leading scorer, first in assists and first in steals (45).

Lynch, a two-sport athlete, also plays football for the Cardinals on the team coached by his father, Bill. Billy Lynch moved into the starting lineup on Dec. 1 and didn't relinquish the spot. His 2.5-to-1.0 assist-to-turnover ratio ranked second in the MAC. As a backup wide receiver for his dad's football Cardinals, he is a two-year letterman with 24 career catches for 202 yards and two touchdowns.

The trio of Jackson, Lynch and 6-4 junior guard **Rob Robbins** (6.6 ppg, 1.5 rpg, .518 3PT) from Muncie, Ind., are hometown products of Delta High School. In 1997 their high school of 900 students fell just short of creating another Hoosiers story. Delta lost in the championship game of Indiana's last single-class state tournament.

Robbins came on strong late, hitting for seven double-figure scoring games in the final nine. He had one double-figure outing before that.

Robbins lit it up from the three-point line during that stretch, making 27-of-41 (.658). For the season he made 43-of-83 (.518).

"Rob Robbins in my opinion is as good a shooter as there is in college basketball," Buckley said.

Others returning for the Cardinals include 6-7 sophomore forward **Robert Owens** (2.9 ppg, 2.3 rpg); 6-8, 275-pound senior center **Brian Burns** (1.6 ppg, 1.2 rpg); 6-5 junior forward **Mark Farris** (2.7 ppg, 1.8 rpg); and 6-8, 237-pound junior center **Corey Harris** (0.7 ppg, 1.1 rpg).

The Cardinals are happy about the return of 6-5 freshman guard Michael Bennett (2.3 ppg, 1.8 rpg). Bennett started the first three games of the year before suffering a season-ending knee injury. He received a medical red-shirt.

A player with a shooter's reputation, 6-3 junior **Chris Williams**, sat out last season as a transfer from Loyola-Chicago. Williams started in 29-of-52 games in two seasons at Loyola-Chicago, averaging 10.6 points as a freshman and 10.8 as a sophomore.

Williams is from Fenwick High School in Chicago.

Andrew White also joins the Cardinals as a 6-3 sophomore guard. White is a MAC transfer from Central Michigan, where he didn't appear in any games. White went to Mishawaka Penn High School in South Bend, Ind., where as a senior he averaged 16.4 points and 6.6 rebounds. White was the South Bend Tribune's Metro Player of the Year.

The biggest loss for the Cardinals was the transfer of starting forward Josh Murray (8.2 ppg, 8.0 rpg) to Indiana University-Purdue University-Indianapolis (IUPUI). Backcourt player Cedric Moodie (10.3 ppg, 3.4 rpg) transferred to the University of Indianapolis. Rawle Marshall (2.4 ppg, 1.2 rpg) also left the program.

"Now we are adding a quality recruiting class of student-athletes that understand what we are all about and that should continue to add to the success of Ball State basketball," Buckley said.

Ball State completed its recruiting class in June by signing 6-6, 205-pound guard **Zach Willingham**, a transfer from Allen County Community College in Kansas. He scored 16 points a game while averaging 6.5 rebounds and 4.9 assists as an All-Jayhawk Conference third team selection. He is a good three-point (.406) and free throw (.784) shooter.

Willingham also played one season at Notre Dame Prep School in Fitchburg, Mass. He is originally from Riverview, Fla., about 30 minutes from Theron Smith's hometown of Auburndale. Ball State coaches first spotted him in a workout where they were scouting Smith.

"He can shoot the ball from deep, handle the ball and he's a very effective passer," Allen County coach Mike Hayes said in a Muncie Star Press newspaper report. "He has a good all-around game. He's very team-oriented. He's an unselfish passer and he's a good decision-maker on the floor. He understands how the game is played."

Two of Ball State's freshmen—6-8, 185-pound **Gabe Miller** and 6-7, 200-pound **Scott Bushong**—were teammates at Carroll High School in Fort Wayne, Ind.

Miller was selected to the Indiana all-state third team with averages of 21.8 points and 4.4 rebounds a game. He set school records in high school for career points (1,196) and points in a season (536).

"He is a very versatile player that will help us in a variety of ways, and he is a winner," Buckley said.

Bushong is a walk-on. He averaged 9.4 points and 7.4 rebounds as a prep senior.

Buckley also signed 6-2 freshman guard **Matt McCollom** out of Mt. Zion, Ill. McCollom was one of three NCAA Division I recruits who led Mt. Zion High School to a 27-4 record and third-place finish in the Class AA state tournament. Teammates Neil Plank signed with Wisconsin while Jake Sams signed with Indiana State. McCollom averaged 14 points, four rebounds and five assists.

"Matt is a natural guard with a great shooting touch who will fill some specific needs for our team," Buckley said.

2001-2002 SCHEDULE

Nov.	19-21	#MAUI Classic
	30	##First Merchants Classic
Dec.	1	##First Merchants Classic
	6	IUPU-FW
	8	@Indiana
	15	@IUPUI
	19	Butler
	22	@Indiana State
	29	*Oklahoma
Jan.	2	@Kent State
	5	@Eastern Michigan
	9	Central Michigan
	12	@Toledo
	16	Bowling Green
	19	Akron
	23	Western Michigan
	26	@Miami
	29	@Marshall
Feb.	2	Eastern Michigan
	5	@Northern Illinois
	9	@Ohio
	13	Buffalo
	16	Toledo
	20	@Western Michigan
	23	Miami
	27	Northern Illinois
March	2	@Central Michigan
	4	###MAC Tournament
	7-9	####MAC Tournament

@Road Games
*Oklahoma City, OK
#Maui, HI (also Ball State, Chaminade, Duke, UCLA, Seton Hall, South Carolina)
##Muncie, IN (vs. Elon first round; also Austin Peay, Binghampton)
###At campus sites
####Gund Arena, Cleveland, OH

BLUE RIBBON ANALYSIS

BACKCOURT	B
BENCH/DEPTH	C+
FRONTCOURT	A
INTANGIBLES	B

Smith, Jones and Jackson return as the three leading scorers on last year's team that played its best basketball in February and March.

Once the Cardinals adapted to Buckley's philosophy, they were hard to beat. Ball State won seven of its final 10 regular-season games and then defeated Northern Illinois and Marshall in the MAC Tournament before falling to Kent State in a semifinal. That momentum will carry over.

Smith and Jones form a formidable duo around the basket. Jackson, Robbins and newcomer Williams are three-point shooters who will keep the defenses from sagging. Willingham is another good shooter who at 6-6 can play point guard and give Ball State another backcourt weapon.

The Cardinals know what their coach expects now, and Buckley knows what his players are capable of. Ball State will be in the upper echelon of the MAC West Division and challenge for the championship.

(R.M.)

 ## Bowling Green

LOCATION	Bowling Green, OH
CONFERENCE	Mid-American (East)
LAST SEASON	15-14 (.517)
CONFERENCE RECORD	10-8 (5th)

STARTERS LOST/RETURNING	1/4
NICKNAME	Falcons
COLORS	Orange & Brown
HOMECOURT	Anderson Arena (5,000)
COACH	Dan Dakich (Indiana '85)
RECORD AT SCHOOL	65-48 (4 years)
CAREER RECORD	65-48 (4 years)
ASSISTANTS	Keith Noftz (Heidelbert '78)
	Artie Pepelea (Wisconsin-Purdue '94)
	Sean Bledsoe (Indianapolis '94)
TEAM WINS (last 5 years)	22-10-18-22-15
RPI (last 5 years)	73-206-70-60-160
2000-01 FINISH	Lost in conference quarterfinal.

Bowling Green, and its head coach in particular, got a lot of mileage out of doing things backward.

With the Falcons mired in a four-game January losing skid, coach Dan Dakich did something completely out of the ordinary. Dakich had the players and his staff begin wearing their practice gear backward. Dakich started coming out for the start of games with his sports coat on backward, too.

"We didn't respect the program and we didn't play hard," Dakich said. "We were disrespectful."

Bowling Green promptly reversed its fortunes, ripping off six consecutive victories and went 8-3 to finish the regular season. Dakich said the bit of strategy caught the players' attention, created some enthusiasm and they started playing with more effort.

The "backward look" probably won't appear in coaching manuals any time soon, but it worked for Bowling Green. In a column Dakich wrote for Collegeinsider.com he said, "The next time you're having a bad day, give it a try."

Dakich said he was going to wear his jacket backward throughout the games, but tried it once and changed his mind.

"If you've ever worn your sports coat backward, which I'm sure most people haven't, it rides up on your neck and it chokes you," he said.

As much as Dakich's bizarre fashion statement called attention to Bowling Green's problems, the turnaround was more a result of better play on defense. At one point during the season, Dakich said the Falcons might have been the worst defensive team in NCAA Division I. But the defense improved, and so did the Falcons.

The only piece missing from last year's team is the top defensive player—guard Trent Jackson (10.5 ppg, 3.8 rpg, 2.1 steals). Jackson led the MAC with 59 steals.

Bowling Green's top returning players are 6-2 senior guard **Keith McLeod** and 6-9, 230-pound senior center **Len Matela**, the MAC's highest-scoring duo in league games. Those two combined for 34.2 points per game in MAC play.

McLeod (18.1 ppg, 3.4 rpg, 2.9 apg, .354 3PT, .813 FT) was voted to the All-MAC second team. He was second in the league in scoring. McLeod is no slouch defensively, either. He has 111 career steals.

"Keith has always been a good scorer," Dakich said. "As he's worried less about scoring and more about playing and let his true personality come out, he's done a wonderful job. You should not go to college as an 18-year-old and leave as a 21-year-old with the same personality. Keith has done a terrific job of letting his true personality come out."

Matela (15.7 ppg, 8.8 rpg, .550 FG, .788 FT) is a two-time All-MAC honorable mention selection. He ranked 12th in the league scoring, third in rebounding and second in field-goal percentage. Matela spent part of the summer touring Australia as a member of the Nacel All-Stars coached by former Marquette coach Mike Deane. He averaged 15.4 points and 6.6 rebounds in seven games while making 60.9 percent of his shots.

The "M&M" boys are both 1,000-point career scorers, McLeod with 1,140 and Matela with 1,002.

Brandon Pardon is the senior point guard who makes the Falcons go. The 6-1 Pardon (10.0 ppg, 3.6 rpg) started every game and became only the third player in school history with more than 200 assists (204).

Pardon led the MAC with 7.0 assists a game. A true ironman, Pardon played 1,065 minutes of a possible 1,165.

As a member of the All-MAC Freshman team, 6-8 hometown product **Josh Almanson** (7.0 ppg, 3.4 rpg) was definitely an impact player. Almanson started only four times but established Bowling Green freshman records for field-goal (.675) and free-throw (.851) percentage. He shared the team lead with 23 blocked shots.

Bowling Green's most colorful, and perhaps its hardest-working player is 6-8, 230-pound senior forward **Brent Klassen** (4.0 ppg, 2.7 rpg), nicknamed "Cowboy" because his roots are in Nebraska. He's an emotional, tenacious player coaches love to have on their side.

"Klassen is arguably the best kid I've ever coached," Dakich said. "The most fun to be around and just everything else."

Junior guard **Cory Ryan** was chosen BG's most improved player. The 6-5 Ryan (6.8 ppg, 2.8 rpg, 1.1 apg) scored 190 points last year after scoring 16 as a freshman. He had seven double-figure scoring games and led the Falcons in three-point field goals (43 for 110, .391).

Two sophomores expected to step up are 6-10, 245-pound center **Kevin Netter** (5.1 ppg, 2.0 rpg, 18 blocks) and 6-0 guard **Jabari Mattox** (0.7 ppg, 0.9). Mattox was ineligible for the second semester after appearing in nine games.

Kris Gerken, a 6-3 junior guard (0.1 ppg, 0.3 rpg), played a total of 37 minutes spread over 14 games.

McLeod, Matela and Pardon are the foundation of the team, but four recruits are expected to be good supporting members.

Freshman **Germain Fitch** is a 6-5, 220-pound addition out of Notre Dame Prep in Fitchburg, Mass., where he averaged 10 points, six rebounds and six assists. He was one of 10 players from a 32-6 team who signed with Division I programs.

Fitch grew up in Cleveland and moved to Huntsville, Ala., as a high school sophomore. He made the all-city team as a junior at Butler High School when he averaged 12 points a game.

"Germain is a great athlete who can play just about anywhere on the floor," Butler coach Jack Doss told the Toledo Blade. "He has outstanding ability, he's an explosive jumper and as far as pure athleticism goes he's the best we've ever had here. He's a scorer, a great passer, a great ball handler and he has a streak in him that will have him take somebody inside just to dunk on them."

Doss has seen 21 of his Butler players go on to Division I.

Freshman **Erik Crawford** from Tartan High School in Minneapolis was a finalist for Mr. Basketball in Minnesota. The 6-4, 210-pound guard was a two time Minneapolis Defensive Player of the Year. He also averaged 21 points for a 27-3 team.

Crawford was a target of several Big Ten schools in football as a wide receiver, but didn't play football as a senior in order to concentrate on basketball.

Bowling Green signed another player, 5-10 guard **Kris Wilson**, from under the nose of MAC rival Marshall at Spring Valley High School in Huntington, W.Va. Wilson made a commitment to Marshall as a junior.

"Through a mutual thing," Wilson and Marshall decided to go separate ways, Spring Valley coach Gary Norris said.

Wilson was slowed by a groin injury early in his senior season. He bounced back to average 17.6 points a game and make all state for the second time. As a four-year starter at Spring Valley, Wilson had 1,739 points and 242 three-pointers. He scored 23 points a game as a junior.

"I think he gives them some quickness and some ball handling skills," Norris said. "I think things will work out for him if he goes in, concentrates and keeps his academics at an acceptable level."

The Falcons also signed 6-8, 225-pound forward **Cory Eyink** from Marion Local High School in Maria Stein, Ohio. Eyink averaged 18 points last year.

Transfer John Reimold sits out this season. Reimold, a 6-6, 215-pound sophomore forward, played last season at Loyola College, where he scored 15.6 points per game as rookie of the year in the Metro Atlantic Athletic Conference.

2001-2002 SCHEDULE

Nov.	15-18	#Top of the World Classic
	24	Defiance
	28	Michigan
Dec.	1	Marist
	5	@Duquesne
	10	UNC Wilmington
	15	@Evansville
	22	Detroit
	29	@Indiana State
Jan.	3	@Central Michigan
	8	Northern Illinois
	12	@Buffalo
	16	@Ball State
	19	Toledo
	23	@Akron
	26	Kent State
	30	@Western Michigan
Feb.	2	Miami
	4	@Kent State
	6	Ohio
	9	Marshall
	13	Eastern Michigan
	18	@Toledo
	20	@Miami
	23	Akron
	27	Buffalo
March	2	@Ohio
	4	##MAC Tournament
	7-9	###MAC Tournament

@Road Games
#Fairbanks, AK (vs. Ole Miss first round; also Washington, Alaska-Fairbanks, Radford, Butler, Wichita State, Delaware)
##At campus sites
###Gund Arena, Cleveland, OH

BLUE RIBBON ANALYSIS

BACKCOURT	A
BENCH/DEPTH	C
FRONTCOURT	B
INTANGIBLES	B

Bowling Green's offense was solid, its defensive play spotty. That's why the Falcons slipped last season to a 15-14 record after going 22-8 and receiving an NIT berth in 1999-2000.

The offense, led by McLeod and Matela, was actually very good. Bowling Green was the second-highest scoring Mid-American Conference team (75.9 ppg) and second-best shooting team (.484 FG) while leading the 13-team league in free throw shooting (.767). Defensively the Falcons ranked 10th in points allowed (72.8).

Overcoming that inconsistency is the key to this season.

McLeod and Matela return, along with some youngsters who played well at times and some promising recruits.

The MAC East Division is strong with defending champion Kent State, Marshall and Ohio expected to challenge for the top. If Dakich gets the kind of tough defensive play he demands, the Falcons will be there, too.

(R.M.)

Buffalo

LOCATION	Buffalo, NY
CONFERENCE	Mid-American (East)
LAST SEASON	4-24 (.143)
CONFERENCE RECORD	2-16 (7th)
STARTERS LOST/RETURNING	1/4
NICKNAME	Bulls
COLORS	Royal Blue & White
HOMECOURT	Alumni Arena (8,500)
COACH	Reggie Witherspoon (Empire State '95)
RECORD AT SCHOOL	7-44 (2 years)
CAREER RECORD	7-44 (2 years)
ASSISTANTS	Jim Kwitchoff (Boston College '89)
	Mike Mennenga (Morehead State '93)
	Chris Hawkins (Radford '92)
TEAM WINS (last 5 years)	17-15-5-5-4
RPI (last 5 years)	134-191-279-255-273
2000-01 FINISH	Lost in conference first round.

For the first time since joining the Mid-American Conference in the 1998-99 season, Buffalo has a realistic shot at success. But first, the school must deal with the NCAA.

Buffalo was placed on NCAA probation in March for a two-year period relating to violations committed under former head coach Tim Cohane from the 1995-96 season through December 1999, when he resigned. The NCAA said Buffalo broke rules on preseason practice, scouting of opponents and extra benefits.

The sanctions limit the Bulls to bringing only eight prospects on campus for official paid visits—the NCAA limit is 12. Buffalo wasn't barred from postseason play.

Buffalo is also limited to 12 scholarships this season, one less than the NCAA maximum.

"In large part, I think this is a lesson in shortcuts," coach Reggie Witherspoon said. "I think it's the shortcuts that get you in trouble. It's not going to be easy or quick to build this program, but we're going to do it and we're going to do it the right way."

Witherspoon got off to a rough start when he moved

across town from a head coaching job at Erie Community College to take over the Buffalo program as interim head coach when Cohane left. Witherspoon lost his first eight games.

This season, his third with the program, Witherspoon just might have enough talent to jump-start the Bulls, who compiled a 6-48 conference record the last three years.

Buffalo welcomes back six of its top eight scorers from a team that lost 12 regular-season games by 10 points or less. The only other NCAA Division I team losing more times by that margin was American University, with 13.

The Bulls lost some talent, most notably Jason Robinson (14.2 ppg, 5.4 rpg) and Damien Foster (10.9 ppg, 2.9 rpg), along with Maliso Libomi (2.8 ppg, 3.6 rpg), O'Tes Alston (3.8 ppg, 3.7 rpg), Karl Rainey (2.0 ppg, 0.6 rpg), Duane Williams (3.5 ppg, 2.0 rpg) and Adam Johnson (0.1 ppg, 1.5 rpg). They'll be replaced with better depth.

"It's a good situation," Witherspoon said. "We have 12 guys that have a chance to get into the game. That makes everybody work that much harder and if they work that much harder then we will be that much better."

Two returning players—6-4, 215-pound senior forward **Robert Brown** and 6-2 senior guard **Louis Campbell**—are all-conference candidates.

Brown (15.3 ppg, 5.7 rpg, .497 FG) might have been All-MAC last year if he was on a better team. He was voted to the All-Juco Transfer team chosen by collegeinsider.com. He scored in double figures 24 times in 28 games with 20 or more five times. Brown started his career in the MAC as a freshman at Central Michigan.

Campbell (13.6 ppg, 4.9 rpg, 4.3 apg, 1.9 steals) is also deserving of more recognition as one of the MAC's top all-around players. Campbell is just the 11th player in school history to score more than 1,000 career points. His 1,045 points rank 10th at Buffalo and he needs only 292 more to break into the top five. He's already the first Buffalo player with more than 1,000 points and 300 assists in a career.

Buffalo's award for most improved player went to senior **Davis Lawrence**. The 5-10 Lawrence (4.3 ppg, 3.1 rpg, 2.0 apg) started in 17 games and averaged 22.4 minutes.

Gabe Cagwin adds experienced depth at point guard, if he stays free of injuries. The 5-10 senior Cagwin (3.7 ppg, 1.3 apg) played in only 19 games after transferring in from Northeastern Junior College in Colorado. He missed nine games from having contusions on his feet and after having oral surgery and losing his front two teeth.

The Bulls welcome back 6-8, 230-pound senior forward **Clement Smith** (3.3 ppg, 4.4 rpg) who was playing his best basketball when he was knocked out Feb. 3 by a partially dislocated left shoulder.

Senior **Kevin Swoffer** (1.9 ppg, 1.9 rpg) is a 6-10, 265-pounder who worked his way into the starting lineup for the final nine games. **Jason Walcott** (0.3 ppg, 0.9 rpg) is a 6-5 sophomore who appeared in only 10 games, but received extra minutes late in the year because of injuries to others.

Forwards **Joe Veal** and **Darcel Williams** are eligible after sitting out last season. The 6-9, 220-pound Veal, a junior, was red-shirted as a transfer from Northern Pioneer Junior College in Arizona, where he averaged 12 points, nine rebounds and 2.5 blocks.

Williams sat out the season after transferring from Eastern Kentucky. The 6-5, 220-pound senior played in 25 games for Eastern Kentucky in the 1999-200 season, averaging 6.6 points and 3.4 rebounds. He also played one year at Polk Community College in Florida and one year at Erie Community College, where Witherspoon was his coach. Williams earned conference player-of-the-year honors and was a third-team junior-college All-American.

"This year we have more players who are capable of scoring, especially in the low post," Witherspoon said. "Now when the game gets close we will be able to go down inside and get some scoring."

Buffalo is building around Brown and Campbell with an impressive crop of newcomers. The most heralded newcomer, 6-3, 175-pound **Turner Battle** from East Forsythe High School in Kernersville, N.C., was rated as one of the top 100 prospects by recruiting expert Bob Gibbons. Battle averaged 17 points, five rebounds and five assists per game

"I think this is the steal of the millennium," Gibbons wrote in his All-Star Sports publication. "Turner Battle could have played for an ACC school."

Battle signed with the Bulls in the fall. Otherwise, they might not have gotten him.

"Turner is a point guard with quickness and speed,"

Witherspoon said. "His abilities stretch out wide enough that he is fully complete coming out of high school. He's played well in a structured situation and prides himself on being able to play defense."

Buffalo also won a recruiting battle with MAC members Central Michigan and Western Michigan along with Detroit, Drake and Marquette for 6-9, 230-pound forward **Mark Bortz** out of Walled Lake Central High School in Commerce Township, Mich. He led his team to a 22-2 record and the regional semifinals with averages of 15.5 points, 14.2 rebounds, 5.0 blocks and 3.1 assists. Bortz was one of the state's top 30 players in Class A (top level). He was also voted All-Metro North by the Detroit Free Press. Bortz had a 3.77 GPA in high school.

"I think it's great that we went into the middle of MAC territory and pulled out a great get," Witherspoon said.

Bortz is a big man who can score, has good hands and doesn't back down from anybody.

Freshman **Jason Bird**, a 6-3, 180-pound guard, averaged 18 points, eight rebounds and eight assists at Ypsilanti High School in Michigan. Bird was the Ann Arbor News co-player of the year and also made the All-Metro West team picked by the Detroit Free Press. Bird is a southpaw wing player who made the transition from point guard as a high school senior.

"Jason is noted as being able to score points," Witherspoon said.

MAC schools Eastern Michigan, Akron and Bowling Green also recruited Bird.

The fourth recruit is **Daniel Gilbert**, a 6-5, 205-pound backcourt player from Cass Technical in Detroit, where he averaged 22 points and 14 rebounds. Gilbert was chosen a Detroit Free Press All-Metro honorable mention.

"Daniel gives us size and a defensive presence on the perimeter," Witherspoon said. "He plays with a great deal of intensity and he rebounds the ball well at both ends of the floor."

2001-2002 SCHEDULE

Nov.	19	@Niagara
	21	@Chicago State
	24	Canisius
	29	@Rhode Island
Dec.	1	New Hampshire
	5	@Cornell
	8	Akron
	20-22	#Yahoo Invitational
	29	@Syracuse
Jan.	2	@Eastern Michigan
	5	@Northern Illinois
	9	Kent State
	12	Bowling Green
	15	Ohio
	19	@Marshall
	22	@Kent State
	26	Northwestern
	28	@Northern Illinois
Feb.	2	@Akron
	6	Miami
	9	Western Michigan
	13	@Ball State
	16	CMU
	20	@Toledo
	23	Marshall
	25	@Miami
	27	@Bowling Green
March	4	##MCC Tournament
	7-9	###MCC Tournament

@Road Games
#At BYU-Hawaii (vs. Tulsa first round; also BYU-Hawaii, Navy, Montana, Valpairaso, New Mexico State, Columbia)
##At campus sites
###Gund Arena, Cleveland, OH

BLUE RIBBON ANALYSIS

BACKCOURT	A
BENCH/DEPTH	C
FRONTCOURT	B
INTANGIBLES	C

Last season Buffalo was one of those teams Mid-American Conference foes hated to face. The Bulls weren't real good, but just good enough to remain a threat. Just ask Miami (Ohio), a late-season, overtime victim.

To build on that, Buffalo must become a more balanced offensive team. Four players—returnees Robert Brown and Louis Campbell, along with departed Jason

Robinson and Damien Foster—accounted for 54 points a game. Buffalo averaged just 65.1.

Buffalo also has to develop a better shooting eye. A .417 percent accuracy mark doesn't cut it. Neither does .651 percent free throw shooting.

This is a team that could be much improved, win more games and still not move out of the MAC East cellar. Building a program from the bottom up takes time.

(R.M.)

Central Michigan

LOCATION	Mount Pleasant, MI
CONFERENCE	Mid-American (West)
LAST SEASON	20-8 (.714)
CONFERENCE RECORD	14-4 (1st)
STARTERS LOST/RETURNING	1/4
NICKNAME	Chippewas
COLORS	Maroon & Gold
HOMECOURT	Rose Arena (5,200)
COACH	Jay Smith (Saginaw Valley '84)
RECORD AT SCHOOL	41-68 (4 years)
CAREER RECORD	41-68 (4 years)
ASSISTANTS	Dave Grube (Kent '66)
	Cornell Mann (Akron '95)
	Jeff Smith (Alma '94)
TEAM WINS (last 5 years)	7-5-10-6-20
RPI (last 5 years)	272-256-219-253-120
2000-01 FINISH	Lost in conference quarterfinal.

All last season as the victories piled up, one of Central Michigan coach Jay Smith's pet phrases was "We're not there yet."

By the end of the season, Central Michigan had arrived. The Chippewas won their first Mid-American Conference regular-season title since 1987.

"We did it," Smith said after his team wrapped up first place in the MAC West Division with a 14-4 record and secured the No. 1 seeding in the conference tournament. "I told everyone all season there was no time to celebrate. Now, this is the time to celebrate. There were people who doubted us and didn't believe in us. I don't think there was any doubt in our players. They believed in one another."

Central Michigan became the only team in MAC history to go from a last-place finish one season to first place the following year. The 14-game improvement from 6-23 to 20-8 reflected the 10th biggest turnaround in NCAA history.

The story book run was halted by Miami in a MAC Tournament quarterfinal. For the second consecutive year the MAC sent only its tournament winner, Kent State, to the NCAA Tournament. Toledo received the MAC's lone NIT berth.

"We were fortunate to win the conference championship," said Smith, voted MAC Coach of the Year. "We were very blessed and very lucky to do it. It's just unfortunate because this is a very tough league and we normally have one, maybe two teams in the tournament."

Smith was rewarded with a contract extension through 2005.

With MAC Player-of-the-Year **David Webber** leading the way, the Chippewas are expected to be right back in the MAC championship hunt this season. Webber, a senior, is no longer only known as the younger brother of NBA All-Star Chris Webber. The 6-2, 210-pound senior (18.4 ppg, 5.2 rpg, 2.5 apg, .430 FG, .345 3PT, .691 FT, 41 steals) is a senior from Farmington Hills, Mich., with an identity all his own.

Purdue coach Gene Keady didn't even mention Chris Webber's name to the Associated Press when he was asked about David after Central Michigan's early-season upset of the Boilermakers.

"Our kids were not ready for him," Keady said after Webber scored 24 points and grabbed 10 rebounds. "But they definitely respected him after the game for what he does for that team."

Webber topped the MAC in scoring and tied for the team lead in rebounding. He was selected to the Associated Press All-America honorable mention list and was one of 16 finalists for the Oscar Robertston Player-of-the-Year Trophy that's presented by the U.S. Basketball Writers Association.

Central Michigan has four starters back, but Webber is being asked to do even more.

"David has to be a consistent, vocal leader for us this season because we lost a great deal of leadership," Smith said. "He knows his role as a scorer and he knows he has to aggressively find a position on the court to score."

Competition for the point-guard spot vacated by senior Tim Kisner (8.2 ppg, 2.0 rpg, 4.6 apg) is led by 5-11 newcomer **Whitney Robinson**, a transfer from Eastern Kentucky. Robinson scored 11.7 points a game as an Eastern Kentucky sophomore. He was selected All-Ohio Valley Conference honorable mention as a freshman, averaging 17.8 points as the fifth-leading rookie scorer in the nation. He made 121 three-pointers in two years at Eastern Kentucky.

Robinson played at Notre Dame High School in Detroit, where he was a teammate of former Toledo star Greg Stempin, and the Chippewas are happy to have him back in the state.

Other point guards in the mix are 6-0 junior **J.R. Wallace** (1.1 ppg, 0.5 rpg) and 6-3 sophomore **T.J. Meerman** (0.8 ppg, 0.4 rpg). Central Michigan's only freshman, 6-3, 210-pound **Herb Goliday**, is another point-guard prospect. Goliday averaged 15.5 points at Ferndale (Mich.) High School. He made the Detroit News All-Metro honorable mention list.

"He's a scorer and a gifted athlete," Smith said. "Herb will have a bright future in our program."

The Chippewas are also enthused about finally having a completely healthy **Mike Manciel** (9.3 ppg, 4.0 rpg, .506 FG, .362 3PT, .638 FT) in the lineup at small forward. Manciel, a 6-5, 225-pound junior, was the MAC's top freshman in 1998-99, then missed the 1999-2000 season because of a broken foot. He played in 26 games last season, 20 as a starter, but wasn't fully recovered from the foot injury. Manciel had the surgical pins removed from his foot in the off-season.

"Mike is totally pain free and feels the best he has in a year and a half," Smith said. "He has improved speed and lateral quickness, and he's working on defense and ball handling."

Workhorse 6-6, 230-pound junior forward **Chad Pleiness** (11.7 ppg, 5.2 rpg, .546 FG, .884 FT) is the other minor scorer. Pleiness was CMU's second-leading scorer and shared the team rebounding lead with Webber during an All-MAC honorable mention season. He led the MAC in free-throw shooting, hitting 76-of-86 (.884).

Smith said he likes the versatility of Pleiness, who can play a variety of positions. Pleiness can defend against quick players on the perimeter and guard post players, too. With his experience, Pleiness also needs to be a team leader.

While featuring more speed than Central Michigan has had in some time, the squad also a nice dose of size with sophomores and MAC All-Freshman team members **Chris Kaman** and **Gerrit Brigitha**. The 7-foot Kaman (9.8 ppg, 4.8 rpg, .574 FG) is up from 225 pounds to 245. Kaman, who started only one game, was fourth in the conference with 45 blocked shots. Brigitha (5.8 ppg, 2.4 rpg, .528 FG), 6-8 and 230 pounds, started all 28 games.

"Gerrit and Chris will be competitive in the post," Smith said. "They each played about half the minutes last year and could see more time on the floor together."

Seven-foot senior **Jon Woods** (0.7 ppg, 0.0 rpg) played only eight minutes in three appearances.

Red-shirt freshman **Tony Bowne**, a 6-3 guard, scored 20.7 points per game as a senior at Hastings High School and was sixth in voting for Michigan Mr. Basketball. **Tom Pantlind**, a 6-8 red-shirt freshman from East Grand Rapids High School in Michigan, averaged 14 points and 5.8 rebounds as a senior.

Sophomore forwards who played sparingly last season are 6-7 **Adam Dentlinger** (1.4 ppg, 0.6 rpg) and 6-5 **Dan Quinn** (0.5 ppg, 0.3 rpg).

"I'm delighted with the core of players we have returning," Smith said. "They have tremendous work ethic and do things the right way. More importantly, these players have been through a championship season and now they understand how one possession can determine the outcome of every game. Each game is an important one when you are challenging for the conference title."

The Chippewas have enough talent to keep the beat going and make up for losing seniors Kisner, Jon Borovich (3.9 ppg, 2.6 rpg), Luke Johnson (2.3 ppg, 1.9 rpg) and Todd Schrotenboer (1.7 ppg, 1.6 rpg).

2001-2002 SCHEDULE

Nov.	18	Tri-State
	21	@Dayton
	24	Georgia State
	28	@Oklahoma
Dec.	2	Loyola-Chicago
	5	@George Mason
	9	@Illinois State
	19	Detroit
Jan.	22	@Northern Iowa
	3	Bowling Green
	5	Miami
	9	@Ball State
	12	@Western Michigan
	16	Marshall
	22	Toledo
	26	@Akron
Feb.	2	Northern Illinois
	4	Western Michigan
	6	@Toledo
	9	Kent State
	13	@Ohio
	16	@Buffalo
	20	Eastern Michigan
	23	@Northern Illinois
	27	@Marshall
March	2	Ball State
	4	#MCC Tournament
	7-9	##MCC Tournament

@Road Games
#At campus sites
##Gund Arena, Cleveland, OH

BLUE RIBBON ANALYSIS

BACKCOURT	A
BENCH/DEPTH	C
FRONTCOURT	B+
INTANGIBLES	B

There hasn't been this much excitement—or success—at Central Michigan since Dan Majerle, who plays for the Miami Heat, took his leaping ability and shooting touch to the NBA in 1988.

A year ago Central Michigan was only looking to improve on a 6-23 season. Now, the Chippewas are defending the Mid-American Conference regular-season championship. The next stop? How about the NCAA Tournament, where the Chippewas haven't been since Majerle led them there in 1987.

Coach Smith has the tools to get there. Webber returns along with three other starters, including Manciel. If completely free of injury, Manciel just might join Webber as an all-conference team member.

Central Michigan also has size and experience. But wait, there's more.

"We're going to be more athletic and quicker than we have been," Smith said in an interview this summer with Andy Katz of ESPN.com.

That's something the rest of the MAC didn't want to hear.

(R.M.)

Eastern Michigan

LOCATION	Ypsilanti, MI
CONFERENCE	Mid-American (West)
LAST SEASON	3-25 (.107)
CONFERENCE RECORD	1-17 (6th)
STARTERS LOST/RETURNING	2/3
NICKNAME	Eagles
COLORS	Green & White
HOMECOURT	Convocation Center (8,429)
COACH	Jim Boone (West Virginia St. '81)
RECORD AT SCHOOL	3-25 (1 year)
CAREER RECORD	48-91 (5 years)
ASSISTANTS	Glenn Gutierrez (West Liberty St. '85)
	Dave Pilpovich (Thiel '86)
	LaMonta Stone (Wayne State '99)
TEAM WINS (last 5 years)	22-20-5-15-3
RPI (last 5 years)	77-67-221-140-305
2000-01 FINISH	Lost in conference first round

Eastern Michigan coach Jim Boone has been down this road before, and he knows where it leads.

The Eagles struggled to a 3-25 record last season, so there's only one direction to go. Four players left the program after former coach Milton Barnes was let go and before Boone was hired. Three others were dismissed for actions off the court. Another player left after just two days of practice.

Through it all, Boone remained upbeat. After all, he's been down the road before.

The West Virginia native went to Eastern Michigan from Robert Morris, where he inherited a team coming off consecutive last-place finishes in the Northeast Conference. In two years Robert Morris climbed to sev-

enth place. Boone's third team jumped to third place, going 18-12, and lost in the conference tournament final.

Boone's philosophy is based on a commitment to excellence on and off the court.

"Unfortunately, it doesn't always work that way," he said. "There are those who are not willing or able to accept our manner of leadership and the direction of our program."

Boone was prepared for last year and along with his staff continued working to build a solid foundation. In order to talk about winning, in order to expect to win, you must first earn the right to win, he said.

"We tell our team that we can easily put on the board that one of our goals is to win 20 games and the Mid-American Conference championship," Boone said. "We can say that, but you have to earn the right to put that expectation on the board."

Melvin Hicks (13.1 ppg, 3.7 rpg, .831 FT) leads a group of only five returning players. On the down side the Eagles could be forced to play the early part of the season without Hicks, a 6-3 senior, who injured his right knee in a May pickup game and had surgery. Hicks is targeted to return in early January.

Sophomore **Ricky Cottrill** also returns to the backcourt after having his college debut season short-circuited by academic troubles. The 6-3 Cottrill (12.3 ppg, 2.1 rpg, .865 FT) was declared ineligible after playing in 11 games for falling short of the Mid-American Conference minimum GPA requirement. Cottrill was EMU's top scorer at the time and had averaged 20 points in a four-game span before his suspension. He went out with a flourish by scoring 20 against Tennessee Tech, 16 against Iona, 23 against Grambling State and 20 against Michigan.

Cottrill recovered nicely, posting a 3.5 GPA in the spring semester. Boone was almost apologetic about the situation because Cottrill isn't a bad student. In fact, he was president of the National Honor Society at his high school.

It seems that Cottrill, who hails from Poca, W.Va., near Boone's hometown of Winfield, just got caught up in college life and fell behind in the classroom. Boone also said the freshman was given a class schedule that was a bit too difficult.

"A couple of the dismissals we made in our program were because of academics," Boone said. "We had some very serious academic problems. We recruited people accordingly. We got Ricky Cottrill, who was taken a little bit for granted."

Cottrill made up for some of the minutes touring France with an all-star team.

The third returning starter is 6-8, 215-pound senior forward **Tyron Radney** who emerged as one of the MAC's best rebounders. Radney (5.2 ppg, 8.3 rpg, .500 FG) doesn't score much, but hits the boards hard. Radney was not able to play as a freshman and received a fourth year of eligibility after meeting NCAA academic standards. Radney had double-figure rebounds in 11 games, including 19 against Wisconsin-Green Bay and 17 against Grambling State.

"He's a good jumper and can run all day long," Boone said. "It seems like he never gets tired."

Forward **Ryan Prillman** (9.8 ppg, 4.4 rpg, .545 FG) comes off a solid season when the 6-9, 235-pound junior scored in double figures 15 times and blocked 33 shots. Prillman's 33 blocks (1.18 per game) ranked fifth in the conference.

Boone said he expects a much-improved version of Prillman, who put on 20 pounds and "increased his strength levels 100 percent."

Guard **Ben Romano** (1.5 ppg, 1.2 rpg) is from Luanda, Angola. The 6-4 senior played on the national team of Angola in the 1996 Olympic Games. His personal highlight was scoring six points against the U.S. Dream Team. Romano, a former walk-on, was awarded a scholarship this year.

One player who knows exactly what the coach wants is 6-8, 235-pound junior forward **Steve Pettyjohn**, who followed Boone from Robert Morris. Pettyjohn, who sat out last season, averaged 12.3 points and 8.4 rebounds at Robert Morris in 1999-2000. He made 46.2 percent of his field goal attempts and .795 percent at the free-throw line.

Pettyjohn also went to France this summer on the same all-star squad as Cottrill.

"He has been in our system for three years and he has an understanding of what our expectations are and how to mold a team together," Boone said.

Sophomore **James "Boo" Jackson** was academically ineligible as a freshman and made the most of his wait, growing an inch to 6-9 and putting on 30 pounds to 215. Jackson averaged 21 points and 15 rebounds as an all-city first-team player for Perry Academy in Pittsburgh, Pa.

Eastern Michigan expects immediate production from a freshman class that includes 6-6, 215-pound forward **Markus Austin** from White Plains, N.Y. Austin averaged 28 points and nine rebounds for a 27-2 team at White Plains High School. Austin was a prospect who might have fallen through the cracks because he didn't go to the big-time summer camps or play in a prominent AAU program.

Freshman guard **Michael Ross**, at 5-9, is another intriguing recruit. Ross was selected to all-state teams in basketball and football at one of West Virginia's perennial basketball powerhouses, Beckley High School. Very quick and extremely athletic, Ross had college offers in both sports.

Ross averaged 17 points and eight assists for the Flying Eagles, who were 24-4. This summer at the West Virginia North-South All-Star Game, he won the three-point shooting and slam dunk contests. He scored 64 points in one AAU game.

As a football standout, Ross rushed for 1,200 yards and scored 21 touchdowns.

Adam Sommer, 6-5 and 225 pounds, was chosen MVP of his Pickerington (Ohio) High School team where he averaged 18 points and eight rebounds as an All-Ohio Central District first-team player.

The fourth freshman, 6-10, 220-pound **Ryan Stennett** played at Kimball High School in Royal Oak, Mich. Stennett averaged 15 points, nine rebounds and three blocks as a member of the Royal Oak Daily Tribune All-Area Dream Team and all-state honorable mention selection.

Eastern Michigan lost seven players from last season including starters C.J. Grantham (10.0 ppg, 2.9 rpg) and Rod Wells (3.3 ppg, 1.5 rpg) along with Shamar Herron (4.9 ppg, 2.9 rpg) and Mosi Barnes (4.3 ppg, 1.1 rpg). Ryan Hopkins (3.8 ppg, 1.0 rpg) and Mats Nordin (0.0 ppg, 0.7 rpg) transferred and Dante Darling (8.4 ppg, 2.9 rpg) was dismissed after seven games.

2001-2002 SCHEDULE

Nov.	17-20	#Paradise Jam
	26	Maryland-Eastern Shore
Dec.	1	Tennessee Tech
	3	Detroit
	8	Delaware State
	11	@Wisconsin-Green Bay
	19	Concordia
	22	@Michigan
Jan.	2	Buffalo
	5	Ball State
	7	@Akron
	9	Toledo
	12	@Marshall
	16	@Miami
	19	Central Michigan
	22	Ohio
	26	@Northern Illinois
	29	Kent State
Feb.	2	@Ball State
	6	@Western Michigan
	9	Northern Illinois
	13	@Bowling Green
	16	Akron
	20	@Central Michigan
	27	Western Michigan
March	2	@Toledo
	4	##MAC Tournament
	7-9	###MAC Tournament

@Road Games
#St. Thomas, Virgin Islands (vs. UAB, first round; also Clemson, Morris Brown, LaSalle, Miami, FL)
##At campus sites
###Gund Arena, Cleveland, OH

BLUE RIBBON ANALYSIS

BACKCOURT	B+
BENCH/DEPTH	C
FRONTCOURT	C
INTANGIBLES	C

Being picked to finish at the bottom of the Mid-American Conference again is a motivator for Eastern Michigan. Boone actually wants it that way because he thinks the Eagles need to grow at their own speed and not try to live up to someone else's standards.

Boone isn't looking for short-term success. Winning is a byproduct of traveling many miles down the road to success, he said.

Eastern Michigan has a good foundation with returning starters Hicks, Cottrill and Radney, plus some promising newcomers.

The one player who brings the Eagles together, however, might be transfer forward Pettyjohn, who played two good years under Boone at Robert Morris.

It's a safe bet the Eagles will be better than last season and even better in years to come as Boone's program matures.

(R.M)

Kent State

LOCATION	Kent, OH
CONFERENCE	Mid-American (East)
LAST SEASON	24-10 (.706)
CONFERENCE RECORD	13-5 (1st)
STARTERS LOST/RETURNING	1/4
NICKNAME	Golden Flashes
COLORS	Navy Blue & Gold
HOMECOURT	Memorial Athletic and Convocation Cener (6,327)
COACH	Stan Heath (Eastern Michigan '88)
RECORD AT SCHOOL	First year
CAREER RECORD	First year
ASSISTANTS	Jim Christian (Rhode Island '88)
	Klint Pleasant (Lipscomb '98)
	Oronde Taliaferro (Wayne State '94)
TEAM WINS (last 5 years)	9-13-23-23-24
RPI (last 5 years)	206-204-31-36-83
2000-01 FINISH	Lost in NCAA second round.

Back in the spring, Sports Illustrated ran a story recognizing "five college coaches waiting in the wings."

The list that appeared on March 19 included Iowa State assistant Leonard Perry, Florida assistant John Pelphrey, Iona head coach Jeff Ruland, Michigan State assistant Stan Heath and Hofstra assistant Jay Wright.

Perry left the list the next day when he was hired as head coach at Idaho, and Wright exited a week later when he was chosen to head the Villanova program.

Heath was still available a month later, and Kent State snagged him as the successor for Gary Waters, who was selected head coach at Rutgers after leading the Golden Flashes to new heights the past five seasons.

"I feel like this is an excellent fit for me as well as the returning team members and the future of Kent State basketball," the 36-year-old Heath said.

Waters left behind most of the ingredients from the best team in school history. Kent State emerged on the national scene under Waters, who was 92-60 in five years and led the Golden Flashes to postseason appearances in the last three years (NCAA in 1999 and 2001, NIT in 2000).

Last year's team won a school-record 24 games after posting 23 wins in each of the two previous years. Before that Kent State had only two 20-win seasons ever. Kent State also recorded its first-ever NCAA Tournament victory, beating Indiana in the West Regional before falling to Cincinnati in the second round.

Only the storybook season enjoyed by Jay Smith at Central Michigan prevented Waters from being selected Mid-American Conference Coach of the Year for the third time in a row.

Heath spent five seasons on Tom Izzo's staff at Michigan State, where the Spartans won the 2000 national championship, made three consecutive trips to the NCAA Final Four and won four consecutive Big Ten regular-season titles.

Before that, he spent two seasons in the MAC as an assistant on the staff of Jim Larranaga, now head coach at George Mason. He also played in the MAC as a three-year letterman at Eastern Michigan.

"There's no question Stan is ready for this job," Izzo said. "In his five years at Michigan State he's helped us go from start to finish with three Final Four appearances and one national championship. We've built it and maintained it, and he's been a big part of that on the court and on the recruiting trail.

"Gary Waters did an incredible job. Now it's Stan's job to maintain and build upon that, and he's been part of the blueprint of how we've done it here. We wouldn't be where we are today without the job Stan did."

All-MAC first-team selection Trevor Huffman (16.8 ppg, 2.9 rpg, 4.5 assists, .849 FT) is one of four starters back. The 6-1 senior was the only MAC player ranked in the top 10 for scoring and assists.

Huffman, who was invited this summer to participate in USA Basketball Team Trials, is seventh in school history with 1,243 career points and on pace to break the 23-year-old record of 1,710 set by Burrell McGhee. He can score and play defense. In one game last season Huffman outscored MAC Player of the Year David Webber from Central Michigan, 27-19. In another outing, he held Marshall star Tamar Slay to five points, his season low.

"I don't think there's another player in the league who can score the way he does and also take the [opposing team's] best player out on the floor and shut him down," Waters said.

Huffman received MVP honors in the MAC Tournament.

Kent State's most underrated player is 5-11, 160-pound senior **Andrew Mitchell** (12.2 ppg, 2.4 rpg, 3.3 apg, .404 3PT, .848 FT) who scores, shoots well from the outside, distributes and takes care of the basketball and plays good defense. Mitchell has started all 95 games of his college career. Heath once invited Mitchell, who is from Detroit, to walk-on at Michigan State.

Completing a three-guard lineup is 6-3, 195-pound senior **Demetric Shaw** (10.0 ppg, 6.9 rpg, .826 FT) who was voted the MAC's "best pound for pound" in a poll of conference team captains conducted by the Cleveland Plain Dealer.

At his size, Shaw led the Golden Flashes and was eighth in the league in rebounding. In MAC games only, he averaged 8.2 rebounds with a high of 17 against Eastern Michigan. And, he was also chosen conference defensive player of the year by the MAC News Media Association. He averaged 1.68 steals.

Mitchell and Shaw both received All-MAC honorable mention honors. Shaw was also selected to the Academic District IV team.

One thing opposing teams need to remember about the Kent State guards: Don't foul them. Huffman, Mitchell and Shaw combined to shoot .843 percent at the line.

Center **Mike Perry** (5.3 ppg, 3.5 rpg) is Kent State's fourth returning starter, but the 6-9, 230-pound senior was placed on academic suspension and can't play in games for the first semester. Perry is a defensive specialist who worked his way into the lineup for the final 20 games.

Seven-footer **John Edwards** (2.0 ppg, 1.7 rpg, 1.0 blocks) might be ready to step in at center. The big sophomore played an average of 6.8 minutes per game and had one blocked shot for every 6.7 minutes played.

Other returning players are 6-4 sophomore **Bryan Bedford** (2.1 ppg, 2.0 rpg), 6-0 sophomore **Eric Haut** (3.1 ppg, 1.5 rpg) and 6-4 senior **Eric Thomas** (2.0 ppg, 1.3 rpg). Thomas missed most of the season because of a stress fracture in his right foot and appeared in just seven games, but returned in time for the conference tournament.

Kent State's lost players include its second-leading scorer, Kyrem Massey (12.7 ppg, 4.6 rpg). Others not back this year are Rashaun Warren (6.1 ppg, 3.5 rpg), Matt Smriga (0.5 ppg, 0.6 rpg) and Seth Coblentz (0.6 ppg, 0.3 rpg).

With plenty of guards on the roster, Waters was able to red-shirt 6-7, 210-pound junior **Anthony Wilkins** last year after he transferred from Gulf Coast Community College in Florida. Wilkins, a native of nearby Cleveland, is a distant relative of former NBA stars Dominique and Gerald Wilkins. Wilkins averaged 10 points and seven rebounds as a sophomore point guard at Gulf Coast and was considered one of the Top 50 junior college prospects in the nation.

Transfer **Brian Howard**, a 6-5 sophomore, played in four games at Austin Peay as a freshman walk-on in the first part of last season. Howard enrolled at Kent State in January and is eligible at the end of the first semester.

Heath proved once again that recruiting never ends when much-traveled **Antonio Gates** enrolled at Kent State this fall. Gates, am athletic 6-3, 220-pound junior, is enrolled in classes but as of mid-September the school was still going over transcripts to determine his eligibility.

Gates was a first team All-Michigan basketball and football player at Detroit Central High School and signed with Michigan State, intending to continue in both sports. Michigan State's defensive coordinator at the time of Gates' signing was Dean Pees, now Kent State's head coach. Heath was also at Michigan State when Pees worked there.

Gates averaged 27 points and 12 rebounds on a Detroit Central team coached by Oronde Taliaferro, now one of Heath's assistants. He led Detroit Central to a Class A state championship. Gates was a partial qualifier as a Michigan State freshman, so he transferred to Eastern Michigan for the 1999-2000 season.

Gates was an academic casualty at Eastern Michigan, where in a brief stay he averaged 10.2 points and 7.4 rebounds in 18 games. He attended College of the Sequoias in Visalia, Calif., for a semester, then enrolled at Henry Ford Community College in Michigan last spring, but didn't play sports at either school. Now he's on Kent State's basketball team and might end up playing football, too.

Less than a week after Heath accepted the job, he signed 6-7, 210-pound **Jonathan Merritt**, one of Prep Spotlight's top 10 Michigan players from West Bloomfield High School. Merritt, a 3.0 student, averaged 18 points, 15 rebounds and seven blocks.

"Jonathan is a perfect fit for the university and our basketball program," Heath said. "There is no question he'll be an impact player during his career at Kent State. To get a player of his caliber this late in the year is huge."

Pittsburgh standout **Nate Gerwig**, a 6-9, 250-pound center, averaged 14 points per game as an all-city league player who shattered two backboards in practices at Schenley High School. Gerwig scored more than 1,000 points as a four-year starter.

Gerwig and 6-7, 235-pound freshman **Brandon Roach** both signed with Waters. Roach averaged 15 points at Bedford Heights High School in the Cleveland area. The eligibility of Roach was also still undecided in mid-September. Kent State is hoping he'll at least be a partial qualifier who can practice but not participate in games.

Bryan Pellegrino is a 6-3 red-shirt freshman from Solon, Ohio.

2001-2002 SCHEDULE

Nov.	23-25	#Robert Morris Tournament
	28	*Kentucky
Dec.	1	Tennessee-Chattanooga
	15	@Youngstown State
	20	@Xavier
	22	@Illinois State
	29	**Cleveland State
	31	St. Bonaventure
Jan.	2	Ball State
	5	@Marshall
	9	@Buffalo
	12	Ohio
	16	@Akron
	19	Western Michigan
	22	Buffalo
	26	@Bowling Green
	29	@Eastern Michigan
Feb.	2	Toledo
	4	Bowling Green
	9	@Central Michigan
	13	@Northern Illinois
	16	Miami
	19	Marshall
	23	@Ohio
	25	Akron
March	2	@Miami
	4	##MAC Tournamnet
	7-9	###MAC Tournament

@Road Games
*Cincinnati, OH
**Gund Arena
#Moon Township, PA (vs. Hofstra first round; also Pittsburgh, Oakland, UC Irvine, Illinois State, Robert Morris, South Florida)
##At campus sites
###Gund Arena, Cleveland, OH

BLUE RIBBON ANALYSIS

BACKCOURT	A
BENCH/DEPTH	C
FRONTCOURT	C
INTANGIBLES	B

Kent State is a guard-oriented team, but its guards are very good. Huffman, Mitchell and Shaw are proven Mid-American Conference performers and seniors with NCAA Tournament experience who will carry this team far.

It's a tough act to follow for Heath coming off Kent State's best season ever, but the Golden Flashes are once again among the MAC favorites and one of the league's best hopes for receiving an NCAA Tournament berth—if not as the league champion then as an at-large entry.

Heath is fully aware of what his predecessor, Waters, did at Kent State, and said it's time to raise the bar even higher. He plans to do it with an up-tempo style and pressure defense, which both are perfectly suited to the team he inherited.

(R.M.)

 Marshall

LOCATION	Huntington, WV
CONFERENCE	Mid-American (East)
LAST SEASON	18-9 (.667)
CONFERENCE RECORD	12-6 (t-2nd)
STARTERS LOST/RETURNING	2/3
NICKNAME	Thundering Herd
COLORS	Green & White
HOMECOURT	Cam Henderson Center (9,043)
COACH	Greg White (Marshall '82)
RECORD AT SCHOOL	86-54 (5 years)
CAREER RECORD	86-54 (5 years)
ASSISTANTS	Jeff Burkhamer (Alderson-Broaddus '84)
	Jeff Boals (Ohio '95)
	Kevin Keatts (Ferrum '95)
TEAM WINS (last 5 years)	20-11-16-21-18
RPI (last 5 years)	98-213-134-97-107
2000-01 FINISH	Lost in conference quarterfinal.

Marshall head coach Greg White is a strong believer that great players lead their teams to championships. If so, a Mid-American Conference pennant might be hanging next spring from the rafters of Cam Henderson Center.

Guard **Tamar Slay** and center **J.R. VanHoose**, both seniors, are the cornerstones of this Marshall squad.

"I'm pretty excited about our team," White said. "VanHoose was first team all-league. Slay has been first team and was second team last year. We've never had that before."

Nobody was happy about how the Marshall season ended. Marshall was picked to win the MAC last season and fell short, losing to Ball State in a conference tournament quarterfinal.

"It was a sudden end and we were disappointed because we thought we could go farther," White said.

Slay, VanHoose and power forward **Latece Williams**, another senior, are returning starters.

The 6-9, 210-pound Slay (17.3 ppg, 5.4 rpg, .405 FG, .327 3PT, .816 FT) led Marshall in scoring and was ranked among the league leaders in free-throw percentage, steals per game (1.44) and three-point shooting percentage. He was the MAC's 17th-best rebounder.

Slay had a very interesting off-season, starting when he toyed with the idea of declaring for the NBA draft, (he eventually opted to stay at Marshall for another year). Then he was arrested April 29 near the Marshall campus and charged with DUI and driving without a license. Slay's attorney said a plea agreement is being worked on with the Cabell County prosecutor. If convicted, Slay would face up to six months in jail and up to a $500 fine on each misdemeanor.

Fortunately for the Herd, things got better for Slay. In August he made it to the final cut for the USA team that won a bronze medal in the World University Games in Beijing, China. And, Slay was selected as one of 50 preseason candidates for the John R. Wooden Award. Slay is the only MAC player on the Wooden list.

"Tamar is very deserving," White said. "He has worked extremely hard to get to this point."

Marshall needs Slay to develop more consistency in his game, but the Herd always knows what it's getting from VanHoose. VanHoose (16.6 ppg, 11.1 rpg, .578 FG, .762 FT) was seventh in the conference in scoring, first in rebounding and first in field-goal percentage. He was the third-leading rebounder in the nation. The 6-10, 255-pounder had 20 double-doubles in 27 games, second in the nation to Iowa's Reggie Evans with 22 in 35 games.

The Herd center carries a consecutive game streak of 10 consecutive double-doubles into the season.

"He's a big, wide body with a soft shooting touch," former Northern Illinois coach Andy Greer said. "What makes him even more difficult to defend is that he can step out around 15 or 17 feet and nail the jumper as well."

VanHoose is one of only five players in school history with career totals of more than 1,300 points and more than 700 rebounds. He has 1,353 and 767 respectively. The other four players were Herd standouts Russell Lee, George Stone, Charlie Slack and Hal Greer.

This summer VanHoose spent a week at the big man camp in Honolulu conducted by former NBA and U.S. Olympic coach Pete Newell. The Kentucky Association of Basketball Coaches selected VanHoose as one of 50 players on its all-time Sweet 16 state tournament team. VanHoose led Paintsville High School to a Sweet 16 title in 1996, the semifinals in 1997 and a runner-up finish in 1998.

VanHoose leads the Herd back into Rupp Arena in Lexington, Ky., where the Sweet 16 is played, for an early-season appearance in the NABC Classic and a possible match-up against Kentucky, the school that overlooked him as a prep star.

Williams (10.5 ppg, 6.5 rpg, .542 FG) provides a strong inside presence.

"Latece is huge," said White, and he wasn't only talking about the player's physical presence. Williams led the team with 48 blocked shots and usually draws the toughest defensive assignment in the frontcourt. He fouled out only twice in 27 games.

Sophomore **Ardo Armpalu**, a 6-10, 260-pound center from Estonia, was mentioned in a series of articles done by the Dayton Daily News about foreign players being shuttled to the United States by an Estonian sports agent, Maarten van Gent. The Daily News reported that Armpalu said he was aware of contracts players had with van Gent, but that he didn't sign one. Marshall officials conducted their own investigation.

"I have no reason to believe Ardo isn't telling the truth," White said.

Armpalu (1.6 ppg, 1.7 rpg) chose not to be red-shirted as a freshman and appeared in 17 games. He could provide a nice boost inside.

Monty Wright (2.5 ppg, 0.9 rpg) is a 6-4, 205-pound junior guard who will get a chance to compete for quality playing time. The backcourt mix also includes 6-0 red-shirt freshman point guard **Enoch Bunch**, a two-time high school Mr. Basketball runner-up in Tennessee. Bunch worked against senior point guard Cornelius Jackson every day in practice and held his own. Bunch is a good floor leader and has a nice outside shot.

Forward **William Butler**, a 6-7 senior, is the forgotten member of this year's squad. Butler enrolled at Marshall in 1999 as a transfer from Santa Fe Community College in Florida, where he played for Herd assistant coach Jeff Burkhamer, and sat out the 1999-2000 season.

Butler was looking good and challenging for a starting position last October when he tore up his knee during a layup drill in MU's first public practice. After a year of rehab, Butler is back.

"I think he's going to be fine," White said. "I am excited about what I've seen."

Joe Dressel (0.0 ppg, 0.2 rpg) is a 6-4 sophomore who had five game appearances.

Marshall is excited about its recruits, especially Temple transfer **Ronald Blackshear**, a 6-5, 210-pound guard with sophomore eligibility beginning at the end of the fall semester. Blackshear left Temple looking for more playing time. He'll probably find it at Marshall, which lost its top three guards.

Blackshear played in 10 games last season at Temple, averaging 10.4 minutes, 3.4 points and 0.7 rebounds. In his final game for the Owls, against Wisconsin, he scored 15 points in 20 minutes of action. Temple coach John Chaney once described Blackshear as an offensive weapon. White says he's "the real deal" for the Herd.

Blackshear dominated squad workouts with his ability to score from long range.

"He can get his own," White said. "I've never seen anybody shoot the ball as deep as he can on the college level."

Blackshear was the Class AA state player of the year at Mitchell-Baker High School in Camilla, Ga., in 1998 when he averaged 19 points a game. He was a consensus Top 40 prospect and Recruiting USA ranked him as the seventh-best shooting guard in the nation.

He went to Hargrave Military Academy in Chatham, Va., and averaged 29 points on a team loaded with Division I signees. Marshall assistant coach Kevin Keatts was on the Hargrave staff then.

Clemson signed him, but Blackshear didn't qualify academically, so Temple took him and he sat out the 1999-2000 season.

"The best thing about Ronald is he's a 22-year-old man," White said. "We were fortunate to get him. He's capable of getting 20, 30 points a night. He'll open it up inside."

Freshman recruit **Ronny Dawn**, a 6-3 guard out of Newport Central Catholic High School in northern Kentucky, scored 20.2 points a game as the Cincinnati Enquirer's Northern Kentucky Player of the Year, an award he also won as a junior. Dawn also averaged 3.5 rebounds and 4.1 assists. He made 45 percent of three-point attempts as a senior and 43 percent for his career.

"Ronny Dawn brings the total package," White said.

Dawn scored 2,124 career points at Newport Central Catholic, breaking the record held by former Marshall player John Brannen.

The newcomer at point guard is 6-4, 200-pound junior transfer **Richard Wilson** from Cowley County Community College in Kansas. Wilson averaged 12.8 points, 8.1 assists, 4.0 rebounds and 1.7 steals in an All-Jayhawk Conference season. He was a .790 percent free-throw shooter.

"Wilson is an absolute warrior who is a great defender and an unbelievable passer that makes big shots," Cowley County assistant coach Brian Jackson said.

A report from The Sporting News on Wilson's performance at the Jayhawk Conference Shootout said, "Terribly under-rated because he is not flashy. Simply runs the team. Thinks 'We' is 'I'."

Freshman walk-on **Keith Archie** sent videos of himself in action to several schools, including Marshall and Central Michigan in the MAC. The 6-6, 230-pound power forward from the Chicago area averaged 10 points and eight rebounds at Thornridge High School, but was only lightly recruited. Archie said he chose Marshall to get a little farther away from home.

Marshall also added another walk-on this year, 6-7 freshman **Nelson Guerin** from Keyser High School in West Virginia.

In addition to the loss of Jackson (9.4 ppg, 3.3 rpg, 5.7 assists) the Herd also has to replace starting guard Travis Young (13.4 ppg, 4.2 rpg) along with Joda Burgess (7.9 ppg, .364 3PT), Marques Evans (1.5 ppg, 2.1 rpg), Sean Wuller (0.3 ppg, 0.6 rpg) and Jason Pyles (0.8 ppg, 0.2 rpg).

2001-2002 SCHEDULE

Nov.	15-16	#NABC Classic
	23	Troy State
	26	Shepherd
Dec.	3	@Winthrop
	6	@Radford
	8	Northern Illinois
	15	*Auburn
	22	@Western Michigan
	29	Massachusetts
Jan.	5	Kent State
	9	@Miami
	12	Eastern Michigan
	16	@Central Michigan
	19	Buffalo
	23	**West Virginia
	26	@Toledo
	29	Ball State
Feb.	2	@Ohio
	5	Akron
	9	@Bowling Green
	14	Miami
	16	Ohio
	19	@Kent State
	23	@Buffalo
	27	Central Michigan
March	2	@Akron
	4	##MAC Tournament
	7-9	###MAC Tournament

@Road Games
*Mobile, AL
**Charleston. WV
#Lexington, KY (vs. George Washington first round; also Kentucky, Western Kentucky)
##At campus sites
###Gund Arena, Cleveland, OH

BLUE RIBBON ANALYSIS

BACKCOURT	A
BENCH/DEPTH	B
FRONTCOURT	A
INTANGIBLES	C

Marshall begins the season with a question mark. Two unidentified basketball players were among 14 student-athletes (the other 12 are on the football team) suspended by the NCAA for receiving extra work benefits. An appeal was denied and the basketball players must sit out eight games that can be staggered throughout the season.

Who the suspended players are could directly affect the season. Names of the players and specific details of the allegations will not be released by the school in compliance with the federal Family Educational Rights and Privacy Act, also known as the "Buckley Amendment."

As long as the suspensions weren't handed to Tamar Slay or J.R. VanHoose, the Thundering Herd is in pretty good shape to challenge for the Mid-American Conference championship. Expectations for this team are high.

(R.M.)

Miami (Ohio)

LOCATION	Oxford, OH
CONFERENCE	Mid-American (East)
LAST SEASON	17-16 (.515)
CONFERENCE RECORD	10-8 (t-4th)
STARTERS LOST/RETURNING	2/3
NICKNAME	RedHawks
COLORS	Red & White
HOMECOURT	Millett Hall (9,200)
COACH	Charlie Coles (Miami '65)
RECORD AT SCHOOL	94-60 (5 years)
CAREER RECORD	186-144 (11 years)
ASSISTANTS	James Whitford (Wisconsin '94)
	Jermaine Henderson (Miami '97)
	Frankie Smith (Eastern Kentucky '88)
TEAM WINS (last 5 years)	21-17-24-15-17
RPI (last 5 years)	71-116-19-87-118
2000-01 FINISH	Lost in conference final.

Miami is definitely on a roll, with a record five consecutive appearances in the Mid-American Conference Tournament final and a string of 11 straight seasons at or above .500.

Along the way to the MAC championship game last year, the RedHawks stepped outside the league to record early upsets of No. 17 Temple and No. 10 Notre Dame.

For the last five seasons, the driving force has been head coach Charlie Coles, who also grabbed the Miami spotlight as an All-MAC player there in the mid-1960s. Coles, 59, received a contract extension through the 2003-04 season.

Maybe then, just maybe, he'll consider retirement. Right now, however, he isn't slowing down.

"Charlie is a tremendous person and coach," Miami athletic director Joel Maturi said. "He certainly epitomizes Miami and its 'Cradle of Coaches.' We're fortunate to have him leading our program into the new century."

Actually, the school is fortunate to have Coles at all after the events of March 1998, when he collapsed during a game at Western Michigan, suffering cardiac arrest.

Coles, who also coached at Central Michigan from 1986-91, is the fifth-winningest coach in MAC history.

"I'll accept that, but I'm kind of like the guy who got a hundred yards but it took a hundred carries," the always colorful Coles said.

With more than 65 percent of its scoring and 60 percent of its rebounding back this year, there's no sign of a letup at Miami.

Forward **Alex Shorts** (15.7 ppg, 5.5 rpg, .486 FG, .801 FT) was voted All-MAC second team in his NCAA Division I debut season after transferring from San Jacinto Junior College. Shorts, a 6-8, 239-pound senior, was Miami's leading scorer and second-leading rebounder.

Despite being slowed first by a strained tendon in his foot and later by a dislocated toe, point guard **Doug Davis** (9.8 ppg, 1.7 rpg, 2.3 apg) led the RedHawks with 30 steals and played his best basketball toward the end of the season. Davis, a 6-3 senior, also joined the team last season. He played two seasons at Michigan State behind All-American Mateen Cleaves.

The third returning starter is 6-5 sophomore guard **Julius "Juby" Johnson** (6.6 ppg, 2.7 rpg, 1.3 spg), a MAC All-Freshman team member.

Miami has its best group of returning starters since the 1999 NCAA Sweet 16 team led by Wally Szczerbiak and Damon Frierson.

"We've got our best player coming back in Alex Shorts, Then, we have Doug Davis, who, if you take away the injuries, played really well last year," Coles said. "We also return Julius Johnson, who I feel was probably one of the top freshmen in the league last year. It really helps us to return a strong group of starters."

The RedHawks lost only three players—seniors Mike Ensminger (6.1 ppg, 5.9 rpg), Jason Grunkemeyer (11.3 ppg, 3.2 rpg) and Rich Allendorf 6-10 (3.3 ppg, 3.5 rpg).

One of last year's recruits, 6-2 sophomore guard **Chester Mason** is now academically eligible to play. As a partial qualifier "The Jet" was able to practice with the team, but not see game action.

Mason was selected Ohio's Division I Co-Mr. Basketball as a senior at Cleveland South High School. He averaged a triple-double of 25 points, 13 rebounds and 11 assists.

"We really missed Chester last year, but we've got him now," Coles said. "He will finally be able to make his mark. I have a lot of faith in him as a ball player. He's a tough competitor."

Miami is also counting on the continued development of 6-5 junior forward **Larry Drake** (3.0 ppg, 1.2 rpg) and 6-1 junior guard **Matt Jameson** (2.7 ppg, 1.5 rpg).

Jameson started 15 games at point guard, including eight in conference play. He played the entire 40 minutes at Notre Dame when Davis was injured and had seven points and six rebounds while committing just two turnovers.

Forward **Eugene Seals** (4.0 ppg, 2.5 rpg) is a 6-6 sophomore with a nice future.

"And don't forget **Brian Edwards**," said Coles about the 6-7, 251-pound senior who averaged 1.3 points and 1.0 rebounds. "We've waited a long time for Brian. He's worked hard and I think it's going to pay off. I think he's going to have a fine senior season."

Other returning lettermen are 6-1 senior **Ben Helmers** (0.9 ppg, 0.3 rpg), 6-6 junior **Bryan Reed** (1.3 ppg, 1.4 rpg) and 6-4 swing man **Doug Williams** (0.4 ppg, 0.3 rpg).

Miami brought in three recruits. Forward **Danny Horace** is a 6-5, 220-pound freshman out of Cincinnati's Western Hills High School. Horace scored 21.9 points per game and averaged 12.1 rebounds. He played in the Ohio/West Virginia All-Star Games, scoring 29 and 21 points in the series.

"Danny is a ferocious rebounder and competitor," Coles said. "He can hit the 15-foot jump shot and also drive to the basket. He's a hard worker and good player."

Horace was ranked No. 128 on a list of the nation's Top 300 seniors compiled by Brick Oettinger of Prep Stars Recruiters Handbook.

Nate VanderSluis, a 6-11, 310-pound freshman, averaged 19.9 points and 12.0 rebounds at Oak Harbor High School in Ohio. Coles said VanderSluis is a versatile player for his size and isn't limited to the low post only. Miami hasn't had a player with the size of VanderSluis since the great Wayne Embry, a Naismith Memorial Basketball Hall of Fame member, left the Oxford campus in 1958.

"We were looking for some inside help and we got it in these two players," Coles said. "I expect them to make the same impact as Julius [Johnson] and Eugene [Seals] did as freshmen. Last year Julius and Eugene really added to our team, and I expect the same of Danny and Nate."

Another standout from Cincinnati, 6-7 freshman **Tim Schenke** from Elder High School, also signed with Miami. Schenke averaged 12 points and seven rebounds as a senior.

To be successful when March rolls around, Coles starts getting ready in November. Miami's non-conference schedule features four 2001 NCAA Tournament teams (George Mason, Xavier, Notre Dame, Boston College) and two NIT participants (UNC-Wilmington, Dayton).

Coles said he lines up tough competition to (a) give his players a chance to face the best players in the nation; (b) enhance Miami's reputation; and (c) to make his team better.

"The best way for your team to improve is to play teams that do good things," he said. "This is probably the most difficult schedule in my six years, and I think it will really help prepare us for the rest of our season."

2001-2002 SCHEDULE

Nov.	17	@UNC Wilmington
	19	George Mason
	28	Xavier
Dec.	1	Wright State
	3	@Evansville
	8	Notre Dame
	16	@USC
	19-22	#Rainbow Classic
	29	@Dayton
Jan.	2	@Western Michigan
	5	@Central Michigan
	9	Marshall
	12	Akron
	16	Eastern Michigan
	19	@Ohio
	22	@Northern Illinois
	26	Ball State
Feb.	2	@Bowling Green
	6	@Buffalo
	9	Toledo
	11	Ohio
	14	@Marshall
	16	@Kent State
	20	Bowling Green
	23	@Ball State

	25	Buffalo
March	2	Kent State
	4	##MAC Tournament
	7-9	###MAC Tournament

@Road Games
#At Hawaii (vs. Boston College first round; also Hawaii, Portland, Iona, Holy Cross, Georgia, Arkansas State)
##At campus sites
###Gund Arena, Cleveland, OH

BLUE RIBBON ANALYSIS

BACKCOURT	A
BENCH/DEPTH	B
FRONTCOURT	A
INTANGIBLES	A

Miami will be right back in the thick of the Mid-American Conference championship picture.

Last year's team had three seniors and a lot of inexperienced players. This year Miami has four seniors and several others with a lot of experience. Coles likes the balance of the squad.

"Our blend this year is just much better than it was a year ago," Coles said. "We've got a couple of freshmen and some seniors, but then we also have experienced sophomores and juniors, which is what we were missing last year."

It sounds as though Coles thinks the RedHawks are pretty good. He's right.

(R.M.)

 ## Northern Illinois

LOCATION	DeKalb, IL
CONFERENCE	Mid-American (West)
LAST SEASON	5-23 (.179)
CONFERENCE RECORD	4-14 (5th)
STARTERS LOST/RETURNING	3/2
NICKNAME	Huskies
COLORS	Cardinal & Black
HOMECOURT	Chick Evans Fieldhouse (6,044)
COACH	Rob Judson (Illinois '80)
RECORD AT SCHOOL	First year
CAREER RECORD	First year
ASSISTANTS	Mike Shepard (Kansas State '90)
	Donald Whiteside (Northern Illinois '94)
	Carl Armato (Northern Illinois '84)
TEAM WINS (last 5 years)	12-10-6-13-5
RPI (last 5 years)	211-234-276-171-290
2000-01 FINISH	Lost in conference first round.

When Brian Hammel walked off the court on Dec. 6, 2000, he knew he'd had enough. Hammel, the coach who led Northern Illinois into the Mid-American Conference in 1997, abruptly announced his resignation that night.

Hammel said he was physically, emotionally and mentally drained and that it was time for a change.

Northern Illinois actually won that game, drubbing Rockford College by 33 points to end a season-opening six-game losing skid, but couldn't muster many more victories for interim coach Andy Greer. The Huskies limped in with a 5-23 record, the worst in the school's 100-year men's basketball history.

Less than 24 hours after the season ended, Northern Illinois selected University of Illinois assistant Rob Judson as its new head coach. Judson, 43, was at Northern Illinois in the 1989-90 and 1990-91 seasons on Jim Molinari's staff.

"The transition has been great," Judson said. "This is a very natural fit for me. I've worked hard and prepared all my career for this. It's a situation that fits me very well and I feel very comfortable."

Judson also worked for Molinari at Bradley from 1991-96, then joined Lon Kruger's staff at Illinois for four seasons from 1996-2000. He remained with the Illini last season when Bill Self took over for Kruger.

Illinois was in the NCAA Tournament four times in the last five years, including a spot in last season's Elite Eight. So Judson knows what the big time is all about.

"He is a tireless worker, a great communicator and will be a tremendous ambassador for Northern Illinois University," Self said. "Basketball-wise, there's no person in the state of Illinois as well-connected as he is. I know his move will be very successful."

While watching individual workouts last spring, Judson saw some Northern Illinois players who were hungry for success, but needed direction and a structure that will allow them to be successful. He definitely has some work to do.

Northern Illinois lost three starters in guards Mike "Downtown" Brown (12.5 ppg, 2.4 apg) and Stephen Jones (9.8 ppg, 7.3 rpg) and forward Steve Determan (3.7 ppg, 2.4 rpg). Brown's outside shooting (188 career three-point field goals) will be missed.

Other lost lettermen are forward Jerry Sanders (9.3 ppg, 4.3 rpg) and guards Markus Jankus (1.1 ppg, 1.2 apg) and Morgan Thompson (2.2 ppg).

The two returning starters are solid. Forward **Leon Rodgers**, a 6-6, 222-pound senior, comes off an All MAC honorable mention season. Rodgers (16.6 ppg, 6.3 rpg, 2.0 apg) is a career 1,000-point scorer and shared last year's team MVP award with Brown.

Rodgers is a good-shooting big man (.439 FG). He shot .407 percent from the three-point line, sinking 55-of-135. Against Rockford he was 13-for-13 from the field and scored 27 points.

In an article written by Dick Vitale for ESPN Magazine, he described Rodgers as the most versatile player in the conference.

"For Leon it's a matter of being consistent day in and day out in practice so he can be more consistent in games," Judson said. "This year we're challenging him to attack the basket more so he can make more trips to the free-throw line."

Center **Matt Nelson**, a 6-9, 237-pound senior, developed into a steady force in the middle. Nelson (7.5 ppg, 5.3 rpg) ranked ninth in the MAC with 26 blocked shots. Nelson's best scoring game was 16 points against Ohio University.

Sean Ezell (6.6 ppg, 2.5 rpg, 1.5 apg), a 6-4 sophomore, is the leading returning scorer among the remaining players. **Mike Morrison** (2.3 ppg, 1.6 rpg) is a 6-9 junior center.

Few players in the MAC are quicker off the floor than 6-6 sophomore forward **Marcus Smallwood** (5.0 ppg, 3.7 rpg). Smallwood led the Huskies and was sixth in the conference with 30 blocks, including three games with four. Smallwood was selected NIU's best defensive player.

Another player who gained valuable experience is 6-4 sophomore guard **Al Sewasciuk** (5.4 ppg, 2.3 rpg). Sewasciuk set a school freshman record with 36 three-pointers in 127 attempts (.283). Sewasciuk had his best game at Wisconsin when he hit five three-pointers and scored 21 points.

Walter Thompson, a 5-10 sophomore, averaged 0.7 points and 1.3 assists in 12 game appearances.

Transfer guard **Perry "P.J." Smith** is eligible after sitting out last season and has three years to play. The 6-4 Smith averaged 9.1 points 4.2 rebounds a game at Illinois State as a member of the Missouri Valley Conference All-Freshman team.

"Perry is athletic and he can shoot the ball," Judson said. "That is an excellent combination for a wing player in college basketball. The biggest adjustment he will have to make is to the intensity of practice and games after a red-shirt year."

Judson said his recruiting will focus on players with quickness and skill who can provide an exciting style of basketball for the fans. His first signee was 6-6 freshman point guard **Julian McElroy** from Gordon Tech in Chicago. Judson's father, Phil, coached McElroy's father, David, in the 1960s at North Chicago High School.

"Once we knew Julian would be our first signee, it made the whole situation special," Judson said.

The signing of McElroy wasn't just a favor, because he brings some impressive credentials. McElroy averaged 17 points, seven rebounds and 10 assists as a senior member of Chicago's All-Catholic League North first team.

Judson said he's a good player and student with an unlimited upside.

"With Julian's size, along with his ability to handle the ball and see the floor, he can add a lot to our team right away," Judson said. "He's very unselfish, he thinks pass first then shoot, and that's what we're looking for in our point guard."

Eugene Bates is also a Chicago product, a 6-1 junior transfer from Lincoln College. Bates averaged 14.9 points and 3.7 assists last year. He also shot .600 from the field.

Hammel left behind two freshman recruits he signed during the early period. **Chris Lawson**, 6-3, averaged 18 points, six assists, six rebounds and two steals as an all-city guard who led Harlan High School to a 22-3 record in the Chicago Blue South Conference. **Jamel Staten**, a 6-6 forward, is from Minneapolis North High School.

2001-2002 SCHEDULE

Nov.	24	@Loyola-Chicago
	27	Valpairaiso
	30	#Marquette Blue and Gold Classic
Dec.	1	#Marquette Blue and Gold Classic
	4	South Florida
	8	@Marshall
	15	@Illinois-Chicago
	22	@Drake
	29	Eastern Illinois
Jan.	2	Ohio
	5	Buffalo
	8	@Bowling Green
	12	@Lipscomb
	16	@Toledo
	22	Miami
	26	Eastern Michigan
	28	@Buffalo
	30	Toledo
Feb.	2	@Central Michigan
	5	Ball State
	9	@Eastern Michigan
	13	Kent State
	16	Western Michigan
	20	@Akron
	23	Central Michigan
	27	@Ball State
March	2	@Western Michigan
	4	##MAC Tournament
	7-9	###MAC Tournament

@Road Games
#Milwaukee, WI (vs. Marquette first round; also Texas Southern, Sam Houston State)
##At campus sites
###Gund Arena, Cleveland, OH

BLUE RIBBON ANALYSIS

BACKCOURT	C+
BENCH/DEPTH	C
FRONTCOURT	A
INTANGIBLES	C

Judson is one of three first-year head coaches in the Mid-American Conference. There's no question he has the toughest job of the three. Stan Heath at Kent State and Tim O'Shea at Ohio both stepped into better situations.

Judson isn't accustomed to losing and he'll work as hard as humanly possible to right the ship in a hurry. This year's team might not have the firepower to do it, however.

Big men Rodgers and Nelson form a strong inside duo, but some players need to step up at the guard positions. If Smith can shake off the rust from sitting out last season, he'll be a nice addition at shooting guard or small forward. The recruits provide a lot of athleticism.

It will probably be at least another year until Judson gets his program firmly in place.

(R.M.)

 ## Ohio

LOCATION	Athens, OH
CONFERENCE	Mid-American (East)
LAST SEASON	19-11 (.633)
CONFERENCE RECORD	12-6 (t-2nd)
STARTERS LOST/RETURNING	2/3
NICKNAME	Bobcats
COLORS	Hunter Green & White
HOMECOURT	Convocation Center (13,000)
COACH	Tim O'Shea (Boston College '84)
RECORD AT SCHOOL	First year
CAREER RECORD	First year
ASSISTANTS	John Rhodes (Ohio '88)
	Gary Manchel (Vermont '85)
	Kevin Kuwik (Notre Dame '96)
TEAM WINS (last 5 years)	17-5-18-20-19
RPI (last 5 years)	94-250-75-72-108
2000-01 FINISH	Lost in conference semifinal.

Ohio won 39 games the last two seasons and lost only two players who contributed much last year, so new head coach Tim O'Shea jumps in at a good time.

Athletic director Thomas Boeh brought four candidates to campus for interviews in his search to replace highly successful Larry Hunter, whose contract wasn't renewed. O'Shea, the associate head coach at Boston College, was selected March 29 from a group that included North Carolina assistant Doug Wojcik, Georgetown assistant Ronnie Thompson and University of Charleston head coach Jayson Gee, a former Ohio assistant.

"Tim is a great recruiter," Boeh said. "He knows talent—where to find it and how to get kids to come. He is a great floor coach and was a part of the rebuilding of a program at Boston College."

It's interesting that Boeh mentioned "rebuilding" in his statement, because Ohio certainly isn't in that mode.

O'Shea has a tough act to follow. All Hunter did was win games and graduate players in his 12 seasons at Ohio, and he was swept out the door. Hunter directed the Bobcats to a 204-148 record and postseason appearances in 1994 (NCAA) and 1995 (NIT). His 1993-94 team won the Preseason NIT championship. A press release from North Carolina State, where Hunter caught on as an assistant coach, said 28 of the 34 players he coached at Ohio received degrees.

The one thing Hunter didn't do was take Ohio to the postseason recently.

"We are very appreciative of the many years coach Hunter dedicated to our men's basketball team and its student-athletes," Boeh said on March 15. "However, at this time we feel it is in the best interest of the program to secure new leadership in our effort to return the team to national postseason play as well as the exceptional competitive level that is commensurate with the quality of Ohio University."

O'Shea, who turns 40 on Sept. 22, worked for the last 13 years under Al Skinner at Rhode Island and Boston College, which won last year's Big East championship and earned a No. 3 seeding for the NCAA East Regional. O'Shea was with Skinner at Rhode Island nine seasons and the Rams made two NCAA appearances and earned two NIT berths.

Jay Bilas of ESPN.com placed O'Shea on his list of the nation's "Undervalued Coaches" who is a good teacher and has a real eye for talent.

"O'Shea was instrumental in building the Rhode Island program by finding diamonds in the rough and polishing what others had overlooked," Bilas said. "Skinner and O'Shea did the same thing at Boston College, turning a forgotten program around in the same manner."

Ohio will play a fast-paced, up-tempo game set up by pressure defense, O'Shea said. He believes in a balanced attack, saying it's harder to stop a team that has five players in double figures versus one that has one big scorer.

Junior forward **Brandon Hunter** can certainly be a big scorer, and Ohio will be pretty good if O'Shea can develop the right combination of players around the 6-7, 260-pounder. Hunter (18.1 ppg, 9.4 rpg, .510 FG) was selected to the All Mid-American Conference first team and finished runner-up in player-of-the-year voting to Central Michigan guard David Webber. Hunter was the only player in the top four of the MAC statistics for scoring, rebounding and field-goal percentage.

He had 13 games with 20 or more points and recorded 14 double-doubles, second most in the league behind Marshall center J.R. VanHoose.

"You try to limit his touches," Miami coach Charlie Coles said. "He's got those long arms and he just reaches out. We don't have any one player that can guard him. He's really something special."

The Bobcats have a formidable one-two inside punch with Hunter playing alongside 6-9, 205-pound senior **Patrick Flomo** (9.1 ppg, 6.5 rpg, 3.5 bpg, .633 FG). Flomo would have easily led the MAC in field-goal percentage, but fell short of the required number of shots made.

Flomo did top the MAC and was ninth in the country in blocked shots and set a league record with 105. He has 169 career blocks, 92 shy of the school and MAC record of 260 set by former Ohio player John Devereaux (1981-84). Until last season Devereaux also had the MAC season record of 99. Last season Flomo rejected more shots than 10 teams in the conference.

He also showed he can provide some scoring when needed. Hunter struggled in a conference tournament semifinal against Miami (Ohio), going 2-for-9 from the field and scoring nine points, but Flomo had 17 points along with seven rebounds and three blocks.

Forward **Jon Sanderson** (8.9 ppg, 3.8 rpg) had a solid debut with the Bobcats after transferring from Ohio State, where he was a starter in 1999 when the Buckeyes went to the NCAA Final Four. The 6-7, 230-pound senior impressed O'Shea this summer on a trip to Italy, where Ohio went 1-4 in games against some quality club teams.

"Jon is a very talented player who has a chance to be a key contributor for us this season," O'Shea wrote in an online journal for www.ohiobobcats.com. "Jon's biggest challenge is to adopt a blue collar approach to the game. By this I mean he needs to be very physical and aggressive in his approach."

Steve Esterkamp (10.7 ppg, 3.7 rpg, .395 3PT, .800 FT) is a versatile 6-6, 200-pound junior who can do many things to help a team win. Esterkamp was Ohio's third-leading scorer as a starter in 17-of-30 games.

Other returning players include 6-5 sophomore **Jaivon Harris** (2.4 ppg, 1.3 rpg), 6-8 senior **Alex Liatsos** (2.3 ppg, 1.4 rpg), 6-4 senior **Jason Crawford** (0.8 ppg, 0.4 rpg) and 6-3 junior **Adam Howell** (1.2 ppg, 0.2 rpg).

The leading candidate to replace departed Dustin Ford at point guard is probably 6-0 sophomore **Thomas Stephens** (2.4 ppg, 1.1 rpg, 1.5 assists). Stephens is a gifted athlete who also plays cornerback on the Ohio football team.

Along with Ford (7.6 ppg, 2.3 rpg, 2.6 assists) the Bobcats also lost Anthony Jones (12.7 ppg, 3.9 rpg, 3.7 assists), Shaun McVicker (1.0 ppg, 1.4 rpg) and Ryan Smith (0.7 ppg, 0.9 rpg).

Transfer **Sonny Johnson**, a 6-5 junior from Cleveland State, becomes eligible after the fall quarter. Johnson started 22-of-30 games at Cleveland State in 1999-2000, averaging 11.9 points and 4.6 rebounds.

Ohio was able to red-shirt forward **Kevin Shorter** last year and he joins the Bobcats as a 6-8, 200-pound freshman. Shorter averaged 14 points, 11 rebounds and four assists as a senior at Chippewa High School in Clinton Township, Mich. The Prep Spotlight publication ranked him as the fifth-best forward in Michigan.

O'Shea's first recruit was 6-1 freshman guard **Zach Kiekow** out of Osseo High School in Minnesota. Kiekow averaged 12.6 points, six assists and two steals a game. He was selected to the Minneapolis Star Tribune All-State honorable mention list.

"He is an outstanding leader who should provide an immediate impact for our team," O'Shea said.

James Bridgewater is a 6-4 freshman from Pioneer High School in Ann Arbor, Mich. Bridgewater averaged 17.9 points, 12.5 rebounds and 4.2 assists as a senior, his fourth season as a starter. His former teammates include Boston College player Ryan Sidney and LaVell Blanchard at Michigan.

"James is a tremendous athlete and competitor," O'Shea said. "His aggressive style will fit nicely with the way we want to play. He has been extremely well-coached in the fundamentals of the game."

2001-2002 SCHEDULE

Nov.	26	@Navy
	29	Duquesne
Dec.	5	@DePaul
	8	Wisconsin
	12	@St. Bonaventure
	15	Oakland
	27-28	#Florida International Holiday Classic
Jan.	2	@Northern Illinois
	5	@Akron
	9	Western Michigan
	12	@Kent State
	15	@Buffalo
	19	Miami
	22	@Eastern Michigan
	26	@Western Michigan
	30	Akron
Feb.	2	Marshall
	6	@Bowling Green
	9	Ball State
	11	@Miami
	13	Central Michigan
	16	@Marshall
	20	@North Carolina
	23	Kent State
	27	Toledo
March	2	Bowling Green
	4	##MAC Tournament
	7-9	###MAC Tournament

@Road Games
#Miami, FL (vs. Long Island first round; also Florida International, Vermont)
##At campus sites
###Gund Arena, Cleveland, OH

BLUE RIBBON ANALYSIS

BACKCOURT	B
BENCH/DEPTH	C
FRONTCOURT	A
INTANGIBLES	B

Ohio's players already know how to win, which puts O'Shea ahead of the game.

The Bobcats played some basketball and did a lot of bonding this summer during a trip to Italy. They went 1-4 on the trip, but O'Shea came away with a good assessment of what he has to work with.

Scoring points won't be a problem with players such as Hunter, Esterkamp, Flomo and Sanderson on the court. Flomo is also a tremendous shot blocker.

O'Shea's biggest concern coming back from Europe was on the defensive end. He said the Bobcats must become a more alert and tougher defensive team to contend for the Mid-American Conference championship.

Ohio rarely loses in the Convocation Center and the Bobcats will win enough on the road to be in the MAC title chase.

(R.M.)

 Toledo

LOCATION	Toledo, OH
CONFERENCE	Mid-American (West)
LAST SEASON	22-11 (.667)
CONFERENCE RECORD	12-6 (2nd)
STARTERS LOST/RETURNING	3/2
NICKNAME	Rockets
COLORS	Midnight Blue & Gold
HOMECOURT	John F. Savage Hall (9,000)
COACH	Stan Joplin (Toledo '79)
RECORD AT SCHOOL	87-59 (5 years)
CAREER RECORD	87-59 (5 years)
ASSISTANTS	Bob Simon (Eastern Michigan '89)
	Mike Jackson (Detroit '95)
	Tim Saliers (Aquinas '92)
TEAM WINS (last 5 years)	13-15-19-18-22
RPI (last 5 years)	170-147-64-74-80
2000-01 FINISH	Lost in NIT second round.

A change in leadership doesn't mean a change in team goals. Sure, Toledo lost three-time all-conference forward Greg Stempin (18.3 ppg, 8.2 rpg, .473 FG), who helped get the Rockets to the NIT twice in the last three seasons and 22 victories last year—the school's first 20-win season in 20 years. But, Stempin didn't lead Toledo to a Mid-American Conference championship.

"Each year our goals are going to remain the same," coach Stan Joplin said. "We'll always want to win the MAC West Division title, have the best overall record in the MAC, win the MAC Tournament and get to the NCAA Tournament."

Joplin will ask 5-9, 180-pound sophomore point guard **Terry Reynolds** to take the lead. Reynolds (12.6 ppg, 4.0 rpg, 4.6 apg, .386 FG, .765 FT) was the MAC Freshman of the Year last season.

Reynolds played 34.4 minutes a game at point guard, a position Joplin considers as important as the quarterback on a football team.

"We asked Terry to do a lot, and I think he did an outstanding job," Joplin said. "That's a very demanding position."

Reynolds is being asked to be more of a leader on and off the court for a team that not only lost Stempin, but also must replace senior starters Robierre Cullars (9.1 ppg, 4.9 rpg) and Craig Rodgers (6.8 ppg, 3.8 rpg). Cullars and Rodgers were starters.

Other players gone from last season are guard Rory Jones (7.7 ppg, 3.2 rpg) and forward Albert Wilson (2.8 ppg, 1.9 rpg).

"I don't know if we can replace them entirely, but we'll have to try to do it by committee," Joplin said. "You don't replace a Greg Stempin, because a player like him only comes along every 15 or 20 years."

Stempin, the third-leading scorer in school history with 1,705 points, played for the Dallas Mavericks' summer league team attempting to get into the NBA.

Reynolds isn't alone in the backcourt. Junior shooting guard **Nick Moore** (10.1 ppg, 2.7 rpg, 2.3 apg) was one of the MAC's best three-point shooting threats. The 6-1 Moore was 72-for-167 on three-point attempts (.431). Joplin said Moore is his most experienced returning player and is a key to this year's success. Moore also showed a deadly touch at the free-throw line, hitting 46-of-49 (.939) as a sophomore.

The addition of 6-3 sophomore **Keith Triplett**, who sat out last season as a partial qualifier, strengthens the backcourt. Triplett is a hometown product from Toledo

Bowsher High School, where he won the City League scoring title three consecutive seasons. He averaged 25.1 points as a senior and 29.8 as a junior.

"Keith is a very good athlete who can do a lot of things for us," Joplin said. "He's a scorer and he should be able to help us out on the defensive end as well."

Joplin anticipates going with a three-guard lineup the majority of the time.

Three others will compete for minutes in the backcourt.

Garwin Patterson (1.8 ppg, 7.9 minutes) is a 5-10 senior.

Recruit **Jim Clement** is a 6-6, 190-pound freshman from St. Ignace High School in Michigan. Clement averaged 22.4 points, 8.4 rebounds, 4.0 blocks and 2.9 assists as a Class C all-state player.

"Jim is a good outside shooter who possesses a lot of versatility," Joplin said of Clements, who set St. Ignace records with a 45-point game, eight three-pointers in a game and 188 career blocked shots. "He's a good athlete who should become a better player as he gets stronger and gains more experience."

The Rockets also signed 6-6, 195-pound **Sammy Villegas** (pronounced vill-LAY-hahs) out of Lima Senior High School in Ohio. Villegas moved to the United States from Catalina, Puerto Rico, in 1999. Joplin said he is a versatile player who can play two or three positions.

Toledo has some talent at the forwards, but it's an inexperienced group led by 6-7, 215-pound junior **Milo Kirsh** (4.3 ppg, 2.6 rpg) who played in all 33 games but started just two. Kirsh did lead the team with 23 blocked shots.

Kirsh, who played at Bradley as a freshman, finished last season strong by averaging 10 points and four rebounds in a pair of MAC Tournament games.

"I hope Milo steps up and takes his game to another level," Joplin said. "When he gets the ball in the low post he's very quick and athletic, but he still needs to improve defensively and be more consistent."

Another transfer forward, 6-7, 217-pound **Ricardo Thomas**, came in from Eastern Kentucky, sat out last season and is now eligible. Thomas averaged 5.0 points and 5.0 rebounds at Eastern Kentucky. He led the Colonels with 38 steals and was second in assists (84) and blocked shots (24).

Thomas is from Detroit, where he was a two-time All-City player at Communication Media Arts High School. He averaged 21.2 points and 11.3 rebounds as a senior.

Joplin also expects incoming freshmen **Anton Currie** and **Kareem Milson** to battle for playing time.

Currie, only 17, is a 6-6, 195-pound forward from Okemos High School in Michigan, where he averaged 16.7 points, 9.8 rebounds and 3.0 blocks on a 23-2 team. He was ranked as the No. 3 wing forward prospect in Michigan by Prep Spotlight magazine.

"He's a good athlete who will be able to do a lot of things for us," Joplin said. "Bob Simon [assistant coach] first spotted him and then I went and saw him play and we both liked what we saw. We believe he has a very bright future."

The 6-7, 215-pound Milson is a native of Toronto, Canada who attended Rayen High School in Youngstown, Ohio. Milson was ruled ineligible for his senior season by the Ohio High School Athletic Association because he played three years of high school ball at Sir Robert Borden High School in Toronto.

Milson was ranked as the No. 5 power forward in the state by Prep Spotlight entering his senior year. He averaged 19 points and 15 rebounds as a junior.

"Kareem is a good athlete, a good rebounder and a fundamentally sound player," Joplin said.

Sophomore **A.J. Shellabarger** gives the Rockets a big body in the middle at 6-9 and 250 pounds. Shellabarger elected to red-shirt last season after appearing in 27-of-31 games as a freshman (1.9 ppg, 2.1 rpg in 1999-2000). He was expected to red-shirt as a freshman but was pressed into action when Toledo had a shortage of big men.

"A.J. has a big body and good skills," Joplin said. "He needs to do a good job on the boards and stay away from foul trouble. I think the extra year of practice was beneficial for him and now he has a better grasp of things."

2001-2002 SCHEDULE

Nov.	18	@Dayton
	21	IUPU-FW
	24	@George Mason
Dec.	1	St. Bonaventure
	4	@Siena
	8	Youngstown State
	10	@Cincinnati
	15	@Detroit
	27	@Oakland
Jan.	5	@Western Michigan
	9	@Eastern Michigan
	12	Ball State
	16	Northern Illinois
	19	@Bowling Green
	22	@Central Michigan
	26	Marshall
	30	@Northern Illinois
Feb.	2	@Kent State
	6	Central Michigan
	9	@Miami
	13	Akron
	16	@Ball State
	18	Bowling Green
	20	Buffalo
	23	Western Michigan
	27	@Ohio
March	2	Eastern Michigan
	4	#MAC Tournament
	7-9	##MAC Tournament

@Road Games
#At campus sites
##Gund Arena, Cleveland, OH

BLUE RIBBON ANALYSIS

BACKCOURT	A
BENCH/DEPTH	C
FRONTCOURT	C
INTANGIBLES	B

Joplin is one of those coaches in a difficult situation coaching at his alma mater, where expectations are higher for someone so well known. He has handled it well, though, and was rewarded this summer with a contract extension through the 2005-06 season.

That's good news for fans of the Rockets. But, can he get Toledo over the NIT hump and into the NCAA Tournament this season? That's doubtful because Toledo is woefully inexperienced in the frontcourt.

Even winning the MAC West Division and returning to the NIT this year will be difficult. The guards, Reynolds and Moore, will have to carry the team, especially early in the season.

But, who knows? By the end of the year Toledo should be hanging around with Central Michigan and Ball State near the top of the West Division standings. Anything can happen in the MAC Tournament.

(R.M.)

Western Michigan

LOCATION	Kalamazoo, MI
CONFERENCE	Mid-American (West)
LAST SEASON	7-21 (.250)
CONFERENCE RECORD	7-11 (4th)
STARTERS LOST/RETURNING	1/4
NICKNAME	Broncos
COLORS	Brown & Gold
HOMECOURT	University Arena (5,800)
COACH	Robert McCullum (Birmingham Southern '76)
RECORD AT SCHOOL	7-21 (1 year)
CAREER RECORD	7-21 (1 year)
ASSISTANTS	Clayton Bates (Florida '95)
	Steve Hawkins (South Alabama '87)
	Lorenzo Neely (Eastern Michigan '91)
TEAM WINS (last 5 years)	14-21-11-10-7
RPI (last 5 years)	145-53-156-186-253
2000-01 FINISH	Lost in conference first round.

WQSN, a sports talk radio station in Kalamazoo, conducted a poll asking the question "Was Robert McCullum the right choice to replace Bob Donewald as men's basketball coach at Western Michigan?"

The answer was overwhelmingly "yes," as 64 percent of the people responding said McCullum was the right man for the job.

It didn't show up in last year's record when McCullum's first team actually lost more games (7-21) than Donewald's team did (10-18) in his final year with the Broncos. It is showing up in other places.

McCullum is working hard to rebuild an image, not just a basketball team, and Western Michigan is a program on the rise. The Broncos won three of their final five games to finish the year with some momentum.

The resume for McCullum is impressive. He worked 18 years as an NCAA Division I assistant, most of it under Lon Kruger. McCullum was with Kruger one season at Kansas State, six years at Florida and four years at Illinois before taking his first head coaching assignment. He spoke often last season about building a foundation.

"I think our guys now have a better understanding of what it takes to be successful," McCullum said late in the season. "We have a better understanding of how we want our program to be perceived."

Four starters return and forward Jon Powell (15.9 ppg, 3.6 rpg, .502 FG, .772 FT) was the only significant loss. Powell was an All-MAC honorable mention selection.

And, the second-year coaching staff's first recruiting class was ranked 19th in the region by MidWestHoops.com.

"Outstanding first effort by new head coach Robert McCullum," Vince Baldwin reported on MidWestHoops.com. "**Ben Reed** is a mid-major steal and **Rickey Willis** is a tough, scrappy leader. **Steve Green** is a 6-10 kid who could surprise down the road."

Stephen Wacaser of The Sporting News rated the Broncos' class at the top of the MAC.

Western Michigan didn't go far to land Reed, a 6-3, 220-pound freshman from Central High School in Battle Creek, Mich. Reed averaged 25.7 points, 12.3 rebounds and 3.2 assists as a senior and graduated with a 3.5 GPA.

McCullum said one of his priorities was to establish a local recruiting base and signing Reed was the best start he could have hoped for. Reed was a member of the Michigan Dream Team selected by the Detroit Free Press.

"There is no doubt he is among the top 100 players in the country and also one of the nation's best-kept secrets," McCullum said.

The Broncos went to Detroit for 6-0, 175-pound freshman point guard Willis, an all-state second team performer from Mackenzie High School who scored 18 points a game and averaged nine assists. If McCullum wants to rev up the running game, Willis is his man. He was a third-place finisher in the city cross-country championships.

From the first time Western Michigan coaches saw him play, Willis was on top of their list of point guard prospects.

"He has tremendous quickness and very good command of the basketball," McCullum said. "He possesses the ability to break down the defense while also having the ability to consistently knock down perimeter shots."

Freshman center Green, 6-10, 210, is by far the tallest Bronco on a roster with nobody else taller than 6-7. Obviously, his size was needed. Green, a product of Lutheran North High School in Macomb, Mich., averaged 17 points, nine rebounds and four blocks as a senior. Also an outstanding student, he carried a 4.0 GPA.

The other freshman on scholarship is 6-6, 215-pound forward **Jeff Bronson** from Countryside High School in Safety Harbor, Fla. No doubt McCullum was familiar with the Clearwater, Fla., area from his days as a Florida assistant.

Bronson was a Florida all-state second team selection last year when he averaged 14.4 points, 9.9 rebounds and 2.5 blocked shots. His team advanced to the Class 5A Sweet 16.

"He is a versatile player with outstanding skills," McCullum said. "While he plays well with his back to the basket, the most impressive aspect of his game may be his ability to shoot the ball from the perimeter."

Nick Evola is an addition at power forward from the junior college ranks. Evola, a 6-7, 235-pound junior, played two years at Schoolcraft Community College near Detroit. He averaged 13 points and eight rebounds. Schoolcraft, an NJCAA tournament participant, averaged 104 points per game. Evola is a graduate of Woods Tower High School in Warren, Mich.

The Broncos also have two invited walk-ons this year—6-0 junior transfer **Antwan Joseph** from Kellogg Community College in Battle Creek, Mich., and 6-2 freshman **Loren Scheu** from nearby Mattawan High School.

With all those new players coming, in Western Michigan should be able to replace Powell, its leading scorer, and create some battles for playing time with the returning starters.

As usually happens when a new coaching staff comes in, Western Michigan had some defections. Three guards, none of them major contributors, transferred out—K.C. Cavette (6.0 ppg, 1.5 rpg) to Southern University, Maverick Carter (2.0 ppg, 1.3 rpg) to Akron as a walk-on and Nate Richie to Drake. Richie played only four minutes last season.

Forward **Steve Reynolds** (14.8 ppg, 4.4 rpg) played

Western Michigan, Chicago State • 253

more minutes and took more shots than anyone on the team. Reynolds shot just .379 percent from the field, making 145-of-383 attempts.

If the 6-7, 210-pound senior shoots the basketball better this season, he's an all-conference candidate.

Taylor Bro, a 6-7 junior forward, is the squad's most experienced player and its only two-year letterman. Bro (5.7 ppg, 5.2 rpg) ended the season with an 11-point, 11-rebound performance against Bowling Green in the MAC Tournament.

In the backcourt 6-4 sophomore **Reggie Berry** (6.1 ppg, 2.1 rpg, .342 FG) showed glimpses of his potential as a starter in 19 games. Six-foot-one junior **Robby Collum** (9.3 ppg, 3.9 rpg, 3.3 apg) was by far the team leader with 90 assists and also led in steals with 44.

Returning lettermen at the forward position are 6-7, 230-pound sophomore forward **Anthony Kann** (5.5 ppg, 5.6 rpg), 6-5 junior forward **Terrance Slater** (5.2 ppg, 1.4 rpg), 6-5 junior **Pat Cleland** (1.5 ppg, 0.5 rpg) and 6-3 junior **Brandon Johnson** (0.6 ppg, 0.9 rpg).

2001-2002 SCHEDULE

Nov.	15	*Long Beach
	16	*Oregon
	17	*Alabama State
	21	Wisconsin-Milwaukee
	23	Michigan
	27	Morgan State
Dec.	1	@Detroit
	12	@Virginia Tech
	15	@Wisconsin-Milwaukee
	22	Marshall
	29	@Oakland
Jan.	2	Miami
	5	Toledo
	9	@Ohio
	12	Central Michigan
	15	IUPUI
	19	@Kent State
	23	@Ball State
	26	Ohio
	30	Bowling Green
Feb.	4	@Central Michigan
	6	Eastern Michigan
	9	@Buffalo
	11	@Akron
	16	@Northern Illinois
	20	Ball State
	23	@Toledo
	27	@Eastern Michigan
March	2	Northern Illinois
	4	#MAC Tournament
	7-9	##MAC Tournament

@Road Games
*America's Youth Classic, Eugene, OR
#At campus sites
##Gund Arena, Cleveland, OH

BLUE RIBBON ANALYSIS

BACKCOURT	B+
BENCH/DEPTH	B
FRONTCOURT	B
INTANGIBLES	B+

Western Michigan's transition period under McCullum is ongoing. McCullum needed immediate help up and down the roster and he recruited some promising players. That, however, is sort of a good-news, bad-news situation because seven of the 15 players are new to the program.

It's little consolation, but Western Michigan was the best team among four 20-game losers last season in the Mid-American Conference. The Broncos finished fourth in the West Division standings and were a No. 10-seeded team in the 13-team conference tournament.

McCullum juggled his lineup a lot, and will probably do that again searching for the right combinations. The Broncos are headed in the right direction, but they're not there yet.

(R.M.)

Chicago State

LOCATION	Chicago, IL
CONFERENCE	Mid-Continent
LAST SEASON	5-22 (.185)

MID-CONTINENT

BLUE RIBBON FORECAST
1. Valparaiso
2. Oakland
3. UMKC
4. Chicago State
5. Western Illinois
6. Oral Roberts
7. IUPUI
8. Southern Utah

ALL-CONFERENCE TEAM
G-Jason Rozycki, SR, Oakland
G-Milo Stovall, SR, Valparaiso
C-Raitis Grafs, JR, Valparaiso
F-Michael Jackson, SR, UMKC
F-Charles Price, SR, IUPUI

PLAYER OF THE YEAR
Raitis Grafs, JR, Valparaiso

NEWCOMER OF THE YEAR
Kevin Smallwood, JR, Chicago State

2001-2002 CONFERENCE TOURNAMENT
March 3-5, Memorial Coliseum, Ft. Wayne, IN

2000-2001 POSTSEASON PARTICIPANTS
Postseason Record: 0-1 (.000)
NCAA
Southern Utah

TOP BACKCOURTS
1. Oakland
2. Valparaiso
3. Oral Roberts

TOP FRONTCOURTS
1. Valparaiso
2. Chicago State
3. UMKC

INSIDE THE NUMBERS
2001-2002 conference RPI: 31st (of 31)
Conference RPI (last five years): 18-23-24-29-22

DID YOU KNOW?
With the exit of Youngstown State, the Mid-Continent is down to eight teams. But Oakland is now eligible for postseason play and will take part in its first Mid-Continent conference tournament this year. Rumors were swirling that the Mid-Continent might be disbanding, but the league's athletic directors recently pledged to work to continue to improve and stabilize the conference. ... Valparaiso center Raitis Grafs had more blocked shots (67) than turnovers (59) last year. ... Valparaiso has quite an international flavor, with players from the Czech Republic, Latvia, Angola, Finland, Puerto Rico and Colombia on its roster. ... Meanwhile, Chicago State has 11 Chicago-area players in the program this year. ... Southern Utah snapped Valpo's six-year conference tournament winning streak with a 62-59 victory in the championship game last season. ... Chicago State is planning a new 6,200-seat on-campus arena. ... Oakland has five fifth-year seniors on the roster who are three-time letter winners. ... UMKC senior Michael Jackson has been a first-team all-Mid-Continent selection in each of his two years in the conference.

(P.D.)

CONFERENCE RECORD	2-14 (9th)
STARTERS LOST/RETURNING	2/3
NICKNAME	Cougars
COLORS	Green & White
HOMECOURT	Jacoby D. Dickens Center (2,500)
COACH	Bo Ellis (Marquette '77)
RECORD AT SCHOOL	18-64 (3 years)
CAREER RECORD	18-64 (3 years)
ASSISTANTS	James Farr (Creighton '89)
	Ty Moesler (Wisconsin-Oshkosh '96)
	William Bailey (UAB '99)
TEAM WINS (last 5 years)	18-21-19-17-13
RPI (last 5 years)	142-63-146-148-257
2000-01 FINISH	Lost in conference first round.

Chicago is undeniably one of the top hotbeds of prep basketball talent in the country. But years of losing prevented Chicago State from keeping its hometown players at home.

When former Marquette star Bo Ellis took over the program in 1998, his goal was to begin to reverse that losing reputation and start showing the local stars why they should consider playing in front of their family and friends in person, rather than on TV.

And three years later, Ellis is beginning to taste the fruits of his hard work. His recruiting efforts have resulted in a roster featuring eight Chicago players, as well as two from nearby Gary, Ind., and one from Joliet, Ill. In all that's 11 Cougars from Chicagoland, which puts a smile on the face of the hometown head coach.

"I'm feeling pretty good about the program," Ellis said. "We're starting to keep some Chicago kids home for a change, starting to shed those images and perceptions as far as Chicago State not being successful.

"The problem with keeping Chicago kids here is they've seen how bad Chicago State has been over the years, and that's thrown up a red flag for them. But they've seen us beat UI-C two years ago, and beat Loyola last year, and taking DePaul down to the wire last year, and they're starting to see that with the right talent, Chicago State can win."

Even as the Cougars struggled to a five-win season

last year, they battled through some adjustments in losing their most experienced players from the previous season and hung tough through a 13-game losing streak. They also managed to sweep IUPUI and give Valpo a tough game in the first round of the Mid-Continent Tournament.

This year, the Cougars will come back strong with a roster balanced by players familiar with the system and some talented newcomers who could make a difference immediately.

"It's going to be very competitive," Ellis said of the battle for starting spots. "Playing time is never promised over the phone—they've got to go out there and earn it. But we've been having 6:45 a.m. weight training and nobody's been late yet. Last year, I always had to be on some of the guys to get there. But I'm getting pretty good vibes from these guys—the kids seem to be getting along pretty well. We're going to be more of a team this year. These kids have known each other for awhile, having played with and against each other in high school, and they're starting to understand what we need to do to win at this level."

Gone from last year are the top three scorers, including forward Tony Jones (14.3 ppg, 7.8 rpg), center Darrel Johns (11.6 ppg, 5.8 rpg) and guard Jason Wesenberg (5.6 ppg, 1.4 apg). With the loss of size up front, this year's Cougars will be expected to run a bit more, which should suit the players just fine, considering the talent joining the program.

The two returning starters are 6-9 junior **Randy Nelson** (4.9 ppg, 3.3. rpg) and 6-0 senior **Terrence West** (4.7 ppg, 3.3 apg), while 6-8 junior **Clark Bone** (4.6 ppg, 3.0 rpg) also started 10 games last year. Ellis said their experience has been invaluable in showing the newcomers what Division I basketball is all about.

"This is the third time around for Bone and Nelson, and you can really see it in their conditioning and attitude," Ellis said. "In our conditioning drills the veterans have been laughing as they see the new kids discovering how hard it is at this level. These kids really understand what we need from them to get where we're going."

Among the new faces creating the biggest stir on

campus is 6-6 junior **Kelvin Smallwood**, a forward from Dunbar High School and Kennedy-King Community College in Chicago. He averaged 16 points and nine rebounds last year, and Ellis said that if Smallwood lives up to his expectations, he could be the newcomer of the year in the Mid-Continent.

Look for 5-11 junior point guard **Jessie Shorts** to push for the starting point guard spot. Shorts comes to Chicago State from Farragut Academy (which also produced Kevin Garnett and Ronnie Fields) via Highland Community College, and is known as a scorer who will push the ball, which should be a good fit in Ellis' system.

Shorts should get support at the point guard spot from 5-11 senior **Jimmy Mack** (3.8 ppg, 1.4 apg), who started seven games last year.

Entering the fray at shooting guard will be 6-2 sophomore **Craig Franklin**, who missed his freshman year because of academics. Another Chicago area player, Franklin helped lead his Westinghouse High School team to a 31-2 record and a second-place finish in the state tournament two years ago.

The fourth new face is actually a player who practiced with the Cougars all last season. **Rubeen Perry** is a 6-9 sophomore who sat out after transferring from Centenary College. Like Ellis, Perry is a graduate of Chicago's Robeson High School, where he was all-area as a senior, averaging 23 points and 12 boards a game in the tough Chicago Public League.

Depth should be a strength for the Cougars this year. In addition to Perry, Smallwood, Bone and Nelson up front, 6-4 senior **Andre Wiggins** (3.7 ppg, 1.9 rpg) and 6-6 sophomore **Rafael Morris** will compete for playing time. Also in the mix is transfer **Marcus Ford**, a 6-6 junior from Joliet (III.) Junior College who could be one of the best of the lot.

"Ford is every bit as athletic as Tony Jones," Ellis said, "and probably a little stronger. He can give us what Tony gave us and maybe more once he understands what it takes to play at this level."

Ellis points to 6-3 senior **Danny Osby** (4.0 ppg) and 5-10 junior **Erick Cooley** (1.0 ppg), a pair of junior-college guards with one season behind them, as two players ready to contribute after seeing Division I ball up close for a year. Also in the backcourt mix are 6-3 junior **Kin Yanders** (4.2 ppg) and 5-8 senior **Brian DiLosa**.

2001-2002 SCHEDULE

Nov.	18	@Marquette
	21	Buffalo
	24	@Northwestern
	27	@Wisconsin-Green Bay
Dec.	1	Youngstown State
	4	Wisconsin-Milwaukee
	13	@Central Florida
	18	@DePaul
	20	Lakeland
	22	@Loyola-Chicago
	29	Wichita State
Jan.	3	@Oakland
	5	@IUPUI
	8	@IUPU-Fort Wayne
	10	Western Illinois
	12	Valparaiso
	19	@Southern Utah
	24	UMKC
	26	Oral Roberts
	31	IUPUI
Feb.	2	Oakland
	7	@Valparaiso
	9	@Western Illinois
	16	Southern Utah
	19	IUPU-Fort Wayne
	21	Oral Roberts
	23	UMKC
March	2-5	#Mid-Continent Tournament

@Road Games
#Memorial Coliseum, Fort Wayne, IN

BLUE RIBBON ANALYSIS

BACKCOURT	B-
BENCH/DEPTH	B
FRONTCOURT	B+
INTANGIBLES	C+

With his Chicago pipeline finally flowing, Ellis clearly has the program headed in the right direction.

"It's my fourth year here and I'm as excited as I've been from the time that I took the job," he said. "It's the first time that I've felt really good about where we're going.

"I think back to something [Valpo coach] Homer Drew said to me when I took over, and coach [Al] McGuire told me the same thing—you've just got to stick with it. It takes a few years to build a program, and as we go forward I'm learning more and more about what it takes."

Team is obviously an important concept to Ellis, and he feels confident that he's got the right mix of people and players in the program to be successful.

"We're only going to be as good as the next man on the team," he said. "As long as we play together, we're going to be alright."

The intangible in question is how quickly Ellis can mesh the new faces with the returning players. The talent is there—if the team comes together, Chicago State fans could look back on 2002 as the year the program turned around.

In a very balanced Mid-Continent, these Cougars could make their first run at the conference title with just a few breaks.

(P.D.)

IUPUI

LOCATION	Indianapolis, IN
CONFERENCE	Mid-Continent
LAST SEASON	11-18 (.379)
CONFERENCE RECORD	6-10 (6th)
STARTERS LOST/RETURNING	3/2
NICKNAME	Jaguars
COLORS	Red, Gold & Black
HOMECOURT	IUPUI Gymnasium (2,000)
COACH	Rod Hunter (Miami, Ohio '86)
RECORD AT SCHOOL	101-95 (7 years)
CAREER RECORD	101-95 (7 years)
ASSISTANTS	Todd Howard (Louisville '93)
	Carlos Knox (IUPUI '01)
TEAM WINS (last 5 years)	18-21-19-17-13
RPI (last 5 years)	142-63-146-148-257
2000-01 FINISH	Lost in conference semifinal.

After four years of watching his team take baby steps, IUPUI coach Ron Hunter thinks his Jaguars are ready to start running. Hunter took over the IUPUI post seven years ago and oversaw its transition from an NAIA program through Division II all the way to Division I in that time. And starting their fourth year at D-I, the Jaguars are showing signs that they're ready to shed the "former NAIA program" tag and be recognized as one of the big boys in the Mid-Continent Conference.

"I feel like we've gone from what I call an advanced intramural program to D-I in just a couple of years," Hunter said. "I was at UW-Milwaukee when they made the transition and I always tell people, 'If you've never done it before, don't try it.' It's tough, but I understand what we need to do to be successful."

One route for that success has been mining the rich in-state talent that Indiana produces every year. This year, seven Jaguars hail from the Hoosier State, and next year they'll be joined by two Indianapolis natives who transferred from other schools.

"We're really trying to build a program," Hunter said. "The best way to do that here is with Indiana kids. We need the media, need the fans, and need a way to separate ourselves from the other state schools. They've done such a wonderful job of recruiting kids from all over—but we're really focused on Indiana kids."

Last year the Jaguars were seeded fifth in the Mid-Continent Tournament and upset No. 4 UMKC, 54-52, in the first round, before falling by 11 to Valparaiso in a semifinal. Three starters were lost from that team, including leading scorer Don Carlisle (15.5 ppg, 8.5 rpg), who finished seventh in the conference in scoring and fourth in rebounding last year and was a first-team all-conference selection.

Other key losses include guards Sylvester Allen (9.2 ppg, 4.1 rpg) and Matt Hermes (7.6 ppg, 1.8 rpg) and forwards Josh Fitzwater (7.6 ppg, 4.0 rpg) and Lonie Holland (5.1 ppg, 1.4 rpg).

The high turnover in the program will be balanced by nine new faces—seven of them from Indiana—including five junior college transfers, two freshmen recruits and the two transfers, Josh Murray from Ball State and Marcus May from Wright State. Both are seniors who will sit out this season, but Hunter expects big contributions from both off the court because of their experience.

The 6-7 Murray was a three-year starter at Ball State, played in the NCAA Tournament and will be a force under the boards, while May—his teammate at Indianapolis' North Central High School—averaged in double figures in scoring as a sophomore. He will push the guards in practice this year and push for playing time next season.

But all these new faces will be joining a steady nucleus that already has most of its building blocks in place for a solid starting lineup. Leading the way will be 6-8 senior forward **Charles Price** (12.5 ppg, 7.0 rpg), who was the second-leading scorer on the team last season.

"Charles Price should be one of the top two or three players in the conference," Hunter said. "He's actually something of a secret weapon for us, because he's played in the shadow of Don Carlisle for the last couple of years, but he's actually got more talent than Don. He's very athletic, with long arms, and he's great in the post."

Price will get help in the leadership department from a 28-year-old sophomore—6-2 guard **Matt Crenshaw** (3.7 ppg, 1.9 rpg). Crenshaw came to IUPUI from the Marines and Hunter said after a feeling-out process last year, he's ready to take charge of his younger teammates this season.

"He stayed here this summer and worked on his agility and his shooting. He's a great leader, really a tough kid—although I guess you can't really call him a 'kid'—with a lot of maturity. Last year he didn't really assert himself as much as I'd like, so this year I expect him to be more of a leader."

Sharing the point with Crenshaw will be 6-1 senior **Taj Hawkins** (4.1 ppg, 1.6 rpg, 2.2 apg). Hunter said Hawkins is a decent shooter and a great defender who takes care of the ball. The graduate of Oak Hill Academy started 12 games last season.

The off-guard will be either 5-11 senior **Lance Williams** (8.7 ppg, 1.6 rpg, 1.4 apg), who was the sixth man most of last year, or 6-3 freshman **Blair Crawford**.

"Williams has made some big shots for us here," Hunter said. "He scored 27 at Valpo [last year] when we snapped the longest home-court winning streak in the country [Feb. 17], and he beat Indiana State at home with a buzzer-beater [last Dec. 20]. We expect big things from him."

Crawford, another in-state recruit from Kokomo, Ind., is what Hunter calls "a typical Indiana kid who can absolutely fill it up, can really stroke it with range. We expect him to push Williams for playing time this year, and if he doesn't take over that spot as a true freshman he will next year as a sophomore."

The other freshman is 6-1 guard **Rashad Pace**, who won a state title at Andrean High School in Gary, Ind.

Up front, look for 6-6 junior college transfer **Dannorris Harvey** to grab a starting position immediately.

"I can't imagine anybody beating him out," Hunter said of the forward from Middle Georgia College. "We were very fortunate to sign him—my assistants did an outstanding job recruiting him."

Other candidates for front line play include 6-5 junior **Josh Mullins**, a transfer from Lincoln Trail (III.) Community College; 6-10 junior **Herb Lambert** (0.3 ppg, 0.8 rpg); senior **Chris Spencer** (0.5 ppg; 0.6 rpg); and 6-6 junior **Rocky Clouse**, who has missed the last two seasons with a variety of injuries but is now healthy and ready to contribute.

Two other junior college transfers might play their way into the forward mix—6-5 junior **Chris Sanders**, who averaged 27 points a game in high school and was a three-point threat at Vincennes (Ind.) University, and 6-7 junior **Antoine Lewis** from Northeastern Nebraska Community College.

The main goal for Hunter this year will be to improve the team's .433 shooting percentage, which he thinks cost the Jaguars a few games last year.

"We have to shoot the ball better," he said. "We've lost so many close games and we have not been a great three-point shooting team. We brought in four guys who can really stroke it and that's an area where we have to improve."

2001-2002 SCHEDULE

Nov.	16	Cleveland State
	21	@Middle Tennessee
	24	Olivet Nazarene
	28	Indiana Tech
Dec.	1	@Indiana State
	9	@Ohio State
	15	Ball State
	18	Morehead State
	21-22	#Sun Bowl Classic
	29	@Georgia Tech
Jan.	3	Southern Utah
	5	Chicago State
	10	@Oral Roberts
	12	@UMKC

	15	@Western Michigan
	19	@Oakland
	24	Valparaiso
	26	Western Illinois
	31	@Chicago State
Feb.	2	@Southern Utah
	7	UMKC
	9	Oral Roberts
	12	IPFW
	16	Oakland
	21	@Western Illinois
	23	@Valparaiso
March	2-5	##Mid-Continent Tournament

@Road Games
#El Paso, TX (vs. Mississippi, first round; also Mississippi Valley State, UTEP)
##War Memorial Coliseum, Fort Wayne, IN

BLUE RIBBON ANALYSIS

BACKCOURT	C-
BENCH/DEPTH	C
FRONTCOURT	B
INTANGIBLES	C+

Hunter will have a lot of new faces on campus to deal with this year, but he'll also have some raw talent to work with, and a horse like Price to build on.

One of his challenges will be getting his team to mesh, and hoping players like Williams and Crenshaw can flourish in their expanded roles. Don't expect much early, especially with trips to Ohio State, Georgia Tech and the UTEP Tournament—where the Jags will face Ole Miss in the first round. But if they put it together, a competitive run at the conference tournament is not out of the question.

(P.D.)

UMKC

LOCATION	Kansas City, MO
CONFERENCE	Mid-Continent
LAST SEASON	14-16 (.467)
CONFERENCE RECORD	9-7 (4th)
STARTERS LOST/RETURNING	1/4
NICKNAME	Kangaroos
COLORS	Blue & Gold
HOMECOURT	Municipal Auditorium (9,827)
COACH	Rich Zvosec (Defiance '83)
RECORD AT SCHOOL	First year
CAREER RECORD	103-146 (10 years)
ASSISTANTS	Ken Dempsey (Moravian '83)
	Jason Ivey (Temple '97)
TEAM WINS (last 5 years)	18-21-19-17-13
RPI (last 5 years)	142-63-146-148-257
2000-01 FINISH	Lost in conference first round.

Rich Zvosec takes over the Kangaroos after a year as associate head coach, and he's inheriting a better situation than most coaches at the mid-major level could ask for. That's because former coach Dean Demopoulos, a long-time assistant to John Chaney at Temple, put his two-year stamp on the program before leaving last spring for an assistant's job with the Seattle Supersonics.

Demopoulos' departure handed Zvosec a veteran team with a legitimate league player-of-the-year candidate. And because Zvosec worked with the players for a year, he's familiar with their tendencies.

"It's been going along very well so far," said Zvosec, who didn't take over the head job until the first week of June. "It's been a smoother transition than in some of my previous stops [which include St. Francis (N.Y.), D-II North Florida and Millersville (Pa.) University] because I didn't have to introduce myself to the players."

Last year the Kangaroos found themselves once again in the upper division of the Mid-Continent with the league's top scoring defense (60.5 points per game) and a conservative offense that took care of the ball. In fact, their 8.1 turnovers per game were second best in the NCAA behind Temple (imagine that), and their Mid-Continent-leading +6.3 turnover margin in conference games was more than double the next-best team.

But for UMKC to take the next step, Zvosec knows he's got to find some help underneath the boards. Last year the Kangaroos were the worst rebounding team in the conference, giving up 8.4 more rebounds per game to their opponents.

"Last year we became very proficient at handling the basketball, but this year we need to work on creating some easier offensive opportunities," said Zvosec, whose squad grabbed a league-worst 9.0 offensive boards a game last year.

He's pushing for improvement with mostly the same cast as last year, hoping that another year of experience will lead to better work on the glass. UMKC returns four starters, and the top seven should include four seniors and two juniors.

The big man on campus will be 6-7 senior forward **Michael Jackson** (15.4 ppg, 4.5 rpg, 1.7 bpg), who was the Mid-Continent Player of the Year and Newcomer of the Year two years ago as a sophomore when he averaged 19.8 points, 5.7 rebounds and 1.7 blocks and shot 59 percent from the field. Last year with teams focusing more on him, Jackson's numbers dipped, but Zvosec is expecting big things from him as a senior.

"He's as good a post player as there is at the mid-major level," Zvosec said. "He can score on the block with a variety of moves, and offensively he can play with anyone in the country. When he's playing one-on-one, he's a major threat."

A two-time all-conference pick, Jackson scored 25 points against Nebraska's Kimani Ffriend—who made the Big 12's all-defensive team—in the Kangaroos' 82-71 victory over the Cornhuskers in Lincoln last year. His season-high was a 27-point effort against Oakland, but he was held to just six points and five boards in UMKC's first-round Mid-Continent Tournament loss to IUPUI.

Jackson should benefit from the return of 6-7 senior forward **Will Palmer** (5.8 ppg, 5.4 rpg), who missed the last five games of last season with appendicitis. "He's a blue-collar guy who can get a lot of the dirty work done," Zvosec said.

Last year Palmer started all 25 games before his illness.

The bulk of Jackson's scoring help should come from 6-0 sophomore guard **Michael Watson**, who pumped in 14.4 points a game as a freshman.

"He's very explosive," Zvosec said. "He's got lots of juice—he can get to the basket and shoot the three."

Watson's 2.6 three pointers made last season were fifth-best in the Mid-Continent.

Senior **Matt Suther** (8.5 ppg, 5.2 rpg, 2.7 apg), 6-4, is moving to the point this season to replace Javin Tindall, who transferred after starting 29 games as a freshman. Zvosec looks for Suther's size (he's five inches taller than Tindall) to help the team's defense overall.

"He gives us a big, strong guard up front—when a team is looking through the zone, he's just a bigger presence," Zvosec said. "He can also knock down the big jumper and run the show."

Last year Suther led the conference with an 88.0 free-throw percentage. But Tindall led the Mid-Continent with a 2.5 assist-to-turnover ratio, numbers Suther will need to match for the Kangaroos to be successful in their offensive set.

Vying for the final starting spot will be 6-8 senior **Marcus Golson** (3.5 ppg, 1.9 rpg) and 6-5 junior **Randall Atchison** (4.9 ppg, 2.4 rpg).

"Golson is long and lean, a good jumper who can score in the post and step out and shoot it from 15-to-17 feet," Zvosec said. "He gives us versatility when he's on the court."

Meanwhile, Atchison did a little bit of everything last year.

"He was our 'utility infielder' last year," Zvosec said. "He can play at the two or the three, in the low post or the high post. But because we've got more size this year, we can play him strictly on the perimeter. He's a very exciting player when he gets it going."

The new big man on the scene is 6-9 junior college transfer **Tom Curtis**, a junior from Grand Rapids (Mich.) Community College. Zvosec is looking for Curtis to have an impact on the boards immediately, but his long-term project is even more intriguing.

That would be sophomore Randall Logan, a 6-10 center who transferred in from D-II Shaw University in North Carolina. Logan is sitting out this season but he'll be the guy you can't miss on the bench.

"When he came to us he was 390 [pounds], but he's down to 320 right now," Zvosec said. "Obviously his best basketball is in front of him—it's just a question of getting him into shape."

Freshman **Brandon Lipsey**, 6-8, is another player who could find himself in the mix. Zvosec was planning to red-shirt Lipsey—from Sumner Academy in Kansas City, Kansas—but after Lipsey had a strong summer of basketball, Zvosec changed his mind.

In the end, Zvosec knows he'll lean on his experienced players to get his team through what could be the toughest schedule in school history.

"I've got four seniors who know this is their last go-round," Zvosec said. "That will make a difference."

2001-2002 SCHEDULE

Nov.	17	@Wisconsin-Green Bay
	24	Maryland-Eastern Shore
	27	Southwest Missouri State
Dec.	1	Northern Iowa
	5	@Robert Morris
	8	@Kansas
	15	Wisconsin-Green Bay
	19	Oklahoma State
	22	Youngstown State
	28	*Arkansas State
	29	*Wayland Baptist
Jan.	5	Oral Roberts
	10	Oakland
	12	IUPUI
	14	Texas A&M-Corpus Christi
	17	@Western Illinois
	19	@Valparaiso
	24	Chicago State
	26	Southern Utah
Feb.	2	@Oral Roberts
	7	@IUPUI
	9	@Oakland
	14	Valparaiso
	16	Western Ilinois
	21	@Southern Utah
	23	@Chicago State
	26	IUPUI
March	3-5	#Mid-Continent Tournament

@Road Games
*Koch Islandere Invitational, Corpus Christi, TX
#War Memorial Coliseum, Fort Wayne, IN

BLUE RIBBON ANALYSIS

BACKCOURT	B-
BENCH/DEPTH	C
FRONTCOURT	B+
INTANGIBLES	B

The Kangaroos could surprise some people if Jackson returns to his sophomore form. He's a horse down low and will continue to draw major attention from opponents. His support beneath the hoop is suspect, but if Watson continues to develop and Suther's transition to the point is a smooth one, Jackson will find more room to work with on the block.

Look for UMKC to be a factor in the Mid-Con race and use its experience to make a run in the league's postseason tournament.

(P.D.)

Oakland

LOCATION	Rochester, MI
CONFERENCE	Mid-Continent
LAST SEASON	12-16 (.428)
CONFERENCE RECORD	8-8 (5th)
STARTERS LOST/RETURNING	0/5
NICKNAME	Golden Grizzlies
COLORS	Black, Gold & White
HOMECOURT	Athletics Center 'O'rena (4,005)
COACH	Greg Kampe (Bowling Green '78)
RECORD AT SCHOOL	289-195 (17 years)
CAREER RECORD	289-195 (17 years)
ASSISTANTS	Eric Stephan (Carthage '86)
	Harold Baber (Oakland '98)
	Jennifer Johnston (Northern Michigan '98)
TEAM WINS (last 5 years)	18-21-19-17-13
RPI (last 5 years)	142-63-146-148-257
2000-01 FINISH	Not eligible for postseason.

The way Oakland coach Greg Kampe sees it, this is the season the Grizzlies have had circled on their long-range calendar for the last four years.

You see, four years ago, the Grizzlies made the jump from Division II, and they've spent the last three years in a postseason probation period ("purgatory" as Kampe calls it). But this year, the Grizzlies are finally eligible for postseason play, and they couldn't be more excited about it.

"Now we've got something to play for," said Kampe, who has been at Oakland for 17 years. "The kids won the league two years ago, but all they got was a ring from that. This is what we've been looking forward to."

Indeed, the Grizzlies do have a 1999 Mid-Continent regular-season title to their credit, and when they started last year with a 97-90 victory over Michigan, it looked like a repeat might be on the horizon.

But a run at a second straight conference title was derailed on Jan. 27 at Valparaiso. The Grizzlies entered the game 6-3 in the Mid-Continent and just a game out of first, but leading scorer **Jason Rozycki** tore the ACL in his left knee and was lost for the season.

Rozycki's injury took the steam out of the Grizzlies' season. They went on to lose five of their last seven conference games and had to settle for a .500 record and a fifth-place finish in the regular-season standings.

This year, Rozycki is back and so is the rest of the starting lineup. High hopes have returned to the Oakland campus.

"Our program was built with this year in mind—for the first year we were eligible for postseason play," Kampe said. "When we made the jump to D-I, we looked at it as an expansion-type club. We brought in a bunch of freshmen, red-shirted them all and built for the first year we were eligible for postseason play."

And now Kampe has an experienced, talented ball club that should make some noise in the conference during the regular season, and has a legitimate shot at an NCAA berth.

The key to the OU attack will once again be a wide-open offense. In their conference-winning season, the Grizzlies led the nation in three-pointers made, and this year Kampe expects them to fire up 25-to-30 shots per game from beyond the arc. Last season they were second in the conference in scoring offense (74.5 points per game), but second worst in scoring defense (76.0).

"We're very wide open," Kampe ssaid. "We are a perimeter oriented jump-shooting offense the plays fast and lets it go. We're going to be able to score—we've got four guys who can really score, there will be nights that they'll all be on and we'll be pretty good on those nights. And the good thing is that it won't be often, if ever, that they'll all have off nights."

Leading the charge once again will be the 6-4 senior Rozycki (18.3 ppg, 3.0 ppg, 2.3 apg), who as a junior jacked up eight long balls a game. But Rozycki isn't just a perimeter player—when he was injured, he was leading the conference in free throws made, so he can get to the basket as well as he can shoot the three.

All eyes will be on that shaky left knee, but Kampe isn't worried that his senior star will be slowed by it.

"He stayed in town over the summer to work with our trainers and physical therapist staff," Kampe said. "He's been very religious about his workouts and feels he's ready to go."

Last season Rozycki scored 36 against Ohio, pumped in 34 at UMKC and dropped 32 on Michigan in the season-opener, so his offense was clearly missed when he went down.

Filling the void was 6-2 sophomore **Mike Helms** (11.3 ppg, 2.3 rpg), who was voted Mid-Continent Freshman of the Year and was the team's leading scorer in eight games, including the first five after Rozycki's injury. He averaged 21 points a game down the stretch when the burden of the offense fell on his shoulders.

"Helms is an athlete," Kampe said. "You just give him the ball and get out of the way. He's the kind of guy you watch play and you say, 'Why is he at Oakland?' He's 6-2, he can jump out of the gym and any way you want to score, he can score it. He's got a chance to be the best player ever to play at Oakland."

Another talented athlete the Grizzlies will rely on is 6-5 senior forward **Brad Buddenborg** (15.1 ppg, 4.6 rpg). He finished second on the team in scoring and third in rebounding a year ago.

"Buddenborg has all the talent in the world," Kampe ssaid. "We just have to harness it. For example, he had 26 in second half versus Michigan, and that was after sitting the whole first half with three quick fouls. All the pro scouts are interested in him—he just needs to develop consistency."

The key player in Kampe's mind will be 6-7 senior forward **Dan Champagne** (12.5 ppg, 4.9 rpg). One focus for the Grizzlies this season will be inside play, and Champagne is the player Kampe says can consistently score with his back to the basket.

Injuries have dogged Champagne since he set foot on the Oakland campus. He dislocated his hip as a freshman and was red-shirted, then petitioned the NCAA for a second red-shirt year after he broke his wrist two years later. Now a sixth-year senior, Champagne's toughness and inside grit will go a long way to determining the team's success.

"He came back with that wrist still broken last year and he was very average until the last seven games or so," Kampe said of Champagne, who still managed to average 12.5 points and 4.9 boards a game.

The fourth senior in the starting lineup will be 6-4 point guard **Mychal Covington** (7.0 ppg, 3.8 rpg), who dished out a team-high 5.5 assists per game last season. He's a four-year starter and his long arms help make him the top defender on the team.

"He came to Oakland as a wing but he wasn't really a scorer, so we moved to point and he's gotten better every year," Kampe said. "He's got a tough job because he's got to make sure the right people have the ball at the right spots, and with all the different types of scorers we've got, that's not easy to do."

Sophomore forward **Kelly Williams** (5.6 ppg, 5.7 rpg), 6-5, also figures to be a key player in the rotation this season. A high school teammate of Helms at Detroit's Martin Luther King High, Williams led the team in rebounding last season.

"He's an athlete who can rebound and play D," Kampe said. "He's probably our top inside defender and he can shoot it. He's an inconsistent scorer, but he's the kind of kid who is really the glue to the team."

The Grizzlies' one true big man will come off the bench. Sophomore **Jordan Sabourin** (1.8 ppg, 2.8 rpg), 7-0 and 262 pounds, is expected to play 20-to-25 minutes per game and provide a solid inside presence to this perimeter-oriented team.

"He's a big kid who was overlooked by a lot of the top schools because of his offensive liabilities," Kampe said. "But he's really learning how to play the game. He played at 240 [pounds] last year, then came in this summer at 262 with eight percent body fat, so he's done the work he needs to get better."

Senior **Ryan Williams** (2.4 ppg, 1.6 rpg), 6-1, should also contribute off the bench, as will newcomer **Adrian Martin**, a 6-8 junior who transferred from Midland College in Texas. "He's a hard-nosed kid," Kampe said of Martin. "When he came in for his visit he had a cut under his eye from playing in a tournament with a Mexican team, and I knew I wanted him immediately.

"His team was 55-11 when he was at Midland, and even though he had two teammates that went to big-time schools, his coach credited him for their victories because he could guard the best player in the post. I'm really excited about him—I think he's just what we need."

Kampe hopes that players like Martin will help shore up the team's inside deficiencies.

"We're very weak at rebounding. We can play the best D in the world, but if they get the rebound and lay it in, what have you got?"

"Our defensive priorities are No. 1 rebounding, and No. 2 toughness. You can berate them, you can hug them, but mostly what we've tried to do is educate them. We tell them to look at the differences between when we won the league two years ago and last year. Sometimes they think they can give up an offensive rebound and a bucket and just go down and fire up a three-pointer, but we're trying to show them that that doesn't always work."

But in the end, Kampe admits it will be up to the players to make the difference between last year's disappointing finish and the success they're hoping for this season.

"I'm not going to fool around much with these kids," Kampe said. If we win, it won't be because of any of my magic from the sidelines—it's all on their shoulders."

2001-2002 SCHEDULE

Nov.	16	@Michigan
	20	St. Mary's
	23-25	#University Hoops Classic
	30	##Purdue Classic
Dec.	1	##Purdue Classic
	6	Detroit
	8	@Air Force
	11	@Wright State
	15	@Ohio
	19	@Michigan State
	27	Toledo
	29	Western Michigan
Jan.	3	Chicago State
	5	Southern utah
	10	@Oral Roberts
	12	@UMKC
	19	IUPUI
	24	Western Illinois
	26	Valparaiso
	28	@IP-Fort Wayne
	31	@Southern Utah
Feb.	2	@Chicago State
	7	Oral Roberts
	9	UMKC
	16	@IUPUI
	21	@Valparaiso
	23	@Western Illinois
March	2-5	###Mid-Continent Tournament

@Road Games
#Moon Township, PA (vs. Pittsburgh first round; also Cal-Irvine, Hofstra, Illinois State, Kent, Robert Morris, South Florida)
##West Lafayette, IN (vs. Akron first round; also Purdue, William & Mary)
###Memorial Coliseum, Fort Wayne, IN

BLUE RIBBON ANALYSIS

BACKCOURT	A
BENCH/DEPTH	C
FRONTCOURT	C
INTANGIBLES	B

This is the big year for Oakland, the year the Grizzlies could make a small splash on the national scene. Their experience and high-flying offense could be just the formula for a run through the conference tournament and the school's first berth in the NCAA Tournament.

They've shown in the last two years that they can play with conference titans like Valpo and Southern Utah. Now it's a matter of staying healthy, tightening the defense and catching a break or two. If it puts the pieces together, Oakland has a great chance to become the media darling of the big dance next March.

(P.D.)

Oral Roberts

LOCATION	**Tulsa, OK**
CONFERENCE	**Mid-Continent**
LAST SEASON	**10-19 (.345)**
CONFERENCE RECORD	**5-11 (t-7th)**
STARTERS LOST/RETURNING	**0/5**
NICKNAME	**Golden Eagles**
COLORS	**Navy Blue, Vegas Gold & White**
HOMECOURT	**Mabee Center (10,575)**
COACH	**Scott Sutton (Oklahoma State '94)**
RECORD AT SCHOOL	**23-26 (2 years)**
CAREER RECORD	**23-26 (2 years)**
ASSISTANTS	**Tom Hankins (Northeastern State '90)**
	Corey Williams (Oklahoma State '92)
	Conley Phipps (Northeastern State '90)
TEAM WINS (last 5 years)	**18-21-19-17-13**
RPI (last 5 years)	**142-63-146-148-257**
2000-01 FINISH	**Lost in conference semifinal.**

It's been 18 long years since Oral Roberts last earned a trip to the NCAA Tournament. But if Golden Eagles head coach Scott Sutton has his way, that streak will be snapped this year.

Last year's team sputtered through a pair of extended losing streaks, but the Golden Eagles won three of their final six games, including a 73-70 upset of third-seeded Youngstown State in the first round of the Mid-Continent Conference Tournament. ORU succumbed to eventual champion Southern Utah in a semifinal, but this year Sutton thinks his team has a shot to be the ones dancing on the court in Ft. Wayne.

"That's what we're going to work on every day, to get to the point where we can cut those nets down and play in the Big Dance," Sutton said.

In what's generally believed to be a balanced conference, that dream is not out of the question, even for a team that finished tied for seventh place last season.

"Last year, that probably wouldn't have been a realistic goal with so many new players," said Sutton, who was forced to play 10 players making the transition to Division I basketball. "But now we feel we're in a position to challenge for the conference title."

Last year ORU started the season 3-0, including an 87-83 home victory over Nebraska in the season opener. But a pair of close conference losses started the Golden Eagles on a nine-game losing skid that included two overtime defeats. They came back to win four straight Mid-Continent games, including a nine-point win over regular-season co-champion Valpo, but that was followed by a seven-game losing streak before their late-season surge.

The Golden Eagles lost only two of their top eight from last year—starting forward Kyan Brown (7.6 ppg and a team-high 6.3 rpg) and backup guard Evan Black (5.3 ppg). But Sutton gave three freshmen extensive playing time last season, and three other key veterans return to welcome four talented newcomers.

"We have just about everybody back," Sutton said. "We lose Kyan and Evan, who were good players for us and great kids, but I think the guys we're bringing in can definitely replace the ones we lost."

Senior **Markius Barnes** (16.0 ppg, 3.8 rpg, 3.2 apg) led the team in scoring and was second in assists last season. The 6-3 guard transferred from Southwest Christian Junior College and was voted to the Mid-Continent All-Newcomer team last season. He also earned all-tournament team honors after scoring 31 points in the Golden Eagles' opening-round upset of Youngstown State.

"Markius proved that on any given night he can take over a game and lead us to a win," Sutton said. "He put the team on his shoulders and won us that game."

Barnes finished fourth in the Mid-Continent in scoring, fifth in free-throw percentage (79.7) and seventh in field-goal percentage (.412), and the Golden Eagles will count on him to provide even more scoring punch with a year of D-I play behind him.

Point guard **Luke Spencer-Gardner** (8.3 ppg, 4.0 apg) returns to run the offense. The 6-1 sophomore was fourth in the conference in assists and fifth in three-point percentage, knocking down 41.9 percent of his attempts behind the arc (44-of-105)—from where he took almost 60 percent of his shots.

The Golden Eagles' second-leading scorer was guard **Josh Atkinson** (11.6 ppg, 2.3 rpg, 1.9 apg). The 6-3 junior was another major threat from three-point land—his .424 percentage was third best in the conference, and almost half of his field-goal attempts came from behind the arc.

The center duties could be shared again by 7-0 junior **Charlie Ludwig** (6.8 ppg, 3.7 rpg) and 6-11 sophomore **Matt Gastel** (7.2 ppg, 3.6 rpg). Last season Ludwig started 17 games while Gastel started 10, earning both players valuable experience that should carry over into this year.

Another player who started 10 games last year was 6-5 sophomore **Ralph Charles** (5.3 ppg, 2.7 rpg), while the final returning letterman is 6-8 senior **Kyle Stewart** (1.6 ppg, 1.2 rpg).

Sutton brought in a handful of junior college transfers to bolster the team's inside play. They include 6-7 junior **Reggie Borges** from Los Angeles Harbor Junior College, 6-7 junior **Richie Myers** from Northern Oklahoma College, and red-shirt junior **Kendrick Moore**, a 6-8 forward from Dawson (Mont.) Community College.

The Golden Eagles also expect 6-1 junior **Tyrone Tiggs** from Okaloosa-Walton (Fla.) Community College to have an immediate impact at point guard. Others in the backcourt mix are 6-4 sophomore **Andy Mathurin**, 6-5 sophomore **Andrew Meloy** and 6-1 junior **Matt Frazier**, a transfer from Pittsburg State.

"There's going to be great depth, which is something we didn't have last year," Sutton said. "We may have 12 guys fighting for playing time."

This year's non-conference schedule includes a couple of imposing road dates—a trip to revenge-minded Nebraska, and "40 minutes of Hell" against the Arkansas Razorbacks in Fayetteville. The Golden Eagles also play in the San Juan Shootout, where they'll face Jacksonville in the first round. Home dates include defending NIT champion Tulsa, as well as Drake, Texas-Arlington and Stephen F. Austin.

2001-2002 SCHEDULE

Nov.	16	Cameron
	18	@Arkansas
	23	Drake
	25	@Colgate
	27	@Binghamton
Dec.	1	Tulsa
	5	Tennessee State
	8	@Nebraska
	14	@SMU
	17	Texas-Arlington
	20-22	#San Juan Shootout
	29	Stephen F. Austin
Jan.	2	@Texas-Arlington
	5	@UMKC
	10	IUPUI
	12	Oakland
	17	@Valparaiso
	19	@Western Illinois
	24	Southern Utah
	26	Chicago State
Feb.	2	UMKC
	7	@Oakland
	9	@IUPUI

	14	Western Illinois
	16	Valparaiso
	21	@Chicago State
	23	@Southern Utah
March	3-5	##Mid-Continent Tournament

@Road Games
#San Juan, Puerto Rico (vs. Jacksonville first round; also Baylor, Puerto Rico, Coppin State, Florida International, Niagara, Texas-Pan American)
##War Memorial Coliseum, Fort Wayne, IN

BLUE RIBBON ANALYSIS

BACKCOURT	B
BENCH/DEPTH	B
FRONTCOURT	C
INTANGIBLES	C+

Things are definitely looking up for ORU. Opposing coaches around the conference have taken notice, listing the Golden Eagles among their favorites in the Mid-Continent race.

Most of the talent is still relatively unproven, but after taking their lumps last season, they could be ready to put it together in 2002.

(P.D.)

Southern Utah

LOCATION	Cedar City, UT
CONFERENCE	Mid-Continent
LAST SEASON	25-6 (.806)
CONFERENCE RECORD	13-3 (t-1st)
STARTERS LOST/RETURNING	4/1
NICKNAME	Thunderbirds
COLORS	Scarlet & White
HOMECOURT	Centrum (5,300)
COACH	Bill Evans (Southern Utah '72)
RECORD AT SCHOOL	138-123 (9 years)
CAREER RECORD	138-123 (9 years)
ASSISTANTS	Barrett Peery (Southern Utah '95)
	Patrick Harrington (Rollins '86)
TEAM WINS (last 5 years)	18-21-19-17-13
RPI (last 5 years)	142-63-146-148-257
2000-01 FINISH	Lost in NCAA first round.

Imagine how Sir Edmund Hillary might have felt if, after reaching the peak of Mt. Everest, his Sherpa guides deserted him and left him to make his way back down the mountain by himself.

Now you have some idea how Southern Utah coach Bill Evans must feel.

Last year, Evans helped guide the Thunderbirds to their first NCAA Tournament appearance, going so far as to push No. 2-seeded Boston College to the final seconds before dropping a 68-65 decision in the first round of the Eastern Regional.

But only one starter returns from that team, meaning that after reaching the peak last year, Evans and his team might be in for some rough sledding.

"We've got to have somebody step up from the guys with just a little playing time, or juco transfers who are playing at a new and different level," Evans said. "The unknown is always a scary thing."

Chief among Evans' priorities for this season is finding a way to replace the 52.4 points per game he lost to graduation last season.

"Who's going to score the ball and how we're going to score the ball is going to be a big concern," Evans said. "I don't have any idea who that's going to be, and that scares me."

Last year, the Thunderbirds had no shortage of options when looking for offense. But the graduation of wings Fred House (17.8 ppg, 5.9 rpg) and Justin Sant (9.9 ppg, 3.0 apg, 2.9 rpg), point guard Jeff Monaco (17.5 ppg, 5.4 apg, 2.3 rpg) and big men John Wheeler (5.2 ppg, 3.3 rpg) and B.J. Chandler (2.0 ppg, 1.4 ppg) leaves a rather sizeable hole in the Southern Utah attack.

"We lost some very talented kids," Evans said, "kids who had a big hand in what we were doing offensively and defensively the past couple of years. Jeff and Fred both had opportunities to make NBA teams as free agents and the other three were good complementary guys who understood the roles they played in our system."

Evans is hoping that the experience gained from the Thunderbirds' run to the Mid-Continent Tournament title

and trip to the NCAA Tournament will be evident when the new starters hit the court this year.

"I think it gives you a sense of accomplishment," he said. "We didn't rebound the ball well at all, but I think it showed our guys that we can play with a lot of teams. The experience of going there and winning games on the road like that is a real positive."

Those road wins last year included victories at Utah, Montana, Cal-Riverside and Idaho State, and a 5-3 road mark in the conference. In one murderous five-game road stretch, the Thunderbirds went 4-1, with their only loss coming by three points at Valpo.

Then in the Mid-Continent Tournament in Fort Wayne, Ind., Southern Utah rattled off three wins in three days—turning the tables on Valpo with a three-point win of its own in the championship game.

This year Evans has put together another challenging schedule, with 10 of the first 13 on the road, including trips to Stanford, Oregon State, Utah and BYU. And as the western-most school in the Mid-Continent, the Thunderbirds will rack up more road miles in conference games than any of their opponents.

"We're doing it for a reason," Evans said. "With all of our young players, we need to show them that we have some long trips to make and some tough places to play. We need them to be tough mentally and physically."

The lone returning member of the starting lineup is senior **Dan Beus** (10.9 ppg, 7.9 rpg). The 6-5 forward was the Mid-Continent Newcomer of the Year after finishing third in the conference in rebounding. He should be the anchor of the team at power forward this year.

"Dan had an exceptional year for us as a junior," Evans said. "I don't know if I've ever been around anyone who is any tougher, and he's a guy who practices like he plays. When he steps on that floor, he is all business. He's got tremendous toughness, tremendous heart, and he will get more scoring opportunities this year with the others gone."

Beus' primary backup will be 6-8 junior **Aaron Miles** (0.8 ppg, 0.9 rpg), who has seen his role begin to develop a bit in his two seasons with the Thunderbirds.

Joining Beus down low will be 6-11 junior **Chris Wallin** (4.3 ppg, 2.8 ppg), who has started 18 games over the last two years, and 6-10 senior **Jeff Dorenbosch** (1.3 ppg, 0.8 rpg), an athletic big man. Dorenbosch began last year recovering from a knee injury but came back strong toward the end of the season.

Wallin led the team with a .743 shooting percentage and filled in nicely when Wheeler went down with a knee injury, putting up 12 points and eight boards at Valpo and posting his first career double-double (10 and 10) at home against Oakland.

"Chris is a player who just continues to improve," Evans said. "He has worked very hard since coming to us and this year we are expecting him to score some points for our basketball team, so we will try to give him opportunities to score. He's a good defender in our match-up defense, but we definitely need more rebounding out of him this year. Chris is one of the guys who needs to take a step up if we are going to be successful this year."

The battle to replace House at small forward appears to be wide open. **Ross Day** (2.1 ppg, 0.6 rpg) is a 6-5 junior who hit on 14-of-40 three-pointers (.350) in limited playing time last year.

"Ross is one of the hardest workers I've ever had and we thought last year would be a breakout year for him," Evans said. "While that didn't quite work out, we're looking for him to continue to improve, particularly with more playing time."

Junior **Tyler Finlanson**, a 6-5 junior college transfer who was red-shirted last year, is the other known commodity to the coaching staff. The other candidates are all newcomers to the program—**Rand Janes**, a 6-6 freshman from Cedar City, Utah who recently returned from a two-year church mission; **Donnie Jackson**, a 6-6 junior who was the team MVP last year at Utah Valley State; and **Kevin Henry**, a 6-4 junior who earned all-tournament honors last year at the NJCAA national tournament while playing for Cochise (Ariz.) Community College.

In the backcourt, the departed Monaco, the Mid-Continent Player of the Year last year, leaves some big shoes to fill, and Evans' options don't have much Division I experience. **Jason Baker** (1.2 ppg, 0.5 apg), a 6-2 sophomore, played in 25 games as a freshman last year and averaged just more than six minutes a game. **Jay Collins**, a 6-3 junior, was Henry's teammate at Cochise last year, scoring 20.0 points and 4.2 assists a game last year in earning NJCAA honorable mention honors. And 5-9 junior **Jordan Mulford** played mostly shooting guard last year as a teammate of Jackson at Utah Valley, where he missed the final eight games with a knee injury.

"We have three guys who could play the point for us this year," Evans said. "None of them have much experience at playing a very key position at this level—which scares me a little, I have to admit—but they're all tough, intelligent, team guys, my kind of guys. I think they all have the ability to play the point and they are all capable of playing off-guard at this level as well."

The top prospects at the shooting guard are 6-2 junior **Stan Johnson** (2.1 ppg, 0.9 rpg) and 6-3 senior **Brian Gardner** (0.6 ppg, 0.4 rpg). Johnson was the team's sixth man last year, while Gardner displayed a nice touch from long range in his limited minutes. Finlanson, Day and any of the point guards could find themselves in the mix at shooting guard as well.

"Stan is the epitome of a team ballplayer," Evans said. "His biggest strength is that he makes those around him better. He is unselfish, works had and is a natural leader. Stan hasn't scored a lot of points for us, but that's because he has understood his role in the past. This year we will look for him to score a little more. Brian may just be the most talented player on our team—he is athletic, he can shoot and he can score, plus he's good in our match-up defense. He didn't get as many opportunities to play last year as he wanted, but he understands what he has to do to change that this year."

2001-2002 SCHEDULE

Nov.	16	Ft. Lewis
	20	@Stanford
	24	@Idaho State
	27	Adams State
	30	@Oregon State
Dec.	3	@Sacramento State
	8	UC Riverside
	10	Idaho State
	15	@Boise State
	18	@Utah
	22	@Weber State
	29	@Brigham Young
Jan.	3	@IUPUI
	5	@Oakland
	10	Valparaiso
	12	Western Illinois
	19	Chicago State
	24	@Oral Roberts
	26	@UMKC
	31	Oakland
Feb.	2	IUPUI
	7	@Western Illinois
	9	@Valparaiso
	16	@Chicago State
	21	UMKC
	23	Oral Roberts
March	1-5	#Mid-Continent Tournament

@Road Games
#Memorial Coliseum, Fort Wayne, IN

BLUE RIBBON ANALYSIS

BACKCOURT	D
BENCH/DEPTH	C-
FRONTCOURT	C+
INTANGIBLES	D+

There are just too many question marks this year for the Thunderbirds to be overly optimistic. Any team that loses as much as they've lost will have its hands full, and when you take into account the number of minutes played by House, Monaco, Sant, Wheeler and Chandler last year, it leaves precious few players with meaningful Division I experience on the roster.

Also, as the defending conference champs, Southern Utah will have a big target on its back as the rest of the Mid-Continent will look to knock the champ off the top of the mountain.

Having a player like Beus is always a reason for hope—he was a junior college transfer himself, like many of the new players on whom the team will be counting to provide meaningful minutes, points and rebounds. Also, Evans is a proven winner, with three conference championships in his nine-year career, and his guidance will be invaluable to a young team.

But in the end, inexperience will be the biggest factor in the Thunderbirds' season. If the junior college players develop faster than expected, they could peak in time for another run at the conference tourney. But don't be shocked if this year is little more than a building block for a return to prominence in 2002-03.

(P.D.)

Valparaiso

LOCATION	Valparaiso, IN
CONFERENCE	Mid-Continent
LAST SEASON	24-8 (.800)
CONFERENCE RECORD	13-3 (t-1st)
STARTERS LOST/RETURNING	2/3
NICKNAME	Crusaders
COLORS	Brown & Gold
HOMECOURT	Athletics-Recreation Center (4,500)
COACH	Homer Drew (William Jewell '66)
RECORD AT SCHOOL	210-177 (13 years)
CAREER RECORD	479-299 (25 years)
ASSISTANTS	Scott Drew (Butler '93)
	William Colon (University of Puerto Rico '81)
	Mark Morefield (Valparaiso '98)
	Craig Brunes (Valparaiso '98)
TEAM WINS (last 5 years)	18-21-19-17-13
RPI (last 5 years)	142-63-146-148-257
2000-01 FINISH	Lost in conference final.

As college basketball dynasties go, you usually have to go pretty far down the list—through North Carolina and Indiana and UCLA and Kentucky—before you get to Valparaiso. But not many schools can match the dominance the Crusaders have held over their conference opponents in the last decade.

Last year Valpo won a share of its sixth Mid-Continent regular-season title in the last seven years. The Crusaders had also won six consecutive conference tournaments, earning the automatic NCAA Tournament berth that went with the title.

But that NCAA streak was snapped last year when Southern Utah knocked off Valpo, 62-59, in the Mid-Continent championship game. The Crusaders were bitten by a bug—specifically, a mono bug that swept through campus late last winter. Of the 100 documented cases at the school, two of them were starters on the basketball team—senior guard Dwayne Toatley and junior guard **Milos Stovall**, both second-team all-Mid-Continent selections.

With Toatley—who coach Homer Drew called "the heart and soul of our team"—and Stovall slowed by the illness, and key reserve **Joaquim Gomes** sidelined with a knee injury, the deep, experienced and talented Southern Utah team took advantage. The Thunderbirds pulled out a close victory in the title game, then did what Valpo traditionally does every March—they gave a higher seeded team a major scare before falling by three points to No. 7 Boston College in the first round of the NCAA Tournament.

But don't expect this to be the beginning of the end for the Valpo dynasty. The Crusaders lost only two key players from last year's team, and a trio of talented recruits should help push them toward another run at the Mid-Continent championship.

Gone are Toatley (8.9 ppg, 4.4 rpg, 2.3 apg), a leader on the court who Drew has retained as the team's strength coach this year, and starting forward Jason Jenkins (8.9 ppg, 4.0 rpg, 2.2 apg), a skilled passer and shooter.

But Drew welcomes back his top three scorers, four players who earned Mid-Continent postseason honors, and five players who started at least seven games last year.

Leading the way is 6-11 junior center **Raitis Grafs** (13.8 ppg, 8.1 rpg, 2.1 bpg), a first-team all-Mid-Continent selection from Lativia Drew calls one of the best big men in the conference.

"He was superb last year," Drew said. "He plays tremendous defense, is quick on his feet and blocks a lot of shots. He also led our team in steals as a freshman, and he's the first center to do that for us."

Close behind Grafs in scoring last year was 6-8 senior forward **Lubos Barton** (13.5 ppg, 6.1 rpg, 3.3. apg), a second-team all-conference pick out of the Czech Republic.

"He's a superb shooter, a real gym rat who worked hard all summer to improve his game," Drew said. "He played in the pro-am league in Chicago this summer and has a chance to play at the next level."

Yet another experienced scoring option is 6-3 senior guard Stovall (11.8 ppg, 3.9 rpg, 2.1 apg), another second-team All-Mid-Continent pick. He led the conference in three-point percentage last year (.439) and is one of the team's top defenders.

"He's gotten over the mono and worked hard on his shot and dribble all summer," Drew said. "He's improved his strength and his all-around game."

Senior guard **Jared Nuness** (5.9 ppg, 2.7 apg), a 5-10 sparkplug, started 22 games last year after recovering from an ankle injury that required surgery. He'll bring experience and leadership to the backcourt as a player who was a key part of Valpo's NCAA Tournament teams in 1999 and 2000.

Also in the backcourt mix are 6-0 sophomore **Mike Nelke** (3.2 ppg, 2.1 apg), who started seven games at the end of last year and played well down the stretch, and 6-3 junior **Greg Tonagel**, who has missed the last two years with knee problems but is back to 100 percent and ready to contribute.

Joining Grafs and Barton up front could be **Antti Nikkila** (2.7 ppg, 2.1 rpg), a 7-0 junior who spent the summer playing on the Finnish national team.

"We just got an e-mail from the Finnish national coach, and he said Antti was playing better than he'd ever seen him," Drew said. "He'll get more minutes this year and should really help us with our inside game."

He'll be joined by Phil Wille, a 6-10 junior who saw limited action last year. But Wille worked on his strength and shot in the off-season and could be ready to contribute this year.

The X-factor down low will be the health of Gomes (6.2 ppg, 4.1 rpg). The 6-8 sophomore from Angola was chosen to the Mid-Continent All-Newcomer team last season, but he missed the conference tournament when he suffered a torn ACL in the final regular-season game.

"We're going to take it slow with Gomes this fall," Drew said. "He's in a full rehab program right now, and we hope to have him back by the first game. He was really playing well at the end of last year, giving us speed and rebounding."

Drew brought in a trio of international recruits who should push for playing time immediately. Freshman **Ali Berdial** is a 6-5 point guard from Puerto Rico who played his senior year of high school in Merrilville, Ind., as an exchange student.

"He really sees the floor well," Drew said. "He is a great shooter, but he's a good team player and if you're open, Ali will get you the ball."

Fellow Puerto Rican Tony Falu, a 6-5 junior from San Jacinto (Texas) College, was a junior college All-American last year. He can play both guard spots, and brings quickness, scoring and defense to the Crusaders.

Finally, 6-3 junior guard **Stalin Ortiz** comes to Valpo from Cali, Colombia, via Three Rivers (Mo.) Community College, where he earned all-conference and honorable mention all-America honors last year. Drew calls him a tenacious defender who can slash to the basket and hit the three-pointer on the other end of the court.

"We've probably got more depth than we've ever had," Drew said of this year's team. "We have three seniors who will provide excellent leadership, and if we learn to play together as a team we'll be tough."

Drew will challenge his players with another difficult schedule that opens at home against Purdue. Other home games include Rhode Island, UW-Milwaukee and former Mid-Continent foe Youngstown State, while road trips include holiday tournaments in Honolulu and Tucson, followed by a Jan. 2 date at Kansas.

2001-2002 SCHEDULE

Nov.	6	Purdue
	19	@Belmont
	21	@Indiana State
	24	Wisconsin-Milwaukee
	27	@Northern Illinois
	29	Youngstown State
Dec.	5	@Charlotte
	8	Rhode Island
	13	Goshen
	20-22	#Yahoo Sports Invitational
	28-30	##Fiesta Bowl Classic
Jan.	2	@Kansas
	10	@Southern Utah
	12	@Chicago State
	17	Oral Roberts
	19	UMKC
	24	@IUPUI
	26	@Oakland
Feb.	2	Western Illinois
	7	Chicago State
	9	Southern Utah
	14	@UMKC
	16	@Oral Roberts
	21	Oakland
	23	IUPUI
March	3-5	###Mid-Continent Tournament

@Road Games
#Laie, HI (vs. New Mexico State first round; also BYU-

Hawaii, Buffalo, Columbia, Montana, Navy, Tulsa)
##Phoenix, AZ (vs. West Virginia first round; also Arizona, Pepperdine)
###Memorial Coliseum, Fort Wayne, IN

BLUE RIBBON ANALYSIS

BACKCOURT	B+
BENCH/DEPTH	A
FRONTCOURT	A-
INTANGIBLES	B+

Valpo will start the season in an unfamiliar position—trying to take back the Mid-Continent crown that slipped away last year. But don't think the rest of the conference will be overlooking the Crusaders. They will remain the hunted, not the hunters.

"Until one of the other schools proves that it can consistently beat them, Valpo will continue to be the team to beat," Chicago State coach Bo Ellis said.

Western Illinois coach Jim Kerwin went one step further.

"Valpo will be outstanding again this year," he said. "They have almost everybody back and they recruited well. They could have one of their best teams ever, and could wind up in the top 30 to 35 teams in the country."

Certainly few teams in the Mid-Continent can match the trio of Grafs, Barton and Stovall, and if the recruits play according to form, this is a team that can not only get back to the NCAA Tournament but possibly pull a couple of shockers to reach the Sweet 16.

(P.D.)

Western Illinois

LOCATION	Macomb, IL
CONFERENCE	Mid-Continent
LAST SEASON	5-23 (.179)
CONFERENCE RECORD	5-11 (t-7th)
STARTERS LOST/RETURNING	1/4
NICKNAME	Leathernecks
COLORS	Purple & Gold
HOMECOURT	Mabee Center (10,575)
COACH	Jim Kerwin (Tulane '64)
RECORD AT SCHOOL	116-137 (9 years)
CAREER RECORD	116-137 (9 years)
ASSISTANTS	Brad Underwood (Kansas State '86)
	Chrys Cornelius (Western Illinois '95)
	Geoff Alexander (Western Illinois '00)
TEAM WINS (last 5 years)	18-21-19-17-13
RPI (last 5 years)	142-63-146-148-257
2000-01 FINISH	Lost in conference quarterfinal.

Ask any college coach and he'll tell you that an experienced roster is a key to winning, especially at the mid-major level.

It's much easier for the Dukes and North Carolinas and UConns of the world to reload with four new McDonald's All-Americans every year. But when you're a small school, it's a distinct advantage to have five players on the court (and a few more on the bench) who are familiar with each other's tendencies, understand the system and are committed to the program.

Western Illinois coach Jim Kerwin is in an enviable position this year for just that reason. Even though the Leathernecks struggled to a 5-23 record last season, he was giving his young players invaluable experience. And now he's got a more veteran team ready to attack the Mid-Continent Conference this season.

"Last year we were starting two freshmen and two juco transfers," Kerwin said. "Now we've got seven of our top eight back, and we're hoping to make some progress from last year."

The Leathernecks graduated two seniors who started a total of 16 games last season, and that's all they lost. The top five scorers are back. The top six rebounders return. The top four in assists and top two in blocked shots are back as well.

In other words, Western Illinois has experience on its side, and that will be a big factor in the team's success this year.

Kerwin is looking for the team to develop some continuity after trying a variety of combinations last year.

"All of our positions are wide open," he said. "We've got a good nine to 10 guys competing for playing time. Last year we played a lot of guys and never really got solid in our top six to eight players. We were always grasping, trying to find players who fit together. This year we want eight to nine guys we can bank on, who know

their roles, so we can set a rotation."

Leading the offense will be 6-2 senior guard **Cory Fosdyck** (10.8 ppg, 2.4 rpg, 2.0 apg), who led the team with 57 three-pointers last year and shot 42.3 percent from behind the arc in conference games.

"He's an outstanding shooter," Kerwin said. "As a freshman and sophomore he didn't penetrate much, but he's added that now. He's also strong on defense and plays an all-around solid game."

Kerwin is looking for 6-2 senior **Brian Williams** (8.4 ppg, 3.5 apg) to take charge and earn the point-guard spot this season after starting 25 games last year.

"He showed a great deal of improvement through the year and did a great job pushing the ball," Kerwin said. "He's got to be the guy to run our basketball team this year."

Senior **Jamal Richardson** (8.7 ppg, 5.4 rpg), a 6-8 forward, could be a force inside if he develops some consistency.

"He was productive at times last year but he had so many up and down games," Kerwin said. "He's got more athletic ability than any big man we've ever had here—he can run, he can jump and he's a pretty good shooter. We're hoping that with experience he'll develop some consistency."

The two freshman who played extensively last year were 6-3 forward **J.D. Summers** (6.8 ppg, 3.5 rpg) and 6-9 forward **Karl Petersen** (6.7 ppg, 5.1 rpg).

"They were not ready play at this level last year but due to need, we had to play them," Kerwin said.

Summers is a strong shooter who hit 42.5 percent of his three-pointers as a freshman.

"He's strong and aggressive, and having a year under his belt, playing in 30 ballgames, will really help him," Kerwin said.

Peterson started a team-high 26 games as a freshman and finished second on the team in rebounding and steals.

"He's solid in a lot of areas but not outstanding in any," Kerwin said. "He's got some size and strength and does a lot of good things. He's probably our best inside defender."

On the wing, Kerwin looks for 6-4 senior **Quentin Mitchell** (5.8 ppg, 2.5 rpg) and 6-3 junior college transfer **Lorenzo Lawrence** to compete for playing time. Another pair of new faces are expected to enter the mix inside—6-6 junior **Shawn Mason** from Seminole (Okla.) Junior College, and 6-7 junior **Luis Rivas**, a transfer from Arkansas State. Meanwhile, 6-0 sophomore guard **Derek Colvin**, another transfer from Seminole, has a chance to step in and play immediately.

The Leathernecks' non-conference schedule this year includes games at Illinois and Nebraska and home games with Bradley, Drake, Hampton and Eastern Illinois, a strong test to see how many lessons Kerwin's young players learned last season.

2001-2002 SCHEDULE

Nov.	18	Cardinal Stritch
	20	@Eastern Kentucky
	24	Bradley
	27	Drake
Dec.	1	@Southeast Missouri
	5	@Nebraska
	8	Eastern Illinois
	16	@Illinois
	19	Eastern Kentucky
	23	Hampton
	30	Youngstown State
Jan.	2	Southeast Missouri State
	5	Vallparaiso
	7	St. Ambrose
	10	@Chicago State
	12	@Southern Utah
	17	UMKC
	19	Oral Roberts
	24	@Oakland
	26	@IUPUI
Feb.	2	@Valparaiso
	7	Southern Utah
	9	Chicago State
	14	@Oral Roberts
	16	@UMKC
	21	IUPUI
	23	Oakland
March	1-5	#Mid-Continent Tournament

@Road Games
#Memorial Coliseum, Fort Wayne, IN

BLUE RIBBON ANALYSIS

BACKCOURT	C+
BENCH/DEPTH	B
FRONTCOURT	C-
INTANGIBLES	B-

The top priority for the Leathernecks this year is shoring up the defense. Last season they allowed the most points in the conference—an average of 77.9 per game. Kerwin wants his team to improve both inside and on the perimeter, although that could be tough with the size—or lack of it—on the roster. With only one player taller than 6-9, the Leathernecks could continue to take a beating inside.

But their smaller lineup could work to their advantage offensively, where players like Fosdyck and Williams could shake free for some high-scoring games. If Western Illinois can find a way to stop teams inside with a bunch of 6-8 and 6-9 guys down low, they'll find themselves back in the middle of the conference and ready to put a scare into some top teams at the league tournament.

(P.D.)

Bethune-Cookman

LOCATION	Daytona Beach, FL
CONFERENCE	Mid-Eastern Athletic
LAST SEASON	10-19 (.345)
CONFERENCE RECORD	5-13 (9th)
STARTERS LOST/RETURNING	2/3
NICKNAME	Wildcats
COLORS	Maroon & Gold
HOMECOURT	Moore Gymnasium (3,000)
	and Ocean Center (9,000)
COACH	Horace Broadnax (Georgetown '86)
RECORD AT SCHOOL	36-76 (5 years)
CAREER RECORD	36-76 (5 years)
ASSISTANTS	Cliff Reed (Bethune-Cookman '91)
	Rick Walrand (Methodist '75)
TEAM WINS (last 5 years)	8-1-12-13-10
RPI (last 5 years)	263-306-224-205-283
2000-01 FINISH	Lost in conference second round.

Bethune-Cookman coach Horace Broadnax refuses to call the 2001-02 season a rebuilding year. It's a building year instead.

Despite graduating their top two scorers from last year's 10-19 team, the Wildcats will be "building" this season.

"This is a building year for us," said Broadnax, who twice has been chosen MEAC Coach of the Year. "This is a try to get better year, better than we were last year."

It sure looks like a rebuilding year, but then again don't bet against Broadax-coached teams. Both times he's been selected coach of the year, he took teams picked near the bottom of the league and competed for the MEAC regular-season titles.

The Wildcats graduated their top two scorers from last year in 6-1 guard Tyree Harris (14.6 ppg) and 6-6 forward Derricus Lockwood (13.8 ppg) but do return three starters and have four other lettermen back.

Five newcomers have been brought in, and all will have a chance to play this year.

"We have five new guys and really don't have any dominant guys coming back to give that leadership," Broadnax said. "We have several guys who are capable of stepping up to that spot, but at this point we don't know who that could be. We will just have to wait and see."

The backcourt should be led by 6-1 senior guard **Brian Cox** (8.1 ppg, 3.0 rpg). Also back is 5-10 senior guard **Moses Cage** (5.3 ppg, 3.1 rpg).

"What we want Moses to do is to distribute the ball and get the ball to our scorers," Broadnax said. "We want him to show some leadership and just not make too make too many mistakes. He struggled a little bit last year, but he should be better because he has a year under his belt.

"Brian did a good job for us last year but fell off a little bit toward the end of the season. I think he felt a little pressure to score for us, but that won't be the case this season because of the players we brought in. If Brian can score what he did last season, we'll be just fine."

Cox and Cage will have to battle for starting spots with a trio of newcomers. They are 6-3 junior guard **Mike Williams**, 6-3 junior guard **Richard Toussaint** and 6-3 junior forward **Maurice Riddick**. Broadnax expects help from all three of those players this season.

"If they do what we recruited them to do, they will be our impact players," Broadnax said. "They should be able to replace Derricus and Tyree."

With these new players, Broadnax believes the strength of his team is in the backcourt.

"Our perimeter game is our strength," Broadnax said. "We brought in three perimeter guys in Riddick, Touissant and Williams. They are good at shooting off the dribble. We hope that on any given night, they can put 20 points on the scoreboard."

Riddick transferred to Bethune-Cookman from Alleghany College of Maryland, where he averaged nine points per game last season.

"He [Riddick] played for a team that played for a national championship last year in junior college," Broadnax said. "He'll add a lot of firepower."

Toussaint enjoyed an excellent junior college career at Hillsborough Community College in Tampa. Last year, he averaged 22.1 points.

"Richard is another guy who can score and he proved that in junior colllege," Broadnax said.

Williams is a 6-3 guard/forward from Eastern Oklahoma State Junior College who averaged 9.1 points and 3.1 rebounds for a team that was ranked nationally throughout his two-year career.

Broadnax points to one big reason why the Wildcats struggled so much last year.

"Two years ago we had a pretty good season and we averaged 78 points per game," Broadnax said. "Last year we struggled and averaged only 63 points. That's a big difference and that's why we went out and got the players we did. These guys should be able to score some points for us and make a real difference.

"We play good defense but when you don't score a lot of points then you put a lot of pressure on your defense," Broadnax said. "If we can get that scoring average up to 70 points per game that could make a real difference for us this coming season.

O'Neal Carter, a 6-2 freshman, could get a chance to play some this season. The rookie point guard played at Morgan Park High School, just outside of Chicago.

"We've got some pretty good depth in the backcourt," Broadnax said. "O'Neal has got some good skills and played against some great competition. He'll get a chance to play a little bit, but he's got a chance to learn this season."

Dwight Lauder (2.6 ppg, 1.1 rpg), a 6-0 sophomore guard, will also provide depth in the backcourt.

The strength of this team, as Broadnax pointed out, is the backcourt. The Wildcats will try and simply make do in the front court.

Heading the returnees up front will be 6-5 sophomore **Diondre Larmond** (5.3 ppg, 3.3 rpg).

"Diondre's learned a lot last year and should be better off for it this season," Broadnax said.

Also back is 6-5 senior forward **Brent King** (3.9 ppg, 4.3 rpg), who Broadnax would like to see bounce back to his freshman form.

"Brent had a great freshman year but has struggled a little bit since then," Broadnax said. "We need him to do what he did his freshman year. If he can do that, that will help us a great deal."

The center spot returns 6-8 sophomore **Jerome Nicholson** (5.1 ppg, 2.9 rpg) and 6-9 junior **Jerry Daniels** (1.5 ppg, 1.7 rpg). Nicholson was the Wildcats' starter last year and should be ready to have a good season.

"Jerome Nicholson had a good year last season and if he can improve, that will be a strength," Broadnax said.

Andre Walsh, a 6-9 freshman, has a shot at receiving significant playing time. He comes to Bethune-Cookman from Brazosport High School in Freeport, Texas. Last year, he averaged 16 points, 11 rebounds and three blocked shots.

"Andre has some good post-up moves and has a nice jump shot from 10 feet out," Broadnax said. "We'll give him a chance to see what he can do this year."

2001-2002 SCHEDULE

Nov.	20	Iona
	24	Florida A&M
	26	Louisiana-Lafayette
	28	@Georgetown
Dec.	1	@Maryland-Eastern Shore
	12	@South Alabama
	17	@Oklahoma
	20	@Louisiana-Lafayette
Jan.	2	@Alabama
	5	South Carolina State
	7	North Carolina A&T
	9	@Savannah State
	12	@Delaware State
	14	@Howard
	19	Coppin State
	21	Morgan State

	26	Hampton
	28	@Norfolk State
Feb.	2	Maryland-Eastern Shore
	9	@South Carolina State
	11	@North Carolina A&T
	16	Delaware State
	18	Howard
	20	South Alabama
	23	@Morgan State
	25	@Coppin State
March	2	@Florida A&M
	4-8	MEAC Tournament

@Road Games
#Richmond Coliseum, Richmond, VA

BLUE RIBBON ANALYSIS

BACKCOURT	C+
BENCH/DEPTH	D+
FRONTCOURT	D+
INTANGIBLES	C

If the Wildcats can get some scoring from its newcomers, they have a chance to be competitive in the MEAC this year. But that's a big if. The Wildcats are having to rely on a lot of new players to try and improve on last year's 10-19 overall record and 5-13 MEAC mark.

We think they'll have a hard time getting to double digits in wins this year. The league is just too good for a team with this amount of inexperience to make a dent in the conference race. But we've said that before and Broadnax-coached teams have surprised the league in the past.

But not this year. Bethune-Cookman will play good

MID-EASTERN

BLUE RIBBON FORECAST
1. North Carolina A&T
2. South Carolina State
3. Hampton
4. Coppin State
5. Howard
6. Norfolk State
7. Delaware State
8. Bethune-Cookman
9. Maryland-Eastern Shore
10. Morgan State
11. Florida A&M

ALL-CONFERENCE TEAM
G-Terrence Winston, SR, Norfolk State
G- Ali Abdullah, SR, Howard
C-Cleveland Davis, JR, Hampton
F-Bruce Jenkins, JR, North Carolina A&T
F-Dexter Hall, SR, South Carolina State

PLAYER OF THE YEAR
Terrence Winston, SR, Norfolk State

NEWCOMER OF THE YEAR
Kyle Williams, JR, Howard

2001-2002 CONFERENCE TOURNAMENT
March 4-8, Richmond Coliseum, Richmond, VA

2000-2001 CHAMPIONS
Hampton and South Carolina State (Regular season)
Hampton (Conference tournament)

2000-2001 POSTSEASON PARTICIPANTS
Post-Season Record 1-1 (.500)
NCAA
Hampton (Second round)

TOP BACKCOURTS
1. Howard
2. South Carolina State
3. Delaware State

TOP FRONTCOURTS
1. South Carolina State
2. Hampton
3. Howard

INSIDE THE NUMBERS
2000-2001 Conference RPI: 27th (of 31)
Conference RPI (last five years): 29-28-28-31-27

DID YOU KNOW?
For the second time in the last five NCAA Tournaments, the MEAC provided a big upset when 15th-seeded Hampton shocked second-seeded Iowa State, 58-57. The sight of Pirate coach Steve Merfeld being carried around the court by one of his players after the upset will be shown for years to come. ... Hampton had a great year on the road last season, going 15-6. ... South Carolina State lost to Hampton in the 2001 MEAC Tournament title game, but that was Bulldogs' fifth straight appearance in the final. ... Two teams from the MEAC will play at ACC power North Carolina this year. Hampton will open the season in Chapel Hill, and in late December, North Carolina A&T coach Curtis Hunter will make a homecoming to Chapel Hill when the Aggies play the Tar Heels for the first time ever. Hunter played with current North Carolina coach Matt Doherty in the early '80s. ... There are two new coaches in the MEAC this year, and both have impressive backgrounds. Florida A&M hired Mike Gillespie, who did a great job at Tallahassee (Fla.) Junior College. Morgan State hired former NBA coach Butch Beard to head up its program. This is the second tour of MEAC duty for Beard, who was the head man at Howard in the early '90s and led the Bison to the NCAA Tournament in 1992. ... Delaware State's 11 league wins last year were a school record. The Hornets' third-place finish was the best league finish for the school in close to 20 years. ... Under veteran coach Frankie Allen, who was in his first season, Howard won 10 games last year, one more than the Bison program had won the previous three seasons.

(M.G.)

defense but just won't have enough to make a real impact in the conference. Look for an eighth- or ninth-place finish.

(M.G.)

 # Coppin State

LOCATION	Baltimore, MD
CONFERENCE	Mid-Eastern Athletic
LAST SEASON	13-15 (.464)
CONFERENCE RECORD	11-8 (5th)
STARTERS LOST/RETURNING	1/4
NICKNAME	Eagles
COLORS	Royal Blue & Gold
HOMECOURT	Coppin Center (1,720)
COACH	Ron "Fang" Mitchell (Edison State '84)
RECORD AT SCHOOL	269-172 (15 years)
CAREER RECORD	269-172 (15 years)
ASSISTANTS	Keith Johnson (Cheyney '83)
	Stephanie Ready (Coppin State '98)
TEAM WINS (last 5 years)	19-22-21-15-15
RPI (last 5 years)	127-107-181-200-207
2000-01 FINISH	Lost in conference quarterfinal.

Could the great Coppin State dynasty be in decline?

For years, the Eagles' program has been either the team to beat or one of the teams to beat in the MEAC. Fang Mitchell has built a program that had been the envy of everyone in the MEAC, at least this side of South Carolina State.

But it's now been five seasons since Coppin State

shocked America with its victory over South Carolina in the first round of the NCAA Tournament and then nearly upset Texas for an improbable Sweet 16 berth.

The Eagles have not gone to the NCAA Tournament since 1997 and last year, Fang's Gang became mediocre. Coppin State staggered to a 13-15 overall record and finished with a very average 11-8 league mark. How bad is that for the Eagles? It was the school's first losing record since 1988. Coppin State lost just 21 league games in the '90s.

But the MEAC is different now than it was in the 90s. New schools such as Hampton and Norfolk State have come into the league and made an immediate impact. And the rest of the league has begun to catch up with the Eagles.

On paper, things could be worse for Coppin State this year. The Eagles graduated their best player in guard Joe Brown. The first team all-conference player averaged 18.4 points last season on a squad that averaged just 64 points. The 6-7 guard who was a transfer from Hofstra scored 827 points during his two years with program.

"When a team that averaged 64 points loses a player like Joe Brown, who gave us 18 a night, that's a lot to lose," Mitchell said.

The veteran coach looks for improvement on offense to come from several sources.

"We'll count on some of the new players to provide some offense," Mitchell said. "I also expect our returning players to have better years than they did last season.

"Balance will play a key role in our success. It will probably be a situation where we're looking for points by committee, but consistency will be important."

Mitchell believes Coppin State has to improve in several other areas besides offense.

"Rebounding and shooting were just some of the problems we had," Mitchell said. "Our decision-making was not good last year and our big men have to play better. I'm hoping with a year of experience they've improved, especially on the boards.

"We also did not play at the intensity level we needed last year," Mitchell said. "That has to change for us to be successful."

Mitchell has four starters back, plus six newcomers who all could help immediately. The recruits are mostly perimeter players and should help the Eagles improve on offense.

"Most of the newcomers come from winning programs," Mitchell said. "We were looking to bring in players who could help in the areas where we had some weaknesses, and I think we were able to do that.

"I'll take a wait-and-see attitude as to how they'll do because most of them are inexperienced at this level. But we're content with this crew, and they certainly give us much better depth."

Heading the list of returnees is 6-2 senior point guard **Rasheem Sims** (11.9 ppg, 85 assists). Sims enjoyed a standout year last season and led the MEAC in free-throw percentage at (.860) and was second on the team in three-pointers made (38).

"Rasheem does it all," Mitchell said. "The fact that he plays 37 minutes a game last year tells you everything you need to know about him. He controls the offense, he's a good passer and he's worked to make himself one of the best shooters in the conference. He's also a good defender. He is extremely valuable to our team."

The Eagles would like Sims not to play 37 minutes per game this year and have brought in two newcomers to help back him up. **Alexy Ferreira**, a 6-3 sophomore, and 6-0 freshman **Robert Smith** will battle for playing time at the point this season and be ready to step in Sims' spot next year.

Ferreira was a non-qualifier last season. He played at Rice High School in New York City and averaged 16 points and seven rebounds per game as a senior two years ago.

Smith is from Northland High School in Columbus, Ohio. Last season, he averaged 10 points, six assists and two steals per game.

The big question for Coppin State this year is who will replace the scoring of Brown at the shooting guard spot. The Eagles have several options at both shooting guard and small forward. Ferreira could see time as a shooting guard.

One of the more interesting options that Mitchell has is 6-4 senior **Larry Tucker**. Tucker (11.9 ppg, 5.6 rpg) has played the small forward spot during his career. He was Coppin State's top rebounder last year and Mitchell believes he can make the transition.

"Larry can score inside and outside, and he definitely has the skills that will allow him to play more on the perimeter this season," Mitchell said. "Larry was one of the guys who came to play every night last season, and I expect a good year from him."

Michael Poster (8.3 ppg, 4.3 rpg), a 6-3 senior guard, could also make an impact at the shooting guard spot. His scoring has improved each season and he was Coppin State's fourth leading scorer last year despite being moved inside halfway through last season to try and bolster the Eagles' inside game. The ex-football player is known as a great athlete who plays great defense.

Two newcomers will be in the mix to play in the backcourt—**Jimmy Boykin**, a 6-7 sophomore transfer from Western Kentucky, and 6-5 junior college transfer Drew Cagle. Boykin averaged 2.0 points per game in a reserve role for the Hilltoppers his only year there. Cagle played at Mitchell College and helped lead the junior college to a Region 21 championship last season. He averaged 21 points and 10 rebounds per game last year and earned all-region, all-conference and All New England honors.

Coppin State will have its tallest team since Mitchell took over 16 years ago. Seven of the 13 players on this year's roster stand 6-7 or taller, which should help the Eagles' inside game. Returnees include 6-8 senior forward **Donnell Thomas**, 6-10 junior forward **DeMond Huff** and 6-11 center **Terek Wright**.

All three played a great deal last season and are expected to lead an improved Coppin State inside attack this year.

Thomas (4.4 ppg, 4.8 rpg) started the first seven games of the year before being replaced at the power forward spot. He still was a key player for the Eagles and capped the season with a 14-point and 11-rebound effort in the final game of the year against Norfolk State. Thomas finished the year as Coppin's third best rebounder but his stats need to improve this season for him to play more.

Huff (4.2 ppg, 5.3 rpg, 29 blocked shots) really came on last year and ended up being the Eagles' starting center at the end of the season. He didn't do much offensively, but his defense was very good—Huff's 1.4 blocked shots per game average was fourth best in the MEAC. Huff was also second on the team in rebounding. If he can improve on offense, then he could be the Eagles' answer at center and compete for all-league honors.

At 6-11, Wright (2.4 ppg, 2.2 rpg) is Coppin State's tallest player. He showed some signs last year of having some strong offensive skills but was sidelined throughout the season with a stress fracture.

Wright is a player who is still learning the game and has only been playing organized basketball for three years. The Eagles hope his development continues this year and he is able to give Coppin some offense and defense.

LeMar Ruffin (1.0 ppg, 0.7 rpg), a 6-8 sophomore, didn't play much last season and will provide depth at the power forward spot this year. He has an effective jump shot but needs to get stronger.

Two newcomers will add to the mix inside and could make a difference for the Eagles this season. First off will be 6-7 sophomore **Jean Pierre**, who is known as a rugged rebounder. He practiced with the team last year but could not play because he was a partial qualifier. Pierre came to Coppin State from El Camino High School in California. Two years ago, he averaged 17 points, 14 rebounds and four blocked shots and led his school to the state title game.

"Jean is athletic and runs the floor very well for a big man," Mitchell said. "He has the ability to score inside and is an aggressive rebounder. He will challenge for playing time."

Harry Colter, a 6-10 center, is expected to add depth in the pivot, but he can also play both forward spots. He is the first player from Texas to play for Coppin State. Colter averaged 10.5 points and two blocked shots per game at Lyndon B. Johnson High School in Austin.

2001-2002 SCHEDULE

Nov.	17-19	#Battle of Baltimore
	24	@Morgan State
	28	@George Mason
Dec.	1	Norfolk State
	3	Hampton
	8	@Cincinnati
	12	@Louisville
	20-22	##San Juan Shootout
	28-29	###Golden Bear Classic
Jan.	2	@Missouri
	5	@Delaware State
	7	@Howard
	14	Maryland-Eastern Shore
	19	@Bethune-Cookman
	21	@Florida A&M
	26	South Carolina State
	28	@North Carolina A&T
Feb.	2	@Norfolk State
	4	@Hampton
	9	Delaware State
	11	Howard
	18	@Maryland-Eastern Shore
	23	Florida A&M
	25	Bethune-Cookman
March	1	Morgan State
	4-9	####MEAC Tournament

@Road Games
#Reitz Arena, Baltimore, MD (vs. Towson, first round; also Loyola, UMBC)
##San Juan, Puerto Rico (vs. Florida International, first round; also Baylor, Jacksonville, Niagara, Oral Roberts, Puerto Rico-Mayaguez, Texas-Pan American)
###Berkeley, CA (vs. Penn State, first round; also California, Harvard)
####Richmond Coliseum, Richmond, VA

BLUE RIBBON ANALYSIS

BACKCOURT	B-
BENCH/DEPTH	C+
FRONTCOURT	C+
INTANGIBLES	C

The days of the Eagles totally dominating the MEAC are over. For the second straight year, the regular-season champ had at least four losses, indicating the balance in the league. Coppin State will still be a factor, but there's plenty of competition to go around. Mitchell knows that.

"The MEAC has gotten to the point that it is so balanced there are a lot of teams capable of contending," Mitchell said. "We'll be fighting to stay in the upper echelon."

If Coppin State can replace Brown and get a little help from its inside game, the Eagles could once again be fighting for the top of the MEAC. Though last season was not a typical Coppin State year, the Eagles still had plenty of impressive victories in league play.

There are plenty of solid players returning, and it appears most of the newcomers should be able to contribute.

Look for the Eagles to finish in second place and make a run at the league championship in the conference tournament. You get the feeling Mitchell didn't like taking a backseat to others in the conference last season.

That being said, this is a big season for the Eagles' program. South Carolina State and Hampton are the teams people are talking about in the MEAC these days. Coppin State needs to have a good season to remind everyone that this program is moving back in the right direction.

(M.G.)

Delaware State

LOCATION	**Dover, DE**
CONFERENCE	**Mid-Eastern Athletic**
LAST SEASON	**13-15 (.464)**
CONFERENCE RECORD	**11-7 (3rd)**
STARTERS LOST/RETURNING	**1/4**
NICKNAME	**Hornets**
COLORS	**Columbia Blue & Red**
HOMECOURT	**Memorial Hall (3,000)**
COACH	**Greg Jackson (St. Paul's '80)**
RECORD AT SCHOOL	**13-15 (1 year)**
CAREER RECORD	**179-92 (10 years)**
ASSISTANTS	**Jarrell Wilkerson (Norfolk State '75)**
	Keith Walker (Clemson '81)
	Arthur Tyson (NC Central '81)
TEAM WINS (last 5 years)	**7-9-7-6-13**
RPI (last 5 years)	**293-281-302-311-226**
2000-01 FINISH	**Lost in conference first round.**

One of the best stories in college basketball last year was the emergence of Delaware State under first-year coach Greg Jackson.

The Hornets, with their fifth coach in the last six years, stunned just about everybody in the MEAC with an 11-7 league record (13-15 overall). Delaware State finished in third place, its highest finish in the MEAC in close to 20 years. The 11 conference wins were a school record and the 13 victories overall were the most for the Hornets since the 1992-93 season.

Not bad for a club that was picked to finish in 10th place by just about everyone (including Blue Ribbon).

The Delaware State program was due for a good coach. The year before Jackson arrived was the worst season of all for DSC, as former coach Tony Sheals was suspended late in the season after an altercation with a player after another Hornets' loss. He was fired right after the season.

Jackson entered the chaos that was Delaware State after building a Division II power at North Carolina Central. He knew he was not inheriting a real positive situation.

"It was hard for the guys to believe in me first because for some of the guys, I was their fourth head coach," Jackson said. "That's a lot of different systems to try and absorb."

Jackson tried a simple approach.

"I told them there two things I wanted to emphasize and that was discipline and patience," Jackson said. "If you use those two principles in life you'll be successful and if you use them in basketball you'll be successful, as well."

Despite a great opening season, the program is nowhere near where Jackson wants it to be.

"The players and assistants worked extremely hard to accomplish what we did last season," Jackson said. "We still have a long way to go to reach the competitive level I believe is possible, but the program is certainly headed in the right direction."

And where does Jackson hope to take the program?

"My goal for this program is to be ranked in the Top 25," Jackson said. "We got a long ways to go before we do that, but that's where I want us to be in a few years."

Where the Hornets go this year will be interesting to see. Delaware State returns four starters and eight lettermen from last year's surprise team. The backcourt should be one of the best in the conference because it returns intact.

Leading the way will be 5-7 sophomore **Miles Davis** (6.1 ppg, 126 assists) and 6-2 senior guard **Marty Bailey** (9.8 ppg, 2.0 rpg, 59 three-pointers).Davis was the MEAC Rookie of the Year and did a great job running the Hornets' offense.

"Miles was simply outstanding last year," Jackson said. "He did a great job running our team and was the glue that kept us together the entire season. Miles was so good that teams stopped pressing us last year because of the way he handled pressure defense. I expect to be even better this season."

Bailey was the Hornets' second leading scorer last year and led the program in three-pointers made. His 59 treys were sixth most in the MEAC last year.

"Marty really did a great job for us last year," Jackson said.

"He had a good attitude and worked well in the backcourt with Miles."

Anthony Dulin (2.6 ppg, 1.5 rpg), a 6-2 junior guard, will provide depth in the backcourt. **Tyrone Johnson** (1.2 ppg, 1.1 rpg), a 6-1 sophomore guard, will back up Davis.

The shooting-guard spot will be backed up by 6-2 junior guard **James Bowen** (8.5 ppg, 2.0 rpg).

"James did a great job for us last season and he'll help us more this year," Jackson said.

At the small-forward spot is 6-4 senior **Carrington Hightower** (7.5 ppg, 2.5 rpg). Hightower finished second with 37 three-pointers made.

"Carrington worked very hard last year and turned out to be very coachable," Jackson said. "He really responded to what we wanted and expected."

Isaiah Nathaniel (2.5 ppg, 1.5 rpg), a 6-5 sophomore forward, was a reserve last year and played sparingly.

"As a freshman, Isaiah did a good job for the most part but at times was a little nervous," Jackson said. "He'll be better this year with a year under his belt."

One of the best players in the MEAC is 6-5 junior forward **Andre Matthews** (14.8 ppg, 4.9 rpg, 55 assists, 40 steals). Matthews, despite his size, was one of the best inside players in the league last year and shot 54 percent from the field (161-of-295).

"Andre Matthews was just outstanding for us last year," Jackson said. ."He's a great person and a hard worker who also provides with superb leadership. Andre should be poised to have another great season this year."

The Hornets struggled for much of the first part of the season and started the MEAC at 1-4. Things began to change when 6-6 senior **Sergey Stephanenkov** (6.1 pg, 4.5 rpg, 30 blocked shots) moved into the starting lineu. Delaware State went on to win 10 of its next 13 games.

"When we put Sergey into the starting lineup, things began to click for us both on offense and defense," Jackson said. "He's an inside player who can knock down a three-pointer and he did great things on defense. He also did a great job blocking shots."

Last year, Jackson said in these pages how he was going to build this program the right way. In the past, Delaware State went almost exclusively with junior college players. Jackson said while his program will take one every now and then, he will build primarily with freshmen. The Hornets did that last year with freshman like Davis.

This year, Jackson's program took two junior college players to help fill some needs inside, where the Hornets are weakest. **Dhamian Hill**, a 6-4 sophomore forward, comes to Delaware State from State Fair (Mo.) Community College, where he averaged 14.9 points per game. Also coming to DSU is 6-7 sophomore forward **Anton James** from Polk (Fla.) Community College. He averaged 13.2 points and 8.4 rebounds last season.

"Dhamian is one of the better athletes we have on this year's team," Jackson said. "He'll help us this season.

"Anton is a player that can play three different positions. And I think he's a guy that can really help us in the MEAC."

While most people in the MEAC were impressed with what Delaware State accomplished last season, there was some talk that the Hornets had snuck up on a lot of teams. Things will be different this year, now that they're somewhat expected to win.

"We might have snuck up on some teams last year but I'm not concerned about what other teams think of us," Jackson said. "We're in the process of building a program, and we still have some work to do.

"This year we just want to keep getting better and make more strides toward being the program we want to be."

2001-2002 SCHEDULE

Nov.	16	Hartford
	20	@Maine
	24	@Maryland
	26	@Old Dominion
Dec.	1	@South Carolina State
	3	@North Carolina A&T
	8	@Eastern Michigan
	19	@Fordham
	22	@Fairleigh Dickinson
	28	@Villanova
Jan.	2	@Towson
	5	Coppin State
	7	Morgan State
	12	Bethune-Cookman
	14	Florida A&M
	19	@Hampton
	21	@Norfolk State
	26	Maryland-Eastern Shore
Feb.	2	South Carolina State
	4	North Carolina A&T
	9	@Coppin State
	11	@Morgan State
	16	@Bethune-Cookman
	18	@Florida A&M
	23	Hampton
	25	Norfolk State
March	2	@Howard
	4-9	#MEAC Tournament

@Road Games
#Richmond Coliseum, Richmond, VA

BLUE RIBBON ANALYSIS

BACKCOURT	B
BENCH/DEPTH	C
FRONTCOURT	C-
INTANGIBLES	B+

Delaware State hard to figure out. No one would have come close to picking the Hornets to finish in third place last year. It will be hard for Delaware State to match what it did last year because the MEAC is just too good from top to bottom.

But there's no question that there's a new team to watch out for in the MEAC. Jackson showed last season that his teams would be well coached, play great defense and not take bad shots. The Hornets will not be fun to play for anybody this year, or as long as Jackson coaches them.

Look for the Hornets to finish in the middle of the pack this season. They shouldn't match last year's win total,

but something special may be brewing over the next few years. Jackson is a winner.

(M.G.)

Florida A&M

LOCATION	Tallahassee, FL
CONFERENCE	Mid-Eastern
LAST SEASON	6-22 (.214)
CONFERENCE RECORD	4-14 (10th)
STARTERS LOST/RETURNING	4/1
NICKNAME	Rattlers
COLORS	Orange & Green
HOMECOURT	Jake Gaither Gymnasium (3,365)
COACH	Mike Gillespie (DePaul '74)
RECORD AT SCHOOL	First year
CAREER RECORD	First year
ASSISTANTS	Shawn Forrest
	(Arkansas Pine-Bluff '98)
	Lamont Franklin (UNC Wilmington '97)
	Matt Chlebek (Florida State '01)
TEAM WINS (last 5 years)	8-13-12-9-6
RPI (last 5 years)	285-261-249-287-303
2000-01 FINISH	Lost in conference first round.

Mike Gillespie had always wanted to be a Division I basketball coach. He finally got the opportunity last spring, and luckily for him he only had to move about five minutes down the road.

Gillespie built one of the best junior college programs in the country at Tallahassee (Fla.) Community College. His program was constantly at or near the top of the JUCO rankings every year. Gillespie's teams supplied a lot of big-time programs with some big-time players.

And when Florida A&M officials let Mickey Clayton go at the end of a disastrous 6-22 season, they turned to Gillespie, who had to move his office only about five minutes down the road to the Florida A&M campus. Though it took the Rattlers' administration a long time to decide on Gillespie, the veteran coach couldn't be happier.

"There are only 320 Division I jobs in the country, and I'm lucky enough to have one of them," Gillespie said. "I think this is a program where we can win, but it will take time. We need to recruit and get some good players in here to try and turn this thing around."

Turning the Rattlers' program around won't be easy. Florida A&M hasn't had a winning season in nine years. Three years ago, the Rattlers had a miracle run in the MEAC Tournament, winning four games in four days to go to the NCAA Tournament. But even that team finished with an overall record of 10-19, and though Clayton got a nice Saturn commercial out of the deal, that team will be remembered as an aberration more than anything else.

The talent level isn't threadbare at Florida A&M, especially in the backcourt. The Rattlers have some good guards returning and Gillespie has plans to use them.

"We might use a lot of four-guard lineups this year to take advantage of the guards we do have," Gillespie said.

Leading the way for the Rattlers this year will be 6-0 sophomore point guard **Demarcus Wilkins** (13.0 ppg, 55 assists, 45 steals).

Wilkins was a bright spot in a dismal season for Florida A&M and earned MEAC all-rookie honors. Also back is 6-3 junior guard **Jason Miles** (12.4 ppg, 76 three-pointers). He was Florida A&M's second leading scorer and was one of the MEAC's top three-point shooters.

"We've got a nice backcourt," Gillespie said. "There's no question that our backcourt is the strength of our team and we're going to try and take advantage of that this year."

Nicholas Ross (9.4 ppg, 2.2 rpg), a 6-2 junior guard, is also back. He was the Rattlers' third-leading scorer a year ago.

Joining that trio will be a pair of talented newcomers. **Michael Griffith**, a 6-2 junior college transfer, and 6-2 freshman **Dominque Jackson** will compete for playing time in the backcourt. Griffith was a late signee from Lincoln Trail (Ill.) Junior College, while Jackson is a Sunshine State product via Glen Mills Prep School in Pennsylvania. He's originally from Immokalle, Fla.

"Michael is an explosive scorer and can score from anywhere on the floor," Gillespie said. "Dominique is a very talented player and he has a chance to make an impact for us this year. He's got a chance to be an all-league player for us pretty soon."

John Cuyler (4.0 ppg, 2.0 rpg), a 6-1 senior guard,

has been a reserve all his career and will provide depth again this season.

While the guard situation is in good shape, the frontcourt is a different story. The good news is the Rattlers have most of their frontcourt players back. The bad news is most of their frontcourt players are back.

"We're going to have really use our guards to our advantage this year," Gillespie said. "We're going to have to try and run some, do some pressing and hope we can get some easy baskets from our defense. I don't anticipate us getting too many baskets on offensive rebounds this year."

The top frontcourt player returning is 6-6 senior forward **Sonny Tudeme** (7.5 ppg, 5.0 rpg). He was Florida A&M's leading rebounder last season.

"Sonny will play either the three or the four for us this year," Gillespie said. "He's got some good quickness and at the four, his quickness could cause some real match-up problems for people. We need Sonny to provide some leadership for us and to have a good year."

Also returning is 6-6 senior forward **Clayton Jenkins** (4.2 ppg, 3.0 rpg). Jenkins showed a nice touch around the basket last year as he made 51 percent of his field-goal attempts.

The center spot should be a battle between three players, two returnees and one newcomer. The returnees are 6-10 junior **Jermaine Hill** (4.2 ppg, 2.9 rpg) and 6-9 junior **Abdelkhardre Cisse** (5.3 ppg, 3.4 rpg). Neither were world beaters last season. The only people Cisse really scared were public address announcers who had to try and pronounce his first name. Gillespie is leaning toward Hill as his starter this year.

"Jermaine has a chance to be a solid post player," Gillespie said. "He's worked hard in the preseason and has shown a lot of improvement from last year.

"Cisse has some work to do," Gillespie said about the Belgian native. "He's not as tough as he needs to be and he still wants to play on the perimeter too much, like a lot of European players. We need him to become more of a power player."

Brian Zamore, a 6-8 freshman, will look for playing time this season. Zamore was an early signee last year by Clayton and Gillespie admits that his best playing days are in the future He is a West Indies' native and played at Berkshire Prep Academy in Miami.

Because Florida A&M took its time hiring Gillespie, the Rattlers will pay the price this year. Gillespie really didn't have a chance to recruit, and Florida A&M's schedule is a disaster waiting to happen. The Rattlers open the season with 12 straight road games and won't play a home game until Jan. 5. The opening schedule includes road games at Georgia Tech, Mississippi State, Northwestern and Miami. Those games and others will help bring in more than $200,000 to the Florida A&M program, which should help the volleyball budget but won't do much for the won-loss record.

"The schedule is very tough and it will be tough not to play a home game for such a long while," Gillespie said. "But that's the way things went this year with me getting here so late."

2001-2002 SCHEDULE

Nov.	16	@Georgia Tech
	19	@Mississippi State
	24	@Bethune-Cookman
	26	@Wofford
	28	@Alabama State
Dec.	3	@Maryland-Eastern Shore
	8	@Central Florida
	15	@Northwestern
	18	@Miami
Jan.	5	North Carolina A&T
	7	South Carolina State
	12	@Howard
	14	@Delaware State
	19	Morgan State
	21	Coppin State
	26	Norfolk State
	28	@Hampton
Feb.	4	Maryland-Eastern Shore
	9	@North Carolina A&T
	11	@South Carolina State
	16	Howard
	18	Delaware State
	23	@Coppin State
	25	@Morgan State
March	2	Bethune-Cookman
	4-9	#MEAC Tournament

@Road Games
#Richmond Coliseum, Richmond, VA

BLUE RIBBON ANALYSIS

BACKCOURT	C+
BENCH/DEPTH	D+
FRONTCOURT	D+
INTANGIBLES	C

Though it took A&M too long to hire Gillespie, his hiring was an excellent choice to get this program moving. Gillespie puts its best when he says the only way to turn the Rattlers around is with good recruiting.

And the move is already paying dividends. Terrence Woods, an excellent three-point shooter who enjoyed some great moments at Tennessee before being kicked off the team this summer, will join the Rattlers' next year. The veteran coach has a lot of contacts from his junior college days, so look for the caliber of talent to improve over the next few years.

But this year will be a tough season for the Rattlers. The schedule early is brutal, which shouldn't help with confidence. And the MEAC should be very good this season, making it a tough year to be rebuilding.

But teams in the MEAC better enjoy beating up on Florida A&M this year. Gillespie will have things turned around here quickly.

This year, though, Florida A&M will have a hard time finishing out of the cellar. Look for the Rattlers to play hard but finish in last place. There are just too many good teams in the MEAC to expect otherwise.

(M.G.)

Hampton

LOCATION	**Hampton, VA**
CONFERENCE	**Mid-Eastern Athletic**
LAST SEASON	**25-6 (.806)**
CONFERENCE RECORD	**14-4 (t-1st)**
STARTERS LOST/RETURNING	**2/3**
NICKNAME	**Pirates**
COLORS	**Royal Blue & White**
HOMECOURT	**Hampton Convocation Center (7,200)**
COACH	**Steve Merfeld (Wisconsin-Lacrosse '84)**
RECORD AT SCHOOL	**64-50 (4 years)**
CAREER RECORD	**64-50 (4 years)**
ASSISTANTS	**Bobby Collins (Eastern Kentucky '89)**
	Ed Huckaby (Toledo '92)
	Bill Old (Randolph-Macon '94)
TEAM WINS (last 5 years)	**8-14-8-17-25**
RPI (last 5 years)	**291-210-283-201-119**
2000-01 FINISH	**Lost in NCAA second round.**

When Hampton made a decision to move up to Division I about eight years ago, many basketball experts questioned the move.

With all the D-I schools in the state of Virginia, how would Hampton even think about getting good players to compete on that level? Hampton was simply another smaller school thinking it could make it in Division I. Most observers thought the program would be better served staying at the D-II level, where it had enjoyed some success.

No one is questioning the upward mobility now. And it's probably a good bet that a lot of people in Ames, Iowa aren't questioning Hampton either.

Hampton gave every little guy in Division I a shot in the arm in last year's NCAA Tournament, when No. 15-seeded Pirates shocked No. 2-seeded Iowa State, 58-57, in the opening round of the NCAA Tournament. Hampton's fun ended in the next round to Georgetown, but the Hoyas had to play their best to hold the Pirates off, 76-57.

Not bad for a program that just became eligible to compete for an NCAA Tournament berth two years earlier.

And the win was no fluke. The Pirates finished with a 25-7 record, shared the MEAC regular-season crown with South Carolina State and then won three impressive games in the MEAC Tournament to win their first but probably not last conference tournament championship. Steve Merfeld's club was outstanding throughout the year, winning its first three games on the road and then pulling off the upset in the NCAA Tournament. The Pirates were an amazing 15-6 on the road last year.

So what do you do for an encore?

"Last year we had a wonderful group of talented kids who understood their roles," Merfeld said. "They made the necessary sacrifices you have to make to win a championship.

"Hopefully we know that last year is behind us. Things are totally different and we have to work hard again to approach what we did last season."

Graduation hit Hampton hard. Last year's MEAC Player of the Yea,r center Tarvis Williams, plus forward LeSean Howard and point guard Marseiles Brown, the heart and soul of the Pirates last year, are all gone.

But there's some talent back. Last year, the Pirates were a true team, and everyone knew their role. Some of those returning players will just have to step up their roles this season. Hampton returns two starters and seven other lettermen back from last year's championship team.

Leading the way back for the Pirates is 6-3 senior shooting guard **Tommy Adams** (10.2 ppg, 2.7 rpg). Adams was Hampton's third-leading scorer and took pressure off the Pirates' inside game with 68 three-pointers made. He led the team in steals with 50. This year will be his chance to shine.

"Tommy is a very consistent player and he's been with us for four years," Merfeld said. "He was an unsung hero for us, [a player] who did a lot of things for us to make the team better."

The big question for the Pirates this year is who will replace Brown and play the point. Hampton has several options. They include 6-0 junior **Jamaal James** (0.5 ppg, 0.5 rpg), 6-2 senior **Mackel Purvis** (1.5 ppg, 1.1 rpg) and 5-10 sophomore guard **Donald Didlake** (1.6 ppg, 0.8 rpg).

"Everyone will get a chance to contribute this year," Merfeld said. "There are no guarantees for any of them. It all depends on which one of them is willing to do what's best for the team.

"One of the keys for us last year was when Marseilles Brown dropped his scoring average from 16 points per game to 12 points per game. By doing that, he got other people involved on offense and made our team better."

C.J. Paul, a 6-1 freshman guard, is a walk-on from West Forsyth High School in Winston-Salem, N.C. and will add depth in the backcourt.

Issac Jefferson (5.4 ppg, 6.7 rpg), a 6-5 junior guard, returns and was another unsung hero for the Pirates last season. He led Hampton in rebounding.

"Issac was such an important player with our team last season," Merfeld said. "As a guard, he led us in rebounding and got some crucial offensive rebounds for us throughout the year. Issac is a player who will do all the little things you need to win."

Two newcomers could help here. They are 6-3 junior guard **Barry Hairston** and 6-4 freshman **Elzie Bibby**. Hairston went to Broome Community College in Supply, N.C.

"Both of them have a chance to help us, but they're going to have to step up their game," Merfeld said. "Barry is an explosive scorer, who can shoot the ball or score on a drive. Elzie is a tremendous shooter."

In the front court, 6-8 junior forward **Cleveland Davis** (8.2 ppg, 6.3 rpg) returns. Davis was another unheralded contributor for the Pirates. He backed up Tarvis Williams, and his play in the MEAC Tournament when Williams was in foul trouble was a big reason Hampton won the tournament championship. He also played well in the NCAA Tournament.

"Cleveland was our best player in March," Merfeld said. "His play had a tremendous impact for us in March and was a big reason we had success. We look for that play to continue this year."

Three other returnees who didn't play much will have an opportunity for playing time. They are 6-7 sophomore **David Johnson** (1.8 ppg, 1.3 rpg), 6-8 sophomore **Dwayne McNeal** (1.5 ppg, 1.4 rpg) and 6-8 sophomore **Maurice Pitts** (0.8 ppg, 0.9 rpg).

"All three of these guys will have a chance to help us," Merfeld said. "It just depends on who steps up and gets the job done. I think David Johnson will be a key factor for us. He sat out his first year and then came back last year and played a little bit. He's lost 30 pounds and really came back in good shape.

"Dwayne had some moments for us last year, and he fits into the game we play. Maurice has practiced with us for two years and not played much, but this year he could play some."

Devin Green, a 6-6 freshman, was an early signee by the Pirates last year. Merfeld is excited about his potential.

"Devin has the potential to be a very, very good player," Merfeld said. "We just don't know how quickly he'll develop. When he does, he has a chance to really help us but we just don't know when that will happen."

2001-2002 SCHEDULE

Nov.	16	@North Carolina

	19	Central Florida
	23-25	#Hawaii Pacific Tournament
Dec.	1	@Morgan State
	3	@Coppin State
	8	Norfolk State
	18	@Old Dominion
	21	@Bradley
	23	@Western Illinois
	29-30	##Montana State Tournament
Jan.	5	Maryland-Eastern Shore
	12	@South Carolina State
	14	@North Carolina A&T
	19	Delaware State
	21	Howard
	25	@Bethune-Cookman
	28	Florida A&M
Feb.	2	Morgan State
	4	Coppin State
	6	@William & Mary
	9	@Maryland-Eastern Shore
	16	South Carolina State
	18	North Carolina A&T
	23	@Delaware State
	25	@Howard
March	2	@Norfolk State
	4-9	###MEAC Tournament

@Road Games
#Honolulu, HI (vs. Vanderbilt, first round; also Akron, Hawaii-Pacific, Liberty, Monmouth, Notre Dame, Tennessee-Chattanooga)
##Bozeman, MT (vs. San Diego, first round; also Montana State, Troy State)
###Richmond Coliseum, Richmond, VA

BLUE RIBBON ANALYSIS

BACKCOURT	C+
BENCH/DEPTH	C+
FRONTCOURT	C+
INTANGIBLES	C+

This will be an interesting year for Hampton, a program that, the last two years, has relied a lot on transfers from other Division I schools. Give Merfeld and his staff a lot of credit for blending those transfers into a cohesive unit.

What Hampton accomplished last year will go down as one of the best seasons in the history of the MEAC. Not many teams anywhere, but especially in the MEAC, go 15-6 on the road.

The Pirates have a lot of question marks this season. Their dominant players have graduated and though there are nine lettermen back, all of them were role players a year ago. There's still some talent, though, and players like Jefferson and Davis will compete for all-conference honors this year.

Hampton will be one of the best teams in the conference this year, but it just won't be the best. Look for the Pirates to finish in third place and perhaps get to the final of the MEAC Tournament.

(M.G.)

Howard

LOCATION	Washington, DC
CONFERENCE	Mid-Eastern Athletic
LAST SEASON	10-18 (.357)
CONFERENCE RECORD	8-10 (8th)
STARTERS LOST/RETURNING	0/5
NICKNAME	Bison
COLORS	Blue, Red & White
HOMECOURT	Burr Gymnasium (2,700)
COACH	Frankie Allen (Roanoke College '71)
RECORD AT SCHOOL	10-18 (1 year)
CAREER RECORD	181-219 (14 years)
ASSISTANTS	Aki Collins (Clark '97)
	Kevin Baggett (St. Joseph's '89)
	Darryl Butler
TEAM WINS (last 5 years)	7-8-2-1-10
RPI (last 5 years)	291-292-315-317-274
2000-01 FINISH	Lost in conference play-in game.

At most places, a 10-18 record is not much to get too excited about. But at Howard, the Bison had one of the happiest 10-18 seasons of all time last year.

Howard surprised just about everybody in the MEAC with its 10-18 record. The program had been one of the worst in Division I before last year, winning just three games in the previous two years.

Two years ago, Howard went 1-27 and fired its coach in the middle of the year because of recruiting violations. The players didn't like the way things were handled and went to the student paper to complain.

Into the Bison mess came veteran coach Frankie Allen. Allen, who had successful teams at Virginia Tech and Tennessee State, came on board in the spring of 2000 and gave the school a calming presence.

Allen didn't have much to work with last year. He had most of the team back from that 1-27 squad, which wasn't really good news. Allen had to weed out some players who weren't working out, and at times last season, the Bison had just eight players on the roster. Not all of them were on scholarship.

But a funny thing happened to Howard on its way to another dismal season. The Bison started winning some games. Howard won two non-conference games over VMI and American and then became competitive in the MEAC. The Bison won eight league games.

It was a rewarding season for Allen, a year he thoroughly enjoyed.

"Last year was a lot of fun for me," Allen said. "We had an opportunity to experiment a little bit and the kids were just great. We had to weed out a few, but the ones that stuck with us did a great job and got the program going in a different direction."

That direction could be toward the top of the MEAC standings. No one is picking Howard to win the MEAC, but the buzz around the league is to watch out for the Bison this year. Howard returns all five of its starters, and Allen has brought in some players who could come in and help right away. There's a scary notion that if Allen won eight league games with the team he had last year, what happens when he gets some more players?

Allen is cautious about the upcoming year, but he is excited.

"We still have a lot of work to do to get the program where we want," Allen said. "Teams will be on the lookout for us this year, maybe more so than they were last season.

"But the big thing we have going for us this year is we have some depth. On paper, we've got two players to put at every position and that's already a lot better than we had last year."

The heart of the Bison team this year will be in its backcourt.

Senior 5-8 point guard **Ali Abdullah** (14.4 ppg, 141 assists) and 6-1 junior shooting guard **Ron Williamson** (19.2 ppg, 3.4 rpg) may be the best duo in the MEAC. Abdullah earned all-conference honors in 2000-2001. Williamson got off to a great start last year, including a monster game against Georgetown when he scored 45 points. But he was ineligible in the second half of the season and didn't play.

"Ali was in a tough situation at the start of last season because I was his fourth coach in three years," Allen said. "But he responded quite well with the way he learned our system and had a great season. We'll need to him to provide us with some senior leadership and just do what he did for us last year.

"We missed Ron in the second half of the season but we're glad he'll be back this year. He has a great stroke and can really shoot the three-pointer."

The backcourt will have some depth in **Heikima Jackson**, a 6-1 sophomore guard, (7.1 ppg, 2.5 rpg). Jackson was a super sub last year and gave the Bison some real offense. He tied for the team lead in three-pointers with 40 and shot a respectable 41 percent from beyond the arc.

Also providing depth will be 5-11 freshman **Gil Goodrich**, who comes to Howard via Newport Prep High School in Virginia.

The Bison used a lot of three-guard offense last season and that could be the case again this year. And the reason for that is 6-3 junior **Jonathan Stokes** (13.1 ppg, 4.5 rpg). Stokes enjoyed a breakout year last season as he knocked down 40 treys.

"Jonathan is an all-purpose player who just did a really good job for us last season," Allen said.

In the frontcourt, 6-5 senior forward **Darren Kennedy** (9.0 ppg, 6.4 rpg) played solidly last year, and without much help. He led the team in rebounding and was Howard's main weapon inside. But this year Kennedy will have some assistance.

Last year the Bison depended primarily on its perimeter game and just hoped its inside players would get a rebound occasionally and play some good defense. That will not be the case this year, thanks in large part to the University of Colorado. Allen brought in two transfers from Boulder and both should make an immediate impact for the Bison this year.

Kyle Williams, a 6-6 junior forward, and 6-8 senior **Aki Thomas** played some at Colorado and Allen is glad the duo have come east. They both averaged 5.6 points

per game two years ago.

"We expect big things both from Kyle and Aki this year," Allen said. "Kyle is a player who can play either guard spot or either forward spot. He'll add a lot to our program this year.

"Aki has a nice shooting touch and he should be a big help to our inside game this season."

Howard will have some depth inside, with some junior college transfer and some returnees. **Shawn Radford**, a 6-6 sophomore forward, comes to Washington, D.C., from Southeast Illinois Junior College. **Mario Grove**, a 6-7 junior, and 6-6 junior **Terry Brannon** both came to Howard from Connor State, Okla.

The returnees include 6-6 sophomore **Seye Aluko** (5.1 ppg, 3.3 rpg) and 6-8 sophomore **Ronald Miller** (3.6 ppg, 2.5 rpg). Both of them took turns playing at center last year and should battle for time in the pivot.

Joining in the mix is 6-10 freshman **Daniel Wright**, who comes from Upper Room Christian High School in Bayshore, N.Y.

2001-2002 SCHEDULE

Nov.	16	*Mercer
	21	@Virginia
	24	@St. Francis NY
	26	Cal State Northridge
	29	@Miami
Dec.	1	@North Carolina A&T
	3	@South Carolina State
	10	American
	15	St. Francis PA
	17	@Georgetown
	20	**Towson
	30	@Lafayette
Jan.	5	Morgan State
	7	Coppin State
	12	Florida A&M
	14	Bethune-Cookman
	19	@Norfolk State
	21	@Hampton
	28	@Maryland-Eastern Shore
Feb.	2	North Carolina A&T
	9	@Morgan State
	11	@Coppin State
	16	@Florida A&M
	18	@Bethune-Cookman
	23	Norfolk State
	25	Hampton
March	2	Delaware State
	4-9	#MEAC Tournament

@Road Games
*Atlanta Tipoff Classic, Morehouse College
**John Thompson Foundation Classic, MCI Center
#Richmond Coliseum, Richmond, VA

BLUE RIBBON ANALYSIS

BACKCOURT	B+
BENCH/DEPTH	C+
FRONTCOURT	C+
INTANGIBLES	B-

Watch out for the Bison in 2001-02. Howard could very well be the surprise team this year, and don't be surprised if it makes a real move to the top in the MEAC.

Howard has some ingredient to have enjoy some upward mobility. The Bison has an excellent backcourt, and if the transfers from Colorado are as good as expected, Allen's team will be very tough to beat this year.

One thing that could hurt Howard is the element of surprise is over. The Bison snuck up on a lot of teams last year and that will not be the case again. When coaches around the MEAC were asked about teams to watch out for, Howard was always mentioned.

Still, to go from one victory to a league championship in just two years would be asking for a lot. Howard may have its first winning season in nine years. Look for a fourth-place finish for the Bison this season and a team no one will want to play in the MEAC Tournament.

(M.G.)

Maryland Eastern Shore

LOCATION	Princess Anne, MD
CONFERENCE	Mid-Eastern Athletic

LAST SEASON	12-16 (.428)
CONFERENCE RECORD	10-8 (5th)
STARTERS LOST/RETURNING	2/3
NICKNAME	Hawks
COLORS	Maroon & Gray
HOMECOURT	Hytche Athletic Center (5,500)
COACH	Thomas Trotter (Wisconsin-Parkside '85)
RECORD AT SCHOOL	12-16 (1 year)
CAREER RECORD	12-16 (1 year)
ASSISTANTS	Paris Parham (Minnesota State '95)
	Steve Goldston (Buena Vista '99)
TEAM WINS (last 5 years)	11-9-10-12-12
RPI (last 5 years)	280-276-277-273-243
2000-01 FINISH	Lost in conference first round.

There were a lot of good coaching jobs turned in last season in the MEAC. The new coaches in the MEAC, Frankie Allen at Howard and Greg Jackson at Delaware State, did sensational jobs getting those programs moving in the right direction for the first time in a long time.

You can also add Maryland-Eastern Shore's Thomas Trotter to that list.

Trotter was hired in mid June after the Hawks' administration took its time recruiting a replacement for Lonnie Williams. It finally settled on Trotter, and it appears he was worth the wait.

Not much was expected from Maryland-Eastern Shore last season, no matter who was coaching. The Hawks had been stuck in mediocrity for the last few years and with Trotter hired so late, it seemed like it would be another mediocre year. Throw in a difficult non-conference schedule that had the Eagles playing seven of their first eight games on the road, and things looked bleak. Predictably, UMES started out 1-7, and it looked like a long year was on the way.

But the Eagles turned things around when the calendar turned to 2001. Trotter's club quickly won five games in a row and would finish the MEAC with a 10-8 league mark and in fifth place. No one predicted that for Maryland-Eastern Shore last year. Even Trotter was a little surprised at the Hawks' performance. The winning record in league play was the first for this program since the 1992-93 season.

"I went into last year just wanting to survive and maybe get to 10 wins," Trotter said. "We ended up with 12 wins and had a winning season in the conference."

Trotter points to several reasons why his team surprised teams last year.

"I was fortunate to sign some players last summer that were able to come into the program and help us right away," Trotter said. "We also shot the ball pretty well last year and hit some big shots in close games that got us wins. If those shots don't go in, things could have been a lot different the other way."

So can the Hawks take the next step and have a winning year this season?

"I think we have some exciting young talent that has some real potential," Trotter said. "I really think we're going in the right direction with the program, but we still have work to do to move to the top of the league."

One of the players Trotter signed last summer was a player he was very familiar with. He didn't have to go very far to find him. His son, **Thomas Trotter**, was the first player signed by the new coach. It turned out to be a very good move.

The 6-0 sophomore Trotter (14.2 ppg) was the Hawks' leading scorer last season. He also led the team in three-pointers made with 51. Trotter, Jr. earned MEAC all-rookie honors for his play and Trotter, Sr. was a proud papa.

"Obviously Thomas played with a lot of pressure on him last season," Trotter said. "He had to start at the point guard spot as a freshman and that's a lot of pressure right there, and then having to play for your dad isn't easy either. Thomas handled things pretty well."

Another late signee, 6-3 senior guard **Tim Smith**, also had an impact season. Smith (8.4 ppg, 5.0 rpg) added some toughness to the Hawks' backcourt.

"I'm glad we were able to get Tim so late and he was a big reason why we were able to turn things around," Trotter said.

The point-guard spot will be shared once again by 5-9 senior **Joshua Hickman** (8.4 ppg, 2.9 rpg, 86 assists, 42 three-pointers). Hickman led the team in assists and was third on the team in three-pointers.

"Joshua is a leader both on and off the floor and I expect him to do that again this year," Trotter said. "He's a great free-throw shooter and led us in charges taken."

Adding depth in the backcourt will be a newcomer who could compete for playing time.

Ka'Reem Horton, a 6-4 junior college transfer, comes to UMES from Roxbury (Mass.) Junior College, where he enjoyed a sensational career. He was a Division III NJCAA All-American who averaged 20.3 points per game last year. In two years at Roxbury, Horton scored more than 1,000 points and became the school's all-time leading scorer.

"A good friend of mine told me about Ka'Reem," Trotter said. "He has the ability to go one on one and create his own shot. We'll see how he adjusts to our system, but he could really help us this year if he can learn quickly."

Trotter is a native of Chicago and still has a lot of contacts in the Windy City. You can tell there's a Chicago to Princess Anne pipeline developing. There are already four players on this year's roster from the Chicago area. One of them is 6-6 senior forward **Andre Newson** (11.2 ppg, 6.2 rpg). All Newson did in his first year with the Hawks was become UMES's second-leading scorer and leading rebounder.

"We need Andre to do exactly what he did last year," Trotter said. "He moved to the four-spot and just did a great job there, rebounding and giving us some scoring."

Also back in the frontcourt is 6-5 senior forward **Kevin Darby** (10.9 ppg, 2.9 rpg). Darby will be a wing player who gave the Eagles some punch from the outside last season with 47 three-pointers.

"Kevin was a real leader last year and we need him to provide us some more leadership this season," Trotter said. "He's got good skills and can make an outside shot."

Ali Troutman (1.1 ppg, 1.4 rpg), a 6-6 junior, will add depth at the forward spot.

Trotter has brought in two freshmen from Chicago who could help inside. They are 6-7 **Justin Bowen** from Marshall High School and 6-8 **Brandon Allen** from Whitney Young High School.

"Both of them played at very good high schools in Chicago and faced some very tough competition," Trotter said. "They both have potential to help us, but it's a big jump from high school to Division I basketball. How long it will take them to adjust will determine how much they'll play."

The center spot could be handled by 6-8 senior **Mohammad N'Diaye** (1.9 ppg, 3.7 rpg). He didn't play much last year, and Trotter expects more from the only center listed on the roster.

"We do expect more from Mohammad this year," Trotter said. "He's worked hard to get stronger and should be a better player this year. We need him to score more and play good defense."

2001-2002 SCHEDULE

Nov.	13-14	#Guardian Classic
	18	@Duquesne
	24	@UMKC
	26	@Eastern Michigan
Dec.	1	Bethune-Cookman
	3	Florida A&M
	8	@Loyola-Chicago
	11	Towson
	13	@Minnesota
	23	@Iowa State
Jan.	5	@Hampton
	7	@Norfolk State
	12	@Morgan State
	14	@Coppin State
	19	South Carolina State
	21	North Carolina A&T
	26	@Delaware State
	28	Howard
Feb.	2	Bethune-Cookman
	4	Florida A&M
	9	Hampton
	11	Norfolk State
	13	@Hartford
	16	Morgan State
	18	Coppin State
	23	North Carolina A&T
	25	@South Carolina State
March	4-9	##MEAC Tournament

@Road Games
#Guardian Classic, Iowa City, IA (If the Fighting Hawks win, they will play either Boston University or New Orleans on Nov. 14; semifinals and final are Nov. 20-21 at Kemper Arena, Kansas City, MO)
##Richmond Coliseum, Richmond, VA

BLUE RIBBON ANALYSIS

BACKCOURT	B-
BENCH/DEPTH	C
FRONTCOURT	C-
INTANGIBLES	C

The Hawks surprised many last year with their 10-8 league mark. But they also won a lot of close games. UMES was 3-1 in overtime games and won four games by four points or less.

This will be a little tougher year for Trotter's club. The Hawks won't be sneaking up on teams, and while the backcourt is sound, the frontcourt has a lot of question marks. We think the ball will bounce a little differently for Maryland-Eastern Shore this year and it will be a tougher season.

Trotter is a good coach who has the program going the right way, but this will be a rebuilding season for the Hawks. The MEAC is simply too good for UMES to make too much noise this year. Look for an eighth or ninth-place finish.

(M.G.)

Morgan State

LOCATION	Baltimore, MD
CONFERENCE	Mid-Eastern Athletic
LAST SEASON	6-23 (.207)
CONFERENCE RECORD	4-15 (11th)
STARTERS LOST/RETURNING	2/3
NICKNAME	Bears
COLORS	Reflex Blue & Orange
HOMECOURT	Hill Field House (4,500)
COACH	Butch Beard (Louisville '69)
RECORD AT SCHOOL	First year
CAREER RECORD	41-66 (4 years)
ASSISTANTS	Lamont Pennick (Cumberland '89)
	Alfred Bears III (Howard '94)
TEAM WINS (last 5 years)	9-12-14-5-6
RPI (last 5 years)	268-216-217-313-306
2000-01 FINISH	Lost in conference second round.

Butch Beard has already rebuilt one MEAC program. Now he wants to rebuild another one.

In the early 1990s, Beard coached at Howard and took the Bison to the NCAA Tournament. The former NBA standout then went to the NBA, first as the head coach of the New Jersey Nets for two seasons (1994-95 and 1995-96).

In June, he decided to come back to the MEAC and Morgan State. Beard worked very hard to turn Howard around. He'll need to work even harder at Morgan State.

The Bears' program seemed to be making progress under the likeable Chris Fuller after the Morgan State program had gone on probation after the 1994-95 season. Fuller had the Bears knocking on the door as late as two years ago. But then came two straight disastrous seasons, including last year's 6-23, and Fuller was let go by the Morgan State administration.

Morgan State took its time looking for his replacement. Really took its time. Beard was finally hired in mid June. And though Beard's hiring took forever, the move was a good one for the Morgan State. The program got some national recognition for the hire and a lot of ink in the Baltimore area. That isn't easy to do for a program like Morgan State when it has to compete with the Baltimore Orioles, Baltimore Ravens, University of Maryland and several other Division I programs in the immediate area.

"It just seemed like the right situation for me," Beard said. "I think we can build something here, like we did at Howard. Now it's going to be quite a challenge, but it can be done here."

Beard knows his program is behind the rest of the MEAC.

"We've got our work cut out for us," Beard said. "Everyone else in the MEAC has improved their program through recruiting, and we didn't really have a chance to do that because we were hired so late. We did sign a couple of players in the summer, but we're behind."

The Bears do return three starters, including 6-0 sophomore guard **Cedrick Barrow** (5.0 ppg, 40 assists) and 6-3 sophomore guard **Randy Dukes** (7.1 ppg, 3.1 rpg). Both will be key players, but both will have to earn playing time under Beard.

"Cedrick will be vying for the point guard spot this year," Beard said. "He has a lot more skills running the game from his experience last season, but time will tell if he'll be our starter this year.

"I look for Randy to have a good year for us. He was a big-time recruit for us from what I understand two years ago but was a Prop 48. He had to sit out his first year and then played for the first time last season. Any time you sit out a year, there's a period of adjustment. I think because he has that year under his belt now, he'll be more effective this year."

Reggie Winkfield (6.6 ppg, 2.7 rpg), a 6-4 junior guard, struggled with his shooting last season as he knocked down just 31 percent of his field-goal attempts.

"I'm hoping Reggie regains his shot because we're going to need him to shoot the ball well for us," Beard said. "He's certainly capable of shooting the ball better than he did last year, and I think he will this season."

The Bears didn't have much time to recruit, but they did land two freshmen in the summer. The first is 6-0 point guard **Stan Grandy** from Valley Forge, Pa.

"Stan is a point guard who played against some great competition in high school and held his own," Beard said. "He also knows how to score, but we'll need him to play the point for us this season."

Cory McNeil (2.4 ppg, 1.3 rpg), a 6-1 senior, is a fifth-year player that Beard wants leadership from this year.

"Cory has been an up-and-down player in the past, and we'll need for him to be more consistent this season," Beard said. "I also expect a lot of leadership from him both on and off the floor. He's a fifth-year senior and he should be able to do that for us."

There may not be a lot of talent on hand, but the Bears do have one of the best forwards in 6-7 senior **Curtis King** (15.6 ppg, 4.6 rpg). King was a bright spot in a dismal season for Morgan State last year.

"Curtis is going to be the key player for us this season, there's little doubt about that," Beard said. "I'd like to see him have double-doubles every night out. He's going to be the guy we're looking for to help us this year. We expect a lot from him this season."

The inside game has two more returning players who both hope to have better years this season than last. **Douglas Sims**, a 6-8 junior forward, (5.6 ppg, 3.5 rpg) and 6-8 senior forward **Brandon Reece** (3.4 ppg, 2.6 rpg) are back and should play a lot this year.

"Douglas does a nice job with his back to the basket and is probably our best inside player," Beard said. "He's got a nice body to play inside and he can play big.

"Brandon has some good size, as well. We'll need him to play even bigger this year."

The other recruit the Bears brought in this summer was 6-6 forward **Steve Snipes** from Schenectady (Pa.) High School. Beard likes his potential.

"I'm really excited that we were able to get Steve," Beard said. "He's an excellent shooter and may have a chance to help us this year."

There could be some additions to the roster in September or October.

"We don't have much depth with our inside game and we don't have much height either," Beard said. "We'll hold some walk-on tryouts and maybe we can some players from there to help us with depth."

2001-2002 SCHEDULE

Nov.	10	Bowie State
	16	@Pittsburgh
	24	Coppin State
	27	@Western Michigan
Dec.	1	Hampton
	3	Norfolk State
	8	@Towson
	10	@Georgetown
	18	@Arkansas-Little Rock
	22	@James Madison
	27-28	#Minnesota Winter Jam
Jan.	5	@Howard
	7	@Delaware State
	9	Canisius
	12	Maryland-Eastern Shore
	19	@Florida A&M
	21	@Bethune-Cookman
	26	North Carolina A&T
	28	South Carolina State
Feb.	2	@Hampton
	4	@Norfolk State
	9	Howard
	11	Delaware State
	16	@Maryland-Eastern Shore
	23	Bethune-Cookman
	25	Florida A&M
March	1	@Coppin State
	4-9	#MEAC Tournament

@Road Games
#Minneapolis, MN (also Alcorn State, Norfolk State, Texas Southern)
##Richmond Coliseum, Richmond, VA

BLUE RIBBON ANALYSIS

BACKCOURT	C
BENCH/DEPTH	C-
FRONTCOURT	D+
INTANGIBLES	C

Beard will probably wish he was back in the NBA about halfway through the year after trying to coach this team. There's a little talent here—behind King, there's not much else. Morgan State took its time in hiring Beard, and that will really haunt the Bears this year. When your coach is talking about adding depth through walk-on tryouts, that is not a good sign.

And though Beard coached at Howard, that was seven years ago and there will be a period of adjustment for him as well. The MEAC is a much different league than it was when he coached there in the early '90s.

It all adds up to a long year for Morgan State. Beard is a good choice for this job because just his name alone will open doors to recruits that a lot of schools the size of Morgan State wouldn't. But that really won't help this season.

Look for a 10th-place finish for the Bears and a fight with Florida A&M to stay out of the cellar.

(M.G.)

Norfolk State

LOCATION	Norfolk, VA
CONFERENCE	Mid-Eastern Athletic
LAST SEASON	12-17 (.414)
CONFERENCE RECORD	11-7 (4th)
STARTERS LOST/RETURNING	4/1
NICKNAME	Spartans
COLORS	Green & Gold
HOMECOURT	Echols Hall (5,000)
COACH	Wil Jones (American '64)
RECORD AT SCHOOL	24-33 (2 years)
CAREER RECORD	256-178 (22 years)
ASSISTANTS	Fred Burroughs (Air Force CC)
	Jim Hammond (Otterbein '73)
TEAM WINS (last 5 years)	17-6-13-12-12
RPI (last 5 years)	NA-268-222-278-206
2000-01 FINISH	Lost in conference semifinal.

Earlier in this section, you read about the amazing season Hampton had last year. And you read about the great postseason the Pirates had with their stunning upset of Iowa State in the first round of the NCAA Tournament and a respectable showing against Georgetown in the second round.

The Pirates dominated most of the MEAC last season, with the notable exception of the Wil Jones' Norfolk State Spartans. Norfolk beat Hampton twice last year, including an overtime thriller in the last regular-season game of the year to deny the Pirates the regular-season title.

The teams met in the semifinals of the conference tournament, but this time Hampton got the win, 94-67. The Pirates then cruised to the tournament title the next day over South Carolina State and made their mark in the NCAA Tournament. But getting by Norfolk State was a big step for Hampton to make.

It's a loss that Jones still remembers.

"We just hit the wall midway though the first half," Jones said. "We had to play at night the day before and come right back and play the next afternoon. I'm not making any excuses though, they beat us and did a good job in the NCAA Tournament."

Believe Jones when he says he's not making any excuses. He may be the most blunt coach in America and says what's on his mind. He showed that in these pages two years ago when he just got hired and he declared that his program would be among the best.

"I ain't here to compete; I'm here to dominate," Jones said two years ago. "I just need to get my players in here, and when we do we're going to look to dominate the league."

The Spartans didn't dominate the MEAC last year but they were pretty good. Norfolk State finished with an overall record of 12-17 but was a more than respectable 11-7 in the conference. There were the two wins over Hampton, two wins over Coppin State and a win over South Carolina State. The Spartans then took care of Coppin in a MEAC Tournament quarterfinal before falling the next day to Hampton.

"We're definitely on the right track," Jones said. "Last

year, we put ourselves in position to have a chance at the title. I'm starting to get mostly my players in the program and that's what you want to have.

"And what I like about this year is we got a lot of competition for playing time. And baby I love competition. You want to play, you've got to earn your playing time. When you have that kind of competition, then you got a chance to be really good because everybody can't help but get better with competition."

The Spartans graduated four starters from last season but the starter back is one of the best players in the MEAC. Just ask Jones.

"**Terrence Winston** is one of the best players in the conference and he's ready to have a great year," Jones said. "Teams in the MEAC are recruiting players specifically to try and stop him."

Winston (14.6 ppg 2.5 rpg, 102 assists), a 6-0 senior, led Norfolk State in scoring and assists last season, but despite those fine stats, he didn't earn first- or second team all-conference honors. And Jones still isn't pleased about that.

"It was unbelievable that Terrence didn't earn all-conference, simply unbelievable and wrong," Jones said. "But that's just going to motivate him more for this season."

Joining the talented Winston in the backcourt will be 6-4 sophomore **Derrick Smith** (11.0 ppg, .6 rpg). Smith was the Spartans' second leading scorer last year and also knocked down 39 treys.

"Derrick is a great shooter," Jones said. "He's still coming and is only going to get better this year."

Slated to back up Winston this year is 6-0 sophomore **Nicholas Byrd** (0.4 ppg, 9 assists). He didn't play much last year but should see more time in 2001-2002 because he's a good defender.

The Spartans believe they've also signed some players who can really help here. They include 6-4 junior guard **Daryl Towe** and a pair of brothers—6-2 freshman **Joemi Byrd** and 6-4 freshman **Hirami Byrd**. And Jones believes all three are going to be good players, maybe even great players.

Towe played at Alleghany Junior College and averaged 17 points per game last season.

"Daryl has the experience to really complement Terrence in the backcourt," Jones saidd. "He knows how to score, but to play he's going to face some great competition in our backcourt. But he had a great summer and we're glad he's with us."

Both Byrds played at Hopewell High School in Hopewell, Va., and had great careers there. Jones expects the duo to have great careers for him, as well.

"Hirami can really shoot the ball," Jones said. "He was a first-team all-state player and averaged close to 23 points per game. He's got such a nice stroke and I'm anxious to see him out there.

"And I'm really high on Joemi. I think we got a sleeper with this guy and I think some bigger schools really missed out on him. He was just awesome in the Virginia All-Star game, where he scored 30 points and didn't miss a shot. I've been watching this game a long time, and I've never seen anybody do that."

One of the forward spots could be handled by 6-7 junior **Michael Boyd** (5.8 ppg, 5.2 rpg). Boyd started in three games last season and was the Spartans' second leading rebounder.

"Mike is a tremendous rebounder and he just knows how to go get the ball," Jones said. "He just needs to grow up a little bit and he'll be a good player for us."

Jamal Mills (4.4 ppg, 3.1 rpg), a 6-9 senior forward, started on about half the season a year ago at the power-forward spot.

"Jamal's matured some and he's got a chance to help us even more than he did last season," Jones said.

Gregory Quick (2.4 ppg, 1.7 rpg), a 6-8 junior forward, played sparingly last season but could play more this year.

"Greg's got the ability to be super because he's so quick," Jones said. "He just needs to working to get better."

The center spot could be handled by 6-9 sophomore **Edward Seward** (2.4 ppg, 2.7 rpg).

"Let me tell you now, Edward is coming on like wildfire," Jones said. "He showed some flashes last year and gave Tarvis Williams [the MEAC Player of the Year last season at Hampton] some trouble in the conference tournament. Look for him to really step up this year."

The Spartans may be the tallest team in the MEAC this year with the centers they have brought into the program. Two junior college transfers—6-10 **Thomas Aladi** and 7-1 **C.J. Young**—could make Norfolk State tough to defend in the pivot.

Aladi is originally from Nigeria but played at Three Rivers (Mo.) Community College. And Jones really believes he's got a good player in Aladi.

"Thomas reminds of a 6-10 Charles Oakley," Jones said. "He's a Nigerian Warrior who comes to play every night. He's a little raw yet but baby he wants to get better and better. Thomas is just perfect for us."

Young is a native of Olympia, Wash., and played at Midland (Texas) Community College.

"C.J. has great hands and has a great touch from the free throw line," Jones said. "He's a big man who's getting better and better. I just fell in love with him when I saw him."

Jones believes his team can be pretty good this year. But attitudes could determine a lot.

"If the kids have good attitudes, we've got a chance to win a lot of games this year," Jones said. "I like the way this team in lining up. We've got two players who are 6-0, but everybody else is 6-4 and above. I believe you can have a lot of success with a roster like that in the MEAC."

Jones issues a bit of a warning to the MEAC that this won't be his best team, not yet.

"I'm getting there with this program but I think I'm a year away from having all the pieces in place to be really, really good," Jones said. "But let me tell you this, I got of lot of pieces in place this year."

2001-2002 SCHEDULE

Nov.	16-18	#Nike Tip-Off Tournament
	21	@San Diego State
	24	@Tulane
	26	@New Orleans
Dec.	1	@Coppin State
	3	@Morgan State
	8	@Hampton
	11	Maine
	20	@UNC Greensboro
	27-28	##Minnesota Winter Jam Classic
Jan.	3	@Maryland
	7	Maryland-Eastern Shore
	12	@North Carolina A&T
	14	@South Carolina State
	19	Howard
	21	Delaware State
	26	@Florida A&M
	28	Bethune-Cookman
Feb.	2	Coppin State
	4	Morgan State
	11	@Maryland-Eastern Shore
	16	North Carolina A&T
	18	South Carolina State
	23	@Howard
	25	@Delaware State
March	2	Hampton
	4-9	MEAC Tournament

@Road Games
#Honolulu, HI (vs. Hawaii, first round; Also Drake and Sam Houston State)
##Minneapolis, MN (also Alcorn State, Morgan State, Texas Southern)
###Richmond Coliseum, Richmond, VA

BLUE RIBBON ANALYSIS

BACKCOURT	B+
BENCH/DEPTH	C+
FRONTCOURT	C
INTANGIBLES	B-

Jones has plenty to say about his program, but in the two years he has been at Norfolk State, the Spartans have been very competitive in the MEAC. Last year, if the Spartans could have beaten Delaware State and Howard, they might have been the top-seeded team in the league's postseason tournament.

Coppin State may not be the program it once was but Norfolk beat the Eagles three times last year. Not many MEAC teams can accomplish that.

It's hard to pick against the Spartans after talking to Jones, but there's a lot to work to be done here. The backcourt looks in good shape with Winston, a first-team preseason All-MEAC pick by Blue Ribbon.

But the frontcourt has a lot of question marks. Players who didn't play much last year and newcomers are going to have to play right away. It will take time for these guys to jell.

The Spartans will be plenty competitive this year in the MEAC. We look for them to finish in fifth place, but if some of those new frontcourt players start producing, Norfolk State could be a year ahead of Jones' timetable.

(M.G.)

North Carolina A&T

LOCATION	Greensboro, NC
CONFERENCE	Mid-Eastern Athletic
LAST SEASON	13-17 (.433)
CONFERENCE RECORD	8-10 (t-3rd)
STARTERS LOST/RETURNING	2/3
NICKNAME	Aggies
COLORS	Blue & Gold
HOMECOURT	Corbett Sports Center (6,700)
COACH	Curtis Hunter (North Carolina '87)
RECORD AT SCHOOL	27-32 (2 years)
CAREER RECORD	27-32 (2 years)
ASSISTANTS	Bill Sutton (North Carolina '57)
	Adam Chaskin (Michigan '92)
	Tarrell Robinson (North Carolina A&T '01)
TEAM WINS (last 5 years)	15-8-9-14-13
RPI (last 5 years)	230-279-238-260-247
2000-01 FINISH	Lost in conference semifinal.

All Curtis Hunter wants is a healthy season.

North Carolina A&T has been hard to figure out over the last few years. The Aggies have had some great wins, but also some strange losses. And though A&T is a dangerous team in the MEAC, it has simply not been a consistent one.

Last year was another one of those years. The Aggies finished with a 13-17 overall record and had a disappointing 8-10 league mark, good for a seventh-place finish. However, at the end of the season, North Carolina A&T played its best basketball, winning two games in the MEAC Tournament and just missing a trip to the league championship game when it lost to South Carolina State, 57-53, in a semifinal.

But a big reason for the Aggies' inconsistencies last year was injuries.

"We really did pretty well when you consider all the injuries we had last year," Hunter said. "Our two top players were hurt all year, so we had to go with a lot of different lineups."

That's why Hunter is really looking for a year without injuries.

"We've got a chance to have a real good year barring injuries," Hunter said. "We've got a good team back and if we can just stay healthy, I think we've got a chance to be pretty good."

Leading the way for the Aggies in the backcourt is 6-2 senior point guard **Marque Carrington**, who missed most of last year with a herniated disk. Two years ago, Carrington averaged 8.5 points per game and led the team in assists with 84.

"We're glad Marque is back this year because we really missed him last season," Hunter said. "He's a good point guard and a strong defensive player."

One of the big questions for the Aggies this year is who will join Carrington in the backcourt. A&T has to replace leading scorer J.J. Miller (16.1 ppg) who enjoyed a great career and was a real outside threat.

Anthony Debro (11.1 ppg, 4.9 rpg), a 6-5 senior guard, is the leading candidate to step in for Miller. The fifth-year senior is an explosive offensive player who Hunter thinks will have a good season.

"Anthony is a consistent shooter who can give us points in a hurry," Hunter said.

The backcourt should be bolstered by 5-10 freshman guard **Tyrone Green**, who had a great high school career at Creedmor Christian Faith Academy in Washington, N.C.

"Tyrone has a chance to be a special player," Hunter said. "He reminds me a lot of J.J. Miller and he's better than J.J. at this point in his career. Now we'll see how much he improves as his career goes on, but we're really excited about getting him. He has a chance to be a great player for us."

Another newcomer should add to the mix in the backcourt and could make the Aggies very big here. **Victor Carter**, a 6-7 freshman, is an older freshman who played at Marine Military Academy. He hasn't played in two years, but Hunter thinks he can help the Aggies pretty quickly.

"Victor is a big-time player that we're really thrilled to get into our program," Hunter said. "He's got to get the rust out of his game because he hasn't played in two years. But once he gets that rust off, he could be special for us. He can score in a lot of different ways and he makes us very big in the backcourt."

A returnee who could help in the backcourt is 6-2 sophomore guard **Landon Beckwith** (3.0 ppg, 0.8 rpg).

"Landon is a real threat to shoot the ball," Hunter said.

"He'll give us another outside threat this year."

Steven Koger, a 6-3 freshman guard, was a teammate of Green's at Creedmor Christian Faith Academy. Hunter looks for him to be a player who can play either the shooting-guard spot or small forward.

"Steven has a lot of athletic ability and is a strong penetrator," Hunter said. "We'll see how much he learns but he's got a chance to be a factor for us this year."

Providing depth in the backcourt will be 6-3 freshman guard **Reehood Carter**, and 5-9 walk-on guard **Cornelius Toliver** (1.5 ppg).

The small-forward spot should be handled by one of the top players in the MEAC in 6-6 junior forward **Bruce Jenkins** (14.0 ppg, 9.9 rpg), who enjoyed an outstanding year last season and earned second team all-conference honors. He's also a preseason Black College second-team selection. He was the Aggies' second leading scorer a year ago and led the club in rebounding.

"Bruce should be one of the best players in the league this year," Hunter said. "He had a great year for us last season and I hope he has similar production for us this season."

Hunter is also high on 6-6 freshman forward **Adam Hefner** from North Iredell High School in Statesville, N.C.

"Adam is another freshman who has a chance to be special," Hunter said. "He's a player who is fundamentally sound and knows how to play defense. We think he's a dynamite player who can give us some minutes this year."

Chris Ferguson, a 6-7 sophomore forward, is a transfer from Campbell who will be eligible in December. Hunter wants Ferguson to help the Aggies on the boards this year.

The center spot will have four different players competing for playing time, including 6-8 junior center **Jafar Taalib** (7.9 ppg, 4.8 rpg).

"Jafar shoots the three very well and is a good [all-around] shooter," Hunter said

Hunter expects 6-8 junior center **Travis Totten**, who played in only one game last season, to be a factor for the Aggies. Two seasons ago, Totten averaged 2.2 points and 1.4 rebounds in limited playing time.

"Travis has potential skills to do some big things for us," Hunter said.

Abraham Traore (0.8 ppg, 1.0 rpg), a 6-10 sophomore center, is just in his third year of playing organized basketball.

"Abraham had a wake-up call last year and learned a lot about basketball," Hunter said. "I hope this season is a coming-out party for him because he has all the potential in the world."

David Morris, a 6-8 freshman center, is a native of Jos, Nigeria who will provide some depth this year.

"David rebounds well and knows how to block shots," Hunter said. "We'll just have to see how much he learns this year."

The Aggies will play another tough schedule this year that will be highlighted by a two-game stretch in December that will see North Carolina A&T play defending national champion Duke and a homecoming game for Hunter at North Carolina. Hunter played with current North Carolina coach Matt Doherty in the early 80's.

"I'm excited about playing at North Carolina and making my first trip back to the Smith Center," Hunter said. "I'm honored that they've agreed to play us and I'm looking forward to having our guys playing at North Carolina."

Hunter doesn't mince words when he thinks how the Aggies should do this year.

"We have the talent, and we have enough depth to have a great season," Hunter said. "If the guys can get together as a unit and get production from everybody, then we have a chance to be pretty good.

"How good we'll be will depend on how far our senior class takes us. We need our seniors to produce great leadership and show the way for us this year. Some of our seniors have been with us for five years. It's their time to shine and get the job done."

2001-2002 SCHEDULE

Nov.	16	@Elon
	18	@Creighton
	20	@Nebraska
	29	@VCU
Dec.	1	Howard
	3	Delaware State
	7	American
	16	@Duke
	27	@North Carolina
Jan.	5	@Florida A&M
	7	@Bethune-Cookman
	12	Norfolk State

	14	Hampton
	16	@UNC Greensboro
	20	*North Carolina Central
	21	@Maryland-Eastern Shore
	26	@Morgan State
	28	Coppin State
	30	South Carolina State
Feb.	2	@Howard
	4	@Delaware State
	9	Florida A&M
	11	Bethune-Cookman
	16	@Norfolk State
	18	@Hampton
	23	Maryland-Eastern Shore
March	2	@South Carolina State
	4-9	#MEAC Tournament

@Road Games
*Charlotte Coliseum, Charlotte, NC
#Richmond Coliseum, Richmond, VA

BLUE RIBBON ANALYSIS

BACKCOURT	B-
BENCH/DEPTH	A-
FRONTCOURT	B-
INTANGIBLES	B+

The Aggies are Blue Ribbon's pick to win the MEAC this year. There will be plenty of competition in the wild, wacky world of the MEAC, but it just seems like it's North Carolina A&T's time to win the league title again.

The Aggies won it all the time in the '80s and then slipped back in the '90s, only to win it coming out of nowhere in 1994 and '95.

Hunter did a nice job last year keeping his team focused despite all the injuries, and he had his club playing its best ball at the end of the season when A&T nearly sneaked into the title game against Hampton.

The Aggies don't have one superstar, but they have a lot of depth and if Carrington and Jenkins stay healthy, they will be the team to beat in March.

(M.G.)

South Carolina State

LOCATION	Orangeburg, SC
CONFERENCE	Mid-Eastern Athletic
LAST SEASON	19-14 (.576)
CONFERENCE RECORD	7-7 (t-1st)
STARTERS LOST/RETURNING	2/3
NICKNAME	Bulldogs
COLORS	Garnett & Blue
HOMECOURT	Smith-Hammond Center (3,200)
COACH	Cy Alexander (Catawba '75)
RECORD AT SCHOOL	242-175 (14 years)
CAREER RECORD	242-175 (14 years)
ASSISTANTS	Francis Simmons (Voorhees '71)
	Jamal Brown (South Carolina State '97)
	Tim Gates (Allen '71)
TEAM WINS (last 5 years)	14-22-20-20-19
RPI (last 5 years)	209-103-183-204-153
2000-01 FINISH	Lost in conference finals.

It was business as usual for South Carolina State last year.

Cy Alexander's team marched to a 19-14 overall record, shared the MEAC regular-season championship with Hampton and advanced to the league championship game for the fifth straight year. It's been 1997 since South Carolina State failed to make the finals. The Bulldogs are as much a part of championship week on ESPN as Dick Vitale and Digger Phelps.

Last year might have been one of Alexander's best coaching jobs since coming to Orangeburg, S.C. The Bulldogs had 10 new players on the roster, had to replace five starters from the previous season and then got struck with some tough injuries midway through the year. They were injuries that didn't sideline players but caused them to play in a lot of pain.

Through it all, the Bulldogs hung tough, battled and somehow got to the MEAC championship game again before falling to a great Hampton team in the final.

Though South Carolina State didn't win the title again, it continued another amazing streak for the Bulldog program. S.C. State has either finished first or second in the MEAC during the regular season the last nine years. In Alexander's 14 years at S.C. State, the Bulldogs have never finished lower than fourth. They've

gone to five NCAA Tournaments and will certainly be a threat to do it again this year.

"We achieved a lot last year," Alexander said. "When you consider we had so many new faces plus some injuries down the stretch, I was really pleased with how last year went. We got as much as we could out of last year's team and that should make us even better this season."

What's scary for the MEAC is that a lot of those new players from last season will be coming back this year. Those injured players are all healthy now and the Bulldogs should be pointing toward another league championship.

Heading the list of returnees is 6-3 senior point guard **LaRon Mapp** (10.4 ppg, 2.4 rpg). Mapp is one of the MEAC's best and was one of the Bulldogs who struggled with injuries late last season.

"LaRon has got to be the leader of this year's team, and I'm confident he'll be able to do that this year," Alexander said. "Last year, he lost his ability to make an outside shot but he's come back in great shape and should be ready to have a great year."

Andre Riviere (8.9 ppg, 2.5 rpg), a 6-3 senior guard, had some success last season, but Alexander would like to see more consistency from him this year.

"Andre is a tough kid from New York City and is a great scorer but he's got to learn to be a little more structured," Alexander said. "We need him to be a true field general this season."

One of the most versatile players in the conference is 6-6 senior guard/forward **Greg Grey** (12.8 ppg, 5.4 rpg). Grey can play both guard spots and either forward position. He played in a lot of pain the last part of the season with a dislocated tendon in his foot.

"Greg was a warrior last year because of the pain he played in the last part of the season," Alexander said. "He's so versatile and can play four different positions. We'll use him at all four spots throughout the year and that versatility makes us a much better team."

Providing depth in the backcourt will be 6-1 junior **Najia Taylor** (4.1 ppg, 1.5 rpg).

"Najia's a two-guard in a point-guard's body," Alexander said. "He can really shoot the ball, and we will bring him off the bench to knock down shots against zones."

Alexander has brought in some newcomers who could make this the top backcourt in the MEAC this season. **Demeco Haith**, a 6-2 freshman, comes to Orangeburg form Kinston (N.C.) High School.

"Demeco is the point guard of the future and we plan to bring him along slowly," Alexander said. "He's a big-time competitor who played for a great high school program in Kinston."

The other new player in the backcourt for the Bulldogs has a pretty familiar name to basketball fans everywhere. Six-foot-four junior guard **Moses Malone, Jr.** comes to South Carolina State after playing two years at Texas Tech.

"Moses comes from a pretty good bloodline of basketball players, " said Alexander, referring to Malone's father Moses Malone, who was the NBA's MVP in 1983 and one of the greatest rebounders in the history of the game.

"We look for Moses to be a two-guard for us and provide us with some high-quality offensive minutes this year," Alexander said. "We think he can play a major role for us this season."

Will Jones, a 6-3 walk-on junior guard, could be a surprise, as well. Jones transfers to S.C. State from nearby Division II school Erskine.

"Will will be a great addition because he can shoot the ball so well," Alexander said. "He's a tremendous shooter and he'll play when teams try to play zones against us."

The frontcourt will be led by two seniors in 6-9 forward **Louis Radford** (6.2 ppg, 3.5 rpg) and 6-8 forward **Dexter Hall** (7.5 ppg, 8.3 rpg).

"Louis is our best defensive player and worked very hard to improve his game," Alexander said. "He's another player who is very versatile and can play both the backcourt and the front court. We'll probably start him as a small forward this year and with his height that could give us some real advantages."

The fact that Hall is back is a pleasant surprise for the Bulldogs and not-so-pleasant surprise for the MEAC. Hall was a Prop 48 his freshman year, but because he graduated over the summer, he was awarded an extra year of eligibility. Hall is also healthy after suffering a broken wrist midway through last season. He still played and was a key reason the Bulldogs went to another MEAC championship game as he led the squad in rebounding.

"Getting Dexter back is a big plus for us," Alexander

said. "He's got a chance to be an all-conference player this season."

Xerxes Sabb (1.1 ppg, 1.0 rpg), a 6-7 junior forward, will provide depth, as will 6-9 junior college transfer **Hassan Diabi**. Diabi is another New York City player on the Bulldogs' roster. He's from Brooklyn and went to Monroe Community College in New York.

"Hassan plays with a warrior mentality and has a very good chance to help us this season" Alexander said. "He can make a mid-range jumper and we're glad to have him."

2001-2002 SCHEDULE

Nov.	20	@Tennessee Tech
	23-25	#Hawaii-Hilo Tournament
Dec.	1	Delaware State
	3	Howard
	7	@Wake Forest
	9	@Coastal Carolina
	15	@Kansas
	18	@South Carolina
	21-22	##Winthrop Tournament
Jan.	2	The Citadel
	5	@Bethune-Cookman
	7	@Florida A&M
	12	Hampton
	14	Norfolk State
	19	@Maryland-Eastern Shore
	26	@Coppin State
	28	Morgan State
	30	@North Carolina A&T
Feb.	2	@Delaware State
	4	@Howard
	9	Bethune-Cookman
	11	Florida A&M
	16	@Hampton
	18	@Norfolk State
	25	Maryland-Eastern Shore
March	2	North Carolina A&T
	4-9	MEAC Tournament

@Road Games
#Hilo, HI (vs. Colorado State first round; also Hawaii, Hawaii-Hilo, Mercer, LSU, Weber State, Wisconsin)
##Rock Hill, SC (vs. West Virginia State first round; also Tennessee-Martin, Winthrop)
###Richmond Coliseum, Richmond, VA

BLUE RIBBON ANALYSIS

BACKCOURT	B+
BENCH/DEPTH	B-
FRONTCOURT	B
INTANGIBLES	B

The only thing the Bulldogs don't have on this year's team is a marquee player. A player like Vincent Whitt from last year or a Roderick Blakney, the MEAC Player of the Year in 1998.

But they have everything else—an experienced backcourt, an experienced front court and depth everywhere. Throw in a winning tradition and an excellent coach in Alexander and you have a very tough team in the MEAC. One of the mysteries in college basketball is why Alexander has not moved on to a bigger program. This is a man who can coach anywhere against anybody.

We think the Bulldogs will battle North Carolina A&T for first place in the MEAC this year. And it's almost a safe bet South Carolina State will be in the MEAC title game—again.

(M.G.)

Bradley

LOCATION	Peoria, IL
CONFERENCE	Missouri Valley
LAST SEASON	19-12 (.613)
CONFERENCE RECORD	2-6 (t-2nd)
STARTERS LOST/RETURNING	3/2
NICKNAME	Braves
COLORS	Red & White
HOMECOURT	Carver Arena (11,300)
COACH	Jim Molinari (Illinois Wesleyan '77)
RECORD AT SCHOOL	165-132 (10 years)
CAREER RECORD	207-149 (12 years)
ASSISTANTS	Al Biancalana (Elmhurst '82)
	Duane Broussard (Bradley '93)

Howard Moore (Wisconsin '95)
TEAM WINS (last 5 years) 17-15-17-14-19
RPI (last 5 years) 102-159-69-112-99
2000-01 FINISH Lost in conference title game.

MISSOURI VALLEY

After a year of great expectations that came up well short and incited civil unrest—and more importantly, the protest of empty seats—among the throngs of impatient and impassioned Bradley fans, coach Jim Molinari and his Braves delivered.

A rebuilding year was expected from a team comprised of four freshmen, three seniors who had previously underachieved, and a former walk-on among the 10 players left from a summer bloodletting when four players were dismissed. But the Braves, picked for eighth place in the Missouri Valley, surprised everyone by going 19-12, tying for second in the Valley and reaching the championship game of the league tournament before losing by six to Indiana State. Bradley then was invited to the National Invitation Tournament, but fell in the first round to eventual NIT Final Four participant Detroit Mercy.

"Last year was an important one for our program," said Molinari, who in his 11th year at BU is the dean of Valley coaches. "It restored some credibility we had lost the year before. We lost that year [14-16 overall and fifth place after being picked to win the league] because of a combination of factors. We overscheduled, we had some upperclassmen who didn't come through, we lost some confidence and I didn't blend 'em as well as I should have. So doing what we did last year meant a lot to our program."

Last year's seniors —guard Jerome Robinson, forward Eddie Cage and center Jeffrey Rabey—all registered seasons far above expectations. Robinson, who averaged just 6.2 points the year before, became one of the league's dominant players, scoring 16.9 points per game and being voted the league's defensive player of the year. Cage posted career bests of 9.0 points and 5.9 rebounds and the 6-11 Rabey set a school record for blocked shots with 79 while establishing a great presence in the middle, averaging 7.0 points and 7.3 rebounds.

"Those three had tremendous years," Molinari said. "Besides producing on the court, they produced off the court and helped the young players along."

That was significant, because several of those young players—particularly freshmen **James Gillingham**, **Phillip Gilbert** and **Marcello Robinson** and sophomore Andre Corbitt—were major contributors in the Braves' resurrection.

Gilbert, a 6-3 guard from East St. Louis, finished as the team's second-leading scorer at 12.5, the highest average for a BU freshman since Hersey Hawkins averaged 14.6 points in 1984-85. Gilbert was selected to the Valley's All-Newcomer and All-Freshman teams.

"Phillip has the right raw materials, but we had to provide the right environment for him to mature," Molinari said. "Maturity has been everything for Phillip—mentally, physically and emotionally. He's going to be a very strong player for years to come."

Gillingham was recruited as a shooting guard, but with Jerome Robinson and Gilbert filling that role ably, the 6-4 Canadian was shifted to point guard when expected point guard starter Robinson's initial adjustment to college ball was slow. Gillingham, also chosen to the league's all-freshman team, averaged 6.1 points and 2.2 assists while shooting a BU freshman record .840 from the free-throw line. Gillingham was selected to Team Canada this summer and participated in the World University Games.

"James' summer experience will greatly help him," Molinari said. "He hit the wall toward the end of last year and he needs to become more of a three-point threat for us."

Robinson, a 5-10 sophomore from Kankakee, Ill., is likely the point guard of the future for the Braves. He finished strong during the season's stretch run, averaging 11.7 points and 3.7 assists, and then equaled his season high with five assists in the NIT game.

"Marcello finished the best of any of the freshmen and that's a credit to his toughness," Molinari said. "He's our quickest player, but he still needs to become a more consistent shooter and learn to play through his mistakes."

Junior Andre Corbitt, the Braves' top returning rebounder and second-leading returning scorer, was dismissed from the team soon after arriving on campus for fall semester for repeated violations of team rules.

Corbitt, a 6-4 small forward who averaged 4.9 rebounds and 7.3 points last season, had been plagued by suspensions and disciplinary problems throughout his BU career. As a freshman, he was suspended twice for

BLUE RIBBON FORECAST
1. Illinois State
2. Creighton
3. Southern Illinois
4. Bradley
5. Indiana State
6. Drake
7. Southwest Missouri State
8. Evansville
9. Wichita State
10. Northern Iowa

ALL-CONFERENCE TEAM
G - Tarise Bryson, SR, Illinois State
G - Kent Williams, JR, Southern Illinois
G - Kelyn Block, SR, Indiana State
F - Kyle Korver, JR, Creighton
F - Mike Wallace, SR, Southwest Missouri State

PLAYER OF THE YEAR
Tarise Bryson, SR, Illinois State

NEWCOMER OF THE YEAR
Rolan Roberts, JR, Southern Illinois

2001-2002 CONFERENCE TOURNAMENT
March 1-4, Savvis Center, St. Louis, MO

2000-2001 POSTSEASON PARTICIPANTS
Postseason Record 1-4 (.200)
NCAA
Indiana State (Second Round)
Creighton
NIT
Bradley
Illinois State

TOP BACKCOURTS
1 Illinois State
2 Bradley
3 Southern Illinois

TOP FRONTCOURTS
1 Indiana State
2 Southwest Missouri State
3 Creighton

INSIDE THE NUMBERS
2000-2001 conference RPI: 12th (of 31)
Conference RPI (last 5 years): 10-12-8-11-12

DID YOU KNOW?
League champion Creighton advanced to the NCAA Tournament for the third consecutive year, a first in school history. ... The Bluejays' first-round loss to Iowa marked the eighth consecutive year in which the MVC regular-season champion earned an at-large bid to the Big Dance. ... Indiana State earned back-to-back NCAA bids for the first time in school history. ... For the fifth consecutive year, Bradley led the Missouri Valley in attendance, averaging 9,112 for its 15 home games, including an NIT game against Detroit. The Braves have ranked among the NCAA's top 50 in attendance the last eight years. ... Northern Iowa's Joe Breakenridge captured the league's rebounding title for the third year in a row, joining an illustrious group of three Valley greats—Xavier McDaniel, Bob Elmore and Wes Unseld—who have accomplished the feat. ... Illinois State's Tarise Bryson, the Valley's scoring champion and player of the year, finished fourth nationally with his 22.8 points per game average. That marked just the third time in the last 15 seasons that an MVC player has ranked among the nation's top 10. Bradley's Hersey Hawkins led the nation in 1988 and Wichita State's Maurice Evans was ninth in 1999. ... Drake sophomore Luke McDonald, the Missouri Valley Freshman of the Year, indicated a desire to transfer after the season, but changed his mind during the summer and will remain a Bulldog. McDonald established an MVC freshman record with 86 treys. ... Of first- and second-team all-conference selections, those departed are Bradley's Jerome Robinson, Indiana State's Matt Renn and Michael Menser, Breakenridge, Creighton's Ryan Sears and Ben Walker and Evansville's Craig Snow. Returning are Bryson, a two-time first-teamer, and second-teamers Southern Illinois' Kent Williams and Creighton's Kyle Korver. ... Northern Iowa's Greg McDermott is the league's only new coach, replacing Sam Weaver, who was 30-55 in three years. McDermott played at Northern Iowa, graduating in 1988. He has been a head coach at Wayne State and North Dakota State the last seven seasons, compiling a record of 131-64. ... Bradley's Jim Molinari, beginning his 11th year at the school, is the dean of Valley coaches although Evansville's Jim Crews, whose team has been an MVC member for just eight years, is starting his 17th year as the Aces' head coach. ... Bradley guard James Gillingham played for Team Canada in the World University Games this summer.

(D.R.)

insubordination and he was suspended for the season opener in his sophomore season after getting into a fist fight at a campus party.

"It's really disappointing," Molinari said. "Andre knew there was a certain level of conduct he had to follow and he didn't do it."

Corbitt's departure will give freshmen small forwards **Joah Tucker** and **Michael Suggs** a greater opportunity to step into the perimeter rotation, although Gillingham and freshman power forward **Danny Granger** can also play the position.

Also returning to the guard corps is **Brian Hogue**, originally a walk-on who earned a scholarship with the player defections of last summer. He played just 14 minutes all season.

Newcomers on the perimeter are both freshmen and sizeable small forwards—the 6-6 Suggs of Grace King High in Metairie. La., and the 6-5, 210-pound Tucker of Milwaukee Nicolet High. As high school seniors, Suggs averaged 22 points, 9.0 rebounds and 4.5 assists, while Tucker averaged 17.7 points and 10.8 rebounds.

"Mike is fearless," Molinari said. "He's got to become one of those knockdown three-point shooters for us. Joah is a very thick, strong player who's a great competitor."

As talented and deep as the Braves are in the backcourt, they are as green inside. The half-dozen big guys

include a backup senior, three freshmen, a junior college transfer and an inexperienced sophomore coming off surgery.

The senior is 6-6 **Reggie Hall**, who has had a disappointing career. Last year, he averaged just 1.8 points and 1.4 rebounds.

"Reggie has always been a very good practice player and a great team person," Molinari said. "He produces a lot of activity in games, but hasn't had a lot of accomplishment. He's got to find the confidence and take the next step."

The transfer is **Michael Stewart**, a 6-8, 230-pounder who averaged 10 points and 7.5 rebounds at Olney Central College in 1999-00. Stewart sat out last year for academic reasons, but has two seasons of eligibility remaining.

"Michael is strong and a good athlete," Molinari said. "He has a high basketball IQ and will need to step up on the front line."

Sophomore **Jason Faulknor** suffered through a freshman year plagued by ankle injuries. The 6-6 Faulknor underwent surgery on the ankle this summer, but is expected to be ready to open the season.

"Jason is an unproven product," Molinari said. "He's a good character guy and a great team person who had a really tough adjustment to the intensity of college basketball last year."

The three freshmen include 7-foot **Brandon Heemskerk** of Grand Rapids (Mich.) Christian High School; the 6-8 Granger of Metairie (La.) Grace King High and 6-8 **Antoine Tisby** of Kansas City (Kan.) Schlagle High.

Heemskerk averaged 13.1 points, 8.1 rebounds and 1.3 blocked shots as a senior. Granger's numbers were 23.8 points and 12.5 rebounds, while Tisby averaged 15.2 points and 7.4 rebounds.

"Brandon will take time to develop, but he has a good work ethic and runs great for a big guy," Molinari said. "Danny needs strength, but he has skills and is a good athlete. Antoine is athletic and can really rebound. He's long and has a chance to be a good shot blocker."

Molinari sees the development of the frontcourt as the key to the Braves this year.

"Our backcourt seems to be in good hands this year, but we have no proven entities in the frontcourt," he said. "We face the same challenge with them that we faced with our backcourt last year. We have a physically good team and I'm excited about the direction our program is going."

2001-2002 SCHEDULE

Nov.	19	Louisiana-Lafayette
	24	@Western Illinois
	27	@UAB
Dec.	1	Southern Cal
	8	Northern Iowa
	11	@Louisiana-Lafayette
	21	Hampton
	29-30	#Dr Pepper Classic
Jan.	2	@Wichita State
	5	Drake
	10	@Southwest Missouri State
	13	@Evansville
	16	Southern Illinois
	23	Illinois State
	27	Wichita State
	31	Indiana State
Feb.	2	@Northern Iowa
	5	@Illinois State
	9	Evansville
	13	@Indiana State
	16	@Drake
	20	Southwest Missouri State
	23	Creighton
	25	@Southern Illinois
March	1-4	##Missouri Valley Tournament

@Road Games
#Chattanooga, TN McKenzie Arena (vs. Weber State first round; also Chattanooga, Sam Houston State)
##Savvis Center, St. Louis, MO

BLUE RIBBON ANALYSIS

BACKCOURT	B+
BENCH/DEPTH	C+
FRONTCOURT	C
INTANGIBLES	B-

After an underachieving year in 1999-00, Molinari redeemed himself last season, turning in perhaps his best coaching job in 10 years at Bradley. Limited to a roster of 10 players that often became just nine because of injuries, Molinari was forced to be more patient with his young players instead of yanking them quickly after mistakes. The new approach paid off handsomely as two BU freshmen were voted to the league's all-freshman team en route to a second-place MVC finish.

With a full roster again this year, Molinari will certainly have more options. He also has five freshmen and a largely inexperienced frontcourt, so the potential for a return to his old impatient style is possible. But a talented, while still young, backcourt should help ease the new big guys' transition.

If the freshmen in the frontcourt can adapt quickly, there is enough talent on hand at Bradley for another run at the Valley championship. If they can't, the league is balanced enough that a second-division finish for the Braves is quite conceivable.

(D.R.)

Creighton

LOCATION Omaha, NE
CONFERENCE Missouri Valley

LAST SEASON	24-8 (.750)
CONFERENCE RECORD	14-4 (1st)
STARTERS LOST/RETURNING	3/2
NICKNAME	Bluejays
COLORS	Blue & White
HOMECOURT	Omaha Civic Auditorium (9,493)
COACH	Dana Altman (Eastern New Mexico '80)
RECORD AT SCHOOL	123-86 (7 years)
CAREER RECORD	206-153 (12 years)
ASSISTANTS	Greg Grensing (SW Texas State '79)
	Len Gordy (Arizona '77)
	Darian DeVries (Northern Iowa '98)
TEAM WINS (last 5 years)	15-18-22-23-24
RPI (last 5 years)	138-89-34-63-30
2000-01 FINISH	Lost in NCAA first round.

It's the end of an era.

That's the only way to describe what Creighton fans are feeling as their team embarks on a season for the first time in five years without their sterling backcourt of Ryan Sears and Ben Walker.

The pair led the Jays to four consecutive postseason bids—the last three years were capped by appearances in the NCAA Tournament. Creighton won 86 games during those four years and last season captured its first Missouri Valley Conference championship in a decade.

"Ben and Ryan were very productive for us," Creighton coach Dana Altman said. "Athletically, we'll be able to replace 'em. But it won't be so easy to replace the intangibles they brought to us—their leadership, competitiveness and work ethic."

Altman isn't blowing smoke about the Bluejays' more athletic look this year. Aside from Walker and Sears, other lesser athletes who made big contributions to this team—Alan Huss, Justin Haynes and John Klein—have been replaced by players who are faster, quicker and better jumpers.

The best include 6-8, 240-pound **Brody Deren**, a sophomore transfer from Northwestern (3.5 ppg, 2.4 rpg); 6-4 **Larry House**, a junior transfer from Colby (Kansas) Community College (17.7 ppg, 7.6 rpg); 6-7 **Austin Collier**, a medical red-shirt transfer from Scottsdale (Ariz.) Community College (14.4 ppg, 9.0 rpg) and 6-0 point guard **DeAnthony Bowden**, a junior transfer from Jacksonville (Texas) College (14.1 ppg, 6.3 apg, 3.7 spg).

Other newcomers include red-shirt forward Dan Bresnahan, a 6-8 freshman who averaged 16 points and eight rebounds for Lourdes High in Rochester, Minn.; 6-2 freshman guard **Tyler McKinney** of Urbandale, Iowa (21.5 ppg, 5.4 rpg and Iowa's Mr. Basketball); 6-7 freshman forward **Jimmy Motz** of Lincoln, Neb. (19.5 ppg, 6.0 rpg at Northeast High) and 6-3 freshman guard **T.J. Freeman**, a walk-on from Marshall High in Duluth, Minn., where he averaged 21.8 points.

"Brody is a very good athlete for our league, but his skills still need a lot of refinement," Altman said. "Larry House is really athletic, not a great shooter, but he drives well to the hole. DeAnthony is quick and he penetrates well.

"We've tried to get a little more athletic. You're always trying to improve things. Ryan and Ben gave us a lot of things, but we thought by becoming a little more athletic we could mask some of that loss. We won't change our style, but maybe we'll put a little more teeth into our press and bite into our break."

The Bluejays' full-court defensive pressure was plenty effective last season. Creighton led the MVC in steals, turnover margin and scoring defense. Offensively, the Bluejays also led the league in three-point field goals made with nearly eight per game.

The two returning starters—juniors **Kyle Korver** and **Terrell Taylor**—had much to do with all of those numbers. Korver, a 6-7 small forward who was forced to play the power forward last season after Collier broke his leg in pre-season drills, led the team in scoring at 14.6 points per game. He also topped the Valley in three-point field goals made with 100 (3.1 per game) and ranked third in three-point percentage (.452). The Pella, Iowa native also was sixth in the league in steals at 1.75 per game. Korver, a second-team All-MVC selection last year, enters this season as a lock for preseason first-team honors and may challenge for the league's player of the year.

Taylor, a 6-3 small forward/shooting guard, averaged 10.4 points, 2.6 rebounds and 1.3 steals. His athleticism and jumping ability created havoc on both ends of the court for the Jays.

Other returnees with experience as backups in Altman's everybody-plays system are 6-10 sophomore center **Joe Dabbert**, who averaged 4.1 points and 1.8 rebounds; **Ismael Caro**, a 5-11 sophomore point guard who spelled Sears and averaged 2.5 points and 1.2

assists; **Mike Grimes**, a 6-6 sophomore forward who averaged 2.0 points and 1.6 rebounds; and 6-6 sophomore forward **Michael Lindeman**, who averaged 1.2 points and 1.4 rebounds.

"After Kyle and Terrell, we have a lot of guys we brought off the bench who made contributions for us throughout the season," Altman said. "I like the work some of them put in over the summer. They know what the expectations are now."

Those team expectations won't be what they were last season when the Bluejays were picked to win the conference in the preseason and delivered a title come late February. These Jays, with eight newcomers on their roster, have more question marks and likely won't be nearly as targeted by MVC opponents.

"If I had my choice, I'd still like to be picked No. 1," Altman said. "You always want to have a good team. Sometimes it's not as easy when you're picked No. 1 because teams take more time to prepare for you. We hope we're competitive. We won't be picked at the top of the league, but we'll still be swinging away."

2001-2002 SCHEDULE

Nov.	18	North Carolina A&T
	27	Western Kentucky
	29	Grambling
Dec.	4	@TCU
	8	@BYU
	12	Nebraska
	16	Indiana State
	19	@Western Kentucky
	22	Xavier
	29	Mississippi Valley State
Jan.	2	@Illinois State
	5	@Northern Iowa
	9	Evansville
	13	@Southwest Missouri State
	16	Illinois State
	19	Bradley
	22	@Wichita State
	26	@Evansville
	30	Southwest Missouri State
Feb.	3	Southern Illinois
	6	@Indiana State
	9	Northern Iowa
	13	@Drake
	17	Wichita State
	20	@Southern Illinois
	23	@Bradley
	25	Drake
March	1-4	#Missouri Valley Tournament

@Road Games
#Savvis Center, St. Louis, MO

BLUE RIBBON ANALYSIS

BACKCOURT	C+
BENCH/DEPTH	B
FRONTCOURT	B
INTANGIBLES	A

In the last four years, Dana Altman has retooled this team around Sears and Walker and increased the Bluejays' win total each year. With Sears and Walker graduated, this season will be one of Altman's greatest challenges in his seven years in Omaha.

But he has plenty of options from which to choose. This team is more athletic than any of Altman's Creighton clubs and boasts plenty of size as well. Newcomers like Deren, House and Collier should provide frontcourt production to complement the established outside games of Korver and Taylor.

As usual, a challenging non-conference schedule awaits with games against Xavier, Nebraska, TCU, BYU and two against Western Kentucky. So should the season break right, the Jays' RPI stands a good chance to remain in decent shape.

Despite their heavy personnel losses, don't count the Bluejays out. With their constant full-court pressure, changing defenses and up-tempo offense, they play more differently than anyone else in the league, thus are more difficult to prepare for. And with Altman, the Valley's best tactician and coach of the year last season, prowling the sidelines, look for the Jays to be in the thick of the conference race come February.

(D.R.)

Drake

LOCATION	Des Moines, IA
CONFERENCE	Missouri Valley
LAST SEASON	12-16 (.429)
CONFERENCE RECORD	8-10 (t-7th)
STARTERS LOST/RETURNING	2/3
NICKNAME	Bulldogs
COLORS	Blue & White
HOMECOURT	Knapp Center (7,000)
COACH	Kurt Kanaskie (LaSalle '80)
RECORD AT SCHOOL	38-101 (5 years)
CAREER RECORD	38-101 (5 years)
ASSISTANTS	Marty Ball (South Carolina '85)
	Kevin Reynolds (Bloomsburg '91)
	Chris Davis (Michigan '83)
TEAM WINS (last 5 years)	2-3-10-11-12
RPI (last 5 years)	255-293-173-193-195
2000-01 FINISH	Lost in conference play-in game.

Drake was the feel-good story in the Missouri Valley Conference last season as the Bulldogs bolted from the shackles of four consecutive years in the league's dungeon.

But the true essence of the Bulldogs' progress wasn't the mere ascent of three spots in the standings. It was the team's gallant accomplishments after four key players became academically ineligible at mid-season.

In those final 15 games, reduced to just seven scholarship players, Drake managed to snap a five-year, 43-game road conference losing streak at, of all places, the home of league runners-up and NIT-bound Illinois State.

Three days later, the plucky Bulldogs won at Southwest Missouri State for the first time in the 10 years the Bears have been members of the Valley. Also coming in that second-half stretch was a 12-point home win over defending league champion Indiana State, which would go on to reach the second round of the NCAA Tournament.

DU coach Kurt Kanaskie finished a close second to Creighton's Dana Altman for the Valley's Coach of the Year, became the first coach in Drake history to post improved records four years in a row and was rewarded with a new four-year contract after the season. But Kanaskie was a reluctant recipient of all the praise heaped upon his team and the job he did pulling his short-handed troops through such adversity.

"Those guys we had left really bought into what we wanted them to do," Kanaskie said. "But it was still disappointing that we finished where we did. If everyone had stayed together, we could have had a real nice year."

Still, the strides made by this perpetual also-ran program, which has finished in the league's first division just once in the last 15 years (a fifth-place finish in 1992-93), signify enough progress for encouragement this season.

"I think we can continue to build on last season," Kanaskie said. "Our returning players had to play a lot more minutes than we probably anticipated going into the season. But they responded well and that should help their confidence as we enter play this year."

Certainly, the Bulldogs should again boast one of the Valley's top perimeter shooting attacks. Behind the league's freshman-of-the-year **Luke McDonald**, a 6-5 sophomore guard who averaged a team-high 14.7 points, and **Andry Sola**, a 6-7 junior forward who averaged 11.8 points and 6.0 rebounds, Drake led the MVC in three-point field-goal percentage (.398) last year. The Bulldogs connected on a school-record 201 treys, while setting single-game records for three-point field-goal percentage of .762 and 17 treys against Wichita State.

The Drake program is particularly pleased that McDonald, whose .460 field-goal percentage for three-pointers was the highest of any Division I freshman last year, will find his way back to Des Moines after three months of soul-searching as he considered transferring closer to his home in Texas.

"It was a difficult time for Luke," Kanaskie said. "He was a home-schooled kid and was far from home. I don't think he really wanted to leave, but his [family] circle wanted him to make a move. But he expressed a desire to stay and we're happy he's staying."

Sola, who transferred from George Washington, was a member of the Valley's All-Newcomer team along with McDonald.

"Andry is a unique player in that he can shoot threes and also score with his back to the basket," Kanaskie said. "He's had a good summer and worked really hard in the weight room."

Other key returnees are 6-9 junior center **Greg Danielson** (9.3 ppg, 6.2 rpg) and senior sixth man **Aaron Knight**, a 6-3 guard who returned from a torn ACL to average 4.8 points.

"Greg was up and down last year and we need much greater consistency out of him," Kanaskie said. "Aaron has fully recovered now from his surgery. He finally has full confidence in his leg and we feel he can have a good year for us."

Also back is **Mike O'Neill**, the 6-10 center who was one of those ineligible players at mid-season last year. O'Neill averaged 2.6 points and 1.6 rebounds.

"We're hoping Mike can be the real surprise of our team," Kanaskie said. "He dropped a lot of weight and picked up in skill development."

The Bulldogs welcome seven newcomers, three of whom are juniors who should provide an immediate impact.

Junior point guard **David Newman**, a 6-0 transfer from Northwestern where he started for his first two years (4.4 ppg, 2.5 apg in 1999-00), was Iowa's Mr. Basketball when he was a senior at Des Moines Hoover.

"David gives us leadership and experience in the backcourt," Kanaskie said. "He's really fiery in our practices and gives maximum effort."

Junior college transfers **J.J. Sola**, a 6-7 junior forward from Fullerton (Calif.) Junior College (18.2 ppg, 7.4 rpg) and **Armon Tillman**, a 6-4 junior from Midland (Texas) Junior College (9.4 ppg, 2.7 rpg) provide strength and athleticism. Sola, no relation to Andry, began his career at Loyola Marymount where he averaged 6.9 points and 4.0 rebounds as a freshman.

"Sola is very skilled as an inside scorer and is a good passer," Kanaskie said. "Tillman is a tough, hard-nosed competitor who really gets after it defensively and on the boards."

T.J. Welton, a 6-6 junior red-shirt forward who averaged 17.9 points and 7.5 rebounds at Kirkwood (Iowa) Community College in 1999-00, has re-broken the same foot that kept him sidelined last year.

"If he gets healthy, he can help us," Kanaskie said.

A trio of freshmen round out the team—6-9 forward **Dave Bancroft** (22.3 ppg, 13.8 rpg, 4.8 bpg) from Marshfield, (Mo.) High; 6-5 forward **Quantel Murphy** (16.3 ppg, 7.5 rpg, 3.2 spg) from George Washington High School in Denver; and 6-1 guard **Lonnie Randolph** (16.7 ppg, 4.9 rpg, 4.4 apg) from Merrillville (Ind.) High.

"Murphy is a superior athlete," Kanaskie said. "He had 56 dunks last year, which is a dimension we haven't had before. Randolph is a very quick, intelligent player and Bancroft is an excellent jumper and shooter who needs physical strength and maturity and may red-shirt."

Kanaski likes his blend of talent, and is glad to have some depth at his disposal.

"This is probably one of the most talented teams we've had," Kanaskie said. "We will be able to shoot the ball and we'll be deeper. Hopefully, we'll play a little faster offensively, but we'll still have the same focus of what we're trying to do."

2001-2002 SCHEDULE

Nov.	16-18	#Nike Tip-Off Tournament
	23	@Oral Roberts
	27	@Western Illinois
Dec.	6	Arkansas-Pine Bluff
	9	Indiana State
	12	@Iowa
	15	Iowa State
	22	Northern Illinois
	27	@Florida Atlantic
	30	Denver
Jan.	2	@Northern Iowa
	5	@Bradley
	10	Illinois State
	12	@Wichita State
	16	@Evansville
	20	Northern Iowa
	24	Southern Illinois
	26	@Illinois State
	30	Wichita State
Feb.	2	Evansville
	6	@Southwest Missouri State
	9	@Southern Illinois
	13	Bradley
	19	@Indiana State
	23	SW Missouri State
	25	@Creighton
March	1-4	##Missouri Valley Tournament

@Road Games
#Honolulu, HI (vs. Sam Houston State first round; also

Norfolk State, Hawaii)
##Savvis Center, St. Louis, MO

BLUE RIBBON ANALYSIS

BACKCOURT	B
BENCH/DEPTH	C
FRONTCOURT	C
INTANGIBLES	C

McDonald's decision to stay at Drake was a huge positive for the program, which could challenge for its first winning season in 16 years. The adversity the returnees went through a year ago should also help build some much-needed toughness into this team.

The real question of how successful the Bulldogs will be this season revolves around how effective a supporting cast some of the seven newcomers and O'Neill can be. Newman needs to become a take-charge point guard and set up scoring opportunities for McDonald and Andry Sola. And at least a couple of the others must step forward consistently as solid contributors.

It has taken Kanaskie five long years to resuscitate a nearly dead program. The patient got out of bed last year and took some tentative steps down the hallway, but found the path strewn with obstacles. This is the year the obstacles need to be pushed aside and the pace picked up to at least a brisk walk.

(D.R.)

Evansville

LOCATION	Evansville, IN
CONFERENCE	Missouri Valley
LAST SEASON	14-16 (.467)
CONFERENCE RECORD	9-9 (6th)
STARTERS LOST/RETURNING	3/2
NICKNAME	Purple Aces
COLORS	Purple & Orange
HOMECOURT	Roberts Stadium (12,300)
COACH	Jim Crews (Indiana '76)
RECORD AT SCHOOL	287-188 (16 years)
CAREER RECORD	287-188 (16 years)
ASSISTANTS	Lennox Forrester (Evansville '92)
	Kirk Sarff (Millikin '84)
	Marty Simmons (Evansville '87)
TEAM WINS (last 5 years)	17-15-23-18-14
RPI (last 5 years)	89-190-50-123-162
2000-01 FINISH	Lost in conference quarterfinal.

Everything seemed in place as last season began for Evansville to return to the top of the Missouri Valley Conference. In 1998-99, the sophomore-dominated Aces captured their first league regular-season title and earned an NCAA Tournament bid. The loss of MVC Player-of-the- Year Marcus Wilson and a slew of injuries caused a drop-off to sixth place the following year.

But entering last season, the Aces were healthy and boasted the league's most experienced team. Valley prognosticators took note, picking them for second in the preseason poll.

Evansville proceeded to start the season 0-3, surfaced above .500 just once at 8-7 and then dropped nine of its last 15 to again land in sixth. The Aces' 14-16 record marked just the second time in the last 15 years the program had been below the break-even mark for a season.

"It was a very disappointing season," UE coach Jim Crews said. "We did not respond to the things we needed to respond to in a more productive fashion. We didn't respond well to injuries, the getting beat, to winning a couple of games in a row, to travel problems. There are always a million variables in a season and good teams respond to them. We didn't. It was surprising because we responded better when we were younger."

The Aces' personnel problems began after six games when center **Faruk Mujezinovic** was lost for the season because of injury and guard Clint Keown, the team's third-leading scorer as a sophomore, quit the team. Point guard Jeremy Stanton missed four games with an ankle sprain and senior forward Kyle Runyan continued to battle injuries that had plagued him throughout his career. Then, leading scorer Craig Snow, the MVC Preseason Player of the Year, hit a shooting slump that affected the rest of his game and was benched by Crews. Snow eventually returned to the lineup and ended up as the team's leading scorer at 14.6 points per game.

"Kyle is the one I feel really bad for," Crews said. "He could have been an exceptional player for us but had injury problems for four straight years. He's a kid who could really score and no one got to see him at his best for an extended period."

Through it all, the Aces still managed to lead the Valley in field-goal percentage at .484 and were second in three-point percentage at .389. But the Aces' defense was woeful, giving up 71.5 points, second most in the league. And in each of the statistics that reflect athleticism—steals, blocked shots and offensive rebounds—Evansville was near the bottom.

"People don't think we were athletic and they've thought that for 16 years," Crews said. "You get stuck with that reputation. Last year, people would say, 'You need to be more athletic.' Well, we had guys who were plenty good athletically. We just didn't play athletically."

Nevertheless, Crews made it a point to recruit players who more fit a mold of athleticism rather than the small-town Indiana jump shooters that traditionally dominate his roster.

The most promising include junior college transfer forwards **Larry Ferguson** and **Tobias Brinkley**. The 6-6 Ferguson averaged 17 points and 11 rebounds for Jacksonville (Texas) College and Brinkley, 6-5, averaged 15.6 points at Eastern Oklahoma State College.

"We probably aren't known for bringing in many JC kids," Crews said. "But we had a little gap in classes and needed to fill in there. Ferguson is a tough kid who plays very hard defensively and goes to the boards extremely well. Brinkley scores well and scores in different ways. He's also been very well schooled defensively."

Other newcomers include 6-6 junior **Ian Hanavan**, a transfer from Illinois-Chicago (5.1 ppg, 4.2 rpg in two years at UIC) and three freshmen—**Eric Ottens** of Fulton, Ill., **Lucious Wagner** of Leavenworth, Kan., and **Jordan Watson** of Galesburg, Ill.

Ottens, a 6-7 forward, averaged 20.1 points and 10.2 rebounds at Fulton High; Wagner, a red-shirt, averaged 10.4 points and 4.5 assists for state champion Leavenworth High; and Watson averaged 17.2 points and 5.0 rebounds at Galesburg High.

"Hanavan we think will bring a lot of energy," Crews said. "He's a very good rebounder and has a chance to be a very good player. You never know about freshmen, but we think both Jordan and Eric are guys with the athletic ability to be pretty good defensive players."

Senior guard **Adam Seitz** and sophomore center **Dan Lytle** are the returning starters. Seitz, a 6-4 dynamo, was the Aces' second-leading scorer at 11.9 points. He also grabbed 3.3 rebounds per game. Lytle averaged 10.6 points and 4.0 rebounds and was chosen to the Valley's All-Freshman team.

"We need more consistency out of those guys," Crews said. "Dan showed he could score 19 or 20 points and then would follow it up with zero. He had a real tendency to get in foul trouble last year [fouling out of 11 games]."

Other primary returnees are 6-8 senior forward **Chuck Hedde** (8.0 ppg, 3.5 rpg), 6-6 sophomore forward **Clint Cuffle** (6.9 ppg, 3.4 rpg), 6-2 senior guard **Mark Allaria** (2.4 ppg, 2.4 apg) and Mujezinovic, a 6-9 sophomore who averaged 3.5 points and 1.7 rebounds in six games.

"We really felt good about Clint last year," Crews said. "We were going to red-shirt him, but we needed to play him and he showed good basketball savvy and good poise. Faruk is aggressive and has a real zest for playing. It's a shame he's been hurt for the last year and a half. We're real excited about having him back."

2001-2002 SCHEDULE

Nov.	17	Youngstown State
	20	@Western Kentucky
	24	@Tennessee State
	27	@Illinois-Chicago
Dec.	3	Miami (Ohio)
	5	Eastern Illinois
	8	@Butler
	15	Bowling Green
	22	Wisconsin-Green Bay
	30	Southwest Missouri State
Jan.	2	Southern Illinois
	5	@Indiana State
	9	@Creighton
	13	Bradley
	16	Drake
	19	@Wichita State
	21	@Southwest Missouri State
	26	Creighton
	30	@Southern Illinois
Feb.	2	@Drake
	5	Northern Iowa
	9	@Bradley
	13	Illinois State
	16	Indiana State
	19	@Northern Iowa
	23	Wichita State
	25	@Illinois State
March	1-4	#Missouri Valley Tournament

@Road Games
#Savvis Center, St. Louis, MO

BLUE RIBBON ANALYSIS

BACKCOURT	C+
BENCH/DEPTH	C
FRONTCOURT	C
INTANGIBLES	C

Evansville lost a large share of its production with the graduations of Snow, Stanton and Runyan. But after an MVC championship two years ago with those three playing key roles as sophomores, the Aces have finished a disappointing sixth in each of the last two seasons.

So maybe some new blood was in order. More athletic players like Brinkley and Ferguson promise to give Evansville a different look. It's doubtful, however, that Crews' deliberate motion offense and half-court man-to-man defense will change much.

If Lytle can become more consistent and stay out of foul trouble and if Ferguson and Hanavan can improve the league's worst rebounding squad and if some of the newcomers can help Seitz and Cuffle with the program's usually excellent outside attack, the Aces could surprise. But those are a lot of ifs. And there are several Valley teams with fewer question marks. A sixth-place finish by Evansville this season, it would seem, would not be as discouraging as it was the last two years.

(D.R.)

Illinois State

LOCATION	Norman, IL
CONFERENCE	Missouri Valley
LAST SEASON	21-9 (.700)
CONFERENCE RECORD	12-6 (t-2nd)
STARTERS LOST/RETURNING	1/4
NICKNAME	Redbirds
COLORS	Red & White
HOMECOURT	Redbird Arena (10,200)
COACH	Tom Richardson (St. Xavier '78)
RECORD AT SCHOOL	31-29 (2 years)
CAREER RECORD	31-29 (2 years)
ASSISTANTS	Chad Altadonna (Illinois State '96)
	Doug Novsek (Southern Illinois '87)
TEAM WINS (last 5 years)	24-25-16-10-21
RPI (last 5 years)	42-27-96-211-83
2000-01 FINISH	Lost in NIT first round.

Major rebuilding jobs for new coaches in college basketball usually take years and tiny steps to complete. If the Illinois State Redbirds accomplish what Blue Ribbon and many others are predicting for them this season—a Missouri Valley Conference championship—it will have taken Tom Richardson exactly two years and two giant leaps to go from the outhouse to the penthouse.

When Richardson inherited the Redbirds from his former mentor, Kevin Stallings, entering the 1999-00 season, the program quickly came unglued through defection and injury. ISU finished 10-20, the school's second-worst record in 30 years of Division I membership.

The addition of some key recruits and some much-needed maturity of the holdovers allowed the Redbirds to make their first big jump last season, emerging from a tie for eighth in the league to a tie for second, going 21-9. They became the first team in the nearly century-long history of the MVC to follow a 20-loss season with a 20-win year.

"We had a young team last year and scheduled a lot of home games," Richardson said of his team's 8-1 start, six of which were at Redbird Arena. "It gave us some confidence early on."

Last year is history, but enough firepower returns to make the Redbirds the odds-on pick to return to the top of the conference where they took up residence much of the 1990s. In the nine seasons from 1989-1998, Illinois State finished first or second seven times.

It all starts with 6-1 senior guard **Tarise Bryson**, the Valley's Player of the Year last season when his 22.8 points per game scoring average led the league for the second consecutive season and ranked fourth nationally. Bryson, who officially became eligible for this season over the summer when he fulfilled academic requirements to earn back his fourth year of basketball, needs just 513 points to pass former Olympian and NBA great Doug Collins for the Redbird career scoring record.

"Tarise might beat Doug Collins' scoring record and lead the conference in scoring again," Richardson said. "But the best statistic is winning the championship and he's not done that yet. That's what he can do for an encore. He needs to continue to make the guys around him better, delivering them the ball if he's covered.

"Tarise doesn't need to score 22 points a game for us. He needs to get other guys some layups. He did better at that last year. Of course, there will be times he'll need to take over, too."

Bryson will have plenty of experienced help in the backcourt. Six-foot-two senior **Shawn Jeppson**, who averaged 12.5 points and shot an uncanny 55 percent from the field last season, was a major reason for the Birds' turnaround. The combination of Bryson and Jeppson is far and away the best offensive backcourt in the Valley.

"Shawn takes good shots and benefits from the attention Tarise gets," Richardson said. "Hopefully, though, both of them will get better defensively. I've told both of them, 'What good is it if you get 20 points and you give up 18?'"

The unsung returnee in the guard corps is 6-0 senior point guard **Randy Rice**, who averaged just 3.7 points, but contributed 4.7 assists and was the team's top defender. Rice will have an awfully talented understudy in **Vince Greene**, a 5-9 Prop 42 sophomore from Chicago's Brother Rice High School who averaged 18.9 points and 3.5 assists as a senior.

"Randy makes everything happen out there for us," said Richardson. "Vince is really a good shooter, which Randy had problems with last year. That was more of a confidence thing, especially when teams started leaving him open. He just needs to relax and hit the open shot."

The other perimeter newcomer is 6-4 freshman swingman **Gregg Alexander**, who averaged 26.5 points and 5.0 rebounds at Lincoln (Ill.) High School.

"Gregg is really going to push some of our guys for playing time," Richardson said. "He's a real competitive, fiery kid who can score."

Shedrick Ford, a 6-5 senior small forward, is the top inside returnee, having averaged 12.1 points and 5.8 rebounds last season.

"We're looking for Shed to do the things he did last year and then some," Richardson said. "He needs to rebound more and play better defense. He's a good outside shooter (19-for-47 on three-pointers) and we'll move him out on the perimeter more.'"

The rest of the frontcourt is largely unproven. Returning are 6-6 senior **Chad Mazanowski** (0.6 ppg, 0.8 rpg), 6-8 sophomore **Dirk Williams** (3.6 ppg, 3.1 rpg) and 6-11 junior **Andy Strandmark** (1.2 ppg, 2.0 rpg).

"Chad is a good role player for us," Richardson said. "Dirk is really a talented kid and should pop onto the scene more this year. He has added about 10 pounds of muscle. Andy is a key guy for us in a lot of ways. He did not have a good season last year and he's determined to make sure that doesn't happen again. He needs to be a presence for us, but right now, he's the 'X' factor."

Two junior college transfers are expected to log heavy minutes in the frontcourt. **Baboucarr Bojang**, a 6-9 junior out of Southwest Missouri State-West Plains Community College, where he averaged 15.4 points and 10.2 rebounds, and 6-7 junior Casey Reid of Scottsdale (Ariz.) Community College (22.0 ppg, 12.0 rpg) should both be productive inside players.

"Bojang is long and athletic, he can run and score and plays very hard with a lot of energy," Richardson said. "Reid could be an impact player for us because he's very skilled. They should complement each other well."

The Redbirds suffered some key losses in the frontcourt in the off-season. Starting power forward Rich Beyers (5.6 ppg, 3.1 rpg) graduated and three players—Cedric Knight (5.1 ppg, 3.4 rpg), Traves Wilson (6.9 ppg, 3.8 rpg) and Jason Hammock (2.6 ppg, 1.5 rpg)—quit the team.

"I'm disappointed in any personnel turnover, but unfortunately, this is sometimes the nature of our business," Richardson said. "These guys leaving allowed us to recruit a couple of kids [Bojang and Reid] I think will be better."

For all its offensive prowess last season, one of this team's weaknesses last year was on the defensive end. Despite ranking second in the Valley in steals, the Redbirds were eighth in the league in scoring defense. In the season's final four games, Illinois State yielded 78 points per game.

"Guys got comfortable and that showed at the end of last year when our defense really tailed off," Richardson said. "Guys paced themselves on defense knowing they were playing lots of minutes. That's why we didn't win a championship and that's why we lost to Bradley in the [MVC] tournament.

"That's one of the good things about this year's team. We will have depth and competition we didn't have last year. It will be my challenge to use that depth to our best advantage."

Of course, when a team is improving by leaps and bounds like Illinois State, there are major challenges everywhere. The biggest one this season for all involved is to learn to win a championship. More challenging still is that, this time around, great things are expected.

2001-2002 SCHEDULE

Nov.	16	Weber State
	23	#University Hoops Classic
	29	@Georgia Southern
Dec.	1	@Texas-San Antonio
	8	Samford
	15	@Tennessee-Chattanooga
	18	@Illinois
	22	Kent State
Jan.	2	Creighton
	5	@Southern Illinois
	7	Wichita State
	10	@Drake
	12	Indiana State
	16	@Creighton
	19	Southwest Missouri State
	23	@Bradley
	26	Drake
	30	Northern Iowa
Feb.	2	@Southwest Missouri State
	5	Bradley
	9	@Indiana State
	13	@Evansville
	16	Southern Illinois
	20	@Wichita State
	23	@Northern Iowa
	25	Evansville
March	1-4	##Missouri Valley Tournament

@Road Games
#Pittsburgh, PA (vs. Cal-Irvine first round; also Hofstra, Kent State, Oakland, Pittsburgh, Robert Morris, South Florida)
##Savvis Center, St. Louis, MO

BLUE RIBBON ANALYSIS

BACKCOURT	A
BENCH/DEPTH	B
FRONTCOURT	B
INTANGIBLES	A-

Returning four starters—including the league's 2000-2001 player of the year in Bryson—from a team that finished in a surprising tie for second place last season may be reason enough to pick Illinois State to return to the top of the MVC after a two-year absence.

But Richardson appears to have had an outstanding recruiting year besides, lending more credence to the Redbirds' title claims.

Still, there are some nagging questions facing this program. Can an offensive-oriented group, which overwhelmingly led the league in scoring last year, improve a porous defense? Can a frontcourt made up of little-used returnees and a couple of junior college transfers be productive enough to keep opponents from concentrating most of their efforts on stopping Bryson and Jeppson? Is there enough strength and bulk in that seemingly thin frontline to weather the long season and battle the big boys come March?

Despite the uncertainties, the Redbirds boast more proven commodities than anyone else in the Valley. And when one of those commodities is the league's returning player of the year, picking them for first is a no-brainer.

(D.R.)

 **Indiana State**

LOCATION	Terre Haute, IN
CONFERENCE	Missouri Valley
LAST SEASON	22-12 (.647)

CONFERENCE RECORD	10-8 (t-4th)
STARTERS LOST/RETURNING	2/3
NICKNAME	Sycamores
COLORS	Blue & White
HOMECOURT	Hulman Center (10,200)
COACH	Royce Waltman (Slippery Rock '64)
RECORD AT SCHOOL	75-45 (4 years)
CAREER RECORD	75-45 (4 years)
ASSISTANTS	Dick Bender (Western Michigan '86)
	Rick Ray (Grand View College '94)
	Kareem Richardson (Evansville '96)
TEAM WINS (last 5 years)	12-16-15-22-22
RPI (last 5 years)	163-111-103-53-78
2000-01 FINISH	Lost in NCAA first round.

Check out the progression of team wins and RPI just above and you get a pretty good idea where Royce Waltman has brought this program in his four years.

But consider some of the numbers that don't appear: Before Waltman arrived, the Sycamores hadn't had a winning season for 18 years. They were permanent residents in the bottom half of the Missouri Valley Conference and their RPIs were consistently in the high 200s. The Sycamores' NCAA Tournament history consisted of the one bright shining season of 1978-79, when Larry Bird carried the team to the championship game against Michigan State.

It had been since the Bird days that the Sycamores had posted back-to-back winning seasons. They accomplished that in Waltman's second year. It had been since Bird's senior year that the Sycamores had won the MVC regular-season and tournament titles. They accomplished those feats in Waltman's third and fourth seasons, respectively. They had never been to the NCAA Tournament more than once. They accomplished that feat in each of the last two seasons. Last March, Indiana State upset Oklahoma in overtime in the first round before falling to Gonzaga.

"I think we've turned the corner as far as the perception of our program, how people look at it, how recruits look at it," Waltman said. "We've had four winning seasons and two championship seasons. Having said that, we'll have lost all five kids we've built it on after this year.

"So we're at sort of an important juncture. Are we a flash in the pan or a consistent, successful program?"

Two of those players—four-year starters Matt Renn and Michael Menser—graduated after last season. The pair—Waltman's first two recruits at Terre Haute—were instrumental in the Sycamores' success.

Renn was a 6-6 forward who led the team in scoring two of the last three years and in rebounding all three seasons. For his career, Renn averaged 11.4 points and 6.7 rebounds. The 5-11 Menser was the consummate point guard, starting 115 of the 116 games he played in over four seasons and averaging 3.7 assists and 11.2 points for his career. As a senior, he posted an astounding assist-to-turnover ratio of 4.0, the best mark among Division I players.

"Those two were clearly the heart and soul of our program," Waltman said. "Their basketball IQs were off the chart, so we'll definitely miss them. At the same time, it leaves the door open for other guys to step forward. Djibril Kante and Kelyn Block are the likely guys to take over those leadership roles."

Both seniors have already had excellent careers. Block, a 6-2 guard, averaged 14.6 points last year and has a career mark of 10.9 per game. The Kansas City native shot .526 from the field, impressive for a guard.

Kante (9.3 ppg, 5.8 rpg), a 6-7, 235-pound center, averaged shot .561 and blocked 61 shots as he rebounded well from an injury-plagued sophomore season. Kante has a good chance of becoming the school's all-time leader in blocked shots this year.

"Some people said that Block disappeared some last year," Waltman said. "But it was more because Menser and Renn had the ball in their hands most of the time. Kelyn really responds to every opportunity he has. As good as Michael and Matt were, they couldn't always create a shot on their own and Kelyn has always been able to do that.

"Djibril is quiet, but he's the hardest worker on our team. He really inspires guys by how hard he plays."

Indiana State returns one more starter—sophomore swingman **Marcus Howard**, who averaged 4.7 points for the season, but came on strong in the postseason, averaging 9.5 points in the Valley and NCAA Tournaments.

"Marcus Howard is the best defender in the league," Waltman said. "He got much more forceful down the stretch and I look for him to assert himself more offensively. He's a very smart, good player."

Three key subs last year will take on more significant roles this season for the Sycamores. **Terence Avery**, a

6-9 senior center, averaged 8.2 points and 4.4 rebounds off the bench. **Matt Berry**, a 6-5 sophomore swingman, averaged 3.2 points and 1.5 rebounds. And junior **Matt Broermann**, a 6-5 three-point specialist, averaged 2.4 points.

"Terence was sporadic last year and needs to be a more consistent scorer for us," Waltman said. "When he scored, he gave us an inside threat. He needs to build on those scoring flashes.

"Matt Berry is a role player who helps us on the boards and is a hard worker. Matt Broermann we rely on mostly as a shooter."

Other returnees are 6-11, 190-pound sophomore forward **Michael Kernan** (0.8 ppg, 0.5 rpg), 6-5 junior guard **Andy Williamson** (1.5 ppg, 0.6 rpg) and 6-0 sophomore guard **Barry Welsh** (0.8 ppg).

"Michael was too thin and weak to play last year, but he'll have to play some this year," Waltman said. "He's a very good shooter. Barry can defend and is good in transition."

Welsh is one of the three candidates facing the unenviable task of replacing Menser at the point. He's joined by newcomers **Batiste Haywood**, a 6-1 walk-on junior transfer from Northeast (Ind.) Community College, and **Lamar Grimes**, a 5-11 freshman from Chicago Gage Park. A year ago, Haywood averaged 18.0 points and 5.0 rebounds, while Grimes averaged 26.0 points and 10.0 assists.

"Point guard is the biggest gap to fill," Waltman said. "No knock on these three guys, but I may coach another 10 years and not have anybody fill that spot the way Michael did in terms of taking care of the ball."

The other Sycamore newcomers are all frontcourt freshmen. **Jake Sams**, a 6-8 forward from Mount Zion (Ill.) High School (14.0 ppg, 8.5 rpg) is joined by 6-9 forward **Jerod Adler** of Monroe (Ind.) Adams Central High (14.0 ppg, 11.3 rpg) and 6-6 **Darron Evans** of Chicago Providence St. Mel High (13.5 ppg, 9.0 rpg).

"Sams is an outstanding player, a four man who is a good perimeter shooter," Waltman said. "Adler will have to come off the bench and play some in the post. Evans is an outstanding athlete who defends, blocks shots and rebounds. We've always hung our hat on recruiting kids with good attitudes and work habits. I think we've brought in kids like that again, although none of them will probably make a big splash this year."

Waltman described his non-conference schedule as "too hard," but is cooperating with the league's new edict about averaging a 150 RPI among non-league opponents. The Sycamores play Illinois-Chicago, Valparaiso, Butler, Eastern Illinois, Murray State, Wyoming, Ball State, Bowling Green and IUPUI in their nine non-conference games.

"That should make the conference office happy," Waltman said. "I know there are mixed feelings around the league about the new policy. But I don't see anything wrong with us setting a minimum standard for scheduling."

The one possible casualty may be the Sycamores' run of 20-win seasons, currently at two. Only three times in school history—and not since 1977-79—has Indiana State won 20 or more three years in a row.

2001-2002 SCHEDULE

Nov.	18	@Illinois-Chicago
	21	Valparaiso
	25	@Butler
	28	@Eastern Illinois
Dec.	1	IUPUI
	3	Murray State
	9	@Drake
	16	@Creighton
	19	@Wyoming
	22	Ball State
	29	Bowling Green
Jan.	5	Evansville
	10	Northern Iowa
	12	@Illinois State
	16	Wichita State
	19	@Southern Illinois
	23	@Northern Iowa
	27	Southwest Missouri State
	31	@Bradley
Feb.	3	@Wichita State
	6	Creighton
	9	Illinois State
	13	Bradley
	16	@Evansville
	19	Drake
	23	Southern Illinois
	25	@Southwest Missouri State
March	1-4	#Missouri Valley Tournament

@Road Games
#Savvis Center, St. Louis, MO

BLUE RIBBON ANALYSIS

BACKCOURT	B-
BENCH/DEPTH	C
FRONTCOURT	B
INTANGIBLES	B

The Sycamores became more offensive-oriented last season, improving their points per game average by more than four points and their field-goal percentage from .435 to .460. But they've also lost their top two offensive weapons in Renn and Menser, whose team influence extended far beyond putting the ball in the basket. They will be sorely missed and difficult to replace.

Menser's absence, in particular, leaves a big hole at point guard because there is little experience to draw from. Little-used sophomore Welsh and freshman Grimes appear to be the top candidates for the spot.

Overall though, a solid nucleus, a savvy coach and a newfound winning attitude return, making Indiana State a middle-of-the-pack MVC team at worst.

(D.R.)

Northern Iowa

LOCATION	Cedar Falls, IA
CONFERENCE	Missouri Valley
LAST SEASON	7-24 (.226)
CONFERENCE RECORD	3-15 (9th)
STARTERS LOST/RETURNING	2/3
NICKNAME	Panthers
COLORS	Purple & Old Gold
HOMECOURT	UNI Dome (10,000)
COACH	Greg McDermott (Northern Iowa '88)
RECORD AT SCHOOL	First year
CAREER RECORD	First year
ASSISTANTS	Ron Smith (Illinois State '76)
	Ben Jacobson (North Dakota '94)
	Kyle Green (Hamline '92)
TEAM WINS (last 5 years)	14-16-10-9-7
RPI (last 5 years)	122-85-226-168-248
2000-01 FINISH	Lost in conference quarterfinal.

When Greg McDermott was hired as head coach at Northern Iowa last spring, some comments he made at the press conference had folks wondering if the school had just hired the world's greatest optimist.

"I'm the luckiest man alive," McDermott said. "When we win a Missouri Valley championship, which we will, then all my dreams will come true."

Bold words for a man with no Division I head coaching experience taking over a program that has posted just two winning league seasons in its 10 years as a Valley member and no finish above fourth place. And last year, the Panthers bottomed out with their 7-24 record and last-place 3-15 mark in the conference.

Not only did UNI post an abysmal 30-55 record in the just-completed three-year reign of coach Sam Weaver, but the program earned a bad reputation as a revolving door for players. In those three seasons, 16 underclassmen left UNI, most of them dismissed by Weaver or the school.

Enter McDermott, who played for the Panthers in the '80s and has served as a Division II head coach for the last seven years—six at Wayne State, where he was 116-53, and last season at North Dakota State, where his team finished 15-11.

"I don't see any reason why the men's basketball program here can't achieve the same success the other programs at Northern Iowa have achieved," McDermott said. "The promise of a new basketball facility sometime in the near future has created some momentum for our program and we have a great product to sell academically. There's no reason we can't compete."

It might be asking too much for it to happen this season, though. While 5-11 senior guard Robbie Sieverding, the team's 1999-00 leading scorer, returns after missing all of last season with major knee surgery, the Panthers suffered a big loss with the graduation of All-MVC forward Joe Breakenridge, who led the Valley in rebounding three years in a row.

The Panthers' top three-point threat, guard Martin Coon, graduated early and won't return for his final year. And three transfers expected to make an impact last season—center Damond Gregory and forwards Corey

Hill and Booker Warren—encountered limited success before all became academic casualties and have since departed.

Joining Sieverding in the backcourt will be 6-2 senior guard Erik Smith, who averaged 8.7 points last season, 5-10 point guard Andy Woodley, who led the Valley in steals last season and was third in assists, and 5-9 Chris Foster, a red-shirt freshman who was sidelined by illness a year ago.

"It's certainly key for us to have Robbie back healthy," McDermott said. "He gives us a proven scorer in the Valley. With Woodley and Smith back, we'll have a lot of experience in the backcourt and that always gives you a chance.

"I've liked what I've seen from Erik Smith in the individual workouts and Woodley does a great job of running the show. We're going to ask him to shoot that three-point shot more often than he has in the past."

By comparison, the frontcourt experience level is low. Among the returnees, only 6-5 senior small forward Aaron Middendorf played more than a dozen minutes per game last year. He averaged 8.8 points and 4.7 rebounds.

"We'll play Aaron both at small and power forward depending on how teams match up against us," McDermott said. "He's tough to match up against. He's very effective off the dribble."

Senior Octav Moraiu, a 6-11, 250-pounder from Romania, started seven games and averaged 2.5 points and 2.4 rebounds.

"Octav is really a key to how good we can be," McDermott said. "There's not many players his size in the Missouri Valley. He just needs some experience. He's playing with the Romanian National Team this summer, so hopefully playing against that kind of experience will give him the confidence he needs going into [the] season."

Blake Anderson, a 6-7 sophomore who averaged 1.8 points and 1.3 rebounds in limited play last season, will likely be the power forward, but will get stiff competition from 6-7 sophomore transfer David Gruber, who averaged 12.7 points and 8.5 rebounds at Kirkwood (Iowa) Community College last season.

"Gruber should make the biggest impact for us among our newcomers," McDermott said. "He's most effective with his back to the basket. It'll be tough to replace all of Breakenridge's rebounds, but we're hoping Gruber can help us."

Another forward, 6-7 senior Trey Austin, will miss the first seven games because of academic ineligibility.

The other scholarship newcomers are all freshmen—Adam Jacobson, a 6-6 forward from Fargo, N.D., where he averaged 21 points and 8.5 rebounds for Shanley High; Michael Miller, a 6-7 forward from Ames, Iowa, where he averaged 18.2 points and 10.9 rebounds for Ames High; and Matt Bennett, a 6-6 forward from Woodbury, Minn., where he averaged 20.5 points and 9.8 rebounds for Woodbury High.

"Either Jacobson or Bennett will play at the small forward," McDermott said. "And the other probably will red-shirt. That will play itself out."

Three transfers join the program, but won't be eligible until the 2002-03 season. They include Utah transfer Jon Godfread, a highly-regarded 6-11 center; 6-8 Matt Schneiderman, a junior via Morningside College; and Northern Michigan transfer Scott Mueller, a 6-2 guard.

Improving his team's shooting is a top priority for McDermott didn't take long to notice the Panthers were last in the Valley in scoring offense (60.2), scoring margin (-7.1), field-goal percentage (.418) and free-throw percentage (.628).

"You're going to have a hard time winning games when you're last in all those shooting categories," he said. "Last year's team was in a lot of games, but seemed to run out of gas and have a hard time getting good looks in the last five minutes of games. I'd like for us to be up tempo, play a lot of people and be very aggressive defensively. The three-point shot has certainly been a big part of my teams of the past and I'd like to have four guys on the floor who can shoot the three."

2001-2002 SCHEDULE

Nov.	16-17	#Red Raider Classic
	20	Montana
	25	@Wisconsin-Green Bay
	29	Texas-Pan American
Dec.	1	@UMKC
	4	Iowa
	8	@Bradley
	15	@Butler
	22	Central Michigan

	29	@Iowa State
Jan.	2	Drake
	5	Creighton
	10	@Indiana State
	12	@Southern Illinois
	16	Southwest Missouri State
	20	@Drake
	23	Indiana State
	26	Southern Illinois
	30	@Illinois State
Feb.	2	Bradley
	5	@Evansville
	9	@Creighton
	12	Wichita State
	16	@Southwest Missouri State
	19	Evansville
	23	Illinois State
	25	@Wichita State
March	1-4	##Missouri Valley Tournament

@Road Games
#Lubbock, TX (vs. San Diego State, first round; also Texas Tech, William & Mary)
##Savvis Center, St. Louis, MO

BLUE RIBBON ANALYSIS

BACKCOURT	C+
BENCH/DEPTH	D
FRONTCOURT	D
INTANGIBLES	D

The season-ending knee injury to Sieverding in the season opener last season and the subsequent unraveling of a rudderless team of transfers doomed those Panthers to a horrible fate—a 7-24 record and a last-place finish in the Missouri Valley.

Much of the dead weight has been cleared away, the energetic McDermott is in place and Sieverding is healthy for his senior year. But compared to the rest of the league, the Panthers appear to be seriously overmatched. Sieverding, Smith and Woodley form a decent backcourt, but there is little size or experience in the frontcourt.

Look for another bleak season in the cellar for the Panthers. But with a new arena on the horizon and a new coach with a UNI degree and a plan, at least the program seems to have hope for the future.

(D.R.)

Southern Illinois

LOCATION	Carbondale, IL
CONFERENCE	Missouri Valley
LAST SEASON	16-14 (.533)
CONFERENCE RECORD	10-8 (t-4th)
STARTERS LOST/RETURNING	2/3
NICKNAME	Salukis
COLORS	Maroon & White
HOMECOURT	SIU Arena (10,000)
COACH	Bruce Weber (Wisconsin-Milwaukee '74)
RECORD AT SCHOOL	51-39 (3 years)
CAREER RECORD	51-39 (3 years)
ASSISTANTS	Matt Painter (Purdue '94)
	Chris Lowery (Southern Illinois '94)
	Rodney Watson (Eastern Illinois '82)
TEAM WINS (last 5 years)	13-14-15-20-16
RPI (last 5 years)	140-157-78-58-124
2000-01 FINISH	Lost in conference quarterfinal.

In each of his three seasons at Southern Illinois, coach Bruce Weber's teams have been knocking at the Missouri Valley Conference title door. But each year the Salukis were left out in the cold, finishing fifth, third and fourth, respectively.

With some key players returning along with some talented newcomers, this is the season that SIU may knock that door down.

"We'd like to make the next step now," Weber said. "We feel we have a chance to be pretty good. [Winning a championship] won't be easy. I think the league is very, very balanced."

The Salukis' hopes start with 6-2 junior guard Kent Williams, the Valley's second-leading returning scorer at 17.6 points per game. The league's newcomer and freshman of the year in 1999-00, Williams improved his game in several areas last season. And Weber is looking for even more improvement this year.

"Last year, Kent increased his free-throw shooting

percentage, he made a big jump in three-point shooting before he wore out late in the year and he led us in total assists," Weber said. "We'd like for Kent to make a little of a transition to the point. If he played more of a combination guard, he can create more of his own shots. The biggest improvement for him can be defensively. Also, I've talked with him about averaging the same number of points as last year, but taking four or five fewer shots because we'll have some more offensive options."

The two most potent options will be inside. **Jermaine Dearman**, a 6-8 junior, averaged 11.6 points and 6.4 rebounds last season. He'll get big-time help in the SIU interior from 6-6, 240-pound **Rolan Roberts**, a senior transfer who averaged 13.1 points and 6.1 rebounds for Virginia Tech two years ago.

Roberts, a native of Woodbridge, Va., transferred to Carbondale for his final season after Virginia Tech officials suspended him for a year after an off-season, off-court incident.

"Rolan and his family decided he needed a new look, a getaway," Weber said. "So we decided he was a good enough player to take a gamble on. The year of sitting may have made him a little rusty, but it really helped him appreciate it more. Rolan will be one of the strongest kids in the league."

Roberts' presence will allow Dearman to pursue, to some degree, the face-the-basket game he prefers.

"Jermaine would like to improve his skills all over the court," Weber said. "And Roberts will free him up some inside. Roberts is a back-to-the-basket guy who can step out, but mainly he's a power player. I'd still like Jermaine to become one of the best rebounders in the league."

Sylvester Willis, a 6-6 sophomore who averaged 3.7 points and 3.1 rebounds as a freshman and started 16 games, should also be a big contributor to the Salukis. Another 6-6 returnee, senior **Tyrese Buie**, adds quality frontcourt depth. He averaged 6.6 points and 3.7 rebounds off the bench.

"Besides Kent, our strength will be our front line," Weber said. "Our goal will be to get the ball inside more and make it tougher on people to defend us. Willis is a guy who gives us a lot of little things. Buie played a lot last year and we're hoping he can step up more this year."

Another frontcourt player who will help is 6-9 **Brad Korn**, a slender red-shirt freshman who can light it up from behind the arc. Other big guys on the squad are 6-8 sophomore **Josh Warren** (0.5 ppg, 0.3 rpg), 6-6 senior **Jason Ward** (0.3 ppg, 1.4 rpg) and 6-10 freshman **Stefan Jabkiewicz**, who played at Notre Dame Prep in Greenfield, Wis.

"Brad Korn can really shoot and is really an active player," Weber said. "He's one of those unknowns for us."

Joining Williams in the backcourt is point guard **Marcus Belcher**, a 6-0 senior who wrested the position from Brandon Mells last year after Mells suffered through an injury-plagued season and eventually left the team. Belcher averaged 4.4 points and 2.3 assists.

"Marcus got the crash course at the point last year," Weber said. "He wasn't great, but he did a decent job. Hopefully, he can be a little more of a seasoned veteran for us this year."

David McGlown, a 5-10 Schoolcraft (Mich.) Community College transfer, will begin the season backing up Belcher. Other guards expected to contribute in backup roles are 6-3 freshman **Stetson Hairston**, who prepped at Bridgeton (Ill.) Academy and 6-3 freshman red-shirt **Darren Brooks**, who averaged 25 points and 6.2 rebounds at St. Louis Jennings High School two years ago.

"McGlown is a key because he gives us good depth at that position," Weber said. "Hairston gives us some athleticism and also a defensive stopper we need in the backcourt. Brooks is very talented."

Walk-on junior guard **David Carney**, who averaged 0.7 points in eight games last year, rounds out the squad.

Forward Toshay Harvey, who scored 4.4 points and grabbed 2.7 rebounds last season, has transferred to NAIA Southern New Orleans.

The Salukis' two graduated starters are forwards Joshua Cross (10.6 ppg, 6.3 rpg) and Abel Schrader (9.2 ppg, 3.3 rpg).

"A lot of people say we're not going to miss those guys," Weber said. "But they did some good things in a quiet way. Both had good careers here."

Cross and Schrader provided experienced leadership last season to a young team.

"I didn't realize how much experience meant until we went through last year," Weber said. "It started with the first day of practice. There are so many things you have to explain to an inexperienced team. It was the middle of January before they started figuring it out. Then, down the stretch, we won three games on last-second shots and three in overtime. That [close-game] experience will definitely help us this year."

The Salukis have compiled a tough non-conference schedule that should keep their RPI in good stead. They play four games against non-league teams that made the NCAA Tournament—Indiana, Iowa State, George Mason and Cal State-Northridge—as well as Conference USA rival Saint Louis.

2001-2002 SCHEDULE

Nov.	16	Belmont
	19	#@Saint Louis
	22-24	##Las Vegas Tournament
	29	Illinois-Chicago
Dec.	1	Indiana
	8	@George Mason
	16	@Cal State-Northridge
	18	@Colorado State
	22	Southeast Missouri State
	29	@Murray State
Jan.	2	@Evansville
	5	Illinois State
	7	Southwest Missouri State
	10	@Wichita State
	12	Northern Iowa
	16	@Bradley
	19	Indiana State
	24	@Drake
	26	@Northern Iowa
	30	Evansville
Feb.	3	@Creighton
	6	Wichita State
	9	Drake
	13	@Southwest Missouri State
	16	@Illinois State
	20	Creighton
	23	@Indiana State
	25	Bradley
March	1-4	###Missouri Valley Tournament

@Road Games
#First round Las Vegas Tournament
##Las Vegas, NV (schedule determined after first-round games; Pool 1 includes Georgia Tech, Illinois, Eastern Illinois, Pennsylvania. Pool 2 includes Iowa State, Saint Louis, Hartford, Southern Illinois)
###Savvis Center, St. Louis, MO

BLUE RIBBON ANALYSIS

BACKCOURT	B-
BENCH/DEPTH	B
FRONTCOURT	B-
INTANGIBLES	B-

As if returning their top two players in Williams and Dearman and some decent role players in Buie, Willis and Belcher weren't enough to make the Salukis contenders, add to the mix skilled strongman Roberts, the Virginia Tech transfer, and SIU wields an inside force virtually unmatched in the Missouri Valley.

So while the Salukis may surpass their second-place 73-point scoring average, the real question of this team remains the defense. Last year's club was the worst in the Valley, yielding 72.2 points.

Other significant question marks center on the Salukis' chemistry and leadership. Can this team blend more cohesively than it did a year ago? Will the addition of Roberts help or hinder that process?

SIU has won 32 conference games (of 54) in Weber's three years, finishing in the first division each year. This is the season the Salukis could finally push their way to the top.

(D.R.)

Southwest Missouri State

LOCATION	**Springfield, MO**
CONFERENCE	**Missouri Valley**
LAST SEASON	**13-16 (.448)**
CONFERENCE RECORD	**8-10 (t-7th)**
STARTERS LOST/RETURNING	**1/4**
NICKNAME	**Bears**
COLORS	**Maroon & White**
HOMECOURT	**Hammons Student Center (8,846)**
COACH	**Barry Hinson (Oklahoma State '83)**
RECORD AT SCHOOL	**36-27 (2 years)**
CAREER RECORD	**72-50 (8 years)**
ASSISTANTS	**Tommy Deffebaugh (Drury '85)**
	Ric Wesley (Central Michigan '80)
	Steve Lynch (Manchester '93)
TEAM WINS (last 5 years)	**24-16-22-23-13**
RPI (last 5 years)	**51-118-27-37-155**
2000-01 FINISH	**Lost in conference quarterfinal.**

Southwest Missouri State Coach Barry Hinson has heard the old good news-bad news joke about a college team returning all of its players. Good sport that he is, he's even willing to repeat it with cameras rolling and tape recorders running.

"The good news is we've got everybody back," Hinson said. "The bad news is we've got everybody back. This is the same team that finished eighth in the Missouri Valley last year and we still have great improvement to make. We don't deserve to be picked higher than fifth."

That's all well and good, but the diminutive coach, whose folksy twang is a dead ringer for Ross Perot's, has left out a couple of pertinent details in that broad stroke just as ol' Ross was wont to do. The Bears' biggest problem last year was production from their backcourt. These stats bear that out: SMS was last in the league in steals, turnover margin, three-point field goals made and finished ninth of the 10 MVC teams in assists.

And that's where guard recruits **Jason Gilbert**, a 5-11 junior transfer from Arkansas and **Terrance McGee**, a 6-0 Kirkwood (Iowa) Community College transfer, come in.

Gilbert, a native of Mountain View, Ark., is a three-point artist who left the Arkansas program toward the end of his sophomore year. After transferring to SMS, he suffered a torn ACL and underwent knee surgery last fall. He was cleared to play in June.

Gilbert, a McDonald's All-American at Mountain View where he averaged 27 points per game, scored 2.8 points as an Arkansas freshman and 6.1 as a sophomore, leading the Razorbacks in scoring twice.

McGee, a native of Milwaukee, averaged 17 points, 4.6 assists and 2.2 steals per game last season at Kirkwood, where he was selected second team NJCAA Division II All-America.

"Those two should help us dramatically in our backcourt, which was our Achilles heel all year long," Hinson said. "I'm confident that should give us much more depth and flexibility on both offense and defense.

"Everyone we've talked to about Terrance McGee emphasizes how tough a competitor he is. He's a very effective leader when he's on the floor and very competitive. He's played both guard positions and is a good shooter who does a good job running a ball club on the floor in addition to his scoring. He has good speed and quickness and he can shoot the three."

Senior guard **Robert Yanders** made some big contributions as the Bears' point guard last year in his first season after transferring from SMS-West Plains. He averaged 3.6 assists and 9.8 points. But he shot just 39 percent from the floor and only 32 percent from three-point range. Backing him up was **Donnie Williams**, now a sophomore, who averaged 1.8 points.

The Bears' shooting guard spot was a weak area all season. Two returnees—6-1 sophomore **Luke Dobbins** (4.0 ppg), 6-6 junior **Travis Walk** (2.7 ppg)—and departed Josh Hume (2.0 ppg) handled most of the duty, but that trio combined to shoot an anemic 31 percent from the field.

The frontcourt was a different story. Southwest Missouri boasted plenty of quality depth, led by junior college transfer **Mike Wallace**, a powerful 6-5 senior forward who was voted the Valley's Newcomer of the Year and Sixth Man award winner with a scoring average of 12.4 and a rebounding mark of 7.2. He also shot a league-best .583 from the field.

Graduated center Matt Rueter, who started 23 games, averaging 6.2 points and 3.5 rebounds, is the only significant player not to return.

Forward **Scott Brakebill**, a 6-8 senior who was the Bears' lone returning starter entering last year, had a frustrating season as he broke his arm at mid-season when he was fouled hard by Southern Illinois' Jermaine Dearman on a breakaway layup. Brakebill, who missed nine games, still led the team in scoring at 12.6 points per game and pulled down 4.8 rebounds.

"We've replaced Gatorade with milk as our official team drink so we can avoid broken bones this year," Hinson joked. "Scott basically didn't have a season last year. Once he broke his arm, he couldn't get it going again when he came back."

Charles Gaines, a 6-7 junior, is back after a solid year averaging 8.3 points and 6.2 rebounds. **Daniel**

Novak, a 6-7 senior who led the Bears in three-point shooting (51-for-117, .436), averaged 8.0 points and 3.8 rebounds.

Sophomore **Monwell Randle** (2.8 ppg, 2.8 rpg), a 6-7 forward, lost his red-shirt year when Brakebill went down. **Matt Engstrom**, a 6-9 red-shirt sophomore who averaged 0.4 points as a freshman, is the other returnee up front.

"We have three guys who had extensive playing time as freshmen—Dobbins, Randle and Engstrom," Hinson said. "The experience they gained was invaluable. In the Missouri Valley, that's a huge difference."

Newcomers in the frontcourt are freshmen forwards **Tamarr Maclin** of St. Louis and 6-5 walk-on **Eric Smith** of Lee's Summit, Mo. Great things are expected from Maclin, a 6-7, 240-pounder.

"Tamarr will bring a great presence," Hinson said. "He can play out on the floor and inside as well."

Freshman red-shirt guard **Trevyor Fisher**, who averaged 21.5 points and 7.0 rebounds at Greenwood High in Springfield two years ago, rounds out the squad.

Considering the Bears suffered just their second losing season last year since joining the Valley in 1990, there was much chagrin across the Ozarks.

"It was an extremely disappointing season because of the expectations we have at our university and our community," Hinson said. "We have a great basketball tradition and any time you go through something like we did, it's not advantageous to your program. But we're hoping for better times ahead this year."

2001-2002 SCHEDULE

Nov.	16	@North Texas
	24	Southeast Missouri State
	27	UMKC
Dec.	1	New Orleans
	4	@Tulsa
	7-8	#SMS Pizza Hut Classic
	17	#Texas A&M
	20-22	##Las Vegas Classic
	30	@Evansville
Jan.	2	Saint Louis
	5	Wichita State
	7	@Southern Illinois
	10	Bradley
	13	Creighton
	16	@Northern Iowa
	19	@Illinois State
	21	Evansville
	27	@Indiana State
	30	@Creighton
Feb.	2	Illinois State
	6	Drake
	9	@Wichita State
	13	Southern Illinois
	16	Northern Iowa
	20	@Bradley
	23	@Drake
	25	@Indiana State
March	1-4	###Missouri Valley Tournament

@Road Games
#Springfield, MO (vs. Southern; also Idaho State, Texas-San Antonio)
#Las Vegas Classic
##Las Vegas, NV (vs. Illinois Chicago or Purdue second round; championship on Dec. 22)
###Savvis Center, St. Louis, MO

BLUE RIBBON ANALYSIS

BACKCOURT	C
BENCH/DEPTH	C
FRONTCOURT	B+
INTANGIBLES	C

Last year, the Bears struggled shooting the ball (.435 field-goal percentage, eighth in the Valley, last in three-point field goals made) and in all of the playmaking categories (last in turnover margin, steals and ninth in assists). The additions of transfer guards Gilbert and McGee should help improve all of those numbers.

But what's needed most on this team is a better chemistry. At times last season, the five Bears on the court seemed to be playing their own games of one-on-one instead of working together. Hinson faced the unenviable task of trying to mix three junior college players with the returnees. Some of those mixtures went awry and it showed on the court.

Can SMS become more team-oriented this year? Or will the new guards clash with the backcourt returnees—Yanders, Dobbins and Williams—as everyone fights for

minutes? With a talented frontcourt in place, the key to this team will be how effectively the guards can not only get the ball inside, but also knock down some three-pointers to loosen up opposing defenses.

The Bears will find the going tough in attempting to improve on their seventh-place finish of '00-01. But there's enough talent here for this usually solid program to climb back to respectability.

(D.R.)

Wichita State

LOCATION	Wichita, KS
CONFERENCE	Missouri Valley
LAST SEASON	9-19 (.321)
CONFERENCE RECORD	4-14 (9th)
STARTERS LOST/RETURNING	2/3
NICKNAME	Shockers
COLORS	Yellow & Black
HOMECOURT	Levitt Arena (10,556)
COACH	Mark Turgeon (Kansas '87)
RECORD AT SCHOOL	9-19 (1 year)
CAREER RECORD	34-48 (3 years)
ASSISTANTS	Tad Boyle (Kansas '85)
	Jean Prioleau (Fordham '92)
	Mike Rohn (McPherson '90)
TEAM WINS (last 5 years)	14-16-13-12-9
RPI (last 5 years)	135-122-167-183-219
2000-01 FINISH	Lost in conference play-in game.

When his first Wichita State team was picked to finish last in the 10-team Missouri Valley Conference before last season, coach Mark Turgeon claimed there was no way his group would finish 10th. He was right, barely.

A late-season surge allowed the Shockers to finish ninth at 4-14, one game ahead of Northern Iowa.

"Last year was a trying year," Turgeon said. "We started pretty well [5-1 with home wins over Kansas State and Oklahoma State], but we just couldn't get it done in the league. We lost our confidence and couldn't get over the hump. We weren't a very good road team (0-12 away from Wichita). But we showed some good signs toward the end of the year when we won two-of-three and then played well at Illinois State in our last game."

A solid nucleus returns from that 9-19 team, including starters **CC McFall**, a 6-4 point guard, **Terrell Benton**, a 6-5 shooting guard and 6-8 **Troy Mack** at center, all seniors. Benton was the Shockers' leading scorer last year at 12.8 points per game. McFall was second at 10.5, and was also the team leader in assists (3.9) and the second-leading rebounder (4.7). Mack averaged 6.6 points and 4.2 rebounds in the middle.

"CC was our team MVP last year and our best player," Turgeon said. "He had a tremendous summer, lost about 20 pounds and looks good and ready to lead our team.

"Terrell carried us early last season, then had some foot problems that really hampered him. He took it easy this summer trying to get his foot right. He's trying to be a leader with this team and I think he's set up to have a good year. I expect him to be a better player.

"I expect a totally different Troy Mack this year, one more focused on basketball. He passed 46 hours last year to earn back his fourth year so as a staff we put more emphasis on academics than basketball."

Also back for Wichita State are top reserves **Duke Tshomba**, a 6-5 senior forward who averaged 7.5 points and 3.0 rebounds, **Adam Grundvig**, a 6-8 senior forward who averaged 7.1 points and 3.6 rebounds and **Matt Clark**, a 6-0 sophomore guard who averaged 2.3 points.

"At times, Duke was our best player in practice, but it never carried over to the games," Turgeon said. "He has a lot of talent and learned a lot last year [as a junior college transfer]. He needs to play better defense and be more sound with the basketball.

"Adam has a natural ability to score and has put on about 15 pounds over the summer. He had off-season knee surgery, but should be full speed by the time the season starts.

"Matt Clark had an OK freshman year and knows how to play the game. He is an excellent shooter who didn't shoot well last year [29 percent from the field]. He's a gym rat who has become a better athlete."

The Shockers are also welcoming back 6-2 junior guard **Craig Steven**, who didn't play last year because of knee and back injuries, but whose scrappiness and

desire earned him a starting spot as a freshman walk-on.

"Craig is a tough kid we really missed last year," Turgeon said. "The month he did practice he helped our toughness. I don't think I've seen the real Craig since I've been here."

Three players with eligibility remaining—6-9 Willie Davis (4.0 ppg, 2.9 rpg), 6-6 Juston White (0.5 ppg) and 6-5 Josh Drumgole (0.9 ppg)—did not return to the program.

The rest of this year's unit is comprised of seven freshmen. Because of the NCAA's 5/8 scholarship rule, the two in-state recruits (**Jamar Howard** and **Brett Begnoche**) have agreed to be walk-ons. Judging by the group's varying size and strengths, it is virtually a team within a team.

"We got a little bit of everything," Turgeon said. "We got a point guard, some guards who can really shoot it, some slashers and some inside bulk. We like this class and feel it has the potential to be successful although we may have to break it up eventually to even out our classes. We really felt the need to add some offense and all of them are scorers. The question is can they do it at the college level."

The two freshman big guys—6-8 **Rob Kampman** (18.9 ppg, 10.8 rpg at Forest City, Iowa High School) and 6-10, 254-pound **Paul Miller** (18.0 ppg, 10.0 rpg, 3.5 bpg at Blair Oaks High in Jefferson City, Mo.) will get thrown into the fire right away, Turgeon said.

"They'll both be ready for it," he said. "Especially in backup roles, although they will compete for starting jobs."

A couple of freshman guards who could make an immediate impact are 5-11 point guard **Randy Burns** of Houston (17.0 ppg, 6.0 apg at Booker T. Washington High) and 6-3 **Dion Sherrell** of Detroit (26.7 ppg at Henry Ford High). Forwards who may see early action are the 6-5 Howard of Shawnee Mission, Kan. (18.9 ppg, 9.0 rpg at Bishop Miege High) and 6-7 **Jamie Sowers** of Newark, N.J. (14.0 ppg, 9.0 rpg at St. Patrick's High).

"Randy was kind of a sleeper recruit," Turgeon said. "He's a better player than we thought. He's a tremendous shooter and has more speed than we thought.

"Dion Sherrell, Jamar Howard and Jamie Sowers are all tremendous athletes who have a chance to play right away. From day one, Howard will be our best defender and has a chance to be one of the best in the league at some point."

Begnoche, a hometown kid who averaged 16.7 points at Kapaun Mount Carmel High, is the seventh freshman.

The young Shockers will be challenged by a decent non-conference schedule that includes games against Oklahoma State, Kansas State and Tulsa as well as a respectable field at the season-opening Top of the World Classic in Fairbanks, Alaska.

"We're rebuilding and trying to get this thing going," Turgeon said. "But there's no question we're headed in the right direction. We have a great administration and we hope to break ground soon on our new athletic offices, practice facility and renovation of Henry Levitt. It will really be phenomenal when it's done.

"We had the second-best attendance in the league last year [averaging 8,026] and that wasn't very good. We're coming off a 9-19 season and we have seven freshmen, so we're trying not to get the cart ahead of the horse. But I do think we're a better basketball team than last year."

Notice he left the predictions this year to the sportswriters.

2001-2002 SCHEDULE

Nov.	16-18	#Top of the World Classic
	24	Georgia Southern
	28	Texas-Arlington
Dec.	1	@Oklahoma State
	5	@Kansas State
	8	Tulsa
	17	Jacksonville
	21	Western Carolina
	29	@Chicago State
Jan.	2	Bradley
	5	@Southwest Missouri State
	7	@Illinois State
	10	Southern Illinois
	12	Drake
	16	@Indiana State
	19	Evansville
	22	Creighton
	27	@Bradley
	30	@Drake
Feb.	3	Indiana State
	6	@Southern Illinois

9	Southwest Missouri State
12	@Northern Iowa
17	@Creighton
20	Illinois State
23	@Evansville
25	Northern Iowa
March 1-4	##Missouri Valley Tournament

@Road Games
#Fairbanks, AK (vs. Delaware first round; also Radford, Butler, Ole Miss, Alaska-Fairbanks, Butler, Bowling Green)
##Savvis Center, St. Louis, MO

BLUE RIBBON ANALYSIS

BACKCOURT	C+
BENCH/DEPTH	D+
FRONTCOURT	D+
INTANGIBLES	C

Turgeon got the league's attention at the start of last season when the Shockers, picked to finish last in the Valley, began 5-1 and sported wins over Kansas State and Oklahoma State. Then came an agonizing 2-13 stretch when they could have folded up shop. But Turgeon kept the team motivated and finished reasonably strong as the Shockers won two of their last five and played competitively in the three losses. The new coach was well received in a basketball-crazy town that has been starved for a winner for more than a decade.

The top two scorers—Benton and McFall—are back along with some decent role players, but this year's Shockers will have to rely strongly on at least some of the seven incoming freshmen, never a winning formula in a league where the top teams are always heavy on experience. Keep in mind the Shockers did not win a road game last year.

So the good folks of Wichita will need to rely again on their well-tested patience. The Shockers have enough talent on hand to produce some exciting moments as Turgeon continues to inculcate the Kansas Jayhawks' system into the program. But they are too young and too thin inside to expect much better than the ninth-place finish of a year ago.

(D.R.)

Air Force

LOCATION	Colorado Springs, CO
CONFERENCE	Mountain West
LAST SEASON	8-21 (.276)
CONFERENCE RECORD	3-11 (8th)
STARTERS LOST/RETURNING	1/4
NICKNAME	Falcons
COLORS	Blue & Silver
HOMECOURT	Clune Arena (6,002)
COACH	Joe Scott (Princeton '87)
RECORD AT SCHOOL	8-21 (1 year)
CAREER RECORD	8-21 (1 year)
ASSISTANTS	Chris Mooney (Princeton '94)
	Mike McKee (Lehigh '94)
	Larry Mangino (Montclair State '83)
TEAM WINS (last 5 years)	7-10-10-8-8
RPI (last 5 years)	250-208-179-224-232
2000-01 FINISH	Lost in conference quarterfinal.

Joe Scott knew he had a difficult task ahead of him when he took over the Air Force program last year. Air Force has been the doormat of the Mountain West Conference and former Western Athletic Conference ever since the Academy left independent status in 1980.

One of Scott's first goals was easy—to upgrade the Falcons' schedule to eliminate all non-Division I games. That took longtime patsies like Regis College and Adams State off the schedule and eliminated a couple of automatic wins from the Falcons' ledger.

The next goal was to win more Division I games, and the Falcons did that by winning eight, two more than the year before.

Another thing Scott wanted to accomplish was to be competitive every game, and for the most part the Falcons were in 2000-2001. Looking back, Scott can point to nine games the Falcons had a legitimate shot at winning in the second half.

Scott isn't putting any numbers goals on this year's squad, but he wants the Falcons to be better mentally so they can win the close games they lost last year.

"I know we're a better team, but are we better men-

tally?" he said. "I know we were more competitive and were in every game last year. At the start of the season our players expected to lose. But by the end of the season they started expecting to win."

One of the Falcons' biggest wins came in the final week of the regular season when they dominated Utah in a 71-60 home win, keeping the Utes from winning the MWC outright and perhaps knocking them from the NCAA Tournament. Two nights later they lost to co-champion BYU by one point in the final seconds, then were eliminated by the Cougars in the first round of the MWC Tournament after leading at halftime.

The Falcons will miss Jarvis Croff, their leading scorer the last two seasons and an All-MWC selection as a junior. Croff averaged 13.0 points last year, actually down four from the previous year, as his shooting fell to 41.7 percent and 38.2 percent from three-point range.

But Croff is the only loss, as two other graduating seniors hardly played last year. Two other players who "didn't want to play," Scott said—center Josh Wallace and forward Bryan Summers—aren't returning either. The 6-9 Wallace had started nine games last year and averaged 3.2 points and 2.0 rebounds per game.

"Everybody else is back," Scott said. "Last year we only had six players we'd use in games and who could practice with us. With all the returning players and the freshmen we have coming in, I expect spirited practices every day with competition for spots. These guys expect to play, and I think that brings healthy respect and raises

the level of the program."

Lamoni Yazzie the only senior expected to play much this year, has been chosen captain. Yazzie, a 6-1, 180-pound guard, started 20 games and averaged 8.8 points. Yazzie is a fine outside shooter, averaging 43.7 percent from three-point range. But where he really excels is at the free-throw line, where he shot 88.0 percent last year, best in the Mountain West Conference.

Yazzie was buried on the Falcon bench before Scott arrived—he played in only 15 games the previous year and averaged just 1.3 points. But Scott saw something in the young man from a family of eight in Tuba City, Ariz., and now sees him as a big part of the Falcons' plans this year.

"Yazzie has really improved his passing ability," Scott said. "He's a very competitive player."

Tom Bellairs was MWC co-freshman of the year two years ago and big things were expected from him in 2000-2001. Unfortunately he missed the first five games with an injury and took a while to get back in the flow. He ended up leading the team in rebounding with 7.2 per game, an average that ranked fifth in the Mountain West Conference. He was also third on the team in scoring at 9.7 points per game.

"Bellairs is getting better all the time," Scott said. "He's a very good rebounder, but he's not your typical center per se. We need him to be more of a perimeter player for us. We need him to make threes in our system. He's dribbling the ball more and I like what I see in him."

MOUNTAIN WEST

BLUE RIBBON FORECAST
1. Wyoming
2. Utah
3. New Mexico
4. San Diego State
5. BYU
6. UNLV
7. Colorado State
8. Air Force

TOP 40
Utah and Wyoming are ranked among the 2001-2002 Blue Ribbon Top 40. Extended profiles can be found in the Top 40 section of Blue Ribbon.

ALL-CONFERENCE TEAM
G - Ruben Douglas, JR, New Mexico
G - Marcus Bailey, JR, Wyoming
F - Britton Johnsen, JR, Utah
F - Josh Davis, SR, Wyoming
C - Tom Bellairs, JR, Air Force

PLAYER OF THE YEAR
Josh Davis, Wyoming

NEWCOMER OF THE YEAR
Tony Bland, JR, San Diego State

2001-2002 CONFERENCE TOURNAMENT
March 7-9, Thomas and Mack Center, Las Vegas, NV

2000-2001 CHAMPIONS
Utah, BYU and Wyoming (Regular season)
BYU (Conference tournament)

2000-2001 POSTSEASON PARTICIPANTS
NCAA
BYU
NIT
New Mexico (Third Round)
Utah
Wyoming

TOP BACKCOURTS
1. New Mexico
2. Utah
3. Wyoming

TOP FRONTCOURTS
1. Wyoming
2. Utah
3. San Diego State

INSIDE THE NUMBERS
2000-2001 conference RPI: 2nd (of 31)
Conference RPI (last five years): 6-2-4-1-2

DID YOU KNOW?
Because of the Winter Olympics being contested in Utah in February, the MWC schedule had to be worked around the two-week event. Utah and BYU will go out of town the weekend of the opening ceremonies and the weekend of the closing ceremonies and will each play host to New Mexico and Air Force the middle weekend, Feb. 16-18. The Air Force team will be housed at Hill Air Force Base 30 miles north of Salt Lake City because of the lack of hotel space, but New Mexico's plans are uncertain. ... The MWC postseason tournament has been played in Las Vegas the last two years and three years before that when the MWC teams were part of the Western Athletic Conference. But starting in 2004, the tournament will be played at a neutral site at the Pepsi Center in Denver. That contract runs through 2006. ... Utah's Rick Majerus has been at his school for 12 years, one year less than the rest of the league's coaches have been at their schools combined. BYU's Steve Cleveland is second in seniority with four years, followed by Wyoming's Steve McClain (3), New Mexico's Fran Fraschilla (2), San Diego State's Steve Fisher (2), Air Force's Joe Scott (1) and Colorado State's Dale Layer (1). UNLV's Charlie Spoonhour is starting his first year. ... For the second straight year, the MWC put half of its teams into postseason play in 2000-2001, with BYU in the NCAA and New Mexico, Wyoming and Utah in the NIT. ... Utah had its longest-in-the-nation home winning streak broken last year with two home losses, but still has the longest league home winning streak with 44 straight wins. ... BYU led the nation in free-throw shooting at 78.0 percent last year. ... Utah found secondary NCAA violations in its program during an internal audit this summer and imposed penalites, including a cutback in recruiting by the coaching staff. ... Mountain West teams will play 16 games on national television, including 10 on ESPN, four on ABC and two on ESPN2. ... Las Vegas native Demetrius Hunter has transferred from Georgetown to UNLV and will be eligible for the 2002-2003 season.

(M.S.)

Bellairs made 9-of-34 three-pointers last year and shot 46.1 from the field.

Vernard Jenkins was the only player to start every game for the Falcons last year after starting most games the year before. Although Scott doesn't like to label his guards, Jenkins essentially is the point guard as he averaged nearly four assists per game, more than double anyone else on the team. He also scored 6.7 points per game, up from his 4.6 average the year before. Jenkins needs to improve his shooting, however, after he shot just 28.4 percent from three-point range and just 37.4 percent overall after shooting 34 percent the year before from both three-point range and overall.

Two 6-6 sophomores, **Joel Gerlach** and **Robert Todd**, were pleasant surprises as freshmen last year and both are likely to start this year. Gerlach was voted MWC freshman of the year in a media poll and Scott believes Todd could have earned the honor if he hadn't sat out the last eight games.

Gerlach started the last 20 games and scored 8.6 points per game on 51.2 percent shooting. His best outing came against Wyoming, when he scored 26 points on 9-of-13 from the field.

"He's well-rounded, he's fast, athletic, he can make the three-point shot," Scott said. "He poses match-up problems for other teams."

Todd had to miss the last eight games because of a violation of Academy rules, but he's back in full standing for this season. Todd finished second on the team in scoring with a 10.7 average and led all MWC freshmen in scoring. He also led the MWC in three-pointers per game. His best game came against Long Beach State, when he scored 25 points on 10-of-11 shooting.

"He's a very good three-point shooter (45.7 percent) and has worked on his driving," Scott said. "He's one of those players who benefited a lot from having played last year."

Scott wants Todd to go to the basket more and draw some fouls. He attempted only 19 free throws last year, despite playing 27 minutes a game.

Bellairs has played center much of the last two years, but Scott would like to develop a true center this season, even though Bellairs will still see time in the middle.

"You can't play 40 minutes with a 6-7 center in this league," Scott said.

Tysen Pina, a 6-8, 202-pound sophomore, who played in 11 games last year, has been impressive, and he'll get a look along with three freshmen—6-9 **Jarrett Hess**, 6-8 **David Peterson** and 6-8 **Shawn McDanal**.

"I don't know which of the four guys is going to do it, but we need one of them to step up," Scott said.

Another freshman who will play a lot is **Tim Keller**, a 6-3, 175-pound guard from Austin, Texas, who played on the AFA Prep School team last year.

"Tim is long-armed, he's fast and he's a good shooter," Scott said. "He'll definitely play a lot for us."

Other freshmen who will see time for the Falcons this year are **Eric Lang**, a 6-4 forward and **Dan Stock**, a 5-9 guard from Wyoming, both of whom played for the AFA Prep School last year.

A.J. Kuhle, a 6-3 sophomore swingman, didn't have great numbers as a freshman (28.1 field-goal shooting), but he'll be in the mix after playing in 26 games with five starts last year. So could **Selwyn Mansell**, another 5-9 guard, who played in 19 games last year with four early starts.

One other player who will get a chance is **Donny Legans**, a 6-2 guard who worked his way up from the junior varsity to play the final four games last year. In his second game, he hit a pair of key baskets near the end of an upset win over Utah.

Whoever he ends up playing, Scott says it may not have anything to do with what the positions are.

"My philosophy is you play your best guys," Scott said. "I'd rather go out with three 6-6 guys who battle and scrap and fight."

2001-2002 SCHEDULE

Nov.	13	#Yale
	18	Denver
	24	@Navy
	30	##Fresno State Tournament
Dec.	1	##Fresno State Tournament
	5	Arkansas State
	8	Oakland
	12	@Denver
	22	@Liberty
	29	Tennessee Tech
Jan.	2	@Northern Arizona
	7	UNLV
	10	@Texas-Pan American
	14	@New Mexico
	19	Utah
	21	Brigham Young
	26	@Colorado State
	28	@Wyoming
Feb.	4	San Diego State
	9	New Mexico
	16	@Utah
	18	@Brigham Young
	23	@Wyoming
	25	Colorado State
	28	@UNLV
March	2	@San Diego State
	7-10	###MWC Tournament

@Road Games
#Guardians Classic (if Air Force wins, it will play again on Nov. 14; Semifinals and final are Nov. 20-21 at Kemper Arena, Kansas City, MO)
##Fresno, CA (vs. Montana State first round; also Fresno State, UC Riverside)
###Thomas & Mack Center, Las Vegas, NV

BLUE RIBBON ANALYSIS

BACKCOURT	C
BENCH/DEPTH	C+
FRONTCOURT	B-
INTANGIBLES	C+

There's no doubt Scott has injected some life into the Air Force program. He's weeded out some of the dead wood in the program and by playing a lot of freshmen last year, he'll have some needed experience this year.

The former Princeton assistant believes Air Force is the kind of school that can develop a strong basketball program with smart, disciplined players, and he's determined to prove it.

The Falcons aren't about to turn into a winning program overnight, especially in the competitive Mountain West Conference. Scott knows it will take baby steps, but he also feels strongly that his team can beat anyone else in the league at home and can push anyone to the limit on the road.

This year the Falcons should improve their record slightly, perhaps getting to double-figure wins overall. They'll still struggle to make the first division in the MWC, but watch for them to escape from the cellar this year. If one of their centers can develop, keep on eye on the Falcons in 2002-2003, when they return all but one player from this year's team.

(M.S.)

Brigham Young

LOCATION	**Provo, UT**
CONFERENCE	**Mountain West**
LAST SEASON	**24-9 (.727)**
CONFERENCE RECORD	**10-4 (t-1st)**
STARTERS LOST/RETURNING	**4/1**
NICKNAME	**Cougars**
COLORS	**Blue & White**
HOMECOURT	**Marriott Center (22,700)**
COACH	**Steve Cleveland (UC Irvine '76)**
RECORD AT SCHOOL	**67-57 (5 years)**
CAREER RECORD	**67-57 (5 years)**
ASSISTANTS	**Dave Rose (Houston '83)**
	Andy Toolson (BYU '90)
	John Wardenburg (BYU '86)
TEAM WINS (last 5 years)	**1-9-12-22-24**
RPI (last 5 years)	**261-167-139-41-43**
2000-01 FINISH	**Lost in NCAA first round.**

During his four years as BYU coach, Steve Cleveland has taken the Cougars on a steady upward climb from one of the worst teams in America (1-25 the year before he took over) to a conference championship team that made it to the NCAA Tournament last year.

Talk about going from the outhouse to the penthouse.

After winning nine games his first year and 12 his second, Cleveland led the Cougars to a 22-11 record in 1999-2000 and followed it with last year's sterling 24-9 record that included the Mountain West regular-season co-championship, the league tournament championship and a first-round NCAA Tournament loss to Cincinnati.

It would be hard for any coach to keep moving upward after a season like last year's, and after losing four-of-five starters from last year the Cougars will be looking to keep from sliding too much.

"I think when you lose five seniors, 80 percent of your scoring and your top three recruits leave [on missions and to play baseball], there's probably reason to be concerned," Cleveland said. "Certainly nobody in the league had greater losses than we did."

Not only did the Cougars lose MWC Player of the Year Mekeli Wesley, they also lost all-league guard Terrell Lyday, and guard Trent Whiting, who contributed plenty (14.2 ppg) in his one year in the program. Among the three of them, Wesley, Lyday and Whiting combined to score 48 points per game last year. Also gone are Nathan Cooper, who started 20 games and Nate Knight, who was one of the first men off the bench last year.

On top of that, Garner Meads and Derek Dawes left on Mormon missions and Jake Chrisman decided to take a year off from basketball to find out if a professional baseball career is in his future.

Then there are the injured players. Michael Vranes, a 6-3 junior who started every game in 1999-2000, sat out last year and hasn't played for nearly 18 months because of a foot problem that has plagued him for years. In late September, Vranes decided to leave the team.

"He is having a difficult time walking without pain," Cleveland said. "It's a quality of life issue. It's a matter of maintaining a normal life."

Also, **Jesse Pinegar**, who sat out last year with an injury after missing his senior year of high school, suffered another injury in June and will likely be out until December.

Eric Nielsen is the top returning starter, but he's not the type of player you can build a team around. The 6-9, 215-pound senior is a hard-working forward who gets rebounds and plays tough defense, but has never been much of an offensive force. He's an aggressive player who often gets in foul trouble (nine disqualifications last year), something he needs to avoid this year because of the lack of depth on the front line. At 6.2 points and 3.8 rebounds, Nielsen is the top returning player in both categories and the Cougars need him to double both numbers this year.

"Eric is going to have to be a 15 [points] and 10 [rebounds] guy for us and he hasn't been asked to do that before," Cleveland said. "He may have to play 35 minutes a night for us, which will be hard if he gets in foul trouble like he has."

Mark Bigelow was the leading scorer and rebounder for the Cougars and WAC Freshman of the Year two years ago before he went on a two-year Mormon mission to Florida. Bigelow, who averaged 15.0 points and 6.3 rebounds per game in 1998-99, came back an inch taller at 6-7, but he also weighed less at 185 and will need to bulk up a bit before the season starts. Traditionally, returned missionaries take a few months to get their legs back and the question will be how long it takes Bigelow to round into playing shape after just returning in June.

"We have to expect it will take some time for Mark," Cleveland said. "It's a little easier for guards than big men coming back from missions, but it's still difficult. It probably won't happen for awhile, but I expect by January for him to be a go-to guy."

Daniel Bobik was coming off a mission last year and averaged just 3.5 points in 28 games, shooting just .388 from the field and .267 from three-point range. Bobik, a 6-6 sophomore, was a highly-touted recruit out of high school and over the summer he spent a few weeks in New York, learning the city game at the West 4th Street cage and the Brooklyn YMCA. A New York Post article reported that Bobik "stuck out like a white thread on a black suit," but he also got accolades from several of the players and coaches there.

"This is Daniel's time and I expect him to play a lot for us this year," Cleveland said.

Travis Hansen, a 6-6 junior, started nine games last year, but had his season shortened by a foot injury that caused him to miss nine games. He will need to improve his shooting, (29 percent from three-point range and 41 percent overall).

"Between Eric, Mark, Daniel and Travis—we'll look to those four guys to score for us," Cleveland said. "We might even play all four together sometimes."

Matt Montague, a 6-1 senior, has quite a bit of starting experience, including 12 games last year and 45 his first two years. Although the Kentucky native performs many of the point-guard duties well—such as passing and leading the team—he's never been much of a scorer, especially from the outside. Last year he made just 40 percent of his field goals in averaging just 2.2 points per game.

Vranes would provide valuable experience if he is able to return. In 1999-2000, Vranes started every game and averaged 8.0 points, 4.1 rebounds and 2.7 assists, and the year before he started 25-of-27 games. Although his natural position is the off-guard, he started several games at the point.

Challenging Montague in the backcourt is **Shawn Opunui**, a 5-11 freshman who returned from his mission earlier this year. Playing at Orem High School, not far from the BYU campus, Opunui averaged 21.7 points and 6.1 assists per game as a senior.

The Cougars lost three members of last year's heralded freshman class, at least temporarily. Chrisman, who played in 28 games and averaged 2.8 points, will red-shirt this year while he decides whether to pursue a baseball career. Chrisman pitched for the Cougar baseball team and is considered a good professional prospect.

The 6-10 Dawes would likely have been the starting center this year, but decided after the season to leave on a church mission. Meads, who was coveted by both Utah and Stanford, left for a mission in January after suffering an injury in preseason practice.

The other member of last year's freshman class, the 6-9 Pinegar, missed last season because of an injury and will be out until at least December recovering from shoulder surgery.

Cleveland said the center position would be handled "by committee" this year, with no standouts ready to step in for Wesley.

Seven-foot sophomore **Dan Howard** is one candidate for the open center position, but he doesn't have a lot of experience after scoring just 12 points in 14 games last year. **Bart Jepsen**, a 6-9, 235-pound sophomore, sat out last year with an injury after having returned from a mission. He could see some time inside after starting nine games as a freshman.

Jon Carlisle, a 6-10, 260-pound junior, was the backup center behind Michael Doleac on Utah's 1998 NCAA runner-up team and he transferred after his mission. He had some serious health problems during his mission, however, and may not be ready to contribute this season.

Since Cleveland has been coach, he hasn't shown any hesitation about playing freshman and besides Opunui, center **Jared Jensen**, 6-9, 240, should see some significant minutes. Jensen was selected Mr. Basketball in Utah by the Desert News after starring for Fremont High School, where he averaged 26 points and 13 rebounds per game. Cleveland said Jensen might already have the best post moves of any of his centers.

Another freshman is 6-5 guard **Jimmy Balderson**, who averaged 34.5 points at Magrath High School in Alberta, but Cleveland expects him to sit out as a red-shirt this year.

Two Division I transfers, guard Rick Bower (Wisconsin) and forward Jake Shoff (Weber State), will red-shirt this year and be eligible for the 2002-2003 season.

Last year the Cougars led the nation in free throw shooting, thanks mainly to the big three of Wesley, Whiting and Lyday, who all made more than 80 percent of their free throws. No one else on the team shot more than 78 percent, so that could be a factor in close games.

The loss of the three top scorers is the most obvious blow to the program, but just as key could be the loss of assistant coaches Heath Schroyer and Jeff Judkins. Schroyer, who was credited with implementing the Cougars' strong defense under Cleveland, left to become an assistant at Wyoming, while Judkins, who brought a wealth of experience as a 10-year assistant to Rick Majerus at Utah, has taken over as head coach of the BYU women's team.

Taking over as assistant coaches this year are Andy Toolson—a former star for the Cougars who has played professional ball overseas for most of the last decade and also spent some time in the NBA—and John Wardenburg, who coached high school basketball in southern Utah.

2001-2002 SCHEDULE

Nov.	17	@San Diego
	24	Arizona State
	28	@UC Santa Barbara
Dec.	1	@Utah State
	5	Weber State
	8	Creighton
	12	Fort Lewis
	15	Idaho
	22	*Stanford
	27	Cal State Northridge
	29	Southern Utah
Jan.	2	San Francisco
	5	@Pepperdine
	10	UNLV
	12	San Diego State
	19	@New Mexico
	21	@Air Force
	28	@Utah
	31	Colorado State
Feb.	2	Wyoming
	9	@UNLV
	11	@San Diego State
	14	Air Force
	16	New Mexico
	23	Utah
	28	@Wyoming
March	2	@Colorado State
	7-9	#MWC Tournament

@Road Games
*Las Vegas Shootout, Las Vegas
#Thomas & Mack Center, Las Vegas, NV

BLUE RIBBON ANALYSIS

BACKCOURT	B-
BENCH/DEPTH	C+
FRONTCOURT	B
INTANGIBLES	C+

After consecutive seasons with 22 and 24 victories, the Cougars will be hard-pressed to win 20 games this year. They still have talent in the program, especially at the big guard and small forward spots, but point guard and center will be a big concern for Cleveland this year, as will overall depth.

Church missions have always been a problem for BYU coaches because they never know which players will be leaving and when, and then they don't know how each player will respond when he returns. Losing Dawes and Meads hurts the Cougars in the middle and they won't know perhaps until mid-season how much Bigelow will help them.

With all the uncertainty surrounding the team—the injuries to Vranes and Pinegar, how well Bigelow will come back and who will take over at center—the Cougars could be in for a challenging year. After last year's championship season, the Cougars may have to be content with just an overall winning season and a top-division finish in the Mountain West.

(M.S.)

Colorado State

LOCATION	**Fort Collins, CO**
CONFERENCE	**Mountain West**
LAST SEASON	**15-13 (.536)**
CONFERENCE RECORD	**6-8 (t-5th)**
STARTERS LOST/RETURNING	**4/1**
NICKNAME	**Rams**
COLORS	**Green & Gold**
HOMECOURT	**Moby Arena (8,745)**
COACH	**Dale Layer (Eckerd College '80)**
RECORD AT SCHOOL	**182-100 (10 years)**
CAREER RECORD	**205-87 (10 years)**
ASSISTANTS	**Pat Eberhart (Adams State '89)**
	Bill Peterson (Eckerd '79)
	Buzz Williams (Oklahoma City '94)
TEAM WINS (last 5 years)	**20-20-19-18-15**
RPI (last 5 years)	**69-72-88-105-134**
2000-01 FINISH	**Lost in conference quarterfinal.**

For the last four years, the Colorado State basketball program has been in a bit of a slide. The number of wins has gone down every year while the RPI rating has gotten worse every year. Instability in the program has been part of the reason, as the Rams have gone through three coaches with Stew Morrill leaving to go to Utah State, Ritchie McKay leaving for Oregon State after two years and Dale Layer taking over for McKay last year.

Layer inherited a veteran team with several starters back but no real stars and not a lot of talent in the frontcourt. Still, the team held together well and some called it an overachieving team to get to 15-13. After the season Layer had no complaints, saying his team "couldn't have worked any harder."

The Rams started off 5-0 for the first time since 1971, with a road win at Washington State the most significant, but they came back to earth with a 23-point loss to eventual NCAA Tournament entrant Creighton. After going 9-4 in non-conference play, the Rams started off league play with a tough one-point loss to Wyoming and later lost to the Cowboys by only two on the road. Losses at New Mexico and Air Force were both by one point. Reverse those four losses and the Rams would have tied for the conference crown and finished with 19 overall wins.

Over the last couple of years, the Rams have been one of the nation's best shooting teams, ranking 11th in three-point shooting last year after leading the nation the year before. However, a lack of a productive inside game with no legitimate center hurt them against some of the big, bruising teams in the Mountain West Conference.

With sharpshooters like Jon Sivesind, Ron Grady and Aki Palmer gone, the Rams will have to reload in the backcourt and try to become a more balanced team, instead of relying so much on their outside shooting. Besides the three guards, the Rams also lost 6-10 forward David Fisher, the second-leading scorer last year at 11.7 points per game, and forward Garrett Patik, who started every game but one and led the team in rebounding (6.0), while scoring 7.8 points per game. Forward R'Cell Harris played 25 games but saw limited action, while Buck Hayes left the program after playing in just 12 games.

"With eight new players, there's no question we are rebuilding this year," Layer said. "Any time you lose five guys who started a good bit of the year, you end up being a little nervous about what your team will be like. We have a lot of uncertainties."

The one returning starter is 6-8, 225-pound junior **Brian Greene**, and even he wasn't a full-time starter in 2000-2001. Greene, a home grown star from Horizon High School in Thornton, Colo., started 18-of-27 games and averaged 7.8 points and 5.9 rebounds while shooting 50.9 percent from the field. His best game was a 15-point, 15-rebounds performance against Wyoming, but a sprained knee a couple of games later set him back and hindered him for the rest of the season.

"He's a warrior inside and a ferocious rebounder," Layer said. "He's got a toughness about him and he's just a solid, all-around player."

Andy Birley (5.7 ppg, 1.8 rpg) made an instant impact as a freshman two years ago when he made 48.2 percent of his three-point shots and ranked among the nation's leaders all season. The 6-4 junior combo guard couldn't duplicate his freshman success last year as his shooting fell off to 35.7 percent from three-point range and 39.1 percent from the field, down from 47.5 the year before. He struggled a bit when he had to play the point last year, but still had the second-best assist-to-turnover ratio on the team with 76 assist to 45 turnovers.

"Andy's got excellent size and should fill in for Sivesind," said Layer. "He's really improved his ball-handling skills and his one-on-one moves. He's a very good outside shooter."

The only other returning players are sophomore **Jonathan Sanders** (1.3 ppg, 1.4 rpg) and senior **Matt Brown** (3.8 ppg, 2.0 rpg).

The 6-7, 195-pound Sanders, who was a highly-touted recruit out of Denver, can play two positions, but he's different from most in that the two positions he plays are point guard and small forward. That's because of the way he plays—he's a very good passer who likes to drive and slash to the basket, but he isn't known as a great outside shooter (33 percent field-goal shooting last year). His size is more suited to the small-forward spot, but if his ball-handling skills are solid enough, he can be a valuable weapon as a 6-7 point guard.

"He has very good passing skills and sees the floor well," Layer said. "He'll definitely get some good experience this year."

The 6-9, 215-pound Brown came from Southern Idaho Junior College, where he shot 65 percent from the field, after spending a year at Stephen F. Austin. He saw action in 24 games last year. He's not expected to be a main contributor this year, but he can provide some inside muscle for he Rams.

Among the newcomers, two who might make the biggest impact are junior college transfers **Quantone Smith** and point guard **Joe Macklin**.

Smith is a 6-8, 250-pound junior forward from North Dakota State Junior College, who was ranked among the top 40 junior college players in the nation.

"He's a strong, big-body with a lot of good skills," Layer said. "He can score inside and outside and he ought to be a productive inside guy for us."

Macklin is a 5-11 junior from Barton County (Kansas) Community College who led his team to the NJCAA Tournament. Layer said he has a chance to start or he could back up Birley if he plays the point.

"He showed an ability to be an up-tempo player on a very good team last year," Layer said. "He's a good defender who gives us more quickness on the perimeter and a different dimension than we've had in recent years."

Two red-shirt freshmen who are ready to play after biding their time last year are guard **Jon Rakiecki** and center **Matt Nelson**. Rakiecki is a 6-3 shooting guard who was considered one of Colorado's finest players during his career at Fruita Monument High School. He earned all-state honors twice and led his team to four consecutive state tournament appearances.

"Jon is a very athletic, explosive scoring guard who could have played for us last year if we didn't have two or three guys just like him," Layer said. "He's a very good shooter and should play a lot for us this year."

Nelson is one of the tallest players ever at CSU at 7-0. The only problem is he needs a little more meat on his bones. He gained 15 pounds during his red-shirt year to get up to 227, but Layer would like to see him add another 15 to get him above 240.

"Matt has got some skills and foot quickness for his size," Layer said. "He's definitely going to help us, but needs to get bigger so he can withstand the banging that goes on in our league."

A player who could make an impact for the Rams is 6-5 sophomore forward **Ronnie Clark**, who was the player of the year at Florida Southern College two years ago. Unfortunately, he won't be eligible until after the first semester, which means he'll miss the first nine or 10 games as well as the practices. Layer expects Clark to "definitely be in the rotation" but it may take him awhile for him to get warmed up.

Other newcomers are **Darian Burke**, a 6-10 forward-center who will be a sophomore in eligibility, **Freddy Robinson**, a 6-5 freshman swingman and **Matt Williams**, a 6-6 freshman forward from Temple, Texas, who was ranked among the top 200 prep players last year.

Burke averaged two blocked shots per game at Grayson (Texas) College and during the off-season he was invited to play some games in Iran, of all places. Williams was an all-state player in Texas and ranked among the nation's 200 recruits. Likewise for Robinson, who was also an all-state pick at Central High School in Tulsa, Okla.

"The guys we've signed are more athletic than what we have now," Layer told the Denver Post. "These guys represent a big change for us."

The Rams play seven non-conference games at home, which should help their overall record and give them some confidence before league games start in January. Among the teams coming to Moby Arena are Michigan, Colorado and Southern Illinois, along with patsies such as Montana Tech and Morris Brown. The road schedule includes games at Washington State, Baylor and South Carolina and the Hawaii-Hilo Tournament.

"We are going to be very young and when you have that many young guys, you hope to grow and develop," Layer said. "We're going to an improved team by the time league play starts and we hope to be in the mix."

2001-2002 SCHEDULE

Nov.	17	Montana Tech
	20	@Washington State
	23-25	#Big Island Invitational
	29	@Gardner Webb
Dec.	1	@South Carolina
	5	Colorado
	8	Arkansas-Little Rock
	15	@Denver
	18	Southern Illinois
	20	Indiana-Purdue Fort Wayne
	29	Michigan
Jan.	2	@Baylor
	5	Morris Brown
	12	@Wyoming
	19	@San Diego State
	21	@UNLV
	26	Air Force
	28	New Mexico
	31	@BYU
Feb.	2	@Utah
	9	Wyoming
	16	San Diego State
	18	UNLV
	23	@New Mexico
	25	@Air Force
	28	Utah
March	2	Brigham Young
	7-10	##MWC Tournament

@Road Games
#Hilo, HI (vs. South Carolina State first round; also Hawaii, Hawaii-Hilo, Mercer, LSU, Weber State, Wisconsin)
##Thomas & Mack Center, Las Vegas, NV

BLUE RIBBON ANALYSIS

BACKCOURT	C+
BENCH/DEPTH	C
FRONTCOURT	C+
INTANGIBLES	B-

Replacing four starters and five of your top six players isn't easy for any basketball program and for one that finished barely above .500 last year, it could mean disaster. The Rams will be missing 52 points from last year's team which averaged just 69 per game, with just one starter back in Greene.

Layer did an admirable job coaching last year with his undersized team, but the Rams were able to prevail in several games because of their outstanding shooting. Unfortunately many of those fine shooters have graduated and the Rams will have to find more ways to win ball games with an inexperienced bunch of players this year.

The Rams' record of nine consecutive winning seasons and nine straight years with at least 15 wins could come to an end this year. CSU has some talent coming into the program, but if the new players don't come together in a hurry, the Rams may be fighting to stay out of the Mountain West cellar this year.

(M.S.)

UNLV

LOCATION	Las Vegas, NV
CONFERENCE	Mountain West
LAST SEASON	16-13 (.552)
CONFERENCE RECORD	7-7 (4th)
STARTERS LOST/RETURNING	3/2
NICKNAME	Rebels
COLORS	Scarlet & Gray
HOMECOURT	Thomas & Mack Center (18,500)
COACH	Charlie Spoonhour (Ozarks '61)
RECORD AT SCHOOL	First year
CAREER RECORD	319-171 (16 years)
ASSISTANTS	Deane Martin (Central Missouri '87)
	Jay Spoonhour (Pittsburg State '94)
	Derek Thomas (Missouri-St. Louis '89)
TEAM WINS (last 5 years)	22-20-16-23-16
RPI (last 5 years)	55-47-82-50-98
2000-01 FINISH	Won regular-season finale.

Since Jerry Tarkanian left in 1992, two years after winning an NCAA championship, the UNLV basketball program has gone through four coaches, if you count Max Good, who was the coach for most of last season.

Good took over after Billy Bayno was fired seven games into his sixth season soon after the NCAA put UNLV on probation. Before that, Rollie Massimino came from Villanova and lasted just two years before Tim Grgurich took over for the 1994-95 season.

Looking for some stability and experience, the Rebels hired 62-year-old Charlie Spoonhour, the former Saint Louis and Southwest Missouri State coach after getting spurned by a couple of Ricks—Rick Pitino and Utah coach Rick Majerus.

In becoming the 12th head coach in school history, Spoonhour was actually lured from the comforts of retirement to come to the desert and try to turn the Vegas program back into the national powerhouse it once was. He said he planned to retire in Las Vegas anyway, so what the heck, he might as well coach while he's there.

"The main thing is because the job is in Las Vegas," Spoonhour said, when asked why he took the job. "This is a place that I had planned to live when my coaching was done. I can say without much reservation that this is the only job I considered coming out of retirement for because it is a combination of where I want to live and working with, and for, people that I really enjoy. There is great opportunity here."

Some folks wonder why the UNLV administration would settle for a retired coach who may not be around a lot of years instead of a younger successful coach who might stick around a while and try to build up the program. The feeling among UNLV officials is that they have a proven commodity in Spoonhour and even if he lasts just five years or so, he can raise the level of the program high enough for another top coach to take over.

In some ways, Spoonhour was a consolation prize after UNLV officials went hard after a couple of the best college coaches in America, only to come up empty in both cases.

For awhile it looked like Pitino—who was so successful at Providence and Kentucky before struggling in the NBA with Boston—might be on his way to Las Vegas. He put out some positive feelers and for a while it looked like a done deal before Pitino pulled back and instead started pursuing the Louisville job, which he

eventually took.

Then UNLV set its sights on Majerus, who had been a candidate twice before, immediately after Tarkanian left and again after Massimino didn't work out.

However, Majerus did what he always does when coaching jobs become open—he listened, got his ego stroked, but ultimately stayed at Utah. Actually this time, Majerus made it clear quite quickly that he wasn't interested in the job.

Like Majerus, Spoonhour is known as a defensive coach, which may not go over too well with the Las Vegas fans, who like to see a run 'n gun product on the floor. After all, the team is called the Runnin' Rebels.

"Defense is where we will start and if our players are going to be on the floor they are obviously going to have to work on the defensive end of the court," said Spoonhour, who brings a 319-171 Division I record. "We hope our defense will be exciting for the fans and I know people in Las Vegas appreciate a great defensive effort."

It won't be easy for Spoonhour, considering the program is on probation for three more years and is denied two scholarships for two recruiting seasons. Fortunately the one-season postseason ban is over for the Rebels.

Spoonhour inherits a team with just one returning starter, two part-time starters and several key backups. However it will be missing All-Mountain West center Kaspars Kambala, a four-year starter in the middle, as well as guard Trevor Diggs, who lit up Wyoming for 49 points in the season finale and forward Danny Brotherson, a hard-nosed player who performed a variety of roles for the Rebels.

One of the top offensive threats for the Rebels in 2001-2002 will be 6-9 junior forward **Dalron Johnson**, who averaged 12.3 points and 7.6 rebounds last year while blocking 58 shots, which ranks seventh in UNLV history for most blocks in a season. Johnson ranked second in the Mountain West in blocks and was fourth in rebounding. The year before he was voted MWC Co-Freshman of the Hear after averaging 11.1 points and 6.9 rebounds.

"Dalron is very talented," Spoonhour said. "Our mission as coaches is to show him how to use all his skill and to make him someone that we can rely upon. In this setting this year we expect Dalron to be the man that we go through, so I would hope that he would have a really good year."

Another Johnson, **Lafonte Johnson**, ended up starting 11 games at point guard after coming from Baltimore as a freshman. The 5-10 sophomore averaged just 4.4 points and 2.2 assists, but he could blossom this season with a year under his belt.

"I really like his approach to the game," Spoonhour said. "He has played on great teams and I think he could be a really good player. He can really shoot the basketball and he does things the way coaches like."

Vince Booker, a 6-1 senior guard, started 17-of-23 games after walking on the team and averaged 3.8 points. He's not a flashy player and he may not hold the starting spot long if the Rebels are looking to the future.

Two other point-guard possibilities are **Jevon Banks** and **Marcus Banks**, who are not related.

Jevon Banks, a 6-foot senior, returns after appearing in 13 games last year. He missed several games because of an ankle injury. He played at Texas Tech before transferring to UNLV.

Marcus Banks, 6-1, comes to this Rebel program from another Rebel program—Dixie College in St. George, Utah—after attending high school at Las Vegas' Cimarron-Memorial. Last year he was voted player of the year for Region 18 and was a first-team NJCAA All-American. He could well end up in the starting lineup this year.

"I have seen Marcus play more than anyone on our squad because he was in the junior college tournament and played against my son Jay's team in the semifinals," Spoonhour said. "I like everything about him. I especially like his approach to the game, his strength and his quickness. He has a chance to be a special player."

At the big guard and small forward positions, UNLV has **Lou Kelly**, **Lamar Bigby**, **Ernest Turner** and possibly, **Jermaine Lewis**, who is recovering from a severe knee injury suffered last year.

Kelly, a 6-5 senior guard/forward, returns for his third season at UNLV, but he's seen very little action after coming to Vegas with much hype.

Last year he appeared in 18 games and averaged 6.5 points and 2.2 rebounds. He missed the first eight games of the season after fracturing a bone in his foot and he missed all but one game of his first season with an injury to the same foot.

"Lou has been somewhat of a mystery because of his injuries," Spoonhour said. "He hasn't had a season since he has been here where he has been healthy the whole year. He is someone that has some size and can do things on the inside and on the outside, which is what we need from him."

Bigby, a 6-4 junior guard, comes to UNLV from Schoolcraft College in Livonia, Mich., where he averaged 17.5 points, six rebounds and four assists.

Turner, a 6-2 freshman guard, comes to UNLV from Sterling High School in Summerdale, N.J., where he averaged 28 points and seven rebounds per game.

Lewis, a 6-4 senior guard, appeared in 26 games last year and averaged 9.3 points and 3.2 rebounds before tearing his right ACL with two games left in the season. He had surgery in the off-season and isn't expected to be ready for the start of the year.

The other returnees in the Rebels' frontcourt are **Chris Richardson**, **Omari Pearson** and **Noel Bloom**, none of whom has much experience.

Richardson, a 6-6 senior forward, appeared in 22 games a year ago and averaged 4.7 points and 3.5 rebounds. Pearson, a 6-8 sophomore forward, returns for his second season at UNLV after appearing in just 12 games last year and averaging 4.7 minutes per game. Bloom, a 6-7 senior forward, played in just one game last year.

A player who could move into a starting role in his first season is 6-9 junior forward/center **Jamal Holden**, who comes from Westark College in Fort Smith, Ark. He averaged 11 points and six rebounds, while shooting 62 percent from the field last year as his team was 30-4 and finished fifth at the National Junior College Tournament.

"Jamal will be our big guy this year," Spoonhour said. "He has the capability to go in and play off the block and he also has athleticism. He can handle the basketball and go out and face the goal as well. He has been well coached and has a chance to really step up and help us."

One more frontcourt player for the Rebels is **Louis Amundson**, a 6-7 freshman forward from Monarch High School in Louisville, Colo. Last year he averaged 18 points, 9 rebounds, 3.1 blocks and 1.7 steals for a team that went 19-3.

2001-2002 SCHEDULE

Nov.	17	Wisconsin
	20	Nicholls State
	24	@Cincinnati
	28	@Washington
Dec.	1	Georgia Southern
	8	*UAB
	15	@Loyola Marymount
	20	Nevada
	22	**Texas
	28	Tennessee State
	30	Old Dominion
Jan.	5	Wyoming
	7	@Air Force
	12	@Utah
	15	@BYU
	21	Colorado State
	26	@San Diego State
Feb.	3	DePaul
	5	@New Mexico
	9	BYU
	11	Utah
	13	Florida International
	16	@Wyoming
	18	@Colorado State
	23	San Diego State
	28	Air Force
March	2	New Mexico
	7-9	#MWC Tournament

@Road Games
*Arby's Hardwood Classic, Birmingham, AL
**Las Vegas Shootout, Las Vegas, NV
#Thomas & Mack Center, Las Vegas, NV

BLUE RIBBON ANALYSIS

BACKCOURT	B-
BENCH/DEPTH	C+
FRONTCOURT	B-
INTANGIBLES	B-

Spoonhour may wonder what he got himself in to by the time he gets through with his first tour of the Mountain West Conference. It's not easy winning games at Utah, Wyoming, BYU and New Mexico and with the team he's been left with, it may be tough beating those teams at home.

A non-conference schedule that includes opponents such as Wisconsin, Cincinnati, Texas and DePaul won't help the Rebels gain confidence in the early part of the schedule, especially with a new coach and a lot of inexperienced players.

Last year, the Rebels had little to play for because of the postseason ban. Spoonhour might inject some life into the program, but its going to be tough for the Rebels to get back to the 20-win plateau and challenge for the MWC title.

(M.S.)

New Mexico

LOCATION	Albuquerque, NM
CONFERENCE	Mountain West
LAST SEASON	21-13 (.618)
CONFERENCE RECORD	6-8 (t-5th)
STARTERS LOST/RETURNING	2/3
NICKNAME	Lobos
COLORS	Cherry & Silver
HOMECOURT	University Arena (18,018)
COACH	Fran Fraschilla (Brooklyn College '80)
RECORD AT SCHOOL	39-27 (2 years)
CAREER RECORD	159-86 (8 years)
ASSISTANTS	Joe Dooley (George Washington '88)
	Darren Savino (Jersey City State '94)
	Travis Lyons (Manhattan '98)
	Rodney Belcher (North Texas '87)
TEAM WINS (last 5 years)	25-24-25-18-21
RPI (last 5 years)	14-17-62-83-50
2000-01 FINISH	Lost in NIT third round.

Under Dave Bliss, New Mexico enjoyed unrivaled success, with seven NCAA appearances in 11 years, including four straight before the 1998-99 season.

But all that success wasn't good enough for Lobo fans, who wanted more than annual appearances in the NCAA Tournament. They wanted WINS in the NCAA Tournament and perhaps a few conference titles to boot, so Bliss resigned in 1999 and left to build a program at Baylor.

New York native Fran Fraschilla was hired to move the New Mexico program to the next level, but so far all Fraschilla has to show are some are a few wins in the NIT, something the Lobos used to make a habit of back in the 1980s and early '90s.

Fraschilla wants to put his own mark on the program and it is getting close to the point where he can't blame any lack of success on his predecessor's players. Only two players are left from the Bliss era as most have run out of eligibility, but some left on their own accord or by mutual agreement.

In Fraschilla's first year, the Lobos went 18-14 and last year they improved to 21-13, although most observers agree the team wasn't any better than the year before, as evidenced by its 6-8, fifth-place finish in the Mountain West Conference, the Lobos' first losing league season since 1982-83.

This year Fraschilla hopes his team finally has what it takes to get back into the Big Dance. His 2000 recruiting class was considered one of the Top 15 in the country, and he also brought in several top players in his latest recruiting class.

"Our system is finally in place," Fraschilla said. "It has taken us two years to recruit the kind of guys that not only want to be good players on the court, but also want to be successful off the court."

The Lobos return three talented guards and will likely play the same three-guard offense they did last year in order to get their best players on the floor at the same time. The best of the newcomers is also a guard, so the Lobos will need to develop their inside players to be an improved team this year.

"The strength of this year's team is definitely the experience in the backcourt, although I think by the middle of the season the strength will be depth at every position," Fraschilla said.

Marlon Parmer (11.6 ppg, 4.0 rpg), a 6-2 junior, was inconsistent during his freshman season when he started nine games and averaged 7.8 points per game on 41 percent shooting, but he got better and better as his sophomore season progressed. He finished the season leading the Mountain West Conference in assists with 5.4 per game and improved his shooting percentage to 45 percent. Parmer is known for his ability to slash to the basket, but can also can the long jumpers.

This year he'll get more help in the backcourt from transfer **Senque Carey** after averaging 34 minutes per game last year.

"Marlon Parmer has matured on and off the court as much as any player I have coached in eight years," Fraschilla said. "He finished last season as one of the best point guards in our conference. Over the next two years he has a chance to establish himself as one of the better point guards in the country."

Ruben Douglas (16.3 ppg, 5.8 rpg), a 6-4 junior, came to New Mexico after starting his career at Arizona. Although he started there, he became disenchanted and transferred to New Mexico, where he had to sit out six games last year. Once he got in gear, Douglas blossomed and ended up leading the Lobos in scoring and earning second-team all-league honors.

Douglas is known as pure shooter who can also penetrate to the basket. He was at his best late in the season when he averaged 23 points per game in three NIT games and hit nine-of-18 three-pointers.

"Reuben had an outstanding start to his UNM career," Fraschilla said. "He has done everything we thought he could do and he loves to keep improving. He enters his junior year as already one of the best players in the Mountain West."

After coming to New Mexico as a junior college transfer from Angelina (Texas) College, 6-3 senior **Eric Chatfield** started off with a bang and quickly established himself as one of the Lobos' top players. He started all 34 games at the two-guard spot and finished the season with a 12.9 average after starting out with a 19.2 average through the first half of the schedule.

Heath issues (flu and kidney stones) and some minor injuries were part of the reason for his drop in production in the second half of the season, but Chatfield hopes to match his fast start of last year.

"Eric is probably our best defensive guard," Fraschilla said. "He was set back last year with some injuries that really affected his production. He is healthy now though and goes into his senior season as a guy that is an outstanding penetrator."

With three established guards, it may be hard for Carey, a 6-4 junior, to crack the starting lineup after transferring from Washington. Carey played mostly point guard as he averaged 9.6 points and 4.1 assists over two seasons while starting 45-of-59 games. Last year he practiced with the Lobos as a red-shirt and impressed his coaches and teammates.

"Senque has established himself on our team as one of our guys who players look to in terms of leadership," Fraschilla said. "He can handle the ball, but also shoot it and he knows how to get in the lane and he knows how to make other people better. He just adds to the versatility of our backcourt."

Tim Lightfoot (7.6 ppg, 1.5 rpg), a 6-3 senior, is one of the two leftover players from the Bliss era and as a senior he may find his playing time diminish with the addition of Carey. Lightfoot saw his most action last year when he started six games. He's a good shooter—40 percent each of the last two years from three-point range—but he'll be lucky to average 19 minutes a game as he did last year.

Other guards who will try to find some time on the talented guard line are three local players—6-2 sophomore **Michael Jordan** (0.4 ppg, 0.5 rpg), who has the name but not the game, 6-2 sophomore **Ryan Ashcraft** (0.7 ppg, 0.0 rpg) and 6-2 freshman **Mark Walters**.

Jordan played in 10 games and scored four points, while Ashcraft played in just three games. Fraschilla called Walters "one of the best pure athletes I have recruited in 22 years," but says he's likely to red-shirt this year, while getting valuable experience.

The frontcourt is where all the questions are for the Lobos. Gone are both Wayland White and Brian Smith, who started 30 and 33 games, respectively, last year. White was a leaper who could score inside but had very little range. He was also a liability at the free-throw line (37.9 percent average last year).

Smith was a banger who did most of his work inside, but wasn't much of a rebounder as evidenced by the fact that he ranked sixth on the team in rebounding, despite being the tallest player.

Sophomores **Patrick Dennehy** and **Alvin Broussard** played in every game as freshmen and each showed promise late in the year when they got more playing time. The 6-9, 220-pound Dennehy averaged just 2.5 points per game, but led the team in rebounds per minute as he averaged 4.2 boards per game in just 12.6 minutes.

The 6-6, 215-pound Broussard averaged just 1.6 points and 1.9 rebounds per game. He needs to stick to the inside more this year. Last year he missed all 16 of his three-point shots.

Pat Kelly (0.5 ppg, 0.3 rpg), a 6-6 senior swingman, is the only other player left from the Bliss regime and he isn't likely to see many minutes after getting in just four games last year.

Four new players have the chance to play a lot, given the shortage of bodies inside. **Cody Payne** is a 6-7, 235-pound junior power forward from Collin County Community College in Texas, who averaged 15.2 points and 12.6 rebounds last year. He is an all-around player who can muscle inside, but also can jump well and shoot from the outside.

Moustapha Diagne, a 7-0, 235-pound junior, comes to New Mexico from Senegal, by way of Trinity Valley (Texas) Community College, where he averaged 14.8 points and 8.2 rebounds. He's still a relative newcomer to the game, but seems to have a tremendous upside.

Two California freshmen who will help the Lobos down the line are **Chad Bell** and **Jamaal Williams**. The 6-11 Bell had agility for his size and comes from a winning program (Westchester). The 6-6 Williams was rated as one of the top 75 high school players in the nation last year and was co-player of the year in southern California while playing for Centennial High School. He averaged 21.8 points and 8.0 rebounds per game.

"This team provides the most depth in our frontcourt of any of the three teams I have coached," Fraschilla said. "It starts with Pat Dennehy, who comes into this season with a solid year of experience. He certainly has the ability to become an impact player in the Mountain West during his career. He is a shot blocker, a rebounder, he runs the court well and his offensive game is going to continue to improve."

Dennehy could get the start at power forward with Diagne at center, because he is the only true center on the team. However, Fraschilla won't be afraid to tinker with his lineup and use various combinations.

"Our desire to come into this season and compete for a Mountain West title is probably more evident now than it has been at any time in my tenure at UNM," Fraschilla said. "We have a team that has a great deal of character and has a commitment to be successful both on and off the court."

2001-2002 SCHEDULE

Nov.	17	Stanford
	19	Texas Southern
	23-24	#Hispanic College Fund Classic
	28	@California
Dec.	1	Alcorn State
	5	@New Mexico State
	8	Tennessee Tech
	16	New Mexico State
	22	UNC Greensboro
	28-29	##Lobo Invitational
Jan.	5	Northern Arizona
	7	Gonzaga
	14	Air Force
	19	BYU
	21	Utah
	26	@Wyoming
	28	@Colorado State
Feb.	2	San Diego State
	5	UNLV
	9	@Air Force
	16	@BYU
	18	@Utah
	23	Colorado State
	25	Wyoming
	28	@San Diego State
March	2	@UNLV
	7-10	###Mountain West Tournament

@Road Games
#Albuquerque, NM (vs. Pacific first round; also Southern Miss, West Virginia)
##Albuquerque, NM (vs. St. Mary's first round; also Dartmouth, SE Louisiana)
###Thomas & Mack Center, Las Vegas, NV

BLUE RIBBON ANALYSIS

BACKCOURT	B+
BENCH/DEPTH	B
FRONTCOURT	B-
INTANGIBLES	B

With a bunch of home games in their noisy Pit, the Lobos should certainly pad their overall record this year and hit the 20-win mark again. The Lobos have just two road games in the preseason and both of those are winnable, at California and New Mexico State.

With their first three Mountain West Conference games at home, the Lobos will play an incredible 15 of their first 17 games at The Pit. By the time late January hits, the Lobos should have a pretty glossy record. The question will be whether all those early games will give

the young Lobos confidence going into the tough part of the schedule (seven of final 11 on the road) or if the lack of road games will come back to haunt them.

The Lobos should surely make it to the postseason for the 18th time in the last 19 years, but this time the Lobos won't be satisfied with an NIT appearance. For Fraschilla, it's time to start making regular appearances in the NCAA tournament as he promised when he arrived in Albuquerque.

(M.S.)

 # San Diego State

LOCATION	San Diego, CA
CONFERENCE	Mountain West
LAST SEASON	14-14 (.500)
CONFERENCE RECORD	4-10 (7th)
STARTERS LOST/RETURNING	1/4
NICKNAME	Aztecs
COLORS	Scarlet & Black
HOMECOURT	Cox Arena (12,414)
COACH	Steve Fisher (Illinois State '67)
RECORD AT SCHOOL	19-37 (2 years)
CAREER RECORD	203-119 (10 years)
ASSISTANTS	Brian Dutcher (Minnesota '82)
	Marvin Menzies (UCLA '86)
	Jim Tomey (Michigan '81)
TEAM WINS (last 5 years)	12-13-4-5-14
RPI (last 5 years)	198-158-285-265-159
2000-01 FINISH	Lost in conference quarterfinal.

The word around San Diego State last year was that two red-shirts were teaming with three walk-ons and regularly beating the Aztec starting five in team scrimmages.

That may say something about the lack of overall talent at SDSU last year, or it might tell you how good these red-shirts are who will be eligible to play for the Aztecs this year.

Tony Bland, a two-year starter at Syracuse and **Brandon Smith**, a former starter at Michigan, will be joining an experienced Aztec team that lost very little from last year's group that finished a respectable 14-14.

It has taken awhile, but the San Diego State basketball program looks like it might finally be ready to turn the corner under third-year coach Steve Fisher in 2001-2002.

"We've gone from survival to competitive and this year we expect to win," said Fisher, who won a national title at Michigan and twice took teams to the finals.

The former Michigan coach took over the moribund program that had won just four games the year before he arrived and had just one winning season in the previous 15 years. Fisher's first year wasn't fun, as the Aztecs won just five games and suffered through a 17-game losing streak.

However, Fisher jettisoned several players in the program and brought in his own talent from several four-year programs and began to turn things around last year. The Aztecs started 10-3 last year with wins over Arizona State, Oklahoma State and New Mexico State and two of their losses were by three points.

Then reality hit when the Aztecs headed into Mountain West Conference play and BYU beat them by 29, Utah won by 19 and Wyoming cruised by 35. The Aztecs limped home with a 4-10 league record, which was much better than the 0-14 mark of a year earlier and good enough to keep them from an overall losing record at 14-14.

When asked to describe his situation at San Diego, Fisher says "progress" is the one word that comes to mind. "We're excited about this season," Fisher said.

Having four starters back at any program is good news. But at San Diego State, the even better news is that two players who sat out last year as red-shirts are as good or better than any of the returning starters. The infusion of new blood along with some experienced starters should result in an improved team in San Diego this year.

The only players gone from last year's squad are center Marcelo Correa, Michael Marion, who played sparingly, averaging just 1.9 points, and David Abramowitz, who is taking a year off from basketball and may return next year after red-shirting.

Correa, a four-year letterman, averaged 6.4 points and 4.0 rebounds in the middle for the Aztecs. Abramowitz started at least five games in each of his three years and was known for his ability to shoot from the outside. His best year was 1999-2000 when he started nine games and averaged 7.6 points and 3.0 assists.

While the Aztecs have most of their team back from a year ago, a lot of folks are talking about the two transfers who played so well in practice last year.

The 6-4 junior Bland played two seasons at Syracuse

and started all 32 games, averaging 6.7 points in 1999-2000 when the Orangemen were the Big East co-champions and advanced to the Sweet 16. The year before he played in all 32 games and averaged 4.4 points in 15.7 minutes per game. Bland was a two-time high school All-American at Westchester High School in Los Angeles and one of the reasons for his transfer is that he wanted to be closer to his family in southern California.

"He brings a great deal to the program as a leader, a winner with a big reputation in the L.A. area," said Fisher. "He's a wonderful addition."

Smith, a 6-7 senior, played three years at Michigan, where he was originally recruited by Fisher. During his sophomore and junior seasons, he averaged 8.1 points and 3.8 rebounds per game.

"He's a long-armed wing player who's very athletic," Fisher said. "He gives us one of the premier athletes in the league."

Two of the best players on last year's team were also transfers from major programs. Senior forward **Randy Holcomb** played a year at Fresno State before transferring, while 5-9 junior point guard **Deandre Moore** began his career at Vanderbilt before coming to San Diego.

The 6-9 Holcomb turned out to be the Aztecs' best player last year as he led the team in both scoring (15.9 ppg) and rebounding (6.6 rpg), ranking sixth in the MWC in both categories. He also averaged just under one steal per game and finished with 19 blocked shots. The Aztecs would like to see his shooting percentages increase after he shot just 29.2 percent from three-point range and 42.2 percent overall.

"Randy is one of the better returning players in our conference," Fisher said. "He's very athletic and does a lot of things for us. He should be a lot better as a senior."

Moore (6.8. ppg, 5.0 apg, 1.5 spg) started 24-of-25 games and made an immediate impact at the point for the Aztecs with his quickness and decision-making. He ranked first in the MWC in assist-to-turnover ratio, second in assists and third in steals. However, he was slowed by a shoulder that became dislocated four times last year and resulted in off-season surgery.

"When Moore was healthy we were a much better team," Fisher said. "By the end of the year, he was just a shell of what he had been earlier in the season. He,s a smart, quick point guard and I expect him to be back into shape for this season."

Myron Epps, a 6-6 senior, has been a three-year starter for the Aztecs, but with the influx of talent, he may be hard-pressed to earn a starting spot again. He averaged 11.8 points as a freshman, 14.4 as a sophomore and 11.1 last year, when he shot 54.9 percent from the floor. He's already up to No. 16 on the all-time SDSU scoring list, not bad for a guy who originally came to SDSU to play baseball. Epps gets most of his points inside and has made just two three-pointers during his career.

"He has more experience than any other player and he's been here longer than I have," Fisher said. "He's a very athletic player and we can use his experience this year."

A surprising starter last year was **Al Faux**, a 6-2 junior guard who walked on after playing at Shoreline (Wash.) Community College. Faux averaged 10.5 points while shooting 42 percent from three-point range and from the field. He finished third in the MWC in three-point percentage and 11th in three-point field goals made. In a win over Oklahoma State, he sank a record nine three-pointers and finished with 28 points.

"Al surprised a lot of people last year, but this year he won't be a surprise," Fisher said.

Karlo Kovacic (5.3 ppg, 1.8 rpg), a 6-5 senior, came to San Diego from Modesto (Calif.) Community College, where he led the state in three-point percentage at 46.3. However, his shooting was a disappointment to the Aztecs as he shot 36.3 percent from the field, 36.5 percent from three-point range and only 41.4 percent from the foul line.

"Karlo was sporadic last year," Fisher said. "His strength is supposed to be his shooting, but last year he didn't shoot the way we expected."

Chris Walton, the youngest son of former NBA star Bill Walton, is a 6-8 sophomore forward. He played in all 28 games last year and his production increased as the season progressed as he finished with a 4.3 scoring average in league play and 3.3 overall and also pulled down 2.5 rebounds per game.

"He made big improvements as the season went along and I expect the same this year," Fisher said.

Another transfer is junior **Mike Mackell**, the only true center on the team at 6-9, 230 pounds. He was selected California's junior college player of the year after averaging 22.4 points and 10.6 rebounds for Porterville Junior College last year.

"He's a big, tough, player with a lot of skills in the high and low post," Fisher said. "He's a strong athlete who will help us against the bigger players in the league."

Aerick Sanders (3.8 ppg, 3.8 rpg), a 6-8 sophomore, had his freshman season cut short by a stress fracture in his right foot in mid-January, just after he had scored a career-high nine points against BYU. He's a versatile performer who can help the Aztecs inside.

Jim Roban, a 6-6 senior, might play if the NCAA grants him another year of eligibility after he sat out with an injury last year.

Among the freshmen coming in are forward **Trimaine Davis**, guard **Tommie Johnson**, both from California and guard **Steve Sir** from Minnesota. Fisher likes all three, but says they may not see a lot of time with all the experienced players already in the program.

Johnson from Crenshaw High School in Los Angeles, averaged 17 points and six rebounds two years ago, when he was ranked by several recruiting services as the No. 2 shooting guard in the 2000 southern California prep class, behind DeShawn Stevenson, who bypassed college and went directly from Washington Union High in Fresno, Calif., the Utah Jazz. He originally signed with Washington State, but sat out last year to concentrate on academics.

The 6-8 Davis, from Pittsburg High School in Bay Point, Calif., averaged 20.6 points, 14.7 rebounds and 5.7 blocked shots s a year ago.

Given this array of talent, who will end up logging the most minutes year? Not even Fisher claims to know that, although you'd have to figure Epps, Holcomb, Moore, Bland and Smith will get a lot of time.

That lineup would be talented but small with Holcomb having to play in the middle. Fisher said he has nine or 10 players who can all play and will be fighting for playing time.

"It's nice to have depth, something we have not had in the past," he said.

Like last year, the Aztecs should be able to compile a winning record with a non-conference schedule that keeps them at Cox Arena most of the time. They do have a game at Duke on Dec. 29, which will give them some national exposure at best, and games at New Mexico State and Hawaii as well as a tournament at Texas Tech, Bobby Knight's new school, to open the season.

"We're going to expect to win this year," Fisher said. "We won only four league games last year and we need to find ways to win, especially when we go on the road. We've become competitive at home and now we need to win on the road."

2001-2002 SCHEDULE

Nov.	16-17	#Red Raider Classic
	21	Norfolk State
	24	@New Mexico State
	27	UC San Diego
Dec.	1	Cal State Northridge
	5	@San Diego
	8	Fresno State
	15	@Hawaii
	17	Houston
	23	Eastern Washington
	29	@Duke
	31	Columbia
Jan.	2	Indiana Purdue-Fort Wayne
	8	@Texas A&M-Corpus Christi
	12	@Brigham Young
	14	@Utah
	19	Colorado State
	21	Wyoming
	26	UNLV
Feb.	2	@New Mexico
	4	@Air Force
	9	Utah
	11	Brigham Young
	16	@Colorado State
	18	@Wyoming
	23	@UNLV
	28	New Mexico
March	2	Air Force
	7-9	##Mountain West Tournament

@Road Games
#Lubbock, TX (vs. Northern Iowa first round; also Texas Tech, William & Mary)
##Thomas & Mack Center, Las Vegas, NV

BLUE RIBBON ANALYSIS

BACKCOURT	B
BENCH/DEPTH	B+
FRONTCOURT	B
INTANGIBLES	B-

NORTHEAST

BLUE RIBBON FORECAST
1. Monmouth
2. Wagner
3. Maryland-Baltimore County
4. Central Connecticut State
5. Long Island
6. Mount St. Mary's
7. Robert Morris
8. Fairleigh Dickinson
9. St. Francis (NY)
10. Quinnipiac
11. Sacred Heart
12. St. Francis (Pa.)

ALL-CONFERENCE TEAM
G-Rashaan Johnson, SR, Monmouth
G-Antawn Dobie, SR, Long Island
F-Jermaine Hall, JR, Wagner
F-Wesley Fluellen, SR, Robert Morris
C-Corsley Edwards, SR, Central Connecticut State

PLAYER OF THE YEAR
Rashaan Johnson, SR, Monmouth

NEWCOMER OF THE YEAR
Darshan Luckey, FR, St. Francis (Pa.)

2001-2002 CONFERENCE TOURNAMENT
March 1-2, Spiro Sports Center, Staten Island, NY
March 4, Championship game at site of higher remaining seed

2000-2001 POSTSEASON PARTICIPANTS
St. Francis (N.Y.) (Regular season)
Monmouth (Conference tournament)

TOP BACKCOURTS
1. Long Island
2. Wagner
3. Monmouth

TOP FRONTCOURTS
1. Maryland-Baltimore County
2. Central Connecticut State
3. Monmouth

For now Fisher has rebuilt his program with the aid of four-year transfers, who will keep the Aztecs competitive with most teams in the Mountain West Conference. Eventually Fisher would like to maintain the program with freshmen and not have to rely on transfers as he is this year. But he says he may always have a few in the program.

This year the Aztecs should be as talented as any team in the MWC, on paper at least. They'll win some games on sheer athleticism alone, but it may not hold up every week, particularly with a lack of post men. Whether the Aztecs will be able to compete week in and week out with the Utahs, Wyomings and New Mexicos of the Mountain West Conference remains to be seen.

Still, watch for the Aztecs to emerge with a winning overall record this year and finish in the top half of the league standings for a change. They should also see their first postseason action, probably to the NIT, for the first time since 1985.

(M.S.)

Central Connecticut State

LOCATION	New Britain, CT
CONFERENCE	Northeast
LAST SEASON	14-14 (500)
CONFERENCE RECORD	11-9 (t-5th)

INSIDE THE NUMBERS
2000-01 conference RPI: 29 (of 31)
Conference RPI (last five years): 20-22-21-25-29

DID YOU KNOW?
With Sacred Heart now being eligible for the conference tournament, the number of qualifying teams has been raised from seven to eight. ... Last season the Northeast Conference celebrated its 20th anniversary. Former Marist star and 12-year Indiana Pacer Rik Smits was chosen the Anniversary MVP. ... The NEC has yet to win an NCAA Tournament game (0-20). ... The league schedule will change next year with conference games for each team in 2002-03 getting reduced from 20 to 18. Each team will still play 20 this season. ... Four conference games will be played on Nov. 29, the earliest start in NEC history. ... The league will also be changing the tournament venue. After two years of playing the event at the Sovereign Bank Arena in Trenton, N.J., it will move back to the Wagner campus, where it was in 1999 for the quarterfinals and semifinals. The championship game will be hosted by the highest remaining seed. ... Central Connecticut State's appearance in the Preseason NIT is the NEC's first since Wagner lost to Arizona State in 1997. ... Monmouth's Rashaan Johnson and Central Connecticut State's Corsley Edwards went over the 1,000 career point mark last season and should be joined this season by Wagner's Jermaine Hall (982) and Qunnipiac's Bill Romano (932) and Jared Grasso (887). ... Hall has a scoring average of 23.2 points in games against Penn State, Michigan, Seton Hall, and Fresno State. ... Sacred Heart's 7-2 Mading Mading is the second tallest player in NEC history behind the 7-4 Smits. ... Quinnipiac freshman forward C.J. Vick is a cousin of Atlanta Falcons' first round pick and backup quarterback Michael Vick. ... Long Island coach Ray Martin was an assistant coach under Jim Valvano on the 1983 North Carolina State NCAA championship team on which Wagner coach Dereck Whittenburg starred. ... Four NEC teams (Long Island, St. Francis (Pa.), Mount St. Mary's, Robert Morris) failed to win a non-conference game last season.

(C.C.)

STARTERS LOST/RETURNING	2/3
NICKNAME	Blue Devils
COLORS	Blue & White
HOMECOURT	William E. Detrick Gym (3,200)
COACH	Howie Dickenman (Central Conn. '70)
RECORD AT SCHOOL	70-64 (5 years)
CAREER RECORD	70-64 (5 years)
ASSISTANTS	Patrick Sellers (Central Conn. '90)
	Anthony Latina (Brandeis '95)
	Chris Casey (Western Conn. St '87)
TEAM WINS (last 5 years)	8-4-19-25-14
RPI (last 5 years)	264-295-180-96-246
2000-01 FINISH	Lost in conference quarterfinal.

Now two seasons removed from perhaps the best performance ever by an NEC team in the NCAA Tournament, Central Connecticut State sixth-year head coach Howie Dickenman enters the next phase in re-making the Blue Devils for another trip to March's greatest sports spectacle.

CCSU lost three starters off the team that pushed second-seeded Iowa State to the limit in the 1999 Midwest sub-regional and now Dickenman must replace two more double-digit scorers from last year's 14-14 club. Gone are forward John Tice (13.2 ppg, 3.7 rpg) and guard Dean Walker (13.3 ppg, 5.1 rpg), key members of both the successful 1999-2000 team and the schizophrenic 2000-01 edition. Plenty has changed since that 10-point loss to the Cyclones, most notably the faces. Yet, one in particular remains. While it's not his face that other NEC teams are concerned about, they sure wish senior **Corlsey Edwards** had changed, too, perhaps into Gary Coleman, instead of remaining the imposing and dominant 6-9, 270-pounder that he is.

At one time Dickenman said Edwards had the ability to be the best player in the league. That day may arrive this season. Edwards (16.2 ppg, 7.9 rpg) graduated to the first-team all-NEC last year after making the second team as a sophomore and if Monmouth's Rahsaan Johnson suddenly came down with an allergy to gymnasiums, then Edwards would be a heavy favorite for player of the year.

"We need Corsley to be the dominant big man in the league and to be our go-to-guy in crucial situations," Dickenman said.

Edwards has become the rebounder Dickenman hoped he would, and that has led to monster-game potential every time out, like the 36-point, 17-rebound effort last year against UMBC or, perhaps the even more impressive 30-point, nine-rebound performance at then nationally-ranked Seton Hall. In all Edwards collected a league-high six double-doubles and he scored in double figures in 25 of the Blue Devils' 28 games.

"He's always had very good games against us," UMBC assistant Doug Nicholas said. "We say don't let him get position and he gets position. We say make him turn to his right because he's lefty and the next thing you know he's going that way anyway and dunking. He'll definitely play at least overseas somewhere next year."

The chore for Dickenman is to find enough satellites to stay in proper orbit with his Jupiter-sized big man. The backcourt will have a distinctly different look and Dickenman hopes Polk Community College (Fla.) transfer John Alexander can shore up the point-guard spot. The 6-0 junior has Division I experience, playing as a freshman at Northeastern, where he averaged 1.4 points in 21 games. The Blue Devils lacked a true point man last season and Dickenman went with more a committee approach. The result was the third-worst team assist-to-turnover ratio in the conference.

"He may be the best one-on-one player we have on the team. He can beat you off the dribble and create open shots for teammates. We haven't had anyone here that can do that for a long time," Dickenman said of Alexander.

Sharp-shooting 6-1 senior Lee Guinn (9.8 ppg, 1.9 rpg) should join Alexander in the starting lineup, giving CCSU the shortest backcourt in the conference. Guinn, a junior college transfer himself from Champlain (Vt.) Junior College, played through injuries much of his inaugural season as a Blue Devil and was finally done for good after breaking his wrist in the second to last game of the regular season. In effect that also meant the end of Central Connecticut State. The Blue Devils scored just 44 points in a 15-point loss to UMBC in the first round of the NEC Tournament. Guinn made six three-pointers in game twice and was sixth in the league in long-range accuracy.

Damian Battles (5.2 ppg, 2.4 rpg), a 6-3 junior, made great strides last season and could be ready to move into the starting lineup. He went from just playing 100 minutes his rookie season to appearing in all 28 games (22.5 minutes per game) a year ago, starting 18. Battles' ability to play two or three positions gives Dickenman more options. He could spell Alexander at the point or play the wing as the third man in a three-guard lineup.

Most of Edwards' interior help will come from 6-6 sophomore Ron Robinson (5.5 ppg, 7.6 rpg), who became a terror on the boards after breaking into the starting lineup at mid-season. Robinson averaged nearly 10 rebounds a game from mid-January on, including a 21-rebound night against Mt. St. Mary's on Feb. 5. Almost solely on his talents as a relentless rebounder, Robinson found himself on the NEC All-Rookie team. The Blue Devils hope to get more offense from him this year.

"I expect him to effective out to 15 feet this year," Dickenman said.

Ricardo Scott (6.2 ppg, 3.3 rpg), a 6-4 guard, joined Guinn on the injured list with a separated shoulder just before the start of the conference tournament, but will be back to full strength for his sophomore season.

Scott came to New Britain physically mature for a freshman and immediately displayed some offensive ability. His defensive skills lagged behind, though, limiting slightly what remained a productive career beginning.

"Ricardo has perhaps the best offensive skills on the team, but he must continue to work on his defense," Dickenman said in a familiar refrain for young players.

Scott will likely be the first wing off the bench, spelling Guinn and Battles. The flip side to Scott might be 6-5 sophomore forward Gerry McNair (1.1 ppg, 1.1 rpg, 16 games), who is at his best trying to stop opponents. His playing time last season was limited by the presence of two many veterans at the big guard/small forward spots.

Dickenman would like to use McNair as a defensive stopper who enters the game to shut down a hot scorer.

Edwards has a sturdy and capable backup in 6-9 senior Jason Smith (0.2 ppg, 0.1 rpg). Playing behind one of the league's best, minutes have been few and far between for Smith, but he is one of those rugged big men coaches love to have—willing to mix it up underneath, always hustling, and never giving in.

Alexander is the headliner of the four-man recruiting class, but guard Jonathan Popofski could also work his way into the rotation. The 6-3 freshman from Guelph Centennial High School in Ontario, Canada can play all three perimeter positions and spent the summer playing for the Canadian Junior National team. Dickenman likes Popofski's instincts as a passer and called him a "gym rat."

Richard Pittman, a 6-6 freshman forward, is a three-sport athlete from Thayer Academy in Mattapan, Mass. A three-year starter, Pittman averaged 18 points, 11 rebounds and four blocks during his career and was also a conference champion in the high jump.

He'll also be in the fight for froncourt minutes with 6-7 freshman forward Robert Barrett and 6-9 red-shirt freshman center Ryan Murphy. Barrett averaged 15 points and 10 rebounds over his career at Christ the King High School in Brooklyn, N.Y. Murphy sat out last year to bulk up. His strengths lie on the offensive end.

Michael Dukes (0.4 ppg, 0.4 rpg), a 6-2 junior guard, will again be a deep reserve in the backcourt.

2001-2002 SCHEDULE

Nov.	13	#@Oklahoma
	16-17	##Mohegan Sun Classic
	29-30	###Phoenix Classic
Dec.	3	St. Francis NY
	6	@Mount St. Mary's
	8	@UMBC
	12	@Long Island
	15	Massachusetts
	22	Loyola
	30	Providence
Jan.	10	Sacred Heart
	12	Wagner
	16	@Quinnipiac
	19	UMBC
	23	Monmouth
	26	Quinnipiac
	28	@Sacred Heart
Feb.	2	@St. Francis PA
	4	@Robert Morris
	7	Fairleigh Dickinson
	9	@Monmouth
	15	@Wagner
	17	Long Island
	20	@Fairleigh Dickinson
	23	St. Francis PA
	25	Robert Morris
March	1-2	####NEC Tournament
	6	#####NEC Tournament

@Road Games
#Preseason NIT (if Central Connecticut State wins, it will play Detroit or Michigan on Nov. 14 or 16; semifinals and final Nov. 21 and 23 at Madison Square Garden, NY)
##New Britain, CT (vs. Bucknell first round; also Brown, Vermont)
###Phoenix, AZ (vs. Hartford first round; also Niagara, Winthrop)
####Quarterfinals, semifinals at Wagner
#####Championship at highest seeded team

BLUE RIBBON ANALYSIS

BACKCOURT	B-
BENCH/DEPTH	B-
FRONTCOURT	B+
INTANGIBLES	C

Central Connecticut State struggled with its consistency last season and that gave the Blue Devils little chance to overcome injures to Guinn and Scott just before the NEC Tournament. The year ended with a whimper, very unlike the excitement of the previous year's NCAA Tournament scare CCSU put into Iowa State.

Avoiding those injuries is just the first step in the Blue Devils re-establishing themselves as an NEC power. Then comes Edwards. Dickenman wants his center to be the dominant big man in the league and he should be. He'll also need to be, at least until someone else shows a consistent ability to score. That shouldn't be too far off though.

Guinn and newcomer Alexander give CCSU one of the quickest backcourts in the NEC and Guinn is a good shooter who should be even better with Edwards taking up space and defenders down low.

Battles and Scott give Dickenman flexibility on the perimeter, Robinson could be even more productive than Edwards on the backboards and McNair is a defensive stopper off the bench. The pieces for success and improving upon last season's .500 record are in place. Then comes the execution and CCSU won't have much time to get that worked out.

The Blue Devils open the year at Oklahoma in the Pre-season NIT. After hosting their own tournament, they are in Phoenix for another, then begin a run of four conference games in nine days, three of which are on the road.

CCSU also mixes in games against UMass and Providence. The Blue Devils have enough veteran experience to benefit from a pre-2002 schedule like this, and it should pay dividends in January and February.

CCSU may not get all the way back to the top of the NEC standings, but this year the Blue Devils should contend and be a factor down the stretch.

(C.C.)

Fairleigh Dickinson

LOCATION	Teaneck, NJ
CONFERENCE	Northeast
LAST SEASON	13-15 (.464)
CONFERENCE RECORD	10-10 (7th)
STARTERS LOST/RETURNING	3/2
NICKNAME	Knights
COLORS	Blue, Black & White
HOMECOURT	Rothman Center (5,000)
COACH	Tom Green (Syracuse '71)
RECORD AT SCHOOL	302-216 (18 years)
CAREER RECORD	302-216 (18 years)
ASSISTANTS	Ellonya Green (Upsala '80)
	Jim Carr (York College '90)
	Jim Hill (Upsala College '70)
TEAM WINS (last 5 years)	18-23-12-17-13
RPI (last 5 years)	105-92-207-158-223
2000-01 FINISH	Lost in conference first round.

In many ways it's a case of starting over at Fairleigh Dickinson. Tom Green is in his 19th year on the Teaneck campus and figures this edition of the Knights will be among his greatest challenges.

"It's going to be interesting because I have a lot of new faces, probably more so than I've had in the past, with a lot of inexperience," said Green, who has the second-longest tenure of any NEC coach behind Mt. St. Mary's Jim Phelan.

With four starters back after a 17-win season in 1999-2000, last season should have been a success. Injuries and academic problems ensured that it wasn't. FDU went into the second game of the season at Rutgers with just seven scholarship players. The Knights barely kept their heads above water during the non-conference schedule and the lack of depth never allowed them to see over the top of the mountain.

To its credit Fairleigh Dickinson never had a losing streak of more than two, but also topped out with only one three-win string. It may even be considered a small victory to have played .500 ball in the league and at least qualified for the NEC Tournament, but that was no solace to a coach who had hoped for much more.

"Last year was one of the craziest years I've ever been associated with, maybe even the craziest. We probably had the best conditioned assistant coaches in America and my manager had to have a physical every month just to make sure he could stay with us," Green said.

Only three Knights were able to play in all 28 games and two of them are now gone.

Green hopes he can rely on 6-10 senior James Felton as his foundation, but with that there are no guarantees. Felton's career compares to a wooden wheel in a mud pit—it keeps starting, but never gets going. After a semester at St. John's in 1997, Felton transferred to Florida State and then St. Peter's, but never played. He spent two years on the sideline before landing at FDU and then spent most of last season out with a broken foot.

Outside of the seven games Felton was able to play at the end of 2000-01, he hasn't played college basketball in three years. Fortunately for the Knights, those seven games were promising. Felton (13.3 ppg, 5.4 rpg) contributed almost immediately with 21 points in his second game and 24 points and 12 rebounds five days later.

"We thought he would have a pretty good year and what he gave us at the end was about what we expected out of him," Green said. "It was tough on him mentally, going through the entire preseason and getting in shape and then having the broken foot just before the start of the season."

The loss of the graduated center Chris Ekwe (15.7 ppg, 9.1), last year's best and most consistent player, makes Felton's health and production that much more important. The same holds true for 6-8 senior forward **Matt Hammond** (8.8 ppg, 4.3 rpg, 1.3 apg), who made huge strides a year ago. As a sophomore, Hammond was merely a spot player, not even averaging a point a game. Last season he started all but one game and is the only returning Knight to have played in every game.

"He was probably one of the most improved players in our league," Green said of Hammond, whose ability on the perimeter can make him a match-up problem for other power forwards.

After Hammond and Felton, Green is stuck with nothing but unknowns. **Greg McBain** (0.9 ppg, 0.9 rpg, eight games), a 6-9 sophomore, is expected to be Felton's primary backup, but was rarely used a year ago. His longest stint was a nine-minute run against St. Francis (Pa.) in early January. However, McBain's experience dwarfs that of senoir center **Joern Grundmann** (0.5 ppg, 1.0 rpg, six games). The 7-0 native of Germany has played in a total of eight games and 21 minutes in two seasons. Injuries have curtailed his progress and Grundmann has just never improved enough to be of any service.

That means Green will have to hope a pair of athletic newcomers—6-9 junior **Doug Whitler** and 6-5 freshman **Ryshaun Sunkins**—can be immediate impact players. Whitler is a finesse player who likes it in the open court, and that's the way Green likes to play. Whitler's modest junior college numbers were eight points and six rebounds for Howard (Texas) Junior College. Sunkins is a local product from North Brunswick High School.

"Ryshaun is an really good athlete who shoots it pretty good and can put it on the floor. Obviously, he's just lacking that experience," Green said.

Sunkins will swing between the guard and forward spots and is set to play behind 6-4 junior **Lionel Bomayako** on the wing. Bomayako (10.9 ppg, 1.4 rpg, .390 3PT) was FDU's best long-range threat (64 three-pointers) and like Hammond, made big strides a year ago. A native of the Republic of Central Africa, Bomayako never played in high school and got minimal playing time as a freshman. Just two seasons later he joins Felton and Hammond as Green's key veterans.

Transfer **Iman Mattox** will also spell Bomayako at the two-guard. Mattox comes east after a high school and junior college career in Hayward, Calif. The 6-3 junior averaged 17.6 points for Chabot Junior College last season and was a first-team All-Coast Conference pick.

Green's most difficult, and probably most important, decision comes at the point, where he'll have three players to replace the departed Jarvis Mitchell (11.6 ppg, 2.3 rpg, 3.4 apg) from which to choose. None of the three have much experience.

Mensah Peterson (2.3 ppg, 0.8 rpg), a 6-2 sophomore, is the most accomplished, playing in 26 games with five starts as a freshman, but is more suited to play off the ball. Peterson was a point guard at North Brunswick (N.J.) High School and will probably get the call at point if the other two fail.

The other two are 5-9 sophomore **Marcus Whitaker** and 6-1 freshman **Richard Chavez**. Whitaker (1.3 ppg, 0.9 rpg) played in just 14 games as a rookie with little to show for it, but the job is his if he's ready. Chavez averaged 12.3 points and 4.1 assists in his final season at Wichita Northwest (Kansas) High School.

"I think Marcus will get the first look at the point, but Richard will play," Green said. "Marcus is very quick, can penetrate and is more of the scorer of the two. Richard is much more of a run-the-club point guard and is an outstanding passer."

Brad Green (0.1 ppg, 0.2 rpg, 16 games), Green's son and a 6-0 sophomore, will continue his roll as a deep reserve and valuable practice player.

2001-2002 SCHEDULE

Nov.	14-16	#BCA Classic
	24	@American
	26	Loyola MC
	29	Wagner
Dec.	1	Sacred Heart
	8	@Hartford
	13	@Seton Hall
	22	Delaware State
	29	@Kansas State
Jan.	4	@St. Francis NY
	6	@Long Island
	10	UMBC
	12	Mount St. Mary's
	16	@Sacred Heart
	19	Robert Morris
	23	@Quinnipiac
	26	@Mount St. Mary's
	28	@UMBC
Feb.	2	St. Francis NY
	4	Monmouth
	7	@Central Connecticut State
	9	Quinnipiac
	14	@Robert Morris
	16	@St. Francis PA
	20	Central Connecticut State
	23	Long Island
	25	@Monmouth
March	1-2	##NEC Tournament
	6	###NEC Tournament

@Road Games
#Raleigh, NC (vs. San Jose State first round; also East Carolina, Rutgers, Northwestern, VCU, North Carolina State, Prairiew View A&M)
##Quarterfinals and semifinals at Wagner
###Championship at highest seeded team

BLUE RIBBON ANALYSIS

BACKCOURT	D+
BENCH/DEPTH	D
FRONTCOURT	C
INTANGIBLES	C

Green has found a home at Fairleigh Dickinson and the school and its fans have been happy to have him. Before his arrival, FDU hadn't had a 20-win season since 1953. The Knights have had five since and made three trips to the NCAA Tournament.

As with any mid-to-low major, there have been ups and downs, but Green has stuck it out and been rewarded for his loyalty. After an up period in 1997 and '98, FDU is again in a down cycle, one that always tests the resolve of a coach and the fans.

If the injuries that befell Fairleigh Dickinson last season happen again, Green thinks his emotions will also be tested.

"It was just a crazy, crazy year. I don't want to do that again," Green said.

This Knight team isn't nearly as experienced either and would be unlikely to even muster the 10-10 conference mark of a year ago.

If healthy, FDU still has a number of questions. The team's best player, Felton, has played only seven games in the last three seasons. Hammond is greatly improved, but is the only froncourt player with any real experience. Bomayako is a solid shooting guard, but his backcourt partner—either Whitaker, Peterson, or Chavez—and his backups are only lacking significant experience.

"We are going to circle the wagons and pray a lot," Green said. "We've gotta walk before we can run."

Green will look to play with even a little more pace and press more often than in the past to take advantage of Whitaker's quickness and the athleticism freshman Sunkins and junior college transfers Whitler and Mattox bring to the program. The immediate contributions of Whitler and Mattox may be the key elements to how quickly Green's metaphor plays out and his team can start running.

Last season was a struggle and it's likely 2001-02 will follow suit, but perhaps for different reasons. Injuries were the cause last year, inexperience the likely culprit this time around.

With another difficult non-conference schedule that includes an appearance in the BCA Invitational and games at Seton Hall and Kansas State, the overall record may go backward. With the conference tournament field expanding by one team to eight, the Knights should still be fighting for a berth by late February.

(C.C.)

Long Island

LOCATION	Brooklyn, NY
CONFERENCE	Northeast

LAST SEASON	12-16 (.429)
CONFERENCE RECORD	12-8 (4th)
STARTERS LOST/RETURNING	2/3
NICKNAME	Blackbirds
COLORS	Black, Silver & Royal Blue
HOMECOURT	Schwartz Athletic Center (1,000)
COACH	Ray Martin (Notre Dame '77)
RECORD AT SCHOOL	30-52 (3 years)
CAREER RECORD	30-52 (3 years)
ASSISTANTS	Ron Brown (John Jay '76)
	Carlton Screen (Providence '90)
TEAM WINS (last 5 years)	21-21-10-8-12
RPI (last 5 years)	81-97-223-283-242
2000-01 FINISH	Lost in conference first round.

What Magic was to the Lakers and Bird was to the Celtics in the beginning of the '80s, **Antawn Dobie** was to the Long Island Blackbirds last season.

Obviously, this is not to say Dobie is the same caliber player as the aforementioned legends, but the 6-0 senior made that kind of profound and immediate impact upon his return in mid-January from academic troubles.

On Jan. 19, LIU was sputtering along at 3-12, averaging just over 60 points per game. The next day Dobie stepped onto the floor for the first time in 2000-01 and fortunes changed. A win over St. Francis (Pa.) began a stretch of eight wins in nine games. Long Island finished the regular season winning nine-of-12, raised its scoring average to just under a 75 point a game clip and qualified for the NEC Tournament with a fourth-place finish.

"He made a heck of a difference, there's no question about it. He probably was the deciding factor that turned our season around," fourth-year coach Ray Martin said. "He's a hard to guard type player and his ability to penetrate and made it so much easier for the other guys and that also made us better. He also caught the attention of a lot of opposing coaches and became the focus of their tape sessions and scouting reports."

One of those coaches was Monmouth's Dave Calloway.

"Dobie is quick and talented. He has a chance to be something very special in this league," Calloway said.

Dobie added 16.9 points and two steals a game to the mix over the final 13 games (which included a first-round loss to Wagner in the NEC Tournament). That kind of production helped establish that he and 6-0 junior point guard **Maurice Yearwood** (11.2 ppg, 2.7 rpg, 2.9 apg, 1.7 spg, .352 3PT) might just become the conference's most explosive and dangerous backcourt in 2001-02.

In many ways Long Island's backcourt is a throwback. Neither Dobie nor Yearwood are strictly defined. In today's vernacular they would be called combo guards. They both handle the ball well and each can shoot the three, taking pressure off the other to always excel in a particular phase of the game.

"I'll say it to anyone who is willing to listen and yell it off the highest mountain, I won't give my guards up for anybody. I think we have the best pair of guards in the league. There may be some dispute, but I won't give them up for anybody in the country," Martin said.

The 12-8 NEC mark and fourth-place finish were the best in Martin's three seasons in Brooklyn. To continue the climb, Martin will need his ultra-quick backcourt to force the tempo to help offset for a relative lack of size and inside muscle. The Blackbirds lost their three top rebounders from a team that was already the NEC's second worst in rebounding margin (-5.8).

"There is no question and, it is a concern, that rebounding and play along the baseline is the key to our season," Martin said.

JaJa Bey (10.4 ppg, 3.8 rpg, 1.3 apg), a 6-7 junior forward, is Long Island's top returnee in that department, but he's more of a slasher.

Martin is hoping newcomers **Craig Taylor** and **Derek Bell** can make a difference on the glass. A 6-8 junior, Taylor arrives at LIU from Westchester Community College in Valhalla, New York. He was a 62 percent shooter and averaged 13.7 points and 5.5 rebounds last season.

Bell, a 6-7 freshman, is a homegrown Brooklyn product who played the last two seasons at Milford (Conn.) Academy. He averaged 14.4 points and 9.5 rebounds for the 21-3 New England Prep School runners-up. Both Taylor and Bell should push for immediate playing time next to Bey and 6-6 junior **Dawan Gary** (5.6 ppg, 4.4 rpg).

"This is a breakout year for Ja Ja. He has two years experience and knows what to expect. He has to give us consistent play all season, offensively, rebounding-wise, and defensively. That will be a critical position for us to get production out of," Martin said.

The athletic Gary made 13 starts last season and may work himself into a full-time job alongside Bey. He's at his best when the Blackbirds are running and pressing. Taylor will also vie for one of the starting forward jobs.

Martin is hoping **Raymond Edwards** helps solidify the baseline play as well. The 6-7, 225-pound sophomore is a tough, physical player who sat out last season as a partial qualifier. He averaged 18 points and eight rebounds at John F. Kennedy High School in the Bronx two seasons ago.

Dobie and Yearwood will log most of the minutes, but unlike the frontcourt, the Blackbird backcourt has some depth. **LaForest Knox** (4.1 ppg, 1.6 rpg, 1.8 apg), a 5-11 sophomore, was productive playing behind Yearwood last season and 6-1 sophomore guard **Walter Price** is back from a shoulder separation suffered on the first day of practice last year that delayed the start of his career. Price had been expected to contribute right away after averaging 15 points a game for St. Patrick's (N.J.) High School.

"Walter is just champing at the bit and can't wait to get out there," Martin said. "Both guys [Knox and Price] will challenge and compete with Antawn and Mo [Maurice Yearwood] for playing time and that's the way it should be," Martin said.

Martin will also be able to bring 6-3 senior guard **Keith Leslie** (4.9 ppg, 0.8 rpg, 1.4 apg) off the bench. Leslie made seven starts a year ago.

2001-2002 SCHEDULE

Nov.	17	Colgate
	26	Manhattan
	29	@Quinnipiac
Dec.	5	@Xavier
	12	Central Connecticut State
	16	@DePaul
	27-28	#Florida International Classic
Jan.	4	Monmouth
	6	Fairleigh Dickinson
	10	@St. Francis PA
	12	@Robert Morris
	16	@UMBC
	19	Mount St. Mary's
	23	@St. Francis PA
	28	Robrert Morris
Feb.	2	@Monmouth
	4	Wagner
	7	Sacred Heart
	9	@Wagner
	15	UMBC
	17	@Central Connecticut State
	20	@Sacred Heart
	23	@Fairleigh Dickinson
	25	St. Francis NY
March	1-2	##NEC Tournament
	6	###NEC Tournament

@Road Games
#Miami, FL (vs. Ohio first round; also Florida International, Vermont)
##Quarterfinals and semifinals at Wagner
###Championship at highest seeded team

BLUE RIBBON ANALYSIS

BACKCOURT	B
BENCH/DEPTH	C
FRONTCOURT	C-
INTANGIBLES	B

Can momentum carry over from one year to the next? That is the question Martin will be asking himself throughout the first part of the 2001-02 season. And it's unlikely he'll easily find the answer.

"If I knew I put it in a bottle, sell it to every coach, and get out of the business," Martin said.

The Blackbirds second half was almost a reversal of their first half a year ago— a 3-12 to start and 9-3 to finish the regular season. The revival came, not coincidentally, at the same time Dobie returned from his academic woes and injected a new energy and offensive presence to a team that was struggling to score.

"Our season was like a round of golf," Martin said. "On the front nine we had a lot of bogeys and doublebogeys and were having a tough time. Then on the back nine we were lucky enough to get a couple of pars, a few birdies, and a Dobie."

LIU will miss the 14.5 points a game of Rivera, but with Dobie back for entire season to start in the backcourt with the equally versatile Yearwood, the Blackbirds should not go through any long stretches averaging just 60 points per game like last season.

The big men are the mystery. Other than Bey there isn't a truly proven player on the baseline. Taylor, Bell, and Edwards will all play significant minutes and the trio has played a total of zero Division I basketball games.

With that in mind, Martin's club will probably press

and run more to offset a lack of size. Long Island's tallest player is the 6-8 Taylor, and the Blackbirds were not a good rebounding team a year ago.

"I don't deny that our size concerns me. I talk about it with my staff all the time and it keeps me up at night a little. It will be something we watch all season," Martin said.

Fortunately for Martin and the Blackbirds, the NEC is a guard-oriented league, and for the most part, guard-dominated league. And in that category, LIU can match up with anyone. It's a big pre-game conversation piece of television analysts, but it really is worth noting with Long Island this year: Watch the pace of the games early. If the Blackbirds can dictate how the game flows from the beginning more often than they can't, then a winning season should follow.

Don't expect the Jekyll and Hyde season for Long Island again this year, but a similar end result is a reasonable expectation.

(C.C.)

Maryland-Baltimore County

LOCATION	Baltimore, MD
CONFERENCE	Northeast
LAST SEASON	18-11 (.621)
CONFERENCE RECORD	13-7 (3rd)
STARTERS LOST/RETURNING	2/3
NICKNAME	Retrievers
COLORS	Black & Gold with Red
HOMECOURT	Retriever Activities Center (4,024)
COACH	Tom Sullivan (Fordham '72)
RECORD AT SCHOOL	72-96 (6 years)
CAREER RECORD	226-221 (16 years)
ASSISTANTS	Randy Monroe (Cheyney '85)
	Doug Nicholas (Gettysburg '89)
	Bill Zotti (Seton Hall '95)
TEAM WINS (last 5 years)	5-14-19-11-18
RPI (last 5 years)	297-254-113-242-186
2000-01 FINISH	Lost in conference semifinal.

It isn't often that a team can lose three players that formed its foundation for two seasons and still have a well-formed and talented nucleus to step right to the forefront.

Led by NEC Rookie-of-the-Year **Peter Mulligan**, UMBC head coach Tom Sullivan has exactly that. Gone are guard Terrence Ward (15.7 ppg, 2.3 rpg), forward Kennedy Okafor (11.8 ppg, 9.2 rpg), and Brad Martin, but Mulligan, 6-9 sophomore forward/center **Will McClurkin** and 6-0 junior point guard **Justin Wilson** are right there to be the new Three Musketeers for the Retrievers.

UMBC will be relying on that nucleus to overcome the disappointing end to an otherwise successful season. The Retrievers won 11-of-13 conference games and seven in a row at one point during a stretch in January and February, including a win at Monmouth in the final week of the regular season. However, Monmouth returned the favor two weeks later in the NEC Tournament and the season was over for UMBC.

"It was disappointing in the semis because we just couldn't make our shots. Not to take anything away from Monmouth, but we just couldn't score. One of these years it's going to be us," eight-year UMBC assistant Doug Nicholas said of a program that has the second-best record in the NEC (37 wins) over the last three seasons (UMBC's first three since leaving the Big South), but no postseason appearances.

Ironically, the Retrievers will not have a single senior this season, but by no means do they lack experience. For instance, Wilson is just a junior, but has been a full-time starter for two years. And of course there is Mulligan, who played in all 29 games as a freshman and was the clear choice for rookie honors. In fact, Mulligan (15.5 ppg, 5.5 rpg, 2.4 apg, .465 FG, .714 FT) is working on something of a streak of postseason awards. Two seasons ago he was New York State's Mr. Basketball.

"He had a great year, putting up points, which we needed," Nicholas said. "Peter could get a little bit more involved with the defense. But that's a team thing, especially for younger players."

While Mulligan is more of a perimeter player and is cagey around the offensive glass, McClurkin (10.4 ppg, 6.4 rpg, .494 FG, .738 FT) is more of a post-up player with a range of 15 feet and a good turnaround jumper. On a team where Ward and Mulligan got most of the opponent's attention, McClurkin quietly led UMBC in scoring five times and joined Mulligan on the all-rookie

team.

The Retrievers will clearly miss Ward, who at times was their do-everything shooting guard. He made eight three-pointers in that win over Monmouth.

"He just had incredible range and could come off screens and hit from anywhere," Nicholas said. "When he found his rhythm, forget about it. We don't have anybody that can shoot like that. We have scorers, but not that kind of shooter."

One of those scorers is 6-2 junior guard **Malik Wallace**, a native of Camden, N.J., and a transfer from Allegany Community College in Maryland. Wallace averaged 15.1 points during the NJCAA National Tournament, leading Allegheny to a runner-up finish.

"Wallace isn't the three-point shooter that Ward is. He can shoot them, but his game is more getting to the basket. He can really defend and do some things in the open floor," Nicholas said.

Wallace will probably slide right into Ward's vacated two-guard spot, and he may also see some time backing up Wilson at the point. At this time last year, that job belonged to 6-4 sophomore guard **Ron Yates** (3.2 ppg, 1.6 rpg, 1.6 apg). However, Yates, more accustomed to playing off the ball, struggled in that role. He finished the year at the wing and played much better.

"He got more comfortable with that and showed us he can slash and score. He could be someone to get us eight or 10 points a game," Nicholas said.

Wilson (6.0 ppg, 1.9 rpg, 2.8 apg, .437 FG, .317 3PT, .614 FT) is not a big scorer from the point, but he has established himself as a solid floor leader. His 1.68 assist-to-turnover ratio would have placed Wilson fourth in the NEC if he had enough assists to qualify.

"After playing just about every minute of every game his freshman year, I think Justin came in his sophomore year thinking the same thing was going to happen and he wasn't in the best shape. It turned out we had more guards to give him competition and he struggled a bit," Nicholas said. "But he got into shape as the year went on and by January he was playing very well."

Wilson spent 10 days this summer playing in France as part of a touring all-star team, which should help prevent another slow start.

UMBC may have to look at a pair of freshmen to help negate the loss of Ward as a long-range threat. **Rob Gogerty**, a 6-1 guard, and 6-2 guard **Mike Snyder** both put up big numbers as high school seniors. Gogerty was selected third-team All-New Jersey at Cedar Grover High School, averaging 25 points, eight rebounds, and eight assists. Snyder was second-team all state in New Jersey at Cranford High School with 23.7 points, 7.8 rebounds, and 4.5 assists per game.

"Mulligan's shot is coming around and Wilson is improving and these two freshmen are pretty good shooters, but right now there's a little bit of unknown in that department," Nicholas said. "Right now I'd have to call it a weakness. It's definitely an area we'll have to improve upon."

Andre Williams (1.2 ppg, 1.3 rpg, 16 games), a 6-4 junior forward, and 6-7 sophomore forward **Eugene Young** (0.4 ppg, 0.5 rpg, 17 games) should get more of an opportunity up front with Okafor or Martin gone.

Kareem Washington (1.4 ppg, 0.4 rpg, in five games), a 6-3 junior, is a shooting guard who finds himself behind Yates, Wallace and perhaps Gogerty and Snyder.

Andrew Feeley, a 6-9 freshman forward/center from New Jersey, may have to wait a year before he makes an impact.

2001-2002 SCHEDULE

Nov.	17, 19	#Battle of Baltimore
	29	@St. Francis PA
Dec.	1	@Robert Morris
	6	Quinnipiac
	8	Central Connecticut State
	11	@Bucknell
	15	@Rutgers
	22	Towson
	28-29	##Calbe Car Classic
Jan.	10	@Fairleigh Dickinson
	12	@Monmouth
	16	Long Island
	19	@Central Connecticut State
	23	@Mount St. Mary's
	26	Monmouth
	28	Fairleigh Dickinson
Feb.	2	@Sacred Heart
	4	@St. Francis NY
	7	St. Francis NY
	9	Robert Morris
	15	@Long Island

	17	@Wagner
	20	Mount St. Mary's
	23	Wagner
	25	Sacred Heart
March	1-2	###NEC Tournament
	6	####NEC Tournament

@Road Games
#Baltimore, MD (vs. Loyola College first round; also Coppin State, Towson)
##Santa Clara, CA (vs. Santa Clara first round; also Detroit, UC Santa Barbara)
###Quarterfinals and semifinals at Wagner
####Championship at highest-seeded team

BLUE RIBBON ANALYSIS

BACKCOURT	C
BENCH/DEPTH	D+
FRONTCOURT	B
INTANGIBLES	B

In the world of low-major college basketball, teams generally get just one shot a year. For UMBC and the rest of the NEC, that shot comes in the conference tournament. Last year it was Monmouth's time to shine. The Retrievers have not yet had their moment since joining the league four years ago, despite being one of the Northeast Conference's dominant teams.

"I wouldn't pick us one, but we should be in the mix among the top four. Monmouth has to be the favorite, but I think it's fairly wide open," Nicholas said.

UMBC will have to find a shooter to replace the first-team all-league Ward or learn to play without the three-pointer as a weapon, but otherwise are as solid as anyone in the NEC. Mulligan and McClurkin are probably the best scoring frontcourt duo in the conference and Wilson gives the Retrievers steady and reliable play at the point. Wallace could be the wildcard. If he plays up to expectations, then UMBC could again be one of the most potent and athletic teams in the NEC.

The lack of seniors should matter very little with 65 starts from the returnees last year.

"Team chemistry will be big with us. I think we have enough scoring power and talent, but it's just a matter of gelling, putting egos aside maybe," Nicholas said. "We relied a lot on Mulligan and McClurkin last year as freshmen, so they should only be helped by more experience."

Perhaps that experience will spell the difference for the Retrievers in March. Expect them to be there again among the final four still standing at the NEC Tournament. Then it's anybody's guess.

(C.C.)

Monmouth

LOCATION	West Long Branch, NJ
CONFERENCE	Northeast
LAST SEASON	21-10 (.677)
CONFERENCE RECORD	15-5 (2nd)
STARTERS LOST/RETURNING	1/4
NICKNAME	Hawks
COLORS	Blue & White
HOMECOURT	Baylan Gymnasium (2,500)
COACH	Dave Calloway (Monmouth '91)
RECORD AT SCHOOL	41-57 (4 years)
CAREER RECORD	41-57 (4 years)
ASSISTANTS	Mark Calzonetti (Bentley '85)
	Geoff Billet (Rutgers '99)
	Ron Krayl (Sioux Falls '68)
TEAM WINS (last 5 years)	18-4-5-12-21
RPI (last 5 years)	118-288-286-209-132
2000-01 FINISH	Lost in conference quarterfinal.

Monmouth head coach Dave Calloway seems to have a philosophy that says, "Look to the future without forgetting the past."

With four returning starters, including the NEC's reigning player of the year, from a team that won 21 games and played in the NCAA Tournament, Calloway has every reason to point forward. Yet he doesn't forget recent history in the NEC, a conference where there hasn't been a repeat tournament winner since 1994.

"It's nice to be one of the favorites, but in this conference over the last five or six years, the team that has been the favorite hasn't won it," Calloway said. "Someone has always come out of nowhere in this league. Last year it was us."

Calloway also doesn't quickly forget what it was like to begin 0-19 in 1998-99, his first full season. That makes the swift ascent that much sweeter.

"Once we got that first one, we got some confidence and it just grew. We went 5-2 the rest of that year and just kept getting better," said Calloway, whose Monmouth clubs went from 5-21 to 12-16 to 21-10. "I didn't think we'd get to this point this quickly, but I always thought we'd get there."

Not coincidentally, the rapid development of 6-0 senior point guard **Rashaan Johnson** has coincided with Monmouth's rocket ride up the NEC standings last year, capped by an even more improbable 20-point second-half comeback in the NEC title game against St. Francis (N.Y.). Johnson scored 14 points in that game on his way to tournament MVP honors. That followed the hardware Johnson had already taken home as the NEC's Player of the Year.

As Monmouth's lead guard, Johnson has the ball in his hands on every possession. Add that to his ability to penetrate, score and find teammates and it makes not only the conference MVP, but also the league's most influential, and possibly, most dominant player.

"He's very good with the basketball. He's a little guy, but he's extremely explosive," St. Francis (Pa.) coach Bobby Jones said of Johnson. "He's very good at breaking down [defenders] in the open court, but if you get too far off of him, he can shoot the basketball. Frankly, he's just a very, very good player because he was first-team all-defense too."

Johnson finished third in the conference in scoring (19.1 ppg,) and steals (2.1), first in assists (5.7 apg), and was in the top 15 in free-throw percentage (.768), rebounding (6.1) and assist-to-turnover ratio (1.31).

"Where he has come from his first year to last year is amazing. If we could have that much improvement as a team, we'd be great," Calloway said. "The thing that really helped was that Rashaan still scored the same, but his shooting percentage was better. He took fewer shots and his shot selection was much better. Also his turnovers were down. If he can keep improving there, he'll be even better."

But perhaps the most impressive part of Johnson's season was that he found himself atop the league in assists.

"The year before last Rashaan scored 40 in our last game against St. Francis and we lost," Calloway said. "Then he started last year with 28 and 29 in two of our first three games and we lost those, too. I think at that point, he realized he had to get guys involved for us to be successful."

One teammate Johnson learned to trust regularly, Gerry Crosby, graduated, but Johnson is still surrounded by plenty of experienced talent.

Johnson's backcourt partner, **Cameron Milton**, is back for his senior season. Milton (4.0 ppg, 2.7 rpg, 1.5 apg) is not the typical two-guard, instead deferring to Johnson in the areas of scoring and shooting. The 6-3 Milton, who was only seventh among the Hawks in shots taken, is more the steadying influence.

"Cameron and Rashaan complement each other nicely. Rashaan is fiery, aggressive, and so talented we just let him go. Cameron knows him and can see what's going on to keep it all under control," Calloway said.

Monmouth has the benefit of a third senior starter in **Steve Bridgemohan**. The 6-8 power forward and two-year starter does most of his damage near the basket and put up relatively modest offensive numbers until the two biggest games of the season. In the NEC championship, Bridgemohan (5.5 ppg, 4.3 rpg, .598 FG) paced the Hawks with 16 points and then he scored 12 against Duke in the NCAA Tournament.

"Bridgemohan was great down the stretch. He found more confidence and stayed out of foul trouble and it made him a much better player," Calloway said.

As reliable as Milton and Bridgemohan have been, the keys to Monmouth maintaining or surpassing last season's results, may just be junior center **Kevin Owens** and sophomore **Jason Krayl**.

"Kevin improved a lot from his freshman to sophomore years, but he needs to step it up again," Calloway said. "He can get 14 points and 10 rebounds, but we need him do that every night. He has a chance to be a really special player in this league."

The 6-10 Owens (9.4 ppg, 5.8 rpg, 1.0 bpg, .557 FG) became a starter immediately upon his arrival in West Long Branch from Haddonfield and has heard his name called before all but one of Monmouth's 59 games in the last two seasons.

The 6-5 Krayl, whose father Ron is a Monmouth assistant, will be the only new starter. Playing behind Crosby and a little out of position, Krayl struggled at times in his rookie season, yet still put up respectable

numbers (7.6 ppg, 2.8 rpg, 1.8 apg, .393 3PT). Now the wing-forward spot is all his, and Calloway expects bigger production from the sharp-shooting Krayl.

"Gerry was what put us over the top last year. We never expected to get 16 points a game from him," Calloway said. "We think Jason is more than capable of giving us that kind of production."

Krayl will get perimeter shooting help from 6-7 junior **Russ Anderson** (5.4 ppg, 3.0 rpg, .368 3PT), who should return to his role as Calloway's sixth man. That kind of size filters down to the rest of the frontline reserves.

Calloway can bring 6-9 **Nick Barnes**, 6-6 **Jay Dooley**, and 6-8 **Phil Bonczewski** off his bench. Barnes (1.9 ppg, 0.8 rpg) also checks in at 260 pounds and the sophomore will again serve as Owens' primary backup. Dooley 1.9 ppg, 1.4 rpg), a junior, and Bonczewski (0.8 ppg, 0.8 rpg), a sophomore, mainly played spot minutes a year ago and will have similar roles, but may see more floor time with the added experience.

They may also be pushed back in the rotation by 6-7 freshman **Blake Hamilton**, a strong 225-pound forward from Central Dauphin High School in Harrisburg, Pa. Hamilton averaged 19.9 points, 9.8 rebounds, two blocks and two steals per game, earning all-Pennsylvania honorable mention honors.

"Blake is a big kid and he could be very, very good," Calloway said. "But we are so deep up front, that could hurt his chances to play a lot."

The other two members of the Monmouth freshman class have some significant credentials as well. The 6-1 **Dwayne Bifield**, out of Elmont, N.Y., posted 17.5 points and 3.2 assists a game for a St. Mary's team that went 25-1 and won the New York Federation state title.

Brandon Owens, 5-9, helped lead St. Thomas More to the New England Prep Class A championship while scoring 15.5 points, grabbing 3.7 rebounds, and handing out 5.3 assists per game.

Bifield and Owens will be competing with 6-5 sophomore **Tom Kaplan** (0.3 ppg, 0.9 rpg) for playing time behind Milton and Krayl, and for those precious few minutes Johnson isn't on the floor.

2001-2002 SCHEDULE

Nov.	17	Rider
	23-25	#Hawaii Pacific Thanksgiving Classic
	29	@Seton hall
Dec.	1	Wagner
	8	@Princeton
	11	@Maryland
	14	@St. Peter's
	16	Sacred Heart
	29	Gonzaga
Jan.	4	@Long Island
	6	@St. Francis NY
	10	Mount St. Mary's
	12	UMBC
	16	@Wagner
	19	St. Francis PA
	23	@Central Connecticut State
	26	@UMBC
	28	@Mount St. Mary's
Feb.	2	Long Island
	4	@Fairleigh Dickinson
	7	@Quinnipiac
	9	Central Connecticut State
	14	@St. Francis PA
	16	@Robert Morris
	20	Quinnipiac
	23	St. Francis NY
	25	Fairleigh Dickinson
March	1-2	##NEC Tournament
	6	###NEC Tournament

@Road Games
#Honolulu, HI (vs. Akron first round; also Chattanooga, Hampton, Hawaii Pacific, Liberty, Notre Dame, Vanderbilt)
Quarterfinals and semifinals at Wagner
###Championship a highest seeded team

BLUE RIBBON ANALYSIS

BACKCOURT	B+
BENCH/DEPTH	B+
FRONTCOURT	B
INTANGIBLES	B

Calloway and his players were none too happy with how they acquitted themselves in a 95-52 thrashing at the hands of top-seeded and eventual national champion Duke in the first round of the NCAA Tournament. That makes the goal this year simple: Get better so as not be in that situation again.

"By getting there, the guys got hungry to go back. They enjoyed the entire experience—the week before, the media attention, drawing a team like Duke," Calloway said. "But it also showed us we have a lot of room to improve to try to get back and get a higher seed."

If the Hawks can deliver against their tough schedule, then a higher RPI ranking and seeding are possible. In November, Monmouth plays in a Hawaii Pacific Tournament that includes Vanderbilt, Notre Dame, and 2001 NCAA Tournament darling Hampton. Four days later the Hawks visit Seton Hall. They also have road games at Maryland and Princeton and host Gonzaga.

"The schedule is very tough and demanding. If the kids are overconfident, the schedule should knock them back to reality," Calloway said.

In the NEC, the entire season comes down to those three conference tournament games. St. Francis (N.Y.) learned that the hard way after Monmouth's 20-point rally ended what had been an outstanding season. Calloway is well aware of how narrow that margin is.

"Playing our schedule will help get us ready for the conference and the experience and confidence that last year brought us will help, too. We are deeper and have a lot of veterans, but in this league, anybody can become a contender like we did last year," Calloway said.

Expect Calloway's cautious confidence to be well placed. His club will be at or near the top the entire regular season, but come NEC Tournament time it's anyone's guess.

(C.C.)

Mount St. Mary's

LOCATION	Emmitsburg, MD
CONFERENCE	Northeast
LAST SEASON	7-20 (.250)
CONFERENCE RECORD	7-13 (t-9th)
STARTERS LOST/RETURNING	1/4
NICKNAME	Mountaineers
COLORS	Blue & White
HOMECOURT	Knott Arena (3,196)
COACH	Jim Phelan (La Salle '51)
RECORD AT SCHOOL	816-484 (47 years)
CAREER RECORD	816-484 (47 years)
ASSISTANTS	Don Anderson (Franklin & Marshall '82)
	Lamont Franklin (UNC Wilmington '97)
	Jack McLatchy (Cheyney '60)
TEAM WINS (last 5 years)	14-13-15-9-7
RPI (last 5 years)	171-200-158-256-306
2000-01 FINISH	Lost regular-season finale.

Jim Phelan is about as closely associated with Mount St. Mary's as any coach can possibly be with a school.

When one thinks Penn State, Joe Paterno comes to mind. North Carolina. it's still Dean Smith. Florida State instantly means Bobby Bowden. The Mountaineers will never be big-time in college basketball, but the link is the same. Jim Phelan is what anyone conjures up as an image when Mount St. Mary's is mentioned, and that's a notion the 47th-year head coach is not always comfortable with.

"Fortunately we're in the country and we don't get the same kind of coverage you might get in New York and that helps," Phelan said. "We get coverage when we hit milestone marks or when we win and then people come around and say, 'Hey, this guy is 72 years old. What is he still doing coaching?' "

Phelan and the Mountaineers haven't done much winning in the last two seasons, and that has generally kept everyone but the Frederick New Post and the Gettysburg Times away, but that may be ready to turn around if they can avoid the bad luck of 1999 and 2000.

Phelan was part of that bad luck. He was waging a fight against prostate cancer and was receiving radiation treatment throughout the first half of last season. He is fully recovered and back to good health. The other piece of good news involves the second-most talked about figure in Mount St. Mary's basketball—**Melvin Whitaker.**

The roller-coaster ride that has been Whitaker's career has mostly been untracked for two years. After helping the Mountaineers to the NCAA Tournament in 1999, Whitaker broke his right ankle and missed the entire 1999-00 season. As it turns out, the 6-10 center needed as much rehabilitation in his academics as he did for his ankle. Poor grades left Whitaker ineligible for the first semester last season. He came back to average 12.8 points and 8.6 rebounds in 11 games. Then on Feb. 15, just as he was getting rid of the layers of rust, Whitaker broke his left ankle.

Two years, two broken ankles, one academic suspension and very little basketball for a player, who when healthy and on the floor, could be the NEC's best.

The 25-year-old Whitaker is listed as a junior. A career that has already seemed to last forever—from Oak Hill Academy, to Virginia, to prison for the assault of a Cavalier football player with a box cutter, to Mount St. Mary's—still has two more collegiate seasons remaining.

"He's back and looks good and says he feels good. Melvin still has a big bolt in his ankle from two years ago, but he seems ready to be a big help to us," Phelan said. "He never had any serious injury before this and then all of a sudden he has two broken ankles. You figure the law of averages is with him and it won't happen this year. At least you hope so."

Phelan hopes so more than anyone. The Mountaineers with Whitaker take on a completely different look than without him. Even with a bad ankle and probably too much extra weight, Whitaker blocked 30 shots in those 11 games. He's a dominant inside force in a league and at a school that rarely sees that.

A healthy Whitaker makes sophomore forward **Pat Atangana** a different player. The 6-6 Atangana (10.0 ppg, 7.9 rpg), the Mount's top returning scorer and rebounder, would be forced to play some center without Whitaker around. Now he has a little more freedom.

"He gives us a scorer and rebounder who we really expect to improve on last year," Phelan said of the Cameroon native.

Atangana joins the rest of his teammates in desperately needing to upgrade their marksmanship. A 39.8 percent shooter, Atangana was actually a sharpshooter on a team that hit just 38.6 percent of its shots.

"When you shot as poorly as we did, you can't really say anyone had a decent year," Phelan said. "But some of that goes back to teams being able to play up tight on the outside guys because without Melvin we didn't have much of an inside game."

One of those outside guys is 5-11 senior **Jerry Lloyd** (9.0 ppg, 1.4 rpg, 1.3 rpg), who is a better shooter than last year's 29.1 three-point percentage would indicate. After coming off the bench most of last season, Lloyd could grab a starting job if his long-range game is closer to the 36.3 percent of his sophomore season.

Keith Price (9.6 ppg, 3.3 rpg, 1.4 apg), a 6-5 sophomore, managed 11 starts on the wing and it may come down to Price and Lloyd as to who gets the nod this time around. Price has more size but isn't as good a shooter and doesn't have as much experience. Lloyd played a supporting role on the 1999 NEC Tournament championship team. In either case, both Price and Lloyd will have key roles.

Lloyd could also play some point, but Phelan would prefer to go with 6-1 sophomore **Shawn Mark** as his lead guard. Mark, who hails from Brooklyn, originally committed to Manhattan, but was late getting his qualifying SAT score. The Jaspers couldn't wait and moved on. Mark landed at Palm Beach (Fla.) Community College, where he played last year to the tune of seven points and six assists per game.

"His goal is to lead the nation in assists, which is always pleasant for a coach to hear. The big guys will like a guy like that too," Phelan said.

Another one of those big guys and the probable third starter up front with Whitaker and Atangana is 6-8 junior **Angel Rivera** (7.4 ppg, 5.2 rpg, .432 FG), whose 22 starts a year ago was the most for any returning Mountaineer.

"Angel has filled out nicely. He has excellent speed and we are looking for him to have a breakout year," Phelan said. "He's big enough, he's strong enough, he's a good shot blocker. He has all the ingredients."

The reserves up front are a pair of newcomers—6-8 freshman **Jason Epps** and 6-6 freshman **Jason Carbone**. Epps, a sturdy 230 pounds, is from Lovejoy High School in Atlanta and will likely play right away. Carbone, from South Windsor High School in Connecticut, is more of a shooter and scored 22.2 points and grabbed 10 rebounds per game as a senior.

"Jason Epps runs the floor pretty well and actually defends pretty well. He looks like a good prospect. Jason Carbone could come in and pressure the people who are here," Phelan said.

Jamion Christian (2.4 ppg, 0.8 rpg), a 6-2 sophomore guard, actually made more starts (13) than both Price and Lloyd, but didn't make nearly as much use of the opportunity. Christian played just 9.8 minutes each time out, but still figures to be the fourth guard in the rotation.

Six-foot-1 senoir **Esmond Marvray** (4.3 ppg, 2.8 rpg, 2.1 apg) figures to push Christian for those minutes. **Donte Alexander** (1.8 ppg, 0.4 rpg, 14 games), a 6-3 sophomore, and 6-4 junior **Michael Bajornas** (1.3 ppg, 1.4 rpg in 15 games), will likely have a longer road to significant playing time.

2001-2002 SCHEDULE

Nov.	24	@Virginia Tech
	29	@Robert Morris
Dec.	1	@St. Francis PA
	6	Central Connecticut State
	8	Quinnipiac
	15	Loyola College
	17	Butler
	21	@California
	22	@San Jose State
	30	@Navy
Jan.	2	Bucknell
	10	@Monmouth
	12	@Fairleigh Dickinson
	16	St. Francis NY
	19	@Long Island
	23	UMBC
	26	Fairleigh Dickinson
Feb.	2	@Wagner
	4	@Sacred Heart
	7	Robert Morris
	9	St. Francis PA
	14	@St. Francis PA
	16	@Quinnipiac
	20	@UMBC
	23	Sacred Heart
	25	Wagner
March	1-2	#NEC Tournament
	6	##NEC Tournament

@Road Games
#Quarterfinals and semifinals at Wagner
##Championship at highest seeded team

BLUE RIBBON ANALYSIS

BACKCOURT	D
BENCH/DEPTH	C
FRONTCOURT	B
INTANGIBLES	B

Phelan is 72-years-old and has been the head coach at Mount St. Mary's for nearly half a century, but has no intention of ending the ride.

"You just keep going and see how things go. As long as I can still do it right and still communicate with the players, I'm not planning on going anywhere," said Phelan, whose 48 seasons will equal Phog Allen's recor. (His 47 seasons at one school is also a record).

Reversing the fortunes of the last two seasons would go a long way to keeping his energy up and a lot of that depends on the health of Whitaker at center.

Upon his arrival, Phelan said that Whitaker had a chance to perhaps be the greatest player the NEC has ever seen. That time will have to be now. Phelan may not be getting any younger, but neither is Whitaker, now 25.

The big man's presence should be a big boost to a team that was last in the NEC in rebounding margin (-6.8), a situation made much worse considering Mount St. Mary's was also the conference's least accurate shooting team (.386). Phelan is depending on forwards Rivera and Atangana to help Whitaker change that and new point guard Mark joins a team that had the league's fewest assists.

No one is guessing why 2000-2001 was a tough year in Emmitsburg. Recent history says the Mountaineers should not depend on Whitaker being there all season. The laws of fair balance say he will. Reality says he needs to be. With the 6-10 shot blocker on the court for 27 games, the Mountaineers are a potential top-four NEC team and a certain conference tournament qualifier. If Whitaker goes down again, then Mount St. Mary's will be in for another single digit win total.

In either case, Phelan certainly won't catch Dean Smith's 879 wins this year, but the college basketball world will still think about Jim Phelan every time it hears the name Mount St. Mary's.

(C.C.)

Quinnipiac

LOCATION	Hamden, CT
CONFERENCE	Northeast

LAST SEASON	6-21 (.222)
CONFERENCE RECORD	3-17 (12th)
STARTERS LOST/RETURNING	2/3
NICKNAME	Braves
COLORS	Blue & Gold
HOMECOURT	Burt Kahn Court (1,500)
COACH	Joe DeSantis (Fairfield '79)
RECORD AT SCHOOL	42-92 (5 years)
CAREER RECORD	42-92 (5 years)
ASSISTANTS	Steve Baker (Towson '89)
	Mitch Oliver (So. Connecticut St. '97)
	Ed Younng (Lock Haven '80)
TEAM WINS (last 5 years)	5-4-9-18-6
RPI (last 5 years)	NA-NA-252-166-313
2000-01 FINISH	Lost regular-season finale.

Will the real Quinnipiac basketball team please stand up?

Two seasons ago the Braves, just a couple of years removed from playing at the Division II level, sent a minor ripple of surprise through the NEC by winning 12 conference games, 18 overall, and finishing fourth in the league.

Then just as quickly as Quinnipiac rose through the standings, the elevator reversed direction. It didn't stop until the Braves reached the basement, one season and only three league wins later.

"Regardless of the wins and losses, it was disappointing because our expectation was to play better," sixth-year coach Joe DeSantis said. "Last year we had six seniors and they were all good kids, but it was problem trying to please all of them with playing time. The chemistry was never really there, we just didn't make the right plays at the right time and it started to snowball. We didn't stop trying and were in every game, but we just couldn't win."

DeSantis was exactly right. The Braves just couldn't win—the close ones anyway. The Braves lost 12 of their 16 games that were decided by 10 points or less and were 2-5 when the margin was under five.

"They were in every ball game. I remember watching them early in the year and they gave Connecticut a hell of a run," Long Island coach Ray Martin said, referring to the Braves' eventual 86-72 season-opening loss to the Huskies. "With about three or four minutes to go it's a three-possession game, so for them it was just the little breaks that can go either way and spell gloom or doom for you."

To reverse those close-game fortunes, DeSantis will rely on veterans **Jared Grasso** and **Bill Romano**. After two years as the starting lead guard, Grasso, a 6-3 senior, slid off the ball to make room for Colin Charles (17.5 ppg, 3.0 rpg, 3.1 apg), who was one-year-and-done after his transfer from St. John's.

Grasso (11.7 ppg, 2.0 rpg, 3.9 apg, .390 3PT, .855 FT) will return to the point, where he was slightly more productive and was more accurate from deep (.431 3PT) two seasons ago.

"I like my point guards to be able to score and he was the point guard when we won 18 games," DeSantis said. "Jared has a good understanding of tempo and he understands the game. He knows my system. He's not the fastest guy, but he has quickness and smarts."

Romano (10.0 ppg, 5.2 rpg, .411 FG) resumes his place in the middle of the Braves' front line, where he has been nothing but steady for three seasons. The 6-8, 250-pound senior maximizes the use of his wide body and has developed solid offensive skills around the basket. DeSantis would like to see Romano's field-goal percentage get back closer to the .522 he shot as a sophomore. He also needs his center on the floor more. Foul trouble has plagued Romano throughout his career. He tied for second with six disqualifications last season and was able play just 24 minutes per game.

"They are the ones that are going to have to make the big shots and the big decisions on and off the court. They are the leaders. They are going to have to be," DeSantis said.

Both Romano (932 points) and Grasso (887) will likely both join the 1,000-point club this season.

The brightest surprise of a year ago was 6-3 sophomore guard **Kason Mims** (7.5 ppg, 3.6 rpg, 2.1 apg, .317 3PT), who eventually worked his way into the starting lineup and became the Braves fourth-leading scorer.

"I'm looking for him to improve on his driving game and his defense. I really think he'll be a better player," DeSantis said of Mims. "Now with Kason, even though he didn't start all year, I feel like I do have three returning starters. He played well enough to be a starter."

DeSantis also got valuable production from 6-1 junior guard **Kareem Lee** (5.0 ppg, 1.7 rpg, 1.0 apg, .344 3PT) off the bench. The one-time first-team all-state player in Connecticut played one year at Drake before returning to his home state.

However, Lee could get an even bigger battle for playing time from sophomore forward **Rashaun Banjo** (2.7 ppg, 1.1 rpg). After Grasso and Mims, DeSantis figures to throw out any other combination of perimeter players, meaning even the 6-6 Banjo could steal away minutes from the 6-1 Lee. Now that Banjo has been through a year of college basketball, DeSantis will likely begin the season with the sophomore in the starting lineup.

DeSantis prefers to use perimeter-oriented players to surround Romano in his motion offense, even including the power-forward spot. DeSantis figures he's got that perfect fit in junior college transfer **Jeremy Bishop**. The 6-8 junior from Champlain (Vt.) Junior College averaged 16.5 points and a staggering-at-any-level 15.3 rebounds per game last season.

"I don't want to build anyone up, but he's probably the key new guy," DeSantis said. "I'm constantly in a search for what I call a perimeter four-man and last year I didn't have that. Now I think I do in Jeremy Bishop."

Bishop figures to have the biggest impact of the four newcomers, but it's 6-8 **C.J. Vick** who has the name recognition. Vick, a freshman from Springfield, Va. who played at Notre Dame Academy in Massachusetts last year, is the cousin of the NFL's first overall draft pick in 2001, Atlanta Falcons quarterback Michael Vick. C.J. averaged 9.2 points last season.

"I try to recruit players who can play more than one position," DeSantis said. "His strength right now indicates that he's a small forward. His height indicates that he can be that perimeter four once he builds up. He's a sound kid fundamentally and will be good in my system because he has skills."

Another 6-8 forward comes by way Sullivan (N.Y.) Community College. Junior **Kris Ibezim** helped Sullivan to the Division III NJCAA National Tournament, scoring 13.9 points and grabbing 8.2 rebounds per game.

The well-traveled **Rob Monroe** rounds out DeSantis' recruiting class. The 5-10 Monroe played last year at the Berkshire School in Massachusetts after spending two high school seasons at St. John's-Prospect Hall and two more at Montrose Chrisitian in Maryland. The freshman was a 22.4-points-per-game scorer with 7.2 assists and 3.1 steals at Berkshire.

Ryan Kelly (1.0 ppg, 1.5 rpg, 17 games), a 6-6 senior center, and 6-4 sophomore guard **John Baja** (1.2 ppg, 0.4 rpg, 9 games) both have good size to fill in on the wings, but lost out on the competition for meaningful minutes in 2000-01.

Vernon Thompson (2.9 ppg, 0.8 rpg, 12 games), a 6-4 junior forward, will also have a tough time breaking into a rotation DeSantis plans to keep tighter and more regular than a year ago.

2001-2002 SCHEDULE

Nov.	20	@Army
	24	Albany
	29	Long Island
Dec.	1	St. Francis NY
	6	@UMBC
	8	@Mount St. Mary's
	18	Dartmouth
	21	*@Connecticut
	29	@St. John's
Jan.	4	@Binghamton
	10	@Wagner
	12	Sacred Heart
	16	Central Connecticut State
	19	@St. Francis NY
	23	Fairleigh Dickinson
	26	@Central Connecticut State
	28	Wagner
Feb.	2	@Robert Morris
	4	@St. Francis PA
	7	Monmouth
	9	@Fairleigh Dickinson
	14	@Sacred Heart
	16	Mount St. Mary's
	20	@Monmouth
	23	Robert Morris
	25	St. Francis PA
March	1-2	#NEC Tournament
	6	##NEC Tournament

@Road Games
*Hartford Civic Center
#Quarterfinals and semifinals at Wagner
##Championship at highest seeded team

BLUE RIBBON ANALYSIS

BACKCOURT	C
BENCH/DEPTH	C
FRONTCOURT	C
INTANGIBLES	C+

Last season gave Quinnipiac a look at the other end of the spectrum—the bad end. Losing begot losing and created additional chemistry problems that never resolved themselves.

The Braves went from 18 wins after just two seasons in Division I down to six.

"It's funny how expectations went from nothing to maybe winning the league or being in the top three or four. But that's over with now and we've all learned," DeSantis said. "I have two, three, four guys who've experienced the 18-win season and the six-win season. If you asked them a multiple choice question on how they want the season to end, they're all going to try to get back to 18 wins because that felt a lot better. So I think we are going to turn this into a positive."

Last season DeSantis tried to accommodate his seniors, but with six to appease, the plan backfired. He's going to do the same this season, but this time there are only two—four-year starters Grasso and Romano—to worry about. And DeSantis needs them as much as they need him.

"I won't mind going into the locker room this year and saying Jared and Bill are the guys and if anyone has a problem with that should come see me," DeSantis, the one-time second-round pick of the Washington Bullets said.

Both Mims and Banjo will need to go to the next level in their development, because DeSantis will be relying on them to play pivotal roles and Bishop should be an impact freshman.

"I like my starting five to average between nine and 16 or eight and 20 points a game, or something like that," DeSantis said. "When you play a motion offense, the ball touches everyone's hand, but by the same token I want them to know who will be getting the big shots and what everyone's role is."

The Braves aren't as bad as last year's 6-21. They probably aren't another 18-win team this year either. But that doesn't bother DeSantis, who figures he'll always keep perspective.

"Hubie Brown used to give this one foot from the gutter lecture that I follow," DeSantis said. "I think when you lose it helps you appreciate the winning. I just want to put myself in a position to, at the end of the year, sit in my office and say this team overachieved and played well. Now if that means an NEC championship or an eighth-place finish, so be it."

(C.C.)

Robert Morris

LOCATION	Moon Township, PA
CONFERENCE	Northeast
LAST SEASON	7-22 (.241)
CONFERENCE RECORD	7-13 (t-9th)
STARTERS LOST/RETURNING	1/4
NICKNAME	Colonials
COLORS	Blue & White
HOMECOURT	Charles L. Sewall Center (3,056)
COACH	Mark Schmidt (Boston College '85)
RECORD AT SCHOOL	First year
CAREER RECORD	First year
ASSISTANTS	Todd Kalsey (Xavier '99)
	Eddie Benton (Vermont '97)
	Steve Curran (Merrimack '92)
TEAM WINS (last 5 years)	4-8-15-18-7
RPI (last 5 years)	287-283-193-150-288
2000-01 FINISH	Lost regular-season finale.

Danny Nee said all the right things when he arrived at Robert Morris a year ago. He wanted to re-establish the Colonial program as a perennial NCAA Tournament contender and eventually be a big winner.

Then 12 months and a mere seven wins later, cross-town Duquesne came calling. The allure of the Atlantic 10 was more than enough and the love fest was over. Nee was on his way to bigger (not necessarily greener) pastures.

That meant for the third time in three years, Robert Morris would have a new coach and this time Director of Athletics Susan Hofacre went for a long-time assistant rather than the big-time resume and hired Mark Schmidt, who spent the last seven seasons on Skip Prosser's staff at Xavier.

"A lot of guys in this business never get the opportunity to be a head coach, so I feel a little blessed and honored to coach at the Division I level," Schmidt said. "I think the success we had at Xavier with coach Prosser really helped me."

During those seven years under Prosser, the Musketeers made four NCAA Tournaments and two NITs, and Schmidt was instrumental in the recruitment of NBA players James Posey and Torraye Braggs. Before his time at Xavier, Schmidt spent one season as an assistant at Loyola (Md.), two under Bruce Parkhill at Penn State and three at St. Michael's College in Vermont. That followed a four-year playing career at Boston College under two highly successful coaches, Tom Davis and Gary Williams. In other words, Schmidt has influences aplenty.

"In many ways I'm a reflection of all of those guys," Schmidt said. "I'm an aggressive personality. I really believe in pressure and trying to get things in the open court and when we miss a shot we are going to send four guys to the backboard. It's a fun style and it has been successful. For the last seven years at Xavier we had a lot of success with it. You need athletic kids to do that and I think we have some here and will recruit more."

Schmidt's transition from assistant to boss is made much easier by the fact that Robert Morris lost as many players as it did head coaches. Point guard Naron Jackson (8.3 ppg, 3.4 rpg, 4.3 apg) is the only Colonial gone from Nee's team and Schmidt inherits a roster of five seniors.

Leading the way is 6-5 senior **Wesley Fluellen** (16.7 ppg, 4.9 rpg, 1.6 apg, .549 FG), who a year ago may have been the NEC's most improved player and was a second-team all-league pick. He averaged just 6.2 points per game as a sophomore part-time player, but blossomed after becoming a starter. Now the Colonials hope he takes the next step to NEC star and unquestionable go-to guy.

"Wesley Fluellen is a good kid and a very good player," Schmidt said. "I think he has the respect of his teammates and will be a guy that will be vocal and get the guys to buy into what we are trying to sell."

Fluellen's partner at forward, **Aaron Thomas** (9.0 ppg, 3.6 rpg, 1.1 apg), is most comfortable on the perimeter. The 6-7 sophomore forward led the Colonials and was seventh in the NEC in three-point field-goal percentage. His 39.1 percent accuracy was especially impressive on a team that without Thomas made just 71-of-266 (.266) from beyond the arc. Even with Thomas' contribution, Robert Morris was last in the league in three-point accuracy and three-pointers made.

Matt Smith (7.5 ppg, 5.1 rpg, 1.0 apg, .533 FG), a 6-9 senior center, is unspectacular but steady in the middle. A two-year starter, Smith gets the most out of his bulk and strength. He led Robert Morris with 56 offensive rebounds, an area from where much of his scoring production comes.

Schmidt's time in the Queen City did more than help him land his first head-coaching job. He was also able to bring with him from Cincinnati the Colonials' top recruit, 6-8 freshman **Pierre Darden**. Schmidt recruited him to go to Xavier and then hitched him to the moving van when Robert Morris came calling.

"He's athletic and can run and he can play the style we want to play." Schmidt said. "He's a little raw and needs to be a little stronger, but I think he'll be a very good player in this league. He's got as good a chance as anybody to get playing time. It's tough for any freshman at the Division I level, but I wouldn't be shocked if he had an immediate impact."

Darden averaged 11 points, 10 rebounds, and six blocks per game last season at Withrow High School in Cincinnati.

The other two newcomers will also have the opportunity to play right away because 6-1 junior **DaMarcus Ellis** and 5-11 freshman **Maurice Carter** are both point guards, and otherwise, the Colonials have none.

"The first thing we did when we got the job was go out and find a point guard," Schmidt said. "The way we play the point guard is crucial. He's going to have the ball in his hands 90 percent of the time. If we don't anybody we can rely on then we have big trouble."

Ellis is a Dallas native who played at Los Angeles Valley Community College last year. He's a true playmaker and averaged 4.7 assists per game. Carter hails from Richmond, but played last season at Eleanor Roosevelt High School in Maryland, where he teamed with two other Division I recruits—Eddie Basden (Charlotte) and Delonte West (St. Joseph's). Carter averaged 14.5 points, 5.5 assists, and 3.0 rebounds per game, helping Eleanor Roosevelt to the Class 4A State title.

Schmidt also has a trio of combo guards in 6-1 sophomore **Liviti Clarke** (4.3 ppg, 1.2 rpg, 1.9 apg), 6-0 junior **John Caruso** (2.7 ppg, 2.2 rpg, 12 games) and 6-4

sophomore **Chaz McCrommon**, who could be fighting for reserve point guard duty. Clarke played in all 29 games a year ago and has the upper hand in terms of experience. Caruso's minutes dwindled as the season progressed and McCrommon sat out last year as a non-qualifier.

On the wing, Nee got far more than he expected from 5-10 senior guard **Ricky Richburg** (7.1 ppg, 2.8 rpg, 1.7 apg, .373 3 PT) and much less from 6-4 senior guard **Tyler Bacon** (4.3 ppg, 2.2 rpg). Richburg had played very little as a sophomore, but emerged from a pack of shooting guards that also includes 6-5 senior **Eric Casey-Ford** (6.7 ppg, 2.8 rpg, 1.8 rpg) to start 19 times. Casey-Ford got 18 starts and the two are the most likely candidates to start next to one of the new point guards. Richburg is more of the shooter and Casey-Ford likes to go to the basket.

Bobby Davenport (3.6 ppg, 2.2 rpg, nine games), a 6-8 sophomore forward, will be a primary reserve in relatively thin frontcourt.

2001-2002 SCHEDULE

Nov.	20	@Pittsburgh
	23-25	#Robert Morris Hoops Classic
	29	Mount St. Mary's
Dec.	1	UMBC
	5	UMKC
	15	@West Virginia
	19	@Youngstown State
	23	Albany
	29	@Purdue
Jan.	3	@Sacred Heart
	5	@Wagner
	10	St. Francis NY
	12	Long Island
	15	St. Francis PA
	19	@Fairleigh Dickinson
	23	Sacred Heart
	26	@St. Francis NY
	28	@Long Island
Feb.	2	Quinnipiac
	4	Central Connecticut State
	7	@Mount St. Mary's
	9	@UMBC
	14	Fairleigh Dickinson
	16	Monmouth
	23	@Quinnipiac
	25	@Central Connecticut State
March	1-2	##NEC Tournament
	6	###NEC Tournament

@Road Games
#Moon Township, PA (vs.South Florida first round; also UC Irvine, Illinois State, Kent State, Hofstra, Pittsburgh, Oakland)
##Quarterfinals and semifinals at Wagner
###Championship at highest seeded team

BLUE RIBBON ANALYSIS

BACKCOURT	D
BENCH/DEPTH	D+
FRONTCOURT	C+
INTANGIBLES	C

After consecutive seasons of 15 and 18 wins under Jim Boone, Robert Morris slumped badly last year in Nee's one and only season. When Nee jumped ship to Duquesne, stability quickly became the No. 1 issue for the Colonial basketball program.

Enter Schmidt, finally getting his chance to become a head coach after a long career as an assistant.

"One of the reasons why I was hired and why they didn't go after a head coach is because they need stability," Schmidt said. "They know for me to move on, I've got to win and it's going to take a number of years to do that. I'm in a situation where we can build this the right way. Hopefully I'll be here a long time and have our guys get comfortable with what we're trying to teach."

What Schmidt wants to teach is the fullcourt pressure, up-tempo, high-intensity style that he learned as a player under Davis and Williams and as an assistant under Prosser. The Colonials have a handful of athletic players to hit the ground running with Schmidt's philosophy, but perhaps not enough.

One who should be ready is Fluellen, who emerged as Robert Morris' clear-cut top gun a year ago. A wiry forward, Fluellen can get up and down the floor and is effective in the lane. Schmidt will hope to enjoy Fluellen's final year, while he grooms Darden as his next scoring for-

ward.

Smith helps create space for Fluellen and takes care of any misses and Richburg provides some solid deep shooting.

Those three are all seniors and should help Schmidt ease into the job, but there are holes that could become headaches. Someone in the group of Richburg, Thomas, or Casey-Ford will need to emerge as a dependable second scorer and either Ellis or Carter will have to be the answer at the point.

This is likely to be another transition year at Robert Morris, but one that could produce more than last season's seven wins.

"I think we have good kids and kids who want to get better and now it's my job to push them to go beyond what they did last year," Schmidt said.

That's entirely possible, but it's doubtful the Colonials will be competing for a title.

(C.C.)

Sacred Heart

LOCATION	Fairfield, CT
CONFERENCE	Northeast
LAST SEASON	7-21 (.333)
CONFERENCE RECORD	6-14 (11th)
STARTERS LOST/RETURNING	3/2
NICKNAME	Pioneers
COLORS	Scarlet & White
HOMECOURT	William H. Pitt Center (2,100)
COACH	Dave Bike (Sacred Heart '69)
RECORD AT SCHOOL	384-291 (23 years)
CAREER RECORD	384-291 (3 years)
ASSISTANTS	Johnny Kidd (Cent. Conn. St. '85)
	Keith Bike (Hartford '98)
	Terrence Kirker (Providence '00)
TEAM WINS (last 5 years)	12-15-11-3-7
RPI (last 5 years)	NA-NA-NA-308-286
2000-01 FINISH	Won regular-season finale.

College sports' top dogs in Indianapolis might not like the analogy, but indulge us for just a moment. Picture the world of NCAA basketball as one big college fraternity, say Delta House, everyone's favorite fictional home of collegiate shenanigans. Following the analogy a step further, that might make Sacred Heart the hoops version of Flounder, and, bare with us, we mean that with all respect in mind.

After making the leap from Division II two seasons ago (much like the naive Flounder leaving mom, dad, and high school behind), the Pioneers had their own version of pledge week (with Notre Dame and Stanford playing the roles of D-Day and Niedermayer) that lasted 38 games. Nobody had their car wrecked, but some confidences took a beating.

Yet, just as Flounder persevered to become an accepted member of Delta House, so too did Sacred Heart, entering its third year in Division I, to become a legitimate member at college basketball's highest level (we told you this analogy had a happy ending).

Of course, the hardwood and Hollywood are two different places, and no rebuilding process has an ending wrapped up as tight as a movie script.

Sacred Heart still has a long way to go, yet progress was noticeable in 2000-01. After losing 35 of those first 38 games, pledging was over as the calendar turned to a new year.

On Jan. 3, 2001, Sacred Heart ended its 10-game losing streak that began the season by beating Holy Cross and embarked on what turned out to be 7-11 finish, certainly not what Final Fours are made of, but also a far cry from 3-35.

"I don't know what acceptable progress is, but we have made progress," 24th-year head coach Dave Bike said. "It shows a little character that these kids were pretty good to hang in there. We think that got us to the corner. Now we have to turn it and go up the street."

The Pioneers took a few major strides down NEC Boulevard with a win over regular-season conference champion St. Francis (N.Y.) in February and hope to proceed through the green light with seniors **Andrew Hunter** and **Tim Welch** driving the bus.

The 6-7 Hunter (12.2 ppg, 5.8 rpg, 1.2 apg, .442 FG) was Sacred Heart's top scorer a year ago and the onus will be on the Ontario native to take his game to the next level.

"Some people will ask me how good I think so-and-so is going to be and I tell them it's not important how good I think he can be. What's important is how he feels he's going to be," Bike said. "Andrew is right there and he needs to get over that hump. He needs to set his goals higher and not look back."

The 6-10, 285-pound Welch (9.5 ppg, 6.6 rpg, .516 FG) is a far more grounded player compared to the high-flying excitement contained in Hunter's game. He does most of his damage close to the basket, using bulk and space, rather than leaping ability, to his advantage.

"He's in better shape and has a good feel for the game. He's another guy who just needs to believe in himself a little more," Bike said of Welch, who was once a non-qualifier, but is now in graduate school as a fifth-year senior.

Welch leads a pack of Pioneer giants. Unusual for a program at this stage of development, Sacred Heart has four players who stand 6-10 or taller.

"We'll look good in warmups," Bike joked.

The downside for Bike is that Welch is the only big man with any real experience. **Zach Spivey** (1.8 ppg, 1.4 rpg), a 6-10 sophomore, did play in 22 games as a rookie, but was never a regular part of the rotation. He will be given more of an opportunity, but will also have to compete with 7-2 sophomore **Mading Mading** and 6-10 freshman **Kibwe Trim**.

Mading, the tallest player in the NEC since 7-4 Rik Smits toiled for Marist, is a native of the Sudan and has very little American basketball experience. He played just one year at Bridgton Academy in Maine, has lived in this country only three years and is coming off a lost year because of knee surgery. Nonetheless, Bike is hopeful and impressed.

"It's nice when you have a 7-2 kid who is willing to be in the gym working by himself. Mading is a really hard worker and I think his recovery from the injury can be attributed to his work ethic," Bike said.

Bike noticed Trim at the Metro Classic Shootout at Seton Hall this summer and immediately offered Trim his last remaining scholarship. Trim came to the United States from St. Mary's school in Trinidad and became familiar with Sacred Heart via the Internet. He averaged 25 points and 13 rebounds last year.

On the other end of the size scale is 5-10 sophomore **Omar Wellington**, Sacred Heart's smallest player but perhaps its most important. Wellington (5.7 ppg, 1.7 rpg, 2.8 apg, .368 3PT) spent much of last year playing behind and learning from the now departed Kurt Reis, all the while establishing himself early in his career as a leader.

"A basketball team needs a personality like Omar's," Bike said. "I told him last year, 'Omar we recruited you for basketball, but we also recruited your personality.'

"He did a good job and was one of the leaders last year, but it's tough as a freshman point guard with a senior point guard there, too."

Wellington was at his best near season's end when he led the Pioneers in scoring in two of the final four games, including the program's biggest win as a Division I member to date over St. Francis (N.Y.), when he had 19 points.

Just who earns significant minutes alongside Hunter, Welch, and Wellington is a question that may take a while to answer. The opportunity to emerge from the pack will be there every night.

Max Yokono (2.4 ppg, 2.2 rpg), a 6-7 sophomore, and 6-6 sophomore **Justin James** (5.5 ppg, 2.2 rpg) may be the leading candidates at forward. Yokono made 11 starts a year ago, while James could be the sleeper. He attended high school at the Pentecostal Church of God Christian Academy in Tampa, Fla., which didn't have a basketball team. James played for a year at Lutheran Academy in Philadelphia and Bike snatched him up.

Bike is also high on a pair of freshmen wing players— 6-4 **James Samuels** and 6-6 **Mike Queenan**. Samuels is an athletic swingman who averaged 18 points and seven rebounds at Uniondale (N.Y.) High School and has defensive instincts that may give him an edge in the fight for minutes in the backcourt next to Wellington. Samuels' chief competition may be 6-1 sophomore **Chris Assel** (4.8 ppg, 1.1 rpg). Assel was second on the team with 29 three pointers last season and will be the Pioneers primary deep threat.

Bike is also impressed with athleticism of Queenan, a West Chester, Pa., native who scored 16 points and pulled 10 rebounds a game at the Hun School in New Jersey.

Chris Hairfield (2.5 ppg, 1.0 rpg), a 6-6 sophomore and explosive leaper, and 6-4 junior **Jannik Tuffel** (0.3 ppg, 0.2 rpg) will also be in the mix.

"Somebody has to play. It's up for grabs as to who wants to be a full-time player," Bike said.

2001-2002 SCHEDULE

Nov.	19	Stony Brook
	24	@Baylor
	28	@Yale
Dec.	1	@Fairleigh Dickinson
	5	Vermont
	8	Maine
	16	@Monmouth
	19	@Providence
	21	@Harvard
Jan.	3	Robert Morris
	5	St. Francis PA
	10	@Central Connecticut State
	12	@Quinnipiac
	16	Fairleigh Dickinson
	23	@Robert Morris
	26	@Wagner
	28	Central Connecticut State
Feb.	2	UMBC
	4	Mount St. Mary's
	7	@Long Island
	9	@St. Francis NY
	14	Quinnipiac
	16	St. Francis NY
	20	Long Island
	23	@Mount St. Mary's
	25	@UMBC
March	1-2	#NEC Tournament
	6	##NEC Tournament

@Road Games
#Quarterfinals and semifinals at Wagner
##Championship at highest seeded team

BLUE RIBBON ANALYSIS

BACKCOURT	D
BENCH/DEPTH	C-
FRONTCOURT	C
INTANGIBLES	C

Progress is one thing, but contending for a championship, or even an upper-division finish is another. Sacred Heart made the move from three wins its first year in Division I to seven in its second, but it may be another few seasons before anyone can talk about the Pioneers supplanting any of the other, more established NEC programs at the top. Before that can happen a few more subtle improvements must come.

"I don't know what comes first, the confidence or a few wins," Bike said. "If you can measure confidence, I hope that the confidence level will grow. I think some of our guys have been a little unsure of themselves. The mental approach is as important as the physical here."

Any rise in self-esteem might be best applied to the defensive end, where Sacred Heart allowed an NEC-high 78.6 points per game and 48.1 shooting percentage.

"We've got to reverse our percentages" said Bike, whose team also shot only 41.9 percent from the field. "That difference is huge. If you take 60 shots a game, that's about 3.6 shots more a game that are going in."

To help change that, Bike and his staff spent a second straight year trying to recruit more Division I caliber athletes and more size. With freshmen Samuels and Queenan and sophomores James, Hairfield, and Yokono joining senior Hunter, Sacred Heart now has a core group of runners and jumpers to play more aggressively. Adding Mading and Trim to Welch and Spivey, the Pioneers also have the size to cover up defensive mistakes.

Point guard Omar Wellington will be the one to make it all go.

"Omar will have to be more aggressive, but I think he will. He's already becoming a leader," Bike said.

The puzzle still has some missing pieces, but that number is much smaller than it was two seasons ago, when the Pioneers began this Division I quest. Sacred Heart stayed out of the NEC cellar last season and should have every opportunity to take a few more steps toward the first floor this year. The Pioneers will still take their lumps, and a berth in the NEC upper-division and in the conference tournament are unlikely, but they are no longer that out-of-place frat boy. Flounder is no more.

(C.C.)

St. Francis (N.Y.)

LOCATION	Brooklyn Heights, NY
CONFERENCE	Northeast
LAST SEASON	18-11 (.621)
CONFERENCE RECORD	16-4 (1st)
STARTERS LOST/RETURNING	4/1
NICKNAME	Terriers
COLORS	Red & Blue
HOMECOURT	Pope Physical Education Center (1,250)
COACH	Ron Ganulin (Long Island '68)
RECORD AT SCHOOL	127-153 (10 years)
CAREER RECORD	154-176 (12 years)
ASSISTANTS	Glen Braica (Queens College '88)
	Ed Custodio (St. Francis NY '98)
	Larry Wingate (St. Francis NY '78)
TEAM WINS (last 5 years)	13-15-20-18-18
RPI (last 5 years)	242-189-112-168-155
2000-01 FINISH	Lost in conference final.

The Dodgers may be long gone, but for the last four years there has been a rebirth of the "Wait 'til next year" call to arms in Brooklyn. The turn of the century model comes by way of the St. Francis basketball team.

The Terriers are certainly not "dem bums," but the frustration can't be erased. St. Francis has accumulated an NEC-best 54-20 conference record since the 1997-98 season. The Terriers also have regular-season finishes of third, second, fourth, and first during that span, yet added up, none of it equals a single NCAA Tournament appearance.

The icing on the "Missed Again" cake came last March, when St. Francis let a 20-point second half lead on Monmouth in the NEC championship game get away and had to watch the Hawks skip away to college basketball bliss.

"It was devastating. It was one of the worst locker rooms I'd ever seen," 11-year head coach Ron Ganulin said, referring to the immediate aftermath of the loss to Monmouth. "I couldn't get [then-senior point guard] Greg Nunn dressed for about two hours. I couldn't even console my assistants. It was tough."

The climb back to having such an opportunity again looks to be more difficult in 2001-02. Nunn (5.1 ppg, 5.6 apg) was just one of four starters who departed, leaving some big holes. Wings Stephen Howard (20.2 ppg, 4.0 rpg) and Richy Dominguez (19.3 ppg, 7.4 rpg) were both first-team all-conference players and, along with Nunn and center Hebreth Reyes (7.6 ppg, 6.6 rpg), were the foundation that generated all the recent success in Brooklyn.

"That's what hurt more than anything about not getting to the NCAA Tournament. That they didn't have the chance to go and put the cherry on top of the sundae after all they had done for us," Ganulin said.

The top dessert on this season's menu is 6-7 senior **Clifford Strong**, the lone returning starter and one of the most dependable players in the conference.

"He's always right there with his 13 points and seven rebounds no matter what. Cliff is so consistent. He reminds me a little of Larry Johnson because he's so strong inside, but can step out and shoot it a little too," said Ganulin, who was an assistant coach at UNLV during Johnson's collegiate playing days. "Even when Cliff has what looks like a bad game he delivers that production. We'll need even a little bit more out of him this season."

Strong (14.5 ppg, 7.1 rpg, .548 FG) joined the Terriers in December after transferring from Loyola (Md.) and sitting out a year and became the final piece to the puzzle as NEC play began in earnest.

Karl Sanders, a 5-9 senior, is expected to be the full-time point guard after playing behind Nunn last season. Sanders (1.9 ppg, 0.9 rpg, 1.9 apg) played in 28 games a year ago, but had trouble getting his offense on track. He shot a meager 25.8 percent from the floor, something Ganulin figures will improve with an increase in floor time.

"I think Karl actually has better overall point guard skills than Greg had," Ganulin said. "But I'm not sure Karl is the same kind of leader. That was Greg's strength."

Very quietly, 6-4 senior **Jason Morgan** (9.4 ppg, 2.6 rpg, .372 3PT) became a valuable weapon off the bench last season. Morgan ended up the team's fourth-leading scorer and its best three-point shooter. He will be the Terriers' chief perimeter threat this season.

With Strong, Mason and Sanders, Ganulin still has a solid nucleus to rely upon, but he also immediately restocked with a five-man recruiting class that might be the best in the league. Having an influx of new players changes not only the Terriers' dynamic, but also the coach's philosophy and approach.

"I enjoy the practices much more than the games. If you like to teach, then that is where you like to be," Ganulin said. "The last few years it's been repeating things and brushing up. Here it will be like going back to the fundamentals. It should be a lot of fun. The last few years we've been picked at the top of the conference and that puts a lot of pressure on you. You end up playing not to lose. We won't have that this year."

Four of those five new faces are junior college transfers, perhaps making the transition from a veteran team to a reshaped roster a bit easier.

"Like they say in the draft, sometimes you need to take the best player available and sometimes the junior college kids are easier because they've been through much of this before," Ganulin said.

The best of that bunch might be 6-2 junior **Jonathan Burge** from Lakeland (Ohio) Community College. Burge, a lefty shooting guard, was a 22.3 points-per-game scorer and was a first-team NJCAA Division II All-American. Expect him to play immediately.

"He sort of reminds me of Johnny Dawkins. He's a scorer and a slasher. He'll be a very good player here," Ganulin said.

Chris Sockwell, a 6-8 junior, is the tallest in the class, but he's more of a face up jump shooter. Ganulin's years as an assistant paid off here. Sockwell played for Jerry Tarkanian's son, George, at the College of the Sequoias in California. It also helped that Sockwell, born in Brooklyn and raised in Pennsylvania, wanted to return East.

Bronski Dockery is another recruit coming home. After a career at Rice High School in New York, Dockery went to Tallahassee (Fla.) Community College, where he averaged 16.4 points and 4.8 rebounds last season. The 6-3 Dockery, who teamed with prize St. John's recruit Marcus Hatten at Tallahassee, is a tough-nosed, do-a-little-of everything guard.

"He just helps you win," Ganulin said.

The best references of the bunch come from 6-2 junior **Omar Hatcher**, who is the son of former UCLA and NBA player Omar McCarter and was a high school teammate of Kobe Bryant at Lower Merion in Philadelphia. Hatcher is another hard-nosed guard moving back closer to home after two years at Oxnard (Calif.) Community College.

Damien Herard, 6-6, is the only freshman in the recruiting class. Herard, who hails from Jamaica, New York and Francis Lewis High School, prefers to play inside and should supply the Terriers with some interior muscle.

"He's the strong, tough kid that we are looking for. Damien, Omar, and Bronski are especially tough kids and that will help them right away," Ganulin said.

At center, **Paul Kowalczuk** (3.0 ppg, 1.7 rpg), a 6-9 junior, will be given every opportunity to build on his seven starts of a year ago. Kowalczuk offers a nice complement to Strong, who would prefer to play close to and with his back to the basket. Kowalczuk's ability to shoot with some range frees some space inside.

Patrice Thevenot (0.9 ppg, 1.4 rpg), a 6-6, 230-pound sophomore, is tough inside, but lacks significant offensive skills. He played in 26 games all the while shaking off the effects of asthma that limited him in high school. With much of that problem now better controlled, Thevenot, Ganulin thinks, could be a surprise. He showed a glimpse with seven rebounds in a game at Syracuse early last season.

Eric Thompson (1.9 ppg, 1.6 rpg, 24 games), a 6-8 sophomore, spent much of his rookie year getting stronger. His height and overall skills should open the door for a little more playing time if any of the newcomers don't work out.

2001-2002 SCHEDULE

Nov.	16	Lehigh
	21	St. Peter's
	24	Howard
Dec.	1	@Quinnipiac
	3	@Central Connecticut State
	11	@Fairfield
	20	@St. John's
	29	@Pittsburgh
Jan.	4	Fairleigh Dickinson
	6	Monmouth
	10	@Robert Morris
	12	@St. Francis PA
	16	@Mount St. Mary's
	19	Quinnipiac
	23	Long Island
	26	Robert Morris
	28	St. Francis PA
Feb.	2	@Fairleigh Dickinson
	4	UMBC
	9	Sacred Heart
	11	@Wagner
	14	Mount St. Mary's
	16	@Sacred Heart
	20	Wagner
	21	Binghamton
	23	@Monmouth
	25	@Long Island
March	1-2	#NEC Tournament
	6	##NEC Tournament

@Road Games
#Quarterfinals and semifinals at Wagner
##Championship at highest seeded team

BLUE RIBBON ANALYSIS

BACKCOURT	C
BENCH/DEPTH	B
FRONTCOURT	C+
INTANGIBLES	B

At one time Ganulin tried to build his program with nothing but high school recruits, and it didn't seem to work. He failed again going the junior-college route. Then foreign players began to catch his eye, and he had his formula.

Only one player—Kowalczuk from Poland—on the current roster hails from outside the United States, but the success of the last few years was built largely on players like Richy Dominguez from Columbia and Hebreth Reyes from Venezuela.

That success brought St. Francis the best conference record of any team in the NEC over the last four seasons, but no berths in the NCAA Tournament and the look of the team is now a definite mix.

Leading returning scorer Strong is a transfer from Loyola (Md.). There are five players Ganulin recruited out of high school and five more who come by the junior-college route.

Ganulin is hoping his recent run of success isn't interrupted too much by the fact that he needs to replace four starters, two of whom were All-NEC.

"I'm really excited. I can't wait to see how this moves along. I think we can be pretty good," the 11th-year coach said. "The only thing I worry about is how everyone accepts their roles. And the other thing is the experience factor and the difference between this and high school or junior college ball. Or even just going to a new gym to play and going through the league once."

Initially, the Terriers will have to lean heavily on Strong and hope he can thrive as the focal point of both the St. Francis offense and the opponent's defense. That should dictate how many open shots Morgan can get and how comfortable Sanders is as a distributor. If that is in sync, then Ganulin will have an easier time letting the talented but inexperienced newcomers get adjusted to Division I.

Ganulin said he is looking forward to the challenge of more coaching and more teaching this season and that's exactly what he will have. Gone are the expectations to win, but coming in through the other door are the pressures of the unknown and if the new players will ever have the chance to approach the results by the last group.

The Terriers will likely take a bit of a tumble and roll back to the middle of the pack in the NEC, but if the new guys are as talented as Ganulin hopes, the tumble might not be that far.

(C.C)

St. Francis (Pa.)

LOCATION	Loretto, PA
CONFERENCE	Northeast
LAST SEASON	9-18 (.333)
CONFERENCE RECORD	9-11 (8th)
STARTERS LOST/RETURNING	4/1
NICKNAME	Red Flash
COLORS	Red & White
HOMECOURT	DeGol Arena/Stokes Center (3,500)
COACH	Bobby Jones (Western Kentucky '84)
RECORD AT SCHOOL	19-36 (2 years)
CAREER RECORD	19-36 (2 years)

ASSISTANTS Jacob Morton (Miami-Fla. '93)
Mike Summey (North Carolina State '97)
Rob Krimmel (St.Francis-Pa. '00)
TEAM WINS (last 5 years)	12-17-9-10-9
RPI (last 5 years)	216-172-253-262-269
2000-01 FINISH	Lost regular-season finale.

Coaches hate words that start with "re." RE-build, RE-load, RE-place.

Perhaps the only "re" they do like is RE-turners, and St. Francis (Pa.) third-year coach Bobby Jones doesn't have many of those. He'll be doing a lot more of the first three with just two players back who played more than 20 minutes per game. But starting over isn't so bad when a team is coming off consecutive 18-loss seasons. That meant that Jones got to do another one of those "re's." RE-cruit.

Jones also figured if he's going to win games, he'll need players who already know what that entails. His five-man recruiting class, all of whom are freshmen, is fill with players from big-name, traditional high schools, the likes of which don't usually find their way into the NEC.

"What we were trying to do is get kids from winning programs that have a winning attitude," Jones said. "They are not just big-name high schools, but ones that have been very successful for a number of years."

Leading the pack is 6-4 **Darshan Luckey**, who was a teammate of North Carolina-bound Melvin Scott at Baltimore's Southern High School and averaged 17.5 points, eight rebounds and eight assists. Luckey got some serious looks from Georgetown, Providence, Duquesne, and Delaware and could turn out to be a real find for Jones. He can play either guard spot and, with no experienced veterans in front of him on the wing, will play right away.

"Darshan has great size and is rangy and athletic with a lot of confidence. I don't want to put any undo pressure on him, but he should be a very, very good player in his league," Jones said.

Sonny Benton, 5-11, who was a high school teammate of Red Flash forward **Pete Fox**, helped St. Ignatius in Cleveland to the Ohio state title as a senior and can also play either guard spot. He has point-guard size and a scoring guard's mentality.

"Sonny will bring tenacity from an offensive standpoint and he is a very good defender," Jones said. "Of all of our guards, Sonny probably has the best range on his jump shot."

Jones also lured Washington D.C. and Gonzaga High School product **Joey Goodson** to Loretto. The 6-3 Goodson has a solid mid-range game and is a good rebounding guard.

"Joey is the kind of player who can grab a rebound, go the length of the floor, and finish the play," Jones said. "He'll give us some solid minutes at that two-guard position."

Rodney Gibson, a 6-5 small forward, was the Baltimore Catholic League MVP a year ago at Saint Maria Goretti High School. He scored 18.1 points and grabbed 7.7 rebounds per game as a senior. Of all the freshmen, Gibson is the only one with his path to instant playing time blocked by a veteran. The 6-5 junior Fox is St. Francis' top returning player, but Jones figures Gibson will get his chances.

"Rodney can create his own shot and he rebounds the ball well, so he'll see some quality minutes for us this year," Jones said.

The final piece to the Freshmen Five is big man **Guy Saragba**. Luckey may have the best credentials and the most talent in the group, but the 6-9, 235-pound Saragba could be the most important of the first-year players. Saragba, who brings a solid back-to-the-basket game from Notre Dame prep in Leesburg, Va., replaces leading scorer and two-year starter Melvin Scott (13.0 ppg, 8.2 rpg, 70 blocks) and is the only center on the roster.

"Guy brings toughness to the program and we really need that, losing Melvin Scott," Jones said. "Overall we need to get tougher as a program and all of the young guys will help us in that area."

With Fox (7.4 ppg, 2.9 rpg, 1.5 apg, .438 3PT) and 5-10 junior guard **Dan Swoger** (5.4 ppg, 2.1 rpg, 2.7 apg, .410 3PT) back, Jones will still have reliable veterans to ease the program's transition to the younger group.

"Both those guys have been through it and they can both really shoot the basketball," Jones said.

Fox (first) and Swoger (fifth) were the most accurate three-point shooting tandem in the conference. Fox did his damage playing on a bad knee most of the year, and Swoger came off the bench as a backup to four-year starting point guard Jamal Ragland (12.6 ppg, 3.3 rpg). With Fox now healthy, both should be mainstays in the lineup this season. Swoger, who was Jones' first recruit, will take over full-time at the point.

Jones is also expecting a big bump in production from 6-7 senior forward **Reiner Mougnol** (7.4 ppg, 4.5 rpg). Mougnol was a different player down the stretch than he was in the first two-thirds of the season. He averaged 15.0 points and 8.1 rebounds over the final nine games and not surprisingly, that was St. Francis' best stretch of the year (5-4). Mougnol will play the power-forward spot, combining with Fox to give the Red Flash some frontcourt experience to surround Saragba in the middle.

Bryan Martin (5.1 ppg, 1.6 rpg), a 6-5 senior forward, may be the most likely of the remaining veterans to hold off the freshmen for playing time, but he could get pushed by 6-6 sophomore forward **Carl Ulmer** (3.8 ppg, 2.7 rpg) as Mougnol's primary backup. Ulmer is a hustling, aggressive player who is willing to give up his body for loose balls and rebounds.

Matt Augustin, a 5-10 sophomore guard who sat out last season to concentrate on academics, now has more competition for minutes, but he too has a big-name background. Augustin helped New York City's St. Raymond's High School to the city championship two years ago. He brings some toughness Jones is looking for.

Steveroy Daley (1.8 ppg, 1.1 rpg), a 6-4 sophomore forward, and **Chad Clifford** (1.7 ppg, 0.5 rpg, 16 games), a 6-4 sophomore guard, will have their work cut out to get into the rotation.

2001-2002 SCHEDULE

Nov.	17	Wright State
	20	American
	24	Bucknell
	29	UMBC
Dec.	1	Mount St. Mary's
	5	@Pittsburgh
	15	@Howard
	19	@Wake Forest
	30	@Miami
Jan.	3	@Wagner
	5	@Sacred Heart
	10	Long Island
	12	St. Francis NY
	15	@Robert Morris
	19	@Monmouth
	23	Wagner
	26	@Long Island
	28	@St. Francis NY
Feb.	2	Central Connecticut State
	4	Quinnipiac
	7	@UMBC
	9	@Mount St. Mary's
	14	Monmouth
	16	Fairleigh Dickinson
	19	Robert Morris
	23	@Central Connecticut State
	25	@Quinnipiac
March	1-2	#NEC Tournament
	6	##NEC Tournament

@Road Games
#Quarterfinals and semifinals at Wagner
##Championship at highest seeded team

BLUE RIBBON ANALYSIS

BACKCOURT	D
BENCH/DEPTH	D
FRONTCOURT	D
INTANGIBLES	D

Jones isn't starting over at St. Francis, but he's close. He has surrounded his veteran trio of Fox, Swoger, and Mougnol with five talented freshmen, many of whom come from nationally known high school programs, and he hopes that success on the scholastic level will eventually beget collegiate success.

"I'm really excited about the young talent, but it's tough to win with young guys. In some ways it is going to be another rebuilding year, but I have every intention of playing the young guys and allowing them to get game experience," Jones said, not minding the "re" words at least for one more year. "I truly believe in building a program with high school players. They are going to play and learn and they are going to have to."

Luckey is the best of the bunch and could be an NEC impact freshmen and is a strong candidate for league rookie-of-the-year honors.

Saragba will have to absorb a lot quickly because he is the only true answer in the middle playing for a coach who will emphasize rebounding and defense.

"We've got to be the best conditioned team and we have to defend," Jones said. "Our talent is better, but young guys are going to be inconsistent offensively. The effort on the defensive can't be inconsistent. Conditioning, rebounding, and guarding people will determine whether we are successful or unsuccessful.

The 2001-2002 season will be one of experimentation for St. Francis. Jones will play around with different defenses and different combinations. That, coupled with the general inexperience, could make for a long year. The foundation has been built, but the rest of the house will have to wait for a season or two. If Jones can get his troops to stay the course, he could have himself a luxury home, but for now matching even last year's nine wins could be a lofty goal.

(C.C.)

Wagner

LOCATION	Staten Island, NY
CONFERENCE	Northeast
LAST SEASON	16-13 (.551)
CONFERENCE RECORD	11-9 (5th)
STARTERS LOST/RETURNING	1/4
NICKNAME	Seahawks
COLORS	Green & White
HOMECOURT	Spiro Sports Center (2,100)
COACH	Dereck Whittenberg (N.C. State '84)
RECORD AT SCHOOL	27-29 (2 years)
CAREER RECORD	27-29 (2 years)
ASSISTANTS	Darryl Bruce (Towson '90)
	Ross Burns (UMass '99)
TEAM WINS (last 5 years)	10-13-9-11-16
RPI (last 5 years)	238-236-245-267-211
2000-01 FINISH	Lost in conference semifinal.

The buzzword in the NEC is Wagner.

"I think Wagner is going to be very good," St. Francis (N.Y.) coach Ron Ganulin said. "They have everyone back and they are a tough team that plays hard and is very quick."

Said Sacred Heart coach Dave Bike, "You take Wagner. They were the highest scoring team in the league and they return all their points. That's a good place to start. They're going to be tough."

And it doesn't end there.

"Wagner is a team I keep on eye on. Dereck [Whittenburg] has done a great job," St. Francis (Pa.) coach Bobby Jones said.

The reasons Wagner is suddenly getting everyone's attention are few, but precise.

Third-year coach Whittenburg's style might top the list. Upon his arrival three years ago, the one-time N.C. State gunslinger has instituted his own form of the Wild, Wild West. The Seahawks will run, press, swarm, attack and shoot from anywhere. Whittenburg had 10 players average double figures in minutes last season. That allowed the frenzy to have its full effect. Wagner posted the NEC's best turnover margin by an average of nearly two a game. The Seahawks also launched 123 more shots than their nearest competitor and the most three-pointers in the league.

But these weren't just any shots. They often went in. Wagner was second in the conference with 37.4 percent accuracy from three-point range and was fourth in overall field-goal percentage (.449). It all added up to another NEC-leading statistic—82.5 points per game.

Yet there is an irony in all of this, and that brings us to reason number two why last year Wagner enjoyed its first winning season since 1993-94. The Seahawks' best player is 6-5 junior forward **Jermaine Hall**, who, by no definition is a deep shooter, or even a perimeter-oriented player.

Hall would prefer to use his versatile post game to get his 18.4 points per game. Only Monmouth's Rashaan Johnson scored more among returning NEC players. Hall is like the queen bee. He remains solid and in his place while everyone and everything else is buzzing around him. In the end the honey is his.

"Jermaine Hall is a special player. He's just so consistent. He always seems to get his points," Monmouth coach Dave Calloway said.

Scoring is not all that Hall does. He was also Wagner's leading rebounder (5.8 rpg) and blocked one shot every game (1.2 bpg). His 58.8 field-goal percentage was second in the league.

Most of Hall's help and the catalysts for the Wagner pressure game is a deep group of guards and wing players. In particular it is **Courtney Pritchard**, **Dedrick Dye**, and **Jeff Klauder** that have the NEC's other coaches looking over their shoulders a bit.

Pritchard (10.7, 3.9 rpg, 4.5 apg, .329 3PT) assumed the starting point-guard duties almost immediately and affirmed Whittenburg's confidence in him with a NEC all-rookie team season. The 6-0 sophomore, while quarterbacking Wagner's running game, emerged with an assist-to-turnover of 1.39. Only the league's senior point guards and teammate Dye ranked ahead of him in the conference.

Dye (12.8 ppg, 3.5 rpg, 3.1 apg, 2.2 spg, .425 3PT) led the NEC in that category for the second straight year (2.57), but that was only a small part of his contribution. The 6-0 junior was willing to come off the bench most of the season, making just nine starts, but only Hall played more minutes or scored more points. He, along with Klauder were the Seahawks' prime deep shooting threats. The two took more three-pointers than any other tandem in the conference. Dye was also the NEC's top thief.

The 6-4 Klauder (9.7 ppg, 2.8 rpg, .386 3PT, .818 FT) has put together back-to-back seasons of more than 65 threes. For the hat trick, Klauder will again have to overcome lower back pain that stayed with him all last season and prevented the senior from making an August trip to Mexico with his teammates. The injury may be a herniated disc and cortisone shots may be needed to get Klauder through the season.

Hassan Wilkerson (5.6 ppg, 1.6 rpg), a 6-4 senior forward, is the fourth starter back, but he generally took a back seat to Dye. Wilkerson played a mere 12 minutes per game and will probably find himself in the same situation in his final season.

Wilkerson's chance to contribute may also be diminished by the continued emergence of 6-2 sophomore guard **Teoine Carroll** (3.1 ppg, 1.4 rpg), who was more impressive to Whittenburg on the Mexico trip than he was at any point last season.

"He played more like the way we thought he could when we recruited him," Whittenburg said.

As strong as Wagner is in the backcourt, the Seahawks may be just as vulnerable in the frontcourt. Hall didn't get much help last year and his rebounding average of 5.8 is still pretty low for a team leader.

As his rookie season progressed, 6-9 forward **Nigel Wyatte** (5.7 ppg, 4.3 rpg) became more of a factor and has the potential to be key defensive presence.

"He helped us far beyond our expectations," said Whittenburg of the sophomore who increased those averages to eight points and seven rebounds over the final eight games. "Nigel really came on. He was better than his numbers. But he still has a long, long way to go."

Still needing more depth up fron,t Whittenburg brought in two more big men to push Wyatte. **Kevin Martin**, a 6-10 freshman, and 6-9 junior **Cory Underwood** give Wagner much more size than it had last year and should help reduce or erase a minus-3.4 rebounding margin.

Underwood, who played at Westchester (N.Y.) Community College last season, is probably the more likely of the two to play right away. He is a familiar with the NEC, having spent a year at St. Francis (N.Y.) before landing at Westchester, where averaged 13 points, six rebounds, and two blocks.

"I'm very impressed with Cory. He runs and handles the ball well for someone his size. We think he can help us right away and that he also still has a lot of up side to his game," Whittenburg said

Martin is from Columbia High School in Maplewood, N.J., and could be what Wyatte was a year ago—someone who Whittenburg will get more from as the season wears on.

"We targeted size this recruiting season," the former Georgia Tech, West Virginia, and Colorado assistant said. "It was a goal of ours. And I think we're considerably better with the players we've brought in. First we were able to get Kevin [Martin], who is going to be good."

Whittenburg also used some of those southern ties to lure another swing player and the third member of the recruiting class—**Ralfael Golden**, a 6-4 freshman from Trezvant High School in Memphis. Golden may have a tough time wrestling playing time away from Dye, Klauder, and Carroll, but, like Martin, he may be more valuable once the calendar turns to 2002.

Whittenburg also has the reliable and productive 6-7 senior forward **Chris Jackson** (6.8 ppg, 3.8 rpg) to turn to as a key reserve on the baseline. Jackson was a double-figure scorer two years ago, but took on a more supporting role last season. He still managed nine starts and more than 17 minutes per game in Whittenburg's revolving lineup.

Less likely to build on his playing time is 6-0 guard **Yves Kabroce** (4.0 ppg, 1.3 rpg).

Jason Allen (0.5 ppg, 0.1 rpg, 12 games), a 6-1 junior guard, and 6-0 junior guard **Jeff Johnson** (0.3 ppg, 0.0 rpg, 10 games) are walk-ons who will again have a difficult time breaking into the deep rotation in the backcourt.

2001-2002 SCHEDULE

Nov.	16	@Virginia
	20	@Lehigh
	24	@Brown
	29	@Fairleigh Dickinson
Dec.	1	@Monmouth
	4	Iona
	8	@Rutgers
	29	@American
Jan.	3	St. Francis PA
	5	Robert Morris
	10	Quinnipiac
	12	@Central Connecticut State
	16	Monmouth
	19	@Sacred Heart
	23	@St. Francis PA
	26	Sacred Heart
	28	@Quinnipiac
Feb.	2	Mount St. Mary's
	4	@Long Island
	9	Long Island
	11	St. Francis NY
	15	Central Connecticut State
	17	UMBC
	20	@St. Francis NY
	23	@UMBC
	25	@Mount St. Mary's
March	1-2	#NEC Tournament
	6	##NEC Tournament

@Road Games
#Quarterfinals and semifinals at Wagner
##Championship at highest seeded team

BLUE RIBBON ANALYSIS

BACKCOURT	B
BENCH/DEPTH	C+
FRONTCOURT	C+
INTANGIBLES	B

Like the grades above, Whittenburg has his own evaluation process and he may be more difficult to impress.

"We get an A for effort," Whittenburg said. "But only a C in defense and poise, and a C-plus in offense."

He didn't mention rebounding either, which may have been the Seahawks' weakest area. The additions of Underwood and Martin, plus the emergence of Wyatte late last season give Whittenburg reason to believe his team will be better on the glass.

The Seahawks made strides during their Mexico trip this August, posting a 3-1 record despite having just eight scholarship players. Klauder stayed home with his bad back and NCAA rules prohibited the newcomers from going.

Neither the strong off-season showing nor last year's success has Whittenburg ready to acknowledge his team is ready to make a move in the NEC.

"We had a good season, but we're still a middle-of-the-road team in our conference. Until people say you're a good team, you're not a good team," Whittenburg said, obviously not hearing the refrain from the NEC's other coaches. "We had a good season, but good teams consistently have good seasons."

Wagner did finish just 2-6 against the teams ahead of it in last year's conference standings (St. Francis [N.Y.], Monmouth, and UMBC), so the work still needs to be done.

On the other hand, no team in the league returns more players who contributed so substantially last year. And Whittenburg seems to have filled his biggest hole with the signing of big men Underwood and Martin.

Monmouth may still be the team to beat in the NEC, but it's not unreasonable to believe second place is a distinct possibility. Wagner plays its up-tempo style in such a way that clearly makes the NEC's other teams uncomfortable. Now Whittenburg has sprinkled talent into the mix. The Seahawks will continue to get better.

(C.C.)

OHIO VALLEY

BLUE RIBBON FORECAST
1. Tennessee Tech
2. Murray State
3. Eastern Illinois
4. Tennessee-Martin
5. Morehead State
6. Austin Peay
7. Eastern Kentucky
8. Southeast Missouri State
9. Tennessee State

ALL-CONFERENCE TEAM
G - Leigh Gayden, JR, Tennessee Tech
G - Nick Stapleton, SR, Austin Peay
F - Henry Domercant, JR, Eastern Illinois
F - Brian Foster, SR, Tennessee-Martin
C - Kyle Umberger, SR, Morehead State

PLAYER OF THE YEAR
Henry Domercant, JR, Eastern Illinois

NEWCOMER OF THE YEAR
Damien Kinloch, JR, Tennessee Tech

2001-2002 CONFERENCE TOURNAMENT
Feb. 27, top four seeds host first round at campus sites. March 2-3, International Convention Center, Louisville, KY

2000-2001 CHAMPIONS
Tennessee Tech (Regular season)
Eastern Illinois (Conference tournament)

2000-2001 POSTSEASON PARTICIPANTS
Postseason record 0-1 (.000)
NCAA
Eastern Illinois

TOP BACKCOURTS
1. Tennessee Tech
2. Murray State
3. Morehead State

TOP FRONTCOURTS
1. Tennessee-Martin
2. Murray State
3. Tennessee Tech

DID YOU KNOW?
The OVC Tournament moves from Nashville's Gaylord Entertainment Center to the International Convention Center in Louisville, Ky., where the league was founded in 1948. Louisville hosted the first 11 OVC Tournaments. ... ESPN will televise the men's final for the 16th straight year. ... Austin Peay's Trenton Hassell and Eastern Illinois' Kyle Hill were both picked in the 2001 NBA draft. Hassell, the OVC Player of the Year, was chosen by Chicago with the first pick of the second round (No. 30 overall). Hill was the 15th pick of the second round (No. 44 overall) and was chosen by Dallas. ... For the first time since the 1992-93 season, Murray State did not earn at least a share of the OVC regular-season title. ... Tennessee Tech won the regular season for the first time since the 1984-85 season. ... Domercant and Austin Peay point guard Nick Stapleton are the league's top two returning scorers. Domercant, who averaged 22.8 points, was second last year behind Hill, who led the league with a 23.8 average. Stapleton averaged 17.8 points last season. Murray State's Antione Whelchel is the top returning rebounder after averaging 7.8 per game last season. ... Tennessee Tech opens the season against the University of Tennessee, where Golden Eagles coach Jeff Lebo interviewed for the head coaching job last spring. ... Southeast Missouri has added a 7-footer, Kostas Avgerinos of Greece, to its roster this season. Murray State's Andi Hornig, a 7-foot center from Germany, also returns. ... Eastern Illinois' NCAA appearance was its first since it won the Mid-Continent Conference Tournament in 1992 and lost to Indiana in the first round of the NCAA. The Panthers lost to Arizona, 101-76, in the 2001 NCAA Tournament.

(D.L.)

AP Austin Peay

LOCATION	Clarksville, TN
CONFERENCE	Ohio Valley
LAST SEASON	22-10 (.688)
CONFERENCE RECORD	10-6 (4th)
STARTERS LOST/RETURNING	3/2
NICKNAME	Governors
COLORS	Red & White
HOMECOURT	Dunn Center (9,000)
COACH	Dave Loos (Memphis State '70)
RECORD AT SCHOOL	161-155 (11 years)
CAREER RECORD	242-208 (15 years)
ASSISTANTS	Tony Collins (Virginia State '79)
	Scott Combs (Austin Peay '97)
	Jay Bowen (Christian Brothers '84)
TEAM WINS (last 5 years)	17-17-11-18-22
RPI (last 5 years)	199-159-236-155-111
2000-01 FINISH	Lost in conference final.

For months, Austin Peay coaches and fans awaited the decision of Trenton Hassell, the 2000-01 Ohio Valley Conference Player of the Year.

Would he stay in college or go to the NBA? Finally, on July 20, Hassell made the announcement that will have a profound effect on OVC basketball this season. Hassell, who declared himself eligible for the NBA draft in early summer, decided to remain in the draft and forego his final year at Austin Peay.

As the rest of the OVC breathed a sigh of relief, Austin Peay coaches began plans for the post-Hassell days. One of the most talented and productive players in

school history was gone.

Hassell, a 6-5 swing player, was a three-time All-OVC first team player who averaged 19.4 points, 8.2 rebounds and 4.5 assists during his career. Last season, Hassell (21.7 ppg, 7.8 rpg, 5.2 apg) was believed to be the only player in the nation ranking among his conference's top five in scoring, rebounding and assists for the second straight year. He was third in the conference in scoring and rebounding and fourth in assists.

In the NBA draft, Hassell was the first pick of the second round (No. 30 overall) by the Chicago Bulls.

"There's no way to replace a guy like that, especially with one player," Govs coach Dave Loos said. "That can't happen. He had a huge impact and we will certainly miss him."

Hassell's career ended with a heartbreaking loss to Eastern Illinois in the championship game of the OVC Tournament. The Govs blew a 21-point lead with less than nine minutes left and lost, 84-83, when Theanthony Haymon was called for goal tending at the buzzer. Austin Peay had led by 18 with 6:30 left.

Not only is Hassell gone, but so are Haymon (10.1 ppg, 5.8 rpg) and Joe Williams (13.9 ppg, 8.0 rpg), the two starters in the frontcourt. Williams was chosen to the to the All-OVC second team, while Haymon led the league in field-goal percentage (.667).

"We got more mileage out of those two in two years than any junior college players we've had," Loos said.

Also gone is shooting guard Matt Jakeway (7.1 ppg, 2.6 rpg), who started the first 22 games last season. Jakeway, a sophomore last season, transferred to Kent State.

With Hassell gone, 6-1 senior guard **Nick Stapleton** will assume the role as the team's marquee player. Stapleton (17.8 ppg, 1.8 rpg, 3.4 apg) is a scoring point guard who can pour on the points in a number of ways.

He was fourth in the conference in scoring, 10th in three-pointers per game (2.16) and shot .366 from three-point range. He was chosen to the All-OVC second team.

Stapleton and Hassell sat out their first seasons at Austin Peay as non-qualifiers, and both graduated on time in May, allowing them the option of returning for a fourth year of eligibility.

Look for Stapleton to step up his game with the departure of Hassell. Two years ago, Stapleton had two of his best games when Hassell went down with ankle injuries, scoring 29 against Murray State and 26 against Southeast Missouri State.

In summer-league ball in his hometown of Flint, Mich., Stapleton averaged about 35 points while playing against some top-notch competition, including Detroit Pistons guard Mateen Cleaves.

"Nick will have a good year, no question about it," Loos said. "He's primed to give it a real all-conference type of effort. I think he understands his role. At the same time, I think he'll see a lot of different defenses and people will try to take him out of the game. He'll have to be ready for that.

"Nick has no problem getting a pretty good look at the basket most of the time. It's nice to have a guy who is creative enough and athletic enough to get a pretty good look on most occasions."

Two players vying for the job as Stapleton's backup will be 6-0 sophomore **Gerrell Webster** and 6-0 freshman **Levi Carmichael**. Webster (1.5 ppg, 0.8 rpg, 0.8 apg) played in 29 games last season, averaging 5.6 minutes.

Carmichael will certainly push for the backup job. Last season, Carmichael averaged 23.8 points and 7.2 assists at East Greene High School in Bloomfield, Ind. He shot 40 percent from three-point range and 85 percent from the free-throw line while earning all-state honors.

If Carmichael can make a quick adjustment or if Webster can get a grip on the job, the Govs may at times play Stapleton at the shooting guard position.

"I think Carmichael is a guy who knows how to run a basketball team from the point guard position," Loos said. "He has a good feel for how to play the position. I like his ability to penetrate and pitch the basketball. Obviously he also is a guy who is capable of scoring from the point guard position. He is a good shooter."

Loos has big plans for 6-2 guard **Anthony Davis**, a first-team all-state player last year at Inglewood (Calif.) High School. Davis averaged 18 points, nine rebounds and six assists as Inglewood went 28-7 and lost in the Bay Conference championship game to a Diminguez Hills team that was led by Tyson Chandler, who was acquired by the Bulls after entering the NBA Draft.

Davis was recruited by several Pac-10 schools, including Arizona, Arizona State and Oregon. He was setting up visits to Oregon and Saint Louis when he committed to play for the Govs. He has no doubt he could have played at a Pac-10 school.

"Most definitely I could," Davis said. "I just didn't want to go to a really big school where I'd have to sit behind somebody and wait until my junior or senior year to play. I wanted to come in as a freshman and shine."

Davis, who shot 46 percent from the field and 38 percent from three-point range last season, will likely get his chance to shine this season.

"Anthony is a guy who is very skilled and athletic," Loos said. "He plays a lot bigger than he is. He plays like he's 6-5. He also brings something to our two-guard position that we don't really have right now, someone who can penetrate and finish. I also believe with his athletic ability and mindset that he can be a very good defensive player."

Rhet Wierzba, a 6-4 sophomore, and 6-1 senior **Kevin Easley** will again battle for minutes at shooting guard. Wierzba (1.0 ppg, 0.3 rpg) averaged only 2.6 minutes in 21 games. Easley (0.7 ppg, 0.2 rpg) played in 21 games and averaged 4.6 minutes.

Adrian Henning, a 6-6 sophomore, moved into the starting lineup for the last 10 games of the 2000-01 season. Henning (3.6 ppg, 2.3 rpg) replaced Jakeway in a move that allowed Hassell to play shooting guard. He can play either forward position, and with the departures of Williams, Haymon and Hassell, his scoring and rebounding numbers could have a sharp rise.

"Stapleton is not a secret, and I'm sure people will try to take him out of the game," Loos said. "That's where I think Henning will need to have a breakout year. Last year he did a nice job and really improved. Now he's got to be more of a factor. He's got to be part of the real foundation for our team."

Fred Marshall, a 6-6 freshman, will make a push for the starting job or at least quality minutes at small forward. Marshall averaged 17 points, 15 rebounds and five

assists as a senior at Atlanta's Paideia High School and earned all-state honors. During high school, Marshall played every position at one time or another.

In the summer, Marshall was chosen most valuable player in Georgia's North-South All-Star game when he scored a game-high 26 points. An outstanding athlete, Marshall spent much of the summer on the Austin Peay campus, playing against current and former Govs, including Hassell and Williams.

"Fred has a pretty good mid-range game," Loos said. "He's pretty good at putting it on the floor and he can raise up on you from 15-to-17 feet. He needs to improve his three-point shooting. Like most high school players coming in, I think he has a long way to go defensively."

Igor Macura, a 6-7 junior, wasn't as much a factor as expected last season, but that could also change this year. Macura (0.8 ppg, 1.2 rpg) can be a physical player at either forward position.

Loos says the off-season work of **Josh Lewis**, a 6-8 sophomore center, could pay off greatly this year. Lewis (1.3 ppg, 1.9 rpg) was eighth in the OVC in blocked shots per game (26 in 29 games) despite averaging only 9.1 minutes per game.

Since last year, Lewis has bulked up and improved his conditioning, which was his biggest drawback last season as a red-shirt freshman. He also stayed on campus in the summer and played pickup games with current and former Govs, including his good friend, Hassell.

"Josh Lewis has had as good work habits as any player we've had here in a long time," Loos said. "He really did a great job working on his conditioning, getting stronger and working on his game. Last year he'd play three minutes and hit a wall. I hope his conditioning and work habits will help him play through that."

Loos is counting on two junior college transfers, 6-7 forward **Sean Prather** and 6-8 forward/center **Bobbye Hill**, to take up some of the void left by the departures of Williams and Haymon.

Hill, a former tight end in high school, is a bruising post player who weighs 240 pounds. As a high school senior in Tyler, Texas, Hill was offered a football scholarship at Texas Christian but turned it down to pursue a basketball career. He played two years at Tyler Junior College, where he averaged 12 points and seven rebounds last season.

"He will give us a real physical presence," Loos said. "I hope he's a better offensive player player than his numbers in junior college indicate, and I think he is. He played on a junior college team that had five Division I signees. That spreads the shots around."

Prather, who is from Gaithersburg, Md., averaged 18 points and nine rebounds last season at Brown Mackie College in Salina, Kan. He shot 56 percent from the floor and 72 percent from the line.

"Sean is very athletic and runs the floor very well," Loos said. "I think he can help us inside and out. He has a very solid post game but is athletic enough to go out on the floor and play away from the basket. He goes to the boards very hard and has a good touch around the basket."

Morten Szmiedowicz, a 6-10 sophomore forward/center, returns after limited playing time last season. Szmiedowicz (0.4 ppg, 0.2 rpg) played in only eight games, averaging 2.8 minutes.

2001-2002 SCHEDULE

Nov.	17	#@Oklahoma State
	19-21	##Las Vegas Tournament
	26	Marian, IN
	30	###First Merchants Classic
Dec.	1	###First Merchants Classic
	5	@Arkansas-Little Rock
	8	Western Kentucky
	15	Arkansas-Little Rock
	18	@Dayton
	20	Webster
	22	@Memphis
	29	@Eastern Kentucky
Jan.	3	Eastern Illinois
	5	@Western Kentucky
	10	Tennessee-Martin
	12	Murray State
	17	Tennessee Tech
	19	Tennessee State
	24	@Eastern Illinois
	26	@Southeast Missouri
	31	@Tennessee-Martin
Feb.	2	Eastern Kentucky
	4	Morehead State
	9	@Murray State
	14	@Tennessee State
	16	@Tennessee Tech
	18	@Morehead State
	23	Southeast Missouri
	26	####OVC Tournament
March	2-3	#####OVC Tournament

@ Road Games
# First round Las Vegas Tournament
Las Vegas, NV (also UTEP, Providence, TCU, Northwestern State, Oklahoma State)
Muncie, IN (vs. Binghamton first round; also Ball State, Elon)
Campus sites
Kentucky International Convention Center, Louisville, KY

BLUE RIBBON ANALYSIS

BACKCOURT	B+
BENCH/DEPTH	C
FRONTCOURT	C
INTANGIBLES	B

Last season, Loos had a good idea what to expect from each of his starters. That has changed this year.

Loos knows what Stapleton can do, but there are big questions to be answered at almost every other position.

Can junior college transfers Prather and Hill put up good numbers in their first seasons of Division I ball? Can guard Davis and forward Marshall be impact players as freshmen? Can starting forward Henning raise his averages considerably?

"We're going to have to count on a number of new players and young guys to come in and play critical roles," Loos said. "They'll get a significant amount of playing time. That's always an iffy proposition because you never know how they're going to respond, but our young guys and new people are talented enough. I think our success or lack of it will depend on how our new people fit in and what kind of factor they are."

Loos assembled one of the best recruiting classes in the OVC, and that bodes well for the future. As for this year, it may be an adjustment period. There is plenty of talent on this team, but it might be a year away from contending for the OVC title.

(D.L.)

Eastern Illinois

LOCATION	Charleston, IL
CONFERENCE	Ohio Valley
LAST SEASON	21-10 (.677)
CONFERENCE RECORD	11-5 (t-2nd)
STARTERS LOST/RETURNING	2/3
NICKNAME	Panthers
COLORS	Blue & Gray
HOMECOURT	Lantz Gym (5,300)
COACH	Rick Samuels (Chadron State '71)
RECORD AT SCHOOL	313-292 (21 years)
CAREER RECORD	313-292 (21 years)
ASSISTANTS	Steve Weemer (Eastern Illinois '94)
	Troy Collier (Eastern Illinois '94)
	Mike Church (Northeast Missouri '73)
TEAM WINS (last 5 years)	12-16-13-17-21
RPI (last 5 years)	251-151-218-147-115
2000-01 FINISH	Lost in NCAA first round.

In many ways, Eastern Illinois' amazing victory over Austin Peay in the championship game of the OVC Tournament was a microcosm of the Panthers' season.

It was a magical season, perhaps the most memorable in school history, highlighted by an 84-83 victory over the Governors in the OVC title game at Nashville's Gaylord Entertainment Center.

The Panthers rallied from a 21-point deficit with less than nine minutes remaining. It was a stunning finish when Kyle Hill drove the lane, missed a 14-foot shot, and **Jan Thompson** tossed up a follow shot that was blocked by the Govs' Theanthony Haymon.

When Haymon was called for goal tending, the Panthers had pulled off the stunning comeback and were headed to the NCAA Tournament. It was only their second NCAA berth since attaining NCAA Division I status in 1981.

"Frankly, I thought the championship game kind of typified the season in that it was a group of kids who refused to quit, had great chemistry and really supported one another," veteran coach Rick Samuels said.

"That wasn't the only game where we came from a deficit to win. We could go back and find key games throughout the season. One that sticks out in my mind was at Morehead State when we were down seven with 42 seconds left and won by three in regulation. It was a never-give-up attitude within that team."

Hill, a 6-2 guard, sparked the comeback, scoring 13 of his 31 points in the last nine minutes. Hill (23.8 ppg, 4.9 rpg) finished as the nation's second-leading scorer and was drafted by Dallas in the second round (No. 44 overall pick).

Hill, who scored 20 or more points in 23-of-27 games, was seventh in the OVC in assists (4.0 per game), ninth in steals (1.6 per game), 17th in rebounds, third in free-throw percentage (.839) and sixth in three-point percentage (.432). He finished his career as the school's third-leading scorer.

Combined with point guard Matt Britton (13.2 ppg, 5.1 rpg, 5.2 apg) and small forward **Henry Domercant** (22.8 ppg, 6.8 rpg, 2.1 apg), the Panthers had the most dangerous backcourt in the OVC. Now, only Domercant, a 6-4 junior, remains of that backcourt.

"They certainly will be hard to replace," Samuels said. "It's obvious with Kyle Hill. Here's a kid who's second in the nation in scoring. His stats are real solid. Plus we saw him at his peak level take over a game, but we can't overlook Matt Britton. He may have epitomized the toughness of our team, the refuse-to-lose attitude. He was our third-leading scorer. He made us hard to guard in that we had three perimeter guys you had to defend. We have a large hole to fill in replacing those two players."

Domercant and Hill both earned All-OVC first-team honors, while Britton was chosen to the second team.

Domercant led the OVC in scoring for much of the season, but was overtaken by Hill late in the season. He was runner-up in voting for OVC Player of the Year, finishing behind Austin Peay's Trenton Hassell, and was second in the league in scoring and third in three-point shooting (.441).

"I think he's become a shooter," Samuels said of Domercant. "His mentality is more that of a scorer. He's really worked hard to become an efficient three-point shooter and a kid who can catch and shoot off the pass. He's always been good at scoring off the dribble, but he's a worker. There is no one in the country that works harder on his game than Henry. I literally mean that. He is in the gym every day, 7 or 7:30 in the morning. He works very hard at his game."

This year, Domercant should again be one of the OVC's premier players. NBA scouts will keep a close eye on his progress. Over the summer, Domercant was a counselor at one of Michael Jordan's camps in Chicago.

One television clip had Domercant being guarded by Jordan, and vice versa, during a pickup game. Because of his size, athleticism and backcourt talents, his NBA chances seem good.

"I would think so," Samuels said. "We play him at small forward. He's very capable of playing the two-guard. He's a little bigger than Kyle. He's probably two to two-and-a- half inches taller than Kyle. He's an athlete in his own right, not as explosive as Kyle but an athlete in his own right. I think he's got a legit chance [in the NBA].

"He's not as fluid a shooter from a distance as Kyle. It's so easy for Kyle to jump up and shoot the ball, but Henry's strength, where Kyle doesn't have the strength, is Henry can score with contact. He can take it right at you and right at the basket and score with contact."

Several players will look to fill the voids left by the departures of Hill and Britton.

Jason Wright, a 5-9 freshman point guard from DeKalb, Ill., sat out last season as a non-qualifier.

"Jason Wright is a very good athlete," Samuels said. "He was on campus last year and watched us practice frequently so he has an understanding of what we're doing. He may be the truest point guard we have in our system, so there's a great need there. His chances are good."

Chris Herrera, a 5-9 sophomore guard, could also play point guard. Herrera (1.2 ppg, 0.3 rpg) played in 26 games last year.

Ramone Taylor, a 5-10 junior from Louisville, Ky., played at Southeastern (Ill.) Community College last season. Taylor can play either guard spot.

"He's a combination guard," Samuels said of Taylor. "We hope he's to the point that he can play a lot of minutes. He's very explosive. He will give us a dimension that we didn't have last year in that he can really push the ball. The idea there is that we can create shots for Henry by ball penetration where the defense is forced to help, and we can get the ball out to Henry."

J.R. Reynolds, a 6-3 junior swing player, was a teammate of Taylor's last season at Southeastern.

"We think he fits into our system well," Samuels said. "He's a very good catch-and-shoot kid. He has a good

feel for the game and he looks like he has a good feel for the motion concepts that we use."

Two returning guards, 6-1 junior **Craig Lewis** and 6-3 sophomore **Rod Henry**, will look to make more of an impact this season.

Samuels said it's time for Lewis (3.1 ppg, 1.8 rpg) to show what he can do, especially with the departures of Domercant and Britton.

"This is coach speak: It's time. He's talented, and he's got to take advantage of the opportunity," Samuels said.

Henry (2.6 ppg, 1.0 rpg) played in 28 games last season. "Rod Henry is a young kid who is really developing and working hard," Samuels said. "He could have sort of a breakout season in terms of really helping our basketball team."

Jake Sinclair, a 6-3 freshman forward, is a walk-on from Pana, Ill.

Two of the three returning starters are post players—6-8 senior forward **Todd Bergmann** and Thompson, the 6-11 center.

Bergmann (5.8 ppg, 3.1 rpg) and Thompson (3.6 ppg, 3.9 rpg) both started all 31 games last season and were used mostly to set screens in the Panthers' motion offense. They were satisfied to let the three backcourt players do most of the scoring.

"We can't overlook [Bergmann's and Thompson's] contributions," Samuels said. "They're very selfless. They were willing to just get the other people open and play key roles for us without scoring. I think part of the hole we have to fill in replacing Kyle and Matt will be picked up by our inside guys. That's more than Todd and Jan. I think our two [sophomores], Ryan Kelly and Jesse Mackinson, are kids who are very capable of scoring points for us. It will just give us a little different look."

The 6-8 Mackinson (5.5 ppg, 3.8 rpg), who's listed as a forward/center, played in 31 games, and although he didn't start played valuable minutes.

"At the end of the year Mackinson was playing 18 or 19 minutes," Samuels said. "At the end of the year he and Jan were about splitting time."

Kelly averaged 1.4 points and 1.4 rebounds in 29 games last season.

John Thorsen, a 6-7 sophomore forward, played sparingly in 13 games, averaging 0.9 points and one rebound.

2001-2002 SCHEDULE

Nov.	16	St. Joseph's
	19	#@Illinois
	22-24	##Las Vegas Invitational
	28	Indiana State
Dec.	1	Augustana
	5	@Evansville
	8	@Western Illinois
	15	Loyola
	18	@Oklahoma
	22	@Ohio State
	29	@Northern Illinois
Jan.	3	@Austin Peay
	5	Southeast Missouri
	10	Morehead State
	12	Eastern Kentucky
	14	Illinois Benedictine
	17	@Murray State
	19	@Tennessee-Martin
	24	Austin Peay
	31	@Tennessee Tech
Feb.	2	@Tennessee State
	7	@Eastern Kentucky
	9	@Morehead State
	14	Murray State
	16	Tennessee-Martin
	18	@Southeast Missouri
	21	Tennessee State
	23	Tennessee Tech
	26	###OVC Tournament
March	1-2	####OVC Tournament

@Road Games
#First round, Las Vegas Invitational
##Las Vegas, NV (schedule determined after first-round games; Pool 1 includes Georgia Tech, Illinois, Eastern Illinois, Pennsylvania. Pool 2 includes Iowa State, Saint Louis, Hartford, Southern Illinois)
###At campus sites
####Kentucky International Convention Center, Louisville, KY

BLUE RIBBON ANALYSIS

BACKCOURT	C+

BENCH/DEPTH	B
FRONTCOURT	B-
INTANGIBLES	A

Samuels, a master at the motion offense, had all the tools to make it work last season. With point guard Britton and shooting guard Hill gone, Samuels must try to find replacements in the backcourt.

Samuels won't change styles this year, but he will be looking for more frontcourt scoring than a year ago. After all, Hill and Britton averaged a combined 37 points last season.

"We have to develop scoring from somewhere else," Samuels said. "Again, we'd like to have it from more than just one other position. I think our big guys will help there by giving us some scoring. We also signed two junior college kids [backcourt players Reynolds and Taylor] that we would anticipate helping us pick up that scoring slack, too."

The Panthers have experience in the frontcourt with the return of starters Bergmann and Thompson, plus backup forward/center Mackinson, who played as much as Thompson for most of the OVC season.

Samuels will have one of the best players in the OVC in Domercant. He turned his ankle in the NCAA Tournament game against Arizona with about eight minutes left in the half. At the time, the Panthers were within striking distance. Domercant went to the sideline for the rest of the half, and by the time he limped back for the second half, the Wildcats had pulled away.

Domercant is fine now, and that means trouble for the rest of the OVC. Despite the loss of Domercant's partners in the backcourt, the Panthers will be a dangerous team.

(D.L.)

Eastern Kentucky

LOCATION	Richmond, KY
CONFERENCE	Ohio Valley
LAST SEASON	7-19 (.269)
CONFERENCE RECORD	1-15 (9th)
STARTERS LOST/RETURNING	3/2
NICKNAME	Colonels
COLORS	Maroon & White
HOMECOURT	McBrayer Arena (6,500)
COACH	Travis Ford (Kentucky '94)
RECORD AT SCHOOL	7-19 (1 year)
CAREER RECORD	74-50 (4 years)
ASSISTANTS	Chad Dollar (Milligan '95)
	Jerry Pelphrey (East Tennessee State '94)
	John Brannen (Marshall '97)
TEAM WINS (last 5 years)	8-10-3-6-7
RPI (last 5 years)	275-211-303-299-298
2000-01 FINISH	Lost in regular-season finale.

For the Eastern Kentucky Colonels, the Ohio Valley Conference season was like watching the same film over and over again.

The Colonels would hang around for most of the game, then fade in the last six or eight minutes. Game after game, the Colonels would repeat the scenario.

"We got blown out in two games," second-year coach Travis Ford said. "Every conference game we were in until the last six or seven minutes and then we just got worn down."

Eastern Kentucky's only OVC victory came on Feb. 15 when it beat Tennessee-Martin, 75-62, in Richmond, Ky. The Colonels were then competitive in their last three games, losing by five at home to Murray, by 11 at Southeast Missouri and by nine at Eastern Illinois.

Of the Colonels' 19 losses, eight were by 10 or fewer points.

Such was the plight of a rebuilding team. Ford, the former point guard at Kentucky, had seven scholarship players last year, but basically played only six.

"We were just trying to survive last year," Ford said. "When I got here there were 12 players returning and we only ended up keeping two of them. Different players went different directions for certain reasons, but our first year we were just trying to survive.

"Seven games is what we won and that was probably four more than we expected to win. Guys played hard and that's what we asked of them."

Only five players return from last year's team, including starting guards **Spanky Parks** and **Clinton Sims**. **Ben Rushing**, a 5-11 guard, also returns after blowing out his knee after two exhibition games.

With the influx of new players, all starting jobs are up

for grabs.

Parks, a 6-3 swing player, played shooting guard and small forward last season. Parks (13.4 ppg, 3.8 rpg) started 13 games and finished strong. He shot 42.8 percent from the field, 34.1 percent from three-point range, and was the team's second-leading scorer.

"He's very athletic, a great one-on-one player," Ford said. "At the end of the season, the last four games he shot like 50 percent from the three-point line, which was something he really worked on. His outside shooting was really consistent at the end of the year and he's continued to work on that over the summer."

Sims, a 6-3 senior, is versatile enough to play either guard position or small forward. Sims has played for four different programs since his days as an all-state player at Paris (Ky.) High School.

His first stop was at Maine Central Institute, where he averaged 18.1 points for a 35-0 team. He then went to Boston College where he averaged 8.7 points and 5.2 rebounds and was one of the top players in the Big East. His next stop was at St. Catharine (Ky.) College, where he averaged 18.2 points, 7.3 rebounds and 5.4 assists, earning second-team NJCAA All-America honors.

Last season, Sims (10.3 ppg, 5.3 rpg, 2.7 apg) started 14 games and shot 44.2 percent from the field. At the end of the year, Sims was effective at a position he had never played.

"We started playing him at the end of the year at the point," Ford said. "It was really surprising to us and to him that he did so well because he had never played that position. Clinton's the type of player who is very versatile. At the end of the game he's going to have 12 points, seven or eight rebounds, six or seven assists. If we can just get him to stop turning the ball over he could be very productive."

With the departure of point guard John White (12.6 ppg, 3.3 rpg, 4.2 apg), a senior last season, Sims could get more minutes at the point.

"He can play the one, two or three," Ford said. "He'll get a chance to play the point again."

Also contending for the starting point guard job will be 6-1 junior **Kenyatta Dix**, a transfer from Frank Phillips (Texas) Community College. A native of Gainesville, Fla., Dix averaged 17.2 points and 4.3 assists last season in junior college. He averaged 6.3 points at Kansas State in 1999-2000 before leaving for junior college.

"He's scheduled to hopefully start at the point," Ford said. "He's a player who's played at the highest level at Kansas State. He started half the year and with the coaching change (Jim Woolridge replacing Tom Asbury) he left and went to junior college and now we have him. He scored 20 points against [Missouri's] Keyon Dooling head to head. He's more of a two-guard but this past year at junior college he did play the point so that got us encouraged that he had a year under his belt as a point guard."

Dix averaged 19.5 points as a senior at Buchholz High in Gainesville and finished his career with a school-record 1,964 points, breaking the record held by Vernon Maxwell.

A great athlete, Dix won the dunk contest at the Alonzo Mourning Summer Groove Camp after his senior year of high school.

"He's more of a scoring point, but I want to teach him to pass first and score second," Ford said, "and I think he can definitely learn that very easily because he has great basketball savvy."

Rushing, a native of Clinton, Ky., led the Colonels in scoring in their first two exhibition games last year, scoring 27 and 22 points in the two games. The red-shirt freshman averaged 25.4 points as a high school senior two years ago.

"He's back at 100 percent and he's already shown what he can do," Ford said. "He's a great perimeter shooter, a knock-down shooter. We were probably going to start him at the two last year but he could see a lot of action at the point or the two."

Shawn Fields, a 6-3 junior and native of nearby Lexington, will also figure into the backcourt plans. Fields, a transfer from Georgia, practiced with the Colonels last season. He was a spot starter at Georgia, but Ford thinks he can be a much bigger factor in Richmond.

"He started 12 games at Georgia," Ford said. "I think he'll be one of the best players in the conference. He was tremendous in practice last year and he'll probably start at the two-guard spot. He can be one of the best players in the conference without a doubt. He scored 29 against Mississippi State in the SEC and had some big games for Georgia. He just wanted to be closer to home."

Brett Howell, a 6-1 freshman guard from Auburn (Ala.) High School, will be used strictly as a backup. Howell averaged 15.2 points and 4.3 assists last year as a senior.

Jon Bentley, a 6-9 transfer from Marshall, can play either forward postition and will contend for a starting job. He was red-shirted at Marshall two years ago and practiced with the Colonels last year. As a senior at Hazard (Ky.) High School, Bentley averaged 26.9 points and 13.9 rebounds.

"He's a great perimeter shooter with long arms, can block shots in the post and again, he's a very versatile player who can play inside-outside," Ford said. "I expect big things out of him."

Chris Carswell, a 6-7 senior forward, will be one of the leaders on the team. Carswell (4.5 ppg, 5.4 rpg) started 11 games last season and was the team's second-leading rebounder.

"If he keeps improving his outside shot he can play the three or the four," Ford said of Carswell. "He played primarily in the post last year but he can step out and play the perimeter. We'll look at him for some leadership and I think he'll be a great role player for us."

Two others will vie for starting jobs in the post—6-10 sophomore **Tim Volpenhein** and 6-10 junior **Johnny Hardwick**.

Hardwick, a transfer from Compton (Calif.) Community College, averaged 10.2 points, 8.4 rebounds and 4.3 blocks last season and as Compton went 26-4. He led the conference in blocked shots and was one of the league's top defenders. He was one of the Colonels' late signees in the spring.

"He's one of the most athletic 6-10 players I've seen," Ford said. "All I want him to do is block shots and rebound. If he can do that he'll get good minutes. He can score around the basket because he's so explosive. He's going to be great in our press."

Volpenhein (3.2 ppg, 3.2 rpg) played in 25 games last season with two starts. Since then, Volpenhein has worked hard to assure himself of a bigger role.

"We're really high on him," Ford said of Volpenhein. "He's gained 25 pounds of strength and muscle. He's really worked hard on his game. I'm expecting big things about him in the future. His biggest asset as a scorer is his outside shooting. He's a great perimeter shooter."

Two freshmen, 6-6 forward **Michael Haney** and 6-9 forward **Richard Sadler**, will also get a good look from Ford.

Haney averaged 21.2 points and 12.4 rebounds last season at North Hopkins High School in Madisonville, Ky. Sadler averaged 22.4 points and 9.3 rebounds at Habersham Central High School in Mt. Airy, Ga.

"Haney has a chance to start and so does Sadler," Ford said. "They're two players who had great high school careers that prepared them for college and we're not extremely deep in the post as far as returning players. We've got a lot of post players but none of them played significant minutes last year, so they'll definitely see great minutes and both could start. They could both hold down the four or five position."

2001-2002 SCHEDULE

Nov.	17	UNC Wilmington
	20	Western Illinois
	24	@Wyoming
	27	Marietta
Dec.	1	@Memphis
	4	@High Point
	8	@Dayton
	15	Transylvania
	19	@Western Illinois
	26	@Louisville
	29	Austin Peay
Jan.	3	Tennessee Tech
	5	Tennessee State
	10	@Southeast Missouri
	12	@Eastern Illinois
	15	IUPU
	19	@Morehead State
	24	Tennesse-Martin
	26	Murray State
Feb.	2	@Austin Peay
	4	@Tennessee Tech
	7	Eastern Illinois
	9	Southeast Missouri
	11	@Tennessee State
	16	Morehead State
	21	@Murray State
	23	@Tennessee-Martin
	26	#OVC Tournament
March	1-2	##OVC Tournament

@Road Games
#At campus sites
##Kentucky International Convention Center, Louisville, KY

BLUE RIBBON ANALYSIS

BACKCOURT	B
BENCH/DEPTH	C+
FRONTCOURT	C
INTANGIBLES	C+

Ford has a lot more to work with this year, and that should be a welcome relief. Now, it's up to Ford to get the team to mesh and keep everybody happy.

Transfers Fields from Georgia and Bentley from Marshall should have an impact. Junior college transfer Dix looks like the point guard for the next couple of years, and he should make returnees Parks and Sims more effective.

Perhaps the biggest question is in the frontcourt, which must be solidified by newcomers and role players from last year's team.

"Obviously we should be much improved," Ford said. "What gets me excited is we've improved our talent level and we will be much deeper than we were last year."

Don't expect the Colonels to get to the top of the OVC this season, but look for them to make a move upward.

(D.L.)

Morehead State

LOCATION	**Morehead, KY**
CONFERENCE	**Ohio Valley**
LAST SEASON	**12-16 (.429)**
CONFERENCE RECORD	**6-10 (7th)**
STARTERS LOST/RETURNING	**1/4**
NICKNAME	**Eagles**
COLORS	**Blue & Gold**
HOMECOURT	**Johnson Arena (6,500)**
COACH	**Kyle Macy (Kentucky '80)**
RECORD AT SCHOOL	**37-72 (5 years)**
CAREER RECORD	**37-72 (5 years)**
ASSISTANTS	**Wayne Breeden (Kentucky '83)**
	David Marshall (Northern Kentucky '95)
	Troy Thomas (Morehead State '97)
TEAM WINS (last 5 years)	**8-3-13-9-12**
RPI (last 5 years)	**288-296-226-285-230**
2000-01 FINISH	**Lost in conference quarterfinal.**

When he was hired as Morehead State's coach five years ago, Kyle Macy knew it wouldn't be an easy job getting the Eagles into the upper tier of the Ohio Valley Conference.

His second team made a good run, riding Erik Brown's 19.3-point average and finishing in a four-way tie for third in the 1998-99 season. When Brown departed for Louisville after his freshman year, the Eagles took a dive and finished ninth two years ago and seventh last season.

Now they seem ready to make a move toward the top.

"It's the first time since I've been here that we've been to the full scholarship allotment, so that's encouraging," Macy said. "They really hadn't recruited for seven or eight years [before Macy's arrival]. For an outsider looking in, they really don't know what all we've had to do and build here, but I think now we're to the point that we're not looking at it as a building process but as an accomplishing goals process.

"We have players coming back that were in the system. We've got guys coming in now to where we can hopefully see some definite improvement and accomplish some of those goals."

Macy has two of the better players in the OVC in sophomore swing player **Ricky Minard** and senior forward **Kyle Umberger**.

The 6-4 Minard wasn't a secret for long around the OVC. An exceptional athlete, Minard can score in a number of ways, from three-point shooting to short-range jumpers and drives to the basket for dunks.

Minard (16.7 ppg, 4.8 rpg), chosen as the OVC Freshman of the Year and to the All-OVC second team, was eighth in the league in scoring, tied for seventh in three-point percentage (.400) and sixth in three-pointers per game (27 in 62 games, 2.30 per game). He was also quick on the defensive end, ranking fourth in steals per game (27 in 49 games, 1.81 per game).

His freshman season ended on a low note because of injuries, and that certainly didn't help the Eagles' chances in their 102-80 quarterfinal loss to Eastern Illinois in the tournament.

"[Minard] got banged up late in the year," Macy said.

"Really about the last five games he had a deep thigh bruise on his left leg and we just couldn't get him healthy. We sat him for a couple of games."

Minard spent the summer at his hometown of Mansfield, Ohio, and is fine now. His versatility and competitiveness makes Minard dangerous.

"He can penetrate and he shot it very well last year," Macy said. "He likes to compete, which is obviously a plus."

Marquis Sykes, a 5-11 junior and Minard's teammate at Mansfield High School, returns as the Eagles' starting point guard. Sykes (7.3 ppg, 2.1 apg, 5.3 apg) ranked second in the OVC in assists last season and fifth in steals (1.79).

As a freshman, Sykes took over the starting point guard job at mid-season, so he has almost two years of starting experience.

"We don't really look for him to score that much, but I think he has that capability with his penetration and quickness," Macy said. "He gained some good experience over the last two years."

Several players will battle for the starting job at shooting guard. Two of them are 6-3 freshman **Kyle Hankins** and 6-4 freshman **Ramon Kelly**. Both are versatile players.

Last season, Hankins averaged 22.5 points and 4.5 rebounds at Bloomington (Ind.) South High School.

"He's versatile enough that he can play (shooting guard or point guard)," Macy said.

Kelly averaged 19 points and 5.0 rebounds at Belleville (Ill.) High School last year.

"Kelly is an outstanding player," Macy said. "He has real good size and can play point guard or the two or three."

Two returning players will also be factors in the backcourt.

Andy Keating, a 6-4 senior who played one season of football at West Virginia University, was expected to be more of a factor last year, but averaged only 3.0 points and 1.3 rebounds. Before coming to Morehead State, Keating averaged 15.7 points and 7.6 rebounds at Sinclair (Ohio) Junior College. He was expected to compete for a starting job last season and can play shooting guard or small forward.

Casey Lowe, a 6-2 sophomore guard, averaged 2.7 points and 1.0 rebounds last season. Lowe, who averaged 21 points and 4.7 rebounds as a senior at Columbus (Ind.) North High School, can play point guard or shooting guard.

"They came in and were solid contributors last season," Macy said of Keating and Lowe.

Chez Marks, a 6-2 junior guard, played only eight games last season before his season ended with a knee injury. He averaged 6.9 points and less than a rebound per game. Marks was a big-time scorer in high school three years ago, averaging 24.2 points at Paris (Ky.) High School.

While Sykes appears to have a hold on point guard, there will be plenty of competition at shooting guard.

"That's one thing I'm kind of excited about too," Macy said. "Practices should be more competitive this year. We really haven't had that depth. Once we got past six or seven, it really dropped off, but with the players coming back and the new class we've got coming in, we'll have some competition. We'll have a little bit of versatility in the backcourt and perimeter."

The only departed starter was Greg Hendricks (11.5 ppg, 3.5 rpg). He arrived at Morehead as a point guard, was replaced by Sykes midway through his junior year, and started at shooting guard last year.

One newcomer who could play a key role will be **Kalilou Kamara**, a 6-6 swing player from France. Kamara averaged 25 points and 8.5 rebounds at Lycee Paul-Langevin Deauvis High School.

"Again, he's a foreign player," Macy said. "It will take some time for him to adjust to American basketball. If he can make that transition it will obviously be a big plus. He's a very athletic type player. That could make it a possibility to move Minard to a two position."

Macy has both starters in the post, led by the 6-7, 220-pound Umberger, who makes the most of his abilities.

Umberger (13.3 ppg, 5.1 rpg) was among the OVC's top-20 scorers and ranked seventh in field-goal percentage (.495). He has great moves around the basket, a soft touch, and a knack for the basketball down low.

"He's very deceiving," Macy said. "You look at him with his size, or lack of (size for a low post), and his build, and doesn't really look like a basketball player, but he's been very successful because he knows how to use his body and the angles. We've had three strong years from him. He's real good pinning in the block and using his girth, beating guys behind him and using those angles."

Umberger was chosen to the All-OVC third team last season.

Iker "Ike" Lopez, a 6-8 junior, returns as the starting

power forward. Lopez (8.2 ppg, 4.8 rpg), a Spaniard, has benefited from a year of playing Division I college ball.

"I think any time you have a player from a foreign country who comes over to the U.S. to play, I think it takes a little longer for them to make that adjustment just because it's kind of a different brand of basketball than they've grown up with," Macy said. "Obviously I think with that year under his belt he knows a little more what to expect and how the year will progress."

David Aliu, a 6-6 sophomore forward from Liverpool, England, averaged 5.8 points and 3.3 rebounds for the Eagles last season, his first in the program. Aliu should be more of a factor this season.

Two freshmen, 6-7 **Chad McKnight** and 6-9 **Cory Burris**, will give backup support in the post. McKnight averaged 16.3 points and 9.0 rebounds last season at Lancaster (Ohio) High School. Burns averaged 16.8 points and 9.2 rebounds at Maconaquah High School in Peru, Ind.

2001-2002 SCHEDULE

Nov.	16	@IUPU-Fort Wayne
	19	Shawnee State
	24	@Kentucky
	28	VMI
Dec.	1	@Dayton
	5	Wright State
	8	Asbury
	18	@IUPUI
	21	@Samford
	29	@Vanderbilt
Jan.	3	Tennessee State
	5	Tennessee Tech
	10	@Eastern Illinois
	12	@Southeast Missouri
	15	Ohio Dominican
	19	Eastern Kentucky
	24	Murray State
	26	Tennessee-Martin
	28	@Tennessee State
Feb.	4	@Austin Peay
	7	Southeast Missouri
	9	Eastern Illinois
	12	@Tennessee Tech
	16	Eastern Kentucky
	18	Austin Peay
	21	@Tennessee-Martin
	23	@Murray State
	26	#OVC Tournament
March	2-3	##OVC Tournament

@Road Games
#Home sites
##Kentucky International Convention Center, Louisville, KY

BLUE RIBBON ANALYSIS

BACKCOURT	B+
BENCH/DEPTH	C+
FRONTCOURT	B-
INTANGIBLES	C

Morehead State looks solid with four starters returning. The Eagles have All-OVC candidates in swing player Minard and post player Umberger, plus an experienced point guard in Sykes.

Macy has more depth than he has had in four previous seasons at Morehead, and competition in practice should make the returnees even better.

"We're excited about the fact this will be one of the first years since I've been here that we've got a little experience coming back," Macy said. "We only had one senior graduate last year and we played a lot of freshmen last year. Add that experience and the fact we felt we signed some good young players, now we can maybe see some of the development we've been trying to accomplish here at Morehead State."

The Eagles should at least contend for a top-four finish in the OVC. With a good recruiting class of freshmen, Morehead's move toward the upper half of the OVC may not be temporary. The Eagles might be there for a few years.

(D.L.)

Murray State

LOCATION	Murray, KY
CONFERENCE	Ohio Valley
LAST SEASON	17-12 (.586)
CONFERENCE RECORD	11-5 (t-2nd)
STARTERS LOST/RETURNING	1/4
NICKNAME	Racers
COLORS	Navy & Gold
HOMECOURT	Regional Special Events Center (8,600)
COACH	Tevester Anderson (Arkansas AM&N '62)
RECORD AT SCHOOL	67-27 (3 years)
CAREER RECORD	67-27 (3 years)
ASSISTANTS	Jim Hatfield (East Tennessee State '65)
	Chris Woolard (UCLA '96)
	Anthony Boone (Mississippi '99)
TEAM WINS (last 5 years)	20-29-27-23-17
RPI (last 5 years)	161-58-66-77-129
2000-01 FINISH	Lost in conference semifinal.

When the 2000-01 regular season ended, Murray State's Racers found themselves in a strange place.

For the first time in eight seasons, the Racers didn't have at least a share of the Ohio Valley Conference championship. They were close—tied for second—but in Racer country, close isn't good enough.

Nor could Murray State rectify its finish in the OVC Tournament. In fact, it didn't come close to knocking off Eastern Illinois, which routed the Racers, 97-71, in a tournament semifinal.

The Racers never seemed to recover from some off-the-court turmoil early in the season. Ray Cunningham, who was arrested in the preseason, was eventually dismissed from the team by a school disciplinary board after playing two games. Cunningham, a 6-5 swing player, averaged 11.3 points and 6.8 rebounds in 1999-2000 and was one of two returning starters.

Even three-time OVC first-team forward Isaac Spencer couldn't help the Racers extend their run of first-place finishes.

"We had Isaac back, but we didn't have Ray Cunningham back," Racers coach Tevester Anderson said. "If we had both of those guys together we would have had an excellent chance of tying for it or winning the conference. We kind of waited for Cunningham all year long and we never could use him. We did consider it a rebuilding year."

Spencer, one of the league's most feared players during his career, has finally departed, only after being granted a fourth year of eligibility by the NCAA last year. Spencer, who sat out his first season under NCAA Proposition 48 guidelines, was granted another year of eligibility because he was diagnosed with a learning disability after he came to Murray State.

Once again, Spencer was among the league's top players, ranking fourth in the league in scoring (21.6) and tied for fifth in rebounding (7.1). Spencer didn't just put up big numbers, either; he was a warrior, the guy who had that aura of invincibility about him.

"Losing Isaac Spencer will hurt us a lot," Anderson said. "We've got basically the same team as last year and a few recruits, but you never know how those guys are going to play. Their first time playing Division I ball, you never know."

Anderson tried to upgrade his backcourt with a recruiting class and appears to have achieved that goal. Several returnees must battle for their minutes.

Kevin Paschel, a 5-11 junior, took over as the starting point guard after 17 games last season. Paschel (5.1 ppg, 1.1 rpg, 2.4 apg) was the Racers' only true point guard, but that won't be the case again. His job is in no way secure.

"I thought [Paschel] underachieved last year," Anderson said. "He didn't do as well as we thought he would do. We thought he had a very, very mediocre year. How much he's matured and how much better he's gotten, I don't know. He was very erratic from what we expected of him."

It was a drastic drop off at point guard from previous years when Aubrey Reece, the 1999-2000 OVC Player of the Year, ran the team.

"We've been used to some fine point guards," Anderson said. "That was my sixth year here [his first three were as an assistant coach] and ever since I've been here we've had some pretty good guards. I thought we took a step down last year."

Perhaps the top returning backcourt player is 6-1 senior **Justin Burdine**, who started the first 17 games at point guard. After losing his starting job, Burdine (15.3 ppg, 3.2 ppg) seemed more at ease coming off the bench and playing mostly shooting guard. He is the top returning scorer and was Murray's second-leading scorer last season.

Burdine, chosen to the All-OVC third team, has excellent range and ranked sixth in the league in three-point shooting percentage (.403) and fourth in three-pointers per game (2.59).

"Justin is a very talented player who has been behind some great players during his career," Anderson said. "He fulfilled a lot of expectations last season and will be counted on to provide more leadership for us this year."

In a recruiting class of five players, Anderson landed four guards. However, one of them, 6-0 freshman Mark Borders of Dr. Phillips High School in Orlando, Fla., is a partial qualifier and won't play this season.

Rashard Harris, a 6-1 junior point guard from Atlanta Metro Community College, will certainly challenge Paschel for the starting job. Harris, a native of Greenville, S.C., averaged 19.6 points, 3.7 rebounds and 4.3 assists in junior college last season. He shot 46 percent from the field, 42 percent from three-point range and became eligible only after passing summer school classes.

"He's a pretty good point guard, he really is," Anderson said. "He can score some too and he can do some things for us."

One player who could emerge as an OVC star is 6-1 sophomore **Rick Jones**, a well-traveled player. Jones, who played high school ball in Georgetown, Ky., at first planned to continue his career at Eastern Kentucky after being dismissed from Vanderbilt, then resurfaced at Murray after a brush with the law. He was a point guard in high school and is equally talented as a shooting guard.

Jones played in all 30 Vanderbilt games in 1999-2000 and led the team in three-point percentage, shooting 48.2 percent. He averaged 5.7 points. Against Mississippi State in the first round of the SEC Tournament, Jones scored 24 points, making 8-of-9 three-point shots. He was cleared to play late in the summer.

"We think he's put everything behind him now and got his act together," Anderson said. "He seems to be on the right track to being very successful on and off the court right now."

Yet another newcomer, 6-1 guard **Antonio Henderson**, will make his bid for the starting job at shooting guard. Henderson, also a combination guard, averaged 28 points and 7.9 rebounds two years ago at Atlanta Metro Community College. He spent the last year at Somerset (Ky.) Community College but didn't play basketball.

"He's a good shooter and he's athletic," Anderson said. "He's a guy who could be a really fine guard for us before the season's over."

Murray has experience returning at the wings with 6-5 junior swing player **Chris Shumate**, 6-5 junior forward **Antione Whelchel** and 6-5 sophomore forward **Cuthbert Victor**. Whelchel and Victor can also play power forward.

Shumate (12.9 ppg, 4.3 rpg) started all 29 games and ranked second in the OVC in three-point percentage (.458) and 11th in three-pointers per game (1.9).

"I expect Shumate to play some two and three this year," Anderson said. "He's a complete player. I think he's more of a three than a two, but we played him at two last year. He's a good shooter. He's probably one of our better shooters, kind of streaky but one of our better shooters."

Whelchel (11.2 ppg, 7.8 rpg) led the Racers in rebounding last year and ranked fourth in the OVC. With the departure of Spencer, Whelchel will be the top candidate to start at power forward.

Victor (6.2 ppg, 4.3 rpg) started 17 games and averaged 16.3 minutes per game. He is a defensive specialist and could play either forward spot. Victor shot 56.5 percent from the field, which would have ranked among the top five in the OVC, but he didn't meet the minimum of four field goals per game to be listed in the league statistics.

"He's really athletic," Anderson said. "He's an average shooter but he rebounds the ball very well and he's very athletic. He's probably one of our better defenders."

In the low post, the Racers are anchored by 7-0, 268-pound sophomore **Andi Hornig**, a native of Idstein, Germany who started as a freshman. Hornig (5.0 ppg, 6.1 rpg) started all 29 games and averaged 21.8 minutes. He ranked second in the league in blocked shots with 51. Hornig spent the summer in Germany.

"I expect him to start again," Anderson said. "I thought for a guy coming in as a freshman and being a foreign player, he played consistent for us. You hope that he improved over the summer months and got better and comes in stronger and more experienced."

Rod Thomas, a 6-8 senior, will also vie for time in the frontcourt. Thomas averaged 1.7 points and 2.2 rebounds last season.

Jamar Avant, a 6-8, 230-pound sophomore, sat out last season under Proposition 48 guidelines. Avant was a three-time all-state player at Murphysboro (Ill.) High

School, where he averaged 17 points and 15 rebounds as a senior. As a senior, Avant was rated as the 76th-best player in the nation and No. 3 in Illinois by Hoop Scoop.

"You just don't know what to expect from a guy who's been away from the game for a year," Anderson said. "He has great potential as a four man. He's about [6-8] and jumps very well, runs well, shoots the ball well. He could be an impact player."

The only newcomer to the frontcourt, 6-8 junior **James Singleton**, should also have an impact. Singleton averaged 13.9 points and 13.8 rebounds last season at Pearl River (Miss.) Community College. He shot 61.3 percent from the field and 68.3 percent from the line. He had game-highs of 27 points, 25 rebounds and 11 blocks and went to junior college from Hirsch High School in Chicago.

"He's a good rebounder and shot blocker," Anderson said. "He jumps real well and blocks shots and runs the floor very well. He's not much of an offensive player.

"Jamar and James give us two very athletic power forwards who are versatile enough to run the floor and play away from the basket, but could also play the post for us."

Chiwale Bedeau, a 6-7 junior forward, also returns. Bedeau (1.5 ppg, 1.7 rpg) played in 11 games and averaged 8.7 minutes per game.

2001-2002 SCHEDULE

Nov.	17	West Florida
	19	Colorado-Colorado Springs
	24	@Western Kentucky
	29	Tennessee-Chattanooga
Dec.	1	UAB
	3	@Indiana State
	7-8	#Jim Thorpe Tournament
	11	@DePaul
	20	Tennessee State
	22	@Tennessee-Chattanooga
	29	Southern Illinois
Jan.	3	Tennessee-Martin
	5	Gardner-Webb
	10	@Tennessee Tech
	12	@Austin Peay
	17	Eastern Illinois
	19	Southeast Missouri
	24	@Morehead State
	26	@Eastern Kentucky
Feb.	2	@Tennessee-Martin
	4	@Tennessee State
	7	Tennessee Tech
	9	Austin Peay
	14	@Eastern Illinois
	16	@Southeast Missouri
	21	Eastern Kentucky
	23	Morehead State
	27	##OVC Tournament
March	2-3	###OVC Tournament

@Road Games
#Louisville, KY (vs. Virginia Tech first round; also Louisville, Wisconsin-Milwaukee)
##First-round games at campus sites
###Kentucky International Convention Center, Louisville, KY

BLUE RIBBON ANALYSIS

BACKCOURT	A-
BENCH/DEPTH	A-
FRONTCOURT	B+
INTANGIBLES	A-

Anderson had one of the best recruiting classes in the OVC, and combined with the returning players he should have one of the league's best teams.

Now loaded with guards, the Racers will look to push the ball as they did so effectively a couple a years ago.

Anderson may have lost Spencer, but he has athleticism in the frontcourt to go with Hornig. And his backcourt is talented and deep. Vanderbilt transfer Jones and junior college transfers Harris and Henderson will solve any backcourt problems the Racers had last season.

"We hope that even with Ike gone, we can move forward this year and the rebuilding process will be further along," Anderson said.

Murray State won't be the league favorite, but it should give Tennessee Tech and the other top teams all they want.

(D.L.)

Southeast Missouri State

LOCATION	Cape Girardeau, MO
CONFERENCE	Ohio Valley
LAST SEASON	18-12 (.600)
CONFERENCE RECORD	8-8 (5th)
STARTERS LOST/RETURNING	4/1
NICKNAME	Indians
COLORS	Red & Black
HOMECOURT	Show Me Center (7,000)
COACH	Gary Garner (Missouri '65)
RECORD AT SCHOOL	76-41 (4 years)
CAREER RECORD	324-204 (18 years)
ASSISTANTS	Keno Davis (Iowa '95)
	Gary Abner (Wichita State '98)
	John Daniel (Missouri-Rolla)
TEAM WINS (last 5 years)	12-14-20-24-18
RPI (last 5 years)	223-198-115-61-178
2000-01 FINISH	Lost in conference quarterfinal.

Only two years ago, Southeast Missouri State was celebrating an OVC Tournament championship and NCAA berth. Since then, the Indians have taken a fall.

Despite having one of the league's best backcourts last season, the Indians tumbled to fifth in the OVC regular season and were knocked out of the conference tournament by Austin Peay in overtime.

This season, the Indians will have trouble matching that fifth-place finish. For the first time in a couple of years, Indians coach Gary Garner won't have a team expected to contend for the title.

"We definitely won't be picked at the top," Garner said. "Late in the year we might have a good basketball team. It's just going to take a while."

Not only did the Indians lose five seniors, including four starters, they also lost two players who would potentially have been among their better players this season. Post player Terry Rogers (4.9 ppg, 3.4 rpg), who started eight games and averaged 14.3 minutes, and point guard Bobby Smith, who sat out the 2000-01 season after transferring from Villanova, were dismissed from the team after running into trouble with the law.

Suddenly, the youthful Indians looked even younger.

"This is my fifth year, and this will be the youngest team we've had," Garner said. "That's the No. 1 thing. We're going to really be young. So much of our season depends on our young kids.

"Some young kids can come in and play pretty good fairly quick. Others it takes them all year before they get going, so that's going to be a big concern and a big issue of ours—just how good are they and how quick can they be pretty good players."

Replacing the backcourt production of point guard Michael Stokes (15.0 ppg, 4.0 rpg, 4.8 apg), shooting guard Antonio Short (10.3 ppg, 3.7 rpg) and small forward Emmanuel McCuthison (11.9 ppg, 5.0 rpg) will be almost impossible with the newcomers. The three were the team's top scorers.

Also gone is 6-11 post player Nyah Jones, who never became the dominant force the Indians had hoped to see. Jones (4.3 ppg, 2.9 rpg) started 13 games, and although he had some good moments in the second half of the year, he was never able to become a major player.

Backup guard Amory Sanders (8.2 ppg, 2.0), one of the league's top three-point shooters, was also a senior last year.

So where does that leave the Indians? Well, they're looking for answers.

Drew DeMond, a 6-7 junior power forward, is the only returning starter. DeMond (5.8 ppg, 4.3 rpg) started 23 games and averaged 24.5 minutes. He spent part of the summer playing in China for Sports Reach. Also on the team was Eastern Illinois guard Henry Domercant.

"He's a four man who can score around the basket," Garner said of DeMond. "He's a pretty good athlete, runs and jumps pretty good, and he's really a good shot blocker. He's just a good athlete."

Garner may find a starting spot for 6-7 junior forward **Tim Scheer** (6.8 ppg, 3.0 rpg), who started five games last season and averaged 16.2 minutes in 28 games.

"Tim can shoot the ball from the perimeter," Garner said. "He could play some three. We're going to take a look at several positions and combinations. Our nonconference season, we may have a different starting lineup out there every game."

Daniel Weaver, a 6-8 sophomore forward, will also figure into the frontcourt plans. Weaver (4.0 ppg, 2.1 rpg) started nine games and shot 50 percent from the floor.

"He's a smart player," Garner said of Weaver. "He can help us, there's no question about that, and Daniel could wind up starting. He's a good passer, shoots good from 15 feet on in and he plays very intelligently."

Monte Gordan (3.2 ppg, 2.6 rpg), a 6-5 senior forward, will likely be a backup again.

Garner is hoping for a quick adjustment to college ball by 7-1 center **Kostas Avgerinos**, a sophomore from Greece. Avgerinos took a roundabout road to Cape Girardeau after signing with the Indians out of high school.

After failing to qualify academically, Avgerinos went to Southern Idaho in 1999-2000, but played on a team loaded with frontcourt players. In preseason practices last fall, Avgerinos suffered a severe concussion and missed the season. He averaged 15 points, 11 rebounds and five blocks in the European Junior League three years ago.

"Not getting to see him play last year, I don't know how much he's progressed," Garner said, "but I do know he has very good skills. He can catch it, he can pass it, he can shoot it. He's thin, 7-1 or 7-2 and 220 pounds, but he's got the skills to be a good player. How much that year off [affected him], how much he's developed, I don't know. And he needs to get stronger, but we're definitely planning on him fitting into our team and playing a lot."

Adam Crader, a 6-11 freshman center, averaged 20.6 points, 12.5 rebounds and 6.5 blocks last season at Doniphan (Mo.) High School. He shot 61 percent from the field.

"Crader has good size at 6-11 and 230 and he has a body frame that will allow him to add more size and strength with a good weight program," Garner said. "He has good hands, a good shooting touch around the basket and he is really aggressive. He's an excellent student and was aggressively recruited by Kansas State, Southern Illinois, Illinois State and New Orleans, so we beat out some good schools to sign him."

After two seasons at Southeast Missouri, 6-6 sophomore swingman **Damarcus Hence** is still looking for a breakout year. Now would be a good time for it.

Hence, an outstanding player at Memphis Fairly High School, was injured as a freshman and red-shirted. Last season, Hence (3.1 ppg, 1.4 rpg) didn't have an impact early, but Garner hopes his play late in the year will carry over into this season.

"Last year was really like his freshman year and he really started coming on late," Garner said. "I'm guessing. but the last 10 or 12 games of the year he probably averaged 15 minutes a game. You could see his confidence starting to come. We're sure hoping he has a good year. We're planning on him being our three man."

Joel Shelton, the backup point guard last season, will stay at the point or could move to shooting guard. Shelton (2.4 ppg, 0.6 rpg), a 5-9 sophomore, played in 25 games and averaged 10.4 minutes.

Two freshmen, 6-2 **Derek Winans** and 6-2 **Brett Hale**, will also contend for the job at shooting guard. Winans, who averaged 27 points, 10 rebounds and four assists as a senior at Shawnee (Ill.) High School, was red-shirted last year.

Hale, a freshman, averaged 29 points last season at Dexter (Mo.) High School.

"They're both going to be good players," Garner said. "Again, it's just how quick [they adjust]. Both of them are very good shooters."

Also returning is 6-2 senior guard **Matt Morris**, who was red-shirted after missing the season with mononucleosis. He averaged 1.9 points and 0.7 rebounds two years ago as a walk-on.

Garner is planning on 6-0 junior **Kenny Johnson**, a transfer from Penn Valley Junior College, to be the starting point guard. Johnson averaged 12 points and 7.5 assists last season.

"Johnson is a true point guard who can also play the two guard," Garner said. "He is very quick and is an excellent ball handler and passer. Johnson is very competitive and he can really distribute the ball."

Kevin Roberts, a 6-3 guard, is the Indians' other freshman. Roberts, a walk-on, averaged 12 points last season at DeSmet High School in St. Louis.

Justin Smith, a 6-3 sophomore, will be eligible at the end of the fall semester. He transferred last year from Arkansas State, where he played sparingly during the fall semester in 2000.

"I won't hesitate at all to play three guards," Garner said. "When you give up size at the three spot, you gain something for it. I like our ability to shoot the ball, like Hale and Winans. We may wind up seeing some [three-guard lineups]."

2001-2002 SCHEDULE

Nov.	16	Birmingham Southern
	24	@Southwest Missouri
	27	Arkansas-Little Rock
Dec.	1	Western Illinois
	5	@Vanderbilt
	8	North Alabama
	15	@Saint Louis
	17	Mississippi Valley
	22	@Southern Illinois
	29	Lincoln University
Jan.	2	@Western Illinois
	5	@Eastern Illinois
	7	Tennessee State
	10	Eastern Kentucky
	12	Morehead State
	17	@Tennessee-Martin
	19	@Murray State
	24	Tennessee Tech
	26	Austin Peay
	31	@Tennessee State
Feb.	2	@Tennessee Tech
	7	@Morehead State
	9	@Eastern Kentucky
	14	Tennessee-Martin
	16	Murray State
	18	Eastern Illinois
	23	@Austin Peay
	26	#OVC Tournament
March	1-2	##OVC Tournament

@Road Games
#At campus sites
##Kentucky International Convention Center, Louisville, KY

BLUE RIBBON ANALYSIS

BACKCOURT	C-
BENCH/DEPTH	C
FRONTCOURT	C-
INTANGIBLES	B

Perhaps the Indians will surprise some people. Garner is a proven winner, and he's a coach who can mold a team together. Clearly, Garner has his work cut out this year.

The Indians' only returnees were role players last season, guys who did what they could while Stokes, Short and McCuthison did the scoring.

The roles of several players must change in order for the Indians to be successful. DeMond, Scheer, and Weaver need to play more of a prominent role in the frontcourt.

Swing player Hence will get the chance to show what he did in high school. Avgerinos is a 7-footer, but lacks Division I experience. Even the high school signees will get a chance to show their stuff.

"We've got a nucleus of kids who played some coming back," Garner said. "When you lose five seniors, maybe we should have gone the junior college route. We brought in one junior college player [point guard Kenny Johnson]. We got these freshmen signed in the fall and liked them and that's the route we decided to go."

With that in mind, Indian fans can count on this being a rebuilding year.

(D.L.)

Tennessee State

LOCATION	**Nashville, TN**
CONFERENCE	**Ohio Valley**
LAST SEASON	**10-19 (.345)**
CONFERENCE RECORD	**7-9 (6th)**
STARTERS LOST/RETURNING	**3/2**
NICKNAME	**Tigers**
COLORS	**Royal Blue & White**
HOMECOURT	**Gentry Complex (10,500)**
COACH	**Nolan Richardson III (Langston '90)**
RECORD AT SCHOOL	**10-19 (1 year)**
CAREER RECORD	**10-19 (1 year)**
ASSISTANTS	**Hosea Lewis (LaVerne '87)**
TEAM WINS (last 5 years)	**9-13-12-7-10**
RPI (last 5 years)	**239-196-243-274-261**
2000-01 FINISH	**Lost in conference quarterfinal.**

Once again, Tennessee State is the mystery team of the OVC.

The Tigers have only three scholarship players returning. They have a bunch of new faces. Tennessee State has a turnover rate among its players that can't be matched by any team in the league.

Coach Nolan Richardson III hopes to change that, although several of his newcomers are junior-college transfers who will be around only two years. Richardson has loaded the team with athletic players whose forte is versatility.

"Basically this whole team, every one of them, is almost the same," said Richardson, son of Arkansas coach Nolan Richardson. "They can play inside or outside and they all can shoot."

Richardson's nephew, **Garrett Richardson**, is one of two returning starters. The younger Richardson (11.4 ppg, 3.1 rpg, 3.1 apg), a 6-3 sophomore, will likely start at point guard.

Last season, Richardson was the team's fourth-leading scorer and was second in assists. He will replace starter Terrick Brown (8.0 ppg, 2.8 rpg, 4.4 apg) as the starting point guard. Last season, Richardson played both guard positions.

"Garrett had a tremendous year," coach Richardson said, "but I think he's a lot better than he showed, even though he had a great year. He played in a summer league and all that. I see him playing 10 times better than [last season]. He can score, defend, [hand out] assists. He's very unselfish."

Garrett Richardson shot 34.4 percent from three-point range last season and was third on the team in three-pointers made (42-of-122). Coach Richardson will give his nephew the green light this season.

"I've got to make him shoot," the coach said. "That's going to be an emphasis this year. He's going to get to shoot a lot."

Kyle Rolston, a 6-4 senior guard from Nashville, returns after starting 23 games last season and averaging 28.4 minutes per game. Rolston (11.8 ppg, 3.9 rpg) shot 36.8 percent from three-point range last season and 50 percent from the field. He was the second-leading scorer on a team that had five players average double-figure scoring.

Josh Cooperwood, a 6-3 junior guard, can play anywhere in the backcourt. Cooperwood averaged 20 points last season at Chattanooga State (Tenn.) Community College. He is a former player at Hillwood High School in Nashville.

"He's kind of like Garrett," Richardson said. "They're both very similar. They can score inside, outside, shoot it deep, run and defend. It's going to be fun watch those guys go at it."

Richardson plans to find a spot for **Antonio Cook**, a 6-5 swing player from Jefferson Davis Community College in Brewton, Ala. Cook, who averaged 15 points last season, played in the frontcourt in junior college, but will probably move to the perimeter this year.

"He's a true two-three player but in junior college they played him at the four because of his size and jumping ability," Richardson said. "He's 6-5, 195 pounds. His strength is a guard spot but he can play on the post, and that's a great addition for us because of the way we play. Sometimes I post a lot of my guards up, so that's going to help us tremendously."

After sitting out last season, 6-5 senior swing player **Darnai Thomas** looks to make an impact. Thomas, who played high school ball at Hamilton High in Los Angeles, played two years at Santa Monica (Calif.) Community College before sitting out last season. He is a tremendous leaper and good shooter. In his second year of junior college, Thomas averaged 21 points.

"Thomas was one of the top players coming out of his junior college," Richardson said. "He's a good player."

Rounding out the backcourt are 6-2 senior guard **Rodrick James**, 5-9 senior guard **Damon Ross**, and 6-0 sophomore **Brandon Lockridge**. All played sparingly last season.

James (1.9 ppg, 0.7 rpg) played in 21 games last season, starting two, and averaged 4.7 minutes. Ross (0.9 ppg, 0.7 rpg) played in 18 games and averaged 5.9 minutes. Lockridge (1.1 ppg, 0.6 rpg) played in 10 games last season and averaged 3.7 minutes.

Olushula Ajannaku, a 6-5 junior forward, looks to build on a solid sophomore season. As a high school player at Northside in Memphis, Ajannaku wasn't able to break into the starting lineup, but he did just that last year at Tennessee State. Ajannaku (2.8 ppg, 1.7 rpg) joined the team after Richardson saw him playing pickup ball in Tennessee State's gym shortly after getting the job in 1999.

"He's going to be very instrumental on our team," Richardson said. "He's a 6-5 guard that played center for me last year and did well. He's another combination type player that can go inside or outside. He's one of those kids that was second string on his high school team and wanted to go to Tennessee State, so that's where he went. When I got the job, I saw him playing and pulled him over."

The only freshmen signees are both forwards—6-7 **Brandon Turner** of Jo Byrns High School in Cedar Hill, Tenn., and 6-6 **Roshaun Bowens** from McGavock High School in Nashville.

Of those two, Bowens seems more likely to see significant playing time this year.

"Bowens is a tremendous freshman coming in," Richardson said. "He's more of a finesse-type player, a slasher who can shoot the ball from the outside."

Sophomore **Kellen Brandon**, a 6-7 forward, was a backup last season. Brandon (1.7 ppg, 0.6 rpg) played in 12 games, starting two, and averaged 7.3 points.

After spending much of his junior college career in junior playing out of position, 6-6 junior forward **Thad Jones** will get to move to his natural small forward position. Jones played in the post in junior college.

"Thad Jones is probably the most athletic player we have," Richardson said. "He's 6-6 and can jump to the moon. He's another three man who played four and five on his junior college team. The beauty of it all is he gets to play his position now, so that's a big plus for us."

Arvid Caldwell, a 6-7 junior, is probably the only pure post player on the team.

"He can come out but he's probably more comfortable around the basket," Richardson said. "Mostly he'll be under the basket, and **Will Hendricks** will be under the basket a lot."

Hendricks, a 6-7, 225-pound junior from Seattle, sat out last season after transferring from Lon Morris (Texas) Community College. Hendricks is the strongest of the Tiger frontcourt players.

2001-2002 SCHEDULE

Nov.	16	Trevecca
	24	Evansville
	26	@Kansas State
	29	@Wright State
Dec.	1	@Louisville
	3	Fisk
	5	@Oral Roberts
	8	@Middle Tennessee State
	20	@Murray State
	28	@UNLV
	30	@Houston
Jan.	3	@Morehead State
	5	@Eastern Kentucky
	7	@Southeast Missouri
	12	Tennessee-Martin
	14	Lipscomb
	19	@Austin Peay
	26	Tennessee Tech
	28	Morehead State
Feb.	2	Eastern Illinois
	4	Murray State
	7	@Tennessee-Martin
	11	Eastern Kentucky
	14	Austin Peay
	18	@Tennessee Tech
	21	@Eastern Illinois
	26	#OVC Tournament
March	2-3	##OVC Tournament

@Road Games
#Home sites
##Kentucky International Convention Center, Louisville, KY

BLUE RIBBON ANALYSIS

BACKCOURT	B-
BENCH/DEPTH	C
FRONTCOURT	D
INTANGIBLES	D

Tennessee State will employ the "40 Minutes of Hell" approach this season, a style Richardson learned under his father at Arkansas.

With the personnel on the Tigers' roster, that's the best approach for this team. It is a roster full of guards and swing players.

"Because of our style of play, I don't play position players," Richardson said. "My guys that can play the five, they can also play the two."

That means the Tigers will try to run and press and trap their way to victory this season. Forget the halfcourt stuff.

"I've played different ways as a player," Richardson said. "I recruit players to play. I know if I change styles and slow it down, some players aren't going to get to play as much. I need to open it up and play to their abilities."

Maybe that strategy will work this season. With so

many new players, there are lots of questions on this team. Perhaps the Tigers will surprise some people.

(D.L.)

Tennessee Tech

LOCATION	Cookeville, TN
CONFERENCE	Ohio Valley
LAST SEASON	20-9 (.690)
CONFERENCE RECORD	13-3 (1st)
STARTERS LOST/RETURNING	1/4
NICKNAME	Golden Eagles
COLORS	Purple & Gold
HOMECOURT	Eblen Center (10,152)
COACH	Jeff Lebo (North Carolina '89)
RECORD AT SCHOOL	48-36 (3 years)
CAREER RECORD	48-36 (3 years)
ASSISTANTS	John Shulman (East Tennessee State '89)
	Tracy Garrick (Furman '91)
	Dave Lebo (Elizabethton College '66)
TEAM WINS (last 5 years)	15-9-12-16-20
RPI (last 5 years)	221-270-247-167-116
2000-01 FINISH	Lost in conference semifinal.

It took only three years for Tennessee Tech coach Jeff Lebo to attain one of his primary goals. After the 2000-2001 season was complete, Lebo was able to hang an Ohio Valley Conference championship banner from the rafters of the Eblen Center.

For the first time since the 1984-85 season, the Golden Eagles were champions of the OVC.

"It's going to help our confidence and help our demeanor," Lebo said. "It's like, 'Hey, we've done this. We've won the championship.' We put so much emphasis on trying to hang a banner, which hadn't been done since the '80s, and then it was one, and then you have to go back to the '60s [for the previous OVC title, in the 1962-63 season]."

"It took a lot out of our kids. I think we have a good understanding of how hard it is to win a championship and how tough day in and day out this league is and what kind of sacrifices have to be made to win."

Lebo lost his best player from last year's team, All-OVC forward Larrie Smith (16.3 ppg, 8.8 rpg), but has replaced him with three quality post players.

Smith and backup guard Trey Ferguson were the only departed players from last year's team, and with the newcomers, the Golden Eagles should be even better than the 2000-01 team.

They look ready to take the next step: win not only the OVC regular-season title but the postseason tournament. Tech's last NCAA appearance was in 1963, when it lost to Loyola (Ill.), 111-42.

"We'll move that goal up and move that bar up higher this year," Lebo said. "We will not be able to sneak up on people this year. We will take everybody's best shot and we will have to raise the level of our game to combat that. I think we've come a long way in this program from when we first got here. We're in position to have a good year."

No doubt about that.

Smith, who earned All-OVC second team honors two years ago and was the league's Newcomer of the Year, spent last season practicing against South Carolina transfer **Damien Kinloch**, a 6-8 junior from Charleston, S.C. Smith was on the All-OVC first team last year when he led the league in rebounding and was ninth in scoring.

Kinloch, who averaged 3.9 points and 4.2 points for the Gamecocks two years ago, reportedly gave Smith all he wanted in practice last season. In one game at South Carolina, Kinloch had 13 points and seven rebounds against Michigan State. He won't be eligible until January.

"He will step in and fill Larrie's shoes," Lebo said. "Damien has experience playing at a high level, starting at South Carolina and playing 20 minutes a game his sophomore year. He's bigger and more athletic than Larry at 6-8 and about 220 pounds. He has a chance to come in and make a major impact. He's as talented a big guy as there is in this league. He's tough, he can defend, he's smart and he can score. We're going to rely a lot on him stepping in and playing and giving us more of a physical presence around the basket."

Adonis Hart, a 6-8, 250-pound senior center, is also a physical presence in the paint. Hart, however, has spent his career battling knee injuries. He has sustained torn anterior cruciate ligaments on both of his knees and

had two surgeries. His last knee injury happened in mid-January of the 1999-2000 season against Austin Peay and ended his season.

Last season, Hart (3.8 ppg, 2.8 rpg) played in 27 games and averaged 13.3 minutes.

"He didn't come back as quick as we had hoped from the second [ACL injury]," Lebo said. "Adonis had been playing very well when he went down with his second knee injury. That really had taken him back. It's so hard to come back from one of those, let alone two of them. We're going to go hard at him when he comes back and get him in shape and give him confidence. He's a big mule around the basket area and we'll need him in there to anchor down some things."

Two junior college transfers, 6-9, 220-pound **Antwyon Jones** and 6-8, 215-pound **Greg Morgan**, also factor heavily into Lebo's frontcourt plans. Both can play power forward and center.

"In our system, four and five are very similar [positions]," Lebo said, "so they can both play both positions. Damien Kinloch can do the same thing. All three are very athletic and can move."

Jones averaged 12.5 points and 6.0 rebounds last season at Dodge City (Kansas) Community College, shooting 55 percent from the field. He shot 78 percent from the foul line in his first season of junior college, but shot 66 percent from the line last year.

"Antwyon Jones is a terrific athlete with the ability to score with his back to the basket and from within 15 feet," Dodge City coach Brian Hoberecht said. "He can block shots with either hand and always plays extremely hard."

Morgan averaged 13.5 points and 7.0 rebounds in two years at Parkland (Ill.) Community College.

"Morgan is more of a scorer," Lebo said. "He's left-handed, he can score in a variety of different ways and he can face the basket and shoot a little bit. Jones is a shot blocker, long and athletic and can run. We've lost one post player [Smith] but added three."

Lebo also anticipates more production from 6-9 junior **Rusty Strange** (1.9 ppg, 1.0 rpg), who played in 21 games but averaged only 5.1 minutes.

"He's really worked hard in the off-season," Lebo said. "He's up to 240 pounds and dedicated himself in the summer to getting better. He went to some camps and played in the summer league and had a good summer. I think he can step up and play some big minutes."

The Golden Eagles have an experienced forward in 6-6 senior **Joey Westmoreland**, who can play either forward position. Westmoreland (6.9 ppg, 4.8 rpg), who should start for the fourth year, is a blue-collar type player.

"You can't measure in statistics what he means to the team," Lebo said. "He makes all the big plays. He's a competitor, a very good rebounder. He'll get the big rebound, dive on the floor and get the big jump ball. He's tough. He's been through the wars. You need guys like that if you're going to be successful."

Perhaps the most versatile Golden Eagle is 6-6 senior **DeAntoine Beasley**, who came to Tech as a point guard and can now play either forward position. Beasley (8.5 ppg, 5.2 rpg) started all 29 games last season. He sat out the 1999-2000 season while having chemotherapy for Hodgkins disease.

"He causes matchup problems because he can play some four and he plays like a guard," Lebo said. "He has guard skills and can post. He can come out on the perimeter and beat you off the dribble. He's a great passer with an unbelievable feel for the game. At times he can score for us. He gets a lot of garbage baskets here and there. He can run, he can pass, he hits the open man and he has become a very good defender."

Jason Harrell, a 6-7 sophomore, can play shooting guard or small forward. Harrell (8.9 ppg, 3.7 rpg) started only three games last season but averaged 21 minutes. He was the team's fourth-leading scorer.

"Of all the players, he probably has the biggest upside," Lebo said. "Jason is long, athletic and can shoot it at 6-7 or 6-8. He's gotten a lot stronger and he's gotten a lot better at putting the ball on the floor. He was inconsistent as a freshman last year, but he had some big games. He can rebound and block shots at the guard spot."

Damien Perkins, a 6-7 junior forward, sat out last season. Like Harrell, Perkins is a swing player. Perkins averaged 12.1 points, 8.7 rebounds and 3.9 assists two years ago at Holmes (Miss.) Junior College. He is an outstanding defender.

"He's very athletic and can defend and he's also an excellent offensive rebounder," Lebo said. "He's gotten stronger and he can defend anybody on the court. He can defend a big player or a point guard."

Running the team is 5-10 junior point guard **Leigh**

Gayden, chosen to the All-OVC third team last season.

Gayden (13.4 ppg, 2.2 rpg, 4.0 apg, 2.0 tpg), seventh in the OVC in assists, has the ability to take over a game with his long-range shooting. He shot 40 percent from three-point range and led the OVC in three-pointers per game (2.76 per game).

"There's not a guy that I've coached or been around who has worked harder at his game than Leigh Gayden," Lebo said. "Leigh takes a thousand shots a day in the summer. He's a basketball junkie. It's good to see guys do well who have paid the price, and Leigh has paid the price and continues to pay the price.

"His leadership this year will move to another level ... I like my point guard to be able to score. The more players we have on the court that can put the ball in the basket, the harder it is for us to be guarded. He runs our team and he gets the ball up the court very quick. He's really improved defensively. He couldn't guard my daughter when he first came here and he's learned the principles and improved defensively."

Backing up Gayden will be 6-3 sophomore **Cameron Crisp** (3.0 ppg, 0.8 rpg), who played in 29 games last season and averaged 9.2 minutes.

Crisp, who can play either guard position, has better size and strength than Gayden but is not as quick.

"He's really gotten stronger," Lebo said. "I think he could have a coming out year this year."

Brent Jolly, a 6-5 junior, returns as the starting shooting guard. Jolly (12.6 ppg, 2.7 rpg), former Mr. Basketball at White County (Tenn.) High School, was 10th in the OVC in three-point percentage (.381) and tied for eighth in three-pointers per game (2.21). He led the OVC in free-throw percentage (.931).

"He's a great scorer, not the most athletic guy in the world but he will beat you with his brain and can make the open shots," Lebo said. "He's gotten bigger and stronger in the off-season."

Ahmad Richardson, a 6-5 sophomore, had ankle surgery in the off-season. Richardson (2.4 ppg, 1.4 rpg) will play small forward or shooting guard.

"We're in position to have a good year," Lebo said. "That doesn't necessarily mean we will, but we've got some new players coming in along with some veteran guys who have played a lot of minutes and been around the league and played against a high level of competition. I don't think when we step on the floor we'll be in awe of anybody."

2001-2002 SCHEDULE

Nov.	16	@Tennessee
	20	South Carolina State
	24	Bluefield College
	27	Loyola
Dec.	1	@Eastern Michigan
	4	Reinhardt College
	8	@New Mexico
	17	@Louisville
	21	@North Texas
	29	@Air Force
Jan.	3	@Eastern Kentucky
	5	@Morehead State
	10	Murray State
	12	King College
	17	@Austin Peay
	21	Tennessee-Martin
	24	@Southeast Missouri
	26	@Tennessee State
	31	Eastern Illinois
Feb.	2	Southeast Missouri State
	4	Eastern Kentucky
	7	@Murray State
	9	@Tennessee-Martin
	12	Morehead State
	16	@Austin Peay
	18	Tennessee State
	23	@Eastern Kentucky
	27	#OVC Tournament
March	2-3	##OVC Tournament

@Road Games
#First-round games at campus sites
##Kentucky International Convention Center, Louisville, KY

BLUE RIBBON ANALYSIS

BACKCOURT	A
BENCH/DEPTH	B+
FRONTCOURT	A
INTANGIBLES	A

The Golden Eagles suffered a huge disappointment last season when they were beaten by Austin Peay, 83-63, in the semifinals of the OVC Tournament.

Surely, they haven't forgotten it.

"I think we were a little emotionally drained at the end of the season after winning the regular-season championship," Lebo said. "We put a lot into that. We weren't sharp. We had beaten Austin Peay a couple of times in a row. They emotionally had more energy and were emotionally more prepared to play than we were. We've got to be prepared when we're not playing our best basketball to find ways to win."

With the personnel on this year's team, the Golden Eagles should be able to do that on a consistent basis.

Despite the loss of Smith, the Golden Eagles appear to be even stronger in the frontcourt. With the addition of Kinloch, Jones and Morgan, Tech will be more physical in the post.

"We're going to be different in the frontcourt," Lebo said. "We'll have some depth and we'll have a different kind of inside player. Larrie was a finesse guy. I think we'll be able to do some finesse but we'll also be able to get some baskets with the power game."

Tech also has a dangerous perimeter game, led by point guard Gayden and shooting guard Jolly, and two big guards, and Harrell, who can create big matchup problems.

The Golden Eagles have an abundance of talent, experience, and a championship to defend. It will be difficult for anybody to wrestle that title away from them.

(D.L.)

Tennessee-Martin

LOCATION	Martin, TN
CONFERENCE	Ohio Valley
LAST SEASON	10-18 (.357)
CONFERENCE RECORD	5-11 (8th)
STARTERS LOST/RETURNING	1/4
NICKNAME	Skyhawks
COLORS	Royal Blue, Orange & White
HOMECOURT	Skyhawk Arena (6,700)
COACH	Bret Campbell (Valdosta State '83)
RECORD AT SCHOOL	20-37 (2 years)
CAREER RECORD	20-37 (2 years)
ASSISTANTS	David James (Harding '90)
	Tommy Tormohlen (Berry '93)
	Trent Becker (Buena Vista '95)
TEAM WINS (last 5 years)	11-7-8-10-10
RPI (last 5 years)	252-278-284-210-250
2000-01 FINISH	Lost in conference quarterfinal.

Bret Campbell isn't afraid to put a little pressure on himself and his team. In his third season as a head coach, Campbell says it's time for the Skyhawks to make a move in the Ohio Valley Conference.

"I think we've got a chance," Campbell said. "We've got seven seniors on the team. I obviously like that. They've been in our program, and I think any time you go into your third year, that's kind of a measuring stick of where you should be with your program."

After spending seven years as the top assistant at Austin Peay, Campbell was hired as the Skyhawks' coach in 1999.

His first team went 10-19 overall and finished seventh in the OVC with a 7-11 record. The Skyhawks flirted with an upset in an OVC Tournament quarterfinal before losing to eventual champion Southeast Missouri State, 76-74.

Last season, the Skyhawks faded late in the season, losing their last five OVC regular-season games, and finished eighth at 5-11. They were thumped by top-seeded Tennessee Tech, 69-58, in a tournament quarterfinal.

Campbell has an athletic, experienced frontcourt returning, but his concern is the backcourt. Can it improve enough to get Skyhawks into the upper tier of the OVC? That will be Campbell's task.

"I think the biggest key for our success will be our backcourt," Campbell said. "That's still the question mark. I think our frontcourt is as good as anybody's in the league. We've got three guys who averaged double figures in the conference that will be back in **Okechi [Egbe]**, **[Brian] Foster** and **Jeremy Sargent**, but I think the No. 1 concern will be our play out front."

Egbe, Foster and Sargent are three of the better players in the OVC. Egbe, a 6-5 junior swing player, was the OVC Freshman of the Year in 1999-2000. Last season, Egbe (13.2 ppg, 3.8 rpg) earned All-OVC honorable mention honors, starting all 28 games. He shot 48 percent from the field and was the team's top three-point shooter, making 32-of-85 (37 percent).

Campbell says Egbe, who will start at small forward, may be better than ever this season and the next.

"He's gotten bigger and stronger since the spring started," Campbell said. "It will be interesting to see how he develops. I would think by this year and his senior year, he could be one of the premier players in the league ... He is athletic and has a lot of different ways he can score."

Perhaps one of the biggest surprises in the OVC last season was Foster, a senior power forward. Foster (13.8 ppg, 4.9 rpg) was the team's leading scorer and earned the OVC's Newcomer of the Year award. He shot 52 percent from the field—ranking fourth in the OVC—but his free throw shooting (51 percent) must improve.

More impressive than his basketball talents were his intangibles. Foster, a strong, muscular player, is a battler with great instinct for basketball.

"He's got the uncanny ability around the basket to score," Campbell said. "He uses both hands very well and he understands the game extremely well. He will fight you and he's very strong inside."

Sargent, a 6-8 senior, will be the starter in the low post. He is not a big scorer, but Sargent (9.9 ppg, 7.1 rpg) is one of the better rebounders in the league. Last season, he was fifth in the OVC in rebounding, and he is the OVC's second-leading returning rebounder. He shot .579 from the field, which would have tied for second in the OVC had Sargent met the required minimum of four field goals per game to be included in league statistics.

Sargent, who led the OVC with 51 blocks (1.86 per game), is also an intimidator in the middle.

"He rebounds as well as anybody in the league and he alters a lot of shots," Campbell said. "He's just another kid who can go get rebounds, not just the ones that come to him. He's long, 6-8, and extremely bouncy."

With those three making up a solid frontcourt, 7-0 senior post **Ned Rolsma** will again be pushed into a backup role. Rolsma (3.1 ppg, 2.4 rpg) played in 25 games last season, starting three, and averaged 11.6 minutes per game.

Byron Benton, a 6-5 post player, was academically ineligible last season and again did not qualify. Benton was on the All-OVC honorable mention team two years ago when he led the team with a 14.3-point average and grabbed 4.9 rebounds per game.

All four of the Skyhawks' newcomers are guards or wings. **Joey Walker**, a 6-6 wing from Dickson, Tenn., averaged 17.2 points and 9.5 rebounds last season at Southeastern Illinois Junior College. He could also play some power forward.

"He's going to get some playing time right away," Campbell said. "He's a 6-5 wing who led [his junior college] in scoring and rebounding. He's extremely athletic. He's a smaller version of Sargent."

In the backcourt, Campbell will likely try moving a couple of players to different spots.

Michael Jackson, a 6-1 senior, split time at point guard last season with 5-9 senior **Jermi Hampton**, a scholarship running back on the Skyhawks' football team.

Jackson (7.0 ppg, 1.6 rpg, 4.0 apg) will move to shooting guard. Last season, Jackson started 20 of the 28 games and averaged 20.4 minutes.

Hampton (5.0 ppg, 1.6 rpg, 2.9 apg), who started 14 games and averaged 20.7 minutes, will also get a chance to play shooting guard. Jackson and Hampton played both guard positions at times last season.

"We kind of rotated our point guards last year because we couldn't find one with consistency," Campbell said. "I think the only thing that was consistent [with our guard play] was our inconsistency."

Brooks Smith, a junior college transfer from Snow (Utah) College, and 5-9 senior **Jair Peralta** will battle for the starting point guard job.

Smith comes from the same junior college league as Sargent and Hayden Prescott (11.3 ppg, 6.4 rpg), one of the Skyhawks key players in the frontcourt last season. Sargent also played at Snow College.

Last season, Smith averaged 10.4 points and 4.3 assists.

"[Smith] was second team all-conference in the Scenic West League," Campbell said. "That league has been pretty good to us. We got Prescott, who started for us, and Sargent, who started for us, and of course I'm hoping this kid will start for us.

"He's kind of a scoring point guard. He's a 23-year-old kid who is very heady and understands the game. He kind of gives you that John Stockton look with his deceptive quickness, and he can really shoot the ball."

Peralta, a senior, began the 1999-2000 season at Tennessee State and left at the Christmas break. He sat out last season. Peralta spent the summer playing for the Panama National team.

"He led them in scoring and assists," Campbell said.

"I think he's got a chance to be a pretty good player in this league."

One potential starter at shooting guard is 6-9 sophomore **Kenan Asceric** (3.2 ppg, 1.8 rpg), a Bosnian who played well in the second half last season. Asceric, who played in 18 games and started six last season, has great size for a perimeter player.

"He's really had a good summer," Campbell said. "I would think that [the shooting guard job] will be between Jackson and Hampton and possibly Asceric."

The two freshman signees, 6-1 **Adrian Higgs** and 6-4 **Jeremy Kelly**, will probably have to wait a year to get some quality minutes.

Higgs averaged 26.6 points last season at Greenfield (Tenn.) High School. Kelly averaged 18 points at Pleasure Ridge (Ky.) High School in Louisville.

"Kelly and Higgs are both two guards," Campbell said. "They're both athletic kids. Both were on all-state teams in their states. Having seniors, I think a lot of the playing time will fall on them."

Two players from last year's team have transferred. Jared Bledsoe, a 6-3 junior swing player, left for Moorhead (Minn.) State, an NCAA Division II school. Bledsoe (3.0 ppg, 1.4. rpg) played in 21 games last season and started three.

Robert James, a 6-3 guard and the Skyhawks' only freshman last year, left for West Plains (Mo.) Junior College. James (3.7 ppg, 0.5 rpg) played in 24 games and averaged 7.0 minutes.

2001-2002 SCHEDULE

Nov.	13-14	#Legends Classic
	19	Lipscomb
	28	Saint Mary's
Dec.	3	Bethel
	6	*Middle Tennessee
	8	Northern Arizona
	16	@Mississippi
	21-22	##Winthrop Holiday Tournament
	28	@Memphis
Jan.	3	@Murray State
	7	Berry College
	10	@Austin Peay
	12	@Tennessee State
	17	Southeast Missouri
	19	Eastern Illinois
	24	@Eastern Kentucky
	26	@Morehead State
	31	Austin Peay
Feb.	2	Murray State
	7	Tennessee State
	9	Tennessee Tech
	14	@Southeast Missouri
	16	@Eastern Illinois
	21	Morehead State
	23	Eastern Kentucky
	26	###OVC Tournament
March	2-3	####OVC Tournament

@Road Games
*Oman Arena, Jackson, TN
#Columbia, MO (vs. Missouri first round; also Air Force, Yale)
##Rock Hill, SC (vs. Winthrop first round; also South Carolina State, West Virginia State)
###First-round games at campus sites
####Kentucky International Convention Center, Louisville, KY

BLUE RIBBON ANALYSIS

BACKCOURT	C-
BENCH/DEPTH	B-
FRONTCOURT	A-
INTANGIBLES	B

When the Skyhawks lost starting point guard Andrae Betts and shooting guard Steve Sensabaugh last year, it proved to be costly. Betts didn't qualify academically and Sensabaugh decided to get a job.

With an inconsistent backcourt, the Skyhawks endured an up-and-down season that ended on a down note.

Now, Campbell is in a similar situation as last year—searching for answers in the backcourt. Not only do the Skyhawks need a point guard, they also seem to lack perimeter shooters.

Campbell thinks he has a couple of solutions in junior Smith and senior Peralta.

"I think out of those two, our point guard needs will be taken care of," Campbell said. "If that's taken care of, I think we could be pretty good."

That's because the Skyhawks are as solid in the

PAC-10

BLUE RIBBON FORECAST
1. UCLA
2. USC
3. Stanford
4. Arizona
5. Arizona State
6. Cal
7. Oregon State
8. Oregon
9. Washington State
10. Washington

TOP 40
Arizona, Stanford, UCLA and USC are ranked among the 2001-2002 Blue Ribbon Top 40. Extended profiles can be found in the Top 40 section of Blue Ribbon.

ALL-CONFERENCE TEAM
G - Jason Gardner, JR, Arizona
G - Casey Jacobsen, JR, Stanford
F - Jason Kapono, JR, UCLA
F - Sam Clancy, SR, USC
C - Dan Gadzuric, SR, UCLA

PLAYER OF THE YEAR
Casey Jacobsen, JR, Stanford

NEWCOMER OF THE YEAR
Cedric Bozeman, FR, UCLA

2000-2001 CHAMPIONS
Stanford (Regular season)

2000-2001 POSTSEASON PARTICIPANTS
Post-Season Record: 13-5 (.722)
NCAA
Arizona (National finals)
USC (Regional finals)
Stanford (Regional finals)
UCLA (Sweet 16)
Cal (First round)

TOP BACKCOURTS
1. Oregon
2. USC
3. Stanford

TOP FRONTCOURTS
1. UCLA
2. USC
3. Stanford

INSIDE THE NUMBERS
2000-2001 conference RPI: 4th (of 31)
Conference RPI (past five years): 5-5-3-6-4

DID YOU KNOW?
The Pac-10 will resume a conference tournament for the first time since 1990. The event will be staged at the Staples Center in Los Angeles, with which the Pac-10 signed a six-year contract, and will be a three-day affair featuring only the top eight finishers in the conference standings. ... The Pac-10 played a conference tournament for just four years in its original incarnation, with UCLA capturing the 1987 event and Arizona winning the next three, by an average margin of more than 21 points per game. ... The return of the Pac-10 Tournament means that teams were forced to schedule two conference games before Christmas. The exceptions are Cal and Stanford, which managed to schedule both games of their home-and-home series the first week of January. ... Stanford won its third straight Pac-10 title last season, becoming the first team other than UCLA, Arizona or Oregon State to assemble such a streak since Cal in 1958-59-60. ... The Pac-10 had five teams finish the regular season with at least 20 victories for the first time since 1939. As a result, all five were awarded berths in the NCAA Tournament, marking just the second time the conference sent half its members to the event. A Pac-10 team has reached the national championship game each of those three years, with UCLA and Arizona winning titles in 1995 and '97, respectively, and Arizona reaching the finals against Duke last spring. . ... The Pac-10 was not represented in the NIT for the first time since 1981. ... Cal senior Sean Lampley, who led the league in scoring (19.7 ppg) and became the Bears' career scoring leader, was the fourth Cal player in eight years to win Pac-10 Player-of-the-Year honors. ... Chicago was represented on the All-Pac-10 first team by three players—Lampley, Oregon's Bryan Bracey and Arizona's Michael Wright—while a fourth Chicagoan, Arizona State's Awvee Storey, was chosen honorable mention. ... Eleven Pac-10 players were selected in the two-round NBA draft, although only Arizona's Richard Jefferson and Stanford's Jason Collins went in the first round. ... Oregon will celebrate the 75th anniversary of McArthur Court with a Jan. 15 rematch against Willamette, the school it faced in the building's opening game. The Ducks beat Willamette, a Salem, Ore., school that now plays NCAA Division III ball, 38-10 on Jan. 14, 1927, but Willamette actually won the most recent meeting, beating Oregon 55-43 during the 1948-49 season. ... The best line of the off-season came from Alanna Taylor, the eight-year-old daughter of former Stanford assistant Blaine Taylor, after he accepted a five-year contract as head coach at Old Dominion. "Are we still going to beat Duke?" she asked her father.

(J.F.)

starting frontcourt as any team in the OVC with the return of Foster, Sargent, and Egbe. Campbell will need Rolsma to play up to his size because the Skyhawks are somewhat thin in numbers down low.

Campbell hopes the team's experience last year will give it the edge needed to make a move toward the top of the OVC.

"Time will tell," he said. "I think we were in a lot of games last year. I think the difference last year from the first year was we proved we could beat some of the top teams on a consistent basis. But again, we didn't show we could win on the road, and I think a lot of that can be attributed to not having a point guard."

If Smith or Peralta can fill that need, Campbell and the Skyhawks could be flying high.

(D.L.)

Arizona State

LOCATION	Tempe, AZ
CONFERENCE	Pac-10
LAST SEASON	13-16 (.448)
CONFERENCE RECORD	5-13 (t-6th)
STARTERS LOST/RETURNING	1/4
NICKNAME	Sun Devils
COLORS	Maroon & Gold
HOMECOURT	Wells Fargo Arena (14,198)
COACH	Rob Evans (New Mexico State '68)
RECORD AT SCHOOL	46-45 (3 years)
CAREER RECORD	132-126 (9 years)
ASSISTANTS	Tony Benford (Texas Tech '86)
	Russ Pennell (Pittsburg State '89)
	Dan O'Dowd (Bethany College '86)
TEAM WINS (last 5 years)	10-18-14-19-13
RPI (last 5 years)	187-63-101-62-86
2000-01 FINISH	Lost in regular-season finale.

Last spring, Arizona State made a spring trip to Australia, where the players attended an Aussie Rules football game, snorkeled at the Great Barrier Reef and climbed the Sydney Harbour Bridge.

The Sun Devils also won all five of their games on the tour, equaling the number of victories they totaled during the entire Pac-10 season a year ago. This year, they're expecting more.

ASU's performance dip from 19-13 in 2000 to 13-16 last season is not hard to explain. First of all, the Sun Devils had to adjust without conference scoring champ

Eddie House, who had taken his game to the NBA.

Then there was injury and illness, the likes of which no one could anticipate. Sophomore wing **Tanner Shell**, who might have been the team's top perimeter shooter, played a total of 12 minutes all season, shelved by back and hand injuries. And sophomore forward **Justin Allen** sat out the year after being diagnosed in September with Hodgkin's disease.

Meanwhile, the rest of the Devils' promising sophomore class progressed unevenly, never truly meshing after a misleading 8-3 non-conference effort against overmatched competition. In his fourth season at ASU, coach Rob Evans believes most of what ailed the Sun Devils will be fixed this season.

"If we stay healthy, we should have quite a bit of depth. We should have balance and be a pretty versatile basketball team," Evans said. "We'll be a better shooting team, but we also have guys who can get it to them in position to score. We've added some pieces we had to have and depending on our chemistry, we've got a chance to be a very good team."

ASU returns four starters, having lost only senior point guard **Alton Mason**, who started all 29 games and led the team in scoring (13.4 ppg) and assists (3.8 apg). Additionally, the Sun Devils have back seven other lettermen, including Allen, Shell and sophomore guard **Kenny Crandall**, who spent the last two years on a Mormon mission in Eugene, Ore.

Three newcomers include junior guard **Curtis Millage**, a junior college transfer, and freshman point guard **Jason Braxton**, both of whom will compete for starting jobs.

In all, the Sun Devils will field a squad with a promising mix of experience and new blood, and enough bodies to perhaps approach the game somewhat differently on occasion.

"We haven't been able to play the way I'd like to, not at all, because we haven't had the numbers or guys with versatility," Evans said. "I'd like to think we've got it now. We like to trap but we haven't been able to because we couldn't afford to foul.

"Now we can do some things to try to create turnovers, and transform that into wins."

The buzz in Tempe is that the club's best player may wind up being someone who was not a full-time starter last year. Junior **Tommy Smith** (9.3 ppg, 4.5 rpg, 1.0 spg, .568 FG, .615 FT) started just nine games last season and averaged barely 19 minutes per outing. His biggest obstacle: 120 personal fouls and 10 games in which he fouled out.

At 6-9, Smith can play either forward position and is ready to blossom, Evans thinks.

"I think people are going to be surprised by Tommy," Evans said. "He can be one of the better players in the league this year. He has really extended range on his shot and he's got his confidence up."

Smith played his best ball late last season, averaging 12.0 points and 5.5 rebounds and shooting 66 percent over the final six games.

Smith, who also toured Greece on a summer all-star team, said the international experience he gained will contribute in a big way this season.

"Basically, I'll be at the beginning of the season where everyone else will be in February. It puts me ahead of everyone in conditioning and gives me more experience," Smith told ESPN.com. "This will be a breakthrough season for me."

Evans expects Smith's development to be so profound he could wrestle the starting power forward spot away from 6-6, 221-pound senior **Awvee Storey** (13.1 ppg, 9.1 rpg, .498 FG, .602 FT), who led the Pac-10 in rebounding and posted 11 double-doubles.

"Both guys can play either spot," Evans said. "Awvee's going to give you 15-to-18-foot range and we want to take advantage of his abilities, which are attacking the basket, rebounding and defending. The biggest thing with Awvee is he played too many minutes (26.5 per game). When you play on athletic ability, the more minutes you play, the slower you get."

Also back at forward is 6-7 junior **Sean Redhage** (8.1 ppg, 4.2 rpg, .404 FG, .816 FT), who started 24 games and had 19-point outbursts against Tulsa and Charlotte. However, Redhage averaged just 4.2 points over the final eight games of the season, and finished the season coming off the bench.

The likely starter at the small forward spot is 6-7 junior **Donnell Knight** (9.8 ppg, 4.6 rpg, 2.1 apg, .415 FG, .306 3PT, .684 FT), who started 25 games last season (most of them out of position at shooting guard) and scored in double figures 18 times. Knight is a slasher with good quickness who scored a season-high 21 points against Southern Utah, but has been up and down his first two seasons.

"He's worked hard and gotten better. He's still got half his career ahead of him, and it's time for him to step to the plate," Evans said.

Behind Knight is Shell, who demonstrated on the Australian tour that he's over his hand and back injuries of a year ago. The 6-6 sophomore, who averaged 9.1 points in Pac-10 play as a freshman two years ago and had 24 points in a game at USC, made seven three-pointers Down Under.

Evans said Shell's return is critical for a team that ranked last in the Pac-10 in three-point accuracy last season at .295.

"He brings a lot to the table for us," Evans said.

The starting center will again be 6-9, 241-pound senior **Chad Prewitt** (10.1 ppg, 4.9 rpg, .481 FG, .351 3PT, .637 FT), regarded as a strong passer and post defender. Prewitt scored 23 points against Charlotte and 20 against BYU, and had a 15-point, 11-rebound performance against Kent State.

"I expect to get more scoring out of Chad," Evans said. "He was injured a lot last year and wasn't in the greatest condition. He's moving well now, and he can really shoot the basketball."

Junior **Chris Osborne**, a 6-9, 240-pound junior college transfer, will provide depth at both center and power forward. Osborne originally signed with ASU in the fall of 1998, but spent the last two years at Compton College in Los Angeles.

Also available at center is 7-foot junior **Tyson Johnston** (1.4 ppg, 1.5 rpg, .390 FG, .238 FT), who two years ago transferred from Utah. Johnston considered leaving the ASU program in the off-season, and now is playing as a non-scholarship walk-on.

With Knight moving back to small forward, the Sun Devils will send a new starting backcourt onto the floor. There are plenty of candidates, led by newcomers Millage and Braxton.

Millage is a 6-3 shooting guard who earned California Junior College Player-of-the-Year honors last season at L.A. Southwest Junior College.

"He can score and he can shoot the basketball," Evans said. "The aspect of his game that can help us most is he can create his own shot. He is very energetic and competitive, and that can be very contagious, especially with younger players."

Braxton, a 6-3 point guard from Canyon Springs High School in Moreno Valley, Calif., was a Top 100 recruit last season.

"Jason is very athletic, quick and fast," Evans said. "He can push the ball under control and makes great decisions. It's difficult to teach things he can do. He gets the ball to people when they can do something with it."

Junior **Kyle Dodd** (4.8 ppg, 2.2 rpg, 2.1 apg, .368 FG, .321 3PT, .710 FT) returns as a contender for the point guard spot. At 6-0, 165 pounds, Dodd still relies more on guile than strength, but he has become stronger.

"His experience is really going to help him and he understands that we're looking for," said Evans, alluding to the fact that Dodd turned the ball over just once every 23.5 minutes last season.

Sophomore **Jonathan Howard** (2.6 ppg, .360 FG, .217 3PT, .400 FT), at 6-4, saw action at both the point and shooting guard on the Australian trip. He doesn't make many mistakes, but does not shoot well and lacks great explosiveness.

Back from his Mormon mission, 6-4 sophomore Crandall brings maturity and shooting ability. He averaged 5.9 points and started 23 games as a freshman in 1998-99, and added 25 pounds of muscle during his two years away.

"I thin it'll take him a while to adjust," Evans said, "but a guy who can shoot the ball can shoot the ball. He doesn't have to come in here and play 30 minutes a game."

The team's most welcome returnee is Allen, the 6-7 sophomore whose future was in doubt when he contracted Hodgkin's disease, the same form of cancer that afflicted NHL star Mario Lemieux. Allen's weight temporarily dropped 40 pounds from 230 during six months of chemotherapy, a program that was followed by radiation treatment.

Allen said from the beginning he expected to return to the team, and last spring he joined the Sun Devils in Australia, averaging 8.3 points and leading the club with 11 three-pointers in five games. As a freshman, Allen averaged 2.1 points.

"It surprised me how well he did in Australia," Evans said. "It really means a lot to him to battle back the way he did, and it meant a lot to all of us. He'd come to practice last year and I'd know he was dead tired, but I'd say, 'How you doin' Justin?' and he said, 'I'm doing fine.' I knew he wasn't. He just wanted to be treated the same as everybody else.

"I don't know exactly what Justin was going through, but I have a good idea. He is an inspiration, not only to us, but to everybody around the country. I'm always talking to the players about the fact that they're going to face adversity in their lives, but with Justin it's right there in front of your eyes."

Rounding out the backcourt are three walk-ons, including 6-4 senior **Brad Nahra** (2.4 ppg, 1.1 rpg). Junior **Jonathan Bray**, who played 12 minutes last season, and junior **Brandon Goldman** will contribute during practice.

2001-2002 SCHEDULE

Nov.	17	Stephen F. Austin
	20	Portland State
	24	@BYU
	27	UC Riverside
Dec.	4	*Utah
	13	Montana State
	20	@Oregon
	22	@Oregon State
	28-29	#ASU Holiday Classic
Jan.	4	Oregon State
	6	Oregon
	10	@Washington
	12	@Washington State
	17	UCLA
	19	Southern Cal
	23	Arizona
	31	@Stanford
Feb.	2	@California
	7	Washington State
	9	Washington
	14	@Southern Cal
	16	@UCLA
	20	@Arizona
	28	California
March	2	Stanford
	7-9	##Pac-10 Tournament

@Road Games
*America West Arena, Phoenix
#Tempe, AZ (vs. Canisius, first round; also Louisiana-Lafayette, Northwestern)
##Staples Center, Los Angeles

BLUE RIBBON ANALYSIS

BACKCOURT	B-
BENCH/DEPTH	A-
FRONTCOURT	B
INTANGIBLES	B-

The Sun Devils believe they have remedied many of their glaring problems from a year ago. They expect to shoot the ball much better and improved depth should allow them to survive fouls and play the aggressive style of defense they favor.

It's an intriguing team with a lot of parts, many of them interchangeable. But the Sun Devils must show they can put it together after losing nine Pac-10 games by double-digit margins.

"Our biggest concerns are staying healthy and getting these guys to play better defensively," Evans said. "I think we'll be a good rebounding team and if our point guard play is as solid as I think it can be in time, we've got a chance."

A chance for the NCAA Tournament? Evans believes so.

"Every year we expect to be an NCAA team," he said. "If we do the things we need to, I think we can be."

Don't count the Sun Devils out.

(J.F.)

California

LOCATION	Berkeley, CA
CONFERENCE	Pac-10
LAST SEASON	20-11 (.645)
CONFERENCE RECORD	11-7 (t-4th)
STARTERS LOST/RETURNING	1/4
NICKNAME	Golden Bears
COLORS	Blue & Gold
HOMECOURT	Haas Pavilion (12,172)
COACH	Ben Braun (Wisconsin '75)
RECORD AT SCHOOL	95-61 (5 years)
CAREER RECORD	280-193 (16 years)
ASSISTANTS	Louis Reynaud (San Francisco St. '82)

Jon Wheeler (California '87)
Joe Pasternack (Indiana '99)
TEAM WINS (last 5 years)   23-12-22-18-20
RPI (last 5 years)   15-124-38-68-35
2000-01 FINISH   Lost in NCAA first round.

The hard reality is that the most significant day of Cal's 2001-02 basketball season may have been Aug. 30—2 1/2 months before the start of the Golden Bears' season. That's when the NCAA turned down an appeal by Cal on the initial eligibility of incoming star freshman forward **Julian Sensley**.

Sensley is a 6-8, 230-pound native of Kailua, Hawaii, who spent the last two years at St. Thomas More School in Oakdale, Conn., polishing his basketball and academic skills. There is no doubting his hoops acumen. Sensley has been rated among the top half-dozen forward prospects in the nation.

He averaged 21 points and nine rebounds last season on a team with six college-bound prospects, and led St. Thomas More to a 59-7 record and a pair of championships in the tough New England Prep School League.

Said UCLA coach Steve Lavin of Sensley and Cal's other big-name frontcourt recruit, center **Jamal Sampson**, "If they have Sensley and Sampson healthy, and those guys play to their ability, they're a potential monster. They're two of the top 10 [incoming] frontline players in the entire country."

But academics are difficult for Sensley, who has a diagnosed learning disability. Cal coach Ben Braun said Sensley compiled a grade-point average of better than 2.5 at St. Thomas More, but test-taking has been a problem. Sensley did not have the required SAT score to be fully academically qualified.

Cal—hoping that Sensley might help fill the void of graduated senior Sean Lampley, the reigning Pac-10 Player of the Year and the school's career scoring leader—filed an appeal to the NCAA on the basis of Sensley's learning disability. The NCAA said no.

Sensley responded to the NCAA's decision by vowing to continue pursuing his eligibilty for this season. He planned to file a personal appeal to the NCAA which, if approved, could make him eligible to play after the conclusion of the fall semester at Cal. In that case, Sensley would be allowed to make his debut Dec. 21 when the Bears play at home against Mount St. Mary's.

"My goal is to pursue all avenues available to me to become eligible and be at Cal," Sensley said on the day the NCAA announced its decision.

"Julian has not wavered on his commitment to Cal and he intends to pursue his options to become a full qualifier," Braun said.

There was some precedent for optimism. Cal junior guard Donte Smith faced a similar scenario three years ago when the NCAA turned down his initial eligibility appeal. Smith won a second appeal and has gone on to become a very capable student at Berkeley.

Sensley's loss for the season would be a significant blow to the Bears. He committed to Cal in the summer of 1999, before leaving for prep school, and is regarded as a player able to dominate from the perimeter or near the basket. Without much argument, he was the highest-rated recruit Braun has landed for Cal.

The Bears lost the best player Braun has developed at Cal when Lampley graduated and was selected in the second round of the NBA draft by his hometown Chicago Bulls. The 6-7 Lampley, a talented but erratic player early in his career, was superb as a senior, averaging a league-leading 19.5 points along with 7.2 rebounds and 3.3 assists to power the Bears to a 20-11 record and their first NCAA Tournament appearance since Braun's debut season in 1997.

"Sean was kind of a luxury," Braun said, "because you always knew you had a go-to guy. I think we'll find a way to replace his points. The question mark will be how do you replace his experience and his leadership. Those are the two areas I'm concerned about."

Even without Sensley, the Bears have plenty of personnel options.

Lampley was the only significant player lost from last year's squad, and the Bears feature seven juniors and seniors with extensive experience among their scholarship players.

The most obvious choice as the club's leader is 5-10 junior point guard **Shantay Legans** (9.5 ppg, 2.7 rpg, 4.8 apg, 1.4 spg, 30.0 minutes, .429 FG, .382 3PT, .785 FT). Legans is an excellent shooter whom the Bears will encourage to shoot more, and a selfless playmaker. Braun wants to see Legans become a more aggressive player.

"Shantay has got to lead our team, and that's got to start on the defensive end," Braun said. "I think he can increase ball pressure—I think he was a little conserva-

tive last year. His theme right now would be aggressiveness on both ends."

Junior **Brian Wethers** (8.5 ppg, 2.3 rpg, 21.5 minutes, .517 FG, .439 3PT, .727 FT) figures to maintain the shooting-guard assignment after starting 23 times last season. The 6-5 Wethers has shown flashes of great potential, such as when he erupted for a career-high 27 points against Arizona State last year. What he needs is confidence he can do it on a nightly basis.

"Brian is probably our most explosive player, and there are so many ways he can be effective for our team," Braun said. "He's made big improvements on his jump shot and his range, and that sets up his drive. I'd like to see Brian be more aggressive on the boards for us.

"When you have Sean Lampley on your team, other players naturally aren't as aggressive as they could be. With Brian, it's a combination of confidence and settling into a role."

On the other wing, the Bears will go with 6-5 senior **Ryan Forehan-Kelly** (7.2 ppg, 2.7 rpg, 26.2 minutes, .464 FG, .418 3PT, .784 FT), a steady, well-rounded player. A one-time walk-on, Forehan-Kelly scored 18 points against Arizona State, notched 17 against Yale and had 16-point performances against UCLA, Arizona and Albany.

"He's probably our most solid player," Braun said. "Whether he starts or comes off the bench, I'm not concerned. He'll be the same player, either way. He's very dependable."

The most versatile of Cal's remaining wing players is 6-5 junior **Joe Shipp** (8.4 ppg, 2.8 rpg, 23.8 minutes, .440 FG, .315 3PT, .700 FT), who has played shooting guard and small forward. Shipp's perimeter shooting accuracy slipped a bit last year, and it's important he continues to work on taking the ball to the basket as a counter to his outside shot.

"Joe worked hard this summer and he's the kind of guy who can give you some versatility," Braun said. "The only thing missing is what the Stanford guys ended up doing well. When [Ryan] Mendez and [Casey] Jacobsen started putting it down, their three-point shot become a weapon. It's something Joe has to prove, because they jam him."

Also available at shooting guard is fiery 6-3 senior **Dennis Gates** (3.4 ppg, 0.9 rpg, 11.3 minutes, .366 FG, .293 3PT, .903 FT), an erratic shooter but an aggressive defender.

"Through his leadership and tenacity, he's been one of our most aggressive players," Braun said. "That's something our team can follow. His shot selection was much better last year, and it's not like Dennis can't shoot. He just wants to put his mark in there. It's a matter of not forcing things."

The Bears also expect a boost from 6-7 freshman wing **Erik Bond**, who averaged 20.8 points, 7.5 rebounds and 2.5 assists last season at Seattle Prep High School. Bond, a 46-percent shooter from three-point range, has a 37-inch vertical leap and placed second in the Washington state track meet, scaling 6-8 in the high jump. He was MVP of the Washington state tournament as a junior, averaging 22.5 points in the postseason as Seattle Prep won the state crown. His dad, Jay Bond, was a 6-10 center at Washington in the late 1960s, and his older brothers played at Gonzaga and St. Mary's College.

"The great thing about Erik is he's a winner and a tremendous team guy," Braun said.

Back as a walk-on guard is 6-3 sophomore **Ronnie West** (0.4 ppg), the half-brother of former Cal great Kevin Johnson, who saw action in 12 games last season. Freshman **Tayshaun Forehan-Kelly**, a 6-3 guard, will join his big brother on the roster as a walk-on.

Backing Legans at the point will be Smith, a 6-2 junior, or 5-10 sophomore walk-on **A.J. Diggs**.

Smith (2.4 ppg, 9.1 minutes, .362 FG, .233 -PT, .800 FT) is a former Washington D.C. Prep Player of the Year who has yet to get comfortable in the college game. He shows brief glimpses of his potential, but often plays without much confidence and has not shot well.

"I really believe Donte has capabilities to help our team," Braun said. "If Donte is an aggressive player, he can help us. It's something he's going to have to prove."

Diggs (1.2 ppg, 7.8 minutes, .500 FG, .684 FT) got playing time when Smith struggled and provided a defensive catalyst with his hustling quickness.

"He became a sparkplug for us," Braun said.

The likely absence of Sensley leaves a hole up front that Braun might decide to fill by going with two true post players. Certainly one of the starters will be 6-11 senior **Solomon Hughes** (8.2 ppg, 4.0 rpg, 1.0 bpg, 18.3 minutes, .629 FG, .426 FT), who made marked improvement last season and has improved both his strength

and stamina.

"The best thing that can happen is Solomon will have people breathing down his neck," Braun said. "He's going to be challenged, and I think that will push him."

The primary challenge will come from Sampson, the 6-11, 225-pound cousin of former Virginia All-America and NBA All-Star Ralph Sampson. Sampson averaged 15.5 points, 10.0 rebounds and 2.4 blocks last year at Mater Dei High School in Santa Ana, Calif., teaming with UCLA freshman Cedric Bozeman to lift the club to a 33-2 record, the California large-school state title and a No. 4 final national ranking by USA Today.

Sampson, the first Parade magazine All-America player signed by Braun, was rated the No. 15 prospect overall in the nation by FoxSports.com and the No. 26 prospect by The Sporting News.

"Jamal is such a presence on the court," Braun said. "He's going to alter your game from a defensive standpoint because he can block shots, and offensively he's a legitimate threat on the block and he can step out to the high post."

Sampson underwent surgery in July to remove bone spurs in his ankle that prevented him from practicing much between games his senior season. He was expected to be fully recovered well in advance of the start of practice.

UCLA's Lavin, who watched Sampson developed as a high schooler and tried recruiting him to Westwood, believes the Bears got a good one.

"Jamal Sampson is as talented a player as has come into our league in a long time," Lavin said. "What's unique is he enjoys passing the ball, making his teammates better. His basketball IQ is pretty exceptional. He's been living in the shadow of Tyson Chandler, but longterm, if he stays healthy and his work ethic and attitude are in line, he has a chance to be as good as anybody in the country in his class for that position."

The Bears also will need a contribution from 6-10 sophomore **Gabriel Hughes**, Solomon's younger brother. As a freshman last season, Hughes (0.4 ppg, 0.6 rpg) played just 53 minutes spread over 19 games. But he has a natural assertiveness on the floor the Bears hope to harness.

The Bears anxiously were awaiting final word on the eligibility status of 6-11, 250-pound freshman **Amit Tamir**, a native of Israel who committed during the summer. Tamir played last year on an Israeli professional team and, despite the fact that Braun said he was not paid anything more than allowable expenses, a new NCAA crackdown on foreign professionals may sideline him.

The Bears also welcome back 6-6 walk-on power forward **Conor Famulener** (0.6 ppg, 0.3 rpg), who saw action in 10 games last season.

Gone after one forgettable season is 6-11 forward Saulius Kuzminskas, who scored a total of six points as a freshman and decided to return to his native Lithuania to play professionally.

2001-2002 SCHEDULE

Nov.	15-16	#BCA Classic
	20	Santa Clara
	28	New Mexico
Dec.	1	@South Florida
	6	Saint Louis
	11	Fresno State
	21	Mount Saint Mary's
	28-29	##Golden Bear Classic
Jan.	4	@Stanford
	6	Stanford
	10	@Oregon
	12	@Oregon State
	17	Washington
	19	Washington State
	24	@Southern Cal
	26	@UCLA
	31	Arizona
Feb.	2	Arizona State
	7	Oregon State
	9	Oregon
	14	@Washington State
	16	@Washington
	21	UCLA
	23	Southern Cal
	28	@Arizona State
March	2	@Arizona
	7-9	###Pac-10 Tournament

@Road Games
#Berkeley, CA (vs. Princeton, first round; also Eastern Washington and St. Joseph's)
##Berkeley, CA (vs. Harvard, first round; also Coppin

State and Penn State)
###Staples Center, Los Angeles

BLUE RIBBON ANALYSIS

BACKCOURT	B
BENCH/DEPTH	B-
FRONTCOURT	C+
INTANGIBLES	B-

Cal is a team with lots of experience and perimeter depth, but also lots of questions. Will the Bears ever see Sensley in a Cal uniform? Is there enough depth in the frontcourt? Can a leader emerge in the wake of Lampley's departure? Are there go-to players ready to step forward?

"I like our potential," Braun said before the NCAA's ruling on Sensley. "There are some question marks we're going to have to answer [including] can we step up collectively? Is there a steady place we're going to get points? We'd like to establish that consistency. We want aggressiveness to be out there this year."

Sensley might have helped answer a few of those questions, certainly providing a potential go-to scorer. Now that assignment likely falls in the laps of players such as Legans, Wethers and Hughes, who didn't need to carry a heavy load last year, when Lampley led the team in scoring 23 times. Now they assume prime-time roles.

If Sampson emerges quickly and meshes well with Hughes, and the Bears' perimeter players show maturity, the Bears might be able to battle for an NCAA Tournament bid. Without question, however, there is more guesswork to this team now.

(J.F.)

 **Oregon**

LOCATION	Eugene, OR
CONFERENCE	Pac-10
LAST SEASON	14-14 (.500)
CONFERENCE RECORD	5-13 (t-6th)
STARTERS LOST/RETURNING	2/3
NICKNAME	Ducks
COLORS	Green & Yellow
HOMECOURT	McArthur Court (9,087)
COACH	Ernie Kent (Oregon '77)
RECORD AT SCHOOL	68-49 (4 years)
CAREER RECORD	158-129 (10 years)
ASSISTANTS	Greg Graham (Oregon '78)
	Scott Duncan (College of Wooster '78)
	Fred Litzenberger (Northern Colorado '68)
TEAM WINS (last 5 years)	17-13-19-22-14
RPI (last 5 years)	61-108-36-29-110
2000-01 FINISH	Won regular-season finale.

Two for seven. That's what Ernie Kent needs from his big men. The equivalent of a .286 batting average, and he'll be content. Huh? Just listen up.

"I think we have one of the most experienced perimeter games in the conference and maybe even on the West Coast," Kent said. "The key to our season will be **Freddie Jones** having a great year ... and if two of our seven big guys can emerge and be steady for us, we have a chance to be a surprise team. With that, we can battle with the best teams."

Two for seven. That's all Kent asks. The Ducks' roster will feature three returning big men and four newcomers standing between 6-8 and 7-feet. If two of them deliver, Kent believes his club will improve on its 5-13 record in Pac-10 play last year.

"That's our key, right there," Kent said. "I know it will happen. The key is when it will happen."

While he awaits the development of his interior game, Kent will rely on a perimeter group that should excel from the start.

Jones, a senior, has started 59 games in his Oregon career and has the fabled NBA body. Point guard **Luke Ridnour** was the Pac-10 Freshman of the Year last season, and wing **Luke Jackson** joined him on the league's all-freshman squad.

Senior **Anthony Lever** officially changed his name from Norwood to honor his biological father, former NBA standout Lafayette Lever, and returns with great long-range shooting and open-court skills. And the Ducks expect sophomore **James Davis** to evolve into a dangerous three-point threat.

At 6-4 and 209 pounds, Jones (14.8 ppg, 5.6 rpg, 3.4 apg, 1.1 spg, 31.9 minutes, .472 FG, .306 3PT, .806 FT)

seemingly has few limits. Kent's first great in-state recruit, the Gresham, Ore., native scored in double figures 20 times last season and, at times, can be a dominant player. Kent wants to see that much more often.

"The biggest thing I expect out of him is consistency," Kent said. "He doesn't need to explode, he just needs to be consistent and score in the 16-to 20-point range. He can't have two great games and then not show up for a game. He needs to be a guy who, night-in and night-out, we can count on."

Kent saw a welcome change in Jones' approach to workouts, even in the off-season.

"He's had his most productive spring and summer," Kent said. "A lot of it has been his understanding of the work ethic you have to have on a day-to-day basis."

Ridnour (7.4 ppg, 3.8 apg, 2.5 rpg, 1.0 spg, 30.3 minutes, .339 FG, .293 3PT, .792 FT) started all 28 games last season and gave the Ducks a remarkably steady floor leader for a rookie. The 6-2 sophomore had a 1.6-to-1 assist-to-turnover ratio, and had a superb game with a career-high 17 points, seven rebounds and three steals in a 79-67 upset of No. 7 Arizona at McArthur Court.

Ridnour had 15 points and five assists in a win at Louisville, and eight assists and no turnovers in a near-upset of USC. Kent, who acknowledges Ridnour may have become physically worn down late in the year, expects improvement in two primary areas.

"He's got a different body on him—he's bigger and stronger—and I think you're going to see a very effective, confident basketball player," Kent said. "We want him to shoot the ball and be able to feel he has the green light to shoot it anytime."

The 6-7 sophomore Jackson (7.8 ppg, 4.1 rpg, 2.0 apg, 18.1 minutes, .424 FG, .360 3PT, .740 FT) showed the range in his game when he recorded Oregon's first triple-double in 28 years, collecting 14 points, 11 rebounds and 10 assists in a win at Washington.

"That says a lot about his game. He's a versatile guy," said Kent, who believes he can use a much stronger Jackson at virtually any position except center. "In the two Lukes, what you see are two eager players who can't wait for the start of the season because of what they know now."

The 6-3 Lever (9.9 ppg, 2.0 rpg, 2.1 apg, 25.8 minutes, .386 FG, .354 3PT, .794 FT) is "probably the best shooter on the team," said Kent, who wants to see more consistency.

The Ducks were 10-1 last year when Lever shot at least 50 percent from the field.

"When his shooting went down, that's when we struggled," Kent said. "He has to shoot that ball for us, particularly in transition."

At 5-10, Davis (3.9 ppg, 0.6 rpg, 9.1 minutes, .306 FG, .317 3Pt, .750 FT) was touted last year as potentially one of the great shooters ever to come to Oregon. He struggled in the transition to college ball, hitting three three-pointers in each of three games, but a total of just 11 the rest of the season.

"He's still a great shooter ... it's just the intensity, size, strength, the defense ... learning all that stuff," Kent said. "The biggest thing is if he jump-starts his confidence by coming in ready to go. He's certainly a huge part of [our] arsenal just because he can shoot the ball so well."

The remaining backcourt veteran is 6-4 senior **Ben Lindquist** (3.5 ppg, 1.1 rpg, 12.7 minutes, .403 FG, .381 3PT, .850 FT), a steady player who turned the ball over just 17 times in 26 games last season.

"He understands our system very well," Kent said, "and has made himself a much better defender."

Joining the club as a walk-on freshman is 6-4, 230-pound wing **Marcus Kent**, the coach's son who missed most of his senior season at Eugene's Churchill High because of a knee injury.

The Ducks' most experienced big man—and the Pac-10's biggest player—is 7-2, 280-pound senior center **Chris Christoffersen** (3.3 ppg, 2.5 rpg, 9.0 minutes, .403 FG, .429 FT). A native of Denmark, Christoffersen has played 58 games for the Ducks and expects a quantum leap in performance after attending the Pete Newell Big Man Camp over the summer.

"He can run the floor with our forwards and he should cause some problems for someone to match up with," Kent said. "His biggest thing is to stay out of foul trouble. [Christoffersen had one foul every 3.75 minutes last season]. Offensively, he's starting to become a presence."

Senior **Mark Michaelis** (1.2 ppg, 0.7 rpg, 4.2 minutes in 12 games) is a 6-10 forward who began his career at BYU. He actually scored 14 points for the Cougars in a loss to Oregon three years ago.

The Ducks' other returning interior player is 6-9 sophomore center Jay Anderson (1.8 ppg, 0.9 rpg, 5.2 minutes in 21 games), who has good mid-range shooting

ability.

Kent hopes to get immediate help from a couple of his frontcourt newcomers. Junior **Robert Johnson** is a 6-8, 235-pound power forward who averaged 12 points and 14 rebounds last season for a Santa Rosa (Calif.) Junior College team that posted a 29-3 record.

"He has that Dennis Rodman mentality of going to get the ball. I like that part of his game," Kent said.

Johnson is not a great shooter, but is a capable passer.

Another junior college transfer is 6-9, 285-pound junior center **Brian Helquist**, who averaged 14.7 points and 8.8 rebounds at Florida Community College in Jacksonville. Helquist began his career at LSU, but transferred after red-shirting as a freshman.

"He's a big low-post presence who plays physical basketball," Kent said. "He can score and he's an excellent defender in the low block."

Oregon could get an international boost from **Ian Crosswhite**, a 6-11, 225-pound freshman forward from Sydney, Australia who is considered one of his country's most promising young prospects. He was a member of Australia's 21-under national team last summer until ankle surgery sidelined him.

"He's got perimeter skills—he can pass, shoot and he's crafty with the ball," said Kent, who played against Crosswhite's father, Perry, when the Aussie national team toured the U.S. in 1975 and played against the Ducks at Mac Court.

Freshman **Matt Short** is a 7-foot, 220-pounder who averaged 16 points as a senior at Yreka High in the upper reaches of Northern California. Short was rated the fifth-best center prospect on the West Coast by PacWest Hoops.

Kent said Short could possibly be red-shirted as a freshman.

Depending on how quickly the new big men adjust, Jackson could be shifted into the power-forward slot, giving the Ducks a smaller, quicker lineup. But Kent would prefer a more traditional setup, which would match up better defensively against most Pac-10 opponents.

Defense is a concern for Kent after last year when Oregon ranked fourth in the conference in scoring (78.1 ppg) but last in scoring defense (77.3). Oregon also was a mediocre rebounding team, highlighting the need for improved interior play.

Kent also added assistant Fred Litzenberger from the Oregon women's staff. He has a strong defensive background and worked with Kent on the staff at Colorado State some years back.

2001-2002 SCHEDULE

Nov.	15	*Alabama State
	16	*Western Michigan
	17	*Long Beach State
	24	**Louisville
	27	***Massachusetts
Dec.	2	@Portland
	10	@Minnesota
	14	Pepperdine
	16	Northern Arizona
	20	Arizona State
	22	Arizona
	27	Morris Brown
Jan.	4	@Arizona
	6	@Arizona State
	10	California
	12	Stanford
	15	Williamette
	19	@Oregon State
	24	@Washington
	26	@Washington State
	31	UCLA
Feb.	2	Southern Cal
	7	@Stanford
	9	@California
	16	Oregon State
	21	Washington State
	23	Washington
	28	@Southern Cal
March	2	UCLA
	7-9	#Pac-10 Tournament.

@Road Games
*America's Youth Classic, Eugene, OR
**Rose Garden, Portland, OR
***Springfield Civic Center, Springfield, MA
#Staples Center, Los Angeles

BLUE RIBBON ANALYSIS

BACKCOURT	A-

BENCH/DEPTH	B-
FRONTCOURT	C
INTANGIBLES	B-

Kent spent several weeks last summer on the coaching staff of the USA 21-under team that won a gold medal in international competition in Japan. He came away with a warm feeling about representing his country and with some new ideas, picked up from his fellow coaches and rival teams.

What he really could have used was some experienced, productive frontcourt help. Oregon's backcourt is quite good and has a chance to be excellent. If the two Lukes make progress as sophomores, the Ducks should feel very good about their perimeter.

How well the team competes in the Pac-10, however, is more likely to be dictated by its frontcourt performance. To be blunt, the Ducks have no big man in their program who has demonstrated he can produce at this level.

Maybe it will happen, but there is no track record.

The Ducks must play better defense and must rebound better to make a step toward cracking the upper division in the Pac-10. Sounds like an imposing assignment, but Kent believes it requires nothing more than a two-for-seven effort from his big guys.

(J.F.)

Oregon State

LOCATION	Corvillas, OR
CONFERENCE	Pac-10
LAST SEASON	10-20 (.333)
CONFERENCE RECORD	4-14 (t-9th)
STARTERS LOST/RETURNING	3/2
NICKNAME	Beavers
COLORS	Orange & Black
HOMECOURT	Gill Coliseum (10,400)
COACH	Ritchie McKay (Seattle Pacific '87)
RECORD AT SCHOOL	10-20 (1 year)
CAREER RECORD	72-72 (5 years)
ASSISTANTS	Brad Soucie (Christian Heritage '92)
	Scott Didrickson (Washington '95)
	Lance Richardson (Samford '96)
TEAM WINS (last 5 years)	7-13-13-13-10
RPI (last 5 years)	190-180-130-139-163
2000-01 FINISH	Lost in regular-season finale.

Perhaps no one associated with Oregon State basketball is more excited about the program's improved depth than the Beavers' three assistant coaches. With the club's roster reduced to as few as seven healthy players at times last season, the coaching staff was forced to suit up to help meet practice needs.

"I have never seen anything like the setbacks this team experienced last season," second-year head coach Ritchie McKay said.

It was a season that began with high hopes and expectations, and quickly disintegrated. Although the Beavers hadn't enjoyed a winning season since Gary Payton was a senior in 1989-90, the return of four starters and the arrival of a new coach and potential star power forward prompted optimism.

Even Blue Ribbon envisioned good things, picking the Beavers fifth in the Pac-10 and No. 40 in its national rankings.

Injuries, suspensions and plain old bad chemistry plagued Oregon State. Junior college transfer **Philip Ricci**, a would-be star at power forward, underwent arthroscopic knee surgery before the season and never played a game. And his injury was merely the start of a virtual epidemic.

Forward **Brian Jackson** suffered through an unexpectedly rough sophomore season, senior point guard Deaundra Tanner was erratic and even suspended for one weekend, and senior shooting guard Josh Steinthal converted just 33 percent from three-point range.

"I really think our team was a trendy pick last year," McKay said. "The bottom line: we had bad chemistry and the buttons I pushed didn't work."

Far from seeing the glass half-empty, McKay is more enthused than ever about this team. Center Jason Heide, who enjoyed a productive senior season, is among four players who have departed, but an infusion of young, talented newcomers should gave OSU new life.

"I like this team," McKay said. "We're much more committed, and if we can get some confidence early, I think we can make a little bit of noise."

Three starters return, including the backcourt duo of sophomore point guard **Jimmie Haywood** and senior shooting guard **Adam Masten**. The 6-2 Haywood (8.9 ppg, 2.8 rpg, 1.8 apg, .453 FG, .352 3-PT, .767 FT) is a hybrid guard who still is getting comfortable at the point. But he improved his shooting from 36 percent as a freshman and started 14 games last season after figuring out what his coach wanted.

"Jimmie was out of the rotation in early January because of his lack of submitting to the role I wanted him to have," McKay said. "If Jimmie takes good shots, he can be one of the best guards in this league, and I mean that. He's quick, he can shoot, he can get to the rim, and he's been one of our hardest workers."

Masten (8.4 ppg, 4.5 rpg, 3.0 apg, .519 FG, .421 3-PT, .726 FT) started all 30 games last season. The 6-5, 200-pounder improved his shooting accuracy from 38 percent the year before and doubled his scoring average and minutes played. His assist-to-turnover ratio of 1.84-to-1 was fifth best in the Pac-10.

"He's really kind of our glue," McKay said. "He started being a better leader at the end of last year. If he can guard the Jacobsens and the Kaponos of the world—not shut them down but at least be a presence—he really can be a complete guard."

Four newcomers add great versatility in the backcourt. Foremost among them is a name familiar to OSU fans.

Brandon Payton—half-brother to the former Pac-10 Player of the Year—is ready to go after sitting out last season as a transfer from UC Santa Barbara. The 6-0 senior, who averaged 8.9 points in three seasons with the Gauchos, can play either guard position and already has proven to be a vocal leader.

"He's the key to our success," McKay said. "He's the best guard we had in practice all last year, hands down. Brandon gives us the ability to play in transition, he's an excellent decision-maker and can score. He gives us commitment and confidence. His confidence is going to make us a better team."

Three freshmen guards will all get the chance to play from day one. McKay has called 6-footer **Joe See** the team's point guard of the future. See averaged 18 points, five assists and shot 60 percent last year for two-time California state finalist De La Salle High School, the alma mater of Payton and another ex-OSU star, Brent Barry.

"See's a great shooter who doesn't get credit for how quick he is," said McKay, who compared him to former Georgia Tech star Mark Price. "He's been coached as well as any kid in America at De La Salle and his four-year record is 110-11."

J.S. Nash averaged 32 points last season at Rancho Verde High School, his second straight season as the top scorer in Southern California's Riverside County. At 6-2, Nash is regarded as a superb shooter and smart player.

Floyd North III, a 6-5 wing player from suburban San Diego, averaged 23.6 points and 9.2 rebounds as a senior at St. Augustine High School. North became just the fifth player in San Diego County history to score more than 2,000 career points.

Rounding out the backcourt is 5-8 junior **Mike Cokley** (2.0 ppg, .450 FG), who started 12 games last season when the Beavers were strapped for personnel. His playing time is likely to greatly diminish this season.

The frontcourt should be improved with the much-awaited arrival of Ricci, a 6-7, 252-pound forward, who two seasons ago averaged 25 points and 10 rebounds at San Joaquin Delta Junior College in California.

"He is the best big man I have ever coached, period," McKay said. "He's got power and he's explosively athletic. He's unselfish, but still competitive. I don't want to say he's the franchise because he still hasn't done it at the Pac-10 level, but he can have the same impact as Brian Scalabrine at USC or Michael Wright at Arizona."

The other key piece to the puzzle up front is Jackson, the 6-9 junior who averaged 12.5 points and 5.1 rebounds during an encouraging freshman season, then slipped to 9.7 points and 4.2 rebounds a year ago. At the heart of his problems: 110 fouls and 11 disqualifications.

"When he gets into foul trouble, the aggressiveness he starts out with changes because he wants to stay in the game," McKay said.

Videotape study showed Jackson had trouble maintaining proper balance, so during the summer he enrolled in yoga and karate classes to help remedy the problem.

"Brian looks so much better, the difference has been amazing," McKay said.

The Beavers also recruited 6-9 sophomore forward **Jarman Sample**, who averaged 11.1 points and 7.9 rebounds as a freshman at Colby Community College in

Kansas. Another long-term prospect at forward is 6-7 freshman walk-on **David Lucas**, the son of former NBA strongman guard Maurice Lucas.

Red-shirt freshman center **Derek Potter**, a 6-11, 217-pounder from Vancouver, B.C., is available after breaking a toe and sitting out last season. **Chris Manker** (1.6 ppg, 2.0 rpg, .286 FG) is a 6-11 sophomore forward/center who will see limited action.

2001-2002 SCHEDULE

Nov.	17	Northern Colorado
	22-24	#Great Alaska Shootout
	26	San Diego
	30	Southern Utah
Dec.	12	@Portland State
	15	@Cal Poly
	20	Arizona
	22	Arizona State
	27	Indiana-Purdue Fort Wayne
	31	Lehigh
Jan.	4	@Arizona State
	6	@Arizona
	10	Stanford
	12	California
	19	Oregon
	24	@Washington State
	26	@Washington
	31	Southern Cal
Feb.	2	UCLA
	7	@California
	9	@Stanford
	16	@Oregon
	18	Portland
	21	Washington
	23	Washington State
	28	@UCLA
March	2	@Southern Cal
	7-9	##Pac-10 Tournament

@Road Games
#Anchorage, AK (vs. Texas, first round; also Alaska-Anchorage, Gonzaga, Indiana, Marquette, St. John's, Tennessee)
##Staples Center, Los Angeles.

BLUE RIBBON ANALYSIS

BACKCOURT	B-
BENCH/DEPTH	B-
FRONTCOURT	B
INTANGIBLES	C

The first battle the Beavers must win is with themselves.

"We have to shed the negativity that has grown around this program since the last winning season (1990)," McKay said.

He saw signs of that happening during off-season workouts, but knows a good start to the season at the Great Alaska Shootout will create confidence that can have a lasting effect.

A year ago, OSU lost six games by four points or fewer.

"That's the difference between 10-20 and 16-14, even with the problems we had," McKay said.

McKay expects some of those problems to be resolved. The Beavers ranked last in the Pac-10 in rebounding margin at minus-5.8 per game and shot just 33 percent from three-point range. Personnel changes should benefit both areas.

The center spot is very shaky, so don't be surprised if McKay utilizes Ricci and Jackson as the two post players and surrounds them with a three-guard set. That will allow him to play more of the up-tempo style that he prefers.

The Beavers may not be a trendy pick this year, but they ought to be better.

(J.F.)

Washington

LOCATION	Seattle, WA
CONFERENCE	Pac-10
LAST SEASON	10-20 (.333)
CONFERENCE RECORD	4-14 (t-9th)
STARTERS LOST/RETURNING	3/2
NICKNAME	Huskies
COLORS	Purple & Gold

HOMECOURT	Edmundson Pavilion (10,000)	
COACH	Bob Bender (Duke '80)	
RECORD AT SCHOOL	105-124 (8 years)	
CAREER RECORD	165-181 (12 years)	
ASSISTANTS	Byron Boudreaux (Tulsa '87)	
	Eric Hughes (Cal State Hayward '89)	
	Al Hairston (Washington '72)	
TEAM WINS (last 5 years)	17-20-17-10-10	
RPI (last 5 years)	84-35-33-164-154	
2000-01 FINISH	Won regular-season finale.	

Coach Ben Bender feels as though he's been down this road before at Washington.

"Even in rebuilding things the first two years (1994 and '95), we were in this same position," said Bender, whose squad is coming off back-to-back 10-20 seasons. "We felt very confident we were getting better. But at the same time, so was the league."

But this time there's a twist. A new coach is greeted by a honeymoon period when any progress earns a pat on the back. After all, he's fixing someone else's mess.

Now, in his ninth season, Bender must start the Huskies back toward the level they maintained from 1996 through '99, when they averaged 18 victories and twice reached the NCAA Tournament.

"We've had two losing seasons and we've got to get back to winning basketball games," he said. "Our veterans have that sense of urgency and we certainly need to get the new kids coming in to have that same sense of urgency."

The good news for Husky fans is that the club's talent level is higher, and there is more of it. Washington returns two starters, two other veterans who should secure starting assignments and a home grown red-shirt in **Doug Wrenn**, who likely will be the Huskies' top player.

In addition, Bender brought in three scholarship freshmen, a junior college transfer and two walk-ons he believes can make an impact.

No question about it, the Huskies will have a different look to them.

"This is by far the most talented roster we've ever had," Bender said. "We have a lot of inexperience and question marks as far as how we'll put it together. But we have athletic ability, ability to score in different ways and run the floor and create mismatches."

And better depth, with at least two potentially capable bodies at virtually every position.

"When you go into a season with questions about who's going to be on the floor, one thing that will get you those answers more quickly is competition," Bender said.

The most-anticipated of the new arrivals is Wrenn, a 6-6 sophomore forward who made his name as a Parade magazine All-American at O'Dea High School in Seattle four years ago, even briefly offering the Huskies a commitment.

He changed his mind, attended a year of prep school in the East, then enrolled at the University of Connecticut. Those Huskies weren't a good fit, so Wrenn returned home and spent last season as a transfer red-shirt.

Bender's biggest concern is that Wrenn might try to make up for lost time in the season opener against Alaska Fairbanks at the Top of the World Classic. "You know he's going to try to make up for basically two years in the first 20 minutes," Bender said. "We just don't want him to get frustrated."

Wrenn was a pleasant surprise for the coaching staff even last season, while only practicing with the team.

"I thought [his effort] would be a little inconsistent," Bender said, "but he competed on a daily basis, playing with a purpose."

Bender said Wrenn arrived early for practice, improved his perimeter shooting and became a role model for his teammates.

"Every day he would bring a high energy level to practice," Bender said. "He's doing everything that you ask of him."

Joining Wrenn in the lineup are two returning starters—6-11 senior center **David Dixon** and 6-0 sophomore point guard **Curtis Allen**.

Dixon (4.7 ppg, 3.2 rpg, .574 FG, .367 FT) is in his third year at UW, and Bender believes he's finally ready to blossom. Excessive weight limited Dixon's endurance and mobility the last two years, but he trimmed down to the 270-pound range over the summer.

"With players, the light comes on at different times. For David, I think, everything's coming together," Bender said. "He knows what the league is all about, knows what we need from him. It's not that sort of thing where he's thinking, 'I hope I can.' He really knows he can produce for us on a consistent basis."

That will be critical because the program's only other center is 6-10 senior **Marlon Shelton** (4.2 ppg, 3.8 rpg, .362 FG, .5514 FT), who tore his ACL in the team's second-to-last game back on March 8. The son of former Oregon State star and NBA standout Lonnie Shelton, Shelton spent the off-season rehabbing and was expected to be ready for practice in October.

Allen (7.0 ppg, 2.0 rpg, 2.2 apg, .388 FG, .247 3-PT, .767 FT) earned a spot on the Pac-10 All-Freshman team. He made two big shots at Oregon last season, the first to force overtime, the second to win the game.

"Curtis from Day One assimilated into the point guard role and prospered in it," Bender said. "We want him to utilize his quickness and make better decisions. When you have that kind of quickness and the chance to break a defense down, how do you know when to turn those things on and off?"

Allen likely will be paired in the backcourt with fellow sophomore **C.J. Massingale** (5.9 ppg, 1.5 rpg, .388 FG, .425 3-PT, .629 FT), who saw action at both guard spots last year. The coaching staff initially envisioned Massingale, 6-3, as a point guard and Allen on the wing, but quickly decided the two should flip-flop those roles.

Massingale had a breakout game with 25 points at UCLA, and had 18 points and three steals at Oregon.

"C.J. has a real understanding of what we want to do," Bender said. "He picked up motion offense off the ball great. He's good at using screens and is in constant motion, finding ways to get open. Now his shooting percentage must go up."

Junior college transfer **Josh Barnard**, a 6-6 wing from Tacoma (Wash.) Community College, should compete for significant playing time. Barnard made 99 three-point shots last season, averaging 17.3 points.

"He certainly has the ability to stretch the defense and we have got to make more efficient use of the three-point line," Bender said. "But he doesn't have solely a shooter's mentality. If people start flying at him, he's more than capable of shot-faking and finding somebody else open."

Bender also has high hopes for instant contribution from 6-6 freshman guard **Erroll Knight**, who averaged 19.6 points and 7.0 rebounds last season at Chief Stealth High School in Seattle.

"Knight's got a lion's heart," Bender said. "He competes every time on the floor. Defensively, intensity-wise, he doesn't have any adjustments to make."

Sophomore walk-on **Sterling Brown** (1.5 ppg, 0.7 rpg) completes the wing corps.

Two walk-ons are likely to provide depth at the point. **Will Conroy** is a 6-footer from Garfield High School in Seattle who helped lead his team to a 27-2 record and a No. 1 ranking in the state for much of the season. **Charles Frederick** is also a 6-foot freshman who comes to Washington on a football scholarship from Boca Raton, Fla. Frederick, a top-50 recruit in both sports, will play wide receiver for the football team fall, likely joining the basketball team in January.

The power forward spot will feature a battle between senior team captain **Grant Leep** and freshman **Mike Jensen**.

At 6-7, 220 pounds, Leep (3.1 ppg, 1.8 rpg, .384 FG, .643 FT) is probably better suited for small forward, but he will move closer to the basket, where the Huskies need an experienced man. He'll be pushed by the 6-8, 210-pound Jensen, who once dunked over Tyson Chandler but whose senior season at Kentwood High School in suburban Seattle was cut short when he was convicted for his involvement in a shoplifting incident.

Jensen, rated the No. 66 prospect in the nation by The Sporting News, was not personally involved in stealing beer from a convenience market, but drove the vehicle occupied by a number of his Kentwood teammates.

"Mike's a very good person who made a mistake," Bender said. "He accepted it and handled the punishment without any excuse."

Freshmen **Jeffrey Day**, a 6-9, 215-pounder from Seattle Prep, and **Anthony Washington**, a 6-9, 200-pound teammate of Conroy's at Garfield, both provide depth at the power forward position. Depending on Shelton's health, both could also see some time backing up Dixon.

2001-2002 SCHEDULE

Nov.	15-18	#Top of the World Classic
	24	Santa Clara
	28	UNLV
Dec.	1	@San Diego
	6	@Texas-El Paso
	8	@New Mexico State
	11	Gonzaga
	20	UCLA
	27	Southern Cal
	29	@Saint Louis
Jan.	4	@UCLA
	6	*Southern Cal
	10	Arizona State
	12	Arizona
	17	@California
	19	@Stanford
	24	Oregon
	26	Oregon State
	31	@Washington State
Feb.	7	@Arizona
	9	@Arizona State
	14	Stanford
	16	California
	21	@Oregon State
	23	@Oregon
	28	Washington State
March	7-9	###Pac-10 Tournament

@Road Games
*The Forum, Los Angeles
#Fairbanks, AK (vs. Alaska Fairbanks, first round; also Bowling Green, Butler, Delaware, Ole Miss, Radford, Wichita State)
##Staples Center, Los Angeles

BLUE RIBBON ANALYSIS

BACKCOURT	B-
BENCH/DEPTH	C+
FRONTCOURT	C
INTANGIBLES	C

Three Huskies in particular will be closely scrutinized this season. Can Wrenn live up to the hype that has followed him since his beginnings in Seattle? Can Dixon become the player the Huskies have long awaited?

Will Jensen make fans remember him for his exploits on the court, rather than in the courtroom?

At the same time, Bender and his program will be watched as they try to turn things around after back-to-back 10-win seasons. Without a doubt, there is more talent here than in recent seasons, but much of it is young or inexperienced at the Division I level.

Fitting together the pieces will require some deft handling by Bender.

"We've put ourselves in a position as a coaching staff where we've got to push and certainly demand, but we also have to be patient," Bender said. "We have a great deal of teaching to do, but we also have to demand consistency. It's a fine line."

If the Huskies can keep their balance on that line, they may just turn the corner and build for the future. But this year is unlikely to be much more than just that—a step in the right direction.

(J.F.)

 # Washington State

LOCATION	Pullman, WA
CONFERENCE	Pac-10
LAST SEASON	12-16 (.429)
CONFERENCE RECORD	5-13 (t-6th)
STARTERS LOST/RETURNING	0/5
NICKNAME	Cougars
COLORS	Crimson & Gray
HOMECOURT	Friel Court (12,085)
COACH	Paul Graham (North Texas '74)
RECORD AT SCHOOL	18-38 (2 years)
CAREER RECORD	18-38 (2 years)
ASSISTANTS	Randall Dickey (Ouachita Baptist '83)
	Gary Stewart (La Verne '84)
	Chris Croft (Southern Mississippi '95)
TEAM WINS (last 5 years)	13-10-10-6-12
RPI (last 5 years)	144-184-137-225-165
2000-01 FINISH	Lost in regular-season finale.

Paul Graham is willing to be patient, but don't call him wishy-washy. In his second year last season, the Cougars coach drew a line in the sand and got the attention of his players. Now he hopes WSU is ready to continue its march toward respectability.

Late on the evening of Jan. 19, Graham received a phone call in his Eugene, Ore., hotel room, informing him that a half-dozen of his players had slipped out of their rooms and were enjoying the nightlife at a local western bar.

Graham went back to sleep, but the next morning,

after getting verification of those involved, greeted his team at a morning shoot-around with a surprise announcement. All six had immediate plane flights home and would be suspended from that night's game against Oregon for violation of team curfew rules.

Among those sent home was starting senior forward Eddie Miller and Graham's sophomore son, **Nick Graham**. The Cougars, predictably, lost to the Ducks that night.

Back home on Sunday, Graham sat down with the guilty parties to discuss further sanctions. It was agreed the players would do extra running before rejoining the team. It was agreed by all, except for Miller, who was promptly dismissed from the team.

Graham believes the incident may serve the Cougars well over the long haul.

"Guys understood if we're going to have a basketball program that represents the university, we're going to try to do it right," Graham said. "What those guys did was wrong, and we punished them for it. That makes guys understand coach is committed to doing what is right."

The lesson may have sunk in sooner than Graham expected. Oregon and Oregon State visited Pullman four weeks later, and WSU pulled off a sweep, its first against the Oregon schools in four years.

In fact, the Cougars made significant strides on most fronts last season, starting with the bottom line. From 6-22 the year before, they improved to 12-16, doubling their win total. They claimed 10 victories on their home floor, rallied from 17 points down on the road to beat Arizona State in the biggest comeback of the Pac-10 season, and wound up in a tie for sixth place for their highest conference finish in six years.

"The first year was tough," Graham said. "Last year we made a big improvement with our team. If we can make as big a step on the ladder as we did the second year, then we can be a pretty good basketball team. It's difficult because we live in an impatient society, and we're in a tough league."

WSU's greatest strength this season will be its backcourt, which should eventually consist of a pair of talented 6-6 athletes in sophomore **Marcus Moore** at the point and senior **Mike Bush** at shooting guard. The Cougars will have to wait for football season to end before getting back Bush, who will play wide receiver in the fall.

Bush (15.9 ppg, 5.2 rpg, .399 FG, .333 3-PT, .703 FT) missed the first semester of last season, too, sidelined by academic shortcomings. He wound up earning honorable mention All-Pac-10 honors.

"Mike's going to play football, and I don't have a problem with that," Graham said. "The way Mike plays, we know what he's going to give us—leadership and toughness. He missed the while preseason last year and the first game back he played 30-plus minutes and scored 29 points."

Moore (10.4 ppg, 3.6 rpg, 3.6 apg, .376 FG, .299 3-PT, .754 FT) flourished as a freshman after sitting out the previous year to put his classroom work in order. He won a spot on the Pac-10's All-Freshman team and created matchup problems for smaller point guards.

"Marcus is not the prototype point guard who is 6-foot, 6-1," Graham said. "Marcus is 6-6, also he's left-handed. He's very clever with the basketball ... drives me nuts sometimes. Early in the season he really struggled, but once he got going and began to understand what you need to do, he was a good point guard."

If Moore can improve his erratic perimeter shooting, Graham suggested, "He's got a chance to be really good."

Would-be senior shooting guard David Adams, who started 17 games last season, surprised the coaching staff when he decided to transfer. Guard Kendall Minor also transferred.

But there are plenty of choices in the backcourt. While Bush is playing football, fans will get a good look at returning 6-2 junior **Jerry McNair** and 6-6 newcomer **Justin Lyman**. McNair (9.4 ppg, 1.7 rpg, .467 FG, .396 FT, .581 FT) turned heads in a game at Stanford when he scored 29 points and helped the Cougars to a nine-point lead they couldn't hold.

"McNair's a tough kid who will compete," Graham said. "Once he got going against Stanford, he did very, very well every night out. Jerry's a little thin, but he's very quick and he's got great range on his jump shot."

Lyman red-shirted last season at Blinn (Texas) Junior College, the year after averaging 21 points and shooting 44 percent from three-point range. Originally a signee with Houston and coach Clyde Drexler, Lyman comes to WSU with two years of eligibility.

"Justin is an outstanding shooter," Graham said. "He is very athletic and has good size."

Freshman **Thomas Kelati**, a 6-6 wing from Walla

Walla, Wash., likely will see limited action early.

Graham's son will try to earn the backup point guard job. The younger Graham (0.6 ppg in 12 games) has been limited by an ankle injury his first season, then chest pains last year. Likewise, the Cougars are looking for a bigger contribution from combo guard **E.J. Harris**, a 6-1 sophomore who played just one game last year before suffering a stress fracture in his leg.

The front line is experienced, but somewhat limited and not quite as deep as the backcourt group. The anchor is 6-10, 235-pound senior center **J Locklier** (9.5 ppg, 6.1 rpg, .455 FG, .692 FT), who won Pac-10 Newcomer-of-the-Year honors last season.

"He's tough, physical and plays his butt off every night," Graham said. "He's not a great offensive player, but he gets you eight [points] and eight [rebounds] every night and defends those other big guys. All he's got to do is show he can score down there and that will help our perimeter game."

Junior **Milton Riley** (5.3 ppg, 3.5 rpg, .510 FG, .648 FT) returns as a willing but undersized (6-9, 197) power forward. His lack of muscle caused him to collect 99 personal fouls and foul out of nine games last season.

"He's one of the best athletes on the team, but he's not a physical player and he's just got to stay out of foul trouble," Graham said. "What he can do is he's a very good offensive rebounder because he's so quick to the bucket."

The fifth returning starter would have been 6-4 senior small forward Framecio Little (7.0 ppg, 4.6 rpg, .475 FG, .692 FT), but he is academically ineligible for the fall semester.

If he is able to return in December, Little should benefit from playing at his more natural position after being forced to man the power forward spot at times last year. "He's tough and competitive and just makes us a better basketball team," Graham said.

WSU also hopes to get an immediate lift from 6-8, 225-pound freshman forward **Shaminder Gill**, who averaged 24 points and 14 rebounds last year at Philip Pocock High School in Toronto, Ontario. Gill was rated the country's top prep big man by Hoops Canada.

The Cougars' final newcomer is 6-11, 220-pound junior **Pawel Stasiak**, a native of Poland who played the last two seasons at Cloud County Community College in Kansas. Graham called him a typical European big man, with good shooting range and strong ball skills. Stasiak had seriously considered going to South Carolina before coach Eddie Fogler resigned last February.

The Cougars added two wing players to their roster just as school began in the fall.

Cedrick Hughey, a 6-6, 195-pound sophomore guard from Westark (Ark.) College and Chris Schlatter, a 6-7, 190-pound sophomore guard from St. Mary's of California, both transferred to WSU.

Hughey, who is eligible to play this season, averaged 13 points and six rebounds last season after scoring 20 points per game as an all-state selection at Waldo High School in Waldo, Ark. Little's forced absence should give Hughey an immediate opportunity to find a place in the rotation.

Schlatter, who will sit out as a transfer this season, averaged 8.0 points and 2.9 rebounds last season as a freshman at St. Mary's. He started 17 games, scored in double figures 11 times and had a season-high 17 points against Gonzaga. Schlatter comes to WSU as a nonscholarship walkon.

Walk-on senior **Justin Murray**, a 6-4 forward, rounds out the roster.

2001-2002 SCHEDULE

Nov.	20	*Colorado State
	24	Prairie View A&M
	28	Montana-Missoula
Dec.	1	Arkansas-Pine Bluff
	4	Idaho
	7	Texas-Pan American
	10	@Texas
	15	@Gonzaga
	22	UCLA
	29	Southern Cal
Jan.	4	**Southern Cal
	6	@UCLA
	10	Arizona
	12	Arizona State
	17	@Stanford
	19	@California
	24	Oregon State
	26	Oregon
	31	Washington
Feb.	7	@Arizona State
	9	@Arizona
	14	California
	16	Stanford
	21	@Oregon
	23	@Oregon State
	28	@Washington
March	2	Centenary
	7-9	#Pac-10 Tournament

@Road Games
* Spokane, WA
** The Forum, Los Angeles
#Staples Center, Los Angeles

BLUE RIBBON ANALYSIS

BACKCOURT	B
BENCH/DEPTH	C
FRONTCOURT	C
INTANGIBLES	C+

Step by step, Graham is rebuilding the Cougars' program. It's not an easy job. Recruiting to Pullman, Wash., is a challenge, and the rest of the Pac-10 has elevated play in recent years, as well.

"We went from finishing last in a great league to finishing sixth," Graham said. "I'm really encouraged."

But big questions remain with the Cougars.

"I think we proved our guards are pretty good," Graham said. "We've got to be able to rebound and defend people inside. Sometimes it seemed like we needed an act of Congress to score inside.

"We're not there yet, and we've got a hell of a long way to go. But we're working at it."

(J.F.)

 **American**

LOCATION	Washington, DC
CONFERENCE	Patriot
LAST SEASON	7-20 (.259)
CONFERENCE RECORD	3-13 (9th CAA)
STARTERS LOST/RETURNING	3/2
NICKNAME	Eagles
COLORS	AU Red & Blue
HOMECOURT	Bender Arena (4,500)
COACH	Jeff Jones (Virginia '82)
RECORD AT SCHOOL	7-20 (1 year)
CAREER RECORD	153-124 (9 years)
ASSISTANTS	Kelvin Jefferson (Southern Connecticut State '95)
	Ryan Odom (Hampden-Sydney '96)
	Kieran Donohue (Virginia '97)
TEAM WINS (last 5 years)	11-9-7-11-7
RPI (last 5 years)	194-192-280-231-256
2000-01 FINISH	Won regular-season finale.

Despite winning only seven games last year in the Colonial Athletic Association, American coach Jeff Jones believes his team can have success as the newest member of the Patriot League.

"I feel very strongly that we can achieve a high level on the basketball court in the years to come," Jones said. "We are going to have a challenging road ahead, but with attention to details, this can get turned around and American will become one of the beacons of the Patriot League."

What else would you expect of Jones? From his days as a star point guard at the University of Virginia, Jones has been a winner. And he was a successful head coach, serving eight seasons at his alma mater. Jones was also an assistant at Rhode Island before becoming American's 17th head coach in April of 2000.

"When you have a league that is as balanced and competitive as the Patriot League, your team has to be focused each time it takes the floor," Jones said. "There is never a break on the schedule, and especially in our case being the new kid on the block, teams are going to be keyed up to play us."

Five players are back from last season, and a lot of newcomers dot the roster. There is also a new coach on Jones' staff—Kelvin Jefferson, who was previously at the University of Vermont.

"We are excited to have Kelvin join our staff," Jones said. "He brings a tireless work ethic, and has a great background in recruiting the Northeast. He will be a valuable member of our staff."

The key returnee for American is 6-9 center/forward **Patrick Doctor** (16.1 ppg, 7.3 rpg, 1.4 apg), a senior who was selected to the league's preseason all-conference team. He was a All-CAA second team selection last season and will be counted on to lead the Eagles in scoring and rebounding.

Also returning in the frontcourt are 6-6 senior **Vladimir Buscaglia** (9.3 ppg, 3.4 rpg, 1.6 apg), 6-8 senior **Keith Gray** (6.3 ppg, 6.2 rpg, 0.4 apg) and 6-8 senior **Brian Williams** (5.3 ppg, 3.0 rpg, 1.0 apg).

Buscaglia played in 21 games last year after transferring from Wabash Valley Community College in Mount Carmel, Ill. Gray played in 27 games last year, getting nine starts. Williams will provide depth in the middle.

The only other returnee is 6-0 junior guard **Demek Adams** (2.2 ppg, 1.6 rpg, 2.0 apg), a product of Carroll High School in Washington, D.C.

Expected to start at point guard is newcomer **Glenn Stokes**, a 5-9 junior who averaged 9.7 points and 4.1 assists last year at Tallahassee (Fla.) Community College. A 24-year-old product of Silver Spring, Md., Stokes was chosen to the All-Panhandle Conference first team.

"Glenn does a lot of good things on the court," Jones said. "The greatest ability that he will bring to the program, though, is his ability to lead. He is a very mature player and has great court awareness."

At Einstein High in Silver Spring, Stokes averaged 16 points, eight assists and 3.5 steals his senior season.

Another newcomer could become an outstanding player in the Patriot League. **Steven Miles**, a 6-4 junior guard, begins his first season with the program after transferring from Coastal Carolina, where he was the Big South Conference Rookie of the Year in 1999-2000. He averaged 9.1 points and 5.0 rebounds at Coastal Carolina.

Also expecting to see playing time in the backcourt are **Corey Tabron** and **Andres Rodriguez**. Tabron, a 6-4 junior, averaged 12.6 points last year in leading Hagerstown (Md.) Community College to the NJCAA regions.

"The first thing that jumps out about Corey is his ability to shoot the basketball," Jones said. "He is a solid all-around player, but his perimeter shooting skills will fill a void."

Rodriguez, a 6-0 sophomore from Louisville, will be eligible at the conclusion of the fall semester.

The frontcourt is also full of new faces, including 6-10 senior center **Joe Casper**, 6-7 junior forward **Nick Boyd**, 6-9 freshman forward **Matej Cresnik** and 6-7 freshman forward **Patrick Okpwae**.

Casper joins the program from Rhode Island after sitting out last season. He will add depth in the frontcourt. His averages two years ago at Rhode Island were 0.6 points, 1.0 rebounds and 0.8 assists.

Boyd comes to American from Essex Community College in Newark, N.J. He will bring athleticism to the frontcourt.

Cresnik comes from the Univerza V Ljubljani in Slovenia, where he studied for the last year.

"Matej really knows how to play the game," Jones said. "He has been extremely well coached, and is very smart and tough. He will be able to blend in immediately and help us from day one."

Okpwae comes from The Berkshire School in Homestad, Fla. The program went 16-2 and was ranked No. 5 nationally by ESPN last year.

"No. 1, Patrick is a tremendous young man with a refreshing outlook on life," Jones said. "As a basketball player, Patrick is raw, but has exceptional athletic ability. He has the potential to be an outstanding player in the Patriot League."

2001-2002 SCHEDULE

Nov.	17	@Maryland
	20	@St. Francis (Pa.)
	24	Fairleigh Dickinson
	28	College of Charleston
Dec.	1	Pennsylvania
	4	@Radford
	7	@North Carolina A&T
	10	@Howard
	20	@Vanderbilt
	22	@Florida State
	29	Wagner
Jan.	2	Liberty
	5	Fairfield
	9	@Colgate
	12	Army
	16	Lafayette
	19	Bucknell
	23	@Lehigh
	26	@Holy Cross
	30	Navy

PATRIOT

BLUE RIBBON FORECAST

1. Holy Cross
2. Navy
3. Colgate
4. Lehigh
5. Bucknell
6. American
7. Lafayette
8. Army

ALL-CONFERENCE TEAM

G - Bryan Bailey, SR, Bucknell
G - Chris Spatola, SR, Army
F - Pat Campolieta, SR, Colgate
F - Tim Szatko, JR, Holy Cross
C - Patrick Doctor, SR, America

PLAYER OF THE YEAR

Tim Szatko, JR, Holy Cross

NEWCOMER OF THE YEAR

Steven Miles, JR, American

2001-2002 CONFERENCE TOURNAMENT

March 2-3, The Show Place Arena, Upper Marlboro, MD
March 8, Championship game at homecourt of highest-seeded team

2000-2001 CHAMPIONS

Holy Cross (Regular season)
Holy Cross (Conference tournament)

2000-2001 POSTSEASON PARTICIPANTS

Postseason Record: 0-1 (.000)
NCAA
Holy Cross

TOP BACKCOURTS

1. Holy Cross
2. Navy
3. Bucknell

Feb.	2	Colgate
	6	@Army
	9	@Lafayette
	13	@Bucknell
	16	Lehigh
	20	@Navy
	23	Holy Cross
March	2,3, 8	#Patriot League Tournament

@Road Games
#Show Place Arena, Upper Marlboro, MD

BLUE RIBBON ANALYSIS

BACKCOURT	B
BENCH/DEPTH	C
FRONTCOURT	B
INTANGIBLES	B-

The Patriot League Council of Presidents voted unanimously last spring to formally accept American University as the league's eighth full member. The American Eagles will begin competing this fall in a full league schedule in 18 sports.

"We are proud to join the outstanding institutions of the Patriot League as their new colleague and athletics competitor," AU President Benjamin Ladner said. "American University supports the goals of the league in striving to achieve the very best of what higher education offers with both academic and athletic excellence."

So how will American compete?

The Patriot League coaches and sports information directors think the Eagles will be OK. In the preseason poll, American was picked to finish sixth in the league, ahead of Lafayette and Army.

Still, it will be difficult for American to win more than

TOP FRONTCOURTS

1. Holy Cross
2. Colgate
3. American

INSIDE THE NUMBERS

2000-2001 Conference RPI: 23rd (of 31)
Conference RPI (last five years): 28-27-23-25-23

DID YOU KNOW?

Six Patriot League games will be broadcast nationally this year, including the second Army-Navy game on Feb. 23. CBS will do the honors. ESPN will be on hand for the Jan. 7 Wake Forest at Navy game and the league's tournament championship game March 8 at the homecourt of the highest-seeded team. ... Army's Spatola brothers (senior Chris and sophomore J.P.) are believed to be the first siblings in Division I history to win a league's weekly honors on the same week. On Jan. 29, 2001, Chris was chosen the Patriot's Player of the Week, and J.P. its Rookie of the Week. ... Holy Cross coach Ralph Willard has guided three teams into postseason tournaments. Before the Crusaders' NCAA Tournament trip last season, Willard had taken Western Kentucky to the NCAAs and the NIT and Pittsburgh to the NIT. Likewise, Don DeVoe has coached postseason teams at Navy (NCAA), Tennessee (NCAA and NIT) and Virginia Tech (NIT). American's Jeff Jones previously led Virginia to five NCAA appearances and one trip to the NIT. ... DeVoe is the winningest active coach in the PL. He needs 11 wins to reach the 500 mark for his career. ... Bucknell is the only team to reach the double-figure victory mark in each of the Patriot's 11 seasons. ... Last season, for the second time in three years, Colgate placed two players on the Patriot's All-Rookie team and one of them was chosen's the league's top newcomer. That honor went to guard Mark Linebaugh. He was joined on the all-rookie team by center Howard Blue.

(S.C.)

the seven games it won last year in the Colonial Athletic Association. The schedule includes road games at Maryland, Vanderbilt, Florida State, Radford and North Carolina AT&T. Non-conference home games are against College of Charleston, Pennsylvania, Fairfield, Fairleigh Dickinson, Liberty and Wagner.

For a roster that feature only five returnees, Jones will have a tough time molding the old with the new.

(S.C.)

Army

LOCATION	West Point, NY
CONFERENCE	Patriot
LAST SEASON	9-19 (.322)
CONFERENCE RECORD	3-9 (7th)
STARTERS LOST/RETURNING	0/5
NICKNAME	Black Knights, Cadets
COLORS	Black, Gold & Gray
HOMECOURT	Christl Arena (5,043)
COACH	Pat Harris (USMA '79)
RECORD AT SCHOOL	30-80 (4 years)
CAREER RECORD	30-80 (4 years)
ASSISTANTS	Robert Brickey (Duke '90)
	Denny Carroll (Dayton '71)
	Marty Coyne (USMA '92)
TEAM WINS (last 5 years)	10-8-8-5-9
RPI (last 5 years)	290-285-290-307-291
2000-01 FINISH	Lost in regular-season finale.

Pat Harris remembers how it feels to be part of a winning basketball program at Army. He did it years ago with

Mike Krzyzewski when the Duke coach was coaching the Black Knights.

During his undergraduate days at the Academy, Harris helped lead Coach K's team to a 19-9 record in 1977-78 and a berth in the National Invitation Tournament. Harris, a point guard, was also a member of the last Army team to win 20 games in a season (1976-77).

Now, Harris wants that feeling again after winning only 31 games in his first five years as head coach at West Point.

"I know a lot of people may be upset with me when I say this, but I really felt as though when I was here that we were the pride of West Point," Harris said. "We were a very, very popular team because I think we embodied the values of the Academy.

"It was a great opportunity for me to be part of an outstanding family. Still today we get together—every year six or seven of us go down to the Duke basketball camp. It was a great experience to be part of that program."

That same experience is what Harris wants to instill in his young players. He will stress that this year to a group that has a chance to succeed because 17-of-19 players who played last year are back, including five starters.

"All of our players have at least one year together under their belts," Harris said. "They are starting to gel and have a better understanding of what it takes to be a competitive and better basketball team.

"We want to continue instilling the 'Army attitude' in our players. That means diving for the loose ball, hustling for 40 minutes and taking the charge if the opportunity presents itself. It also includes communication, trust and a 100 percent commitment every time you take the floor. Those are the ingredients that you need to build a successful program."

In order for the Cadets to be successful this season, Harris will look to the position he played—guard. And he has a couple of good ones in brothers Chris and J.P. Spatola, one of three sets of brother combinations to start for the same team in Division I last year.

"A lot of people think we have the best returning backcourt in the Patriot League," Harris said. "I would certainly say we have 'one of the best.'

"That's a legitimate assessment. When Chris shoots the ball, you think it's going in every time. And J.P. is a true leader who is becoming more and more aware of his role as an extension of the coach on the floor."

Chris Spatola, a 6-1 senior voted second-team All-Patriot League last year, led the Black Knights in scoring (18.5), three-point field goals (149) and free-throw shooting (.898). He ranked among the national leaders in free throw shooting (seventh) and scoring (62nd).

J.P. Spatola, a 6-0 sophomore, led Army in assists (3.42 per game) while ranking fourth on the team in scoring (7.8). He also grabbed 2.8 rebounds per game as the team's point guard.

Also looking for playing time in the backcourt will be 6-1 senior **Joe Quinn** (2.9 ppg), 5-8 senior **Jerry Crockett** (0.4 ppg), 5-9 junior **Ray Frederick** (1.1 ppg), 6-2 junior **Mike Canty** (2.1 ppg), 6-3 sophomore **Andy Smith** (4.6 ppg), 6-4 sophomore **Andy Pawling** (1.0 ppg), 6-4 sophomore **Sean O'Keefe** (0.0 ppg) and 6-1 freshman **Joey Payton** from Ft. Leavenworth, Kan.

Harris calls Smith "the best shooter in our program." He will back up Chris Spatola at off-guard. He shot .468 from beyond the arc last year, leading the league in that category. Quinn can play either guard position and Harris brings versatility to the backcourt. Crockett is a respected off-court leader with a strong work ethic.

"With so much competition for playing time, players will need to know their roles," Harris said. "For some, it might be coming to practice and pushing the others. That's what makes a team better. Joe brings a wealth of experience to the team while Jerry is greatly respected by the rest of our players."

Canty started 26 games as a freshman but moved into a reserve role last year. Fredrick gives the Black Knights quickness at point guard while O'Keefe and Pawling saw limited time last year. Payton, a freshman, can play either guard position. Harris likes his athleticism and defensive intensity.

"We have depth and experience, two indicators that our program is headed in the right direction," Harris said. "Now, we need to concentrate on getting better every day and being ready when the season begins.

"Last year, we had nine wins and seven other games that could have gone either way. Those are the types of games we need to win this year, and I think we are ready to do that."

Three starters return in the front court, including 6-6 senior **Dax Pearson** (9.5 ppg, 5.5 rpg) and 6-5 senior **Charles Woodruff** (11.8 ppg, 4.6y rpg) inside and 6-6 senior **Jonte Harrell** (4.2 ppg, 4.6 rpg) at small forward. They combined for 63 starts last year.

Pearson has added around 15 pounds this year, which should help him when guarding the opposition's center. Woodruff is one of the most underrated players in the Patriot League and Harrell is a slasher and great leaper.

"We have a lot of depth and experience up front," Harris said. "I think that is very important for us to be successful in the Patriot League. We have a bunch of players in contention, but we return three seniors in the starting lineup and it's their job to lose.

"Jonte needs to be comfortable in his position and for him that means just playing more. He is possibly one of the most physically talented players in the league. We are looking for Jonte to create easy shots for himself, rebound and play great defense."

Depth in the frontcourt will come from 6-9 senior **Matt Rutledge** (2.4 ppg, 1.6 rpg), 6-5 junior **Matt Collins** (1.0 ppg, 0.6 rpg), 6-6 sophomore **Josh Wilson** (2.3 ppg, 1.8 rpg), 6-6 sophomore **Kenny Doleac** (2.3 ppg, 0.8 rpg), 6-7 sophomore **Chris Sexton** (who didn't play last year), 6-7 sophomore **Bill Mohr** (5.0 ppg, 2.0 rpg) and 6-8 freshman **Greg Wallace** from Tomball (Texas) High School.

Rutledge is the biggest player in the program at 6-9, 265 pounds.

"Matt is a big body and he seems to be coming into his own as a player," Harris said. "Missing the first semester last year [academic suspension] really hurt him. His presence inside certainly is a boost."

Collins is a solid rebounder and hard worker while Wilson is an exciting player who can score from the outside and create inside. During Army's last nine games a year ago, Collins averaged 3.8 points and 2.2 rebounds.

"There is no tougher kid in the Patriot League than Matt Collins," Harris said. "Right now, he just needs to be playing every day. He needs to gain more confidence, but Matt is the type of player who can give us quality minutes off the bench because he brings an added dimension of toughness.

Doleac is a solid long-range shooter while Mohr played mostly with the junior varsity last year. In his only appearance with the varsity, Mohr had five points and two rebounds against Bethany.

Sexton is a transfer from Lincoln Memorial (Tenn.) University who practiced with the team last year. He started in 17 games for LMU, averaging 3.7 points and 3.2 rebounds.

"Chris is one of the most fundamentally sound post players we have," Harris said. " His biggest obstacle now is that he has not played competitively in more than a year, so it will take him a while to adjust. However, he has the potential to give us a boost at the four."

Wallace played last year at the U.S. Military Academy Prep School.

"Greg is the type of freshman who would have been thrust into a key role in this program several years ago and been asked to carry the load," Harris said. "Now, he won't have such high expectations placed on his shoulders because we are so deep. But, we think he can be a vital contributor for us and could see a lot of playing time."

2001-2002 SCHEDULE

Nov.	17	Coast Guard
	20	Quinnipiac
	24	New York Maritime
	28	@Notre Dame
Dec.	1	@Yale
	5	Columbia
	8	Binghamton
	11	@Albany
	13	Stony Brook
	30	Marist
Jan.	2	@Brown
	5	@Cornell
	7	@New Hampshire
	9	Lehigh
	12	@American
	16	@Bucknell
	19	Lafayette
	23	Holy Cross
	26	@Navy
	30	@Colgate
Feb.	2	@Lehigh
	6	American
	9	Bucknell
	13	@Lafayette
	16	@Holy Cross
	20	Colgate
	23	Navy
March	2-3, 8	#Patriot League Tournament

@Road Games
#Show Place Arena, Upper Marlboro, MD

BLUE RIBBON ANALYSIS

BACKCOURT	B+
BENCH/DEPTH	C
FRONTCOURT	C
INTANGIBLES	C+

The Black Knights could make some noise in the Patriot League this year if they continue to adhere to Harris' philosophy, but this is the 100th basketball season in the history of the school and there has yet to be an appearance in the NCAA Tournament.

Harris does have a good nucleus of players with five starters returning. The Spatola brothers will be the key as they try to bring a winning record back to West Point. They would love to have the same kind of success that Harris enjoyed while playing for Krzyzewski.

Still, don't expect too much from the Cadets. In a preseason poll of Patriot League coaches and sports information directors, Army was finished to finish last in the eight-team league.

(S.C.)

Bucknell

LOCATION	**Lewisburg, PA**
CONFERENCE	**Patriot**
LAST SEASON	**14-15 (.483)**
CONFERENCE RECORD	**4-8 (6th)**
STARTERS LOST/RETURNING	**1/4**
NICKNAME	**Bison**
COLORS	**Orange & Blue**
HOMECOURT	**Davis Gymnasium (2,300)**
COACH	**Pat Flannery (Bucknell '80)**
RECORD AT SCHOOL	**108-90 (8 years)**
CAREER RECORD	**209-133 (13 years)**
ASSISTANTS	**Don Friday (Lebanon Valley '90)**
	Bryan Goodman (Barat '96)
	Sean McAloon (Randolph Macon '99)
TEAM WINS (last 5 years)	**18-13-16-17-14**
RPI (last 5 years)	**193-219-201-151-228**
2000-01 FINISH	**Lost in conference semifinal.**

Facing a season without five seniors, including four starters, from the year before, Bucknell coach Pat Flannery could have considered 2000-2001 a rebuilding year.

But instead of looking ahead, Flannery concentrated on the present and guided the Bison to a 14-15 season. With just a little more consistency Bucknell could easily have finished above .500.

"We were such a developing team last season that I think a little bit of inconsistency was inevitable," Flannery said. "But the end result was that we got a lot of young guys much-needed experience, which should make us deeper and better this season."

Bucknell avoided a disastrous rebuilding season because of the play of point guard **Bryan Bailey** and a tenacious defense. Bucknell ranked second in the Patriot League in scoring defense (68.8 ppg in league games). But the offense managed a league-low 64.2 points in league games.

"I think [the offensive struggles] have partly been a product of trying to develop young players," Flannery said. "We would like to do a little more scoring in transition and possibly find a few more scorers.

"You might see a team that looks to get shots up a little quicker. This year, with a more experienced team we ought to be able to open it up a bit more, but I still think a good staple for us will always be to be a good defensive team."

Bailey (17.7 ppg, 3.3 rpg), a 6-0 senior, was a first-team All-Patriot League selection last year and is a member of the preseason first team. He scored in double figures in 25-of-27 games last year.

"Bryan has really come into his own," Flannery said. "He will certainly be a leader of this team. He is a great scorer. He is quick, he defends and he really sets the tone in a lot of ways."

Starting alongside Bailey in the backcourt will be defensive stopper **Dan Blankenship** (8.1 ppg, team-high 81 assists). The 6-2 junior may be asked for more offensive production this season.

"Dan brings an important dimension to our team with his toughness," Flannery said. "He has to make his open jumpers and continue to take the ball to the basket consistently, but it's his intangibles that we count on day-to-day."

Three sophomores will battle for playing time in the backcourt—6-5 Matt Quinn, 6-3 Roland Webber and 6-2 Chris Rodgers. Quinn (1.5 ppg, 1.1 rpg) was slowed last year by a deep thigh bruise, but still played in 20 games. He made 4-of-15 three-point shots and was 9-of-10 from the free-throw line. Webber (1.3 ppg, 0.9 rpg) started two games, but was also slowed by injuries. Rodgers (1.0 ppg, 0.4 rpg) will be the backup at point guard.

A late signee at guard was Antario Glover, a 6-3 freshman from Stephens (Ark.) High School.

On the perimeter, veterans Peter Santos, Jordan Hardenbergh and Jack Namvou will compete for playing time. Santos (2.2 ppg, 1.9 rpg), a 6-5 senior, is known for his quickness, while Hardenbaugh (2.3 ppg, 2.1 rpg) is a solid complementary player who could move into a starting position. Namvou (1.6 ppg, 1.3 rpg), from Cameroon, prepped at Georgetown Prep. He played in only 16 games last year before suffering a broken foot.

Also on the perimeter is 6-6 freshman Chris Niesz, from Middletown, N.J. Flannery believes Niesz could be an impact player at the three spot.

Two starters return in the frontcourt—6-6 junior Boakai Lalugba (14.5 ppg, 7.9 rpg) and 6-8 junior Brian Werner (9.0 ppg, 5.7 rpg). Lalugba was another reason Bucknell was able to win 14 games in a rebuilding season. He started all 29 games and led the league in field-goal percentage at (.548). He was voted to the all-tournament team.

"We didn't really know how much to expect from Boakai," Flannery said. "He didn't start playing basketball until late in his high school career, but we really thought highly of him as a tremendous athlete.

"He needs to learn to be consistent. There are nights when he is just outstanding, and others where he isn't, but that's not from a lack of effort but from a lack of experience."

Werner started in 26 games last year and turned in a 23-point, seven-steal effort in an overtime victory over Lehigh that included a 63-foot buzzer beater that sent the game into overtime.

Also in the mix in the frontcourt are 6-9 sophomore Jeremiah Bennett (1.9 ppg, 2.5 rpg), 6-11 sophomore Davorin Skornik (0.5 ppg, 1.4 rpg) and 6-6 sophomore Ben Slater (2.3 ppg, 2.2 rpg).

Bennett has good range for a big man, while Skornik is a true center who broke his hand late in the year. Slater is a good scorer from the low post.

2001-2002 SCHEDULE

Nov.	16-17	#Mohegan Sun Classic
	20	@Rider
	24	@St Francis (Pa.)
	26	Cornell
Dec.	1	@Villanova
	5	Albany
	11	UMBC
	22	@Penn State
	28-29	##South Florida Tournament
Jan.	2	@Mount St. Mary's
	5	@Canisius
	9	Lafayette
	12	@Navy
	16	Army
	19	@American
	23	@Colgate
	26	Lehigh
	30	Holy Cross
Feb.	2	@Lafayette
	6	Navy
	9	@Army
	13	American
	16	Colgate
	20	@Holy Cross
	23	@Lehigh
March	2-3,8	###Patriot League Tournament

@Road Games
#New Britain, CT (vs. Central Connecticut, first round; also Brown, Vermont)
##At South Florida, Tampa, FL (vs. South Florida, first round; also Hofstra, Illinois-Chicago)
###Show Place Arena, Upper Marlboro, MD

BLUE RIBBON ANALYSIS

BACKCOURT	B+

BENCH/DEPTH	B
FRONTCOURT	C
INTANGIBLES	B

Bucknell's early schedule features road games at Villanova and Penn State, home dates against Cornell and UMBC and two tournament appearances. Also on the schedule is new league member American.

"American has a whole new group of kids coming in, but they are sure to be very athletic again," Flannery said. "It will be interesting to see them go through the league for the first time.

"It seems like the prevailing rule of thumb around the rest of the league is that everyone has good players coming back. Lafayette, Lehigh and Army all have a lot returning. Holy Cross has the player of the year back [Tim Szaltko] and certainly a lot of confidence after their run last season. Navy is always going to be deep and physical."

Flannery and his team gained a lot of confidence last year by beating third-seeded Colgate, 75-68, in the opening round of the Patriot League Tournament. Bucknell also won the last three games of the regular season.

"I can't say there is one trip in the league that I fear, but I can't say that there is one trip that I feel really good about walking in and getting an easy win," Flannery said. "So when you feel that way as a coach, you feel that this thing is very wide open. Whoever can use the summer to improve the most and keep it going into February and March has the best shot."

The league is wide open and Bucknell has been picked to finish fifth by the league's coaches and sports writers behind Holy Cross, Navy, Colgate and Lehigh. Don't be surprised if the Bison overachieves once again.

(S.C.)

Colgate

LOCATION	Hamilton, NY
CONFERENCE	Patriot
LAST SEASON	13-15 (.464)
CONFERENCE RECORD	6-6 (t-3rd)
STARTERS LOST/RETURNING	0/5
NICKNAME	Red Raiders
COLORS	Maroon, Gray & White
HOMECOURT	Cotterell Court (3,100)
COACH	Emmett Davis (St. Lawrence '81)
RECORD AT SCHOOL	40-45 (3 years)
CAREER RECORD	40-45 (3 years)
ASSISTANTS	Dennis Csensits (Allentown '90)
	Kevin Curley (Penn State '93)
	Cory Conklin (Genesco '90)
TEAM WINS (last 5 years)	12-10-14-13-13
RPI (last 5 years)	210-246-177-235-254
2000-01 FINISH	Lost in conference quarterfinal.

Before his team left for a European trip in August, Colgate coach Emmett Davis said, "We should know a lot about ourselves by the time we return from the trip."

After his team returned home with a 3-3 record and victories in its last two games, Davis said, "The trip to Europe was a huge success."

Davis was able to play many different combinations of players on the trip.

"Our 3-3 record included five very solid performances and only one poorly played game, which probably was more a result of travel fatigue than anything else," Davis said. "The trip provided this year's Colgate team with a starting point for the season ahead, but more importantly, it created a strong bond among teammates and memories that will last a lifetime."

Davis believes the chemistry developed in Europe will pay rich dividends.

"I'd be very disappointed if we didn't finish in the top four of the Patriot League and challenge for the championship," he said. "The league is going to be very competitive once again."

Colgate will have chemistry, aided greatly by the trip, but it doesn't hurt that five starters are back from a team that finished 13-15 last year with a third-place finish in the league. The Raiders were also three overtime losses from posting their first winning season since 1994-95.

"This is certainly the most experienced team we've had since I've been here," Davis said. "I think this is a group of young men that have a chance to do some special things this year.

"I think it's a great thing to have [five starters back] because the guys have played a lot of minutes and have

been experienced players. All five of them were right around or at double figures. There's better than 50 points coming back in the starting lineup."

Davis is also excited about having a competitive team while being able to bring his freshmen signees along slowly.

"For the first time, our freshmen aren't going to be in a position where one of them is going to have to be a starter or play major minutes," Davis said. "Each one of them is talented enough that if they prove to me that they deserve to play major minutes, they will.

"It's not a situation where we have to put one of those guys in the starting lineup like we have in the past."

The Raiders' starter at point guard will be Dave Hardy (9.8 ppg, 2.4 rpg, 3.8 apg), a 6-2 junior who led the league in assists and turnover/assist ratio (1.85). Hardy has developed into a point guard capable of taking care of the basketball while making solid decisions.

Backing up Hardy will be 5-11 junior Jeremy Ballard (1.5 ppg, 0.4 rpg), 5-11 senior Bill Kern (1.8 ppg, 0.8 rpg) and 6-0 senior Devon Tuohey (2.8 ppg, 0.9 rpg). Ballard has improved over the last two seasons while Kern served as a defensive stopper last season against teams with bigger guards. Tuohey has started during his career and is considered an outstanding shooter.

Tim Sullivan (10.8 ppg, 3.4 rpg), a 6-5 junior, will start at shooting guard. An excellent shooter (.439 percent), Sullivan was second in the league last year from beyond the arc. He is capable of playing the three spot if Davis inserts 6-2 sophomore Mark Linebaugh (10.1 ppg, 3.0 rpg) into the starting lineup.

Linebaugh was the Patriot League Rookie of the Year last year while averaging 25.7 minutes off the bench. He was the leading scorer among first-year players in the league and the team's best free-throw shooter (.882).

Also in the mix at shooting guard is 6-3 sophomore Casey Langel (1.5 ppg). He played in only two games last year before suffering a season-ending shoulder injury.

If Linebaugh doesn't start at small forward, the likely starter is 6-5 junior Marques Green (2.0 ppg, 1.0 rpg). He must shoot better this year and play better defensively in order to contribute. The other contenders are 6-5 sophomore Josh Humphrey (0.3 ppg, 1.2 rpg) and 6-4 freshman Keith Williams. Humphrey could develop into a starter. Williams played last year for Poly Prep in Brooklyn, N.Y., which won the state championship his junior season.

The power forward for the Raiders for the fourth straight year will be 6-6 senior Pat Campolieta (14.4 ppg, 6.0 rpg), who was All-Patriot League first team the last two years. He needs to improve from the free-throw line this year and stay out of foul trouble for Colgate to contend for a league championship.

Backing up Campolieta will be 6-5 senior LaMarr Datcher (2.5 ppg, 2.0 rpg) and 6-8 sophomore Matt Shirley (0.3 ppg, 0.8 rpg). Datcher has been a strong player off the bench in the past and is capable of guarding bigger players in the post. Shirley could see more minutes this year because he is a good shooter and rebounder.

Two freshmen could see time at power forward—6-7 LaBraun Andrew from Memphis, Tenn., and 6-8 Andrew Zidar from Plantation, Fla. Andrew played post-graduate ball last year at Lawrenceville Prep, while Zidar played on a championship team at St. Thomas Aquinas.

Expected to start at center is 6-7 sophomore Howard Blue (9.7 ppg, 5.9 rpg), who made the league's all-rookie team last year. He was inconsistent at times and underwent foot surgery in May.

Martin Marek (5.0 ppg, 2.7 rpg), a 6-9 forward/center, could see considerable playing time this year at the four- and five spots. Hard-luck Chris Fox (1.7 ppg, 1.3 rpg), a 6-9 junior, will also challenge for playing time at center. He has had two shoulder surgeries in the last two years, but has good potential. He was MVP of the New York state tournament his senior year at McQuaid Jesuit in Rochester, N.Y.

The final player in the picture at center is 6-9 sophomore Peter Kyte (0.5 ppg, 0.3 rpg), who is a good shot blocker with a nice shooting touch.

2001-2002 SCHEDULE

Nov.	17	@Long Island
	21	Northern Arizona
	25	Oral Roberts
	27	@Syracuse
Dec.	1	@Cornell
	3	Yale
	8	@Harvard
	18	Hobart
	21	Dartmouth

	30	@Notre Dame
Jan.	3	Bethany
	5	@New Hampshire
	9	American
	12	@Lehigh
	16	@Holy Cross
	19	Navy
	23	Bucknell
	26	@Lafayette
	28	@Binghamton
	30	Army
Feb.	2	@American
	6	Lehigh
	9	Holy Cross
	13	@Navy
	16	@Bucknell
	20	@Army
	23	Lafayette
March	2,3, 8	#Patriot League Tournament

@Road Games
#Show Place Arena, Upper Marlboro, MD

BLUE RIBBON ANALYSIS

BACKCOURT	B
BENCH/DEPTH	B
FRONTCOURT	B+
INTANGIBLES	B

The Colgate schedule features road games against Notre Dame and Syracuse from the Big East Conference. Also on the schedule are home games against Northern Arizona and Oral Roberts and games against Cornell, Dartmouth, Harvard and Yale from the Ivy League.

The Raiders will also add two games with new league member American as well as a home-and-home series against New Hampshire from the America East Conference.

In a preseason poll of conference coaches and sports information directors, Colgate was picked to finish third behind Holy Cross and Navy. Colgate received one first-place vote.

The leader of this team will be Campolieta, who was voted to the preseason all-conference team. If he has a season worthy of player-of-the-year honors, Colgate could battle for the league championship.

The Raiders would like nothing better than to return to the top of the Patriot League for the first time since back-to-back championships in 1994 and '95.

(S.C.)

Holy Cross

LOCATION	Worcester, MA
CONFERENCE	Patriot
LAST SEASON	22-8 (.733)
CONFERENCE RECORD	10-2 (1st)
STARTERS LOST/RETURNING	2/3
NICKNAME	Crusaders
COLORS	Royal Purple
HOMECOURT	Hart Center (3,600)
COACH	Ralph Willard (Holy Cross '67)
RECORD AT SCHOOL	32-26 (2 years)
CAREER RECORD	176-150 (11 years)
ASSISTANTS	Sean Doherty (Worcester State '92)
	Tony Newsom (Niagara '93)
	Eric Eaton (UMass-Dartmouth '97)
TEAM WINS (last 5 years)	8-7-7-10-22
RPI (last 5 years)	296-291-295-284-93
2000-01 FINISH	Lost in NCAA first round.

Ralph Willard still fondly recalls his four years at Western Kentucky, when the Hilltoppers advanced to the NCAA Tournament his last two seasons, including a magical march to the Sweet 16 in 1992-93.

Despite winning 81 games in those four years and also going to the NIT one season, Willard decided he'd done all he could in Bowling Green and sought out another challenge, at Pittsburgh of the mighty Big East. In five years there, however, his team never made an appearance in the NCAA Tournament.

"I probably never should have left Western Kentucky," Willard said. "It was fun being there, and I still have lots of great friends there."

Though the Pitt gig wasn't everything he'd imagined, things turned out OK for Willard. That's because he's home now—at Holy Cross. The same school where

Willard was a three-year letter winner and team captain in 1966-67.

"It's great to be doing this for my alma mater," Willard said. "I'm very pleased to be here. I'm very happy."

And why not?

Willard guided the Crusaders to a 10-18 record in 1999-2000 and then last year his team went 22-8 and earned a berth in the NCAA Tournament. It was the first trip to the Big Dance for Holy Cross since 1993-94 and tied the school record for the best turnaround in school history.

For his efforts last year, Willard was chosen Patriot League Coach of the Year as the Crusaders won both the regular season and tournament titles.

Willard said his coaching style has changed very little since his days at Western Kentucky.

"Really, there's not that much difference," Willard said. "At Holy Cross, I've had to adjust my style due to our lack of athleticism.

"But we will always be up-tempo and keep playing defense. And I'm still as hungry as I ever was. Maybe I'm trying to atone for past transgressions."

The outlook for the 2001-02 season is good, as Willard and the Crusaders try to continue their march back to national prominence. This is what returns in the numbers game for Willard: scoring (63.2 percent), rebounding (53.9 percent), assists (68.8 percent) and minutes (59.6 percent).

"We have only one senior starter (**Ryan Serravalle**) and could be very good by the end of the year," Willard said. "We've got a tough early schedule."

The Crusaders begin the season with four road games before Christmas and an appearance in the Rainbow Classic. Iona is first up in that tournament.

"We were No. 1 in field-goal defense in the nation last year," Willard said. "That's what we have to do again. We defended especially well. Our wings really locked up their guys last year.

"That's the challenge for this year. We will be better offensively, but we've got to have some people really step up on defense."

Serravalle (11.2 ppg), a 6-0 senior, returns at point guard as a four-year starter for the Crusaders. He ranked third on the team in scoring last year and led HC in three-point field-goal percentage (.392) and free-throw percentage (.789). He made two three-pointers in overtime in helping lead the Crusaders to the Patriot League Tournament title. He will be counted on for leadership and clutch play again this year.

"Ryan really stepped up last year," Willard said. "We're looking for him to increase his scoring this season."

Starting at two-guard will be 6-1 **Jave Meade** (7.3 ppg, 3.1 apg), who earned Patriot League All-Rookie team honors last year. He recorded a team-best 50 steals and was a key in helping the Crusaders handle the press.

"Meade had a great freshman year," Willard said. "We just hope he builds on that. He's a fantastic slasher, penetrator."

Starting at the three-spot will be 6-2 junior **Brian Wilson** (4.9 ppg, 1.2 rpg), who has started in 35 games the last two seasons. A Patriot League All-Rookie team performer two seasons ago, Wilson has 47 steals and 42 three-point field goals in his two years with the Crusaders.

"Brian has been a steady performer for us," Willard said. "We're expecting him to have a big year."

Also in the rotation at guard will be 6-0 senior **Guillermo Sanchez** (0.3 ppg), 6-0 junior **Mark Jerz** (0.7 ppg) and 6-5 sophomore **John Bucaro** (1.4 ppg). Sanchez is a former walk-on who has 12 starts at point guard. Jerz has played in 26 games the last two seasons, while Bucaro connected on 30.0 percent of his shots from three-point range last year.

Willard and his staff also brought in freshman guards **Greg Kinsey** from Philadelphia, Pa., and **Michael Smiley** from Swampscott, Ma. Kinsey, 6-5, spent last season at Mercersburg Academy after a successful career at Hatsboro-Horsham High School, where he averaged 14.0 points, 5.0 rebounds and 3.0 assists per game. Smiley, 6-3, played at Brewster Academy last year, where he averaged 18.0 points, 7.0 rebounds and 20 assists.

Starting at the four-spot for the Crusaders will be 6-8 junior **Tim Szatko** (11.4 ppg, 6.5 rpg), who was voted league player of the year last year, becoming only the second sophomore in Patriot history to receive the award. He led the Crusaders in scoring, rebounding and free-throw percentage in league games. He was chosen by league coaches and sports writers as the preseason league player of the year.

"Tim just has a great work ethic and keeps getting

better ever year," Willard said.

Also in the mix will be 6-7, 230-pound red-shirt freshman **Greg Richter**, who missed last season with mononucleosis. He averaged 21 points, 17 rebounds and three blocked shots as a senior at Quince Orchard High School in Gaithersburg, Md.

Freshman **John Hurley** from South Boston, Mass., averaged 13.0 points, 5.0 rebound sand 4.0 assists last year at Thayer Academy. The 6-7, 190-pounder needs to develop physically.

A key for the Crusaders this year will be replacing center Josh Sankes. The leading candidate is 6-9, 245 junior **Patrick Whearty** (62 ppg, 5.1 rpg), who started 16 games last year. He ranked second on the team with 27 blocked shots and had two double-doubles, including a 23-point, 13-rebound effort against Manhattan.

"Patrick has a great body," Willard said. "He really needs to stay out of foul trouble this year and be more consistent.

"Actually, he is more mobile than Sankes and that should help us defensively."

The tallest Crusader is 6-11, 220-pound freshman **Nate Lufkin** from Austin, Texas. He is a young shot blocker with good potential who was the 26th-ranked senior in the Texas last year. He averaged 20.0 points and 10.0 rebounds during the district playoffs.

2001-2002 SCHEDULE

Nov.	20	Harvard
	23	@Manhattan
	27	@Dartmouth
Dec.	1	Boston University
	4	@Massachusetts
	6	Brown
	16	@Boston College
	19-22	#Rainbow Classic
	28-29	##State Farm Good Neighbor Classic
Jan.	2	Fordham
	5	@Princeton
	9	Navy
	12	@Lafayette
	16	Colgate
	19	@Lehigh
	23	@Army
	26	American
	30	@Bucknell
Feb.	2	@Navy
	6	Lafayette
	9	@Colgate
	13	Lehigh
	16	Army
	20	Bucknell
	23	@American
March	2-3	###Patriot League Tournament

@Road Games
#At Hawaii (vs. Iona first game; also Arkansas State, Boston College, Georgia, Hawaii, Miami [OH], Portland)
##At Holy Cross (vs. Radford first game; also College of Charleston, Louisiana-Monroe)
####Show Place Arena, Upper Marlboro, MD

BLUE RIBBON ANALYSIS

BACKCOURT	B+
BENCH/DEPTH	B
FRONTCOURT	B+
INTANGIBLES	A

It should come as no surprise that Holy Cross has been picked by the league's coaches and sports writers to repeat as Patriot League champion.

Holy Cross received 10-of-16 first-place votes to repeat, while Navy had three, Lehigh two and Colgate one.

"That's a shocker," Willard said. "But I'd rather have the bulls-eye than no respect."

With Willard stressing defense, the Crusaders will be tough to knock from the top spot in the Patriot League. Szatko is a premier player in the league and Serravalle, Meade and Wilson are solid. The key to another title is Whearty, a mobile player who could help the Crusaders be even better defensively.

Although Navy, Colgate and Lehigh could emerge as the Patriot League champion, our choice to take the league title has to be Holy Cross.

(S.C.)

Lafayette

LOCATION	Easton, PA
CONFERENCE	Patriot
LAST SEASON	12-16 (.428)
CONFERENCE RECORD	4-8 (5th)
STARTERS LOST/RETURNING	3/2
NICKNAME	Leopards
COLORS	Maroon & White
HOMECOURT	Allan P. Kirby Sports Center (3,500)
COACH	Fran O'Hanlon (Villanova '70)
RECORD AT SCHOOL	95-77 (6 years)
CAREER RECORD	95-77 (6 years)
ASSISTANTS	Pat Brogan (Dickinson '90)
	Mike Longabardi (Frostburg State '96)
	John O'Connor (Penn State '83)
TEAM WINS (last 5 years)	11-19-22-24-12
RPI (last 5 years)	267-143-98-115-263
2000-01 FINISH	Lost in conference first round.

Although Lafayette finished only 12-16 last year, it marked the end of a memorable run for the most successful men's basketball classes in school history.

The Class of 2001 finished its career with three Patriot League championships, two NCAA Tournament berths and 77 victories.

That success is a reflection of the job that coach Fran O'Hanlon has done since taking over seven years ago. He inherited a non-scholarship program coming off a 2-25 season and turned it into a consistent contender for Patriot League honors.

Last year could have been even better if not for two key players missing significant action. Still, the Leopards earned victories over Princeton and eventual conference champion Holy Cross.

O'Hanlon, a 1970 graduate of Villanova and captain of the 1969-70 team, earned Patriot League Coach-of-the-Year honors for the 1997-98 and 1998-99 seasons.

In order to return to prominence in the league this season, O'Hanlon will rely on the play of senior captains **Brian Burke** (14.0 ppg, 1.9 rpg) and **Rob Worthington** (3.7 ppg, 2.87 rpg).

"We are really going to rely on the leadership of our co-captains," O'Hanlon said. "They were both part of successful seasons in the past and I hope that they can relay that winning experience to our younger players."

Burke will be counted on to be the offensive leader for the Leopards. He came off the bench last year in 14-of-15 games that he played. He missed a good portion of the season with a punctured lung suffered on Dec. 11 at Fordham. Without Burke, the Leopards went 3-9.

He led the team in assists as a junior and is shooting 88 percent for his career from the free-throw line.

"Our strength is going to be our perimeter play," O'Hanlon said. "Brian Burke has made key contributions in each of his three seasons, and with him healthy I expect even more."

Senior **Reggie Guy** (4.5 ppg, 1.7 rpg) started in 18 games last season and is a defensive standout. Guy, 6-3, needs to increase his scoring output this season but is expected to be a starter.

Sophomore **Justin DeBerry** (5.8 ppg, 2.2 rpg) started several games last year when four-year starter Tim Bieg torned his ACL. DeBerry, 6-3, averaged 13.7 points the last three games, including the Patriot League Tournament. **Ben Saxton** (6.4 ppg, 1.7 rpg), a 6-5 sophomore, scored in double figures in six games last year.

"Justin DeBerry started the final eight games of last season and was able to get experience in the point-guard role," O'Hanlon said.

Another player who should see extensive playing time in the backcourt is junior **Andrew Pleick**, a transfer from Drake. The 6-5, 207-pounder will be eligible to play on Dec. 19. If Pleick comes through offensively, it should take some of the scoring load off Burke.

Also in the mix in the backcourt will be 5-10 junior **Drew Dawson** (0.9 ppg, 0.1 rpg) and 6-5 sophomore **Winston Davis** (1.9 ppg, 1.0 rpg). Davis is a talented player who took a medical red-shirt as a freshman and missed most of last season with stress fractures.

Two freshmen will also be in the picture in the backcourt—6-1 **Kenny Grant** and 6-5 **Eric Mugavero**.

Grant played at St. Mary's in Manhasset, N.Y., where he averaged 9.5 points and 11.0 assists last year in leading his team to the Long Island Catholic League championship. He played point guard on the 30-1 team.

Mugavero finished his career as the fifth all-time leading scorer at Phillipsburg (N.J.) High School with 1,061 points. He shot 54 percent from the field and 32 percent

from beyond the arc.

In the frontcourt, All-Patriot selection Frank Barr and power forward Nash Ablo must be replaced.

Worthington started 12-of-28 games last year and 20-of-31 games in 1999-2000. He is known for his back-door cuts, especially while slipping off screens. Also, 6-10, 230-pound senior **Mick Kuberka** (13 three-pointers last year) is a solid threat from three-point land.

Three sophomores will see time in the frontcourt as well—6-9 **Rob Dill** (1.7 ppg, 2.1 rpg), 6-8 **Mike Farrell** (4.1 ppg, 2.7 rpg) and 6-5 **Greg McCleary**, who took a medical red-shirt last season.

Dill may be in the starting lineup after blocking 31 shots in only 10 minutes per game as a freshman. Farrell started four games last year and led the Leopards in field-goal percentage (.506).

"The key for us will be how we play in the post," O'Hanlon said. "Rob Dill improved dramatically in the 2000-01 season and has continued to improve his game by playing in upper level international competitions in Europe. Mike Farrell and Rob Worthington will compete for time at the power-forward slot."

Two freshmen could see playing time in the frontcourt—7-2, 275-pound **James Hughes** and 6-11, 225-pound **Brad Anderson**.

Hughes prepped at Mercersburg Academy in Mechanicsville, Va., where he helped his team finish 18-7. He averaged 5.5 points, 6.7 rebounds and 2.0 blocks. Anderson, from Ontario-Choate, helped his team to a Founds League championship game by averaging 8.5 points, 7.0 rebounds and 2.0 blocks.

"We're really excited about the four players we have coming in as part of the Class of 2005," O'Hanlon said. "They all come from winning programs and will be able to strengthen our squad over the next four years."

2001-2002 SCHEDULE

Nov.	17	@Albany
	21	@Penn State
	24	@Miami
	27	St. Peter's
	29	Marist
Dec.	1	@Columbia
	5	@Drexel
	8	Cornell
	19	Scranton
	21	@Princeton
	30	Howard
Jan.	2	Rider
	9	@Bucknell
	12	Holy Cross
	16	@American
	19	@Army
	21	@Pennsylvania
	23	@Navy
	26	Colgate
	30	@Lehigh
Feb.	2	Bucknell
	6	@Holy Cross
	9	American
	13	Army
	16	Navy
	20	Lehigh
	23	@Colgate
March	2,3,8	#Patriot League Tournament

@Road Games
#Show Place Arena, Marlboro, MD

BLUE RIBBON ANALYSIS

BACKCOURT	B-
BENCH/DEPTH	B
FRONTCOURT	C
INTANGIBLES	C

O'Hanlon would deserve coach-of-the-year honors once again if he develops this team into a championship contender. Four players who started 10 or more games last year were lost to graduation, so Hanlon will be depending on a few upperclassmen, a talented sophomore class and possibly some contributions from the freshman class.

The Leopards were picked by league coaches and sports information directors to finish seventh in the eight-team league, ahead of only Army.

Lafayette can finish higher depending on the play of its co-captains—Burke and Worthington. They are outstanding players who could lift the Leopards into the top half of the league standings. Dill could be a big factor as well.

More than likely, this will be a rebuilding year.

(S.C.)

Lehigh

LOCATION	Bethlehem, PA
CONFERENCE	Patriot
LAST SEASON	13-16 (.448)
CONFERENCE RECORD	6-6 (t-3rd)
STARTERS LOST/RETURNING	1/4
NICKNAME	Mountain Hawks, Engineers
COLORS	Brown & White
HOMECOURT	Stabler Arena (5,600)
COACH	Sal Mentesana (Providence '69)
RECORD AT SCHOOL	38-102 (5 years)
CAREER RECORD	156-207 (14 years)
ASSISTANTS	Jeff Wilson (East Stroudsburg '86)
	Jon Deeb (Pace '93)
	Glenn Noack (Bloomsburg '86)
TEAM WINS (last 5 years)	1-10-6-8-13
RPI (last 5 years)	304-264-300-282-241
2000-01 FINISH	Lost in conference semifinal.

After winning only 25 games the previous four years, Lehigh picked up 13 victories last year and a third-place finish in the Patriot League.

Funny how much confidence can be gained from 13 wins, a nice finish in the regular season and a berth in a conference tournament semifinal.

The optimism is dripping from this letter written to prospective Lehigh basketball players from 2001-02 Lehigh co-captains **Scott Taylor** and **Matt Logie**: "The foundation has been built. It is now our job as members of the Lehigh basketball program to make sure that this foundation strengthens and success becomes a habit, not a surprise. If you're a dedicated and hard-working player who sets his goals high and stops at nothing to achieve them, then come join us in our efforts to build a winning tradition at Lehigh."

That is the kind of mentality that coach Sal Mentesana, selected the best dressed college coach in 2000 by College Hoops Insider, instills in his players. Since taking over the Lehigh program in 1996, Mentesana has brought a strong work ethic and determination to succeed both on and off the court.

"Coach Sal is a motivational speaker who thrives on pressure and wants to make a difference," former Lehigh captain Edil Lacayo said. "He started from the bottom and built himself to the top."

Mentesana, announced as Lehigh's 25th head coach in April of 1996, guided the Mountain Hawks to a 13-16 record last year—the school's best since the 1991-92 season.

"I think this is a very exciting time to be a part of the Lehigh basketball program," Mentesana said. "We are still a very young team with a bright future. We are on solid ground academically and I am very proud of the quality of individuals in our program.

"Last season was a good season, but I think it's now time to take a dramatic step forward. We have all of the elements in place; it's time to put it all together."

With four starters returning and nine lettermen, there are great expectations.

"I expect us to be a contender and a factor in the tournament," Mentesana said. "I am not saying I expect us to win the Patriot League or even be a favorite to win, but I do expect us to be a dangerous team that could surprise a few people."

Returning to lead the team at point guard is 6-2 sophomore **Alex Jensen** (7.1 ppg), who finished second in the league in assists with 107, fourth in assist-to-turnover ratio at 1.43, and scored in double figures nine times. Jensen moved into the starting lineup the fourth game of the season last year.

Backing up Jensen will be 5-11 sophomore **Ra Tiah** (1.2 ppg), who handed out 30 assists in 20 games last year. Freshman **Jamal Williams**, a 6-3 standout who averaged 15 points and five assists per game last year at Cherokee High School in Marlton, N.J., will provide depth at point guard.

At shooting guard will be co-captain Logie (14.1 ppg, 2.1 rpg), a 6-5 junior who was a second team all-league selection last year. The sharpshooter led Lehigh in scoring last year and was second in the league in three-pointers made with 78. He was also fourth in the nation in free throw shooting at 91.7 percent, and scored in double figures 21 times.

"If I had to describe this year's captains, I would call them fire and ice," Mentesana said. "Scott Taylor is the fire and Matt Logie is the ice. Scott brings a tremendous work ethic and emotional approach to the game.

"Matt is more cerebral and calm and leads by example. I think this dual approach will really benefit our team both on and off the court."

Alan Goff (8.4 ppg, 3.2 rpg), a 6-4 junior, also returns to the starting lineup at small forward. He is a defensive standout who was second in the league in steals with 61 and second on his team in assists with 80.

Jense, Logie and Goff will give the Mountain Hawks three shooters who can provide instant offense and help Mentesana and his group establish a winning tradition.

"In order to have tradition, you have to become a constant winner," Mentesana said. "If you look at all the top programs, they all have a winning tradition.

"Everything is in place for a winning tradition, all we have to do is start beating people that are better than us. We have to start winning."

Backing up Logie and Goff will be 6-3 junior **Zlatko Savovic** (4.2 ppg, 3.1 rpg), who is making the transition from point guard to more of a shooting role this year. Last year, Savovic handed out 61 assists—third on the team. Also seeking playing time will be 6-4 sophomore **Steve Callahan** (0.9 ppg) and four talented freshmen—6-6 **Kevin Murawinski**, 6-5 **Nick Monserez**, 6-4 **Curtis Allen** and 6-1 **Brad Szalachowski**.

The versatile Murawinski may also play some at power forward. He averaged 18 points and seven rebounds per game at Middletown South High School in Lincroft, N.J.

"Kevin has the size and strength to play at the Division I level as a freshman," Mentesana said. "He can create mismatches for our opponents at both positions."

Monserez averaged 14 points and 7.5 rebounds at Archbishop Moeller High School in Cincinnati. Allen led the Southern Tier Athletic Conference in scoring for three years at Chenango Valley High School in Binghamton, N.Y. He averaged 27.5 points per game last year. Szalachowski played at Parkland High School in Allentown, Pa., where he set school records for three-pointers made in a game (seven), in a season (104) and in a career (209).

With the loss of captain Edil Lacayo at power forward, the 6-7 senior Taylor (5.9 ppg, 3.2 rpg) will be expected to step in and fill the void. Taylor started two games last year and improved his numbers in the last 10 games to averages of 7.4 points and 3.4 rebounds.

Providing depth and looking for significant playing time behind Taylor will be 6-8 freshman **Eric Heil**, a McDonald's All-America nominee. Heil averaged 15.0 points at Pleasant Valley High School in Bettendorf, Iowa.

"Eric has the potential to be an impact player for us," Mentesana said. "He has terrific skills for a player his size. He can make three-pointers and handles the ball very well. We are thrilled to have a player of Eric's caliber in our program."

The fourth returning starter is 6-10 junior center **Matt Crawford** (7.5 ppg, 6.0 rpg), who finished second in the league in blocked shots with 65. He averaged 10.3 points and 7.8 rebounds in league play.

Backing up Crawford will be 6-5 senior **Bobby Mbom** (6.9 ppg, 3.2 rpg) and 6-8 freshman **Dayne Mickelson**. Mbom is a strong player who finished fifth in the nation last year in field-goal percentage at 61.7 percent. Mickelson averaged 15.0 points and 10.0 rebounds last year at Woodinville (Va.) High School.

2001-2002 SCHEDULE

Nov.	16	St. Francis, NY
	20	Wagner
	24	Harvard
	27	@Columbia
	30	@Dartmouth
Dec.	2	@Vermont
	5	@Penn State
	8	New Hampshire
	10	Swarthmore
	22	@Cornell
	29	@Portland
	31	@Oregon State
Jan.	5	Pennsylvania
	9	@Army
	12	Colgate
	16	@Navy
	19	Holy Cross
	23	American
	30	Lafayette
Feb.	2	Army
	6	@Colgate
	9	Navy
	13	@Holy Cross
	16	@American
	20	@Lafayette
	23	Bucknell

| March | 2-3, 8 | #Patriot League Tournament |

@Road Games
#Show Place Arena, Upper Marlboro, MD

BLUE RIBBON ANALYSIS

BACKCOURT	B+
BENCH/DEPTH	B
FRONTCOURT	B
INTANGIBLES	B+

When Mickelson signed with Lehigh, he said, "Everyone spoke of how the team has been improving and I wanted to be a part of taking the program to another level."

That is exactly what Mentesana expects.

"We are asking our players to make a number of sacrifices to play for us, but it is a two-way street," the colorful Lehigh coach said. "I'm not in this for the wins on the court. Sure they help, but when a player calls you 10 years down the road and tells you about his life experiences, that is a much bigger win."

With four starters back and Taylor and Logie ready to provide leadership, Lehigh may forge above the .500 mark this season. Although Holy Cross will be favored to win the league again, Lehigh could nudge ahead of Navy and Colgate for second.

"This league continues to get better and better each year," Mentesana said. "It is a tough and exciting league with every game being a war. The league is one of competitive balance, but Holy Cross is the champion until someone knocks them off."

(S.C.)

 # Navy

LOCATION	Annapolis, MD
CONFERENCE	Patriot
LAST SEASON	19-12 (.612)
CONFERENCE RECORD	9-3 (2nd)
STARTERS LOST/RETURNING	4/1
NICKNAME	Midshipmen or Mids
COLORS	Navy, Blue & Gold
HOMECOURT	Alumni Hall (5,710)
COACH	Don DeVoe (Ohio State '64)
RECORD AT SCHOOL	161-98 (9 years)
CAREER RECORD	489-326 (28 years)
ASSISTANTS	Jimmy Allen (Emory & Henry '93)
	Nathan Davis (Randolph-Macon '97)
	Victor Mickel (Navy '94)
TEAM WINS (last 5 years)	20-19-20-23-19
RPI (last 5 years)	147-165-119-126-145
2000-01 FINISH	Lost in conference championship game.

When a college basketball program averages 20 wins a year for a five-year stretch, it tends to earn respect.

Navy is the perfect example.

Even though veteran coach Don DeVoe returns only one starter, his team was picked to finish second in the Patriot League behind Holy Cross by the league's coaches and sports information directors. The Midshipmen even received three first-place votes.

DeVoe is a big reason Navy has earned respect.

Stressing rebounding and fundamental basketball, especially on the defensive end, DeVoe in 1999 became only the 29th active coach to collect 450 career victories. And now, DeVoe is looking at another facet of the game.

"When I first started coaching, I thought defense was everything," he said. "But now, I am putting more stress on offense."

In 31 games last year, Navy averaged 75.4 points while limiting its opponents to 70.6. The result was another berth in the Patriot League championship game, where the Midshipmen lost to Holy Cross, 68-64, in overtime.

It could be difficult this season for Navy and DeVoe to maintain that 20-win average, as only 6-1 senior point guard **Demond Shepard** (5.0 ppg, 1.5 rpg, 1.6 apg) returns to the starting lineup.

"Demond has the ability to lead by example as both a scorer as well as an excellent defender," DeVoe said. "As our point guard, he controls the game.

"While he averaged about five points a game last season, he's proven to my staff many times that he can put down the three."

Shepard, a tenacious defensive standout, will be

expected to score more this season. He is a career 74 percent free-throw shooter, so he can get creative in increasing his point production.

"Demond certainly has the ability to contribute more scoring from both the field and the free-throw line," DeVoe said. "It all flows together. If he looks to score more, he will likely get fouled more often."

Backing up Shepard will be 5-11 sophomore **Kwame Ofori** (0.3 ppg, 0.3 rpg) and 6-0 sophomore **Jason Fernandez** (0.6 ppg).

"Jason is a gifted shooter who emerged as he gained experience," DeVoe said. "Like Jason, Kwame's time last season was limited. He's a very athletic player who has a strong defensive prowess. I'd like to see him look to score from the perimeter a little more and penetrate the middle."

At shooting guard, 6-3 **Jehiel Lewis** (8.6 ppg, 3.9 rpg) returns for his senior season. Although limited by injuries in the past, Lewis is accurate from beyond the arc. An aggressive player, Lewis made 100 trips to the free-throw line last year, shooting 68 percent. He also had 29 steals last season.

"Last year, Jehiel finally got the chance to emerge as the player we thought he could be," DeVoe said. "He had been injured much of his first two years, but last year he was able to contribute to the team on both ends of the court. I think this year he will have the ability to take us places."

Another wing candidate will be junior 6-3 **Jason Jeanpierre** (5.7 ppg, 1.3 rpg), who has also been slowed by injuries. He made 22 three-point shots as a sophomore and is considered an excellent playmaker. He can also play the point.

"Jason has the chance to be one of the premier scorers in the Patriot League," DeVoe said. "He's blessed with shooting range, strength and the ability to take the ball to the bucket.

"Patience may be the key to Jason's game this season, but he will be an integral part of the success of this team."

Filling backup roles will be relative newcomers—6-5 sophomore **Jeff Charles** (0.9 ppg), 6-3 junior **Nate Jennings** and 6-3 sophomore **Ryan Bailey**.

Charles saw action in seven games last season while Jennings has fine-tuned his game through the junior varsity ranks. Bailey played exclusively with the junior varsity last season.

"Jeff has the ability to read the opponent's next move and is a great defender," DeVoe said. "Nate's quickness and lateral ability have developed him into quite a defender. I think the summer league he played in will pay dividends when the season rolls around."

After being slowed last year by mononucleosis, 6-6 junior **Scott Long** (3.1 ppg, 1.6 rpg) returns to full strength at small forward. He is a physical player who can post up or shoot the three-point shot.

"We, as a staff, have a great deal of confidence in Scott," DeVoe said. "He started as a freshman here, which is rare, so that is a good indication of our confidence in Scott.

"If he can remain healthy this season, I believe he will have a fine year. He needs to be a bit more patient in looking for his shot, but he certainly fits the mold of a great team player."

Also returning at small forward is 6-6 junior **Quintrell McCreary** (0.6 ppg, 0.7 rpg), who played in 17 games last year.

"I'd like to see Quintrell unleash some of his innate ability and strength on our opponents," DeVoe said. "He will get his share of rebounds and he has a feel for scoring."

Also back is 6-7 senior **Jamie Nero**, who has seen action in only 14 varsity games.

The starter at power forward will be 6-7 junior **Kyle Barker** (8.2 ppg, 2.8 rpg), who shot 35.8 percent from three-point range last year and 88.5 percent from the free-throw line. He can also play with his back to the basket.

"Kyle is unquestionably one of the best scorers in recent years at the Naval Academy," DeVoe said. "He is the epitome of a great scorer. He doesn't rush his shot and he's rarely off balance.

"He plays with a great deal of confidence, whether it's shooting the three-pointer, posting up in the paint or making the trip to the free-throw line. We look for him to have some big nights, but he needs to be consistent through the entire season."

Providing depth at power forward will be 6-8 sophomore **Sonny Lewis** (3.1 ppg, 1.6 rpg), He will give Navy some height and strength if he fully recovers from the broken ankle he suffered a year ago.

Starting at center will be 6-8 junior **Francis Ebong** (5.3 ppg, 4.0 rpg), who is also capable of playing both small and power forward.

"Francis has put on weight in the off-season and has worked on his scoring," DeVoe said. "I really can see him emerging into one of Navy's great shot blockers, as Mike Cunningham did a year ago."

Backing up Ebong will be 6-8 junior **Mitch Moore** (0.0 ppg, 0.3 rpg) and 6-10 sophomore **Mike Wheeler**, who played on the junior varsity last year.

"Mitch is one of the many rising juniors who can make a mark this season," DeVoe said. "Mike is a bit of an unknown, but I think he will help add depth to the center position."

2001-2002 SCHEDULE

Nov.	16	@Rice
	18	@SMU
	24	Air Force
	26	Ohio
	29	@The Citadel
Dec.	1	@Davidson
	16	Gettysburg
	20-22	#Montana
	28	Belmont
	30	Mount St. Mary's
Jan.	2	Coastal Carolina
	5	@Brown
	7	Wake Forest
	9	@Holy Cross
	12	Bucknell
	16	Lehigh
	23	Lafayette
	26	Army
	30	@American
Feb.	2	Holy Cross
	6	@Bucknell
	9	@Lehigh
	13	Colgate
	16	@Lafayette
	20	American
	23	@Army
March	2-3, 8	##Patriot League Tournament

@Road Games
#Yahoo Sports Invational, Lale, HI (also Buffalo, BYU, Columbia, Hawaii, New Mexico State, Tulsa and Valparaiso).
##Show Place Arena, Upper Marlboro, MD

BLUE RIBBON ANALYSIS

BACKCOURT	B+
BENCH/DEPTH	B
FRONTCOURT	B-
INTANGIBLES	B-

With only one starter returning, Navy may get off to a slow start. And it doesn't help that four of the first six games are on the road, followed by a trip to Hawaii for the Yahoo Sports Invitational.

Many experts believe Navy should be picked fourth instead of second in the league behind Holy Cross, Colgate and Lehigh. Still, Navy gets respect because DeVoe has kept the Midshipmen at the top of the league for years.

Shepard has the ability to lead this team back to the championship game if the players around him mature. As for DeVoe, well, he will continue to weave his magic toward another 20-victory season.

(S.C.)

 **Auburn**

LOCATION	Auburn, AL
CONFERENCE	Southeastern (Western)
LAST SEASON	18-14 (.562)
CONFERENCE RECORD	7-9 (t-4th)
STARTERS LOST/RETURNING	1/4
NICKNAME	Tigers
COLORS	Burnt Orange & Navy Blue
HOMECOURT	Beard-Eaves Memorial Coliseum (12,500)
COACH	Cliff Ellis (Florida State '68)
RECORD AT SCHOOL	138-83 (7 years)
CAREER RECORD	564-307 (29 years)
ASSISTANTS	Shannon Weaver (Middle Tenn. '93)
	Mike Wilson (SE Louisiana '86)
	Charlton Young (Middle Tennessee '93)
TEAM WINS (last 5 years)	16-16-29-24-18

SOUTHEASTERN

BLUE RIBBON FORECAST

East Division
1. Kentucky
2. Florida
3. Tennessee
4. South Carolina
5. Vanderbilt
6. Georgia

West Division
1. Arkansas
2. Ole Miss
3. Alabama
4. Auburn
5. Mississippi State
6. LSU

TOP 40

Arkansas, Alabama, Florida, Kentucky, Ole Miss and Tennessee are ranked among the 2001-2002 Blue Ribbon Top 40. Extended profiles can be found in the Top 40 section of Blue Ribbon.

ALL-CONFERENCE TEAM

G-Brett Nelson, JR, Florida
G-Keith Bogans, JR, Kentucky
C-Udonis Haslem, SR, Florida
F-Rod Grizzard, JR, Alabama
F-Tayshaun Prince, SR, Kentucky

PLAYER OF THE YEAR

Tayshaun Prince, SR, Kentucky

NEWCOMER OF THE YEAR

Maurice Williams, FR, Alabama

2001-2002 CONFERENCE TOURNAMENT

March 7-10, Georgia Dome, Atlanta, GA

2000-2001 CHAMPIONS

Kentucky, Florida (Eastern Division and overall)
Ole Miss (Western Division)
Kentucky (Conference tournament)

2000-2001 POSTSEASON PARTICIPANTS

Postseason record: 12-10 (.545)
NCAA
Kentucky (Sweet 16)
Ole Miss (Sweet 16)
Florida (Second round)
Arkansas
Georgia
Tennessee

NIT
Alabama (Runner-up)
Mississippi State (Third round)
Auburn (Second round)
South Carolina

TOP BACKCOURTS

1. Florida
2. Arkansas
3. Ole Miss

TOP FRONTCOURTS

1. Kentucky
2. Tennessee
3. Alabama

INSIDE THE NUMBERS

2000-2001 conference RPI: 2nd (of 31)
Conference RPI (last five years): 6-2-4-1-2

DID YOU KNOW?

Two new coaches join the league this season. Dave Odom bolted Wake Forest for South Carolina, and Buzz Peterson left behind an NIT championship team at Tulsa to take over at Tennessee. … In the last nine NCAA Tournaments (1993-2001), the SEC's nine Final Four appearances is tied with the ACC for the most by any conference. With Florida returning to the Final Four in 2000, the SEC has placed four teams in the national semifinals, one behind the Big Ten's five. … Since the 1980-81 season, each of the 12 SEC schools has won an SEC divisional, overall or tournament title and 10 schools have won or shared the SEC Championship since the league's inception in 1933. The SEC once again had co-regular-season champions in 2000-2001, with Florida and Kentucky claiming a share. During the last 13 seasons, four schools captured their first SEC title. Florida began the string by winning the school's first championship in 1989. Georgia followed in 1990 with Mississippi State tying LSU for the 1991 title, Arkansas winning the 1992 title in its first season in the SEC and Vanderbilt earning the top spot in 1993. … Last season, the SEC led the nation with the best non-conference record at 119-28 (.810) entering the NCAA and NIT tournaments. The SEC's 81.0 winning percentage was 4.3 percentage points better than the next closest conference, the Big East, at 76.7 percent. The league also was second in the nation with 119 non-conference wins.

(C.D.)

| RPI (last 5 years) | 100-58-8-26-59 |
| 2000-01 FINISH | Lost in NIT second round. |

Like so many of his fellow Southeastern Conference coaches, Auburn's Cliff Ellis can only wonder what kind of team he would have put on the floor this season had the NBA not intervened.

Florida's Billy Donovan, Alabama's Mark Gottfried, Arkansas' Nolan Richardson and LSU's John Brady knew just how Ellis felt last spring when former Auburn point guard Jamison Brewer announced he was giving up his final two years of eligibility to enter the NBA draft. Brewer wasn't a great shooter, but he was a true lead guard and perhaps the most versatile player in the league.

Auburn might have been the favored team in the SEC's Western Division with Brewer, who was taken in the second round by the Cleveland Cavaliers. But Ellis doesn't want to ponder that for long. If misery does indeed love company, he's got plenty in the SEC, particularly in the Tigers' own division. Donovan (Kwame Brown), Gottfried (Gerald Wallace), Richardson (Joe Johnson) and Brady (Kedrick Brown) will wonder how their teams could have fared if their own star players had

either stayed in school or honored their scholarships.

"The situation with Jamison kind of caught us off guard," said Ellis, no pun intended. "He opted for the draft on the last day, and we didn't recruit a point guard. With Brewer on the squad, we felt like we were two deep at every position. I felt like this was going to be our deepest team and most talented team."

No, Ellis hasn't forgotten how good Auburn was two years ago, when Doc Robinson and Chris Porter transformed the Tigers from SEC also-rans to SEC champions.

"That team a couple of years ago was a great team, solid to the core," Ellis said. "[But] I don't think there was as much talent as there is on this team, and it wasn't as deep. With Jamison, we could have really made a run. [Brewer's departure] really threw us a curve. We've got to get through it the best we can. It's our only question mark."

The point-guard spot really became a question mark in early September, when it was announced that 5-10 senior **Lincoln Glass** was suspended indefinitely because of academics.

"Lincoln is still a part of this basketball team and will have an opportunity to rejoin the team at the appropriate time," Ellis said. "Academics will always be the first priority with our basketball team."

Glass made some significant contributions after transferring from junior college last season. He's a point guard by trade. But Ellis got spoiled with the 6-5 Brewer running the show, and now tends to favor taller point guards. Thus his willingness to try 6-6 junior **Marquis Daniels** at the point.

Daniels (15.7 ppg, 7.0 rpg, 2.2 spg) had enjoyed a breakout season a year ago, earning All-SEC third-team honors. Daniels led Auburn in scoring and steals and was second in rebounding. He paced the SEC in steals and was fourth in field-goal percentage (.522). But even though Daniels did most of his damage from a wing position, Ellis isn't the least bit hesitant to move him the point.

The Auburn coaching staff would have loved to let Daniels have a trial run at point guard during the team's trip to Spain in August. But a foot injury prevented him from making the trip.

"Marquis isn't unfamiliar with the point," Ellis said. "He played it until his junior year of high school. Marquis knows the game. He's not a true point guard, but he knows the game."

Daniels put together several strong performances a year ago. He scored a career-high 29 points—in just 29 minutes—against Grambling, notched 26 points, seven rebounds, a career-high five steals and four assists versus Louisiana-Lafayette and scored 24 points and grabbed a career-high 13 boards against LSU.

Daniels led Auburn in double-figure scoring games (29), 20-point games (nine) and double-doubles (six).

If Glass (7.2 ppg, 1.6 rpg, 2.2 apg) returns, he could take over the point if the Daniels experiment doesn't work. Glass has the requisite skills for a point guard. He's quick, can handle the ball and knows how to make plays. He shoots well enough (.319 from three-point range) to keep defenses honest and can put games away in the late going with his free-throw shooting (team-high .891 a year ago).

"He's a small point guard, but he shoots the ball extremely well," Ellis said of Glass. "The big thing there is size, but he has heart and all the characteristics. He dribbles, passes and shoots it well and defends well."

Glass showed his scoring prowess on the trip to Spain, scoring 33 points in a game against the Spanish National team. Then came the suspension. Auburn needs Glass, especially if Daniels can't play the point.

Newcomer **Dwayne Mitchell**, a 6-4 freshman, can also play the point in a pinch, but Ellis would rather have him looking for shots rather than setting up teammates. As a senior at John F. Kennedy High School in New Orleans, Mitchell averaged 28 points, five rebounds, six assists and four steals while shooting 60 percent from the field. He was a consensus Top 100 player.

"Dwayne Mitchell is a guy who can score," Ellis said. "He can break you down both ways. He is very good in the open floor, like Jamison Brewer."

If the point-guard spot is uncertain, the shooting guard position is the exact opposite. **Adam Harrington** (15.5 ppg, 4.3 rpg), a 6-5 junior, was chosen to the All-SEC third team last season, his first at Auburn after transferring from North Carolina State. Harrington, a willing shooter who hoisted a team-high 211 three-pointers, was eighth in the SEC in scoring and fifth in three-pointers per game (2.3).

Harrington, a solid shooter who can also get to the basket with his excellent leaping ability, reached double figures 26 times, with a career high of 32 coming against Detroit. He also scored 27 against Kentucky, 25 against Tennessee and 23 against Jacksonville State.

Auburn is loaded at the wing positions. Besides Daniels, Mitchell and Harrington, newcomer **Derrick Bird** can also play either small forward or big guard. Bird, a 6-4 junior from Schoolcraft (Mich.) College, averaged 20.3 points and 5.0 rebounds a year ago. He shot .450 from three-point range. As an added bonus, Daniels can defend.

"He is a young man who can score and defend," Ellis said. "I like that. His defense is going to tremendously help our press game."

Auburn's frontcourt will benefit greatly from the return of 6-7, 250-pound senior **Mack McGadney**, if he returns. In late September, McGadney was the second Auburn player in less than a month to be suspended. McGadney's suspension was for disciplinary reasons.

"Mack has been suspended indefinitely and will have the opportunity to rejoin the team subject to the progress he makes personally," Ellis said.

McGadney (15.0 ppg, 8.3 rpg in eight games) was averaging nearly a double-double (16.9 ppg, 9.3 rpg) before tearing the anterior cruciate ligament in his left knee in the season's eighth game, against Louisiana-Lafayette. McGadney was lost for the season, and

worse, had played in too many games to earn a medical red-shirt.

The loss of McGadney could have been crippling, considering he was one of the Tigers' few veteran players. That the Tigers earned a postseason tournament (NIT) berth without him was impressive.

McGadney is a typical Ellis player in that he's a blue-collar type who doesn't mind doing the dirty work. At the time of his injury, he was eighth in the SEC in rebounding.

McGadney showed how valuable he could be against Toledo, when he torched the Rockets for 33 points and a career-high 19 rebounds.

If McGadney, who played pickup games in the summer, is anywhere near full strength, he will claim the starting power forward job. That leaves center to 6-10, 220-pound sophomore **Kyle Davis**, (4.8 ppg, 5.3 rpg, 2.8 bpg), who had an excellent freshman season.

Davis isn't a stiff offensively—he shot .518 from the field a year ago—but his primary value is on defense. Last season he blocked 84 shots, tops in the SEC. Davis turned back an amazing 13 shots against Miami in the first round of the NIT. That was the second-highest single-game total in NCAA history (Navy's David Robinson, BYU's Shawn Bradley, Arizona's Loren Woods and Alabama's Roy Rogers share the record of 14). The 13 blocks were the second highest in SEC history.

Davis had five game-saving blocks on the year, against Oregon, Detroit, South Carolina, Alabama and Vanderbilt.

Davis can do other things. He scored a career-high 19 points against Purdue in the second round of the NIT and grabbed a career-high 15 boards against LSU.

"Kyle held his own last year," Ellis said. "McGadney was gone and he took a pounding inside, but he stood his ground. That's a very good sign. Kyle's the kind of kid who is hungry. I think you can look for an even more positive impact from his freshman year to his sophomore year."

Auburn has another slender sophomore frontcourt player in 6-9, 210-pound **Abdou Diame** (7.0 ppg, 3.3 rpg). The native of Sengal showed real promise as a rookie, playing in all 32 games, starting seven and averaging 21 minutes. He led Auburn in field-goal percentage (.542) and was second in blocked shots (30).

Like Davis, Diame had some impressive games. He scored a career-high 25 points (on 12-of-15 shooting) and had seven rebounds in 24 minutes against Grambling and 15 points against Florida. In the NIT, he scored 13 points against Miami. Against Tennessee in the regular season, Diame had his first double-double with 12 points and a career-high 12 boards.

Diame is quick, runs well and can get to the rim in a hurry. He doesn't mind rebounding, either.

Auburn shored up its depth with a recruiting class that one analyst rated the third-best in the nation. Besides Mitchell and Bird, Ellis and his staff brought in two frontcourt players who should have an immediate impact.

The first is first-team Parade All-American **Marco Killingsworth**, a 6-8, 240-pound freshman power forward from Central Park Christian Academy in Birmingham, Ala. That's the same school that produced Alabama star Rod Grizzard.

In his final season at Central Park, Killingsworth averaged 30 points, 13 rebounds and seven blocked shots while shooting 67 percent from the field. He's the prototypical power forward who can post, rebound, block shots and confound defenders with his left-handed shot. He can also run.

"Marco Killingsworth brings us strength," Ellis said. "He brings us more depth inside, but he is powerful and strong. I like his strength and I like his game. He can do a lot of things."

Another versatile big man is 6-8 freshman **Brandon Robinson**, a native of New Market, Ala. who has strong Auburn ties. He's a cousin of former Auburn All-SEC forward Bryant Smith, and he patterns his game after former Auburn All-SEC forward Chris Porter.

Robinson, who played last year for Notre Dame (Mass.) Prep, averaged 17 points, 11 rebounds and four blocked shots, earning first-team Prep School All-America honors. He has an inside-outside game in that he's an excellent rebounder but can shoot from the perimeter. He's also quick, athletic and plays hard, just like his idol Porter. Like Killingsworth, he's left-handed.

"Brandon Robinson is a tremendous athlete," Ellis said. "He has a nose for the ball. With time, he is going to be a very good one."

Auburn has yet another young frontcourt player in 7-0, 235-pound sophomore **Marin Bota** (0.7 ppg, 1.0 rpg). The native of Croatia wasn't asked to do much last year, averaging just 4.9 minutes in the 27 games he played.

Walk-ons **Charlton Barker** (2.0 ppg, 1.0 rpg), a 5-11

senior, and **Donny Calton** (0.7 ppg, 1.7 rpg), a 6-6 junior, round out the team.

2001-2002 SCHEDULE

Nov.	16	High Point
	18	Jacksonville State
	24	@Rutgers
	27	McNeese State
	30	Florida International
Dec.	4	Louisiana Tech
	8	*Virginia
	15	**Marshall
	20	UNC Asheville
	29	Southern Mississippi
Jan.	5	Arkansas
	9	@Ole Miss
	12	Alabama
	16	@Vanderbilt
	19	@LSU
	22	Kentucky
	27	@Tennessee
	30	Mississippi State
Feb.	2	@Arkansas
	9	Georgia
	13	Ole Miss
	16	@Mississippi State
	20	@Florida
	23	South Carolina
	27	@Alabama
March	2	LSU
	7-10	#SEC Tournament

@Road Games
*Arby's Hardwood Classic, Birmingham, AL
**Coors Classic, Mobile, AL
#Georgia Dome, Atlanta, GA

BLUE RIBBON ANALYSIS

BACKCOURT	B
BENCH/DEPTH	B
FRONTCOURT	B
INTANGIBLES	B

After a brief side trip to the NIT last year, Auburn seems capable of returning to the NCAA Tournament, where the Tigers played in 1998-99 and 1999-00. Those teams, led by veteran guard Doc Robinson and All-SEC forward Chris Porter, were deep, talented and athletic. Even without Brewer, coach Ellis thinks he has a team that could rival the best he's produced at Auburn.

Though Brewer's leadership, versatility and playmaking will be missed, Auburn has at least three players who have, at one time in their careers, played point guard. Ellis would rather have an abundance of candidates than none at all. One of the point guard hopefuls could well be Daniels, who elevated his game as a sophomore and was chosen All-SEC while playing a wing position.

Up front, the Tigers will get a boost by the return of McGadney, who injured his knee in the seasons' eighth game. McGadney was headed for an All-SEC season before his injury, and if he's anywhere near that form this year, Auburn will be strong up front.

That's because the Tigers also have two sophomores with star potential in Davis and Diame, plus two freshmen who will also make their presence known quickly.

Auburn is clearly a postseason tournament team. Whether it's the NIT or the NCAAs depends on if someone can approximate Brewer's contributions at the point.

(C.D.)

 Georgia

LOCATION	Athens, GA
CONFERENCE	Southeastern (Eastern)
LAST SEASON	16-15 (.516)
CONFERENCE RECORD	9-7 (3rd)
STARTERS LOST/RETURNING	3/2
NICKNAME	Bulldogs
COLORS	Red & Black
HOMECOURT	Stegeman Coliseum (10,523)
COACH	Jim Harrick (Morris Harvey '60)
RECORD AT SCHOOL	26-35 (2 years)
CAREER RECORD	429-217 (21 years)
ASSISTANTS	James Holland (USC-Spartanburg '85)
	Jim Harrick, Jr. (Pepperdine '87)
	Jeff Dunlap (UCLA '86)
TEAM WINS (last 5 years)	24-20-15-10-16

RPI (last 5 years)   **27-45-79-143-31**
2000-01 FINISH   **Lost in NCAA first round.**

Georgia's Jim Harrick is college basketball's resident jet-setter. He has coached on the West Coast, coached in the Northeast, and most recently, has settled in the deep South.

His 429 wins are a testament to his staying power, and a quick scan of his resume reveals something else: He's a fast worker.

At Pepperdine, Harrick had the Waves in the NIT during his first season and in the NCAA Tournament by his third season. He took UCLA to the NCAA Tournament all eight seasons he was there and won a national championship in 1995.

But after the 1996 season, Harrick was fired at UCLA for what the school's chancellor said was an attempt by Harrick to mislead the university in its investigation of a recruiting violation.

Down but not out, Harrick resurfaced at Rhode Island a year later and promptly led the Rams to NCAA Tournament berths both seasons he was there.

It should come as no surprise then that the 63-year-old Harrick did it again last season, guiding Georgia to the NCAA Tournament in only his second year on the job. Harrick became one of only three coaches in history to take four different teams to the NCAA Tournament. Lefty Driesell and Eddie Sutton were the other two.

For the Bulldogs, it was their first NCAA Tournament appearance in four years. They managed to negotiate their way through the nation's toughest schedule and finished third in the SEC's Eastern Division with a 9-7 record.

"It was important that we have that kind of success," Harrick said. "We don't have a lot of kids from that team coming back, but I think the confidence now is so much better. There's a sense of achievement there."

As good as the 21-year coaching veteran was last season, he'll need to be even better this season. Gone are five of the top seven scorers from a year ago, including Georgia's entire frontcourt and the top reserve in the post. Making matters worse, all three of Georgia's freshmen recruits were academically ineligible, two of them at the very least for the first semester.

"I don't think I've ever had a season like this, with this many questions and this many unknowns," Harrick said. "Two years ago when I got here, there were a lot of questions. But there seems to be even more now, and we're coming off a team that went to the tournament."

Indeed, after the carnage that took out Harrick's recruiting class, he'll have just eight scholarship players to work with.

It was hard enough for the Bulldogs to lose the inside scoring tandem of Anthony Evans (11.5 ppg, 7.5 rpg) and Shon Coleman (10.0 ppg, 5.2 rpg, 1.0 bpg) to graduation. But their leading scorer—All-SEC guard D.A. Layne (16.8 ppg, 3.0 rpg, 3.4 apg)—shocked everyone by deciding to turn pro. The frustrating part (for Layne and for the Bulldogs) was that he wasn't even drafted and lasted all of one day on Memphis' summer league team.

"He's looking for a job, like a lot of guys," said Harrick, who tried to dissuade Layne from giving up his senior season.

The loss of Layne became even more magnified when two freshmen guards, Michael Dean Liggons and Jarrod Gerald, weren't admitted to school. The third recruit who couldn't enroll was center Larry Turner.

The Bulldogs played three guards a year ago, and two of those players are back—6-1 sophomore **Rashad Wright** and 6-4 junior **Ezra Williams**.

Wright (4.7 ppg, 3.0 rpg, 3.3 apg) took over the point guard duties in December last season and kept the job the remainder of the year. He was the first Georgia freshman since Litterial Green to hand out more than 100 assists in his first season. Wright, who's not a great shooter, made up for it with his ability to take care of the ball.

During SEC play, Wright ranked third among the league leaders in assist/turnover ratio (plus-1.85). Only three times in 16 games did he have a negative ratio.

Williams (12.0 ppg, 4.2 rpg, 2.3 apg) returns as the starter at one of the wing positions. Williams was streaky last season. He pumped in 30 points against Auburn and 25 against Mississippi State. But he was also prone to disappear. He failed to reach double figures in five of his last seven games.

Nonetheless, Williams is the kind of player that's difficult to defend. He can beat teams from the perimeter and also has the ability to attack the basket. Paramount, though, will be improving on his .297 three-point percentage from last season.

"Wright and Williams have had a year to grow," Harrick said. "They've adjusted. They're more mature and will be better."

A concern in the backcourt will be depth, especially in light of the travails of Gerald and Liggons. Junior college signee Tony Cole could be the answer. The 5-10 junior played last season for NJCAA national champion Wabash Valley (Ill.) College and is a blur up and down the court. He's originally from Baton Rouge, La., and signed with Harrick at Rhode Island two years ago before heading for junior college.

"He can run your break, penetrate and get inside," Harrick said of Cole. "I don't know anybody in our league that will have the quickness he has."

Ideally, Harrick would like to push the tempo more than the Bulldogs did a year ago. Evans and Coleman were not the kind of post players who could effectively run the floor. On top of that, Wright was just a freshman.

"That's the way we like to play, forcing the issue, and we haven't been able to do that the last two years," Harrick said. "I think you'll see more of that this year."

In many of the Bulldogs' practices last season, one of the best players on the court was 6-6 sophomore forward **Jarvis Hayes**, a transfer from Western Carolina who was sitting out. He's ready to go this season and will inherit the other wing spot opposite Williams.

Hayes, a big-time leaper and versatile performer, was the Southern Conference Freshman of the Year in 2000. He averaged 17.1 points and 5.4 rebounds for the Catamounts and was the first freshman in 40 years to lead the Southern Conference in scoring.

"Jarvis gives us several dimensions on offense that we didn't have in the past," Harrick said. "He can shoot from long range or slash to the basket. I think he'll be an exciting player for us."

Another newcomer who could have seen immediate playing time was 6-1 freshman guard Liggons of Rome, Ga. Dean averaged 31.3 points last season for Coosa High School and was selected to the Atlanta Journal-Constitution's "Terrific Ten" of top in-state talent. But Liggons had his academic transcript flagged by the NCAA's Clearinghouse. The transcript apparently didn't reflect all Liggon's grades, but Georgia has appealed and hopes the NCAA will accept an updated version.

Another freshman guard, Gerald, failed to qualify academically and enrolled in a prep school. Gerald, from Mullins, S.C., could have played the point.

Former walk-on **Mike Patrick**, a 6-4 junior, is back after playing sparingly down the stretch last season. He averaged 1.4 points and played in just three SEC games. Senior swingman **Ryan Pevey** (1.6 ppg) will provide additional depth on the wing.

On the interior, Georgia will be bigger and more athletic than it was a year ago with 6-8 sophomore **Steve Thomas** (2.1 ppg, 2.9 rpg) and 6-7 sophomore **Chris Daniels** (3.5 ppg, 2.6 rpg). Neither, though, is as accomplished scoring in the post as Evans or Coleman.

"I think both of those guys will be a lot quicker than Coleman and Evans and will be able to get up and down the floor a little better," Harrick said. "It's a trade-off."

Thomas, at 230 pounds, is the team's best rebounder and a solid post defender. Daniels showed flashes toward the end of last season and always seemed to come up with timely plays. Harrick loves his instincts for the game.

Harrick was also counting on Turner, of Milledgeville, Ga., to provide a presence in the post, especially with 7-1 center Robb Dryden gone. Turner averaged 17.1 points, 8.0 rebounds and 4.7 blocks last season at Baldwin High School. He was voted the MVP at the prestigious 5-Star Camp in Pennsylvania in June of 2000.

But like Liggons and Gerald, Turner will be on the sidelines this season, at least for the first semester. His score on the ACT was flagged by the ACT board. He'll retake the test, and hope to regain eligibility by the winter semester. He had gotten through an earlier academic hurdle by passing the Georgia high school exit exam before the bad news came from the ACT board.

The other half of the Hayes combination, identical twin **Jonas Hayes**, will play a backup role to Daniels at the power forward spot. Like Jarvis, Jonas sat out last season after transferring from Western Carolina, but was allowed to practice with the team.

Another transfer is on the way. Damien Wilkins, the son of Gerald Wilkins and nephew of former Georgia great Dominique Wilkins, is transferring from North Carolina State. Wilkins, who has two years of eligibility remaining, will have to sit out this season.

"I envision this being a more balanced team, where it's not just two or three guys doing all of the scoring," Harrick said. "I certainly hope we have five guys in double figures. That's when you become hard to guard."

2001-2002 SCHEDULE

Nov.	16	Furman
	19	*Georgetown
	21	@Georgia Southern
	26	Samford
Dec.	1	Colorado
	4	*Georgia State
	7	Minnesota
	9	Georgia Tech
	15	@South Alabama
	17	@Pepperdine
	19-22	#Rainbow Classic
Jan.	5	Vanderbilt
	9	@Kentucky
	12	Tennessee
	16	Alabama
	19	@Florida
	23	Arkansas
	26	@Vanderbilt
	30	@South Carolina
Feb.	2	Ole Miss
	6	@Mississippi State
	9	@Auburn
	12	Florida
	16	Kentucky
	23	@LSU
	27	South Carolina
March	2	@Tennessee
	7-10	##SEC Tournament

@Road Games
*Tip-Off Classic, Springfield, MA
**Georgia Dome, Atlanta, GA
#Honolulu, HI (vs. Arkansas State, first round; also Boston College, Hawaii, Holy Cross, Iona, Miami, Portland)
##Georgia Dome, Atlanta, GA

BLUE RIBBON ANALYSIS

BACKCOURT	C
BENCH/DEPTH	C-
FRONTCOURT	C+
INTANGIBLES	B

In truth, Georgia could suffer its share of growing pains this year, although Harrick isn't conceding anything.

Layne made so many clutch baskets the last couple of years for the Bulldogs. It remains to be seen who takes those shots this season. And better yet, who's going to be the one to make them?

That's probably where Jarvis Hayes comes in. His development will be critical.

"He's got to pick up the slack that Layne gave us," Harrick said. "That and our inside guys have really got to come through for us with defense and rebounding, and a little bit of scoring."

Avoiding the cellar in the East will be a chore, especially if there are any injuries or other casualties. But if Georgia can't get any of its recruits eligible, the Bulldogs could suffer through a long season. With only eight bodies on hand to deal with the rigors of the SEC season, a last-place finish is likely (see LSU, 2000-2001).

(C.L.)

LSU

LOCATION	Baton Rouge, LA
CONFERENCE	Southeastern (Western)
LAST SEASON	13-16 (.448)
CONFERENCE RECORD	2-14 (6th)
STARTERS LOST/RETURNING	1/4
NICKNAME	Tigers
COLORS	Purple & Gold
HOMECOURT	Pete Maravich Assembly Center (14,164)
COACH	John Brady (Belhaven '76)
RECORD AT SCHOOL	63-55 (4 years)
CAREER RECORD	151-132 (10 years)
ASSISTANTS	Kermit Davis (Mississippi State '82)
	Butch Pierre (Mississippi State '84)
	Mike Giorlando (Spring Hill '80)
TEAM WINS (last 5 years)	10-9-12-28-13
RPI (last 5 years)	114-161-124-13-104
2000-01 FINISH	Lost in conference second round.

If John Brady can ever get the NBA to stop plundering his program, he might be able to put together a sustained run of success.

After the 1999-2000 season, the play-for-pay league snatched away Stromile Swift, who had been a big reason LSU went 28-6, won the SEC Western Division championship and advanced to the NCAA Tournament's Sweet 16. Swift's premature departure—he played all of a season and half for the Tigers—was also a big reason the Tigers pulled a first-to-worst turnaround, finishing sixth in the West last year. Swift's presence would surely have reversed LSU's fortunes in enough games to give the Tigers a winning record.

It would have been difficult to replace Swift, but Brady would have liked to at least try. But because of NCAA scholarship restrictions placed on the program before he arrived, Brady couldn't sign another player after Swift turned pro.

Thus, LSU went into last season with eight scholarship players, a scary proposition in any conference, let alone one as tough as the SEC. The Tigers had to get lucky and hope everyone stayed healthy, but that didn't happen.

First, starting center **Brad Bridgewater** went down for the season with a knee injury in preseason practice. After eleven games, starting guard Lamont Roland also suffered a season-ending knee injury. Thus the Tigers' 2-14 SEC record was understandable—they often played great for a half but simply didn't have the energy or depth to sustain their effort. To their credit, they didn't quit, even knocking off Western Division champion Ole Miss in the second-to-last game of the regular season.

Suffice to say Brady wasn't sad to see last year come to an end. He has higher hopes for this season, but again, the NBA has made his job just a bit tougher. It was expected that Swift would leave early, but the departure of junior college signee Kedrick Brown was a bit more surprising. Brown, a 6-7, 220-pound forward from Okaloosa-Walton (Fla.) Community College, had been the Tigers' premier recruit. But when Brown became convinced last spring he would be chosen in the NBA draft, he signed with an agent. Brown was eventually chosen by the Boston Celtics with the 11th pick in the first round, the highest a junior college player had ever been taken.

Brown would probably have become the SEC's newcomer of the year, but Brady has had to purge him from memory. Of some consolation is the fact LSU will have 11 scholarship players this season, the most in Brady's five years in Baton Rouge.

"I like our talent, and for the first time, we've got some numbers," Brady said. "But you can't help but think what we'd be like if we had Stromile Swift and Kedrick Brown on this team. I liked our chances to win the West with Kedrick and **Ronald Dupree**.

"We've had back-to-back years where we've had major blows losing significant talents early to the NBA. I'm happy for both kids. But for the program, especially with the scholarship restrictions we've had, it's been tough."

As Brady said, he does have some talent. It starts with the 6-6 junior Dupree (17.3 ppg, 8.8 rpg), who had to shoulder a huge load last season and handled it without complaint, drastically improving his game as he went along. Playing nearly 35 minutes a game, Dupree led the league in scoring and was second in rebounding, all while playing out of position at center.

Dupree, who averaged just five points as a freshman, impressed other SEC coaches with his dramatic improvement.

"He's fantastic," Georgia coach Jim Harrick said. "He's so athletic on the offensive end. He can play for anybody in this league, heck, anybody in the country for that matter. He's the genuine article."

Said Mississippi State coach Rick Stansbury, who recruited Dupree, a Mississippi native, "He's always had the talent and athleticism. Now he's blending it with work ethic."

Dupree, a third-team All-SEC pick a year ago, continued working hard in the off-season. He improved his vertical leap from 36 inches to 41, and worked on his perimeter game. With the return of Bridgewater and the addition of some junior college big men, he'll be freed from his post duties and returned to the perimeter.

"If Ronald improves as much from his sophomore to his junior year as he did from his freshman to his sophomore year, he'll make a run at MVP of this league," Brady said. "We'll move him on the perimeter this year, but also ask him to drive the ball to the goal and incorporate a mid-range game into his overall game. He's a tremendous athlete—very explosive."

With Dupree, 6-7 junior **Collis Temple III** and 6-7 senior **Jermaine Williams**, LSU has plenty of size and scoring punch at the wing positions. The Tigers will probably run a four-out, one-in offense most of the time. That means opposing defenses will have their hands full trying to stop all the perimeter shooters, especially given Brady's motion offense, which incorporates a dizzying amount of cuts and some crafty screening, all designed to get open jump shots.

Temple (14.1 ppg, 4.6 rpg, 2.2 apg) was another of LSU's iron men a year ago, logging 32 minutes a game. He wound up 12th in the SEC in scoring, eighth in free-throw percentage (.733) and ninth in three-point percentage (.363).

Temple put together some big games, torching Tennessee for 30 points and Mississippi State for 27. He scored 20 or more in six games.

Williams (7.4 ppg, 3.9 rpg) reached double figures 10 times. He wasn't nearly as reliant on the three-pointer as some of his teammates, taking just 17 shots from behind the arc. Williams did most of his damage closer to the basket. He shot .497 from the field, tops among LSU regulars.

LSU should be set at guard. **Torris Bright** (10.8 ppg, 2.8 rpg, 4.0 apg), a 6-4 junior, returns for his third season as a starter. Bright was third in the SEC in assists last season, but drove Brady crazy with his turnovers (110, tops among SEC point guards).

Brady would love for Bright to cut down on his turnovers and become a bit more solid. With depth, Brady now has options, which might get Bright's attention.

"We've got a little pressure on Torris," Brady said. "I always like to put it on players. It's their responsibility to earn a spot. With challenges from other players who can play the point, it will be on Torris. In the past, it's been on me because I've had nobody to put pressure on players. Now we've got a more competitive situation."

Freshman **Xavier Whipple** might be the one to put a little heat on Bright. The 6-3 Whipple played last year for Wilkinson County High School in McIntyre, Ga., where he averaged 20 points, six rebounds, seven assists and four steals.

Whipple was also a quarterback for Wilkinson County's football team, passing for 26 touchdowns and 1,900 yards as a senior. He's used to being a leader.

"He's a true point guard with size," Brady said. "He brings great stability at the point guard position, a position we have needed stability at."

Another rookie talent at guard is 6-4 sophomore **JueMichael Young**, who was ineligible a year ago, which also contributed to LSU's depth crisis. Young, a Top 100 player two years ago at Hammond (La.) High School, knows what to do with the basketball.

"He's a scorer," Brady said. "He can drive it to the goal, shoot it from past the [three-point] arc and has a good mid-range game. He's better than Lamont Roland was as a senior."

After Bridgewater went down a year ago, the Tigers were practically defenseless in the post. The return of the 6-8, 260-pound junior is welcomed.

"He'll be a good addition," Brady said. "He's extremely athletic, and he'll block some shots, get some rebounds and dunk some balls for us that we couldn't have done a year ago."

Other than Brown, LSU recruited two more highly regarded junior college transfers, but only one is eligible this season. Shawnson Brown is a 6-9, 240-pound junior from Lee (Texas) College by way of Shreveport did not officially graduate from Lee and can't play for the Tigers this season.

Johnson did not meet Lee's Aug. 15 deadline for completing and turning in all course work. So, he won't graduate from the school until Dec. 14.

"We are disappointed his work was not completed at the appropriate time, but respect and understand the Lee College policy," Brady said.

Johnson will enroll at LSU in the spring, but mid-term graduates are not eligible to play.

"With that being the case, our plan is for Shawnson to be at LSU in the second semester, practice with our team, but not play in games. He will then play the following two seasons with this year counting as a redshirt."

Junior **Thomas Davis**, a Pineville, La. native who played last season at Kilgore (Texas) Junior College, averaged 14.7 points and six rebounds as a sophomore. The 6-8, 225-pound Davis brings more than just size.

"Thomas is an athletic forward who can play different positions," Brady said. "He can play around the goal and defend the opponent's power forward, and on offense, he can face the basket and move around on the floor, which can make him very difficult to defend."

Still another newcomer is 6-4 freshman **Antonio Hudson**, who scored 30.3 points last year for Grambling (La.) Lab. Hudson, chosen the state's 1A player of the year, also averaged 9.2 rebounds and 6.5 assists.

"He's very talented," Brady said. "We felt he was without question the best player in Louisiana last year. We think he's got an opportunity to come in and play right away."

Jason Wilson (3.7 ppg, 3.5 rpg), a 6-8, 250-pound junior who walked on last year, has been given a scholarship, a just reward for his heroism. Wilson could have taken a scholarship at TCU or Texas Tech, but knew LSU, a team he had rooted for all his life, needed help. Wilson wound up playing 17 minutes a game and shooting a respectable .506 (44-of-87) from the field.

He won't play as much as he did a year ago, but Wilson will provide depth in a frontcourt that suddenly has size and numbers again.

2001-2002 SCHEDULE

Nov.	17	Campbell
	19	Southern
	23-25	#Big Island Invitational
	28	Towson
Dec.	2	Northwestern State
	4	Louisiana-Lafayette
	15	McNeese State
	18	*New Orleans
	20	Houston
	27	**Miami
	30	Nicholls State
Jan.	5	@Alabama
	13	Arkansas
	16	@Florida
	19	Auburn
	23	@Ole Miss
	26	@Mississippi State
	30	Tennessee
Feb.	2	Alabama
	6	@Vanderbilt
	9	Kentucky
	13	Mississippi State
	16	@Arkansas
	20	@South Carolina
	23	Georgia
	27	Ole Miss
March	2	@Auburn
	7-10	##SEC Tournament

@Road Games
*Lakefront Arena, New Orleans, LA
**Sugar Bowl Classic, New Orleans, LA
#Hilo, HI (vs. Weber State, first round; also Colorado State, Hawaii, Hawaii-Hilo, Mercer, Pepperdine, Wisconsin)
##Georgia Dome, Atlanta, GA

BLUE RIBBON ANALYSIS

BACKCOURT	C
BENCH/DEPTH	C
FRONTCOURT	B
INTANGIBLES	B

Brady experienced the best and worst college basketball has to offer in the span of a year. Two years ago, he was the SEC Coach of the Year after leading his team to 28 wins and a trip to the NCAA Tournament's Sweet 16. Last season, his roster gutted by the NBA draft and injuries, Brady watched his team plummet to the bottom of the SEC West standings.

Now, with NCAA scholarship restrictions lifted, Brady can begin to play with a full deck. This season, the Tigers have 11 scholarship players, and next year they'll have the full 13. To Brady, who struggled last year with six scholarship players, 11 will seem like an army.

Brady has a nice mix of talent, starting with Dupree. LSU has plenty of scoring punch and athleticism, good overall size, and a lot more bulk in the post than it did a year ago. The Tigers managed to win 13 games with a depleted roster. This year, we look for that number to rise to 16 or more.

What to make of LSU in the crowded and talented SEC West? Now that's a good one. The loss in September of junior college recruit Johnson hurt the inside game. If the Tigers can get lucky and suffer no additional personnel losses, they have enough talent to fashion a winning record. A upper-division finish in the West might be too much to ask this season.

(C.D.)

Mississippi State

LOCATION	Starkville, Miss.
CONFERENCE	Southeastern
LAST SEASON	18-13 (.581)
CONFERENCE RECORD	7-9 (t-4th West)
STARTERS LOST/RETURNING	3/2
NICKNAME	Bulldogs
COLORS	Maroon & White
HOMECOURT	Humphrey Coliseum (10,500)
COACH	Rick Stansbury (Campbellsville '82)
RECORD AT SCHOOL	52-42 (3 years)
CAREER RECORD	52-42 (3 years)
ASSISTANTS	Robert Kirby (Pan American '83)
	Phil Cunningham (Campbellsville '90)
	Stan Jones (Memphis State '84)
TEAM WINS (last 5 years)	12-15-20-14-18
RPI (last 5 years)	120-112-95-128-34
2000-01 FINISH	Lost in NIT quarterfinal.

Rick Stansbury has grown weary of coming close.

In two of his first three seasons as the Mississippi State head coach, the Bulldogs have beaten on the door of the NCAA Tournament. But they've yet to kick it in.

"Naturally, you look back over the last three years, and there's two of those three years we'd like to have made the NCAA Tournament," said Stansbury, whose Bulldogs lost to eventual NIT tournament champion Tulsa in a quarterfinal in Starkville a year ago.

Even more difficult for Stansbury to swallow was that Mississippi State entered postseason competition last season with a No. 40 RPI, earning the Bulldogs the sobering distinction of owning the highest RPI of any school not selected to the NCAA Tournament.

"This past season, I wasn't pleased to make the quarterfinals of the NIT and win 18 games. That's not what our goals are," said Stansbury, who spent eight years as an assistant at MSU before getting the head job. "Again, it comes down to what a fine line it was, you were one win away from making the (NCAA) Tournament.

"But what I love about it is if you look at years past, winning 20 or 18 games would have been terrific. Now we have the expectations up, up where I want them."

Never mind that this will be one of Stansbury's younger teams, a roster that includes eight freshmen and sophomores. From a chemistry standpoint, overall basketball skill and ability to defend in the post, Stansbury thinks the Bulldogs have a chance to be better than a year ago.

And that was a team he thinks could have easily won 22 or 23 games and been a factor in the NCAA Tournament. But the Bulldogs simply failed to close the deal in two or three key games during the regular season.

"We won't be as experienced as we have been, but I think we will be tougher mentally in a couple of areas," Stansbury told CBS Sportsline.

In some ways, Mississippi State is still feeling the effects of Jonathan Bender opting for the NBA in 1999. Bender, who had signed with the Bulldogs, was the fifth pick in the draft that year and would have obviously been a force at the college level.

"I've moved on past that," Stansbury said. "I've never used that as an excuse, but we all know how that affected us."

When it comes to young talent, the Bulldogs will be as stocked as any team in the SEC. **Mario Austin**, a 6-9 sophomore, has All-SEC potential after showing it in spurts last season. The former McDonald's High School All-American averaged 7.9 points, 3.6 rebounds and shot .478 from the field. He's an extremely effective scorer from 12 feet in and has an array of moves.

Austin has also lost some of his baby fat and will move to his natural position of power forward this season.

"Getting weight off Mario will help him move out there the way a power forward has to move," Stansbury said. "He's never guarded out much on the floor, one, and getting that weight last summer made it that much more difficult.

"No question he'll be so much better as a power forward-type player for us, not just from a skill standpoint, but understanding what it takes."

Austin, unable to attend summer school last year, blew up to 280 pounds before he entered Mississippi State, and that slowed his progress.

With MSU fans hoping that Austin takes flight this season, the overriding key will be the development of junior point guard **Derrick Zimmerman** (4.6 ppg, 2.9

apg, 2.7 rpg). Gone is two-year starter Antonio Jackson.

The Bulldogs, who didn't sign any other point guards during the off-season, need for the 6-2 Zimmerman to continue on the same track he was on during their NIT run last season. He averaged 13.3 points, 5.3 rebounds and 3.0 assists during those three games. He also shot 59 percent from the field.

"I think Derrick Zimmerman can do it," Stansbury told CBS Sportsline. "He really played well for us late last year, and he is a young man that we are looking to turn the ball over to. He is going to be our point guard. He is athletic and as talented as they come. He is a young player who came to our place and matured a lot, has grown up a lot and really settled in.

"I think he'll have a big year for us, and if he does, I think our team will be really good."

Paramount for Zimmerman is not allowing his confidence to wane. That was a problem a year ago. But he's a great athlete (40-inch vertical leap) and plays suffocating on-the-ball defense.

The most likely backup to Zimmerman is 6-3 sophomore **Roy Goffer** (2.0 ppg, 1.1 apg, .353 3PT). The 23-year-old Goffer served in the Israeli army for three years before enrolling at MSU. He started the final seven games at shooting guard last season, but will probably be needed more at the point this season. He can play both positions.

Walk-on **Guy Gardner**, a 6-2 senior, started in six games last season at point guard. He averaged 3.2 points and 1.3 assists and shot .444 from the three-point line.

Marckell Patterson, a 6-5 senior, is the Bulldogs' leading returning scorer. He averaged 12.2 points, 4.4 rebounds and 2.0 assists last season in a swingman's role.

Patterson led MSU a year ago with 21 double-digit scoring games.

The Bulldogs struggled from the perimeter at times last season. Stansbury is counting on Patterson to make people pay from out there this season. The same goes for junior college transfer **Michal Ignerski**, a 6-9 junior who comes to MSU from Eastern Oklahoma State College.

Originally from Poland, Ignerski shot 47 percent from three-point range last season, while averaging 17.3 points. He will be a tough match-up for teams at power forward, but can also step out and play on the wing.

The other returning senior perimeter player is 6-5 **Michael Gholar**, who averaged 2.9 points and 3.7 rebounds last season. Gholar struggled through injuries a year ago and shot just .291 from the field and .204 from three-point range.

Someone else to watch on the wing is 6-5 sophomore **Ontario Harper** (0.8 ppg), who Stansbury thinks can be one of the surprises this season.

Stansbury is also hoping to get 6-2 sophomore guard **Timmy Bowers** a few more looks this season. Bowers (2.5 ppg, .240 3PT) has added strength during the off-season.

Freshman **Winsome Frazier** may wind up being the best of the Bulldogs' wing players. A dynamic athlete, the 6-4 Frazier averaged 18.3 points and 8.9 rebounds last season while playing for Northwestern High School in Miami, Fla. He's a complete player who will pay dividends on both ends of the court.

"He's a great athlete, he has the ability to go get a basket," Stansbury said. "Defensively, most young kids struggle, but I think for him that adjustment is going to be minimized because of his ability to play defense right now."

On the inside, Stansbury went out and signed a pair of 7-footers. One of those, 7-1 freshman **Marcus Campbell** of Albany, Ga., will contend right away for the starting center position. Having Campbell in the fold allows Mississippi State to move Austin to power forward. Departed senior Tang Hamilton was the starter there last season.

Clemson and Georgia both wanted Campbell, rated among the Top 50 high school prospects, but Stansbury was able to win the recruiting battle. The left-handed Campbell is nimble for a big man and equally skilled as a shot-blocker. He showed his promise in late July in the Tennessee-Georgia High School All-Star game in Chattanooga, Tenn., playing against a team loaded with SEC signees, Campbell scored 23 points, 17 in the first half, and grabbed a game-high 17 rebounds.

Stansbury also signed 7-2 freshman **Wesley Holmes** of Gallatin, Tenn., but Holmes is a red-shirt candidate.

The odds-on favorite to win the center job is 6-9 sophomore **Lincoln Smith**, who red-shirted last season after playing as a freshman. At one time, Smith weighed more than 300 pounds after playing high school football.

But he's now down to 270, and while still raw as a basketball player, should make an impact this season.

Last year's starter at center, Robert Jackson, disagreed with Stansbury as to what his role should be in the offense and left the team. Jackson, who quit toward the end of last season, is transferring to Marquette.

"I think we're going to have the ability to guard the post guy one-on-one, something we haven't had basically since Tyrone (Washington) left," Stansbury said. "We had a six-year stretch with Erick Dampier and Tyrone where we had the big guy who could guard the block, protect the basket and block a shot. That's an area we're going to be better in."

2001-2002 SCHEDULE

Nov.	17	Nicholls State
	19	Florida A&M
	21	Arkansas-Little Rock
	24	@Louisiana-Lafayette
	28	Alabama A&M
Dec.	1	South Alabama
	5	@Richmond
	8	Arkansas State
	15	#Las Vegas Classic
	16	**Georgia State
	20-22	##Las Vegas Classic
	29	@Tulane
Jan.	5	Kentucky
	8	@Arkansas
	12	@Ole Miss
	16	Tennessee
	19	@Alabama
	26	LSU
	30	@Auburn
Feb.	2	@Florida
	6	Georgia
	9	Alabama
	13	@LSU
	16	Auburn
	20	@Vanderbilt
	23	Ole Miss
	27	Arkansas
March	2	@South Carolina
	7-10	###SEC Tournament

@Road Games
**Chick-fil-A Peach Bowl Classic, Philips Arena, Atlanta, GA
#Southaven, MS (vs. Louisiana-Monroe)
##Las Vegas, NV (Pool A will consist of Illinois-Chicago, Purdue, Southwest Missourit StateTexas A&M; Pool B will consist of Mississippi State, Louisiana-Monroe, Cincinnati and Richmond)
#Georgia Dome, Atlanta, GA

BLUE RIBBON ANALYSIS

BACKCOURT	C+
BENCH/DEPTH	B-
FRONTCOURT	B
INTANGIBLES	B

This Mississippi State team needs to find an identity, something the last couple never did.

There's plenty of potential with the young players, and Stansbury just keeps bringing talented prospects into the program. But developing that talent will be critical.

"We've got some good kids coming in and how good we will be will depend on how quick those guys fit in," Stansbury told CBS Sportsline. "There is no question we have good size."

The best-case scenario is that Zimmerman plays with great confidence all season and develops into a prime leader and that Austin explodes into one of the top power forwards in the conference. He certainly has the ability.

Depth in the backcourt is a concern, not to mention a lack of proven players who can consistently make big jump shots. Is it too much to ask Ignerski and Frazier to be those guys this season?

Stansbury, whose contract is up after this season, needs to get this club over that proverbial hump. The inexperience will show early, but talent should prevail to again put the Bulldogs in position for an NCAA Tournament berth.

Whether this is the year they finally kick the door in remains to be seen. Competition is awfully tough in the SEC's Western Division.

(C.L.)

South Carolina

LOCATION	Columbia, S.C.
CONFERENCE	Southeastern
LAST SEASON	15-15 (.500)
CONFERENCE RECORD	6-10 (5th East)
STARTERS LOST/RETURNING	1/4
NICKNAME	Gamecocks
COLORS	Garnet & black
HOMECOURT	Carolina Coliseum (12,401)
COACH	Dave Odom (Guilford '65)
RECORD AT SCHOOL	First year
CAREER RECORD	278-174 (15 years)
ASSISTANTS	Barry Sanderson (Alabama '90)
	Ernie Nestor (Alderson-Broaddus '68)
	Rick Duckett (North Carolina '79)
TEAM WINS (last 5 years)	24-23-8-15-15
RPI (last 5 years)	25-12-147-82-69
2000-01 FINISH	Lost in NIT first round.

Dave Odom wanted another challenge, and Eddie Fogler wanted out.

Odom, after 12 years of building Wake Forest into a national contender, left the glamour of the ACC for South Carolina last April. It's a move that raised some eyebrows, but one that's understandable when you consider the landscape on Tobacco Road.

For all of the Deacons' success under Odom, they often times languished in the shadow of Duke and North Carolina, and occasionally, even North Carolina State. And the stringent academic standards at Wake Forest, a small private school, weren't always tailor-made for bringing in the top basketball talent.

At South Carolina, where Fogler grew increasingly disillusioned the last couple of years, those standards will be much more forgiving. Just as important, the 58-year-old Odom seems refreshed and ready to take on a conference he says is every bit as good as the ACC.

He's certainly proven his worth as a basketball coach, even if he wasn't the first choice of South Carolina athletic director Mike McGee. The Gamecocks were turned down by Kentucky's Tubby Smith and Connecticut's Jim Calhoun. They also made overtures to Buzz Peterson, who left Tulsa to take the Tennessee job.

Odom, who led the Deacons to 11 consecutive post-season appearances, hardly seemed offended that he wasn't at the front of the pack.

"They're great coaches. If they were talked to, it didn't work out. Nobody needs to apologize," Odom said when he was introduced as the Gamecocks' coach.

He takes over for Fogler, one of the more respected coaches in the country when it came to getting the most out of his players and running a clean program. But Fogler and McGee didn't exactly see eye-to-eye on the subject of expectations at South Carolina. McGee said making the NCAA or NIT tournament every year should be the rule. Fogler said it should be more the goal.

So after three straight non-winning seasons in Columbia, Fogler resigned.

It's up to Odom to get the South Carolina ship steered back toward the top of the SEC. The Gamecocks compiled a 26-6 record in SEC play during the 1997 and '98 seasons, but were upset in the first round of the NCAA Tournament each year by a No. 15-seeded team in '97 and a No. 14-seeded team in '98.

"I'm not going to put a bad team on the court," said Odom, who earned national coach-of-the-year honors in '95. "I'm going to put a good team on that court, somehow, some way."

This year would be as good as any, especially with the Gamecocks saying goodbye to the 33-year-old Carolina Coliseum. They will move to a new 18,600-seat arena in time for the 2002-03 season.

"That motivates me. I want to close that coliseum out the best we can be," Odom said. "Let's finish this one up the right way."

One thing's for certain. The Gamecocks, coming off a 15-15 finish a year ago, have ample experience returning and a veteran backcourt that's been through the wars.

Seniors **Aaron Lucas** and **Jamel Bradley** are both back. They started in every game they appeared in a year ago and complement each other well.

The 5-11 Lucas (10.3 ppg, 3.9 apg) is a steady point guard who loves getting everybody else involved. He needs to cut down on his turnovers after committing 88 a year ago. Still, he was fifth in the SEC in assists and led the Gamecocks in minutes played. He's also a proven leader.

The day after Odom was introduced as South Carolina's new coach, he met with the team. One of his first questions was "Who's the leader here?"

Everybody immediately pointed at Lucas, who welcomes that role.

"It's my responsibility to pass along what I've learned," he told the Columbia State. "I mean, that's how life works."

Backing up Lucas at point guard will once again be sophomore **Michael Boynton** (2.2 ppg, 1.5 apg). He had a respectable freshman season, but like Lucas, turned it over too many times. They combined for 132 turnovers.

The 6-2 Bradley spent last summer playing for the United States team in the 19th Deaflympics in Rome, Italy. Bradley (11.5 ppg, 2.2 apg) led the Gamecocks in scoring last season. He possesses a sweet shooting stroke, but didn't shoot it particularly well a year ago (.383 FG, .355 3-PT).

Gone are departed seniors Antonio Grant and David Ross, a pair of wing players who weren't dynamic basketball players. But they were instrumental in holding things together last season during some of the tough times.

"A lot of experience went out the door with those two guys," Odom said. "When you lose seniors, hopefully there's just a temporary void in leadership. Replacing them is going to be one of the prime objectives early on."

Offense was a problem across the board last season. The Gamecocks were last in the league in scoring offense (68.1 ppg), field-goal percentage (.417) and three-point field-goal percentage (.302). They were also 10th in assists.

The best news coming out of the off-season was the progress of junior swingman **Chuck Eidson**, who tore ligaments in his knee last season and underwent surgery. One of the most versatile players in the league, the 6-7 Eidson resumed playing pickup games toward the end of July.

Odom is optimistic that Eidson (9.0 ppg, 5.3 rpg, 3.1 apg) will make a full recovery, and so is Eidson. He dropped out of school for a semester to rehabilitate in Charleston, S.C. There was speculation that he might transfer when Fogler stepped down.

For Eidson, simply being back on the court is a blessing.

"It was real tough because I wanted a chance to turn things around and I wasn't allowed to have that," he told the Columbia State. "I think it's made me real hungry for this next season because I've never gone more than a week or two weeks without basketball. It's been one of the worst things.

"In 20 years of basketball, I'd never missed a game."

The Gamecocks missed him desperately last season. After he went down, they were 5-10 and lost seven of those games by seven points or less. But even before the injury, Eidson was not playing to the level of his freshman season, when he was voted to the SEC's all-freshman team and set a South Carolina record with 93 steals.

The problem was his shot. He tweaked it to get a quicker release after his freshman season and shot just .321 from the field and .184 from the three-point line before injuring his knee.

South Carolina needs the trio of Lucas, Bradley and Eidson to shoot better from the perimeter this season, especially now that Travis Kraft—the team's best pure shooter—has transferred.

Ideally, Odom would like to push the tempo, which means an array of three-point shooters playing the inside-out game with the big men. To do that, though, the Gamecocks must improve on their accuracy from long distance.

"We don't have flame throwers waiting to throw up threes," Odom said. "We've either got to develop our three-point shooters or get some people in here that can shoot with range. Maybe both."

If the Gamecocks get their shooting woes straightened out, they have a chance to do some real damage in the post.

Rolando Howell, a 6-9 sophomore, could be braced for a breakout season. He has unlimited athletic ability and showed it in flashes as a freshman. Howell (8.5 ppg, 5.1 rpg, .528 FG) averaged 12 points and 6.9 rebounds and shot .625 from the field during the last month of the season a year ago.

It was a sign he was starting to figure out the college game, and he should be that much better this season. Even better for Howell, who gave some consideration to turning pro, is that Odom is known for developing big men.

Remember how nicely Tim Duncan developed when he was at Wake Forest?

What's more, Howell will have proven people playing around him. **Tony Kitchings**, a 6-10 junior center, will look to be more consistent this season on the offensive end. Kitchings (10.0 ppg, 6.6 rpg, .515 FG) is still evolving as a low-post scorer, but eats up space and can rebound. He's also an effective passer in the post.

The other big body down low is 6-10 junior **Marius Petravicius** (8.5 ppg, 4.7 rpg, .487 FG). Petravicius, originally from Lithuania, is at his best on the defensive end and can also rebound.

"One of the things a new head coach finds when he goes to a new program is that usually there's a void in the post, not many accomplished big players," Odom said. "I don't think that's true here at South Carolina. We have some post players, and that's a welcome find."

The one casualty was 6-7 forward Calvin Clemmons, who decided to transfer. Odom said it was a case of Clemmons being lost in the shuffle behind Howell, Kitchings and Petravicius.

"The ones we needed to stay have re-committed themselves to Gamecock basketball, and I couldn't be more pleased with that," Odom said.

Off the bench, Odom will look to 6-7 sophomore forward **Ivan Howell** for depth.

Howell, the older brother of Rolando Howell, sat out last season because of all the numbers at small forward. He still needs to prove that he can hit the perimeter jumper. **Greg Taylor**, a 6-5 sophomore, also returns on the wing.

Of the newcomers, junior college transfer **Chris Warren** may be the most equipped to step in and contribute right away. Warren, a 6-5 junior who loves to shoot off the dribble, averaged 17.1 points last season for Collin County (Texas) Community College.

Issa Konare and **Carlos Powell**, a pair of 6-7 freshmen, will provide depth at the small forward position. Powell, who played for Wilson High School in Florence, S.C., averaged 20 points, 11 rebounds and four assists last season, when he was selected Region 6-AAA Player of the Year and was runnerup as state AAA player of the year. Recruiting guru Bob Gibbons says Powell could be the surprise of South Carolina's class.

Konare, a native of Senegal, will be 20 years old when he shows up on campus. He's played basketball just three years, but has showed extreme promise. Last season at Bridgton (Maine) Academy, he averaged 14 points, eight rebounds, three steals and two blocked shots.

"He's extremely versatile," Bridgton coach Whit Lesure told The State. "He scores in a bunch of different ways. He's not a great jump shooter, but he can catch and finish. He has to define his offensive game, but he has the explosiveness you'd look for. Defensively, he's super. He's the most fundamentally sound player I've had on the defensive end."

The lone freshman post player Odom brought in was 6-10 **John Chappell**, whose father, Len Chappell, led Wake Forest to the Final Four in 1962. Chappell played high school basketball at New Berlin (Wisc.) West, but a year ago played a postgraduate season at Fork Union (Va.) Military Academy, where he averaged 10 points and 10 rebounds. He's a solid rebounder and defender who can run and pass from the high post.

2001-2002 SCHEDULE

Nov.	19-21	#Maui Invitational
	26	East Tennessee State
	28	@Wofford
Dec.	1	Colorado State
	3	Providence
	6	Georgetown
	8	@Clemson
	18	South Carolina State
	20	The Citadel
	28	Charleston Southern
	30	Mercer
Jan.	5	@Florida
	12	Kentucky
	16	@Arkansas
	19	Vanderbilt
	23	@Tennessee
	26	@Ole Miss
	30	Georgia
Feb.	2	@Kentucky
	5	Florida
	9	Tennessee
	13	Alabama
	16	@Vanderbilt
	20	LSU
	23	@Auburn
	27	@Georgia
March	2	Mississippi State

7-10	##SEC Tournament

@Road Games
#Lahaina, HI (vs. Chaminade, first round; also Ball State, Duke, Houston, Kansas, Seton Hall, UCLA)
##Georgia Dome, Atlanta, GA

BLUE RIBBON ANALYSIS

BACKCOURT	B
BENCH/DEPTH	C
FRONTCOURT	B
INTANGIBLES	B

By no means was Wake Forest an easy job, but Odom more than got it done there. Before his arrival in Winston-Salem, N.C., the Deacons had suffered through four consecutive losing seasons.

His new challenge is to stop the bleeding at South Carolina. The Gamecocks are just 14-34 in SEC regular-season games the last three years, which places them at the very bottom of the league during that stretch.

In the ACC, Odom had to battle Duke, North Carolina, Maryland, Virginia ... well, you get the idea. In the SEC's East Division, it's not much easier. Kentucky and Florida are both Top 10 teams, and Tennessee has been a Top 25 program for much of the last four years.

Still, Odom thinks he has the nucleus to win right away.

Finding a few more outside shooters will be critical, and the recovery of Eidson will be equally so. If he makes it all the way back this season, it's reasonable to think South Carolina could push Tennessee for the third spot in the East and make a run for an NCAA Tournament berth.

And if Howell makes the kind of jump from his freshman to sophomore year that many in Columbia are anticipating, look out. He has all the makings of a star.

(C.L.)

Vanderbilt

LOCATION	Nashville, TN
CONFERENCE	Southeastern (Eastern)
LAST SEASON	15-15 (.500)
CONFERENCE RECORD	4-12 (6th)
STARTERS LOST/RETURNING	1/4
NICKNAME	Commodores
COLORS	Black & Gold
HOMECOURT	Memorial Gym (14,168)
COACH	Kevin Stallings (Purdue '82)
RECORD AT SCHOOL	34-26 (2 years)
CAREER RECORD	157-89 (8 years)
ASSISTANTS	Tim Jankovich (Kansas State '82)
	Jeff Jackson (Cornell '84)
	Brad Frederick (North Carolina '99)
TEAM WINS (last 5 years)	19-20-14-19-15
RPI (last 5 years)	43-46-109-43-77
2000-01 FINISH	Lost in conference first round.

It was a dark day on the Vanderbilt campus last April 10 after prized recruit David Harrison announced he would sign with Colorado.

For two years, ever since Kevin Stallings had taken over the program, most Commodore fans assumed Harrison, who played for Nashville's Brentwood Academy, would sign with Vanderbilt. The presence of Stallings and Harrison's proximity to the school weren't the only factors Vandy fans thought they had in their favor. Harrison's father Dennis is an assistant coach for Vanderbilt's football team.

But Harrison, a 7-0, 240-pound center who averaged 28.5 points, 13.1 rebounds and 5.6 blocks last year in being chosen to the Parade and McDonald's All-America teams, traded one family tie for another. He signed with Colorado in large part because his brother, D.J., plays there.

Obviously, Stallings desperately wanted Harrison, a franchise center who played virtually in Vanderbilt's back yard. Harrison would have filled a glaring void in the post. But it wasn't to be, and after Harrison's decision, Stallings quickly went about his business.

"I don't waste much time worrying about people we don't get," Stallings said. "We have other guys."

Make that young guys. Of Vanderbilt's 13 scholarship players, 10 are freshmen or sophomores.

Stallings is philosophic about the Commodores' inexperience.

"We're probably too young to be taken seriously," he said.

As long as Stallings is coaching this team, it will have to be taken seriously. True, most of the Commodores haven't started shaving yet. And Vandy could stand to find a low-post presence who can score and defend in the paint. But Stallings will make do with what he has. He always does.

Two players have a chance to emerge from the pack of youngsters and become stars. The first is 6-9, 226-pound sophomore **Matt Freije** (10.4 ppg, 4.4 rpg, 1.0 bpg), who started 18 games as a freshman and was the team's third-leading scorer. He was only the fifth Vanderbilt player to be chosen to the SEC's All-Freshman team.

Though Freije has decent size, he's more of a perimeter threat than an inside scorer, not unlike former Vandy star Dan Langhi, to whom Freije is sometimes compared. Freije led the Commodores in three-point percentage (.390, 23-of-59) a year ago.

"Matt Freije is a guy who has a chance to be really good," Stallings said. "He showed as a freshman he was someone people would have to deal with in this league. He's big and long and athletic, and can put the ball on the floor, shoot it from the perimeter and post up pretty well."

The question is whether Freije can absorb pounding and dish it back out in the post.

Vandy's other potential star is 6-5 sophomore **Billy Richmond** (8.8 ppg, 2.4 rpg, 2.2 apg), who can play three positions but will have to settle on one. That would probably be small forward, where he wound up playing most of last season. Richmond showed signs of his ability—such as when he scored 21 points against Boston College and 15 in the second half against Kentucky—but like most freshmen was inconsistent.

"We would like to see Billy emerge," Stallings said. "He has the talent level to be an impact player in this league. It's all about his ability to adjust and learn the college game. As he matures and realizes how hard you have to work, he'll get that consistency we're looking for."

Richmond had off-season surgery on both legs and wasn't able to work much in the spring and early summer. But he's expected back at full strength.

A newcomer who could see some frontcourt minutes right away is 6-11, 223-pound freshman **David Pzrybyszewski**, a native of Poland who signed in late June.

"He isn't physical enough yet," Stallings said. "He needs a great deal of court time as well as significant strength training before he reaches his potential, but we think he can be very good."

Stallings is hoping Pzrybyszewski or 6-10, 235-pound red-shirt freshman **Martin Schnedlitz** can handle the center position, which illustrates Vanderbilt's problems there. Pzrybyszewski has played basketball only four years and needs game experience and strength. Schnedlitz, after tearing the ACL in his left knee twice, hasn't played much since the first semester of his junior year in high school. Last year, he tore the ACL a second time in as many years on the first day of practice. Schnedlitz could have used a red-shirt season to work on strength, conditioning and basketball skills. Instead he had to burn it on rehab.

Darius Coulibaly (1.0 ppg, 1.0 rpg), a 7-1, 245-pound senior, was signed by former Vandy coach Jan van Breda Kolff as a project and has remained a project. He played in 28 games a year ago, but averaged just 6.8 minutes. Coulibaly fouls too much to be effective for long stretches and lacks any real offensive skills. But he can alter shots. That might earn him some time if the freshmen can't defend in the middle.

Stallings and his staff signed a couple of freshmen who can provide some size, if not great height, to the frontcourt. **Brian Thornton**, who is 6-8 and weighs 235 pounds, averaged 20 points, 13 rebounds and three blocks last season at duPont Manual High School in Louisville, Ky. The Louisville Courier-Journal made Thornton a second-team all-state pick.

Stallings is counting on Thornton to become a rebounder. "If he is able to improve his body like we expect he will, he could be a tenacious player who will be able to get the tough rebounds for us," Stallings said.

Another bulky newcomer is 6-5, 230-pound **Corey Smith**, who averaged 15 points and seven boards last season for Lamar High School in Houston. Smith's game is on the perimeter, but he has the size to post up smaller defenders.

"He brings a physical element to our perimeter game," Stallings said.

Vanderbilt has more experience in the backcourt. Seniors **Chuck Moore** (12.0 ppg, 3.5 rpg, 1.7 apg) and **Sam Howard** (6.4 ppg, 1.8 rpg) will probably share the shooting-guard spot. The 6-3 Moore, a Seton Hall transfer, led the Commodores in scoring last year after sitting out the season before.

Moore came to Vandy with the reputation of a shooter, and he didn't disappoint, launching 157 three-pointers, tops on the team. He made a respectable 35 percent of his shots from behind the arc. In SEC games only, Moore was fifth with his average of 2.3 three-pointers per game and sixth in three-point percentage (.394).

Moore shook off some early season injury problems and came into his own in the latter part of the SEC schedule. He led the Commodores in scoring in seven of their last nine games.

"Once Chuck got healthy, he put together a good year for us," Stallings said.

Howard's playing time, scoring average and shooting percentage slipped a year ago. Howard has trouble defending the quicker guards in the SEC, which has cut into his playing time under the defensive-minded Stallings. And the addition of other perimeter players has given Stallings other options besides Howard.

Last year, Howard broke his foot before the season began, but he still played in all 30 games, starting 11 times. Howard is known as a three-point shooter, but a year ago he struggled from behind the arc (.292). He'll have to shoot better, or his playing time could decline further with the addition of high-scoring freshman **Jason Holwerda**.

Other players who could take some of Howard's minutes are sophomores **Brendan Plavich** and **Scott Hundley**.

The 6-2 Plavich (5.3 ppg, 0.8 rpg) originally signed with Georgia Tech, but was released from his scholarship after former coach Bobby Cremins resigned. That allowed him to attend Vanderbilt, and he was a welcome addition. He played in 30 games, started five and averaged 13 minutes.

Plavich found time to toss up 140 three pointers, second on the team, and he made a decent number of them (.340). Plavich drained two huge threes in the final minute in leading Vandy to a come-from-behind win at Florida, which was ranked No. 7 at the time.

Hundley (3.3 ppg, 2.3 rpg), a 6-5 swingman, was inconsistent as a freshman, but he had two games that gives Stallings hope for the future. Hundley scored a career-high 20 points against Boston College in late December, but didn't come close to scoring in double figures again until the Commodores' last game, a loss to Alabama in the SEC Tournament.

Hundley scored 17 points against the Crimson Tide, knocking down 3-of-4 three-point shots. Stallings would love it if the former Kentucky Mr. Basketball could produce double-figure scoring efforts off the bench.

The man who will make the Vanderbilt offense go is 6-0 sophomore **Russell Lakey** (5.4 ppg, 3.0 rpg, 3.1 apg, 1.8 spg), who claimed the starting point guard job as a rookie and kept it all season. Lakey played in 30 games and started 27 of them, learning as he went along. Lakey wound up with the third most assists (94) by a freshman and 10th most steals (54) in Vanderbilt history. In SEC games only, Lakey was second in steals (1.8 spg). He was 10th in the league in assists.

"Lakey was steady all year," Stallings said. "But by the end of the year, he was very solid, especially for a freshman."

Lakey is a decent shooter (.363 from three-point range) but will have to make more free throws if he's going to have the ball in his hands in the late stages of games. A year ago, Lakey made just 23-of-51 free throws (.451).

Vanderbilt signed the 6-5 Holwerda away from, among others, arch rival Tennessee and Florida. He's an athletic swingman who averaged 29 points per game at Chattanooga Christian High School.

"I think Jason has a chance to impact this team," Stallings said. "He's got great court awareness and is very athletic."

Holwerda's shot is inconsistent, but he's a great leaper who can finish plays. If he takes care of the basketball, he'll play.

2001-2002 SCHEDULE

Nov.	16	Liberty
	19	*Connecticut
	23-25	#Thanksgiving Classic
	29	Caly Poly
Dec.	2	Western Kentucky
	5	Southeast Missouri
	8	Centenary
	10	@Tulane
	20	American
	22	East Tennessee State
	29	Morehead State
Jan.	5	@Georgia

	9	@Alabama
	12	Florida
	16	Auburn
	19	@South Carolina
	26	Georgia
	30	@Ole Miss
Feb.	2	Tennessee
	6	LSU
	9	@Florida
	13	@Kentucky
	16	South Carolina
	20	Mississippi State
	23	@Tennessee
	27	Kentucky
March	2	@Arkansas
	7-10	##SEC Tournament

@Road Games
*Hartford Civic Center, Hartford, CT
#Honolulu, HI (vs. Hampton, first round; also Akron, Hawaii-Pacific, Liberty, Notre Dame, Monmouth, Tennessee-Chattanooga)
##Georgia Dome, Atlanta, GA

BLUE RIBBON ANALYSIS

BACKCOURT	B
BENCH/DEPTH	C
FRONTCOURT	C
INTANGIBLES	B

The retooling efforts of Stallings would have been assisted in large measure with the addition of blue-chip freshman Harrison. But it wasn't to be. After a two-year courtship with hometown Vanderbilt, Harrison chose to sign with Colorado. Understandably disappointed after he and his staff had waged a fierce recruiting battle for Harrison, Stallings nevertheless didn't waste a lot of time agonizing over the big one that got away. It takes more than one player to run a program.

Still, a low-post scorer would have complemented Vandy's talent nicely. Without Harrison in the middle, Stallings will have to find a combination of players who can give his team some semblance of an inside game.

Vanderbilt isn't hurting for perimeter threats. So if any combination of Pzrybyszeweski, Freije and Schnedlitz can take the defensive heat off the Commodores' shooters, they would be a lot tougher to defend.

Stallings knows this season could be trying, because of all the young players on his roster. As these youngsters learn the game and Stallings' system, they'll evolve into a competitive group. Until then, the Commodores will be looking up at probably four other teams in the SEC East. Vanderbilt has a chance to move up one spot from last season, but realistically, it might be a year or two before it advances higher.

(C.D.)

Appalachian State

LOCATION	Boone, NC
CONFERENCE	Southern
LAST SEASON	11-20 (.355)
CONFERENCE RECORD	7-9 (t-3rd North)
STARTERS LOST/RETURNING	0/5
NICKNAME	Mountaineers
COLORS	Black & Gold
HOMECOURT	Holmes Convocation Center (8,300)
COACH	Houston Fancher (Middle Tennessee '88)
RECORD AT SCHOOL	11-20 (1 year)
CAREER RECORD	55-61 (4 years)
ASSISTANTS	Lavell Hall (Western Carolina '79)
	Joel Haskins (Appalachian State '81)
	John Braswell (Appalachian State '99)
TEAM WINS (last 5 years)	14-21-21-23-11
RPI (last 5 years)	152-109-89-107-267
2000-01 FINISH	Lost in conference quarterfinal.

Houston Fancher's first year as Appalachian State's coach was a long one. How long?

"It was the longest 10 years of my life last year," Fancher said. "It was unbelievable the things we went through, but we weathered the storm and lived to tell about it. We've put it in the rear-view mirror."

In his fourth season as a head coach, Fancher had to deal with more than many coaches experience in a decade.

Before his players reported to campus, Fancher lost guard Rufus Leach, who drowned in nearby Watauga

SOUTHERN

BLUE RIBBON FORECAST

North Division
1. UNC Greensboro
2. Davidson
3. East Tennessee State
4. Appalachian State
5. Western Carolina
6. Virginia Military Institute

South Division
1. Georgia Southern
2. Chattanooga
3. College of Charleston
4. Furman
5. The Citadel
6. Wofford

ALL-CONFERENCE TEAM

G-Courtney Eldridge, SR, UNC Greensboro
G-Dimeco Childress, SR, East Tennessee State
F-Jeff Bolton, SR, College of Charleston
F-Karim Souchu, JR, Furman
C-Kashien Latham, SR, Georgia Southern

PLAYER OF THE YEAR

Courtney Eldridge, SR, UNC Greensboro

NEWCOMER OF THE YEAR

Graham Bunn, JR, Appalachian State

2001-2002 CONFERENCE TOURNAMENT

Feb. 28-March 1-3, North Charleston Coliseum, Charleston, SC

2000-2001 CHAMPIONS

East Tennessee State (North Division)
College of Charleston (South Division)
UNC Greensboro (Conference tournament)

2000-2001 POSTSEASON PARTICIPANTS

Postseason record 0-1 (.000)
NCAA
UNC Greensboro

TOP BACKCOURTS

1. UNC Greensboro
2. Georgia Southern
3. East Tennessee State

TOP FRONTCOURTS

1. Georgia Southern
2. Appalachian State
3. UNC Greensboro

INSIDE THE NUMBERS

2000-01 conference RPI: 24th (of 31)
Conference RPI (last 5 years): 19-24-20-22-24

DID YOU KNOW?

Furman and the Southern Conference will co-host an NCAA Sub-Regional on March 14 and March 16. The games will be played at the BI-LO Center in Greenville, S.C. ... After a two-year stay at the BI-LO Center in Greenville, the Southern Conference Tournament moves to the North Charleston Coliseum in Charleston, S.C. ... Six players on the coaches' all-conference team return. They are forwards Karim Souchu of Furman and Kashien Latham of Georgia Southern and guards Courtney Eldridge of UNC Greensboro, Jeff Bolton of College of Charleston, Julius Jenkins of Georgia Southern and Dimeco Childress of East Tennessee State. ... Souchu is the league's top returning scorer, averaging 18.9 points last season. Wofford's Ian Chadwick won the scoring title last year as a senior when he averaged 20.4 points. Souchu was second behind Chadwick. ... Latham is the top returning rebounder, averaging 9.7 per game last season, second only to VMI's Eric Mann, who averaged 10.5 as a senior. ... Mann, who averaged 13.5 points, was the first player in the conference to average a double-double since Appalachian State's Chad McClendon (18.4 ppg, 10.1 rpg) in 1994-95. ... For the first time in the seven seasons that the league has gone to North and South Divisions, neither of the No. 1 seeds from the divisions advanced to the championship game. South Division champion College of Charleston lost to Davidson in the quarterfinals and North Division champion East Tennessee State lost to Georgia Southern in the quarterfinals. ... Both No. 2 seeded teams advanced to the championship, with UNC Greensboro of the North beating Chattanooga from the South, 67-66, on David Schuck's layup with less than a second remaining. ... The league's 12 teams have 47 of the 60 starters returning from last year. Appalachian State, Davidson, Georgia Southern, and Western Carolina return all five starters. Four other teams return four starters. They are College of Charleston, The Citadel, Furman and UNC Greensboro. East Tennessee State, Chattanooga and Wofford each return three starters. ... Seven of the league's top 10 scorers return this season. The league's assist leader, Georgia Southern's Sean Peterson (6.23 apg), blocks leader Rans Brempong of Western Carolina (3.0 bpg) and steals leader Courtney Eldridge of UNC Greensboro (2.7 spg) also return.

(D.L.)

Lake in the summer of 2000. Leach, who set the school's single-season record by making 103 three-pointers in 1999-2000, was chosen to the coaches' All-SoCon first team.

"Rufus Leach was the best guard in the league," Fancher said. "When we lost him, it was a big blow to us."

It was the first and by far the most tragic of the Mountaineers' losses.

In addition, two freshmen left the program and one player flunked out. Early in the season, starting center Corey Cooper and starting guard Shawn Alexander were dismissed for violations of team rules. Midway through the season, junior guard **Charles Dearmon** went down with a knee injury and missed several games.

When that happened, Fancher was down to seven players. The Mountaineers lost four straight games entering the SoCon Tournament.

"We just didn't have enough players to finish games," Fancher recalls.

That shouldn't be a problem this year.

Fancher has reloaded with six newcomers, including

Graham Bunn, a 5-11 junior point guard who transferred from Bowling Green. Bunn, who averaged 2.3 points and 1.4 assists at Bowling Green, practiced with the Mountaineers last season.

"He was a starting point guard at Bowling Green," Fancher said. "He's a really good point guard. We're excited about him and we feel fortunate to get him here with us."

Also returning is starting point guard **Jonathan Butler** (7.3 ppg, 3.2 rpg, 3.3 apg), a 5-11 senior from Winston-Salem, N.C.

Corwin Davis, a 6-0 freshman from Selma, N.C., will also battle for playing time at the point. Davis averaged 21.1 points, 5.1 rebounds and 5.2 assists last season at Ravenscroft High School.

"I think our point guard position will be our most heated competition," Fancher said. "I'm really excited about our depth. Butler started and averaged 30-something minutes a game and Graham, who is obviously a very good player, was great for us in practice and already knows the system, and we're really high on Davis, who will be right there in the mix. It will be interesting to see how that plays out."

Noah Brown, a 6-1 sophomore, started at shooting guard last season as a freshman. Brown (7.9 ppg, 3.4 rpg, 3.1 apg) was chosen to the SoCon Coaches' All-Freshman team. He enters the preseason as the likely starter at that position.

"He had a good season for us," Fancher said. "He was up and down as most freshmen are. He had 26 one night at Chattanooga and zero against Greensboro the next night. He's gotten bigger and stronger and really worked on his game."

Brown will be pushed by 5-9 junior **Shawn Hall**, a transfer from Kankakee (Ill.) Community College. Hall averaged 15.1 points, 4.3 rebounds and 3.8 assists last season.

"He can really shoot it," Fancher said. "That's one thing we were lacking. We didn't really shoot the ball well from the three-point line [App's .304 percentage was 10th in the league]."

Dearmon, a walk-on last year, is more of a scorer than shooter. Dearmon (4.3 ppg, 1.9 rpg), a 6-2 senior, is a very quick and athletic player who can get to the rim.

Hal Kivette, a 6-1 sophomore from Boone, will be a backup. Kivette (0.0 ppg, 0.0 rpg) is a walk-on. **Brett Huckle**, a 6-0 guard, is a freshman walk-on from Brookwood High School in Snellville, Ga.

Matt Jones, a 6-3 sophomore, is back after starting at small forward last year. Jones (5.3 ppg, 3.0 rpg) is probably the Mountaineers' best perimeter defender.

"He's a really good slasher-type player with a strong body," Fancher said. "His perimeter shot has gotten better since last year. That was something we really worked on with him. He's going to be a much better player. Here's a kid who was thrown into the fire as a freshman walk-on and earned a starting spot. He will be an impact player this year but people will push him."

One of those players pushing Jones will be 6-6 junior **Nate Carson**, who averaged 13.5 points, 5.0 rebounds and 3.7 assists last season at Dodge City (Kansas) Community College. Carson is big enough and strong enough to play power forward, but Fancher plans to play him at small forward.

"We think he'll be a good one for us," Fancher said. "He has a good frame for our league and he's a very intelligent player who knows how to play. He's a big perimeter player who can go inside and do some things. He's a great rebounder from the perimeter and a good defender as well. He could be the sleeper of the signing class."

Freshman **Chris McFarland**, a 6-5 forward, will also play on the wing. McFarland averaged 19 points, nine rebounds and 4.5 assists last season at Riverdale High in Jonesboro, Ga.

Before McFarland committed to Appalachian State, he took a visit to South Carolina, where he was the first recruit brought in by coach Dave Odom. McFarland also cancelled visits to College of Charleston and Tulane and took an unoffical visit to Auburn. Fancher said recruiting analyst Bob Gibbons planned to rate McFarland as the preseason freshman newcomer in the league.

"He's a very, very explosive kid," Fancher said. "If he continues to shoot with more consistency he will be awfully hard to guard in this league."

Junior college transfer **Ahmad Smith** will also be in the forward mix. Smith, 6-4 and 225 pounds, averaged 17.2 points and 5.5 rebounds last season for Cedar Valley (Texas) Junior College, a Division III national power.

"He's an absolute warrior, a tank," Fancher said.

Donald Payne, a 6-6 senior, was chosen to the all-conference third team by the league's media. Payne (8.8 ppg, 5.6 rpg) fits the mold of former Mountaineer power forwards Marshall Phillips and Cedric Holmes.

Fancher hopes that Payne's season of Division I ball has prepared him for an outstanding season, like the ones Phillips and Holmes enjoyed.

"Payne is the prototypical power forward for Appalachian State, an undersized guy who plays bigger than what he is," Fancher said. "I think he's going to have a wonderful senior year. He's worked hard all summer and prepared himself and now he's more comfortable with the system and his role. I think he's a guy you'll see put up potential double-double numbers every night. He's a good defender, he's athletic, and he rebounds like crazy. He plays as hard as he can all the time."

Backing up Payne will be **Buddy Davis**, a 6-6 senior who can also play the low post. Davis (5.0 ppg, 3.9 rpg) and Butler are the team's only fourth-year seniors.

Josh Shehan, a 6-9, 235-pound junior, started at center last season and should retain the job. Shehan played sparingly as a freshman, and when Cooper was dismissed last season, he moved into the starting lineup. Shehan (11.3 ppg, 4.8 rpg) was chosen as the team's most valuable player and was a member of the media's all-conference third team.

"He's very strong and has gotten stronger," Fancher

said. "He's added pounds and muscle. He's been to big man camps this summer. He's one of those guys who tasted some success and liked it."

Brian Boxler, a 7-0, 240 sophomore, is in his third year with the program. Boxler (3.6 ppg, 2.2 rpg) has added weight and grown an inch since last season and should be more of a factor.

Lennox Marshall, a 6-8 freshman center, came to Appalachian State from Independence High in Charlotte, N.C. Marshall wasn't recruited much out of high school because he missed most of the year with pneumonia. He averaged 10 points and seven rebounds in the games he played and will be a walk-on this year.

"I think he's got a chance to be a very good player," Fancher said.

2001-2002 SCHEDULE

Nov.	16	@Richmond
	19	East Carolina
	24	Barton
	26	@Charlotte
	29	@Tennessee
Dec.	1	Liberty
	5	@Clemson
	13	North Greenville
	20	@TCU
	30	@UNC Asheville
Jan.	2	@East Tennessee
	5	@UNC Greensboro
	7	Georgia Southern
	12	Chattanooga
	19	@Furman
	21	VMI
	23	Gardner-Webb
	26	@The Citadel
	28	@Western Carolina
Feb.	2	Davidson
	4	@VMI
	9	@College of Charleston
	11	Wofford
	16	@Davidson
	18	UNC Greensboro
	23	East Tennessee State
	28	#SoCon Tournament
March	1-3	#SoCon Tournament

@Road Games
#North Charleston Coliseum, Charleston, SC

BLUE RIBBON ANALYSIS

BACKCOURT	B+
BENCH/DEPTH	B+
FRONTCOURT	B
INTANGIBLES	B

Last year, Fancher saw his roster dwindle to seven players at one point in the season. When he looked down his bench, he had very few options.

Fancher won't have that problem this year. On the contrary, his biggest task will be finding enough playing time to satisfy all his players.

With six newcomers and several walk-ons joining five returning starters and four returning lettermen (two walk-ons), Fancher must figure out how to fit all the pieces together.

"I would much rather have this problem than have the problem I faced last year when we didn't have as many options," Fancher said. "Now we're going to turn the tempo up, we're going to try to play more people, get up and down the floor. When we were good [in previous years], we were causing and creating turnovers. Last year we were making turnovers.

"This year we want to turn that around and get back to the up-tempo style of play that was good to us in the past and not have to be so methodical and half-court oriented as last year."

The Mountaineers seem to have the personnel to make a run at the North Division title. Can they do it? If Fancher can find the right chemistry and combinations, they probably can.

(D.L.)

Chattanooga

LOCATION	Chattanooga, TN
CONFERENCE	Southern (South)

LAST SEASON	17-13 (.567)
CONFERENCE RECORD	9-7 (t-2nd)
STARTERS LOST/RETURNING	2/3
NICKNAME	Mocs
COLORS	Navy Blue & Old Gold
HOMECOURT	McKenzie Arena (11,218)
COACH	Henry Dickerson (Morris Harvey '73)
RECORD AT SCHOOL	56-59 (4 years)
CAREER RECORD	56-59 (4 years)
ASSISTANTS	John Gibson (Chattanooga '88)
	L.J. Kilby (Lincoln Memorial '75)
	Kenny Seifert (Oakland City '86)
TEAM WINS (last 5 years)	24-13-16-10-17
RPI (last 5 years)	111-205-146-239-150
2000-01 FINISH	Lost in conference final.

Chattanooga coach Henry Dickerson, one of the nice guys in college basketball, had his team within 2.6 seconds of an NCAA Tournament berth last March.

The Mocs led UNC Greensboro by one with a couple of ticks left on the clock in the Southern Conference Tournament championship. Then the unthinkable happened.

Greensboro's Jay Joseph threw a baseball-style pass that sailed three-quarters of the court. It was caught by David Schuck, whose uncontested layup gave the Spartans a 67-66 victory and stole the Big Dance ticket from the Mocs.

When point guard **Clyde McCully** drove the lane and made a layup for a 66-65 lead, the Mocs thought their NCAA Tournament dreams would be realized.

"Our guys, they just thought the game was over," Dickerson said. "I didn't have another timeout. If I had another timeout, I could have rallied them and gotten them settled down a little more. I think they went back out playing not to lose, not to foul anybody."

For much of the 2000-01 season, rumors swirled about Dickerson's future. With 2.6 seconds left, Dickerson's job was secure. Then came the pass. Then the layup by Schuck, and folks were talking about Dickerson's contract, which was up at the end of the season.

Dickerson's contract was extended through the 2001-02 season, but his future may depend on another tournament run.

"If we win that game, you wouldn't even ask me about my contract," Dickerson said.

With one of the most athletic teams in the conference, Dickerson should have another contender this season.

Two solid players were seniors last year. Oliver Morton (12.1 ppg, 6.2 rpg), a 6-10 center, was on the coaches' all-conference first team and media's all-conference second team, and 6-3 guard Idris Harper (9.4 ppg, 3.3 rpg) was a starter for most of his career.

Despite the loss of Harper, the Mocs will have one of the better backcourts in the league.

McCully (8.4 ppg, 2.8 rpg, 4.8 apg), a 6-0 senior, returns after starting all 30 games and leading the team in minutes (30.2 per game). He was fourth in the conference in assists and seventh in steals (1.73 per game).

Coming out of North Iowa Area Community College last year, McCully quickly took on a leadership role. His teammates voted him a team captain even before he had played a game for the Mocs.

"That was pretty unusual for a guy who had never played a game here," Dickerson said. "He's a strong kid, an athletic kid who knows how to win and wants to win. As the season went on he really turned it on and really played well. He's a very good ball handler, passes the ball well, but is a suspect jump shooter. But he has really worked extremely hard on his jump shooting. I think that will make him a better player."

Petie Spaulding, a 6-0 junior point guard, will contend for a starting job. Spaulding averaged 11.6 points and 4.8 assists last season at Moberly (Mo.) Junior College. He shot 39 percent from three-point range and 75 percent from the free-throw line.

"He's a heck of a point guard who could slide into the two-guard," Dickerson said. "I think right now Clyde probably has the advantage because he's been in the system for a year, but they're going to push each other and make each other better, so I don't know who will start. But the way we plan on playing they're both going to have to play some quality minutes."

Brian Dickerson, a 5-11 point guard, will probably be red-shirted. Dickerson (1.5 ppg, 0.8 rpg), the son of coach Dickerson, played in 14 games last season and averaged 5.1 minutes.

Toot Young, a 6-3 senior shooting guard, started 25 games last season. Young (12.5 ppg, 4.0 rpg) was one of the league's top three-point shooters, ranking second in three-point percentage (.417) and second in three-pointers per game (2.6). He was chosen to the SoCon All-Tournament team.

Young is the younger brother of Willie Young, a starting guard on the Mocs' 1996-97 team that reached the NCAA Sweet 16.

"He started off slow but was solid the whole year and really got better at the end of the year," Dickerson said. "He's a very, very talented player. He's a good shooter who can guard you and you can slide him into the point-guard spot, but it takes so much away from his scoring when you put him at the point."

Bryan Richardson, a 6-5 sophomore guard, gives the Mocs good size on the perimeter. Richardson (4.2 ppg, 1.9 rpg) averaged 11 minutes in 24 games.

The Mocs are loaded with forwards who can play on the wings or in the paint.

Michael Townsend, a 6-7 senior, started 17 games last season but averaged only 11.7 minutes. Townsend (2.2 ppg, 2.1 rpg) could have a battle holding his starting job with the influx of newcomers.

Tim Parker, a 6-4 junior, is one of the team's better perimeter shooters. Two years ago, Parker played in the post as a power forward, but that wasn't his natural spot. Last season, Parker (7.7 ppg, 3.0 rpg) shot 37.4 percent from three-point range while playing mostly on the wing.

Dickerson said Parker doesn't mind being a role player and that he won three or four games last season with his shooting.

"With the athletic-type kids we have, Tim can come in and just play hard and shoot the basketball," Dickerson said. "That's what he does best. He's a good rebounder, not very quick but he plays extremely hard. He's a kid that will be a role player and he understands that."

Look for **Neil Ashby**, a 6-8 senior forward, to make an impact when he returns this year. Ashby (8.6 ppg, 5.3 rpg) started the first 12 games last season before being ruled academically ineligible in late December.

A transfer from Alabama, Ashby has the tools to be a standout in the Southern Conference. He is a tremendous leaper whose athleticism makes him one of the Mocs' most versatile players.

"He's as athletic as athletic can be," Dickerson said. "He's an emotional kid, a kid who plays hard. He can play the four, the three, could play the five but you run into the strength factor there. Defensively he gives you a presence as a shot blocker."

Two other transfers came from Moberly Junior College, along with Moberly head coach Kenny Seifert, who joined Dickerson's staff. **Nick Benson**, a 6-5 forward, and **Aaron Morgan**, a 6-9 center, arrived in Chattanooga along with Spaulding and their coach.

When they did, most everybody was thinking the Mocs got a package deal from Moberly. Not so, says Dickerson.

"Kenny was the head coach at Sullivan Junior College in Louisville where we got Tim Brooks, Gary Robb and Keith Nelson," said Dickerson, who recruited those players as a UTC assistant. "Then he took the Moberly job. We've always stayed in touch and we're just pretty good friends. Of course, everybody thinks we hired Kenny for his players. That's the way it looks, but Kenny was coming no matter what. We were already on the players. ... They're all pretty good players. They'll push players for starting spots, that's for sure."

Townsend, who signed with the Mocs in 2000, also came from Moberly.

Benson can play either forward spot. Last season, he averaged 16.2 points and 7.4 rebounds for a team that went 28-5 and was ranked No. 1 nationally at one time in the NJCAA rankings. He shot 50 percent from the floor and 70 percent from the line.

Tim Harris, a 6-6 junior, came from Vincennes University, where he averaged 13.2 points and 8.0 rebounds last season. He led the 26-5 team in rebounding and was second in scoring. Harris will play either forward spot.

"He's a decent shooter from 15 feet who can shoot the three," Dickerson said. "Hopefully he's worked hard [on his shot] this summer and will be a better shooter, but he's more of a slasher type player."

Dusty Pulliam, a 6-8 senior forward, set a school and SoCon record by shooting 72.1 percent from the field last season. Pulliam (8.7 ppg, 6.9 rpg) started four games and played practically starter minutes, averaging 23.9 points per game.

"He's a blue-collar player that just gets the job done and goes unnoticed until you look at his stats," Dickerson said. "He just knows how to play."

Morgan will try to fill some of the void left by Morton's departure. Last season, Morgan averaged 6.2 points and 5.7 rebounds, shooting more than 60 percent from the field. He split time with another post player at Moberly.

"He's a left-handed kid. He's not the offensive player that Oliver was, but he's a tough kid who can rebound and has a long wing span," Dickerson said. "He's not a great athlete but a good athlete that will give us more defense than Oliver did, but with our other people perimeter-wise we won't expect him to score a lot."

Chris Bishop, a 6-6 forward, sat out last season. He will be a red-shirt freshman. Also contending for time will be 6-6 forward **Norm Cain**, a transfer from Brevard (Fla.) Junior College, and 6-8 senior forward **Diamory Sylla** (1.4 ppg, 1.5 rpg), who averaged 5.2 minutes in 11 games last season.

Cain sat out last year for academic reasons, and won't be eligible until the second semester. He averaged 17 points and 9.5 rebounds for Brevard in 1999-2000.

2001-2002 SCHEDULE

Nov.	17	Tennessee Wesleyan
	21-26	#Hawaii Pacific Tournament
	29	@Murray State
Dec.	1	@Kent State
	3	@Alabama
	15	Illinois State
	18	Bluefield State
	20	@Arkansas
	22	Murray State
	29-30	##Dr Pepper Classic
Jan.	2	UNC Greensboro
	5	College of Charleston
	8	@Davidson
	12	@Appalachian State
	14	Wofford
	19	@The Citadel
	21	Furman
	26	@ETSU
	28	@Georgia Southern
Feb.	2	The Citadel
	4	@Wofford
	9	@Furman
	11	VMI
	16	@College of Charleston
	18	Georgia Southern
	23	Western Carolina
	28	###Southern Conf. Tournament
March	1-3	###Southern Conf. Tournament

@Road Games
#Honolulu, HI (vs. Liberty first round; also Akron, Hampton, Hawaii Pacific, Monmouth, Notre Dame, Vanderbilt)
##Chattanooga, TN (vs. Sam Houston first round; also Weber State, Bradley)
###Charleston Colliseum, Charleston SC

BLUE RIBBON ANALYSIS

BACKCOURT	A
BENCH/DEPTH	A-
FRONTCOURT	B
INTANGIBLES	B

For most of the 1980s and early '90s, Chattanooga was in contention for the Southern Conference title, and it wasn't afraid to use junior college players.

Dickerson, an assistant under former Mocs coach Mack McCarthy from 1989-97, has gone back to that formula in pursuit of the title.

Chattanooga now has 10 junior-college transfers, including five newcomers, on its roster this year. The Mocs' backcourt is good. The frontcourt is athletic. About the only thing Dickerson doesn't have is a big man to replace Morton.

Regardless, the Mocs have an abundance of weapons. After coming so close to the SoCon Tournament title last season, Dickerson has reloaded for another run.

"I was a little disappointed because we lost the championship, but I'm really looking forward to this year with all the kids we have coming back and the new kids we have," Dickerson said. "With this year's team, I think we'll be more athletic and I think we'll be deeper. We'll be able to take one athletic kid out and put another one in and not lose anything, and maybe we gain something."

Clearly, there is talent on this team. Dickerson must find the right combinations, and there are plenty of those. When he does, the Mocs will be tough to beat.

(D.L.)

The Citadel

LOCATION	**Charleston, SC**
CONFERENCE	**Southern (South)**
LAST SEASON	**16-12 (.571)**
CONFERENCE RECORD	**9-7 (t-2nd)**
STARTERS LOST/RETURNING	**1/4**
NICKNAME	**Bulldogs**
COLORS	**Blue & White**
HOMECOURT	**McAlister Field House (6,000)**
COACH	**Pat Dennis (Washington & Lee '79)**
RECORD AT SCHOOL	**104-142 (9 years)**
CAREER RECORD	**104-142 (9 years)**
ASSISTANTS	**Michael Hopkins (Coastal Carolina '83)**
	Chris Cowart (Florida '97)
	Chris Gerlufsen (Randolph-Macon '98)
TEAM WINS (last 5 years)	**13-15-9-9-16**
RPI (last 5 years)	**203-222-292-297-224**
2000-01 FINISH	**Lost in conference first round.**

In his 10th season as The Citadel's coach, Pat Dennis says his program has turned the corner. That may seem like a slow progression, but building a winning program at a military school is no easy task.

Last season, the Bulldogs finished in a three-way tie for second in the Southern Conference South Division, but lost in the tournament opener to Western Carolina, 67-57.

"We've been able to attract quality kids," Dennis said. "We had excellent chemistry on the team last year. The guys get along on and off the court. We have a good mix of athletic players and real smart players. I think we have a team that's going to compete and play very hard night in and night out.

"We know we can't take a night off and beat anybody. We're a team that's got to do everything near perfect and we were fortunate last year. We won 16 games and won a lot of close games, which really helped us have a good season, especially at a military school. We felt we had a very fine season."

The Bulldogs' only key departure this year is point guard Mike Roy (6.1 ppg, 3.0 rpg, 4.3 apg), and that certainly is a big loss. Roy has been the starter at the point the last two years.

Dennis will be counting on 6-0 junior **Kenny Milford** and 6-0 sophomore **Erick Wilson** to take over for Roy. Milford has played in 43 games at The Citadel and Wilson has played in 19, all last season as a freshman.

Milford (1.7 ppg, 0.5 rpg) played in 16 games last season and averaged 5.8 minutes per game. Wilson (0.6 ppg, 0.2 rpg) averaged 4.9 minutes.

"Both sort of backed up Mike Roy but neither of them played a tremendous amount of minutes," Dennis said. "Wilson is probably a little better at running our halfcourt set and he's a very strong, tough guard and he's got a very good handle and shoots the ball a little bit.

"Milford gives us a lot of quickness and he can put great defensive pressure on you. The biggest thing with Kenny is he's got to learn to play under control more. That's one thing, we're not an up-and-down, fast-paced team and he's got to be able to push it when it's there but he's got to really be able to run the offense.

"I think the biggest thing we look at is being able to show leadership on the court and run what we want to run. That's where Mike Roy was very good. He was just real solid."

The Bulldogs return their leading scorer, 6-3 senior **Travis Cantrell** (12.7 ppg, 2.8 rpg), who was second in the league in free-throw shooting (.837) and third in three-pointers per game (2.39). Cantrell has NBA range and isn't afraid to use it.

"He's really good," Dennis said. "He's got a lot of mental toughness and he's willing to take the big shot. There's no question he will step up and take the big shot at the end of the game and he'll hit a lot of them."

Backing up Cantrell will be 6-4 junior **Clyde Wormley**, perhaps the best athlete on the team. Wormley (2.7 ppg, 1.4 rpg) played in 27 games last season with one start and averaged 10 minutes per game.

His numbers should increase this year.

"He's a very athletic young man," Dennis said. "He's got skills. He can just play. He's got to do it on a consistent basis. If he comes back ready to play he will fight Travis for minutes."

The Bulldogs' only signee, 6-4, 190-pound freshman **Michael Vega**, is also slotted in the shooting guard slot. Vega was a good catch by Dennis.

Last season, Vega averaged 13.4 points, 5.4 rebounds, 2.6 assists and 1.3 steals for Brookwood High

School in Lilburn, Ga. Brookwood, a Class 5A school, went 27-2 and was ranked No. 1 in Georgia for six weeks and was nationally ranked by USA Today. Vega, who had 26 dunks last season, earned all-region honors by the Atlanta Tip-Off Club.

"I think we got a real steal," Dennis said. "Time will tell. He's a 6-4 wing who is very athletic, can really shoot the ball, and plays with a lot of toughness. He's got a chance to be a really nice player. He's a real gym rat."

Cantrell has a dangerous counterpart on the perimeter with the return of 6-3 senior **Alan Puckett**, who will start at small forward. Puckett (10.6 ppg, 3.1 rpg) was third in the league in three-point percentage (.403) and fifth in three-pointers per game (2.21). Cantrell had 67 three-pointers last season and Puckett had 62.

Puckett is on pace to break the school's three-point record this season.

"He's another dead-eye shooter," Dennis said of Puckett. "He's been a real mainstay for us. He's actually been one of the best three-point shooters in the country."

One of the most versatile players on the team is 6-4 junior **Michael Joseph** (8.0 ppg, 3.9 rpg), who started 13 games last season. Joseph, who averaged 19 minutes per game, is a good ball handler and passer who can drive to the basket and score.

Dennis said Joseph will push Puckett for the starting job.

"We can go with a lineup with Travis at point, Alan at two and Mike at three," Dennis said. "We did that at times last year. Mike Joe will get a lot of minutes. He's a young man we recruited as an under-sized post man in high school and we made him a three man. He has good skills. He's a strong, tough kid and a good athlete."

Sewell Setzer, a 6-6 red-shirt freshman, benefited from a year of practicing with the team. Sewell, another athletic player, will be a backup small forward.

Dennis has a couple of options at power forward with the return of 6-6 junior **Romas Krywonis** and 6-8 sophomore **Max Mombollet**. Both weigh about 215.

Krywonis (6.4 ppg, 4.4 rpg) started 12 games last season and averaged 21 minutes, while Mombollet started three games and averaged 17.2 minutes. Both played in all 28 games.

Krywonis was born in Baltimore, but his parents are from Lithuania.

"Romas is very skilled, but maybe a little under-sized at the four spot," Dennis said. "He's very tough and has a great feel for basketball. He just gives us a lot of toughness. He's a real competitor. He's a gym rat. He's gotten better every year. All he does in the summer is lift and play basketball. He won't back down from anybody."

Mobollet, who is from Central African Republic, played for his national team during the summer at a tournament in Morocco. "He's got a big upside," Dennis said. "He's very athletic, runs exceptionally well, is bouncy and pretty skilled. He just needs to continue to learn to play. We expect big things from him."

Ben Tobias, a 6-6 junior, will again be a backup at power forward. Tobias (2.1 ppg, 1.1 rpg) played in nine games last season and averaged 4.6 minutes.

The Bulldogs are solid at the low post with 6-6 senior **Cliff Washburn** and 6-7 junior **Gregg Jones**.

Washburn (10.3 ppg, 5.5 rpg) started 26 games last season and was the team's third-leading scorer. At about 240 pounds, Washburn gives the Bulldogs plenty of muscle inside. He will start for the fourth year.

"I always say he's the nicest kid off the court but he's as mean as a snake on the court," Dennis said. "He is tough. He won't back down from anybody. He's exceptionally competitive and he has improved offensively. He's made himself into a very fine player. He gives us a defensive presence and he can rebound."

Jones (5.2 ppg, 3.6 rpg) started 13 games last season. During the summer, Jones hit the weights and gained about 10 pounds. He now weighs about 215.

Occasionally, Dennis may play Jones and Washburn at the same time, giving the Bulldogs finesse and power in the post.

"Jones is very athletic, a bouncy kid," Dennis said. "He's got to continue to get stronger. He gives us a very athletic guy around the basket and he has really improved on the offensive end."

2001-2002 SCHEDULE

Nov.	19	Flagler
	23	@North Carolina State
	26	William & Mary
	29	Navy
Dec.	1	*Charleston Southern
	5	Emmanuel
	8	Davidson
	10	@Philander Smith College
	17	Greensboro College
	20	@South Carolina
	29	Coastal Carolina
Jan.	2	@SC State
	5	East Tennessee State
	7	@Wofford
	12	@Western Carolina
	14	Georgia Southern
	19	Chattanooga
	21	@College of Charleston
	26	Appalachian State
	28	@Furman
Feb.	2	@Chattanooga
	4	College of Charleston
	9	@UNC Greensboro
	11	Furman
	16	@Georgia Southern
	18	@VMI
	23	Wofford
Feb.	28	#SoCon Tournament
March	1-3	#So Con Tournament

@Road Games
*Lowcountry Shootout, North Charleston Coliseum
#North Charlesotn Coliseum, Charleston, SC

BLUE RIBBON ANALYSIS

BACKCOURT	B-
BENCH/DEPTH	B
FRONTCOURT	B
INTANGIBLES	B

If the Bulldogs can replace Roy, they have a chance to be very good. But that's a big if.

"That's the key to us having a good season," Bulldogs coach Pat Dennis said. "I think we can be OK anyway, but if we want to have another good season that's the area we need to have somebody really step up."

It will be up to Milford and Wilson to take over the point guard job. Both have been used only as backups.

Elsewhere, the Bulldogs are solid at each position. Cantrell and Puckett are outstanding perimeter shooters, and Wormley, Joseph and Vega give the Bulldogs athleticism on the perimeter.

In the frontcourt, the Bulldogs have depth and experience.

Can the Bulldogs make a run in the South? Again, it's up to the point guard.

"I think we can be in that mix again," Dennis said. "Whether we do much better really depends on our point guard and whether we do worse depends on the point guard situation. If somebody steps up we can be better than we were last season. That's the biggest question mark, but every other position I feel we're solid."

(D.L.)

College of Charleston

LOCATION	**Charleston, SC**
CONFERENCE	**Southern (South)**
LAST SEASON	**22-7 (.759)**
CONFERENCE RECORD	**12-4 (1st)**
STARTERS LOST/RETURNING	**1/4**
NICKNAME	**Cougars**
COLORS	**Maroon & White**
HOMECOURT	**John Kresse Arena (3,500)**
COACH	**John Kresse (St. John's '64)**
RECORD AT SCHOOL	**539-134 (22 years)**
CAREER RECORD	**539-134 (22 years)**
ASSISTANTS	**Ben Betts (Roanoke '90)**
	Marty McGillan (UNC Wilmington '90)
	Phil Kahn (Spring Hill '92)
TEAM WINS (last 5 years)	**29-24-28-24-22**
RPI (last 5 years)	**49-78-37-96-91**
2000-01 FINISH	**Lost in conference quarterfinal.**

For the second straight year, College of Charleston went into the Southern Conference as a No. 1 seeded team, only to have its NCAA Tournament hopes dashed.

Two seasons ago, the Cougars lost to Appalachian State in the championship game. In the 2001 tournament, the Cougars were beaten by Davidson, 57-54, in the first round. The Cougars also lost to Davidson by three in the regular-season finale.

After coming up short of tournament bids the last two years, the Cougars will be hungry in 2002.

"Davidson came on real strong at the end of last season and knocked us out in the first round," coach John Kresse said. "That loss cost us an NIT bid because we had 22 wins and I think one or two more would have gotten us in the NIT if we had not won the Southern Conference championship.

"We have 12 teams in our league all vying for that Big Dance ticket and we're going to fight as hard as anyone to try to reclaim that title."

This year, the Cougars will be fighting without center Jody Lumpkin, voted the SoCon Player of the Year by the coaches and media after his senior season. Lumpkin (17.1 ppg, 7.9 rpg, 2.7 blg), 6-8 and 250 pounds, was third in the league in scoring, fourth in rebounding, third in shooting percentage (.580) and second in blocks. He is playing pro ball in Belgium.

"Jody Lumpkin won a bunch of games for us by himself," Kresse said. "He was very dominant. We just can't replace him because of his size and tremendous abilities."

Lumpkin was the only senior on last year's team that posted the program's eighth straight season with 22 or more victories.

With his departure, Kresse will look for the only senior on the team, 6-3 senior guard **Jeff Bolton**, to assume the leadership role. Bolton (16.1 ppg, 4.8 rpg) was fifth in the league in scoring last season and third in free-throw percentage (.833). He was 15th in three-pointers per game (1.72) and shot 35 percent (50-of-143) from three-point range.

Bolton was chosen to the coaches' All-SoCon first team and was on the media's all-conference second team.

"We'll build this year around our lone senior, Jeff Bolton," Kresse said. "He's a dynamic swing player."

Kresse says he has several options at shooting guard and small forward, and you can bet Bolton is in the thick of the plans.

Troy Wheless, a 6-3 junior, was a mainstay in the backcourt last season, starting 26-of-28 games and averaging 29.1 minutes. Wheless (6.7 ppg, 3.0 rpg) will be pushed by several players for minutes at shooting guard, including 6-2 sophomore **Quinton Hollis** (2.0 ppg, 1.1 rpg) and 6-2 freshman **Stanley Jackson**. Hollis averaged 8.2 minutes in 27 games last season.

Last year, Jackson averaged 25.6 points at Dunnellon (Fla.) High School and finished with more than 3,000 career points.

"Troy Wheless has played there [at shooting guard] quite a bit," Kresse said. "Quinton Hollis was a freshman last year and will look at playing time. Stanley Jackson will also be a player we look at for some playing time at the two spot."

Thomas Mobley (4.9 ppg, 2.3 rpg), a 6-4 sophomore, will also get a chance to play shooting guard or small forward. Mobley played in 28 games last season with three starts and averaged 14.2 minutes.

"We're counting on Thomas Mobley," Kresse said. "He played sparingly as a rookie but he's got a wealth of talent at the forward position. We're counting on him for scoring and rebounding in the forward spot this season."

Joe Weurding, a 6-6 sophomore, can also play either forward position. Weurding (1.9 ppg, 1.4 rpg) averaged 7.3 minutes in 29 games last season with one start.

A.J. Harris (1.3 ppg, 1.2 rpg, 4.1 apg) returns after starting at point guard in 19 games last season. Harris, a 6-0 junior, will have to beat out 5-11 freshman **Tony Mitchell** for the starting job.

Mitchell was a star at Josey High School in Augusta, Ga., where he averaged 26 points, 11 assists, five rebounds and four steals last season.

"A.J. Harris has started for the last two seasons but will be dramatically pushed by Mitchell," Kresse said. "He scored 42 points in the Georgia-Florida all-star game in the spring and was most valuable player of that ball game. He's a very complete guard who's going to push A.J. Harris for sure."

Orloff Civil, a 6-0 junior walk-on, hasn't played since high school at Port Charlotte (Fla.) High School. Civil will have a tough time earning quality minutes.

Kresse will likely fill a starting spot with 6-6 junior **Leighton Bowie** (9.8 ppg, 4.9 rpg), who started all but one game last season and was the team's third-leading scorer.

Last season, Bowie started started at power forward.

"One thing is we have players who play multiple positions this season," Kresse said. "We can do a lot of jigsawing of our lineup to make it work in our favor. We have multi-dimensional players and they can play a few positions. That's going to help us."

Kresse hopes Bowie can overcome the inconsistency that plagued him last year. Bowie averaged 12 points and 6.6 rebounds as a freshman.

"Leighton Bowie had a tremendous freshman year

and somewhat of an up and down sophomore year," Kresse said. "He is as quick as a cat and we expect him to progress well this year in his third year in the program."

Rob Masters (0.6 ppg, 1.1 rpg), a 6-5 sophomore, will be a backup again after playing little last season. Walk-on **Tom McCloskey**, a 6-6 sophomore, is a transfer from Navy. McCloskey played in only four games at Navy last year before leaving and averaged 0.5 points and 1.8 rebounds.

It has been a tough recovery for 6-6 red-shirt freshman **Shannon Chambers**, who collided with Lumpkin two years ago and sustained a serious neck injury. Chambers missed all of last season, but will try to add something to the power forward spot this season.

Obviously, the biggest question is at low post, where 6-8 junior **Rudy Rothseiden** backed up Lumpkin last season. Rothseiden (3.1 ppg, 2.3 rpg) played in 29 games, but averaged only 11.3 minutes.

Mike Benton, a 6-9 sophomore, was red-shirted last season and will battle Rothseiden for the starting job at low post. Benton averaged 2.1 points and 1.6 rebounds two years ago.

Bernard Jackson, a 6-6 sophomore, transferred from Tallahassee (Fla.) Community College. He could be a factor. Jackson averaged 6.4 points and 3.0 rebounds last season. Despite those low averages, Jackson, who's strong and physical, is expected to make a significant contribution.

"He's a powerful inside player who can play both the power forward and the center slot," Kresse said. "He is a very physical inside presence who will help us immediately."

2001-2002 SCHEDULE

Nov.	16	Charleston Southern
	19	Stetson
	24	Francis Marion
	28	@American
Dec.	1	Coastal Carolina
	8	Belmont Abbey
	15	@UNC Wilimgton
	21-22	#Tournament of Champions
	28-29	##State Farm Good Neighbor Classic
Jan.	2	Wofford
	5	@Chattanooga
	7	East Tennessee State
	12	@Wofford
	14	@Furman
	19	@VMI
	21	The Citadel
	26	Georgia Southern
	28	@NC Greensboro
Feb.	2	Furman
	4	@The Citadel
	9	Appalachian State
	11	@Western Carolina
	16	Chattanooga
	19	Davidson
	23	@Georgia Southern
Feb.	28	###Southern Conference Tournament
March	1-3	###Southern Conference Tournament

@Road Games
#Charlotte, NC (vs. Charlotte, first round; also Georgia State, St. Joseph's)
##Charleston, SC (vs. Louisiana-Monroe, first round; also Holy Cross, Radford)
###North Charleston Coliseum, Charleston, SC

BLUE RIBBON ANALYSIS

BACKCOURT	A-
BENCH/DEPTH	B
FRONTCOURT	C
INTANGIBLES	A

For the last three seasons, College of Charleston has been a fixture in the Southern Conference title chase. Don't look for that to change this year, even with the departure of Lumpkin, the SoCon's Player of the Year last season.

The Cougars won't have the dominant big man again this year, but they will have an abundance of guards and forwards.

"We've got plenty of depth, but it's still basically a young team with again only one senior [Bolton]," Kresse said. "We're still fairly young but we're experienced and we're talented. Not only Jeff Bolton, but other players will really have to rise to the occasion to step up and fulfill Jody Lumpkin's points, rebounds and defense. We're

looking for a number of players to step up."

Bolton, a candidate for SoCon Player of the Year, will be the team's feature player.

The Cougars will again rely on their defense, a trademark of Kresse teams. They allowed only 60 points per game last season and ranked among the nation's top 13 in scoring defense for the ninth time in 10 seasons. Charleston, however, may pick up the tempo this season.

"It always starts with defense in our program and that's been very solid, so hopefully we'll stay very strong defensively," Kresse said. "We have to open up our game. With Jody Lumpkin's departure, we need to get easy baskets by pressing, running and penetrating more."

(D.L.)

Davidson

LOCATION	Davidson, NC
CONFERENCE	Southern (North)
LAST SEASON	15-17 (.469)
CONFERENCE RECORD	7-9 (4th)
STARTERS LOST/RETURNING	0/4
NICKNAME	Wildcats
COLORS	Black & Red
HOMECOURT	Belk Arena (5,700)
COACH	Bob McKillop (Hofstra '72)
RECORD AT SCHOOL	184-161 (12 years)
CAREER RECORD	184-161 (12 years)
ASSISTANTS	Matt Matheny (Davidson '93)
	Jason Zimmerman (Davidson '94)
	Mike Kelly (St. Joseph's College '93)
TEAM WINS (last 5 years)	18-20-16-15-15
RPI (last 5 years)	110-93-143-169-225
2000-01 FINISH	Lost in conference semifinal.

OK, so the Wildcats' fourth-place finish in the North wasn't the greatest regular season for their program. But their late-season run made up for some of the disappointments earlier in the season.

After knocking off The Citadel and College of Charleston in the last two games of the regular season, the Wildcats beat Wofford and Charleston (again) in the Southern Conference Tournament.

Only after a 73-68 loss to UNC Greensboro were the Wildcats finished.

Clearly, the Wildcats were playing some of their best ball at the end of the season, and with almost their entire team returning, there is plenty of optimism on campus.

"We're returning an extremely experienced team, a team that has quite a bit of versatility from the standpoint of guys playing varying roles during the past season as well as during their career," Wildcats coach Bob McKillop said. "With that being said, we've had a lot of pieces that we could fit into the puzzle to make ourselves a very competitive team. Having them all fit and making that fit successful is the challenge we face in September, October and November."

Davidson is a team of good players, not all-stars. That was the case last season when none of the Wildcats were chosen to the 10-player All-SoCon team by the league's coaches or the first, second or third All-SoCon teams by the media. **Wayne Bernard**, a 6-3 junior shooting guard, was on the all-tournament second team.

Bernard (13.7 ppg, 2.9 rpg) returns along with two solid point guards, 5-10 senior **Fernando Tonella** (5.0 ppg, 2.2 rpg, 2.5 apg) and 6-0 senior **Michael Bree** (5.4 ppg, 2.8 rpg, 3.2 apg).

Tonella started 22 games and averaged 21.3 minutes; Bree started 11 games and averaged 20.8 minutes. McKillop considers both starters.

"Both of them have started 50 percent of the games that they've competed in and both are seniors," McKillop said, "and when you become a senior there's something that happens in that transition period that can really spur you on to something that perhaps you couldn't do as an inexperienced sophomore or even as a mature junior. The senior year somehow ties it together."

McKillop says the two point guards have different talents.

"I think Fern has more of a scoring mentality," McKillops said. "Michael has more of a passing mentality. Fern shoots it much better and Michael has had a terrific off-season, so we're optimistic that he's going to step into the forefront."

Bernard should stay in the forefront as the starter at shooting guard, but he will have competition for the job

from 6-5 sophomore **Nick Booker**, 6-1 junior **Peter Anderer** and 6-3 freshman **Eric Blancett**.

Booker (4.3 ppg, 3.5 rpg) was actually a starter in 23 of the 31 games in which he played. He was in the line-up because of numerous injuries to 6-5 senior small forward Emeke Erege. Booker averaged 21.7 minutes.

Anderer (6.0 ppg, 1.4 rpg) played in 32 games with eight starts and averaged 14.4 mintues.

With those three returning, McKillop has players with starting experience, which will make for a competitive preseason.

"Bernard is more of a slasher-scorer than a shooter, but he's very effective at all those responsibilities," McKillop said. "He is the frontrunner now. Wayne had an exceptional sophomore year and we feel well backed up there with Peter Anderer, who starter eight or nine games as a sophomore. We also feel Nick Booker can play either the shooting guard spot or the small-forward spot. Again, he's another guy who started a number of games as a freshman. It gives us a little bit of flexibility."

Blancett averaged 15.1 points, 5.1 rebounds, and 2.4 assists last season at DeSmet High School in St. Louis. He shot 50 percent from the floor, 32.7 percent from three-point range and 75.5 percent from the line.

"Blancett is very similar in that he can bridge the gap between the shooting guard and small forward positions, which are basically interchangeable in our system," McKillop said.

McKillop hopes Erege can avoid the injuries that have plagued him in his career at Davidson. As a freshman, he broke his leg, missed almost half the season and had a rod put in his leg. Last season, he played in 19 games with 15 starts, but missed the rest of the games with a broken bone in his foot.

"Erege is probably our best player," McKillop said. "He has had a variety of injuries. ... He's a guy that when he's on the court and he's healthy he's as good a player as we can get. I consider him a slasher, someone who can create points for himself with his ability to put it on the floor, make the medium-range jump shot and get some garbage points inside."

Players who will be backups in the backcourt are 6-1 sophomore **Jason Ford** (4.7 ppg, 1.4 rpg), 6-1 sophomore **Terrell Ivory** (0.0 ppg, 0.5 rpg) and 6-1 junior **Jarred Cochran** (0.5 ppg, 0.5 rpg).

Of those players, only Ford played significant minutes last season. Ford averaged 11.5 minutes in 23 games.

In the frontcourt, 6-9 junior **Chris Pearson** returns after starting all but one game last year. Pearson (7.8 ppg, 6.8 rpg), who plays the power forward, was the team's leading rebounder.

Another player competing for time in the backcourt is 6-6 sophomore **Jouni Eho** (4.1 ppg, 1.9 rpg), who played in all 32 games with two starts and averaged 13 minutes.

"[Pearson] is athletic and has improved dramatically during the last two years," McKillop said. "We'll back him up with Jouni Eho. [Eho] had some outstanding performances last year and then some not-so-outstanding performances. It's typically a bug that attacks most freshmen. He had that bug."

Eho (4.1 ppg, 1.9 rpg), a 6-6 sophomore, averaged 13 minutes in 32 games and started twice.

At center, 7-2 senior **Martin Ides** (8.8 ppg, 6.8 rpg) will get the start. Ides, who weighs 280, averaged 23.2 minutes and started 21 games.

"He's a big, wide body," McKillop said. "He has a very good shooting touch and excellent hands and passing ability. He doesn't have the athleticism and mobility that the great players have, but he makes up for that with his basketball know-how."

Two others will be backups in the frontcourt.

Michael Lusakueno, a 6-10 junior, played in 31 games last season and averaged 8.0 minutes, 1.8 points and 2.0 rebounds.

Conor Grace, a 6-8, 215 freshman from Dublin, Ireland, played prep ball at Bridgton Academy in Maine, where he averaged 11 points, 6.9 rebounds and 2.1 assists for a team that went 27-6 and reached the championship game of the New England Prep School Athletic Conference.

2001-2002 SCHEDULE

Nov.	16	@Charlotte
	20	@North Carolina
	23	Oglethorpe
	26	@Texas A&M
Dec.	1	Navy
	4	Elon
	8	@The Citadel
	16	Washington & Jefferson
	19	Georgia Tech

	22	@Pennsylvania
	29	Hamilton
Jan.	2	Duke
	5	@Western Carolina
	8	Chattanooga
	12	@Furman
	16	VMI
	19	East Tennessee State
	23	@UNC Greensboro
	26	Western Carolina
	30	Wofford
Feb.	2	@Appalachian State
	5	UNC Greensboro
	9	@East Tennessee State
	13	Georgia Southern
	16	Appalachian State
	19	@College of Charleston
	23	@VMI
	28	#Southern Conf. Tournament
March	1-3	#Southern Conf. Tournament

@Road Games
#Charleston Coliseum, Charleston, SC

BLUE RIBBON ANALYSIS

BACKCOURT	B+
BENCH/DEPTH	B
FRONTCOURT	B+
INTANGIBLES	A

McKillop says the Southern Conference is full of contenders this season, thanks to an abundance of returning starters. His team fits that mold perfectly.

The Wildcats have two good point guards in seniors Tonella and Bree, a very good shooting guard in Bernard and experienced post players in Pearson and Ides.

If small forward Erege can avoid the injuries that have plagued him throughout his career, he could be one of the league's best players. McKillop says Erege is probably the best player on the Wildcats' roster.

Davidson has a number of versatile players, and McKillop is just the coach who can make the team click.

"We think there are a lot of teams in the North Division and a lot of teams in the South Division that can contend for the championship," McKillop said.

Davidson should be one of those teams.

(D.L.)

East Tennessee State

LOCATION	Johnson City, TN
CONFERENCE	Southern (North)
LAST SEASON	18-10 (.643)
CONFERENCE RECORD	13-3 (1st)
STARTERS LOST/RETURNING	2/3
NICKNAME	Buccaneers
COLORS	Navy Blue & Old Gold
HOMECOURT	Memorial Center (13,000)
COACH	Ed DeChellis (Penn State '82)
RECORD AT SCHOOL	67-72 (5 years)
CAREER RECORD	67-72 (5 years)
ASSISTANTS	Tom Conrad (Old Dominion '79)
	Hillary Scott (Roanoke '94)
	Scott Wagers (Tennessee Wesleyan '89)
TEAM WINS (last 5 years)	7-11-17-14-18
RPI (last 5 years)	273-267-174-213-174
2000-01 FINISH	Lost in conference quarterfinal.

For the first time since the 1991-92 season, East Tennessee State returns to the basketball court as a defending champion. Last season, sixth-year coach Ed DeChellis was able to bring back memories of the program's glory days in the late '80s and early '90s.

When DeChellis was hired, he took over a team that was at the bottom of the North. His first team struggled, going 7-20 and 2-12 in the league, but from that low point, the Bucs have made a steady rise to the top.

Despite their upset loss to Georgia Southern in last year's tournament quarterfinals, the Bucs' season will be remembered as a championship year.

If anything, the 72-64 loss to the Eagles left the Bucs hungry to take the next step.

"We have to follow up last year's accomplishments with another great season," DeChellis said. "We haven't fulfilled our ultimate goal of making the NCAA Tournament."

In pursuit of that goal, DeChellis will be counting on his experience and talent on the perimeter.

Dimeco Childress, a 6-3 senior shooting guard/small forward, returns after being chosen to the all-conference first team by the league's coaches last season. Childress (13.2 ppg, 4.0 rpg) led the team in scoring and three-pointers (54) last season. He ranked 11th in the conference in three-point percentage (.370).

"He's a senior who's a great shooter and really has a knack for scoring," DeChellis said. "He's kind of made every big shot for us throughout his career."

Joining Childress in the backcourt is 6-1 senior point guard **Cliff Decoster** (9.3 ppg, 3.4 rpg, 2.7 apg), who ranked 13th in the league in assists and third in steals (2.19).

Decoster is one of the league's best perimeter defenders, and DeChellis will look for him to increase his role as a team leader and make better decisions.

"He's just strong," DeChellis said. "He's a very strong player and he's pretty athletic. He's worked hard. He works hard every day. He works hard in the off-season. He's a very conditioned guy, takes pride in what he does. Sometimes he gets a little too fast and sometimes his decisions are somewhat questionable, but I know he's going to give me everything he has."

Decoster's backups are young. **Sam Oatman** (2.3 ppg, 1.0 rpg, 1.9 apg), a 6-1 sophomore, played in 24 games last season and averaged 12 minutes per game.

James Anthony, a 6-3 freshman, can play either guard spot. Anthony averaged 22 points, seven rebounds and six assists as a senior at Armwood High School in Tampa last year. He was a McDonald's All-America nominee.

"James Anthony is a very athletic guard with the ability to play the point or the two-guard," DeChellis said. "He is very good at creating off the dribble. Anthony can score off the dribble as well as from the outside."

Ryan Lawson, a 6-2 junior, is the third guard in the three-guard starting lineup. Lawson (7.6 ppg, 2.0 rpg) started 21 games last season and was second on the team in three-pointers (39.). He was sixth in the league in three-point shooting percentage (.386).

Once DeChellis put Lawson in the starting lineup, he had no reason to take him out.

"When we inserted him into the starting lineup we won like 11 or 12 games and had an eight-game winning streak, so it was tough to move him out," DeChellis said. "Ryan's a kid that can make open shots. He works extremely hard on the defensive end and tries to make things happen on the defensive end.

"He's just one of those players you like to have on your team but you hate to play against. He's always diving on the floor, taking charges, that kind of stuff. He really kind of sets the tone for us."

Jon Perry, a 6-1 senior guard, was strictly a backup last season and his role won't likely change. Perry (1.8 ppg, 0.9 rpg), who played in eight games and averaged 4.4 minutes, will have to battle freshmen **Keeton Brooks** and **Michael Tolliver** for playing time on the perimeter.

The 6-4 Brooks was a high school teammate of 6-7 freshman **Tiras Wade** at Tampa Tech High School. Brooks averaged 18.2 points and 3.5 assists last season.

"Keeton is a very strong guard who has the ability to play both wing positions," DeChellis said. "He is an outstanding shooter and perimeter scorer."

Tolliver, a 6-1 combination guard, is from Bremo Bluff, Va., and played last season at Fork Union (Va.) Military. He fits the mold of former Bucs guard D.J. McDuffie (8.7 ppg, 2.5 rpg), a senior last season.

As a senior at Fluvanna (Va.) High School, Tolliver averaged 21 points, eight rebounds and five assists. He averaged 10 points and five assists last season for a Fork Union team that went 28-2.

"Michael is a good shooter," DeChellis said. "He has a knack of getting other people a shot."

Wade gives the Bucs good size on the wing. Last season, Wade averaged 29.9 points and 8.2 rebounds at Tampa Tech.

"Tiras has the ability to score while being a great defender," DeChellis said. "Once he learns the system he could see quality time."

DeChellis' biggest challenge will be replacing frontcourt starters Renaldo Johnson (8.8 ppg, 6.4 rpg) and Adrian Meeks (7.8 ppg, 5.4 rpg).

"They were two seniors who had a lot of game experience," DeChellis said.

The likely replacements for Johnson and Meeks will be 6-6 sophomore **Jerald Fields** and 6-9 sophomore **Cory Seels**.

Fields (6.5 ppg, 4.3 rpg) averaged 19 minutes in 23 games last season and will probably start at power forward. Seels (2.8 ppg, 2.4 rpg) averaged 8.7 minutes in 27 games with one start.

"Fields played extremely well for us and actually got about 20 minutes a game," DeChellis said. "Now he's got to be ready to step into more of a starting role. Jerald's pretty athletic and he can step out on the perimeter, too. We're going to try to use Jerald on the perimeter as well as in the post. He's got perimeter skills. He can put it on the floor, he can shoot the three. We're going to try to do some things where we step him away from the basket and try to use his perimeter skills.

"Cory will basically be a low-block guy and the kind of guy who plays high-post, low-post. Those two guys need to be solid for us."

Probable backups for Fields will be 6-6 junior **Isaac Potter**, 6-6 sophomore **Zakee Wadood**, and 6-7 junior **Shannon Huffstetler**.

Potter (3.3 ppg, 1.6 rpg) played in 18 games last year and averaged 7.0 minutes. Wadood (2.8 ppg, 3.0 rpg) played slightly more, averaging 9.0 minutes in 22 games.

Huffstetler comes to the Bucs from Brunswick (Ga.) Community College, where he averaged 16.8 points and 11.5 rebounds last year. He made the Dean's List for two years in junior college.

"We hope he's going to be a solid guy for us," DeChellis said of Huffstetler. "You never know how a kid's going to make that adjustment. He has the tools to be a kid who can come in and be solid for us."

DeChellis says the newcomers and backups from last season will fill the roles of Johnson and Meeks.

"Hopefully by committee we'll be OK on the front line," DeChellis said.

2001-2002 SCHEDULE

Nov.	16	Guilford College
	18	@Virginia
	20	@Virginia Commonwealth
	26	@South Carolina
	28	@UNC Asheville
Dec.	4	@Coastal Carolina
	8	Radford
	15	James Madison
	17	Shenandoah
	19	Virginia-Wise
	22	@Vanderbilt
Jan.	2	Appalachian State
	5	@The Citadel
	7	@College of Charleston
	12	VMI
	14	@UNC Greensboro
	19	@Davidson
	23	Wofford
	26	Chattanooga
	30	@VMI
Feb.	2	Georgia Southern
	4	@Western Carolina
	9	Davidson
	12	UNC Greensboro
	16	Western Carolina
	18	@Furman
	23	@Appalachian State
	28	#Southern Conf. Tournament
March	1-3	#Southern Conf. Tournament

@Road Games
###North Charleston Coliseum, Charleston, SC

BLUE RIBBON ANALYSIS

BACKCOURT	A
BENCH/DEPTH	B-
FRONTCOURT	C
INTANGIBLES	B

The Bucs will have one of the best backcourts in the Southern Conference, but the frontcourt is the big question. Fields and Seels were backups last season, and their ability to take over starting jobs in the frontcourt will be critical. Decoster combines with Childress and Lawson to make a dangerous backcourt.

Coach Ed DeChellis doesn't work with a star system, but looks to win with balance.

"In our system we don't need a guy to go out and get 10, 12, or 14 points a night," DeChellis said. "We're just asking them to be solid and rebound and play defense for us, and if they do that, I think their averages will come naturally.

"I think that's what's positive about us. We don't need one guy to do a certain thing. I think we've got enough weapons that it can be a different guy every night, and that's how we won so many games in the league. We were a very balanced team and you didn't really know who was going to hurt you each night."

DeChellis will be counting on some young players this season, but his senior guards will be the backbone of the team.

"We need to have big years from our young players," DeChellis said. "One or two of our freshmen have to step up and play some quality minutes."

The Bucs won't be favored to win the North again, but they'll be a dangerous bunch.

(D.L.)

Furman

LOCATION	Greenville, SC
CONFERENCE	Southern (South)
LAST SEASON	10-16 (.385)
CONFERENCE RECORD	5-11 (6th)
STARTERS LOST/RETURNING	1/4
NICKNAME	Paladins
COLORS	Purple & White
HOMECOURT	Timmons Arena (5,000)
COACH	Larry Davis (Asbury '78)
RECORD AT SCHOOL	45-70 (4 years)
CAREER RECORD	45-70 (4 years)
ASSISTANTS	Ken Potosnak (Randolph-Macon '90)
	Chris Keeling (Maine '97)
	Niko Medved (Minnesota '97)
TEAM WINS (last 5 years)	10-19-12-14-10
RPI (last 5 years)	258-290-233-245-271
2000-01 FINISH	Lost in conference first round.

For the first time in his four years at Furman, Paladins coach Larry Davis has his own team in place. He has a veteran team returning, and with some added size in the frontcourt, Davis believes this year's team can make a move in the Southern Conference South Division.

"We've got almost everybody back," Davis said. "I think it's the first year since I've been here that we've have a veteran group returning. The first two years, we had veteran guys returning but they were guys we took over with. They just weren't very talented.

"Now we have a group that has played in our system, our guys, who are finally getting into their junior and senior years."

Marcus Dilligard (5.3 ppg, 4.4 rpg), a 6-5 guard/forward, is the only starter gone from last year's team, and he wasn't in the starting lineup at the end of the year.

Davis has two experienced point guards returning in 6-3 junior Guilherme Da Luz (11.2 ppg, 4.9 rpg, 5.9 apg) and 6-1 senior Paul Foster (1.5 ppg, 1.9 rpg). Foster will be the backup, but when he runs the point Da Luz can play shooting guard.

Da Luz will be starting at the point for the third year. Last season he ranked second in the league in assists.

"He's raised his shooting percentage from his freshman to his sophomore year," Davis said. "He's worked extremely hard on his shooting. I think his shooting percentage is going to go up from [three-point range]. That's really the missing ingredient of his game [he shot 30.1 percent last season].

"He's a great decision-maker and can really get in the lane. He's a great post-up guard. The thing he's really lacked is consistency from three. If he raises his shooting percentage like he did last year, he can be shooting in the high 30s and low 40s from three."

Anthony Thomas, a 6-4 senior, is the likely starter at shooting guard. Thomas (11.1 ppg, 2.2 rpg) was the team's third-leading scorer—a tenth of a point behind Da Luz—and started 25 games. He has started for most of the last three years.

"He's another one whose percentage has raised every year he's been here from [three-point range]," Davis said, "and his scoring average has raised every year. He's gotten stronger and made good progress. He's not a super athlete, but an OK athlete. He's a prelaw major and a smart player. He's got a great mid-range game, can hit the little runner and that stuff. He came in and weighed 165 and now he's at 205. He's gotten bigger and stronger."

Jason Patterson, a 6-4 freshman guard, will provide depth. Patterson averaged 16 points and seven rebounds last season at Lithonia (Ga.) High School. Matt Sides (0.0 ppg, 0.0 rpg), a 6-2 sophomore guard, and 6-1 sophomore Evan Aldrich (2.0 ppg, 0.0 rpg) will be practice players, for the most part. Both played in only one game last season.

Backing up Thomas will be 6-5 swing player Jorge Seraphim (2.1 ppg, 2.1 rpg) and 6-2 junior Ryan Chancler, a transfer from New Mexico Junior College. Chancler averaged 17.8 points in junior college last sea-

son and shot better than 40 percent from three-point range.

"[Chancler] will vie for time at that spot and I'm sure at times we'll play a three-guard lineup and he'll be in there," Davis said. "He can really shoot."

The Paladins' best player is 6-7 junior Karim Souchu, who is from Paris, France. Souchu (18.9 ppg, 5.3 rpg), an All-SoCon first-team player, was second in the league in scoring last season. He can also play power forward but us more suited for small forward.

"He's a multi-dimensional player," Davis said. "He can score inside, shoot the three, he's got a knack for driving the ball ... Last year he developed into a really good defender."

Davis said Souchu had an "OK year, but had sophomore-itis, but had a great freshman year. We expect even bigger things from him this year from the standpoint if he comes along maturity-wise. He needs to take it to another level."

At power forward, 6-5 junior Kenny Zeigler (10.2 ppg, 7.5 rpg) returns as the starter. Zeigler was fifth in the SoCon in rebounding last season and was the Paladins' fourth-leading scorer.

For about half the year, Zeigler played out of position at the low post because of recurring foot problems to starter Darrell Arbaugh. Arbaugh, who weighed 255, was the only bulky player in the frontcourt, and when he went down the Paladins had a serious shortage of strength in the post.

"Kenny has put on some weight, and now weighs 215 or 220," Davis said. "He had a good year last year. He came on and averaged almost a double-double. He's a kid who can really rebound the ball and with added size, he won't have to be outmatched so much sizewise. He creates a little bit of a problem when he's at power forward because he can go out and shoot it from 15 to 18 feet and go out and drive it from out there."

Zeigler will be pushed for the job by 6-8 sophomore Maleye Ndoye (3.5 ppg, 2.8 rpg), who started six games and averaged 14.9 minutes per game. Ndoye is from Dakar, Senegal.

"He started some games at center, but he's not a center," Davis said. "He's a forward who plays the three or the four and with his national team he played point guard because they didn't have anybody [at point guard]. He's a real versatile kid who can shoot it. Again, he's a kid who weighed 180 last year and he was [almost] 6-9. He's gotten a lot stronger and is over 200 now. That will help him."

Ndoye could end up at center at times this season.

Others who will play in the post include 6-9 freshman Cedrick Price, 6-7 freshman Paco Gonzalez, and 6-10 sophomore Marijan Pojatina.

Pojatina (2.1 ppg, 2.1 rpg) played in 20 games last season with five starts and averaged 13.9 minutes. He started at the end of the season and was second on the team in blocks with 21. He has bulked up from about 190 pounds to about 215.

"That will help him," Davis said. "He's a lot stronger. He's a very good shot blocker."

Gonzalez averaged 22 points and nine rebounds last season at Coral Gables (Fla.) High School. Price played at Fork Union (Va.) Military last season.

"Price will play some," Davis said. "They all split time [at Fork Union]. He probably averaged double figures, but just barely. He's a good player."

Nick Sanders, a 6-7 freshman forward from Leavenworth (Kan.) High School, tore his anterior cruciate ligament during the last week of his senior season and may be red-shirted.

2001-2002 SCHEDULE

Nov.	16	@Georgia
	20	Asbury
	26	@Campbell
	28	Methodist
Dec.	1	Campbell
	4	UNC Asheville
	8	Emory
	15	@Wisconsin
	19	@Saint Louis
	28-29	#Poinsettia Holiday Classic
Jan.	2	Georgia Southern
	5	@Wofford
	7	@Western Carolina
	12	Davidson
	14	College of Charleston
	19	Appalachian State
	21	@Chattanooga
	26	@VMI
	28	The Citadel
Feb.	2	@College of Charleston
	4	@Georgia Southern
	9	Chattanooga
	11	@The Citadel
	16	Wofford
	18	ETSU
	23	@UNC Greensboro
	28	#SoCon Tournament
March	1-3	#SoCon Tournament

@Road Games
#Greenville, SC (vs. Macalester first round; also Gardner-Webb, Yale)
##North Charleston Coliseum, Charleston, SC

BLUE RIBBON ANALYSIS

BACKCOURT	A-
BENCH/DEPTH	B-
FRONTCOURT	C
INTANGIBLES	C

Furman lacked size in the frontcourt last season, so Davis recruited just that for this season. Davis hopes that will solve the Paladins' frontcourt woes.

"We've got a veteran group on the perimeter in particular and we've got some size, which we did not have last year," Davis said. "Last year when [Darrell] Arbaugh went down, the heaviest guy on the floor for us was our point guard, and he was 205."

Still, the Paladins' frontcourt is the biggest question. In a league with lots of sizeable low-post players, the Paladins must be able to do some banging underneath the basket.

Furman has one of the league's marquee players in small forward Souchu, and the backcourt is solid.

If the newcomers and added muscle on returnees can bolster the frontcourt, the Paladins should make a sharp climb from the South's cellar.

"We've added some much-needed bulk on the front line and got another shooter or two," Davis said. "I'm excited about this team. I think we'll be pretty good."

The Paladins will only be as good as their frontcourt, though.

(D.L.)

Georgia Southern

LOCATION	Statesboro, GA
CONFERENCE	Southern (South)
LAST SEASON	15-15 (.500)
CONFERENCE RECORD	9-7 (t-2nd)
STARTERS LOST/RETURNING	0/5
NICKNAME	Eagles
COLORS	Blue, Gold & White
HOMECOURT	Hanner Fieldhouse (4,378)
COACH	Jeff Price (Pikeville '81)
RECORD AT SCHOOL	31-27 (2 years)
CAREER RECORD	167-69 (8 years)
ASSISTANTS	Carl Nash (Fort Lewis '82)
	Garrick Respress (Georgia Southern '97)
	Tom Spencer (Lynn '97)
TEAM WINS (last 5 years)	10-10-11-16-15
RPI (last 5 years)	271-273-257-174-218
2000-01 FINISH	Lost in conference semifinal.

At a school known for its football, Georgia Southern's basketball team is finding its own niche.

The Eagles have finished in second place in the Southern Conference's South Division the last two seasons. Last year, they were one of three teams tied for second.

With five starters returning, the Eagles seemed poised to take the next step this season.

"Physically, I think we're finally there in terms of being able to compete for a conference championship," third-year coach Jeff Price said. "We have the kind of talent it takes to win this league. This year will be more mental in that we've got to be able to handle being looked at as one of the favorites. Hopefully, we will be looked at that way."

Price won't have to worry about that. The rest of the league knows his team is loaded.

The Eagles are led by 6-2 junior shooting guard Julius Jenkins and 6-9 senior post Kashien Latham. Both earned all-conference honors last season.

Jenkins (16.7 ppg, 4.2 rpg, 2.5 apg) was chosen to the All-SoCon second team last season after earning all-freshman honors his first year.

In each of his first two seasons, Jenkins has been the

team's leading scorer. He was 13th in the league in three-pointers per game last season (1.86), but shot only 31 percent from long range. Look for that percentage to improve this year.

Jenkins will be joined in the backcourt by starting point guard **Sean Peterson** (13.6 ppg, 3.8 rpg, 6.2 apg, 2.4 spg), a 6-1 senior who led the league in assists and was second in steals.

It took half the season for Peterson to make the adjustment from junior-college ball at Pasco-Hernando (Fla.) Junior College, but once he did, he became a team leader. He led the team in scoring 11 times—the most of any player on the team—and was on the SoCon All-Tournament first team.

"There's no doubt Sean was one of our best players last year," Price said. "When he played well, we played well. He took over in the tournament. We think he's one of the top point guards in the country.

"Julius had really good numbers, but he knows and we know they could have been a lot better. His shooting percentage (.370) went down, but that was from trying to do so much early on. We know he'll bounce back. He's got a chance to be a very special player here."

Terry Williams, a 6-1 freshman, will be a backup at point guard and shooting guard. Williams was a big-time scorer at P.K. Yonge High School in Gainesville, Fla., where he averaged 29.5 points, 5.5 assists, 5.4 steals and 4.5 rebounds.

Kenny Faulk returns for his sophomore season and could start at the third guard spot. The 6-3 Faulk (6.2 ppg, 2.4 rpg) started the last 17 games of the season. He led the team in three-point percentage (.400), making 26-of-65.

Frank Bennett, a 6-7 sophomore forward, was also pushed into a starting job early in his career. Bennett (8.6 ppg, 6.2 rpg) moved into the lineup in the seventh game and stayed there the rest of the season. He was the team's second-leading rebounder and was chosen to the league's all-freshman team.

"You couldn't have asked for any more out of those two [Faulk and Bennett]," Price said. "We threw them right into the fire. They had to learn on the job and they still produced. Frank had some great moments as a freshman, and Kenny came up big for us several times. He hit some huge shots down the stretch. Both of them have outstanding futures. It's going to be fun seeing how much they've improved from their first to second year."

Sam Cox, a 6-7 senior swing player, will give the Eagles some punch off the bench. Cox (3.2 ppg, 1.8 rpg) started two games last season and averaged 9.2 minutes in 26 games. He scored 11 points in the Eagles' tournament quarterfinal victory over East Tennessee State.

"Sam showed what kind of player he can be in the conference tournament," Price said. "He's so athletic, he can cause a lot of problems."

Willie Puckett, a 6-5 junior forward, is a transfer from Odessa (Texas) Junior College. Puckett, from Griffin, Ga., averaged 17.5 points and 8.5 rebounds in junior college last season.

Kordel Gibson, a 6-4 sophomore, can also play either forward position. Gibson, who was red-shirted last season, played one season at Palm Beach (Fla.) Community College, where he averaged 17.5 points and 3.9 rebounds two years ago.

Latham will be the leader in the frontcourt. Last season, Latham (13.4 ppg, 9.7 rpg) was chosen to the 10-player all-conference first team by the league's coaches and was a member of the media's second team. He was second in the SoCon in rebounding and seventh in field-goal percentage (.522).

In conference games, Latham averaged a double-double (12.3 ppg, 10.3 rpg), and his 291 total rebounds were the most by a Georgia Southern player since the 1969-70 season.

"Kashien was very solid for us," Price said. "We need him to raise his game a notch. When he played well, we were a different team. Seniors have a way of finding that little extra, that sense of urgency that puts them over the top. I think you'll see that with him this season."

Adding quality depth to the frontcourt will be senior post players **Edward "Bobo" Keith** and **Wayne Wooley** and sophomore forward **Marcus Byams**.

The 6-7 Wooley (3.9 ppg, 4.6 rpg) played in 14 games with three starts before suffering a shoulder injury that required surgery. He averaged 17.2 minutes per game.

Byams (2.4 ppg, 1.9 rpg), 6-6, averaged 10.1 minutes in 17 games. His role became much greater when Wooley went out with the injury.

"Wayne and Bobo give us a ton of experience in the post," Price said. "Those two have been through the wars and know what to expect. Bobo is as tough as they come and Wayne should be all the way back from his surgery. Marcus gave us some productive minutes after we lost Wayne. His hustle and effort was contagious."

The 6-7 Keith was in the starting lineup early in the season but became a backup after four games. Keith (3.1 ppg, 3.1 rpg) averaged 11.4 minutes and played in 27 games.

Sean Olivier, a 6-9 freshman, will benefit from playing and practicing with the veteran post players. Olivier averaged 16.8 points, 10.4 rebounds and 4.6 steals last season for St. Cloud (Fla.) High School.

Price does not plan for any of his newcomers to sit on the bench all season.

"All those guys will get a chance to help us," Price said. "Willie [Puckett] gives us some real size and toughness at the wing and Terry [Williams] is as fine a shooter as I've seen in a long time. Sean [Olivier] is a real sleeper with a very, very bright future. Kordel [Gibson] sat out last year, but he was able to practice and pick up the system. He's also a real solid shooter."

2001-2002 SCHEDULE

Nov.	16	North Georgia
	19	Gardner-Webb
	21	@Georgia
	24	@Wichita State
	29	Illinois State
Dec.	1	UNLV
	4	@Gardner-Webb
	6	@Savannah State
	8	Mercer
	17	Albany State
Jan.	2	@Furman
	5	VMI
	7	@Appalachian State
	12	UNC Greensboro
	14	@The Citadel
	19	Wofford
	21	Western Carolina
	26	@College of Charleston
	28	Chattanooga
	30	Savannah State
Feb.	2	@ETSU
	4	Furman
	9	@Wofford
	13	@Davidson
	16	The Citadel
	23	College of Charleston
	28	#SoCon Tournament
March	1-3	#SoCon Tournament

@Road Games
#North Charleston Coliseum, Charleston, SC

BLUE RIBBON ANALYSIS

BACKCOURT	A
BENCH/DEPTH	B+
FRONTCOURT	A-
INTANGIBLES	B

The Eagles have an all-conference player in both the frontcourt and backcourt—Jenkins at shooting guard and Latham in the post.

They also have an outstanding point guard in Peterson. Those three are surrounded by solid players and talented backups. It seems the Eagles have all the ingredients of a winning team.

"This is the deepest, most athletic team we've had in our three years here," third-year coach Jeff Price said. "That's what I like the most right now about our team. We've got a bunch of experience. Some of it is young experience, when you consider how many games Julius [Jenkins] has played the last two years and how much Frank [Bennett] and Kenny [Faulk] played last season. They have been in the heat of battle."

Price is a proven winner. He averaged almost 23 victories per season at Lynn (Fla.) University and built the team into a Division II national contender. His 1997 team went 28-3 and became the first school in NCAA history to reach a national semifinal in its first year of NCAA competition. It earned him national coach-of-the-year honors.

With the experience the team gained from last year, Georgia Southern should be the favorite in the South Division.

"We haven't finished first and we haven't won the conference tournament yet, so there are still goals left to be achieved," Price said. "That has to be the ultimate goal, capturing a championship."

That goal isn't far-fetched.

(D.L.)

UNC Greensboro

LOCATION	Greensboro, NC
CONFERENCE	Southern (North)
LAST SEASON	19-12 (.613)
CONFERENCE RECORD	10-6 (2nd)
STARTERS LOST/RETURNING	1/4
NICKNAME	Spartans
COLORS	Gold, White & Navy
HOMECOURT	Fleming Gym (2,320)
COACH	Fran McCaffery (Pennsylvania '82)
RECORD AT SCHOOL	34-25 (2 years)
CAREER RECORD	83-64 (5 years)
ASSISTANTS	Billy Taylor (Notre Dame '95)
	Dick Stewart (Rutgers '69)
	Bill Reinson (Phoenix '00)
TEAM WINS (last 5 years)	10-9-7-15-19
RPI (last 5 years)	232-229-282-188-173
2000-01 FINISH	Lost in NCAA first round.

It took a perfect pass, a perfect play, and a perfect finish for the UNC Greensboro Spartans to win the Southern Conference Tournament championship last year.

With 2.6 seconds left, **Jay Joseph** threw a three-quarters court pass to **David Schuck**, whose layup with less than a second left lifted the Spartans to a 67-66 victory over Chattanooga and into the NCAA Tournament.

It was a stunning moment for a team that made a remarkable turnaround in two seasons. Only three years ago, the Spartans went 7-20 and finished fifth in the SoCon North Division with a 5-11 record.

Fran McCaffery, who spent the previous 11 years as an assistant at Notre Dame, was hired as the Spartans' head coach in 1999-2000 to jump-start the program. He has done just that.

"My first year we win 15 games, which was a good step, and then we turn around and win 19 games and go to the [NCAA] Tournament," McCaffery said. "The fact that we could go from the bottom of the barrel to win the conference championship and go to the NCAA Tournament I think says a lot about this program and the institution.

"This is a great place to go to school and a lot is offered here that is attractive to a prospect. We've really come a long way."

It doesn't look like the Spartans will be dropping out of sight anytime soon, either.

Four starters and 10 lettermen return from last year's team. The only key loss was shooting guard Nathan Jameson (10.7 ppg, 1.7 rpg), who started all but one game last season. Jameson was a 1,000-point scorer and four-year starter.

His spot will be filled by Joseph, a 6-4 sophomore and the SoCon's Freshman of the Year last season. Joseph (13.3 ppg, 4.9 rpg) set a school scoring record for freshmen last season after hitting double-figure scoring in 24-of-31 games.

Surprisingly, Joseph was recruited as a shooting guard, but with Jameson in the lineup, he played small forward once **James Maye** went out with an injury.

"That [shooting guard] spot is open and Jay is a natural fit there because he can really shoot the ball, he can put it on the floor, and he's a powerful two-guard," McCaffery said. "James has been a very good rebounding small forward and a very good scorer. He averaged 13.5 points as a sophomore.

"That was the plan, to play Jay at the two and James at the three last year, not necessarily with Jay as the starter but with Jay coming in to fill in at two or three. It probably worked to Jay's benefit that he was able to just assimilate into college basketball without having to dribble the ball as much. He could just run off the screens and shoot the ball in the hole for us."

Maye (9.2 ppg, 4.8 rpg), a 6-6 junior, played in six games with three starts before missing the rest of the season with a stress fracture in his foot. Two years ago, Maye was the team's second-leading scorer (13.7 ppg) and rebounder (5.9 rpg).

The Spartans return one of the top point guards in the league in 5-10 senior **Courtney Eldridge** (14.6 ppg, 3.1 rpg, 4.8 apg). He was seventh in the league in scoring and third in assists. He led the league in steals with 2.65 per game and was chosen to the coaches' and media's all-conference first team.

Eldridge was also on the all-tournament first team.

"He's got a chance to rewrite the record books in a lot of different areas here," McCaffery said. "Anytime you have the general coming back who is a proven winner, that certainly makes you feel good as a coach."

Ronnie Taylor, a 6-1 sophomore, can play either guard position. Taylor (9.0 ppg, 1.7 rpg) played in all 31 games and averaged 21.5 minutes.

"Taylor is a fantastic player," McCaffery said. "I treat him more or less as a starter. He played starter minutes last year, especially in the second half of the season. What happened is Courtney would start and Jay and Ronnie would come in for either one. A lot of times we played Courtney and Ronnie together and defensively they just swarmed people, and they both can break their man down off the dribble.

"They can both get their own shot. They both can get it to the rim and they both can shoot from the outside. It really puts a lot of pressure on the defense when those two guys are playing together."

Danny Hargrove, a 6-4 freshman guard, will be a backup on the perimeter, as will 6-3 junior forward **Brian Fitzgerald**, 6-3 junior forward **Brandon Beck**, and 6-6 freshman forward Josh Gross.

Of those players, Gross and Hargrove will have the best chance to make an impact. Gross could also play either forward spot.

Hargrove averaged 26 points, 10 rebounds, four assists and three blocks last season at Faith Christian Academy in Allentown, Penn.

Last year, Gross averaged 18.2 points, 10 rebounds, and 3.4 blocks for Long Reach High School in Columbia, Md. He was the Baltimore Sun's Howard County Player of the Year.

"Josh is an outstanding athlete who has continued to improve throughout his career," McCaffery said. "He brings versatility as a multiple-position player who can score, rebound and run the floor."

Fitzgerald (1.6 ppg, 0.5 rpg) played in 11 games for the Spartans last season and averaged 3.6 minutes. Beck (0.0 ppg, 0.0 rpg) played in only three games last season.

In the frontcourt, McCaffery has plenty of options.

Schuck (14.5 ppg, 8.3 rpg), a 6-7 senior power forward, started all 31 games last season and led the team in minutes per game (33.7). He was third in the league in rebounding and 15th in field-goal percentage (.475).

A transfer from Air Force, Schuck sat out the 1999-2000 season. He was fifth in the WAC in rebounding in 1998-99, averaging 8.7 per game.

Tizzo Johnson, a 6-6 sophomore, returns after missing last season with a knee injury. Johnson averaged 12 points and 10 rebounds two years ago at Millersburg (Ky.) Military Academy.

"In Jay Joseph's class, Tizzo Johnson was our top frontcourt recruit," McCaffery said. "He's somebody we're really counting on. He's very athletic and very skilled and really played for the first time in Scandinavia the last two weeks [in mid-summer] and showed that he's a really talented player."

Also contending for time will be 6-7 freshman **Ronnie Burrell**, who averaged 18 points, 11 rebounds and three blocks as a senior last year at Montclair (N.J.) High School.

"He's very talented and figures into the mix," McCaffery said. "He's definitely going to play. He's an athletic combination forward."

Luke Boythe, a 6-7 junior, will also be in the mix. Boythe (3.6 ppg, 2.5 rpg) started eight games last season and averaged 13.5 minutes.

In the off-season, Boythe bulked up to about 250 pounds, and the added strength should make a big difference this year. He started early in the season, but often ran into foul trouble. Once he started coming off the bench, Boythe seemed more comfortable.

"In the second half of the season he was a scoring force for us in the frontcourt and really developed confidence," McCaffery said.

McCaffery expects to see 6-8 sophomore **Peter Tsampas** (1.2 ppg, 1.0 rpg) play more this season. Tsampas averaged 6.5 minutes in 23 games last season.

In the low post, the Spartans return starter **Nathan Popp** and backup **Sean McCarthy**. Both are sophomores.

The 7-2, 258-pound Popp is a load in the middle. Last season, Popp (1.7 ppg, 3.1 rpg) started 18 games and averaged 16.4 minutes.

As a freshman, Popp made big improvements, and if he progresses the next three years, McCaffery expects him to get some NBA attention.

"He'd be a force at any level but in particular at this level," McCaffery said. "There aren't a lot of people his size. He can clog up the lane. I thought as the season went on he became a much more effective rebounder. He started getting the rebounds that were coming off the rim that weren't necessarily coming to him."

"Offensively I thought he was more of a force [later in the year]. He's a very good passer and very good face-up shooter. He scores pretty much on put-backs and face-up jump shots."

The 6-11 McCarthy (2.0 ppg, 2.2 rpg) played in 31 games with two starts and averaged 9.7 minutes.

"We've got a lot of bodies in the frontcourt," McCaffery said.

2001-2002 SCHEDULE

Nov.	19	@UNC Asheville
	24	@Middle Tennessee
	27	@Elon
Dec.	1	Saint Peters
	5	East Carolina
	8	Delaware
	10	@Arkansas
	20	Norfolk State
	22	@New Mexico
	29	@Ohio State
Jan.	2	@Chattanooga
	5	Appalachian State
	8	@VMI
	12	@Georgia Southern
	14	East Tennessee
	16	North Carolina A&T
	19	@Western Carolina
	23	Davidson
	26	@Wofford
	28	College of Charleston
Feb.	2	Western Carolina
	5	@Davidson
	9	The Citadel
	12	@East Tennessee State
	16	VMI
	18	@Appalachian State
	23	Furman
	28	#Southern Conference Tournament
March	1-3	#Southern Conference Tournament

@Road Games
#North Charleston Coliseum, Charleston, SC

BLUE RIBBON ANALYSIS

BACKCOURT	A
BENCH/DEPTH	B
FRONTCOURT	B+
INTANGIBLES	A

Everything seems in place for the Spartans to make another run at the Southern Conference title. Most of the 2000-01 team that lost to Stanford, 89-60, in the NCAA Tournament returns.

Leading the way is Eldridge and Joseph. If Maye comes back full speed from his foot injury, the Spartans will have a backcourt that will be hard to beat.

McCaffery has size, experience and depth in the frontcourt.

"I think we have a tremendous amount of experience coming back," McCaffery said. "Obviously you start with your point guard [Eldridge], who basically will be a four-year starter. He's kind of been the backbone of the team."

McCaffery returns three players of all-conference caliber in Eldridge, Joseph and Schuck. With that as the nucleus, the Spartans are set.

"We've got a good chance," McCaffery said. "A lot of teams have everybody back and there's only one bid [to the NCAAs]. That makes our tournament fun, but there's a lot of pressure. This should be as competitive as the Southern Conference has been in a long time."

Still, UNC Greensboro looks like the team to beat.

(D.L.)

Virginia Military Academy

LOCATION	Lexington, VA
CONFERENCE	Southern (North)
LAST SEASON	9-19 (.321)
CONFERENCE RECORD	5-11 (5th)
STARTERS LOST/RETURNING	3/2
NICKNAME	Keydets
COLORS	Red, Yellow & White
HOMECOURT	Cameron Hall (5,029)
COACH	Bart Bellairs (Warren Wilson '79)
RECORD AT SCHOOL	81-113 (7 years)

CAREER RECORD	102-130 (9 years)
ASSISTANTS	Ramon Williams (VMI '90)
	Kirby Dean (Eastern Mennonite '92)
	Mark Hanks (Emory & Henry '83)
TEAM WINS (last 5 years)	12-14-12-6-9
RPI (last 5 years)	208-221-210-309-301
2000-01 FINISH	Lost in conference first round

Wanted: A big man. VMI coach Bart Bellairs has never been more optimistic about the future of his program, but the missing ingredient is a low-post player.

"If we can secure one more really good big man, the future is really, really bright," Bellairs said.

For now, the Keydets are without that really strong inside presence. Bellairs' biggest task this season will be replacing the production of starting post players Eric Mann (13.5 ppg, 10.5 rpg) and Nick Richardson (12.9 ppg, 6.1 rpg), the top two scorers and rebounders from last year's team. Mann earned all-conference first-team honors from the coaches and media.

While the low post is in question, the Keydets have plenty of young talent at every other position.

Zach Batte, a 6-9 junior, will likely be the starting center. Batte started for the Keydets three years ago and transferred to Skyline (Calif.) Junior College the next year.

"He thought about it and decided to transfer because the military lifestyle wasn't for him," Bellairs said. "He went to a junior college and played, then called me back and said, 'I was wrong. Now that I've been out I see that I really like [VMI].' He had a couple of other scholarship offers and still wanted to come back."

Batte returned last year and received a medical redshirt. He is a talented forward, but lacks the muscle of many Southern Conference low-post players. When Batte was a freshman, the Keydets won 14 games with him playing the center spot. Since then, Batte has gotten stronger.

"He's fairly athletic, but he's a very good shooter," Bellairs said. "He'll mix it up, but he weighs maybe 225 and he'll be playing people inside who are 250 or better."

Batte is listed as a forward. **Tim Cole**, a 6-9 senior, and 6-8 freshman **Tim Allmond** are the only centers on the roster.

Cole (0.3 ppg, 0.2 rpg) played only 2.5 minutes in 16 games last season.

Allmond was the leading scorer his last two years at Massaponax High School in Fredericksburg, Va., where he averaged 13 points and 7.7 rebounds. He set school records for scoring (682 points), rebounding (444) and shot blocking (358). His father, Tim Sr., played basketball at Nebraska before a pro career in South America.

Another option at low post is 6-8 junior **Mike Gilbert** (1.5 ppg, 1.0 rpg), who played in 22 games last season and averaged 5.8 minutes. "Mike's kind of untested," Bellairs said.

Gilbert could also play power forward, a spot where Bellairs will have lots of options.

Radee Skipworth, a 6-6 sophomore, will be a frontrunner for the starting job and two freshmen—6-6 **Sam Mielnik** and 6-6 **Preston Beverly**—will also contend for time there.

Skipworth (9.9 ppg, 4.7 rpg) was the team's third-leading scorer last season when he started 25 games and averaged 26.9 minutes. He was on the SoCon's All-Freshman team.

Beverly averaged 12 points and 11 rebounds as a senior at Metuchen (N.J.) High School. His father, Randy Sr., is a former defensive back for the New York Jets and a member of the 1969 Super Bowl championship team.

Mielnik averaged 13 points and 12 rebounds at Abraham Lincoln High School in Brooklyn last year. He can play inside or outside.

"Mielnik is an under-sized four man but he's just a very good rebounder," Bellairs said. "He's a tough, tough kid from Brooklyn. We think he's going to help us."

Jason Conley, a 6-4 red-shirt freshman, sat out last season and could be the starter at small forward. Conley averaged 23 points and six rebounds two years ago at Millersburg (Md.) Military Academy. As a senior in high school, Conley averaged 17.5 points and eight rebounds at Montrose Christian Academy.

"Bob Gibbons rated [Conley] in the top 80 players in the country [out of high school]," Bellairs said. "He's a talent. He'll be worth the price of admission to come in.

"We could slide Radee Skipworth to the four because Conley is now eligible. We can move some guys around in that spot. If we decided we want to go scoring and be real quick, we'll move Skipworth to the four. He did some of that last year, and that means we move Conley to the three. We also brought in two freshmen who can really fill it up at the three spot."

Those two players are 6-7 **Esau Eatman** and 6-5

Clint Zwayer. Eatman averaged 10.5 points and 7.5 rebounds last year at South Durham (N.C.) High School, which went 25-4. Eatman shot 47 percent from the floor, 35 percent from three-point range and 79 percent from the line as a senior while averaging three assists and two steals.

Zwayer averaged 19.7 points and 10.8 rebounds as a senior at Sebring (Fla.) High School, shooting 50.6 percent from the floor and 38.8 percent from three-point range. He was a 78.4-percent shooter from the line and averaged four assists and two steals for a team that went 22-6 and was ranked No. 9 among Florida's Class 4A schools. He was a McDonald's All-America candidate. His brother Eric is a starting center at the University of Richmond.

"Eatman is a legit 6-7 who can really put it on the floor and is just long, long," Bellairs said, "and he can play the two-three, and so can Clint Zwayer. He can really shoot it. I don't know whether he'll be a two or a three or both."

Daron Pressley, a 6-0 sophomore guard, earned some quality time last season as a freshman, averaging 21.9 minutes in 23 games with three starts. Pressley (8.8 ppg, 2.4 rpg) led the Keydets in three-point percentage (.360) and three-pointers (45).

"He was a part-time starter and he can flat fill it up," Bellairs said. "If we want to go with a small shooting guard, we'll go with him, but if not, we'll have Conley and we're excited about the two freshmen, Eatman and Zwayer."

Bellairs has three solid point guards in 5-11 sophomore **Ben Rand**, 5-7 senior **Renard Phillips** and 5-10 sophomore **Richard Little**.

Little (3.9 ppg, 2.0 rpg, 3.5 apg) started 24 games last season, but his starting job will be challenged by Rand, who sat out last season after transferring from VCU. Little led the team in assists last season.

"Rand will be a big factor in the mix," Bellairs said. "He's a smart kid. Our kids say he's hard to guard, and he really distributes the ball well. He'll probably exclusively play the one."

Phillips (1.2 ppg, 1.1 rpg, 2.6 apg) played in 24 games, averaging 16.6 minutes, and started three games. He was second on the team in assists.

"We're real, real young but we're very athletic," Bellairs said. "We're excited. I think the future looks really bright."

Chad Kenna (1.0 ppg, 0.7 rpg), a 6-4 senior forward, and 6-2 senior guard **Mark Grigsby** (0.3 ppg, 0.4 rpg) will again play limited minutes.

2001-2002 SCHEDULE

Nov.	16	Mary Washington
	28	@Morehead State
Dec.	3	@Virginia Tech
	5	@Kentucky
	8	St. Mary's
	12	Charleston Southern
	15	Eastern Mennonite
	22	@Villanova
	28-29	#Spider Invitational
Jan.	2	Western Carolina
	5	@Georgia Southern
	8	UNC Greensboro
	12	@ETSU
	16	@Davidson
	19	College of Charleston
	21	@Appalachian State
	24	@Virginia
	26	Furman
	30	ETSU
Feb.	4	Appalachian State
	9	@Western Carolina
	11	@Chattanooga
	16	@UNC Greensboro
	18	The Citadel
	23	Davidson
	28	##SoCon Tournament
March	1-3	##SoCon Tournament

@Road Games
#Richmond, VA (vs.Richmond first round; also Cornell, James Madison)
##North Charleston Coliseum, Charleston, SC

BLUE RIBBON ANALYSIS

BACKCOURT	B
BENCH/DEPTH	C
FRONTCOURT	C-
INTANGIBLES	C

Bellairs says he has more athleticism this year than in any of his previous seven seasons.

"We'll play above the rim as much as we've ever played here and I think we have a pretty good shooting team," Bellairs said. "We have the depth I want. Last year we went a little bit back to our helter-skelter style, but this year I'm committed to it."

Rand and Little will vie for the point guard job, and the rest of the backcourt is solid led by Conley and Skipworth and freshmen Eatman and Zwayer.

"If you're going to play the run-gun style, it's always great to have great wing men as long as you have enough point guards who can push it, and we feel we have three point guards who can play," Bellairs said. "We brought in a couple more shooters. Really the only question is going to be is our rebounding and inside play. We're really going to work hard to try to develop that."

Bellairs will play that run-and-gun style that fits his personnel.

"We won 19 games my second year and that's the way we really played," Bellairs said. "Our starting center was 6-4 and a half. We think we've got so much depth that we might even go to Dean Smith's platoon system where we play five guys at a time. The reason there is we want to develop some of these young guys because maybe our top 10 players are freshmen or sophomores."

For that reason, the Keydets may be a year or so away from making a strong push toward the top.

(D.L.)

Western Carolina

LOCATION	Cullowhee, NC
CONFERENCE	Southern
LAST SEASON	6-25 (.194)
CONFERENCE RECORD	3-13 (6th North)
STARTERS LOST/RETURNING	0/5
NICKNAME	Catamounts
COLORS	Purple & Gold
HOMECOURT	Ramsey Center (7,826)
COACH	Steve Shurina (St. John's '88)
RECORD AT SCHOOL	6-25 (1 year)
CAREER RECORD	6-25 (1 year)
ASSISTANTS	Duggar Baucom (UNC Charlotte '95)
	Michael Craft (Wingate '90)
	Stacey Palmore (Livingstone '93)
TEAM WINS (last 5 years)	14-12-8-14-6
RPI (last 5 years)	201-247-267-230-302
2000-01 FINISH	Lost in conference quarterfinal.

When you win six games in a season, the good times are few and far between. Fortunately for Western Carolina, the good times came at the end of the 2000-01 season.

The Catamounts upset UNC Greensboro, 63-58, in the last game of the regular season, then knocked off The Citadel, 67-57, in the first round of the Southern Conference Tournament. Their season ended with a 91-69 loss to tournament champion UNC Greensboro in a quarterfinal.

"There were two positives from last year," Catamounts coach Steve Shurina said. "One, guys got to play a lot. They got unbelievable experience. The other positive thing for this team was the fact that we played really well late in the year and just kept coming up short.

"We played at Davidson and were beating them the whole game and they came back and beat us (69-63). We played really well against Chattanooga and they beat us right at the end (76-71). We played really well late in the year. The best thing about all of that was we beat Greensboro to finish the season and then beat The Citadel to open the tournament. Our guys were able to go home over the summer with some confidence, like 'Yeah, we're doing it right. We believe in it.' "

With five starters returning and five newcomers, Shurina and the Catamounts started individual workouts in late summer with plenty of optimism.

Of course, Shurina doesn't expect his counterparts in the league to be in awe of his team. "We've got everybody back," Shurina said. "We were 6-25 last year, so the jokes among coaches will be, 'There's good news and bad news.' "

Western Carolina has at least two all-conference candidates in 6-7 senior forward **Cory Largent** and 6-0 senior guard **Casey Rogers**.

Last year, Rogers moved from point guard to shooting guard out of necessity. A former SoCon Freshman of the Year, Rogers (11.4 ppg, 3.7 rpg, 4.5 apg) had a solid

year despite playing out of position. At one time two years ago, Rogers ranked seventh nationally in assists.

Shurina will move Rogers back to the point this year.

"He's a senior who has been through the wars," Shurina said. "I screwed him up last year, but I had no choice. I put him at two, and he was thinking score. He can score when he's not thinking about it, when he has an open shot. He's a great hustle guy, he's great at setting up the team and making the right passes. That's his game."

Rogers will have two backups at the point—5-9 junior **Kori Hatcher** (6.5 ppg, 2.4 rpg, 3.3 apg) and 5-9 freshman **L.T. Lockett**. Hatcher started 17-of-31 games at point guard last year.

Lockett can play either guard position. While at Sandy Creek High School in Fairburn, Ga., Lockett played shooting guard and set the school record for scoring with 1,680 points. He earned Class 4A second-team all-state honors. In AAU ball, Lockett played point guard.

"When I saw him in the summer and recruited him, he played solely the point," Shurina said. "I didn't know if he could shoot because he never did. In the camps and in AAU he basically played point, and in school he played two. He's physically strong enough at only 6-foot to play the two.

"That's sort of the question mark [at shooting guard]. Every other position we've got experience. The two-guard we don't."

Two other shooting guards are 6-3 sophomore **Emre Atsure** (2.5 ppg, 0.6 rpg) and 6-5 freshman **Kevin Martin**.

Atsure played in 19 games last year, averaging 10.2 minutes, with two starts.

"He broke his leg last summer right before he came to school and was always behind the whole year," Shurina said. "He rehabbed again this summer. His leg is 100 percent now. He's a good shooter, a connector kind of guy. When you put him on the floor he really knows how to play and is always in the right place at the right time and connects everybody together."

Martin averaged 22.1 points and 5.9 rebounds as a senior at Zanesville (Ohio) High School. During individual workouts, Martin was one of the team's most impressive players.

"We thought he was going to be pretty good and so far in the preseason he's way better than we thought he was," Shurina said. "He has great size for a two guard. He's good. He shoots it really well, he's got great athleticism and great instincts for the game."

James Johnson, a 6-1 freshman guard from Mequon High in Mequon, Wisc., will be red-shirted this year.

Largent (15.8 ppg, 5.6 rpg) will get the start at small forward. Last season, Largent was sixth in the league in scoring, 18th in scoring, eighth in three-point percentage (.384) and sixth in three-pointers per game (2.03). He was chosen to the media's all-conference second team.

Largent and Rogers were teammates at Freedom High School in Morganton, N.C.

"When I came in last year, I said, 'Cory, you've got to be the first option,' " Shurina said. "He never had that responsibility before and at times he struggled with it during the year. At the end of the year, he was the key when we beat The Citadel in the tournament.

"When they started making a big run and we needed somebody to step up, he just took the team on his shoulders and had like 27 points. He just totally took the game over. He has good size, 6-7. He's one of our better returning players on paper. He's pretty athletic, another all-around guy, shoots the three well, and he can also go down and post you up."

Terrence Woodyard, a 6-9 freshman from Mt. Zion High School in Jonesboro, Ga., will be red-shirted this year. Woodyard averaged 10 points, seven rebounds and 4.4 blocks last season.

Shurina plans to rotate four players in the frontcourt—6-8 sophomore center **Rans Brempong**, 6-9 junior center **Lamont Speaks**, 6-6 senior forward **Willie Freeman**, and 6-7 senior forward **Kelvin Wiley**.

Wylie sat out last season after transferring from Gardner-Webb, where he averaged 14.2 points and 8.2 rebounds two years ago. He ranked second among NCAA Division II players in shooting percentage (.653) that year.

Freeman (11.8 ppg, 7.3 rpg) was the Catamounts' second-leading scorer and top rebounder last year. He shot 46.4 percent from the floor and is a team captain this year.

Brempong (7.4 ppg, 5.7 rpg) was second on the team in rebounding, but his forte is shot blocking. He led the league in blocks with 93 (3.0 per game) and was chosen to the coaches' all-freshman team.

A native of Thornhill, Ontario, Brempong played more

than 20 games against international competition over the summer for Canadian national junior teams.

"He came back a lot stronger with a lot more confidence in his game," Shurina said. "He needs to get better offensively. He's clearly the class of the league defensively. He's had as good a summer as anybody could hope to have."

Speaks is the Catamounts' muscle man inside. He played two years at Cincinnati State Community College.

"He's 285 or 290 and very well-proportioned," Shurina said. "He's one of the biggest human beings I've ever been around. There won't be anybody in the league as big as him. He'll defend, screen for us, take up space, rebound and score close to the basket.

"He's a great contrast to Rans, who's 6-8, 185 pounds, a sleek, shot-blocking runner, and Kelvin's the same thing. Kelvin's probably 215 to 220 pounds and he's athletic, a jumping, sleek athlete."

Just exactly where 6-8 sophomore **Alexander Osipovitch** fits into the equation will be determined throughout the season.

Osipovitch, from Minsk, Belarus, suffered a severe concussion in the summer of 2000 and never made it to Western Carolina. He went to school in his home country and is therefore a sophomore. He will play small forward or power forward.

"I've watched him shoot and he's got great range and great athleticism," Shurina said. "My guys over there [in Belarus] have been swearing he's a stud."

2001-2002 SCHEDULE

Nov.	19	Tennessee Wesleyan
	24	@Coastal Carolina
	26	Toccoa Falls
	28	Emmanuel
Dec.	1	UNC Asheville
	6	@Stetson
	8	@Florida State
	11	Guilford
	19	@Kansas State
	21	@Wichita State
	29	@Eastern Michigan
Jan.	2	@VMI
	5	Davidson
	7	Furman
	12	The Citadel
	14	@Appalachian State
	19	UNC Greensboro
	21	@Georgia Southern
	26	@Davidson
	28	Appalachian State
Feb.	2	@UNC Greensboro
	4	ETSU
	9	VMI
	11	College of Charleston
	16	@ETSU
	18	@Wofford
	23	@Chattanooga
	28	#SoCon Tournament
March	1-3	#SoCon Tournament

@Road Games
#North Charleston Coliseum, Charleston, SC

BLUE RIBBON ANALYSIS

BACKCOURT	C+
BENCH/DEPTH	C
FRONTCOURT	B
INTANGIBLES	C

Western Carolina could be the sleeper of the North. Unlike last year, the Catamounts have some depth, thanks to several newcomers and the nucleus of last year's team returning. How well the new guys play will determine if the Catamounts can make a big jump out of the cellar.

"I think you can win with seniors and we've got four seniors," Shurina said. "I think we've got a chance to be good. How everybody jells together, how well our younger guys play, how Alexander Osipovitch plays, those are the X-factors."

Rogers will be one of the league's better point guards and Largent one of the better small forwards. Both are seniors. The Catamounts must find a shooting guard, and freshman Kevin Martin may get the starting job. Early in individual workouts, Martin looked like one of the team's best players.

"We're excited," Shurina said. "There's a lot of ifs for us, but at the same time we've got solid players and we know what they're about."

With those solid players and some new talent, the Catamounts may surprise some people this year.

(D.L.)

Wofford

LOCATION	Spartanburg, SC
CONFERENCE	Southern (South)
LAST SEASON	12-16 (.429)
CONFERENCE RECORD	7-9 (5th)
STARTERS LOST/RETURNING	2/3
NICKNAME	Terriers
COLORS	Old Gold & Black
HOMECOURT	Johnson Arena (3,500)
COACH	Richard Johnson (The Citadel '76)
RECORD AT SCHOOL	225-212 (16 years)
CAREER RECORD	225-212 (16 years)
ASSISTANTS	Mike Young (Emory & Henry '86)
	Bob Johnson (Washington '68)
	Alex Peavey (Virginia '99)
TEAM WINS (last 5 years)	7-9-11-14-12
RPI (last 5 years)	300-274-240-217-234
2000-01 FINISH	Lost in conference first round.

Wofford enters the post-Ian Chadwick era with quite a bit of uncertainty.

Chadwick (20.4 ppg, 3.2 rpg), a 6-4 guard, was a three-time All-SoCon player and last season was runner-up in the league's player of the year award. He led the conference in scoring and in three-pointers per game (2.92) while shooting 33 percent from that range. He finished his career as the league's career leader in three-pointers with 299.

"It's a huge loss," Terriers coach Richard Johnson said. "It's about as big a loss as you can have."

With the loss of Chadwick, the Terriers have a big void to fill, but they should be in decent shape at point guard with the return of 6-3 junior **Mike Lenzly**, chosen to the media's all-conference third team. Lenzly (9.6 ppg, 4.1 rpg, 2.0 apg) started seven games and finished strong.

In the last seven games, Lenzly averaged 18.1 points, 6.7 rebounds and 4.3 assists. During that stretch, he shot 55.6 percent from the field and was 17-of-33 from three-point range (51.5 percent). A left-handed shooter, Lenzly posted Wofford's first-ever triple-double with 21 points, 12 assists and 10 rebounds in a 105-69 victory over Chattanooga on Feb. 13.

"Mike is a big guard, 6-2 or 6-3," Johnson said. "He's an exceptional player. I think Mike is as good a point guard as there is in this league."

LSU transfer **Edmond Davis**, a 5-10 sophomore, will battle Lenzly for the job and minutes. Davis is the younger brother of former Wofford point guard Donald Davis, who played from 1997-99. Edmond Davis is an excellent defender and a player who can push the ball up the floor. He practiced with the Terriers last season, but his time was limited because of a couple of injuries. If Davis can become a quick fit at point guard, Johnson has the option of moving Lenzly to shooting guard.

"His older brother was a very good point guard and we think Edmond has that potential," Johnson said. "He doesn't shoot it as well as Donald, but Donald didn't shoot it that well until he was really a senior and then he had a fantastic senior year."

David Eaton (1.8 ppg, 0.2 rpg), a 6-2 sophomore, will battle two freshmen, 6-0 **Adrien Borders** and 6-2 **Justin Stephens**, for the shooting guard job. Eaton, a walk-on, played in only 12 games last year and averaged 4.4 minutes.

Borders averaged 15 points and four assists last season at Berkmar High School in Lilburn, Ga.

"He played on a great Berkmar team in Atlanta," Johnson said. "Adrien is a tremendous athlete. He's not real tall, but he's a gifted, gifted athlete. He's quick as a cat and could possibly play some point. He's a two who can shoot it and penetrate and he had the benefit of playing on a great team with a good coach."

Stephens averaged 13 points and four assists at Saint Thomas More (Conn.) Prep School. Stephens averaged 22.5 points and six assists as a senior at East Coweta (Ga.) High School.

"He's a two and maybe a three," Johnson said. "Because he went to a prep school, we think he has a chance to make a contribution as well. That's what we're relying on."

Lee Nixon, a 6-4 junior, is projected as the starter at small forward, but he could also fit into the shooting guard slot. Nixon (10.1 ppg, 2.2 rpg) was the team's sec-

ond-leading scorer and made a strong push at the end of the season, along with Lenzly.

In the last seven games, Nixon averaged 16.9 points and had a career-high 31 in an 83-73 victory over Davidson on Feb. 5. He is one of the team's best perimeter defenders and was second on the team in three-pointers with 32, shooting 31.4 percent from behind the arc.

"Leigh is a great penetrator and great shooter," Johnson said.

Wilky Colon, a 6-5 sophomore, will likely be Nixon's backup at small forward.

At power forward, 6-7 junior **Grant Sterley** is the likely starter, replacing Bishop Ravenel (7.8 ppg, 5.7 rpg), who tied for the team-high in rebounding last season with **Kenny Hastie**.

Sterley was plagued by tendinitis in his thumb last season. As a freshman, he set a Wofford record by making nine consecutive three-point shots during a five-game stretch.

"If his thumb is adequately healed, he gives us an exceptional shooter," Johnson said. "He is a better shooter on the perimeter than Bishop, but he did not bring the penetration off the dribble that Bishop brought us, and then the question would be defensively. Bishop was an excellent defender."

Jeff Tarr, a 6-7 freshman, will also contend for time at either forward position. Tarr averaged 12.5 points and 4.5 rebounds at Fork Union (Va.) Military last year. He averaged 22 points and 13 rebounds as a senior at Yadkinville (N.C.) High School.

"Jeff brings us some versatility," Johnson said.

Hastie (5.9 ppg, 5.7 rpg), a 6-8 senior, returns as the starter in the low post. Hastie started all 28 games last year and set a single-season school record with 49 blocks. He was fourth in the league in blocks per game (1.75). He is one of the team leaders.

"He's an athletic player," Johnson said. "Kenny has never been a big scorer. He's always been a defender, a shot blocker, an excellent passer. We've got to get more scoring out of Kenny. We've got to turn Kenny into more of a selfish player."

Two others, 6-9 freshman **Sam Daniels** and 6-10 junior **Edvin Masic**, will battle for time in the frontcourt.

Daniels averaged 17.6 points and 11.6 rebounds last year at Carolina Day High School in Asheville, N.C.

"I think Sam is a great catch and will be a very good player," Johnson said. "You worry about the development of players when you have to throw them in there, but I'm afraid Sam's going to get tossed in. I think on paper he has a chance of playing because that's one of our critical needs."

Masic (1.9 ppg, 1.7 rpg) played in 21 games last season and averaged 8.3 minutes. He was slowed by a knee injury. If he's healthy, the 250-pound Masic can be a force inside.

"He's 6-10 and the best post player I've ever recruited in terms of talent, but he has had all kinds of problems with his knee," Johnson said. "We haven't been able to get anything out of him. They're trying different treatments with him. His cartilage is just a wreck in there."

2001-2002 SCHEDULE

Nov.	13	#Memphis
	17	Toccoa Falls
	24	@Clemson
	26	Florida A&M
	29	South Carolina
Dec.	2	@Nebraska
	5	@North Carolina State
	8	Emmanuel
	15	Virginia Intermont
	17	Reinhardt
	21	@Georgia Tech
Jan.	2	@College of Charleston
	5	Furman
	7	The Citadel
	12	College of Charleston
	14	@Chattanooga
	19	@Georgia Southern
	23	@East Tennessee
	26	UNC Greensboro
	30	@Davidson
Feb.	2	VMI
	4	Chattanooga
	9	Georgia Southern
	11	@Appalachian State
	16	@Furman
	18	Western Carolina
	23	@The Citadel
	28	##Southern Conf. Tournament
March	1-3	##Southern Conf. Tournament

@Road Games
#Guardians Classic at Memphis (if Wofford wins, it will play Old Dominion or Sacramento Stte on Nov. 14. Semifinals and final on Nov. 21 at Kemper Arena, Kansas City, MO)
##Chaleston Colliseum, Charleston SC

BLUE RIBBON ANALYSIS

BACKCOURT	C+
BENCH/DEPTH	C-
FRONTCOURT	C
INTANGIBLES	B-

For the first time in a couple of years, Johnson enters the season searching for answers at several positions.

Gone is Chadwick, a 6-3 guard and one of the Southern Conference's premier players last year. Also gone is starting power forward Bishop Ravenel, a solid player in the frontcourt.

"We have a lot of uncertainty," Johnson said. "From a team that two years ago was very, very deep—10 players easily—to a team that last year had some depth to a team this year that depth is a real question.

"We have some talent but so much of it is untested. I've been in this long enough to know that that's a problem."

One key player will be Davis, a transfer from LSU. Davis could solidify the backcourt if he can take over as the starter, which would allow Lenzly to move to shooting guard and Nixon to move to small forward. Lenzly started at the point last year and Nixon was very impressive at the end of last season.

In the frontcourt, Johnson must replace Ravenel, and he needs more production from Hastie.

"We've got a lot of questions," Johnson said. "Historically, we've had guys literally seize the opportunity and fill the voids. We need that trend to continue. We need some surprises, and if the past is any indication, we'll have that occur."

(D.L.)

Lamar

LOCATION	Beaumont, TX
CONFERENCE	Southland
LAST SEASON	9-18 (.333)
CONFERENCE RECORD	7-13 (9th)
STARTERS LOST/RETURNING	4/1
NICKNAME	Cardinals
COLORS	Red & White
HOMECOURT	Montage Center (10,080)
COACH	Mike Deane (Potsdam State '74)
RECORD AT SCHOOL	24-34 (2 years)
CAREER RECORD	314-191 (17 years)
ASSISTANTS	Dan Theiss (Plattsburgh State '81)
	Leonard Drake (Central Michigan '78)
	Brian Bidlingmyer (Siena '95)
TEAM WINS (last 5 years)	15-15-17-15-9
RPI (last 5 years)	169-178-215-176-284
2000-01 FINISH	Won regular-season finale.

Lamar came crashing back down to earth last season. A year after surprising the league by winning the Southland Conference Tournament and advancing to the NCAAs, the Cardinals failed to even make the SLC Tournament last year.

"We played a lot of young players last year and we took our lumps," third-year coach Mike Deane said. "The year of experience should make us a better team, especially on the road."

However, Deane will be without two key cogs from last year. Kenyon Spears finished an outstanding four-year Lamar career with a modestly successful (9.7 ppg, 3.4 rpg, 82 assists) senior year.

"His numbers won't be so hard to replace," Deane said. "But what's hard to replace is his leadership. He was one good basketball player."

Also gone is Joey Ray, who led his team in scoring (11.3 ppg) as a freshman coming off the bench in 2000.

"He decided to get closer to home [Indiana]," Deane said. "I understand that."

Still, the Cardinals have four starters back, led by 6-6 junior **Lewis Arline** (8.6 ppg, 8.9 rpg), the conference's second-leading rebounder a year ago.

"Arline is hard working and has a quick temper," Deane said. "He has a nose for the ball. I think his numbers will improve this year."

SOUTHLAND

BLUE RIBBON FORECAST
1. Texas-San Antonio
2. Louisiana-Monroe
3. Texas-Arlington
4. McNeese State
5. Southwest Texas State
6. Northwestern State
7. Lamar
8. Sam Houston State
9. Stephen F. Austin
10. Nicholls State
11. Southeastern Louisiana

ALL-CONFERENCE TEAM
G - Steven Barber, SR, Texas-Arlington
G - Michael Byars-Dawson, SR, Northwestern State
F - Devin Brown, SR, Texas-San Antonio
F - Brian Lubeck, SR, Louisiana-Monroe
C - Wojciech Myrda, JR, Louisiana-Monroe

PLAYER OF THE YEAR
Devin Brown, SR, Texas-San Antonio

NEWCOMER OF THE YEAR
Jay Oliphant, JR, Sam Houston State

2001-2002 CONFERENCE TOURNAMENT
March 4, 6 and 9 at home sites of higher seeds

2000-2001 CHAMPIONS
McNeese State (Regular season)
Northwestern State (Conference tournament)

2000-2001 POSTSEASON PARTICIPANTS
Postseason Record: 1-2 (.333)
NCAA
Northwestern State (Second Round)
NIT
McNeese State

TOP BACKCOURTS
1. Sam Houston State
2. Louisiana-Monroe
3. Texas-San Antonio

TOP FRONTCOURTS
1. Louisiana-Monroe
2. McNeese State
3. Texas-San Antonio

INSIDE THE NUMBERS
2000-2001 conference RPI: 26th (of 31)
Conference RPI (last five years): 26-26-27-23-26

DID YOU KNOW?
Southland Conference champions have struggled in the league's postseason tournament in recent years.

The last two years, the SLC Tournament champion has been a seven seed, meaning in both years the conference representative in the NCAA tournament has been a 16 seed (2001 tournament winner Northwestern State had to play a play-in game). That won't happen this year. The SLC voted to reduce the tournament from eight teams to six teams and try a unique new format, where the higher-seed teams enjoy a home-court advantage throughout the three-round tournament, which is stretched out over six days. The top two seeds will get a first-round bye, then host semifinal games. In recent years, the league has played the postseason event in the Shreveport-Bossier City, La. area, but has failed to attract much fan support in the neutral city. Most league coaches like the idea of the top seed enjoying a home-court advantage throughout. "The best thing about it is we know we are going to have a crowd," one coach said. "I think it helps the league to have a large crowd for the TV game, and I think having the game at the home of the highest remaining seed guarantees that." On the flip side, many coaches complained about the field having just more than half of the league's members. "This guarantees that some pretty good teams won't be there," one coach said. "I'm never for leaving teams out of the tournament." The change was actually a compromise. The original proposal was for the tournament to have only five teams, with the top seed getting a bye to the championship game, which it would have hosted. ... The Southland Conference may be an all-sport league soon. The conference's football teams fly under the banner of the Southland Football League, which is technically a seperate entity from the SLC. However, the final football-only member of the SFL, Jacksonville State, will leave the SFL after the 2002 season, leaving only six members, all of which are SLC schools in all sports. That would eliminate the need for a seperate football organization. Of course, the SFL is looking for new associate members, because six teams would put it in danger of losing its automatic playoff bid in Division I-AA. Among the ideas to keep the football part of the league above water is to get basketball schools to add football. Southeastern Louisiana appears to be on its way to reinstating the sport. Lamar and Texas-Arlington, two more schools that had had and dropped football programs, have both had discussions about reinstating the sport. ... Only one school had to find a new coach during the off-season. League champion McNeese hired former Memphis and New Orleans head coach Tic Price to replace Ron Everhart, who took the head coaching job at Northeastern University in Boston. ... It may be called the Southland Conference, but you might as well call it the International League now. ... McNeese State, Louisiana-Monroe, Stephen F. Austin, Southwest Texas State, Nicholls State and Texas-Arlington have players from places like Poland, Russia, Australia, Yugoslavia, Kenya, Canada, Turkey and Croatia.

(D.L.)

Deane said he would like to see Arline become more of a consistent scoring threat, but he likes his forward's attitude.

Also back are starting guards **Ron Austin** (10.0 ppg), a 6-3 junior, and **Eddie Robinson** (6.2 ppg, 79 assists), a 6-3 junior. **Terrell Petteway** (5.3 ppg, 4.5 rpg), a 6-7 junior, is back next to Arline on the starting front line.

Austin and Robinson will again push for time in the backcourt, but Petteway will be challenged by a talented recruiting class Deane has assembled.

"We might red-shirt him," Deane said of Petteway. "I'm thinking long-term on him. That would be the best thing for him."

Deane is confident in newcomers like 6-6 sophomore **Krunti Hester**, a Marquette transfer, 6-7 **Ben Jacobson** and 6-7 junior **Damany Hendrix**. Hendrix averaged 24 points and 11 rebounds as a sophomore last year at Santa Rosa (Calif.) Junior College.

"Hendrix is a real scoring threat inside much like

Landon Rowe was [on the 1999 NCAA Tournament team]," Deane said. "He's big, strong, he can shoot the three, he can put the ball on the floor."

Jacobson, a red-shirt freshman who prepped at Omaha (Neb.) Central High, represented the USA at the World Maccabiah Games in Israel last summer. He averaged 20.1 points and 10.2 rebounds as a senior in high school.

"He can score," Deane said.

Hester, a 235-pounder, gives the Cardinals inside strength. He played for Deane at Marquette before coming to Beaumont with his old coach last year.

"That's something we didn't have last year," Deane said. "We struggled when we played the big, powerful teams."

Also back in the front line are 6-8 senior **Joe Adande**, 6-10 sophomore **Brian Rowan**, 6-8 sophomore **Brian McCormack** and 6-6 sophomore **Michael Ridgeway**.

Adande (2.5 ppg, 2.5 rpg) had off-season back surgery and is questionable coming into the year.

"Adande's status is very much up in the air," Deane said. "I just don't know if he is going to be cleared or what his status will be."

Most of the Cardinals' front-line players are lithe forward types, and that makes the presence of Rowan (2.9 ppg, 2.3 rpg, 18 blocks) valuable for Lamar.

"He's our one guy who can go against guys like Raynell Brewer (McNeese State's 7-1 center) and Wojiech (Myrda, Louisiana-Monroe's 7-2 center)," Deane said. "He's developing strength wise and hopefully he'll develop into a good player."

Ridgeway (2.5 ppg, 2.4 rpg) plays inside and shoots from the outside. McCormack had just six appearances as a freshman.

In the backcourt, the Cardinals have the slashing Austin, who led the team in free throws attempted (105) and makes (70), a testament to his ability to go to the basket. Austin also made 23 three-pointers.

Robinson was second on the team in assists behind Spears and looks to assume more point-guard duty. However, he could be pushed by freshman **Isaac Hines**, a 5-11 dynamo who averaged 24 points at Dallas Molina High School. He represented America at the Global Youth games during the summer.

"He's a point guard that brings a different dimension," Deane said. "He's the kind of point guard I had success with at Marquette."

Also back in the backcourt is 6-3 sophomore **Tyler Hackstadt** (4.7 ppg), a shooter who made 21 three-pointers a season ago. Deane also signed 6-2 guard **Hayes Grooms** of Detroit, Mich. Brother Rice High School.

2001-2002 SCHEDULE

Nov.	20	@Rice
	24	Texas A&M
	27	Texas Southern
	30	#Michigan State Tournament
Dec.	1	#Michigan State Tournament
	13	@Texas-Pan American
	15	@Texas A&M-Corpus Christi
	20	@Texas-San Antonio
	22	@Southwest Texas
	29	Northwestern State
Jan.	5	McNeese State
	7	Sam Houston State
	10	@Stephen F. Austin
	12	@Texas-Arlington
	17	Nicholls State
	19	Southeastern Louisiana
	24	@Northwestern State
	26	@Louisiana-Monroe
	31	Texas-San Antonio
Feb.	2	Southwest Texas
	7	@Nicholls State
	9	@Southeastern Louisiana
	14	Stephen F. Austin
	16	Texas-Arlington
	21	@McNeese State
	27	Louisiana-Monroe
March	2	@Sam Houston State
	4-9	##SLC Tournament

@Road Games
#East Lansing, MI (vs. Maine first round; also IUPU-Fort Wayne, Michigan State)
##Home sites

BLUE RIBBON ANALYSIS

BACKCOURT	C
BENCH/DEPTH	B-
FRONTCOURT	B
INTANGIBLES	B

Lamar was once a Southland Conference power and seemed close to returning to glory when the roof caved in last year.

This year, Deane's team joins teams like Stephen F. Austin, Southeastern Louisiana and Nicholls State as teams whose success relies on the impact of newcomers.

If first-year players like Hendrix, Jacobson and Hester give solid contributions, the Cardinals can compete with the best in the league.

If Lamar plays at a high level, look out. Beaumont supports its team better than any school in the SLC.

"We have the best home-court advantage in the league," Deane saidd.

If the Cardinals ever become a high-seeded team in the SLC Tournament, they will be hard to beat at

Montagne Center. For now, however, Lamar will settle for just getting into the postseason tournament.

(G.L.)

Louisiana-Monroe

LOCATION	Monroe, LA
CONFERENCE	Southland
LAST SEASON	11-17 (.393)
CONFERENCE RECORD	8-12 (8th)
STARTERS LOST/RETURNING	0/5
NICKNAME	Indians
COLORS	Maroon & Gold
HOMECOURT	Ewing Coliseum (8,000)
COACH	Mike Vining (ULM '67)
RECORD AT SCHOOL	350-236 (20 years)
CAREER RECORD	350-236 (20 years)
ASSISTANTS	John Gullatt (LSU '88)
	Keith Brown (Belhaven '81)
	Terry Martin (ULM '84)
TEAM WINS (last 5 years)	18-7-13-6-11
RPI (last 5 years)	180-286-213-281-235
2000-01 FINISH	Lost in conference first round.

Mike Vining, the dean of Southland Conference coaches, is hoping to turn around a disastrous 2001 season. He has plenty of reason to think it will happen.

Vining, who has piled up 350 wins in his 20 years in Monroe, has all five starters and all but one player from last year's team returning. He's enthused about the possibilities this experienced team carries into the season.

"After only having two players back last year and a bunch of new faces, this will be different," Vining said. "People here are excited."

Adding fuel to the optimism was a strong finish a year ago. The Indians went 5-3 over their last eight games, with two of the losses coming at runaway league champion McNeese State by a combined 13 points.

"We lost to McNeese once, then lost again in a game that was very close [McNeese pulled out an 83-78 win]," Vining said. "That has people here very excited."

It also helps to have star power, and the Indians do not lack it. Leading the way is 7-2 senior center **Wojciech Myrda** (11.5 ppg, 6.3 rpg). The native of Poland has been among the nation's top shot blockers ever since he arrived in Monroe as a freshman and with 363 career rejections, he is within 130 of Adonal Foyle's NCAA career record.

Myrda can own the record if he increases his 2000-2001 pace a bit. A year ago, he blocked 123 shots and was tied with Seton Hall's Eddie Griffin for No. 2 in the NCAA's statistics (4.4 bpg), barely behind Hampton's Tarvis Williams, who led the country (4.6 bpg).

"He has a chance at the record and hopefully, he'll get better on the offensive end," Vining said.

That is something the Indians have hoped for before. After losing several players from the 2000 team, last year's team started the season trying to run the offense through the big man.

"It just didn't work," Vining said. "We had to go through a more team-oriented game and that's when things started to turn around. Wojciech is better in a team-oriented game. Hopefully, he'll be more of a factor."

As Myrda's offensive role diminished, the star rose for 6-6 senior forward **Brian Lubeck**, who enters this season as a leading candidate for SLC Player of the Year. A tough-as-nails 220 pounder, Lubeck led the league in rebounding (9.0 rpg) and was the team's leading scorer with a 13.7 average. Lubeck can score inside or step outside, where he made 42 three-point shots last season.

"He's just a good player," Vining said. "He's someone who can play back to the basket or shoot the three, he's strong and on the boards he has great timing and leaping ability."

Completing the Indians' starting front line is **Kevin Paige** (11.5 ppg, 5.0 rpg), an athletic 6-7 senior power forward.

"We're looking for a better year from Kevin," Vining said. "He's a kid with tremendous athletic ability. He started last year strong, but after conference started, his scoring sort of tailed off. We look for him to step it up."

Nick Coln, a 6-3 senior sharpshooter, leads the backcourt. Coln's production increased as the year went on, and he finished the season averaging 11.3 points per game, including a team-high 85 three-pointers.

"Nick is a stroker," Vining said. "He can fill it up. We started last season with him on the bench with the idea being we'd have a guy coming off the bench giving us

offense, but we wound up starting him."

Rounding out the returning starting five is 5-11 senior point guard **Michael Hardaway** (4.1 ppg, 105 assists), a "true" point guard whose primary concern is ball distribution.

He split time with 6-0 sophomore **Brandon Horn** (4.9 ppg), who promises to push Hardaway for playing time again this year.

"Brandon is a better shooter," Vining said. "Hardaway doesn't usually look to shoot, but it's nice to know that we can put a shooter in the game if they leave him open too much."

Sixth-man Charles Sanders did not return to the team, but there is still experience coming off the bench. Swingman **Mark Keith**, a 6-5 sophomore, returns after averaging 4.1 points per game last year.

"He got better as the year went on and he settled in," Vining said. "He made great strides."

Radoslaw Ciszkiewicz, a 6-5 sophomore guard from the same Polish town as Myrda, is back after averaging just 1.2 points per game last year.

"He can help us," Vining said. "He can really shoot it. But he missed some practice last year and he just seemed lost when he came back."

Vining added two junior college transfers. **Kirby Lemons**, a 6-7 forward, comes to Monroe from power Garden City (Kansas). **Reggie Griffith**, a 6-5 swingman, comes to ULM after averaging 20.7 points and 7.7 rebounds at Cedar Valley (Texas) Community College.

"These are two really athletic forwards," Vining said. "They are the kind of players we used to win with."

Vining also brought in a pair of high school guard prospects in 6-3 **Aaron Branch** of West Monroe, La., and 6-1 **Brian Rusley** from Shreveport (La.) Booker T. Washington High.

"Branch went from a small school to West Monroe [which competes at Louisiana's highest enrollment class] and he did fine," Vining said. "He's big and strong and can shoot. Rusley is so athletic. He can play point and the two. He's quick and he can shoot."

2001-2002 SCHEDULE

Nov.	17	@Samford
	20	Tougaloo
	25	@TCU
Dec.	1	@McNeese State
	3	@Ole Miss
	13	@Sam Houston
	15	#@Mississippi State
	20-22	#Las Vegas Classic
	28	@College of Charleston
Jan.	5	Stephen F. Austin
	7	Texas-Arlington
	10	@Southeastern Louisiana
	12	@Nicholls State
	14	@McNeese State
	17	Texas-San Antonio
	19	Southwest Texas
	24	Sam Houston
	26	Lamar
	31	@Northwestern State
Feb.	8	@Texas-San Antonio
	10	@Southwest Texas
	14	Southeastern Louisiana
	16	Nicholls State
	21	@Texas-Arlington
	23	@Stephen F. Austin
	27	@Lamar
March	2	Northwestern State
	4-9	###SLC Tournament

@Road Games
#First round Las Vegas Classic
##Las Vegas, NV (vs. Cincinnati second round; final on Dec. 22)
###Home sites

BLUE RIBBON ANALYSIS

BACKCOURT	B
BENCH/DEPTH	B
FRONTCOURT	A
INTANGIBLES	B

Vining's last Louisiana-Monroe has all the makings of a contender. The Indians have size, quickness, shooting ability, defense and experience.

The one thing ULM lacks is experience at winning. Several of the players from last year's team were junior college transfers playing their first year of Division I.

Still it's hard to ignore talent. If Myrda makes himself a consistent scoring threat, the Indians will have two SLC player- of-the-year candidates in he and Lubeck. Even if he remains a role player on the offensive end, Myrda's name will be mentioned among the best defensive big men in the history of the league.

The Indians also have last year's late-season success to build off. It all adds up to a big season in Monroe.

(G.L)

McNeese State

LOCATION	Lake Charles, LA
CONFERENCE	Southland
LAST SEASON	22-9 (.710)
CONFERENCE RECORD	17-3 (1st)
STARTERS LOST/RETURNING	2/3
NICKNAME	Cowboys
COLORS	Blue & Gold
HOMECOURT	Burton Center (8,000)
COACH	Tic Price (Virginia Tech '79)
RECORD AT SCHOOL	First year
CAREER RECORD	93-54 (5 years)
ASSISTANTS	David Dumars (Louisiana-Monroe '80)
	John Dillard (Lindsey Wilson College '91)
	Jamie Eagles (Louisiana Tech '99)
TEAM WINS (last 5 years)	18-7-13-6-22
RPI (last 5 years)	180-286-213-281-103
2000-01 FINISH	Lost in conference semifinal.

McNeese State had a dream season in 2001, winning 15 straight games at one point to win the conference title, go 22-9 and reach the NIT.

This year's Cowboys will have a far different look, however. Gone are not only the team's two leading scorers, but the conference's top scorers in guards Demond Mallet (21.3 ppg) and Tierre Brown (20.1 ppg), the key performers in last year's high-powered three-guard offense.

Also gone is head coach Ron Everhart, who accepted a lucrative offer to become head coach at Northeastern University in Boston. Everhart was succeeded by assistant Tic Price, the former Memphis and New Orleans head coach who resigned from Memphis after admitting to an affair with a student after the 1999 season.

He spent last season as Everhart's top assistant and now has a chance to get back into the head-coaching fold.

"I'm thankful for the opportunity McNeese is giving me," Price said. "Coach Everhart and McNeese believed in me in a time where a lot of other people didn't."

Along with a new coach comes a team with a new look. No longer will the Cowboys be able to lean on the exploits of its free-wheeling gunners of last year.

"Our attitude is a bit different," Price said. "We'll score more in transition and in halfcourt we'll be more of an inside-out team."

The inside game looks solid with the return of muscular senior power forward **Fred Gentry**, who at 6-6 and 225 pounds is an Adonis-like figure in the post who was the team MVP in 2000 before his numbers (8.9 ppg, 6.3 rpg) slid last year.

"I don't think Fred was ever able to get in synch last year," Price said. "We've got to get the big fella more touches this year. I'm a believer that if you give the big guy the ball more, he'll rebound for you more, too."

On the wing is 6-6 senior **Ben Perkins** (7.3 ppg, 4.6 rpg), the team's super sixth man last year after he transferred from Providence. Perkins is an outstanding athlete who can step outside to shoot, slash to the basket and score in the post. Perkins started last season slowly before finishing the year with a flourish of strong performances.

"The sky's the limit with Ben," Price said. "I really think he has a chance to be special. If he picks up where he left off last year, he'll be an all-league player."

Gentry and Perkins lead a deep and talented core of rangy forwards that also includes junior former starter **Adrian Johnson** (6-6, 4.1 ppg), 6-6 junior **Paul Beik**, and athletic 6-6 junior college transfer **Damond Williams**.

Center **Raynell Brewer** (6.3 ppg, 5.2 rpg), a rail-thin 7-1 shot blocker (68 in 26 games last year), returns and will be pushed by rapidly improving 6-11 senior **Dmitri Khorokorin** and 6-11, 280-pound junior college transfer **Larry Jackson**.

"We will kind of go center by committee," Price said.

While the scorers are gone in the backcourt, McNeese will be solid at point guard with 5-8 senior **Chauncey Bryant** back to start for a fourth straight year.

Bryant, described as the "prototype" point guard by Price, rarely scores, but shows the savvy of a player from legendary prep coach Bob Hurley's program at Jersey City, N.J. St. Anthony's High School.

Bryant's understudy, 5-9 sophomore **Eldridge Lewis**, also returns after showing promise in limited playing time last year.

The shooting guard spot will be inherited by 6-4 junior **Jason Coleman** (5.0 ppg), a former SLC Freshman of the Year who has outstanding range on his jumper. He will be pushed by newcomer **Ed Garriet**, a 6-0 sophomore who sat out two years trying to get academically eligible after a stellar career at Beaumont (Texas) Central High.

McNeese suffered a blow in the off-season when highly-touted junior college transfer Jaeson Maravich, the son of Pete Maravich, decided not to return to the Cowboys and instead enrolled at Clearwater Christian College in Florida.

Maravich was among the nation's leading scorers in junior college before sitting out last year with a back injury.

2001-2002 SCHEDULE

Nov.	17	@Louisiana-Lafayette
	19	Loyola, New Orleans
	27	@Auburn
	29	@Alabama
Dec.	1	@Louisiana-Monroe
	3	Nicholls State
	5	@Jackson State
	8	Southwest Texas
	15	@LSU
	19	@Texas
	22	Southeastern Louisiana
	29	Texas-San Antonio
Jan.	3	@Sam Houston
	5	@Lamar
	10	@Texas-San Antonio
	12	@Southwest Texas State
	14	Louisiana-Monroe
	19	Texas-Arlington
	26	@Southeastern Louisiana
	28	@Nicholls State
Feb.	2	@Northwestern State
	9	@Stephen F. Austin
	11	@Texas-Arlington
	21	Lamar
	23	Sam Houston State
	28	Northwestern State
March	2	Stephen F. Ausitn
	4-9	#SLC Tournament

@Road Games
#Home sites

BLUE RIBBON ANALYSIS

BACKCOURT	C+
BENCH/DEPTH	B
FRONTCOURT	B
INTANGIBLES	B

The loss of Mallet, Brown and Everhart will hurt, but few are discounting the defending champions. There is plenty of talent coming back and recent successes have yielded the Cowboys some bumper recruiting crops, meaning there are plenty of talented younger players (like Garriet and Maravich) ready to fill some voids.

With the return of a lot of front line talent (few teams at the mid-major level have the front line size and depth of McNeese) and a veteran point guard in Bryant, the Cowboys are hardly a team that's rebuilding after massive losses.

Price will be spending more time learning the ins and outs of the Southland, but he has had experience coaching in a similar league while coaching at the University of New Orleans in the Sun Belt Conference. Despite his off-the-court problems at Memphis, Price is a proven winner at this level and has been greeted with an enthusiastic welcome in Lake Charles.

In short, there are certainly pitfalls that come with losing players the caliber of Brown and Mallet, and coaching transitions are always tricky, especially with teams that have enjoyed success. However, it's not far-fetched to see the Cowboys successfully defend their title.

(G.L)

Nicholls State

LOCATION	Thibodaux, LA
CONFERENCE	Southland
LAST SEASON	14-14 (.500)
CONFERENCE RECORD	12-8 (t-2nd)
STARTERS LOST/RETURNING	2/3
NICKNAME	Colonels
COLORS	Red & Gray
HOMECOURT	Stopher Gym (3,800)
COACH	Ricky Broussard (Louisiana-Lafayette '71)
RECORD AT SCHOOL	148-158 (11 years)
CAREER RECORD	148-158 (11 years)
ASSISTANTS	Quinn Strander (Nicholls State '95)
	Sheldon Jones (Southern '97)
	Chris Oney (Mississippi '98)
TEAM WINS (last 5 years)	10-19-14-11-14
RPI (last 5 years)	244-141-214-249-215
2000-01 FINISH	Lost in conference first round.

Nicholls State coach Rickey Broussard has been here before. Twice in his 11 years in Thibodaux, Broussard has had dominant, senior-laden Colonels teams that won the league, only to go through rebuilding years the following season.

Broussard is there again. "Only this time, we didn't win the league last year," he said.

Gone are the top three scorers off a Colonels team that went 14-14 in 2001. Departed is perhaps the league's best front line in power forward Arthur Haralson (18.1 ppg, 8.3 rpg) and center Chris Bacon (15.8 ppg, 7.4 rpg), along with the leading outside threat, Marlon Green (10.5 ppg).

"It's going to be tough," Broussard said. "We lost some productive people. But we are going to compete."

Nicholls will try to do so with a team that will de-emphasize its front line scorers and put more emphasis on an experienced, talented backcourt.

That only stands to reason. The Colonels have no player taller than 6-8 junior **Clifton Jones** (2.3 ppg, 1.0 rpg), the projected starter at center. However, Nicholls does have plenty of returning guards.

A star on the rise is 6-4 junior **Earnest Porter** (8.3 ppg, 2.2 rpg), the team's leading returning scorer. If he becomes the player Broussard is hoping for, his will be one of the league's best stories. After completing his career at Port Allen (La.) High School, Porter seemed destined to play at a junior college before Broussard discovered him playing a pickup game on the Nicholls campus.

Broussard encouraged Porter to pay his way to Nicholls for a year to get academically eligible. He did, then played well as a sophomore last year, scoring in double figures in six of Nicholls' last eight games.

"He is already a success story," Broussard said, "and he still has a couple of years to play."

Porter will be joined in the backcourt by 5-10 junior **Sean Hughley** (6.4 ppg, 3.4 rpg 109 assists), a lightning-quick playmaker. Hughley needs to be more sure-handed this season; a year ago, he made 104 turnovers.

Ronnie Price, a 5-10 true freshman out of Houston Clear Brook High School, is expected to push Hughley for playing time. Price was recruited, but wound up without a scholarship offer. He was invited to walk on at Nicholls, which had already reached its scholarship limit.

Also back in the backcourt is 6-1 senior **Shane Beaudean**, a walk-on who has earned a scholarship for this year; 6-4 senior **Zach Ray** (2.2 ppg, 1.1 rpg), a two-year letterman; and former starter **Beau O'Quin** (2.7 ppg, 1.3 rpg), a 6-2 junior.

Those three will have early opportunities to show their stuff because Hughley will be academically ineligible for the first semester. They will be pressed for playing time by 6-6 junior college transfer **Damien Lennon** and 6-2 freshman **Larry Jones**. Lennon, a native of Australia who played last season at Porterville (Calif.) College, gives Nicholls an outside scoring threat. He can also play the small forward. Jones was highly regarded out of Port Arthur (Texas) Lincoln High.

"Larry can help out a lot," Broussard said. "It's hard counting on freshmen because obviously they don't know what the college game and college life is all about. But he is going to be a player."

With all of the talent stockpiled at guard, Broussard said it's not out of the question to see some non-traditional lineups.

"You might even see us going with four guards on the floor at once," Broussard said.

That depends on how well the big men develop.

Clifton Jones, who is a rail-thin 185 pounds, showed some flashes in an injury-prone sophomore season but was not productive. **Reggie Williams** (2.3 ppg, 1.9 rpg), a 6-6 junior saw limited action at forward last year.

Broussard added another freshman in 6-5 **Dominique Geason**, who's from the suburbs west of New Orleans.

"We won't be that good on paper," Broussard said. "We certainly won't be ranked very high. But I think we can compete. I think we'll be in the mix."

2001-2002 SCHEDULE

Nov.	17	@Mississippi State
	20	@UNLV
	24	New Orleans
	28	Loyola-New Orleans
Dec.	3	McNeese State
	9	@Michigan State
	15	@Troy State
	19	Stephen F. Austin
	22	Texas-Arlington
	30	@LSU
Jan.	3	@Southwest Texas
	5	@Texas-San Antonio
	10	Northwestern State
	12	Louisiana-Monroe
	17	@Lamar
	19	@Sam Houston State
	24	@Southeastern Louisiana
	28	McNeese State
	31	@Stephen F. Austin
Feb.	2	@Texas-Arlington
	7	Lamar
	9	Sam Houston State
	14	@Northwestern State
	16	@Louisiana-Monroe
	21	Texas-San Antonio
	23	Southwest Texas
	28	Southeastern Louisiana
March	4-9	#SLC Tournament

@Road Games
#Home sites.

BLUE RIBBON ANALYSIS

BACKCOURT	B
BENCH/DEPTH	C
FRONTCOURT	D
INTANGIBLES	C

Broussard is a patient man who is willing to go through rebuilding years. This might be one of those years.

Unless Nicholls lands a late impact recruit, the Colonels will have a young, small and unproven group of big men. When the Colonels are good under Broussard, they usually have quality up front like they had last year.

If it happens this year, it will have to be with guards. There is plenty of experience and some talent at that position.

More than likely, this will be a down year. But don't count out Broussard, who has done more with less than most coaches in the league.

(G.L.)

 # Northwestern State

LOCATION	Natchitoches, LA
CONFERENCE	Southland
LAST SEASON	19-13 (.594)
CONFERENCE RECORD	11-9 (1st)
STARTERS LOST/RETURNING	2/3
NICKNAME	Demons
COLORS	Purple, White & Orange Trim
HOMECOURT	Prather Center (3,900)
COACH	Mike McConnathy (Louisiana Tech '77)
RECORD AT SCHOOL	36-26 (2 years)
CAREER RECORD	36-26 (2 years)
ASSISTANTS	David Simmons (Louisiana Tech '82)
	Micah Coleman (Northwestern State '99)
	Mark Slessinger (Aurora '96)
TEAM WINS (last 5 years)	18-7-13-6-22
RPI (last 5 years)	224-232-250-182-164
2000-01 FINISH	Lost in NCAA first round.

The bad news for the defending conference tournament champion Northwestern State Demons is that they lost four seniors, including two of their best players, from last year's 19-13 team that beat Winthrop in an NCAA opening-round "play-in" game.

Included in the losses were forward Chris Thompson, the team's second-leading scorer and leading rebounder, and starting point guard Josh Hancock.

"We really did lose the core of our team," third-year head coach Mike McConnathy said. "But we played a lot of people and they have experience. We have some good young players too."

McConnathy played so many players last season, there are still plenty of veterans to build this season's team on, including four of the top five scorers and seven seniors. It wasn't unusual for 11 or 12 Demons to see meaningful playing time in a game. That paid off as Northwestern gelled late in the year.

"That's the way we are," McConnathy said. "With all the people we play, we might start slow, but we finish strong as everybody gets comfortable in their rolls. Hopefully, we'll be able to springboard off last season's success and do better early."

Among the returnees is SLC Tournament MVP **Michael Byars-Dawson** (13.2 ppg, 3.2 rpg, 66 assists, 55 steals), a 5-11 senior bulldog who can score from the two-guard spot and handle the ball at the point if necessary. Byars-Dawson, a transfer from Miami, was the hero of the postseason. His two free-throws in the final minute helped Northwestern to a 72-71 victory over McNeese State in the SLC Tournament championship game. That earned the Demons a berth in the NCAA Tournament's play-in game.

"It goes back further than the last minute," said Byars-Dawson after he iced the McNeese game. "Coming into the [SLC] tournament, I told these guys I wasn't going to let them lose. I told them we were going to the NCAA if I had anything to do with it."

Once Byars-Dawson got his team into the NCAAs, he did his best to keep it there a while. In the play-in game against Winthrop, Byars-Dawson made a pair of key plays down the stretch as Northwestern State won, 71-67.

With his team leading 69-67, Byars-Dawson blocked Winthrop's Tywan Harris' three-point attempt with 10 seconds left. Two free throws by Byars-Dawson with two seconds to go provided the final margin.

The victory earned Northwestern a shot against mighty Illinois, but Byars-Dawson's magic wore off. He was 1-for-8 from the field and made four turnovers as the Illini won, 96-54.

Also back is 6-6 forward **Chris Lynch** (7.8 ppg, 4.2 rpg), 6-2 point guard **Ryan Duplessis** (7.2 ppg) and 6-7 forward **Melvin Roberts** (6.5 ppg, 2.7 rpg). All three are seniors. They ranked third through fifth on the team in scoring behind Byars-Dawson and Thompson last year.

Another returnee is 6-3 senior guard **Alann Polk**, who is coming off a red-shirt year after undergoing his second knee surgery in as many years last year. Polk was the team's leading returning scorer (9.1 ppg) before the injury ended his season last year.

Kory Wilson (4.0 ppg, 1.4 rpg), a 6-3 senior, **Jerrold McRae** (2.4 ppg, 2.3 rpg), a 6-5 senior, and **Michael Edwards** (0.8 ppg, 0.4 rpg), a 6-1 sophomore, were also in McConnathy's regular rotation a year ago. **B.J. Netterfield** (1.1 ppg, 0.3 rpg), a 5-10 junior, also saw limited action.

However, the most intriguing of the returning players may be 6-11 sophomore center **D'Or Fischer** (5.1, 4.0 rpg). Fischer showed flashes of dominance last year, getting a triple-double (11 points, 14 rebounds, 13 blocks) against Southwest Texas and nearly getting another against Winthrop (10 points, 11 rebounds, nine blocks). Fischer finished with 69 blocks and was fourth in the SLC with his average of 2.1 blocks per game.

This was from a player who never completed a season of high school basketball, but became a prospect when a late growth spurt pushed him to his current height after he finished high school.

Fischer will have some big bodies around him this year. McConnathy is high on a trio of new recruits—6-5 sophomore **Darnell Bradley**, who sat out last year as an academic casualty; 6-9 junior college transfer **Carl Jones**, and 6-7, 260-pound freshman **Byron Allen**.

"With the guys we have coming in, we can match big bodies with nearly anybody in college basketball," McConnathy said. "With the big guys we have coming back, we won't have to rush them into the lineup."

McConnathy had high praise for Bradley, who comes from the same high school (Leesville, La.) that produced 2001 SLC Player of the Year Demond Mallet of McNeese State.

"I think he will do a lot of the things Chris Thompson did for us," McConnathy said. "He's not as big as Thompson, but he'll rebound for you and he'll score inside. He's a workhorse-type guy."

McConnathy also recruited another true center in 6-11 Tim Van, who will have to sit out his freshman season as an academic casualty. He also recruited two freshman guards in 6-2 **Steven Burch** from Stanley, La. and 6-2 **D.J. Ross** of Northwood High in Lena, La.

2001-2002 SCHEDULE

Nov.	17	@TCU
	21	@Southern
Dec.	5	*Oral Roberts
	16	@Oklahoma State
	18	@Oral Roberts
	20	@Arkansas
	28	Sam Houston State
	30	Lamar
Jan.	4	@Louisiana-Monroe
	8	McNeese State
	11	@Texas-Arlington
	13	@Stephen F. Austin
	18	Southwest Texas State
	20	Texas-San Antonio
	22	Southwest Texas
	25	@Nicholls State
	27	Louisiana-Monroe
	29	@Southeastern Louisiana
Feb.	3	@Sam Houston State
	5	@Lamar
	10	Southeastern Louisiana
	12	Nicholls State
	15	@Texas-San Antonio
	17	@Southwest Texas State
	21	@Centenary
	24	@McNeese State
Mardh	1	Stephen F. Austin
	6-10	#SLC Tournament

@Road Games
*Bossier City, LA
#Home sites

BLUE RIBBON ANALYSIS

BACKCOURT	B
BENCH/DEPTH	A
FRONTCOURT	B
INTANGIBLES	B

McConnathy does things a different way and it's starting to pay off in Natchitoches.

The Demons use more players than most teams in college basketball. While that may make chemistry slow to come around and limits the star power of some players, it also means the Demons have a plethora of players back with meaningful experience.

That experience includes an upset of a superior McNeese State team in the SLC Tournament final, a win over Winthrop in an NCAA opening-round game and a first-round NCAA game against Illinois. Not only are there a lot of Demons who have played, there are a lot who have the big games under their belt.

McConnathy is a proven winner. His record in junior college was outstanding and he's off to a solid start at Northwestern. It wouldn't be surprising to see Northwestern become a power in this league in a hurry.

(G.L.)

 # Sam Houston State

LOCATION	Huntsville, TX
CONFERENCE	Southland
LAST SEASON	16-13 (.552)
CONFERENCE RECORD	11-9 (4th)
STARTERS LOST/RETURNING	3/2
NICKNAME	Bearkats
COLORS	Orange & White
HOMECOURT	Johnson Coliseum (6,100)
COACH	Bob Marlin (Mississippi State '81)
RECORD AT SCHOOL	48-36 (4 years)
CAREER RECORD	48-36 (4 years)
ASSISTANTS	Darby Rich (Alabama '92)
	Neil Hardin (West Florida '95)
	Joe Hicks (Sam Houston '98)
TEAM WINS (last 5 years)	8-9-10-22-16
RPI (last 5 years)	260-265-258-110-192
2000-01 FINISH	Lost in conference semifinal.

While few are picking Sam Houston State to be in

contention for the Southland Conference title this season, they shouldn't be surprised if the Bearkats make a move in the league. After all, they have been the closest thing to a bully the league has had in the last few years.

That's right, Sam Houston State.

Since Bob Marlin arrived in Huntsville for the 1998-99 season, no SLC school has had a better conference won-lost record than the Bearkats' 33-23 mark.

Before Marlin's arrival, Sam Houston had never had a winning season in Division I. The Bearkats won their first-ever league title in 2000.

"I'm proud of that," Marlin said. "We've worked hard for that."

However, a couple of the main players who have been the leaders of recent Sam Houston teams have departed. After 2000, posts David Amaya and Ricky Fernandez were finished. Now, Sam Houston will start life without talented wings Senecca Wall and Jeremy Burkhalter. Burkhalter was the team's all-time leading scorer, finishing his career with a 14.6 scoring average as a senior. Wall was first-team All-SLC as a senior, averaging 19.1 points and grabbing 6.5 boards a night. He finished fourth in the league in scoring.

"We lost two really good ones in Senecca Wall and Jeremy Burkhalter," Marlin said. "Senecca had an outstanding season. Nobody scored more points in Division I here than Jeremy. We are just going to have to get our points from different sources."

Marlin admitted those sources might not be among the returning cast. Two starters come back. Point guard **Eddy Barlow** (7.9 ppg, 4.9 apg), a 6-0 junior, is more likely to pass the ball. A year ago, he led the conference in assists. Post **Eddie Fobbs** (6.1 ppg, 4.9 rpg), a 6-11 sophomore, is a shot blocker, but not a huge scoring threat.

The best scorer coming back is senior guard **Demetrice "Meechie" Sims**, a muscular 6-2 senior who gave the Bearkats instant offense off the bench a year ago, scoring 9.7 points a night while playing just over a half every game.

"Here's a guy that scored 15 points in 1:27 in one game [against Texas-Arlington]," Marlin said. "He had five three-pointers in 1:27. That's the kind of scoring he is capable of."

While Sims will get more shots, Marlin has gone the junior college route to find most of his new "go-to" threats, turning up a trio of in-state JUCO recruiting steals.

Donald Cole is a 6-7 forward who averaged 18 points and 12 rebounds at Navarro (Texas) Junior College last season.

"He's a guy that can score inside and go outside," Marlin said. "He's a high-post, low-post type player. He's really good."

Also coming in is 6-4 wing **Felton Freeman** from Panola (Texas) Junior College. He averaged 18 points and 10 boards a game in his career.

"He's a really hard-nosed defender," Marlin said. "He's really good. He might not be as athletic as Senecca was, but he may be a better overall player."

The third candidate is Blinn (Texas) Junior College transfer **Jay Oliphant**, a 6-5 forward who scored 20 points and grabbed nine rebounds a night, using his savvy and physical strength inside. Oliphant led the nation in field-goal percentage at Blinn.

"He is a lot like Arthur Haralson who played at Nicholls last year," said Marlin, referring to the muscular but short power forward who starred for Sam Houston's SLC rival a season ago. "He isn't as heavy as Haralson, but he finishes inside. He played against much bigger kids in his junior college league and he held his own."

The junior college trio will join Fobbs and three returning lettermen on a deep front line. The other returning lettermen are **Vince Brown** (3.3 ppg, 2.7 rpg), a 6-8, 260-pound senior bull; **Brian Jordy** (0.6 ppg, 1.1 rpg), a 6-7 senior; and **Roderick Winters** (2.2 ppg, 2.9 rpg), a 6-5 sophomore wing. Also back is 6-8 junior **Nick Christopher**, who red-shirted last year.

"We are deep on the front line," Marlin said.

The key may be Fobbs, who is one of an increasing number of talented, raw big men who have entered the league in recent years. A year ago, he blocked 66 shots, but was a liability on the offensive end, where he shot 37 percent, a low number for a player who mainly shoots around the basket.

One valuable player who might not return is **Keith Heinrich** (0.6 ppg, 1.1 rpg). The 6-7, 255-pounder entered his senior year in the fall as a preseason Division I-AA all-American tight end on the Bearkats football team.

"He has a lot of [NFL] scouts looking at him," Marlin said. "He might decide not to play and concentrate on getting ready for the draft. If he comes out, he is more

than welcome."

Marlin said there might be a swap of football players. Quarterback **Josh McCown**, who transferred to Sam Houston from SMU this year, has shown an interest in playing.

"But he's a [football] prospect, too, so he might end up in the same boat a Heinrich," Marlin said.

Barlow and Sims stabilize a backcourt that also includes 6-2 sophomore **Jason Stephenson** (4.8 ppg), a sharpshooter who will eventually inherit the starting point-guard position. Also back is 5-11 senior **Antwon Parker** (1.0 apg) and 5-11 red-shirt freshman **Wes Hawthorne**.

Marlin also recruited two freshman guards. **Tremaine Harrison** is a 6-1 point guard from Kountz, Texas and Chris Jordan is a 6-4 guard who averaged 16.4 points at Hitchcock (Texas) High.

Marlin was particularly high on Jordan.

"He's really good," Marlin said. "He's a kid that played in a small town and if he had played in the city of Houston, I don't know if we would have had a shot at him. He has a chance to have a great career here."

2001-2002 SCHEDULE

Nov.	16-17	#Hawaii Nike Classic
	24	@Texas Tech
	30	##Marquette Blue Gold Classic
Dec.	1	##Marquette Blue Gold Classic
	13	Louisiana-Monroe
	15	@Nebraska
	20	@Southwest Texas
	22	@Texas-San Antonio
	29-30	###Dr Pepper Classic
Jan.	3	McNeese
	7	@Lamar
	10	@Texas-Arlington
	12	@Stephen F. Austin
	17	Southeastern Louisiana
	19	Nicholls State
	24	@Louisiana-Monroe
	26	@Northwestern State
	31	Southwest Texas
Feb.	2	Texas-San Antonio
	4	Northwestern State
	7	@Southeastern Louisiana
	9	@Nicholls State
	14	Texas-Arlington
	16	Stephen F. Austin
	23	@McNeese State
March	2	Lamar
	4-9	####Southland Tournament

@Road Games
#Honolulu, HI (vs. Drake first round; also Norfolk State, Hawaii)
##Milwaukee, WI (vs. Texas Southern first round; also Northern Illinois, Marquette)
###Chattanooga, TN (vs. Chattanooga first round; also Bradley, Weber State)
####Home sites

BLUE RIBBON ANALYSIS

BACKCOURT	B
BENCH/DEPTH	B-
FRONTCOURT	C
INTANGIBLES	B

Sam Houston has had a remarkable run of success under Marlin, who would be considered one of the nation's hot young coaches if he wasn't toiling in the obscurity of the Southland Conference.

However, this year Marlin's Bearkats will be going at it without the likes of Burkhalter and Wall, two of the best players in the league for the last two years. Clearly, this season will be a huge test for the Bearkats' ability to maintain success even with turnover on the roster.

The three junior college transfers all have the promise to fill the shoes of the departed stars. How Sam Houston does may directly correlate with the kinds of seasons those players have.

The best news for Sam Houston is that Barlow and Sims promise to be one of the league's better starting backcourts and Fobbs is one of the better defensive big men in the league.

(G.L.)

Southeastern Louisiana

LOCATION	Hammond, LA
CONFERENCE	Southland
LAST SEASON	8-21 (.276)
CONFERENCE RECORD	5-15 (11th)
STARTERS LOST/RETURNING	2/3
NICKNAME	Lions
COLORS	Green & Gold
HOMECOURT	University Center (7,500)
COACH	Billy Kennedy (SLU '86)
RECORD AT SCHOOL	18-38 (2 years)
CAREER RECORD	42-72 (4 years)
ASSISTANTS	William Small (Bellhaven '95)
	Steve Prohm (Alabama '97)
TEAM WINS (last 5 years)	10-6-6-10-8
RPI (last 5 years)	298-302-294-259-292
2000-01 FINISH	Lost in regular-season finale.

Billy Kennedy is used to having questions in his backcourt. A year ago, his Southeastern Louisiana Lions had one of the better backcourts in the Southland Conference coming into the year with senior play maker Lee Carney and senior shooting guard Marcus Kemp. But injuries robbed both players of their chance to have a good seasons.

Carney appeared in only six games. Kemp played in 24, but was plagued by a broken shooting hand that resulted in his scoring average dipping from double figures as a junior to 6.9 points per game a year ago.

Now Carney and Kemp are gone, along with Jamaal Wolfe and Jaron Singletary (10.0 ppg), the players who got the bulk of the backcourt playing time after the injuries. As a result, the Lions slipped to last place in the SLC.

"The injuries really hurt us," Kennedy said. "These were people we were counting on."

Without Carney and with Kemp's abilities seriously compromised, the Lions struggled, losing several close games while averaging just under 58 points per game.

"We just couldn't score," Kennedy said.

So Kennedy made it a priority to find replacements ready to step in.

"We went out and got four guards that I really feel good about," Kennedy said. "I think right now we have 10 legitimate Division I players and that's the first time I've been able to say it."

Included in those 10 are four senior front-line players who received significant playing time. **Donald Ceasar** (7.1 ppg, 4.4 rpg), a 6-6 former pitcher in the Atlanta Braves system, is the Lions' leading returning scorer. **Derrick Franklin** (5.9 ppg, 4.5 rpg), an athletic 6-3 wing who is the team's leading returning rebounder.

Also back is former Marquette player **Harold Juluke** (2.8 ppg, 3.0 rpg), a 6-6, 243-pound man-child down low, along with **Curtis Walker** (2.7 ppg, 2.2 rpg), a 6-7, 235 pounder. Those two give SLU bulk to defend the goal and rebound.

Besides those four, the only other front-line player is 6-10 red-shirt freshman **Travis Benton**, meaning Kennedy will have to reload with big men after this season.

"The thing is, those four guys we have coming back were all first-year guys last year," Kennedy said. "They will be more comfortable in our system this year."

The top returning guard is sophomore wing **Lane Frey** (2.8 ppg), a 6-4 shooter who seemed to turn the corner late in the season. Frey dropped in a career-high 16 points in the Lions' second-to-last game of the year against Southwest Texas.

"Lane finished strong last year," Kennedy said. "We have a lot of confidence in him."

Frey will battle for time at shooting guard with **Amir Abdur-Rahim**, a 6-3 transfer from Garden City (Kansas) Junior College via Atlanta. Abdur-Rahim averaged 13.6 points per game as a freshman. He once scored 41 points in a junior college game.

"He comes from a high-profile program in Garden City and he was able to average double figures," Kennedy said. "We expect him to be a factor at the two-guard."

Also at the off-guard spot is 6-2 sophomore **Neill Berry** (0.9 ppg), who made 18 appearances last season, starting once.

At point, the Lions have 5-9 junior **Dyron Clark** (3.3 ppg, 36 steals), a former walk-on who has been given a scholarship this year. Clark started three games last season.

He will get competition from **Marcus Smith**, a 6-0 transfer from Middle Georgia College, where he received all-conference and all-state recognition.

SLU also recruited a pair of high school guards in 6-

4 **Adrian Scott** from Tuscaloosa, Ala. Hillcrest High and 6-2 **Dee Gadsden** of Wheeler High in Marietta, Ga.

2001-2002 SCHEDULE

Nov.	16	Louisiana College
	24	@Memphis
	28	@South Alabama
Dec.	5	@Texas A&M
	8	New Orleans
	17	Stephen F. Austin
	20	Texas-Arlington
	22	@McNeese State
	28-29	#New Mexico Classic
Jan.	3	@Texas-San Antonio
	5	@Southwest Texas
	10	Louisiana-Monroe
	12	Northwestern State
	17	@Sam Houston
	19	@Lamar
	24	Nicholls State
	26	McNeese State
	31	@Texas-Arlington
Feb.	2	@Stephen F. Austin
	7	Sam Houston
	9	Lamar
	14	@Louisiana-Monroe
	16	@Northwestern State
	21	Southwest Texas
	23	Texas-San Antonio
	28	@Nicholls State
March	4-9	##SLC Tournament

@Road Games
#Albuquerque, NM (vs. Dartmouth first round; also New Mexico, St. Mary's)
##Home sites

BLUE RIBBON ANALYSIS

BACKCOURT	D
BENCH/DEPTH	C
FRONTCOURT	C+
INTANGIBLES	C

Kennedy's third Southeastern Louisiana team returns no players who averaged double figures in scoring and no players who pulled down at least five rebounds a game. With that in mind, it's hard to envision a much-better finish than last year's last-place ending.

However, basketball at the mid-major level can be influenced heavily by an influx of quality junior college transfers. The Lions can be good, but only if its recruiting class is as good as Kennedy hopes.

If the success Smith and Abdur-Rahim enjoyed in junior college translates to this level, the Lions will have a quality backcourt to go with an experienced front line.

Until that is proven, however, it's hard seeing SLU climbing out of the second division.

(G.L.)

Southwest Texas State

LOCATION	San Marcos, TX
CONFERENCE	Southland
LAST SEASON	13-15 (.464)
CONFERENCE RECORD	10-10 (7th)
STARTERS LOST/RETURNING	1/4
NICKNAME	Bobcats
COLORS	Maroon & Gold
HOMECOURT	Strahan Coliseum (7,200)
COACH	Dennis Nutt (TCU '86)
RECORD AT SCHOOL	13-15 (1 year)
CAREER RECORD	13-15 (1 year)
ASSISTANTS	Greg Young (Howard Payne '86)
	Dionne Phelps (TCU '89)
	Clark Sheehy (John Brown '98)
TEAM WINS (last 5 years)	16-17-19-12-13
RPI (last 5 years)	175-154-138-246-240
2000-01 FINISH	Lost in conference first round.

That Southwest Texas State has four starters back is not all that remarkable in the Southland Conference, where schools like Texas-Arlington, Texas-San Antonio and Louisiana-Monroe all boast at least four returning starters. Several other teams have three starters back.

Still, there is ample reason for optimism in San Marcos. The Bobcats have six seniors and, as Texas-

San Antonio coach Tim Carter put it, "this is a senior-oriented league."

That, plus the fact that SWT won six-of-seven games in one stretch late in the season, gives second-year head coach Dennis Nutt reason to enter the season with what he calls "cautious optimism."

"These are veterans with a lot of playing experience," Nutt said. "I feel better about them and I like the new pieces we've added."

The only starter missing from last season's team is point guard Manny Flores. Back are the other four starters, plus four players who contributed heavily off the bench.

Even with all the seniors, leading the way is 6-5 junior wing **David Sykes** (12.7 ppg, 6.6 rpg, 3.4 apg). The Duncanville, Texas native led the Bobcats in scoring and was second in both rebounding and assists a year ago.

"David has had a great summer," Nutt said. "I feel good about where he is."

Like a lot of the top players in the SLC, Sykes is a dangerous athlete on the wing. He's big enough and athletic enough to score and rebound inside, but can step out, where he made 27 three-pointers a year ago, although his percentage (28 percent) was not great.

The other wing player is **Clay Click** (12.1 ppg), a 6-3 senior who is among the league's premier three-point shooters. He made 64-of-165 from long range a season ago. Also back in the starting lineup are 6-7 senior power forward **Byron Hobbs** (8.5 ppg, 6.8 rpg), the team's leading rebounder a year ago, and **Melih Yavasner** (7.0 ppg, 5.3 rpg, 1.4 bpg), a 6-11, 250-pound senior space eater inside.

"Clay has also had a great summer and so has Hobbs," Nutt said. "We'll get some pretty good games out of them."

The Bobcats should have depth inside, with Hobbs leading the way. Yavasner, a native of Turkey, has grown accustomed to the grind of the American season.

"Last year, he lost a lot of weight during the season," Nutt said. "He got down to around 230. This year, we hope to keep the meat on him. He has great feet and hands, if he can just learn to be more aggressive."

The Bobcats' depth starts with 6-6 senior forward **Dain Ervin** (9.1 ppg, 4.1 rpg), an athletic native of the Bronx via Angelina (Texas) Junior College.

"Dain played well early, then toward the end he kind of tapered off," Nutt said. "He's a versatile kid. He can play inside or out."

Gerald Scott (3.9 ppg, 1.9 rpg), a 6-8, 240-pound senior, rounds out a big and experienced returning front line. But Nutt didn't stop there. He recruited 6-8 forward **Moses Aguko** of Seminole (Okla.) Junior College.

"He's raw, but he gives us toughness and a blue-collar attitude," Nutt said of Aguko.

The one place Nutt was pursuing immediate help was at point guard, where only **Brady Richeson** (2.5 ppg), a 5-11 junior, is back. Sykes also played a lot of point guard last year and will push for starting duty.

There are plenty of newcomers who will contend for playing time at the point. **Marcus Johnson**, a 6-2 combo guard out of Trinity Valley (Texas) Community College will have a shot.

"He's athletic, he has speed and he's a good shooter," Nutt said. "He can play the point and off."

Nutt also recruited freshman **Brady Brickens**, a 6-4 product of Austin (Texas) Bowie High, to compete for the job.

"He's talented," Nutt said. "He sees the floor and he can pass. I think he'll grow up well in our system."

Nutt said he hopes the competition between the four point-guard candidates will produce the desired results.

"We are going to give all four of these guys a shot and see what happens," he said.

Nutt also returns two other guards, **Slaven Smiljanic** (4.8 ppg), a 6-4 senior who was second on the team behind Click with 31 three-pointers, and **Shane Wright**, a 6-0 junior transfer from Coastal Carolina.

"I feel much better about this team this year," Nutt said. "I feel much better than last year when we had a bunch of new guys who hadn't been through the wars."

SWT has another potential contributor sitting out this season in Texas transfer Roosevelt Brown. Brown, 6-3, played for the Longhorns the last two seasons. The combo guard played in 12 games in 2000-2001 as a reserve and averaged 1.7 points and 0.5 assists in 6.6 minutes per game. His best game of the year came against Southwest Texas in December, when he posted 10 points on four of six shooting (two of three threes), two rebounds, two steals and one assist in 14 minutes.

2001-2002 SCHEDULE

Nov.	17	Schreiner
	19	@Texas-Pan American
	25	@Texas-Corpus Christi
	25	@TCU
Dec.	1	@Stephen F. Austin
	4	@Arkansas
	8	@McNeese State
	16	@Houston
	20	Sam Houston
	22	Lamar
Jan.	3	Nicholls State
	5	Southeastern Louisiana
	8	Texas-Pan American
	12	McNeese State
	17	@Northwestern State
	19	@Louisiana-Monroe
	24	Stephen F. Austin
	26	Texas-Arlington
	31	@Sam Houston
Feb.	2	@Lamar
	8	Northwestern State
	10	Louisiana-Monroe
	16	@Texas-San Antonio
	21	@Southeastern Louisiana
	23	@Nicholls State
	26	@Texas-Arlington
March	2	Texas-San Antonio
	4-9	#SLC Tournament

@Road Games
#Home sites

BLUE RIBBON ANALYSIS

BACKCOURT	B-
BENCH/DEPTH	B
FRONTCOURT	C+
INTANGIBLES	B-

If experience means a lot, then it should mean that Nutt's Bobcats will be in the thick of the Southland Conference title race in late February.

However, there are questions. The two best SWT players are wings, but in a league that has traditionally been dominated by two guards and small forwards (see Demond Mallet and Tierre Brown last year at McNeese State), are Sykes and Click the kind of players it takes to win a championship?

Also, the Bobcats have plenty of experience up front, but don't have a player who has been consistently strong inside.

For Nutt's team to win, it would seem like his best players will have to step up a notch to a higher level. With six seniors, there are plenty of candidates to do that in their final year.

(G.L.)

Stephen F. Austin

LOCATION	Nacogdoches, TX
CONFERENCE	Southland
LAST SEASON	9-17 (.346)
CONFERENCE RECORD	6-14 (10th)
STARTERS LOST/RETURNING	3/2
NICKNAME	Lumberjacks
COLORS	Purple & White
HOMECOURT	Johnson Coliseum (7,200)
COACH	Danny Kaspar (North Texas '78)
RECORD AT SCHOOL	9-17 (1 year)
CAREER RECORD	228-68 (10 years)
ASSISTANTS	Rennie Bailey (Louisiana Tech '85)
	Steve Lutz (Texas Lutheran '95)
	T.J. Marcum (Texas A&M '99)
TEAM WINS (last 5 years)	12-10-4-6-9
RPI (last 5 years)	181-249-306-305-287
2000-01 FINISH	Lost regular-season finale.

Losing is not something Stephen F. Austin coach Danny Kaspar is used to. In nine years at NAIA power Incarnate Word, Kaspar's teams never failed to win at least 21 games.

Before that, he was an assistant coach on successful teams at Lamar, Midwestern State, Stephen F. Austin and Baylor.

But 2001 proved to be a humbling year for Kaspar in his first season as head coach at a Division I program. His SFA Lumberjacks barely avoided the Southland Conference cellar in what was his toughest season as a head coach and his second worst season as either a head coach or an assistant.

"We just had two kids who were hurt and one who left the team," Kaspar said. "After that, we just didn't score enough."

The most costly loss was guard Kevin Daniels, who played in only seven games last year and averaged 19 points in the two SLC games. Without him, the 'Jacks lost six games by three or fewer points.

The Lumberjacks stayed in games by playing slow and defending well. SFA allowed only 61.4 points per game, but scored only 59.4

"We did play tough defense," Kaspar said. "Hopefully this year, we'll also be able to score."

It helps that Kaspar has his most prolific offensive weapon in shooting guard **Skip Jackson**. A deadly shooter spotting up and coming off screens, the 5-11 junior from Beaumont, Texas averaged 14.6 points per game and sank 55 three-pointers, 35 more than the next player on the team. He earned third-team All-SLC recognition.

"With McNeese losing its two guards [Demond Mallet and Tierre Brown], Skip is probably one of the two or three best players coming back in this league," Kaspar said.

Jackson was chosen Texas Class 5A all state as a senior in high school before playing his freshman year for current Lumberjacks assistant Rennie Bailey at Panola.

Jackson is the leader of a backcourt that Kaspar calls the strength of his team. **Edwin Tatum** (5.5 ppg, 3.7 rpg), a 6-4 junior, started three games at guard last season and averaged 18 minutes a game. Tatum, who checks in at a muscular 205 pounds, is strong enough to play on the front line and agile enough to perform in the backcourt.

"Tatum will be a bigger factor this year," Kaspar said.

Another swingman who lettered a year ago is 6-5 senior **Scott Spradlin** (5 ppg, 2.7 rpg), who came to SFA from Incarnate Word with Kaspar. However, he was only able to show flashes of what he is capable of because of the effects of off-season knee surgery.

"He was in a lot of pain last year," Kaspar said. "He did have some big games against Loyola and Texas-San Antonio. But I feel he will play a bigger role this year."

Kaspar said Spradlin's ailing knee will be close to 100 percent when practice begins.

"Scott could play a huge role for us this season if he continues to recover from his surgery," Kaspar said.

Jason Gast, a 6-3 swingman, is a second transfer from Incarnate Word. Gast was ineligible last season, but worked out with the team.

"He is a great shooter, knows the system and his familiarity with the system will help his chances at the start of the season," Kaspar said.

Kaspar also recruited four new guards. One who could make an immediate impact is 6-0 freshman point guard **Tim Simon** of Houston Klein Forest High. Simon has a chance to be a first-year starter because last year's starter, Ji Thomas, has departed.

"Tim Simon could have a great four-year career here," Kaspar said. "He is quick, strong and can really shoot the ball well."

Ben Hunt, a 6-2 Australian, should make an immediate impact as a junior. His experience thus far has been in international ball, including stints with a touring team from Australia.

"He's older than the other players and he is very mature," Kaspar said. "He is a great outside shooter."

Rashard Wright, a 6-4 junior transfer from Blinn (Texas) Junior College, is an athletic player who could be a factor at the two or the three.

While there is plenty of depth in the backcourt, Kaspar is concerned about the numbers on the front line.

"Our inside game is a question mark," Kaspar said. "Some new people will have to play well for us."

One starter does return. **Ransom White**, a 6-7 senior power forward, was 11th in the conference in rebounding last year (6.5 rpg, along with 6.2 ppg). He had 15 boards in a game against McNeese State.

"Ransom is an excellent athlete and has the potential to be one of the best defenders in the Southland Conference this year," Kaspar said.

What Kaspar is looking for is a scoring threat to replace the departed Ron Banks (13.0 ppg) up front. That could come from 6-7 junior **Percy Green**, a transfer from Garden City (Kansas) Community College. Kaspar said the Oklahoma City native has the strength to rebound and defend and the skill to score down low.

"Percy is a very good sign for us," Kaspar said.

Two front line players return. **Stephen Cobb**, a little-used 6-11 senior center, improved during the off-season, Kaspar said. **Stevin Ozier**, a 6-7 red-shirt freshman from Brazosport, Texas, made the most of his year off.

"He has improved a great deal through his work in the weight room," Kaspar said.

SFA also signed **Taylor Moore**, a 6-8, 225-pound freshman from Fort Worth (Texas) Polytech High. He was rated as one of the state's top 40 players as a high

school senior.

2001-2002 SCHEDULE

Nov.	17	@Arizona State
	21	@Jackson State
	24	Texas Lutheran
	27	Rice
Dec.	1	Southwest Texas
	5	Centenary
	8	Texas Southern
	17	@Southeastern Louisiana
	19	@Nicholls State
	29	@Oral Roberts
Jan.	3	@Northwestern State
	5	Louisian-Monroe
	10	Lamar
	12	Sam Houston
	17	@UT-Arlington
	24	@Southwest Texas
	26	@UT-San Antonio
	31	Nicholls State
Feb.	2	Southeastern Louisiana
	7	UT-Arlington
	9	McNeese State
	14	@Lamar
	16	@Sam Houston
	21	Northwestern State
	23	Louisiana-Monroe
	26	UT-San Antonio
March	2	@McNeese State
	4-9	#SLC Tournament

@Road Games
#Home sites

BLUE RIBBON ANALYSIS

BACKCOURT	B
BENCH/DEPTH	C
FRONTCOURT	C-
INTANGIBLES	C

In Jackson, Stephen F. Austin has a bona fide star in this league. However, there are few proven players aside from him.

If Green is as good as advertised and White continues to crash the boards with his relentless attitude, the Lumberjacks may have a competitive front line. With the recruiting he did in the backcourt, Kaspar has plenty of reasons to think he will find reliable people to put next to Jackson.

However, most of these players are new and unproven. In a league where teams like Texas-San Antonio, McNeese State, Louisiana-Monroe and Texas-Arlington are loaded with veterans, it's hard to imagine SFA matching up with players of similar ability and superior experience.

(G.L.)

Texas-Arlington

LOCATION	Arlington, TX
CONFERENCE	Southland
LAST SEASON	13-15 (.464)
CONFERENCE RECORD	11-9 (6th)
STARTERS LOST/RETURNING	1/4
NICKNAME	Mavericks
COLORS	Royal Blue & White
HOMECOURT	Texas Hall (4,200)
COACH	Eddie McCarter (UAB '75)
RECORD AT SCHOOL	107-140 (10th year)
CAREER RECORD	107-140 (10th year)
ASSISTANTS	Anthony Anderson (McNeese St. '95)
	Scott Cross (UTA '98)
	Matt Daniel (Harding '98)
TEAM WINS (last 5 years)	12-13-10-15-13
RPI (last 5 years)	240-240-261-190-237
2000-01 FINISH	Lost in conference quarterfinal.

Texas-Arlington was nothing if not fun to watch last year. A team full of perimeter shooters, the Mavericks' wide-open style often saw them go on unbelievable runs or go into depressing droughts.

It wasn't a dull style of ball, and it even brought UTA modest success. However, veteran coach Eddie McCarter would like to see more consistency from his team this year.

"I feel good about this team," said McCarter, who brings back four starters, but will miss sharp-shooting

guard Jabari Johnson (17.9 ppg). "I know this league is very competitive top to bottom and a lot of people return key players though."

The top returnee for UTA is exciting lead guard **Steven Barber**. The 5-10 senior was second on the team in scoring with a 16.4 scoring average while finishing second to the departed Jason Arbuckle in assists (80) last year. He was a second-team all-conference player.

"Barber had a phenomenal second half of the year," McCarter said. "I just hope he can keep it up."

Barber made 61 three-pointers while Johnson hit 66, making them the SLC's "other" explosive backcourt tandem aside from McNeese's dynamic duo of Demond Mallet and Tierre Brown.

The Mavericks established themselves as contenders a year ago and as a team of the future. McCarter landed two of the league's best freshmen in 6-7 forward **Derrick Obasohan** (8.8 ppg, 3.9 rpg), who was voted the league's freshman of the year, and 6-5 forward **Donny Beacham** (5.9 ppg, 5.9 rpg).

Both started as freshmen and had the beginnings of what promises to be four solid years as starters for the Mavericks.

"I just hope they get better as sophomores," McCarter said. "Sometimes, these guys get sophomore bliss. But they are playing with a lot of confidence right now. If they keep playing with intensity they will continue to improve."

Obasohan and Beacham aren't the only good, young returning players. Junior **Mack Callier** (11.6 ppg, 8.7 rpg), a 6-7 forward, was third in the league in rebounding last year. Three sophomore reserves—6-9 **Roy Johnson** (4.6 ppg, 4.5 rpg), 6-8 **Achille Ngounou** (2.9 ppg, 2.6 rpg) and 6-8 **Milos Nikolic** (1.9 ppg, 1.5 rpg)—were all part of McCarter's prize freshman class of a year ago.

With the departure of Arbuckle, the only true point guard a season ago, McCarter brought in junior college transfer **Josh Daniels**, a 6-2 junior and native of Jonesboro, Ark., who played at Southwest Missouri State-West Plains Junior College last year.

Daniel led his team to a 54-10 record over the last two years, including a school-record 27 wins last season. In addition, Southwest Missouri State-West Plains claimed a share of the Region 16 championship in 2000-01, while climbing the NJCAA rankings to as high as third. Two years ago, the Grizzlies were ranked as high as second.

Daniel, the younger brother of UTA assistant Matt Daniel, averaged 7.5 points, 3.1 assists, 2.1 rebounds and 1.5 steals last year. He was also chosen the school's "Scholar-Athlete of the Year" and recipient of the Grizzlies' "110 Percent Award."

Also capable of playing the point is **Clifton Palmer**, a 6-3 transfer from Howard (Texas) Junior College. McCarter brought in plenty of help to shore up the backcourt with 6-4 Butler transfer **Mike Hicks** and freshmen **Emmanuel Adigun**, a 6-5 wing out of Houston Wheatley and **Luca Jackovic**, a Canadian who was added to the roster late.

The key to the recruiting class may be strapping 6-8, 240-pound Midland (Texas) Junior College transfer **Hamilton Rucker**, who is being brought in to add much-needed muscle up front. He averaged 12 points and eight rebounds as a sophomore last season.

"We had trouble with big strong players up front like [Fred] Gentry at McNeese or [Arthur] Haralson at Nicholls," McCarter said. "We just had trouble matching up with them. We hope Hamilton can help us in those situations."

Even with Callier inside, UTA was out-rebounded by two boards a game and allowed opponents to score 76 points a game, numbers McCarter would like to see improved this year.

2001-2002 SCHEDULE

Nov.	17	New Mexico State
	21	@Baylor
	28	@Wichita State
Dec.	3	@Texas Tech
	17	@Oral Roberts
	20	@Southeastern Louisiana
	22	@Nicholls State
	29	Hardin-Simmons
Jan.	2	Oral Robertts
	5	Northwestern State
	7	@Louisiana-Monroe
	10	Sam Houston State
	12	Lamara
	17	Stephen F. Austin
	19	@McNeese State

	24	@Texas-San Antonio
	26	@Southwest Texas State
	31	Southeastern Louisiana
Feb.	2	Nicholls State
	4	Texas-San Antonio
	7	@Stephen F. Austin
	11	McNeese State
	14	@Sam Houston State
	16	@Lamar
	21	Louisiana-Monroe
	23	@Northwestern State
	26	Southwest Texas State
March	4-9	#SLC Tournament

@Road Games
#Home sites

BLUE RIBBON ANALYSIS

BACKCOURT	B
BENCH/DEPTH	B
FRONTCOURT	C+
INTANGIBLES	B

Texas-Arlington has most of the ingredients to contend for the SLC title this year. In Barber, the Mavericks have a scintillating scorer and lead guard. In Callier, UTA has an inside threat and a rebounder.

But there are questions. The Mavericks will miss Johnson, who had the ability to change games in a hurry with his outstanding shooting range. Also, it's unclear how tough UTA will be inside in a league that has an increasing number of talented big men.

Still, UTA has as many starters back as anyone in the league but Louisiana-Monroe. The best part is that two of those starters were freshmen last year and Callier was a sophomore, so if you believe in the natural progression of skills, then they should all improve this year.

If Rucker gives UTA an inside threat and if McCarter can find someone to provide the "true" point-guard abilities of an Arbuckle, watch out for the Mavs.

(G.L.)

Texas-San Antonio

LOCATION	San Antonio, TX
CONFERENCE	Southland
LAST SEASON	14-15 (.483)
CONFERENCE RECORD	12-8 (2nd)
STARTERS LOST/RETURNING	1/4
NICKNAME	Roadrunners
COLORS	Orange, Navy Blue & White
HOMECOURT	Convocation Center (5,100)
COACH	Tim Carter (Kansas '79)
RECORD AT SCHOOL	86-81 (6 years)
CAREER RECORD	97-97 (7 years)
ASSISTANTS	Owen Miller (Mississippi College '94)
	Roland Ware (Oklahoma '92)
	Lloyd Williams (UTSA '00)
TEAM WINS (last 5 years)	9-16-18-15-14
RPI (last 5 years)	294-215-152-179-200
2000-01 FINISH	Lost in conference semifinal.

McNeese State won the Southland Conference championship last season with Demond Mallet and Tierre Brown, a pair of dominant wing players. Sam Houston State won the league the year before with Jeremy Burkhalter and Seneca Wall, another pair of outstanding wings.

All four of the above-mentioned athletes have completed their eligibility. Now seems the time for Texas-San Antonio, with its star wing, Devin Brown, to take the title.

Brown, a 6-5 senior, is the leading candidate to be the SLC's Player of the Year coming off a season where he averaged 19.9 points and 7.6 rebounds while earning first-team All-SLC honors.

It's been a storybook career for Brown, who was one of the biggest recruiting steals in UTSA history after he set the all-time career scoring record in the history of San Antonio prep basketball. He's about to do the same at the local college. He needs 283 points to become the No. 1 scorer in Roadrunners history.

"Devin seems like he's been here forever," coach Tim Carter said. "But I tell you what, I wish I had him four more years. He's a great player and what I've always liked about him is he really cares about his team."

Brown is a multi-talented scorer who can shoot from the outside, drive inside to finish and has the confidence to get his points in the toughest situations.

"He's an aggressive kid," Carter said. "Sometimes he's too aggressive. But like John Cheney said, I'd rather have my best player taking a bad shot than a guy who can't shoot taking a good shot."

Brown isn't the only reason UTSA will likely be the league's favorite. Carter returns three other starters, plus four lettermen who played significant minutes. Of the returning players, five are seniors. He has also brought in five newcomers.

However, being picked to win in a lot of corners is not necessarily where Carter wants to be.

"I've been in this league seven years now," he said, "and the team that is picked to win never seems to win it."

Also back in the starting lineup is rugged 6-8 senior forward **McEverett Powers** (10.0 ppg, 6.8 rpg), a blue-collar worker who tends to get his production the hard way inside.

"He'll be a three-year starter," Carter said. "We expect a good year from him."

Senior **Reggie Minnieweather** (9.0 ppg, 5.9 rpg), a prototypical SLC guard-sized wing at 6-3, is another returning stalwart.

"Devin, McEverett and Reggie, those are our three mainstays," Carter said. "Those three will be called to step up for us."

Carter also returns 6-2 junior point guard **Jon Havens** (9.3 ppg, 112 assists, 46 three-pointers). However, the son of a high school coach will likely play more off the ball this year.

"A lot of people really didn't know that we finished second in the league last year and we really didn't have a true point guard," Carter said. "We may have been the only team in America who finished second in their league without a point guard. Jon played the whole year there for us and did a good job, but we'll slide him over to the two."

To take the point spot, UTSA has recruited three newcomers—6-0 junior **Keary Brownlee** of Meridian (Miss.) Community College, 6-0 junior **Kerry Willis** of Grayson County (Texas) Community College and 6-1 freshman **David President** of Temple, Texas High.

"Brownlee is a one or a two but President and Willis are true points," Carter said.

Brownlee and Havens on the wing will create a logjam there.

"We are very deep on the wing," Carter said.

The Roadrunners lost center Mahcoe Parker, but return 6-11 sophomore **Juan Valdez** (4.5 ppg, 3.8 rpg), 6-7 senior **James Joseph** (5.6 ppg, 4.7 rpg), 6-5 junior **Ike Atotaobi** (3.9 ppg) and 6-6 senior **Robert Bell** (4.3 ppg, 3.4 rpg).

Joseph can step out to the wing. Bell is an aggressive offensive rebounder and Atotaobi is a phenomenal athlete who has been plagued with knee problems. Valdez will likely start in the middle.

"The sky is the limit for Juan," Carter said. "He can be as good as he wants to be."

Carter also brought in two big men—6-9 **Michael Watkins** of Pratt (Kansas) Community College and 6-7 **Raymond Biggs** of Soward County (Kansas) Community College to add depth inside.

LeRoy Hurd, a 6-7, 215-pound forward who played his first two seasons at Miami, will sit out this season after transferring to UTSA.

In his two seasons in Miami, Hurd appeared in 62 games, four as a starter, averaging 4.3 points as a freshman and 5.8 points as a sophomore. In addition to two double figure scoring outings last season, Hurd also pulled down 2.8 rebounds and dished out 1.1 assists per game while ranking third on the team with nine dunks.

2001-2002 SCHEDULE

Nov.	16-17	#Florida International Tournament
	28	@Nebraska
Dec.	1	Illinois State
	7-8	##SW Missouri State Tournament
	15	@TCU
	20	Lamar
	22	Sam Houston State
	29	@McNeese State
Jan.	3	Southeastern Louisiana
	5	Nicholls State
	10	McNeese State
	17	@Louisiana-Monroe
	19	@Northwestern State
	24	Texas-Arlington
	26	Stephen F. Austin
	31	@Lamar
Feb.	2	@Sam Houston State
	4	@Texas-Arlington
	8	Louisiana-Monroe
	10	Northwestern State
	16	Southwest Texas State
	21	@Nicholls State
	23	@Southeastern Louisiana
	26	@Stephen F. Austin
March	2	@Southwest Texas State
	5-9	###SLC Tournament

@Road Games
#Miami, FL (vs. Maine first round; also Florida International, St. Peter's)
##Springfield, MO (vs. Idaho State first round; also Southwest Missouri State, Southern)
###Home sites

BLUE RIBBON ANALYSIS

BACKCOURT	B
BENCH/DEPTH	A-
FRONTCOURT	B+
INTANGIBLES	B

Texas-Arlington coach Eddie McCarter noted that the Southland Conference is a league won and lost on the wing. If that's the case, the Roadrunners are your team in 2001.

Brown is a tough kid who is a match-up problem anywhere in college basketball because of his ability to score inside, shoot outside, drive or score the hard basket on the offensive glass. He's the leading candidate to be the conference player of the year.

Minnieweather is also a solid wing and the move of Havens to the two-guard only makes UTSA stronger. The questions are whether Carter's recruiting class has produced a reliable point guard and whether there is enough inside production.

Still, this is the team many will expect to be hosting the SLC Tournament championship game in March.

(G.L.)

Alabama A&M

LOCATION	Normal, AL
CONFERENCE	Southwestern Athletic
LAST SEASON	17-11 (.607)
CONFERENCE RECORD	13-5 (t-3rd)
STARTERS LOST/RETURNING	1/4
NICKNAME	Bulldogs
COLORS	Maroon & White
HOMECOURT	T.M. Elmore Gym (6,000)
COACH	Vann Pettaway (Alabama A&M '80)
RECORD AT SCHOOL	326-121 (15 years)
CAREER RECORD	326-121 (15 years)
ASSISTANTS	Willie Hayes (Alabama A&M '89)
	Sammy Jackson (Montevallo)
TEAM WINS (last 5 years)	24-18-10-18-17
RPI (last 5 years)	NA-NA-NA-207-202
2000-01 FINISH	Won regular-season finale.

Alabama State, Alcorn State and Mississippi Valley State were expected to contend for the Southwestern Athletic Conference regular-season title a year ago.

Alabama A&M wasn't—the Bulldogs were picked sixth in the coaches preseason poll. Yet coach Vann Pettaway's scrappy bunch won 13 conference games and finished in a tie for third place with two-time defending regular season champ Alcorn. With seven games remaining, Alabama A&M was tied for first.

The year before, the Bulldogs—in their first full season in the SWAC—won 14 conference games and finished in a tie for second after being picked to finish at or near the bottom of the pack. That's 27 conference wins and a second and a third-place finish in the last two years for those of you keeping record at home. No wonder the Bulldogs feel like the Rodney Dangerfield of the SWAC.

"We're still relatively new to the league so we don't get much respect," Pettaway said. "We certainly don't get the kind of respect these kids deserve. Some people around the league still don't know us. But we've held our own. We're going to be competitive.

"When you look at it, we've been successful but we haven't won anything yet. So in a way I guess we haven't earned it. But most people in the SWAC know now that Alabama A&M isn't going to lay down for anybody."

As hard as the Bulldogs have played night in and night out in their first couple of years in the SWAC—and make no mistake, they play hard—they may play with even more reckless abandon this season. The reason? For the first time since entering the league, Alabama A&M is eligible for the SWAC Tournament.

"Oh yes! Oh yes!" Pettaway said. "I think it's the

biggest thing to happen to this program in the last five years or so. It gives these kids something to play for. I can tell already that the kids are more upbeat. They're already talking about it. It's right down the road in Birmingham, too. The thing about it is, now that we're going to get that opportunity we have to be ready. And I think we will be."

Pettaway's teams usually are. During his 15-year tenure at Alabama A&M, he has guided the Bulldogs to eight NCAA Division II playoff appearances, seven Southern Intercollegiate Athletic Conference championships, six SIAC Tournament titles and an average of 21 wins per season. Alabama A&M has won 20 or more games seven times under Pettaway.

With four starters returning, including first-team All-SWAC performer **Desmond Cambridge**, another 20-win season isn't out of the question. And as their short track record in the SWAC suggests, neither is another finish at or near the top of the league standings.

"We should be a better team," Pettaway said. "We should be deeper, stronger and we'll definitely be more athletic. We really helped ourselves in recruiting by bringing in some people that we think can step in and play right away.

"We finished second one year and we finished third last year. The only thing we haven't kept is first. Maybe this will be the year."

To do so, Alabama A&M will have to find the basket with more regularity. The Bulldogs finished eighth in the league in field-goal percentage (.391), eighth in three-point field-goal percentage (.290) and ninth in free-throw percentage (.626). The defense will be there—Alabama A&M's trapping, scrambling, in-your-face "D" came up with a league-leading 12 steals per game and forced a league-high 24 turnovers per game. So will the hustle—Alabama A&M led the league in offensive rebounds at 17.8 per game.

Now if the shooting could come around to match that defensive intensity.

"We've got to be able to shoot the ball better as a team," Pettaway said. "That's a big key. We did a good job on defense. You look at it, and our opponents averaged 24 turnovers a game for the second year in a row."

Three players who played a part in that statistic won't be around this season—forward Ryan Jones and guards Damian Crayton and Dwaynius Harris.

Pettaway kicked off Jones and Crayton in December, about the same time Harris was lost because of academic reasons. Jones was the Bulldogs' leading scorer and rebounder at the time. Harris and Crayton were averaging nearly 14 points, four steals and two assists between them. Even without those three players, the Bulldogs were able to reel off eight straight wins in January and vault into a tie for first place alongside eventual champ Alabama State.

Alabama A&M lost its next three games, however, and despite winning its last four couldn't make up the lost ground.

"Losing three of our best players in December was tough," Pettaway said. "But if you're not going to do things the right way, you're not going to be a part of this program."

One player Pettaway can't afford to lose is Cambridge. The 6-1 senior ranked first in the league in steals (3.82 spg), second in the league in scoring (18.6 ppg), fifth in assists (3.64 apg) and sixth in free-throw percentage (.771). He led the team in scoring in the last 11 games, including a 41-point outing against Prairie View and a 40-point performance against Jackson State.

"He's our leader," Pettaway said. "He makes things go. He did it all for us. I'll tell you, Desmond plays hard all the time. He brings his "A" game every night. He's not a real vocal leader, but he [leads] by example. If we need a basket, he does that. If we need a defensive stop, he does that. And he's very unselfish. When the game is over, he's left it all on the floor."

Joining Cambridge in the backcourt is 6-3 senior **Steve Ward** (14.2 ppg, 4.4 rpg). "He's our main perimeter presence," Pettaway said. "He has to come out shooting the basketball again like he's capable. He's one of the top shooters in the league."

Other returning guards include 6-3 junior **Nigel Moore** (5.4 ppg, 3.9 rpg), 6-3 sophomore **Terry Horton** (2.3 ppg, 2.3 rpg) and 5-11 sophomore **Lorenzo Burks** (1.4 ppg, 0.7 rpg). Moore and Horton split time at the three-spot last season.

"Moore is more of a banger, and Horton is more of a finesse player," Pettaway said. "Lorenzo will get more minutes this season. He did a great job for us last year playing backup point guard."

Besides improved shooting, the other big key for Alabama A&M is getting production from its front line players. Outside of Cambridge and Ward, the Bulldogs

SOUTHWESTERN

BLUE RIBBON FORECAST
1. Alcorn State
2. Alabama State
3. Alabama A&M
4. Jackson State
5. Prairie View
6. Grambling State
7. Mississippi Valley State
8. Southern
9. Texas Southern
10. Arkansas-Pine Bluff

ALL-CONFERENCE TEAM
G - Desmond Cambridge, SR, Alabama A&M
G - Gregory Burks, JR, Prairie View
C - Alvin Pettway, JR, Alabama State
F - Marcus Fleming, SR, Alcorn State
F - Tyrone Levett, SR, Alabama State

PLAYER OF THE YEAR
Tyrone Levett, SR, Alabama State

NEWCOMER OF THE YEAR
Tim Henderson, JR, Jackson State

2001-2002 CONFERENCE TOURNAMENT
March 5-10, Fair Park Arena, Birmingham, AL

2000-2001 CHAMPIONS
Alabama State (regular season)
Alabama State (Conference Tournament)

2000-2001 POSTSEASON PARTICIPANTS
Postseason record: 0-1 (.000)
NCAA
Alabama State

TOP BACKCOURTS
1. Alabama A&M
2. Prairie View
3. Jackson State

TOP FRONTCOURTS
1. Alabama State
2. Alcorn State
3. Alabama A&M

INSIDE THE NUMBERS
2000-2001 conference RPI: 30th (of 31)
Conference RPI (last five years:) 31-30-29-32-30

DID YOU KNOW?
Alabama State coach Rob Spivery, who last season led the Hornets to the first SWAC championship and NCAA appearance in school history, hasn't had much free time on his hands lately. The reason: In May, Spivery took over as Alabama State's athletic director. "It's a lot of extra work, I'll tell you," Spivery said. "I've got a lot of extra duties. Basketball will be my refuge this season."... Alabama State ranked second in the nation behind Holy Cross in field-goal percentage

defense (.382) last season. ... Alabama State's loss to No. 1 seeded team Michigan State in the South Regional opening round game last year dropped to the SWAC to 4-21 all time in the NCAA Tournament. The SWAC's last NCAA Tournament win came in 1993 when Southern stunned Georgia Tech, 93-78. ... Alabama State ranked first in the league in average home attendance (2,659); Texas Southern ranked last (1,335). ... After this season, legendary Alcorn State Davey Whitney is calling it quits after 25 seasons and two separate stints on The Reservation. Whitney is the SWAC's all-time winningest coach. "I'd like to go out on top," Whitney said. ... Alcorn has won 40 of its last 44 games at home over the last four seasons. ... Grambling snapped Alcorn's 32-game home winning streak with a 76-74 win on Feb. 5. ... Alcorn is a league-best 44-10 in league play over the last three seasons. ... Jackson State was counting heavily on 6-8 forward Eric Chess this season. However, the Grand Rapids Community College standout didn't have enough credits to be eligible this season. Chess originally signed with Alcorn out of high school. "It's was a big blow for us," JSU coach Andy Stoglin said. ... Jackson State signee Tommie Hunter, brother of former JSU star and current Milwaukee Bucks guard Lindsey Hunter, was killed in a one-car accident in Bolton, MS., in June. A 5-11 guard, Tommie Hunter spent the early portion of the summer playing pickup games at JSU's Athletics and Assembly Center. ... Arkansas-Pine Bluff's Elander Holmes, a sophomore-to-be, was killed in a car accident on Father's Day. His father and brother were banged up but survived. "It was really a tragedy," UAPB coach Harold Blevins said. ... Prairie View guard Greg Burks, who suffered a season-ending knee injury in the Panthers' sixth game last season, is healthy once again. He's also put on 10 pounds of muscle thanks to his work with a personal trainer. ... Grambling's ancient Memorial Gym is still undergoing renovations, meaning the Tigers may play their home games at nearby Ruston High. ... Grambling coach Larry Wright has used the ties he established while as a scout for the Detroit Pistons to help bring players from Michigan into his program. Nearly half of the players on the Tigers' roster hail from the state of Michigan. ... Ben Jobe, who led Southern's program to rare heights in late 1980s and early 1990s, has been rehired. Jobe replaces Tommy Green, who replaced Jobe in August of 1996. Jobe is 68-years-old. ... Southern's Clark Activity Center is undergoing renovations meaning the Jaguars may have to play their home games at another site. ... Ronnie Courtney, a highly successful high school coach in Houston, replaces long-time coach Bob Moreland at Texas Southern. Courtney won two state titles and 100 games in four seasons at Sugarland Willowridge High. ... Nobody was happier to see the SWAC portion of the schedule arrive than the players and coaches around the league. The 10 SWAC teams had a combined record of 11-50 (a winning percentage of .180) heading into the first full weekend of conference play. Five teams were winless.

(M.A.)

didn't have any one player that struck fear in opponents.

"Our guards had to go out and play because we weren't getting any production down low," Pettaway said.

He hopes that changes this season in the return to form of 6-7 junior **Garik Nicholson** (6.7 ppg, 4.0 rpg) and 6-8 junior **Rodney Kellum** (2.2 ppg, 1.9 rpg).

"Hopefully those guys are going to play better for us this year," Pettaway said. "We need them to come on in order to help us be more physical in the paint. They both kind of went through a sophomore jinx last season.

"Garik did an admirable job, but we were expecting more out of him. He's got to provide some scoring, rebounding and defense for this team this season. Rodney needs to play big and give us a low scoring presence."

Another player Pettaway is counting on to do that is 6-7 sophomore **Otis Walker** (1.6 ppg, 0.9 rpg).

"He might be our most improved player over the summer," Pettaway said. "He's gotten bigger and stronger and it looks like he's out to contribute something this year. He's really stepped it up. We feel like he can get the job done. Last year he played like a freshman. He really wasn't focused. But we think he can be a big, physical presence for us."

Perhaps no coach in the league helped himself more in recruiting than did Pettaway. Newcomers include 6-4 junior swingman **Anthony Hayes**, 6-8 junior forward **Jarvis Smith**, 6-3 freshman guard **Ricky Ricketts** and 6-1 freshman guard **Jacques Curry**.

Pettaway expects Hayes, a Faulkner State transfer,

to start at small forward. He expects Smith, a Texas junior college transfer, to start at the four-spot.

"He's a highlight reel waiting to happen," Pettaway said. "He gets up and down the floor and can really jump. And Smith is tough."

Ricketts averaged 21 points per game at Atlanta's Dundwoody High last season.

"He's a hired gun," Pettaway said. "I had to bring a shooter in and he's the guy. I expect him to play a lot."

Curry, from Stratford, Tenn., averaged 26 points.

"I call him 'Mr. Tennessee,' " Pettaway said. "He'll play the one and the two as a freshman. I really like him. This kid can play.

"We feel like we've brought in some guys that are going to be able to help us right away. "We feel good about them. And we've got enough veterans. It's a good balance."

2001-2002 SCHEDULE

Nov.	17	Tuskegee
	24	@Detroit
	28	@Mississippi State
Dec.	1	Athens State
	15	@Jackson State
	17	@Grambling
	21	@Alabama
Jan.	5	Arkansas-Pine Bluff
	7	Mississippi Valley State
	12	@Alabama State
	14	@Savannah State
	19	@Southern
	21	@Alcorn A&M
	26	Prairie View A&M
	28	Texas Southern
	30	@Morris Brown
Feb.	2	@Arkansas-Pine Bluff
	4	@Mississippi Valley State
	9	Alabama State
	11	Savannah State
	16	Southern
	18	Alcorn State
	20	Morris Brown
	23	@Prairie View A&M
	25	@Texas Southern
	28	Jackson State
March	6-9	#SWAC Tournament

@Road Games
#Fair Park Arena, Birmingham, AL

BLUE RIBBON ANALYSIS

BACKCOURT	A
BENCH/DEPTH	B
FRONTCOURT	B-
INTANGIBLES	A

This is one of the most entertaining teams in the SWAC, definitely worth the price of admission. Why Alabama A&M continues to get picked low in the coaches' poll year after year remains a mystery. Maybe the coaches get just as confused when it comes time to vote as they do when they're trying to find ways to solve the wide variety of presses and traps thrown at them by the Bulldogs.

Alabama A&M has finished in the top three in the league the last two years and this year figures to be no different, especially with Cambridge at the controls. The key, as Pettaway pointed out, is improved shooting and improved post play. If the newcomers are good as advertised, the Bulldogs could be really dangerous come March. And this year, Cambridge and Co. won't be back home in Normal come SWAC Tournament time.

(M.A.)

Alabama State

LOCATION	Montgomery, AL
CONFERENCE	Southwestern Athletic
LAST SEASON	22-10 (.688)
CONFERENCE RECORD	15-3 (1st)
STARTERS LOST/RETURNING	1/4
NICKNAME	Hornets
COLORS	Gold & Black
HOMECOURT	Joe L. Reed Acadome (8,000)
COACH	Rob Spivery (Ashland '72)
RECORD AT SCHOOL	65-79 (5 years)
CAREER RECORD	239-224 (16 years)

ASSISTANTS	Joe Proctor (Memphis '71)
	Calvin Cochran (Tennessee-Chattanooga '83)
TEAM WINS (last 5 years)	9-8-11-13-22
RPI (last 5 years)	281-287-266-258-150
2000-01 FINISH	Lost in NCAA first round.

Alabama State began last season with three goals: win 20 games, win the Southwestern Athletic Conference regular season and go to the NCAA Tournament.

Those were lofty goals considering that before last season, the Hornets had never won a SWAC championship, much less gone to the NCAA Tournament.

Yet Alabama State was indeed able to accomplish all three of those goals and in the process created a basketball frenzy never before witnessed in Montgomery.

"It was a very exciting year to say the least," said Alabama State coach Rob Spivery, who is entering his sixth season. "It generated so much excitement and recognition to the university. I really didn't realize that our success would create so much interest. It's been overwhelming to see the joy and the excitement that everybody here has shown.

"And we were the only team in the state of Alabama in the NCAA Tournament so that added to the excitement and the exposure."

Alabama State had finished fifth in the conference two years ago and in a three-way tie for fourth in 2000. But Spivery knew he had a young team, and he was waiting for them to mature into champions. Last year was that year.

The Hornets, who were expecting big things with the return of all five starters, won a school-record 22 games games and lost just three times inside the conference.

"We knew that by the time our first class became seniors that we would be competitive," Spivery said. "That's how we had envisioned things. To watch it develop, to watch it all come together and be successful like that made it even more rewarding."

Back-to-back SWAC titles and NCAA Tournament appearances would be even more rewarding. And with four starters returning, including first-team All-SWAC forward Tyrone Levett and second-team All-SWAC center/forward Alvin Pettway, that's a distinct possibility. Spivery knows the expectations will be such.

"Rightfully so," Spivery said. "Any time you win the conference championship and you have four starters back the expectations at the beginning of the season are going to be very high. I'm sure there are a lot of people around here even more excited about the season, and so are our players. We've got most of the same players back, and they've got one more year of experience now. Plus, we think we've added some depth. So I feel like we've got a chance to be just as good or better than last year.

"If we can get our point-guard situation settled, and if some of our players come off the bench and play well, I feel like we've got a chance to be pretty good again."

The Hornets won with defense and balanced offense a year ago. They led the SWAC in scoring defense (64.4 ppg.), field-goal percentage defense (.385), three-point field-goal percentage defense (.308) and also ranked first in the league in field-goal percentage (.449).

Spivery would like to see his team score a few more points—Alabama State averaged 69 points per game. But don't expect a radical change in approach this season from the defensive-oriented Hornets.

"I don't see any reason why we should go away from that," Spivery said. "We might change up a few things because our point guards are different type players than what we had last year. They are a little bit quicker, a little bit more offensive-minded. So we'll have to make some adjustments accordingly. But we're still going to play good defense and, for the most part, run our offense through [Alvin] Pettway in the post.

Pettway, a 6-9 power forward/center, and 6-5 forward Levett form one of the most formidable 1-2 combinations in the SWAC. Levett, a senior, is one of the toughest players in the league to defend. He's also perhaps the most versatile player in the league. Levett ranked seventh in the league in scoring (16.3 ppg), seventh in free-throw percentage (.762), fourth in rebounding (8.3 rpg.) and recorded 10 double-doubles.

"You're talking about a guy who was our leading scorer and leading rebounder," Spivery said. "He's very versatile; he can score inside and he can score outside. He's a tremendous player."

Pettway, a junior, emerged last season as one of the best post players in the league. Some thought he was the best. Without a doubt Pettway is one of the strongest players in the league and is tough to stop once he gets the ball on the block. He ranked ninth in the league in scoring (14.5 ppg.) and second in field-goal percentage (.554).

"We went through him on the offensive end," Spivery said. "Our goal was to get it to him as much as possible. And the good thing about Alvin is that he'll throw it back out if it's not there for him. He's not selfish. His work ethic, his unselfishness and his determination make him a terrific player."

Michael Green, a 6-11 junior center, also returns after averaging two points and two rebounds per game last season.

"He's matured a lot," Spivery said.

A couple of players who need to step up on the front line include 6-7 senior Angel Branch and 6-7 sophomore Xavier Oliver. The two combined for just five points and five rebounds per game last season.

"Xavier played sparingly last season, but he's capable of helping us out in the paint," Spivery said. "He adds to our strength down low. And he's the best leaper on the team.

"Angel is a JUCO transfer who really didn't start to play like we thought he would play until the end of the season. People aren't really going to be thinking about him too much, so I think he can really surprise some people."

In 6-2 senior guard Joey Ball (10.8 ppg, 3.0 rpg) and 6-5 junior swingman Keith Gamble (10.1 ppg., 3.7 rpg.), Alabama State has a couple of the most athletic guard types in the league, although they are sometimes overshadowed by the exploits of Levett and Pettway.

"Joey is very explosive," Spivery said. "He's quick off the dribble, and he can score in a variety of ways. Plus, he's an excellent defensive player.

"And Keith is a threat from the outside, plus he can put the ball on the floor."

The biggest question is at point guard, where Spivery must replace four-year starter Tobarie Burton. Burton ranked first in the league in three-point field-goal percentage, second in steals, second in assist/turnover ratio and third in assists.

"He brought everything together for us," Spivery said. "Our chemistry went through him. He was a very good player over the time he was here. He didn't score a lot, but we didn't ask him to score a lot. He knew what his role was and he accepted that role. We're going to miss him."

The two players in the running to fill the void left behind by Burton are 5-11 sophomore Malcolm Campbell (2.4 ppg) and 5-11 sophomore Kevin Harris (1.6 ppg).

"They're a little smaller than Tobarie, but they're a little quicker," Spivery said. "And they should provide a little more scoring. It just depends on which one comes around. It's a matter of how they adjust. The question is which one of them will provide the leadership we're looking for out of that position."

Alabama State wasn't very deep last year—the five starters each averaged 30 minutes or more per game. Those minutes could be less this season if some of the newcomers can come in and contribute as Spivery expects.

One of the Hornets' top newcomers is 6-9 red-shirt freshman forward Derrick Russell, who sat out last season after a solid career at Benjamin Russell High in Alexander City, Ala.

"I really like him," Spivery said. "I like his athletic ability. As he gains experience he'll get better and better. He can be intimidating, blocking shots and that sort of thing. It's just hard to say how he's going to react to that first amount of playing time. But I feel like he can help us."

Other newcomers are 6-3 sophomore guard Johnny Mitchell and 6-5 sophomore swingman Lamar Clark.

Mitchell, a transfer from Murray State, won't be eligible until mid-December. The same is true for Clark, who transferred from a Texas junior college.

"Mitchell is an excellent scorer," Spivery said. "He gives us another deep threat. He's going to add a lot at the guard position.

"Lamar is a a tremendous athlete. He'll probably be the best athlete we have on our team. He can run and jump. He's not a great shooter, but he's good inside the arc."

2001-2002 SCHEDULE

Nov.	15	*Oregon
	16	*Long Beach State
	17	*Western Michigan
	24	Mobile
	28	Florida A&M
	30	#Hawkeye Challenge
Dec.	1	#Hawkeye Challenge
	5	Montevallo
	8	@Morris Brown
	15	@Grambling Stte

	17	@Jackson State
	22	Morris Brown
Jan.	2	@Birmingham Southern
	5	Mississippi Valley State
	7	Arkansas-Pine Bluff
	12	Alabama A&M
	19	@Alcorn State
	21	@Southern
	26	Texas Southern
	28	Prairie View A&M
Feb.	2	@Mississippi Valley State
	4	@Arkansas-Pine Bluff
	9	@Alabama A&M
	16	Alcorn State
	18	Southern
	23	@Texas Southern
	25	@Prairie View A&M
	28	Grambling State
March	2	Jackson State
	5-9	##SWAC Tournament

@Road Games
*America's Youth Classic, Eugene, OR
#Iowa City, IA (vs. Iowa first round; also LaSalle, SMU)
##Fair Park Arena, Birmingham, AL

BLUE RIBBON ANALYSIS

BACKCOURT	B
BENCH/DEPTH	C
FRONTCOURT	A
INTANGIBLES	A

Alabama State returns four starters, including two of the best players in the league in Levett and Pettway. It's hard to imagine the Hornets not competing for the league title again this season. Also, Alabama State is well coached and plays good defense—two good constants to fall back on. And last year's title will give Levett and Co. more confidence going into this season. The Hornets didn't know how to win games before, now they do. The biggest key is whether Spivery can find an able replacement for departed point guard Tobarie Burton, who meant more to last year's team than most people realized until late in the year.

Even with Burton, the Hornets had trouble scoring at times. Without him, will Levett and Pettway get the ball in the right spots on the floor at the right time to do their thing? One or more non-starters also have to step up. If not, Alabama State's bid to repeat could fall short, especially because Alcorn State and Alabama A&M figure to be better than last year.

(M.A.)

Alcorn State

LOCATION	**Lorman, MS**
CONFERENCE	**Southwestern Athletic**
LAST SEASON	**15-15 (.500)**
CONFERENCE RECORD	**13-5 (t-3rd)**
STARTERS LOST/RETURNING	**0/5**
NICKNAME	**Braves**
COLORS	**Purple & Gold**
HOMECOURT	**Davey L. Whitney Complex (7,000)**
COACH	**Davey Whitney (Kentucky State '53)**
RECORD AT SCHOOL	**475-264 (25 years)**
CAREER RECORD	**530-327 (30 years)**
ASSISTANTS	**Sammy West (Texas Southern '77)**
	Maurice Buie (Arkansas-Little Rock '99)
TEAM WINS (last 5 years)	**11-12-23-19-15**
RPI (last 5 years)	**247-269-114-187-215**
2000-01 FINISH	**Lost in conference final.**

Alcorn State finished tied for third in the Southwestern Athletic Conference last season. That might not be too bad for most programs. But when you're the league's two-time defending regular-season champion and picked to win a third as the Braves were entering the 2000-01 season, tied for third doesn't sound quite so good.

"Very disappointing," said Alcorn coach Dave Whitney, who is entering his 26th and final season on The Reservation. "The chemistry didn't come around until the last four of five games of the season. We had so many new players, they didn't understand their roles completely.

"But we came a long way from where we started [2-9] to where we finished [15-15]. We didn't fall off too far."

If Alcorn is to regain its spot atop the league standings and better its 0-9 non-conference mark, it will have to do a much better job of taking care of the basketball. The Braves averaged 19.2 turnovers per game—unheard of for Whitney-coached teams—and finished eighth in the league in assist/turnover ratio. **Marcus Fleming**, the team's leading scorer and rebounder, also led the team in turnovers with 110.

Never was the Braves' inability to take care of the ball more evident than in the SWAC Tournament championship game. Leading Alabama State by double digits early in the second half, Alcorn threw away its chance at a NCAA Tournament trip by committing one costly turnover after another down the stretch.

"They had 20 points off our turnovers in that game," Whitney said. "That was the difference between us winning and losing.

"Inconsistent guard play was our downfall all last season. Our assist-to-turnover ratio was too poor for us to be a consistent ball club. We've got to do a better job in that area."

Alcorn won its first six SWAC games and was sitting in first place until hitting a stretch where it lost four-of -six. The Braves regrouped after a 17-point home loss to Alabama State, winning five straight games before falling to the Hornets in the tournament final.

The outlook for the 2001-'02 season is bright, with all five starters (11 lettermen) returning. Fleming, who came to Alcorn as an academic non-qualifier, was listed as a senior a year ago. But thanks to the NCAA rule that allows non- as well as partial qualifiers to regain a fourth year of eligibility if the player graduates on time, Fleming is expected to return.

The 6-8, 215-pound Fleming led the Braves in scoring (16.7 ppg) and rebounding (7.7 rpg) and made the All-SWAC team for the second straight season.

"Marcus getting that year back is big," Whitney said. "I was a little disappointed overall in the year Marcus had last year. But he sees where he could've done a better job. And you've got to consider he didn't have the kind of help he needed. He thought he had to win it by himself and he started pressing. He won't have to do it by himself this year."

That's good news for the 71-year old Whitney, who would like to add one last SWAC championship to his resume in what will be his final season. And what a resume it is. Whitney, affectionately called the "Wiz," has compiled 530 wins, 11 SWAC regular-season titles, five conference tournament titles and five NCAA Tournament appearances.

In addition, he has won two games in the NCAA Tournament, including the first victory by a historically black college or university—Alcorn beat South Alabama in 1980. He earned even more notoriety for narrow losses to programs like Kansas, Stanford, Indiana and LSU in postseason play.

"I would certainly like to go out on top, no question," Whitney said. "It would be nice. But I would go into this season with the same philosophy whether I was going out or not. I want to win. I'm not going to place any more or any less emphasis on this season. It's not going to be any different."

Fleming will be joined on the front line by 6-8 senior center **Walter Harper**. A four-year starter, Harper averaged 9.3 points and 6.6 rebounds as a junior.

"He came back bigger and stronger," Whitney said. "He became a little more offensive-minded last year, but we're looking for him to be even more offensive-minded this year. We've got to get more points out of him. We're going to try to get the ball to him more."

Other returning baseline players are 6-6 junior forward **Brian Jackson** (10.6 ppg, 5.2 rpg), 6-8 senior forward **Larry Robinson** (2.0 rpg, 1.6 rpg) and 6-8 junior **Dion Callans** (2.4 ppg, 2.2 rpg).

Jackson sat out as a freshman but burst on the SWAC scene last year and emerged as one of the most versatile players in the league. He was arguably the SWAC's top sixth man.

"He's much bigger because he worked all summer in the LSU weight room," Whitney said. "Looking back on last season, Brian was a real pleasant surprise. He played extremely well. He did a tremendous job. I thought he should have been newcomer of the year in our league last year. I wouldn't be surprised if he started for us some this year."

Robinson was a big body if nothing else a year ago. He could play a bigger role this season, however.

"Much improved," Whitney said. "I don't know what he did this summer. He must have gone to see a scientist or something. I don't know. But he came back and all of a sudden is knocking down 12-14 footers."

Callans didn't get many minutes last season, but when he did get in the game he was active.

"He was thrown into a situation last year that he's never been thrown into before," Whitney said. "He showed some flashes of being a good player. He puts the ball on the floor well."

Alcorn's top returning guards are 6-2 junior **Jason Cable** (11.8 ppg, 2.9 rpg) and 6-4 junior **Tori Harris** (11.7 ppg, 4.4 rpg). Walk-on **Travis Norris** (2.8 ppg, 1.0 rpg) will also see some playing time.

"Jason is a streak shooter," Whitney said. "When he's on he can really shoot it. If we can get good point-guard play, get somebody to give him the ball at the proper time, I'm expecting him to really arrive this year. He's capable of having some 20-30-point scoring nights."

"Tori's going to have to work real hard to keep his spot. We're even looking at possibly moving him to the two-spot. He shoots the ball pretty well, but he's a streak shooter, too."

Junior point guard **Jeff Cammon** (3.6 ppg, 2.1 rpg), 5-11, also returns but will be hard pressed to keep his job because of an influx of talented newcomers at that position.

"He's really going to have to step up," Whitney said. "He's been an overachiever.

"Our point guard wasn't stable last year. That was the biggest weakness we had. That contributed to the inconsistency. But we hope we solved that problem."

One of the players looking to take Cammon's spot is freshman **Corey Jackson**. The 6-2 Jackson averaged 20.2 points, seven rebounds and 6.7 assists last season at Dulles High in Houston, Texas.

"He's going to cause all kinds of problems for people," Whitney said. "He's going to be a real surprise. He's so quick. And he can shoot it, he can penetrate, he plays solid defense and he loves to push the ball up the floor."

Other guard newcomers are 6-4 freshman **Quentin Fairman** of Maret High in Washington, D.C., and 6-3 junior **Rudy Bell**, a transfer from East Central (Miss.) Community College.

Fairman averaged 20 points, 10 rebounds and five assists. He'll play both guard spots.

"He's not as quick as Jackson, but he's a solid basketball player," Whitney said.

Bell averaged 14 points and four assists last season.

"I'll tell you what, this kid can run all day," Whitney said. "And he can jump. Man, can he jump. He's got a 42 or 43 inch vertical."

The Braves will also welcome newcomers **Lee Cook**, a 6-10 player who can play three positions, 6-6 junior small forward **Steven Wallace** and 6-5 guard **Miles Howard**.

Cook, who sat out last year, could have as much impact as any newcomer in the league. He averaged 25.5 points, 7.8 rebounds and five blocks at Benson High in Omaha, Neb., two years ago.

"There's no doubt, he could be our best player if he adjusts to what we're trying to do," Whitney said. "He runs the floor well, he's got extremely good hands and he jumps well. He's just got to get in basketball shape and learn our offense."

Wallace red-shirted last season after getting injured early on. Two years ago, he averaged 17.2 points and six rebounds per game at Olive-Harvey Junior College in Chicago.

"He could help us," Whitney said.

Whitney found Howard—a Syracuse transfer who is attending school on a football scholarship—in the intramural gym.

"He can really jump," Whitney said. "He can touch the top of the square."

No doubt, with Cook and Co., Whitney will have one of the tallest teams in the SWAC. He also has one of the most experienced.

"We'll be much stronger next season," Whitney said. "I'm excited about this ball club. We've got a lot of depth, and we're bigger than we've ever been. We've got three or four 6-8s, a couple of 6-7s and a 6-10, and our guards are going to be big. We've got a lot of talent. Now a lot of coaches don't like to say that, but we do.

"We'll be a much more offensive-minded ball club, and I don't expect our defense to suffer. And these kids have come back hungry. We'll be right there."

2001-2002 SCHEDULE

Nov.	19	@New Mexico State
	27	@Southern Miss
Dec.	1	@New Mexico
	10	@Hawaii
	15	@Prairie View A&M
	17	@Texas Southern
	27-29	#Minnesota Winter Jam
Jan.	5	Jackson State
	7	Grambling State
	12	@Mississippi Valley State

	14	@Arkansas-Pine Bluff
	19	Alabama State
	21	Alabama A&M
	23	@Morris Brown
	26	@Southern
	28	@UTEP
Feb.	2	@Jackson State
	4	@Grambling
	9	Mississippi Valley State
	11	Arkansas-Pine Bluff
	16	@Alabama State
	18	@Alabama A&M
	23	Southern
	25	Morris Brown
	28	Texas Southern
March	2	Prairie View A&M
	7-9	##SWAC Tournament

@Road Games
#Minneapolis, MN (also Morgan State, Norfolk State, Texas Southern)
##Fair Park Arena, Birmingham, AL

BLUE RIBBON ANALYSIS

BACKCOURT	B
BENCH/DEPTH	B
FRONTCOURT	A
INTANGIBLES	A

Alcorn has assembled so much talent on The Reservation that Whitney is hedging on his pending retirement. The conventional pick in the SWAC this year is defending champ Alabama State, but don't be surprised to see the Braves holding the trophy come March. Alcorn didn't have that great of a team last year and still came within one second-half collapse of making it back to the NCAA Tournament.

And this year, Whitney has many more weapons at his disposal. He'll also have one of if not the tallest teams in the league. Cook, who has been dominant in pickup games, is a big addition. The key is whether one of the newcomers can step in and perform at point guard. If so, Alcorn can send Whitney out in appropriate fashion—as a winner.

(M.A.)

Arkansas-Pine Bluff

LOCATION	Pine Bluff, AR
CONFERENCE	Southwestern Athletic
LAST SEASON	2-25 (.074)
CONFERENCE RECORD	2-16 (10th)
STARTERS LOST/RETURNING	2/3
NICKNAME	Golden Lions
COLORS	Black & Gold
HOMECOURT	HYPER Complex (8,000)
COACH	Harold Blevins (UAPB '65)
RECORD AT SCHOOL	34-121 (6 years)
CAREER RECORD	34-121 (6 years)
ASSISTANTS	Van Holt (Arkansas AM&N '70)
	Lamong Daniels (Portland '96)
TEAM WINS (last 5 years)	10-4-3-6-2
RPI (last 5 years)	NA-NA-309-312-319
2000-01 FINISH	Lost in conference first round.

Last season, Arkansas-Pine Bluff was eligible to play in the Southwestern Athletic Conference Tournament for the first time since rejoining the league four years ago.

Not that it mattered. Only the top eight teams in the league played in the tournament and the Golden Lions finished last. Matter of fact, UAPB not only finished last in the league, it was also the worst Division I-A team in the country according to the final RPI. That's right, No. 319.

"It was definitely not the year we were looking for," UAPB coach Harold Blevins said.

How bad was it? UAPB won just two games—by a combined margin of six points—and finished last in the league in scoring (61.5 ppg.), scoring margin (-23.1) free-throw percentage (.588), field-goal percentage defense (.473), three-point field goal percentage (.361.), rebound margin (-8.3) and assist/turnover ratio.

The Golden Lions were next to last in the league in field-goal percentage (.368) and three-point field-goal percentage (.276). They scored 56 points or less nine times, including a season-low 40 points in a 85-40 loss to Baylor.

Considering it was UAPB's sixth straight losing sea-

son in as many years under Blevins, rumors circulated around the league that he might be on his way out. Instead, he returned for a seventh season.

"We tried not to look at last year as a total loss," said Blevins, who saw his team lose five games by six points or less. "We were in a lot of games, we just couldn't drive down that final nail. A couple of baskets here, a couple of baskets there, and we win a few more games. We didn't have a point guard that could spread the floor and make things happen down the stretch. It's hard for us to get over that hump right now. Hopefully it will get better.

"We're fighting a battle not in our control. We need more talented players to compete. But we're going to keep fighting. We're not going to back out of this thing. We've just got to quit making mistakes at crucial times, and we've got to be able to shoot the ball better."

To that end, Blevins once again sought shooters while out on the recruiting trail. He did the same thing last year, and thought he had helped his situation. Two of the three guards he signed combined for 12 points per game, but they didn't have the type of impact Blevins was seeking. The third is no longer on the team.

"We tried to recruit some help to help fill some of the voids we have," Blevins said.

The good news is that Blevins isn't starting from scratch like a year ago, when he had to replace 10 players who had accounted for nearly 50 points and 25 rebounds. He did lose second-leading scorer Michael Vickers, but seven lettermen and two starters return.

Any conversation about UAPB beings with **Jeremy Jefferson**. The 6-7 senior forward led the Golden Lions in scoring (12.3 ppg) and rebounding (10.7 rpg). He was the only player in the SWAC to average a double-double, and he tied for the league-lead in that category with 14. This despite the fact that he's often matched up against taller players down low.

Perhaps the best leaper in the league, Jefferson ranked 15th in the league in scoring, first in rebounding, fifth in blocked shots (1.30 bpg) and sixth in field-goal percentage (.491). He scored a season-high 25 points against Arkansas-Little Rock and hauled down a season-high 17 rebounds in UAPB's 67-64 win over Southern University.

Jefferson missed the last three games of last season with an ankle injury, but he is back and primed for a big senior season.

"In my opinion he's one of the top five players in this league," Blevins said. "He can be a dominating player in the SWAC when he performs up to his capabilities. That's just the kind of player he is. Obviously, we've got a lot riding on him. He'll be a very important part of whatever success we may have."

So too will point guard **Thaddeaus Hackworth**. The 6-0 senior averaged 7.2 points, 2.7 rebounds and 2.3 assists last season in his first year in a Golden Lion uniform. Hackworth led UAPB in scoring five times, including a season-high 18 points against Alabama State.

"He's going to be our leader," Blevins said. "He's got a lot of talent. I thought he was a little better shooter than what he showed last season, but I think it's just a matter of him regaining some confidence. He really started to come on at the end of last year, so we're looking for a big year out of him."

Other returning forwards include 6-6 junior **Charles Almond** (3.9 ppg, 2.0 rpg), 6-7 sophomore **Arlondo Holder** (1.0 ppg, 1.2 rpg), 6-7 junior **Justin Loyd** (0.6 ppg, 0.8 rpg) and 6-9 senior **Corey Williams** (0.5 ppg, 1.3 rpg). Almond is expected to start at small forward.

"He's a big kid," Blevins said. "He didn't perform the way we thought he would when we recruited him. But this is his third year, and he showed some signs last year. He can shoot it a little. He's going to help us.

"Holder will, too. He'll play just because of his size. He's a little thin but he runs the floor well. He's got some skills."

Antwan Emsweller, who started at center last season, won't be eligible the first semester. Blevins hopes to have his big man back the second semester. The chiseled 6-8 junior averaged 7.7 points and 5.7 rebounds per game last season.

"He's in school," Blevins said. "We should have him the second semester. You talk about a talented young man."

Other returning guards include 6-3 sophomore **Brandon Jones** (7.3 ppg, 1.3 rpg), 6-3 sophomore **Billy Hall** (5.1 ppg, 1.2 rpg), 6-4 senior **James Williams** (1.5 ppg, 0.7 rpg) and 6-1 senior **Wesley Norris** (1.3 ppg, 0.9 rpg).

Jones had a career-high 25 points in UAPB's 67-64 win over Southern. He was slowed the first part of the season by foot problems, but played better the second half.

"He gained some valuable experience last year,"

Blevins said. "I feel like he's a better shooter than he showed."

Hall's brightest moment was a 15-point outing at Alabama State.

"I'm looking for him to play some ball this year," Blevins said.

Williams didn't play much a year ago, but that could change this season. Norris also should see more playing time.

"It's our fault he [Williams] didn't play more," Blevins said. "He can score. I expect him to push Almond at the three-spot.

"We brought Norris in last year to run the point, but he never really came around like we expected."

Blevins brought in five newcomers—**Mik Balance**, a 6-2 junior guard from Northeast Missouri Community College; **Lamaquis Blake**, a 5-11 guard from Melbourne (Fla.) High; **Don Fleming**, a 6-6 junior from New Mexico Community College; **Kory McKee**, a 6-7 junior from Hinds (Miss.) Community College; and **Clifford Washington**, a 6-1 junior guard from Labette (Kansas) Community Colllege.

Blevins says Balance is "a shooter" who will "bring some shooting to the table."

Blake averaged 19 points per game.

"He's a small guy, but he's a talent," Blevins said. "It's unreal how he can shoot it."

Fleming averaged 12 points and six rebounds last season.

"He's a nice basketball player," Blevins said. "He's so smooth it looks like he's not working hard. But he'll rebound for us. He's going to be the man."

McKee's forte is rebounding, Blevins said.

Washington averaged 16 points, five rebounds and five assists as a sophomore.

"He's going to be Mr. Excitement coming into the SWAC," Blevins said. "I really like him. There's no doubt he's going to be a good player. We've got Jones penciled in at No. 2, but there's no way he's going to hold that. I've never seen a guard his size that can tomahawk dunk the way he does.

"These five kids we brought in, on paper at least, all are capable of scoring. They're all going to play a lot of basketball for us."

Blevins hopes it's good enough to help his team avoid another disastrous season like last year.

"I think we've got a good mix," Blevins said. "We're hoping that we'll be a much basketball team than last season. We're looking to kick the door in. The main thing we've got to do is improve our shooting and cut back on the mistakes. Those are the two areas that hurt us severely. We've got to be able to knock down the open jump shot."

2001-2002 SCHEDULE

Nov.	17	@Colorado
	19	@Wyoming
	21	@Arkansas State
	24	@Arkansas-Little Rock
	29	@Gonzaga
Dec.	1	@Washington State
	4	@Iowa State
	6	@Drake
	15	@Mississippi Valley State
	19	@Marquette
	29	@Ole Miss
Jan.	5	@Alabama A&M
	7	@Alabama State
	12	Southern
	14	Alcorn State
	19	@Prairie View A&M
	21	@Texas Southern
	26	Grambling State
	28	Jackson State
Feb.	2	Alabama A&M
	4	Alabama State
	9	@Southern
	11	@Alcorn State
	16	Prairie View A&M
	18	Texas Southern
	23	@Grambling
	25	@Jackson State
March	2	Mississippi Valley State
	5-9	#SWAC Tournament

@Road Games
#Fair Park Arena, Birmingham, AL

BLUE RIBBON ANALYSIS

BACKCOURT	C+
BENCH/DEPTH	C-

FRONTCOURT	C
INTANGIBLES	D

Arkansas-Pine Bluff figures to be better, especially if the five newcomers are as good as advertised. But the question is, how much better? The Golden Lions are quickly becoming to SWAC basketball what Prairie View is to SWAC football.

The league figures to be better this year, making UAPB's mission even harder. A move to the middle of the pack in the league would have to be considered a success. A more likely scenario: Another finish at or near the bottom of the league.

If so, school officials will be hard-pressed to bring Blevins back for another season. The Golden Lions are a scrappy bunch, but the talent just isn't there for them to compete. Some people try to make basketball more complicated than it really is. You still have to put the ball in the basket, and UAPB has problems doing that.

(M.A.)

 **Grambling**

LOCATION	Grambling, LA
CONFERENCE	Southwestern Athletic
LAST SEASON	8-18 (.308)
CONFERENCE RECORD	7-11 (t-5th)
STARTERS LOST/RETURNING	1/4
NICKNAME	Tigers
COLORS	Black & Gold
HOMECOURT	Memorial Gym (4,000)
COACH	Larry Wright (Grambling '75)
RECORD AT SCHOOL	9-48 (2 years)
CAREER RECORD	9-48 (2 years)
ASSISTANTS	Theodia Johnson (Grambling '78)
	Willie Simmons (Grambling '78)
TEAM WINS (last 5 years)	10-16-6-1-8
RPI (last 5 years)	282-230-299-318-287
2000-01 FINISH	Lost in conference first round.

Memorial Gymnasium isn't the only thing on Grambling's campus undergoing renovations these days. So too is the men's basketball team that calls the aging building home.

Two years ago—in coach Larry Wright's first season—Grambling won just one game. Last year, the Tigers—led mostly by players Wright brought into the program after that initial dismal season—won eight games. It's a small step in rebuilding the program, but at least it's a start.

"We feel pretty good about it, although we're certainly not satisfied," said Wright, a former Grambling star in the mid-1970s who went on to play in the NBA. "We were able to win a few more games and we showed that we can compete with some of the top teams in the league. That's a step we wanted to take. But we've still got a long way to go before we get this program where we want it.

"That first year was like a wasted year, really. Last year we were unable to bring in what you would call our players. And the kids responded well. Now we're back at it again. We feel like we should be better this year because these players have one year under their belts together."

After finishing last in the Southwestern Athletic Conference (1-30 overall, 0-18 in league play), Grambling jumped to a tie for fifth along with in-state rival Southern U. Armed with more athletic personnel, last year's Tigers looked nothing like the slow-the-pace, milk-the-clock team of the previous year. Wright ran players in and out, pressed at times, and loosened the reigns, making for a much more enjoyable brand of basketball.

Grambling ranked third in the league in scoring (75.1 ppg) and third in the league in three-pointers made per game (6.08). Four players averaged double figures; two more averaged nine points.

"That's the style we like to play," Wright said. "The kids like it because it gives them a chance to show off their athleticism. We recruit players who fit that style and we work hard to get in shape so that we can play uptempo."

Like most teams in the SWAC, Grambling struggled out of the gate against upper Division I teams. The Tigers lost by 46 at Alabama, 44 at Auburn, 37 at Georgetown and 55 at Arkansas. There's a reason, other than the money, those games are called "guarantee games."

That struggle continued in the early portion of SWAC play. The Tigers started 1-6, a stretch that was capped by an embarrassing 66-53 home loss to Jackson State.

Making matters worse, or so it seemed at the time, was the fact that William Howell and Julius Hall were lost that night—Howell to academics, Hall to an ankle injury. Howell and Hall were averaging 23 points between them.

The Tigers then won seven of their next eight games, including an eye-opening 76-74 win at Alcorn—snapping the Braves' 32-game home winning streak—and a 107-84 win over Mississippi Valley State.

"Maybe I should've been playing some of those other guys all along," Wright said with a laugh. "When those two guys went down the other guys on the team picked their games up.

"That [Alcorn] was a big win. It's not easy going into Alcorn and winning. That was major because it gave our kids a lot of confidence. Our guys think they can win anywhere now."

Grambling lost its last four games, including a disappointing 85-68 loss to Southern in the opening round of the SWAC Tournament. However, the mid-season success is something Wright can build on.

"That run we had showed our kids something," Wright said. "It showed them that if they keep working hard, good things will happen."

Grambling's best player was 6-7 freshman **Paul Haynes**, who led the Tigers in scoring (13.9 ppg) and rebounding (5.9 rpg). He scored 23 points in his first college game against Alabama, 22 in his second game against Auburn and went on to become the SWAC's Freshman of the Year.

"Here's a kid who led us in scoring and rebounding as a freshman," Wright said. "He had to come in and play right away, and he responded well to that challenge. He loves the game. Paul shoots the ball well, and he's very versatile. He can stay out on the perimeter or he can go inside."

Another newcomer who contributed greatly to the cause was junior **William McDonald**. The 6-9 McDonald averaged 9.6 points and 5.4 rebounds per game and ranked second in the league in blocked shots with 62 as a sophomore. He was selected the SWAC's Newcomer of the Year.

"That was the type of year we expected him to have," Wright said. "We felt like he the athletic ability to get the job done. He's about 6-9, he runs the floor well, he can block shots and he's got a nice jump hook."

Other returning frontcourt players include 6-4 junior **Randy Hymes** (9.1 ppg, 6.0 rpg), 6-5 junior **Gershone Jesse** (4.0 ppg, 4.3 rpg), 6-7 junior **Jarrod Jones** (1.9 ppg, 1.4 rpg) and 6-4 **Ashico Wilson** (0.0 ppg, 0.0 rpg).

Hymes and Jesse play football and won't join the team until their season is over. Hymes, a quarterback, is the best athlete on Grambling's campus and one of the league's top leapers. He led the league in field-goal percentage last season (.574).

"Randy's very athletic," Wright said. "He gives us a lot of different things when he's out there on the floor. We're looking forward to the day those guys join us."

Forward Keith Howell, who averaged 10.2 points per game, transferred to Texas-Arlington.

"He said he wanted to be closer to home," Wright said.

The Tigers' sparkplug is **Nick Mitchell**. The 5-10 junior averaged 6.1 points, 2.3 rebounds and three assists per game last season. It was Mitchell's runner in the lane in the waning seconds that gave Grambling a 83-82 win at Jackson State.

"He as the guy that fueled the fire," Wright said. "He was our leader on the floor, the one who made us go. Nick initiated our offense and defense. He did a great job, and we're expecting the same type of things from him this year."

Other returning guards include 6-4 sophomore **Paris Bernard** (4.7 ppg, 1.7 rpg); 6-2 sophomore **Darius Whiteside** (3.3 ppg, 1.3 rpg); 6-3 freshman **Ronald Ellis** (medical red-shirt); and 6-3 sophomore **Terry Russ** (1.0 ppg, 0.5 rpg).

"We're looking for Paris to really step up and play the way we know he can," Wright said. "He can shoot it. And he's a hard worker. We're probably going to play 10 people and I expect him to be in that number."

Ellis broke his wrist against Alabama and red-shirted.

"He [Ellis] was doing a great job for us before he got hurt," Wright said. "He had won a starting job. The injury doesn't seem to have slowed him down much. If he can regain form, that will really help us out."

The Haynes or McDonald of this year for Grambling could be newcomer **Jamel Goodin**, a talented 6-6, 240-pound junior forward who sat out last year after transferring from Southeastern Iowa Community College.

"He's a mixture of power and finesse," Wright said. "He can play inside and outside. We're getting a quality player with him. He's going to help us from a physical

standpoint. Jamel will more than make up for what we lost."

Other newcomers are 6-1 junior combo guard **Nick Hall** from Lee (Texas) Community College; 6-8 freshman forward **Steve Taylor** from Centennial High in Atlanta; and 5-11 junior guard **Rashad Moore** from Pontiac Northern.

"Hall is an athlete," Wright said. "Taylor, he's not there yet, but he gives us another 6-8 kid. And Moore's a kid that sat out last year. He's got potential."

Wright has a fairly young team, one that will have to improve on defense if it hopes to bring Grambling its first SWAC title since 1989. The Tigers ranked last in the league in defense (85.6 ppg) and next-to-last in field-goal percentage defense (.467).

It should be noted that Grambling did rank second in the league in steals (8.69 spg) and second in blocked shots (4.19).

"We have to be more physical inside where people won't just be able to push us around," Wright said. "I don't really know how everything's going to shake out. It should be an interesting year. All we can do is control Grambling, though. That's the attitude we're taking. Right now we're in the middle of the pack. I'd like for us to hold our ground and maybe improve some."

2001-2002 SCHEDULE

Nov.	17	Wiley College
	19	@Tulsa
	26	@Georgetown
	29	@Creighton
Dec.	1	@Missouri
	8	Northwestern Louisiana
	15	Alabama State
	17	Alabama A&M
	21	Arkansas-Little Rock
	30	@Virginia
Jan.	5	@Southern
	7	@Alcorn State
	12	Prairie View A&M
	14	Texas Southern
	19	@Jackson State
	26	@Arkansas Pine Bluff
	28	@Mississippi Valley State
Feb.	2	Southern
	4	Alcorn State
	9	@Prairie View A&M
	11	@Texas Southern
	16	Jackson State
	23	Arkansas Pine Bluff
	25	Mississippi Valley State
	28	@Alabama State
March	2	@Alabama A&M
	5-9	#SWAC Tournament

@Road Games
#Fair Park Arena, Birmingham, AL

BLUE RIBBON ANALYSIS

BACKCOURT	B
BENCH/DEPTH	B-
FRONTCOURT	C+
INTANGIBLES	C

Grambling was one of the surprise teams in the league last year. No team was hotter in February. Wright, without question, has upgraded the talent level on this team.

Haynes is a nice player, McDonald is super athletic, as is Hymes. Mitchell showed he's quite capable of running the point, too.

This is still a young team lacking in size. And the loss of Howell and seniors Devin Ewing and Michael Daniels will hurt. The Tigers had a nice balance and nice chemistry last season. The key will be to regain those ingredients and maintain them. Picking up the defensive intensity is also a must.

The keys here could be Goodin and Ellis. If Goodin is as good as advertised, he and McDonald could form a good 1-2 punch down low. Haynes needs some help on the perimeter, and that's where Ellis comes in.

(M.A.)

 **Jackson State**

LOCATION	Jackson, MS
CONFERENCE	Southwestern Athletic

LAST SEASON	7-23 (.233)
CONFERENCE RECORD	7-11 (7th)
STARTERS LOST/RETURNING	0/5
NICKNAME	Tigers
COLORS	Blue & White
HOMECOURT	Assembly Cener (8,000)
COACH	Andy Stoglin (UTEP '65)
RECORD AT SCHOOL	178-179 (12 years)
CAREER RECORD	211-202 (14 years)
ASSISTANTS	Chris Giles (UAB '82)
	Eric Stothers (JSU '91)
TEAM WINS (last 5 years)	14-14-16-17-7
RPI (last 5 years)	200-227-205-214-294
2000-01 FINISH	Lost in conference first round.

The 2000-2001 season won't go down as one to remember for Jackson State.

The Tigers started the season by losing a school-record 16 consecutive games and finished 7-23 overall and 7-12 in the Southwestern Athletic Conference. It was JSU's worst record since a 6-24 mark in 1982-83.

This just one season removed from a SWAC Tournament title and NCAA Tournament trip. The Tigers' three leading scorers and leading rebounder from that team were no longer around, leaving coach Andy Stoglin with a depleted deck.

Stoglin and his staff figured they were in for a long year, and they were right. Complicating matters even more: Starting guards Roy Dixon (ankle) and Eric Large (knee) missed most of the season because of injuries.

Not only was JSU lacking a presence of any kind in the post, it also lacked perimeter shooters. The Tigers ranked seventh in the league in three-point field-goal percentage (.300), last in three-pointers made per game (3.63) and finished the season ranked eighth in scoring at 67.1 points per game. They scored 61 points or fewer 10 times, including a season-low 48 points on Dec. 16 at Alabama State. The Tigers' best outside shooter was a walk-on who made most of his three-pointers at home—the majority of which came on the same goal.

To their credit, JSU scratched and clawed on the defensive end, and during one stretch actually won four-of-six games. Included in that stretch was an impressive 70-53 win against eventual champion Alabama State.

"We were one of the best defensive teams in the league last season, but we couldn't score," said Stoglin, entering his 13th season. "We didn't have any shooters."

With virtually every player returning, including leading scorer and rebounder Richard Bradley, and a host of talented newcomers ready to join the mix, the Tigers should be a much-improved team in 2001-02. And yes, they should have more outside scoring punch.

"There's no question," Stoglin said. "I'll have shooters this year, maybe the best group of shooters I've ever had."

Those shooters will need to come through big time for a couple of reasons. First, Stoglin—in the final year of a two-year contract—finds himself on the hot seat once again. It's no secret that he probably has to won and win big this year to keep his job. Second, JSU will again be without a true big man. The Tigers' top recruit—6-8 Eric Chess, who averaged 19 points and 14 rebounds last season at Grand Rapids (Mich.) Community College—failed to meet eligibility requirements.

"We were really counting on him to give us that inside presence that we didn't have last year," Stoglin said. "Now we still don't have it. We've got a real shortage of big men."

As for his job security?

"My job is on the line," Stoglin said. "I know I have to win this year. My back is up against the wall, but with the players I have, I feel good about my situation."

Much of Stoglin's optimism surrounds the development of several key returnees and three players who sat out last season—guards Tim Henderson, Damion Smith and Reggie Taylor.

Combined, the three guards averaged 63 points per game two years ago—just four less than JSU averaged as a team last season.

"Those three guys can play for anybody," Stoglin said. "They can all play in the SEC. They're that good. We've had problems shooting the ball. That's solved. People don't know what we have here."

Henderson, an explosive 6-2 junior swingman, signed with JSU out of Coahoma (Miss.) Community College, where he averaged 21.5 points and five rebounds per game. A first-team All-North pick, Henderson ranked among the scoring leaders in Mississippi's junior college league.

Smith, a 6-2 combo guard, averaged 27.5 points as a junior and a senior at Spearsville, (La.) High.

Taylor, a 6-0 point guard, averaged 14.1 points and 4.2 assists as a senior at Brandon (Miss.) High despite

playing most of the season on a sore ankle. He was a two-time All-Metro selection.

"I've never had three guys together that can shoot, play defense and have the instincts that those three guys have," Stoglin said.

The addition of Henderson, Smith and Taylor should take some of the load off Bradley, who was forced into a starring role last year. The 6-4 senior responded, leading JSU in scoring (15.3 ppg) and rebounding (8.0 rpg). He played mostly at the three spot and improved his perimeter skills, although he is better suited to play the four spot despite his lack of size.

No returning player in the league is harder to keep off the offensive boards—Bradley ranked second in the league with 3.43 offensive rebounds per game.

"Richard was our offense in some games last year, and that was with two people on him at times," Stoglin said. "We'll probably move him back to the four-spot this season, and I expect him to be even more effective there. With Tim and Damion, teams aren't going to be able to double Richard any more."

Other returnees along the front line are 6-9 senior Brian Nichols (5.4 ppg, 3.4 rpg), 6-5 sophomore Cliff Walker (6.4 ppg, 5.9 rpg), 6-7 senior Roy Maxwell (3.9 ppg, 2.0 rpg) and 6-5 senior Cedric Gilbert (0.9 ppg, 0.7 rpg). Kelly Ross (6-8, 225), who red-shirted last season, will also see some playing time.

One player Stoglin was counting on down low, 6-7, 240-pound junior Leonard Taylor (3.1 ppg, 3.1 rpg), didn't return.

Walker isn't a big scorer, but is a decent rebounder and can shoot the ball from 16-17 feet.

"He really came on last year and turned into one of my top players," Stoglin said.

Maxwell, a Grambling transfer, is one of the most athletic players on the team. He showed signs of being a good player last year, although he needs to toughen up.

"He runs the floor like a guard," Stoglin said. "He could be one of our best players. He has the ability ... he's real quick and athletic. He just didn't play very smart last season."

As for the guards? Heck, Stoglin's got more guards than President Bush. Returnees include 6-3 senior Raymond Appleberry (10.2 ppg, 3.7 rpg), 5-11 senior Kendell Noel (9.7 ppg, 1.6 rpg), 6-1 senior Eric Large (6.7 ppg, 2.8 rpg), 6-3 sophomore John Chandler (6.2 ppg, 0.8 rpg), and 5-11 senior Lawrence Myers (1.8 ppg, 1.5 rpg).

Appleberry, a track standout, emerged as the Tigers' second-leading scorer after becoming eligible in mid-December. He excels in the open floor and is a good finisher. His best game was a 20-point performance in the Tigers' 66-53 win at Grambling.

Noel, who has a knack for creating his own shot on an array of slashing moves and pull-up jumpers, was perhaps JSU's biggest surprise last season.

"The thing about Kendell was we didn't know how to use him," Stoglin said. "We didn't know how good he was until late in the season. He was kind of nonchalant in practice, and really had a hard time picking up on things we were trying to do. But he's very talented. He's got instincts you can't teach. I think he's one of the best guards in the conference."

Large came to JSU highly regarded but has been plagued by injuries throughout his career. Two years ago, he missed most of the season with a hip injury and last year was slowed by hip and knee injuries. When he's healthy, Large can be pretty good, as evidenced by his 21-point scoring night at Arkansas and 22-point performance three nights later against Arkansas State.

"If we had had Roy [Dixon] and Eric [Large] healthy last season we might have won five or six more games," Stoglin said. "Eric's capable of being a leader, we just need for him to stay healthy for an entire season."

Chandler is the aforementioned walk-on, who as it turned out has one of the sweetest shooting strokes in the SWAC. The left-hander hit six three-pointers for a game-high 18 points in a home win over Arkansas-Pine Bluff and later connected on four three-pointers in a home win over Prairie View.

"When he's on he can really shoot it," Stoglin said.

Myers started at point guard the majority of the season, although he didn't play as well as he did the year before.

One player who figures to push for playing time at the point guard spot is junior Robin Lucas. A terrific penetrator, the 6-1 Lucas averaged 14 points and six assists a year ago at East Central (Mo.) Junior College.

"He's going to play a great deal," Stoglin said.

With so much depth at guard, Stoglin plans to press and run more, a la Arkansas. Stoglin has spent a lot of time picking the brain of Arkansas coach and good friend Nolan Richardson on the finer points of the Razorbacks'

famed "40 minutes of hell" attack.

"Half of my phone bill this summer was from talking to him so much," Stoglin said with a laugh. "We're going to get after people. We're going to press from the get-go. I think we have to with what we have. It would be a mistake not to.

"And I'm going to let these guys shoot it, We're going to play up-tempo. This will be the most fun to watch team that I've ever had."

2001-2002 SCHEDULE

Nov.	17	@Southern Miss
	21	Stephen F. Austin
	26	Arkansas State
	29	@Missouri
Dec.	1	Louisiana Tech
	5	McNeese State
	8	@Oklahoma State
	15	Alabama A&M
	17	Alabama State
	22	@Louisiana Tech
	29	@UAB
Jan.	5	@Alcorn State
	7	@Southern
	12	Texas Southern
	14	Prairie View A&M
	19	Grambling
	26	@Mississippi Valley State
	28	@Arkansas-Pine Bluff
Feb.	2	Alcorn State
	4	Southern
	9	@Texas Southern
	11	@Prairie View A&M
	16	@Grambling
	23	Mississippi Valley State
	25	Arkansas-Pine Bluff
	28	@Alabama A&M
March	2	@Alabama State
	5-9	#SWAC Tournament

@Road Games
#Fair Park Arena, Birmingham, AL

BLUE RIBBON ANALYSIS

BACKCOURT	A
BENCH/DEPTH	B
FRONTCOURT	C
INTANGIBLES	B

As Stoglin said, this will be a fun team to watch. Henderson, who could make a run for newcomer of the year in the league, is a very explosive player who will make a big difference.

With Henderson at three and Bradley at four, JSU has two of the better players in the league at their respective positions. The key is whether Smith, Lucas or Taylor play as well as advertised.

Stoglin is making the right move in cutting this team loose. The Tigers played a halfcourt, slow-it-down brand of basketball last season that wasn't very effective. Besides, what does he have to lose? The loss of Chess hurt, although JSU should be all right on most nights as the SWAC is more of a guard league than a big man league.

Against the likes of Alcorn and Alabama State, the lack of a big man could be a deciding factor, however. JSU could make some noise this season. The question is, will it be enough noise for Stoglin to return for a 14th season?

(M.A.)

Mississippi Valley State

LOCATION	Itta Bena, MS
CONFERENCE	Southwestern Athletic
LAST SEASON	18-9 (.666)
CONFERENCE RECORD	14-4 (2nd)
STARTERS LOST/RETURNING	3/2
NICKNAME	Delta Devils
COLORS	Green & White
HOMECOURT	Harrison HPER Complex (5,500)
COACH	LaFayette Stribling
	(Miss. Industrial College '57)
RECORD AT SCHOOL	255-265 (18 years)
CAREER RECORD	255-265 (18 years)
ASSISTANTS	George Ivory (Mississippi Valley '87)

Harvey Wardell (Alcorn State)

TEAM WINS (last 5 years)	19-6-14-7-18
RPI (last 5 years)	189-298-227-289-197
2000-01 FINISH	Lost in conference first round.

It has been more than half a year since Mississippi Valley State's surprising 59-58 upset loss to Texas Southern in the opening round of the Southwestern Athletic Conference Tournament.

The Delta Devils have moved on, with an eye on the upcoming season. But they can't help but ponder that off night in Itta Bena that put a not-so-storybook ending to what was otherwise a highly successful season.

"It's still tough to this day," Valley coach Lafayette Stribling said during the summer. "I've thought about it a lot. But I came to the conclusion that things happen for a reason. What I don't know."

Valley, which finished 18-9 overall and 14-4 in the SWAC and one game behind champion Alabama State, came into the tournament riding an eight-game winning streak. Many believed the Delta Devils, who had beaten Alabama State twice, were the team to beat.

Instead, Valley suffered through a bad shooting night, got beat at the buzzer by a seventh-place team that had struggled down the stretch and saw its NCAA Tournament hopes dashed.

"It was one of those nights where we couldn't shoot the ball," said Stribling, who is entering his 19th season at Valley. "But I'm not going to let that one loss determine what type of season we had. We finished second in the conference, and with a break here or there could have won the thing. We beat Alabama State twice. When I look back at last season, it was a very fruitful season. Our guys gave our fans something to be thrilled about and proud of."

The 18 wins represented the most in the last four seasons for Valley, which posted its highest league finish since winning the SWAC in 1997. The Delta Devils went 12-0 at home during the regular season, including non-conference wins over Drake and Southeast Missouri State. And they did it in entertaining fashion, leading the league in scoring (80 ppg) and three-pointers made (9.26 per game) and attempted (26 per game).

The bad news for Valley fans is that six seniors, including SWAC Player of the Year DeWayne Jefferson and first-team All-SWAC center Henry Jordan, must be replaced. Jefferson averaged a league-best 24 points per game; Jordan led the league in blocked shots.

In all, those six seniors accounted for nearly 50 points and 30 rebounds per game.

"Under no circumstances do I expect us to be picked any higher than seventh or eighth in the preseason," Stribling said. "Now we're not intending to finish there, but I'm being realistic. We're the only team in the league that lost a lot of people, and we lost big. We lost a heckuva lot. I mean you're talking about losing a guy who was second in the nation in scoring. You're talking about losing a guy who led the league in blocked shots. Those type caliber kids you can't replace.

"Not only that, we lose our second string center, both of our power forwards and one of our guards, James Pruitt, transferred to Kentucky State. So we're going to be an entirely different team. The guys we do have back are just going to have to step up."

Leading the way will be senior point guard **Ashley Robinson**. The 5-9 Robinson averaged 9.8 points, 4.1 rebounds and a league-leading 7.4 assists per game a year ago. There's not a point guard anywhere in the country capable of pushing the ball up the floor any quicker than Robinson.

As a sophomore, Robinson sometimes played out of control and made questionable decisions with the ball. Last year he became the consummate floor leader. He led the league in assist/turnover ratio, ranked third in the league in free-throw percentage (.865) and ranked among the league leaders in minutes played.

"He had a great year last year, and I'm expecting an even better year from Ashley this season," Stribling said. "Of course, he's not going to have guys like Jefferson and Jordan to throw the ball to anymore. He's going to have to take this team on his shoulders and be a coach on the floor. He's such a big part of what we do.

"I thought he was the best point guard in this league last year. He's got such a big heart, and his decision-making improved a great deal. If you get open he's going to get the ball to you, and he'll get up in your face if you don't finish."

One of the players Robinson will be looking for a lot this season will be 6-6 senior swingman **D'Jamel Jackson** (11.9 ppg, 4.3 rpg). A former high school teammate of Robinson's at Murrah (Miss.) High, Jackson earned the reputation as one of the best spot-up shooters in the league by leading the league in three-point field-goal percentage (40.6).

"He'll be one of our mainstays again," Stribling said. "He's certainly one of the best shooters in this league. We're going to ask him to do a few more things for us this year. He's going to have to. We need for him to become a little better off the dribble, and we need him to help us rebound more."

Robinson and Jackson were spotted many a day this summer running laps under the hot Mississippi sun. One night, Stribling got a call from campus security notifying him that Robinson and Jackson were on the track.

"They had broken in and the security guard called me to let me know about it," Stribling said. "I told him 'They're fine, they're just working' and that was the end of it.

"That's how those two guys are. They're not cocky, they just want to be the best."

Other returning guards are 6-2 junior **Kevin Conley** (3.6 ppg, 0.5 rpg) and 6-4 sophomore **Elvis Robinson** (0.6 ppg, 1.0 rpg). **Steven Redd**, a 6-0 sophomore who sat out last season after averaging 30 points a game as a senior at Florence (Miss.) High, also should be in the guard mix.

If there was ever a player who never found a shot he didn't like—or pass up—it's the free-firing Conley.

"Kevin had some pretty big games for us, but he went stale down the stretch," Stribling said. "He's not the fastest guy in the world, but he can shoot the basketball. It's true Kevin needs to be a little more selective with his shots. But we're expecting him to have a big year. We need it."

With the backcourt crowded a year ago with the likes of Jefferson and Co., Redd opted to red-shirt. Now he's ready to step into the Delta Devils' up-and-down, let-it-rip offensive attack.

"We're expecting him to do some things," Stribling said. "There's no doubt he has the offense to play. He's just got to improve on the defensive end. And he realizes that. When he's on, he can really shoot it. He's capable of getting 20 points on any given night."

A pair of 6-7 junior forwards—**Attarrius Norwood** (3.5 ppg, 1.8 rpg) and **Willie Neal** (2.0 ppg, 1.5 rpg)—head the list of returning forwards. Neither played a big role last year, but Stribling expects that to change.

"Norwood may be the most improved player on the team," Stribling said. "He can play all over the floor, and he's a great leaper. The thing about Norwood is he can score inside and he can take you outside. He can do it all. I feel like he'll be a tremendous basketball player before he leaves here."

Neal isn't as versatile as Norwood, but he's capable of scoring around the basket.

"Neal's going to come in and help us," Stribling said. "He's got a big body. Last year he was a little on the lazy side, but I think he's eliminated that. If so, he could do some things he's capable of doing and become an integral part of this basketball team."

James Nelson, a 6-4 senior, also returns after averaging just 2.1 points and 1.6 rebounds last season.

"He's going to have to help out this team," Stribling said. "He's got a nose for the ball."

Stribling brought in six newcomers, led by Solomon Forbes of Jackson (Miss.) Lanier High and **Adrian Harper** of Clinton (Miss.) High.

Unfortunately, Forbes and Harper failed to meet NCAA freshmen eligibility requirements. The 6-4 Forbes, a first-team all-state pick, averaged 18.5 points per game. He scored a team-high 23 points in the Alabama/Mississippi All Star Classic in leading Mississippi to an 87-83 win. Harper, an All-Metro pick, averaged 17.2 points per game.

"With a little seasoning those guys could've helped us tremendously," Stribling said. "Our future would've looked a whole lot better."

One newcomer Stribling is looking forward to seeing in a Delta Devil uniform this year is **Michael Archie**. The 6-4 jumping jack averaged 17 points, nine rebounds, four assists and three steals per game at Greenwood (Miss.) High. A Dandy Dozen selection, Archie was one of the best athletes in the state.

"He's a tremendous jumper, and he can really run the floor," Stribling said. "I think he's going to give us a lot of service. He's a kid with a lot of heart. He plays hard all the time."

Other newcomers are 6-3 guard **James Lewis**, of East Mississippi Community College, 6-0 guard **Derrick Melton** of Lanier (Miss.) High and 6-6 power forward **Michael Wilson** of North Panola (Miss.) High.

"Lewis will come in and give us some minutes," Stribling said. "He's not the greatest shooter in the world, but he can score. He'll nickel and dime you to death.

"One thing I like about Wilson is that he's got a big body. It's just going to depend on how quickly he picks up on our system."

Stribling has been around too long to know better than to expect another season like last year, considering all the firepower he lost. But he also knows his team will show up and play hard.

"We've just got to get enough parts and find a way to put things back together," Stribling said. "It's going to be pretty tough. But this is a hard-nosed group. They are going to compete. What we might lack in size and talent, we'll make up for it with attitude. We're just going to have to take what we have and make the most of it."

2001-2002 SCHEDULE

Nov.	28	Arkansas State
Dec.	8	Delta State
	10	@Arkansas State
	15	Arkansas-Pine Bluff
	17	@Southeast Missouri
	21-22	#Sun Bowl Tournament
	29	@Creighton
Jan.	5	@Alabama State
	7	@Alabama A&M
	12	Alcorn State
	14	Southern
	19	@Texas Southern
	21	@Prairie View A&M
	26	Jackson State
	28	Grambling
Feb.	2	Alabama State
	4	Alabama A&M
	9	@Alcorn State
	11	@Southern
	16	Texas Southern
	18	Prairie View A&M
	23	@Jackson State
	25	@Grambling
March	2	@Arkansas-Pine Bluff
	6-9	#SWAC Tournament

@Road Games
#Fair Park Arena, Birmingham, AL

BLUE RIBBON ANALYSIS

BACKCOURT	B
BENCH/DEPTH	C-
FRONTCOURT	D
INTANGIBLES	B-

Clearly, Mississippi Valley won't have the talent it had last year. That's a given because Jefferson and Co. are no longer around. And the Delta Devils won't have much experience outside of Robinson and Jackson.

It will be tough for the Delta Devils to move into the upper tier for those very reasons. But don't sell Stribling short. He's usually at his best when not much is expected out of his team.

Jackson will likely play more two-guard this season, giving Valley a good backcourt. And any time you have good guards, you've got a chance to win in college basketball, especially in the guard-laden SWAC.

(M.A.)

Prairie View

LOCATION	Prairie View, TX
CONFERENCE	Southwestern Athletic
LAST SEASON	6-22 (.214)
CONFERENCE RECORD	5-13 (t-8th)
STARTERS LOST/RETURNING	1/4
NICKNAME	Panthers
COLORS	Purple & Gold
HOMECOURT	Williams Nicks Arena (5,000)
COACH	Elwood Plummer (Jackson State '66)
RECORD AT SCHOOL	153-337 (17 years)
CAREER RECORD	329-443 (27 years)
ASSISTANTS	Ed Phillips (Alabama A&M '73)
TEAM WINS (last 5 years)	10-13-6-7-6
RPI (last 5 years)	278-252-305-314-314
2000-01 FINISH	Lost in conference first round.

Before last season started, many followers of Southwestern Athletic Conference basketball thought it might have been the year Prairie View made a run at the regular-season title.

The Panthers, with four starters returning led by all-everything guard **Greg Burks**, were picked to finish fourth in the coaches' preseason poll. They even got one first-place vote.

Instead, Prairie View again finished near the bottom of the league standings, was on the outside looking in by the time the conference postseason tournament rolled around and was left wondering what if. As in, what if three key players hadn't been lost to season-ending knee injuries early in the season.

"We'll never know," Prairie View coach Elwood Plummer said.

Prairie View lost 6-foot-11 center **Roderick Riley**, Iowa State transfer **William Tucker** and Burks. Riley's injury occurred before the season started, Tucker's in the first game and Burks' in the sixth game.

"I've been coaching 34 years and prior to that [last year] I think I had only two players go down with knee injuries," Plummer said. "Last year we had three. I thought we were going to have a pretty good team, but … "

It didn't help matters that Plummer was suspended four games because of a violation of conference rules. It also didn't help matters that prized recruits Mike Lambert and Ben Paxon withdrew from school. Lambert was expected to step in at point guard; Paxon, the cousin of former NBA players Jim and John Paxon, was expected to provide points from the perimeter.

"I was really counting on them," Plummer said.

The most devastating blow was the loss of Burks, a first-team All-SWAC selection and arguably the league's most exciting player, was averaging 21.3 points and 4.5 assists per game before the injury. He averaged 18 points and 4.3 assists per game as a sophomore. That year Burks scored 20 or more points 14 times, including a career-high 32 against Wichita State.

"Obviously, that hurt us tremendously," Plummer said. "There was no way we could replace him. It's like having a Rolls-Royce and taking the motor out. I mean, he was our go-to-man. We had to re-arrange everything we were doing, offensively and defensively.

"Not only is he an outstanding player and a tremendous scorer, he's our team leader. He's the best guard in this conference."

The Burks-less Panthers went on to win just five more games after he went down—two against cellar-dwelling Arkansas-Pine Bluff.

"I'm pleased with the way we competed considering we lost three guys we were counting on," Plummer said.

Burks, Riley and Tucker are back and healthy. So are four starters and a host of returning lettermen, making Plummer's bunch among the most experienced in the league. Barring injury, Prairie View could have the year many expected last year, albeit one season later.

Prairie View last won the SWAC regular-season championship in 1961-62, the second of back-to-back titles.

"It's always good when you have experience," said Plummer, who led the Panthers to a SWAC Tournament title and NCAA Tournament appearance in 1998. "And we'll have good size. We'll be big. These guys are very optimistic. They think they have a chance to win the conference."

To do so, Prairie View will have to step it up on the defensive end of the floor. The Panthers ranked eighth in the SWAC in scoring defense a year ago, allowing 82.9 points per game. They allowed 90 or more points nine times, including 115 points against Tulsa, 104 against Texas A&M-Corpus Christi and 100 against Southern.

"We'll be able to score," Plummer said. "And we should be a pretty good rebounding team. The area where we need to improve the most is team defense. That's our weakest link."

Plummer will also have to find a way to replace 6-4 forward Xavier Lee, who ranked third in the SWAC in scoring last season at 17.7 points per game. Guard Sadit Montgomery (8.6 ppg., 3.7 rpg.) and forward Reginald Walton (2.4 ppg., 4.5 rpg.) are also gone.

Some of that scoring slack will be picked up by Burks, who has put on about 10 pounds of much-needed muscle thanks to months of work with a personal trainer.

The 5-8 Burks will be joined in the backcourt by 6-0 junior **Blannon Campbell**. A Mississippi Valley transfer, Campbell averaged 9.9 points, 3.8 rebounds and 4.0 assists after becoming eligible in mid-December. Against Alabama A&M, Campbell poured in a season-high 25 points. He's slated to play the point with Burks moving to the two-spot.

"He's a good leader, he can score, and we usually put him on the other team's leading scorer," Plummer said. "He was a good addition to the team."

Other returning guards include 5-11 sophomore **Christian Sonier** (1.9 ppg, 0.6 rpg.) and 5-11 sophomore **Chad Bowden** (1.6 ppg, 0.8 rpg.). **Jamar Miles**, an Alabama A&M transfer, is slated to start at small forward. The 6-6 junior averaged 9.1 points and 3.8 rebounds last season—his first in a Prairie View uniform.

"He's one of our scoring weapons," Plummer said. "He's an outstanding outside shooter."

Miles will be joined on the front line by 6-8 senior **Ivan Coulter** (6.6 ppg, 6.2 rpg) and 6-5 wide-body **Ray Lark** (12.6 ppg, 6.1 rpg). The 6-11, 315-pound Riley, nicknamed "Baby Shaq" will also see significant playing time and could start if he becomes more aggressive.

"He's got a nice touch around the basket," said Plummer of Riley, who is the biggest player in the league.

Coulter isn't a big scorer, but that's not is role anyway.

"He's the quickest forward in the conference," Plummer said. "He's quick as a cat. And he's very aggressive, sometimes too aggressive. We're counting on him to defend and rebound for us."

Lark, nicknamed "Sugar Ray," certainly made his presence felt after becoming eligible in mid-December. With an array of post moves at his disposal, the 250-pound Lark quickly gained notoriety for his low-post game. He had a season-high 25 points against Texas Southern and had 21 points and 11 rebounds against a formidable Alabama State frontline.

"Sugar Ray is a guy I've been trying to get a long time, and we finally got him," Plummer said. "He can really score around the basket."

Chris Garwood, a slender 6-10 sophomore forward, also should see considerable playing time. He averaged 3.2 points and 2.6 rebounds as a freshman.

"He's really improved this summer," Plummer said. "He's left-handed … good around the basket. And it looks like he's extended his range some."

Other returning forwards are 6-6 senior **Keith Toney** (0.8 ppg., 0.8 rpg.) and Tucker.

No doubt, Campbell and Lark proved to be good additions after joining the team after the first semester. Plummer hopes **Brandon Moore** and **Marc Robey**—each becomes eligible in mid-December—can have a similar impact. The 6-8, 220-pound Moore averaged averaged 16 points and 10 rebounds at Compton (Calif.) Community College last season. The 6-2, 185-pound Robey averaged 14 points and two assists at Incarnate Word.

"He's [Brandon] a scorer and a rebounder," Plummer said. "He can really jump, and he's not a bad defender. He's certainly going to push Miles for a starting spot once he joins the team. Robey will play the one and and two."

While most men's basketball programs in Division I award the maximum 13 scholarships, Prairie View offers only four. That said, if there's any school that can't afford a rash of injuries like a year ago, it's Prairie View.

"No, we certainly don't want that to happen again," Plummer said.

2001-2002 SCHEDULE

Nov.	14-16	#BCA Invitational
	19	Huston-Tillotson
	24	@Washington State
	28	@South Florida
Dec.	1	@Arizona State
	4	Paul Quinn
	15	Alcorn State
	17	Southern
	20	@Wright State
	22	@Cleveland State
Jan.	12	@Grambling
	14	@Jackson State
	19	Arkansas-Pine Bluff
	21	Mississippi Valley State
	26	@Alabama A&M
	28	@Alabama State
Feb.	2	Texas Southrn
	5	@Texas Southern
	9	Grambling
	11	Jackson State
	16	@Arkansas-Pine Bluff
	18	@Mississippi Valley State
	23	Alabama A&M
	25	Alabama State
	28	@Southern
March	2	@Alcorn State
	6-9	##SWAC Tournament

@Road Games
#Raleigh, NC (vs. North Carolina State, first round; also East Carolina, Rutgers, Northwestern, VCU, San Jose State, Fairleigh Dickinson, High Point)
##Fair Park Arena, Birmingham, AL

BLUE RIBBON ANALYSIS

BACKCOURT	B+
BENCH/DEPTH	C
FRONTCOURT	B
INTANGIBLES	C

Assuming Burks and Co. stay healthy, Prairie View could make some noise in the SWAC this season. It's hard to envision the Panthers being better than Alcorn, Alabama State or Alabama A&M for that matter, but a top five finish certainly isn't out of the question. That's especially true considering the experience factor.

Burks is one of, if not the best guard in the conference, and he's quite capable of putting a team on his shoulders. With Burks, Campbell and Lark, Prairie View should have no trouble scoring points. Riley's presence should help on the defensive end. Still, the Panthers probably won't be world-beaters on defense.

Plummer has the option of playing Riley and Lark together, which could pose problems for other SWAC teams.

(M.A.)

Southern

LOCATION	**Baton Rouge, LA**
CONFERENCE	**Southwestern Athletic**
LAST SEASON	**11-16 (.407)**
CONFERENCE RECORD	**8-10 (t-5th)**
STARTERS LOST/RETURNING	**1/4**
NICKNAME	**Jaguars**
COLORS	**Columbia Blue & Gold**
HOMECOURT	**F.G. Clark Activity Center (7,500)**
COACH	**Ben Jobe (Fisk '56)**
RECORD AT SCHOOL	**193-101 (10 years)**
CAREER RECORD	**506-297 (28 years)**
ASSISTANTS	**Roman Banks (Northwestern St. '91)**
	Otis Hughley (Livingston '89)
TEAM WINS (last 5 years)	**10-14-21-18-11**
RPI (last 5 years)	**299-280-150-227-278**
2000-01 FINISH	**Lost in conference semifinal.**

He's baaaaack.

Ben Jobe, at age 68 and out of basketball for the last season, has returned to head the Southern University program he left five years ago. Jobe was introduced as the Jaguars' new head coach in April.

"I hope we can rekindle some of the relationships we had," Jobe said. "I want to do a little better job of getting involved in the community. … I hope we can work together to produce a good team for us, not for me, but the entire Southern University family.

"It's always been my feeling that this is somewhat hallowed ground. If you can't win here, you can't win anywhere."

Jobe has a career mark of 506-297 in 28 seasons, including 194-100 in 10 at Southern from 1986-87 through 1995-96. He coached the Jaguars to three regular-season Southwestern Athletic Conference titles and four tournament championships.

The highlight of his first tenure at Southern came in 1993, when the 16th-seeded Jaguars shocked the college basketball world by upsetting No. 4 seeded Georgia Tech in the opening round of the NCAA Tournament. But Jobe left the school in August of 1996 with two years left on his contract to take a job at Division II Tuskegee University. Jobe went 37-70 in four seasons there, including the only three losing seasons in his career, and was out of coaching this past season.

"I've had much more success here than any other place I've ever been," Jobe said. "The climate is fantastic. There are people who want to win and are willing to support the problem.

"I hope I can do the job. If I can do anything like I did the last time, I'll be happy. I really want [Southern fans] to enjoy a championship. If I can do that for you, then I will feel real good. I would hate not to do a good job the second time around. We'll try to see if we can make lightning strike twice."

Jobe has a two-year contract with a one-year option for a third year. Interestingly enough, Jobe will make $79,000 in base pay, $17,000 more than the man he replaced, Tommy Green, was paid last year in the first year of a three-year contract. Green, Jobe's assistant for all 10 years during his first stint at Southern, went 74-64 in five years. Southern was 11-16 last season after finishing as the SWAC runner-up in both the regular season and tournament each of the previous two years.

Southern's decision to bring back Jobe is similar to what Alcorn State did a few years ago when it brought back Davey Whitney. The 70-year old Whitney—the SWAC's all-time winningest coach—enjoyed mega-success at Alcorn in the 1980s but was fired in 1989 after three straight losing seasons.

The school renamed the basketball arena in Whitney's honor in 1994, and two years later he was re-hired by the school. He's led the Braves to two regular-season titles and one tournament title since returning.

The question is, can Jobe enjoy that type of success? And can he bring back the fast-paced, up-tempo style that made the Jags so fun to watch in the late 1980s? He was 59 when Southern knocked off Georgia Tech. He's 68 now. In May, Jobe had a series of surgeries he says cure the sleep apnea that's plagued him for more than three decades.

"I may have to learn how to do a little rapping," Jobe said. "Nowadays you have to deal with Master P and 'Slip Sloppy Hog' and all the others."

That's Snoop Doggy Dog, coach. But hey, who cares. Southern didn't bring back Jobe to name off the names of popular rap artists properly. The school brought him back to rebuild the basketball program.

And that won't be easy. Southern lost four seniors off last year's 11-16 team, including the starting backcourt of Courtney Henderson (16.5 ppg) and Devan Clark (11.2 ppg, 5.7 apg). Two other players—Keith Dixon and Zebton Wells—transferred.

Jobe said he had not followed Southern's basketball team much and knew little of his team other than what he saw in the first half of the Jaguars' 81-56 loss to Alabama State in a SWAC Tournament semifinal.

"I've always been able to find players, but you don't want to lose the ones you've got," said Jobe, who point-ed out that the only job he's ever had where he didn't turn the program around in his first year was Denver.

If he is to win in his first season back at Southern he'll likely have to get a big year out of 6-5 junior swingman **Brian Johnson**. The ultra-athletic Johnson was the Jaguars' second-leading scorer last season at 14.1 points per game, including a 25-point performance against Grambling in the opening round of the SWAC Tournament.

Johnson, who has good hops, can take a player off the dribble or just as easily pull up and launch a jumper from long range. He ranked seventh in the league in field-goal percentage (.488) and 11th in three-point field-goal percentage (.342).

"He killed us when we played them here," Jackson State coach Andy Stoglin said. "He can play."

After Johnson, it's anybody's guess who will start. However, 5-9 junior point guard **Victor Tarver** figures to be in the mix. Tarver quit the team in mid-January last season in part because of a lack of playing time. A high-ly touted high school prospect two years ago, the cat-quick Tarver was averaging just 5.1 points per game at the time.

"We've asked him to come back with us," Jobe said of Tarver, who is the son of Southern system president Dr. Leon Tarver.

Other returning players are 6-3 junior guard **Jonathan Oliver** (2.6 ppg, 0.3 rpg); 6-4 senior swing-man **DeAndre Bell** (4.4 ppg, 2.1 rpg); 6-4 junior forward **DeJuan Goston** (2.8 ppg, 0.6 rpg); and 6-5 senior for-ward **Carl Alexander** (1.8 ppg, 1.1 rpg).

"I'm going to have to look at film galore," Jobe said. "I don't know much about the guys returning."

There was some discussion that burly forward Greg Martin, who teamed with two-time SWAC player of the year Adarrial Smylie to form one of the most feared front-court tandems in the league two years ago, might return after sitting out last season. But Southern assistant coach Roman Banks, who served as interim coach after Green was fired, said that's not the case.

"He's going to school at Florida State," Banks said.

It was Banks who helped reel in Jobe's first recruiting class of Stint No. 2. That class includes 6-8 freshman for-ward **Peter Cipriano** of famed St. Anthony's High in New Jersey; 6-5 freshman forward **Nicholas England** of Boston High in Lake Charles, La.; 6-1 freshman **Trayvian Scott** of Southern Lab in Baton Rouge; 6-8 center **Jerrid Campbell** of Patterson High in Dayton, Ohio; 5-11 guard **Randall Anderson** of Parker High in Birmingham, Ala.; and 6-0 guard **Nicholas McGee** of Peabody High in Alexandria, La.

"We brought in seven players, but only five of those are scholarship players," Banks said. "That's all the NCAA allows. These guys can be good. It's tough to find freshmen of this caliber. I'd say this is one of the best freshmen classes we've ever had."

Banks is really high on England, an all-state player who can play the three or the four. He averaged 20 points per game.

"There were a lot of people after him," Banks said. "He's mature enough to help us right away. He can score."

Banks also likes Cipriano, who averaged 13 points and eight rebounds last season.

"We were lucky to get him," Banks said. "He's very fundamentally sound, and he can step out on the floor."

Scott enrolled at Texas Southern, but stayed there only two days before opting to transfer to Southern, which is much closer to home.

"I'm expecting him to come in and play right away," Banks said. "He's a very good basketball player."

Banks thinks Campbell has a great upside.

"He a very good athlete," Banks said. "He can score on the inside and he defends well in the post."

Banks calls Anderson "a tremendous shooter" and says McGee "can shoot the three, and is not shy about shooting it."

"We're missing a lot of points from last season, but we think these guys can come in and pick up some of the slack," Banks said.

2001-2002 SCHEDULE

Nov.	19	@LSU
	26	West Alabama
Dec.	1	@Centenary
	8	@Missouri-Columbia
	13	@Colorado
	15	@Texas Southern
	17	@Prairie View
	20	San Francisco
Jan.	5	Grambling
	7	Jackson State
	12	Arkansas-Pine Bluff
	14	@Mississippi Valley
	17	Morris Brown
	19	Alabama A&M
	21	Alabama State
	26	Alcorn State
	28	@Morris Brown
Feb.	2	@Grambling
	9	Arkansas-Pine Bluff
	11	Mississippi Valley State
	16	@Alabama A&M
	18	@Alabama State
	23	@Alcorn State
	28	Prairie View
March	2	Texas Southern
	5-9	#WAC Tournament

@Road Games
#Fair Park Arena, Birmingham, AL

BLUE RIBBON ANALYSIS

BACKCOURT	B
BENCH/DEPTH	C-
FRONTCOURT	C
INTANGIBLES	C-

There are so many question marks for this Southern team. The first is whether Jobe can find away to rekindle the fire for a program that has lost some of its luster over the last several years. The second is how many of the newcomers are going to be called upon, and how many of them can log quality minutes once league play begins. Winning with freshmen isn't easy at any level, unless you are Duke.

Last year, internal strife played a part in the Jaguars' demise. That shouldn't be the case this season. However, replacing Henderson and Clark won't be easy. Johnson is a good player, but he'll have to play well night in and night out for this team to make much noise.

(M.A.)

Texas Southern

LOCATION	Houston, TX
CONFERENCE	Southwestern Athletic
LAST SEASON	7-22 (.241)
CONFERENCE RECORD	5-13 (t-8th)
STARTERS LOST/RETURNING	3/2
NICKNAME	Tigers
COLORS	Maroon & Gray
HOMECOURT	Health & PE Arena (7,500)
COACH	Ronnie Courtney (McMurry '81)
RECORD AT SCHOOL	First year
CAREER RECORD	First year
ASSISTANTS	John Howie (SW Texas State '92)
	James Wilhemi (Wisconsin-Whitewater '97)
TEAM WINS (last 5 years)	12-15-8-15-7

| RPI (last 5 years) | 256-214-287-268-305 |
| 2000-01 FINISH | Lost in conference semifinal. |

Out with the old, in with the new.

That was the approach Texas Southern officials took last April when they fired long-time coach Bob Moreland and replaced him with Ronnie Courtney, a highly suc-cessful high school coach in Houston.

"This falls into our athletic department's vision in mak-ing inroads in the Greater Houston area and national scene," Texas Southern athletic director Alois Blackwell said. "Coach Courtney is a tremendous find for our ath-letic department, and we're looking for exciting times from him both off and on the court."

There were plenty of exciting times during Moreland's 26-year stint. Texas Southern won or shared seven SWAC titles in the 1990s—four regular season, three tournament. He also led the Tigers to regular season titles in 1976-'77, '82-83, and '88-89 and three NCAA Tournament appearances.

But those good times have been few and far in between the last three years as Moreland's teams amassed only 30 wins in that time. Even Texas Southern's 59-58 upset of No. 2-seeded Mississippi Valley State in the opening round of the SWAC Tournament wasn't enough for Moreland to save his job.

In stepped the 43-year old Courtney, who led Houston's Sugarland Willowridge High to two consecu-tive 5A state championships and built the program into a national contender during his four years there.

He has coached high school basketball for 20 years, including eight years as a head coach at Houston's Davis High. During his high school career, Courtney was chosen district coach of the year four times and three times was chosen Greater Houston Area Coach of the Year. USA Today selected him its national coach of the year last year.

"The transition has been very smooth," said Courtney, who averaged 25 wins per season at Willowridge. "I'm extremely excited to have this opportu-nity. The reception from the players has been very posi-tive.

"It's an awkward situation [replacing Moreland]. I have a great deal of respect for coach Moreland. I'm not expecting to replace him. I'm going to bring my own style, my own ideas."

Courtney knows it's going to be a learning process as he makes his first trek through the Southwestern Athletic Conference. He began watching film and evaluating the talent on hand as soon as he was hired.

"As we get a little deeper into that evaluation process, I'll know more about what type of team we'll be," said Courtney, who attended a handful of Texas Southern's games over the last couple of years. "We just want to be competitive. I'm not going to say we're going to win the SWAC or anything like that. We're going to play hard and let the chips fall where they may."

Courtney prefers an up-tempo brand of basketball, like the product he put on the floor at Willowridge.

"But I'm a flexible coach," he said.

Courtney may have to be flexible, as graduation, defections and academics have left the cupboard rather bare. Oft-injured big man Rahmeen Underwood gradu-ated, leading scorer Chris Miller isn't eligible and second leading scorer Ricky Bennett transferred. Those three players combined for 40.7 points per game.

"We're going to be totally different," Courtney said.

Even with Miller, Bennett and Underwood, Texas Southern ranked next-to-last in the SWAC in scoring offense (65.4 ppg), last in field-goal percentage (.352) and three-point field-goal percentage (.256).

The versatile 6-3 Miller not only led the Tigers in scor-ing but rebounding as well. He had a SWAC-best 14 double-doubles.

"He didn't have the grades," Courtney said of Miller, who ranked sixth in the SWAC in scoring and second in rebounding.

Bennett, who averaged 15.8 points and 5.4 rebounds per game, transferred to New Orleans. He's from nearby Picayune, Miss.

That leaves Courtney with 13 players, four of whom are walk-ons, and no true big man.

"It's my job to find out what these guys can and can't do," Courtney said.

One player Courtney knows can play is **Rakim Hollis**. The 6-2 junior guard averaged 14 points, 3.8 rebounds and 2.6 assists last season as a sophomore after sitting out as a freshman. He really picked his game up the latter portion of the season when Bennett was out with an injury, averaging nearly 20 points per game over the Tigers' last 12 games.

It was Hollis' 28 points, including a late three-pointer, that keyed Texas Southern's upset at Mississippi Valley in the opening round of the SWAC Tournament. The Tigers had lost eight of nine before that win.

"He's got a lot of talent," Courtney said. "And he's a leader. We're going to look to him to keep us going emotionally. He's that kind of player."

Hollis will likely play more at the off-guard spot, leaving the point-guard duties to 6-2 senior **Steve Hoyer**. Hoyer played in only five games last season, averaging 8.8 points and 2.6 rebounds.

"He didn't a chance to play that much last year, but he's got tremendous skills," Courtney said. "He's very athletic."

Other returning guards are 5-11 junior **Marquel Timmons** (3.9 ppg, 2.7 rpg); 5-5 junior walk-on guard **Jason Roland** (0.0 ppg, 0.6 rpg); 6-0 junior walk-on guard **Leveil Lander** (0.4 ppg, 0.5 rpg); 6-0 senior walk-on **Terell Goff** (1.2 ppg, 0.5 rpg); and 6-0 sophomore guard **Brian Brown** (0.5 ppg, 0.4 rpg).

Courtney has been impressed with Timmons.

"He's got good quickness and speed," Courtney said.

Gregory Grady, a 6-8 senior who averaged 3.9 points and 3.3 rebounds, figures to start somewhere along the front line. So too does 6-8 sophomore **Akil Butler** (6.2 ppg, 4.5 rpg) and 6-8 sophomore **Jamaal Clark** (2.8 ppg, 2.4 rpg).

"Grady and Butler are probably going to play a lot," Courtney said. Grady is an extremely hard worker.

Newcomers include 6-6, 210-pound sophomore **Jerome Bell** and 6-0 freshman point guard **Donald Hogan**, both of whom helped Courtney win his first state championship at Suglarland Willowridge. Bell won't be eligible until after Christmas.

"Jerome's one of those guys that has amazing speed and quickness," Courtney said. "And he jumps extremely well. He may be the best rebounder I have on the team."

Courtney said he expects Hogan to battle for the starting point-guard job.

"He knows the game extremely well," Courtney said. "He's very smart."

2001-2002 SCHEDULE

Nov.	19	@New Mexico
	24	@Texas-Pan American
	27	Lamar
	30	#Blue and Gold Classic
Dec.	1	#Blue and Gold Classic
	4	Houston
	8	@Stephen F. Austin
	15	Southern
	17	Alcorn State
	27-29	#Minnesota Winter Jam
Jan.	12	@Jackson State
	14	@Grambling
	19	Mississippi Valley State
	21	Arkansas-Pine Bluff
	26	@Alabama State
	28	@Alabama A&M
Feb.	2	@Prairie View
	5	Prairie View
	9	Jackson State
	11	Grambling
	16	@Mississippi Valley State
	18	@Arkansas-Pine Bluff
	23	Alabama State
	25	Alabama A&M
	28	@Alcorn State
March	2	@Southern
	6-9	##SWAC Tournament

@Road Games
#Milwaukee, WI (vs. Sam Houston State first round; also Marquette, Northern Illinois)
##Minneapolis, MN (also Morgan State, Alcorn State, Norfolk State)
###Fair Park Arena, Birmingham, AL

BLUE RIBBON ANALYSIS

BACKCOURT	B
BENCH/DEPTH	D
FRONTCOURT	C-
INTANGIBLES	C

It's hard to imagine a Texas Southern team taking the floor without Moreland on the sideline. Moreland had been a fixture in the SWAC for so long. Moreland has moved on, even if it wasn't on his own accord, and so too must the Tigers. Courtney was a highly successful high school coach, but he inherits a team that is depleted talent-wise. Hollis is a nice player, but there's not much returning if you go by past stats alone. There's no proven

point guard, no proven big man and absolutely no depth to speak of. It's hard to imagine this team finishing anywhere but near the bottom of the league—that is unless Courtney has a few talented players that we don't know about, which is always a distinct possibility in the sometimes secretive, information-starved SWAC.

(M.A.)

Arkansas State

LOCATION	Jonesboro, AR
CONFERENCE	Sun Belt (East)
LAST SEASON	17-13 (.567)
CONFERENCE RECORD	10-6 (t-2nd)
STARTERS LOST/RETURNING	2/3
NICKNAME	Indians
COLORS	Scarlet & Black
HOMECOURT	Convocation Center (10,563)
COACH	Dickey Nutt (Oklahoma State '82)
RECORD AT SCHOOL	89-82 (6 years)
CAREER RECORD	89-82 (6 years)
ASSISTANTS	Charlie Fenske (Wisc.-Stout '74)
	Tony Madlock (Memphis '92)
	Micah Marsh (Arkansas State '88)
TEAM WINS (last 5 years)	15-20-18-10-17
RPI (last 5 years)	164-85-129-184-177
2000-01 FINISH	Lost in conference semifinal.

The metamorphosis continues at Arkansas State.

In the last of the '90s, the Indians found success in small places, using a host of quality guards and wing players to put together back-to-back 20-9 and NCAA Tournament-qualifying 18-12 marks between 1997-99.

Last year, though, ASU grew up—literally—and now it is a strong inside game that Indian fans hope will help keep their favorites as a factor in the Sun Belt Conference's East Division.

In other words, as 7-0 senior **Jason Jennings** goes, so goes the Tribe.

"There's no question that we're playing a new game," ASU head coach Dickey Nutt said. "In the era when we had guys like Chico [Fletcher] and Antonio [Harvey], we were very guard-oriented and got up and down the floor as fast as we could to use our quickness.

"Now we've got guys 7-0 and 6-9 that can really play. We didn't make a conscious change away from a fast-paced game, but we made it pretty clear that with a guy like Jason in there, he's going to touch the ball every time down the floor."

Jennings (13.9 ppg, 7.1 rpg) broke ASU's season record for blocked shots before January even ended, and finished as the Sun Belt's top shot blocker with 102 rejections in his first season with the Indians. The rangy Jennings, who transferred from the University of Arkansas after his sophomore year, was an All-Sun Belt pick after shooting 52.8 percent from the field and 71.8 percent from the line.

He and teammate **Kolin Weaver** were both invited to the prestigious Pete Newell Big Man Camp, the first two players from the school ever to attend.

Including Jennings and Weaver, eight lettermen return.

"We've still got a lot of work to do," said Nutt, the dean of Sun Belt coaches and the winningest active coach in the league, "but the good thing is that we were able to do all of that last year with mostly underclassmen. The bulk of our team's back, and that's always exciting for a coach.

"Last year, we had nine newcomers, and seven of them had never played Division I basketball. That was really a challenge. This year's just the opposite, and hopefully we can reap the benefits from that."

The player who may have been the Indians' MVP coming down the stretch was shooting guard **Nick Rivers** (13.5 ppg, 1.9 rpg, 1.5 apg), a 6-1 senior who averaged 16.6 points per game in league play on the way to being voted the Sun Belt's Newcomer of the Year. He scored double figures in 17 of his final 20 games and gunned in 30 in the regular-season finale against Arkansas-Little Rock.

"He just found a way to get his points late in the year," Nutt said. "He was inconsistent at times, but when he was on he became a very explosive player for us."

After Rivers, though, the next three top returning scorers for the Indians are the big fellows, and that group will likely carry a heavy load on both ends of the floor once again.

Jennings is obviously the man to watch, but the 6-9 senior Weaver (11.5 ppg, 6.5 rpg) has steadily improved

in his two years at ASU after transferring from Siena. He had 18 double-figure scoring games and led the team on the boards nine times. He was the only Indian to score in double digits in each of ASU's two games in the Sun Belt Tournament.

"He just got better and better as the year went along," Nutt said of Weaver. "When you put him out there with the number one shot blocker in the league, we have the potential to be good on the front line."

The likely man to round out that front line is 6-8 sophomore **Kim Adams** (4.9 ppg, 6.0 rpg), who played in all 30 games last year as a sixth man. Adams, Arkansas' "Mr. Basketball" one year earlier, was capable of big things—including 10 rebounds in his first college game and a 15-point, 14-board effort against Jackson State—but he drew more raves for his defensive play.

Add in the other front line spark off the bench provided by 6-8 junior **Josh Sokolewicz** (2.2 ppg, 1.2 rpg), and the Indians should be very solid near the basket.

"Kim Adams just has a great work ethic," Nutt said. "He gives us everything we need … toughness, defense, rebounding, athleticism. Josh didn't play a lot last year, but he's really improved in two years."

One of the keys to the Tribe's success this year is the return to form of 6-3 junior guard **Odie Williams** (5.0 ppg, 2.7 apg, 2.5 rpg), who had a "sophomore jinx" season after a stellar freshman year. In his defense, Williams struggled with the passing of his mother during the year but still finished second on the team in both assists and steals despite starting only five games.

"He came on strong for us toward the end of the year," Nutt said of Williams. "It was certainly a difficult year for him, but at the end of the year he was playing his best basketball."

Two other guards, 6-0 junior **Jon Beck** (3.6 ppg) and 6-5 sophomore **DeWayne Hart** (3.6 ppg, 2.5 rpg), are also back to provide help in the backcourt. Hart saw his first action after missing virtually two full years with knee injuries.

Also back is **Tony Brown** (5.0 ppg), a 6-3 senior who started the first three games of last season before being sidelined the rest of the season with major foot surgery.

"Jon's won some games for us with the way he shoots the basketball," Nutt said. "Tony's back 100 percent now, and he feels like he can bring us a lot of experience even though he hasn't been on the floor a lot."

With all of that experience available in the backcourt, though, it's very likely that there'll be a new face in the Indians' three-guard starting lineup. That's because **Terrance Saulsberry** (15.4 ppg), a 6-5 junior from Moberly Junior College, joins the ASU program after being ranked in the top five among the nation's junior-college players by two different publications last year. He was also named as the top defensive player in his junior college region.

"It seems like everybody wants to talk about Terrance," Nutt said. "He was obviously one of the top guards in the country last year, and he can play a couple of different positions for us. We feel like he's going to be a great addition to us, and will really fit in an area where we need help."

Nutt is also high on 6-0 junior **Jonathan Reed** (9.0 ppg, 7.0 apg), a two-time all-conference selection for Division III junior-college national champion Cedar Valley (Texas) College.

Two highly regarded freshmen are also new in the Indian program: 6-9 forward **Yevgeny Sokolov** (9.1 ppg, 5.6 rpg), who came from Russia and led Melbourne (Fla.) to a state title, and 6-7 forward **Lucious Lenear** (14.0 ppg, 8.0 rpg, 6.0 blocks), who led his Turrell (Ark.) team to back-to-back state championships and is also a sprinter in track. With the wealth of experience already on the front line, though, both are red-shirt candidates.

"We may not have to depend on those guys this season," Nutt said, "and that's a terrific opportunity to maybe sit a guy out that can help us in the future. I'm open to them playing if they can help us, but they need to prove to me they can do something to help us this season."

2001-2002 SCHEDULE

Nov.	16	Central Methodist
	17	Briar Cliff
	21	Arkansas-Pine Bluff
	24	Nevada
	26	@Jackson State
	28	@Mississippi Valley
Dec.	1	Southern Mississippi
	5	@Air Force
	8	@Mississippi State
	10	Mississippi Valley
	20-22	#Rainbow Classic
	29	Texas A&M-Corpus Christi

Jan.	3	Denver
	5	North Texas
	10	Arkansas-Little Rock
	12	@South Alabama
	16	@Florida International
	19	New Orleans
	24	@Middle Tennessee
	26	@Western Kentucky
Feb.	2	@Arkansas-Little Rock
	7	Middle Tennessee
	9	Western Kentucky
	14	@Louisiana-Lafayette
	16	@New Mexico State
	21	Florida International
	28	##Sun Belt Tournament
March	1-5	##Sun Belt Tournament

@Road Games
#At Honolulu, HI (vs. Georgia first round; also Boston College, Hawaii, Holy Cross, Iona, Miami (OH), Portland)
##Lakefront Arena, New Orleans, LA

BLUE RIBBON ANALYSIS

BACKCOURT	B
BENCH/DEPTH	B+
FRONTCOURT	A-
INTANGIBLES	B

Nutt now admits it … you have to have an inside game if you're going to be consistently successful. But that doesn't mean you have to sacrifice a fast-paced offense. ASU still ranked in the top third of the league in scoring last year even with a plethora of new faces.

That inside game is still there, with Jennings ranking among the nation's top big men. If it weren't for Chris Marcus at Western Kentucky, Jennings would be getting a lot more notice regionally and nationally. But if the Indians continue their improvement this year, it will be because of a big improvement in overall guard play.

"We think our guards have made a big jump in getting where we want to go," Nutt said. "Time will tell, but I think we're going to be a lot better on the perimeter, especially defensively."

If that's the case, maybe Western Kentucky will face a little challenge in the East Division after all.

(D.M.)

Arkansas-Little Rock

LOCATION	Little Rock, AR
CONFERENCE	Sun Belt (East)
LAST SEASON	18-11 (.621)
CONFERENCE RECORD	9-7 (4th)
STARTERS LOST/RETURNING	3/2
NICKNAME	Trojans
COLORS	Maroon & Silver
HOMECOURT	ALLTEL Arena (18,000)
COACH	Porter Moser (Creighton '90)
RECORD AT SCHOOL	18-11 (1 year)
CAREER RECORD	18-11 (1 year)
ASSISTANTS	Steve Shields (Baylor '88)
	Joe Harge (Oregon State '89)
	Kevin Fricke (Nebraska '84)
TEAM WINS (last 5 years)	18-15-12-4-18
RPI (last 5 years)	141-160-235-303-184
2000-01 FINISH	Lost in conference quarterfinal.

One year ago, the rags-to-riches success story in the Sun Belt Conference was provided by Arkansas-Little Rock. Second-year coach Porter Moser is now looking to get a sequel published.

It will be pretty much impossible to duplicate the kind of improvement the Trojans made last season. Actually, it is mathematically possible, but to do that UALR would have to go 34-0 this year.

Moser will have to be content with continuing to build a program that had nearly hit bottom in the 1999-2000 season with a 4-24 record. He took over a team that had three solid seniors and a world of unproven undergraduates, and he wasn't sure what course to take.

"We had the three seniors," he said, "and we had a choice to make. After the four wins a year earlier, we didn't have a lot of pressure, and we could have played the underclassmen and gotten the young kids all the minutes. Or we could have gone with the seniors and filled in with the young kids.

"That's what we did, and we were able to get some wins and build some excitement about the program."

BLUE RIBBON FORECAST

East Division
1. Western Kentucky
2. Arkansas State
3. Florida International
4. Arkansas-Little Rock
5. Middle Tennessee

West Division
1. New Mexico State
2. Louisiana-Lafayette
3. South Alabama
4. Denver
5. New Orleans
6. North Texas

TOP 40

Western Kentucky is ranked among the 2001-2002 Blue Ribbon Top 40. An extended profile can be found in the Top 40 section of Blue Ribbon.

ALL-CONFERENCE TEAM

G - Eric Channing, SR, New Mexico State
G - Chris Davis, JR, North Texas
F - Anthony Johnson, JR, Louisiana-Lafayette
C - Chris Marcus, SR, Western Kentucky
C - Jason Jennings, SR, Arkansas State

PLAYER OF THE YEAR

Chris Marcus, SR, Western Kentucky

NEWCOMER OF THE YEAR

Rodrigo Viegas, JR, Florida International

2001-2002 CONFERENCE TOURNAMENT

Feb. 28-March 5, Lakefront Arena, New Orleans, LA

2000-2001 CHAMPIONS

Western Kentucky (East)
South Alabama (West)
Western Kentucky (Conference tournament)

2000-2001 POSTSEASON PARTICIPANTS

Postseason Record 0-2 (.000)
NCAA
Western Kentucky
NIT
South Alabama

TOP BACKCOURTS

1. Louisiana-Lafayette
2. New Mexico State
3. Western Kentucky

TOP FRONTCOURTS

1. Western Kentucky
2. Arkansas State
3. Florida International

INSIDE THE NUMBERS

2000-2001 Conference RPI: 20th (of 31)
Conference RPI (last five years): 16-1615-18-20

DID YOU KNOW?

The league drops from 12 to 11 basketball-playing members this year, with Louisiana Tech moving to the Western Athletic Conference. Only 11 of last year's 12 members were eligible for the league tournament and postseason play, with New Mexico State serving a self-sanctioned penalty during an NCAA investigation into violations dating back to the 1996-97 season. … NMSU, Middle Tennessee and North Texas are in their second year in the conference, joining the league before the 2000-01 season. The three came in with a league expansion that included the addition of football as a championship sport beginning this fall and the birth of the New Orleans Bowl that will include the league's football champion. … Arkansas-Little Rock tied for the nation's biggest improvement record-wise during the 2000-01 season. The Trojans' jump from a 4-24 mark to an 18-11 record last year represented an improvement of 13 games, which is also the largest in Sun Belt history. … Three new coaches will be on league sidelines, with two of them (Terry Carroll at Denver and Monte Towe at New Orleans) in their first four-year head coaching post. Johnny Jones, the new boss at North Texas, served as interim head coach at Memphis during the 1999-2000 season. … Three members of last year's all-conference team—Western Kentucky's Chris Marcus, Eric Channing of New Mexico State and Arkansas State's Jason Jennings—return this season. Marcus was also MVP at the conference tournament, and Louisiana-Lafayette's Blane Harmon also returns from that all-tournament team. … For the second year in a row, the league will hold its men's and women's tournaments simultaneously at the same site. The combined tournament at New Orleans' Lakefront Arena runs six days and includes 20 games. The tournament host team has reached the finals 13 times, winning five titles, but no host team has won the tournament since 1991. … The Sun Belt championship game will air on ESPN for the 23rd consecutive year. The Sun Belt is the only conference to have its championship televised on ESPN every year since the network's inception. … Guard Eric Channing of NMSU was a first-team Verizon Academic All-America selection by the College Sports Information Directors of America. The business major has been a first-team selection two straight years. … Middle Tennessee coach Randy Wiel was head coach of the Dutch National Team in the 1992 Olympic Games.

(D.M.)

What the Trojans also did was make themselves a major factor in the Sun Belt race, compiling an 18-11 overall mark and a 9-7 record in the East Division. A four-game win streak and a run of seven wins in eight games in the middle of the league wars made people sit up and take notice.

"The people here were great," Moser said. "As the year went along, more and more people started coming out. We had about 8,000 when we played Arkansas State and over 7,000 when Western Kentucky came in. As we started winning, people got behind us, and in turn our guys started realizing what they were capable of doing."

The final tally was an improvement of 13 games, a Sun Belt record for the best turnaround in one season. The 13-game improvement also tied for the top turnaround in the nation last year.

School officials were so pleased with the job Moser did that they extended his contract for seven years.

Now, about that sequel …

"It's going to be very different in a lot of ways," said Moser, who spent two seasons one seat over on the

UALR bench as an assistant coach before taking over last year. "We've lost a lot in terms of leadership. But I like a lot of the new faces we have and I like the guys that are back."

A talented group of seniors—forward Stan Blackman and guards Alan Barksdale and Laverne Smith—led that program rebound. All three were full-time starters for the Trojans for at least two years.

Only one full-time starter is back, that being 6-10 sophomore forward **Jake Yancey** (3.8 ppg, 2.8 rpg), but five other returnees all saw some starting duty during the year.

Those numbers of starters and returnees would be higher, but junior point guard Alex Finger left the team to concentrate on school. Finger started all 29 games last year, averaging 3.0 points and 2.4 rebounds along with leading the Trojans in assists.

"That leaves us in a little bit of a bind," Moser said, "and we're probably going to have to count on freshmen there."

The other guard slot does not carry nearly that many question marks. Sophomore **Nick Zachery** (10.4 ppg,

1.9 rpg, 1.5 apg) came on strong during the latter half of his freshman season and wound up starting the final three games of the year. The 6-1 Zachery is the leading returning scorer and also paced the team with a nearly 47 percent success rate from three-point range.

He and the new-and-improved Yancey will likely carry the leadership roles.

"They're both much stronger than they were at this time last year," Moser said. "Yancey's really gotten his strength up, and Nick came on at the end and gave us somebody that could score."

Three other forwards played extensive roles last year. Sophomore **Columbus Willis** (3.1 ppg, 2.3 rpg), 6-5, provided valuable assistance on both ends of the floor.

The versatile **Damion Ninkovic** (4.6 ppg, 3.6 rpg), a 6-5 senior who came from Wisconsin-Milwaukee a year ago, is an offensive threat and also finished second on the team in rebounding last season.

And **Darius Eason** (2.1 ppg, 2.1 rpg), a 6-9 sophomore, showed improvement throughout his freshman year, starting eight games and finishing with 25 blocked shots to lead the squad.

That type of defense became UALR's calling card last season. The Trojans, who allowed opponents to shoot just a fraction under 50 percent and score almost 80 points a game one year earlier, led the Sun Belt in team defense. Trojan opponents shot only 40.4 percent from the floor last season.

"We never answered the question of how many games we were going to win," Moser said. "All we said was that we were going to defend, pressure the ball and play hard. That defense was a huge difference from previous years."

Junior **Mark Green** (7.9 ppg, 3.5 rpg), 6-2, provided scoring for the second straight season—at least until a practice session on New Year's Eve when he broke a bone in his right foot and was out for the rest of the year. He's back after starting nine of the Trojans' first 10 games last season.

Aside from Green and Zachery, the only other backcourt returnee is seldom-used 6-2 sophomore **Jermain Speights** (0.6 ppg), who played 22 minutes in 12 games.

Fortunately, backcourt help is on the way in a newcomer class that includes a major offensive threat in 6-2 junior guard **Jibrahn Ike** from Southeastern Community College.

"Jibrahn can really score it," Moser said of the 6-2 Minneapolis product. "He scored about 35 a game in high school and led the state of Minnesota, and then he led his juco district in scoring and helped them win a national title."

Last season, Ike averaged 15.9 points for a team that went 25-8.

The point-guard dilemma may be solved with a freshman, 6-2 **Rory Green** of Memphis Oak Haven High School. A year ago, Green, playing for his father, averaged 21 points, five rebounds, four assists and two steals.

"Rory is the total package," Moser said of Green. "He excels both on the floor and in the classroom. He is the valedictorian of his high school class and a coach's son who knows the game well. He can play two positions, both the point guard and the two guard, because he shoots the ball so well. I just love how fearless he is when he plays."

Three other new faces will help on the front line, and one of them also comes with the reputation as a prolific scorer. Transfer **Nick Jones**, a 6-7 junior forward from Aquinas (Tenn.) College, is a combination inside-outside threat who could provide punch to an attack that lost almost 51 points per game from last season.

Last year, Jones averaged 18 points and 8.8 rebounds. At 220 pounds, he has the size to work inside, but Jones can also knock down three-pointers. He shot 40 percent from behind the arc last year, once making seven threes in a half.

"Nick is an extremely versatile player," Moser said. "The things that stuck out when we watched Nick was how well he shot the ball and how hard he played. He's athletic and he's very skilled. And we like the fact that he comes from a winning program and knows the amount of work it takes to win."

Moser, though, may be the highest on a hometown product, 6-7 junior **Danny McCall** of North Little Rock and Westark College.

"He's just a warrior," Moser said. "He's a true power forward that's played on nothing but winning programs."

Incoming 6-6 freshman **Josh Jacobs** (22.0 ppg, 8.0 rpg, 4.0 apg) of Mesquite, Texas, and returning 6-6 sophomore forward **Richard Hardman** will also be available for front-line duty.

The Trojans may need all those bodies in an East

Division that harbors just about all of the size in the league.

"Western Kentucky and Arkansas State both have a lot of size and a lot of quickness," Moser said. "I think they're head and shoulders above the rest of us on our side, and they're the ones that we're going to have to take a run at."

2001-2002 SCHEDULE

Nov.	16	@Massachusetts
	19	Arkansas Tech
	21	@Mississippi State
	24	Arkansas-Pine Bluff
	27	@Southeast Missouri
	30	@Saint Louis
Dec.	3	Central Arkansas
	5	Austin Peay
	8	@Colorado State
	10	The Citadel
	15	@Austin Peay
	18	Morgan State
	21	@Grambling State
	30	@Florida International
Jan.	3	North Texas
	5	Denver
	10	@Arkansas State
	14	@New Orleans
	19	South Alabama
	24	@Western Kentucky
	26	@Middle Tennessee
Feb.	2	Arkansas State
	7	Western Kentucky
	9	Middle Tennessee
	14	@New Mexico State
	16	@Louisiana-Lafayette
	23	Florida International
	28	#Sun Belt Tournament
March	1-5	#Sun Belt Tournament

@Road Games
#Lakefront Arena, New Orleans, LA

BLUE RIBBON ANALYSIS

BACKCOURT	B-
BENCH/DEPTH	B-
FRONTCOURT	C+
INTANGIBLES	B

The Trojans came a long way last season, much further than anyone, maybe themselves included, expected. But it's hard to replace guys like Blackmon, a unanimous all-league selection, and the offensive production that Barksdale and Smith provided.

Nobody expected much last year, either.

"We could have said that there was no pressure last year," Moser said, "but we always put the pressure on ourselves. We know we've got to keep doing the same things … we have to defend, change defenses, take advantage of things. We're not going to have one guy to step in and do what Stan Blackmon or any of those other guys did."

Then again, UALR learned the value of defense last year and had all the teams in the league looking over their collective shoulders. They're still there.

(D.M.)

 **Denver**

LOCATION	Denver, CO
CONFERENCE	Sun Belt (West)
LAST SEASON	10-18 (.357)
CONFERENCE RECORD	5-11 (5th)
STARTERS LOST/RETURNING	2/3
NICKNAME	Pioneers
COLORS	Crimson & Gold
HOMECOURT	Magness Arena (7,200)
COACH	Terry Carroll (Northern Iowa '78)
RECORD AT SCHOOL	First year
CAREER RECORD	First year
ASSISTANTS	Greg Lackey (Southern Miss '82)
	Byron Jones (Central Oklahoma '95)
	Matt Woodley (Drake '00)
TEAM WINS (last 5 years)	14-7-10-6-10
RPI (last 5 years)	NA-NA-NA-290-265
2000-01 FINISH	Lost in conference first round.

The growing pains continue for the University of

Denver in the Pioneers' fourth season as a Division I member and their third year in the Sun Belt Conference. But don't think that Denver hasn't made strides in that time.

The Pioneers went 10-18 last year against a second straight rugged schedule, showing an improvement of four wins over the previous season. Denver also won five Sun Belt games, two more than it posted in its first season in the league, and went on the road to take three of those wins, including a double-digit job against an Arkansas State team that finished tied for second in the East Division.

Apparently, that wasn't enough for the powers that be, as four-year head coach Marty Fletcher—who holds more Sun Belt career wins than any coach outside of Gene Bartow—was given the axe after the season.

Enter Terry Carroll, who brings a history of phenomenal success at his last two coaching stops. This, though, could be his toughest coaching challenge.

"It's our job to determine what direction we want this program to go," he said. "This program's been in Division I for three years, and the biggest thing we have to do is make sure everybody knows who DU is."

Carroll was able to do that at his last two stops. At Indian Hills Community College in Ottumwa, Iowa, he led his team to a national-record 72 straight victories at one point. That string included a pair of national titles and two national coach-of-the-year honors.

From there, he went to Iowa State as an assistant, eventually becoming associate head coach and a key part of that program's advance to the Elite Eight in the 1999-2000 season. He's hoping he can bring the same type of magic to the mountains.

"I hope we have guys that want to come in here and be a part of something," he said. "We've tried to develop a sense of urgency about it. This summer was absolutely huge for us, and it'll be interesting to see how much the off-season work helps us."

Carroll has already made one major move, shifting senior forward **Wahhab Carter** back to the power-forward slot after a year at small forward. The 6-6 Carter (9.6 ppg, 4.0 rpg) had his production drop off noticeably from a sophomore season when he earned All-Sun Belt honors and was heralded as one of the league's rising young stars.

"He made a position change, and he just wasn't comfortable," Carroll said. "We're putting him back at the four spot, and hopefully he'll establish himself a lot like he did two years ago."

That year, Carter did it all for the Pioneers, averaging 17.4 points and 7.5 rebounds and displaying one of the league's top all-around floor games. He ranked second in the Sun Belt in scoring and third in rebounding and was one of only two sophomores on the all-league squad, along with Western Kentucky's Chris Marcus.

But Denver went 6-22 that year despite those efforts, mostly because the squad shot under 37 percent from the floor. The Pioneers bettered that mark last season even with the struggles of Carter, who slipped to a 38.1 shooting mark and hit only 44.7 percent from the line after shooting 66 percent as a sophomore.

Carroll, for one, expects the El Reno, Okla., product to return to form for his final season.

"We're counting on him for a lot of leadership," he said. "He's got to be the guy that sets the tone for us in the preseason, leads us in practice and gets us ready for that first ball game."

Two other starters return, but the player who drew the most attention and ended up having Denver's most successful individual season wasn't a part of that regular starting group. **B.J. Pratt** (16.2 ppg, 3.2 rpg, 2.4 apg), a 6-2 junior started only once, but played more than 27 minutes per game off the bench and ended the season as the squad's leading scorer.

Pratt, who had shown signs of freshman greatness a year earlier with a 37-point night against Louisiana Tech, became a more consistent scorer as a sophomore. He hit almost 40 percent from three-point range, making 75 shots behind the arc, and was voted to the U.S. Basketball Writers Association All-District 8 team.

Like Carter, he will also go through a position switch this year.

"He's a proven scorer," Carroll said. "We're going to take him from a shooting guard and make him more of a combo guard, let him play both spots. We expect to let him run the show some, but to also score from whichever position he's at."

Change is also the name of the game for 6-5 senior forward **Sherman Rochell** (7.1 ppg, 4.5 rpg, 4.0 apg), a solid player who can play several different positions—and did last year. That was borne out by his team-leading 110 assists to go with earning a reputation as one of the league's best defensive players.

"We're going to play him at the three spot most of the time," Carroll said. "We're going to try to play to fit his game better. We need to take advantage of his abilities, and the small forward spot may really fit him in this offense."

The other returning starter is 6-9 senior center **Steve Simmons** (8.1 ppg, 9.0 rpg, 1.0 bpg), who improved his scoring and rebounding numbers greatly last season, along with his shooting. He shot 55 percent last year, 35 percent the season before.

He proved last year he can play in this league," Carroll said after Simmons averaged 9.4 points and 9.9 rebounds in Sun Belt play [ranking second in the conference in the latter]. "We need for he and Sherman to have big senior seasons for us since they're experienced guys that have been around."

Experience is not short for the Pioneers. Carter, Pratt, Rochell and Simmons have a combined eight letters, and five other players saw action in at least 15 games last season.

"We came in here with not a lot of time to recruit, and only recruited one guy," Carroll said. "So we're going to try to mold what we do around these guys' talents and see where our best chance to win is. We're going to play a four-man motion offense so it doesn't matter much if you're the two, three or four guy. It's much more important who you're covering on defense."

Denver also improved on defense last year. Opponents shot better than 48 percent from the field and out-rebounded the Pioneers by six per game two years ago, but DU allowed foes to shoot only 43.2 percent last year and took a season rebound advantage over its opposition for the first time in the Division I ranks.

Two of the reasons for that was the inside improvement of 6-9 sophomores **Brett Starkey** (2.4 ppg, 4.3 rpg) and **Jamaal Ramey** (1.8 ppg, 2.3 rpg). The two played double-figure minutes each in a reserve role and threw their weight around. Starkey weights 260, Ramey 230.

"They're going to have to step up and be front-line guys for us," Carroll said. "One of those two will have to prove that he can get after it, and our new guys will also have to step up."

Three other players—5-11 senior **Phillip Heath** (2.0 ppg, 0.9 rpg), 5-10 senior **Tyrone Turner** (1.4 ppg, 0.8 rpg, 1.0 apg) and 6-0 sophomore **Ryan Goral** (1.4 ppg)—saw limited backcourt time last season. Their roles will likely be limited to spot duty again this year, especially with the arrival of highly regarded junior college swingman **Leslie Richardson** (19.0 ppg, .460 3PT), a 6-3 product of Aurora, Colo., and Lamar (Colo.) Community College.

"He's proven in junior college that he can shoot it," Carroll said. "That's something we felt we desperately needed, an experienced type guy who could take some of the pressure off the other guys to score. Hopefully he'll give us a little more scoring punch."

With the late recruiting start, Carroll and his staff have only two other new faces on the roster, those being 6-3 freshman guard **Adam Warren** of Richland Hills, Texas, and 6-7 freshman forward **Taylor Lay** of Oklahoma City, Okla. Whether they will make an impact remains to be seen, but Carroll already knows that the Sun Belt can be a tough league for new players.

"It's a great basketball conference," he said, "and we know it's a challenge to compete night in and night out. Our focus the entire spring was on toughness because we knew we had to get stronger, and I think we did that."

2001-2002 SCHEDULE

Nov.	16	Montana Tech
	18	@Air Force
	26	Wyoming
	30	@Manhattan
Dec.	6	@Morris Brown
	9	@Saint Louis
	12	Air Force
	15	Colorado State
	21	@Texas A&M-Corpus Christi
	27	New Mexico State
	30	@Drake
Jan.	3	@Arkansas State
	5	@Arkansas-Little Rock
	7	Morris Brown
	13	Florida International
	17	North Texas
	19	Western Kentucky
	24	@New Mexico State
	26	@Louisiana-Lafayette
Feb.	2	@North Texas
	5	Texas A&M-Corpus Christi
	7	South Alabama
	10	New Orleans
	14	@South Alabama
	16	@Middle Tennessee
	18	Louisiana-Lafayette
	23	@New Orleans
	28	#Sun Belt Tournament
Feb.	1-5	#Sun Belt Tournament

@Road Games
#Lakefront Arena, New Orleans, LA

BLUE RIBBON ANALYSIS

BACKCOURT	B-
BENCH/DEPTH	C
FRONTCOURT	C
INTANGIBLES	C

Denver was 10th in the Sun Belt in scoring and turnover margin and 11th in field-goal percentage last year and also finished last in the league from the free-throw line. So it's not surprising that the Pioneers have worked to re-tool themselves offensively.

Carter remains the key. Teams playing Denver used to worry about him first and everybody else as an afterthought. Hey, maybe they did that too well, and the rest of the Pioneers got a chance to shine a little more. But if Carter can return to his sophomore form, and DU fulfills its new coach's desires to toughen up, the steady improvement could continue.

"We lost games down the stretch last year just from not being tough," Carroll said, "so that's the first priority ahead of everything else. We have to get them to understand how tough and physical this game is."

(D.M.)

Florida International

LOCATION	**Miami, FL**
CONFERENCE	**Sun Belt (East)**
LAST SEASON	**8-21 (.276)**
CONFERENCE RECORD	**5-11 (5th)**
STARTERS LOST/RETURNING	**2/3**
NICKNAME	**Golden Panthers**
COLORS	**Blue & Gold**
HOMECOURT	**Golden Panther Arena (5,000)**
COACH	**Donnie Marsh (Franklin & Marshall '79)**
RECORD AT SCHOOL	**8-21 (1 year)**
CAREER RECORD	**84-54 (6 years)**
ASSISTANTS	**Don Kelbick (Boston '77)**
	Sergio Roucco (Nova Southeastern '87)
	Lonnie Williams (Eastern Washington '80)
TEAM WINS (last 5 years)	**16-21-13-16-18-8**
RPI (last 5 years)	**177-87-163-165-252**
2000-01 FINISH	**Lost in conference quarterfinal.**

Sure, Florida International has got six players who started at least seven games back from last year, and the Golden Panthers won four games at the end of the 2000-01 season before a tournament loss with those guys playing key roles.

But to listen to all the talk coming from the southern tip of Florida, those guys are just an afterthought … passe … yesterday's news.

All of the excitement in the Panther camp surrounds the new faces, faces who have come from a lot of new places and who have yet to put a single point in FIU's scorebook.

But, make no mistake about it. The combination of transfer players becoming eligible for this season and a big-time recruiting class make the Panthers' newcomer group among the nation's best—easily enough to vault FIU back into the Sun Belt Conference's upper echelon.

It should make for a much happier season for second-year coach Donnie Marsh, who struggled with a team that finished 8-21 last season and mostly stood around and watched standout guard Carlos Arroyo do his thing.

The now-graduated and two-time all-league pick Arroyo did his part, averaging 21.2 points and more than four assists per game, but many times the FIU offense ground to a halt when the Puerto Rican standout was off his game.

"It's going to be a heck of a chore to replace him," Marsh said, "because he was everything to us. But we're gong to change our focus a lot and pick the tempo up. We're going to be a much more fast-paced team and play a lot more guys."

He's going to be able to do that because of a combination of the six returning lettermen who each started between seven and 20 games last year, and the ultra-talented newcomers. The only question is how quickly the two groups assimilate.

"Winning those games at the end of the year was a real boost for us," said Marsh, a former third-round NBA draft choice whose varied background includes work in collegiate admissions, high school district coordination and even a stint as baseball coach at his Franklin & Marshall alma mater. "We did some things at the end of the year that we really wanted and needed to do."

Marsh admits that one thing he and his staff needed to do was increase the overall talent level to compete with the league's top teams, and they've done that with a combination of four transfers and four highly-regarded high school signees.

"We're really excited about this group," Marsh said. "We feel good that they're pretty young but very talented, and the only question is how quickly we mature as a team … how quickly we forget playing like individuals."

Three members of that group already have Division I experience. **Al Harris**, a 6-8 sophomore forward, becomes eligible on Dec. 15 after transferring from Seton Hall. **Todd Smith**, a 6-4 junior swingman, began his career at Nebraska before transferring to Daytona Beach Community College and eventually to the FIU campus.

And **Rodrigo Viegas**, a 6-6 junior forward, played at Virginia Tech while Marsh was on staff there.

"Harris has played a year in the Big East and Rodrigo has two years in the Atlantic 10," Marsh said," so those guys have been there. They may be a little rusty, but they did a great job last year of helping us just with the way they played in practice. They know our system, and they know the demands.

"Rodrigo really knows me, and what he does is head off a lot of things in the locker room that never get to me. He's a leader already for us."

Those three join with junior college transfer **Nikola Novakovic**, a 6-8, 235-pound Yugoslavian strongman who came from Gulf Coast (Fla.) Community College to give FIU a quick infusion of experience.

"He brings us the inside, low-post presence that we don't have," Marsh said. "He's a lot more pure low post that your typical European guy."

The freshman group could also make an impact. **Taurance Johnson** is 6-9 but could be at a guard slot after a strong career at Faith Christian High in New Jersey. He was on virtually all of the nation's listings of top prep recruits. Brick Oettinger of Prep Stars Recruiters Handbook and CNN/Sports Illustrated.com chose Johnson as his No. 39 recruit in the nation. And Oettinger selected Johnson as his No. 1 "non-power conference" recruit last fall. The Sporting News rated Johnson the No. 78 high school senior in the country and ESPN rated him the No. 12 power forward in the country.

"He's a major, major prospect," Marsh said. "He brings a lot of versatility to the table. I think he could play all five positions if we needed it."

Carlos Morgan, a 6-3 guard from Miami Christian High by way of the Dominican Republic was one of the top prep player in Florida last year. He was Oettinger's No. 120 prospect, and No. 11 "non-power conference" recruit last fall.

David Luber, a 5-10 point guard, came out of a Pennsylvania prep program—Hattboro-Horsham—that had five players sign college scholarships. And **John Boney**, at 6-5 and 240 pounds, is a wild card after playing high school ball four years ago and no organized competition since then.

Boney played at Bishop Loughlin High School in New York. He signed with UNLV in 1996, but never enrolled there.

Instead, Boney stayed in the New York City area playing AAU basketball with the Brooklyn Gauchos Club team. It was through a relationship with Gauchos' Coach Chuck Austin, that Marsh first had contact with Boney, who enrolled at FIU last fall and spent the year working on academics.

"It's been a hard road for John," Marsh said. "After four years away from the classroom, he has had to pay his own way down here and work to get himself eligible to play. He's proven that he wants to make this happen and I'm glad we're here to give him the opportunity."

Marsh was very pleased with his recruiting class, which Oettinger ranked No. 1 last fall among non-power conference classes.

"There's a lot of versatility in this group," Marsh said. "They're going to have a chance to impact us right away because there are some minutes to be had."

Where those minutes will come from isn't certain, because that solid returnee corps isn't going to step back and let the young turks take over.

Guard and hometown Miami product **Haven Jackson** (7.6 ppg, 2.9 rpg), a 6-2 senior, became eligible at mid-term and started the final 20 games of the season for the Panthers, ranking as the team's leading returning scorer.

Guard mate **Fab Fisher** (3.3 ppg, 1.4 rpg, 1.4 apg), a 5-9 junior, played in all 29 games, but FIU appeared to jell late in the year when he stepped into the starting lineup at point guard.

"That might have been the turnaround for us," Marsh said. "Fab started doing what we needed at the point, and **[Chris] Carter** ended up starting most of the time down the stretch."

The 6-6 senior Carter (2.5 ppg, 2.5 rpg) also became eligible at mid-season, and he and Bulgaria native **Slavcho Slavtchev** (5.9 ppg, 0.8 rpg), a 6-4 sophomore who shot better than 47 percent from three-point range, became regular fixtures over the final half of the season. Carter, who led the team in field goal percentage, developed a reputation as one of the Sun Belt's most intense defensive stoppers.

"We only had seven players for the first eight games last year," Marsh said, "so a lot of guys had a chance to play a lot of minutes for us."

Ten different players started at least five games for the Panthers last season, and the most surprising of that group may have been 6-4 junior **Javier Cuenca** and 6-7 junior **Carlos Fernandez**, both also Miami products. Cuenca (1.9 ppg, 2.0 rpg) started nine of the first 10 games.

Fernandez (2.5 ppg, 2.9 rpg), who was a walk-on football player at the University of Miami before switching to basketball, hadn't played the game since high school. Nevertheless, he wound up starting 15 games.

FIU will need all its new firepower this season. The Golden Panthers play a rugged non-conference schedule that includes Princeton, Auburn, Miami, West Virginia, Penn and UNLV to go with an appearance in the San Juan Shootout.

2001-2002 SCHEDULE

Nov.	16-17	#FIU Tip-Off Classic
	20	Florida Tech
	24	Princeton
	26	Indiana-Fort Wayne
	30	@Auburn
Dec.	3	@Miami
	8	@West Virginia
	20-22	##San Juan Shootout
	27-28	###FIU Holiday Classic
	30	Arkansas-Little Rock
Jan.	2	@Western Kentucky
	5	Middle Tennessee
	7	@Pennsylvania
	10	@North Texas
	13	@Denver
	16	Arkansas State
	23	South Alabama
	26	New Orleans
	31	@Western Kentucky
Feb.	2	@Middle Tennessee
	6	@New Mexico State
	9	Louisiana-Lafayette
	13	@UNLV
	21	@Arkansas State
	23	@Arkansas-Little Rock
	28	####Sun Belt Tournament
March	1-5	####Sun Belt Tournament

@Road Games
#Miami, FL (vs. St. Peter's first round; also Maine, Texas-San Antonio)
##San Juan, Puerto Rico (vs. Coppin State first round; also Baylor, Jacksonville, Niagara, Oral Roberts, Puerto Rico, Texas-Pan American)
###Miami, FL (vs. Vermont first round; also Long Island, Ohio)
####Lakefront Arena, New Orleans, LA

BLUE RIBBON ANALYSIS

BACKCOURT	B-
BENCH/DEPTH	A-
FRONTCOURT	B-
INTANGIBLES	B+

Potential is just that … it's something that hasn't happened yet. The Golden Panthers have potential by the boatload, but there will be skeptics until FIU proves on the floor that it belongs among the Sun Belt's elite.

But the soft-spoken Marsh lights up when he talks about the combination of returning veterans and a newcomer group that will have a huge task in just living up to its preseason hype.

"We started competing and playing hard and playing smart late last year," he said. "Put that together with our entering group and we have the makings of something special."

The non-conference schedule should provide a severe test, a learning environment … or maybe a proving ground. If it becomes the latter, the rest of the Sun Belt better beware of panthers screaming in the night.

(D.M.)

Louisiana-Lafayette

LOCATION	**Lafayette, LA**
CONFERENCE	**Sun Belt (West)**
LAST SEASON	**16-13 (.552)**
CONFERENCE RECORD	**10-6 (t-2nd)**
STARTERS LOST/RETURNING	**2/3**
NICKNAME	**Ragin' Cajuns**
COLORS	**Vermilion & White**
HOMECOURT	**Cajundome (12,800)**
COACH	**Jessie Evans (Eastern Michigan '80)**
RECORD AT SCHOOL	**72-51 (4 years)**
CAREER RECORD	**72-51 (4 years)**
ASSISTANTS	**Robert Lee (Nicholls State '91)** **Paul Johnson (Harding '97)** **Eddie Vaughn (Southeastern Louisiana '76)**
TEAM WINS (last 5 years)	**12-18-13-25-16**
RPI (last 5 years)	**185-130-185-67-138**
2000-01 FINISH	**Lost in conference semifinal.**

You could almost take a ruler and divide Louisiana Lafayette's team.

On one side, there are nine lettermen, all of whom have seen action even though two of them are back after a year's absence. More importantly, all are backcourt and wing players, and the tallest of that group is 6-6.

On the other side, there's the beef—six new faces in the program, four freshmen and two transfers, and every one of them stands 6-8—or taller.

It will make for an eclectic mix.

"This is the most that our squad has changed in a while," coach Jessie Evans said. "My second year here it changed a lot when inherited seniors were gone and other players came in. Unfortunately, we didn't have the upperclassman leadership and took a step back. The next year, things fell more into place."

That "next year" was the 1999-2000 season, when the Cajuns went 25-9 on the way to the Sun Belt Conference title and the NCAA Tournament. Many of the main cogs from that unit were back last year, but the squad slipped to a 16-13 mark.

"Every time we've had awesome senior leadership," Evans said, "we've had seasons like we did two years ago. Last year, no one really stepped forward and provided that, even though we had a big senior class. That's what we're looking for from this team ... someone to step forward and take charge."

He'll also need someone to point the way to the gym for the newcomer group, and make sure they don't bump their heads on the doorjamb on the way in. That's the kind of size the group has.

"There's a little concern because the guys down low haven't been here," Evans said, "but we are certainly going to have the size and strength on the interior, and I have no question that a lot of these guys can step right in and be big contributors immediately."

The Cajuns will be the strongest and most experienced on the perimeter, and that's where big things will need to happen if the squad is going to be in the thick of the league race down the stretch—just like UL has in every one of Evans' five seasons.

"The one thing that I'm maybe the most proud of is that we've been consistently in the mix every year," he said. "We've had a chance to win the league in the last two weeks of the season. I hope that's the case this year, and I think we have a chance to do that."

One of the keys to that success is 6-2 senior guard **Blane Harmon** (9.7 ppg, 2.8 apg), who received an added year of NCAA eligibility for this season after sitting out his freshman year. Harmon averaged double figures in each of his first two seasons before the Cajuns spread scoring responsibilities around more last year. But, he's still capable of explosions, like his 26 points against Western Kentucky in a tough 82-75 loss in a conference tournament semifinal.

Tournament time has been good for Harmon; his selection to the All-Sun Belt Tournament team makes him the only player in school history picked twice to the league's all-tournament squad.

"It's great to have him on the floor because I know he's going to do everything we ask him to do," Evans said. "But we need him to step up, take charge and be enthusiastic and a leader in everything we do. We need him to be a vocal leader both on and off the floor."

Harmon, who has led the squad in three-pointers each of the last two years, heads up a deep backcourt that also returns regular starter **Kenneth Lawrence** at point guard. The 6-0 junior Lawrence (6.6 ppg, 3.2 apg) also had his season-high game in the league tournament with 16 points in a quarterfinal win over Louisiana Tech.

But, when the Cajuns need points in a bundle and in a hurry, the name that jumps out (jump being the key word) is 6-6 junior wingman **Anthony Johnson** (15.5 ppg, 5.5 rpg), who in his first season might have been the most athletic player in the conference. The high-flying Chicago product finished in the Sun Belt's top 10 in scoring and led the league in field-goal percentage. He also probably topped the Sun Belt in rim-rattling dunks—six of them came in one game against North Texas on his way to a 33-point night.

"He's impressive, and you look at a player like him and you want more," Evans said. "He can be even better and reach his true potential if he keeps working and taking care of the little things on and off the floor. But he's capable just because of his athletic ability."

The Cajuns have solid support for all three perimeter spots. Local product **Brad Boyd** (4.9 ppg) at 6-5 is a streak shooter with deep three-point range, and Evans said that 6-5 sophomore **Laurie Bridges** (2.0 ppg, 1.4 rpg) may be the most improved player on the team since the end of last season.

Robert Jupiter, a 6-3 junior who sat out last year after a promising freshman year (4.1 ppg), is also available at the second guard and wing slots, and 5-11 sophomore **Antoine Landry** (3.1 ppg) got game experience at both guard slots in his first year.

"A lot of these guys have developed a lot," Evans said. "Antoine's really a combo guard despite his size, and all the players have talked about how Laurie has played in free play. This is a big year for Robert Jupiter, and he's in for a lot of competition."

Also back after red-shirting last season is 6-6 senior wing **Shea Whiting** (5.5 ppg, 2.7 rpg in 1999-2000), who will provide athleticism when he returns in the second semester. And 6-6 senior **Darryl Robins** (4.5 ppg, 3.5 rpg) returns as the closest thing UL has to a low-post presence among the returning class.

Robins plays bigger than his size but has not been consistent.

"Daryl's going to have to emerge now for us," Evans said. "He's had upperclassmen in front of him for a while, and it's his time to step up and play now. Shea's also going to help us tremendously just to give us some experience in the middle."

The Cajuns will not lack for numbers inside, or for size, as a sextet of big bodies checks into the program. The biggest two in that group are a pair of freshmen—6-11 Australian product **Chris Cameron** and 6-10 1/2 **Michael Southall**, who Evans expects to have immediate impact.

"Chris is very capable of posting up and also stepping out and shooting the mid-range jumper," Evans said. "Michael will be a force on the interior, and will be the type of forward that will be a power player early and could develop into a face-the-basket player."

UL is a landing point for Southall, whose off-court brushes with the law caused scholarship offers from Kentucky and Georgia Tech to be pulled before and during a year at Hargrave Military Academy in Virginia.

Highly-regarded 6-8 Chicago freshman **Johnathan Byrd** (18.0 ppg, 12.0 rpg), from Morgan Park High School, will also make immediate waves on the front line, as could 6-9 freshman **Cedric Williams** (16.0 ppg, 12.0 rpg) of Houston North Shore High School. Byrd led his team to the city championship and a third-place finish in the Illinois state tournament.

Evans also expects 6-9, 245-pound Senegal native and Trinity Valley Junior College product **Khadim Khandji** (8.0 ppg, 9.0 rpg) to see action on the front line along with 6-8 junior **Chris Williams**, a transfer from Missouri-Kansas City.

"We're going to find a way to use all of their talents and abilities," Evans said. "Basketball is still a game of speed and quickness, and even with their size these guys still give us a lot of quickness and athletic ability. And they'll get a lot of opportunities to get a baptism this year."

A strong non-conference schedule includes a historic

meeting with nearby LSU, the first such encounter in 57 years.

"It's going to challenge us before the opening of conference play," Evans said, "but that's nothing but good for this team. We do have pretty good balance, and that will be a great barometer of where we're at before the conference starts."

2001-2002 SCHEDULE

Nov.	17	McNeese State
	19	@Bradley
	24	Mississippi State
Dec.	4	@LSU
	9	Birmingham Southern
	11	Bradley
	13	Loyola, New Orleans
	17	@Texas Tech
	26	@Bethune-Cookman
	28-29	#Arizona State Tournament
Jan.	3	South Alabama
	5	New Orleans
	10	@Western Kentucky
	12	@Middle Tennessee State
	19	@New Mexico State
	24	North Texas
	26	Denver
	31	@South Alabama
Feb.	2	@New Orleans
	7	Centenary
	9	@Florida International
	11	@North Texas
	14	Arkansas State
	16	Arkansas-Little Rock
	18	@Denver
	23	New Mexico State
	28	##Sun Belt Tournament
March	1-5	##Sun Belt Tournament

@Road Games
#Tempe, AZ (vs. Northwestern first round; also Canisius, Arizona State)
##Lakefront Arena, New Orleans, LA

BLUE RIBBON ANALYSIS

BACKCOURT	B+
BENCH/DEPTH	B-
FRONTCOURT	B-
INTANGIBLES	B

Many Sun Belt teams had heralded and nationally-ranked recruiting years. UL's was much more quiet, and Evans likes it that way. That being said, the incoming Cajun class may be the league's most valuable and most important, because it has almost total responsibility for the inside game this season.

Still, the experienced players will have to come through outside in order for the youngsters to show their talents inside.

"We will be as good as our veterans allow us to be," Evans said.

That could be very good. Johnson is a mercurial talent and Harmon and Lawrence have worlds of game experience. If that group sharpens its focus, leaders step forward and the newcomers mature down low, a team that was a couple of plays away from a second straight league tournament title last season will be right there again.

(D.M.)

Middle Tennessee

LOCATION	Murfreesboro, TN
CONFERENCE	Sun Belt (East)
LAST SEASON	5-22 (.185)
CONFERENCE RECORD	1-15 (6th)
STARTERS LOST/RETURNING	2/3
NICKNAME	Blue Raiders
COLORS	Royal Blue & White
HOMECOURT	Murphy Center (11,520)
COACH	Randy Wiel (North Carolina '79)
RECORD AT SCHOOL	70-75 (5 years)
CAREER RECORD	102-125 (8 years)
ASSISTANTS	Jim Ryan (Montclair State '90)
	Andy Herzer (UNC Asheville '84)
	Pat Sullivan (North Carolina '95)
TEAM WINS (last 5 years)	19-19-12-15-5
RPI (last 5 years)	156-136-232-170-309

2000-01 FINISH   **Lost in conference first round.**

Middle Tennessee wanted to make a major splash in its first year in the newly expanded Sun Belt Conference. That was before the freak accident that sidelined most of the Blue Raiders' key players.

No, just kidding … there was no such freak accident. But it may have seemed like that, because MTSU went through a series of injuries that would send just about any team on a downward spiral. And those injuries are still having their effects.

"We were really looking forward to our first season in the league," coach Randy Wiel said. "The Sun Belt was going to be a great league for us."

That was before the squad's inside power man, 6-10, 240-pound center **Les Nosse** (9.3 ppg, 3.5 rpg), went down four games into the schedule with a stress fracture in his right leg and was lost for the season, and leading scorer Fernando Ortiz failed to recover from two off-season knee surgeries and was forced to the sideline after 14 games.

"The doctors pretty much shut him down for the year," said Wiel, whose team struggled to a 5-22 season, its worst in more than 60 years.

It didn't help that **Iiro Tenngren** (9.6 ppg, 3.7 rpg), a 6-8, 240-pound senior forward, hobbled through most of the season on sore ankles, both of which were operated on immediately after the season mercifully ended.

Will this year be any better, enough to get Wiel off the hot seat after last year's atrocity and two previous so-so seasons on the heels of 19-win seasons in his first two years in 1997 and '98? Again, it depends on the injury factor.

Tenngren had surgery four days after last season ended, but a follow-up procedure was still necessary and he was still in a cast at the start of the fall semester and facing rehabilitation before the opening of preseason drills. Nosse, meanwhile, was expected to continue rehab until practice begins.

"He's still not doing everything full steam," Wiel said of Nosse, one of four seniors on the MTSU roster. "He's done conditioning drills, but he hasn't had any kind of contact, any hard defensive slides. We don't want him to do anything until he's pain free."

The return of that pair will help solidify a lineup, and the silver lining to their absence is that a lot of players ended up gaining experience—as rugged as it was in conference play—during their first sojourn through the Sun Belt.

The most notable of that group is 6-3 sophomore shooting guard **Tommy Gunn** (9.2 ppg, 3.0 rpg), who took over the graduated Ortiz' slot as a freshman and finished as the team's second-leading scorer while compiling 13 double-figure games. Even with those numbers and his experience, though, he'll be challenged for that spot by junior college second-team All-America selection **John Humphrey**, a 6-2 junior sharpshooter who averaged 24.6 points per game at Louisburg (N.C.) Junior College last season.

The Raiders also have **Derek Glasper** (19.6 ppg, 3.5 rpg), a 6-3 junior from Neosho (Kansas) Junior College, available at that slot.

"The two-guard is our deepest position," Wiel said, "but that's also our biggest challenge. It's going to really be competitive and we'll have to see who works the best with the rest of our guys."

Tenngren ended up as MTSU's leading scorer despite limping through the latter part of the season. The Helsinki, Finland, product, who played at Vanderbilt as a freshman before transferring, had to take over much of the inside role after Nosse's departure and will now be allowed to shift back to his natural power-forward slot.

Joining Gunn and Tenngren as returning starters is 5-9 senior point guard **D'Marius Wilkes** (4.7 ppg, 3.3 apg), an in-state (Memphis) product who came out of Hiwassee (Tenn.) Junior College and moved into the starting role at mid-season. But his job isn't secure either, with 5-11 junior **Eric Parham** (15.6 ppg, 9.0 apg) of Aquinas (Tenn.) Junior College joining the squad and 5-10 sophomore walk-on **Jermale Wilkerson** (1.1 ppg) showing continued improvement.

"Parham's a little bigger than D'Marius and is a very explosive point guard," Wiel said. "He could give us a lot of speed and quickness."

Nosse averaged 10.0 points and 4.4 rebounds while setting a school record with an 89.2 free-throw percentage in his junior year in 1999-00, and was shooting better than 60 percent from the field before leaving with the stress fracture last November. He received a medical red-shirt year, but Wiel said it will take him some time to round into form after such a major injury.

"He's anxious to get back and play," Wiel said. "He'd never had an injury of any consequence, and suddenly

he's out for the whole year, so he's going to be a little tentative. There's a psychological part of it he's got to overcome, but he realizes what he means to this team with his size and strength.

"The biggest difference in the Sun Belt and the Ohio Valley [where MTSU held membership for 52 years before last season] is that the Sun Belt's got some dominant big men. The OVC was more guard and wing-oriented."

Backup center **Demario Watson** (3.4 ppg, 2.1 rpg), a 6-8 senior, returns to provide depth in the middle, but the team's leading rebounder last year was 6-7 junior forward **Bryant Mitchell** (8.6 ppg, 4.9 rpg). Mitchell was in the sixth-man role and will be in a mix of power forwards that Wiel hopes will fill what was a big hole for the Raiders last year.

Mitchell had double-figure rebounds twice and scored twin digits in 11 games, while 6-6 sophomore **Steven Jackson** (2.1 ppg, 1.2 rpg) saw his playing time increase as his first season progressed.

Two noteworthy newcomers will also be available there, including highly regarded freshman **Charles Anderson** (19.5 ppg, 11.4 rpg), a 6-8 post from Chattanooga City High School, and 6-8 junior **William Pippen** (16.0 ppg, 7.2 rpg), the nephew of NBA standout Scottie Pippen. Pippen played last season for Connors State (Okla.) Junior College.

"Anderson has really shown flashes of brilliance in individual drills," Wiel said, "but he has a lot to learn. He's a hard worker and we may have to throw him to the sharks, but he's played a lot of AAU ball so it's not like he hasn't been in the wars.

"Pippen's more of a wing guy but he can swing inside, and when he does that he gives us good size at the small forward. He's kind of built like Scottie."

2001-2002 SCHEDULE

Nov.	17	Bryan College
	21	IUPUI
	24	UNC Greensboro
	26	@Belmont
Dec.	1	@Radford
	4	Rice
	6	@Tennessee-Martin
	8	Tennessee State
	15	@Texas-Pan American
	19	@East Carolina
	28	@South Alabama
	30	@New Orleans
Jan.	5	@Florida International
	10	New Mexico State
	12	Louisiana-Lafayette
	16	Western Kentucky
	19	@North Texas
	21	@Tennessee
	24	Arkansas State
	26	Arkansas-Little Rock
	31	@IUPUI-Fort Wayne
Feb.	2	Florida International
	4	Texas-Pan American
	7	@Arkansas State
	9	@Arkansas-Little Rock
	16	Denver
	23	@Western Kentucky
	28	#Sun Belt Tournament
March	1-5	#Sun Belt Tournament

@Road Games
#Lakefront Arena, New Orleans, LA

BLUE RIBBON ANALYSIS

BACKCOURT	C
BENCH/DEPTH	B-
FRONTCOURT	B-
INTANGIBLES	B

The Raiders have a lot more bodies available at every position, but whether quantity will translate into quality remains to be seen. Even though 64 percent of last year's point production returns, no returning player managed a 20-point game last year, so the influx of potential scorers can do nothing but help there.

Of the 22 losses last year, only nine of them were by single-digit margins. In a season-ending 15-game losing streak—all in Sun Belt play—nine of the last 12 losses were by an average of more than 21 points.

"We were in a lot of games that got away from us at the end," Wiel said. "We were just constantly fighting an uphill battle all year that we just got worn down at the end of games. I know I really want to get the bad taste out of my mouth and see how we can compete in the Sun Belt with a fully healthy team."

Whether this team can mesh together is a major question, but if Nosse and Tenngren can round back into shape and the newcomers can provide the scoring that their numbers indicate, there's no question the Blue Raiders can be much more of a factor in the league. Even if all of that falls into place, though, MTSU is still likely a Murfreesboro mile away from contending for conference honors.

(D.M.)

New Mexico State

LOCATION	Las Cruces, NM
CONFERENCE	Sun Belt (West)
LAST SEASON	14-14 (.500)
CONFERENCE RECORD	10-6 (t-2nd)
STARTERS LOST/RETURNING	2/3
NICKNAME	Aggies
COLORS	Crimson & White
HOMECOURT	Pan American Center (13,071)
COACH	Lou Henson (New Mexico State '55)
RECORD AT SCHOOL	250-117 (13 years)
CAREER RECORD	740-377 (39 years)
ASSISTANTS	Tony Stubblefield (Nebraska-Omaha '95)
	Elmer Chavez (Lubbock Christian '80)
	Chris Crutchfield (Nebraska-Omaha '92)
TEAM WINS (last 5 years)	19-18-23-22-14
RPI (last 5 years)	78-150-71-71-204
2000-01 FINISH	Won regular-season finale.

All dressed up, and no place to go.

New Mexico State's Aggies were playing as well as any team in the Sun Belt Conference at the end of their first season in the league last year, winning nine of their last 10 regular-season games with the one loss coming by only four points. NMSU also won five straight conference road games during that stretch.

Legendary head coach Lou Henson said that his team was playing as close to its potential as any team he'd been around in a career that spans almost four decades.

Unfortunately, when that regular season ended, so did the Aggies' surge.

Because of NCAA rules violations that occurred under previous head coach Neil McCarthy, the university declared itself ineligible for the league tournament, and therefore ineligible for any chance at playing in the postseason.

All of the infractions took place before Henson returned for his second stint of coaching at New Mexico State in the 1997-98 season, but one of the players involved was still on the squad and played that year.

"I think it was a shock when the players first heard about it," Henson said of his club's non-involvement in the postseason. "I think we could have been a good club in the tournament."

The Aggies knew that their season would end on Feb. 24, and one month before that date NMSU was stumbling along with a 5-13 record and was mired in a four-game losing streak. Facing that record, and knowing that they didn't even have the league tournament available to get a second chance at success, it would have been very easy for the Aggies to go quietly into the New Mexico desert.

All they did from that point on was start whipping everybody. Five of the last nine wins came by double-digit margins, and NMSU took two out of three games from eventual conference tournament semifinalists in that successful run.

"It was tough on those guys, but they adjusted," said Henson, who goes into his 39th season as a head coach needing only 10 victories to reach the NCAA's all-time Division I Top 10 in career wins. "Our young men had a lot of character, I knew that, and they showed it late in the year. It was a real tribute to the young men that we have."

The good thing for Henson and the NMSU faithful is that a lot of those young men are back this year, and the lingering death that was the NCAA investigation is history. The Aggies are eligible for any and all berths in postseason play, and they're expected to do well once they get that "second-season" opportunity that was denied a year ago.

"You never know what's going to happen," said Henson, whose 722 wins ranks fifth among active coaches. "But I expect us to be much stronger this year. If they come along and play like they can, we can have a very good season."

It won't take much for the Aggies to be better than they were at the start of the 2000-01 season, when departures left the squad in a lurch.

"We'd lost four guys from the previous season," Henson said, "and then we had a player flunk out, another one quit and another one mess up a knee. We struggled early with all of that going on."

The Aggies also struggled to lock in a point guard, and wound up manning the position by committee for most of the season. A couple of sophomores, 6-3 **Dennis Trammell** (6.2 ppg, 1.8 apg) and 6-1 **Emanuel Dildy** (4.8 ppg, 1.5 apg) saw most of the time, but returning swingman **Brandon Mason** actually led the team in assists with 82.

"All those guys got a lot better as the year went along," Henson said. "That's one of the biggest reasons we started playing better."

The biggest reason for what success NMSU had last year, though, was the presence of 6-4 junior **Eric Channing**, who became one of the league's most respected/feared point producers in the Aggies' first run through the Sun Belt.

Channing (18.6 ppg, 3.4 rpg) ranked second in the Sun Belt in scoring and led the Aggies in three-point percentage (42.7) and free-throw percentage (84.6). He also became a clutch scorer in several games during NMSU's victory streak.

"He's just a tremendous shooter," Henson said, "but more importantly he's a leader. He's one of the finest shooters I've ever coached, but the key is that we've got some guys to go with him. No question that he makes a big difference to our squad."

Channing was an easy all-league pick and also added first-team Academic All-America honors.

Mason (9.8 ppg, 3.4 rpg, 3.0 apg), a 6-4 junior, was Channing's running mate outside for most of his sophomore season and returns as the team's third leading scorer.

The other key to the Aggies' late run was the rapid improvement of 6-8 sophomore forward **James Moore** (11.7 ppg, 5.9 rpg), who led the team in field-goal percentage and blocks. He was second in scoring and rebounding on the way to being voted freshman of the year in the Sun Belt. His 52 blocked shots set an NMSU single-season record.

"When he came on and played like we thought he could," Henson said, "that's when we really started getting production from a lot of places. His improvement helped solidify our lineup."

With the departure of solid senior baseliner Daveeno Hines (9.4 ppg, 9.1 rpg) to graduation, the Aggies are short on game experience on the front line. **Kelsey Crooks** (2.6 ppg, 2.6 rpg), a 6-6 sophomore, averaged 11 minutes per game last year and is the only returnee other than Moore at those spots.

James Felder, a 6-8 sophomore, will be seeing his first collegiate action this year after tearing an anterior cruciate ligament in his right knee in a summer pickup game and missing the whole season. He averaged 13.8 points and a league-leading 9.8 rebounds in his only year at New Mexico Junior College.

Another player will also be in an Aggie uniform for the first time, through a circuitous route. **Lamar Hill**, a 6-8 junior forward, attended Dayton for one semester before heading to Tyler (Texas) Junior College, then enrolled at NMSU last year and will be eligible at mid-season. He averaged 18 points and 14 boards as a sophomore at Tyler.

Two other junior-college transfers will also make major impacts, including one that will help on the thin front line. **Chris Jackson** (18.0 ppg, 12.0 rpg) is a 6-10 presence who was a standout at Garden City (Kansas) Community College along with being invited to a tryout for the NJCAA/USA Basketball team that competed in the Tournament of the Americas. Last season, Jackson had high games of 43 points and 26 rebounds.

Will Morris, a 6-4 junior who averaged 23.8 points, 6.7 rebounds and 2.0 steals at Riverside (Calif.) Junior College last season, will also get a chance to contribute right away. Morris has previous Division I experience. Before attending Riverside, Morris played at Eastern Kentucky, where he averaged 8.9 points and 3.3 rebounds as a freshman. Morris played in 27 games, starting seven, and averaged 20.3 minutes. He scored a season-high 22 points against Tennessee Tech and grabbed a season-best eight rebounds versus Loyola-Chicago and Cal State Fullerton.

Twins **Jason** and **James Fontenot** of Phoenix, Ariz., will add depth to the backcourt. Jason, who's 5-10, and James, 6-1, helped lead St. Mary's High School to the Arizona 5-A state championship.

Jason, a point guard, was the more highly regarded of the twins. Last year he was the Arizona Republic state

Big Schools Player of the Year and a first-team all-state pick after averaging 20.6 points, 7.0 assists and 4.0 steals. James was a second-team all-state pick and averaged 14 points.

"Jason needs to come along at the point for us," Henson said. "Having Hill back will help at midterm and we're going to be solid at the wings. But we've got to have a couple of guys come through at the point, because that's where we were weak last year and where we're going to concentrate in the fall."

2001-2002 SCHEDULE

Nov.	17	@Texas-Arlington
	19	Alcorn State
	24	San Diego State
	28	Texas Tech
Dec.	1	UTEP
	5	New Mexico
	8	Washington
	16	@New Mexico
	20-22	#Yahoo Sports Festival
	27	@Denver
	29	@North Texas
Jan.	3	New Orleans
	5	South Alabama
	10	@Middle Tennessee
	13	@Western Kentucky
	15	Eastern New Mexico
	19	Louisiana-Lafayette
	24	Denver
	26	North Texas
	31	@New Orleans
Feb.	2	@South Alabama
	6	Florida International
	9	Western New Mexico
	11	@Texas-Pan American
	14	Arkansas-Little Rock
	16	Arkansas State
	20	@Texas-El Paso
	23	@Louisiana-Lafayette
	28	##Sun Belt Tournament
March	1-5	##Sun Belt Tournament

@Road Games
#Laie, HI (vs. Valparaiso first round; also Buffalo, BYU-Columbia, Hawaii, Montana, Navy, Tulsa)
##Lakefront Arena, New Orleans, LA

BLUE RIBBON ANALYSIS

BACKCOURT	B
BENCH/DEPTH	B-
FRONTCOURT	B-
INTANGIBLES	B

The Aggies found themselves at midterm last year when they had nothing to play for but pride, and now that they're motivated with the promise of postseason play coming at the end of the year, they should be even better.

But the preseason schedule is a make-or-break one, with home-and-home games against big-time rivals UTEP and New Mexico and outings against Texas Tech, Washington and San Diego State.

"That will do a lot to help the new guys get ready," Henson said. "We should be in pretty good shape experience-wise when the league games come around, and that's good since the Sun Belt's a very underrated league."

If NMSU survives that stretch, figure on the Aggies getting out to a much quicker start in league play. Channing, Moore and Mason alone will make the Aggies competitive with just about anybody, and any contribution at all from the supporting cast could make the school's first Sun Belt Tournament outing a memorable one.

(D.M.)

New Orleans

LOCATION	New Orleans, LA
CONFERENCE	Sun Belt (West)
LAST SEASON	17-12 (.586)
CONFERENCE RECORD	10-6 (t-2nd)
STARTERS LOST/RETURNING	5/0
NICKNAME	Privateers
COLORS	Royal Blue &Silver
HOMECOURT	Lakefront Arena (10,000)

COACH Monte Towe (North Carolina State '76)
RECORD AT SCHOOL First year
CAREER RECORD First year
ASSISTANTS Patrick Harrington (Rollins College '86)
Nikita Johnson (West Georgia '89)
Mark Downey (Charleston ('95)
TEAM WINS (last 5 years) 22-15-14-11-17
RPI (last 5 years) 75-155-197-229-185
2000-01 FINISH Lost in conference quarterfinal.

The city of New Orleans has been described in many terms, but boring has never been one of them.

Apparently, that agrees with Monte Towe, who swept into town as the new basketball coach at the University of New Orleans last March.

"This is a great city," the former sparkplug guard for North Carolina State's 1974 national championship team said. "It fits me perfectly. I can be who I am and coach a basketball team."

That coaching has pretty much kept him off Bourbon Street since he took over a squad that went 17-12 last year and earned former mentor Joey Stiebing coach-of-the-year honors in the Sun Belt Conference—before he was unceremoniously relieved of his position by the university.

Towe's first four-year head coaching position after three assistant stops and two junior college head jobs puts him into a situation where all five starters have departed and fan apathy is rampant. Even including two games against cross-town foes Tulane and Loyola, the Privateers still averaged only 787 fans in their 16 home games last year.

"The first thing you have to do is have a good basketball team," Towe said of resurrecting interest in the UNO program. "Then, you have to get out and do things. I served ice cream on campus our first day of school. I tell our kids that the people sitting with them in class are potential fans. Our alumni base here is staggering, so we're going to work on those people and do what we can do."

That attitude fits with this season's team motto "Taking it to the Streets," and the Privateers will take that literally in playing one of their home games in another local arena, the Pontchartrain Center. Towe is hoping those efforts will make Lakefront Arena more of a home-court advantage, especially when New Orleans plays host to the Sun Belt Tournament in March.

"We're trying to let people see us as much as we can," he said. "We're going to get people involved."

While Towe will be introducing his team to the public, he'll also be introducing himself to them. Of course, maybe the Privateers should introduce themselves to each other, because all regular starters are gone and no returnee averaged more than 3.5 points per game last year.

"I haven't seen them play," Towe said, "but then again they haven't played very much. But that's going to make for an exciting preseason for me because everything is open. We're kind of young and inexperienced, but the opportunity is there for everybody to play."

It's not like the whole Privateer roster will need directions to the arena. Five returning lettermen saw action in at least 24 games, and 6-3 junior guard Kyle Smith (1.9 ppg, 3.4 apg) started seven of his 17 appearances before missing the rest of the year with a knee injury that will also likely sideline him for this season.

In all, nine lettermen return—every player other than last year's normal starting five—and that group will be boosted by what has been ranked by several sources as one of the nation's top 25 recruiting classes.

"The recruiting class isn't so young," Towe said. "They've played on a very high level."

Speaking of high—that's where one of the team's two seniors is height-wise and academics-wise. Corey Sanders (3.3 ppg, 2.7 rpg) at 6-11 is the team's second-leading returning scorer and top returning rebounder, and is already enrolled in graduate school after receiving his degree last spring.

"He's a mobile 6-11 guy that can pass, can get out on the front end of the zone press and can trap," Towe said of the former Cal State Fullerton player. "He can really move for a guy his size."

He could be joined on the front line by fellow senior Jason Mann (3.5 ppg, 2.5 rpg), a 6-8 forward who transferred from Duquesne before his junior season and has fought his way through nagging injuries.

"This will be the healthiest he's been in three years," Towe said. "He's going to be a really good defender for us."

Most of the other returnees are in the backcourt, with Smith's absence figuring to give 6-0 sophomore A.J. Meredith (2.8 ppg, 2.0 apg) the lead at the point. Meredith averaged 16 minutes per game in a backup role last season.

Sophomore Kyle Buggs (2.7 ppg, 1.4 rpg), 6-3, could also see action at the point, giving Towe some choices heading into the season.

"Kyle's a good shooter and can score for us," he said, "but he may have to play the point early. He and Meredith will get the best look early and we'll see. Meredith sometimes gets a little out of control, but if he can cut down on his turnovers he can really help us."

There's also some experience at the other outside slot in 6-3 sophomore Ben Wilson (1.7 ppg), who played in 24 games last season and has already impressed the new staff with his spot-up shooting (he hit 44.4 percent on three-point tries last year). Sophomores Shelton Little (1.6 ppg) at 6-4 and Brian Hamilton (1.1 ppg) at 6-3 saw limited action in their freshman seasons.

One key returnee could be slashing swingman John Ashalou (2.7 ppg, 1.2 rpg), a 6-6 sophomore.

"I think he's going to be a big offensive threat," Towe said. "He tries to get to the basket and score. Somebody's going to have to get points for us, and he's a guy that looks to score."

Points should also be coming from the talented group of newcomers, and even more would be anticipated if one of Towe's most talented players from his last coaching stop was available. Guard Johnell Smith, a 6-2 junior, broke a handful of scoring records at Santa Fe Community College last year on the way to a 30.2 average (86 in one game) and the No. 1 combo guard rating by one national scouting service. Unfortunately for UNO, he has to complete academic work and will not be eligible this season.

"I sure wish we had him this year," said Towe, who coached at Santa Fe the last two seasons, "just because he's a guy I'm familiar with."

Even without Smith, the newcomer group is talented and big. With the exception of fellow Santa Fe product Kentrell Martin at 6-4, the rest of the group of four junior college transfers and one prep signee are all 6-8 or taller.

The Privateer staff had to make only one stop to get the two tallest transfers—6-10 Lithuanian native Nerijus Lisauskas and 6-11 Ukraine product Andryi Sukhotin, both juniors, played last season for Mississippi Gulf Coast Junior College.

"Nerijus was really rated high and then had a torn ACL," Towe said, "but he's coming back from that. He's a big kid, about 245 pounds with good post moves, and should help us down low because we really need somebody there.

"Andryi is a different kind of player. He's 6-11 but he's really a perimeter guy. He's going to be very interesting to watch."

Last season, Lisauskas averaged 13.3 points and 7.0 rebounds while shooting 57 percent from the field. Sukhotin had similar numbers: 13.7 points, 7.0 rebounds and 3.0 blocked shots. The two have been close since enrolling in junior college as freshmen.

"I think they'll do a great job at UNO," veteran Gulf Coast coach Bob Weathers said. "They're just now coming into their own as far as the American style of basketball is concerned. They have bright futures in the sport."

The most impressive player in the new group, though, may be Venezuelan native Hector Romero, a 6-7 junior power forward who was a standout at Independence (Kansas) Community College for two years. Towe, who coached in Venezuela during the mid-'90s, has crossed paths with Romero before.

"He was about 13 and used to come to our games," Towe said. "He was a double-double guy on a good team at Independence, and in our players' pickup games he's the first guy picked every time."

Last season, Romero averaged 21 points and 10.5 boards. He scored 30 or more points five times and 40 or more twice. He broke the 1,000-point barrier in his two seasons at Independence. Romero played for Venezuela in the World Junior Games in 1999.

"Hector can flat out play," Towe said. "He's an all-around athlete who can rebound and distribute the ball. He is tenacious at both ends of the floor and can score inside and out."

Freshman Victor Brown at 6-8 and 240 pounds, and Martin give UNO flexibility. Towe said that Martin is the most versatile player he's coached and can play anywhere from point guard to power forward, and that Brown could be one of the Sun Belt's top freshmen.

Brown averaged 24 points and 10 rebounds last season at Edgewater High School in Orlando, Fla.

2001-2002 SCHEDULE

Nov.	13-14	#Boston
	17	Rollins
	19	@Jacksonville
	24	@Nicholls State
	26	Norfolk State
	29	@Oklahoma State
Dec.	1	@Southwest Missouri State
	5	@Tulane
	8	@Southeastern Louisiana
	18	LSU
	22	@Florida
	28	Western Kentucky
	30	Middle Tennessee
Jan.	3	@New Mexico State
	5	@Louisiana-Lafayette
	14	Arkansas-Little Rock
	17	@South Alabama
	19	@Arkansas State
	24	@Texas A&M-Corpus Christi
	26	@Florida International
	31	New Mexico State
Feb.	2	Louisiana-Lafayette
	7	@North Texas
	10	@Denver
	16	South Alabama
	21	North Texas
	23	Denver
	28	##Sun Belt Tournament
March	1-5	##Sun Belt Tournament

@Road Games
#Guardians Classic, Iowa City, IA (If New Orleans wins, it will play either Maryland Eastern Shore or Iowa on Nov. 14; Semifinals and final are Nov. 20-21 at Kemper Arena, Kansas City, MO)
##Lakefront Arena, New Orleans, LA

BLUE RIBBON ANALYSIS

BACKCOURT	B-
BENCH/DEPTH	B
FRONTCOURT	B-
INTANGIBLES	A-

The Privateers have annually been one of the Sun Belt's most difficult teams to rate, mostly because of the number of new faces in the program. That hasn't changed this year, and that's also compounded with a new coaching staff in place.

UNO normally played nine to 11 players in virtually every game last season, so that should be a benefit to the new staff. More of a benefit, though, may be the untapped talents of a recruiting class that on paper fills all the major holes in the Privateer lineup.

"We're kind of the wild card in this thing," Towe said. "If we can put this thing together and adjust to all of this, I think we can be competitive and give ourselves a chance to win every night."

That group will be battle-tested before the conference season rolls around after a non-league schedule that includes Florida, Oklahoma State, LSU and Iowa. And, don't forget, the Sun Belt Conference will crown its champion at UNO's Lakefront Arena, site of the league tournament. If the Privateers can somehow create a homecourt advantage there, anything can happen.

(D.M.)

North Texas

LOCATION	Denton, TX
CONFERENCE	Sun Belt (West)
LAST SEASON	4-24 (.143)
CONFERENCE RECORD	1-15 (6th)
STARTERS LOST/RETURNING	1/4
NICKNAME	Eagles, Mean Green
COLORS	Green & White
HOMECOURT	The Super Pit (10,000)
COACH	Johnny Jones (LSU '84)
RECORD AT SCHOOL	First year
CAREER RECORD	15-16 (1 year)
ASSISTANTS	Fred Rike (West Texas State '89)
	Alvin Brooks (Lamar '81)
	Charlie Leonard (Christian Brothers '75)
TEAM WINS (last 5 years)	10-5-4-7-4
RPI (last 5 years)	226-233-256-241-295
2000-01 FINISH	Lost in conference first round.

Johnny Jones didn't know it at the time, but he had a view of his future last December, and it wasn't a pretty one.

Jones, who takes over as coach at North Texas this

season, was serving as an assistant coach at Alabama last year, and the Crimson Tide faced the Mean Green in the Coors Classic Tournament in Mobile, Ala.

Alabama rolled to a 94-55 victory in that game, a loss compounded by point guard **Terrance White** going down with a leg injury and missing North Texas' next 15 games including the bulk of the Sun Belt Conference season.

"I guess it was a little bit of an advantage," Jones said of meeting his future employer. "I got the chance to see tape of some of their games and become familiar with the guys a little bit. Even after we played them, I kind of kept up with what they were doing. They had just come off tough back-to-back games with Arkansas and Oklahoma when we played them at Alabama."

Now he takes over a program that last year went 4-24, beat just two Division I opponents and lost 15 in a row to end the season on the way to a 1-15 Sun Belt record.

"It's been interesting, to say the least," said Jones, a 17-year coaching veteran and a long-time assistant to Dale Brown at LSU before spending the last four years at Memphis—where he was interim head coach in 1999-2000—and Alabama. "But I'm excited about the transition, the opportunity and the challenge we'll be presented with.

"I'm familiar with most of the coaches in the league, and while I was at LSU, Memphis and Alabama we had the opportunity to play a lot of the Sun Belt teams. I've always thought it was a very good basketball conference."

The biggest challenge for Jones may be finding a successful trainer, because injuries became a fact of life for UNT last year. In addition to White, three other regular performers missed significant playing time last year with various ailments, and one other player is coming back from an medical red-shirt season.

In addition, one of the team's top signees, 6-10 freshman **Justin Barnett** of Arlington, missed his entire senior prep season with a variety of ailments.

With the Eagle squad resembling a M*A*S*H unit for much of the season, a lot of the UNT bench had a chance to see extensive action. Jones said that could be a positive for this year's squad as it looks for its first double-digit win season since 1997.

"That should help us down the road," he said. "These guys got an opportunity to get a great deal of experience last year when they weren't expecting it."

One player that Jones doesn't have to worry much about in the area of experience is 6-6 junior guard **Chris Davis** (18.0 ppg, 4.4 rpg, 2.1 apg), who averaged 20.6 points in Sun Belt play and was only 0.6 per game away from leading the conference in league-game scoring.

One year earlier, Davis was the Big West Conference's Freshman of the Year in North Texas' final year in that league, and led the Big West in scoring as a freshman with a 21.7 average, good enough to rank 14th nationally.

"He's a very solid player," Jones said, "but the thing that impresses me is that he's worked very hard this summer in preparing himself for this year. He's shown that he's excited about this year, and he knows that if he continues to progress as a player he'll have the opportunity to play at the next level when he's finished here."

Davis also improved his shooting percentage between his freshman and sophomore seasons—though his .266 effort from three-point range still needs work—and with the injuries at point guard actually finished as the Mean Green's assist leader last year.

He's hoping not to have to do that again, and he probably won't because UNT will be deeper at the point than perhaps any other position.

White (5.8 ppg, 4.0 apg), a 6-2 senior, was on his way to a solid season in his first year out of Blinn Junior College before suffering a deep thigh bruise in the Alabama game. White came back for the final five games, but by that time the Eagles' season was a lost cause.

Jerome Rogers (5.2 ppg, 2.2 apg), a 5-10 sophomore, saw most of the action at the point during White's absence, starting 11 of his 25 appearances.

"He was thrown in the fire," Jones said, "and had to play a lot earlier than he expected. He had a tough early part of the year, but toward the end of the year he came on and started to play better. He'll be a better player with that experience. Terrance is also definitely a good point man with good quickness and speed, and he's also a good defender."

The Eagles also signed 6-3 junior **Lee Green** (10.0 ppg, 3.0 rpg, 5.0 apg) out of Allegany (Md.) Junior College, and all Green did last year was help lead his team to the runner-up slot in the NJCAA tournament. He also finished No. 2 on the school's career three-point field goal list.

"Lee is a very solid point guard," Jones said. "He's very capable of handling the ball, taking care of the ball and getting you into your offense and getting the ball into the hands of the right people. We're very fortunate to sign a player of his caliber."

Suffice to say the battle for minutes at the point will be competitive.

"The point guard position's definitely going to be stronger than it was last year," Jones said. "We've got two guys that have played and were here last year and one guy that was obviously very effective at his junior college. We could be very good out there."

UNT should be good across the entire perimeter, especially if another injury heals in time. **Kenneth Mangrum** (8.5 ppg, 3.2 rpg), a 6-4 senior, started the first 22 games of the season before tearing an ACL in early February and missing the rest of the year.

"I think he'll be ready to play by October," Jones said, "but we're not certain there. He worked hard in the off-season."

Freshman guard **Leonard Hopkins**, 6-4, played only three games last year before shin splints and a knee injury sidelined him. He was granted a medical red-shirt season.

The ugliest of all the injuries, though, may have been the one that 6-3 junior **Wes Allen** (3.1 ppg, 1.1 rpg) suffered when he fell on the back of his neck in a home game against Denver. He suffered a concussion and a separated shoulder and missed the season's final 12 games.

"Leonard's a very explosive player on the offensive end," Jones said, "and if he's healthy he and Davis can complement each other well."

They all may have to, because the perimeter will have to carry the Eagles because of a front line short on depth and experience. The already-thin group was dealt a huge blow when two-year letterman Jason Miller (12.8 ppg, 6.8 rpg) decided to transfer at the start of the fall semester.

The only returning lettermen near the basket are a still-raw 6-7 sophomore **Will Smith** (3.5 ppg, 2.6 rpg) and 6-9 sophomore **Unjel Masters**, who averaged only 1.2 points and 0.8 rebounds two years ago before red-shirting last year.

"Will's still learning how to play, but he's very aggressive," Jones said. "He's a good defender and capable of finishing around the basket. Unjel's going to have to play at lot at center with the people we've lost."

Barnett and 6-7 junior signee **Jermaine Green** (16.0 ppg) from Temple (Texas) Junior College will also likely be thrown into the mix early.

"Our biggest question mark is going to be inside play," Jones said. "Nobody's played really significant minutes, and they're going to have to step in for us in a hurry."

2001-2002 SCHEDULE

Nov.	16	Southwest Missouri State
	24	@Oklahoma State
	27	@Lipscomb
Dec.	1	@Houston
	4	SMU
	15	@Kansas State
	19	Lipscomb
	21	Tennessee Tech
	23	@TCU
	29	New Mexico State
Jan.	3	@Arkansas-Little Rock
	5	@Arkansas State
	10	Florida International
	12	Texas A&M-Kingsville
	17	@Denver
	19	Middle Tennessee
	24	@Louisiana-Lafayette
	26	@New Mexico State
	30	St. Edwards
Feb.	2	Denver
	7	New Orleans
	9	South Alabama
	11	Louisiana-Lafayette
	16	@Western Kentucky
	21	@New Orleans
	23	@South Alabama
	28	#Sun Belt Tournament
March	1-5	#Sun Belt Tournament

@Road Games
#Lakefront Arena, New Orleans, LA

BLUE RIBBON ANALYSIS

BACKCOURT	B+
BENCH/DEPTH	C
FRONTCOURT	D
INTANGIBLES	B-

Jones has his work cut out for him. The last four North Texas squads have combined to win only 20 games, and the Eagles have won 17 games in a season only twice since 1978. So the first order of business may be to install a winning attitude.

The backcourt won't be a problem. Davis is one of the league's most underrated talents and is capable of big things, and he'll have a solid supporting cast on the perimeter. The frontcourt is a different story, with problems on both ends of the floor making the squad less Mean Green and more Lean Green. North Texas has only three and one-half points per game returning on the front line, and as a team the Eagles were last in the Sun Belt in both scoring defense (88.2 ppg) and field-goal defense.

"Hopefully," Jones said, "our perimeter players can make up the slack where we're lacking in the post area, and our post guys can come around by the time the conference season begins."

They have a long way to come.

(D.M.)

South Alabama

LOCATION	**Mobile, AL**
CONFERENCE	**Sun Belt (West)**
LAST SEASON	**22-11 (.667)**
CONFERENCE RECORD	**11-5 (1st)**
STARTERS LOST/RETURNING	**3/2**
NICKNAME	**Jaguars**
COLORS	**Blue, Red & White**
HOMECOURT	**Mitchell Center (10,000)**
COACH	**Bob Weltlich (Ohio State '67)**
RECORD AT SCHOOL	**74-44 (4 years)**
CAREER RECORD	**293-314 (21 years)**
ASSISTANTS	**Chris Jones (Indiana State '93)**
	Dwight Evans (Birmingham Southern '84)
	Mark Coffman (Western New Mexico '80)
TEAM WINS (last 5 years)	**23-21-11-20-22**
RPI (last 5 years)	**82-60-202-114-94**
2000-01 FINISH	**Lost in NIT first round.**

One day, people are going to stop betting against South Alabama's Jaguars.

Last season, South Alabama won the Sun Belt's West Division, lost to Western Kentucky in the league tournament championship game and earned an NIT berth. Despite all that, prognosticators are again calling for the decline of the Jaguars.

Why? Just because eight of last season's 11 players departed, and the three returnees combined for only 17.5 points and 8.1 rebounds per game a year ago, is that any reason to write USA off?

Those who do don't know their history. South Alabama and head coach Bob Weltlich have won more than 20 games in four of the last five seasons, and have done it mostly after being picked to finish somewhere other than at the top of the conference race.

They probably won't be picked first once again, but maybe the predictors should heed Weltlich's words.

"I like this team," he said. "I don't have a good handle on it yet since we have so many newcomers, but this team's going to be a lot of fun to be around."

The Jaguars finished with a 22-11 record last season—going 11-5 to win a tight division race by one game over three teams deadlocked at 10-6—and won six of their eight road games in league play, so it was probably fun to be around last year.

This year could be, too, but it will again take a lot of work. The Jags return only one full-time starter, one part-time starter and a role player who averaged less than four minutes per game. In other words, a lot of new faces will be in a lot of new places.

All-conference selections Virgil Stanescu (14.0 ppg, 8.4 rpg) and Ravonte Dantzler (12.7 ppg, 4.8 rpg, 2.4 apg) departed through graduation, as did regular starter Brett Gravitt and defensive stopper Ericson Beck.

Then, USA took two more hits over the summer when junior regular Michael Bollman (3.5 ppg, 2.8 rpg) transferred and sophomore forward Emmett Thomas (9.5 ppg, 3.8 rpg) also left the program just before the start of the fall semester.

Thomas would have been the team's leading returning scorer and the second-leading rebounder, after improving by leaps and bounds during his freshman season.

"Really, that's six of our first eight players that we've lost," Weltlich said. "That's most of our scoring and rebounding, so we're kind of starting over and that's not what you want to be doing at this point."

With all of the departures, the Jaguars have only nine scholarship players on the season-opening roster despite a full—and potentially talented—recruiting class.

"The scholarship rule hurt us," Weltlich said of the short roster. "The unexpected departures have made it very difficult."

It has also put a big burden on the few returnees the Jaguars have, and has thrust junior guard **Demetrice Williams** and junior forward **Henry Williams** (no relation) into a sudden leadership role.

"The nature of our program is that the kids that have been here feel like we're going to compete for championships," Weltlich said. "We've been successful, and there's now an expectation level regardless of how many kids are back. Henry and Demetrice know that, and they've worked hard in the off-season so we're looking for them to step up and be even better players than they were last year."

The 6-2 junior Demetrice Williams (9.2 ppg, 3.2 apg) led the Jags in assists and ranked fourth in the Sun Belt in steals as one of the most consistent players on the team. He'll likely start the season at the point once again, but even that could change, especially because he ranked third on the squad in scoring last season.

"He's obviously the heir apparent there," Weltlich said, "but he's worked hard on his shot, and it wouldn't be surprising to me if he also played at lot at the two guard. That's where he was when we recruited him, and he's probably going to share responsibilities at both positions."

Henry Williams (7.7 ppg, 5.4 rpg) was one of the team's biggest surprises in his first season. The 6-6 junior forward, who had to sit out his freshman season as a partial qualifier, finished the season as the team's top shooter with a 56.3 field goal mark. He also was the team's top shot blocker along with ranking second in rebounding to the departed Stanescu.

The latter Williams started 16 games last year, including the last six when he averaged 13 points and six boards as a boost to the Jags' postseason run.

Past that, though, the only other player on the roster ever to don a red, white and blue game jersey is 7-1 sophomore **Matt Forget** (0.6 ppg, 0.9 rpg) of Bordeaux, France, whom Jaguar fans hope, like fine wine, improves with age. Forget missed last season's first eight games because of transfer rules after attending Seward County Community College for one semester, and played in 18 games off the bench but averaged only 3.9 minutes per game.

At least one of the new players is familiar to the program. Sophomore 6-2 guard **Benjamin Sormonte** of Laverune, France was on the USA squad a year ago, but left the team before the season began to care for an ill grandmother.

He will be part of the guard picture, but a bigger part of that portrait will likely be painted by 6-2 junior **Larry Thompson** (13.0 ppg, 4.0 rpg) of Fort Scott (Kansas) Community College. Thompson shot 36 percent on three-point shots in junior college, and averaged 18 as a freshman at Atlanta Metro Community College before going to Fort Scott.

"He can really shoot it," Weltlich said. "We feel like he can step in and give us some very solid play, a lot like Ravonte gave us last year."

The other newcomer guard is late signee **Jamaicus Ricks** (16.5 ppg, 8.0 apg, 4.5 spg), a 5-9 product of Independence (Kansas) Community College who was the most valuable player in the Region VI tournament as a freshman.

"We signed him late," Weltlich said, "but he's going to be a good player for us. He's not the biggest guy, but he's a solid kid and a true point, where we need help to back up Demetrice."

Three other newcomers will help on the front line, and with the limited number of bodies all will have to contribute heavily. The one who may contribute the most is 6-6 sophomore **Marques Ivy** (12.4 ppg, 5.4 rpg), who played one year at Cloud County (Kansas) Community College after missing his natural freshman year with a knee injury. He will have three years of eligibility with the Jaguars.

"He's going to be a special player and a guy that's really created a lot of anticipation for us," Weltlich said. "He's shown an athleticism and a feel for the game that should let him make an immediate impact."

The other new faces on the front line are freshman center signee **Justin White** (22.5 ppg, 11.5 rpg, 5.0 blocks), a 6-10 product of Inman, Kansas, and freshman forward **Adam Salow** (19.0 ppg, 10.9 rpg, 4.9 blocks), a

6-8 product of West Delaware High in Manchester, Iowa.

"They both have a lot of up side," Weltlich said, "but how ready they're going to be is really hard to determine right now."

That could probably describe most of the Jaguar roster, and compounding that problem is a rugged early-season schedule. USA provides the opposition for Rick Pitino's coaching debut at Louisville in front of a national television audience to open the season, and will also face Mississippi State, Georgia and Auburn before Sun Belt play opens.

2001-2002 SCHEDULE

Nov.	18	@Louisville
	21	@Marist
	24	Valdosta State
	28	Southeastern Louisiana
Dec.	1	@Mississippi State
	5	Southern Miss
	12	Bethune-Cookman
	15	Georgia
	18	@Auburn
	21	Gardner Webb
	28	Middle Tennessee
	30	Western Kentucky
Jan.	3	@Louisiana-Lafayette
	5	@New Mexico State
	12	Arkansas State
	17	New Orleans
	19	@Arkansas-Little Rock
	23	@Florida International
	26	Georgia Southwestern
	31	Louisiana-Lafayette
Feb.	2	New Mexico State
	7	@Denver
	9	@North Texas
	14	Denver
	16	@New Orleans
	20	@Bethune-Cookman
	23	North Texas
	28	#Sun Belt Tournament
March	1-5	#Sun Belt Tournament

@Road Games
#Lakefront Arena, New Orleans, LA

BLUE RIBBON ANALYSIS

BACKCOURT	B+
BENCH/DEPTH	C
FRONTCOURT	B-
INTANGIBLES	B

The Jaguars have won or shared Sun Belt titles in four of the last five seasons and made three postseason appearances in that time, so they have tradition on their side. As to how much that means, well …

"The new guys, they hear all about the last few years and how much is expected of them," Weltlich said, "but do they really understand it? We're going to find out quick when we open up at Louisville. We'll know how quickly they understand the situation. I guess nobody really understands something like that until they go through it."

Don't bet against the Jags, though. The lack of depth will be hard to overcome, as will the loss of some standout defensive players—a major concern, because USA annually ranks among the league leaders defensively. But if the new faces fit into their assigned places, the Jags could have the last growl.

(D.M.)

Gonzaga

LOCATION	Spokane, WA
CONFERENCE	West Coast
LAST SEASON	26-7 (.787)
CONFERENCE RECORD	13-1 (1st)
STARTERS LOST/RETURNING	2/3
NICKNAME	Bulldogs
COLORS	Blue, White & Red
HOMECOURT	The Kennel in Martin Centre (4,000)
COACH	Mark Few (Oregon '85)
RECORD AT SCHOOL	52-16 (2 years)
CAREER RECORD	52-16 (2 years)
ASSISTANTS	Bill Grier (Oregon '90)
	Leon Rice (Washington State '86)
	Tommy Lloyd (Whitman '98)

TEAM WINS (last 5 years)	15-24-28-26-26
RPI (last 5 years)	184-65-30-31-63
2000-01 FINISH	Lost in NCAA Sweet 16.

Mark Few refuses to waste his time worrying about what he doesn't have—Casey Calvary, in particular.

Instead, Gonzaga's third-year head coach prefers to center his attention on what he does have.

Which, in this case, is three returning starters from a team that finished 26-7 last year, won its fifth WCC regular-season title in seven seasons and joined Duke and Michigan State as the only three teams to advance to the Sweet 16 in each of the last three NCAA Tournaments.

"You can never replace a player like Casey," Few said of Calvary, last year's WCC Player of the Year who averaged a team-best 19.0 points and 6.7 rebounds. "But you have to move on, and I think we've got enough talent and experience to do that successfully."

At the core of Few's confidence is the best backcourt in the conference. And at the core of that backcourt is senior point guard **Dan Dickau**, who burst upon the scene last winter after sitting out the 1999-2000 season under the NCAA's transfer rule. Dickau, despite missing nine early season games with a broken finger, averaged 18.9 points, 6.25 assists and had an assist-to-turnover ration of 1.70 in his first year as a Bulldog. He also shot 48 percent from three-point range and 86 percent from the free-throw line while earning first-team All-WCC honors.

"Statistically, you could make a strong case for Dan being the best point guard ever to play here," Few said of Dickau, who played his first two seasons at the University of Washington. That might sound like a bit of a stretch, considering one of GU's most famous alums is Utah Jazz point guard John Stockton, the NBA's all-time assist leader. But it should also be noted that the Zags were a gaudy 21-3—losing only to Arizona, Santa Clara and Michigan State, in the semifinals of the NCAA South Regional—with the 6-0 Dickau, a Wooden Award nominee, in the starting lineup.

"And I've always said the best way to rate a point guard is by his wins and losses," Few said.

Joining Dickau in the backcourt is 6-4 sophomore **Blake Stepp** (10.3 ppg, 3.6 rpg, 3.5 apg), who filled in at the point in Dickau's absence last year and was later voted the WCC's Freshman of the Year. Stepp, however, underwent off-season knee surgery to repair a hole in the cartilage in his right knee, and might not be at full strength when practice starts. Few said he anticipates a full recovery, which would seem to be crucial to the Zags' chances of winning another WCC title and making a fourth-consecutive trip to the NCAA Tournament.

If Stepp doesn't heal in time to start the season, Few has several other options, including 6-0 junior **Germayne Forbes** (3.9 ppg, 1.4 rpg) and 6-3 sophomore walk-on **Kyle Bankhead** (5.6 ppg, 1.1 apg), who shot a team-best .507 per cent from three-point range by draining 37-of-73 shots.

In addition, the Bulldogs picked up a couple of high-profile backcourt recruits in **Winston Brooks** and **Josh Reisman**, a couple of 6-footers who can both play the point. Brooks, a junior transfer, averaged 8.6 points, 7.8 assists and 1.9 steals for North Idaho College last winter. He is a quick, disruptive defender who likes to get out and run. Reisman, who will red-shirt under ideal circumstances, averaged 15.0 points and 4.0 assists in leading his unbeaten Mount Vernon team to the Washington State 3A title.

The Zags also have a couple of experienced wings in 6-4 senior **Alex Hernandez** (6.8 ppg, 2.6 rpg, 1.1 apg) and 6-5 senior **Anthony Reason** (4.5 ppg, 3.5 rpg, 1.4 apg), who both played key minutes as first-year transfers last winter. Hernandez is a slasher who can get to the basket and Reason is one of the best leapers in the WCC.

Both will need to contribute on the boards if the Bulldogs hope to make up for the absence of Calvary and Mark Spink, who was voted the league's top defender after averaging 7.5 points and 5.6 rebounds as a senior last year.

Few thought he had the answer to his front-line graduation losses in 7-0 Croatian Mario Kasun, who spent last year as a foreign exchange student in GU's English as a Second Language program. Kasun, however, opted to return to Europe and pursue a professional career rather than wait for the NCAA to sort out his eligibility status.

Kasun's decision left the Bulldogs short-handed on the front line. But the two experienced players returning—6-8 junior **Zach Gourde** (8.5 ppg, 3.9 rpg) and 6-8 sophomore **Cory Violette** (3.6 ppg, 2.9 rpg)—both made major contributions last year, especially during GU's strong stretch run.

Gourde, after undergoing off-season knee surgery, opened the season in a bit of funk. But he started the final 24 games and will enter the 2001-02 season as the Zags' go-to guy inside. Violette, Few said, made massive strides in the off-season and should be ready to build substantially on his rookie numbers.

The rotation after Gourde and Violette could be a bit of a crapshoot, however. **Jay Sherrell** (1.4 ppg, 1.3 rpg), a 6-8 sophomore, played only sparingly as a red-shirt freshman, and the only other big men on the Zags' roster—6-8 **Dustin Villepigue** and 6-10 Frenchman **Ronny Turiaf**—are rookies.

Villepigue, a slender 215-pounder, was a three-year letter winner at Simi Valley (Calif.) High, where he averaged 23.0 points and 12.7 rebounds as a senior. He is tough and aggressive, much like Calvary, but needs to add some weight and muscle.

"I don't think anybody will be in Casey's mold," Few said. "But Dustin is somebody that plays physical, is tough and competes on the same level. He doesn't shy away from being physical, and he has a great knack for scoring and rebounding."

Turiaf, a late signee from Martinique, via France's National Institute for Sport and Physical Education, remains a bit of a mystery.

The key to how GU's frontcourt stacks up in the physical WCC could be Sherrell, who was hampered the last two seasons by injuries.

"Jay needs to come on and have a good year," Few said of the 220-pound Sherrell. "He needs to play the type of basketball we believe he's capable of playing.

"He's had it tough, playing behind Casey Calvary, but I think he's learned a lot. Now it's time for him to take the next step as far becoming a complete player."

2001-2002 SCHEDULE

Nov.	16	@Illinois
	18	Montana
	22-24	#Great Alaska Shootout
	29	Arkansas-Pine Bluff
Dec.	1	Portland State
	4	Eastern Washington
	7	*Fresno State
	11	@Washington
	15	Washington State
	21	Eastern Oregon State
	29	@Monmouth
	31	@St. Joseph's
Jan.	7	@New Mexico
	11	Santa Clara
	13	San Diego
	18	@Pepperdine
	19	@Loyola Marymount
	24	San Francisco
	26	Saint Mary's
	30	Portland
Feb.	2	@Portland
	7	@San Diego
	9	@Santa Clara
	14	Loyola Marymount
	16	Pepperdine
	22	@St. Mary's
	23	@San Francisco
	28	##WCC Tournament
March	1-4	##WCC Tournament

@Road Games
*Fab Four Double-header, The Forum, Los Angeles, CA
#Anchorage, AK (vs. St. John's first round; also Indiana, Alaska-Anchorage, Tennessee, Marquette, Oregon State, Texas)
##Jenny Craig Pavilion, San Diego, CA

BLUE RIBBON ANALYSIS

BACKCOURT	A-
BENCH/DEPTH	C+
FRONTCOURT	B
INTANGIBLES	B+

Gonzaga lost a real warrior in Calvary, and a emotional leader in Spink. But with Dickau and Stepp back to anchor a backcourt that should be as good as any in the Pacific Northwest, don't look for the Bulldogs to disappear.

The Zags, who have averaged 26 wins over the last four seasons, have grown accustomed to rubbing elbows with the best programs in the country, and they have no intentions of letting things slide.

Few enters his third season armed with a new long-term contract, the promise of a new arena and plenty of returning talent in a league that lost many of last year's

WEST COAST

BLUE RIBBON FORECAST
1. Gonzaga
2. Santa Clara
3. Pepperdine
4. San Francisco
5. San Diego
6. Loyola Marymont
7. Portland
8. Saint Mary's

ALL-CONFERENCE TEAM
G - Dan Dickau, SR, Gonzaga
G - Andre Laws, SR, San Diego
F - Darrell Tucker, JR, San Francisco
F - Steve Ross, SR, Santa Clara
C - San Francisco SR Hondre Brewer

PLAYER OF THE YEAR
Dan Dickau, SR, Gonzaga

NEWCOMER OF THE YEAR
Winston Brooks, JR, Gonzaga

2001-2002 CONFERENCE TOURNAMENT
March 2-4, Jenny Craig Pavilion, San Diego, CA

2000-2001 CHAMPIONS
Gonzaga (Regular season)
Gonzaga (Conference tournament)

2000-2001 POSTSEASON PARTICIPANTS
Postseason Record: 3-2 (.600)
NCAA
Gonzaga (Sweet 16)
NIT
Pepperdine (Second round)

TOP BACKCOURTS
1. Gonzaga
2. Santa Clara
3. San Diego

TOP FRONTCOURTS
1. San Francisco
2. Gonzaga
3. Santa Clara

INSIDE THE NUMBERS
2000-2001 conference RPI: 16th (of 31)
Conference RPI (last five years): 17-11-12-14-16

DID YOU KNOW?
The West Coast Conference, which was formed in 1952, is celebrating its 50th anniversary this year. Charter members of the league included San Francisco, Saint Mary's, Santa Clara, San Jose State and Pacific. ... By advancing to the Sweet 16 of last year's NCAA Tournament, Gonzaga joined defending champion Duke and 2000 champion Michigan State as the only three schools to make it that far in each of the last three seasons. ... Because of a rash of off-season coaching changes, there will be several new faces on the sidelines at West Coast Conference games this winter. Former Portland assistant Michael Holton will take over the Pilots' reins from his former boss, Rob Chavez. Randy Bennett, a top assistant under Lorenzo Romar at Saint Louis, replaces Dave Bollwinkel at St. Mary's. And Paul Westphal, the former head coach of the NBA's Phoenix Suns and Seattle SuperSonics, steps in at Pepperdine in place of Jan van Breda Kolff, who moved on to St. Bonaventure. ... Gonzaga is coming off an unprecedented sweep of all major WCC postseason awards last winter. Mark Few was chosen coach of the year, senior Casey Calvary was honored as player of the year, senior Mark Spink was chosen defender of the year and sophomore Blake Stepp was selected freshman of the year. ... With Pepperdine's Brandon Armstrong having decided to forego his senior season to play in the NBA, and with Portland center Tim Frost having opted to transfer to Utah in the wake of a coaching change, the WCC is left with Gonzaga's Dan Dickau as its only returning first-team all-conference player from last season. ... Dick Davey, in his 10th season at Santa Clara, is the dean of WCC coaches. Only two other coaches, San Diego's Brad Holland and San Francisco's Philip Mathews, have held their current positions for more than three seasons. ... The WCC Tournament returns to San Diego's 5,000-seat Jenny Craig Pavilion (March 2-4) for the second straight year. The tournament had been played at Santa Clara's Toso Pavilion five of the previous six years. ... The host team of the WCC Tournament has never won it. ... Gonzaga has won the last three WCC Tournaments and has won or shared the regular-season crown four of the last six seasons.

(S.B.)

top stars to graduation.

Another run to the Sweet 16 of the NCAA Tournament seems unlikely, but the Bulldogs should at least get the chance.

(S.B.)

Loyola Marymount

LOCATION	Los Angeles, CA
CONFERENCE	West Coast
LAST SEASON	9-19 (.321)
CONFERENCE RECORD	5-9 (t-5th)
STARTERS LOST/RETURNING	2/3
NICKNAME	Lions
COLORS	Crimson & Navy Blue
HOMECOURT	Gersten Pavilion (4,156)
COACH	Steve Aggers (Chadron State '71)
RECORD AT SCHOOL	9-19 (1 year)
CAREER RECORD	60-101 (6 years)
ASSISTANTS	Brian Preibe (Washington '95)
	Byron Jenson (Pepperdine '93)
	Dedrique Taylor (UC-Davis '97)
TEAM WINS (last 5 years)	7-7-11-2-9
RPI (last 5 years)	254-255-184-316-262
2000-01 FINISH	Lost in conference quarterfinal.

Year Two of Steve Aggers' rebuilding efforts at Loyola Marymount is not unfolding exactly as planned.

Injuries to three key players and prize recruit Oscar Forman's decision to play professionally back in his Australian homeland have forced Aggers to adjust his goals rather dramatically heading into the 2001-02 season.

"When you're rebuilding, it always seems to be like that—one step forward and two steps back," said Aggers, who took over at LMU last year after successfully reviving a critically ill program at Eastern Washington.

The three players coming off injury rehab are 6-9 senior forward **Greg Lakey** and newcomers **Kent Dennis** and **Miroslav Neskovic**.

Lakey, who averaged 10.3 points and 4.4 rebounds as a junior, broke his foot during last year's West Coast Conference Tournament and had a metal screw inserted into his heel to help the healing process. He was on crutches for eight weeks after the surgery and didn't start working out again until late June.

"That's the bad news," Aggers said in trying to put a positive spin on a bad situation. "The good news is, all he could do while the bone was healing was lift and eat, so he got bigger—from about 210 pounds to 238—and that's a plus."

Dennis, a 6-4 junior guard who sat out last season after transferring from West Virginia, underwent off-season knee surgery to repair some old cartilage damage and was on crutches nearly all summer.

And Neskovic, a 6-9, 230-pound junior transfer from Belgrade, Yugolslavia via Casper (Wyo.) Junior College, was limited to only light workouts throughout much of the off-season after undergoing shoulder surgery, also to repair an existing problem.

"There's no question that injuries have taken a toll," said Aggers, who took over a Lions program that did not win a Division I game in 1999-2000 and went a respectable 9-19 and 5-9 in his debut season in the WCC. "How those guys heal up and how they come along this fall will determine how good a team we're going to be."

Still, the biggest blow of all might have been Forman's decision to return to return to Australia to play for his hometown Adelaide 36ers. Forman, a 6-9, 230-pounder, signed with the Lions as a 19-year-old freshman with four years of college eligibility remaining. He had been penciled in as the starting power forward on a team that lost its two top front liners—All-WCC forward Elton Mashack and center Pablo Machado—from last season.

"For us, that was a huge loss," Aggers said. "We were really excited about his potential. His leaving means we suddenly have a lot less size and depth in the frontcourt."

Without Forman, Mashack and Machado, the Lions will be thin and inexperienced up front. Lakey is a proven talent who should benefit from the weight he put on over the summer. But he will be surrounded on the low blocks by players with little or no Division I experience.

Neskovic put up some decent junior college numbers last winter, averaging 16.9 points and 6.6 rebounds in earning Wyoming Conference Player-of-the-Year honors, and is the leading candidate to start alongside Lakey in the post.

The other forward spot will probably go to either 6-6 junior **Keith Kincade**, another West Virginia transfer who sat out last season under the NCAA's transfer rule, or highly touted freshman **Andy Osborn**, a 6-9, 220-pounder from Longmont, Colo. Osborn was runner-up for Colorado Prep Player-of-the-Year honors last winter after averaging 24 points, 10 rebounds and four blocked shots.

Front line depth will come from 6-7 junior **Sean Mollins** (4.3 ppg, 2.9 rpg), 6-6 senior **Philipp Czernin** (5.9 ppg, 3.0 rpg), 6-7 sophomore **Sherman Gay** (1.6 ppg, 1.8 rpg) and little-used 6-8 junior walk-on **Jason Dickens**.

"We lost two really solid front line performers in Elton and Pablo," Aggers said. "And for us to be any good this year, we need somebody to step up and score for us in the paint."

If that kind of player emerges, things might not be as bleak as they appear, because the Lions have some talent in the backcourt.

Robert Davis, a 6-2 senior, averaged a team-high 11.9 points and 4.3 rebounds last winter, but he will be hard-pressed by Dennis and 6-0 senior **Marcus Smith** (8.0 ppg, 2.0 rpg, 2.3 apg) for the starting off-guard spot.

"Robert didn't really have a very good year last year," Aggers said of Davis, who shot just 38.8 percent (109-281) from the field as a junior. "He has a lower back problem that flares up and gives him problems, especially with his shooting.

"His inconsistency is something he's going to have to correct this year."

Aggers said he expects a heated battle between Davis, Smith and Dennis for the No. 2 spot. But he also has the option of going with a three-guard look and putting at least two of the three on the court together.

Eurskine Robinson, a 6-0 senior, returns at the point after averaging 5.3 points, 3.2 rebounds and 2.9 assists last year. He will probably retain his starting job early in the year, but Aggers looks for freshman Charles Brown to push for playing time once he learns the Lions' system.

Brown, a 6-0, 170-pounder, averaged 11 points and five assists as a senior at De La Salle (Calif.) High School, where he went 88-7 as a starting point guard.

"He's young and all of that," Aggers said of Brown, "but he comes from a quality high school program and he knows how to win. It's hard to start as a freshman early but I'm hoping that by January, Charles can be a real factor."

The other two guards on Aggers' roster are 6-0 senior walk-on **Tyler McClenahan** (3.0 ppg, 1.0 rpg, 1.1 apg) and **Chris Trumpy**, a 6-2 sophomore transfer from the University of Victoria in Victoria, British Columbia.

"We played all season with just eight scholarship guys and three walk-ons last year," Aggers said. "This year, we'll have more depth and solid contributors. But we need some of our guys to get healthy and improve if

we're going to take that next step."

2001-2002 SCHEDULE

Nov.	13	#Guardians Classic
	17	Idaho State
	24	@Cal State Fullerton
	28	UC Irvine
Dec.	2	@Texas A&M
	5	UC Santa Barbara
	8	Sacramento State
	15	UNLV
	18	@Long Beach State
	22	USC
	30	@Montana
Jan.	2	Occidental
	5	@Portland State
	11	@San Francisco
	12	@Saint Mary's
	18	Portland
	19	Gonzaga
	24	@San Diego
	26	@Santa Clara
	30	@Pepperdine
Feb.	2	Pepperdine
	8	Saint Mary's
	9	San Francisco
	14	@Gonzaga
	16	@Portland
	22	Santa Clara
	23	San Diego
	28	##WCC Tournament
March	1-4	##WCC Tournament

@Road Games
#Coleman Coliseum, Tuscaloosa, AL (vs. Samford first round; vs. Iona or Maryland-Eastern Shore on Nov. 14; semifinals and final Nov. 20-21 at Kemper Arena, Kansas City, MO)
##Jenny Craig Pavilion, San Diego, CA

BLUE RIBBON ANALYSIS

BACKCOURT	C
BENCH/DEPTH	C-
FRONTCOURT	C-
INTANGIBLES	C+

Aggers is fast earning a reputation as a master rebuilder. The job he did at Eastern Washington, where he built the Eagles into a perennial Big Sky Conference contender, was nothing short of remarkable.

And now he seems intent on doing the same thing at Loyola Marymount. This could be the toughest of the two assignments, considering the overall strength of the West Coast Conference. But don't be surprised if the Lions make some noise in the league race this winter—especially if Lakey, Dennis and Neskovic recover from their off-season surgeries.

"I'm happy with where we are after only one season," Aggers said. "We have more bodies than we had last year, but we obviously have to get recruiting. We have some talent, but we're not physically big enough yet to complete in our league. We probably need at least one more recruiting class."

(S.B.)

Pepperdine

LOCATION	Malibu, CA
CONFERENCE	West Coast
LAST SEASON	22-9 (.710)
CONFERENCE RECORD	12-2 (2nd)
STARTERS LOST/RETURNING	3/2
NICKNAME	Waves
COLORS	Blue, Orange & White
HOMECOURT	Firestone Fieldhouse (3,104)
COACH	Paul Westphal (Southern Cal '72)
RECORD AT SCHOOL	First year
CAREER RECORD	First year
ASSISTANTS	Gib Arnold (BYU '95)
	Jim Nielsen (Washington State '72)
	Wyking Jones (Loyola Marymount '95)
TEAM WINS (last 5 years)	6-17-19-25-22
RPI (last 5 years)	262-114-110-45-75
2000-01 FINISH	Lost in NIT second round.

When it comes to changing coaches, few schools do it better than Pepperdine.

In the last seven years, the Malibu-based university has changed coaches four times. But unlike many programs that take a step or two backward each time the reins are placed in unfamiliar hands, the Waves seem to thrive with each new nameplate that is tacked on the door of the head coach's office.

When Lorenzo Romar took over in 1996, Pepperdine was coming off a miserable 10-18 season that had produced a 2-12 record and eighth-place finish in the West Coast Conference. The Waves went 6-21 in Romar's rookie season, but won 36 games the next two years and made it to the NIT in 1999.

Romar left for St. Louis later that spring and was succeeded by Jan van Breda Kolff, who debuted with a 25-9 record that included a WCC regular-season title and an at-large NCAA berth. Last year, the Waves finished 22-9 and made it to the second round of the NIT, which was good enough to earn van Breda Kolff a ticket out of town and a five-year contract at St. Bonaventure.

To replace him, Pepperdine tapped into the long list of former NBA coaches who were looking for work and landed Paul Westphal, a 12-year NBA veteran player and former head coach of the Seattle SuperSonics and Phoenix Suns.

And with eight letter winners returning, there seems to be little reason to think the Waves will back off even a smidgen in their relentless pursuit to overtake Gonzaga as the model program in the WCC.

"I am absolutely thrilled about the opportunity to coach at Pepperdine," Westphal said. "The university's basketball tradition is outstanding. I'm anxious to roll up my sleeves and get things started."

Westphal's first order of business will be finding some offense to help ease the losses of departed seniors Kelvin Gibbs (14.9 ppg, 8.0 rpg), Derrick Anderson (6.8 ppg, 3.7 rpg) and David Lalazarian (10.1 ppg, 4.3 rpg) and WCC scoring leader Brandon Armstrong, who left school a year early for the NBA.

Armstrong, the 23rd overall pick in the NBA draft, averaged 22.1 points as a junior and, along with Gibbs, was voted to the All-WCC team.

"I saw a few games in person last year and watched others on television," said Westphal, whose son, **Mike Westphal**, saw limited action as a walk-on junior guard for the Waves last season, "and I know we're losing some key guys. As far as I'm concerned, though, we're starting fresh. And that is a good situation from a player's perspective."

Westphal would appear to have decent depth in the backcourt, where 6-3 senior **Craig Lewis** and 6-3 sophomore **Micah McKinney** return. Lewis averaged 9.2 points and 2.6 assists last season, while McKinney (3.5 ppg, 2.9 apg) was picking up valuable experience as a rookie point guard.

In addition, the Waves added several new faces to their backcourt mix, including junior college transfers **Devin Montgomery** and **Gary Colbert**, both of whom have previous Division I experience.

Montgomery, a 6-0 junior from Moorpark (Calif.) Community College, played at Duquesne as a freshman and was voted the Atlantic 10's top freshman after averaging 7.7 points, 3.1 rebounds and 3.8 assists.

The 6-3 Colbert spent a year at Utah before transferring to Dixie (Utah) Community College.

But the most intriguing of Westphal's new backcourt prospects is red-shirt freshman **Robert Turner**, a versatile 6-9, 190-pounder who averaged 24.8 points, 9.3 rebounds and 6.0 blocks as a senior at Western High School in Buena Park, Calif.

Turner is an excellent outside shooter and will probably get a good look at starting on the wing.

The Waves' frontcourt is also well stocked with veteran players, including 6-7 junior **Boomer Brazzle** (3.5 ppg, 3.3 rpg), 6-9 sophomore **Will Kimble** (2.0 ppg, 2.1 rpg) and 6-11 senior **Cedric Suitt** (1.5 ppog, 2.6 rpg).

Brazzle and Suitt, who blocked a team-high 33 shots as a junior, each started several games last year. Both will be pressed for playing time by 6-8 sophomore **Glen McGowan** (1.9 ppg, 1.1 rpg), 6-7 junior **Dustin Johnson** (0.2 ppg, 0.3 rpg), 6-6 junior transfer **Jimmy Miggins** and 6-5 freshman **Terrance Johnson**, who averaged 15.0 points and 8.0 rebounds as a senior at Duncanville (Texas) High School last winter.

Westphal said he plans to employ the same kind of fast-paced offense and pressing defense that van Breda Kolff put in place during his short tenure at Pepperdine.

"I prefer a pressing, up-tempo style of play, with an assortment of defenses," Westphal said. "My expectation is to build on what was accomplished by the previous coaching staff."

Westphal got a chance to introduce himself and his coaching philosophy to his players over the summer when the Waves made a 12-day trip to Spain, where they finished 5-0 in exhibition games. The experience, Westphal said, gave him an excellent opportunity to "evaluate our personnel and get a gauge on where we stand as a team."

There will be plenty of other early season challenges as well, thanks to another taxing non-conference schedule that includes road games at UCLA, UC Irvine, UC Santa Barbara and Utah, along with a match-up against Southern California at the Great Western Forum in LA. USC advanced to the Elite Eight of last year's NCAA Tournament, while Irvine and Utah were both members of the NIT's 32-team field.

"Our non-conference schedule will provide plenty of difficult tests, but that should better prepare the team for the rigors of conference play," said Westphal, in his first season as a Division I head coach. "We play eight non-conference games on the road, so the team will certainly be battle-tested in hostile environments."

2001-2002 SCHEDULE

Nov.	17	Cal State Fullerton
	20	@UC Irvine
	28	@UCLA
Dec.	1	@Utah
	4	Long Beach State
	6	*USC
	8	@UC Santa Barbara
	14	@Oregon
	17	Georgia
	21	Point Loma
	28-30	#Fiesta Bowl Classic
Jan.	5	Brigham Young
	11	@Saint Mary's
	12	@San Francisco
	18	Gonzaga
	19	Portland
	24	@Santa Clara
	26	@San Diego
	30	Loyola Marymount
Feb.	2	@Loyola Marymount
	8	San Francisco
	9	Saint Mary's
	14	@Portland
	16	@Gonzaga
	22	San Diego
	23	Santa Clara
	28	##WCC Tournament
March	1-4	##WCC Tournament

@Road Games
*Fab Four Double-header, The Forum, Los Angeles, CA
#Tuscon, AZ (vs. Arizona first round; also Valparaiso, West Virginia)
##Jenny Craig Pavilion, San Diego, CA

BLUE RIBBON ANALYSIS

BACKCOURT	B+
BENCH/DEPTH	B-
FRONTCOURT	C+
INTANGIBLES	B

There aren't many teams in the West Coast Conference that could withstand the early departure of a shot creator and scoring machine like Armstrong. But Pepperdine, after a brief fall from it customary spot among the league's elite, has re-established itself as one that can.

Westphal inherited a roster that is a bit short on experience, but loaded with talent.

And another strong recruiting class, headed by heralded 6-9 freshman guard Turner, should help make the Waves' latest coaching transition as smooth and successful as the previous two.

Look for Westphal to keep the pressure on opponents defensively as the Waves make a run at Gonzaga and the WCC title.

(S.B.)

Portland

LOCATION	Portland, OR
CONFERENCE	West Coast
LAST SEASON	11-17 (.393)
CONFERENCE RECORD	4-10 (7th)
STARTERS LOST/RETURNING	4/1
NICKNAME	Pilots
COLORS	Purple & White

HOMECOURT	Chiles Center (5,000)
COACH	Michael Holton (UCLA '92)
RECORD AT SCHOOL	First year
CAREER RECORD	First year
ASSISTANTS	Eddie Hill (Washington State '94)
	Rich Wold (Oregon State '90)
	Matt Gordon (UCLA '99)
TEAM WINS (last 5 years)	11-10-9-14-9
RPI (last 5 years)	246-187-246-266-245
2000-01 FINISH	Lost in conference quarterfinal.

Michael Holton wasn't expecting much when he returned to Portland this spring to take over the Pilots' sagging program.

Having served as an assistant at UP under his predecessor, Rob Chavez, during the 1994-95 season, Holton was all too familiar with the Pilots' recent struggles. He knew about the dramatic decline in fortunes from the 21-8 NCAA Tournament team he had helped coach to last year's 11-17 team that finished 4-10 and in seventh place in the West Coast Conference.

Yet, once he arrived on campus, he found even less than he expected.

In the wake of Chavez's departure, four regulars from last year's team—including all-conference center and leading scorer Tim Frost (14.9 ppg, 7.0 rpg)—decided to quit the team, leaving Holton with only four returning letter winners on his roster.

"With those four guys not coming back, we lost over 70 percent of our offense and 80 percent of our rebounding," said Holton, who takes over his first Division I program after having spent the previous five seasons as an assistant at UCLA, his alma mater.

"We lost large numbers in every statistical category, along with a lot of leadership. We're rebuilding, I guess, is the right way to put it. But that being said, I like the guys we have. Every one of them is committed to being here and wants to help put this program back on top."

Despite signing on late in the recruiting process, Holton still managed to sell his vision to six newcomers. His first recruiting class, which Holton admitted was "signed on the scramble," was still ranked No. 1 in the WCC by Hoop Scoop Online, a leading national recruiting service.

"I feel great about every kid we signed," Holton said. "Every one of them has a chance to have an immediate impact. But I've been in this league before and I know it's hard to win with young players."

Leading Portland's short list of returning players is 6-1 sophomore point guard Adam Quick, who averaged 4.2 points and a team-high 4.2 assists as a freshman last year.

"Adam has a very solid rookie season," Holton said of the Australian native, who started 27-of-28 games and finished with an assist-to-turnover ratio of 2-1. "We're counting on him to come back and continue to build on the numbers he put up last year."

If he doesn't, the Pilots could be in big trouble in the backcourt, where 6-1 senior Ross Jorgusen (4.6 ppg, 1.8 rpg, 1.5 apg) and little-used 6-3 sophomore Casey Frandsen are the only returning players with Division I experience.

Last year's starting off-guard, Ryan Jones, who averaged 12.9 points and 2.4 rebounds, quit school, and his backup, Brian Mills (2.6 ppg, 2.1 rpg, 1.7 apg), transferred to a Division II school in Florida.

That means any other backcourt help will have to come from the three guards Holton managed to recruit.

Karl Aaker, a 6-5 freshman who was signed by Chavez, is the most highly touted of the three. As a senior at McQueen High in Reno, Nev., Aaker averaged 21 points and seven rebounds after missing the early part of the year with a broken foot.

"He's one of the guys I'm really excited about," Holton said of Aaker. "He's got a good outside shot, and he can play inside and out."

Aaker, who weighs 210 pounds, could end up on the wing, however, leaving 6-2 junior transfer Eric Knight and 6-4 freshman Brian Kim to battle for backup duty at the point and off-guard positions.

Knight, who averaged 19.6 points for Los Angeles Southwest Community College last winter, can play either position and brings some much-needed maturity and experience to the lineup. Kim, from Langley, British Columbia, was ranked among the top ten prospects in B.C., but remains a bit of an unknown commodity.

The outlook in the frontcourt is even more uncertain. With the 7-0 Frost having decided to transfer to Utah and 6-7 forward Diaby Kamara (4.0 ppg, 3.7 rpg) having opted to transfer to Cal Poly, there is very little to recommend about the Pilots' inside game.

Coky Rochin, a 6-8, 265-pound senior, averaged 7.0 points and 4.1 rebounds last year but played in only 21 games and averaged less than 17 minutes a game.

"He played on the Mexican National team, though, and had a great summer," Holton said of Rochin. "We're counting on him to bring an inside presence to the low blocks."

Ghislain Sema, a 6-8 sophomore, and Matt Towsley, a 6-11 freshman, red-shirted last year. Sema, says Holton, is a "live-body, athletic-type of guy, who should be able to some rebounding for us. But he's not a very seasoned player."

Of Towsley, Holton said, "We really don't know what to expect."

Among the other frontcourt hopefuls are freshmen Patrick Galos, Erick Soderberg and Porter Troup.

Galos is a 6-7 forward who averaged 18 points, 11 rebounds, four assists and three blocks in leading Wilcox High to the Santa Clara (Calif.) Valley League title last winter. The 6-9 Soderberg, another Californian, started his prep career at Mater Dei, but lettered the last two seasons a Centennial High in Corona.

Holton seems most intrigued by Galos, a 210-pounder who needs to become a more frequent visitor to the weight room.

"He needs to get stronger," Holton said. "If we had the luxury, we'd probably red-shirt him, but he's one of our more skilled frontline guys."

Troupe was a standout at La Jolla High, but slipped through the recruiting cracks after being courted initially by Fresno State and San Jose State.

"We're definitely counting on him being an impact player," Holton said. "He just ended up being available and kind of gravitated toward a private-school education.

"We certainly had a need for a player of his caliber, so it ended up being a very good get for us."

2001-2002 SCHEDULE

Nov.	17	UC Riverside
	21	Idaho State
	25	@Duke
	28	@Idaho
Dec.	2	Oregon
	15	Eastern Washington
	19-22	#Rainbow Classic
	20	Lehigh
Jan.	5	Montana State
	11	San Diego
	13	Santa Clara
	18	@Loyola Marymount
	19	@Pepperdine
	24	Saint Mary's
	26	San Francisco
	30	@Gonzaga
Feb.	2	Gonzaga
	7	@Santa Clara
	9	@San Diego
	14	Pepperdine
	16	Loyola Marymount
	18	@Oregon State
	22	@San Francisco
	23	@Saint Mary's
	28	##WCC Tournament
March	1-4	##WCC Tournament

@Road Games
#At Honolulu, HI (vs. Hawaii first round; also Iona, Holy Cross, Boston College, Miami OH, Georgia, Arkansas State)
##Jenny Craig Pavilion, San Diego, CA

BLUE RIBBON ANALYSIS

BACKCOURT	B
BENCH/DEPTH	D
FRONTCOURT	C-
INTANGIBLES	D

Holton is a proven recruiter, but he is still a recruiting class or two away from building Portland back into the kind of WCC power it was in the first two years of Chavez's seven-year tenure.

The transfer loss of Frost was huge, and Jones' decision to quit school will have a major impact on the Portland's ability to score.

Quick was one of the best freshmen in league last winter, despite playing at the most demanding position on the floor. He is the real deal and a legitimate all-conference prospect, but his supporting cast is young and inexperienced—which means the Pilots will probably find themselves mired deep in the second division of the WCC again this year.

(S.B.)

Saint Mary's

LOCATION	Moraga, CA
CONFERENCE	West Coast
LAST SEASON	2-26 (.071)
CONFERENCE RECORD	0-14 (8th)
STARTERS LOST/RETURNING	3/2
NICKNAME	Gaels
COLORS	Red & Blue
HOMECOURT	McKeon Pavilion (3,500)
COACH	Randy Bennett (Idaho '96)
RECORD AT SCHOOL	First year
CAREER RECORD	First year
ASSISTANTS	Kyle Smith (Hamilton '92)
	Lamont Smith (San Diego '99)
	Dan Shell (California '98)
TEAM WINS (last 5 years)	2-10-9-14-9
RPI (last 5 years)	92-187-204-269-314
2000-01 FINISH	Lost in conference quarterfinal.

Randy Bennett is a glass-half-full kind of guy. His unbridled optimism should serve him well as he tackles his first Division I coaching assignment and attempts to pump life back into a dormant Saint Mary's program.

Unfortunately for Bennett, the glass he was handed at SMC doesn't qualify as being either half full or half empty. In fact, the talent Bennett inherited in the wake of Dave Bollwinkel's off-season resignation barely covers the bottom.

Granted, the Gaels' return eight players—including three starters—from last year's team. But that team finished a miserable 2-26 overall and failed to win a game in the West Coast Conference. Which makes the restoration of confidence a top priority.

"Any time you struggle the way they did last year, it beats you up a little bit," said Bennett, who spent the last two seasons as Lorenzo Romar's top assistant at Saint Louis. "Our players' confidence and self esteem were a little bit down, and that's been a concern."

It didn't help when last year's leading scorer, sophomore guard Jovan Harris (15.1 ppg, 3.2 rpg, 2.1 apg), was ruled academically ineligible and left school during the summer. Or when forward Chris Schlatter, who averaged 7.7 points and 2.8 rebounds as a freshman last season, decided to transfer to Washington State.

But Bennett is determined to keep his focus on what few positives he found when he first arrived on campus.

"I'm not making any bold predictions or anything," Bennett said, "but I honestly thought the talent level was better than what you might expect in a case like this."

Among the returning players that Bennett likes the most are 6-5 junior Tyler Herr, 6-3 senior Teohn Conner and 6-6 senior Ethnie Stubbs.

Herr (6.2 ppg, 3.3 rpg, 1.4 apg) was a key reserve last season and is the third-leading returning scorer. Conner (5.9 ppg, 4.2 rpg, 1.9 apg), was a part-time starter, and Stubbs (4.1 ppg, 1.4 rpg) had his moments as a first-year junior college transfer.

"All three of those guys can give you points," Bennett said. "That's what they do best—make baskets."

The problem is that all three are best suited to play the wing, so getting them on the floor at the same time will take some imagination.

"We'll play three guards at times," Bennett said. "And if we have to, we'll downsize and play four with either Stubbs or Herr as our power forward."

Bennett will have plenty of other options in the backcourt, thanks to a roster that is loaded with guards. But deciding on who plays point guard might take some time.

Ryan Nelson, a 6-0 freshman who averaged 18 points and 10 assists at Westview High School in Phoenix, Ariz., last year, and Samuel Saint-Jean, a 6-1 junior transfer from Foothill College in Los Altos Hills, Calif., are the only true point guards and could share time at that position.

Everyone else, including newcomers Antony Woodards, a 6-2 junior transfer from Skyline (Calif.) Junior College, and Adam Caporn, a 6-3 freshman from Australia, is a combo guard.

"We'll have a lot of options in the backcourt," Bennett said. "I got through it every single night, trying to figure out who will play where. I just figure time will tell and it will all get sorted out eventually."

Capon averaged 14 points and five rebounds for the Australian Institute of Sports last season and was a good late recruiting get. Any other backcourt help will have to come from returning veteran Paul Marigney or walk-on Scott O'Hara. Marigney, a 6-3 sophomore, played in only 12 games as a rookie, but averaged 4.3 points and

is considered by Bennett to be one of the Gaels' most aggressive players.

"He's talented and pretty versatile, too," Bennett said of Marigney. "If he gets it all under control, he could help us."

The Gaels' aren't nearly as deep in the frontcourt, but again, Bennett likes the caliber of the players who are retuning. Ross Benson, a 6-9 junior, averaged 8.5 points and 4.4 rebounds and is penciled in as the starting center.

"He's got a chance to be a good player," Bennett said. "Obviously, he's got to make some improvement from last year and he's got to learn to be more consistent. But he's been in the league awhile, and he's got the tools."

Bennett is also intrigued by 6-8, 230-pound sophomore Chase Poole, who averaged 2.1 points and 3.1 rebounds as a freshman, despite seeing limited playing time.

"I like Chase," Bennett said. "He's probably put on 25 pounds since last year and he's got a really good basketball body. He's really athletic and bouncy, and he's got a chance to be good. It's just hard to make that jump to being a really good player in this league as a sophomore."

The Gaels have another experienced front liner in 6-9 senior Chris Baert, who averaged 6.4 points and 3.3 rebounds as a junior after transferring from Chemeketa (Ore.) Community College. And Ervin Anderson, a 6-8 senior who played only sparingly after transferring from Cecil (Md.) College last year, could see some minutes once he gets back in shape after being shelved most of the summer with a stress fracture in his foot.

"He's another bouncy, athletic type of guy," Bennett said of Anderson. "And if he gets healthy, he'll contribute."

Still, the Gaels have to learn how to win. And they have to do it in a tough league that doesn't get him kind of national exposure it probably deserves.

"We are missing that winning experience," Bennett said. "These guys have gone through [losing] for a lot of years now, and it's going to take some time to get their confidence built back up. But I like the kids we have, and I'm ready to get started."

2001-2002 SCHEDULE

Nov.	16	@UC Irvine
	19	@Cal Poly
	21	Nevada
	28	Sacramento State
Dec.	1	@UC Santa Barbara
	5	@San Jose State
	9	UC Santa Cruz
	18	Loyola-Chicago
	28-29	#New Mexico Tournament
Jan.	2	@Colorado
	7	Utah
	11	Pepperdine
	12	Loyola Marymount
	16	San Francisco
	19	@San Francisco
	24	@Portland
	26	@Gonzaga
Feb.	1	Santa Clara
	2	San Diego
	8	@Loyola Marymount
	9	@Pepperdine
	14	@San Diego
	16	@Santa Clara
	22	Gonzaga
	23	Portland
	28	##WCC Tournament
March	1-4	##WCC Tournament

@Road Games
#Albuquerque, NM (vs. New Mexico first round; also Dartmouth, Southeast Louisiana)
##Jenny Craig Pavilion, San Diego, CA

BLUE RIBBON ANALYSIS

BACKCOURT	C-
BENCH/DEPTH	D
FRONTCOURT	B
INTANGIBLES	D-

Bennett spent 12 of his 16 years as an assistant in the West Coast Conference and knows the landscape. He remains well connected and will eventually be able to recruit the area as well as anyone in the league, but he faces a difficult task in rebuilding a Saint Mary's program that has slipped dramatically in recent years.

There is reason for optimism on the front line, thanks to the return of Benson and Poole, and the Gaels should be able to score from the wings. But uncertainty at the point-guard position, coupled with a lack of overall experience at the off-guard spot, leaves Saint Mary's with little hope of challenging for a first-division finish.

(S.B.)

San Diego

LOCATION	San Diego, CA
CONFERENCE	West Coast
LAST SEASON	16-13 (.552)
CONFERENCE RECORD	7-7 (4th)
STARTERS LOST/RETURNING	3/2
NICKNAME	Toreros
COLORS	Columbia, Navy & White
HOMECOURT	Jenny Craig Pavilion (5,100)
COACH	Brad Holland (UCLA '79)
RECORD AT SCHOOL	110-86 (7 years)
CAREER RECORD	133-117 (9 years)
ASSISTANTS	David Fitzdale (San Diego '96)
	Steve Flint (UC San Diego '84)
	Sam Scholl (San Diego '99)
TEAM WINS (last 5 years)	16-20-18-14-17
RPI (last 5 years)	146-163-126-109-152
2000-01 FINISH	Lost in conference semifinal.

It's been a while since any major retooling has been necessary at San Diego.

Last year, for instance, the Toreros returned their top 11 scorers from a team that finished 20-9 overall and 10-4 in the West Coast Conference. But this year, coach Brad Holland has some work to do. Three starters—point guard Dana White, power forward Cameron Rigby and center Tyler Field—were lost to graduation. So was super-sub Nick Greene.

Those four seniors accounted for 32 points and nearly 19 rebounds per game on a team that was as balanced as any in the WCC. And Holland, in his eighth season at USD, is troubled by their absence.

"We lost a ton of rebounds," he said. "And that's been a major part of our defense the last several years. We're going to have to find a way to replace that, and it isn't going to be easy."

The biggest loss, perhaps, was Field, a 6-9, 245-pound banger who averaged 9.4 points, 6.1 rebounds and a couple of TKOs per game.

"We lost a significant inside presence with Tyler," said Holland, who is desperately hoping that 6-10, 250-pound senior Kevin Hanson is finally ready to mix it up on the low blocks. Hanson led the team in blocks as a freshman and sophomore, despite playing limited minutes. But last year he struggled in Field's considerable shadow and averaged just 3.6 points and 2.6 rebounds while blocking only nine shots.

"We need Kevin Hanson to be ready," Holland said. "He's never been in a starting role before, but he's going to be relied upon to play maybe 25 minutes a game this year. And we need him to be ready to perform for all 25 minutes."

Hanson is not as physical at Field, but he possesses nice short-range shooting touch, along with a wide body that is hard to move. Unfortunately for the Toreros, who finished a disappointing 16-13 last season, they don't have much in the way of experienced hands to complement Hanson on the low blocks.

Tom Lippold, a 6-6 senior, averaged 6.2 points and 3.2 rebounds last winter but spent most of his time on the wing. That means the power forward spot will probably be manned by either Jason Blair, a 6-7 sophomore who sat out the 2000-01 season after transferring from Southwest Texas State, or 6-10 sophomore Ryan Hegerty, who red-shirted last year because of an assortment of leg and foot injuries.

Blair, who averaged 13.7 points as a freshman at SWTS, is considered the favorite.

"He's a proven Division I guy and a solid power-forward type," Holland said. "After losing Green and Rigby, we're obviously looking for him to come in and fill the void."

The Toreros also have a freshman front-liner with plenty of potential in Nick Lewis, a former standout at Brophy Prep in Phoenix, Ariz.

"He's fairly slight," Holland said of the 6-9, 210-pound Lewis, "but he's getting stronger. We'll look to get some minutes out of him as a freshman."

Lippold has played some power forward and has been a top reserve for the past two seasons. But Holland would like to keep him on the wing, if possible.

The backcourt is loaded with returning players, including last year's leading scorer **Andre Laws** (10.3 ppg, 3.1 rpg, 2.5 apg), a 6-1 senior combo guard who can play the point in an emergency.

Laws may be forced into that role because of **Roy Morris**' lingering problems with a broken foot. Morris, a 6-2 junior, backed up White at the point last year and averaged 3.9 points and 1.2 assists. But he underwent a second surgery on his foot late in the summer to re-insert a screw in the broken bone.

"Point guard is a problem," Holland said. "We lost an all-conference player in Dana White. You simply couldn't press him, and we'll miss that.

"Morris was ready to step in, but because of his surgery, Andre Laws is probably going to be asked to step in and play the point at the beginning of the year, at least."

Mike McGrain, a 6-2 freshman from Jesuit High in Portland, Ore., might also see time at the point.

The shooting-guard position will be handled by committee, with 6-2 senior **Matt Delzell** (4.2 ppg, 1.9 rpg, 1.5 apg), 6-4 junior **Scott Boardman** (2.1 ppg, 0.7 rpg, 0.5 apg) and 6-4 senior **Sam Adamo** (9.2 ppg, 2.3 rpg, 0.7 apg) all expected to get their share of minutes.

Delzell, however, was on crutches most of the summer after undergoing off-season knee surgery to reconstruct the patella tendon in his left knee.

"We have a lot of pieces that have to come together," Holland said in assessing his team's chances this winter. "We lost four starters and the majority of our rebounding, but I do think we have a quality group of veterans returning.

"We also have a some young players that are going to be called upon for some productive minutes, and if they can execute and produce we can be a quality team."

Holland is also hoping his team will feel more at home in 5,100-seat Jenny Craig Pavilion, which opened last year. The Toreros, who had been nearly unbeatable in the dark, cramped confines of their previous Sports Center digs, finished a disappointing 7-5 at home last year.

"We were getting used to the new visual and acoustical environment, just like our opponents," Holland said "I hope like crazy that we're going to feel much more at home in our own building this year."

2001-2002 SCHEDULE

Nov.	17	Brigham Young
	20	UC San Diego
	24	@Portland State
	26	@Oregon State
Dec.	1	Washington
	5	San Diego State
	8	Boise State
	11	UC Irvine
	20	USC
	22	Southern Oregon
	29-30	#Montana State Tournament
Jan.	3	@Northridge
	11	@Portland
	13	@Gonzaga
	16	@Santa Clara
	19	Santa Clara
	24	Loyola Marymount
	26	Pepperdine
Feb.	1	@San Francisco
	2	@Saint Mary's
	7	Gonzaga
	9	Portland
	14	Saint Mary's
	16	San Francisco
	22	@Pepperdine
	23	Loyola Marymount
	28	##WCC Tournament
March	1-4	##WCC Tournament

@Road Games
#Bozeman, MT (vs. Hampton first round; also Montana State, Troy State)
##Jenny Craig Pavilion, San Diego, CA

BLUE RIBBON ANALYSIS

BACKCOURT	B+
BENCH/DEPTH	B
FRONTCOURT	B-
INTANGIBLES	B+

Holland, the West Coast Conference Coach of the Year in 1998-99 and 1999-2000, has built a reputation

for getting the most out of his players. In the minds of many, however, last year's veteran-laden team underachieved on its way to a 7-7 record and fourth-place finish in the WCC.

There is enough returning talent to suggest that the Toreros will make amends this winter. But for that to happen, they need a big senior season from Hanson and a return to health from shooting guard Delzell and point guard Morris.

Unlike past seasons, USD is thin on the front line and won't have its customary 15-20 fouls to throw around.

(S.B.)

San Francisco

LOCATION	San Francisco, CA
CONFERENCE	West Coast
LAST SEASON	12-18 (.400)
CONFERENCE RECORD	5-9 (5th)
STARTERS LOST/RETURNING	2/3
NICKNAME	Dons
COLORS	Green & Gold
HOMECOURT	War Memorial Gymnasium (5,300)
COACH	Philip Mathews (Irvine '72)
RECORD AT SCHOOL	94-80 (6 years)
CAREER RECORD	94-80 (6 years)
ASSISTANTS	Billy Reid (San Francisco '79)
	Justin Piergrossi (Pennsylvania '97)
	Paul Trevor (Sonoma State '97)
TEAM WINS (last 5 years)	12-19-12-19-16
RPI (last 5 years)	158-94-182-132-227
2000-01 FINISH	Lost in conference quarterfinal.

Since **Darrell Tucker** first stepped on campus back in the fall of 1999, expectations surrounding the University of San Francisco program have soared—often to unrealistic levels.

Those expectations are hovering in the stratosphere again heading into the 2001-02 season. Only now, it appears that Tucker, an immensely gifted 6-9 junior, and his supporting cast of upperclassmen might finally have the experience and maturity to live up to them.

If they do, the Dons will be able to run with the best in the West Coast Conference and, perhaps, snap their streak of four consecutive second-division finishes.

The key is Tucker, a chiseled 220-pounder, who has been plagued by inconsistency in this first two seasons at USF. As a rookie in 1999-2000, the former Bay Area Prep Player of the Year from McClymonds High School in Oakland, Calif., averaged 13.2 points and 7.0 rebounds and was selected the WCC's Freshman of the Year. He closed with a rush, scoring 20 or more points in the Dons' last six games, and was also a first-team All-WCC selection.

But he followed his breakout freshman season with a disappointing sophomore year that left him in coach Philip Mathews' doghouse much of the winter.

Tucker's scoring average increased to 16.5 last year, but his rebounding averaged dropped to 6.8, while his turnovers increased from 47 to 79. He started only 23-of-30 games and didn't make the all-conference team as USF closed an injury plagued season by losing 14 of its last 20 games.

Mathews remains hopeful, however, that Turner can shake his sophomore funk and team with 7-0 senior **Hondre Brewer** to help form one of the most dominant front lines in the conference. Brewer (8.5 ppg, 6.2 rpg), burst into the spotlight last winter as a shot-blocking machine. The slender 225-pounder, who was also recruited out of Oakland, rejected a WCC-record 114 shots as a junior and enters his final season with 201 career blocks, just six short of the league record of 207 held by Gonzaga's Casey Calvary.

"If those two guys can produce like they can up front," Mathews said, "we can play with anyone on our schedule.

"Tucker can score with anyone on a given night, while Brewer makes opponents think twice before stepping in the lane."

The only concern up front is depth. **Tayo Akinsete**, a 6-6, 230-pound senior, averaged 6.7 points and 5.0 rebounds last season and will once again serve as an exciting, capable frontline backup—and three-point threat—wherever he is needed.

Eugene Brown (1.6 ppg, 1.5 rpg), a 6-10 junior, is another defensive whiz who specializes in blocking shots. But beyond those four, there are no proven inside threats.

That means Mathews will go almost exclusively with

a three-guard lineup, built around returning 6-0 senior point guard **LyRyan Russell**, who missed the 2000-01 season with a hip injury he sustained during a preseason workout.

Russell started 22 games as a junior in 1999-2000 and averaged 4.9 points and 4.1 assists. He will be spelled at the point this year by 6-0 red-shirt freshman **Jason Gaines**, a former prep standout at Deer Valley High School in Antioch, Calif., who also missed all but two games of his rookie season after suffering a knee injury.

The Dons also return off-guard **John Cox**, a 6-4 sophomore, who sat out last year after having bone spurs removed from his foot. Cox, the son of former USF star Chubby Cox and a cousin of NBA standout Kobe Bryant, played in 28 games as a freshman and averaged 4.9 points and 2.0 rebounds.

With LyRyan, Gaines and Cox all on the shelf, USF led the WCC in turnovers last winter with 550. The Dons also suffered defensively by not being able to apply the kind of full-court, in-your-face pressure that has become their trademark.

"Without solid backcourt play, it is impossible to establish yourself at either end of the court," Mathews said. "The ball ends up in the wrong places at the wrong times, leaving you with poor shots and your opponents with good ones."

The one backcourt player who did manage to stay healthy last year was 6-5 junior **Shamell Stallworth** (8.0 ppg, 3.3 rpg), who shot .407 (35-86) from three-point range. Stallworth is a great leaper who can run the floor with anyone in the league. He will probably get his share of minutes, considering the other four backcourt players on the Dons' roster are either Division I rookies or seldom-used walk-ons.

Still, Mathews likes his depth at guard, especially at the point.

"It will certainly help us get the ball into the post where we can get some easy baskets," Mathews said. "And we will definitely do a better job of pressuring the ball. This should make a huge difference, and we should have one of the league's better turnover margins instead of the worst."

Among the newcomers in the backcourt are freshmen **Jerome Gumbs**, **DeWayne Morris** and **Mike Chambers** and junior **Scepter Brownlee**, who will all get a chance to earn a spot in the guard rotation.

Gumbs, a 6-4, 185-pounder from Barren County High School in Glaskow, Ky., averaged 24.0 points and 14.0 rebounds as a prep senior and shot 65 percent from the floor. Morris, also 6-4, averaged 17.0 points, 5.0 assists and 6.0 rebounds for Mira Costa High School in Manhattan Beach, Calif., last year. And Chambers, a 6-2 standout at Wood High in Vacaville, CA, averaged 21.8 points, 6.0 rebounds and 5.0 assists last winter.

The 6-1 Brownlee could see considerable time at the point after averaging 15.0 points and 7.0 assists as a sophomore at Glen Oaks (Ind.) Community College last year.

"Scepter is an excellent, all-around point guard," Mathews said. "He will add great defensive pressure, as well as lead our offense. He is a very physically strong player."

The Dons' other two backcourt prospects are walk-ons **Eddy Harris**, a 6-1 sophomore, and **Tony Hickman**, a 5-10 junior, who combined to play in only five games last year.

Mathews' team, with so many new faces from last season, should benefit greatly from the seven-game tour of the Canary Islands and Spain that it took during the summer.

2001-2002 SCHEDULE

Nov.	16	Seton Hall
	19	@Cal State Fullerton
	24	UC Santa Barbara
	28	@Nevada
Dec.	1	*Xavier
	4	@Fresno State
	8	Cal State Hayward
	15	Pacific
	18	@Texas A&M
	20	@Southern
	29	**Michigan
Jan.	2	@Brigham Young
	5	Texas A&M
	11	Loyola Marymount
	12	Pepperdine
	16	@Saint Mary's
	19	Saint Mary's
	24	@Gonzaga
	26	@Portland

Feb.	1	San Diego
	2	Santa Clara
	8	@Pepperdine
	9	@Loyola Marymount
	14	@Santa Clara
	16	@San Diego
	22	Portland
	23	Gonzaga
	28	#WCC Tournament
March	1-4	#WCC Tournament

@Road Games
*Northwestern Mutual Mayor's Game
**Pete Newell Challenge, Oakland, CA
#Jenny Craig Pavilion, San Diego, CA

BLUE RIBBON ANALYSIS

BACKCOURT	B
BENCH/DEPTH	B-
FRONTCOURT	A
INTANGIBLES	C-

Several coaches around the WCC are convinced that this will be the year Mathews finally puts everything together at San Francisco. The Dons' summer trip to the Canary Islands and Spain should help familiarize newcomers like Brownlee and Morris with Mathews' demanding system, but chemistry could still be a problem. With so many guards on board, it could be difficult finding enough minutes to keep them all happy.

That shouldn't be a problem up front, however, and if Tucker, a leading candidate for WCC Player of the Year honors, can play up to his vast potential, look for the Dons to return to the first division and challenge for the league title. Especially if shot-blocking sensation Brewer can develop the other aspects of his game.

(S.B.)

Santa Clara

LOCATION	Santa Clara, CA
CONFERENCE	West Coast
LAST SEASON	20-12 (.625)
CONFERENCE RECORD	10-4 (4th)
STARTERS LOST/RETURNING	2/3
NICKNAME	Broncos
COLORS	Red & White
HOMECOURT	Leavey Event Center (5,000)
COACH	Dick Davey (Pacific '64)
RECORD AT SCHOOL	160-102 (9 years)
CAREER RECORD	160-102 (9 years)
ASSISTANTS	Steve Seandel (San Jose State '81)
	Sam Scuilli (Stanford '94)
	Antonio Veloso (Santa Clara '96)
TEAM WINS (last 5 years)	20-19-14-18-16
RPI (last 5 years)	109-80-145-106-81
2000-01 FINISH	Lost in conference final.

Dick Davey isn't big on sugarcoating. The dean of West Coast Conference coaches, now in his 10th season as the man in charge at Santa Clara, knows his Broncos are going to miss point guard Brian Jones.

And he's not afraid to admit as much.

"I don't think we see anybody on our roster right now who is going to be able to step right in and take over all the things he did," Davey said of Jones, who closed his distinguished career as the first player in WCC history to record 1,500 points, 500 rebounds and 500 assists.

"Brian was truly valuable to us—not only as a point-guard leader, but also because of his ability to rebound the ball, his court sense, his effort and his strength."

The 6-3 Jones, who signed with SCU hoping to make Bronco fans forget Steve Nash, might not have lived up to everyone's expectations. But he left having started more games (113) than any player in school history, and he finished second in career assists (506) and steals (218), and fifth in career scoring (1,666 points).

Despite missing the 1998-99 season with a horrific knee injury, Jones managed to finish in style, averaging 15.8 points, 5.0 rebounds, 4.18 assists and a WCC-best 2.11 steals as a senior. He was a first-team All-WCC selection for the third time, and was the offensive and defensive leader of an over-achieving Broncos team that won 20 games for the first time in six seasons.

Yet, the thing the Broncos might miss more than anything is Jones' physical and mental toughness. He and departed All-WCC forward Jamie Holmes, who averaged 13.6 points and 7.4 rebounds as a senior last year,

brought a touch of orneriness to the court night in and night out.

And Davey isn't sure this year's team has anyone of that same ilk.

"We lost our two strongest and most physical players in Brian and Jamie," Davey said. "We try to survive by being physical, at times, and we're just not going to be as physical this year as we've been in the past."

So where does Davey turn for finesse? To 6-2 sophomore guard Kyle Bailey, for starters. Bailey, from Fairbanks, Alaska, proved to be one of the big surprises in the WCC last winter, averaging 9.1 points, 2.8 rebounds and 2.6 assists while making a strong case for league freshman-of-the-year honors. He is the player most likely to inherit Jones' point-guard duties.

"Kyle played a lot as a freshman at that position," said Davey, who was rewarded during the off season with a contract extension through the 2004-05 season. "He's a guy that we're counting on to be a big factor for us down the road and a guy we're hoping will be able to take over a lot of the load."

In addition, the Broncos are bringing in freshman Bakari Altheimer, a former prep standout at St. Elizabeth High School in Oakland, Calif. Altheimer, a 5-10, 175-pounder, averaged 22 points, four assists, four rebounds and three steals as a high school senior.

"We expect him to contribute right away," Davey said, "but that still means we'll have a sophomore and a freshman at the point-guard position."

The Broncos seem well stocked at the other guard spot, where 6-2 senior Brian Vaka (4.5 ppg, 2.9 rpg, 1.8 apg) returns, along with 6-4 sophomore Jason Morrissette and 6-4 red-shirt freshman Ethan Rohde.

"Vaka, being a senior, would get the nod right away as the starter," Davey said. "We feel good with those two at that position, and we also have a probable backup in Steve Ross, although he'll probably have a great chance to start at the three [position]."

Ross, a 6-5 senior, emerged as one of the WCC's most versatile players last year after transferring from San Diego. He played in 24 games and averaged 12.2 points, 5.5 rebounds and 1.3 assists.

"He was a little bit of a surprise," Davey said of Ross, who hails from Victoria, British Columbia. "He's a guy that's worked real hard to make himself a player. He's spent a lot of extra hours—more than most kids do—in the gym, and he's enhanced his game, basically, in all areas.

"He was not a very good defender, initially, but he's improved in that area. And he can drive the ball and he's a good rebounder. He's a player who has a chance, if he continues to improve like he has, to maybe play somewhere beyond college."

Things are much less settled on the front line, where as many as nine players are expected to get looks.

"We have a multitude of players we can throw in there," Davey said.

David Emslie, a 6-11 senior, will probably start at center after averaging 4.4 points and 3.6 rebounds last season. Other experienced frontliners include 6-6 senior Jason Westphal (1.0 ppg, 2.0 rpg), 6-7 senior Justin Holbrook (8.2 ppg, 2.8 rpg), 6-8 sophomore Jim Howell (1.6 ppg, 3.0 rpg) and Brad and Cord Anderson, a pair of little-used 6-4 juniors. None, however, is a physical as Holmes.

"David Emslie has improved his game to the point where we can count on him for a lot of minutes in the post area," Davey said. "Again, he's not very physical, but he's a good shooter and he's long, which present some problems for some guys."

Howell, at 230 pounds, is the most physical of Davey's returning post players and will probably back up Emslie.

And there is also a trio of freshmen, 6-10 Linden Tibbets, 6-9 Jordan Legge and 6-8 Scott Borchart, who have come on board to add depth.

Borchart, from Newbury Park, Calif., averaged 20 points and seven rebounds for Chaminade Prep last winter, while Legge, from Mesa, Ariz., averaged 18.3 points and 9.0 rebounds.

Tibbets, who will probably redshirt, averaged five points, four rebounds and two blocks per game at Duncanville, Texas.

"We're hoping that one of our freshmen can emerge and give us some quality time at either the four or five," Davey said. "Ideally, we'd like to red-shirt one or two of them, but we probably won't know if we can do that until we go through November.

"If a guy's not quite ready, we'll talk about that possibility, but if a guy is ready, we're going to want him to contribute right away."

2001-2002 SCHEDULE

Nov.	17	Pacific
	20	@California
	24	@Washington
	27	San Jose State
Dec.	1	@Nevada
	12	@Ohio State
	15	@Wright State
	18-19	#Stanford Invitational
	22	Chico State
	28-29	##Cable Car Classic
Jan.	4	Loyola, MD
	11	@Gonzaga
	12	Portland
	16	San Diego
	19	@San Diego
	24	Pepperdine
	26	Loyola Marymount
Feb.	1	@St. Mary's
	2	@San Francisco
	7	Portland
	9	Gonzaga
	14	San Francisco
	16	St. Mary's
	22	@Loyola Marymount
	23	@Pepperdine
	28	###WCC Tournament

@Road Games
#Maples Pavilion (vs. Portland State first round; also Belmont, Stanford)
##San Francisco, CA (vs. Maryland-Baltimore County first round; also Detroit, UC Santa Barbara)
###Jenny Craig Pavilion, San Diego, CA

BLUE RIBBON ANALYSIS

BACKCOURT	B+
BENCH/DEPTH	B
FRONTCOURT	C+
INTANGIBLES	B

Santa Clara might not look like a legitimate contender on paper, but Davey is a master at getting his players to play to their potential.

Replacing Jones will be difficult. Bailey won't bring the same kind of toughness and athleticism to the point, but he could prove to be more consistent than his predecessor.

Davey bemoans that fact that this year's team won't be as physical as those that came before it. Granted, the Broncos are lacking experience up front, but there are plenty of bodies—and plenty of fouls—available if Davey needs them.

The Broncos might start slowly, because of another killer schedule that has them playing at California, Washington and Stanford. But look for them to finish strong like they did last year when they won six straight games before losing to Gonzaga in the final of the WCC Tournament.

(S.B.)

Boise State

LOCATION	Boise, ID
CONFERENCE	Western Athletic
LAST SEASON	17-14 (.548)
CONFERENCE RECORD	8-8 (t-5th Big West)
STARTERS LOST/RETURNING	1/4
NICKNAME	Broncos
COLORS	Blue & Orange
HOMECOURT	BSU Pavilion (12,380)
COACH	Rod Jensen (Redlands '75)
RECORD AT SCHOOL	96-76 (6 years)
CAREER RECORD	96-76 (6 years)
ASSISTANTS	Ed Boyce (Pacific Lutheran '84)
	Mark Folsom (Seattle Pacific '96)
	Jeff Drinkwine (Eastern Oregon '87)
TEAM WINS (last 5 years)	14-15-20-12-17
RPI (last 5 years)	148-163-106-186-130
2000-01 FINISH	Lost in conference semifinal.

Boise State is one of those basketball programs still feeling a little dazed and confused since stepping on the fast track of Division I. Not that the Broncos mind this sudden transition.

They wanted to make the two moves over the last six

seasons that have them shifting from Big Sky to Big West to Western Athletic Conference.

True, Boise State has suffered the growing pains of increasing the caliber of competition. They haven't been invited to the big NCAA dance since 1994 and don't figure to get back this year unless the four returning starters make the major adjustment to the WAC.

Of all the things seventh-year head coach Rod Jensen has thought about since Boise State joined the underrated WAC, how quickly the Broncos can get comfortable in their new corral heads the list. He knows a middle-of-the-pack finish in the Big West Conference last year doesn't exactly give him bragging rights this time around.

He also saw what former Big West partner Nevada went through during its first tour of WAC duty in 2000-2001. But if senior forward **Abe Jackson** can remain as effective down low and sophomore guard **Booker Nabors** keeps it together out front, the Broncos should be more effective than the Wolf Pack proved to be during its rookie season in the No. 7-rated conference by CollegeRPI.com last year.

"Naturally, this is a big move up for us," Jensen said. "They had four teams go to the postseason last year, which tells you something right there. The transition may be difficult at times, but to me, it will be worth it for Boise State basketball in the long run."

The short run might be a different matter, but not because Jensen doesn't have a player or two. He does. Starting with the 6-7 Jackson (17.4 ppg, 5.7 rpg) at small forward and swinging around to the 6-3 Nabors (9.6 ppg, 2.8 rpg, 3.3 apg) out front, there are some promising prospects waiting to show their new WAC neighbors they belong on the block.

"But for that to happen, everybody has to be ready to take it up a notch," Jensen said. "We've got some experience, which is exciting for us. But we also have to be aware that the level of competition has been bumped up. We have to respond to the kind of athletic teams and talented coaches we'll be facing this season."

Jackson believes he can answer the call. Twice an All-Big West selection, including first team last year, the Boise, Idaho, native has the bulk to battle on the boards and the outside shot that leaves defenders wondering why they gave him such an open look.

Jackson set a school record last year with 83 three-pointers (.403), 11 better than his sophomore season. The man possesses a quick release. But if opponents guard him too close or charge him on the perimeter, he can take it to the basket just as easily.

"His gaining 20 pounds the last three years makes him one of the most dangerous inside-outside guys around," Jensen said. "Now, he'll be facing some better guys in the post, but he's such a pure outside shooter, we feel like he'll still be very effective."

Joining them in the frontcourt will be senior power forward **Richard Morgan** (7.2 ppg, 3.3 rpg). At 6-8 and 240 pounds, Morgan will be better suited setting picks on the perimeter for Jackson than trying to compete as an undersized center as he has done the last three seasons.

The move to his more natural position should make the Broncos even that more effective in the paint.

Senior center **Trever Tillman** (4.9 ppg, 2.8 rpg) will see more starting minutes this year, which should translate to good things for the 6-11, 260-pounder. Once he establishes position down low in the post, he's hard to get out of there, which is just what Jensen is looking for.

Last year, Jensen backed down on his defensive intensity, believing the NCAA was about to get whistle happy. It cost the team 11 points a season over the 1999-2000 season, prompting Jensen to take a more hard-line approach.

"We're going to play defense like we have in the past, which should work well in the WAC," Jensen said. "We've always tried to be defensive-minded because that creates fast-break points.

"That's one reason why I'm putting Trever at center. He blocked 38 shots for us last year. He really came on strong for us late, so I'm hoping he'll pick up where he left off and become even more effective this year. We need him and Rich to have breakout seasons."

Those three starters provide the experience. They have combined to play 244 games in four years. Throw in the fact that starting power forward of a year ago Kejuan Woods (14.6 ppg, 3.6 rpg) and backup forward Delvin Armstrong (9.5 ppg, 3.0 rpg) are gone, and it's easy to see that depth at forward could pose a problem.

Sophomores **Scott Fraser-Dauphinee** and **Kenney Gainous** will try to help fill the void. The 6-7 Fraser-Dauphinee (1.7 ppg, 1.2 rpg) red-shirted last year after playing in 20 games his freshman season. The 6-8 Gainous (1.4 ppg, 1.4 rpg) is a perfect small forward who

WESTERN ATHLETIC

BLUE RIBBON FORECAST
1. Fresno State
2. Tulsa University
3. Hawaii
4. UTEP
5. Louisiana Tech
6. SMU
7. Boise State
8. Rice
9. Nevada
10. San Jose State

ALL-CONFERENCE TEAM
G Gerrod Henderson, SR, Louisiana Tech
G Predrag Savovic, SR, Hawaii
C Melvin Ely, SR, Fresno State
F Chris Jefferies, JR, Fresno State
F Kevin Johnson, JR, Tulsa

PLAYER OF THE YEAR
Melvin Ely, SR, Fresno State

NEWCOMER OF THE YEAR
Hiram Fuller, JR, Fresno State

2001-2002 CONFERENCE TOURNAMENT
March 5-9, Reynolds Center, Tulsa, OK

2000-2001 CHAMPIONS
Fresno State (Regular season)
Hawaii (Conference tournament)

2000-2001 POSTSEASON PARTICIPANTS
Postseason Record 7-3 (.700)
NCAA
Fresno State (Second Round)
Hawaii

NIT
Tulsa (Champion)
UTEP (Second Round)

TOP BACKCOURTS
1. SMU
2. Tulsa
3. Hawaii

TOP FRONTCOURTS
1. Fresno State
2. Tulsa
3. Boise State

INSIDE THE NUMBERS
2000-2001 conference RPI: 7th (of 31)
Conference RPI (last five years): 7-9-9-8-7

DID YOU KNOW?
Fresno State senior center Melvin Ely was selected by a national poll of the Wooden Award Committee to be one of the top 50 preseason candidates for the 2001-2002 All-American team. So was Bulldog guard Tito Maddox, but he has since been asked to leave the building by Fresno State head coach Jerry Tarkanian for accepting a gift from an agent. ... Last year was Tulsa's eighth trip to the NIT, dating back to 1953. The Golden Hurricane is 13-6 in the postseason event, including championship runs last year and in 1981. ... Fresno State advanced to the second round of the NCAA Tournament, assuring the WAC its seventh consecutive season of having a team make it at least that far. ... Fresno State head coach Jerry Tarkanian is 38-18 (.679) lifetime in the NCAA Tournament, including four Final Four appearances with UNLV. He won the national championship in 1990. ... The WAC has a rather average 61-79 mark in 73 appearances in the NCAA Tournament. Utah's 1998 advancement to the national title game against Kentucky is as far as a WAC team has ever gone in the Big Dance. ... Hawaii set the WAC Tournament record in assists last year with 26 in the opening-round win over TCU. The old mark of 25 was set by New Mexico in 1996. ... Fresno State center Melvin Ely has the eighth-best career field-goal percentage (.584) in WAC history. New Mexico's George Scott set the previous record (.622) in 1982-85. ... SMU's Jeryl Sasser exited the WAC scene in style. One reason Orlando selected Sasser in the first round of the NBA draft was his willingness to look for his shot. The guard finished fifth all-time in field goals attempted with 1,711. He still trailed front-runner Danny Ainge by plenty. The former Cougar guard attempted 1,875 shots from 1978-81. Sasser is also sixth all-time in free-throws attempted (720) and No. 11 in rebounds with 976. ... Hawaii currently has six foreign athletes who figure to compete for starting jobs this season, including all-everything guard Predrag Savovic. If he isn't ruled ineligible for possibly playing with professionals in a European League, he could be one of the premier swingmen in the country.

(P.A.)

should see some quality minutes this season.

Joining them are fresh faces **Robby Gerichs**, a 6-9 transfer from Treasure Valley (Oregon) Community College, who sat out last year. Freshman **Jason Ellis** is a 6-7 forward (16.0 ppg, 13.0 rpg) from Kentridge High in Kent, Wash., who could see playing time right away. He was the MVP of the South Puget Sound League last year, something not lost on Jensen.

"Jason is one of several solid recruits joining our program," Jensen said. "I really like our frontcourt. We have three players with a lot of experience who should help the younger guys develop as they get minutes on the floor. We've got size, which should help us because we're not as quick and athletic as we might need to be at this level."

That shouldn't be a problem out front. Jensen has three point guards from which to choose, including **Bryan DeFares**, last year's backup to starter **Joe Skiffer**, and **C.J. Williams**, who sat out last year after being the starting point man his first two times through the program.

The 6-2 junior Skiffer (3.5 ppg, 2.5 rpg, 3.2 apg) is a solid assist man for Jensen. He did a better job of taking care of the ball last season. He had 97 assists and only 61 turnovers, and can also play the two-guard when necessary. The 6-3 DeFares (1.8 ppg, 1.4 rpg, 0.7 apg) lives

in Holland and is only getting better with his exposure to Division I hoops.

Should he falter, the 6-0 junior Williams (4.3 ppg, 2.2 rpg, 3.2 apg), who red-shirted last year because of a bad knee injury, should be able to step right in. This three-way punch gives Jensen plenty of options out front.

"Each guy brings something different to the table," Jensen said. "A head coach loves deciding how to attack each defense. This is a luxury for us."

Nabors' freshman rise helps soften the blow of losing Clint Hordemann. The 6-3 graduating senior (7.1 ppg, 4.8 rpg) had a nice outside touch and an ability to move the ball quickly around the perimeter. His loss will be felt should Nabors, another Boise resident, succumb to the sophomore jinx.

Nabors was the starter last year. He could shoot from the outside (.480) and also led the team in assists with 103. He can play either guard spot if necessary, but look for him to be at the two spot for most of the season.

His backup is Fraser-Dauphinee, who is an excellent swingman. Transfer **Cory Ortiz**, a 6-4 walk-on from Santa Rosa (Calif.) Junior College, should provide some much-needed depth at the two-guard. Overall, the backcourt should be able to more than hold its own.

"Having Joe and Booker back can only help us," Jensen said. "Both are very versatile athletes on both ends of the court. They are a perfect complement to our frontcourt. I think our inside-outside game will be one of our strong points this season."

2001-2002 SCHEDULE

Nov.	17	Portland State
	20	@Utah
	24	Idaho
	26	@Eastern Washington
Dec.	1	@Idaho
	5	Lewis-Clark State College
	8	@San Diego
	12	Wyoming
	15	Southern Utah
	18	Northern Arizona
	28	@SMU
	30	@Louisiana Tech
Jan.	3	San Jose State
	5	Hawaii
	10	@Rice
	12	@Tulsa
	17	Fresno State
	19	Nevada
	26	@UTEP
	31	@Hawaii
Feb.	2	@San Jose State
	7	Tulsa
	9	Rice
	14	@Nevada
	16	@Fresno State
	23	UTEP
	28	Louisiana Tech
March	2	SMU
	5-9	#WAC Tournament

@Road Games
#Reynolds Center, Tulsa, OK

BLUE RIBBON ANALYSIS

BACKCOURT	C+
BENCH/DEPTH	B-
FRONTCOURT	B
INTANGIBLES	C+

Judging by how difficult it was for Nevada to be competitive in the WAC its first time around last year, it stands to reason that Boise State won't be battling for the conference crown just yet. Not that the Broncos can't make some noise—they can, especially at home.

The big test will be how athletic Boise State is in a league where talent abounds. Fresno State, Tulsa and Hawaii are all more athletic than Jensen's club and are used to the rigors of competing against top Division I talent.

One thing that could help the Broncos is getting back to basics defensively. Two years ago, the Broncos were in the top 25 nationally in scoring defense, yielding a stingy 62.2 points a game. If Boise State can play that tenacious style at this level, look out, the Broncos could cause the upper echelon teams some trouble.

"Being consistent will be a big challenge for us," Jensen said. "Our seniors need to give us the kind of leadership necessary to be a winning program on and off the floor. We believe they'll do that for us."

The problem may be depth. While there are four returning starters, the experience level takes a dive after that. It will be up to Jackson underneath and Nabors out front to keep Boise State from struggling mightily as former Big West Conference partner Nevada did last season. Who knows, the Broncos could be the dark horse in the WAC.

(P.A.)

Hawaii

LOCATION	Honolulu, HI
CONFERENCE	Western Athletic
LAST SEASON	17-14 (.548)
CONFERENCE RECORD	8-8 (t-5th)
STARTERS LOST/RETURNING	2/3
NICKNAME	Rainbow Warriors
COLORS	Green & White
HOMECOURT	Stan Sheriff Center (10,300)
COACH	Riley Wallace (Centenary '64)
RECORD AT SCHOOL	216-198 (14 years)
CAREER RECORD	231-225 (16 years)
ASSISTANTS	Bob Nash (Hawaii '84)

Jackson Wheeler (Loyola Marymount '82)
Scot Rigot (South Carolina '88)

TEAM WINS (last 5 years)	21-21-6-17-17
RPI (last 5 years)	50-45-215-111-55
2000-01 FINISH	Lost in NCAA first round.

In a land where vowels are king, Hawaii basketball coach Riley Wallace decided names with consonants is the wave of the future for his Pacific Island program.

For years, Wallace has tried— with limited success— to recruit top junior college players on the West Coast. Granted, he landed starting point guard Anthony Carter, who later played for for the Miami Heat, during a successful run in the late 1990s.

"But you can't go against the top schools in the Pac-10 and expect to win too many of those," Wallace said. "So, we decided to recruit foreign players who are mature and can handle playing away from home. It has been a good strategy for us the past few years."

Unfortunately for Wallace, the NCAA took a long, hard look at the foreign influx, trying to determine how many, if any, are professional players in disguise. Over the summer, Hawaii was part of a 60-school Division I review by the NCAA.

Last year, projected starting center Haim Shimonovich was suspended by the NCAA for 22 games for competing in an Israeli league with other professionals. While he was not paid, the NCAA thought the 22 games he played in with pros should be deducted from his freshman season.

That decision is likely to haunt any other schools who discover any past transgressions among international players, including Hawaii. This summer, the NCAA asked the Rainbows to supply information on four foreign athletes, including first team All-WAC performer Predgrag Savovic (17.6 ppg, 4.7 rpg, 3.5 apg, 1.3 spg), a 6-6 senior.

Before Hawaii's first round NCAA Tournament game against Syracuse in Dayton, Ohio, the local newspaper ran an article about eligibility problems for foreign athletes.

"And their poster child was Savo," Wallace said. "The article questioned whether Savo played in a professional league while playing in Europe. We looked into that during the off-season and feel like he may have played in 10 games. We're hopeful if there is a suspension, it will be similar to that of Haim's.

"The thing that bothers me is it's unfair. We allow collegiate golfers to play with professionals in tournaments every weekend. As long as they don't get paid, nobody says anything about it. Well, this situation with our foreign athletes is the same. They didn't get paid even though some of the guys they played with did."

For Hawaii to be a legitimate contender, the Rainbows can ill-afford to lose Savovic for an extended period of time. Wallace believed three things could happen to Savovic: He could be suspended for a determined amount of games, he won't be suspended or he will be suspended for the season.

Last year, Savovic led the Rainbows and was ranked third in the league in scoring. In 28-of-31 games, Savo scored at least 10 points, and 10 times he managed 20 or more. The problem is he had a penchant for giving up points on the defensive end, often relying on a bad European flop in hopes of drawing a charge. Usually, all this routine incurred was the wrath of the referees, who regarded it with disdain. But after seeing Savovic the first day of school, Wallace is convinced his top off-guard means this to be his money season.

"He is in outstanding shape," Wallace said. "He has worked hard on his footwork, his shooting, his conditioning and his decision-making. He wants to play at the next level and in order to do that, he has things he needs to work on. He is key for us."

Joining him in the backcourt will be 6-3 senior Mike McIntyre (7.1 ppg, 2.2 apg, 1.6 rpg), something of an enigma for Wallace. At times, McIntyre plays on a higher plane, only to come down hard for unexplainable stretches. Injuries last year not only kept him out of three games but hampered him the middle part of the season.

Still, he started 11 games, including the final nine of UH's strong 7-2 finish. He provides some much-needed senior leadership. McIntyre was the team's best at the free-throw line, hitting a blistering .829. What Wallace likes about this team is its closeness with McIntyre and Savocic serving as the leaders of the pack.

"I'm counting on those guys to help keep us where we were at the end of last season," Wallace said. "We had several freshmen come on for us late, particularly Carl English (4.9 ppg, 3.1 rpg, 1.6 apg) and Phil Martin (8.8 ppg, 4.2 rpg). We've got several more young guys coming in, so we need to stay together on and off the court."

English, a 6-4 red-shirt sophomore, is one of those fresh faces who will be hard-pressed to match his closing act as a freshman in the WAC Tournament.

Voted MVP in leading Hawaii to the improbable title, English scored 44 points, pulled 15 rebounds and managed 11 assists in the three wins over Texas Christian, Fresno State and eventual NIT champion Tulsa on the Golden Hurricane's home floor.

All that production was off the bench, something that could happen again this year if Savovic and McIntyre hold their starting roles.

"Even if we wind up losing Savo for part of the season, I feel like Mike and Carl can carry us through the non-conference," Wallace said. "We've got to continue to work hard to improve, but I like our backcourt."

Wallace also went out and signed a point guard, Mark Campbell, a 6-4 junior from Clackamas (Ore.) Community College who Wallace says will challenge for playing time. Last year, Clackamas (14.5 ppg, 10.2 apg) earned MVP honors, partly for leading the league in assists. He has a chance to play right away, no matter how well English, Savovic and McIntyre are clicking.

Reserves Lance Takaki (0.2 ppg, 0.2 rpg), a 5-4 junior, and Ryne Holliday (0.0 ppg, 0.0 rpg), a 5-10 senior, round out a solid, if not potentially dangerous backcourt. The hard part will be replacing three effective players in the frontcourt, including center Troy Ostler (15.5 ppg, 5.9 rpg) and small forward Nerijus Puida (9.3 ppg, 5.8 rpg, 4.4 apg).

This twosome made everyone around them that much more effective, putting a lot of pressure on center Shimonovich, and fellow sophomores Martin and Mindaugas Burneika at forward to produce.

While English is from Canada, Shimonovich from Israel and Burneika calls Lithuania home, Wallace believes the common denominator among these foreign athletes is a will to win on the court.

"You hear all kinds of languages when you come to one of our practices," Wallace said. "It's kind of interesting to listen to Savo and Bosko [Radovic] because they're both from Yugoslavia. But all of these guys speak English well enough to know what to do on the court."

Martin, a 6-7 sophomore, is also from Canada. He played well enough last year to lead the WAC in field-goal accuracy (.627). Not exactly a power forward or a swing man, Martin can fool you with his quickness and ability to go hard to the basket.

He'll get plenty of help from Shimonovich (2.1 ppg, 2.6 rpg), a 6-10, 245-pound sophomore, and Burneika (7.4 ppg, 2.7 rpg), a 6-7 senior. This twosome only figures to get stronger as they gain experience in the collegiate game.

Radovic (5.8 ppg, 3.4 rpg), a 6-9 freshman, red-shirted after having his season cut short with a broken leg. He played in the first five games, starting three of those, and gives Wallace a good experienced mix in the paint.

"We've got a lot of depth there, but they're still young," Wallace said. "The game over in the USA is different from that in Europe, but they're learning. I think we showed that toward the end of the season when we got everybody back and playing."

There are several newcomers who also figure to vie for playing time. Chief among them are junior college transfers LucArthur Vebobe (11.9 ppg, 4.5 rpg, 2.5 apg) and Paul Jesinskis (13.9 ppg, 10.0 rpg). Jesinskis, a 6-7 junior, played at Skyline (Calif) Community College, but had his season cut short with a knee injury. He was a member of the South African junior national team.

Vebobe, a 6-9 junior, attended two junior colleges before settling on Hawaii. He was voted to two all-tournament teams, including the San Jose Christmas event, where he averaged 17.8 points and 7.8 rebounds a game.

Add Nigerian Nkerunem Akpan (17.5 ppg, 13.1 rpg), a 6-8, 230-pound freshman, to the mix and it's truly an international cast. Akpan is a graduate of Central Park Christian High School in Birmingham, Ala., where he played with two other Division I signees, Marco Killingsworth (Auburn) and Lucky Williams (Alabama).

2001-2002 SCHEDULE

Nov.	16,18	#Nike Tip-Off Tournament
	23-25	##Big Island Tournament
	27	Northwestern State
Dec.	10	Alcorn State
	14	San Diego State
	19-22	###Rainbow Classic
	27	Fresno State
	29	Nevada
Jan.	3	@UTEP
	5	@Boise State
	10	Louisiana Tech

	12	SMU
	19	@San Jose State
	24	@Rice
	26	@Tulsa
	31	Boise State
Feb.	2	UTEP
	7	@SMU
	9	@Louisiana Tech
	16	San Jose State
	21	Tulsa
	23	Rice
	28	@Nevada
March	2	@Fresno State
	5-9	####WAC Tournament

@Road Games
#Honolulu, HI (vs. Norfolk State first round; also Drake, Sam Houston State)
##Hilo, HI (vs. Mercer first round; also Colorado State, South Carolina State, Hawaii-Hilo, Wisconsin, LSU, Weber State)
###At Honolulu, HI (vs. Portland first round; also Iona, Holy Cross, Boston College, Miami OH, Georgia, Arkansas State)
####Reynolds Center, Tulsa, OK

BLUE RIBBON ANALYSIS

BACKCOURT	B+
BENCH/DEPTH	B
FRONTCOURT	B-
INTANGIBLES	B+

Just how well this team performs this season depends on how kind or unkind a cut the NCAA makes into the foreign mix. There were as many as four players being looked at by the NCAA, including veterans and incoming recruits. But none is more important than Savovic.

If the NCAA follows a similar formula to the 22-game suspension handed down last year to Shimonovich, then Savovic could miss a third of the season, perhaps more. He is key for Hawaii's postseason success.

Without him, the backcourt is not ordinary, but certainly not as dynamic as it would be with him. English and McIntyre can more than hold their own at either guard spot. They have a big, raw-boned frontcourt to dump the ball into in the half-court game. It won't be pretty—no rim-rattling dunks—just old-fashioned screens, picks and back cuts to the basket to take advantage of over-playing defenses like Fresno State's.

Of Fresno State's seven losses a year ago, two were to Hawaii. That bodes well for Wallace as he tries to parlay last year's 7-2 finish and NCAA Tournament appearance into an even better regular season.

"The key for us is how well we play on the road," Wallace said. "We proved to ourselves that we could win on the road, but we have to do it again. If we have success away from the islands, I look for us to be a very competitive basketball team."

(P.A.)

Louisiana Tech

LOCATION	**Ruston, LA**
CONFERENCE	**Western Athletic**
LAST SEASON	**17-12 (.586)**
CONFERENCE RECORD	**10-6 (2nd-Sun Belt East)**
STARTERS LOST/RETURNING	**1/4**
NICKNAME	**Bulldogs**
COLORS	**Red & Columbia Blue**
HOMECOURT	**Thomas Assembly Center (8,000)**
COACH	**Keith Richard (Louisiana-Monroe '82)**
RECORD AT SCHOOL	**57-29 (3 years)**
CAREER RECORD	**57-29 (3 years)**
ASSISTANTS	**Steve Forbes (Southern Ark. '88)**
	Johnny Simmons (Louisiana Tech '84)
	Kevin Caballero (Louisiana-Monroe '89)
TEAM WINS (last 5 years)	**14-12-19-21-17**
RPI (last 5 years)	**145-175-148-126-172**
2000-01 FINISH	**Lost in conference semifinal.**

You get the feeling Louisiana Tech isn't too worried about moving out of the Sun Belt and into the Western Athletic Conference. Unlike fellow WAC first-timer Boise State, the Bulldogs are accustomed to playing top-caliber teams from around the nation.

This year alone, the Bulldogs are playing 11 teams that advanced to the postseason in 2000-2001, including Iowa, Auburn and Oklahoma, which should help them as they prepare for the long road trips in the WAC.

True enough, the Tech men are lost in the shadow of the nationally ranked women's program that has focused attention to this school located off the main highway. As well as fourth-year head coach Keith Richard has done since taking over the men's program, it hasn't been enough to land the Bulldogs an invitation to the NCAA Tournament.

Not since 1988 have the men been a part of that postseason parade, something Richard would like to remedy right away. Starting with the fortunate return of **Gerrod Henderson**, who earned an extra year of eligibility by graduating on time, and ending with perhaps the best recruiting class since the days of Karl Malone, Richard is confident Louisiana Tech will make a smooth transition into a league rated No. 7 overall among Division I conferences a year ago.

Henderson will be a key component for the Bulldogs' success. The leading scorer for Louisiana Tech the last two seasons, the 6-4 Henderson (18.4 ppg, 5.0 rpg) had some NBA feelers come his way, but believes returning to Ruston was the right decision for him and the basketball team.

"We couldn't have been happier for Gerrod in working hard in school and earning that fourth year of eligibility," Richard said.

Henderson sat out his freshman season as a Proposition 48 athlete, known today as a partial qualifier.

"It's says a lot about him and his character to develop as a student and a player," Richard said. "I'm glad we'll have him on the floor this season because he's the kind of leader you want out on the floor during crunch time."

Henderson was voted the Sun Belt Conference's Player of the Year in 1999-2000. He also was first team all-league last season and had a chance to see if the pro life was for him over the summer. Fortunately for Louisiana Tech, graduation was more important.

"Gerrod was invited to the pre-NBA draft camp in Massachusetts, which says a lot about him," Richard said. "He had a choice to make and he decided to stick with us, which is great. What he has managed to do academically is an even better achievement for him and his family."

Henderson is not the only guard in the station house for Richard. He could suit up as many as 10 this season. Some could slip in at the three-spot and give a guard look similar to what the Mustangs run at Southern Methodist. There will be times when Richard wants to go big.

He welcomes back **Marco Cole**, who will also see plenty of playing time in the Louisiana Tech backcourt. The 6-5 senior is a big guard (12.3 ppg, 5.0 rpg), who can not only score from the outside, but drive hard to the basket. Cole is solid on the boards and is a perfect complement for the flashy Henderson.

How it shakes out from here is anyone's guess. Richard has a pair of players with some Division I experience, which always comes in handy. Senior **Lawrence Williams** (2.0 ppg, 0.4 rpg) has so-so numbers, but the 6-3 guard may not be strong enough to hold off Richard's youth movement.

Brian Martin might be a steady backup at the point. The 6-1 junior (3.1 ppg, 1.5 rpg) has recorded some serious minutes, but look for several of the young guns to make a play in what many believe is the best recruiting class in these parts in recent memory. One recruiting service said Tech's class is among the top 25 nationally.

Junior college transfer **Michael Wilder** is near the head of the class. The 6-2 junior from Chipola (Fla.) Junior College is considered quite a catch for the Bulldogs.

Recruiting USA considered Wilder (22.3 ppg, 4.6 rpg) among the top 20 players in junior college last year. He is good on both ends of the floor and was voted first team All-Region, which comprises the entire state of Florida. He's what coaches call instant offense.

"We're glad we could convince Michael to come play for us," Richard said. "He's a very exciting player."

Local Ruston High star **Corey Dean** is in the guard mix, as are fellow newcomers **Bruce Edwards** of New Orleans Carver High, **Lavelle Felton** of Chipola, **Daryl Ford** of Summerfield (La.) High and Ole Miss transfer **Darrian Brown**. All have good size, especially the 6-5 Brown and 6-4 Felton. It's going to make for some very interesting practices in the early going.

"We need to get competitive as soon as we can because we open the season with Iowa," Richard said. "They won the Big Ten Tournament last year and are always an outstanding basketball team. We've got a lot of guards competing, but we also have several very good players in the frontcourt. A lot of our talent will be down low."

Richard welcomes back starting forwards **Antonio Meeking** and **Zach Johnson**. The 6-8, 250-pound Meeking (14.0 ppg, 7.6 rpg) is a powerful junior with a wide body who can set picks out high and crash the boards down low. The 6-9 junior Johnson (7.6 ppg, 5.3 rpg) is equally effective in the paint.

Neither guy is a true center, which could open a spot for one of the two talented newcomers who will be batting the establishment for playing time. In Richard's mind, this is healthy competition. He knows Meeking will be on the floor a majority of the time this season. Johnson is going to garner his fair share of minutes, too, because they understand the offense and defense Richard likes to run.

But given the opportunity, 6-9 post **Wayne Powell** (22.0 ppg, 15.0 rpg 3.0 bpg) is going to make some noise as well. The Peabody High School sensation from Alexandria, La., learned he was one of 30 prep players taking part in the Louisiana High School All-Star basketball game the day he signed his national letter of intent.

Powell was considered one of the top 100 prep prospects in the country by ESPN.com.

Marshalltown (Iowa) Junior College transfer **Joe Sykes**, a 6-10 junior, will be the tallest man in the Louisiana Tech huddle. But how big of a role he plays remains to be seen.

"Wayne is the kind of good, young prospect you need to build your program," Richard said. "We're going to need to get bigger in order to compete in the WAC. It will be more of a factor for us than it has my first three years here.

"I know there have been some outstanding individual players go through here over the years. But if you look at the group of players we have coming back and the new guys coming in, you can't help but get a little excited. We think we'll be ready to take this big step into the WAC."

2001-2002 SCHEDULE

Nov.	17	@Iowa
	20	Harding
	27	Arkansas-Monticello
Dec.	1	@Jackson State
	4	@Auburn
	8	@Oklahoma
	15	Centenary
	19	@UAB
	22	Jackson State
	28	UTEP
	30	Boise State
Jan.	5	SMU
	10	@Hawaii
	12	@San Jose State
	17	Tulsa
	19	Rice
	24	@Nevada
	26	@Fresno State
	30	@Centenary
Feb.	2	@SMU
	7	San Jose Stte
	9	Hawaii
	14	@Rice
	16	@Tulsa
	21	Fresno State
	23	Nevada
	28	@Boise State
March	2	@UTEP
	5-9	#WAC Tournament

@Road Games
#Reynolds Center, Tulsa, OK

BLUE RIBBON ANALYSIS

BACKCOURT	B
BENCH/DEPTH	B
FRONTCOURT	B
INTANGIBLES	B+

This may be the first time the Louisiana Tech men's program has an opportunity to steal some of the highlights usually reserved for the nationally ranked women.

Through the years, they have given Ruston, La., an identity that far exceeds the city limits of this ideal college town.

Before Keith Richard was hired as head coach in 1998, he served as an assistant for the Bulldogs in 1994 and was chosen the associate head coach the following season. But despite seeing his fair share of talent come and go through the program, he hasn't laid eyes on anything quite like this group.

In terms of talent and experience, returning starters

Henderson, Cole and Meeking are as good a threesome as you will find in the WAC. Fresno State's Melvin Ely and Chris Jefferies are better known, but they'll be hard pressed to beat Louisiana Tech in Ruston.

So will anybody else, which is why Richard is quietly confident Louisiana Tech's first tour of duty through the WAC may be a memorable one, similar to when the Bulldogs won the Sun Belt Conference title in Richard's first year as head coach.

"We play 22-of-28 teams that competed in one of the top eight conferences in the country," Richard said. ""That could be a good thing or a bad thing, depending on how well we respond to the challenge of taking a step up."

With Henderson back for another senior season, Richard might have the proper ingredients to lead Louisiana Tech straight to the top of the WAC.

"I've told my coaches that I really like this team," Richard said. "We're all anxious to see how well we do our first year in the WAC."

(P.A.)

 **Nevada**

LOCATION	Reno, NV
CONFERENCE	Western Athletic
LAST SEASON	10-18 (.357)
CONFERENCE RECORD	3-13 (9th)
STARTERS LOST/RETURNING	1/4
NICKNAME	Wolf Pack
COLORS	Blue & Silver
HOMECOURT	Lawlor Events Center (11,200)
COACH	Trent Johnson (Boise State '83)
RECORD AT SCHOOL	19-38 (2nd year)
CAREER RECORD	19-38 (2nd year)
ASSISTANTS	Andy McClouskey (Oregon State '82)
	David Carter (Saint Mary's '89)
	Mark Fox (Eastern New Mexico '91)
TEAM WINS (last 5 years)	19-15-7-8-10
RPI (last 5 years)	76-131-266-235-204
2000-01 FINISH	Lost in WAC play-in game.

Last season began well enough for the University of Nevada. The Wolf Pack closed out its eight-year run in the Big West by advancing to the semifinals of that conference's tournament, then turned around and won seven of its first 10 to start the second season of young coach Trent Johnson.

There was an air of confidence permeating the Wolf Pack camp. Perhaps they were ready to play in the rapidly improving WAC, after all. Maybe Nevada was a league rookie. But this team had some young talent blending with the seasoned veterans.

Unfortunately for Johnson, that didn't prove to be enough as the Wolf Pack finished last in the WAC with a 3-13 mark. They were eliminated by Rice in the play-in game of the conference tournament, further demonstrating moving up in the Division I world comes with a learning curve.

Not that Nevada was blown out of every game. The Wolf Pack lost six league meetings by six points or less. Often enough, Nevada held comfortable leads in the second half, only to let them slip away in the waning moments, including a home game against nationally ranked Fresno State.

"Those come down to making big plays at the right moments," Johnson said. "We didn't do that often enough in the conference and we struggled as a result."

Nevada also begins its second season in the WAC without three experienced players, including small forward Richard Stirgus (7.9 ppg, 8.0 rpg) and point guard Adrian McCullough (6.2 ppg, 1.1 rpg, 2.0 apg). These two regulars helped develop the young talent coming up through the ranks as Johnson continues to rebuild a program that had hit rock bottom.

Before to his takeover in 1999-2000, the Wolf Pack had won only 15 games the two previous seasons. This forced him to use young players such as returning starters **Terrance Green**, **Andre Hazel** and **Sean Paul** before they were comfortable in their Division I setting. Now these three underclassmen form the backbone of a team Johnson believes is better suited to play in the athletic WAC.

"Any time you play in a league that's rated the seventh-best in the nation, you're going to experience some growing pains," Johnson said. "We were competitive, but we want to be more than that this year. We have a good nucleus, but we need everybody to work hard and continue to grow as a team."

One area Johnson feels comfortable with is his backcourt. Returning are Hazel, a 5-11 sophomore point guard (8.9 ppg, 2.2 rpg, 3.7 apg, 1.8 spg) with pizzazz, and 6-2 junior Green, a two-year starter (11.8 ppg, 3.1 rpg), who has something to prove to himself and the team after fading somewhat down the stretch last season.

As a freshman, Hazel began his journey with a career-high 12 assists in the season-opener at San Francisco. He can score when needed, but looks to pass first on offense and get the fast break started with his steals out front on defense.

"I can't say enough about the way Andre played last year," Johnson said. "He got better as the year went along. We're counting on him to continue that level of play this season."

With McCullough gone, Johnson needed a solid backup at the point. He signed junior transfer **Jerry Petty** of North Idaho College. The 5-11 Petty (14.6 ppg, 4.8 apg, 3.9 spg) sat out last season but is being counted on to be Hazel's understudy.

Green is penciled in as the top shooting guard. He has led the team in scoring the last two seasons. That's the good news. The bad news is he didn't always connect with the big bucket.

Still, he was the Wolf Pack's go-to man often enough. He started 23-of-28 games, and in his career has scored 20 or more points a dozen times and 30 or more four times. Should he falter, **Garry Hill-Thomas** (7.2 ppg, 2.2 rpg) is more than just an adequate backup. The 6-3 sophomore has a deft outside touch and is also a veteran of sorts, starting 10 games as a freshman. He scored in double figures in nine of his last 11 games, giving Johnson the kind of options he needs to build depth and be successful.

"We're counting on both of those guys to play with more consistency," Johnson said. "Terrance has had some big games for us. So did Garry the last part of the year. If they can hit consistently from the outside, it opens up so much for our guys in the frontcourt."

Much like the backcourt, the frontcourt has a good blend of youth and experience. True, replacing Stirgus will be a challenge. He was first in the Big West in rebounding two years ago and was second last year in the WAC. He made everyone around him that much better, which leaves Johnson wondering how sophomore center **Sean Paul** and forwards **James Bayless**, **Corey Jackson** and **Matt Ochs** will respond without Stirgus by their sides.

"You don't lose a hard worker like Richard and not notice he's gone," Johnson said of Stirgus, who started 56 games the last two seasons. "He was a good leader for us, on and off the floor. But I like the guys we have coming back."

They will be led by the 6-7, 230-pound Jackson (5.1 ppg, 4.8 rpg), the only senior on this rebuilt team, and 6-8 juniors Bayless (6.2 ppg, 3.0 rpg) and Ochs (1.6 ppg, 1.8 rpg). Jackson was on the floor only about 13 minutes a game as Stirgus' backup. But he still produced big enough numbers to get Johnson's attention.

"He always gave us a lift when he was on the floor," Johnson said. "He has survived a lot of changes around here because he can do a lot of things."

Bayless and Ochs have had their moments as well. Bayless once scored 24 points in a game at UNLV and had his first career double-double a month later against Washington State, while Ochs started 32-of-56 games his first two years. There is untapped potential here.

"All three of these guys have produced and not always with a lot of minutes on the floor," Johnson said. "We ask our players to do a lot when they're in there. It gives us a balanced offense and builds depth."

The 6-9, 240-pound sophomore Paul is another young player being asked to mature beyond his years. As a freshman, Paul (5.2 ppg, 4.0 rpg) wound up third on the team in shooting (.475) and first in blocked shots (16).

Was he ready for the rigors of Division I? Probably not. But the experience he gained last year can't only be measured in points and rebounds. Johnson expects his play on both ends of the floor to be improved.

Backing him up is fellow sophomore **Jason Eversteyn**. The 7-1 center (8.0 ppg, 6.0 rpg, 4.0 bpg) from Australia transferred from Hill College in Hillsboro, Texas. If he is able to adjust to the next level, this big man could allow the smaller Paul to shift to his more natural position of power forward.

"We also have a pair of young high school players who we think could see some playing time," Johnson said. "We think we have things moving in the right direction."

Incoming forwards **Kevinn Pinkney** (21.0 ppg, 13.0 rpg, 5.0 bpg) and **Kirk Snyder** (20.0 ppg, 10.3 rpg, 4.5 apg, 3.3 bpg) could be proof of that. The 6-9 Pinkney of Colton (Calif.) High School was chosen first team all-conference and honorable mention all-state. He scored a career-high 46 points his senior season.

Snyder has some impressive honors of his own. The 6-6 small forward was selected the CIF's I-AAA Player of the Year last season. He could also be a shooting guard in certain offenses Nevada will run this year.

2001-2002 SCHEDULE

Nov.	17	Cal State Northridge
	21	@Saint Mary's
	24	@Arkansas State
	28	San Francisco
Dec.	1	Santa Clara
	5	@Montana
	8	Cal State Northridge
	12	Southern Oregon
	15	Portland State
	20	@UNLV
	27	@San Jose State
	29	@Hawaii
Jan.	3	Tulsa
	5	Rice
	12	Fresno State
	17	@UTEP
	19	@Boise State
	24	Louisiana Tech
	26	SMU
	31	@Rice
Feb.	2	@Tulsa
	7	@Fresno State
	14	Boise State
	16	UTEP
	21	@SMU
	23	@Louisiana Tech
	28	Hawaii
March	2	San Jose State
	5-9	#WAC Tournament

@Road Games
#Reynolds Center, Tulsa, OK

BLUE RIBBON ANALYSIS

BACKCOURT	C+
BENCH/DEPTH	B-
FRONTCOURT	B-
INTANGIBLES	B+

You have to give Trent Johnson credit for taking over a shaky program and returning it to a model of stability in only two seasons. The changes he has made are expected to pay off in a major way for Johnson, who sees this team as much more competitive than it was in the WAC last year.

One reason is youth will be served for Johnson. He has only one senior and several sophomores who figure to play major roles in the continued turnaround of the Wolf Pack.

This is a team with several potential stars among the veterans and young recruits alike. Johnson is attracting major talent, but may still be a year away from being one of the teams in the top half of the league.

Hazel and Green will probably start, but can they lead by example? Hazel can pass, shoot and run the team with the best of them. Green has shown the capability of filling it up on any given night.

The frontcourt has some young starters returning and is blessed with several good players on the bench, including a pair of talented high school stars. But how that all comes together remains to be seen for Johnson, who signed a two-year contract extension in the off-season.

"For me, it all begins with defense and that's what we teach here," Johnson said. "We also like to spread things around with each guy contributing. We've made some good progress the last two years. Hopefully, that will be reflected in our record this year."

(P.A.)

 Rice

LOCATION	Houston, TX
CONFERENCE	Western Athletic
LAST SEASON	14-16 (.467)
CONFERENCE RECORD	5-11 (8th)
STARTERS LOST/RETURNING	2/3

NICKNAME	Owls
COLORS	Blue & Gray
HOMECOURT	Autry Court (5,000)
COACH	Willis Wilson (Rice '82)
RECORD AT SCHOOL	117-136 (8 years)
CAREER RECORD	117-136 (8 years)
ASSISTANTS	Marty Gross (Jacksonville '77)
	Todd Smith (Valparaiso '89)
	Marty Gillespie (Iowa State '79)
TEAM WINS (last 5 years)	10-5-16-3-14
RPI (last 5 years)	124-200-87-282-115
2000-01 FINISH	Lost in conference first round.

If there is one coach favored by most of his league peers for his perseverance, it's Rice University's Willis Wilson. For the last several seasons, the Owls have made U-turns similar to those practiced by the mob to give the feds the slip.

Two years ago, Rice won three games. Two years before that, only five. But sandwiched between these dismal seasons is a 16 win-season. Last year, the Owls won 14, meaning if the trend continues, this time around should be another turn for the worse.

"We're going to try to break that cycle this year if we can," Wilson said. "Part of the reason for our problems have been injuries. We're not using that as an excuse, but when you lose key players, it makes it difficult to win in our league."

Since the 1994-95 season, the Owls have missed 421 player games for an average of 60 games lost to injury per year. The 2000-2001 season was no exception. True, Wilson wasn't wiped out as he was in 1999-2000. During that grueling 3-24 campaign, every starter was sidelined for extended periods of time with a significant injury.

Last year, promising guard **Omar-Seli Mance** was lost early to stress fractures in each knee. Soon after, top center **T.J McKenzie** went down with an ACL tear in his right knee. Rice was 9-4 with them in the lineup. With them off the court, only 5-12.

Their return is crucial because all everything seniors Mike Wilks and Erik Cooper are gone. The 5-foot-11 Wilks (20.1 ppg, 4.9 rpg, 3.0 apg) was a first team All-WAC standout who did a little bit of this and that for Rice out front. The 6-6 Cooper (13.2 ppg, 6.0 rpg) was an excellent swingman with a deft outside touch and a talent for going hard to the boards.

"You don't start out the season without feeling the loss of those two guys," Wilson said. "But you don't dwell on it, either. You move forward and play with the guys you have. The secret for us is staying healthy. If we do, then we can build some consistency with our younger players."

Returning three starters is a good place to begin in the frontcourt. In addition to the 6-11 senior McKenzie (6.1 ppg, 6.4 rpg) at center, top forwards **Shawn Tyndell** (10.5 ppg, 3.2 rpg, 1.9 apg) and 6-9, 250-pound junior **Brandon Evans** (2.7 ppg, 5.3 rpg) are also back to mix it up in the paint.

One problem with McKenzie and Tyndell is durability. The 6-5 senior Tyndell missed 25 games in 1999-2000 with a broken foot. McKenzie was sidelined for 13 last year with his knee injury. They are battle tested and provide the kind of fifth-year leadership Wilson believes will keep the Owls from slipping off the radar.

"These two guys deserve everything they get because they worked so hard to get here," Wilson said. "Shawn is a great outside shooter and T.J. is strong underneath. This combination is what we need to be successful. Our big guys are much better at the start of this year than we were at the start of last year, and that can only help us."

It will start with Tyndell, who can move from shooting guard to small forward this year with the return of Mance in the backcourt. Tyndell is the leading returning scorer for the Owls. He hit at least two three-pointers in 21-of-30 games last year and has the kind of strength to be able to pound the boards down low.

Evans is a perfect complement at power forward for Tyndell. Over the last seven games of the season, he averaged nearly eight rebounds. He started 10-of-28 games as a sophomore and should see even more playing time this season.

Yamar Diene (2.7 ppg, 2.8 rpg), a 6-9, 230-pound sophomore, promises to have Evans' back whenever possible. He will look to be more offensive-minded, but it's his defensive capabilities that caught Wilson's eye for talent. Last year, Diene managed 24 blocked shots, the second most ever by a Rice freshman.

Fellow sophomore **Christian Kollik** (0.6 ppg, 0.6 rpg), 6-7, is similar to Diene in size and scope, but lacks any real experience. He played fewer than four minutes a game last season in 17 appearances and will have to improve his skills on both ends of the floor to merit any

more playing time this year. He can shoot the three-pointer (.375) if given an open look.

Freshman **Michael Harris** (26.8 ppg, 18.7 rpg, 4.5 bpg) from Hillsboro High in the Texas town of the same name will be given every opportunity to play. The 6-6 forward will have to adjust to the rigors of Division I, but so far, Wilson likes what he sees.

"Michael is one of our younger players we hope can contribute right away," Wilson said. "We like how hard he plays on both ends of the floor. He's going to be a good one."

Center looks strong as well for Rice. In addition to the oft-injured McKenzie, Wilson can turn to 6-10 junior **Ferron Morgan** (2.5 ppg, 2.8 rpg) for support. Spelling McKenzie will be important in developing depth.

With as much experience as the frontcourt has, the backcourt is as green as the Monster at Fenway Park. That doesn't bother Wilson. He believes by season's end, the backcourt could be better than the frontcourt. And that could spell trouble for Rice's opponents this season.

It all starts with the 6-2 junior Mance (4.8 ppg, 3.2 rpg, 2.5 apg), who will move from the point to shooting guard this year. If the transfer from LSU can stay healthy and the lanky 6-3 sophomore **Rashid Smith** (1.4 ppg, 0.6 rpg) can handle the point, Wilson's problems of replacing Wilks may be over with very quickly. Of course, that's no given just yet.

"We've got a long way to go before those two guys will be comfortable with their positions," Wilson said. "But if they can grow into them during the course of the season, we'll be a better basketball team for it."

Michael Walton will provide some immediate help off the bench. The 6-0 junior (2.5 ppg, 0.6 rpg) can play both guard spots. Last year, he set a single-game assist mark for Rice with 11 against Texas Christian. Walton also can shoot. He had a 10-game stretch during the season when he connected on 13-of-25 three-pointers.

"He's the perfect guy to come off the bench and give our team a spark," Wilson said. "He has great energy out there."

Joining the guard crew are 6-0 **Brock Gillespie** (18.5 ppg, 5.0 apg, 3.0 spg), a freshman from Clarksville High in Tennessee, and **Jason McKrieth**, a 6-4 freshman from Schenectady High in New York. McKrieth led his team to the state final, where the Patriots suffered their only defeat in 29 games. He averaged 18.5 points his senior season and is expected to play right away.

"We look for Jason to be our best athlete," Wilson said. "He has a great feel for finishing off a play. He's very talented."

Swingman **Nick Robinson** (0.7 ppg, 0.7 rpg) was better as a freshman than a sophomore, but look for the 6-6 junior to expand his minutes on the floor, giving Rice potentially more depth than in recent years.

"I like this group," Wilson said. "We are very athletic with a good blend of experience and youth. By the time the WAC starts, I look for us to be competitive."

2001-2002 SCHEDULE

Nov.	16	Navy
	20	Lamar
	27	@Stephen F. Austin
	29	@Houston
Dec.	1	Baylor
	4	@Middle Tennessee
	8	Birmingham Southern
	21	Centenary
	27	Texas-Pan American
	29	Siena
Jan.	3	@Fresno State
	5	@Nevada
	10	Boise State
	12	UTEP
	17	@SMU
	19	@Louisiana Tech
	24	Hawaii
	26	San Jose State
	28	@Tulsa
	31	Nevada
Feb.	2	Fresno State
	7	@UTEP
	9	@Boise State
	14	Louisiana Tech
	16	SMU
	21	@San Jose State
	23	@Hawaii
	28	Tulsa
March	5-9	#WAC Tournament

@Road Games
#Reynolds Center, Tulsa, OK

BLUE RIBBON ANALYSIS

BACKCOURT	B-
BENCH/DEPTH	B
FRONTCOURT	B+
INTANGIBLES	B-

Rice has been one of the more interesting teams in the WAC the last five seasons. When the Owls are good, they aren't bad, but when they're injured, they're awful.

Wilson hopes the injuries are a thing of the past and Rice can come out, play hard, stay healthy and maybe finish above .500 for a change.

"We'll have to be patient and wait for our young guys to get comfortable playing at this level," Wilson said. "I think our practices will be very competitive. We'll be able to build from there a very good team if we stay healthy."

The Owls have a good non-conference schedule with most of their games at home. It's here Wilson plans to lay the foundation. He has three returning starters in the backcourt and a host of guards vying for the two starting roles.

McKenzie and Tyndell will be called upon to whip the young guards into shape. Look for incoming freshman McKrieth to make a name for himself as he tries to fill the shoes of the dearly departed Wilks. It won't happen overnight, but Wilson believes it could in time.

Rice has never been a serious contender for the WAC crown. And even competing with the top five in the league will prove challenging, no matter how healthy or well the young guys respond during the course of the season.

"This is the best league nobody knows about," Wilson said. "That's why I know we have a long way to go before we can run with the Fresno States and the Tulsas. But given a chance, we might surprise some teams this season, especially if our perimeter game comes together."

(P.A.)

San Jose State

LOCATION	San Jose, CA
CONFERENCE	Western Athletic
LAST SEASON	14-14 (.500)
CONFERENCE RECORD	6-10 (7th)
STARTERS LOST/RETURNING	5/0
NICKNAME	Spartans
COLORS	Gold & Blue
HOMECOURT	The Event Center (5,000)
COACH	Steve Barnes (Azusa Pacific College '81)
RECORD AT SCHOOL	29-29 (2 years)
CAREER RECORD	29-29 (2 years)
ASSISTANTS	Patrick Springer (Iowa '88)
	Don Funk (Ohio Northern '59)
	Richad Lucas (Oregon '91)
TEAM WINS (last 5 years)	13-3-12-15-14
RPI (last 5 years)	122-253-209-161-136
2000-01 FINISH	Lost in conference first round.

The cover of the 2000-2001 San Jose State media guide tells the story. On the front, there's Billy Landram, Cory Powell and Darnell Williams. Flip it over and there's Mike Garrett. All four were starters. All four were seniors. All four are gone.

Add fifth starter David Granucci to the graduated list and no one in America will have a more complete makeover than the Spartans as they prepare for the new 10-team WAC. Joining in the fun are Louisiana Tech and Boise State, two universities that might hang around in San Jose State's neighborhood for a while, but don't count on them remaining in the second tier of the league standings for long.

They are upwardly mobile with the likes of Fresno State, Tulsa, Texas-El Paso and Hawaii. San Jose State would like to be heading in the same direction, but unlike most coaches entering their third year in the program, main man Steve Barnes isn't expecting a payoff.

Remember, Barnes inherited a team that lost its coach to the NBA just weeks before the start of the 1999-2000 season. He bravely stepped into this hornet's nest and got stung a little bit, but he managed to piece together a team that played stellar defense, but not much offense.

Players came and went in Barnes' rookie season as he deftly guided San Jose State to a 15-15 mark. What was left of the program was a group of upperclassmen that didn't have as many options as its younger counterparts.

This veteran contingent played well enough to finish 14-14 last year. Once again, the Spartans could defend, but often not score enough to take advantage of their one gift.

They were coachable. They bought into Barnes' way of doing things. And they wound up winning half the time. Now, they have left the building and taken nearly all the offense with them. Four of the starters—the 6-1 Garrett (12.2 ppg, 2.8 rpg); the 6-6 Landram (9.0 ppg, 3.0 rpg), the 6-5 Powell (13.6 ppg, 7.1 rpg) and the 6-7 Williams (12.5 ppg, 7.3 rpg)—did what was asked of them and did it well enough to finish 6-10 in league play.

All that's left is a plate of leftovers and a service tray of recruits that some say is among the best classes in the nation. Regardless, Barnes will need a program to keep everyone straight through the early practice sessions.

Continuity will be a problem, leadership a must. Just who steps forward in the first part of the season and who's still standing in WAC play is something Barnes can only wonder about. He does have senior **Scott Sonnenberg** at the point. The 5-11 transfer (4.8 ppg, 0.8 rpg, 1.8 rpg) from BYU is the only returning player remotely acquainted with the starting lineup and even he couldn't crack the top five consistently last season.

He's part of an unproven backcourt that will have to grow day by day, not only with Sonnenberg and fellow returnee **Akimbola Okunrinboye** on the floor, but a bevy of newcomers as well.

Like Sonnenberg, the 5-11 Okunrinboye (1.0 ppg, 0.6 rpg) has seen limited action and may not figure heavily into Barnes' plans in the long run. In the short haul, Barnes will count on both seniors to provide leadership that will allow the young guys to shine.

Among the half-dozen newcomers on board, two of them are guards who arrived during the early signing period last November. They are junior **Moises Alvarez** from Mt. San Jacinto (Calif.) Junior College and junior **Phil Calvert**. Both are 6-2, with Calvert making a name for himself last season at Cloud County (Kansas) Community College.

Neither one will likely push themselves into the starting lineup right away, although Alvarez was an all-conference guard at Mt. San Jacinto. He gives the Spartans a little more size than the two senior returnees.

"They will have a chance to play right away because this is as wide open as it gets," Barnes said. "Usually after three years you want to believe this is your payoff season, but that probably won't happen for us because we have so many new players on the team.

"It's going to take a little time to get it all together. We won't be on the same page every day, but I feel like we've got some players coming in who will make a difference for us once they get used to playing at this level. The problem is, there are a lot of good teams in our league. We want to have as much in place as possible once we begin league play."

By then, 6-3 guard **Brandon Hawkins** will be able to join the shaky backcourt. The transfer from Iowa State via Los Angeles shows some promise for Barnes, but will have to sit out the fall semester. **Gary Black** from Indian Hills (Calif.) Community College is another hired gun, who at 6-3, gives the Spartans a big look out front.

"You never know how a guard is going to fit in until they actually get on the floor," Barnes said. "Part of the reason why our class has been so highly rated is because of the collection of guards we've got coming in."

For the third consecutive year and second for Barnes, San Jose State's recruiting class is ranked in the top 30 nationally. Hoop Scoop rated the class the 13th best, tied with the boys Bobby Knight was able to sign at Texas Tech.

The key component of the class is transfer **Carlton "Oudie" Baker** from Barton (Kansas) Community College. The 6-6 forward will make the Spartans' frontcourt far more formidable than without him.

The East Chicago Central High School sensation was a preseason All-America selection as a senior by Blue Ribbon and Street & Smith's. He was a three-time AAU All-American standout and was rated one of the top 2001 junior college transfers by Recruiting USA. He finished seventh nationally in scoring (22.7 ppg) last year and 14th (9.2 rpg) in rebounding. Baker led his Barton County team to a 29-9 mark in 2000-2001. You can hear the excitement in Barnes' voice whenever he mention's Baker's name.

"You can't help but be excited signing one of the top junior college prospects in the country," Barnes said. "We obviously have a lot of holes to fill with the loss of all our seniors. Four of those guys averaged in double figures, so Oudie will be very important to us on the boards and in scoring. He also is strong defensively, which fits in well with what we want to continue doing here."

Joining him in the paint is fellow Barton County standout **Eric Washington**. He too is a sturdy 6-7, but isn't quite as dominant as Baker. Still, Washington was rated among the top 40 forwards coming out of junior college, so he should help down low as well.

"We also have a couple of guys coming back in the frontcourt who we think will make a difference for us," Barnes said of senior power forward **Marion Thurmond** (5.6 ppg, 3.9 rpg) and small forward **Andre Valentine** (4.5 ppg, 2.0 rpg). The 6-4 senior Valentine is a good swingman who could slip into the two-guard spot if called upon to do so. Thurmond is a frontcourt man all the way at 6-8 and a paint-filling 276 pounds. He and Baker could make for a troubling twosome in the lane.

"We have a chance to be very strong in the frontcourt," Barnes said. "We have some muscle and we have some finesse. These guys can go hard if they need to and step out and make a good jumper from 15 feet. I like what I see here."

And it doesn't end there. Center **Garvin Davis** is a 6-11 standout from Georgia Perimeter College. He was rated among the top 300 players nationwide and can give Barnes the kind of dominant presence down low needed in a league where big men abound. There are a lot of guards in the WAC, but the teams with the big frontcourt will likely rule.

2001-2002 SCHEDULE

Nov.	14-16	#BCA Classic
	21	Cal State Sacramento
	27	@Santa Clara
	30	##Cyclone Challenge
Dec.	1	##Cyclone Challenge
	5	Saint Mary's
	8	@Pacific
	12	Menlo College
	22	Mount Saint Mary's
	27	Nevada
	29	Fresno State
Jan.	3	@Boise State
	5	@UTEP
	10	SMU
	12	Louisiana Tech
	19	Hawaii
	24	@Tulsa
	26	@Rice
	31	UTEP
Feb.	2	Boise State
	7	@Louisiana Tech
	9	@SMU
	16	@Hawaii
	21	Rice
	23	Tulsa
	28	@Fresno State
March	2	@Nevada
	5-9	###WAC Tournament

@Road Games
#Raleigh, NC (vs. Fairleigh Dickinson first round; also North Carolina State, Rutgers, Northwestern, VCU, East Carolina, Prairiew View)
##Ames, IA (vs. Nebraska-Omaha first round; also Iowa State, Wisconsin-Milwauee)
###Reynolds Center, Tulsa, OK

BLUE RIBBON ANALYSIS

BACKCOURT	C
BENCH/DEPTH	C-
FRONTCOURT	B+
INTANGIBLES	C

There are too many new faces in the crowd replacing too many good veterans to believe San Jose State will be able to better its .500 record under the direction of third-year head coach Steve Barnes. While he did a remarkable job of recruiting and coaching the last two years, having to mend a patch-work quilt before this season has left Barnes with very little proven experience or leadership.

True enough, the signing of Baker goes a long way in finding a go-to player. He has been sought after since his high school playing days in Chicago. He's not physically imposing at 6-7, but he plays a lot like former UNLV star Larry Johnson, which can only mean good things for Barnes this season.

"We know there's a lot of work to be done in all phases of our game," Barnes said. "And in some ways, it will be like we're starting over as guys try to learn what we expect of them on both ends of the floor. We can be good, but when that happens depends on how well everybody comes together that first month of practice."

(P.A.)

Southern Methodist

LOCATION	Dallas, TX
CONFERENCE	Western Athletic
LAST SEASON	18-12 (.600)
CONFERENCE RECORD	8-8 (t-5th)
STARTERS LOST/RETURNING	2/3
NICKNAME	Mustangs
COLORS	Red & Blue
HOMECOURT	Moody Coliseum (8,998)
COACH	Mike Dement (East Carolina '76)
RECORD AT SCHOOL	96-78 (6 years)
CAREER RECORD	218-201 (15 years)
ASSISTANTS	Jimmy Tubbs (Bishop College '72)
	Robert Lineburg (Roanoke College '91)
	Simon Cote (Tennessee '95)
TEAM WINS (last 5 years)	15-17-14-21-18
RPI (last 5 years)	115-102-110-49-98
2000-01 FINISH	Lost in conference first round.

If you were SMU coach Mike Dement, you could look at the last two years and feel pretty good about your program. You have 39 victories, produced the first first-round NBA draft pick at the school in 16 years and won the most games over the course of two seasons since 1987-1988.

But somehow, if you're Mike Dement, you feel a little left out and let down. What once looked like sure-fire trips on the tracks to the Final Four were derailed by late-season collapses you can't possibly explain.

Not that you would articulate any of that outside the safety of your office. You don't want the troops to despair, especially considering you have the top returning scoring tandem in the WAC.

True, Jeryl Sasser is gone; taken as the 22nd pick overall by the Orlando Magic, a team that sees the upside in Sasser—points, passing and rebounds—not the down, the one who couldn't lead the Mustangs around the NCAA dance floor.

But now, it's someone else's turn. And although Sasser and Willie Davis are gone—two guys who produced too many big nights to count—Dement refuses to lament over their departure. It's part of the natural order of things in college basketball. And anyway, he believes he has two guys who can take SMU where they all want to go.

"Obviously, losing two guys like that who were a key part of our offense, won't be easy to replace," Dement said of Sasser and Davis. "But we welcome back two very talented players in **Damon Hancock** and **Quinton Ross**. And that's a very exciting prospect for me."

So is the idea of building on a five-year run where Dement is averaging 17 wins a season. He does it with a three-guard offense that attacks the basket on the drive or the use of the three-point shot. One guard is almost a small forward in disguise. The big men are used more to set screens and take up space in the paint. They rarely crash the boards as hard as the guards.

That's why the 6-6 Sasser (17.0 ppg, 8.3 rpg) and 6-6 Davis (11.9 ppg, 7.3 rpg) had all the numbers in their corners. Sasser wound up the all-time leading scorer for SMU. Davis won't be in the NBA, but is still playing professionally in Europe with his unique brand of rebounding.

Not that the 6-3 senion Hancock (16.7 ppg, 3.5 rpg, 3.2 apg) and 6-6 junior Ross (14.2 ppg, 5.1 rpg) don't offer some solid numbers of their own. They do. And that core is what Dement is counting on as he prepares to challenge Fresno State and Tulsa for the league title.

Dement also has one of the best recruiting classes in the WAC after the signing of five fresh faces. They should give SMU the kind of enthusiasm that went missing as it lost the final six games of the 2000-2001 season.

"We'll build our team around Ross and Hancock because they can do so many things and fit well in our offensive scheme," Dement said. "We also have a lot of young guys coming in who we believe will help us make a difference this season. But we need Damon and Quinton to step up and set the tone."

The tone is up-tempo, and it's music to Hancock's ears. He not only could pass, but had a decent outside shot from beyond the three-point line (.344). If you came out on him, he made you pay by driving to the basket and either securing a layup or drawing a foul. He hit 133-of-177 free throws last year, tops on the team.

"We feel like Damon could go the way of the NBA just like Jeryl did," Dement said. "He's that good. The scouts watching Sasser said they'd be back this year to see how Damon is developing on both ends of the floor. This guy has it all. He can defend as well as anyone on the team."

How well teams defend Ross could go a long way in determining how free Hancock will be this season. Ross is the better shooter of the two. He knocked down 48 three-pointers (.372) and can drive to the basket as well.

"And he's not even our best shooter," Dement said. "That's the kind of depth we had last year. Everybody was so busy worrying about Jeryl and Willie, they forgot to watch out for Quinton. There were a lot of nights when he was our best player."

Don't be surprised if top returning three-point artist **Lavardicus Atkins** (4.4 ppg, 0.9 rpg) works his way into the starting lineup as the third guard. The 6-3 sophomore was slowed by a bad knee last season, but still has the kind of outside eye to die for, leading the team in shooting (.513). He's could provide the energetic force Dement looks for in a starter.

If Atkins can't stay healthy, there is a pair of freshmen recruits waiting for their opportunity to start. **Justin Isham** hails from Lancaster, Texas, where Hancock started on his path to fame and glory.

The 6-5 Isham cut up high school defenses with his blazing first step. At Lancaster, Isham (21.7 ppg, 7.0 rpg) led his team to a four-year record of 109-21. He has great speed and leaping abilities that make him a perfect fit for Dement's offense. He loves to rebound, and that brings a smile to Dement's face.

So does **Brian Miller**. The 6-5 freshman from Lewisville, Texas, was also considered a Top 10 prospect in the Lone Star State. He has a great outside shot, one that allowed him to score 21.5 points per game as a senior in high school. If he can stroke the long ball, he'll be the perfect complement to the men in the paint.

SMU has plenty of depth in the post, but no proven center, something not lost on Dement.

"This is the one spot I feel is wide open," Dement said. "I know we have a guard-oriented attack, but every team needs a competent center to get things started and to make them go."

Two seniors and one junior will get the hardest looks at center. They are **Jon Forinash**, **Mike Niemi** and **Nigel Smith**. All three could potentially fit the big shoes in the lane, but injuries played a vital role in keeping any of them from filling them last year.

Most believed the 6-11, 270-pound senior Forinash (0.9 ppg, 1.8 rpg) would be the man, but a slow start left him in the gate. Dement believes this post needs to score at least six points and garner 10 rebounds per game in order for the team to be successful. In his mind, Forinash can be that man.

"He is also a force on defense because of his size," Dement said. "Not too many players will want to take him one-on-one."

Niemi, a senior, tries in practice and as a result, was fairly productive on the floor. The 6-9, 270-pound wide body produced the best results (3.9 ppg, 2.5 rpg) of the big post men last year. But his lack of height and leaping ability hurt against taller opponents. He can play when called upon.

So can Smith (1.2 ppg, 1.3 rpg), if nagging ailments don't slow him down. The problem is, the junior has never made it back to form since undergoing sinus surgery two years ago.

Power forward is another post position that could give Dement cause for concern. Junior **Jibran Kelley** returns, which is the best news of all. The 6-8 wide body (3.4 ppg, 3.9 rpg) needs to attack the basket to produce more points. But Dement thinks another year of experience will give him the kind of confidence necessary to be a WAC force.

If he falters, figure **Kris Rowe** to see more playing time. The 6-6 sophomore (2.3 ppg, 1.1 rpg) played in 29 games last year and was the kind of shooter from the field (.500) and at the free-throw line (.778) who gives a coach confidence, especially in a tight game down the stretch.

"Kris and Jibran each bring something good to the court," Dement said. "But ball handling can be a problem for the big men, especially in a quick-paced game like the one we play. That's what made Willie Davis so good for us."

Dement believes he has a 6-9 freshman in **Patrick Simpson** who might make people forget about Davis some day. Dement said Simpson is more skilled than Davis, which is frightening for opponents, especially considering the other young talent expected to make Dallas their home.

Simpson was considered among the Top 100 prep recruits nationwide. Born in Houston, Simpson played his prep ball at George Washington High in Denver. Simpson (23.9 ppg, 13.5 rpg) has a wingspan equal to

that of a man 7-2 and was selected the Colorado Player of the Year by USA Today.

"This kid can play," Dement said. "In a few years, he could be another player of ours headed to the NBA. He's that good in my mind."

Two other newcomers should make their presence felt as well. They are 6-8 **Eric Castro** of Mt. St. Mary's High School in Oklahoma City and junior college transfer **Billy Pharis**. The 6-8 forward played two seasons at Westark College (Ark.) and his high school ball in Van Buren, Ark.

Castro (19.2 ppg, 12.3 rpg) led his Class 2A team to the state title. He is wide and carries the kind of load necessary to set screens and go hard for offensive rebounds. Throw in Pharis (14.0 ppg and 7.0 rpg), who signed late and would like nothing better than to enroll in SMU's famed law school when he's done.

"I'm excited about this ball club," Dement said. "In time, we may be able to take that next step to the NCAA postseason, which is the toughest one of all."

2001-2002 SCHEDULE

Nov.	16	Savannah State
	18	Navy
	20	Texas South
	27	@Baylor
	30	#Hawkeye Challenge
Dec.	1	#Hawkeye Challenge
	4	@North Texas
	6	Tennessee
	14	Oral Roberts
	18	@TCU
	28	Boise State
	30	UTEP
Jan.	5	@Louisiana Tech
	10	@San Jose State
	12	@Hawaii
	17	Rice
	19	Tulsa
	24	@Fresno State
	26	@Nevada
Feb.	2	Louisiana Tech
	7	Hawaii
	9	San Jose State
	14	@Tulsa
	16	@Rice
	21	Nevada
	23	Fresno State
	28	@UTEP
March	2	@Boise State
	5-9	##WAC Tournament

@Road Games
#Iowa City, IA (vs. LaSalle first round; also Alabama A&M, Iowa)
##Reynolds Center, Tulsa, OK

BLUE RIBBON ANALYSIS

BACKCOURT	A-
BENCH/DEPTH	B
FRONTCOURT	C+
INTANGIBLES	C

SMU has been something of a mystery the last two years. At mid-season, the Mustangs appeared to be headed to the NCAA Tournament, only to collapse late and exit early from the WAC Tournament.

Something tells Dement that won't happen this time around. Gone are Sasser and Davis, true, but in their places is a plethora of young talent waiting to be born on the floor. This gives SMU some hope that history won't be repeating itself.

Still, the Mustangs could play as many as 11 teams that made it to the postseason in 2000-2001. Perhaps in playing well or even beating some of these teams, SMU can emerge as a title contender. It's time for Dement to go beyond all the numbers and reach his destiny at the Big Dance.

"Our schedule should help us know where we are," Dement said. "We could be a very competitive basketball team by the end of the season. And that will be one of our goals, to reach that potential."

(P.A.)

UTEP

LOCATION	El Paso, TX
CONFERENCE	Western Athletic
LAST SEASON	23-9 (.719)
CONFERENCE RECORD	10-6 (t-2nd)
STARTERS LOST/RETURNING	1/4
NICKNAME	Miners
COLORS	Orange & Blue
HOMECOURT	Don Haskins Center (11,500)
COACH	Jason Rabedeaux (UC Davis '88)
RECORD AT SCHOOL	36-24 (2nd year)
CAREER RECORD	36-24 (2nd year)
ASSISTANTS	Ryan Carr (Indiana '96)
	Willard Cotten (Utah State '94)
	Silvey Dominguez (New Mexico '75)
TEAM WINS (last 5 years)	10-10-15-13-23
RPI (last 5 years)	98-150-103-137-62
2000-01 FINISH	Lost in NIT second round.

Jason Rabedeaux must possess a little John Wayne in his walk for having the courage to step in for the suddenly retiring Don Haskins.

Two years ago, the man whose name is on the side of the center where the Miners play decided it was time to walk out of the locker room as head coach for the final time. True, it was only a couple of months before the start of the 1999-2000 season, but Haskins believed the last-minute decision would be best for UTEP in the long run.

Finding someone willing to walk a mile or two in the legend's shoes would be difficult. But anyone willing to try must be worth something to the program that hasn't been to the NCAA Tournament in nearly a decade.

Enter Rabedeaux, a young, vibrant coach who claps a lot on the sideline to burn the nervous energy that spills out of him regularly. You can't help but like the guy. He's so positive, you wonder why he doesn't have one of those early morning infomercials about making it big overnight. He certainly has, taking the program to the NIT last year before being eliminated in the second round on the court of Memphis, home of the king.

Rabedeaux is something of a royal himself in the West Texas town of El Paso. During years of anonymity in football, UTEP fans could always count on basketball to give them a lift. Haskins brought the bright lights of the NCAA to his doorstep with his distinctive personality and style of play. The Miners were often successful, even winning a national championship in the mid-1960s.

But things and people have a way of changing. And Haskins proved no exception to the sands of time. Perhaps he lost a step or two, but he still left Rabedeaux with several good players, including all-everything power forward Brandon Wolfram. His departure this season leaves Rabedeaux with a big hole in the middle as he prepares for a season that still should have the Miners within rebounding distance of WAC frontrunners Fresno State and Tulsa.

That's because four starters return, including talented 5-10 senior point guard **Eugene Costello**. True, he had some off-the-court problems to settle over the summer, but Costello promises his past transgressions are just there—in the past—leaving UTEP with one of the best point men in the business. He is joined by three other returning starters.

"But replacing Brandon will still be a challenge, even with four starters back," Rabedeaux said. "He was our go-to guy when we needed a basket. He was there to grab the big rebound. He not only had the numbers, but the leadership to go with it. He will be missed."

It's hard to argue that point. The 6-9 postman (22.3 ppg, 7.6 rpg) was WAC Player of the Year as a junior and finished runner-up to Fresno State center Melvin Ely in last season's voting. He could play center, but was more comfortable and effective at power forward. That just means Costello (14.2 ppg, 3.9 rpg, 4.6 apg) will have to play even bigger out front. In Rabedeaux's mind, the little guy with the big heart can do it.

"But there are some things he needs to work on night in and night out in order for us to be successful," Rabedeaux said. "Consistency is what we need from Eugene anytime he's running the team. We need him to eliminate the turnovers and be a more consistent shooter."

That's saying something, considering Costello's numbers. As a newcomer, no one in 33 years had a bigger scoring impact at UTEP than Costello. The Midland (Texas) College transfer managed to score 20 points or more nine times last year, including high-caliber performances in wins over Texas Tech and Washington.

If he hit 45 percent of his shots from the field, UTEP was 12-3. If he committed two turnovers or less, the Miners were 15-1. Costello is one of five returning seniors Rabedeaux is counting on to lead this team back to the postseason.

His backcourt mate is fellow senior **Chris Neal**. The 6-2 shooting guard can take pressure off Costello, who was second team All-WAC last year, out front and give the Miners a more balanced attack. Neal (7.3 ppg, 2.1 rpg, 2.6 apg) scored in double figures seven times last year. Not coincidentally, the Miners won all those games.

"He is another senior who needs to step it up this year and play with more consistency," Rabedeaux said. "We need his outside shot to be there to help open things up offensively underneath. He has the capability to be the best three-point shooter (.397) on the team. His defense needs to improve to make him a more complete player."

Rabedeaux is also expecting a lot from senior guard **Victor Luces** (2.7 ppg, 0.8 rpg). He is one of the few current players to be in the program three years and while his statistical data isn't on the high end point-wise, he can shoot well enough from the field (.489) and the free-throw line (.722) to draw some interest from the opposition. His minutes on the floor should increase as long as he brings the kind of energy he did last year in several critical games. Rabedeaux is counting on him to spend time with several of the new recruits signed in the off-season.

Chief among them are Hitchcock (Texas) High standout **T.J. Fontenette** (18.4 ppg, 13.5 rpg) and fellow freshman guard **Luke Martin**. The 5-11 Martin (10.1 ppg, 7.0 apg) won't be eligible until December. The Australian was highly recruited from St. John's Catholic Prep in Concord. These two newcomers should add some depth once they are comfortable competing at the Division I level.

"T.J. has the chance to be one of the top guys ever to wear a UTEP uniform," Rabedeaux said. "And that's saying something. You can't teach a 42-inch vertical leap. That kind of athleticism gives him a big advantage."

UTEP isn't only big in the backcourt. The Miners' frontcourt returns starting forward **Roy Smallwood** and center **Brian Stewart**. Stewart, 6-10, will miss having Wolfram by his side, but Rabedeaux still has faith in the senior big man (11.8 ppg, 6.7 rpg) down low.

"We didn't have anyone more effective the last half of the season than Brian," Rabedeaux said of the center who averaged 14.3 points and 8.3 rebounds in that stretch. "He is a very effective shot blocker (1.5 bpg) and is the kind of player we need to emerge as one of the leaders on this team, both on the floor and in the locker room."

Last year, Stewart produced six double-doubles and was ranked third in the WAC in shooting (.583). Whether he can produce those kind of numbers again without Wolfram will depend strongly on forwards Smallwood and **Leonard Owens**. The 6-6 Owens performed well in several areas. Last year, the senior (5.9 ppg, 4.2 rpg, 3.2 apg) was second on the team in blocked shots, assists and steals. There are a lot of the pieces of the puzzle that have to fit, but in Rabedeaux's opinion, perhaps none more than Owens.

"If all of our players were as consistent as Leonard, we would be tough to beat," Rabedeaux said. "He is very mature and capable of producing even bigger numbers than last year now that Brandon is gone."

Smallwood, a junior, figures to produce some numbers of his own. WAC Freshman of the Year in 2000, the 6-6 Smallwood (10.5 ppg, 6.1 rpg. 2.0 apg) was forced to move from the power position to swingman last year, and it worked wonderfully for him and the team.

Like Owens, Smallwood can do a lot of things. He finished third on the team in blocked shots (1.0) and was among the top 15 in the WAC in three key statistical categories.

"Roy has to be one of our go-to guys," Rabedeaux said. "All of our returning starters have to contribute more this year in order for us to not only do as well as last year, but maybe even get into the NCAA Tournament."

Other post players expected to make a contribution are sophomores **Nick Enzweiler** and **Antone Jarrell**. The 6-6 Enzweiler (5.2 ppg, 2.6 rpg) and 6-6 Jarrell (2.0 ppg, 1.4 rpg) learned a lot as freshmen. They will try to help develop incoming junior **Justinio Victoriano** (14.3 ppg, 8.6 rpg) from Western Nebraska Community College and El Paso native **Joe Devance** (27 ppg, 14 rpg, 4.5 bpg and 2.0 spg).

Both newcomers are 6-7 forwards who have got game. Devance, who was born in Honolulu, played his prep ball at Burgess High School. The continued recruiting success should keep the Miners up top for years to come.

2001-2002 SCHEDULE

Nov.	16	#Las Vegas Classic
	19-21	##Las Vegas Classic
	26	Texas Tech
Dec.	1	@New Mexico State
	6	Washington
	8	Texas A&M-Corpus Christi
	18	@Charlotte
	21-22	###Sun Bowl Classic
	28	@Louisiana Tech
	30	@SMU
Jan.	3	Hawaii
	5	San Jose State
	10	@Tulsa
	12	@Rice
	17	Nevada
	19	Fresno State
	26	Boise State
	28	Alcorn State
	31	@San Jose State
Feb.	2	@Hawaii
	7	Rice
	9	Tulsa
	14	@Fresno State
	16	@Nevada
	20	New Mexico State
	23	@Boise State
	28	SMU
March	2	Louisiana Tech
	5-9	####WAC Tournament

@Road Games
#First-round TBA
##Las Vegas, NV (also Providence, Austin Peay, TCU, Northwestern State, Oklahoma State)
###El Paso, TX (vs. Mississippi Valley State, first round; also IUPUI, Ole Miss)
####Reynolds Center, Tulsa, OK

BLUE RIBBON ANALYSIS

BACKCOURT	B
BENCH/DEPTH	B
FRONTCOURT	B+
INTANGIBLES	B-

There's little question that Rabedeaux has brought back belief in the UTEP program. Not only did he take the inherited players and make them better, he recruited well enough to lead the Miners to the Final 16 of the NIT last spring.

Now, he eyes an even bigger prize—the WAC title and a possible NCAA Tournament berth that goes with it. This isn't just a preseason goal anymore, it's a real possibility. Even without departing Wolfram, UTEP welcomes back four starters who produced 72 percent of the scoring and 79 percent of the rebounding last year.

This is a good basketball team that has the proper blend of scoring and rebounding that could make it a title contender once again. The Miners will need to find added scoring in the paint and more consistency from their guards, but don't be surprised if UTEP is still around when the 64-team field is announced next spring.

(P.A.)

Tulsa

LOCATION	Tulsa, OK
CONFERENCE	Western Athletic
LAST SEASON	26-22 (.703)
CONFERENCE RECORD	10-6 (t-2nd)
STARTERS LOST/RETURNING	2/3
NICKNAME	Golden Hurricane
COLORS	Gold & Blue
HOMECOURT	Reynolds Center (8,355)
COACH	John Phillips (Oklahoma State '73)
RECORD AT SCHOOL	First year
CAREER RECORD	First year
ASSISTANTS	Steve Cooper (NE Oklahoma St. '78)
	Kwanza Johnson (Tulsa '95)
	Alvin Williamson (Tulsa '96)
TEAM WINS (last 5 years)	23-18-22-29-26
RPI (last 5 years)	15-98-29-21-61
2000-01 FINISH	Won NIT championship.

This is one of those jobs John Phillips wants to hold onto tighter than the dreams that led him to Tulsa long

ago. Unlike his predecessors, current head coaches Bill Self of Illinois and Buzz Peterson of Tennessee, Phillips sees this as one of those stops that hopefully ends in retirement a quarter-century from now.

True, there are those who may question whether the former assistant to Self and Peterson has risen above his station. All rookie head coaches face that inevitable question, even Peterson a season ago.

In Self's last time through the WAC, Tulsa made it to the doorstep of the Final Four, before losing to North Carolina in an Elite Eight meeting in Austin, Texas. Peterson took over last fall and faced a few questions of his own after the Golden Hurricane broke from the gate, then stumbled to a 6-4 start.

Tulsa finished strong enough, only to lose to Hawaii in the WAC Tournament title game in front of the home folk, costing the Golden Hurricane an NCAA Tournament bid. Tulsa took the snub personally—only two WAC teams were selected—and promptly pounded out its frustrations on the entire NIT field.

Peterson closed out Alabama in the NIT final and quickly volunteered to be the new head coach at troubled Tennessee. Some would say Tulsa has been a better representative in the NCAA Tournament the last decade, but Peterson was intrigued by the potential of the Southeastern Conference program.

For Phillips, this is a position he has aspired to for a long, long time. He not only learned a lot from Self and Peterson and their different styles of coaching, he helped recruit most of the players on the current team.

Despite the loss of two key players, Tulsa should still contend with Fresno State for the WAC championship.

"We've got a good nucleus of players coming back," Phillips said.

"Obviously, we've got to replace two of our better players from a year ago, but that's the nature of the college game. It's always changing."

There's little doubt filling the shoes of steady stars Marcus Hill and David Shelton will be challenging. Hill was a deadly defender and shooter from the outside who played in more games than anyone in Tulsa history. The 6-5 guard had some impressive numbers (12.7 ppg, 4.7 rpg, 2.9 apg) and was aided by the play of the 6-6 Shelton (11.9 ppg, 5.2 rpg) as a power forward down low.

This team didn't quite have the flair of the one in 1999-2000. That one quietly went along, taking care of business before the sticky Tar Heels stopped Tulsa in its Final Four tracks. This year's model may be a step slower still.

Senior **Greg Harrington** is the old man on this team and a key component for Phillips. He was often lost in Hill's headlines, relegated to the fine print, but without his quick hands, pinpoint passes and ability to punish sagging defenses with a good outside shot, Hill wouldn't have embraced so much success.

The 6-2 point guard (10.8 ppg, 2.8 rpg, 5.4 apg) will need to be a dominant force out front. Without Hill by Harrington's side, it may prove more challenging to create off the dribble or find the clear passing lanes he has enjoyed the last two seasons.

Still, Harrington's experience as a two-year starter should serve him well enough. He became only the seventh player in Tulsa history to surpass the 300 career-assist mark. Harrington starts the season third on the career list with 375 and needs only 82 more to set the all-time Tulsa record. His 201 assists last year are a single-season best for the school. He also led the WAC in three-point shooting (.468).

"Having a guy like Greg running the team is something every coach wants," Phillips said. "He is the consummate point guard. He can not only score, pass and direct traffic, he can create fast breaks out front off of turnovers he causes. Greg is a vital member to this team."

It starts with experience. Harrington has played in 11 postseason tournament games. He is averaging 11.1 points, 2.6 rebounds and 2.8 assists in those high-profile encounters. He also is averaging 2.0 steals in NCAA Tournament games and shooting a blistering .470 from the field.

Joining him in the backcourt are **Antonio Reed** and **Dante Swanson**. Reed and Swanson are both juniors, both 5-10 and both well rounded enough to help ease the loss of Hill. Reed (7.6 ppg, 2.6 rpg, 2.6 apg) is a good outside shooter who can hit the boards hard and dish it out when necessary. The same can be said of Swanson (9.8 ppg, 3.6 rpg, 2.6 apg), who may be the more valuable of the two.

Not all three guards will be on the floor all the time, but there are certain situations where Phillips may field a three-guard lineup. He likes the speed this trio brings to the game and their ability to make the frontcourt that much more effective in the paint.

Newcomer **Kyle Blankenship** of Byrd High School in Shreveport, La., should be able to lend his support once he grows accustomed to the rigors of Division I basketball. The 6-0 guard is a lot like Harrington. He can pass, shoot and create out front. Jason Parker, a 6-2 sophomore, also figures into the mix. Last year, Parker (2.9 ppg, 1.4 apg) didn't see a lot of playing time, but that may change this season.

"We're going to need everyone to contribute in our backcourt," Phillips said. "The strength for us the last two years is we played as a team. No one individual made us go. It was a group effort. We were very balanced."

The same can be said of the frontcourt. Sure, Shelton is gone. The talented sixth man made everyone on the front line that much better, which means small forward **Kevin Johnson** will have to make some adjustments. The 6-7 junior (13.9 ppg, 7.0 rpg) was a second team All-WAC performer last year.

Not only can he score and rebound, but defend down low as well. His 104 career blocks ranks third on the school's all-time list. Johnson needs only 32 more to slip into second. If there is a go-to guy this year, Johnson figures to be that man. He was voted to the all-tournament team in last year's NIT after averaging 17.4 points, 7.0 rebounds and 2.0 blocks. Johnson is one of the best forwards in the WAC and will need to live up to that expectation in order for Tulsa to be successful.

Johnson had a productive summer, leading the NIT All-Stars to a 4-1 record on their tour of Europe. Johnson averaged 14.6 points, 8.0 rebounds, 3.2 blocked shots and shot 63 percent from the field (31-of-49) in the five games.

"Kevin had a tremendous year for us, especially the last half of the season," Phillips said. "We feel like Kevin is a difference-maker who fits well within our team concept."

Fellow forward **Marqus Ledoux** figures to make some noise as well. The 6-8 junior transfer (1.5 ppg, 1.0 rpg) from LSU didn't see that much action until the NIT, where he averaged 2.0 points and 4.0 rebounds. With Shelton gone, Ledoux needs to step it up big time in order to complement Johnson in the paint.

He will probably be sharing time with 6-10 sophomore **Jack Ingram**, who can also shift to center if necessary. Ingram (3.1 ppg, 2.5 rpg) played well as a freshman last year, starting 11 games. His numbers weren't eye opening, but he did block 26 shots, second only to Johnson and he did score 12 points in a close loss to North Carolina.

Sophomore center **J.T. Ivie** and junior small forward **Charlie Davis** also figure into Phillips' plans. Like Ingram, Ivie (1.0 ppg, 0.5 rpg) has good size at 6-10. He received a medical hardship after playing in only two games last year.

Davis (3.1 ppg, 3.6 rpg) has a lot more experience and figures to see playing time at both forward spots. At 6-7, he has good size for a perimeter player. His season high of 10 points came in the NIT championship win over Alabama and he also grabbed 11 rebounds in a win over UTEP.

"We've got some young players coming up who we believe will help us," Phillips said. "They just need the experience and playing time with our starters. Their contributions are important to us."

Rounding out the Tulsa lineup are small forwards **Glenn Jarius** and **Trevor Meier**. The two freshmen had big numbers in high school. Jarius (25.4 ppg, 10.6 rpg, 3.3 apg, 3.3 bpg, 2.0 spg) was first team all-state player at Avondale High in Decatur, Ga. The 6-6 swingman was rated among the Top 100 seniors nationwide in several recruiting services. He expects to play right away.

So does Meier, a 6-6 forward from Alva High School in Alva, Okla. Meier (19.6 ppg, 7.3 rpg, 3.2 apg) has excellent range from the field. He was an all-state player himself, capable of cracking the lineup as the season progresses.

2001-2002 SCHEDULE

Nov.	19	Grambling
	24	Morris Brown
	28	Arkansas
Dec.	1	@Oral Roberts
	4	Southwest Missouri State
	14	*Texas A&M
	20-22	#Yahoo Sports Invitational
	29	**Kansas
Jan.	3	@Nevada
	5	@Fresno State
	10	UTEP
	12	Boise State
	17	@Louisiana Tech
	19	@SMU
	24	San Jose State
	26	Hawaii
	28	Rice
	31	Fresno State
Feb.	2	Nevada
	7	@Boise State
	9	@UTEP
	14	SMU
	16	Louisiana Tech
	21	@Hawaii
	23	@San Jose State
	28	@Rice
March	5-9	##WAC Tournament

@Road Games
*Houston, TX
**Kansas City, MO
#Laie, HI (vs. Buffalo first round; also BYU-Hawaii, Columbia, Montana, Navy, New Mexico State, Valparaiso)
##Reynolds Center, Tula, OK

BLUE RIBBON ANALYSIS

BACKCOURT	B+
BENCH/DEPTH	B
FRONTCOURT	B+
INTANGIBLES	B-

Tulsa University has been one of the premier programs few basketball fans know that much about. The Golden Hurricane should have been in the NCAA Tournament last year, but lost the WAC title game in overtime to upstart Hawaii.

After the disappointed Golden Hurrican regrouped to win the NIT, former coach Peterson resigned to be the head coach at Tennessee, leaving the program in limbo. New head coach Phillips has been an assistant through much of Tulsa's recent success. He learned his lessons well and believes he's ready to take the helm.

Tulsa fans hope he is as successful as previous coaches, and will stick around long enough to build a lasting legacy. His problems will be replacing two talent-

INDEPENDENTS*

BLUE RIBBON FORECAST
1. Texas-Pan American
2. Centenary
3. Morris Brown
4. Savannah State

ALL-CONFERENCE TEAM
G-Michael Gale, SO, Centenary
G-Mire Chatman, SR, Texas-Pan American
G-Anthony Adams, SR, Morris Brown
F-DeMario Hooper, JR, Centenary
F-Alvin Payton, SR, Savannah State

PLAYER OF THE YEAR
Mire Chatman, SR, Texas-Pan American

NEWCOMER OF THE YEAR
DeMario Hooper, SO, Centenary

2000-2001 POSTSEASON PARTICIPANTS
NCAA
None
NIT
None

TOP BACKCOURTS
1. Texas-Pan American
2. Centenary
3. Morris Brown

TOP FRONTCOURTS
1. Texas-Pan American
2. Centenary
3. Morris Brown

DID YOU KNOW?
*No official standings for independent schools are kept by the NCAA. Blue Ribbon's preseason rankings seek only to rate the four schools playing as independents. … The list of independents said goodbye to three members and added two more. Albany and Stony Brook left to join the retooled America East and Belmont joined the newly named Atlantic Sun Conference (formally the Trans America Athletic Conference). … The independents are also bidding farewell to three players who at one time or another scored over more than 20 points per game in their careers. Texas-Pan Am's Brian Merriweather scored 20.4 in 1999-2000 before slipping to 18.0 last year. Meanwhile, Centenary's Ronnie McCollum (28.8) and Texas A&M-Corpus Christi's Michael Hicks (26.3) would have been 1-2 in the nation last season had Corpus Christi been a full-fledged Division I school. The Islanders are only half-way through a four-year NCAA probationary watch period. … New additions Morris Brown and Savannah State played a number of Division I opponents last season in preparation for the jump, but managed to finish only a combined 10-43. … Centenary appears the closest of the remaining independents to joining a conference. The Gents have been talking to the Southland and Sun Belt Conferences. … Not only are Morris Brown and Savannah State starting over in Division I, each is starting over with essentially new coaches. Morris Brown's Dereck Thompson is in his first year after serving as an assistant, and Savannah State's Jack Grant is in his second after also having been promoted.

(C.C.)

ed seniors who averaged 24.6 points and 9.9 rebounds between them.

Tulsa is young, starting only one senior, and will have to learn its third system in as many seasons. Johnson at forward and point guard Harrington should help make the transition a smooth one. They are both potential first team All-WAC performers who possess the skills and experience to keep the Golden Hurricane among the top teams in the WAC.

Whether they can match the success of the last two seasons remains to be seen.

There are several newcomers who could make a difference right away given the opportunity and the time to develop. This may not be the best Tulsa team in recent memory, but the Golden Hurricane aren't half bad.

(P.A.)

Centenary

LOCATION	Shreveport, LA
CONFERENCE	Independent
LAST SEASON	8-19 (.296)
CONFERENCE RECORD	NA
STARTERS LOST/RETURNING	2/3
NICKNAME	Gentlemen, Gents
COLORS	Maroon & White
HOMECOURT	Gold Dome (3,000)
COACH	Kevin Johnson (Texas-Pan American '88)
RECORD AT SCHOOL	18-37 (2 years)
CAREER RECORD	18-37 (2 years)
ASSISTANTS	Arturo Ormond (Texas-Pan Am. '89)
	Roy Garcia (Texas-Pan American '96)
	Harris Adler (Philadelphia College of Pharmacy '98)
TEAM WINS (last 5 years)	9-10-14-10-8
RPI (last 5 years)	269-263-196-271-294
2000-01 FINISH	Lost in regular-season finale.

Year one as an independent wasn't easy for Centenary. Year two may have been a little easier, but ended less successful. Now into year three, the Gents face some big changes.

Centenary's first season on its own came in 1999-00 after leaving the Trans America Athletic Conference. It was also Kevin Johnson's first as head coach. Clearly big changes, but neither may have the same impact as losing Ronnie McCollum.

Through the transition, McCollum was a constant, as in constantly scoring. As he gained experience as head coach, Johnson could always turn to one man in the game's crucial moments. McCollum's talents could help mask other deficiencies. The 6-4 wing was the nation's third most prolific scorer (23.8 ppg) as a junior. He led the country (29.1 ppg) in his final season. The completion of his eligibility leaves a big hole and drastically changes Johnson's design.

"Losing a guy that averaged 29 points a game will be tough, tough to replace," the third-year coach said. "I think we'll have more balance. I think we have a better caliber of player top to bottom than we had last year. While we probably don't have a guy on our roster who will average 25 points a game, hopefully we'll have four or five who can get between 10 and 15."

Johnson hopes that from a group of three returning starters and six transfers, he finds that scoring.

Michael Gale's (8.2 ppg, 4.3 rpg, .469 FG) freshman year was enough to convince Johnson that the 6-4 sophomore can be the Gents' next go-to guy.

"Michael worked very hard this summer and really started to establish himself toward the end of last season as someone who could get to the basket. He's where we'll start," Johnson said.

Gale's outside game will be something to watch, however. Last season, while McCollum launched 252 three-pointers, Gale took just three. In fact, only one Gent came within 200 three-point attempts of McCollum. That was 6-0 senior guard **Kevin Atamah** (7.3 ppg, 2.2 rpg, 2.5 apg, 1.0 spg, .322 3PT), who should offer the needed on-court stability for a team which will have eight newcomers. Atamah eventually won the job last year from Warren Harris because he was more productive. However, Atamah did turn the ball over more and will have to distance his assist numbers (67) from those turnovers (63).

"The big thing is that he will be a senior," Johnson said.

The third and final returning starter will not be among the group of scorers that Johnson is looking for to replace McCollum's production. That's because in 26 games (13 starts) 6-9 senior center **Brien Rabenhorst** averaged only 2.3 points. Rabenhorst didn't even have much impact on the glass with just 3.0 rebounds an outing, but is Centenary's best post defender. That in itself makes Rabenhorst a major key on a team whose personnel is overflowing with perimeter players.

Two of those are Division I transfers **DeMario Hooper** and **Andrew Wisniewski**, whom Johnson is relying to join Gale in the quest to fill the void left by McCollum.

Hooper, a 6-4 sophomore, was a member of Tulsa's Elite Eight team and was a Top 100 recruit of Bill Self. However, playing time was not easy to come by and Hooper averaged just 1.2 points in 21 games for the Golden Hurricane.

"He definitely has the all the ability to score. He just hasn't gotten the opportunity at this level," Johnson said.

The 6-2 Wisniewski will also have three years of eligibility after leaving St. Peter's after a coaching change there. While Wisniewski played sparingly at St. Peter's, he was a 20.2 point per game scorer as a senior in 1998-99 at St. Peter's High School on Staten Island. It's likely that either Hooper or Wisniewski will be coming off the bench even in Johnson's three-guard alignment with Gale and Atamah settled in as the first two starters.

In **DeAndre Cornelius**, Johnson may have found the physical replacement for McCollum. At 6-6, Cornelius stands two inches taller than Centenary's second all-time leading scorer and packs a similarly powerful 200-pound build. Cornelius will be a junior after spending two seasons at Carl Albert College in Oklahoma, where he averaged 24 points and was a Region II junior college All-American.

Johnson also figures to get immediate help from 6-0 junior guard **Cornelius Riley**, a transfer from Kennedy King Junior College in Chicago. Riley once played high school ball with Kevin Garnett at Farragut and was an 11- points and five-assists per game performer last season at Kennedy King. Riley should push Atamah much the same way Atamah pushed Harris a year ago.

With Gale, Hooper, Wisniewski and Cornelius, Centenary remains pretty well stocked on the wings. What it lacked last year and continues to have in short supply this season are bona fide low post threats. The

addition of 6-5 junior **Melvin Dews** should help a little in that area. Dews spent the last two years at Jacksonville (Texas) College after a 1,989-point career at Oakwood (Texas) High School.

"Melvin gives us someone we didn't have last year and that's someone that can score inside. You to have a low post presence to be successful," Johnson said. "In Dews, Riley, and Cornelius, we brought in three more guys who can possibly help us right away to go with the three starters and the two young men we had sitting out. That gives us a pretty solid group."

It also means that a few more newcomers will have their work cut out for them. **Jason Zimmer**, a 6-10 freshman center, has the size Centenary needs, but may not be quite ready to take minutes away from his more experienced teammates. Zimmer averaged 15 points, 15 rebounds, and five blocks at Perris High School in Nuevo, Calif., and was second-team All-Riverside County.

Chad Maclies, a 6-6 freshman forward, was an even bigger scorer in high school, going over the 20-point mark in 16 of Kingwood (Texas) High School's 34 games and averaging 18 points and 10 rebounds.

Ronald Mickel, a 6-5 sophomore forward, follows Cornelius from Carl Albert College and will also join the crop of big guards and small forwards Johnson will have at his disposal.

In his quest for more post offense beyond Dews, Johnson is hoping for more from 6-9 junior center **Kresimir Tomorad** (2.7 ppg, 2.5 rpg), who shared the center spot with Rabenhorst last season and was equally unproductive on the offensive end.

2001-2002 SCHEDULE

Nov.	17	East Texas Baptist
	20	@Tulane
	27	LeTourneau
Dec.	1	Southern
	5	Stephen F. Austin
	8	@Vanderbilt
	15	@Louisiana Tech
	17	@Baylor
	21	@Rice
	28-29	#Gossner Foods Classic
Jan.	3	Texas A&M
	7	Northwestern State
	10	Gardner-Webb
	12	Texas A&M-Corpus Christi
	16	Texas College
	24	@Lipscomb
	26	@Gardner-Webb
	30	Louisiana Tech
Feb.	2	Texas Pan American
	5	Lipscomb
	7	@Louisiana-Lafayette
	16	Arkansas Baptist
	19	@Northwestern State
	23	@Texas A&M-Corpus Christi
	25	@Texas Pan American
March	2	@Washington State

@Road Games
#Logan, UT (vs. Utah State first round; also Idaho State, Birmingham Southern)

BLUE RIBBON ANALYSIS

BACKCOURT	C
BENCH/DEPTH	C
FRONTCOURT	C
INTANGIBLES	C+

Life as a major college independent has very little upside. It usually means a very difficult time lining up games. It often means playing a very unbalanced schedule. Either the opponent is too good to realistically challenge or comes with very little power-rating worthiness.

Most importantly, it means going on the road plenty and never getting a quality opponent to come to your place.

Last season Centenary played Arkansas, Marquette, Kent State, Tulane, Iowa, Minnesota, Texas A&M, UAB and LSU, and every one of those games was away from the Gold Dome.

"We're in a situation where our budget is funded by the money we raise and a large portion of that is done by guarantees. It often means we have to put things in perspective," Johnson said.

Eventually that takes its toll. The Gents didn't win a single road game last season and lost seven of their last eight overall.

"There was a point last year where we were playing

really good basketball in January, but then, because of our lack of depth, we got tired in February," Johnson said. "I was really disappointed in the way we played away from home.

The Southland and Sun Belt Conferences continue to be possible future homes for Centenary and, says Johnson, staying an independent too much longer just isn't going to work.

"In order for us to get this thing turned around, we are going to have to be in a league," Johnson said.

Until then Johnson will rely on a roster turnover and, what he believes to be more talented depth, to make the Gents as competitive as possible.

Returning guards Gale and Atamah get help from Division I transfers Wisniewski and Hooper and JUCO transfers Dews, Cornelius, and Riley as Centenary moves on after the departure of McCollum, the nation's leading scorer.

"If you look at the three starters we have coming back and the two young men sitting out, and they are definitely the two most talented on our team, we have the makings of being able to have a better team than we had last year," Johnson said.

The schedule is just a bit softer, especially after the New Year and Centenary even gets Texas A&M to play at the Gold Dome. Nonetheless, Johnson's goal of a .500 season seems to be the ceiling as the Gents wait for a conference to come calling.

(C.C.)

Morris Brown

LOCATION	Atlanta, GA
CONFERENCE	Independent
LAST SEASON	6-22 (.214)
CONFERENCE RECORD	NA
STARTERS LOST/RETURNING	2/3
NICKNAME	Wolverines
COLORS	Purple & Black
HOMECOURT	John H. Lewis Gymnasium (2,000)
COACH	Dereck Thompson (Morris Brown '96)
RECORD AT SCHOOL	First year
CAREER RECORD	First year
ASSISTANTS	Travis Gordon (Jackson State '96)
	Eric Rashad (Guilford '85)
TEAM WINS (last 5 years)	NA-NA-NA-19-6
RPI (last 5 years)	NA-NA-NA-NA-NA
2000-01 FINISH	Lost regular-season finale.

Remember that day at the amusement park when your head finally rose beyond the extended finger of the wooden-carved clown and it was OK to go for it—your first roller coaster ride. You were excited, but oh so scared.

Balancing the need to try something new and thrilling was the thought that, "This ground is pretty good, why should I chance it?"

You get to your seat with great hesitation, but knowing there is no turning back now. Mom and Dad were so proud. Your wise cracking big brother is watching, just waiting for you to chicken out. You also realize there has to be a first time at some point, so let's get it over now, knowing, without a shadow of a doubt, it's going to be a bumpy ride.

Well, that's exactly what jumping from low division college basketball to the top dog Division I feels like. Those teams know they have to go through it in order for the program to make any strides, but realize it's as bumpy a ride as it gets.

Fortunately Morris Brown dealt with much of the turbulence last season, playing its final season in Division II, but competing against mainly Division I competition.

Now the Wolverines will get to run with the big boys in name, too.

And the firsts don't end there. Dereck Thompson debuts as the Morris Brown head coach after four years each as both a player and an assistant coach at the school.

Thompson won't be alone. Nearly half the players will be playing their first games at Morris Brown. Thompson and his staff, after living through a 6-22 season, playing the likes of West Virginia, Pittsburgh, Minnesota, Texas A&M, and Michigan for the first time, brought in five junior college transfers for a quick injection of ready-to-go talent.

A pair of teammates from Florida's Polk Community College—6-2 junior guard **Jamaal Turner** and 6-7 junior forward **Rashad Davis**—expect to play right away.

Davis totes a well-rounded game to go with his 240-

pound frame. As a point guard growing up, Davis developed ball-handling skills that Gordon figures will make him the Wolverines' primary weapon against full-court pressure. He averaged 8.2 points and 6.4 rebounds at Polk.

Turner, who averaged 10.5 points and 4.4 rebounds last season, is a combo guard who will probably find most of his duty off the ball because of his talents as a deep shooter.

"We are looking for some things from Jamaal because he can also play the point, but his greatest asset is his ability to fill it up from long range," assistant coach Travis Gordon said.

Turner joins holdovers **Anthony Adams** (14.2 ppg, 3.3 rpg, 3.0 apg, .372 3 PT) and **Joseph Dunn** (5.8 ppg, 2.3 rpg, 1.1 apg) to form a solid rotation on the wings. Adams and Dunn are both 6-3 seniors.

The man trying to get that trio the ball will be another JUCO transfer, 6-4 junior **Sam Daniels**, who played at Monroe College in the Bronx last season.

Daniels averaged 14.2 points, 2.4 rebounds, and 1.8 assists playing almost exclusively at the two-guard. Daniels' coach at Monroe, Charles Jackson, said even he will be watching how his former star makes the adjustment to the point.

The Wolverines are less certain about the contributions of the final two newcomers, but there's no disputing the size of 6-8, 240-pound junior **Jeff Singleton** and 6-9, 250-pound junior **Eric Love**. Morris Brown sorely lacked any muscle last season. This year the Wolverines hope they will be able to push back a little.

"Last year we were just overmatched every game. That's why we needed guys like Jeff and Eric to give us a little bulk," Gordon said.

Singleton will be looked to for rebounding and interior defense off the bench. He averaged nine points and eight rebounds playing for Phillip Wallace at Andrews College (Ga.) last season. Gordon likened Singleton's style to that of Eugene Edgerson, referencing the former Arizona forward and card-carrying member of the hard-hat union.

"Jeff is hard worker and a very intelligent young man," Wallace said. "He turned out to be a valuable player for us last season."

Love's situation isn't nearly as concrete. He has missed the last two seasons with injuries. First he suffered an ACL tear early in his first season at Olive Harvey Junior College in Chicago. Then a car accident took away last year. Love's health and basketball shape may need some time to come around.

Adams was Morris Brown's best player a year ago, leading the Wolverines in scoring, assists, and three-point shooting, and he did it playing out of position at the point. With Daniels in the fold, Adams should be even more valuable back at his natural two-guard spot.

"Anthony loves contact and that's what I love about him. He's very aggressive and can finish. We'll expect a lot of leadership and scoring out of Anthony," Gordon said.

Dunn was a part-time starter a year ago and will have his work cut out for him to increase that to full-time status. More than likely Dunn will come off the bench, playing behind Adams, a role he was more comfortable in a year ago.

It may be even tougher for 6-2 **Chris Thomas** (1.2 ppg, 0.8 rpg) and 6-2 **Larry Washington** (1.7 ppg, 0.6 rpg) to make the leap from seldom used freshman to productive sophomores. Thomas plays the point and could have an opportunity if the Daniels experiment is a bust. As a wing, Washington is stuck in a position where there may be too many veterans ahead of him.

"Larry might be the hardest worker on the team. It was unbelievable the strides he showed in the preseason conditioning drills," Gordon said. "Chris is probably our most athletic player and now has gone through that freshman year learning curve, learning how to think on this level."

If the junior college big men aren't quite ready to take on important roles, the Wolverines can lean on 6-6 junior **Amien Hicks** (8.9 ppg, 8.0 rpg, .505 FG) and 6-8 sophomore **Akiem Claborn** (6.4 ppg, 5.2 rpg). Hicks was the team's top rebounder and third-leading scorer, but it was Morris Brown's lack of size that forced Hicks, a natural small forward, into the center spot. Claborn was a spot starter who is most effective as a "spark of energy off the bench," Gordon said. Claborn was a much better player in the second half of the season and should be ready to make a much bigger impact as a sophomore.

2001-2002 SCHEDULE

Nov.	15-20	#Paradise Jam
	21	Lipscomb
	28	Ole Miss
Dec.	4	@Boston College
	6	Denver
	8	Alabama State
	15	@Southern Miss
	22	@Alabama State
	27	@Oregon
	31	@Iowa State
Jan.	2	@Marquette
	5	@Colorado State
	7	@Denver
	9	@Colorado
	12	@Savannah State
	14	Clark-Atlanta
	17	Southern
	23	Alcorn State
	28	Southern
	30	Alabama A&M
Feb.	3	@Western Kentucky
	11	Jacksonville State
	13	@Clark-Atlanta
	18	@Jacksonville State
	20	@Alabama A&M
	25	@Alcorn State

@Road Games
#St. Thomas, Virgin Islands (vs. Clemson first round; also UAB, Eastern Michigan, LaSalle, Miami FL)

BLUE RIBBON ANALYSIS

BACKCOURT	D
BENCH/DEPTH	D
FRONTCOURT	F
INTANGIBLES	D

Morris Brown is in for some lumps in its first official season in Division I. In preparation for the upgrade, 64 percent of the roster has been turned over in the last two seasons and there is a new coaching staff to lead the charge.

The core of the team is still Adams, but the Wolverines will be relying heavily on a collection of junior college transfers. The most important in that group may be Daniels, who will not only be learning at a new level, but also a new position. An off-guard at Monroe College, Daniels is now being asked to take over the vital job as the Wolverines' point guard.

The schedule is just as challenging and, like any independent must endure, all the tough games are on the road. Trips to Tulsa, Mississippi, Boston College, Southern Mississippi, Oregon and Iowa State, plus an appearance in a tournament in St. Thomas that includes at least games against Clemson and La Salle all before the New Year, are likely to put Morris Brown in a huge early hole.

"When we got the letter that made us full-fledged Division I it took our guys to another level," assistant coach Gordon said. "It really pushed these guys to bust their tails even more. It's too early to predict what's going to happen, but they are ready to face challenge."

That challenge will be immense, but that's never a surprise when a team makes this jump.

(C.C.)

Savannah State

LOCATION	**Savannah, GA**
CONFERENCE	**Independent**
LAST SEASON	**4-21 (.160)**
CONFERENCE RECORD	**NA**
STARTERS LOST/RETURNING	**0/5**
NICKNAME	**Tigers**
COLORS	**Orange & Reflex Blue**
HOMECOURT	**Tiger Arena (5,000)**
COACH	**Jack Grant (Savannah State '88)**
RECORD AT SCHOOL	**4-21 (1 year)**
CAREER RECORD	**4-21 (1 year)**
TEAM WINS (last 5 years)	**10-11-9-8-4**
RPI (last 5 years)	**NA**
2000-01 FINISH	**Lost in regular-season finale.**

As Savannah State takes the unfamiliar plunge into full-fledged Division I status, at least second-year head coach Jack Grant can go to practice and see some familiar faces.

The Tigers return seven players, including five starters, from 2000-01. Of course, that is the same group that took some severe lumps during its preparatory season.

Playing a schedule that was probably not as difficult as fellow Division II leaper Morris Brown, Savannah State was still outscored by an average of 23.4 points, scored just under 60 per game and didn't have a player of significance shoot above 45 percent from the field. That may be an ominous sign now that the likes of Augusta State, Montevallo, and Paine have been replaced by Florida State, Pittsburgh, and Iowa State. Clearly, the Tigers will have to hope that one does, truly, learn from his mistakes.

"We are excited about the opportunity, but we'll a lot of work to do to build the program," Grant said.

Although the majority of the Tigers' production a year ago came from its starting backcourt of **Maurice Belle** (11.6 ppg, 2.7 rpg, 2.3 apg, .359 3 PT) and **Toyian Williams** (11.6 ppg, 3.0 rpg, 1.3 apg), Grant focused much of his recruiting efforts on guards, guaranteeing nothing for the returnees.

Belle, a 6-3 senior, was Savannah State's top three-point threat, but played most of the year out of position at the point. With incoming freshmen 5-10 **Carlos Smalls** and 6-1 **Jasmin Lowe** and the development of 6-0 sophomore **Taurean Spann**, Grant has more pure point-guard options. That pushes Belle to his more natural two-guard spot where **Toyian Williams** and **Levi Williams** already occupy most of the minutes. Chances are something has to give and Grant thinks that perhaps his top player from a year ago could be the odd man out.

"Toyian has been a three-year starter so it will be difficult for Maurice to break in there and I do have a lot of point guards, although I don't know which one I would single out right now," Grant said.

Spann (1.3 ppg, 1.0 rpg) could be the one. He spent most of last season watching, but that played mainly to Grant's reluctance to throw a freshman into the fire at such a key position.

The aptly named Smalls is a local product from Savannah High School. He's a quick penetrator whose ability to shoot, if not his size, will also allow for the possibility of some time at the two. Interestingly, Smalls did not play last season. He attended Shaws University in North Carolina before transferring to Savannah State.

"Carlos is very, very quick and a very good defender. I like to pressure the ball, so that could be where Carlos fits in," Grant said.

Lowe is a combo guard from Groves High School, also in Savannah, who appears to have just too many veterans ahead of him on the wing. His best chance to play right away will be if Lowe impresses early at the point.

Another possibility in the guard rotation is 6-0 senior **Darris Kelly** (8.5 ppg, 2.0 rpg, 2.5 apg) who sat out much of last season under a Grant-imposed suspension for disciplinary reasons. Kelly is back and Grant figures to have him for the entire season.

The 6-4 **Levi Williams** (5.8 ppg, 2.9 rpg, 1.5 apg) could find himself in a battle with fellow senior Belle for immediate playing time at the wing opposite Toyian Williams. Levi didn't prove to be the same caliber shooter that Belle was last season, but Grant figures to give him more opportunity this time around.

He and Belle will also get a push from 6-0 freshman **Raphael Sharper** from Dunwoody High School in Atlanta. Sharper is purely a shooting guard, much in the same mold as last year's sixth man, 6-3 junior **Marcus Boyd**. Boyd (5.6 ppg, 5.8 rpg) is the club's best leaper and was something of a sparkplug off the bench. His role should be similar this season. Boyd can also play the forward spot, where he may even see the majority of his minutes.

"We expect big things from Raphael right away as far as his ability to score from the perimeter and Marcus is very athletic and can help us in a lot of areas," Grant said.

Those backcourt choices for Grant are plenty and will create some heated competition all season long. For better or for worse, the second-year coach doesn't have nearly that many options along the baseline.

Alvin Payton (10.7 ppg, 5.2 rpg), a 6-5 senior, is the Tigers' best all-around player. He's a decent ball-handler who can also play in the post. He'll be needed to raise his production.

The Tigers also return their man in the middle, junior **Brian Fisher** (6.2 ppg, 5.9 rpg, 1.4 bpg). At 6-9 Fisher is the team's tallest player and will be asked to carry a big load defensively and on the boards.

"Brian is definitely our best inside player and we'll really need him every night this year," Grant said.

A pair of freshmen round out the abbreviated front-court rotation. **Armand Burnett**, 6-8, will definitely play immediately. He sat out last season as a non-qualifier, but the native of Macon and former Southwest High

School standout is ready to go.

"Armand can run the floor and is very aggressive. We'll need that and his ability to shoot it well from 15 feet," Grant said.

Sherrod Reddick, 6-5, is an equally athletic forward from Windsor Forest High School in Savannah.

"Sherrod should help us out inside. His athleticism allows him to play with bigger guys underneath," Grant said.

Vincent Lynn (2.0 ppg, 1.7 rpg, 3 games), a 6-2 senior, and 6-5 sophomore **Thomas Simpson** (0.0 ppg, 0.5 rpg, 2 games) didn't play much a year ago and figure to face the same fate this season.

Terrence Moses, a 5-9 freshman walk-on, could get more of an opportunity, but with the situation as crowded as it is in the backcourt, he may have to wait a year. Moses attended Savannah State last year, but did not play basketball. He hails from Ft. Lauderdale.

2001-2002 SCHEDULE

Nov.	16	@SMU
	20	@Florida State
	27	@Ohio State
Dec.	1	@Pittsburgh
	4	@Armstrong
	6	Georgia Southern
	8	@Jacksonville
	10	Armstrong
	18	@Weber State
	20	@Fresno State
	29	Jacksonville
Jan.	2	@Nebraska
	4	Lipscomb
	9	Bethune-Cookman
	12	Morris Brown
	14	Alabama A&M
	24	Jacksonville State
	26	Birmingham Southern
	30	@Georgia Southern
Feb.	2	@Jacksonville State
	5	Gardner-Webb
	9	@Morris Brown
	11	@Alabama A&M
	13	Texas A&M-Corpus Christi
	19	@Gardner Webb
	23	@Birmingham Southern
	28	@Texas A&M-Corpus Christi

@Road Games

BLUE RIBBON ANALYSIS

BACKCOURT	D
BENCH/DEPTH	D
FRONTCOURT	F
INTANGIBLES	D

Even with five starters back, Savannah State is a long way from being a competitive Division I program. Even with a schedule that contained plenty of remaining Division II opponents, the Tigers struggled mightily in 2000-01. A new year and new status won't change that, especially with the schedule nearly devoid of those lower-division opponents.

Grant has a very top-heavy roster. He is loaded with guards and very thin up front. He also has his core group of seniors led by Toyian Williams, Levi Williams, Alvin Payton and then a large contingent freshman (two of whom didn't even play basketball last year) and inexperienced sophomores. So with good reason, Grant's expectations are realistic.

"My main goal is just for the team to play hard every night and improve on a game-by-game basis. That's the only pressure I'm putting on them. We just want to play hard, especially on the defensive end," Grant said.

With his abundant backcourt and thin frontcourt, Grant would like to use plenty of pressure and run the ball up and down that court. Much of that will depend on the Tigers—most specifically the ability of Fisher, Payton and Burnett to improve on a minus-5.8 rebounding margin from a year ago.

"If we let too many teams get into their set offenses then we are going to be in some trouble," Grant said in what might contend for the title of understatement of the year. "We need to create turnovers and apply pressure."

(C.C.)

Texas-Pan American

LOCATION	Edinburg, TX
CONFERENCE	Independent
LAST SEASON	12-17 (.414)
CONFERENCE RECORD	NA
STARTERS LOST/RETURNING	4/1
NICKNAME	Broncs, Gents
COLORS	Green & White
HOMECOURT	UPTA Fieldhouse (5,000)
COACH	Bob Hoffman (Oklahoma Baptist '79)
RECORD AT SCHOOL	24-33 (2 years)
CAREER RECORD	355-128 (14 years)
ASSISTANTS	Robert Davenport (Okla. Baptist '88)
	Spencer Wright (Oklahoma Baptist '95)
	Mark Van Curen (Oklahoma Baptist '88)
TEAM WINS (last 5 years)	3-3-5-12-12
RPI (last 5 years)	303-258-278-247-285
2000-01 FINISH	Lost in regular-season finale.

When Bob Hoffman says he's been at Texas-Pan American for two years but is starting his third season, he's not kidding. Hired on Sept. 24, 1999 to take over a program that had reached rock bottom, Hoffman had three weeks to get a whistle, grab some balls, and learn his roster before starting practice.

"I barely had enough time to learn the names and figure out how to use the phones," said Hoffman, who coached Oklahoma Baptist to the NAIA title games in 1993 and 1997 and led Southern Nazarene's women's team to a NAIA championship in 1989.

Even three years later it's tough to determine the most damaging aspect of Delray Brooks' tenure as coach. Was it the $25,000 check owed the school from an in-season tournament that he tried to deposit in his own account or was it his mere eight wins in two seasons?

In either case it has been Hoffman's job to bury that chapter in Texas-Pan Am basketball history, and he has done an admirable job.

"I'm really encouraged about our situation. We've come leaps and bounds because the players that were here bought into what we were doing. They helped make this what it is," Hoffman said.

The first hurdle was ending an NCAA-record 64-game road losing streak, which the Broncs did in Hoffman's first season by winning at Oral Roberts.

It certainly hasn't been a Hollywood script since, but Texas-Pan American has climbed back to respectability with back-to-back 12-win seasons. Taking the next step to .500 will have to come without four starters from last season and with eight newcomers to the active roster. Bridging the waters of change is 6-2 senior guard **Mire Chatman** (18.0 ppg, 4.3 rpg, 2.6 apg, 2.7 spg, .435 3PT).

With the departed Brian Merriweather (18.1 ppg, 2.6 rpg, 108 three-pointers) playing the role of go-to guy, Chatman thrived in a subordinate role, even coming off the bench in all but one of the Broncs' 29 games. Yet, playing eight minutes per game fewer (25.6) than Merriweather, Chatman still averaged as many points and was ranked 12th nationally in steals.

"Mire has a chance to do something pretty special. He's a special player. He's definitely someone to keep an eye on," Hoffman said. "Even last year we wanted to get the ball in his hands because something good usually happened."

While Merriweather was a pure shooter, Chatman is more aggressive. He was the Broncs' most accurate three-point shooter, but also likes to get to the basket and led the team in free-throw attempts (139).

Chatman will have a new backcourt running mate in 6-2 junior **Kevin Mitchell**, who takes over at the point after two seasons at McLennan Community College in Waco, Texas. Mitchell averaged 8.4 points and 3.4 assists and was a 38.0 percent shooter from three-point range last season.

"Kevin was a Presidential Scholar and is really sharp. We run a lot of different sets, so we think he has great chance to run this team," Hoffman said.

Another JUCO transfer, 6-4 junior forward **Jonathan Nubine**, could be playing regularly on the wing opposite Chatman. Nubine spent much of last season at Carl Albert State (Oka.) Junior College injured, but he still scored 16.5 points and grabbed eight rebounds a game.

"Jon is really strong, athletic and physical. We think he can really take up a lot of the scoring slack we lost with Brian Merriweather," Hoffman said.

Hoffman will also depend on another transfer coming off an injury to be one of his top perimeter weapons off the bench. **Tomas Sitnikovas**, a 6-6 junior guard, was averaging 17 points a game at Mid-Plains (Neb.) Community College before going down about midway through last season. A native of Panevezys, Lithuania, Sitnikovas can fill in at both wings and can even play some point.

The final two members of the recruiting class play up front. **Andruis Sakalys**, a 6-6 junior forward, once played on the same club team in Lithuania as Sitnikovas but isn't as talented. Sakalys is more of a grinder and hustler, a player his former coach at Eastern Oklahoma, Jimmy Voight, said would be, "a fan and crowd favorite because of his worth ethic and hustle."

With averages of 11.4 points and 4.7 rebounds, Sakalys helped Eastern Oklahoma to a top-10 ranking last season and a 47-17 two-year mark.

Forward **Derrick East** is the only high school player in the class and Hoffman says there is a possibility East could be red-shirted. The 6-8 freshman played for a 27-3 Lookeba-Sickles (Okla.) High School squad last season and averaged 21.1 points, 12.9 rebounds, and 6.1 blocks.

If East is red-shirted, he'll have plenty of people to ask about the experience. **Eric Montalvo**, a 6-3 freshman guard, 6-2 sophomore guard **Nick Traylor**, and 6-10 freshman center **Josh Autenrieth**, all sat on the sideline a year ago.

"They all have a chance to contribute depending on the situation. We'll just have to wait and see on that," Hoffman said.

Montalvo is a local from nearby LaJoya High School in Texas. He averaged 22.5 points, seven rebounds and five assists as a senior. Traylor already has one season of college ball behind him. He scored eight points a game at Northwestern Oklahoma two seasons ago as a freshman.

The 280-pound Autenrieth, a "big boy" said Hoffman, played scholastically at West Columbia (Texas) High School. He was an honorable mention McDonald's All-American and academic all-state after a 16.5-point, 9.8-rebound, and five-block per game senior season, but walked on last season.

Autenrieth would provide some welcomed beef to a frontline that isn't nearly as deep and versatile as Hoffman's perimeter corp.

Oddly, the club's only returning starter comes from this bunch, but 6-7 junior forward **Terrell Hill** (5.7 ppg, 5.8 rpg) was only modestly productive and shot just 47.2 percent from the field.

Marcus Quinn (5.4 ppg, 3.0 rpg), a 6-9 senior center, put up similar numbers in a more limited role. Hill and Quinn should join Sakalys as the heart of the Broncs' interior game.

DeFrance Gurley (1.7 ppg, 1.1 rpg), a 6-7 senior forward, may have an opportunity to improve upon his six minutes a game, as may 6-4 senior **Joey Tate** (1.8 ppg, 1.8 rpg), who averaged seven minutes in his 25 games.

James Davis (0.5 ppg, 0.4 rpg, 17 games), a 5-10 junior guard, 6-1 senior guard **Quin Canada** (0.9 ppg, 0.2 rpg, 10 games), 6-3 sophomore **Mark Bills** (1.3 ppg, 1.3 rpg, four games), 6-1 sophomore **Gabriel Cortez** (0.5 ppg, 0.0 rpg, four games), and 6-1 sophomore guard **Matt Hall** (0.8 ppg, 0.2 rpg) all played sparingly a year ago and may have an equally difficult time breaking into the deep guard rotation again this season.

"We are a lot deeper than we've been since I've been here and we're excited about that. One to 12 we could be a lot better," Hoffman said.

2001-2002 SCHEDULE

Nov.	17	Sul Ross State
	19	Southwest Texas State
	21	Texas College
	24	Texas Southern
Dec.	1	@Minnesota
	5	@Portland
	7	@Washington State
	13	Lamar
	15	Middle Tennessee State
	20-22	#San Juan Shootout
	27	@Rice
	29	LeTourneau
	30	Schreiner
Jan.	2	@Texas
	8	@SW Texas State
	10	Air Force
	17	Lipscomb
	19	Gardner-Webb
	23	@Wright State
	26	Texas A&M-Corpus Christi
Feb.	2	@Centenary
	4	@Middle Tennessee State
	9	@Texas A&M-Corpus Christi
	11	New Mexico State
	14	@Lipscomb
	16	@Gardner-Webb
	25	Centenary

@Road Games
#San Juan, Puerto Rico (vs. Niagara first round; also Baylor, Puerto Rico, Coppin State, Florida International, Jacksonville, Oral Roberts)

BLUE RIBBON ANALYSIS

BACKCOURT	C
BENCH/DEPTH	C
FRONTCOURT	C
INTANGIBLES	C+

Texas-Pan American is full of new faces as the restructuring process continues. Third year head coach

Hoffman inherited what appeared to be an untenable situation, but somehow has made it work.

His reputation and background of running high-character programs at Oklahoma Baptist and the women's team at Southern Nazarene has helped. So has a lot of work on the recruiting roads. Now comes the chore of making the off-season efforts of the last two years into one functioning unit that can exceed what, considering the circumstances, has been a remarkable first two seasons.

"It'll just be blending everyone together and understanding they have a common purpose. We've been blessed in the past to get guys to buy into that and I think we'll be able to do that again," Hoffman said. "With the character of the kids we have and the ones we've recruited, we figure the blending should work."

That blending is made easier if Chatman takes the role of wooden spoon. No longer overshadowed by Merriweather, Chatman is unquestionably the Broncs' main man. How he performs in that role could be a measuring stick to Texas-Pan Am's season. He should get most of his help from a talented group of junior college transfers who will be given every opportunity to play key parts immediately.

The Broncs' have shaken that NCAA record 64-game road losing streak and even managed to win at Air Force last season, just before the Falcons knocked off Utah. Hoffman has turned Texas-Pan American into a rock solid home team (9-2 in Edinburgh last year). He has even managed to schedule 14 games at the UPTA Fieldhouse this season, the most since he took over the program.

There is no reason to believe the Broncs' quality play at home won't continue, but the road is a problem. That probably means more of the same in 2001-02 with anywhere from 12-15 wins a realistic outcome.

(C.C.)

2000-2001 Division I Individual Statistics

SCORING

		CL	HT	G	TFG	3FG	FT	PTS.	AVG.
1.	Ronnie McCollum, Centenary	SR	6-4	27	244	85	214	787	29.1
2.	Kyle Hill, Eastern Ill.	SR	6-2	31	250	86	151	737	23.8
3.	DeWayne Jefferson, Miss. Va	SR	6-3	27	216	107	98	637	23.6
4.	Tarise Bryson, Illinois St.	SR	6-1	30	208	62	207	685	22.8
5.	Henry Domercant, E. Ill.	SO	6-4	31	256	79	115	706	22.8
6.	Rashad Phillips, Detroit	SR	5-10	35	232	136	185	785	22.4
7.	Brandon Wolfram, UTEP	SR	6-9	32	251	6	206	714	22.3
8.	Rasual Butler, La Salle	JR	6-8	29	231	97	82	641	22.1
9.	Brandon Armstrong, Pepperdi	JR	6-4	31	240	76	128	684	22.1
10.	Marvin O'Connor, St. Joseph	JR	6-4	32	240	99	127	706	22.1
11.	Tarvis Williams, Hampton	SR	6-9	32	259	0	184	702	21.9
12.	Troy Murphy, Notre Dame	JR	6-11	30	223	30	177	653	21.8
13.	Trenton Hassell, Austin Pea	SR	6-5	32	246	53	148	693	21.7
14.	Isaac Spencer, Murray St.	SR	6-6	29	225	6	170	626	21.6
15.	Jason Williams, Duke	SO	6-2	39	285	132	139	841	21.6
16.	Demond Mallet, McNeese St.	SR	6-1	31	216	107	121	660	21.3

REBOUNDING

		CL	HT	G	NO.	AVG.
1.	Chris Marcus, Western Ky.	JR	7-1	31	374	12.1
2.	Reggie Evans, Iowa	JR	6-8	35	416	11.9
3.	J.R. VanHoose, Marshall	JR	6-10	27	299	11.1
4.	David West, Xavier	SO	6-8	29	316	10.9
5.	Eddie Griffin, Seton Hall	FR	6-9	30	323	10.8
6.	Jeremy Jefferson, Ark.Pne-Blf	JR	6-7	23	246	10.7
7.	Brian Carroll, Loyola (Md.)	SR	6-8	27	286	10.6
8.	Eric Mann, VMI	SR	6-9	28	294	10.5
8.	Joe Breakenridge, N. Iowa	SR	6-6	28	294	10.5
10.	Alvin Jones, Georgia Tech	SR	6-11	30	312	10.4
11.	Kelly Wise, Memphis	JR	6-10	36	363	10.1
12.	Erwin Dudley, Alabama	SO	6-8	36	361	10.0
13.	Andy Savtchenko, Radford	JR	7-0	29	290	10.0
14.	Chris Miller, Texas Southern	SO	6-3	26	259	10.0
15.	Bruce Jenkins, N.C. A&T	JR	6-6	27	266	9.9
16.	Michael Bradley, Villanova	JR	6-10	31	303	9.8
17.	Calvin Bowman, W. Virginia	SR	6-9	29	282	9.7
18.	Kashien Latham, Ga. So.	JR	6-9	30	291	9.7
19.	Ajmal Basit, Delaware	SR	6-9	30	289	9.6
20.	Ian McGinnis, Dartmouth	SR	6-8	27	260	9.6

FG PCT.

MIN 5 FG MADE PER GAME

		CL	HT	G	FG	FGA	PCT.
1.	Michael Bradley, Villanova	JR	6-10	31	254	367	69.2
2.	Nakiea Miller, Iona	SR	6-9	27	163	244	66.8
3.	Kimani Ffriend, Nebraska	SR	6-11	28	144	231	62.3
4.	Andre Hutson, Michigan St.	SR	6-8	32	173	278	62.2
5.	George Evans, Geo. Mason	SR	6-7	30	233	380	61.3
6.	Carlos Boozer, Duke	SO	6-9	32	160	265	60.4
7.	Steffon Bradford, Nebraska	SR	6-6	30	155	257	60.3
8.	Terry Black, Baylor	SR	6-5	31	191	317	60.3
9.	Joe Linderman, Drexel	SR	6-9	24	146	244	59.8
10.	Nick Collison, Kansas	SO	6-9	33	187	313	59.7
11.	Udonis Haslem, Florida	JR	6-8	31	188	315	59.7
12.	Michael Wright, Arizona	JR	6-7	36	202	340	59.4
13.	Brandon Wolfram, UTEP	SR	6-9	32	251	425	59.1
14.	Jermaine Hall, Wagner	SO	6-5	29	211	359	58.8
15.	Melvin Ely, Fresno St.	SR	6-10	33	208	357	58.3
16.	Joe Breakenridge, N. Iowa	SR	6-6	28	150	258	58.1

FT PCT

MIN 2.5 FG MADE PER GAME

		CL	HT	G	FT	FTA	PCT.
1.	Gary Buchanan, Villanova	SO	6-4	31	97	103	94.2
2.	Brent Jolly, Tennessee Tech	SO	6-5	29	95	102	93.1
3.	Ryan Mendez, Stanford	SR	6-7	34	94	101	93.1
4.	Rashad Phillips, Detroit	SR	5-10	35	185	202	91.6
5.	Ronnie McCollum, Centenary	SR	6-4	27	214	236	90.7
6.	Titus Ivory, Penn St.	SR	6-4	33	125	139	89.9
7.	Chris Spatola, Army	JR	6-1	28	149	166	89.8
8.	Albert Mouring, Connecticut	SR	6-3	32	104	117	88.9
8.	Scott Knapp, Siena	SR	6-3	31	80	90	88.9
10.	Dominic Smith, Houston	JR	5-10	29	142	160	88.8
11.	Roger Mason, Virginia	SO	6-5	29	122	138	88.4
12.	Chad Pleiness, Central Mich.	SO	6-6	28	76	86	88.4
13.	Mark Linebaugh, Colgate	FR	6-2	28	90	102	88.2
14.	Adam Lopez, Northern Ariz.	JR	6-0	29	89	101	88.1
15.	Steve Logan, Cincinnati	JR	6-0	34	132	150	88.0
16.	Joe Crispin, Penn St.	SR	6-1	33	144	165	87.3

ASSISTS

		CL	HT	G	NO.	AVG.
1.	Markus Carr, C.St. Northridge	JR	6-1	32	286	8.9
2.	Omar Cook, St. John's (N.Y.)	FR	6-1	29	252	8.7
3.	Sean Kennedy, Marist	JR	6-2	27	219	8.1
4.	Tito Maddox, Fresno St.	SO	6-4	25	200	8.0
5.	Ashley Robinson, Mississippi Val.	JR	5-9	27	201	7.4
6.	Brandon Pardon, Bowling Green	JR	6-1	29	204	7.0
7.	Jeremy Stanton, Evansville	SR	6-1	26	181	7.0
8.	Kirk Hinrich, Kansas	SO	6-3	33	229	6.9
9.	Steve Blake, Maryland	SO	6-3	36	248	6.9
10.	Allen Griffin, Syracuse	SR	6-1	34	220	6.5
11.	Jose Winston, Colorado	JR	5-11	30	194	6.5
12.	Jameer Nelson, St. Joseph's	FR	6-0	33	213	6.5
13.	Martin Ingelsby, Notre Dame	SR	6-0	30	193	6.4
14.	Elliott PrasseFreeman, Harvard	SO	6-3	26	164	6.3
15.	Jamal Brown, Texas Tech	JR	6-0	28	175	6.3
16.	Sean Peterson, Ga. Southern	JR	6-1	30	187	6.2

BLOCKED SHOTS

		CL	HT	G	NO.	AVG.
1.	Tarvis Williams, Hampton	SR	6-9	32	147	4.6
2.	Eddie Griffin, Seton Hall	FR	6-9	30	133	4.4
3.	Wojciech Myrda, La.Monroe	JR	7-2	28	123	4.4
4.	Kris Hunter, Jacksonville	SR	6-11	28	114	4.1
5.	Ken Johnson, Ohio St.	SR	6-11	31	125	4.0
6.	Hondre Brewer, San Francisco	JR	7-0	30	114	3.8
7.	Brendan Haywood, N. Carolina	SR	7-0	33	120	3.6
8.	Jason Jennings, Arkansas St.	JR	7-0	29	102	3.5
9.	Patrick Flomo, Ohio	JR	6-9	30	105	3.5
10.	Alvin Jones, Georgia Tech	SR	6-11	30	101	3.4
11.	Chris Marcus, Western Ky.	JR	7-1	31	97	3.1
12.	Nakiea Miller, Iona	SR	6-9	27	84	3.1
13.	Rans Brempong, Western Caro.	FR	6-8	31	93	3.0
14.	Henry Jordan, Mississippi Val.	SR	6-10	27	80	3.0
15.	Loren Woods, Arizona	SR	7-1	29	84	2.9
16.	Kyle Davis, Auburn	FR	6-10	30	84	2.8

STEALS

		CL	HT	G	NO.	AVG.
1.	Greedy Daniels, TCU	JR	6-1	25	108	4.3
2.	Desmond Cambridge, Ala. A&M	JR	6-1	28	107	3.8
3.	Senecca Wall, Sam Houston St.	SR	6-4	29	103	3.6
4.	John Linehan, Providence	JR	5-9	26	81	3.1
5.	Fred House, Southern Utah	SR	6-5	31	93	3.0
6.	Andy Woodley, Northern Iowa	JR	5-9	27	80	3.0
7.	Kevin Braswell, Georgetown	JR	6-2	33	94	2.8
8.	Andrew Gellert, Harvard	JR	6-1	26	72	2.8
9.	Cookie Belcher, Nebraska	SR	6-4	30	82	2.7
10.	Mire Chatman, Tex-Pan Am	JR	6-2	29	78	2.7
11.	Greg Gray, South Carolina St.	JR	6-7	31	82	2.6
11.	Courtney Eldridge, UNC Gmsbro	JR	5-10	31	82	2.6
13.	Juan Dixon, Maryland	JR	6-3	36	95	2.6
14.	Robert Rushing, Troy St.	JR	6-1	31	81	2.6
15.	Troy Bell, Boston College	SO	6-1	32	83	2.6
16.	Beau Wallace, Liberty	SR	6-2	28	72	2.6

3PT FG PCT

MIN 1.5 P/G AND 40%

		CL	HT	G	FG	FGA	PCT.
1.	Amory Sanders, SE Missouri St	SR	6-1	24	53	95	55.8
2.	David Falknor, Akron	JR	6-7	22	47	87	54.0
3.	Cary Cochran, Nebraska	JR	6-1	30	78	165	47.3
4.	Casey Jacobsen, Stanford	SO	6-6	34	84	178	47.2
5.	Tim Erickson, Idaho St.	SR	6-3	28	82	177	46.3
6.	Justin Brown, Montana St.	JR	6-5	30	60	130	46.2
7.	Luke McDonald, Drake	FR	6-5	28	86	187	46.0
8.	Sean Jackson, UC Irvine	SR	6-5	30	62	135	45.9
9.	Brian Chase, Virginia Tech	SO	5-10	23	60	131	45.8
10.	Jason Kapono, UCLA	SO	6-7	32	84	184	45.7
11.	Brett Nelson, Florida	SO	6-3	31	81	179	45.3
12.	Kyle Korver, Creighton	SO	6-7	32	100	221	45.2
13.	Alan Barksdale, Ark.Little Ro	SR	6-4	29	80	178	44.9
14.	Kareem Rush, Missouri	SO	6-6	26	69	154	44.8
15.	Cory Schwab, Northern Ariz.	SR	6-5	29	105	235	44.7
16.	Ravonte Dantzler, South Ala.	SR	6-2	33	69	155	44.5

3PT FG MADE PER GAME

		CL	HT	G	NO.	AVG.
1.	DeWayne Jefferson, Miss. Val.	SR	6-3	27	107	4.0
2.	Rashad Phillips, Detroit	SR	5-10	35	136	3.9
3.	Brian Merriweather, Tex-Pan Am	SR	6-3	29	108	3.7
4.	Cory Schwab, Northern Ariz.	SR	6-5	29	105	3.6
5.	Demond Mallet, McNeese St.	SR	6-1	31	107	3.5
6.	Tony Orciari, Vermont	SR	6-3	27	92	3.4
7.	Jason Williams, Duke	SO	6-2	39	132	3.4
8.	Rasual Butler, La Salle	JR	6-8	29	97	3.3
9.	Darius Lane, Seton Hall	JR	6-4	31	103	3.3
10.	Wes Burtner, Belmont	JR	6-5	28	93	3.3
10.	E.J. Gallup, Albany (N.Y.)	FR	6-4	28	93	3.3
12.	Lamar Plummer, Pennsylvania	JR	6-1	29	96	3.3
13.	Monty Mack, Massachusetts	SR	6-3	29	95	3.3
14.	Joe Crispin, Penn St.	SR	6-1	33	108	3.3
15.	Clarence Gilbert, Missouri	JR	6-2	32	102	3.2
16.	Shane Battier, Duke	SR	6-8	39	124	3.2

1999-2000 Division I Team Statistics

SCORING OFFENSE

		G	(W-L)	PTS.	AVG.
1.	TCU	31	(20-11)	2902	93.6
2.	Duke	39	(35-4)	3538	90.7
3.	Maryland	36	(25-11)	3067	85.2
4.	Virginia	29	(20-9)	2464	85.0
5.	McNeese St.	31	(22-9)	2580	83.2
6.	Stanford	34	(31-3)	2829	83.2
7.	Cal St. Northridge	32	(22-10)	2650	82.8
8.	Eastern Ill.	31	(21-10)	2564	82.7
9.	Wagner	29	(16-13)	2393	82.5
10.	Gonzaga	33	(26-7)	2720	82.4
11.	Kansas	33	(26-7)	2707	82.0
12.	Fresno St.	33	(26-7)	2689	81.5
13.	Arizona	36	(28-8)	2926	81.3

SCORING DEFENSE

		G	(W-L)	PTS.	AVG.
1.	Wisconsin	29	(18-11)	1641	56.6
2.	Utah St.	34	(28-6)	1959	57.6
3.	Princeton	27	(16-11)	1569	58.1
4.	UNC Wilmington	30	(19-11)	1751	58.4
5.	Miami (Ohio)	33	(17-16)	1928	58.4
6.	Columbia	27	(12-15)	1591	58.9
7.	Col. of Charleston	29	(22-7)	1739	60.0
8.	UMKC	30	(14-16)	1815	60.5
9.	Richmond	29	(22-7)	1763	60.8
10.	Butler	32	(24-8)	1946	60.8
11.	Western Ky.	31	(24-7)	1889	60.9
12.	Stephen F. Austin	26	(9-17)	1595	61.3
13.	Michigan St.	33	(28-5)	2039	61.8

SCORING MARGIN

		OFF.	DEF.	MAR.
1.	Duke	90.7	70.5	20.2
2.	Stanford	83.2	65.5	17.7
3.	Michigan St.	77.4	61.8	15.6
4.	Arizona	81.3	66.3	15.0
5.	Florida	80.9	67.1	13.8
6.	Gonzaga	82.4	68.8	13.6
7.	Western Ky.	74.3	60.9	13.4
8.	Utah St.	70.7	57.6	13.1
9.	Boston College	79.6	66.5	13.1
10.	Maryland	85.2	72.4	12.8
11.	Kansas	82.0	69.3	12.8
12.	Illinois	77.9	65.9	11.9
13.	TCU	93.6	82.3	11.4

WON-LOST PERCENTAGE

		W-L	PCT.
1.	Stanford	31-3	.912
2.	Duke	35-4	.897
3.	Georgia St.	29-5	.853

4.	Michigan St.	28-5	.848
5.	Boston College	27-5	.844
6.	Hofstra	26-5	.839
7.	UC Irvine	25-5	.833
8.	Utah St.	28-6	.824
9.	Iowa St.	25-6	.806
9.	Southern Utah	25-6	.806
11.	Fresno St.	26-7	.788
11.	Gonzaga	26-7	.788
11.	Kansas	26-7	.788
11.	North Carolina	26-7	.788

FIELD GOAL PERCENTAGE

		FG	FGA	PCT.
1.	Stanford	953	1865	51.1
2.	Gonzaga	915	1793	51.0
3.	Austin Peay	935	1845	50.7
4.	Kansas	1002	1996	50.2
5.	Villanova	845	1708	49.5
6.	Cal St. Northridge	910	1842	49.4
7.	UTEP	878	1786	49.2
8.	Michigan St.	957	1957	48.9
9.	Southern Utah	783	1602	48.9
10.	Central Mich.	669	1370	48.8
11.	Nebraska	775	1591	48.7
12.	Montana St.	771	1588	48.6
13.	Utah St.	852	1755	48.5

FIELD GOAL PERCENTAGE DEFENSE

		FG	FGA	PCT.
1.	Kansas	782	2069	37.8
2.	Holy Cross	628	1642	38.2
3.	Illinois	748	1936	38.6
4.	Georgetown	745	1922	38.8
5.	Texas	734	1889	38.9
6.	Alabama St.	728	1869	39.0
7.	Columbia	525	1344	39.1
8.	North Carolina	859	2196	39.1
9.	Michigan St.	716	1823	39.3
10.	Notre Dame	781	1988	39.3
11.	Indiana	761	1930	39.4
12.	Utah St.	708	1795	39.4
13.	Gonzaga	794	2009	39.5

FREE THROW PERCENTAGE

		FT	FTA	PCT.
1.	Brigham Young	651	835	78.0
2.	Eastern Ill.	504	650	77.5
3.	UNC Greensboro	552	718	76.9
4.	Bowling Green	546	712	76.7
5.	Penn St.	587	768	76.4
6.	Kent St.	564	739	76.3
7.	Manhattan	471	618	76.2
8.	Drake	428	562	76.2

9.	UMKC	315	414	76.1
10.	Col. of Charleston	467	615	75.9
11.	Long Island	354	467	75.8
12.	Centenary (La.)	483	641	75.4
13.	Idaho St.	421	559	75.3

REBOUND MARGIN

		OFF.	DEF.	MAR.
1.	Michigan St.	42.5	27.1	15.4
2.	Western Ky.	40.0	30.4	9.6
3.	Georgetown	44.9	35.6	9.2
4.	Iowa St.	39.6	30.8	8.8
5.	Mississippi St.	41.2	33.3	7.9
6.	Holy Cross	38.5	30.8	7.7
7.	Kansas	42.6	35.0	7.6
8.	Stanford	36.6	29.2	7.4
9.	Valparaiso	37.5	30.3	7.3
10.	Alabama	42.2	35.0	7.2
11.	Illinois	40.0	33.0	7.0
12.	Central Conn. St.	38.9	32.2	6.8
13.	Iowa	38.6	31.9	6.7

3PT FG PC

MIN 3.0 P/G AND 40%

		G	FG	FGA	PCT.
1.	Akron	28	189	436	43.3
2.	Stanford	34	252	587	42.9
3.	New Orleans	29	186	444	41.9
4.	Iowa St.	31	182	436	41.7
5.	Montana St.	30	226	544	41.5
6.	Northern Ariz.	29	237	571	41.5
7.	Butler	32	251	617	40.7
8.	Ark.Little Rock	29	200	492	40.7
9.	Ball St.	30	193	477	40.5
10.	Gonzaga	33	245	606	40.4
11.	Colorado St.	28	183	454	40.3
12.	Providence	31	249	622	40.0
13.	Southern Utah	31	197	493	40.0

3PT FG MADE PER GAME

		G	NO.	AVG.
1.	Duke	39	407	10.4
2.	Belmont	28	288	10.3
3.	Samford	29	284	9.8
4.	Mississippi Val.	27	250	9.3
5.	Charlotte	33	305	9.2
6.	Tennessee St.	29	260	9.0
7.	Arkansas	31	273	8.8
8.	Wis.Milwaukee	28	244	8.7
9.	Georgia Tech	30	260	8.7
10.	TCU	31	268	8.6
11.	Siena	31	266	8.6
12.	Missouri	33	279	8.5
13.	Troy St.	31	262	8.5

Division I Coaching Changes for 2001-2002

SCHOOL	FORMER COACH	NEW COACH
Butler	Thad Matta	Todd Lickliter
Cal Poly	Jeff Schneider	Kevin Bromley
Denver	Martin Fletcher	Terry Carroll
Drexel	Steve Seymour	Bruiser Flint
Duquesne	Darelle Porter	Danny Nee
Florida A&M	Mickey Clayton	Mike Gillespie
George Washington	Tom Penders	Karl Hobbs
Hofstra	Jay Wright	Tom Pecora
Idaho	David Farrar	Leonard Perry
Kent State	Gary Waters	Stan Heath
LaSalle	Speedy Morris	Billy Hahn
Louisville	Denny Crum	Rick Pitino
Massachusetts	Bruiser Flint	Steve Lappas
McNeese State	Ron Everhart	Tic Price
Michigan	Brian Ellerbe	Tommy Amaker
Mo.-Kansas City	Dean Demopoulos	Rich Zvosec
Morgan State	Chris Fuller	Butch Beard
New Orleans	Joey Stiebling	Monte Towe
North Texas	Vic Trilli	Johnny Jones
Northeastern	Rudy Keeling	Ron Everhart
Northern Illinois	Andy Greer	Rob Judson
Northern Iowa	Sam Weaver	Greg McDermott
Ohio	Larry Hunter	Tim O'Shea
Old Dominion	Jeff Capel	Blaine Taylor

SCHOOL	FORMER COACH	NEW COACH
Pepperdine	Jan van Breda Kolff	Paul Westphal
Portland	Rob Chavez	Michael Holton
Rhode Island	Jerry DiGregorio	Jim Baron
Robert Morris	Danny Nee	Mark Schmidt
Rutgers	Kevin Bannon	Gary Waters
St. Bonaventure	Jim Baron	Jan van Breda Kolff
St. Mary's, Calif.	David Bollwinkel	Randy Bennett
Seton Hall	Tommy Amaker	Louis Orr
Siena	Louis Orr	Rob Lanier
South Carolina	Eddie Fogler	Dave Odom
Southern	Tommy Green	Ben Jobe
Stetson	Murray Arnold	Derek Waugh
Tennessee	Jerry Green	Buzz Peterson
Texas Southern	Robert Moreland	Ronnie Courtney
Texas Tech	James Dickey	Bob Knight
Towson	Mike Jakulski	Michael Hunt
Tulsa	Buzz Peterson	John Phillips
UNLV	Max Good	Charlie Spoonhour
Villanova	Steve Lappas	Jay Wright
Wake Forest	Dave Odom	Skip Prosser
Wisconsin	Brad Soderberg	Bo Ryan
Wis.-Milwaukee	Bo Ryan	Bruce Pearl
Xavier	Skip Prosser	Thad Matta

2000-2001 Division I Conference Standings

AMERICA EAST CONFERENCE

TEAM	CONFERENCE			FULL SEASON		
	W	L	PCT.	W	L	PCT.
Hofstra#	16	2	.889	26	5	.839
Delaware	14	4	.778	20	10	.667
Drexel	12	6	.667	15	12	.556
Maine	10	8	.556	18	11	.621
Boston U.	9	9	.500	14	14	.500
Northeastern	8	10	.444	10	19	.345
Towson	7	11	.389	12	17	.414
Vermont	7	11	.389	12	17	.414
New Hampshire	6	12	.333	7	21	.250
Hartford	1	17	.056	4	24	.143

ATLANTIC COAST CONFERENCE

TEAM	CONFERENCE			FULL SEASON		
	W	L	PCT.	W	L	PCT.
Duke#	13	3	.813	35	4	.897
North Carolina	13	3	.813	26	7	.788
Maryland	10	6	.625	25	11	.694
Virginia	9	7	.563	20	9	.690
Wake Forest	8	8	.500	19	11	.633
Georgia Tech	8	8	.500	17	13	.567
North Carolina St.	5	11	.313	13	16	.448
Florida St.	4	12	.250	9	21	.300
Clemson	2	14	.125	12	19	.387

ATLANTIC 10 CONFERENCE

TEAM	CONFERENCE			FULL SEASON		
	W	L	PCT.	W	L	PCT.
St. Joseph's	14	2	.875	26	7	.788
Xavier	12	4	.750	21	8	.724
Temple#	12	4	.750	24	13	.649
Massachusetts	11	5	.688	15	15	.500
Dayton	9	7	.563	21	13	.618
St. Bonaventure	9	7	.563	18	12	.600
George Washington	6	10	.375	14	18	.438
La Salle	5	11	.313	12	17	.414
Fordham	4	12	.250	12	17	.414
Duquesne	3	13	.188	9	21	.300
Rhode Island	3	13	.188	7	23	.233

BIG EAST CONFERENCE

TEAM	CONFERENCE			FULL SEASON		
	W	L	PCT.	W	L	PCT.
East						
Boston College#	13	3	.813	27	5	.844
Providence	11	5	.688	21	10	.677
Connecticut	8	8	.500	20	12	.625
Villanova	8	8	.500	18	13	.581
Miami (Fla.)	8	8	.500	16	13	.552
St. John's (N.Y.)	8	8	.500	14	15	.483
Virginia Tech	2	14	.125	8	19	.296
West						
Notre Dame	11	5	.688	20	10	.667
Georgetown	9	6	.600	25	8	.758
Syracuse	9	6	.600	25	9	.735
West Virginia	8	8	.500	17	12	.586
Pittsburgh	6	9	.400	19	14	.576
Seton Hall	5	11	.313	16	15	.516
Rutgers	3	13	.188	11	16	.407

BIG SKY CONFERENCE

TEAM	CONFERENCE			FULL SEASON		
	W	L	PCT.	W	L	PCT.
Cal St. Northridge#	13	3	.813	22	10	.688
Eastern Wash.	11	5	.688	17	11	.607
Idaho St.	10	6	.625	14	14	.500
Montana St.	8	8	.500	16	14	.533
Northern Ariz.	8	8	.500	15	14	.517
Weber St.	8	8	.500	15	14	.517
Montana	6	10	.375	11	16	.407
Portland St.	6	10	.375	9	18	.333
Cal St. Sacramento	2	14	.125	5	22	.185

BIG SOUTH CONFERENCE

TEAM	CONFERENCE			FULL SEASON		
	W	L	PCT.	W	L	PCT.
Radford	12	2	.857	19	10	.655
Winthrop#	11	3	.786	18	13	.581
UNC Asheville	9	5	.643	15	13	.536
Charleston So.	6	8	.429	10	19	.345
Coastal Caro.	6	8	.429	8	20	.286
Liberty	5	9	.357	13	15	.464
Elon	4	10	.286	9	20	.310
High Point	3	11	.214	8	20	.286

BIG TEN CONFERENCE

TEAM	CONFERENCE			FULL SEASON		
	W	L	PCT.	W	L	PCT.
Michigan St.	13	3	.813	28	5	.848
Illinois	13	3	.813	27	8	.771
Ohio St.	11	5	.688	20	11	.645
Indiana	10	6	.625	21	13	.618
Wisconsin	9	7	.563	18	11	.621
Iowa#	7	9	.438	23	12	.657
Penn St.	7	9	.438	21	12	.636
Purdue	6	10	.375	17	15	.531
Minnesota	5	11	.313	18	14	.563
Michigan	4	12	.250	10	18	.357
Northwestern	3	13	.188	11	19	.367

BIG 12 CONFERENCE

TEAM	CONFERENCE			FULL SEASON		
	W	L	PCT.	W	L	PCT.
Iowa St.	13	3	.813	25	6	.806
Kansas	12	4	.750	26	7	.788
Oklahoma	12	4	.750	26	7	.788
Texas	12	4	.750	25	9	.735
Oklahoma St.	10	6	.625	20	10	.667
Missouri	9	7	.563	20	13	.606
Nebraska	7	9	.438	14	16	.467
Baylor	6	10	.375	19	12	.613
Colorado	5	11	.313	15	15	.500
Kansas St.	4	12	.250	11	18	.379
Texas A&M	3	13	.188	10	20	.333
Texas Tech	3	13	.188	9	19	.321

BIG WEST CONFERENCE

TEAM	CONFERENCE			FULL SEASON		
	W	L	PCT.	W	L	PCT.
UC Irvine	15	1	.938	25	5	.833
Utah St.#	13	3	.813	28	6	.824
Long Beach St.	10	6	.625	18	13	.581
UC Santa Barbara	9	7	.563	13	15	.464
Pacific (Cal.)	8	8	.500	18	12	.600
Boise St.	8	8	.500	17	14	.548
Cal Poly	3	13	.188	9	19	.321
Idaho	3	13	.188	6	21	.222
Cal St. Fullerton	3	13	.188	5	23	.179

COLONIAL ATHLETIC ASSOCIATION

TEAM	CONFERENCE			FULL SEASON		
	W	L	PCT.	W	L	PCT.
Richmond	12	4	.750	22	7	.759
UNC Wilmington	11	5	.688	19	11	.633
George Mason#	11	5	.688	18	12	.600
Va. Commonwealth	9	7	.563	16	14	.533
Old Dominion	7	9	.438	13	18	.419
William & Mary	7	9	.438	11	17	.393
East Caro.	6	10	.375	14	14	.500
James Madison	6	10	.375	12	17	.414
American	3	13	.188	7	20	.259

CONFERENCE USA

TEAM	CONFERENCE			FULL SEASON		
	W	L	PCT.	W	L	PCT.
American						
Cincinnati	11	5	.688	25	10	.714
Charlotte#	10	6	.625	22	11	.667
Marquette	9	7	.563	15	14	.517
St. Louis	8	8	.500	17	14	.548
Louisville	8	8	.500	12	19	.387
DePaul	4	12	.250	12	18	.400
National						
Southern Miss.	11	5	.688	22	9	.710
Memphis	10	6	.625	21	15	.583
South Fla.	9	7	.563	18	13	.581
UAB	8	8	.500	17	14	.548
Houston	6	10	.375	9	20	.310
Tulane	2	14	.125	9	21	.300

IVY LEAGUE

TEAM	CONFERENCE			FULL SEASON		
	W	L	PCT.	W	L	PCT.
Princeton	11	3	.786	16	11	.593
Brown	9	5	.643	15	12	.556
Pennsylvania	9	5	.643	12	17	.414
Harvard	7	7	.500	14	12	.538
Columbia	7	7	.500	12	15	.444
Yale	7	7	.500	10	17	.370
Dartmouth	3	11	.214	8	19	.296
Cornell	3	11	.214	7	20	.259

METRO ATLANTIC ATHLETIC CONFERENCE

TEAM	CONFERENCE			FULL SEASON		
	W	L	PCT.	W	L	PCT.
Iona#	12	6	.667	22	11	.667
Siena	12	6	.667	20	11	.645
Niagara	12	6	.667	15	13	.536
Rider	11	7	.611	16	12	.571
Marist	11	7	.611	17	13	.567
Manhattan	11	7	.611	14	15	.483
Canisius	9	9	.500	20	11	.645
Fairfield	8	10	.444	12	16	.429
Loyola (Md.)	2	16	.111	6	23	.207
St. Peter's	2	16	.111	4	24	.143

MID-AMERICAN CONFERENCE

TEAM	CONFERENCE			FULL SEASON		
	W	L	PCT.	W	L	PCT.
East						
Kent St.#	13	5	.722	24	10	.706
Marshall	12	6	.667	18	9	.667
Ohio	12	6	.667	19	11	.633
Bowling Green	10	8	.556	15	14	.517
Miami (Ohio)	10	8	.556	17	16	.515
Akron	9	9	.500	12	16	.429
Buffalo	2	16	.111	4	24	.143
West						
Central Mich.	14	4	.778	20	8	.714
Toledo	12	6	.667	22	11	.667
Ball St.	12	6	.667	18	12	.600
Western Mich.	7	11	.389	7	21	.250
Northern Ill.	4	14	.222	5	23	.179
Eastern Mich.	1	17	.056	3	25	.107

MID-CONTINENT CONFERENCE

TEAM	CONFERENCE			FULL SEASON		
	W	L	PCT.	W	L	PCT.
Southern Utah#	13	3	.813	25	6	.806
Valparaiso	13	3	.813	24	8	.750
Youngstown St.	11	5	.688	19	11	.633
UMKC	9	7	.563	14	16	.467
Oakland	8	8	.500	12	16	.429
IUPUI	6	10	.375	11	18	.379
Oral Roberts	5	11	.313	10	19	.345
Western Ill.	5	11	.313	5	23	.179
Chicago St.	2	14	.125	5	23	.179